A TREASURY OF THE THEATRE

[FROM HENRIK IBSEN TO EUGENE IONESCO]

Third College Edition

EDITED BY

JOHN GASSNER

STERLING PROFESSOR OF PLAYWRITING AND DRAMATIC LITERATURE

YALE UNIVERSITY

Distributed By

HOLT, RINEHART AND WINSTON

Published By

SIMON AND SCHUSTER

NEW YORK, NEW YORK

Copyright, 1935, 1940, 1950, 1960, by SIMON AND SCHUSTER, INC.

23052-0510

Manufactured in the United States of America

May, 1962

The editor and publishers of A TREASURY OF THE THEATRE are grateful to the following publishers, playwrights, and translators for permission to reprint many of the plays in this volume:

To Charles Scribner's Sons for their consent to the inclusion of *Ghosts* and *Hedda Gabler* by Henrik Ibsen, as translated by William Archer and Edmund Gosse. Published by Charles Scribner's Sons, New York.

To John W. Luce and Company for their consent to the inclusion of *The Father* by August Strindberg, as translated by Edith and Warner Oland. Copyright 1907 by John W. Luce and Company, Boston, Mass.

To The Viking Press, Inc., for their consent to the inclusion of *The Weavers* by Gerhart Hauptmann, as translated by Mary Morison, and published as Volume I of *The Dramatic Works of Gerhart Hauptmann.* Copyright 1912 and published by The Viking Press, Inc., New York.

To George Rapall Noyes and George Z. Patrick for their consent to the inclusion of their translation of *The Power of Darkness* by Leo Tolstoy. Reprinted by permission of George Rapall Noyes from *Masterpieces of the Russian Drama* by George Rapall Noyes, D. Appleton & Co., 1933. *Caution:* No performance, professional or amateur, no public reading, no radio broadcast, and no television performance may be given without permission from and payment of royalty to Mr. George R. Noyes, 1486 Greenwood Terrace, Berkeley, Calif.

To Morris Gest for his consent to the inclusion of the Jenny Covan translation of *The Lower Depths* by Maxim Gorki, and to Oliver M. Sayler for consent to the inclusion, in part, of his introduction to the same play.

To Random House, Inc., for their consent to the inclusion of *The Intruder* by Maurice Maeterlinck.

To Holt, Rinehart and Winston, Inc., for their consent to the inclusion of *Cyrano de Bergerac* by Edmond Rostand, as translated by Brian Hooker. Reprinted by permission of the publishers Copyright, 1923, by Holt, Rinehart and Winston, Inc., New York.

To Charles Scribner's Sons for their consent to the inclusion of *There Are Crimes and Crimes.* Reprinted from *Plays, Second Series* by August Strindberg, translated by Edwin Bjorkman; copyright 1913 by Charles Scribner's Sons, 1942 by Edwin Bjorkman; used by permission of the publishers, Charles Scribner's Sons, New York.

To Liveright Publishing Corporation, for their consent to the inclusion of *Liliom* by Ferenc Molnár. Copyright 1921 by Boni and Liveright, Inc., New York.

To E. P. Dutton and Company, Inc., for their consent to the inclusion of *Six Characters in Search of an Author* by Luigi Pirandello, as translated by Edward Storer. Copyright 1922 by E. P. Dutton and Company, Inc., New York.

To Samuel French for consent to the inclusion of *R. U. R.* by Karel Capek, English version by Paul Selver and Nigel Playfair. Copyright, 1923, by Doubleday, Page & Co. All Rights Reserved. *Caution:* Professionals and amateurs are hereby warned that *R. U. R.,* being fully protected under the copyright laws of the United States of America, the British Empire, including the Dominion of Canada, and all other countries of the Copyright Union, is subject to a royalty. All rights, including professional, amateur, motion pictures, recitation, public reading, radio broadcasting, televising, and the rights of translation into foreign languages are strictly reserved. Amateurs may produce this play upon payment of a royalty of Twenty-Five Dollars for each performance, payable one week before the play is to be given, to Samuel French, at 25 West 45th Street, New York 19, or 7623 Sunset Blvd., Hollywood 46, Calif., or, if in Canada, to Samuel French (Canada) Ltd., 480 University Ave., Toronto.

To New Directions for their consent to the inclusion of *Blood Wedding* by Federico García Lorca. Copyright, 1947, by New Directions, Norfolk, Conn.

To New Directions for their permission to include excerpts of *The Private Life of the Master Race* by Bertolt Brecht, as translated by Eric R. Bentley. Copyright 1944 by E. R. Bentley. Published by New Directions, Norfolk, Conn.

To Alfred A. Knopf, Inc., for their consent to the inclusion of *The Flies* by Jean-Paul Sartre, as translated by Stuart Gilbert. Copyright 1946 by Stuart Gilbert. Also to Hamish Hamilton, Ltd., London, for Canadian distribution permission. Reprinted from *No Exit and The Flies,* by Jean-Paul Sartre, by permission of Alfred A. Knopf, Inc.

To George Bernard Shaw and Dodd, Mead & Company, Inc., for their consent to the inclusion of *Candida* by George Bernard Shaw. Copyright 1898 by Herbert S. Stone and copyright renewed in 1926 by Dodd, Mead & Company, Inc., New York.

To Charles Scribner's Sons for their consent to the inclusion of *The Admirable Crichton* by James M. Barrie. Reprinted from *The Admirable Crichton* by James M. Barrie; copyright 1918 by James M. Barrie, 1946 by Peter Llewelyn Davies; used by permission of the publishers, Charles Scribner's Sons.

To Charles Scribner's Sons for their consent to the inclusion of *Escape* by John Galsworthy. Copyright 1926 and published by Charles Scribner's Sons, New York.

To G. P. Putnam's Sons for their consent to the inclusion of *The Workhouse Ward* by Lady Gregory. Copyright 1909 by Lady Gregory. Reprinted from *Seven Short Plays* by Lady Gregory. Published by G. P. Putnam's Sons, New York.

To Random House, Inc., for their consent to the inclusion of *Riders to the Sea* by John Millington Synge.

To The Macmillan Company and Sean O'Casey for their consent to the inclusion of *The Plough and the Stars* by Sean O'Casey. Copyright, 1926, by Sean

and amateur production, recitations, readings, radio broadcasting, televised performance, and motion pictures are to be addressed to Mr. Arvid Paulson, in care of Simon and Schuster, 630 Fifth Avenue, New York 20, N.Y.

To Grove Press for consent to the inclusion of *The Chairs* by Eugène Ionesco, translated by Donald M. Allen. Copyright © by Grove Press, Inc., 1958. All rights reserved, including the right of reproduction in whole or part in any form. Permission for any use of these plays must be obtained in writing from the author's agents, Marie Rodell and Joan Davis, Inc., 15 East 48th Street, New York 17, N.Y.

To Grove Press for consent to the inclusion of *The Maids* by Jean Genet, translated by Bernard Frechtman. Copyright © by Grove Press, Inc., 1954. All rights reserved, including the right of reproduction in whole

or part in any form. Permission for any use of this play must be obtained in writing from Grove Press, Inc., 64 University Place, New York 3, N.Y.

CAUTION:

CONTENTS

MODERN AMERICAN DRAMA

MODERNIST DIRECTIONS

A REPRESENTATIVE LIST OF MODERN PLAYS

PREFACE

TEACHERS FAMILIAR with the 1940 "Ibsen to Odets" edition of *A Treasury of the Theatre* need only examine pages vii-viii to observe the departures offered by this REVISED EDITION. In view of the extensiveness of the changes, a word of explanation is in order.

The number of plays has been increased—a change urged upon us by requests from teachers who have adopted *A Treasury of the Theatre* in hundreds of colleges and universities. That there is today a decided preference for a single volume sufficient in range to serve as a core textbook, there is little doubt. The new plays in the REVISED EDITION have been chosen in order to afford this range.

The editorial introductions have been proportionately enlarged to provide an accompanying critical treatment of the modern drama. Nobody faced with thirty-nine works by modern dramatists can wholly appreciate their respective qualities without some understanding of the relation of each play to the others and to the time in which it emerged. Following the general introduction (p. xi), which briefly relates modern drama to the three great earlier periods of drama, there is a four-part division which corresponds to the major lines of development: (1) Realism and Naturalism, (2) Departures from Realism, (3) Modern Drama in England and Ireland, and (4) Modern American Drama. A rather extensive discussion introduces each of these parts, to enable the student to approach the plays in their sociocultural context. A briefer introduction, preceding each play, gives detailed attention to the author and attempts some critical analysis of his work.

Taken as a whole, the two kinds of introduction constitute a synoptic survey of the modern drama. Even though the discussions are necessarily brief and may leave room for lively disagreement, the student may find them helpful. No amount of editorial comment should discourage independent analysis or compel a reader to take pleasure in every play in the anthology, and the introductions, indeed, often invite an exchange of opinion.

Although this anthology does not include a table of contents arranged by types, such a tabulation can readily be made. There are tragedies in the more or less traditional sense (*The Power of Darkness, Blood Wedding, Riders to the Sea, Elizabeth the Queen*) and approximations of tragedy (such as *Hedda Gabler, The Father, The Plough and the Stars,* and *Death of a Salesman*). There are also numerous examples of intermediate tragic drama (*Ghosts, The Weavers, The Cherry Orchard, The Lower Depths, The Intruder, Liliom, Escape, Journey's End, Anna Christie, The Hairy Ape, The Green Pastures, Our Town, The Little Foxes,* and *The Glass Menagerie*).

Comedy and farce are represented with clearly definable or traditional examples (*The Importance of Being Earnest, Candida, The Circle, Blithe Spirit, The Admirable Crichton, The Workhouse Ward*). There are also more or less intermediate types (*The Vultures, The Tenor, There Are Crimes and Crimes, Six Characters in Search of an Author, What Price Glory?, My Heart's in the Highlands,* and *Cyrano de Bergerac*). Among both groups of plays are found the modern variant of comedy of ideas as well as satire and romantic comedy.

In such classifications as the foregoing there is always room for some argument; and the same can be said of melodrama and social drama. The latter can, of course, be traced throughout the volume, from *Ghosts* to *Death of a Salesman*. If we construe *R. U. R.* and *The Flies* as melodrama in an honorable sense, then this anthology also offers melodrama, but with a special flavoring of drama of ideas and discussion.

The REVISED EDITION offers full scope for a similar investigation of the styles of drama. The European section, in fact, presents a sharp cleavage between realistic drama and various stylistic and structural departures from realism, and the plays in the British and American sections can be fitted into either classification. There are distinct examples of naturalism and of naturalism fused with a non-realistic technique. Folk drama appears in various guises, and fantasy is mixed with other elements. We find expressionism as well as a persistence of romanticism. Despite the prevalence of prose, there are at least five—or even seven—examples of poetic drama. We are dealing with a highly eclectic theatre after the first solidification of realism and naturalism; an anthology inevitably reflects this eclecticism.

In preparing this REVISED EDITION, the editor has been given invaluable assistance by his wife, Mollie Gassner, and by his friend Stanley Burnshaw. To them he is deeply indebted. And since this edition required unusually generous collaboration on the part of the publishers, he gratefully acknowledges the assistance of Simon and Schuster, Inc., given in this instance especially by M. Lincoln Schuster, Richard Simon, Albert Rice Leventhal, Henry Simon, and Peter Schwed.

New York, N. Y.
March 1950

J. G.

PREFATORY NOTE TO THIRD COLLEGE EDITION

The present revised edition is essentially an amplification intended to take the student of the modern drama closer to contemporary directions and enlarge his knowledge of the origins of these directions. The amplification appears in a section, *Modernist Directions,* on pages 1102–1256. It is necessarily limited in extent by problems of space and of permission clearances. I trust that the instructor who misses a favorite recent play in this section will understand that even the most fortunate anthologist is apt to run out of space and luck. Even in the present revision, however, it has been possible to attend to some noteworthy tendencies in modernistic playwriting, and the examples given in the new section can be instructively augmented with some of the plays (such as *There Are Crimes and Crimes, Liliom, Six Characters in Search of an Author, Blood Wedding, The Flies, The Hairy Ape,* and *Our Town*) included in the preceding sections. The new and old material can be amalgamated without serious difficulty in any study of the advanced styles and techniques of modern drama.

J. G.

New York, N.Y.
January 1960

Introduction

THE DRAMA OF MODERN TIMES has been a literature of the valleys and plateaus rather than of the heights. This has been its chief limitation, but it has also been its greatest strength, for humanity will be found mostly in the valleys and on the plateaus. One of America's earliest pioneers in modern drama, Arthur Hopkins, once expressed a conviction that the theatre can "ultimately reach a place where it helps mankind to a better human understanding, to a deeper social pity, and to a wider tolerance of all that is life." That much, although in artistry a good deal more than that, has been attained by the theatre of modern times. Even in its intellectualism and skepticism it has remained a humanistic enterprise.

Until the modern age there were only three truly major periods of dramatic art in some twenty-four centuries of Western theatre: the fifth-century B.C. Athenian, the Elizabethan, and the seventeenth-century French. Ours is the fourth great period. It began during the last quarter of the nineteenth century and has not yet ended. The modern period has already lasted as long as the Greek, longer than the seventeenth-century French, and twice as long as the Elizabethan. And it has already established its main claims to importance.

Among these is the very extensiveness of modern drama. Classic tragedy was the achievement of a few men in one city; great Renaissance drama was mainly the work of Englishmen during the reigns of Elizabeth and James I; memorable neoclassic drama was the product of three French writers of the age of Louis XIV. Significant modern playwriting has come from virtually all Europe and the United States.

After preliminary efforts chiefly in France, the modern drama took shape as a critical and analytical instrument of realism in Scandinavia, largely in the hands of Henrik Ibsen and August Strindberg. It was simultaneously and subsequently employed in France by a number of able practitioners of less stature—Henry Becque, Eugène Brieux, François de Curel, Georges de Porto-Riche, and Paul Hervieu; in Central Europe, by Gerhart Hauptmann, Frank Wedekind, and Arthur Schnitzler; in Russia, by Leo Tolstoy, Anton Chekhov, and Maxim Gorki; in Southern Europe, by Jacinto Benavente and other Spaniards and Italians; and, finally, in England, Ireland, and America. In each instance, moreover, the realistic style underwent some modification or augmentation as it spread across the Western world. It acquired precision in France, humanization in Russia, poetic intensification in Ireland, robustness in America, intellectual nimbleness in England. The possibility of variation was inherent in modern realism and was made apparent by writers so different in temperament and endowment as Becque, Chekhov, George Bernard Shaw, Sean O'Casey, and Eugene O'Neill. This cannot be said of Greek tragedy, which was only vulgarized and sterilized in Rome; of Elizabethan drama, which was not for export and lost vitality very quickly even in England; of seventeenth-century French tragedy, which shriveled when exposed to a different national climate.

A similar capacity for dissemination and variation appeared in the second and, after 1890, parallel movement of dramatic modernism, which diverged from realism. The movement away from realism began in France with the Belgian symbolist Maurice Maeterlinck and the romanticist Edmond Rostand. It spread to Scandinavia, affecting the later work of Ibsen and Strindberg as well as their successors in the North. It drew Central European playwrights such as Hauptmann

Wedekind, Ferenc Molnár, Bertolt Brecht, and a variety of "expressionists" into its orbit. It moved east toward Russia and south to Italy and Spain, where it found a memorable response from Luigi Pirandello and Federico García Lorca. It advanced to the Irish drama of William Butler Yeats, John Millington Synge, and O'Casey; to the English theatre of James M. Barrie; and to the American stage of O'Neill, Thornton Wilder, Tennessee Williams, and Arthur Miller. No Western nation, in fact, failed to respond to the possibilities of imaginative theatre. Although it remained poorer in poetic texture than the older major dramatic literatures, the modern drama acquired poetic overtones everywhere in its course. Realistic writing, too, became interpenetrated with poetry. And, as a result of imaginative techniques, a poetry of the theatre came into being.

The varied interests of modern playwrights led to a vast exploration of dramatic forms and styles. By comparison with the modern theatre's readiness to experiment, the older theatres had been conservative. Whoever wishes to call the state of the modern stage anarchic may do so, but we may also call it remarkably exploratory. We need point only to a few representative developments—the one-act play as an art form; the discussion piece; the naturalistic but also poetic "slice-of-life" play, free from contrived plotting; the "mass drama," or group drama; the "memory play"; the theatricalist form, which presents the staging of a play, or the "play within the play." To this list we must add the various other styles represented in this anthology, such as symbolism and expressionism. If the modern theatre did not actually invent any or all of these forms of the drama, it employed and developed them with freedom and skill.

With these and other means, the modern drama swept into its orbit an extensive knowledge of man and his world, including the multiple advances of modern times in the fields of sociology and psychology. The creators of modern playwriting were men whose horizons were broad and not confined to the theatre. Many, indeed, received their training in other fields. (Ibsen had studied pharmacy; Hauptmann, science and astronomy; John Galsworthy, law; Chekhov, Schnitzler, and Somerset Maugham, medicine; Pirandello, Karel Capek, and Jean-Paul Sartre, philosophy and psychology. Shaw had cut his eyeteeth on music and economics.) Many were also intensely occupied at one time or another with politics. Playwrights brought into the theatre the intellectual seeds of Schopenhauer, Nietzsche, Kierkegaard, Darwin, Marx, the Webbs, Freud, and other leaders of Western thought. A cartoon intended by Max Beerbohm as a jest at Shaw's expense may stand as a summary of the dramatists' responsiveness to the busy world of modern ideas. Beerbohm shows Shaw presenting a parcel of clothes to the famous nineteenth-century critic Georg Brandes, who is called a *marchand d'idées*. The "merchant of ideas" asks Shaw what he wants for the parcel. The latter sanguinely answers, "Immortality." Brandes protests, "Come, I've handled these goods before! Coat, Mr. Schopenhauer's; waistcoat, Mr. Ibsen's; Mr. Nietzsche's trousers. . . ." Shaw's rejoinder is, "Ah, but look at the patches." In the work of most playwrights, perhaps even the patches had been taken from the thinkers of the age. Yet the combined effect was frequently interesting and exciting.

There also entered into the drama some of the qualities and elements of the novel, the major literary medium of modern times. It was the nineteenth-century writers of fiction who taught the best lessons of naturalness, documentation, psychological probing, and clinical reporting. It was from the novel, and not from the weak eighteenth-century examples of bourgeois drama, that playwrights could discover the true possibilities of commonplace characters and environments.

Flaubert alone supplied a conclusive example with *Madame Bovary*. It was from the novel, too, that playwrights could learn the art of letting the small events of life express human experience without theatrical fireworks or *coups de théâtre*. Some extremely effective theatre was created by these means, from 1890, when Maeterlinck wrote *The Intruder* as evidence that uneventful drama could be tremendously moving, to 1950, when Carson McCullers transferred her warm novel of adolescence, *The Member of the Wedding,* to the stage. Dramatists learned, in short, that untheatrical theatre could make good theatre.

The grand manner of romanticism and later the more efficient theatricality of the "well-made play" were discredited chiefly by the example of the powerful novelists of the nineteenth century. It was to the naturalistic novel that Emile Zola pointed in the eighteen-seventies when he tried to inculcate a new approach to playwriting. Not only were naturalness and verisimilitude furthered by the lessons of the novel but dramatists were enabled to introduce new material that did not suit the grand manner and the contrived dramaturgy of Ibsen's forerunners. There was room now for sociology, for clinical data, for the interchange of ideas, for the evaluation and transvaluation of values. When fiction became experimental in a nonrealistic manner, moreover, with Conrad, Proust, Kafka, and Joyce, dramatists had new lessons to learn.

There is surely some interest in the fact that the modern theatre should have played host to so many dramatizations of novels, not only because it indicates an enrichment of the drama by the most ample and progressive medium of modern literature but because it shows the modern stage capable of assimilating the rich matter of modern fiction. It was apparently unable to do so in the Victorian period, for example, when fiction made much progress while the theatre floundered in a morass of banality. It is remarkable, indeed, how many modern playwrights began as novelists and short-story writers or wrote fiction and drama concurrently. (Among them were Tolstoy, Chekhov, Gorki, Strindberg, Zola, Barrie, Galsworthy, Maugham, Pirandello, Sartre, Molnár, Capek, Wilder, and William Saroyan.) It is also noteworthy how many novelists made forays into the theatre, from Henry James to James Joyce, Thomas Wolfe, Ernest Hemingway, John Steinbeck, Gertrude Stein, and André Gide.

Virtually everything in modern culture found its way, in fact, into the theatre. The poets came into it—directly, as in the case of Yeats, T. S. Eliot, Robinson Jeffers, Lorca, and Brecht, and indirectly. (The influence of poetry on symbolist drama is an obvious example.) Modern music contributed its advances, not merely in serving as accompaniment or in playing an important part in musical comedy and music drama but in enlarging the possibilities of a poetry of the theatre. Nor has this contribution been limited to an enrichment of texts that would otherwise have made banal theatre. A musical element is potent in Shaw's and Chekhov's plays, for example; we may observe the undulation of arguments and themes in Shavian drama and the counterpointing of characters and situations in Chekhovian drama. And an even stronger influence radiated from the emphasis on nuance, atmosphere, and unification of the play and the stage production by mood in Wagner's music-drama cycle *The Ring of the Nibelung*. Nor can it be said that modern developments in the fine arts, from nineteenth-century impressionism to twentieth-century surrealism, failed to make an impression on playwriting and stage art.

Enrichment and provocation, as well as considerable confusion, came, then, into the modern theatre. The fourth major phase of Western drama owes its importance largely to its comprehensiveness. Only a small portion of the culture and social reality of Roman civilization found expression in Roman comedy and tragedy. Hardly anything pertinent to the age of Darwin, Faraday, Huxley, Mill, Dickens, and George Eliot will be found in the work of the Victorian playwrights. In few periods did the drama assimilate the substance that made the age historically and culturally important. Even the medieval drama, so close to the interests and religion of the masses, failed to express medieval culture and life as did Dante's *Divine Comedy*. Only the major dramatic literatures provide a sufficient summation and distillation of their times. This is true of Greek tragedy and comedy and of Elizabethan playwriting. It is also true of the modern drama. From the plays included in *A Treasury of the Theatre* and from the others dealt with in the introductions and the appendix we may derive not only a picture of our age but perspectives on its civilization.

The modern passion for showing things just as they are—that is, for veri-similitude—has indeed had many consequences. It has, for one thing, made our dramatic literature prose, if not necessarily prosaic. Modern playwrights have not written any sublime masterpieces in which the greatest dramatic insights and con-flicts find expression in the greatest poetry. Because the drama, unlike the novel, is a concentrated form and a highly selective art, it aspires inherently to the state of poetry. The greatest drama has also been great poetry. Modern poets have written in both prose and verse, but they have not reached the towering heights of an Aeschylus, Sophocles, or Shakespeare. It may also be said that there is less memorable writing in many good modern plays than in many poor ones written in Athens or in Elizabethan England. The use of prose, however, has not only helped to give modern plays verisimilitude and the effect of authenticity but it has discouraged the reliance on rant and rhetoric that vitiated the work of many earlier playwrights. It has also compelled modern writers to dramatize rather than to narrate events. Our theatre has been an imitation of an action in the form of action more completely than much of the playwriting of the past, and dramatists have found it necessary to build plays more logically and convincingly than when they could dazzle audiences with verbal pyrotechnics. Prose, admittedly a deterrent to the highest flights of dramatic art, has served as a discipline and a challenge.

The concern with verisimilitude has had also an effect on dramatic style for which the term "realism" is inadequate. In the past, a realism of content and thought was often achieved without the instrumentality of a realistic technique. Who shall say that there is a less realistic attitude and understanding in the tragedies of Euripides and Shakespeare than in the plays of Ibsen, Strindberg, and Chekhov? Yet the former employed such formal devices as choruses, narrations, soliloquies, and asides to signify experience instead of presenting it as it would appear in a photographic and phonographic record. Modern play-wrights have generally tried, however, to create the illusion that we are watching events exactly as they occurred. The older playwrights distilled experience, whereas most recent writers have reproduced it. To use the terms introduced by the critic Alexander Bakshy, modern playwrights have *represented* dramatic experience whereas the older playwrights *presented* it. The older theatre tended to be a rite; the modern theatre has been, as a rule, a picture.

Even poetic plays, such as those of Maeterlinck and Rostand, have been essentially *representational,* and their action is meant to be staged as a picture unveiled for the spectator. The effort to project or signify rather than actually to reproduce experience has been the unconventional procedure in our theatre. Although some of the results, as in *Our Town,* have been singularly effective, the *presentational* style has been the secondary one in our drama. It has also been more or less at odds with our picture-frame stage, which, lacking a forestage, creates a physical gulf between the actor and the spectator, who is invited to look on and overhear rather than to participate in the dramatic action. The history of the modern drama, as well as of the stage, has been, to a degree, a battle between realism and antirealism and, more especially, between the representational and presentational styles.

In our unstable age we observe, finally, as we might well have expected, much erosion of boundaries between the types of drama created in the past; that is, many plays are not sharply distinguishable as comedy or tragedy. Tragicomedy may be as old as some of the plays of Euripides (to the well-known Elizabethan vogue of tragicomedy even Shakespeare succumbed), and sentimental comedy (*comédie larmoyante,* or "tearful comedy") was a middle-class creation of the eighteenth century. But the mixed drama of modern times has a different quality. It often consists of an analysis or challenge carried to a consistent conclusion. It offers no happy endings as a salve for suffering characters or as an evasion of an issue; nor does it substitute sentimentality for stern confrontations of reality. Yet, whether it concludes in victory or disaster for the protagonist, this type of drama falls between the provinces of comedy and tragedy.

Even high seriousness on the part of the modern playwright is not apt to be exalting or has been exalting only to those who are roused by its message. No one is likely to be uplifted by *The Little Foxes*—or, for that matter, by *Ghosts,* although it was possible enough in the eighteen-eighties to become excited over the issue it presented. Characters in a play may command the full range of our sympathy, as they do in *The Cherry Orchard* and *The Lower Depths,* without exhilarating us. For this intermediate kind of play no entirely adequate term has yet been discovered. "Tragicomedy" can apply accurately only to plays that develop tragically but conclude happily. "Drama," the term generally favored, is perhaps broad enough to be serviceable.

Since most people are neither comic nor tragic, neither heroes nor villains, they fall into intermediate classifications. There is much truth in the modern playwrights' observation of such personalities, but it is the kind of truth that produces drama of intermediate effect. So does the veracious playwriting that shows us small men falling from small heights or characters vitiated by their environment (as is the young prize fighter in *Golden Boy*), destroyed by a pathological condition, or doomed to stalemate and disintegration. Intermediate, too, is the play in which the author is more interested in discussing a subject or in demonstrating a situation than in providing a unitary experience of joy or grief.

Truthful observation, verisimilitude, and common reality have led playwrights away from the glory that was Greek, Elizabethan, and seventeenth-century French tragedy. Even greatly tried characters—such as Ibsen's Mrs. Alving in *Ghosts,* the starved workers of *The Weavers,* the derelicts of *The Lower Depths,* or the bewildered stoker of *The Hairy Ape*—suffer with vastly more genuineness than magnificence of mind and spirit. Modern drama is not heroic drama in the high tragic sense of the other great ages of the theatre. The language of prose, although it can be poetically colored, suits the characters of modern drama best, just as the language of poetry suits Antigone and Hamlet.

If poetry has not been altogether absent from the modern theatre, it is partly because some playwrights have cast backward glances at a romantic past and rejected the workaday world, as did Rostand, or because they have found sources of poetic feeling and language in a people not yet completely drawn into the modern world, as did Synge in Ireland and Lorca in Spain. For the most part, however, the poetry of the moderns has been wrung from the plain life they have observed with tender or passionate awareness. They have found little grandeur in modern reality; but in feeling the common pulse, they have found that it somehow throbbed with the splendor of all life that seeks and suffers, and that feels lost in the world and nonetheless tries to find meaning and purpose in it. As they have listened to men and women, they have heard no thunderous symphonies of the universe, but they have heard the still, small voice of humanity. Sometimes that voice has become a song. And the song has risen at times to a higher pitch and become impassioned. If it has celebrated no glories of a traditional heroic nature, who shall say that it has not been heroic in the unassuming manner in which a great deal of common life is, and is compelled to be, heroic?

A symbolistic stage design by Jo Mielziner for Anderson's *Winterset* (see pp. 864 f.), making expressive use of a bridge which casts a foreboding shadow on the tragic action. (*Photo: Peter A. Juley & Son*)

An example of symbolist style (see p. 260). The "plastic" setting by Norman Bel Geddes for O'Neill's *Lazarus Laughed* provides for the playing of different scenes without realistic settings.

An expressionist setting (see p. 777). The courtroom scene from the Theatre Guild production of Rice's *The Adding Machine*. Note the expressive distortion. Design by Lee Simonson.

Above: The "sunrise scene" (p. 37) from Act III of the Alla Nazimova production of Ibsen's *Ghosts*. Lighting by Feder. (*Photo: Vandamm*)

Below: Strindberg's *The Father* (p. 94). Robert L. Joseph production. Raymond Massey as the Captain, Mady Christians as Laura. (*Photo: George Korgei*)

Above: A scene from Act II (pp. 213 ff.) of Chekhov's *The Cherry Orchard*, with Alla Nazimova (third from left) as Mme. Ranevsky (Lyubov). (*Photo: Van-damm*)

Below: Setting of the Moscow Art Theatre production of Gorki's *The Lower Depths* (p. 229). A famous example of naturalism on the stage (see pp. 7-9).

Top: Scene vii (p. 382) of the Theatre Guild production of Molnár's *Liliom,* showing Liliom offering Louise the star. Design by Lee Simonson.

Bottom: Epilogue (p. 431) of the Theatre Guild production of Capek's *R. U. R.,* showing the robots demanding to be taught to reproduce. Design by Lee Simonson. (*Photos:* Vandamm)

Right: Act I of the Erwin Piscator Dramatic Workshop production of Sartre's *The Flies* (pp. 469 ff.). The skeletal and symbolic setting is dominated by the blood-smeared statue of Zeus, who in this scene appears in disguise at the right. (*Photo: Balcombe*)

Below: Act III, scene ii (p. 454) of the Boris Tumarin New Stages production of Lorca's *Blood Wedding*. The choreographic arrangement of the actors intensifies the lament for the dead. (*Photo: Fritz Hock*)

Above: Act III, scene ii (p. 766) of the John C. Wilson production of Coward's *Blithe Spirit*, showing Madame Arcati (Mildred Natwick) using the maid as a medium. (*Photo: K. W. Herrmann*)

Below: Part I, scene x (p. 912) of the Broadway production of Connelly's *The Green Pastures.* An example of theatricalist stylization (see p. 260). (*Photo: Vandamm*)

Realism and Naturalism

Realism and Naturalism

The first important advances in modern drama and theatre were made in the direction variously known as realism and naturalism. "Realism" was the general tendency; "naturalism," the specialized, extreme style developed by militant champions of realism who created a program and a movement. Neither realism nor naturalism was a new style in literature when dramatists and stage directors promoted it during the last quarter of the nineteenth century. But the stage had lagged considerably behind the other literary culture of Europe. Consequently, principles were trumpeted in the theatre as though they had never been heard before, and vanguards marched out to do battle with the entrenched proprietors of the old-fashioned stage. When the clash of arms ended and the smoke receded, the first battalion of "modernists" could claim complete victory.

Almost immediately, many Europeans began to wonder whether the victory had been worth winning. Realism and naturalism were decried as commonplace or arid, and a second battalion of "modernists," dedicated to recovering poetry and imagination for dramatic art, swept over the stage. Nevertheless, the pioneering realists had not labored in vain, and their victories were never actually dissipated by later experimentation, so that today the dominant theatre of the Western world is still realistic. Before 1895, realism brought forth masterpieces that have rarely been equaled by the nonrealistic plays of the twentieth century. And in spite of successive waves of theatrical stylization since 1895, most of the durable dramas since then have been essentially realistic or have owed much of their power to elements introduced into the theatre during the eighteen-seventies and 'eighties.

The world since then has belonged to the middle classes and the working classes, for whom the facts of daily life are immediate and momentous. In no previous period have both ordinary citizens and artists been so greatly occupied with science and sociology, and with political and economic realities. No other age has been so materialistic in its thinking, even though science lost a good deal of its nineteenth-century mechanistic philosophy and sociology was invaded by conflicting ideologies heatedly maintained by their socialist, communist, and fascist proponents.

Concreteness became the modern passion. And the theatre, in which things must always be shown and shouted or they simply do not exist, in which a hint is illuminated with thousand-watt power and a whisper reaches every ear—the theatre lent itself to the presentation of the concrete more than any of the other arts before the photographic medium of motion pictures reached maturity. Whether or not we approve of a dramatic art devoted to the prose of life, that is what we receive from the realists and from the naturalists.

THE ARRIVAL OF DRAMATIC REALISM

Until the advent of realistic styles and techniques, the nineteenth-century stage was a flimsy anachronism, made tolerable by some brilliant virtuoso acting. Up to the eighteen-seventies, most of the plays clung to the conventions of a decadent romanticism, even when they dealt with contemporary characters and problems. Alert and earnest men of the theatre could not fail to realize that a wide rift had occurred between these conventions and the realities of the nineteenth century. It was time to end the cleavage, as John Mason Brown has said, "between the grotesque and the commonplace, the picturesque and the factual, the Gothic revival and the scientific spirit, the cloak and swords of yesteryear and the slums of today." The novelists were already facing the modern world, as anyone could see in the work of such masters as Balzac, Flaubert, and Tolstoy. The dramatists could not trail behind them any longer.

Adapting the drama to reality was more difficult than attuning the novel to modern times, because a playwright is dependent upon the stage for which he is writing. And the stage held on to antiquated styles of production. Its stock scenery represented the vested interests of playhouse proprietors, and the acting profession would not willingly, and could not easily, unlearn lifetime habits of theatrical declamation and ostentatious performance. Dramaturgy, moreover, presents more intricate problems than narrative art. No matter how strongly the playwright tries to make his play conform to life, he has to provide effective exits and entrances, convincing time-covering scenes, and act endings that will bring the audience back into the theatre after the intermissions. He must also telescope events that the novelist would present in separate chapters, and intermingle characters whom a novelist would keep separate. Kitty and Anna, for example, can live apart for long periods in Tolstoy's *Anna Karenina* and still belong to the same book, whereas a stage version in which their lives merely ran parallel to each other would disintegrate and fail to sustain interest. In truth, the dramatist had, and still has, a hard time of it whenever he tries to realize standards of absolute realism. Nevertheless, playwrights began to infuse their work with the breath of life and to give their art a greater degree of verisimilitude than earlier dramatists had usually attained or had considered necessary.

From their effort to approximate reality, moreover, the drama acquired more or less special at-

Above: Scene VII (p. 1057) of the Eddie Dowling and Louis J. Singer production of Williams' *The Glass Menagerie.* Julie Haydon plays the part of Laura. *Below:* The Elia Kazan production of Miller's *Death of a Salesman* (p. 1063). Jo Mielziner's skeletal setting represents various parts of the interior and exterior simultaneously. An example of stylization. (*Photo: Eileen Darby*)

Above: Act III (p. 946) of the Jed Harris production of Wilder's *Our Town*, Emily joins the dead, seated on chairs, as her funeral proceeds. The background of this sceneryless production consists of the bare stage walls. No attempt is made to create verisimilitude at the left, and the funeral, held in the rain, is merely suggested by the group holding umbrellas. (*Photo: Vandamm*)

Below: Herbert Andrews' semisurrealistic design for the Group Theatre production of Saroyan's *My Heart's in the Highlands* (p. 1022). The production style conveys a fairy-tale simplicity. (*Photo: Valente*)

tributes, and these are of signal importance in differentiating the modern realistic play from the dramatic work of previous ages. Not even the casual reader or playgoer can overlook the emphatic contrasts between plays written for the realistic stage and those written for the romantic theatre of Schiller and Goethe, for the renaissance theatre of Shakespeare and Lope de Vega, or for the classic theatre of Sophocles and Euripides.

Poetry, the dominant vehicle for high drama in earlier periods, gave way to prose dialogue. Prose had entered the theatre long before the middle of the last century, but now it became the medium for exalted feeling as well as for commonplace experience, for tragedy as well as for comedy. Authentic dialect also came into frequent use, and was employed not merely for comic effect, as it was in Shakespearean drama. Whether the theatre suffered a setback from the triumph of prose has been a subject for debate for many decades and will probably remain so for a long time to come.

Playwrights began to introduce detailed stage directions into their work in order to authenticate the background and behavior of their characters, as well as to voice opinions they could no longer relegate to declamation by the actor as in the more artificially written earlier drama. The audience would not, of course, hear directions and undramatized comments of the author. Yet their effect could be felt in the stage productions, insofar as the stage director and the scene designer carried out the intentions thus indicated by the playwright. The reader —and plays began to be read on a larger scale than hitherto, except for national classics or the Greek and Latin drama taught in school—could re-create the dramatist's world more faithfully when he followed descriptions of the setting, costuming, and appearance of the characters; and he could acquaint himself more closely with the playwright's mind. He now received a printed text that bore a closer resemblance to a novel than to a dramatic poem. (What intelligent reader would forego the pleasure of Shaw's directions and comments?) More important, however, was the fundamental approach of the playwright, for he was now dominated by the consuming desire to study life more scientifically and more specifically than hitherto. He began to document his work, to present his material objectively, and to pay close attention to the role of instinct and milieu in human behavior. The study of so-called instinct gave rise to modern psychological drama, the study of background to modern social drama.

No one familiar with the drama since Sophocles would maintain that "psychological drama" was invented by realists and naturalists. Not even in the clinical sense of the term was psychology unknown in the theatre until the advent of modern playwrights such as Strindberg and O'Neill. The intuitions of Sophocles, Euripides, and Shakespeare were just as valid and penetrating as O'Neill's schematizations, if not indeed more so. (As Freud himself pointed out, the world's artists had discovered the "unconscious" long before clinicians, including himself, found a place for it in their case reports.) But the realistic dramatists were the first to represent psychological deviations or complexities directly rather than suggestively or symbolically and to locate them in familiar, contemporary backgrounds rather than to imply them in the context of myth or history.

If authors, in addition, often tended to view their subjects with a disconcerting indifference to moral judgments, this, too, reflected an essentially new attitude. Once playwrights conceived the notion of bringing a scientific view into the theatre, they could no more hesitate to fill the stage with unappetizing exhibitions than an anatomist would to perform a dissection in the operating room of a hospital or a medical school. The modernists who called themselves naturalists were dedicated to the cause of evolving a "natural science" of human behavior and considered themselves "determinists." Men, the writers tended to imply, behave as they must; that is, their hereditary traits and their instincts shape and determine their character and frequently overpower their reason or moral scruples. If this is so, man is not responsible for his actions, and moral indignation is out of order. For a dramatist to register disapproval of a person who succumbs to his sexual or criminal drives would be as absurd as for a physician to upbraid a patient for developing a cancer. This was the extreme view, and its illogicality became transparent to all writers but those who refused to make a distinction between inorganic matter or animal life and human beings. But the scientific attitude made itself generally felt in the playwright's concern with psychology, heredity, and instinct, in his matter-of-fact treatment of these matters, and in his air of playing the role of a detached observer.

As important as the growth of psychological and clinical studies, finally, was the advent of modern social drama, and here too the scientific attitude of the age of Darwin and Marx played a part. Enthusiasts of naturalistic doctrine proposed to study man as a creature inexorably determined by his social situation, or milieu. The earlier romantic playwrights had introduced "local color" into the drama. The realists went one great step further and introduced environment.

Writers now tended to treat the environment not merely as the background for a dramatic complication but as the foreground itself. They regarded society as a reality interesting and important in its own right. If the idea that character is to a great degree a product of social factors already existed in European thought, it was still new in the theatre. And if romantic dramatists had already pitted characters against social convention as long ago as the third quarter of the eighteenth century, it was nonetheless an innovation for the new playwrights to treat the subject with attention to contemporary life and with sociological interest. The problem play that maintains a thesis directly and the drama of social agitation that openly promotes a cause won more and more adherents in the modern theatre.

In an increasing number of instances, moreover, social drama no longer presented an individual as the central character. From such early plays as Haupt- mann's *The Weavers* and Gorki's *The Lower Depths* to such comparatively recent examples as Rice's *Street Scene* and Odets' *Waiting for Lefty,* one can trace a trend toward representing a collective char- acter or "mass hero"—a group of weavers, sailors, taxicab drivers, and the like. In such instances, we may well wonder how much has been lost or gained by the change of focus. If "the proper study of mankind is man," is he better understood or more meaningfully presented as a singular individual or as a collective entity? Debate over these questions can range far and wide. But the "collective character" has remained important in the theatre since *The Weavers* appeared in 1892.

As an inevitable consequence of the new social outlook, it was the common man who came to hold "stage center"—not merely in comedies of intrigue and sentimental pieces, but in tragedy and in serious plays concerned with his problems. The "little man," who had been usually presented in the older drama as the roguish servant, the lumpish peasant, or the upstart and absurd bourgeois, acquired dignity and importance in the new democratic theatre. He was not entirely new to his honors, it is true. He had been invested with them to some degree in Eliza- bethan plays such as *Arden of Feversham* and *The Yorkshire Tragedy,* and in such peasant dramas as Lope de Vega's *The Sheep-Well* and Calderon's *The Mayor of Zalamea.* The French encyclopedist of the eighteenth century, Diderot, had promulgated the need for "middle-class tragedy," and had written ineffectual samples himself. Other writers of "bour- geois" or of "liberal" persuasion—such as Lillo in England and Lessing and Schiller in Germany—had followed his example. But their plays had been ex- ceptions to the unwritten, and also written, rule that only the highborn were worthy of heroic treatment. It was the realists who made the commoner com- pletely at home in the theatre and gave him the tragic stature hitherto reserved for the aristocracy, insofar as it was within the province of realism to endow anyone with such stature. In time, too, the lowly hero was apt to be found more and more in working-class circles and among the peasantry rather than in middle-class circumstances.

FROM REALISM TO NATURALISM

The stages by which dramatic realism moved to supremacy would have to be traversed through many centuries. The conscientious chronicler would carry

us as far back as the farces and religious dramas of the Middle Ages. (We have already noted the appearance of peasant drama in Spain's Golden Age and of middle-class drama in Shakespeare's day and in the eighteenth century.) Then he would deposit us on the threshold of modern drama in France. Here, shortly after Victor Hugo won a signal victory for romanticism with his *Hernani* in 1830, the in- creasingly bourgeois world of Louis Philippe and Louis Napoleon found a remarkably proficient en- tertainer in Eugène Scribe (1791–1861). His char- acters belonged to this workaday world, even if they only went through the motions of life as their author dangled them from the strings of artificial plots. Scribe, however, managed to create the illusion of reality on the stage with surface effects, and he taught a generation how to hold audiences with any kind of material. He did so by spinning out intrigues, by tangling up and then unwinding situations, and by producing discoveries and unexpected twists of circumstance. He turned playwriting into a virtuoso performance like tightrope-walking and sword-swal- lowing. The artificial pattern he evolved has been aptly named "the well-made play," for it was made rather than lived, and it was made well in the sense that it "worked" on the playgoer by keeping him on emotional tenterhooks. Scribe's clever craftsman- ship was adopted by such younger playwrights as Emile Augier (1820–1889) and Alexandre Dumas *fils* (1824–1895), the illegitimate son of the great ro- mancer of *The Three Musketeers.* They were fol- lowed by the most proficient of all the contrivers, Victorien Sardou (1831–1908). It must be remem- bered that all these manufacturers of plot found adapters and imitators throughout the Western world. The young Ibsen himself served an appren- ticeship in Scribe's workshop when he stage-man- aged twenty-one plays by Scribe at the theatre in Bergen where he got his first practical experience. The Scribian technique of surprise discoveries and turns of intrigue appeared in Ibsen's work as late as 1877, when he composed his social drama *The Pillars of Society.*

Within the artificial circle of the well-made play, Augier (alone and in collaboration) painted ob- jective pictures of his times such as *The Son-in-Law of Monsieur Poirier* (1854) and *The Marriage of Olympia* (1855), and Dumas *fils* delivered sermons on social reform after having first created a sensa- tion with his famous tragedy—or pseudo tragedy— of a courtesan, *The Lady of the Camellias* (1852). Augier and the younger Dumas were, in fact, full- fledged realists, according to their own view, and what we call their artificial technique struck them as simply good craftsmanship. They dealt with facets of the life of their times that they considered im- portant, employed prose dialogue, and made their plots revolve around ordinary people instead of knights of old or creatures of fancy. They regarded themselves as modernists and held what they believed to be advanced ideas, although these may strike us today as singularly old-fashioned, quaint, and narrow. Augier appointed himself the arch-defender of middle-class values that we now call mid-Victorian. He thought he was treating a momentous issue when he showed courtesans snaring youths of good family in marriage and thus infiltrating respectable society. Dumas' zeal for moral edification and for "useful theatre," as he called it, led him to lecture the public on a variety of then current problems ranging from illegitimacy to corrupt journalism.

Whether the well-made play was always an evil is arguable. Insofar as construction was concerned, the plays were assuredly not an abomination but a boon to the theatre. No one who is aware of the chaotic character of much Elizabethan and romantic drama can think otherwise. The multiple plots, static narrations, and long declamations in these nonrealistic plays could cause only confusion and boredom except in the hands of very able craftsmen. Indeed, with the advent of realism, dramatists tended to favor classic clarity and order. The well-made play assured effectiveness. Any number of admirable modern plays—*The Father, Hedda Gabler, The Power of Darkness, Loyalties, Desire Under the Elms,* and *The Little Foxes,* for example—are "well made." The adjective acquired a pejorative meaning as a result of the practice of superficial playwrights who strove only for theatrical effect and of didactic dramatists who were more intent upon delivering a message than upon presenting life on the stage.

In a bumbling fashion, another current of realism also began when Balzac produced his unflattering study of finance and usury, *Mercadet,* in 1851. The De Goncourt brothers left the security of the novel to write a play about a daughter who falls in love with her mother's lover, *Henriette Maréchal* (1865). The poet Villiers de L'Isle Adam anticipated *A Doll's House* with *The Revolt* in 1870, and the great Flaubert floundered with a drama, *Le Candidat,* in 1874. None of the authors belonged to the theatre by profession. Nor did Emile Zola (1840–1902), who, having already started his study of heredity and environment in the celebrated "Rougon-Macquart" series of family novels, wrote a sordid case history of adultery, *Thérèse Raquin,* in 1867, dramatized it in 1873, and defended it with a proclamation of principles for a new dramatic art. None of these plays won any immediate success, but they indicated a trend toward naturalism. They were not as contrived as the plays of Dumas and Augier, if only because their authors were less skillful in the theatre. The material was for the most part unsavory and was presented without the spice of moralization. The treatment of social reality or human nature was regarded as naturalistic because the objective reporting could be said to parallel the methods of the natural sciences.

In the meantime, there were stirrings in the theatre elsewhere: all the way from Russia, where Gogol's stinging satire on bureaucracy, *The Inspector General,* was produced as early as 1836, to England, where Thomas William Robertson (1829–1871) presented the tepid social dramas *Society* in 1865 and *Caste* in 1867. In Germany, the short-lived genius George Büchner (1813–1837) left a fragment that is a curious naturalistic masterpiece, *Wozzeck,* in 1836. (It remained unknown for many decades and was first produced in 1913.) In Germany, too, Friedrich Hebbel (1813–1863) developed his theory that tragedy is the product of the individual's clash with his society and wrote the powerful middle-class prose tragedy *Maria Magdalena* (1845). With *The League of Youth* published in 1869 and *The Pillars of Society* in 1877, Ibsen was on the way to turning his individual genius into the channels of genuinely modern realism, as was that other individualist, Henry Becque, when he wrote *The Vultures* in the same year, 1877, in Paris. Neither of these men needed any prodding from proclamations by Zola. They did need a new style of theatre for their plays, but would have to wait some ten years before it came into being.

A program was nonetheless needed to bring the formative drama into focus, and Zola, who had a gift for polemics among his varied talents, provided it first in the preface he wrote for the published version of *Thérèse Raquin* in 1873, then in prefaces to other unsuccessful plays the next year, and in his collected essays, *Le Naturalisme au théâtre,* printed in 1881. Zola was particularly impressed with the researches of Claude Bernard, who was investigating the relationship between the nervous system and nutrition in experiments on living animals and had published his *Introduction to the Study of Experimental Medicine* in 1865. Making extravagant claims for a truly modern drama, Zola took his stand on the side of what he called "nature" and found a suitable name for his conception of "scientific" realism in the term "naturalism," already familiar in other fields.

In order to "bring the theatre into closer relation with the great movement toward truth and experimental science," Zola maintained that the drama would have to apply the "new methods of science" to the study of human nature and behavior. Natural laws were in operation throughout the universe and applied to man as well as to the rest of creation. "A like determinism," wrote Zola, "will govern the stones of a highway and the brain of man." The moral life was no exception to this rule, and the French critic Taine had already expressed this view in declaring that "vice and virtue are products like sugar and vitriol."

Zola's notions of determinism were no sounder than his understanding of scientific method, and his attempt to apply animal reflexes to human behavior was a flagrant oversimplification. He had merely picked up scraps of materialistic philosophy and mechanistic science as a means for justifying an un-varnished picture of raw passion in *Thérèse Raquin.* He stated that "given a strong man and unsatisfied woman," he had tried "to see in them the beast [or animal], to see nothing but the beast, to throw them into a violent drama and note scrupulously the sensations and acts of these creatures." He concluded with a flourish, "I have simply done on two living bodies the work which surgeons do on corpses." This was, however, only his way of justifying a clinical approach that was soon to become frequent in dramatic realism; and in spite of making excessive claims for his procedure in the play, he did strike a blow in behalf of the modern dramatist's right to uncover sordid realities in the interest of truth.

It may be noted, too, that Zola extended the range of observation beyond the narrow limits of the clinic, just as he himself went beyond them in *Thérèse Raquin* when he allowed his murdering couple to be overcome with devastating remorse; the "beast" he proposed to study turned into a human creature after all. Zola expressed his crusade for naturalism most satisfactorily when he stated it most flexibly, as when he proposed to submit "man and his work to a system of precise analysis, taking into account all circumstances, environment, and 'organic causes.' " If the phrase "system of precise analysis" is dropped from these lines as a procedure impossible to art, Zola's sentence leaves room for considerable variation in the drama. It was the variation or deviation from rigid naturalism that was generally interesting or successful in the theatre. The variations grew in number and the deviations multiplied, leaving pure Zolaism in the lurch. Truly creative playwrights did not feel tethered to the program of Zola, and even those who thought they followed it merely approximated it. If Hauptmann, for example, thought he had written a completely dispassionate play when he composed *The Weavers,* that was not the effect it had on its audiences, who were roused to pity and revolutionary ardor by his account of the miseries of the Silesian weavers.

Zola's polemics helped to put an end to the rule of the degenerate romantic drama and discredited the "well-made plays" of sheer artifice. He incited, instead, and gave honorable status to, the uncontrived document of reality that he called a *lambeau d'existence,* or fragment of life, which a younger minor dramatist, Jean Jullien, popularized under the term *tranche de vie,* or slice of life. Dramatists, not excluding Zola himself, in spite of his fulminations against *any* kind of "arrangement," continued to "arrange" life more or less. To be an art, how could the drama fail to be an arrangement? The same question would arise when enthusiasts of stage naturalism thought that they were creating a completely natural art of theatre, free of all conventions. How could the theatre fail to abide by some degree and some kind of convention? A realistic, even naturalistic, stage production only created its own conven-tion. It based its acting style on the hypothesis that the large open space framed by the proscenium arch was a "fourth wall" that shut the actor off completely from the audience. If the front of the set had been an *actual* fourth wall, how could an actor have been seen or heard from the auditorium? Nevertheless, the natural, "unarranged" (that is, inconspicuously arranged) dramatic style was to give us after Zola's trumpetings such persuasive and affecting works as the best plays of Chekhov and O'Casey. And the "unconventional" (that is, inconspicuously conventional) theatre was to yield the memorable productions of the Moscow Art Theatre and the early Abbey Theatre in Dublin.

No program is more valuable than the uses to which it is put. Zola's propaganda challenged the old romantic and contrived styles of the drama and justified a more natural art of playwriting, as well as greater fidelity to life, than had been considered desirable in dramatic writing before 1870. The playwrights and stage producers who put his proposals into successful practice in their own way were the genuine artists of the theatre. Their creativity at its best was always individual, sometimes intensely personal.

Always, indeed, it was the personal talent of an Ibsen, Strindberg, or Chekhov that made realism and naturalism important on the stage and between the covers of a book. Realism was undoubtedly promoted by a change in the theatre audiences of the nineteenth century, which became increasingly middle class after 1830. Understandably, they favored plays that dealt with the world they knew and that presented a real environment on the stage. Naturalism was unquestionably aided in Europe by advances in science (Zola wanted the French intellect to keep in step with scientific advances being made throughout Europe, especially in Germany). The decline of idealism as a consequence of political corruption during the reign of Louis Philippe and the failure of the revolutionary movements of 1848 no doubt inclined men toward the deterministic and unemotional view of reality held by the naturalists. But it was the creativity of playwrights and stage directors in response to these and other developments that gave us a theatre vital enough to deserve our interest and respect.

THE NEW THEATRE

A new drama requires a new theatre, and a new theatre was born by the last decade of the nineteenth century. Its history, like that of the drama, consists of at first half-understood, gradual advances within the province of the older theatre itself, of some skirmishing at the borders by a hardy forerunner of new stagecraft (the Duke of Saxe-Meiningen), and, finally, of decisive victories by leaders who were articulate and wholly aware of their mission.

As for the initial trends, they may be summarized best as responses to the failure of romantic theatre in the nineteenth century. Ever since the Renaissance in Italy, the European theatre had tried to simulate backgrounds by combining architecture and painting on the stage. "Side wings" of painted canvas stretched on wooden frames were placed in grooves at the sides of the stage. They were arranged in accordance with the laws of perspective so as to form a stage picture, which was completed by the addition of a painted backdrop. The feats of Renaissance and seventeenth-century scene designers were often extraordinarily beautiful, especially when viewed from the front rows center in the auditorium. These "wing-and-backdrop" settings were in effect architectural forms in the contemporary Baroque style and created illusion conventionally. Most of the acting took place in front of the setting, so that there was no great discrepancy between the real actors and the simulated street scene or interior on the stage. In the nineteenth century, the platform in front of the setting began to disappear and the actors played more and more within the set. But they continued to indulge in soliloquies and asides, to act in a declamatory style, and to address themselves to the audience, as though they were not sitting and moving within the scenic environment. This alone would have made the performance flagrantly artificial, and the formal style of acting actually became absurd when the subject was middle-class life and the characters were ordinary persons.

The artificiality of the theatre was made transparent by the nature of the settings themselves. These continued to be built of canvas, yet the flats were now used to create the impression of real rooms instead of being arranged by means of a backdrop and side wings to create an essentially formal effect. The flats were put together to form the walls of a room. Since these walls were made of canvas, however, they were flimsy and the actors had to be warned not to lean against them lest they destroy the illusion by shaking the set. Canvas doors with the cloth shivering on them when they were opened or closed could reduce an entrance or an exit to an absurdity. Worse still, some doors and part of the furniture were painted on the walls, and sometimes entire scenes were painted on backdrops. If the actor backed up far enough he might tower over the objects diminished in perspective, and there would also be a discrepancy between the shadows the living person cast under the lights and the painted shadows. Here, then, was a theatre that tried to create illusion with illusion-destroying means. It was doomed by its own ineptitude.

Meanwhile the trend toward making stage production more realistic was already under way. It started with an antiquarian movement that introduced authentic costuming into the theatre and tried to make the painted setting an accurate re-production of a classic background or a medieval scene. Producers were indeed so proud of such achievements that they publicized them, citing authorities to prove that their costumes, stage properties, scenery, spectacles, and dances were authentic. In time, too, the old painted flats vanished and were supplanted by solid scenery, and when ceilings were placed across the walls of the setting, the theatre acquired the "box set" still in use when interiors are represented. Once the old "apron," or forestage, was eliminated, all the acting was cut off from the audience. A distinct environment became possible for the performance on the stage, and the presentation of environment assumed increasing importance to realists and naturalists. Stock scenery was discarded, and special scenery which was solid and practical was constructed for each play.

Once the box set came into use, it was plain, too, that a new convention had arisen. Since the setting was now enclosed on three sides by walls, a "fourth wall" had to be assumed. Inevitably, given the stage, the empty space framed by the proscenium arch had to be assumed to represent the fourth wall of a room, and, in time, the actor was expected to treat it as such. He had to perform as though he were living not in the theatre but in privacy behind the "wall." Much as it distressed the old-time actor, he could no longer ogle the audience and declaim to it. He could not even take "stage center" on every occasion without violating the naturalness expected of actions behind the "wall." A modern director would actually expect him to turn his back to the public from time to time, as if oblivious that he was being observed by an audience "out front," and the scene designer might place a piece of furniture against the imaginary partition. The playwright was also importantly affected by the new convention. He became conscious of the absurdity of writing the time-honored soliloquies and asides of the older styles of drama once the actor was no longer on terms of intimacy with the public and could not take it into his confidence concerning his state of mind or secret intentions. Acting and stage production consequently became increasingly "natural." These changes, accelerated by the introduction of gas and electric illumination, were tantamount to a revolution in the theatre.

The important changes were effectuated by far-seeing leaders who created their own acting companies while the established theatre held on to outworn practices as long as possible. Among the pioneers, four or five were particularly influential, and the history of realism on the stage is largely the history of their efforts. In chronological order, they are the Duke of Saxe-Meiningen, André Antoine, Otto Brahm, Constantin Stanislavsky, and his associate, Vladimir Nemirovitch-Dantchenko.

In the eighteen-seventies the Duke of Saxe-Meiningen created an acting company for the court theatre of his little duchy, and for seventeen seasons between 1874 and 1890 the troupe made notable advances in authentic costuming, carefully designed scenery, and effective ensemble acting. In staging a battle scene, for example, the Duke went so far in his passion for realism as to place a stuffed horse on the stage. He employed the famous realistic painters Israels and Liebermann as scenic artists. For exterior scenes the Duke broke up the stage floor into different levels, creating a realistic effect of uneven ground. But his crowning achievement was his meticulous treatment of crowds on the stage. He was so intent upon individualizing these that he would even place important members of his company in the mob whenever they were not playing major roles. When a prominent actress refused to do "mob duty" she was summarily dismissed. By emphasizing ensemble performances, the Duke actually abolished the time-honored "star" system, and he gave full sway to the stage director as the autocrat of the stage, responsible for a unified production. There was nothing regimental about the Meiningen crowds; symmetrical arrangements were abolished; the actors were ordered to look at one another or at the events transpiring in their presence instead of facing the audience. Antoine, who saw a performance of the Meiningen company in Brussels in the summer of 1888, was particularly impressed with the crowd scenes and tableaux. Although the Duke also produced some of Ibsen's dramas (Pillars of Society and A Doll's House), his repertory consisted mostly of plays by Shakespeare and later romantic works by Schiller, Kleist, and others. But his stagecraft marked the first major advance toward realistic theatre. Among those who were stimulated by the Meiningen company's achievements were Antoine and Stanislavsky, who saw its performances in Moscow in 1885. Since the Duke made every effort to display his troupe outside his own little territory (his capital city had no more than eight thousand inhabitants), he was a remarkably effective missionary for early realism. He brought the company to Berlin on May 1, 1874, and to Vienna and Budapest in 1875. Between 1874 and 1890 the Meiningen group played 385 times in Berlin and 2,206 times on tours through Germany, Switzerland, Poland, Russia, Denmark, Sweden, Holland, Belgium, and England.

Antoine's contributions to realistic theatrical art occurred in Paris, the capital of European culture. An employee of the Paris Gas Company, he had trained himself for an acting career and joined a small amateur group, the Cercle Gaulois. At first he had only vague aspirations and no program, but when he tried to produce a realistic one-act play based on a story by Zola he found it necessary to break with the Cercle Gaulois. He formed his own group, named it Le Théâtre Libre (The Free Theatre) and presented a first bill of one-acters on May 30, 1887. As Zola and his followers gave the project their support, the Théâtre Libre became the outpost of French naturalism. Soon Antoine produced the work of Ibsen, Strindberg, Tolstoy, and Hauptmann, among others; his little subscription theatre became the seat of European naturalism. Subsequently he founded another, larger theatre for the general public, the Théâtre Antoine, and ran it for nine years (1897–1906). He also took charge of the state theatre, the Odéon, for some eight years, until 1914. He won fame as an actor and became an effective drama critic.

Antoine's influence continued long after he resigned from the Théâtre Libre in 1894, but it was there that he inaugurated realistic stagecraft. In the course of his work as manager, actor, and stage director he banished the false theatricality of the conventional French theatre. He abolished the declamatory style, introduced realistic settings, going so far as to hang real meat on hooks in a butcher-shop scene, and he even had his actors now and then turn their backs on the audience. He was willing to grant that the stage setting was a matter of secondary importance for the performance of a classic drama, but he considered it of major significance in the staging of "works written in the vein of realism and naturalism, where the theory of environment and the influence of exterior things have become so important." "Should it not assume on the stage," he added, "the same importance as a description in a novel?" Antoine's work at the Théâtre Libre, as well as its extension into the larger theatres of France and its dissemination in other little theatres, was the second round of the battle for a realistic stage.

The third round was fought under the leadership of a critic turned director, Otto Brahm, who opened a little theatre in Berlin on September 29, 1889, in imitation of Antoine's project. The Freie Bühne (literally the Free Stage) began by producing Ibsen's Ghosts. Then followed a native naturalistic play, Hauptmann's Before Sunrise, the De Goncourt brothers' Henriette Maréchal, Tolstoy's The Power of Darkness, and three other native dramas. In its second season, the Freie Bühne gave seven plays, including Zola's Thérèse Raquin, Becque's The Vultures, Strindberg's The Father, and Hauptmann's Lonely Lives. When this last play was accepted in 1892 by the citadel of conventional art, the Deutsches Theater of Berlin, victory was in sight. In 1894, Otto Brahm was made the director of the Deutsches Theater, the new realistic style triumphed, and Brahm completed the renovation of theatrical art in Germany. The Freie Bühne ceased operations, having accomplished its pioneering task.

Brahm introduced into Central Europe practically the same realistic innovations that Antoine had developed in France. He achieved many triumphs with his famous "Brahm style" of plain and natural stagecraft, which made the actors underplay their roles and speak as casually as the scene permitted. A declared enemy of theatricalism and artifice, he strove for authenticity rather than theatrical effect, forbidding his cast to indulge in any emphases not absolutely required by a situation. Brahm got rewarding results whenever he staged a realistic play. He failed only when he mistakenly applied the principles of realism to Shakespearean drama.

The widening arc of the free-theatre movement in Europe reached its farthest points when it touched Moscow and London. The Independent Theatre, founded in London in 1891 by Jacob T. Grein, a native of Holland, is less important for its founder's innovations of theatrical art than for its hospitality to the new drama. Grein's theatre never had more than 175 supporters, but among these were such important men as George Meredith, Thomas Hardy, George Moore, Frank Harris, William Archer, Bernard Shaw, Arthur Wing Pinero, and Henry Arthur Jones. The Independent Theatre lasted from 1891 to 1897 and produced twenty-six plays. Like Brahm, Grein selected *Ghosts* for his opening salvo. His second production was Zola's *Thérèse Raquin,* and to Grein goes the credit for having introduced Shaw as a playwright with *Widowers' Houses* (1893). In Moscow, six years after the establishment of a free theatre in London, there was born an enterprise of greater and more lasting importance, the Moscow Art Theatre, which developed the art of inner realism in addition to adopting external realism in the stage picture.

Stanislavsky and Dantchenko's theatre became notable on many counts. Founded in 1897, it has lasted up to the present time. It reached large audiences in Russia and it also toured Europe and the United States extensively. It fathered other enterprises, including a second studio devoted to musical productions. It also made Anton Chekhov a dramatist of international renown after successfully reviving his failure *The Sea Gull,* and it introduced Maxim Gorki to the world with *The Lower Depths.* Its most important achievement, however, was its development of the art of acting. Largely owing to the genius of Stanislavsky as a director and teacher

of acting, the Moscow company carried realistic performance beyond mimicry and verisimilitude.

Actors were trained to achieve an "inner justification" for their roles, to make a complete identification with the characters they played. Step by step, an actor was expected to lose his own personality as something that stands apart from the role. But this was to be done not by destroying the individuality of the performer but by exploring it for elements of experience and emotion that would enable him to re-create himself as a character in the play. And for this purpose, the Moscow Art Theatre actors followed processes in preparing their parts that have come to be known as the "Stanislavsky system," although the word "system" must be employed with the widest possible latitude. The preparation of a role included exercises before and during rehearsals: "sense memory," by means of which the actor gained mastery of the physical actions he was expected to perform; "affective memory," through which he made his feeling genuine by drawing upon memories of his own experience, emotions, or states of mind which paralleled the feelings he was expected to express on the stage; and "improvisations," with which he imagined or performed actions that he would not exhibit on the stage after the rehearsals but that he would have performed if he had been the same character outside the text of the play. By means of such intensive preparation over a period of many months, the actors were fully justified in calling their art "a theatre of inner feeling." In becoming the world's foremost theatre, in maintaining that position for half a century, inspiring other groups with its example, and revolutionizing the training of actors, the Moscow Art Theatre brought the advances of the earlier pioneers of the stage to their ultimate realization.

A revolution was needed in theatrical art before the revolution in playwriting could be made complete and effectual. The free-theatre movement effected this revolution between 1887 and 1900, concluding the first major phase of the modernization of the stage and drama.

Henrik Ibsen

(1828–1906)

'To the unwary, Ibsen can be one of the most deceptive of dramatists. He was an advocate of causes who was apt to reverse himself disconcertingly. A flouter of middle-class convention in his writings, he was nevertheless very much of the middle class himself. He dressed meticulously, liked to display the orders of merit that governments and royalty bestowed on him, and invested his royalties in railroad securities and other sound businesses with the care of a conservative banker. For a cosmopolitan artist who spent much of his adult life in foreign lands, he was singularly provincial in many respects. As a political thinker, he gave comfort at different times to both the liberals and conservatives of his native Norway, and both were mistaken in claiming his undivided allegiance. A poet of distinction, he wrote some of the most outwardly prosaic masterpieces of the drama, and he continued to write lyric poetry during the decisive period when he made the prose play the norm for modern playwriting. He injected realism into his early, romantic dramas, and introduced symbolism into his late, realistic work. Ibsen was uniquely a writer who could sing like a thrush and croak like a raven—sometimes simultaneously. Only a full-length study can chart the contradictions of the man and the artist.

If Ibsen was nonetheless portrayed by many of his champions as a modern realist with a reformer's zeal and simple sociological outlook, the reason is that there was a need to create this concept of a fighting realist in the late nineteenth century. The simplified Ibsen was an invention, or "construct," of history as a result of the interest in science and sociology, the emancipation of women, and the liberalization of religion and government that started well before 1875 but became particularly marked after that date. Since Ibsen responded intensely to his times, he collaborated with history in the style and content of about a dozen of his plays, even if the collaboration was on his own terms as man and artist. Especially after 1875, he wrote a series of plays that were explicit enough, at least on the surface, to be praised or denounced as realistic vehicles of modern problems and ideas.

For convenience his plays may be divided into three categories: romantic drama, from his first play, *Catiline,* in 1850, to *Emperor and Galilean* in 1873; realistic drama, from *The Pillars of Society* in 1877 to *Hedda Gabler* in 1890; and symbolist drama, from *The Lady from the Sea* in 1888 to his last work, *When We Dead Awaken,* in 1899. He was as much an artist in one phase as he was in another, but it was the Ibsen of the middle period who was, and still is, singled out as the dramatist important, for better or worse, to society and the theatre. Of the plays in this segment of his career, moreover, there were several—*Pillars of Society, A Doll's House, Ghosts,* and *An Enemy of the People*—that presented social problems of importance to their times and did so in an unorthodox manner that could not be ignored. Ibsen became a hero to progressives and Antichrist to the conservatives. He kept his own counsel more often than either side realized, but this did not matter to his supporters and enemies. He became the central figure of the modern drama because he incorporated modern tensions. *Peer Gynt,* a play that belongs essentially to the romantic theatre, is his greatest work. But it is *Ghosts* that made Ibsen the most influential dramatist of the modern theatre.

Born and reared in the town of Skien in southeastern Norway, Ibsen was to experience the narrowness of provincial society from the moment his wealthy merchant family lost its fortune when he was eight years old. Poverty brought social ostracism in its wake, and the lad, who had to be sent to a poor people's school where he received an inferior education, became ingrown and embittered. Nor did he find much sympathy in his family—in later life he maintained virtually no connection with its members except for one sister, Hedwig. His father was always absorbed in his own troubles, and his mother's religious dogmatism created a gulf which her son was disinclined to bridge.

Ibsen began to reveal a talent for painting, dreamed of going to Dresden or Rome to study art, and took some instruction from a local landscape painter. Since art was no career for a poor boy, he fixed his eyes on medicine, but lacking both the means and the educational prerequisites, he became apprenticed in 1844 to a pharmacist in Grimstad, a small town in the south, a day's travel by steamer from Skien. He was fifteen, thin and undersized, when he left his parents, and he returned to Skien for a visit only once in his life, six years later.

A community lacking cultural activities, with only one teacher for over a hundred children, Grimstad was no improvement upon Skien. For three years Ibsen lived alone with his dreams, growing into the taciturn and dour individual he remained even in the days when he was feted by royalty and pursued by admirers of both sexes. But Grimstad was on the sea and on its shores Ibsen fed poetry into his soul, besides, the town had a little lending library which enabled him to immerse himself in the Danish comedies of Holberg and the romantic literature of Goethe, Schiller, and Heine. He grew a huge black seaman's beard and began to write verse. In his fourth year in Grimstad he found a congenial friend in a young customs inspector, Christopher Due, who in turn introduced him to a law student, Schulerud. They soon formed a little circle of radicals and called for a Scandinavian union against Prussian expansionism, then threatening to wrest the province of Schleswig-Holstein from Denmark. Ibsen's contribution to the cause consisted of impassioned tirades and the poem "Awake, Ye Scandinavians" (1849). Less innocent were his pranks on Grimstad citizens, his drinking and card parties, and his consorting with a servant girl whose illegitimate child he had to support for fourteen years. It was in Grimstad, moreover, that he began to think of a literary career; he was encouraged by Due, who had his nature poem "In Autumn" published in the *Christiania Post.*

Revolution was in the air in 1848 and the failure of the uprisings that broke out at the time in Germany and Hungary strengthened his conviction that he was called upon to express the momentous struggles of the day. "Deeper I must thrust and lower, Till I hear the ring of ore," he wrote in a poem entitled "The Miner." And taking his cue from his reading in Cicero and Sallust, he wrote his first verse drama, *Catiline,* under the pen name of Brynjolf Bjarme. It was a historical play in the romantic vein that glorified the Roman traitor as an enemy of convention and a man who "burns in freedom's holy zeal." His law-student friend Schulerud took it to Christiania, but was unable to place it with either a theatre or a publisher; he finally printed it at his own expense as a token of his faith in Ibsen, who was then in despair over an unsuccessful love affair. Confident of his friend's future, Schulerud also encouraged him to leave Grimstad and enroll at the University of Christiania.

To prepare for the entrance examinations he entered a "student factory," where he met other young men with literary ambitions, among them Björnstjerne Björnson, who became Norway's leading man of letters while Ibsen still lived in obscurity. Unable to matriculate at the University, however, he gave up his ambition to study medicine, and enrolled only for special lectures given by a prominent poet. He joined a short-lived liberal weekly, to which he contributed sarcastic articles and caricatures. He signed political protests and joined a secret revolutionary society, whose leaders were arrested within the year and sentenced to long prison terms. Ibsen was shocked by this turn of events and, never possessing much physical courage, thereafter refrained scrupulously from political activities. He finished a romantic medieval play, *The Warrior's Barrow,* and saw it performed three times in Christiania in September and October 1850. Attracting attention with a patriotic verse prologue written for the opening of a national theatre in Bergen, the young playwright suddenly found himself launched upon a career that was to make him world famous.

Invited to serve as theatre poet and stage manager at the Bergen theatre by its founder and director, the famous Norwegian violinist and national hero Ole Bull, Ibsen left Christiania in the fall of 1851. He spent six years at Bergen, learning more about the theatre from his experience there than he could teach the more or less inexperienced actors whom he timidly directed. Fortunately, too, the trustees of the theatre subsidized him to study the stage in Copenhagen and Dresden the next year, on the condition that he would obligate himself to stage-manage in Bergen for a period of five years. He returned from his travels a well-informed young man and brought with him the first of the plays he wrote for the National Theatre, a fairy play, *St. John's Night,* inspired by a continental production of *A Midsummer Night's Dream.* Henceforth, his work as stage manager was notable for efficiency, as he prepared each scene for the stage in "production books" with illustrations of the background and notations for the stage movement. As he put into production 145 plays by Holberg, Scribe, Shakespeare, and others, assigning the roles to the actors and supervising their rehearsals, he acquired a practical knowledge possessed by few important playwrights since Molière. As his contract also required him to write one play a year for performance on the anniversary of the theatre, he had, in addition, an unusual incentive for playwriting. The national idealism of his historical play *Lady Inger of Ostrat* won favor in 1855, and the piece he wrote for the season of 1856, *The Feast at Solhoug,* a lyrical drama based on medieval Norwegian balladry, proved successful not only in Bergen but subsequently in Christiania. In that same happy year he met and proposed to Susannah Thoresen, daughter of the dean of a church in Bergen, who was to prove a staunch companion during the rest of his life. The young woman became the model for the *femme fatale* of his next drama, *The Vikings of Helgeland,* produced in Christiania in 1857 and considered the outstanding Norwegian play of its time.

During that summer, Ibsen became director of the Norwegian Theatre in Christiania, and in this capacity he spent his next five years until the theatre went bankrupt in 1862. In Christiania, Ibsen married his fiancée (1858), and became the father of a son, Sigurd. Throwing himself wholeheartedly into the world of the large city, he founded with Björnson a Norwegian society for the promotion of national culture, joined an iconoclastic literary circle that called itself "The Hollanders," and participated in its alcoholic and intellectual revelries, neglecting his stage duties and his writing. He did not publish another play till 1862, when *Love's Comedy* appeared. Regarded as scandalous, it proved a fiasco, although this verse satire on conventional love and marriage later came to be considered the first important step in Ibsen's development as a realist and social critic. On top of this fiasco came the bankruptcy of the Norwegian Theatre, and Ibsen found himself in desperate straits. He became shabby and moody, took to drink, and was often found lying in the gutter late at night.

Fortunately his spirits rallied and, fired by his dream of a Scandinavian union against Prussia, he composed a historical drama, *The Pretenders,* in two months of excited writing during 1863. The production at the Christiania Theatre was successful, and this profound drama won him a government stipend of four hundred dollars for travel. He began to envision himself once more as his nation's bard and conscience, publishing a fiery poem in favor of aid to Denmark; but the failure of Norway to rise to his heroic demands, and the defeat of the Danes by Prussia depressed him when he left the country in the spring of 1864. He remained a voluntary exile from Norway for twenty-seven years.

Brooding in Rome on the cautious Philistinism of his countrymen, and stirred by the liberation movement in Italy under Garibaldi, Ibsen wrote his ringing verse drama *Brand,* whose clerical hero rejects all compromise and tries to lead his flock to the heights regardless of consequences. The entire Scandinavian world, which could hardly have missed the implications of this dramatic epic, was excited when *Brand* was published in 1866. Its author was voted a lifelong pension by the Norwegian parliament, and the demand for the book was so great that it had to be republished numerous times. Relieved of financial pressure, Ibsen wrote a reverse treatment of the theme of heroism in *Peer Gynt,* whose hero never commits himself to anything and is deficient in integrity. In *Peer Gynt,* published in 1867 with tremendous success, Ibsen produced an amalgam of humor and pathos, folklore and fantasy. The careless hero of the play became the incarnation of the spinelessness and opportunism that Ibsen deplored in his country, and, by extension, the play became the classic indictment of the antiheroic modern man. For a romantic drama it was an unusually devastating social exposé, and it remains a modern masterpiece. For a satire, however, it was a singularly imaginative and poetic drama, and it towers above the topical plays of the modern theatre engendered largely by Ibsen's own later social dramas. With this work, moreover, he brought the long first period of his career to its peak. After 1867, he wrote only two more verse plays, the uneven philosophical double-drama *Emperor and Galilean* (1873), which called for a fusion of Christian and pagan ideals, and *When We Dead Awaken* (1899), a feeble last effort before illness incapacitated him for the rest of his life.

After *Peer Gynt,* Ibsen was to establish a second claim to fame, this time as a realist rather than as a dramatic poet whose ideas were modern but whose artistic ties were with the older theatre of romanticism. In 1869 came his prose satire on political opportunism or pseudo liberalism, *The League of Youth,* and its reception indicated that Ibsen had started on a difficult new road. The riots that greeted the play in Norway were dress rehearsals for the fury that was to be unleashed by Ibsen's later social problem plays. *The Pillars of Society* (1877), an attack on the unscrupulous practices of shipbuilders and on the shaky foundations of respectability in general, was the exception. Five theatres played it simultaneously in Berlin early in 1878, and it was with this play that Ibsen became the most popular modern dramatist in Germany. The years 1876 to 1878 were, indeed, roseate for Ibsen; in 1876 *Peer Gynt,* with incidental music by the young Edvard Grieg, enjoyed an unprecedented run in Christiania, and in 1877 the University of Upsala awarded Ibsen an honorary doctor's degree, so that he proudly could list himself henceforth as "Doctor" Henrik Ibsen. And it is just as well that he collected his harvest of reputation and royalties at that time. Two years later, in 1879, his name was anathema to conservatives as the author of *A Doll's House;* and four years later, when he published *Ghosts,* he was pilloried as the perpetrator of the greatest scandal of modern times.

A Doll's House was the fruit of reflection on woman's dependent status in society and a response to the growing clamor for "women's rights," a subject to which Ibsen had been introduced ten years earlier by Georg Brandes' translation of John Stuart Mill's treatise *The Subjection of Women.* The production of *A Doll's House* in Christiania drew a storm of protest against his heroine Nora's leaving her husband, and other managements refused to produce the play at all until Ibsen obliged them by composing an alternate ending in which Nora stayed home for the sake of her children. (Ibsen, incidentally, left an unfinished play, hitherto unpublished, which traces Nora's career after she left her "doll's house.") To the opposition, it seemed as if Ibsen had taken an ax not merely to the "doll's house" Nora abandoned in search of self-realization but to the foundations of the church and state. Nevertheless, Ibsen won a victory for himself and for realism in the theatre. The Christiania playhouse gave twenty-five performances of the work in the winter of 1879–1880 and it was triumphantly staged, without the alternate ending, at Munich in March 1880.

Ghosts (1881) was a logical sequel to *A Doll's House.* In the earlier play a wife had left her home after discovering that she was the useless property of her husband and had been reared in ignorance of the world outside her household. And for this Nora had been roundly denounced, especially by clergymen, as having behaved "unnaturally." 12

Ghosts, Ibsen reversed the situation. In heeding the clergyman, Pastor Manders, and not leaving her husband, Mrs. Alving had been guilty of an act far more "unnatural" than anything that could have been charged against Nora. Irony could go no further than Mrs. Alving's reward for obeying conventional precepts. The wages of "virtue" here are paresis for the son and desperation for the mother. It is not difficult to understand why the play should have outraged the circumspect, for whom the mere mention of Oswald's "social disease" on the stage would have been sufficient provocation.

In the perspective of time, *Ghosts* is important for reasons other than the scandal it caused. Ibsen was under the influence of Zola when he wrote the play. By incorporating environment and heredity as decisive factors in his drama, and by admitting the scientific knowledge of his day into the theatre, Ibsen gave naturalism its most controversial work. No other stage piece disseminated the naturalists' program so widely or so arrestingly. Ibsen proved himself a greater craftsman than any of the confirmed modernists. "Natural" dramaturgy was as much a part of the naturalist program as the candid presentation of life, no matter how sordid the details. But no one else except Henry Becque (whose exemplary drama *The Vultures* was still unproduced in 1881) was as yet capable of dispensing entirely with artificial dialogue, suspensive intrigue, and theatrical trickery.

Ibsen went so far toward abolishing "plot" that he eliminated all events antecedent to the critical situation. He dramatized only the harvest of Mrs. Alving's conformity to the conventional code. The past is shown dramatically in those parts of the play in which Mrs. Alving reacts to drastic developments and exposes her situation to the pastor who sent her back to a dissipated husband. Ibsen's procedure was, in fact, radical even for the naturalists who congregated in Antoine's theatre nine years later. When, at Zola's suggestion, Antoine produced the play at the Théâtre Libre on May 30, 1890, the playwright Henry Céard complained that it was too obscure "for our Latin brains." He suggested using a prologue in which Oswald's father would be surprised by the young Mrs. Alving in the act of making love to Regina's mother. After this, "a French public would enter into the significance of the play perfectly."

That was not, of course, the "significance" that Ibsen strove for in *Ghosts,* any more than he was particularly concerned with venereal disease or with the question of mercy killing. (When asked whether Mrs. Alving administered the lethal pills to her imbecile son after the final curtain, Ibsen invariably replied that he did not know.) As a work of art, indeed, Ibsen's drama still eludes the superficial reader and stage director. *Ghosts* became famous as a model naturalistic document and social-problem play, but it is both less and more than that. As a "problem play" about heredity and disease, it has been outdated for many decades and, for all its realism, it is not a mere slice-of-life exercise, since Ibsen contrived the action to enforce his argument. His skill is so great that everything seems entirely natural in the play, and yet it consists of coincidences like the fire in the orphan asylum, the revelation that Regina is Oswald's illegitimate half sister, and the discovery of Oswald's ailment. Blow after blow is struck by the hammer of dramaturgy in order to destroy the rotten edifice that convention had reared. Behind the mask of Ibsen's prosaic dialogue and pretence of ordinariness hides the face of an ironist and poet.

The ironist, who mocks Pastor Manders on every occasion, becomes as mordant as Jonathan Swift in piling up the sequence of events. Mrs. Alving does not want to touch the money left by her husband, therefore she erects an orphan asylum in his name—a curious monument to a man who was a profligate all his life and whose illegitimate child is a servant girl in Mrs. Alving's household. The dedication ceremony is to be performed by the same Pastor Manders who has congratulated himself for many years on having saved Mrs. Alving's marriage! The institution must not be insured against fire, according to Manders, because it is under the protection of God. And it burns down! The late Alving's legacy goes up in smoke. But he has left another legacy—in the diseased bloodstream of his son. Mrs. Alving erected a last façade of respectability for her unhappy marriage, and it vanishes in a few minutes, whereas her "reward" for submission to convention is a grief that will endure to the end of her days. The traditionalists who were outraged by *Ghosts* had more reason than we are apt to concede today. If they complained that the play was cynical, they were actually more penetrative than latter-day innocents for whom it is a very simple tract.

The poet in Ibsen transmutes the simple idea of heredity into the Nemesis or Fate of Greek tragedy, and a bleak background and sultry weather brood over the proceedings; the atmosphere is that of the "haunted house" theme of romanticism. Ibsen here recalls the Aeschylus of the Oresteian trilogy and the Sophocles of *Oedipus Rex,* as well as the Poe of *The Fall of the House of Usher.* And the poetry has a dry, modern quality, for the haunted house is a bourgeois home in provincial Norway and the classic Fury or "domestic Ate" is now a streptococcus in the circulatory system. This is "bourgeois tragedy," antiheroic drama. The poet, moreover, transcends the simple social reformer with his grisly symbolism of the orphan asylum as the vain façade of respectability and of Oswald's ailment as the hidden reality. The very title of the play is symbolic and its story carries us beyond the manifest drama of hereditary disease. Mrs. Alving is haunted by the "ghosts" of the past—not only by Regina, the child of Alving's indiscretions, and by the unfortunate

Oswald, but by all the conformities she finally recognizes as unfortunate and evil. One of these ghosts of convention even goes as far back as her girlhood, for it was her early training that made her an inadequate wife and started Alving on his extramarital adventures. Even if Mrs. Alving had left her husband permanently after the first year of marriage there would have been ghosts of miseducation and false values to haunt her. The dark tones of the play, in sum, are overtones never present in humdrum topical plays that offer us a simple demonstration of a problem and one specific remedy.

Curiously enough, the first production of *Ghosts* was given in America, where not a single earlier play of Ibsen's had yet been produced. It was performed in 1882 by a company playing in Danish and Norwegian in Chicago, Minneapolis, and other cities of the Midwest. (The first American production of an Ibsen play in English was a bowdlerized version of *A Doll's House* under the title of *Thora.*) The European *première* of *Ghosts* was in Helsingborg, Sweden, in 1883. That year, too, a provincial company gave performances in Denmark, and another production materialized in the Dramatic Theatre in Stockholm.

The violent attacks on *Ghosts* from all quarters in Norway, its rejection by Norwegian theatres, and the refusal of booksellers to stock copies of the published play drew eloquent rejoinders from Björnson and the great Danish critic Georg Brandes. In April 1886, an enthusiastic Viennese playwright, Felix Philippi, gave the first German production of the play in the Bavarian city of Augsburg, northwest of Munich. It was a private performance, since *Ghosts*

was then still banned in Germany as a revolutionary play "with destructive tendencies." Next, the Duke of Saxe-Meiningen, the pioneer of stage realism in Europe, gave the play in his ducal theatre at Meiningen in December 1886 and signalized the occasion by knighting the author. Elsewhere the play became a rallying point for such vigorous modernists as the young Bernard Shaw and Emile Zola, and the critic turned director, Otto Brahm, defiantly started the first season of his Berlin progressive theatre, the Freie Bühne, with *Ghosts* on the afternoon of September 29, 1889. Antoine himself played the part of Oswald seven months later in his Théâtre Libre production. Public productions of *Ghosts* were forbidden in England as late as 1891, but J. T. Grein gave one private performance for the subscribers of his Independent Theatre in London on March 13, 1891.

BIBLIOGRAPHY: William Archer, Introductions to *The Collected Works of Henrik Ibsen*, 1906–1912; Eric Bentley, *The Playwright as Thinker* (pp. 92–94, 102–135, 140–144), 1946; Anita Block, *The Changing World in Plays and Theatre* (pp. 22–33), 1939; Barrett H. Clark and George Freedley, *A History of Modern Drama* (pp. 1–20), 1947; John Gassner, *Masters of the Drama* (pp. 354–386), 1945; Edmund Gosse, *Henrik Ibsen* (with essays by Edward Dowden and James Huneker), 1917; James Huneker, *Iconoclasts* (pp. 1–138), 1905; Halvdan Koht, *The Life of Ibsen*, 1931; A. E. Zucker, *Ibsen the Master-Builder*, 1929.

For additional commentary, see pages 40–41.

GHOSTS

By Henrik Ibsen

TRANSLATED FROM THE NORWEGIAN BY WILLIAM ARCHER [1]

CHARACTERS

MRS. HELEN ALVING, *widow of Captain Alving, late Chamberlain to the King*
OSWALD ALVING, *her son, a painter*
PASTOR MANDERS

JACOB ENGSTRAND, *a carpenter*
REGINA ENGSTRAND, *Mrs. Alving's maid*
The action takes place at Mrs. Alving's country house, beside one of the large fjords in Western Norway.

ACT I

A spacious garden-room, with one door to the left, and two doors to the right. In the middle of the room a round table, with chairs about it. On the table lie books, periodicals, and newspapers. In the foreground to the left a window, and by it a small sofa, with a work-table in front of it. In the background, the room is continued into a somewhat narrower conservatory, the walls of which are formed by large panes of glass. In the right-hand wall of the conservatory is a door leading down into the garden. Through the glass wall a gloomy fjord-landscape is faintly visible, veiled by steady rain. Engstrand, the carpenter, who has a club foot, stands by the garden door. His left leg is somewhat bent; he has a clump of wood under the sole of his boot. Regina, with an empty garden syringe in her hand, hinders him from advancing.

REGINA: [*In a low voice*] What do you want? Stop where you are. You're positively dripping.

ENGSTRAND: It's the Lord's own rain, my girl.

REGINA: It's the devil's rain, *I* say.

ENGSTRAND: Lord, how you talk, Regina. [*Limps a step or two forward into the room*] It's just this as I wanted to say—

REGINA: Don't clatter so with that foot of yours, I tell you! The young master's asleep upstairs.

ENGSTRAND: Asleep? In the middle of the day?

REGINA: It's no business of yours.

ENGSTRAND: I was out on the loose last night—

REGINA: I can quite believe that.

ENGSTRAND: Yes, we're weak vessels, we poor mortals, my girl—

REGINA: So it seems.

ENGSTRAND: —and temptations are manifold in this world, you see. But all the same, I was hard at work, God knows, at half-past five this morning.

REGINA: Very well; only be off now. I won't stop here and have *rendezvous* with you.

[1] Entirely revised by William Archer.

ENGSTRAND: What do you say you won't have?

REGINA: I won't have any one find you here; so just you go about your business.

ENGSTRAND: [*Advances a step or two*] Blest if I go before I've had a talk with you. This afternoon I shall have finished my work at the school-house, and then I shall take to-night's boat and be off home to the town.

REGINA: [*Mutters*] Pleasant journey to you!

ENGSTRAND: Thank you, my child. To-morrow the Orphanage is to be opened, and then there'll be fine doings, no doubt, and plenty of intoxicating drink going, you know. And nobody shall say of Jacob Engstrand that he can't keep out of temptation's way.

REGINA: Oh!

ENGSTRAND: You see, there's to be heaps of grand folks here to-morrow. Pastor Manders is expected from town, too.

REGINA: He's coming to-day.

ENGSTRAND: There, you see! And I should be cursedly sorry if he found out anything against me, don't you understand?

REGINA: Oho! is that your game?

ENGSTRAND: Is what my game?

REGINA: [*Looking hard at him*] What are you going to fool Pastor Manders into doing, this time?

ENGSTRAND: Sh! sh! Are you crazy? Do *I* want to fool Pastor Manders? Oh no! Pastor Manders has been far too good a friend to me for that. But I just wanted to say, you know—that I mean to be off home again to-night.

REGINA: The sooner the better, say I.

ENGSTRAND: Yes, but I want you with me, Regina.

REGINA: [*Open-mouthed*] You want me—? What are you talking about?

ENGSTRAND: I want you to come home with me, I say.

REGINA: [*Scornfully*] Never in this world shall you get me home with you.

ENGSTRAND: Oh, we'll see about that.

REGINA: Yes, you may be sure we'll see about it!

15

Me, that have been brought up by a lady like Mrs. Alving! Me, that am treated almost as a daughter here! Is it me you want to go home with you?—to a house like yours? For shame!

ENGSTRAND: What the devil do you mean? Do you set yourself up against your father, you hussy?

REGINA: [*Mutters without looking at him*] You've said often enough I was no concern of yours.

ENGSTRAND: Pooh! Why should you bother about that—

REGINA: Haven't you many a time sworn at me and called me a—? *Fi donc!*

ENGSTRAND: Curse me, now, if ever I used such an ugly word.

REGINA: Oh, I remember very well what word you used.

ENGSTRAND: Well, but that was only when I was a bit on with drink. Temptations are manifold in this world, Regina.

REGINA: Ugh!

ENGSTRAND: And besides, it was when your mother was that aggravating—I had to find something to twit her with, my child. She was always setting up for a fine lady. [*Mimics*] "Let me go, Engstrand; let me be. Remember I was three years in Chamberlain Alving's family at Rosenvold." [*Laughs*] Mercy on us! She could never forget that the Captain was made a Chamberlain while she was in service here.

REGINA: Poor mother! you very soon tormented her into her grave.

ENGSTRAND: [*With a twist of his shoulders*] Oh, of course! I'm to have the blame for everything.

REGINA: [*Turns away; half aloud*] Ugh—! And that leg too!

ENGSTRAND: What do you say, my child?

REGINA: *Pied de mouton.*

ENGSTRAND: Is that English, eh?

REGINA: Yes.

ENGSTRAND: Ay, ay; you've picked up some learning out here; and that may come in useful now, Regina.

REGINA: [*After a short silence*] What do you want with me in town?

ENGSTRAND: Can you ask what a father wants with his only child? A'n't I a lonely, forlorn widower?

REGINA: Oh, don't try on any nonsense like that with me! Why do you want me?

ENGSTRAND: Well, let me tell you, I've been thinking of setting up in a new line of business.

REGINA: [*Contemptuously*] You've tried that often enough, and much good you've done with it.

ENGSTRAND: Yes, but this time you shall see, Regina! Devil take me—

REGINA: [*Stamps*] Stop your swearing!

ENGSTRAND: Hush, hush; you're right enough there, my girl. What I wanted to say was just this—I've laid by a very tidy pile from this Orphanage job.

REGINA: Have you? That's a good thing for you.

ENGSTRAND: What can a man spend his ha'pence on here in this country hole?

REGINA: Well, what then?

ENGSTRAND: Why, you see, I thought of putting the money into some paying speculation. I thought of a sort of a sailor's tavern—

REGINA: Pah!

ENGSTRAND: A regular high-class affair, of course; not any sort of pig-sty for common sailors. No! damn it! it would be for captains and mates, and—and—regular swells, you know.

REGINA: And I was to—?

ENGSTRAND: You were to help, to be sure. Only for the look of the thing, you understand. Devil a bit of hard work shall you have, my girl. You shall do exactly what you like.

REGINA: Oh, indeed!

ENGSTRAND: But there must be a petticoat in the house; that's as clear as daylight. For I want to have it a bit lively-like in the evenings, with singing and dancing, and so on. You must remember they're weary wanderers on the ocean of life. [*Nearer*] Now don't be a fool and stand in your own light, Regina. What's to become of you out here? Your mistress has given you a lot of learning; but what good is that to you? You're to look after the children at the new Orphanage, I hear. Is that the sort of thing for you, eh? Are you so dead set on wearing your life out for a pack of dirty brats?

REGINA: No; if things go as I want them to— Well there's no saying—there's no saying.

ENGSTRAND: What do you mean by "there's no saying"?

REGINA: Never you mind.—How much money have you saved?

ENGSTRAND: What with one thing and another, a matter of seven or eight hundred crowns.

REGINA: That's not so bad.

ENGSTRAND: It's enough to make a start with, my girl.

REGINA: Aren't you thinking of giving me any?

ENGSTRAND: No, I'm blest if I am!

REGINA: Not even of sending me a scrap of stuff for a new dress?

ENGSTRAND: Come to town with me, my lass, and you'll soon get dresses enough.

REGINA: Pooh! I can do that on my own account, if I want to.

ENGSTRAND: No, a father's guiding hand is what you want, Regina. Now, I've got my eye on a capital house in Little Harbour Street. They don't want much ready-money; and it could be a sort of a Sailors' Home, you know.

REGINA: But I will not live with you! I have nothing whatever to do with you. Be off!

ENGSTRAND: You wouldn't stop long with me, my girl. No such luck! If you knew how to play your cards, such a fine figure of a girl as you've grown in the last year or two—

REGINA: Well?

ENGSTRAND: You'd soon get hold of some mate—or maybe even a captain—

REGINA: I won't marry any one of that sort. Sailors have no *savoir vivre*.

ENGSTRAND: What's that they haven't got?

REGINA: I know what sailors are, I tell you. They're not the sort of people to marry.

ENGSTRAND: Then never mind about marrying them. You can make it pay all the same. [*More confidential*] He—the Englishman—the man with the yacht—he came down with three hundred dollars, he did; and she wasn't a bit handsomer than you.

REGINA: [*Making for him*] Out you go!

ENGSTRAND: [*Falling back*] Come, come! You're not going to hit me, I hope.

REGINA: Yes, if you begin talking about mother I shall hit you. Get away with you, I say! [*Drives him back towards the garden door*] And don't slam the doors. Young Mr. Alving—

ENGSTRAND: He's asleep; I know. You're mightily taken up about young Mr. Alving— [*More softly*] Oho! you don't mean to say it's him as—?

REGINA: Be off this minute! You're crazy, I tell you! No, not that way. There comes Pastor Manders. Down the kitchen stairs with you.

ENGSTRAND: [*Towards the right*] Yes, yes, I'm going. But just you talk to him as is coming there. He's the man to tell you what a child owes its father. For I am your father all the same, you know. I can prove it from the church register.

[*He goes out through the second door to the right, which* Regina *has opened, and closes again after him.* Regina *glances hastily at herself in the mirror, dusts herself with her pocket handkerchief, and settles her necktie; then she busies herself with the flowers.* Pastor Manders, *wearing an overcoat, carrying an umbrella, and with a small travelling-bag on a strap over his shoulder, comes through the garden door into the conservatory*]

MANDERS: Good-morning, Miss Engstrand.

REGINA: [*Turning round, surprised and pleased*] No, really! Good-morning, Pastor Manders. Is the steamer in already?

MANDERS: It is just in. [*Enters the sitting-room*] Terrible weather we have been having lately.

REGINA: [*Follows him*] It's such blessed weather for the country, sir.

MANDERS: No doubt; you are quite right. We townspeople give too little thought to that. [*He begins to take off his overcoat*]

REGINA: Oh, mayn't I help you?—There! Why, how wet it is! I'll just hang it up in the hall. And your umbrella, too—I'll open it and let it dry.

[*She goes out with the things through the second door on the right.* Pastor Manders *takes off his travelling-bag and lays it and his hat on a chair. Meanwhile* Regina *comes in again*]

MANDERS: Ah, it's a comfort to get under cover. I hope everything is going on well here?

REGINA: Yes, thank you, sir.

MANDERS: You have your hands full, I suppose, in preparation for to-morrow?

REGINA: Yes, there's plenty to do, of course.

MANDERS: And Mrs. Alving is at home, I trust?

REGINA: Oh dear, yes. She's just upstairs, looking after the young master's chocolate.

MANDERS: Yes, by-the-bye—I heard down at the pier that Oswald had arrived.

REGINA: Yes, he came the day before yesterday. We didn't expect him before to-day.

MANDERS: Quite strong and well, I hope?

REGINA: Yes, thank you, quite; but dreadfully tired with the journey. He has made one rush right through from Paris—the whole way on one train, I believe. He's sleeping a little now, I think; so perhaps we'd better talk a little quietly.

MANDERS: Sh!—as quietly as you please.

REGINA: [*Arranging an arm-chair beside the table*] Now, do sit down, Pastor Manders, and make yourself comfortable. [*He sits down; she places a footstool under his feet*] There! Are you comfortable now, sir?

MANDERS: Thanks, thanks, extremely so. [*Looks at her*] Do you know, Miss Engstrand, I positively believe you have grown since I last saw you.

REGINA: Do you think so, sir? Mrs. Alving says I've filled out too.

MANDERS: Filled out? Well, perhaps a little; just enough. [*Short pause*]

REGINA: Shall I tell Mrs. Alving you are here?

MANDERS: Thanks, thanks, there is no hurry, my dear child.—By-the-bye, Regina, my good girl, tell me: how is your father getting on out here?

REGINA: Oh, thank you, sir, he's getting on well enough.

MANDERS: He called upon me last time he was in town.

REGINA: Did he, indeed? He's always so glad of a chance of talking to you, sir.

MANDERS: And you often look in upon him at his work, I daresay?

REGINA: I? Oh, of course, when I have time, I—

MANDERS: Your father is not a man of strong character, Miss Engstrand. He stands terribly in need of a guiding hand.

REGINA: Oh, yes; I daresay he does.

MANDERS: He requires some one near him whom he cares for, and whose judgment he respects. He frankly admitted as much when he last came to see me.

REGINA: Yes, he mentioned something of the sort to me. But I don't know whether Mrs. Alving can spare me; especially now that we've got the new Orphanage to attend to. And then I should be so sorry to leave Mrs. Alving; she has always been so kind to me.

MANDERS: But a daughter's duty, my good girl— Of course, we should first have to get your mistress's consent.

REGINA: But I don't know whether it would be

quite proper for me, at my age, to keep house for a single man.

MANDERS: What! My dear Miss Engstrand! When the man is your own father!

REGINA: Yes, that may be; but all the same— Now, if it were in a thoroughly nice house, and with a real gentleman—

MANDERS: Why, my dear Regina—

REGINA: —one I could love and respect, and be a daughter to—

MANDERS: Yes, but my dear, good child—

REGINA: Then I should be glad to go to town. It's very lonely out here; you know yourself, sir, what it is to be alone in the world. And I can assure you I'm both quick and willing. Don't you know of any such place for me, sir?

MANDERS: I? No, certainly not.

REGINA: But, dear, dear sir, do remember me if—

MANDERS: [*Rising*] Yes, yes, certainly, Miss Engstrand.

REGINA: For if I—

MANDERS: Will you be so good as to tell your mistress I am here?

REGINA: I will, at once, sir. [*She goes out to the left*]

MANDERS: [*Paces the room two or three times, stands a moment in the background with his hands behind his back, and looks out over the garden. Then he returns to the table, takes up a book, and looks at the title-page; starts, and looks at several books*] Ha—indeed!

[Mrs. Alving *enters by the door on the left; she is followed by* Regina, *who immediately goes out by the first door on the right*]

MRS. ALVING: [*Holds out her hand*] Welcome, my dear Pastor.

MANDERS: How do you do, Mrs. Alving? Here I am as I promised.

MRS. ALVING: Always punctual to the minute.

MANDERS: You may believe it was not so easy for me to get away. With all the Boards and Committees I belong to—

MRS. ALVING: That makes it all the kinder of you to come so early. Now we can get through our business before dinner. But where is your portmanteau?

MANDERS: [*Quickly*] I left it down at the inn. I shall sleep there to-night.

MRS. ALVING: [*Suppressing a smile*] Are you really not to be persuaded, even now, to pass the night under my roof?

MANDERS: No, no, Mrs. Alving; many thanks. I shall stay at the inn, as usual. It is so conveniently near the landing-stage.

MRS. ALVING: Well, you must have your own way. But I really should have thought we two old people—

MANDERS: Now you are making fun of me. Ah, you're naturally in great spirits to-day—what with to-morrow's festival and Oswald's return.

MRS. ALVING: Yes; you can think what a delight it is to me! It's more than two years since he was

home last. And now he has promised to stay with me all the winter.

MANDERS: Has he really? That is very nice and dutiful of him. For I can well believe that life in Rome and Paris has very different attractions from any we can offer here.

MRS. ALVING: Ah, but here he has his mother, you see. My own darling boy—he hasn't forgotten his old mother!

MANDERS: It would be grievous indeed, if absence and absorption in art and that sort of thing were to blunt his natural feelings.

MRS. ALVING: Yes, you may well say so. But there's nothing of that sort to fear with him. I'm quite curious to see whether you know him again. He'll be down presently; he's upstairs just now, resting a little on the sofa. But do sit down, my dear Pastor.

MANDERS: Thank you. Are you quite at liberty—?

MRS. ALVING: Certainly. [*She sits by the table*]

MANDERS: Very well. Then let me show you— [*He goes to the chair where his travelling-bag lies, takes out a packet of papers, sits down on the opposite side of the table, and tries to find a clear space for the papers*] Now, to begin with, here is— [*Breaking off*] Tell me, Mrs. Alving, how do these books come to be here?

MRS. ALVING: These books? They are books I am reading.

MANDERS: Do you read this sort of literature?

MRS. ALVING: Certainly I do.

MANDERS: Do you feel better or happier for such reading?

MRS. ALVING: I feel, so to speak, more secure.

MANDERS: That is strange. How do you mean?

MRS. ALVING: Well, I seem to find explanation and confirmation of all sorts of things I myself have been thinking. For that is the wonderful part of it, Pastor Manders—there is really nothing new in these books, nothing but what most people think and believe. Only most people either don't formulate it to themselves, or else keep quiet about it.

MANDERS: Great heavens! Do you really believe that most people—?

MRS. ALVING: I do, indeed.

MANDERS: But surely not in this country? Not here among us?

MRS. ALVING: Yes, certainly; here as elsewhere.

MANDERS: Well, I really must say—!

MRS. ALVING: For the rest, what do you object to it these books?

MANDERS: Object to in them? You surely do not suppose that I have nothing better to do than to study such publications as these?

MRS. ALVING: That is to say, you know nothing of what you are condemning?

MANDERS: I have read enough about these writings to disapprove of them.

MRS. ALVING: Yes; but your own judgment—

MANDERS: My dear Mrs. Alving, there are many occasions in life when one must rely upon others.

Things are so ordered in this world; and it is well that they are. Otherwise, what would become of society?

MRS. ALVING: Well, well, I daresay you're right there.

MANDERS: Besides, I of course do not deny that there may be much that is attractive in such books. Nor can I blame you for wishing to keep up with the intellectual movements that are said to be going on in the great world—where you have let your son pass so much of his life. But—

MRS. ALVING: But?

MANDERS: [Lowering his voice] But one should not talk about it, Mrs. Alving. One is certainly not bound to account to everybody for what one reads and thinks within one's own four walls.

MRS. ALVING: Of course not; I quite agree with you.

MANDERS: Only think, now, how you are bound to consider the interests of this Orphanage, which you decided on founding at a time when—if I understand you rightly—you thought very differently on spiritual matters.

MRS. ALVING: Oh, yes; I quite admit that. But it was about the Orphanage—

MANDERS: It was about the Orphanage we were to speak; yes. All I say is: prudence, my dear lady! And now let us get to business. [Opens the packet, and takes out a number of papers] Do you see these?

MRS. ALVING: The documents?

MANDERS: All—and in perfect order. I can tell you it was hard work to get them in time. I had to put on strong pressure. The authorities are almost morbidly scrupulous when there is any decisive step to be taken. But here they are at last. [Looks through the bundle] See! here is the formal deed of gift of the parcel of ground known as Solvik in the Manor of Rosenvold, with all the newly constructed buildings, schoolrooms, master's house, and chapel. And here is the legal fiat for the endowment and for the By-laws of the Institution. Will you look at them? [Reads] "By-laws for the Children's Home to be known as 'Captain Alving's Foundation.' "

MRS. ALVING: [Looks long at the paper] So there it is.

MANDERS: I have chosen the designation "Captain" rather than "Chamberlain." "Captain" looks less pretentious.

MRS. ALVING: Oh, yes; just as you think best.

MANDERS: And here you have the Bank Account of the capital lying at interest to cover the current expenses of the Orphanage.

MRS. ALVING: Thank you; but please keep it—it will be more convenient.

MANDERS: With pleasure. I think we will leave the money in the Bank for the present. The interest is certainly not what we could wish—four per cent. and six months' notice of withdrawal. If a good mortgage could be found later on—of course it must

be a first mortgage and an unimpeachable security—then we could consider the matter.

MRS. ALVING: Certainly, my dear Pastor Manders. You are the best judge in these things.

MANDERS: I will keep my eyes open at any rate.—But now there is one thing more which I have several times been intending to ask you.

MRS. ALVING: And what is that?

MANDERS: Shall the Orphanage buildings be insured or not?

MRS. ALVING: Of course they must be insured.

MANDERS: Well, wait a moment, Mrs. Alving. Let us look into the matter a little more closely.

MRS. ALVING: I have everything insured; buildings and movables and stock and crops.

MANDERS: Of course you have—on your own estate. And so have I—of course. But here, you see, it is quite another matter. The Orphanage is to be consecrated, as it were, to a higher purpose.

MRS. ALVING: Yes, but that's no reason—

MANDERS: For my own part, I should certainly not see the smallest impropriety in guarding against all contingencies—

MRS. ALVING: No, I should think not.

MANDERS: But what is the general feeling in the neighbourhood? You, of course, know better than I.

MRS. ALVING: Well—the general feeling—

MANDERS: Is there any considerable number of people—really responsible people—who might be scandalised?

MRS. ALVING: What do you mean by "really responsible people"?

MANDERS: Well, I mean people in such independent and influential positions that one cannot help attaching some weight to their opinions.

MRS. ALVING: There are several people of that sort here, who would very likely be shocked if—

MANDERS: There, you see! In town we have many such people. Think of all my colleagues' adherents! People would be only too ready to interpret our action as a sign that neither you nor I had the right faith in a Higher Providence.

MRS. ALVING: But for your own part, my dear Pastor, you can at least tell yourself that—

MANDERS: Yes, I know—I know; my conscience would be quite easy, that is true enough. But nevertheless we should not escape grave misinterpretation; and that might very likely react unfavourably upon the Orphanage.

MRS. ALVING: Well, in that case—

MANDERS: Nor can I entirely lose sight of the difficult—I may even say painful—position in which I might perhaps be placed. In the leading circles of the town, people take a lively interest in this Orphanage. It is, of course, founded partly for the benefit of the town, as well; and it is to be hoped it will, to a considerable extent, result in lightening our Poor Rates. Now, as I have been your adviser, and have had the business arrangements in my hands,

I cannot but fear that I may have to bear the brunt of fanaticism—

MRS. ALVING: Oh, you mustn't run the risk of that.

MANDERS: To say nothing of the attacks that would assuredly be made upon me in certain papers and periodicals, which—

MRS. ALVING: Enough, my dear Pastor Manders. That consideration is quite decisive.

MANDERS: Then you do not wish the Orphanage to be insured?

MRS. ALVING: No. We will let it alone.

MANDERS: [Leaning back in his chair] But if, now, a disaster were to happen? One can never tell— Should you be able to make good the damage?

MRS. ALVING: No; I tell you plainly I should do nothing of the kind.

MANDERS: Then I must tell you, Mrs. Alving—we are taking no small responsibility upon ourselves.

MRS. ALVING: Do you think we can do otherwise?

MANDERS: No, that is just the point; we really cannot do otherwise. We ought not to expose ourselves to misinterpretation; and we have no right whatever to give offence to the weaker brethren.

MRS. ALVING: You, as a clergyman, certainly should not.

MANDERS: I really think, too, we may trust that such an institution has fortune on its side; in fact, that it stands under a special providence.

MRS. ALVING: Let us hope so, Pastor Manders.

MANDERS: Then we will let it take its chance?

MRS. ALVING: Yes, certainly.

MANDERS: Very well. So be it. [Makes a note] Then—no insurance.

MRS. ALVING: It's odd that you should just happen to mention the matter to-day—

MANDERS: I have often thought of asking you about it—

MRS. ALVING: —for we very nearly had a fire down there yesterday.

MANDERS: You don't say so!

MRS. ALVING: Oh, it was a trifling matter. A heap of shavings had caught fire in the carpenter's workshop.

MANDERS: Where Engstrand works?

MRS. ALVING: Yes. They say he's often very careless with matches.

MANDERS: He has so much on his mind, that man —so many things to fight against. Thank God, he is now striving to lead a decent life, I hear.

MRS. ALVING: Indeed! Who says so?

MANDERS: He himself assures me of it. And he is certainly a capital workman.

MRS. ALVING: Oh, yes so long as he's sober—

MANDERS: Ah, that melancholy weakness! But he is often driven to it by his injured leg, he says. Last time he was in town I was really touched by him. He came and thanked me so warmly for having got him work here, so that he might be near Regina.

MRS. ALVING: He doesn't see much of her.

MANDERS: Oh, yes; he has a talk with her every day. He told me so himself.

MRS. ALVING: Well, it may be so.

MANDERS: He feels so acutely that he needs some one to keep a firm hold on him when temptation comes. That is what I cannot help liking about Jacob Engstrand: he comes to you so helplessly, accusing himself and confessing his own weakness. The last time he was talking to me— Believe me, Mrs. Alving, supposing it were a real necessity for him to have Regina home again—

MRS. ALVING: [Rising hastily] Regina!

MANDERS: —you must not set yourself against it.

MRS. ALVING: Indeed I shall set myself against it. And besides—Regina is to have a position in the Orphanage.

MANDERS: But, after all, remember he is her father—

MRS. ALVING: Oh, I know very well what sort of a father he has been to her. No! She shall never go to him with my goodwill.

MANDERS: [Rising] My dear lady, don't take the matter so warmly. You sadly misjudge poor Engstrand. You seem to be quite terrified—

MRS. ALVING: [More quietly] It makes no difference. I have taken Regina into my house, and there she shall stay. [Listens] Hush, my dear Mr. Manders; say no more about it. [Her face lights up with gladness] Listen! there is Oswald coming downstairs. Now we'll think of no one but him.

[Oswald Alving, in a light overcoat, hat in hand, and smoking a large meerschaum, enters by the door on the left; he stops in the doorway]

OSWALD: Oh, I beg your pardon; I thought you were in the study. [Comes forward] Good-morning, Pastor Manders.

MANDERS: [Staring] Ah—! How strange—!

MRS. ALVING: Well now, what do you think of him, Mr. Manders?

MANDERS: I—I—can it really be—?

OSWALD: Yes, it's really the Prodigal Son, sir.

MANDERS: [Protesting] My dear young friend—

OSWALD: Well, then, the Lost Sheep Found.

MRS. ALVING: Oswald is thinking of the time when you were so much opposed to his becoming a painter.

MANDERS: To our human eyes many a step seems dubious, which afterwards proves— [Wrings his hand] But first of all, welcome, welcome home! Do not think, my dear Oswald—I suppose I may call you by your Christian name?

OSWALD: What else should you call me?

MANDERS: Very good. What I wanted to say was this, my dear Oswald—you must not think that I utterly condemn the artist's calling. I have no doubt there are many who can keep their inner self unharmed in that profession, as in any other.

OSWALD: Let us hope so.

MRS. ALVING: [Beaming with delight] I know one who has kept both his inner and his outer self unharmed. Just look at him, Mr. Manders.

OSWALD: [*Moves restlessly about the room*] Yes, yes, my dear mother; let's say no more about it.

MANDERS: Why, certainly—that is undeniable. And you have begun to make a name for yourself already. The newspapers have often spoken of you, most favourably. Just lately, by-the-bye, I fancy I haven't seen your name quite so often.

OSWALD: [*Up in the conservatory*] I haven't been able to paint so much lately.

MRS. ALVING: Even a painter needs a little rest now and then.

MANDERS: No doubt, no doubt. And meanwhile he can be preparing himself and mustering his forces for some great work.

OSWALD: Yes.—Mother, will dinner soon be ready?

MRS. ALVING: In less than half an hour. He has a capital appetite, thank God.

MANDERS: And a taste for tobacco, too.

OSWALD: I found my father's pipe in my room—

MANDERS: Aha—then that accounts for it!

MRS. ALVING: For what?

MANDERS: When Oswald appeared there, in the doorway, with the pipe in his mouth, I could have sworn I saw his father, large as life.

OSWALD: No, really?

MRS. ALVING: Oh, how can you say so? Oswald takes after me.

MANDERS: Yes, but there is an expression about the corners of the mouth—something about the lips —that reminds one exactly of Alving: at any rate, now that he is smoking.

MRS. ALVING: Not in the least. Oswald has rather a clerical curve about his mouth, I think.

MANDERS: Yes, yes; some of my colleagues have much the same expression.

MRS. ALVING: But put your pipe away, my dear boy; I won't have smoking in here.

OSWALD: [*Does so*] By all means. I only wanted to try it; for I once smoked it when I was a child.

MRS. ALVING: You?

OSWALD: Yes. I was quite small at the time. I recollect I came up to father's room one evening when he was in great spirits.

MRS. ALVING: Oh, you can't recollect anything of those times.

OSWALD: Yes, I recollect it distinctly. He took me on his knee, and gave me the pipe. "Smoke, boy," he said; "smoke away, boy!" And I smoked as hard as I could, until I felt I was growing quite pale, and the perspiration stood in great drops on my forehead. Then he burst out laughing heartily—

MANDERS: That was most extraordinary.

MRS. ALVING: My dear friend, it's only something Oswald has dreamt.

OSWALD: No, mother, I assure you I didn't dream it. For—don't you remember this?—you came and carried me out into the nursery. Then I was sick, and I saw that you were crying.—Did father often play such practical jokes?

MANDERS: In his youth he overflowed with the joy of life—

OSWALD: And yet he managed to do so much in the world; so much that was good and useful; although he died so early.

MANDERS: Yes, you have inherited the name of an energetic and admirable man, my dear Oswald Alving. No doubt it will be an incentive to you—

OSWALD: It ought to, indeed.

MANDERS: It was good of you to come home for the ceremony in his honour.

OSWALD: I could do no less for my father.

MRS. ALVING: And I am to keep him so long! That is the best of all.

MANDERS: You are going to pass the winter at home, I hear.

OSWALD: My stay is indefinite, sir.—But, ah! it is good to be at home!

MRS. ALVING: [*Beaming*] Yes, isn't it, dear?

MANDERS: [*Looking sympathetically at him*] You went out into the world early, my dear Oswald.

OSWALD: I did. I sometimes wonder whether it wasn't too early.

MRS. ALVING: Oh, not at all. A healthy lad is all the better for it; especially when he's an only child. He oughtn't to hang on at home with his mother and father, and get spoilt.

MANDERS: That is a very disputable point, Mrs. Alving. A child's proper place is, and must be, the home of his fathers.

OSWALD: There I quite agree with you, Pastor Manders.

MANDERS: Only look at your own son—there is no reason why we should not say it in his presence— what has the consequence been for him? He is six or seven and twenty, and has never had the opportunity of learning what a well-ordered home really is.

OSWALD: I beg your pardon, Pastor; there you're quite mistaken.

MANDERS: Indeed? I thought you had lived almost exclusively in artistic circles.

OSWALD: So I have.

MANDERS: And chiefly among the younger artists?

OSWALD: Yes, certainly.

MANDERS: But I thought few of those young fellows could afford to set up house and support a family.

OSWALD: There are many who cannot afford to marry, sir.

MANDERS: Yes, that is just what I say.

OSWALD: But they may have a home for all that. And several of them have, as a matter of fact; and very pleasant, well-ordered homes they are, too.

[Mrs. Alving *follows with breathless interest; nods, but says nothing*]

MANDERS: But I'm not talking of bachelors' quarters. By a "home" I understand the home of a family, where a man lives with his wife and children.

OSWALD: Yes; or with his children and his children's mother.

MANDERS: [*Starts; clasps his hands*] But, good heavens—

OSWALD: Well?

MANDERS: Lives with—his children's mother!

OSWALD: Yes. Would you have him turn his children's mother out of doors?

MANDERS: Then it is illicit relations you are talking of! Irregular marriages, as people call them!

OSWALD: I have never noticed anything particularly irregular about the life these people lead.

MANDERS: But how is it possible that a—a young man or young woman with any decency of feeling can endure to live in that way?—in the eyes of all the world!

OSWALD: What are they to do? A poor young artist—a poor girl—marriage costs a great deal. What are they to do?

MANDERS: What are they to do? Let me tell you, Mr. Alving, what they ought to do. They ought to exercise self-restraint from the first; that is what they ought to do.

OSWALD: That doctrine will scarcely go down with warm-blooded young people who love each other.

MRS. ALVING: No, scarcely!

MANDERS: [*Continuing*] How can the authorities tolerate such things! Allow them to go on in the light of day! [*Confronting* Mrs. Alving] Had I not cause to be deeply concerned about your son? In circles where open immorality prevails, and has even a sort of recognised position—!

OSWALD: Let me tell you, sir, that I have been in the habit of spending nearly all my Sundays in one or two such irregular homes—

MANDERS: Sunday of all days!

OSWALD: Isn't that the day to enjoy one's self? Well, never have I heard an offensive word, and still less have I witnessed anything that could be called immoral. No; do you know when and where I have come across immorality in artistic circles?

MANDERS: No, thank heaven, I don't!

OSWALD: Well, then, allow me to inform you. I have met with it when one or other of our pattern husbands and fathers has come to Paris to have a look round on his own account, and has done the artists the honour of visiting their humble haunts. They knew what was what. These gentlemen could tell us all about places and things we had never dreamt of.

MANDERS: What! Do you mean to say that respectable men from home here would—?

OSWALD: Have you never heard these respectable men, when they got home again, talking about the way in which immorality runs rampant abroad?

MANDERS: Yes, no doubt—

MRS. ALVING: I have too.

OSWALD: Well, you may take their word for it. They know what they are talking about! [*Presses his hands to his head*] Oh! that that great, free, glorious life out there should be defiled in such a way!

MRS. ALVING: You mustn't get excited, Oswald. It's not good for you.

OSWALD: Yes; you're quite right, mother. It's bad for me, I know. You see, I'm wretchedly worn out. I shall go for a little turn before dinner. Excuse me, Pastor: I know you can't take my point of view; but I couldn't help speaking out. [*He goes out by the second door to the right*]

MRS. ALVING: My poor boy!

MANDERS: You may well say so. Then this is what he has come to! [Mrs. Alving *looks at him silently*]

MANDERS: [*Walking up and down*] He called himself the Prodigal Son. Alas! alas!

[Mrs. Alving *continues looking at him*]

MANDERS: And what do you say to all this?

MRS. ALVING: I say that Oswald was right in every word.

MANDERS: [*Stands still*] Right? Right! In such principles?

MRS. ALVING: Here, in my loneliness, I have come to the same way of thinking, Pastor Manders. But I have never dared to say anything. Well! now my boy shall speak for me.

MANDERS: You are greatly to be pitied, Mrs. Alving. But now I must speak seriously to you. And now it is no longer your business manager and adviser, your own and your husband's early friend, who stands before you. It is the priest—the priest who stood before you in the moment of your life when you had gone farthest astray.

MRS. ALVING: And what has the priest to say to me?

MANDERS: I will first stir up your memory a little. The moment is well chosen. To-morrow will be the tenth anniversary of your husband's death. To-morrow the memorial in his honour will be unveiled. To-morrow I shall have to speak to the whole assembled multitude. But to-day I will speak to you alone.

MRS. ALVING: Very well, Pastor Manders. Speak.

MANDERS: Do you remember that after less than a year of married life you stood on the verge of an abyss? That you forsook your house and home? That you fled from your husband? Yes, Mrs. Alving—fled, fled, and refused to return to him, however much he begged and prayed you?

MRS. ALVING: Have you forgotten how infinitely miserable I was in that first year?

MANDERS: It is the very mark of the spirit of rebellion to crave for happiness in this life. What right have we human beings to happiness? We have simply to do our duty, Mrs. Alving! And your duty was to hold firmly to the man you had once chosen, and to whom you were bound by the holiest ties.

MRS. ALVING: You know very well what sort of life Alving was leading—what excesses he was guilty of.

MANDERS: I know very well what rumours there were about him; and I am the last to approve the life he led in his young days, if report did not wrong him. But a wife is not appointed to be her husband's judge. It was your duty to bear with humility the cross which a Higher Power had, in its wisdom, laid upon you. But instead of that you rebelliously throw away the cross, desert the back-slider whom you should have supported, go and risk your good name and reputation, and—nearly succeed in ruining other people's reputation into the bargain.

MRS. ALVING: Other people's? One other person's, you mean.

MANDERS: It was incredibly reckless of you to seek refuge with me.

MRS. ALVING: With our clergyman? With our intimate friend?

MANDERS: Just on that account. Yes, you may thank God that I possessed the necessary firmness; that I succeeded in dissuading you from your wild designs; and that it was vouchsafed me to lead you back to the path of duty, and home to your lawful husband.

MRS. ALVING: Yes, Pastor Manders, that was certainly your work.

MANDERS: I was but a poor instrument in a Higher Hand. And what a blessing has it not proved to you, all the days of your life, that I induced you to resume the yoke of duty and obedience! Did not everything happen as I foretold? Did not Alving turn his back on his errors, as a man should? Did he not live with you from that time, lovingly and blamelessly, all his days? Did he not become a benefactor to the whole district? And did he not help you to rise to his own level, so that you, little by little became his assistant in all his undertakings? And a capital assistant, too—oh, I know, Mrs. Alving, that praise is due to you.—But now I come to the next great error in your life.

MRS. ALVING: What do you mean?

MANDERS: Just as you once disowned a wife's duty, so you have since disowned a mother's.

MRS. ALVING: Ah—!

MANDERS: You have been all your life under the dominion of a pestilent spirit of self-will. The whole bias of your mind has been towards insubordination and lawlessness. You have never known how to endure any bond. Everything that has weighed upon you in life you have cast away without care or conscience, like a burden you were free to throw off at will. It did not please you to be a wife any longer, and you left your husband. You found it troublesome to be a mother, and you sent your child forth among strangers.

MRS. ALVING: Yes, that is true. I did so.

MANDERS: And thus you have become a stranger to him.

MRS. ALVING: No! no! I am not.

MANDERS: Yes, you are; you must be. And in what state of mind has he returned to you? Bethink yourself well, Mrs. Alving. You sinned greatly against your husband;—that you recognise by raising yonder memorial to him. Recognise now, also, how you have sinned against your son—there may yet

be time to lead him back from the paths of error. Turn back yourself, and save what may yet be saved in him. For [*With uplifted forefinger*] verily, Mrs. Alving, you are a guilt-laden mother!—This I have thought it my duty to say to you. [*Silence*]

MRS. ALVING: [*Slowly and with self-control*] You have now spoken out, Pastor Manders; and to-morrow you are to speak publicly in memory of my husband. I shall not speak to-morrow. But now I will speak frankly to you, as you have spoken to me.

MANDERS: To be sure; you will plead excuses for your conduct—

MRS. ALVING: No. I will only tell you a story.

MANDERS: Well—?

MRS. ALVING: All that you have just said about my husband and me, and our life after you had brought me back to the path of duty—as you called it—about all that you know nothing from personal observation. From that moment you, who had been our intimate friend, never set foot in our house again.

MANDERS: You and your husband left the town immediately after.

MRS. ALVING: Yes; and in my husband's lifetime you never came to see us. It was business that forced you to visit me when you undertook the affairs of the Orphanage.

MANDERS: [*Softly and hesitatingly*] Helen—if that is meant as a reproach, I would beg you to bear in mind—

MRS. ALVING: —the regard you owed to your position, yes; and that I was a runaway wife. One can never be too cautious with such unprincipled creatures.

MANDERS: My dear—Mrs. Alving, you know that is an absurd exaggeration—

MRS. ALVING: Well well, suppose it is. My point is that your judgment as to my married life is founded upon nothing but common knowledge and report.

MANDERS: I admit that. What then?

MRS. ALVING: Well, then, Pastor Manders—I will tell you the truth. I have sworn to myself that one day you should know it—you alone!

MANDERS: What is the truth, then?

MRS. ALVING: The truth is that my husband died just as dissolute as he had lived all his days.

MANDERS: [*Feeling after a chair*] What do you say?

MRS. ALVING: After nineteen years of marriage, as dissolute—in his desires at any rate—as he was before you married us.

MANDERS: And those—those wild oats—those irregularities—those excesses, if you like—you call "a dissolute life"?

MRS. ALVING: Our doctor used the expression.

MANDERS: I do not understand you.

MRS. ALVING: You need not.

MANDERS: It almost makes me dizzy. Your whole married life, the seeming union of all these years, was nothing more than a hidden abyss!

MRS. ALVING: Neither more nor less. Now you know it.

MANDERS: This is—this is inconceivable to me. I cannot grasp it! I cannot realize it! But how was it possible to——? How could such a state of things be kept secret?

MRS. ALVING: That has been my ceaseless struggle, day after day. After Oswald's birth, I thought Alving seemed to be a little better. But it did not last long. And then I had to struggle twice as hard, fighting as though for life or death, so that nobody should know what sort of man my child's father was. And you know what power Alving had of winning people's hearts. Nobody seemed able to believe anything but good of him. He was one of those people whose life does not bite upon their reputation. But at last, Mr. Manders—for you must know the whole story—the most repulsive thing of all happened.

MANDERS: More repulsive than what you have told me!

MRS. ALVING: I had gone on bearing with him, although I knew very well the secrets of his life out of doors. But when he brought the scandal within our own walls——

MANDERS: Impossible! Here!

MRS. ALVING: Yes; here in our own home. It was there [Pointing towards the first door on the right], in the dining-room, that I first came to know of it. I was busy with something in there, and the door was standing ajar. I heard our housemaid come up from the garden, with water for those flowers.

MANDERS: Well——?

MRS. ALVING: Soon after, I heard Alving come in too. I heard him say something softly to her. And then I heard—[With a short laugh]—oh! it still sounds in my ears, so hateful and yet so ludicrous—I heard my own servant-maid whisper, "Let me go, Mr. Alving! Let me be!"

MANDERS: What unseemly levity on his part! But it cannot have been more than levity, Mrs. Alving; believe me, it cannot.

MRS. ALVING: I soon knew what to believe. Mr. Alving had his way with the girl; and that connection had consequences, Mr. Manders.

MANDERS: [As though petrified] Such things in this house! in this house!

MRS. ALVING: I had borne a great deal in this house. To keep him at home in the evenings, and at night, I had to make myself his boon companion in his secret orgies up in his room. There I have had to sit alone with him, to clink glasses and drink with him, and to listen to his ribald, silly talk. I have had to fight with him to get him dragged to bed——

MANDERS: [Moved] And you were able to bear all this!

MRS. ALVING: I had to bear it for my little boy's sake. But when the last insult was added; when my own servant-maid——; then I swore to myself: This shall come to an end! And so I took the reins into my own hand—the whole control—over him and everything else. For now I had a weapon against him, you see; he dared not oppose me. It was then I sent Oswald away from home. He was nearly seven years old, and was beginning to observe and ask questions, as children do. That I could not bear. It seemed to me the child must be poisoned by merely breathing the air of this polluted home. That was why I sent him away. And now you can see, too, why he was never allowed to set foot inside his home so long as his father lived. No one knows what that cost me.

MANDERS: You have indeed had a life of trial.

MRS. ALVING: I could never have borne it if I had not had my work. For I may truly say that I have worked! All the additions to the estate—all the improvements—all the labour-saving appliances, that Alving was so much praised for having introduced—do you suppose he had energy for anything of the sort?—he, who lay all day on the sofa, reading an old Court Guide! No; but I may tell you this too: when he had his better intervals, it was I who urged him on; it was I who had to drag the whole load when he relapsed into his evil ways, or sank into querulous wretchedness.

MANDERS: And it is to this man that you raise a memorial?

MRS. ALVING: There you see the power of an evil conscience.

MANDERS: Evil——? What do you mean?

MRS. ALVING: It always seemed to me impossible but that the truth must come out and be believed. So the Orphanage was to deaden all rumours and set every doubt at rest.

MANDERS: In that you have certainly not missed your aim, Mrs. Alving.

MRS. ALVING: And besides, I had one other reason. I was determined that Oswald, my own boy, should inherit nothing whatever from his father.

MANDERS: Then it is Alving's fortune that——?

MRS. ALVING: Yes. The sums I have spent upon the Orphanage, year by year, make up the amount—I have reckoned it up precisely—the amount which made Lieutenant Alving "a good match" in his day.

MANDERS: I don't understand——

MRS. ALVING: It was my purchase-money. I do not choose that that money should pass into Oswald's hands. My son shall have everything from me—everything.

[Oswald Alving enters through the second door to the right; he has taken off his hat and overcoat in the hall]

MRS. ALVING: [Going towards him] Are you back again already? My dear, dear boy!

OSWALD: What can a fellow do out of doors in this eternal rain? But I hear dinner is ready. That's capital!

REGINA: [With a parcel, from the dining-room] A parcel has come for you, Mrs. Alving. [Hands it to her]

MRS. ALVING: [*With a glance at* Mr. Manders] No doubt copies of the ode for to-morrow's ceremony.

MANDERS: H'm—

REGINA: And dinner is ready.

MRS. ALVING: Very well. We will come directly. I will just—[*Begins to open the parcel*]

REGINA: [*To* Oswald] Would Mr. Alving like red or white wine?

OSWALD: Both, if you please.

REGINA: *Bien.* Very well, sir. [*She goes into the dining-room*]

OSWALD: I may as well help to uncork it. [*He also goes into the dining room, the door of which swings half open behind him*]

MRS. ALVING: [*Who has opened the parcel*] Yes, I thought so. Here is the Ceremonial Ode, Pastor Manders.

MANDERS: [*With folded hands*] With what countenance I am to deliver my discourse to-morrow—!

MRS. ALVING: Oh, you will get through it somehow.

MANDERS: [*Softly, so as not to be heard in the dining-room*] Yes; it would not do to provoke scandal.

MRS. ALVING: [*Under her breath, but firmly*] No. But then this long, hateful comedy will be ended. From the day after to-morrow, I shall act in every way as though he who is dead had never lived in this house. There shall be no one here but my boy and his mother.

[*From the dining-room comes the noise of a chair overturned, and at the same moment is heard*]

REGINA: [*Sharply, but in a whisper*] Oswald! take care! are you mad? Let me go!

MRS. ALVING: [*Starts in terror*] Ah—!

[*She stares wildly towards the half-open door. Oswald is heard laughing and humming. A bottle is uncorked*]

MANDERS: [*Agitated*] What can be the matter? What is it, Mrs. Alving?

MRS. ALVING: [*Hoarsely*] Ghosts! The couple from the conservatory—risen again!

MANDERS: Is it possible! Regina—? Is she—?

MRS. ALVING: Yes. Come. Not a word—!

[*She seizes* Pastor Manders *by the arm, and walks unsteadily towards the dining-room*]

CURTAIN

ACT II.

The same room. The mist still lies heavy over the landscape. Manders *and* Mrs. Alving *enter from the dining-room.*

MRS. ALVING: [*Still in the doorway*] *Velbekomme,*[1] Mr. Manders. [*Turns back towards the dining-room*] Aren't you coming too, Oswald?

[1] A phrase equivalent to the German *Prosit die Mahlzeit*—"May good digestion wait on appetite."

OSWALD: [*From within*] No, thank you. I think I shall go out a little.

MRS. ALVING: Yes, do. The weather seems a little brighter now. [*She shuts the dining-room door, goes to the hall door, and calls:*] Regina!

REGINA: [*Outside*] Yes, Mrs. Alving?

MRS. ALVING: Go down to the laundry, and help with the garlands.

REGINA: Yes, Mrs. Alving.

[Mrs. Alving *assures herself that* Regina *goes; then shuts the door*]

MANDERS: I suppose he cannot overhear us in there?

MRS. ALVING: Not when the door is shut. Besides, he's just going out.

MANDERS: I am still quite upset. I don't know how I could swallow a morsel of dinner.

MRS. ALVING: [*Controlling her nervousness, walks up and down*] Nor I. But what is to be done now?

MANDERS: Yes; what is to be done? I am really quite at a loss. I am so utterly without experience in matters of this sort.

MRS. ALVING: I feel sure that, so far, no mischief has been done.

MANDERS: No; heaven forbid! But it is an unseemly state of things, nevertheless.

MRS. ALVING: It is only an idle fancy on Oswald's part; you may be sure of that.

MANDERS: Well, as I say, I am not accustomed to affairs of the kind. But I should certainly think—

MRS. ALVING: Out of the house she must go, and that immediately. That is as clear as daylight—

MANDERS: Yes, of course she must.

MRS. ALVING: But where to? It would not be right to—

MANDERS: Where to? Home to her father, of course.

MRS. ALVING: To whom did you say?

MANDERS: To her— But then, Engstrand is not—? Good God, Mrs. Alving, it's impossible! You must be mistaken after all.

MRS. ALVING: Unfortunately there is no possibility of mistake. Johanna confessed everything to me; and Alving could not deny it. So there was nothing to be done but to get the matter hushed up.

MANDERS: No, you could do nothing else.

MRS. ALVING: The girl left our service at once and got a good sum of money to hold her tongue for the time. The rest she managed for herself when she got to town. She renewed her old acquaintance with Engstrand, no doubt let him see that she had money in her purse and told him some tale about a foreigner who put in here with a yacht that summer. So she and Engstrand got married in hot haste. Why, you married them yourself.

MANDERS: But then how to account for—? I recollect distinctly Engstrand coming to give notice of the marriage. He was quite overwhelmed with contrition and bitterly reproached himself for the misbehaviour he and his sweetheart had been guilty of.

MRS. ALVING: Yes; of course he had to take the blame upon himself.

MANDERS: But such a piece of duplicity on his part! And towards me too! I never could have believed it of Jacob Engstrand. I shall not fail to take him seriously to task; he may be sure of that.—And then the immorality of such a connection! For money—! How much did the girl receive?

MRS. ALVING: Three hundred dollars.

MANDERS: Just think of it—for a miserable three hundred dollars to go and marry a fallen woman!

MRS. ALVING: Then what have you to say of me? I went and married a fallen man.

MANDERS: Why—good heavens!—what are you talking about! A fallen man!

MRS. ALVING: Do you think Alving was any purer when I went with him to the altar than Johanna was when Engstrand married her?

MANDERS: Well, but there is a world of difference between the two cases—

MRS. ALVING: Not so much difference after all—except in the price:—a miserable three hundred dollars and a whole fortune.

MANDERS: How can you compare such absolutely dissimilar cases? You had taken counsel with your own heart and with your natural advisers.

MRS. ALVING: [Without looking at him] I thought you understood where what you call my heart had strayed to at the time.

MANDERS: [Distantly] Had I understood anything of the kind I should not have been a daily guest in your husband's house.

MRS. ALVING: At any rate, the fact remains that with myself I took no counsel whatever.

MANDERS: Well then, with your nearest relatives —as your duty bade you—with your mother and your two aunts.

MRS. ALVING: Yes, that is true. Those three cast up the account for me. Oh, it's marvellous how clearly they made out that it would be downright madness to refuse such an offer. If mother could only see me now, and know what all that grandeur has come to!

MANDERS: Nobody can be held responsible for the result. This, at least, remains clear: your marriage was in full accordance with law and order.

MRS. ALVING: [At the window] Oh, that perpetual law and order! I often think that is what does all the mischief in this world of ours.

MANDERS: Mrs. Alving, that is a sinful way of talking.

MRS. ALVING: Well, I can't help it; I must have done with all this constraint and insincerity. I can endure it no longer. I must work my way out to freedom.

MANDERS: What do you mean by that?

MRS. ALVING: [Drumming on the window-frame] I ought never to have concealed the facts of Alving's life. But at that time I dared not do anything else—

I was afraid, partly on my own account. I was such a coward.

MANDERS: A coward?

MRS. ALVING: If people had come to know anything, they would have said—"Poor man! with a runaway wife, no wonder he kicks over the traces."

MANDERS: Such remarks might have been made with a certain show of right.

MRS. ALVING: [Looking steadily at him] If I were what I ought to be, I should go to Oswald and say, "Listen, my boy: your father led a vicious life—"

MANDERS: Merciful heavens—!

MRS. ALVING: —and then I should tell him all I have told you—every word of it.

MANDERS: You shock me unspeakably, Mrs. Alving.

MRS. ALVING: Yes; I know that. I know that very well. I myself am shocked at the idea. [Goes away from the window] I am such a coward.

MANDERS: You call it "cowardice" to do your plain duty? Have you forgotten that a son ought to love and honour his father and mother?

MRS. ALVING: Do not let us talk in such general terms. Let us ask: Ought Oswald to love and honour Chamberlain Alving?

MANDERS: Is there no voice in your mother's heart that forbids you to destroy your son's ideals?

MRS. ALVING: But what about the truth?

MANDERS: But what about the ideals?

MRS. ALVING: Oh—ideals, ideals! If only I were not such a coward!

MANDERS: Do not despise ideals, Mrs. Alving; they will avenge themselves cruelly Take Oswald's case: he, unfortunately, seems to have few enough ideals as it is; but I can see that his father stands before him as an ideal.

MRS. ALVING: Yes, that is true.

MANDERS: And this habit of mind you have yourself implanted and fostered by your letters.

MRS. ALVING: Yes; in my superstitious awe for duty and the properties, I lied to my boy, year after year. Oh, what a coward—what a coward I have been!

MANDERS: You have established a happy illusion in your son's heart, Mrs. Alving; and assuredly you ought not to undervalue it.

MRS. ALVING: H'm; who knows whether it is so happy after all—? But, at any rate, I will not have any tampering with Regina. He shall not go and wreck the poor girl's life.

MANDERS: No; good God—that would be terrible!

MRS. ALVING: If I knew he was in earnest, and that it would be for his happiness—

MANDERS: What? What then?

MRS. ALVING: But it couldn't be; for unfortunately Regina is not the right sort of woman.

MANDERS: Well, what then? What do you mean?

MRS. ALVING: If I weren't such a pitiful coward, I should say to him, "Marry her, or make what arrangement you please, only let us have nothing underhand about it."

MANDERS: Merciful heavens, would you let them marry! Anything so dreadful—! so unheard of—

MRS. ALVING: Do you really mean "unheard of"? Frankly, Pastor Manders, do you suppose that throughout the country there are not plenty of married couples as closely akin as they?

MANDERS: I don't in the least understand you.

MRS. ALVING: O yes, indeed you do.

MANDERS: Ah, you are thinking of the possibility that— Alas! yes, family life is certainly not always so pure as it ought to be. But in such a case as you point to, one can never know—at least with any certainty. Here, on the other hand—that you, a mother, can think of letting your son—

MRS. ALVING: But I cannot—I wouldn't for anything in the world; that is precisely what I am saying.

MANDERS: No, because you are a "coward," as you put it. But if you were not a "coward," then—? Good God! a connection so shocking!

MRS. ALVING: So far as that goes, they say we are all sprung from connections of that sort. And who is it that arranged the world so, Pastor Manders?

MANDERS: Questions of that kind I must decline to discuss with you, Mrs. Alving; you are far from being in the right frame of mind for them. But that you dare to call your scruples "cowardly"—!

MRS. ALVING: Let me tell you what I mean. I am timid and faint-hearted because of the ghosts that hang about me, and that I can never quite shake off.

MANDERS: What do you say hangs about you?

MRS. ALVING: Ghosts! When I heard Regina and Oswald in there, it was as though ghosts rose up before me. But I almost think we are all of us ghosts, Pastor Manders. It is not only what we have inherited from our father and mother that "walks" in us. It is all sorts of dead ideas, and lifeless old beliefs, and so forth. They have no vitality, but they cling to us all the same, and we cannot shake them off. Whenever I take up a newspaper, I seem to see ghosts gliding between the lines. There must be ghosts all the country over, as thick as the sands of the sea. And then we are, one and all, so pitifully afraid of the light.

MANDERS: Aha—here we have the fruits of your reading. And pretty fruits they are, upon my word! Oh, those horrible, revolutionary, freethinking books!

MRS. ALVING: You are mistaken, my dear Pastor. It was you yourself who set me thinking; and I thank you for it with all my heart.

MANDERS: I!

MRS. ALVING: Yes—when you forced me under the yoke of what you called duty and obligation; when you lauded as right and proper what my whole soul rebelled against as something loathsome. It was then that I began to look into the seams of your doctrines. I wanted only to pick at a single knot; but when I had got that undone, the whole thing ravelled out. And then I understood that it was all machine-sewn.

MANDERS: [Softly, with emotion] And was that the upshot of my life's hardest battle?

MRS. ALVING: Call it rather your most pitiful defeat.

MANDERS: It was my greatest victory, Helen—the victory over myself.

MRS. ALVING: It was a crime against us both.

MANDERS: When you went astray, and came to me crying, "Here I am; take me!" I commanded you, saying, "Woman, go home to your lawful husband." Was that a crime?

MRS. ALVING: Yes, I think so.

MANDERS: We two do not understand each other.

MRS. ALVING: Not now, at any rate.

MANDERS: Never—never in my most secret thoughts have I regarded you otherwise than as another's wife.

MRS. ALVING: Oh—indeed?

MANDERS: Helen—!

MRS. ALVING: People so easily forget their past selves.

MANDERS: I do not. I am what I always was.

MRS. ALVING: [Changing the subject] Well well well; don't let us talk of old times any longer. You are now over head and ears in Boards and Committees, and I am fighting my battle with ghosts, both within me and without.

MANDERS: Those without I shall help you to lay. After all the terrible things I have heard from you today, I cannot in conscience permit an unprotected girl to remain in your house.

MRS. ALVING: Don't you think the best plan would be to get her provided for?—I mean, by a good marriage.

MANDERS: No doubt. I think it would be desirable for her in every respect. Regina is now at the age when— Of course I don't know much about these things, but—

MRS. ALVING: Regina matured very early.

MANDERS: Yes, I thought so. I have an impression that she was remarkably well developed, physically, when I prepared her for confirmation. But in the meantime, she ought to be at home, under her father's eye— Ah! but Engstrand is not— That he—that he—could so hide the truth from me!

[A knock at the door into the hall]

MRS. ALVING: Who can this be? Come in!

ENGSTRAND: [In his Sunday clothes, in the doorway] I humbly beg your pardon, but—

MANDERS: Aha! H'm—

MRS. ALVING: Is that you, Engstrand?

ENGSTRAND: —there was none of the servants about, so I took the great liberty of just knocking.

MRS. ALVING: Oh, very well. Come in. Do you want to speak to me?

ENGSTRAND: [Comes in] No, I'm obliged to you,

ma'am; it was with his Reverence I wanted to have a word or two.

MANDERS: [*Walking up and down the room*] Ah—indeed! You want to speak to me, do you?

ENGSTRAND: Yes, I'd like so terrible much to—

MANDERS: [*Stops in front of him*] Well; may I ask what you want?

ENGSTRAND: Well, it was just this, your Reverence: we've been paid off down yonder—my grateful thanks to you, ma'am,—and now everything's finished, I've been thinking it would be but right and proper if we, that have been working so honestly together all this time—well, I was thinking we ought to end up with a little prayer-meeting to-night.

MANDERS: A prayer-meeting? Down at the Orphanage?

ENGSTRAND: Oh, if your Reverence doesn't think it proper—

MANDERS: Oh yes, I do; but—h'm—

ENGSTRAND: I've been in the habit of offering up a little prayer in the evenings, myself—

MRS. ALVING: Have you?

ENGSTRAND: Yes, every now and then—just a little edification, in a manner of speaking. But I'm a poor, common man, and have little enough gift, God help me!—and so I thought, as the Reverend Mr. Manders happened to be here, I'd—

MANDERS: Well, you see, Engstrand, I have a question to put to you first. Are you in the right frame of mind for such a meeting? Do you feel your conscience clear and at ease?

ENGSTRAND: Oh, God help us, your Reverence! we'd better not talk about conscience.

MANDERS: Yes, that is just what we must talk about. What have you to answer?

ENGSTRAND: Why—a man's conscience—it can be bad enough now and then.

MANDERS: Ah, you admit that. Then perhaps you will make a clean breast of it, and tell me—the real truth about Regina?

MRS. ALVING: [*Quickly*] Mr. Manders!

MANDERS: [*Reassuringly*] Please allow me—

ENGSTRAND: About Regina! Lord, what a turn you gave me! [*Looks at* Mrs. Alving] There's nothing wrong about Regina, is there?

MANDERS: We will hope not. But I mean, what is the truth about you and Regina? You pass for her father, eh?

ENGSTRAND: [*Uncertain*] Well—h'm—your Reverence knows all about me and poor Johanna.

MANDERS: Come now, no more prevarication! Your wife told Mrs. Alving the whole story before quitting her service.

ENGSTRAND: Well, then, may—! Now, did she really?

MANDERS: You see we know you now, Engstrand.

ENGSTRAND: And she swore and took her Bible oath—

MANDERS: Did she take her Bible oath?

ENGSTRAND: No; she only swore; but she did it that solemn-like.

MANDERS: And you have hidden the truth from me all these years? Hidden it from me, who have trusted you without reserve, in everything.

ENGSTRAND: Well, I can't deny it.

MANDERS: Have I deserved this of you, Engstrand? Have I not always been ready to help you in word and deed, so far as it lay in my power? Answer me. Have I not?

ENGSTRAND: It would have been a poor look-out for me many a time but for the Reverend Mr. Manders.

MANDERS: And this is how you reward me! You cause me to enter falsehoods in the Church Register, and you withhold from me, year after year, the explanations you owed alike to me and to the truth. Your conduct has been wholly inexcusable, Engstrand; and from this time forward I have done with you!

ENGSTRAND: [*With a sigh*] Yes! I suppose there's no help for it.

MANDERS: How can you possibly justify yourself?

ENGSTRAND: Who could ever have thought she'd have gone and made bad worse by talking about it? Will your Reverence just fancy yourself in the same trouble as poor Johanna—

MANDERS: I!

ENGSTRAND: Lord bless you, I don't mean just exactly the same. But I mean, if your Reverence had anything to be ashamed of in the eyes of the world, as the saying goes. We menfolk oughtn't to judge a poor woman too hardly, your Reverence.

MANDERS: I am not doing so. It is you I am reproaching.

ENGSTRAND: Might I make so bold as to ask your Reverence a bit of a question?

MANDERS: Yes, if you want to.

ENGSTRAND: Isn't it right and proper for a man to raise up the fallen?

MANDERS: Most certainly it is.

ENGSTRAND: And isn't a man bound to keep his sacred word?

MANDERS: Why, of course he is; but—

ENGSTRAND: When Johanna had got into trouble through that Englishman—or it might have been an American or a Russian, as they call them—well, you see, she came down into the town. Poor thing, she'd sent me about my business once or twice before: for she couldn't bear the sight of anything as wasn't handsome; and I'd got this damaged leg of mine. Your Reverence recollects how I ventured up into a dancing saloon, where seafaring men was carrying on with drink and devilry, as the saying goes. And then, when I was for giving them a bit of an admonition to lead a new life—

MRS. ALVING: [*At the window*] H'm—

MANDERS: I know all about that, Engstrand; the ruffians threw you downstairs. You have told me of the affair already. Your infirmity is an honour to you.

ENGSTRAND: I'm not puffed up about it, your Reverence. But what I wanted to say was, that when she came and confessed all to me, with weeping and gnashing of teeth, I can tell your Reverence I was sore at heart to hear it.

MANDERS: Were you indeed, Engstrand? Well, go on.

ENGSTRAND: So I says to her, "The American, he's sailing about on the boundless sea. And as for you, Johanna," says I, "you've committed a grievous sin, and you're a fallen creature. But Jacob Engstrand," says I, "he's got two good legs to stand upon, he has—" You see, your Reverence, I was speaking figurative-like.

MANDERS: I understand quite well. Go on.

ENGSTRAND: Well, that was how I raised her up and made an honest woman of her, so as folks shouldn't get to know how as she'd gone astray with foreigners.

MANDERS: In all that you acted very well. Only I cannot approve of your stooping to take money—

ENGSTRAND: Money? I? Not a farthing!

MANDERS: [*Inquiringly to* Mrs. Alving] But—

ENGSTRAND: Oh, wait a minute!—now I recollect. Johanna did have a trifle of money. But I would have nothing to do with that. "No," says I, "that's mammon; that's the wages of sin. This dirty gold— or notes, or whatever it was—we'll just fling that back in the American's face," says I. But he was off and away, over the stormy sea, your Reverence.

MANDERS: Was he really, my good fellow?

ENGSTRAND: He was indeed, sir. So Johanna and I, we agreed that the money should go to the child's education; and so it did, and I can account for every blessed farthing of it.

MANDERS: Why, this alters the case considerably.

ENGSTRAND: That's just how it stands, your Reverence. And I make so bold as to say as I've been an honest father to Regina, so far as my poor strength went; for I'm but a weak vessel, worse luck!

MANDERS: Well, well, my good fellow—

ENGSTRAND: All the same, I bear myself witness as I've brought up the child, and lived kindly with poor Johanna, and ruled over my own house, as the Scripture has it. But it couldn't never enter my head to go to your Reverence and puff myself up and boast because even the likes of me had done some good in the world. No, sir; when anything of that sort happens to Jacob Engstrand, he holds his tongue about it. It don't happen so terrible often, I daresay. And when I do come to see your Reverence, I find a mortal deal that's wicked and weak to talk about. For I said it before, and I say it again—a man's conscience isn't always as clean as it might be.

MANDERS: Give me your hand, Jacob Engstrand.

ENGSTRAND: Oh, Lord! your Reverence—

MANDERS: Come, no nonsense. [*Wrings his hand*] There we are!

ENGSTRAND: And if I might humbly beg your Reverence's pardon—

MANDERS: You? On the contrary, it is I who ought to beg your pardon—

ENGSTRAND: Lord, no, sir!

MANDERS: Yes, assuredly. And I do it with all my heart. Forgive me for misunderstanding you. I only wish I could give you some proof of my hearty regret, and of my good-will towards you—

ENGSTRAND: Would your Reverence do it?

MANDERS: With the greatest pleasure.

ENGSTRAND: Well then, here's the very chance. With the bit of money I've saved here, I was thinking I might set up a Sailors' Home down in the town.

MRS. ALVING: You?

ENGSTRAND: Yes; it might be a sort of Orphanage, too, in a manner of speaking. There's such a many temptations for seafaring folk ashore. But in this Home of mine, a man might feel like as he was under a father's eye, I was thinking.

MANDERS: What do you say to this, Mrs. Alving?

ENGSTRAND: It isn't much as I've got to start with, Lord help me! But if I could only find a helping hand, why—

MANDERS: Yes, yes; we will look into the matter more closely. I entirely approve of your plan. But now, go before me and make everything ready, and get the candles lighted, so as to give the place an air of festivity. And then we will pass an edifying hour together, my good fellow; for now I quite believe you are in the right frame of mind.

ENGSTRAND: Yes, I trust I am. And so I'll say good-bye, ma'am, and thank you kindly; and take good care of Regina for me—[*Wipes a tear from his eye*]—poor Johanna's child. Well, it's a queer thing, now; but it's just like as if she'd growd into the very apple of my eye. It is, indeed. [*He bows and goes out through the hall*]

MANDERS: Well, what do you say of that man now, Mrs. Alving? That was a very different account of matters, was it not?

MRS. ALVING: Yes, it certainly was.

MANDERS: It only shows how excessively careful one ought to be in judging one's fellow creatures. But what a heartfelt joy it is to ascertain that one has been mistaken! Don't you think so?

MRS. ALVING: I think you are, and will always be, a great baby, Manders.

MANDERS: I?

MRS. ALVING: [*Laying her two hands upon his shoulders*] And I say that I have half a mind to put my arms round your neck, and kiss you.

MANDERS: [*Stepping hastily back*] No, no! God bless me! What an idea!

MRS. ALVING: [*With a smile*] Oh, you needn't be afraid of me.

MANDERS: [*By the table*] You have sometimes such an exaggerated way of expressing yourself. Now, let me just collect all the documents, and put them in my bag. [*He does so*] There, that's all right. And now, good-bye for the present. Keep your eyes open when Oswald comes back. I shall look in again later. [*He takes his hat and goes out through the hall door*]

MRS. ALVING: [*Sighs, looks for a moment out of the window, sets the room in order a little, and is about to go into the dining-room, but stops at the door with a half-suppressed cry*] Oswald, are you still at table?

OSWALD: [*In the dining room*] I'm only finishing my cigar.

MRS. ALVING: I thought you had gone for a little walk.

OSWALD: In such weather as this?

[*A glass clinks. Mrs. Alving leaves the door open, and sits down with her knitting on the sofa by the window*]

OSWALD: Wasn't that Pastor Manders that went out just now?

MRS. ALVING: Yes; he went down to the Orphanage.

OSWALD: H'm. [*The glass and decanter clink again*]

MRS. ALVING: [*With a troubled glance*] Dear Oswald, you should take care of that liqueur. It is strong.

OSWALD: It keeps out the damp.

MRS. ALVING: Wouldn't you rather come in here, to me?

OSWALD: I mayn't smoke in there.

MRS. ALVING: You know quite well you may smoke cigars.

OSWALD: Oh, all right then; I'll come in. Just a tiny drop more first.—There! [*He comes into the room with his cigar, and shuts the door after him. A short silence*] Where has the pastor gone to?

MRS. ALVING: I have just told you; he went down to the Orphanage.

OSWALD: Oh, yes; so you did.

MRS. ALVING: You shouldn't sit so long at table, Oswald.

OSWALD: [*Holding his cigar behind him*] But I find it so pleasant, mother. [*Strokes and caresses her*] Just think what it is for me to come home and sit at mother's own table, in mother's room, and eat mother's delicious dishes.

MRS. ALVING: My dear, dear boy!

OSWALD: [*Somewhat impatiently, walks about and smokes*] And what else can I do with myself here? I can't set to work at anything.

MRS. ALVING: Why can't you?

OSWALD: In such weather as this? Without a single ray of sunshine the whole day? [*Walks up the room*] Oh, not to be able to work—!

MRS. ALVING: Perhaps it was not quite wise of you to come home?

OSWALD: Oh, yes, mother; I had to.

MRS. ALVING: You know I would ten times rather forego the joy of having you here, than let you—

OSWALD: [*Stops beside the table*] Now just tell me, mother: does it really make you so very happy to have me home again?

MRS. ALVING: Does it make me happy!

OSWALD: [*Crumpling up a newspaper*] I should have thought it must be pretty much the same to you whether I was in existence or not.

MRS. ALVING: Have you the heart to say that to your mother, Oswald?

OSWALD: But you've got on very well without me all this time.

MRS. ALVING: Yes; I have got on without you. That is true.

[*A silence. Twilight slowly begins to fall. Oswald paces to and fro across the room. He has laid his cigar down*]

OSWALD: [*Stops beside Mrs. Alving*] Mother, may I sit on the sofa beside you?

MRS. ALVING: [*Makes room for him*] Yes, do, my dear boy.

OSWALD: [*Sits down*] There is something I must tell you, mother.

MRS. ALVING: [*Anxiously*] Well?

OSWALD: [*Looks fixedly before him*] For I can't go on hiding it any longer.

MRS. ALVING: Hiding what? What is it?

OSWALD: [*As before*] I could never bring myself to write to you about it; and since I've come home—

MRS. ALVING: [*Seizes him by the arm*] Oswald, what is the matter?

OSWALD: Both yesterday and to-day I have tried to put the thoughts away from me—to cast them off; but it's no use.

MRS. ALVING: [*Rising*] Now you must tell me everything, Oswald!

OSWALD: [*Draws her down to the sofa again*] Sit still; and then I will try to tell you.—I complained of fatigue after my journey—

MRS. ALVING: Well? What then?

OSWALD: But it isn't that that is the matter with me; not any ordinary fatigue—

MRS. ALVING: [*Tries to jump up*] You are not ill, Oswald?

OSWALD: [*Draws her down again*] Sit still, mother. Do take it quietly. I'm not downright ill, either; not what is commonly called "ill." [*Clasps his hands above his head*] Mother, my mind is broken down—ruined—I shall never be able to work again! [*With his hands before his face, he buries his head in her lap, and breaks into bitter sobbing*]

MRS. ALVING: [*White and trembling*] Oswald! Look at me! No, no; it's not true.

OSWALD: [*Looks up with despair in his eyes*] Never to be able to work again! Never!—never! A living death! Mother, can you imagine anything so horrible!

MRS. ALVING: My poor boy! How has this horrible thing come upon you?

OSWALD: [*Sitting upright again*] That's just what I cannot possibly grasp or understand. I have never led a dissipated lif —never, in any respect. You mustn't believe that of me, mother! I've never done that.

MRS. ALVING: I am sure you haven't, Oswald.

OSWALD: And yet this has come upon me just the same—this awful misfortune!

MRS. ALVING: Oh, but it will pass over, my dear, blessed boy. It's nothing but over-work. Trust me, I am right.

OSWALD: [Sadly] I thought so too, at first; but it isn't so.

MRS. ALVING: Tell me everything, from beginning to end.

OSWALD: Yes, I will.

MRS. ALVING: When did you first notice it?

OSWALD: It was directly after I had been home last time, and had got back to Paris again. I began to feel the most violent pains in my head—chiefly in the back of my head, they seemed to come. It was as though a tight iron ring was being screwed round my neck and upwards.

MRS. ALVING: Well, and then?

OSWALD: At first I thought it was nothing but the ordinary headache I had been so plagued with while I was growing up—

MRS. ALVING: Yes, yes—

OSWALD: But it wasn't that. I soon found that out. I couldn't work any more. I wanted to begin upon a big new picture, but my powers seemed to fail me; all my strength was crippled; I could form no definite images; everything swam before me— whirling round and round. Oh, it was an awful state! At last I sent for a doctor—and from him I learned the truth.

MRS. ALVING: How do you mean?

OSWALD: He was one of the first doctors in Paris. I told him my symptoms; and then he set to work asking me a string of questions which I thought had nothing to do with the matter. I couldn't imagine what the man was after—

MRS. ALVING: Well?

OSWALD: At last he said: "There has been something worm-eaten in you from your birth." He used that very word—vermoulu.

MRS. ALVING: [Breathlessly] What did he mean by that?

OSWALD: I didn't understand either, and begged him to explain himself more clearly. And then the old cynic said—[Clenching his fist] Oh—!

MRS. ALVING: What did he say?

OSWALD: He said, "The sins of the fathers are visited upon the children."

MRS. ALVING: [Rising slowly] The sins of the fathers—!

OSWALD: I very nearly struck him in the face—

MRS. ALVING: [Walks away across the room] The sins of the fathers—

OSWALD: [Smiles sadly] Yes; what do you think of that? Of course I assured him that such a thing was out of the question. But do you think he gave

in? No, he stuck to it; and it was only when I produced your letters and translated the passages relating to father—

MRS. ALVING: But then—?

OSWALD: Then of course he had to admit that he was on the wrong track; and so I learned the truth— the incomprehensible truth! I ought not to have taken part with my comrades in that light-hearted, glorious life of theirs. It had been too much for my strength. So I had brought it upon myself!

MRS. ALVING: Oswald! No, no; do not believe it!

OSWALD: No other explanation was possible, he said. That's the awful part of it. Incurably ruined for life—by my own heedlessness! All that I meant to have done in the world—I never dare think of it again—I'm not able to think of it. Oh! if I could only live over again, and undo all I have done! [He buries his face in the sofa. Mrs. Alving wrings her hands and walks, in silent struggle, backwards and forwards]

OSWALD: [After a while, looks up and remains resting upon his elbow] If it had only been something inherited—something one wasn't responsible for! But this! To have thrown away so shamefully, thoughtlessly, recklessly, one's own happiness, one's own health, everything in the world—one's future, one's very life—!

MRS. ALVING: No, no, my dear, darling boy; this is impossible! [Bends over him] Things are not so desperate as you think.

OSWALD: Oh, you don't know—[Springs up] And then, mother, to cause you all this sorrow! Many a time I have almost wished and hoped that at bottom you didn't care so very much about me.

MRS. ALVING: I, Oswald? My only boy! You are all I have in the world! The only thing I care about!

OSWALD: [Seizes both her hands and kisses them] Yes, yes, I see it. When I'm at home, I see it, of course; and that's almost the hardest part for me.— But now you know the whole story; and now we won't talk any more about it to-day. I daren't think of it for long together. [Goes up the room] Get me something to drink, mother.

MRS. ALVING: To drink? What do you want to drink now?

OSWALD: Oh, anything you like. You have some cold punch in the house.

MRS. ALVING: Yes, but my dear Oswald—

OSWALD: Don't refuse me, mother. Do be kind, now! I must have something to wash down all these gnawing thoughts. [Goes into the conservatory] And then—it's so dark here! [Mrs. Alving pulls a bell-rope on the right] And this ceaseless rain! It may go on week after week, for months together. Never to get a glimpse of the sun! I can't recollect ever having seen the sun shine all the times I've been at home.

MRS. ALVING: Oswald—you are thinking of going away from me.

OSWALD: H'm—[Drawing a heavy breath] I'm not

thinking of anything. I cannot think of anything!
[*In a low voice*] I let thinking alone.

REGINA: [*From the dining-room*] Did you ring,
ma'am?

MRS. ALVING: Yes; let us have the lamp in.

REGINA: Yes, ma'am. It's ready lighted. [*Goes out*]

MRS. ALVING: [*Goes across to* Oswald] Oswald,
be frank with me.

OSWALD: Well, so I am, mother. [*Goes to the
table*] I think I have told you enough.

[Regina *brings the lamp and sets it upon the
table*]

MRS. ALVING: Regina, you may bring us a small
bottle of champagne.

REGINA: Very well, ma'am. [*Goes out*]

OSWALD: [*Puts his arm round* Mrs. Alving's *neck*]
That's just what I wanted. I knew mother wouldn't
let her boy go thirsty.

MRS. ALVING: My own, poor, darling Oswald;
how could I deny you anything now?

OSWALD: [*Eagerly*] Is that true, mother? Do you
mean it?

MRS. ALVING: How? What?

OSWALD: That you couldn't deny me anything.

MRS. ALVING: My dear Oswald—

OSWALD: Hush!

REGINA: [*Brings a tray with a half-bottle of
champagne and two glasses, which she sets on the
table*] Shall I open it?

OSWALD: No, thanks. I will do it myself.

[Regina *goes out again*]

MRS. ALVING: [*Sits down by the table*] What was it
you meant—that I mustn't deny you?

OSWALD: [*Busy opening the bottle*] First let us
have a glass—or two. [*The cork pops; he pours wine
into one glass. and is about to pour it into the other*]

MRS. ALVING: [*Holding her hand over it*] Thanks;
not for me.

OSWALD: Oh! won't you? Then I will! [*He empties
the glass, fills, and empties it again; then he sits
down by the table*]

MRS. ALVING: [*In expectancy*] Well?

OSWALD: [*Without looking at her*] Tell me—I
thought you and Pastor Manders seemed so odd—
so quiet—at dinner to-day.

MRS. ALVING: Did you notice it?

OSWALD: Yes. H'm— [*After a short silence*] Tell
me: what do you think of Regina?

MRS. ALVING: What do I think?

OSWALD: Yes; isn't she splendid?

MRS. ALVING: My dear Oswald, you don't know
her as I do—

OSWALD: Well?

MRS. ALVING: Regina, unfortunately, was allowed
to stay at home too long. I ought to have taken her
earlier into my house.

OSWALD: Yes, but isn't she splendid to look at,
mother? [*He fills his glass*]

MRS. ALVING: Regina has many serious faults—

OSWALD: Oh, what does that matter? [*He drinks
again*]

MRS. ALVING: But I am fond of her, nevertheless,
and I am responsible for her. I wouldn't for all the
world have any harm happen to her.

OSWALD: [*Springs up*] Mother, Regina is my only
salvation!

MRS. ALVING: [*Rising*] What do you mean by that?

OSWALD: I cannot go on bearing all this anguish
of soul alone.

MRS. ALVING: Have you not your mother to share
it with you?

OSWALD: Yes; that's what I thought; and so I
came home to you. But that will not do. I see it
won't do. I cannot endure my life here.

MRS. ALVING: Oswald!

OSWALD: I must live differently, mother. That is
why I must leave you. I will not have you looking
on at it.

MRS. ALVING: My unhappy boy! But, Oswald
while you are so ill as this—

OSWALD: If it were only the illness, I should stay
with you, mother, you may be sure; for you are the
best friend I have in the world.

MRS. ALVING: Yes, indeed I am, Oswald; am I
not?

OSWALD: [*Wanders restlessly about*] But it's all the
torment, the gnawing remorse—and then, the great,
killing dread. Oh—that awful dread!

MRS. ALVING: [*Walking after him*] Dread? What
dread? What do you mean?

OSWALD: Oh, you mustn't ask me any more. I
don't know. I can't describe it.

[Mrs. Alving *goes over to the right and pulls
the bell*]

OSWALD: What is it you want?

MRS. ALVING: I want my boy to be happy—that
is what I want. He sha'n't go on brooding over
things. [*To* Regina, *who appears at the door:*] More
champagne—a large bottle.

[Regina *goes*]

OSWALD: Mother!

MRS. ALVING: Do you think we don't know how
to live here at home?

OSWALD: Isn't she splendid to look at? How beautifully she's built! And so thoroughly healthy!

MRS. ALVING: [*Sits by the table*] Sit down, Oswald;
let us talk quietly together.

OSWALD: [*Sits*] I daresay you don't know, mother,
that I owe Regina some reparation.

MRS. ALVING: You!

OSWALD: For a bit of thoughtlessness, or whatever
you like to call it—very innocent, at any rate. When
I was home last time—

MRS. ALVING: Well?

OSWALD: She used often to ask me about Paris,
and I used· to tell her one thing and another. Then
I recollect I happened to say to her one day,
"Shouldn't you like to go there yourself?"

MRS. ALVING: Well?

OSWALD: I saw her face flush, and then she said, "Yes, I should like it of all things." "Ah, well," I replied, "it might perhaps be managed"—or something like that.

MRS. ALVING: And then?

OSWALD: Of course I had forgotten all about it; but the day before yesterday I happened to ask her whether she was glad I was to stay at home so long—

MRS. ALVING: Yes?

OSWALD: And then she gave me such a strange look, and asked, "But what's to become of my trip to Paris?"

MRS. ALVING: Her trip!

OSWALD: And so it came out that she had taken the thing seriously; that she had been thinking of me the whole time, and had set to work to learn French—

MRS. ALVING: So that was why—!

OSWALD: Mother—when I saw that fresh, lovely, splendid girl standing there before me—till then I had hardly noticed her—but when she stood there as though with open arms ready to receive me—

MRS. ALVING: Oswald!

OSWALD: —then it flashed upon me that in her lay my salvation; for I saw that she was full of the joy of life.

MRS. ALVING: [Starts] The joy of life—? Can there be salvation in that?

REGINA: [From the dining-room, with a bottle of champagne] I'm sorry to have been so long, but I had to go to the cellar. [Places the bottle on the table]

OSWALD: And now bring another glass.

REGINA: [Looks at him in surprise] There is Mrs. Alving's glass, Mr. Alving.

OSWALD: Yes, but bring one for yourself, Regina. [Regina starts and gives a lightning-like side glance at Mrs. Alving] Why do you wait?

REGINA: [Softly and hesitatingly] Is it Mrs. Alving's wish?

MRS. ALVING: Bring the glass, Regina.

[Regina goes out into the dining-room]

OSWALD: [Follows her with his eyes] Have you noticed how she walks?—so firmly and lightly!

MRS. ALVING: This can never be, Oswald!

OSWALD: It's a settled thing. Can't you see that? It's no use saying anything against it.

[Regina enters with an empty glass, which she keeps in her hand]

OSWALD: Sit down, Regina.

[Regina looks inquiringly at Mrs. Alving]

MRS. ALVING: Sit down. [Regina sits on a chair by the dining-room door, still holding the empty glass in her hand] Oswald—what were you saying about the joy of life?

OSWALD: Ah, the joy of life, mother—that's a thing you don't know much about in these parts. I have never felt it here.

MRS. ALVING: Not when you are with me?

OSWALD: Not when I'm at home. But you don't understand that.

MRS. ALVING: Yes; yes; I think I almost understand it—now.

OSWALD: And then, too, the joy of work! At bottom, it's the same thing. But that, too, you know nothing about.

MRS. ALVING: Perhaps you are right. Tell me more about it, Oswald.

OSWALD: I only mean that here people are brought up to believe that work is a curse and a punishment for sin, and that life is something miserable, something it would be best to have done with, the sooner the better.

MRS. ALVING: "A vale of tears," yes; and we certainly do our best to make it one.

OSWALD: But in the great world people won't hear of such things. There, nobody really believes such doctrines any longer. There, you feel it a positive bliss and ecstasy merely to draw the breath of life. Mother, have you noticed that everything I have painted has turned upon the joy of life?—always, always upon the joy of life?—light and sunshine and glorious air—and faces radiant with happiness. That is why I'm afraid of remaining at home with you.

MRS. ALVING: Afraid? What are you afraid of here, with me?

OSWALD: I'm afraid lest all my instincts should be warped into ugliness.

MRS. ALVING: [Looks steadily at him] Do you think that is what would happen?

OSWALD: I know it. You may live the same life here as there, and yet it won't be the same life.

MRS. ALVING: [Who has been listening eagerly, rises, her eyes big with thought, and says:] Now I see the sequence of things.

OSWALD: What is it you see?

MRS. ALVING: I see it now for the first time. And now I can speak.

OSWALD: [Rising] Mother, I don't understand you.

REGINA: [Who has also risen] Perhaps I ought to go?

MRS. ALVING: No. Stay here. Now I can speak. Now, my boy, you shall know the whole truth. And then you can choose. Oswald! Regina!

OSWALD: Hush! The Pastor—

MANDERS: [Enters by the hall door] There! We have had a most edifying time down there.

OSWALD: So have we.

MANDERS: We must stand by Engstrand and his Sailors' Home. Regina must go to him and help him—

REGINA: No thank you, sir.

MANDERS: [Noticing her for the first time] What—? You here? And with a glass in your hand!

REGINA: [Hastily putting the glass down] Pardon!

OSWALD: Regina is going with me, Mr. Manders.

MANDERS: Going! With you!

OSWALD: Yes; as my wife—if she wishes it.

MANDERS: But, merciful God—!

REGINA: I can't help it, sir.

OSWALD: Or she'll stay here, if I stay.

REGINA: [Involuntarily] Here!

MANDERS: I am thunderstruck at your conduct, Mrs. Alving.

MRS. ALVING: They will do neither one thing nor the other; for now I can speak out plainly.

MANDERS: You surely will not do that! No, no, no!

MRS. ALVING: Yes, I can speak and I will. And no ideals shall suffer after all.

OSWALD: Mother—what is it you are hiding from me?

REGINA: [Listening] Oh, ma'am, listen! Don't you hear shouts outside. [She goes into the conservatory and looks out]

OSWALD: [At the window on the left] What's going on? Where does that light come from?

REGINA: [Cries out] The Orphanage is on fire!

MRS. ALVING: [Rushing to the window] On fire!

MANDERS: On fire! Impossible! I've just come from there.

OSWALD: Where's my hat? Oh, never mind it— Father's Orphanage—! [He rushes out through the garden door]

MRS. ALVING: My shawl, Regina! The whole place is in a blaze!

MANDERS: Mrs. Alving, it is a judgment upon this abode of lawlessness.

MRS. ALVING: Yes, of course. Come, Regina. [She and Regina hasten out through the hall]

MANDERS: [Clasps his hands together] And we left it uninsured! [He goes out the same way]

ACT III.

The room as before. All the doors stand open. The lamp is still burning on the table. It is dark out of doors; there is only a faint glow from the conflagration in the background to the left. Mrs. Alving, with a shawl over her head, stands in the conservatory, looking out. Regina, also with a shawl on, stands a little behind her.

MRS. ALVING: The whole thing burnt!—burnt to the ground!

REGINA: The basement is still burning.

MRS. ALVING: How is it Oswald doesn't come home? There's nothing to be saved.

REGINA: Should you like me to take down his hat to him?

MRS. ALVING: Has he not even got his hat on?

REGINA: [Pointing to the hall] No; there it hangs.

MRS. ALVING: Let it be. He must come up now. I shall go and look for him myself. [She goes out through the garden door]

MANDERS: [Comes in from the hall] Is not Mrs. Alving here?

REGINA: She has just gone down the garden.

MANDERS: This is the most terrible night I ever went through.

REGINA: Yes; isn't it a dreadful misfortune, sir?

MANDERS: Oh, don't talk about it! I can hardly bear to think of it.

REGINA: How can it have happened—?

MANDERS: Don't ask me, Miss Engstrand! How should I know? Do you, too—? Is it not enough that your father—?

REGINA: What about him?

MANDERS: Oh, he has driven me distracted—

ENGSTRAND: [Enters through the hall] Your Reverence—

MANDERS: [Turns round in terror] Are you after me here, too?

ENGSTRAND: Yes, strike me dead, but I must—! Oh, Lord! what am I saying? But this is a terrible ugly business, your Reverence.

MANDERS: [Walks to and fro] Alas! alas!

REGINA: What's the matter?

ENGSTRAND: Why, it all came of this here prayer-meeting, you see. [Softly] The bird's limed, my girl. [Aloud] And to think it should be my doing that such a thing should be his Reverence's doing!

MANDERS: But I assure you, Engstrand—

ENGSTRAND: There wasn't another soul except your Reverence as ever laid a finger on the candles down there.

MANDERS: [Stops] So you declare. But I certainly cannot recollect that I ever had a candle in my hand.

ENGSTRAND: And I saw as clear as daylight how your Reverence took the candle and snuffed it with your fingers, and threw away the snuff among the shavings.

MANDERS: And you stood and looked on?

ENGSTRAND: Yes; I saw it as plain as a pike-staff, I did.

MANDERS: It's quite beyond my comprehension. Besides, it has never been my habit to snuff candles with my fingers.

ENGSTRAND: And terrible risky it looked, too, that it did! But is there such a deal of harm done after all, your Reverence?

MANDERS: [Walks restlessly to and fro] Oh, don't ask me!

ENGSTRAND: [Walks with him] And your Reverence hadn't insured it, neither?

MANDERS: [Continuing to walk up and down] No, no, no; I have told you so.

ENGSTRAND: [Following him] Not insured! And then to go straight away down and set light to the whole thing! Lord, Lord, what a misfortune!

MANDERS: [Wipes the sweat from his forehead] Ay, you may well say that, Engstrand.

ENGSTRAND: And to think that such a thing should happen to a benevolent Institution, that was to have been a blessing both to town and country, as the saying goes! The newspapers won't be for handling your Reverence very gently, I expect.

MANDERS: No; that is just what I am thinking of. That is almost the worst of the whole matter. All the malignant attacks and imputations—! Oh, it makes me shudder to think of it!

MRS. ALVING: [*Comes in from the garden*] He is not to be persuaded to leave the fire.

MANDERS: Ah, there you are, Mrs. Alving.

MRS. ALVING: So you have escaped your Inaugural Address, Pastor Manders.

MANDERS: Oh, I should so gladly—

MRS. ALVING: [*In an undertone*] It is all for the best. That Orphanage would have done no one any good.

MANDERS: Do you think not?

MRS. ALVING: Do you think it would?

MANDERS: It is a terrible misfortune, all the same.

MRS. ALVING: Let us speak of it plainly, as a matter of business.—Are you waiting for Mr. Manders, Engstrand?

ENGSTRAND: [*At the hall door*] That's just what I'm a-doing of, ma'am.

MRS. ALVING: Then sit down meanwhile.

ENGSTRAND: Thank you, ma'am; I'd as soon stand.

MRS. ALVING: [*To* Manders] I suppose you are going by the steamer?

MANDERS: Yes; it starts in an hour.

MRS. ALVING: Then be so good as to take all the papers with you. I won't hear another word about this affair. I have other things to think of—

MANDERS: Mrs. Alving—

MRS. ALVING: Later on I shall send you a power of attorney to settle everything as you please.

MANDERS: That I will very readily undertake. The original destination of the endowment must now be completely changed, alas!

MRS. ALVING: Of course it must.

MANDERS: I think, first of all, I shall arrange that the Solvik property shall pass to the parish. The land is by no means without value. It can always be turned to account for some purpose or other. And the interest of the money in the Bank I could, perhaps, best apply for the benefit of some undertaking of acknowledged value to the town.

MRS. ALVING: Do just as you please. The whole matter is now completely indifferent to me.

ENGSTRAND: Give a thought to my Sailors' Home, your Reverence.

MANDERS: Upon my word, that is not a bad suggestion. That must be considered.

ENGSTRAND: Oh, devil take considering—Lord forgive me!

MANDERS: [*With a sigh*] And unfortunately I cannot tell how long I shall be able to retain control of these things—whether public opinion may not compel me to retire. It entirely depends upon the result of the official inquiry into the fire—

MRS. ALVING: What are you talking about?

MANDERS: And the result can by no means be foretold.

ENGSTRAND: [*Comes close to him*] Ay, but it can though. For here stands old Jacob Engstrand.

MANDERS: Well well, but—?

ENGSTRAND: [*More softly*] And Jacob Engstrand isn't the man to desert a noble benefactor in the hour of need, as the saying goes.

MANDERS: Yes, but my good fellow—how—?

ENGSTRAND: Jacob Engstrand may be likened to a sort of a guardian angel, he may, your Reverence.

MANDERS: No, no; I really cannot accept that.

ENGSTRAND: Oh, that'll be the way of it, all the same. I know a man as has taken others' sins upon himself before now, I do.

MANDERS: Jacob! [*Wrings his hand*] Yours is a rare nature. Well, you shall be helped with your Sailors' Home. That you may rely upon.

[Engstrand *tries to thank him, but cannot for emotion*]

MANDERS: [*Hangs his travelling-bag over his shoulder*] And now let us set out. We two will go together.

ENGSTRAND: [*At the dining-room door, softly to* Regina] You come along too, my lass. You shall live as snug as the yolk in an egg.

REGINA: [*Tosses her head*] Merci! [*She goes out into the hall and fetches* Manders' *overcoat*]

MANDERS: Good-bye, Mrs. Alving! and may the spirit of Law and Order descend upon this house, and that quickly.

MRS. ALVING: Good-bye, Pastor Manders. [*She goes up toward the conservatory, as she sees* Oswald *coming in through the garden door*]

ENGSTRAND: [*While he and* Regina *help* Manders *to get his coat on*] Good-bye, my child. And if any trouble should come to you, you know where Jacob Engstrand is to be found. [*Softly*] Little Harbour Street, h'm—! [*To* Mrs. Alving *and* Oswald] And the refuge for wandering mariners shall be called "Chamberlain Alving's Home," that it shall! And if so be as I'm spared to carry on that house in my own way, I make so bold as to promise that it shall be worthy of the Chamberlain's memory.

MANDERS: [*In the doorway*] H'm—h'm!—Come along, my dear Engstrand. Good-bye! Good-bye! [*He and* Engstrand *go out through the hall*]

OSWALD: [*Goes towards the table*] What house was he talking about?

MRS. ALVING: Oh, a kind of Home that he and Pastor Manders want to set up.

OSWALD: It will burn down like the other.

MRS. ALVING: What makes you think so?

OSWALD: Everything will burn. All that recalls father's memory is doomed. Here am I, too, burning down. [Regina *starts and looks at him*]

MRS. ALVING: Oswald! You oughtn't to have remained so long down there, my poor boy.

OSWALD: [*Sits down by the table*] I almost think you are right.

MRS. ALVING: Let me dry your face, Oswald; you

are quite wet. [*She dries his face with her pocket-handkerchief*]

OSWALD: [*Stares indifferently in front of him*] Thanks, mother.

MRS. ALVING: Are you not tired, Oswald? Should you like to sleep?

OSWALD: [*Nervously*] No, no—not to sleep! I never sleep. I only pretend to. [*Sadly*] That will come soon enough.

MRS. ALVING: [*Looking sorrowfully at him*] Yes, you really are ill, my blessed boy.

REGINA: [*Eagerly*] Is Mr. Alving ill?

OSWALD: [*Impatiently*] Oh, do shut all the doors! This killing dread—

MRS. ALVING: Close the doors, Regina.

[*Regina shuts them and remains standing by the hall door. Mrs. Alving takes her shawl off. Regina does the same. Mrs. Alving draws a chair across to Oswald's and sits by him*]

MRS. ALVING: There now! I am going to sit beside you—

OSWALD: Yes, do. And Regina shall stay here too. Regina shall be with me always. You will come to the rescue, Regina, won't you?

REGINA: I don't understand—

MRS. ALVING: To the rescue?

OSWALD: Yes—when the need comes.

MRS. ALVING: Oswald, have you not your mother to come to the rescue?

OSWALD: You? [*Smiles*] No, mother; that rescue you will never bring me. [*Laughs sadly*] You! ha ha! [*Looks earnestly at her*] Though, after all, who ought to do it if not you? [*Impetuously*] Why can't you say "thou" to me, Regina? Why don't you call me "Oswald"?

REGINA: [*Softly*] I don't think Mrs. Alving would like it.

MRS. ALVING: You shall have leave to, presently. And meanwhile sit over here beside us.

[*Regina seats herself demurely and hesitatingly at the other side of the table*]

MRS. ALVING: And now, my poor suffering boy, I am going to take the burden off your mind—

OSWALD: You, mother?

MRS. ALVING: —all the gnawing remorse and self-reproach you speak of.

OSWALD: And you think you can do that?

MRS. ALVING: Yes, now I can, Oswald. A little while ago you spoke of the joy of life; and at that word a new light burst for me over my life and everything connected with it.

OSWALD: [*Shakes his head*] I don't understand you.

MRS. ALVING: You ought to have known your father when he was a young lieutenant. He was brimming over with the joy of life!

OSWALD: Yes, I know he was.

MRS. ALVING: It was like a breezy day only to look at him. And what exuberant strength and vitality there was in him!

OSWALD: Well—?

MRS. ALVING: Well then, child of joy as he was— for he was like a child in those days—he had to live at home here in a half-grown town, which had no joys to offer him—only dissipations. He had no object in life—only an official position. He had no work into which he could throw himself heart and soul; he had only business. He had not a single comrade that could realise what the joy of life meant —only loungers and boon-companions—

OSWALD: Mother—!

MRS. ALVING: So the inevitable happened.

OSWALD: The inevitable?

MRS. ALVING: You told me yourself, this evening, what would become of you if you stayed at home.

OSWALD: Do you mean to say that father—?

MRS. ALVING: Your poor father found no outlet for the overpowering joy of life that was in him. And I brought no brightness into his home.

OSWALD: Not even you?

MRS. ALVING: They had taught me a great deal about duties and so forth, which I went on obstinately believing in. Everything was marked out into duties—into my duties, and his duties, and—I am afraid I made his home intolerable for your poor father, Oswald.

OSWALD: Why have you never spoken of this in writing to me?

MRS. ALVING: I have never before seen it in such a light that I could speak of it to you, his son.

OSWALD: In what light did you see it, then?

MRS. ALVING: [*Slowly*] I saw only this one thing: that your father was a broken-down man before you were born.

OSWALD: [*Softly*] Ah—! [*He rises and walks away to the window*]

MRS. ALVING: And then, day after day, I dwelt on the one thought that by rights Regina should be at home in this house—just like my own boy.

OSWALD: [*Turning round quickly*] Regina—!

REGINA: [*Springs up and asks, with bated breath*] I—?

MRS. ALVING: Yes, now you know it, both of you.

OSWALD: Regina!

REGINA: [*To herself*] So mother was that kind of woman.

MRS. ALVING: Your mother had many good qualities, Regina.

REGINA: Yes, but she was one of that sort, all the same. Oh, I've often suspected it; but— And now, if you please, ma'am, may I be allowed to go away at once?

MRS. ALVING: Do you really wish it, Regina?

REGINA: Yes, indeed I do.

MRS. ALVING: Of course you can do as you like; but—

OSWALD: [*Goes towards Regina*] Go away now? Your place is here.

REGINA: *Merci*, Mr. Alving!—or now, I suppose, I may say Oswald. But I can tell you this wasn't at all what I expected.

MRS. ALVING: Regina, I have not been frank with you—

REGINA: No, that you haven't indeed. If I'd known that Oswald was an invalid, why— And now, too, that it can never come to anything serious between us— I really can't stop out here in the country and wear myself out nursing sick people.

OSWALD: Not even one who is so near to you?

REGINA: No, that I can't. A poor girl must make the best of her young days, or she'll be left out in the cold before she knows where she is. And I, too, have the joy of life in me, Mrs. Alving!

MRS. ALVING: Unfortunately, you have. But don't throw yourself away, Regina.

REGINA: Oh, what must be, must be. If Oswald takes after his father, I take after my mother, I daresay.—May I ask, ma'am, if Pastor Manders knows all this about me?

MRS. ALVING: Pastor Manders knows all about it.

REGINA: [Busied in putting on her shawl] Well then, I'd better make haste and get away by this steamer. The Pastor is such a nice man to deal with; and I certainly think I've as much right to a little of that money as he has—that brute of a carpenter.

MRS. ALVING: You are heartily welcome to it, Regina.

REGINA: [Looks hard at her] I think you might have brought me up as a gentleman's daughter, ma'am; it would have suited me better. [Tosses her head] But pooh—what does it matter! [With a bitter side glance at the corked bottle] I may come to drink champagne with gentlefolks yet.

MRS. ALVING: And if you ever need a home, Regina, come to me.

REGINA: No, thank you, ma'am. Pastor Manders will look after me, I know. And if the worst comes to the worst, I know of one house where I've every right to a place.

MRS. ALVING: Where is that?

REGINA: "Chamberlain Alving's Home."

MRS. ALVING: Regina—now I see it—you are going to your ruin.

REGINA: Oh, stuff! Good-bye. [She nods and goes out through the hall]

OSWALD: [Stands at the window and looks out] Is she gone?

MRS. ALVING: Yes.

OSWALD: [Murmuring aside to himself] I think it was a mistake, this.

MRS. ALVING: [Goes up behind him and lays her hands on his shoulders] Oswald, my dear boy—has it shaken you very much?

OSWALD: [Turns his face towards her] All that about father, do you mean?

MRS. ALVING: Yes, about your unhappy father. I am so afraid it may have been too much for you.

OSWALD: Why should you fancy that? Of course it came upon me as a great surprise; but it can make no real difference to me.

MRS. ALVING: [Draws her hands away] No difference! That your father was infinitely unhappy!

OSWALD: Of course I can pity him, as I would anybody else; but—

MRS. ALVING: Nothing more! Your own father!

OSWALD: [Impatiently] Oh, "father,"—"father"! I never knew anything of father. I remember nothing about him, except that he once made me sick.

MRS. ALVING: This is terrible to think of! Ought not a son to love his father, whatever happens?

OSWALD: When a son has nothing to thank his father for? has never known him? Do you really cling to that old superstition?—you who are so enlightened in other ways?

MRS. ALVING: Can it be only a superstition—?

OSWALD: Yes; surely you can see that, mother. It's one of those notions that are current in the world, and so—

MRS. ALVING: [Deeply moved] Ghosts!

OSWALD: [Crossing the room] Yes; you may call them ghosts.

MRS. ALVING: [Wildly] Oswald—then you don't love me, either!

OSWALD: You I know, at any rate—

MRS. ALVING: Yes, you know me; but is that all!

OSWALD: And, of course, I know how fond you are of me, and I can't but be grateful to you. And then you can be so useful to me, now that I am ill.

MRS. ALVING: Yes, cannot I, Oswald? Oh, I could almost bless the illness that has driven you home to me. For I see very plainly that you are not mine: I have to win you.

OSWALD: [Impatiently] Yes, yes, yes; all these are just so many phrases. You must remember that I am a sick man, mother. I can't be much taken up with other people; I have enough to do thinking about myself.

MRS. ALVING: [In a low voice] I shall be patient and easily satisfied.

OSWALD: And cheerful too, mother!

MRS. ALVING: Yes, my dear boy, you are quite right. [Goes towards him] Have I relieved you of all remorse and self-reproach now?

OSWALD: Yes, you have. But now who will relieve me of the dread?

MRS. ALVING: The dread?

OSWALD: [Walks across the room] Regina could have been got to do it.

MRS. ALVING: I don't understand you. What is this about dread—and Regina?

OSWALD: Is it very late, mother?

MRS. ALVING: It is early morning. [She looks out through the conservatory] The day is dawning over the mountains. And the weather is clearing, Oswald. In a little while you shall see the sun.

OSWALD: I'm glad of that. Oh, I may still have much to rejoice in and live for—

MRS. ALVING: I should think so, indeed!

OSWALD: Even if I can't work—

MRS. ALVING: Oh, you'll soon be able to work

again, my dear boy—now that you haven't got all
those gnawing and depressing thoughts to brood over
any longer.

OSWALD: Yes, I'm glad you were able to rid me
of all those fancies. And when I've got over this one
thing more— [*Sits on the sofa*] Now we will have a
little talk, mother—

MRS. ALVING: Yes, let us. [*She pushes an arm-
chair towards the sofa, and sits down close to him*]

OSWALD: And meantime the sun will be rising.
And then you will know all. And then I shall not
feel this dread any longer.

MRS. ALVING: What is it that I am to know?

OSWALD: [*Not listening to her*] Mother, did you
not say a little while ago, that there was nothing in
the world you would not do for me, if I asked you?

MRS. ALVING: Yes, indeed I said so!

OSWALD: And you'll stick to it, mother?

MRS. ALVING: You may rely on that, my dear and
only boy! I have nothing in the world to live for
but you alone.

OSWALD: Very well, then; now you shall hear—
Mother, you have a strong, steadfast mind, I know.
Now you're to sit quite still when you hear it.

MRS. ALVING: What dreadful thing can it be—?

OSWALD: You're not to scream out. Do you hear?
Do you promise me that? We will sit and talk about
it quietly. Do you promise me, mother?

MRS. ALVING: Yes, yes; I promise. Only speak!

OSWALD: Well, you must know that all this fatigue
—and my inability to think of work—all that is not
the illness itself—

MRS. ALVING: Then what is the illness itself?

OSWALD: The disease I have as my birthright—
[*He points to his forehead and adds very softly*]—
is seated here.

MRS. ALVING: [*Almost voiceless*] Oswald! No—no!

OSWALD: Don't scream. I can't bear it. Yes,
mother, it is seated here—waiting. And it may break
out any day—at any moment.

MRS. ALVING: Oh, what horror—!

OSWALD: Now, quiet, quiet. That is how it stands
with me—

MRS. ALVING: [*Springs up*] It's not true, Oswald!
It's impossible! It cannot be so!

OSWALD: I have had one attack down there already. It was soon over. But when I came to know
the state I had been in, then the dread descended
upon me, raging and ravening; and so I set off home
to you as fast as I could.

MRS. ALVING: Then this is the dread—!

OSWALD: Yes—it's so indescribably loathsome,
you know. Oh, if it had only been as ordinary mortal
disease—! For I'm not so afraid of death—though
I should like to live as long as I can.

MRS. ALVING: Yes, yes, Oswald, you must!

OSWALD: But this is so unutterably loathsome. To
become a little baby again! To have to be fed! To
have to— Oh, it's not to be spoken of!

MRS. ALVING: The child has his mother to nurse
him.

OSWALD: [*Springs up*] No, never that! That is just
what I will not have. I can't endure to think that
perhaps I should lie in that state for many years—
and get old and grey. And in the meantime you
might die and leave me. [*Sits in* Mrs. Alving's *chair*]
For the doctor said it wouldn't necessarily prove
fatal at once. He called it a sort of softening of the
brain—or something like that. [*Smiles sadly*] I think
that expression sounds so nice. It always sets me
thinking of cherry-colored velvet—something soft
and delicate to stroke.

MRS. ALVING: [*Shrieks*] Oswald!

OSWALD: [*Springs up and paces the room*] And
now you have taken Regina from me. If I could
only have had her! She would have come to the
rescue, I know.

MRS. ALVING: [*Goes to him*] What do you mean
by that, my darling boy? Is there any help in the
world that I would not give you?

OSWALD: When I got over my attack in Paris, the
doctor told me that when it comes again—and it
will come—there will be no more hope.

MRS. ALVING: He was heartless enough to—

OSWALD: I demanded it of him. I told him I had
preparations to make— [*He smiles cunningly*] And
so I had. [*He takes a little box from his inner breast
pocket and opens it*] Mother, do you see this?

MRS. ALVING: What is it?

OSWALD: Morphia.

MRS. ALVING: [*Looks at him horror-struck*] Oswald—my boy—

OSWALD: I've scraped together twelve pilules—

MRS. ALVING: [*Snatches at it*] Give me the box,
Oswald.

OSWALD: Not yet, mother. [*He hides the box again
in his pocket*]

MRS. ALVING: I shall never survive this!

OSWALD: It must be survived. Now if I'd had Regina here, I should have told her how things stood
with me—and begged her to come to the rescue at
the last. She would have done it. I know she would.

MRS. ALVING: Never!

OSWALD: When the horror had come upon me,
and she saw me lying there helpless, like a little new-
born baby, impotent, lost, hopeless—past all saving—

MRS. ALVING: Never in all the world would Regina have done this!

OSWALD: Regina would have done it. Regina was
so splendidly light-hearted. And she would soon have
wearied of nursing an invalid like me.

MRS. ALVING: Then heaven be praised that Regina
is not here—

OSWALD: Well then, it is you that must come to the
rescue, mother.

MRS. ALVING: [*Shrieks aloud*] I!

OSWALD: Who should do it if not you?

MRS. ALVING: I! your mother!

OSWALD: For that very reason.

MRS. ALVING: I, who gave you life!

OSWALD: I never asked you for life. And what sort of a life have you given me? I will not have it! You shall take it back again!

MRS. ALVING: Help! Help! [*She runs out into the hall*]

OSWALD: [*Going after her*] Do not leave me! Where are you going?

MRS. ALVING: [*In the hall*] To fetch the doctor, Oswald! Let me pass!

OSWALD: [*Also outside*] You shall not go out. And no one shall come in.

[*The locking of a door is heard*]

MRS. ALVING: [*Comes in again*] Oswald! Oswald—my child!

OSWALD: [*Follows her*] Have you a mother's heart for me—and yet can see me suffer from this unutterable dread?

MRS. ALVING: [*After a moment's silence, commands herself, and says:*] Here is my hand upon it.

OSWALD: Will you—

MRS. ALVING: If it should ever be necessary. But it will never be necessary. No, no; it is impossible.

OSWALD: Well, let us hope so. And let us live together as long as we can. Thank you, mother.

[*He seats himself in the arm-chair which Mrs. Alving has moved to the sofa. Day is breaking. The lamp is still burning on the table*]

MRS. ALVING: [*Drawing near cautiously*] Do you feel calm now?

OSWALD: Yes.

MRS. ALVING: [*Bending over him*] It has been a dreadful fancy of yours, Oswald—nothing but a fancy. All this excitement has been too much for you. But now you shall have a long rest; at home with your mother, my own blessed boy. Everything you point to you shall have, just as when you were a little child.—There now. The crisis is over. You see how easily it passed! Oh, I was sure it would. —And do you see, Oswald, what a lovely day we are going to have? Brilliant sunshine! Now you can really see your home.

[*She goes to the table and puts out the lamp. Sunrise. The glacier and the snow-peaks in the background glow in the morning light*]

OSWALD: [*Sits in the arm-chair with his back towards the landscape, without moving. Suddenly he says:*] Mother, give me the sun.

MRS. ALVING: [*By the table, starts and looks at him*] What do you say?

OSWALD: [*Repeats, in a dull, toneless voice*] The sun. The sun.

MRS. ALVING: [*Goes to him*] Oswald, what is the matter with you?

[Oswald *seems to shrink together in the chair; all his muscles relax; his face is expressionless, his eyes have a glassy stare*]

MRS. ALVING: [*Quivering with terror*] What is this? [*Shrieks*] Oswald! what is the matter with you? [*Falls on her knees beside him and shakes him*] Oswald! Oswald! look at me! Don't you know me?

OSWALD: [*Tonelessly as before*] The sun.—The sun.

MRS. ALVING: [*Springs up in despair, entwines her hands in her hair and shrieks*] I cannot bear it! [*Whispers, as though petrified*] I cannot bear it! Never! [*Suddenly*] Where has he got them? [*Fumbles hastily in his breast*] Here! [*Shrinks back a few steps and screams:*] No; no; no!—Yes!—No; no!

[*She stands a few steps away from him with her hands twisted in her hair, and stares at him in speechless horror*]

OSWALD: [*Sits motionless as before and says*] The sun.—The sun.

THE END

Henrik Ibsen

(1828–1906)

After the publication of *Ghosts,* Ibsen replied to the critics who had denounced him as an offender against society with a vehement polemic, *An Enemy of the People* (1883). He pitted his idealist Dr. Stockmann against the "compact majority" of the selfish, the timid, and the opportunistic. Ibsen was, indeed, so outspoken at the time that he impressed acquaintances as a thoroughgoing anarchist. But having discharged his spleen with this satire on vested interests, he proceeded to write one of the most sympathetic and beautiful of his plays, *The Wild Duck.* On the surface, it would even appear that he recanted his views in this drama, since he reduced the passion for reform to an absurdity in the case of a provincial Hamlet who destroys people's happiness with "the call of the ideal." Actually, Ibsen's procedure in the play was ironical, since it proposed that morality was relative rather than absolute and that illusions were a necessary part of happiness. Nevertheless, *The Wild Duck* represents an important change in direction for Ibsen. Thereafter he was to concentrate upon the drama of character rather than of social ideas. Social issues and problems still appeared in several of his plays, but they were qualified by the wisdom of one who treats such matters as a student of human nature. Beginning with *The Wild Duck* in 1884, Ibsen, who had introduced the social-problem play into the theatre of realism through his earlier prose works, created modern character drama in play after play—in *Rosmersholm, The Lady from the Sea, Hedda Gabler, The Master Builder, Little Eyolf,* and *John Gabriel Borkman.*

All these works locate the conflict within the characters. This quality does not by itself, of course, indicate any particular modernity to readers familiar with such classics as *Hamlet* and *Phaedra.* But Ibsen presented his character dramas in modern dress by means of prose dialogue, contemporary rather than historical backgrounds, and ordinary persons engaged in prosaic, nonheroic activities. And to these elements he added his concern with the general problem of self-realization and with specific social questions. The "woman question," that is, the problems raised by the so-called liberation of women, is implied in all but two of his last works. *Rosmersholm,* in addition, presents the problem of religious reform, and *John Gabriel Borkman* delineates a Napoleon of modern finance. Ibsen expressed his aims clearly when he wrote that his intention in *Hedda Gabler* had been to present characters, emotions, and human destinies "upon a groundwork of certain of the social conditions and principles [ideas] of the present day."

In most of the late plays, Ibsen relied a good deal on symbolism, and not always successfully. To see character drama in the clearest light we must turn to *Hedda Gabler* (1890), written without benefit of symbolism. Those who insist upon reading symbolism into the play are straining a point. The recurrent references to Hedda's pistols and "vine leaves in one's hair" are essentially punctuation marks in the characterization.

As was his habit, Ibsen based his work on observation of real people; in this case, of young women who considered themselves emancipated without finding proper outlets for their desires or notions of themselves. They thought of themselves as "new women," "Ibsen women," but achieved nothing themselves; posed as superior and mysterious personalities, but had no depths; spoke of freedom in love but were too egotistical to make either freedom or love fruitful. Often, too, they became "harpy women," Ibsen's phrase for those who tried to gratify themselves parasitically by making extreme demands upon men without giving anything substantial in return. Ibsen was not a little disturbed by them, for they were the products of a changing society, and he himself had advocated the change. Were the spiritual daughters of his Nora to be fundamentally unwomanly, sterile, and destructive? Ibsen found himself particularly involved with one of these "modern" girls, the eighteen-year-old Austrian, Emilie Bardach, who once confessed to him that she had no desire to marry but intended to take married men away from their wives. It is not too much to say that the sixty-year-old author was himself captivated for a time. But he was also able to resist her and to study her objectively, and he drew upon his observations to delineate Hedda. His younger contemporary, Strindberg, had warned the world against the "new woman" in *The Father, Comrades,* and *Miss Julie* in 1887 and 1888, and had attacked Ibsen for promoting a vicious "gynolatry." *Hedda Gabler* was in a sense a major qualification of Ibsen's previous championship of the "new woman." He did not, however, turn the qualification into an issue or debate, but made it implicit in the story of Hedda. The result was one of the most rounded characterizations of the modern drama, which has attracted most of the great and, unfortunately, many of the less than great actresses of the theatre.

Because her sisters are to be found everywhere

in the Western world, Hedda deserves more study than is usually given her. Restlessness without direction, self-regard combined with uselessness, desire for a rich life without willingness to enrich her own and others' lives, bold ideas of "living dangerously" nullified by a cold heart—these are some of the elements that went into the making of Ibsen's highly individualized yet decidedly representative portrait. For a complete understanding of the play, moreover, Hedda must be viewed within the constellation of the supplementary characters that Ibsen supplied with more calculation than may be suspected. Judge Brack is her male counterpart, and may serve to remind us that Hedda draws her frailties not merely from woman but from the human race. Tesman, who belongs to a species of pedant less familiar here than in Europe, is significant in several ways. That Hedda married a Tesman instead of joining her fate to the Dionysian Lövborg is surely indicative of fundamental Philistinism. Like so many of her sisters, she plays safe. She is an aristocrat by birth who lacks aristocracy of the spirit, a second-rate Brunhild in furbelows, a very pale shadow of the heroic women of Norse legend whom Ibsen had celebrated in his romantic dramas, even if she rides horses and shoots off pistols. She might have had a different life if she had married someone who was not a Tesman, but would she have been able to marry a man of different mettle? That she repulsed Lövborg and did marry Tesman, is carrying a child by the latter, and must live with him on a social level wounding to her vanity—these are essential factors in her drama.

Hedda's situation stems from her character, a

fact Ibsen enforces upon us by drawing her opposite in Mrs. Elvsted. The once mousy girl who claims neither social nor individual superiority is Hedda's superior as a human being. The sophisticated Hedda is cowardly, whereas the "unemancipated," feminine Mrs. Elvsted behaves like a brave "new woman." She leaves husband and children in order to protect the man she saved from drink and despair and inspired to write an important book. It is the "bourgeois" Mrs. Elvsted, who, moved by love, is the free person. Because she has inner resources, moreover, she can continue to live after Lövborg's suicide, and finds self-realization in reconstructing his masterpiece. Hedda can only die.

Ibsen may be charged with returning to old-fashioned dramaturgy in making Hedda commit suicide. He may be defended, it is true, on the ground that Hedda is at the end of her resources, and that she has not been in full command of herself since her pregnancy. Also, she finds herself entirely superfluous when Tesman and Mrs. Elvsted start restoring the manuscript she threw into the fire, and her particular self-esteem makes her incapable of accepting Brack as a lover and buying his silence. Nevertheless, women like Hedda fail more usually, as well as more crushingly, by hanging on to life and avenging their frustration on others. The tragedy of a Hedda in real life, Bernard Shaw remarked, "is not that she commits suicide but that she continues to live."

For additional commentary and bibliography, see pages 10–14.

HEDDA GABLER

By Henrik Ibsen

TRANSLATED FROM THE NORWEGIAN BY EDMUND GOSSE AND WILLIAM ARCHER

CHARACTERS

GEORGE TESMAN
HEDDA TESMAN, *his wife*
MISS JULIANA TESMAN, *his aunt*

MRS. ELVSTED
JUDGE BRACK

EILERT LÖVBORG
BERTA, *servant at the Tesmans*

The scene of the action is Tesman's villa, in the west end of Christiania.

ACT I.

A spacious, handsome, and tastefully furnished drawing-room, decorated in dark colors. In the back, a wide doorway with curtains drawn back, leading into a smaller room decorated in the same style as the drawing-room. In the right-hand wall of the front room, a folding door leading out to the hall. In the opposite wall, on the left, a glass door, also with curtains drawn back. Through the panes can be seen part of a veranda outside, and trees covered with autumn foliage. An oval table, with a cover on it, and surrounded by chairs, stands well forward. In front, by the wall on the right, a wide stove of dark porcelain, a high-backed arm-chair, a cushioned foot-rest, and two footstools. A settee, with a small round table in front of it, fills the upper right-hand corner. In front, on the left, a little way from the wall, a sofa. Further back than the glass door, a piano. On either side of the doorway at the back a whatnot with terra-cotta and majolica ornaments.— Against the back wall of the inner room a sofa, with a table, and one or two chairs. Over the sofa hangs the portrait of a handsome elderly man in a General's uniform. Over the table a hanging lamp, with an opal glass shade.—A number of bouquets are arranged about the drawing-room, in vases and glasses. Others lie upon the tables. The floors in both rooms are covered with thick carpets.—Morning light. The sun shines in through the glass door.

Miss Juliana Tesman, *with her bonnet on and carrying a parasol, comes in from the hall, followed by* Berta, *who carries a bouquet wrapped in paper.* Miss Tesman *is a comely and pleasant-looking lady of about sixty-five. She is nicely but simply dressed in a gray walking-costume.* Berta *is a middle-aged woman of plain and rather countrified appearance.*

MISS TESMAN: [*Stops close to the door, listens, and says softly*] Upon my word, I don't believe they are stirring yet!

BERTA: [*Also softly*] I told you so, Miss. Remember how late the steamboat got in last night. And then, when they got home!—good Lord, what a lot the young mistress had to unpack before she could get to bed.

MISS TESMAN: Well, well—let them have their sleep out. But let us see that they get a good breath of the fresh morning air when they do appear.

[*She goes to the glass door and throws it open*]

BERTA: [*Beside the table, at a loss what to do with the bouquet in her hand*] I declare there isn't a bit of room left. I think I'll put it down here, Miss.

[*She places it on the piano*]

MISS TESMAN: So you've got a new mistress now, my dear Berta. Heaven knows it was a wrench to me to part with you.

BERTA: [*On the point of weeping*] And do you think it wasn't hard for me, too, Miss? After all the blessed years I've been with you and Miss Rina.

MISS TESMAN: We must make the best of it, Berta. There was nothing else to be done. George can't do without you, you see—he absolutely can't. He has had you to look after him ever since he was a little boy.

BERTA: Ah, but, Miss Julia, I can't help thinking of Miss Rina lying helpless at home there, poor thing. And with only that new girl, too! She'll never learn to take proper care of an invalid.

MISS TESMAN: Oh, I shall manage to train her. And, of course, you know I shall take most of it upon myself. You needn't be uneasy about my poor sister, my dear Berta.

BERTA: Well, but there's another thing, Miss. I'm so mortally afraid I shan't be able to suit the young mistress.

MISS TESMAN: Oh, well—just at first there may be one or two things——

BERTA: Most like she'll be terrible grand in her ways.

MISS TESMAN: Well, you can't wonder at that— General Gabler's daughter! Think of the sort of life she was accustomed to in her father's time. Don't you remember how we used to see her riding down the road along with the General? In that long black habit—and with feathers in her hat?

BERTA: Yes, indeed—I remember well enough!— But, good Lord, I should never have dreamt in those days that she and Master George would make a match of it.

MISS TESMAN: Nor I.—But by-the-bye, Berta— while I think of it: in future you mustn't say Master George. You must say Dr. Tesman.

BERTA: Yes, the young mistress spoke of that, too —last night—the moment they set foot in the house. Is it true then, Miss?

MISS TESMAN: Yes, indeed it is. Only think, Berta —some foreign university has made him a doctor— while he has been abroad, you understand. I hadn't heard a word about it, until he told me himself upon the pier.

BERTA: Well, well, he's clever enough for anything, he is. But I didn't think he'd have gone in for doctoring people, too.

MISS TESMAN: No, no, it's not that sort of doctor he is. [Nods significantly] But let me tell you, we may have to call him something still grander before long.

BERTA: You don't say so! What can that be, Miss?

MISS TESMAN: [Smiling] H'm—wouldn't you like to know! [With emotion] Ah, dear, dear—if my poor brother could only look up from his grave now, and see what his little boy has grown into! [Looks around] But bless me, Berta—why have you done this? Taken the chintz covers off all the furniture?

BERTA: The mistress told me to. She can't abide covers on the chairs, she says.

MISS TESMAN: Are they going to make this their everyday sitting-room then?

BERTA: Yes, that's what I understood—from the mistress. Master George—the doctor—he said nothing.

[George Tesman comes from the right into the inner room, humming to himself, and carrying an unstrapped empty portmanteau. He is a middle-sized, young-looking man of thirty-three, rather stout, with a round, open, cheerful face, fair hair and beard. He wears spectacles, and is somewhat carelessly dressed in comfortable indoor clothes]

MISS TESMAN: Good morning, good morning, George.

TESMAN: [In the doorway between the rooms] Aunt Julia! Dear Aunt Julia! [Goes up to her and shakes hands warmly] Come all this way—so early! Eh?

MISS TESMAN: Why, of course I had to come and see how you were getting on.

TESMAN: In spite of your having had no proper night's rest?

MISS TESMAN: Oh, that makes no difference to me.

TESMAN: Well, I suppose you got home all right from the pier? Eh?

MISS TESMAN: Yes, quite safely, thank goodness. Judge Brack was good enough to see me right to my door.

TESMAN: We were so sorry we couldn't give you a seat in the carriage. But you saw what a pile of boxes Hedda had to bring with her.

MISS TESMAN: Yes, she had certainly plenty of boxes.

BERTA: [To Tesman] Shall I go in and see if there's anything I can do for the mistress?

TESMAN: No thank you, Berta—you needn't. She said she would ring if she wanted anything.

BERTA: [Going towards the right] Very well.

TESMAN: But look here—take this portmanteau with you.

BERTA: [Taking it] I'll put it in the attic. [She goes out by the hall door]

TESMAN: Fancy, Auntie—I had the whole of that portmanteau chock full of copies of documents. You wouldn't believe how much I have picked up from all the archives I have been examining—curious old details that no one has had any idea of——

MISS TESMAN: Yes, you don't seem to have wasted your time on your wedding trip, George.

TESMAN: No, that I haven't. But do take off your bonnet, Auntie. Look here! Let me untie the strings —eh?

MISS TESMAN: [While he does so] Well well— this is just as if you were still at home with us.

TESMAN: [With the bonnet in his hand, looks at it from all sides] Why, what a gorgeous bonnet you've been investing in!

MISS TESMAN: I bought it on Hedda's account.

TESMAN: On Hedda's account? Eh?

MISS TESMAN: Yes, so that Hedda needn't be ashamed of me if we happened to go out together.

TESMAN: [Patting her cheek] You always think of everything, Aunt Julia. [Lays the bonnet on a chair beside the table] And now, look here—suppose we sit comfortably on the sofa and have a little chat, till Hedda comes.

[They seat themselves. She places her parasol in the corner of the sofa]

MISS TESMAN: [Takes both his hands and looks at him] What a delight it is to have you again, as large as life, before my very eyes, George! My George—my poor brother's own boy!

TESMAN: And it's a delight for me, too, to see you again, Aunt Julia! You, who have been father and mother in one to me.

MISS TESMAN: Oh yes, I know you will always keep a place in your heart for your old aunts.

TESMAN: And what about Aunt Rina? No improvement—eh?

MISS TESMAN: Oh no—we can scarcely look for any improvement in her case, poor thing. There she lies, helpless, as she has lain for all these years. But heaven grant I may not lose her yet awhile. For if

I did, I don't know what I should make of my life, George—especially now that I haven't you to look after any more.

TESMAN: [*Patting her back*] There there there——!

MISS TESMAN: [*Suddenly changing her tone*] And to think that here are you a married man, George! —And that you should be the one to carry off Hedda Gabler—the beautiful Hedda Gabler! Only think of it—she, that was so beset with admirers!

TESMAN: [*Hums a little and smiles complacently*] Yes, I fancy I have several good friends about town who would like to stand in my shoes—eh?

MISS TESMAN: And then this fine long wedding-tour you have had! More than five—nearly six months——

TESMAN: Well, for me it has been a sort of tour of research as well. I have had to do so much grubbing among old records—and to read no end of books too, Auntie.

MISS TESMAN: Oh yes, I suppose so. [*More confidentially, and lowering her voice a little*] But listen now, George,—have you nothing—nothing special to tell me?

TESMAN: As to our journey?

MISS TESMAN: Yes.

TESMAN: No, I don't know of anything except what I have told you in my letters. I had a doctor's degree conferred on me—but that I told you yesterday.

MISS TESMAN: Yes, yes, you did. But what I mean is—haven't you any—any—expectations——?

TESMAN: Expectations?

MISS TESMAN: Why you know, George—I'm your old auntie!

TESMAN: Why, of course I have expectations.

MISS TESMAN: Ah!

TESMAN: I have every expectation of being a professor one of these days.

MISS TESMAN: Oh yes, a professor——

TESMAN: Indeed, I may say I am certain of it. But my dear Auntie—you know all about that already!

MISS TESMAN: [*Laughing to herself*] Yes, of course I do. You are quite right there. [*Changing the subject*] But we were talking about your journey. It must have cost a great deal of money, George?

TESMAN: Well, you see—my handsome traveling-scholarship went a good way.

MISS TESMAN: But I can't understand how you can have made it go far enough for two.

TESMAN: No, that's not so easy to understand—eh?

MISS TESMAN: And especially travelling with a lady—they tell me that makes it ever so much more expensive.

TESMAN: Yes, of course—it makes it a little more expensive. But Hedda had to have this trip, Auntie! She really had to. Nothing else would have done.

MISS TESMAN: No no, I suppose not. A wedding-tour seems to be quite indispensable nowadays.—

But tell me now—have you gone thoroughly over the house yet?

TESMAN: Yes, you may be sure I have. I have been afoot ever since daylight.

MISS TESMAN: And what do you think of it all?

TESMAN: I'm delighted! Quite delighted! Only I can't think what we are to do with the two empty rooms between this inner parlor and Hedda's bed-room.

MISS TESMAN: [*Laughing*] Oh my dear George, I daresay you may find some use for them—in the course of time.

TESMAN: Why of course you are quite right, Aunt Julia! You mean as my library increases—eh?

MISS TESMAN: Yes, quite so, my dear boy. It was your library I was thinking of.

TESMAN: I am specially pleased on Hedda's account. Often and often, before we were engaged, she said that she would never care to live anywhere but in Secretary Falk's villa.

MISS TESMAN: Yes, it was lucky that this very house should come into the market, just after you had started.

TESMAN: Yes, Aunt Julia, the luck was on our side, wasn't it—eh?

MISS TESMAN: But the expense, my dear George! You will find it very expensive, all this.

TESMAN: [*Looks at her, a little cast down*] Yes, I suppose I shall, Aunt!

MISS TESMAN: Oh, frightfully!

TESMAN: How much do you think? In round numbers?—Eh?

MISS TESMAN: Oh, I can't even guess until all the accounts come in.

TESMAN: Well, fortunately, Judge Brack has secured the most favorable terms for me,—so he said in a letter to Hedda.

MISS TESMAN: Yes, don't be uneasy, my dear boy. —Besides, I have given security for the furniture and all the carpets.

TESMAN: Security? You? My dear Aunt Julia—what sort of security could you give?

MISS TESMAN: I have given a mortgage on our annuity.

TESMAN: [*Jumps up*] What! On your—and Aunt Rina's annuity!

MISS TESMAN: Yes, I knew of no other plan, you see.

TESMAN: [*Placing himself before her*] Have you gone out of your senses, Auntie! Your annuity—it's all that you and Aunt Rina have to live upon.

MISS TESMAN: Well well—don't get so excited about it. It's only a matter of form you know—Judge Brack assured me of that. It was he that was kind enough to arrange the whole affair for me. A mere matter of form, he said.

TESMAN: Yes, that may be all very well. But nevertheless——

MISS TESMAN: You will have your own salary to depend upon now. And, good heavens, even if we did have to pay up a little——! To eke things out a bit at the start——! Why, it would be nothing but a pleasure to us.

TESMAN: Oh Auntie—will you never be tired of making sacrifices for me!

MISS TESMAN: [*Rises and lays her hand on his shoulders*] Have I any other happiness in this world except to smooth your way for you, my dear boy? You, who have had neither father nor mother to depend on. And now we have reached the goal, George! Things have looked black enough for us, sometimes; but, thank heaven, now you have nothing to fear.

TESMAN: Yes, it is really marvelous how everything has turned out for the best.

MISS TESMAN: And the people who opposed you—who wanted to bar the way for you—now you have them at your feet. They have fallen, George. Your most dangerous rival—his fall was the worst.—And now he has to lie on the bed he has made for himself—poor misguided creature.

TESMAN: Have you heard anything of Eilert? Since I went away, I mean.

MISS TESMAN: Only that he is said to have published a new book.

TESMAN: What! Eilert Lövborg! Recently—eh?

MISS TESMAN: Yes, so they say. Heaven knows whether it can be worth anything! Ah, when your new book appears—that will be another story, George! What is it to be about?

TESMAN: It will deal with the domestic industries of Brabant during the Middle Ages.

MISS TESMAN: Fancy—to be able to write on such a subject as that!

TESMAN: However, it may be some time before the book is ready. I have all these collections to arrange first, you see.

MISS TESMAN: Yes, collecting and arranging—no one can beat you at that. There you are my poor brother's own son.

TESMAN: I am looking forward eagerly to setting to work at it; especially now that I have my own delightful home to work in.

MISS TESMAN: And, most of all, now that you have got the wife of your heart, my dear George.

TESMAN: [*Embracing her*] Oh yes, yes, Aunt Julia. Hedda—she is the best part of it all! [*Looks towards the doorway*] I believe I hear her coming—eh?

[*Hedda enters from the left through the inner room. She is a woman of nine-and-twenty. Her face and figure show refinement and distinction. Her complexion is pale and opaque. Her steel-gray eyes express a cold, unruffled repose. Her hair is of an agreeable medium brown, but not particularly abundant. She is dressed in a tasteful, somewhat loose-fitting morning gown*]

MISS TESMAN: [*Going to meet Hedda*] Good morning, my dear Hedda! Good morning, and a hearty welcome!

HEDDA: [*Holds out her hand*] Good morning, dear Miss Tesman! So early a call! That is kind of you.

MISS TESMAN: [*With some embarrassment*] Well —has the bride slept well in her new home?

HEDDA: Oh yes, thanks. Passably.

TESMAN: [*Laughing*] Passably! Come, that's good, Hedda! You were sleeping like a stone when I got up.

HEDDA: Fortunately. Of course one has always to accustom one's self to new surroundings, Miss Tesman—little by little. [*Looking towards the left*] Oh —there the servant has gone and opened the veranda door, and let in a whole flood of sunshine.

MISS TESMAN: [*Going towards the door*] Well, then we will shut it.

HEDDA: No no, not that! Tesman, please draw the curtains. That will give a softer light.

TESMAN: [*At the door*] All right—all right.— There now, Hedda, now you have both shade and fresh air.

HEDDA: Yes, fresh air we certainly must have, with all these stacks of flowers——. But—won't you sit down, Miss Tesman?

MISS TESMAN: No, thank you. Now that I have seen that everything is all right here—thank heaven! —I must be getting home again. My sister is lying longing for me, poor thing.

TESMAN: Give her my very best love, Auntie; and say I shall look in and see her later in the day.

MISS TESMAN: Yes, yes, I'll be sure to tell her. But by the by, George—[*Feeling in her dress pocket*] —I had almost forgotten—I have something for you here.

TESMAN: What is it, Auntie? Eh?

MISS TESMAN: [*Produces a flat parcel wrapped in newspaper and hands it to him*] Look here, my dear boy.

TESMAN: [*Opening the parcel*] Well, I declare!— Have you really saved them for me, Aunt Julia! Hedda! isn't this touching—eh?

HEDDA: [*Beside the whatnot on the right*] Well, what is it?

TESMAN: My old morning-shoes! My slippers.

HEDDA: Indeed. I remember you often spoke of them while we were abroad.

TESMAN: Yes, I missed them terribly. [*Goes up to her*] Now you shall see them, Hedda!

HEDDA: [*Going towards the stove*] Thanks, I really don't care about it.

TESMAN: [*Following her*] Only think—ill as she was, Aunt Rina embroidered these for me. Oh you can't think how many associations cling to them.

HEDDA: [*At the table*] Scarcely for me.

MISS TESMAN: Of course not for Hedda, George.

TESMAN: Well, but now that she belongs to the family, I thought——

HEDDA: [*Interrupting*] We shall never get on with this servant, Tesman.

MISS TESMAN: Not get on with Berta?

TESMAN: Why, dear, what puts that in your head? Eh?

HEDDA: [*Pointing*] Look there! She has left her old bonnet lying about on a chair.

TESMAN: [*In consternation, drops the slippers on the floor*] Why, Hedda——

HEDDA: Just fancy, if any one should come in and see it!

TESMAN: But Hedda—that's Aunt Julia's bonnet.

HEDDA: Is it!

MISS TESMAN: [*Taking up the bonnet*] Yes, indeed it's mine. And, what's more, it's not old, Madam Hedda.

HEDDA: I really did not look closely at it, Miss Tesman.

MISS TESMAN: [*Trying on the bonnet*] Let me tell you it's the first time I have worn it—the very first time.

TESMAN: And a very nice bonnet it is too—quite a beauty!

MISS TESMAN: Oh, it's no such great thing, George. [*Looks around her*] My parasol——? Ah, here. [*Takes it*] For this is mine too—[*mutters*]—not Berta's.

TESMAN: A new bonnet and a new parasol! Only think, Hedda!

HEDDA: Very handsome indeed.

TESMAN: Yes, isn't it? Eh? But Auntie, take a good look at Hedda before you go! See how handsome she is!

MISS TESMAN: Oh, my dear boy, there's nothing new in that. Hedda was always lovely.

[*She nods and goes towards the right*]

TESMAN: [*Following*] Yes, but have you noticed what splendid condition she is in? How she has filled out on the journey?

HEDDA: [*Crossing the room*] Oh, do be quiet——!

MISS TESMAN: [*Who has stopped and turned*] Filled out?

TESMAN: Of course you don't notice it so much now that she has that dress on. But I, who can see——

HEDDA: [*At the glass door, impatiently*] Oh, you can't see anything.

TESMAN: It must be the mountain air in the Tyrol——

HEDDA: [*Curtly, interrupting*] I am exactly as I was when I started.

TESMAN: So you insist; but I'm quite certain you are not. Don't you agree with me, Auntie?

MISS TESMAN: [*Who has been gazing at her with folded hands*] Hedda is lovely—lovely—lovely. [*Goes up to her, takes her head between both hands, draws it downwards, and kisses her hair*] God bless and preserve Hedda Tesman—for George's sake.

HEDDA: [*Gently freeing herself*] Oh——! Let me go.

MISS TESMAN: [*In quiet emotion*] I shall not let a day pass without coming to see you.

TESMAN: No you won't, will you, Auntie? Eh?

MISS TESMAN: Good-bye—good-bye!

[*She goes out by the hall door. Tesman accompanies her. The door remains half open. Tesman can be heard repeating his message to Aunt Rina and his thanks for the slippers*]

[*In the meantime, Hedda walks about the room, raising her arms and clenching her hands as if in desperation. Then she flings back the curtains from the glass door, and stands there looking out*]

[*Presently* Tesman *returns and closes the door behind him*]

TESMAN: [*Picks up the slippers from the floor*] What are you looking at, Hedda?

HEDDA: [*Once more calm and mistress of herself*] I am only looking at the leaves. They are so yellow—so withered.

TESMAN: [*Wraps up the slippers and lays them on the table*] Well you see, we are well into September now.

HEDDA: [*Again restless*] Yes, to think of it!—Already in—in September.

TESMAN: Don't you think Aunt Julia's manner was strange, dear? Almost solemn? Can you imagine what was the matter with her? Eh?

HEDDA: I scarcely know her, you see. Is she not often like that?

TESMAN: No, not as she was to-day.

HEDDA: [*Leaving the glass door*] Do you think she was annoyed about the bonnet?

TESMAN: Oh, scarcely at all. Perhaps a little, just at the moment——

HEDDA: But what an idea, to pitch her bonnet about in the drawing-room! No one does that sort of thing.

TESMAN: Well you may be sure Aunt Julia won't do it again.

HEDDA: In any case, I shall manage to make my peace with her.

TESMAN: Yes, my dear, good Hedda, if you only would.

HEDDA: When you call this afternoon, you might invite her to spend the evening here.

TESMAN: Yes, that I will. And there's one thing more you could do that would delight her heart.

HEDDA: What is it?

TESMAN: If you could only prevail on yourself to say *du* to her. For my sake, Hedda? Eh?

HEDDA: No no, Tesman—you really mustn't ask that of me. I have told you so already. I shall try to call her "Aunt"; and you must be satisfied with that.

TESMAN: Well well. Only I think now that you belong to the family, you——

HEDDA: H'm—I can't in the least see why——

[*She goes up towards the middle doorway*]

TESMAN: [*After a pause*] Is there anything the matter with you, Hedda? Eh?

HEDDA: I'm only looking at my old piano. It doesn't go at all well with all the other things.

TESMAN: The first time I draw my salary, we'll see about exchanging it.

HEDDA: No, no—no exchanging. I don't want to part with it. Suppose we put it there in the inner room, and then get another here in its place. When it's convenient, I mean.

TESMAN: [*A little taken aback*] Yes—of course we could do that.

HEDDA: [*Takes up the bouquet from the piano*] These flowers were not here last night when we arrived.

TESMAN: Aunt Julia must have brought them for you.

HEDDA: [*Examining the bouquet*] A visiting-card. [*Takes it out and reads*] "Shall return later in the day." Can you guess whose card it is?

TESMAN: No. Whose? Eh?

HEDDA: The name is "Mrs. Elvsted."

TESMAN: Is it really? Sheriff Elvsted's wife? Miss Rysing that was.

HEDDA: Exactly. The girl with the irritating hair, that she was always showing off. An old flame of yours I've been told.

TESMAN: [*Laughing*] Oh, that didn't last long; and it was before I knew you, Hedda. But fancy her being in town!

HEDDA: It's odd that she should call upon us. I have scarcely seen her since we left school.

TESMAN: I haven't seen her either for—heaven knows how long. I wonder how she can endure to live in such an out-of-the-way hole—eh?

HEDDA: [*After a moment's thought, says suddenly*] Tell me, Tesman—isn't it somewhere near there that he—that—Eilert Lövborg is living?

TESMAN: Yes, he is somewhere in that part of the country.

[Berta *enters by the hall door*]

BERTA: That lady, ma'am, that brought some flowers a little while ago, is here again. [*Pointing*] The flowers you have in your hand, ma'am.

HEDDA: Ah, is she? Well, please show her in.

[Berta *opens the door for* Mrs. Elvsted, *and goes out herself.—*Mrs. Elvsted *is a woman of fragile figure, with pretty, soft features. Her eyes are light blue, large, round, and somewhat prominent, with a startled, inquiring expression. Her hair is remarkably light, almost flaxen, and unusually abundant and wavy. She is a couple of years younger than* Hedda. *She wears a dark visiting dress, tasteful, but not quite in the latest fashion*]

HEDDA: [*Receives her warmly*] How do you do, my dear Mrs. Elvsted? It's delightful to see you again.

MRS. ELVSTED: [*Nervously, struggling for self-control*] Yes, it's a very long time since we met.

TESMAN: [*Gives her his hand*] And we too—eh?

HEDDA: Thanks for your lovely flowers——

MRS. ELVSTED: Oh, not at all—— I would have

come straight here yesterday afternoon; but I heard that you were away——

TESMAN: Have you just come to town? Eh?

MRS. ELVSTED: I arrived yesterday, about midday. Oh, I was quite in despair when I heard that you were not at home.

HEDDA: In despair! How so?

TESMAN: Why, my dear Mrs. Rysing—I mean Mrs. Elvsted——

HEDDA: I hope that you are not in any trouble?

MRS. ELVSTED: Yes, I am. And I don't know another living creature here that I can turn to.

HEDDA: [*Laying the bouquet on the table*] Come—let us sit here on the sofa——

MRS. ELVSTED: Oh, I am too restless to sit down.

HEDDA: Oh no, you're not. Come here.

[*She draws* Mrs. Elvsted *down upon the sofa and sits at her side*]

TESMAN: Well? What is it, Mrs. Elvsted——?

HEDDA: Has anything particular happened to you at home?

MRS. ELVSTED: Yes—and no. Oh—I am so anxious you should not misunderstand me——

HEDDA: Then your best plan is to tell us the whole story, Mrs. Elvsted.

TESMAN: I suppose that's what you have come for —eh?

MRS. ELVSTED: Yes, yes—of course it is. Well then, I must tell you—if you don't already know— that Eilert Lövborg is in town, too.

HEDDA: Lövborg——!

TESMAN: What! Has Eilert Lövborg come back? Fancy that, Hedda!

HEDDA: Well well—I hear it.

MRS. ELVSTED: He has been here a week already. Just fancy—a whole week! In this terrible town, alone! With so many temptations on all sides.

HEDDA: But, my dear Mrs. Elvsted—how does he concern you so much?

MRS. ELVSTED: [*Looks at her with a startled air, and says rapidly*] He was the children's tutor.

HEDDA: Your children's?

MRS. ELVSTED: My husband's. I have none.

HEDDA: Your step-children's, then?

MRS. ELVSTED: Yes.

TESMAN: [*Somewhat hesitatingly*] Then was he— I don't know how to express it—was he—regular enough in his habits to be fit for the post? Eh?

MRS. ELVSTED: For the last two years his conduct has been irreproachable.

TESMAN: Has it indeed? Fancy that, Hedda!

HEDDA: I hear it.

MRS. ELVSTED: Perfectly irreproachable, I assure you! In every respect. But all the same—now that I know he is here—in this great town—and with a large sum of money in his hands—I can't help being in mortal fear for him.

TESMAN: Why did he not remain where he was? With you and your husband? Eh?

MRS. ELVSTED: After his book was published he was too restless and unsettled to remain with us.

TESMAN: Yes, by the by, Aunt Julia told me he had published a new book.

MRS. ELVSTED: Yes, a big book, dealing with the march of civilization—in broad outline, as it were. It came out about a fortnight ago. And since it has sold so well, and been so much read—and made such a sensation——

TESMAN: Has it indeed? It must be something he has had lying by since his better days.

MRS. ELVSTED: Long ago, you mean?

TESMAN: Yes.

MRS. ELVSTED: No, he has written it all since he has been with us—within the last year.

TESMAN: Isn't that good news, Hedda? Think of that.

MRS. ELVSTED: Ah yes, if only it would last!

HEDDA: Have you seen him here in town?

MRS. ELVSTED: No, not yet. I have had the greatest difficulty in finding out his address. But this morning I discovered it at last.

HEDDA: [Looks searchingly at her] Do you know, it seems to me a little odd of your husband—h'm——

MRS. ELVSTED: [Starting nervously] Of my husband! What?

HEDDA: That he should send you to town on such an errand—that he does not come himself and look after his friend.

MRS. ELVSTED: Oh no, no—my husband has no time. And besides, I—I had some shopping to do.

HEDDA: [With a slight smile] Ah, that is a different matter.

MRS. ELVSTED: [Rising quickly and uneasily] And now I beg and implore you, Mr. Tesman—receive Eilert Lövborg kindly if he comes to you! And that he is sure to do. You see you were such great friends in the old days. And then you are interested in the same studies—the same branch of science—so far as I can understand.

TESMAN: We used to be, at any rate.

MRS. ELVSTED: That is why I beg so earnestly that you—you too—will keep a sharp eye upon him. Oh, you will promise me that, Mr. Tesman—won't you?

TESMAN: With the greatest of pleasure, Mrs. Rysing——

HEDDA: Elvsted.

TESMAN: I assure you I shall do all I possibly can for Eilert. You may rely upon me.

MRS. ELVSTED: Oh, how very, very kind of you! [Presses his hands] Thanks, thanks, thanks! [Frightened] You see, my husband is so very fond of him!

HEDDA: [Rising] You ought to write to him, Tesman. Perhaps he may not care to come to you of his own accord.

TESMAN: Well, perhaps it would be the right thing to do, Hedda? Eh?

HEDDA: And the sooner the better. Why not at once?

MRS. ELVSTED: [Imploringly] Oh, if you only would!

TESMAN: I'll write this moment. Have you his address, Mrs.—Mrs. Elvsted?

MRS. ELVSTED: Yes. [Takes a slip of paper from her pocket, and hands it to him] Here it is.

TESMAN: Good, good. Then I'll go in—— [Looks about him] By the by—my slippers? Oh, here.

[Takes the packet, and is about to go]

HEDDA: Be sure you write him a cordial, friendly letter. And a good long one too.

TESMAN: Yes, I will.

MRS. ELVSTED: But please, please don't say a word to show that I have suggested it.

TESMAN: No, how could you think I would? Eh?

[He goes out to the right, through the inner room]

HEDDA: [Goes up to Mrs. Elvsted, smiles, and says in a low voice] There! We have killed two birds with one stone.

MRS. ELVSTED: What do you mean?

HEDDA: Could you not see that I wanted him to go?

MRS. ELVSTED: Yes, to write the letter——

HEDDA: And that I might speak to you alone.

MRS. ELVSTED: [Confused] About the same thing?

HEDDA: Precisely.

MRS. ELVSTED: [Apprehensively] But there is nothing more, Mrs. Tesman! Absolutely nothing!

HEDDA: Oh yes, but there is. There is a great deal more—I can see that. Sit here—and we'll have a cosy, confidential chat.

[She forces Mrs. Elvsted to sit in the easy-chair beside the stove, and seats herself on one of the footstools]

MRS. ELVSTED: [Anxiously, looking at her watch] But, my dear Mrs. Tesman—I was really on the point of going.

HEDDA: Oh, you can't be in such a hurry.—Well? Now tell me something about your life at home.

MRS. ELVSTED: Oh, that is just what I care least to speak about.

HEDDA: But to me, dear——? Why, weren't we schoolfellows?

MRS. ELVSTED: Yes, but you were in the class above me. Oh, how dreadfully afraid of you I was then!

HEDDA: Afraid of me?

MRS. ELVSTED: Yes, dreadfully. For when we met on the stairs you used always to pull my hair.

HEDDA: Did I, really?

MRS. ELVSTED: Yes, and once you said you would burn it off my head.

HEDDA: Oh, that was all nonsense, of course.

MRS. ELVSTED: Yes, but I was so silly in those days.—And since then, too—we have drifted so far—far apart from each other. Our circles have been so entirely different.

HEDDA: Well then, we must try to drift together again. Now listen! At school we said *du* to each other; and we called each other by our Christian names——

MRS. ELVSTED: No, I am sure you must be mistaken.

HEDDA: No, not at all! I can remember quite distinctly. So now we are going to renew our old friendship. [*Draws the footstool closer to* Mrs. Elvsted] There now! [*Kisses her cheek*] You must say *du* to me and call me Hedda.

MRS. ELVSTED: [*Presses and pats her hands*] Oh, how good and kind you are! I am not used to such kindness.

HEDDA: There, there, there! And I shall say *du* to you, as in the old days, and call you my dear Thora.

MRS. ELVSTED: My name is Thea.

HEDDA: Why, of course! I meant Thea. [*Looks at her compassionately*] So you are not accustomed to goodness and kindness, Thea? Not in your own home?

MRS. ELVSTED: Oh, if I only had a home! But I haven't any; I have never had a home.

HEDDA: [*Looks at her for a moment*] I almost suspected as much.

MRS. ELVSTED: [*Gazing helplessly before her*] Yes—yes—yes.

HEDDA: I don't quite remember—was it not as housekeeper that you first went to Mr. Elvsted's?

MRS. ELVSTED: I really went as governess. But his wife—his late wife—was an invalid,—and rarely left her room. So I had to look after the housekeeping as well.

HEDDA: And then—at last—you became mistress of the house.

MRS. ELVSTED: [*Sadly*] Yes, I did.

HEDDA: Let me see—about how long ago was that?

MRS. ELVSTED: My marriage?

HEDDA: Yes.

MRS. ELVSTED: Five years ago.

HEDDA: To be sure; it must be that.

MRS. ELVSTED: Oh those five years——! Or at all events the last two or three of them! Oh, if you [1] could only imagine——

HEDDA: [*Giving her a little slap on the hand*] De? Fie, Thea!

MRS. ELVSTED: Yes, yes, I will try—— Well, if you could only imagine and understand——

HEDDA: [*Lightly*] Eilert Lövborg has been in your neighborhood about three years, hasn't he?

MRS. ELVSTED: [*Looks at her doubtfully*] Eilert Lövborg? Yes—he has.

HEDDA: Had you known him before, in town here?

MRS. ELVSTED: Scarcely at all. I mean—I knew him by name of course.

[1] Mrs. Elvsted here uses the formal pronoun *De*, whereupon Hedda rebukes her. In her next speech Mrs. Elvsted says *du*.

HEDDA: But you saw a good deal of him in the country?

MRS. ELVSTED: Yes, he came to us every day. You see, he gave the children lessons; for in the long run I couldn't manage it all myself.

HEDDA: No, that's clear.—And your husband——? I suppose he is often away from home?

MRS. ELVSTED: Yes. Being sheriff, you know, he has to travel about a good deal in his district.

HEDDA: [*Leaning against the arm of the chair*] Thea—my poor, sweet Thea—now you must tell me everything—exactly as it stands.

MRS. ELVSTED: Well then, you must question me.

HEDDA: What sort of a man is your husband, Thea? I mean—you know—in everyday life. Is he kind to you?

MRS. ELVSTED: [*Evasively*] I am sure he means well in everything.

HEDDA: I should think he must be altogether too old for you. There is at least twenty years' difference between you, is there not?

MRS. ELVSTED: [*Irritably*] Yes, that is true, too. Everything about him is repellent to me! We have not a thought in common. We have no single point of sympathy—he and I.

HEDDA: But is he not fond of you all the same? In his own way?

MRS. ELVSTED: Oh I really don't know. I think he regards me simply as a useful property. And then it doesn't cost much to keep me. I am not expensive.

HEDDA: That is stupid of you.

MRS. ELVSTED: [*Shakes her head*] It cannot be otherwise—not with him. I don't think he really cares for any one but himself—and perhaps a little for the children.

HEDDA: And for Eilert Lövborg, Thea.

MRS. ELVSTED: [*Looking at her*] For Eilert Lövborg? What puts that into your head?

HEDDA: Well, my dear—I should say, when he sends you after him all the way to town—— [*Smiling almost imperceptibly*] And besides, you said so yourself, to Tesman.

MRS. ELVSTED: [*With a little nervous twitch*] Did I? Yes, I suppose I did. [*Vehemently, but not loudly*] No—I may just as well make a clean breast of it at once! For it must all come out in any case.

HEDDA: Why, my dear Thea——?

MRS. ELVSTED: Well, to make a long story short: My husband did not know that I was coming.

HEDDA: What! Your husband didn't know it!

MRS. ELVSTED: No, of course not. For that matter, he was away from home himself—he was traveling. Oh, I could bear it no longer, Hedda! I couldn't indeed—so utterly alone as I should have been in future.

HEDDA: Well? And then?

MRS. ELVSTED: So I put together some of my things—what I needed most—as quietly as possible. And then I left the house.

HEDDA: Without a word?

MRS. ELVSTED: Yes—and took the train straight to town.

HEDDA: Why, my dear, good Thea—to think of you daring to do it!

MRS. ELVSTED: [*Rises and moves about the room*] What else could I possibly do?

HEDDA: But what do you think your husband will say when you go home again?

MRS. ELVSTED: [*At the table, looks at her*] Back to him?

HEDDA: Of course.

MRS. ELVSTED: I shall never go back to him again.

HEDDA: [*Rising and going towards her*] Then you have left your home—for good and all?

MRS. ELVSTED: Yes. There was nothing else to be done.

HEDDA: But then—to take flight so openly.

MRS. ELVSTED: Oh, it's impossible to keep things of that sort secret.

HEDDA: But what do you think people will say of you, Thea?

MRS. ELVSTED: They may say what they like, for aught *I* care. [*Seats herself wearily and sadly on the sofa*] I have done nothing but what I had to do.

HEDDA: [*After a short silence*] And what are your plans now? What do you think of doing?

MRS. ELVSTED: I don't know yet. I only know this, that I must live here, where Eilert Lövborg is —if I am to live at all.

HEDDA: [*Takes a chair from the table, seats herself beside her, and strokes her hands*] My dear Thea —how did this—this friendship—between you and Eilert Lövborg come about?

MRS. ELVSTED: Oh it grew up gradually. I gained a sort of influence over him.

HEDDA: Indeed?

MRS. ELVSTED: He gave up his old habits. Not because I asked him to, for I never dared do that. But of course he saw how repulsive they were to me; and so he dropped them.

HEDDA: [*Concealing an involuntary smile of scorn*] Then you have reclaimed him—as the saying goes— my little Thea.

MRS. ELVSTED: So he says himself, at any rate. And he, on his side, has made a real human being of me—taught me to think, and to understand so many things.

HEDDA: Did he give you lessons too, then?

MRS. ELVSTED: No, not exactly lessons. But he talked to me—talked about such an infinity of things. And then came the lovely, happy time when I began to share in his work—when he allowed me to help him!

HEDDA: Oh he did, did he?

MRS. ELVSTED: Yes, he never wrote anything without my assistance.

HEDDA: You were two good comrades, in fact?

MRS. ELVSTED: [*Eagerly*] Comrades! Yes, fancy, Hedda—that is the very word he used!—Oh, I ought to feel perfectly happy; and yet I cannot; for I don't know how long it will last.

HEDDA: Are you no surer of him than that?

MRS. ELVSTED: [*Gloomily*] A woman's shadow stands between Eilert Lövborg and me.

HEDDA: [*Looks at her anxiously*] Who can that be?

MRS. ELVSTED: I don't know. Some one he knew in his—in his past. Some one he has never been able wholly to forget.

HEDDA: What has he told you about—about this?

MRS. ELVSTED: He has only once—quite vaguely —alluded to it.

HEDDA: Well! And what did he say?

MRS. ELVSTED: He said that when they parted, she threatened to shoot him with a pistol.

HEDDA: [*With cold composure*] Oh, nonsense! No one does that sort of thing here.

MRS. ELVSTED: No. And that is why I think it must have been that red-haired singing-woman whom he once——

HEDDA: Yes, very likely.

MRS. ELVSTED: For I remember they used to say of her that she carried loaded firearms.

HEDDA: Oh—then of course it must have been she.

MRS. ELVSTED: [*Wringing her hands*] And now just fancy, Hedda—I hear that this singing-woman— that she is in town again! Oh, I don't know what to do——

HEDDA: [*Glancing towards the inner room*] Hush! Here comes Tesman. [*Rises and whispers*] Thea— all this must remain between you and me.

MRS. ELVSTED: [*Springing up*] Oh yes—yes! For heaven's sake——!

[George Tesman, *with a letter in his hand, comes from the right through the inner room*]

TESMAN: There now—the epistle is finished.

HEDDA: That's right. And now Mrs. Elvsted is just going. Wait a moment—I'll go with you to the garden gate.

TESMAN: Do you think Berta could post the letter, Hedda dear?

HEDDA: [*Takes it*] I will tell her to.

[Berta *enters from the hall*]

BERTA: Judge Brack wishes to know if Mrs. Tesman will receive him.

HEDDA: Yes, ask Judge Brack to come in. And look here—put this letter in the post.

BERTA: [*Taking the letter*] Yes, ma'am.

[*She opens the door for* Judge Brack *and goes out herself.* Brack *is a man of forty-five; thickset, but well-built and elastic in his movements. His face is roundish with an aristocratic profile. His hair is short, still almost black, and carefully dressed. His eyes are lively and sparkling. His eyebrows thick. His moustaches are also thick, with short-cut ends. He wears a well-cut walking-suit, a little too youthful for his age. He uses an eye-glass, which he now and then lets drop*]

JUDGE BRACK: [*With his hat in his hand, bowing*] May one venture to call so early in the day?

HEDDA: Of course one may.

TESMAN: [*Presses his hand*] You are welcome at any time. [*Introducing him*] Judge Brack—Miss Rysing——

HEDDA: Oh——!

BRACK: [*Bowing*] Ah—delighted——

HEDDA: [*Looks at him and laughs*] It's nice to have a look at you by daylight, Judge!

BRACK: Do you find me—altered?

HEDDA: A little younger, I think.

BRACK: Thank you so much.

TESMAN: But what do you think of Hedda—eh? Doesn't she look flourishing? She has actually——

HEDDA: Oh, do leave me alone. You haven't thanked Judge Brack for all the trouble he has taken——

BRACK: Oh, nonsense—it was a pleasure to me——

HEDDA: Yes, you are a friend indeed. But here stands Thea all impatience to be off—so *au revoir* Judge. I shall be back again presently.

[*Mutual salutations.* Mrs. Elvsted *and* Hedda *go out by the hall door*]

BRACK: Well,—is your wife tolerably satisfied——

TESMAN: Yes, we can't thank you sufficiently. Of course she talks of a little rearrangement here and there; and one or two things are still wanting. We shall have to buy some additional trifles.

BRACK: Indeed!

TESMAN: But we won't trouble you about these things. Hedda says she herself will look after what is wanting.—Shan't we sit down? Eh?

BRACK: Thanks, for a moment. [*Seats himself beside the table*] There is something I wanted to speak to you about, my dear Tesman.

TESMAN: Indeed? Ah, I understand! [*Seating himself*] I suppose it's the serious part of the frolic that is coming now. Eh?

BRACK: Oh, the money question is not so very pressing; though, for that matter, I wish we had gone a little more economically to work.

TESMAN: But that would never have done, you know! Think of Hedda, my dear fellow! You, who know her so well——. I couldn't possibly ask her to put up with a shabby style of living!

BRACK: No, no—that is just the difficulty.

TESMAN: And then—fortunately—it can't be long before I receive my appointment.

BRACK: Well, you see—such things are often apt to hang fire for a time.

TESMAN: Have you heard anything definite? Eh?

BRACK: Nothing exactly definite—— [*Interrupting himself*] But by the by—I have one piece of news for you.

TESMAN: Well?

BRACK: Your old friend, Eilert Lövborg, has returned to town.

TESMAN: I know that already.

BRACK: Indeed! How did you learn it?

TESMAN: From that lady who went out with Hedda.

BRACK: Really? What was her name? I didn't quite catch it.

TESMAN: Mrs. Elvsted.

BRACK: Aha—Sheriff Elvsted's wife? Of course—he has been living up in their regions.

TESMAN: And fancy—I'm delighted to hear that he is quite a reformed character!

BRACK: So they say.

TESMAN: And then he has published a new book—eh?

BRACK: Yes, indeed he has.

TESMAN: And I hear it has made some sensation!

BRACK: Quite an unusual sensation.

TESMAN: Fancy—isn't that good news! A man of such extraordinary talents——. I felt so grieved to think that he had gone irretrievably to ruin.

BRACK: That was what everybody thought.

TESMAN: But I cannot imagine what he will take to now! How in the world will he be able to make his living? Eh?

[*During the last words,* Hedda *has entered by the hall door*]

HEDDA: [*To* Brack, *laughing with a touch of scorn*] Tesman is for ever worrying about how people are to make their living.

TESMAN: Well you see, dear—we were talking about poor Eilert Lövborg.

HEDDA: [*Glancing at him rapidly*] Oh, indeed? [*Seats herself in the arm-chair beside the stove and asks indifferently*] What is the matter with him?

TESMAN: Well—no doubt he has run through all his property long ago; and he can scarcely write a new book every year—eh? So I really can't see what is to become of him.

BRACK: Perhaps I can give you some information on that point.

TESMAN: Indeed!

BRACK: You must remember that his relations have a good deal of influence.

TESMAN: Oh, his relations, unfortunately, have entirely washed their hands of him.

BRACK: At one time they called him the hope of the family.

TESMAN: At one time, yes! But he has put an end to all that.

HEDDA: Who knows? [*With a slight smile*] I hear they have reclaimed him up at Sheriff Elvsted's——

BRACK: And then this book that he has published——

TESMAN: Well well, I hope to goodness they may find something for him to do. I have just written to him. I asked him to come and see us this evening, Hedda dear.

BRACK: But my dear fellow, you are booked for my bachelors' party this evening. You promised on the pier last night.

HEDDA: Had you forgotten, Tesman?

TESMAN: Yes, I had utterly forgotten.

BRACK: But it doesn't matter, for you may be sure he won't come.

TESMAN: What makes you think that? Eh?

BRACK: [With a little hesitation, rising and resting his hands on the back of his chair] My dear Tesman—and you too, Mrs. Tesman—I think I ought not to keep you in the dark about something that—that——

TESMAN: That concerns Eilert——?

BRACK: Both you and him.

TESMAN: Well, my dear Judge, out with it.

BRACK: You must be prepared to find your appointment deferred longer than you desired or expected.

TESMAN: [Jumping up uneasily] Is there some hitch about it? Eh?

BRACK: The nomination may perhaps be made conditional on the result of a competition——

TESMAN: Competition! Think of that, Hedda!

HEDDA: [Leans further back in the chair] Aha—aha!

TESMAN: But who can my competitor be? Surely not——?

BRACK: Yes, precisely—Eilert Lövborg.

TESMAN: [Clasping his hands] No, no—it's quite inconceivable! Quite impossible! Eh?

BRACK: H'm—that is what it may come to, all the same.

TESMAN: Well but, Judge Brack—it would show the most incredible lack of consideration for me. [Gesticulates with his arms] For—just think—I'm a married man! We have married on the strength of these prospects, Hedda and I; and run deep into debt; and borrowed money from Aunt Julia too. Good heavens, they had as good as promised me the appointment. Eh?

BRACK: Well, well, well—no doubt you will get it in the end; only after a contest.

HEDDA: [Immovable in her arm-chair] Fancy, Tesman, there will be a sort of sporting interest in that.

TESMAN: Why, my dearest Hedda, how can you be so indifferent about it?

HEDDA: [As before] I am not at all indifferent. I am most eager to see who wins.

BRACK: In any case, Mrs. Tesman, it is best that you should know how matters stand. I mean—before you set about the little purchases I hear you are threatening.

HEDDA: This can make no difference.

BRACK: Indeed! Then I have no more to say. Good-bye! [To Tesman] I shall look in on my way back from my afternoon walk, and take you home with me.

TESMAN: Oh yes, yes—your news has quite upset me.

HEDDA: [Reclining, holds out her hand] Good-bye, Judge; and be sure you call in the afternoon.

BRACK: Many thanks. Good-bye, good-bye!

TESMAN: [Accompanying him to the door] Good-bye, my dear Judge! You must really excuse me——

[Judge Brack goes out by the hall door]

TESMAN: [Crosses the room] Oh Hedda—one should never rush into adventures. Eh?

HEDDA: [Looks at him, smiling] Do you do that?

TESMAN: Yes, dear—there is no denying—it was adventurous to go and marry and set up house upon mere expectations.

HEDDA: Perhaps you are right there.

TESMAN: Well—at all events, we have our delightful home, Hedda! Fancy, the home we both dreamed of—the home we were in love with, I may almost say. Eh?

HEDDA: [Rising slowly and wearily] It was part of our compact that we were to go into society—to keep open house.

TESMAN: Yes, if you only knew how I had been looking forward to it! Fancy—to see you as hostess—in a select circle! Eh? Well, well, well—for the present we shall have to get on without society, Hedda—only to invite Aunt Julia now and then.—Oh, I intended you to lead such an utterly different life, dear——!

HEDDA: Of course I cannot have my man in livery just yet.

TESMAN: Oh no, unfortunately. It would be out of the question for us to keep a footman, you know.

HEDDA: And the saddle-horse I was to have had——

TESMAN: [Aghast] The saddle-horse!

HEDDA: ——I suppose I must not think of that now.

TESMAN: Good heavens, no!—that's as clear as daylight.

HEDDA: [Goes up the room] Well, I shall have one thing at least to kill time with in the meanwhile.

TESMAN: [Beaming] Oh thank heaven for that! What is it, Hedda? Eh?

HEDDA: [In the middle doorway, looks at him with covert scorn] My pistols, George.

TESMAN: [In alarm] Your pistols!

HEDDA: [With cold eyes] General Gabler's pistols.

[She goes out through the inner room, to the left]

TESMAN: [Rushes up to the middle doorway and calls after her] No, for heaven's sake, Hedda darling—don't touch those dangerous things! For my sake, Hedda! Eh?

ACT II.

The room at the Tesmans as in the first act, except that the piano has been removed, and an elegant little writing-table with book-shelves put in its place. A smaller table stands near the sofa on the left. Most of the bouquets have been taken away. Mrs. Elvsted's bouquet is upon the large table in front.—It is afternoon

Hedda, *dressed to receive callers, is alone in the room. She stands by the open glass door, loading a revolver. The fellow to it lies in an open pistol-case on the writing-table.*

HEDDA: [*Looks down the garden, and calls*] So you are here again, Judge!

BRACK: [*Is heard calling from a distance*] As you see, Mrs. Tesman!

HEDDA: [*Raises the pistol and points*] Now I'll shoot you, Judge Brack!

BRACK: [*Calling unseen*] No, no, no! Don't stand aiming at me!

HEDDA: This is what comes of sneaking in by the back way.[1] [*She fires*]

BRACK: [*Nearer*] Are you out of your senses!——

HEDDA: Dear me—did I happen to hit you?

BRACK: [*Still outside*] I wish you would let these pranks alone!

HEDDA: Come in then, Judge.

[Judge Brack, *dressed as though for a men's party, enters by the glass door. He carries a light overcoat over his arm*]

BRACK: What the deuce—haven't you tired of that sport, yet? What are you shooting at?

HEDDA: Oh, I am only firing in the air.

BRACK: [*Gently takes the pistol out of her hand*] Allow me, Madam! [*Looks at it*] Ah—I know this pistol well! [*Looks around*] Where is the case? Ah, here it is. [*Lays the pistol in it, and shuts it*] Now we won't play at that game any more to-day.

HEDDA: Then what in heaven's name would you have me do with myself?

BRACK: Have you had no visitors?

HEDDA: [*Closing the glass door*] Not one. I suppose all our set are still out of town.

BRACK: And is Tesman not at home either?

HEDDA: [*At the writing-table, putting the pistol-case in a drawer which she shuts*] No. He rushed off to his aunt's directly after lunch; he didn't expect you so early.

BRACK: H'm—how stupid of me not to have thought of that!

HEDDA: [*Turning her head to look at him*] Why stupid?

BRACK: Because if I had thought of it I should have come a little—earlier.

HEDDA: [*Crossing the room*] Then you would have found no one to receive you; for I have been in my room changing my dress ever since lunch.

BRACK: And is there no sort of little chink that we could hold a parley through?

HEDDA: You have forgotten to arrange one.

BRACK: That was another piece of stupidity.

HEDDA: Well, we must just settle down here—and wait. Tesman is not likely to be back for some time yet.

¹ *Bagveje* means both "back ways" and "underhand courses."

BRACK: Never mind; I shall not be impatient.

[Hedda *seats herself in the corner of the sofa. Brack lays his overcoat over the back of the nearest chair, and sits down, but keeps his hat in his hand. A short silence. They look at each other*]

HEDDA: Well?

BRACK: [*In the same tone*] Well?

HEDDA: I spoke first.

BRACK: [*Bending a little forward*] Come, let us have a cosy little chat, Mrs. Hedda.

HEDDA: [*Leaning further back in the sofa*] Does it not seem like a whole eternity since our last talk? Of course I don't count those few words yesterday evening and this morning.

BRACK: You mean since our last confidential talk? Our last *tête-à-tête?*

HEDDA: Well, yes—since you put it so.

BRACK: Not a day has passed but I have wished that you were home again.

HEDDA: And I have done nothing but wish the same thing.

BRACK: You? Really, Mrs. Hedda? And I thought you had been enjoying your tour so much!

HEDDA: Oh, yes, you may be sure of that!

BRACK: But Tesman's letters spoke of nothing but happiness.

HEDDA: Oh, Tesman! You see, he thinks nothing so delightful as grubbing in libraries and making copies of old parchments, or whatever you call them.

BRACK: [*With a spice of malice*] Well, that is his vocation in life—or part of it at any rate.

HEDDA: Yes, of course; and no doubt when it's your vocation——. But *I!* Oh, my dear Mr. Brack, how mortally bored I have been.

BRACK: [*Sympathetically*] Do you really say so? In downright earnest?

HEDDA: Yes, you can surely understand it——! To go for six whole months without meeting a soul that knew anything of our circle, or could talk about the things we are interested in.

BRACK: Yes, yes—I, too, should feel that a deprivation.

HEDDA: And then, what I found most intolerable of all——

BRACK: Well?

HEDDA: ——was being everlastingly in the company of—one and the same person——

BRACK: [*With a nod of assent*] Morning, noon, and night, yes—at all possible times and seasons.

HEDDA: I said "everlastingly."

BRACK: Just so. But I should have thought, with our excellent Tesman, one could——

HEDDA: Tesman is—a specialist, my dear Judge.

BRACK: Undeniably.

HEDDA: And specialists are not at all amusing to travel with. Not in the long run at any rate.

BRACK: Not even—the specialist one happens to love?

HEDDA: Faugh—don't use that sickening word!

BRACK: [*Taken aback*] What do you say, Mrs. Hedda?

HEDDA: [*Half laughing, half irritated*] You should just try it! To hear of nothing but the history of civilization morning, noon and night——

BRACK: Everlastingly.

HEDDA: Yes, yes, yes! And then all this about the domestic industry of the middle ages——! That's the most disgusting part of it!

BRACK: [*Looks searchingly at her*] But tell me— in that case, how am I to understand your——? H'm——

HEDDA: My accepting George Tesman, you mean?

BRACK: Well, let us put it so.

HEDDA: Good heavens, do you see anything so wonderful in that?

BRACK: Yes and no—Mrs. Hedda.

HEDDA: I had positively danced myself tired, my dear Judge. My day was done—— [*With a slight shudder*] Oh, no—I won't say that; nor think it, either!

BRACK: You have assuredly no reason to.

HEDDA: Oh, reasons—— [*Watching him closely*] And George Tesman—after all, you must admit that he is correctness itself.

BRACK: His correctness and respectability are beyond all question.

HEDDA: And I don't see anything absolutely ridiculous about him.—Do you?

BRACK: Ridiculous? N—no—I shouldn't exactly say so——

HEDDA: Well—and his powers of research, at all events, are untiring.—I see no reason why he should not one day come to the front, after all.

BRACK: [*Looks at her hesitatingly*] I thought that you, like every one else, expected him to attain the highest distinction.

HEDDA: [*With an expression of fatigue*] Yes, so I did.—And then, since he was bent, at all hazards, on being allowed to provide for me—I really don't know why I should not have accepted his offer?

BRACK: No—if you look at it in that light——

HEDDA: It was more than my other adorers were prepared to do for me, my dear Judge.

BRACK: [*Laughing*] Well, I can't answer for all the rest; but as for myself, you know quite well that I have always entertained a—a certain respect for the marriage tie—for marriage as an institution, Mrs. Hedda.

HEDDA: [*Jestingly*] Oh, I assure you I have never cherished any hopes with respect to you.

BRACK: All I require is a pleasant and intimate interior, where I can make myself useful in every way, and am free to come and go as—as a trusted friend——

HEDDA: Of the master of the house, do you mean?

BRACK: [*Bowing*] Frankly—of the mistress first of all; but, of course, of the master, too, in the second place. Such a triangular friendship—if I may call it

so—is really a great convenience for all parties, let me tell you.

HEDDA: Yes, I have many a time longed for some one to make a third on our travels. Oh—those railway-carriage *tête-à-têtes*——!

BRACK: Fortunately your wedding journey is over now.

HEDDA: [*Shaking her head*] Not by a long—long way. I have only arrived at a station on the line.

BRACK: Well, then the passengers jump out and move about a little, Mrs. Hedda.

HEDDA: I never jump out.

BRACK: Really?

HEDDA: No—because there is always some one standing by to——

BRACK: [*Laughing*] To look at your ankles, do you mean?

HEDDA: Precisely.

BRACK: Well, but, dear me——

HEDDA: [*With a gesture of repulsion*] I won't have it. I would rather keep my seat where I happen to be—and continue the *tête-à-tête*.

BRACK: But suppose a third person were to jump in and join the couple.

HEDDA: Ah—that is quite another matter!

BRACK: A trusted, sympathetic friend——

HEDDA: ——with a fund of conversation on all sorts of lively topics——

BRACK: ——and not the least bit of a specialist!

HEDDA: [*With an audible sigh*] Yes, that would be a relief, indeed.

BRACK: [*Hears the front door open, and glances in that direction*] The triangle is completed.

HEDDA: [*Half aloud*] And on goes the train.

[*George Tesman in a gray walking-suit, with a soft felt hat, enters from the hall. He has a number of unbound books under his arm and in his pockets*]

TESMAN: [*Goes up to the table beside the corner settee*] Ouf—what a load for a warm day—all these books. [*Lays them on the table*] I'm positively perspiring, Hedda. Hallo—are you there already, my dear Judge? Eh? Berta didn't tell me.

BRACK: [*Rising*] I came in through the garden.

HEDDA: What books have you got there?

TESMAN: [*Stands looking them through*] Some new books on my special subjects—quite indispensable to me.

HEDDA: Your special subjects?

BRACK: Yes, books on his special subjects, Mrs. Tesman.

[*Brack and Hedda exchange a confidential smile*]

HEDDA: Do you need still more books on your special subjects?

TESMAN: Yes, my dear Hedda, one can never have too many of them. Of course, one must keep up with all that is written and published.

HEDDA: Yes, I suppose one must.

TESMAN: [*Searching among his books*] And look

here—I have got hold of Eilert Lövborg's new book, too. [*Offering it to her*] Perhaps you would like to glance through it, Hedda? Eh?

HEDDA: No, thank you. Or rather—afterwards perhaps.

TESMAN: I looked into it a little on the way home.

BRACK: Well, what do you think of it—as a specialist?

TESMAN: I think it shows quite remarkable soundness of judgment. He never wrote like that before. [*Putting the books together*] Now I shall take all these into my study. I'm longing to cut the leaves——! And then I must change my clothes. [*To Brack*] I suppose we needn't start just yet? Eh?

BRACK: Oh, dear, no—there is not the slightest hurry.

TESMAN: Well, then, I will take my time. [*Is going with his books, but stops in the doorway and turns*] By the by, Hedda—Aunt Julia is not coming this evening.

HEDDA: Not coming? Is it that affair of the bonnet that keeps her away?

TESMAN: Oh, not at all. How could you think such a thing of Aunt Julia? Just fancy——! The fact is, Aunt Rina is very ill.

HEDDA: She always is.

TESMAN: Yes, but to-day she is much worse than usual, poor dear.

HEDDA: Oh, then it's only natural that her sister should remain with her. I must bear my disappointment.

TESMAN: And you can't imagine, dear, how delighted Aunt Julia seemed to be—because you had come home looking so flourishing!

HEDDA: [*Half aloud, rising*] Oh, those everlasting Aunts!

TESMAN: What?

HEDDA: [*Going to the glass door*] Nothing.

TESMAN: Oh, all right.

[*He goes through the inner room, out to the right*]

BRACK: What bonnet were you talking about?

HEDDA: Oh, it was a little episode with Miss Tesman this morning. She had laid down her bonnet on the chair there—[*looks at him and smiles*]—and I pretended to think it was the servant's.

BRACK: [*Shaking his head*] Now, my dear Mrs. Hedda, how could you do such a thing? To that excellent old lady, too!

HEDDA: [*Nervously crossing the room*] Well, you see—these impulses come over me all of a sudden; and I cannot resist them. [*Throws herself down in the easy-chair by the stove*] Oh, I don't know how to explain it.

BRACK: [*Behind the easy-chair*] You are not really happy—that is at the bottom of it.

HEDDA: [*Looking straight before her*] I know of no reason why I should be—happy. Perhaps you can give me one?

BRACK: Well—amongst other things, because you have got exactly the home you had set your heart on.

HEDDA: [*Looks up at him and laughs*] Do you, too, believe in that legend?

BRACK: Is there nothing in it, then?

HEDDA: Oh, yes, there is something in it.

BRACK: Well?

HEDDA: There is this in it, that I made use of Tesman to see me home from evening parties last summer——

BRACK: I, unfortunately, had to go quite a different way.

HEDDA: That's true. I know you were going a different way last summer.

BRACK: [*Laughing*] Oh fie, Mrs. Hedda! Well, then —you and Tesman——?

HEDDA: Well, we happened to pass here one evening; Tesman, poor fellow, was writhing in the agony of having to find conversation; so I took pity on the learned man——

BRACK: [*Smiles doubtfully*] You took pity? H'm——

HEDDA: Yes, I really did. And so—to help him out of his torment—I happened to say, in pure thoughtlessness, that I should like to live in this villa.

BRACK: No more than that?

HEDDA: Not that evening.

BRACK: But afterwards?

HEDDA: Yes, my thoughtlessness had consequences, my dear Judge.

BRACK: Unfortunately that too often happens, Mrs. Hedda.

HEDDA: Thanks! So you see it was this enthusiasm for Secretary Falk's villa that first constituted a bond of sympathy between George Tesman and me. From that came our engagement and our marriage, and our wedding journey, and all the rest of it. Well, well, my dear Judge—as you make your bed so you must lie, I could almost say.

BRACK: This is exquisite! And you really cared not a rap about it all the time?

HEDDA: No, heaven knows I didn't.

BRACK: But now? Now that we have made it so homelike for you?

HEDDA: Uh—the rooms all seem to smell of lavender and dried rose-leaves.—But perhaps it's Aunt Julia that has brought that scent with her.

BRACK: [*Laughing*] No, I think it must be a legacy from the late Mrs. Secretary Falk.

HEDDA: Yes, there is an odor of mortality about it. It reminds me of a bouquet—the day after the ball. [*Clasps her hands behind her head, leans back in her chair and looks at him*] Oh, my dear Judge— you cannot imagine how horribly I shall bore myself here.

BRACK: Why should not you, too, find some sort of vocation in life, Mrs. Hedda?

HEDDA: A vocation—that should attract me?

BRACK: If possible, of course.

HEDDA: Heaven knows what sort of a vocation

that could be. I often wonder whether—— [*Breaking off*] But that would never do, either.

BRACK: Who can tell? Let me hear what it is.

HEDDA: Whether I might not get Tesman to go into politics, I mean.

BRACK: [*Laughing*] Tesman? No, really now, political life is not the thing for him—not at all in his line.

HEDDA: No, I daresay not.—But if I could get him into it all the same?

BRACK: Why—what satisfaction could you find in that? If he is not fitted for that sort of thing, why should you want to drive him into it?

HEDDA: Because I am bored, I tell you! [*After a pause*] So you think it quite out of the question that Tesman should ever get into the ministry?

BRACK: H'm—you see, my dear Mrs. Hedda— to get into the ministry, he would have to be a tolerably rich man.

HEDDA: [*Rising impatiently*] Yes, there we have it! It is this genteel poverty I have managed to drop into——! [*Crosses the room*] That is what makes life so pitiable! So utterly ludicrous!—For that's what it is.

BRACK: Now *I* should say the fault lay elsewhere.

HEDDA: Where, then?

BRACK: You have never gone through any really stimulating experience.

HEDDA: Anything serious, you mean?

BRACK: Yes, you may call it so. But now you may perhaps have one in store.

HEDDA: [*Tossing her head*] Oh, you're thinking of the annoyances about this wretched professorship! But that must be Tesman's own affair. I assure you I shall not waste a thought upon it.

BRACK: No, no, I daresay not. But suppose now that what people call—in elegant language—a solemn responsibility were to come upon you? [*Smiling*] A new responsibility, Mrs. Hedda?

HEDDA: [*Angrily*] Be quiet! Nothing of that sort will ever happen!

BRACK: [*Warily*] We will speak of this again a year hence—at the very outside.

HEDDA: [*Curtly*] I have no turn for anything of the sort, Judge Brack. No responsibilities for me!

BRACK: Are you so unlike the generality of women as to have no turn for duties which——?

HEDDA: [*Beside the glass door*] Oh, be quiet, I tell you!—I often think there is only one thing in the world I have any turn for.

BRACK: [*Drawing near to her*] And what is that, if I may ask?

HEDDA: [*Stands looking out*] Boring myself to death. Now you know it. [*Turns, looks towards the inner room, and laughs*] Yes, as I thought! Here comes the Professor.

BRACK: [*Softly, in a tone of warning*] Come, come, come, Mrs. Hedda!

[George Tesman, *dressed for the party, with his gloves and hat in his hand, enters from the right through the inner room*]

TESMAN: Hedda, has no message come from Eilert Lövborg? Eh?

HEDDA: No.

TESMAN: Then you'll see he'll be here presently.

BRACK: Do you really think he will come?

TESMAN: Yes, I am almost sure of it. For what you were telling us this morning must have been a mere floating rumor.

BRACK: You think so?

TESMAN: At any rate, Aunt Julia said she did not believe for a moment that he would ever stand in my way again. Fancy that!

BRACK: Well, then, that's all right.

TESMAN: [*Placing his hat and gloves on a chair on the right*] Yes, but you must really let me wait for him as long as possible.

BRACK: We have plenty of time yet. None of my guests will arrive before seven or half-past.

TESMAN: Then meanwhile we can keep Hedda company, and see what happens. Eh?

HEDDA: [*Placing Brack's hat and overcoat upon the corner settee*] And at the worst Mr. Lövborg can remain here with me.

BRACK: [*Offering to take his things*] Oh, allow me, Mrs. Tesman!—What do you mean by "at the worst"?

HEDDA: If he won't go with you and Tesman.

TESMAN: [*Looks dubiously at her*] But, Hedda, dear—do you think it would quite do for him to remain with you? Eh? Remember, Aunt Julia can't come.

HEDDA: No, but Mrs. Elvsted is coming. We three can have a cup of tea together.

TESMAN: Oh, yes, that will be all right.

BRACK: [*Smiling*] And that would perhaps be the safest plan for him.

HEDDA: Why so?

BRACK: Well, you know, Mrs. Tesman, how you used to gird at my little bachelor parties. You declared they were adapted only for men of the strictest principles.

HEDDA: But no doubt Mr. Lövborg's principles are strict enough now. A converted sinner——

[Berta *appears at the hall door*]

BERTA: There's a gentleman asking if you are at home, ma'am——

HEDDA: Well, show him in.

TESMAN: [*Softly*] I'm sure it is he! Fancy that!

[Eilert Lövborg *enters from the hall. He is slim and lean; of the same age as* Tesman, *but looks older and somewhat worn-out. His hair and beard are of a blackish brown, his face long and pale, but with patches of color on the cheek-bones. He is dressed in a well-cut black visiting suit, quite new. He has dark gloves and a silk hat. He stops near the door, and makes a rapid bow, seeming somewhat embarrassed*]

TESMAN: [*Goes up to him and shakes him warmly by the hand*] Well, my dear Eilert—so at last we meet again!

EILERT LÖVBORG: [*Speaks in a subdued voice*] Thanks for your letter, Tesman. [*Approaching Hedda*] Will you, too, shake hands with me, Mrs. Tesman?

HEDDA: [*Taking his hand*] I am glad to see you, Mr. Lövborg. [*With a motion of her hand*] I don't know whether you two gentlemen——?

LÖVBORG: [*Bowing slightly*] Judge Brack, I think.

BRACK: [*Doing likewise*] Oh, yes,—in the old days——

TESMAN: [*To Lövborg, with his hands on his shoulders*] And now you must make yourself entirely at home, Eilert! Mustn't he, Hedda?—For I hear you are going to settle in town again? Eh?

LÖVBORG: Yes, I am.

TESMAN: Quite right, quite right. Let me tell you, I have got hold of your new book; but I haven't had time to read it yet.

LÖVBORG: You may spare yourself the trouble.

TESMAN: Why so?

LÖVBORG: Because there is very little in it.

TESMAN: Just fancy—how can you say so?

BRACK: But it has been very much praised, I hear.

LÖVBORG: That was what I wanted; so I put nothing into the book but what every one would agree with.

BRACK: Very wise of you.

TESMAN: Well, but, my dear Eilert——!

LÖVBORG: For now I mean to win myself a position again—to make a fresh start.

TESMAN: [*A little embarrassed*] Ah, that is what you wish to do? Eh?

LÖVBORG: [*Smiling, lays down his hat, and draws a packet, wrapped in paper, from his coat pocket*] But when this one appears, George Tesman, you will have to read it. For this is the real book—the book I have put my true self into.

TESMAN: Indeed? And what is it?

LÖVBORG: It is the continuation.

TESMAN: The continuation? Of what?

LÖVBORG: Of the book.

TESMAN: Of the new book?

LÖVBORG: Of course.

TESMAN: Why, my dear Eilert—does it not come down to our own days?

LÖVBORG: Yes, it does; and this one deals with the future.

TESMAN: With the future! But, good heavens, we know nothing of the future!

LÖVBORG: No; but there is a thing or two to be said about it all the same. [*Opens the packet*] Look here——

TESMAN: Why, that's not your handwriting.

LÖVBORG: I dictated it. [*Turning over the pages*] It falls into two sections. The first deals with the civilizing forces of the future. And here is the second—[*running through the pages towards the end*]—forecasting the probable line of development.

TESMAN: How odd now! I should never have thought of writing anything of that sort.

HEDDA: [*At the glass door, drumming on the pane*] H'm—— I daresay not.

LÖVBORG: [*Replacing the manuscript in its paper and laying the packet on the table*] I brought it, thinking I might read you a little of it this evening.

TESMAN: That was very good of you, Eilert. But this evening——? [*Looking at Brack*] I don't quite see how we can manage it——

LÖVBORG: Well, then, some other time. There is no hurry.

BRACK: I must tell you, Mr. Lövborg—there is a little gathering at my house this evening—mainly in honor of Tesman, you know——

LÖVBORG: [*Looking for his hat*] Oh—then I won't detain you——

BRACK: No, but listen—will you not do me the favor of joining us?

LÖVBORG: [*Curtly and decidedly*] No, I can't—thank you very much.

BRACK: Oh, nonsense—do! We shall be quite a select little circle. And I assure you we shall have a "lively time," as Mrs. Hed—as Mrs. Tesman says.

LÖVBORG: I have no doubt of it. But nevertheless——

BRACK: And then you might bring your manuscript with you, and read it to Tesman at my house. I could give you a room to yourselves.

TESMAN: Yes, think of that, Eilert,—why shouldn't you? Eh?

HEDDA: [*Interposing*] But, Tesman, if Mr. Lövborg would really rather not! I am sure Mr. Lövborg is much more inclined to remain here and have supper with me.

LÖVBORG: [*Looking at her*] With you, Mrs. Tesman?

HEDDA: And with Mrs. Elvsted.

LÖVBORG: Ah—— [*Lightly*] I saw her for a moment this morning.

HEDDA: Did you? Well, she is coming this evening. So you see you are almost bound to remain, Mr. Lövborg, or she will have no one to see her home.

LÖVBORG: That's true. Many thanks, Mrs. Tesman —in that case I will remain.

HEDDA: Then I have one or two orders to give the servant——

[*She goes to the hall door and rings. Berta enters. Hedda talks to her in a whisper, and points towards the inner room. Berta nods and goes out again*]

TESMAN: [*At the same time, to Lövborg*] Tell me, Eilert—is it this new subject—the future—that you are going to lecture about?

LÖVBORG: Yes.

TESMAN: They told me at the bookseller's that

you are going to deliver a course of lectures this autumn.

LÖVBORG: That is my intention. I hope you won't take it ill, Tesman.

TESMAN: Oh no, not in the least! But——?

LÖVBORG: I can quite understand that it must be disagreeable to you.

TESMAN: [Cast down] Oh, I can't expect you, out of consideration for me, to——

LÖVBORG: But I shall wait till you have received your appointment.

TESMAN: Will you wait? Yes, but—yes, but—are you not going to compete with me? Eh?

LÖVBORG: No; it is only the moral victory I care for.

TESMAN: Why, bless me—then Aunt Julia was right after all! Oh, yes—I knew it! Hedda! Just fancy—Eilert Lövborg is not going to stand in our way!

HEDDA: [Curtly] Our way? Pray leave me out of the question.

[She goes up towards the inner room, where Berta is placing a tray with decanters and glasses on the table. Hedda nods approval, and comes forward again. Berta goes out.]

TESMAN: [At the same time] And you, Judge Brack—what do you say to this? Eh?

BRACK: Well, I say that a moral victory—h'm—may be all very fine——

TESMAN: Yes, certainly. But all the same——

HEDDA: [Looking at Tesman with a cold smile] You stand there looking as if you were thunderstruck——

TESMAN: Yes—so I am—I almost think——

BRACK: Don't you see, Mrs. Tesman, a thunderstorm has just passed over?

HEDDA: [Pointing towards the inner room] Will you not take a glass of cold punch, gentlemen?

BRACK: [Looking at his watch] A stirrup-cup? Yes, it wouldn't come amiss.

TESMAN: A capital idea, Hedda! Just the thing! Now that the weight has been taken off my mind——

HEDDA: Will you not join them, Mr. Lövborg?

LÖVBORG: [With a gesture of refusal] No, thank you. Nothing for me.

BRACK: Why bless me—cold punch is surely not poison.

LÖVBORG: Perhaps not for every one.

HEDDA: I will keep Mr. Lövborg company in the meantime.

TESMAN: Yes, yes, Hedda dear, do.

[He and Brack go into the inner room, seat themselves, drink punch, smoke cigarettes, and carry on a lively conversation during what follows. Eilert Lövborg remains standing beside the stove. Hedda goes to the writing-table]

HEDDA: [Raising her voice a little] Do you care to look at some photographs, Mr. Lövborg? You

know Tesman and I made a tour in the Tyrol on our way home?

[She takes up an album, and places it on the table beside the sofa, in the further corner of which she seats herself. Eilert Lövborg approaches, stops, and looks at her. Then he takes a chair and seats himself to her left, with his back towards the inner room]

HEDDA: [Opening the album] Do you see this range of mountains, Mr. Lövborg? It's the Ortler group. Tesman has written the name underneath. Here it is: "The Ortler group near Meran."

LÖVBORG: [Who has never taken his eyes off her, says softly and slowly:] Hedda—Gabler!

HEDDA: [Glancing hastily at him] Ah! Hush!

LÖVBORG: [Repeats softly] Hedda Gabler!

HEDDA: [Looking at the album] That was my name in the old days—when we two knew each other.

LÖVBORG: And I must teach myself never to say Hedda Gabler again—never, as long as I live.

HEDDA: [Still turning over the pages] Yes, you must. And I think you ought to practise in time. The sooner the better, I should say.

LÖVBORG: [In a tone of indignation] Hedda Gabler married? And married to—George Tesman!

HEDDA: Yes—so the world goes.

LÖVBORG: Oh, Hedda, Hedda—how could you [1] throw yourself away!

HEDDA: [Looks sharply at him] What? I can't allow this!

LÖVBORG: What do you mean?

[Tesman comes into the room and goes towards the sofa]

HEDDA: [Hears him coming and says in an indifferent tone] And this is a view from the Val d'Ampezzo, Mr. Lövborg. Just look at these peaks! [Looks affectionately up at Tesman] What's the name of these curious peaks, dear?

TESMAN: Let me see. Oh, those are the Dolomites.

HEDDA: Yes, that's it!—Those are the Dolomites, Mr. Lövborg.

TESMAN: Hedda, dear,—I only wanted to ask whether I shouldn't bring you a little punch after all? For yourself, at any rate—eh?

HEDDA: Yes, do, please; and perhaps a few biscuits.

TESMAN: No cigarettes?

HEDDA: No.

TESMAN: Very well.

[He goes into the inner room and out to the right. Brack sits in the inner room, and keeps an eye from time to time on Hedda and Lövborg]

LÖVBORG: [Softly, as before] Answer me, Hedda—how could you go and do this?

HEDDA: [Apparently absorbed in the album] If you continue to say du to me I won't talk to you.

LÖVBORG: May I not say du even when we are alone?

[1] He uses the familiar du.

HEDDA: No. You may think it; but you mustn't say it.

LÖVBORG: Ah, I understand. It is an offence against George Tesman, whom you [1]—love.

HEDDA: [*Glances at him and smiles*] Love? What an idea!

LÖVBORG: You don't love him then!

HEDDA: But I won't hear of any sort of unfaithfulness! Remember that.

LÖVBORG: Hedda—answer me one thing——

HEDDA: Hush!

[Tesman *enters with a small tray from the inner room*]

TESMAN: Here you are! Isn't this tempting?

[*He puts the tray on the table*]

HEDDA: Why do you bring it yourself?

TESMAN: [*Filling the glasses*] Because I think it's such fun to wait upon you, Hedda.

HEDDA: But you have poured out two glasses. Mr. Lövborg said he wouldn't have any——

TESMAN: No, but Mrs. Elvsted will soon be here, won't she?

HEDDA: Yes, by the by—Mrs. Elvsted——

TESMAN: Had you forgotten her? Eh?

HEDDA: We were so absorbed in these photographs. [*Shows him a picture*] Do you remember this little village?

TESMAN: Oh, it's that one just below the Brenner Pass. It was there we passed the night——

HEDDA: ——and met that lively party of tourists.

TESMAN: Yes, that was the place. Fancy—if we could only have had you with us, Eilert! Eh?

[*He returns to the inner room and sits beside* Brack]

LÖVBORG: Answer me this one thing, Hedda——

HEDDA: Well?

LÖVBORG: Was there no love in your friendship for me, either? Not a spark—not a tinge of love in it?

HEDDA: I wonder if there was? To me it seems as though we were two good comrades—two thoroughly intimate friends. [*Smilingly*] You especially were frankness itself.

LÖVBORG: It was you that made me so.

HEDDA: As I look back upon it all, I think there was really something beautiful, something fascinating—something daring—in—in that secret intimacy—that comradeship which no living creature so much as dreamed of.

LÖVBORG: Yes, yes, Hedda! Was there not?— When I used to come to your father's in the afternoon—and the General sat over at the window reading his papers—with his back towards us——

HEDDA: And we two on the corner sofa——

LÖVBORG: Always with the same illustrated paper before us——

HEDDA: For want of an album, yes.

LÖVBORG: Yes, Hedda, and when I made my confessions to you—told you about myself, things that

[1] From this point onward Lövborg uses the formal *De.*

at that time no one else knew! There I would sit and tell you of my escapades—my days and nights of devilment. Oh, Hedda—what was the power in you that forced me to confess these things?

HEDDA: Do you think it was any power in me?

LÖVBORG: How else can I explain it? And all those—those roundabout questions you used to put to me——

HEDDA: Which you understood so particularly well——

LÖVBORG: How could you sit and question me like that? Question me quite frankly——

HEDDA: In roundabout terms, please observe.

LÖVBORG: Yes, but frankly nevertheless. Cross-question me about—all that sort of thing?

HEDDA: And how could you answer, Mr. Lövborg?

LÖVBORG: Yes, that is just what I can't understand—in looking back upon it. But tell me now, Hedda—was there not love at the bottom of our friendship? On your side, did you not feel as though you might purge my stains away—if I made you my confessor? Was it not so?

HEDDA: No, not quite.

LÖVBORG: What was your motive, then?

HEDDA: Do you think it quite incomprehensible that a young girl—when it can be done—without any one knowing——

LÖVBORG: Well?

HEDDA: ——should be glad to have a peep, now and then, into a world which——

LÖVBORG: Which——?

HEDDA: ——which she is forbidden to know anything about?

LÖVBORG: So that was it?

HEDDA: Partly. Partly—I almost think.

LÖVBORG: Comradeship in the thirst for life. But why should not that, at any rate, have continued?

HEDDA: The fault was yours.

LÖVBORG: It was you that broke with me.

HEDDA: Yes, when our friendship threatened to develop into something more serious. Shame upon you, Eilert Lövborg! How could you think of wronging your—your frank comrade?

LÖVBORG: [*Clenching his hands*] Oh, why did you not carry out your threat? Why did you not shoot me down?

HEDDA: Because I have such a dread of scandal.

LÖVBORG: Yes, Hedda, you are a coward at heart.

HEDDA: A terrible coward. [*Changing her tone*] But it was a lucky thing for you. And now you have found ample consolation at the Elvsteds'.

LÖVBORG: I know what Thea has confided to you.

HEDDA: And perhaps you have confided to her something about us?

LÖVBORG: Not a word. She is too stupid to understand anything of that sort.

HEDDA: Stupid?

LÖVBORG: She is stupid about matters of that sort.

HEDDA: And I am cowardly. [*Bends over towards*

him, without looking him in the face, and says more softly:] But now I will confide something to you.

LÖVBORG: [*Eagerly*] Well?

HEDDA: The fact that I dared not shoot you down——

LÖVBORG: Yes!

HEDDA: ——that was not my most arrant cowardice—that evening.

LÖVBORG: [*Looks at her a moment, understands, and whispers passionately*] Oh, Hedda! Hedda Gabler! Now I begin to see a hidden reason beneath our comradeship! You and I——! After all, then, it was your craving for life——

HEDDA: [*Softly, with a sharp glance*] Take care! Believe nothing of the sort!

[*Twilight has begun to fall. The hall door is opened from without by* Berta]

HEDDA: [*Closes the album with a bang and calls smilingly:*] Ah, at last! My darling Thea,—come along!

[*Mrs. Elvsted enters from the hall. She is in evening dress. The door is closed behind her*]

HEDDA: [*On the sofa, stretches out her arms towards her*] My sweet Thea—you can't think how I have been longing for you!

[*Mrs. Elvsted, in passing, exchanges slight salutations with the gentlemen in the inner room, then goes up to the table and gives Hedda her hand. Eilert Lövborg has risen. He and Mrs. Elvsted greet each other with a silent nod*]

MRS. ELVSTED: Ought I to go in and talk to your husband for a moment?

HEDDA: Oh, not at all. Leave those two alone. They will soon be going.

MRS. ELVSTED: Are they going out?

HEDDA: Yes, to a supper-party.

MRS. ELVSTED: [*Quickly, to Lövborg*] Not you?

LÖVBORG: No.

HEDDA: Mr. Lövborg remains with us.

MRS. ELVSTED: [*Takes a chair and is about to seat herself at his side*] Oh, how nice it is here!

HEDDA: No, thank you, my little Thea! Not there! You'll be good enough to come over here to me. I will sit between you.

MRS. ELVSTED: Yes, just as you please.

[*She goes round the table and seats herself on the sofa on* Hedda's *right.* Lövborg *re-seats himself on his chair*]

LÖVBORG: [*After a short pause, to* Hedda] Is not she lovely to look at?

HEDDA: [*Lightly stroking her hair*] Only to look at?

LÖVBORG: Yes. For we two—she and I—we are two real comrades. We have absolute faith in each other; so we can sit and talk with perfect frankness——

HEDDA: Not round about, Mr. Lövborg?

LÖVBORG: Well——

MRS. ELVSTED: [*Softly clinging close to* Hedda]

Oh, how happy I am, Hedda! For, only think, he says I have inspired him, too.

HEDDA: [*Looks at her with a smile*] Ah! Does he say that, dear?

LÖVBORG: And then she is so brave, Mrs. Tesman!

MRS. ELVSTED: Good heavens—am I brave?

LÖVBORG: Exceedingly—where your comrade is concerned.

HEDDA: Ah, yes—courage! If one only had that!

LÖVBORG: What then? What do you mean?

HEDDA: Then life would perhaps be livable, after all. [*With a sudden change of tone*] But now, my dearest Thea, you really must have a glass of cold punch.

MRS. ELVSTED: No, thanks—I never take anything of that kind.

HEDDA: Well, then, you, Mr. Lövborg.

LÖVBORG: Nor I, thank you.

MRS. ELVSTED: No, he doesn't, either.

HEDDA: [*Looks fixedly at him*] But if I say you shall?

LÖVBORG: It would be no use.

HEDDA: [*Laughing*] Then I, poor creature, have no sort of power over you?

LÖVBORG: Not in that respect.

HEDDA: But seriously, I think you ought to—for your own sake.

MRS. ELVSTED: Why, Hedda——!

LÖVBORG: How so?

HEDDA: Or rather on account of other people.

LÖVBORG: Indeed?

HEDDA: Otherwise people might be apt to suspect that—in your heart of hearts—you did not feel quite secure—quite confident in yourself.

MRS. ELVSTED: [*Softly*] Oh, please, Hedda——!

LÖVBORG: People may suspect what they like—for the present.

MRS. ELVSTED: [*Joyfully*] Yes, let them!

HEDDA: I saw it plainly in Judge Brack's face a moment ago.

LÖVBORG: What did you see?

HEDDA: His contemptuous smile, when you dared not go with them into the inner room.

LÖVBORG: Dared not? Of course I preferred to stop here and talk to you.

MRS. ELVSTED: What could be more natural, Hedda?

HEDDA: But the Judge could not guess that. And I saw, too, the way he smiled and glanced at Tesman when you dared not accept his invitation to this wretched little supper-party of his.

LÖVBORG: Dared not! Do you say I dared not?

HEDDA: I don't say so. But that was how Judge Brack understood it.

LÖVBORG: Well, let him.

HEDDA: Then you are not going with them?

LÖVBORG: I will stay here with you and Thea.

MRS. ELVSTED: Yes, Hedda—how can you doubt that?

HEDDA: [*Smiles and nods approvingly to* Lövborg]

Firm as a rock! Faithful to your principles, now and forever! Ah, that is how a man should be! [*Turns to* Mrs. Elvsted *and caresses her*] Well, now, what did I tell you, when you came to us this morning in such a state of distraction——

LÖVBORG: [*Surprised*] Distraction!

MRS. ELVSTED: [*Terrified*] Hedda—oh, Hedda——!

HEDDA: You can see for yourself! You haven't the slightest reason to be in such mortal terror—— [*Interrupting herself*] There! Now we can all three enjoy ourselves!

LÖVBORG: [*Who has given a start*] Ah—what is all this, Mrs. Tesman?

MRS. ELVSTED: Oh, my God, Hedda! What are you saying? What are you doing?

HEDDA: Don't get excited! That horrid Judge Brack is sitting watching you.

LÖVBORG: So she was in mortal terror! On my account!

MRS. ELVSTED: [*Softly and piteously*] Oh, Hedda —now you have ruined everything!

LÖVBORG: [*Looks fixedly at her for a moment. His face is distorted*] So that was my comrade's frank confidence in me?

MRS. ELVSTED: [*Imploringly*] Oh, my dearest friend—only let me tell you——

LÖVBORG: [*Takes one of the glasses of punch, raises it to his lips, and says in a low, husky voice*] Your health, Thea!

[*He empties the glass, puts it down, and takes the second*]

MRS. ELVSTED: [*Softly*] Oh, Hedda, Hedda—how could you do this?

HEDDA: *I* do it? *I*? Are you crazy?

LÖVBORG: Here's to your health, too, Mrs. Tesman. Thanks for the truth. Hurrah for the truth!

[*He empties the glass and is about to re-fill it.*]

HEDDA: [*Lays her hand on his arm*] Come, come —no more for the present. Remember you are going out to supper.

MRS. ELVSTED: No, no, no!

HEDDA: Hush! They are sitting watching you.

LÖVBORG: [*Putting down the glass*] Now, Thea— tell me the truth——

MRS. ELVSTED: Yes.

LÖVBORG: Did your husband know that you had come after me?

MRS. ELVSTED: [*Wringing her hands*] Oh, Hedda— do you hear what he is asking?

LÖVBORG: Was it arranged between you and him that you were to come to town and look after me? Perhaps it was the Sheriff himself that urged you to come? Aha, my dear—no doubt he wanted my help in his office! Or was it at the cardtable that he missed me?

MRS. ELVSTED: [*Softly, in agony*] Oh, Lövborg, Lövborg——!

LÖVBORG: [*Seizes a glass and is on the point of filling it*] Here's a glass for the old Sheriff, too!

HEDDA: [*Preventing him*] No more just now. Remember, you have to read your manuscript to Tesman.

LÖVBORG: [*Calmly, putting down the glass*] It was stupid of me all this, Thea—to take it in this way, I mean. Don't be angry with me, my dear, dear comrade. You shall see—both you and the others—that if I was fallen once—now I have risen again! Thanks to you, Thea.

MRS. ELVSTED: [*Radiant with joy*] Oh, heaven be praised——!

[*Brack has in the meantime looked at his watch. He and Tesman rise and come into the drawing room*]

BRACK: [*Takes his hat and overcoat*] Well, Mrs. Tesman, our time has come.

HEDDA: I suppose it has.

LÖVBORG: [*Rising*] Mine too, Judge Brack.

MRS. ELVSTED: [*Softly and imploringly*] Oh, Lövborg, don't do it!

HEDDA: [*Pinching her arm*] They can hear you!

MRS. ELVSTED: [*With a suppressed shriek*] Ow!

LÖVBORG: [*To* Brack] You were good enough to invite me.

BRACK: Well, are you coming after all?

LÖVBORG: Yes, many thanks.

BRACK: I'm delighted——

LÖVBORG: [*To Tesman, putting the parcel of MS. in his pocket*] I should like to show you one or two things before I send it to the printers.

TESMAN: Fancy—that will be delightful. But, Hedda dear, how is Mrs. Elvsted to get home? Eh?

HEDDA: Oh, that can be managed somehow.

LÖVBORG: [*Looking towards the ladies*] Mrs. Elvsted? Of course, I'll come again and fetch her. [*Approaching*] At ten or thereabouts, Mrs. Tesman? Will that do?

HEDDA: Certainly. That will do capitally.

TESMAN: Well, then, that's all right. But you must not expect me so early, Hedda.

HEDDA: Oh, you may stop as long—as long as ever you please.

MRS. ELVSTED: [*Trying to conceal her anxiety*] Well, then, Mr. Lövborg—I shall remain here until you come.

LÖVBORG: [*With his hat in his hand*] Pray do, Mrs. Elvsted.

BRACK: And now off goes the excursion train, gentlemen! I hope we shall have a lively time, as a certain fair lady puts it.

HEDDA: Ah, if only the fair lady could be present unseen——!

BRACK: Why unseen?

HEDDA: In order to hear a little of your liveliness at first hand, Judge Brack.

BRACK: [*Laughing*] I should not advise the fair lady to try it.

TESMAN: [*Also laughing*] Come, you're a nice one, Hedda! Fancy that!

BRACK: Well, good-bye, good-bye, ladies.

LÖVBORG: [*Bowing*] About ten o'clock, then.

[Brack, Lövborg, *and* Tesman *go out by the hall door. At the same time,* Berta *enters from the inner room with a lighted lamp, which she places on the drawing-room table; she goes out by the way she came*]

MRS. ELVSTED: [*Who has risen and is wandering restlessly about the room*] Hedda—Hedda—what will come of all this?

HEDDA: At ten o'clock—he will be here. I can see him already—with vine-leaves in his hair—flushed and fearless——

MRS. ELVSTED: Oh, I hope he may.

HEDDA: And then, you see—then he will have regained control over himself. Then he will be a free man for all his days.

MRS. ELVSTED: Oh, God!—if he would only come as you see him now!

HEDDA: He will come as I see him—so, and not otherwise! [*Rises and approaches* Thea] You may doubt him as long as you please; *I* believe in him. And now we will try——

MRS. ELVSTED: You have some hidden motive in this, Hedda!

HEDDA: Yes, I have. I want for once in my life to have power to mould a human destiny.

MRS. ELVSTED: Have you not the power?

HEDDA: I have not—and have never had it.

MRS. ELVSTED: Not your husband's?

HEDDA: Do you think that is worth the trouble? Oh, if you could only understand how poor I am. And fate has made you so rich! [*Clasps her passionately in her arms*] I think I must burn your hair off, after all.

MRS. ELVSTED: Let me go! Let me go! I am afraid of you, Hedda!

BERTA: [*In the middle doorway*] Tea is laid in the dining-room, ma'am.

HEDDA: Very well. We are coming.

MRS. ELVSTED: No, no, no! I would rather go home alone! At once!

HEDDA: Nonsense! First you shall have a cup of tea, you little stupid. And then—at ten o'clock—Eilert Lövborg will be here—with vine-leaves in his hair.

[*She drags* Mrs. Elvsted *almost by force towards the middle doorway*]

ACT III.

The room at the Tesmans'. *The curtains are drawn over the middle doorway, and also over the glass door. The lamp, half turned down, and with a shade over it, is burning on the table. In the stove, the door of which stands open, there has been a fire, which is now nearly burnt out.*

Mrs. Elvsted, *wrapped in a large shawl, and with her feet upon a foot-rest, sits close to the stove,* sunk back in the armchair. Hedda, *fully dressed, lies sleeping upon the sofa, with a sofa-blanket over her.*

MRS. ELVSTED: [*After a pause, suddenly sits up in her chair, and listens eagerly. Then she sinks back again wearily, moaning to herself*] Not yet!— Oh, God—oh, God—not yet!

[Berta *slips cautiously in by the hall door. She has a letter in her hand*]

MRS. ELVSTED: [*Turns and whispers eagerly*] Well —has any one come?

BERTA: [*Softly*] Yes, a girl has just brought this letter.

MRS. ELVSTED: [*Quickly, holding out her hand*] A letter! Give it to me!

BERTA: No, it's for Dr. Tesman, ma'am.

MRS. ELVSTED: Oh, indeed.

BERTA: It was Miss Tesman's servant that brought it. I'll lay it here on the table.

MRS. ELVSTED: Yes, do.

BERTA: [*Laying down the letter*] I think I had better put out the lamp. It's smoking.

MRS. ELVSTED: Yes, put it out. It must soon be daylight now.

BERTA: [*Putting out the lamp*] It is daylight already, ma'am.

MRS. ELVSTED: Yes, broad day! And no one come back yet——!

BERTA: Lord bless you, ma'am—I guessed how it would be.

MRS. ELVSTED: You guessed?

BERTA: Yes, when I saw that a certain person had come back to town—and that he went off with them. For we've heard enough about that gentleman before now.

MRS. ELVSTED: Don't speak so loud. You will waken Mrs. Tesman.

BERTA: [*Looks towards the sofa and sighs*] No, no —let her sleep, poor thing. Shan't I put some wood on the fire?

MRS. ELVSTED: Thanks, not for me.

BERTA: Oh, very well.

[*She goes softly out by the hall door*]

HEDDA: [*Is awakened by the shutting of the door, and looks up*] What's that——?

MRS. ELVSTED: It was only the servant——

HEDDA: [*Looking about her*] Oh, we're here—! Yes, now I remember. [*Sits erect upon the sofa, stretches herself, and rubs her eyes*] What o'clock is it, Thea?

MRS. ELVSTED: [*Looks at her watch*] It's past seven.

HEDDA: When did Tesman come home?

MRS. ELVSTED: He has not come.

HEDDA: Not come home yet?

MRS. ELVSTED: [*Rising*] No one has come.

HEDDA: Think of our watching and waiting here till four in the morning——

MRS. ELVSTED: [*Wringing her hands*] And how I watched and waited for him!

HEDDA: [*Yawns, and says with her hand before her mouth*] Well, well—we might have spared ourselves the trouble.

MRS. ELVSTED: Did you get a little sleep?

HEDDA: Oh, yes; I believe I have slept pretty well. Have you not?

MRS. ELVSTED: Not for a moment. I couldn't, Hedda!—not to save my life.

HEDDA: [*Rises and goes towards her*] There, there, there! There's nothing to be so alarmed about. I understand quite well what has happened.

MRS. ELVSTED: Well, what do you think? Won't you tell me?

HEDDA: Why, of course, it has been a very late affair at Judge Brack's——

MRS. ELVSTED: Yes, yes—that is clear enough. But all the same——

HEDDA: And then, you see, Tesman hasn't cared to come home and ring us up in the middle of the night. [*Laughing*] Perhaps he wasn't inclined to show himself either—immediately after a jollification.

MRS. ELVSTED: But in that case—where can he have gone?

HEDDA: Of course, he has gone to his aunts' and slept there. They have his old room ready for him.

MRS. ELVSTED: No, he can't be with them; for a letter has just come for him from Miss Tesman. There it lies.

HEDDA: Indeed? [*Looks at the address*] Why, yes, it's addressed in Aunt Julia's own hand. Well, then, he has remained at Judge Brack's. And as for Eilert Lövborg—he is sitting, with vine-leaves in his hair, reading his manuscript.

MRS. ELVSTED: Oh, Hedda, you are just saying things you don't believe a bit.

HEDDA: You really are a little blockhead, Thea.

MRS. ELVSTED: Oh, yes, I suppose I am.

HEDDA: And how mortally tired you look.

MRS. ELVSTED: Yes, I am mortally tired.

HEDDA: Well, then, you must do as I tell you. You must go into my room and lie down for a little while.

MRS. ELVSTED: Oh, no, no—I shouldn't be able to sleep.

HEDDA: I am sure you would.

MRS. ELVSTED: Well, but your husband is certain to come soon now; and then I want to know at once——

HEDDA: I shall take care to let you know when he comes.

MRS. ELVSTED: Do you promise me, Hedda?

HEDDA: Yes, rely upon me. Just you go in and have a sleep in the meantime.

MRS. ELVSTED: Thanks; then I'll try to.

[*She goes off through the inner door*]

[Hedda *goes up to the glass door and draws back the curtains. The broad daylight streams into* the room. *Then she takes a little hand-glass from the writing-table, looks at herself in it, and arranges her hair. Next she goes to the hall door and presses the bell-button*]

[Berta *presently appears at the hall door*]

BERTA: Did you want anything, ma'am?

HEDDA: Yes; you must put some more wood in the stove. I am shivering.

BERTA: Bless me—I'll make up the fire at once. [*She rakes the embers together and lays a piece of wood upon them; then stops and listens*] That was a ring at the front door, ma'am.

HEDDA: Then go to the door. I will look after the fire.

BERTA: It'll soon burn up.

[*She goes out by the hall door*]

[Hedda *kneels on the foot-rest and lays some more pieces of wood in the stove*]

[*After a short pause,* George Tesman *enters from the hall. He looks tired and rather serious. He steals on tiptoe towards the middle doorway and is about to slip through the curtains*]

HEDDA: [*At the stove, without looking up*] Good morning.

TESMAN: [*Turns*] Hedda! [*Approaching her*] Good heavens—are you up so early? Eh?

HEDDA: Yes, I am up very early this morning.

TESMAN: And I never doubted you were still sound asleep! Fancy that, Hedda!

HEDDA: Don't speak so loud. Mrs. Elvsted is resting in my room.

TESMAN: Has Mrs. Elvsted been here all night?

HEDDA: Yes, since no one came to fetch her.

TESMAN: Ah, to be sure.

HEDDA: [*Closes the door of the stove and rises*] Well, did you enjoy yourselves at Judge Brack's?

TESMAN: Have you been anxious about me? Eh?

HEDDA: No, I should never think of being anxious. But I asked if you had enjoyed yourself.

TESMAN: Oh, yes,—for once in a way. Especially the beginning of the evening; for then Eilert read me part of his book. We arrived more than an hour too early—fancy that! And Brack had all sorts of arrangements to make—so Eilert read to me.

HEDDA: [*Seating herself by the table on the right*] Well? Tell me, then——

TESMAN: [*Sitting on a footstool near the stove*] Oh, Hedda, you can't conceive what a book that is going to be! I believe it is one of the most remarkable things that have ever been written. Fancy that!

HEDDA: Yes, yes; I don't care about that—

TESMAN: I must make a confession to you, Hedda. When he had finished reading—a horrid feeling came over me.

HEDDA: A horrid feeling?

TESMAN: I felt jealous of Eilert for having had it in him to write such a book. Only think, Hedda!

HEDDA: Yes, yes, I am thinking!

TESMAN: And then how pitiful to think that he—with all his gifts—should be irreclaimable, after all.

HEDDA: I suppose you mean that he has more courage than the rest?

TESMAN: No, not at all—I mean that he is incapable of taking his pleasures in moderation.

HEDDA: And what came of it all—in the end?

TESMAN: Well, to tell the truth, I think it might best be described as an orgy, Hedda.

HEDDA: Had he vine-leaves in his hair?

TESMAN: Vine-leaves? No, I saw nothing of the sort. But he made a long, rambling speech in honor of the woman who had inspired him in his work—that was the phrase he used.

HEDDA: Did he name her?

TESMAN: No, he didn't; but I can't help thinking he meant Mrs. Elvsted. You may be sure he did.

HEDDA: Well—where did you part from him?

TESMAN: On the way to town. We broke up—the last of us at any rate—all together; and Brack came with us to get a breath of fresh air. And then, you see, we agreed to take Eilert home; for he had had far more than was good for him.

HEDDA: I daresay.

TESMAN: But now comes the strange part of it, Hedda; or, I should rather say, the melancholy part of it. I declare I am almost ashamed—on Eilert's account—to tell you——

HEDDA: Oh, go on——!

TESMAN: Well, as we were getting near town, you see, I happened to drop a little behind the others. Only for a minute or two—fancy that!

HEDDA: Yes, yes, yes, but——?

TESMAN: And then, as I hurried after them—what do you think I found by the wayside? Eh?

HEDDA: Oh, how should I know!

TESMAN: You mustn't speak of it to a soul, Hedda! Do you hear! Promise me, for Eilert's sake. [Draws a parcel, wrapped in paper, from his coat pocket] Fancy, dear—I found this.

HEDDA: Is not that the parcel he had with him yesterday?

TESMAN: Yes, it is the whole of his precious, irreplaceable manuscript! And he had gone and lost it, and knew nothing about it. Only fancy, Hedda! So deplorably——

HEDDA: But why did you not give him back the parcel at once?

TESMAN: I didn't dare to—in the state he was then in——

HEDDA: Did you not tell any of the others that you found it?

TESMAN: Oh, far from it! You can surely understand that, for Eilert's sake, I wouldn't do that.

HEDDA: So no one knows that Eilert Lövborg's manuscript is in your possession?

TESMAN: No. And no one must know it.

HEDDA: Then what did you say to him afterwards?

TESMAN: I didn't talk to him again at all; for when we got in among the streets, he and two or three of the others gave us the slip and disappeared. Fancy that!

HEDDA: Indeed! They must have taken him home then.

TESMAN: Yes, so it would appear. And Brack, too, left us.

HEDDA: And what have you been doing with yourself since?

TESMAN: Well, I and some of the others went home with one of the party, a jolly fellow, and took our morning coffee with him; or perhaps I should rather call it our night coffee—eh? But now, when I have rested a little, and given Eilert, poor fellow, time to have his sleep out, I must take this back to him.

HEDDA: [Holds out her hand for the packet] No—don't give it to him! Not in such a hurry, I mean. Let me read it first.

TESMAN: No, my dearest Hedda, I mustn't, I really mustn't.

HEDDA: You must not?

TESMAN: No—for you can imagine what a state of despair he will be in when he wakens and misses the manuscript. He has no copy of it, you must know! He told me so.

HEDDA: [Looking searchingly at him] Can such a thing not be reproduced? Written over again?

TESMAN: No, I don't think that would be possible. For the inspiration, you see——

HEDDA: Yes, yes—I suppose it depends on that—— [Lightly] But, by the by—here is a letter for you.

TESMAN: Fancy——!

HEDDA: [Handing it to him] It came early this morning.

TESMAN: It's from Aunt Julia! What can it be? [He lays the packet on the other footstool, opens the letter, runs his eye through it, and jumps up] Oh, Hedda—she says that poor Aunt Rina is dying!

HEDDA: Well, we were prepared for that.

TESMAN: And that if I want to see her again, I must make haste. I'll run in to them at once.

HEDDA: [Suppressing a smile] Will you run?

TESMAN: Oh, my dearest Hedda—if you could only make up your mind to come with me! Just think!

HEDDA: [Rises and says wearily, repelling the idea] No, no, don't ask me. I will not look upon sickness and death. I loathe all sorts of ugliness.

TESMAN: Well, well, then——! [Bustling around] My hat——? My overcoat——? Oh, in the hall——. I do hope I mayn't come too late, Hedda! Eh?

HEDDA: Oh, if you run——

[Berta appears at the hall door]

BERTA: Judge Brack is at the door, and wishes to know if he may come in.

TESMAN: At this time! No, I can't possibly see him.

HEDDA: But I can. [To Berta] Ask Judge Brack to come in.

[Berta *goes out*]

HEDDA: [*Quickly, whispering*] The parcel, Tesman! [*She snatches it up from the stool*]

TESMAN: Yes, give it to me!

HEDDA: No, no, I will keep it till you come back. [*She goes to the writing-table and places it in the bookcase.* Tesman *stands in a flurry of haste, and cannot get his gloves on*]

[Judge Brack *enters from the hall*]

HEDDA: [*Nodding to him*] You are an early bird, I must say.

BRACK: Yes, don't you think so? [*To* Tesman] Are you on the move, too?

TESMAN: Yes, I must rush off to my aunts'. Fancy —the invalid one is lying at death's door, poor creature.

BRACK: Dear me, is she indeed? Then on no account let me detain you. At such a critical moment——

TESMAN: Yes, I must really rush—— Good-bye! Good-bye!

[*He hastens out by the hall door*]

HEDDA: [*Approaching*] You seem to have made a particularly lively night of it at your rooms, Judge Brack.

BRACK: I assure you I have not had my clothes off, Mrs. Hedda.

HEDDA: Not you, either?

BRACK: No, as you may see. But what has Tesman been telling you of the night's adventures?

HEDDA: Oh, some tiresome story. Only that they went and had coffee somewhere or other.

BRACK: I have heard about that coffee-party already. Eilert Lövborg was not with them, I fancy?

HEDDA: No, they had taken him home before that.

BRACK: Tesman too?

HEDDA: No, but some of the others, he said.

BRACK: [*Smiling*] George Tesman is really an ingenuous creature, Mrs. Hedda.

HEDDA: Yes, heaven knows he is. Then is there something behind all this?

BRACK: Yes, perhaps there may be.

HEDDA: Well then, sit down, my dear Judge, and tell your story in comfort.

[*She seats herself to the left of the table.* Brack *sits near her, at the long side of the table*]

HEDDA: Now then?

BRACK: I had special reasons for keeping track of my guests—or rather of some of my guests—last night.

HEDDA: Of Eilert Lövborg among the rest, perhaps?

BRACK: Frankly—yes.

HEDDA: Now you make me really curious——

BRACK: Do you know where he and one or two of the others finished the night, Mrs. Hedda?

HEDDA: If it is not quite unmentionable, tell me.

BRACK: Oh no, it's not at all unmentionable. Well, they put in an appearance at a particularly animated *soirée*.

HEDDA: Of the lively kind?

BRACK: Of the very liveliest——

HEDDA: Tell me more of this, Judge Brack——

BRACK: Lövborg, as well as the others, had been invited in advance. I knew all about it. But he declined the invitation; for now, as you know, he has become a new man.

HEDDA: Up at the Elvsteds', yes. But he went after all, then?

BRACK: Well, you see, Mrs. Hedda—unhappily the spirit moved him at my rooms last evening——

HEDDA: Yes, I hear he found inspiration.

BRACK: Pretty violent inspiration. Well, I fancy that altered his purpose; for we menfolk are unfortunately not always so firm in our principles as we ought to be.

HEDDA: Oh, I am sure you are an exception, Judge Brack. But as to Lövborg——?

BRACK: To make a long story short—he landed at last in Mademoiselle Diana's rooms.

HEDDA: Mademoiselle Diana's?

BRACK: It was Mademoiselle Diana that was giving the soirée, to a select circle of her admirers and her lady friends.

HEDDA: Is she a red-haired woman?

BRACK: Precisely.

HEDDA: A sort of a—singer?

BRACK: Oh yes—in her leisure moments. And moreover a mighty huntress—of men—Mrs. Hedda. You have no doubt heard of her. Eilert Lövborg was one of her most enthusiastic protectors—in the days of his glory.

HEDDA: And how did all this end?

BRACK: Far from amicably, it appears. After a most tender meeting, they seem to have come to blows——

HEDDA: Lövborg and she?

BRACK: Yes. He accused her or her friends of having robbed him. He declared that his pocket-book had disappeared—and other things as well. In short, he seems to have made a furious disturbance.

HEDDA: And what came of it all?

BRACK: It came to a general scrimmage, in which the ladies as well as the gentlemen took part. Fortunately the police at last appeared on the scene.

HEDDA: The police too?

BRACK: Yes. I fancy it will prove a costly frolic for Eilert Lövborg, crazy being that he is.

HEDDA: How so?

BRACK: He seems to have made a violent resistance—to have hit one of the constables on the head and torn the coat off his back. So they had to march him off to the police-station with the rest.

HEDDA: How have you learnt all this?

BRACK: From the police themselves.

HEDDA: [*Gazing straight before her*] So that is what happened. Then he had no vine-leaves in his hair.

BRACK: Vine-leaves, Mrs. Hedda?

HEDDA: [*Changing her tone*] But tell me now

Judge—what is your real reason for tracking out Eilert Lövborg's movements so carefully?

BRACK: In the first place, it could not be entirely indifferent to me if it should appear in the police-court that he came straight from my house.

HEDDA: Will the matter come into court then?

BRACK: Of course. However, I should scarcely have troubled so much about that. But I thought that, as a friend of the family, it was my duty to supply you and Tesman with a full account of his nocturnal exploits.

HEDDA: Why so, Judge Brack?

BRACK: Why, because I have a shrewd suspicion that he intends to use you as a sort of blind.

HEDDA: Oh, how can you think such a thing!

BRACK: Good heavens, Mrs. Hedda—we have eyes in our head. Mark my words! This Mrs. Elvsted will be in no hurry to leave town again.

HEDDA: Well, even if there should be anything between them, I suppose there are plenty of other places where they could meet.

BRACK: Not a single home. Henceforth, as before, every respectable house will be closed against Eilert Lövborg.

HEDDA: And so ought mine to be, you mean?

BRACK: Yes. I confess it would be more than painful to me if this personage were to be made free of your house. How superfluous, how intrusive, he would be, if he were to force his way into——

HEDDA: ——into the triangle?

BRACK: Precisely. It would simply mean that I should find myself homeless.

HEDDA: [Looks at him with a smile] So you want to be the one cock in the basket[1]—that is your aim.

BRACK: [Nods slowly and lowers his voice] Yes, that is my aim. And for that I will fight—with every weapon I can command.

HEDDA: [Her smile vanishing] I see you are a dangerous person—when it comes to the point.

BRACK: Do you think so?

HEDDA: I am beginning to think so. And I am exceedingly glad to think—that you have no sort of hold over me.

BRACK: [Laughing equivocally] Well well, Mrs. Hedda—perhaps you are right there. If I had, who knows what I might be capable of?

HEDDA: Come, come now, Judge Brack! That sounds almost like a threat.

BRACK: [Rising] Oh, not at all! The triangle, you know, ought, if possible, to be spontaneously constructed.

HEDDA: There I agree with you.

BRACK: Well, now I have said all I had to say; and I had better be getting back to town. Good-bye, Mrs. Hedda. [He goes towards the glass door]

HEDDA: [Rising] Are you going through the garden?

BRACK: Yes, it's a short cut for me.

[1] Eneste hane i kurven—a proverbial saying.

HEDDA: And then it is a back way, too.

BRACK: Quite so. I have no objection to back ways. They may be piquant enough at times.

HEDDA: When there is ball practice going on, you mean?

BRACK: [In the doorway, laughing to her] Oh, people don't shoot their tame poultry, I fancy.

HEDDA: [Also laughing] Oh, no, when there is only one cock in the basket——

[They exchange laughing nods of farewell. He goes. She closes the door behind him]

[Hedda, who has become quite serious, stands for a moment looking out. Presently she goes and peeps through the curtain over the middle doorway. Then she goes to the writing-table, takes Lövborg's packet out of the bookcase, and is on the point of looking through its contents. Berta is heard speaking loudly in the hall. Hedda turns and listens. Then she hastily locks up the packet in the drawer, and lays the key on the inkstand]

[Eilert Lövborg, with his greatcoat on and his hat in his hand, tears open the hall door. He looks somewhat confused and irritated]

LÖVBORG: [Looking towards the hall] And I tell you I must and will come in! There!

[He closes the door, turns, sees Hedda, at once regains his self-control, and bows]

HEDDA: [At the writing-table] Well, Mr. Lövborg, this is rather a late hour to call for Thea.

LÖVBORG: You mean rather an early hour to call on you. Pray pardon me.

HEDDA: How do you know that she is still here?

LÖVBORG: They told me at her lodgings that she had been out all night.

HEDDA: [Going to the oval table] Did you notice anything about the people of the house when they said that?

LÖVBORG: [Looks inquiringly at her] Notice anything about them?

HEDDA: I mean, did they seem to think it odd?

LÖVBORG: [Suddenly understanding] Oh yes, of course! I am dragging her down with me! However, I didn't notice anything.—I suppose Tesman is not up yet?

HEDDA: No—I think not——

LÖVBORG: When did he come home?

HEDDA: Very late.

LÖVBORG: Did he tell you anything?

HEDDA: Yes, I gathered that you had had an exceedingly jolly evening at Judge Brack's.

LÖVBORG: Nothing more?

HEDDA: I don't think so. However, I was so dreadfully sleepy——

[Mrs. Elvsted enters through the curtains of the middle doorway]

MRS. ELVSTED: [Going towards him] Ah, Lövborg! At last——!

LÖVBORG: Yes, at last. And too late!

MRS. ELVSTED: [*Looks anxiously at him*] What is too late?

LÖVBORG: Everything is too late now. It is all over with me.

MRS. ELVSTED: Oh no, no—don't say that!

LÖVBORG: You will say the same when you hear——

MRS. ELVSTED: I won't hear anything!

HEDDA: Perhaps you would prefer to talk to her alone? If so, I will leave you.

LÖVBORG: No, stay—you too. I beg you to stay.

MRS. ELVSTED: Yes, but I won't hear anything, I tell you.

LÖVBORG: It is not last night's adventures that I want to talk about.

MRS. ELVSTED: What is it then——?

LÖVBORG: I want to say that now our ways must part.

MRS. ELVSTED: Part!

HEDDA: [*Involuntarily*] I knew it!

LÖVBORG: You can be of no more service to me, Thea.

MRS. ELVSTED: How can you stand there and say that! No more service to you! Am I not to help you now, as before? Are we not to go on working together?

LÖVBORG: Henceforward I shall do no work.

MRS. ELVSTED: [*Despairingly*] Then what am I to do with my life?

LÖVBORG: You must try to live your life as if you had never known me.

MRS. ELVSTED: But you know I cannot do that!

LÖVBORG: Try if you cannot, Thea. You must go home again——

MRS. ELVSTED: [*In vehement protest*] Never in this world! Where you are, there will I be also! I will not let myself be driven away like this! I will remain here! I will be with you when the book appears.

HEDDA: [*Half aloud, in suspense*] Ah yes—the book!

LÖVBORG: [*Looks at her*] My book and Thea's; for that is what it is.

MRS. ELVSTED: Yes, I feel that it is. And that is why I have a right to be with you when it appears! I will see with my own eyes how respect and honor pour in upon you afresh. And the happiness—the happiness—oh, I must share it with you!

LÖVBORG: Thea—our book will never appear.

HEDDA: Ah!

MRS. ELVSTED: Never appear!

LÖVBORG: Can never appear.

MRS. ELVSTED: [*In agonized foreboding*] Lövborg—what have you done with the manuscript?

HEDDA: [*Looks anxiously at him*] Yes, the manuscript——?

MRS. ELVSTED: Where is it?

LÖVBORG: Oh Thea—don't ask me about it!

MRS. ELVSTED: Yes, yes, I will know. I demand to be told at once.

LÖVBORG: The manuscript——. Well then—I have torn the manuscript into a thousand pieces.

MRS. ELVSTED: [*Shrieks*] Oh no, no——!

HEDDA: [*Involuntarily*] But that's not——

LÖVBORG: [*Looks at her*] Not true, you think?

HEDDA: [*Collecting herself*] Oh well, of course—since you say so. But it sounded so improbable——

LÖVBORG: It is true, all the same.

MRS. ELVSTED: [*Wringing her hands*] Oh God—oh God, Hedda—torn his own work to pieces!

LÖVBORG: I have torn my own life to pieces. So why should I not tear my life-work too——?

MRS. ELVSTED: And you did this last night?

LÖVBORG: Yes, I tell you! Tore it into a thousand pieces—and scattered them on the fjord—far out. There there is cool sea-water at any rate—let them drift upon it—drift with the current and the wind. And then presently they will sink—deeper and deeper—as I shall, Thea.

MRS. ELVSTED: Do you know, Lövborg, that what you have done with the book—I shall think of it to my dying day as though you had killed a little child.

LÖVBORG: Yes, you are right. It is a sort of child-murder.

MRS. ELVSTED: How could you, then——! Did not the child belong to me too?

HEDDA: [*Almost inaudibly*] Ah, the child——

MRS. ELVSTED: [*Breathing heavily*] It is all over then. Well well, now I will go, Hedda.

HEDDA: But you are not going away from town?

MRS. ELVSTED: Oh, I don't know what I shall do. I see nothing but darkness before me. [*She goes out by the hall door*]

HEDDA: [*Stands waiting for a moment*] So you are not going to see her home, Mr. Lövborg?

LÖVBORG: I? Through the streets? Would you have people see her walking with me?

HEDDA: Of course I don't know what else may have happened last night. But is it so utterly irretrievable?

LÖVBORG: It will not end with last night—I know that perfectly well. And the thing is that now I have no taste for that sort of life either. I won't begin it anew. She has broken my courage and my power of braving life out.

HEDDA: [*Looking straight before her*] So that pretty little fool has had her fingers in a man's destiny. [*Looks at him*] But all the same, how could you treat her so heartlessly?

LÖVBORG: Oh, don't say that it was heartless!

HEDDA: To go and destroy what has filled her whole soul for months and years! You do not call that heartless!

LÖVBORG: To you I can tell the truth, Hedda.

HEDDA: The truth?

LÖVBORG: First promise me—give me your word —that what I now confide to you Thea shall never know.

HEDDA: I give you my word.

LÖVBORG: Good. Then let me tell you that what I said just now was untrue.

HEDDA: About the manuscript?

LÖVBORG: Yes. I have not torn it to pieces—nor thrown it into the fjord.

HEDDA: No, no——. But—where it is then?

LÖVBORG: I have destroyed it none the less—utterly destroyed it, Hedda!

HEDDA: I don't understand.

LÖVBORG: Thea said that what I had done seemed to her like a child-murder.

HEDDA: Yes, so she said.

LÖVBORG: But to kill his child—that is not the worst thing a father can do to it.

HEDDA: Not the worst?

LÖVBORG: No. I wanted to spare Thea from hearing the worst.

HEDDA: Then what is the worst?

LÖVBORG: Suppose now, Hedda, that a man—in the small hours of the morning—came home to his child's mother after a night of riot and debauchery, and said: "Listen—I have been here and there—in this place and in that. And I have taken our child with me—to this place and to that. And I have lost the child—utterly lost it. The devil knows into what hands it may have fallen—who may have had their clutches on it."

HEDDA: Well—but when all is said and done, you know—this was only a book——

LÖVBORG: Thea's pure soul was in that book.

HEDDA: Yes, so I understand.

LÖVBORG: And you can understand, too, that for her and me together no future is possible.

HEDDA: What path do you mean to take then?

LÖVBORG: None. I will only try to make an end of it all—the sooner the better.

HEDDA: [A step nearer him] Eilert Lövborg—listen to me.—Will you not try to—to do it beautifully?

LÖVBORG: Beautifully? [Smiling] With vine-leaves in my hair, as you used to dream in the old days——?

HEDDA: No, no. I have lost my faith in the vine-leaves. But beautifully nevertheless! For once in a way!—Good-bye! You must go now—and do not come here any more.

LÖVBORG: Good-bye, Mrs. Tesman. And give George Tesman my love. [He is on the point of going]

HEDDA: No, wait! I must give you a memento to take with you.

[She goes to the writing-table and opens the drawer and the pistol-case; then returns to Lövborg with one of the pistols]

LÖVBORG: [Looks at her] This? Is this the memento?

HEDDA: [Nodding slowly] Do you recognize it? It was aimed at you once.

LÖVBORG: You should have used it then.

HEDDA: Take it—and do you use it now.

LÖVBORG: [Puts the pistol in his breast pocket] Thanks!

HEDDA: And beautifully, Eilert Lövborg. Promise me that!

LÖVBORG: Good-bye, Hedda Gabler.

[He goes out by the hall door]

[Hedda listens for a moment at the door. Then she goes up to the writing-table, takes out the packet of manuscript, peeps under the cover, draws a few of the sheets half out, and looks at them. Next she goes over and seats herself in the arm-chair beside the stove, with the packet in her lap. Presently she opens the stove door, and then the packet]

HEDDA: [Throws one of the quires into the fire and whispers to herself] Now I am burning your child, Thea!—Burning it, curly-locks! [Throwing one or two more quires into the stove] Your child and Eilert Lövborg's. [Throws the rest in] I am burning—I am burning your child.

ACT IV.

The same rooms at the Tesmans'. It is evening. The drawing-room is in darkness. The back room is lighted by the hanging lamp over the table. The curtains over the glass door are drawn close.

Hedda, dressed in black, walks to and fro in the dark room. Then she goes into the back room and disappears for a moment to the left. She is heard to strike a few chords on the piano. Presently she comes in sight again, and returns to the drawing-room.

Berta enters from the right, through the inner room, with a lighted lamp, which she places on the table in front of the corner settee in the drawing-room. Her eyes are red with weeping, and she has black ribbons in her cap. She goes quietly and circumspectly out to the right. Hedda goes up to the glass door, lifts the curtain a little aside, and looks out into the darkness.

Shortly afterwards, Miss Tesman, in mourning, with a bonnet and veil on, comes in from the hall. Hedda goes towards her and holds out her hand.

MISS TESMAN: Yes, Hedda, here I am, in mourning and forlorn; for now my poor sister has at last found peace.

HEDDA: I have heard the news already, as you see. Tesman sent me a card.

MISS TESMAN: Yes, he promised me he would. But nevertheless I thought that to Hedda—here in the house of life—I ought myself to bring the tidings of death.

HEDDA: That was very kind of you.

MISS TESMAN: Ah, Rina ought not to have left us just now. This is not the time for Hedda's house to be a house of mourning.

HEDDA: [*Changing the subject*] She died quite peacefully, did she not, Miss Tesman?

MISS TESMAN: Oh, her end was so calm, so beautiful. And then she had the unspeakable happiness of seeing George once more—and bidding him good-bye.—Has he not come home yet?

HEDDA: No. He wrote that he might be detained. But won't you sit down?

MISS TESMAN: No thank you, my dear, dear Hedda. I should like to, but I have so much to do. I must prepare my dear one for her rest as well as I can. She shall go to her grave looking her best.

HEDDA: Can I not help you in any way?

MISS TESMAN: Oh, you must not think of it! Hedda Tesman must have no hand in such mournful work. Nor let her thoughts dwell on it either—not at this time.

HEDDA: One is not always mistress of one's thoughts——

MISS TESMAN: [*Continuing*] Ah yes, it is the way of the world. At home we shall be sewing a shroud; and here there will soon be sewing too, I suppose—but of another sort, thank God!

[*George Tesman enters by the hall door*]

HEDDA: Ah, you have come at last!

TESMAN: You here, Aunt Julia? With Hedda? Fancy that!

MISS TESMAN: I was just going, my dear boy. Well, have you done all you promised?

TESMAN: No; I'm really afraid I have forgotten half of it. I must come to you again to-morrow. To-day my brain is all in a whirl. I can't keep my thoughts together.

MISS TESMAN: Why, my dear George, you mustn't take it in this way.

TESMAN: Mustn't——? How do you mean?

MISS TESMAN: Even in your sorrow you must rejoice, as I do—rejoice that she is at rest.

TESMAN: Oh yes, yes—you are thinking of Aunt Rina.

HEDDA: You will feel lonely now, Miss Tesman.

MISS TESMAN: Just at first, yes. But that will not last very long, I hope. I daresay I shall soon find an occupant for poor Rina's little room.

TESMAN: Indeed? Who do you think will take it? Eh?

MISS TESMAN: Oh, there's always some poor invalid or other in want of nursing, unfortunately.

HEDDA: Would you really take such a burden upon you again?

MISS TESMAN: A burden! Heaven forgive you, child—it has been no burden to me.

HEDDA: But suppose you had a total stranger on your hands——

MISS TESMAN: Oh, one soon makes friends with sick folk; and it's such an absolute necessity for me to have some one to live for. Well, heaven be praised, there may soon be something in *this* house, too, to keep an old aunt busy.

HEDDA: Oh, don't trouble about anything here.

TESMAN: Yes, just fancy what a nice time we three might have together, if——?

HEDDA: If——?

TESMAN: [*Uneasily*] Oh, nothing. It will all come right. Let us hope so—eh?

MISS TESMAN: Well well, I daresay you two want to talk to each other. [*Smiling*] And perhaps Hedda may have something to tell you too, George. Good-bye! I must go home to Rina. [*Turning at the door*] How strange it is to think that now Rina is with me and with my poor brother as well!

TESMAN: Yes, fancy that, Aunt Julia! Eh? [*Miss Tesman goes out by the hall door*]

HEDDA: [*Follows Tesman coldly and searchingly with her eyes*] I almost believe your Aunt Rina's death affects you more than it does your Aunt Julia.

TESMAN: Oh, it's not that alone. It's Eilert I am so terribly uneasy about.

HEDDA: [*Quickly*] Is there anything new about him?

TESMAN: I looked in at his rooms this afternoon, intending to tell him the manuscript was in safe keeping.

HEDDA: Well, did you not find him?

TESMAN: No. He wasn't at home. But afterwards I met Mrs. Elvsted, and she told me that he had been here early this morning.

HEDDA: Yes, directly after you had gone.

TESMAN: And he said that he had torn his manuscript to pieces—eh?

HEDDA: Yes, so he declared.

TESMAN: Why, good heavens, he must have been completely out of his mind! And I suppose you thought it best not to give it back to him, Hedda?

HEDDA: No, he did not get it.

TESMAN: But of course you told him that we had it?

HEDDA: No. [*Quickly*] Did you tell Mrs. Elvsted?

TESMAN: No; I thought I had better not. But you ought to have told him. Fancy, if, in desperation, he should go and do himself some injury! Let me have the manuscript, Hedda! I will take it to him at once. Where is it?

HEDDA: [*Cold and immovable, leaning on the arm-chair*] I have not got it.

TESMAN: Have not got it? What in the world do you mean?

HEDDA: I have burnt it—every line of it.

TESMAN: [*With a violent movement of terror*] Burnt! Burnt Eilert's manuscript!

HEDDA: Don't scream so. The servant might hear you.

TESMAN: Burnt! Why, good God——! No, no, no! It's impossible!

HEDDA: It is so, nevertheless.

TESMAN: Do you know what you have done, Hedda? It's unlawful appropriation of lost property. Fancy that! Just ask Judge Brack, and he'll tell you what it is.

HEDDA: I advise you not to speak of it—either to Judge Brack, or to any one else.

TESMAN: But how could you do anything so unheard-of? What put it into your head? What possessed you? Answer me that—eh?

HEDDA: [*Suppressing an almost imperceptible smile*] I did it for your sake, George.

TESMAN: For my sake!

HEDDA: This morning, when you told me about what he had read to you——

TESMAN: Yes yes—what then?

HEDDA: You acknowledged that you envied him his work.

TESMAN: Oh, of course I didn't mean that literally.

HEDDA: No matter—I could not bear the idea that any one should throw you into the shade.

TESMAN: [*In an outburst of mingled doubt and joy*] Hedda! Oh, is this true? But—but—I never knew you show your love like that before. Fancy that!

HEDDA: Well, I may as well tell you that—just at this time—— [*Impatiently, breaking off*] No, no; you can ask Aunt Julia. She will tell you, fast enough.

TESMAN: Oh, I almost think I understand you, Hedda! [*Clasps his hands together*] Great heavens! do you really mean it! Eh?

HEDDA: Don't shout so. The servant might hear.

TESMAN: [*Laughing in irrepressible glee*] The servant! Why, how absurd you are, Hedda. It's only my old Berta! Why, I'll tell Berta myself.

HEDDA: [*Clenching her hands together in desperation*] Oh, it is killing me,—it is killing me, all this!

TESMAN: What is, Hedda? Eh?

HEDDA: [*Coldly, controlling herself*] All this—absurdity—George.

TESMAN: Absurdity! Do you see anything absurd in my being overjoyed at the news! But after all—perhaps I had better not say anything to Berta.

HEDDA: Oh——why not that too?

TESMAN: No, no, not yet! But I must certainly tell Aunt Julia. And then that you have begun to call me George too! Fancy that! Oh, Aunt Julia will be so happy—so happy!

HEDDA: When she hears that I have burnt Eilert Lövborg's manuscript—for your sake?

TESMAN: No, by the by—that affair of the manuscript—of course nobody must know about that. But that you love me so much, Hedda—Aunt Julia must really share my joy in that! I wonder, now, whether this sort of thing is usual in young wives? Eh?

HEDDA: I think you had better ask Aunt Julia that question too.

TESMAN: I will indeed, some time or other. [*Looks uneasy and downcast again*] And yet the manuscript —the manuscript! Good God! it is terrible to think what will become of poor Eilert now.

[Mrs. Elvsted, *dressed as in the first act, with hat and cloak, enters by the hall door*]

MRS. ELVSTED: [*Greets them hurriedly, and says in evident agitation*] Oh, dear Hedda, forgive my coming again.

HEDDA: What is the matter with you, Thea?

TESMAN: Something about Eilert Lövborg again—eh?

MRS. ELVSTED: Yes! I am dreadfully afraid some misfortune has happened to him.

HEDDA: [*Seizes her arm*] Ah,—do you think so?

TESMAN: Why, good Lord—what makes you think that, Mrs. Elvsted?

MRS. ELVSTED: I heard them talking of him at my boarding-house—just as I came in. Oh, the most incredible rumors are afloat about him to-day.

TESMAN: Yes, fancy, so I heard too! And I can bear witness that he went straight home to bed last night. Fancy that!

HEDDA: Well, what did they say at the boarding-house?

MRS. ELVSTED: Oh, I couldn't make out anything clearly. Either they knew nothing definite, or else——. They stopped talking when they saw me; and I did not dare to ask.

TESMAN: [*Moving about uneasily*] We must hope —we must hope that you misunderstood them, Mrs. Elvsted.

MRS. ELVSTED: No, no; I am sure it was of him they were talking. And I heard something about the hospital or——

TESMAN: The hospital?

HEDDA: No—surely that cannot be!

MRS. ELVSTED: Oh, I was in such mortal terror! I went to his lodgings and asked for him there.

HEDDA: You could make up your mind to that, Thea!

MRS. ELVSTED: What else could I do? I really could bear the suspense no longer.

TESMAN: But you didn't find him either—eh?

MRS. ELVSTED: No. And the people knew nothing about him. He hadn't been home since yesterday afternoon, they said.

TESMAN: Yesterday! Fancy, how could they say that?

MRS. ELVSTED: Oh, I am sure something terrible must have happened to him.

TESMAN: Hedda dear—how would it be if I were to go and make inquiries——?

HEDDA: No, no—don't you mix yourself up in this affair.

[Judge Brack, *with his hat in his hand, enters by the hall door, which* Berta *opens, and closes behind him. He looks grave and bows in silence*]

TESMAN: Oh, is that you, my dear judge? Eh?

BRACK: Yes. It was imperative I should see you this evening.

TESMAN: I can see you have heard the news about Aunt Rina?

BRACK: Yes, that among other things.

TESMAN: Isn't it sad—eh?

BRACK: Well, my dear Tesman, that depends on how you look at it.

TESMAN: [*Looks doubtfully at him*] Has anything else happened?

BRACK: Yes.

HEDDA: [*In suspense*] Anything sad, Judge Brack?

BRACK: That, too, depends on how you look at it, Mrs. Tesman.

MRS. ELVSTED: [*Unable to restrain her anxiety*] Oh! it is something about Eilert Lövborg!

BRACK: [*With a glance at her*] What makes you think that, Madam? Perhaps you have already heard something——?

MRS. ELVSTED: [*In confusion*] No, nothing at all, but——

TESMAN: Oh, for heaven's sake, tell us!

BRACK: [*Shrugging his shoulders*] Well, I regret to say Eilert Lövborg has been taken to the hospital. He is lying at the point of death.

MRS. ELVSTED: [*Shrieks*] Oh God! oh God——!

TESMAN: To the hospital! And at the point of death!

HEDDA: [*Involuntarily*] So soon then——

MRS. ELVSTED: [*Wailing*] And we parted in anger, Hedda!

HEDDA: [*Whispers*] Thea—Thea—be careful!

MRS. ELVSTED: [*Not heeding her*] I must go to him! I must see him alive!

BRACK: It is useless, Madam. No one will be admitted.

MRS. ELVSTED: Oh, at least tell me what has happened to him? What is it?

TESMAN: You don't mean to say that he has himself—— Eh?

HEDDA: Yes, I am sure he has.

TESMAN: Hedda, how can you——?

BRACK: [*Keeping his eyes fixed upon her*] Unfortunately you have guessed quite correctly, Mrs. Tesman.

MRS. ELVSTED: Oh, how horrible!

TESMAN: Himself, then! Fancy that!

HEDDA: Shot himself!

BRACK: Rightly guessed again, Mrs. Tesman.

MRS. ELVSTED: [*With an effort at self-control*] When did it happen, Mr. Brack?

BRACK: This afternoon—between three and four.

TESMAN: But, good Lord, where did he do it? Eh?

BRACK: [*With some hesitation*] Where? Well—I suppose at his lodgings.

MRS. ELVSTED: No, that cannot be; for I was there between six and seven.

BRACK: Well then, somewhere else. I don't know exactly. I only know that he was found——. He had shot himself—in the breast.

MRS. ELVSTED: Oh, how terrible! That he should die like that!

HEDDA: [*To Brack*] Was it in the breast?

BRACK: Yes—as I told you.

HEDDA: Not in the temple?

BRACK: In the breast, Mrs. Tesman.

HEDDA: Well, well—the breast is a good place, too.

BRACK: How do you mean, Mrs. Tesman?

HEDDA: [*Evasively*] Oh, nothing—nothing.

TESMAN: And the wound is dangerous, you say—eh?

BRACK: Absolutely mortal. The end has probably come by this time.

MRS. ELVSTED: Yes, yes, I feel it. The end! The end! Oh, Hedda——!

TESMAN: But tell me, how have you learnt all this?

BRACK: [*Curtly*] Through one of the police. A man I had some business with.

HEDDA: [*In a clear voice*] At last a deed worth doing!

TESMAN: [*Terrified*] Good heavens, Hedda! what are you saying?

HEDDA: I say there is beauty in this.

BRACK: H'm, Mrs. Tesman——

TESMAN: Beauty! Fancy that!

MRS. ELVSTED: Oh, Hedda, how can you talk of beauty in such an act!

HEDDA: Eilert Lövborg has himself made up his account with life. He has had the courage to do—the one right thing.

MRS. ELVSTED: No, you must never think that was how it happened. It must have been in delirium that he did it.

TESMAN: In despair!

HEDDA: That he did not. I am certain of that.

MRS. ELVSTED: Yes, yes! In delirium! Just as when he tore up our manuscript.

BRACK: [*Starting*] The manuscript? Has he torn that up?

MRS. ELVSTED: Yes, last night.

TESMAN: [*Whispers softly*] Oh, Hedda, we shall never get over this.

BRACK: H'm, very extraordinary.

TESMAN: [*Moving about the room*] To think of Eilert going out of the world in this way! And not leaving behind him the book that would have immortalized his name.

MRS. ELVSTED: Oh, if only it could be put together again!

TESMAN: Yes, if it only could! I don't know what I would not give——

MRS. ELVSTED: Perhaps it can, Mr. Tesman.

TESMAN: What do you mean?

MRS. ELVSTED: [*Searches in the pocket of her dress*] Look here. I have kept all the loose notes he used to dictate from.

HEDDA: [*A step forward*] Ah——!

TESMAN: You have kept them, Mrs. Elvsted! Eh?

MRS. ELVSTED: Yes, I have them here. I put them in my pocket when I left home. Here they still are——

TESMAN: Oh, do let me see them!

MRS. ELVSTED: [*Hands him a bundle of papers*] But they are in such disorder—all mixed up.

TESMAN: Fancy, if we could make something out of them, after all! Perhaps if we two put our heads together——

MRS. ELVSTED: Oh yes, at least let us try——

TESMAN: We will manage it! We must! I will dedicate my life to this task.

HEDDA: You, George? Your life?

TESMAN: Yes, or rather all the time I can spare. My own collections must wait in the meantime. Hedda—you understand, eh? I owe this to Eilert's memory.

HEDDA: Perhaps.

TESMAN: And so, my dear Mrs. Elvsted, we will give our whole minds to it. There is no use in brooding over what can't be undone—eh? We must try to control our grief as much as possible, and——

MRS. ELVSTED: Yes, yes, Mr. Tesman. I will do the best I can.

TESMAN: Well then, come here. I can't rest until we have looked through the notes. Where shall we sit? Here? No, in there, in the back room. Excuse me, my dear Judge. Come with me, Mrs. Elvsted.

MRS. ELVSTED: Oh, if only it were possible!

[Tesman *and* Mrs. Elvsted *go into the back room. She takes off her hat and cloak. They both sit at the table under the hanging lamp, and are soon deep in an eager examination of the papers. Hedda* crosses to the stove and sits in the arm-chair. Presently Brack *goes up to her*]

HEDDA: [*In a low voice*] Oh, what a sense of freedom it gives one, this act of Eilert Lövborg's.

BRACK: Freedom, Mrs. Hedda? Well, of course, it is a release for him——

HEDDA: I mean for me! It gives me a sense of freedom to know that a deed of deliberate courage is still possible in this world,—a deed of spontaneous beauty.

BRACK: [*Smiling*] H'm—my dear Mrs. Hedda——

HEDDA: Oh, I know what you are going to say. For you are a kind of specialist, too, like—you know!

BRACK: [*Looking hard at her*] Eilert Lövborg was more to you than perhaps you are willing to admit to yourself. Am I wrong?

HEDDA: I don't answer such questions. I only know that Eilert Lövborg has had the courage to live his life after his own fashion. And then—the last great act, with its beauty! Ah! that he should have the will and the strength to turn away from the banquet of life—so early.

BRACK: I am sorry, Mrs. Hedda,—but I fear I must dispel an amiable illusion.

HEDDA: Illusion?

BRACK: Which could not have lasted long in any case.

HEDDA: What do you mean?

BRACK: Eilert Lövborg did not shoot himself—voluntarily.

HEDDA: Not voluntarily?

BRACK: No. The thing did not happen exactly as I told it.

HEDDA: [*In suspense*] Have you concealed something? What is it?

BRACK: For poor Mrs. Elvsted's sake I idealized the facts a little.

HEDDA: What are the facts?

BRACK: First, that he is already dead.

HEDDA: At the hospital?

BRACK: Yes—without regaining consciousness.

HEDDA: What more have you concealed?

BRACK: This—the event did not happen at his lodgings.

HEDDA: Oh, that can make no difference.

BRACK: Perhaps it may. For I must tell you—Eilert Lövborg was found shot in—in Mademoiselle Diana's boudoir.

HEDDA: [*Makes a motion as if to rise, but sinks back again*] That is impossible, Judge Brack! He cannot have been there again to-day.

BRACK: He was there this afternoon. He went there, he said, to demand the return of something which they had taken from him. Talked wildly about a lost child——

HEDDA: Ah—so that was why——

BRACK: I thought probably he meant his manuscript; but now I hear he destroyed that himself. So I suppose it must have been his pocket-book.

HEDDA: Yes, no doubt. And there—there he was found?

BRACK: Yes, there. With a pistol in his breast-pocket, discharged. The ball had lodged in a vital part.

HEDDA: In the breast—yes.

BRACK: No—in the bowels.

HEDDA: [*Looks up at him with an expression of loathing*] That, too! Oh, what curse is it that makes everything I touch turn ludicrous and mean?

BRACK: There is one point more, Mrs. Hedda—another disagreeable feature in the affair.

HEDDA: And what is that?

BRACK: The pistol he carried——

HEDDA: [*Breathless*] Well? What of it?

BRACK: He must have stolen it.

HEDDA: [*Leaps up*] Stolen it! That is not true! He did not steal it!

BRACK: No other explanation is possible. He must have stolen it—— Hush!

[Tesman *and* Mrs. Elvsted *have risen from the table in the back room, and come into the drawing-room*]

TESMAN: [*With the papers in both his hands*] Hedda, dear, it is almost impossible to see under that lamp. Think of that!

HEDDA: Yes, I am thinking.

TESMAN: Would you mind our sitting at your writing-table—eh?

HEDDA: If you like [*Quickly*] No, wait! Let me clear it first!

TESMAN: Oh, you needn't trouble, Hedda. There is plenty of room.

HEDDA: No, no, let me clear it, I say! I will take these things in and put them on the piano. There!

[*She has drawn out an object, covered with sheet music, from under the bookcase, places several other pieces of music upon it, and carries the whole into the inner room, to the left.* Tesman *lays the scraps of paper on the writing-table, and moves the lamp there from the corner table. He and* Mrs. Elvsted *sit down and proceed with their work.* Hedda *returns*]

HEDDA: [*Behind* Mrs. Elvsted's *chair, gently ruffling her hair*] Well, my sweet Thea,—how goes it with Eilert Lövborg's monument?

MRS. ELVSTED: [*Looks dispiritedly up at her*] Oh, it will be terribly hard to put in order.

TESMAN: We must manage it. I am determined. And arranging other people's papers is just the work for me.

[Hedda *goes over to the stove, and seats herself on one of the footstools.* Brack *stands over her, leaning on the arm-chair*]

HEDDA: [*Whispers*] What did you say about the pistol?

BRACK: [*Softly*] That he must have stolen it.

HEDDA: Why stolen it?

BRACK: Because every other explanation ought to be impossible, Mrs. Hedda.

HEDDA: Indeed?

BRACK: [*Glances at her*] Of course, Eilert Lövborg was here this morning. Was he not?

HEDDA: Yes.

BRACK: Were you alone with him?

HEDDA: Part of the time.

BRACK: Did you not leave the room whilst he was here?

HEDDA: No.

BRACK: Try to recollect. Were you not out of the room a moment?

HEDDA: Yes, perhaps just a moment—out in the hall.

BRACK: And where was your pistol-case during that time?

HEDDA: I had it locked up in——

BRACK: Well, Mrs. Hedda?

HEDDA: The case stood there on the writing-table.

BRACK: Have you looked since, to see whether both the pistols are there?

HEDDA: No.

BRACK: Well, you need not. I saw the pistol found in Lövborg's pocket, and I knew it at once as the one I had seen yesterday—and before, too.

HEDDA: Have you it with you?

BRACH: No; the police have it.

HEDDA: What will the police do with it?

BRACK: Search till they find the owner.

HEDDA: Do you think they will succeed.

BRACK: [*Bends over her and whispers*] No, Hedda Gabler—not so long as I say nothing.

HEDDA: [*Looks frightened at him*] And if you do not say nothing,—what then?

BRACK: [*Shrugs his shoulders*] There is always the possibility that the pistol was stolen.

HEDDA: [*Firmly*] Death rather than that.

BRACK: [*Smiling*] People say such things—but they don't do them.

HEDDA: [*Without replying*] And supposing the pistol was not stolen, and the owner is discovered? What then?

BRACK: Well, Hedda—then comes the scandal.

HEDDA: The scandal!

BRACK: Yes, the scandal—of which you are so mortally afraid. You will, of course, be brought before the court—both you and Mademoiselle Diana. She will have to explain how the thing happened—whether it was an accidental shot or murder. Did the pistol go off as he was trying to take it out of his pocket, to threaten her with? Or did she tear the pistol out of his hand, shoot him, and push it back into his pocket? That would be quite like her; for she is an able-bodied young person, this same Mademoiselle Diana.

HEDDA: But *I* have nothing to do with all this repulsive business.

BRACK: No. But you will have to answer the question: Why did you give Eilert Lövborg the pistol? And what conclusions will people draw from the fact that you did give it to him?

HEDDA: [*Lets her head sink*] That is true. I did not think of that.

BRACK: Well, fortunately, there is no danger, so long as I say nothing.

HEDDA: [*Looks up at him*] So I am in your power, Judge Brack. You have me at your beck and call, from this time forward.

BRACK: [*Whispers softly*] Dearest Hedda—believe me—I shall not abuse my advantage.

HEDDA: I am in your power none the less. Subject to your will and your demands. A slave, a slave then! [*Rises impetuously*] No, I cannot endure the thought of that! Never!

BRACK: [*Looks half-mockingly at her*] People generally get used to the inevitable.

HEDDA: [*Returns his look*] Yes, perhaps. [*She crosses to the writing-table. Suppressing an involuntary smile, she imitates* Tesman's *intonations*] Well? Are you getting on, George? Eh?

TESMAN: Heaven knows, dear. In any case it will be the work of months.

HEDDA: [*As before*] Fancy that! [*Passes her hands softly through* Mrs. Elvsted's *hair*] Doesn't it seem strange to you, Thea? Here are you sitting with Tesman—just as you used to sit with Eilert Lövborg?

MRS. ELVSTED: Ah, if I could only inspire your husband in the same way!

HEDDA: Oh, that will come, too—in time.

TESMAN: Yes, do you know, Hedda—I really

think I begin to feel something of the sort. But won't you go and sit with Brack again?

HEDDA: Is there nothing I can do to help you two?

TESMAN: No, nothing in the world. [*Turning his head*] I trust to you to keep Hedda company, my dear Brack.

BRACK: [*With a glance at* Hedda] With the very greatest of pleasure.

HEDDA: Thanks. But I am tired this evening. I will go in and lie down a little on the sofa.

TESMAN: Yes, do dear—eh?

[Hedda *goes into the back room and draws the curtains. A short pause. Suddenly she is heard playing a wild dance on the piano*]

MRS. ELVSTED: [*Starts from her chair*] Oh—what is that?

TESMAN: [*Runs to the doorway*] Why, my dearest Hedda—don't play dance-music to-night! Just think of Aunt Rina! And of Eilert, too!

HEDDA: [*Puts her head out between the curtains*] And of Aunt Julia. And of all the rest of them.— After this, I will be quiet. [*Closes the curtains again*]

TESMAN: [*At the writing-table*] It's not good for her to see us at this distressing work. I'll tell you what, Mrs. Elvsted,—you shall take the empty room at Aunt Julia's, and then I will come over in the evenings, and we can sit and work there—eh?

HEDDA: [*In the inner room*] I hear what you are saying, Tesman. But how am *I* to get through the evenings out here?

TESMAN: [*Turning over the papers*] Oh, I daresay Judge Brack will be so kind as to look in now and then, even though I am out.

BRACK: [*In the arm-chair, calls out gaily*] Every blessed evening, with all the pleasure in life, Mrs. Tesman! We shall get on capitally together, we two!

HEDDA: [*Speaking loud and clear*] Yes, don't you flatter yourself we will, Judge Brack? Now that you are the one cock in the basket——

[*A shot is heard within.* Tesman, Mrs. Elvsted, *and* Brack *leap to their feet*]

TESMAN: Oh, now she is playing with those pistols again.

[*He throws back the curtains and runs in, followed by* Mrs. Elvsted. Hedda *lies stretched on the sofa, lifeless. Confusion and cries.* Berta *enters in alarm from the right*]

TESMAN: [*Shrieks to* Brack] Shot herself! Shot herself in the temple! Fancy that!

BRACK: [*Half-fainting in the arm-chair*] Good God!—people don't do such things.

August Strindberg

(1849–1912)

When the British actor-manager Robert Lorraine read *The Father* to his wife, she was on her knees before him at the end of the second act, assuring him that all their children were his own and that he was not to believe a single word of Strindberg's play. This appears to have convinced him that one could give a successful production of this formidable drama even in England, which he proceeded to do in 1927. Strindberg's furious onslaught on the emotions, however, had enabled him to overcome the diffidence of audiences elsewhere as early as the eighteen-eighties and 'nineties—in Germany and France, as well as in his own country, Sweden, which came to acknowledge him as its greatest writer. Ever since the Théâtre Libre produced his drama *Miss Julie* (1892), the European theatre has been fully aware of its debt to this author of some seventy long and short plays. It has even tended to approve the prediction of Ibsen, who, though often berated by his junior colleague, once declared, "He will be greater than I."

Strindberg's fame spread as far east as Japan, where he found imitators, and as far west as America, where O'Neill, his debtor, claimed him in 1924 as "the most modern of moderns, the greatest interpreter of the characteristic spiritual conflicts that constitute the drama." It was during the period of O'Neill's close association with the Provincetown Playhouse that Strindberg was introduced to its small but faithful audiences with one of his most experimental plays, *The Spook Sonata*. Although his virulent dramas were never received with open arms in the English-speaking world, the impression they made upon leaders of the American and English theatre makes Strindberg important to us. His example can be traced in many an O'Neill success and failure. His importance was dinned into the ears of American writers by important critics like James Huneker and H. L. Mencken. Huneker, who predicted in 1905 that the antifeminist Strindberg would find no popularity in America, "a land peopled with gynolatrists," thought of him as a "culture hero" who had "brought us the history of experiences not to be forgotten." Later, when Shaw received the Nobel Prize, which had been withheld from Strindberg himself by the enmity of a committee member, he converted it into a trust fund for English translations of Strindberg's writings—fifty-five volumes of plays, stories, novels, autobiographies, and miscellaneous writings—from the standard Swedish edition.

Johan August Strindberg was born in Stockholm, the fourth of eleven children. His mother had been a barmaid in the city, and his father, a small businessman whose family deplored the *mésalliance,* had married her only a few months before August's birth. Cradled in poverty and reared in an overcrowded three-room household harassed by many births and deaths, August became an oversensitive and rebellious lad. He became even more irritable and suspicious when, in his thirteenth year, his mother died and his father promptly remarried. Fixated on his mother by love and hatred, made insecure for life, and filled with aggressive drives compounded of desire and fear, Strindberg was primed from the start for a life of furious conflict with the world and with himself. He froze and starved at the University of Upsala for a semester in 1867, tried the University of Stockholm for a time, left it to teach at the same grammar school where he had suffered childhood humiliations, served for a while as a physician's assistant, and made a vain attempt to become an actor. Returning in 1870 to the University of Stockholm, he studied literature and science avidly; but winning a stipend from King Charles V of Sweden for a short romantic play, he abandoned his studies in 1872 to pursue a literary career.

Fortunately, although his first full-length drama, *Master Olof,* was rejected by both publishers and theatres, Strindberg received an appointment as assistant in the Royal Library in Stockholm, and here, from 1874 to 1882, he brooded and browsed, studied philosophy, tried to master the Chinese language, produced a scholarly study, and wrote the first naturalistic social novel in Swedish, *The Red Room* (1879), under the influence of Flaubert. During this period he also fell fatefully in love with the wife of a baron, Siri von Essen, whom he married and with whom he had three children before becoming embroiled in as violent a domestic conflict as any ever aired in literature. Leaving his librarian's post, he traveled about Europe with his family between 1883 and 1889, publishing a collection of realistic short stories on marriage, *Married* (1884). The volume was confiscated and its publisher arraigned for blasphemy, but Strindberg won popularity with the Swedish public by hastening home to assume full responsibility for the book. He gained an acquittal from the court and the following year published a second and even more trenchant collection of stories, also entitled *Married*. It contained all the familiar elements of Strindberg's later ultra-realistic plays, including their misogyny and their attack on the cult of feminism which had been promoted by *A Doll's House.* Here first appeared his strange attraction-repulsion pattern in his relations with women, which had been no doubt implanted in him by childhood experiences with a mother of lowly origins who could give him scant attention and died when he was still a boy.

Thereafter "the battle of the sexes" was to consume much of his energy and to find notable expression in *The Father* (1887), *Comrades* (1888), *Miss Julie* (1888), *The Link* (1893), and *The Dance of Death* (1901), as well as in searing, if embarrassing, autobiographical novels. He was finally divorced in 1891 after overpublicized bickerings, but since he married for a second time (1893) and for a third time (1901), there was never any lack of fuel for his analytical and recriminatory studies of marriage. In the war of the sexes, Strindberg contended, "the less honest and more perverse would come out conqueror"; that is, the woman would win, the man being handicapped "by an inbred respect for women." Of Ibsen and the "Ibsenites," or feminists, he declared, "My superior intelligence revolts against the gynolatry which is the latest superstition of the freethinkers," and he expressed a fear that society was going back to a state of matriarchy. His antifeminism often verged on hysteria; nor was it consistent with his own practice as the husband of three wives, each of whom was an "emancipated" woman. Although he made penetrative observations, he hardly qualified as a sociologist. His findings were obviously too colored by personal animus to be accepted as considered judgments. It is for his talent as a dramatist and not as an ineffectual eccentric that Strindberg is remembered.

A number of his plays devoted directly to the sex duel are masterworks of analysis. Although he did not follow naturalism slavishly, he went far toward making it enduringly memorable, and the psychological conflicts in which he specialized led modern playwrights into one of the rewarding channels of their craft. Strindberg advanced dramatic art by writing more probingly and more tautly than Ibsen generally did. He went further than Ibsen in turning out a species of drama in which hardly anything remains of exposition and nearly everything is simply the dramatized climax. To this end, he abolished intermissions and act divisions, virtually giving rise to the modern one-act drama, which is to be distinguished as an art form from the "vaudevilles" or inconsequential curtain-raisers of the popular theatre. (He was anticipated by the authors of short plays for Antoine's Théâtre Libre, it is true, but these precursors had neither his breadth nor his depth.) The masterpiece of this kind of concentrated dramaturgy is the hour-and-a-half-long uninterrupted drama *Miss Julie,* in which the sexual instinct thrusts a fastidious and neurotic noblewoman into a disastrous affair with her father's footman.

In another long one-acter, *The Creditor,* in which he exposed a woman's parasitism, he transferred all the conflict to the psychological plane and conveyed it entirely through analytical conversation before moving on to a shattering conclusion. The extreme example of simplification was *The Stronger,* which is no more than a betrayed but ultimately victorious woman's monologue in the presence of her rival.

Without exemplifying any breadth of vision or sweetness of spirit in his realistic pieces, Strindberg concerned himself with the subject of human relations, especially with the intensified competitiveness of men and women in modern society and their loss of emotional security. Since he placed in the arena of the sex duel "exceptional people in conflict with exceptional circumstance," as the novelist Storm Jameson has noted, the sparks that fly from the collisions illuminate the scene and excite the onlooker. And if Strindberg was often so extreme in utterance as to seem to exceed the bounds of rationality, there is no evidence of a clouded mind in his observations and logic. The difference between him and more relaxed writers is that his lucidity happened to be charged with lightning. His works were more than mere displays of "the sorrows of a hen-pecked Blue Beard," as the British critic Desmond MacCarthy called them; and plays like *The Father* and *Miss Julie* are something else and something more than his pronouncements on women and marriage. His best work distributes justice between its antagonists, takes account of human contradictions, and crackles with sardonic humor. Like other good artists, Strindberg wrote more richly and better than he perhaps knew or intended. In *The Link* and *The Dance of Death* he presented a husband whose behavior was just as deplorable as the wife's, and in *Miss Julie* he made the drama revolve around a girl who was the victim of sexuality welling up from suppression. Miss Julie's compulsively offensive behavior toward a suitor of her own class and her attraction to a valet is fundamentally pitiable in the light of clinical understanding, whereas real ruthlessness emerges in the valet's exploitation of her weakness. Mrs. X, heroine of *The Stronger,* is a wife who managed to retrieve her husband from the clutches of a sterile seductress and proved herself "the stronger woman" by doing what the "emancipated" woman could not do—that is, holding her man. No doubt Strindberg approved of her "unemancipated" conduct, but he was sufficiently objective to refrain from making her lovable. His animosities, in short, did not often lessen his power to create character, whereas many playwrights far more agreeable than he have not hesitated to turn characters into puppets of their argument. Even so relentless a treatment of domestic war as *The Father* reveals at the helm of Strindberg's dramaturgy a steady hand not always noticed by this dramatist's detractors.

In *The Father* Strindberg championed the husband in his struggle against the wife, and, indeed, the husband is more sinned against than sinning. Yet the Captain is hardly a reasonable man either in his dealings with his wife Laura or in his frantic obsession with the possibility that their daughter may not be his own. The old nurse who puts him in a straitjacket is a compassionate woman, and even the ruthless Laura is not an unmitigated serpent of subtlety and evil. For all her diabolical scheming, she is ignorant and obtuse, as well as conventionally religious; she can be, besides, as considerate to others as she is inconsiderate toward her husband when balked by him. Even in the all-consuming struggle of *The Father*, we find the contradictions and divagations that distinguish life from the closed syllogism of argument. Next to the power of a ruling passion, we find here, as in other Strindberg plays, creative flexibility and multifaceted reality.

Although *The Father* follows the dramatic line of an intrigue and has act divisions, so that it is less originally constructed than either *Miss Julie* or *The Creditor,* it exhibits most of the qualities we associate with its author's genius. It is a remarkably compact play, and everything that occurs in it forms a climax in the relations of husband and wife. The quarrel over the education of the daughter is only the spark that explodes the powder keg. We can hardly fail to realize that the domestic struggle has been going on for some time and that the hatred of the couple has been mounting in countless details of daily experience. The man's irritability has been compounding itself and now it pays a heavy interest on its capital; otherwise, he would be nothing but a fool, and he is no fool. The woman has

been smouldering before she becomes demoniacal in the play; otherwise her attitude toward the husband would be inexplicable. An unwritten novel, but one fully traced in Strindberg's distressingly candid autobiographies, underlies *The Father*.

Above all, Strindberg approaches a new concept of tragedy or, more precisely, approximates comparatively new variations on it. More than in the work of any earlier dramatist, man is destroyed in *The Father* (as in other Strindberg dramas, especially in *The Creditor* and in the second-rate one-acter *Simoon*) by his neuroses, and it is by inciting or encouraging a neurotic condition that Laura works her will. Strindberg's destroyed character, moreover, is no longer a hero in the classic or Elizabethan sense of the term, and he falls ignominiously. Miss Julie cuts her throat, the husband in *The Dance of Death* gets an apoplectic stroke, and the Father collapses in a straitjacket, after having waged a struggle over more or less picayune or unheroic matters that became momentous only in his disturbed mind. Nevertheless, because of the substantial amount of passion and will invested by the characters, the effect of the action in Strindberg's work is not inconsequential or devoid of a certain degree of tragic exaltation. For, unlike the followers of Zolaist naturalism, from which Strindberg learned a good deal while living in the Paris of the eighteen-eighties and 'nineties, Strindberg made no virtue of scientific detachment. Strindberg was the dramatist of division in the modern soul, and it splits apart explosively in his characters as it often did in his own person.

For additional commentary and bibliography, see pages 328–329.

THE FATHER

By August Strindberg

TRANSLATED FROM THE SWEDISH BY EDITH AND WARNER OLAND

CHARACTERS

A CAPTAIN OF CAVALRY   DOCTOR ÖSTERMARK   NÖJD
LAURA, *his wife*   THE PASTOR   AN ORDERLY
BERTHA, *their daughter*   THE NURSE

ACT I.

The sitting-room at the Captain's. *There is a door a little to the right at the back. In the middle of the room, a large, round table strewn with newspapers and magazines. To right a leather-covered sofa and table. In the right-hand corner a private door. At left there is a door leading to the inner room and a desk with a clock on it. Gamebags, guns and other arms hang on the walls. Army coats hang near door at back. On the large table stands a lighted lamp.*

CAPTAIN: [*Rings, an orderly comes in*]
ORDERLY: Yes, Captain.
CAPTAIN: Is Nöjd out there?
ORDERLY: He is waiting for orders in the kitchen.
CAPTAIN: In the kitchen again, is he? Send him in at once.
ORDERLY: Yes, Captain.
  [*Goes*]
PASTOR: What's the matter now?
CAPTAIN: Oh, the rascal has been cutting up with the servant-girl again; he's certainly a bad lot.
PASTOR: Why, Nöjd got into the same trouble year before last, didn't he?
CAPTAIN: Yes, you remember? Won't you be good enough to give him a friendly talking to and perhaps you can make some impression on him. I've sworn at him and flogged him, too, but it hasn't had the least effect.
PASTOR: And so you want me to preach to him? What effect do you suppose the word of God will have on a rough trooper?
CAPTAIN: Well, it certainly has no effect on me.
PASTOR: I know that well enough.
CAPTAIN: Try it on *him,* anyway.
  [Nöjd *comes in*]
CAPTAIN: What have you been up to now, Nöjd?
NÖJD: God save you, Captain, but I couldn't talk about it with the Pastor here.
PASTOR: Don't be afraid of me, my boy.
CAPTAIN: You had better confess or you know what will happen.

NÖJD: Well, you see it was like this; we were at a dance at Gabriel's, and then—then Ludwig said—
CAPTAIN: What has Ludwig got to do with it? Stick to the truth.
NÖJD: Yes, and Emma said "Let's go into the barn——"
CAPTAIN: ——Oh, so it was Emma who led you astray, was it?
NÖJD: Well, not far from it. You know that unless the girl is willing nothing ever happens.
CAPTAIN: Never mind all that: Are you the father of the child or not?
NÖJD: Who knows?
CAPTAIN: What's that? Don't you know?
NÖJD: Why no—that is, you can never be sure.
CAPTAIN: Weren't you the only one?
NÖJD: Yes, that time, but you can't be sure for all that.
CAPTAIN: Are you trying to put the blame on Ludwig? Is that what you are up to?
NÖJD: Well, you see it isn't easy to know who is to blame.
CAPTAIN: Yes, but you told Emma you would marry her.
NÖJD: Oh, a fellow's always got to say that—
CAPTAIN: [*To* Pastor] This is terrible, isn't it?
PASTOR: It's the old story over again. See here, Nöjd, you surely ought to know whether you are the father or not?
NÖJD: Well, of course, I was mixed up with the girl—but you know yourself, Pastor, that it needn't amount to anything for all that.
PASTOR: Look here, my lad, we are talking about you now. Surely you won't leave the girl alone with the child. I suppose we can't compel you to marry her, but you should provide for the child—that you shall do!
NÖJD: Well, then, so must Ludwig, too.
CAPTAIN: Then the case must go to the courts. I cannot ferret out the truth of all this, nor is it to my liking. So now be off.
PASTOR: One moment, Nöjd. H'm—don't you think it dishonorable to leave a girl destitute like that with her child? Don't you think so? Don't you see that such conduct——h'm—h'm——

78

NÖJD: Yes, if I only knew for sure that I was father of the child, but you can't be sure of that, Pastor, and I don't see much fun slaving all your life for another man's child. Surely you, Pastor, and the Captain can understand for yourselves.

CAPTAIN: Be off.

NÖJD: God save you, Captain.

[Goes]

CAPTAIN: But keep out of the kitchen, you rascal! [To Pastor] Now, why didn't you get after him?

PASTOR: What do you mean?

CAPTAIN: Why, you only sat and mumbled something or other.

PASTOR: To tell the truth I really don't know what to say. It is a pity about the girl, yes, and a pity about the lad, too. For think if he were not the father. The girl can nurse the child for four months at the orphanage, and then it will be permanently provided for, but it will be different for him. The girl can get a good place afterwards in some respectable family, but the lad's future may be ruined if he is dismissed from the regiment.

CAPTAIN: Upon my soul I should like to be in the magistrate's shoes and judge this case. The lad is probably not innocent, one can't be sure, but we do know that the girl is guilty, if there is any guilt in the matter.

PASTOR: Well, well, I judge no one. But what were we talking about when this stupid business interrupted us? It was about Bertha and her confirmation, wasn't it?

CAPTAIN: Yes, but it was certainly not in particular about her confirmation but about her whole welfare. This house is full of women who all want to have their say about my child. My mother-in-law wants to make a Spiritualist of her. Laura wants her to be an artist; the governess wants her to be a Methodist, old Margret a Baptist, and the servant-girls want her to join the Salvation Army! It won't do to try to make a soul in patches like that. I, who have the chief right to try to form her character, am constantly opposed in my efforts. And that's why I have decided to send her away from home.

PASTOR: You have too many women trying to run this house.

CAPTAIN: You're right! It's like going into a cage full of tigers, and if I didn't hold a red-hot iron under their noses they would tear me to pieces any moment. And you laugh, you rascal! Wasn't it enough that I married your sister, without your palming off your old stepmother on me?

PASTOR: But, good heavens, one can't have stepmothers in one's own house!

CAPTAIN: No, you think it is better to have mothers-in-law in some one else's house!

PASTOR: Oh well, we all have some burden in life.

CAPTAIN: But mine is certainly too heavy. I have my old nurse into the bargain, who treats me as if I ought still to wear a bib. She is a good old soul, to be sure, and she must not be dragged into such talk.

PASTOR: You must keep a tight rein on the women folk. You let them run things too much.

CAPTAIN: Now will you please inform me how I'm to keep order among the women folk?

PASTOR: Laura was brought up with a firm hand, but although she is my own sister, I must admit she was pretty troublesome.

CAPTAIN: Laura certainly has her faults, but with her it isn't so serious.

PASTOR: Oh, speak out—I know her.

CAPTAIN: She was brought up with romantic ideas, and it has been hard for her to find herself, but she is my wife——

PASTOR: And because she is your wife she is the best of wives? No, my dear fellow, it is she who really wears on you most.

CAPTAIN: Well, anyway, the whole house is topsy-turvy. Laura won't let Bertha leave her, and I can't allow her to remain in this bedlam.

PASTOR: Oh, so Laura won't? Well, then, I'm afraid you are in for trouble. When she was a child if she set her mind on anything she used to play dead dog till she got it, and then likely as not she would give it back, explaining that it wasn't the thing she wanted, but having her own way.

CAPTAIN: So she was like that even then? H'm—she really gets into such a passion sometimes that I am anxious about her and afraid she is ill.

PASTOR: But what do you want to do with Bertha that is so unpardonable? Can't you compromise?

CAPTAIN: You mustn't think I want to make a prodigy of her or an image of myself. I don't want to be a procurer for my daughter and educate her exclusively for matrimony, for then if she were left unmarried she might have bitter days. On the other hand, I don't want to influence her toward a career that requires a long course of training which would be entirely thrown away if she should marry.

PASTOR: What do you want, then?

CAPTAIN: I want her to be a teacher. If she remains unmarried she will be able to support herself, and at any rate she wouldn't be any worse off than the poor schoolmasters who have to share their salaries with a family. If she marries she can use her knowledge in the education of her children. Am I right?

PASTOR: Quite right. But, on the other hand, hasn't she shown such talent for painting that it would be a great pity to crush it?

CAPTAIN: No! I have shown her sketches to an eminent painter, and he says they are only the kind of thing that can be learned at schools. But then a young fop came here in the summer who, of course, understands the matter much better, and he declared that she had colossal genius, and so that settled it to Laura's satisfaction.

PASTOR: Was he quite taken with Bertha?

CAPTAIN: That goes without saying.

PASTOR: Then God help you, old man, for in that case I see no hope. This is pretty bad—and, of course, Laura has her supporters—in there?

CAPTAIN: Yes, you may be sure of that; the whole house is already up in arms, and, between ourselves, it is not exactly a noble conflict that is being waged from that quarter.

PASTOR: Don't you think I know that?

CAPTAIN: You do?

PASTOR: I do.

CAPTAIN: But the worst of it is, it strikes me that Bertha's future is being decided from spiteful motives. They hint that men better be careful, because women can do this or that now-a-days. All day long, incessantly, it is a conflict between man and woman. Are you going? No, stay for supper. I have no special inducements to offer, but do stay. You know I am expecting the new doctor. Have you seen him?

PASTOR: I caught a glimpse of him as I came along. He looked pleasant and reliable.

CAPTAIN: That's good. Do you think it possible he may become my ally?

PASTOR: Who can tell? It depends on how much he has been among women.

CAPTAIN: But won't you really stay?

PASTOR: No thanks, my dear fellow; I promised to be home for supper, and the wife gets uneasy if I am late.

CAPTAIN: Uneasy? Angry, you mean. Well, as you will. Let me help you with your coat.

PASTOR: It's certainly pretty cold tonight. Thanks. You must take care of your health, Adolf, you seem rather nervous.

CAPTAIN: Nervous?

PASTOR: Yes, you are not really very well.

CAPTAIN: Has Laura put that into your head? She has treated me for the last twenty years as if I were at the point of death.

PASTOR: Laura? No, but you make me uneasy about you. Take care of yourself—that's my advice! Good-bye, old man; but didn't you want to talk about the confirmation?

CAPTAIN: Not at all! I assure you that matter will have to take its course in the ordinary way at the cost of the clerical conscience for I am neither a believer nor a martyr.

PASTOR: Good-bye. Love to Laura.

[Goes]

[The Captain opens his desk and seats himself at it. Takes up account books]

CAPTAIN: [Figuring] Thirty-four—nine, forty-three—seven, eight, fifty-six—

LAURA: [Coming in from inner room] Will you be kind enough?——

CAPTAIN: Just a moment! Sixty-six—seventy-one, eighty-four, eighty-nine, ninety-two, a hundred. What is it?

LAURA: Am I disturbing you?

CAPTAIN: Not at all. Housekeeping money, I suppose?

LAURA: Yes, housekeeping money.

CAPTAIN: Put the accounts down there and I will go over them.

LAURA: The accounts?

CAPTAIN: Yes.

LAURA: Am I to keep accounts now?

CAPTAIN: Of course you are to keep accounts. Our affairs are in a precarious condition, and in case of a liquidation, accounts are necessary, or one is liable to punishment for being careless.

LAURA: It's not my fault that our affairs are in a precarious condition.

CAPTAIN: That is exactly what the accounts will decide.

LAURA: It's not my fault that our tenant doesn't pay.

CAPTAIN: Who recommended this tenant so warmly? You! Why did you recommend a—good-for-nothing, we'll call him?

LAURA: But why did you rent to this good-for-nothing?

CAPTAIN: Because I was not allowed to eat in peace, nor sleep in peace, nor work in peace, till you women got that man here. You wanted him so that your brother might be rid of him, your mother wanted him because I didn't want him, the governess wanted him because he reads his Bible, and old Margret because she had known his grandmother from childhood. That's why he was taken, and if he hadn't been taken, I'd be in a madhouse by now or lying in my grave. However, here is the housekeeping money and your pin money. You may give me the accounts later.

LAURA: [Curtsies] Thanks so much. Do you too keep an account of what you spend besides the housekeeping money?

CAPTAIN: That doesn't concern you.

LAURA: No, that's true—just as little as my child's education concerns me. Have the gentlemen come to a decision after this evening's conference?

CAPTAIN: I had already come to a decision, and therefore it only remained for me to talk it over with the one friend I and the family have in common. Bertha is to go to boarding school in town, and starts in a fortnight.

LAURA: To which boarding school, if I may venture to ask?

CAPTAIN: Professor Säfberg's.

LAURA: That free thinker!

CAPTAIN: According to the law, children are to be brought up in their father's faith.

LAURA: And the mother has no voice in the matter?

CAPTAIN: None whatever. She has sold her birthright by a legal transaction, and forfeited her rights in return for the man's responsibility of caring for her and her children.

LAURA: That is to say she has no rights concerning her child.

CAPTAIN: No, none at all. When once one has sold

one's goods, one cannot have them back and still keep the money.

LAURA: But if both father and mother should agree?

CAPTAIN: Do you think that could ever happen? I want her to live in town, you want her to stay at home. The arithmetical result would be that she remain at the railway station midway between town and home. This is a knot that cannot be untied, you see.

LAURA: Then it must be broken. What did Nöjd want here?

CAPTAIN: That is an official secret.

LAURA: Which the whole kitchen knows!

CAPTAIN: Good, then you must know it.

LAURA: I do know it.

CAPTAIN: And have your judgment ready-made?

LAURA: My judgment is the judgment of the law.

CAPTAIN: But it is not written in the law who the child's father is.

LAURA: No, but one usually knows that.

CAPTAIN: Wise minds claim that one can never know.

LAURA: That's strange. Can't one ever know who the father of a child is?

CAPTAIN: No; so they claim.

LAURA: How extraordinary! How can the father have such control over the children then?

CAPTAIN: He has control only when he has assumed the responsibilities of the child, or has had them forced upon him. But in wedlock, of course, there is no doubt about the fatherhood.

LAURA: There are no doubts then?

CAPTAIN: Well, I should hope not.

LAURA: But if the wife has been unfaithful?

CAPTAIN: That's another matter. Was there anything else you wanted to say?

LAURA: Nothing.

CAPTAIN: Then I shall go up to my room, and perhaps you will be kind enough to let me know when the doctor arrives. [Closes desk and rises]

LAURA: Certainly.

[Captain goes through the private door right]

CAPTAIN: As soon as he comes. For I don't want to seem rude to him, you understand.

[Goes]

LAURA: I understand. [Looks at the money she holds in her hands]

MOTHER-IN-LAW'S VOICE: [Within] Laura!

LAURA: Yes.

MOTHER-IN-LAW'S VOICE: Is my tea ready?

LAURA: [In doorway to inner room] In just a moment.

[Laura goes toward hall door at back as the orderly opens it]

ORDERLY: Doctor Ostermark.

DOCTOR: Madam!

LAURA: [Advances and offers her hand] Welcome. Doctor—you are heartily welcome. The Captain is out, but he will be back soon.

DOCTOR: I hope you will excuse my coming so late, but I have already been called upon to pay some professional visits.

LAURA: Sit down, won't you?

DOCTOR: Thank you.

LAURA: Yes, there is a great deal of illness in the neighborhood just now, but I hope it will agree with you here. For us country people living in such isolation it is of great value to find a doctor who is interested in his patients, and I hear so many nice things of you, Doctor, that I hope the pleasantest relations will exist between us.

DOCTOR: You are indeed kind, and I hope for your sake my visits to you will not often be caused by necessity. Your family is, I believe, as a rule in good health——

LAURA: Fortunately we have been spared acute illnesses, but still things are not altogether as they should be.

DOCTOR: Indeed?

LAURA: Heaven knows, things are not as might be wished.

DOCTOR: Really, you alarm me.

LAURA: There are some circumstances in a family which through honor and conscience one is forced to conceal from the whole world——

DOCTOR: Excepting the doctor.

LAURA: Exactly. It is, therefore, my painful duty to tell you the whole truth immediately.

DOCTOR: Shouldn't we postpone this conference until I have had the honor of being introduced to the Captain?

LAURA: No! You must hear me before seeing him.

DOCTOR: It relates to him then?

LAURA: Yes, to him, my poor, dear husband.

DOCTOR: You alarm me, indeed, and believe me, I sympathize with your misfortune.

LAURA: [Taking out handkerchief] My husband's mind is affected. Now you know all, and may judge for yourself when you see him.

DOCTOR: What do you say? I have read the Captain's excellent treatises on mineralogy with admiration, and have found that they display a clear and powerful intellect.

LAURA: Really? How happy I should be if we should all prove to be mistaken.

DOCTOR: But of course it is possible that his mind might be affected in other directions.

LAURA: That is just what we fear, too. You see he has sometimes the most extraordinary ideas which, of course, one might expect in a learned man, if they did not have a disastrous effect on the welfare of his whole family. For instance, one of his whims is buying all kinds of things.

DOCTOR: That is serious; but what does he buy?

LAURA: Whole boxes of books that he never reads.

DOCTOR: There is nothing strange about a scholar's buying books.

LAURA: You don't believe what I am saying?

DOCTOR: Well, Madam, I am convinced that you believe what you are saying.

LAURA: Tell me, is it reasonable to think that one can see what is happening on another planet by looking through a microscope?

DOCTOR: Does he say he can do that?

LAURA: Yes, that's what he says.

DOCTOR: Through a microscope?

LAURA: Through a microscope, yes.

DOCTOR: This is serious, if it is so.

LAURA: If it is so! Then you have no faith in me, Doctor, and here I sit confiding the family secret to——

DOCTOR: Indeed, Madam, I am honored by your confidence, but as a physician I must investigate and observe before giving an opinion. Has the Captain ever shown any symptoms of indecision or instability of will?

LAURA: Has he! We have been married twenty years, and he has never yet made a decision without changing his mind afterward.

DOCTOR: Is he obstinate?

LAURA: He always insists on having his own way, but once he has got it he drops the whole matter and asks me to decide.

DOCTOR: This is serious, and demands close observation. The will, you see, is the mainspring of the mind, and if it is affected the whole mind goes to pieces.

LAURA: God knows how I have taught myself to humor his wishes through all these long years of trial. Oh, if you knew what a life I have endured with him—if you only knew.

DOCTOR: Your misfortune touches me deeply, and I promise you to see what can be done. I pity you with all my heart, and I beg you to trust me completely. But after what I have heard I must ask you to avoid suggesting any ideas that might make a deep impression on the patient, for in a weak brain they develop rapidly and quickly turn to monomania or fixed ideas.

LAURA: You mean to avoid arousing suspicions?

DOCTOR: Exactly. One can make the insane believe anything, just because they are receptive to everything.

LAURA: Indeed? Then I understand. Yes—yes. [A bell rings within] Excuse me, my mother wishes to speak to me. One moment—— —Ah, here is Adolf.

[Captain comes in through private door]

CAPTAIN: Oh, here already, Doctor? You are very welcome.

DOCTOR: Captain! It is a very great pleasure to me to make the acquaintance of so celebrated a man of science.

CAPTAIN: Oh, I beg of you. The duties of service do not allow me to make any very profound investigations, but I believe I am now really on the track of a discovery.

DOCTOR: Indeed?

CAPTAIN: You see, I have submitted meteoric stones to spectrum analysis, with the result that I have found carbon, that is to say, a clear trace of organic life. What do you say to that?

DOCTOR: Can you see that with a microscope?

CAPTAIN: Lord, no—with the spectroscope.

DOCTOR: The spectroscope! Pardon. Then you will soon be able to tell us what is happening on Jupiter.

CAPTAIN: Not what is happening, but what has happened. If only the confounded book-sellers in Paris would send me the books; but I believe all the book-sellers in the universe have conspired against me. Think of it, for the last two months not a single one has ever answered my communications, neither letters nor abusive telegrams. I shall go mad over it, and I can't imagine what's the matter.

DOCTOR: Oh, I suppose it's the usual carelessness; you mustn't let it vex you so.

CAPTAIN: But the devil of it is I shall not get my treatise done in time, and I know they are working along the same lines in Berlin. But we shouldn't be talking about this—but about you. If you care to live here we have rooms for you in the wing, or perhaps you would rather live in the old quarters?

DOCTOR: Just as you like.

CAPTAIN: No, as you like. Which is it to be?

DOCTOR: You must decide that, Captain.

CAPTAIN: No, it's not for me to decide. You must say which you prefer. I have no preference in the matter, none at all.

DOCTOR: Oh, but I really cannot decide.

CAPTAIN: For heaven's sake, Doctor, say which you prefer. I have no choice in the matter, no opinion, no wishes. Haven't you got character enough to know what you want? Answer me, or I shall be provoked.

DOCTOR: Well, if it rests with me, I prefer to live here.

CAPTAIN: Thank you—forgive me, Doctor, but nothing annoys me so much as to see people undecided about anything. [Nurse comes in] Oh, there you are, Margret. Do you happen to know whether the rooms in the wing are in order for the Doctor?

NURSE: Yes, sir, they are.

CAPTAIN: Very well. Then I won't detain you, Doctor; you must be tired. Good-bye, and welcome once more. I shall see you tomorrow, I hope.

DOCTOR: Good evening, Captain.

CAPTAIN: I daresay that my wife explained conditions here to you a little, so that you have some idea how the land lies?

DOCTOR: Yes, your excellent wife has given me a few hints about this and that, such as were necessary to a stranger. Good evening, Captain.

CAPTAIN: [To Nurse] What do you want, you old dear? What is it?

NURSE: Now, little Master Adolf, just listen——

CAPTAIN: Yes, Margret, you are the only one I can listen to without having spasms.

NURSE: Now, listen, Mr. Adolf. Don't you think you should go half-way and come to an agreement with Mistress in this fuss over the child? Just think of a mother——

CAPTAIN: Think of a father, Margret.

NURSE: There, there, there. A father has something besides his child, but a mother has nothing but her child.

CAPTAIN: Just so, you old dear. She has only one burden, but I have three, and I have her burden, too. Don't you think that I should hold a better position in the world than that of a poor soldier if I had not had her and her child?

NURSE: Well, that isn't what I wanted to talk about.

CAPTAIN: I can well believe that, for you wanted to make it appear that I am in the wrong.

NURSE: Don't you believe, Mr. Adolf, that I wish you well?

CAPTAIN: Yes, dear friend, I do believe it; but you don't know what is for my good. You see it isn't enough for me to have given the child life, I want to give her my soul, too.

NURSE: Such things I don't understand. But I do think you ought to be able to agree.

CAPTAIN: You are not my friend, Margret.

NURSE: I? Oh, Lord, what are you saying, Mr. Adolf? Do you think I can forget that you were my child when you were little?

CAPTAIN: Well, you dear, have I forgotten it? You have been like a mother to me, and always have stood by me when I had everybody against me, but now, when I really need you, you desert me and go over to the enemy.

NURSE: The enemy!

CAPTAIN: Yes, the enemy! You know well enough how things are in this house! You have seen everything from the beginning.

NURSE: Indeed I have seen! But, God knows, why two people should torment the life out of each other; two people who are otherwise so good and wish all others well. Mistress is never like that to me or to others——

CAPTAIN: Only to me, I know it. But let me tell you, Margret, if you desert me now, you will do wrong. For now they have begun to weave a plot against me, and that doctor is not my friend.

NURSE: Oh, Mr. Adolf, you believe evil about everybody. But you see it's because you haven't the true faith; that's just what it is.

CAPTAIN: Yes, you and the Baptists have found the only true faith. You are indeed lucky!

NURSE: Anyway, I'm not unhappy like you, Mr. Adolf. Humble your heart and you will see that God will make you happy in your love for your neighbor.

CAPTAIN: It's a strange thing that you no sooner speak of God and love than your voice becomes hard and your eyes fill with hate. No, Margret, surely you have not the true faith.

NURSE: Yes, go on being proud and hard in your learning, but it won't amount to much when it comes to the test.

CAPTAIN: How mightily you talk, humble heart. I know very well that knowledge is of no use to you women.

NURSE: You ought to be ashamed of yourself. But in spite of everything old Margret cares most for her great big boy, and he will come back to the fold when it's stormy weather.

CAPTAIN: Margret! Forgive me, but believe me when I say that there is no one here who wishes me well but you. Help me, for I feel that something is going to happen here. What it is, I don't know, but something evil is on the way. [*Scream from within*] What's that? Who's that screaming?

[Bertha *enters from inner room*]

BERTHA: Father! Father! Help me; save me.

CAPTAIN: My dear child, what is it? Speak!

BERTHA: Help me. She wants to hurt me.

CAPTAIN: Who wants to hurt you? Tell me! Speak!

BERTHA: Grandmother! But it's my fault for I deceived her.

CAPTAIN: Tell me more.

BERTHA: Yes, but you mustn't say anything about it. Promise me you won't.

CAPTAIN: Tell me what it is then.

[Nurse *goes*]

BERTHA: In the evening she generally turns down the lamp and then she makes me sit at a table holding a pen over a piece of paper. And then she says that the spirits are to write.

CAPTAIN: What's all this—and you have never told me about it?

BERTHA: Forgive me, but I dared not, for Grandmother says the spirits take revenge if one talks about them. And then the pen writes, but I don't know whether I'm doing it or not. Sometimes it goes well, but sometimes it won't go at all, and when I am tired nothing comes, but she wants it to come just the same. And tonight I thought I was writing beautifully, but then Grandmother said it was all from Stagnelius, and that I had deceived her, and then she got terribly angry.

CAPTAIN: Do you believe that there are spirits?

BERTHA: I don't know.

CAPTAIN: But I know that there are none.

BERTHA: But Grandmother says that you don't understand, Father, and that you do much worse things —you who can see to other planets.

CAPTAIN: Does she say that! Does she say that? What else does she say?

BERTHA: She says that you can't work witchery.

CAPTAIN: I never said that I could. You know what meteoric stones are—stones that fall from other heavenly bodies. I can examine them and learn whether they contain the same elements as our world. That is all I can tell.

BERTHA: But Grandmother says that there are things that she can see which you cannot see.

CAPTAIN: Then she lies.

BERTHA: Grandmother doesn't tell lies.

CAPTAIN: Why doesn't she?

BERTHA: Then Mother tells lies, too.

CAPTAIN: H'm!

BERTHA: And if you say that Mother lies, I can never believe in you again.

CAPTAIN: I have not said so, and so you must believe in me when I tell you that it is for your future good that you should leave home. Will you? Will you go to town and learn something useful?

BERTHA: Oh, yes, I should love to go to town, away from here, anywhere. If I can only see you sometimes—often. Oh, it is so gloomy and awful in there all the time, like a winter night, but when you come home, Father, it is like a morning in spring when they take off the double windows.

CAPTAIN: My beloved child! My dear child!

BERTHA: But, Father, you'll be good to Mother, won't you? She cries so often.

CAPTAIN: H'm—then you want to go to town?

BERTHA: Yes, yes.

CAPTAIN: But if Mother doesn't want you to go?

BERTHA: But she must let me.

CAPTAIN: But if she won't?

BERTHA: Well, then, I don't know what will happen. But she must! She must!

CAPTAIN: Will you ask her?

BERTHA: You must ask her very nicely; she wouldn't pay any attention to my asking.

CAPTAIN: H'm! Now if you wish it, and I wish it, and she doesn't wish it, what shall we do then?

BERTHA: Oh, then it will all be in a tangle again! Why can't you both——

[Laura *comes in*]

LAURA: Oh, so Bertha is here. Then perhaps we may have her own opinion as the question of her future has to be decided.

CAPTAIN: The child can hardly have any well-grounded opinion about what a young girl's life is likely to be, while we, on the contrary, can more easily estimate what it may be, as we have seen so many young girls grow up.

LAURA: But as we are of different opinions Bertha must be the one to decide.

CAPTAIN: No, I let no one usurp my rights, neither women nor children. Bertha, leave us.

[Bertha *goes out*]

LAURA: You were afraid of hearing her opinion, because you thought it would be to my advantage.

CAPTAIN: I know that she wishes to go away from home, but I know also that you possess the power of changing her mind to suit your pleasure.

LAURA: Oh, am I really so powerful?

CAPTAIN: Yes, you have a fiendish power of getting your own way; but so has anyone who does not scruple about the way it is accomplished. How did you get Doctor Norling away, for instance, and how did you get this new doctor here?

LAURA: Yes, how did I manage that?

CAPTAIN: You insulted the other one so much that he left, and made your brother recommend this fellow.

LAURA: Well, that was quite simple and legitimate. Is Bertha to leave home now?

CAPTAIN: Yes, she is to start in a fortnight.

LAURA: That is your decision?

CAPTAIN: Yes.

LAURA: Then I must try to prevent it.

CAPTAIN: You cannot.

LAURA: Can't I? Do you really think I would trust my daughter to wicked people to have her taught that everything her mother has implanted in her child is mere foolishness? Why, afterwards, she would despise me all the rest of her life!

CAPTAIN: Do you think that a father should allow ignorant and conceited women to teach his daughter that he is a charlatan?

LAURA: It means less to the father.

CAPTAIN: Why so?

LAURA: Because the mother is closer to the child, as it has been discovered that no one can tell for a certainty who the father of a child is.

CAPTAIN: How does that apply to this case?

LAURA: You do not know whether you are Bertha's father or not.

CAPTAIN: I do not know?

LAURA: No; what no one knows, you surely cannot know.

CAPTAIN: Are you joking?

LAURA: No; I am only making use of your own teaching. For that matter, how do you know that I have not been unfaithful to you?

CAPTAIN: I believe you capable of almost anything, but not that, nor that you would talk about it if it were true.

LAURA: Suppose that I was prepared to bear anything, even to being despised and driven out, everything for the sake of being able to keep and control my child, and that I am truthful now when I declare Bertha is my child, but not yours. Suppose——

CAPTAIN: Stop now!

LAURA: Just suppose this. In that case your power would be at an end.

CAPTAIN: When you had proved that I was not the father.

LAURA: That would not be difficult! Would you like me to do so?

CAPTAIN: Stop!

LAURA: Of course I should only need to declare the name of the real father, give all details of place and time. For instance—when was Bertha born? In the third year of our marriage.

CAPTAIN: Stop now, or else——

LAURA: Or else, what? Shall we stop now? Think carefully about all you do and decide, and whatever you do, don't make yourself ridiculous.

CAPTAIN: I consider all this most lamentable.

LAURA: Which makes you all the more ridiculous.

CAPTAIN: And you?

LAURA: Oh, we women are really too clever.

CAPTAIN: That's why one cannot contend with you.

LAURA: Then why provoke contests with a superior enemy?

CAPTAIN: Superior?

LAURA: Yes, it's queer, but I have never looked at a man without knowing myself to be his superior.

CAPTAIN: Then you shall be made to see your superior for once, so that you shall never forget it.

LAURA: That will be interesting.

NURSE: [Comes in] Supper is served. Will you come in?

LAURA: Very well.

[Captain lingers; sits down with a magazine in an arm chair near table]

LAURA: Aren't you coming in to supper?

CAPTAIN: No, thanks. I don't want anything.

LAURA: What, are you annoyed?

CAPTAIN: No, but I am not hungry.

LAURA: Come, or they will ask unnecessary questions—be good now. You won't? Stay there then.

[Goes]

NURSE: Mr. Adolf! What is this all about?

CAPTAIN: I don't know what it is. Can you explain to me why you women treat an old man as if he were a child?

NURSE: I don't understand it, but it must be because all you men, great and small, are women's children, every man of you.

CAPTAIN: But no women are born of men. Yes, but I am Bertha's father. Tell me, Margret, don't you believe it? Don't you?

NURSE: Lord, how silly you are. Of course you are your own child's father. Come and eat now, and don't sit there and sulk. There, there, come now.

CAPTAIN: Get out, woman. To hell with the hags. [Goes to private door] Svärd, Svärd!

[Orderly comes in]

ORDERLY: Yes, Captain.

CAPTAIN: Hitch into the covered sleigh at once.

NURSE: Captain, listen to me.

CAPTAIN: Out, woman! At once!

[Orderly goes]

NURSE: Good Lord, what's going to happen now? [Captain puts on his cap and coat and prepares to go out]

CAPTAIN: Don't expect me home before midnight.

[Goes]

NURSE: Lord preserve us, whatever will be the end of this!

ACT II.

The same scene as in previous act. A lighted lamp is on the table; it is night. The Doctor and Laura are discovered at rise of curtain.

DOCTOR: From what I gathered during my conversation with him the case is not fully proved to me. In the first place you made a mistake in saying that he had arrived at these astonishing results about other heavenly bodies by means of a microscope. Now that I have learned that it was a spectroscope, he is not only cleared of any suspicion of insanity, but has rendered a great service to science.

LAURA: Yes, but I never said that.

DOCTOR: Madam, I made careful notes of our conversation, and I remember that I asked about this very point because I thought I had misunderstood you. One must be very careful in making such accusations when a certificate in lunacy is in question.

LAURA: A certificate in lunacy?

DOCTOR: Yes, you must surely know that an insane person loses both civil and family rights.

LAURA: No, I did not know that.

DOCTOR: There was another matter that seemed to me suspicious. He spoke of his communications to his booksellers not being answered. Permit me to ask if you, through motives of mistaken kindness, have intercepted them?

LAURA: Yes, I have. It was my duty to guard the interests of the family, and I could not let him ruin us all without some intervention.

DOCTOR: Pardon me, but I think you cannot have considered the consequences of such an act. If he discovers your secret interference in his affairs, he will have grounds for suspicions, and they will grow like an avalanche. And besides, in doing this you have thwarted his will and irritated him still more. You must have felt yourself how the mind rebels when one's deepest desires are thwarted and one's will is crossed.

LAURA: Haven't I felt that!

DOCTOR: Think, then, what he must have gone through.

LAURA: [Rising] It is midnight and he hasn't come home. Now we may fear the worst.

DOCTOR: But tell me what actually happened this evening after I left. I must know everything.

LAURA: He raved in the wildest way and had the strangest ideas. For instance, that he is not the father of his child.

DOCTOR: That is strange. How did such an idea come into his head?

LAURA: I really can't imagine, unless it was because he had to question one of the men about supporting a child, and when I tried to defend the girl, he grew excited and said no one could tell who was the father of the child. God knows I did everything to calm him, but now I believe there is no help for him. [Cries]

DOCTOR: But this cannot go on. Something must be done here without, of course, arousing his suspicions. Tell me, has the Captain ever had such delusions before?

LAURA: Six years ago things were in the same state, and then he, himself, confessed in his own letter to the doctor that he feared for his reason.

DOCTOR: Yes, yes, yes, this is a story that has deep roots and the sanctity of the family life—and so on—of course I cannot ask about everything, but must limit myself to appearances. What is done can't be undone, more's the pity, yet the remedy should be based upon all the past.—Where do you think he is now?

LAURA: I have no idea, he has such wild streaks.

DOCTOR: Would you like to have me stay until he returns? To avoid suspicion, I could say that I had come to see your mother who is not well.

LAURA: Yes, that will do very nicely. Don't leave us, Doctor; if you only knew how troubled I am! But wouldn't it be better to tell him outright what you think of his condition?

DOCTOR: We never do that unless the patient mentions the subject himself, and very seldom even then. It depends entirely on the case. But we mustn't sit here; perhaps I had better go into the next room; it will look more natural.

LAURA: Yes, that will be better, and Margret can sit here. She always waits up when he is out, and she is the only one who has any power over him. [Goes to the door left] Margret, Margret!

NURSE: Yes, Ma'am. Has the master come home?

LAURA: No; but you are to sit here and wait for him, and when he does come you are to say my mother is ill and that's why the doctor is here.

NURSE: Yes, yes. I'll see that everything is all right.

LAURA: [Opens the door to inner rooms] Will you come in here, Doctor?

DOCTOR: Thank you.

[Nurse seats herself at the table and takes up a hymn book and spectacles and reads]

NURSE: Ah, yes, ah, yes! [Reads half aloud]

Ah woe is me, how sad a thing
Is life within this vale of tears,
Death's angel triumphs like a king,
And calls aloud to all the spheres—
Vanity, all is vanity.

Yes, yes! Yes, yes!

[Reads again]

All that on earth hath life and breath
To earth must fall before his spear,
And sorrow, saved alone from death,
Inscribes above the mighty bier.
Vanity, all is vanity.

Yes, Yes.

BERTHA: [Comes in with a coffee-pot and some embroidery. She speaks in a low voice] Margret, may I sit with you? It is so frightfully lonely up there.

NURSE: For goodness sake, are you still up, Bertha?

BERTHA: You see I want to finish Father's Christmas present. And here's something that you'll like.

NURSE: But bless my soul, this won't do. You must be up in the morning, and it's after midnight now.

BERTHA: What does it matter? I don't dare sit up there alone. I believe the spirits are at work.

NURSE: You see, just what I've said. Mark my words, this house was not built on a lucky spot. What did you hear?

BERTHA: Think of it, I heard some one singing up in the attic!

NURSE: In the attic? At this hour?

BERTHA: Yes, it was such a sorrowful, melancholy song! I never heard anything like it. It sounded as if it came from the store-room, where the cradle stands, you know, to the left——

NURSE: Dear me, dear me! And such a fearful night. It seems as if the chimneys would blow down. "Ah, what is then this earthly life. But grief, affliction and great strife? E'en when fairest it has seemed, Nought but pain it can be deemed." Ah, dear child, may God give us a good Christmas!

BERTHA: Margret, is it true that Father is ill?

NURSE: Yes, I'm afraid he is.

BERTHA: Then we can't keep Christmas Eve? But how can he be up and around if he is ill?

NURSE: You see, my child, the kind of illness he has doesn't keep him from being up. Hush, there's some one out in the hall. Go to bed now and take the coffeepot away or the master will be angry.

BERTHA: [Going out with tray] Good night, Margret.

NURSE: Good night, my child. God bless you.

[Captain comes in, takes off his overcoat]

CAPTAIN: Are you still up? Go to bed.

NURSE: I was only waiting till——

[Captain lights a candle, opens his desk, sits down at it and takes letters and newspapers out of his pocket]

NURSE: Mr. Adolf.

CAPTAIN: What do you want?

NURSE: Old mistress is ill and the doctor is here.

CAPTAIN: Is it anything dangerous?

NURSE: No, I don't think so. Just a cold.

CAPTAIN: [Gets up] Margret, who was the father of your child?

NURSE: Oh, I've told you many and many a time; it was that scamp Johansson.

CAPTAIN: Are you sure that it was he?

NURSE: How childish you are; of course I'm sure when he was the only one.

CAPTAIN: Yes, but was he sure that he was the only one? No, he could not be, but you could be sure of it. There is a difference, you see.

NURSE: Well, I can't see any difference.

CAPTAIN: No, you cannot see it, but the difference exists, nevertheless. [Turns over the pages of a photograph album which is on the table] Do you think Bertha looks like me?

NURSE: Of course! Why, you are as like as two peas.

CAPTAIN: Did Johansson confess that he was the father?

NURSE: He was forced to!

CAPTAIN: How terrible! Here is the Doctor. [Doctor comes in] Good evening, Doctor. How is my mother-in-law?

DOCTOR: Oh, it's nothing serious; merely a slight sprain of the left ankle.

CAPTAIN: I thought Margret said it was a cold.

There seem to be different opinions about the same case. Go to bed, Margret.

[Nurse *goes. A pause*]

CAPTAIN: Sit down, Doctor.

DOCTOR: [*Sits*] Thanks.

CAPTAIN: Is it true that you obtain striped foals if you cross a zebra and a mare?

DOCTOR: [*Astonished*] Perfectly true.

CAPTAIN: Is it true that the foals continue to be striped if the breed is continued with a stallion?

DOCTOR: Yes, that is true, too.

CAPTAIN: That is to say, under certain conditions a stallion can be sire to striped foals or the opposite?

DOCTOR: Yes, so it seems.

CAPTAIN: Therefore an offspring's likeness to the father proves nothing?

DOCTOR: Well——

CAPTAIN: That is to say, paternity cannot be proven.

DOCTOR: H'm——well——

CAPTAIN: You are a widower, aren't you, and have had children?

DOCTOR: Ye-es.

CAPTAIN: Didn't you ever feel ridiculous as a father? I know of nothing so ludicrous as to see a father leading his children by the hand around the streets, or to hear a father talk about his children. "My wife's children," he ought to say. Did you ever feel how false your position was? Weren't you ever afflicted with doubts, I won't say suspicions, for, as a gentleman, I assume that your wife was above suspicion.

DOCTOR: No, really, I never was; but, Captain, I believe Goethe says a man must take his children on good faith.

CAPTAIN: It's risky to take anything on good faith where a woman is concerned.

DOCTOR: Oh, there are so many kinds of women.

CAPTAIN: Modern investigations have pronounced that there is only one kind! Lately I have recalled two instances in my life that make me believe this. When I was young I was strong and, if I may boast, handsome. Once when I was making a trip on a steamer and sitting with a few friends in the saloon, the young stewardess came and flung herself down by me, burst into tears, and told us that her sweetheart was drowned. We sympathized with her, and I ordered some champagne. After the second glass I touched her foot; after the fourth her knee, and before morning I had consoled her.

DOCTOR: That was just a winter fly.

CAPTAIN: Now comes the second instance—and that was a real summer fly. I was at Lysekil. There was a young married woman stopping there with her children, but her husband was in town. She was religious, had extremely strict principles, preached morals to me, and was, I believe, entirely honorable. I lent her a book, two books, and when she was leaving, she returned them, strange to say! Three months later, in those very books I found her card with a declaration on it. It was innocent, as innocent as a declaration of love can be from a married woman to a strange man who never made any advances. Now comes the moral. Just don't have too much faith.

DOCTOR: Don't have too little faith, either.

CAPTAIN: No, but just enough. But, you see, Doctor, that woman was so unconsciously dishonest that she talked to her husband about the fancy she had taken to me. That's what makes it dangerous, this very unconsciousness of their instinctive dishonesty. That is a mitigating circumstance, I admit, but it cannot nullify judgment, only soften it.

DOCTOR: Captain, your thoughts are taking a morbid turn, and you ought to control them.

CAPTAIN: You must not use the word morbid. Steam boilers, as you know, explode at a certain pressure, but the same pressure is not needed for all boiler explosions. You understand? However, you are here to watch me. If I were not a man I should have the right to make accusations or complaints, as they are so cleverly called, and perhaps I should be able to give you the whole diagnosis, and, what is more, the history of my disease. But unfortunately, I am a man, and there is nothing for me to do but, like a Roman, fold my arms across my breast and hold my breath till I die.

DOCTOR: Captain, if you are ill, it will not reflect upon your honor as a man to tell me all. In fact, I ought to hear the other side.

CAPTAIN: You have had enough in hearing the one, I imagine. Do you know when I heard Mrs. Alving eulogizing her dead husband, I thought to myself what a damned pity it was the fellow was dead. Do you suppose that he would have spoken if he had been alive? And do you suppose that if any of the dead husbands came back they would be believed? Good night, Doctor. You see that I am calm, and you can retire without fear.

DOCTOR: Good night, then, Captain. I'm afraid I can be of no further use in this case.

CAPTAIN: Are we enemies?

DOCTOR: Far from it. But it is too bad we cannot be friends. Good night.

[*Goes. The* Captain *follows the* Doctor *to the door at back and then goes to the door at left and opens it slightly*]

CAPTAIN: Come in, and we'll talk. I heard you out there listening. [Laura, *embarrassed*. Captain *sits at desk*] It is late, but we must come to some decision. Sit down. [*Pause*] I have been at the post office tonight to get my letters. From these it appears that you have been keeping back my mail, both coming and going. The consequence of which is that the loss of time has as good as destroyed the result I expected from my work.

LAURA: It was an act of kindness on my part, as you neglected the service for this other work.

CAPTAIN: It was hardly kindness, for you were quite sure that some day I should win more honor from that than from the service; but you were particularly anxious that I should not win such honors, for fear your own insignificance would be emphasized by it. In consequence of all this I have intercepted letters addressed to you.

LAURA: That was a noble act.

CAPTAIN: You see, you have, as you might say, a high opinion of me. It appears from these letters that for some time past you have been arraying my old friends against me by spreading reports about my mental condition. And you have succeeded in your efforts, for now not more than one person exists from the Colonel down to the cook, who believes that I am sane. Now these are the facts about my illness; my mind is sound, as you know, so that I can take care of my duties in the service as well as my responsibilities as a father; my feelings are more or less under my control, as my will has not been completely undermined; but you have gnawed and nibbled at it so that it will soon slip the cogs, and then the whole mechanism will slip and go to smash. I will not appeal to your feelings, for you have none; that is your strength; but I will appeal to your interests.

LAURA: Let me hear.

CAPTAIN: You have succeeded to such an extent that my judgment is no longer clear, and my thoughts begin to wander. This is the approaching insanity that you are waiting for, which may come at any time now. So you are face to face with the question whether it is more to your interest that I should be sane or insane. Consider. If I go under I shall lose the service, and where will you be then? If I die, my life insurance will fall to you. But if I take my own life, you will get nothing. Consequently, it is to your interest that I should live out my life.

LAURA: Is this a trap?

CAPTAIN: To be sure. But it rests with you whether you will run around it or stick your head into it.

LAURA: You say that you will kill yourself! You won't do that!

CAPTAIN: Are you sure? Do you think a man can live when he has nothing and no one to live for?

LAURA: You surrender, then?

CAPTAIN: No, I offer peace.

LAURA: The conditions?

CAPTAIN: That I may keep my reason. Free me from my suspicions and I give up the conflict.

LAURA: What suspicions?

CAPTAIN: About Bertha's origin.

LAURA: Are there any doubts about that?

CAPTAIN: Yes, I have doubts, and you have awakened them.

LAURA: I?

CAPTAIN: Yes, you have dropped them like henbane in my ears, and circumstances have strengthened them. Free me from the uncertainty; tell me outright that it is true and I will forgive you beforehand.

LAURA: How can I acknowledge a sin that I have not committed?

CAPTAIN: What does it matter when you know that I shall not divulge it? Do you think a man would go and spread his own shame broadcast?

LAURA: If I say it isn't true, you won't be convinced; but if I say it is, then you will be convinced. You seem to hope it is true!

CAPTAIN: Yes, strangely enough; it must be, because the first supposition can't be proved; the latter can be.

LAURA: Have you any ground for your suspicions?

CAPTAIN: Yes, and no.

LAURA: I believe you want to prove me guilty, so that you can get rid of me and then have absolute control over the child. But you won't catch me in any such snare.

CAPTAIN: Do you think that I would want to be responsible for another man's child, if I were convinced of your guilt?

LAURA: No, I'm sure you wouldn't, and that's what makes me know you lied just now when you said that you would forgive me beforehand.

CAPTAIN: [Rises] Laura, save me and my reason. You don't seem to understand what I say. If the child is not mine I have no control over her and don't want to have any, and that is precisely what you do want, isn't it? But perhaps you want even more—to have power over the child, but still have me to support you.

LAURA: Power, yes! What has this whole life and death struggle been for but power?

CAPTAIN: To me it has meant more. I do not believe in a hereafter; the child was my future life. That was my conception of immortality, and perhaps the only one that has any analogy in reality. If you take that away from me, you cut off my life.

LAURA: Why didn't we separate in time?

CAPTAIN: Because the child bound us together; but the link became a chain. And how did it happen; how? I have never thought about this, but now memories rise up accusingly, condemningly perhaps. We had been married two years, and had no children; you know why. I fell ill and lay at the point of death. During a conscious interval of the fever I heard voices out in the drawing-room. It was you and the lawyer talking about the fortune that I still possessed. He explained that you could inherit nothing because we had no children, and he asked you if you were expecting to become a mother. I did not hear you reply. I recovered and we had a child. Who is its father?

LAURA: You.

CAPTAIN: No, I am not. Here is a buried crime that begins to stench, and what a hellish crime! You women have been compassionate enough to free the black slaves, but you have kept the white ones. I have worked and slaved for you, your child, your mother, your servants; I have sacrificed promotion and career; I have endured torture, flagellation, sleeplessness, worry for your sake, until my hair has grown gray; and all that you might enjoy a life without care, and when you grew old, enjoy life over again in your child. I have borne everything withou complaint, because I thought myself the father of your child. This is the commonest kind of theft, the most brutal slavery. I have had seventeen years of penal servitude and have been innocent. What can you give me in return for that?

LAURA: Now you are quite mad.

CAPTAIN: That is your hope!—And I see how you have labored to conceal your crime. I sympathized with you because I did not understand your grief. I have often lulled your evil conscience to rest when I thought I was driving away morbid thoughts. I have heard you cry out in your sleep and not wanted to listen. I remember now night before last—Bertha's birthday—it was between two and three in the morning, and I was sitting up reading; you shrieked, "Don't, don't!" as if someone were strangling you; I knocked on the wall—I didn't want to hear any more. I have had my suspicions for a long time but I did not dare to hear them confirmed. All this I have suffered for you. What will you do for me?

LAURA: What can I do? I will swear by God and all I hold sacred that you are Bertha's father.

CAPTAIN: What use is that when you have often said that a mother can and ought to commit any crime for her child? I implore you as a wounded man begs for a death-blow, to tell me all. Don't you see I'm as helpless as a child? Don't you hear me complaining as to a mother? Won't you forget that I am a man, that I am a soldier who can tame men and beasts with a word? Like a sick man I only ask for compassion. I lay down the tokens of my power and implore you to have mercy on my life.

[Laura *approaches him and lays her hand on his brow*]

LAURA: What! You are crying, man!

CAPTAIN: Yes, I am crying although I am a man. But has not a man eyes? Has not a man hands, limbs, senses, thoughts, passions? Is he not fed with the same food, hurt by the same weapons, warmed and cooled by the same summer and winter as a woman? If you prick us do we not bleed? If you tickle us do we not laugh? And if you poison us, do we not die? Why shouldn't a man complain, a soldier weep? Because it is unmanly? Why is it unmanly?

LAURA: Weep then, my child, as if you were with your mother once more. Do you remember when I first came into your life, I was like a second mother? Your great strong body needed nerves; you were a giant child that had either come too early into the world, or perhaps was not wanted at all.

CAPTAIN: Yes, that's how it was. My father's and my mother's will was against my coming into the world, and consequently I was born without a will. I thought I was completing myself when you and I became one, and therefore you were allowed to rule, and I, the commander at the barracks and before the troops, became obedient to you, grew through you, looked up to you as to a more highly-gifted being, listened to you as if I had been your undeveloped child.

LAURA: Yes, that's the way it was, and therefore I loved you as my child. But you know, you must have seen, when the nature of your feelings changed and you appeared as my lover that I blushed, and your embraces were joy that was followed by a remorseful conscience as if my blood were ashamed. The mother became the mistress. Ugh!

CAPTAIN: I saw it, but I did not understand. I believed you despised me for my unmanliness, and I wanted to win you as a woman by being a man.

LAURA: Yes, but there was the mistake. The mother was your friend, you see, but the woman was your enemy, and love between the sexes is strife. Do not think that I gave myself; I did not give, but I took—what I wanted. But you had one advantage. I felt that, and I wanted you to feel it.

CAPTAIN: You always had the advantage. You could hypnotize me when I was wide awake, so that I neither saw nor heard, but merely obeyed; you could give me a raw potato and make me imagine it was a peach; you could force me to admire your foolish caprices as though they were strokes of genius. You could have influenced me to crime, yes, even to mean, paltry deeds. Because you lacked intelligence, instead of carrying out my ideas you acted on your own judgment. But when at last I awoke, I realized that my honor had been corrupted and I wanted to blot out the memory by a great deed, an achievement, a discovery, or an honorable suicide. I wanted to go to war, but was not permitted. It was then that I threw myself into science. And now when I was about to reach out my hand to gather in its fruits, you chop off my arm. Now I am dishonored and can live no longer, for a man cannot live without honor.

LAURA: But a woman?

CAPTAIN: Yes, for she has her children, which he has not. But, like the rest of mankind, we lived our lives unconscious as children, full of imagination, ideals, and illusions, and then we awoke; it was all over. But we awoke with our feet on the pillow, and he who waked us was himself a sleep-walker. When women grow old and cease to be women, they get beards on their chins; I wonder what men get when they grow old and cease to be men. Those who crowed were no longer cocks, but capons, and the pullets answered their call, so that when we thought the sun was about to rise we found ourselves in the bright moonlight amid ruins, just as in the good old times. It had only been a little morning slumber with wild dreams, and there was no awakening.

LAURA: Do you know, you should have been a poet!

CAPTAIN: Who knows.

LAURA: Now I am sleepy, so if you have any more fantastic visions keep them till tomorrow.

CAPTAIN: First, a word more about realities. Do you hate me?

LAURA: Yes, sometimes, when you are a man.

CAPTAIN: This is like race hatred. If it is true that we are descended from monkeys, at least it must be from two separate species. We are certainly not like one another, are we?

LAURA: What do you mean to say by all this?

CAPTAIN: I feel that one of us must go under in this struggle.

LAURA: Which?

CAPTAIN: The weaker, of course.

LAURA: And the stronger will be in the right?

CAPTAIN: Always, since he has the power.

LAURA: Then I am in the right.

CAPTAIN: Have you the power already, then?

LAURA: Yes, and a legal power with which I shall put you under the control of a guardian.

CAPTAIN: Under a guardian?

LAURA: And then I shall educate my child without listening to your fantastic notions.

CAPTAIN: And who will pay for the education when I am no longer here?

LAURA: Your pension will pay for it.

CAPTAIN: [Threateningly] How can you have me put under a guardian?

LAURA: [Takes out a letter] With this letter of which an attested copy is in the hands of the board of lunacy.

CAPTAIN: What letter?

LAURA: [Moving backward toward the door left] Yours! Your declaration to the doctor that you are insane. [The Captain stares at her in silence] Now you have fulfilled your function as an unfortunately necessary father and breadwinner, you are not needed any longer and you must go. You must go, since you have realized that my intellect is as strong as my will, and since you will not stay and acknowledge it.

[The Captain goes to the table, seizes the lighted lamp and hurls it at Laura, who disappears backward through the door]

CURTAIN DROP.

ACT III.

Same Scene. Another lamp on the table. The private door is barricaded with a chair.

LAURA: [To Nurse] Did he give you the keys?

NURSE: Give them to me, no! God help me, but I took them from the master's clothes that Nöjd had out to brush.

LAURA: Oh, Nöjd is on duty today?

NURSE: Yes, Nöjd.

LAURA: Give me the keys.

NURSE: Yes, but this seems like downright stealing. Do you hear him walking up there, Ma'am? Back and forth, back and forth.

LAURA: Is the door well barred?

NURSE: Oh, yes, it's barred well enough!

LAURA: Control your feelings, Margret. We must be calm if we are to be saved. [Knock] Who is it?

NURSE: [Opens door to hall] It is Nöjd.

LAURA: Let him come in.

NÖJD: [Comes in] A message from the Colonel.

LAURA: Give it to me. [Reads] Ah!—Nöjd, have you taken all the cartridges out of the guns and pouches?

NÖJD: Yes, Ma'am.

LAURA: Good, wait outside while I answer the Colonel's letter.

[Nöjd goes. Laura writes]

NURSE: Listen. What in the world is he doing up there now?

LAURA: Be quiet while I write.

[The sound of sawing is heard]

NURSE: [Half to herself] Oh, God have mercy on us all! Where will this end!

LAURA: Here, give this to Nöjd. And my mother must not know anything about all this. Do you hear?

[Nurse goes out, Laura opens drawers in desk and takes out papers. The Pastor comes in, he takes a chair and sits near Laura by the desk]

PASTOR: Good evening, sister. I have been away all day, as you know, and only just got back. Terrible things have been happening here.

LAURA: Yes, brother, never have I gone through such a night and such a day.

PASTOR: I see that you are none the worse for it all.

LAURA: No, God be praised, but think what might have happened!

PASTOR: Tell me one thing, how did it begin? I have heard so many different versions.

LAURA: It began with his wild idea of not being Bertha's father, and ended with his throwing the lighted lamp in my face.

PASTOR: But this is dreadful! It is fully developed insanity. And what is to be done now?

LAURA: We must try to prevent further violence and the doctor has sent to the hospital for a straitjacket. In the meantime I have sent a message to the Colonel, and I am now trying to straighten out the affairs of the household, which he has carried on in a most reprehensible manner.

PASTOR: This is a deplorable story, but I have always expected something of the sort. Fire and powder must end in an explosion. What have you got in the drawer there?

LAURA: [Has pulled out a drawer in the desk] Look, he has hidden everything here.

PASTOR: [Looking into drawer] Good Heavens, here is your doll and here is your christening cap and Bertha's rattle; and your letters; and the locket. [Wipes his eyes] After all he must have loved you very dearly, Laura. I never kept such things!

LAURA: I believe he used to love me, but time— time changes so many things.

PASTOR: What is that big paper? The receipt for a grave! Yes, better the grave than the lunatic asylum! Laura, tell me, are you blameless in all this?

LAURA: I? Why should I be to blame because a man goes out of his mind?

PASTOR: Well, well, I shan't say anything. After all, blood is thicker than water.

LAURA: What do you dare to intimate?

PASTOR: [*Looking at her penetratingly*] Now, listen!

LAURA: Yes?

PASTOR: You can hardly deny that it suits you pretty well to be able to educate your child as you wish?

LAURA: I don't understand.

PASTOR: How I admire you!

LAURA: Me? H'm!

PASTOR: And I am to become the guardian of that free-thinker! Do you know I have always looked on him as a weed in our garden.

[Laura *gives a short laugh, and then becomes suddenly serious*]

LAURA: And you dare say that to me—his wife?

PASTOR: You are strong, Laura, incredibly strong. You are like a fox in a trap, you would rather gnaw off your own leg than let yourself be caught! Like a master thief—no accomplice, not even your own conscience. Look at yourself in the glass! You dare not!

LAURA: I never use a looking glass!

PASTOR: No, you dare not! Let me look at your hand. Not a tell-tale blood stain, not a trace of insidious poison! A little innocent murder that the law cannot reach, an unconscious crime—unconscious! What a splendid idea! Do you hear how he is working up there? Take care! If that man gets loose he will make short work of you.

LAURA: You talk so much, you must have a bad conscience. Accuse me if you can!

PASTOR: I cannot.

LAURA: You see! You cannot, and therefore I am innocent. You take care of your ward, and I will take care of mine! Here's the doctor.

[Doctor *comes in*]

LAURA: [*Rising*] Good evening, Doctor. You at least will help me, won't you? But unfortunately there is not much that can be done. Do you hear how he is carrying on up there? Are you convinced now?

DOCTOR: I am convinced that an act of violence has been committed, but the question now is whether that act of violence can be considered an outbreak of passion or madness.

PASTOR: But apart from the actual outbreak, you must acknowledge that he has "fixed ideas."

DOCTOR: I think that your ideas, Pastor, are much more fixed.

PASTOR: My settled views about the highest things are——

DOCTOR: We'll leave settled views out of this. Madam, it rests with you to decide whether your husband is guilty to the extent of imprisonment and fine or should be put in an asylum! How do you class his behavior?

LAURA: I cannot answer that now.

DOCTOR: That is to say you have no decided opinion as to what will be most advantageous to the interests of the family? What do you say, Pastor?

PASTOR: Well, there will be a scandal in either case. It is not easy to say.

LAURA: But if he is only sentenced to a fine for violence, he will be able to repeat the violence.

DOCTOR: And if he is sent to prison he will soon be out again. Therefore we consider it most advantageous for all parties that he should be immediately treated as insane. Where is the nurse?

LAURA: Why?

DOCTOR: She must put the straitjacket on the patient when I have talked to him and given the order! But not before. I have—the garment out here. [*Goes out into the hall and returns with a large bundle*] Please ask the nurse to come in here.

[Laura *rings*]

PASTOR: Dreadful! Dreadful!

[Nurse *comes in*]

DOCTOR: [*Takes out the straitjacket*] I want you to pay attention to this. We want you to slip this jacket on the Captain, from behind, you understand, when I find it necessary to prevent another outbreak of violence. You notice it has very long sleeves to prevent his moving and they are to be tied at the back. Here are two straps that go through buckles which are afterwards fastened to the arm of a chair or the sofa or whatever is convenient. Will you do it?

NURSE: No, Doctor, I can't do that; I can't.

LAURA: Why don't you do it yourself, Doctor?

DOCTOR: Because the patient distrusts me. You, Madam, would seem to be the one to do it, but I fear he distrusts even you.

[Laura's *face changes for an instant*]

DOCTOR: Perhaps you, Pastor——

PASTOR: No, I must ask to be excused.

[Nöjd *comes in*]

LAURA: Have you delivered the message already?

NÖJD: Yes, Madam.

DOCTOR: Oh, is it you, Nöjd? You know the circumstances here, you know that the Captain is out of his mind and you must help us to take care of him.

NÖJD: If there is anything I can do for the Captain, you may be sure I will do it.

DOCTOR: You must put this jacket on him——

NURSE: No, he shan't touch him. Nöjd might hurt him. I would rather do it myself, very, very gently. But Nöjd can wait outside and help me if necessary. He can do that.

[*There is loud knocking on the private door*]

DOCTOR: There he is! Put the jacket under your shawl on the chair, and you must all go out for the time being and the Pastor and I will receive him, for that door will not hold out many minutes. Now go.

NURSE: [*Going out left*] The Lord help us!

[Laura *locks desk, then goes out left. Nöjd goes out back. After a moment the private door is forced open, with such violence that the lock is broken and the chair is thrown into the middle of the room. The* Captain *comes in with a pile of books under his arm, which he puts on the table]*

CAPTAIN: The whole thing is to be read here, in every book. So I wasn't out of my mind after all! Here it is in the *Odyssey,* book first, verse 215, page 6, of the Upsala translation. It is Telemachus speaking to Athene. "My mother indeed maintains that he, Odysseus, is my father, but I myself know it not, for no man yet hath known his own origin." And this suspicion is harbored by Telemachus about Penelope, the most virtuous of women! Beautiful, eh? And here we have the prophet Ezekiel: "The fool saith; behold here is my father, but who can tell whose loins engendered him." That's quite clear! And what have we here? The *History of Russian Literature* by Mersläkow. Alexander Pushkin, Russia's greatest poet, died of torture from the reports circulated about his wife's unfaithfulness rather than by the bullet in his breast from a duel. On his death-bed he swore she was innocent. Ass, ass! How could he swear to it! You see, I read my books. Ah, Jonas, are you here? and the doctor, naturally. Have you heard what I answered when an English lady complained about Irishmen who used to throw lighted lamps in their wives' faces? "God, what women," I cried. "Women," she gasped. "Yes, of course," I answered. "When things go so far that a man, a man who loved and worshipped a woman, takes a lighted lamp and throws it in her face, then one may know."

PASTOR: Know what?

CAPTAIN: Nothing. One never knows anything. One only believes. Isn't that true, Jonas? One believes and then one is saved! Yes, to be sure. No, I know that one can be damned by his faith. I know that.

DOCTOR: Captain!

CAPTAIN: Silence! I don't want to talk to you; I won't listen to you repeating their chatter in there, like a telephone! In there! You know! Look here, Jonas; do you believe that you are the father of your children? I remember that you had a tutor in your house who had a handsome face, and the people gossiped about him.

PASTOR: Adolf, take care!

CAPTAIN: Grope under your toupee and feel if there are not two bumps there. By my soul, I believe he turns pale! Yes, yes, they will talk; but, good Lord, they talk so much. Still we are a lot of ridiculous dupes, we married men. Isn't that true, Doctor? How was it with your marriage bed? Didn't you have a lieutenant in the house, eh? Wait a moment and I will make a guess—his name was— [*Whispers in the* Doctor's *ear*] You see he turns pale, too! Don't be disturbed. She is dead and buried and what is done can't be undone. I knew him well, by the way, and he is now—look at me, Doctor— No, straight in my eyes—a major in the cavalry!

By God, if I don't believe he has horns, too.

DOCTOR: [*Tortured*] Captain, won't you talk about something else?

CAPTAIN: Do you see? He immediately wants to talk of something else when I mention horns.

PASTOR: Do you know, Adolf, that you are insane?

CAPTAIN: Yes; I know that well enough. But if I only had the handling of your illustrious brains for awhile I'd soon have you shut up, too! I am mad, but how did I become so? That doesn't concern you, and it doesn't concern anyone. But you want to talk of something else now. [*Takes a photograph album from the table*] Good Lord, that is my child! Mine? We can never know. Do you know what we would have to do to make sure? First, one should marry to get the respect of society, then be divorced soon after and become lovers, and finally adopt the children. Then one would at least be sure that they were one's adopted children. Isn't that right? But how can all that help us now? What can keep me now that you have taken my conception of immortality from me, what use is science and philosophy to me when I have nothing to live for, what can I do with life when I am dishonored? I grafted my right arm, half my brain, half my marrow on another trunk, for I believed they would knit themselves together and grow into a more perfect tree, and then someone came with a knife and cut below the graft, and now I am only half a tree. But the other half goes on growing with my arm and half my brain, while I wither and die, for they were the best parts I gave away. Now I want to die. Do with me as you will. I am no more.

[*Buries his head on his arms on table. The* Doctor *whispers to the* Pastor, *and they go out through the door left. Soon after* Bertha *comes in]*

BERTHA: [*Goes up to* Captain] Are you ill, Father?

CAPTAIN: [*Looks up dazed*] I?

BERTHA: Do you know what you have done? Do you know that you threw the lamp at Mother?

CAPTAIN: Did I?

BERTHA: Yes, you did. Just think if she had been hurt.

CAPTAIN: What would that have mattered?

BERTHA: You are not my father when you talk like that.

CAPTAIN: What do you say? Am I not your father? How do you know that? Who told you that? And who is your father, then? Who?

BERTHA: Not you at any rate.

CAPTAIN: Still not I? Who, then? Who? You seem to be well informed. Who told you? That I should live to see my child come and tell me to my face that I am not her father! But don't you know that you disgrace your mother when you say that? Don't you know that it is to her shame if it is so?

BERTHA: Don't say anything bad about Mother; do you hear?

CAPTAIN: No; you hold together, every one of

you, against me! and you have always done so.

BERTHA: Father!

CAPTAIN: Don't use that word again!

BERTHA: Father, father!

CAPTAIN: [*Draws her to him*] Bertha, dear, dear child, you are my child! Yes. Yes; it cannot be otherwise. It is so. The other was only sickly thoughts that come with the wind like pestilence and fever. Look at me that I may see my soul in your eyes!—But I see her soul, too! You have two souls and you love me with one and hate me with the other. But you must only love me! You must have only one soul, or you will never have peace, nor I either. You must have only one mind, which is the child of my mind and one will, which is my will.

BERTHA: But I don't want to, I want to be myself.

CAPTAIN: You must not. You see, I am a cannibal, and I want to eat you. Your mother wanted to eat me, but she was not allowed to. I am Saturn who ate his children because it had been prophesied that they would eat him. To eat or be eaten! That is the question. If I do not eat you, you will eat me, and you have already shown your teeth! But don't be frightened, my dear child; I won't harm you. [*Goes and takes a revolver from the wall*]

BERTHA: [*Trying to escape*] Help, Mother, help, he wants to kill me.

NURSE: [*Comes in*] Mr. Adolf, what is it?

CAPTAIN: [*Examining revolver*] Have you taken out the cartridges?

NURSE: Yes, I put them away when I was tidying up, but sit down and be quiet and I'll get them out again!

> [*She takes the* Captain *by the arm and gets him into a chair, into which he sinks feebly. Then she takes out the straitjacket and goes behind the chair.* Bertha *slips out left*]

NURSE: Mr. Adolf, do you remember when you were my dear little boy and I tucked you in at night and used to repeat: "God who holds his children dear" to you, and do you remember how I used to get up in the night and give you a drink, how I would light the candle and tell you stories when you had bad dreams and couldn't sleep? Do you remember all that?

CAPTAIN: Go on talking, Margret, it soothes my head so. Tell me some more.

NURSE: O yes, but you must listen then! Do you remember when you took the big kitchen knife and wanted to cut out boats with it, and how I came in and had to get the knife away by fooling you? You were just a little child who didn't understand, so I had to fool you, for you didn't know that it was for your own good. "Give me that snake," I said, "or it will bite you!" and then you let go of the knife. [*Takes the revolver out of the* Captain's *hand*] And then when you had to be dressed and didn't want to, I had to coax you and say that you should have a coat of gold and be dressed like a prince. And then I took your little blouse that was just made of green wool and held it in front of you

and said: "In with both arms," and then I said, "Now sit nice and still while I button it down the back," [*She puts the straitjacket on*] and then I said, "Get up now, and walk across the floor like a good boy so I can see how it fits." [*She leads him to the sofa*] And then I said, "Now you must go to bed."

CAPTAIN: What did you say? Was I to go to bed when I was dressed—damnation! what have you done to me? [*Tries to get free*] Ah! you cunning devil of a woman! Who would have thought you had so much wit. [*Lies down on sofa*] Trapped, shorn, outwitted, and not to be able to die!

NURSE: Forgive me, Mr. Adolf, forgive me, but I wanted to keep you from killing your child.

CAPTAIN: Why didn't you let me? You say life is hell and death the kingdom of heaven, and children belong to heaven.

NURSE: How do you know what comes after death?

CAPTAIN: That is the only thing we do know, but of life we know nothing! Oh, if one had only known from the beginning.

NURSE: Mr. Adolf, humble your hard heart and cry to God for mercy; it is not yet too late. It was not too late for the thief on the cross, when the Saviour said, "Today shalt thou be with me in Paradise."

CAPTAIN: Are you croaking for a corpse already, you old crow?

> [Nurse *takes a hymn book out of her pocket*]

CAPTAIN: [*Calls*] Nöjd, is Nöjd out there?

> [Nöjd *comes in*]

CAPTAIN: Throw this woman out! She wants to suffocate me with her hymnbook. Throw her out of the window, or up the chimney, or anywhere.

NÖJD: [*Looks at* Nurse] Heaven help you, Captain, but I can't do that, I can't. If it were only six men, but a woman!

CAPTAIN: Can't you manage one woman, eh?

NÖJD: Of course I can—but—well, you see, it's queer, but one never wants to lay hands on a woman.

CAPTAIN: Why not? Haven't they laid hands on me?

NÖJD: Yes, but I can't, Captain. It's just as if you asked me to strike the Pastor. It's second nature, like religion, I can't!

> [Laura *comes in, she motions* Nöjd *to go*]

CAPTAIN: Omphale, Omphale! Now you play with the club while Hercules spins your wool.

LAURA: [*Goes to sofa*] Adolf, look at me. Do you believe that I am your enemy?

CAPTAIN: Yes, I do. I believe that you are all my enemies! My mother was my enemy when she did not want to bring me into the world because I was to be born with pain, and she robbed my embryonic life of its nourishment, and made a weakling of me. My sister was my enemy when she taught me that I must be submissive to her. The first woman I embraced was my enemy, for she gave me ten years of illness in return for the love I gave her. My daughter became my enemy when she had to choose between me and you. And you, my wife, you have been my arch enemy, because you never let up on me till I lay here lifeless.

LAURA: I don't know that I ever thought or even intended what you think I did. It may be that a dim desire to get rid of you as an obstacle lay at the bottom of it, and if you see any design in my behavior, it is possible that it existed, although I was unconscious of it. I have never thought how it all came about, but it is the result of the course you yourself laid out, and before God and my conscience I feel that I am innocent, even if I am not. Your existence has lain like a stone on my heart—lain so heavily that I tried to shake off the oppressive burden. This is the truth, and if I have unconsciously struck you down, I ask your forgiveness.

CAPTAIN: All that sounds plausible. But how does it help me? And whose fault is it? Perhaps spiritual marriages! Formerly one married a wife, now, one enters into partnership with a business woman, or goes to live with a friend—and then one ruins the partner, and dishonors the friend!—What has become of love, healthy sensuous love? It died in the transaction. And what is the result of this love in shares, payable to the bearer without joint liability? Who is the bearer when the crash comes? Who is the fleshly father of the spiritual child?

LAURA: And as for your suspicions about the child, they are absolutely groundless.

CAPTAIN: That's just what makes it so horrible. If at least there were any grounds for them, it would be something to get hold of, to cling to. Now there are only shadows that hide themselves in the bushes, and stick out their heads and grin; it is like fighting with the air, or firing blank cartridges in a sham fight. A fatal reality would have called forth resistance, stirred life and soul to action; but now my thoughts dissolve into air, and my brain grinds a void until it is on fire.—Put a pillow under my head, and throw something over me, I am cold. I am terribly cold!

[Laura *takes her shawl and spreads it over him. Nurse goes to get a pillow*]

LAURA: Give you your hand, friend.

CAPTAIN: My hand! The hand that you have bound! Omphale! Omphale!—But I feel your shawl against my mouth; it is as warm and soft as your arm, and it smells of vanilla, like your hair when you were young! Laura, when you were young, and we walked in the birch woods, with the primroses and the thrushes—glorious, glorious! Think how beautiful life was, and what it is now. You didn't want to have it like this, nor did I, and yet it happened. Who then rules over life?

LAURA: God alone rules——

CAPTAIN: The God of strife then! Or the Goddess perhaps, nowadays.—Take away the cat that is lying on me! Take it away!

[Nurse *brings in a pillow and takes the shawl away*]

CAPTAIN: Give me my army coat!—Throw it over me! [Nurse *gets the coat and puts it over him*] Ah, my rough lion skin that you wanted to take away from me! Omphale! Omphale! You cunning woman, champion of peace and contriver of man's disarmament. Wake, Hercules, before they take your club away from you! You would wile our armor from us too, and make believe that it is nothing but glittering finery. No, it was iron, let me tell you, before it ever glittered. In olden days the smith made the armor, now it is the needle woman. Omphale! Omphale! Rude strength has fallen before treacherous weakness.—Out on you infernal woman, and damnation on your sex. [He *raises himself to spit but falls back on the sofa*] What have you given me for a pillow, Margret? It is so hard, and so cold, so cold. Come and sit near me. There. May I put my head on your knee? So!—This is warm! Bend over me so that I can feel your breast! Oh, it is sweet to sleep against a woman's breast, a mother's or a mistress', but the mother's is sweetest.

LAURA: Would you like to see your child, Adolf?

CAPTAIN: My child? A man has no children, it is only woman who has children, and therefore the future is hers when we die childless. Oh, God, who holds his children dear!

NURSE: Listen, he is praying to God.

CAPTAIN: No, to you to put me to sleep, for I am tired, so tired. Good night, Margret, and blessed be you among women.

[He *raises himself, but falls with a cry on the Nurse's lap. Laura goes to the left and calls the Doctor, who comes in with the Pastor*]

LAURA: Help us, Doctor, if it isn't too late. Look, he has stopped breathing.

DOCTOR: [*Feels the* Captain's *pulse*] It is a stroke.

PASTOR: Is he dead?

DOCTOR: No, he may yet come back to life, but to what an awakening we cannot tell.

PASTOR: "First death, and then the judgment."

DOCTOR: No judgment, and no accusations. You who believe that a God shapes man's destiny must go to him about this.

NURSE: Ah, Pastor, with his last breath he prayed to God.

PASTOR: [*To* Laura] Is that true?

LAURA: It is.

DOCTOR: In that case, which I can understand as little as the cause of his illness, my skill is at an end. You try yours now, Pastor.

LAURA: Is that all you have to say at this deathbed, Doctor?

DOCTOR: That is all! I know no more. Let him speak who knows more.

[Bertha *comes in from left and runs to her mother*]

BERTHA: Mother, Mother!

LAURA: My child, my own child!

PASTOR: Amen.

CURTAIN.

Henry Becque

(1837–1899)

It was Henry Becque's ironic destiny to be neglected while he was laying the foundations of dramatic realism in France and to be unable to complete a single long play once the theatre recognized his merit and was eager to do him justice. In the eighteen-seventies, Emile Zola was thundering precepts for a new dramatic art and searching for saviors of the French stage. His eyes lighted readily enough on the De Goncourt brothers, fellow novelists who shared his credo of naturalism and whose wretched play *Henriette Maréchal* had been hissed off the stage. He also glanced appreciatively at himself while writing some half-dozen plays which he hoped would serve as good examples to a new generation. Zola, indeed, looked in every direction except that of Becque, who was then making desperate efforts to win a place for himself in the theatre and was developing an irascible temper in the process. When the long-frustrated dramatist came to write his memoirs in *Souvenirs d'un auteur dramatique* (1885), he remarked glumly that Zola was "an excellent lawmaker who wrote superb programmes and miserable plays." No love was lost between the two men even after they came to be regarded as the twin deities of the naturalistic theatre.

Upon graduation from the Lycée Bonaparte, Henry-François Becque, the son of a lowly government clerk in Paris, first found employment in a railroad office. But encouraged by a maternal uncle who had collaborated on a comedy with the successful playwright Labiche and wrote short farces, the young man turned eagerly to the theatre. Bored by his humdrum work in the railroad company, he took a minor position in the chancellery of the Legion of Honor, and from there graduated to the household of the influential Polish diplomat Count Potoczki, doubling as tutor and private secretary. Here he found his first opportunity to emerge as a writer when the Count introduced him to a young composer, Victorien Joncières. A collaboration ensued, with Becque contributing the libretto to Joncières' opera *Sardanapale* in 1865. In the same year, Becque started writing dramatic criticism for the newspaper *Le Peuple,* and in 1866 he had the good fortune of seeing his little farce *The Prodigal Son* produced successfully.

Encouraged by this first taste of success, the young author resolved to rely solely on his literary labors for a livelihood. The rash decision was to cost him a lifetime of struggle with producers and critics. He staged his first full-length serious play, *Michel Pauper,* at his own expense in 1870 only to encounter a crushing failure, and his next attempt, *The Elopement,* fared no better in 1871, although it was a problem play composed in the popular didactic vein of Dumas *fils.* Seven years were to elapse before another play of his was to appear on the stage. Twice defeated, the financially depleted author returned to the chancellery of the Legion of Honor, and, from there, moved to the more practical world of a stockbroker's office. He remained in the stockmarket for several years before venturing once more upon the insecure career of a playwright and free-lance journalist. Some measure of success did come to Becque in 1878 with the production of a short play, *The Shuttle,* and in 1880 with *The Virtuous Women,* which was ultimately included in the repertory of the Comédie Française. But neither play greatly improved his financial condition, and his temper was sorely tried by failure to obtain a production for his masterpiece *The Vultures (Les Corbeaux),* written in 1877. It took him five years to win a hearing, and its acceptance by the Comédie Française was only the beginning of a protracted struggle with the directors of the theatre.

Stubbornly rejecting all their demands for changes in the text, Becque finally saw *The Vultures* on the stage in 1882 exactly as he had written it. The artificial style of staging then in vogue brought only a qualified success, and the hisses that greeted his unpleasant picture of middle-class life were as loud as the applause of the progressives who welcomed his realism. The *première* threatened to become another pitched battle in the theatre, like the "battle of *Hernani*" half a century earlier when romanticists had fought classicists on behalf of Hugo's romantic melodrama. Nor did Becque gain enough prestige at the time to be able to place his next work, *The Parisian Woman (La Parisienne),* without encountering many rejections. The first production (1885) proved a sensation but failed to attract large audiences, and when the Comédie Française finally condescended to revive this candid description of Parisian immorality five years later, it nearly turned a masterpiece into a complete fiasco with its inept staging methods.

Becque needed a theatre capable of conveying his detached art of representing reality. The entire point of both *The Vultures* and *The Parisian Woman* lay in their revelation of moral turpitude through the natural behavior of his characters. They were drawn by Becque as people who consider their questionable morals beyond reproach and regard themselves as proper men and women. Their conduct and sentiments are norms of the social level on which they live and thrive—or so they believe. Becque's masterpieces derive their sharp humor, as well as their implicit indictment, entirely from the discrepancy between what the characters think of themselves and our judgment of them. The "little foxes" of Becque's picture of the middle class (and Lillian Hellman's *The Little Foxes* strongly recalls *The Vultures* with its portraits of predatory people) call themselves realistic businessmen when they cheat a widow and three orphaned daughters of their inheritance. They are only acting sensibly in conformity with the law of the survival of the fittest! It is regrettable that the weak and helpless must become their prey, they believe, but that is how the world is ordered and the spoils belong to the strong. They are "social Darwinists," so to speak. The family's lawyer in *The Vultures* is, indeed, so great a believer in the doctrine that whoever has the upper hand should take advantage of the opportunity that he urges the daughter Marie to compel Teissier to settle half his estate on her before she marries him. Previously the advocate was on the side of Teissier; but since the elderly Teissier hankers for a young girl, the advantage has passed into Marie's hands and it is only proper that she make full use of it!

Becque's characters condemn themselves in our eyes even when they are consistent, but it is their inconsistency that completely annihilates them. The adulterous Clotilde in *The Parisian Woman*, for example, believes herself to be a loyal wife when she wins political advancement for her husband with her infidelity. She possesses so strong a sense of propriety and so little sense of morality that she can seriously reprove her lover for his lack of religion: "You even pass for a freethinker," she declares, "and no doubt you would get along famously with a mistress who had no religion at all, perish the thought!" The lover Lafont, whose squabble with her in the first scene would pass for a quarrel between husband and wife, is equally self-righteous. "Remember one thing," he warns her, "that a folly once committed can never be undone. . . . Remain loyal to me, and keep your honor and self-respect." In *The Vultures* the despoilers of the weak are extremely alert to the villainies of others and voice their indignation in no uncertain terms. Irony can go no further than the conclusion, when Teissier, the worst of the birds of prey, who has married the daughter of the family he has impoverished, proceeds to drive off the other vultures, remarking to the girl that her family has been surrounded by a pack of scoundrels ever since her father's death.

The effectiveness of such writing depends entirely on the objectivity of the playwright, and the proper staging of such plays must be equally objective. To allow the actor to play to the audience and address his remarks to it instead of to other characters, to declaim his lines as in the classic drama, and to solicit applause from the spectators with well-timed pauses—these were the unpardonable sins that the old-fashioned theatre committed against Becque's plays. A major revolution in theatrical art was needed to make the revolution in playwriting effective, and this did not materialize until after Antoine founded the Théâtre Libre in 1887. It was as natural that Becque should rally to its support as it was that Antoine should cherish Becque's merits as a playwright. It was Antoine who gave *The Parisian Woman* its first satisfactory production at the Théâtre Antoine, a theatre he founded in 1897, two years before the author's death.

With the triumph of the new naturalistic stagecraft Becque finally came into his own, without being able, however, to profit from his opportunities. He wrote nothing of significance after 1885 except the two short pieces *The Start* and *Widowed*, both in 1897. The former was a naturalistic sketch of a shopgirl's induction into vice by a "respectable" employer who discharges her for refusing to yield to his son. *Widowed* was a sequel to *The Parisian Woman* which presented Clotilde widowed at last but otherwise unchanged. A few other one-acters were only slight sketches; a promising full-length drama, *The Puppets*, an exposé of the world of finance, was left unfinished at Becque's death. Although he was admitted to the Legion of Honor in 1886, lionized in society for his acrid wit, and invited to lecture in Italy, where his plays had won appreciation, he remained a poor and unsociable man. His admirers racked their brains for ways of stimulating him to create more masterpieces, and Antoine even lured him to Brittany for a summer vacation in order to induce him to write again. A fire that the solitary man started in his bedroom with a lighted cigar caused him a severe shock, and he had to be placed in a sanatorium by his friends. He never recovered. His death on May 15, 1899, was a deep blow to the men of the theatre who gratefully remembered his struggle to modernize the French drama.

Writing about Becque in 1905, James Huneker declared that *The Vultures* was "the bible of the dramatic realists." The statement is substantially correct if we remember to distinguish between the surface realism of the contrived "well-made plays" and the slice-of-life technique of Becque to which his contemporaries applied the term "naturalism." By no means a theorist of naturalism like Zola, Becque offered no program for playwrights. He did not even evince any enthusiasm for Ibsen, and the only realist who affected him was Tolstoy, whose peasant tragedy *The Power of Darkness* impressed him greatly. With curious inconsistency, apparently for reasons of personal gratitude, he maintained a lifelong admiration for Victorien Sardou, the playwright who was scorned by all confirmed naturalists and whose extreme theatricality was dismissed by the young Bernard Shaw as "Sardoodledom." In writing a preface to *The Vultures,* Becque disassociated himself from the naturalists' fondness for sordid drama and from their pet doctrine that man should be studied scientifically in terms of conditioning and heredity. He wrote: "I have never entertained much liking for assassins, hysterical and alcoholic characters, or for the martyrs of heredity and victims of evolution." Concerning his own encounters with conservative critics and managers, he maintained only that there were no conventions that originality could not destroy or displace, and that "the history of art is nothing but a struggle between original talents and routine-bound minds."

All that Becque intended to do was to set down reality as he saw it without comment or preachment. "Make what you will of it," he seemed to say, "but this is how people behave in our time and place, this is how they think, and this is how they speak." He tried, moreover, to create a natural flow of life instead of chopping up a play with mechanical calculation into "exposition," "climax" or "crisis," and "dénouement" or "resolution." Nor would he cater to the audiences of his time with tricks of the trade by composing high-flown declamatory passages for which the actor could be applauded, building "big" scenes with which to stun

the spectators, or writing act endings calculated to bring the curtain down with a dramatic flourish. Theatrical expediency, which was honored in Becque's time as it too often still is in our own, was anathema to his uncompromising and formidable spirit. In such a play as *The Vultures,* as well as in the more brilliantly executed but also more narrowly Parisian comedy *The Parisian Woman,* it is not a naturalistic formula, scientific or sociological, that thrusts itself forward. The power of the play, still undiminished for all its occasional prolixity, lies in the hard integrity of the writing and the structure. It is this virtue, for which there has never been sufficient regard in the practical theatre, which accounts for the influence that *The Vultures* exerted on the formative modern drama.

BIBLIOGRAPHY: James Huneker, *Iconoclasts,* 1905; Matthew Josephson, *Zola and His Time,* 1928; Edmond Sée, *Henry Becque,* 1920; Adolphe Thalasso, *Le Théâtre Libre,* 1909; Samuel Montefiore Waxman, *Antoine and the Théâtre Libre,* 1926. See also Becque's nondramatic writings: *Querelles littéraires, Notes d'album,* and *Souvenirs d'un auteur dramatique.*

THE VULTURES

By Henry Becque

TRANSLATED FROM THE FRENCH BY FREEMAN TILDEN

CHARACTERS

VIGNERON, *a manufacturer*
MRS. VIGNERON
MRS. DE SAINT-GENIS
MARIE
BLANCHE } *the Vignerons' daughters*
JUDITH
GASTON, *the Vignerons' son*

TEISSIER, *formerly a small banker, now Vigneron's partner*
BOURDON, *a lawyer*
MERCKENS, *a music-teacher*
LEFORT, *an architect*
DUPUIS, *a dealer in house furnishings*

AUGUSTE, *the Vignerons' butler*
A DOCTOR
GEORGE DE SAINT-GENIS
LENORMAND
GENERAL FROMENTIN
ROSALIE, *the Vignerons' old servant*

The action takes place at Paris in our own day.[1]

ACT I.

A luxuriously furnished drawing-room. There are three double doors at the rear, and double doors on the sides. At the right, in the foreground, there is a piano; and at the left, against the wall, a writing-table. Behind this writing-table is a fireplace. At the rear, on the right, a table; at the left, in the fore-ground, a couch. Other furniture, mirrors, flowers, etc.

When the curtain rises, Vigneron *is seen asleep on the couch. He is in a dressing-gown, and has a newspaper in his hands.* Marie, *seated near him, is engaged in needle-work.* Judith *is at the piano.* Blanche *is writing at the table.*

MRS. VIGNERON: Don't play any more, Judith; your father is asleep. [*Going over to the table*] Blanche.
BLANCHE: Yes, Mama.
MRS. VIGNERON: Is it finished?
BLANCHE: Just one minute.
MRS. VIGNERON: Have you gone over them? How many will there be at table?
BLANCHE: Sixteen.
MRS. VIGNERON: That's good.
   [*She brings a chair and sits down beside* Blanche]
BLANCHE: Do you think the dinner will be any better for putting a menu at each plate?
MRS. VIGNERON: It won't be any the worse for it, anyhow.
BLANCHE: What a queer custom! But are you quite sure it is the proper thing?
MRS. VIGNERON: Absolutely sure. I saw it in the *Ladies' Home Companion.*
BLANCHE: Shall we run over the places together?

---

1 The time would be any year between 1877 and 1882.

MRS. VIGNERON: Let's go over the list first. Mrs. de Saint-Genis?
BLANCHE: I've got her down.
MRS. VIGNERON: Her son?
BLANCHE: You needn't be afraid of my forgetting him.
MRS. VIGNERON: Father Mouton?
BLANCHE: The dear old man! He baptized me, and confirmed me—and now he is going to marry me.
MRS. VIGNERON: If you are going to gossip about every name we come to, we won't be through by next week. Mr. Teissier?
BLANCHE: I've got him down. I could get along very well without him, though.
VIGNERON: [*Waking*] What's that I hear? Is Miss Blanche giving orders in my house?
BLANCHE: Goodness, yes, Papa; it's little Blanche.
VIGNERON: And may we know what Mr. Teissier has done to you, miss?
BLANCHE: To me? Nothing. But he is old, and ugly, and boorish, and a miser. And he never looks anybody in the face; that's reason enough why I don't like him around me.
VIGNERON: Fine! Bully! I'll fix things all right. Mrs. Vigneron, you needn't save a place at the table for this young lady. She is going to have dinner in her room.
BLANCHE: You'll be saying soon that the wedding will go ahead without me.
VIGNERON: If you say another word, you shan't be married——— Oh!
   [*A pause*]
MARIE: [*Rising*] Listen, Daddy dear, and give me a serious answer—which you never do when anybody speaks to you about your health. How do you feel?
VIGNERON: Oh, not bad.
MARIE: But your face is red.

VIGNERON: Red! That'll go away as soon as I get outdoors.

MARIE: If your dizziness comes back, we shall have to call in a doctor.

VIGNERON: A doctor! Do you want me to die?

MARIE: You know that kind of joking hurts me. We won't talk any more about it.

[*She starts away, and he catches her by the bottom of her gown and pulls her down into his arms*]

VIGNERON: Does she love her old daddy?

MARIE: I love you so, so, so much . . . but you don't do a thing I want you to, or a thing you should do. Why don't you work less, get some fun out of your money, and look out for yourself when you are sick?

VIGNERON: But I am not sick, little girl. I know what's the matter with me. I'm a bit tired, and there's too much blood in my head. It's just the same every year about this time, after I have finished taking inventory. The inventory of the house of Teissier, Vigneron, and Company! Do you know what Teissier and I were offered for our factory, only a week ago? Six hundred thousand francs!

MARIE: Well, sell it.

VIGNERON: Ten years from now, I am going to sell for a million. And in the meantime it will bring us in that much.

MARIE: How old will you be then?

VIGNERON: How old? Ten years from now? I shall be just the age of my grandchildren; and we shall have fine times together. [Auguste *enters*] What is it, Auguste?

AUGUSTE: Your architect, sir. He wants only a word with you.

VIGNERON: Tell Mr. Lefort if he wants to speak to me he should see me at the factory.

AUGUSTE: He has just come from there, sir.

VIGNERON: Let him go back there. I am at home here, with my wife and children, and I shan't be bothered by my contractors. [Auguste *goes out*] Let me get up.

[Marie *steps aside;* Vigneron *rises with an effort; then he is seized with dizziness and walks a few steps unsteadily*]

MARIE: [*Returning to him*] Why won't you see a doctor?

VIGNERON: Isn't that question settled?

MARIE: No; it is not settled. There's no use talking—you are not well, and it makes me uneasy. Take care of yourself; do something; perhaps a little dieting for seven or eight days would make you all right again.

VIGNERON: Sly puss! I see through you and your little dieting. I eat too much, eh? Come, speak right out; I don't mind. I eat too much. Well, little girl, what do you expect? I haven't always had a table full of good things. Ask your mother; she will tell you that when we began keeping house I went to bed many a time without my supper. Now I'm mak-

ing up for it. It's stupid, beastly, it hurts me, but I can't resist the temptation. [*Leaving* Marie] And then, I suppose I shouldn't read the newspaper after luncheon; it hurts my digestion. [*He crumples up the newspaper and going back to the couch throws himself upon it; then his glance falls upon* Judith, *who, seated at the piano, her back turned to her father, is in a brown study; he tiptoes over to her and shouts in her ear*] Judith!

JUDITH: Oh, Father, you know I don't like such jokes!

VIGNERON: Don't be angry, missy, I won't do it again. Judith, tell me something about what's going on—in the moon.

JUDITH: Now make fun of me.

VIGNERON: How do you make that out? I have a daughter named Judith. Is she here? Is she somewhere else? How can I know? We never hear from her.

JUDITH: I haven't anything to say.

VIGNERON: That doesn't bother most people.

JUDITH: What fun is there in teasing me all the time about it? I see you, hear you, love you, and I am happy.

VIGNERON: Are you happy?

JUDITH: Quite.

VIGNERON: Well, then, little girl, you're right and I'm wrong. Have you got a kiss for me?

JUDITH: [*Rising*] Have I? A hundred of them, Daddy.

[*They embrace;* Auguste *enters*]

VIGNERON: Now what is it? I don't seem to be able to kiss my children in peace, nowadays.

AUGUSTE: Mr. Dupuis, sir.

VIGNERON: Dupuis? Dupuis, the house furnisher? What does he want? I settled his bill long ago.

AUGUSTE: Mr. Dupuis stopped in to see if you wished anything, sir.

VIGNERON: Tell Mr. Dupuis for me that I don't buy twice of a swindler like him. Go ahead. [Auguste *goes out;* Vigneron *walks over to the table*] Well, what have you got your heads together about?

MRS. VIGNERON: Let us alone, that's a dear. We're busy with this evening's dinner.

VIGNERON: Oh!—Come and let me whisper just a few words in your ear. [Mrs. Vigneron *rises and joins her husband at the front of the stage*] So it's all settled that we are going to marry our daughter to that popinjay?

MRS. VIGNERON: Did you interrupt me just to say that?

VIGNERON: Now listen: I haven't any prejudice against this marriage. Mrs. de Saint-Genis impresses me as a first-rate woman. It isn't her fault if she hasn't a cent. Her son is a lovely little boy, very pleasant and polite, and he certainly does curl his hair nicely. For a long while, now, I've hardly been able to keep from telling him that he uses too much hair-oil. His government job carries a good salary with it, for a chap of his age. But at the last moment, I can't help wondering whether this marriage is well-advised, and whether Blanche will be really happy with that young fellow, even if he does belong to one of the oldest families.

MRS. VIGNERON: But Blanche is crazy about him.

VIGNERON: Blanche is only a child. It's easy to see that the first young fellow she met turned her head.

MRS. VIGNERON: What have you got up your sleeve? What's the use of talking that way about a marriage which is done and over with, one might say? You aren't reproaching me, are you, with Mrs. de Saint-Genis' financial position? Ours wasn't always what it is now. Then what are you complaining of? Because George is a good-looking young fellow, well-brought-up, and of a good family? If he comes from one of the best families, so much the better for him.

VIGNERON: It flatters you to have a son-in-law from one of the oldest families.

MRS. VIGNERON: Yes, I admit it does flatter me; but I wouldn't sacrifice one of my girls to mere vanity. [*Coming nearer and speaking in a lower tone*] Do you want me to tell you the whole truth? It is true that Blanche is a child, as modest and innocent—the dear little girl—as can be; but her feelings are unusually powerful for a girl of her age, and we shan't regret having her married early. And then, our friend, Father Mouton, who has known us twenty years, wouldn't interest himself in the marriage if it were not for the best all around.

VIGNERON: Who said he would? But no matter, we are going ahead too fast. In the first place, it isn't a priest's business to make matches. And then, I'd like to have you tell me how it is that Mrs. de Saint-Genis—who hasn't a cent, I repeat—has such good connections. I thought that her son's witnesses would be common-place people; gracious, she's found some smarter than our own! A high government official and a general! The government official I can account for—George works in his office—but the general!

MRS. VIGNERON: What's that? Oh, the general? Surely, you know that Mr. de Saint-Genis was a captain in the army. Run along to your work, dear. [*She turns away from him*] Blanche, give your father his coat.

[*She goes out at the right, leaving the door open behind her*]

VIGNERON: [*Taking off his dressing-gown and putting on the coat brought by* Blanche] So here you are, you ingrate!

BLANCHE: Ingrate! Why do you call me that?

VIGNERON: Why? Now that we are rich, and are going to let you be married, and give you a dowry, why shouldn't we marry you to Mr. Teissier?

BLANCHE: No, Papa.

VIGNERON: "No, Papa." Why not? I reckon it's Teissier and his factory that have made me what I am.

BLANCHE: You mean that you have made Mr.

Teissier's factory what it is. Without you, it would have cost him money enough; with you, heaven only knows how much money it has brought him in. Now see here, Papa, if Mr. Teissier were anybody else—if he were a fair man—here is what he would say, after all the work you have done and the pains you have taken: "This factory first belonged to me; then it belonged to both of us; now it belongs to you."

VIGNERON: Her kind little heart puts sentiment into everything. It's a good thing to have sentiment, but not to count too much on other people's having it. [*He kisses her*]

MRS. VIGNERON: [*Entering*] What, are you still here?

VIGNERON: Answer this question: Am I under obligation to Teissier, or is Teissier under obligations to me?

MRS. VIGNERON: Neither.

VIGNERON: How is that?

MRS. VIGNERON: Do you really want me to go all over that story again?

VIGNERON: Yes.

MRS. VIGNERON: Well, children, Mr. Teissier was a banker in a small way, on the street where we used to live. We knew him, and yet we didn't. We had been under obligations to him at certain times when we were in need, and he had taken our note without much hesitation, because our reputation was good. Later on, in the course of his business, he found that he had a factory on his hands. He remembered your father and offered him the management, but with a salary. At that time we were getting along pretty well because your father had a good position with a good business house, and the wisest thing to do was to keep it. Fifteen months passed. We had thought nothing more of it for a long time, when one evening at exactly half-past nine—I remember the hour—when your father and I were looking through the door that led into your room, and watching you as you lay asleep, somebody rang. It was Mr. Teissier, and it was the first time he had ever climbed the five flights to our floor. He had made up his mind at last. The truth was, his works were not working, and he came to ask your father to come to his assistance by joining forces with him. Your father thanked him politely and asked him to wait till the following day for an answer. As soon as Mr. Teissier had gone, your father said to me—now listen to this—your father said to me: "Here is an opportunity, my dear. It comes rather late, and just when we are beginning to take things easy. It's going to be a lot of work for me, and you will always be in a state of terror until I make a go of it—if I do make a go of it! But we have four children, and perhaps this is their chance." [*She weeps and clutches her husband's hand; the children gather around them, amid general emotion*] To come back to the question you asked, it seems to me easily answered. Mr. Teissier and Mr. Vigneron went into business together. It was a good thing for both of them, and they owe each other nothing.

VIGNERON: There, children, is a model woman! Pattern after this woman, measure up to her standard, and nothing more can be expected of you. [*He kisses his wife*]

MRS. VIGNERON: You do it beautifully, but it isn't natural to you, my dear. Do you feel ill?

VIGNERON: No, sweetheart; on the contrary, I feel better. I believe I have wholly recovered. Now I am going to ask Miss Judith, the g-r-r-reat musician of the family, to play me something, and then I'll relieve you of my company.

JUDITH: What do you want me to play? *Il Trovatore?*

VIGNERON: Find *Il Trovatore.* [*To* Blanche] That's fine, that *Trovatore* piece. Is it by Rossini?

BLANCHE: No; Verdi.

VIGNERON: Oh, Verdi, the author of the *Huguenots.*

BLANCHE: No; the *Huguenots* was written by Meyerbeer.

VIGNERON: That's so. The great Meyerbeer. How old is Meyerbeer, now?

BLANCHE: He's dead.

VIGNERON: What? My goodness, did he die without my knowing it? [*To* Judith] Can't you find *Il Trovatore?* Never mind, don't take the trouble to look for it. Listen: play me—just play me—*La Dame Blanche.*

JUDITH: I don't know it.

VIGNERON: You don't know *La Dame Blanche?* Say that again. You don't know——? What's the good, then, of the lessons I'm having you take at ten francs an hour? What *does* your music-teacher teach you? Tell me, now, what *does* he teach you?

JUDITH: He teaches me music.

VIGNERON: Well? Isn't *La Dame Blanche* music?

MARIE: [*Leading* Judith *to the piano*] Come, big sister, play Daddy what he wants to hear. [*Judith seats herself at the piano and begins the famous selection*]

"From here behold that fair domain
Whose lofty turrets touch the sky;
A strange and spectral chatelaine
Guards that old castle ceaselessly.
Perfidious and faithless knight
Weaving your plots of shame and spite,
          Take care!
La Dame Blanche sees you there,
She hears—the woman in white!" [2]

[Vigneron *begins to sing, then his wife joins him, then his daughters follow suit; half-way through the verse* Gaston *enters, having first stuck his head in at one of the rear doors. Then* Gaston *goes to the fireplace, takes the shovel and tongs, and contributes to the hubbub*]

VIGNERON: [*Going toward his son, when the verse*

[2] Translated by Allan Updegraff.

is sung] Where did you come from, you young rascal? Why weren't you at luncheon with us?

GASTON: I lunched with one of my friends.

VIGNERON: What's that friend's name?

GASTON: You don't know him.

VIGNERON: I know well enough that I don't know him. Stand there while I have a look at you. [*He draws off a few steps, the better to survey his son.* Gaston *still has the shovel and tongs in his hands.* Vigneron *takes them away and puts them back in their place; then he goes back toward his son and regards him tenderly*] Stand up straight! [*He goes over to him and strokes his hair*] Show me your tongue! Good! Put it out a little farther. Farther than that. That's all right. [*In a low tone*] I hope you're not tiring yourself out too much.

GASTON: Doing what, Dad? I haven't been doing anything.

VIGNERON: Now you're talking nonsense. When I said, "You're not tiring yourself out too much," I knew what I meant, and so did you, you scamp. Do you need any money?

GASTON: No.

VIGNERON: Open your hand.

GASTON: What's the use?

VIGNERON: [*Speaking louder*] Open your hand.

GASTON: I don't want to.

VIGNERON: Papa Vigneron brought this boy up, so he did! Here, put this money in your pocket, and be quick about it! Have a good time, son—I want you to have the best kind of a time. Cut loose and raise the dickens. But remember—away from here you are your own boss—but here, among your sisters, mind how you act! Be careful what you say; and above all, no mushy letters! If you want to confide in anybody, I'm the one.

JUDITH: We're waiting for you to join in the second verse, Dad.

VIGNERON: [*Looking at his watch*] You'll have to sing the second verse without me. [*He takes his hat and goes toward the door. Then, pausing and looking around at his family, he comes back like a man who is happy where he is, and does not want to go away*] Come here a minute, old lady! [Mrs. Vigneron *comes over to him, and he puts one arm under hers*] Judith, get up! [*He does the same to* Judith] Come here, you other girls! If I had my own way, dearies, I'd get back into my dressing-gown and stay here until dinner time. But unfortunately my work won't do itself; and I haven't money enough yet to live without working. Perhaps I shall have some day, when I am the owner of the factory. But I must wait for two things—till my new buildings are finished, and until my children are provided for. Who could have thought that this little minx Blanche, the youngest of you, would be the first to get married? Whose turn is it next? Judith? Oh, Judith is a young lady hard to please. Unless she meets a prince, she'll die an old maid. Well, then, let some prince come along, and I'll buy him for her. As for you, you young scamp, standing over there laughing while I am talking—you can have your fling, but it won't be for long. Some fine day I'm going to take you to work with me, and you are going to start in by sweeping the factory, from top to bottom—until I make an errand boy of you. After that we'll see whether you are good for anything. Of you all, I'm the least worried about Marie. She isn't a dreamer [*Looking at* Judith] like you; nor a sentimentalist [*Looking at* Blanche] like you. She'll marry some good fellow, some healthy chap, a hard worker and tough as a knot, who will make you think of your father when he's not here any more. [*To his wife*] I haven't mentioned you, sweetheart, because at our age, we don't have any great longings or needs. We're happy if the kids are happy. I don't think these children of ours would have been any happier anywhere else. Well, and what next? Just let the old man put in a few more years to ensure the future of this little family, and then he'll have earned the right to take a rest. Now, then, I'm off!

THE CHILDREN: Good-by, Papa. Kiss me. Good-by.

[Vigneron *escapes from them and goes out quickly*]

MRS. VIGNERON: Now, girls, get yourselves ready. [*To* Blanche] I want you to wait a minute; I've got something to say to you. [*To* Marie] Look in at the kitchen, dear, and tell Rosalie to be sure not to keep us waiting; hurry her up a little. Rosalie is very fond of us, but she's always late with dinner. Gaston, let your sister go to her room—you can take your music lesson some other time. [*There is a hustle and bustle as all the children except* Blanche *go out*] Now pay attention, dearie; I haven't time to talk much. I want you to make use of what I'm going to tell you; and don't interrupt me. I don't like the way you conduct yourself when your future husband is here. You look at him too much; when he gets up, you get up; you get into little corners to do your talking. I don't like those things; and to-day, when we have visitors, I should like it less than ever. If you admire George, and if you love each other, so much the better, since you are going to be married—but you are not married yet. Until you are, I want you to be more careful, and I want you to keep your feelings to yourself, as a nice girl should do. There's no sense in crying about it! It's all said and done. Now dry your eyes, give me a kiss, and go and get yourself ready. [Blanche *leaves her mother and is going out at the door when* Auguste *enters at the rear and announces* Mrs. de Saint-Genis; Blanche *pauses*] Go and get ready!

MRS. DE SAINT-GENIS: How do you do, dear. Come, kiss me. It's not only the style, it's a perfect mania now, for people to kiss every five minutes. I'm here early, but don't let me disturb you. If I bother you the least bit, just say so. I'll stay or go, just as you please.

MRS. VIGNERON: Oh, stay, by all means.

MRS. DE SAINT-GENIS: Perhaps you have calls to make?

MRS. VIGNERON: Not one.

MRS. DE SAINT-GENIS: Then maybe you expect to receive some?

MRS. VIGNERON: No.

MRS. DE SAINT-GENIS: Shall I take off my hat?

MRS. VIGNERON: If you don't I'll put mine on.

MRS. DE SAINT-GENIS: It isn't often nowadays, Mrs. Vigneron, that one finds a woman like you—a woman who can be seen any time. I wouldn't want to risk such a thing with some of my most intimate friends.

MRS. VIGNERON: Sit down and tell me: how are you?

MRS. DE SAINT-GENIS: I'm well; quite well. I don't remember ever feeling better. I was saying this morning, at my toilet, that I had got back my color and figure.

MRS. VIGNERON: There is a question I've been wanting to ask you, ever so long. It shouldn't make any difference between us. How old are you?

MRS. DE SAINT-GENIS: Why, Mrs. Vigneron, I never try to hide my age. Even if I wanted to, I couldn't; on account of my son. He will be twenty-three years old in a few days; I was seventeen when he was born; you can figure it out.

MRS. VIGNERON: Then you don't mind my curiosity?

MRS. DE SAINT-GENIS: It is quite natural, between two old women.

MRS. VIGNERON: You know we are two rash mothers—you, in letting your son marry so young, at twenty-three, and I, in letting my daughter marry him!

MRS. DE SAINT-GENIS: Don't worry about that, my dear. George has obeyed me so far, and I certainly count on keeping him straight after he is married. I have brought up my son very strictly, as I think I have already told you, and there are few children like him. He has never gone into debt; and what is just as unusual, he has never frittered away his time with women. All the same, I know some women who wouldn't have asked anything better. My son has had a very thorough education; he speaks three languages, he plays, he bears a good name, has good manners and religious principles. So, with all that, he won't go far wrong, unless the world changes a good deal. [*Changing her tone*] Tell me, now that we are talking about George, and since I am looking out for his interest, does your husband know that I asked my lawyer to rectify an omission in the marriage contract?

MRS. VIGNERON: I can't say as to that.

MRS. DE SAINT-GENIS: You remember that Mr. Vigneron, after having fixed Blanche's marriage portion at two hundred thousand francs, asked us to let him pay it in the form of an annuity.

MRS. VIGNERON: That's not so, Mrs. de Saint-Genis. From the very first my husband said that he wanted time to settle his daughter's dowry. It was then that you spoke of some guarantee, a mortgage on the buildings under construction; and he refused to do that. Finally, the amount and the time of payment was fully agreed upon.

MRS. DE SAINT-GENIS: Very well. It seemed to me only natural and fair that until the young couple come into the whole sum, it should pay them interest of five or six per cent—say, six per cent. However, in making out the contract Mr. Vigneron showed such kind spirit toward all my little whims, that there will be no trouble between us. Let us talk about something else. Your dinner, for instance. Are you going to have many here?

MRS. VIGNERON: There are your witnesses, and ours, and my eldest daughter's music-teacher——

MRS. DE SAINT-GENIS: Oh, you have invited him——

MRS. VIGNERON: Yes; we invited the young fellow. He is a musician, I know; but really we didn't want to make him feel his position.

MRS. DE SAINT-GENIS: Well, Mrs. Vigneron, perhaps you will think I am meddling with what doesn't concern me, but if I were in your place I'd let him come this once, and then see no more of him.

MRS. VIGNERON: Why, Mrs. de Saint-Genis? My daughter has never had reason to complain either of him or his work.

MRS. DE SAINT-GENIS: Well, never mind. Who else is there?

MRS. VIGNERON: Mr. Teissier—that's all.

MRS. DE SAINT-GENIS: So I am going to meet this Mr. Teissier, whom I have heard so much of, but whom I have never yet seen! [*She rises and goes over to* Mrs. Vigneron, *taking her by the hand in a friendly way*] Why is it, Mrs. Vigneron, we have never seen your husband's partner?

MRS. VIGNERON: My daughters don't like him.

MRS. DE SAINT-GENIS: Surely your daughters do not lay down the law in your house? I should think Mr. Vigneron would have his partner come here regardless of childish whims.

MRS. VIGNERON: But the men see each other every day at the factory, and when they have talked over their business affairs, they have nothing more to say to each other.

MRS. DE SAINT-GENIS: Now see here, Mrs. Vigneron, I am not the kind of a woman to betray anybody's confidence; but if I guessed a secret, that would be different. Now own up—for some reason or other, it's you who have kept Mr. Teissier from coming here.

MRS. VIGNERON: I? You are entirely wrong about that. In the first place I do whatever my family wishes; besides, if I don't exactly like Mr. Teissier, at least I don't absolutely dislike him.

MRS. DE SAINT-GENIS: You—just feel indifferent toward him?

MRS. VIGNERON: That's exactly it—indifferent.

MRS. DE SAINT-GENIS: Then I must say that you are either very shortsighted, or altogether too unselfish. Isn't Mr. Teissier extremely wealthy?

MRS. VIGNERON: Yes.

MRS. DE SAINT-GENIS: And past sixty?

MRS. VIGNERON: Long past.

MRS. DE SAINT-GENIS: He has no wife or children.

MRS. VIGNERON: That's right.

MRS. DE SAINT-GENIS: It isn't known that he has a mistress?

MRS. VIGNERON: A mistress! Mr. Teissier! Good Lord, what would he be doing with a mistress?

MRS. DE SAINT-GENIS: Now listen; it's no laughing matter. Here you have, right in your grasp, a big unclaimed legacy which may come any day. It could fall to you without making talk and without underhanded means. Doesn't such a legacy mean anything to you? Either you don't care for money, or you think that it would be buying it too dearly if you showed some semblance of affection for an old man.

MRS. VIGNERON: What you say is true enough, Mrs. de Saint-Genis, and you are not the first one who has said as much. I'll explain my position. If we should be indebted to a stranger, our home wouldn't be quite the same; my husband couldn't hold up his head, and we shouldn't be as happy. But this reason doesn't apply to you. There's nothing to keep you from trying your luck with Mr. Teissier, after the children are married. If he takes an interest in this marriage, so much the better. I would be only too glad if Blanche and her husband could benefit in that way. Well, I'm drifting away from the point. If Mr. Teissier, who must be tired of living alone at his age, should succumb to your charms, I should be quite pleased to see you married to him. Of course, there would be certain disadvantages on your side, but the compensations would be great.

MRS. DE SAINT-GENIS: You don't know men, Mrs. Vigneron, and you're talking nonsense. In a pinch, Mr. Teissier wouldn't be too old for me; the trouble is I'm not young enough for him.

AUGUSTE: [*Entering*] Mr. Merckens has just come, ma'am. Shall I show him into the other parlor?

MRS. VIGNERON: Which would you rather do, Mrs. de Saint-Genis—stay here and talk with Mr. Merckens or come and help me dress?

MRS. DE SAINT-GENIS: Just as you please.

MRS. VIGNERON: Then come with me. I'll show you some things I have bought, and you must tell me whether they are the latest style.

MRS. DE SAINT-GENIS: With pleasure.

MRS. VIGNERON: Bring Mr. Merckens in and ask him to wait a few moments.

[*They go out at the left*]

AUGUSTE: Come in and have a chair, Mr. Merckens; I'm the only one here just at the moment.

MERCKENS: All right; go ahead with your work, Auguste, don't let me disturb you. [*Going down the* stage] The servant is a good fellow, but this treatment is intolerable.

AUGUSTE: [Coming back again] No lessons today, Mr. Merckens. You're here to have a good time.

MERCKENS: Is Miss Judith dressing?

AUGUSTE: Probably. But you know, with her it's one, two, three—done!

MERCKENS: Please tell Miss Judith that I'm here and have brought the music she wanted.

[At this moment Judith enters]

AUGUSTE: Now what did I tell you! [To Judith] You weren't long dressing, miss, but you put in your time pretty well.

JUDITH: Thank you, Auguste.

[Auguste takes up Vigneron's dressing-gown and goes out]

MERCKENS: Your servant took that compliment out of my mouth; and I don't know what to say.

JUDITH: Well, it isn't worth bothering about.

MERCKENS: [Unrolling some sheets of music] Here is your composition, Miss Judith.

JUDITH: Let me have it.

MERCKENS: The name of the composer isn't on it, but I can have it put on.

JUDITH: You must keep it to yourself.

MERCKENS: Are you satisfied?

JUDITH: I don't know what to do. I know so well that the family, and particularly Mama, wouldn't like our little conspiracy.

MERCKENS: I repeat what I told you about this little piece. It is distinctive and interesting. It's a little bit melancholy; perhaps you had a cold in the head that day. We had it printed because it was worth it; that's all there is to it.

JUDITH: Now understand, Mr. Merckens, I reserve the right to show my composition or to say nothing about it, just as I please.

MERCKENS: Why?

JUDITH: Because a girl of my age must live very quietly, without letting herself indulge in unbecoming fancies.

MERCKENS: The young ladies I know are not so particular.

JUDITH: All the more reason. [She opens the music and reads the title tenderly] "Farewell to the Bride and Groom." I'm not surprised that this piece is sad. I felt deeply while I was writing it. I was thinking of my little sister whom we all love so much and who is so soon to leave us. Who knows what she is giving up, and what fate awaits her!

MERCKENS: To tell the truth, wasn't there something underhanded about this marriage?

JUDITH: No. Why do you ask?

MERCKENS: Mrs. de Saint-Genis had her pick. She could have asked for the oldest rather than the youngest.

JUDITH: That would have been too bad. He and my sister make a fine couple, and that wouldn't have been the case—otherwise.

MERCKENS: Don't be impatient; your turn will come.

JUDITH: I don't let that worry me.

MERCKENS: Yet you do wish a little that you were married?

JUDITH: As late as possible. I'm getting along first-rate, and I don't care to make any change.

MERCKENS: Composing satisfies you?

JUDITH: You are right, it does.

MERCKENS: It seems too bad that such a delightful young women, so gifted, should lack just a little something which would make her work worth while.

JUDITH: What is that something?

MERCKENS: [In a low tone] A little of the devil.

JUDITH: Mama wouldn't be pleased if she heard you say that; she'd think I was already running wild.

MERCKENS: Does your mother scold you sometimes?

JUDITH: Yes, sometimes. But worse than that, when she is angry she locks up my piano; and she has told father not to take us to the Opera.

MERCKENS: Where do you go, then?

JUDITH: To the Circus. I don't blame Mama, though. She thinks the Opera is bad for me; and perhaps she is right. It's true; the wonders of the scenery, the allurement of the acting, and the splendid singing—why, it's a week before I am myself again.

MERCKENS: These great singers get high prices, you know.

JUDITH: They are all great to me.

MERCKENS: Perhaps you envy them?

JUDITH: I'm wild about them.

MERCKENS: Why don't you be one?

JUDITH: What! I go on the stage?

MERCKENS: Why not? You have a good contralto voice, and there are very few contraltos. You have the presence, and vivacity, and, above all, you have feeling—a great deal of it. The world will never miss one housekeeper, and it will rejoice in one more artist.

JUDITH: Hush! don't say any more about it. I am going to stick to your lessons. They seem to me better than your advice. Have you an engagement for this evening? Will you stay a little while after dinner?

MERCKENS: A little while. I still count on hearing your composition.

JUDITH: And you will play something for us, too?

MERCKENS: Don't ask that. I don't stand on ceremony with you; you and I speak right out. When I am talking I can be witty and amusing; but my music doesn't resemble my conversation the least bit.

JUDITH: We're going to dance.

MERCKENS: Nonsense!

JUDITH: Yes, we are. Blanche wanted to. The least she can do is to dance once or twice with her future husband before she is married. And then

Gaston has a surprise for us. He insists he is going to dance a quadrille with his father, and that we won't be able to tell them apart.

MERCKENS: How so?

JUDITH: You'll see. You don't know how my brother can imitate Papa to the very life. It's wonderful how much like him he seems at those times —his voice, his gestures, his way of joking.

MERCKENS: I can see you are going to have a good time. Thank you for asking me to be here.

JUDITH: Now you're making fun of me, Mr. Artist. I don't want to be too severe, but I fancy that many of your parties aren't worth all the fuss you make about them. Our folks would consider them ridiculous, too, to say the least. There's one thing we can say, anyway; here you will be among respectable people.

[Mrs. Vigneron, and Mrs. de Saint-Genis re-enter]

MRS. DE SAINT-GENIS: [Aside] I knew we'd find them together.

[Judith goes over to her and they greet each other affectionately]

MRS. VIGNERON: [Dressed loudly and covered with jewelry] Pardon me, Mr. Merckens, for making you wait. Women never do get dressed. Do you think I look well?

MERCKENS: Dazzling!

MRS. VIGNERON: Perhaps I have too much jewelry on. Mrs. de Saint-Genis advised me to take off some of it.

MERCKENS: Why, Mrs. Vigneron? Princess Limperani wore three hundred thousand francs' worth at the dinner she gave yesterday.

MRS. VIGNERON: Three hundred thousand francs! Then I can keep on what I have.

[Marie and Blanche enter]

MRS. VIGNERON: [Going to Judith] Your father is late. He won't be here to receive his guests.

BLANCHE: [To Mrs. de Saint-Genis] Why didn't your son come with you?

MRS. DE SAINT-GENIS: George is working, dear. You mustn't expect me to keep him from his duties.

BLANCHE: He has more than one kind of duty now. He must love me as much as I love him.

MRS. DE SAINT-GENIS: That's easy. He won't have to forget his other duties to do that. I warn you we are going to pull hair if you begin to spoil my boy.

MRS. VIGNERON: [To Mrs. de Saint-Genis] I suppose George's witnesses will arrive together.

MRS. DE SAINT-GENIS: No. Mr. Lenormand and my son will leave the office and come here together; the general will come alone. The general and Mr. Lenormand know each other, because they have met at our house, but I have never tried to bring about any closer relationship between them.

AUGUSTE: [Announcing] Mr. Teissier!

TEISSIER: [Entering] How do you do, Mrs. Vigneron?

MRS. VIGNERON: Let me take your hat, Mr. Teissier.

TEISSIER: Never mind. I'll put it somewhere myself, so as to be sure of finding it again.

MRS. VIGNERON: Just as you like. Won't you sit here, in this armchair?

TEISSIER: I will in a few minutes. It's so cold outdoors and so warm in here that I'm going to stay on my feet until I get used to the temperature of the room.

MRS. VIGNERON: I hope you are not ill?

TEISSIER: I try to keep from being ill.

MRS. VIGNERON: How do you think my husband has been lately?

TEISSIER: Very well. Vigneron takes better care of himself, now that he's got some money ahead. He's right, too. A man's life is worth more when he's got something laid by. You can attend to your guests, Mrs. Vigneron; I'll sit in the corner until dinner time. [He leaves her]

MRS. VIGNERON: [Going over to Mrs. de Saint-Genis] Well, that's Mr. Teissier! What do you think of him?

MRS. DE SAINT-GENIS: He has the eyes of a fox and the face of a monkey.

AUGUSTE: [Announcing] Mr. Bourdon!

MRS. VIGNERON: I forgot to tell you that our lawyer will dine with us.

BOURDON: How do you do, ladies—young people——— [Greetings]

MRS. VIGNERON: [Presenting Bourdon] Mrs. de Saint-Genis; Mr. Merckens, my eldest daughter's music-teacher. You are one of the first to come, Mr. Bourdon; that's very nice of you.

[Bourdon bows]

MRS. DE SAINT-GENIS: Mr. Bourdon is setting a good example for his brother lawyers. They don't usually pride themselves on their punctuality.

BOURDON: Yes, we do sometimes keep people waiting—but never at dinner. [Going over to Mrs. de Saint-Genis] I have been asked to congratulate you, Mrs. de Saint-Genis.

MRS. DE SAINT-GENIS: Mr. Testelin?

BOURDON: Yes. We were talking about your son's marriage to Miss Vigneron, and I happened to say that I was going to have dinner with you. "There will be a delightful woman there," he said. "Give her my best regards."

MRS. DE SAINT-GENIS: Mr. Testelin has been my lawyer for twenty years.

BOURDON: So he said. [In a lower tone, coming nearer to her] Testelin is a courteous fellow, with considerable weakness for pretty women.

MRS. DE SAINT-GENIS: [Dryly] It's the first time I ever heard that. [She leaves him, smiling]

BOURDON: [To Mrs. Vigneron] Is Teissier dining here?

MRS. VIGNERON: [Pointing out Teissier to him] There he is, if you want to talk to him.

BOURDON: How are you, Teissier?

TEISSIER: Oh, it's you, Bourdon! Come here a minute; I want to tell you something. [*In a low tone*] I was at the Lawyer's Club to-day on business. I was speaking to the President about my long acquaintance with you, and he got rather confidential about you. "I know Bourdon," he said. "He's got brains enough; he's as shrewd as they make them; but sometimes he overplays his hand. We've got to squelch him."

BOURDON: What do I care for the Lawyer's Club? They're a crowd of stiff-necks who want to give the Club a goody-goody tone. The Club is meant to be a protection for us—not for the public.

TEISSIER: Now listen, Bourdon: I haven't repeated this conversation to keep you from doing business. I just thought I would be doing you a favor by letting you know.

BOURDON: So I take it, friend Teissier. I'm much obliged.

AUGUSTE: [*Announcing*] Mr. Lenormand and Mr. George de Saint-Genis!

MRS. DE SAINT-GENIS: [*To* Mrs. Vigneron] I want you to meet Mr. Lenormand.

[*This presentation and those following take place at the rear*. George *alone goes to the front of the stage*]

BLANCHE: [*Speaking in a low tone to* George] Don't say anything to me, and don't come too near me. Mama has given me a dressing down. I was terribly afraid; I didn't know just what she was going to say.

AUGUSTE: [*Announcing*] General Fromentin!

BOURDON: [*To* Merckens] You are a pianist?

MERCKENS: A composer.

BOURDON: A musician—that's what I should have said. Do you like to go into society?

MERCKENS: I can't help myself; I'm dragged into it.

BOURDON: You might remember my name and address, "Mr. Bourdon, lawyer, 22 St. Anne Street." We have a few friends with us every Sunday evening. I ought to warn you there's nothing fancy about it. The people come at nine o'clock, we have a little music, sing a few songs, have a cup of tea, and by midnight everybody is in bed.

MERCKENS: I couldn't promise to come every Sunday.

BOURDON: Come when you can; we'll be glad to see you any time.

AUGUSTE: [*Announcing*] Mr. Vigneron!

MRS. DE SAINT-GENIS: [*To* Mrs. Vigneron] What! Is your husband in the habit of announcing his arrival?

MRS. VIGNERON: The servant has made a mistake, of course.

[Gaston *enters, with his father's dressing-gown on. He imitates his father's voice and walk*]

GASTON: [*Approaching* Mrs. de Saint-Genis] How is the lovely Mrs. de Saint-Genis?

MRS. DE SAINT-GENIS: [*Taking the joke in good part*] I'm very well, thank you, Mr. Vigneron.

GASTON: Mr. Bourdon, I am your humble servant. [*To* Merckens] How do you do, young man. [*To* Lenormand *and the* General] Delighted to meet you, gentlemen.

MRS. VIGNERON: That's what we get for spoiling children! This young rascal is caricaturing his father.

GASTON: [*To* Mrs. Vigneron] Well, old lady, is dinner ready? By heavens, we haven't spared any expense to give you a good time; we don't have a marriage in the family every day. [*To his sisters*] Which one of you is it? I don't remember. It strikes me that while we are waiting for dinner Miss Judith ought to play us something—*La Dame Blanche,* for instance.

MRS. VIGNERON: Come, Gaston, that's enough. Take off that dressing-gown and act properly.

GASTON: Yes, old lady.

[*The sisters help him off with the gown, amid general laughter*]

AUGUSTE: [*Approaching* Mrs. Vigneron] There's a gentleman here who wasn't invited to dinner and wants to speak with you.

MRS. VIGNERON: What gentleman, Auguste? Is this some new joke of my sons's?

AUGUSTE: If you order me to admit him you will see whether it is or not.

MRS. VIGNERON: Don't admit any one. Tell the gentleman I can't see him.

AUGUSTE: If he insists, ma'am?

MRS. VIGNERON: Then send him about his business.

AUGUSTE: [*Returning*] Here he is, ma'am.

THE DOCTOR: [*Coming forward*] Mrs. Vigneron!

MRS. VIGNERON: Yes, sir.

THE DOCTOR: [*Coming close to her and speaking in a very low voice*] Have you children here, Mrs. Vigneron?

MRS. VIGNERON: Yes, sir.

THE DOCTOR: Send them out of the room. Please do it at once.

MRS. VIGNERON: [*Disturbed, and speaking quickly*] Go into the other parlor, girls. Run along, now; do as I tell you; go into the other parlor. Gaston, you go along with your sisters. Mrs. de Saint-Genis, will you please take the girls in?

[*She opens the door at the right, and the children pass out*]

THE DOCTOR: [*Speaking to the men, who have risen*] You can stay, gentlemen. Are you relatives of Mr. Vigneron?

BOURDON: No, just his friends.

THE DOCTOR: Well, gentlemen, your friend has just had a stroke of apoplexy.

[Vigneron *is brought in at the rear.* Mrs. Vigneron *cries out and throws herself upon her husband's body*]

CURTAIN

ACT II.

The scene is the same as in the preceding act.

MRS. VIGNERON: [*Weeping with handkerchief in hand*] Do forgive me, Mrs. de Saint-Genis; I'm ashamed to weep like this before you, but I can't help it. To think that only one month ago he was sitting there right where you are now, and that I shall never see him again! You knew him; he was so good, so happy; he was too happy, and so were we all; it couldn't last. Do talk to me; it will give me a chance to control myself. I know I ought to make the best of it. He had to die sometime. But many a time I used to ask God to let me be the first to go. Don't you think men as good as my husband go to heaven?

MRS. DE SAINT-GENIS: There's no doubt about it, Mrs. Vigneron.

MRS. VIGNERON: Tell me about your son. I have scarcely laid eyes on him since our misfortune. He's good, too; Blanche told me he wept.

MRS. DE SAINT-GENIS: George is well, thank you.

MRS. VIGNERON: What a setback it is for the poor dears! And they love each other so much!

MRS. DE SAINT-GENIS: This marriage is exactly what I should have talked of if I had found you composed. You are not sensible or courageous, my dear. I know what it is to lose a husband. I've been all through it. Only I had more reason to complain than you. When Mr. de Saint-Genis died he left me nothing but debts and a four-year-old child on my hands. Your daughters are old enough to be a consolation to you; they are grown up; and you don't have to worry about their future or your own. [*Changing her tone*] I suppose now, in the condition you are in, you haven't given thought to your business affairs?

MRS. VIGNERON: What business affairs?

MRS. DE SAINT-GENIS: You ought to know that Mr. Vigneron's estate won't settle itself. You will have to have the apportionment settled, and perhaps there will be some difficulties to meet.

MRS. VIGNERON: Oh, no, Mrs. de Saint-Genis, no difficulties. My husband was too honest a man ever to have business difficulties.

MRS. DE SAINT-GENIS: They could arise after his death. Now listen to me. It isn't Mr. Vigneron's uprightness I'm questioning; it's that of the other people. Have you seen Mr. Teissier yet?

MRS. VIGNERON: Mr. Teissier has stayed at home as usual. I needed money, and he sent it to me after a little urging; that is the extent of our dealings.

MRS. DE SAINT-GENIS: Now listen to what I tell you, Mrs. Vigneron. Even if my advice should be wrong in this case, adopt it as a general rule: Keep an eye on Mr. Teissier.

MRS. VIGNERON: All right, I will keep an eye on him. But just suppose he should have bad intentions: it's my lawyer, not I, who should bring him to terms.

MRS. DE SAINT-GENIS: Keep an eye on your lawyer.

MRS. VIGNERON: Oh, Mrs. de Saint-Genis!

MRS. DE SAINT-GENIS: There's no use saying "Oh!" I know these lawyers, Mrs. Vigneron. You never know whether they are going to save you or be the undoing of you; and according to their ideas you are always in the wrong.

MRS. VIGNERON: What would you say if I should tell you that my lawyer, Mr. Bourdon, is also Mr. Teissier's lawyer?

MRS. DE SAINT-GENIS: I would advise you to get another.

MRS. VIGNERON: No; I have a blind confidence in Mr. Bourdon, and I shan't get rid of him till I lose it.

MRS. DE SAINT-GENIS: It will be too late then.

AUGUSTE: [*Entering and speaking to* Mrs. Vigneron] Mr. Lefort sends his regards and wants to know if you have looked over his memorandum.

MRS. VIGNERON: His memorandum! Did he give me one?

AUGUSTE: Yes, ma'am.

MRS. VIGNERON: Where did I put it? I don't know anything about it.

AUGUSTE: Mr. Lefort will call sometime during the day.

MRS. VIGNERON: Very well, tell him I will see him. [Auguste *goes out*] Mr. Lefort is our architect.

MRS. DE SAINT-GENIS: Keep an eye on your architect!

MRS. VIGNERON: I don't know where you got such a bad opinion of other people, Mrs. de Saint-Genis; but if I were you, I shouldn't display it.

MRS. DE SAINT-GENIS: It's the least I can do to put you on your guard. Everybody looks honest to you.

MRS. VIGNERON: And nobody looks honest to you.

MRS. DE SAINT-GENIS: [*Rising*] I don't wish you any harm, Mrs. Vigneron, and I hope with all my heart, for your sake and the sake of your daughters, who are really delightful girls, that everything goes smoothly in settling Mr. Vigneron's estate. But in business nothing goes smoothly. What seems simple is complicated, and what seems complicated is beyond understanding. Take my word for it, you will be wise to stop thinking a little while of him who is gone, in order to think of yourself and your children instead. Unfortunately I don't know whether Mr. Vigneron left you an annuity or government bonds. He didn't, did he? I dare say his fortune was in that factory, owned by him and Mr. Teissier together? He had land, true enough; but he had bought most of it with borrowed money and on mortgage. I tell you all this with the best of feeling. Women ought to warn and help each other. As for self-interest, it looks as though I no longer had any. We had a very nice plan, to marry our children. I must say it is not merely postponed, but really in danger. It doesn't seem possible for you to fulfill the financial obligations you undertook, and I wouldn't let my son make a poor marriage for anything—and have him blame me for it afterwards.

MRS. VIGNERON: Just as you please, Mrs. de Saint-Genis.

[*A pause and embarrassed silence*]

MRS. DE SAINT-GENIS: [*Speaking quickly*] Good-by, Mrs. Vigneron. Do as I tell you; look out for your interests, and we can talk about our children some other time. But for heaven's sake, Mrs. Vigneron, get this into your head—it is the most useful and the friendliest advice I can give you: Keep an eye on everybody—*everybody!* [*She goes toward the door at the rear,* Mrs. Vigneron *coldly escorting her. The door opens and* Teissier *enters*] Stay here; you needn't go to the door with me. [*She goes out*]

MRS. VIGNERON: [*Weeping, handkerchief in hand*] What a terrible thing this is, Mr. Teissier! My poor husband! It was work that killed him! Why did he work so hard? He didn't care for money; he spent nothing on himself. Oh, he wanted to see his children happy while he was living, and to leave them rich!

[*A silence*]

TEISSIER: Mrs. Vigneron, did you authorize Mrs. de Saint-Genis to come to my house to find out how things stand in regard to your husband's estate?

MRS. VIGNERON: I know nothing about it, and I should not have sanctioned it.

TEISSIER: I did my duty on the double-quick. I took the lady by the arm and showed her the door.

MRS. VIGNERON: That's all she deserved. Mrs. de Saint-Genis was here when you came, Mr. Teissier, and was talking about my husband's affairs. You know all about them and understand them better than anybody else. Won't you enlighten me?

TEISSIER: When I have a few minutes of leisure, I'll take pleasure in drawing up a statement of your husband's estate. What do you want most to know? Whether it will be settled at a loss or profit? [Mrs. Vigneron *waves her hand deprecatingly*] From off-hand calculations I have made, the situation in general looks something like this—now pay attention: when the factory is sold——

MRS. VIGNERON: Why sell it?

TEISSIER: We shall have to. When your real estate and the unfinished buildings, also, are sold——

MRS. VIGNERON: I'm going to keep my real estate.

TEISSIER: You can't. When your current debts are liquidated——

MRS. VIGNERON: But I have no debts.

TEISSIER: I figure them at about forty thousand francs. In that sum I haven't included your architect, who will have to be paid after your real estate is sold. Let me go on. After the registry tax is paid——

MRS. VIGNERON: What! Does a person have to pay for inheriting money?

TEISSIER: Certainly you have to pay, Mrs. Vigneron. Now, when the usual expenses have been met—I include under the head of "usual expenses" such things as the lawyers' fees, and those of his associates, unforeseen bills, carriage hire, postage, *etc*. In

a word, when you have closed the account which you must open under the head of "Settlement of the estate of the late Mr. Vigneron, my husband," there will be left about fifty thousand francs.

MRS. VIGNERON: Fifty thousand francs a year income.

TEISSIER: What, income? Don't you hear what I'm telling you? How do you see in what Vigneron left the capital necessary to provide an income of fifty thousand francs?

MRS. VIGNERON: [*Leaves him abruptly, and, having rung, opens the writing-desk in a hurry and writes*] "My dear Mr. Bourdon. Please come and see me as soon as you can. I shall not rest till I have seen you. Mrs. Vigneron." Fifty thousand francs! [*To* Auguste, *who has just come in*] Deliver this letter at once.

TEISSIER: [*Having taken out a pocketbook cram-full of papers*] Now if you will pay better attention while I am reading——

MRS. VIGNERON: Fifty thousand francs! [*Turning to* Teissier *and making him stuff the papers back into his pocketbook*] Keep your papers, Mr. Teissier; I want nothing more to do with you. [*She goes out at the left hurriedly*]

TEISSIER: [*Stuffing the papers back*] Ignorance, incompetence, impulsiveness—that's a woman, all over. What's she thinking of, I'd like to know? She wants to keep her lands. Well, she can't. Bourdon will have to make her understand that. If Bourdon can handle this case as he promised me he could—quickly and quietly—I can get my hands on real estate worth twice what it will cost me. But we can't lose a minute's time. Delay will bring around a crowd of prospective buyers, and that puts prices up. When Bourdon finds out that I have struck the first blow, he'll do the rest in a hurry.

[*He is going out when* Marie *enters at the left*]

MARIE: Don't go away, Mr. Teissier, before making up with my mother. She has cried so much, poor thing, that she doesn't know which end her head is on.

TEISSIER: [*Coming back*] You stopped me just in time, young woman. I was going to have your mother summoned into court, in order to recover the money I have advanced to her. For my part, I'd rather not leave your mother in this mess. [*He takes out his pocketbook again and selects a different paper from it*] Please give your mother this little bill. She can verify it easily enough: "On the seventh of January, advanced to Mrs. Vigneron 4,000 francs to pay the expenses of your father's funeral; on the fifteenth of January, advanced to Mrs. Vigneron 5,000 francs for household expenses" (at least that's what she said it was for); "on the same day"—the fifteenth, understand?—"paid out, in taking up a bill of exchange signed by your brother and drawn to the order of a money-lender named Lefébure, 10,000 francs." Your brother being under age, his signature was worthless. But your mother, knowing that your brother deceived the man about his age and personal resources, didn't want the money-lender to be cheated. [*He folds up the paper and puts it back in the pocketbook*] Now, what can I do for you?

MARIE: Please stay awhile, Mr. Teissier. It wasn't this bill that upset my mother and made her lose her temper with you. On the contrary, she would have thanked you for honoring my brother's signature. She put the blame on him, where it belongs.

TEISSIER: [*Surprised, and smiling*] Then you know what a signature is?

MARIE: My father told me.

TEISSIER: He would have done better by telling your brother.

MARIE: Sit down, Mr. Teissier. Perhaps I am rather young to talk business with you.

TEISSIER: [*Remaining standing, smiling all the while*] Go ahead, talk; I'm listening.

MARIE: Speaking for myself, I am looking for a great change in our social condition, but I don't think that we shall lose everything. In any case, Mr. Teissier, you would not advise us to be either too yielding or too rash, would you? Then what are we to do? Why, we must find out just where we stand, ask for advice, and not take a single step without knowing the why and wherefore of our condition.

TEISSIER: Ah!—Leaving aside the real estate, which doesn't concern me, what would you do with the factory, while you are waiting?

MARIE: What will happen, Mr. Teissier, if we want to keep it, and you want to sell it?

TEISSIER: It will be sold. The law provides for such a case.

MARIE: There is a law about it?

TEISSIER: [*Smiling all the while*] Yes, miss, there is a law on the subject. Article 815 of the Statutes authorizes either one of two partners to dissolve a partnership that has been broken by the death of one of them. I can prove it to you on the spot. [*Taking a book from his pocket*] You see the title of this book: "Collected Laws and Regulations in Force throughout French Territory." I always carry a copy with me. I advise you to do the same. [*He passes her the book with a certain page indicated. While she is reading he watches her with a look in which are mingled interest, pleasure, and mockery*] Do you understand it?

MARIE: Perfectly.

[*A pause*]

TEISSIER: Your name is Marie, and you are the second daughter?

MARIE: Yes, Mr. Teissier. Why?

TEISSIER: Your father had a marked preference for you.

MARIE: My father loved all his children alike.

TEISSIER: Nevertheless, he considered you cleverer than your sisters.

MARIE: He used to say so sometimes, to console me for not being as good-looking as they are.

TEISSIER: What's the matter with you? You have pretty eyes, rosy cheeks, a well-rounded figure, everything that goes to indicate a healthy woman.

MARIE: I am not worried about my appearance. All I ask is not to be noticed.

TEISSIER: Of course, you are the one that helps your mother run the house. In a pinch you would make a good private secretary.

MARIE: There has never been any necessity for it so far.

TEISSIER: Now is the time. I don't believe your mother is capable of disentangling herself alone. You will be a great help to her. Have you any taste for business?

MARIE: I understand as much of it as I have to.

TEISSIER: You're not afraid to take care of correspondence?

MARIE: No; I know what has to be said.

TEISSIER: Are you good at figures? Come, yes or no? You don't want to tell? [*Leaving her*] She ought to be a wonder at figures.

MARIE: Mr. Teissier, what do you think our real estate is worth?

TEISSIER: Your lawyer can tell you that better than I can. [*Going back toward her, after taking up his hat*] I must get back to business now, miss. I know what you are thinking of; that the factory is a fine property, and you can keep a hold on it. Who is going to assure me that it won't fall down some night? Who is going to convince me that you yourselves, by some slick trick, might not sell it so that you could buy it up at half price?

MARIE: Why should you anticipate that, Mr. Teissier?

TEISSIER: I anticipate only what I would do myself, if I were forty years old instead of sixty odd. To sum up, your need of money on the one hand, and on the other hand my knowledge of where my best interests lie, are going to end in the sale of the factory. Its condition is very prosperous. The death of its manager is a good excuse, and one that doesn't often happen along, to sell out at a profit. Have you got anything else to say to me?

MARIE: Don't go away, Mr. Teissier, without seeing my mother again. She is calmer now, and will listen to you very willingly.

TEISSIER: It's no use. I told your mother what I had to say. You are intelligent enough to explain the rest to her.

MARIE: [*Having rung*] Do what I ask, Mr. Teissier. My mother could not help losing her temper; by going in to see her, you will give her a chance to apologize.

TEISSIER: Well, just as you say. So you want us to be on good terms? I'll tell you right now, you can't gain anything by it. How old are you, Miss Marie? Scarcely turned twenty! And already a modest, sensible little woman, who is able to express herself very clearly. [*Leaving her*] And what her father did not tell me, a very tempting creature.

[Auguste *enters*]

MARIE: Go with Auguste, please; he will take you in to my mother.

TEISSIER: My best wishes for you, miss.

[*He goes out at the left, at a signal from Auguste to follow him*]

MARIE: [*Bursting into tears*] Oh, Father, Father!

BLANCHE: [*Entering and going slowly over to her sister*] What's the matter, dear?

MARIE: Mr. Teissier.

BLANCHE: Is it that scoundrel you've been with such a long while?

MARIE: Hush, dear, hush! We must be careful now and not talk indiscreetly.

BLANCHE: Why?

MARIE: Why? I don't want to tell you; but whether you know to-day or to-morrow, it will be just as hard for you.

BLANCHE: What do you mean by that?

MARIE: We may be ruined.

BLANCHE: Ruined!

[Marie *lowers her head.* Blanche *bursts into tears, and the two girls put their arms around each other. Then they separate, but* Blanche *continues to weep, and is greatly affected*]

MARIE: I shouldn't have told you about a misfortune that may not happen. Here is the whole truth: I don't yet see very clearly into our situation, but it doesn't look promising. Nevertheless, it may all come out right, on one condition: that we are reasonable, prudent, careful in our dealings with everybody, and make up our minds from this moment to overlook many distasteful things.

BLANCHE: You can do as you please, Mama, Judith and you; but I shall have nothing to do with it. I should like to sleep until after I am married.

MARIE: Until after your marriage, dear!

BLANCHE: Now what have you on your mind?

MARIE: I'm sorry to think that this marriage, which means so much to you, may not take place, after all.

BLANCHE: You are wrong, if you think Mr. de Saint-Genis thinks more about a dowry than he does about a loving heart.

MARIE: Men want both when they marry. But even if Mr. de Saint-Genis were the most disinterested man in the world, he has a mother who will do the calculating for him.

BLANCHE: His mother is his mother. If she has faults, I don't want to see them. But she has been married, and she would not want her son to be disloyal to another woman.

MARIE: Let's not be unreasonable and unjust in our misfortune, dear. Both families have promised certain things; if we cannot keep ours, Mr. de Saint-Genis will be released from his.

BLANCHE: You are wrong, you are wrong, I am sure of it. If I should say the word to-morrow, or a year from now, or ten years from now, George would marry me, just as he ought to do, if I wished

it. You see, dear, my marriage is not like so many others, which can take place or not, without doing harm. You don't know how you are hurting me by having the least doubt about its taking place. [*Pause*] Tell me something about how we are ruined.

MARIE: Later on; I don't know myself, yet.

BLANCHE: Who told you about it?

MARIE: Mr. Teissier. I must tell you again to be careful. Mr. Teissier is in the other room with Mama. I have just made it up between them.

BLANCHE: Were they angry with each other?

MARIE: Yes, they were. Mama lost her temper and told him to get out.

BLANCHE: She did right.

MARIE: She did wrong; and she knew it right away. Our situation is bad enough without making it worse by hasty and thoughtless actions. Bear in mind, Blanche, the very existence of all of us, you as well as the rest of us, is at stake. No matter how sure you may feel of Mr. de Saint-Genis, a man looks twice before marrying a woman who hasn't a cent. You are the sweetest little woman in the world; you are all heart and feelings; for you money doesn't exist; but you will find it exists for other people. You will find that out wherever you go. In business, for instance; and we are engaged in business with Mr. Teissier. In marriages, too, as perhaps you are going to learn to your cost. Money certainly has its price. Otherwise there would not be so many misfortunes coming from the lack of it, or so many vile deeds committed because of it.

BLANCHE: [*Aside*] Is it possible that a young man like him, loving and beloved as he is, would stoop to such a base act rather than sacrifice his money interests?

MARIE: You know what I would like, don't you, dear? You know I want this marriage to take place, because you see happiness in it. But if I were in your place, I should be prepared for anything. I should be in raptures if it took place; and if it didn't I should be resigned.

BLANCHE: Resigned! If I thought that Mr. de Saint-Genis had sought me out for my money, I shouldn't be able to hold up my head again. And if he refused to marry me because I had lost my money, I should either go crazy or I should die.

MARIE: Then you do love him a great deal?

BLANCHE: Yes, I do. If you want to know, I worship him! He is kind and loving, and childlike, just as I am. I am positive he has a big heart and couldn't bring himself to do a wrong thing. You can see, can't you, how much I want to marry him? But even if I should be deceived in him; if I should find out that he was not worthy of either love or respect; if he should prove to be the vilest creature in the world, I should still have to marry him——

MARIE: [*Aside*] The poor girl is suffering so much she doesn't know what she is saying.

BLANCHE: [*Aside*] Oh, what a mistake! What a mistake!——You know me, sister dear. We have lived together for twenty years without any secrets from each other. Haven't I been a good girl? I have been very affectionate, I know; but haven't I been good, too? I have never had a single thought that I couldn't tell. If I had met Mr. de Saint-Genis in the street, I shouldn't have even looked at him. But he came here arm in arm with my father. We liked each other immediately, and so we were engaged. Mama told me to keep an eye on the future, but I couldn't see any great harm or wrong in trusting him.

MARIE: Come, don't go on that way; you are exaggerating, as you always do. You told Mr. de Saint-Genis that you loved him, I suppose? Well, you are going to marry him, so that's excusable. You held hands sometimes? Perhaps you let him kiss you? You shouldn't have done that; but it doesn't call for all the reproaches you are heaping on yourself.

BLANCHE: [*After a little hesitation*] I am his wife, do you hear? I am his wife!

MARIE: [*Very innocently*] I don't see what you mean.

BLANCHE: [*At first overcome with amazement*] Oh, forgive me, dearie. You are as pure as an angel. I shouldn't have spoken to you that way. Forget what I have just said; don't try to understand it; and please don't say anything about it to Mama or Judith.

MARIE: Either you are slightly out of your head or I am rather stupid.

BLANCHE: Yes, that's it; I am out of my head. And you are the dearest and sweetest sister any one ever had. [*She kisses her passionately*]

BOURDON: [*Entering*] How do you do? Your mother is in, isn't she? Will you please tell her that I am here?

MARIE: You go, dear.

[Blanche *goes out at the left*]

BOURDON: Your mother just wrote me that she was very eager to see me; and I can readily believe it. I have been at my office every day, waiting for her to call me.

MARIE: My mother has been so afflicted, Mr. Bourdon, and has suffered so much——

BOURDON: I understand perfectly, my dear young lady, that a woman who has had such a blow as your mother can't enjoy paying visits or going shopping. But it is no more than proper to see your lawyer, or at least to ask him to drop in. Fortunately, your father's estate does not offer very great difficulties. Nevertheless, your father left considerable real estate which ought to be inspected at once and turned into cash as soon as possible. Understand me, as soon as possible.

MARIE: Here's Mother.

MRS. VIGNERON: [*Weeping, handkerchief in hand*] What a terrible blow, Mr. Bourdon! What a dreadful thing! My poor husband! I don't seem to be able to weep enough. I just know I shall never live through it.

[*A silence*]

BOURDON: Tell me, Mrs. Vigneron, while I happen to think of it: did you give Mrs. de Saint-Genis permission to call on me to learn how things stand in regard to your husband's estate?

MRS. VIGNERON: She had no permission from me. And so Mrs. de Saint-Genis paid you a visit too——!

BOURDON: Don't worry about that. The way I treated her she won't want to come again. You wanted to see me, Mrs. Vigneron. Please speak quickly and clearly, and make it brief.

MRS. VIGNERON: I won't detain you long, Mr. Bourdon. I have only one question to ask you. Is it true—is it possible that my husband left all told only fifty thousand francs?

BOURDON: Who told you that?

MRS. VIGNERON: Mr. Teissier.

BOURDON: Fifty thousand francs! Teissier was too quick about it. You know him; he isn't a bad man, but he is brutal when it comes to a matter of money. I hope you will get more than that out of it, Mrs. Vigneron, and I will do all I can, you may be sure. [Mrs. Vigneron *bursts into tears and sinks upon the couch;* Bourdon *goes over to her*] So, you were hoping that Mr. Vigneron's estate would amount to a great deal? What was your estimate?

MRS. VIGNERON: I don't know, Mr. Bourdon.

BOURDON: But you should have figured up what your husband left. When a woman loses her husband, that's the first thing she should think of. [*He walks away*] However, it was none the less wrong on Teissier's part—and I'll tell him so, too—to name an amount at random. Business isn't conducted that way. In a settlement, the way to begin is at the beginning, taking up the most urgent matters: then advancing step by step until the end is reached —and then you have what you have. [*Returning to* Mrs. Vigneron] Have you made any decision, Mrs. Vigneron, about your real estate? There your necessity is manifest; it must be sold.

MARIE: How much do you think it would bring us?

BOURDON: [*Going over to* Marie] How much? Nothing. You can't count on anything.

MRS. VIGNERON: [*Rising*] Then what is the advantage of getting rid of it?

BOURDON: [*Returning to* Mrs. Vigneron] What advantage, Mrs. Vigneron? By doing so you remove the shackles from your feet. Believe me, I am not usually so downright in my advice as I am at this moment. Each day's delay is filled with grave consequences for you. While you are deliberating, Catiline is at the gates of Rome; Catiline being, in this case, the mortgages that are eating you up, your architect with his bill, and the civil authorities, with their taxes and fees.

[Teissier *reenters at the left;* Blanche *comes in behind him*]

TEISSIER: How are you, Bourdon?

BOURDON: How do you do, Teissier? I was just

explaining to Mrs. Vigneron and her daughter the impossibility of their holding on to their real estate.

TEISSIER: I have nothing to say as to that. The ladies couldn't find a better adviser than you. They are in good hands.

BOURDON: Mrs. Vigneron, please look at the thing from my point of view, so that we won't misunderstand each other. I don't want to be reproached later on for what wasn't my fault. I restrict myself to this principle: the *status quo* being deadly against you, you must get rid of the *status quo*. I can't say that your real estate is well situated, or that this is the best time to put it up at auction. Far from it. But, by having the sale at the most favorable time—and I'll look out for that—and getting rid of certain obstacles, together with some smooth work and clever advertising, we may get something good out of it.

TEISSIER: [*Aside*] What's that? What's that? [*In a low voice to* Bourdon] Then we're not working together in this?

BOURDON: [*In a low tone to* Teissier] Let me go ahead. [*Going over to* Mrs. Vigneron] Now, then, Mrs. Vigneron, think it over; but think it over quickly, I urge you. When you have made up your mind, please let me know. [*He makes a move as if to go*]

TEISSIER: Don't go, Bourdon, without saying something about the factory.

BOURDON: The factory can wait, friend Teissier. I want to help Mrs. Vigneron get rid of her real estate before we do anything else. We see here a widow and four children who are growing poorer every day. That's a mighty important state of things; we mustn't forget that.

[Teissier *smiles*]

AUGUSTE: [*Entering, and in a low voice to* Mrs. Vigneron] Mr. Lefort is here, ma'am.

MRS. VIGNERON: Please wait for a minute, Mr. Bourdon. After hearing what our architect has to say you may change your mind.

BOURDON: Just as you say, madam.

MRS. VIGNERON: [*To* Auguste] Bring Mr. Lefort in, and ask Judith to come here.

[Lefort *enters*]

MRS. VIGNERON: [*Weeping, her handkerchief in her hand*] What a terrible blow, Mr. Lefort! What a dreadful thing! My poor husband! I shall never get over his loss.

LEFORT: [*Has vulgar manners and a powerful voice*] Come, madam, don't cry like that. With a little nerve and perseverance you can fill your husband's boots. [*He goes up stage*]

TEISSIER: Hello, Lefort!

LEFORT: Glad to see you, Teissier.

[Judith *enters*]

MARIE: [*To* Lefort] Were you very much interested, Mr. Lefort, in the buildings entrusted to you?

LEFORT: Yes, miss. Vigneron was more like a brother than a client.

MARIE: We are on the eve of making an important decision——

LEFORT: Ask me anything you want to. My time is yours, my money is at your service. Vigneron's children are my children.

MARIE: If you had some explanations, or even some project, to let us hear, please tell us in the presence of these gentlemen.

LEFORT: I am ready, miss. These gentlemen don't scare me. It's a way of mine to stand right up to everybody.

MRS. VIGNERON: Sit there, Mr. Lefort.

LEFORT: [*Seated*] Have you looked at my memorandum, madam? No? That's bad. It contained a little account of Mr. Vigneron's real estate, showing the whole business from A to Z. If I had that account right here before me, I could be briefer and make you understand better.

MARIE: I can give it to you, Mr. Lefort. I put it away myself.

LEFORT: If you please.

[Marie *goes to the writing-desk, passing in front of her mother and* Teissier, *who are seated side by side*]

TEISSIER: [*To* Mrs. Vigneron] Is your daughter methodical?

MRS. VIGNERON: Very.

TEISSIER: She's likely to grow up to be a clever woman, isn't she?

MRS. VIGNERON: Yes, I think so.

TEISSIER: Is she good at figures?

[*No reply*]

BOURDON: [*Having taken the memorandum from* Marie, *detaches part of it and hands it to* Lefort] That's what you want, undoubtedly. If you don't mind, I'll run over your memorandum while I'm listening to you.

[*The two exchange hostile glances*]

LEFORT: [*Stressing each phrase*] In the first place, Mr. Vigneron's real estate, situated on the outskirts of Paris near a railway station, and on that account under a thousand disadvantages, was, at the price he paid for it, a sorry bargain. To speak plainly, he was a sucker.

BOURDON: Stop! Nobody had any reason to deceive Mr. Vigneron. He bought this land hoping it would be taken by eminent domain.

LEFORT: By whom?

BOURDON: By the railroad.

LEFORT: Great joke, that is! It was the railroad that sold it to him.

BOURDON: Are you sure of that?

LEFORT: Absolutely sure.

BOURDON: Well, even so. Then he must have supposed that the city, which had undertaken some big work in the neighborhood, would need that land. I remember, now; he expected to do business with the city.

LEFORT: Huh! With the city or with the Turks! You can't tell me anything about real estate. I know the lay of Paris land from A to Z. Well, I'll go on. Mr. Vigneron having been caught for a sucker—I say it again—very quickly realized his foolishness and wanted to dodge the consequences. How could he do it? By building on the land. Then he sent for me. He knew of old that I was square and straightforward, and before I left him he had given me the work of making plans. Unfortunately, I had scarcely begun the work, and the foundations had hardly been laid [*He accompanies his words with a comical pantomime*] when Vigneron moved on to the next world.

BOURDON: We know all these details, my dear fellow. You are wasting our time in telling them over again.

LEFORT: The heirs are in a bad fix; but they can get out of it and make something, too. They can command the services of a man who is faithful, intelligent and highly esteemed throughout the building profession in Paris. That man is the architect who served the deceased. He is now their architect. Will they listen to him? If they ignore his advice and management [*Another comical pantomime*] their goose is cooked.

BOURDON: Now, sir, cutting out phraseology, what's your plan?

LEFORT: Let's reason it out from the least favorable hypothesis. Leave Lefort out of it. He put in an honest bill, without quibbling over each item. He asked for nothing more for himself. Now what's going to become of the real estate? I repeat that it is situated far from the center of the city, and I add that it suffers from numerous other defects. It is encumbered with mortgages. These are just so many points which some unknown purchaser could turn against the owners. [*Volubly*] It would be like this: somebody would depreciate the property, precipitate a public sale, get rid of any honest prospective buyers, fool the courts into granting a judgment at some miserably small sum, pack the auction [*More pantomime*] and there you have a property reduced to nothing.

BOURDON: I demand, sir, that you be more precise. You say somebody would do this, that, and the other. Who would do it, pray? Do you know that only one person could do it, and that you are slandering the lawyer who has charge of the settlement of the estate?

LEFORT: That's you, ain't it?

BOURDON: I am not speaking for myself, sir, but for all my brother lawyers, whom you are libelling. You are attacking, offhand, the most respectable body of men I know of. You are bringing under suspicion the Law itself, in the persons of the officers sworn to execute it. Sir, you are doing worse, if it be possible. You are disturbing the security of families. Really, now, it's rather stiff to make an accusation like this, and then bring in a bill of thirty-seven thousand francs!

LEFORT: I should like to be present when you present *your* bill.

BOURDON: Enough, sir! Now, briefly, what do you propose?

LEFORT: I'm coming to my proposal. I propose that the Vigneron heirs carry out the building——

BOURDON: Well, now, that's what I thought you were getting at. You are the architect, and you propose to continue the building operations.

LEFORT: Let me go on, sir.

BOURDON: It isn't worth while. If Mrs. Vigneron wants to listen to you, she may; but I can't bear such rambling talk any longer. How much money can you sink in it? Mrs. Vigneron has no money; of that I warn you. Where is yours? In three months we should be back at the same point, with this difference—that your bill, now thirty-seven thousand francs, would be doubled, at the rate you are going. Don't force me to say any more. I take your offers in the spirit they are made. I don't want to witness any such shady transaction, which would hand the ownership over to you for a song.

LEFORT: Do you know what you are saying, sir? Look me in the eye. Do I look like a man who would indulge in shady transactions? Upon my soul, I never saw such a clown as you in my life.

BOURDON: [*Restraining himself, and speaking just above a whisper*] What did you call me? You humbug!

[Mrs. Vigneron *rises to intervene*]

TEISSIER: Let 'em go on, madam; don't say anything. Never interrupt a business conversation.

LEFORT: [*To* Mrs. Vigneron] I give in, madam. If you want to know my plan and the resources at my disposal, you can call me again. In the other event, you will please settle my bill as soon as possible. I have to advance money to my clients; while lawyers juggle with their clients' money. [*He goes out*]

TEISSIER: Wait for me, Lefort. We'll go up street together. [*To* Mrs. Vigneron] I leave you in Bourdon's hands, Mrs. Vigneron. Profit by his advice.

LEFORT: [*Returning*] I forgot to say, madam— was it with your permission that Mrs. de Saint-Genis came to my place——?

MRS. VIGNERON: She has been everywhere! I gave nobody permission to go to see you, Mr. Lefort; nobody. And if she comes again——

LEFORT: She won't. She went down the stairs quicker than she came up.

TEISSIER: [*To* Marie] Good-by, Miss Marie, and good health to you. [*He leaves her, and then comes back*] Stay as you are. You won't lack lovers. If I were not so old, I'd get in line.

[*He and* Lefort *go out together*]

BOURDON: Well, madam?

MRS. VIGNERON: What have I done, Mr. Bourdon, to have such a scene?

BOURDON: I shall not regret that discussion, madam, if it shows you where your interests lie.

MRS. VIGNERON: Putting aside what has just passed, let's look at things as they are. I agree that Mr. Lefort is a man who lacks good breeding, but he has a good deal of common sense and a knack of getting things done. After all, what he proposes is nothing more than what my husband would have done, if he had lived.

BOURDON: Are you serious, madam, in what you are saying? Haven't you learned to appraise that architect's offers at their real value?

MRS. VIGNERON: By taking somebody else we could——

BOURDON: You are not satisfied yet? [A pause] Come here, young ladies; you are not in the way. Your mother is wandering in cloudland; help me get her back on earth. Mrs. Vigneron, I am not going to present the matter in its best light. Admitting, for the sake of argument, that the real estate belongs to you—forgetting the creditors and mortgagees who have claims on it—do you know what it would cost to finish those buildings of yours, of which the foundations have hardly been put in? Four to five hundred thousand francs! You know well that Mr. Lefort hasn't that amount. You cannot count on me to get it for you. And then, even if you could get it through me or any one else, would it look well for a woman, I ask, to place herself at the head of a large establishment and throw herself into an enterprise that nobody could see the end of? This question that I am asking you is so serious that if it were brought up before the civil authorities, whose duty it is to help you bring up your minor children, it could be opposed on the ground that the children's inheritances—what little they have—were being risked in mere speculation. [Speaking solemnly] As a member of that civil board, pledged to look out for the best interest of minor children—the greatest duty in existence—I should oppose it myself. [Silence] Take heed, madam. I will not overstep the bounds of my duty by saying anything more. You know where my office is; I will await further orders there. [He goes out]

MRS. VIGNERON: Let's talk awhile, children. Don't all speak at once, and try to listen. Mr. Lefort——

JUDITH: [Interrupting] Oh, Mr. Lefort!

MRS. VIGNERON: You don't know yet what I was going to say. Perhaps Mr. Lefort did express himself very clumsily, but I believe he has a good and loyal heart.

JUDITH: I don't believe so.

MRS. VIGNERON: Why?

JUDITH: I think he has the manner of a swindler.

MRS. VIGNERON: Oh! And you, Blanche; do you think Mr. Lefort has a swindler's manner?

BLANCHE: Yes, somewhat. I agree with Judith.

MRS. VIGNERON: So! Anyhow, his advice seems better to me than Mr. Bourdon's. All Mr. Bourdon's amounts to is that we shall sell our property. What do you think, Marie?

MARIE: I haven't anything to say just yet.

MRS. VIGNERON: We're making a splendid headway, are we not?—Well, then, what do you think about Mr. Teissier?

MARIE: It seems to me that if we don't offend him, but show him a little regard, we may get help from Mr. Teissier.

BLANCHE: What's that, Marie? Mr. Teissier is the most treacherous and dangerous man in the world.

MRS. VIGNERON: Judith?

JUDITH: I don't know who is right, Marie or Blanche; but the way I look at it, we can't count on getting help from any one but Mr. Bourdon.

MRS. VIGNERON: I don't agree with you, dear. Mr. Bourdon! Mr. Bourdon! There is one question that Mr. Bourdon should have asked me right off, and he never seemed once to think of it. Then I noticed something obscure about his words. What did he mean by saying: "Catiline is at the gates of Rome"? [To Marie] Did you understand that?

MARIE: Yes, I understood it.

MRS. VIGNERON: You did? Is that so? We won't talk about it any more; you are wiser than I am. But Mr. Bourdon could have spoken to me about Catiline some other time. Why didn't he ask if we needed money? Now listen, children. If we must sell the real estate, we must. What we shall lose, we shall lose. But remember what your mother says; once and forever, as long as I live: they shall not touch the factory.

MARIE: You are wrong there, Mama.

MRS. VIGNERON: As long as I live they shan't touch the factory!

MARIE: Mr. Teissier could sell it to-day. He has a legal right to do it.

MRS. VIGNERON: As long as I live——

MARIE: There is a law——

BLANCHE AND JUDITH: If there is a law!

MRS. VIGNERON: Come, don't bother me about your law. If I should go through many days like this, I couldn't stand it; you would soon be without either father or mother. [She falls upon the couch, weeping]

AUGUSTE: [Entering] Here are some letters for you, ma'am.

MRS. VIGNERON: [To Marie] Take these and read them, dear.

MARIE: This one is a letter from your dressmaker: "Dear Madam: We take the liberty of sending you your bill, and beg to remind you that it has passed the ordinary credit limit. Our cashier will call upon you to-day. Believe us, madam, yours very truly. P.S. May we call your attention to a brand new dress-goods called 'short-term mourning,' which looks well on young women, and can be worn by misses with equally good effect." [She opens and reads another letter:] "Dear Madam: Mr. Dubois hereby gives you permission to sub-let your apartment, which will not be difficult, provided you make a small sacrifice. Mr. Dubois would like to do more, but he cannot. If he should permit you to break a lease on account of the death of the lessee, he would be establishing a precedent which would cause him much trouble." [*Third letter:*] "Dear Madam: I sent to your house last week concerning my bill against you, and my young lady representative was rudely treated by your servants, and could not make collection. Not being able to reach you, I do not know how to understand a delay which must not be further prolonged. I do not run after business, and as you know, madam, I do not advertise in the papers; I leave that to the big Parisian houses that charge you more on that account. If I am able to make hats at a surprisingly low price, at the same time showing originality and superior workmanship, it is merely because of my large business and regular collections."

[Marie *prepares to read a fourth letter.* Mrs. Vigneron *stops her and begins to weep. The young girls look on without a word, with bowed heads, saddened and frightened*]

CURTAIN

ACT III.

The scene is the same as in the first and second acts.

ROSALIE: Sit down, ma'am.

MRS. DE SAINT-GENIS: [*Hesitating and annoyed*] I don't know.

ROSALIE: Do as I tell you, ma'am. Sit down there and be comfortable, with your pretty little feet on this hassock.

MRS. DE SAINT-GENIS: Don't urge me, Rosalie. I am wondering whether it would be wiser to wait or to come again.

ROSALIE: Do as I say, ma'am. Wait. You'll get me in trouble with Blanchy if I let you go away without seeing her.

MRS. DE SAINT-GENIS: Blanche will see me a little later. She is just the one I came to see, and I want to talk to her about a very serious matter. I didn't think Mrs. Vigneron would have company at luncheon.

ROSALIE: Not company; no, there's no company.

MRS. DE SAINT-GENIS: The ladies of the house are at luncheon; is that what you mean?

ROSALIE: Yes.

MRS. DE SAINT-GENIS: They are not alone, are they?

ROSALIE: No.

MRS. DE SAINT-GENIS: Then there is somebody with them?

ROSALIE: Yes. [*In a low voice*] Mr. Teissier.

MRS. DE SAINT-GENIS: Oh, Mr. Teissier! [*Coming close to* Rosalie] He comes here now, does he?

ROSALIE: Oftener than folks like to have him.

MRS. DE SAINT-GENIS: But they give him a welcome?

ROSALIE: They have to. The young ladies are right in not liking him, but the need of being on good terms with him overcomes that feeling.

MRS. DE SAINT-GENIS: On good terms with him? What for?

ROSALIE: For the sake of their fortune.

MRS. DE SAINT-GENIS: Yes, Rosalie, for the sake of their fortune [*Moving away*] or his.

ROSALIE: You're going to stay, aren't you, ma'am?

MRS. DE SAINT-GENIS: No, I'm going. I've made up my mind. Mr. Teissier is here, and the ladies have business with him. What business? I don't want to embarrass anybody, or pry into any secrets. [*She goes toward the door*]

ROSALIE: Will you call again, ma'am?

MRS. DE SAINT-GENIS: I'll call again.

ROSALIE: Surely?

MRS. DE SAINT-GENIS: Surely. Listen, Rosalie. If Mrs. Vigneron and her daughters—except Blanche, you understand—wish to go out, let them go; don't let them put themselves out for me. Blanche is the only one who need wait in for me. I want to speak with her once and for all. You are her old nurse; so you tell her to keep calm—to think it all over—to make up her mind to the inevitable—that it isn't my fault that her father is dead—that she must take into account her financial condition—and my son can't be responsible—that he can't—not by any means—— Now, Rosalie, do you understand what I'm asking you to say?

ROSALIE: Certainly I understand, ma'am. But you mustn't expect me to say anything that would distress my little Blanchy.

MRS. DE SAINT-GENIS: There, that's your bell. See what's wanted, and I'll find my own way out. [*She leaves*]

ROSALIE: She gives me the creeps, that woman does. I cross myself every time she comes in and goes out.

[*The third door at the rear opens.* Teissier *comes in with* Marie *on his arm, and* Mrs. Vigneron *behind them. Then come* Judith, *and finally* Blanche. Rosalie *steps aside to let them pass; she stops* Blanche, *arranges her dress and embraces her, then goes out through the open door, closing it behind her*]

TEISSIER: Do you mind if I lean on you a little? I'm not used to eating so much at luncheon, and with such nice people. [*Stopping*] What did I say at the table?

MARIE: Different things.

TEISSIER: What about?

MARIE: About life in general.

TEISSIER: Did we say anything about your affairs?

MARIE: The subject didn't come up.

[*They proceed, going toward the right; then* Marie *disengages herself and walks away*]

TEISSIER: [*Following her*] Your sisters are nice;

the oldest one, especially, is well built. Yet I prefer you. I haven't always been old. I can still tell a blonde from a brunette. I'm very much pleased with you, understand?

MARIE: Pay a little attention to my mother.

TEISSIER: Why is it, Mrs. Vigneron, that Gaston, the boy that writes such fine I. O. U.'s, didn't have luncheon with us?

MRS. VIGNERON: [*With some emotion*] My son is engaged.

TEISSIER: He's gone soldiering. That's the best thing he could do. A soldier is lodged, fed, and warmed at the expense of the government. What risk does he take? None but being killed. And then he doesn't need anything.

MRS. VIGNERON: My son did what he wished; but he will be sorry for it later. I wanted to arrange with you, Mr. Teissier, to put him in the factory; and if the factory, as I believe, doesn't go out of your hands or ours, Gaston would take his father's place in a few years.

[*Silence*]

TEISSIER: Have you seen Bourdon?

MRS. VIGNERON: No. Should we see him?

TEISSIER: [*Embarrassed and making no reply, but turning to* Marie] Your sisters are nice; but they are city women. You can see that at a glance. No color. Looking at you, nobody would ever say that you had been brought up with them. In the summer I have roses in my garden, but they haven't the bloom your cheeks have. You and your mother and sisters must come and visit my country house. You are no longer children, so you won't hurt anything. You can have luncheon at home before you start, and be back in time for dinner. You haven't many diversions; that will be one for us.

MARIE: You mustn't expect us to come to see you, Mr. Teissier, before our position is easier. You know we haven't progressed a bit, just got more tangled up, that's all. We are being tormented now by our old tradesmen. They have become very impatient creditors.

TEISSIER: [*Embarrassed, and making no reply, but turning to* Mrs. Vigneron] If you want to go on with your work, madam, don't bother about me. Your girls will keep me company until I go.

MRS. VIGNERON: Stay as long as you please; we shan't send you away. [*Going over to* Marie] Have you spoken to Mr. Teissier?

MARIE: No, not yet.

MRS. VIGNERON: Are you ashamed to?

MARIE: Yes, I am ashamed to. Twelve thousand francs is a big sum to ask for.

MRS. VIGNERON: Let's not ask for it.

MARIE: And where shall we be to-morrow if that dressmaker puts her bill in the hands of a sheriff? She will do just as she said.

MRS. VIGNERON: Do you want me to take Mr. Teissier aside and save you from doing it?

MARIE: No. This is the time to show courage, and I am going to show it.

TEISSIER: [*Seated on the couch beside* Judith] Do you get along well with your sisters?

JUDITH: Very well.

TEISSIER: Who is the cleverest of you three?

JUDITH: Marie.

TEISSIER: Miss Marie. [*He looks at her*] Does she think very much about getting married?

JUDITH: She never says anything about it.

TEISSIER: Yet people think she is pretty.

JUDITH: She is more than pretty; she is charming.

TEISSIER: Exactly. [*He looks again at* Marie] She isn't a living skeleton, like so many of the young girls, and she isn't a heavyweight, either. Has she a firm character?

JUDITH: Very.

TEISSIER: Simple tastes?

JUDITH: Very simple.

TEISSIER: Is she the kind of woman who would stay at home and like to take care of an old person?

JUDITH: Maybe.

TEISSIER: Could a person give her the keys of a house, without being uneasy about it? [Judith *looks at him in astonishment*] Then what's she thinking of? Why doesn't she have a talk with me? [*Rising and speaking to* Judith] I don't want to keep you, miss. Go over there [*Pointing at* Blanche] where your sister is sitting, looking as though she were doing penance. [Marie *approaches him. He joins her and they come out to the front of the stage*] What do you call that little thing you have there?

MARIE: Just a purse.

TEISSIER: What for?

MARIE: A charity bazaar.

TEISSIER: For the poor? I see. You're working for them while they are loafing.

MARIE: Mr. Teissier, my mother wants me to ask something of you that she herself doesn't dare to ask.

TEISSIER: What is it?

MARIE: As I was telling you just now, it seems that our tradesmen have got their heads together. Where we once couldn't get them to send in their bills, now it is a question of which can get his money first.

TEISSIER: These people are within their rights in claiming their due.

MARIE: Unfortunately we haven't the amount necessary to settle with them. A pretty round sum. Twelve thousand francs. Mr. Teissier, please lend us this much more; you will be relieving us of many little embarrassments, which are sometimes worse than big ones.

[*A pause*]

TEISSIER: Have you seen Bourdon?

MARIE: No. Do we have to see Bourdon?

TEISSIER: You know well that this state of things can't last, either for you or for me. Twelve thousand francs that you want and twenty thousand that you owe me make thirty-two thousand francs that have come out of my pocket. I am not risking anything, of course. I know where to get back that money. But it certainly must come back to me. You won't be surprised to learn that I have taken steps toward that end. Don't cry; don't cry. You have time enough ahead of you to get sunken eyes and hollow cheeks. Keep your twenty-year-old advantages; a little girl of your age, blooming and flourishing, is unhappy only when she wants to be. Understand me? Only when she wants to be. [*He quits her suddenly, takes his hat and goes over to* Mrs. Vigneron] Your second daughter has just told me that you need twelve thousand francs. You needn't add anything to what she said; it isn't necessary. Just you wait while I go and get the money. [*He goes out abruptly*]

MRS. VIGNERON: Thanks, Marie dear. It makes one feel so silly and shamefaced to have to take money from that old codger! At the last minute I really came near deciding not to ask him for it.

MARIE: It's done.

MRS. VIGNERON: Judith—where are you going, child?

JUDITH: I'm going to leave you; I need sleep.

MRS. VIGNERON: Stay here, please do.

JUDITH: But, Mama——

MRS. VIGNERON: [*Commandingly*] Stay here! [Judith *obeys, and goes over to her mother*] Isn't our situation serious? Doesn't it interest you? We can't talk about it half enough.

JUDITH: What's the use talking about it? We are always saying over the same things without making the slightest decision. Don't you see it requires a different kind of woman than you to get us out of the scrape we are in?

MRS. VIGNERON: Soon you'll be saying that I am not doing my duty.

JUDITH: I don't say that. It isn't your fault that you don't understand anything about business.

MRS. VIGNERON: Then why don't you take charge of our business affairs?

JUDITH: Excuse me! I can't add a column of figures.

MRS. VIGNERON: Nobody is asking you to add a column of figures. We are asking you to be here, to take part in the discussion, and give us your opinion when you have any.

JUDITH: You know what my opinion is; and it won't change. We can't do anything, and there is nothing to do.

MRS. VIGNERON: But suppose they are robbing us?

JUDITH: Well, then they'll rob us. You can't stop them and I can't. Neither can Marie. She ought to see plainly that we must wait for something to turn up. As for me, I should like a thousand times better —yes, a thousand times—to settle the whole thing to-day and take what they leave us, because they really *are* willing to leave us something. Then, when we no longer had to think about the past, we could think about the future.

MRS. VIGNERON: You talk very glibly about the future, Judith.

JUDITH: It worries me, but it doesn't frighten me. I think Blanche is by far the most unfortunate of us. She is going to lose the man she loves.

MARIE: Nobody said she was going to lose him.

JUDITH: On the contrary, everybody says so. It's as clear as daylight that Blanche won't be married. If I were in her place, I shouldn't wait for Mr. de Saint-Genis to ask for his release; I'd throw him over myself.

MRS. VIGNERON: Now just see, Judith, what silly things you've been saying in the last five minutes. First you hurt me, and now you have discouraged one of your sisters and made the other one cry.

JUDITH: [*Going over to* Blanche] Are you angry with me?

BLANCHE: No, I'm not angry with you. You don't know Mr. de Saint-Genis, or you wouldn't say such things. I was very glad to be able to bring him a dowry, but he won't love me less because I have lost it, and he will have just the same desire to marry me. All the trouble comes from his mother. But sooner or later mothers have to give in, and Mrs. de Saint-Genis will do just as the rest. She will find that the wisest thing is to give her consent, when she sees that we would marry without it. You are right, Judith, when you say that we are not defending ourselves very well. But though we may lack decision in dealing with our business affairs, I don't lack any in regard to my marriage.

MRS. VIGNERON: Oh, dear! I don't understand you, girls. You are always talking about decision: we lack decision; we must have decision. You don't say anything else. And when I propose some real idea, you are the first ones to throw cold water on it. Come now, yes or no: do you want me to dismiss Mr. Bourdon and get another lawyer?

MARIE: Who?

MRS. VIGNERON: Who? The first one that comes along. [*To* Judith] That man, for instance, who sent us his card.

JUDITH: Take him; I'd just as lief.

MARIE: I'm opposed to it.

MRS. VIGNERON: Well, children, I'll have to settle it. If Mr. Bourdon says one more word to me—just one more word—that seems out of place to me, I'll get rid of him and send for this other man. But first of all, where is this man's card? [*Silence*] Look in the desk for it, Judith, and look carefully. Marie, you look on the piano, perhaps it's over there. Blanche, you look, too. Do something! Look on the shelf over the fireplace. [*Another silence*] You needn't look any more, children. I have it in my pocket. [*To* Judith] What are you laughing about?

JUDITH: I had to laugh. I was thinking that our enemies know what they do with *their* things.

MRS. VIGNERON: [*Sadly*] Are you going to begin again?

JUDITH: No; I'm not going to, and I'm sorry for

what I said. If I said anything wrong, I didn't mean to. I wish this whole business was over with. It makes us irritable and sour-tempered; and instead of fighting our enemies we quarrel with one another. One might think that we should have loved each other more when we were happier; but the contrary is true.

[*She kisses her mother.* Marie *and* Blanche *make up. All are greatly affected*]

ROSALIE: [*Entering*] Mr. Bourdon, ma'am.

JUDITH: This time I *am* going.

MRS. VIGNERON: Go to bed, children. I'll talk with Mr. Bourdon.

[*The three girls leave*]

BOURDON: [*Entering*] Seeing how useless my previous advice proved, Mrs. Vigneron, I had intended to let matters take their course and not come to see you until you were ready for me. Believe me, I have no hand in the bad news I have been asked to bring you.

MRS. VIGNERON: I am beginning to get used to bad news, Mr. Bourdon.

BOURDON: You must, madam, you must. In your position, courage and resignation are of prime necessity.

MRS. VIGNERON: It strikes me, Mr. Bourdon, that my affairs give you a good deal of trouble, considering the little you get out of them. I have just heard of a man, very upright and intelligent, who will take charge of them.

BOURDON: Very well, madam, very well. Perhaps it would have been a little more seemly to have saved me this visit by letting me know of your decision earlier. Never mind. Shall I send all your papers here, or will they call at my office for them?

MRS. VIGNERON: [*Disconcerted*] But I haven't made any arrangements with this man yet. Wait awhile; there's no hurry.

BOURDON: On the contrary, madam, there is hurry. And since you have found, as you say, a capable, true and tried man, he shouldn't lose any time getting acquainted with the details of your estate—a matter of which he knows absolutely nothing. He is a business man, I suppose?

MRS. VIGNERON: Who told you he was a business man?

BOURDON: I guessed as much. Would it be indiscreet of me to ask who this man is? [Mrs. Vigneron, *after some hesitation, takes the card from her pocket and hands it to him; he returns it, smiling*] One last piece of advice, Mrs. Vigneron, which you may take or not, as you please. Duhamel, whose card this is, is an old lawyer who was debarred for embezzlement. Perhaps you do not know that in the legal profession black sheep are summarily expelled. After that setback, Duhamel set up a business office near the Court Buildings. It isn't my business to tell you what goes on in his office; but you will come to me with news about it before long.

MRS. VIGNERON: Tear up that card, Mr. Bourdon, and tell me what you came to see me about.

BOURDON: Mrs. Vigneron, you really deserve to be left in this man Duhamel's clutches. All he would have to do would be to come to an understanding with another scoundrel like himself—Lefort, for instance—and that would be the last of Mr. Vigneron's estate. You are angry with me because I spoil your illusions. Am I wrong to do so? Judge for yourself. In the face of your obstinate resolve to keep your real estate—a resolve I do not favor—I had to make an accurate survey of the situation. Well, in going over the bundle of mortgages, I found that one of them had fallen due. I wrote immediately to ask for a renewal. This request was refused. We need sixty-odd thousand francs to take up this mortgage, and we need it right now.

MRS. VIGNERON: What are we going to do?

BOURDON: That's what I am asking you. And that isn't all. Time is passing; are you ready to pay the inheritance taxes?

MRS. VIGNERON: But, Mr. Bourdon, according to you, our real estate is worth nothing; and where there is nothing, the authorities can't claim anything.

BOURDON: You are wrong. The authorities, in dealing with an estate, chase no wild geese. They collect taxes where they see the chance, regardless of who ought to be paying them.

MRS. VIGNERON: Are you sure of that?

BOURDON: What a question, Mrs. Vigneron! Why, my office-boy, a twelve-year-old boy, knows those things as well as I do. Now you can just see what a hard time we have with clients like you—entirely respectable, of course, but also entirely ignorant. If by some inadvertence we had not taken up this point together, and then, later on—in going over the accounts after the inevitable sale of your real estate—you had found set down "Inheritance tax: so much," who knows but you might have said: "Mr. Bourdon put that money in his own pocket."

MRS. VIGNERON: Such an idea never would have occurred to me.

BOURDON: Well, Mrs. Vigneron, you are a little suspicious that I am not fulfilling my duty toward you in all respects; and that accusation is grave enough. But let it go. While you are floundering about, doing nothing, waiting for something or other to turn up, that won't turn up, Teissier, like the business man he is, has gone right ahead. He has put experts into the factory. They have finished their report. In short, Teissier has just sent me instructions to put your factory up for sale.

MRS. VIGNERON: I don't believe you.

BOURDON: What, madam, you don't believe me? [*He takes a letter from his pocket and hands it to her*] Teissier's letter is clear enough; right to the point, just as he always writes.

MRS. VIGNERON: Will you leave that letter with me, Mr. Bourdon?

BOURDON: I don't see what you could do with it, and it ought to remain in my files.

MRS. VIGNERON: I'll return it to you to-morrow, if Mr. Teissier persists in his determination.

BOURDON: As you please.

MRS. VIGNERON: You don't know, Mr. Bourdon, that our dealings with Mr. Teissier have become very friendly.

BOURDON: Why shouldn't they be?

MRS. VIGNERON: He likes my daughters.

BOURDON: That's fine, Mrs. Vigneron, that's very fine.

MRS. VIGNERON: Why, he even took luncheon with us to-day.

BOURDON: I should be more surprised if you had taken luncheon with him.

MRS. VIGNERON: Well, we have let Mr. Teissier know about our straitened circumstances, and he has consented to lend us a pretty round sum of money; and it isn't the first, either.

BOURDON: Why do you ask Teissier for money? Am I not here? I told you, Mrs. Vigneron, that you could not look to me for four or five hundred thousand francs for imaginary building operations. Teissier wouldn't let you have it either, I'm dead sure of that. But it is I, your lawyer, who ought to provide for your everyday needs, and you would have pleased me if you had not waited for me to tell you so.

MRS. VIGNERON: I beg your pardon, Mr. Bourdon; I did doubt you for a moment. You mustn't be angry with me; my head is whirling in the midst of these complications; and you were right when you said that I am ignorant. If I could do as I wished, I would stay in my bedroom and mourn for my husband; but what would people say of a mother who did not defend her children as best she could? [She sobs and throws herself down on the couch]

BOURDON: [Going over to her, and speaking softly] I will try hard to get Teissier to put off the sale of the factory, but on one condition: that you give up your real estate. [She looks at him fixedly] You certainly must understand why I suggest this condition, which is wholly to your advantage. I can't think of spending useless energy and serving your interests on one point only to have you getting me in hot water on another.

[Silence]

MRS. VIGNERON: [To Rosalie, who comes in] What is it, Rosalie?

ROSALIE: Mr. Merckens wishes to see you, ma'am.

MRS. VIGNERON: [Rising] Very well. Show him in. [To Bourdon] Do you mind having Mr. Merckens with you a moment, while I talk this over with my daughters?

BOURDON: Go ahead, Mrs. Vigneron; go and talk it over with your daughters.

[She goes out at the left]

MERCKENS: [Entering] How d'ye do, Mr. Bourdon?

BOURDON: How are you, young man? How have you been since that unlucky dinner when I saw you last?

MERCKENS: The dinner wasn't bad, but unfortunately we had to eat it on top of a rather nasty spectacle.

BOURDON: Right you are. Poor Vigneron was brought in right under our noses. . . .

MERCKENS: What did you have in mind when you took me to the restaurant that day?

BOURDON: That was your idea. You said to me, as we were coming out of the house: "I don't like the idea of going home with a white necktie and an empty stomach." I said: "Let's dine somewhere, and then think up something to do during the rest of the evening." Well, we had a half-hearted meal, and the only thing we wanted to do was to go to bed. You see, people are always more sensitive to the death of others than they imagine, and it is particularly the case with a violent death. In spite of yourself you can't help thinking that the same thing might happen to you the very next day; and you don't feel much like laughing about it.

MERCKENS: Are you waiting to see Mrs. Vigneron?

BOURDON: Yes. I ought not to wait, but Mrs. Vigneron is no ordinary client of mine, and I spoil her. You don't give lessons here any more, I suppose?

MERCKENS: Miss Judith hasn't taken any since her father died.

BOURDON: If you'll take my advice, you won't count on having her for a pupil any more, and you'll look somewhere else.

MERCKENS: Why?

BOURDON: I know what I'm talking about. This family's new circumstances are going to force them to economize.

MERCKENS: No?

BOURDON: Yes.

MERCKENS: Really?

BOURDON: Really.

[A pause]

MERCKENS: But Mr. Vigneron was wealthy.

BOURDON: He wasn't wealthy; he made a lot of money, that's all.

MERCKENS: He didn't spend it on himself.

BOURDON: He speculated with it, and that's often worse.

MERCKENS: I thought that husky chap was going to leave his wife and children a fortune.

BOURDON: A fortune! You'll do me a favor if you'll show me where it is. Any minute, now, the Vigneron family are likely to find themselves in a bad predicament; and I can tell you, without shouting about my devotion to their interests, that they'll owe it to me if they save a loaf of bread.

MERCKENS: Impossible!

BOURDON: That's just where it stands, young man. Keep this news confidential, and make what use you can of it.

[*A pause*]

MERCKEN: [*In a low voice*] What do they say about it here?

BOURDON: What would you expect them to say?

MERCKENS: These women can't be in very good spirits.

BOURDON: Well, what has happened to them hasn't been any cause for rejoicing.

MERCKENS: Tears?

BOURDON: Tears!

MERCKENS: [*Going over to him with a smile*] Do me a slight favor, will you? Be good enough to tell Mrs. Vigneron that I only had a minute to spare, that I didn't want to bother her, and that I'll call again shortly.

BOURDON: You *will* call again?

MERCKENS: Not very likely.

BOURDON: Stay awhile, then, now that you are here, young man. You'll be repaid in listening to the poor woman, and she'll be thankful for a little kindness. She is really beginning to doubt whether any one is interested in her misfortunes.

MERCKENS: It's certain that Miss Judith won't continue with her lessons?

BOURDON: That's very certain.

MERCKENS: You don't see anything ahead which could put Mrs. Vigneron and her daughters on their feet?

BOURDON: I do not.

MERCKENS: Then you bet I'm off. That suits me better. No jabbering nonsense such as I could talk to Mrs. Vigneron would make her feel any better. I know myself too well. I should probably make some awful break; while you, with your great command of language, can find some excuse for me. How's that?

BOURDON: Just as you say.

MERCKENS: Thanks. Good-by, Mr. Bourdon.

BOURDON: Good-by.

MERCKENS: [*Returning*] Up to what time are you at your office?

BOURDON: Till seven o'clock.

MERCKENS: I'm coming after you one of these days, and we'll go to the theater together. Is that all right?

BOURDON: Indeed it is.

MERCKENS: Which do you like best, grand opera or musical comedy?

BOURDON: Musical comedy.

MERCKENS: Musical comedy! You want something light. All right, we'll see that kind of a show. Say, I hope this time we shan't have our evening spoiled by an apoplectic fit. So long!

BOURDON: So long, young man.

[Merckens *goes out at the rear while* Mrs. Vigneron *is coming in at the left*]

MRS. VIGNERON: Why did Mr. Merckens go away without waiting for me?

BOURDON: The young man was very much embarrassed, Mrs. Vigneron. When he saw me here, he understood that you were already occupied, and he thought best to postpone his visit until some more convenient time.

MRS. VIGNERON: He shouldn't have gone. I just told my daughters he was here, and they were going to entertain him.

BOURDON: Well, Mrs. Vigneron, what is the result of your conference with your daughters?

MRS. VIGNERON: Nothing, Mr. Bourdon.

BOURDON: What are you going to wait for now?

MRS. VIGNERON: We shan't do anything until we have seen Mr. Teissier.

BOURDON: And what do you expect he will say to you?

MRS. VIGNERON: There is no doubt about his intentions, that's true. He wants to sell our factory as much as he did yesterday. But this move would be so disastrous for us that he wouldn't dare to have a finger in it. We are going to have a straight talk with Mr. Teissier and we shan't hide the fact from him that he isn't treating us square.

BOURDON: Not square? That's rather strong talk. I doubt very much, Mrs. Vigneron, whether you can change his mind by using that kind of language to him.

MRS. VIGNERON: I'm not going to do the talking to Mr. Teissier. I lost my temper the first time, and I could easily do so again. Besides, considering the turn our affairs have taken, I would let them go as they please now, were it not for the fact that one of my daughters shows more perseverance than the rest of us—her sisters and myself. Mr. Teissier really seems to be well disposed toward her; so perhaps she can succeed in making him change his mind.

BOURDON: Excuse me—you say Teissier has taken a liking to one of your daughters?

MRS. VIGNERON: At least, we think so.

BOURDON: Which one?

MRS. VIGNERON: My second daughter, Marie.

BOURDON: And does Miss Marie reciprocate this kindly feeling shown by Mr. Teissier?

MRS. VIGNERON: What in the world are you thinking about, Mr. Bourdon? You're not figuring on making a match, are you?

BOURDON: Wait a minute, Mrs. Vigneron. If Teissier were disposed to marry this young lady, she wouldn't do a bad stroke of business in accepting him; but I had something else in mind. You know Teissier is no longer young; he has reached an age where the slightest sickness might carry him off. If this very sudden affection he is showing toward your daughter should lead him, later on, to make some provisions for her, perhaps it would be just as well if you didn't antagonize the old man at this point.

MRS. VIGNERON: We expect nothing from Mr. Teissier. Let him live as long as he can and do what he pleases with his money. But this factory he wants to sell belongs to both of us, and not to him alone. To do as he pleases with my husband's work and my children's property would be to abuse the rights given him by the law.

BOURDON: I won't argue further.

ROSALIE: [Entering] Mr. Teissier is here, ma'am.

MRS. VIGNERON: Just a minute, Rosalie. [To Bourdon] Is it necessary for you to meet?

BOURDON: Yes; I should prefer it. Please understand perfectly, Mrs. Vigneron, that I am working for Teissier as well as you. I make no difference between you. All I want is for you to come to some decision, so that I may know what to do.

MRS. VIGNERON: Very well. I'll send my daughter in.

[She goes out at the left, gesturing to Rosalie to have Teissier come in. Teissier enters]

BOURDON: You here—you?

TEISSIER: Yes, I'm here.

BOURDON: What's this I've been hearing? Nobody sees you anywhere else but here.

TEISSIER: I have been here several times. What of it?

BOURDON: You are hostile to the interests of this family, and yet you sit at their table?

TEISSIER: What are you kicking about, as long as what I do doesn't interfere with you?

BOURDON: My position isn't an easy one as it is. You are making it more difficult.

TEISSIER: Go right ahead as we agreed, Bourdon—do you understand? Don't bother yourself about my doings.

BOURDON: Miss Marie will get what she wants out of you.

TEISSIER: Miss Marie will get nothing.

BOURDON: It seems you have a weakness for this young lady.

TEISSIER: Who told you so?

BOURDON: Her mother.

TEISSIER: What is she meddling for?

BOURDON: You had better get ready for a carefully planned siege on the part of your simple maiden. I warn you they are looking to her to bring you to terms.

TEISSIER: Take your hat, Bourdon, and go back to your office.

BOURDON: All right; just as you say. [Returning to Teissier] I needn't wait any longer, eh? Shall I start the thing going?

TEISSIER: Sure! [Calling Bourdon back] Listen, Bourdon! I told you about my talk with Lefort, didn't I? He's an ugly customer, and he's right after us. The wise thing will be to go easy with him, don't you think? He is still in charge of the building operations.

BOURDON: What? Have you had dealings with Lefort, after that wretched scene when he insulted both of us?

TEISSIER: Still thinking about that, are you? If we should refuse to see people just because a few strong words had passed between us, then we couldn't see anybody at all.

BOURDON: Well, it's your business, after all. I don't know why I should mix into it. I promised you should get the real estate, and you shall. The rest doesn't worry me. [Marie enters, he goes over to her and speaks in a low tone] I leave you with Teissier, my dear young lady. Try to convince him; a woman sometimes succeeds where we fail. If you get anything out of him, you will be more fortunate and cleverer than I am. [He goes out]

TEISSIER: Here is the money you asked me for. You told me it was intended for your tradespeople. Meet them yourself. Look sharp at the bills they render; don't be afraid to beat them down as much as you can; and, above all, take good care not to pay the same bill twice. [Detaining her] Where is my receipt?

MARIE: I'll give it to you by and by.

TEISSIER: I ought to take it in one hand while I am handing over the money with the other. Just this minute I am flustered. [She goes to the writing-desk and puts the banknotes in a drawer; then she comes back. There is a moment of silence] You have something to tell me, and I have something to tell you, too. Come sit beside me, won't you, and have a nice friendly talk. [They sit down] What do you figure on doing?

MARIE: I don't understand your question.

TEISSIER: My question is simple enough, nevertheless. I told you before that there would be fifty thousand francs coming to you; no more. You can't think of holding on to this apartment and keeping open house until your last cent is gone. What do you figure on doing?

MARIE: A relative of my mother's who lives in the country has invited us to come and settle near him.

TEISSIER: Your mother's relative is like all relatives. He made that suggestion thinking to get an invitation in return; he won't cling to the idea when it will be his turn to carry out the suggestion.

MARIE: Then we'll stay in Paris.

TEISSIER: What are you going to do in Paris?

MARIE: My oldest sister is ready to give music lessons, when the time comes.

TEISSIER: Good. Your oldest sister, if she carries out that idea, will promptly let the rest of the family support themselves. She will want her money herself, and she will be right.

MARIE: But I count on getting something to do, too.

TEISSIER: What?

MARIE: That's it, what? I don't know yet. It's so hard for a woman to find work, and she gets so little for it.

TEISSIER: That brings us to what I wanted to say. [A pause; he continues with some hesitation and embarrassment] I know of a house where, if you want to, you can come to live. You will get your room and board there, and every month a small sum which you can save up for a rainy day. You will not have to look any further for a place.

MARIE: Whose house? Yours?

TEISSIER: [*With an equivocal half-smile*] Mine.

MARIE: [*After a display of emotion; not knowing how she ought to interpret his words, nor how she ought to reply*] What you propose is impossible. In the first place, my mother would not let me leave her.

TEISSIER: Yes; I had an idea your mother might interpose some opposition. But you are of age now and can consider your best interests without consulting anybody.

MARIE: I told you no, Mr. Teissier; *no!*

TEISSIER: Wouldn't you be mighty glad to let your family stay in the ditch and go out and do something on your own account? That's the way I should feel, if I were in your place.

MARIE: That isn't the way I feel.

TEISSIER: What good do you see in all scrambling around together, instead of going your separate ways?

MARIE: Just the advantage of not being separated. [*Leaving him*] Sometimes it is good to have consolation nearby. That way you are not troubled so much with certain events that would otherwise be disconcerting.

[*A pause*]

TEISSIER: It is some time now since I began coming here. I don't stay away from my business without a good reason. You aren't stupid—you have a quick wit. You ought to be able to see through it.

MARIE: I was thinking of something else.

TEISSIER: What?

MARIE: I was thinking only of my family. I can think only of the fate that awaits them, now that they have lost everything.

TEISSIER: [*With a smile*] So you are trying to get the best of me and worm something out of me for them?

MARIE: Oh, Mr. Teissier! I have enough sorrow without your adding anything to it. You want to know what I thought; I will tell you. I was thinking that you are no longer young, that you live a very dreary and lonely life, that you have no children, and so you like the company of other people—those were my thoughts. Yet you were right, I admit. We did not have you coming here before my father died; and we shouldn't have begun afterward. We shall have to take things as they come, meeting our difficulties courageously, and telling ourselves that after all women are never unhappy when they love each other, and are brave, and stand by one another.

[*A pause*]

TEISSIER: How many are there of you? You, your mother and your two sisters?

MARIE: And Rosalie.

TEISSIER: Where does Rosalie come in?

MARIE: She is a saint. She brought us all up.

TEISSIER: What do you do to keep your servants? I could never get one attached to me. There are

four of you—Rosalie doesn't count. Unfortunately, four is too many; you can understand that. Even to please a little friend I want to have with me, I can't be responsible for a whole family. They would bore me to death.

MARIE: Nobody asked you to; and nobody dreamed of such a thing.

TEISSIER: I didn't want to tell you, but you guessed it. A fellow doesn't complain of being alone as long as he is young; but at my age it is tiresome and unsafe.

MARIE: If you are alone, it's because you prefer to be.

TEISSIER: I ought to get married?

MARIE: It isn't necessary to get married to have people around you. You still have your parents.

TEISSIER: I don't see them any more, because I wanted to get out of reach of their demands for money; they are starving. I want very much to get hold of a little woman of simple tastes, kind and trustworthy, who will conduct herself decently in my house, and who won't steal everything in sight. Perhaps later on I'll see whether I ought to marry her. But you women are all lambs before marriage, and God knows what afterward. I would regulate my conduct according to hers; she would not be badly off while I was living, and she'd have no cause to complain after I died. Married or not, it would be just the same for her.

MARIE: Take your hat, Mr. Teissier, and go away. I don't want to have you near me another minute. I believe you are unhappy, and I pity you. I believe your proposal was an honest and proper one, and I thank you for it. But it could have another meaning, a meaning so loathsome that my heart trembles at the very thought of it. Go away.

TEISSIER: [*Standing, embarrassed, blubbering*] Just stop and think of what you are saying to me.

MARIE: No more! Not a word! I ought to be ashamed of having spoken to you about my family; I ought to be ashamed for them as well as for myself. Think it over. Consider what kind of man my father was, and what you owe to his honesty, to his work, to his memory. [*She goes hurriedly to the desk, takes out the banknotes and hands them back to him*] Take your money. Don't be embarrassed; take it. Mr. Bourdon has just offered to help us, and we shall get from him what we could not have asked of you. Go now! Go, before I call Rosalie to show you out. [*A pause; Rosalie enters*] Here she is now. What is it, Rosalie?

ROSALIE: Mrs. de Saint-Genis is here.

MARIE: Very well, show her in.

ROSALIE: What's the matter, dearie; you are blushing? [*Looking alternately from* Marie *to* Teissier] I hope nobody has said anything to you they shouldn't?

MARIE: Show Mrs. de Saint-Genis in.

TEISSIER: I'll go. I'll stop in and see Bourdon on my way, as to whether there is still a way to fix

things up; but don't count too much on it. Good-
by!

ROSALIE: It isn't wise to leave such a child with a
man of his age!

[Mrs. de Saint-Genis, *entering, encounters*
Teissier *on his way out*]

MRS. DE SAINT-GENIS: How do you do, Miss
Vigneron? I never come here these days without
meeting Mr. Teissier. Is that a good sign? Are you
going to come to terms with him?

MARIE: No, Mrs. de Saint-Genis.

MRS. DE SAINT-GENIS: Pshaw! I thought you were.

MARIE: Why?

MRS. DE SAINT-GENIS: An old man ought to find
it pleasant to be in a house like yours.

MARIE: Mr. Teissier came to-day for the last time.

MRS. DE SAINT-GENIS: Then I can sincerely say I
am sorry for you. Is your sister at home?

MARIE: Yes.

MRS. DE SAINT-GENIS: Please have her come here.
Don't bother your mother; it isn't necessary; I can
see her another time. I want to talk with Blanche.

MARIE: She'll be right in. [*Goes out*]

MRS. DE SAINT-GENIS: It is decidedly better to
have a talk with this young woman and tell her
straight out that the marriage is not postponed, but
broken off. It is better for her to know where she
stands, and it will clear my own mind, too. For the
first time in his life George was going contrary to
my wishes. He clung to his sweetheart, and wanted
to marry her. Fortunately another good match came
along, and I gave him his choice—to obey me or
never see me again. He gave in. But what a brigand
a young man twenty-three years old can be! And as
for this giddy miss, who couldn't wait until she was
married—well, so much the worse for her.

BLANCHE: [*Entering*] Oh, I am so glad to see you,
Mrs. de Saint-Genis!

MRS. DE SAINT-GENIS: How do you do, child; how
do you do?

BLANCHE: Give me a good hug!

MRS. DE SAINT-GENIS: Of course I will.

BLANCHE: You know I love you so much.

MRS. DE SAINT-GENIS: Come, Blanche, dear, don't
get so excited. I have come to-day to talk seriously
with you; so listen to me like the great big woman
you are. It is time, at your age, to use a little reason.
[*She sits down*] My son loves you, child; I tell you
very frankly, he loves you a great deal. Don't interrupt me. I know, too, that you feel somewhat the
same toward him—a light, thoughtless affection such
as young girls often have when they meet a nice
young man.

BLANCHE: Oh, Mrs. de Saint-Genis, you are dis-
paraging a feeling which goes very much deeper than
that.

MRS. DE SAINT-GENIS: Well, I was wrong, then.
Love is a very fine thing, very vague and poetic; but
a passion, however great it may be, never lasts very
long, and never gets anywhere. I know what I am

talking about. You can't pay the rent and the baker's
bill with that kind of currency. You know I am not
rich; my son's position is not yet assured; and certain
deplorable circumstances have endangered your domestic situation, and perhaps will ruin you. Now,
my child, I want to ask you if under these circumstances it would be very discreet to go on with a
marriage which promises so unfavorably?

BLANCHE: [*Quickly*] We ought to be married, Mrs.
de Saint-Genis, and we are going to be.

MRS. DE SAINT-GENIS: [*Sweetly*] You are, if I
say so.

BLANCHE: You will give your consent.

MRS. DE SAINT-GENIS: I don't think so.

BLANCHE: Yes, Mrs. de Saint-Genis; yes, you will!
There are affections so sincere that even a mother
has no right to come between them. There are
promises so sacred that a man is dishonored if he
does not fulfil them.

MRS. DE SAINT-GENIS: What promises are you talking about? [*Silence*] I admit, if that suits you, that
a marriage was planned between you and my son;
but it was subject to certain conditions, and it is not
my fault if you cannot live up to them. I was hoping,
child, you would think of that yourself. I was hoping you would bow in submission before a changed
situation which is nobody's fault, but which necessarily alters the expectations of you both.

BLANCHE: George does not talk that way, Mrs.
de Saint-Genis. His expectations are the same as
ever. The loss of our money hasn't affected him in
the least bit, and I think he is only more eager to
marry me.

MRS. DE SAINT-GENIS: Leave my son out of the
matter, won't you? I tell him every day he is too
young yet to know what he does or says.

BLANCHE: George is twenty-three.

MRS. DE SAINT-GENIS: Twenty-three! Indeed!

BLANCHE: At that age, Mrs. de Saint-Genis, a man
has passions, and will-power, and certain rights.

MRS. DE SAINT-GENIS: You insist on talking about
my son—very well, we'll talk about him. Are you so
sure of his feelings? I don't see them in the same
light as you. Placed, as he is, between an affection
which is dear to him and a future in which he is
interested, the poor boy is uncertain, hesitating.

BLANCHE: [*Rising suddenly*] You are deceiving
me, Mrs. de Saint-Genis.

MRS. DE SAINT-GENIS: No, child, I am not deceiving you—no, indeed! I have given my son the benefit
of my serious reflection, and I should be sorry for
him if he did not make good use of it. Another
thing: do we ever know what is going on in a man's
brain? George is no more sincere than the next
man. Perhaps he is only waiting for my order to get
out of an embarrassing situation.

BLANCHE: Well, give him that order.

MRS. DE SAINT-GENIS: He would obey it.

BLANCHE: No, Mrs. de Saint-Genis.

MRS. DE SAINT-GENIS: I assure you he would, even if reluctantly.

BLANCHE: If it comes to that, Mrs. de Saint-Genis, your son would decide to confess to you something he has withheld out of respect for me.

MRS. DE SAINT-GENIS: What confession? [*Silence*] So! I thought you would be the first one to break the reserve on that subject. You may spare yourself any delicate confidence. I know all about it. [Blanche, *confused and blushing, runs to* Mrs. de Saint-Genis *and throws herself at her feet, with her head on the older woman's knees;* Mrs. de Saint-Genis *rebukes her, caressing her all the while*] I don't care to inquire, child, whether you or George was responsible. It is your mother and I who are at fault, for leaving you two children together when you should have been watched. You see, I do not attach any undue importance to the result of a moment of forgetfulness, justified by your youth, and all the surrounding circumstances. You ought to want your fault to remain a secret; my son is an honorable man who would never betray you. So much said, the next question is: is it necessary for both of you to sacrifice your whole lives for the sake of a slip? Wouldn't it be better to forget it?

BLANCHE: [*Rising*] Never.

[*A pause*]

MRS. DE SAINT-GENIS: [*Has risen and her tone changes*] You will not be surprised, Blanche, if my son doesn't come here any more.

BLANCHE: I want to hear that from *him*.

MRS. DE SAINT-GENIS: Are you hoping he will disobey his mother?

BLANCHE: Yes; to do his duty.

MRS. DE SAINT-GENIS: You should not have forgotten yours, in the first place.

BLANCHE: Go ahead, wound me, humiliate me; I know I deserve it.

MRS. DE SAINT-GENIS: I feel more like pitying you, Blanche, than hurting you. But it seems to me that a young girl, after a misfortune like yours, should bow her head and submit.

BLANCHE: You shall see, Mrs. de Saint-Genis, what a young girl can do toward getting the reparation due her.

MRS. DE SAINT-GENIS: Well, what will you do?

BLANCHE: I'll find out first whether your son has two kinds of talk, one for you and another for me. I don't say yet that he has. He knows what you want, and so he conceals his own thoughts from you. But if I am dealing with a coward who hides behind his mother's skirts, he needn't think he can get rid of me so easily. Everywhere, everywhere he goes, I shall injure him. I'll ruin his standing, and spoil his future.

MRS. DE SAINT-GENIS: You'll get yourself talked about that way; that's all. Perhaps that's what you want to do. Fortunately, your mother will stop that. She'll think a stain on the family's name is enough without adding a scandal to it. Good day, Blanche.

BLANCHE: [*Holding her*] Don't go, Mrs. de Saint-Genis.

MRS. DE SAINT-GENIS: [*Sweetly*] We have nothing more to say.

BLANCHE: Stay here. See, I am weeping! I am suffering! Feel my hand; I am burning up with fever.

MRS. DE SAINT-GENIS: Yes; I understand the frame of mind you are in; but that will pass. Whereas, if you should be married to my son, your regrets and his would last forever.

BLANCHE: We love each other.

MRS. DE SAINT-GENIS: To-day, yes—but to-morrow?

BLANCHE: Give us your consent, I implore you.

MRS. DE SAINT-GENIS: Must I repeat that word you just said to me? Never!

[Blanche *leaves her and walks back and forth across the stage in a state of great emotion and violent grief; then she drops into an armchair*]

MRS. DE SAINT-GENIS: [*Going up to* Blanche] I am very sorry, child, to seem so cruel and to leave you in this condition. But I am right; absolutely right. A woman of my age and experience, who has seen all there is to see in this world, knows the true value of things and doesn't exaggerate one thing at the expense of another.

BLANCHE: [*Throwing herself on her knees*] Listen, Mrs. de Saint-Genis. What will become of me if your son does not marry me? It is his duty. There is nothing nobler or kinder in a man than to cling to the woman he loves. Believe me, if it were an ordinary engagement, I shouldn't humiliate myself to the extent of holding him back. Yes, I should break my heart rather than offer it to one who disdained it, or was unworthy of it. But your son must marry me; I say again it is his duty. Everything gives way before that fact. You speak about the future. The future will be as he pleases. I am thinking only of the past. I should die of shame and sorrow.

MRS. DE SAINT-GENIS: Child that you are, to speak of dying at your age! Come, get up and listen to me now. I see that you really do love my son more than I thought, if you still cling to a boy who is almost poverty-stricken. But if I should consent to this marriage, in a year—yes, in six months, you would bitterly reproach me for my weakness. Love would pass, but you would have a household still. What do you think would be your lot then? Shabby, worried, vulgar, nursing your children yourself, while your discontented husband would be reproaching you all the time on account of the sacrifice he had made for you. Do what I ask. Make the sacrifice yourself instead. Can't you see how different all will be then? George will not have abandoned you; it will be you who have dismissed him generously. He will be under obligation to you. You will hold forever a place way down deep in his heart. Men always remain sensitive to the memory of a woman they have truly loved, even for an hour. It is so rare! And what will happen to you after that? I'll tell you. Little by little the love for my son, which seems so tremendous to you just now, will disappear. Yes; quicker than you think. You are young, pretty, full of charm for young men. Ten, yes, twenty, young fellows will come along. You will choose, not the most attractive, but the one who is best off. And on your wedding day you will think of me and say to yourself: "Mrs. de Saint-Genis was right."

BLANCHE: What kind of a woman are you, Mrs. de Saint-Genis, to give me such advice as that? What would your son say if he knew it? I would rather be his mistress than the wife of another man.

MRS. DE SAINT-GENIS: His mistress! Pretty words to come from you! My son shall know what you have just said. It's one more sign of your waywardness.

BLANCHE: No, no, Mrs. de Saint-Genis; don't repeat that awful word. I blushed when I said it.

MRS. DE SAINT-GENIS: His mistress! Evidently you can stand anything; so I am going to tell you all. I should never have broken off your marriage for a matter of dollars and cents. But I want my son to have a wife whose past is above suspicion, and who will give him no anxiety for the future. [She goes toward the door]

BLANCHE: Oh, oh, oh! You insult me, Mrs. de Saint-Genis, without any reason—without pity!

MRS. DE SAINT-GENIS: Let me go, young woman. His mistress! Why, that's the talk of a fallen woman!

[She repulses Blanche gently and goes out]

BLANCHE: A fallen woman! She dares to call me—— Oh, God! [She bursts into tears] Oh, it's all over now! George is weak, his mother controls him . . . he will obey her. A fallen woman! [She weeps increasingly] A fine fellow like him! Not at all like that woman! And yet under her thumb! . . . I can't stand it. A little while ago my hands were burning hot; now they are cold as ice. [She rings and comes to the front of the stage; she speaks in a broken voice] He is young . . . barely twenty-three . . . gentle, refined, charming . . . some other woman will love him and marry him.

ROSALIE: [Entering] Is it you, dearie, who rang for me?

BLANCHE: [Going to her sadly] I'm cold, nursey. Throw something over me.

ROSALIE: [Having scrutinized her] I'm going to put you to bed; that'll be much better.

BLANCHE: No.

ROSALIE: Do as I tell you, if you don't want to be sick.

BLANCHE: Oh, yes; I am going to be sick.

ROSALIE: Come, Rosalie is going to undress you. It won't be the first time.

BLANCHE: Call Mama.

ROSALIE: You don't need your mother; I'm here.

BLANCHE: I'm not going to be married, Rosalie.

ROSALIE: Well, it's an ill wind that blows no good!

We've spoiled you; but not enough to make you prefer that she-devil and her monkey. That's what they are. That marriage, I tell you, wasn't the right kind for you. If they had listened to your father and me, it wouldn't have been considered a minute.

BLANCHE: [Out of her head] My father! I see my father now! He's reaching out his arms to me and beckoning me to come with him.

ROSALIE: Come and lie down, Blanchy.

BLANCHE: Your Blanchy is a fallen woman! You didn't know it. I'm a fallen woman!

ROSALIE: Don't talk that way, dearie; it isn't nice. Come, come with your old nursey.

BLANCHE: Oh, I can't bear it! [She cries out] Marie! Marie! Marie!

[She grows weak in Rosalie's arms and slips little by little to the floor]

MARIE: [Entering and throwing herself down by her sister] Blanche! Blanche!

ROSALIE: Keep still, girlie; it's no use, she can't hear. Take her up gently, poor lamb, and we'll put her to bed.

BLANCHE: [Murmuring] Fallen woman!

MRS. VIGNERON: [Appearing] What's the matter? [She throws herself down by Blanche]

ROSALIE: Come away from her, ma'am; you'll bother us more than you'll help.

[Judith appears]

MRS. VIGNERON: Judith, come here. [They walk aside together] You were right, Judith. We've got nothing in the world. They're putting your sister to bed; to-morrow it will be your turn, and the next day mine. You still think the best way is to settle everything?

JUDITH: Yes; I still think so.

MRS. VIGNERON: Good. Take Rosalie with you and go to see Mr. Bourdon. Tell him I accept everything, approve everything, and all I want now is to have it over with. You can add that we are just as much in a hurry as he is. That's your idea, too?

JUDITH: That's my idea.

MRS. VIGNERON: Go ahead then. [They separate] I should like to keep what belongs to me; but the first thing is to save my children.

CURTAIN

ACT IV.

A cheaply furnished dining-room, with a shabby-genteel look. Here and there a few chairs; in one place everything is reminiscent of the furniture of the previous acts, and plainly not fitting these new surroundings. There are two single doors, one at the left and the other at the back. At the rear, to the right, a mahogany table covered with red oil-

cloth stands against the wall; on this table appears a loaf of bread; also cups and other dishes.

ROSALIE: Come in, Mr. Merckens. They'll be glad to see somebody they know.

MERCKENS: [*Having looked about him*] Well, well! The lawyer wasn't lying to me. This is poverty, sure enough!

ROSALIE: You're looking at our new home? Yes, it isn't very much! Oh, Lord; yesterday and to-day are two different things.

MERCKENS: What's happened to the family?

ROSALIE: Ruined, Mr. Merckens. My poor missus and the girls have lost everything. I'm not saying how it happened, but I've got my opinion, and I'll keep it, too. You see, when business men get into a house where a person has just died, you may as well say: "Here come the vultures." They don't leave anything they can carry away.

MERCKENS: It isn't a pleasant place any more, eh, Rosalie?

ROSALIE: Not for anybody, Mr. Merckens, not for anybody.

MERCKENS: Why don't you find another place?

ROSALIE: How can the girls get along without me, any more than I can without them? I'm one more mouth to be fed, true enough; but you bet I earn what I eat. You mustn't think you can stay to luncheon with us, Mr. Merckens. In the old days, when I saw you coming at this hour, I didn't need any orders to know what to do; you'd find your place ready at the table; but things are different now. I'll go and tell Mrs. Vigneron you are here.

MERCKENS: No; don't bother Mrs. Vigneron. Just tell Miss Judith I am here.

[*Judith enters*]

ROSALIE: Here she is now.

JUDITH: How do you do, Mr. Merckens?

[*Merckens bows*]

ROSALIE: But of course, if a good cup of coffee will do you, we can still offer you that.

JUDITH: Leave us, Rosalie——

[*Rosalie goes out*]

JUDITH: [*To Merckens*] First of all, I've a little bone to pick with you, and then that'll be out of the way. I wrote to you twice asking you to come and see me. Once ought to be enough.

MERCKENS: [*Awkwardly*] Are you sure you wrote me twice?

JUDITH: You know well I did.

MERCKENS: No, really; your first letter didn't reach me.

JUDITH: Well, never mind. I don't need to tell you the conditions we are reduced to; you saw the moment you came in.

MERCKENS: [*Half serious, half joking*] Tell me about it.

JUDITH: It's a story you wouldn't be interested in, and it wouldn't be pleasant for me to tell. In a word, we didn't have money enough to fight for our

rights; we had to have a hundred thousand francs in cash.

MERCKENS: Why didn't you tell me? I would have found the money.

JUDITH: It's too late now. Please sit down. Mr. Merckens, you have seen, and you remember, our family life. We were very happy; very fond of one another; we knew very few people outside, and cared to know none. We didn't think that some day we should have need of acquaintances, and that then we shouldn't have any. [Merckens *looks at his watch*] Are you in a hurry?

MERCKENS: Yes; I am. Will you please cut the story short? You wanted to see me; here I am. You want to ask me something. What is it? Perhaps it would be just as well for me to tell you that I am not a very obliging person.

JUDITH: Shall I go on?

MERCKENS: Yes, certainly; go ahead.

JUDITH: Here is what I first thought of; I'll start with the simplest and surest thing. I am thinking of turning to account the fine lessons you have given me, by giving lessons myself.

MERCKENS: [*Touching her knee*] What, poor child—you've got down to that?

JUDITH: Come, come, Mr. Merckens; please call me "Miss," as you have been used to do, and answer me seriously.

MERCKENS: Lessons! In the first place, are you capable of giving lessons? I'm not so sure of it. But let's suppose you are. Would you do what is necessary to get pupils? To get them, you have to play the part of a beggar. You don't get any by being dignified and putting on airs. But it is possible that people might take pity on you, and in four or five years—not before—you might have enough pupils. Your pupils would as often as not be disagreeable; their parents would nearly always be brutes. What is a poor little music teacher to a lot of Philistines that don't even know what C major is? You needn't look any farther, for instance, than your dad. . . .

JUDITH: We won't speak of my father.

MERCKENS: Surely a fellow can laugh a little— he didn't leave you anything.

[*A pause*]

JUDITH: Let's put aside the question of music lessons a minute; we can come back to that. Now in what I am going to say to you, Mr. Merckens, please don't think I am prompted by vanity or presumption; I am just trying to make use of what talent I have for music. I have composed a good deal; you know that. With the little things I've already written, and others I can produce, can't I get a living for my family?

MERCKENS: [*After laughing*] Look at me. [*He laughs again*] Never, never say that again; understand? I mean what you have just said to me. You'd be the laughing-stock of the whole world. [*He laughs again*] Earn a living! Is that all?

JUDITH: No, it isn't. We were talking once about a profession that didn't strike me favorably then, and still doesn't more than half appeal to me. But the way my family is fixed, I ought not to hesitate at anything to help them out. The stage?

MERCKENS: Too late.

JUDITH: Why can't I do as others have—women who felt undecided at first, but summoned up their courage and went into it?

MERCKENS: Too late.

JUDITH: Perhaps I have natural qualities—and lack only work and experience?

MERCKENS: Too late. It's no use thinking of the stage without preparing for it a long time. You'll never be an artist. It isn't in you. As you are now, all you'd find on the stage would be disillusionment . . . or adventures; and that isn't what you are after, is it?

JUDITH: But what can I do, then?

MERCKENS: Nothing. I see the fix you are in. You're not the first one I've seen in the same situation, and made the same reply to. There are no resources for a woman; or, at least, only one. Now I'll tell you the whole truth in one sentence. If you are good, people will respect you without doing anything for you; and if you're not, they'll do things for you without respecting you. There's no other way about it. Are you going to take up the subject of giving lessons again?

JUDITH: It's no use. I'm sorry to have bothered you.

MERCKENS: You want me to go?

JUDITH: I shan't stop you.

MERCKENS: Good-by, Miss Judith.

JUDITH: Good-by, Mr. Merckens.

MERCKENS: [At the door] There was nothing else to tell her.

MARIE: [Entering] Well?

JUDITH: Well, if Mr. Merckens is right, and if things are as he says, we aren't out of our difficulties yet. Meanwhile, here are all my plans upset; those you know of, and another one I had kept to myself.

MARIE: What other?

JUDITH: What's the use telling you?

MARIE: Tell me, anyway.

JUDITH: I did think, for a while, of making use of my voice, by going on the stage.

MARIE: You, sister, on the stage!

JUDITH: Well, why not? We must be doing something, and we've got to take what comes. We can't wait till we have got down to our last cent. Mama isn't able to go to work, and furthermore we don't want her to. Who knows whether poor Blanche will ever recover her reason? Well, then, there's just you and me; and what is there you can do, dearie? You would have to work twelve hours a day to earn a franc and a half.

MARIE: Tell me, really and truly, what you think of Blanche's condition? How do you find her?

JUDITH: One day better and the next day worse. We expect her to recognize us any moment; but as yet she doesn't seem to see any one or hear anything. I've been thinking over this misfortune; and perhaps we have escaped a worse one. If Blanche, in that condition, had heard of the marriage of Mr. de Saint-Genis, might it not have killed her? She is alive. That's the main thing. We have her still with us. If we must always take care of her, we will. If we must go hungry for her, we'll do that, too. She isn't our sister now—she's our little girl.

MARIE: How good you are, sister; I love you so much!

[They embrace]

JUDITH: I love you, too. At times I am blunt; but I always have you here, in my heart. It seems to me that I, the eldest sister—"big sister," as you call me—I am the one who should find a way out of our troubles. I don't know how to do it. I've looked, and I can't find a way. If the only thing needed were to go through fire and water for the rest of you, I should have done that before now.

[A pause]

MARIE: Has Mama said anything about a visit from Mr. Bourdon?

JUDITH: No. What was he doing here?

MARIE: Mr. Teissier sent him to ask me to be his wife.

JUDITH: I'm not surprised. It was easy enough to see that Mr. Teissier took a liking to you, and sooner or later the idea of marriage was bound to come to him.

MARIE: Would you advise me to accept him?

JUDITH: You mustn't ask my advice on that point. You are the one concerned; it is for you to decide. Think it over well, look at it from all sides, but by all means think only of yourself. If you are frightened at our situation, and you look back regretfully to the times when we had plenty of money, marry Mr. Teissier. He will make you pay dearly enough for your comfort and security. But if I understand you, and the way you love your mother and sisters, and how you could do for them what would be repulsive if you alone were concerned, we should be very wrong—all the guiltier—to advise you to make the greatest sacrifice a woman can make.

MARIE: What you say is right from the heart; kiss me again.

[Rosalie *enters at the rear; in one hand she carries a coffee-pot, in the other a casserole full of milk; she places them on the table, and then draws near the two sisters and watches them, sighing;* Marie *and* Judith *separate*]

JUDITH: Is luncheon ready?

ROSALIE: Yes, miss. I'll serve it whenever you wish.

MARIE: Judith is going to help you with the table, Rosalie.

[Judith *and* Rosalie *carry the table to the front of the stage, placing it at the right;* Rosalie *arranges the cups and serves the coffee while* Judith *places the chairs.* Marie *meanwhile, goes to the door at the left and opens it.* Blanche *comes in, followed by her mother.* Blanche *is pale, limp, and stares stupidly, her attitude being that of a harmless insane person.* Mrs. Vigneron *is aged and whitened.* Marie *helps* Blanche *to a place, and then they sit down one by one, except* Rosalie, *who takes her coffee standing. There is a prolonged silence, and an atmosphere of utter desolation*]

MRS. VIGNERON: [*Suddenly bursting out*] Oh, children; if your father could see us!

[*Tears and sobbing. At that moment* Bourdon *steps quietly into the room*]

ROSALIE: [*To* Bourdon] How did you get in?

BOURDON: By the open door. You ought not leave your outside door open. Thieves could steal everything you've got.

ROSALIE: [*Speaking directly at him*] No fear of that. That job has been done—and done brown.

BOURDON: [*To* Mrs. Vigneron, *who has risen*] Don't let me disturb you, madam; I'll wait until you have finished luncheon.

MRS. VIGNERON: [*Going to him*] What have you got to say to me, Mr. Bourdon?

BOURDON: [*In a low tone*] This time, madam, I've come for Teissier, regarding a matter very dear to him. I assume you have let your daughter know about the offer I spoke about?

MRS. VIGNERON: Certainly.

BOURDON: Do I have your permission to renew the offer to her, in your presence?

MRS. VIGNERON: Very well, you have my consent. Judith, dear, take your sister away. Marie, Mr. Bourdon wishes to speak with us.

[Judith *leads* Blanche *out*]

BOURDON: [*To* Marie] You mother has told you, young lady, of the desire expressed by Mr. Teissier?

MARIE: Yes, sir.

BOURDON: Of your own free will you have declined this proposal of marriage?

MARIE: Of my own free will.

BOURDON: Good! Good! I'm glad it's that way. For a moment, I was afraid, when you refused such a handsome offer, that your mother and sisters had conspired to keep you with them—not out of jealousy, but in a spirit of misdirected affection. If you have come to a definite, unalterable decision, of your own accord, I don't see any use in going further into the matter.

[*A silence*]

MRS. VIGNERON: Don't be afraid, dear; answer frankly just what you think. [*Another silence*]

BOURDON: In case you regret your first decision, young lady—and that's easy to explain—I am offering you a chance to change your mind. You had better take advantage of it.

MARIE: You must tell Mr. Teissier for me that I like him better for his persistence, but that I still wish some time to think it over.

BOURDON: Well! That's a reasonable answer,

madam—very sensible, indeed.—That doesn't look like the categorical refusal you gave me.

MRS. VIGNERON: My daughter may have changed her mind. But she should know that I don't approve of it.

BOURDON: Say no more, madam. Leave the young lady to her own devices. Later on she might reproach you because she followed your wishes. [*Returning to* Marie] I understand perfectly, young lady, why this marriage must present some objectionable features to you, and why you have been in no hurry to enter it. Unfortunately, Teissier is not twenty years old, like yourself—indeed, that is your greatest cause for complaint—and at his age, a man isn't willing to have things delayed.

MARIE: Mr. Bourdon, I want to know, and I beg you will tell me sincerely, whether Mr. Teissier is an honest man.

BOURDON: An honest man! What do you mean by that? In case you should marry Mr. Teissier, I should not advise you to place implicit confidence in a simple promise; but there are lawyers to draw up contracts establishing the rights of the parties concerned. Have I answered your question?

MARIE: No; you didn't understand me. When a young woman says "an honest man," she thinks of a good many things.

BOURDON: Do you want to know whether Teissier has made his money in an honorable way?

MARIE: Yes; I want to be assured on that point, as well as some others.

BOURDON: Why should that worry you? If you were to look into all the fortunes in France, there aren't a hundred—no, not fifty—that would stand a close examination. I speak as a man who has been through the mill. Teissier has been in business all his life; he has amassed a considerable sum, and nobody would dream of attacking his right to it. That's all you need to know.

MARIE: What is Mr. Teissier's ordinary conduct? What are his tastes and his habits?

BOURDON: Just the tastes and habits of any man of his age. I don't think you have anything to fear on that score. I see now what you are driving at. Believe me, as a husband Teissier will have rather too much than too little virtue. I leave it to your mother.

MRS. VIGNERON: It occurs to me, to ask what interest you have in this marriage, Mr. Bourdon?

BOURDON: What interest, madam? Only the welfare of this young lady, and yours, at the same time.

MRS. VIGNERON: It's rather late, isn't it, to show such devotion for us?

BOURDON: Madam, you are still thinking of that wretched business. I know everything went about as badly as it could. But was it my fault that you were unable to fight for your husband's estate? You had to give way to the law of the strongest, that's all. To-day, this law has shifted in your favor. It happens that your daughter has made a conquest of an old man, who will grant anything to be able to spend his remaining days with her. The whole situation favors you. You've got the trumps. Play 'em. Do I need to tell you, madam, that we lawyers know neither the weak nor the strong; that absolute impartiality is a duty we never depart from? Nevertheless, I don't think I do wrong, even though I am Teissier's attorney, to stipulate for your daughter all the advantages she is in a position to demand. [*Returning to* Marie] You heard what I have just said to your mother, miss. Put whatever questions you wish to me; but particularly the question which is really the most important—the question of money. I'm listening.

MARIE: No; you speak.

BOURDON: [*With a half-smile*] I'm here to listen to you, and advise you.

MARIE: It would be painful for me to talk about it.

BOURDON: [*Smiling*] Nonsense! What you want to know is what Mr. Teissier is worth, down to a cent, isn't it?

MARIE: It's enough, I know, without being told.

BOURDON: Right you are. Teissier is rich, very rich. Why, he's richer, the old fox, than he himself knows. Come, now, miss, I'm waiting for you.

MARIE: Of course Mr. Teissier has told you of his intentions?

BOURDON: Yes; but I must know yours, too. It's always fun for us lawyers to see the parties fighting tooth and nail over the terms.

MARIE: Please don't add to my embarrassment. If this marriage must take place, I had rather run my chances than make the conditions.

BOURDON: [*Smiling continually*] Really! [Marie *looks at him fixedly*] I don't doubt your scruples, miss. When they are so plainly shown, we are forced to believe them sincere. But Teissier doesn't think you are marrying him for his beauty. So he is already willing to make a settlement on you. But this settlement, I hasten to tell you, is not sufficient. You are making a bargain, are you not? Or, if that word hurts you, at any rate a speculation. And you ought to reap all the benefits of it. So it is only just—and you can insist—that when Teissier marries you, he shall make you half-owner of all he possesses, irrevocably and incontestably, so that you will receive one-half after he dies. Then all you would have to do would be to pray that the time would not be too long deferred. [*Turning to* Mrs. Vigneron] You heard what I have just told your daughter, madam?

MRS. VIGNERON: I heard.

BOURDON: What do you think?

MRS. VIGNERON: If you want to know, Mr. Bourdon, I think instead of promising my daughter half Mr. Teissier's fortune, you would have done better to have saved her father's for her.

BOURDON: Can't get away from that subject, eh, madam? [*Returning to* Marie] Well, miss, now you know the great advantages in store for you in the near future. I am wondering what objections you can find now. I can't think of any. Sentimental objections? I am speaking, I think, to a sensible young woman, well brought up, without foolish notions. You ought to know there is no such thing as love. I never met with it. This world is made up of businesses. Marriage is a business, just like the rest, and the chances offered you to-day will never come your way again.

MARIE: In the conversations you have had with Mr. Teissier, has he said anything about my family?

BOURDON: About your family? No. [*In a low tone*] Do they want something, too?

MARIE: Mr. Teissier ought to know that I would never consent to separate from them.

BOURDON: Why should you? Your sisters are nice girls, and your mother is very agreeable. Besides, Teissier has every reason not to want to leave a young wife with idle moments on her hands. Now, miss, be ready for what remains for me to tell you. Teissier came here with me. He is outside. He is waiting for a reply, and this time it must be a definite answer. You will take long chances in doing otherwise. So it is a "yes" or "no" that I am asking for.

MRS. VIGNERON: That's enough of that, Mr. Bourdon. I was willing enough for you to tell my daughter whatever propositions were made to her. Whether she accepts them or not, is her business. But I don't intend that she shall be surprised into acceptance, or do anything in a moment of weakness or emotion. Moreover, you must know that I reserve the right to have a talk with her and tell her certain things which would be out of place with you here—things a mother can tell her child, and must tell, when they are alone. One thing I can tell you: I haven't brought up a girl to be twenty—a girl full of health and fine spirit—only to hand her over to an old man.

BOURDON: To whom are you going to give her? To hear you talk, madam, anyone might think you had your pockets full of sons-in-law, and that your daughters' only trouble was to choose between them. Why was it that the marriage of one of them—a marriage that seemed practically settled—fell through? Lack of money. And lack of money, madam, is just what will keep every one of your daughters an old maid.

MRS. VIGNERON: You're wrong. I had nothing, and neither did my husband. He married me all the same, and we have been very happy.

BOURDON: It is true you have had four children. But if your husband were still in this world, madam, he would disagree with you—perhaps for the first time. When he saw the situation of his daughters, he would be frightened—for, whatever you may think of it, it is perplexing and dangerous. He would put a true value on Mr. Teissier's proposal. To be sure, it is not perfect; but it is more than acceptable. It is reassuring for the present and

[*Looking at* Marie] full of dazzling prospects for the future. I know well enough that it's easy to say what dead people might or mightn't do, but this young lady's father, whose heart was just as big as yours, had all the experience that you lack. He knew life. He knew that you pay for what you get in this world. And, in the end, his thoughts to-day would be something like this: "I have lived for my family; I died for them; surely my daughter can sacrifice a few years for them."

MARIE: [*With her eyes full of tears*] Tell Mr. Teissier I accept.

BOURDON: Come now, young lady, you're giving yourself a great deal of trouble over making your fortune. Here is your contract. I drew it up in advance, without knowing whether I should be paid for my trouble. Read it over carefully and soberly. All it needs is Teissier's signature; and I'll attend to that. I was your father's lawyer, and I'm hoping to be yours. I'll go find Teissier and bring him here. [*He goes out*]

MARIE: [*To her mother*] Kiss me—but don't say anything. Don't take away my courage. I've no more than I need, as it is. You must see that Mr. Bourdon is right. This marriage is our salvation. I'm ashamed —oh, so ashamed!—to do it; but I should always feel guilty if I did not. Mother dear, could you, at your age, begin to live another life of misery and privation? Yes, yes, I know—you are full of courage! But Blanche—Blanche, the poor child—we can't ask her to have courage—not her. What remorse I should have to suffer later, if her health were to demand care that we couldn't give her! And Judith! Oh, I'm thinking of Judith, too. Who knows what would become of a young girl, the best, the highest-minded girl in the world, if she should be driven to extremes, and should lose her fear—of things. Come, I feel a weight off my shoulders now that it's done. It will be just as he wishes—a dishonest, self-seeking marriage—and a sad one, too. But still I prefer a little shame and regret that I know about to a host of terrors of all kinds that might end in a terrible misfortune. Don't cry any more; don't let them see that you have been crying.

[*Bourdon comes in, followed by* Teissier. Teissier, *smiling, goes toward* Marie; *but* Bourdon *stops him and motions that he must first speak to* Mrs. Vigneron]

TEISSIER: How do you do, madam? [*Going to* Marie] Is it really true, what Bourdon just told me —that you will be my wife?

MARIE: It is true.

TEISSIER: A mighty good decision—you won't change your mind by to-morrow, will you? [*She offers him her hand; he kisses her on both cheeks*] Don't blush. That's the way we do in the village I came from. A man kisses his bride-to-be first on the right cheek, saying, "Here's one for the Mayor"; and then one on the left cheek, saying, "Here's one for the priest." [Marie *smiles*: Teissier *goes over to* Mrs. Vigneron] If you are willing, madam, we'll publish the banns to-morrow. Bourdon will make us a little contract—won't you, Bourdon? [Bourdon *replies with a significant gesture*] And three weeks from now your second daughter will be Mrs. Teissier.

[Rosalie *enters*]

MRS. VIGNERON: What is it, Rosalie?

ROSALIE: Will you see Mr. Dupuis, ma'am?

MRS. VIGNERON: Mr. Dupuis? The house-furnisher?

ROSALIE: Yes, ma'am.

MRS. VIGNERON: What does he want of us?

ROSALIE: You owe him money, ma'am. At least, he says so. Another vulture, sure as you live!

MRS. VIGNERON: We owe Mr. Dupuis nothing—do you hear?—nothing! Tell him I don't want to see him.

TEISSIER: Yes, madam, yes; you must see Mr. Dupuis. Either there is really something due him, in spite of what you think, or Mr. Dupuis is mistaken, in which case it won't be out of place to show him his error. You are not alone; you have a man with you now. Show Mr. Dupuis in. Miss Marie is going to receive him. She will soon be mistress of a house, and I want to see how she will act. Come, Bourdon. Let's leave your daughter with Mr. Dupuis.

[Mrs. Vigneron *and* Bourdon *go out at the left*]

TEISSIER: [*To* Marie] I'll be here, behind this door; I won't miss a word. [*He hides behind the door*]

DUPUIS: [*Entering*] How do you do, Miss Marie?

MARIE: How do you do, Mr. Dupuis?

DUPUIS: Is your mother well?

MARIE: Pretty well, thank you.

DUPUIS: Your sisters are well?

MARIE: Yes.

DUPUIS: I don't need to ask how you are; you're as fresh and rosy as a new-born babe.

MARIE: My mother told me to receive you for her, Mr. Dupuis. Tell me as soon as possible what brings you here.

DUPUIS: Can't you make a little guess as to what brings me here?

MARIE: No, really.

DUPUIS: Is that so? Don't you say to yourself, that if I come here, after so long a time has passed, it must be that I need money?

MARIE: Explain yourself.

DUPUIS: I would have given a whole lot—yes, I would, young lady—not to have to make this visit. When I heard of your father's death, I said to my wife: "I believe Mr. Vigneron still owes us something—but what of it?—it isn't much, and we won't die if we set it down to profit and loss." That's the way I do with my good customers. Mr. Vigneron was a good customer; never had the least trouble with him; that's the way things ought to be between honest folks. Unfortunately, you know how business is—up one day and down the next; well, it isn't good just now. Understand?

MARIE: I'm pretty certain, Mr. Dupuis, that my father settled everything with you.

DUPUIS: Don't say that—you hurt me.

MARIE: Nevertheless, I'm as sure as any one can be that my father squared his account with you.

DUPUIS: Be careful; you'll get me angry. It's only a matter of two thousand francs. The amount isn't worth the trouble. Perhaps you are embarrassed at this moment. Then say so. I haven't come to take your last cent. Just let your mother give me a note for two thousand francs, at three months. Her signature is the same as ready money to me.

MARIE: I'll tell my mother you are here to collect two thousand francs. But I tell you again you are mistaken. I'm certain we don't owe it.

DUPUIS: Well, young lady, I don't leave here till I get it. I came politely, with my hat in my hand [He puts it on] and you seem to be treating me like a robber. Those ways don't go with me. You'd better find your mother and make her give me two thousand francs—or a note—I'm still willing to take her note—or Mr. Dupuis will have a fit of anger that will shake the house.

[Teissier enters; Dupuis, surprised and quickly intimidated by his appearance, takes off his hat again]

TEISSIER: Keep your hat on. There's no ceremony in business. You've got your bill with you?

DUPUIS: Certainly, sir, I have my bill.

TEISSIER: Let's have it.

DUPUIS: Shall I give my bill to this gentleman, miss?

MARIE: Do as he says.

TEISSIER: [Reading the bill] "Received of Mrs. Vigneron, two thousand francs to settle her account in full." What kind of bill is this? Don't you usually give an itemized account?

DUPUIS: We can't make out the same bill five or six times, sir. The first one I rendered to Mr. Vigneron contained all the necessary specifications.

TEISSIER: All right. I'm going to pay you. I'll verify the bill when I get home.

DUPUIS: Go ahead, sir, and verify it. Mr. Vigneron should have left his papers in order.

TEISSIER: Yes, he did. [Holding the bill close to his eyes] Dupuis is the name, eh? Is this signature yours? You are Mr. Dupuis?

DUPUIS: Yes, sir.

TEISSIER: I am going to give you your two thousand francs.

DUPUIS: Verify it, sir, if you can. I'll wait till then.

TEISSIER: You're very sure that when Mr. Vigneron died, he still owed you two thousand francs?

DUPUIS: Yes, sir—yes, sir. My wife may have made a mistake in her figures; but I don't think so.

TEISSIER: Your wife has nothing to do with it. It's you who would be liable if you received the same amount twice.

DUPUIS: I don't demand it, sir, if it isn't due me. I am an honest man.

TEISSIER: [Offering him the money] Here's your two thousand francs.

DUPUIS: No; verify it first. I'd rather you would.

TEISSIER: Get out of here! And don't let me see you inside these doors again. Do you hear?

DUPUIS: What's that, sir?

TEISSIER: I tell you not to come back here. Don't be fresh, or you'll regret it.

DUPUIS: Give me back my bill, anyway.

TEISSIER: Look out, or you'll see it again in a courtroom.

DUPUIS: Now that's too much! How dare you—I don't even know who you are—how dare you talk to me like that! I'm going, miss; but you'll hear from me again—and soon! [He puts on his hat and goes out]

TEISSIER: Child, since your father died you've been surrounded by a lot of scoundrels. . . . Let's go and join your family.

CURTAIN

Gerhart Hauptmann

(1862–1946)

The career of Hauptmann, long considered Germany's greatest modern playwright, is a record of many successes and distinctions, including the Nobel Prize in 1912 and honorary degrees from the universities of Oxford, Leipzig, Prague, and Columbia. But there is also a history of fluctuations in his work that has made us suspect the quality of his talent; if anything, we have tended to underrate this writer who was for many years overrated. One sharp critic accused him of having no more constancy than a weather vane, and the charge was vigorously maintained against the man himself, as well as the artist, when, after 1933, Hauptmann allowed his reputation to serve as window dressing for the Hitler regime. No particular importance can be attached to the plays written during the last twenty-five years of his life, and today even the bulk of his work before 1921 rings hollow outside, and apparently also inside, Germany. Hauptmann, nevertheless, went as far in the direction of international importance between 1889 and 1912 as a writer can be carried by keen responsiveness to literary and social currents and by virtuosity.

Hauptmann was largely responsible for giving the naturalist style its high estate in Central Europe for a decade or longer. And more than that, he enlarged the scope of dramatic naturalism in the Western world, directing it into the channels of class-conflict drama with *The Weavers* and of comedy of peasant and proletarian life with such plays as *The Beaver Coat* and *The Conflagration*. Social drama, which came to the fore earlier and was made impressive by Ibsen, was led into the unexplored world of working-class problems by the example of *The Weavers*, Hauptmann's account of an uprising of the Silesian weavers in the eighteen-forties. Since the writing of *The Weavers* in 1892, the modern theatre has represented conflicts between capital and labor with great frequency, and the plays have run the gamut from such moderate studies as Galsworthy's *Strife* to such inflammatory documents as Odets' *Waiting for Lefty*.

Hauptmann, the son of a prosperous innkeeper, was born in the village of Obersalzbrunn in Silesia, and was exposed early in life to the mystical pietism of the Moravian sect. He was in delicate health for many years, and it took him some time to find himself as a young man. After failing in preparatory studies for the university, he turned to science, pursued agronomy for a time on an uncle's estate, and then veered toward the arts. He attended the Art School of Breslau and studied sculpture in Rome,

evidently with no great success, before turning to literature. Marriage to a wealthy girl, who supported him during the four years of their engagement, gave him the leisure to unfold as a writer, to experiment with various types of writing, and to make careful notations on dialect which were to prove useful when he adopted naturalism. His marriage at twenty-three, which lasted ten years, was unhappy, and Hauptmann remarried in 1905.

Hauptmann was attracted as early as 1885 to the scientific realism of the liberal "youngest Germany" group and the Social-Democratic movement. He was also one of many young Germans to feel the attraction of Ibsen and Zola. In Berlin, a literary club called "Through" made strides, and Hauptmann was active in its membership, which included scientists, liberal theologians, and journalists. Finally, he aligned himself with the Freie Bühne, or Free Stage, founded in Berlin by Otto Brahm.

Hauptmann's *Before Sunrise* was produced during the new theatre's first season in 1889. It created a sensation with its study of degeneracy among the Silesian peasants who had been enriched but not improved by the discovery of coal in the area. The style was severely naturalistic in its frankness and its use of dialogue appropriate to the characters. The educated people spoke high German, one character from the German capital talked in the Berlin dialect, and the peasants used the Silesian patois. In content and point of view the play observed Zolaist tenets. Hauptmann placed such great importance on the role of heredity that he made his young hero refuse to marry the heroine whose germ plasm carried a tendency toward alcoholism. Next, between 1890 and 1892, came such plays as *The Reconciliation* and *Lonely Lives*, middle-class studies of domestic misery that recalled Ibsen's social plays, just as *Before Sunrise* recalled Tolstoy's peasant tragedy *The Power of Darkness*. Then Hauptmann struck out in a new direction with *The Weavers* (1892), which won him world-wide fame; and in still another direction with *The Beaver Coat* (1893), a picaresque comedy noteworthy for its satire on Prussian bureaucracy and for the character of Mrs. Wolff, a Falstaff among women.

As though he had not yet displayed all the virtuosity of which he was capable, he started on a new romantic-symbolist track with *The Assumption of Hannele* (1893). This drama of a poor girl's suicide and delirious fantasy was a transitional work. Starting with a grossly naturalistic picture of life in the poorhouse, Hauptmann proceeded to make rich use of the symbolism that was beginning to be favored in literary circles under the influence of French poetry. The child's dying delirium, rendered in terms of her reading of fairy tales and the Bible, was an unusual innovation for a playwright hitherto considered Germany's chief exponent of naturalism.

The poetic plays that followed ranged from *The Sunken Bell,* an allegory on the artist's struggle between commonplace duty and desire for freedom, to legendary or historical dramas such as *Schluck und Jau* (1899), *Poor Henry* (1902), and *The White Savior* (1920). In between, moreover, Hauptmann returned to naturalism with works of varying quality, the best of which are *Drayman Henschel* (1898) and *Rose Bernd* (1903), the tragedy of a girl in the grip of the sexual instinct; and, finally, in *The Rats* (1911), Hauptmann added a half-humorous, half-tragic justification of naturalistic art.

Of the great number of plays—he wrote continuously—*The Weavers* is undoubtedly his most significant. Hauptmann attempted to achieve an air of detachment in his treatment of the starving weavers who go berserk, wreck their employer's home, and then proceed to destroy the newly introduced machines upon which they blame their misfortunes. But in *The Weavers,* perhaps by identification with a grandfather who had been one of the weavers, as well as with the insurgent German Social-Democratic movement, Hauptmann managed to make naturalism not only exciting but compassionate. James Huneker, one of its many admirers, correctly described the play as "a symphony in five movements with one grim, leading motive—hunger."

It is to be regretted that Hauptmann did not find it to his purpose to round out his characters and that his slice-of-life chronicle presents the miseries of the people three times (in the first, second, and fifth acts) and the weavers' revolt twice. It is also true that the play falls back upon the past and that the weavers' course of action contributes nothing to an intelligent treatment of modern realities. Hauptmann, however, could justify his brutish representation of the people on the ground that starvation is not conducive to the development of rich personalities, and that the Silesian workers of the eighteen-forties had too limited an understanding of the Industrial Revolution to resort to anything but elemental revenge and destruction of the machines. As for the repetitiveness of the drama, it could be argued that the grievances of the unfortunates had to be represented as pervasive and as cumulative in effect.

Historically, *The Weavers* is memorable for Hauptmann's use of a collective hero of some seventy characters. Here we find the drama of a group rather than of an individual. Ibsen and the other precursors dealt with the single person, Hauptmann with the mass. In this play, moreover, the group is moved by economic forces, and these are primary in the drama, although they translate themselves into emotion through the characters' suffering and protest. We may well wonder whether Hauptmann himself realized when he wrote *The Weavers* what important innovations he was making; how many subsequent plays would represent the working class; and how many would present the group rather than the individual hero. "If Hauptmann had died after writing *The Weavers,*" wrote Huneker, "he would have been acclaimed a great dramatist."

Staged at the Freie Bühne on February 26, 1893, after a year's litigation with the authorities, the play took the theatre by storm. Shortly thereafter the large Berlin Deutsches Theater signalized its conversion to naturalism by reviving the work with a famous ensemble. Kaiser Wilhelm II removed his imperial arms from the theatre in protest. But the *première* was the occasion of one of the greatest demonstrations ever accorded a play. The audience, led by the Socialist leader August Bebel, punctuated the performance with cheers for the weavers and sang their song "Bloody Justice" with them. The production became a rallying ground for the partisans of labor, even if it would appear that Hauptmann's own convictions were neither strong nor long lasting. The play was also produced with great success at the Théâtre Libre on May 29, 1893. The entire Parisian audience in the orchestra stood up in the fourth act when the weavers entered the manufacturer Dreissiger's house. Antoine was so enthusiastic over his production that he acclaimed the play "the masterpiece of a social drama which is still in its infancy."

BIBLIOGRAPHY: Anita Block, *The Changing World in Plays and Theatre* (pp. 33–39), 1939; Frank W. Chandler, *Modern Continental Writers* (pp. 268–298), 1931; Barrett Clark and George Freedley, *A History of Modern Drama* (pp. 78–85), 1947; John Gassner, *Masters of the Drama* (pp. 446–466), 1945; *Columbia Dictionary of Modern European Literature* (pp. 369–371), 1947; James Huneker, *Iconoclasts* (pp. 182–210); Ludwig Lewisohn, *The Modern Drama* (pp. 110–128), 1921.

THE WEAVERS

By Gerhart Hauptmann

TRANSLATED FROM THE GERMAN BY MARY MORISON

COMPLETE LIST OF CHARACTERS

DREISSIGER, *fustian manufacturer*
MRS. DREISSIGER
PFEIFER, *manager*
NEUMANN, *cashier*
AN APPRENTICE
JOHN, *coachman*
A MAID
  in DREISSIGER'S *employment*
WEINHOLD, *tutor to* DREISSIGER'S *sons*

PASTOR KITTELHAUS
MRS. KITTELHAUS
HEIDE, *Police Superintendent*
KUTSCHE, *policeman*
WELZEL, *publican*
MRS. WELZEL
ANNA WELZEL
WIEGAND, *joiner*

A COMMERCIAL TRAVELER
A PEASANT
A FORESTER
SCHMIDT, *surgeon*
HORNIG, *rag-dealer*
WITTIG, *smith*

WEAVERS

BECKER
MORITZ JAEGER
OLD BAUMERT
MOTHER BAUMERT
BERTHA
EMMA   } BAUMERT
FRITZ, EMMA'S *son (four years old)*

AUGUST BAUMERT
OLD ANSORGE
MRS. HEINRICH
OLD HILSE
MOTHER HILSE
GOTTLIEB HILSE
LUISE, GOTTLIEB'S *wife*

MIELCHEN, *their daughter (six years old)*
REIMANN, *weaver*
HEIBER, *weaver*
A WEAVER'S WIFE
A number of weavers, young and old, of both sexes

The action passes in the forties, at Kaschbach, Peterswaldau and Langenbielau, in the Eulengebirge.

ACT I.

A large whitewashed room on the ground floor of Dreissiger's *house at Peterswaldau, where the weavers deliver their finished webs and the fustian is stored. To the left are uncurtained windows, in the back wall there is a glass door, and to the right another glass door, through which weavers, male and female, and children are passing in and out. All three walls are lined with shelves for the storing of the fustian. Against the right wall stands a long bench, on which a number of weavers have already spread out their cloth. In the order of arrival each presents his piece to be examined by* Pfeifer, Dreissiger's *manager, who stands, with compass and magnifying-glass, behind a large table, on which the web to be inspected is laid. When* Pfeifer *has satisfied himself, the weaver lays the fustian on the scale, and an office apprentice tests its weight. The same boy stores the accepted pieces on the shelves.* Pfeifer *calls out the payment due in each case to* Neumann, *the cashier, who is seated at a small table.*

It is a sultry day toward the end of May. The clock is on the stroke of twelve. Most of the waiting work-people have the air of standing before the bar of justice in torturing expectation of a decision that means life or death to them. They are marked, too, by the anxious timidity characteristic of the receiver of charity, who has suffered many humiliations, and, conscious that he is barely tolerated, has acquired the habit of self-effacement. Add to this an expression on every face that tells of constant, fruitless brooding. There is a general resemblance among the men. They have something about them of the dwarf, something of the schoolmaster. The majority are flat-breasted, short-winded, sallow, and poor-looking—creatures of the loom, their knees bent with much sitting. At a first glance the women show fewer typical traits. They look over-driven, worried, reckless, whereas the men still make some show of a pitiful self-respect; and their clothes are ragged, while the men's are patched and mended. Some of the young girls are not without a certain charm, consisting in a wax-like pallor, a slender figure, and large, projecting, melancholy eyes.

NEUMANN: [*Counting out money*] Comes to one and sevenpence halfpenny.

WEAVER'S WIFE: [*About thirty, emaciated, takes up the money with trembling fingers*] Thank you, sir.

NEUMANN: [*Seeing that she does not move on*] Well, something wrong this time, too?

WEAVER'S WIFE: [*Agitated, imploringly*] Do you think I might have a few pence in advance, sir? I need it that bad.

NEUMANN: And I need a few pounds. If it was only a question of needing it—! [*Already occupied in counting out another weaver's money, shortly*] It's Mr. Dreissiger who settles about pay in advance.

WEAVER'S WIFE: Couldn't I speak to Mr. Dreissiger himself, then, sir?

PFEIFER: [*Now manager, formerly weaver. The type is unmistakable, only he is well fed, well dressed, clean-shaven; also takes snuff copiously. He calls out roughly*] Mr. Dreissiger would have enough to do if he had to attend to every trifle himself. That's what we are here for. [*He measures, and then examines through the magnifying-glass*] Mercy on us! what a draught! [*Puts a thick muffler round his neck*] Shut the door, whoever comes in.

APPRENTICE: [*Loudly to* Pfeifer] You might as well talk to stocks and stones.

PFEIFER: That's done—Weigh! [*The weaver places his web on the scales*] If you only understood your business a little better! Full of lumps again. . . . I hardly need to look at the cloth to see them. Call yourself a weaver, and "draw as long a bow" as you've done there!

[Becker *has entered. A young, exceptionally powerfully-built weaver; off-hand, almost bold in manner.* Pfeifer, Neumann, *and the* Apprentice *exchange looks of mutual understanding as he comes in*]

BECKER: Devil take it! This is a sweating job, and no mistake.

FIRST WEAVER: [*In a low voice*] This blazing heat means rain.

[Old Baumert *forces his way in at the glass door on the right, through which the crowd of weavers can be seen, standing shoulder to shoulder, waiting their turn. The old man stumbles forward and lays his bundle on the bench, beside* Becker's. *He sits down by it, and wipes the sweat from his face*]

OLD BAUMERT: A man has a right to a rest after that.

BECKER: Rest's better than money.

OLD BAUMERT: Yes, but we needs the money, too. Good-mornin' to you, Becker!

BECKER: Morning, Father Baumert! Goodness knows how long we'll have to stand here again.

FIRST WEAVER: And what does that matter? What's to hinder a weaver waitin' for an hour, or for a day if need be? What else is he there for?

PFEIFER: Silence there! We can't hear our own voices.

BECKER: [*In a low voice*] This is one of his bad days.

PFEIFER: [*To the weaver standing before him*] How often have I told you that you must bring cleaner cloth? What sort of mess is this? Knots, and straw, and all kinds of dirt.

REIMANN: It's for want of a new picker, sir.

APPRENTICE: [*Has weighed the piece*] Short weight, too.

PFEIFER: I never saw such weavers. I hate to give out the yarn to them. It was another story in my day! I'd have caught it finely from my master for work like that. The business was carried on in different style then. A man had to know his trade—that's the last thing that's thought of nowadays. Reimann, one shilling.

REIMANN: But there's always a pound allowed for waste.

PFEIFER: I've no time. Next man!—What have you to show?

HEIBER: [*Lays his web on the table. While* Pfeifer *is examining it, he goes close up to him; eagerly in a low tone*] Beg pardon, Mr. Pfeifer, but I wanted to ask you, sir, if you would perhaps be so very kind as do me the favor an' not take my advance money off this week's pay.

PFEIFER: [*Measuring and examining the texture; jeeringly*] Well! What next, I wonder? This looks very much as if half the weft had stuck to the bobbins again.

HEIBER: [*Continues*] I'll be sure to make it all right next week, sir. But this last week I've had to put in two days' work on the estate. And my missus is ill in bed. . . .

PFEIFER: [*Giving the web to be weighed*] Another piece of real slop-work. [*Already examining a new web*] What a selvage! Here it's broad, there it's narrow; here it's drawn in by the wefts goodness knows how tight, and there it's torn out again by the temples. And hardly seventy threads weft to the inch. What's come of the rest? Do you call this honest work? I never saw anything like it.

[Heiber, *repressing tears, stands humiliated and helpless*]

BECKER: [*In a low voice to* Baumert] To please that brute you would have to pay for extra yarn out of your own pocket.

[*The* Weaver's Wife, *who has remained standing near the cashier's table, from time to time looking around appealingly, takes courage and once more comes forward*]

WEAVER'S WIFE: [*To cashier imploringly*] I don't know what's to come of me, sir, if you won't give me a little advance this time—O Lord, O Lord!

PFEIFER: [*Calls across*] It's no good whining, or dragging the Lord's name into the matter. You're not so anxious about Him at other times. You look after your husband and see that he's not to be found so often lounging in the public house. We can give no pay in advance. We have to account for every penny. It's not our money. People that are industrious, and understand their work, and do it in the fear of God, never need their pay in advance. So now you know.

NEUMANN: If a Bielau weaver got four times as much pay, he would squander it four times over and be in debt into the bargain.

WEAVER'S WIFE: [*In a loud voice, as if appealing to the general sense of justice*] No one can't call me idle, but I'm not fit now for what I once was. I've twice had a miscarriage. And as to John, he's but a poor creature. He's been to the shepherd at Zerlau, but he couldn't do him no good, and . . . you can't do more than you've strength for. . . . We works as hard as ever we can. This many a week I've been at it till far on into the night. An' we'll keep our heads above water right enough if I can just get a bit of strength into me. But you must have pity on us, Mr. Pfeifer, sir. [*Eagerly, coaxingly*] You'll please be so very kind as to let me have a few pence on the next job, sir?

PFEIFER: [*Paying no attention*] Fiedler, one and twopence.

WEAVER'S WIFE: Only a few pence, to buy bread with. We can't get no more credit. We've a lot of little ones.

NEUMANN: [*Half aside to the* Apprentice, *in a serio-comic tone*] "Every year brings a child to the linen-weaver's wife, heigh-ho, heigh-ho, heigh."

APPRENTICE: [*Takes up the rhyme, half singing*] "And the little brat it's blind the first weeks of its life, heigh-ho, heigh-ho, heigh."

REIMANN: [*Not touching the money which the cashier has counted out to him*] We've always got one and fourpence for the web.

PFEIFER: [*Calls across*] If our terms don't suit you, Reimann, you have only to say so. There's no scarcity of weavers—especially of your sort. For full weight we give full pay.

REIMANN: How anything can be wrong with the weight is past . . .

PFEIFER: You bring a piece of fustian with no faults in it, and there will be no fault in the pay.

REIMANN: It's not possible that there's too many knots in this web.

PFEIFER: [*Examining*] If you want to live well, then be sure you weave well.

HEIBER: [*Has remained standing near* Pfeifer, *so as to seize any favorable opportunity. He laughs at* Pfeifer's *little witticism, then steps forward and again addresses him*] I wanted to ask you, sir, if you would perhaps have the great kindness not to take my advance of six-pence off to-day's pay? My missus has been bedridden since February. She can't do a hand's turn for me, and I've to pay a bobbin girl. And so . . .

PFEIFER: [*Takes a pinch of snuff*] Heiber, do you think I have no one to attend to but you? The others must have their turn.

REIMANN: As the warp was given me I took it home and fastened it to the beam. I can't bring back better yarn than I get.

PFEIFER: If you are not satisfied, you need come for no more. There are plenty ready to tramp the soles off their shoes to get it.

NEUMANN: [*To* Reimann] Do you not want your money?

REIMANN: I can't bring myself to take such pay.

NEUMANN: [*Paying no further attention to* Reimann] Heiber, one shilling. Deduct sixpence for pay in advance. Leave sixpence.

HEIBER: [*Goes up to the table, looks at the money, stands shaking his head as if unable to believe his eyes, then slowly takes it up*] Well, I never!—[*Sighing*] Oh, dear, oh, dear!

OLD BAUMERT: [*Looking into* Heiber's *face*] Yes, Franz, that's so. There's matter enough for sighing.

HEIBER: [*Speaking with difficulty*] I've a girl lying sick at home, too, an' she needs a bottle of medicine.

OLD BAUMERT: What's wrong with her?

HEIBER: Well, you see, she's always been a sickly bit of a thing. I don't know. . . . I needn't mind tellin' you—she brought her trouble with her. It's in her blood, and it breaks out here, there, and everywhere.

OLD BAUMERT: It's always the way. Let folks be poor, and one trouble comes to them on the top of another. There's no help for it and there's no end to it.

HEIBER: What are you carryin' in that cloth, Father Baumert?

OLD BAUMERT: We haven't so much as a bite in the house, and so I've had the little dog killed. There's not much on him, for the poor beast was half starved. A nice little dog he was! I couldn't kill him myself. I hadn't the heart to do it.

PFEIFER: [*Has inspected* Becker's *web—calls*] Becker, one and threepence.

BECKER: That's what you might give to a beggar: it's not pay.

PFEIFER: Every one who has been attended to must clear out. We haven't room to turn round in.

BECKER: [*To those standing near, without lowering his voice*] It's a beggarly pittance, nothing else. A man works his treadle from early morning till late at night, an' when he has bent over his loom for days an' days, tired to death every evening, sick with the dust and the heat, he finds he's made a beggarly one and threepence!

PFEIFER: No impudence allowed here.

BECKER: If you think I'll hold my tongue for your telling, you're much mistaken.

PFEIFER: [*Exclaims*] We'll see about that! [*Rushes to the glass door and calls into the office*] Mr. Dreissiger, Mr. Dreissiger, will you be good enough to come here?

[*Enter* Dreissiger. *About forty, full-bodied, asthmatic. Looks severe*]

DREISSIGER: What is it, Pfeifer?

PFEIFER: [*Spitefully*] Becker says he won't be told to hold his tongue.

DREISSIGER: [*Draws himself up, throws back his head, stares at* Becker; *his nostrils tremble*] Oh, indeed!—Becker. [*To* Pfeifer] Is he the man? . . . [*The clerks nod*]

BECKER: [*Insolently*] Yes, Mr. Dreissiger, yes! [*Pointing to himself*] This is the man. [*Pointing to* Dreissiger] And that's a man, too!

DREISSIGER: [*Angrily*] Fellow, how dare you?

PFEIFER: He's too well off. He'll go dancing on the ice once too often, though.

BECKER: [*Recklessly*] You shut up, you Jack-in-the-box. Your mother must have gone dancing once too often with Satan to have got such a devil for a son.

DREISSIGER: [*Now in a violent passion, roars*] Hold your tongue this moment, sir, or . . .

[*He trembles and takes a few steps forward*]

BECKER: [*Holding his ground steadily*] I'm not deaf. My hearing's quite good yet.

DREISSIGER: [*Controls himself, asks in an apparently cool business tone*] Was this fellow not one of the pack? . . .

PFEIFER: He's a Bielau weaver. When there's any mischief going, they are sure to be in it.

DREISSIGER: [*Trembling*] Well, I give you all warning: if the same thing happens again as last night—a troop of half-drunken cubs, marching past my windows singing that low song . . .

BECKER: Is it "Bloody Justice" you mean?

DREISSIGER: You know well enough what I mean. I tell you that if I hear it again I'll get hold of one of you, and—mind, I'm not joking—before the justice he shall go. And if I can find out who it was that made up that vile doggerel . . .

BECKER: It's a beautiful song, that's what it is!

DREISSIGER: Another word and I send for the police on the spot, without more ado. I'll make short work with you young fellows. I've got the better of very different men before now.

BECKER: I believe you there. A real thoroughbred manufacturer will get the better of two or three hundred weavers in the time it takes you to turn round—swallow them up, and not leave as much as a bone. He's got four stomachs like a cow, and teeth like a wolf. That's nothing to him at all!

DREISSIGER: [*To his clerks*] That man gets no more work from us.

BECKER: It's all the same to me whether I starve at my loom or by the roadside.

DREISSIGER: Out you go, then, this moment! . . .

BECKER: [*Determinedly*] Not without my pay.

DREISSIGER: How much is owing to the fellow, Neumann?

NEUMANN: One and threepence.

DREISSIGER: [*Takes the money hurriedly out of the cashier's hand, and flings it on the table, so that some of the coins roll off on the floor*] There you are, then; and now, out of my sight with you!

BECKER: Not without my pay.

DREISSIGER: Do you not see it lying there? If you don't take it and go . . . It's exactly twelve now . . . The dyers are coming out for their dinner. . . .

BECKER: I get my pay into my hand—here. [*Points with the fingers of his right hand at the palm of his left*]

DREISSIGER: [*To the* Apprentice] Pick up the money, Tilgner.

[*The* Apprentice *lifts the money and puts it into* Becker's *hand*]

BECKER: Everything in proper order. [*Deliberately takes an old purse out of his pocket and puts the money into it*]

DREISSIGER: [*As* Becker *still does not move away*] Well? Do you want me to come and help you?

[*Signs of agitation are observable among the crowd of weavers. A long, loud sigh is heard, and then a fall. General interest is at once diverted to this new event*]

DREISSIGER: What's the matter there?

CHORUS OF WEAVERS AND WOMEN: "Some one's fainted."—"It's a little sickly boy." —"Is it a fit, or what?"

DREISSIGER: What do you say? Fainted?

[*He goes nearer*]

OLD WEAVER: There he lies, any way.

[*They make room. A boy of about eight is seen lying on the floor as if dead*]

DREISSIGER: Does any one know the boy?

OLD WEAVER: He's not from our village.

OLD BAUMERT: He's like one of Weaver Heinrich's boys. [*Looks at him more closely*] Yes, that's Heinrich's little Philip.

DREISSIGER: Where do they live?

OLD BAUMERT: Up near us in Kaschbach, sir. He goes round playin' music in the evenings, and all day he's at the loom. They've nine children an' a tenth a-coming.

CHORUS OF WEAVERS AND WOMEN: "They're terrible put to it."—"The rain comes through their roof."—"The woman hasn't two shirts among the nine."

OLD BAUMERT: [*Taking the boy by the arm*] Now then, lad, what's wrong with you? Wake up, lad.

DREISSIGER: Some of you help me, and we'll get him up. It's disgraceful to send a sickly child this distance. Bring some water, Pfeifer.

WOMAN: [*Helping to lift the boy*] Surely you're not going to die, lad!

DREISSIGER: Brandy, Pfeifer, brandy will be better.

BECKER: [*Forgotten by all, has stood looking on. With his hand on the door-latch, he now calls loudly and tauntingly*] Give him something to eat, an' he'll soon be all right.

[*Goes out*]

DREISSIGER: That fellow will come to a bad end.—Take him under the arm, Neumann. Easy now, easy; we'll get him into my room. What?

NEUMANN: He said something, Mr. Dreissiger. His lips are moving.

DREISSIGER: What—what is it, boy?

BOY: [*Whispers*] I'm h—hungry.

WOMAN: I think he says . . .

DREISSIGER: We'll find out. Don't stop. Let us get him into my room. He can lie on the sofa there. We'll hear what the doctor says.

[Dreissiger, Neumann, *and the woman lead the boy into the office. The weavers begin to behave like school-children when their master has left the classroom. They stretch themselves, whisper, move from one foot to the other, and in the course of a few moments are conversing loudly*]

OLD BAUMERT: I believe as how Becker was right.

CHORUS OF WOMEN AND WEAVERS: "He did say something like that."—"It's nothing new here to fall down from hunger."—"God knows what's to come of them in winter if this cutting down of wages goes on."—"An' this winter the potatoes aren't no good at all."—"Things'll get worse and worse till we're all done for together."

OLD BAUMERT: The best thing a man could do would be to put a rope round his neck and hang hisself on his own loom, like Weaver Nentwich. [*To another old weaver*] Here, take a pinch. I was at Neurode yesterday. My brother-in-law, he works in the snuff factory there, and he gave me a grain or two. Have you anything good in your handkercher?

OLD WEAVER: Only a little pearl barley. I was coming along behind Ulbrich the miller's cart, and there was a slit in one of the sacks. I can tell you we'll be glad of it.

OLD BAUMERT: There's twenty-two mills in Peterswaldau, but of all they grind, there's never nothing comes our way.

OLD WEAVER: We must keep up heart. There's always something comes to help us on again.

HEIBER: Yes, when we're hungry, we can pray to all the saints to help us, and if that don't fill our bellies we can put a pebble in our mouths and suck it. Eh, Baumert?

[*Reënter* Dreissiger, Pfeifer, *and* Neumann]

DREISSIGER: It was nothing serious. The boy is all right again. [*Walks about excitedly, panting*] But all the same it's a disgrace. The child's so weak that a puff of wind would blow him over. How people, how any parents can be so thoughtless is what passes my comprehension. Loading him with two heavy pieces of fustian to carry a good six miles! No one would believe it that hadn't seen it. It simply means that I shall have to make a rule that no goods brought by children will be taken over. [*He walks up and down silently for a few moments*] I sincerely trust such a thing will not occur again.—Who gets all the blame for it? Why, of course the manufacturer. It's entirely our fault. If some poor little fellow sticks in the snow in winter and goes to sleep, a special correspondent arrives posthaste, and in two days we have a blood-curdling story served up in all the papers. Is any blame laid on the father, the parents, that send such a child?—Not a bit of it. How should they be to blame? It's all the manu-

facturer's fault—he's made the scapegoat. They flatter the weaver, and give the manufacturer nothing but abuse—he's a cruel man, with a heart like a stone, a wicked fellow, at whose calves every cur of a journalist may take a bite. He lives on the fat of the land, and pays the poor weavers starvation wages. In the flow of his eloquence the writer forgets to mention that such a man has his cares too and his sleepless nights; that he runs risks of which the workman never dreams; that he is often driven distracted by all the calculations he has to make, and all the different things he has to take into account; that he has to struggle for his very life against competition; and that no day passes without some annoyance or some loss. And think of the manufacturer's responsibilities, think of the numbers that depend on him, that look to him for their daily bread. No, no! none of you need wish yourselves in my shoes—you would soon have enough of it. [*After a moment's reflection*] You all saw how that fellow, that scoundrel Becker, behaved. Now he'll go and spread about all sorts of tales of my hard-heartedness, of how my weavers are turned off for a mere trifle, without a moment's notice. Is that true? Am I so very unmerciful?

CHORUS OF VOICES: No, sir.

DREISSIGER: It doesn't seem to me that I am. And yet these ne'er-do-wells come round singing low songs about us manufacturers—prating about hunger, with enough in their pockets to pay for quarts of bad brandy. If they would like to know what want is, let them go and ask the linen-weavers: they can tell something about it. But you here, you fustian-weavers, have every reason to thank God that things are no worse than they are. And I put it to all the old, industrious weavers present: Is a good workman able to gain a living in my employment, or is he not?

MANY VOICES: Yes, sir; he is, sir.

DREISSIGER: There now! You see! Of course such a fellow as that Becker can't. I advise you to keep these young lads in check. If there's much more of this sort of thing, I'll shut up shop—give up the business altogether, and then you can shift for yourselves, get work where you like—perhaps Mr. Becker will provide it.

FIRST WEAVER'S WIFE: [*Has come close to* Dreissiger, *obsequiously removes a little dust from his coat*] You've been an' rubbed ag'in' something, sir.

DREISSIGER: Business is as bad as it can be just now, you know that yourselves. Instead of making money, I am losing it every day. If, in spite of this, I take care that my weavers are kept in work, I look for some little gratitude from them. I have thousands of pieces of cloth in stock, and don't know if I'll ever be able to sell them. Well, now, I've heard how many weavers hereabouts are out of work, and—I'll leave Pfeifer to give the particulars —but this much I'll tell you, just to show you my good will. . . . I can't deal out charity all round;

I'm not rich enough for that; but I can give the people who are out of work the chance of earning at any rate a little. It's a great business risk I run by doing it, but that's my affair. I say to myself: Better that a man should work for a bite of bread than that he should starve altogether. Am I not right?

CHORUS OF VOICES: Yes, yes, sir.

DREISSIGER: And therefore I am ready to give employment to two hundred more weavers. Pfeifer will tell you on what conditions.

[*He turns to go*]

FIRST WEAVER'S WIFE: [*Comes between him and the door, speaks hurriedly, eagerly, imploringly*] Oh, if you please, sir, will you let me ask you if you'll be so good . . . I've been twice laid up for . . .

DREISSIGER: [*Hastily*] Speak to Pfeifer, good woman. I'm too late as it is.

[*Passes on, leaving her standing*]

REIMANN: [*Stops him again. In an injured, complaining tone*] I have a complaint to make, if you please, sir. Mr. Pfeifer refuses to . . . I've always got one and two-pence for a web . . .

DREISSIGER: [*Interrupts him*] Mr. Pfeifer's my manager. There he is. Apply to him.

HEIBER: [*Detaining Dreissiger; hurriedly and confusedly*] O sir, I wanted to ask if you would p'r'aps, if I might p'r'aps . . . if Mr. Pfeifer might . . . might . . .

DREISSIGER: What is it you want?

HEIBER: That advance pay I had last time, sir; I thought p'r'aps you would kindly . . .

DREISSIGER: I have no idea what you are talking about.

HEIBER: I'm awful hard up, sir, because . . .

DREISSIGER: These are things Pfeifer must look into—I really have not the time. Arrange the matter with Pfeifer.

[*He escapes into the office. The supplicants look helplessly at one another, sigh, and take their places again among the others*]

PFEIFER: [*Resuming his task of inspection*] Well, Annie, let us see what yours is like.

OLD BAUMERT: How much are we to get for the web, then, Mr. Pfeifer?

HEIBER: One shilling a web.

OLD BAUMERT: Has it come to that!

[*Excited whispering and murmuring among the weavers*]

ACT II.

A small room in the house of Wilhelm Ansorge, *weaver and house-owner in the village of Kaschbach, in the Eulengebirge.*

In this room, which does not measure six feet from the dilapidated wooden floor to the smoke-blackened rafters, sit four people. Two young girls, Emma *and* Bertha Baumert, *are working at their looms;* Mother Baumert, *a decrepit old woman, sits on a stool beside the bed, with a winding-wheel in front of her; her idiot son* August *sits on a footstool, also winding. He is twenty, has a small body and head, and long, spider-like legs and arms.*

Faint, rosy evening light makes its way through two small windows in the right wall, which have their broken panes pasted over with paper or stuffed with straw. It lights up the flaxen hair of the girls, which falls loose on their slender white necks and thin bare shoulders, and their coarse chemises. These, with a short petticoat of the roughest linen, form their whole attire. The warm glow falls on the old woman's face, neck, and breast—a face worn away to a skeleton, with shriveled skin and sunken eyes, red and watery with smoke, dust, and working by lamplight; a long goitre neck, wrinkled and sinewy; a hollow breast covered with faded, ragged shawls.

Part of the right wall is also lighted up, with stove, stove-bench, bedstead, and one or two gaudily colored sacred prints. On the stove-rail rags are hanging to dry, and behind the stove is a collection of worthless lumber. On the bench stand some old pots and cooking-utensils, and potato-parings are laid out on it, on paper, to dry. Hanks of yarn and reels hang from the rafters; baskets of bobbins stand beside the looms. In the backwall there is a low door without fastening. Beside it a bundle of willow wands is set up against the wall, and beyond them lie some damaged quarter-bushel baskets.

The room is full of sound—the rhythmic thud of the looms, shaking floor and walls, the click and rattle of the shuttles passing back and forward, and the steady whirr of the winding-wheels, like the hum of gigantic bees.

MOTHER BAUMERT: [*In a querulous, feeble voice, as the girls stop weaving and bend over their webs*] Got to make knots again already, have you?

EMMA: [*The elder of the two girls, about twenty-two, tying a broken thread*] It's the plaguyest web, this!

BERTHA: [*Fifteen*] Yes, it's real bad yarn they've given us this time.

EMMA: What can have happened to father? He's been away since nine.

MOTHER BAUMERT: You may well ask. Where in the wide world can he be?

BERTHA: Don't you worry yourself, mother.

MOTHER BAUMERT: I can't help it, Bertha lass.

[*Emma begins to weave again*]

BERTHA: Stop a minute, Emma!

EMMA: What is it!

BERTHA: I thought I heard some one.

EMMA: It'll be Ansorge coming home.

[*Enter* Fritz, *a little, barefooted, ragged boy of four*]

FRITZ: [*Whimpering*] I'm hungry, mother.

EMMA: Wait, Fritzel, wait a bit! Gran'father will

be here very soon, an' he's bringin' bread along with him, an' coffee, too.

FRITZ: But I'm awful hungry, mother.

EMMA: Be a good boy now, Fritz. Listen to what I'm tellin' you. He'll be here this minute. He's bringin' nice bread an' nice corn-coffee; an' when we stop working mother'll take the tater peelin's and carry them to the farmer, and the farmer'll give her a drop o' good skim milk for her little boy.

FRITZ: Where's grandfather gone?

EMMA: To the manufacturer, Fritz, with a web.

FRITZ: To the manufacturer?

EMMA: Yes, yes, Fritz; down to Dreissiger's at Peterswaldau.

FRITZ: Is it there he gets the bread?

EMMA: Yes; Dreissiger gives him money, and then he buys the bread.

FRITZ: Does he give him a heap of money?

EMMA: [Impatiently] Oh, stop that chatter, boy.

[She and Bertha go on weaving for a time, and then both stop again]

BERTHA: August, go and ask Ansorge if he'll give us a light.

[August goes out accompanied by Fritz]

MOTHER BAUMERT: [Overcome by her childish apprehension, whimpers] Emma! Bertha! where can father be?

BERTHA: He'll have looked in to see Hauffen.

MOTHER BAUMERT: [Crying] What if he's sittin' drinkin' in the public house?

EMMA: Don't cry, mother! You know well enough father's not the man to do that.

MOTHER BAUMERT: [Half distracted by a multitude of gloomy forebodings] What . . . what . . . what's to become of us if he doesn't come home? —if he drink the money, and brings us nothin' at all? There's not so much as a handful of salt in the house—not a bite o' bread, nor a bit o' wood for the fire.

BERTHA: Wait a bit, mother! It's moonlight just now. We'll take August with us and go into the wood and get some sticks.

MOTHER BAUMERT: Yes, an' be caught by the forester.

[Ansorge, an old weaver of gigantic stature, who has to bend down to get into the room, puts his head and shoulders in at the door. Long, unkempt hair and beard]

ANSORGE: What's wanted?

BERTHA: Light, if you please.

ANSORGE: [In a muffled voice, as if speaking in a sick-room] There's good daylight yet.

MOTHER BAUMERT: Are we to sit in the dark next?

ANSORGE: I've to do the same myself. [Goes out]

BERTHA: It's easy to see that he's a miser.

EMMA: Well, there's nothin' for it but to sit an' wait his pleasure.

[Enter Mrs. Heinrich, a woman of thirty, enceinte; an expression of torturing anxiety and apprehension on her worn face]

MRS. HEINRICH: Good-evenin' t' you all.

MOTHER BAUMERT: Well, Jenny, and what's your news?

MRS. HEINRICH: [Who limps] I've got a piece o' glass into my foot.

BERTHA: Come an' sit down, then, an' I'll see if I can get it out.

[Mrs. Heinrich seats herself. Bertha kneels down in front of her, and examines her foot]

MOTHER BAUMERT: How are you all at home, Jenny?

MRS. HEINRICH: [Breaks out despairingly] Things is in a terrible way with us! [She struggles in vain against a rush of tears; then weeps silently]

MOTHER BAUMERT: The best thing as could happen to the likes of us, Jenny, would be if God had pity on us an' took us away out o' this weary world.

MRS. HEINRICH: [No longer able to control herself, screams, still crying] My children's starvin'. [Sobs and moans] I'm at my wits' ends. Let me work till I fall down—I'm more dead than alive—it's all no use. Am I able to fill nine hungry mouths? We got a bit o' bread last night, but it wasn't enough even for the two smallest ones. Who was I to give it to, eh? They all cried: Me, me, mother! give it to me! . . . An' if it's like this while I'm still on my feet, what'll it be when I've to take to bed? Our few taters was washed away. We haven't a thing to put in our mouths.

BERTHA: [Has removed the bit of glass and washed the wound] We'll put a rag around it. Emma, see if you can find one.

MOTHER BAUMERT: We're no better off than you, Jenny.

MRS. HEINRICH: You have your girls, anyway. You've a husband as can work. Mine was taken with one of his fits last week again—so bad that I didn't know what to do with him, and was half out o' my mind with fright. And when he's had a turn like that, he can't stir out of bed under a week.

MOTHER BAUMERT: Mine's no better. His breathin' 's bad now as well as his back. An' there's not a farthin' nor a farthin's worth in the house. If he don't bring a few pence with him to-day, I don't know what we're to do.

EMMA: It's the truth she's tellin' you, Jenny. We had to let father take the little dog with him to-day, to have him killed, that we might get a bite into our stomachs again!

MRS. HEINRICH: Have you not got as much as a handful of flour to spare?

MOTHER BAUMERT: And that we have not, Jenny. There's not as much as a grain of salt in the house.

MRS. HEINRICH: Oh, whatever am I to do? [Rises; stands still, brooding] I don't know what'll be the end of this! It's more nor I can bear. [Screams in rage and despair] I would be contented if it was nothin' but pigs' food!—But I can't go home again empty-handed—that I can't. God forgive me, I see no other way out of it. [She limps quickly out]

MOTHER BAUMERT: [*Calls after her in a warning voice*] Jenny, Jenny! don't you be doin' anything foolish, now!

BERTHA: She'll do herself no harm, mother. You needn't be afraid.

EMMA: That's the way she always goes on. [*Seats herself at the loom and weaves for a few seconds*]

[August *enters, carrying a tallow candle, and lighting his father,* Old Baumert, *who follows close behind him, staggering under a heavy bundle of yarn*]

MOTHER BAUMERT: Oh, father, where have you been all this long time? Where have you been?

OLD BAUMERT: Come now, mother, don't fall on a man like that. Give me time to get my breath first. An' look who I've brought with me.

[Moritz Jaeger *comes stooping in at the low door. Reserve soldier, newly discharged. Middle height, rosy-cheeked, military carriage. His cap on the side of his head, hussar fashion, whole clothes and shoes, a clean shirt without collar. Draws himself up and salutes*]

JAEGER: [*In a hearty voice*] Good-evening, Auntie Baumert!

MOTHER BAUMERT: Well, well, now! And to think you've got back! An' you've not forgotten us? Take a chair, then, lad.

EMMA: [*Wiping a wooden chair with her apron, and pushing it toward* Moritz] An' so you've come to see what poor folks are like again, Moritz?

JAEGER: I say, Emma, is it true that you've got a boy nearly old enough to be a soldier? Where did you get hold of him, eh?

[Bertha, *having taken the small supply of provisions which her father has brought, puts meat into a saucepan, and shoves it into the oven, while* August *lights the fire*]

BERTHA: You knew Weaver Finger, didn't you?

MOTHER BAUMERT: We had him here in the house with us. He was ready enough to marry her; but he was too far gone in consumption; he was as good as a dead man. It didn't happen for want of warning from me. But do you think she would listen? Not she. Now he's dead an' forgotten long ago, an' she's left with the boy to provide for as best she can. But now tell us how you've been gettin' on, Moritz.

OLD BAUMERT: You've only to look at him, mother, to know that. He's had luck. It'll be about as much as he can do to speak to the likes of us. He's got clothes like a prince, an' a silver watch, an' thirty shillings in his pocket into the bargain.

JAEGER: [*Stretching himself consequentially, a knowing smile on his face*] I can't complain. I didn't get on at all badly in the regiment.

OLD BAUMERT: He was the major's own servant. Just listen to him—he speaks like a gentleman.

JAEGER: I've got so accustomed to it that I can't help it.

MOTHER BAUMERT: Well, now, to think that such a good-for-nothing as you were should have come to be a rich man. For there wasn't nothing to be made of you. You would never sit still to wind more than a hank of yarn at a time, that you wouldn't. Off you went to your tom-tit boxes an' your robin redbreast snares—they was all you cared about. Is it not the truth I'm telling?

JAEGER: Yes, yes, auntie, it's true enough. It wasn't only redbreasts. I went after swallows, too.

EMMA: Though we were always tellin' you that swallows were poison.

JAEGER: What did I care?—But how have you all been getting on, Auntie Baumert?

MOTHER BAUMERT: Oh, badly, lad, badly these last four years. I've had the rheumatics—just look at them hands. And it's more than likely as I've had a stroke o' some kind, too, I'm that helpless. I can hardly move a limb, an' nobody knows the pains I suffers.

OLD BAUMERT: She's in a bad way, she is. She'll not hold out long.

BERTHA: We've to dress her in the mornin' an' undress her at night, an' to feed her like a baby.

MOTHER BAUMERT: [*Speaking in a complaining, tearful voice*] Not a thing can I do for myself. It's far worse than bein' ill. For it's not only a burden to myself I am, but to every one else. Often and often do I pray to God to take me. For oh! mine's a weary life. I don't know . . . p'r'aps they think . . . but I'm one that's been a hard worker all my days. An' I've always been able to do my turn, too; but now, all at once, [*She vainly attempts to rise*] I can't do nothing.—I've a good husband an' good children, but to have to sit here and see them! . . . Look at the girls! There's hardly any blood left in them—faces the color of a sheet. But on they must work at these weary looms whether they earn enough to keep theirselves or not. What sort o' life is it they lead? Their feet never off the treadle from year's end to year's end. An' with it all they can't scrape together as much as'll buy them clothes that they can let theirselves be seen in; never a step can they go to church, to hear a word of comfort. They're liker scarecrows than young girls of fifteen and twenty.

BERTHA: [*At the stove*] It's beginnin' to smoke again!

OLD BAUMERT: There now; look at that smoke. And we can't do nothin' for it. The whole stove's goin' to pieces. We must let it fall, and swallow the soot. We're coughin' already, one worse than the other. We may cough till we choke, or till we cough our lungs up—nobody cares.

JAEGER: But this here is Ansorge's business; he must see to the stove.

BERTHA: He'll see us out of the house first; he has plenty against us without that.

MOTHER BAUMERT: We've only been in his way this long time past.

OLD BAUMERT: One word of complaint an' out we go. He's had no rent from us this last half-year.

MOTHER BAUMERT: A well-off man like him needn't be so hard.

OLD BAUMERT: He's no better off than we are, mother. He's hard put to it, too, for all he holds his tongue about it.

MOTHER BAUMERT: He's got his house.

OLD BAUMERT: What are you talkin' about, mother? Not one stone in the wall is the man's own.

JAEGER: [*Has seated himself, and taken a short pipe with gay tassels out of one coat-pocket, and a quart bottle of brandy out of another*] Things can't go on like this. I'm dumbfoundered when I see the life the people live here. The very dogs in the towns live better.

OLD BAUMERT: [*Eagerly*] That's what I say! Eh? eh? You know it, too! But if you say that here, they'll tell you that it's only bad times.

[*Enter* Ansorge, *an earthenware pan with soup in one hand, in the other a half-finished quarter-bushel basket*]

ANSORGE: Glad to see you again, Moritz!

JAEGER: Thank you, Father Ansorge—same to you!

ANSORGE: [*Shoving his pan into the oven*] Why, lad, you look like a duke!

OLD BAUMERT: Show him your watch, Moritz! An' he's got a new suit of clothes besides them he's on, an' thirty shillings in his purse.

ANSORGE: [*Shaking his head*] Is that so? Well, well!

EMMA: [*Puts the potato-parings into a bag*] I must be off; I'll maybe get a drop o' skim milk for these. [*Goes out*]

JAEGER: [*The others hanging on his words*] You know how you all used to be down on me. It was always: Wait, Moritz, till your soldiering time comes—you'll catch it then. But you see how well I've got on. At the end of the first half-year I had got my good conduct stripes. You've got to be willing—that's where the secret lies. I brushed the sergeant's boots; I groomed his horse; I fetched his beer. I was as sharp as a needle. Always ready, accoutrements clean and shining—first at stables, first at roll-call, first in the saddle. And when the bugle sounded to the assault—why, then, blood and thunder, and ride to the devil with you!! I was as keen as a pointer. Says I to myself: There's no help for it now, my boy, it's got to be done; and I set my mind to it and did it. Till at last the major said before the whole squadron: There's a hussar now that shows you what a hussar should be!

[*Silence. He lights his pipe*]

ANSORGE: [*Shaking his head*] Well, well, well! You had luck with you, Moritz. [*Sits down on the floor, with his willow twigs beside him, and continues mending the basket, which he holds between his legs*]

OLD BAUMERT: Let's hope you've brought some of it to us.—Are we to have a drop to drink your health in?

JAEGER: Of course you are, Father Baumert. And when this bottle's done, we'll send for more. [*He flings a coin on the table*]

ANSORGE: [*Open-mouthed with amazement*] Oh, my! Oh, my! What goings on to be sure! Roast meat frizzlin' in the oven! A bottle o' brandy on the table! [*He drinks out of the bottle*] Here's to you, Moritz!—Well, well, well!

[*The bottle circulates freely after this*]

OLD BAUMERT: If we could anyway have a bit o' meat on Sundays and holidays, instead of never seein' the sight of it from year's end to year's end! Now we'll have to wait till another poor little dog finds its way into the house like this one did four weeks gone by—an' that's not likely to happen soon again.

ANSORGE: Have you killed the little dog?

OLD BAUMERT: We had to do that or starve.

ANSORGE: Well, well!

MOTHER BAUMERT: A nice, kind little beast he was, too!

JAEGER: Are you as keen as ever on roast dog hereabouts?

OLD BAUMERT: My word, if we could only get enough of it!

MOTHER BAUMERT: A nice little bit o' meat like that does you a lot o' good.

OLD BAUMERT: Have you lost the taste for it, Moritz? Stay with us a bit, and it'll soon come back to you.

ANSORGE: [*Sniffing*] Yes, yes! That will be a tasty bite—what a good smell it has!

OLD BAUMERT: [*Sniffing*] Splendid!

ANSORGE: Come, then, Moritz, tell us your opinion, you that's been out and seen the world. Are things at all like improving for us weavers, eh?

JAEGER: They would need to.

ANSORGE: We're in an awful state here. It's not livin' an' it's not dyin'. A man fights to the bitter end, but he's bound to be beat at last—to be left without a roof over his head, you may say without ground under his feet. As long as he can work at the loom he can earn some sort o' poor, miserable livin'. But it's many a day since I've been able to get that sort o' job. Now I tries to put a bite into my mouth with this here basket-makin'. I sits at it late into the night, and by the time I tumbles into bed I've earned three-halfpence. I put it to you if a man can live on that, when everything's so dear? Nine shillin' goes in one lump for house tax, three shillin' for land tax, nine shillin' for mortgage interest—that makes one pound one. I may reckon my year's earnin' at just double that money, and that leaves me twenty-one shillin' for a whole year's food, an' fire, an' clothes, an' shoes; and I've got to keep up some sort of a place to live in. Is it any wonder if I'm behind-hand with my interest payments?

OLD BAUMERT: Some one would need to go to Berlin an' tell the King how hard put to it we are.

JAEGER: Little good that would do, Father Baumert. There's been plenty written about it in the newspapers. But the rich people, they can turn and twist things round . . . as cunning as the devil himself.

OLD BAUMERT: [*Shaking his head*] To think they've no more sense than that in Berlin!

ANSORGE: And is it really true, Moritz? Is there no law to help us? If a man hasn't been able to scrape together enough to pay his mortgage interest, though he's worked the very skin off his hands, must his house be taken from him? The peasant that's lent the money on it, he wants his rights—what else can you look for from him? But what's to be the end of it all, I don't know.—If I'm put out o' the house. . . . [*In a voice choked by tears*] I was born here, and here my father sat at his loom for more than forty year. Many was the time he said to mother: Mother, when I'm gone, the house'll still be here. I've worked hard for it. Every nail means a night's weaving, every plank a year's dry bread. A man would think that . . .

JAEGER: They're quite fit to take the last bite out of your mouth—that's what they are.

ANSORGE: Well, well, well! I would rather be carried out than have to walk out now in my old days. Who minds dyin'? My father, he was glad to die. At the very end he got frightened, but I crept into bed beside him, an' he quieted down again. I was a lad of thirteen then. I was tired and fell asleep beside him—I knew no better—and when I woke he was quite cold.

MOTHER BAUMERT: [*After a pause*] Give Ansorge his soup out o' the oven, Bertha.

BERTHA: Here, Father Ansorge, it'll do you good.

ANSORGE: [*Eating and shedding tears*] Well, well, well!

[Old Baumert *has begun to eat the meat out of the saucepan*]

MOTHER BAUMERT: Father, father, can't you have patience an' let Bertha serve it up properly?

OLD BAUMERT: [*Chewing*] It's two years now since I took the Sacrament. I went straight after that an' sold my Sunday coat, an' we bought a good bit o' pork, an' since then never a mouthful of meat has passed my lips till to-night.

JAEGER: How should *we* need meat? The manufacturers eat it for us. It's the fat of the land *they* live on. Whoever doesn't believe that has only to go down to Bielau and Peterswaldau. He'll see fine things there—palace upon palace, with towers and iron railings and plate-glass windows. Who do they all belong to? Why, of course, the manufacturers! No signs of bad times there! Baked and boiled and fried—horses and carriages and governesses—they've money to pay for all that and goodness knows how much more. They're swelled out to bursting with pride and good living.

ANSORGE: Things was different in my young days. Then the manufacturers let the weaver have his share. Now they keep everything to theirselves. An'

would you like to know what's at the bottom of it all? It's that the fine folks nowadays believes neither in God nor devil. What do they care about commandments or punishments? And so they steal our last scrap of bread, an' leave us no chance of earnin' the barest living. For it's their fault. If our manufacturers was good men, there would be no bad times for us.

JAEGER: Listen, then, and I'll read you something that will please you. [*He takes one or two loose papers from his pocket*] I say, August, run and fetch another quart from the public-house. Eh, boy, do you laugh all day long?

MOTHER BAUMERT: No one knows why, but our August's always happy—grins an' laughs, come what may. Off with you, then, quick! [*Exit August with the empty brandy-bottle*] You've got something good now, eh, father?

OLD BAUMERT: [*Still chewing; spirits rising from the effect of food and drink*] Moritz, you're the very man we want. You can read an' write. You understand the weavin' trade, and you've a heart to feel for the poor weavers' sufferin's. You should stand up for us here.

JAEGER: I'd do that quick enough! There's nothing I'd like better than to give the manufacturers round here a bit of a fright—dogs that they are! I'm an easygoing fellow, but let me once get worked up into a real rage, and I'll take Dreissiger in the one hand and Dittrich in the other, and knock their heads together till the sparks fly out of their eyes.—If we could only arrange all to join together, we'd soon give the manufacturers a proper lesson . . . without help from King or Government . . . all we'd have to do would be to say: We want this and that, and we don't want the other thing. There would be a change of days then. As soon as they see that there's some pluck in us, they'll cave in. I know the rascals; they're a pack of cowardly hounds.

MOTHER BAUMERT: There's some truth in what you say. I'm not an ill-natured woman. I've always been the one to say as how there must be rich folks as well as poor. But when things come to such a pass as this. . . .

JAEGER: The devil may take them all, for what I care. It would be no more than they deserve.

[Old Baumert *has quietly gone out*]

BERTHA: Where's father?

MOTHER BAUMERT: I don't know where he can have gone.

BERTHA: Do you think he's not been able to stomach the meat, with not gettin' none for so long?

MOTHER BAUMERT: [*In distress, crying*] There, now, there! He's not even able to keep it down when he's got it. Up it comes again, the only bite o' good food as he's tasted this many a day.

[*Reënter* Old Baumert, *crying with rage*]

OLD BAUMERT: It's no good! I'm too far gone! Now that I've at last got hold of somethin' with a taste in it, my stomach won't keep it. [*He sits down on the bench by the stove crying*]

JAEGER: [*With a sudden violent ebullition of rage*] And yet there are people not far from here, justices they call themselves too, over-fed brutes, that have nothing to do all the year round but invent new ways of wasting their time. And these people say that the weavers would be quite well off if only they weren't so lazy.

ANSORGE: The men as say that are no men at all, they're monsters.

JAEGER: Never mind, Father Ansorge; we're making the place hot for 'em. Becker and I have been and given Dreissiger a piece of our mind, and before we came away we sang him "Bloody Justice."

ANSORGE: Good Lord! Is that the song?

JAEGER: Yes; I have it here.

ANSORGE: They call it Dreissiger's song, don't they?

JAEGER: I'll read it to you.

MOTHER BAUMERT: Who wrote it?

JAEGER: That's what nobody knows. Now listen. [*He reads, hesitating like a schoolboy, with incorrect accentuation, but unmistakably strong feeling. Despair, suffering, rage, hatred, thirst for revenge, all find utterance*]

> The justice to us weavers dealt
> Is bloody, cruel, and hateful;
> Our life's one torture, long drawn out:
> For Lynch law we'd be grateful.
> Stretched on the rack day after day,
> Hearts sick and bodies aching,
> Our heavy sighs their witness bear
> To spirits slowly breaking.

[*The words of the song make a strong impression on* Old Baumert. *Deeply agitated, he struggles against the temptation to interrupt* Jaeger. *At last he can keep quiet no longer*]

OLD BAUMERT: [*To his wife, half laughing, half crying, stammering*] Stretched on the rack day after day. Whoever wrote that, mother, wrote the truth. You can bear witness . . . eh, how does it go? "Our heavy sighs their witness bear" . . . what's the rest?

JAEGER: "To spirits slowly breaking."

OLD BAUMERT: You know the way we sigh, mother, day and night, sleepin' and wakin'.

[*Ansorge has stopped working, and cowers on the floor, strongly agitated.* Mother Baumert *and* Bertha *wipe their eyes frequently during the course of the reading*]

JAEGER: [*Continues to read*]

> The Dreissigers true hangmen are,
> Servants no whit behind them;
> Masters and men with one accord
> Set on the poor to grind them.
> You villains all, you brood of hell . . .

OLD BAUMERT: [*Trembling with rage, stamping on the floor*] Yes, brood of hell!!!

JAEGER: [*Reads*]

> You fiends in fashion human,
> A curse will fall on all like you,
> Who prey on man and woman.

ANSORGE: Yes, yes, a curse upon them!

OLD BAUMERT: [*Clenching his fist threateningly*] You prey on man and woman.

JAEGER: [*Reads*]

> The suppliant knows he asks in vain,
> Vain every word that's spoken.
> "If not content, then go and starve—
> Our rules cannot be broken."

OLD BAUMERT: What is it? "The suppliant knows he asks in vain"? Every word of it's true . . . every word . . . as true as the Bible. He knows he asks in vain.

ANSORGE: Yes, yes! It's all no good.

JAEGER: [*Reads*]

> Then think of all our woe and want,
> O ye who hear this ditty!
> Our struggle vain for daily bread
> Hard hearts would move to pity.
> But pity's what *you've* never known,—
> You'd take both skin and clothing,
> You cannibals, whose cruel deeds
> Fill all good men with loathing.

OLD BAUMERT: [*Jumps up, beside himself with excitement*] Both skin and clothing. It's true, it's all true! Here I stand, Robert Baumert, master-weaver of Kaschbach. Who can bring up anything against me? I've been an honest, hard-working man all my life long, an' look at me now! What have I to show for it? Look at me! See what they've made of me! Stretched on the rack day after day. [*He holds out his arms*] Feel that! Skin and bone! "You villains all, you brood of hell!!" [*He sinks down on a chair, weeping with rage and despair*]

ANSORGE: [*Flings his basket from him into a corner, rises, his whole body trembling with rage, gasps*] And the time's come now for a change, I say. We'll stand it no longer! We'll stand it no longer! Come what may!

ACT III.

The common room of the principal public house in Peterswaldau. A large room with a raftered roof supported by a central wooden pillar, round which a table runs. In the back wall, a little to the right of the pillar, is the entrance door, through the opening of which the spacious lobby or outer room is seen, with barrels and brewing utensils. To the right of this door, in the corner, is the bar—a high wooden counter with receptacles for beermugs, glasses, etc.; a cupboard with rows of brandy and liqueur bottles on the wall behind, and between counter and cupboard a narrow space for the barkeeper. In front of the bar stands a table with a gay-colored cover, a pretty lamp hanging above it, and several cane chairs placed around it. Not far off, in the right wall, is a door with the inscription: Bar Parlor. Nearer the front on the same side an old eight-day clock stands ticking. At the back, to the left of the entrance door, is a table with bottles and glasses, and beyond this, in the corner, is the great stove. In the left wall there are three small windows. Below them runs a long bench; and in front of each stands a large oblong wooden table, with the end towards the wall. There are benches with backs along the sides of these tables, and at the end of each facing the window stands a wooden chair. The walls are washed blue and decorated with advertisements, colored prints and oleographs, among the latter a portrait of Frederick William III.

Welzel, *the publican, a good-natured giant, upwards of fifty, stands behind the counter, letting beer run from a barrel into a glass.*

Mrs. Welzel *is ironing by the stove. She is a handsome, tidily dressed woman in her thirty-fifth year.*

Anna Welzel, *a good-looking girl of seventeen, with a quantity of beautiful, fair, reddish hair, sits, nicely dressed, with her embroidery, at the table with the colored cover. She looks up from her work for a moment and listens, as the sound of a funeral hymn sung by school-children is heard in the distance.*

Wiegand, *the joiner, in his working clothes, is sitting at the same table, with a glass of Bavarian beer before him. His face shows that he understands what the world requires of a man if he is to attain his ends—namely, craftiness, sharpness, and relentless determination.*

A Commercial Traveler *is seated at the pillar-table, vigorously masticating a beefsteak. He is of middle height, stout and thriving-looking, inclined to jocosity, lively, and impudent. He is dressed in the fashion of the day, and his portmanteau, pattern-case, umbrella, overcoat, and traveling-rug lie on chairs beside him.*

WELZEL: [*Carrying a glass of beer to the* Traveler, *but addressing* Wiegand] The devil's loose in Peterswaldau to-day.

WIEGAND: [*In a sharp, shrill voice*] That's because it's delivery day at Dreissiger's.

MRS. WELZEL: But they don't generally make such an awful row.

WIEGAND: It's maybe because of the two hundred new weavers that he's going to take on.

MRS. WELZEL: [*At her ironing*] Yes, yes, that'll be it. If he wants two hundred, six hundred's sure to have come. There's no lack of *them.*

WIEGAND: You may well say that. There's no fear of their dying out, let them be ever so badly off. They bring more children into the world than we know what to do with. [*The strains of the funeral hymn are suddenly heard more distinctly*] There's a funeral to-day, too. Weaver Nentwich is dead, as no doubt you know.

WELZEL: He's been long enough about it. He's been goin' about like a livin' ghost this many a long day.

WIEGAND: You never saw such a little coffin, Welzel; it was the tiniest, miserablest little thing I ever glued together. And what a corpse! It didn't weigh ninety pounds.

TRAVELER: [*His mouth full*] What I don't understand's this. . . . Take up whatever paper you like and you'll find the most heartrending accounts of the destitution among the weavers. You get the impression that three-quarters of the people in this neighborhood are starving. Then you come and see a funeral like what's going on just now. I met it as I came into the village. Brass band, schoolmaster, school-children, pastor, and such a procession behind them that you would think it was the Emperor of China that was getting buried. If the people have money to spend on this sort of thing, well! . . . [*He takes a drink of beer; puts down the glass; suddenly and jocosely*] What do you say to it, miss? Don't you agree with me?

[Anna *gives an embarrassed laugh, and goes on working busily*]

TRAVELER: Now, I'll take a bet that these are slippers for papa.

WELZEL: You're wrong, then; I wouldn't put such things on my feet.

TRAVELER: You don't say so! Now, I would give half of what I'm worth if these slippers were for me.

MRS. WELZEL: Oh, you don't know nothing about such things.

WIEGAND: [*Has coughed once or twice, moved his chair, and prepared himself to speak*] You were saying, sir, that you wondered to see such a funeral as this. I tell you, and Mrs. Welzel here will bear me out, that it's quite a small funeral.

TRAVELER: But, my good man . . . what a monstrous lot of money it must cost! Where does that all come from?

WIEGAND: If you'll excuse me for saying so, sir, there's a deal of foolishness among the poorer working-people hereabouts. They have a kind of inordinate idea, if I may say so, of the respect an' duty an' honor they're bound to show to such as are taken from their midst. And when it comes to be a case of parents, then there's no bounds whatever to their superstitiousness. The children and the nearest family scrapes together every farthing they can call their own, an' what's still wanting, that they borrow from some rich man. They run themselves into debt over head and ears; they're owing money to the pastor, to the sexton, and to all concerned. Then there's the victuals an' the drink, an' such like. No, sir, I'm far from speaking against dutifulness to parents; but it's too much when it goes the length of the mourners having to bear the weight of it for the rest of their lives.

TRAVELER: But surely the pastor might reason them out of such foolishness.

WIEGAND: Begging your pardon, sir, but I must mention that every little place hereabouts has its church an' its respected pastor to support. These honorable gentlemen has their advantages from big funerals. The larger the attendance is, the larger the offertory is bound to be. Whoever knows the circumstances connected with the working classes here, sir, will assure you that the pastors are strong against quiet funerals.

[Enter Hornig, the rag-dealer, a little bandy-legged old man, with a strap round his chest]

HORNIG: Good-mornin', ladies and gentlemen! A glass of schnapps, if you please, Mr. Welzel. Has the young mistress anything for me to-day? I've got beautiful ribbons in my cart, Miss Anna, an' tapes, an' garters, an' the very best of pins an' hairpins an' hooks an' eyes. An' all in exchange for a few rags. [He changes his voice] An' out of them rags fine white paper's to be made, for your sweetheart to write you a letter on.

ANNA: Thank you, but I've nothing to do with sweethearts.

MRS. WELZEL: [Putting a bolt into her iron] No, she's not that kind. She'll not hear of marrying.

TRAVELER: [Jumps up, affecting delighted surprise, goes forward to Anna's table, and holds out his hand to her across it] That's right, miss. You and I think alike in this matter. Give me your hand on it. We'll both remain single.

ANNA: [Blushing scarlet, gives him her hand] But you are married already!

TRAVELER: Not a bit of it. I only pretend to be. You think so because I wear a ring. I only have it on my finger to protect my charms against shameless attacks. I'm not afraid of you, though. [He puts the ring into his pocket] But tell me, truly, miss, are you quite determined never, never, never, to marry?

ANNA: [Shakes her head] Oh, get along with you!

MRS. WELZEL: You may trust her to remain single unless something very extra good turns up.

TRAVELER: And why should it not? I know of a rich Silesian proprietor who married his mother's lady's maid. And there's Dreissiger, the rich manufacturer, his wife is an innkeeper's daughter, too, and not half so pretty as you, miss, though she rides in her carriage now, with servants in livery. And why not? [He marches about, stretching himself, and stamping his feet] Let me have a cup of coffee, please.

[Enter Ansorge and Old Baumert, each with a bundle. They seat themselves meekly and silently beside Hornig, at the front table to the left]

WELZEL: How are you, Father Ansorge? Glad to see you once again.

HORNIG: Yes, it's not often as you crawl down from that smoky old nest.

ANSORGE: [Visibly embarrassed, mumbles] I've been fetchin' myself a web again.

BAUMERT: He's going to work at a shilling the web.

ANSORGE: I wouldn't have it, but there's no more to be made now by basket-weavin'.

WIEGAND: It's always better than nothing. He does it only to give you employment. I know Dreissiger very well. When I was up there taking out his double windows last week we were talking about it, him and me. It's out of pity that he does it.

ANSORGE: Well, well, well! That may be so.

WELZEL: [Setting a glass of schnapps on the table before each of the weavers] Here you are, then. I say, Ansorge, how long is it since you had a shave? The gentleman over there would like to know.

TRAVELER: [Calls across] Now, Mr. Welzel, you know I didn't say that. I was only struck by the venerable appearance of the master-weaver. It isn't often one sees such a gigantic figure.

ANSORGE: [Scratching his head, embarrassed] Well, well!

TRAVELER: Such specimens of primitive strength are rare nowadays. We're all rubbed smooth by civilization . . . but I can still take pleasure in nature untampered with. . . . These bushy eyebrows! That tangled length of beard!

HORNIG: Let me tell you, sir, that these people haven't the money to pay a barber, and as to a razor for themselves, that's altogether beyond them. What grows, grows. They haven't nothing to throw away on their outsides.

TRAVELER: My good friend, you surely don't imagine that I would. . . . [Aside to Welzel] Do you think I might offer the hairy one a glass of beer?

WELZEL: No, no; you mustn't do that. He wouldn't take it. He's got some queer ideas in that head of his.

TRAVELER: All right, then, I won't. With your permission, miss. [He seats himself at Anna's table] I declare, miss, that I've not been able to take my eyes off your hair since I came in—such glossy softness, such a splendid quantity! [Ecstatically kisses his finger-tips] And what a color! . . . like ripe wheat. Come to Berlin with that hair and you'll create no end of a sensation. On my honor, with hair like that you may go to Court. . . . [Leans back, looking at it] Glorious, simply glorious!

WIEGAND: They've given her a name because of it.

TRAVELER: And what may that be?

HORNIG: The chestnut filly, isn't it?

WELZEL: Come, now, we've had enough o' this. I'm not goin' to have the girl's head turned altogether. She's had a-plenty of silly notions put into it already. She'll hear of nothing under a count to-day, and to-morrow it'll be a prince.

MRS. WELZEL: You let her alone, father. There's no harm in wantin' to rise in the world. It's as well that people don't all think as you do, or nobody would get on at all. If Dreissiger's grandfather had been of your way of thinkin', they would be poor weavers still. And now they're rollin' in wealth. An' look at old Tromtra. He was nothing but a weaver, too, and now he owns twelve estates, an' he's been made a nobleman into the bargain.

WIEGAND: Yes, Welzel, you must look at the thing fairly. Your wife's in the right this time. I can answer for that. I'd never be where I am, with seven workmen under me, if I had thought like you.

HORNIG: Yes, you understand the way to get on; that your worst enemy must allow. Before the weaver has taken to bed, you're gettin' his coffin ready.

WIEGAND: A man must attend to his business if he's to make anything of it.

HORNIG: No fear of you for that. You know before the doctor when death's on the way to knock at a weaver's door.

WIEGAND: [Attempting to laugh, suddenly furious] And you know better than the police where the thieves are among the weavers, that keep back two or three bobbins full every week. It's rags you ask for, but you don't say No, if there's a little yarn among them.

HORNIG: An' your corn grows in the churchyard. The more that are bedded on the sawdust, the better for you. When you see the rows of little children's graves, you pats yourself on the belly, and says you: This has been a good year; the little brats have fallen like cockchafers off the trees. I can allow myself a quart extra in the week again.

WIEGAND: And supposing this is all true, it still doesn't make me a receiver of stolen goods.

HORNIG: No; perhaps the worst you do is to send in an account twice to the rich fustian manufacturers, or to help yourself to a plank or two at Dreissiger's when there's building goin' on and the moon happens not to be shinin'.

WIEGAND: [Turning his back] Talk to any one you like, but not to me. [Then suddenly] Hornig the liar!

HORNIG: Wiegand the coffin-jobber!

WIEGAND: [To the rest of the company] He knows charms for bewitching cattle.

HORNIG: If you don't look out, I'll try one of 'em on you.

[Wiegand turns pale]

MRS. WELZEL: [Had gone out; now returns with the Traveler's coffee; in the act of putting it on the table] Perhaps you would rather have it in the parlor, sir?

TRAVELER: Most certainly not! [With a languishing look at Anna] I could sit here till I die.

[Enter a Young Forester and a Peasant, the latter carrying a whip. They wish the others "Good-Morning," and remain standing at the counter]

PEASANT: Two brandies, if you please.

WELZEL: Good-morning to you, gentlemen. [He pours out their beverage; the two touch glasses, take a mouthful, and then set the glasses down on the counter]

TRAVELER: [To Forester] Come far this morning, sir?

FORESTER: From Steinseiffersdorf—that's a good step.

[Two old Weavers enter, and seat themselves beside Ansorge, Baumert, and Hornig]

TRAVELER: Excuse me asking, but are you in Count Hochheim's service?

FORESTER: No. I'm in Count Keil's.

TRAVELER: Yes, yes, of course—that was what I meant. One gets confused here among all the counts and barons and other gentlemen. It would take a giant's memory to remember them all. Why do you carry an ax, if I may ask?

FORESTER: I've just taken this one from a man who was stealing wood.

OLD BAUMERT: Yes, their lordships are mighty strict with us about a few sticks for the fire.

TRAVELER: You must allow that if every one were to help himself to what he wanted. . . .

OLD BAUMERT: By your leave, sir, but there's a difference made here as elsewhere between the big an' the little thieves. There's some here as deals in stolen wood wholesale, and grows rich on it. But if a poor weaver . . .

FIRST OLD WEAVER: [Interrupts Baumert] We're forbid to take a single branch; but their lordships, they take the very skin off of us—we've assurance money to pay, an' spinning money, an' charges in kind—we must go here an' go there, an' do so an' so much field work, all willy-nilly.

ANSORGE: That's just how it is—what the manufacturer leaves us, their lordships takes from us.

SECOND OLD WEAVER: [Has taken a seat at the next table] I've said it to his lordship himself. By your leave, my lord, says I, it's not possible for me to work on the estate so many days this year. For why—my own bit of ground, my lord, it's been next to carried away by the rains. I've to work both night and day if I'm to live at all. For oh, what a flood that was! . . . There I stood an' wrung my hands, an' watched the good soil come pourin' down the hill, into the very house! And all that dear, fine seed! . . . I could do nothing but roar an' cry until I couldn't see out o' my eyes for a week. And then I had to start an' wheel eighty heavy barrowloads of earth up that hill, till my back was all but broken.

PEASANT: [Roughly] You weavers here make such an awful outcry. As if we hadn't all to put up with what Heaven sends us. An' if you are badly off just now, whose fault is it but your own? What did you do when trade was good? Drank an' squandered all you made. If you had saved a bit then, you'd have it to fall back on now when times is bad, and not need to be goin' stealin' yarn and wood.

FIRST YOUNG WEAVER: [Standing with several comrades in the lobby or outer room, calls in at the door] What's a peasant but a peasant, though he lies in bed till nine?

FIRST OLD WEAVER: The peasant an' the count, it's the same story with 'em both. Says the peasant when a weaver wants a house: I'll give you a little bit of a hole to live in, an' you'll pay me so much rent in money, an' the rest of it you'll make up by helpin' me to get in my hay an' my corn—an' if that doesn't please you, why, then you may go elsewhere. He tries another, and the second he says the same as the first.

BAUMERT: [Angrily] The weaver's like a bone that every dog takes a gnaw at.

PEASANT: [Furious] You starving curs, you're no good for anything. Can you yoke a plough? Can you draw a straight furrow or throw a bundle of sheaves on to a cart? You're fit for nothing but to idle about an' go after the women. A pack of scoundrelly ne'er-do-wells!

[He has paid and now goes out. The Forester follows, laughing. Welzel, the Joiner, and Mrs. Welzel laugh aloud; the Traveler laughs to himself. Then there is a moment's silence]

HORNIG: A peasant like that's as stupid as his own ox. As if I didn't know all about the distress in the villages round here. Sad sights I've seen! Four and five lyin' naked on one sack of straw.

TRAVELER: [In a mildly remonstrative tone] Allow me to remark, my good man, that there's a great difference of opinion as to the amount of distress here in the Eulengebirge. If you can read . . .

HORNIG: I can read straight off, as well as you. An' I know what I've seen with my own eyes. It would be queer if a man that's traveled the country with a pack on his back these forty years an' more didn't know something about it. There was Fullern, now. You saw the children scraping about among the dung-heaps with the peasants' geese. The people up there died naked, on the bare stone floors. In their sore need they ate the stinking weavers' glue. Hunger carried them off by the hundred.

TRAVELER: You must be aware, since you are able to read, that strict investigation has been made by the Government, and that . . .

HORNIG: Yes, yes, we all know what that means. They send a gentleman that knows all about it already better nor if he had seen it, an' he goes about a bit in the village, at the lower end, where the best houses are. He doesn't want to dirty his shining boots. Thinks he to himself: All the rest'll be the same as this. An' so he steps into his carriage, an' drives away home again, an' then writes to Berlin that there's no distress in the place at all. If he had but taken the trouble to go higher up into a village like that, to where the stream comes in, or across the stream on to the narrow side—or, better still, if he'd gone up to the little out-o'-the-way hovels on the hill above, some of 'em that black an' tumble-down as it would be the waste of a good match to set fire to 'em—it's another kind of report he'd have sent to Berlin. They should have come to me, these government gentlemen that wouldn't believe there was no distress here. I would have shown them something. I'd have opened their eyes for 'em in some of these starvation holes.

[The strains of the Weavers' Song are heard, sung outside]

WELZEL: There they are, roaring at that devil's song again.

WIEGAND: They're turning the whole place upside down.

MRS. WELZEL: You'd think there was something in the air.

[Jaeger and Becker arm in arm, at the head of a troop of young weavers, march noisily through the outer room and enter the bar]

JAEGER: Halt! To your places!

[The new arrivals sit down at the various tables, and begin to talk to other weavers already seated there]

HORNIG: [Calls out to Becker] What's up now, Becker, that you've got together a crowd like this?

BECKER: [Significantly] Who knows but something may be going to happen? Eh, Moritz?

HORNIG: Come, come, lads. Don't you be a-gettin' of yourselves into mischief.

BECKER: Blood's flowed already. Would you like to see it? [He pulls up his sleeve and shows bleeding tattoo-marks on the upper part of his arm. Many of the other young weavers do the same]

BECKER: We've been at Father Schmidt's gettin' ourselves vaccinated.

HORNIG: Now the thing's explained. Little wonder there's such an uproar in the place, with a band of young rapscallions like you paradin' round.

JAEGER: [Consequentially, in a loud voice] You may bring two quarts at once, Welzel! I pay. Perhaps you think I haven't got the needful. You're wrong, then. If we wanted we could sit an' drink your best brandy an' swill coffee till to-morrow morning with any bagman in the land.

[Laughter among the young weavers]

TRAVELER: [Affecting comic surprise] Is the young gentleman kind enough to take notice of me?

[Host, hostess, and their daughter, Wiegand, and the Traveler all laugh]

JAEGER: If the cap fits wear it.

TRAVELER: Your affairs seem to be in a thriving condition, young man, if I may be allowed to say so.

JAEGER: I can't complain. I'm a traveler in made-up goods. I go shares with the manufacturers. The nearer starvation the weaver is, the better I fare. His want butters my bread.

BECKER: Well done, Moritz! You gave it to him that time. Here's to you!

[Welzel has brought the corn-brandy. On his way back to the counter he stops, turns round slowly, and stands, an embodiment of phlegmatic strength, facing the weavers]

WELZEL: [Calmly but emphatically] You let the gentleman alone. He's done you no harm.

YOUNG WEAVERS: And we're doing him no harm.

[Mrs. Welzel *has exchanged a few words with the* Traveler. *She takes the cup with the remains of his coffee and carries it into the parlor. The* Traveler *follows her amidst the laughter of the weavers*]

YOUNG WEAVERS: [*Singing*]

"The Dreissigers the hangmen are,
    Servants no whit behind them."

WELZEL: Hush-sh! Sing that song anywhere else you like, but not in my house.

FIRST OLD WEAVER: He's quite right. Stop that singin', lads.

BECKER: [*Roars*] But we must march past Dreissiger's boys, and let them hear it once more.

WIEGAND: You'd better take care—you may march once too often.

[*Laughter and cries of Ho, ho!*]

[Wittig *has entered; a gray-haired old smith, bareheaded, with leather apron and wooden shoes, sooty from the smithy. He is standing at the counter waiting for his schnapps*]

YOUNG WEAVER: Wittig, Wittig!

WITTIG: Here he is. What do you want with him?

YOUNG WEAVERS: "It's Wittig!"—"Wittig, Wittig!" —"Come here, Wittig."—"Sit beside us, Wittig."

WITTIG: Do you think I would sit beside a set of rascals like you?

JAEGER: Come and take a glass with us.

WITTIG: Keep your brandy to yourselves. I pay for my own drink. [*Takes his glass and sits down beside* Baumert *and* Ansorge. *Clapping the latter on the stomach*] What's the weavers' food so nice? Sauerkraut and roasted lice!

OLD BAUMERT: [*Excitedly*] But what would you say now if they'd made up their minds as how they would put up with it no longer.

WITTIG: [*With pretended astonishment, staring open-mouthed at the old weaver*] Heinerle! you don't mean to tell me that that's you? [*Laughs immoderately*] O Lord, O Lord! I could laugh myself to death. Old Baumert risin' in rebellion! We'll have the tailors at it next, and then there'll be a rebellion among the baa-lambs, and the rats and the mice. Damn it all, but we'll see some sport. [*He nearly spits with laughter*]

OLD BAUMERT: You needn't go on like that, Wittig. I'm the same man I've always been. I still say 't would be better if things could be put right peaceably.

WITTIG: Peaceably! How could it be done peaceably? Did they do it peaceably in France? Did Robespeer tickle the rich men's palms? No! It was: Away with them, everyone! To the gilyoteen with them! Allongs onfong! You've got your work before you. The geese'll not fly ready roasted into your mouths.

OLD BAUMERT: If I could make even half a livin'—

FIRST OLD WEAVER: The water's up to our chins now, Wittig.

SECOND OLD WEAVER: We're afraid to go home.

It's all the same whether we works or whether we lies abed; it's starvation both ways.

FIRST OLD WEAVER: A man's like to go mad at home.

OLD ANSORGE: It's that length with me now that I don't care how things go.

OLD WEAVERS: [*With increasing excitement*] "We've no peace anywhere."—"We've no spirit left to work."—"Up with us in Steenkunzendorf you can see a weaver sittin' by the stream washin' hisself the whole day long, naked as God made him. It's driven him clean out of his mind."

THIRD OLD WEAVER: [*Moved by the spirit, stands up and begins to "speak with tongues," stretching out his hand threateningly*] Judgment is at hand! Have no dealings with the rich and the great! Judgment is at hand! The Lord God of Sabaoth . . .

[*Some of the weavers laugh. He is pulled down on his seat*]

WELZEL: That's a chap that can't stand a simple glass—he gets wild at once.

THIRD OLD WEAVER: [*Jumps up again*] But they— they believe not in God, not in hell, not in heaven. They mock at religion . . .

FIRST OLD WEAVER: Come, come now, that's enough!

BECKER: You let him do his little bit o' preaching. There's many a one would be the better for taking it to heart.

VOICES: [*In excited confusion*] "Let him alone!"— "Let him speak!"

THIRD OLD WEAVER: [*Raising his voice*] But hell is opened, saith the Lord; its jaws are gaping wide, to swallow up all those that oppress the afflicted and pervert judgment in the cause of the poor. [*Wild excitement*]

THIRD OLD WEAVER: [*Suddenly declaiming, schoolboy fashion*]

When one has thought upon it well,
It's still more difficult to tell
Why they the linen-weaver's work despise.

BECKER: But we're fustian-weavers, man.

[*Laughter*]

HORNIG: The linen-weavers is ever so much worse off than you. They're wandering about among the hills like ghosts. You people here have still got the pluck left in you to kick up a row.

WITTIG: Do you suppose the worst's over here? It won't be long till the manufacturers drain away that little bit of strength they still have left in their bodies.

BECKER: You know what he said: It will come to the weavers working for a bit of bread.

[*Uproar*]

SEVERAL OLD AND YOUNG WEAVERS: Who said that?

BECKER: Dreissiger said it.

A YOUNG WEAVER: The damned rascal should be hung up by the heels.

JAEGER: Look here, Wittig. You've always jawed

such a lot about the French revolution, and a good deal too about your own doings. A time may be coming, and that before long, when every one will have a chance to show whether he's a braggart or a true man.

WITTIG: [*Flaring up angrily*] Say another word if you dare! Have you heard the whistle of bullets? Have you done outpost duty in an enemy's country?

JAEGER: You needn't get angry about it. We're comrades. I meant no harm.

WITTIG: None of your comradeship for me, you impudent young fool.

[*Enter* Kutsche, *the policeman*]

SEVERAL VOICES: Hush—sh! Police!

[*This calling goes on for some time, till at last there is complete silence, amidst which* Kutsche *takes his place at the central pillar-table*]

KUTSCHE: A small brandy, please.

[*Again complete silence*]

WITTIG: I suppose you've come to see if we're all behaving ourselves, Kutsche?

KUTSCHE: [*Paying no attention to* Wittig] Good-morning, Mr. Wiegand.

WIEGAND: [*Still in the corner in front of the counter*] Good-morning t' you, sir.

KUTSCHE: How's trade?

WIEGAND: Thank you, much as usual.

BECKER: The chief constable's sent him to see if we're spoiling our stomach on these big wages we're getting.

[*Laughter*]

JAEGER: I say, Welzel, you will tell him how we've been feasting on roast pork an' sauce an' dumplings and sauerkraut, and now we're sitting at our champagne wine.

[*Laughter*]

WELZEL: The world's upside down with them today.

KUTSCHE: An' even if you had the champagne wine and the roast meat, you wouldn't be satisfied. I've to get on without champagne wine as well as you.

BECKER: [*Referring to* Kutsche's *nose*] He waters his beet-root with brandy and gin. An' it thrives upon it, too.

[*Laughter*]

WITTIG: A p'liceman like that has a hard life. Now it's a starving beggar boy he has to lock up, then it's a pretty weaver girl he has to lead astray; then he has to get roarin' drunk an' beat his wife till she goes screamin' to the neighbors for help; and there's the ridin' about on horseback and the lyin' in bed till nine—nay, faith, but it's no easy job!

KUTSCHE: Jaw away; you'll jaw a rope round your neck in time. It's long been known what sort of a fellow you are. The magistrates know all about that dangerous tongue of yours. I know who'll drink wife and child into the poorhouse an' himself into jail before long, who it is that'll go on agitatin' and

agitatin' till he brings down judgment on himself and all concerned.

WITTIG: [*Laughs bitterly*] It's true enough—no one knows what'll be the end of it. You may be right yet. [*Bursts out in fury*] But if it does come to that, I know who I've got to thank for it, who it is that's blabbed to the manufacturers an' all the gentlemen round, an' blackened my character to that extent that they never give me a hand's turn of work to do—an' set the peasants an' the millers against me, so that I'm often a whole week without a horse to shoe or a wheel to put a tire on. I know who's done it. I once pulled the damned brute off his horse, because he was givin' a little stupid boy the most awful flogging for stealin' a few unripe pears. But I tell you this, Kutsche, and you know me—if you get me put into prison, you may make your own will. If I hear as much as a whisper of it, I'll take the first thing as comes handy, whether it's a horseshoe or a hammer, a wheel-spoke or a pail; I'll get hold of you if I've to drag you out of bed from beside your wife, and I'll beat in your brains, as sure as my name's Wittig. [*He has jumped up and is going to rush at* Kutsche]

OLD AND YOUNG WEAVERS: [*Holding him back*] Wittig, Wittig! Don't lose your head!

KUTSCHE: [*Has risen involuntarily, his face pale. He backs toward the door while speaking. The nearer the door the higher his courage rises. He speaks the last words on the threshold, and then instantly disappears*] What are you goin' on at me about? I didn't meddle with you. I came to say something to the weavers. My business is with them an' not with you, and I've done nothing to you. But I've this to say to you weavers: The Superintendent of Police herewith forbids the singing of that song—Dreissiger's song, or whatever it is you call it. And if the yelling of it on the streets isn't stopped at once, he'll provide you with plenty of time and leisure for going on with it in jail. You may sing there, on bread and water, to your hearts' content. [*Goes out*]

WITTIG: [*Roars after him*] He's no right to forbid it—not if we were to roar till the windows shook an' they could hear us at Reichenbach—not if we sang till the manufacturers' houses tumbled about their ears an' all the Superintendents' helmets danced on the top of their heads. It's nobody's business but our own.

[Becker *has in the meantime got up, made a signal for singing, and now leads off, the others joining in*]

　　The justice to us weavers dealt
　　　　Is bloody, cruel, and hateful;
　　Our life's one torture, long drawn out;
　　　　For Lynch law we'd be grateful.

[Welzel *attempts to quiet them but they pay no attention to him.* Wiegand *puts his hands to his ears and rushes off. During the singing of the next verse the weavers rise and form into procession behind* Becker *and* Wittig, *who have given pantomimic signs for a general break-up*]

    Stretched on the rack, day after day,
      Hearts sick and bodies aching,
    Our heavy sighs their witness bear
      To spirit slowly breaking.

[*Most of the weavers sing the following verse out on the street, only a few young fellows, who are paying, being still in the bar. At the conclusion of the verse no one is left in the room except* Welzel *and his wife and daughter,* Hornig, *and* Old Baumert]

    You villains, all you brood of hell,
      You fiends in fashion human,
    A curse will fall on all like you
      Who prey on man and woman.

WELZEL: [*Phlegmatically collecting the glasses*] Their backs are up to-day, and no mistake.

HORNIG: [*To* Old Baumert, *who is preparing to go*] What in the name of Heaven are they up to, Baumert?

BAUMERT: They're goin' to Dreissiger's to make him add something on to the pay.

WELZEL: And are you joining in these foolish on-goings?

OLD BAUMERT: I've no choice, Welzel. The young men may an' the old men must. [*Goes out rather shamefacedly*]

HORNIG: It'll not surprise me if this ends badly.

WELZEL: To think that even old fellows like him are goin' right off their heads!

HORNIG: We all set our hearts on something!

ACT IV.

Peterswaldau. *Private room of* Dreissiger, *the fustian manufacturer—luxuriously furnished in the chilly taste of the first half of this century. Ceiling, doors, and stove are white, and the wall paper with its small, straight-lined floral pattern, is dull and cold in tone. The furniture is mahogany, richly-carved, and upholstered in red. On the right, between two windows with crimson damask curtains, stands the writing-table, a high bureau with falling flap. Directly opposite to this is the sofa, with the strong-box beside it; in front of the sofa a table, with chairs and easy-chairs arranged about it. Against the back wall is a gun-cupboard. All three walls are decorated with bad pictures in gilt frames. Above the sofa is a mirror with a heavily gilt rococo frame. On the left an ordinary door leads into the hall. An open fold-ing-door at the back shows the drawing-room, over-furnished in the same style of comfortless splendor. Two ladies,* Mrs. Dreissiger *and* Mrs. Kittelhaus, *the Pastor's wife, are seen in the drawing-room, looking at pictures. Pastor Kittelhaus is there too, engaged in conversation with* Weinhold, *the tutor, a theological graduate.*

KITTELHAUS: [*A kindly little elderly man, enters the front room, smoking and talking to the tutor, who is also smoking; he looks round and shakes his head in surprise at finding the room empty*] You are young, Mr. Weinhold, which explains everything. At your age we old fellows held—well, I won't say the same opinions—but certainly opinions of the same tendency. And there's something fine about youth—youth with its grand ideals. But unfortunately, Mr. Weinhold, they don't last; they are as fleeting as April sunshine. Wait till you are my age. When a man has said his say from the pulpit for thirty years—fifty-two times every year, not in-cluding saints' days—he has inevitably calmed down. Think of me, Mr. Weinhold, when you come that length.

WEINHOLD: [*Nineteen, pale, thin, tall, with lanky fair hair; restless and nervous in his movements*] With all due respect, Mr. Kittelhaus—I can't think —people have such different natures.

KITTELHAUS: My dear Mr. Weinhold, however restless-minded and unsettled a man may be—[*in a tone of reproof*]—and you are a case in point—however violently and wantonly he may attack the existing order of things, he calms down in the end. I grant you, certainly, that among our professional brethren individuals are to be found, who, at a fairly advanced age, still play youthful pranks. One preaches against the drink evil and founds temper-ance societies, another publishes appeals which un-doubtedly read most effectively. But what good do they do? The distress among the weavers, where it does exist, is in no way lessened—but the peace of society is undermined. No, no; one feels inclined in such cases to say: Cobbler, stick to your last; don't take to caring for the belly, you who have the care of souls. Preach the pure Word of God, and leave all else to Him who provides shelter and food for the birds, and clothes the lilies of the field. But I should like to know where our good host, Mr. Dreissiger, has suddenly disappeared to.

[Mrs. Dreissiger, *followed by* Mrs. Kittelhaus, *now comes forward. She is a pretty woman of thirty, of a healthy, florid type. A certain dis-cordance is noticeable between her deportment and way of expressing herself and her rich, ele-gant toilette*]

MRS. DREISSIGER: That's what I want to know, too, Mr. Kittelhaus. But it's what William always does. No sooner does a thing come into his head than off he goes and leaves me in the lurch. I've said enough about it, but it does no good.

KITTELHAUS: It's always the way with business men, my dear Mrs. Dreissiger.

WEINHOLD: I'm almost certain that something has happened downstairs.

[Dreissiger *enters, hot and excited*]

DREISSIGER: Well, Rosa, is coffee served?

MRS. DREISSIGER: [*Sulkily*] Fancy your needing to run away again!

DREISSIGER: [*Carelessly*] Ah! these are things you don't understand.

KITTELHAUS: Excuse me—has anything happened to annoy you, Mr. Dreissiger?

DREISSIGER: Never a day passes without that, my dear sir. I am accustomed to it. What about that coffee, Rosa?

[Mrs. Dreissiger *goes ill-humoredly and gives one or two violent tugs at the broad embroidered bell-pull*]

DREISSIGER: I wish you had been down stairs just now, Mr. Weinhold. You'd have gained a little experience. Besides . . . But now let us have our game of whist.

KITTELHAUS: By all means, sir. Shake off the dust and burden of the day, Mr. Dreissiger; forget it in our company.

DREISSIGER: [*Has gone to the window, pushed aside a curtain, and is looking out*] Vile rabble!! Come here, Rosa! [*She goes to the window*] Look . . . that tall red-haired fellow there! . . .

KITTELHAUS: That's the man they call Red Becker.

DREISSIGER: Is he the man that insulted you the day before yesterday? You remember what you told me—when John was helping you into the carriage?

MRS. DREISSIGER: [*Pouting, carelessly*] I'm sure I don't know.

DREISSIGER: Come now, what's the use of being cross? I must know. If he's the man, I mean to have him arrested. [*The strains of the Weavers' Song are heard*] Listen to that! Just listen!

KITTELHAUS: [*Highly incensed*] Is there to be no end to this nuisance? I must acknowledge now that it is time for the police to interfere. Permit me. [*He goes forward to the window*] See, see, Mr. Weinhold! These are not only young people. There are numbers of steady-going old weavers among them, men whom I have known for years and looked upon as most deserving and God-fearing. There they are, taking part in this intolerable uproar, trampling God's law under foot. Do you mean to tell me that you still defend these people?

WEINHOLD: Certainly not, Mr. Kittelhaus. That is, sir . . . *cum grano salis*. For after all, they are hungry and they are ignorant. They are giving expression to their dissatisfaction in the only way they understand. I don't expect that such people . . .

MRS. KITTELHAUS: [*Short, thin, faded, more like an old maid than a married woman*] Mr. Weinhold, Mr. Weinhold, how can you?

DREISSIGER: Mr. Weinhold, I am sorry to be obliged to . . . I didn't bring you into my house to give me lectures on philanthropy, and I must request that you will confine yourself to the education of my boys, and leave my other affairs entirely to me—entirely! Do you understand?

WEINHOLD: [*Stands for a moment rigid and deathly pale, then bows, with a strained smile. In a low voice*] Certainly, of course I understand. I have seen this coming. It is my wish too. [*Goes out*]

DREISSIGER: [*Rudely*] As soon as possible then, please. We require the room.

MRS. DREISSIGER: William, William!

DREISSIGER: Have you lost your senses, Rosa, that you're taking the part of a man who defends a low, blackguardly libel like that song?

MRS. DREISSIGER: But, William, he didn't defend it.

DREISSIGER: Mr. Kittelhaus, did he defend it or did he not?

KITTELHAUS: His youth must be his excuse, Mr. Dreissiger.

MRS. KITTELHAUS: I can't understand it. The young man comes of such a good, respectable family. His father held a public appointment for forty years, without a breath on his reputation. His mother was overjoyed at his getting this good situation here. And now . . . he himself shows so little appreciation of it.

PFEIFER: [*Suddenly opens the door leading from the hall and shouts in*] Mr. Dreissiger, Mr. Dreissiger! they've got him! Will you come, please? They've caught one of them.

DREISSIGER: [*Hastily*] Has some one gone for the police?

PFEIFER: The Superintendent's on his way upstairs.

DREISSIGER: [*At the door*] Glad to see you, sir. We want you here.

[Kittelhaus *makes signs to the ladies that it will be better for them to retire. He, his wife, and* Mrs. Dreissiger *disappear into the drawing-room*]

DREISSIGER: [*Exasperated, to the* Police Superintendent, *who has now entered*] I have at last had one of the ringleaders seized by my dyers. I could stand it no longer—their insolence was beyond all bounds —quite unbearable. I have visitors in my house, and these blackguards dare to . . . They insult my wife whenever she shows herself; my boys' lives are not safe. My visitors run the risk of being jostled and cuffed. Is it possible that in a well-ordered community incessant public insult offered to unoffending people like myself and my family should pass unpunished? If so . . . then . . . then I must confess that I have other ideas of law and order.

SUPERINTENDENT: [*A man of fifty, middle height, corpulent, full-blooded. He wears cavalry uniform with a long sword and spurs*] No, no, Mr. Dreissiger . . . certainly not! I am entirely at your disposal. Make your mind easy on the subject. Dispose of me as you will. What you have done is quite right. I am delighted that you have had one of the ringleaders arrested. I am very glad indeed that a settling day has come. There are a few disturbers of the peace here whom I have long had my eye on.

DREISSIGER: Yes, one or two raw lads, lazy vagabonds, that shirk every kind of work, and lead a life of low dissipation, hanging about the public-houses until they've sent their last halfpenny down their throats. But I'm determined to put a stop to the trade of these professional blackguards once and for all. It's in the public interest to do so, not only my private interest.

SUPERINTENDENT: Of course it is! Most undoubt-edly, Mr. Dreissiger! No one can possibly blame you. And everything that lies in my power . . .

DREISSIGER: The cat-o'-nine tails is what should be taken to the beggarly pack.

SUPERINTENDENT: You're right, quite right. We must make an example.

[Kutsche, *the policeman, enters and salutes. The door is open, and the sound of heavy steps stumbling up the stair is heard*]

KUTSCHE: I have to inform you, sir, that we have arrested a man.

DREISSIGER: [*To* Superintendent] Do you wish to see the fellow?

SUPERINTENDENT: Certainly, most certainly. We must begin by having a look at him at close quarters. Oblige me, Mr. Dreissiger, by not speaking to him at present. I'll see to it that you get complete satisfac-tion, or my name's not Heide.

DREISSIGER: That's not enough for me, though. He goes before the magistrates. My mind's made up.

[Jaeger *is led in by five dyers, who have come straight from their work—faces, hands, and clothes stained with dye. The prisoner, his cap set jauntily on the side of his head, presents an appearance of impudent gayety; he is excited by the brandy he has just drunk*]

JAEGER: Hounds that you are!—Call yourselves workingmen!—Pretend to be comrades! Before I would do such a thing as lay my hands on a mate, I'd see my hand rot off my arm!

[At a sign from the Superintendent, Kutsche *orders the dyers to let go their victim. Jaeger straightens himself up, quite free and easy. Both doors are guarded*]

SUPERINTENDENT: [*Shouts to* Jaeger] Off with your cap, sir. [Jaeger *takes it off, but very slowly, still with an impudent grin on his face*] What's your name!

JAEGER: What's yours? I'm not your swineherd.

[*Great excitement is produced among the audi-ence by this reply*]

DREISSIGER: This is too much of a good thing.

SUPERINTENDENT: [*Changes color, is on the point of breaking out furiously, but controls his rage*] We'll see about this afterwards.—Once more, what's your name? [*Receiving no answer, furiously*] If you don't answer at once, fellow, I'll have you flogged on the spot.

JAEGER: [*Perfectly cheerful, not showing by so much as the twitch of an eyelid that he has heard the* Superintendent's *angry words, calls over the heads of those around him to a pretty servant girl,*

who has brought in the coffee and is standing open-mouthed with astonishment at the unexpected sight] Hullo, Emmy, do you belong to this company now? The sooner you find your way out of it, then, the better. A wind may begin to blow here, an' blow everything away overnight.

[*The girl stares at* Jaeger, *and as soon as she comprehends that it is to her he is speaking, blushes with shame, covers her eyes with her hands, and rushes out, leaving the coffee things in confusion on the table. Renewed excitement among those present*]

SUPERINTENDENT: [*Half beside himself, to* Dreis-siger] Never in all my long service . . . such a case of shameless effrontery . . .

[Jaeger *spits on the floor*]

DREISSIGER: I'll thank you to remember that this is not a stable.

SUPERINTENDENT: My patience is at an end now. For the last time: What's your name?

[Kittelhaus, *who has been peering out at the partly opened drawing-room door, listening to what has been going on, can no longer refrain from coming forward to interfere. He is trembling with excitement*]

KITTELHAUS: His name is Jaeger, sir. Moritz . . . is it not? Moritz Jaeger. [*To* Jaeger] And, Jaeger, you know me.

JAEGER: [*Seriously*] You are Pastor Kittelhaus.

KITTELHAUS: Yes, I am your pastor, Jaeger! It was I who received you, a babe in swaddling clothes, into the Church of Christ. From my hands you took for the first time the body of the Lord. Do you remember that, and how I toiled and strove to bring God's Word home to your heart? Is this your grati-tude?

JAEGER: [*Like a scolded schoolboy, in a surly voice*] I paid my half-crown like the rest.

KITTELHAUS: Money, money . . . Do you imag-ine that the miserable little bit of money . . . Such utter nonsense! I'd much rather you kept your money. Be a good man, be a Christian! Think of what you promised. Keep God's law. Money, money! . . .

JAEGER: I'm a Quaker now, sir. I don't believe in anything.

KITTELHAUS: Quaker! What are you talking about? Try to behave yourself, and don't use words you don't understand. Quaker, indeed! They are good Christian people, and not heathens like you.

SUPERINTENDENT: Mr. Kittelhaus, I must ask you . . . [*He comes between the* Pastor *and* Jaeger] Kutsche! tie his hands!

[*Wild yelling outside: "Jaeger, Jaeger! come out!"*]

DREISSIGER: [*Like the others, slightly startled, goes instinctively to the window*] What's the mean-ing of this next?

SUPERINTENDENT: Oh, I understand well enough. It means that they want to have the blackguard out among them again. But we're not going to oblige them. Kutsche, you have your orders. He goes to the lock-up.

KUTSCHE: [*With the rope in his hand, hesitating*] By your leave, sir, but it'll not be an easy job. There's a confounded big crowd out there—a pack of raging devils. They've got Becker with them, and the smith . . .

KITTELHAUS: Allow me one more word!—So as not to rouse still worse feeling, would it not be better if we tried to arrange things peaceably? Perhaps Jaeger will give his word to go with us quietly, or . . .

SUPERINTENDENT: Quite impossible! Think of my responsibility. I couldn't allow such a thing. Come, Kutsche! lose no more time.

JAEGER: [*Putting his hands together, and holding them out*] Tight, tight, as tight as ever you can! It's not for long.

[Kutsche, *assisted by the workmen, ties his hands*]

SUPERINTENDENT: Now, off with you, march [*To* Dreissiger] If you feel anxious, let six of the weavers go with them. They can walk on each side of him, I'll ride in front, and Kutsche will bring up the rear. Whoever blocks the way will be cut down.

[*Cries from below:* "Cock-a-doodle-doo-oo-oo! ow, wow, wow!"]

SUPERINTENDENT: [*With a threatening gesture in the direction of the window*] You rascals, I'll cock-a-doodle-doo and bow-wow you! Forward! March! [*He marches out first, with drawn sword; the others, with* Jaeger, *follow*]

JAEGER: [*Shouts as he goes*] An' Mrs. Dreissiger there may play the lady as proud as she likes, but for all that she's no better than us. Many a hundred times she's served my father with a half penny-worth of schnapps. Left wheel—march! [*Exit laughing*]

DREISSIGER: [*After a pause, with apparent calmness*] Well, Mr. Kittelhaus, shall we have our game now? I think there will be no further interruption. [*He lights a cigar, giving short laughs as he does so; when it is lighted, bursts into a regular fit of laughing*] I'm beginning now to think the whole thing very funny. That fellow! [*Still laughing nervously*] It really is too comical: first came the dispute at dinner with Weinhold—five minutes after that he takes leave—off to the other end of the world; then this affair crops up—and now we'll proceed with our whist.

KITTELHAUS: Yes, but . . . [*Roaring is heard outside*] Yes, but . . . that's a terrible uproar they're making outside.

DREISSIGER: All we have to do is to go into the other room; it won't disturb us in the least there.

KITTELHAUS: [*Shaking his head*] I wish I knew what has come over these people. In so far I must agree with Mr. Weinhold, or at least till quite lately I was of his opinion, that the weavers were a patient, humble, easily-led class. Was it not your idea of them, too, Mr. Dreissiger?

DREISSIGER: Most certainly that is what they used to be—patient, easily managed, peaceable people. They were that as long as these so-called humanitarians let them alone. But for ever so long now they've had the awful misery of their condition held up to them. Think of all the societies and associations for the alleviation of the distress among the weavers. At last the weaver believes in it himself, and his head's turned. Some of them had better come and turn it back again, for now he's fairly set a-going there's no end to his complaining. This doesn't please him, and that doesn't please him. He must have everything of the best.

[*A loud roar of* "Hurrah!" *is heard from the crowd*]

KITTELHAUS: So that with all their humanitarianism they have only succeeded in almost literally turning lambs into wolves.

DREISSIGER: I won't say that, sir. When you take time to think of the matter coolly, it's possible that some good may come of it yet. Such occurrences as this will not pass unnoticed by those in authority, and may lead them to see that things can't be allowed to go on as they are doing—that means must be taken to prevent the utter ruin of our home industries.

KITTELHAUS: Possibly. But what is the cause, then, of this terrible falling off of trade?

DREISSIGER: Our best markets have been closed to us by the heavy import duties foreign countries have laid on our goods. At home the competition is terrible, for we have no protection, none whatever.

PFEIFER: [*Staggers in, pale and breathless*] Mr. Dreissiger, Mr. Dreissiger!

DREISSIGER: [*In the act of walking into the drawing-room, turns round, annoyed*] Well, Pfeifer, what now?

PFEIFER: Oh, sir! Oh, sir! . . . It's worse than ever!

DREISSIGER: What are they up to next?

KITTELHAUS: You're really alarming us—what is it?

PFEIFER: [*Still confused*] I never saw the like. Good Lord!—The Superintendent himself . . . they'll catch it for this yet.

DREISSIGER: What's the matter with you, in the devil's name? Is any one's neck broken?

PFEIFER: [*Almost crying with fear, screams*] They've set Moritz Jaeger free—they've thrashed the Superintendent and driven him away—they've thrashed the policeman and sent him off too—without his helmet . . . his sword broken . . . Oh dear, oh dear!

DREISSIGER: I think you've gone crazy, Pfeifer.

KITTELHAUS: This is actual riot.

PFEIFER: [*Sitting on a chair, his whole body trembling*] It's turning serious, Mr. Dreissiger! Mr. Dreissiger, it's serious now!

DREISSIGER: Well, if that's all the police . . .

PFEIFER: Mr. Dreissiger, it's serious now!

DREISSIGER: Damn it all, Pfeifer, will you hold your tongue?

MRS. DREISSIGER: [*Coming out of the drawing-room with* Mrs. Kittelhaus] This is really too bad, William. Our whole evening's being spoiled. Here's Mrs. Kittelhaus saying that she'd better go home.

KITTELHAUS: You mustn't take it amiss, dear Mrs. Dreissiger, but perhaps, under the circumstances, it *would* be better . . .

MRS. DREISSIGER: But, William, why in the world don't you go out and put a stop to it?

DREISSIGER: Go you and try if you can do it. Try! Go and speak to them! [*Standing helplessly in front of the* Pastor] Am I such a tyrant? Am I a cruel master?

[*Enter* John *the coachman*]

JOHN: If you please, m'm, I've put to the horses. Mr. Weinhold's put Georgie and Charlie into the carriage. If it comes to the worst, we're ready to be off.

MRS. DREISSIGER: If what comes to the worst?

JOHN: I'm sure I don't know, m'm. But the crowd's gettin' bigger and bigger, an' they've sent the Superintendent an' the p'liceman to the right-about.

PFEIFER: It's serious now, Mr. Dreissiger! It's serious!

MRS. DREISSIGER: [*With increasing alarm*] What's going to happen?—What do the people want?— They're never going to attack us, John?

JOHN: There's some rascally hounds among 'em, ma'am.

PFEIFER: It's serious now! serious!

DREISSIGER: Hold your tongue, fool!—Are the doors barred?

KITTELHAUS: I ask you as a favor, Mr. Dreissiger . . . as a favor . . . I am determined to . . . I ask you as a favor . . . [*To* John] What demands are the people making?

JOHN: [*Awkwardly*] It's higher wages they're after, the blackguards.

KITTELHAUS: Good, good!—I shall go out and do my duty. I shall speak seriously to these people.

JOHN: Oh, sir, please, sir, don't do any such thing. Words is quite useless.

KITTELHAUS: One little favor, Mr. Dreissiger. May I ask you to post men behind the door, and to have it closed at once after me?

MRS. KITTELHAUS: Oh Joseph, Joseph! you're not really going out?

KITTELHAUS: I am. Indeed I am. I know what I'm doing. Don't be afraid. God will protect me.

[Mrs. Kittelhaus *presses his hand, draws back, and wipes tears from her eyes*]

KITTELHAUS: [*While the murmur of a great, excited crowd is heard uninterruptedly outside*] I'll go . . . I'll go out as if I were simply on my way home. I shall see if my sacred office . . . if the

people have not sufficient respect for me left to . . . I shall try . . . [*He takes his hat and stick*] Forward, then, in God's name!

[*Goes out accompanied by* Dreissiger, Pfeifer, *and* John]

MRS. KITTELHAUS: Oh, dear Mrs. Dreissiger! [*She bursts into tears and embraces her*] I do trust nothing will happen to him.

MRS. DREISSIGER: [*Absently*] I don't know how it is, Mrs. Kittelhaus, but I . . . I can't tell you how I feel. I didn't think such a thing was possible. It's . . . it's as if it was a sin to be rich. If I had been told about all this beforehand, Mrs. Kittelhaus, I don't know but what I would rather have been left in my own humble position.

MRS. KITTELHAUS: There are troubles and disappointments in every condition of life, Mrs. Dreissiger.

MRS. DREISSIGER: True, true, I can well believe that. And suppose we have more than other people . . . goodness me! we didn't steal it. It's been honestly got, every penny of it. It's not possible that the people can be going to attack us! If trade's bad, that's not William's fault, is it?

[*Loud, confused yelling is heard outside. While the two women stand gazing at each other, pale and startled,* Dreissiger *rushes in*]

DREISSIGER: Quick, Rosa—put on something, and get into the carriage. I'll be after you this moment. [*He rushes to the strong box, and takes out papers and various articles of value*]

[*Enter* John]

JOHN: We're ready to start. But come quickly, before they get round to the back door.

MRS. DREISSIGER: [*In a transport of fear, throwing her arms around* John's *neck*] John, John, dear, good John! Save us, John. Save my boys! Oh, what is to become of us?

DREISSIGER: Rosa, try to keep your head. Let John go.

JOHN: Yes, yes, ma'am! Don't you be frightened. Our good horses'll soon leave them all behind; an' whoever doesn't get out of the way'll be driven over.

MRS. KITTELHAUS: [*In helpless anxiety*] But my husband . . . my husband? But, Mr. Dreissiger, my husband?

DREISSIGER: He's in safety now, Mrs. Kittelhaus. Don't alarm yourself; he's all right.

MRS. KITTELHAUS: Something dreadful has happened to him. I know it. You needn't try to keep it from me.

DREISSIGER: You mustn't take it to heart—they'll be sorry for it yet. I know exactly whose fault it was. Such a detestable, shameful outrage will not go unpunished. A community laying hands on its own pastor and maltreating him—abominable! Mad dogs they are—raging brutes—and they'll be treated as such. [*To his wife who still stands petrified*] Go, for my sake, Rosa, go quickly! [*The clatter of window panes being smashed on the ground floor is heard*] They've gone quite mad. There's nothing for it but to get away as fast as we can.

[*Cries of "Pfeifer, come out!"—"We want Pfeifer!"—"Pfeifer, come out!" are heard*]

MRS. DREISSIGER: Pfeifer, Pfeifer, they want Pfeifer!

PFEIFER: [*Dashes in*] Mr. Dreissiger, there are people at the back gate already, and the house door won't hold much longer. The smith's battering it in with a stable pail.

[*The cry sounds louder and clearer: "Pfeifer! Pfeifer! Pfeifer! come out!" Mrs. Dreissiger rushes off as if pursued. Mrs. Kittelhaus follows. Pfeifer listens, and changes color as he hears what the cry is. A perfect panic of fear seizes him; he weeps, entreats, whimpers, writhes, all at the same moment. He overwhelms Dreissiger with childish caresses, strokes his cheeks and arms, kisses his hands, and at last, like a drowning man, throws his arms round him and prevents him moving*]

PFEIFER: Dear, good, kind Mr. Dreissiger, don't leave me behind. I've always served you faithfully. I've always treated the people well. I couldn't give them more wages than the fixed rate. Don't leave me here—they'll do for me. If they find me, they'll kill me. O God! O God! My wife, my children!

DREISSIGER: [*Making his way out, vainly endeavoring to free himself from Pfeifer's clutch*] Can't you let me go, fellow? It'll be all right; it'll be all right.

[*For a few seconds the room is empty. Windows are broken in the drawing-room. A loud crash resounds through the house, followed by shouts of "Hurrah!" For an instant there is silence. Then gentle, cautious steps are heard on the stair, then timid, hushed ejaculations: "To the left!"—"Up with you!"—"Hush!"—"Slow, slow!"—"Don't shove like that!"—"It's a wedding we're goin' to!"—"Stop that crowding"—"You go first!"—"No, you go!"*]

[*Young weavers and weaver girls appear at the door leading from the hall, not daring to enter, but each trying to shove the other in. In the course of a few moments their timidity is overcome, and the poor, thin, ragged or patched figures, many of them sickly-looking, disperse themselves through Dreissiger's room and the drawing-room, first gazing timidly and curiously at everything, then beginning to touch things. Girls sit down on the sofas, whole groups admire themselves in the mirrors, men stand up on chairs, examine the pictures and take them down. There is a steady influx of miserable-looking creatures from the hall*]

FIRST OLD WEAVER: [*Entering*] No, no, this is carryin' it too far. They've started smashing things downstairs. There's no sense nor reason in that. There'll be a bad end to it. No man in his wits would do that. I'll keep clear of such ongoings.

[*Jaeger, Becker, Wittig carrying a wooden pail, Baumert, and a number of other old and young weavers, rush in as if in pursuit of something, shouting hoarsely*]

JAEGER: Where has he gone?

BECKER: Where's the cruel brute?

BAUMERT: If we can eat grass, he may eat sawdust.

WITTIG: We'll hang him whenever we catch him.

FIRST YOUNG WEAVER: We'll take him by the legs and fling him out at the window, onto the stones. He'll never get up again.

SECOND YOUNG WEAVER: [*Enters*] He's off!

ALL: Who?

SECOND YOUNG WEAVER: Dreissiger.

BECKER: Pfeifer too?

VOICES: Let's get hold of Pfeifer. Look for Pfeifer!

BAUMERT: Yes, yes! Pfeifer! Tell him there's a weaver here for him to starve.

[*Laughter*]

JAEGER: If we can't lay hands on that brute Dreissiger himself . . . we'll at any rate make a poor man of him.

BAUMERT: As poor as a church mouse . . . we'll see to that!

[*All, bent on the work of destruction, rush towards the drawing-room door*]

BECKER: [*Who is leading, turns round and stops the others*] Halt! Listen to me! This is nothing but a beginning. When we're done here, we'll go straight to Bielau, to Dittrich's, where the steam power-looms are. The whole mischief's done by these factories.

OLD ANSORGE: [*Enters from hall. Takes a few steps, then stops and looks round, bewildered; shakes his head, taps his forehead*] Who am I? Weaver Anton Ansorge. Has he gone mad, Old Ansorge? My head's goin' round like a humming-top, sure enough. What's he doing here? He'll do whatever he's a mind to. Where is Ansorge? [*He taps his forehead repeatedly*] Something's wrong! I'm not answerable! I'm off my head! Off with you, off with you, rioters that you are! Heads off, legs off, hands off! If you take my house, I take your house. Forward, forward!

[*Goes yelling into the drawing-room, followed by a yelling, laughing mob*]

ACT V.

Langenbielau. Old Weaver Hilse's work-room. On the left a small window, in front of which stands the loom. On the right a bed, with a table pushed close to it. Stove, with stove-bench, in the right-hand corner. Family worship is going on. Hilse, his old, blind, and almost deaf wife, his son Gottlieb, and Luise, Gottlieb's wife, are sitting at the table, on the bed and wooden stools. A winding-wheel and bob-

bins on the floor between table and loom. Old spinning, weaving, and winding implements are disposed
of on the smoky rafters; hanks of yarn are hanging down. There is much useless lumber in the low
narrow room. The door, which is in the back wall,
and leads into the big outer passage, or entry-room
of the house, stands open. Through another open
door on the opposite side of the passage, a second,
in most respects similar weaver's room is seen. The
large passage, or entry-room of the house, is paved
with stone, has damaged plaster, and a tumble-down
wooden staircase leading to the attics; a washing-
tub on a stool is partly visible; dirty linen of the most
miserable description and poor household utensils
lie about untidily. The light falls from the left into
all three apartments.

Old Hilse is a bearded man of strong build, but
bent and wasted with age, toil, sickness, and hardship. He is an old soldier, and has lost an arm. His
nose is sharp, his complexion ashen-gray, and he
shakes; he is nothing but skin and bone, and has the
deep-set, sore weaver's eyes.

OLD HILSE: [Stands up, as do his son and daughter-
in-law; prays] O Lord, we know not how to be
thankful enough to Thee, for that Thou hast spared
us this night again in thy goodness . . . an' hast
had pity on us . . . an' hast suffered us to take no
harm. Thou art the All-Merciful, an' we are poor,
sinful children of men—that bad that we are not
worthy to be trampled under thy feet. Yet Thou art
our loving Father, an' Thou will look upon us an'
accept us for the sake of thy dear Son, our Lord and
Saviour Jesus Christ. "Jesus' blood and righteousness,
Our covering is and glorious dress." An' if we're
sometimes too sore cast down under thy chastening
—when the fire of thy purification burns too raging
hot—oh, lay it not to our charge; forgive us our sin.
Give us patience, heavenly Father, that after all
these sufferin's we may be made partakers of thy
eternal blessedness. Amen.

MOTHER HILSE: [Who has been bending forward,
trying hard to hear] What a beautiful prayer you
do say, father!

[Luise goes off to the wash-tub, Gottlieb to the
room on the other side of the passage]

OLD HILSE: Where's the little lass?

LUISE: She's gone to Peterswaldau, to Dreissiger's.
She finished all she had to wind last night.

OLD HILSE: [Speaking very loud] You'd like the
wheel now, mother, eh?

MOTHER HILSE: Yes, father, I'm quite ready.

OLD HILSE: [Setting it down before her] I wish I
could do the work for you.

MOTHER HILSE: An' what would be the good of
that, father? There would I be, sittin' not knowin'
what to do.

OLD HILSE: I'll give your fingers a wipe, then,
so that they'll not grease the yarn. [He wipes her
hands with a rag]

LUISE: [At her tub] If there's grease on her hands,
it's not from what she's eaten.

OLD HILSE: If we've no butter, we can eat dry
bread—when we've no bread, we can eat potatoes
—when there's no potatoes left, we can eat bran.

LUISE: [Saucily] An' when that's all eaten, we'll
do as the Wenglers did—we'll find out where the
skinner's buried some stinking old horse, an' we'll
dig it up an' live for a week or two on rotten carrion
—how nice that'll be!

GOTTLIEB: [From the other room] There you are,
letting that tongue of yours run away with you again.

OLD HILSE: You should think twice, lass, before
you talk that godless way. [He goes to his loom,
calls] Can you give me a hand, Gottlieb?—there's a
few threads to pull through.

LUISE: [From her tub] Gottlieb, you're wanted to
help father.

[Gottlieb comes in, and he and his father set
themselves to the troublesome task of "drawing and slaying," that is, pulling the strands of
the warp through the "heddles" and "reed" of
the loom. They have hardly begun to do this
when Hornig appears in the outer room]

HORNIG: [At the door] Good luck to your work!

HILSE AND HIS SON: Thank you, Hornig.

GOTTLIEB: I say, Hornig, when do you take your
sleep? You're on your rounds all day, and on watch
all night.

HORNIG: Sleep's gone from me nowadays.

LUISE: Glad to see you, Hornig!

OLD HILSE: And what's the news?

HORNIG: It's queer news this mornin'. The weavers
at Peterswaldau have taken the law into their own
hands, an' chased Dreissiger an' his whole family out
of the place.

LUISE: [Perceptibly agitated] Hornig's at his lies
again.

HORNIG: No, missus, not this time, not to-day.—
I've some beautiful pinafores in my cart.—No, it's
God's truth I'm telling you. They've sent him to the
right-about. He came down to Reichenbach last
night, but, Lord love you! they daren't take him in
there, for fear of the weavers—off he had to go
again, all the way to Schweidnitz.

OLD HILSE: [Has been carefully lifting threads of
the web and approaching them to the holes, through
which, from the other side, Gottlieb pushes a wire
hook, with which he catches them and draws them
through] It's about time you were stopping now,
Hornig!

HORNIG: It's as sure as I'm a livin' man. Every
child in the place'll soon tell you the same story.

OLD HILSE: Either your wits are a-wool-gatherin'
or mine are.

HORNIG: Not mine. What I'm telling you's as true
as the Bible. I wouldn't believe it myself if I hadn't
stood there an' seen it with my own eyes—as I see
you now, Gottlieb. They've wrecked his house from
the cellar to the roof. The good china came flyin'

out at the garret windows, rattlin' down the roof. God only knows how many pieces of fustian are lying soakin' in the river! The water can't get away for them—it's running over the banks, the color of washin'-blue with all the indigo they've poured out at the window—it was flyin' like clouds of sky-blue dust. Oh, it's a terrible destruction they've worked! And it's not only the house—it's the dyeworks, too —an' the stores! They've broken the stair rails, they've torn up the fine flooring—smashed the look-in'-glasses—cut an' hacked an' torn an' smashed the sofas an' the chairs.—It's awful—it's worse than war.

OLD HILSE: An' you would have me believe that my fellow weavers did all that? [*He shakes his head incredulously. Other tenants of the house have collected at the door and are listening eagerly*]

HORNIG: Who else, I'd like to know? I could put names to every one of 'em. It was me took the sheriff through the house, an' I spoke to a whole lot of 'em, an' they answered me back quite friendly like. They did their business with little noise, but my word! they did it well. The sheriff spoke to them, and they answered him mannerly, as they always do. But there wasn't no stoppin' of them. They hacked on at the beautiful furniture as if they were workin' for wages.

OLD HILSE: *You* took the sheriff through the house?

HORNIG: An' what would I be frightened of? Every one knows me. I'm always turning up, like a bad penny. But no one has anything agin' me. They're all glad to see me. Yes, I went the rounds with him, as sure as my name's Hornig. An' you may believe me or not as you like, but my heart's sore yet from the sight—an' I could see by the sheriff's face that he felt queer enough, too. Not a living word did we hear—they were doin' their work and holdin' their tongues. It was a solemn an' a woeful sight to see the poor starving creatures for once in a way takin' their revenge.

LUISE: [*With irrepressible excitement, trembling, wiping her eyes with her apron*] An' right they are! It's only what should be!

VOICES AMONG THE CROWD AT THE DOOR: "There's some of the same sort here."—"There's one no farther away than across the river."—"He's got four horses in his stable an' six carriages, an' he starves his weavers to keep them."

OLD HILSE: [*Still incredulous*] What was it set them off?

HORNIG: Who knows? Who knows? One says this, another says that.

OLD HILSE: What do they say?

HORNIG: The story as most of them tells is that it began with Dreissiger sayin' that if the weavers were hungry they might eat grass.

[*Excitement at the door, as one person repeats this to the other, with signs of indignation*]

OLD HILSE: Well, now, Hornig—if you was to say

to me: Father Hilse, says you, you'll die to-morrow, I would answer back: That may be—an' why not? You might even go to the length of saying: You'll have a visit to-morrow from the King of Prussia. But to tell me that weavers, men like me an' my son, have done such things as that—never! I'll never in this world believe it.

MIELCHEN: [*A pretty girl of seven, with long, loose flaxen hair, carrying a basket on her arm, comes running in, holding out a silver spoon to her mother*] Mammy, mammy! look what I've got! An' you're to buy me a new frock with it.

LUISE: What d'you come tearing in like that for, girl? [*With increased excitement and curiosity*] An' what's that you've got hold of now? You've been runnin' yourself out o' breath, an' there—if the bobbins aren't in her basket yet? What's all this about?

OLD HILSE: Mielchen, where did that spoon come from?

LUISE: She found it, maybe.

HORNIG: It's worth its seven or eight shillin's at least.

OLD HILSE: [*In distressed excitement*] Off with you, lass—out of the house this moment—unless you want a lickin'! Take that spoon back where you got it from. Out you go! Do you want to make thieves of us all, eh? I'll soon drive that out of you. [*He looks round for something to beat her with*]

MIELCHEN: [*Clinging to her mother's skirts, crying*] No, grandfather, no! don't lick me! We—we did find them. All the other bob—bobbin . . . girls has . . . has them too.

LUISE: [*Half frightened, half excited*] I was right, you see. She found it. Where did you find it, Mielchen?

MIELCHEN: [*Sobbing*] At—at—Peterswaldau. We —we found them in front of—in front of Drei—Dreissiger's house.

OLD HILSE: This is worse an' worse! Get off with you this moment, unless you would like me to help you.

MOTHER HILSE: What's all the to-do about?

HORNIG: I'll tell you what, Father Hilse. The best way'll be for Gottlieb to put on his coat an' take the spoon to the police office.

OLD HILSE: Gottlieb, put on your coat.

GOTTLIEB: [*Pulling it on, eagerly*] Yes, an' I'll go right in to the office an' say they're not to blame us for it, for what can a child like that understand about it? an' I brought the spoon back at once. Stop your crying now, Mielchen!

[*The crying child is taken into the opposite room by her mother, who shuts her in and comes back*]

HORNIG: I believe it's worth as much as nine shillin's.

GOTTLIEB: Give us a cloth to wrap it in, Luise, so that it'll take no harm. To think of the thing bein' worth all that money. [*Tears come into his eyes while he is wrapping up the spoon*]

LUISE: If it was only ours, we could live on it for many a day.

OLD HILSE: Hurry up, now! Look sharp! As quick as ever you can. A fine state o' matters, this! Get that devil's spoon out o' the house.

[Gottlieb *goes off with the spoon*]

HORNIG: I must be off now, too. [*He goes, is seen talking to the people in the entry-room before he leaves the house*]

SURGEON SCHMIDT: [*A jerky little ball of a man, with a red, knowing face, comes into the entry-room*] Good-morning, all! These are fine goings on! Take care! Take care! [*Threatening with his finger*] You're a sly lot—that's what you are. [*At* Hilse's *door without coming in*] Morning, Father Hilse. [*To a woman in the outer room*] And how are the pains, mother? Better, eh? Well, well. And how's all with you, Father Hilse? [*Enters*] Why the deuce! what's the matter with mother?

LUISE: It's the eye veins, sir—they've dried up, so as she can't see at all now.

SURGEON SCHMIDT: That's from the dust and weaving by candle-light. Will you tell me what it means that all Peterswaldau's on the way here? I set off on my rounds this morning as usual, thinking no harm; but it wasn't long till I had my eyes opened. Strange doings, these! What in the devil's name has taken possession of them, Hilse? They're like a pack of raging wolves. Riot—why, it's revolution! they're plundering and laying waste right and left . . . Mielchen! where's Mielchen? [Mielchen, *her face red with crying, is pushed in by her mother*] Here, Mielchen, put your hand into my coat pocket. [Mielchen *does so*] The ginger-bread nuts are for you. Not all at once, though, you baggage! And a song first! The fox jumped up on a . . . come, now . . . The fox jumped up . . . on a moonlight . . . Mind, I've heard what you did. You called the sparrows on the churchyard hedge a nasty name, and they're gone and told the pastor. Did any one ever hear the like? Fifteen hundred of them agog—men, women, and children. [*Distant bells are heard*] That's at Reichenbach—alarm-bells! Fifteen hundred people! Uncomfortably like the world coming to an end!

OLD HILSE: An' is it true that they're on their way to Bielau?

SURGEON SCHMIDT: That's just what I'm telling you. I've driven through the middle of the whole crowd. What I'd have liked to do would have been to get down and give each of them a pill there and then. They were following on each other's heels like grim death, and their singing was more than enough to turn a man's stomach. I was nearly sick, and Friedrich was shaking on the box like an old woman. We had to take a stiff glass at the first opportunity. I wouldn't be a manufacturer, not though I could drive my carriage and pair. [*Distant singing*]

Listen to that! It's for all the world as if they were beating at some broken old boiler. We'll have them here in five minutes, friends. Good-bye! Don't you be foolish. The troops will be upon them in no time. Keep your wits about you. The Peterswaldau people have lost theirs. [*Bells ring close at hand*] Good gracious! There are our bells ringing too! Every one's going mad. [*He goes upstairs*]

GOTTLIEB: [*Comes back. In the entry-room, out of breath*] I've seen them, I've seen them! [*To a woman*] They're here, auntie, they're here! [*At the door*] They're here, father, they're here! They've got bean-poles, an' ox-goads, an' axes. They're standin' outside the upper Dittrich's kickin' up an awful row. I think he's payin' them money. O Lord! whatever's goin' to happen? What a crowd! Oh, you never saw such a crowd! Dash it all—if once they make a rush, our manufacturers'll be hard put to it.

OLD HILSE: What have you been runnin' like that for? You'll go racin' till you bring on your old trouble, and then we'll have you on your back again, strugglin' for breath.

GOTTLIEB: [*Almost joyously excited*] I had to run, or they would have caught me an' kept me. They were all roarin' to me to join them. Father Baumert was there too, and says he to me: You come an' get your sixpence with the rest—you're a poor starving weaver, too. An' I was to tell you, father, from him, that you were to come an' help to pay out the manufacturers for their grindin' of us down. Other times is coming, he says. There's going to be a change of days for us weavers. An' we're all to come an' help to bring it about. We're to have our half-pound of meat on Sundays, and now and again on a holiday sausage with our cabbage. Yes, things is to be quite different, by what he tells me.

OLD HILSE: [*With repressed indignation*] An' that man calls himself your godfather! and he bids you take part in such works of wickedness? Have nothing to do with them, Gottlieb. They've let themselves be tempted by Satan, an' it's his works they're doin'.

LUISE: [*No longer able to restrain her passionate excitement, vehemently*] Yes, Gottlieb, get into the chimney corner, an' take a spoon in your hand, an' a dish of skim milk on your knee, an' put on a petticoat an' say your prayers, an' then father'll be pleased with you. And *he* sets up to be a man!

[*Laughter from the people in the entry-room*]

OLD HILSE: [*Quivering with suppressed rage*] An' you set up to be a good wife, eh? You call yourself a mother, an' let your evil tongue run away with you like that? You think yourself fit to teach your girl, you that would egg on your husband to crime an' wickedness?

LUISE: [*Has lost all control of herself*] You an' your piety an' religion—did they serve to keep the life in my poor children? In rags an' dirt they lay, all the four—it didn't as much as keep them dry.

Yes! I set up to be a mother, that's what I do—an' if you'd like to know it, that's why I would send all the manufacturers to hell—because I'm a mother!—Not one of the four could I keep in life! It was cryin' more than breathin' with me from the time each poor little thing came into the world till death took pity on it. The devil a bit you cared! You sat there prayin' and singin', and let me run about till my feet bled, tryin' to get one little drop o' skim milk. How many hundred nights have I lain an' racked my head to think what I could do to cheat the churchyard of my little one? What harm has a baby like that done that it must come to such a miserable end—eh? An' over there at Dittrich's they're bathed in wine an' washed in milk. No! you may talk as you like, but if you begin here, ten horses won't hold me back. An' what's more—if there's a rush on Dittrich's, you'll see me in the forefront of it—an' pity the man as tries to prevent me—I've stood it long enough, so now you know it.

OLD HILSE: You're a lost soul—there's no help for you.

LUISE: [*Frenzied*] It's you that there's no help for! Tater-breeched scarecrows—that's what you are—an' not men at all. Whey-faced gutter-scrapers that take to your heels at the sound of a child's rattle. Fellows that say "thank you" to the man as gives you a hidin'. They've not left that much blood in you as that you can turn red in the face. You should have the whip taken to you, an' a little pluck flogged into your rotten bones. [*She goes out quickly*]

[*Embarrassed pause*]

MOTHER HILSE: What's the matter with Liesl, father?

OLD HILSE: Nothin', mother! What should be the matter with her?

MOTHER HILSE: Father, is it only me that's thinkin' it, or are the bells ringin'?

OLD HILSE: It'll be a funeral, mother.

MOTHER HILSE: An' I've got to sit waitin' here yet. Why must I be so long a-dyin', father?

[*Pause*]

OLD HILSE: [*Leaves his work, holds himself up straight; solemnly*] Gottlieb!—you heard all your wife said to us. Look here, Gottlieb! [*He bares his breast*] Here they cut out a bullet as big as a thimble. The King knows where I lost my arm. It wasn't the mice as ate it. [*He walks up and down*] Before that wife of yours was ever thought of, I had spilled my blood by the quart for King an' country. So let her call what names she likes—an' welcome! It does me no harm.—Frightened? Me frightened? What would I be frightened of, will you tell me that? Of the few soldiers, maybe, that'll be comin' after the rioters? Good gracious me! That would be a lot to be frightened at! No, no, lad; I may be a bit stiff in the back, but there's some strength left in the old bones; I've got the stuff in me yet to make a stand against a few rubbishin' bay'nets.—An' if it

came to the worst! Willin', willin' would I be to say good-bye to this weary world. Death would be welcome—welcomer to me to-day than to-morrow. For what is it we leave behind? That old bundle of aches an' pains we call our body, the care an' the oppression we call by the name of life. We may be glad to get away from it.—But there's something to come after, Gottlieb!—an' if we've done ourselves out of that too—why, then it's all over with us!

GOTTLIEB: Who knows what's to come after? Nobody's seen it.

OLD HILSE: Gottlieb! don't you be throwin' doubts on the one comfort us poor people have. Why have I sat here an' worked my treadle like a slave this forty year an' more?—sat still an' looked on at him over yonder livin' in pride an' wastefulness—why? Because I have a better hope, something as supports me in all my troubles. [*Points out at the window*] You have your good things in this world—I'll have mine in the next. That's been my thought. An' I'm that certain of it—I'd let myself be torn in pieces. Have we not His promise? There's a Day of Judgment coming; but it's not us as are the judges—no: vengeance is mine, saith the Lord.

[*A cry of "Weavers, come out!" is heard outside the window*]

OLD HILSE: Do what you will for me. [*He seats himself at his loom*] I stay here.

GOTTLIEB: [*After a short struggle*] I'm going to work, too—come what may. [*Goes out*]

[*The Weavers' Song is heard, sung by hundreds of voices quite close at hand; it sounds like a dull monotonous wail*]

INMATES OF THE HOUSE: [*In the entry-room*] "Oh, mercy on us! there they come swarmin' like ants!"—"Where can all these weavers be from?"—"Don't shove like that, I want to see too."—"Look at that great maypole of a woman leadin' on in front!"—"Gracious! they're comin' thicker an' thicker."

HORNIG: [*Comes into the entry-room from outside*] There's a theayter play for you now! That's what you don't see every day. But you should go up to the other Dittrich's an' look what they've done there. It's been no half work. He's got no house now, nor no factory, nor no wine-cellar, nor nothing. They're drinkin' out of the bottles—not so much as takin' the time to get out the corks. One, two, three, an' off with the neck, an' no matter whether they cut their mouths or not. There's some of them runnin' about bleedin' like stuck pigs.—Now they're goin' to do for this Dittrich.

[*The singing has stopped*]

INMATES OF THE HOUSE: There's nothin' so very wicked-like about them.

HORNIG: You wait a bit! you'll soon see! All they're doin' just now is makin' up their minds where they'll begin. Look, they're inspectin' the palace from every side. Do you see that little stout man there, him with the stable pail? That's the smith from Peterswaldau—an' a dangerous little chap he is. He batters in the thickest doors as if they were made o' pie-crust. If a manufacturer was to fall into his hands it would be all over with him!

INMATES OF THE HOUSE: "That was a crack!"— "There went a stone through the window!"— "There's old Dittrich, shakin' with fright."—"He's hangin' out a board."—"Hangin' out a board?"— "What's written on it?"—"Can you not read?"—"It would be a bad job for me if I couldn't read!"— "Well, read it, then!"—" 'You—shall have—full— satisfaction! You—shall have full satisfaction.' "

HORNIG: He might ha' spared himself the trouble —*that* won't help him. It's something else they've set their minds on here. It's the factories. They're goin' to smash up the power-looms. For it's them that are ruinin' the hand-loom weaver. Even a blind man might see that. No! the good folks know what they're after, an' no sheriff an' no p'lice superin-tendent'll bring them to reason—much less a bit of a board. Him as has seen them at work already knows what's comin'.

INMATES OF THE HOUSE: "Did any one ever see such a crowd?"—"What can these ones be wantin'?" —[*Hastily*] "They're crossin' the bridge!"—[*Anxiously*] "They're never comin' over on this side, are they?"—[*In excitement and terror*] "It's to us they're comin'!"—"They're comin' to us!"—"They're comin' to fetch the weavers out of their houses!'

[*General flight. The entry-room is empty. A crowd of dirty, dusty rioters rush in, their faces scarlet with brandy and excitement; tattered, untidy-looking, as if they had been up all night. With the shout: "Weavers, come out!" they disperse themselves through the house. Becker and several other young weavers, armed with cudgels and poles, come into* Old Hilse's *room. When they see the old man at his loom they start, and cool down a little*]

BECKER: Come, Father Hilse, stop that. Leave your work to them as wants to work. There's no need now for you to be doin' yourself harm. You'll be well taken care of.

FIRST YOUNG WEAVER: You'll never need to go hungry to bed again.

SECOND YOUNG WEAVER: The weaver's goin' to have a roof over his head and a shirt on his back once more.

OLD HILSE: An' what's the devil sendin' you to do now, with your poles an' axes?

BECKER: These are what we're goin' to break on Dittrich's back.

SECOND YOUNG WEAVER: We'll beat them red hot an' stick them down the manufacturers' throats, so as they'll feel for once what burnin' hunger tastes like.

THIRD YOUNG WEAVER: Come along, Father Hilse! We'll give no quarter.

SECOND YOUNG WEAVER: No one had mercy on us—neither God nor man. Now we're standin' up for our rights ourselves.

[Old Baumert *enters, somewhat shaky on the legs, a newly killed cock under his arm*]

OLD BAUMERT: [*Stretching out his arms*] My brothers—we're all brothers! Come to my arms, brothers!

[*Laughter*]

OLD HILSE: And that's the state you're in, Willem?

OLD BAUMERT: Gustav, is it you? My poor starvin' friend! Come to my arms, Gustav!

OLD HILSE: [*Mutters*] Let me alone.

OLD BAUMERT: I'll tell you what, Gustav. It's nothin' but luck that's wanted. You look at me. What do I look like? Luck's what's wanted. Do I not look like a lord? [*Pats his stomach*] Guess what's in there! There's food fit for a prince in that belly. When luck's with him a man gets roast hare to eat an' champagne wine to drink.—I'll tell you some-thing: We've made a big mistake—we must help ourselves.

ALL: [*Speaking at once*] We must help ourselves, hurrah!

OLD BAUMERT: As soon as we get the first good bite inside us we're different men. Damn it all! but you feel the power comin' into you till you're like an ox, an' that wild with strength that you hit out right an' left without as much as takin' time to look. Dash it, but it's grand!

JAEGER: [*At the door, armed with an old cavalry sword*] We've made one or two first-rate attacks.

BECKER: We know how to set about it now. One, two, three, an' we're inside the house. Then, at it like lightning—bang, crack, shiver! till the sparks are flyin' as if it was a smithy.

FIRST YOUNG WEAVER: It wouldn't be half bad to light a bit o' fire.

SECOND YOUNG WEAVER: Let's march to Reichen-bach an' burn the rich folks' houses over their heads!

JAEGER: That would be nothing but butterin' their bread. Think of all the insurance money they'd get.

[*Laughter*]

BECKER: No, from here we'll go to Freiburg, to Tromtra's.

JAEGER: What would you say to givin' all them as holds Government appointments a lesson? I've read somewhere as how all our troubles come from them birocrats, as they call them.

SECOND YOUNG WEAVER: Before long we'll go to Breslau, for more an' more'll be joining us.

OLD BAUMERT: [*To* Hilse] Won't you take a drop, Gustav?

OLD HILSE: I never touches it.

OLD BAUMERT: That was in the old world; we're in a new world to-day, Gustav.

FIRST YOUNG WEAVER: Christmas comes but once a year.

[*Laughter*]

OLD HILSE: [*Impatiently*] What is it you want in my house, you limbs of Satan?

OLD BAUMERT: [*A little intimidated, coaxingly*]

I was bringin' you a chicken, Gustav. I thought it would make a drop o' soup for mother.

OLD HILSE: [*Embarrassed, almost friendly*] Well, you can tell mother yourself.

MOTHER HILSE: [*Who has been making efforts to hear, her hand at her ear, motions them off*] Let me alone. I don't want no chicken soup.

OLD HILSE: That's right, mother. An' I want none, an' least of all that sort. An' let me say this much to you, Baumert: The devil stands on his head for joy when he hears the old ones jabberin' and talkin' as if they was infants. An' to you all I say—to every one of you: Me and you, we've got nothing to do with each other. It's not with my will that you're here. In law an' justice you've no right to be in my house.

A VOICE: Him that's not with us is against us.

JAEGER: [*Roughly and threateningly*] You're a cross-grained old chap, and I'd have you remember that we're not thieves.

A VOICE: We're hungry men, that's all.

FIRST YOUNG WEAVER: We want to *live*—that's all. An' so we've cut the rope we were hung up with.

JAEGER: And we were in our right! [*Holding his fist in front of the old man's face*] Say another word, and I'll give you one between the eyes.

BECKER: Come now, Jaeger, be quiet. Let the old man alone.—What we say to ourselves, Father Hilse, is this: Better dead than begin the old life again.

OLD HILSE: Have I not lived that life for sixty years an' more?

BECKER: That doesn't help us—there's got to be a change.

OLD HILSE: On the Judgment Day.

BECKER: What they'll not give us willingly we're going to take by force.

OLD HILSE: By force. [*Laughs*] You may as well go an' dig your graves at once. They'll not be long showin' you where the force lies. Wait a bit, lad!

JAEGER: Is it the soldiers you're meaning? We've been soldiers, too. We'll soon do for a company or two of them.

OLD HILSE: With your tongues, maybe. But supposin' you did—for two that you'd beat off, ten'll come back.

VOICES: [*Call through the window*] The soldiers are comin'! Look out!

[*General, sudden silence. For a moment a faint sound of fifes and drums is heard; in the ensuing silence a short, involuntary exclamation, "The devil! I'm off!" followed by general laughter*]

BECKER: Who was that? Who speaks of running away?

JAEGER: Which of you is it that's afraid of a few paltry helmets? You have me to command you, and I've been in the trade. I know their tricks.

OLD HILSE: An' what are you goin' to shoot with? Your sticks, eh?

FIRST YOUNG WEAVER: Never mind that old chap; he's wrong in the upper story.

SECOND YOUNG WEAVER: Yes, he's a bit off his head.

GOTTLIEB: [*Has made his way unnoticed among the rioters; catches hold of the speaker*] Would you give your impudence to an old man like him?

SECOND YOUNG WEAVER: Let me alone. 'Twasn't anything bad I said.

OLD HILSE: [*Interfering*] Let him jaw, Gottlieb. What would you be meddlin' with him for? He'll soon see who it is that's been off his head to-day, him or me.

BECKER: Are you comin', Gottlieb?

OLD HILSE: No, he's goin' to do no such thing.

LUISE: [*Comes into the entry-room, calls*] What are you puttin' off your time with prayin' hypocrites like them for? Come quick to where you're wanted! Quick! Father Baumert, run all you can! The Major's speakin' to the crowd from horseback. They're to go home. If you don't hurry up, it'll be all over.

JAEGER: [*As he goes out*] That's a brave husband of yours.

LUISE: Where is he? I've got no husband!

[*Some of the people in the entry-room sing*]

> Once on a time a man so small,
>   Heigh-ho, heigh!
> Set his heart on a wife so tall,
>   Heigh diddle-di-dum-di!

WITTIG, THE SMITH: [*Comes downstairs, still carrying the stable pail; stops on his way through the entry-room*] Come on! all of you that are not cowardly scoundrels!—hurrah! [*He dashes out, followed by Luise, Jaeger, and others, all shouting "Hurrah!"*]

BECKER: Good-bye, then, Father Hilse; we'll see each other again. [*Is going*]

OLD HILSE: I doubt that. I've not five years to live, and that'll be the soonest you'll get out.

BECKER: [*Stops, not understanding*] Out o' what, Father Hilse?

OLD HILSE: Out of prison—where else?

BECKER: [*Laughs wildly*] Do you think I would mind that? There's bread to be had there anyhow! [*Goes out*]

OLD BAUMERT: [*Has been cowering on a low stool, painfully beating his brains; he now gets up*] It's true, Gustav, as I've had a drop too much. But for all that I know what I'm about. You think one way in this here matter; I think another. I say Becker's right: even if it ends in chains an' ropes—we'll be better off in prison than at home. You're cared for there, an' you don't need to starve. I wouldn't have joined them, Gustav, if I could have let it be; but once in a lifetime a man's got to show what he feels. [*Goes slowly toward the door*] Good-bye, Gustav. If anything happens, mind you put in a word for me in your prayers. [*Goes out*]

[*The rioters are now all gone. The entry-room gradually fills again with curious onlookers from the different rooms of the house. Old Hilse knots at his web. Gottlieb has taken an ax from behind the stove and is unconsciously feeling its edge. He and the old man are silently agitated. The hum and roar of a great crowd penetrate into the room*]

MOTHER HILSE: The very boards is shakin', father —what's goin' on? What's goin' to happen to us?

[*Pause*]

OLD HILSE: Gottlieb!

GOTTLIEB: What is it?

OLD HILSE: Let that ax alone.

GOTTLIEB: Who's to split the wood, then? [*He leans the ax against the stove*]

[*Pause*]

MOTHER HILSE: Gottlieb, you listen to what father says to you.

[*Some one sings outside the window*]
    Our little man does all that he can,
        Heigh-ho, heigh!
    At home he cleans the pots an' the pan,
        Heigh-diddle-di-dum-di!

[*Passes on*]

GOTTLIEB: [*Jumps up, shakes his clenched fist at the window*] Brute that you are, would you drive me crazy?

[*A volley of musketry is heard*]

MOTHER HILSE: [*Starts and trembles*] Good Lord! is that thunder again?

OLD HILSE: [*Instinctively folding his hands*] Oh, our Father in heaven! defend the poor weavers, protect my poor brothers!

[*A short pause ensues*]

OLD HILSE: [*To himself, painfully agitated*] There's blood flowing now.

GOTTLIEB: [*Had started up and grasped the ax when the shooting was heard; deathly pale, almost beside himself with excitement*] And am I to lie to heel like a dog still?

A GIRL: [*Calls from the entry-room*] Father Hilse, Father Hilse! get away from the window. A bullet's just flown in at ours upstairs. [*Disappears*]

MIELCHEN: [*Puts her head in at the window, laughing*] Gran'father, gran'father, they've shot with their guns. Two or three's been knocked down, an' one of them's turnin' round and round like a top, an' one's twistin' himself like a sparrow when its head's bein' pulled of. An' oh, if you saw all the blood that came pourin'—! [*Disappears*]

A WEAVER'S WIFE: Yes, there's two or three'll never get up again.

AN OLD WEAVER: [*In the entry-room*] Look out! They're goin' to make a rush on the soldiers.

A SECOND WEAVER: [*Wildly*] Look, look, look at the women!—skirts up, an' spittin' in the soldiers' faces already!

A WEAVER'S WIFE: [*Calls in*] Gottlieb, look at your wife. She's more pluck in her than you. She's jumpin' about in front o' the bay'nets as if she was dancin' to music.

[*Four men carry a wounded rioter through the entry-room. Silence, which is broken by some one saying in a distinct voice, "It's Weaver Ulbrich." Once more silence for a few seconds, when the same voice is heard again: "It's all over with him; he's got a bullet in his ear." The men are heard climbing the wooden stair. Sudden shouting outside: "Hurrah, hurrah!"*]

VOICES IN THE ENTRY-ROOM: "Where did they get the stones from?"—"Yes, it's time you were off!"— "From the new road."—"Ta-ta, soldiers!"—"It's raining paving-stones."

[*Shrieks of terror and loud roaring outside, taken up by those in the entry-room. There is a cry of fear, and the house door is shut with a bang*]

VOICES IN THE ENTRY-ROOM: "They're loading again."—"They'll fire another volley this minute."— "Father Hilse, get away from that window."

GOTTLIEB: [*Clutches the ax*] What! are we mad dogs? Are we to eat powder an' shot now instead of bread? [*Hesitating an instant: to the old man*] Would you have me sit here an' see my wife shot? Never! [*As he rushes out*] Look out! I'm coming!

OLD HILSE: Gottlieb, Gottlieb!

MOTHER HILSE: Where's Gottlieb gone?

OLD HILSE: He's gone to the devil.

VOICES FROM THE ENTRY-ROOM: Go away from the window, Father Hilse.

OLD HILSE: Not I! Not if you all go crazy together! [*To Mother Hilse, with rapt excitement*] My heavenly Father has placed me here. Isn't that so, mother? Here we'll sit, an' do our bounden duty— ay, though the snow was to go on fire. [*He begins to weave*]

[*Rattle of another volley. Old Hilse, mortally wounded, starts to his feet and then falls over the loom. At the same moment loud shouting of "Hurrah!" is heard. The people who till now have been standing in the entry-room dash out, joining in the cry. The old woman repeatedly asks: "Father, father, what's wrong with you?" The continued shouting dies away gradually in the distance. Mielchen comes rushing in*]

MIELCHEN: Gran'father, gran'father, they're drivin' the soldiers out of the village; they've got into Dittrich's house, an' they're doin' what they did at Dreissiger's. Gran'father!

[*The child grows frightened, notices that something has happened, puts her finger in her mouth, and goes up cautiously to the dead man*]

Gran'father!

MOTHER HILSE: Come now, father, can't you say something? You're frightenin' me.

Frank Wedekind

(1864–1918)

Frank Wedekind, christened Benjamin Franklin, was born in the city of Hanover, shortly after his parents returned to Germany from the United States. It is ironical that but for chance he might have been born on American soil, since few important writers of the European stage are less known to the American public. For an actor-playwright who rebelled against convention and combined romantic and scientific attitudes in his work, Wedekind, we may add, was introduced to the world by an "appropriate" set of parents. His mother was a young German actress sojourning in San Francisco when she met the considerably older man who became her husband. He was a physician, an adventurer who left Germany and moved from Turkey to California, and a passionate democrat who detested Bismarck as intensely as he revered Washington and Franklin. The father's political convictions apparently descended to the son. Wedekind was imprisoned in 1899 for publishing certain political poems in the satirical periodical *Simplicissimus*.

It was mostly with plays, however, that Wedekind stirred the hornet's nest of the old German monarchy, its bureaucracy, and its conservative adherents. He was a strong admirer of Ibsen and, upon turning actor, toured Germany giving effective professional readings from Ibsen's works. By the time he reached his twenty-fifth birthday, the naturalistic movement was in full swing in Munich and Berlin, and it was intensified in the German empire by the political agitation of the Social-Democratic movement, which Germany's "iron chancellor" Bismarck tried vainly to suppress. The young writer aligned himself with the naturalists to the extent of concerning himself with the operations of the sexual instinct and exhibiting it in situations extremely shocking to the sensibilities of staid citizens. He started his career of iconoclasm in 1890 with *The World of Youth*, a picture of conditions in a girls' boarding school, and became increasingly devastating in *The Awakening of Spring* (1892), *Earth Spirit* (1894), and *Pandora's Box* (1903). He continued to write variations on erotic subjects long after they ceased to be novel, and he did so with decreasing effectiveness. As a lyricist of the flesh, Wedekind placed himself in the vanguard of the anti-Philistine progressives. He also came to be regarded as one of the progenitors of nudism and eurythmics, both of which enjoyed a great vogue in Germany. Wedekind knew that slavery to eroticism results in enervation and depression, and declared it in his work; hence it is an error to consider him a simple-minded propagandist for free love. But it was inevitable that he should be alternately denounced as a mere pornographer and acclaimed as a liberator.

Hauptmann and other naturalists were tame by comparison with Wedekind in his excursions into the tabooed field of sexual problems. Yet Wedekind was not a consistent naturalist. An original artist who was not apt to follow fashions, he helped himself to much naturalistic detail to support his personal crusade for frankness about the elemental power of the sexual instinct. Absolute candor, which the English-speaking world still finds too strong for its stomach, was an essential quality of his talent. As a result, some of his work gives the impression of having been written expressly according to Zola's formula for naturalistic "scientism"—"to see the beast [animal] in man, and only the beast." No prurience, but a primal amorality, characterizes his studies of Lulu, the heroine of *Earth Spirit* and *Pandora's Box*, who destroys man after man, only to be destroyed herself by a male counterpart. And sexual awakening in adolescence has a melancholy and hypnotic quality in *The Awakening of Spring*, the play that first brought its author international renown.

Because he was an overintense and highly imaginative person (and partly, no doubt, because his subject lay beneath surface reality) Wedekind also followed antirealistic directions. In *The Awakening of Spring* he even added a spectral fantasy to his story of the inner torments and suicide of his adolescents, who find themselves in the grip of the sexual instinct without proper guidance from their convention-bound, obtuse elders. Wedekind wrote the play in short, jerky scenes, and he shifted the background frequently—a procedure not favored in realistic circles. The weird—now and then macabre—and explosive dramaturgy and style of much of his work made Wedekind, indeed, a precursor of "expressionism." He brought the naturalistic tendencies of the theatre to their logical conclusion with his subjects and his uncompromising treatment, but he also introduced us to a nervous, subjective style of drama. When Hauptmann and other contemporaries of Wedekind departed from naturalism they turned toward a somewhat effete romanticism. Although himself impatient with the commonplace and leisurely spirit of standard naturalistic plays, Wedekind was too explosive to content himself with lyricism, legend, and gentle allegories such as Max Reinhardt's spectacle *The Miracle*.

Like other writers, Wedekind was, of course, not always at his best; and never a particularly disciplined person, in many ill-conceived and disordered plays he failed to do justice to his talent. But his importance in the modern theatre cannot be underestimated. Nor is it based entirely on his studies of "the tyranny of sex," the title of the only collection of his plays in English. He was also a master of a wry kind of comedy dedicated to characters who live outside the pale of middle-class life either as swindlers, like the hero of his tantalizing masterpiece *The Marquis of Keith* (1901), or as artists, like the singer Gerardo in *The Tenor* (1899). Wedekind himself stood outside the pale, unable to remain at peace with the secure world of respectability, which he tended to bait on the grounds that it was stupid, smug, and hypocritical. He was therefore strongly attracted to characters who would not or could not lead easy, conventional lives. Since he was a penetrative artist, however, his approach to his subject tended to be antiheroic, quizzical, and a trifle blighting.

The Tenor was Wedekind's most popular work. It is also frequently regarded as his best. Although it does not represent the full scope of his talent and lacks the profundity of several of his longer pieces, it is his most thoroughly integrated play. If its technique is in no respect expressionistic, its picture of the life of the singer who is slave to his profession is curiously unreal. That, indeed, is the point of this ironic little comedy, and Wedekind is all the more realistic in presenting the unreality of this public idol. Gerardo dreads yielding to real emotions because he belongs to the Philistines he is paid to entertain. Wedekind's powers of incisive observation and style are all impacted here. His play would have been welcomed as an ultranaturalistic masterpiece by the playwrights who began to supply Antoine's Théâtre Libre in 1887 with cynical one-acters known as *comédies rosses*. Since *The Tenor* happens to be better than anything of the kind they wrote in the service of naturalism, Wedekind's mordant masterpiece can be allowed to represent their *avant-garde* shockers, as well as its author's often uneven but always striking work.

BIBLIOGRAPHY: Eric Bentley, *The Playwright as Thinker* (pp. 64–67, 318–321), 1946; Anita Block, *The Changing World in Plays and Theatre* (pp. 39–45), 1939; Samuel Eliot, *Tragedies of Sex*, 1923; Arthur Kutscher, *Frank Wedekind, sein Leben und seine Werke*, 1931; Raimund Pissin, *Frank Wedekind*, volume 53 of *Moderne Essays*, 1905(?).

THE TENOR

By Frank Wedekind

TRANSLATED FROM THE GERMAN BY ANDRÉ TRIDON

CHARACTERS

GERARDO, *Wagnerian tenor, thirty-six years old*
HELEN MAROVA, *a beautiful dark-haired woman of twenty-five*
PROFESSOR DUHRING, *sixty, the typical "misunderstood genius"*
MISS ISABEL CŒURNE, *a blond English girl of sixteen*
MULLER, *hotel manager*
A VALET   A BELL BOY   AN UNKNOWN WOMAN

TIME: *The present.*   PLACE: *A city in Austria.*

SCENE: *A large hotel room. There are doors at the right and in the center, and at the left a window with heavy portières. Behind a grand piano at the right stands a Japanese screen which conceals the fireplace. There are several large trunks, open; bunches of flowers are all over the room; many bouquets are piled up on the piano.*

VALET: [*Entering from the adjoining room carrying an armful of clothes which he proceeds to pack in one of the trunks. There is a knock at the door*] Come in.

BELL BOY: There is a lady who wants to know if the Maestro is in.

VALET: He isn't in. [*Exit Bell Boy. The Valet goes into the adjoining room and returns with another armful of clothes. There is another knock at the door. He puts the clothes on a chair and goes to the door*] What's this again? [*He opens the door and some one hands him several large bunches of flowers, which he places carefully on the piano; then he goes back to his packing. There is another knock. He opens the door and takes a handful of letters. He glances at the addresses and reads aloud:*] "Mister Gerardo. Monsieur Gerardo. Gerardo Esquire. Signor Gerardo." [*He drops the letters on a tray and resumes his packing*]

[*Enter Gerardo*]

GERARDO: Haven't you finished packing yet? How much longer will it take you?

VALET: I'll be through in a minute, sir.

GERARDO: Hurry! I still have things to do. Let me see. [*He reaches for something in a trunk*] God Almighty! Don't you know how to fold a pair of trousers? [*Taking the trousers out*] This is what you call packing! Look here! You still have something to learn from me, after all. You take the trousers like this. . . . You lock this up here. . . . Then you take hold of these buttons. Watch these buttons here, that's the important thing. Then—you pull them straight. . . . There. . . . There. . . . Then you fold them here. . . . See. . . . Now these trousers would keep their shape for a hundred years.

VALET: [*Respectfully, with downcast eyes*] You must have been a tailor once, sir.

GERARDO: What! Well, not exactly. . . . [*He gives the trousers to the* Valet] Pack those up, but be quick about it. Now about that train. You are sure this is the last one we can take?

VALET: It is the only one that gets you there in time, sir. The next train does not reach Brussels until ten o'clock.

GERARDO: Well, then, we must catch this one. I will just have time to go over the second act. Unless I go over that. . . . Now don't let anybody. . . . I am out to everybody.

VALET: All right, sir. There are some letters for you, sir.

GERARDO: I have seen them.

VALET: And flowers!

GERARDO: Yes, all right. [*He takes the letters from the tray and throws them on a chair before the piano. Then he opens the letters, glances over them with beaming eyes, crumples them up and throws them under the chair*] Remember! I am out to everybody.

VALET: I know, sir. [*He locks the trunks*]

GERARDO: To everybody.

VALET: You needn't worry, sir. [*Giving him the trunk keys*] Here are the keys, sir.

GERARDO: [*Pocketing the keys*] To everybody!

VALET: The trunks will be taken down at once. [*He goes out*]

GERARDO: [*Looking at his watch*] Forty minutes, [*He pulls the score of "Tristan" from underneath the flowers on the piano and walks up and down humming*] "Isolde! Geliebte! Bist du mein? Hab' ich dich wieder? Darf ich dich fassen?" [*He clears his throat, strikes a chord on the piano and starts again*] "Isolde! Geliebte! Bist du mein? Hab' ich dich wieder? . . ."* [*He clears his throat*] The air is dead

166

here. [*He sings*] "Isolde! Geliebte. . . ." It's oppressive here. Let's have a little fresh air. [*He goes to the window at the left and fumbles for the curtain cord*] Where is the thing? On the other side! Here! [*He pulls the cord and throws his head back with an annoyed expression when he sees* Miss Cœurne]

MISS CŒURNE: [*In three-quarter length skirt, her blonde hair down her back, holding a bunch of red roses; she speaks with an English accent and looks straight at* Gerardo] Oh, please don't send me away.

GERARDO: What else can I do? God knows, I haven't asked you to come here. Do not take it badly, dear young lady, but I have to sing to-morrow night in Brussels. I must confess, I hoped I would have this half-hour to myself. I had just given positive orders not to let any one, whoever it might be, come up to my rooms.

MISS CŒURNE: [*Coming down stage*] Don't send me away. I heard you yesterday in "Tannhäuser," and I was just bringing you these roses, and—

GERARDO: And—and what?

MISS CŒURNE: And myself. . . . I don't know whether you understand me.

GERARDO: [*Holding the back of a chair; he hesitates, then shakes his head*] Who are you?

MISS CŒURNE: My name is Miss Cœurne.

GERARDO: Yes. . . . Well?

MISS CŒURNE: I am very silly.

GERARDO: I know. Come here, my dear girl. [*He sits down in an armchair and she stands before him*] Let's have a good earnest talk, such as you have never had in your life—and seem to need. An artist like myself—don't misunderstand me; you are—how old are you?

MISS CŒURNE: Twenty-two.

GERARDO: You are sixteen or perhaps seventeen. You make yourself a little older so as to appear more—tempting. Well? Yes, you are very silly. It is really none of my business, as an artist, to cure you of your silliness. . . . Don't take this badly. . . . Now then! Why are you staring away like this?

MISS CŒURNE: I said I was very silly, because I thought you Germans liked that in a young girl.

GERARDO: I am not a German, but just the same. . . .

MISS CŒURNE: What! I am not as silly as all that.

GERARDO: Now look here, my dear girl—you have your tennis court, your skating club; you have your riding class, your dances; you have all a young girl can wish for. What on earth made you come to me?

MISS CŒURNE: Because all those things are awful, and they bore me to death.

GERARDO: I will not dispute that. Personally, I must tell you, I know life from an entirely different side. But, my child, I am a man; I am thirty-six. The time will come when you, too, will claim a fuller existence. Wait another two years and there will be some one for you, and then you won't need to—hide yourself behind curtains, in my room, in the room

of a man who—never asked you, and whom you don't know any better than—the whole continent of Europe knows him—in order to look at life from his—wonderful point of view. [Miss Cœurne *sighs deeply*] Now then. . . . Many thanks from the bottom of my heart for your roses. [*He presses her hand*] Will this do for to-day?

MISS CŒURNE: I had never in all my life thought of a man, until I saw you on the stage last night in "Tannhäuser." And I promise you—

GERARDO: Oh, don't promise me anything, my child. What good could your promise do me? The burden of it would all fall upon you. You see, I am talking to you as lovingly as the most loving father could. Be thankful to God that with your recklessness you haven't fallen into the hands of another artist. [*He presses her hand again*] Let this be a lesson to you and never try it again.

MISS CŒURNE: [*Holding her handkerchief to her face but shedding no tears*] Am I so homely?

GERARDO: Homely! Not homely, but young and indiscreet. [*He rises nervously, goes to the right, comes back, puts his arm around her waist and takes her hand*] Listen to me, child. You are not homely because I have to be a singer, because I have to be an artist. Don't misunderstand me, but I can't see why I should simply, because I am an artist, have to assure you that I appreciate your youthful freshness and beauty. It is a question of time. Two hundred, maybe three hundred, nice, lovely girls of your age saw me last night in the rôle of Tannhäuser. Now if every one of those girls made the same demands upon me which you are making— what would become of my singing? What would become of my voice? What would become of my art?

[Miss Cœurne *sinks into a seat, covers her face and weeps*]

GERARDO: [*Leaning over the back of her chair, in a friendly tone*] It is a crime for you, child, to weep over the fact that you are still so young. Your whole life is ahead of you. Is it my fault if you fell in love with me? They all do. That is what I am for. Now won't you be a good girl and let me, for the few minutes I have left, prepare myself for to-morrow's appearance?

MISS CŒURNE: [*Rising and drying her tears*] I can't believe that any other girl would have acted the way I have.

GERARDO: [*Leading her to the door*] No, dear child.

MISS CŒURNE: [*With sobs in her voice*] At least, not if—

GERARDO: If my valet had stood before the door.

MISS CŒURNE: If—

GERARDO: If the girl had been as beautiful and youthfully fresh as you.

MISS CŒURNE: If—

GERARDO: If she had heard me only once in "Tannhäuser."

MISS CŒURNE: [*Indignant*] If she were as respectable as I am!

GERARDO: [*Pointing to the piano*] Before saying good-by to me, child, have a look at all those flowers. May this be a warning to you in case you feel tempted again to fall in love with a singer. See how fresh they all are. And I have to let them wither, dry up, or I give them to the porter. And look at those letters. [*He takes a handful of them from a tray*] I don't know any of these women. Don't worry; I leave them all to their fate. What else could I do? But I'll wager with you that every one of your lovely young friends sent in her little note.

MISS CŒURNE: Well, I promise not to do it again, not to hide myself behind your curtains. But don't send me away.

GERARDO: My time, my time, dear child. If I were not on the point of taking a train! I have already told you, I am very sorry for you. But my train leaves in twenty-five minutes. What do you expect?

MISS CŒURNE: A kiss.

GERARDO: [*Stiffening up*] From me?

MISS CŒURNE: Yes.

GERARDO: [*Holding her around the waist and looking very serious*] You rob Art of its dignity, my child. I do not wish to appear an unfeeling brute, and I am going to give you my picture. Give me your word that after that you will leave me.

MISS CŒURNE: Yes.

GERARDO: Good. [*He sits at the table and autographs one of his pictures*] You should try to become interested in the operas themselves instead of the men who sing them. You would probably derive much greater enjoyment.

MISS CŒURNE: [*To herself*] I am too young yet.

GERARDO: Sacrifice yourself to music. [*He comes down stage and gives her the picture*] Don't see in me a famous tenor but a mere tool in the hands of a noble master. Look at all the married women among your acquaintances. All Wagnerians. Study Wagner's works; learn to understand his *leit motifs*. That will save you from further foolishness.

MISS CŒURNE: I thank you.

[Gerardo *leads her out and rings the bell. He takes up his piano score again. There is a knock at the door*]

VALET: [*Coming in out of breath*] Yes, sir.

GERARDO: Are you standing at the door?

VALET: Not just now, sir.

GERARDO: Of course not! Be sure not to let anybody come up here.

VALET: There were three ladies who asked for you, sir.

GERARDO: Don't you dare to let any one of them come up, whatever she may tell you.

VALET: And then here are some more letters.

GERARDO: Oh, all right. [*The* Valet *places the letters on a tray*] And don't you dare to let any one come up.

VALET: [*At the door*] No, sir.

GERARDO: Even if she offers to settle a fortune upon you.

VALET: No, sir. [*He goes out*]

GERARDO: [*Singing*] "Isolde! Geliebte! Bist du . . ." Well, if women don't get tired of me— Only the world is so full of them; and I am only one man. Every one has his burden to carry. [*He strikes a chord on the piano*]

[*Prof.* Duhring, *dressed all in black, with a long white beard, a red hooked nose, gold spectacles, Prince Albert coat and silk hat, an opera score under his arm, enters without knocking*]

GERARDO: What do you want?

DUHRING: Maestro—I—I—have—an opera.

GERARDO: How did you get in?

DUHRING: I have been watching for two hours for a chance to run up the stairs unnoticed.

GERARDO: But, my dear good man, I have no time.

DUHRING: Oh, I will not play the whole opera for you.

GERARDO: I haven't the time. My train leaves in forty minutes.

DUHRING: You haven't the time! What should I say? You are thirty and successful. You have your whole life to live yet. Just listen to your part in my opera. You promised to listen to it when you came to this city.

GERARDO: What is the use? I am not a free agent—

DUHRING: Please! Please! Please! Maestro! I stand before you an old man, ready to fall on my knees before you; an old man who has never cared for anything in the world but his art. For fifty years I have been a willing victim to the tyranny of art—

GERARDO: [*Interrupting him*] Yes, I understand; I understand, but—

DUHRING: [*Excitedly*] No, you don't understand. You could not understand. How could you, the favorite of fortune, you understand what fifty years of bootless work means? But I will try to make you understand it. You see, I am too old to take my own life. People who do that do it at twenty-five, and I let the time pass by. I must now drag along to the end of my days. Please, sir, please don't let these moments pass in vain for me, even if you have to lose a day thereby, a week even. This is in your own interest. A week ago, when you first came for your special appearances, you promised to let me play my opera for you. I have come here every day since; either you had a rehearsal or a woman caller. And now you are on the point of going away. You have only to say one word: I will sing the part of Hermann—and they will produce my opera. You will then thank God for my insistence. . . . Of course you sing Siegfried, you sing Florestan—but you have no rôle like Hermann in your repertoire, no rôle better suited to your middle register.

[Gerardo *leans against the mantelpiece; while drumming on the top with his right hand, he discovers something behind the screen; he suddenly stretches out his arm and pulls out a woman in a gray gown, whom he leads out of the room through the middle door; after closing the door, he turns to* Duhring]

GERARDO: Oh, are you still there?

DUHRING: [*Undisturbed*] This opera is good; it is dramatic; it *is* a financial success. I can show you letters from Liszt, from Wagner, from Rubinstein, in which they consider me as a superior man. And why hasn't my opera ever been produced? Because I am not crying wares on the market-place. And then you know our directors: they will revive ten dead men before they give a live man a chance. Their walls are well guarded. At thirty you are in. At sixty I am still out. One word from you and I shall be in, too. This is why I have come, and [*Raising his voice*] if you are not an unfeeling brute, if success has not killed in you the last spark of artistic sympathy, you will not refuse to hear my work.

GERARDO: I will give you an answer in a week. I will go over your opera. Let me have it.

DUHRING: No, I am too old, Maestro. In a week, in what you call a week, I shall be dead and buried. In a week—that is what they all say; and then they keep it for years.

GERARDO: I am very sorry but—

DUHRING: To-morrow perhaps you will be on your knees before me; you will boast of knowing me . . . and today, in your sordid lust for gold, you cannot even spare the half-hour which would mean the breaking of my fetters.

GERARDO: No, really, I have only thirty-five minutes left, and unless I go over a few passages . . . . You know I sing Tristan in Brussels to-morrow night. [*He pulls out his watch*] I haven't even half an hour. . . .

DUHRING: Half an hour. . . . Oh, then, let me play to you your big aria at the end of the first act. [*He attempts to sit down on the piano bench. Gerardo restrains him*]

GERARDO: Now, frankly, my dear sir . . . I am a singer; I am not a critic. If you wish to have your opera produced, address yourself to those gentlemen who are paid to know what is good and what is not. People scorn and ignore my opinions in such matters as completely as they appreciate and admire my singing.

DUHRING: My dear Maestro, you may take it from me that I myself attach no importance whatever to your judgment. What do I care about your opinions? I know you tenors; I would like to play my score for you so that you could say: "I would like to sing the rôle of Hermann."

GERARDO: If you only knew how many things I would like to do and which I have to renounce, and how many things I must do for which I do not care in the least! Half a million a year does not repay me for the many joys of life which I must sacrifice for the sake of my profession. I am not a free man. But you were a free man all your life. Why didn't you go to the market-place and cry your wares?

DUHRING: Oh, the vulgarity of it. . . . I have tried it a hundred times. I am a composer, Maestro, and nothing more.

GERARDO: By which you mean that you have exhausted all your strength in the writing of your operas and kept none of it to secure their production.

DUHRING: That is true.

GERARDO: The composers I know reverse the process. They get their operas written somehow and then spend all their strength in an effort to get them produced.

DUHRING: That is the type of artist I despise.

GERARDO: Well, I despise the type of man that wastes his life in useless endeavor. What have you done in those fifty years of struggle, for yourself or for the world? Fifty years of useless struggle! That should convince the worst blockhead of the impracticability of his dreams. What have you done with your life? You have wasted it shamefully. If I had wasted my life as you have wasted yours—of course I am only speaking for myself—I don't think I should have the courage to look any one in the face.

DUHRING: I am not doing it for myself; I am doing it for my art.

GERARDO: [*Scornfully*] Art, my dear man! Let me tell you that art is quite different from what the papers tell us it is.

DUHRING: To me it is the highest thing in the world.

GERARDO: You may believe that, but nobody else does. We artists are merely a luxury for the use of the *bourgeoisie*. When I stand there on the stage I feel absolutely certain that not one solitary human being in the audience takes the slightest interest in what we, the artists, are doing. If they did, how could they listen to "Die Walküre," for instance? Why, it is an indecent story which could not be mentioned anywhere in polite society. And yet, when I sing Siegmund, the most puritanical mothers bring their fourteen-year-old daughters to hear me. This, you see, is the meaning of whatever you call art. This is what you have sacrificed fifty years of your life to. Find out how many people came to hear me sing and how many came to gape at me as they would at the Emperor of China if he should turn up here to-morrow. Do you know what the artistic wants of the public consist in? To applaud, to send flowers, to have a subject for conversation, to see and be seen. They pay me half a million, but then I make business for hundreds of cabbies, writers, dressmakers, restaurant keepers. It keeps money circulating; it keeps blood running. It gets girls engaged, spinsters married, wives tempted, old cronies supplied with gossip; a woman loses her pocketbook in the crowd, a fellow becomes insane during the performance. Doctors, lawyers made. . . . [*He coughs*] And with this I must sing Tristan in Brussels to-morrow night! I tell you all this, not out of vanity, but to cure you of your delusions. The measure of a man's worth is the world's opinion of him, not the inner belief which one finally adopts after brooding over it for years. Don't imagine that you are a misunderstood genius. There are no misunderstood geniuses.

DUHRING: Let me just play to you the first scene of the second act. A park landscape as in the painting, "Embarkation for the Isle of Cythera."

GERARDO: I repeat to you I have no time. And furthermore, since Wagner's death the need for new operas has never been felt by any one. If you come with new music, you set against yourself all the music schools, the artists, the public. If you want to succeed just steal enough out of Wagner's works to make up a whole opera. Why should I cudgel my brains with your new music when I have cudgeled them cruelly with the old?

DUHRING: [Holding out his trembling hand] I am afraid I am too old to learn how to steal. Unless one begins very young, one can never learn it.

GERARDO: Don't feel hurt. My dear sir—if I could. . . . The thought of how you have to struggle. . . . I happen to have received some five hundred marks more than my fee. . . .

DUHRING: [Turning to the door] Don't! Please don't! Do not say that. I did not try to show you my opera in order to work a touch. No, I think too much of this child of my brain. . . . No, Maestro.

[He goes out through the center door]

GERARDO: [Following him to the door] I beg your pardon. . . . Pleased to have met you.

[He closes the door and sinks into an armchair. A voice is heard outside: "I will not let that man step in my way." Helen rushes into the room followed by the Valet. She is an unusually beautiful young woman in street dress]

HELEN: That man stood there to prevent me from seeing you!

GERARDO: Helen!

HELEN: You knew that I would come to see you.

VALET: [Rubbing his cheek] I did all I could, sir, but this lady actually—

HELEN: Yes, I slapped his face.

GERARDO: Helen!

HELEN: Should I have let him insult me?

GERARDO: [To the Valet] Please leave us.

[The Valet goes out]

HELEN: [Placing her muff on a chair] I can no longer live without you. Either you take me with you or I will kill myself.

GERARDO: Helen!

HELEN: Yes, kill myself. A day like yesterday, without even seeing you—no, I could not live through that again. I am not strong enough. I beseech you, Oscar, take me with you.

GERARDO: I couldn't.

HELEN: You could if you wanted to. You can't leave me without killing me. These are not mere words. This isn't a threat. It is a fact: I will die if I can no longer have you. You must take me with you—it is your duty—if only for a short time.

GERARDO: I give you my word of honor, Helen, I can't—I give you my word.

HELEN: You must, Oscar. Whether you can or not, you must bear the consequences of your acts. I love life, but to me life and you are one and the same thing. Take me with you, Oscar, if you don't want to have my blood on your hands.

GERARDO: Do you remember what I said to you the first day we were together here?

HELEN: I remember, but what good does that do me?

GERARDO: I said that there couldn't be any question of love between us.

HELEN: I can't help that. I didn't know you then. I never knew what a man could be to me until I met you. You knew very well that it would come to this, otherwise you wouldn't have obliged me to promise not to make you a parting scene.

GERARDO: I simply cannot take you with me.

HELEN: Oh, God! I knew you would say that! I knew it when I came here. That's what you say to every woman. And I am just one of a hundred. I know it. But, Oscar, I am lovesick; I am dying of love. This is your work, and you can save me without any sacrifice on your part, without assuming any burden. Why can't you do it?

GERARDO: [Very slowly] Because my contract forbids me to marry or to travel in the company of a woman.

HELEN: [Disturbed] What can prevent you?

GERARDO: My contract.

HELEN: You cannot . . .

GERARDO: I cannot marry until my contract expires.

HELEN: And you cannot . . .

GERARDO: I cannot travel in the company of a woman.

HELEN: That is incredible. And whom in the world should it concern?

GERARDO: My manager.

HELEN: Your manager! What business is it of his?

GERARDO: It is precisely his business.

HELEN: Is it perhaps because it might—affect your voice?

GERARDO: Yes.

HELEN: That is preposterous. Does it affect your voice?

[Gerardo chuckles]

HELEN: Does your manager believe that nonsense?

GERARDO: No, he doesn't.

HELEN: This is beyond me. I can't understand how a decent man could sign such a contract.

GERARDO: I am an artist first and a man next.

HELEN: Yes, that's what you are—a great artist—an eminent artist. Can't you understand how much I must love you? You are the first man whose superiority I have felt and whom I desired to please, and you despise me for it. I have bitten my lips many a time not to let you suspect how much you meant to me; I was so afraid I might bore you. Yesterday, however, put me in a state of mind which

no woman can endure. If I didn't love you so in-
sanely, Oscar, you would think more of me. That is
the terrible thing about you—that you must scorn
a woman who thinks the world of you.

GERARDO: Helen!

HELEN: Your contract! Don't use your contract as
a weapon to murder me with. Let me go with you,
Oscar. You will see if your manager ever mentions
a breach of contract. He would not do such a thing.
I know men. And if he says a word, it will be time
then for me to die.

GERARDO: We have no right to do that, Helen.
You are just as little free to follow me, as I am to
shoulder such a responsibility. I don't belong to
myself; I belong to my art.

HELEN: Oh, leave your art alone. What do I care
about your art? Has God created a man like you
to make a puppet of himself every night? You
should be ashamed of it instead of boasting of it.
You see, I overlooked the fact that you were merely
an artist. What wouldn't I overlook for a god like
you? Even if you were a convict, Oscar, my feelings
would be the same. I would lie in the dust at your
feet and beg for your pity. I would face death as I
am facing it now.

GERARDO: [Laughing] Facing death, Helen!
Women who are endowed with your gifts for enjoying life don't make away with themselves. You
know even better than I do the value of life.

HELEN: [Dreamily] Oscar, I didn't say that I would
shoot myself. When did I say that? Where would I
find the courage to do that? I only said that I will
die, if you don't take me with you. I will die as I
would of an illness, for I only live when I am with
you. I can live without my home, without my
children, but not without you, Oscar. I cannot live
without you.

GERARDO: Helen, if you don't calm yourself. . . .
You put me in an awful position. . . . I have only
ten minutes left. . . . I can't explain in court that
your excitement made me break my contract. . . .
I can only give you ten minutes. . . . If you don't
calm yourself in that time . . . I can't leave you
alone in this condition. Think all you have at stake!

HELEN: As though I had anything else at stake!

GERARDO: You can lose your position in society.

HELEN: I can lose you!

GERARDO: And your family

HELEN: I care for no one but you.

GERARDO: But I cannot be yours.

HELEN: Then I have nothing to lose but my life.

GERARDO: Your children!

HELEN: Who has taken me from them, Oscar?
Who has taken me from my children?

GERARDO: Did I make any advances to you?

HELEN: [Passionately] No, no. I have thrown myself at you, and would throw myself at you again.
Neither my husband nor my children could keep
me back. When I die, at least I will have lived;

thanks to you, Oscar! I thank you, Oscar, for revealing me to myself. I thank you for that.

GERARDO: Helen, calm yourself and listen to me.

HELEN: Yes, yes, for ten minutes.

GERARDO: Listen to me. [Both sit down on the
divan]

HELEN: [Staring at him] Yes, I thank you for it.

GERARDO: Helen!

HELEN: I don't even ask you to love me. Let me
only breathe the air you breathe.

GERARDO: [Trying to be calm] Helen—a man of
my type cannot be swayed by any of the bourgeois
ideas. I have known society women in every country
of the world. Some made parting scenes to me, but
at least they all knew what they owed to their
position. This is the first time in my life that I have
witnessed such an outburst of passion. . . . Helen,
the temptation comes to me daily to step with some
woman into an idyllic Arcadia. But every human
being has his duties; you have your duties as I have
mine, and the call of duty is the highest thing in
the world. . . .

HELEN: I know better than you do what the
highest duty is.

GERARDO: What, then? Your love for me? That's
what they all say. Whatever a woman has set her
heart on winning is to her good; whatever crosses her
plans is evil. It is the fault of our playwrights. To
draw full houses they set the world upside down,
and when a woman abandons her children and her
family to follow her instincts they call that—oh,
broad-mindedness. I personally wouldn't mind living
the way turtle doves live. But since I am a part of
this world I must obey my duty first. Then whenever
the opportunity arises I quaff of the cup of joy.
Whoever refuses to do his duty has no right to make
any demands upon another fellow being.

HELEN: [Staring absent-mindedly] That does not
bring the dead back to life.

GERARDO: [Nervously] Helen, I will give you back
your life. I will give you back what you have sacrificed for me. For God's sake take it. What does it
come to, after all? Helen, how can a woman lower
herself to that point? Where is your pride? What
am I in the eyes of the world? A man who makes a
puppet of himself every night! Helen, are you going
to kill yourself for a man whom hundreds of women
loved before you, whom hundreds of women will
love after you without letting their feelings disturb
their life one second? Will you, by shedding your
warm blood, make yourself ridiculous before God
and the world?

HELEN: [Looking away from him] I know I am
asking a good deal, but—what else can I do?

GERARDO: Helen, you said I should bear the consequences of my acts. Will you reproach me for not
refusing to receive you when you first came here,
ostensibly to ask me to try your voice? What can
a man do in such a case? You are the beauty of this
town. Either I would be known as the bear among

artists who denies himself to all women callers, or I might have received you and pretended that I didn't understand what you meant and then pass for a fool. Or the very first day I might have talked to you as frankly as I am talking now. Dangerous business. You would have called me a conceited idiot. Tell me, Helen—what else could I do?

HELEN: [*Staring at him with imploring eyes, shuddering and making an effort to speak*] O God! O God! Oscar, what would you say if to-morrow I should go and be as happy with another man as I have been with you? Oscar—what would you say?

GERARDO: [*After a silence*] Nothing. [*He looks at his watch*] Helen—

HELEN: Oscar! [*She kneels before him*] For the last time, I implore you. . . . You don't know what you are doing. . . . It isn't your fault—but don't let me die. . . . Save me—save me!

GERARDO: [*Raising her up*] Helen, I am not such a wonderful man. How many men have you known? The more men you come to know, the lower all men will fall in your estimation. When you know men better you will not take your life for any one of them. You will not think any more of them than I do of women.

HELEN: I am not like you in that respect.

GERARDO: I speak earnestly, Helen. We don't fall in love with one person or another; we fall in love with our type, which we find everywhere in the world if we only look sharply enough.

HELEN: And when we meet our type, are we sure then of being loved again?

GERARDO: [*Angrily*] You have no right to complain of your husband. Was any girl ever compelled to marry against her will? That is all rot. It is only the women who have sold themselves for certain material advantages and then try to dodge their obligations who try to make us believe that nonsense.

HELEN: [*Smiling*] They break their contracts.

GERARDO: [*Pounding his chest*] When I sell myself at least I am honest about it.

HELEN: Isn't love honest?

GERARDO: No! Love is a beastly bourgeois virtue. Love is the last refuge of the mollycoddle, of the coward. In my world every man has his actual value, and when two human beings make up a pact they know exactly what to expect from each other. Love has nothing to do with it, either.

HELEN: Won't you lead me into your world, then?

GERARDO: Helen, will you compromise the happiness of your life and the happiness of your dear ones for just a few days' pleasure?

HELEN: No.

GERARDO: [*Much relieved*] Will you promise me to go home quietly now?

HELEN: Yes.

GERARDO: And will you promise me that you will not die. . . .

HELEN: Yes.

GERARDO: You promise me that?

HELEN: Yes.

GERARDO: And you promise me to fulfill your duties as mother and—as wife?

HELEN: Yes.

GERARDO: Helen!

HELEN: Yes. What else do you want? I will promise anything.

GERARDO: And now may I go away in peace?

HELEN: [*Rising*] Yes.

GERARDO: A last kiss?

HELEN: Yes, yes, yes. [*They kiss passionately*]

GERARDO: In a year I am booked again to sing here, Helen.

HELEN: In a year! Oh, I am glad!

GERARDO: [*Tenderly*] Helen!

[Helen *presses his hand, takes a revolver out of her muff, shoots herself and falls*]

GERARDO: Helen! [*He totters and collapses in an armchair*]

BELL BOY: [*Rushing in*] My God! Mr. Gerardo! [Gerardo *remains motionless; the* Bell Boy *rushes toward* Helen]

GERARDO: [*Jumping up, running to the door and colliding with the manager of the hotel*] Send for the police! I must be arrested! If I went away now I should be a brute, and if I stay I break my contract. I still have [*Looking at his watch*] One minute and ten seconds.

MANAGER: Fred, run and get a policeman.

BELL BOY: All right, sir.

MANAGER: Be quick about it. [*To* Gerardo] Don't take it too hard, sir. Those things happen once in a while.

GERARDO: [*Kneeling before* Helen's *body and taking her hand*] Helen! . . . She still lives—she still lives! If I am arrested I am not wilfully breaking my contract. . . . And my trunks? Is the carriage at the door?

MANAGER: It has been waiting twenty minutes, Mr. Gerardo. [*He opens the door for the porter, who takes down one of the trunks*]

GERARDO: [*Bending over her*] Helen! [*To himself*] Well, after all. . . . [*To* Muller] Have you called a doctor?

MANAGER: Yes, we had the doctor called at once. He will be here at any minute.

GERARDO: [*Holding her under the arms*] Helen! Don't you know me any more? Helen! The doctor will be here right away, Helen. This is your Oscar.

BELL BOY: [*Appearing in the door at the center*] Can't find any policeman, sir.

GERARDO: [*Letting* Helen's *body drop back*] Well, if I can't get arrested, that settles it. I must catch that train and sing in Brussels to-morrow night. [*He takes up his score and runs out through the center door, bumping against several chairs*]

CURTAIN

Leo Nikolayevich Tolstoy

(1828–1910)

Although Tolstoy is best known to the world as a novelist, his genius can also be legitimately claimed by the theatre, for the author of *War and Peace* and *Anna Karenina* is the dramatist of *The Power of Darkness* and of other more or less distinguished works for the stage. It was with the 1888 production of *The Power of Darkness* that the Théâtre Libre and its director Antoine had their epoch-making debut as an international influence instead of remaining a local phenomenon in Paris. The French saw this peasant tragedy even before *Ghosts,* and it made a deeper impression than Ibsen's play on France's pioneer in dramatic realism, Henry Becque. Since Otto Brahm also staged the play a year later in his Freie Bühne in Berlin, Tolstoy's drama was quickly established as a classic of the progressive naturalistic movement in Western Europe. The greater part of the author's lifetime lay behind the composition of *The Power of Darkness*. Tolstoy was able to fill it with all the understanding of the peasantry that he had amassed in the course of a varied career as a landowner, writer, and social reformer.

Tolstoy's restless spirit carried him through a period of wayward university studies, furious dissipations, experiments in scientific farming, and military adventures in the Caucasus Mountains before he became a professional writer with the publication of his first book, *Childhood* (1852). Two years later, he enlarged his reputation with his realistic *Sevastopol* sketches inspired by the Crimean war, during which he had commanded an exposed bastion at the siege of Sevastopol. Disillusioned with war and his military career, he retired to private life, published the second and third parts of his autobiographical novel *Childhood, Boyhood, and Youth,* traveled extensively in Europe, and finally settled down on his estate, Yasnaya Polyana (1860). Here he devoted himself to educating the children of the peasantry with modern methods, and he made an unsuccessful attempt to convert his serfs into free farmers. Upon marrying the eighteen-year-old daughter of a physician in 1862, he threw himself wholeheartedly into domestic life, rearing a large family of sons and daughters. For a period of some sixteen years Tolstoy led a life that any man of letters could have envied—a useful and essentially unclouded life, during which he turned out such masterpieces as *War and Peace* (1865–1869) and *Anna Karenina* (1875–1877).

In 1876, however, Tolstoy lost his confidence in the values that had brought him gratifications as a family man and artist. Shocked by the death of a brother into reviewing the meaning of his life, he began to search for spiritual comfort and moral direction. He embraced religion with such fervor that before long he found himself excommunicated by the Greek Orthodox Church for propounding heretical doctrines, and he became an apostle of a highly idealistic faith that brought him into conflict with the state and his own family as well as with the Russian Church. Resolved to communicate his views to the common man, he began to write instructive stories for the peasantry and tracts for the educated classes, such as *What Then Must We Do?*, in which he condemned war, private property, and the economic exploitation of man by man. The stories were beautiful folk tales, although there is no evidence that they made much impression on the largely illiterate public for which they were intended; but the tracts brought Tolstoy a horde of disciples, among them Romain Rolland and Gandhi. "Tolstoyism," with its doctrine of pacifism and passive resistance, absorbed much of its author's time and energy. His creative faculties, however, were not materially diminished by his crusading activities, and it is to this reformist period, which lasted until his death, that we owe the great novelist's contributions to the theatre.

Tolstoy wrote *The Power of Darkness* in 1886, mastering a new medium. Playwriting continued to be one of his strong interests in close to two and a half decades of writing, of attempting to pattern his life after unworldly Christian principles, and of quarreling with a hysterical wife embittered by his effort to divest himself of earthly possessions and well-earned royalties. When he died on November 8, 1910, after running away from home in his eighty-second year, he left a collection of dramatic work which is impressive even if it ranks below his greatest novels. In 1889 appeared his satirical comedy about the bumbling aristocracy, *The Fruits of Enlightenment,* which Bernard Shaw, writing in 1921, called "the first of the Heartbreak Houses." It anticipated by a decade Chekhov's obituaries on the Russian upper classes.

The rest of Tolstoy's dramatic work awaited posthumous publication. *The Cause of It All,* a short drama with which he had hoped to wean the peasantry from vodka, is considerably more poignant than most problem dramas, and the Enoch Arden play *The Living Corpse* has had many successful productions under a variety of titles. (It is better known in America as *Redemption,* the title under which it was produced in 1919 with John Barry-more in the role of the ne'er-do-well who pretends to be dead in order to relieve his wife of his presence.) Finally, Tolstoy left an uncompleted masterpiece patterned after his own idealistic efforts and inner contradictions, *The Light That Shines in Darkness,* the last act of which exists only in outline.

The Power of Darkness contains all the vibrancy of humanization that makes Tolstoy one of the major writers of all time. He brought to bear on the drama all the heavy artillery we associate with "naturalism"—the raw passions, the sordid life and action, and the authentic colloquial speech upon which the naturalists prided themselves. Tolstoy, however, did not write according to any of their practices, or, for that matter, according to the practices of any of his predecessors in the modern theatre. Dramatic technique was not even a practical calculation in his case, as he had never had an opportunity to see his earlier plays on the stage. He did not, for example, pay any particular attention to the art of concentration that Ibsen started refining with *A Doll's House; The Power of Darkness* starts fully two acts before the "point of attack" that the Norwegian dramatist would have chosen. (Tolstoy, indeed, expressed no particular fondness for Ibsen; he liked neither Ibsen's *An Enemy of the People* nor *When We Dead Awaken,* according to the Moscow Art Theatre's codirector, Dantchenko.) Nor did he seem aware of the "fourth-wall convention," which would have made him avoid soliloquies. Scene after scene in *The Power of Darkness* is a triumph of dramatic art without the least exertion of theatrical virtuosity, because here, as in Tolstoy's best fiction, the thing felt is also the thing plainly spoken and clearly seen. Drama in *The Power of Darkness* was only a specialization of the qualities of genius present in his narrative writing. In one important respect, moreover, he could have no traffic with the theorists and practitioners of naturalism: he was constitutionally, as well as in principle, incapable of viewing men as animalcules conveniently placed under the lens of a microscope. For all the lusts of the flesh, man for Tolstoy was a spiritual entity in a universe ruled by spirit. Like all true tragedy, his great play affirms the distinctive humanity of the species.

Nevertheless, *The Power of Darkness* is no more an exercise in easy optimism than it is a preachment pure and simple. It is "the power of darkness" that constitutes the basis of the play, and the light of redemption with which it glows in the last act not only needs the "darkness" to set it off but would have been dramatically ineffective without it. Whereas the naturalistic scientism, for which Zola proselytized so zealously, produced mostly cold-storage passions, Tolstoy's natural energy infused his drama with burning life.

It is not farfetched to believe that had Russia developed a free theatre early enough to attract Tolstoy's allegiance, the world would have been the richer by several dramatic masterpieces. In his most creative years, he could hope at most for amateur productions, for even the representation of mild intellectual revolt and feminism in *The Progressives,* which he read to friends in 1865, was enough to prevent its production in Russia. Tolstoy had no stage to write for until the advent of the Moscow Art Theatre, by which time he was already an aged man, a harassed zealot, and an institution.

Stanislavsky and Dantchenko produced *The Power of Darkness* at their Art Theatre in their fifth season, on November 5, 1902, after some remarkable experiences when they brought a peasant woman from the provinces to help them stage the play with maximum authenticity. (She proved to be so realistic in every role she was given that she made the rest of the great Moscow cast seem woefully unauthentic.) Some seven years earlier, Tolstoy had said to Stanislavsky, who had given an amateur production of *The Fruits of Enlightenment,* "Make an old man happy; free *The Power of Darkness* from censorship and play it," and he proceeded to discuss revisions for the stage production. But when the Art Theatre's production eventuated, it had too much surface naturalism. Stanislavsky himself expressed dissatisfaction with the staging of the drama in later years because it failed to fuse the detailed village realism "with the more important line of the intuition of feelings." It was only with the staging of *The Living Corpse* that the Art Theatre did justice to Tolstoy's genius, and this took place on September 23, 1911, after the author's death.

In conclusion, it should be noted that after *The Power of Darkness* had been sent to press, Tolstoy wrote variant scenes for the end of Act IV upon being informed that the original ending would be too gruesome in the theatre. Candidly confessing to ignorance of the practical theatre, he even requested the young Stanislavsky to assist him in combining the two variants to the greatest advantage. These scenes appear on pages 196–199, and it will be apparent to the reader that Tolstoy, in the hope of seeing his play staged, effected a compromise without the least sacrifice of artistic integrity and dramatic force. The scene which merely reports the murder of the infant is the one which has been used in most productions.

BIBLIOGRAPHY: Vladimir Nemirovitch-Dantchenko, *My Life in the Russian Theatre* (English translation, 1936), pp. 338–340, 343–441; Aylmer Maude, *Life of Tolstoy,* 1910; George R. Noyes, *Tolstoy,* 1918; Ernest J. Simmons, *Leo Tolstoy,* 1946; Constantin Stanislavsky, *My Life in Art* (English translation, 1924), pp. 217–225, 400–403.

THE POWER OF DARKNESS

By Leo Nikolayevich Tolstoy

TRANSLATED FROM THE RUSSIAN BY
GEORGE RAPALL NOYES AND GEORGE Z. PATRICK

CHARACTERS

PETR, *a rich peasant, forty-two years old, married for a second time, in poor health*

ANISYA, *his wife, thirty-two years old, smartly dressed (in Acts I and II)*

AKULINA, *daughter of* Petr *by his first marriage, sixteen years old, hard of hearing and feeble-minded*

ANYUTKA, *daughter of* Petr *and* Anisya, *ten years old*

NIKITA, *their workman, twenty-five years old, smartly dressed*

AKIM, *father of* Nikita, *fifty years old, a pious peasant, unattractive in external appearance*

MATRENA, *his wife, fifty years old*

MARINA, *an orphan girl, twenty-two years old*

FRIEND *of* Anisya

MARFA, *sister of* Petr

MITRICH, *an old laborer, a soldier retired because of age*

NEIGHBOR *(woman)*

MATCHMAKER *(man), a glum peasant*

HUSBAND *of* Marina

FIRST GIRL

SECOND GIRL

POLICEMAN

COACHMAN

MATCHMAKER *(woman)*

BRIDEGROOM *of* Akulina

BEST MAN *(at wedding)*

VILLAGE ELDER

Peasants: men, women, and girls

ACT I.

The action takes place in autumn in a large peasant village. The stage represents Petr's *spacious cottage.* Petr *is seated on a bench, repairing a horse-collar.* Anisya *and* Akulina *are spinning and singing together.*

PETR: [*Glancing out of the window*] The horses have got loose again. They'll kill the colt before you know it. Nikita! Hey, Nikita! He's deaf! [*Listens for a moment. To the women*] Keep still, will you! I can't hear anything.

NIKITA: [*From the yard, off stage*] What?

PETR: Drive in the horses.

NIKITA: [*Same*] I'll drive 'em in. Give me time.

PETR: [*Shaking his head*] Drat these hired men! If I was well, I'd never think of keeping one. They do nothing but make trouble. [*Rises and sits down again*] Nikita! I can't make him hear.— One of you go, will you? Akulina, go and drive 'em in.

AKULINA: The horses?

PETR: What do you suppose?

AKULINA: Right away. [*Goes out*]

PETR: The fellow's a loafer, no good on the farm. If he'd only stir himself!

ANISYA: You're mighty spry yourself—just crawl from the stove to the bench. All you do is boss the rest of us.

PETR: If I didn't boss you, the whole farm'd be ruined in a year. Oh, what a lot you are!

ANISYA: You give us a dozen jobs and then growl. It's easy to lie on the stove and give orders.

PETR: [*Sighing*] Oh, if this sickness didn't have hold of me, I wouldn't keep him for a day.

AKULINA: [*Off stage*] Shoo! shoo! shoo! [*One can hear the colt whinny and the horses run into the yard. The gate creaks*]

PETR: Fancy talk is all he's good for. Honest, I wouldn't keep him.

ANISYA: [*Mimicking him*] "I won't keep him." If you'd only get a move on yourself, you might talk.

AKULINA: [*Coming in*] I had hard work to drive 'em in. The roan kept—

PETR: Where's that Nikita?

AKULINA: Nikita? He's standing in the street.

PETR: What's he standing there for?

AKULINA: What for? He's standing round the corner and chatting.

PETR: Can't get sense out of her! Who's he chatting with?

AKULINA: [*Not catching his words*] What?

[Petr *brandishes his arm at* Akulina; *she sits down at her spinning*]

ANYUTKA: [*Running in. To her mother*] Nikita's father and mother have come to see him. They're taking him home to marry him—just think!

ANISYA: Aren't you lying?

ANYUTKA: Honest and true, may I die if it ain't! [*Laughs*] I was going by, and Nikita says to me: "Now good-by, young lady," he says; "come and have some fun at my wedding. I'm leaving you," he says. And then he just laughed.

ANISYA: [*To her husband*] Folks haven't much need of you. You see he was getting ready to leave himself. And you were saying: "I'll turn him out"!

PETR: Let him go; can't I find other men?

175

ANISYA: But haven't you paid him in advance?

[Anyutka *goes toward the door, listens to their words for a moment, and goes out*]

PETR: [*Frowning*] He can work off the money next summer if necessary.

ANISYA: Yes, you're glad to let him go—one less mouth to feed. But during the winter I'll have to tend to things all alone, like a work horse. The girl ain't awful eager to work, and you'll just lie on the stove. I know you!

PETR: What's the use of wagging your tongue for nothing when you ain't heard anything yet?

ANISYA: The place is crowded with the animals. You haven't sold the cow and you've taken in all the sheep for the winter—it'll be hard enough to store up feed for all of 'em, and to water 'em. And now you want to let the hired man go. I won't do a man's work! I'll lie down on the stove just like you and let things go to smash—and you can do what you please about it.

PETR: [*To* Akulina] Go for the fodder, will you? It's time.

AKULINA: For the fodder? All right. [*Puts on her coat and takes a rope*]

ANISYA: I won't work for you. I've had enough of it—I won't! Work for yourself.

PETR: Shut up! What are you mad about? You're like a wet hen.

ANISYA: You're a mad dog yourself! There's no work or joy to be got out of you. You're just sucking the life out of me. A mad dog, that's what you are.

PETR: [*Spits and puts on his coat*] Plague take you—Lord forgive me! I'll go and find out how things are. [*Goes out*]

ANISYA: [*Shouts after him*] Rotten, long-nosed devil!

AKULINA: What are you scolding dad for?

ANISYA: Shut up, you fool!

AKULINA: [*Going toward the door*] I know what you're scolding him for. You're a fool yourself, you cur. I ain't afraid of you.

ANISYA: What's that? [*Jumps up and looks for something with which to strike her*] Look out or I'll take the poker to you.

AKULINA: [*Opening the door*] You're a cur, you're a devil; that's what you are. Devil, cur, cur, devil! [*Runs out*]

ANISYA: [*Meditates*] "Come to the wedding," says he. So that's what they're up to—marrying him? Look out, Nikita, if that's your doings, I'll have my say too. . . . I can't live without him. I won't let him go.

NIKITA: [*Comes in and glances about. Seeing that* Anisya *is alone, he approaches her quickly. Whispers*] Well, my girl, I'm in trouble! My father's come and wants to take me away—tells me I must go home. "We're marrying you off for good and all," says he, "and you'll have to stay at home."

ANISYA: Well then, marry. What do I care?

NIKITA: Oh, re-ally! I thought it'd be better to talk things over; but this is what he says: he tells me I must marry. What does this mean? [*Winks*] Have you forgotten?

ANISYA: Go ahead and marry. You needn't—

NIKITA: What are you snorting at? You won't even let me pet you a bit.—Well, what's wrong with you?

ANISYA: I think you want to desert me. And if you do want to desert me, then I've no use for you either. That's the whole story!

NIKITA: Oh, stop, Anisya. Do you think I want to forget you?—Not so long as I live. So I won't leave you for good and all. This is the way I figure it; let 'em marry me, but then I'll come back to you— if only they don't make me stay at home.

ANISYA: Much I'll care for you if you're married.

NIKITA: But remember, my dear girl: I simply can't go against my father's will.

ANISYA: You put the blame on your father, but the scheme's your own. You've been plotting for a long time with your sweetheart, with Marina. She put you up to this. She didn't run over here the other day for nothing.

NIKITA: Marina? Much I care for her! . . . Many of her kind fall for me!

ANISYA: Why did your father come? You told him to! You've been deceiving me! [*Weeps*]

NIKITA: Anisya, do you believe in God or not? I never even dreamed of any such thing. Honestly, I never thought of it. My old man made the plan out of his own head.

ANISYA: If you don't want to get married yourself, can any one pull you to it like a jackass?

NIKITA: All the same, I figure a fellow can't oppose his father. And I don't want to.

ANISYA: Just say you won't, and stick to it.

NIKITA: One fellow refused, and they thrashed him in the village jail. Then he understood. I don't want to go through that. I tell you, it's ticklish.

ANISYA: Quit your fooling. Listen, Nikita: if you're going to marry Marina, I don't know what I'll do to myself. . . . I'll kill myself! I've sinned and broken the law, but now I can't turn back. Just as soon as you leave me, I'll do it.

NIKITA: Why should I leave? If I wanted to leave I'd have gone long ago. The other day Ivan Semenych offered me a job as coachman . . . and what an easy life! Yet I didn't take it. I think that everybody likes me. If you didn't love me, I'd act differently.

ANISYA: Just remember this. The old man may die any day; then I think we can cover up all our sins. I've planned to marry you; then you'll be the master of the house.

NIKITA: No use guessing. What do I care? I do the work as if it was for my own self. The master likes me, and his wife—well, she's in love with me. And if women love me, I'm not to blame; it's a simple matter.

ANISYA: Will you love me?

NIKITA: [*Embracing her*] Just this way! You've always been in my heart.

[Matrena *comes in and for some time stands before the ikon in the corner of the room, crossing herself.* Nikita *and* Anisya *move away from each other*]

MATRENA: Oh, what I've seen, I didn't see; what I've heard, I didn't hear. Been having fun with a nice little woman, have you? What of it? Even calves have their fun, you know. Why shouldn't you? You're still young. But the master is asking for you in the yard, my son.

NIKITA: I came in to get the ax.

MATRENA: I know, my boy; I know what sort of an ax you came for. You're likely to find that kind near a woman.

NIKITA: [*Bends down and picks up an ax*] Well, mother, are you really going to marry me? I think there's no reason for that at all. And then I don't want to marry.

MATRENA: Oh, my darling, why should we marry you? You're living and having a good time; it's only the old man's plan. Go ahead, my boy; we'll settle the whole business without your help.

NIKITA: This is queer: first you want to marry me, and then you say there's no need of it. I can't understand things at all. [*Goes out*]

ANISYA: Well, Auntie Matrena, do you really want to marry him?

MATRENA: Why should we marry him, my precious? You know what our family's like. My old man keeps mumbling foolish stuff: "Marry him, must marry him." But he hasn't enough sense to judge. Horses don't run away from oats, you know, men don't quit one good thing for another: that's the way to look at it. Don't I see [*Winks*] the turn things are taking?

ANISYA: It's no use for me to hide from you, Auntie Matrena. You know everything. I have sinned; I have fallen in love with your son.

MATRENA: Well, this is news! And Auntie Matrena didn't know! Oh, girlie, Auntie Matrena is an old bird, a sly old bird. Auntie Matrena, I can tell you, darling, can see a yard underground. I know everything, precious! I know why young wives need sleeping powders. I've brought some. [*Unties a corner of her kerchief and takes out a packet of powders*] What I need to, I see; and what I don't need to, I don't know and don't want to know. That's the way. Auntie Matrena was young once herself. I've had to find out how to live with my own fool, you see. I know the whole seventy-seven tricks. I see your old man's withering away, darling, withering away. What sort of life can you have? Stick a pitchfork into him and the blood won't flow. I tell you: you'll be burying him next spring!

You must get some one else to be the boss. And ain't my son up to the job? He's no worse than others. So what use would it be for me to pull my son away from a good soft place? Am I my own child's enemy?

ANISYA: If only he don't leave us!

MATRENA: He won't leave you, birdie. That's all nonsense. You know my old man. His wits are all gone by now; but sometimes, when he gets a notion into his noodle, you can't knock it out with a mallet.

ANISYA: But how did the business start?

MATRENA: You see, darling; you know yourself the lad is daft on women; and he's handsome too, I must say. Well, he was living on the railroad, you know, and there they had an orphan girl as cook. Well, that hussy began to chase after him.

ANISYA: Marina?

MATRENA: Yes, plague take her! Well, whether anything happened or not, my old man only knows. Whether people talked, or whether the girl herself got round him—

ANISYA: What impudence, the bold thing!

MATRENA: So my silly old fool got on his ear and kept saying: "We must marry him, marry him to cover up the sin. Let's take the lad home," says he, "and marry him." I argued all I could, but it was no use. "All right," thinks I, "I'll play another game." You have to know how to manage those fools, darling. Just pretend to agree, but when the time comes you can turn things your own way. You know a woman can fly up in the air and think seven and seventy thoughts, and how's a man to guess 'em! "Well, old man," says I, "it's a good plan, but we must think it over. Let's go call on our son," says I, "and ask the advice of Petr Ignatych. Let's see what he'll say." So we've come.

ANISYA: Oh, auntie, how's this? What if his father orders him?

MATRENA: Orders him? Stick his orders under a dog's tail! Don't you worry: this thing won't come off. I'll talk over the whole business with your old man right away; I'll sift it so there won't be anything left of it. I came along just to fix it up. Think of it: my son's living in happiness and expecting more —and I'm to marry him off to a vagabond girl! Do you think I'm a fool?

ANISYA: She's even been running over here to see him, that Marina.—Will you believe it, auntie: when they told me he was to be married, I felt a knife run through my heart? I thought that his heart was with her.

MATRENA: Eh, darling! Do you think he's a fool? He's not the man to love a homeless trollop. Nikita, you know, is a lad of some sense. He knows whom it's worth while to love. And don't you worry, darling. We'll never take him away as long as he lives. And we won't marry him. Just hand us a little money, and we'll let him stay here.

ANISYA: If Nikita left, I think I'd die.

MATRENA: Yes, you're young. Hard lines! For a

woman like you, fresh and rosy, to live with that old scarecrow—

ANISYA: Believe me, auntie, I'm sick to death of that man of mine, that long-nosed cur; I don't want ever to see him again.

MATRENA: Yes, such is your lot. But look here. [*In a whisper, glancing around*] I went to that old man for powders, you know, and he gave me two different kinds. Just look here. "This is a sleeping powder," says he. "Give him one of 'em," says he, "and he'll fall asleep so sound you could walk on him. And this," says he "is a sort that she must have him drink—there's no smell to it, but it's awful strong. Give it seven times over," says he, "one pinch at a time. Give it to him seven times. And then," says he, "she'll soon be free from him."

ANISYA: Oh ho ho! What's that!

MATRENA: "It won't leave any traces," says he. He charged a whole ruble. "Can't let you have 'em for less," says he, "for it's hard to get 'em, you know." I paid my own money for 'em, darling. I thought you could use 'em; if you can't, I'll take 'em to Mikhaylovna.

ANISYA: Oh! oh! But maybe there's something bad about 'em.

MATRENA: What's bad about it, darling? It'd be different if your man was in strong health, but now he just makes a bluff at being alive. He don't belong to the living, he don't. There are a lot of men like him.

ANISYA: Oh! oh! poor me! Auntie, I'm afraid it may be sinful. Oh, what have I come to!

MATRENA: I can take 'em back.

ANISYA: Do you dissolve the second sort in water, like the others?

MATRENA: It's better in tea, he says. "You don't notice 'em at all," he says, "there's no smell to 'em, not a bit." He's a clever man.

ANISYA: [*Taking the powders*] Oh! oh! poor me! I'd never meddle with such things if my life wasn't a torment worse than prison.

MATRENA: And don't forget the ruble; I promised to take it to the old man. He has troubles of his own.

ANISYA: Sure! [*Goes to the chest and hides the powders*]

MATRENA: And keep 'em tight, darling, so that people won't know. And if he finds 'em—God forbid!—say that they're for cockroaches. [*Takes the ruble*] They're good for cockroaches too. . . . [*Stops suddenly*]

[Akim *comes in and crosses himself before the ikon*; Petr *comes in and sits down*]

PETR: Well, how goes it, Uncle Akim?

AKIM: A bit better, Ignatych, a bit better, y'see; a bit better. Because I was afraid that there might— Foolery, you know. I'd like, y'see, I'd like to get the lad down to business. And if you'd agree, y'see, then we might. It'd be better if—

PETR: All right, all right. Sit down and let's talk.

[Akim *sits down*] Well then? So you want to marry him?

MATRENA: We can wait about marrying him, Petr Ignatych. You know how hard up we are, Ignatych. If we marry him, we can't make a living ourselves. How can we marry him!

PETR: Decide for yourselves what's better.

MATRENA: Well, there's no haste about the marrying. It'll wait. She's no raspberry; she won't fall off the bush.

PETR: Of course, it'd be a good thing if you married him.

AKIM: I'd like to, y'see. Because, y'see, I've some work in town; I struck a good job, y'see.

MATRENA: Fine job! Cleaning cesspools. When he came home the other day, I puked and puked. Ugh!

AKIM: That's true; at first it just knocks you over, y'see, the smell of it. But when you get used to it, it's no worse than malt dregs, and after all it suits me. And about the smell, y'see— Men like me needn't mind it. And then we can change our clothes.— I wanted to have Nikita at home, you know; he can tend to things there. He can tend to things at home, and I'll make some money in town, y'see.

PETR: You want to keep your son at home: very well then. But how about the pay he took in advance?

AKIM: That's right, Ignatych, that's right; you told the truth there, y'see. He's hired himself out and sold himself, so let the bargain stand. But we must just marry him, y'see; so you just let him off for a while.

PETR: Well, that's possible.

MATRENA: But we two don't agree about it. Petr Ignatych, I'll tell you the truth as I'd tell it to God. You judge between me and my old man. He keeps saying, "Marry him, marry him." But marry him to whom, may I ask? If she was a decent girl, I'd not stand in my boy's way, but she's a low-lived hussy.

AKIM: That's all wrong. You're wrong in slandering the girl, y'see; you're wrong. Because she— that girl, I say—has been injured by my son; she's been injured, I tell you. The girl has, you know.

PETR: What was the injury?

AKIM: She got mixed up with my son, Nikita, y'see. With Nikita, you know.

MATRENA: Don't you speak of it; my tongue's softer, I'll tell the story. Before he came to you, you know, our lad was living on the railroad. And there a girl got hold of him; you know, a stupid hussy named Marina—she was cook for the railroad gang. So she accused him, that hussy did, our own son, and said that it was he, Nikita, that deceived her.

PETR: That's a bad business.

MATRENA: But she's a low-lived creature herself, runs after the men. She's just a streetwalker.

AKIM: Old woman, you're telling wrong stories again, y'see; it ain't a bit so. I tell you it ain't, y'see.

MATRENA: All my old boy can say is, "y'see,

y'see"; but what he means by it he don't know himself. Don't ask me about the hussy, Petr Ignatych, ask other folks; anybody'll tell you. She's just a homeless vagrant.

PETR: [*To* Akim] Well, Uncle Akim, if that's the case, then there's no use marrying him. The business ain't an old shoe that you can kick off by making him marry her.

AKIM: [*Getting excited*] It's an injury to the girl, y'see, old woman, an injury, y'see. Because the girl is a very decent sort, y'see, a very decent sort; and I'm sorry for her, sorry for the girl, you know.

MATRENA: You're just like a silly old woman; you waste your sorrow on the whole world, while your own folks go hungry. You're sorry for the girl, but you ain't sorry for your son. Tie her round your own neck and walk with her! Quit talking nonsense!

AKIM: No, it ain't nonsense.

MATRENA: Don't you get on your ear: I'll say my say.

AKIM: [*Interrupting*] No, it ain't nonsense. You turn things your own way—maybe about the girl, maybe about yourself—you turn things your own way, as it's best for you; but, y'see, God will turn 'em his way. That's how it stands.

MATRENA: Bah! No use wasting words on you.

AKIM: The girl's a hard worker, a decent sort, and she knows how to look out for herself, y'see. And we're poor, and she'll be an extra hand, y'see; and the wedding won't cost much. But the main thing's the injury done the girl, you know; she's an orphan, y'see, the girl is. And she's been injured.

MATRENA: Any girl'd say that.

ANISYA: Just you listen to us women, Uncle Akim. We can tell you things.

AKIM: But God, I tell you, God! Ain't she a human being, that girl? So, y'see, God cares for her. What do you think about that?

MATRENA: Oh, he's off again!

PETR: See here, Uncle Akim, you can't much believe those hussies either. And the lad's alive. He's close by! Let's send and ask him straight out whether it's true. He won't perjure his soul. Call the lad here! [Anisya *rises*] Tell him his father's calling for him. [Anisya *goes out*]

MATRENA: You've settled the business, my dear, you've cleaned it up: let the lad speak for himself. And these times you can't marry off a lad by force. We must ask him what he thinks. He'll never want to marry her and shame himself. What I think is: he'd better stay with you and work for his master. Even in summer we won't need to take him; we can hire somebody. Just give us ten rubles and he can stay here.

PETR: We'll talk about that later: take things in order. Finish one job before you start another.

AKIM: I'm talking this way, Petr Ignatych, you know, because such things happen sometimes, y'see. You keep trying to better yourself, and you forget about God, y'see; you think it'd be better—you go

your own gait, and find the load's on your own shoulders. We think it'll be better for us, you know; and then it's much worse, for we've left out God.

PETR: Of course! We must remember God.

AKIM: All of a sudden it's worse. But if you act according to the law, and as God wills, then, y'see, somehow everything makes you happy. So that's how you want to do. So I struck the idea, you know: I'll marry the lad and keep him out of sin. He'll be at home, y'see, just as he should be by rights; and I'll just go to work in the town, y'see. It's a pleasant job. Suits me. Do as God wills, y'see, and things are better. And then she's an orphan. For instance, last summer they stole some wood from the clerk— what a trick! They thought they'd fool him. They did fool the clerk, but y'see, they didn't fool God: so, y'see—

[*Enter* Nikita *and* Anyutka]

NIKITA: Did you ask for me? [*Sits down and takes out his tobacco*]

PETR: [*In a low voice, reproachfully*] Look here, don't you know how to behave? Your father is going to ask you questions, and you're fooling with your tobacco, and you've sat down. Get up and come over here.

[Nikita *takes his stand by the table, jauntily leaning against it, and smiling*]

AKIM: Well, y'see, there's a complaint against you, Nikita; a complaint, y'see.

NIKITA: Who complained?

AKIM: Who complained? A girl, an orphan complained. It was she, that same Marina, who complained on you, y'see.

NIKITA: [*Grinning*] Mighty queer. What's the complaint? Who told you about it? Was it she?

AKIM: Now I'm asking you questions, y'see, and you've got to answer, you know. Did you get mixed up with the girl? Did you get mixed up with her, I say?

NIKITA: I simply don't understand what you're talking about.

AKIM: I mean, was there any foolery, y'see, between you and her? Foolery, foolery, you know.

NIKITA: Of course there was. You have fun with the cook to pass the time away; you play the accordion and she dances. What more foolery do you want?

PETR: Nikita, don't shuffle around: answer straight out what your father's asking you.

AKIM: [*Solemnly*] Nikita, you can hide things from men, but you can't hide 'em from God. Nikita, just think it over, y'see; don't you tell me lies! She's an orphan, y'see; it's easy to injure her. An orphan, you know. Tell me plain how it was.

NIKITA: But there's nothing to tell. I'm telling you the whole story, because there's nothing to tell. [*Getting excited*] She'll say anything. She can spread all the stories she wants, as if a man was dead. What stories didn't she tell of Fedka Mikishkin? So I suppose nowadays you can't have any fun! Let her talk!

AKIM: Eh, Nikita, look out! The truth will be known. Was there something or wasn't there?

NIKITA: [Aside] They're pressing me hard. [To Akim] I tell you there wasn't anything. There was nothing between me and her. [Angrily] I swear to Christ, may I die on the spot if there was! [Crosses himself] I don't know anything about the business. [Silence. Nikita continues still more excitedly] How did you get the idea of marrying me to her! What's all this anyhow? It's an outrage. Nowadays you've no right to marry a man by force. It's simple enough. I've just sworn to you—I don't know a thing about it.

MATRENA: [To her husband] That's it, you silly old fool: whatever rubbish they tell you, you believe it all. You've just put the lad to shame for nothing. And he'd better just stay on living here with the master. Now the master will give us ten rubles to help us out. And when the time comes—

PETR: Well then, Uncle Akim?

AKIM: [Clucks with his tongue. To his son] Look out, Nikita; the tear of an injured girl don't flow in vain, y'see; it drops on a man's head. Look out for what's coming.

NIKITA: What's there to look out for? Look out yourself. [Sits down]

ANYUTKA: I'll go tell mama. [Goes out]

MATRENA: [To Petr] That's how it always is, Petr Ignatych. My old man just makes trouble with his talk; when he gets a notion in his nut, you can't knock it out. We've just bothered you for nothing. Let the lad stay on living here as he has done. Keep the lad—he's your servant.

PETR: How about it, Uncle Akim?

AKIM: Well, y'see, I didn't want to force the lad— I was just afraid—Y'see, I'd like to have—

MATRENA: You don't know yourself what you're meddling with. Let him live here just as he has. The lad himself don't want to leave. And what use have we for him? We'll manage alone.

PETR: Just one thing, Uncle Akim: if you're going to take him in the summer, I don't want him this winter. If he's to say here, it must be for a year.

MATRENA: He'll promise for the whole year. At home, when the working time comes, if we need anybody we'll hire him; and let the lad stay here. And now you give us ten rubles.

PETR: Well then, for a year more?

AKIM: [Sighing] Well, seems like, y'see; I suppose it's so.

MATRENA: One year more, from the feast of St. Dmitry. You won't beat us down on the price—and now give us ten rubles. You'll do us that favor. [Rises and bows]

[Anisya comes in with Anyutka and sits down at one side]

PETR: Well? If that's all right, then—then let's go to the tavern and wet down the bargain. Come on, Uncle Akim, and have a drink of vodka.

AKIM: I don't drink vodka, I don't.

PETR: Well, you'll have some tea.

AKIM: Tea's my sin. Tea, sure.

PETR: The women will have some tea too. Nikita, see that you don't drive the sheep too fast—and rake up the straw.

NIKITA: All right.

[All go out except Nikita. Darkness is falling]

NIKITA: [Lights a cigarette] They nagged and nagged me to tell about my doings with the girls. Those'd make a long story. He told me to marry her. If I married 'em all, I'd have a lot of wives. No use of my marrying; I'm as well off now as a married man: people envy me. And how lucky it was that something or other just put me up to go and cross myself before the ikon. That way I cut the whole business short. They say it's scary to swear to what ain't true. That's all bosh. Nothing but words anyhow. It's simple enough.

AKULINA: [Comes in, lays down the rope, takes off her coat, and goes to the storeroom] You might give us a light, anyhow.

NIKITA: To look at you? I can see you without it.

AKULINA: Drat you!

ANYUTKA: [Runs in and whispers to Nikita] Nikita, hurry up; somebody's asking for you. Can you imagine!

NIKITA: Who is it?

ANYUTKA: Marina from the railroad. She's standing round the corner.

NIKITA: You lie.

ANYUTKA: Honest!

NIKITA: What's she want?

ANYUTKA: Wants you to come. "I just need to speak one word to Nikita," she says. I began to ask questions, but she won't tell. She just asked if it was true that you're leaving us. "It ain't true," says I, "his father wanted to take him away and marry him, but he refused and he's going to stay another year with us." And she says: "Just send him to me, for Christ's sake. I just must say one word to him," she says. She's been waiting a long time. You go to her.

NIKITA: Plague take her! Why should I go?

ANYUTKA: "If he don't come," she says, "I'll come into the cottage for him. Honest I'll come," she says.

NIKITA: Don't worry: she'll stand there a while and then go away.

ANYUTKA: "Do they want to marry him to Akulina?" she says.

AKULINA: [Still spinning, goes up to Nikita] Marry whom to Akulina?

ANYUTKA: Nikita.

AKULINA: Really? Who says so?

NIKITA: Some people say so. [Looks at her and laughs] Akulina, will you marry me?

AKULINA: You? Maybe I'd have married you a little while ago, but now I won't.

NIKITA: Why won't you now?

AKULINA: 'Cause you won't love me.

NIKITA: Why won't I?

AKULINA: They won't let you. [Laughs]

NIKITA: Who won't?

AKULINA: Stepmother, of course. She keeps scolding; she watches you all the time.

NIKITA: [Laughing] Bright girl! What sharp eyes you have!

AKULINA: I? Course I see. Am I blind? She blew up dad sky-high to-day. She's a witch with a big snout. [Goes into the storeroom]

ANYUTKA: Nikita, just look! [She looks out of the window] She's coming. Honest, it's she. I'll clear out. [Goes out]

MARINA: [Coming in] What's this you're doing to me?

NIKITA: What am I doing? I'm not doing anything.

MARINA: You're going to desert me.

NIKITA: [Rising angrily] Well, what do you mean by coming here?

MARINA: Oh, Nikita!

NIKITA: You girls are a queer lot. . . . What have you come for?

MARINA: Nikita!

NIKITA: Nikita, you say? I'm Nikita. What do you want? Get out, I tell you.

MARINA: I see you mean to desert me, to forget me.

NIKITA: Why should I remember you? You don't know yourself. You were standing round the corner and sent Anyutka to me, and I didn't come to you. So I haven't any use for you; that's all. Now get out.

MARINA: No use for me! You've no use for me now. I believed you when you said you'd love me. And now you've done this with me and haven't any use for me.

NIKITA: This talk of yours is all no use, don't amount to anything. You even blabbed to my father. Clear out, please!

MARINA: You know yourself that I never loved anybody but you. You might marry me or not, as you please; I shouldn't care. Have I done you any wrong that you've stopped loving me? Why did you?

NIKITA: There's no use of our wasting time talking. Clear out! . . . These senseless girls!

MARINA: What hurts ain't that you deceived me and promised to marry me, but that you don't love me any more. And it don't hurt that you don't love me, but that you've changed me off for another woman. For whom? I know!

NIKITA: [Steps towards her angrily] No use talking with girls like you; they won't listen to reason. Clear out, I tell you, or you'll make me do something bad.

MARINA: Something bad? Well, are you going to beat me? Go on, do! What are you turning away your mug for? Oh, Nikita!

NIKITA: Of course, it won't do; people'd come. But talking's no use.

MARINA: Well, this is the end; what's done is done. You tell me to forget it all! Well, Nikita, remember this. I guarded my honor more than my very eyes. You just ruined me and deceived me. You had no pity for an orphan [Weeps]; you deserted me. You've killed me, but I don't bear you any grudge. Good-by; I don't care. If you find a better one, you'll forget me; if you find a worse one, you'll remember. You'll remember, Nikita! Good-by, if I must go. But how I loved you! Good-by for the last time! [Tries to embrace him and clasp his head]

NIKITA: [Tearing himself free] Bah! I'm sick of talking with you. If you won't go, I'll go myself and you can stay here.

MARINA: [Screams] You're a beast! [In the doorway] God won't give you happiness! [Goes out, weeping]

AKULINA: [Coming out of the storeroom] You're a cur, Nikita!

NIKITA: Well?

AKULINA: How she yelled! [Weeps]

NIKITA: What's the matter with you?

AKULINA: What? You wronged her. You'll wrong me the same way—you cur! [Goes out into the store-room]

NIKITA: [After an interval of silence] It's all a puzzle to me. I love those women like sugar; but if a man sins with them—there's trouble!

ACT II.

The stage represents a street and Petr's cottage. On the spectators' left, a cottage with a porch in the center, and on each side of this a living room; on the right, the yard fence, with a gate. Near the fence Anisya is stripping hemp. Six months have passed since the first act.

ANISYA: [Stopping and listening] He's growling once more. Most likely he's got off the stove.[1]

[Akulina *comes in, carrying pails on a yoke*]

ANISYA: He's calling. Go and see what he wants. Hear him yell!

AKULINA: Why don't you go yourself?

ANISYA: Go along, I tell you!

[Akulina *goes into the cottage*]

ANISYA: He's worn me out: he won't tell where the money is; that's all there is to it. The other day he was in the entry way; most likely he'd hid it there. Now I don't know myself where it is. It's lucky he's afraid to part with it. It's still in the house. If I could only find it! It wasn't on him yesterday. Now I don't know where it is myself. He's clean worn me out.

[Akulina *comes out, tying on her kerchief*]

[1] In a Russian peasant cottage the best couch is on top of the oven. It is generally reserved for the old or infirm.

ANISYA: Where are you going?

AKULINA: Where? He told me to call Auntie Marfa. "Send for my sister," he says. "I'm dying," he says, "and I need to tell her something."

ANISYA: [To herself] Sending for his sister! Oh, poor me! Oh! oh! Most likely he wants to give it to her. What shall I do? Oh! [To Akulina] Don't you go! Where are you going?

AKULINA: For auntie.

ANISYA: Don't you go, I tell you; I'll go myself. And you go to the brook with the wash. Otherwise you won't finish it before night.

AKULINA: But he told me to.

ANISYA: Go where I'm sending you. I'll go for Marfa myself, I tell you. Take the shirts off the fence.

AKULINA: The shirts? But I'm afraid you won't go. He told me to.

ANISYA: I've told you I'll go. Where's Anyutka?

AKULINA: Anyutka? She's herding the calves.

ANISYA: Send her here; they won't stray.

[Akulina gathers up the clothes and goes out]

ANISYA: If I don't go, he'll scold at me. If I go, he'll give his sister the money. All my toil will go for nothing. I don't know myself what to do. My head's all mixed up. [Continues her work]

[Matrena comes in with a staff and a small bundle, equipped for traveling on foot]

MATRENA: God help you, darling.

ANISYA: [Looks around, drops her work, and claps her hands for joy] Well, I never expected you, auntie. God has sent me such a guest just in time.

MATRENA: Well then?

ANISYA: I was just going crazy. Trouble!

MATRENA: Well, he's still alive, they tell me?

ANISYA: Don't speak of it. He's half alive and half dead.

MATRENA: Has he given the money to anybody?

ANISYA: He's just sending for Marfa, his own sister. Must be about the money.

MATRENA: Sure thing. But ain't he given it to somebody without your knowing it?

ANISYA: Not much! I've been watching him like a hawk.

MATRENA: But where is it?

ANISYA: He won't tell. And I can't find out anyhow. He hides it first one place and then another. And Akulina hampers me. She's only a silly fool, but she too keeps spying round and watching. Oh, poor me! I'm all worn out.

MATRENA: Eh, darling, if he gives the money to some one without your knowing it, you'll weep forever. They'll turn you out of the house empty-handed. You've worn yourself out, my precious, worn yourself out all your life with a man you don't love, and when you're a widow you'll have to go begging.

ANISYA: Don't speak of it, auntie. My heart aches and I don't know what to do and I've nobody to advise me. I told Nikita. But he's afraid to meddle

with the business. He just told me yesterday that it was under the floor.

MATRENA: Well, did you look to see?

ANISYA: I couldn't; he was there himself. I notice, sometimes he carries it on him, sometimes he hides it.

MATRENA: Just remember, girlie: if you slip up once, you'll never get straight again. [In a whisper] Well, have you given him the strong tea?

ANISYA: O-oh! [Is about to reply, but sees her friend, and stops short]

[Another housewife, a friend of Anisya, walks past the cottage, and stops to listen to the shouts from within it]

FRIEND: [To Anisya] Hey, friend! Anisya, Anisya, I say! Your man seems to be calling you.

ANISYA: He keeps coughing that way, and it sounds as if he was calling. He's pretty low by now.

FRIEND: [Coming up to Matrena] Good day, old woman, where in the world did you come from?

MATRENA: From home, of course, my dear. I came to see my son. I've brought him some shirts. He's my boy, you know, and I'm sorry for him.

FRIEND: That's natural. [To Anisya] I was going to bleach my linen, friend, but I think it's too soon. People haven't begun yet.

ANISYA: No use of hurrying.

MATRENA: Well, have they given him the Communion?

ANISYA: Sure; the priest was here yesterday.

FRIEND: [To Matrena] I had a look at him yesterday myself, my dear; and he seemed hardly alive. He'd just wasted away. And the other day, my friend, he seemed on the point of death; they laid him out under the holy ikons. They were already wailing for him, and getting ready to wash the body.

ANISYA: He's come to life again—got out of bed; now he's walking again.

MATRENA: Well, will you give him extreme unction?

ANISYA: People are urging me to. If he's alive, we're going to send for the priest to-morrow.

FRIEND: Eh, it must be pretty hard for you, Anisya dear. It's a true saying: The bed's soft for the sick man, but hard for those that tend him.

ANISYA: That's so, but there's more to it.

FRIEND: Of course, he's been dying for most a year. He's tied you hand and foot.

MATRENA: A widow's lot is hard too. It's all right when you're young, but when you're old nobody will pity you. Old age is no joy. Take me for instance. I haven't walked far; but I'm tired out—my legs are numb.—— Where's my son?

ANISYA: Plowing.—— But come in, we'll start the samovar. The tea'll refresh you.

MATRENA: [Sitting down] I'm certainly tired, my dears. But you simply must give him the unction. People say that it's good for the soul.

ANISYA: Yes, we'll send to-morrow.

MATRENA: That's right.— But we're having a wedding down our way, girlie.

FRIEND: What, in the spring?

MATRENA: It's a good old proverb: "A poor man hurries to marry before the night's over." Semyon Matveyevich is going to take Marina.

ANISYA: She's in great luck!

FRIEND: He must be a widower; she'll have to look out for the children.

MATRENA: There are four of 'em. What decent girl would marry him? Well, he took her. And she's glad enough. They were drinking, you know, and the glass was cracked—they spilled the wine.

FRIEND: Just think! Was there gossip? And has the man some property?

MATRENA: They get along pretty well.

FRIEND: It's true, hardly any girl will marry a man with children. . . . Just take our Mikhaylo. My dear, he's a man who—

PEASANT: [Off stage] Hey, Mavra, what the devil are you up to? Go and drive home the cow.

[Friend goes out]

MATRENA: [While the Friend is going out, she speaks in a calm voice] They've got her out of harm's way, girlie; at any rate my old fool won't think any more about Nikita. [Suddenly changes her voice to a whisper] She's gone! [Whispers] Well, I say, did you give him the tea?

ANISYA: Don't speak of it. He'd better die all by himself. He's not dying anyhow; I've just got the sin of it on my conscience. O-oh, poor me! Why did you give me those powders?

MATRENA: Powders? They were sleeping powders, girlie; why shouldn't I give 'em to you? They won't do any harm.

ANISYA: I don't mean the sleeping powders; I mean the others, the white ones.

MATRENA: Well, darling, those powders were medicine.

ANISYA: [Sighs] I know, but I'm afraid. He's worn me out.

MATRENA: Have you used much of it?

ANISYA: I gave it to him twice.

MATRENA: Well, he didn't notice?

ANISYA: I tasted it a bit in the tea, myself; it's a trifle bitter. And he drank it with the tea and said: "I can't stand that tea." And says I, "Everything's bitter to a sick man." And I felt my heart sink, auntie.

MATRENA: Don't think about it; thinking makes things worse.

ANISYA: I wish you hadn't given 'em to me and led me into sin. When I remember it, it makes me shiver. And why did you give 'em to me?

MATRENA: Eh, what do you mean, darling! Lord help you! Why do you throw the blame on me? Look out, girlie, don't shift the blame to some one else's shoulders. If any questions are asked, I'm not concerned; I don't know a thing about it: I'll kiss the cross and say I never gave her powders, never

saw any, never even heard that there were such powders. Just think for yourself, girlie. We were talking about you the other day, saying how the precious woman was just tormented to death. Her step-daughter's a fool, and her husband's no good, just skin and bones. Such a life'd make a woman do anything.

ANISYA: Well, I don't deny it. My life'd make me do worse things than these; I'm ready to hang myself or strangle him. 'Tain't being alive.

MATRENA: That's just the point. No time to stand and yawn. Somehow you must find the money and give him some more tea.

ANISYA: O-oh! Poor me! What to do now I don't know myself; it makes me shiver. I wish he'd die all by himself. I don't want to have the guilt on my soul.

MATRENA: [Angrily] But why don't he tell where the money is? Does he expect to take it with him and not let anybody have it? Is that right and proper? God forbid that such a lot of money should be wasted. Ain't that a sin? What's he doing? May I have a look at him?

ANISYA: I don't know myself. He's worn me out.

MATRENA: What don't you know? It's a clear case. If you make a slip now, you'll repent of it forever. He'll give the money to his sister, and you'll be left out.

ANISYA: O-oh, he was sending for her—I must go.

MATRENA: Don't go yet awhile: we'll start the samovar first thing. We'll give him the tea and between us we'll find where the money is—we'll manage to get it.

ANISYA: O-oh! Something may happen.

MATRENA: What's the matter? What are you staring at? Are you just going to roll your eyes at the money and not get it in your hands? Get to work.

ANISYA: Then I'll go and start the samovar.

MATRENA: Go on, darling; do the business right, so that you won't be sorry afterwards. That's the way. [Anisya moves away, Matrena urging her] Be sure and not tell Nikita about all this business. He's sort of silly. God forbid he find out about the powders. God knows what he'd do. He's very tender-hearted. You know, he never would kill a chicken for me. Don't you tell him. Trouble is, he won't understand it. [She stops in horror; Petr makes his appearance on the threshold]

[Petr, holding to the wall, crawls out on the porch and calls in a weak voice]

PETR: Why can't I make you hear? O-oh! Anisya, who's here? [Falls on the bench]

ANISYA: [Coming in from around the corner] What have you come out for? You ought to lie where you were.

PETR: Well, has the girl gone for Marfa? . . . I feel bad. . . . Oh, if death would only hurry up!

ANISYA: She's busy; I sent her to the brook. Give me time and I'll attend to it. I'll go myself.

PETR: Send Anyutka. Where is she? Oh, I feel bad! Oh, my death!

ANISYA: I've sent for her already.

PETR: O-oh! Where is she?

ANISYA: Where can she be? Plague take her!

PETR: O-oh, I can't stand it! My inside is burning. Seems like an auger was boring me. Why have you deserted me like a dog? . . . There's no one even to give me a drink. . . . O-oh! . . . Send Anyutka to me.

ANISYA: Here she is.—Anyutka, go to your father.

[Anyutka *runs in and* Anisya *retires around the corner*]

PETR: Go and tell—o-oh!—your Aunt Marfa that your father wants to see her; tell her to come here.

ANYUTKA: Is that all?

PETR: Wait. Tell her to hurry up. Tell her I'm almost dead. O-oh!

ANYUTKA: I'll just get my kerchief and go right away. [*Runs out*]

MATRENA: [*Winking*] Now girlie, get down to work. Go into the cottage and rummage everywhere. Look for it like a dog looks for fleas; turn over everything, and I'll search him right away.

ANISYA: [*To* Matrena] With you seems like I have more courage. [*Goes towards the porch. To* Petr] Shan't I start a samovar for you? Auntie Matrena's come to see her son; you'll have tea with her.

PETR: Go ahead and start it. [Anisya *goes into the cottage.* Matrena *comes towards the porch*]

PETR: Hello!

MATRENA: Good day, my benefactor! Good day, my precious! I see you're still sick. And my old man is so sorry for you. "Go and inquire," says he. He sent his regards. [*Bows once more*]

PETR: I'm dying.

MATRENA: Well, when I look at you, Ignatych, I can see that trouble haunts men and not the forest. You've wasted away, my precious, all wasted away; I can see that. Sickness don't bring beauty, I suppose?

PETR: My death's near.

MATRENA: Well, Petr Ignatych, it's God's will. They've given you the Communion, and now, God willing, they'll give the unction. Thank God, your wife's a sensible woman; she'll bury you and have prayers said, all as is proper. And my son too, while he's needed, he'll tend to things about the house.

PETR: There's no one that I can give orders to! The woman's heedless and spends her time on foolery; I know all about it—I know. The girl's half-witted, and young at that. I've gathered a good property, and there's nobody to attend to it. It's too bad. [*Snivels*]

MATRENA: Well, if it's money or anything like that, you can give directions.

PETR: [*Calls into the house, to* Anisya] Has Anyutka gone yet?

MATRENA: [*Aside*] Oh my, he still remembers!

ANISYA: [*From indoors*] She went right off. Come into the house; I'll help you.

PETR: Let me sit here for the last time. It's close in there. I feel bad. . . . Oh, my heart's burning! . . . If only death would come!

MATRENA: When God won't take a soul, the soul won't leave of itself. God's the judge of life and death, Petr Ignatych. You can never tell when death will come. Sometimes you recover. For instance in our village a peasant was just on the point of death—

PETR: No! I feel that I'll die to-day; I feel it. [*Leans against the wall and closes his eyes*]

ANISYA: [*Coming out of the cottage*] Well, are you coming in or not? Don't keep me waiting. Petr! Petr, I say!

MATRENA: [*Walking away and beckoning to* Anisya] Well, how about it?

ANISYA: [*Coming down from the porch, to* Matrena] Not there.

MATRENA: But did you look everywhere? Under the floor?

ANISYA: Not there either. Maybe in the shed. He went there yesterday.

MATRENA: Search, search, I tell you. Lick things clean. And it's my notion he'll die to-day anyhow: his nails are blue and his face like earth. Is the samovar ready?

ANISYA: It'll boil right off.

[Nikita *comes in from the other side of the stage—if possible on horseback, he comes up to the gate without seeing* Petr]

NIKITA: [*To his mother*] Hello, mother; are you all well at home?

MATRENA: Thanks to the Lord God, we're still alive; we can still eat.

NIKITA: Well, how's the boss?

MATRENA: Shh—he's sitting there. [*Points to the porch*]

NIKITA: Well, let him sit. What do I care?

PETR: [*Opening his eyes*] Nikita; hey, Nikita, come here!

[Nikita *goes to him.* Anisya *and* Matrena *whisper*]

PETR: Why have you come home so early?

NIKITA: I finished the plowing.

PETR: Did you plow the strip beyond the bridge?

NIKITA: It was too far to go there.

PETR: Too far? It's still farther from the house. You'll have to go there specially. You ought to have finished it at the same time.

[Anisya *listens to the conversation without showing herself*]

MATRENA: [*Approaching them*] Oh, sonny, why don't you try to please the master? The master is ill and relies on you; you ought to work for him as for your own father. Just stir yourself and work hard for him as I've told you to so often.

PETR: Then—ugh!—haul out the potatoes; the women—o-oh!—will sort them over.

ANISYA: [*To herself*] Well, I won't budge. He's

trying to send everybody away from him once more; most likely he has the money on him. He wants to hide it somewhere.

PETR: Otherwise—o-oh!— It'll be time to plant 'em, and they'll have sweated. O-oh, I'm exhausted. [Rises]

MATRENA: [Runs up on the porch and supports Petr] Shall I take you into the room?

PETR: Yes. [Stops] Nikita!

NIKITA: [Angrily] What next?

PETR: I shan't see you again. . . . I shall die to-day. . . . Forgive me for Christ's sake if I've sinned against you. . . . Whether in word or deed . . . if I ever sinned. There were many times. Forgive me.

NIKITA: No need to forgive; I'm a sinner myself.

MATRENA: Oh, sonny, take this to heart!

PETR: Forgive me, for Christ's sake! . . . [Weeps]

NIKITA: [In a choked voice] God will forgive you, Uncle Petr. I've no cause to bear you a grudge. I've never been ill treated by you. You forgive me; maybe I've sinned more against you. [Weeps]

[Petr goes out, sniffling, supported by Matrena]

ANISYA: Oh, poor me! He didn't think of that for nothing; it's clear that— [Goes up to Nikita] Well, you said that the money was under the floor.— It ain't there.

NIKITA: [Sobs, without replying] He was always fair and square to me—and see what I've done!

ANISYA: Well, stop it. Where's the money?

NIKITA: [Angrily] How should I know? Look for yourself.

ANISYA: You seem to be awful sorry for him?

NIKITA: Yes, I am sorry for him, mighty sorry. How he wept! O-oh!

ANISYA: How kind you are—found somebody to pity! He treated you like a dog, like a dog. Just now he was telling us to turn you out. You might be sorry for me instead.

NIKITA: Why should I be sorry for you?

ANISYA: He'll die and hide the money. . . .

NIKITA: Maybe he won't hide it. . . .

ANISYA: Oh, Nikita dear! He's sent for his sister and wants to give it to her. Bad luck for us! How can we live if he gives away the money? They'll drive me out of the house. You might do something about it. Didn't you tell me he went to the shed last evening?

NIKITA: I saw him coming out of there, but nobody knows where he hid it.

ANISYA: Oh, poor me, I'll go and look there. [Nikita walks away]

[Matrena comes out of the cottage and goes over to Anisya and Nikita]

MATRENA: [Whispers] You needn't go anywhere. The money's on him: I felt it; it's on a string around his neck.

ANISYA: Oh, poor me!

MATRENA: If you let it out of your sight now, you can look for it next door to nowhere. His sister'll come and you're done for.

ANISYA: She'll come and he'll give it to her. What shall we do? Oh, poor me!

MATRENA: What shall you do? See here: the samovar's boiling; go make the tea and pour it out for him, and [In a whisper] sprinkle in all the powder out of the paper and make him drink it. When he's drunk a cupful, just pull the string. Don't worry; he'll never tell about it.

ANISYA: Oh, I'm afraid!

MATRENA: Don't argue, hurry up about it; and I'll take care of the sister if she comes. Don't make a slip. Pull out the money and bring it here, and Nikita will hide it.

ANISYA: Oh, poor me! How can I ever dare to . . . and . . . and . . .

MATRENA: Don't argue, I tell you; do as I say, Nikita!

NIKITA: What?

MATRENA: Stay here; sit down on the bench close to the house, in case—you're needed.

NIKITA: [With a wave of his hand] Those women are crafty. They make a man dizzy. Plague take you! I'll go haul out the potatoes.

MATRENA: [Clutching his arm] Stay here, I tell you.

[Anyutka comes in]

ANISYA: [To Anyutka] Well?

ANYUTKA: She was at her daughter's in the garden; she'll come right away.

ANISYA: If she comes, what'll we do?

MATRENA: [To Anisya] Don't bother about her now; do as I tell you.

ANISYA: I don't know myself—I don't know anything; my head's all mixed up. Anyutka, girlie, run off for the calves; they must have strayed away. Oh, I'll never dare!

[Anyutka runs out]

MATRENA: Go along; the samovar's boiling over, most likely.

ANISYA: Oh, poor me! [Goes out]

MATRENA: [Going up to her son] Well, sonny! [Sits down beside him on the earth bench around the house] Now we must think over your business, not just let it drift.

NIKITA: What business?

MATRENA: Why, how you're going to get along and make your living.

NIKITA: Get along? Other people do, and so can I.

MATRENA: The old man's sure to die to-day.

NIKITA: If he dies, let him go to heaven! What do I care?

MATRENA: [During her speech she keeps glancing at the porch] Eh, sonny! The living must think of life. Here you need a lot of sense, my precious. Just think, for your sake I've run around everywhere; I've trotted my legs off working for you. And mind you: don't forget me later.

NIKITA: What sort of work were you doing?

MATRENA: For your sake, for your future. If you don't take pains in time, nothing ever succeeds. You know Ivan Moseich? I called on him too. I went over the other day, you know, and told him about a certain matter; I sat there and we got to talking. "Ivan Moseich," says I, "how could a case like this be fixed up? Suppose," says I, "a peasant is a widower, and suppose he takes another wife; and just suppose," says I, "he has children, one daughter by his first wife and one by the second. Well," says I, "if that peasant dies, is it possible," says I, "for another peasant to marry the widow and get the farm? Is it possible," says I, "for that peasant to marry off the daughters and stay on the farm himself?" "It's possible," says he, "only you need to take a lot of pains; and," says he, "you need to use money to fix things up. Without money," says he, "there's no use meddling with it."

NIKITA: [Laughing] You needn't tell me that; just give 'em money. Everybody needs money.

MATRENA: Well, darling, I explained everything to him. "First of all," says he, "your son must get himself enrolled legally as a member of that village commune: for this he'll need money, to give a drink to the old men of the village. Then they'll agree to it and sign the paper. Only," says he, "you must do everything with some sense." Look here [Takes a paper from her kerchief] he wrote out a paper. Read it—you're smart.

[Nikita reads, and Matrena listens]

NIKITA: The paper is a legal order, of course. No great amount of sense needed here.

MATRENA: But just hear what Ivan Moseich had to say. "The main thing is, auntie," says he, "look out and don't let the money slip past you. If she don't grab the money," says he, "they won't let her marry off her daughter. The money's the root of the whole matter," says he. So look out. The time's coming to act, sonny.

NIKITA: What do I care: the money's hers, let her worry about it.

MATRENA: Is that what you think, sonny! Can a woman make plans? Even if she gets the money, she won't know how to manage it. She's nothing but a woman, and you're a man. So you can hide it and do anything you choose. Anyhow, you have more sense if any hitch comes.

NIKITA: Oh, you women don't understand anything!

MATRENA: Don't we though? You get hold of the money. Then the woman will be in your hands. If she ever happens to growl or grumble, then you can take her down.

NIKITA: Oh, you make me tired! I'm going.

[Anisya runs out of the cottage, all pale, and goes around the corner to Matrena]

ANISYA: It was on him. There it is. [Points under her apron]

MATRENA: Give it to Nikita; he'll hide it. Nikita,

take it and hide it somewhere.

NIKITA: Well, give it here!

ANISYA: O-oh, poor me! Maybe I'd better do it myself. [Goes towards the gate]

MATRENA: [Clutching her by the arm] Where are you going? They'll miss it; his sister's coming. Give it to him; he knows what to do. How silly you are!

ANISYA: [Stops, undecided] Oh, poor me!

NIKITA: Well, give it here; I'll hide it somewhere.

ANISYA: Where'll you hide it?

NIKITA: Are you afraid? [Laughs]

[Akulina comes in with the clothes]

ANISYA: O-oh, poor me, poor me! [Hands him the money] Look out, Nikita!

NIKITA: What're you afraid of? I'll tuck it away where I can't find it myself. [Goes out]

ANISYA: [Stands terrified] O-oh, what if he—

MATRENA: Well, is he dead?

ANISYA: Yes, seems dead. I pulled it out, and he didn't feel it.

MATRENA: Go inside; there's Akulina coming.

ANISYA: Well, I've sinned—and now he's got the money.—

MATRENA: That'll do; go inside: there's Marfa coming.

ANISYA: Well, I trusted him. What'll come of it? [Goes out]

[Marfa comes in from one side; Akulina approaches from the other]

MARFA: [To Akulina] I'd have come long ago, but I'd gone to my daughter's.— Well, how's the old man? Is he dying?

AKULINA: [Sorting out the clothes] How should I know? I've been at the brook.

MARFA: [Pointing to Matrena] Where's she from?

MATRENA: I'm from Zuyev; I'm Nikita's mother, from Zuyev, dearie. Good day to you! Your dear brother is very sick, very sick. He came out here himself. "Send for my sister," says he, "because," says he— Oh! Maybe he's dead already?

[Anisya runs out of the cottage with a cry, clutches the post of the porch, and begins to wail]

ANISYA: O-o-oh! O-o-oh! Why have you left— o-o-oh!—and why have you deserted—o-o-oh!—your wretched widow?— Forever and ever, he has closed his bright eyes!—

[Friend comes in. The Friend and Matrena support Anisya under the arms. Akulina and Marfa go into the cottage. Peasants, both men and women, come in]

VOICE FROM THE CROWD: Call the old women; they must lay him out.

MATRENA: [Rolling up her sleeves] Is there any water in the kettle? And I don't believe the samovar's been emptied. I'll help in the work myself.

ACT III.

Petr's *cottage. Winter. Nine months have passed
since Act II.* Anisya, *dressed in shabby workaday
clothes, is seated at the loom, weaving.* Anyutka *is
perched on the stove.* Mitrich, *an old laborer, comes
in.*

MITRICH: Oh, the Lord be with you! Well, hasn't
the master come home?

ANISYA: What?

MITRICH: Hasn't Nikita come home from town?

ANISYA: No.

MITRICH: Seems like he's been on a spree. Oh,
Lord!

ANISYA: Have you fixed up the threshing floor?

MITRICH: Sure. I fixed it all up proper, covered
it with straw. I don't like a halfway job. Oh, Lord!
Gracious St. Nicholas! [*Pecks at his callouses*] Yes,
it's high time for him to be here.

ANISYA: Why should he hurry? He has money; I
suppose he's on a spree with some hussy.

MITRICH: He has money; so why shouldn't he go
on a spree? What did Akulina go to town for?

ANISYA: Ask her why the devil took her there!

MITRICH: Why should she go to town? There are
all kinds of things in town, if you only have the
money. Oh, Lord!

ANYUTKA: Mama, I heard why. "I'll buy you a
little shawl," says he, just think; "you can pick it out
yourself," says he. And she dressed up just fine; put
on her plush wrap and a French kerchief.

ANISYA: That's just it: maiden's modesty as far as
the threshold; but when she's crossed it she forgets
everything. She's a shameless hussy.

MITRICH: Really! Why be modest? If you have
money, go on a spree! Oh, Lord! Is it too soon for
supper? [Anisya *is silent*] I'll go warm myself meanwhile. [*Climbs on the stove*] Oh, Lord! Holy Virgin
Mother! St. Nicholas the Martyr!

FRIEND: [*Coming in*] I see your man ain't back
yet?

ANISYA: No.

FRIEND: Time for him. Hasn't he gone to our
tavern? Sister Fekla said, my dear, that a lot of
sleighs from town were standing there.

ANISYA: Anyutka! Hey, Anyutka!

ANYUTKA: What?

ANISYA: Run over to the tavern, Anyutka, and
take a look. See if he's got drunk and gone there.

ANYUTKA: [*Jumping down from the stove and putting on her coat*] Right away.

FRIEND: Did he take Akulina with him?

ANISYA: Otherwise he'd have no reason to go. It's
she who keeps him busy in town. "I must go to the
bank," says he, "there's some money due me"——but
she's really the cause of all this mess.

FRIEND: [*Shaking her head*] You don't say! [*Silence*]

ANYUTKA: [*At the door*] If he's there, what shall
I say!

ANISYA: Just see if he's there.

ANYUTKA: All right, I'll fly like a bird. [*Goes out.
A long silence*]

MITRICH: [*Bellows*] Oh, Lord! Gracious St. Nicholas!

FRIEND: [*Starts from fright*] Oh, he scared me!
Who's that?

ANISYA: Mitrich, our laborer.

FRIEND: O-oh, how he frightened me! I forgot
about him. Well, friend, they say people have made
proposals for Akulina?

ANISYA: [*Coming out from behind the loom and
sitting down at the table*] People from Dedlov hinted
about it, but they must have heard something—they
hinted and then shut up, so the matter dropped.
Who wants her?

FRIEND: How about the Lizunovs from Zuyev?

ANISYA: They sent to inquire. But that too came
to nothing. He wouldn't receive them.

FRIEND: But you ought to marry her off.

ANISYA: We sure ought. I can hardly wait to get
her out of the house, friend, but I've no luck. He
don't want to, nor she either. You see he's not had
fun enough yet with that beauty of his.

FRIEND: Eh-eh-eh! Sins! The idea of it! Why, he's
her stepfather.

ANISYA: Ah, friend! They tied me hand and foot
too cleverly for words. Fool that I was, I didn't
notice anything, didn't even think of it—and so I
married him. I didn't guess one single thing, but
they already had an understanding.

FRIEND: O-oh, how sad things are!

ANISYA: More and more, I see, they're hiding
things from me. Oh, friend, my life has been miserable, just miserable. It'd be all right if I only didn't
love him.

FRIEND: You needn't tell me!

ANISYA: And it hurts me, friend, it hurts me to
suffer such an insult from him. Oh, how it hurts!

FRIEND: Well, they say he's even getting rough
with his hands. Is that so?

ANISYA: Rough every kind of way. When he was
drunk he used to be gentle; even in old times he
used to take a drop, but it never made him turn
against me. But now, when he gets liquor in him,
he just flies at me and wants to trample on me. The
other day he got his hands into my hair, and I had
hard work to break loose. And the hussy is worse
than a snake; I wonder how the earth can bear such
spiteful creatures.

FRIEND: O-o-oh! You're in hard luck, friend, the
more I think of it! How can you stand it? You took
in a beggar, and now he's going to make sport of
you like that. Why don't you take him down a bit?

ANISYA: Oh, my dear friend, with a heart like
mine what can I do! My dead husband was mighty
severe, but all the same I could manage him whatever way I wanted to; but here I can't, friend. When

I see him, my heart just melts. Against him I haven't any courage; he makes me feel like a wet hen.

FRIEND: O-oh, friend, I can see that somebody's bewitched you. That Matrena—they say she practices such things. Must be she.

ANISYA: I think so myself, friend. Sometimes I'm fairly ashamed of myself. I feel as if I'd like to tear him in pieces. But when I see him, no, my heart won't rise against him.

FRIEND: There must be a spell on you. It's easy enough to ruin a person, my precious. When I look at you, I can see that something's happened.

ANISYA: My legs are thin as bean poles. But look at that fool Akulina. She was a frowsy, sluttish hussy, and now look at her! What's the reason of this change? He's given her finery. She's swelled up and puffed up like a bubble on water. And then, no matter if she is a fool, she's got notions into her head. "I'm the mistress here," she says, "the house is mine. Dad wanted to marry me to him." And what a temper! God save us! When she gets mad, she fairly tears the straw off the roof.

FRIEND: O-oh, I see what a life you have, friend! And yet people envy you! "They're rich," they say; but, my dear, tears flow even through gold, you know.

ANISYA: Much there is to envy! And even the wealth will scatter like dust. He squanders money something awful.

FRIEND: But haven't you given him a pretty free rein, friend? The money's yours.

ANISYA: If you only knew the whole story! I made one big mistake.

FRIEND: In your place, friend, I'd go straight to the chief of police. The money's yours. How can he squander it? He's no right to.

ANISYA: Nowadays rights don't matter.

FRIEND: Oh, friend, I can see that you've grown weak.

ANISYA: Yes, darling, weak as a rag. He's bound me hand and foot. And I can't see any way out of it. O-oh, poor me!

FRIEND: Isn't somebody coming? [*She listens. The door opens and* Akim *comes in*]

AKIM: [*Crossing himself, knocking the snow off his bast shoes, and taking off his coat*] Peace to this house! Are you all well? Good evening, auntie.

ANISYA: Good evening, daddy. Have you come from home?

AKIM: I thought, y'see, I'd come see my son, y'see; I'd call on my son, you know. I didn't start early, had my dinner, you know; I started and it was deep snow, y'see, hard going, hard going; and so, y'see, I'm pretty late, you know. But is sonny at home? Is he home?

ANISYA: No, in town.

AKIM: [*Sitting down on the bench*] I have some business with him, y'see; a bit of business. I was telling him the other day, you know; telling him about our needs, y'see: the old horse has given out,

you know, the old horse. So we must get some sort of nag, y'see; some kind of nag. And so, y'see, I've come.

ANISYA: Nikita told me: when he comes, you can talk with him. [*Rises and goes to the oven*] Have supper, and he'll come. Mitrich, hey, Mitrich, come and have supper.

MITRICH: Oh, Lord, merciful St. Nicholas!

ANISYA: Come and have supper.

FRIEND: I'll be going; good-by. [*Goes out*]

MITRICH: [*Climbing down*] I never noticed how I went to sleep. Oh, Lord, St. Nicholas the Martyr!—Good evening, Uncle Akim.

AKIM: Huh! Mitrich! What're you doing here?

MITRICH: I'm working for Nikita now; I'm living with your son.

AKIM: Do say! So, y'see, you're working for my son. Do say!

MITRICH: I was living with a merchant in town, but I ruined myself by drink there. So I came to the country. I'd no home to go to, so I hired myself out. [*Yawns*] Oh, Lord!

AKIM: Well, y'see, well, what's Nikita doing himself? Is he so fixed, y'see, that he has to hire a workman, you know?

ANISYA: How's he fixed? First he managed by himself, but now he don't want to: so he's hired a laborer.

MITRICH: He has money, so what does he care?

AKIM: That's wrong, y'see; that's all wrong, y'see. It's wrong. He's just lazy.

ANISYA: Yes, he's got lazy, got lazy: that's the trouble.

AKIM: That's it, y'see; you think it'll be better, and, y'see, it turns out worse. When a man's wealthy, he gets lazy, gets lazy.

MITRICH: Fat makes a dog go mad, so why shouldn't fat make a man lazy! Fat was what was the ruin of me. I drank for three weeks without stopping. I drank up my last pair of pants. When I'd nothing more, I just quit. Now I've sworn off. Plague take the stuff!

AKIM: And where's your old woman now, y'see?

MITRICH: My old woman, friend, has found a place of her own. She's in town; sits in the taverns and begs. She's a beauty, too: one eye pulled out and the other knocked in and her mouth twisted sidewise. And—may she always have cakes and pie! —she's never sober.

AKIM: Oh ho! What's that?

MITRICH: But where's there a place for a soldier's wife? She's found her job. [*Silence*]

AKIM: [*To* Anisya] What did Nikita go to town for? Did he take something, y'see? Did he take something to sell, you know?

ANISYA: [*Setting the table and passing the food*] He went empty-handed. He went for money, to get some money in the bank.

AKIM: [*Eating*] What do you want the money for, y'see? Are you going to make some new use of it?

ANISYA: No, we don't spend much. Only twenty or thirty rubles. We ran short, so we had to get some.

AKIM: Had to get some? What's the use of taking it, y'see, that money? To-day you take some, you know; to-morrow you take some, y'see: that way you'll use it all up, you know.

ANISYA: This was just extra. But the money's all there.

AKIM: All there? How can it be all there, y'see? You take it and still it's all there? See here: if you pour meal, y'see, or something, you know, into a chest, y'see, or a storehouse, and then go take the meal out of there—will it still be all there, y'see? That means something is wrong, you know; they're cheating you. You see to it, or they'll cheat you. Much it's all there! You keep on taking it, and it's all there.

ANISYA: I don't know about such things. Ivan Moseich gave us some advice then. "Put your money in the bank," says he, "and the money'll be safer, and you'll get interest."

MITRICH: [Finishing his meal] That's right. I lived with a merchant. They all do that way. Put your money in and lie on the stove and earn more.

AKIM: That's queer talk of yours, y'see. You say, "earn more," y'see, "earn more," but how do they earn that money, you know; who do they earn it from?

ANISYA: They give 'em the money from the bank.

MITRICH: What a notion! Women can't understand things. Look here and I'll explain the whole thing to you. You pay attention. You, for instance, have money; and I, for instance, when spring comes, have an empty field and nothing to sow on it, or I can't pay my taxes, maybe. So I just come to you, you know: "Akim," says I, "give me ten rubles; and when I harvest my crop, I'll return it to you on St. Mary's Day in October, and I'll help you to harvest your field for your kindness." You, for instance, see that I have something to use as security, a horse or a cow, maybe, and you say: "Give me two or three rubles extra for my kindness and let it go at that." I have the halter round my neck and can't help myself. "All right," says I, "I'll take the ten rubles." In the autumn I make a turnover and bring you the money, and you skin me of those three rubles extra.

AKIM: That means, y'see, those peasants are acting crooked, y'see; that's how it is when a man forgets God, y'see; 'tain't right, you know.

MITRICH: Wait a bit. It'll work out the same way over again. Remember now, that's what you've done, skinned me, you know: well, Anisya too, for instance, has some money on hand. She's nowhere to put it; and, just like a woman, you know, don't know what to do with it. She comes to you and says: "Can't you make some use of my money too?" she says. "Sure I can," says you. And you just wait. Then I come again next spring. "Give me another ten," says I, "and I'll pay you for it." So you just

look and see if the skin ain't all peeled off of me, maybe you can tear off a bit more, and you give me Anisya's money. But if, for instance, I haven't a rag left, nothing to seize on, you just know it at a glance, and see that there's nothing to squeeze out of me, and you say right away, "Go somewhere else, my dear man, and may God help you!" and you look for some other fellow: then you lend him your own money once more and Anisya's too, and so you skin him. That's what a bank amounts to. It just goes round and round. It's a clever scheme, friend.

AKIM: [Getting excited] What's that? That's just nasty work, y'see. Peasants do that way; but the peasants, y'see, they feel it's sinful. That ain't lawful, y'see; it ain't lawful. It's nasty work. How do those learned men, y'see—?

MITRICH: That's just what they like best, my friend. Just remember this. If there's a man stupider than the rest of us, or a woman, and he can't make any use of the money himself, he just takes it to the bank; and they—it's fine bread and butter for them —just grab at it; and with that money they skin the people. It's a clever scheme.

AKIM: [Sighing] Eh, I see, it's hard not to have money, y'see; and it's twice as hard if you have it, y'see. Anyhow God bids us toil. But you, y'see, just put your money in the bank and go to sleep; and the money, y'see, will feed you while you lie idle. That's nasty work, you know; 'tain't lawful.

MITRICH: Not lawful? That ain't what folks think nowadays, my friend. And how they do strip a man bare. That's the point.

AKIM: [Sighing] That's the kind of times we're coming to, y'see. I've seen privies in town, you know. The new kind, y'see. All polished and polished, you know; made fine as a tavern. But it's no use, no use at all. Oh, they've forgotten God! They've forgotten him, you know! We've forgotten God, forgotten God!— Thank you, friend Anisya, I'm full; I've had enough. [Gets up and leaves the table; Mitrich climbs on the stove]

ANISYA: [Putting away the dishes and eating] If only his father would make him repent of his sins —but I'm ashamed to tell him.

AKIM: What?

ANISYA: I was just talking to myself.

[Anyutka comes in]

AKIM: [To Anyutka] Hello, girlie! Always busy? Got chilled, didn't you?

ANYUTKA: Just awful chilled. Hello, grandpa!

ANISYA: Well? Is he there?

ANYUTKA: No. Only Andrian was there, just come from town; he said he'd seen 'em in town, in a tavern. He said dad was drunk, drunk as a fish.

ANISYA: Are you hungry? There's something for you.

ANYUTKA: [Going to the stove] I'm so cold. My hands are numb.

[Akim takes off his bast shoes, Anisya washes the dishes]

ANISYA: Daddy!

AKIM: What do you want?

ANISYA: Tell me: is Marina getting on well?

AKIM: All right. She's getting on. She's a sensible, quiet little woman, y'see; she gets on, y'see; she tries hard. She's a good sort of woman, you know; clever and hard-working and patient, y'see. She's a good sort of little woman, you know.

ANISYA: Well, people from your village tell me, the kinsfolk of Marina's husband want to ask for our Akulina in marriage. Have you heard of it?

AKIM: The Mironovs? The women were saying something about it. But I didn't pay attention, you know. I don't know whether it's true, y'see. The old women were talking about it. But I've a poor memory, poor memory, y'see. Well, the Mironovs, y'see, are decent sort of folks, y'see.

ANISYA: I wish that we could marry her off in a hurry.

AKIM: Why so?

ANYUTKA: [Listening] They've come.

ANISYA: Well, let 'em alone. [Continues to wash the dishes, without turning her head. Enter Nikita]

NIKITA: Anisya, wife, who's come?

[Anisya glances at him and turns away in silence]

NIKITA: [Threateningly] Who's come? Have you forgotten?

ANISYA: Quit your bullying. Come in.

NIKITA: [Still more threateningly] Who's come?

ANISYA: [Going to him and taking his arm] Well, my husband's come. Come into the room.

NIKITA: [Resisting] So that's it! Your husband. And what's your husband's name? Say it right.

ANISYA: Confound you: Nikita.

NIKITA: So that's it! Booby! Say the full name.

ANISYA: Akimych. Well!

NIKITA: [Still in the doorway] So that's it! No, tell me what's the last name.

ANISYA: [Laughing and pulling at his arm] Chilikin. How drunk you are!

NIKITA: That's so! [Holds to the door jam] No, tell me what foot Chilikin puts into the room first.

ANISYA: Oh, stop, you'll cool off the room.

NIKITA: Say what foot he puts into the room first. You must tell me.

ANISYA: [To herself] I'm sick of this. [Aloud] Well, the left. Come in, will you?

NIKITA: So that's it!

ANISYA: Just see who's in the room.

NLKITA: Father? Well, I don't despise my father. I can show respect to my father. Good evening, daddy. [Bows to him and offers his hand] My respects to you!

AKIM: [Not replying to him] Liquor, liquor, that's what it does. Nasty business.

NIKITA: Liquor? Have I had a drink? I'm certainly guilty; I had a drink with a friend—drank his health.

ANISYA: You'd better go lie down.

NIKITA: Wife, where am I standing? Tell me!

ANISYA: Oh, that's all right. Go lie down.

NIKITA: I'm going to have some tea with my father. Start the samovar. Akulina, come in, will you?

[Akulina, gayly dressed, comes in with packages she has bought and goes to Nikita]

AKULINA: You've mislaid everything. Where's the yarn?

NIKITA: The yarn? The yarn's over there.— Hey, Mitrich, what're you doing there? Gone to sleep? Go and unharness the horse.

AKIM: [Without noticing Akulina, looks at his son] Just see how he's acting. The old man's tired out, y'see; been thrashing, you know; and he's showing his authority, you know. "Unharness the horse!" Bah! nasty!

MITRICH: [Climbs down from the stove and puts on his felt boots] Oh, merciful Lord! Is the horse in the yard? It sure must be tired. How drunk he is, confound him! Beats all! Oh, Lord! St. Nicholas the Martyr! [Puts on his sheepskin and goes outdoors]

NIKITA: [Sitting down] Forgive me, daddy. I had a drink, that's true; but how can a man help it? Even a hen drinks. Ain't that so? And you forgive me? What about Mitrich? He don't take it ill; he'll unharness.

ANISYA: Shall I really start the samovar?

NIKITA: Yes. My father's come, I want to talk with him; I'll have tea. [To Akulina] Have you brought in all the packages?

AKULINA: Packages? I took my own, but there are some left in the sleigh.— Here, this ain't mine. [She tosses a bundle on the table and puts away the rest of the packages in the chest. Anyutka watches her do so. Akim, without looking at his son, sets his leg wrappers and bast shoes on the stove]

ANISYA: [Going out with the samovar] The chest was full already, and he's bought more.

NIKITA: [Assuming a sober air] Don't be cross with me, dad. You think I'm drunk? I'm equal to anything whatever, because I can drink and not lose my senses. I can talk things over with you this very minute, dad. I remember the whole business. You gave directions about money; the horse was worn out —I remember. I can do the whole thing. I have it right on hand. If you needed a huge sum of money, then you might have to wait a bit; but I can attend to all this! Here it is!

AKIM: [Continues to fuss with the leg wrappers] Eh, my boy, y'see, spring's coming on, y'see; bad traveling.

NIKITA: What're you saying that for? There's no talking with a man that's drunk. But don't you worry; we'll have some tea. And I can do everything; I can fix up absolutely the whole business.

AKIM: [Shaking his head] Eh-eh-eh!

NIKITA: Here's the money. [Puts his hand in his pocket and takes out his purse; he turns over the bills and pulls out a ten-ruble note] Take that for the horse. Take it for the horse; I can't neglect my father. I certainly won't desert you, for you're my father. Here, take it. It's easy enough; I don't grudge it.

[*He comes up and thrusts the money at* Akim; Akim *does not take the money*]

NIKITA: [*Clutching his hand*] Take it, I say, when I give it to you—I don't grudge it.

AKIM: I can't take it, my boy, y'see; and I can't talk with you, you know, because there's no decency in you, y'see.

NIKITA: I won't let you off. Take it. [*Stuffs the money into* Akim's *hands*]

ANISYA: [*Comes in and stops suddenly*] Go ahead and take it. He won't let up, you know.

AKIM: [*Taking the money and shaking his head*] Oh, that liquor! A drunkard's not a man, you know.

NIKITA: There, that's better. If you return it, all right; and if you don't return it, I don't care. That's my way! [*Sees* Akulina] Akulina, show 'em your presents.

AKULINA: What?

NIKITA: Show 'em your presents.

AKULINA: Presents? Why should I show 'em? I've put 'em away already.

NIKITA: Get 'em out, I tell you; Anyutka'll like to see 'em. Show 'em to Anyutka, I tell you. Untie that little shawl. Give it here.

AKIM: O-oh, makes me sick to watch! [*Climbs on the stove*]

AKULINA: [*Getting her presents and laying them on the table*] There! What's the use of looking at 'em?

ANYUTKA: That's pretty! Good as Stepanida's.

AKULINA: Stepanida's? Stepanida's is nothing to this. [*Becoming animated and spreading out the things*] Look here at the quality! It's French.

ANYUTKA: And what gay chintz! Mashutka has one like it, only hers is lighter-colored, with a blue background. That's awful pretty.

NIKITA: That's right.

[Anisya *goes angrily into the storeroom, comes back with the tablecloth and the chimney for the samovar, and goes to the table*]

ANISYA: Confound you! You've covered up all the table.

NIKITA: Just look here!

ANISYA: Why should I look! Haven't I seen 'em? Take 'em away. [*Brushes off the shawl on the floor with her hand*]

AKULINA: What are you slinging round? Sling round your own things. [*Picks it up*]

NIKITA: Anisya! Look out!

ANISYA: What should I look out for?

NIKITA: Do you think I forgot you? Look here! [*Shows her the roll and sits down on it*] There's a present for you. Only you must earn it. Wife, where am I sitting?

ANISYA: Quit your bullying. I'm not afraid of you.

Whose money have you spent on your spree, and on your presents for your fat hussy? Mine.

AKULINA: Much it's yours! You wanted to steal it and couldn't. Get out of my way. [*Tries to pass by her and bumps into her*]

ANISYA: Who are you shoving? I'll give you a push.

AKULINA: A push? Come on now! [*Pushes against her*]

NIKITA: Here, women, women! Stop it! [*Stands between them*]

AKULINA: She picks on me. She'd better shut up and remember what she did. Do you think people don't know?

ANISYA: What do they know? Tell us, tell us what they know.

AKULINA: They know something about you.

ANISYA: You're a slut; you're living with another woman's husband.

AKULINA: And you put yours out of the way.

ANISYA: [*Rushes at* Akulina] You lie!

NIKITA: [*Holding her back*] Anisya! Have you forgotten?

ANISYA: Are you trying to scare me? I'm not afraid of you.

NIKITA: Get out! [*Turns* Anisya *around and starts to push her out*]

ANISYA: Where'll I go? I won't leave my own house.

NIKITA: Get out, I tell you! And don't you dare come back!

ANISYA: I won't go. [Nikita *pushes her;* Anisya *weeps and shrieks, clutching at the door*] What, are you going to kick me out of my own house? What are you doing, you villain? Do you think there's no law for you? You just wait!

NIKITA: Come, come!

ANISYA: I'll go to the village elder, to the policeman.

NIKITA: Get out, I tell you. [*Pushes her out*]

ANISYA: [*Outside*] I'll hang myself!

NIKITA: Don't worry!

ANYUTKA: Oh, oh, oh! Dear, darling mother. [*Weeps*]

NIKITA: Well, I was awful scared of her. What are you crying for? She'll come home all right! Go and see to the samovar. [Anyutka *goes out*]

AKULINA: [*Gathing up and folding the presents*] Nasty woman, how she dirtied it! Just you wait, I'll slit her frock for her. I sure will.

NIKITA: I've turned her out. What more do you want?

AKULINA: She's soiled my new shawl. The bitch— if she hadn't left I'd sure have clawed her eyes out.

NIKITA: Just calm down. What's there for you to be angry at? Think I love her?

AKULINA: Love her? Could anybody love that broad mug? If you'd only quit her then, nothing'd have happened. You ought to have sent her to the devil. But the house is mine anyhow and the money's mine. And then she says she's the mistress. Mistress! She was a fine mistress for her husband! She's a murderess; that's what she is. She'll do the same to you!

NIKITA: Oh, you can't stop up a woman's throat. Do you know yourself what you're talking about?

AKULINA: Yes, I know. I won't live with her. I'll turn her off the place. She can't live with me. She the mistress! She ain't the mistress; she's a prison rat.

NIKITA: Stop it. You needn't meddle with her. Don't even look at her. Look at me. I'm the master. What I wish, I do. I don't love her any more; I love you. I love whoever I want to. I'm the boss. And she'll have to mind. That's where I've got her. [*Points under his feet*] Oh, I haven't my accordion! [*Sings*]

On the stove are buns,
Porridge in the oven;
Now we'll live gaily,
We'll take our pleasure.
And then when death comes,
Then we'll just be dying.
On the stove are buns,
Porridge in the oven.

[*Mitrich comes in, takes off his coat, and climbs on the stove*]

MITRICH: I see the women have been fighting again! Another quarrel! Oh, Lord! Gracious St. Nicholas!

AKIM: [*Sits up on the edge of the stove, gets his leg wrappers and bast shoes, and puts them on*] Crawl in, crawl into the corner there.

MITRICH: [*Crawls in*] I see they're still arguing over their property. Oh, Lord!

NIKITA: Get out the brandy; we'll drink it with the tea.

ANYUTKA: [*Coming in, to Akulina*] Sister, the samovar's going to boil over.

NIKITA: Where's your mother?

ANYUTKA: She's standing in the hall, crying.

NIKITA: All right: call her in, tell her to bring the samovar. And give us the dishes, Akulina.

AKULINA: Dishes? Well, all right. [*Takes out the dishes*]

NIKITA: [*Brings brandy, biscuits, and salt herring*] This is for me, this is yarn for the woman, the kerosene's there in the hall. And here's the money. Wait. [*Takes the counting frame*] I'll reckon it up right away. [*Moves the counters on the frame*] Wheat flour eighty kopecks, vegetable oil . . . Ten rubles for dad. Dad, come and have tea.

[*Silence. Akim sits on the stove and puts on his leg wrappers*]

ANISYA: [*Bringing in the samovar*] Where shall I put it?

NIKITA: Put it on the table. Well, did you go to the village elder? Now, then, talk ahead and have a bit to eat. Just quit being cross. Sit down and drink. [*He pours her out a glass of brandy*] And

here I've brought a present for you. [*Hands her the roll on which he has been sitting. Anisya takes it in silence, shaking her head*]

AKIM: [*Climbs down and puts on his coat. Goes to the table and puts the ten-ruble note on it*] Here, that's your money. Take it.

NIKITA: [*Not seeing the note*] Where're you going to now you're all dressed?

AKIM: I'm going, I'm going, y'see. Bid me good-by, for Christ's sake. [*Takes his hat and girdle*]

NIKITA: Do say! Where are you going by night?

AKIM: I can't stay in your house, y'see; I can't stay, you know. Bid me good-by.

NIKITA: But you are running away from tea?

AKIM: [*Tying on his girdle*] I'm going, y'see, because it ain't good in your house, you know; it ain't good in your house, Nikita, you know. Your life is bad, Nikita, y'see; it's bad. I'm going.

NIKITA: Come, quit your talk; sit down and have tea.

ANISYA: Why, daddy, we'll be ashamed to face folks. What're you taking offense at?

AKIM: I'm not offended at all, y'see, not at all; but I can just see, you know, that my son's going to ruin, you know, going to ruin.

NIKITA: What ruin? Show me.

AKIM: To ruin, to ruin, you're ruined now. What did I tell you last summer?

NIKITA: You told me a lot of stuff.

AKIM: I told you, y'see, about the orphan; that you injured the orphan: you injured Marina, you know.

NIKITA: The old story! Don't talk twice about last year's snow: that thing's past and gone.

AKIM: Past and gone? No, my boy, it ain't gone. One sin brings another, you know; it brings more; and you're stuck fast in sin, Nikita boy. You're stuck fast in sin, I see. You're stuck fast, deep in it, you know.

NIKITA: Sit down and drink tea; that's all I have to say.

AKIM: I can't drink tea, y'see. Because your wicked ways make me sick, you know, awful sick. I can't drink tea with you, y'see.

NIKITA: Oh! . . . He's just talking silly. Sit down at the table.

AKIM: Your wealth, y'see, has caught you in a net; in a net, you know. Ah, Nikita, you need a soul.

NIKITA: What sort of right have you to reproach me in my own house? And what are you bothering me for anyhow? Am I just a kid for you to pull my hair? The time for such things has past.

AKIM: That's true; I've heard that nowadays, y'see, men pull their fathers' beards, you know; and that brings ruin, you know, brings ruin.

NIKITA: [*Angrily*] We make our living and don't beg of you, and you come to us in distress.

AKIM: Money? There's your money. I'll go begging, you know; but that money I won't take, y'see.

NIKITA: Stop that. What are you cross for, breaking up the party? [*Holds him back by the arm*]

AKIM: [*Screaming*] Let me go; I won't stay. I'd rather spend the night under a fence than in this filth of yours. Bah, God forgive me! [*Goes out*]

NIKITA: Well, well!

AKIM: [*Opening the door*] Come to your senses, Nikita! You need a soul. [*Goes out*]

AKULINA: [*Taking the cups*] Well, shall I pour the tea? [*All are silent*]

MITRICH: [*Bellows*] O Lord, be merciful to me a sinner! [*All start with terror*]

NIKITA: [*Lying down on the bench*] Oh, life is hard, hard! Akulina! Where's my accordion?

AKULINA: Your accordion? Don't you know that you took it to be fixed? I've poured the tea. Drink it.

NIKITA: I don't want it. Put out the light. . . . Oh, life is hard for me, awful hard! [*Weeps*]

ACT IV.

A moonlight evening in autumn. The yard behind the cottage. In the center of the stage is the hall, to the right the warm side of the house and a gate, to the left the cold side of the house and the cellar. From within the house can be heard talking and drunken shouts. A Neighbor comes out of the house and beckons to her Anisya's Friend.

NEIGHBOR: Why hasn't Akulina joined the company?

FRIEND: Why not? She'd have been glad to, but it was no time for her, believe me. The matchmakers have come to look at the bride; and she, my dear woman, just lies in the cold room and don't show herself at all, the darling.

NEIGHBOR: Why so?

FRIEND: They say the evil eye has lighted on her belly.

NEIGHBOR: Really!

FRIEND: And you know— [*Whispers in her ear*]

NEIGHBOR: What? That's a sin. But the matchmakers will find out.

FRIEND: How can they find out? They're all drunk. And they're mostly concerned with the dowry. It's no small amount, my dear, they're giving with the hussy: two coats, six silk gowns, a French shawl, and then a whole lot of linen, and—so they say—two hundred in cash.

NEIGHBOR: Well, in a case like this even money won't make a man happy. Such a disgrace!

FRIEND: Sh! There's the matchmaker. [*They stop talking and withdraw into the vestibule of the cottage*]

MATCHMAKER: (*man*) [*Coming out of the vestibule, alone, hiccuping*] I'm all in a sweat. Awful hot! I want to cool off a bit. [*Stands and catches his breath*] And the Lord knows—! Something's wrong.

It don't make me happy. Well, here's the old woman.

[*Matrena comes out of the vestibule*]

MATRENA: And I was gazing round! "Where's the matchmaker? Where's the matchmaker?" says I. So here's where you are, my man. Well, friend, thank the Lord, all's going fine. Wooing's not boasting. And I never learned how to boast. But as you came on a good errand, so, God grant, you'll always be grateful. And the bride, you know, is a marvel. Hard to find such a girl in the district.

MATCHMAKER: That's all right, but we mustn't forget about the money.

MATRENA: Don't you worry about the money. All her parents ever gave her, she still has. By now it must amount to a hundred and fifty.

MATCHMAKER: We're well enough satisfied; but he's our own child, you know. We must do the best we can for him.

MATRENA: I'm telling you the truth, friend: if it wasn't for me, you'd never have found the girl. There was a party from the Kormilins that wanted to get her, but I held out against it. And as for the money I can tell you true and honest: When the deceased—heaven's peace be with him!—was dying, he gave directions that his widow should take Nikita into the house—I know all this through my son— but that the money should be Akulina's. Another man would have made his profit out of the thing, but Nikita is giving them up, every kopek. Just think what a lot of money!

MATCHMAKER: Folks say she was left more money. He's a sly fellow.

MATRENA: Oh, fiddle-faddle! The other man's slice always looks big: they're giving you all there was. I tell you: quit your reckonings. Make it a firm bargain. The girl's pretty as a spring cherry.

MATCHMAKER: That's so. My old woman and I were wondering about one thing in the girl: Why didn't she show herself? We think she may be sickly.

MATRENA: Huh? She sickly? There ain't her like in the district. The girl's so plump you can't pinch her. You saw her the other day yourself. And she's a marvel at working. She's a bit deaf, that's true. Well, one little wormhole don't spoil a red apple. And the reason she didn't show herself, you know, was because of the evil eye. There's a spell on her. I know what bitch contrived it. They knew a charm, you see, and worked it on her. But I know a cure for it. The girl will get up to-morrow. Don't you worry about the girl.

MATCHMAKER: Well, the bargain's made.

MATRENA: That's right—and now don't go back on it. And don't forget me. I worked hard on it too. Don't you leave me out.

[*The voice of a woman is heard from the vestibule: "We must be going: come along, Ivan."*]

MATCHMAKER: Right away. [*Goes out. Peasants throng the vestibule and take their departure. A* yutka *runs out of the vestibule and beckons* Anisya *to follow her*]

ANYUTKA: Mama!

ANISYA: [*From the vestibule*] What?

ANYUTKA: Mama, come here, or they'll hear us. [*Goes off with her to the side of the cart shed*]

ANISYA: Well, what? Where's Akulina?

ANYUTKA: She's gone into the grain shed. It's awful what she's doing there! Just think, "No," says she, "I can't stand it. I'll scream with all my might," she says. Just think!

ANISYA: She can wait. We must see the guests off, you know.

ANYUTKA: Oh, mama! It's so hard for her. And she's cross. "They needn't drink me out of the house," she says. "I won't marry," she says. "I'm going to die," she says. Mama, what if she died? It's awful! I'm afraid!

ANISYA: It ain't likely she'll die; don't you go near her. Get along.

[Anisya *and* Anyutka *go out.* Mitrich *comes in from the gate and sets to raking up the hay that is strewn about*]

MITRICH: Oh, Lord! Merciful St. Nicholas! What a lot of liquor they put down! And they did raise a smell. Stinks even out of doors. No, I won't—I won't touch it. See how they've scattered the hay! They're like a dog in the manger. Just look at this bundle! What a smell! Right under your nose. Plague take it! [*Yawns*] Time to go to sleep! But I don't want to go into the room. It fills up a man's nose. How it smells, damn it! [*One can hear the guests driving away*] Well, they've gone. Oh, Lord! Merciful St. Nicholas! They hug each other and make fools of each other. But it don't amount to nothing.

NIKITA: [*Coming in*] Mitrich! Go lie down on the stove; I'll rake it up.

MITRICH: All right; give some to the sheep.— Well, did you see 'em off?

NIKITA: We saw 'em off, but things didn't go well. I don't know what'll happen.

MITRICH: Rotten business! Too bad we have it here; that's what the Foundling Asylum's for. There you can spill anything you like, they'll pick it up. Give 'em anything; they ask no questions. And they give money too. But the girl has to turn wet nurse. It's simple nowadays.

NIKITA: Look out, Mitrich: if anything happens, don't blab.

MITRICH: What do I care? Cover your tracks as you like. Eh, how you stink of liquor! I'll go in the house. [*Goes out, yawning*] Oh, Lord!

NIKITA: [*After a long silence, sitting down on a sleigh*] What a life!

ANISYA: [*Coming out of the house*] Where are you?

NIKITA: Here!

ANISYA: What are you sitting still for? There's no time to wait. You must take it away right off.

NIKITA: What are we going to do?

ANISYA: I'll tell you what—and you do it.

NIKITA: You women might take it to the Foundling Asylum, maybe.

ANISYA: Take it and carry it, if you want to. You're ready enough to do anything nasty, but you don't know how to get rid of it. I can see that.

NIKITA: Well, what's to be done?

ANISYA: Go in the cellar, I tell you, and dig a hole.

NIKITA: But you women might manage somehow.

ANISYA: [*Mimicking*] Yes, "somehow." You can't let things just slide. You ought to have thought of it in time. Go where you're sent.

NIKITA: Oh, what a life! What a life!

[*Enter* Anyutka]

ANYUTKA: Mama! Grandma's calling you. Sister must have a baby; just think—it cried.

ANISYA: What lies are you telling, plague take you! The kittens are squealing in there. Go into the house and go to sleep. Or I'll thrash you!

ANYUTKA: Mama dear, honest to God!

ANISYA: [*Brandishing her arm at her*] I'll give it to you. Get out of here and don't show yourself again. [Anyutka *runs out*] Go and do what you're told. Otherwise, look out! [*Goes out*]

NIKITA: [*After a long silence*] What a life! Oh, those women! What a mess! "Ought to have thought of it in time," she says. How could I have thought of it in time? When could I have thought of it? Well, last summer, when that Anisya began to nag me about it. What of it? Am I a monk? The master died, and so then I covered up the sin as was proper. I wasn't to blame for that. Such things often happen. And then those powders. Did I set her up to that? If I'd known of it, I'd have killed her on the spot, the bitch. I'd sure have killed her! She made me her partner in that dirty work, the good-for-nothing! And from that time on she was hateful to me. When my mother told me of it at the time, I began to hate her, to hate her; I didn't want to look at her. Well, how could I live with her? And then this thing started! . . . That hussy began to make up to me. What did I care? If it hadn't been me, it'd been somebody else. And this business now! Again I'm not to blame for it a bit. Oh, what a life! [*He sits down and reflects*] Those women are nervy—see what they've thought of! But I won't join in.

[Matrena *comes in out of breath, with a lantern and spade*]

MATRENA: What're you sitting here for like a hen on a perch? What did your wife tell you? Get down to work.

NIKITA: What're you women going to do?

MATRENA: We know what to do. You just attend to your share.

NIKITA: You're getting me mixed up in it.

MATRENA: What's that? Do you think of backing out? So it's come to this: you're trying to back out!

NIKITA: But think what this means! It's a living soul.

MATRENA: Eh, a living soul! Anyhow, it's barely alive. And what can we do with it? If you go and carry it to the Foundling Asylum, it'll die all the same, and there'll be talk; they'll spread the news and that girl'll be left on our hands.

NIKITA: But what if they find out?

MATRENA: We can do what we like in our own house. We'll do it so there won't be a trace. Just do what I tell you. It's our woman's work, but we can't manage it without a man. Here's the spade: now climb down and attend to things there. I'll hold the lantern.

NIKITA: What shall I do?

MATRENA: [Whispers] Dig a hole. And then we'll bring it out and stuff it in there quick. There she is calling again. Go on, will you! And I'll be going.

NIKITA: Well, is it dead?

MATRENA: Of course it's dead. Only you must hurry up. Folks haven't gone to bed yet. They may hear and see; the scoundrels meddle with everything. And the policeman passed by this evening. This is for you. [Hands him the spade] Get down into the cellar. Dig a hole there in the corner, the earth's soft, and you can even it off again. Mother earth won't tell any one; she'll lick it clean as a cow with her tongue. Go on, go on, my boy.

NIKITA: You're getting me mixed up in it. Plague take you! I'm going off. Do the thing alone, as you please.

ANISYA: [From the door] Well, has he dug the hole?

MATRENA: What've you come out for? Where did you put it?

ANISYA: Covered it with some burlap. Nobody'll hear it. Well, has he dug it?

MATRENA: He don't want to!

ANISYA: [Pushing out in a rage] Don't want to! Does he want to feed lice in prison? . . . I'll go right away and tell the whole thing to the policeman. We can go to ruin together. I'll tell it all right off!

NIKITA: [Panic-stricken] What'll you tell?

ANISYA: What? I'll tell everything! Who took the money? You! [Nikita is silent] And who gave him the poison? I gave it to him! But you knew it, knew it! I was in conspiracy with you!

MATRENA: Oh, stop it! Nikita, why are you so stubborn? See here, what's to be done? You must get to work. Come on, darling.

ANISYA: Look what an innocent you are! Don't want to! You've been abusing me long enough. You've been riding over me, but my turn's come now. Go along, I tell you, or I'll do what I said! . . . Here's the spade: take it! Get along!

NIKITA: Well, what are you nagging me for? [Takes the spade, but falters] If I don't want to, I won't go.

ANISYA: Won't go? [Begins to shout] Hey, folks!

MATRENA: [Stopping her mouth] What are you doing? Are you daft! He'll go. . . . Go along, sonny; go along, my dear boy.

ANISYA: I'll cry for help right off.

NIKITA: Stop it! Oh, what a lot you women are! But you'd better hurry up. The sooner the better. [Goes toward the cellar]

MATRENA: Yes, that's the way it is, darling; if you've had your fun, you must know how to cover up your tracks.

ANISYA: [Still agitated] He and his hussy have been taking out their spite on me, and I've had enough of it! I'm not going to be the only one. Let him be a murderer too. He'll find out how it feels.

MATRENA: Well, well, you're excited. Now, girlie, don't be cross: take it slow and easy, and it'll be better. You go in to the hussy. He'll do the work. [She follows Nikita with the lantern; he climbs down into the cellar]

ANISYA: I'll tell him to strangle his dirty brat. [Still excited] I had my torture all alone, pulling Petr's bones. Let him find out, too. I'll do my best to make him; I tell you, I will.

NIKITA: [From the cellar] Give me a light, will you!

MATRENA: [Holding the light, to Anisya] He's digging; go and bring it.

ANISYA: You just watch him. Otherwise he'll run away, the wretch. And I'll go bring it out.

MATRENA: See that you don't forget to put a cross on it. Or I'll attend to that. Is there a cross for it?

ANISYA: I'll find one; I know about that. [Goes out] [2]

MATRENA: How the woman did get worked up! And I must say, it was rough on her. Well, thank God, we'll just hush up this business and hide the traces. We'll get rid of the girl without scandal. My son will rest easy now. The house, thank God, is rich and well-stocked. He won't forget me either. They couldn't get along without Matrena. They couldn't attend to things. [Calls into the cellar] All ready, sonny?

NIKITA: [Climbs up; only his head can be seen] What are you doing there? Bring it, will you! What are you dawdling for? If you're going to do it, go ahead.

[Matrena goes towards the house door and meets Anisya. Anisya comes out with the baby, wrapped in rags]

MATRENA: Well, did you put the cross on?

ANISYA: Sure! I had hard work to get the brat; she wouldn't give it to me. [Comes up and holds out the baby to Nikita]

NIKITA: [Not taking it] Bring it down here yourself.

ANISYA: Here, take it, I tell you. [Throws the baby to him]

NIKITA: [Picking it up] It's alive! Darling mother, it's moving! It's alive! What shall I do with it?

2 For variant ending of Act IV, see p. 196.

ANISYA: [*Snatching the baby out of his hands and throwing it into the cellar*] Hurry up and strangle it and it won't be alive. [*Pushing* Nikita *down*] It's your business; you finish it.

MATRENA: He's too kind-hearted. It's hard for him, the dear boy. Well, no help for it! It's his sin too. [Anisya *stands over the cellar.* Matrena *sits down on the house step, watches her, and reflects*] Eh, eh, eh! How scared he was! Well, even if it is hard, you couldn't do anything ·else. No way out. And then just think how sometimes people beg for children! And then, y'see, God don't give 'em; they're all born dead. Take the priest's wife for instance. . . . But here it wasn't wanted, and it's alive. [*Looks toward the cellar*] He must have finished. [*To* Anisya] Well?

ANISYA: [*Looking into the cellar*] He's covered it with a board and sat down on the board. Must've finished.

MATRENA: O-oh! He'd be glad not to sin, but what can you do?

NIKITA: [*Climbing out, shaking all over*] It's still alive! I can't! It's alive!

ANISYA: If it's alive, where are you going? [*Tries to stop him*]

NIKITA: [*Rushing at her*] Get out; I'll kill you! [*He clutches her by the arm, she tears herself free; he runs after her with the spade.* Matrena *rushes toward him and stops him.* Anisya *runs off to the house.* Matrena *tries to take away the spade from* Nikita]

NIKITA: [*To* Matrena] I'll kill you; I'll kill you too! Get out! [Matrena *runs to the house, to* Anisya. Nikita *stops*] I'll kill you; I'll kill you all!

MATRENA: That's because he's scared. Never mind; it'll pass off!

NIKITA: What's this they've done? What have they done to me? How it wailed! . . . How it cracked underneath me! What have they done to me! And it's still alive, alive sure enough! [*Is silent and listens*] It's wailing! . . . Hear it wail! [*He runs towards the cellar*]

MATRENA: [*To* Anisya] He's going; he must mean to bury it. Nikita, you need a lantern.

NIKITA: [*Listens at the cellar, without answering her*] I can't hear it. I just fancied. [*Walks away and stops*] And how the little bones cracked underneath me! . . . Krr . . . krr. . . . What have they done to me? [*Listens once more*] It's wailing again; it's sure wailing. What's this? Mother! Mother, I say! [*Goes up to her*]

MATRENA: What, sonny?

NIKITA: Mother, darling, I can't do any more. I can't do anything. Mother, darling, have pity on me!

MATRENA: Oh, you're frightened, my dear boy. Come, come, drink a drop to give you courage.

NIKITA: Mother, darling, my time must have come. What have you done to me? How those little bones cracked, and how it wailed! Mother, darling,

what have you done to me! [*Goes off and sits down on a sleigh*]

MATRENA: Go have a drink, my lad. It's true enough, nighttime makes you shiver. But just wait, the dawn will come; and then, you know, a day or two will pass, and you'll forget to think about it. Just wait, we'll get rid of the girl and forget to think about it. But you have a drink, go have a drink. I'll attend to things in the cellar myself.

NIKITA: [*Shaking himself*] Is any liquor left in there? Can't I drink this down! [*He goes out.* Anisya, *who has been standing by the door all this time, silently stands aside to let him pass*]

MATRENA: Come, come, darling, I'll get to work myself; I'll climb down and bury it. Where did he throw the spade? [*She finds the spade and descends half way into the cellar*] Anisya, come here; give me a light.

ANISYA: But what's the matter with him?

MATRENA: He got awful scared. You gave it to him pretty hard. Don't meddle with him; he'll come to himself. Let him alone; I'll get to work myself. Set the lantern here. Then I can see. [Matrena *disappears into the cellar*]

ANISYA: [*Shouts at the door by which* Nikita *has departed*] Well, is your fun over? You've had your fling: now just wait, you'll find out yourself how it feels. You won't be so lofty.

[Nikita *rushes out of the house towards the cellar*]

NIKITA: Mother! Hey, mother!

MATRENA: [*Emerging from the cellar*] What, sonny?

NIKITA: [*Listening*] Don't bury it; it's alive! Don't you hear it? It's alive! There, it's wailing! . . . There . . . plainly. . . .

MATRENA: How could it wail? You squashed it into a pancake. You crushed all its head.

NIKITA: What's that? [*Stops his ears*] It's still wailing! I've ruined my life, ruined it! What have they done to me? . . . Where shall I go! . . . [*Sits down on the steps*]

VARIANT ENDING FOR ACT IV

The same scene as in Act I.

Anyutka, *undressed, is lying on a bench with a coat spread over her.* Mitrich *is sitting on a bunk at the head of the room, smoking.*

MITRICH: Pah! They've raised a smell, good luck to 'em for it! They spilled the goods. You can't drown it with tobacco. It gets into a man's nose. Oh, Lord! I'd better go to sleep. [*Goes to the lamp and is about to turn it out*]

ANYUTKA: [*Sitting up with a start*] Granddad, dear, don't put it out.

MITRICH: Why not put it out?

ANYUTKA: They're up to something in the yard.

[*Listens*] Do you hear? They've gone into the grain shed again.

MITRICH: What do you care? They aren't asking you about it. Lie down and go to sleep. And I'll turn down the light. [*Turns it down*]

ANYUTKA: Granddad, precious! Don't put it way out. Leave just a tiny bit, or I'll feel creepy.

MITRICH: [*Laughing*] All right, all right. [*Sits down beside her*] What makes you creepy?

ANYUTKA: I can't help feeling creepy, granddad! How sister struggled. She kept knocking her head against the chest. [*Whispers*] I know—she's going to have a baby. . . . Maybe it's born already.

MITRICH: What a little imp, confound you! You want to know everything. Lie down and go to sleep. [Anyutka *lies down*] That's the way. [*Covers her up*] That's the way. If you know too much, you'll grow old too soon.

ANYUTKA: Are you going up on the stove?

MITRICH: Of course I am. . . . You're a silly little girl, I see. You want to know everything. [*Covers her up and rises to go*] Just lie there like that and go to sleep. [*Goes to the stove*]

ANYUTKA: It cried just once, but now I can't hear it.

MITRICH: Oh, Lord! Merciful St. Nicholas! . . . What can't you hear?

ANYUTKA: The baby.

MITRICH: There isn't any, so you can't hear it.

ANYUTKA: But I heard it; just think, I heard it. A little shrill voice.

MITRICH: You heard a lot. Did you hear how the bogy-man put a naughty little girl like you in a sack and carried her off?

ANYUTKA: What's the bogy-man?

MITRICH: Just the bogy-man. [*Climbs on the stove*] The stove's fine and warm now. Nice! Oh, Lord! Merciful St. Nicholas!

ANYUTKA: Granddad! Are you going to sleep?

MITRICH: What do you think? That I'm going to sing songs? [*Silence*]

ANYUTKA: Granddad! Oh, granddad! They're digging! Honest to God they're digging! Do you hear? Just think, they're digging!

MITRICH: What notions you have! Digging? Digging at night? Who's digging? It's the cow scratching herself. And you say, digging! Go to sleep, I tell you, or I'll put out the light right away.

ANYUTKA: Granddad, darling, don't put it out. I'll stop. Honest to God, I'll stop. It scares me.

MITRICH: Scares you? Don't you be afraid of anything, and then you won't be scared. Now you just feel afraid and you say that it scares you. Of course it scares you when you're afraid. What a silly little girl!

[*Silence. The cricket chirps*]

ANYUTKA: [*Whispers*] Granddad! Hey, granddad! Are you asleep?

MITRICH: Well, what do you want?

ANYUTKA: What's the bogy-man like?

MITRICH: I'll tell you what he's like. Whenever there's any little girl, like you, who won't go to sleep, he comes along with his sack, and he pops the little girl into the sack; and then he pops his own head in and lifts up her little shirtie, and he gives her a spanking.

ANYUTKA: What does he spank her with?

MITRICH: He takes a broom.

ANYUTKA: But he can't see, himself, can he, in the sack?

MITRICH: He'll see all right.

ANYUTKA: But I'll bite him.

MITRICH: No, girlie, you won't bite him.

ANYUTKA: Granddad, somebody's coming! Who is it? Oh, holy saints, who is it?

MITRICH: If somebody's coming, let him come. What do you care? . . . I think it's your mother coming.

[Anisya *comes in*]

ANISYA: Anyutka! [Anyutka *pretends to be asleep*] Mitrich!

MITRICH: What?

ANISYA: What have you a light burning for? We'll go to bed in the cold half.

MITRICH: I've just finished my work. I'll put it out.

ANISYA: [*Searching in the chest and grumbling*] When you want something, you can't find it.

MITRICH: What are you looking for?

ANISYA: I'm looking for a cross, I must put one on him. He'll die unchristened, God have mercy on him! Without a cross! It's a sin, you know!

MITRICH: Of course, you must do things properly. . . . Well, have you found it?

ANISYA: Yes. [*Goes out*]

MITRICH: That's lucky—otherwise I'd have given her my own. Oh, Lord!

ANYUTKA: [*Jumps up, trembling*] O-oh, granddad! Don't go to sleep, for Christ's sake! I'm so scared!

MITRICH: What are you scared of?

ANYUTKA: Won't the baby die, most likely? Grandma put a cross on Auntie Arina's too—and it died.

MITRICH: If it dies, they'll bury it.

ANYUTKA: But maybe it wouldn't die if Grandma Matrena wasn't here. You know I heard what grandma was saying; just think, I heard it.

MITRICH: What did you hear? Go to sleep, I tell you. Pull things over your head: that's all.

ANYUTKA: But if it was alive, I'd nurse it.

MITRICH: [*Bellows*] Oh, Lord!

ANYUTKA: Where'll they put it?

MITRICH: They'll put it where it's proper. It's not your business. Go to sleep, I tell you. Your mother'll come—she'll give it to you! [*Silence*]

ANYUTKA: Granddad! That little girl you were telling about—they didn't kill her?

MITRICH: That one? Oh, that girl came out all right.

ANYUTKA: How was it you were telling me they found her, granddad?

MITRICH: They just found her.

ANYUTKA: But where did they find her? Tell me.

MITRICH: They found her in a house over there. The soldiers came to a village and began to search the house; and there that same little girl was lying on her belly. They were going to smash her. But I just felt lonesome and I took her in my arms—she struggled. She was as heavy as if she had two hundred pounds inside her; and she clutched at everything with her hands—you could hardly tear her away. Well, I took her and stroked her head, stroked her head. And she was bristly as a hedgehog. I stroked her and stroked her, and she quieted down. I soaked a biscuit and gave it to her. She caught on. She chewed it. What could we do with her? We took her with us. We took her and just fed her and fed her; and she got so used to us we took her with us on the march: she just went with us. She was a nice little girl.

ANYUTKA: Well, she wasn't christened, was she?

MITRICH: Nobody knows. Not altogether, they said. For her people weren't ours.

ANYUTKA: Germans?

MITRICH: "Germans," you say? Not Germans, but Asiatics. They are just the same as Jews, but they aren't Jews either. They're Poles, but they're Asiatics. They're called Krudly or Krugly: I've forgotten the name.— We called the little girl Sashka. Sashka—and she was pretty. I've forgotten everything else, you see; but that little girl—Lord bless her!—I can see before my eyes right now. That's all I remember of life in the army. I recollect how they flogged me, and then I remember that little girl. She used to hang round your neck when you carried her. You couldn't have found a nicer little girl nowhere. Later we gave her away. The sergeant's wife adopted her as her daughter. And she came out all right. How sorry the soldiers were!

ANYUTKA: See here, granddad, I remember how daddy died too. You hadn't come to live with us then. He called Nikita and says to him: "Forgive me, Nikita," he says—and he began to cry himself. [Sighs] That made me sad too.

MITRICH: Well, that's the way things go.

ANYUTKA: Granddad; oh, granddad! They're making a noise again in the cellar. Oh, dearie me, holy saints! Oh, granddad, they'll do something to him. They'll destroy him. He's just a little thing.—Oh! oh! [Pulls the clothes over her head and weeps]

MITRICH: [Listening] They really are up to something nasty—curse 'em! Those women are a nasty lot. The men ain't much to boast of, but the women—they're like beasts of the woods. They ain't afraid of anything.

ANYUTKA: [Getting up] Granddad! Hey, granddad!

MITRICH: Well, what next?

ANYUTKA: The other day, a passer-by spent the night here. He was saying that when a child dies its soul goes straight to heaven. Is that true?

MITRICH: How should I know? Most likely. What of it?

ANYUTKA: Why, then I'd like to die too. [Whimpers]

MITRICH: If you die, nobody'll miss you.

ANYUTKA: Till you're ten years old you're still a child, and maybe your soul'll still go to God. After that you get spoiled, you know.

MITRICH: You certainly do get spoiled! How can girls like you help getting spoiled? Who teaches you anything? What do you ever see? What do you hear? Nothing but nastiness. I'm not very learned, but still I know something; not very well, but anyhow better than a village woman.— What is a village woman? Just mud. There's huge millions of your sort in Russia, and you're all like blind moles—don't know anything. How to keep cows safe from the evil eye—all kinds of charms—how to cure children by putting 'em under the hen roost—that's what women know how to do.

ANYUTKA: Mama used to put 'em there.

MITRICH: That's just it. How many millions of you women and girls there are, and you're all like beasts of the forest. You grow up and then you die. You don't see anything and don't hear anything. A man—even if it's in a tavern, or maybe in a fortress, accidentally, or in the army, like me—he learns something or other. But what about a woman? Don't ask her about God and what's right! She don't even know sensibly what Good Friday is. Friday's Friday, but ask her anything about it and she don't know. They crawl round just like blind pups and stick their noses in the manure.— All they know is their silly songs: "Ho, ho! Ho, ho!" And they don't know themselves what "Ho, ho!" means.

ANYUTKA: But, granddad, I know "Our Father" halfway through.

MITRICH: You know a lot! But then one can't expect much of you. Who teaches you? Only a drunken peasant teaches you now and then with a strap. That's all your training. I don't know who'll ever answer for you. They put a sergeant in charge of recruits and hold him responsible for 'em. But nobody's responsible for you girls. So you women are just like a herd of cattle—without a herdsman—that run wild; your kind is the stupidest that's made. Your kind is just hopeless.

ANYUTKA: But what can you do about it?

MITRICH: Not much. . . . Now pull the clothes over your head and go to sleep. Oh, Lord! [Silence. The cricket chirps]

ANYUTKA: [Jumping up] Granddad! Somebody's shouting, somebody's just yelling! Honest to God, he's shouting. Granddad, dear, he's coming this way.

MITRICH: I tell you, pull the clothes over your head.

NIKITA: [Coming in] What have they done to me? What have they done to me!

MATRENA: Have a drink, have a drink, darling. What's the matter? [*Gets liquor and sets it before him*]

NIKITA: Give it here: I guess I'd better take some.

MATRENA: Shh! They aren't asleep, you know. Here, drink it.

NIKITA: What does this mean? Why did you want to act that way? You might have carried it off.

MATRENA: [*In a whisper*] Sit here, sit here; have another drink, and then smoke a bit. That'll divert your thoughts.

NIKITA: Mother darling, my time must have come. When it wailed, and when those little bones cracked, krr . . . krr . . . my strength gave out.

MATRENA: E-eh! You're just talking silly stuff. It's true enough, nighttime makes you shiver. But just wait till the day comes; a day or two will pass and you'll forget to think about it. [*Goes to* Nikita *and puts her hand on his shoulder*]

NIKITA: Get away from me! What have you done to me?

MATRENA: What do you mean, sonny, anyhow? [*Takes him by the hand*]

NIKITA: Get away from me! I'll kill you! I don't care for anything now. I'll kill you!

MATRENA: Oh, oh, how scared you are! Now go away and go to bed.

NIKITA: I've nowhere to go to. I'm a lost man.

MATRENA: [*Shaking her head*] Oh! oh! I'd better go fix things up myself; and let him sit here for a while till he gets rid of all this. [*Goes out*]

[Nikita *sits still, covering his face with his hands.* Mitrich *and* Anyutka *are stiff with terror*]

NIKITA: It's wailing, it's sure wailing: hark, hark, you can hear it. . . . She'll bury it, she'll bury it! [*Runs to the door*] Mother, don't bury it, it's alive! . . .

MATRENA: [*Returning, in a whisper*] What do you mean, Christ help you! What fancies you have! How can it be alive! All its bones are crushed.

NIKITA: Give me some more liquor! [*Drinks*]

MATRENA: Go along, sonny. Now you'll go to sleep and it'll be all right.

NIKITA: [*Standing and listening*] It's still alive. . . . Hark! . . . It's wailing. Don't you hear it? Hark!

MATRENA: [*In a whisper*] Not a bit of it!

NIKITA: Mother dear! I've ruined my life. What have you done to me? Where shall I go? [*Runs out of the house,* Matrena *following him*]

ANYUTKA: Granddad, dear, darling, they've strangled him!

MITRICH: [*Angrily*] Go to sleep, I tell you! Bother you, confound you! I'll take a broom to you! Go to sleep, I tell you.

ANYUTKA: Granddad, precious. Somebody's grabbing me by the shoulders, somebody's grabbing me, grabbing me with his paws. Dear granddad, just think: I'll be gone right away. Granddad, precious, let me up on the stove! Let me up for Christ's sake! . . . He's grabbing me . . . grabbing. . . . O-o-oh! [*Runs to the stove*]

MITRICH: See how they've scared the poor little girl—those nasty women, confound 'em! Well, come up if you want to.

ANYUTKA: [*Climbing on the stove*] And don't you go away.

MITRICH: Where should I go to? Climb up, climb up! Oh, Lord! St. Nicholas the Martyr! Holy Virgin Mother of Kazan! . . . How they scared the little girl! [*Covers her up*] You're a little fool, just a little fool. . . . They sure scared you, those nasty women, much good may it do 'em!

ACT V. SCENE I.

In the foreground, on the left, a threshing floor, and near it a stack of straw; on the right, a cart shed. The doors of the shed are open; straw is scattered about in the doorway. In the background farm buildings can be seen; songs and the tinkling of tambourines are heard. Two peasant girls come walking along the path past the shed towards the farm buildings.

FIRST GIRL: You see how well we got across, we didn't even soil our boots; but on the road it was awful, so dirty! [*They stop and wipe their feet with straw*]

FIRST GIRL: [*Looks at the straw and sees something*] What's that there?

SECOND GIRL: [*Taking a look*] It's Mitrich, their workman. He's dead drunk.

FIRST GIRL: But he didn't use to drink at all, did he?

SECOND GIRL: Not till to-day, so it seems.

FIRST GIRL: Just look: he must have come here for straw. You see he has a rope in his hands, but he just went to sleep.

SECOND GIRL: [*Listening*] They're still singing the wedding songs. Most likely they haven't given 'em the blessing yet. They say Akulina didn't wail a bit.

FIRST GIRL: Mama told me she didn't want to be married. Her stepfather threatened her; otherwise she'd never have consented. You know what talk there was about her!

MARINA: [*Overtaking the girls*] Hello, girls!

GIRLS: Hello, auntie!

MARINA: Going to the wedding, darlings?

FIRST GIRL: It must be over by now. We just came to look around.

MARINA: Call my old man for me, Semyon of Zuyev. You know him, don't you?

FIRST GIRL: Of course we know him. He's some relative of the bridegroom, it seems.

MARINA: Sure: the bridegroom is a nephew of my boss.

SECOND GIRL: Why don't you go yourself? How can you miss the wedding!

MARINA: I don't feel like going, girlie; and then I haven't the time. I must be riding off. We weren't on our way to the wedding. We were carting oats to town. We stopped to feed the horses, and they called in my old man.

FIRST GIRL: Whose house did you stop at? Fedorych's?

MARINA: Yes. So I'll stand here a bit, and you go call my old man, darling. Make him come, precious. Say: "Your wife Marina says you must be going; the fellows are harnessing already."

FIRST GIRL: All right, very well, if you won't go yourself.

[*The girls go out along the path towards the farm buildings. Songs and the tinkling of tambourines are heard*]

MARINA: [*Muses*] It'd be all right to go, but I don't want to, for I haven't seen him since the very time that he refused me. That's more than a year ago. But I'd like to peep in and see how he gets along with his Anisya. Folks say they don't agree. She's a coarse, ill-tempered woman. He's remembered me many a time, I'll warrant. He must have had a liking for an easy life. He gave me the go-by. Well, God help him, I bear no grudge. It hurt then. Oh, how it pained me! But now it's worn off and I've forgotten. But I'd like to see him. . . . [*Looks towards the house and sees* Nikita] Just look! What's he coming here for? Did the girls tell him? Why's he left the guests? I'll be going.

[Nikita *comes in, at first hanging his head, waving his arms, and muttering to himself*]

MARINA: How gloomy he looks!

NIKITA: [*Seeing* Marina *and recognizing her*] Marina! My dear, darling Marina! What are you here for?

MARINA: I've come for my old man.

NIKITA: Why didn't you come to the wedding? You'd have looked on and laughed at me.

MARINA: What do I want to laugh for? I've come for my boss.

NIKITA: Oh Marina dear! [*Tries to embrace her*]

MARINA: [*Turning away angrily*] Nikita, you quit those tricks. That's been and gone. I've come for my boss. Is he at your house?

NIKITA: So we can't call to mind old times? You won't let me?

MARINA: No use remembering old times. That's been and gone.

NIKITA: So you can't bring it back?

MARINA: It won't come back. But what have you strayed off for? You're the master, and you've deserted the wedding.

NIKITA: [*Sitting down on the straw*] Why have I strayed off? Oh, if you only knew and understood! . . . My life's hard, Marina, so hard that I don't want to look at it. I got up from the table and came away, came away from people so that I needn't see anybody.

MARINA: [*Coming nearer to him*] How's that?

NIKITA: Well, it's that I have no joy in food or drink, no rest in sleep. Oh, I'm sick of life, just sick of it! And what makes me sickest of all, Marina dear, is that I'm all alone, and have nobody that I can share my grief with.

MARINA: You can't live without grief, Nikita. I cried over mine and now it's gone.

NIKITA: You're talking about old, old times. Just think, dear! You've done crying over yours, and now it's come my turn.

MARINA: But how's that?

NIKITA: It's that I loathe my whole life. I loathe myself. Ah, Marina, you could not hold me fast, and so you ruined me and yourself too! Well, is this a life worth living?

MARINA: [*Stands by the shed, weeps, but restrains herself*] I don't complain of my own life, Nikita. God grant that everybody had as good as mine! I don't complain. I confessed right off to my old man. He forgave me. And he don't reproach me. I'm satisfied with my own life. He's a gentle old man. And I like him; I wash and dress his children! And he's kind to me too. I've no reason to complain. It must be what God intended for me.— But what about your life? You're a rich man.

NIKITA: My life! . . . I just don't want to break up the wedding, or I'd take a rope—this one [*Takes up a rope from the straw*], and I'd throw it right over that crossbeam. And I'd fix up a nice noose, and I'd climb on the crossbeam and put my head in it. That's what my life is like!

MARINA: Stop, Christ help you!

NIKITA: You think I'm joking? You think I'm drunk? I'm not drunk. Nowadays even liquor don't affect me. But I'm sick of life, sick to death of it! I'm done for, in such misery that I care for nothing! Oh, Marina dear, do you remember how we lived together, how we spent happy nights on the railroad?

MARINA: Nikita, don't rub my sore spot. I'm married now and you are too. My sin's forgiven; don't bring back the past.

NIKITA: What can I do with my heart? To whom can I give it?

MARINA: What should you do? You have a wife: don't lust after other women, but care for your own. You loved Anisya; keep on loving her.

NIKITA: Ah, that Anisya is bitter wormwood to me. She's just tangled up my legs like witchgrass.

MARINA: Whatever she is, she's your wife.— But it's no use talking! You'd better go to the guests and call my husband.

NIKITA: Oh, if you knew everything!— But why talk about it!

HUSBAND: [*Coming in from the farm buildings, red-faced and drunken, accompanied by* Anyutka] Marina! Wife! Old lady! Are you here?

NIKITA: Here's your boss coming and calling for you. Go along!

MARINA: And what'll you do?

NIKITA: I? I'll lie down here. [*Lies down in the straw*]

HUSBAND: Where is she?

ANYUTKA: There she is, uncle, close to the shed.

HUSBAND: What are you standing here for? Come to the wedding! The hosts want you to come and pay your respects. The marriage party will soon start out: then we'll go.

MARINA: [*Coming to meet her husband*] But I didn't want to.

HUSBAND: Come on, I tell you. We'll have a glass; you'll congratulate that rogue Petrunka. The hosts are taking offense—and we'll have time enough for everything.

[Marina's Husband *embraces her and goes out with her, staggering*]

NIKITA: [*Sitting up on the straw*] Oh, when I saw her, I felt sicker than ever. The only real life I ever had was with her. I've wasted my days for nothing at all; I've ruined my happiness! [*Lies down*] What shall I do with myself? Oh, if only damp mother earth would open!

ANYUTKA: [*Sees Nikita and runs to him*] Daddy! Oh, daddy! They're looking for you. Godfather and everybody have given their blessing. Just think, they've given their blessing; they're cross.

NIKITA: [*To himself*] What shall I do with myself?

ANYUTKA: What's that? What are you saying?

NIKITA: I'm not saying anything. Don't bother me!

ANYUTKA: Daddy! Come on, will you! [Nikita *is silent;* Anyutka *pulls at his arm*] Daddy, go and give your blessing! Honest, they're cross; they're scolding.

NIKITA: [*Pulls away his arm*] Let me alone!

ANYUTKA: Come on!

NIKITA: [*Threatening her with the rope*] Get out, I tell you. I'll give it to you!

ANYUTKA: Then I'll send mother. [*Runs out*]

NIKITA: [*Sitting up*] How can I go in there? How can I take the holy ikon in my hands? How can I look her in the eyes? [*Lies down again*] Oh, if there were a hole in the earth, I'd crawl into it. People wouldn't see me; I'd see nobody. [*Sits up again*] But I won't go. . . . Let 'em go to thunder. I won't go. [*Removes his boots and takes up the rope; he makes a noose and puts it around his neck*] That's the way.

[Matrena *comes in hurriedly*. Nikita *sees her, takes the rope off his neck, and again lies down on the straw*]

MATRENA: Nikita! Hey, Nikita! There you are, and you won't answer. Nikita, what's the matter with you? Are you drunk? Come on, Nikita dear; come on, my precious! Folks are tired of waiting.

NIKITA: Oh, what have you done to me? I'm no longer a man.

MATRENA: What do you mean? Come on, my boy; give the blessing as is proper, and then it'll all be over. Folks are waiting for you.

NIKITA: How can I give a blessing?

MATRENA: Just as usual. Don't you know how?

NIKITA: I know, I know. But who am I going to bless? What have I done to her?

MATRENA: What have you done? The idea of remembering that! Nobody knows: not the cat, nor the mouse, nor the louse in the house. And then the girl herself is willing to marry.

NIKITA: But how is she willing?

MATRENA: Of course, she's doing it out of fear. But she's willing all the same. What else can she do? She ought to have thought of it then. But now she has no other choice. And the matchmakers feel satisfied. They've seen the girl twice, and the money goes with her. All's covered up clean.

NIKITA: But what's in the cellar?

MATRENA: [*Laughing*] What's in the cellar? Cabbage, mushrooms, and potatoes, I suppose. Let bygones be bygones.

NIKITA: I'd be glad to, but I can't. Whenever you make me think, I can hear things. Oh, what have you women done to me?

MATRENA: What are you acting so queer for anyhow?

NIKITA: [*Turning over flat on his face*] Mother, don't torture me! I can't stand it any longer.

MATRENA: But you must, all the same. There's talk among the people anyhow—and then all of a sudden the father goes off and won't come back, don't dare give his blessing. They'll put two and two together right away. If you shrink from it, they'll guess what's up right away. If you walk the beaten path, nobody thinks you a thief. But if you run away from a wolf, you run into a bear. Above all, don't betray yourself; don't be timid, my boy, or they'll think worse of it.

NIKITA: Oh, you've tied me tight!

MATRENA: Stop it, come along. Come into the company and give your blessing; everything must be as is proper and usual, and then the thing's over.

NIKITA: [*Still lying on his face*] I can't.

MATRENA: [*To herself*] What's happened? Everything was all right, all right, and all of a sudden it struck him. There must be a spell on him.— Nikita, get up! Look, there's Anisya coming; she's left the guests.

[Anisya *comes in gayly dressed and flushed with drink*]

ANISYA: Ain't this fine, mother! So fine and proper! And how happy folks are over it! . . . Where is he?

MATRENA: Here, darling, here. He lay down in the straw and there he lies. He won't come.

NIKITA: [*Looking at his wife*] Huh, she's drunk too. When I see her, it makes my heart sick. How can I live with her? [*Turns over on his face*] I'll kill her some day. It'll be still worse!

ANISYA: Look where he is, buried in the straw!

Has he got over his drunk? [*Laughs*] I'd like to lie down there with you, but I haven't the time. Come on; I'll lead you. And it's so nice in the house! It's a pleasure to see 'em. And the accordion! The women are singing songs, just splendid. Everybody's drunk; all's fine and proper!

NIKITA: What's fine?

ANISYA: The wedding, the merry wedding. Everybody says that it's just a marvel of a wedding. Everything's so fine and lovely. Come on! We'll go together. . . . I've had a drink, but I can lead you. [*Takes his arm*]

NIKITA: [*Pulling away from her, with revulsion*] Go on alone. I'll come later.

ANISYA: What're you in such a temper for! All our troubles are over, we've got rid of the girl that stood between us, we can just live and enjoy ourselves. All's nice and proper, according to the law. I'm so happy over it that I can't tell you. It's just as if I was marrying you a second time. Ha ha! Folks are so pleased! They'll all thank us. And the guests are all nice people. Ivan Moseich is there too, and the policeman. They joined in on the songs.

NIKITA: Well, go sit with them. What did you come out here for?

ANISYA: But you must come along. Otherwise it ain't decent: the hosts have left and deserted the guests. And the guests are all nice people.

NIKITA: [*Rising and brushing off the straw*] Go on; I'll come directly.

MATRENA: The night cuckoo sings louder than the day bird. He wouldn't heed me, but he followed his wife right away.

[Matrena *and* Anisya *move away*]

MATRENA: Are you coming?

NIKITA: I'll come right away. You go along, and I'll follow. I'll come and give my blessing. . . . [*The women pause*] Go on, and—I'll follow. Go along.

[*The women go out. Nikita gazes after them, musing*]

NIKITA: [*Sitting down and taking off his boots*] Not much I won't go! No indeed! No, you'd better look for me on the crossbeam. I'll straighten the noose and jump from the crossbeam, and then you can look for me. And here are some rope reins, that's lucky. [*Meditates*] I'd get over my grief, however heavy it was; I'd get over it. But it's right here, it's in my heart; I can't drive it out. [*Looks towards the house*] Looks like she was coming again. [*Mimics Anisya*] "Fine, just fine! I'll lie down with you!" Ugh! the nasty hag! Wait a bit: embrace me when they take me off the beam! That's all that's left. [*Seizes the rope and pulls it*]

MITRICH: [*Drunken, sits up, but does not let go of the rope*] I won't let you have it. I won't let anybody have it. I'll bring it myself. I said I'd bring the straw, and I'll bring it. Is that you, Nikita? [*Laughs*] Oh, the devil! Did you come for straw?

NIKITA: Give me the rope.

MITRICH: No, you wait. The folks sent me. I'll bring it. . . . [*He rises to his feet and begins to rake up the straw, but staggers, recovers himself, and finally falls down*] The liquor's got the best of me. Too much for me!

NIKITA: Give me the reins.

MITRICH: I told you I wouldn't. Oh, Nikita, you're stupid as a blind jackass. [*Laughs*] I like you, but you're stupid. You think I've been drinking. To hell with you! You think I need you. . . . Just look at me! I'm a corporal! You fool, you can't even say it, "Corporal of Her Majesty's very First Regiment of Grenadiers." I served tsar and country with faith and truth. But who am I? You think I'm a soldier? No, I'm not a soldier, but the very least of men; I'm an orphan, a vagrant. I swore off drinking. And now I've started in again! . . . Well, do you think I'm afraid of you? Not much! I ain't afraid of nobody. When I start to drink, I drink! Now I'll swill for two weeks and raise the devil. I'll drink away everything down to my cross, I'll drink away my hat, I'll pawn my passport—and I ain't afraid of nobody! They flogged me in the regiment to keep me from drinking! They laid it on and laid it on. "Well," says they, "will you drink any more?" "Yes," says I. Why should I be afraid of 'em: that's the kind of man I am! I'm the way God made me. I swore off drinking, and I didn't drink. Now I've started again, and I drink! And I ain't afraid of nobody. I'm not lying; that's the way it is. . . . Why should I be afraid of 'em, such rot! "There," says I, "that's the kind of man I am!" A priest was telling me: "The devil is the worst boaster. As soon as you begin to boast," says he, "then you'll feel afraid right away. And when you begin to be afraid of people, then the devil, with his cloven hoof, will snatch you up right away and stick you wherever he wants to." But seeing I'm not afraid of people, it's easy for me. I spit on his beard, the lame cuss, the son of a swine. He won't harm me. "Does my fist taste good?" says I.

NIKITA: [*Crossing himself*] But what's this I'm doing, anyhow? [*Throws away the rope*]

MITRICH: What?

NIKITA: [*Getting up*] You say not to be afraid of people?

MITRICH: Much you need to be afraid of 'em, such rot! Just you look at 'em in the bath. They're all of the same dough. One has a fatter belly, and the other a thinner; that's all the difference between 'em. They're a fine lot to be afraid of, good luck to 'em!

[Matrena *approaches from the house*]

MATRENA: [*Shouts*] Well, are you coming?

NIKITA: Ugh! It *is* better that way. I'm coming! [*Goes off towards the house*]

CHANGE OF SCENE

The cottage of Act I, filled with people, some sitting at tables, others standing. In the front corner are Akulina *and the* Bridegroom. *On the table are the ikons and bread. Among the guests are* Marina, *her* Husband, *and the* Policeman. *The women are singing songs.* Anisya *is passing wine. The songs subside.*

Anisya, Marina *and her* Husband, Akulina, *the* Bridegroom, Coachman, Policeman, Matchmaker (*woman*), *Bridegroom's* Best Man, Matrena, Guests, Peasants.

COACHMAN: It's high time we were going; the church is a long way off.

BEST MAN: Just wait a while; the stepfather will give his blessing. But where is he?

ANISYA: He's coming, he's coming directly, my dears. Have another glass all round; don't hurt our feelings.

MATCHMAKER: (*woman*) What makes him so slow? We've been waiting a long time already.

ANISYA: He's coming. He's coming directly. He'll be here in two shakes of a lamb's tail. Have some more, my dears. [*Passes wine*] He'll be here, directly. Sing some more, my beauties, while you wait.

COACHMAN: They've sung all their songs while we've been waiting.

[*The women sing; in the middle of the song* Nikita *and* Akim *come in*]

NIKITA: [*Holding* Akim *by the arm and pushing him in front of him*] Go on, daddy; I can't do it without you.

AKIM: I don't like it, y'see.

NIKITA: [*To the women*] That's enough; keep still. [*Looks around at everybody in the room*] Marina, are you here?

MATCHMAKER: (*woman*) Come, take the ikon and give us your blessing.

NIKITA: Wait a while, give me time. [*Looking around*] Akulina, are you here?

MATCHMAKER: (*woman*) What are you calling the roll for? Where should she be?— What a freak he is!

ANISYA: Holy saints! Why's he taken off his boots?

NIKITA: Daddy! Are you here? Look at me! Orthodox people, you are here, and I'm here! Here I am! [*Falls on his knees*]

ANISYA: Nikita dear, what are you up to? Oh, poor me!

MATCHMAKER: (*woman*) Well, well!

MATRENA: I'll tell you what: he's had too much of that French wine. Come to your senses, will you? [*She tries to raise him up. He pays no attention to anybody, but looks straight ahead*]

NIKITA: Orthodox people! I am guilty; I wish to repent.

MATRENA: [*Pulling him by the shoulder*] What's the matter with you? Have you gone crazy? Friends, his head's turned; we must take him away.

NIKITA: [*Shoving her aside with his shoulder*] Let me alone! And you, daddy, listen to me. To begin with! Marina, look here! [*He bows down to her feet and rises again*] I did you wrong; I promised to marry you, I seduced you. I deceived you, I cast you off: forgive me for Christ's sake! [*Bows down to her feet once more*]

ANISYA: What are you prating about? This ain't decent. Nobody's questioning you. Get up: what are you making a row for?

MATRENA: O-oh, he's bewitched! How did it happen? He's out of his head.— Get up, what are you talking nonsense for? [*Pulls at him*]

NIKITA: [*Shaking his head*] Don't touch me! Forgive me, Marina! Forgive my sins against you for Christ's sake!

[Marina *covers her face with her hands and is silent*]

ANISYA: Get up, I tell you: what are you making a row for? No use mentioning bygones. Stop your foolery. Shame on you! Oh, poor me! He's gone clean daft.

NIKITA: [*Pushing away his wife and turning to* Akulina] Akulina, I'll talk to you now. Listen, orthodox people! I am an accursed man. Akulina, I did you wrong! Your father did not die a natural death. He was poisoned.

ANISYA: [*Shrieks*] Poor me! What does he mean?

MATRENA: The man's out of his head. Take him away, will you! [*Several men approach and are about to seize him*]

AKIM: [*Shielding him with his arms*] Wait! Here, fellows, wait, y'see; wait, I tell you!

NIKITA: Akulina, I poisoned him. Forgive me, for Christ's sake!

AKULINA: [*Jumping up*] He lies! I know who did it.

MATCHMAKER: (*woman*) What are you doing? Sit still.

AKIM: Oh, Lord! What a sin! What a sin!

POLICEMAN: Seize him! And send for the village elder, and witnesses. We must draw up the document. Get up and come here.

AKIM: [*To the* Policeman] But you, you know— Brass Buttons, y'see—just wait a bit, you know. Just let him tell the story, y'see.

POLICEMAN: [*To* Akim] Look out, old man; don't meddle. I must draw up the document.

AKIM: What a fellow you are, y'see. Wait, I tell you. Don't fuss about the document, y'see. God's work's going on here, you know. A man is repenting, y'see; and you talk about a document, you know.

POLICEMAN: Call the elder!

AKIM: Let God's work go on, you know; when it's over, y'see, then you do your business, y'see.

NIKITA: I did you another great wrong, Akulina; I seduced you. Forgive me for Christ's sake! [*Bows down to her feet*]

AKULINA: [*Coming out from behind the table*] Let me go; I won't get married. He told me to, but now I won't.

POLICEMAN: Repeat what you have said.

NIKITA: Wait, please, policeman; let me finish.

AKIM: [*In ecstasy*] Speak on, my lad; tell it all; it'll be easier for you. Repent in the sight of God; do not fear men. God! God! This is His work!

NIKITA: I poisoned the father; I ruined, cur that I am, the daughter. I had power over her; I ruined her and her baby.

AKULINA: It's true, it's true.

NIKITA: I crushed her child in the cellar with a plank. I sat on it. . . . I crushed it . . . and the little bones in it cracked. [*Weeps*] And I buried it in the earth. I did it, nobody but me!

AKULINA: He lies! I told him to. . . .

NIKITA: Don't shield me! I'm not afraid of anybody now! Forgive me, orthodox people! [*Bows down to the earth. Silence*]

POLICEMAN: Bind him. Your marriage is broken up, that's plain.

[*Men approach* Nikita *with sashes*]

NIKITA: Wait, you'll have time. . . . [*Bows down to his father's feet*] Dearest father! Forgive me, accursed sinner that I am—you also! You said to me in the very beginning, when I began to meddle with this nasty whoredom, you said to me: "If a claw is caught, the whole bird is lost." I did not listen to you, cur that I was, and it has come out as you said. Forgive me, for Christ's sake!

AKIM: [*In ecstasy*] God will forgive you, my beloved child! [*Embraces him*] You have not spared yourself, He will spare you. God! God! This is His work!

ELDER: [*Coming in*] There are plenty of witnesses here already.

POLICEMAN: We'll have the examination right away. [*They bind* Nikita]

AKULINA: [*Coming up and standing beside him*] I'll tell the truth. Question me too.

NIKITA: [*Bound*] No use questioning. I did it all by myself. I planned it and I did it. Lead me wherever you want to. I shall say nothing more.

Anton Chekhov

(1860–1904)

Anyone familiar only with the short stories that first made Chekhov famous would find it difficult to believe that the author was, or could ever have become, one of the greatest playwrights of the modern world. Certainly few of the thousand and more stories reveal any interest in action and plot. At times, in fact, Chekhov himself found it difficult to believe that he could have any serious traffic with the stage. He had a retiring disposition, and detested all self-dramatization and exhibitionism. He declared once that he regarded the narrative form as "a lawful wife" and the drama as "a showy, noisy, impertinent, and tiresome mistress." He advised a friend, "Don't write a single line for the theatre unless it is a thousand miles away from you." Nevertheless, Chekhov was enchanted with the stage from boyhood on, became the Moscow Art Theatre's favorite dramatist, fell in love with its ablest actress, Olga Knipper, and married her about two years before his untimely death.

The son of an ex-serf who attained some prosperity for a time and then lost it, Anton Chekhov knew enough about common life to be able to write numerous tales about the country and small town with memorable realism. His knowledge grew materially when he became a physician, practiced medicine among the peasantry, often without charging a fee, and went to eastern Siberia to investigate conditions in the convict camps on Sakhalin. But possibly because of his delicate health (the result of having contracted tuberculosis while studying at the University of Moscow) he acquired a gentleness quite unusual among writers who presented reality as candidly as he did. Most remarkable of all, however, was his almost disconcerting simplicity. It gained him the love of the elderly but still tempestuous Tolstoy, who treated him with a tenderness reserved for women, and it won the admiration of the rugged Gorki, who wrote in his *Reminiscences*, "I think that in Anton Chekhov's presence everyone involuntarily felt in himself a desire to be simple, more truthful, more one's self."

On receiving his medical degree in 1884, Chekhov decided to refrain from practice, because he found story writing a lucrative profession. He published his first collection two years later and won the coveted Pushkin Prize. But it was as early as the year of his graduation that he wrote his first, and only serious, one-act play, *On the High Road,* a poignant scene of devastated souls which could have served as a preliminary sketch for just the sort of play that Gorki wrote in *The Lower Depths* and

O'Neill in *The Iceman Cometh.* In 1887, he composed his first full-length drama, *Ivanov,* the tragedy of a Hamlet of the provinces whose unconventional marriage proved a failure. (The play failed dismally at first in a provincial performance, but was later carried to success by a popular actor at the St. Petersburg Imperial Theatre.) Next Chekhov worked an entire year (1888–1889) on a play unsuccessfully produced under the title of *The Wood Demon* and later published in revised form under the title of *Uncle Vanya.* Putting the manuscript aside as a failure, he continued to write only one-acters of the farcical variety, then called vaudevilles, several of which—*The Boor* (1888), *The Proposal,* and *The Wedding* (1889)—are still played by amateur and professional companies. Except for an unfinished melodrama about a provincial Don Juan *(That Worthless Fellow Platonov),* Chekhov refrained from serious playwriting for some six years. Then the disastrous fate of *The Sea Gull* at the St. Petersburg Alexandrinsky Theatre in 1896 threatened to divorce him permanently from the theatre. Chekhov left the Alexandrinsky before the curtain fell, vowing to leave playwriting alone forever, a resolution that could be applauded only by those who considered his muted artistry ill adapted to the stage. "Never will I write these plays or try to produce them," he wrote, "not if I live to be 700 years old."

Fortunately the Moscow Art Theatre was able to induce him to reconsider his decision, and he allowed Stanislavsky and Dantchenko to revive *The Sea Gull.* Both Chekhov and the new actors' company were saved for the theatre by the *première* of the revival on December 17, 1898. Congratulatory telegrams were showered on the author, then living in Yalta for his health, and in a postscript to a letter describing the triumph Dantchenko asked him for *Uncle Vanya.* After some difficulties when a rival company got hold of the play, the group produced this absorbing tragicomedy with great success on October 26, 1899, and thereafter Chekhov and the Art Theatre never parted. He wrote *The Three Sisters* for the company, with special attention to the talents of certain of its members, and the production on January 31, 1901, was, in Dantchenko's opinion, the best ever given by the Art Theatre. Then, on January 17, 1904, came *The Cherry Orchard,* Chekhov's last as well as most notable play, for Chekhov succumbed to his malady at a German health resort in July of the same year.

From *Ivanov* to *The Cherry Orchard,* Chekhov's

development as a dramatist was a steady ascent. In the melancholy *Ivanov,* he dramatized the failure of a morbid individual with considerable feeling and insight. In the sensitive tragedy *The Sea Gull,* he added a lyric component, using evocative atmosphere, the device of a play within a play, and delicate symbolism to present the failures of a girl with theatrical ambitions and of a young author who strives to create literature out of his unhappiness as a son and lover. In *Uncle Vanya,* Chekhov succeeded in writing a touching antiheroic drama of wasted lives. The search for happiness was next dramatized with enriched vitality in *The Three Sisters,* and here Chekhov's writing not only deepened but became affirmative through the resolve of his unhappy characters to dedicate themselves to a fruitful way of life even if they themselves were not to enjoy any of the fruits. Finally, in *The Cherry Orchard,* Chekhov broke the impasse of his customary social situation of upper-class decadence by representing a change in society and giving his play a forward direction.

If *The Cherry Orchard* may be construed as an augury of a new order in Russia, at that time on the eve of the Revolution of 1905, the play is also a universal drama of destiny. It speaks for all orders that are fated to pass away, for the humanity that suffers in the course of a transition from an old way of life to a new one, and for all individuals in whom the capacity for adaptation to new conditions is undeveloped—for all "victims of history," so to speak. Gorki's *Yegor Bulychov,* the Soviet playwright Bulgakov's *Days of the Turbins,* Denis Johnston's *The Moon in the Yellow River,* Paul Green's *The House of Connelly,* and Shaw's *Heartbreak House*—these are only a few of the many modern plays that represent a society in the process of transition. Among these studies *The Cherry Orchard* stands out as the most affecting drama and the one most firmly rooted in the life that people hold in common regardless of the interests of contending classes. Chekhov maintained a sensitive equilibrium between regret for the loss of old values and jubilation over the dawn of a new day. And it is the quality of detachment that also enabled him to equalize pathos and humor, and to render a probing account of the contradictions of human character.

The Cherry Orchard holds in solution all of the stylistic and technical attributes of Chekhov's dramatic artistry. Here we find his artful artlessness in presenting the flow and commingling of lives. The characters are often so absorbed in themselves that they are unaware of the trend of a conversation or a situation. Being largely directionless, they fly off at a tangent from their own and other characters' action or thoughts. Chekhov manages to make drama of this very trait and to shape a complete play out of scattered fragments of human reality. It is for this quality that his technique has been designated as "centrifugal." And since people's lives meet only to fly apart or fly apart only to meet, since they cross and recross one another's orbits, Chekhov's method of creating dramatic experience has been aptly called "contrapuntal." As this method of writing is a fascinating problem for playwrights, it has been attempted by others since his day, but rarely with his effectiveness. Only a master can sustain counterpoint interestingly for any length of time in drama, as in music.

It may also be noted that, by creating a new kind of catastrophe, Chekhov, almost alone, introduced into the theatre a new kind of tragedy, a tragedy of attrition. Instead of showing noble people as eventfully destroyed, he generally represented them as being eroded. His characters are seen rusting away in disuse, eventlessly stalemated, or permanently dislocated. Although *Uncle Vanya* and *The Three Sisters* provide the supreme examples, attrition is also the fate of the gentry of *The Cherry Orchard.* The dispersed family has no future, for there is no reason to believe that its members will make a successful adaptation to reality.

If, nevertheless, the effect is not actually depressing, this is due not only to the bountiful humanity of the play but to the realization that if the old order must pass it will not leave a vacuum. The axes that fell the trees of the cherry orchard are clearing the ground for more vital, if less refined, men and women. The summer bungalows will accommodate adults who make a civilization instead of living parasitically on it, and they will probably teem with the common man's brood of children, among whom will be the heroes, saints, scientists, and poets of tomorrow. Stanislavsky, who must have understood Chekhov's plays better than anyone else, found them fundamentally "positive" and rejected the view that they were the elegies of a world-weary man.

BIBLIOGRAPHY: Anton Chekhov, *Note-Book of Anton Chekhov,* 1921; Chekhov, *Letters of A. Tchekov to His Family and Friends,* translated by Constance Garnett, 1920; Chekhov, *The Life and Letters of A. Tchekhov,* translated by S. S. Koteliansky and Philip Tomlinson, 1925; Chekhov, *The Personal Papers of Anton Chekhov, 1948;* Vladimir Nemirovitch-Dantchenko, *My Life in the Russian Theatre* (pp. 139–142, 161–164, 165–167), 1931; John Gassner, *Masters of the Drama,* (pp. 508–520), 1945; William Gerhardi, *Anton Chekhov; A Critical Study,* 1923; Maxim Gorki, *Reminiscences of Tolstoy, Chekhov and Andreyev* (Dover Publications, 1946 edition); Constantin Stanislavsky, *My Life in Art* (pp. 345–375, 415–419), 1924, 1928; Leo Wiener, *The Contemporary Drama of Russia,* 1924.

THE CHERRY ORCHARD

By Anton Chekhov

TRANSLATED FROM THE RUSSIAN BY CONSTANCE GARNETT

CHARACTERS IN THE PLAY

MADAME RANEVSKY (LYUBOV AN-
DREYEVNA), *the owner of the
Cherry Orchard*
ANYA, *her daughter, aged 17*
VARYA, *her adopted daughter, aged
24*
GAEV (LEONID ANDREYEVITCH),
brother of Madame Ranevsky

LOPAHIN (YERMOLAY ALEXEYE-
VITCH), *a merchant*
TROFIMOV (PYOTR SERGEYEVITCH),
a student
SEMYONOV-PISHTCHIK, *a landowner*
CHARLOTTA IVANOVNA, *a governess*
EPIHODOV (SEMYON PANTALEYE-
VITCH), *a clerk*

DUNYASHA, *a maid*
FIRS, *an old valet, aged 87*
YASHA, *a young valet*
A WAYFARER
THE STATION MASTER
A POST-OFFICE CLERK
VISITORS, SERVANTS

The action takes place on the estate of Madame
Ranevsky.

ACT I.

*A room, which has always been called the nur-
sery. One of the doors leads into* Anya's *room.
Dawn, sun rises during the scene. May, the cherry
trees in flower, but it is cold in the garden with
the frost of early morning. Windows closed.
Enter* Dunyasha *with a candle and* Lopahin *with
a book in his hand.*

LOPAHIN: The train's in, thank God. What time
is it?

DUNYASHA: Nearly two o'clock. [*Puts out the
candle*] It's daylight already.

LOPAHIN: The train's late! Two hours, at least.
[*Yawns and stretches*] I'm a pretty one; what a
fool I've been. Came here on purpose to meet them
at the station and dropped asleep. . . . Dozed off
as I sat in the chair. It's annoying. . . . You might
have waked me.

DUNYASHA: I thought you had gone. [*Listens*]
There, I do believe they're coming!

LOPAHIN: [*Listens*] No, what with the luggage and
one thing and another. [*A pause*] Lyubov Andreyevna has been abroad five years; I don't know what
she is like now. . . . She's a splendid woman. A
good-natured, kind-hearted woman. I remember
when I was a lad of fifteen, my poor father——he used
to keep a little shop here in the village in those days
——gave me a punch in the face with his fist and
made my nose bleed. We were in the yard here, I
forget what we'd come about——he had had a drop.
Lyubov Andreyevna——I can see her now——she was
a slim young girl then——took me to wash my face,
and then brought me into this very room, into the
nursery. "Don't cry, little peasant," says she, "it

will be well in time for your wedding day." . . .
[*A pause*] Little peasant. . . . My father was a
peasant, it's true, but here am I in a white waistcoat
and brown shoes, like a pig in a bun shop. Yes, I'm
a rich man, but for all my money, come to think, a
peasant I was, and a peasant I am. [*Turns over the
pages of the book*] I've been reading this book and I
can't make head or tail of it. I fell asleep over it.
[*A pause*]

DUNYASHA: The dogs have been awake all night,
they feel that the mistress is coming.

LOPAHIN: Why, what's the matter with you, Dunyasha?

DUNYASHA: My hands are all of a tremble. I feel
as though I should faint.

LOPAHIN: You're a spoilt soft creature, Dunyasha.
And dressed like a lady too, and your hair done up.
That's not the thing. One must know one's place.

[*Enter* Epihodov *with a nosegay; he wears a
pea-jacket and highly polished creaking top-
boots; he drops the nosegay as he comes in*]

EPIHODOV: [*Picking up the nosegay*] Here! the
gardener's sent this, says you're to put it in the
dining-room. [*Gives* Dunyasha *the nosegay*]

LOPAHIN: And bring me some kvass.

DUNYASHA: I will. [*Goes out*]

EPIHODOV: It's chilly this morning, three degrees
of frost, though the cherries are all in flower. I
can't say much for our climate. [*Sighs*] I can't. Our
climate is not often propitious to the occasion. Yermolay Alexeyevitch, permit me to call your attention to the fact that I purchased myself a pair of
boots the day before yesterday, and they creak, I
venture to assure you, so that there's no tolerating
them. What ought I to grease them with?

LOPAHIN: Oh, shut up! Don't bother me.

EPIHODOV: Every day some misfortune befalls
me. I don't complain, I'm used to it, and I wear
a smiling face.

[Dunyasha *comes in, hands* Lopahin *the kvass*]

EPIHODOV: I am going. [*Stumbles against a chair,*

which falls over] There! [*As though triumphant*] There you see now, excuse the expression, an accident like that among others. . . . It's positively remarkable. [*Goes out*]

DUNYASHA: Do you know, Yermolay Alexeyevitch, I must confess, Epihodov has made me a proposal.

LOPAHIN: Ah!

DUNYASHA: I'm sure I don't know. . . . He's a harmless fellow, but sometimes when he begins talking, there's no making anything of it. It's all very fine and expressive, only there's no understanding it. I've a sort of liking for him too. He loves me to distraction. He's an unfortunate man; every day there's something. They tease him about it—two and twenty misfortunes they call him.

LOPAHIN: [*Listening*] There! I do believe they're coming.

DUNYASHA: They are coming! What's the matter with me? . . . I'm cold all over.

LOPAHIN: They really are coming. Let's go and meet them. Will she know me? It's five years since I saw her.

DUNYASHA: [*In a flutter*] I shall drop this very minute. . . . Ah, I shall drop.

[*There is a sound of two carriages driving up to the house.* Lopahin *and* Dunyasha *go out quickly. The stage is left empty. A noise is heard in the adjoining rooms.* Firs, *who has driven to meet* Madame Ranevsky, *crosses the stage hurriedly leaning on a stick. He is wearing old-fashioned livery and a high hat. He says something to himself, but not a word can be distinguished. The noise behind the scenes goes on increasing. A voice: "Come, let's go in here." Enter* Lyubov Andreyevna, Anya, *and* Charlotta Ivanovna *with a pet dog on a chain, all in traveling dresses.* Varya *in an out-door coat with a kerchief over her head,* Gaev, Semyonov-Pishtchik, Lopahin, Dunyasha *with bag and parasol, servants with other articles. All walk across the room*]

ANYA: Let's come in here. Do you remember what room this is, mamma?

LYUBOV: [*Joyfully, through her tears*] The nursery!

VARYA: How cold it is, my hands are numb [*To* Lyubov Andreyevna] Your rooms, the white room and the lavender one, are just the same as ever, mamma.

LYUBOV: My nursery, dear delightful room. . . . I used to sleep here when I was little. . . . [*Cries*] And here I am, like a little child. . . . [*Kisses her brother and* Varya, *and then her brother again*] Varya's just the same as ever, like a nun. And I knew Dunyasha. [*Kisses* Dunyasha]

GAEV: The train was two hours late. What do you think of that? Is that the way to do things?

CHARLOTTA: [*To* Pishtchik] My dog eats nuts, too.

PISHTCHIK: [*Wonderingly*] Fancy that!

[*They all go out except* Anya *and* Dunyasha]

DUNYASHA: We've been expecting you so long. [*Takes* Anya's *hat and coat*]

ANYA: I haven't slept for four nights on the journey. I feel dreadfully cold.

DUNYASHA: You set out in Lent, there was snow and frost, and now? My darling! [*Laughs and kisses her*] I *have* missed you, my precious, my joy. I must tell you . . . I can't put it off a minute. . . .

ANYA: [*Wearily*] What now?

DUNYASHA: Epihodov, the clerk, made me a proposal just after Easter.

ANYA: It's always the same thing with you. . . . [*Straightening her hair*] I've lost all my hairpins. [*She is staggering from exhaustion*]

DUNYASHA: I don't know what to think, really. He does love me, he does love me so!

ANYA: [*Looking towards her door, tenderly*] My own room, my windows just as though I had never gone away. I'm home! To-morrow morning I shall get up and run into the garden. . . . Oh, if I could get to sleep! I haven't slept all the journey, I was so anxious and worried.

DUNYASHA: Pyotr Sergeyevitch came the day before yesterday.

ANYA: [*Joyfully*] Petya!

DUNYASHA: He's asleep in the bath house, he has settled in there. I'm afraid of being in their way, says he. [*Glancing at her watch*] I was to have waked him, but Varvara Mihalovna told me not to. Don't you wake him, says she.

[*Enter* Varya *with a bunch of keys at her waist*]

VARYA: Dunyasha, coffee and make haste. . . . Mamma's asking for coffee.

DUNYASHA: This very minute. [*Goes out*]

VARYA: Well, thank God, you've come. You're home again. [*Petting her*] My little darling has come back! My precious beauty has come back again!

ANYA: I have had a time of it!

VARYA: I can fancy.

ANYA: We set off in Holy Week—it was so cold then, and all the way Charlotta would talk and show off her tricks. What did you want to burden me with Charlotta for?

VARYA: You couldn't have traveled all alone, darling. At seventeen!

ANYA: We got to Paris at last, it was cold there—snow. I speak French shockingly. Mamma lives on the fifth floor, I went up to her and there were a lot of French people, ladies, an old priest with a book. The place smelt of tobacco and so comfortless. I felt sorry, oh! so sorry for mamma all at once, I put my arms round her neck, and hugged her and wouldn't let her go. Mamma was as kind as she could be, and she cried. . . .

VARYA: [*Through her tears*] Don't speak of it, don't speak of it!

ANYA: She had sold her villa at Mentone, she had nothing left, nothing. I hadn't a farthing left either we only just had enough to get here. And mamma doesn't understand! When we had dinner at the stations, she always ordered the most expensive things and gave the waiters a whole rouble. Charlotta's just the same. Yasha too must have the same as we do; it's simply awful. You know Yasha is mamma's valet now, we brought him here with us.

VARYA: Yes, I've seen the young rascal.

ANYA: Well, tell me—have you paid the arrears on the mortgage?

VARYA: How could we get the money?

ANYA: Oh, dear! Oh, dear!

VARYA: In August the place will be sold.

ANYA: My goodness!

LOPAHIN: [Peeps in at the door and moos like a cow] Moo! [Disappears]

VARYA: [Weeping] There, that's what I could do to him. [Shakes her fist]

ANYA: [Embracing Varya, softly] Varya, has he made you an offer? [Varya shakes her head] Why, but he loves you. Why is it you don't come to an understanding? What are you waiting for?

VARYA: I believe that there never will be anything between us. He has a lot to do, he has no time for me . . . and takes no notice of me. Bless the man, it makes me miserable to see him. . . . Everyone's talking of our being married, everyone's congratulating me, and all the while there's really nothing in it; it's all like a dream. [In another tone] You have a new brooch like a bee.

ANYA: [Mournfully] Mamma bought it. [Goes into her own room and in a light-hearted childish tone] And you know, in Paris I went up in a balloon!

VARYA: My darling's home again! My pretty is home again!

[Dunyasha returns with the coffee-pot and is making the coffee]

VARYA: [Standing at the door] All day long, darling, as I go about looking after the house, I keep dreaming all the time. If only we could marry you to a rich man, then I should feel more at rest. Then I would go off by myself on a pilgrimage to Kiev, to Moscow . . . and so I would spend my life going from one holy place to another. . . . I would go on and on. . . . What bliss!

ANYA: The birds are singing in the garden. What time is it?

VARYA: It must be nearly three. It's time you were asleep, darling. [Going into Anya's room] What bliss!

[Yasha enters with a rug and a traveling bag]

YASHA: [Crosses the stage, mincingly] May one come in here, pray?

DUNYASHA: I shouldn't have known you, Yasha. How you have changed abroad.

YASHA: H'm! . . . And who are you?

DUNYASHA: When you went away, I was that high. [Shows distance from floor] Dunyasha, Fyodor's daughter. . . . You don't remember me!

YASHA: H'm! . . . You're a peach! [Looks round

and embraces her: she shrieks and drops a saucer. Yasha goes out hastily]

VARYA: [In the doorway, in a tone of vexation] What now?

DUNYASHA: [Through her tears] I have broken a saucer.

VARYA: Well, that brings good luck.

ANYA: [Coming out of her room] We ought to prepare mamma: Petya is here.

VARYA: I told them not to wake him.

ANYA: [Dreamily] It's six years since father died. Then only a month later little brother Grisha was drowned in the river, such a pretty boy he was, only seven. It was more than mamma could bear, so she went away, went away without looking back. [Shuddering] . . . How well I understand her, if only she knew! [A pause] And Petya Trofimov was Grisha's tutor, he may remind her.

[Enter Firs: he is wearing a pea-jacket and a white waistcoat]

FIRS: [Goes up to the coffee-pot, anxiously] The mistress will be served here. [Puts on white gloves] Is the coffee ready? [Sternly to Dunyasha] Girl! Where's the cream?

DUNYASHA: Ah, mercy on us! [Goes out quickly]

FIRS: [Fussing round the coffee-pot] Ech! you good-for-nothing! [Muttering to himself] Come back from Paris. And the old master used to go to Paris too . . . horses all the way. [Laughs]

VARYA: What is it, Firs?

FIRS: What is your pleasure? [Gleefully] My lady has come home! I have lived to see her again! Now I can die. [Weeps with joy]

[Enter Lyubov Andreyevna, Gaev and Semyonov-Pishtchik; the latter is in a short-waisted full coat of fine cloth, and full trousers. Gaev, as he comes in, makes a gesture with his arms and his whole body, as though he were playing billiards]

LYUBOV: How does it go? Let me remember. Cannon off the red!

GAEV: That's it—in off the white! Why, once, sister, we used to sleep together in this very room, and now I'm fifty-one, strange as it seems.

LOPAHIN: Yes, time flies.

GAEV: What do you say?

LOPAHIN: Time, I say, flies.

GAEV: What a smell of patchouli!

ANYA: I'm going to bed. Good-night, mamma. [Kisses her mother]

LYUBOV: My precious darling. [Kisses her hands] Are you glad to be home? I can't believe it.

ANYA: Good-night, uncle.

GAEV: [Kissing her face and hands] God bless you! How like you are to your mother! [To his sister] At her age you were just the same, Lyuba.

[Anya shakes hands with Lopahin and Pishtchik, then goes out, shutting the door after her]

LYUBOV: She's quite worn out.

PISHTCHIK: Aye, it's a long journey, to be sure.

VARYA: [*To* Lopahin *and* Pishtchik] Well, gentlemen? It's three o'clock and time to say good-bye.

LYUBOV: [*Laughs*] You're just the same as ever, Varya. [*Draws her to her and kisses her*] I'll just drink my coffee and then we will all go and rest. [Firs *puts a cushion under her feet*] Thanks, friend. I am so fond of coffee, I drink it day and night. Thanks, dear old man. [*Kisses* Firs]

VARYA: I'll just see whether all the things have been brought in. [*Goes out*]

LYUBOV: Can it really be me sitting here? [*Laughs*] I want to dance about and clap my hands. [*Covers her face with her hands*] And I could drop asleep in a moment! God knows I love my country, I love it tenderly; I couldn't look out of the window in the train, I kept crying so. [*Through her tears*] But I must drink my coffee, though. Thank you, Firs, thanks, dear old man. I'm so glad to find you still alive.

FIRS: The day before yesterday.

GAEV: He's rather deaf.

LOPAHIN: I have to set off for Harkov directly, at five o'clock. . . . It is annoying! I wanted to have a look at you, and a little talk. . . . You are just as splendid as ever.

PISHTCHIK: [*Breathing heavily*] Handsomer, indeed. . . . Dressed in Parisian style . . . completely bowled me over.

LOPAHIN: Your brother, Leonid Andreyevitch here, is always saying that I'm a low-born knave, that I'm a money-grubber, but I don't care one straw for that. Let him talk. Only I do want you to believe in me as you used to. I do want your wonderful tender eyes to look at me as they used to in the old days. Merciful God! My father was a serf of your father and of your grandfather, but you—you—did so much for me once, that I've forgotten all that; I love you as though you were my kin . . . more than my kin.

LYUBOV: I can't sit still, I simply can't. . . .

[*Jumps up and walks about in violent agitation*] This happiness is too much for me. . . . You may laugh at me, I know I'm silly. . . . My own bookcase. [*Kisses the bookcase*] My little table.

GAEV: Nurse died while you were away.

LYUBOV: [*Sits down and drinks coffee*] Yes, the Kingdom of Heaven be hers! You wrote me of her death.

GAEV: And Anastasy is dead. Squinting Petruchka has left me and is in service now with the police captain in the town.

[*Takes a box of caramels out of his pocket and sucks one*]

PISHTCHIK: My daughter, Dashenka, wishes to be remembered to you.

LOPAHIN: I want to tell you something very pleasant and cheering. [*Glancing at his watch*] I'm going directly . . . there's no time to say much . . . well, I can say it in a couple of words. I needn't tell you your cherry orchard is to be sold to pay your debts; the 22nd of August is the date fixed for the sale; but don't you worry, dearest lady, you may sleep in peace, there is a way of saving it. . . . This is what I propose. I beg your attention! Your estate is not twenty miles from the town, the railway runs close by it, and if the cherry orchard and the land along the river bank were cut up into building plots and then let on lease for summer villas, you would make an income of at least 25,000 roubles a year out of it.

GAEV: That's all rot, if you'll excuse me.

LYUBOV: I don't quite understand you, Yermolay Alexeyevitch.

LOPAHIN: You will get a rent of at least 25 roubles a year for a three-acre plot from summer visitors, and if you say the word now, I'll bet you what you like there won't be one square foot of ground vacant by the autumn, all the plots will be taken up. I congratulate you; in fact, you are saved. It's a perfect situation with that deep river. Only, of course, it must be cleared—all the old buildings, for example, must be removed, this house too, which is really good for nothing and the old cherry orchard must be cut down.

LYUBOV: Cut down? My dear fellow, forgive me, but you don't know what you are talking about. If there is one thing interesting—remarkable indeed—in the whole province, it's just our cherry orchard.

LOPAHIN: The only thing remarkable about the orchard is that it's a very large one. There's a crop of cherries every alternate year, and then there's nothing to be done with them, no one buys them.

GAEV: This orchard is mentioned in the *Encyclopædia*.

LOPAHIN: [*Glancing at his watch*] If we don't decide on something and don't take some steps, on the 22nd of August the cherry orchard and the whole estate too will be sold by auction. Make up your minds! There is no other way of saving it, I'll take my oath on that. No, No!

FIRS: In old days, forty or fifty years ago, they used to dry the cherries, soak them, pickle them, make jam too, and they used——

GAEV: Be quiet, Firs.

FIRS: And they used to send the preserved cherries to Moscow and to Harkov by the wagon-load. That brought the money in! And the preserved cherries in those days were soft and juicy, sweet and fragrant. . . . They knew the way to do them then. . . .

LYUBOV: And where is the recipe now?

FIRS: It's forgotten. Nobody remembers it.

PISHTCHIK: [*To* Lyubov Andreyevna] What's it like in Paris? Did you eat frogs there?

LYUBOV: Oh, I ate crocodiles.

PISHTCHIK: Fancy that now!

LOPAHIN: There used to be only the gentlefolks and the peasants in the country, but now there are these summer visitors. All the towns, even the small ones, are surrounded, nowadays by these summer villas. And one may say for sure, that in another twenty years there'll be many more of these people and that they'll be everywhere. At present the summer visitor only drinks tea in his verandah, but maybe he'll take to working his bit of land too, and then your cherry orchard would become happy, rich and prosperous. . . .

GAEV: [*Indignant*] What rot!

[*Enter* Varya *and* Yasha]

VARYA: There are two telegrams for you, mamma [*Takes out keys and opens an old-fashioned bookcase with a loud crack*] Here they are.

LYUBOV: From Paris [*Tears the telegrams, without reading them*] I have done with Paris.

GAEV: Do you know, Lyuba, how old that bookcase is? Last week I pulled out the bottom drawer and there I found the date branded on it. The bookcase was made just a hundred years ago. What do you say to that? We might have celebrated its jubilee. Though it's an inanimate object, still it is a *book* case.

PISHTCHIK: [*Amazed*] A hundred years! Fancy that now.

GAEV: Yes. . . . It is a thing. . . . [*Feeling the bookcase*] Dear, honored, bookcase! Hail to thee who for more than a hundred years hast served the pure ideals of good and justice; thy silent call to fruitful labor has never flagged in those hundred years, maintaining [*in tears*] in the generations of man, courage and faith in a brighter future and fostering in us ideals of good and social consciousness [*A pause*]

LOPAHIN: Yes. . . .

LYUBOV: You are just the same as ever, Leonid.

GAEV: [*A little embarrassed*] Cannon off the right into the pocket!

LOPAHIN: [*Looking at his watch*] Well, it's time I was off.

YASHA: [*Handing* Lyubov Andreyevna *medicine*] Perhaps you will take your pills now.

PISHTCHIK: You shouldn't take medicines, my dear madam . . . they do no harm and no good. Give them here . . . honored lady [*Takes the pillbox, pours the pills into the hollow of his hand, blows on them, puts them in his mouth and drinks off some kvass*] There!

LYUBOV: [*In alarm*] Why, you must be out of your mind!

PISHTCHIK: I have taken all the pills.

LOPAHIN: What a glutton! [*All laugh*]

FIRS: His honor stayed with us in Easter week, ate a gallon and a half of cucumbers. . . . [*Mutters*]

LYUBOV: What is he saying?

VARYA: He has taken to muttering like that for the last three years. We are used to it.

YASHA: His declining years!

[Charlotta Ivanovna, *a very thin, lanky figure in a white dress with a lorgnette in her belt, walks across the stage*]

LOPAHIN: I beg your pardon, Charlotta Ivanovna,

I have not had time to greet you. [*Tries to kiss her hand*]

CHARLOTTA: [*Pulling away her hand*] If I let you kiss my hand, you'll be wanting to kiss my elbow, and then my shoulder.

LOPAHIN: I've no luck to-day! [*All laugh*] Charlotta Ivanovna, show us some tricks!

LYUBOV: Charlotta, do show us some tricks!

CHARLOTTA: I don't want to. I'm sleepy. [*Goes out*]

LOPAHIN: In three weeks' time we shall meet again. [*Kisses* Lyubov Andreyevna's *hand*] Good-bye till then—I must go. [*To* Gaev] Good-bye. [*Kisses* Pishtchik] Good-bye. [*Gives his hand to* Varya, *then to* Firs *and* Yasha] I don't want to go. [*To* Lyubov Andreyevna] If you think over my plan for the villas and make up your mind, then let me know; I will lend you 50,000 roubles. Think of it seriously.

VARYA: [*Angrily*] Well, do go, for goodness sake.

LOPAHIN: I'm going, I'm going. [*Goes out*]

GAEV: Low-born knave! I beg pardon, though . . . Varya is going to marry him, he's Varya's fiancé.

VARYA: Don't talk nonsense, uncle.

LYUBOV: Well, Varya, I shall be delighted. He's a good man.

PISHTCHIK: He is, one must acknowledge, a most worthy man. And my Dashenka . . . says too that . . . she says . . . various things. [*Snores, but at once wakes up*] But all the same, honored lady, could you oblige me . . . with a loan of 240 roubles . . . to pay the interest on my mortgage to-morrow?

VARYA: [*Dismayed*] No, no.

LYUBOV: I really haven't any money.

PISHTCHIK: It will turn up. [*Laughs*] I never lose hope. I thought everything was over, I was a ruined man, and lo and behold—the railway passed through my land and . . . they paid me for it. And something else will turn up again, if not to-day, then to-morrow . . . Dashenka'll win two hundred thousand . . . she's got a lottery ticket.

LYUBOV: Well, we've finished our coffee, we can go to bed.

FIRS: [*Brushes* Gaev, *reprovingly*] You have got on the wrong trousers again! What am I to do with you?

VARYA: [*Softly*] Anya's asleep. [*Softly opens the window*] Now the sun's risen, it's not a bit cold. Look, mamma, what exquisite trees! My goodness! And the air! The starlings are singing!

GAEV: [*Opens another window*] The orchard is all white. You've not forgotten it, Lyuba? That long avenue that runs straight, straight as an arrow, how it shines on a moonlight night. You remember? You've not forgotten?

LYUBOV: [*Looking out of the window into the garden*] Oh, my childhood, my innocence! It was in this nursery I used to sleep, from here I looked out into the orchard, happiness waked with me every morning and in those days the orchard was just the same, nothing has changed. [*Laughs with delight*] All, all white! Oh, my orchard! After the dark gloomy autumn, and the cold winter; you are young again, and full of happiness, the heavenly angels have never left you. . . . If I could cast off the burden that weighs on my heart, if I could forget the past!

GAEV: H'm! and the orchard will be sold to pay our debts; it seems strange. . . .

LYUBOV: See, our mother walking . . . all in white, down the avenue! [*Laughs with delight*] It is she!

GAEV: Where?

VARYA: Oh, don't, mamma!

LYUBOV: There is no one. It was my fancy. On the right there, by the path to the arbor, there is a white tree bending like a woman. . . .

[*Enter* Trofimov *wearing a shabby student's uniform and spectacles*]

LYUBOV: What a ravishing orchard! White masses of blossom, blue sky. . . .

TROFIMOV: Lyubov Andreyevna! [*She looks round at him*] I will just pay my respects to you and then leave you at once. [*Kisses her hand warmly*] I was told to wait until morning, but I hadn't the patience to wait any longer. . . .

[*Lyubov Andreyevna looks at him in perplexity*]

VARYA: [*Through her tears*] This is Petya Trofimov.

TROFIMOV: Petya Trofimov, who was your Grisha's tutor. . . . Can I have changed so much?

[*Lyubov Andreyevna embraces him and weeps quietly*]

GAEV: [*In confusion*] There, there, Lyuba.

VARYA: [*Crying*] I told you, Petya, to wait till to-morrow.

LYUBOV: My Grisha . . . my boy . . . Grisha . . . my son!

VARYA: We can't help it, mamma, it is God's will.

TROFIMOV: [*Softly through his tears*] There . . . there.

LYUBOV: [*Weeping quietly*] My boy was lost . . . drowned. Why? Oh, why, dear Petya? [*More quietly*] Anya is asleep in there, and I'm talking loudly . . . making this noise. . . . But, Petya? Why have you grown so ugly? Why do you look so old?

TROFIMOV: A peasant-woman in the train called me a mangy-looking gentleman.

LYUBOV: You were quite a boy then, a pretty little student, and now your hair's thin—and spectacles. Are you really a student still? [*Goes towards the door*]

TROFIMOV: I seem likely to be a perpetual student.

LYUBOV: [*Kisses her brother, then* Varya] Well, go to bed. . . . You are older too, Leonid.

PISHTCHIK: [*Follows her*] I suppose it's time we were asleep. . . . Ugh! my gout. I'm staying the night! Lyubov Andreyevna, my dear soul, if you could . . . to-morrow morning . . . 240 roubles.

GAEV: That's always his story.

PISHTCHIK: 240 roubles . . . to pay the interest on my mortgage.

LYUBOV: My dear man, I have no money.

PISHTCHIK: I'll pay it back, my dear . . . a trifling sum.

LYUBOV: Oh, well, Leonid will give it you. . . . You give him the money, Leonid.

GAEV: Me give it him! Let him wait till he gets it!

LYUBOV: It can't be helped, give it him. He needs it. He'll pay it back.

[*Lyubov Andreyevna, Trofimov, Pishtchik and Firs go out. Gaev, Varya and Yasha remain*]

GAEV: Sister hasn't got out of the habit of flinging away her money. [*To Yasha*] Get away, my good fellow, you smell of the hen-house.

YASHA: [*With a grin*] And you, Leonid Andreyevitch, are just the same as ever.

GAEV: What's that? [*To Varya*] What did he say?

VARYA: [*To Yasha*] Your mother has come from the village; she has been sitting in the servants' room since yesterday, waiting to see you.

YASHA: Oh, bother her!

VARYA: For shame!

YASHA: What's the hurry? She might just as well have come to-morrow. [*Goes out*]

VARYA: Mamma's just the same as ever, she hasn't changed a bit. If she had her own way, she'd give away everything.

GAEV: Yes. [*A pause*] If a great many remedies are suggested for some disease, it means that the disease is incurable. I keep thinking and racking my brains; I have many schemes, a great many, and that really means none. If we could only come in for a legacy from somebody, or marry our Anya to a very rich man, or we might go to Yaroslavl and try our luck with our old aunt, the Countess. She's very, very rich, you know.

VARYA: [*Weeps*] If God would help us.

GAEV: Don't blubber. Aunt's very rich, but she doesn't like us. First, sister married a lawyer instead of a nobleman. . . .

[*Anya appears in the doorway*]

GAEV: And then her conduct, one can't call it virtuous. She is good, and kind, and nice, and I love her, but, however one allows for extenuating circumstances, there's no denying that she's an immoral woman. One feels it in her slightest gesture.

VARYA: [*In a whisper*] Anya's in the doorway.

GAEV: What do you say? [*A pause*] It's queer, there seems to be something wrong with my right eye. I don't see as well as I did. And on Thursday when I was in the district Court . . .

[*Enter* Anya]

VARYA: Why aren't you asleep, Anya?

ANYA: I can't get to sleep.

GAEV: My pet. [*Kisses* Anya's *face and hands*] My child. [*Weeps*] You are not my niece, you are my angel, you are everything to me. Believe me, believe. . . .

ANYA: I believe you, uncle. Everyone loves you and respects you . . . but, uncle dear, you must be silent . . . simply be silent. What were you saying just now about my mother, about your own sister? What made you say that?

GAEV: Yes, yes. . . . [*Puts his hand over his face*] Really, that was awful! My God, save me! And to-day I made a speech to the bookcase . . . so stupid! And only when I had finished, I saw how stupid it was.

VARYA: It's true, uncle, you ought to keep quiet. Don't talk, that's all.

ANYA: If you could keep from talking, it would make things easier for you, too.

GAEV: I won't speak. [*Kisses* Anya's *and* Varya's *hands*] I'll be silent. Only this is about business. On Thursday I was in the district Court; well, there was a large party of us there and we began talking of one thing and another, and this and that, and do you know, I believe that it will be possible to raise a loan on an I.O.U. to pay the arrears on the mortgage.

VARYA: If the Lord would help us!

GAEV: I'm going on Tuesday; I'll talk of it again. [*To* Varya] Don't blubber. [*To* Anya] Your mamma will talk to Lopahin; of course, he won't refuse her. And as soon as you're rested you shall go to Yaroslavl to the Countess, your great-aunt. So we shall all set to work in three directions at once, and the business is done. We shall pay off arrears, I'm convinced of it. [*Puts a caramel in his mouth*] I swear on my honor, I swear by anything you like, the estate shan't be sold. [*Excitedly*] By my own happiness, I swear it! Here's my hand on it, call me the basest, vilest of men, if I let it come to an auction! Upon my soul I swear it!

ANYA: [*Her equanimity has returned, she is quite happy*] How good you are, uncle, and how clever! [*Embraces her uncle*] I'm at peace now! Quite at peace! I'm happy!

[*Enter* Firs]

FIRS: [*Reproachfully*] Leonid Andreyevitch, have you no fear of God? When are you going to bed?

GAEV: Directly, directly. You can go, Firs. I'll . . . yes, I will undress myself. Come, children, bye-bye. We'll go into details to-morrow, but now go to bed. [*Kisses* Anya *and* Varya] I'm a man of the eighties. They run down that period, but still I can say I have had to suffer not a little for my convictions in my life, it's not for nothing that the peasant loves me. One must know the peasant! One must know how. . . .

ANYA: At it again, uncle!

VARYA: Uncle dear, you'd better be quiet!

FIRS: [*Angrily*] Leonid Andreyevitch!

GAEV: I'm coming. I'm coming. Go to bed. Potted the shot—there's a shot for you! A beauty! [*Goes out,* Firs *hobbling after him*]

ANYA: My mind's at rest now. I don't want to go to Yaroslavl, I don't like my great-aunt, but still my mind's at rest. Thanks to uncle. [*Sits down*]

VARYA: We must go to bed. I'm going. Something unpleasant happened while you were away. In the old servants' quarters there are only the old servants, as you know—Efimyushka, Polya and Yevstigney—and Karp too. They began letting stray people in to spend the night—I said nothing. But all at once I heard they had been spreading a report that I gave them nothing but pease pudding to eat. Out of stinginess, you know. . . . And it was all Yevstigney's doing. . . .Very well, I said to myself. . . . If that's how it is, I thought, wait a bit. I sent for Yevstigney. . . . [*Yawns*] He comes. . . . "How's this, Yevstigney," I said, "you could be such a fool as to? . . ." [*Looking at* Anya] Anitchka! [*A pause*] She's asleep. [*Puts her arm around* Anya] Come to bed . . . come along! [*Leads her*] My darling has fallen asleep! Come . . . [*They go*]

[*Far away beyond the orchard a shepherd plays on a pipe.* Trofimov *crosses the stage and, seeing* Varya *and* Anya, *stands still*]

VARYA: 'Sh! asleep, asleep. Come, my own.

ANYA: [*Softly, half asleep*] I'm so tired. Still those bells. Uncle . . . dear . . . mamma and uncle. . . .

VARYA: Come, my own, come along.

[*They go into* Anya's *room*]

TROFIMOV: [*Tenderly*] My sunshine! My spring.

CURTAIN.

ACT II.

The open country. An old shrine, long abandoned and fallen out of the perpendicular; near it a well, large stones that have apparently once been tombstones, and an old garden seat. The road to Gaev's house is seen. On one side rise dark poplars; and there the cherry orchard begins. In the distance a row of telegraph poles and far, far away on the horizon there is faintly outlined a great town, only visible in very fine clear weather. It is near sunset. Charlotta, Yasha and Dunyasha are sitting on the seat. Epihodov is standing near, playing something mournful on a guitar. All sit plunged in thought. Charlotta wears an old forage cap; she has taken a gun from her shoulder and is tightening the buckle on the strap.

CHARLOTTA: [*Musingly*] I haven't a real passport of my own, and I don't know how old I am, and I always feel that I'm a young thing. When I was a little girl, my father and mother used to travel about to fairs and give performances—very good ones. And I used to dance *salto mortale* and all sorts of things. And when papa and mamma died, a German lady took me and had me educated. And so I grew up and became a governess. But where I came from, and who I am, I don't know. . . . Who my parents were, very likely they weren't married. . . . I don't know. [*Takes a cucumber out of her pocket and eats*] I know nothing at all. [*A pause*] One wants to talk and has no one to talk to. . . . I have nobody.

EPIHODOV: [*Plays on the guitar and sings*] "What care I for the noisy world! What care I for friends or foes!" How agreeable it is to play on the mandoline!

DUNYASHA: That's a guitar, not a mandoline. [*Looks in a hand-mirror and powders herself*]

EPIHODOV: To a man mad with love, it's a mandoline. [*Sings*] "Were her heart but aglow with love's mutual flame."

[*Yasha joins in*]

CHARLOTTA: How shockingly these people sing! Foo! Like jackals!

DUNYASHA: [*To Yasha*] What happiness, though, to visit foreign lands.

YASHA: Ah, yes! I rather agree with you there. [*Yawns, then lights a cigar*]

EPIHODOV: That's comprehensible. In foreign lands everything has long since reached full complexion.

YASHA: That's so, of course.

EPIHODOV: I'm a cultivated man, I read remarkable books of all sorts, but I can never make out the tendency I am myself precisely inclined for, whether to live or to shoot myself, speaking precisely, but nevertheless I always carry a revolver. Here it is. . . . [*Shows revolver*]

CHARLOTTA: I've had enough, and now I'm going. [*Puts on the gun*] Epihodov, you're a very clever fellow, and a very terrible one too, all the women must be wild about you. Br-r-r! [*Goes*] These clever fellows are all so stupid; there's not a creature for me to speak to. . . . Always alone, alone, nobody belonging to me . . . and who I am, and why I'm on earth, I don't know. [*Walks away slowly*]

EPIHODOV: Speaking precisely, not touching upon other subjects, I'm bound to admit about myself, that destiny behaves mercilessly to me, as a storm to a little boat. If, let us suppose, I am mistaken, then why did I wake up this morning, to quote an example, and look round, and there on my chest was a spider of fearful magnitude . . . like this. [*Shows with both hands*] And then I take up a jug of kvass, to quench my thirst, and in it there is something in the highest degree unseemly of the nature of a cockroach. [*A pause*] Have you read Buckle? [*A pause*] I am desirous of troubling you, Dunyasha, with a couple of words.

DUNYASHA: Well, speak.

EPIHODOV: I should be desirous to speak with you alone. [*Sighs*]

DUNYASHA: [*Embarrassed*] Well—only bring me my mantle first. It's by the cupboard. It's rather damp here.

EPIHODOV: Certainly. I will fetch it. Now I know what I must do with my revolver. [*Takes guitar and goes off playing on it*]

YASHA: Two and twenty misfortunes! Between ourselves, he's a fool. [*Yawns*]

DUNYASHA: God grant he doesn't shoot himself! [*A pause*] I am so nervous, I'm always in a flutter. I was a little girl when I was taken into our lady's house, and now I have quite grown out of peasant ways, and my hands are white, as white as a lady's. I'm such a delicate, sensitive creature, I'm afraid of everything. I'm so frightened. And if you deceive me, Yasha, I don't know what will become of my nerves.

YASHA: [*Kisses her*] You're a peach! Of course a girl must never forget herself; what I dislike more than anything is a girl being flighty in her behavior.

DUNYASHA: I'm passionately in love with you, Yasha; you are a man of culture—you can give your opinion about anything. [*A pause*]

YASHA: [*Yawns*] Yes, that's so. My opinion is this: if a girl loves anyone, that means that she has no principles. [*A pause*] It's pleasant smoking a cigar in the open air. [*Listens*] Someone's coming this way . . . it's the gentlefolk. [Dunyasha *embraces him impulsively*] Go home, as though you had been to the river to bathe; go by that path, or else they'll meet you and suppose I have made an appointment with you here. That I can't endure.

DUNYASHA: [*Coughing softly*] The cigar has made my head ache. . . . [*Goes off*]

[Yasha *remains sitting near the shrine. Enter* Lyubov Andreyevna, Gaev *and* Lopahin]

LOPAHIN: You must make up your mind once for all—there's no time to lose. It's quite a simple question, you know. Will you consent to letting the land for building or not? One word in answer: Yes or no? Only one word!

LYUBOV: Who is smoking such horrible cigars here? [*Sits down*]

GAEV: Now the railway line has been brought near, it's made things very convenient. [*Sits down*] Here we have been over and lunched in town. Cannon off the white! I should like to go home and have a game.

LYUBOV: You have plenty of time.

LOPAHIN: Only one word! [*Beseechingly*] Give me an answer!

GAEV: [*Yawning*] What do you say?

LYUBOV: [*Looks in her purse*] I had quite a lot of money here yesterday, and there's scarcely any left to-day. My poor Varya feeds us all on milk soup for the sake of economy; the old folks in the kitchen get nothing but pease pudding, while I waste my money in a senseless way. [*Drops purse, scattering gold pieces*] There, they have all fallen out! [*Annoyed*]

YASHA: Allow me, I'll soon pick them up. [*Collects the coins*]

LYUBOV: Pray do, Yasha. And what did I go off to the town to lunch for? Your restaurant's a wretched place with its music and the tablecloth smelling of soap. . . . Why drink so much, Leonid? And eat so much? And talk so much? To-day you talked a great deal again in the restaurant, and all so inappropriately. About the era of the seventies, about the decadents. And to whom? Talking to waiters about decadents!

LOPAHIN: Yes.

GAEV: [*Waving his hand*] I'm incorrigible; that's evident. [*Irritably to* Yasha] Why is it you keep fidgeting about in front of us!

YASHA: [*Laughs*] I can't help laughing when I hear your voice.

GAEV: [*To his sister*] Either I or he. . . .

LYUBOV: Get along! Go away, Yasha.

YASHA: [*Gives* Lyubov Andreyevna *her purse*] Directly. [*Hardly able to suppress his laughter*] This minute. . . . [*Goes off*]

LOPAHIN: Deriganov, the millionaire, means to buy your estate. They say he is coming to the sale himself.

LYUBOV: Where did you hear that?

LOPAHIN: That's what they say in town.

GAEV: Our aunt in Yaroslavl has promised to send help; but when, and how much she will send, we don't know.

LOPAHIN: How much will she send? A hundred thousand? Two hundred?

LYUBOV: Oh, well! . . . Ten or fifteen thousand, and we must be thankful to get that.

LOPAHIN: Forgive me, but such reckless people as you are—such queer, unbusiness-like people—I never met in my life. One tells you in plain Russian your estate is going to be sold, and you seem not to understand it.

LYUBOV: What are we to do? Tell us what to do.

LOPAHIN: I do tell you every day. Every day I say the same thing. You absolutely must let the cherry orchard and the land on building leases; and do it at once, as quick as may be—the auction's close upon us! Do understand! Once make up your mind to build villas, and you can raise as much money as you like, and then you are saved.

LYUBOV: Villas and summer visitors—forgive me saying so—it's so vulgar.

GAEV: There I perfectly agree with you.

LOPAHIN: I shall sob, or scream, or fall into a fit. I can't stand it! You drive me mad! [*To* Gaev] You're an old woman!

GAEV: What do you say?

LOPAHIN: An old woman! [*Gets up to go*]

LYUBOV: [*In dismay*] No, don't go! Do stay, my dear friend! Perhaps we shall think of something.

LOPAHIN: What is there to think of?

LYUBOV: Don't go, I entreat you! With you here it's more cheerful, anyway. [*A pause*] I keep expecting something, as though the house were going to fall about our ears.

GAEV: [*In profound dejection*] Potted the white! It fails—a kiss.

LYUBOV: We have been great sinners. . . .

LOPAHIN: You have no sins to repent of.

GAEV: [*Puts a caramel in his mouth*] They say I've eaten up my property in caramels. [*Laughs*]

LYUBOV: Oh, my sins! I've always thrown my money away recklessly like a lunatic. I married a man who made nothing but debts. My husband died of champagne—he drank dreadfully. To my misery I loved another man, and immediately—it was my first punishment—the blow fell upon me, here, in the river . . . my boy was drowned and I went abroad—went away for ever, never to return, not to see that river again . . . I shut my eyes, and fled, distracted, and *he* after me . . . pitilessly, brutally. I bought a villa at Mentone, for *he* fell ill there, and for three years I had no rest day or night. His illness wore me out, my soul was dried up. And last year, when my villa was sold to pay my debts, I went to Paris and there he robbed me of everything and abandoned me for another woman; and I tried to poison myself. . . . So stupid, so shameful! . . . And suddenly I felt a yearning for Russia, for my country, for my little girl. . . . [*Dries her tears*] Lord, Lord, be merciful! Forgive my sins! Do not chastise me more! [*Takes a telegram out of her pocket*] I got this to-day from Paris. He implores forgiveness, entreats me to return. [*Tears up the telegram*] I fancy there is music somewhere. [*Listens*]

GAEV: That's our famous Jewish orchestra. You remember, four violins, a flute and a double bass.

LYUBOV: That still in existence? We ought to send for them one evening, and give a dance.

LOPAHIN: [*Listens*] I can't hear. . . . [*Hums softly*] "For money the Germans will turn a Russian into a Frenchman." [*Laughs*] I did see such a piece at the theater yesterday! It was funny!

LYUBOV: And most likely there was nothing funny in it. You shouldn't look at plays, you should look at yourselves a little oftener. How gray your lives are! How much nonsense you talk.

LOPAHIN: That's true. One may say honestly, we live a fool's life. [*Pause*] My father was a peasant, an idiot; he knew nothing and taught me nothing, only beat me when he was drunk, and always with his stick. In reality I am just such another blockhead and idiot. I've learnt nothing properly. I write a wretched hand. I write so that I feel ashamed before folks, like a pig.

LYUBOV: You ought to get married, my dear fellow.

LOPAHIN: Yes . . . that's true.

LYUBOV: You should marry our Varya. she's a good girl.

LOPAHIN: Yes.

LYUBOV: She's a good-natured girl, she's busy all day long, and what's more, she loves you. And you have liked her for ever so long.

LOPAHIN: Well? I'm not against it. . . . She's a good girl. [Pause]

GAEV: I've been offered a place in the bank: 6,000 roubles a year. Did you know?

LYUBOV: You would never do for that! You must stay as you are.

[Enter Firs with overcoat]

FIRS: Put it on, sir, it's damp.

GAEV: [Putting it on] You bother me, old fellow.

FIRS: You can't go on like this. You went away in the morning without leaving word. [Looks him over]

LYUBOV: You look older, Firs!

FIRS: What is your pleasure?

LOPAHIN: You look older, she said.

FIRS: I've had a long life. They were arranging my wedding before your papa was born. . . . [Laughs] I was the head footman before the emancipation came. I wouldn't consent to be set free then; I stayed on with the old master. . . . [A pause] I remember what rejoicings they made and didn't know themselves what they were rejoicing over.

LOPAHIN: Those were fine old times. There was flogging anyway.

FIRS: [Not hearing] To be sure! The peasants knew their place, and the masters knew theirs; but now they're all at sixes and sevens, there's no making it out.

GAEV: Hold your tongue, Firs. I must go to town to-morrow. I have been promised an introduction to a general, who might let us have a loan.

LOPAHIN: You won't bring that off. And you won't pay your arrears, you may rest assured of that.

LYUBOV: That's all his nonsense. There is no such general.

[Enter Trofimov, Anya and Varya]

GAEV: Here come our girls.

ANYA: There's mamma on the seat.

LYUBOV: [Tenderly] Come here, come along. My darlings! [Embraces Anya and Varya] If you only knew how I love you both. Sit beside me, there, like that. [All sit down]

LOPAHIN: Our perpetual student is always with the young ladies.

TROFIMOV: That's not your business.

LOPAHIN: He'll soon be fifty, and he's still a student.

TROFIMOV: Drop your idiotic jokes.

LOPAHIN: Why are you so cross, you queer fish?

TROFIMOV: Oh, don't persist!

LOPAHIN: [Laughs] Allow me to ask you what's your idea of me?

TROFIMOV: I'll tell you my idea of you. Yermolay Alexeyevitch: you are a rich man, you'll soon be a millionaire. Well, just as in the economy of nature a wild beast is of use, who devours everything that comes in his way, so you too have your use.

[All laugh]

VARYA: Better tell us something about the planets, Petya.

LYUBOV: No, let us go on with the conversation we had yesterday.

TROFIMOV: What was it about?

GAEV: About pride.

TROFIMOV: We had a long conversation yesterday, but we came to no conclusion. In pride, in your sense of it, there is something mystical. Perhaps you are right from your point of view; but if one looks at it simply, without subtlety, what sort of pride can there be, what sense is there in it, if man in his-physiological formation is very imperfect, if in the immense majority of cases he is coarse, dull-witted, profoundly unhappy? One must give up glorification of self. One should work, and nothing else.

GAEV: One must die in any case.

TROFIMOV: Who knows? And what does it mean —dying? Perhaps man has a hundred senses, and only the five we know are lost at death, while the other ninety-five remain alive.

LYUBOV: How clever you are, Petya!

LOPAHIN: [Ironically] Fearfully clever!

TROFIMOV: Humanity progresses, perfecting its powers. Everything that is beyond its ken now will one day become familiar and comprehensible; only we must work, we must with all our powers aid the seeker after truth. Here among us in Russia the workers are few in number as yet. The vast majority of the intellectual people I know, seek nothing, do nothing, are not fit as yet for work of any kind. They call themselves intellectual, but they treat their servants as inferiors, behave to the peasants as though they were animals, learn little, read nothing seriously, do practically nothing, only talk about science and know very little about art. They are all serious people, they all have severe faces, they all talk of weighty matters and air their theories, and yet the vast majority of us—ninety-nine per cent.— live like savages, at the least thing fly to blows and abuse, eat piggishly, sleep in filth and stuffiness, bugs everywhere, stench and damp and moral impurity. And it's clear all our fine talk is only to divert our attention and other people's. Show me where to find the crèches there's so much talk about, and the reading-rooms? They only exist in novels: in real life there are none of them. There is nothing but filth and vulgarity and Asiatic apathy. I fear and dislike very serious faces. I'm afraid of serious conversation. We should do better to be silent.

LOPAHIN: You know, I get up at five o'clock in the morning, and I work from morning to night; and I've money, my own and other people's, always passing through my hands, and I see what people are made of all round me. One has only to begin to do anything to see how few honest decent people there are. Sometimes when I lie awake at night, I think: "Oh! Lord, thou hast given us immense forests, boundless plains, the widest horizons, and living here we ourselves ought really to be giants."

LYUBOV: You ask for giants! They are no good except in story-books; in real life they frighten us.

[Epihodov *advances in the background, playing on the guitar*]

LYUBOV: [*Dreamily*] There goes Epihodov.

ANYA: [*Dreamily*] There goes Epihodov.

GAEV: The sun has set, my friends.

TROFIMOV: Yes.

GAEV: [*Not loudly, but, as it were, declaiming*] O nature, divine nature, thou art bright with eternal luster, beautiful and indifferent! Thou, whom we call mother, thou dost unite within thee life and death! Thou dost give life and dost destroy!

VARYA: [*In a tone of supplication*] Uncle!

ANYA: Uncle, you are at it again!

TROFIMOV: You'd much better be cannoning off the red!

GAEV: I'll hold my tongue, I will.

[*All sit plunged in thought. Perfect stillness. The only thing audible is the muttering of* Firs. *Suddenly there is a sound in the distance, as it were from the sky—the sound of a breaking harp-string, mournfully dying away*]

LYUBOV: What is that?

LOPAHIN: I don't know. Somewhere far away a bucket fallen and broken in the pits. But somewhere very far away.

GAEV: It might be a bird of some sort—such as a heron.

TROFIMOV: Or an owl.

LYUBOV: [*Shudders*] I don't know why, but it's horrid. [*A pause*]

FIRS: It was the same before the calamity—the owl hooted and the samovar hissed all the time.

GAEV: Before what calamity?

FIRS: Before the emancipation. [*A pause*]

LYUBOV: Come, my friends, let us be going; evening is falling. [*To* Anya] There are tears in your eyes. What is it, darling? [*Embraces her*]

ANYA: Nothing, mamma; it's nothing.

TROFIMOV: There is somebody coming.

[*The* Wayfarer *appears in a shabby white forage cap and an overcoat; he is slightly drunk*]

WAYFARER: Allow me to inquire, can I get to the station this way?

GAEV: Yes. Go along that road.

WAYFARER: I thank you most feelingly. [*Coughing*] The weather is superb. [*Declaims*] My brother, my suffering brother! . . . Come out to the Volga! Whose groan do you hear? . . . [*To* Varya] Mademoiselle, vouchsafe a hungry Russian thirty kopecks.

[Varya *utters a shriek of alarm*]

LOPAHIN: [*Angrily*] There's a right and a wrong way of doing everything!

LYUBOV: [*Hurriedly*] Here, take this. [*Looks in her purse*] I've no silver. No matter—here's gold for you.

WAYFARER: I thank you most feelingly! [*Goes off*] [*Laughter*]

VARYA: [*Frightened*] I'm going home—I'm going. . . . Oh, mamma, the servants have nothing to eat, and you gave him gold!

LYUBOV: There's no doing anything with me. I'm so silly! When we get home, I'll give you all I possess. Yermolay Alexeyevitch, you will lend me some more! . . .

LOPAHIN: I will.

LYUBOV: Come, friends, it's time to be going. And Varya, we have made a match of it for you. I congratulate you.

VARYA: [*Through her tears*] Mamma, that's not a joking matter.

LOPAHIN: "Ophelia, get thee to a nunnery!"

GAEV: My hands are trembling; it's a long while since I had a game of billiards.

LOPAHIN: "Ophelia! Nymph, in thy orisons be all my sins remember'd."

LYUBOV: Come, it will soon be supper-time.

VARYA: How he frightened me! My heart's simply throbbing.

LOPAHIN: Let me remind you, ladies and gentlemen: on the 22nd of August the cherry orchard will be sold. Think about that! Think about it!

[*All go off, except* Trofimov *and* Anya]

ANYA: [*Laughing*] I'm grateful to the wayfarer! He frightened Varya and we are left alone.

TROFIMOV: Varya's afraid we shall fall in love with each other, and for days together she won't leave us. With her narrow brain she can't grasp that we are above love. To eliminate the petty and transitory which hinder us from being free and happy—that is the aim and meaning of our life. Forward! We go forward irresistibly towards the bright star that shines yonder in the distance. Forward! Do not lag behind, friends.

ANYA: [*Claps her hands*] How well you speak! [*A pause*] It is divine here to-day.

TROFIMOV: Yes, it's glorious weather.

ANYA: Somehow, Petya, you've made me so that I don't love the cherry orchard as I used to. I used to love it so dearly. I used to think that there was no spot on earth like our garden.

TROFIMOV: All Russia is our garden. The earth is great and beautiful—there are many beautiful places in it. [*A pause*] Think only, Anya, your grandfather, and great-grandfather, and all your ancestors were slave-owners—the owners of living souls—and from every cherry in the orchard, from every leaf, from every trunk there are human creatures looking at you. Cannot you hear their voices? Oh, it is awful! Your orchard is a fearful thing, and when in the evening or at night one walks about the orchard, the old bark on the trees glimmers dimly in the dusk, and the old cherry trees seem to be dreaming of centuries gone by and tortured by fearful visions. Yes! We are at least two hundred years behind, we have really gained nothing yet, we have no definite attitude to the past, we do nothing but theorize or complain of depression or drink vodka. It is clear that to begin to live in the present, we must first expiate our past; we must break with it; and we can expiate it only by suffering, by extraordinary unceasing labor. Understand that, Anya.

ANYA: The house we live in has long ceased to be our own, and I shall leave it, I give you my word.

TROFIMOV: If you have the house keys, fling them into the well and go away. Be free as the wind.

ANYA: [*In ecstasy*] How beautifully you said that!

TROFIMOV: Believe me, Anya, believe me! I am not thirty yet, I am young, I am still a student, but I have gone through so much already! As soon as winter comes I am hungry, sick, careworn, poor as a beggar, and what ups and downs of fortune have I not known! And my soul was always, every minute, day and night, full of inexplicable forebodings. I have a foreboding of happiness, Anya. I see glimpses of it already.

ANYA: [*Pensively*] The moon is rising.

[*Epihodov is heard playing still the same mournful song on the guitar. The moon rises. Somewhere near the poplars* Varya *is looking for* Anya *and calling* "Anya! where are you?"]

TROFIMOV: Yes, the moon is rising. [*A pause*] Here is happiness—here it comes! It is coming nearer and nearer; already I can hear its footsteps. And if we never see it—if we may never know it—what does it matter? Others will see it after us.

VARYA'S VOICE: Anya! Where are you?

TROFIMOV: That Varya again! [*Angrily*] It's revolting!

ANYA: Well, let's go down to the river. It's lovely there.

TROFIMOV: Yes, let's go. [*They go*]

VARYA'S VOICE: Anya! Anya!

CURTAIN.

ACT III.

A drawing-room divided by an arch from a larger drawing-room. A chandelier burning. The Jewish orchestra, the same that was mentioned in Act II, is heard playing in the ante-room. It is evening. In the larger drawing-room they are dancing the grand chain. The voice of Semyonov-Pishtchik: "Promenade à une paire!" *Then enter the drawing-room in couples first* Pishtchik *and* Charlotta Ivanova, *then* Trofimov *and* Lyubov Andreyevna, *thirdly* Anya *with the* Post-Office Clerk, *fourthly* Varya *with the* Station Master, *and other guests.* Varya *is quietly weeping and wiping away her tears as she dances. In the last couple is* Dunyasha. *They move across the drawing-room.* Pishtchik *shouts:* "Grand rond, balancez!" *and* "Les Cavaliers à genou et remerciez vos dames."

Firs *in a swallow-tail coat brings in seltzer water on a tray.* Pishtchik *and* Trofimov *enter the drawing-room.*

PISHTCHIK: I am a full-blooded man; I have already had two strokes. Dancing's hard work for me, but as they say, if you're in the pack, you must bark with the rest. I'm as strong, I may say, as a horse. My parent, who would have his joke—may the Kingdom of Heaven be his!—used to say about our origin that the ancient stock of the Semyonov-Pishtchiks was derived from the very horse that Caligula made a member of the senate. [*Sits down*] But I've no money, that's where the mischief is. A hungry dog believes in nothing but meat. [*Snores, but at once wakes up*] That's like me . . . I can think of nothing but money.

TROFIMOV: There really is something horsy about your appearance.

PISHTCHIK: Well . . . a horse is a fine beast . . . a horse can be sold.

[*There is the sound of billiards being played in an adjoining room.* Varya *appears in the arch leading to the larger drawing-room*]

TROFIMOV: [*Teasing*] Madame Lopahin! Madame Lopahin!

VARYA: [*Angrily*] Mangy-looking gentleman!

TROFIMOV: Yes, I am a mangy-looking gentleman, and I'm proud of it!

VARYA: [*Pondering bitterly*] Here we have hired musicians and nothing to pay them! [*Goes out*]

TROFIMOV: [*To* Pishtchik] If the energy you have wasted during your lifetime in trying to find the money to pay your interest had gone to something else, you might in the end have turned the world upside down.

PISHTCHIK: Nietzsche, the philosopher, a very great and celebrated man . . . of enormous intellect . . . says in his works, that one can make forged bank-notes.

TROFIMOV: Why, have you read Nietzsche?

PISHTCHIK: What next . . . Dashenka told me. . . . And now I am in such a position, I might just as well forge banknotes. The day after to-morrow I must pay 310 roubles—130 I have procured. [*Feels in his pockets, in alarm*] The money's gone! I have lost my money! [*Through his tears*] Where's the money? [*Gleefully*] Why, here it is behind the lining. . . . It has made me hot all over.

[*Enter* Lyubov Andreyevna *and* Charlotta Ivanova]

LYUBOV: [*Hums the* Lezginka] Why is Leonid so long? What can he be doing in town? [*To* Dunyasha] Offer the musicians some tea.

TROFIMOV: The sale hasn't taken place, most likely.

LYUBOV: It's the wrong time to have the orchestra, and the wrong time to give a dance. Well, never mind. [*Sits down and hums softly*]

CHARLOTTA: [*Gives* Pishtchik *a pack of cards*] Here's a pack of cards. Think of any card you like.

PISHTCHIK: I've thought of one.

CHARLOTTA: Shuffle the pack now. That's right. Give it here, my dear Mr. Pishtchik. *Ein, zwei, drei* —now look, it's in your breast pocket.

PISHTCHIK: [*Taking a card out of his breast pocket*] The eight of spades! Perfectly right! [*Wonderingly*] Fancy that now!

CHARLOTTA: [*Holding pack of cards in her hands, to* Trofimov] Tell me quickly which is the top card.

TROFIMOV: Well, the queen of spades.

CHARLOTTA: It is! [*To* Pishtchik] Well, which card is uppermost?

PISHTCHIK: The ace of hearts.

CHARLOTTA: It is! [*Claps her hands, pack of cards disappears*] Ah! what lovely weather it is to-day!

[*A mysterious feminine voice which seems coming out of the floor answers her.* "Oh, yes, it's magnificent weather, madam"]

CHARLOTTA: You are my perfect ideal.

VOICE: And I greatly admire you too, madam.

STATION MASTER: [*Applauding*] The lady ventriloquist—bravo!

PISHTCHIK: [*Wonderingly*] Fancy that now! Most enchanting Charlotta Ivanovna. I'm simply in love with you.

CHARLOTTA: In love? [*Shrugging shoulders*] What do you know of love, *guter Mensch, aber schlechter Musikant.*

TROFIMOV: [*Pats* Pishtchik *on the shoulder*] You dear old horse. . . .

CHARLOTTA: Attention, please! Another trick! [*Takes a traveling rug from a chair*] Here's a very good rug; I want to sell it. [*Shaking it out*] Doesn't anyone want to buy it?

PISHTCHIK: [*Wonderingly*] Fancy that!

CHARLOTTA: *Ein, zwei, drei!* [*Quickly picks up rug she has dropped; behind the rug stands* Anya; *she makes a curtsey, runs to her mother, embraces her and runs back into the larger drawing-room amidst general enthusiasm*]

LYUBOV: [*Applauds*] Bravo! Bravo!

CHARLOTTA: Now again! *Ein, zwei, drei!* [*Lifts up the rug; behind the rug stands* Varya, *bowing*]

PISHTCHIK: [*Wonderingly*] Fancy that now!

CHARLOTTA: That's the end. [*Throws the rug at* Pishtchik, *makes a curtsey, runs into the larger drawing-room*]

PISHTCHIK: [*Hurries after her*] Mischievous creature! Fancy! [*Goes out*]

LYUBOV: And still Leonid doesn't come. I can't understand what he's doing in the town so long! Why, everything must be over by now. The estate is sold, or the sale has not taken place. Why keep us so long in suspense?

VARYA: [*Trying to console her*] Uncle's bought it. I feel sure of that.

TROFIMOV: [*Ironically*] Oh, yes!

VARYA: Great-aunt sent him an authorization to buy it in her name, and transfer the debt. She's doing it for Anya's sake, and I'm sure God will be merciful. Uncle will buy it.

LYUBOV: My aunt in Yaroslavl sent fifteen thousand to buy the estate in her name, she doesn't trust us—but that's not enough even to pay the arrears. [*Hides her face in her hands*] My fate is being sealed to-day, my fate. . . .

TROFIMOV: [*Teasing* Varya] Madame Lopahin.

VARYA: [*Angrily*] Perpetual student! Twice already you've been sent down from the University.

LYUBOV: Why are you angry, Varya? He's teasing you about Lopahin. Well, what of that? Marry Lopahin if you like, he's a good man, and interesting; if you don't want to, don't! Nobody compels you, darling.

VARYA: I must tell you plainly, mamma, I look at the matter seriously; he's a good man, I like him.

LYUBOV: Well, marry him. I can't see what you're waiting for.

VARYA: Mamma. I can't make him an offer myself. For the last two years, everyone's been talking to me about him. Everyone talks; but he says nothing or else makes a joke. I see what it means. He's growing rich, he's absorbed in business, he has no thoughts for me. If I had money, were it ever so little, if I had only a hundred roubles, I'd throw everything up and go far away. I would go into a nunnery.

TROFIMOV: What bliss!

VARYA: [*To* Trofimov] A student ought to have sense! [*In a soft tone with tears*] How ugly you've grown, Petya! How old you look! [*To* Lyubov Andreyevna, *no longer crying*] But I can't do without work, mamma; I must have something to do every minute.

[*Enter* Yasha]

YASHA: [*Hardly restraining his laughter*] Epihodov has broken a billiard cue! [*Goes out*]

VARYA: What is Epihodov doing here? Who gave him leave to play billiards? I can't make these people out. [*Goes out*]

LYUBOV: Don't tease her, Petya. You see she has grief enough without that.

TROFIMOV: She is so very officious, meddling in what's not her business. All the summer she's given Anya and me no peace. She's afraid of a love affair between us. What's it to do with her? Besides, I have given no grounds for it. Such triviality is not in my line. We are above love!

LYUBOV: And I suppose I am beneath love. [*Very uneasily*] Why is it Leonid's not here? If only I could know whether the estate is sold or not! It seems such an incredible calamity that I really don't know what to think. I am distracted . . . I shall scream in a minute . . . I shall do something stupid. Save me, Petya, tell me something, talk to me!

TROFIMOV: What does it matter whether the estate

is sold to-day or not? That's all done with long ago. There's no turning back, the path is overgrown. Don't worry yourself, dear Lyubov Andreyevna. You mustn't deceive yourself; for once in your life you must face the truth!

LYUBOV: What truth? You see where the truth lies, but I seem to have lost my sight, I see nothing. You settle every great problem so boldly, but tell me, my dear boy, isn't it because you're young—because you haven't yet understood one of your problems through suffering? You look forward boldly, and isn't it that you don't see and don't expect anything dreadful because life is still hidden from your young eyes? You're bolder, more honest, deeper than we are, but think, be just a little magnanimous, have pity on me. I was born here, you know, my father and mother lived here, my grandfather lived here, I love this house. I can't conceive of life without the cherry orchard, and if it really must be sold, then sell me with the orchard. [*Embraces* Trofimov, *kisses him on the forehead*] My boy was drowned here. [*Weeps*] Pity me, my dear kind fellow.

TROFIMOV: You know I feel for you with all my heart.

LYUBOV: But that should have been said differently, so differently. [*Takes out her handkerchief, telegram falls on the floor*] My heart is so heavy to-day. It's so noisy here, my soul is quivering at every sound, I'm shuddering all over, but I can't go away; I'm afraid to be quiet and alone. Don't be hard on me, Petya . . . I love you as though you were one of ourselves. I would gladly let you marry Anya—I swear I would—only, my dear boy, you must take your degree, you do nothing—you're simply tossed by fate from place to place. That's so strange. It is, isn't it? And you must do something with your beard to make it grow somehow. [*Laughs*] You look so funny!

TROFIMOV: [*Picks up the telegram*] I've no wish to be a beauty.

LYUBOV: That's a telegram from Paris. I get one every day. One yesterday and one to-day. That savage creature is ill again, he's in trouble again. He begs forgiveness, beseeches me to go, and really I ought to go to Paris to see him. You look shocked, Petya. What am I to do, my dear boy, what am I to do? He is ill, he is alone and unhappy, and who'll look after him, who'll keep him from doing the wrong thing, who'll give him his medicine at the right time? And why hide it or be silent? I love him, that's clear. I love him! I love him! He's a millstone about my neck, I'm going to the bottom with him, but I love that stone and can't live without it. [*Presses* Trofimov's *hand*] Don't think ill of me, Petya, don't tell me anything, don't tell me. . . .

TROFIMOV: [*Through his tears*] For God's sake forgive my frankness: why, he robbed you!

LYUBOV: No! No! No! You mustn't speak like that. [*Covers her ears*]

TROFIMOV: He is a wretch! You're the only person that doesn't know it! He's a worthless creature! A despicable wretch!

LYUBOV: [*Getting angry, but speaking with restraint*] You're twenty-six or twenty-seven years old, but you're still a schoolboy.

TROFIMOV: Possibly.

LYUBOV: You should be a man at your age! You should understand what love means! And you ought to be in love yourself. You ought to fall in love! [*Angrily*] Yes, yes, and it's not purity in you, you're simply a prude, a comic fool, a freak.

TROFIMOV: [*In horror*] The things she's saying!

LYUBOV: I am above love! You're not above love, but simply as our Firs here says, "You are a good-for-nothing." At your age not to have a mistress!

TROFIMOV: [*In horror*] This is awful! The things she is saying! [*Goes rapidly into the larger drawing-room clutching his head*] This is awful! I can't stand it! I'm going. [*Goes off, but at once returns*] All is over between us! [*Goes off into the ante-room*]

LYUBOV: [*Shouts after him*] Petya! Wait a minute! You funny creature! I was joking! Petya! [*There is a sound of somebody running quickly downstairs and suddenly falling with a crash.* Anya *and* Varya *scream, but there is a sound of laughter at once*]

LYUBOV: What has happened?

[Anya *runs in*]

ANYA: [*Laughing*] Petya's fallen downstairs! [*Runs out*]

LYUBOV: What a queer fellow that Petya is!

[*The* Station Master *stands in the middle of the larger room and reads* The Magdalene, *by Alexey Tolstoy. They listen to him, but before he has recited many lines strains of a waltz are heard from the ante-room and the reading is broken off. All dance.* Trofimov, Anya, Varya *and* Lyubov Andreyevna *come in from the ante-room*]

LYUBOV: Come, Petya—come, pure heart! I beg your pardon. Let's have a dance! [*Dances with* Petya]

[Anya *and* Varya *dance.* Firs *comes in, puts his stick down near the side door.* Yasha *also comes into the drawing-room and looks on at the dancing*]

YASHA: What is it, old man?

FIRS: I don't feel well. In old days we used to have generals, barons and admirals dancing at our balls, and now we send for the post-office clerk and the station master and even they're not overanxious to come. I am getting feeble. The old master, the grandfather, used to give sealing-wax for all complaints. I have been taking sealing-wax for twenty years or more. Perhaps that's what's kept me alive.

YASHA: You bore me, old man! [*Yawns*] It's time you were done with.

FIRS: Ach, you're a good-for-nothing! [*Mutters*]

[Trofimov *and* Lyubov Andreyevna *dance in larger room and then on to the stage*]

LYUBOV: *Merci.* I'll sit down a little. [*Sits down*] I'm tired.

[*Enter* Anya]

ANYA: [*Excitedly*] There's a man in the kitchen has been saying that the cherry orchard's been sold to-day.

LYUBOV: Sold to whom?

ANYA: He didn't say to whom. He's gone away.

[*She dances with* Trofimov, *and they go off into the larger room*]

YASHA: There was an old man gossiping there, a stranger.

FIRS: Leonid Andreyevitch isn't here yet, he hasn't come back. He has his light overcoat on, *demi-saison,* he'll catch cold for sure. *Ach!* Foolish young things!

LYUBOV: I feel as though I should die. Go, Yasha, find out to whom it has been sold.

YASHA: But he went away long ago, the old chap. [*Laughs*]

LYUBOV: [*With slight vexation*] What are you laughing at? What are you pleased at?

YASHA: Epihodov is so funny. He's a silly fellow, two and twenty misfortunes.

LYUBOV: Firs, if the estate is sold, where will you go?

FIRS: Where you bid me, there I'll go.

LYUBOV: Why do you look like that? Are you ill? You ought to be in bed.

FIRS: Yes. [*Ironically*] Me go to bed and who's to wait here? Who's to see to things without me? I'm the only one in all the house.

YASHA: [*To* Lyubov Andreyevna] Lyubov Andreyevna, permit me to make a request of you; if you go back to Paris again, be so kind as to take me with you. It's positively impossible for me to stay here. [*Looking about him; in an undertone*] There's no need to say it, you see for yourself—an uncivilized country, the people have no morals, and then the dullness! The food in the kitchen's abominable, and then Firs runs after one muttering all sorts of unsuitable words. Take me with you, please do!

[*Enter* Pishtchik]

PISHTCHIK: Allow me to ask you for a waltz, my dear lady. [Lyubov Andreyevna *goes with him*] Enchanting lady, I really must borrow of you just 180 roubles, [*dances*] only 180 roubles. [*They pass into the larger room*]

[*In the larger drawing-room, a figure in a gray top hat and in check trousers is gesticulating and jumping about. Shouts of* "Bravo, Charlotta Ivanovna"]

DUNYASHA: [*She has stopped to powder herself*] My young lady tells me to dance. There are plenty of gentlemen, and too few ladies, but dancing makes me giddy and makes my heart beat. Firs, the post-office clerk said something to me just now that quite took my breath away.

[*Music becomes more subdued*]

FIRS: What did he say to you?

DUNYASHA: He said I was like a flower.

YASHA: [*Yawns*] What ignorance! [*Goes out*]

DUNYASHA: Like a flower. I am a girl of such delicate feelings, I am awfully fond of soft speeches.

FIRS: Your head's being turned.

[*Enter* Epihodov]

EPIHODOV: You have no desire to see me. Dunyasha. I might be an insect. [*Sighs*] Ah! life!

DUNYASHA: What is it you want?

EPIHODOV: Undoubtedly you may be right. [*Sighs*] But, of course, if one looks at it from that point of view, if I may so express myself, you have, excuse my plain speaking, reduced me to a complete state of mind. I know my destiny. Every day some misfortune befalls me and I have long ago grown accustomed to it, so that I look upon my fate with a smile. You gave me your word, and though I——

DUNYASHA: Let us have a talk later, I entreat you, but now leave me in peace, for I am lost in reverie. [*Plays with her fan*]

EPIHODOV: I have a misfortune every day, and if I may venture to express myself, I merely smile at it, I even laugh.

[Varya *enters from the larger drawing-room*]

VARYA: You still have not gone, Epihodov. What a disrespectful creature you are, really! [*To* Dunyasha] Go along, Dunyasha! [*To* Epihodov] First you play billiards and break the cue, then you go wandering about the drawing-room like a visitor!

EPIHODOV: You really cannot, if I may so express myself, call me to account like this.

VARYA: I'm not calling you to account, I'm speaking to you. You do nothing but wander from place to place and don't do your work. We keep you as a counting-house clerk, but what use you are I can't say.

EPIHODOV: [*Offended*] Whether I work or whether I walk, whether I eat or whether I play billiards, is a matter to be judged by persons of understanding and my elders.

VARYA: You dare to tell me that! [*Firing up*] You dare! You mean to say I've no understanding. Begone from here! This minute!

EPIHODOV: [*Intimidated*] I beg you to express yourself with delicacy.

VARYA: [*Beside herself with anger*] This moment! get out! away! [*He goes towards the door, she following him*] Two and twenty misfortunes! Take yourself off! Don't let me set eyes on you! [Epihodov *has gone out, behind the door his voice,* "I shall lodge a complaint against you"] What! You're coming back? [*Snatches up the stick* Firs *has put down near the door*] Come! Come! Come! I'll show you! What! you're coming? Then take that! [*She swings the stick, at the very moment that* Lopahin *comes in*]

LOPAHIN: Very much obliged to you!

VARYA: [*Angrily and ironically*] I beg your pardon!

LOPAHIN: Not at all! I humbly thank you for your kind reception!

VARYA: No need of thanks for it. [*Moves away, then looks round and asks softly*] I haven't hurt you?

LOPAHIN: Oh, no! Not at all! There's an immense bump coming up, though!

VOICES FROM LARGER ROOM: Lopahin has come! Yermolay Alexeyevitch!

PISHTCHIK: What do I see and hear? [*Kisses Lopahin*] There's a whiff of cognac about you, my dear soul, and we're making merry here too!

[*Enter Lyubov Andreyevna*]

LYUBOV: Is it you, Yermolay Alexeyevitch? Why have you been so long? Where's Leonid?

LOPAHIN: Leonid Andreyevitch arrived with me. He is coming.

LYUBOV: [*In agitation*] Well! Well! Was there a sale? Speak!

LOPAHIN: [*Embarrassed, afraid of betraying his joy*] The sale was over at four o'clock. We missed our train—had to wait till half-past nine. [*Sighing heavily*] Ugh! I feel a little giddy.

[*Enter Gaev. In his right hand he has purchases, with his left hand he is wiping away his tears*]

LYUBOV: Well, Leonid? What news? [*Impatiently, with tears*] Make haste, for God's sake!

GAEV: [*Makes her no answer, simply waves his hand. To* Firs, *weeping*] Here, take them; there's anchovies, Kertch herrings. I have eaten nothing all day. What I have been through! [*Door into the billiard room is open. There is heard a knocking of balls and the voice of* Yasha *saying "Eighty-seven."* Gaev's *expression changes, he leaves off weeping*] I am fearfully tired. Firs, come and help me change my things. [*Goes to his own room across the larger drawing-room*]

PISHTCHIK: How about the sale? Tell us, do!

LYUBOV: Is the cherry orchard sold?

LOPAHIN: It is sold.

LYUBOV: Who has bought it?

LOPAHIN: I have bought it. [*A pause.* Lyubov *is crushed; she would fall down if she were not standing near a chair and table*]

[Varya *takes keys from her waistband, flings them on the floor in middle of drawing-room and goes out*]

LOPAHIN: I have bought it! Wait a bit, ladies and gentlemen, pray. My head's a bit muddled, I can't speak. [*Laughs*] We came to the auction. Deriganov was there already. Leonid Andreyevitch only had 15,000 and Deriganov bid 30,000, besides the arrears, straight off. I saw how the land lay. I bid against him. I bid 40,000, he bid 45,000, I said 55, and so he went on, adding 5 thousands and I adding 10. Well . . . So it ended. I bid 90, and it was knocked down to me. Now the cherry orchard's mine! Mine! [*Chuckles*] My God, the cherry or-

chard's mine! Tell me that I'm drunk, that I'm out of my mind, that it's all a dream. [*Stamps with his feet*] Don't laugh at me! If my father and my grandfather could rise from their graves and see all that has happened! How their Yermolay, ignorant, beaten Yermolay, who used to run about barefoot in winter, how that very Yermolay has bought the finest estate in the world! I have bought the estate where my father and grandfather were slaves, where they weren't even admitted into the kitchen. I am asleep, I am dreaming! It is all fancy, it is the work of your imagination plunged in the darkness of ignorance. [*Picks up keys, smiling fondly*] She threw away the keys; she means to show she's not the housewife now. [*Jingles the keys*] Well, no matter. [*The orchestra is heard tuning up*] Hey, musicians! Play! I want to hear you. Come, all of you, and look how Yermolay Lopahin will take the ax to the cherry orchard, how the trees will fall to the ground! We will build houses on it and our grandsons and great-grandsons will see a new life springing up there. Music! Play up!

[*Music begins to play.* Lyubov Andreyevna *has sunk into a chair and is weeping bitterly*]

LOPAHIN: [*Reproachfully*] Why, why didn't you listen to me? My poor friend! Dear lady, there's no turning back now. [*With tears*] Oh, if all this could be over, oh, if our miserable disjointed life could somehow soon be changed!

PISHTCHIK: [*Takes him by the arm, in an undertone*] She's weeping, let us go and leave her alone. Come. [*Takes him by the arm and leads him into the larger drawing-room*]

LOPAHIN: What's that? Musicians, play up! All must be as I wish it. [*With irony*] Here comes the new master, the owner of the cherry orchard! [*Accidentally tips over a little table, almost upsetting the candelabra*] I can pay for everything! [*Goes out with* Pishtchik. *No one remains on the stage or in the larger drawing-room except* Lyubov, *who sits huddled up, weeping bitterly. The music plays softly.* Anya *and* Trofimov *come in quickly.* Anya *goes up to her mother and falls on her knees before her.* Trofimov *stands at the entrance to the larger drawing-room*]

ANYA: Mamma! Mamma, you're crying, dear, kind, good mamma! My precious! I love you! I bless you! The cherry orchard is sold, it is gone, that's true, that's true! But don't weep, mamma! Life is still before you, you have still your good, pure heart! Let us go, let us go, darling, away from here! We will make a new garden, more splendid than this one; you will see it, you will understand. And joy, quiet, deep joy, will sink into your soul like the sun at evening! And you will smile, mamma! Come, darling, let us go!

CURTAIN.

ACT IV.

SCENE: *Same as in First Act. There are neither curtains on the windows nor pictures on the walls: only a little furniture remains piled up in a corner as if for sale. There is a sense of desolation; near the outer door and in the background of the scene are packed trunks, traveling bags, etc. On the left the door is open, and from here the voices of* Varya *and* Anya *are audible.* Lopahin *is standing waiting.* Yasha *is holding a tray with glasses full of champagne. In front of the stage* Epihodov *is tying up a box. In the background behind the scene a hum of talk from the peasants who have come to say good-bye. The voice of* Gaev: *"Thanks, brothers, thanks!"*

YASHA: The peasants have come to say good-bye. In my opinion, Yermolay Alexeyevitch, the peasants are good-natured, but they don't know much about things.

[*The hum of talk dies away. Enter across front of stage* Lyubov Andreyevna *and* Gaev. *She is not weeping, but is pale; her face is quivering—she cannot speak*]

GAEV: You gave them your purse, Lyuba. That won't do—that won't do!

LYUBOV: I couldn't help it! I couldn't help it!

[*Both go out*]

LOPAHIN: [*In the doorway, calls after them*] You will take a glass at parting? Please do. I didn't think to bring any from the town, and at the station I could only get one bottle. Please take a glass [*A pause*] What? You don't care for any? [*Comes away from the door*] If I'd known, I wouldn't have bought it. Well, and I'm not going to drink it. [Yasha *carefully sets the tray down on a chair*] You have a glass, Yasha, anyway.

YASHA: Good luck to the travelers, and luck to those that stay behind! [*Drinks*] This champagne isn't the real thing, I can assure you.

LOPAHIN: It cost eight roubles the bottle. [*A pause*] It's devilish cold here.

YASHA: They haven't heated the stove to-day—it's all the same since we're going. [*Laughs*]

LOPAHIN: What are you laughing for?

YASHA: For pleasure.

LOPAHIN: Though it's October, it's as still and sunny as though it were summer. It's just right for building! [*Looks at his watch; says in doorway*] Take note, ladies and gentlemen, the train goes in forty-seven minutes; so you ought to start for the station in twenty minutes. You must hurry up!

[Trofimov *comes in from out of doors wearing a great-coat*]

TROFIMOV: I think it must be time to start, the horses are ready. The devil only knows what's become of my goloshes; they're lost. [*In the doorway*] Anya! My goloshes aren't here. I can't find them.

LOPAHIN: And I'm getting off to Harkov. I am going in the same train with you. I'm spending all the winter at Harkov. I've been wasting all my time gossiping with you and fretting with no work to do. I can't get on without work. I don't know what to do with my hands, they flap about so queerly, as if they didn't belong to me.

TROFIMOV: Well, we're just going away, and you will take up your profitable labors again.

LOPAHIN: Do take a glass.

TROFIMOV: No, thanks.

LOPAHIN: Then you're going to Moscow now?

TROFIMOV: Yes. I shall see them as far as the town, and to-morrow I shall go on to Moscow.

LOPAHIN: Yes, I daresay, the professors aren't giving any lectures, they're waiting for your arrival.

TROFIMOV: That's not your business.

LOPAHIN: How many years have you been at the University?

TROFIMOV: Do think of something newer than that—that's stale and flat. [*Hunts for goloshes*] You know we shall most likely never see each other again, so let me give you one piece of advice at parting: don't wave your arms about—get out of the habit. And another thing, building villas, reckoning up that the summer visitors will in time become independent farmers—reckoning like that, that's not the thing to do either. After all, I am fond of you: you have fine delicate fingers like an artist, you've a fine delicate soul.

LOPAHIN: [*Embraces him*] Good-bye, my dear fellow. Thanks for everything. Let me give you money for the journey, if you need it.

TROFIMOV: What for? I don't need it.

LOPAHIN: Why, you haven't got a half-penny.

TROFIMOV: Yes, I have, thank you. I got some money for a translation. Here it is in my pocket, [*anxiously*] but where can my goloshes be!

VARYA: [*From the next room*] Take the nasty things! [*Flings a pair of goloshes on to the stage*]

TROFIMOV: Why are you so cross, Varya? h'm! . . . but those aren't my goloshes.

LOPAHIN: I sowed three thousand acres with poppies in the spring, and now I have cleared forty thousand profit. And when my poppies were in flower, wasn't it a picture! So here, as I say, I made forty thousand, and I'm offering you a loan because I can afford to. Why turn up your nose? I am a peasant—I speak bluntly.

TROFIMOV: Your father was a peasant, mine was a chemist—and that proves absolutely nothing whatever. [Lopahin *takes out his pocket-book*] Stop that—stop that. If you were to offer me two hundred thousand I wouldn't take it. I am an independent man, and everything that all of you, rich and poor alike, prize so highly and hold so dear, hasn't the slightest power over me—it's like so much fluff fluttering in the air. I can get on without you. I can pass by you. I am strong and proud. Humanity is advancing towards the highest truth, the highest happiness, which is possible on earth, and I am in the front ranks.

LOPAHIN: Will you get there?

TROFIMOV: I shall get there. [*A pause*] I shall get there, or I shall show others the way to get there.

[*In the distance is heard the stroke of an ax on a tree*]

LOPAHIN: Good-bye, my dear fellow; it's time to be off. We turn up our noses at one another, but life is passing all the while. When I am working hard without resting, then my mind is more at ease, and it seems to me as though I too know what I exist for; but how many people are in Russia, my dear boy, who exist, one doesn't know what for. Well, it doesn't matter. That's not what keeps things spinning. They tell me Leonid Andreyevitch has taken a situation. He is going to be a clerk at the bank—6,000 roubles a year. Only, of course, he won't stick to it—he's too lazy.

ANYA: [*In the doorway*] Mamma begs you not to let them chop down the orchard until she's gone.

TROFIMOV: Yes, really, you might have the tact. [*Walks out across the front of the stage*]

LOPAHIN: I'll see to it! I'll see to it! Stupid fellows! [*Goes out after him*]

ANYA: Has Firs been taken to the hospital?

YASHA: I told them this morning. No doubt they have taken him.

ANYA: [*To* Epihodov, *who passes across the drawing-room*] Semyon Pantaleyevitch, inquire, please, if Firs has been taken to the hospital.

YASHA: [*In a tone of offence*] I told Yegor this morning—why ask a dozen times?

EPIHODOV: Firs is advanced in years. It's my conclusive opinion no treatment would do him good; it's time he was gathered to his fathers. And I can only envy him. [*Puts a trunk down on a cardboard hat-box and crushes it*] There, now, of course—I knew it would be so.

YASHA: [*Jeeringly*] Two and twenty misfortunes!

VARYA: [*Through the door*] Has Firs been taken to the hospital?

ANYA: Yes.

VARYA: Why wasn't the note for the doctor taken too?

ANYA: Oh, then, we must send it after them. [*Goes out*]

VARYA: [*From the adjoining room*] Where's Yasha? Tell him his mother's come to say good-bye to him.

YASHA: [*Waves his hand*] They put me out of all patience! [Dunyasha *has all this time been busy about the luggage. Now, when* Yasha *is left alone, she goes up to him*]

DUNYASHA: You might just give me one look, Yasha. You're going away. You're leaving me. [*Weeps and throws herself on his neck*]

YASHA: What are you crying for? [*Drinks the champagne*] In six days I shall be in Paris again. To-morrow we shall get into the express train and

roll away in a flash. I can scarcely believe it! *Vive la France!* It doesn't suit me here—it's not the life for me; there's no doing anything. I have seen enough of the ignorance here. I have had enough of it. [*Drinks champagne*] What are you crying for? Behave yourself properly, and then you won't cry.

DUNYASHA: [*Powders her face, looking in a pocket-mirror*] Do send me a letter from Paris. You know how I loved you, Yasha—how I loved you! I am a tender creature, Yasha.

YASHA: Here they are coming!

[*Busies himself about the trunks, humming softly. Enter* Lyubov Andreyevna, Gaev, Anya *and* Charlotta Ivanovna]

GAEV: We ought to be off. There's not much time now. [*Looking at* Yasha] What a smell of herrings!

LYUBOV: In ten minutes we must get into the carriage. [*Casts a look about the room*] Farewell, dear house, dear old home of our fathers! Winter will pass and spring will come, and then you will be no more; they will tear you down! How much those walls have seen! [*Kisses her daughter passionately*] My treasure, how bright you look! Your eyes are sparkling like diamonds! Are you glad? Very glad?

ANYA: Very glad! A new life is beginning, mamma.

GAEV: Yes, really, everything is all right now. Before the cherry orchard was sold, we were all worried and wretched, but afterwards, when once the question was settled conclusively, irrevocably, we all felt calm and even cheerful. I am a bank clerk now —I am a financier—cannon off the red. And you, Lyuba, after all, you are looking better; there's no question of that.

LYUBOV: Yes. My nerves are better, that's true. [*Her hat and coat are handed to her*] I'm sleeping well. Carry out my things, Yasha. It's time. [*To* Anya] My darling, we shall soon see each other again. I am going to Paris. I can live there on the money your Yaroslavl auntie sent us to buy the estate with—hurrah for auntie!—but that money won't last long.

ANYA: You'll come back soon, mamma, won't you? I'll be working up for my examination in the high school, and when I have passed that, I shall set to work and be a help to you. We will read all sorts of things together, mamma, won't we? [*Kisses her mother's hands*] We will read in the autumn evenings. We'll read lots of books, and a new wonderful world will open out before us. [*Dreamily*] Mamma, come soon.

LYUBOV: I shall come, my precious treasure. [*Embraces her*]

[*Enter* Lopahin. Charlotta *softly hums a song*]

GAEV: Charlotta's happy; she's singing!

CHARLOTTA: [*Picks up a bundle like a swaddled baby*] Bye, bye, my baby. [*A baby is heard crying: "Ooah! ooah!"*] Hush, hush, my pretty boy! [*Ooah! ooah!*] Poor little thing! [*Throws the bundle back*]

You must please find me a situation. I can't go on like this.

LOPAHIN: We'll find you one, Charlotta Ivanovna. Don't you worry yourself.

GAEV: Everyone's leaving us. Varya's going away. We have become of no use all at once.

CHARLOTTA: There's nowhere for me to be in the town. I must go away. [Hums] What care I . . .

[Enter Pishtchik]

LOPAHIN: The freak of nature.

PISHTCHIK: [Gasping] Oh . . . let me get my breath. . . . I'm worn out . . . my most honored . . . Give me some water.

GAEV: Want some money, I suppose? Your humble servant! I'll go out of the way of temptation. [Goes out]

PISHTCHIK: It's a long while since I have been to see you . . . dearest lady. [To Lopahin] You are here . . . glad to see you . . . a man of immense intellect . . . take . . . here [gives Lopahin] 400 roubles. That leaves me owing 840.

LOPAHIN: [Shrugging his shoulders in amazement] It's like a dream. Where did you get it?

PISHTCHIK: Wait a bit . . . I'm hot . . . a most extraordinary occurrence! Some Englishmen came along and found in my land some sort of white clay. [To Lyubov Andreyevna] And 400 for you . . . most lovely . . . wonderful. [Gives money] The rest later. [Sips water] A young man in the train was telling me just now that a great philosopher advises jumping off a house-top. "Jump!" says he; "the whole gist of the problem lies in that." [Wonderingly] Fancy that, now! Water, please!

LOPAHIN: What Englishmen?

PISHTCHIK: I have made over to them the rights to dig the clay for twenty-four years . . . and now, excuse me . . . I can't stay . . . I must be trotting on. I'm going to Znoikovo . . . to Kardamanovo. . . . I'm in debt all round. [Sips] . . . To your very good health! . . . I'll come in on Thursday.

LYUBOV: We are just off to the town, and to-morrow I start for abroad.

PISHTCHIK: What! [In agitation] Why to the town? Oh, I see the furniture . . . the boxes. No matter . . . [Through his tears] . . . no matter . . . men of enormous intellect . . . these Englishmen. . . . Never mind . . . be happy. God will succor you . . . no matter . . . everything in this world must have an end. [Kisses Lyubov Andreyevna's hand] If the rumor reaches you that my end has come, think of this . . . old horse, and say: "There once was such a man in the world . . . Semyonov-Pishtchik . . . the Kingdom of Heaven be his!" . . . most extraordinary weather . . . yes. [Goes out in violent agitation, but at once returns and says in the doorway] Dashenka wishes to be remembered to you. [Goes out]

LYUBOV: Now we can start. I leave with two cares in my heart. The first is leaving Firs ill. [Looking at her watch] We have still five minutes.

ANYA: Mamma, Firs has been taken to the hospital. Yasha sent him off this morning.

LYUBOV: My other anxiety is Varya. She is used to getting up early and working; and now, without work, she's like a fish out of water. She is thin and pale, and she's crying, poor dear! [A pause] You are well aware, Yermolay Alexeyevitch, I dreamed of marrying her to you, and everything seemed to show that you would get married. [Whispers to Anya and motions to Charlotta and both go out] She loves you—she suits you. And I don't know—I don't know why it is you seem, as it were, to avoid each other. I can't understand it!

LOPAHIN: I don't understand it myself, I confess. It's queer somehow, altogether. If there's still time, I'm ready now at once. Let's settle it straight off, and go ahead; but without you, I feel I shan't make her an offer.

LYUBOV: That's excellent. Why, a single moment's all that's necessary. I'll call her at once.

LOPAHIN: And there's champagne all ready too. [Looking into the glasses] Empty! Someone's emptied them already. [Yasha coughs] I call that greedy.

LYUBOV: [Eagerly] Capital! We will go out. Yasha, allez! I'll call her in. [At the door] Varya, leave all that; come here. Come along! [Goes out with Yasha]

LOPAHIN: [Looking at his watch] Yes.

[A pause. Behind the door, smothered laughter and whispering, and, at last, enter Varya]

VARYA: [Looking a long while over the things] It is strange, I can't find it anywhere.

LOPAHIN: What are you looking for?

VARYA: I packed it myself, and I can't remember. [A pause]

LOPAHIN: Where are you going now, Varvara Mihailova?

VARYA: I? To the Ragulins. I have arranged to go to them to look after the house—as a housekeeper.

LOPAHIN: That's in Yashnovo? It'll be seventy miles away. [A pause] So this is the end of life in this house!

VARYA: [Looking among the things] Where is it? Perhaps I put it in the trunk. Yes, life in this house is over—there will be no more of it.

LOPAHIN: And I'm just off to Harkov—by this next train. I've a lot of business there. I'm leaving Epihodov here, and I've taken him on.

VARYA: Really!

LOPAHIN: This time last year we had snow already, if you remember; but now it's so fine and sunny. Though it's cold, to be sure—three degrees of frost.

VARYA: I haven't looked. [A pause] And besides, our thermometer's broken. [A pause]

[Voice at the door from the yard: "Yermolay Alexeyevitch!"]

LOPAHIN: [As though he had long been expecting this summons] This minute!

[Lopahin goes out quickly. Varya sitting on the floor and laying her head on a bag full of *clothes, sobs quietly. The door opens.* Lyubov Andreyevna *comes in cautiously*]

LYUBOV: Well? [*A pause*] We must be going.

VARYA: [*Has wiped her eyes and is no longer crying*] Yes, mamma, it's time to start. I shall have time to get to the Ragulins to-day, if only you're not late for the train.

LYUBOV: [*In the doorway*] Anya, put your things on.

[*Enter* Anya, *then* Gaev *and* Charlotta Ivanovna. Gaev *has on a warm coat with a hood. Servants and cabmen come in.* Epihodov *bustles about the luggage*]

LYUBOV: Now we can start on our travels.

ANYA: [*Joyfully*] On our travels!

GAEV: My friends—my dear, my precious friends! Leaving this house for ever, can I be silent? Can I refrain from giving utterance at leave-taking to those emotions which now flood all my being?

ANYA: [*Supplicatingly*] Uncle!

VARYA: Uncle, you mustn't!

GAEV: [*Dejectedly*] Cannon and into the pocket . . . I'll be quiet. . . .

[*Enter* Trofimov *and afterwards* Lopahin]

TROFIMOV: Well, ladies and gentlemen, we must start.

LOPAHIN: Epihodov, my coat!

LYUBOV: I'll stay just one minute. It seems as though I have never seen before what the walls, what the ceilings in this house were like, and now I look at them with greediness, with such tender love.

GAEV: I remember when I was six years old sitting in that window on Trinity Day watching my father going to church.

LYUBOV: Have all the things been taken?

LOPAHIN: I think all. [*Putting on overcoat, to* Epihodov] You, Epihodov, mind you see everything is right.

EPIHODOV: [*In a husky voice*] Don't you trouble, Yermolay Alexeyevitch.

LOPAHIN: Why, what's wrong with your voice?

EPIHODOV: I've just had a drink of water, and I choked over something.

YASHA: [*Contemptuously*] The ignorance!

LYUBOV: We are going—and not a soul will be left here.

LOPAHIN: Not till the spring.

VARYA: [*Pulls a parasol out of a bundle, as though about to hit someone with it.* Lopahin *makes a gesture as though alarmed*] What is it? I didn't mean anything.

TROFIMOV: Ladies and gentlemen, let us get into the carriage. It's time. The train will be in directly.

VARYA: Petya, here they are, your goloshes, by that box. [*With tears*] And what dirty old things they are!

TROFIMOV: [*Putting on his goloshes*] Let us go, friends!

GAEV: [*Greatly agitated, afraid of weeping*] The train—the station! Double baulk, ah!

LYUBOV: Let us go!

LOPAHIN: Are we all here? [*Locks the sidedoor on left*] The things are all here. We must lock up. Let us go!

ANYA: Good-bye, home! Good-bye to the old life!

TROFIMOV: Welcome to the new life!

[Trofimov *goes out with* Anya. Varya *looks round the room and goes out slowly.* Yasha *and* Charlotta Ivanovna, *with her dog, go out*]

LOPAHIN: Till the spring, then! Come, friends, till we meet! [*Goes out*]

[Lyubov Andreyevna *and* Gaev *remain alone. As though they had been waiting for this, they throw themselves on each other's necks, and break into subdued smothered sobbing, afraid of being overheard*]

GAEV: [*In despair*] Sister, my sister!

LYUBOV: Oh, my orchard!—my sweet, beautiful orchard! My life, my youth, my happiness, good-bye! good-bye!

VOICE OF ANYA: [*Calling gaily*] Mamma!

VOICE OF TROFIMOV: [*Gaily, excitedly*] Aa—oo!

LYUBOV: One last look at the walls, at the windows. My dear mother loved to walk about this room.

GAEV: Sister, sister!

VOICE OF ANYA: Mamma!

VOICE OF TROFIMOV: Aa—oo!

LYUBOV: We are coming. [*They go out*]

[*The stage is empty. There is the sound of the doors being locked up, then of the carriages driving away. There is silence. In the stillness there is the dull stroke of an ax in a tree, clanging with a mournful lonely sound. Footsteps are heard.* Firs *appears in the doorway on the right. He is dressed as always—in a pea-jacket and white waistcoat, with slippers on his feet. He is ill*]

FIRS: [*Goes up to the doors, and tries the handles*] Locked! They have gone . . . [*Sits down on sofa*] They have forgotten me. . . . Never mind . . . I'll sit here a bit. . . . I'll be bound Leonid Andreyevitch hasn't put his fur coat on and has gone off in his thin overcoat. [*Sighs anxiously*] I didn't see after him. . . . These young people . . . [*Mutters something that can't be distinguished*] Life has slipped by as though I hadn't lived. [*Lies down*] I'll lie down a bit. . . . There's no strength in you, nothing left you—all gone! Ech! I'm good for nothing. [*Lies motionless*]

[*A sound is heard that seems to come from the sky, like a breaking harp-string, dying away mournfully. All is still again, and there is heard nothing but the strokes of the ax far away in the orchard*]

CURTAIN.

Maxim Gorki

(1868–1936)

Paying tribute to the man whose pen-name means "Maxim the Bitter," Romain Rolland called Gorki "the man who, like Dante, emerged from hell, but not alone, and brought with him his companions in torment, his comrades in salvation." Gorki did precisely this in *The Lower Depths,* for which James Huneker found an apt description in the quotation from the Vulgate *"de profundis ad te clamavi."* "Out of the depths I cry unto Thee" might have been accepted by the playwright himself as a definition of his intent in much of his work, especially if the "Thee" is allowed to stand for the spirit of humanity instead of some supernatural agency. His humanitarianism early took the form of social protest and led him in time to engage in revolutionary activities that made him a fugitive from his country until the Russian Revolution turned him into the grand old man of Soviet letters. Today both his birthplace, the renamed industrial city of Nizhni-Novgorod, and the Moscow Art Theatre "in the Name of Gorki" bear witness to the esteem in which he came to be held in his homeland.

Alexei Maximovitch Pyeshkov, as he was called before he began to sign himself Maxim Gorki, knew the worst about humanity by the time he attracted attention as a writer of unusual powers. Orphaned in childhood, he grew up in the household of a tyrannical grandfather who bullied him and apprenticed him to unpleasant trades. Escaping from a detestable employer, he wandered over the steppes, a frequently starving young tramp in the company of pilgrims, thieves, and all the flotsam and jetsam of Russian society. With knowledge came pity, and it is the combination of grime-stained realism and compassion that made him the spokesman of the outcasts he called "the creatures that once were men." In his writings he was to remember, for example, the bruised harlot who forgot her own desperation to mother him when a storm drove him to take shelter under an overturned boat; the half-wit he met during his wanderings who was "more hunted than an animal"; the madwoman he found rearing seven subnormal children; and the peasant woman he impetuously defended from her husband. (His intervention resulted in his having to be taken to a hospital by a good Samaritan who found him lying half-dead in the bushes.) In his eighth year, he had hurled himself at his stepfather with a breadknife when he found him beating his consumptive mother. Ever since that childhood episode Gorki had raged against injustice. He became one of the seekers after salvation with which the Russia of the eighteen-nineties teemed, and he needed only an introduction to literature to find an outlet for his social passion.

Introduced to the mysteries of the alphabet by a philosophical cook whose helper he had been on a Volga steamboat, Gorki began educating himself with the aid of members of the provincial intelligentsia who were then attempting to enlighten the masses. His first short story, written in 1892, attracted the attention of a prominent literary figure, Korolenko, who sent it to a periodical. Its publication aroused interest in literary circles, and soon Gorki's sketches of workers and outcasts were hailed as the ultimate in realism. They introduced fresh material into Russian literature, which was already well acquainted, if not surfeited, with the middle classes and the peasantry but had yet to discover the proletariat. As a result, his stories and novels were, if anything, overrated. It was none other than Tolstoy who told the young author that he had serious limitations as an artist because he was apt to become "literary" and to sentimentalize reality. It is the Gorki of a series of candid autobiographies (*My Childhood, In the World, My University Days,* and various *Reminiscences*) and of *The Lower Depths* who is likely to weather time.

Chekhov attracted Gorki to the theatre by introducing him to members of the Moscow Art Theatre, and the actors promptly wrung the promise of a play from him. At first suspicious of them because they were "middle class" people, the laureate of the common man obliged with his first drama, *The Smug Citizen,* and the Art Theatre produced it in a strained atmosphere. As the radical author's election to the Imperial Academy of Russian Artists had just been annulled by the government, a squadron of Cossacks surrounded the playhouse to suppress an expected demonstration. There was no demonstration within the theatre itself only because the management requested self-control from the public "in order that Gorki may continue to write for the theatre," although one enthusiast did climax the last performance with a stentorian "Down with the Grand Duke!" Censorship had also compelled the deletion of such passages in *The Smug Citizen* as "He who works is the master" and "In Russia it is more comfortable to be a drunkard or a tramp than to be a sober and hard-working man." The play, a highly charged account of decadence and rebellion in middle-class life, was an explosive commodity for the then politically neutral theatre, whose program had moved no further left than a production of Ibsen's *An Enemy of the People.* Nevertheless, the actors busied themselves preparing a second Gorki play for production while the first was still running.

The new work was *The Lower Depths,* also known in English as *A Night's Lodging* as well as by other titles. Under the author's expert guidance, the company made trips to the disreputable Khitrov market-place to acquaint itself with the life presented in a drama so uncompromisingly naturalistic that James Huneker was hardly exaggerating when he wrote that Zola "might have gone to school to learn the alphabet of his art at the knees of the young man from Nizhni-Novgorod." Gorki even naïvely offered to bring a streetwalker to stay with the Art Theatre's leading actress, Olga Knipper (Chekhov's wife), who played Nastya. On December 18, 1902, as a result of such scrupulous realism, *The Lower Depths* became one of the Art Theatre's most triumphant productions. Never before had the company thrown itself so wholeheartedly into a play whose matter was so foreign to its own experience. The actors performed as if they walked through a world of half-lights interrupted by sudden flashes of lightning. For a long time the play remained one of the Moscow Art Theatre's most inspired productions.

Gorki provided a rare dramatic experience by taking as sordid a slice of life as it was possible to find and electrifying it with pity rather than revulsion and with hope rather than despair. And to these qualities the author, here not unaided by the memorable first production, added a natural fluidity well described by the historian of the Art Theatre Oliver Sayler when he wrote that Gorki's work is "not so much a matter of utterable line and recountable gesture as it is of the intangible flow of human souls in endlessly shifting contact with one another."

Although it does not appear that *The Lower Depths* was ever again presented on the stage as effectively as in the Moscow company's performances, its unique quality attracted attention throughout the Western world. The Stage Society of London produced it less than a year after its *première* and again in 1911, and Arthur Hopkins gave it for the first time in English on Broadway in 1919, while performances in German and other European languages multiplied over the years. Its great success in Russia, moreover, encouraged Gorki to write a number of other plays, such as *Summer Folk, Children of the Sun,* and *Enemies,* before the Russian Revolution, and afterward two parts of an intended trilogy, *Dostigaev and Others* (1933) and *Yegor Bulychov* (1932). Most of these plays were uneven in quality and owed their importance largely to the social protest imbedded in them. In *Summer Folk* and *Children of the Sun,* for example, Gorki denounced the "intelligentsia" for failing to range itself on the side of social reform, and in *Enemies* he proclaimed that there could be no meeting ground between even well-intentioned employers and workers. *Yegor Bulychov* presented the end of middle-class society through the lingering death of a merchant who reviews the failure of his life on the eve of the Russian Revolution. But even this play, his best after *The Lower Depths,* failed to equal its author's achievement in his memorable picture of "creatures that once were men."

Gorki was himself aware of his shortcomings as a dramatist, and regretted that he tended to become didactic. Admitting that characters should be permitted to act independently of the author's will in accordance with their individuality and environment, he declared himself incapable of abiding by this principle in practice. Nor did he believe that any other European playwright had done so, which is a debatable conclusion. *The Lower Depths* did, however, bring him as close to the ideal of objectivity as a man of his convictions could come. Although the faith-healer Luka constantly preaches in the first three acts, it is plain that Gorki was not using him as his mouthpiece. The climactic action actually demonstrates the futility of Luka's illusion-peddling. Even the tribute to truth by Satine in the last act, which may be taken to express the author's own views, is presented as the wisdom of a tipsy failure whose only regret when the alcoholic actor hangs himself is that he has spoiled the singing.

A national hero after throwing his influence on the side of Lenin, Gorki tried to mitigate the rigors of the Bolshevik terror in the early years of the revolution. He devoted his last years to encouraging and guiding young Russian writers. He also wrote a series of turgid, if vivid, novels reviewing Russian life from 1880 to 1924 and celebrating the rise of an insurgent spirit.

Gorki died after an illness in 1936, under the aura of revolutionary sanctity. He was allegedly murdered by an anti-Stalinist physician who was subsequently executed in the purge of the Trotsky faction. In essence, however, Gorki belongs to no party. His compassion for mankind, his hopes for its ultimate freedom, and his faith have been expressed in an essay in which he wrote that the "true Shekinah"—the "Holy of Holies"—is Man. For all his readiness to present the squalor into which men could sink, he was possessed of romantic fervor. He insisted only on drawing a distinction between the "passive romanticism" that reconciles men to reality by disguising it and the "active romanticism" which strengthens men's will to live and rouses them to action.

BIBLIOGRAPHY: Vladimir Nemirovitch-Dantchenko, *My Life in the Russian Theatre* (pp. 241–243, 237–241, etc.), 1936; John Gassner, *Masters of the Drama* (pp. 526–533), 1945; Maxim Gorky, *Reminiscences of Tolstoy, Chekhov, and Andreyev* (Dover Publications, 1946 edition); Alexander Kaun, *Maxim Gorky and His Russia,* 1931; Constantin Stanislavsky, *My Life in Art* (pp. 367–369, 390–399), 1924, 1938; Leo Wiener, *The Contemporary Drama of Russia,* 1924.

THE LOWER DEPTHS

By Maxim Gorki

TRANSLATED FROM THE RUSSIAN BY JENNY COVAN

CAST OF CHARACTERS

MIKHAIL IVANOFF KOSTILYOFF, *keeper of a night lodging*
VASSILISA KARPOVNA, *his wife*
NATASHA, *her sister*
MIEDVIEDIEFF, *her uncle, a policeman*
VASKA PEPEL, *a young thief*

ANDREI MITRITCH KLESHTCH, *a locksmith*
ANNA, *his wife*
NASTYA, *a street-walker*
KVASHNYA, *a vendor of meat-pies*
BUBNOFF, *a cap-maker*
THE BARON

SATINE
THE ACTOR
LUKA, *a pilgrim*
ALYOSHKA, *a shoemaker*
KRIVOY ZOB ⎱ *Porters*
THE TARTAR ⎰
NIGHT LODGERS, TRAMPS AND OTHERS

The action takes place in a Night Lodging and in "The Waste," an area in its rear.

ACT I.

A cellar resembling a cave. The ceiling, which merges into stone walls, is low and grimy, and the plaster and paint are peeling off. There is a window, high up on the right wall, from which comes the light. The right corner, which constitutes Pepel's room, is partitioned off by thin boards. Close to the corner of this room is Bubnoff's wooden bunk. In the left corner stands a large Russian stove. In the stone wall, left, is a door leading to the kitchen where live Kvashnya, the Baron, and Nastya. Against the wall, between the stove and the door, is a large bed covered with dirty chintz. Bunks line the walls. In the foreground, by the left wall, is a block of wood with a vise and a small anvil fastened to it, and another smaller block of wood somewhat further towards the back. Kleshtch is seated on the smaller block, trying keys into old locks. At his feet are two large bundles of various keys, wired together, also a battered tin samovar, a hammer, and pincers. In the center are a large table, two benches, and a stool, all of which are of dirty, unpainted wood. Behind the table Kvashnya is busying herself with the samovar. The Baron sits chewing a piece of black bread, and Nastya occupies the stool, leans her elbows on the table, and reads a tattered book. In the bed, behind curtains, Anna lies coughing. Bubnoff is seated on his bunk, attempting to shape a pair of old trousers with the help of an ancient hat shape which he holds between his knees. Scattered about him are pieces of buckram, oilcloth, and rags. Satine, just awakened, lies in his bunk, grunting. On top of the stove, the Actor, invisible to the audience, tosses about and coughs.

It is an early spring morning.

THE BARON: And then?

KVASHNYA: No, my dear, said I, keep away from me with such proposals. I've been through it all, you see—and not for a hundred baked lobsters would I marry again!

BUBNOFF: [*To* Satine] What are you grunting about? [Satine *keeps on grunting*]

KVASHNYA: Why should I, said I, a free woman, my own mistress, enter my name into somebody else's passport and sell myself into slavery—no! Why —I wouldn't marry a man even if he were an American prince!

KLESHTCH: You lie!

KVASHNYA: Wha-at?

KLESHTCH: You lie! You're going to marry Abramka. . . .

THE BARON: [*Snatching the book out of* Nastya's *hand and reading the title*] "Fatal Love". . . [*Laughs*]

NASTYA: [*Stretching out her hand*] Give it back— give it back! Stop fooling!

[The Baron *looks at her and waves the book in the air*]

KVASHNYA: [*To* Kleshtch] You crimson goat, you —calling me a liar! How dare you be so rude to me?

THE BARON: [*Hitting* Nastya *on the head with the book*] Nastya, you little fool!

NASTYA: [*Reaching for the book*] Give it back!

KLESHTCH: Oh—what a great lady . . . but you'll marry Abramka just the same—that's all you're waiting for . . .

KVASHNYA: Sure! Anything else? You nearly beat your wife to death!

KLESHTCH: Shut up, you old bitch! It's none of your business!

KVASHNYA: Ho-ho! can't stand the truth, can you?

THE BARON: They're off again! Nastya, where are you?

NASTYA: [*Without lifting her head*] Hey—go away!

ANNA: [*Putting her head through the curtains*]

229

The day has started. For God's sake, don't row!

KLESHTCH: Whining again!

ANNA: Every blessed day . . . let me die in peace, can't you?

BUBNOFF: Noise won't keep you from dying.

KVASHNYA: [Walking up to Anna] Little mother, how did you ever manage to live with this wretch?

ANNA: Leave me alone—get away from me. . . .

KVASHNYA: Well, well! You poor soul . . . how's the pain in the chest—any better?

THE BARON: Kvashnya! Time to go to market. . . .

KVASHNYA: We'll go presently. [To Anna] Like some hot dumplings?

ANNA: No, thanks. Why should I eat?

KVASHNYA: You must eat. Hot food—good for you! I'll leave you some in a cup. Eat them when you feel like it. Come on, sir! [To Kleshtch] You evil spirit!

[Goes into kitchen]

ANNA: [Coughing] Lord, Lord . . .

THE BARON: [Painfully pushing forward Nastya's head] Throw it away—little fool!

NASTYA: [Muttering] Leave me alone—I don't bother you . . .

[The Baron follows Kvashnya, whistling]

SATINE: [Sitting up in his bunk] Who beat me up yesterday?

BUBNOFF: Does it make any difference who?

SATINE: Suppose they did—but why did they?

BUBNOFF: Were you playing cards?

SATINE: Yes!

BUBNOFF: That's why they beat you.

SATINE: Scoundrels!

THE ACTOR: [Raising his head from the top of the stove] One of these days they'll beat you to death!

SATINE: You're a jackass!

THE ACTOR: Why?

SATINE: Because a man can die only once!

THE ACTOR: [After a silence] I don't understand—

KLESHTCH: Say! You crawl from that stove—and start cleaning house! Don't play the delicate primrose!

THE ACTOR: None of your business!

KLESHTCH: Wait till Vassilisa comes—she'll show you whose business it is!

THE ACTOR: To hell with Vassilisa! To-day is the Baron's turn to clean. . . . Baron!

[The Baron comes from the kitchen]

THE BARON: I've no time to clean . . . I'm going to market with Kvashnya.

THE ACTOR: That doesn't concern me. Go to the gallows if you like. It's your turn to sweep the floor just the same—I'm not going to do other people's work . . .

THE BARON: Go to blazes! Nastya will do it. Hey there—fatal love! Wake up! [Takes the book away from Nastya]

NASTYA: [Getting up] What do you want? Give it

back to me! You scoundrel! And that's a nobleman for you!

THE BARON: [Returning the book to her] Nastya! Sweep the floor for me—will you?

NASTYA: [Goes to kitchen] Not so's you'll notice it!

KVASHNYA: [To the Baron through kitchen door] Come on—you! They don't need you! Actor! You were asked to do it, and now you go ahead and attend to it—it won't kill you . . .

THE ACTOR: It's always I . . . I don't understand why. . . .

[The Baron comes from the kitchen, across his shoulders a wooden beam from which hang earthen pots covered with rags]

THE BARON: Heavier than ever!

SATINE: It paid you to be born a Baron, eh?

KVASHNYA: [To Actor] See to it that you sweep up! [Crosses to outer door, letting the Baron pass ahead]

THE ACTOR: [Climbing down from the stove] It's bad for me to inhale dust. [With pride] My organism is poisoned with alcohol. [Sits down on a bunk, meditating]

SATINE: Organism—organon. . . .

ANNA: Andrei Mitritch. . . .

KLESHTCH: What now?

ANNA: Kvashnya left me some dumplings over there—you eat them.

KLESHTCH: [Coming over to her] And you—don't you want any?

ANNA: No. Why should I eat? You're a workman —you need it.

KLESHTCH: Frightened, are you? Don't be! You'll get all right!

ANNA: Go and eat! It's hard on me. . . . I suppose very soon . . .

KLESHTCH: [Walking away] Never mind—maybe you'll get well—you can never tell! [Goes into kitchen]

THE ACTOR: [Loud, as if he had suddenly awakened] Yesterday the doctor in the hospital said to me: "Your organism," he said, "is entirely poisoned with alcohol . . ."

SATINE: [Smiling] Organon . . .

THE ACTOR: [Stubbornly] Not organon—organism!

SATINE: Sibylline. . . .

THE ACTOR: [Shaking his fist at him] Nonsense! I'm telling you seriously . . . if the organism is poisoned . . . that means it's bad for me to sweep the floor—to inhale the dust . . .

SATINE: Macrobistic . . . hah!

BUBNOFF: What are you muttering?

SATINE: Words—and here's another one for you —transcendentalistic . . .

BUBNOFF: What does it mean?

SATINE: Don't know—I forgot . . .

BUBNOFF: Then why did you say it?

SATINE: Just so! I'm bored, brother, with human

words—all our words. Bored! I've heard each one of them a thousand times surely.

THE ACTOR: In Hamlet they say: "Words, words, words!" It's a good play. I played the grave-digger in it once. . . .

[Kleshtch *comes from the kitchen*]

KLESHTCH: Will you start playing with the broom?

THE ACTOR: None of your business. [*Striking his chest*] Opheiia! O—remember me in thy prayers!

[*Back stage is heard a dull murmur, cries, and a police whistle. Kleshtch sits down to work, filing screechily*]

SATINE: I love unintelligible, obsolete words. When I was a youngster—and worked as a telegraph operator—I read heaps of books. . . .

BUBNOFF: Were you really a telegrapher?

SATINE: I was. There are some excellent books—and lots of curious words . . . Once I was an educated man, do you know?

BUBNOFF: I've heard it a hundred times. Well, so you were! That isn't very important! Me—well—once I was a furrier. I had my own shop—what with dyeing the fur all day long, my arms were yellow up to the elbows, brother. I thought I'd never be able ever to get clean again—that I'd go to my grave, all yellow! But look at my hands now—they're plain dirty—that's what!

SATINE: Well, and what then?

BUBNOFF: That's all!

SATINE: What are you trying to prove?

BUBNOFF: Oh, well—just matching thoughts—no matter how much dye you get on yourself, it all comes off in the end—yes, yes—

SATINE: Oh—my bones ache!

THE ACTOR: [*Sits, nursing his knees*] Education is all rot. Talent is the thing. I knew an actor—who read his parts by heart, syllable by syllable—but he played heroes in a way that . . . why—the whole theater would rock with ecstasy!

SATINE: Bubnoff, give me five kopecks.

BUBNOFF: I only have two—

THE ACTOR: I say—talent, that's what you need to play heroes. And talent is nothing but faith in yourself, in your own powers—

SATINE: Give me five kopecks and I'll have faith that you're a hero, a crocodile, or a police inspector—Kleshtch, give me five kopecks.

KLESHTCH: Go to hell! All of you!

SATINE: What are you cursing for? I know you haven't a kopeck in the world!

ANNA: Andrei Mitritch—I'm suffocating—I can't breathe—

KLESHTCH: What shall I do?

BUBNOFF: Open the door into the hall.

KLESHTCH: All right. You're sitting on the bunk, I on the floor. You change places with me, and I'll let you open the door. I have a cold as it is.

BUBNOFF: [*Unconcernedly*] I don't care if you open the door—it's your wife who's asking—

KLESHTCH: [*Morosely*] I don't care who's asking—

SATINE: My head buzzes—ah—why do people have to hit each other over the heads?

BUBNOFF: They don't only hit you over the head, but over the rest of the body as well. [*Rises*] I must go and buy some thread—our bosses are late to-day—seems as if they've croaked. [*Exit*]

[Anna *coughs; Satine is lying down motionless, his hands folded behind his head*]

THE ACTOR: [*Looks about him morosely, then goes to* Anna] Feeling bad, eh?

ANNA: I'm choking—

THE ACTOR: If you wish, I'll take you into the hallway. Get up, then, come! [*He helps her to rise, wraps some sort of a rag about her shoulders, and supports her toward the hall*] It isn't easy. I'm sick myself—poisoned with alcohol . . .

[Kostilyoff *appears in the doorway*]

KOSTILYOFF: Going for a stroll? What a nice couple—the gallant cavalier and the lady fair!

THE ACTOR: Step aside, you—don't you see that we're invalids?

KOSTILYOFF: Pass on, please! [*Hums a religious tune, glances about him suspiciously, and bends his head to the left as if listening to what is happening in* Pepel's *room*. Kleshtch *is jangling his keys and scraping away with his file, and looks askance at the other*] Filing?

KLESHTCH: What?

KOSTILYOFF: I say, are you filing? [*Pause*] What did I want to ask? [*Quick and low*] Hasn't my wife been here?

KLESHTCH: I didn't see her.

KOSTILYOFF: [*Carefully moving toward* Pepel's *room*] You take up a whole lot of room for your two rubles a month. The bed—and your bench—yes—you take up five rubles' worth of space, so help me God! I'll have to put another half ruble to your rent—

KLESHTCH: You'll put a noose around my neck and choke me . . . you'll croak soon enough, and still all you think of is half rubles—

KOSTILYOFF: Why should I choke you? What would be the use? God be with you—live and prosper! But I'll have to raise you half a ruble—I'll buy oil for the ikon lamp, and my offering will atone for my sins, and for yours as well. You don't think much of your sins—not much! Oh, Andrushka, you're a wicked man! Your wife is dying because of your wickedness—no one loves you, no one respects you—your work is squeaky, jarring on every one.

KLESHTCH: [*Shouts*] What do you come here for—just to annoy me?

[Satine *grunts loudly*]

KOSTILYOFF: [*With a start*] God, what a noise!

[The Actor *enters*]

THE ACTOR: I've put her down in the hall and wrapped her up.

KOSTILYOFF: You're a kindly fellow. That's good. Some day you'll be rewarded for it.

THE ACTOR: When?

KOSTILYOFF: In the Beyond, little brother—there all our deeds will be reckoned up.

THE ACTOR: Suppose you reward me right now?

KOSTILYOFF: How can I do that?

THE ACTOR: Wipe out half my debt.

KOSTILYOFF: He-ho! You're always jesting, darling—always poking fun . . . can kindliness of heart be repaid with gold? Kindliness—it's above all other qualities. But your debt to me—remains a debt. And so you'll have to pay me back. You ought to be kind to me, an old man, without seeking for reward!

THE ACTOR: You're a swindler, old man! [Goes into kitchen]

[Kleshtch rises and goes into the hall]

KOSTILYOFF: [To Satine] See that squeaker—? He ran away—he doesn't like me!

SATINE: Does anybody like you besides the Devil.

KOSTILYOFF: [Laughing] Oh—you're so quarrelsome! But I like you all—I understand you all, my unfortunate downtrodden, useless brethren . . . [Suddenly, rapidly] Is Vaska home?

SATINE: See for yourself—

KOSTILYOFF: [Goes to the door and knocks] Vaska!

[The Actor appears at the kitchen door, chewing something]

PEPEL: Who is it?

KOSTILYOFF: It's I—I, Vaska!

PEPEL: What do you want?

KOSTILYOFF: [Stepping aside] Open!

SATINE: [Without looking at Kostilyoff] He'll open—and she's there—

[The Actor makes a grimace]

KOSTILYOFF: [In a low, anxious tone] Eh? Who's there? What?

SATINE: Speaking to me?

KOSTILYOFF: What did you say?

SATINE: Oh—nothing—I was just talking to myself—

KOSTILYOFF: Take care, brother. Don't carry your joking too far! [Knocks loudly at door] Vassily!

PEPEL: [Opening door] Well? What are you disturbing me for?

KOSTILYOFF: [Peering into room] I—you see—

PEPEL: Did you bring the money?

KOSTILYOFF: I've something to tell you—

PEPEL: Did you bring the money?

KOSTILYOFF: What money? Wait—

PEPEL: Why—the seven rubles for the watch—well?

KOSTILYOFF: What watch, Vaska? Oh, you—

PEPEL: Look here. Yesterday, before witnesses, I sold you a watch for ten rubles, you gave me three—now let me have the other seven. What are you blinking for? You hang around here—you disturb people—and don't seem to know yourself what you're after.

KOSTILYOFF: Sh-sh! Don't be angry, Vaska. The watch—it is—

SATINE: Stolen!

KOSTILYOFF: [Sternly] I do not accept stolen goods—how can you imagine—

PEPEL: [Taking him by the shoulder] What did you disturb me for? What do you want?

KOSTILYOFF: I don't want—anything. I'll go—if you're in such a state—

PEPEL: Be off, and bring the money!

KOSTILYOFF: What ruffians! I—I—[Exit]

THE ACTOR: What a farce!

SATINE: That's fine—I like it.

PEPEL: What did he come here for?

SATINE: [Laughing] Don't you understand? He's looking for his wife. Why don't you beat him up once and for all, Vaska?

PEPEL: Why should I let such trash interfere with my life?

SATINE: Show some brains! And then you can marry Vassilisa—and become our boss—

PEPEL: Heavenly bliss! And you'd smash up my household and, because I'm a soft-hearted fool, you'll drink up everything I possess. [Sits on a bunk] Old devil—woke me up—I was having such a pleasant dream. I dreamed I was fishing—and I caught an enormous trout—such a trout as you only see in dreams! I was playing him—and I was so afraid the line would snap. I had just got out the gaff—and I thought to myself—in a moment—

SATINE: It wasn't a trout, it was Vassilisa—

THE ACTOR: He caught Vassilisa a long time ago.

PEPEL: [Angrily] You can all go to the devil—and Vassilisa with you—

[Kleshtch comes from the hall]

KLESHTCH: Devilishly cold!

THE ACTOR: Why didn't you bring Anna back? She'll freeze, out there—

KLESHTCH: Natasha took her into the kitchen—

THE ACTOR: The old man will kick her out—

KLESHTCH: [Sitting down to his work] Well—Natasha will bring her in here—

SATINE: Vassily—give me five kopecks!

THE ACTOR: [To Satine] Oh, you—always five kopecks—Vassya—give us twenty kopecks—

PEPEL: I'd better give it to them now before they ask for a ruble. Here you are!

SATINE: Gibraltar! There are no kindlier people in the world than thieves!

KLESHTCH: [Morosely] They earn their money easily—they don't work—

SATINE: Many earn it easily, but not many part with it so easily. Work? Make work pleasant—and maybe I'll work too. Yes—maybe. When work's a pleasure, life's, too. When it's toil, then life is a drudge. [To the Actor] You, Sardanapalus! Come on!

THE ACTOR: Let's go, Nebuchadnezzar! I'll get as drunk as forty thousand topers! [They leave]

PEPEL: [Yawning] Well, how's your wife?

KLESHTCH: It seems as if soon—[Pause]

PEPEL: Now I look at you—seems to me all that filing and scraping of yours is useless.

KLESHTCH: Well—what else can I do?

PEPEL: Nothing.

KLESHTCH: How can I live?

PEPEL: People manage, somehow.

KLESHTCH: Them? Call them people? Muck and dregs—that's what they are! I'm a workman—I'm ashamed even to look at them. I've slaved since I was a child. . . . D'you think I shan't be able to tear myself away from here? I'll crawl out of here, even if I have to leave my skin behind—but crawl out I will! Just wait . . . my wife'll die . . . I've lived here six months, and it seems like six years.

PEPEL: Nobody here's any worse off than you . . . say what you like . . .

KLESHTCH: No worse is right. They've neither honor nor conscience.

PEPEL: [Indifferently] What good does it do—honor or conscience? Can you get them on their feet instead of on their uppers—through honor and conscience? Honor and conscience are needed only by those who have power and energy . . .

BUBNOFF: [Coming back] Oh—I'm frozen.

PEPEL: Bubnoff! Got a conscience?

BUBNOFF: What? A conscience?

PEPEL: Exactly!

BUBNOFF: What do I need a conscience for? I'm not rich.

PEPEL: Just what I said: honor and conscience are for the rich—right! And Kleshtch is upbraiding us because we haven't any!

BUBNOFF: Why—did he want to borrow some of it?

PEPEL: No—he has plenty of his own . . .

BUBNOFF: Oh—are you selling it? You won't sell much around here. But if you had some old boxes, I'd buy them—on credit.

PEPEL: [Didactically] You're a jackass, Andrushka! On the subject of conscience you ought to hear Satine—or the Baron . . .

KLESHTCH: I've nothing to talk to them about!

PEPEL: They have more brains than you—even if they're drunkards . . .

BUBNOFF: He who can be drunk and wise at the same time is doubly blessed . . .

PEPEL: Satine says every man expects his neighbor to have a conscience, but—you see—it isn't to any one's advantage to have one—that's a fact.

[Natasha enters, followed by Luka who carries a stick in his hand, a bundle on his back, a kettle and a teapot slung from his belt]

LUKA: How are you, honest folks?

PEPEL: [Twisting his mustache] Aha—Natasha!

BUBNOFF: [To Luka] I was honest—up to spring before last.

NATASHA: Here's a new lodger . . .

LUKA: Oh, it's all the same to me. Crooks—I don't mind them, either. For my part there's no bad flea—

they're all black—and they all jump—. . . Well, dearie, show me where I can stow myself.

NATASHA: [Pointing to kitchen door] Go in there, grand-dad.

LUKA: Thanks, girlie. One place is like another—as long as an old fellow keeps warm, he keeps happy . . .

PEPEL: What an amusing old codger you brought in, Natasha!

NATASHA: A hanged sight more interesting than you! . . . Andrei, your wife's in the kitchen with us—come and fetch her after a while. . . .

KLESHTCH: All right—I will . . .

NATASHA: And be a little more kind to her—you know she won't last much longer.

KLESHTCH: I know . . .

NATASHA: Knowing won't do any good—it's terrible—dying—don't you understand?

PEPEL: Well—look at me—I'm not afraid . . .

NATASHA: Oh—you're a wonder, aren't you?

BUBNOFF: [Whistling] Oh—this thread's rotten . . .

PEPEL: Honestly, I'm not afraid! I'm ready to die right now. Knife me to the heart—and I'll die without making a sound . . . even gladly—from such a pure hand . . .

NATASHA: [Going out] Spin that yarn for some one else!

BUBNOFF: Oh—that thread is rotten—rotten—

NATASHA: [At hallway door] Don't forget your wife, Andrei!

KLESHTCH: All right.

PEPEL: She's a wonderful girl!

BUBNOFF: She's all right.

PEPEL: What makes her so curt with me? Anyway—she'll come to no good here . . .

BUBNOFF: Through you—sure!

PEPEL: Why through me? I feel sorry for her . . .

BUBNOFF: As the wolf for the lamb!

PEPEL: You lie! I feel very sorry for her . . . very . . . very sorry! She has a tough life here—I can see that . . .

KLESHTCH: Just wait till Vassilisa catches you talking to her!

BUBNOFF: Vassilisa? She won't give up so easily what belongs to her—she's a cruel woman!

PEPEL: [Stretching himself on the bunk] You two prophets can go to hell!

KLESHTCH: Just wait—you'll see!

LUKA: [Singing in the kitchen] "In the dark of the night the way is black . . ."

KLESHTCH: Another one who yelps!

PEPEL: It's dreary! Why do I feel so dreary? You live—and everything seems all right. But suddenly a cold chill goes through you—and then everything gets dreary . . .

BUBNOFF: Dreary? Hm-hm—

PEPEL: Yes—yes—

LUKA: [Sings] "The way is black . . ."

PEPEL: Old fellow! Hey there!

LUKA: [*Looking from kitchen door*] You call me?

PEPEL: Yes. Don't sing!

LUKA: [*Coming in*] You don't like it?

PEPEL: When people sing well I like it—

LUKA: In other words—I don't sing well?

PEPEL: Evidently!

LUKA: Well, well—and I thought I sang well. That's always the way: a man imagines there's one thing he can do well, and suddenly he finds out that other people don't think so . . .

PEPEL: [*Laughs*] That's right . . .

BUBNOFF: First you say you feel dreary—and then you laugh!

PEPEL: None of your business, raven!

LUKA: Who do they say feels dreary?

PEPEL: I do.

[*The Baron enters*]

LUKA: Well, well—out there in the kitchen there's a girl reading and crying! That's so! Her eyes are wet with tears . . . I say to her: "What's the matter, darling?" And she says: "It's so sad!" "What's so sad?" say I. "The book!" says she.—And that's how people spend their time. Just because they're bored . . .

THE BARON: She's a fool!

PEPEL: Have you had tea, Baron?

THE BARON: Yes. Go on!

PEPEL: Well—want me to open a bottle?

THE BARON: Of course. Go on!

PEPEL: Drop on all fours, and bark like a dog!

THE BARON: Fool! What's the matter with you? Are you drunk?

PEPEL: Go on—bark a little! It'll amuse me. You're an aristocrat. You didn't even consider us human formerly, did you?

THE BARON: Go on!

PEPEL: Well—and now I am making you bark like a dog—and you will bark, won't you?

THE BARON: All right. I will. You jackass! What pleasure can you derive from it, since I myself know that I have sunk almost lower than you. You should have made me drop on all fours in the days when I was still above you.

BUBNOFF: That's right . . .

LUKA: I say so, too!

BUBNOFF: What's over, is over. Remain only trivialities. We know no class distinctions here. We've shed all pride and self-respect. Blood and bone—man—just plain man—that's what we are!

LUKA: In other words, we're all equal . . . and you, friend, were you really a Baron?

THE BARON: Who are you? A ghost?

LUKA: [*Laughing*] I've seen counts and princes in my day—this is the first time I meet a baron—and one who's decaying—at that!

PEPEL: [*Laughing*] Baron, I blush for you!

THE BARON: It's time you knew better, Vassily . . .

LUKA: Hey-hey—I look at you, brothers—the life you're leading . . .

BUBNOFF: Such a life! As soon as the sun rises, our voices rise, too—in quarrels!

THE BARON: We've all seen better days—yes! I used to wake up in the morning and drink my coffee in bed—coffee—with cream! Yes—

LUKA: And yet we're all human beings. Pretend all you want to, put on all the airs you wish, but man you were born, and man you must die. And as I watch I see that the wiser people get, the busier they get—and though from bad to worse, they still strive to improve—stubbornly—

THE BARON: Who are you, old fellow? Where do you come from?

LUKA: I?

THE BARON: Are you a tramp?

LUKA: We're all of us tramps—why—I've heard said that the very earth we walk on is nothing but a tramp in the universe.

THE BARON: [*Severely*] Perhaps. But have you a passport?

LUKA: [*After a short pause*] And what are you—a police inspector?

PEPEL: [*Delighted*] You scored, old fellow! Well, Barosha, you got it this time!

BUBNOFF: Yes—our little aristocrat got his!

THE BARON: [*Embarrassed*] What's the matter? I I was only joking, old man. Why, brother, I haven't a passport, either.

BUBNOFF: You lie!

THE BARON: Oh—well—I have some sort of papers—but they have no value—

LUKA: They're papers just the same—and no papers are any good—

PEPEL: Baron—come on to the saloon with me—

THE BARON: I'm ready. Good-bye, old man—you old scamp—

LUKA: Maybe I am one, brother—

PEPEL: [*Near doorway*] Come on—come on!

[*Leaves,* Baron *following him quickly*]

LUKA: Was he really once a Baron?

BUBNOFF: Who knows? A gentleman—? Yes That much he's even now. Occasionally it sticks out. He never got rid of the habit.

LUKA: Nobility is like small-pox. A man may get over it—but it leaves marks . . .

BUBNOFF: He's all right all the same—occasionally he kicks—as he did about your passport . . .

[*Alyoshka comes in, slightly drunk, with a concertina in his hand, whistling*]

ALYOSHKA: Hey there, lodgers!

BUBNOFF: What are you yelling for?

ALYOSHKA: Excuse me—I beg your pardon! I'm a well-bred man—

BUBNOFF: On a spree again?

ALYOSHKA: Right you are! A moment ago Medyakin, the precinct captain, threw me out of the police station and said: "Look here—I don't want as much as a smell of you to stay in the streets—d'you hear?" I'm a man of principles, and the boss croaks at me—and what's a boss anyway—pah!—

it's all bosh—the boss is a drunkard. I don't make any demands on life. I want nothing—that's all. Offer me one ruble, offer me twenty—it doesn't affect me. [Nastya comes from the kitchen] Offer me a million—I won't take it! And to think that I, a respectable man, should be ordered about by a pal of mine—and he a drunkard! I won't have it—I won't!

[Nastya stands in the doorway, shaking her head at Alyoshka]

LUKA: [Good-naturedly] Well, boy, you're a bit confused—

BUBNOFF: Aren't men fools!

ALYOSHKA: [Stretches out on the floor] Here, eat me up alive—and I don't want anything. I'm a desperate man. Show me one better! Why am I worse than others? There! Medyakin said: "If you show yourself on the streets I smash your face!" And yet I shall go out—I'll go—and stretch out in the middle of the street—let them choke me—I don't want a thing!

NASTYA: Poor fellow—only a boy—and he's already putting on such airs—

ALYOSHKA: [Kneeling before her] Lady! Mademoiselle! Parlez français—? Prix courrant? I'm on a spree—

NASTYA: [In a loud whisper] Vassilisa!

VASSILISA: [Opens door quickly; to Alyoshka] You here again?

ALYOSHKA: How do you do—? Come in—you're welcome—

VASSILISA: I told you, young puppy, that not a shadow of you should stick around here—and you're back—eh?

ALYOSHKA: Vassilisa Karpovna . . . shall I tune up a funeral march for you?

VASSILISA: [Seizing him by the shoulders] Get out!

ALYOSHKA: [Moving towards the door] Wait—you can't put me out this way! I learned this funeral march a little while ago! It's refreshing music . . . wait—you can't put me out like that!

VASSILISA: I'll show whether I can or not. I'll rouse the whole street against you—you foul-mouthed creature—you're too young to bark about me—

ALYOSHKA: [Running out] All right—I'll go—

VASSILISA: Look out—I'll get you yet!

ALYOSHKA: [Opens the door and shouts] Vassilisa Karpovna—I'm not afraid of you—[Hides]

[Luka laughs]

VASSILISA: Who are you?

LUKA: A passer-by—a traveler . . .

VASSILISA: Stopping for the night or going to stay here?

LUKA: I'll see.

VASSILISA: Have you a passport?

LUKA: Yes.

VASSILISA: Give it to me.

LUKA: I'll bring it over to your house—

VASSILISA: Call yourself a traveler? If you'd say a tramp—that would be nearer the truth—

LUKA: [Sighing] You're not very kindly, mother!

[Vassilisa goes to door that leads to Pepel's room. Alyoshka pokes his head through the kitchen door]

ALYOSHKA: Has she left?

VASSILISA: [Turning around] Are you still here?

[Alyoshka disappears, whistling. Nastya and Luka laugh]

BUBNOFF: [To Vassilisa] He isn't here—

VASSILISA: Who?

BUBNOFF: Vaska.

VASSILISA: Did I ask you about him?

BUBNOFF: I noticed you were looking around—

VASSILISA: I am looking to see if things are in order, you see? Why aren't the floors swept yet? How often did I give orders to keep the house clean?

BUBNOFF: It's the actor's turn to sweep—

VASSILISA: Never mind whose turn it is! If the health inspector comes and fines me, I'll throw out the lot of you—

BUBNOFF: [Calmly] Then how are you going to earn your living?

VASSILISA: I don't want a speck of dirt! [Goes to kitchen; to Nastya] What are you hanging round here for? Why's your face all swollen up? Why are you standing there like a dummy? Go on—sweep the floor! Did you see Natalia? Was she here?

NASTYA: I don't know—I haven't seen her . . .

VASSILISA: Bubnoff! Was my sister here?

BUBNOFF: She brought him along.

VASSILISA: That one—was he home?

BUBNOFF: Vassily? Yes—Natalia was here talking to Kleshtch—

VASSILISA: I'm not asking you whom she talked to. Dirt everywhere—filth—oh, you swine! Mop it all up—do you hear? [Exit rapidly]

BUBNOFF: What a savage beast she is!

LUKA: She's a lady that means business!

NASTYA: You grow to be an animal, leading such a life—any human being tied to such a husband as hers . . .

BUBNOFF: Well—that tie isn't worrying her any—

LUKA: Does she always have these fits?

BUBNOFF: Always. You see, she came to find her lover—but he isn't home—

LUKA: I guess she was hurt. Oh-ho! Everybody is trying to be boss—and is threatening everybody else with all kinds of punishment—and still there's no order in life . . . and no cleanliness—

BUBNOFF: All the world likes order—but some people's brains aren't fit for it. All the same—the room should be swept—Nastya—you ought to get busy!

NASTYA: Oh, certainly? Anything else? Think I'm your servant? [Silence] I'm going to get drunk tonight—dead-drunk!

BUBNOFF: Fine business!

LUKA: Why do you want to get drunk, girlie? A

while ago you were crying—and now you say you'll get drunk—

NASTYA: [*Defiantly*] I'll drink—then I cry again—that's all there's to it!

BUBNOFF: That's nothing!

LUKA: But for what reason—tell me. Every pimple has a cause! [Nastya *remains silent, shaking her head*] Oh—you men—what's to become of you? All right—I'll sweep the place. Where's your broom?

BUBNOFF: Behind the door—in the hall—

[Luka *goes into the hall*]

Nastinka!

NASTYA: Yes?

BUBNOFF: Why did Vassilisa jump on Alyoshka?

NASTYA: He told her that Vaska was tired of her and was going to get rid of her—and that he's going to make up to Natasha—I'll go away from here—I'll find another lodging-house—

BUBNOFF: Why? Where?

NASTYA: I'm sick of this—I'm not wanted here!

BUBNOFF: [*Calmly*] You're not wanted anywhere—and, anyway, all people on earth are superfluous—

[Nastya *shakes her head. Rises and slowly, quietly, leaves the cellar.* Miedviedieff *comes in.* Luka, *with the broom, follows him*]

MIEDVIEDIEFF: I don't think I know you—

LUKA: How about the others—d'you know them all?

MIEDVIEDIEFF: I must know everybody in my precinct. But I don't know you.

LUKA: That's because, uncle, the whole world can't stow itself away in your precinct—some of it was bound to remain outside . . . [*Goes into kitchen*]

MIEDVIEDIEFF: [*Crosses to* Bubnoff] It's true—my precinct is rather small—yet it's worse than any of the very largest. Just now, before getting off duty, I had to bring Alyoshka, the shoemaker, to the station house. Just imagine—there he was, stretched right in the middle of the street, playing his concertina and yelping: "I want nothing, nothing!" Horses going past all the time—and with all the traffic going on, he could easily have been run over—and so on! He's a wild youngster—so I just collared him—he likes to make mischief—

BUBNOFF: Coming to play checkers to-night?

MIEDVIEDIEFF: Yes—I'll come—how's Vaska?

BUBNOFF: Same as ever—

MIEDVIEDIEFF: Meaning—he's getting along—?

BUBNOFF: Why shouldn't he? He's able to get along all right.

MIEDVIEDIEFF: [*Doubtfully*] Why shouldn't he? [Luka *goes into hallway, carrying a pail*] M-yes—there's a lot of talk about Vaska. Haven't you heard?

BUBNOFF: I hear all sorts of gossip . . .

MIEDVIEDIEFF: There seems to have been some sort of talk concerning Vassilisa. Haven't you heard about it?

BUBNOFF: What?

MIEDVIEDIEFF: Oh—why—generally speaking.

Perhaps you know—and lie. Everybody knows—[*Severely*] You mustn't lie, brother!

BUBNOFF: Why should I lie?

MIEDVIEDIEFF: That's right. Dogs! They say that Vaska and Vassilisa . . . but what's that to me? I'm not her father. I'm her uncle. Why should they ridicule me? [Kvashnya *comes in*] What are people coming to? They laugh at everything. Aha—you here?

KVASHNYA: Well—my love-sick garrison—? Bubnoff! He came up to me again on the marketplace and started pestering me about marrying him . . .

BUBNOFF: Go to it! Why not? He has money and he's still a husky fellow.

MIEDVIEDIEFF: Me—? I should say so!

KVASHNYA: You ruffian! Don't you dare touch my sore spot! I've gone through it once already, darling. Marriage to a woman is just like jumping through a hole in the ice in winter. You do it once, and you remember it the rest of your life . . .

MIEDVIEDIEFF: Wait! There are different breeds of husbands . . .

KVASHNYA: But there's only one of me! When my beloved husband kicked the bucket, I spent the whole day all by my lonely—just bursting with joy. I sat and simply couldn't believe it was true. . . .

MIEDVIEDIEFF: If your husband beat you without cause, you should have complained to the police.

KVASHNYA: I complained to God for eight years—and he didn't help.

MIEDVIEDIEFF: Nowadays the law forbids to beat your wife . . . all is very strict these days—there's law and order everywhere. You can't beat up people without due cause. If you beat them to maintain discipline—all right . . .

LUKA: [*Comes in with* Anna] Well—we finally managed to get here after all. Oh, you! Why do you, weak as you are, walk about alone? Where's your bunk?

ANNA: [*Pointing*] Thank you, grand-dad.

KVASHNYA: There—she's married—look at her!

LUKA: The little woman is in very bad shape . . . she was creeping along the hallway, clinging to the wall and moaning—why do you leave her by herself?

KVASHNYA: Oh, pure carelessness on our part, little father—forgive us! Her maid, it appears, went out for a walk . . .

LUKA: Go on—poke fun at me . . . but, all the same, how can you neglect a human being like that? No matter who or what, every human life has its worth . . .

MIEDVIEDIEFF: There should be supervision! Suppose she died suddenly—? That would cause a lot of bother . . . we must look after her!

LUKA: True, sergeant!

MIEDVIEDIEFF: Well—yes—though I'm not a sergeant—ah—yet!

LUKA: No! But you carry yourself most martially!

[*Noise of shuffling feet is heard in the hallway. Muffled cries*]

MIEDVIEDIEFF: What now—a row?

BUBNOFF: Sounds like it?

KVASHNYA: I'll go and see . . .

MIEDVIEDIEFF: I'll go, too. It is my duty! Why separate people when they fight? They'll stop sooner or later of their own accord. One gets tired of fighting. Why not let them fight all they want to—freely? They wouldn't fight half as often—if they'd remember former beatings . . .

BUBNOFF: [*Climbing down from his bunk*] Why don't you speak to your superiors about it?

KOSTILYOFF: [*Throws open the door and shouts*] Abram! Come quick—Vassilisa is killing Natasha—come quick.

[*Kvashnya, Miedviedieff, and Bubnoff rush into hallway; Luka looks after them, shaking his head*]

ANNA: Oh God—poor little Natasha . . .

LUKA: Who's fighting out there?

ANNA: Our landladies—they're sisters . . .

LUKA: [*Crossing to Anna*] Why?

ANNA: Oh—for no reason—except that they're both fat and healthy . . .

LUKA: What's your name?

ANNA: Anna . . . I look at you . . . you're like my father—my dear father . . . you're as gentle as he was—and as soft. . . .

LUKA: Soft! Yes! They pounded me till I got soft! [*Laughs tremulously*]

CURTAIN

ACT II.

Same as Act I—Night.

On the bunks near the stove Satine, *the* Baron, Krivoy Zob, *and the* Tartar *play cards.* Kleshtch *and the* Actor *watch them.* Bubnoff, *on his bunk, is playing checkers with* Miedviedieff. Luka *sits on a stool by* Anna's *bedside. The place is lit by two lamps, one on the wall near the card players, the other is on* Bubnoff's *bunk.*

THE TARTAR: I'll play one more game—then I'll stop . . .

BUBNOFF: Zob! Sing! [*He sings*]
"The sun rises and sets . . ."

ZOB: [*Joining in*]
"But my prison is dark, dark . . ."

THE TARTAR: [*To Satine*] Shuffle the cards—and shuffle them well. We know your kind—

ZOB AND BUBNOFF: [*Together*]
"Day and night the wardens
Watch beneath my window . . ."

ANNA: Blows—insults—I've had nothing but that all my life long . . .

LUKA: Don't worry, little mother!

MIEDVIEDIEFF: Look where you're moving!

BUBNOFF: Oh, yes—that's right . . .

THE TARTAR: [*Threatening Satine with his fist*] You're trying to palm a card? I've seen you—you scoundrel . . .

ZOB: Stop it, Hassan! They'll skin us anyway . . . come on, Bubnoff!

ANNA: I can't remember a single day when I didn't go hungry . . . I've been afraid, waking, eating, and sleeping . . . all my life I've trembled—afraid I wouldn't get another bite . . . all my life I've been in rags—all through my wretched life—and why . . . ?

LUKA: Yes, yes, child—you're tired—never you mind!

THE ACTOR: [*To Zob*] Play the Jack—the Jack, devil take you!

THE BARON: And we play the King!

KLESHTCH: They always win.

SATINE: Such is our habit.

MIEDVIEDIEFF: I have the Queen!

BUBNOFF: And so have I!

ANNA: I'm dying . . .

KLESHTCH: Look, look! Prince, throw up the game—throw it up, I tell you!

THE ACTOR: Can't he play without your assistance?

THE BARON: Look out, Andrushka, or I'll beat the life out of you!

THE TARTAR: Deal once more—the pitcher went after water—and got broke—and so did I!

[*Kleshtch shakes his head and crosses to Bubnoff*]

ANNA: I keep on thinking—is it possible that I'll suffer in the other world as I did in this—is it possible? There, too?

LUKA: Nothing of the sort! Don't you disturb yourself! You'll rest there . . . be patient. We all suffer, dear, each in our own way. . . . [*Rises and goes quickly into kitchen*]

BUBNOFF: [*Sings*]
"Watch as long as you please . . ."

ZOB: "I shan't run away . . ."

BOTH: [*Together*]
"I long to be free, free—
Alas! I cannot break my chains. . . ."

THE TARTAR: [*Yells*] That card was up his sleeve!

THE BARON: [*Embarrassed*] Do you want me to shove it up your nose?

THE ACTOR: [*Emphatically*] Prince! You're mistaken—nobody—ever . . .

THE TARTAR: I saw it! You cheat! I won't play!

SATINE: [*Gathering up the cards*] Leave us alone, Hassan . . . you knew right along that we're cheats—why did you play with us?

THE BARON: He lost forty kopecks and he yelps as if he had lost a fortune! And a Prince at that!

THE TARTAR: [*Excitedly*] Then play honest!

SATINE: What for?

THE TARTAR: What do you mean "what for"?

SATINE: Exactly. What for?

THE TARTAR: Don't you know?

SATINE: I don't. Do you?

[The Tartar *spits out, furiously; the others laugh at him*]

ZOB: [*Good-naturedly*] You're a funny fellow, Hassan! Try to understand this! If they should begin to live honestly, they'd die of starvation inside of three days.

THE TARTAR: That's none of my business. You must live honestly!

ZOB: They did you brown! Come and let's have tea. . . . [*Sings*]

"O my chains, my heavy chains . . ."

BUBNOFF: [*Sings*]

"You're my steely, clanking wardens . . ."

ZOB: Come on, Hassanka! [*Leaves the room, singing*]

"I cannot tear you, cannot break you . . ."

[The Tartar *shakes his fist threateningly at the* Baron, *and follows the other out of the room*]

SATINE: [*To* Baron, *laughing*] Well, Your Imperial Highness, you've again sat down magnificently in a mud puddle! You've learned a lot—but you're an ignoramus when it comes to palming a card.

THE BARON: [*Spreading his hands*] The Devil knows how it happened. . . .

THE ACTOR: You're not gifted—you've no faith in yourself—and without that you can never accomplish anything . . .

MIEDVIEDIEFF: I've one Queen—and you've two—oh, well . . .

BUBNOFF: One's enough if she has brains—play!

KLESHTCH: You lost, Abram Ivanovitch?

MIEDVIEDIEFF: None of your business—see? Shut up!

SATINE: I've won fifty-three kopecks.

THE ACTOR: Give me three of them . . . though, what'll I do with them?

LUKA: [*Coming from kitchen*] Well—the Tartar was fleeced all right, eh? Going to have some vodka?

THE BARON: Come with us.

SATINE: I wonder what you'll be like when you're drunk.

LUKA: Same as when I'm sober.

THE ACTOR: Come on, old man—I'll recite verses for you . . .

LUKA: What?

THE ACTOR: Verses. Don't you understand?

LUKA: Verses? And what do I want with verses?

THE ACTOR: Sometimes they're funny—sometimes sad.

SATINE: Well, poet, are you coming? [*Exit with the* Baron]

THE ACTOR: I'm coming. I'll join you. For instance, old man, here's a bit of verse—I forget how it begins—I forget . . . [*Brushes his hand across his forehead*]

BUBNOFF: There! Your Queen is lost—go on, play!

MIEDVIEDIEFF: I made the wrong move.

THE ACTOR: Formerly, before my organism was poisoned with alcohol, old man, I had a good memory. But now it's all over with me, brother. I used to declaim these verses with tremendous success—thunders of applause . . . you have no idea what applause means . . . it goes to your head like vodka! I'd step out on the stage—stand this way—[*Strikes a pose*]—I'd stand there and . . . [*Pause*] I can't remember a word—I can't remember! My favorite verses—isn't it ghastly, old man?

LUKA: Yes—is there anything worse than forgetting what you loved? Your very soul is in the thing you love!

THE ACTOR: I've drunk my soul away, old man—brother, I'm lost . . . and why? Because I had no faith . . . I'm done with . . .

LUKA: Well—then—cure yourself! Nowadays they have a cure for drunkards. They treat you free of charge, brother. There's a hospital for drunkards—where they're treated for nothing. They've owned up, you see, that even a drunkard is a human being, and they're only too glad to help him get well. Well—then—go to it!

THE ACTOR: [*Thoughtfully*] Where? Where is it?

LUKA: Oh—in some town or other . . . what do they call it—? I'll tell you the name presently—only, in the meanwhile, get ready. Don't drink so much! Take yourself in hand—and bear up! And then, when you're cured, you'll begin life all over again. Sounds good, brother, doesn't it, to begin all over again? Well—make up your mind!

THE ACTOR: [*Smiling*] All over again—from the very beginning—that's fine . . . yes . . . all over again . . . [*Laughs*] Well—then—I can, can't I?

LUKA: Why not? A human being can do anything—if he only makes up his mind.

THE ACTOR: [*Suddenly, as if coming out of a trance*] You're a queer bird! See you anon! [*Whistles*] Old man—*au revoir!* [*Exit*]

ANNA: Grand-dad!

LUKA: Yes, little mother?

ANNA: Talk to me.

LUKA: [*Close to her*] Come on—let's chat . . . [Kleshtch, *glancing around, silently walks over to his wife, looks at her, and makes queer gestures with his hands, as though he wanted to say something*]

LUKA: What is it, brother?

KLESHTCH: [*Quietly*] Nothing . . .

[*Crosses slowly to hallway door, stands on the threshold for a few seconds, and exit*]

LUKA: [*Looking after him*] Hard on your man, isn't it?

ANNA: He doesn't concern me much . . .

LUKA: Did he beat you?

ANNA: Worse than that—it's he who's killed me—

BUBNOFF: My wife used to have a lover—the scoundrel—how clever he was at checkers!

MIEDVIEDIEFF: Hm-hm—

ANNA: Grand-dad! Talk to me, darling—I feel so sick . . .

LUKA: Never mind—it's always like this before you die, little dove—never mind, dear! Just have faith! Once you're dead, you'll have peace—always. There's nothing to be afraid of—nothing. Quiet! Peace! Lie quietly! Death wipes out everything. Death is kindly. You die—and you rest—that's what they say. It is true, dear! Because—where can we find rest on this earth?

[Pepel *enters. He is slightly drunk, dishevelled, and sullen. Sits down on bunk near door, and remains silent and motionless*]

ANNA: And how is it—there? More suffering?

LUKA: Nothing of the kind! No suffering! Trust me! Rest—nothing else! They'll lead you into God's presence, and they'll say: "Dear God! Behold! Here is Anna, Thy servant!"

MIEDVIEDIEFF: [*Sternly*] How do you know what they'll say up there? Oh, you . . .

[Pepel, *on hearing* Miedviedieff's *voice, raises his head and listens*]

LUKA: Apparently I do know, Mr. Sergeant!

MIEDVIEDIEFF: [*Conciliatory*] Yes—it's your own affair—though I'm not exactly a sergeant—yet—

BUBNOFF: I jump two!

MIEDVIEDIEFF: Damn—play!

LUKA: And the Lord will look at you gently and tenderly and He'll say: "I know this Anna!" Then He'll say: "Take Anna into Paradise. Let her have peace. I know. Her life on earth was hard. She is very weary. Let Anna rest in peace!"

ANNA: [*Choking*] Grandfather—if it were only so —if there were only rest and peace . . .

LUKA: There won't be anything else! Trust me! Die in joy and not in grief. Death is to us like a mother to small children . . .

ANNA: But—perhaps—perhaps I get well . . .?

LUKA: [*Laughing*] Why—? Just to suffer more?

ANNA: But—just to live a little longer . . . just a little longer! Since there'll be no suffering hereafter, I could bear it a little longer down here . . .

LUKA: There'll be nothing in the hereafter . . . but only . . .

PEPEL: [*Rising*] Maybe yes—maybe no!

ANNA: [*Frightened*] Oh—God!

LUKA: Hey—Adonis!

MIEDVIEDIEFF: Who's that yelping?

PEPEL: [*Crossing over to him*] I! What of it?

MIEDVIEDIEFF: You yelp needlessly—that's what! People ought to have some dignity!

PEPEL: Block-head! And that's an uncle for you—ho-ho!

LUKA: [*To* Pepel, *in an undertone*] Look here—don't shout—this woman's dying—her lips are already grey—don't disturb her!

PEPEL: I've respect for you, grand-dad! You're all right, you are! You lie well, and you spin pleasant yarns. Go on lying, brother—there's little fun in this world . . .

BUBNOFF: Is the woman really dying?

LUKA: You think I'm joking?

BUBNOFF: That means she'll stop coughing. Her cough was very disturbing. I jump two!

MIEDVIEDIEFF: I'd like to murder you!

PEPEL: Abramka!

MIEDVIEDIEFF: I'm not Abramka to you!

PEPEL: Abrashka! Is Natasha ill?

MIEDVIEDIEFF: None of your business!

PEPEL: Come—tell me! Did Vassilisa beat her up very badly?

MIEDVIEDIEFF: That's none of your business, either! It's a family affair! Who are you anyway?

PEPEL: Whoever I am, you'll never see Natashka again if I choose!

MIEDVIEDIEFF: [*Throwing up the game*] What's that? Who are you alluding to? My niece by any chance? You thief!

PEPEL: A thief whom you were never able to catch!

MIEDVIEDIEFF: Wait—I'll catch you yet—you'll see—sooner than you think!

PEPEL: If you catch me, God help your whole nest! Do you think I'll keep quiet before the examining magistrate? Every wolf howls! They'll ask me: "Who made you steal and showed you where?" "Mishka Kostilyoff and his wife!" "Who was your fence?" "Mishka Kostilyoff and his wife!"

MIEDVIEDIEFF: You lie! No one will believe you!

PEPEL: They'll believe me all right—because it's the truth! And I'll drag you into it, too. Ha! I'll ruin the lot of you—devils—just watch!

MIEDVIEDIEFF: [*Confused*] You lie! You lie! And what harm did I do to you, you mad dog?

PEPEL: And what good did you ever do me?

LUKA: That's right!

MIEDVIEDIEFF: [*To* Luka] Well—what are you croaking about? Is it any of your business? This is a family matter!

BUBNOFF: [*To* Luka] Leave them alone! What do we care if they twist each other's tails?

LUKA: [*Peacefully*] I meant no harm. All I said was that if a man isn't good to you, then he's acting wrong. . . .

MIEDVIEDIEFF: [*Uncomprehending*] Now then—we all of us here know each other—but you—who are you? [*Frowns and exit*]

LUKA: The cavalier is peeved! Oh-ho, brothers, I see your affairs are a bit tangled up!

PEPEL: He'll run to complain about us to Vassilisa . . .

BUBNOFF: You're a fool, Vassily. You're very bold these days, aren't you? Watch out! It's all right to be bold when you go gathering mushrooms, but what good is it here? They'll break your neck before you know it!

PEPEL: Well—not as fast as all that! You don't catch us Yaroslavl boys napping! If it's going to be war, we'll fight . . .

LUKA: Look here, boy, you really ought to go away from here—

PEPEL: Where? Please tell me!

LUKA: Go to Siberia!

PEPEL: If I go to Siberia, it'll be at the Tsar's expense!

LUKA: Listen! You go just the same! You can make your own way there. They need your kind out there . . .

PEPEL: My way is clear. My father spent all his life in prison, and I inherited the trait. Even when I was a small child, they called me thief—thief's son.

LUKA: But Siberia is a fine country—a land of gold. Any one who has health and strength and brains can live there like a cucumber in a hot-house.

PEPEL: Old man, why do you always tell lies?

LUKA: What?

PEPEL: Are you deaf? I ask—why do you always lie?

LUKA: What do I lie about?

PEPEL: About everything. According to you, life's wonderful everywhere—but you lie . . . why?

LUKA: Try to believe me. Go and see for yourself. And some day you'll thank me for it. What are you hanging round here for? And, besides, why is truth so important to you? Just think! Truth may spell death to you!

PEPEL: It's all one to me! If that—let it be that!

LUKA: Oh—what a madman! Why should you kill yourself?

BUBNOFF: What are you two jawing about, anyway? I don't understand. What kind of truth do you want, Vaska? And what for? You know the truth about yourself—and so does everybody else . . .

PEPEL: Just a moment! Don't crow! Let him tell me! Listen, old man! Is there a God?

[Luka smiles silently]

BUBNOFF: People just drift along—like shavings on a stream. When a house is built—the shavings are thrown away!

PEPEL: Well? Is there a God? Tell me.

LUKA: [In a low voice] If you have faith, there is; if you haven't, there isn't . . . whatever you believe in, exists . . .

[Pepel looks at Luka in staring surprise]

BUBNOFF: I'm going to have tea—come on over to the restaurant!

LUKA: [To Pepel] What are you staring at?

PEPEL: Oh—just because! Wait now—you mean to say . . .

BUBNOFF: Well—I'm off.

[Goes to door and runs into Vassilisa]

PEPEL: So—you . . .

VASSILISA: [To Bubnoff] Is Natasya home?

BUBNOFF: No. [Exit]

PEPEL: Oh—you've come—?

VASSILISA: [Crossing to Anna] Is she alive yet?

LUKA: Don't disturb her!

VASSILISA: What are you loafing around here for?

LUKA: I'll go—if you want me to . . .

VASSILISA: [Turning towards Pepel's room] Vassily! I've some business with you . . .

[Luka goes to hallway door, opens it, and shuts it loudly, then warily climbs into a bunk, and from there to the top of the stove]

VASSILISA: [Calling from Pepel's room] Vaska—come here!

PEPEL: I won't come—I don't want to . . .

VASSILISA: Why? What are you angry about?

PEPEL: I'm sick of the whole thing . . .

VASSILISA: Sick of me, too?

PEPEL: Yes! Of you, too!

[Vassilisa draws her shawl about her, pressing her hands over her breast. Crosses to Anna, looks carefully through the bed curtains, and returns to Pepel]

Well—out with it!

VASSILISA: What do you want me to say? I can't force you to be loving, and I'm not the sort to beg for kindness. Thank you for telling me the truth.

PEPEL: What truth?

VASSILISA: That you're sick of me—or isn't it the truth? [Pepel looks at her silently. She turns to him] What are you staring at? Don't you recognize me?

PEPEL: [Sighing] You're beautiful, Vassilisa! [She puts her arm about his neck, but he shakes it off] But I never gave my heart to you. . . . I've lived with you and all that—But I never really liked you . . .

VASSILISA: [Quietly] That so? Well—?

PEPEL: What is there to talk about? Nothing. Go away from me!

VASSILISA: Taken a fancy to some one else?

PEPEL: None of your business! Suppose I have—I wouldn't ask you to be my match-maker!

VASSILISA: [Significantly] That's too bad . . . perhaps I might arrange a match . . .

PEPEL: [Suspiciously] Who with?

VASSILISA: You know—why do you pretend? Vassily—let me be frank [With lower voice] I won't deny it—you've offended me . . . it was like a bolt from the blue . . . you said you loved me—and then all of a sudden . . .

PEPEL: It wasn't sudden at all. It's been a long time since I . . . woman, you've no soul! A woman must have a soul . . . we men are beasts—we must be taught—and you, what have you taught me—?

VASSILISA: Never mind the past! I know—no man owns his own heart—you don't love me any longer . . . well and good, it can't be helped!

PEPEL: So that's over. We part peaceably, without a row—as it should be!

VASSILISA: Just a moment! All the same, when I lived with you, I hoped you'd help me out of this swamp—I thought you'd free me from my husband and my uncle—from all this life—and perhaps, Vassya, it wasn't you whom I loved—but my hope—do you understand? I waited for you to drag me out of this mire . . .

PEPEL: You aren't a nail—and I'm not a pair of pincers! I thought you had brains—you are so clever—so crafty . . .

VASSILISA: [*Leaning closely towards him*] Vassa— Let's help each other!

PEPEL: How?

VASSILISA: [*Low and forcibly*] My sister—I know you've fallen for her . . .

PEPEL: And that's why you beat her up, like the beast you are! Look out, Vassilisa! Don't you touch her!

VASSILISA: Wait. Don't get excited. We can do everything quietly and pleasantly. You want to marry her. I'll give you money . . . three hundred rubles—even more than . . .

PEPEL: [*Moving away from her*] Stop! What do you mean?

VASSILISA: Rid me of my husband! Take that noose from around my neck . . .

PEPEL: [*Whistling softly*] So that's the way the land lies! You certainly planned it cleverly . . . in other words, the grave for the husband, the gallows for the lover, and as for yourself . . .

VASSILISA: Vassya! Why the gallows? It doesn't have to be yourself—but one of your pals! And supposing it were yourself—who'd know? Natalia—just think—and you'll have money—you go away somewhere . . . you free me forever—and it'll be very good for my sister to be away from me—the sight of her enrages me. . . . I get furious with her on account of you, and I can't control myself. I tortured the girl—I beat her up—beat her up so that I myself cried with pity for her—but I'll beat her— and I'll go on beating her!

PEPEL: Beast! Bragging about your beastliness?

VASSILISA: I'm not bragging—I speak the truth. Think now, Vassa. You've been to prison twice because of my husband—through his greed. He clings to me like a bed-bug—he's been sucking the life out of me for the last four years—and what sort of a husband is he to me? He's forever abusing Natasha —calls her a beggar—he's just poison, plain poison, to every one . . .

PEPEL: You spin your yarn cleverly . . .

VASSILISA: Everything I say is true. Only a fool could be as blind as you. . . .

[Kostilyoff *enters stealthily and comes forward noisily*]

PEPEL: [*To* Vassilisa] Oh—go away!

VASSILISA: Think it over! [*Sees her husband*] What? You? Following me?

[Pepel *leaps up and stares at* Kostilyoff *savagely*]

KOSTILYOFF: It's I, I! So the two of you were here alone—you were—ah—conversing? [*Suddenly stamps his feet and screams*] Vassilisa—you bitch! You beggar! You damned hag! [*Frightened by his own screams which are met by silence and indifference on the part of the others*] Forgive me, O Lord . . . Vassilisa—again you've led me into the path

of sin. . . . I've been looking for you everywhere. It's time to go to bed. You forgot to fill the lamps— oh, you . . . beggar! Swine! [*Shakes his trembling fist at her, while* Vassilisa *slowly goes to door, glancing at* Pepel *over her shoulder*]

PEPEL: [*To* Kostilyoff] Go away—clear out of here—

KOSTILYOFF: [*Yelling*] What? I? The Boss? I get out? You thief!

PEPEL: [*Sullenly*] Go away, Mishka!

KOSTILYOFF: Don't you dare—I—I'll show you.

[Pepel *seizes him by the collar and shakes him. From the stove comes loud noises and yawns.* Pepel *releases* Kostilyoff *who runs into the hallway, screaming*]

PEPEL: [*Jumping on a bunk*] Who is it? Who's on the stove?

LUKA: [*Raising his head*] Eh?

PEPEL: You?

LUKA: [*Undisturbed*] I—I myself—oh, dear Jesus!

PEPEL: [*Shuts hallway door, looks for the wooden closing bar, but can't find it*] The devil! Come down, old man!

LUKA: I'm climbing down—all right . . .

PEPEL: [*Roughly*] What did you climb on that stove for?

LUKA: Where was I to go?

PEPEL: Why—didn't you go out into the hall?

LUKA: The hall's too cold for an old fellow like myself, brother.

PEPEL: You overheard?

LUKA: Yes—I did. How could I help it? Am I deaf? Well, my boy, happiness is coming your way. Real, good fortune I call it!

PEPEL: [*Suspiciously*] What good fortune—?

LUKA: In so far as I was lying on the stove . . .

PEPEL: Why did you make all that noise?

LUKA: Because I was getting warm . . . it was your good luck . . . I thought if only the boy wouldn't make a mistake and choke the old man . . .

PEPEL: Yes—I might have done it . . . how terrible . . .

LUKA: Small wonder! It isn't difficult to make a mistake of that sort.

PEPEL: [*Smiling*] What's the matter? Did you make the same sort of mistake once upon a time?

LUKA: Boy, listen to me. Send that woman out of your life. Don't let her near you! Her husband— she'll get rid of him herself—and in a shrewder way than you could—yes! Don't you listen to that devil! Look at me! I am bald-headed—know why? Because of all these women. . . . Perhaps I knew more women than I had hair on the top of my head—but this Vassilisa—she's worse than the plague. . . .

PEPEL: I don't understand . . . I don't know whether to thank you—or—well . . .

LUKA: Don't say a word! You won't improve on what I said. Listen: take the one you like by the arm, and march out of here—get out of here—clean out . . .

PEPEL: [*Sadly*] I can't understand people. Who is kind and who isn't? It's all a mystery to me . . .

LUKA: What's there to understand? There's all breeds of men . . . they all live as their hearts tell them . . . good to-day, bad to-morrow! But if you really care for that girl . . . take her away from here and that's all there is to it. Otherwise go away alone . . . you're young—you're in no hurry for a wife . . .

PEPEL: [*Taking him by the shoulder*] Tell me! Why do you say all this?

LUKA: Wait. Let me go. I want a look at Anna . . . she was coughing so terribly . . . [*Goes to* Anna's *bed, pulls the curtains, looks, touches her.* Pepel, *thoughtfully and distraught, follows him with his eyes*] Merciful Jesus Christ! Take into Thy keeping the soul of this woman Anna, new-comer amongst the blessed!

PEPEL: [*Softly*] Is she dead?

[*Without approaching, he stretches himself and looks at the bed*]

LUKA: [*Gently*] Her sufferings are over! Where's her husband?

PEPEL: In the saloon, most likely . . .

LUKA: Well—he'll have to be told . . .

PEPEL: [*Shuddering*] I don't like corpses!

LUKA: [*Going to door*] Why should you like them? It's the living who demand our love—the living . . .

PEPEL: I'm coming with you . . .

LUKA: Are you afraid?

PEPEL: I don't like it . . .

[*They go out quickly. The stage is empty and silent for a few moments. Behind the door is heard a dull, staccato, incomprehensible noise. Then the* Actor *enters*]

THE ACTOR: [*Stands at the open door, supporting himself against the jamb, and shouts*] Hey, old man —where are you—? I just remembered—listen . . . [*Takes two staggering steps forward and, striking a pose, recites*]
"Good people! If the world cannot find
A path to holy truth,
Glory be to the madman who will enfold all humanity
In a golden dream . . ."

[Natasha *appears in the doorway behind the* Actor]
Old man! [*Recites*]
"If to-morrow the sun were to forget
To light our earth,
To-morrow then some madman's thought
Would bathe the world in sunshine. . . ."

NATASHA: [*Laughing*] Scarecrow! You're drunk!

THE ACTOR: [*Turns to her*] Oh—it's you? Where's the old man, the dear old man? Not a soul here, seems to me . . . Natasha, farewell—right—farewell!

NATASHA: [*Entering*] Don't wish me farewell, before you've wished me how-d'you-do!

THE ACTOR: [*Barring her way*] I am going. Spring will come—and I'll be here no longer—

NATASHA: Wait a moment! Where do you propose going?

THE ACTOR: In search of a town—to be cured— And you, Ophelia, must go away! Take the veil! Just imagine—there's a hospital to cure—ah—organisms for drunkards—a wonderful hospital— built of marble—with marble floors . . . light— clean—food—and all gratis! And a marble floor— yes! I'll find it—I'll get cured—and then I shall start life anew. . . . I'm on my way to regeneration, as King Lear said. Natasha, my stage name is . . . Svertchkoff—Zavoloushski . . . do you realize how painful it is to lose one's name? Even dogs have their names . . .

[Natasha *carefully passes the* Actor, *stops at* Anna's *bed and looks*]
To be nameless—is not to exist!

NATASHA: Look, my dear—why—she's dead. . . .

THE ACTOR: [*Shakes his head*] Impossible . . .

NATASHA: [*Stepping back*] So help me God— look . . .

BUBNOFF: [*Appearing in doorway*] What is there to look at?

NATASHA: Anna—she's dead!

BUBNOFF: That means—she's stopped coughing! [*Goes to* Anna's *bed, looks, and returns to his bunk*] We must tell Kleshtch—it's his business to know . . .

THE ACTOR: I'll go—I'll say to him—she lost her name—[*Exit*]

NATASHA: [*In centre of room*] I, too—some day— I'll be found in the cellar—dead. . . .

BUBNOFF: [*Spreading out some rags on his bunk*] What's that? What are you muttering?

NATASHA: Nothing much . . .

BUBNOFF: Waiting for Vaska, eh? Take care— Vassilisa'll break your head!

NATASHA: Isn't it the same who breaks it? I'd much rather he'd do it!

BUBNOFF: [*Lying down*] Well—that's your own affair . . .

NATASHA: It's best for her to be dead—yet it's a pity . . . oh, Lord—why do we live?

BUBNOFF: It's so with all . . . we're born, live, and die—and I'll die, too—and so'll you—what's there to be gloomy about?

[*Enter Luka, the* Tartar, Zob, *and* Kleshtch. *The latter comes after the others, slowly, shrunk up*]

NATASHA: Sh-sh! Anna!

ZOB: We've heard—God rest her soul . . .

THE TARTAR: [*To* Kleshtch] We must take her out of here. Out into the hall! This is no place for corpses—but for the living . . .

KLESHTCH: [*Quietly*] We'll take her out—

[*Everybody goes to the bed,* Kleshtch *looks at his wife over the others' shoulders*]

ZOB: [*To* The Tartar] You think she'll smell? I don't think she will—she dried up while she was still alive . . .

NATASHA: God! If they'd only a little pity . . . if only some one would say a kindly word—oh, you . . .

LUKA: Don't be hurt, girl—never mind! Why and how should we pity the dead? Come, dear! We don't pity the living—we can't even pity our own selves—how can we?

BUBNOFF: [*Yawning*] And, besides, when you're dead, no word will help you—when you're still alive, even sick, it may. . . .

THE TARTAR: [*Stepping aside*] The police must be notified . . .

ZOB: The police—must be done! Kleshtch! Did you notify the police?

KLESHTCH: No—she's got to be buried—and all I have is forty kopecks—

ZOB: Well—you'll have to borrow then—otherwise we'll take up a collection . . . one'll give five kopecks, others as much as they can. But the police must be notified at once—or they'll think you killed her or God knows what not . . .

[*Crosses to* The Tartar's *bunk and prepares to lie down by his side*]

NATASHA: [*Going to* Bubnoff's *bunk*] Now—I'll dream of her . . . I always dream of the dead . . . I'm afraid to go out into the hall by myself—it's dark there . . .

LUKA: [*Following her*] You better fear the living —I'm telling you . . .

NATASHA: Take me across the hall, grandfather.

LUKA: Come on—come on—I'll take you across—

[*They go away. Pause*]

ZOB: [*To* The Tartar] Oh-ho! Spring will soon be here, little brother, and it'll be quite warm. In the villages the peasants are already making ready their ploughs and harrows, preparing to till . . . and we . . . Hassan? Snoring already? Damned Mohammedan!

BUBNOFF: Tartars love sleep!

KLESHTCH: [*In centre of room, staring in front of him*] What am I to do now?

ZOB: Lie down and sleep—that's all . . .

KLESHTCH: [*Softly*] But—she . . . how about . . .

[*No one answers him.* Satine *and* The Actor *enter*]

THE ACTOR: [*Yelling*] Old man! Come here, my trusted Duke of Kent!

SATINE: Miklookha-Maklai is coming—ho-ho!

THE ACTOR: It has been decided upon! Old man, where's the town—where are you?

SATINE: Fata Morgana, the old man bilked you from top to bottom! There's nothing—no towns—no people—nothing at all!

THE ACTOR: You lie!

THE TARTAR: [*Jumping up*] Where's the boss? I'm

going to the boss. If I can't sleep, I won't pay! Corpses—drunkards . . . [*Exit quickly*]

[Satine *looks after him and whistles*]

BUBNOFF: [*In a sleepy voice*] Go to bed, boys—be quiet . . . night is for sleep . . .

THE ACTOR: Yes—so—there's a corpse here. . . . "Our net fished up a corpse. . . ." Verses by Béranger. . . .

SATINE: [*Screams*] The dead can't hear . . . the dead do not feel—Scream!—Roar! . . . the deaf don't hear!

[*In the doorway appears* Luka]

CURTAIN

ACT III.

"The Waste," a yard strewn with rubbish and overgrown with weeds. Back, a high brick wall which shuts out the sight of the sky. Near it are elder-bushes. Right, the dark, wooden wall of some sort of house, barn or stable. Left, the grey tumbledown wall of Kostilyoff's night asylum. It is built at an angle so that the further corner reaches almost to the centre of the yard. Between it and the wall runs a narrow passage. In the grey, plastered wall are two windows, one on a level with the ground, the other about six feet higher up and closer to the brick wall. Near the latter wall is a big sledge turned upside down and a beam about twelve feet long. Right of the wall is a heap of old planks. Evening. The sun is setting, throwing a crimson light on the brick wall. Early spring, the snow having only recently melted. The elder-bushes are not yet in bud.

Natasha *and* Nastya *are sitting side by side on the beam.* Luka *and the* Baron *are on the sledge.* Kleshtch *is stretched on the pile of planks to the right.* Bubnoff's *face is at the ground floor window.*

NASTYA: [*With closed eyes, nodding her head in rhythm to the tale she is telling in a sing-song voice*] So then at night he came into the garden. I had been waiting for him quite a while. I trembled with fear and grief—he trembled, too . . . he was as white as chalk—and he had the pistol in his hand . . .

NATASHA: [*Chewing sun-flower seeds*] Oh—are these students really such desperate fellows? . . .

NASTYA: And he says to me in a dreadful voice: "My precious darling . . ."

BUBNOFF: Ho-ho! Precious—?

THE BARON: Shut up! If you don't like it, you can lump it! But don't interrupt her. . . . Go on . . .

NASTYA: "My one and only love," he says, "my parents," he says, "refuse to give their consent to our wedding—and threaten to disown me because of my love for you. Therefore," he says, "I must take my life." And his pistol was huge—and loaded with ten bullets . . . "Farewell," he says, "beloved comrade! I have made up my mind for good and all . . . I can't live without you . . ." and I replied: "My unforgettable friend—my Raoul. . . ."

BUBNOFF: [Surprised] What? What? Krawl—did you call him—?

THE BARON: Nastka! But last time his name was Gaston. . . .

NASTYA: [Jumping up] Shut up, you bastards! Ah—you lousy mongrels! You think for a moment that you can understand love—true love? My love was real honest-to-God love! [To the Baron] You good-for-nothing! . . . educated, you call yourself—drinking coffee in bed, did you?

LUKA: Now, now! Wait, people! Don't interfere! Show a little respect to your neighbors . . . it isn't the word that matters, but what's in back of the word. That's what matters! Go on, girl! It's all right!

BUBNOFF: Go on, crow! See if you can make your feathers white!

THE BARON: Well—continue!

NATASHA: Pay no attention to them . . . what are they? They're just jealous . . . they've nothing to tell about themselves . . .

NASTYA: [Sits down again] I'm going to say no more! If they don't believe me they'll laugh. [Stops suddenly, is silent for a few seconds, then, shutting her eyes, continues in a loud and intense voice, swaying her hands as if to the rhythm of far music] And then I replied to him: "Joy of my life! My bright moon! And I, too, I can't live without you—because I love you madly, so madly—and I shall keep on loving you as long as my heart beats in my bosom. But—" I say—"don't take your young life! Think how necessary it is to your dear parents whose only happiness you are. Leave me! Better that I should perish from longing for you, my life! I alone! I—ah—as such, such! Better that I should die—it doesn't matter . . . I am of no use to the world—and I have nothing, nothing at all—" [Covers her face with her hand and weeps gently]

NATASHA: [In a low voice] Don't cry—don't!

[Luka, smiling, strokes Nastya's head]

BUBNOFF: [Laughs] Ah—you limb of Satan!

THE BARON: [Also laughs] Hey, old man? Do you think it's true? It's all from that book, Fatal Love . . . it's all nonsense! Let her alone!

NATASHA: And what's it to you? Shut up—or God'll punish you!

NASTYA: [Bitterly] God damn your soul! You worthless pig! Soul—bah!—you haven't got one!

LUKA: [Takes Nastya's hand] Come, dear! It's nothing! Don't be angry—I know—I believe you! You're right, not they! If you believe you had a real love affair, then you did—yes! And as for him—don't be angry with a fellow-lodger . . . maybe he's really jealous, and that's why he's laughing. Maybe he never had any real love—maybe not—come on—let's go!

NASTYA: [Pressing her hand against her breast]

Grandfather! So help me God—it happened! It happened! He was a student, a Frenchman—Gastotcha was his name—he had a little black beard—and patent leathers—may God strike me dead if I'm lying! And he loved me so—My God, how he loved me!

LUKA: Yes, yes, it's all right. I believe you! Patent leathers, you said? Well, well, well—and you loved him, did you? [Disappears with her around the corner]

THE BARON: God—isn't she a fool, though? She's good-hearted—but such a fool—it's past belief!

BUBNOFF: And why are people so fond of lying—just as if they were up before the judge—really!

NATASHA: I guess lying is more fun than speaking the truth—I, too . . .

THE BARON: What—you, too? Go on!

NATASHA: Oh—I imagine things—invent them—and I wait—

THE BARON: For what?

NATASHA: [Smiling confusedly] Oh—I think that perhaps—well—to-morrow somebody will really appear—some one—oh—out of the ordinary—or something'll happen—also out of the ordinary. . . . I've been waiting for it—oh—always . . . But, really, what is there to wait for?

[Pause]

THE BARON: [With a slight smile] Nothing—I expect nothing! What is past, is past! Through! Over with! And then what?

NATASHA: And then—well—to-morrow I imagine suddenly that I'll die—and I get frightened . . . in summer it's all right to dream of death—then there are thunder storms—one might get struck by lightning . . .

THE BARON: You've a hard life . . . your sister's a wicked-tempered devil!

NATASHA: Tell me—does anybody live happily? It's hard for all of us—I can see that . . .

KLESHTCH: [Who until this moment has sat motionless and indifferent, jumps up suddenly] For all? You lie! Not for all! If it were so—all right! Then it wouldn't hurt—yes!

BUBNOFF: What in hell's bit you? Just listen to him yelping!

[Kleshtch lies down again and grunts]

THE BARON: Well—I'd better go and make my peace with Nastinka—if I don't, she won't treat me to vodka . . .

BUBNOFF: Hm—people love to lie . . . with Nastka—I can see the reason why. She's used to painting that mutt of hers—and now she wants to paint her soul as well . . . put rouge on her soul, eh? But the others—why do they? Take Luka for instance—he lies a lot . . . and what does he get out of it? He's an old fellow, too—why does he do it?

THE BARON: [Smiling and walking away] All people have drab-colored souls—and they like to brighten them up a bit . . .

LUKA: [*Appearing from round the corner*] You, sir, why do you tease the girl? Leave her alone—let her cry if it amuses her . . . she weeps for her own pleasure—what harm is it to you?

THE BARON: Nonsense, old man! She's a nuisance. Raoul to-day, Gaston to-morrow—always the same old yarn, though! Still—I'll go and make up with her. [*Leaves*]

LUKA: That's right—go—and be nice to her. Being nice to people never does them any harm . . .

NATASHA: You're so good, little father—why are you so good?

LUKA: Good, did you say? Well—call it that! [*Behind the brick wall is heard soft singing and the sounds of a concertina*] Some one has to be kind, girl—some one must pity people! Christ pitied everybody—and he said to us: "Go and do likewise!" I tell you—if you pity a man when he most needs it, good comes of it. Why—I used to be a watchman on the estate of an engineer near Tomsk—all right—the house was right in the middle of a forest—lonely place—winter came—and I remained all by myself. Well—one night I heard a noise—

NATASHA: Thieves?

LUKA: Exactly! Thieves creeping in! I took my gun—I went out. I looked and saw two of them opening a window—and so busy that they didn't even see me. I yell: "Hey there—get out of here!" And they turn on me with their axes—I warn them to stand back, or I'd shoot—and as I speak, I keep on covering them with my gun, first the one, then the other—they go down on their knees, as if to implore me for mercy. And by that time I was furious—because of those axes, you see—and so I say to them: "I was chasing you, you scoundrels—and you didn't go. Now you go and break off some stout branches!"—and they did so—and I say: "Now—one of you lie down and let the other one flog him!" So they obey me and flog each other—and then they begin to implore me again. "Grandfather," they say, "for God's sake give us some bread! We're hungry!" There's thieves for you, my dear! [*Laughs*] And with an ax, too! Yes—honest peasants, both of them! And I say to them, "You should have asked for bread straight away!" And they say: "We got tired of asking—you beg and beg—and nobody gives you a crumb—it hurts!" So they stayed with me all that winter—one of them, Stepan, would take my gun and go shooting in the forest—and the other, Yakoff, was ill most of the time—he coughed a lot . . . and so the three of us together looked after the house . . . then spring came . . . "Good-bye, grandfather," they said—and they went away—back home to Russia . . .

NATASHA: Were they escaped convicts?

LUKA: That's just what they were—escaped convicts—from a Siberian prison camp . . . honest peasants! If I hadn't felt sorry for them—they might have killed me—or maybe worse—and then there would have been trial and prison and afterwards Siberia—what's the sense of it? Prison teaches no good—and Siberia doesn't either—but another human being can . . . yes, a human being can teach another one kindness—very simply! [*Pause*]

BUBNOFF: Hm—yes—I, for instance, don't know how to lie . . . why—as far as I'm concerned, I believe in coming out with the whole truth and putting it on thick . . . why fuss about it?

KLESHTCH: [*Again jumps up as if his clothes were on fire, and screams*] What truth? Where is there truth? [*Tearing at his ragged clothes*] Here's truth for you! No work! No strength! That's the only truth! Shelter—there's no shelter! You die—that's the truth! Hell! What do I want with the truth? Let me breathe! Why should I be blamed? What do I want with truth? To live—Christ Almighty!—they won't let you live—and that's another truth!

BUBNOFF: He's mad!

LUKA: Dear Lord . . . listen to me, brother—

KLESHTCH: [*Trembling with excitement*] They say: there's truth! You, old man, try to console every one . . . I tell you—I hate every one! And there's your truth—God curse it—understand? I tell you—God curse it!

[*Rushes away round the corner, turning as he goes*]

LUKA: Ah—how excited he got! Where did he run off to?

NATASHA: He's off his head . . .

BUBNOFF: God—didn't he say a whole lot, though? As if he was playing drama—he gets those fits often . . . he isn't used to life yet . . .

PEPEL: [*Comes slowly round the corner*] Peace on all this honest gathering! Well, Luka, you wily old fellow—still telling them stories?

LUKA: You should have heard how that fellow carried on!

PEPEL: Kleshtch—wasn't it? What's wrong with him? He was running like one possessed!

LUKA: You'd do the same if your own heart were breaking!

PEPEL: [*Sitting down*] I don't like him . . . he's got such a nasty, bad temper—and so proud! [*Imitating* Kleshtch] "I'm a workman!" And he thinks everyone's beneath him. Go on working if you feel like it—nothing to be so damned haughty about! If work is the standard—a horse can give us points—pulls like hell and says nothing! Natasha—are your folks at home?

NATASHA: They went to the cemetery—then to night service . . .

PEPEL: So that's why you're free for once—quite a novelty.

LUKA: [*To Bubnoff, thoughtfully*] There—you say—truth! Truth doesn't always heal a wounded soul. For instance, I knew of a man who believed in a land of righteousness . . .

BUBNOFF: In what?

LUKA: In a land of righteousness. He said: "Somewhere on this earth there must be a righteous land—

and wonderful people live there—good people! They respect each other, help each other, and everything is peaceful and good!" And so that man—who was always searching for this land of righteousness—he was poor and lived miserably—and when things got to be so bad with him that it seemed there was nothing else for him to do except lie down and die —even then he never lost heart—but he'd just smile and say: "Never mind! I can stand it! A little while longer—and I'll have done with this life—and I'll go in search of the righteous land!"—it was his one happiness—the thought of that land . . .

PEPEL: Well? Did he go there?

BUBNOFF: Where? Ho-ho!

LUKA: And then to this place—in Siberia, by the way—there came a convict—a learned man with books and maps—yes, a learned man who knew all sorts of things—and the other man said to him: "Do me a favor—show me where is the land of righteousness and how I can get there." At once the learned man opened his books, spread out his maps, and looked and looked and he said—no—he couldn't find this land anywhere . . . everything was correct—all the lands on earth were marked—but not this land of righteousness . . .

PEPEL: [In a low voice] Well? Wasn't there a trace of it?

[Bubnoff roars with laughter]

NATASHA: Wait . . . well, little father?

LUKA: The man wouldn't believe it. . . . "It must exist," he said, "look carefully. Otherwise," he says, "your books and maps are of no use if there's no land of righteousness." The learned man was offended. "My plans," he said, "are correct. But there exists no land of righteousness anywhere." Well, then the other man got angry. He'd lived and lived and suffered and suffered, and had believed all the time in the existence of this land—and now, according to the plans, it didn't exist at all. He felt robbed! And he said to the learned man: "Ah—you scum of the earth! You're not a learned man at all—but just a damned cheat!"—and he gave him a good wallop in the eye—then another one . . . [After a moment's silence] And then he went home and hanged himself!

[All are silent. Luka, smiling, looks at Pepel and Natasha]

PEPEL: [Low-voiced] To hell with this story—it isn't very cheerful . . .

NATASHA: He couldn't stand the disappointment . . .

BUBNOFF: [Sullen] Ah—it's nothing but a fairy-tale . . .

PEPEL: Well—there is the righteous land for you —doesn't exist, it seems . . .

NATASHA: I'm sorry for that man . . .

BUBNOFF: All a story—ho-ho!—land of righteousness—what an idea! [Exit through window]

LUKA: [Pointing to window] He's laughing!

[Pause] Well, children, God be with you! I'll leave you soon . . .

PEPEL: Where are you going to?

LUKA: To the Ukraine—I heard they discovered a new religion there—I want to see—yes! People are always seeking—they always want something better—God grant them patience!

PEPEL: You think they'll find it?

LUKA: The people? They will find it! He who seeks, will find! He who desires strongly, will find!

NATASHA: If only they could find something better —invent something better . . .

LUKA: They're trying to! But we must help them, girl—we must respect them . . .

NATASHA: How can I help them? I am helpless myself!

PEPEL: [Determined] Again—listen—I'll speak to you again, Natasha—here—before him—he knows everything . . . run away with me?

NATASHA: Where? From one prison to another?

PEPEL: I told you—I'm through with being a thief, so help me God! I'll quit! If I say so, I'll do it! I can read and write—I'll work—He's been telling me to go to Siberia on my own hook—let's go there together, what do you say? Do you think I'm not disgusted with my life? Oh—Natasha—I know . . . I see . . . I console myself with the thought that there are lots of people who are honored and respected—and who are bigger thieves than I! But what good is that to me? It isn't that I repent . . . I've no conscience . . . but I do feel one thing: One must live differently. One must live a better life . . . one must be able to respect one's own self . . .

LUKA: That's right, friend! May God help you! It's true! A man must respect himself!

PEPEL: I've been a thief from childhood on. Everybody always called me "Vaska—the thief—the son of a thief!" Oh—very well then—I am a thief— . . . just imagine—now, perhaps, I'm a thief out of spite—perhaps I'm a thief because no one ever called me anything different. . . . Well, Natasha—?

NATASHA: [Sadly] Somehow I don't believe in words—and I'm restless to-day—my heart is heavy . . . as if I were expecting something . . . it's a pity, Vassily, that you talked to me to-day . . .

PEPEL: When should I? It isn't the first time I speak to you . . .

NATASHA: And why should I go with you? I don't love you so very much—sometimes I like you—and other times the mere sight of you makes me sick . . . it seems—no—I don't really love you . . . when one really loves, one sees no fault. . . . But I do see . . .

PEPEL: Never mind—you'll love me after a while! I'll make you care for me . . . if you'll just say yes! For over a year I've watched you . . . you're a decent girl . . . you're kind—you're reliable—I'm very much in love with you . . .

[Vassilisa, *in her best dress, appears at window and listens*]

NATASHA: Yes—you love me—but how about my sister? . . .

PEPEL: [*Confused*] Well, what of her? There are plenty like her . . .

LUKA: You'll be all right, girl! If there's no bread, you have to eat weeds . . .

PEPEL: [*Gloomily*] Please—feel a little sorry for me! My life isn't all roses—it's a hell of a life . . . little happiness in it . . . I feel as if a swamp were sucking me under . . . and whatever I try to catch and hold on to, is rotten . . . it breaks . . . Your sister—oh—I thought she was different . . . if she weren't so greedy after money . . . I'd have done anything for her sake, if she were only all mine . . . but she must have someone else . . . and she has to have money—and freedom . . . because she doesn't like the straight and narrow . . . she can't help me. But you're like a young fir-tree . . . you bend, but you don't break . . .

LUKA: Yes—go with him, girl, go! He's a good lad—he's all right! Only tell him every now and then that he's a good lad so that he won't forget it—and he'll believe you. Just you keep on telling him "Vasya, you're a good man—don't you forget it!" Just think, dear, where else could you go except with him? Your sister is a savage beast . . . and as for her husband, there's little to say of him? He's rotten beyond words . . . and all this life here, where will it get you? But this lad is strong . . .

NATASHA: Nowhere to go—I know—I thought of it. The only thing is—I've no faith in anybody—and there's no place for me to turn to . . .

PEPEL: Yes, there is! But I won't let you go that way—I'd rather cut your throat!

NATASHA: [*Smiling*] There—I'm not his wife yet—and he talks already of killing me!

PEPEL: [*Puts his arms around her*] Come, Natasha! Say yes!

NATASHA: [*Holding him close*] But I'll tell you one thing, Vassily—I swear it before God . . . the first time you strike me or hurt me any other way, I'll have no pity on myself . . . I'll either hang myself . . . or . . .

PEPEL: May my hand wither if ever I touch you!

LUKA: Don't doubt him, dear! He needs you more than you need him!

VASSILISA: [*From the window*] So now they're engaged! Love and advice!

NATASHA: They've come back—oh, God—they saw—oh, Vassily . . .

PEPEL: Why are you frightened? Nobody'll dare touch you now!

VASSILISA: Don't be afraid, Natalia! He won't beat you . . . he don't know how to love or how to beat . . . I know!

LUKA: [*In a low voice*] Rotten old hag—like a snake in the grass . . .

VASSILISA: He dares only with the word!

KOSTILYOFF: [*Enters*] Natashka! What are you doing here, you parasite? Gossiping? Kicking about your family? And the samovar not ready? And the table not cleared?

NATASHA: [*Going out*] I thought you were going to church . . .?

KOSTILYOFF: None of your business what we intended doing! Mind your own affairs—and do what you're told!

PEPEL: Shut up, you! She's no longer your servant! Don't go, Natalia—don't do a thing!

NATASHA: Stop ordering me about—you're commencing too soon! [*Leaves*]

PEPEL: [*To* Kostilyoff] That's enough. You've used her long enough—now she's mine!

KOSTILYOFF: Yours? When did you buy her—and for how much?

[Vassilisa *roars with laughter*]

LUKA: Go away, Vasya!

PEPEL: Don't laugh, you fools—or first thing you know I'll make you cry!

VASSILISA: Oh, how terrible! Oh—how you frighten me!

LUKA: Vassily—go away! Don't you see—she's goading you on . . . ridiculing you, don't you understand? . . .

PEPEL: Yes . . . You lie, lie! You won't get what you want!

VASSILISA: Nor will I get what I don't want, Vasya!

PEPEL: [*Shaking his fist at her*] We'll see . . . [*Exit*]

VASSILISA: [*Disappearing through window*] I'll arrange some wedding for you . . .

KOSTILYOFF: [*Crossing to* Luka] Well, old man, how's everything?

LUKA: All right!

KOSTILYOFF: You're going away, they say—?

LUKA: Soon.

KOSTILYOFF: Where to?

LUKA: I'll follow my nose . . .

KOSTILYOFF: Tramping, eh? Don't like stopping in one place all the time, do you?

LUKA: Even water won't pass beneath a stone that's sunk too firmly in the ground, they say . . .

KOSTILYOFF: That's true for a stone. But man must settle in one place. Men can't live like cockroaches, crawling about wherever they want. . . . A man must stick to one place—and not wander about aimlessly . . .

LUKA: But suppose his home is wherever he hangs his hat?

KOSTILYOFF: Why, then—he's a vagabond—useless . . . a human being must be of some sort of use—he must work . . .

LUKA: That's what you think, eh?

KOSTILYOFF: Yes—sure . . . just look! What's a vagabond? A strange fellow . . . unlike all others. If he's a real pilgrim then he's some good in the world . . . perhaps he discovered a new truth. Well

—but not every truth is worth while. Let him keep it to himself and shut up about it! Or else—let him speak in a way which no one can understand . . . don't let him interfere . . . don't let him stir up people without cause! It's none of his business how other people live! Let him follow his own righteous path . . . in the woods—or in a monastery—away from everybody! He mustn't interfere—nor condemn other people—but pray—pray for all of us—for all the world's sins—for mine—for yours—for everybody's. To pray—that's why he forsakes the world's turmoil! That's so! [*Pause*] But you—what sort of pilgrim are you—? An honest person must have a passport . . . all honest people have passports . . . yes! . . .

LUKA: In this world there are people—and also just plain men . . .

KOSTILYOFF: Don't coin wise sayings! Don't give me riddles! I'm as clever as you . . . what's the difference—people and men?

LUKA: What riddle is there? I say—there's sterile and there's fertile ground . . . whatever you sow in it, grows . . . that's all . . .

KOSTILYOFF: What do you mean?

LUKA: Take yourself for instance . . . if the Lord God himself said to you: "Mikhailo, be a man!"—it would be useless—nothing would come of it—you're doomed to remain just as you are . . .

KOSTILYOFF: Oh—but do you realize that my wife's uncle is a policeman, and that if I . . .

VASSILISA: [*Coming in*] Mikhail Ivanitch—come and have your tea.

KOSTILYOFF: [*To* Luka] You listen! Get out! You leave this place—hear?

VASSILISA: Yes—get out, old man! Your tongue's too long! And—who knows—you may be an escaped convict . . .

KOSTILYOFF: If I ever see sign of you again after to-day—well—I've warned you!

LUKA: You'll call your uncle, eh? Go on—call him! Tell him you've caught an escaped convict—and maybe uncle'll get a reward—perhaps all of three kopecks . . .

BUBNOFF: [*In the window*] What are you bargaining about? Three kopecks—for what?

LUKA: They're threatening to sell me . . .

VASSILISA: [*To her husband*] Come . . .

BUBNOFF: For three kopecks? Well—look out, old man—they may even do it for one!

KOSTILYOFF: [*To* Bubnoff] You have a habit of jumping up like a jack-in-the-box!

VASSILISA: The world is full of shady people and crooks—

LUKA: Hope you'll enjoy your tea!

VASSILISA: [*Turning*] Shut up! You rotten toadstool!

[*Leaves with her husband*]

LUKA: I'm off to-night.

BUBNOFF: That's right. Don't outstay your welcome!

LUKA: True enough.

BUBNOFF: I know. Perhaps I've escaped the gallows by getting away in time . . .

LUKA: Well?

BUBNOFF: That's true. It was this way. My wife took up with my boss. He was great at his trade—could dye a dog's skin so that it looked like a raccoon's—could change cat's skin into kangaroo—muskrats, all sorts of things. Well—my wife took up with him—and they were so mad about each other that I got afraid they might poison me or something like that—so I commenced beating up my wife—and the boss beat me . . . we fought savagely! Once he tore off half my whiskers—and broke one of my ribs . . . well, then I, too, got enraged. . . . I cracked my wife over the head with an iron yard-measure—well—and altogether it was like an honest-to-God war! And then I saw that nothing really could come of it . . . they were planning to get the best of me! So I started planning—how to kill my wife—I thought of it a whole lot . . . but I thought better of it just in time . . . and got away . . .

LUKA: That was best! Let them go on changing dogs into raccoons!

BUBNOFF: Only—the shop was in my wife's name . . . and so I did myself out of it, you see? Although, to tell the truth, I would have drunk it away . . . I'm a hard drinker, you know . . .

LUKA: A hard drinker—oh . . . .

BUBNOFF: The worst you ever met! Once I start drinking, I drink, everything in sight, I'll spend every bit of money I have—everything except my bones and my skin . . . what's more, I'm lazy . . . it's terrible how I hate work!

[*Enter* Satine *and the* Actor, *quarreling*]

SATINE: Nonsense! You'll go nowhere—it's all a damned lie! Old man, what did you stuff him with all those fairy-tales for?

THE ACTOR: You lie! Grandfather! Tell him that he lies!—I am going away. I worked to-day—I swept the streets . . . and I didn't have a drop of vodka. What do you think of that? Here they are—two fifteen-kopeck pieces—and I'm sober!

SATINE: Why—that's absurd! Give it to me—I'll either drink it up—or lose it at cards . . .

THE ACTOR: Get out—this is for my journey . . .

LUKA: [*To* Satine] And you—why are you trying to lead him astray?

SATINE: Tell me, soothsayer, beloved by the gods, what's my future going to be? I've gone to pieces, brother—but everything isn't lost yet, grandfather . . . there are sharks in this world who got more brains than I!

LUKA: You're cheerful, Constantine—and very agreeable!

BUBNOFF: Actor, come over here! [*The* Actor *crosses to window, sits down on the sill before* Bubnoff, *and speaks in a low voice with him*]

SATINE: You know, brother, I used to be a clever

youngster. It's nice to think of it. I was a devil of a fellow . . . danced splendidly, played on the stage, loved to amuse people . . . it was awfully gay . . .

LUKA: How did you get to be what you are?

SATINE: You're inquisitive, old man! You want to know everything? What for?

LUKA: I want to understand the ways of men—I look at you, and I don't understand. You're a bold lad, Constantine, and you're no fool . . . yet, all of a sudden . . .

SATINE: It's prison, grandfather—I spent four years and seven months in prison . . . afterwards —where could I go?

LUKA: Aha! What were you there for?

SATINE: On account of a scoundrel—whom I killed in a fit of rage . . . and despair . . . and in prison I learned to play cards. . . .

LUKA: You killed—because of a woman?

SATINE: Because of my own sister. . . . But look here—leave me alone! I don't care for these cross-examinations—and all this happened a long time ago. It's already nine years since my sister's death. . . . Brother, she was a wonderful girl . . .

LUKA: You take life easily! And only a while ago that locksmith was here—and how he did yell!

SATINE: Kleshtch?

LUKA: Yes—"There's no work," he shouted, "there isn't anything . . ."

SATINE: He'll get used to it. What could I do?

LUKA: [Softly] Look—here he comes!

[Kleshtch walks in slowly, his head bowed low]

SATINE: Hey, widower! Why are you so down in the mouth? What are you thinking?

KLESHTCH: I'm thinking—what'll I do? I've no food—nothing—the funeral ate up all . . .

SATINE: I'll give you a bit of advice . . . do nothing! Just be a burden to the world at large!

KLESHTCH: Go on—talk—I'd be ashamed of myself . . .

SATINE: Why—people aren't ashamed to let you live worse than a dog. Just think . . . you stop work—so do I—so do hundreds, thousands of others —everybody—understand?—everybody'll quit working . . . nobody'll do a damned thing—and then what'll happen?

KLESHTCH: They'll all starve to death . . .

LUKA: [To Satine] If those are your notions, you ought to join the order of Béguines—you know—there's some such organization . . .

SATINE: I know—grandfather—and they're no fools . . .

[Natasha is heard screaming behind Kostilyoff's window: "What for? Stop! What have I done?"]

LUKA: [Worried] Natasha! That was she crying— oh, God . . .

[From Kostilyoff's room is heard noise, shuffling, breaking of crockery, and Kostilyoff's shrill cry: "Ah! Heretic! Bitch!"]

VASSILISA: Wait, wait—I'll teach her—there, there!

NATASHA: They're beating me—killing me . . .

SATINE: [Shouts through the window] Hey—you there— . . .

LUKA: [Trembling] Where's Vassily—? Call Vaska —oh, God—listen, brothers . . .

THE ACTOR: [Running out] I'll find him at once!

BUBNOFF: They beat her a lot these days . . .

SATINE: Come on, old man—we'll be witnesses . . .

LUKA: [Following Satine] Oh—witnesses—what for? Vassily—he should be called at once!

NATASHA: Sister—sister dear! Va-a-a . . .

BUBNOFF: They've gagged her—I'll go and see . . .

[The noise in Kostilyoff's room dies down gradually as if they had gone into the hallway. The old man's cry: "Stop!" is heard. A door is slammed noisily, and the latter sound cuts off all the other noises sharply. Quiet on the stage. Twilight]

KLESHTCH: [Seated on the sledge, indifferently, rubbing his hands; mutters at first indistinguishably, then:] What then? One must live. [Louder] Must have shelter—well? There's no shelter, no roof— nothing . . . there's only man—man alone—no hope . . . no help . . .

[Exit slowly, his head bent. A few moments of ominous silence, then somewhere in the hallway a mass of sounds, which grows in volume and comes nearer. Individual voices are heard]

VASSILISA: I'm her sister—let go . . .

KOSTILYOFF: What right have you . . .?

VASSILISA: Jail-bird!

SATINE: Call Vaska—quickly! Zob—hit him!

[A police whistle. The Tartar runs in, his right hand in a sling]

THE TARTAR: There's a new law for you—kill only in daytime!

[Enter Zob, followed by Miedviedieff]

ZOB: I handed him a good one!

MIEDVIEDIEFF: You—how dare you fight?

THE TARTAR: What about yourself? What's your duty?

MIEDVIEDIEFF: [Running after] Stop—give back my whistle!

KOSTILYOFF: [Runs in] Abram! Stop him! Hold him! He's a murderer—he . . .

[Enter Kvashnya and Nastya supporting Natasha who is disheveled. Satine backs away, pushing away Vassilisa who is trying to attack her sister, while, near her, Alyoshka jumps up and down like a madman, whistles into her ear, shrieking, roaring. Also other ragged men and women]

SATINE: [To Vassilisa] Well—you damned bitch!

VASSILISA: Let go, you jail-bird! I'll tear you to pieces—if I have to pay for it with my own life!

KVASHNYA: [Leading Natasha aside] You—Karpovna—that's enough—stand back—aren't you ashamed? Or are you crazy?

MIEDVIEDIEFF: [*Seizes* Satine] Aha—caught at last!

SATINE: Zob—beat them up! Vaska—Vaska . . . [*They all, in a chaotic mass, struggle near the brick wall. They lead* Natasha *to the right, and set her on a pile of wood.* Pepel *rushes in from the hallway and, silently, with powerful movements, pushes the crowd aside*]

PEPEL: Natalia, where are you . . . you . . .

KOSTILYOFF: [*Disappearing behind a corner*] Abram! Seize Vaska! Comrades—help us get him! The thief! The robber!

PEPEL: You—you old bastard! [*Aiming a terrific blow at* Kostilyoff. Kostilyoff *falls so that only the upper part of his body is seen.* Pepel *rushes to* Natasha]

VASSILISA: Beat Vaska! Brothers! Beat the thief!

MIEDVIEDIEFF: [*Yells to* Satine] Keep out of this—it's a family affair . . . they're relatives—and who are you? . . .

PEPEL: [*To* Natasha] What did she do to you? She used a knife?

KVASHNYA: God—what beasts! They've scalded the child's feet with boiling water!

NASTYA: They overturned the samovar . . .

THE TARTAR: Maybe an accident—you must make sure—you can't exactly tell . . .

NATASHA: [*Half fainting*] Vassily—take me away—

VASSILISA: Good people! Come! Look! He's dead! Murdered!

[*All crowd into the hallway near* Kostilyoff. Bubnoff *leaves the crowd and crosses to* Pepel]

BUBNOFF: [*In a low voice, to* Pepel] Vaska—the old man is done for!

PEPEL: [*Looks at him, as though he does not understand*] Go—for help—she must be taken to the hospital . . . I'll settle with them . . .

BUBNOFF: I say—the old man—somebody's killed him . . .

[*The noise on the stage dies out like a fire under water. Distinct, whispered exclamations: "Not really?" "Well—let's go away, brothers!" "The devil!" "Hold on now!" "Let's get away before the police comes!" The crowd disappears.* Bubnoff, *the* Tartar, Nastya, *and* Kvashnya, *rush up to* Kostilyoff's *body*]

VASSILISA: [*Rises and cries out triumphantly*] Killed—my husband's killed! Vaska killed him! I saw him! Brothers, I saw him! Well—Vasya—the police!

PEPEL: [*Moves away from* Natasha] Let me alone. [*Looks at* Kostilyoff; *to* Vassilisa] Well—are you glad? [*Touches the corpse with his foot*] The old bastard is dead! Your wish has been granted! Why not do the same to you? [*Throws himself at her*]

[Satine *and* Zob *quickly overpower him, and* Vassilisa *disappears in the passage*]

SATINE: Come to your senses!

ZOB: Hold on! Not so fast!

VASSILISA: [*Appearing*] Well, Vaska, dear friend? You can't escape your fate. . . . police—Abram—whistle!

MIEDVIEDIEFF: Those devils tore my whistle off!

ALYOSHKA: Here it is! [*Whistles,* Miedviedieff *runs after him*]

SATINE: [*Leading* Pepel *to* Natasha] Don't be afraid, Vaska! Killed in a row! That's nonsense—only manslaughter—you won't have to serve a long term . . .

VASSILISA: Hold Vaska—he killed him—I saw it!

SATINE: I, too, gave the old man a couple of blows—he was easily fixed . . . you call me as witness, Vaska!

PEPEL: I don't need to defend myself . . . I want to drag Vassilisa into this mess—and I'll do it—she was the one who wanted it . . . she was the one who urged me to kill him—she goaded me on . . .

NATASHA: [*Sudden and loud*] Oh—I understand—so that's it, Vassily? Good people! They're both guilty—my sister and he—they're both guilty! They had it all planned! So, Vassily, that's why you spoke to me a while ago—so that she should overhear everything—? Good people! She's his mistress—you know it—everybody knows it—they're both guilty! She—she urged him to kill her husband—he was in their way—and so was I! And now they've maimed me . . .

PEPEL: Natalia! What's the matter with you? What are you saying?

SATINE: Oh—hell!

VASSILISA: You lie. She lies. He—Vaska killed him . . .

NATASHA: They're both guilty! God damn you both!

SATINE: What a mix-up! Hold on, Vassily—or they'll ruin you between them!

ZOB: I can't understand it—oh—what a mess!

PEPEL: Natalia! It can't be true! Surely you don't believe that I—with her—

SATINE: So help me God, Natasha! Just think . . .

VASSILISA: [*In the passage*] They've killed my husband—Your Excellency! Vaska Pepel, the thief, killed him, Captain! I saw it—everybody saw it . . .

NATASHA: [*Tossing about in agony; her mind wandering*] Good people—my sister and Vaska killed him! The police—listen—this sister of mine—here—she urged, coaxed her lover—there he stands—the scoundrel! They both killed him! Put them in jail! Bring them before the judge! Take me along, too! To prison! Christ Almighty—take me to prison, too!

CURTAIN

ACT IV.

Same as Act I. But Pepel's *room is no longer there, and the partition has been removed. Furthermore, there is no anvil at the place where* Kleshtch *used to sit and work. In the corner, where* Pepel's *room used to be, the* Tartar *lies stretched out, rather restless, and groaning from time to time.* Kleshtch *sits at one end of the table, repairing a concertina and now and then testing the stops. At the other end of the table sit* Satine, *the* Baron, *and* Nastya. *In front of them stand a bottle of vodka, three bottles of beer, and a large loaf of black bread. The* Actor *lies on top of the stove, shifting about and coughing. It is night. The stage is lit by a lamp in the middle of the table. Outside the wind howls.*

KLESHTCH: Yes . . . he disappeared during the confusion and noise . . .

THE BARON: He vanished under the very eyes of the police—just like a puff of smoke . . .

SATINE: That's how sinners flee from the company of the righteous!

NASTYA: He was a dear old soul! But you—you aren't men—you're just—oh—like rust on iron!

THE BARON: [*Drinks*] Here's to you, my lady!

SATINE: He was an inquisitive old fellow—yes! Nastenka here fell in love with him . . .

NASTYA: Yes! I did! Madly! It's true! He saw everything—understood everything . . .

SATINE: [*Laughing*] Yes, generally speaking, I would say that he was—oh—like mush to those who can't chew. . . .

THE BARON: [*Laughing*] Right! Like plaster on a boil!

KLESHTCH: He was merciful—you people don't know what pity means . . .

SATINE: What good can I do you by pitying you?

KLESHTCH: You needn't have pity—but you needn't harm or offend your fellow-beings, either!

THE TARTAR: [*Sits up on his bunk, nursing his wounded hand carefully*] He was a fine old man. The law of life was the law of his heart . . . and he who obeys this law, is good, while he who disregards it, perishes. . . .

THE BARON: What law, Prince?

THE TARTAR: There are a number—different ones —you know . . .

THE BARON: Proceed!

THE TARTAR: Do not do harm unto others—such is the law!

SATINE: Oh—you mean the Penal Code, criminal and correctional, eh?

THE BARON: And also the Code of Penalties inflicted by Justices of the Peace!

THE TARTAR: No. I mean the Koran. It is the supreme law—and your own soul ought to be the Koran—yes!

KLESHTCH: [*Testing his concertina*] It wheezes like all hell! But the Prince speaks the truth—one must live abiding by the law—by the teachings of the Gospels . . .

SATINE: Well—go ahead and do it!

THE BARON: Just try it!

THE TARTAR: The Prophet Mohammed gave to us the law. He said: "Here is the law! Do as it is written therein!" Later on a time will arrive when the Koran will have outlived its purpose—and time will bring forth its own laws—every generation will create its own . . .

SATINE: To be sure! Time passed on—and gave us the Criminal Code . . . It's a strong law, brother— it won't wear off so very soon!

NASTYA: [*Banging her glass on the table*] Why— why do I stay here—with you? I'll go away somewhere—to the ends of the world!

THE BARON: Without any shoes, my lady?

NASTYA: I'll go—naked, if must be—creeping on all fours!

THE BARON: That'll be rather picturesque, my lady —on all fours!

NASTYA: Yes—and I'll crawl if I have to—anything at all—as long as I don't have to see your faces any longer—oh, I'm so sick of it all—the life— the people—everything!

SATINE: When you go, please take the actor along —he's preparing to go to the very same place—he has learned that within a half mile's distance of the end of the world there's a hospital for diseased organons . . .

THE ACTOR: [*Raising his head over the top of the stove*] A hospital for organisms—you fool!

SATINE: For organons—poisoned with vodka!

THE ACTOR: Yes! He will go! He will indeed! You'll see!

THE BARON: Who is he, sir?

THE ACTOR: I!

THE BARON: Thanks, servant of the goddess— what's her name—? The goddess of drama—tragedy —whatever is her name—?

THE ACTOR: The muse, idiot! Not the goddess— the muse!

SATINE: Lachesis—Hera—Aphrodite—Atropos— oh! To hell with them all! You see—Baron—it was the old man who stuffed the actor's head full with this rot . . .

THE BARON: That old man's a fool . . .

THE ACTOR: Ignoramuses! Beasts! Melpomene— that's her name! Heartless brutes! Bastards! You'll see! He'll go! "On with the orgy, dismal spirits!"— poem—ah—by Béranger! Yes—he'll find some spot where there's no—no . . .

THE BARON: Where there's nothing, sir?

THE ACTOR: Right! Nothing! "This hole shall be my grave—I am dying—ill and exhausted . . ." Why do you exist? Why?

THE BARON: You! God or genius or orgy—or whatever you are—don't roar so loud!

THE ACTOR: You lie! I'll roar all I want to!

NASTYA: [*Lifting her head from the table and throwing up her hands*] Go on! Yell! Let them listen to you!

THE BARON: Where is the sense, my lady?

SATINE: Leave them alone, Baron! To hell with the lot! Let them yell—let them knock their damned heads off if they feel like it! There's a method in their madness! Don't you go and interfere with people as that old fellow did! Yes—it's he—the damned old fool—he bewitched the whole gang of us!

KLESHTCH: He persuaded them to go away—but failed to show them the road . . .

THE BARON: That old man was a humbug!

NASTYA: Liar! You're a humbug yourself!

THE BARON: Shut up, my lady!

KLESHTCH: The old man didn't like truth very much—as a matter of fact he strongly resented it—and wasn't he right, though? Just look—where is there any truth? And yet, without it, you can't breathe! For instance, our Tartar Prince over there, crushed his hand at his work—and now he'll have to have his arm amputated—and there's the truth for you!

SATINE: [*Striking the table with his clenched fist*] Shut up! You sons of bitches! Fools! Not another word about that old fellow! [*To the* Baron] You, Baron, are the worst of the lot! You don't understand a thing, and you lie like the devil! The old man's no humbug! What's the truth? Man! Man—that's the truth! He understood man—you don't! You're all as dumb as stones! I understand the old man—yes! He lied—but lied out of sheer pity for you . . . God damn you! Lots of people lie out of pity for their fellow-beings! I know! I've read about it! They lie—oh—beautifully, inspiringly, stirringly! Some lies bring comfort, and others bring peace—a lie alone can justify the burden which crushed a workman's hand and condemns those who are starving! I know what lying means! The weakling and the one who is a parasite through his very weakness—they both need lies—lies are their support, their shield, their armor! But the man who is strong, who is his own master, who is free and does not have to suck his neighbors' blood—he needs no lies! To lie—it's the creed of slaves and masters of slaves! Truth is the religion of the free man!

THE BARON: Bravo! Well spoken! Hear, hear! I agree! You speak like an honest man!

SATINE: And why can't a crook at times speak the truth—since honest people at times speak like crooks? Yes—I've forgotten a lot—but I still know a thing or two! The old man? Oh—he's wise! He affected me as acid affects a dirty old silver coin! Let's drink to his health! Fill the glasses . . . [Nastya *fills a glass with beer and hands it to* Satine, *who laughs*] The old man lives within himself . . . he looks upon all the world from his own angle. Once I asked him: "Grand-dad, why do people live?" [*Tries to imitate* Luka's *voice and gestures*] And he replied: "Why, my dear fellow, people live

in the hope of something better! For example—let's say there are carpenters in this world, and all sorts of trash . . . people . . . and they give birth to a carpenter the like of which has never been seen upon the face of the earth . . . he's way above everybody else, and has no equal among carpenters! The brilliancy of his personality was reflected on all his trade, on all the other carpenters, so that they advanced twenty years in one day! This applies to all other trades—blacksmiths and shoemakers and other workmen—and all the peasants—and even the aristocrats live in the hopes of a higher life! Each individual thinks that he's living for his own self, but in reality he lives in the hope of something better. A hundred years—sometimes longer—do we expect, live for the finer, higher life . . ." [Nastya *stares intently into* Satine's *face.* Kleshtch *stops working and listens. The* Baron *bows his head very low, drumming softly on the table with his fingers. The* Actor, *peering down from the stove, tries to climb noiselessly into the bunk*] "Every one, brothers, every one lives in the hope of something better. That's why we must respect each and every human being! How do we know who he is, why he was born, and what he is capable of accomplishing? Perhaps his coming into the world will prove to be our good fortune . . . Especially must we respect little children! Children—need freedom! Don't interfere with their lives! Respect children!" [*Pause*]

THE BARON: [*Thoughtfully*] Hm—yes—something better?—That reminds me of my family . . . an old family dating back to the time of Catherine . . . all noblemen, soldiers, originally French—they served their country and gradually rose higher and higher. In the days of Nicholas the First my grandfather, Gustave DeBille, held a high post—riches—hundreds of serfs . . . horses—cooks—

NASTYA: You liar! It isn't true!

THE BARON: [*Jumping up*] What? Well—go on—

NASTYA: It isn't true.

THE BARON: [*Screams*] A house in Moscow! A house in Petersburg! Carriages! Carriages with coats of arms!

[Kleshtch *takes his concertina and goes to one side, watching the scene with interest*]

NASTYA: You lie!

THE BARON: Shut up!—I say—dozens of footmen . . .

NASTYA: [*Delighted*] You lie!

THE BARON: I'll kill you!

NASTYA: [*Ready to run away*] There were no carriages!

SATINE: Stop, Nastenka! Don't infuriate him!

THE BARON: Wait—you bitch! My grandfather . . .

NASTYA: There was no grandfather! There was nothing!

[Satine *roars with laughter*]

THE BARON: [*Worn out with rage, sits down on bench*] Satine! Tell that slut—what—? You, too, are laughing? You—don't believe me either? [*Cries out *in despair, pounding the table with his fists*] It's true —damn the whole lot of you!

NASTYA: [*Triumphantly*] So—you're crying? Understand now what a human being feels like when nobody believes him?

KLESHTCH: [*Returning to the table*] I thought there'd be a fight . . .

THE TARTAR: Oh—people are fools! It's too bad . . .

THE BARON: I shall not permit any one to ridicule me! I have proofs—documents—damn you!

SATINE: Forget it! Forget about your grandfather's carriages! You can't drive anywhere in a carriage of the past!

THE BARON: How dare she—just the same—?

NASTYA: Just imagine! How dare I—?

SATINE: You see—she does dare! How is she any worse than you are? Although, surely, in her past there wasn't even a father and mother, let alone carriages and a grandfather . . .

THE BARON: [*Quieting down*] Devil take you—you do know how to argue dispassionately—and I, it seems—I've no will-power . . .

SATINE: Acquire some—it's useful . . . [*Pause*] Nastya! Are you going to the hospital?

NASTYA: What for?

SATINE: To see Natashka.

NASTYA: Oh—just woke up, did you? She's been out of the hospital for some time—and they can't find a trace of her . . .

SATINE: Oh—that woman's a goner!

KLESHTCH: It's interesting to see whether Vaska will get the best of Vassilisa, or the other way around—?

NASTYA: Vassilisa will win out! She's shrewd! And Vaska will go to the gallows!

SATINE: For manslaughter? No—only to jail . . .

NASTYA: Too bad—the gallows would have been better . . . that's where all of you should be sent . . . swept off into a hole—like filth . . .

SATINE: [*Astonished*] What's the matter? Are you crazy?

THE BARON: Oh—give her a wallop—that'll teach her to be less impertinent . . .

NASTYA: Just you try to touch me!

THE BARON: I shall!

SATINE: Stop! Don't insult her! I can't get the thought of the old man out of my head! [*Roars with laughter*] Don't offend your fellow-beings! Suppose I were offended once in such a way that I'd remember it for the rest of my life? What then? Should I forgive? No, no!

THE BARON: [*To* Nastya] You must understand that I'm not your sort . . . you—ah—you piece of dirt!

NASTYA: You bastard! Why—you live off me like a worm off an apple!

[*The men laugh amusedly*]

KLESHTCH: Fool! An apple—?

THE BARON: You can't be angry with her—she's just an ass—

NASTYA: You laugh! Liars? Don't strike you as funny, eh?

THE ACTOR: [*Morosely*] Give them a good beating!

NASTYA: If I only could! [*Takes a cup from the table and throws it on the floor*] That's what I'd like to do to you all!

THE TARTAR: Why break dishes—eh—silly girl?

THE BARON: [*Rising*] That'll do! I'll teach her manners in half a second!

NASTYA: [*Running toward the door*] Go to hell!

SATINE: [*Calling after her*] Hey! That's enough! Whom are you trying to frighten? What's all the row about, anyway?

NASTYA: Dogs! I hope you'll croak! Dogs! [*Runs out*]

THE ACTOR: [*Morosely*] Amen!

THE TARTAR: Allah! Mad women, these Russians! They're bold, wilful; Tartar women aren't like that! They know the law and abide by it . . .

KLESHTCH: She ought to be given a sound hiding!

THE BARON: The slut!

KLESHTCH: [*Testing the concertina*] It's ready! But its owner isn't here yet—that young fellow is burning his life away . . .

SATINE: Care for a drink—now?

KLESHTCH: Thanks . . . it's time to go to bed . . .

SATINE: Getting used to us?

KLESHTCH: [*Drinks, then goes to his bunk*] It's all right . . . there are people everywhere—at first you don't notice it . . . but after a while you don't mind. . . .

[*The* Tartar *spreads some rags over his bunk, then kneels on them and prays*]

THE BARON: [*To* Satine, *pointing at the* Tartar] Look!

SATINE: Stop! He's a good fellow! Leave him alone! [*Roars with laughter*] I feel kindly to-day —the devil alone knows the reason why . . .

THE BARON: You always feel kindly when you're drunk—you're even wiser at such times . . .

SATINE: When I'm drunk? Yes—then I like everything—right—He prays? That's fine! A man may believe or not—that's his own affair—a man is free —he pays for everything himself—belief or unbelief —love—wisdom . . . a man pays for everything— and that's just why he's free! Man is—truth! And what is man? It's neither you nor I nor they—oh, no —it's you and they and I and the old man—and Napoleon—Mohammed—all in one! [*Outlines vaguely in the air the contour of a human being*] Do you understand? It's tremendous! It contains the beginning and the end of everything—everything is in man—and everything exists for him! Man alone exists—everything else is the creation of his hands and his brain! Man! It is glorious! It sounds—oh— so big! Man must be respected—not degraded with pity—but respected, respected! Let us drink to man,

Baron! [*Rises*] It is good to feel that you are a man! I'm a convict, a murderer, a crook—granted!—When I'm out on the street people stare at me as if I were a scoundrel—they draw away from me—they look after me and often they say: "You dog! You humbug! Work!" Work? And what for? to fill my belly? [*Roars with laughter*] I've always despised people who worry too much about their bellies. It isn't right, Baron! It isn't! Man is loftier than that! Man stands above hunger!

THE BARON: You—reason things out. . . . Well and good—it brings you a certain amount of consolation. . . . Personally I'm incapable of it . . . I don't know how. [*Glances around him and then, softly, guardedly*] Brother—I am afraid—at times. Do you understand? Afraid!—Because—what next?

SATINE: Rot! What's a man to be afraid of?

THE BARON: [*Pacing up and down*] You know—as far back as I can remember, there's been a sort of fog in my brain. I was never able to understand anything. Somehow I feel embarrassed—it seems to me that all my life I've done nothing but change clothes—and why? I don't understand! I studied—I wore the uniform of the Institute for the Sons of the Nobility . . . but what have I learned? I don't remember! I married—I wore a frock-coat—then a dressing-gown . . . but I chose a disagreeable wife . . . and why? I don't understand. I squandered everything that I possessed—I wore some sort of a grey jacket and brick-colored trousers—but how did I happen to ruin myself? I haven't the slightest idea. . . . I had a position in the Department of State. . . . I wore a uniform and a cap with insignia of rank. . . . I embezzled government funds . . . so they dressed me in a convict's garb—and later on I got into these clothes here—and it all happened as in a dream—it's funny . . .

SATINE: Not very! It's rather—silly!

THE BARON: Yes—silly! I think so, too. Still—wasn't I born for some sort of purpose?

SATINE: [*Laughing*] Probably—a man is born to conceive a better man. [*Shaking his head*]—It's all right!

THE BARON: That she-devil Nastka! Where did she run to? I'll go and see—after all, she . . . [*Exit; pause*]

THE ACTOR: Tartar! [*Pause*] Prince! [*The Tartar looks round*] Say a prayer for me . . .

THE TARTAR: What?

THE ACTOR: [*Softly*] Pray—for me!

THE TARTAR: [*After a silence*] Pray for your own self!

THE ACTOR: [*Quickly crawls off the stove and goes to the table, pours out a drink with shaking hands, drinks, then almost runs to passage*] All over!

SATINE: Hey, proud Sicambrian! Where are you going?

[*Satine whistles. Miedviedieff enters, dressed in a woman's flannel shirtwaist; followed by Bubnoff. Both are slightly drunk. Bubnoff carries a bunch of pretzels in one hand, a couple of smoked fish in the other, a bottle of vodka under one arm, another bottle in his coat pocket*]

MIEDVIEDIEFF: A camel is something like a donkey—only it has no ears. . . .

BUBNOFF: Shut up! You're a variety of donkey yourself!

MIEDVIEDIEFF: A camel has no ears at all, at all—it hears through its nostrils . . .

BUBNOFF: [*To Satine*] Friend! I've looked for you in all the saloons and all the cabarets! Take this bottle—my hands are full . . .

SATINE: Put the pretzels on the table—then you'll have one hand free—

BUBNOFF: Right! Hey—you donkey—look! Isn't he a clever fellow?

MIEDVIEDIEFF: All crooks are clever—I know! They couldn't do a thing without brains. An honest man is all right even if he's an idiot . . . but a crook must have brains. But, speaking about camels, you're wrong . . . you can ride them—they have no horns . . . and no teeth either . . .

BUBNOFF: Where's everybody? Why is there no one here? Come on out . . . I treat! Who's in the corner?

SATINE: How soon will you drink up everything you have? Scarecrow!

BUBNOFF: Very soon! I've very little this time. Zob—where's Zob?

KLESHTCH: [*Crossing to table*] He isn't here . . .

BUBNOFF: Waughrr! Bull-dog! Br-zz-zz—Turkey-cock! Don't bark and don't growl! Drink—make merry—and don't be sullen!—I treat everybody—Brother, I love to treat—if I were rich, I'd run a free saloon! So help me God, I would! With an orchestra and a lot of singers! Come, every one! Drink and eat—listen to the music—and rest in peace! Beggars—come, all you beggars—and enter my saloon free of charge! Satine—you can have my capital—just like that!

SATINE: You better give me all you have straight away!

BUBNOFF: All my capital? Right now? Well—here's a ruble—here's twenty kopecks—five kopecks—sun-flower seeds—and that's all!

SATINE: That's splendid! It'll be safer with me—I'll gamble with it . . .

MIEDVIEDIEFF: I'm a witness—the money was given you for safe-keeping. How much is it?

BUBNOFF: You? You're a camel—we don't need witnesses . . .

ALYOSHKA: [*Comes in barefoot*] Brothers, I got my feet wet!

BUBNOFF: Go on and get your throat wet—and nothing'll happen—you're a fine fellow—you sing and you play—that's all right! But it's too bad you drink—drink, little brother, is harmful, very harmful . . .

ALYOSHKA: I judge by you! Only when you're drunk do you resemble a human being . . . Kleshtch! Is my concertina fixed? [*Sings and dances*]

"If my mug were not so attractive,
My sweetheart wouldn't love me at all . . ."

Boys, I'm frozen—it's cold . . .

MIEDVIEDIEFF: Hm—and may I ask who's this sweetheart?

BUBNOFF: Shut up! From now on, brother, you are neither a policeman nor an uncle!

ALYOSHKA: Just auntie's husband!

BUBNOFF: One of your nieces is in jail—the other one's dying . . .

MIEDVIEDIEFF: [*Proudly*] You lie! She's not dying —she disappeared—without trace . . .

[Satine *roars*]

BUBNOFF: All the same, brothers—a man without nieces isn't an uncle!

ALYOSHKA: Your Excellency! Listen to the drummer of the retired billygoats' brigade! [*Sings*]

"My sweetheart has money,
I haven't a cent.
But I'm a cheerful,
Merry lad!"

Oh—isn't it cold!

[*Enter Zob. From now until the final curtain men and women drift in, undress, and stretch out on the bunks, grumbling*]

ZOB: Bubnoff! Why did you run off?

BUBNOFF: Come here—sit down—brother, let's sing my favorite ditty, eh?

THE TARTAR: Night was made for sleep! Sing your songs in the daytime!

SATINE: Well—never mind, Prince—come here!

THE TARTAR: What do you mean—never mind? There's going to be a noise—there always is when people sing!

BUBNOFF: [*Crossing to the* Tartar] Count—ah— I mean Prince—how's your hand? Did they cut it off?

THE TARTAR: What for? We'll wait and see—perhaps it won't be necessary . . . a hand isn't made of iron—it won't take long to cut it off . . .

ZOB: It's your own affair, Hassanka! You'll be good for nothing without your hand. We're judged by our hands and backs—without the pride of your hand, you're no longer a human being. Tobacco-carting—that's your business! Come on—have a drink of vodka—and stop worrying!

KVASHNYA: [*Comes in*] Ah, my beloved fellow-lodgers! It's horrible outside—snow and slush . . . is my policeman here?

MIEDVIEDIEFF: Right here!

KVASHNYA: Wearing my blouse again? And drunk, eh? What's the idea?

MIEDVIEDIEFF: In celebration of Bubnoff's birthday . . . besides, it's cold . . .

KVASHNYA: Better look out—stop fooling about and go to sleep!

MIEDVIEDIEFF: [*Goes to kitchen*] Sleep? I can—I want to—it's time—[*Exit*]

SATINE: What's the matter? Why are you so strict with him?

KVASHNYA: You can't be otherwise, friend. You have to be strict with his sort. I took him as a partner. I thought he'd be of some benefit to me— because he's a military man—and you're a rough lot . . . and I am a woman—and now he's turned drunkard—that won't do at all!

SATINE: You picked a good one for partner!

KVASHNYA: Couldn't get a better one. You wouldn't want to live with me . . . you think you're too fine! And even if you did it wouldn't last more than a week . . . you'd gamble me and all I own away at cards!

SATINE: [*Roars with laughter*] That's true, land-lady—I'd gamble . . .

KVASHNYA: Yes, yes. Alyoshka!

ALYOSHKA: Here he is—I, myself!

KVASHNYA: What do you mean by gossiping about me?

ALYOSHKA: I? Speak out everything—whatever my conscience tells me. There, I say, is a wonderful woman! Splendid meat, fat, bones—over four hundred pounds! But brains—? Not an ounce!

KVASHNYA: You're a liar! I've a lot of brains! What do you mean by saying I beat my policeman?

ALYOSHKA: I thought you did—when you pulled him by the hair!

KVASHNYA: [*Laughs*] You fool! You aren't blind, are you? Why wash dirty linen in public? And—it hurts his feelings—that's why he took to drink . . .

ALYOSHKA: It's true, evidently, that even a chicken likes vodka . . .

[Satine *and* Kleshtch *roar with laughter*]

KVASHNYA: Go on—show your teeth! What sort of a man are you anyway, Alyoshka?

ALYOSHKA: Oh—I am first-rate! Master of all trades! I follow my nose!

BUBNOFF: [*Near the* Tartar's *bunk*] Come on! At all events—we won't let you sleep! We'll sing all night. Zob!

ZOB: Sing—? All right . . .

ALYOSHKA: And I'll play . . .

SATINE: We'll listen!

THE TARTAR: [*Smiling*] Well—Bubnoff—you devil —bring the vodka—we'll drink—we'll have a hell of a good time! The end will come soon enough—and then we'll be dead!

BUBNOFF: Fill his glass, Satine! Zob—sit down! Ah—brothers—what does a man need after all? There, for instance, I've had a drink—and I'm happy! Zob! Start my favorite song! I'll sing—and then I'll cry. . . .

ZOB: [*Begins to sing*]
"The sun rises and sets . . ."

BUBNOFF: [*Joining in*]
"But my prison is all dark . . ."

THE BARON: [*On the threshold; yells*] Hey—you—come—come here! Out in the waste—in the yard . . . over there . . . The actor—he's hanged himself. . . .

[*Silence. All stare at the* Baron. *Behind him* appears Nastya, *and slowly, her eyes wide with horror, she walks to the table*]

SATINE: [*In a matter-of-fact voice*] Damned fool—he ruined the song . . . !

CURTAIN.

Departures from Realism

Departures from Realism

There was a time when a particular style of theatre had the opportunity to develop its optimal possibilities. Actors from Betterton to Coquelin could refine their art and make it as personal a possession as an old habit. Such playwrights as Sophocles, Shakespeare, and Molière could grow steadily into greatness. But opportunities for arriving at maturity in a particular style have been meager in the modern theatre. It has adopted and abandoned styles with great celerity, and there has been little stability on the stage since 1890.

No sooner had naturalistic art triumphed after the eighteen-eighties than it was challenged by new romantic playwrights such as Maeterlinck and Rostand. Scene designers such as Gordon Craig and Appia denounced the realistic stage picture and became oracles of imaginative stagecraft. Producers and stage directors such as Lugné-Poë and Max Reinhardt abandoned the peepshow theatre of realism. Then followed the vogues of "expressionism," "formalism," "theatricalism," "constructivism," "futurism," "surrealism," "epic realism," and other antinaturalistic styles, although none of these ever quite displaced realism as the dominant mode of the theatre. The least extreme changes in dramatic style occurred when naturalism was modified and writers, scene designers, and directors achieved verisimilitude with selective realism. But mere modifications did not satisfy the demand for poetry and imagination in dramatic art. A passion for stylization has characterized the modern stage ever since 1890.

EXPERIMENT IN THE THEATRE

The effect of experimentation in poetic and generally nonrealistic drama can be seen in the European section which follows, as well as in the English and American parts of this anthology. We can observe the obvious effects of a return to romanticism, for example, in *Cyrano de Bergerac* and *Elizabeth the Queen*, both based on romantic careers of the past. A "symbolism" of poetic overtones and suggestiveness is strongly marked in Maeterlinck's *The Intruder*, and is realistically fortified in Synge's *Riders to the Sea*. If labels are of convenience to us, we may also find elements of symbolism in the tenderly wry extravaganza of Saroyan's *My Heart's in the Highlands* and in the delicate mood of reminiscence that enfolds Williams' *The Glass Menagerie*, not to mention the more conspicuous symbolization in Strindberg's *There Are Crimes and Crimes*, Molnár's *Liliom*, and Lorca's *Blood Wedding*. The technique of Arthur Miller's *Death of a Salesman* represents a departure from naturalism in spite of its realistic content. Vivacious fantastication charac-

terizes *Blithe Spirit*, which Noel Coward candidly subtitled "An Improbable Farce," and *Liliom* becomes a fantastic drama after the fourth scene. Folk fantasy is celebrated in *The Green Pastures*, and myth forms the groundwork of Sartre's "existentialist" fable *The Flies*. Lorca's *Blood Wedding* is a poetic drama that contains even traditional allegorical figures of the "Moon" and "Death." Capek's *R. U. R.* is a fantasy with some of the depersonalization and telegraphic style that the expressionistic movement popularized in Central Europe after the First World War, and O'Neill's *The Hairy Ape* is both symbolic and expressionistic. Brecht's play *The Private Life of the Master Race* typifies so-called epic realism. Pirandello's *Six Characters in Search of an Author* is representative of a "grotesque" school of theatre in Italy and of frank "theatricalism." It cuts the realistic theatre into shreds, presenting a play in rehearsal and then showing the author's characters asserting their independence by enacting scenes not as he wrote them but as they experienced them in "real life." Thornton Wilder not only combines a real and, in the last part, fantasied world in *Our Town* but adopts Chinese theatricalism for his account of ordinary life in a New England town. There is much overlapping of styles in these and other plays that exemplify a reaction against naturalism. Playgoers and critics have had to adjust their sights continually in trying to make sense of the progressive modern theatre as it has moved from style to style, often with a set of well-publicized if not always clearly defined or conclusively demonstrated principles.

The restlessness of the modern spirit was especially marked in the art of stage production, and the acting profession in particular could report on some bewildering experiences as it submitted to the transmutations of theatrical style. Actors had no sooner adapted themselves to one style of performance than they were expected to adopt a different one. After 1890, many a performer who had just learned to present a fully realized, concrete personality on the realistic stage had to dissolve himself in a mist of poetic implication and become an essence instead of a person—a figment of dream rather than a multidimensional character. When the symbolist *Blue Bird* and *Pelléas and Mélisande* vogue died down and realism proved more tenacious than some enthusiasts of poetic drama had expected, the actor found it necessary to serve reality again. But not for long! Between 1919 and 1925, when expressionism became fashionable, he had to transform himself into a self-charging dynamo by order of such expressionist directors as Leopold Jessner and Jürgen Fehling. In Germany, he was expected to shriek his lines, negotiate flights of stairs at breakneck speed, and strike passionate poses; had he sizzled out of a witches' cauldron he could not have sputtered more than he did in some of the stage productions that eventuated in Central Europe. V. E. Meyerhold, the apostle of "constructivism" in Soviet Russia, made still other demands, and the actor had to become a "biodynamic" automaton swinging from trapeze bars and performing acrobatic stunts on settings that looked like bricklayers' scaffolds or catwalks in an industrial plant. The Russian director Alexander Tairov turned acting into a form of choreography. Still another director, Erwin Piscator, asked the actor to be a character, a lecturer, a harlequin, and a symbol, all in the same body. Even the well-trained actors of the Moscow Art Theatre and the New York Group Theatre could not always respond successfully to the flexibility required of them.

Many a stage production got out of hand while the director displayed his virtuosity. Playwrights, of course, followed suit, impelled by a dissatisfaction with naturalism that affected even its pioneers, Ibsen and Strindberg. Too many of the plays proved distressingly chaotic or pretentious. It is not altogether surprising that there were reactions against so much experimentation and that cautious theatre people clung to the life-belt of simple realism.

There was, nevertheless, often method in the madness of the theatre. In adopting various styles, dramatists responded to insistent social or political pressures and to the new penetrations of psychological science or psychoanalysis, while directors and scenic artists stimulated their creative faculties with the theatrical possibilities of the electric switchboard, the Linnebach projector, the motion picture, the revolving stage, and other technical advances. If the modern theatre brought forth few unassailable dramatic masterpieces, it nevertheless gave us many creditable plays and a great many beautiful and sometimes fascinating stage productions. The modern theatre has been exciting largely because it evolved a succession of experiments and endeavored to find stylized expression on the stage.

SYMBOLIST DRAMA AND THEATRE

The first departures from realism took the form of revived romanticism and of symbolism. Romanticism, which had actually never vanished from the stage, began to reassert its claims with much fanfare after 1890 in scattered works such as *Cyrano de Bergerac* and Sem Benelli's *The Jest,* one of John Barrymore's most popular successes. When romanticism returned creditably it tended, however, to be more disciplined and temperate than in the work of early nineteenth-century romanticists such as Hugo and Schiller, not to mention more erratic writers. The idiom was more brittle, gusty, or colloquial, or the tone was more or less ironic, as in *Cyrano de Bergerac* or in Edwin Justin Mayer's unjustly neglected

tragicomedy *The Children of Darkness.* We may observe the difference of style by turning from the operatic plays of Victor Hugo to Maxwell Anderson's verse dramas *Elizabeth the Queen, Mary of Scotland,* and *Anne of the Thousand Days.* (A meretricious, vulgar romanticism has, besides, been present everywhere in our century, as in other times. It masquerades as prose realism and tries to cheat with false notions. *Abie's Irish Rose* is generally singled out as the prime American example, but only because it won unusual popularity. The world's most hospitable haven for degenerate romanticism has, of course, been Hollywood.) Symbolism was a variant form of romanticism. It arose as a poetic and somewhat vaguely defined movement, strongly influenced by the philosophical idealism of Bergson, the poetry of Baudelaire, Rimbaud, and Verlaine, the painting style of the impressionists, and the music of Wagner.

For a symbolist playwright such as Maeterlinck, Andreyev, or Yeats, the world was full of wonders, and "correspondences" could be found between actual reality and an indefinable spiritual undercurrent. Portentous atmosphere and strange nuances appeared in the symbolist plays of Maeterlinck after 1889. Little was stated and presented directly or plainly. Much was suggested and implied. In many instances, the playwright also told a fanciful story or a fable, as Maeterlinck did in his once very popular *Blue Bird,* Hauptmann in *The Sunken Bell,* James M. Barrie in *Peter Pan,* and Karl Vollmöller in the famous Reinhardt-staged spectacle *The Miracle.* Or the playwright wrote more or less allegorically, like the Austrian poet Hugo von Hofmannsthal in his *Jedermann* (a version of the medieval morality play *Everyman*) and the Russian creator of dreams Leonid Andreyev in *The Life of Man, The Black Maskers,* and *King Hunger.* In some plays, the symbolism was simply an extended and elusive metaphor; in others the symbol was obtrusive, with figures like Death or Hunger appearing on the stage—as in Andreyev's plays. The personification of abstractions, indeed, has persisted to some degree ever since the vogue of symbolism between 1890 and 1914. We may cite such later examples as Alberto Casella's *Death Takes a Holiday,* Paul Osborn's *On Borrowed Time,* in which Death, or Mr. Brink, wears a bowler hat, and Philip Barry's *Here Come the Clowns* in which the Devil is a vaudeville illusionist.

The best and most lasting effect of symbolism, and not only on the nonrealistic but on the realistic theatre of all gradations, came from the efforts of scene designers and stage directors. Artists of the theatre became aware of the illogicality and wastefulness of too much literal procedure in a medium that is essentially make-believe. After all, the "fourth wall" is only empty space. Foreign characters in a play do not speak their own tongue but that of the country in which the production takes place. And even the most natural acting violates actual reality in order to convey an orderly impression of reality. In time, naturalism was supplanted by a "selective realism," and this is the prevailing style today.

The reaction to naturalism in the nineties went much further, however, than mere selectivity in stage design. The word "theatricality," which had been buried with so much opprobrium by the naturalists, was restored to good standing. Opposed to Antoine's Théâtre Libre there arose little "art" theatres which strove to swing the tide back to theatricalism in the name of beauty and spiritual truth. As early as 1890, the French poet Paul Fort established his Théâtre d'Art and dedicated it to the discovery of "the miracle of daily life, the sense of the mysterious." Three years later, Lugné-Poë produced Maeterlinck's penumbral *Pelléas and Mélisande* there, and then founded the Théâtre de l'Oeuvre, where he gave imaginative productions of Ibsen's romantic tale *Peer Gynt,* Hauptmann's symbolist play *The Sunken Bell,* Maeterlinck's *Monna Vanna,* and the French poet Paul Claudel's *The Tidings Brought to Mary.* The art theatres soon spread over Europe, sometimes founded or supervised by the playwrights themselves—by Strindberg and Pirandello, for example.

Efforts to depart from realism led to simplifications and formalizations of the stage. There was even a return to Elizabethan platform staging in Jocza Savits' Shakespeare Theatre in Munich and William Poel's Elizabethan Stage Society in England. Especially effective were the simplifications achieved by Jacques Copeau in his Théâtre du Vieux Colombier, established in Paris in 1913. Here the forestage was lengthened into an "apron" in the Elizabethan manner and the practically bare stage was backed by a permanent set. Other departures brought the nonrealistic painter into the theatre. Just as the Duke of Meiningen had used settings by realistic painters, French producers employed Picasso, Matisse, Derain, Braque, and Léger.

These and many other efforts to "retheatricalize" the theatre were directly or indirectly inspired by the work of the two poets of the physical theatre Adolphe Appia and Gordon Craig. And significantly the first impetus came from music, the least representational of the arts.

Early nineteenth-century romanticists had long ago held the doctrine that music was the ideal of all art and that the theatre could reach its apotheosis only in music. The philosopher Nietzsche stressed the same doctrine in *The Birth of Tragedy,* and his friend Wagner's significant innovations in opera, which he called music-drama, served the romantic ideal of fusing the arts into a single overwhelming theatrical experience. Wagner's formula, "Music is the soul of drama, drama is the body of music,"

announced a synthesis of the arts to which all his major operas were devoted. The great composer regarded himself as primarily a theatrician.

Wagner's far-flung dreams for stagecraft were translated into theatrical design by his Swiss disciple, Adolphe Appia (1862–1928), who had worked with him at Bayreuth. In 1895 appeared Appia's *La mise en scène du drame Wagnérien,* with eighteen superb designs for the Wagnerian operas; in 1899 appeared *Die Musik und die Inszenierung* (translated from a French text); this was followed by a series of shorter studies. Antipathetic to the naturalism that had gained a foothold in Paris a dozen years before, Appia wanted to endow scenic representation with the fluid and suggestive quality of music—that "loftiest expression of the eternal in art," as he called it. The elements of scenic design were to be the scenery, the floor, the moving actor, and the lighted space. The theatre that projects the dramatist's script was to present a perfect synthesis, a single effect. And the unifying element was to be light, which was no longer to provide a blank visibility but was to blend the scene and the actors, thereby creating a unified mood and conveying the "essence" of a dramatic production. Only light, Appia declared, can express "the inner nature of all appearance." Light, with its "infinite capacity for varying nuance," is the "counterpart of a musical score," and it must play as directly upon the emotions as music.

Appia's influence after 1900, especially on Max Reinhardt and on the later expressionists, was to prove tremendous, even though the Wagnerian opera house in Bayreuth did not use his designs and few of them were seen anywhere on the stage. If excesses of grandiosity and pretentious spirituality may be laid at Appia's door, owing to his advocacy of penumbral masses on the stage, his lessons were reflected in the best productions of the present century. Ellen Terry's impulsive son, Gordon Craig, was his spiritual brother, and, being a much more strident pamphleteer, he succeeded in popularizing the doctrine of theatricality. He, too, considered the ideal production of a play to be a single effect that would engage all the senses simultaneously and would address itself directly to the spirit; he convinced stage designers and directors that suggestion is the supreme law of the theatre. "Actuality, accuracy of detail, is useless upon the stage," he declared. But by means of suggestion "you may bring to the stage a sense of all things." The main instrument of suggestion, moreover, is organization, or design, and every production needs a pattern. So concerned was Craig with the inviolability of "design" that at one time he even wanted to banish the living actor as an unreliable agent too easily disturbed by accidental factors like the emotions; the "ideal and tentative solution" proposed by Craig was a "super-marionette." With his magazine *The Mask* and a series of pamphlets and books, the first of which, *The Art of the Theatre,* appeared in 1905, Craig took the theatre by storm.

If Craig was impractical, he nevertheless set up an ideal of production and scenic design. The practical directors and designers who followed parallel paths or caught fire from his ideas at least discarded literal realism. From Appia, moreover, the scenic artists took the basic principle of their art—the use of light as an expressive medium. If Appia the Wagnerian romanticist affected theatrical art only slightly, Appia the practical forerunner of contemporary lighting technique still dominates the theatre, even when this theatre continues to express realism.

The leaders of modern scenic design, however, would have been considerably less influential if they had not found able support from stage directors, and among these Max Reinhardt (1873–1943) assumed undisputed leadership. In starting many projects of imaginative theatre in Germany and Austria before and after the First World War, and in bringing some of his productions as far west as America, Reinhardt became a major influence. He developed a delicate production style in 1922 at the tiny Redoutensaal in Vienna, where he placed a platform at one end of an eighteenth-century ballroom and used nothing but a beautiful rococo screen as a permanent scenic background. He also went to the other extreme, staging great pageants such as *The Miracle* in 1912. (His last spectacle, staged in 1937 in New York, was Franz Werfel's chronicle of the Jewish people *The Eternal Road,* with settings by Norman Bel Geddes.) He gave poetic productions to the romantic plays that were supplanting naturalism at the beginning of his career in 1902. In addition to giving modern poets a hearing by staging poetic works of Maeterlinck and Hofmannsthal, he dusted off Goethe's and Schiller's youthful plays in some spectacular productions. The symbolists won a major victory when Reinhardt was appointed to succeed the naturalist Otto Brahm as director of Berlin's Deutsches Theater in 1905.

Reinhardt brought back the theatricality of the theatre by departing from the peepshow, fourth-wall stage of realism. He renewed the lost connection between the audience and the stage. In producing *Sumurûn,* in 1910, for example, he employed a runway that extended in Japanese theatrical style from the stage well into the audience. For *The Miracle,* two years later, he redesigned the entire theatre building as a cathedral in order to make the public participate in the religious experience of the play. He was not averse, it is true, to employing realism when it served his purposes, but he was willing to resort to any device or to any degree of stylization. An eclectic artist, he did not hesitate to help himself to any older style of theatrical production that suited his taste and his interpretation of a play or to combine a variety of styles. The circus ring or "mass theatre" suited him on some occasions just as well as the most intimate type of staging in a small room. He was adept at employing the simplest devices on the one hand, and the most complicated stage machinery, such as revolving stages, on the other. In his work, the misty impressionism advocated by Appia and Gordon Craig won spectacular victories. Other artists of the stage, especially Jacques Copeau in Paris at his Théâtre du Vieux Colombier, labored with tact and penetration, with grace and understanding. Reinhardt triumphed with effects that publicized the art theatre with Germanic thoroughness and *éclat.*

EXPRESSIONISM AND ITS SEQUELS

Notable after the poetic and spectacular ventures of the symbolists and of Reinhardt the showman was the work of the expressionists. Expressionism was foreshadowed by the dramatic experiments of Strindberg and Wedekind and became full blown after the First World War, especially in Central Europe. Between 1919 and 1925, in fact, the new style promised to effect a challenging transvaluation of dramatic and theatrical values.

Expressionistic techniques were employed not only by undisciplined exhibitionists but by playwrights whose motives were anything but superficial. Writers such as Strindberg and O'Neill endeavored to express personal tensions and problems they considered representative of modern man's alienation in materialistic society. Believing that poetic feeling alone was ineffectual and that realism could project neither inner experience nor the external world as it presented itself to the troubled spirit, they resorted to a fragmentary, constantly dissolving picture. They regarded the inner self not as a fairly orderly organism that moved more or less clearly toward well-defined, attainable ends such as winning a girl in marriage or getting on in business, but as a highly unstable compound of promptings and confusions. The concept of a unified self was a product of eighteenth-century rationalism and nineteenth-century materialism and mechanistic science. Its ideal representatives were the settled people and the career men of the bourgeois world. The rebels against this society were actually no different in spirit or outlook since they too had settled convictions, clear aims, and simple goals realizable by the application of common sense and well-directed efforts. But what if a career or an attainable program of reform was no longer considered a desirable objective? What if it could not be pursued or even entertained by a divided and bedeviled personality? What if the individual's major difficulty was precisely his lack of a unified self that could look out through a clear pane of perceptions at a plainly outlined world?

Such dramatists as Strindberg and O'Neill concerned themselves with the inner fact of psychological division. The form of plays such as *The Dream Play, The Spook Sonata, Emperor Jones,* and *The Hairy Ape* therefore became a whirl of fragmentary events in short scenes. And since the external world is the world formed by the perceiver, it fragmented itself, too. It appeared dislocated, turned out of shape, and exaggerated by the character's state of mind, as well as, of course, by the author, who intended to give us his view of the world as distressingly disordered and of the times as wholly out of joint. Strindberg, for example, made life on this planet look like a nightmare in *The Dream Play,* in support of his more or less Buddhist view in the play that all life was a delusion and a meaningless suffering. Supplementary characters changed their identity again and again or acquired abnormal attributes in Strindberg's expressionist plays. O'Neill's burly stoker in *The Hairy Ape* hurls himself at well-dressed citizens coming out of church only to rebound from them because they represent a society to which he cannot belong.

Making a subjective world out of an objective one ordered by conventional perceptions, playwrights even abolished the conventions of time and place. The Officer in *The Dream Play* changes from youth to middle age to old age with uncanny rapidity. Past and present time mingled freely in expressionist drama; memory scenes intruded into a present situation and not only dominated but altered it. Strindberg's Officer goes back to his childhood school as a teacher only to find himself a pupil again, unable to do simple arithmetic. O'Neill's Emperor Jones is assailed by memories of his past as he tries to escape from his enemies—memories of life on the chain gang in the United States, which he had experienced personally, and "racial" fears of ghosts and of the auction blocks of the slave traffic.

Expressionists, then, found uses not merely for conventional fantasy as old as the theatre but for dream formations and for explosions of the Freudian and Jungian "unconscious." The playwrights' inventions appeared not in the context of stable, everyday consciousness like the story of *A Midsummer Night's Dream* (which lent itself ideally to a romantic Reinhardt production) but in the elusive context of an altered field of consciousness. The significant element in expressionism was the "psychological," by which is meant neither the ordinary probing into the motivations of characters in realistic drama nor the simple, mechanistic psychology of the nineteenth century before the work of Charcot and other forerunners of Freud. Expressionism presented processes of exaggeration, condensation, and distortion that defy Aristotelian logic or have a subconscious logic of their own. The theatre began to play host to the phenomena of "free association," the "stream of consciousness," depersonalization, strange recurrences, "split" personality, schizophrenic

behavior, and mental telepathy. By comparison with the explorations undertaken by expressionist playwrights, Arthur Miller's imaginative treatment of Willy Loman in *Death of a Salesman* is elementary.

Expressionism, however, was applied, not only to psychologically unique experience; both Strindberg and O'Neill, whose primary concerns were psychological and spiritual, employed the expressionist technique for social commentary as well. *The Dream Play* clearly points a finger at the failure of society as well as of individuals, and *The Hairy Ape* is less important as the drama of an individual stoker who went berserk after being snubbed than as the story of humanity's disorientation. Indeed, the application of expressionism to social drama gave us many challenging plays, from Wedekind's first assault on sexual taboos in his tragedy of adolescence *The Awakening of Spring* (1898) to the dramas of social conflict with which the theatre abounded after 1918. To dramas of antiwar protest and social revolt, especially after the First World War, expressionist playwrights brought hortatory and nervous dialogue, high-strung characters, and a general explosiveness. They were also greatly concerned with the theme of modern mechanization, and writers like Georg Kaiser (in *The Coral* and *Gas I* and *II*) and Karel Capek (in *R. U. R.*) foretold disaster for an over-industrialized, overmechanized world, using an appropriate style of stenographic dialogue and depersonalization of characters. For social satire, moreover, the expressionistic style proved particularly effective insofar as extravaganza is more lively and pointed than humdrum slices of life and pedestrian problem plays. Before 1920, the German playwright Carl Sternheim cultivated an acrid antibourgeois satire in comedies such as *Burgher Schippel* and *The Snob,* and Georg Kaiser exposed the shams of society under the Hohenzollern monarchy in animated nightmares when he wrote *From Morn to Midnight* (1916). After 1920, expressionistic satire was adopted even by playwrights in America, and the results were gratifying in Elmer Rice's *The Adding Machine,* Kaufman and Connelly's *Beggar on Horseback,* and John Howard Lawson's *Processional.* Expressionism made the social theatre theatrical; it is not surprising, therefore, that it should have lingered on long after the follies of its enthusiasts cast discredit on the expressionist movement and ushered in a reaction against its excesses of hysteria, irrationality, and confusion.

Expressionism was never given enough time to simmer down to the viable substance of art and become a well-established style of drama. Consequently, after 1925 expressionistic drama was no longer written with much frequency, although its devices have cropped up again and again, and its tone has been borrowed by playwrights more often than is realized. But the antinaturalistic style has continued to challenge the conventional theatre. It has exploded in a variety of exotic movements such as futurism and surrealism, producing oddities, such as the totally incomprehensible but entrancing *tour de force* by Virgil Thomson and Gertrude Stein, *Four Saints in Three Acts.* It has turned somersaults in the work of Jean Cocteau and has displayed an ingratiating madness in the plays of Saroyan. It has found a vital form in epic realism, impressively represented by a number of plays by Bertolt Brecht and by the Federal Theatre's living newspapers, *Power* and *One-Third of a Nation,* in the nineteen-thirties. Lyric drama flared up in the work of Federico García Lorca until his flame was extinguished by a fascist band, and other poets less endowed with theatrical talent, among them T. S.

Eliot and W. H. Auden, have tried to create a modern poetic theatre. And it is significant that even in pragmatic America, playwrights such as Tennessee Williams and Arthur Miller have been applauded for combining realistic with imaginative writing. As for stagecraft, efforts to introduce expressive theatricalism continued to be made with singular success long after expressionism ceased to be a force in the theatre, and it is unlikely that imaginative artists will ever allow themselves to be suppressed by considerations of caution—or of money. The theatre of the twentieth century, facing the crossfire of political struggles and war of unprecedented magnitude and destructiveness, continued, and is likely to continue, to serve the spirit of poetry and imaginative truth.

Maurice Maeterlinck

(1862–1949)

At the beginning of the present century, Maurice Maeterlinck, according to James Huneker, signified to most Americans "a crazy crow masquerading in tail feathers plucked from the Swan of Avon." The scales were more than balanced, however, by the weight of critical opinion in Europe, where he was regarded as the promulgator and creator of a "new drama." Heralded as the messiah of the anti-naturalistic symbolist theatre, he was expected to free dramatic art from bondage to concrete but superficial fact and lead it by the hand into the wonderland of the imagination. By following his guidance, the drama would find itself—and not merely in Poe's misty midregions of Weir but in the forest of symbols where life is a high mystery of the soul and where the truths of life and death are finally revealed to the knight-errant! And there would be related rewards for any stage that would follow his pure vision. It would exfoliate itself from the sordid rags that naturalism had forced it to wear, as well as from the business suits of ordinary, bourgeois realism. The theatre would put on robes of gold and the glowing jewelry of poetry. It would also wear the noble mask of tragedy, and through the mask would be seen the soulful eyes of the Muse that looks upon eternal mystery and universal sorrow. The high art of tragedy would return again to a theatre demeaned by encounters in the cold glare of the workaday world.

Even that irascible genius of naturalism Strindberg, who was not often given to idolatry, became reverential toward Maeterlinck, acclaimed him a master, and paid him the tribute of imitation for a time. And the citadel of naturalistic stagecraft, the Moscow Art Theatre, also succumbed to Maeterlinck's spell, producing his one-act plays *The Blind* and *Interior* on October 2, 1904 (some nine months after presenting the realistic masterpiece *The Cherry Orchard*), and staging *The Blue Bird* on September 30, 1908. Poet, essayist, mystic, entomologist, and philosopher as well as dramatist, Maeterlinck was a potent figure in European culture until after 1910, when the tide of "Maeterlinckism" began to recede.

Maeterlinck was a Belgian, born in Ghent and educated at its university, although his name is linked chiefly with French letters and theatre. After practising law in a desultory fashion, he went to Paris in 1886 and joined the circle of symbolist poets there, publishing in 1889 a collection of dreamful, loosely organized poems, *Serres chaudes,* comparable to the hallucinatory poetry of Arthur Rimbaud. That year he also produced a bizarre tragedy of fear and fate, *La Princesse Maleine,* reminiscent in its violence and moodiness of the plays of Elizabethans such as John Webster and Cyril Tourneur. Its melancholy and its assault on the nervous system with eerie atmosphere and haunting dialogue created a strong impression. The naturalistic writer Octave Mirbeau, writing in the columns of *Figaro* in 1890, called the play the most inspired work of the times and lauded it as "more tragic" than *Macbeth* and superior in meaningfulness to *Hamlet.* These extraordinary overstatements about an overwrought drama of hatred and murder made the twenty-eight-year-old author the most talked-of new playwright in Europe.

This undeserved reputation was soon made more deserving in 1890 by two symbolic short mood pieces, *The Intruder* and *The Blind.* These were followed by *The Seven Princesses* in 1891; the full-length variant of Dante's Paolo and Francesca story, *Pelléas and Mélisande,* in 1892; the affecting one-acter *Interior* and *The Death of Tintagiles,* both in 1894. Their effect communicated itself easily as a dramatic tension and as poetry. The plays also lent themselves admirably to an atmospheric type of staging widely divergent from the precision of realistic stagecraft. And Maeterlinck himself translated his practice into a widely noticed dramatic theory in *The Treasure of the Humble,* published in 1896. In addition to paying tribute to the mysticism and transcendentalism of the men he admired (among whom were the German romanticist Novalis and Ralph Waldo Emerson), Maeterlinck set down thoughts on art that impressed an entire generation with the possibility of creating a new style of dramatic composition.

A play, according to one essay in *The Treasure of the Humble,* should penetrate beneath the surface of reality. Everything concrete and definable is unimportant by comparison with the inner life of man and the universe, and this life is a mystery. Indeed, Maeterlinck believed that ideally his early plays should be acted by marionettes. The human actor would spoil the effect of plays in which atmosphere and vague intimations were intended to convey a universal and largely unutterable experience. The drama should deal with the ultimate reality of the soul rather than with transparent physical reality. For this purpose, moreover, action was to be supplanted by states of feeling. Truth would be served not only to the degree that there is more reality in spirit than in matter, as Plato and Plotinus had taught long ago, but to the degree that much of life is uneventful.

For Maeterlinck there was supreme drama in an externally inactive presentation of an old man sitting in his armchair at night with a lamp beside him, "giving unconscious ear to all the eternal laws that reign about his house, interpreting, without comprehending, the silence of doors and windows and the quivering voice of the light, submitting with bent head to the presence of his soul and his destiny." Such a man, although motionless, lived in reality "a deeper, more human, and more universal life" than the usual characters of the drama—"than the lover who strangles his mistress, the captain who conquers in battle, or the husband who avenges his honor."

From the contemplation of uneventful life, no matter how humble, the dramatist would acquire a high, dignified art and convey a tragic sense of life much more true to fact than the tragedies of violent struggle. Conflict was unnecessary in the drama, and there was no need for showing us the human will constantly engaged in battle. Even dialogue, as normally written for the theatre, was apt to be false because it was always definite and always eloquent. Maeterlinck chose for his slogan an old medieval inscription on a door in Bruges: "Within me there is more." Unspoken dialogue was often more eloquent and significant. There are pregnant silences that teem with inexpressible feeling and thought, and the best modern drama would use silence to good tragic and metaphysical effect. Also, dialogue should be used not only to promote the situation but, as in all great tragedies, to reveal soul states. In great art, it is the dialogue superfluous to the action that draws us closest to beauty and the lofty truths of the spirit. The dialogue that implies rather than states, the mood, or atmosphere, the profound suggestion, and the overtone were to be the most valuable ingredients of dramatic composition. It was not only desirable, then, but possible to create a "static drama" different from the time-honored theatre of primitive violence and brutal passion. Maeterlinck cited the superiority of *Hamlet* to *Othello* as an example, writing that "Othello does not appear to live the august daily life of Hamlet, who has the time to live, inasmuch as he does not act." He added that it was an ancient error to assume that we live our truest lives when we are possessed by some passion. The ideal of dramatic art should be the representation of a "stasis."

One may question all of Maeterlinck's premises, and Maeterlinck himself departed from them, mingling mood and action in *Pelléas and Mélisande* and launching into violently active drama with the romantic Renaissance story of *Monna Vanna* (1902). He came to realize that it was impossible to write long plays effectively without recourse to active events, and years later told his correspondent Barrett Clark not to attach too much weight to his theory of static drama: it was a theory of his youth, "worth what most literary theories are worth—that

is, almost nothing." Maeterlinck, indeed, wrote a good many plays which did not adhere to his pristine notions of a new kind of dramatic poetry. He also began to abandon his pessimistic view of life in 1901, when he made the heroine of his *Ariane and Blue-Beard* free Blue-Beard's prisoners, and when he composed a tribute to triumphant love in *Joyzelle* (1903). In this play, the magician Merlin subjects a girl to every conceivable trial only to find her invincibly devoted in love. Maeterlinck came, indeed, to be regarded as a leader of spiritual "uplift" when he wrote a series of semiscientific, philosophically affirmative books. His search for a ruling spirit led him to engage in occult studies and to write a good deal of pabulum for the popular press.

It must also be admitted that many of his stage pieces were exceedingly tenuous. His *Sister Beatrice* (1900) and *Ariane and Blue-Beard* (1901) are little more than libretti. His medieval cast of mind often caused him to play with horror in an artificially romantic and decorative style, as in *The Seven Princesses*. He cultivated disingenuousness a trifle too strenuously in plays such as *The Seven Princesses* (1891) and *Alladine and Palomides* (1894); the naïveté of *The Blue Bird* (1908), combined with its banal idea that happiness is to be found at home, leaves this once extravagantly esteemed fantasy shelterless except in children's theatres. He often promised more with the portentousness of his atmosphere, as in the theatrically effective *Death of Tintagiles* (1894), than he actually delivered. And even the comparatively active drama *Pelléas and Mélisande*, produced in many countries, is now better known through the Claude Debussy opera of the same title, because the slender story is supersaturated with poetic mood and attenuated by the elfin character of the heroine. It may be accurately said of Maeterlinck's dramatic work in general that there is less in it than meets the eye. Nor would such criticism have troubled Maeterlinck, because he tried to make his plays approximate the state of music and it was the point of his argument that what meets the eye is the least important part of reality. On the whole, his plays had more manner than they had matter.

Nevertheless, during the early part of his career Maeterlinck achieved a pervasive importance in the theatre which was officially acknowledged in 1911 with the Nobel Prize for literature. As a critic of other men's work he drew attention to the presence of poetry even in such masterpieces of naturalism as Ibsen's *Ghosts* and Tolstoy's *The Power of Darkness*, reminding his contemporaries that there was more in these plays than their demonstration of a problem. (He was, indeed, a better critic than many of Ibsen's champions when he wrote in 1901 that in *Ghosts*, "in a stuffy middle-class drawing-room, unbearable, maddening to the characters, there breaks forth one of the most terrible mysteries of human destiny," which took the form of "a law of justice or

injustice, formidable and only recently suspected—
the law of heredity.") His emphasis on the value of
dramatizing inner experience exerted a long-lasting
influence which many an expressionistic or simply
psychological drama reflected after 1900. His idea
of static drama bore fruit in at least one masterpiece, John Millington Synge's *Riders to the Sea,*
and his depreciation of the role of violent action
in plays was vindicated in realistic, rather than romantic, art when Chekhov wrote his masterly
dramas *The Three Sisters* and *The Cherry Orchard.*
The ideal of stasis was echoed in many quarters at
the beginning of the century, and James Joyce was
to recall it memorably (and more sensibly than
Maeterlinck) in his autobiographical novel *Portrait
of the Artist as a Young Man* (1914–1915) when
he made the young hero elaborate a theory of tragedy to a schoolmate. About the same time, Leonid
Andreyev, Maeterlinck's ardent Russian disciple,
asserted in his *Letter on the Theatre* (1914) that
action was unnecessary because in modern times
"life has gone within," having become "psychological." The true contemporary hero, Andreyev maintained and demonstrated in his own plays, was a
character in whom we are interested because he
represents "human thought, with all its sufferings,
joys and struggles." These adumbrations of Maeterlinckian theory bring us a step nearer to the inner
agonies of O'Neill's plays and to the psychological
complications represented by Pirandello.

It is in the early plays, *The Intruder, The Blind,*
and *Interior* that Maeterlinck's artistry is most successful. Among these, *The Intruder* is the purest
expression of his aims. If the play has no external
conflict and approaches a condition of stasis, it
nevertheless progresses from point to point in representing the growing apprehension of the characters.
Although they obviously cannot cope with anything

so intangible as death, their plight does represent the
oldest and most universal of all conflicts. Conflict,
moreover, has its equivalent here in tension; and
tension may be essentially more dynamic than mere
melodramatic excitation. The grandfather makes an
impressive central figure in the penumbral world of
the play, and death, as sensed largely through his apprehensiveness, is an intensely dramatic reality. *The
Intruder* also involves the actuality of a woman
dying in another room after giving birth to a child,
and the playwright presents his characters in an
atmospheric setting without the customary trappings
of medieval romance. There is no pretentious and
anachronistic romanticism in this play. Fortunately,
moreover, Maeterlinck had the good sense not to
overextend and enfeeble his poetic effects. Like *The
Blind* and *Interior, The Intruder* is short enough to
be sustained by its tension. Nor does Maeterlinck
overstrain the mystery he invokes by means of half-
uttered thoughts, haunting repetitions, and still more
haunting silences. Except in *Pelléas and Mélisande,*
Maeterlinck's most impressive triumphs entailed a
short, exquisite flight.

BIBLIOGRAPHY: A. Bailly, *Maeterlinck,* 1931; Eric
Bentley, *The Playwright as Thinker* (pp. 90–94,
96–97, 325–328), 1946; Jethro Bithell, *Life and
Writings of Maurice Maeterlinck,* 1913; *Columbia
Dictionary of Modern European Literature* (p. 501),
1947; James Huneker, *Iconoclasts* (pp. 367–429),
1905; Maurice Maeterlinck, "The Tragical in Daily
Life," in *The Treasure of the Humble,* 1907, and in
Barrett H. Clark, *Chief European Theories of the
Drama* (pp. 411–413), 1918, 1945; Maeterlinck,
"Silence," in *The Treasure of the Humble;* Maeter-
linck, "Preface to the Plays," 1901, in Clark, *Chief
European Theories of the Drama* (pp. 414–416).

THE INTRUDER

By Maurice Maeterlinck

TRANSLATED FROM THE FRENCH

CHARACTERS

THE GRANDFATHER [blind]   THE THREE DAUGHTERS   THE SERVANT
THE FATHER   THE UNCLE

A sombre room in an old Château. A door on the right, a door on the left, and a small concealed door in a corner. At the back, stained-glass windows, in which green is the dominant color, and a glass door giving on to a terrace. A big Dutch clock in one corner. A lighted lamp.

THE THREE DAUGHTERS: Come here, grandfather. Sit down under the lamp.

THE GRANDFATHER: There does not seem to me to be much light here.

THE FATHER: Shall we go out on the terrace, or stay in this room?

THE UNCLE: Would it not be better to stay here? It has rained the whole week, and the nights are damp and cold.

THE ELDEST DAUGHTER: But the stars are shining.

THE UNCLE: Oh the stars—that's nothing.

THE GRANDFATHER: We had better stay here. One never knows what may happen.

THE FATHER: There is no longer any cause for anxiety. The danger is over, and she is saved. . . .

THE GRANDFATHER: I believe she is not doing so well. . . .

THE FATHER: Why do you say that?

THE GRANDFATHER: I have heard her voice.

THE FATHER: But since the doctors assure us we may be easy. . . .

THE UNCLE: You know quite well that your father-in-law likes to alarm us needlessly.

THE GRANDFATHER: I don't see things as you do.

THE UNCLE: You ought to rely on us, then, who can see. She looked very well this afternoon. She is sleeping quietly now; and we are not going to mar, needlessly, the first pleasant evening that chance has put in our way. . . . It seems to me we have a perfect right to peace, and even to laugh a little, this evening, without fear.

THE FATHER: That's true; this is the first time I have felt at home with my family since this terrible confinement.

THE UNCLE: When once illness has come into a house, it is as though a stranger had forced himself into the family circle.

THE FATHER: And then you understand, too, that you can count on no one outside the family.

THE UNCLE: You are quite right.

THE GRANDFATHER: Why couldn't I see my poor daughter to-day?

THE UNCLE: You know quite well—the doctor forbade it.

THE GRANDFATHER: I do not know what to think. . . .

THE UNCLE: It is useless to worry.

THE GRANDFATHER: [*Pointing to the door on the left*] She cannot hear us?

THE FATHER: We will not talk too loud; besides, the door is very thick, and the Sister of Mercy is with her, and she is sure to warn us if we are making too much noise.

THE GRANDFATHER: [*Pointing to the door on the right*] He cannot hear us?

THE FATHER: No, no.

THE GRANDFATHER: He is asleep?

THE FATHER: I suppose so.

THE GRANDFATHER: Some one had better go and see.

THE UNCLE: The little one would cause *me* more anxiety than your wife. It is now several weeks since he was born, and he has scarcely stirred. He has not cried once all the time! He is like a wax doll.

THE GRANDFATHER: I think he will be deaf—dumb too, perhaps—the usual result of a marriage between cousins. . . . [*A reproving silence*]

THE FATHER: I could almost wish him ill for the suffering he has caused his mother.

THE UNCLE: Do be reasonable; it is not the poor little thing's fault. He is quite alone in the room?

THE FATHER: Yes; the doctor does not wish him to stay in his mother's room any longer.

THE UNCLE: But the nurse is with him?

THE FATHER: No; she has gone to rest a little; she has well deserved it these last few days. Ursula, just go and see if he is asleep.

THE ELDEST DAUGHTER: Yes, father. [The Three Sisters *get up, and go into the room on the right, hand in hand*]

THE FATHER: When will your sister come?

THE UNCLE: I think she will come about nine.

THE FATHER: It is past nine. I hope she will come this evening, my wife is so anxious to see her.

267

THE UNCLE: She is sure to come. This will be the first time she has been here?

THE FATHER: She has never been in the house.

THE UNCLE: It is very difficult for her to leave her convent.

THE FATHER: Will she be alone?

THE UNCLE: I expect one of the nuns will come with her. They are not allowed to go out alone.

THE FATHER: But she is the Superior.

THE UNCLE: The rule is the same for all.

THE GRANDFATHER: Do you not feel anxious?

THE UNCLE: Why should we feel anxious? What's the good of harping on that? There is nothing more to fear.

THE GRANDFATHER: Your sister is older than you?

THE UNCLE: She is the eldest.

THE GRANDFATHER: I do not know what ails me; I feel uneasy. I wish your sister were here.

THE UNCLE: She will come; she promised to.

THE GRANDFATHER: Ah, if this evening were only over!

[The Three Daughters *come in again*]

THE FATHER: He is asleep?

THE ELDEST DAUGHTER: Yes, father; he is sleeping soundly.

THE UNCLE: What shall we do while we are waiting?

THE GRANDFATHER: Waiting for what?

THE UNCLE: Waiting for our sister.

THE FATHER: You see nothing coming, Ursula?

THE ELDEST DAUGHTER: [*At the window*] Nothing, father.

THE FATHER: Not in the avenue? Can you see the avenue?

THE DAUGHTER: Yes, father; it is moonlight, and I can see the avenue as far as the cypress wood.

THE GRANDFATHER: And you do not see any one?

THE DAUGHTER: No one, grandfather.

THE UNCLE: What sort of a night is it?

THE DAUGHTER: Very fine. Do you hear the nightingales?

THE UNCLE: Yes, yes.

THE DAUGHTER: A little wind is rising in the avenue.

THE GRANDFATHER: A little wind in the avenue?

THE DAUGHTER: Yes; the trees are trembling a little.

THE UNCLE: I am surprised that my sister is not here yet.

THE GRANDFATHER: I cannot hear the nightingales any longer.

THE DAUGHTER: I think some one has come into the garden, grandfather.

THE GRANDFATHER: Who is it?

THE DAUGHTER: I do not know; I can see no one.

THE UNCLE: Because there is no one there.

THE DAUGHTER: There must be some one in the garden; the nightingales have suddenly ceased singing.

THE GRANDFATHER: But I do not hear any one coming.

THE DAUGHTER: Some one must be passing by the pond, because the swans are ruffled.

ANOTHER DAUGHTER: All the fishes in the pond are diving suddenly.

THE FATHER: You cannot see any one.

THE DAUGHTER: No one, father.

THE FATHER: But the pond lies in the moonlight. . . .

THE DAUGHTER: Yes; I can see that the swans are ruffled.

THE UNCLE: I am sure it is my sister who is scaring them. She must have come in by the little gate.

THE FATHER: I cannot understand why the dogs do not bark.

THE DAUGHTER: I can see the watch-dog right at the back of his kennel. The swans are crossing to the other bank! . . .

THE UNCLE: They are afraid of my sister. I will go and see. [*He calls*] Sister! sister! Is that you? . . . There is no one there.

THE DAUGHTER: I am sure that some one has come into the garden. You will see.

THE UNCLE: But she would answer me!

THE GRANDFATHER: Are not the nightingales beginning to sing again, Ursula?

THE DAUGHTER: I cannot hear one anywhere.

THE GRANDFATHER: But there is no noise.

THE FATHER: There is a silence of the grave.

THE GRANDFATHER: It must be a stranger that is frightening them, for if it were one of the family they would not be silent.

THE UNCLE: How much longer are you going to discuss these nightingales?

THE GRANDFATHER: Are all the windows open, Ursula?

THE DAUGHTER: The glass door is open, grandfather.

THE GRANDFATHER: It seems to be that the cold is penetrating into the room.

THE DAUGHTER: There is a little wind in the garden, grandfather, and the rose-leaves are falling.

THE FATHER: Well, shut the door. It is late.

THE DAUGHTER: Yes, father. . . . I cannot shut the door.

THE TWO OTHER DAUGHTERS: We cannot shut the door.

THE GRANDFATHER: Why, what is the matter with the door, my children?

THE UNCLE: You need not say that in such an extraordinary voice. I will go and help them.

THE ELDEST DAUGHTER: We cannot manage to shut it quite.

THE UNCLE: It is because of the damp. Let us all push together. There must be something in the way.

THE FATHER: The carpenter will set it right tomorrow.

THE GRANDFATHER: Is the carpenter coming to-morrow?

THE DAUGHTER: Yes, grandfather; he is coming to do some work in the cellar.

THE GRANDFATHER: He will make a noise in the house.

THE DAUGHTER: I will tell him to work quietly.

[Suddenly the sound of a scythe being sharpened is heard outside]

THE GRANDFATHER: [With a shudder] Oh!

THE UNCLE: What is that?

THE DAUGHTER: I don't quite know; I think it is the gardener. I cannot quite see; he is in the shadow of the house.

THE FATHER: It is the gardener going to mow.

THE UNCLE: He mows by night?

THE FATHER: Is not to-morrow Sunday?—Yes.—I noticed that the grass was very long round the house.

THE GRANDFATHER: It seems to me that his scythe makes as much noise. . . .

THE DAUGHTER: He is mowing near the house.

THE GRANDFATHER: Can you see him, Ursula?

THE DAUGHTER: No, grandfather. He is standing in the dark.

THE GRANDFATHER: I am afraid he will wake my daughter.

THE UNCLE: We can scarcely hear him.

THE GRANDFATHER: It sounds as if he were mowing inside the house.

THE UNCLE: The invalid will not hear it! There is no danger.

THE FATHER: It seems to me that the lamp is not burning well this evening.

THE UNCLE: It wants filling.

THE FATHER: I saw it filled this morning. It has burnt badly since the window was shut.

THE UNCLE: I fancy the chimney is dirty.

THE FATHER: It will burn better presently.

THE DAUGHTER: Grandfather is asleep. He has not slept for three nights.

THE FATHER: He has been so much worried.

THE UNCLE: He always worries too much. At times he will not listen to reason.

THE FATHER: It is quite excusable at his age.

THE UNCLE: God knows what we shall be like at his age!

THE FATHER: He is nearly eighty.

THE UNCLE: Then he has a right to be strange.

THE FATHER: He is like all blind people.

THE UNCLE: They think too much.

THE FATHER: They have too much time to spare.

THE UNCLE: They have nothing else to do.

THE FATHER: And, besides, they have no distractions.

THE UNCLE: That must be terrible.

THE FATHER: Apparently one gets used to it.

THE UNCLE: I cannot imagine it.

THE FATHER: They are certainly to be pitied.

THE UNCLE: Not to know where one is, not to know where one has come from, not to know whither one is going, not to be able to distinguish midday from midnight, or summer from winter—and always darkness, darkness! I would rather not live. Is it absolutely incurable?

THE FATHER: Apparently so.

THE UNCLE: But he is not absolutely blind?

THE FATHER: He can perceive a strong light.

THE UNCLE: Let us take care of our poor eyes.

THE FATHER: He often has strange ideas.

THE UNCLE: At times he is not at all amusing.

THE FATHER: He says absolutely everything he thinks.

THE UNCLE: But he was not always like this?

THE FATHER: No; once he was as rational as we are; he never said anything extraordinary. I am afraid Ursula encourages him a little too much; she answers all his questions. . . .

THE UNCLE: It would be better not to answer them. It's a mistaken kindness to him.

[Ten o'clock strikes]

THE GRANDFATHER: [Waking up] Am I facing the glass door?

THE DAUGHTER: You have had a nice sleep, grandfather?

THE GRANDFATHER: Am I facing the glass door?

THE DAUGHTER: Yes, grandfather.

THE GRANDFATHER: There is nobody at the glass door?

THE DAUGHTER: No, grandfather; I do not see any one.

THE GRANDFATHER: I thought some one was waiting. No one has come?

THE DAUGHTER: No one, grandfather.

THE GRANDFATHER: [To the Uncle and Father] And your sister has not come?

THE UNCLE: It is too late; she will not come now. It is not nice of her.

THE FATHER: I'm beginning to be anxious about her. [A noise, as of some one coming into the house]

THE UNCLE: She is here! Did you hear?

THE FATHER: Yes; some one has come in at the basement.

THE UNCLE: It must be our sister. I recognized her step.

THE GRANDFATHER: I heard slow footsteps.

THE FATHER: She came in very quietly.

THE UNCLE: She knows there is an invalid.

THE GRANDFATHER: I hear nothing now.

THE UNCLE: She will come up directly; they will tell her we are here.

THE FATHER: I am glad she has come.

THE UNCLE: I was sure she would come this evening.

THE GRANDFATHER: She is a very long time coming up.

THE UNCLE: It must be she.

THE FATHER: We are not expecting any other visitors.

THE GRANDFATHER: I cannot hear any noise in the basement.

THE FATHER: I will call the servant. We shall know how things stand. [*He pulls a bell-rope*]

THE GRANDFATHER: I can hear a noise on the stairs already.

THE FATHER: It is the servant coming up.

THE GRANDFATHER: To me it sounds as if she were not alone.

THE FATHER: She is coming up slowly. . . .

THE GRANDFATHER: I hear your sister's step!

THE FATHER: I can only hear the servant.

THE GRANDFATHER: It is your sister! It is your sister!

[*There is a knock at the little door*]

THE UNCLE: She is knocking at the door of the back stairs.

THE FATHER: I will go and open it myself. [*He opens the little door partly; the* Servant *remains outside in the opening*] Where are you?

THE SERVANT: Here, sir.

THE GRANDFATHER: Your sister is at the door?

THE UNCLE: I can only see the servant.

THE FATHER: It is only the servant. [*To the* Servant] Who was that, that came into the house?

THE SERVANT: Came into the house?

THE FATHER: Yes; some one came in just now?

THE SERVANT: No one came in, sir.

THE GRANDFATHER: Who is it sighing like that?

THE UNCLE: It is the servant; she is out of breath.

THE GRANDFATHER: Is she crying?

THE UNCLE: No; why should she be crying?

THE FATHER: [*To the* Servant] No one came in just now?

THE SERVANT: No, sir.

THE FATHER: But we heard some one open the door!

THE SERVANT: It was I shutting the door.

THE FATHER: It was open?

THE SERVANT: Yes, sir.

THE FATHER: Why was it open at this time of night?

THE SERVANT: I do not know, sir. I had shut it myself.

THE FATHER: Then who was it that opened it?

THE SERVANT: I do not know, sir. Some one must have gone out after me, sir. . . .

THE FATHER: You must be careful.—Don't push the door; you know what a noise it makes!

THE SERVANT: But, sir, I am not touching the door.

THE FATHER: But you are. You are pushing as if you were trying to get into the room.

THE SERVANT: But, sir, I am three yards away from the door.

THE FATHER: Don't talk so loud. . . .

THE GRANDFATHER: Are they putting out the light?

THE ELDEST DAUGHTER: No, grandfather.

THE GRANDFATHER: It seems to me it has grown pitch dark all at once.

THE FATHER: [*To the* Servant] You can go down

again now; but do not make so much noise on the stairs.

THE SERVANT: I did not make any noise on the stairs.

THE FATHER: I tell you that you did make a noise. Go down quietly; you will wake your mistress. And if any one comes now, say that we are not at home.

THE UNCLE: Yes; say that we are not at home.

THE GRANDFATHER: [*Shuddering*] You must not say that!

THE FATHER: . . . Except to my sister and the doctor.

THE UNCLE: When will the doctor come?

THE FATHER: He will not be able to come before midnight. [*He shuts the door. A clock is heard striking eleven*]

THE GRANDFATHER: She has come in?

THE FATHER: Who?

THE GRANDFATHER: The servant.

THE FATHER: No, she has gone downstairs.

THE GRANDFATHER: I thought that she was sitting at the table.

THE UNCLE: The servant?

THE GRANDFATHER: Yes.

THE UNCLE: That would complete one's happiness!

THE GRANDFATHER: No one has come into the room?

THE FATHER: No; no one has come in.

THE GRANDFATHER: And your sister is not here?

THE UNCLE: Our sister has not come.

THE GRANDFATHER: You want to deceive me.

THE UNCLE: Deceive you?

THE GRANDFATHER: Ursula, tell me the truth, for the love of God!

THE ELDEST DAUGHTER: Grandfather! Grandfather! what is the matter with you?

THE GRANDFATHER: Something has happened! I am sure my daughter is worse! . . .

THE UNCLE: Are you dreaming?

THE GRANDFATHER: You do not want to tell me! . . . I can see quite well there is something. . . .

THE UNCLE: In that case you can see better than we can.

THE GRANDFATHER: Ursula, tell me the truth!

THE DAUGHTER: But we have told you the truth, grandfather!

THE GRANDFATHER: You do not speak in your ordinary voice.

THE FATHER: That is because you frighten her.

THE GRANDFATHER: Your voice is changed, too.

THE FATHER: You are going mad! [*He and the* Uncle *make signs to each other to signify the* Grandfather *has lost his reason*]

THE GRANDFATHER: I can hear quite well that you are afraid.

THE FATHER: But what should we be afraid of?

THE GRANDFATHER: Why do you want to deceive me?

THE UNCLE: Who is thinking of deceiving you?

THE GRANDFATHER: Why have you put out the light?

THE UNCLE: But the light has not been put out; there is as much light as there was before.

THE DAUGHTER: It seems to me that the lamp has gone down.

THE FATHER: I see as well now as ever.

THE GRANDFATHER: I have millstones on my eyes! Tell me, girls, what is going on here! Tell me, for the love of God, you who can see! I am here, all alone, in darkness without end! I do not know who seats himself beside me! I do not know what is happening a yard from me! . . . Why were you talking under your breath just now?

THE FATHER: No one was talking under his breath.

THE GRANDFATHER: You did talk in a low voice at the door.

THE FATHER: You heard all I said.

THE GRANDFATHER: You brought some one into the room! . . .

THE FATHER: But I tell you no one has come in!

THE GRANDFATHER: Is it your sister or a priest?—You should not try to deceive me.—Ursula, who was it that came in?

THE DAUGHTER: No one, grandfather.

THE GRANDFATHER: You must not try to deceive me; I know what I know.—How many of us are there here?

THE DAUGHTER: There are six of us round the table, grandfather.

THE GRANDFATHER: You are all round the table?

THE DAUGHTER: Yes, grandfather.

THE GRANDFATHER: You are there, Paul?

THE FATHER: Yes.

THE GRANDFATHER: You are there, Oliver?

THE UNCLE: Yes, of course I am here, in my usual place. That's not alarming, is it?

THE GRANDFATHER: You are there, Geneviève?

ONE OF THE DAUGHTERS: Yes, grandfather.

THE GRANDFATHER: You are there, Gertrude?

ANOTHER DAUGHTER: Yes, grandfather.

THE GRANDFATHER: You are here, Ursula?

THE ELDEST DAUGHTER: Yes, grandfather; next to you.

THE GRANDFATHER: And who is that sitting there?

THE DAUGHTER: Where do you mean, grandfather? —There is no one.

THE GRANDFATHER: There, there—in the midst of us!

THE DAUGHTER: But there is no one, grandfather!

THE FATHER: We tell you there is no one!

THE GRANDFATHER: But you cannot see—any of you!

THE UNCLE: Pshaw! You are joking.

THE GRANDFATHER: I do not feel inclined for joking, I can assure you.

THE UNCLE: Then believe those who can see.

THE GRANDFATHER: [Undecidedly] I thought there was some one . . . I believe I shall not live long. . . .

THE UNCLE: Why should we deceive you? What use would there be in that?

THE FATHER: It would be our duty to tell you the truth . . .

THE UNCLE: What would be the good of deceiving each other?

THE FATHER: You could not live in error long.

THE GRANDFATHER: [Trying to rise] I should like to pierce this darkness! . . .

THE FATHER: Where do you want to go?

THE GRANDFATHER: Over there. . . .

THE FATHER: Don't be so anxious.

THE UNCLE: You are strange this evening.

THE GRANDFATHER: It is all of you who seem to me to be strange!

THE FATHER: Do you want anything?

THE GRANDFATHER: I do not know what ails me.

THE ELDEST DAUGHTER: Grandfather! grandfather! What do you want, grandfather?

THE GRANDFATHER: Give me your little hands, my children.

THE THREE DAUGHTERS: Yes, grandfather.

THE GRANDFATHER: Why are you all three trembling, girls?

THE ELDEST DAUGHTER: We are scarcely trembling at all, grandfather.

THE GRANDFATHER: I fancy you are all three pale.

THE ELDEST DAUGHTER: It is late, grandfather, and we are tired.

THE FATHER: You must go to bed, and grandfather himself would do well to take a little rest.

THE GRANDFATHER: I could not sleep to-night!

THE UNCLE: We will wait for the doctor.

THE GRANDFATHER: Prepare for the truth.

THE UNCLE: But there is no truth!

THE GRANDFATHER: Then I do not know what there is!

THE UNCLE: I tell you there is nothing at all!

THE GRANDFATHER: I wish I could see my poor daughter!

THE FATHER: But you know quite well it is impossible; she must not be awakened unnecessarily.

THE UNCLE: You will see her to-morrow.

THE GRANDFATHER: There is no sound in her room.

THE UNCLE: I should be uneasy if I heard any sound.

THE GRANDFATHER: It is a very long time since I saw my daughter! . . . I took her hands yesterday evening, but I could not see her! . . . I do not know what has become of her. . . . I do not know how she is. . . . I do not know what her face is like now. . . . She must have changed these weeks! . . . I felt the little bones of her cheeks under my hands. . . . There is nothing but the darkness between her and me, and the rest of you! . . . I cannot go on living like this . . . this is not living. . . . You sit there, all of you, looking with open eyes at

my dead eyes, and not one of you has pity on me!
. . . I do not know what ails me. . . . No one tells
me what ought to be told me . . . And everything is
terrifying when one's dreams dwell upon it. . . .
But why are you not speaking?

THE UNCLE: What should we say, since you will
not believe us?

THE GRANDFATHER: You are afraid of betraying
yourselves!

THE FATHER: Come now, be rational!

THE GRANDFATHER: You have been hiding something from me for a long time! . . . Something has
happened in the house. . . . But I am beginning to
understand now. . . . You have been deceiving me
too long!—You fancy that I shall never know anything?—There are moments when I am less blind
than you, you know! . . . Do you think I have not
heard you whispering—for days and days—as if you
were in the house of some one who had been
hanged—I dare not say what I know this evening.
. . . But I shall know the truth! . . . I shall wait
for you to tell me the truth; but I have known it
for a long time, in spite of you!—And now, I feel
that you are all paler than the dead!

THE THREE DAUGHTERS: Grandfather! grandfather!
What is the matter, grandfather?

THE GRANDFATHER: It is not you that I am speaking of, girls. No; it is not you that I am speaking of.
. . . I know quite well you would tell me the truth
—if they were not by! . . . And besides, I feel
sure that they are deceiving you as well. . . . You
will see, children—you will see! . . . Do not I hear
you all sobbing?

THE FATHER: Is my wife really so ill?

THE GRANDFATHER: It is no good trying to deceive
me any longer; it is too late now, and I know the
truth better than you! . . .

THE UNCLE: But we are not blind; we are not.

THE FATHER: Would you like to go into your
daughter's room? This misunderstanding must be
put an end to.—Would you?

THE GRANDFATHER: [Becoming suddenly unde-
cided] No, no, not now—not yet.

THE UNCLE: You see, you are not reasonable.

THE GRANDFATHER: One never knows how much
a man has been unable to express in his life! . . .
Who made that noise?

THE ELDEST DAUGHTER: It is the lamp flickering,
grandfather.

THE GRANDFATHER: It seems to me to be very
unsteady—very!

THE DAUGHTER: It is the cold wind troubling
it. . . .

THE UNCLE: There is no cold wind, the windows
are shut.

THE DAUGHTER: I think it is going out.

THE FATHER: There is no more oil.

THE DAUGHTER: It has gone right out.

THE FATHER: We cannot stay like this in the dark.

THE UNCLE: Why not?—I am quite accustomed
to it.

THE FATHER: There is a light in my wife's room.

THE UNCLE: We will take it from there presently,
when the doctor has been.

THE FATHER: Well, we can see enough here; there
is the light from outside.

THE GRANDFATHER: Is it light outside?

THE FATHER: Lighter than here.

THE UNCLE: For my part, I would as soon talk
in the dark.

THE FATHER: So would I. [Silence]

THE GRANDFATHER: It seems to me the clock
makes a great deal of noise . . .

THE ELDEST DAUGHTER: That is because we are
not talking any more, grandfather.

THE GRANDFATHER: But why are you all silent?

THE UNCLE: What do you want us to talk about?
—You are really very peculiar to-night.

THE GRANDFATHER: Is it very dark in this room?

THE UNCLE: There is not much light. [Silence]

THE GRANDFATHER: I do not feel well, Ursula;
open the window a little.

THE FATHER: Yes, child; open the window a little.
I begin to feel the want of air myself. [The girl
opens the window]

THE UNCLE: I really believe we have stayed shut
up too long.

THE GRANDFATHER: Is the window open?

THE DAUGHTER: Yes, grandfather; it is wide open.

THE GRANDFATHER: One would not have thought
it was open, there was not a sound outside.

THE DAUGHTER: No, grandfather; there is not
the slightest sound.

THE FATHER: The silence is extraordinary!

THE DAUGHTER: One could hear an angel tread!

THE UNCLE: That is why I do not like the country.

THE GRANDFATHER: I wish I could hear some
sound. What o'clock is it, Ursula?

THE DAUGHTER: It will soon be midnight, grandfather. [Here the Uncle begins to pace up and down
the room]

THE GRANDFATHER: Who is that walking round us
like that?

THE UNCLE: Only I! only I! Do not be frightened!
I want to walk about a little. [Silence]—But I am
going to sit down again;—I cannot see where I am
going. [Silence]

THE GRANDFATHER: I wish I were out of this place.

THE DAUGHTER: Where would you like to go,
grandfather?

THE GRANDFATHER: I do not know where—into
another room, no matter where! no matter where!

THE FATHER: Where could we go?

THE UNCLE: It is too late to go anywhere else.
[Silence. They are sitting, motionless, round the
table]

THE GRANDFATHER: What is that I hear, Ursula?

THE DAUGHTER: Nothing, grandfather: it is the

leaves falling.—Yes, it is the leaves falling on the terrace.

THE GRANDFATHER: Go and shut the window, Ursula.

THE DAUGHTER: Yes, grandfather. [*She shuts the window, comes back, and sits down*]

THE GRANDFATHER: I am cold. [*Silence*. The Three Sisters *kiss each other*] What is that I hear now?

THE FATHER: It is the three sisters kissing each other.

THE UNCLE: It seems to me they are very pale this evening. [*Silence*]

THE GRANDFATHER: What is that I hear now, Ursula?

THE DAUGHTER: Nothing, grandfather; it is the clasping of my hands. [*Silence*]

THE GRANDFATHER: And that? . . .

THE DAUGHTER: I do not know, grandfather . . . perhaps my sisters are trembling a little? . . .

THE GRANDFATHER: I am afraid, too, my children.

[*Here a ray of moonlight penetrates through a corner of the stained glass, and throws strange gleams here and there in the room. A clock strikes midnight; at the last stroke there is a very vague sound, as of some one rising in haste*]

THE GRANDFATHER: [*Shuddering with peculiar horror*] Who is that who got up?

THE UNCLE: No one got up!

THE FATHER: I did not get up!

THE THREE DAUGHTERS: Nor I!—Nor I!—Nor I!

THE GRANDFATHER: Some one got up from the table!

THE UNCLE: Light the lamp! . . .

[*Cries of terror are suddenly heard from the child's room, on the right; these cries continue, with gradations of horror, until the end of the scene*]

THE FATHER: Listen to the child!

THE UNCLE: He has never cried before!

THE FATHER: Let us go and see him!

THE UNCLE: The light! The light!

[*At this moment, quick and heavy steps are heard in the room on the left.—Then a deathly silence.—They listen in mute terror, until the door of the room opens slowly; the light from it is cast into the room where they are sitting, and the* Sister of Mercy *appears on the threshold, in her black garments, and bows as she makes the sign of the cross, to announce the death of the wife. They understand, and, after a moment of hesitation and fright, silently enter the chamber of death, while the* Uncle *politely steps aside on the threshold to let the three girls pass. The blind man, left alone, gets up, agitated, and feels his way round the table in the darkness*]

THE GRANDFATHER: Where are you going?— Where are you going?—The girls have left me all alone!

CURTAIN

Edmond Rostand

(1868–1918)

Rostand's masterpiece, *Cyrano de Bergerac,* is subtitled a "Heroic Comedy," and the combination of the adjective and the noun is descriptive not only of this play but of its author's unique power in the theatre. To compose romantic drama successfully in the machine age requires unusual endowment and considerable tact. Rostand was able to blend romantic action and lyricism with humor, and the result was a brief renewal of romanticism on the European continent.

A talent for lyric delight and heroic exaltation appears to have come naturally to this poet. Born in Marseilles to wealthy and distinguished parents who cherished memories of French glory (his mother was the granddaughter of one of Napoleon's marshals), Rostand turned to the writing of poetry and plays at an early age, almost as though a romantic career were his birthright. When he married the poetess Rosemonde Gérard in his twenty-second year, he was able to present his bride with a published volume of verse. Settling in Paris after his marriage in 1890, he quickly made himself at home in theatrical circles, and won the friendship of the superb romantic actor Constant Coquelin, for whom he later wrote the role of Cyrano. It was, in fact, Rostand's good fortune to attract distinguished performers throughout his career.

Rostand's first play to reach the stage, *The Romantics* (1894) proved captivating by virtue of its charming lyricism and its refreshingly frank theatricality. The young hero and heroine, who fall in love lyrically, are first found reading *Romeo and Juliet.* The play was presented as a trifle without apology, and romantic feeling was gaily affirmed by the information that the scene could be laid "wherever you please, provided the costumes are pretty." The action concluded with the actors facing the audience and singing a rondel which lauds the brief tale of "parents, lovers, walled and flowery ways," the rustic "scenes by Watteau," and the poetry as a relief from "all these bitter plays"—presumably, the bleak pictures of life provided by the Zolaist disciples. A year later came *The Faraway Princess,* Rostand's tribute to the Provençal poet Rudel. The play was a celebration of love beyond reason and logic. It bordered on silliness, but there was an engagingly youthful enthusiasm in its story and ecstatic verses. Next, Rostand made an unsuccessful effort to weave a romantic pattern out of Biblical matter in *The Woman of Samaria.* But this failure was quickly followed in the same year of 1897 by the triumphant production of *Cyrano de Bergerac;* and

its author won a second resounding success in 1900 when Sarah Bernhardt, then at the peak of her career, played Napoleon's frail son in the pathetic drama of the eaglet with clipped wings, *L'Aiglon.*

Ill health caused Rostand to retire to the south at the height of his glory and it was there, in the romantic setting of Cambon, at the foot of the Pyrenees, that he made a valiant effort to live up to the high expectations entertained for his next drama. He did, indeed, create a frequently delightful, if uneven, play in *Chantecler.* Mixed with satire on French foibles, it was essentially another affirmation of the heroic spirit that feeds upon intoxicating illusions—such as the rooster's belief that his crowing makes the sun rise—but that can reach new heights when reality brings disenchantment. Having wrested a romantic victory from the facts of life, including the fact of his own illness and retirement, Rostand evidently expected much from his animal fable. *Chantecler,* however, failed on the stage in 1910 and did not attract the French public until 1928, a decade after the playwright's death, when the play received a modernistic production. Deeply disappointed, Rostand remained at Cambon for the rest of his days, writing only the trifle *The Sacred Wood* and an unfinished play about the collapse of Don Juan's amatory career, *The Last Night of Don Juan,* which, published posthumously (1921), came closer to disillusionment than Rostand would have brought himself in the days when he confidently tried to make romance prevail on the modern stage.

Only with *Cyrano de Bergerac,* which had its stirring *première* in Paris on December 28, 1897, when its author was only twenty-nine years old, did Rostand achieve an instantaneous romantic triumph that has not been tarnished by time and the troubled life of the twentieth century. *L'Aiglon* became outmoded because it was compounded of too much pathos and sentimentality, and *Chantecler* presents difficult problems for a stage production, among which the necessity of playing under rooster feathers is not the least. *Cyrano* never fails to exert its spell when performed with tasteful gusto. It has survived translation into English, and it has served American actors extremely well ever since Richard Mansfield, the foremost American actor at the turn of the century, played Rostand's hero to New York audiences in the fall of 1898. Walter Hampden, using the Brian Hooker version, reached the pinnacle of his career with the play in November 1923, and his production was on view for a long time in New

York and other cities. More than two decades later, the play proved just as attractive when it was revived by the young actor-manager José Ferrer.

The secret of *Cyrano's* charm on the stage is an open one. It is one of the most playable of plays, almost superabundant in color and movement, and altogether a work of pure theatre. With his fondness for magnificent gestures, Cyrano is a figure ready-made for the stage in all respects. Yet Rostand's swashbuckling hero also emerges as a human being out of the vividly realized background of the age of Louis XIII. His physical appearance contradicts his spirit and drives him to put on the armor of wit and defiance. The man's triumph of pose and posturing (his "panache") project and compensate an underlying defeat in fact (for he never possesses his Roxane) and in self-esteem (for he never dares to propose to her in his own behalf). Behind his pose lies his pathos, as Cyrano himself well knows. Upon being informed before his death that Molière has stolen a scene from him, he declares that his destiny was always to prompt others. The ironic gods respected by modern man are well served by Rostand, and Cyrano is all the more human, as well as theatrically attractive, for being victimized by them.

Temperament and a love of the theatre helped Rostand escape the pitfalls of the romantic "Wagnerism" that Maeterlinck and the scenic artists Appia and Craig postulated for the theatre. They strove to dissolve dramatic matter into nuances, whereas he accentuated and highlighted drama. They tried to transmute action into elusive music, whereas he translated music—the music of his hero worship and poetry—into exciting action. "With Rostand," as T. S. Eliot noted, "the centre of gravity is in the expression of the emotion, not as with Maeterlinck in the emotion which cannot be expressed." Emotions for Rostand were always significant and strong enough to be exposed on the stage. They were even important enough to carry the full weight of the rhetoric with which he invested them. Few writers have been endurably rhetorical since the seventeenth century. Cyrano's speech on noses is one of the rare acceptable purple patches of the modern drama.

Rostand understood the art of making emotionalism tolerable to the modern world. He made a tragicomedy out of a story that Hugo, sixty years earlier, would have turned into a melodrama masquerading as a tragedy. Hugo, having made the use of grotesque elements a canon of romantic art, lost ironic force by being indiscriminately grandiose. When Rostand selected a grotesque hero, however, he took full advantage of the possibilities of deriving an ironic view of life from grotesqueness, and employed grandiloquence only to characterize Cyrano and to underscore effects. The pyrotechnics of Cyrano's dying speech, for example, can be received all the more gratefully because Rostand heaped the ignominy of a commonplace death on his hero.

It will always be questionable whether the heroic fanfare of *Cyrano de Bergerac* is any more attractive than its antiheroic counterpoint. It is the conjunction of opposites that most absorbs the reader and playgoer, whether he knows it or not. The romanticism of the play Rostand wrote is comparable to Cyrano's "plume." When, as he expects to do, this French Don Quixote sweeps it across the threshold of God's house with a gallant gesture, it is doubtful whether God will regard the feather rather than the man.

The famous Brian Hooker version of *Cyrano de Bergerac* was made especially for Walter Hampden. It was instantly acclaimed as the best, and indeed the only entirely satisfactory, English translation for the stage—the only one that conveyed the brisk theatricality, wit, and rapturous eloquence of the original French. Hooker preserved the meters and rhyme schemes of the incidental lyrics but turned Rostand's Alexandrine couplets into blank verse, which is a more congenial meter in English than the classic French hexameter. Without adding or subtracting lines, the translator took a few liberties in paraphrasing expressions (such as "elegant like Celadon") that would have lacked point for the American public. He also substituted a celebrated quotation from *Dr. Faustus* for a French quotation less known to Americans in Cyrano's tirade on noses.

BIBLIOGRAPHY: Frank W. Chandler, *Modern Continental Playwrights* (pp. 229–236), 1931; T. S. Eliot, *Selected Essays*, 1932; Rosemonde Gérard, *Edmond Rostand*, 1935; Ludwig Lewisohn, *The Modern Drama* (pp. 236–247), 1921.

CYRANO DE BERGERAC

By Edmond Rostand

A NEW VERSION IN ENGLISH VERSE BY BRIAN HOOKER

THE PERSONS

CYRANO DE BERGERAC	CUIGY	TWO MUSICIANS
CHRISTIAN DE NEUVILLETTE	BRISSAILLE	THE POETS
COMTE DE GUICHE	A MEDDLER	THE PASTRYCOOKS
RAGUENEAU	A MUSKETEER	THE PAGES
LE BRET	ANOTHER MUSKETEER	ROXANE
CARBON DE CASTEL-JALOUX	A SPANISH OFFICER	HER DUENNA
THE CADETS	A CAVALIER	LISE
LIGNIÈRE	THE PORTER	THE ORANGE GIRL
VICOMTE DE VALVERT	A CITIZEN	MCTHER MARGUÉRITE DE JÉSUS
A MARQUIS	HIS SON	SISTER MARTHE
SECOND MARQUIS	A CUT-PURSE	SISTER CLAIRE
THIRD MARQUIS	A SPECTATOR	AN ACTRESS
MONTFLEURY	A SENTRY	A SOUBRETTE
BELLEROSE	BERTRANDOU THE FIFER	THE FLOWER GIRL
JODELET	A CAPUCHIN	

The Crowd, Citizens, Marquis, Musketeers, Thieves, Pastrycooks, Poets, Cadets of Gascoyne, Actors, Violins, Pages, Children, Spanish Soldiers, Spectators, Intellectuals, Academicians, Nuns, etc.

[The first four Acts in 1640; the fifth in 1655]

FIRST ACT: *A Performance at the Hôtel de Bourgogne.*
SECOND ACT: *The Bakery of the Poets.*
THIRD ACT: *Roxane's Kiss.*
FOURTH ACT: *The Cadets of Gascoyne.*
FIFTH ACT: *Cyrano's Gazette.*

ACT I.

A Performance at the Hôtel de Bourgogne.
The hall of the Hôtel de Bourgogne in 1640. A sort of tennis court, arranged and decorated for theatrical productions. The hall is a long rectangle; we see it diagonally, in such a way that one side of it forms the back scene, which begins at the first entrance on the right and runs up to the last entrance on the left where it makes a right angle with the stage which is seen obliquely. The stage is provided on either hand with benches placed along the wings. The curtain is formed by two lengths of tapestry which can be drawn apart. Above a Harlequin cloak, the royal arms. Broad steps lead from the stage down to the floor of the hall. On either side of these steps, a place for the musicians. A row of candles serving as footlights. Two tiers of galleries along the side of the hall; the upper one divided into
boxes. *There are no seats upon the floor, which is the actual stage of our theatre; but toward the back of the hall, on the right, a few benches are arranged; and underneath a stairway on the extreme right, which leads up to the galleries, and of which only the lower portion is visible, there is a sort of sideboard, decorated with little tapers, vases of flowers, bottles and glasses, plates of cake, et cetera. Farther along, toward the centre of our stage is the entrance to the hall; a great double door which opens only slightly to admit the audience. On one of the panels of this door, as also in other places about the hall, and in particular just over the sideboard, are playbills in red, upon which we may read the title "La Clorise."*

As the curtain rises, the hall is dimly lighted and still empty. The chandeliers are lowered to the floor, in the middle of the hall, ready for lighting. Sound of voices outside the door. Then a Cavalier enters abruptly.

THE PORTER: [*Follows him*] Halloa there!—Fifteen sols!

THE CAVALIER: I enter free.

THE PORTER: Why?

THE CAVALIER: Soldier of
the Household of the King!

THE PORTER: [*Turns to another* Cavalier *who has
just entered*] You?

SECOND CAVALIER: I pay nothing.

THE PORTER: Why not?

SECOND CAVALIER: Musketeer!

FIRST CAVALIER: [*To the second*]
The play begins at two. Plenty of time—
And here's the whole floor empty. Shall we try
Our exercise?

        [*They fence with the foils which they have
        brought*]

A LACKEY: [*Enters*]—Pst! . . . Flanquin! . . .

ANOTHER: [*Already on stage*] What, champagne?

FIRST LACKEY: [*Showing games which he takes out
of his doublet*] Cards. Dice. Come on. [*Sits on the
floor*]

SECOND LACKEY: [*Same action*] Come on, old
cock!

FIRST LACKEY: [*Takes from his pocket a bit of
candle, lights it, sets it on the floor*] I have stolen
A little of my master's fire.

A GUARDSMAN: [*To a* Flower Girl *who comes forward*]   How sweet
Of you, to come before they light the hall.

        [*Puts his arm around her*]

FIRST CAVALIER: [*Receives a thrust of the foil*] A
hit!

SECOND LACKEY: A club!

THE GUARDSMAN: [*Pursuing the girl*] A kiss!

THE FLOWER GIRL: [*Pushing away from him*]
They'll see us!—

THE GUARDSMAN: [*Draws her into a dark corner*]
No danger!

A MAN: [*Sits on the floor, together with several
others who have brought packages of food*] When
we come early, we have time to eat.

A CITIZEN: [*Escorting his son, a boy of sixteen*]
Sit here, my son.

FIRST LACKEY: Mark the Ace!

ANOTHER MAN: [*Draws a bottle from under his
cloak and sits down with the others*] Here's the spot
For a jolly old sot to suck his Burgundy—

        [*Drinks*]

Here—in the house of the Burgundians!

THE CITIZEN: [*To his son*] Would you not think
you were in some den of vice?

        [*Points with his cane at the drunkard*]

Drunkards—[*In stepping back, one of the cavaliers
trips him up*] Bullies!—[*He falls between the lackeys*]
Gamblers!—

THE GUARDSMAN: [*Behind him as he rises, still
struggling with the* Flower Girl] One kiss—

THE CITIZEN: Good
God!—[*Draws his son quickly away*]

Here!—And to think, my son, that in this hall
They play Rotrou!

THE BOY: Yes father—and Corneille!

THE PAGES: [*Dance in, holding hands and singing*]
Tra-la-la-la-la-la-la-la-lère . . .

THE PORTER: You pages there—no nonsense!

FIRST PAGE: [*With wounded dignity*]   Oh,
monsieur!
Really! How could you?

        [*To the* Second, *the moment the* Porter *turns
        his back*]   Pst!—a bit of string?

SECOND PAGE: [*Shows fishline with hook*] Yes—
and a hook.

FIRST PAGE: Up in the gallery,
And fish for wigs!

A CUT-PURSE: [*Gathers around him several evil-
looking young fellows*] Now then, you picaroons.
Perk up, and hear me mutter. Here's your bout—
Bustle around some cull, and bite his bung . . .

SECOND PAGE: [*Calls to other pages already in the
gallery*]
Hey! Brought your pea-shooters?

THIRD PAGE: [*From above*]   And our peas, too!

        [*Blows, and showers them with peas*]

THE BOY: What is the play this afternoon?

THE CITIZEN: "Clorise."

THE BOY: Who wrote that?

THE CITIZEN: Balthasar Baro.
What a play! . . .

        [*He takes the* Boy's *arms and leads him upstage*]

THE CUT-PURSE: [*To his pupils*] Lace now, on
those long sleeves, you cut it off—

        [*Gesture with thumb and finger, as if using
        scissors*]

A SPECTATOR: [*To another, pointing upward
toward the gallery*] Ah, *Le Cid!*—Yes, the first night,
I sat there—

THE CUT-PURSE: Watches—[*Gesture as of picking a pocket*]

THE CITIZEN: [*Coming down with his son*]   Great
actors we shall see to-day—

THE CUT-PURSE: Handkerchiefs—[*Gesture of
holding the pocket with left hand, and drawing out
handkerchief with right*]

THE CITIZEN: Montfleury—

A VOICE: [*In the gallery*] Lights! Light the lights!

THE CITIZEN: Bellerose, l'Épy, Beaupré, Jodelet—

A PAGE: [*On the floor*] Here comes the orange girl.

THE ORANGE GIRL: Oranges, milk,
Raspberry syrup, lemonade—

        [*Noise at the door*]

A FALSETTO VOICE: [*Outside*] Make way,
Brutes!

FIRST LACKEY: What, the Marquis—on the floor?

        [*The* Marquis *enter in a little group*]

SECOND LACKEY: Not long—
Only a few moments; they'll go and sit
On the stage presently.

FIRST MARQUIS: [*Seeing the hall half empty*] How
now! We enter

Like tradespeople—no crowding, no disturbance!—
No treading on the toes of citizens?
Oh fie! Oh fie!

[*He encounters two gentlemen who have already arrived*] Cuigy! Brissaille!

[*Great embracings*]

CUIGY: The faithful!

[*Looks around him*]

We are here before the candles.

FIRST MARQUIS: Ah, be still!
You put me in a temper.

SECOND MARQUIS: Console yourself,
Marquis—The lamplighter!

THE CROWD: [*Applauding the appearance of the lamplighter*] Ah! . . .

[*A group gathers around the chandelier while he lights it. A few people have already taken their place in the gallery.* Lignière *enters the hall, arm in arm with* Christian de Neuvillette. Lignière *is a slightly disheveled figure, dissipated and yet distinguished looking.* Christian, *elegantly but rather unfashionably dressed, appears preoccupied and keeps looking up at the boxes*]

CUIGY: Lignière!—

BRISSAILLE: [*Laughing*] Still sober—at this hour?

LIGNIÈRE: [*To* Christian] May I present you?

[Christian *assents*]

Baron Christian de Neuvillette. [*They salute*]

THE CROWD: [*Applauding as the lighted chandelier is hoisted into place*] Ah!—

CUIGY: [*Aside to* Brissaille, *looking at* Christian]
Rather a fine head, is it not? The profile . . .

FIRST MARQUIS: [*Who has overheard*] Peuh!

LIGNIÈRE: [*Presenting them to* Christian]
Messieurs de Cuigy . . . de Brissaille . . .

CHRISTIAN: [*Bows*] Enchanted!

FIRST MARQUIS: [*To the second*] He is not ill-looking; possibly a shade
Behind the fashion.

LIGNIÈRE: [*To* Cuigy] Monsieur is recently
From the Touraine.

CHRISTIAN: Yes, I have been in Paris
Two or three weeks only. I join the Guards
To-morrow.

FIRST MARQUIS: [*Watching the people who come into the boxes*] Look—Madame la Présidente
Aubry!

THE ORANGE GIRL: Oranges, milk—

THE VIOLINS: [*Tuning up*] La . . . la . . .

CUIGY: [*To* Christian, *calling his attention to the increasing crowd*] We have
An audience to-day!

CHRISTIAN: A brilliant one.

FIRST MARQUIS: Oh yes, all our own people—the
gay world!

[*They name the ladies who enter the boxes elaborately dressed. Bows and smiles are exchanged*]

SECOND MARQUIS: Madame de Guéméné . . .

CUIGY: De
Bois-Dauphin . . .

FIRST MARQUIS: Whom we adore—

BRISSAILLE: Madame
de Chavigny . . .

SECOND MARQUIS: Who plays with all our hearts—

LIGNIÈRE: Why, there's Corneille returned from
Rouen!

THE BOY: [*To his father*] Are the Academy
All here?

THE CITIZEN: I see some of them . . . there's
Boudu—Boissat—Cureau—Porchères—Colomby—
Bourzeys—Bourdon—Arbaut—
Ah, those great names,
Never to be forgotten!

FIRST MARQUIS: Look—at last!
Our Intellectuals! Barthénoide,
Urimédonte, Félixérie . . .

SECOND MARQUIS: [*Languishing*] Sweet heaven!
How exquisite their surnames are! Marquis,
You know them all?

FIRST MARQUIS: I know them all, Marquis!

LIGNIÈRE: [*Draws* Christian *aside*] My dear boy,
I came here to serve you— Well,
But where's the lady? I'll be going.

CHRISTIAN: Not yet—
A little longer! She is always here.
Please! I must find some way of meeting her.
I am dying of love! And you—you know
Everyone, the whole court and the whole town,
And put them all into your songs—at least
You can tell me her name!

THE FIRST VIOLIN: [*Raps on his desk with his bow*]
Pst— Gentlemen!

[*Raises his bow*]

THE ORANGE GIRL: Macaroons, lemonade—

CHRISTIAN: Then she may be
One of those æsthetes . . . Intellectuals,
You call them— How can I talk to a woman
In that style? I have no wit. This fine manner
Of speaking and of writing nowadays—
Not for me! I am a soldier—and afraid.
That's her box, on the right—the empty one.

LIGNIÈRE: [*Starts for the door*] I am going.

CHRISTIAN: [*Restrains him*] No—wait!

LIGNIÈRE: Not I.
There's a tavern not far away—
And I am dying of thirst.

THE ORANGE GIRL: [*Passes with her tray*] Orange
juice?

LIGNIÈRE: No!

THE ORANGE GIRL: Milk?

LIGNIÈRE: Pouah!

THE ORANGE GIRL: Muscatel?

LIGNIÈRE: Here! Stop! [*To* Christian] I'll stay a
little.

[*To the* Girl] Let me see
Your Muscatel.

[*He sits down by the sideboard. The* Girl *pours out wine for him*]

VOICES: [*In the crowd about the door, upon the entrance of a spruce little man, rather fat, with a beaming smile*] Ragueneau!

LIGNIÈRE: [*To* Christian] Ragueneau, Poet and pastry-cook—a character!

RAGUENEAU: [*Dressed like a confectioner in his Sunday clothes, advances quickly to* Lignière] Sir, have you seen Monsieur de Cyrano?

LIGNIÈRE: [*Presents him to* Christian] Permit me . . . Ragueneau, confectioner, The chief support of modern poetry.

RAGUENEAU: [*Bridling*] Oh—too much honor!

LIGNIÈRE: Patron of the Arts— Mæcenas! Yes, you are—

RAGUENEAU: Undoubtedly, The poets gather round my hearth.

LIGNIÈRE: On credit— Himself a poet—

RAGUENEAU: So they say—

LIGNIÈRE: Maintains The Muses.

RAGUENEAU: It is true that for an ode—

LIGNIÈRE: You Give a tart—

RAGUENEAU: A tartlet—

LIGNIÈRE: Modesty! And for a triolet you give—

RAGUENEAU: Plain bread.

LIGNIÈRE: [*Severely*] Bread and milk! And you love the theatre?

RAGUENEAU: I adore it!

LIGNIÈRE: Well, pastry pays for all. Your place to-day now—Come, between ourselves, What did it cost you?

RAGUENEAU: Four pies; fourteen cakes. [*Looking about*] But— Cyrano not here? Astonishing!

LIGNIÈRE: Why so?

RAGUENEAU: Why— Montfleury plays!

LIGNIÈRE: Yes, I hear That hippopotamus assumes the rôle Of Phédon. What is that to Cyrano?

RAGUENEAU: Have you not heard? Monsieur de Bergerac So hates Montfleury, he has forbidden him For three weeks to appear upon the stage.

LIGNIÈRE: [*Who is, by this time, at his fourth glass*] Well?

RAGUENEAU: Montfleury plays!—

CUIGY: [*Strolls over to them*]   Yes—what then?

RAGUENEAU: Ah! That is what I came to see.

FIRST MARQUIS: This Cyrano— Who is he?

CUIGY: Oh, he is the lad with the long sword.

SECOND MARQUIS: Noble?

CUIGY: Sufficiently; he is in the Guards. [*Points to a gentleman who comes and goes about the hall as though seeking for someone*] His friend Le Bret can tell you more. [*Calls to him*]

Le Bret! [Le Bret *comes down to them*] Looking for Bergerac?

LE BRET: Yes. And for trouble.

CUIGY: Is he not an extraordinary man?

LE BRET: The best friend and the bravest soul alive!

RAGUENEAU: Poet—

CUIGY: Swordsman—

LE BRET: Musician—

BRISSAILLE: Philosopher—

LIGNIÈRE: Such a remarkable appearance, too!

RAGUENEAU: Truly, I should not look to find his portrait By the grave hand of Philippe de Champagne. He might have been a model for Callot— One of those wild swashbucklers in a masque— Hat with three plumes, and a doublet with six points— His cloak behind him over his long sword Cocked, like the tail of strutting Chanticleer— Prouder than all the swaggering Tamburlaines Hatched out of Gascony. And to complete This Punchinello figure—such a nose!— My lords, there is no such nose as that nose— You cannot look upon it without crying: "Oh no, Impossible! Exaggerated!" Then You smile, and say: "Of course— I might have known; Presently he will take it off." But that Monsieur de Bergerac will never do.

LIGNIÈRE: [*Grimly*] He keeps it—and God help The man who smiles!

RAGUENEAU: His sword is one half of the Shears of Fate!

FIRST MARQUIS: [*Shrugs*] He will not come.

RAGUENEAU: Will he not? Sir, I'll lay you A pullet à la Ragueneau!

FIRST MARQUIS: [*Laughing*] Done!

[*Murmurs of admiration;* Roxane *has just appeared in her box. She sits at the front of the box, and her* Duenna *takes a seat toward the rear.* Christian, *busy paying the* Orange Girl, *does not see her at first*]

SECOND MARQUIS: [*With little excited cries*] Ah! Oh! Oh! Sweet sirs, look yonder! Is she not Frightfully ravishing?

FIRST MARQUIS: Bloom of the peach— Blush of the strawberry—

SECOND MARQUIS: So fresh—so cool, That our hearts, grown all warm with loving her, May catch their death of cold!

CHRISTIAN: [*Looks up, sees* Roxane, *and seizes* Lignière *by the arm*] There! Quick—up there— In the box! Look!—

LIGNIÈRE: [*Coolly*] Herself?

CHRISTIAN: Quickly— Her name?

LIGNIÈRE: [*Sipping his wine, and speaking between sips*] Madeleine Robin, called Roxane . . . refined . . . Intellectual . . .

CHRISTIAN: Ah!—

LIGNIÈRE: Unmarried . . .

CHRISTIAN: Oh!—

LIGNIÈRE: No title . . . rich enough . . . an orphan . . . cousin

To Cyrano . . . of whom we spoke just now . . .

[*At this point, a very distinguished looking gentleman, the Cordon Bleu around his neck, enters the box, and stands a moment talking with* Roxane]

CHRISTIAN: [*Starts*] And the man?—

LIGNIÈRE: [*Beginning to feel his wine a little; cocks his eye at them*] Oho! That man? . . . Comte de Guiche . . .

In love with her . . . married himself, however,

To the niece of the Cardinal—Richelieu . . .

Wishes Roxane, therefore, to marry one

Monsieur de Valvert . . . Vicomte . . . friend of his . . .

A somewhat melancholy gentleman . . .

But . . . well, accommodating! . . . She says No . . .

Nevertheless, de Guiche is powerful . . .

Not above persecuting . . .

[*He rises, swaying a little, and very happy*] I have written

A little song about his little game . . .

Good little song, too . . . Here, I'll sing it for you . . .

Make de Guiche furious . . . naughty little song . . .

Not so bad, either— Listen! . . .

[*He stands with his glass held aloft, ready to sing*]

CHRISTIAN: No. Adieu.

LIGNIÈRE: Whither away?

CHRISTIAN: To Monsieur de Valvert!

LIGNIÈRE: Careful! The man's a swordsman . . .

[*Nods toward* Roxane, *who is watching* Christian]

     Wait! Someone

Looking at you—

CHRISTIAN: Roxane! . . .

[*He forgets everything, and stands spellbound, gazing toward* Roxane. *The* Cut-Purse *and his crew, observing him transfixed, his eyes raised and his mouth half open, begin edging in his direction*]

LIGNIÈRE: Oh! Very well,

Then I'll be leaving you . . . Good day . . . Good day! . . .

[Christian *remains motionless*]

Everywhere else, they like to hear me sing!—

Also, I am thirsty.

[*He goes out, navigating carefully.* Le Bret, *having made the circuit of the hall, returns to* Ragueneau, *somewhat reassured*]

LE BRET: No sign anywhere

Of Cyrano!

RAGUENEAU: [*Incredulous*] Wait and see!

LE BRET: Humph! I hope

He has not seen the bill.

THE CROWD: The play!—The play!—

FIRST MARQUIS: [*Observing* de Guiche, *as he descends from* Roxane's *box and crosses the floor, followed by a knot of obsequious gentlemen, the* Vicomte de Valvert *among them*] This man de Guiche—what ostentation!

SECOND MARQUIS: Bah!—

Another Gascon!

FIRST MARQUIS: Gascon, yes—but cold

And calculating—certain to suceed—

My word for it. Come, shall we make our bow?

We shall be none the worse, I promise you . . .

[*They go toward* de Guiche]

SECOND MARQUIS: Beautiful ribbons, Count! That color, now,

What is it—"Kiss-me-Dear" or "Startled-Fawn"?

DE GUICHE: I call that shade "The Dying Spaniard."

FIRST MARQUIS: Ha!

And no false colors either—thanks to you

And your brave troops, in Flanders before long

The Spaniard will die daily.

DE GUICHE: Shall we go

And sit upon the stage? Come, Valvert.

CHRISTIAN: [*Starts at the name*] Valvert!—

The Vicomte— Ah, that scoundrel! Quick—my glove—

I'll throw it in his face—

[*Reaching into his pocket for his glove, he catches the hand of the* Cut-Purse]

THE CUT-PURSE: Oh!—

CHRISTIAN: [*Holding fast to the man's wrist*] Who are you?

I was looking for a glove—

THE CUT-PURSE: [*Cringing*] You found a hand.

[*Hurriedly*] Let me go— I can tell you something—

CHRISTIAN: [*Still holding him*] Well?

THE CUT-PURSE: Lignière—that friends of yours—

CHRISTIAN: [*Same business*] Well?

THE CUT-PURSE: Good as dead—

Understand? Ambuscaded. Wrote a song

About—no matter. There's a hundred men

Waiting for him to-night—I'm one of them.

CHRISTIAN: A hundred! Who arranged this?

THE CUT-PURSE: Secret.

CHRISTIAN: Oh!

THE CUT-PURSE: [*With dignity*] Professional secret.

CHRISTIAN: Where are they to be?

THE CUT-PURSE: Port de Nesle. On his way home.

Tell him so. Save his life.

CHRISTIAN: [*Releases the man*] Yes, but where am I to find him?

THE CUT-PURSE: Go round the taverns. There's the Golden Grape,

The Pineapple, the Bursting Belt, the Two

Torches, the Three Funnels—in every one

You leave a line of writing—understand?

To warn him.

CHRISTIAN: [*Starts for the door*] I'll go! God, what swine—a hundred

Against one man! . . . [*Stops and looks longingly at* Roxane]   Leave *her* here!—

[*Savagely, turning toward* Valvert] And leave *him!*—
[*Decidedly*] I must save Lignière! [*Exit.* De Guiche,
Valvert, *and all the* Marquis *have disappeared
through the curtains, to take their seats upon the
stage. The floor is entirely filled; not a vacant seat
remains in the gallery or in the boxes*]

THE CROWD: The play! The play!
Begin the play!

A CITIZEN: [*As his wig is hoisted into the air on
the end of a fishline, in the hands of a page in the
gallery*] My wig!!

CRIES OF JOY: He's bald! Bravo,
You pages! Ha ha ha!

THE CITIZEN: [*Furious, shakes his fist at the boy*]
Here, you young villain!

CRIES AND LAUGHTER: [*Beginning very loud, then
suddenly repressed*] HA HA! Ha Ha! ha ha. . . .
[*Complete silence*]

LE BRET: [*Surprised*] That sudden hush? . . .
[*A* Spectator *whispers in his ear*]
Yes?

THE SPECTATOR: I was told on good authority . . .

MURMURS: [*Here and there*] What? . . . Here?
. . . No . . . Yes . . . Look—in the latticed box—
The Cardinal! . . . The Cardinal! . . .

A PAGE: The Devil!—
Now we shall all have to behave ourselves!
[*Three raps on the stage. The audience becomes
motionless. Silence*]

THE VOICE OF A MARQUIS: [*From the stage, behind
the curtains*] Snuff that candle!

ANOTHER MARQUIS: [*Puts his head out through the
curtains*] A chair! . . .
[*A chair is passed from hand to hand over the
heads of the crowd. He takes it, and disappears
behind the curtains, not without having blown
a few kisses to the occupants of the boxes*]

A SPECTATOR: Silence!

VOICES: Hssh! . . . Hssh! . . .
[*Again the three raps on the stage. The curtains
part. Tableau. The* Marquis *seated on their
chairs to right and left of the stage, insolently
posed. Back drop representing a pastoral scene,
bluish in tone. Four little crystal chandeliers
light up the stage. The violins play softly*]

LE BRET: [*In a low tone, to* Ragueneau] Montfleury enters now?

RAGUENEAU: [*Nods*] Opens the play.

LE BRET: [*Much relieved*] Then Cyrano is not here!

RAGUENEAU: I lose . . .

LE BRET: Humph!—
So much the better!
[*The melody of a musette is heard.* Montfleury
*appears upon the scene, a ponderous figure in
the costume of a rustic shepherd, a hat garlanded with roses tilted over one ear, playing
upon a beribboned pastoral pipe*]

THE CROWD: [*Applauds*] Montfleury! . . .
Bravo! . . .

MONTFLEURY: [*After bowing to the applause, be-
gins the rôle of* Phédon]
"Thrice happy he who hides from pomp and power
In sylvan shade or solitary bower;
Where balmy zephyrs fan his burning cheeks—"

A VOICE: [*From the midst of the hall*] Wretch!
Have I not forbade you these three weeks?
[*Sensation. Every one turns to look. Murmurs*]

SEVERAL VOICES: What? . . . Where? . . . Who
is it? . . .

CUIGY: Cyrano!

LE BRET: [*In alarm*] Himself!

THE VOICE: King of clowns! Leave the stage—
at once!

THE CROWD: Oh!—

MONTFLEURY: Now,
Now, now—

THE VOICE: You disobey me?

SEVERAL VOICES: [*From the floor, from the boxes*]
Hsh! Go on—
Quiet!—Go on, Montfleury!—Who's afraid?—

MONTFLEURY: [*In a voice of no great assurance*]
"Thrice happy he who hides from . . ."

THE VOICE: [*More menacingly*] Well? Well?
Well? . . .
Monarch of montebanks! Must I come and plant
A forest on your shoulders?
[*A cane at the end of a long arm shakes above
the heads of the crowd*]

MONTFLEURY: [*In a voice increasingly feeble*]
"Thrice hap—"
[*The cane is violently agitated*]

THE VOICE: GO!!!

THE CROWD: Ah! . . .

CYRANO: [*Arises in the center of the floor, erect
upon a chair, his arms folded, his hat cocked ferociously, his moustache bristling, his nose terrible*]
Presently I shall grow angry!
[*Sensation at his appearance*]

MONTFLEURY: [*To the* Marquis] Messieurs,
If you protect me—

A MARQUIS: [*Nonchalantly*] Well—proceed!

CYRANO: Fat swine!
If you dare breathe one balmy zephyr more,
I'll fan your cheeks for you!

THE MARQUIS: Quiet down there!

CYRANO: Unless these gentlemen retain their seats,
My cane may bite their ribbons!

ALL THE MARQUIS: [*On their feet*] That will do!—
Montfleury—

CYRANO: Fly, goose! Shoo! Take to your wings,
Before I pluck your plumes, and draw your gorge!

A VOICE: See here!—

CYRANO: Off stage!!

ANOTHER VOICE: One moment—

CYRANO: What—still there?
[*Turns back his cuffs deliberately*]
Very good—then I enter—*Left—with knife*—
To carve this large Italian sausage.

MONTFLEURY: [*Desperately attempting dignity*] Sir,

When you insult me, you insult the Muse!

CYRANO: [*With great politeness*]

Sir, if the Muse, who never knew your name,
Had the honor to meet you—then be sure
That after one glance at that face of yours,
That figure of a mortuary urn—
She would apply her buskin—toward the rear!

THE CROWD: Montfleury! . . . Montfleury! . . . The play! The play!

CYRANO: [*To those who are shouting and crowding about him*]

Pray you, be gentle with my scabbard here—
She'll put her tongue out at you presently—

[*The circle enlarges*]

THE CROWD: [*Recoiling*] Keep back—

CYRANO: [*To* Montfleury] Begone!

THE CROWD: [*Pushing in closer, and growling*] Ahr! . . . ahr! . . .

CYRANO: [*Turns upon them*] Did someone speak? [*They recoil again*]

A VOICE: [*In the back of the hall, sings*]

    Monsieur de Cyrano
        Must be another Caesar—
    Let Brutus lay him low,
        And play us "La Clorise"!

ALL THE CROWD: [*Singing*] "La Clorise!" "La Clorise!"

CYRANO: Let me hear one more word of that same song,

And I destroy you all!

A CITIZEN: Who might you be? Samson?—

CYRANO: Precisely. Would you kindly lend me Your jawbone?

A LADY: [*In one of the boxes*] What an outrage!

A NOBLE: Scandalous!

A CITIZEN: Annoying!

A PAGE: What a game!

THE CROWD: Kss!

Montfleury! Cyrano!

CYRANO: Silence!

THE CROWD: [*Delirious*] Woof! Woof! Baa! Cockadoo!

CYRANO: I—

A PAGE: Meow!

CYRANO: I say be silent!—

[*His voice dominates the uproar. Momentary hush*]

                          And I offer

One universal challenge to you all!
Approach, young heroes—I will take your names.
Each in his turn—no crowding! One, two, three—
Come, get your numbers—who will head the list—
You sir? No— You? Ah, no. To the first man
Who falls I'll build a monument! . . . Not one?
Will all who wish to die, please raise their hands? . . .
I see. You are so modest, you might blush
Before a sword naked. Sweet innocence! . . .

Not one name? Not one finger? . . . Very well,
Then I go on:

[*Turning back towards the stage, where Montfleury waits in despair*]

                I'd have our theatre cured
Of this carbuncle. Or if not, why then—

[*His hand on his sword hilt*]

The lancet!

MONTFLEURY: I—

CYRANO: [*Descends from his chair, seats himself comfortably in the center of the circle which has formed around him, and makes himself quite at home*]   Attend to me—full moon!

I clap my hands, three times—thus. At the third
You will eclipse yourself.

THE CROWD: [*Amused*] Ah!

CYRANO: Ready? One!

MONTFLEURY: I—

A VOICE: [*From the boxes*] No!

THE CROWD: He'll go— He'll stay—

MONTFLEURY: I really think,
Gentlemen—

CYRANO: Two!

MONTFLEURY: Perhaps I had better—

CYRANO: Three!

[*Montfleury disappears, as if through a trapdoor. Tempest of laughter, hoots and hisses*]

THE CROWD: Yah!—Coward— Come back—

CYRANO: [*Beaming, drops back in his chair and crosses his legs*] Let him—if he dare!

A CITIZEN: The Manager! Speech! Speech!

[*Bellerose advances and bows*]

THE BOXES: Ah! Bellerose!

BELLEROSE: [*With elegance*] Most noble—most fair—

THE CROWD: No! The Comedian— Jodelet!—

JODELET: [*Advances, and speaks through his nose*] Lewd fellows of the baser sort—

THE CROWD: Ha! ha! Not bad! Bravo!

JODELET: No Bravos here!
Our heavy tragedian with the voluptuous bust
Was taken suddenly—

THE CROWD: Yah! Coward!

JODELET: I mean . . .
He had to be excused—

THE CROWD: Call him back— No!— Yes!—

THE BOY: [*To* Cyrano] After all, Monsieur, what reason have you
To hate this Montfleury?

CYRANO: [*Graciously, still seated*] My dear young man,

I have two reasons, either one alone
Conclusive. *Primo*: A lamentable actor,
Who mouths his verse and moans his tragedy,
And heaves up— Ugh!—like a hod-carrier, lines
That ought to soar on their own wings. *Secundo*:—
Well—that's my secret.

THE OLD CITIZEN: [*Behind him*] But you close the
    play—
"La Clorise"—by Baro! Are we to miss
Our entertainment, merely—
    CYRANO: [*Respectfully, turns his chair towards
the old man] My dear old boy,
The poetry of Baro being worth
Zero, or less, I feel that I have done
Poetic justice!
    THE INTELLECTUALS: [*In the boxes*] Really!—our
Baro!—
My dear!—Who ever?—Ah, dieu! The idea!—
    CYRANO: [*Gallantly, turns his chair toward the
boxes*]
Fair ladies—shine upon us like the sun,
Blossom like flowers around us—be our songs,
Heard in a dream— Make sweet the hour of death,
Smiling upon us as you close our eyes—
Inspire, but do not try to criticise!
    BELLEROSE: Quite so!—and the mere money—
        possibly
You would like that returned— Yes?
    CYRANO: Bellerose,
You speak the first word of intelligence!
I will not wound the mantle of the Muse—
Here, catch!—
    [*Throws him a purse*] And hold your tongue.
    THE CROWD: [*Astonished*] Ah! Ah!
    JODELET: [*Deftly catches the purse, weighs it in
his hand*] Monsieur,
You are hereby authorized to close our play
Every night, on the same terms.
    THE CROWD: Boo!
    JODELET: And welcome!
Let us be booed together, you and I!
    BELLEROSE: Kindly pass out quietly . . . .
    JODELET: [*Burlesquing* Bellerose] Quietly . . .
    [*They begin to go out, while* Cyrano *looks
about him with satisfaction. But the exodus
ceases presently during the ensuing scene. The
ladies in the boxes who have already risen and
put on their wraps, stop to listen, and finally sit
down again*]
    LE BRET: [*To* Cyrano] Idiot!
    A MEDDLER: [*Hurries up to* Cyrano] But what a
scandal! Montfleury—
The great Montfleury! Did you know the Duc De
Candale was his patron? Who is yours?
    CYRANO: No one.
    THE MEDDLER: No one—no patron?
    CYRANO: I said no.
    THE MEDDLER: What, no great lord, to cover with
his name—
    CYRANO: [*With visible annoyance*] No, I have
told you twice. Must I repeat?
No sir, no patron—
    [*His hand on his sword*] But a patroness!
    THE MEDDLER: And when do you leave Paris?
    CYRANO: That's as may be.

THE MEDDLER: The Duc de Candale has a long
    arm.
    CYRANO: Mine
Is longer,
    [*Drawing his sword*] by three feet of steel.
    THE MEDDLER: Yes, yes,
But do you dream of daring—
    CYRANO: I do dream
Of daring . . .
    THE MEDDLER: But—
    CYRANO: You may go now.
    THE MEDDLER: But—
    CYRANO: You may go—
Or tell me why are you staring at my nose!
    THE MEDDLER: [*In confusion*] No—I—
    CYRANO: [*Stepping up to him*] Does it astonish
you?
    THE MEDDLER: [*Drawing back*] Your grace
Misunderstands my—
    CYRANO: Is it long and soft
And dangling, like a trunk?
    THE MEDDLER: [*Same business*] I never said—
    CYRANO: Or crooked, like an owl's beak?
    THE MEDDLER: I—
    CYRANO: Perhaps
A pimple ornaments the end of it?
    THE MEDDLER: No—
    CYRANO: Or a fly parading up and down?
What is this portent?
    THE MEDDLER: Oh!—
    CYRANO: This phenomenon?
    THE MEDDLER: But I have been careful not to
look—
    CYRANO: And why
Not, if you please?
    THE MEDDLER: Why—
    CYRANO: It disgusts you, then?
    THE MEDDLER: My dear sir—
    CYRANO: Does its color appear to you
Unwholesome?
    THE MEDDLER: Oh, by no means!
    CYRANO: Or its form
Obscene?
    THE MEDDLER: Not in the least—
    CYRANO: Then why assume
This deprecating manner? Possibly
You find it just a trifle large?
    THE MEDDLER: [*Babbling*] Oh no!—
Small, very small, infinitesimal—
    CYRANO: [*Roars*] What!
How? You accuse me of absurdity?
Small—*my nose*? Why—
    THE MEDDLER: [*Breathless*] My God!—
    CYRANO: Magnificent,
My nose! . . . You pug, you knob, you button-
head,
Know that I glory in this nose of mine,
For a great nose indicates a great man—
Genial, courteous, intellectual,
Virile, courageous—as I am—and such

As you—poor wretch—will never dare to be
Even in imagination. For that face—
That blank, inglorious concavity
Which my right hand finds—
  [*He strikes him*]
  THE MEDDLER: Ow!
  CYRANO: —on top of you,
Is as devoid of pride, of poetry,
Of soul, of picturesqueness, of contour,
Of character, of NOSE in short—as that
  [*Takes him by the shoulders and turns him
  around, suiting the action to the word*]
Which at the end of that limp spine of yours
My left foot—
  THE MEDDLER: [*Escaping*] Help! The Guard!
  CYRANO: Take notice, all
Who find this feature of my countenance
A theme for comedy! When the humorist
Is noble, then my custom is to show
Appreciation proper to his rank—
More heartfelt . . . and more pointed. . . .
  DE GUICHE: [*Who has come down from the stage,
surrounded by the* Marquis] Presently
This fellow will grow tiresome.
  VALVERT: [*Shrugs*] Oh, he blows
His trumpet!
  DE GUICHE: Well—will no one interfere?
  VALVERT: No one? [*Looks round*] Observe. I my-
  self will proceed
To put him in his place.
  [*He walks up to* Cyrano, *who has been watch-
  ing him, and stands there, looking him over
  with an affected air*] Ah . . . your nose . . .
  hem! . . .
Your nose is . . . rather large!
  CYRANO: [*Gravely*] Rather.
  VALVERT: [*Simpering*] Oh well—
  CYRANO: [*Coolly*] Is that all?
  VALVERT: [*Turns away, with a shrug*] Well, of
  course—
  CYRANO: Ah, no, young sir!
You are too simple. Why, you might have said—
Oh, a great many things! Mon dieu, why waste
Your opportunity? For example, thus:—
Aggressive: I, sir, if that nose were mine,
I'd have it amputated—on the spot!
Friendly: How do you drink with such a nose?
You ought to have a cup made specially.
Descriptive: 'Tis a rock—a crag—a cape—
A cape? say rather, a peninsula!
Inquisitive: What is that receptacle —
A razor-case or a portfolio?
Kindly: Ah, do you love the little birds
So much that when they come and sing to you,
You give them this to perch on? Insolent:
Sir, when you smoke, the neighbors must suppose
Your chimney is on fire. Cautious: Take care—
A weight like that might make you topheavy.
Thoughtful: Somebody fetch my parasol—
Those delicate colors fade so in the sun!

Pedantic: Does not Aristophanes
Mention a mythologic monster called
Hippocampelephantocamelos?
Surely we have here the original!
Familiar: Well, old torchlight! Hang your hat
Over that chandelier—it hurts my eyes.
Eloquent: When it blows, the typhoon howls,
And the clouds darken. Dramatic: When it bleeds—
The Red Sea! Enterprising: What a sign
For some perfumer! Lyric: Hark—the horn
Of Roland calls to summon Charlemagne!—
Simple: When do they unveil the monument?
Respectful: Sir, I recognize in you
A man of parts, a man of prominence—
Rustic: Hey? What? Call that a nose? Na, na—
I be no fool like what you think I be—
That there's a blue cucumber! Military:
Point against cavalry! Practical: Why not
A lottery with this for the grand prize?
Or—parodying Faustus in the play—
"Was this the nose that launched a thousand ships
And burned the topless towers of Ilium?"
These, my dear sir, are things you might have said
Had you some tinge of letters, or of wit
To color your discourse. But wit,—not so,
You never had an atom—and of letters,
You need but three to write you down—an Ass.
Moreover,—if you had the invention, here
Before these folk to make a jest of me—
Be sure you would not then articulate
The twentieth part of half a syllable
Of the beginning! For I say these things
Lightly enough myself, about myself,
But I allow none else to utter them.
  DE GUICHE: [*Tries to lead away the amazed* Val-
vert] Vicomte—come.
  VALVERT: [*Choking*] Oh— These arrogant grand
  airs!—
A clown who—look at him—not even gloves!
No ribbons—no lace—no buckles on his shoes—
  CYRANO: I carry my adornments on my soul.
I do not dress up like a popinjay;
But inwardly, I keep my daintiness.
I do not bear with me, by any chance,
An insult not yet washed away—a conscience
Yellow with unpurged bile—an honor frayed
To rags, a set of scruples badly worn.
I go caparisoned in gems unseen,
Trailing white plumes of freedom, garlanded
With my good name—no figure of a man,
But a soul clothed in shining armor, hung
With deeds for decorations, twirling—thus—
A bristling wit, and swinging at my side
Courage, and on the stones of this old town
Making the sharp truth ring, like golden spurs!
  VALVERT: But—
  CYRANO: But I have no gloves! A pity too!
I had one—the last one of an old pair—
And lost that. Very careless of me. Some

Gentleman offered me an impertinence.
I left it—in his face.

VALVERT: Dolt, bumpkin, fool,
Insolent puppy, jobbernowl!

CYRANO: [*Removes his hat and bows*] Ah, yes?
And I—Cyrano-Savinien-Hercule
De Bergerac!

VALVERT: [*Turns away*] Buffoon!

CYRANO: [*Cries out as if suddenly taken with a cramp*] Oh!

VALVERT: [*Turns back*] Well, what now?

CYRANO: [*With grimaces of anguish*]
I must do something to relieve these cramps—
This is what comes of lack of exercise—
Ah!—

VALVERT: What is all this?

CYRANO: My sword has gone to sleep!

VALVERT: [*Draws*] So be it!

CYRANO: You shall die exquisitely.

VALVERT: [*Contemptuously*] Poet!

CYRANO: Why yes, a poet, if you will;
So while we fence, I'll make you a Ballade
Extempore.

VALVERT: A Ballade?

CYRANO: Yes. You know
What that is?

VALVERT: I—

CYRANO: The Ballade, sir, is formed
Of three stanzas of eight lines each—

VALVERT: Oh, come!

CYRANO: And a refrain of four.

VALVERT: You—

CYRANO: I'll compose
One, while I fight with you; and at the end
Of the last line—thrust home!

VALVERT: Will you?

CYRANO: I will.
     [*Declaims*]
"Ballade of the duel at the Hôtel de Bourgogne
  Between de Bergerac and a Boeotian."

VALVERT: [*Sneering*] What do you mean by that?

CYRANO: Oh, that? The title.

THE CROWD: [*Excited*] Come on—

                              A circle—

                              Quiet—

Down in front!

     [*Tableau. A ring of interested spectators in the
     centre of the floor, the Marquis and the Officers
     mingling with the citizens and common folk.
     Pages swarming up on men's shoulders to see
     better; the Ladies in the boxes standing and
     leaning over. To the right, De Guiche and his
     following; to the left, Le Bret, Cuigy, Ragueneau, and others of Cyrano's friends*]

CYRANO: [*Closes his eyes for an instant*]
Stop . . . Let me choose my rimes. . . . Now!
     Here we go—[*He suits the action to the word,
     throughout the following*]
Lightly I toss my hat away,

Languidly over my arm let fall
The cloak that covers my bright array—
Then out swords, and to work withal!
A Launcelot, in his Lady's hall . . .
A Spartacus, at the Hippodrome! . . .
I dally awhile with you, dear jackal,
Then, as I end the refrain, thrust home!
     [*The swords cross—the fight is on*]
Where shall I skewer my peacock? . . . Nay,
Better for you to have shunned this brawl!—
Here, in the heart, thro' your ribbons gay?
—In the belly, under your silken shawl?
Hark, how the steel rings musical!
Mark how my point floats, light as the foam,
Ready to drive you back to the wall,
Then, as I end the refrain, thrust home!

Ho, for a rime! . . . You are white as whey—
You break, you cower, you cringe, you . . . crawl!
Tac!—and I parry your last essay:
So may the turn of a hand forestall
Life with its honey, death with its gall;
So may the turn of my fancy roam
Free, for a time, till the rimes recall,
Then, as I end the refrain, thrust home!
     [*He announces solemnly*]
Refrain:
     Prince! Pray God, that is Lord of all,
Pardon your soul, for your time has come!
Beat—pass—fling you aslant, asprawl—
Then, as I end the refrain . . .
     [*He lunges; Valvert staggers back and falls into
     the arms of his friends. Cyrano recovers, and
     salutes*]—Thrust home!
     [*Shouts. Applause from the boxes. Flowers and
     handkerchiefs come fluttering down. The Offi-
     cers surround Cyrano and congratulate him.
     Ragueneau dances for joy. Le Bret is unable to
     conceal his enthusiasm. The friends of Valvert
     hold him up and help him away*]

THE CROWD: [*In one long cry*] Ah-h!

A CAVALIER: Superb!

A WOMAN: Simply sweet!

RAGUENEAU: Magnelephant!

A MARQUIS: A novelty!

LE BRET: Bah!

THE CROWD: [*Thronging around* Cyrano] Compli-
     ments—regards—
Bravo!—

A WOMAN'S VOICE: Why, he's a hero!

A MUSKETEER: [*Advances quickly to* Cyrano, *with
outstretched hands*] Monsieur, will you
Permit me?—It was altogether fine!
I think I may appreciate these things—
Moreover, I have been stamping for pure joy!
     [*He retires quickly*]

CYRANO: [*To* Cuigy] What was that gentleman's
name?

CUIGY: Oh . . . D'Artagnan.

LE BRET: [*Takes* Cyrano's *arm*] Come here and
tell me—

CYRANO: Let this crowd go first—[*To* Bellerose]
May we stay?

BELLEROSE: [*With great respect*] Certainly!

[*Cries and cat-calls off stage*]

JODELET: [*Comes down from the door where he
has been looking out*] Hark!—Montfleury—
They are hooting him.

BELLEROSE: [*Solemnly*] "Sic transit gloria!"
[*Changes his tone and shouts to the* Porter *and the*
Lamplighter]—Strike! . . . Close the house! . . .
Leave the lights— We rehearse
The new farce after dinner.

[*Jodelet and* Bellerose *go out after elaborately
saluting* Cyrano]

THE PORTER: [*To* Cyrano] You do not dine?

CYRANO: I?—No! [*The* Porter *turns away*]

LE BRET: Why not?

CYRANO: [*Haughtily*] Because—
[*Changing his tone when he sees the* Porter
has gone] Because I have
No money.

LE BRET: [*Gesture of tossing*] But—the purse of
gold?

CYRANO: Farewell,
Paternal pension!

LE BRET: So you have, until
The first of next month—?

CYRANO: Nothing.

LE BRET: What a fool!—

CYRANO: But—what a gesture!

THE ORANGE GIRL: [*Behind her little counter;
coughs*] Hem!
[*Cyrano and* Le Bret *look around; she advances
timidly*] Pardon, monsieur . . .
A man ought never to go hungry . . .
[*Indicating the sideboard*] See,
I have everything here . . . [*Eagerly*] Please!—

CYRANO: [*Uncovers*] My dear child,
I cannot bend this Gascon pride of mine
To accept such a kindness— Yet, for fear
That I may give you pain if I refuse,
I will take . . .
[*He goes to the sideboard and makes his selec-
tion*] Oh, not very much! A grape . . .
[*She gives him the bunch; he removes a single
grape*] One only! And a glass of water . . .
[*She starts to pour wine into it; he stops her*]
Clear!
And . . . half a macaroon!
[*He gravely returns the other half*]

LE BRET: Old idiot!

THE ORANGE GIRL: Please!—Nothing more?

CYRANO: Why yes— Your hand to kiss. [*He kisses
the hand which she holds out, as he would the hand
of a princess*]

THE ORANGE GIRL: Thank you, sir. [*She curtseys*]
Good-night. [*She goes out*]

CYRANO: Now, I am listening.

[*Plants himself before the sideboard and ar-
ranges thereon—*] Dinner!—[*—the macaroon*]
Drink!—[*—the glass of water*]
Dessert!—[*—the grape*]
There—now I'll sit down.
[*Seats himself*]
Lord, I was hungry! Abominably! [*Eating*] Well?

LE BRET: These fatheads with the bellicose grand
airs
Will have you ruined if you listen to them;
Talk to a man of sense and hear how all
Your swagger impresses him.

CYRANO: [*Finishes his macaroon*] Enormously.

LE BRET: The Cardinal—

CYRANO: [*Beaming*] Was he there?

LE BRET: He must have thought you—

CYRANO: Original.

LE BRET: Well, but—

CYRANO: He is himself
A playwright. He will not be too displeased
That I have closed another author's play.

LE BRET: But look at all the enemies you have
made!

CYRANO: [*Begins on the grape*] How many—do
you think?

LE BRET: Just forty-eight
Without the women.

CYRANO: Count them.

LE BRET: Montfleury,
Baro, de Guiche, the Vicomte, the Old Man,
All the Academy—

CYRANO: Enough! You make me
Happy!

LE BRET: But where is all this leading you?
What is your plan?

CYRANO: I have been wandering—
Wasting my force upon too many plans.
Now I have chosen one.

LE BRET: What one?

CYRANO: The simplest—
To make myself in all things admirable!

LE BRET: Hmph!—Well, then, the real reason
why you hate
Montfleury— Come, the truth, now!

CYRANO: [*Rises*] That Silenus,
Who cannot hold his belly in his arms,
Still dreams of being sweetly dangerous
Among the women—sighs and languishes,
Making sheeps' eyes out of his great frog's face—
I hate him ever since one day he dared
Smile upon—
Oh, my friend, I seemed to see
Over some flower a great snail crawling!

LE BRET: [*Amazed*] How,
What? Is it possible?—

CYRANO: [*With a bitter smile*] For me to love? . . .
[*Changing his tone; seriously*] I love.

LE BRET: May I know? You have never said—

CYRANO: Whom I love? Think a moment. Think
of me—

Me, whom the plainest woman would despise—
Me, with this nose of mine that marches on
Before me by a quarter of an hour!
Whom should I love? Why—of course—it must be
The woman in the world most beautiful.

LE BRET: Most beautiful?

CYRANO: In all this world—most sweet;
Also most wise; most witty; and most fair!

LE BRET: Who and what is this woman?

CYRANO: Dangerous
Mortally, without meaning; exquisite
Without imagining. Nature's own snare
To allure manhood. A white rose wherein
Love lies in ambush for his natural prey.
Who knows her smile has known a perfect thing.
She creates grace in her own image, brings
Heaven to earth in one movement of her hand—
Nor thou, O Venus! balancing thy shell
Over the Mediterranean blue, nor thou,
Diana! marching through broad, blossoming woods,
Art so divine as when she mounts her chair,
And goes abroad through Paris!

LE BRET: Oh, well—of course,
That makes everything clear!

CYRANO: Transparently.

LE BRET: Madeleine Robin—your cousin?

CYRANO: Yes; Roxane.

LE BRET: And why not? If you love her, tell her
so!
You have covered yourself with glory in her eyes
This very day.

CYRANO: My old friend—look at me,
And tell me how much hope remains for me
With this protuberance! Oh I have no more
Illusions! Now and then—bah! I may grow
Tender, walking alone in the blue cool
Of evening, through some garden fresh with flowers
After the benediction of the rain;
My poor big devil of a nose inhales
April . . . and so I follow with my eyes
Where some boy, with a girl upon his arm,
Passes a patch of silver . . . and I feel
Somehow, I wish I had a woman too,
Walking with little steps under the moon,
And holding my arm so, and smiling. Then
I dream—and I forget. . . .

          And then I see
The shadow of my profile on the wall!

LE BRET: My friend! . . .

CYRANO: My friend, I have my bitter days,
Knowing myself so ugly, so alone.
Sometimes—

LE BRET: You weep?

CYRANO: [Quickly] Oh, not that ever! No,
That would be too grotesque—tears trickling down
All the long way along this nose of mine?
I will not so profane the dignity
Of sorrow. Never any tears for me!
Why, there is nothing more sublime than tears,

Nothing!—Shall I make them ridiculous
In my poor person?

LE BRET: Love's no more than chance!

CYRANO: [Shakes his head]
No. I love Cleopatra; do I appear
Cæsar? I adore Beatrice; have I
The look of Dante?

LE BRET: But your wit—your courage—
Why, that poor child who offered you just now
Your dinner! She—you saw with your own eyes,
Her eyes did not avoid you.

CYRANO: [Thoughtful] That is true . . .

LE BRET: Well then! Roxane herself, watching
    your duel,
Paler than—

CYRANO: Pale?—

LE BRET: Her lips parted, her hand
Thus, at her breast—I saw it! Speak to her
Speak, man!

CYRANO: Through my nose? She might laugh at
    me;
That is the one thing in this world I fear!

THE PORTER: [Followed by the Duenna, approaches Cyrano respectfully] A lady asking for
    Monsieur.

CYRANO: Mon dieu . . .
Her Duenna!—

THE DUENNA: [A sweeping curtsey] Monsieur . . .
A message for you:
From our good cousin we desire to know
When and where we may see him privately.

CYRANO: [Amazed] To see me?

THE DUENNA: [An elaborate reverence] To see
    you. We have certain things
To tell you.

CYRANO: Certain—

THE DUENNA: Things.

CYRANO: [Trembling] Mon dieu! . . .

THE DUENNA: We go
To-morrow, at the first flush of the dawn,
To hear Mass at St. Roch. Then afterwards,
Where can we meet and talk a little?

CYRANO: [Catching Le Bret's arm] Where?—
I— Ah, mon dieu! . . . mon dieu! . . .

THE DUENNA: Well?

CYRANO: I am thinking . . .

THE DUENNA: And you think?

CYRANO: I . . . The shop of Ragueneau . . .
Ragueneau—pastrycook . . .

THE DUENNA: Who dwells?—

CYRANO: Mon dieu! . . .
Oh, yes . . . Ah, mon dieu! . . . Rue St.-Honoré.

THE DUENNA: We are agreed. Remember—seven
    o'clock. [Reverence]
Until then—

CYRANO: I'll be there. [The Duenna goes out]

CYRANO: [Falls into the arms of Le Bret] Me . . .
    to see me! . . .

LE BRET: You are not quite so gloomy.

CYRANO: After all,
She knows that I exist—no matter why!

LE BRET: So now, you are going to be happy.

CYRANO: Now! . . . [Beside himself]
I—I am going to be a storm—a flame—
I need to fight whole armies all alone;
I have ten hearts; I have a hundred arms; I feel
Too strong to war with mortals—
    [He shouts at the top of his voice] Bring me
    giants!
    [A moment since, the shadows of the comedians
    have been visible moving and posturing upon
    the stage. The violins have taken their places]

A VOICE: [From the stage] Hey—pst—less noise!
    We are rehearsing here!

CYRANO: [Laughs] We are going.
    [He turns up stage. Through the street door
    enter Cuigy, Brissaille, and a number of offi-
    cers, supporting Lignière, who is now thor-
    oughly drunk]

CUIGY: Cyrano!

CYRANO: What is it?

CUIGY: Here—
Here's your stray lamb!

CYRANO: [Recognizes Lignière] Lignière—What's
    wrong with him?

CUIGY: He wants you.

BRISSAILLE: He's afraid to go home.

CYRANO: Why?

LIGNIÈRE: [Showing a crumpled scrap of paper
and speaking with the elaborate logic of profound
intoxication]
This letter—hundred against one—that's me—
I'm the one—all because of little song—
Good song— Hundred men, waiting, understand?
Porte de Nesle—way home— Might be dangerous—
Would you permit me spend the night with you?

CYRANO: A hundred—is that all? You are going
    home!

LIGNIÈRE: [Astonished] Why—

CYRANO: [In a voice of thunder, indicating the
lighted lantern which the Porter holds up curiously
as he regards the scene] Take that lantern!
    [Lignière precipitately seizes the lantern] For-
    ward march! I say
I'll be the man to-night that sees you home.
    [To the officers]
You others follow—I want an audience!

CUIGY: A hundred against one—

CYRANO: Those are the odds
To-night!
    [The Comedians in their costumes are descend-
    ing from the stage and joining the group]

LE BRET: But why help this—

CYRANO: There goes Le Bret
Growling!

LE BRET: —This drunkard here?

CYRANO: [His hand on Le Bret's shoulder] Because this drunkard—
This tun of sack, this butt of Burgundy—

Once in his life has done one lovely thing:
After the Mass, according to the form,
He saw, one day, the lady of his heart
Take holy water for a blessing. So
This one, who shudders at a drop of rain,
This fellow here—runs headlong to the font
Bends down and drinks it dry!

A SOUBRETTE: I say that was
A pretty thought!

CYRANO: Ah, was it not?

THE SOUBRETTE: [To the others] But why
Against one poor poet, a hundred men?

CYRANO: March!
    [To the officers] And you gentlemen, remember
    now,
No rescue— Let me fight alone.

A COMEDIENNE: [Jumps down from the stage]
    Come on!
I'm going to watch—

CYRANO: Come along!

ANOTHER COMEDIENNE: [Jumps down, speaks to a
Comedian costumed as an old man] You, Cassandre?

CYRANO: Come all of you—the Doctor, Isabelle,
Léandre—the whole company—a swarm
Of murmuring, golden bees—we'll parody
Italian farce and Tragedy-of-Blood;
Ribbons for banners, masks for blazonry,
And tambourines to be our rolling drums!

ALL THE WOMEN: [Jumping for joy] Bravo:—My
    hood— My cloak— Hurry!

JODELET: [Mock heroic] Lead on!—

CYRANO: [To the violins] You violins—play us an
    overture—
    [The violins join the procession which is form-
    ing. The lighted candles are snatched from
    the stage and distributed; it becomes a torch-
    light procession]
Bravo!—Officers— Ladies in costume—
And twenty paces in advance. . . .
    [He takes his station as he speaks] Myself,
Alone, with glory fluttering over me,
Alone as Lucifer at war with heaven!
Remember—no one lifts a hand to help—
Ready there? One . . . two . . . three! Porter, the
    doors! . . .
    [The Porter flings wide the great doors. We
    see in the dim moonlight a corner of old Paris,
    purple and picturesque]
Look—Paris dreams—nocturnal, nebulous.
Under blue moonbeams hung from wall to wall—
Nature's own setting for the scene we play!—
Yonder, behind her veil of mist, the Seine,
Like a mysterious and magic mirror
Trembles—
    And you shall see what you shall see!

ALL: To the Porte de Nesle!

CYRANO: [Erect upon the threshold] To the Porte
    de Nesle!
    [He turns back for a moment to the Soubrette]

Did you not ask, my dear, why against one
Singer they send a hundred swords?

[*Quietly, drawing his own sword*]

Because

They know this one man for a friend of mine!

[*He goes out. The procession follows:* Lignière *zigzagging at its head, then the* Comediennes *on the arms of the* Officers, *then the* Comedians, *leaping and dancing as they go. It vanishes into the night to the music of the violins, illuminated by the flickering glimmer of the candles*]

CURTAIN

ACT II.
The Bakery of the Poets

The shop of Ragueneau, *baker and pastrycook: a spacious affair at the corner of the Rue St.-Honoré and the Rue de l'Arbre Sec. The street, seen vaguely through the glass panes in the door at the back, is gray in the first light of dawn. In the foreground, at the left, a counter is surmounted by a canopy of wrought iron from which are hanging ducks, geese, and white peacocks. Great crockery jars hold bouquets of common flowers, yellow sunflowers in particular. On the same side farther back, a huge fireplace; in front of it, between great andirons, of which each one supports a little saucepan, roast fowls revolve and weep into their dripping-pans. To the right at the first entrance, a door. Beyond it, second entrance, a staircase leads up to a little dining-room under the eaves, its interior visible through open shutters. A table is set there and a tiny Flemish candlestick is lighted; there one may retire to eat and drink in private. A wooden gallery, extending from the head of the stairway, seems to lead to other little dining rooms. In the center of the shop, an iron ring hangs by a rope over a pulley so that it can be raised or lowered; adorned with game of various kinds hung from it by hooks, it has the appearance of a sort of gastronomic chandelier. In the shadow under the staircase, ovens are glowing. The spits revolve; the copper pots and pans gleam ruddily. Pastries in pyramids. Hams hanging from the rafters. The morning baking is in progress: a bustle of tall cooks and timid scullions and scurrying apprentices; a blossoming of white caps adorned with cock's feathers or the wings of guinea fowl. On wicker trays or on great metal platters they bring in rows of pastries and fancy dishes of various kinds. Tables are covered with trays of cakes and rolls; others with chairs placed about them are set for guests. One little table in a corner disappears under a heap of papers. At the curtain rise* Ragueneau *is seated there. He is writing poetry.*

A PASTRYCOOK: [*Brings in a dish*] Fruits en gelée!

SECOND PASTRYCOOK: [*Brings dish*] Custard!

THIRD PASTRYCOOK: [*Brings roast peacock ornamented with feathers*] Peacock rôti!

FOURTH PASTRYCOOK: [*Brings tray of cakes*] Cakes and confections!

FIFTH PASTRYCOOK: [*Brings earthen dish*] Beef en casserole!

RAGUENEAU: [*Raises his head; returns to mere earth*]

Over the coppers of my kitchen flows
The frosted-silver dawn. Silence awhile
The god who sings within thee, Ragueneau!
Lay down the lute—the oven calls for thee!

[*Rises; goes to one of the cooks*]

Here's a hiatus in your sauce; fill up
The measure.

THE COOK: How much?

RAGUENEAU: [*Measures on his finger*] One more dactyl.

THE COOK: Huh?

FIRST PASTRYCOOK: Rolls!

SECOND PASTRYCOOK: Roulades!

RAGUENEAU: [*Before the fireplace*] Veil, O Muse, thy virgin eyes

From the lewd gleam of these terrestrial fires!

[*To* First Pastrycook]

Your rolls lack balance. Here's the proper form—
An equal hemistich on either side,
And the caesura in between.

[*To another, pointing out an unfinished pie*]

Your house

Of crust should have a roof upon it.

[*To another, who is seated on the hearth, placing poultry on a spit*]

And you—

Along the interminable spit, arrange
The modest pullet and the lordly Turk
Alternately, my son—as great Malherbe
Alternates male and female rimes. Remember,
A couplet, or a roast, should be well turned.

AN APPRENTICE: [*Advances with a dish covered by a napkin*]

Master, I thought of you when I designed
This, hoping it might please you.

RAGUENEAU: Ah! A lyre—

THE APPRENTICE: In puff-paste—

RAGUENEAU: And the jewels—candied fruit!

THE APPRENTICE: And the strings, barley-sugar!

RAGUENEAU: [*Gives him money*] Go and drink
My health.

[Lise *enters*]

St!—My wife— Circulate, and hide
That money!

[*Shows the lyre to* Lise, *with languid air*]

Graceful—yes?

LISE: Ridiculous! [*She places on the counter a pile of paper bags*]

RAGUENEAU: Paper bags? Thank you . . .

[*He looks at them*] Ciel! My manuscripts!

The sacred verses of my poets—rent
Asunder, limb from limb—butchered to make
Base packages of pastry! Ah, you are one
Of those insane Bacchantes who destroyed
Orpheus!

LISE: Your dirty poets left them here
To pay for eating half our stock-in-trade:
We ought to make some profit out of them!

RAGUENEAU: Ant! Would you blame the locust for
his song?

LISE: I blame the locust for his appetite!
There used to be a time—before you had
Your hungry friends—you never called me Ants—
No, nor Bacchantes!

RAGUENEAU: What a way to use
Poetry!

LISE: Well, what is the use of it?

RAGUENEAU: But, my dear girl, what would you
    do with prose?
    [Two children enter] Well, dears?

A CHILD: Three little patties.

RAGUENEAU: [Serves them] There we are!
All hot and brown.

THE CHILD: Would you mind wrapping them?

RAGUENEAU: One of my paper bags! . . . Oh,
    certainly.
    [Reads from the bag, as he is about to wrap the
    patties in it]
"Ulysses, when he left Penelope"—
Not that one!
    [Takes another bag; reads]
'Phoebus, golden-crowned"—Not that one.

LISE: Well? They are waiting!

RAGUENEAU: Very well, very well!—
The Sonnet to Phyllis . . .
                    Yet—it does seem hard . . .

LISE: Made up your mind—at last! Mph!—Jack-
o'-Dreams!

RAGUENEAU: [As her back is turned, calls back
the children, who are already at the door]
Pst!—Children— Give me back the bag. Instead
Of three patties, you shall have six of them!
    [Makes the exchange. The children go out. He
    reads from the bag, as he smooths it out ten-
    derly]
"Phyllis"—A spot of butter on her name!—
"Phyllis"—

CYRANO: [Enters hurriedly] What is the time?

RAGUENEAU: Six o'clock.

CYRANO: One
Hour more . . .

RAGUENEAU: Felicitations!

CYRANO: And for what?

RAGUENEAU: Your victory! I saw it all—

CYRANO: Which one?

RAGUENEAU: At the Hôtel de Bourgogne.

CYRANO: Oh—the duel!

RAGUENEAU: The duel in Rime!

LISE: He talks of nothing else.

CYRANO: Nonsense!

RAGUENEAU: [Fencing and foining with a spit,
which he snatches up from the hearth]
          "Then, as I end the refrain, thrust home!"
"Then, as I end the refrain"—
                    Gods! What a line!
"Then, as I end"—

CYRANO: What time now, Ragueneau?

RAGUENEAU: [Petrified at the full extent of a
lunge, while he looks at the clock] Five after six—
    [Recovers]
"—thrust home!"
                    A Ballade, too!

LISE: [To Cyrano, who in passing has mechanically shaken hands with her] Your hand—what
have you done?

CYRANO: Oh, my hand?—Nothing.

RAGUENEAU: What danger now—

CYRANO: No danger.

LISE: I believe
He is lying.

CYRANO: Why? Was I looking down my nose?
That must have been a devil of a lie!
    [Changing his tone; to Ragueneau]
I expect someone. Leave us here alone,
When the time comes.

RAGUENEAU: How can I? In a moment,
My poets will be here.

LISE: To break their . . . fast!

CYRANO: Take them away, then, when I give the
    sign.
—What time?

RAGUENEAU: Ten minutes after.

CYRANO: Have you a pen?

RAGUENEAU: [Offers him a pen] An eagle's
    feather!

A MUSKETEER: [Enters, and speaks to Lise in a
stentorian voice] Greeting!

CYRANO: [To Ragueneau] Who is this?

RAGUENEAU: My wife's friend. A terrific warrior.
So he says.

CYRANO: Ah—I see. [Takes up the pen;
waves Ragueneau away]
                    Only to write—
To fold— To give it to her—and to go . . .
    [Throws down the pen]
Coward! And yet—the Devil take my soul
If I dare speak one word to her . . .
    [To Ragueneau] What time now?

RAGUENEAU: A quarter after six.

CYRANO: [Striking his breast]—One little word
Of all the many thousand I have here!
Whereas in writing . . .
    [Takes up the pen] Come, I'll write to her
That letter I have written on my heart,
Torn up, and written over many times—
So many times . . . that all I have to do
Is to remember, and to write it down.
    [He writes. Through the glass of the door ap-
    pear vague and hesitating shadows. The Poets

*enter, clothed in rusty black and spotted with
    mud*]

LISE: [*To* Ragueneau] Here come your scarecrows!

FIRST POET: Comrade!

SECOND POET: [*Takes both* Ragueneau's *hands*]
My dear brother!

THIRD POET: [*Sniffing*]
O Lord of Roasts, how sweet thy dwellings are!

FOURTH POET: Phoebus Apollo of the Silver
    Spoon!

FIFTH POET: Cupid of Cookery!

RAGUENEAU: [*Surrounded, embraced, beaten on
the back*] These geniuses,
They put one at one's ease!

FIRST POET: We were delayed
By the crowd at the Porte de Nesle.

SECOND POET: Dead men
All scarred and gory, scattered on the stones,
Villainous-looking scoundrels—eight of them.

CYRANO: [*Looks up an instant*] Eight? I thought
    only seven—

RAGUENEAU: Do you know
The hero of this hecatomb?

CYRANO: I? . . . No.

LISE: [*To the* Musketeer] Do you?

THE MUSKETEER: Hmm—perhaps!

FIRST POET: They say one man alone
Put to flight all this crowd.

SECOND POET: Everywhere lay
Swords, daggers, pikes, bludgeons—

CYRANO: [*Writing*] "Your eyes . . ."

THIRD POET: As far
As the Quai des Orfèvres, hats and cloaks—

FIRST POET: Why, that man must have been the
    devil!

CYRANO: "Your lips . . ."

FIRST POET: Some savage monster might have
    done this thing!

CYRANO: "Looking upon you, I grow faint with
    fear . . ."

SECOND POET: What have you written lately,
    Ragueneau?

CYRANO: "Your Friend—Who loves you . . ."
                        So. No signature;
I'll give it to her myself.

RAGUENEAU: A Recipe
In Rime.

THIRD POET: Read us your rimes!

FOURTH POET: Here's a brioche
Cocking its hat at me.

    [*He bites off the top of it*]

FIRST POET: Look how those buns
Follow the hungry poet with their eyes—
Those almond eyes!

SECOND POET: We are listening—

THIRD POET: See this cream-puff—
Fat little baby, drooling while it smiles!

SECOND POET: [*Nibbling at the pastry lyre*]
For the first time, the lyre is my support.

RAGUENEAU: [*Coughs, adjusts his cap, strikes an
attitude*]
A Recipe in Rime—

SECOND POET: [*Gives* First Poet *a dig with his elbow*] Your breakfast?

FIRST POET: Dinner!

RAGUENEAU: [*Declaims*]
    A Recipe for Making Almond Tarts

Beat your egg, the yolk and white,
    Very light;
Mingle with their creamy fluff
    Drops of lime-juice, cool and green;
        Then pour in
Milk of Almonds, just enough.

Dainty patty-pans, embraced
    In puff-paste—
Have these ready within reach;
    With your thumb and finger, pinch
        Half an inch
Up around the edge of each—

Into these, a score or more,
    Slowly pour
All your store of custard; so
    Take them, bake them golden-brown—
        Now sit down! . . .
Almond tartlets, Ragueneau!

THE POETS: Delicious! Melting!

A POET: [*Chokes*] Humph!

CYRANO: [*To* Ragueneau] Do you not see
Those fellows fattening themselves?—

RAGUENEAU: I know.
I would not look—it might embarrass them—
You see, I love a friendly audience.
Besides—another vanity—I am pleased
When they enjoy my cooking.

CYRANO: [*Slaps him on the back*] Be off with
    you!—
    [Ragueneau *goes upstage*]
Good little soul! [*Calls to* Lise] Madame!—
    [*She leaves the* Musketeer *and comes down to
    him*]   This musketeer—
He is making love to you?

LISE: [*Haughtily*] If any man
Offends my virtue—all I have to do
Is look at him—once!

CYRANO: [*Looks at her gravely; she drops her
eyes*] I do not find
Those eyes of yours unconquerable.

LISE: [*Panting*]—Ah!

CYRANO: [*Raising his voice a little*]
Now listen—I am fond of Ragueneau;
I allow no one—do you understand?—
To . . . take his name in vain!

LISE: You think—

CYRANO: [*Ironic emphasis*] I think
I interrupt you.

    [*He salutes the* Musketeer, *who has heard with-*

out daring to resent the warning. Lise *goes to
the* Musketeer *as he returns* Cyrano's *salute*]

LISE: You—you swallow that?—
You ought to have pulled his nose!

THE MUSKETEER:　　　　His nose?—His nose! . . .
[*He goes out hurriedly.* Roxane *and the* Duenna
appear outside the door]

CYRANO: [*Nods to* Ragueneau] Pst!—

RAGUENEAU: [*To the* Poets] Come inside—

CYRANO: [*Impatient*] Pst! . . . Pst! . . .

RAGUENEAU:　　　　　　　　We shall be more
Comfortable . . .
[*He leads the* Poets *into inner room*]

FIRST POET: The cakes!

SECOND POET:　　　　　　Bring them along!
[*They go out*]

CYRANO: If I can see the faintest spark of hope,
Then—[*Throws door open—bows*] Welcome!
[Roxane *enters, followed by the* Duenna, *whom*
Cyrano *detains*]
　　　　　　　　　　Pardon me—one word—

THE DUENNA:　　　　　　　　　Take two.

CYRANO: Have you a good digestion?

THE DUENNA:　　　　　　　　Wonderful!

CYRANO: Good. Here are two sonnets, by Ben-
serade—

THE DUENNA: Euh?

CYRANO:　　　　Which I fill for you with éclairs.

THE DUENNA:　　　　　　　　　Ooo!

CYRANO: Do you like cream-puffs?

THE DUENNA:　　　　Only with whipped cream.

CYRANO: Here are three . . . six—embosomed in
a poem
By Saint-Amant. This ode of Chapelin
Looks deep enough to hold—a jelly roll.
—Do you love Nature?

THE DUENNA:　　　　　Mad about it.

CYRANO:　　　　　　　　　　Then
Go out and eat these in the street. Do not
Return—

THE DUENNA: Oh, but—

CYRANO:　　　　　Until you finish them.
[*Down to* Roxane]
Blessed above all others be the hour
When you remembered to remember me,
And came to tell me . . . what?

ROXANE: [*Takes off her mask*] First let me thank
you
Because . . . That man . . . that creature, whom
your sword
Made sport of yesterday— His patron, one—

CYRANO: De Guiche?—

ROXANE:　　—who thinks himself in love with me
Would have forced that man upon me for—
a husband—

CYRANO: I understand—so much the better then!
I fought, not for my nose, but your bright eyes.

ROXANE: And then, to tell you—but before I can
Tell you— Are you, I wonder still the same
Big Brother—almost—that you used to be

When we were children, playing by the pond
In the old garden down there—

CYRANO:　　　　　　　　　I remember—
Every summer you came to Bergerac! . . .

ROXANE: You used to make swords out of bul-
rushes—

CYRANO: Your dandelion-dolls with golden hair—

ROXANE: And those green plums—

CYRANO:　　　　　　And those black mulberries—

ROXANE: In those days, you did everything I
wished!

CYRANO: Roxane, in short skirts, was called Madeleine.

ROXANE: Was I pretty?

CYRANO:　　　　　　　Oh—not too plain!

ROXANE:　　　　　　　　　　Sometimes
When you had hurt your hand you used to come
Running to me—and I would be your mother,
And say— Oh, in a very grown-up voice:
[*She takes his hand*]
"Now, what have you been doing to yourself?
Let me see—"
　　　[*She sees the hand—starts*] Oh! Wait— I said,
"Let me see!"
Still—at your age! How did you do that?

CYRANO:　　　　　　　　　　Playing
With the big boys, down by the Porte de Nesle.

ROXANE: [*Sits at a table and wets her handkerchief
in a glass of water*] Come here to me.

CYRANO:　　　　　—Such a wise little mother!

ROXANE: And tell me, while I wash this blood
away,
How many you—-played with?

CYRANO:　　　　Oh, about a hundred.

ROXANE: Tell me.

CYRANO:　　　No. Let me go. Tell me what you
Were going to tell me—if you dared?

ROXANE: [*Still holding his hand*] I think
I do dare—now. It seems like long ago
When I could tell you things. Yes—I dare . . .
Listen:
I . . . love someone.

CYRANO:　　　　　Ah! . . .

ROXANE:　　　　　Someone who does not know.

CYRANO: Ah! . . .

ROXANE:　　　　　At least—not yet.

CYRANO:　　　　　　　　Ah! . . .

ROXANE:　　　　　　　But he will know
Some day.

CYRANO:　　Ah! . . .

ROXANE:　　　　　A big boy who loves me too,
And is afraid of me, and keeps away,
And never says one word.

CYRANO:　　　　　　Ah! . . .

ROXANE:　　　　　　　Let me have
Your hand a moment—why how hot it is!—
I know. I see him trying . . .

CYRANO:　　　　　　Ah! . . .

ROXANE:　　　　　　　There now!

Is that better?—[*She finishes bandaging the hand with her handkerchief*]

              Besides—only to think—
(This is a secret.) He is a soldier too,
In your own regiment—

CYRANO: Ah! . . .

ROXANE: Yes, in the Guards,
Your company too.

CYRANO: Ah! . . .

ROXANE: And such a man!—
He is proud—noble—young—brave—beautiful—

CYRANO: [*Turns pale; rises*] Beautiful!—

ROXANE: What's the matter?

CYRANO: [*Smiling*] Nothing—this—
My sore hand!

ROXANE: Well, I love him. That is all.
Oh—and I never saw him anywhere
Except the *Comédie*.

CYRANO: You have never spoken?—

ROXANE: Only our eyes . . .

CYRANO: Why, then— How do you know?—

ROXANE: People talk about people; and I hear
Things . . . and I know.

CYRANO: You say he is in the Guards:
His name?

ROXANE: Baron Christian de Neuvillette.

CYRANO: He is not in the Guards.

ROXANE: Yes. Since this morning.
Captain Carbon de Castel-Jaloux.

CYRANO: So soon! . . .
So soon we lose our hearts!—

           —But, my dear child,—

THE DUENNA: [*Opens the door*]
I have eaten the cakes, Monsieur de Bergerac!

CYRANO: Good! Now go out and read the poetry!
[*The* Duenna *disappears*]
—But, my dear child! You, who love only words,
Wit, the grand manner— Why, for all you know,
The man may be a savage, or a fool.

ROXANE: His curls are like a hero from D'Urfé.

CYRANO: His mind may be as curly as his hair.

ROXANE: Not with such eyes. I read his soul in
them.

CYRANO: Yes, all our souls are written in our eyes!
But—if he be a bungler?

ROXANE: Then I shall die—
There!

CYRANO: [*After a pause*] And you brought me here
    to tell me this?
I do not yet quite understand, Madame,
The reason for your confidence.

ROXANE: They say
That in your company— It frightens me—
You are all Gascons . . .

CYRANO: And we pick a quarrel
With any flat-foot who intrudes himself,
Whose blood is not pure Gascon like our own?
Is this what you have heard?

ROXANE: I am so afraid
For him!

CYRANO: [*Between his teeth*] Not without reason!—

ROXANE: And I thought
You . . . You were so brave, so invincible
Yesterday, against all those brutes!—If you,
Whom they all fear—

CYRANO: Oh well— I will defend
Your little Baron.

ROXANE: Will you? Just for me?
Because I have always been—your friend!

CYRANO: Of course . . .

ROXANE: Will you be *his* friend?

CYRANO: I will be his friend.

ROXANE: And never let him fight a duel?

CYRANO: No—never.

ROXANE: Oh, but you are a darling!—I must go—
You never told me about last night— Why,
You must have been a hero! Have him write
And tell me all about it—will you?

CYRANO: Of course . . .

ROXANE: [*Kisses her hand*]
I always did love you!—A hundred men
Against one— Well. . . . Adieu. We are great
    friends,
Are we not?

CYRANO: Of course . . .

ROXANE: He *must* write to me—
A hundred— You shall tell me the whole story
Some day, when I have time. A hundred men—
What courage!

CYRANO: [*Salutes as she goes out*] Oh . . . I have
    done better since!
    [*The door closes after her.* Cyrano *remains motionless, his eyes on the ground. Pause. The other door opens;* Ragueneau *puts in his head*]

RAGUENEAU: May I come in?

CYRANO: [*Without moving*] Yes—
    [Ragueneau *and his friends re-enter. At the same time,* Carbon de Castel-Jaloux *appears at the street door in uniform as Captain of the Guards; recognizes* Cyrano *with a sweeping gesture*]

CARBON: Here he is!—Our hero!

CYRANO: [*Raises his head and salutes*] Our Captain!

CARBON: We know! All our company
Are here—

CYRANO: [*Recoils*] No—

CARBON: Come! They are waiting for you.

CYRANO: No!

CARBON: [*Tries to lead him out*] Only across the
    street— Come!

CYRANO: Please—

CARBON: [*Goes to the door and shouts in a voice of thunder*] Our champion
Refuses! He is not feeling well to-day!

A VOICE OUTSIDE: Ah! Sandious!
    [*Noise outside of swords and trampling feet approaching*]

CARBON: Here they come now!

THE CADETS: [*Entering the shop*] Mille dious!—
Mordious!—Capdedious!—Pocapdedious!

RAGUENEAU: [*In astonishment*] Gentlemen—
You are all Gascons?

THE CADETS: All!

FIRST CADET: [*To* Cyrano] Bravo!

CYRANO: Baron!

ANOTHER CADET: [*Takes both his hands*] Vivat!

CYRANO: Baron!

THIRD CADET: Come to my arms!

CYRANO: Baron!

OTHERS: To mine!—To mine!—

CYRANO: Baron . . . Baron . . . Have mercy—

RAGUENEAU: You are all Barons too?

THE CADETS: *Are* we?

RAGUENEAU: Are they? . . .

FIRST CADET: Our coronets would star the midnight sky!

LE BRET: [*Enters; hurries to* Cyrano] The whole
town's looking for you! Raving mad—
A triumph! Those who saw the fight—

CYRANO: I hope
You have not told them where I—

LE BRET: [*Rubbing his hands*] Certainly
I told them!

CITIZEN: [*Enters, followed by a group*] Listen!
Shut the door!—Here comes
All Paris!

[*The street outside fills with a shouting crowd.
Chairs and carriages stop at the door*]

LE BRET: [*Aside to* Cyrano, *smiling*] And Roxane?

CYRANO: [*Quickly*] Hush!

THE CROWD OUTSIDE: Cyrano!

[*A mob bursts into the shop. Shouts, acclamations, general disturbance*]

RAGUENEAU: [*Standing on a table*]
My shop invaded— They'll break everything—
Glorious!

SEVERAL MEN: [*Crowding about* Cyrano] My
friend! . . . My friend! . . .

CYRANO: Why, yesterday
I did not have so many friends!

LE BRET: Success
At last!

A MARQUIS: [*Runs to* Cyrano, *with outstretched
hands*] My dear—really!—

CYRANO: [*Coldly*] So? And how long
Have I been dear to you?

ANOTHER MARQUIS: One moment—pray!
I have two ladies in my carriage here;
Let me present you—

CYRANO: Certainly! And first,
Who will present you, sir,—to me?

LE BRET: [*Astounded*] Why, what
The devil?—

CYRANO: Hush!

A MAN OF LETTERS: [*With a portfolio*] May I have
the details? . . .

CYRANO: You may not.

LE BRET: [*Plucking* Cyrano's *sleeve*] Theophraste
Renaudot!—Editor
Of the *Gazette*—your reputation! . . .

CYRANO: No.

A POET: [*Advances*] Monsieur—

CYRANO: Well?

THE POET: Your full name? I will compose
A pentacrostic—

ANOTHER: Monsieur—

CYRANO: That will do!
[*Movement. The crowd arranges itself.* De
Guiche *appears, escorted by* Cuigy, Brissaille,
and the other officers who were with Cyrano
at the close of the first act]

CUIGY: [*Goes to* Cyrano] Monsieur de Guiche!—
[*Murmur. Everyone moves*]
A message from the Marshal
De Gassion—

DE GUICHE: [*Saluting* Cyrano] Who wishes to ex-
press
Through me his admiration. He has heard
Of your affair—

THE CROWD: Bravo!

CYRANO: [*Bowing*] The Marshal speaks
As an authority.

DE GUICHE: He said just now
The story would have been incredible
Were it not for the witness—

CUIGY: Of our eyes!

LE BRET: [*Aside to* Cyrano] What is it?

CYRANO: Hush!—

LE BRET: Something is wrong with you;
Are you in pain?

CYRANO: [*Recovering himself*] In pain? Before this
crowd?
[*His moustache bristles. He throws out his
chest*]
I? In pain? You shall see!

DE GUICHE: [*To whom* Cuigy *has been whispering*]
Your name is known
Already as a soldier. You are one
Of those wild Gascons, are you not?

CYRANO: The Guards,
Yes. A Cadet.

A CADET: [*In a voice of thunder*] One of ourselves!

DE GUICHE: Ah! So—
Then all these gentlemen with the haughty air,
These are the famous—

CARBON: Cyrano!

CYRANO: Captain?

CARBON: Our troop being all present, be so kind
As to present them to the Comte de Guiche!

CYRANO: [*With a gesture presenting the* Cadets *to*
De Guiche, *declaims:*]
The Cadets of Gascoyne—the defenders
Of Carbon de Castel-Jaloux:
Free fighters, free lovers, free spenders—
The Cadets of Gascoyne—the defenders
Of old homes, old names, and old splendors—

A proud and a pestilent crew!
The Cadets of Gascoyne, the defenders
Of Carbon de Castel-Jaloux.

Hawk-eyed, they stare down all contenders—
    The wolf bares his fangs as they do—
Make way there, you fat money-lenders!
(Hawk-eyed, they stare down all contenders)
Old boots that have been to the menders,
    Old cloaks that are worn through and through—
Hawk-eyed, they stare down all contenders—
    The wolf bares his fangs as they do!

Skull-breakers they are, and sword-benders;
    Red blood is their favorite brew;
Hot haters and loyal befrienders,
Skull-breakers they are, and sword-benders.
Wherever a quarrel engenders,
    They're ready and waiting for you!
Skull-breakers they are, and sword-benders;
    Red blood is their favorite brew!

Behold them, our Gascon defenders
    Who win every woman they woo!
There's never a dame but surrenders—
Behold them, our Gascon defenders!
Young wives who are clever pretenders—
    Old husbands who house the cuckoo—
Behold them—our Gascon defenders
    Who win every woman they woo!

DE GUICHE: [Languidly, sitting in a chair]
Poets are fashionable nowadays
To have about one. Would you care to join
My following?

CYRANO: No, sir. I do not follow.

DU GUICHE: Your duel yesterday amused my uncle
The Cardinal. I might help you there.

LE BRET: Grand Dieu!

DE GUICHE: I suppose you have written a
    tragedy—
They all have.

LE BRET: [Aside to Cyrano] Now at last you'll
    have it played—
Your "Agrippine!"

DE GUICHE: Why not? Take it to him.

CYRANO: [Tempted] Really—

DE GUICHE: He is himself a dramatist;
Let him rewrite a few lines here and there,
And he'll approve the rest.

CYRANO: [His face falls again] Impossible.
My blood curdles to think of altering
One comma.

DE GUICHE: Ah, but when he likes a thing
He pays well.

CYRANO: Yes—but not so well as I—
When I have made a line that sings itself
So that I love the sound of it—I pay
Myself a hundred times.

DE GUICHE: You are proud, my friend.

CYRANO: You have observed that?

A CADET: [Enters with a drawn sword, along the
whole blade of which is transfixed a collection of
disreputable hats, their plumes draggled, their crowns
cut and torn] Cyrano! See here—
Look what we found this morning in the street—
The plumes dropped in their flight by those fine
    birds
Who showed the white feather!

                            Spoils of the hunt—
Well mounted!

THE CROWD: Ha-ha-ha!

CUIGY: Whoever hired
Those rascals, he must be an angry man
To-day!

BRISSAILLE: Who was it? Do you know?

DE GUICHE: Myself!—
    [The laughter ceases]
I hired them to do the sort of work
We do not soil our hands with—punishing
A drunken poet. . . .
    [Uncomfortable silence]

THE CADET: [To Cyrano] What shall we do with
    them?
They ought to be preserved before they spoil—

CYRANO: [Takes the sword, and in the gesture of
saluting De Guiche with it, makes all the hats slide
off at his feet]
Sir, will you not return these to your friends?

DE GUICHE: My chair—my porters here—imme-
    diately! [To Cyrano violently]
—As for you, sir!—

A VOICE: [In the street] The chair of Monseigneur
Le Comte de Guiche!—

DE GUICHE: [Who has recovered his self-control;
smiling] Have you read Don Quixote?

CYRANO: I have—and found myself the hero.

A PORTER: [Appears at the door] Chair
Ready!

DE GUICHE: Be so good as to read once more
The chapter of the windmills.

CYRANO: [Gravely] Chapter Thirteen.

DE GUICHE: Windmills, remember, if you fight
with them—

CYRANO: My enemies change, then, with every
wind?

DE GUICHE:—May swing round their huge arms
and cast you down
Into the mire.

CYRANO: Or up—among the stars!
    [De Guiche goes out. We see him get into the
    chair. The Officers follow murmuring among
    themselves. Le Bret goes up with them. The
    crowd goes out]

CYRANO: [Saluting with burlesque politeness, those
who go out without daring to take leave of him]
Gentlemen. . . . Gentlemen. . . .

LE BRET: [As the door closes, comes down, shaking his clenched hands to heaven] You have done it
now—
You have made your fortune!

CYRANO: There you go again,
Growling!—

LE BRET: At least this latest pose of yours—
Ruining every chance that comes your way—
Becomes exaggerated—

CYRANO: Very well,
Then I exaggerate!

LE BRET: [*Triumphantly*] Oh, you do!

CYRANO: Yes.
On principle. There are things in this world
A man does well to carry to extremes.

LE BRET: Stop trying to be Three Musketeers in
      one!
Fortune and glory—

CYRANO: What would you have me do?
Seek for the patronage of some great man,
And like a creeping vine on a tall tree
Crawl upward, where I cannot stand alone?
No thank you! Dedicate, as others do,
Poems to pawnbrokers? Be a buffoon
In the vile hope of teasing out a smile
On some cold face? No thank you! Eat a toad
For breakfast every morning? Make my knees
Callous, and cultivate a supple spine,—
Wear out my belly grovelling in the dust?
No thank you! Scratch the back of any swine
That roots up gold for me? Tickle the horns
Of Mammon with my left hand, while my right
Too proud to know his partner's business,
Takes in the fee? No thank you! Use the fire
God gave me to burn incense all day long
Under the nose of wood and stone? No thank you!
Shall I go leaping into ladies' laps
And licking fingers?—or—to change the form—
Navigating with madrigals for oars,
My sails full of sighs of dowagers?
No thank you! Publish verses at my own
Expense? No thank you! Be the patron saint
Of a small group of literary souls
Who dine together every Tuesday? No
I thank you! Shall I labor night and day
To build a reputation on one song,
And never write another? Shall I find
True genius only among Geniuses,
Palpitate over little paragraphs,
And struggle to insinuate my name
Into the columns of the *Mercury?*
No thank you! Calculate, scheme, be afraid,
Love more to make a visit than a poem,
Seek introductions, favors, influences?—
No thank you! No, I thank you! And again
I thank you!—But . . .

                    To sing, to laugh, to dream,
To walk in my own way and be alone,
Free, with an eye to see things as they are,
A voice that means manhood—to cock my hat
Where I choose— At a word, a *Yes,* a *No,*
To fight—or write. To travel any road
Under the sun, under the stars, nor doubt
If fame or fortune lie beyond the bourne—

Never to make a line I have not heard
In my own heart; yet, with all modesty
To say: "My soul, be satisfied with flowers,
With fruit, with weeds even; but gather them
In the one garden you may call your own."
So, when I win some triumph, by some chance,
Render no share to Cæsar—in a word,
I am too proud to be a parasite,
And if my nature wants the germ that grows
Towering to heaven like the mountain pine,
Or like the oak, sheltering multitudes—
I stand, not high it may be—but alone!

LE BRET: Alone, yes!—But why stand against the
      world?
What devil has possessed you now, to go
Everywhere making yourself enemies?

CYRANO: Watching you other people making friends
Everywhere—as a dog makes friends! I mark
The manner of these canine courtesies
And think: "My friends are of a cleaner breed;
Here comes—thank God!—another enemy!"

LE BRET: But this is madness!

CYRANO: Method, let us say.
It is my pleasure to displease. I love
Hatred. Imagine how it feels to face
The volley of a thousand angry eyes—
The bile of envy and the froth of fear
Spattering little drops about me— You—
Good nature all around you, soft and warm—
You are like those Italians, in great cowls
Comfortable and loose— Your chin sinks down
Into the folds, your shoulders droop. But I—
The Spanish ruff I wear around my throat
Is like a ring of enemies; hard, proud,
Each point another pride, another thorn—
So that I hold myself erect perforce.
Wearing the hatred of the common herd
Haughtily, the harsh collar of Old Spain,
At once a fetter and—a halo!

LE BRET: Yes . . .
      [*After a silence, draws* Cyrano's *arm through
      his own*]
Tell this to all the world— And then to me
Say very softly that . . . She loves you not.

CYRANO: [*Quickly*] Hush!
      [*A moment since,* Christian *has entered and
      mingled with the* Cadets, *who do not offer to
      speak to him. Finally, he sits down alone at a
      small table, where he is served by* Lise]

A CADET: [*Rises from a table up stage, his glass
in his hand*] Cyrano!—Your story!

CYRANO: Presently . . .
      [*He goes up, on the arm of* Le Bret, *talking to
      him. The* Cadet *comes down stage*]

THE CADET: The story of the combat! An example
For—
      [*He stops by the table where* Christian *is sit-
      ting*]
—this young tadpole here.

CHRISTIAN: [*Looks up*] Tadpole?

ANOTHER CADET: Yes, you!—
You narrow-gutted Northerner!

CHRISTIAN: Sir?

FIRST CADET: Hark ye,
Monsieur de Neuvillette: You are to know
There is a certain subject—I would say,
A certain object—never to be named
Among us: utterly unmentionable!

CHRISTIAN: And that is?

THIRD CADET: [*In an awful voice*] Look at me! . . .
[*He strikes his nose three times with his finger,
mysteriously*]
                    You understand?

CHRISTIAN: Why, yes; the—

FOURTH CADET: Sh! . . . We never speak that
word—
[*Indicating* Cyrano *by a gesture*]
To breathe it is to have to do with HIM!

FIFTH CADET: [*Speaks through his nose*] He has
exterminated several
Whose tone of voice suggested . . .

SIXTH CADET: [*In a hollow tone; rising from
under the table on all fours*] Would you die
Before your time! Just mention anything
Convex . . . or cartilaginous . . .

SEVENTH CADET: [*His hand on* Christian's
shoulder*] One word—
One syllable—one gesture—nay, one sneeze—
Your handkerchief becomes your winding-sheet!
[*Silence. In a circle around* Christian, *arms
crossed, they regard him expectantly*]

CHRISTIAN: [*Rises and goes to* Carbon, *who is
conversing with an officer, and pretending not to
see what is taking place*] Captain!

CARBON: [*Turns, and looks him over*] Sir?

CHRISTIAN: What is the proper thing to do
When Gascons grow too boastful?

CARBON: Prove to them
That one may be a Norman, and have courage.
[*Turns his back*]

CHRISTIAN: I thank you.

FIRST CADET: [*To* Cyrano] Come—the story!

ALL: The story!

CYRANO: [*Comes down*]   Oh,
My story? Well . . .
[*They all draw up their stools and group them-
selves around him, eagerly.* Christian *places
himself astride of a chair, his arms on the
back of it*]
                    I marched on, all alone
To meet those devils. Overhead, the moon
Hung like a gold watch at the fob of heaven,
Till suddenly some Angel rubbed a cloud,
As it might be his handkerchief, across
The shining crystal, and—the night came down.
No lamps in those back streets— It was so dark—
Mordious! You could not see beyond—

CHRISTIAN: Your nose.

[*Silence. Every man slowly rises to his feet.
They look at* Cyrano *almost with terror. He
has stopped short, utterly astonished. Pause*]

CYRANO: Who is that man there?

A CADET: [*In a low voice*] A recruit—arrived
This morning.

CYRANO: [*Takes a step toward* Christian] A recruit—

CARBON: [*In a low voice*]
                    His name is Christian
De Neuvil—

CYRANO: [*Suddenly motionless*] Oh . . .
[*He turns pale, flushes, makes a movement as
if to throw himself upon* Christian]
I—[*Controls himself, and goes on in a choking voice*]
    I see. Very well,
As I was saying—
[*With a sudden burst of rage*]
                    Mordious! . . .
[*He goes on in a natural tone*]
                    It grew dark,
You could not see your hand before your eyes.
I marched on, thinking how, all for the sake
Of one old souse
[*They slowly sit down, watching him*]
                    who wrote a bawdy song
Whenever he took—

CHRISTIAN: A noseful—
[*Everyone rises.* Christian *balances himself on
two legs of his chair*]

CYRANO: [*Half strangled*] —Took a notion . . .
Whenever he took a notion— For his sake,
I might antagonize some dangerous man,
One powerful enough to make me pay—

CHRISTIAN: Through the nose—

CYRANO: [*Wipes the sweat from his forehead*]
                    —Pay the Piper. After all,
I thought, why am I putting in my—

CHRISTIAN: Nose—

CYRANO:—My oar . . . Why am I putting in my
oar?
The quarrel's none of mine. However—now
I am here, I may as well go through with it.
Come Gascon—do your duty!—Suddenly
A sword flashed in the dark. I caught it fair—

CHRISTIAN: On the nose—

CYRANO: On my blade. Before I knew it,
There I was—

CHRISTIAN: Rubbing noses—

CYRANO: [*Pale and smiling*] Crossing swords
With half a score at once. I handed one—

CHRISTIAN: A nosegay—

CYRANO: [*Leaping at him*] Ventre-Saint-Gris! . . .
[*The Gascons tumble over each other to get a
good view. Arrived in front of* Christian, *who
has not moved an inch,* Cyrano *masters himself again, and continues*] He went down;
The rest gave way; I charged—

CHRISTIAN: Nose in the air—

CYRANO: I skewered two of them—disarmed a
third—
Another lunged— Paf! And I countered—
   CHRISTIAN: Pif!
CYRANO: [*Bellowing*] Tonnerre! Out of here!—All
of you!
   [*All the* Cadets *rush for the door*]
   FIRST CADET: At last—
The old lion wakes!
   CYRANO: All of you! Leave me here
Alone with that man!
   [*The lines following are heard brokenly, in the
confusion of getting through the door*]
   SECOND CADET: Bigre! He'll have the fellow
Chopped into sausage—
   RAGUENEAU: Sausage?—
   THIRD CADET: Mince-meat, then—
One of your pies!—
   RAGUENEAU: Am I pale? You look white
As a fresh napkin—
   CARBON: [*At the door*] Come!
   FOURTH CADET: He'll never leave
Enough of him to—
   FIFTH CADET: Why, it frightens *me.* . . .
To think of what will—
   SIXTH CADET: [*Closing the door*] Something hor-
rible
Beyond imagination . . .
   [*They are all gone: some through the street
door, some by the inner doors to right and left.
A few disappear up the staircase. Cyrano and
Christian stand face to face a moment, and
look at each other*]
   CYRANO: To my arms!
   CHRISTIAN: Sir? . . .
   CYRANO: You have courage!
   CHRISTIAN: Oh, that! . . .
   CYRANO: You are brave—
That pleases me.
   CHRISTIAN: You mean? . . .
   CYRANO: Do you not know
I am her brother? Come!
   CHRISTIAN: Whose?—
   CYRANO: Hers—Roxane!
   CHRISTIAN: Her . . . brother? You? [*Hurries to
him*]
   CYRANO: Her cousin. Much the same.
   CHRISTIAN: And she has told you? . . .
   CYRANO: Everything.
   CHRISTIAN: She loves me?
   CYRANO: Perhaps.
   CHRISTIAN: [*Takes both his hands*] My dear sir—
more than I can say,
I am honored—
   CYRANO: This is rather sudden.
   CHRISTIAN: Please
Forgive me—
   CYRANO: [*Holds him at arms length, looking at
him*] Why, he is a handsome devil,
This fellow!

   CHRISTIAN: On my honor—if you knew
How much I have admired—
   CYRANO: Yes, yes—and all
Those Noses which—
   CHRISTIAN: Please! I apologize.
   CYRANO: [*Change of tone*] Roxane expects a
letter—
   CHRISTIAN: Not from me?—
   CYRANO: Yes. Why not?
   CHRISTIAN: Once I write, that ruins all!
   CYRANO: And why?
   CHRISTIAN: Because . . . because I am a fool!
Stupid enough to hang myself!
   CYRANO: But no—
You are no fool; you call yourself a fool,
There's proof enough in that. Besides, you did not
Attack me like a fool.
   CHRISTIAN: Bah! Any one
Can pick a quarrel. Yes, I have a sort
Of rough and ready soldier's tongue. I know
That. But with any woman—paralyzed,
Speechless, dumb. I can only look at them.
Yet sometimes, when I go away, their eyes . . .
   CYRANO: Why not their hearts, if you should wait
and see?
   CHRISTIAN: No. I am one of those— I know—
those men
Who never can make love.
   CYRANO: Strange. . . . Now it seems
I, if I gave my mind to it, I might
Perhaps make love well.
   CHRISTIAN: Oh, if I had words
To say what I have here!
   CYRANO: If I could be
A handsome little Musketeer with eyes!—
   CHRISTIAN: Besides—you know Roxane—how sen-
sitive—
One rough word, and the sweet illusion—gone!
   CYRANO: I wish you might be my interpreter.
   CHRISTIAN: I wish I had your wit—
   CYRANO: Borrow it, then!—
Your beautiful young manhood—lend me that,
And we two make one hero of romance!
   CHRISTIAN: What?
   CYRANO: Would you dare repeat to
her the words
I gave you, day by day?
   CHRISTIAN: You mean?
   CYRANO: I mean
Roxane shall have no disillusionment!
Come, shall we win her both together? Take
The soul within this leathern jack of mine,
And breathe it into you?
   [*Touches him on the breast*]
                 So—there's my heart
Under your velvet, now!
   CHRISTIAN: But— Cyrano!—
   CYRANO: But— Christian, why not?
   CHRISTIAN: I am afraid—
   CYRANO: I know—

Afraid that when you have her all alone,
You lose all. Have no fear. It is yourself
She loves—give her yourself put into words—
My words, upon your lips!

CHRISTIAN: But . . . but your eyes! . . .
They burn like—

CYRANO: Will you? . . . Will you?

CHRISTIAN: Does it mean
So much to you?

CYRANO: [*Beside himself*] It means—
    [*Recovers, changes tone*]   A comedy,
A situation for a poet! Come,
Shall we collaborate? I'll be your cloak
Of darkness, your enchanted sword, your ring
To charm the fairy Princess!

CHRISTIAN: But the letter—
I cannot write—

CYRANO: Oh yes, the letter.
    [*He takes from his pocket the letter which he
    has written*] Here.

CHRISTIAN: What is this?

CYRANO: All there; all but the address.

CHRISTIAN: I—

CYRANO: Oh, you may send it. It will serve.

CHRISTIAN: But why
Have you done this?

CYRANO: I have amused myself
As we all do, we poets—writing vows
To Chloris, Phyllis—any pretty name—
You might have had a pocketful of them!
Take it, and turn to facts my fantasies—
I loosed these loves like doves into the air;
Give them a habitation and a home.
Here, take it— You will find me all the more
Eloquent, being insincere! Come!

CHRISTIAN: First,
There must be a few changes here and there—
Written at random, can it fit Roxane?

CYRANO: Like her own glove.

CHRISTIAN: No, but—

CYRANO: My son, have faith—
Faith in the love of women for themselves—
Roxane wil' know this letter for her own!

CHRISTIAN: [*Throws himself into the arms of
Cyrano. They stand embraced*] My friend!
    [*The door up stage opens a little. A Cadet steals
    in*]

THE CADET: Nothing. A silence like the tomb . . .
I hardly dare look—
    [*He sees the two*]
            Wha-at?
    [*The other Cadets crowd in behind him and see*]

THE CADET: No!—No!

SECOND CADET: Mon dieu!

THE MUSKETEER: [*Slaps his knee*] Well, well, well!

CARBON: Here's our devil . . . Christianized!
Offend one nostril, and he turns the other.

THE MUSKETEER: Now we are allowed to talk
    about his nose!
    [*Calls*]

Hey, Lise! Come here—
    [*Affectedly*] Snf! What a horrid smell!
What is it? . . .
    [*Plants himself in front of* Cyrano, *and looks
    at his nose in an impolite manner*]
            You ought to know about such things;
What seems to have died around here?

CYRANO: [*Knocks him backward over a bench*]
    Cabbage-heads!
    [*Joy. The* Cadets *have found their old* Cyrano
    again. General disturbance]

CURTAIN

ACT III.

Roxane's Kiss

A little square in the old Marais: old houses, and
a glimpse of narrow streets. On the right, the house
of Roxane and her garden wall, overhung with tall
shrubbery. Over the door of the house a balcony
and a tall window; to one side of the door, a
bench. Ivy clings to the wall; jasmine embraces the
balcony, trembles, and falls away. By the bench and
the jutting stonework of the wall one might easily
climb up to the balcony. Opposite, an ancient house
of the like character, brick and stone, whose front
door forms an entrance. The knocker on this door is
tied up in linen like an injured thumb. At the curtain
rise the Duenna is seated on the bench beside the
door. The window is wide open on Roxane's balcony;
a light within suggests that it is early evening. By the
Duenna stands Ragueneau dressed in what might be
the livery of one attached to the household. He is
by way of telling her something, and wiping his eyes
meanwhile.

RAGUENEAU: —And so she ran off with a Muske-
    teer!
I was ruined— I was alone— Remained
Nothing for me to do but hang myself,
So I did that. Presently along comes
Monsieur de Bergerac, and cuts me down,
And makes me steward to his cousin.

THE DUENNA: Ruined?—
I thought your pastry was a great success!

RAGUENEAU: [*Shakes his head*] Lise loved the sol-
    diers, and I loved the poets—
Mars ate up all the cakes Apollo left;
It did not take long. . . .

THE DUENNA: [*Calls up to window*] Roxane! Are
    you ready?
We are late!

VOICE OF ROXANE: [*Within*] Putting on my cape—

THE DUENNA: [*To* Ragueneau, *indicating the house
opposite*]   Clomire
Across the way receives on Thursday nights—

We are to have a psycho-colloquy
Upon the Tender Passion.
> RAGUENEAU: Ah—the Tender . . .
> THE DUENNA: [*Sighs*]—Passion! . . .
> [*Calls up to window*]
>   Roxane!—Hurry, dear—we shall miss
> The Tender Passion!
> ROXANE: Coming!—
> [*Music of stringed instruments off-stage ap-
> proaching*]
> THE VOICE OF CYRANO: [*Singing*] La, la, la!—
> THE DUENNA: A serenade?—How pleasant—
> CYRANO: No, no, no!—
> F natural, you natural born fool!
> [*Enters, followed by two pages, carrying the-
> orbos*]
> FIRST PAGE: [*Ironically*]
> No doubt your honor knows F natural
> When he hears—
> CYRANO: I am a musician, infant!—
> A pupil of Gassendi.
> THE PAGE: [*Plays and sings*] La, la,—
> CYRANO: Here—
> Give me that—
> [*He snatches the instrument from the* Page *and
> continues the tune*] La, la, la, la—
> ROXANE: [*Appears on the balcony*] Is that you,
> Cyrano?
> CYRANO: [*Singing*] I, who praise your lilies fair,
> But long to love your ro . . . ses!
> ROXANE: I'll be down—
> Wait—[*Goes in through window*]
> THE DUENNA: Did you train these virtuosi?
> CYRANO: No—
> I won them on a bet from D'Assoucy.
> We were debating a fine point of grammar
> When, pointing out these two young nightingales
> Dressed up like peacocks, with their instruments,
> He cries: "No, but I KNOW! I'll wager you
> A day of music." Well, of course he lost;
> And so until to-morrow they are mine,
> My private orchestra. Pleasant at first,
> But they become a trifle—
> [*To the* Pages]   Here! Go play
> A minuet to Montfleury—and tell him
> I sent you!
> [*The* Pages *go up to the exit.* Cyrano *turns to
> the* Duenna]
>   I came here as usual
> To inquire after our friend—
> [*To* Pages]
>   Play out of tune.
> And keep on playing!
> [*The* Pages *go out. He turns to the* Duenna]
>   —Our friend with the great soul.
> ROXANE: [*Enters in time to hear the last words*]
> He is beautiful and brilliant—and I love him!
> CYRANO: Do you find Christian . . . intellectual?
> ROXANE: More so than you, even.
> CYRANO: I am glad.

> ROXANE: No man
> Ever so beautifully said those things—
> Those pretty nothings that are everything.
> Sometimes he falls into a reverie;
> His inspiration fails—then all at once,
> He will say something absolutely . . . Oh! . . .
> CYRANO: Really!
> ROXANE: How like a man! You think a man
> Who has a handsome face must be a fool.
> CYRANO: He talks well about . . . matters of the
> heart?
> ROXANE: He does not talk; he rhapsodizes . . .
> dreams . . .
> CYRANO: [*Twisting his moustache*] He . . . writes
> well?
> ROXANE: Wonderfully. Listen now:
> [*Reciting as from memory*]
> "Take my heart; I shall have it all the more;
> Plucking the flowers, we keep the plant in bloom—"
> Well?
> CYRANO: Pooh!
> ROXANE: And this:
>   "Knowing you have in store
> More heart to give than I to find heart-room—"
> CYRANO: First he has too much, then too little; just
> How much heart does he need?
> ROXANE: [*Tapping her foot*] You are teasing me!
> You are jealous!
> CYRANO: [*Startled*] Jealous?
> ROXANE: Of his poetry—
> You poets are like that . . .
>   And these last lines
> Are they not the last word in tenderness?—
> "There is no more to say: only believe
> That unto you my whole heart gives one cry,
> And writing, writes down more than you receive;
> Sending you kisses through my finger-tips—
> Lady, O read my letter with your lips!"
> CYRANO: H'm, yes—those last lines . . . but he
> overwrites!
> ROXANE: Listen to this—
> CYRANO: You know them all by heart?
> ROXANE: Every one!
> CYRANO: [*Twisting his moustache*] I may call that
> flattering . . .
> ROXANE: He is a master!
> CYRANO: Oh—come.
> ROXANE: Yes—a master!
> CYRANO: [*Bowing*] A master—if you will!
> THE DUENNA: [*Comes down stage quickly*] Mon-
> sieur de Guiche!—
> [*To* Cyrano, *pushing him toward the house*]
> Go inside— If he does not find you here,
> It may be just as well. He may suspect —
> ROXANE: —My secret! Yes; he is in love with me
> And he is powerful. Let him not know—
> One look would frost my roses before bloom.
> CYRANO: [*Going into house*] Very well, very well!
> ROXANE: [*To De Guiche, as he enters*] We were
> just going—

DE GUICHE: I came only to say farewell.

ROXANE: You leave
Paris?

DE GUICHE: Yes—for the front.

ROXANE: Ah!

DE GUICHE: And to-night!

ROXANE: Ah!

DE GUICHE: We have orders to besiege Arras.

ROXANE: Arras?

DE GUICHE: Yes. My departure leaves you . . .
    cold?

ROXANE: [Politely] Oh! Not that.

DE GUICHE: It has left me desolate—
When shall I see you? Ever? Did you know
I was made Colonel?

ROXANE: [Indifferent] Bravo.

DE GUICHE: Regiment
Of the Guards.

ROXANE: [Catching her breath] Of the Guards?—

DE GUICHE: His regiment.
Your cousin, the mighty man of words!—
    [Grimly]
                 Down there
We may have an accounting!

ROXANE: [Suffocating] Are you sure
The Guards are ordered?

DE GUICHE: Under my command!

ROXANE: [Sinks down, breathless, on the bench;
aside] Christian!—

DE GUICHE: What is it?

ROXANE: [Losing control of herself] To the war—
    perhaps
Never again to— When a woman cares,
Is that nothing?

DE GUICHE: [Surprised and delighted] You say this
now—to me—
Now, at the very moment?—

ROXANE: [Recovers—changes her tone]
             Tell me something:
My cousin— You say you mean to be revenged
On him. Do you mean that?

DE GUICHE: [Smiles] Why? Would you care?

ROXANE: Not for him.

DE GUICHE: Do you see him?

ROXANE: Now and then.

DE GUICHE: He goes about everywhere nowadays
With one of the Cadets—de Neuve—Neuville—
Neuvillers—

ROXANE: [Coolly] A tall man?—

DE GUICHE: Blond—

ROXANE: Rosy cheeks?—

DE GUICHE: Handsome!—

ROXANE: Pooh!

DE GUICHE: And a fool.

ROXANE: [Languidly] So he appears . . .
    [Animated]
But Cyrano? What will you do to him?
Order him into danger? He loves that!
I know what I should do.

DE GUICHE: What?

ROXANE: Leave him here
With his Cadets, while all the regiment
Goes on to glory! That would torture him—
To sit all through the war with folded arms—
I know his nature. If you hate that man,
Strike at his self-esteem.

DE GUICHE: Oh woman—woman!
Who but a woman would have thought of this?

ROXANE: He'll eat his heart out, while his Gascon
    friends
Bite their nails all day long in Paris here.
And you will be avenged!

DE GUICHE: You love me then,
A little? . . .
    [She smiles]
          Making my enemies your own,
Hating them—I should like to see in that
A sign of love, Roxane.

ROXANE: Perhaps it is one . . .

DE GUICHE: [Shows a number of folded despatches]
Here are the orders—for each company—
Ready to send . . .
    [Selects one]
          So— This is for the Guards—
I'll keep that. Aha, Cyrano!
    [To Roxane]
             You too,
You play your little games, do you?

ROXANE: [Watching him] Sometimes . . .

DE GUICHE: [Close to her, speaking hurriedly]
And you!—Oh, I am mad over you!—Listen—
I leave to-night—but—let you through my hands
Now, when I feel you trembling?—Listen— Close
by,
In the Rue d'Orléans, the Capuchins
Have their new convent. By their law, no layman
May pass inside those walls. I'll see to that—
Their sleeves are wide enough to cover me—
The servants of my Uncle Cardinal
Will fear his nephew. So—I'll come to you
Masked, after everyone knows I have gone—
Oh, let me wait one day!—

ROXANE: If this be known,
Your honor—

DE GUICHE: Bah!

ROXANE: The war—your duty—

DE GUICHE: [Blows away an imaginary feather]
Phoo!—
Only say yes!

ROXANE: No!

DE GUICHE: Whisper . . .

ROXANE: [Tenderly] I ought not
To let you . . .

DE GUICHE: Ah! . . .

ROXANE: [Pretends to break down] Ah, go!
    [Aside]
           —Christian remains—
    [Aloud—heroically]
I must have you a hero—Antoine . . .

DE GUICHE: Heaven! . . .

So you can love—

ROXANE: One for whose sake I fear.

DE GUICHE: [*Triumphant*]

I go!

Will that content you?

[*Kisses her hand*]

ROXANE: Yes—my friend!

[*He goes out*]

THE DUENNA: [*As* De Guiche *disappears, making a deep curtsey behind his back, and imitating* Roxane's *intense tone*] Yes—my friend!

ROXANE: [*Quickly, close to her*]

                    Not a word to Cyrano—

He would never forgive me if he knew

I stole his war!

[*She calls toward the house*] Cousin!

[Cyrano *comes out of the house; she turns to him, indicating the house opposite*]

                    We are going over—

Alcandre speaks to-night—and Lysimon.

THE DUENNA: [*Puts finger in her ear*]

My little finger says we shall not hear

Everything.

CYRANO: Never mind me—

THE DUENNA: [*Across the street*] Look— Oh, look!

The knocker tied up in a napkin—Yes,

They muzzled you because you bark too loud

And interrupt the lecture—little beast!

ROXANE: [*As the door opens*] Enter . . .

[*To* Cyrano]

                    If Christian comes, tell him to wait.

CYRANO: Oh—

[Roxane *returns*]

                    When he comes, what will you talk about?

You always know beforehand.

ROXANE: About . . .

CYRANO: Well?

ROXANE: You will not tell him, will you?

CYRANO: I am dumb.

ROXANE: About nothing! Or about everything—

I shall say: "Speak of love in your own words—

Improvise! Rhapsodize! Be eloquent!"

CYRANO: [*Smiling*] Good!

ROXANE: Sh!—

CYRANO: Sh!—

ROXANE: Not a word!

[*She goes in; the door closes*]

CYRANO: [*Bowing*] Thank you so much—

ROXANE: [*Opens door and puts out her head*]

He must be unprepared—

CYRANO: Of course!

ROXANE: Sh!—

[*Goes in again*]

CYRANO: [*Calls*] Christian!

[Christian *enters*]

I have your theme—bring on your memory!—

Here is your chance now to surpass yourself,

No time to lose— Come! Look intelligent—

Come home and learn your lines.

CHRISTIAN: No.

CYRANO: What?

CHRISTIAN: I'll wait

Here for Roxane.

CYRANO: What lunacy is this?

Come quickly!

CHRISTIAN: No, I say! I have had enough—

Taking my words, my letters, all from you—

Making our love a little comedy!

It was a game at first; but now—she cares . . .

Thanks to you. I am not afraid. I'll speak

For myself now.

CYRANO: Undoubtedly!

CHRISTIAN: I will!

Why not? I am no such fool—you shall see!

Besides—my dear friend—you have taught me much:

I ought to know something . . . By God, I know

Enough to take a woman in my arms!

[Roxane *appears in the doorway, opposite*]

There she is now . . . Cyrano, wait! Stay here!

CYRANO: [*Bows*] Speak for yourself, my friend!

[*He goes out*]

ROXANE: [*Taking leave of the company*]—Barthénoide!

Alcandre! . . . Grémione! . . .

THE DUENNA: I told you so—

We missed the Tender Passion!

[*She goes into* Roxane's *house*]

ROXANE: Urimédonte!—

Adieu!

[*As the guests disappear down the street, she turns to* Christian]

                    Is that you, Christian? Let us stay

Here, in the twilight. They are gone. The air

Is fragrant. We shall be alone. Sit down

There—so . . .

[*They sit on the bench*]

                    Now tell me things.

CHRISTIAN: [*After a silence*] I love you.

ROXANE: [*Closes her eyes*] Yes,

Speak to me about love . . .

CHRISTIAN: I love you.

ROXANE: Now

Be eloquent! . . .

CHRISTIAN: I love—

ROXANE: [*Opens her eyes*] You have your theme—

Improvise! Rhapsodize!

CHRISTIAN: I love you so!

ROXANE: Of course. And then? . . .

CHRISTIAN: And then . . . Oh, I should be

So happy if you loved me too! Roxane,

Say that you love me too!

ROXANE: [*Making a face*] I ask for cream—

You give me milk and water. Tell me first

A little, how you love me.

CHRISTIAN: Very much.

ROXANE: Oh—tell me how you *feel!*

CHRISTIAN: [*Coming nearer, and devouring her with his eyes*] Your throat . . . If only

I might . . . kiss it—

ROXANE: Christian!

CHRISTIAN: I love you so!

ROXANE: [*Makes as if to rise*] Again?

CHRISTIAN: [*Desperately, restraining her*] No, not again— I do not love you—

ROXANE: [*Settles back*] That is better . . .

CHRISTIAN: I adore you!

ROXANE: Oh!— [*Rises and moves away*]

CHRISTIAN: I know; I grow absurd.

ROXANE: [*Coldly*] And that displeases me As much as if you had grown ugly.

CHRISTIAN: I—

ROXANE: Gather your dreams together into words!

CHRISTIAN: I love—

ROXANE: I know; you love me. Adieu.
[*She goes to the house*]

CHRISTIAN: No, But wait—please—let me— I was going to say—

ROXANE: [*Pushes the door open*] That you adore me. Yes; I know that too. No! . . . Go away! . . .
[*She goes in and shuts the door in his face*]

CHRISTIAN: I . . . I . . .

CYRANO: [*Enters*] A great success!

CHRISTIAN: Help me!

CYRANO: Not I.

CHRISTIAN: I cannot live unless She loves me—now, this moment!

CYRANO: How the devil Am I to teach you now—this moment?

CHRISTIAN: [*Catches him by the arm*]—Wait!— Look! Up there!—Quick—
[*The light shows in* Roxane's *window*]

CYRANO: Her window—

CHRISTIAN: [*Wailing*] I shall die!—

CYRANO: Less noise!

CHRISTIAN: Oh, I—

CYRANO: It does seem fairly dark—

CHRISTIAN: [*Excitedly*] Well?—Well?—Well?—

CYRANO: Let us try what can be done; It is more than you deserve—stand over there, Idiot—there!—before the balcony— Let me stand underneath. I'll whisper you What to say.

CHRISTIAN: She may hear—she may—

CYRANO: Less noise!
[*The* Pages *appear up stage*]

FIRST PAGE: Hep!—

CYRANO: [*Finger to lips*] Sh!—

FIRST PAGE: [*Low voice*] We serenaded Montfleury!—
What next?

CYRANO: Down to the corner of the street— One this way—and the other over there— If anybody passes, play a tune!

PAGE: What tune, O musical Philosopher?

CYRANO: Sad for a man, or merry for a woman— Now go!
[*The* Pages *disappear, one toward each corner of the street*]

CYRANO: [*To* Christian] Call her!

CHRISTIAN: Roxane!

CYRANO: Wait . . . [*Gathers up a handful of pebbles*] Gravel . . . [*Throws it at the window*] There!—

ROXANE: [*Opens the window*] Who is calling?

CHRISTIAN: I—

ROXANE: Who?

CHRISTIAN: Christian.

ROXANE: You again?

CHRISTIAN: I had to tell you—

CYRANO: [*Under the balcony*] Good— Keep your voice down.

ROXANE: No. Go away. You tell me nothing.

CHRISTIAN: Please!—

ROXANE: You do not love me any more—

CHRISTIAN: [*To whom* Cyrano *whispers his words*] No—no— Not any more— I love you . . . evermore . . . And ever . . . more and more!

ROXANE: [*About to close the window—pauses*] A little better . . .

CHRISTIAN: [*Same business*] Love grows and struggles like . . . an angry child . . . Breaking my heart . . . his cradle . . .

ROXANE: [*Coming out on the balcony*] Better still— But . . . such a babe is dangerous; why not Have smothered it new-born? . . .

CHRISTIAN: [*Same business*] And so I do . . . And yet he lives . . . I found . . . as you shall find . . . This new-born babe . . . an infant . . . Hercules!

ROXANE: [*Further forward*] Good!—

CHRISTIAN: [*Same business*] Strong enough . . . at birth . . . to strangle those Two serpents—Doubt and . . . Pride.

ROXANE: [*Leans over balcony*] Why, very well! Tell me now why you speak so haltingly— Has your imagination gone lame?

CYRANO: [*Thrusts* Christian *under the balcony, and stands in his place*] Here— This grows too difficult!

ROXANE: Your words to-night Hesitate. Why?

CYRANO: [*In a low tone, imitating* Christian] Through the warm summer gloom They grope in darkness toward the light of you.

ROXANE: My words, well aimed, find you more readily.

CYRANO: My heart is open wide and waits for them— Too large a mark to miss! My words fly home, Heavy with honey like returning bees, To your small secret ear. Moreover—yours Fall to me swiftly. Mine more slowly rise.

ROXANE: Yet not so slowly as they did at first.

CYRANO: They have learned the way, and you have welcomed them.

ROXANE: [*Softly*] Am I so far above you now?

CYRANO: So far—
If you let fall upon me one hard word,
Out of that height—you crush me!
ROXANE: [*Turns*] I'll come down—
CYRANO: [*Quickly*] No!
ROXANE: [*Points out the bench under the balcony*] Stand you on the bench. Come nearer!
CYRANO: [*Recoils into the shadow*] No!—
ROXANE: And why—so great a *No?*
CYRANO: [*More and more overcome by emotion*]
Let me enjoy
The one moment I ever—my one chance
To speak to you . . . unseen!
ROXANE: Unseen?—
CYRANO: Yes!—yes . . .
Night, making all things dimly beautiful,
One veil over us both— You only see
The darkness of a long cloak in the gloom,
And I the whiteness of a summer gown—
You are all light— I am all shadow! . . . How
Can you know what this moment means to me?
If I was ever eloquent—
ROXANE: You were
Eloquent—
CYRANO: —You have never heard till now
My own heart speaking!
ROXANE: Why not?
CYRANO: Until now,
I spoke through . . .
ROXANE: Yes?—
CYRANO: —through that sweet drunkenness
You pour into the world out of your eyes!
But to-night . . . but to-night, I indeed speak
For the first time!
ROXANE: For the first time— Your voice,
Even, is not the same.
CYRANO: [*Passionately; moves nearer*] How should
it be?
I have another voice to-night—my own,
Myself, daring—
[*He stops, confused; then tries to recover himself*]
Where was I? . . . I forget! . . .
Forgive me. This is all sweet like a dream . . .
Strange—like a dream . . .
ROXANE: How, strange?
CYRANO: Is it not so
To be myself to you, and have no fear
Of moving you to laughter?
ROXANE: Laughter—why?
CYRANO: [*Struggling for an explanation*]
Because . . . What am I . . . What is any man,
That he dare ask for you? Therefore my heart
Hides behind phrases. There's a modesty
In these things too— I come here to pluck down
Out of the sky the evening star—then smile,
And stoop to gather little flowers.
ROXANE: Are they
Not sweet, those little flowers?

CYRANO: Not enough sweet
For you and me, to-night!
ROXANE: [*Breathless*] You never spoke
To me like this . . .
CYRANO: Little things, pretty things—
Arrows and hearts and torches—roses red,
And violets blue—are these all? Come away,
And breathe fresh air! Must we keep on and on
Sipping stale honey out of tiny cups
Decorated with golden tracery,
Drop by drop, all day long? We are alive;
We thirst— Come away, plunge, and drink, and drown
In the great river flowing to the sea!
ROXANE: But . . . Poetry?
CYRANO: I have made rimes for you—
Not now— Shall we insult Nature, this night,
These flowers, this moment—shall we set all these
To phrases from a letter by Voiture?
Look once at the high stars that shine in heaven,
And put off artificiality!
Have you not seen great gaudy hothouse flowers,
Barren, without fragrance?—Souls are like that:
Forced to show all, they soon become all show—
The means to Nature's end ends meaningless!
ROXANE: But . . . Poetry?
CYRANO: Love hates that game of words!
It is a crime to fence with life— I tell you,
There comes one moment, once—and God help
those
Who pass that moment by!—when Beauty stands
Looking into the soul with grave, sweet eyes
That sicken at pretty words!
ROXANE: If that be true—
And when that moment comes to you and me—
What words will you? . . .
CYRANO: All those, all those, all those
That blossom in my heart, I'll fling to you—
Armfuls of loose bloom! Love, I love beyond
Breath, beyond reason, beyond love's own power
Of loving! Your name is like a golden bell
Hung in my heart; and when I think of you,
I tremble, and the bell swings and rings—
"Roxane!" . . .
"Roxane!" . . . along my veins, "Roxane!" . . .
I know
All small forgotten things that once meant You—
I remember last year, the First of May,
A little before noon, you had your hair
Drawn low, that one time only. Is that strange?
You know how, after looking at the sun,
One sees red suns everywhere—so, for hours
After the flood of sunshine that you are,
My eyes are blinded by your burning hair!
ROXANE: [*Very low*] Yes . . . that is . . .
Love—
CYRANO: Yes, that is Love—that wind
Of terrible and jealous beauty, blowing
Over me—that dark fire, that music . . .
Ye

Love seeketh not his own! Dear, you may take
My happiness to make you happier,
Even though you never know I gave it you—
Only let me hear sometimes, all alone,
The distant laughter of your joy! . . .

                    I never
Look at you, but there's some new virtue born
In me, some new courage. Do you begin
To understand, a little? Can you feel
My soul, there in the darkness, breathe on you?
—Oh, but to-night, now, I dare say these things—
I . . . to you . . . and you hear them! . . . It is
  too much!
In my most sweet unreasonable dreams,
I have not hoped for this! Now let me die,
Having lived. It is my voice, mine, my own,
That makes you tremble there in the green gloom
Above me—for you do tremble, as a blossom
Among the leaves— You tremble, and I can feel,
All the way down along these jasmine branches,
Whether you will or no, the passion of you
Trembling . . .
    [*He kisses wildly the end of a drooping spray
    of jasmine*]
  ROXANE: Yes, I do tremble . . . and I
  weep . . .
And I love you . . . and I am yours . . . and you
Have made me thus!
  CYRANO: [*After a pause; quietly*] What is death
  like, I wonder?
I know everything else now . . .
                  I have done
This, to you—I, myself . . .
              Only let me
Ask one thing more—
  CHRISTIAN: [*Under the balcony*] One kiss!
  ROXANE: [*Startled*] One?—
  CYRANO: [*To* Christian] You! . . .
  ROXANE: You ask me
For—
  CYRANO: I . . . Yes, but—I mean—
  [*To* Christian] You go too far!
  CHRISTIAN: She is willing!—Why not make the
  most of it?
  CYRANO: [*To* Roxane] I did ask . . . but I know
  I ask too much . . .
  ROXANE: Only one— Is that all?
  CYRANO: All!—How much more
Than all!—I know—I frighten you—I ask . . .
I ask you to refuse—
  CHRISTIAN: [*To* Cyrano] But why? Why? Why?
  CYRANO: Christian, be quiet!
  ROXANE: [*Leaning over*] What is that you say
To yourself?
  CYRANO: I am angry with myself
Because I go too far, and so I say
To myself: "Christian, be quiet!"—
    [*The theorbos begin to play*]
                    Hark—someone
Is coming—

[Roxane *closes her window.* Cyrano *listens to
the theorbos, one of which plays a gay melody,
the other a mournful one*]
          A sad tune, a merry tune—
Man, woman—what do they mean?—
  [*A* Capuchin *enters; he carries a lantern, and
  goes from house to house, looking at the doors*]
                  Aha!—a priest!
[*To the* Capuchin]
What is this new game of Diogenes?
  THE CAPUCHIN: I am looking for the house of
Madame—
  CHRISTIAN: [*Impatient*] Bah!—
  THE CAPUCHIN: Madeleine Robin—
  CHRISTIAN: What does he want?
  CYRANO: [*To the* Capuchin; *points out a street*]
  This way—
To the right—keep to the right—
  THE CAPUCHIN: I thank you, sir!—
I'll say my beads for you to the last grain.
  CYRANO: Good fortune, father, and my service to
  you!
  [*The* Capuchin *goes out*]
  CHRISTIAN: Win me that kiss!
  CYRANO: No.
  CHRISTIAN: Sooner or later—
  CYRANO: True . . .
That is true . . . Soon or late, it will be so
Because you are young and she is beautiful—
  [*To himself*]
Since it must be, I had rather be myself
  [*The window re-opens.* Christian *hides under
  the balcony*]
The cause of . . . what must be.
  ROXANE: [*Out on the balcony*] Are you still there?
We were speaking of—
  CYRANO: A kiss. The word is sweet—
What will the deed be? Are your lips afraid
Even of its burning name? Not much afraid—
Not too much! Have you not unwittingly
Laid aside laughter, slipping beyond speech
Insensibly, already, without fear,
From words to smiles . . . from smiles to sighs . . .
  from sighing,
Even to tears? One step more—only one—
From a tear to a kiss—one step, one thrill!
  ROXANE: Hush!—
  CYRANO: And what is a kiss, when all is done?
A promise given under seal—a vow
Taken before the shrine of memory—
A signature acknowledged—a rosy dot
Over the *i* of Loving—a secret whispered
To listening lips apart—a moment made
Immortal, with a rush of wings unseen—
A sacrament of blossoms, a new song
Sung by two hearts to an old simple tune—
The ring of one horizon around two souls
Together, all alone!
  ROXANE: Hush! . . .
  CYRANO: Why, what shame?—

There was a Queen of France, not long ago,
And a great lord of England—a queen's gift,
A crown jewel!—

ROXANE: Indeed!

CYRANO: Indeed, like him,
I have my sorrows and my silences;
Like her, you are the queen I dare adore;
Like him I am faithful and forlorn—

ROXANE: Like him,
Beautiful—

CYRANO: [*Aside*] So I am—I forgot that!

ROXANE: Then— Come! . . . Gather your sacred
     blossom . . .

CYRANO: [*To* Christian] Go!—

ROXANE: Your crown jewel . . .

CYRANO: Go on!—

ROXANE: Your old new song . . .

CYRANO: Climb!—

CHRISTIAN: [*Hesitates*] No— Would you?—not
     yet—

ROXANE: Your moment made
Immortal . . .

CYRANO: [*Pushing him*] Climb up, animal!

[Christian *springs on the bench, and climbs by
the pillars, the branches, the vines, until he
bestrides the balcony railing*]

CHRISTIAN: Roxane! . . .

[*He takes her in his arms and bends over her*]

CYRANO: [*Very low*] Ah! . . . Roxane! . . .
     I have won what I have won—
The feast of love—and I am Lazarus!
Yet . . . I have something here that is mine now
And was not mine before I spoke the words
That won her—not for me! . . . Kissing my words
My words, upon your lips!

[*The theorbos begin to play*]

     A merry tune—
A sad tune— So! The Capuchin!

[*He pretends to be running, as if he had arrived
from a distance; then calls up to the balcony*]

     Hola!

ROXANE: Who is it?

CYRANO: I. Is Christian there with you?

CHRISTIAN: [*Astonished*] Cyrano!

ROXANE: Good morrow, Cousin!

CYRANO: Cousin, . . . good
     morrow!

ROXANE: I am coming down.

[*She disappears into the house. The* Capuchin
enters up stage]

CHRISTIAN: [*Sees him*] Oh—again!

THE CAPUCHIN: [*To* Cyrano] She lives *here*, Made-
     leine Robin!

CYRANO: You said RO-LIN.

THE CAPUCHIN: No—
R-O-B-I-N

ROXANE: [*Appears on the threshold of the house,
followed by* Ragueneau *with a lantern, and by* Chris-
tian] What is it?

THE CAPUCHIN: A letter.

CHRISTIAN: Oh! . . .

THE CAPUCHIN: [*To* Roxane]
Some matter profitable to the soul—
A very noble lord gave it to me!

ROXANE: [*To* Christian] De Guiche!

CHRISTIAN: He dares?—

ROXANE: It will not be for long;
When he learns that I love you . . .

[*By the light of the lantern which* Ragueneau
*holds, she reads the letter in a low tone, as if to
herself*]

     "Mademoiselle
The drums are beating, and the regiment
Arms for the march. Secretly I remain
Here, in the Convent. I have disobeyed;
I shall be with you soon. I send this first
By an old monk, as simple as a sheep,
Who understands nothing of this. Your smile
Is more than I can bear, and seek no more.
Be alone to-night, waiting for one who dares
To hope you will forgive . . .—" etcetera—

[*To the* Capuchin]
Father, this letter concerns you . . .

[*To* Christian]

     —and you.
Listen:

[*The others gather around her. She pretends to
read from the letter, aloud*]

     "Mademoiselle:
     The Cardinal
Will have his way, although against your will;
That is why I am sending this to you
By a most holy man, intelligent,
Discreet. You will communicate to him
Our order to perform, here and at once
The rite of . . .

[*Turns the page*]

     —Holy Matrimony. You
And Christian will be married privately
In your house. I have sent him to you. I know
You hesitate. Be resigned, nevertheless,
To the Cardinal's command, who sends herewith
His blessing. Be assured, also of my own
Respect and high consideration—*signed,*
Your very humble and—etcetera—"

THE CAPUCHIN: A noble lord! I said so—never
     fear—
A worthy lord!—a very worthy lord!—

ROXANE: [*To* Christian] Am I a good reader of
     letters?

CHRISTIAN: [*Motions toward the* Capuchin] Care-
     ful!—

ROXANE: [*In a tragic tone*] Oh, this is terrible!

THE CAPUCHIN: [*Turns the light of his lantern on*
Cyrano] You are to be—

CHRISTIAN: *I* am the bridegroom!

THE CAPUCHIN: [*Turns his lantern upon* Christian;
then, as if some suspicion crossed his mind, upon

seeing the young man so handsome] Oh—why,
you . . .

ROXANE: [*Quickly*] Look here—
"Postscript: Give to the Convent in my name
One hundred and twenty pistoles"—

THE CAPUCHIN: Think of it!
A worthy lord—a very worthy lord! . . .

[*To* Roxane, *solemnly*]
Daughter, resign yourself!

ROXANE: [*With an air of martyrdom*] I am resigned . . .

[*While* Ragueneau *opens the door for the*
Capuchin *and* Christian *invites him to enter,*
she turns to Cyrano]
De Guiche may come. Keep him out here with you
Do not let him—

CYRANO: I understand! [*To the* Capuchin] How
long
Will you be?—

THE CAPUCHIN: Oh, a quarter of an hour.

CYRANO: [*Hurrying them into the house*] Hurry—
I'll wait here—

ROXANE: [*To* Christian] Come!

[*They go into the house*]

CYRANO: Now then, to make
His Grace delay that quarter of an hour . . .
I have it!—up here—

[*He steps on the bench, and climbs up the*
wall toward the balcony. The theorbos begin
to play a mournful melody]
                        Sad music— Ah, a man! . . .

[*The music pauses on a sinister tremolo*]
Oh—very much a man!

[*He sits astride of the railing and, drawing*
toward him a long branch of one of the trees
which border the garden wall, he grasps it with
both hands, ready to swing himself down]
                        So—not too high—

[*He peers down at the ground*]
I must float gently through the atmosphere—

DE GUICHE: [*Enters masked, groping in the dark*
toward the house] Where is that cursed, bleating
Capuchin?

CYRANO: What if he knows my voice?—the devil!
—Tic-tac,
Bergerac—we unlock our Gascon tongue;
A good strong accent—

DE GUICHE: Here is the house—all dark—
Damn this mask!

[*As he is about to enter the house,* Cyrano
leaps from the balcony, still holding fast to
the branch, which bends and swings him be-
tween De Guiche *and the door; then he re-*
leases the branch and pretends to fall heavily
as though from a height. He lands flatly on the
ground, where he lies motionless, as if stunned.
De Guiche *leaps back*]
                        What is that?

[*When he lifts his eyes, the branch has sprung*

back into place. He can see nothing but the
sky; he does not understand]
                        Why . . . where did this man
Fall from?

CYRANO: [*Sits up, and speaks with a strong ac-*
cent]—The moon!

DE GUICHE: You—

CYRANO: From the moon, the moon!
I fell out of the moon!

DE GUICHE: The fellow is mad—

CYRANO: [*Dreamily*] Where am I?

DE GUICHE: Why—

CYRANO: What time is it? What place
Is this? What day? What season?

DE GUICHE: You—

CYRANO: I am stunned!

DE GUICHE: My dear sir—

CYRANO: Like a bomb—a bomb—I fell
From the moon!

DE GUICHE: Now, see here—

CYRANO: [*Rising to his feet, and speaking in a*
terrible voice] I say, the moon!

DE GUICHE: [*Recoils*] Very well—if you say so—
[*Aside*]
                        Raving mad!—

CYRANO: [*Advancing upon him*] I am not speaking metaphorically!

DE GUICHE: Pardon.

CYRANO: A hundred years—an hour ago—
I really cannot say how long I fell—
I was in yonder shining sphere—

DE GUICHE: [*Shrugs*] Quite so.
Please let me pass.

CYRANO: [*Interposes himself*] Where am I? Tell the
truth—
I can bear it. In what quarter of the globe
Have I descended like a meteorite?

DE GUICHE: Morbleu!

CYRANO: I could not choose my place to fall—
The earth spun round so fast— Was it the Earth,
I wonder?—Or is this another world?
Another moon? Whither have I been drawn
By the dead weight of my posterior?

DE GUICHE: Sir, I repeat—

CYRANO: [*With a sudden cry, which causes* De
Guiche *to recoil again*] His face! My God—black!

DE GUICHE: [*Carries his hand to his mask*] Oh!—

CYRANO: [*Terrified*] Are you a native? Is this
Africa?

DE GUICHE: —This mask!

CYRANO: [*Somewhat reassured*] Are we in Venice?
Genoa?

DE GUICHE: [*Tries to pass him*] A lady is waiting
for me.

CYRANO: [*Quite happy again*] So this is Paris!

DE GUICHE: [*Smiling in spite of himself*] This fool
becomes amusing.

CYRANO: Ah! You smile?

DE GUICHE: I do. Kindly permit me—

CYRANO: [*Delighted*] Dear old Paris—
Well, well!—
   [*Wholly at his ease, smiles, bows, arranges his dress*]
           Excuse my appearance. I arrive
By the last thunderbolt—a trifle singed
As I came through the ether. These long journeys—
You know! There are so few conveniences!
My eyes are full of star-dust. On my spurs,
Some sort of fur . . . Planet's apparently . . .
   [*Plucks something from his sleeve*]
Look—on my doublet— That's a Comet's hair!
   [*He blows something from the back of his hand*]
Phoo!
   DE GUICHE: [*Grows angry*] Monsieur—
   CYRANO: [*As De Guiche is about to push past, thrusts his leg in the way*] Here's a tooth, stuck in my boot,
From the Great Bear. Trying to get away,
I tripped over the Scorpion and came down
Slap, into one scale of the Balances—
The pointer marks my weight this moment . . .
   [*Pointing upward*]   See?
   [*De Guiche makes a sudden movement. Cyrano catches his arm*]
Be careful! If you struck me on the nose,
It would drip milk!
   DE GUICHE: Milk?
   CYRANO: From the Milky Way!
   DE GUICHE: Hell!
   CYRANO: No, no—Heaven.
   [*Crossing his arms*] Curious place up there—
Did you know Sirius wore a nightcap? True!
   [*Confidentially*]
The Little Bear is still too young to bite.
   [*Laughing*]
My foot caught in the Lyre, and broke a string.
   [*Proudly*]
Well—when I write my book, and tell the tale
Of my adventures—all these little stars
That shake out of my cloak—I must save those
To use for asterisks!
   DE GUICHE: That will do now—
I wish—
   CYRANO: Yes, yes—I know—
   DE GUICHE: Sir—
   CYRANO: You desire
To learn from my own lips the character
Of the moon's surface—its inhabitants
If any—
   DE GUICHE: [*Loses patience and shouts*] I desire no such thing! I—
   CYRANO: [*Rapidly*] You wish to know by what mysterious means
I reached the moon?—well—confidentially—
It was a new invention of my own.
   DE GUICHE: [*Discouraged*] Drunk too—as well as mad!
   CYRANO: I scorned the eagle

Of Regiomontanus, and the dove
Of Archytas!
   DE GUICHE: A learned lunatic!—
   CYRANO: I imitated no one. I myself
Discovered not one scheme merely, but six—
Six ways to violate the virgin sky!
   [*De Guiche has succeeded in passing him, and moves toward the door of* Roxane's *house.* Cyrano *follows, ready to use violence if necessary*]
   DE GUICHE: [*Looks around*] Six?
   CYRANO: [*With increasing volubility*] As for instance—Having stripped myself
Bare as a wax candle, adorn my form
With crystal vials filled with morning dew,
And so be drawn aloft, as the sun rises
Drinking the mist of dawn!
   DE GUICHE: [*Takes a step toward* Cyrano] Yes—
   that makes one.
   CYRANO: [*Draws back to lead him away from the door; speaks faster and faster*]
Or, sealing up the air in a cedar chest,
Rarefy it by means of mirrors, placed
In an icosahedron.
   DE GUICHE: [*Takes another step*] Two.
   CYRANO: [*Still retreating*] Again,
I might construct a rocket, in the form
Of a huge locust, driven by impulses
Of villainous saltpetre from the rear,
Upward, by leaps and bounds.
   DE GUICHE: [*Interested in spite of himself, and counting on his fingers*] Three.
   CYRANO: [*Same business*] Or again,
Smoke having a natural tendency to rise,
Blow in a globe enough to raise me.
   DE GUICHE: [*Same business, more and more astonished*] Four!
   CYRANO: Or since Diana, as old fables tell,
Draws forth to fill her crescent horn, the marrow
Of bulls and goats—to annoint myself therewith.
   DE GUICHE: [*Hypnotized*] Five!—
   CYRANO: [*Has by this time led him all the way across the street, close to a bench*] Finally—seated on an iron plate,
To hurl a magnet in the air—the iron
Follows— I catch the magnet—throw again—
And so proceed indefinitely.
   DE GUICHE: Six!—
All excellent,—and which did you adopt?
   CYRANO: [*Coolly*] Why, none of them. . . . A seventh.
   DE GUICHE: Which was?—
   CYRANO: Guess!—
   DE GUICHE: An interesting idiot, this!
   CYRANO: [*Imitates the sound of waves with his voice, and their movement by large, vague gestures*]
Hoo! . . . Hoo! . . .
   DE GUICHE: Well?
   CYRANO: Have you guessed it yet?
   DE GUICHE: Why, no

CYRANO: [*Grandiloquent*] The ocean! . . .
What hour its rising tide seeks the full moon,
I laid me on the strand, fresh from the spray,
My head fronting the moonbeams, since the hair
Retains moisture—and so I slowly rose
As upon angels' wings, effortlessly,
Upward—then suddenly I felt a shock!—
And then . . .

DE GUICHE: [*Overcome by curiosity, sits down on the bench*] And then?

CYRANO: And then—
[*Changes abruptly to his natural voice*]
                              The time is up!—
Fifteen minutes, your Grace!—You are now free;
And—they are bound—in wedlock.

DE GUICHE: [*Leaping up*] Am I drunk?
That voice . . .
[*The door of* Roxane's *house opens; lackeys appear, bearing lighted candles. Lights up.* Cyrano *removes his hat*]
                              And that nose!—Cyrano!

CYRANO: [*Saluting*] Cyrano! . . .
This very moment, they have exchanged rings.

DE GUICHE: Who?
[*He turns up stage. Tableau: between the lackeys,* Roxane *and* Christian *appear, hand in hand. The* Capuchin *follows them, smiling.* Ragueneau *holds aloft a torch. The* Duenna *brings up the rear, in a negligée, and a pleasant flutter of emotion*]
                              Zounds!
[*To* Roxane]
                              You?—[*Recognizes* Christian]
He?—
[*Saluting* Roxane] My sincere compliments!
[*To* Cyrano]
You also, my inventor of machines!
Your rigmarole would have detained a saint
Entering Paradise—decidedly
You must not fail to write that book some day!

CYRANO: [*Bowing*] Sir, I engage myself to do so.
[*Leads the bridal pair down to* De Guiche *and strokes with great satisfaction his long white beard*]
                              My lord,
The handsome couple you—and God—have joined
Together!

DE GUICHE: [*Regarding him with a frosty eye*]
Quite so.
[*Turns to* Roxane]
                              Madame, kindly bid
Your . . . husband farewell.

ROXANE: Oh!—

DE GUICHE: [*To* Christian] Your regiment
Leaves to-night, sir. Report at once!

ROXANE: You mean
For the front? The war?

DE GUICHE: Certainly!

ROXANE: I thought
The Cadets were not going—

DE GUICHE: Oh yes, they are!
[*Taking out the despatch from his pocket*]
Here is the order—
[*To* Christian] Baron! Deliver this.

ROXANE: [*Throws herself into* Christian's *arms*]
Christian!

DE GUICHE: [*To* Cyrano, *sneering*] The bridal night
is not so near!

CYRANO: [*Aside*] Somehow that news fails to disquiet me.

CHRISTIAN: [*To* Roxane] Your lips again . . .

CYRANO: There . . . That will do now— Come!

CHRISTIAN: [*Still holding* Roxane] You do not
know how hard it is—

CYRANO: [*Tries to drag him away*] I know!
[*The beating of drums is heard in the distance*]

DE GUICHE: [*Up stage*] The regiment—on the
march!

ROXANE: [*As* Cyrano *tries to lead* Christian *away, follows, and detains them*] Take care of him
For me—[*Appealingly*] Promise me never to let him do
Anything dangerous!

CYRANO: I'll do my best—
I cannot promise—

ROXANE: [*Same business*] Make him be careful!

CYRANO: Yes—
I'll try—

ROXANE: [*Same business*] Be sure you keep him
dry and warm!

CYRANO: Yes, yes—if possible—

ROXANE: [*Same business; confidentially, in his ear*] See that he remains
Faithful!—

CYRANO: Of course! If—

ROXANE: [*Same business*] And have him write to
me
Every single day!

CYRANO: [*Stops*] That, I promise you!

CURTAIN

ACT IV.

The Cadets of Gascoyne
The post occupied by the company of Carbon De Castel-Jaloux *at the Siege of Arras. In the background, a rampart traversing the entire scene; beyond this, and apparently below, a plain stretches away to the horizon. The country is cut up with earthworks and other suggestions of the siege. In the distance, against the sky-line, the houses and the walls of Arras. Tents; scattered weapons; drums, et cetera. It is near daybreak, and the east is yellow with approaching dawn. Sentries at intervals. Campfires. Curtain rise discovers the Cadets asleep, rolled in their cloaks.* Carbon De Castel-Jaloux *and* Le Bret *keep watch. They are both very thin and pale.*

Christian *is asleep among the others, wrapped in his cloak, in the foreground, his face lighted by the flickering fire. Silence.*

LE BRET: Horrible!

CARBON: Why, yes. All of that.

LE BRET: Mordious!

CARBON: [*Gesture toward the sleeping* Cadets] Swear gently— You might wake them.
[*To* Cadets]
                              Go to sleep—
Hush! [*To* Le Bret] Who sleeps dines.

LE BRET: I have insomnia.
God! What a famine.
[*Firing off stage*]

CARBON: Curse that musketry!
They'll wake my babies.
[*To the men*] Go to sleep!—

A CADET: [*Rouses*] Diantre!
Again?

CARBON: No—only Cyrano coming home.
[*The heads which have been raised sink back again*]

A SENTRY: [*Off stage*] Halt! Who goes there?

VOICE OF CYRANO: Bergerac!

THE SENTRY ON THE PARAPET: Halt! Who goes?—

CYRANO: [*Appears on the parapet*] Bergerac, idiot!

LE BRET: [*Goes to meet him*] Thank God again!

CYRANO: [*Signs to him not to wake anyone*] Hush!

LE BRET: Wounded?—

CYRANO: No— They always miss me—quite
A habit by this time!

LE BRET: Yes— Go right on—
Risk your life every morning before breakfast
To send a letter!

CYRANO: [*Stops near* Christian] I promised he
should write
Every single day . . .
[*Looks down at him*]
                    Hm— The boy looks pale
When he is asleep—thin too—starving to death—
If that poor child knew! Handsome, none the less . . .

LE BRET: Go and get some sleep!

CYRANO: [*Affectionately*] Now, now—you old bear,
No growling!—I am careful—you know I am—
Every night, when I cross the Spanish lines
I wait till they are all drunk.

LE BRET: You might bring
Something with you.

CYRANO: I have to travel light
To pass through— By the way, there will be news
For you to-day: the French will eat or die,
If what I saw means anything.

LE BRET: Tell us!

CYRANO: No—
I am not sure—we shall see!

CARBON: What a war,
When the besieger starves to death!

LE BRET: Fine war—
Fine situation! We besiege Arras—

The Cardinal Prince of Spain besieges us—
And—here we are!

CYRANO: Someone might besiege *him*.

CARBON: A hungry joke!

CYRANO: Ho, ho!

LE BRET: Yes, you can laugh—
Risking a life like yours to carry letters—
Where are you going now?

CYRANO: [*At the tent door*] To write another.
[*Goes into tent*]
[*A little more daylight. The clouds redden. The town of Arras shows on the horizon. A cannon shot is heard, followed immediately by a roll of drums, far away to the left. Other drums beat a little nearer. The drums go on answering each other here and there, approach, beat loudly almost on the stage, and die away toward the right, across the camp. The camp awakes. Voices of officers in the distance*]

CARBON: [*Sighs*] Those drums!—another good
nourishing sleep
Gone to the devil.
[*The* Cadets *rouse themselves*]
                    Now then!—

FIRST CADET: [*Sits up, yawns*] God! I'm hungry!

SECOND CADET: Starving!

ALL: [*Groan*] Aoh!

CARBON: Up with you!

THIRD CADET: Not another step!

FOURTH CADET: Not another movement!

FIRST CADET: Look at my tongue—
I said this air was indigestible!

FIFTH CADET: My coronet for half a pound of
cheese!

SIXTH CADET: I have no stomach for this war—
I'll stay
In my tent—like Achilles.

ANOTHER: Yes—no bread,
No fighting—

CARBON: Cyrano!

OTHERS: May as well die—

CARBON: Come out here!—You know how to talk
to them.
Get them laughing—

SECOND CADET: [*Rushes up to* First Cadet *who is eating something*] What are you gnawing there?

FIRST CADET: Gun wads and axle-grease. Fat country this
Around Arras.

ANOTHER: [*Enters*] I have been out hunting!

ANOTHER: [*Enters*] I
Went fishing, in the Scarpe!

ALL: [*Leaping up and surrounding the newcomers*]
Find anything?
Any fish? Any game? Perch? Partridges?
Let me look!

THE FISHERMAN: Yes—one gudgeon.
[*Shows it*]

THE HUNTER: One fat . . . sparrow.
[*Shows it*]

ALL: Ah!—See here, this—mutiny!—

CARBON: Cyrano!
Come and help!

CYRANO: [*Enters from tent*] Well?
[*Silence. To the* First Cadet *who is walking
away, with his chin on his chest*]
                    You there, with the long face?

FIRST CADET: I have something on my mind that
    troubles me.

CYRANO: What is that?

FIRST CADET: No doubt   My stomach.

CYRANO: So have I.

FIRST CADET: No doubt
You enjoy this!

CYRANO: [*Tightens his belt*] It keeps me looking
    young.

SECOND CADET: My teeth are growing rusty.

CYRANO: Sharpen them!

THIRD CADET: My belly sounds as hollow as a
    drum.

CYRANO: Beat the long roll on it!

FOURTH CADET: My ears are ringing.

CYRANO: Liar! A hungry belly has no ears.

FIFTH CADET: Oh for a barrel of good wine!

CYRANO: [*Offers him his own helmet*] Your casque.

SIXTH CADET: I'll swallow anything!

CYRANO: [*Throws him the book which he has in
his hand*] Try the "Iliad."

SEVENTH CADET: The Cardinal, he has four meals
    a day—
What does he care!

CYRANO: Ask him; he really ought
To send you . . . a spring lamb out of his flock,
Roasted whole—

THE CADET: Yes, and a bottle—

CYRANO: [*Exaggerates the manner of one speaking
to a servant*] If you please,
Richelieu—a little more of the Red Seal . . .
Ah, thank you!

THE CADET: And the salad—

CYRANO: Of course—Romaine!

ANOTHER: [*Shivering*] I am as hungry as a wolf.

CYRANO: [*Tosses him a cloak*] Put on
Your sheep's clothing.

FIRST CADET: [*With a shrug*] Always the clever
    answer!

CYRANO: Always the answer—yes! Let me die
so—
Under some rosy-golden sunset, saying
A good thing, for a good cause! By the sword,
The point of honor—by the hand of one
Worthy to be my foeman, let me fall—
Steel in my heart, and laughter on my lips!

VOICES HERE AND THERE: All very well— We are
    hungry!

CYRANO: Bah! You think
Of nothing but yourselves.
    [*His eye singles out the old fifer in the back-
    ground*]
                    Here, Bertrandou,

You were a shepherd once— Your pipe now! Come,
Breathe, blow,— Play to these belly-worshippers
The old airs of the South—
                    "Airs with a smile in them,
Airs with a sigh in them, airs with the breeze
And the blue of the sky in them—"
                            Small, demure tunes
Whose every note is like a little sister—
Songs heard only in some long silent voice
Not quite forgotten— Mountain melodies
Like thin smoke rising from brown cottages
In the still noon, slowly— Quaint lullabies,
Whose very music has a Southern tongue—
    [*The old man sits down and prepares his fife*]
Now let the fife, that dry old warrior,
Dream, while over the stops your fingers dance
A minuet of little birds—let him
Dream beyond ebony and ivory;
Let him remember he was once a reed
Out of the river, and recall the spirit
Of innocent, untroubled country days . . .
    [*The fifer begins to play a Provençal melody*]
Listen, you Gascons! Now it is no more
The shrill fife— It is the flute, through woodlands
    far
Away, calling—no longer the hot battle-cry,
But the cool, quiet pipe our goatherds play!
Listen—the forest glens . . . the hills . . . the
    downs . . .
The green sweetness of night on the Dordogne . . .
Listen, you Gascons! It is all Gascoyne! . . .
    [*Every head is bowed; every eye cast down.
    Here and there a tear is furtively brushed
    away with the back of a hand, the corner of a
    cloak*]

CARBON: [*Softly to* Cyrano] You make them
    weep—

CYRANO: For homesickness—a hunger
More noble than that hunger of the flesh;
It is their hearts now that are starving.

CARBON: Yes,
But you melt down their manhood.

CYRANO: [*Motions the drummer to approach*] You
    think so?
Let them be. There is iron in their blood
Not easily dissolved in tears. You need
Only—
    [*He makes a gesture; the drum beats*]

ALL: [*Spring up and rush toward their weapons*]
    What's that? Where is it?—What?—

CYRANO: [*Smiles*] You see—
Let Mars snore in his sleep once—and farewell
Venus—sweet dreams—regrets—dear thoughts of
    home—
All the fife lulls to rest wakes at the drums!

A CADET: [*Looks up stage*] Aha— Monsieur de
    Guiche!

THE CADETS: [*Mutter among themselves*] Ugh! . . .

CYRANO: [*Smiles*] Flattering murmur!

A CADET: He makes me weary!

ANOTHER: With his collar
Of lace over his corselet—

ANOTHER: Like a ribbon
Tied round a sword!

ANOTHER: Bandages for a boil
On the back of his neck—

SECOND CADET: A courtier always!

ANOTHER: The Cardinal's nephew!

CARBON: None the less—a Gascon.

FIRST CADET: A counterfeit! Never you trust that
man—
Because we Gascons, look you, are all mad—
But this fellow is reasonable—nothing more
Dangerous than a reasonable Gascon!

LE BRET: He looks pale.

ANOTHER: Oh, he can be hungry too,
Like any other poor devil—but he wears
So many jewels on that belt of his
That his cramps glitter in the sun!

CYRANO: [Quickly] Is he
To see us looking miserable? Quick—
Pipes!—Cards!—Dice!—

[They all hurriedly begin to play, on their
stools, on the drums, or on their cloaks spread
on the ground, lighting their long pipes mean-
while]

                    As for me, I read Descartes.
[He walks up and down, reading a small book
which he takes from his pocket. Tableau: De
Guiche enters, looking pale and haggard. All
are absorbed in their games. General air of
contentment. De Guiche goes to Carbon.
They look at each other askance, each observing with satisfaction the condition of the other]

DE GUICHE: Good morning!

[Aside] He looks yellow.

CARBON: [Same business] He is all eyes.

DE GUICHE: [Looks at the Cadets]
What have we here? Black looks? Yes, gentlemen—
I am informed I am not popular;
The hill-nobility, barons of Béarn,
The pomp and pride of Périgord—I learn
They disapprove their colonel; call him courtier,
Politician—they take it ill that I
Cover my steel with lace of Genoa.
It is a great offense to be a Gascon
And not to be a beggar!

[Silence. They smoke. They play]
                    Well— Shall I have
Your captain punish you? . . . No.

CARBON: As to that,
It would be impossible.

DE GUICHE: Oh?

CARBON: I am free;
I pay my company; it is my own;
I obey military orders.

DE GUICHE: Oh!
That will be quite enough.

[To the Cadets] I can afford
Your little hates. My conduct under fire

Is well known. It was only yesterday
I drove the Count de Bucquoi from Bapaume,
Pouring my men down like an avalanche,
I myself led the charge—

CYRANO: [Without looking up from his book] And
your white scarf?

DE GUICHE: [Surprised and gratified]
You heard that episode? Yes—rallying
My men for the third time, I found myself
Carried among a crowd of fugitives
Into the enemy's lines. I was in danger
Of being shot or captured; but I thought
Quickly—took off and flung away the scarf
That marked my military rank—and so
Being inconspicuous, escaped among
My own force, rallied them, returned again
And won the day! . . .

[The Cadets do not appear to be listening, but
here and there the cards and the dice boxes remain motionless, the smoke is retained in their
cheeks]
                    What do you say to that?
Presence of mind—yes?

CYRANO: Henry of Navarre
Being outnumbered, never flung away
His white plume.

[Silent enjoyment. The cards flutter, the dice
roll, the smoke puffs out]

DE GUICHE: My device was a success,
However!

[Some attentive pause, interrupting the games
and the smoking]

CYRANO: Possibly . . . An officer
Does not lightly resign the privilege
Of being a target.

[Cards, dice, and smoke fall, roll, and float
away with increasing satisfaction]
                    Now, if I had been there—
Your courage and my own differ in this—
When your scarf fell, I should have put it on.

DE GUICHE: Boasting again!

CYRANO: Boasting? Lend it to me
To-night; I'll lead the first charge, with your scarf
Over my shoulder!

DE GUICHE: Gasconnade once more!
You are safe making that offer, and you know it—
My scarf lies on the river bank between
The lines, a spot swept by artillery
Impossible to reach alive!

CYRANO: [Produces the scarf from his pocket]
                    Yes. Here . . .

[Silence. The Cadets stifle their laughter behind
their cards and their dice boxes. De Guiche
turns to look at them. Immediately they resume
their gravity and their game. One of them
whistles carelessly the mountain air which the
fifer was playing]

DE GUICHE: [Takes the scarf]
Thank you! That bit of white is what I need

To make a signal. I was hesitating—
You have decided me.
> [*He goes up to the parapet, climbs upon it, and waves the scarf at arm's length several times*]

ALL: What is he doing?—
What?—

THE SENTRY ON THE PARAPET: There's a man down there running away!

DE GUICHE: [*Descending*] A Spaniard. Very useful as a spy
To both sides. He informs the enemy
As I instruct him. By his influence
I can arrange their dispositions.

CYRANO: Traitor!

DE GUICHE: [*Folding the scarf*] A traitor, yes; but useful . . .
We were saying? . . .
Oh, yes— Here is a bit of news for you:
Last night we had hopes of reprovisioning
The army. Under cover of the dark,
The Marshal moved to Dourlens. Our supplies
Are there. He may reach them. But to return
Safely, he needs a large force—at least half
Our entire strength. At present, we have here
Merely a skeleton.

CARBON: Fortunately,
The Spaniards do not know that.

DE GUICHE: Oh, yes; they know.
They will attack.

CARBON: Ah!

DE GUICHE: From that spy of mine
I learned of their intention. His report
Will determine the point of their advance.
The fellow asked me what to say! I told him:
"Go out between the lines; watch for my signal;
Where you see that, let them attack there."

CARBON: [*To the* Cadets] Well,
Gentlemen!
> [*All rise. Noise of sword belts and breastplates being buckled on*]

DE GUICHE: You may have perhaps an hour.

FIRST CADET: Oh— An hour!
> [*They all sit down and resume their games once more*]

DE GUICHE: [*To* Carbon] The great thing is to gain time.
Any moment the Marshal may return.

CARBON: And to gain time?

DE GUICHE: You will all be so kind
As to lay down your lives!

CYRANO: Ah! Your revenge?

DE GUICHE: I make no great pretence of loving you!
But—since you gentlemen esteem yourselves
Invincible, the bravest of the brave,
And all that—why need we be personal?
I serve the king in choosing . . . as I choose!

CYRANO: [*Salutes*] Sir, permit me to offer—all our thanks.

DE GUICHE: [*Returns the salute*] You love to fight
a hundred against one;
Here is your opportunity!
> [*He goes up stage with* Carbon]

CYRANO: [*To the* Cadets] My friends,
We shall add now to our old Gascon arms
With their six chevrons, blue and gold, a seventh—
Blood-red!
> [De Guiche *talks in a low tone to* Carbon *up stage. Orders are given. The defense is arranged.* Cyrano *goes to* Christian *who has remained motionless with folded arms*]
Christian? [*Lays a hand on his shoulder*]

CHRISTIAN: [*Shakes his head*] Roxane . . .

CYRANO: Yes.

CHRISTIAN: I should like
To say farewell to her, with my whole heart
Written for her to keep.

CYRANO: I thought of that—
> [*Takes a letter from his doublet*]
I have written your farewell.

CHRISTIAN: Show me!

CYRANO: You wish
To read it?

CHRISTIAN: Of course!
> [*He takes the letter; begins to read, looks up suddenly*] What?—

CYRANO: What is it?

CHRISTIAN: Look—
This little circle—

CYRANO: [*Takes back the letter quickly, and looks innocent*] Circle?—

CHRISTIAN: Yes—a tear!

CYRANO: So it is! . . . Well—a poet while he writes
Is like a lover in his lady's arms,
Believing his imagination—all
Seems true—you understand? There's half the charm
Of writing— Now, this letter as you see
I have made so pathetic that I wept
While I was writing it!

CHRISTIAN: You—wept?

CYRANO: Why, yes—
Because . . . it is a little thing to die,
But—not to see her . . . that is terrible!
And I shall never—
> [Christian *looks at him*]
We shall never—[*Quickly*] You
Will never—

CHRISTIAN: [*Snatches the letter*] Give me that!
> [*Noise in the distance on the outskirts of the camp*]

VOICE OF A SENTRY: Halt—who goes there?
> [*Shots, shouting, jingle of harness*]

CARBON: What is it?—

THE SENTRY ON THE WATCH: Why, a coach.
> [*They rush to look*]

CONFUSED VOICES: What? In the Camp?
A coach? Coming this way— It must have driven

Through the Spanish lines—what the devil— Fire!—
No— Hark! The driver shouting—what does he say?
Wait— He said: "On the service of the King!"
> [*They are all on the parapet looking over. The jingling comes nearer*]

DE GUICHE: Of the King?
> [*They come down and fall into line*]

CARBON: Hats off, all!

DE GUICHE: [*Speaks off stage*] The King! Fall in,
Rascals!—
> [*The coach enters at full trot. It is covered with mud and dust. The curtains are drawn. Two footmen are seated behind. It stops suddenly*]

CARBON: [*Shouts*] Beat the assembly—
> [*Roll of drums. All the* Cadets *uncover*]

DE GUICHE: Two of you,
Lower the steps—open the door—
> [*Two men rush to the coach. The door opens*]

ROXANE: [*Comes out of the coach*] Good morning!
> [*At the sound of a woman's voice, every head is raised. Sensation*]

DE GUICHE: On the King's service— You?

ROXANE: Yes—my own king—
Love!

CYRANO: [*Aside*] God is merciful . . .

CHRISTIAN: [*Hastens to her*] You! Why have you—

ROXANE: Your war lasted so long!

CHRISTIAN: But why?—

ROXANE: Not now—

CYRANO: [*Aside*] I wonder if I dare to look at
her . . .

DE GUICHE: You cannot remain here!

ROXANE: Why, certainly!
Roll that drum here, somebody. . . .
> [*She sits on the drum, which is brought to her*]

                          Thank you— There!
> [*She laughs*]

Would you believe—they fired upon us?
                          —My coach
Looks like the pumpkin in the fairy tale,
Does it not? And my footmen—
> [*She throws a kiss to* Christian]

                          How do you do?
> [*She looks about*]

How serious you all are! Do you know,
It is a long drive here—from Arras?
> [*Sees* Cyrano]

                          Cousin,
I am glad to see you!

CYRANO: [*Advances*] Oh— How did you come?

ROXANE: How did I find you? Very easily—
I followed where the country was laid waste
—Oh, but I saw such things! I had to see
To believe. Gentlemen, is that the service
Of your King? I prefer my own!

CYRANO: But how
Did you come through?

ROXANE: Why, through the Spanish lines
Of course!

FIRST CADET: They let you pass?—

DE GUICHE: What did you say?
How did you manage?

LE BRET: Yes, that must have been
Difficult!

ROXANE: No— I simply drove along.
Now and then some hidalgo scowled at me
And I smiled back—my best smile; whereupon,
The Spaniards being (without prejudice
To the French) the most polished gentlemen
In the world—I passed!

CARBON: Certainly that smile
Should be a passport! Did they never ask
Your errand or your destination?

ROXANE: Oh,
Frequently! Then I drooped my eyes and said:
"I have a lover . . ." Whereupon, the Spaniard
With an air of ferocious dignity
Would close the carriage door—with such a gesture
As any king might envy, wave aside
The muskets that were levelled at my breast,
Fall back three paces, equally superb
In grace and gloom, draw himself up, thrust forth
A spur under his cloak, sweeping the air
With his long plumes, bow very low, and say:
"Pass, Senorita!"

CHRISTIAN: But Roxane—

ROXANE: I know—
I said "a lover"—but you understand—
Forgive me!—If I said "I am going to meet
My husband," no one would believe me!

CHRISTIAN: Yes,
But—

ROXANE: What then?

DE GUICHE: You must leave this place.

CYRANO: At once.

ROXANE: I?

LE BRET: Yes—immediately.

ROXANE: And why?

CHRISTIAN: [*Embarrassed*] Because . . .

CYRANO: [*Same*] In half an hour . . .

DE GUICHE: [*Same*] Or three quarters . . .

CARBON: [*Same*] Perhaps
It might be better . . .

LE BRET: If you . . .

ROXANE: Oh— I see!
You are going to fight. I remain here.

ALL: No—no!

ROXANE: He is my husband—
> [*Throws herself in* Christian's *arms*]

                          I will die with you!

CHRISTIAN: Your eyes! . . . Why do you?—

ROXANE: You know why . . .

DE GUICHE: [*Desperate*] This post
Is dangerous—

ROXANE: [*Turns*] How—dangerous?

CYRANO: The proof
Is, we are ordered—

ROXANE: [*To De Guiche*] Oh—you wish to make
A widow of me?

DE GUICHE: On my word of honor—
ROXANE: No matter. I am just a little mad—
I will stay. It may be amusing.
CYRANO: What,
A heroine—our intellectual?
ROXANE: Monsieur de Bergerac, I am your cousin!
A CADET: We'll fight now! Hurrah!
ROXANE: [*More and more excited*] I am safe with
    you—my friends!
ANOTHER: [*Carried away*] The whole camp
    breathes of lilies!
ROXANE: And I think,
This hat would look well on the battlefield! . . .
But perhaps—
    [*Looks at* De Guiche]
           The Count ought to leave us. Any moment
Now, there may be danger.
DE GUICHE: This is too much!
I must inspect my guns. I shall return—
You may change your mind— There will yet be
    time—
ROXANE: Never! [De Guiche *goes out*]
CHRISTIAN: [*Imploring*] Roxane! . . .
ROXANE: No!
FIRST CADET: [*To the rest*] She stays here!
ALL: [*Rushing about, elbowing each other, brush-
    ing off their clothes*] A comb!—
Soap!—Here's a hole in my— A needle!—Who
Has a ribbon?—Your mirror, quick!—My cuffs—
A razor—
ROXANE: [*To* Cyrano, *who is still urging her*] No!
    I shall not stir one step!
CARBON: [*Having, like the others, tightened his
    belt, dusted himself, brushed off his hat,
    smoothed out his plume and put on his lace
    cuffs, advances to* Roxane *ceremoniously*]
In that case, may I not present to you
Some of these gentlemen who are to have
The honor of dying in your presence?
ROXANE: [*Bows*] Please!—
    [*She waits, standing, on the arm of* Christian,
    while]
CARBON: [*—presents*] Baron de Peyrescous de
    Colignac!
THE CADET: [*Salutes*] Madame . . .
ROXANE: Monsieur . . .
CARBON: [*Continues*] Baron de Casterac
De Cahuzac— Vidame de Malgouyre
Estressac Lesbas d'Escarabiot—
THE VIDAME: Madame . . .
CARBON: Chevalier d'Antignac-Juzet—
Baron Hillot de Blagnac-Saléchan
De Castel-Crabioules—
THE BARON: Madame . . .
ROXANE: How many
Names you all have!
THE BARON: Hundreds!
CARBON: [*To* Roxane] Open the hand
That holds your handkerchief.

ROXANE: [*Opens her hand; the handkerchief falls*]
    Why?
    [*The whole company makes a movement to-
    ward it*]
CARBON: [*Picks it up quickly*] My company
Was in want of a banner. We have now
The fairest in the army!
ROXANE: [*Smiling*] Rather small—
CARBON: [*Fastens the handkerchief to his lance*]
Lace—and embroidered!
A CADET: [*To the others*] With her smiling on me,
I could die happy, if I only had
Something in my—
CARBON: [*Turns upon him*] Shame on you! Feast
    your eyes
And forget your—
ROXANE: [*Quickly*] It must be this fresh air—
I am starving! Let me see . . .
                      Cold partridges,
Pastry, a little white wine—that would do.
Will some one bring that to me?
A CADET: [*Aside*] Will some one!—
ANOTHER: Where the devil are we to find—
ROXANE: [*Overhears; sweetly*] Why, there—
In my carriage.
ALL: Wha-at?
ROXANE: All you have to do
Is to unpack, and carve, and serve things.
                      Oh,
Notice my coachman; you may recognize
An old friend.
THE CADETS: [*Rush to the coach*] Ragueneau!
ROXANE: [*Follows them with her eyes*] Poor fel-
    lows . . .
THE CADETS: [*Acclamations*] Ah!
Ah!
CYRANO: [*Kisses her hand*] Our good fairy!
RAGUENEAU: [*Standing on his box, like a monte-
    bank before a crowd*] Gentlemen!—[*Enthusiasm*]
THE CADETS: Bravo!
Bravo!
RAGUENEAU: The Spaniards, basking in our smiles,
Smiled on our baskets!
    [*Applause*]
CYRANO: [*Aside, to* Christian] Christian!—
RAGUENEAU: They adored
The Fair, and missed—
    [*He takes from under the seat a dish, which he
    holds aloft*]
                      the Fowl!
    [*Applause. The dish is passed from hand to
    hand*]
CYRANO: [*As before, to* Christian] One moment—
RAGUENEAU: Venus
Charmed their eyes, while Adonis quietly
    [*Brandishing a ham*]
Brought home the Boar!
    [*Applause; the ham is seized by a score of
    hands outstretched*]
CYRANO: [*As before*] Pst— Let me speak to you—

ROXANE: [*As the* Cadets *return, their arms full of provisions*] Spread them out on the ground.

[*Calls*]

Christian! Come here;
Make yourself useful.

[Christian *turns to her, at the moment when Cyrano was leading him aside. She arranges the food, with his aid and that of the two imperturbable footmen*]

RAGUENEAU: Peacock, aux truffes!

FIRST CADET: [*Comes down, cutting a huge slice of the ham*] Tonnerre!
We are not going to die without a gorge—

[*Sees Roxane; corrects himself hastily*]

Pardon—a banquet!

RAGUENEAU: [*Tossing out the cushions of the carriage*] Open these— they are full
Of ortolans!

[*Tumult; laughter; the cushions are eviscerated*]

THIRD CADET: Lucullus!

RAGUENEAU: [*Throws out bottles of red wine*]
Flasks of ruby—[*And of white*]
Flasks of topaz—

ROXANE: [*Throws a tablecloth at the head of* Cyrano] Come back out of your dreams!
Unfold this cloth—

RAGUENEAU: [*Takes off one of the lanterns of the carriage, and flourishes it*] Our lamps are bonbonnières!

CYRANO: [*To* Christian] I must see you before you speak with her—

RAGUENEAU: [*More and more lyrical*] My whip-handle is one long sausage!

ROXANE: [*Pouring wine; passing the food*] We
Being about to die, first let us dine!
Never mind the others—all for Gascoyne!
And if De Guiche comes, he is not invited!

[*Going from one to another*]

Plenty of time—you need not eat so fast—
Hold your cup—[*To another*] What's the matter?

THE CADET: [*Sobbing*] You are so good
To us . . .

ROXANE: There, there! Red or white wine?
—Some bread
For Monsieur de Carbon!—Napkins— A knife—
Pass your plate— Some of the crust? A little more—
Light or dark?—Burgundy?—

CYRANO: [*Follows her with an armful of dishes, helping to serve*] Adorable!

ROXANE: [*Goes to* Christian] What would you like?

CHRISTIAN: Nothing.

ROXANE: Oh, but you must!—
A little wine? A biscuit?

CHRISTIAN: Tell me first
Why you came—

ROXANE: By and by. I must take care
Of these poor boys—

LE BRET: [*Who has gone up stage to pass up food to the sentry on the parapet, on the end of a lance*]

De Guiche!—

CYRANO: Hide everything
Quick!—Dishes, bottles, tablecloth—

Now look
Hungry again—

[*To* Ragueneau]

You there! Up on your box—
—Everything out of sight?—

[*In a twinkling, everything has been pushed inside the tents, hidden in their hats or under their cloaks. De Guiche enters quickly, then stops, sniffing the air. Silence*]

DE GUICHE: It smells good here.

A CADET: [*Humming with an air of great unconcern*] Sing ha-ha-ha and ho-ho-ho—

DE GUICHE: [*Stares at him; he grows embarrassed*]
You there—
What are you blushing for?

THE CADET: Nothing—my blood
Stirs at the thought of battle.

ANOTHER: Pom . . . pom . . . pom! . . .

DE GUICHE: [*Turns upon him*] What is that?

THE CADET: [*Slightly stimulated*] Only song—only little song—

DE GUICHE: You appear happy!

THE CADET: Oh yes—always happy
Before a fight—

DE GUICHE: [*Calls to* Carbon, *for the purpose of giving him an order*] Captain! I—

[*Stops and looks at him*]

What the devil—
You are looking happy too!—

CARBON: [*Pulls a long face and hides a bottle behind his back*] No!

DE GUICHE: Here—I had
One gun remaining. I have had it placed

[*He points off stage*]

There—in that corner—for your men.

A CADET: [*Simpering*] So kind!—
Charming attention!

ANOTHER: [*Same business; burlesque*] Sweet solicitude!—

DE GUICHE: [*Contemptuous*] I believe you are both drunk—

[*Coldly*]

Being unaccustomed
To guns—take care of the recoil!

FIRST CADET: [*Gesture*] Ah-h . . . Pfft!

DE GUICHE: [*Goes up to him, furious*] How dare you?

FIRST CADET: A Gascon's gun never recoils!

DE GUICHE: [*Shakes him by the arm*] You *are* drunk—

FIRST CADET: [*Superbly*] With the smell of powder!

DE GUICHE: [*Turns away with a shrug*] Bah!

[*To* Roxane]

Madame, have you decided?

ROXANE: I stay here.

DE GUICHE: You have time to escape—

ROXANE: No!

DE GUICHE: Very well—
Someone give me a musket!

CARBON: What?

DE GUICHE: I stay
Here also.

CYRANO: [Formally] Sir, you show courage!

FIRST CADET: A Gascon
In spite of all that lace!

ROXANE: Why—

DE GUICHE: Must I run
Away, and leave a woman?

SECOND CADET: [To First Cadet] We might give
him
Something to eat—what do you say?
[All the food re-appears, as if by magic]

DE GUICHE: [His face lights up] A feast!

THIRD CADET: Here a little, there a little—

DE GUICHE: [Recovers his self-control; haughtily]
Do you think
I want your leavings?

CYRANO: [Saluting] Colonel—you improve!

DE GUICHE: I can fight as I am!

FIRST CADET: [Delighted] Listen to him—
He has an accent!

DE GUICHE: [Laughs] Have I so?

FIRST CADET: A Gascon!—
A Gascon, after all!
[They all begin to dance]

CARBON: [Who has disappeared for a moment behind the parapet, reappears on top of it] I have
placed my pikemen
Here.
[Indicates a row of pikes showing above the
parapet]

DE GUICHE: [Bows to Roxane] We'll review them;
will you take my arm?
[She takes his arm; they go up on the parapet.
The rest uncover, and follow them up stage]

CHRISTIAN: [Goes hurriedly to Cyrano] Speak
quickly!
[At the moment when Roxane appears on the
parapet the pikes are lowered in salute, and
a cheer is heard. She bows]

THE PIKEMEN: [Off stage] Hurrah!

CHRISTIAN: What is it?

CYRANO: If Roxane . . .

CHRISTIAN: Well?

CYRANO: Speaks about your letters . . .

CHRISTIAN: Yes—I know!

CYRANO: Do not make the mistake of showing . . .

CHRISTIAN: What?

CYRANO: Showing surprise.

CHRISTIAN: Surprise—why?

CYRANO: I must tell you! . . .
It is quite simple—I had forgotten it
Until just now. You have . . .

CHRISTIAN: Speak quickly!—

CYRANO: You
Have written oftener than you think.

CHRISTIAN: Oh—have I!

CYRANO: I took upon me to interpret you;
And wrote—sometimes . . . without . . .

CHRISTIAN: My knowing. Well?

CYRANO: Perfectly simple!

CHRISTIAN: Oh yes, perfectly!—
For a month, we have been blockaded here!—
How did you send all these letters?

CYRANO: Before
Daylight, I managed—

CHRISTIAN: I see. That was also
Perfectly simple!
       —So I wrote to her,
How many times a week? Twice? Three times?
Four?

CYRANO: Oftener.

CHRISTIAN: Every day?

CYRANO: Yes—every day . . .
Every single day.

CHRISTIAN: [Violently] And that wrought you up
Into such a flame that you faced death—

CYRANO: [Sees Roxane returning] Hush—
Not before her!
[He goes quickly into the tent. Roxane comes
up to Christian]

ROXANE: Now—Christian!

CHRISTIAN: [Takes her hands] Tell me now
Why you came here—over these ruined roads—
Why you made your way among mosstroopers
And ruffians—you—to join me here?

ROXANE: Because—
Your letters . . .

CHRISTIAN: Meaning?

ROXANE: It was your own fault
If I ran into danger; I went mad—
Mad with you! Think what you have written me,
How many times, each one more wonderful
Than the last!

CHRISTIAN: All this for a few absurd
Love-letters—

ROXANE: Hush—absurd! How can you know?
I thought I loved you, ever since one night
When a voice that I never would have known
Under my window breathed your soul to me . . .
But—all this time, your letters—every one
Was like hearing your voice there in the dark,
All around me, like your arms around me . . .
[More lightly]
       At last,
I came. Anyone would! Do you suppose
The prim Penelope had stayed at home
Embroidering,—if Ulysses wrote like you?
She would have fallen like another Helen—
Tucked up those linen petticoats of hers
And followed him to Troy!

CHRISTIAN: But you—

ROXANE: I read them
Over and over. I grew faint reading them.
I belonged to you. Every page of them
Was like a petal fallen from your soul—

Like the light and the fire of a great love,
Sweet and strong and true—
    CHRISTIAN: Sweet . . . and strong . . . and true
. . .
You felt that, Roxane?—
    ROXANE: You know how I feel! . . .
    CHRISTIAN: So—you came . . .
    ROXANE: Oh my Christian, oh my king,—
Lift me up if I fall upon my knees—
It is the heart of me that kneels to you,
And will remain forever at your feet—
You cannot lift that!—
                I came here to say
'Forgive me'—(It is time to be forgiven
Now, when we may die presently)—forgive me
For being light and vain and loving you
Only because you were beautiful.
    CHRISTIAN: [Astonished] Roxane! . . .
    ROXANE: Afterwards I knew better. Afterwards
(I had to learn to use my wings) I loved you
For yourself too—knowing you more, and loving
More of you. And now—
    CHRISTIAN: Now? . . .
    ROXANE: It is yourself
I love now: your own self.
    CHRISTIAN: [Taken aback] Roxane!
    ROXANE: [Gravely] Be happy!—
You must have suffered; for you must have seen
How frivolous I was; and to be loved
For the mere costume, the poor casual body
You went about in—to a soul like yours,
That must have been torture! Therefore with words
You revealed your heart. Now that image of you
Which filled my eyes first—I see better now,
And I see it no more!
    CHRISTIAN: Oh!—
    ROXANE: You still doubt
Your victory?
    CHRISTIAN: [Miserably] Roxane!—
    ROXANE: I understand:
You cannot perfectly believe in me—
A love like this—
    CHRISTIAN: I want no love like this!
I want love only for—
    ROXANE: Only for what
Every woman sees in you? I can do
Better than that!
    CHRISTIAN: No—it was best before!
    ROXANE: You do not altogether know me . . .
    Dear,
There is more of me than there was—with this,
I can love more of you—more of what makes
You your own self—Truly! . . . If you were less
Lovable—
    CHRISTIAN: No!
    ROXANE: —Less charming—ugly even—
I should love you still.
    CHRISTIAN: You mean that?
    ROXANE: I do
Mean that!

    CHRISTIAN: Ugly? . . .
    ROXANE: Yes. Even then!
    CHRISTIAN: [Agonized] Oh . . . God! . . .
    ROXANE: Now are you happy?
    CHRISTIAN: [Choking] Yes . . .
    ROXANE: What is it?
    CHRISTIAN: [Pushes her away gently] Only . . .
Nothing . . . one moment . . .
    ROXANE: But—
    CHRISTIAN: [Gesture toward the Cadets] I am
    keeping you
From those poor fellows—Go and smile at them;
They are going to die!
    ROXANE: [Softly] Dear Christian!
    CHRISTIAN: Go—
    [She goes up among the Gascons who gather
    round her respectfully]
Cyrano!
    CYRANO: [Comes out of the tent, armed for the
battle] What is wrong? You look—
    CHRISTIAN: She does not
Love me any more.
    CYRANO: [Smiles] You think not?
    CHRISTIAN: She loves
You.
    CYRANO: No!—
    CHRISTIAN: [Bitterly] She loves only my soul.
    CYRANO: No!
    CHRISTIAN: Yes—
That means you. And you love her.
    CYRANO: I?
    CHRISTIAN: I see—
I know!
    CYRANO: That is true . . .
    CHRISTIAN: More than—
    CYRANO: [Quietly] More than that.
    CHRISTIAN: Tell her so!
    CYRANO: No.
    CHRISTIAN: Why not?
    CYRANO: Why—look at me!
    CHRISTIAN: She would love me if I were ugly,
    CYRANO: [Startled] She—
Said that?
    CHRISTIAN: Yes. Now then!
    CYRANO: [Half to himself] It was good of her
To tell you that . . .
    [Change of tone]
                Nonsense! Do not believe
Any such madness—
             It was good of her
To tell you. . . .
           Do not take her at her word!
Go on—you never will be ugly— Go!
She would never forgive me.
    CHRISTIAN: That is what
We shall see.
    CYRANO: No, no—
    CHRISTIAN: Let her choose between us!—
Tell her everything!
    CYRANO: No—you torture me—

CHRISTIAN: Shall I ruin your happiness, because
I have a cursed pretty face? That seems
Too unfair!

CYRANO: And am I to ruin yours
Because I happen to be born with power
To say what you—perhaps—feel?

CHRISTIAN: Tell her!

CYRANO: Man—
Do not try me too far!

CHRISTIAN: I am tired of being
My own rival!

CYRANO: Christian!—

CHRISTIAN: Our secret marriage—
No witnesses—fraudulent—that can be
Annulled—

CYRANO: Do not try me—

CHRISTIAN: I want her love
For the poor fool I am—or not at all!
Oh, I am going through with this! I'll know,
One way or the other. Now I shall walk down
To the end of the post. Go tell her. Let her choose
One of us.

CYRANO: It will be you.

CHRISTIAN: God—I hope so!
[He turns and calls]
Roxane!

CYRANO: No—no—

ROXANE: [Hurries down to him] Yes, Christian?

CHRISTIAN: Cyrano
Has news for you—important.
[She turns to Cyrano. Christian goes out]

ROXANE: [Lightly] Oh—important?

CYRANO: He is gone . . .
[To Roxane]
              Nothing—only Christian thinks
You ought to know—

ROXANE: I do know. He still doubts
What I told him just now. I saw that.

CYRANO: [Takes her hand] Was it
True—what you told him just now?

ROXANE: It was true!
I said that I should love him even . . .

CYRANO: [Smiling sadly] The word
Comes hard—before me?

ROXANE: Even if he were . . .

CYRANO: Say it—
I shall not be hurt!—Ugly?

ROXANE: Even then
I should love him.
[A few shots, off stage, in the direction in
which Christian disappeared]
            Hark! The guns.

CYRANO: Hideous?

ROXANE: Hideous.

CYRANO: Disfigured?

ROXANE: Or disfigured.

CYRANO: Even
Grotesque?

ROXANE: How could he ever be grotesque—
Ever—to me!

CYRANO: But you could love him so,
As much as?—

ROXANE: Yes—and more!

CYRANO: [Aside, excitedly] It is true!—true!—
Perhaps—God! This is too much happiness . . .
[To Roxane]
I—Roxane—listen—

LE BRET: [Enters quickly; calls to Cyrano in a
low tone] Cyrano—

CYRANO: [Turns] Yes?

LE BRET: Hush! . . .
[Whispers a few words to him]

CYRANO: [Lets fall Roxane's hand] Ah!

ROXANE: What is it?

CYRANO: [Half stunned, and aside] All gone . . .

ROXANE: [More shots] What is it? Oh,
They are fighting!—
[She goes up to look off stage]

CYRANO: All gone. I cannot ever
Tell her, now . . . ever . . .

ROXANE: [Starts to rush away] What has happened?

CYRANO: [Restrains her] Nothing.
[Several Cadets enter. They conceal something
which they are carrying, and form a group so
as to prevent Roxane from seeing their burden]

ROXANE: These men—

CYRANO: Come away . . .
[He leads her away from the group]

ROXANE: You were telling me
Something—

CYRANO: Oh, that? Nothing. . . .
[Gravely]
                    I swear to you
That the spirit of Christian—that his soul
Was—[Corrects himself quickly] That his soul is no
less great—

ROXANE: [Catches at the word] Was?
[Crying out]
                        Oh!—
[She rushes among the men, and scatters them]

CYRANO: All gone . . .

ROXANE: [Sees Christian lying upon his cloak]
Christian!

LE BRET: [To Cyrano] At the first volley.
[Roxane throws herself upon the body of Chris-
tian. Shots; at first scattered, then increasing.
Drums. Voices shouting]

CARBON: [Sword in hand] Here
They come!—Ready!—
[Followed by the Cadets, he climbs over the
parapet and disappears]

ROXANE: Christian!

CARBON: [Off stage] Come on, there, You!

ROXANE: Christian!

CARBON: Fall in!

ROXANE: Christian!

CARBON: Measure your fuse!
[Ragueneau hurries up, carrying a helmet full
of water]

CHRISTIAN: [*Faintly*] Roxane! . . .

CYRANO: [*Low and quick, in* Christian's *ear, while* Roxane *is dipping into the water a strip of linen torn from her dress*] I have told her; she loves you.

[Christian *closes his eyes*]

ROXANE: [*Turns to* Christian] Yes, My darling?

CARBON: Draw your ramrods!

ROXANE: [*To* Cyrano] He is not dead? . . .

CARBON: Open your charges!

ROXANE: I can feel his cheek Growing cold against mine——

CARBON: Take aim!

ROXANE: A letter—— Over his heart——

[*She opens it*]

        For me.

CYRANO: [*Aside*] My letter . . .

CARBON: Fire!

[*Musketry, cries and groans. Din of battle*]

CYRANO: [*Trying to withdraw his hand, which* Roxane, *still upon her knees, is holding*] But Roxane —they are fighting——

ROXANE: Wait a little . . . He is dead. No one else knew him but you . . .

[*She weeps quietly*]

Was he not a great lover, a great man, A hero?

CYRANO: [*Standing, bareheaded*] Yes, Roxane.

ROXANE: A poet, unknown, Adorable?

CYRANO: Yes, Roxane.

ROXANE: A fine mind?

CYRANO: Yes, Roxane.

ROXANE: A heart deeper than we knew—— A soul magnificently tender?

CYRANO: [*Firmly*] Yes, Roxane!

ROXANE: [*Sinks down upon the breast of* Christian] He is dead now . . .

CYRANO: [*Aside; draws his sword*] Why, so am I— For I am dead, and my love mourns for me And does not know . . .

[*Trumpets in distance*]

DE GUICHE: [*Appears on the parapet, disheveled, wounded on the forehead, shouting*] The signal— hark—the trumpets! The army has returned— Hold them now!—Hold them! The army! —

ROXANE: On his letter—blood . . . and tears.

A VOICE: [*Off stage*] Surrender!

THE CADETS: No!

RAGUENEAU: This place is dangerous!—

CYRANO: [*To* De Guiche] Take her away—I am going—

ROXANE: [*Kisses the letter; faintly*] His blood . . . his tears . . .

RAGUENEAU: [*Leaps down from the coach and runs to her*] She has fainted—

DE GUICHE: [*On the parapet; savagely, to the* Cadets] Hold them!

VOICE OFF STAGE: Lay down your arms!

VOICES: No! No!

CYRANO: [*To* De Guiche] Sir, you have proved yourself— Take care of her.

DE GUICHE: [*Hurries to* Roxane *and takes her up in his arms*] As you will—we can win, if you hold on A little longer—

CYRANO: Good!

[*Calls out to* Roxane, *as she is carried away fainting, by* De Guiche *and* Ragueneau]

        Adieu, Roxane!

[*Tumult, outcries. Several* Cadets *come back wounded and fall on the stage.* Cyrano *rushing to the fight, is stopped on the crest of the parapet by* Carbon, *covered with blood*]

CARBON: We are breaking—I am twice wounded——

CYRANO: [*Shouts to* Gascons] Hardi! Reculez pas, Drollos!

[*To* Carbon, *holding him up*]

        So—never fear! I have two deaths to avenge now—Christian's And my own!

[*They come down.* Cyrano *takes from him the lance with* Roxane's *handkerchief still fastened to it*]

        Float, little banner, with her name!

[*He plants it on the parapet; then shouts to the* Cadets]

Toumbé dessus! Escrasas lous!

[*To the fifer*]

        Your fife!

Music!

[*Fife plays. The wounded drag themselves to their feet. Other* Cadets *scramble over the parapet and group themselves around* Cyrano *and his tiny flag. The coach is filled and covered with men, bristling with muskets, transformed into a redoubt*]

A CADET: [*Reels backward over the wall, still fighting. Shouts*] They are climbing over! [*And falls dead*]

CYRANO: Very good— Let them come!— A salute now——

[*The parapet is crowned for an instant with a rank of enemies. The imperial banner of Spain is raised aloft*]

        Fire!

[*General volley*]

VOICE: [*Among the ranks of the enemy*] Fire!

[*Murderous counter-fire; the* Cadets *fall on every side*]

A SPANISH OFFICER: [*Uncovers*] Who are these men who are so fond of death?

CYRANO: [*Erect amid the hail of bullets, declaims*] The Cadets of Gascoyne, the defenders Of Carbon de Castel-Jaloux— Free fighters, free lovers, free spenders—

[*He rushes forward, followed by a few sur-*
vivors]
The Cadets of Gascoyne . . .
[*The rest is lost in the din of battle*]

CURTAIN

ACT V.

Cyrano's Gazette

Fifteen years later, in 1565. The park of the con-
vent occupied by the Ladies of the Cross, at Paris.
Magnificent foliage. To the left, the house upon a
broad terrace at the head of a flight of steps, with
several doors opening upon the terrace. In the center
of the scene an enormous tree alone in the center of
a little open space. Toward the right, in the fore-
ground, among boxwood bushes, a semicircular
bench of stone. All the way across the background of
the scene, an avenue overarched by the chestnut
trees, leading to the door of a chapel on the right,
just visible among the branches of the trees. Beyond
the double curtain of the trees, we catch a glimpse
of bright lawns and shaded walks, masses of shrub-
bery; the perspective of the park; the sky. A little
side door of the chapel opens upon a colonnade,
garlanded with autumnal vines, and disappearing on
the right behind the box-trees. It is late October.
Above the still living green of the turf all the foliage
is red and yellow and brown. The evergreen masses
of box and yew stand out darkly against this au-
tumnal coloring. A heap of dead leaves under every
tree. The leaves are falling everywhere. They rustle
underfoot along the walks; the terrace and the bench
are half covered with them. Before the bench on the
right, on the side toward the tree, is placed a tall
embroidery frame and beside it a little chair. Baskets
filled with skeins and many-colored silks and balls
of wool. Tapestry unfinished on the frame. At the
curtain rise the nuns are coming and going across
the Park; several of them are seated on the Bench
around Mother Marguérite de Jésus. *The leaves are*
falling.

SISTER MARTHE: [*To* Mother Marguérite]
Sister Claire has been looking in the glass
At her new cap; twice!

MOTHER MARGUÉRITE: [*To* Sister Claire] It is
very plain;
Very.

SISTER CLAIRE: And Sister Marthe stole a plum
Out of the tart this morning!

MOTHER MARGUÉRITE: [*To* Sister Marthe] That
was wrong;
Very wrong.

SISTER CLAIRE: Oh, but such a little look!

SISTER MARTHE: Such a little plum!

MOTHER MARGUÉRITE: [*Severely*] I shall tell Monsieur
De Cyrano, this evening.

SISTER CLAIRE: No! Oh, no!—
He will make fun of us.

SISTER MARTHE: He will say nuns
Are so gay!

SISTER CLAIRE: And so greedy!

MOTHER MARGUÉRITE: [*Smiling*] And so good . . .

SISTER CLAIRE: It must be ten years, Mother
Marguérite,
That he has come here every Saturday,
Is it not?

MOTHER MARGUÉRITE: More than ten years; ever
since
His cousin came to live among us here—
Her worldly weeds among our linen veils,
Her widowhood and our virginity—
Like a black dove among white doves.

SISTER MARTHE: No one
Else ever turns that happy sorrow of hers
Into a smile. . .

ALL THE NUNS: He is such fun!—He makes us
Almost laugh!—And he teases everyone—
And pleases everyone— And we all love him—
And he likes our cake, too—

SISTER MARTHE: I am afraid
He is not a good Catholic.

SISTER CLAIRE: Some day
We shall convert him.

THE NUNS: Yes—yes!

MOTHER MARGUÉRITE: Let him be;
I forbid you to worry him. Perhaps
He might stop coming here.

SISTER MARTHE: But . . . God?

MOTHER MARGUÉRITE: You need not
Be afraid. God knows all about him.

SISTER MARTHE: Yes . . .
But every Saturday he says to me,
Just as if he were proud of it: "Well, Sister,
I ate meat yesterday!"

MOTHER MARGUÉRITE: He tells you so?
The last time he said that, he had not eaten
Anything, for two days.

SISTER MARTHE: Mother!—

MOTHER MARGUÉRITE: He is poor;
Very poor.

SISTER MARTHE: Who said so?

MOTHER MARGUÉRITE: Monsieur Le Bret.

SISTER MARTHE: Why does not someone help him?

MOTHER MARGUÉRITE: He would be
Angry; very angry. . .
[*Between the trees up stage,* Roxane *appears,*
all in black, with a widow's cap and long veils.
De Guiche, *magnificently grown old, walks be-*
side her. They move slowly. Mother Marguér-
ite *rises*]
                Let us go in—
Madame Madeleine has a visitor.

SISTER MARTHE: [*To* Sister Claire] The Duc de
Grammont, is it not? The Marshal?

SISTER CLAIRE: [*Looks toward* De Guiche] I think
so—yes.

SISTER MARTHE: He has not been to see her
For months—

THE NUNS: He is busy—the Court!—the Camp!—

SISTER CLAIRE: The world! . . .

[*They go out.* De Guiche *and* Roxane *come
down in silence, and stop near the embroidery
frame. Pause*]

DE GUICHE: And you remain here, wasting all that
gold—
For ever in mourning?

ROXANE: For ever.

DE GUICHE: And still faithful?

ROXANE: And still faithful . . .

DE GUICHE: [*After a pause*] Have you forgiven me?

ROXANE: [*Simply, looking up at the cross of the
Convent*] I am here.

[*Another pause*]

DE GUICHE: Was Christian . . . all that?

ROXANE: If you knew him.

DE GUICHE: Ah? We were not precisely . . .
intimate . . .
And his last letter—always at your heart?

ROXANE: It hangs here, like a holy reliquary.

DE GUICHE: Dead—and you love him still!

ROXANE: Sometimes I think
He has not altogether died; our hearts
Meet, and his love flows all around me, living.

DE GUICHE: [*After another pause*]
You see Cyrano often?

ROXANE: Every week.
My old friend takes the place of my Gazette,
Brings me all the news. Every Saturday,
Under that tree where you are now, his chair
Stands, if the day be fine. I wait for him,
Embroidering; the hour strikes; then I hear,
(I need not turn to look!) at the last stroke,
His cane tapping the steps. He laughs at me
For my eternal needlework. He tells
The story of the past week—

[Le Bret *appears on the steps*]

                         There's Le Bret!—

[Le Bret *approaches*]
How is it with our friend?

LE BRET: Badly.

DE GUICHE: Indeed?

ROXANE: [*To* De Guiche] Oh, he exaggerates!

LE BRET: Just as I said—
Loneliness, misery—I told him so!—
His satires make a host of enemies—
He attacks the false nobles, the false saints,
The false heroes, the false artists—in short,
Everyone!

ROXANE: But they fear that sword of his—
No one dare touch him!

DE GUICHE: [*With a shrug*] H'm—that may be so.

LE BRET: It is not violence I fear for him,
But solitude—poverty—old gray December,
Stealing on wolf's feet, with a wolf's green eyes,
Into his darkening room. Those bravoes yet
May strike our Swordsman down! Every day now,
He draws his belt up one hole; his poor nose
Looks like old ivory; he has one coat
Left—his old black serge.

DE GUICHE: That is nothing strange
In this world! No, you need not pity him
Overmuch.

LE BRET: [*With a bitter smile*] My lord Mar
shal! . . .

DE GUICHE: I say, do not
Pity him overmuch. He lives his life,
His own life, his own way—thought, word, and deed
Free!

LE BRET: [*As before*] My lord Duke! . . .

DE GUICHE: [*Haughtily*] Yes, I know—I have all;
He has nothing. Nevertheless, to-day
I should be proud to shake his hand . . .

[*Saluting* Roxane]

                                   Adieu.

ROXANE: I will go with you.

[De Guiche *salutes* Le Bret, *and turns with*
Roxane *toward the steps*]

DE GUICHE: [*Pauses on the steps, as she climbs*]
                    Yes— I envy him
Now and then . . .
                    Do you know, when a man wins
Everything in this world, when he succeeds
Too much—he feels, having done nothing wrong
Especially, Heaven knows!—he feels somehow
A thousand small displeasures with himself,
Whose whole sum is not quite Remorse, but rather
A sort of vague disgust . . . The ducal robes
Mounting up, step by step, to pride and power,
Somewhere among their folds draw after them
A rustle of dry illusions, vain regrets,
As your veil, up the stairs here, draws along
The whisper of dead leaves.

ROXANE: [*Ironical*] The sentiment
Does you honor.

DE GUICHE: Oh, yes . . .

[*Pausing suddenly*] Monsieur Le Bret!—
[*To* Roxane]
You pardon us?—

[*He goes to* Le Bret, *and speaks in a low tone*]
                    One moment— It is true
That no one dares attack your friend. Some people
Dislike him, none the less. The other day
At Court, such a one said to me: "This man
Cyrano may die—accidentally."

LE BRET: [*Coldly*] Thank you.

DE GUICHE: You may thank me. Keep him at
home
All you can. Tell him to be careful.

LE BRET: [*Shaking his hands to heaven*] Careful!—
He is coming here. I'll warn him—yes, but! . . .

ROXANE: [*Still on the steps, to a* Nun *who approaches her*]

                     Here

I am—what is it?

THE NUN: Madame, Ragueneau
Wishes to see you.

ROXANE: Bring him here.
      [*To* Le Bret *and* De Guiche]

                  He comes

For sympathy—having been first of all
A Poet, he became since then, in turn,
A Singer—

LE BRET: Bath-house keeper—

ROXANE: Sacristan—

LE BRET: Actor—

ROXANE: Hairdresser—

LE BRET: Music-master—

ROXANE: Now,
To-day—

RAGUENEAU: [*Enters hurriedly*] Madame!—
      [*He sees* Le Bret] Monsieur!—

ROXANE: [*Smiling*] First tell your troubles
To Le Bret for a moment.

RAGUENEAU: But Madame—
      [*She goes out, with* De Guiche, *not hearing him.* Ragueneau *comes to* Le Bret]
After all, I had rather— You are here—
She need not know so soon— I went to see him
Just now— Our friend— As I came near his door,
I saw him coming out. I hurried on
To join him. At the corner of the street,
As he passed— Could it be an accident?—
I wonder!—At the window overhead,
A lackey with a heavy log of wood
Let it fall—

LE BRET: Cyrano!

RAGUENEAU: I ran to him—

LE BRET: God! The cowards!

RAGUENEAU: I found him lying there—
A great hole in his head—

LE BRET: Is he alive?

RAGUENEAU: Alive—yes. But . . . I had to carry
him
Up to his room—Dieu! Have you seen his room?—

LE BRET: Is he suffering?

RAGUENEAU: No; unconscious.

LE BRET: Did you
Call a doctor?

RAGUENEAU: One came—for charity.

LE BRET: Poor Cyrano!—We must not tell Roxane
All at once . . . Did the doctor say?—

RAGUENEAU: He said
Fever, and lesions of the— I forget
Those long names— Ah, if you had seen him there,
His head all white bandages!—Let us go
Quickly—there is no one to care for him—
All alone— If he tries to raise his head,
He may die!

LE BRET: [*Draws him away to the right*] This
way— It is shorter—through
The Chapel—

ROXANE: [*Appears on the stairway, and calls to*
Le Bret *as he is going out by the colonnade which
leads to the small door of the Chapel*] Monsieur Le
Bret!—
      [Le Bret *and* Ragueneau *rush off without hearing*] Running away
When I call to him? Poor dear Ragueneau
Must have been very tragic!
      [*She comes slowly down the stair, toward the tree*]

                    What a day! . . .

Something in these bright Autumn afternoons
Happy and yet regretful—an old sorrow
Smiling . . . as though poor little April dried
Her tears long ago—and remembered . . .
      [*She sits down at her work. Two Nuns come
      out of the house carrying a great chair and
      set it under the tree*]

                       Ah—
The old chair, for my old friend!—

SISTER MARTHE: The best one
In our best parlor!

ROXANE: Thank you, Sister—[*The*
Nuns *withdraw*] There—
      [*She begins embroidering. The clock strikes*]
The hour!—He will be coming now—my silks—
All done striking? He never was so late
Before! The sister at the door—my thimble . . .
Here it is—she must be exhorting him
To repent all his sins . . . [*A pause*]

                  He ought to be
Converted, by this time— Another leaf—
      [*A dead leaf falls on her work; she brushes it
      away*]
Certainly nothing could—my scissors—ever
Keep him away—

A NUN: [*Appears on the steps*] Monsieur de Bergerac.

ROXANE: [*Without turning*]
What was I saying? . . . Hard, sometimes, to match
These faded colors! . . .
      [*While she goes on working,* Cyrano *appears
      at the top of the steps, very pale, his hat
      drawn over his eyes. The* Nun *who has brought
      him in goes away. He begins to descend the
      steps leaning on his cane, and holding himself
      on his feet only by an evident effort.* Roxane
      turns to him, with a tone of friendly banter]
               After fourteen years,
Late—for the first time!

CYRANO: [*Reaches the chair, and sinks into it; his
gay tone contrasting with his tortured face*]
              Yes, yes—maddening!
I was detained by—

ROXANE: Well?

CYRANO: A visitor,
Most unexpected.

ROXANE: [*Carelessly, still sewing*] Was your visitor
Tiresome?

CYRANO: Why, hardly that—inopportune,
Let us say—an old friend of mine—at least
A very old acquaintance.

ROXANE: Did you tell him
To go away?

CYRANO: For the time being, yes.
I said: "Excuse me—this is Saturday—
I have a previous engagement, one
I cannot miss, even for you— Come back
An hour from now."

ROXANE: Your friend will have to wait;
I shall not let you go till dark.

CYRANO: [*Very gently*] Perhaps
A little before dark, I must go . . .
    [*He leans back in the chair, and closes his eyes.
    Sister Marthe crosses above the stairway. Rox-
    ane sees her, motions her to wait, then turns to
    Cyrano*]

ROXANE: Look—
Somebody waiting to be teased.

CYRANO: [*Quickly, opens his eyes*] Of course!
    [*In a big, comic voice*] Sister, approach!
    [*Sister Marthe glides toward him*] Beautiful
    downcast eyes!—
So shy!

SISTER MARTHE: [*Looks up, smiling*] You— [*She
sees his face*] Oh!—

CYRANO: [*Indicates Roxane*] Sh!—Careful!
    [*Resumes his burlesque tone*]
                                    Yesterday,
I ate meat again!

SISTER MARTHE: Yes, I know. [*Aside*] That is
why
He looks so pale . . .
    [*To him: low and quickly*]
                        In the refectory,
Before you go—come to me there—
                              I'll make you
A great bowl of hot soup—will you come?

CYRANO: [*Boisterously*] Ah—
Will I come!

SISTER MARTHE: You are quite reasonable
To-day!

ROXANE: Has she converted you?

SISTER MARTHE: Oh, no—
Not for the world!—

CYRANO: Why, now I think of it,
That is so— You, bursting with holiness,
And yet you never preach! Astonishing
I call it. . . .
    [*With burlesque ferocity*]
                        Ah—now I'll astonish you—
I am going to—
    [*With the air of seeking for a good joke and
    finding it*]
                        —let you pray for me
To-night, at vespers!

ROXANE: Aha!

CYRANO: Look at her—
Absolutely struck dumb!

SISTER MARTHE: [*Gently*] I did not wait
For you to say I might.
    [*She goes out*]

CYRANO: [*Returns to* Roxane, *who is bending over
her work*]
                                Now, may the devil
Admire me, if I ever hope to see
The end of that embroidery!

ROXANE: [*Smiling*] I thought
It was time you said that.
    [*A breath of wind causes a few leaves to fall*]

CYRANO: The leaves—

ROXANE: [*Raises her head and looks away through
the trees*]
                                What color—
Perfect Venetian red! Look at them fall.

CYRANO: Yes—they know how to die. A little way
From the branch to the earth, a little fear
Of mingling with the common dust—and yet
They go down gracefully—a fall that seems
Like flying!

ROXANE: Melancholy—you?

CYRANO: Why, no,
Roxane!

ROXANE: Then let the leaves fall. Tell me now
The Court news—my gazette!

CYRANO: Let me see—

ROXANE: Ah!

CYRANO: [*More and more pale, struggling against
pain*]
Saturday, the nineteenth: The King fell ill,
After eight helpings of grape marmalade.
His malady was brought before the court,
Found guilty of high treason; whereupon
His Majesty revived. The royal pulse
Is now normal. Sunday, the twentieth:
The Queen gave a grand ball, at which they burned
Seven hundred and sixty-three wax candles. Note:
They say our troops have been victorious
In Austria. Later: Three sorcerers
Have been hung. Special post: The little dog
Of Madame d'Athis was obliged to take
Four pills before—

ROXANE: Monsieur de Bergerac,
Will you kindly be quiet!

CYRANO: Monday . . . nothing.
Lygdamire has a new lover.

ROXANE: Oh!

CYRANO: [*His face more and more altered*] Tues-
day,
The Twenty-second: All the court has gone
To Fontainebleau. Wednesday: The Comte de Fiesque
Spoke to Madame de Montglat; she said No.
Thursday: Mancini was the Queen of France
Or—very nearly! Friday: La Montglat
Said Yes. Saturday, twenty-sixth. . . .
    [*His eyes close; his head sinks back; silence*]

ROXANE: [*Surprised at not hearing any more, turns, looks at him, and rises, frightened*]
He has fainted—[*She runs to him, crying out*]
Cyrano!

CYRANO: [*Opens his eyes*] What . . . What is it? . . .
[*He sees* Roxane *leaning over him, and quickly pulls his hat down over his head and leans back away from her in the chair*]
          No—oh no—
It is nothing—truly!

ROXANE: But—

CYRANO: My old wound—
At Arras—sometimes—you know. . . .

ROXANE: My poor friend!

CYRANO: Oh it is nothing; it will soon be gone. . . .
[*Forcing a smile*]
There! It is gone!

ROXANE: [*Standing close to him*] We all have our old wounds—
I have mine—here . . . [*Her hand at her breast*] under this faded scrap
Of writing. . . . It is hard to read now—all
But the blood—and the tears. . . .
[*Twilight begins to fall*]

CYRANO: His letter! . . . Did you
Not promise me that some day . . . that some day. . . .
You would let me read it?

ROXANE: His letter?—You . . .
You wish—

CYRANO: I do wish it—to-day.

ROXANE: [*Gives him the little silken bag from around her neck*] Here. . . .

CYRANO: May I . . . open it?

ROXANE: Open it, and read.
[*She goes back to her work, folds it again, re-arranges her silks*]

CYRANO: [*Unfolds the letter; reads*]
"Farewell Roxane, because to-day I die—"

ROXANE: [*Looks up, surprised*] Aloud?

CYRANO: [*Reads*]
          "I know that it will be to-day
My own dearly beloved—and my heart
Still so heavy with love I have not told,
And I die without telling you! No more
Shall my eyes drink the sight of you like wine,
Never more, with a look that is a kiss,
Follow the sweet grace of you—"

ROXANE: How you read it—
His letter!

CYRANO: [*Continues*]
          "I remember now the way
You have, of pushing back a lock of hair
With one hand, from your forehead—and my heart
Cries out—"

ROXANE: His letter . . . and you read it so . . .
[*The darkness increases imperceptibly*]

CYRANO: "Cries out and keeps crying: 'Farewell, my dear,
My dearest—' "

ROXANE: In a voice. . . .

CYRANO: "—My own heart's own,
My own treasure—"

ROXANE: [*Dreamily*] In such a voice. . . .

CYRANO: —"My love—"

ROXANE: —As I remember hearing . . .
[*She trembles*]
          —long ago. . . .
[*She comes near him, softly, without his seeing her; passes the chair, leans over silently, looking at the letter. The darkness increases*]

CYRANO: "—I am never away from you. Even now,
I shall not leave you. In another world,
I shall be still that one who loves you, loves you
Beyond measure, beyond—"

ROXANE: [*Lays her hand on his shoulder*]
          How can you read
Now? It is dark. . . .
[*He starts, turns, and sees her there close to him. A little movement of surprise, almost of fear; then he bows his head. A long pause; then in the twilight now completely fallen, she says very softly, clasping her hands*]
          And all these fourteen years,
He has been the old friend, who came to me
To be amusing.

CYRANO: Roxane!—

ROXANE: It was you.

CYRANO: No, no, Roxane, no!

ROXANE: And I might have known
Every time that I heard you speak my name! . . .

CYRANO: No— It was not I—

ROXANE: It was . . . you!

CYRANO: I swear—

ROXANE: I understand everything now: The letters—
That was you . . .

CYRANO: No!

ROXANE: And the dear, foolish words—
That was you. . . .

CYRANO: No!

ROXANE: And the voice . . . in the dark. . . .
That was . . . you!

CYRANO: On my honor—

ROXANE: And . . . the Soul!—
That was all you.

CYRANO: I never loved you—

ROXANE: Yes,
You loved me!

CYRANO: [*Desperately*] No— He loved you—

ROXANE: Even now,
You love me!

CYRANO: [*His voice weakens*] No!

ROXANE: [*Smiling*] And why . . . so great a "No"?

CYRANO: No, no, my own dear love, I love you
not! . . .
[*Pause*]

ROXANE: How many things have died . . . and
are newborn! . . .
Why were you silent for so many years,
All the while, every night and every day,
He gave me nothing—you knew that— You knew
Here, in this letter lying on my breast,
Your tears— You knew they were your tears—

CYRANO: [*Holds the letter out to her*] The blood
Was his.

ROXANE: Why do you break that silence now,
To-day?

CYRANO: Why? Oh, because—
[Le Bret *and* Ragueneau *enter, running*]

LE BRET: What recklessness—
I knew it! He is here!

CYRANO: [*Smiling, and trying to rise*] Well? Here
I am!

RAGUENEAU: He has killed himself, Madame,
coming here!

ROXANE: He— Oh, God. . . . And that faintness
. . . was that?—

CYRANO: No,
Nothing! I did not finish my Gazette—
Saturday, twenty-sixth: An hour or so
Before dinner, Monsieur de Bergerac
Died, foully murdered.
[*He uncovers his head, and shows it swathed
in bandages*]

ROXANE: Oh, what does he mean?—
Cyrano!—What have they done to you?—

CYRANO: "Struck down
By the sword of a hero, let me fall—
Steel in my heart, and laughter on my lips!"
Yes, I said that once. How Fate loves a jest!—
Behold me ambushed—taken in the rear—
My battlefield a gutter—my noble foe
A lackey, with a log of wood! . . .

                                It seems
Too logical— I have missed everything,
Even my death!

RAGUENEAU: [*Breaks down*] Ah, monsieur!—

CYRANO: Ragueneau,
Stop blubbering! [*Takes his hand*]
                What are you writing nowadays,
Old poet?

RAGUENEAU: [*Through his tears*] I am not a poet
now;
I snuff the—light the candles—for Molière!

CYRANO: Oh—Molière!

RAGUENEAU: Yes, but I am leaving him
To-morrow. Yesterday they played "Scapin"—
He has stolen your scene—

LE BRET: The whole scene—word for word!

RAGUENEAU: Yes: "What the devil was he doing
there"—
That one!

LE BRET: [*Furious*] And Molière stole it all from
you—
Bodily!—

CYRANO: Bah— He showed good taste. . . .
[*To* Ragueneau] The scene
Went well? . . .

RAGUENEAU: Ah, monsieur, they laughed—and
laughed—
How they did laugh!

CYRANO: Yes—that has been my life. . . .
Do you remember that night Christian spoke
Under your window? It was always so!
While I stood in the darkness underneath,
Others climbed up to win the applause—the kiss!—
Well—that seems only justice— I still say,
Even now, on the threshold of my tomb—
"Molière has genius—Christian had good looks—"
[*The chapel bell is ringing. Along the avenue
of trees above the stairway, the* Nuns *pass in
procession to their prayers*]
They are going to pray now; there is the bell.

ROXANE: [*Raises herself and calls to them*] Sister!
—Sister!—

CYRANO: [*Holding on to her hand*] No,—do not
go away—
I may not still be here when you return. . . .
[*The* Nuns *have gone into the chapel. The or-
gan begins to play*]
A little harmony is all I need—
Listen. . . .

ROXANE: You shall not die! I love you!—

CYRANO: No—
That is not in the story! You remember
When Beauty said "I love you" to the Beast
That was a fairy prince, his ugliness
Changed and dissolved, like magic. . . . But you
see
I am still the same.

ROXANE: And I—I have done
This to you! All my fault—mine!

CYRANO: You? Why no,
On the contrary! I had never known
Womanhood and its sweetness but for you.
My mother did not love to look at me—
I never had a sister— Later on,
I feared the mistress with a mockery
Behind her smile. But you—because of you
I have had one friend not quite all a friend—
Across my life, one whispering silken gown! . . .

LE BRET: [*Points to the rising moon which begins
to shine down between the trees*]
Your other friend is looking at you.

CYRANO: [*Smiling at the moon*] I see. . . .

ROXANE: I never loved but one man in my life,
And I have lost him—twice. . . .

CYRANO: Le Bret—I shall be up there presently
In the moon—without having to invent
Any flying machines!

ROXANE: What are you saying? . . .

CYRANO: The moon—yes, that would be the place
   for me—
My kind of paradise! I shall find there
Those other souls who should be friends of mine—
Socrates—Galileo—
   LE BRET: [*Revolting*] No! No! No!
It is too idiotic—too unfair—
Such a friend—such a poet—such a man
To die so—to die so!—
   CYRANO: [*Affectionately*] There goes Le Bret,
Growling!
   LE BRET: [*Breaks down*] My friend!—
   CYRANO: [*Half raises himself, his eye wanders*]
                 The Cadets of Gascoyne,
The Defenders. . . . The elementary mass—
Ah—there's the point! Now, then . . .
   LE BRET: Delirious—
And all that learning—
   CYRANO: On the other hand,
We have Copernicus—
   ROXANE: Oh!
   CYRANO: [*More and more delirious*] "Very well,
But what the devil was he doing there?—
What the devil was he doing there, up there?". . .
   [*He declaims*]
      Philosopher and scientist,
      Poet, musician, duellist—
      He flew high, and fell back again!
   A pretty wit—whose like we lack—
   A lover . . . not like other men. . . .
      Here lies Hercule-Savinien
   De Cyrano de Bergerac—
      Who was all things—and all in vain!
Well, I must go—pardon— I cannot stay!
My moonbeam comes to carry me away. . . .
   [*He falls back into the chair, half fainting. The
   sobbing of* Roxane *recalls him to reality.
   Gradually his mind comes back to him. He
   looks at her, stroking the veil that hides her
   hair*]
I would not have you mourn any the less
That good, brave, noble Christian; but perhaps—
I ask you only this—when the great cold
Gathers around my bones, that you may give
A double meaning to your widow's weeds
And the tears you let fall for him may be
For a little—my tears. . . .
   ROXANE: [*Sobbing*] Oh, my love! . . .
   CYRANO: [*Suddenly shaken as with a fever fit,
he raises himself erect and pushes her away*]
                         —Not here!—
Not lying down! . . .

   [*They spring forward to help him; he motions
   them back*]
                 Let no one help me—no one!—
Only the tree. . . .
   [*He sets his back against the trunk. Pause*]
                 It is coming . . . I feel
Already shod with marble . . . gloved with lead . .
   [*Joyously*]
Let the old fellow come now! He shall find me
On my feet—sword in hand—
   [*Draws his sword*]
   LE BRET: Cyrano!—
   ROXANE: [*Half fainting*] Oh,
Cyrano!
   CYRANO: I can see him there—he grins—
He is looking at my nose—that skeleton
—What's that you say? Hopeless?—Why, very
well!—
But a man does not fight merely to win!
No—no—better to know one fights in vain! . . .
You there— Who are you? A hundred against one—
I know them now, my ancient enemies—
   [*He lunges at the empty air*]
Falsehood! . . . There! There! Prejudice—Compro-
mise—
Cowardice—
   [*Thrusting*] What's that? No! Surrender? No!
Never—never! . . .
                 Ah, you too, Vanity!
I knew you would overthrow me in the end—
No! I fight on! I fight on! I fight on!
   [*He swings the blade in great circles, then
   pauses, gasping. When he speaks again, it is in
   another tone*]
Yes, all my laurels you have riven away
And all my roses; yet in spite of you,
There is one crown I bear away with me,
And to-night, when I enter before God,
My salute shall sweep all the stars away
From the blue threshold! One thing without stain,
Unspotted from the world, in spite of doom
Mine own!—
   [*He springs forward, his sword aloft*]
                 And that is . . .
   [*The sword escapes from his hand; he totters,
   and falls into the arms of* Le Bret *and* Rag-
   ueneau]
   ROXANE: [*Bends over him and kisses him on the
forehead*]
                 —That is . . .
   CYRANO: [*Opens his eyes and smiles up at her*]
                 My white plume. . . .
                 CURTAIN

August Strindberg

(1849–1912)

We left Strindberg (pp. 75–94) as a vastly influential realist in *The Father*. We must now also consider him as one of the major playwrights who carried the drama beyond realism or naturalism, for Strindberg straddled the two main currents of modern theatre. He was not, of course, the only dramatist to restore imagination to the stage before the turn of the century and to bring back atmosphere and suggestiveness; but he was surely one of the most potent pioneers in imaginative drama, as well as the playwright who could least be charged with mental flabbiness and mere theatricality, or "artiness." He did not depart from realism because he was intent on following a new fashion or because he thought it would be clever of him to show how ingenious he could be. He adopted a new style because he felt compelled to express the ineffable and to dramatize personal stresses which the limited scope of dramatic realism could neither encompass nor project. This view is substantiated by the fact that during the period of his subjective dramas he also wrote a series of realistic historical plays (*Gustavus Vasa, Erik XIV,* and *Queen Christina,* for example, after 1899), as well as the inexorably naturalistic drama *The Dance of Death* (1901). The combination of inner compulsion and original talent in his experiments had an important effect on the theatre. He inaugurated a new dramatic style that superseded merely poetic and symbolist styles. It eventuated in Central European expressionism after 1916. It also stimulated the imagination of Eugene O'Neill to create *Emperor Jones* and *The Hairy Ape* before he acquired any familiarity with the German expressionist theatre or any interest in its plays.

In 1893 Strindberg married an Austrian writer, Frida Uhl, and became a father for the fourth time. But this second marriage ended quickly and his troubled mind led him to seek refuge in Swedenborgian mysticism and to make fantastic chemical experiments. (He believed he could make gold and suspected that America cheated him of his invention.) He began to dread a mental collapse even earlier, when, after a weird correspondence with Nietzsche toward the end of 1888, he learned that the philosopher had gone mad. (Nietzsche's last letter to him was signed "The Crucified One.") Fearing that his own state of mind was open to question after his stormy conflict with his first wife, Strindberg had tried to get a certificate of sanity for himself—without success, since he had refused to remain under observation. During and especially after his second marriage, he developed hallucina-tions and delusions of persecution, and felt tormented by invisible spirits. He believed that his food was being poisoned, that gas was being piped into his room, and that an electric girdle was suffocating him. He reached his mental crisis in Paris in 1895–1896. When Swedenborgian mysticism failed to heal him and his nervous crisis became intolerable, Strindberg finally took the precaution of entering a private sanatorium.

He recovered quickly, but never quite shook off his peculiar psychic tendencies, including a belief in rare telepathic powers and a conviction that servants were avenging themselves on their masters by draining their food of nourishing ingredients. A number of his plays reflected both his crisis and its aftereffects. When he dealt with objective material, as in his dramatic chronicles of Swedish history, his mind was crystal clear and gave no indication of aberrant thinking or feeling. In other work (as in the graceful little fairy drama *Swanwhite,* the powerful folk tale *The Bridal Crown,* and the beautiful drama of reconciliation *Easter*), he developed a gentle mysticism tinged at most with melancholia. "One gets more and more humble," wrote the man whose vindictiveness had known no bounds. In some of these plays he also acknowledged the influence of Maeterlinck. He interested himself in a practical theatrical venture, helping a young producer to create an Intimate Theatre for an audience of two hundred. Here he reformed the art of staging, abolishing footlights and using only draperies for the background, and for the small stage of this theatre he wrote a number of simplified works he called "chamber plays," analogous to chamber music as compared with symphonies. In these concentrated dramas, the best of which was *The Spook Sonata* (1907), he sought to strip all pretense from people's lives and expose everything hidden. Along with *The Spook Sonata,* finally, Strindberg wrote several long plays which are among the most original and experimental in the history of Western drama: *To Damascus,* a trilogy on the search for mystic salvation, written between 1898 and 1904; *The Dream Play* (1902), a Buddhistic allegory and fantasy on the misery and failure of life; and *The Great Highway* (1909). To these may be added *There Are Crimes and Crimes* (1898), perhaps the most curious comedy in the modern repertory. Along with equally subjective books like *Inferno* (1897) and *Legends* (1898), with which their author anticipated expressionistic fiction of the stream-of-consciousness variety, these dramas made Strindberg the chief precursor of ultramodernism.

With his "dream plays"—a term that applies with variable appropriateness to the nonrealistic works—Strindberg helped to liberate modern drama from the prosiness to which naturalism had dedicated the theatre. Indeed, his dream plays come to mind whenever we think of the plays of Pirandello, Toller, Kaiser, the Capek brothers, Cocteau, Saroyan, Wilder, and many other contemporary experimentalists, although it is questionable that any later playwright has approximated the compressed passion and anguish that Strindberg had at his command. If the bedlam dance in his expressionistic work often proves confusing, it is largely because Strindberg followed the shifting forms of the dream. He frequently telescoped time and place, made characters undergo numerous changes of identity, allowed symbols to manifest themselves elusively, and presented supersensory and nonrational experience. Above all, he abolished the boundaries between the real and the unreal, and between the objective and the subjective worlds, so that the one blends into the other without warning. In truth, some of this writing was not so much expressionistic as surrealistic. And its ultimate justification was that Strindberg viewed man in modern life as devoid of integration. The world Strindberg placed on the stage had no consistency; it continually disintegrated because he saw it as the nightmare of the divided and bedeviled modern soul.

Representative of the playwright's essays in subjective and symbolic dramaturgy, but less extreme in style and structure than some of the other plays, is *There Are Crimes and Crimes*. Here Strindberg retains considerable realism throughout but allows scope for invisible and indefinable agencies in the dramatic development—agencies malign, sardonic, and moral. The spirit world is present as a functional element, but it is not materialized on the stage; it is left to both the characters and the reader as a matter for wonder and speculation. Perhaps it is unwise, however, to speculate too closely on the identity of these agents of calumny and punishment in this grimly humorous exposé of human egotism and frailty. The excoriation of weakness in the character of his hero, Maurice, needs no explanation. The playwright has merely given the wishes and the "guilt" of Maurice an external dramatic

manifestation in the death of Maurice's child and his persecution for a crime he did not commit except "in thought." A clue for the reader was provided by Strindberg himself when he published *There Are Crimes and Crimes* together with the short "mystery" play *Advent,* under the inclusive title *In a Higher Court.* Since the crimes of Maurice are "not mentioned in the criminal code" because they are crimes against the spirit, he can be tried only "in the higher court" of the spirit. It is enough to follow the play *as if* certain things could happen. With a final *coup de grâce* Strindberg returns us to reality in as sardonic a resolution as any we may conceive, when Maurice makes a final adjustment between conscience and egotism. After noting in one of his autobiographical books, *The Author* (1909), that his mental crisis at the age of fifty had been "revolutions in the life of the soul, desert wanderings, Swedenborgian Heavens and Hells," Strindberg added that this play had been "light after darkness" and productivity with restored certitude, hope, and love. *There Are Crimes and Crimes* was also productivity with "lightness," for it is executed with skillful fantastication and with an air of playfulness, as if both Strindberg and the spirit world were making sport of Maurice and of frail mankind. The conclusion, after the weirdly shattering complications, makes the play technically a comedy. But it certainly provides cold comfort for both moralists and optimists. It is a grim jest with strange overtones, and its mood is no happier than that darkest of Shakespeare's "dark" comedies *Measure for Measure.* It can also remind us of the sultry comedies of Ben Jonson and Henry Becque.

BIBLIOGRAPHY: Eric Bentley, *The Playwright as Thinker* (pp. 60–64, 94–99, 193–221, 316–318, 351–353), 1946; Edwin Bjorkman, Introductions to *Plays by August Strindberg* (4 volumes, 1912–1916); G. A. Campbell, *Strindberg,* 1933; Barrett H. Clark and George Freedley, *A History of the Modern Drama,* (pp. 20–44), 1947; John Gassner, *Masters of the Drama* (pp. 388–395), 1945; John Gassner, "Strindberg in America," in *Theatre Arts,* May 1949 (pp. 49–52); A. Jolivet, *Le Théâtre de Strindberg,* 1931; V. J. McGill, *August Strindberg the Bedeviled Viking,* 1930; Elizabeth Sprigge, *The Strange Life of August Strindberg,* 1949.

For additional commentary, see pages 75–77.

THERE ARE CRIMES AND CRIMES

By August Strindberg

TRANSLATED FROM THE SWEDISH BY EDWIN BJÖRKMAN

CHARACTERS

MAURICE, *a playwright*
JEANNE, *his mistress*
MARION, *their daughter, five years old*
ADOLPHE, *a painter*
HENRIETTE, *his mistress*

EMILE, *a workman, brother of Jeanne*
MADAME CATHERINE
THE ABBÉ
A WATCHMAN
A HEAD WAITER

A COMMISSAIRE
TWO DETECTIVES
A WAITER
A GUARD
A SERVANT GIRL

Act I, Scene 1. The Cemetery
2. The Crêmerie
Act II, Scene 1. The Auberge des Adrets
2. The Bois de Boulogne
Act III, Scene 1. The Crêmerie
2. The Auberge des Adrets
Act IV, Scene 1. The Luxembourg Gardens
2. The Crêmerie

All the scenes are laid in Paris.

ACT I. SCENE I.

The upper avenue of cypresses in the Montparnasse Cemetery at Paris. The background shows mortuary chapels, stone crosses on which are inscribed "O Crux! Ave Spes Unica!" and the ruins of a windmill covered with ivy. A well-dressed woman in widow's weeds is kneeling and muttering prayers in front of a grave decorated with flowers. Jeanne is walking back and forth as if expecting somebody. Marion is playing with some withered flowers picked from a rubbish heap on the ground. The Abbé is reading his breviary while walking along the farther end of the avenue.

WATCHMAN: [*Enters and goes up to* Jeanne] Look here, this is no playground.

JEANNE: [*Submissively*] I am only waiting for somebody who'll soon be here—

WATCHMAN: All right, but you're not allowed to pick any flowers.

JEANNE: [*To* Marion] Drop the flowers, dear.

ABBÉ: [*Comes forward and is saluted by the* Watchman] Can't the child play with the flowers that have been thrown away?

WATCHMAN: The regulations don't permit anybody to touch even the flowers that have been thrown

away, because it's believed they may spread infection—which I don't know if it's true.

ABBÉ: [*To* Marion] In that case we have to obey, of course. What's your name, my little girl?

MARION: My name is Marion.

ABBÉ: And who is your father?

[Marion *begins to bite one of her fingers and does not answer*]

ABBÉ: Pardon my question, madame. I had no intention—I was just talking to keep the little one quiet.

[*The* Watchman *has gone out*]

JEANNE: I understand it, Reverend Father, and I wish you would say something to quiet me also. I feel very much disturbed after having waited here two hours.

ABBÉ: Two hours—for him! How these human beings torture each other! O Crux! Ave spes unica!

JEANNE: What do they mean, these words you read all around here?

ABBÉ: They mean: O cross, our only hope!

JEANNE: Is it the only one?

ABBÉ: The only certain one.

JEANNE: I shall soon believe that you are right, Father.

ABBÉ: May I ask why?

JEANNE: You have already guessed it. When he

lets the woman and the child wait two hours in a cemetery, then the end is not far off.

ABBÉ: And when he has left you, what then?

JEANNE: Then we have to go into the river.

ABBÉ: Oh, no, no!

JEANNE: Yes, yes!

MARION: Mamma, I want to go home, for I am hungry.

JEANNE: Just a little longer, dear, and we'll go home.

ABBÉ: Woe unto those who call evil good and good evil.

JEANNE: What is that woman doing at the grave over there?

ABBÉ: She seems to be talking to the dead.

JEANNE: But you cannot do that?

ABBÉ: She seems to know how.

JEANNE: This would mean that the end of life is not the end of our misery?

ABBÉ: And you don't know it?

JEANNE: Where can I find out?

ABBÉ: Hm! The next time you feel as if you wanted to learn about this well-known matter, you can look me up in Our Lady's Chapel at the Church of St. Germain— Here comes the one you are waiting for, I guess.

JEANNE: [Embarrassed] No, he is not the one, but I know him.

ABBÉ: [To Marion] Good-bye, little Marion! May God take care of you! [Kisses the child and goes out] At St. Germain des Prés.

EMILE: [Enters] Good morning, sister. What are you doing here?

JEANNE: I am waiting for Maurice.

EMILE: Then I guess you'll have a lot of waiting to do, for I saw him on the boulevard an hour ago, taking breakfast with some friends. [Kissing the child] Good morning, Marion.

JEANNE: Ladies also?

EMILE: Of course. But that doesn't mean anything. He writes plays, and his latest one has its first performance to-night. I suppose he had with him some of the actresses.

JEANNE: Did he recognize you?

EMILE: No, he doesn't know who I am, and it is just as well. I know my place as a workman, and I don't care for any condescension from those that are above me.

JEANNE: But if he leaves us without anything to live on?

EMILE: Well, you see, when it gets that far, then I suppose I shall have to introduce myself. But you don't expect anything of the kind, do you—seeing that he is fond of you and very much attached to the child?

JEANNE: I don't know, but I have a feeling that something dreadful is in store for me.

EMILE: Has he promised to marry you?

JEANNE: No, not promised exactly, but he has held out hopes.

EMILE: Hopes, yes! Do you remember my words at the start: don't hope for anything, for those above us don't marry downward.

JEANNE: But such things have happened.

EMILE: Yes, they have happened. But would you feel at home in his world? I can't believe it, for you wouldn't even understand what they were talking of. Now and then I take my meals where he is eating— out in the kitchen is my place, of course—and I don't make out a word of what they say.

JEANNE: So you take your meals at that place?

EMILE: Yes, in the kitchen.

JEANNE: And think of it, he has never asked me to come with him.

EMILE: Well, that's rather to his credit, and it shows he has some respect for the mother of his child. The women over there are a queer lot.

JEANNE: Is that so?

EMILE: But Maurice never pays any attention to the women. There is something square about that fellow.

JEANNE: That's what I feel about him, too, but as soon as there is a woman in it, a man isn't himself any longer.

EMILE: [Smiling] You don't tell me! But listen: are you hard up for money?

JEANNE: No, nothing of that kind.

EMILE: Well, then, the worst hasn't come yet— Look! Over there! There he comes. And I'll leave you. Good-bye, little girl.

JEANNE: Is he coming? Yes, that's him.

EMILE: Don't make him mad now—with your jealousy, Jeanne!

[Goes out]

JEANNE: No, I won't.

[Maurice enters]

MARION: [Runs up to him and is lifted up into his arms] Papa, papa!

MAURICE: My little girl! [Greets Jeanne] Can you forgive me, Jeanne, that I have kept you waiting so long?

JEANNE: Of course I can.

MAURICE: But say it in such a way that I can hear that you are forgiving me.

JEANNE: Come here and let me whisper it to you. [Maurice goes up close to her. Jeanne kisses him on the cheek]

MAURICE: I didn't hear.

[Jeanne kisses him on the mouth]

MAURICE: Now I heard! Well—you know, I suppose that this is the day that will settle my fate? My play is on for to-night, and there is every chance that it will succeed—or fail.

JEANNE: I'll make sure of success by praying for you.

MAURICE: Thank you. If it doesn't help, it can at least do no harm— Look over there, down there in the valley, where the haze is thickest: there lies Paris. To-day Paris doesn't know who Maurice is, but it is going to know within twenty-four hours.

The haze, which has kept me obscured for thirty years, will vanish before my breath, and I shall become visible, I shall assume definite shape and begin to be somebody. My enemies—which means all who would like to do what I have done—will be writhing in pains that shall be my pleasures, for they will be suffering all that I have suffered.

JEANNE: Don't talk that way, don't!

MAURICE: But that's the way it is.

JEANNE: Yes, but don't speak of it— And then?

MAURICE: Then we are on firm ground, and then you and Marion will bear the name I have made famous.

JEANNE: You love me then?

MAURICE: I love both of you, equally much, or perhaps Marion a little more.

JEANNE: I am glad of it, for you can grow tired of me, but not of her.

MAURICE: Have you no confidence in my feelings towards you?

JEANNE: I don't know, but I am afraid of something, afraid of something terrible—

MAURICE: You are tired out and depressed by your long wait, which once more I ask you to forgive. What have you to be afraid of?

JEANNE: The unexpected: that which you may foresee without having any particular reason to do so.

MAURICE: But I foresee only success, and I have particular reasons for doing so: the keen instincts of the management and their knowledge of the public, not to speak of their personal acquaintance with the critics. So now you must be in good spirits—

JEANNE: I can't, I can't. Do you know, there was an Abbé here a while ago, who talked so beautifully to us. My faith—which you haven't destroyed, but just covered up, as when you put chalk on a window to clean it—I couldn't lay hold on it for that reason, but this old man just passed his hand over the chalk, and the light came through, and it was possible again to see that the people within were at home— To-night I will pray for you at St. Germain.

MAURICE: Now I am getting scared.

JEANNE: Fear of God is the beginning of wisdom.

MAURICE: God? What is that? Who is he?

JEANNE: It was he who gave joy to your youth, and strength to your manhood. And it is he who will carry us through the terrors that lie ahead of us.

MAURICE: What is lying ahead of us? What do you know? Where have you learned of this? This thing that I don't know?

JEANNE: I can't tell. I have dreamt nothing, seen nothing, heard nothing. But during these two dreadful hours I have experienced such an infinity of pain that I am ready for the worst.

MARION: Now I want to go home, mamma, for I am hungry.

MAURICE: Yes, you'll go home now, my little darling.

[Takes her into his arms]

MARION: [Shrinking] Oh, you hurt me, papa!

JEANNE: Yes, we must get home for dinner. Good-bye then, Maurice. And good luck to you!

MAURICE: [To Marion] How did I hurt you? Doesn't my little girl know that I always want to be nice to her?

MARION: If you are nice, you'll come home with us.

MAURICE: [To Jeanne] When I hear the child talk like that, you know, I feel as if I ought to do what she says. But then reason and duty protest— Good-bye, my dear little girl!

[He kisses the child, who puts her arms around his neck]

JEANNE: When do we meet again?

MAURICE: We'll meet to-morrow, dear. And then we'll never part again.

JEANNE: [Embraces him] Never, never to part again! [She makes the sign of the cross on his forehead] May God protect you!

MAURICE: [Moved against his own will] My dear, beloved Jeanne!

[Jeanne and Marion go towards the right; Maurice towards the left. Both turn around simultaneously and throw kisses at each other]

MAURICE: [Comes back] Jeanne, I am ashamed of myself. I am always forgetting you, and you are the last one to remind me of it. Here are the tickets for to-night.

JEANNE: Thank you, dear, but—you have to take up your post of duty alone, and so I have to take up mine—with Marion.

MAURICE: Your wisdom is as great as the goodness of your heart. Yes, I am sure no other woman would have sacrificed a pleasure to serve her husband— I must have my hands free to-night, and there is no place for women and children on the battlefield—and this you understand!

JEANNE: Don't think too highly of a poor woman like myself, and then you'll have no illusions to lose. And now you'll see that I can be as forgetful as you —I have bought you a tie and a pair of gloves which I thought you might wear for my sake on your day of honour.

MAURICE: [Kissing her hand] Thank you, dear.

JEANNE: And then, Maurice, don't forget to have your hair fixed, as you do all the time. I want you to be good-looking, so that others will like you, too.

MAURICE: There is no jealousy in you!

JEANNE: Don't mention that word, for evil thoughts spring from it.

MAURICE: Just now I feel as if I could give up this evening's victory—for I am going to win—

JEANNE: Hush, hush!

MAURICE: And go home with you instead.

JEANNE: But you mustn't do that! Go now: your destiny is waiting for you.

MAURICE: Good-bye then! And may that happen which must happen! [Goes out]

JEANNE: [*Alone with* Marion] O Crux! Ave spes unica!

CURTAIN

SCENE II.

The Crêmerie. On the right stands a buffet, on which are placed an aquarium with goldfish and dishes containing vegetables, fruit, preserves, etc. In the background is a door leading to the kitchen, where workmen are taking their meals. At the other end of the kitchen can be seen a door leading out to a garden. On the left, in the background, stands a counter on a raised platform, and back of it are shelves containing all sorts of bottles. On the right, a long table with a marble top is placed along the wall, and another table is placed parallel to the first farther out on the floor. Straw-bottomed chairs stand around the tables. The walls are covered with oil-paintings. Mme. Catherine *is sitting at the counter.* Maurice *stands leaning against it. He has his hat on and is smoking a cigarette.*

MME. CATHERINE: So it's to-night the great event comes off. Monsieur Maurice?

MAURICE: Yes, to-night.

MME. CATHERINE: Do you feel upset?

MAURICE: Cool as a cucumber.

MME. CATHERINE: Well, I wish you luck anyhow, and you have deserved it, Monsieur Maurice, after having had to fight against such difficulties as yours.

MAURICE: Thank you, Madame Catherine. You have been very kind to me, and without your help I should probably have been down and out by this time.

MME. CATHERINE: Don't let us talk of that now. I help along where I see hard work and the right kind of will, but I don't want to be exploited— Can we trust you to come back here after the play and let us drink a glass with you?

MAURICE: Yes, you can—of course, you can, as I have already promised you.

[Henriette *enters from the right.* Maurice *turns around, raises his hat, and stares at* Henriette, *who looks him over carefully*]

HENRIETTE: Monsieur Adolphe is not here yet?

MME. CATHERINE: No, madame. But he'll soon be here now. Won't you sit down?

HENRIETTE: No, thank you, I'd rather wait for him outside.

[*Goes out*]

MAURICE: Who—was—that?

MME. CATHERINE: Why, that's Monsieur Adolphe's friend.

MAURICE: Was—that—her?

MME. CATHERINE: Have you never seen her before?

MAURICE: No, he has been hiding her from me, just as if he was afraid I might take her away from him.

MME. CATHERINE: Ha-ha!— Well, how did you think she looked?

MAURICE: How she looked? Let me see: I can't tell—I didn't see her, for it was as if she had rushed straight into my arms at once and come so close to me that I couldn't make out her features at all. And she left her impression on the air behind her. I can still see her standing there. [*He goes towards the door and makes a gesture as if putting his arm around somebody*] Whew! [*He makes a gesture as if he had pricked his finger*] There are pins in her waist. She is of the kind that stings!

MME. CATHERINE: Oh, you are crazy, you with your ladies!

MAURICE: Yes, it's craziness, that's what it is. But do you know, Madame Catherine, I am going before she comes back, or else, or else— Oh, that woman is horrible!

MME. CATHERINE: Are you afraid?

MAURICE: Yes, I am afraid for myself, and also for some others.

MME. CATHERINE: Well, go then.

MAURICE: She seemed to suck herself out through the door, and in her wake rose a little whirlwind that dragged me along— Yes, you may laugh, but can't you see that the palm over there on the buffet is still shaking? She's the very devil of a woman!

MME. CATHERINE: Oh, get out of here, man, before you lose all your reason.

MAURICE: I want to go, but I cannot— Do you believe in fate, Madame Catherine?

MME. CATHERINE: No, I believe in a good God, who protects us against evil powers if we ask him in the right way.

MAURICE: So there are evil powers after all! I think I can hear them in the hallway now.

MME. CATHERINE: Yes, her clothes rustle as when the clerk tears off a piece of linen for you. Get away now—through the kitchen.

[Maurice *rushes towards the kitchen door, where he bumps into* Emile]

EMILE: I beg your pardon. [*He retires the way he came*]

ADOLPHE: [*Comes in first; after him* Henriette] Why, there's Maurice. How are you? Let me introduce this lady here to my oldest and best friend. Mademoiselle Henriette—Monsieur Maurice.

MAURICE: [*Saluting stiffly*] Pleased to meet you.

HENRIETTE: We have seen each other before.

ADOLPHE: Is that so? When, if I may ask?

MAURICE: A moment ago. Right here.

ADOLPHE: O-oh!— But now you must stay and have a chat with us.

MAURICE: [*After a glance at* Mme. Catherine] If I only had time.

ADOLPHE: Take the time. And we won't be sitting here very long.

HENRIETTE: I won't interrupt, if you have to talk business.

MAURICE: The only business we have is so bad that we don't want to talk of it.

HENRIETTE: Then we'll talk of something else. [Takes the hat away from Maurice and hangs it up] Now be nice, and let me become acquainted with the great author.

[Mme. Catherine signals to Maurice, who doesn't notice her]

ADOLPHE: That's right, Henriette, you take charge of him.

[They seat themselves at one of the tables]

HENRIETTE: [To Maurice] You certainly have a good friend in Adolphe, Monsieur Maurice. He never talks of anything but you, and in such a way that I feel myself rather thrown in the background.

ADOLPHE: You don't say so! Well, Henriette on her side never leaves me in peace about you, Maurice. She has read your works, and she is always wanting to know where you got this and where that. She has been questioning me about your looks, your age, your tastes. I have, in a word, had you for breakfast, dinner, and supper. It has almost seemed as if the three of us were living together.

MAURICE: [To Henriette] Heavens, why didn't you come over here and have a look at this wonder of wonders? Then your curiosity could have been satisfied in a trice.

HENRIETTE: Adolphe didn't want it.

[Adolphe looks embarrassed]

HENRIETTE: Not that he was jealous—

MAURICE: And why should he be, when he knows that my feelings are tied up elsewhere?

HENRIETTE: Perhaps he didn't trust the stability of your feelings.

MAURICE: I can't understand that, seeing that I am notorious for my constancy.

ADOLPHE: Well, it wasn't that—

HENRIETTE: [Interrupting him] Perhaps that is because you have not faced the fiery ordeal—

ADOLPHE: Oh, you don't know—

HENRIETTE: [Interrupting]—for the world has not yet beheld a faithful man.

MAURICE: Then it's going to behold one.

HENRIETTE: Where?

MAURICE: Here.

[Henriette laughs]

ADOLPHE: Well, that's going it—

HENRIETTE: [Interrupting him and directing herself continuously to Maurice] Do you think I ever trust my dear Adolphe more than a month at a time?

MAURICE: I have no right to question your lack of confidence, but I can guarantee that Adolphe is faithful.

HENRIETTE: You don't need to do so—my tongue is just running away with me, and I have to take back a lot—not only for fear of feeling less generous than you, but because it is the truth. It is a bad habit I have of only seeing the ugly side of things,

and I keep it up although I know better. But if I had a chance to be with you two for some time, then your company would make me good once more. Pardon me, Adolphe! [She puts her hand against his cheek]

ADOLPHE: You are always wrong in your talk and right in your actions. What you really think—that I don't know.

HENRIETTE: Who does know that kind of thing?

MAURICE: Well, if we had to answer for our thoughts, who could then clear himself?

HENRIETTE: Do you also have evil thoughts?

MAURICE: Certainly; just as I commit the worst kind of cruelties in my dreams.

HENRIETTE: Oh, when you are dreaming, of course— Just think of it— No, I am ashamed of telling—

MAURICE: Go on, go on!

HENRIETTE: Last night I dreamt that I was coolly dissecting the muscles on Adolphe's breast—you see, I am a sculptor—and he, with his usual kindness, made no resistance, but helped me instead with the worst places, as he knows more anatomy than I.

MAURICE: Was he dead?

HENRIETTE: No, he was living.

MAURICE: But that's horrible! And didn't it make you suffer?

HENRIETTE: Not at all, and that astonished me most, for I am rather sensitive to other people's sufferings. Isn't that so, Adolphe?

ADOLPHE: That's right. Rather abnormally so, in fact, and not the least when animals are concerned.

MAURICE: And I, on the other hand, am rather callous towards the sufferings both of myself and others.

ADOLPHE: Now he is not telling the truth about himself. Or what do you say, Madame Catherine?

MME. CATHERINE: I don't know of anybody with a softer heart than Monsieur Maurice. He came near calling in the police because I didn't give the goldfish fresh water—those over there on the buffet. Just look at them: it is as if they could hear what I am saying.

MAURICE: Yes, here we are making ourselves out as white as angels, and yet we are, taking it all in all, capable of any kind of polite atrocity the moment glory, gold, or women are concerned— So you are a sculptor, Mademoiselle Henriette?

HENRIETTE: A bit of one. Enough to do a bust. And to do one of you—which has long been my cherished dream—I hold myself quite capable.

MAURICE: Go ahead! That dream at least need not be long in coming true.

HENRIETTE: But I don't want to fix your features in my mind until this evening's success is over. Not until then will you have become what you should be.

MAURICE: How sure you are of victory!

HENRIETTE: Yes, it is written on your face that you are going to win this battle, and I think you must feel that yourself.

MAURICE: Why do you think so?

HENRIETTE: Because I can feel it. This morning I was ill, you know, and now I am well.

[Adolphe begins to look depressed]

MAURICE: [Embarrassed] Listen, I have a single ticket left—only one. I place it at your disposal, Adolphe.

ADOLPHE: Thank you, but I surrender it to Henriette.

HENRIETTE: But that wouldn't do!

ADOLPHE: Why not? And I never go to the theatre anyhow, as I cannot stand the heat.

HENRIETTE: But you will come and take us home at least after the show is over.

ADOLPHE: If you insist on it. Otherwise Maurice has to come back here, where we shall all be waiting for him.

MAURICE: You can just as well take the trouble of meeting us. In fact, I ask, I beg you to do so— And if you don't want to wait outside the theatre, you can meet us at the Auberge des Adrets— That's settled then, isn't it?

ADOLPHE: Wait a little. You have a way of settling things to suit yourself, before other people have a chance to consider them.

MAURICE: What is there to consider—whether you are to see your lady home or not?

ADOLPHE: You never know what may be involved in a simple act like that, but I have a sort of premonition.

HENRIETTE: Hush, hush, hush! Don't talk of spooks while the sun is shining. Let him come or not, as it pleases him. We can always find our way back here.

ADOLPHE: [Rising] Well, now I have to leave you—model, you know. Good-bye, both of you. And good luck to you, Maurice. To-morrow you will be out on the right side. Good-bye, Henriette.

HENRIETTE: Do you really have to go?

ADOLPHE: I must.

MAURICE: Good-bye then. We'll meet later.

[Adolphe goes out, saluting Mme. Catherine in passing]

HENRIETTE: Think of it, that we should meet at last!

MAURICE: Do you find anything remarkable in that?

HENRIETTE: It looks as if it had to happen, for Adolphe has done his best to prevent it.

MAURICE: Has he?

HENRIETTE: Oh, you must have noticed it.

MAURICE: I have noticed it, but why should you mention it?

HENRIETTE: I had to.

MAURICE: No, and I don't have to tell you that I wanted to run away through the kitchen in order to avoid meeting you and was stopped by a guest who closed the door in front of me.

HENRIETTE: Why do you tell me about it now?

MAURICE: I don't know.

[Mme. Catherine upsets a number of glasses and bottles]

MAURICE: That's all right, Madame Catherine. There's nothing to be afraid of.

HENRIETTE: Was that meant as a signal or a warning?

MAURICE: Probably both.

HENRIETTE: Do they take me for a locomotive that has to have flagmen ahead of it?

MAURICE: And switchmen! The danger is always greatest at the switches.

HENRIETTE: How nasty you can be!

MME. CATHERINE: Monsieur Maurice isn't nasty at all. So far nobody has been kinder than he to those that love him and trust in him.

MAURICE: Sh, sh, sh!

HENRIETTE: [To Maurice] The old lady is rather impertinent.

MAURICE: We can walk over to the boulevard, if you care to do so.

HENRIETTE: With pleasure. This is not the place for me. I can just feel their hatred clawing at me. [Goes out]

MAURICE: [Starts after her] Good-bye, Madame Catherine.

MME. CATHERINE: A moment! May I speak a word to you, Monsieur Maurice?

MAURICE: [Stops unwillingly] What is it?

MME. CATHERINE: Don't do it! Don't do it!

MAURICE: What?

MME. CATHERINE: Don't do it!

MAURICE: Don't be scared. This lady is not my kind, but she interests me. Or hardly that even.

MME. CATHERINE: Don't trust yourself!

MAURICE: Yes, I do trust myself. Good-bye. [Goes out]

CURTAIN

ACT II. SCENE I.

The Auberge des Adrets: a café in sixteenth-century style, with a suggestion of stage effect. Tables and easy-chairs are scattered in corners and nooks. The walls are decorated with armour and weapons. Along the ledge of the wainscoting stand glasses and jugs. Maurice and Henriette are in evening dress and sit facing each other at a table on which stands a bottle of champagne and three filled glasses. The third glass is placed at that side of the table which is nearest the background, and there an easy-chair is kept ready for the still missing "third man."

MAURICE: [Puts his watch in front of himself on the table] If he doesn't get here within the next five minutes, he isn't coming at all. And suppose in the meantime we drink with his ghost.

[Touches the third glass with the rim of his own]

HENRIETTE: [*Doing the same*] Here's to you, Adolphe!

MAURICE: He won't come.

HENRIETTE: He will come.

MAURICE: He won't.

HENRIETTE: He will.

MAURICE: What an evening! What a wonderful day! I can hardly grasp that a new life has begun. Think only: the manager believes that I may count on no less than one hundred thousand francs. I'll spend twenty thousand on a villa outside the city. That leaves me eighty thousand. I won't be able to take it all in until to-morrow, for I am tired, tired, tired. [*Sinks back into the chair*] Have you ever felt really happy?

HENRIETTE: Never. How does it feel?

MAURICE: I don't quite know how to put it. I cannot express it, but I seem chiefly to be thinking of the chagrin of my enemies. It isn't nice, but that's the way it is.

HENRIETTE: Is it happiness to be thinking of one's enemies?

MAURICE: Why, the victor has to count his killed and wounded enemies in order to gauge the extent of his victory.

HENRIETTE: Are you as bloodthirsty as all that?

MAURICE: Perhaps not. But when you have felt the pressure of other people's heels on your chest for years, it must be pleasant to shake off the enemy and draw a full breath at last.

HENRIETTE: Don't you find it strange that you are sitting here, alone with me, an insignificant girl practically unknown to you—and on an evening like this, when you ought to have a craving to show yourself like a triumphant hero to all the people, on the boulevards, in the big restaurants?

MAURICE: Of course, it's rather funny, but it feels good to be here, and your company is all I care for.

HENRIETTE: You don't look very hilarious.

MAURICE: No, I feel rather sad, and I should like to weep a little.

HENRIETTE: What is the meaning of that?

MAURICE: It is fortune conscious of its own nothingness and waiting for misfortune to appear.

HENRIETTE: Oh my, how sad! What is it you are missing anyhow?

MAURICE: I miss the only thing that gives value to life.

HENRIETTE: So you love her no longer then?

MAURICE: Not in the way I understand love. Do you think she has read my play, or that she wants to see it? Oh, she is so good, so self-sacrificing and considerate, but to go out with me for a night's fun she would regard as sinful. Once I treated her to champagne, you know, and instead of feeling happy over it, she picked up the wine list to see what it cost. And when she read the price, she wept—wept because Marion was in need of new stockings. It is beautiful, of course: it is touching, if you please. But I can get no pleasure out of it. And I do want

a little pleasure before life runs out. So far I have had nothing but privation, but now, now—life is beginning for me. [*The clock strikes twelve*] Now begins a new day, a new era!

HENRIETTE: Adolphe is not coming.

MAURICE: No, now he won't come. And now it is too late to go back to the Crêmerie.

HENRIETTE: But they are waiting for you.

MAURICE: Let them wait. They have made me promise to come, and I take back my promise. Are you longing to go there?

HENRIETTE: On the contrary!

MAURICE: Will you keep me company then?

HENRIETTE: With pleasure, if you care to have me.

MAURICE: Otherwise I shouldn't be asking you. It is strange, you know, that the victor's wreath seems worthless if you can't place it at the feet of some woman—that everything seems worthless when you have not a woman.

HENRIETTE: You don't need to be without a woman—you?

MAURICE: Well, that's the question.

HENRIETTE: Don't you know that a man is irresistible in his hour of success and fame?

MAURICE: No, I don't know, for I have had no experience of it.

HENRIETTE: You are a queer sort! At this moment, when you are the most envied man in Paris, you sit here and brood. Perhaps your conscience is troubling you because you have neglected that invitation to drink chicory coffee with the old lady over at the milk shop?

MAURICE: Yes, my conscience is troubling me on that score, and even here I am aware of their resentment, their hurt feelings, their well-grounded anger. My comrades in distress had the right to demand my presence this evening. The good Madame Catherine had a privileged claim on my success, from which a glimmer of hope was to spread over the poor fellows who have not yet succeeded. And I have robbed them of their faith in me. I can near the vows they have been making: "Maurice will come, for he is a good fellow; he doesn't despise us, and he never fails to keep his word." Now I have made them forswear themselves.

[*While he is still speaking, somebody in the next room has begun to play the finale of Beethoven's Sonata in D-minor (Op. 31, No. 2). The allegretto is first played piano, then more forte, and at last passionately, violently, with complete abandon*]

MAURICE: Who can be playing at this time of the night?

HENRIETTE: Probably some nightbirds of the same kind as we. But listen! Your presentation of the case is not correct. Remember that Adolphe promised to meet us here. We waited for him, and he failed to keep his promise. So that you are not to blame——

MAURICE: You think so? While you are speaking,

I believe you, but when you stop, my conscience begins again. What have you in that package?

HENRIETTE: Oh, it is only a laurel wreath that I meant to send up to the stage, but I had no chance to do so. Let me give it to you now—it is said to have a cooling effect on burning foreheads. [*She rises and crowns him with the wreath; then she kisses him on the forehead*] Hail to the victor!

MAURICE: Don't.

HENRIETTE: [*Kneeling*] Hail to the King!

MAURICE: [*Rising*] No, now you scare me.

HENRIETTE: You timid man! You of little faith who are afraid of fortune even! Who robbed you of your self-assurance and turned you into a dwarf?

MAURICE: A dwarf? Yes, you are right. I am not working up in the clouds, like a giant, with crashing and roaring, but I forge my weapons deep down in the silent heart of the mountain. You think that my modesty shrinks before the victor's wreath. On the contrary, I despise it: it is not enough for me. You think I am afraid of that ghost with its jealous green eyes which sits over there and keeps watch on my feelings—the strength of which you don't suspect. Away, ghost! [*He brushes the third, untouched glass off the table*] Away with you, you superfluous third person—you absent one who has lost your rights, if you ever had any. You stayed away from the field of battle because you knew myself already beaten. As I crush this glass under my foot, so I will crush the image of yourself which you have reared in a temple no longer yours.

HENRIETTE: Good! That's the way! Well spoken, my hero!

MAURICE: Now I have sacrificed my best friend, my most faithful helper, on your altar, Astarte! Are you satisfied?

HENRIETTE: Astarte is a pretty name, and I'll keep it—I think you love me, Maurice.

MAURICE: Of course I do— Woman of evil omen, you who stir up man's courage with your scent of blood, whence do you come and where do you lead me? I loved you before I saw you, for I trembled when I heard them speak of you. And when I saw you in the doorway, your soul poured itself into mine. And when you left, I could still feel your presence in my arms. I wanted to flee from you, but something held me back, and this evening we have been driven together as the prey is driven into the hunter's net. Whose is the fault? Your friend's, who pandered for us!

HENRIETTE: Fault or no fault: what does it matter, and what does it mean?— Adolphe has been at fault in not bringing us together before. He is guilty of having stolen from us two weeks of bliss, to which he had no right himself. I am jealous of him on your behalf. I hate him because he has cheated you out of your mistress. I should like to blot him from the host of the living, and his memory with him—wipe him out of the past even, make him unmade, unborn!

MAURICE: Well, we'll bury him beneath our own memories. We'll cover him with leaves and branches far out in the wild woods, and then we'll pile stone on top of the mound so that he will never look up again. [*Raising his glass*] Our fate is sealed. Woe unto us! What will come next?

HENRIETTE: Next comes the new era— What have you in that package?

MAURICE: I cannot remember.

HENRIETTE: [*Opens the package and takes out a tie and a pair of gloves*] That tie is a fright! It must have cost at least fifty centimes.

MAURICE: [*Snatching the things away from her*] Don't you touch them!

HENRIETTE: They are from her?

MAURICE: Yes, they are.

HENRIETTE: Give them to me.

MAURICE: No, she's better than we, better than everybody else.

HENRIETTE: I don't believe it. She is simply stupider and stingier. One who weeps because you order champagne——

MAURICE: When the child was without stockings. Yes, she is a good woman.

HENRIETTE: Philistine! You'll never be an artist. But I am an artist, and I'll make a bust of you with a shopkeeper's cap instead of the laurel wreath!— Her name is Jeanne?

MAURICE: How did you know?

HENRIETTE: Why, that's the name of all housekeepers.

MAURICE: Henriette!

[Henriette *takes the tie and the gloves and throws them into the fireplace*]

MAURICE: [*Weakly*] Astarte, now you demand the sacrifice of women. You shall have them, but if you ask for innocent children, too, then I'll send you packing.

HENRIETTE: Can you tell me what it is that binds you to me?

MAURICE: If I only knew, I should be able to tear myself away. But I believe it must be those qualities which you have and I lack. I believe that the evil within you draws me with the irresistible lure of novelty.

HENRIETTE: Have you ever committed a crime?

MAURICE: No real one. Have you?

HENRIETTE: Yes.

MAURICE: Well, how did you find it?

HENRIETTE: It was greater than to perform a good deed, for by that we are placed on equality with others; it was greater than to perform some act of heroism, for by that we are raised above others and rewarded. That crime placed me outside and beyond life, society, and my fellow-beings. Since then I am living only a partial life, a sort of dream life, and that's why reality never gets a hold on me.

MAURICE: What was it you did?

HENRIETTE: I won't tell, for then you would get scared again.

MAURICE: Can you ever be found out?

HENRIETTE: Never. But that does not prevent me from seeing, frequently, the five stones at the Place de Roquette, where the scaffold used to stand; and for this reason I never dare to open a pack of cards, as I always turn up the five of diamonds.

MAURICE: Was it that kind of a crime?

HENRIETTE: Yes, it was that kind.

MAURICE: Of course, it's horrible, but it is interesting. Have you no conscience?

HENRIETTE: None, but I should be grateful if you would talk of something else.

MAURICE: Suppose we talk of—love?

HENRIETTE: Of that you don't talk until it is over.

MAURICE: Have you been in love with Adolphe?

HENRIETTE: I don't know. The goodness of his nature drew me like some beautiful, all-but-vanished memory of childhood. Yet there was much about his person that offended my eye, so that I had to spend a long time retouching, altering, adding, subtracting, before I could make a presentable figure of him. When he talked, I could notice that he had learned from you, and the lesson was often badly digested and awkwardly applied. You can imagine then how miserable the copy must appear now, when I am permitted to study the original. That's why he was afraid of having us two meet; and when it did happen, he understood at once that his time was up.

MAURICE: Poor Adolphe!

HENRIETTE: I feel sorry for him, too, as I know he must be suffering beyond all bounds——

MAURICE: Sh! Somebody is coming.

HENRIETTE: I wonder if it could be he?

MAURICE: That would be unbearable.

HENRIETTE: No, it isn't he, but if it had been, how do you think the situation would have shaped itself?

MAURICE: At first he would have been a little sore at you because he had made a mistake in regard to the meeting-place—and tried to find us in several other cafés—but his soreness would have changed into pleasure at finding us—and seeing that we had not deceived him. And in the joy at having wronged us by his suspicions, he would love both of us. And so it would make him happy to notice that we had become such good friends. It had always been his dream—hm! he is making the speech now—his dream that the three of us should form a triumvirate that could set the world a great example of friendship asking for nothing— "Yes, I trust you, Maurice, partly because you are my friend, and partly because your feelings are tied up elsewhere."

HENRIETTE: Bravo! You must have been in a similar situation before, or you couldn't give such a lifelike picture of it. Do you know that Adolphe is just that kind of a third person who cannot enjoy his mistress without having his friend along?

MAURICE: That's why I had to be called in to entertain you— Hush! There is somebody outside— It must be he.

HENRIETTE: No, don't you know these are the hours when ghosts walk, and then you can see so many things, and hear them also. To keep awake at night, when you ought to be sleeping, has for me the same charm as a crime: it is to place oneself above and beyond the laws of nature.

MAURICE: But the punishment is fearful—I am shivering or quivering, with cold or with fear.

HENRIETTE: [Wraps her opera cloak about him] Put this on. It will make you warm.

MAURICE: That's nice. It is as if I were inside of your skin, as if my body had been melted up by lack of sleep and were being remoulded in your shape. I can feel the moulding process going on. But I am also growing a new soul, new thoughts, and here, where your bosom has left an impression, I can feel my own beginning to bulge.

[During this entire scene, the pianist in the next room has been practising the Sonata in D-minor, sometimes pianissimo, sometimes wildly fortissimo; now and then he has kept silent for a little while, and at other times nothing has been heard but a part of the finale: bars 96 to 107]

MAURICE: What a monster, to sit there all night practising on the piano. It gives me a sick feeling. Do you know what I propose? Let us drive out to the Bois de Boulogne and take breakfast in the Pavilion, and see the sun rise over the lakes.

HENRIETTE: Bully!

MAURICE: But first of all I must arrange to have my mail and the morning papers sent out by messenger to the Pavilion. Tell me Henriette: shall we invite Adolphe?

HENRIETTE: Oh, that's going too far! But why not? The ass can also be harnessed to the triumphal chariot. Let him come.

[They get up]

MAURICE: [Taking off the cloak] Then I'll ring.

HENRIETTE: Wait a moment! [Throws herself into his arms]

CURTAIN

SCENE II.

A large, splendidly furnished restaurant room in the Bois de Boulogne. It is richly carpeted and full of mirrors, easy-chairs, and divans. There are glass doors in the background, and beside them windows overlooking the lakes. In the foreground a table is spread, with flowers in the centre, bowls full of fruit, wine in decanters, oysters on platters, many different kinds of wine, glasses, and two lighted candelabra. On the right there is a round table full of newspapers and telegrams. Maurice and Henriette are sitting opposite each other at this small table. The sun is just rising outside.

MAURICE: There is no longer any doubt about it. The newspapers tell me it is so, and these telegrams congratulate me on my success. This is the beginning of a new life, and my fate is wedded to yours by this night, when you were the only one to share my hopes and my triumph. From your hand I received the laurel, and it seems to me as if everything had come from you.

HENRIETTE: What a wonderful night! Have we been dreaming, or is this something we have really lived through?

MAURICE: [*Rising*] And what a morning after such a night! I feel as if it were the world's first day that is now being illumined by the rising sun. Only this minute was the earth created and stripped of those white films that are now floating off into space. There lies the Garden of Eden in the rosy light of dawn, and here is the first human couple— Do you know, I am so happy I could cry at the thought that all mankind is not equally happy— Do you hear that distant murmur as of ocean waves beating against a rocky shore, as of winds sweeping through a forest? Do you know what it is? It is Paris whispering my name. Do you see the columns of smoke that rise skyward in thousand and tens of thousands? They are the fires burning on my altars, and if that be not so, then it must become so, for I will it. At this moment all the telegraph instruments of Europe are clicking out my name. The Oriental Express is carrying the newspapers to the Far East, towards the rising sun; and the ocean steamers are carrying them to the utmost West. The earth is mine, and for that reason it is beautiful. Now I should like to have wings for us two, so that we might rise from here and fly far, far away, before anybody can soil my happiness, before envy has chance to wake me out of my dream—for it is probably a dream!

HENRIETTE: [*Holding out her hand to him*] Here you can feel that you are not dreaming.

MAURICE: It is not a dream, but it has been one. As a poor young man, you know, when I was walking in the woods down there, and looked up to this Pavilion, it looked to me like a fairy castle, and always my thoughts carried me up to this room, with the balcony outside and the heavy curtains, as to a place of supreme bliss. To be sitting here in company with a beloved woman and see the sun rise while the candles were still burning in the candelabra: that was the most audacious dream of my youth. Now it has come true, and now I have no more to ask of life— Do you want to die now, together with me?

HENRIETTE: No, you fool! Now I want to begin living.

MAURICE: [*Rising*] To live; that is to suffer! Now comes reality. I can hear his steps on the stairs. He is panting with alarm, and his heart is beating with dread of having lost what it holds most precious. Can you believe me if I tell you that Adolphe is under this roof? Within a minute he will be standing in the middle of this floor.

HENRIETTE: [*Alarmed*] It was a stupid trick to ask him to come here, and I am already regretting it— Well, we shall see anyhow if your forecast of the situation proves correct.

MAURICE: Oh, it is easy to be mistaken about a person's feelings.

[*The* Head Waiter *enters with a card*]

MAURICE: Ask the gentleman to step in. [*To* Henriette] I am afraid we'll regret this.

HENRIETTE: Too late to think of that now— Hush!

[Adolphe *enters, pale and hollow-eyed*]

MAURICE: [*Trying to speak unconcernedly*] There you are! What became of you last night?

ADOLPHE: I looked for you at the Hôtel des Arrêts and waited a whole hour.

MAURICE: So you went to the wrong place. We were waiting several hours for you at the Auberge des Adrets, and we are still waiting for you, as you see.

ADOLPHE: [*Relieved*] Thank heaven!

HENRIETTE: Good morning, Adolphe. You are always expecting the worst and worrying yourself needlessly. I suppose you imagined that we wanted to avoid your company. And though you see that we sent for you, you are still thinking yourself superfluous.

ADOLPHE: Pardon me: I was wrong, but the night was dreadful.

[*They sit down. Embarrassed silence follows*]

HENRIETTE: [*To* Adolphe] Well, are you not going to congratulate Maurice on his great success?

ADOLPHE: Oh, yes! Your success is the real thing, and envy itself cannot deny it. Everything is giving way before you, and even I have a sense of my own smallness in your presence.

MAURICE: Nonsense!— Henriette, are you not going to offer Adolphe a glass of wine?

ADOLPHE: Thank you, not for me—nothing at all!

HENRIETTE: [*To* Adolphe] What's the matter with you? Are you ill?

ADOLPHE: Not yet, but——

HENRIETTE: Your eyes——

ADOLPHE: What of them?

MAURICE: What happened at the Crêmerie last night? I suppose they are angry with me?

ADOLPHE: Nobody is angry with you, but your absence caused a depression which it hurt me to watch. But nobody was angry with you, believe me. Your friends understood, and they regarded your failure to come with sympathetic forbearance. Madame Catherine herself defended you and proposed your health. We all rejoiced in your success as if it had been our own.

HENRIETTE: Well, those are nice people! What good friends you have, Maurice.

MAURICE: Yes, better than I deserve.

ADOLPHE: Nobody has better friends than he deserves, and you are a man greatly blessed in his friends— Can't you feel how the air is softened today by all the kind thoughts and wishes that stream toward you from a thousand breasts?

[Maurice *rises in order to hide his emotion*]

ADOLPHE: From a thousand breasts that you have rid of the nightmare that had been crushing them during a life-time. Humanity had been slandered—and you have exonerated it: that's why men feel grateful towards you. To-day they are once more holding their heads high and saying: You see, we are a little better than our reputation after all. And that thought *makes* them better.

[Henriette *tries to hide her emotion*]

ADOLPHE: Am I in the way? Just let me warm myself a little in your sunshine, Maurice, and then I'll go.

MAURICE: Why should you go when you have only just arrived?

ADOLPHE: Why? Because I have seen what I need not have seen; because I know now that my hour is past. [*Pause*] That you sent for me, I take as an expression of thoughtfulness, a notice of what has happened, a frankness that hurts less than deceit. You hear that I think well of my fellow-beings, and this I have learned from you, Maurice. [*Pause*] But, my friend, a few moments ago I passed through the Church of St. Germain, and there I saw a woman and a child. I am not wishing that you had seen them, for what has happened cannot be altered, but if you gave a thought or a word to them before you set them adrift on the waters of the great city, then you could enjoy your happiness undisturbed. And now I bid you good-bye.

HENRIETTE: Why must you go?

ADOLPHE: And you ask that? Do you want me to tell you?

HENRIETTE: No, I don't.

ADOLPHE: Good-bye then. [*Goes out*]

MAURICE: The Fall: and lo! "they knew that they were naked."

HENRIETTE: What a difference between this scene and the one we imagined! He is better than we.

MAURICE: It seems to me now as if all the rest were better than we.

HENRIETTE: Do you see that the sun has vanished behind a cloud, and the woods have lost their rose colour?

MAURICE: Yes, I see, and the blue lake has turned to black. Let us flee to some place where the sky is always blue and the trees are always green.

HENRIETTE: Yes, let us—but without any farewells.

MAURICE: No, with farewells.

HENRIETTE: We were to fly. You spoke of wings—and your feet are of lead. I am not jealous, but if you go to say farewell and get two pairs of arms around your neck—then you can't tear yourself away.

MAURICE: Perhaps you are right, but only one pair of little arms is needed to hold me fast.

HENRIETTE: It is the child that holds you then, and not the woman?

MAURICE: It is the child.

HENRIETTE: The child! Another woman's child! And for the sake of it I am to suffer. Why must that child block the way where I want to pass, and must pass?

MAURICE: Yes, why? It would be better if it had never existed.

HENRIETTE: [*Walks excitedly back and forth*] Indeed! But now it does exist. Like a rock on the road, a rock set firmly in the ground, immovable, so that it upsets the carriage.

MAURICE: The triumphal chariot!— The ass is driven to death, but the rock remains. Curse it!
[*Pause*]

HENRIETTE: There is nothing to do.

MAURICE: Yes, we must get married, and then *our* child will make us forget the other one.

HENRIETTE: This will kill this!

MAURICE: Kill! What kind of word is that?

HENRIETTE: [*Changing tone*] Your child will kill our love.

MAURICE: No, girl, our love will kill whatever stands in its way, but it will not be killed.

HENRIETTE: [*Opens a deck of cards lying on the mantelpiece*] Look at it! The five of diamonds—the scaffold! Can it be possible that our fates are determined in advance? That our thoughts are guided as if through pipes to the spot for which they are bound, without chance for us to stop them? But I don't want it, I don't want it!— Do you realise that I must go to the scaffold if my crime should be discovered?

MAURICE: Tell me about your crime. Now is the time for it.

HENRIETTE: No, I should regret it afterwards, and you would despise me—no, no, no!— Have you ever heard that a person could be hated to death? Well, my father incurred the hatred of my mother and my sisters, and he melted away like wax before a fire. Ugh! Let us talk of something else. And, above all, let us get away. The air is poisoned here. To-morrow your laurels will be withered, the triumph will be forgotten, and in a week another triumphant hero will hold the public attention. Away from here, to work for new victories! But first of all, Maurice, you must embrace your child and provide for its immediate future. You don't have to see the mother at all.

MAURICE: Thank you! Your good heart does you honour, and I love you doubly when you show the kindness you generally hide.

HENRIETTE: And then you go to the Crêmerie and say good-bye to the old lady and your friends. Leave no unsettled business behind to make your mind heavy on our trip.

MAURICE: I'll clear up everything, and to-night we meet at the railroad station.

HENRIETTE: Agreed! And then: away from here—away towards the sea and the sun!

CURTAIN

ACT III. SCENE I.

In the Crêmerie. The gas is lit. Mme. Catherine *is seated at the counter,* Adolphe *at a table.*

MME. CATHERINE: Such is life, Monsieur Adolphe. But you young ones are always demanding too much, and then you come here and blubber over it afterwards.

ADOLPHE: No, it isn't that. I reproach nobody, and I am as fond as ever of both of them. But there is one thing that makes me sick at heart. You see, I thought more of Maurice than of anybody else; so much that I wouldn't have grudged him anything that could give him pleasure—but now I have lost him, and it hurts me worse than the loss of her. I have lost both of them, and so my loneliness is made doubly painful. And then there is still something else which I have not yet been able to clear up.

MME. CATHERINE: Don't brood so much. Work and divert yourself. Now, for instance, do you ever go to church?

ADOLPHE: What should I do there?

MME. CATHERINE: Oh, there's so much to look at, and then there is the music. There is nothing commonplace about it, at least.

ADOLPHE: Perhaps not. But I don't belong to that fold, I guess, for it never stirs me to any devotion. And then, Madame Catherine, faith is a gift, they tell me, and I haven't got it yet.

MME. CATHERINE: Well, wait till you get it— But what is this I heard a while ago? Is it true that you have sold a picture in London for a high price, and that you have got a medal?

ADOLPHE: Yes, it's true.

MME. CATHERINE: Merciful heavens!—and not a word do you say about it?

ADOLPHE: I am afraid of fortune, and besides it seems almost worthless to me at this moment. I am afraid of it as of a spectre: it brings disaster to speak of having seen it.

MME. CATHERINE: You're a queer fellow, and that's what you have always been.

ADOLPHE: Not queer at all, but I have seen so much misfortune come in the wake of fortune, and I have seen how adversity brings out true friends, while none but false ones appear in the hour of success— You asked me if I ever went to church, and I answered evasively. This morning I stepped into the Church of St. Germain without really knowing why I did so. It seemed as if I were looking for somebody in there—somebody to whom I could silently offer my gratitude. But I found nobody. Then I dropped a gold coin in the poor-box. It was all I could get out of my church-going, and that was rather commonplace, I should say.

MME. CATHERINE: It was always something; and

then it was fine to think of the poor after having heard good news.

ADOLPHE: It was neither fine nor anything else: it was something I did because I couldn't help myself. But something more occurred while I was in the church. I saw Maurice's girl friend, Jeanne, and her child. Struck down, crushed by his triumphal chariot, they seemed aware of the full extent of their misfortune.

MME. CATHERINE: Well, children, I don't know in what kind of shape you keep your consciences. But how a decent fellow, a careful and considerate man like Monsieur Maurice, can all of a sudden desert a woman and her child, that is something I cannot explain.

ADOLPHE: Nor can I explain it, and he doesn't seem to understand it himself. I met them this morning, and everything appeared quite natural to them, quite proper, as if they couldn't imagine anything else. It was as if they had been enjoying the satisfaction of a good deed or the fulfilment of a sacred duty. There are things, Madame Catherine, that we cannot explain, and for this reason it is not for us to judge. And besides, you saw how it happened. Maurice felt the danger in the air. I foresaw it and tried to prevent their meeting. Maurice wanted to run away from it, but nothing helped. Why, it was as if a plot had been laid by some invisible power, and as if they had been driven by guile into each other's arms. Of course, I am disqualified in this case, but I wouldn't hesitate to pronounce a verdict of "not guilty."

MME. CATHERINE: Well, now, to be able to forgive as you do, that's what I call religion.

ADOLPHE: Heavens, could it be that I am religious without knowing it.

MME. CATHERINE: But then, to *let* oneself be driven or tempted into evil, as Monsieur Maurice has done, means weakness or bad character. And if you feel your strength failing you, then you ask for help, and then you get it. But he was too conceited to do that— Who is this coming? The Abbé, I think.

ADOLPHE: What does he want here?

ABBÉ: [*Enters*] Good evening, madame. Good evening, monsieur.

MME. CATHERINE: Can I be of any service?

ABBÉ: Has Monsieur Maurice, the author, been here to-day?

MME. CATHERINE: Not to-day. His play has just been put on, and that is probably keeping him busy.

ABBÉ: I have—sad news to bring him. Sad in several respects.

MME. CATHERINE: May I ask of what kind?

ABBÉ: Yes, it's no secret. The daughter he had with that girl, Jeanne, is dead.

MME. CATHERINE: Dead!

ADOLPHE: Marion dead!

ABBÉ: Yes, she died suddenly this morning without any previous illness.

MME. CATHERINE: O Lord, who can tell Thy ways!

ABBÉ: The mother's grief makes it necessary that Monsieur Maurice look after her, so we must try to find him. But first a question in confidence: do you know whether Monsieur Maurice was fond of the child, or was indifferent to it?

MME. CATHERINE: If he was fond of Marion? Why, all of us know how he loved her.

ADOLPHE: There's no doubt about that.

ABBÉ: I am glad to hear it, and it settles the matter so far as I am concerned.

MME. CATHERINE: Has there been any doubt about it?

ABBÉ: Yes, unfortunately. It has even been rumoured in the neighbourhood that he had abandoned the child and its mother in order to go away with a strange woman. In a few hours this rumour has grown into definite accusations, and at the same time the feeling against him has risen to such a point that his life is threatened and he is being called a murderer.

MME. CATHERINE: Good God, what is *this*? What does it mean?

ABBÉ: Now I'll tell you my opinion— I am convinced that the man is innocent on this score, and the mother feels as certain about it as I do. But appearances are against Monsieur Maurice, and I think he will find it rather hard to clear himself when the police come to question him.

ADOLPHE: Have the police got hold of the matter?

ABBÉ: Yes, the police have had to step in to protect him against all those ugly rumours and the rage of the people. Probably the Commissaire will be here soon.

MME. CATHERINE: [*To* Adolphe] There, you see what happens when a man cannot tell the difference between good and evil, and when he trifles with vice. God will punish!

ADOLPHE: Then he is more merciless than man.

ABBÉ: What do you know about that?

ADOLPHE: Not very much, but I keep an eye on what happens——

ABBÉ: And you understand it also?

ADOLPHE: Not yet perhaps.

ABBÉ: Let us look more closely at the matter— Oh, here comes the Commissaire.

COMMISSAIRE: [*Enters*] Gentlemen—Madame Catherine—I have to trouble you for a moment with a few questions concerning Monsieur Maurice. As you have probably heard, he has become the object of a hideous rumour, which, by the by, I don't believe in.

MME. CATHERINE: None of us believes in it either.

COMMISSAIRE: That strengthens my own opinion, but for his own sake I must give him a chance to defend himself.

ABBÉ: That's right, and I guess he will find justice, although it may come hard.

COMMISSAIRE: Appearances are very much

against him, but I have seen guiltless people reach the scaffold before their innocence was discovered. Let me tell you what there is against him. The little girl, Marion, being left alone by her mother, was secretly visited by the father, who seems to have made sure of the time when the child was to be found alone. Fifteen minutes after his visit the mother returned home and found the child dead. All this makes the position of the accused man very unpleasant— The post-mortem examination brought out no signs of violence or of poison, but the physicians admit the existence of new poisons that leave no traces behind them. To me all this is mere coincidence of the kind I frequently come across. But here's something that looks worse. Last night Monsieur Maurice was seen at the Auberge des Adrets in company with a strange lady. According to the waiter, they were talking about crimes. The Place de Roquette and the scaffold were both mentioned. A queer topic of conversation for a pair of lovers of good breeding and good social position! But even this may be passed over, as we know by experience that people who have been drinking and losing a lot of sleep seem inclined to dig up all the worst that lies at the bottom of their souls. Far more serious is the evidence given by the head waiter as to their champagne breakfast in the Bois de Boulogne this morning. He says that he heard them wish the life out of a child. The man is said to have remarked that, "It would be better if it had never existed." To which the woman replied: "Indeed! But now it does exist." And as they went on talking, these words occurred: "This will kill this!" And the answer was: "Kill! What kind of word is that?" And also: "The five of diamonds—the scaffold, the Place de Roquette." All this, you see, will be hard to get out of, and so will the foreign journey planned for this evening. These are serious matters.

ADOLPHE: He is lost!

MME. CATHERINE: That's a dreadful story. One doesn't know what to believe.

ABBÉ: This is not the work of man. God have mercy on him!

ADOLPHE: He is in the net, and he will never get out of it.

MME. CATHERINE: He had no business to get in.

ADOLPHE: Do you begin to suspect him also, Madame Catherine?

MME. CATHERINE: Yes and no. I have got beyond having an opinion in this matter. Have you not seen angels turn into devils just as you turn your hand, and then become angels again?

COMMISSAIRE: It certainly does look queer. However, we'll have to wait and hear what explanations he can give. No one will be judged unheard. Good evening, gentlemen. Good evening, Madame Catherine. [*Goes out*]

ABBÉ: This is not the work of man.

ADOLPHE: No, it looks as if demons had been at work for the undoing of man.

ABBÉ: It is either a punishment for secret misdeeds, or it is a terrible test.

JEANNE: [*Enters, dressed in mourning*] Good evening. Pardon me for asking, but have you seen Monsieur Maurice?

MME. CATHERINE: No, madame, but I think he may be here any minute. You haven't met him then since——

JEANNE: Not since this morning.

MME. CATHERINE: Let me tell you that I share in your great sorrow.

JEANNE: Thank you, madame. [*To the* Abbé] So you are here, Father.

ABBÉ: Yes, my child. I thought I might be of some use to you. And it was fortunate, as it gave me a chance to speak to the Commissaire.

JEANNE: The Commissaire! He doesn't suspect Maurice also, does he?

ABBÉ: No, he doesn't, and none of us here do. But appearances are against him in a most appalling manner.

JEANNE: You mean on account of the talk the waiters overheard—it means nothing to me, who has heard such things before when Maurice had had a few drinks. Then it is his custom to speculate on crimes and their punishment. Besides it seems to have been the woman in his company who dropped the most dangerous remarks. I should like to have a look into that woman's eyes.

ADOLPHE: My dear Jeanne, no matter how much harm that woman may have done you, she did nothing with evil intention—in fact, she had no intention whatever, but just followed the promptings of her nature. I know her to be a good soul and one who can very well bear being looked straight in the eye.

JEANNE: Your judgment in this matter, Adolphe, has great value to me, and I believe what you say. It means that I cannot hold anybody but myself responsible for what has happened. It is my carelessness that is now being punished. [*She begins to cry*]

ABBÉ: Don't accuse yourself unjustly! I know you, and the serious spirit in which you have regarded your motherhood. That your assumption of this responsibility had not been sanctioned by religion and the civil law was not your fault. No, we are here facing something quite different.

ADOLPHE: What then?

ABBÉ: Who can tell?

[Henriette *enters, dressed in travelling suit*]

ADOLPHE: [*Rises with an air of determination and goes to meet* Henriette] You here?

HENRIETTE: Yes, where is Maurice?

ADOLPHE: Do you know—or don't you?

HENRIETTE: I know everything. Excuse me, Madame Catherine, but I was ready to start and absolutely had to step in here a moment. [*To* Adolphe] Who is that woman?—Oh!

[Henriette *and* Jeanne *stare at each other.*

Emile *appears in the kitchen door*]

HENRIETTE: [*To* Jeanne] I ought to say something, but it matters very little, for anything I can say must sound like an insult or a mockery. But if I ask you simply to believe that I share your deep sorrow as much as anybody standing closer to you, then you must not turn away from me. You mustn't, for I deserve your pity if not your forbearance. [*Holds out her hand*]

JEANNE: [*Looks hard at her*] I believe you now—and in the next moment I don't. [*Takes* Henriette's *hand*]

HENRIETTE: [*Kisses* Jeanne's *hand*] Thank you!

JEANNE: [*Drawing back her hand*] Oh, don't! I don't deserve it! I don't deserve it!

ABBÉ: Pardon me, but while we are gathered here and peace seems to prevail temporarily at least, won't you, Mademoiselle Henriette, shed some light into all the uncertainty and darkness surrounding the main point of accusation? I ask you, as a friend among friends, to tell us what you meant with all that talk about killing, and crime, and the Place de Roquette. That your words had no connection with the death of the child, we have reason to believe, but it would give us added assurance to hear what you were really talking about. Won't you tell us?

HENRIETTE: [*After a pause*] That I cannot tell! No, I cannot!

ADOLPHE: Henriette, do tell! Give us the word that will relieve us all.

HENRIETTE: I cannot! Don't ask me!

ABBÉ: This is not the work of man!

HENRIETTE: Oh, that this moment had to come! And in this manner! [*To* Jeanne] Madame, I swear that I am not guilty of your child's death. Is that enough?

JEANNE: Enough for us, but not for Justice.

HENRIETTE: Justice! If you knew how true your words are!

ABBÉ: [*To* Henriette] And if you knew what you were saying just now!

HENRIETTE: Do you know that better than I?

ABBÉ: Yes, I do.

[Henriette *looks fixedly at the* Abbé]

ABBÉ: Have no fear, for even if I guess your secret, it will not be exposed. Besides, I have nothing to do with human justice, but a great deal with divine mercy.

MAURICE: [*Enters, hastily, dressed for travelling. He doesn't look at the others, who are standing in the background, but goes straight up to the counter, where* Mme. Catherine *is sitting*] You are not angry at me, Madame Catherine, because I didn't show up? I have come now to apologise to you before I start for the South at eight o'clock this evening.

[Mme. Catherine *is too startled to say a word*]

MAURICE: Then you are angry at me? [*Looks around*] What does all this mean? Is it a dream, or what is it? Of course, I can see that it is all real, but it looks like a wax cabinet— There is Jeanne, looking like a statue and dressed in black— And Henriette looking like a corpse— What does it mean?

[*All remain silent*]

MAURICE: Nobody answers. It must mean something dreadful. [*Silence*] But speak, please! Adolphe, you are my friend, what is it? [*Pointing to* Emile] And there is a detective!

ADOLPHE: [*Comes forward*] You don't know then?

MAURICE: Nothing at all. But I must know!

ADOLPHE: Well, then—Marion is dead.

MAURICE: Marion—dead?

ADOLPHE: Yes, she died this morning.

MAURICE: [*To* Jeanne] So that's why you are in mourning. Jeanne, Jeanne, who has done this to us?

JEANNE: He who holds life and death in his hand.

MAURICE: But I saw her looking well and happy this morning. How did it happen? Who did it? Somebody must have done it? [*His eyes seek* Henriette]

ADOLPHE: Don't look for the guilty one here, for there is none to be found. Unfortunately, the police have turned their suspicion in a direction where none ought to exist.

MAURICE: What direction is that?

ADOLPHE: Well—you may as well know that your reckless talk last night and this morning has placed you in a light that is anything but favorable.

MAURICE: So they were listening to us. Let me see, what were we saying—I remember!— Then I am lost!

ADOLPHE: But if you explain your thoughtless words we will believe you.

MAURICE: I cannot! And I will not! I shall be sent to prison, but it doesn't matter. Marion is dead! Dead! And I have killed her!

[*General consternation*]

ADOLPHE: Think of what you are saying! Weigh your words! Do you realise what you said just now?

MAURICE: What did I say?

ADOLPHE: You said that you had killed Marion.

MAURICE: Is there a human being here who could believe me a murderer, and who could hold me capable of taking my own child's life? You who know me, Madame Catherine, tell me; do you believe, can you believe——

MME. CATHERINE: I don't know any longer what to believe. What the heart thinketh the tongue speaketh. And your tongue has spoken evil words.

MAURICE: She doesn't believe me!

ADOLPHE: But explain your words, man! Explain what you meant by saying that "your love would kill everything that stood in its way".

MAURICE: So they know that too— Are you willing to explain it, Henriette?

HENRIETTE: No, I cannot do that.

ABBÉ: There is something wrong behind all this and you have lost our sympathy, my friend. A while

ago I could have sworn that you were innocent, and I wouldn't do that now.

MAURICE: [*To* Jeanne] What you have to say means more to me than anything else.

JEANNE: [*Coldly*] Answer a question first: who was it you cursed during that orgy out there?

MAURICE: Have I done that, too? Maybe. Yes, I am guilty, and yet I am guiltless. Let me go away from here, for I am ashamed of myself, and I have done more wrong than I can forgive myself.

HENRIETTE: [*To* Adolphe] Go with him and see that he doesn't do himself any harm.

ADOLPHE: Shall I——?

HENRIETTE: Who else?

ADOLPHE: [*Without bitterness*] You are nearest to it— Sh! A carriage is stopping outside.

MME. CATHERINE: It's the Commissaire. Well, much as I have seen of life, I could never have believed that success and fame were such short-lived things.

MAURICE: [*To* Henriette] From the triumphal chariot to the patrol wagon!

JEANNE: [*Simply*] And the ass—who was that?

ADOLPHE: Oh, that must have been me.

COMMISSAIRE: [*Enters with a paper in his hands*] A summons to Police Headquarters—to-night, at once—for Monsieur Maurice Gérard—and for Mademoiselle Henriette Mauclerc—both here?

MAURICE *and* HENRIETTE: Yes.

MAURICE: Is this an arrest?

COMMISSAIRE: Not yet. Only a summons.

MAURICE: And then?

COMMISSAIRE: We don't know yet.

[Maurice *and* Henriette *go towards the door*]

MAURICE: Good-bye to all!

[*Everybody shows emotion. The* Commissaire, Maurice, *and* Henriette *go out*]

EMILE: [*Enters and goes up to* Jeanne] Now I'll take you home, sister.

JEANNE: And what do you think of all this?

EMILE: The man is innocent.

ABBÉ: But as I see it, it is, and must always be, something despicable to break one's promise, and it becomes unpardonable when a woman and her child are involved.

EMILE: Well, I should rather feel that way, too, now when it concerns my own sister, but, unfortunately, I am prevented from throwing the first stone because I have done the same thing myself.

ABBÉ: Although I am free from blame in that respect, I am not throwing any stones either, but the act condemns itself and is punished by its consequences.

JEANNE: Pray for him! For both of them!

ABBÉ: No, I'll do nothing of the kind, for it is an impertinence to want to change the counsels of the Lord. And what has happened here is, indeed, not the work of man.

CURTAIN

SCENE II.

The Auberge des Adrets. Adolphe *and* Henriette *are seated at the same table where* Maurice *and* Henriette *were sitting in the second act. A cup of coffee stands in front of* Adolphe. Henriette *has ordered nothing.*

ADOLPHE: You believe then that he will come here?

HENRIETTE: I am sure. He was released this noon for lack of evidence, but he didn't want to show himself in the streets before it was dark.

ADOLPHE: Poor fellow! Oh, I tell you, life seems horrible to me since yesterday.

HENRIETTE: And what about me? I am afraid to live, dare hardly breathe, dare hardly think even, since I know that somebody is spying not only on my words but on my thoughts.

ADOLPHE: So it was here you sat that night when I couldn't find you?

HENRIETTE: Yes, but don't talk of it. I could die from shame when I think of it. Adolphe, you are made of a different, a better, stuff than he or I—

ADOLPHE: Sh, sh, sh!

HENRIETTE: Yes, indeed! And what was it that made me stay here? I was lazy; I was tired; his success intoxicated me and bewitched me—I cannot explain it. But if you had come it would never have happened. And to-day you are great, and he is small—less than the least of all. Yesterday he had one hundred thousand francs. To-day he has nothing, because his play has been withdrawn. And public opinion will never excuse him, for his lack of faith will be judged as harshly as if he were the murderer, and those that see farthest hold that the child died from sorrow, so that he was responsible for it anyhow.

ADOLPHE: You know what my thoughts are in this matter, Henriette, but I should like to know that both of you are spotless. Won't you tell me what those dreadful words of yours meant? It cannot be a chance that your talk in a festive moment like that dealt so largely with killing and the scaffold.

HENRIETTE: It was no chance. It was something that had to be said, something I cannot tell you—probably because I have no right to appear spotless in your eyes, seeing that I am not spotless.

ADOLPHE: All this is beyond me.

HENRIETTE: Let us talk of something else— Do you believe there are many unpunished criminals at large among us, some of whom may even be our intimate friends?

ADOLPHE: [Nervously] Why? What do you mean?

HENRIETTE: Don't you believe that every human being at some time or another has been guilty of some kind of act which would fall under the law if it were discovered?

ADOLPHE: Yes, I believe that is true, but no evil act escapes being punished by one's own conscience at least. [Rises and unbuttons his coat] And—nobody· is really good who has not erred. [Breathing heavily] For in order to know how to forgive, one must have been in need of forgiveness—I had a friend whom we used to regard as a model man. He never spoke a hard word to anybody; he forgave everything and everybody; and he suffered insults with a strange satisfaction that we couldn't explain. At last, late in life, he gave me his secret in a single word: I am a penitent! [He sits down again]

[Henriette remains silent, looking at him with surprise]

ADOLPHE: [As if speaking to himself] There are crimes not mentioned in the Criminal Code, and these are the worse ones, for they have to be punished by ourselves, and no judge could be more severe than we are against our own selves.

HENRIETTE: [After a pause] Well, that friend of yours, did he find peace?

ADOLPHE: After endless self-torture he reached a certain degree of composure, but life had never any real pleasures to offer him. He never dared to accept any kind of distinction; he never dared to feel himself entitled to a kind word or even well-earned praise: in a word, he could never quite forgive himself.

HENRIETTE: Never? What had he done then?

ADOLPHE: He had wished the life out of his father. And when his father suddenly died, the son imagined himself to have killed him. Those imaginations were regarded as signs of some mental disease, and he was sent to an asylum. From this he was discharged after a time as wholly recovered—as they put it. But the sense of guilt remained with him, and so he continued to punish himself for his evil thoughts.

HENRIETTE: Are you sure the evil will cannot kill?

ADOLPHE: You mean in some mystic way?

HENRIETTE: As you please. Let it go at mystic. In my own family—I am sure that my mother and my sisters killed my father with their hatred. You see, he had the awful idea that he must oppose all our tastes and inclinations. Wherever he discovered a natural gift, he tried to root it out. In that way he aroused a resistance that accumulated until it became like an electrical battery charged with hatred. At last it grew so powerful that he languished away, became depolarised, lost his will-power, and, in the end, came to wish himself dead.

ADOLPHE: And your conscience never troubled you?

HENRIETTE: No, and furthermore, I don't know what conscience is.

ADOLPHE: You don't? Well, then you'll soon learn. [Pause] How do you believe Maurice will look when he gets here? What do you think he will say?

HENRIETTE: Yesterday morning, you know, he and I tried to make the same kind of guess about you while we were waiting for you.

ADOLPHE: Well?

HENRIETTE: We guessed entirely wrong.

ADOLPHE: Can you tell me why you sent for me?

HENRIETTE: Malice, arrogance, outright cruelty!

ADOLPHE: How strange it is that you can admit your faults and yet not repent of them.

HENRIETTE: It must be because I don't feel quite responsible for them. They are like the dirt left behind by things handled during the day and washed off at night. But tell me one thing: do you really think so highly of humanity as you profess to do?

ADOLPHE: Yes, we are a little better than our reputation—and a little worse.

HENRIETTE: That is not a straightforward answer.

ADOLPHE: No, it isn't. But are you willing to answer me frankly when I ask you: do you still love Maurice?

HENRIETTE: I cannot tell until I see him. But at this moment I feel no longing for him, and it seems as if I could very well live without him.

ADOLPHE: It's likely you could, but I fear you have become chained to his fate—Sh! Here he comes.

HENRIETTE: How everything repeats itself. The situation is the same, the very words are the same, as when we were expecting you yesterday.

MAURICE: [Enters, pale as death, hollow-eyed, unshaven] Here I am, my dear friends, if this be me. For that last night in a cell changed me into a new sort of being.

[Notices Henriette and Adolphe]

ADOLPHE: Sit down and pull yourself together, and then we can talk things over.

MAURICE: [To Henriette] Perhaps I am in the way?

ADOLPHE: Now don't get bitter.

MAURICE: I have grown bad in these twenty-four hours, and suspicious also, so I guess I'll soon be left to myself. And who wants to keep company with a murderer?

HENRIETTE: But you have been cleared of the charge.

MAURICE: [Picks up a newspaper] By the police, yes, but not by public opinion. Here you see the murderer Maurice Gérard, once a playwright, and his mistress, Henriette Mauclerc——

HENRIETTE: O my mother and my sisters—my mother! Jesus, have mercy!

MAURICE: And can you see that I actually look like a murderer? And then it is suggested that my play was stolen. So there isn't a vestige left of the victorious hero from yesterday. In place of my own, the name of Octave, my enemy, appears on the bill-boards, and he is going to collect my one hundred thousand francs. O Solon, Solon! Such is fortune, and such is fame! You are fortunate, Adolphe, because you have not yet succeeded.

HENRIETTE: So you don't know that Adolphe has made a great success in London and carried off the first prize?

MAURICE: [Darkly] No, I didn't know that. Is it true, Adolphe?

ADOLPHE: It is true, but I have returned the prize.

HENRIETTE: [With emphasis] That I didn't know! So you are also prevented from accepting any distinction—like your friend?

ADOLPHE: My friend? [Embarrassed] Oh, yes, yes!

MAURICE: Your success gives me pleasure, but it puts us still farther apart.

ADOLPHE: That's what I expected, and I suppose I'll be as lonely with my success as you with your adversity. Think of it—that people feel hurt by your fortune! Oh, it's ghastly to be alive!

MAURICE: You say that! What am I then to say? It is as if my eyes had been covered with a black veil, and as if the colour and shape of all life had been changed by it. This room looks like the room I saw yesterday, and yet it is quite different. I recognise both of you, of course, but your faces are new to me. I sit here and search for words because I don't know what to say to you. I ought to defend myself, but I cannot. And I almost miss the cell, for it protected me, at least, against the curious glances that pass right through me. The murderer Maurice and his mistress. You don't love me any longer, Henriette, and no more do I care for you. To-day you are ugly, clumsy, insipid, repulsive.

[Two men in civilian clothes have quietly seated themselves at a table in the background]

ADOLPHE: Wait a little and get your thoughts together. That you have been discharged and cleared of all suspicion must appear in some of the evening papers. And that puts an end to the whole matter. Your play will be put on again, and if it comes to the worst, you can write a new one. Leave Paris for a year and let everything become forgotten. You who have exonerated mankind will be exonerated yourself.

MAURICE: Ha-ha! Mankind! Ha-ha!

ADOLPHE: You have ceased to believe in goodness!

MAURICE: Yes, if I ever did believe in it. Perhaps it was only a mood, a manner of looking at things, a way of being polite to the wild beasts. When I, who was held among the best, can be so rotten to the core, what must then be the wretchedness of the rest?

ADOLPHE: Now I'll go out and get all the evening papers, and then we'll undoubtedly have reason to look at things in a different way.

MAURICE: [Turning towards the background] Two detectives!—It means that I am released under surveillance, so that I can give myself away by careless talking.

ADOLPHE: Those are not detectives. That's only your imagination. I recognise both of them. [Goes towards the door]

MAURICE: Don't leave us alone, Adolphe. I fear that Henriette and I may come to open explanations.

ADOLPHE: Oh, be sensible, Maurice, and think of your future. Try to keep him quiet, Henriette. I'll be back in a moment. [Goes out]

HENRIETTE: Well, Maurice, what do you think now of our guilt or guiltlessness?

MAURICE: I have killed nobody. All I did was to talk a lot of nonsense while I was drunk. But it is your crime that comes back, and that crime you have grafted on to me.

HENRIETTE: Oh, that's the tone you talk now!— Was it not you who cursed your own child, and wished the life out of it, and wanted to go away without saying good-bye to anybody? And was it not I who made you visit Marion and show yourself to Madame Catherine?

MAURICE: Yes, you are right. Forgive me! You proved yourself more human than I, and the guilt is wholly my own. Forgive me! But all the same I am without guilt. Who has tied this net from which I can never free myself? Guilty and guiltless: guiltless and yet guilty! Oh, it is driving me mad— Look, now they sit over there and listen to us— And no waiter comes to take our order. I'll go out and order a cup of tea. Do you want anything?

HENRIETTE: Nothing.

[Maurice goes out]

FIRST DETECTIVE: [Goes up to Henriette] Let me look at your papers.

HENRIETTE: How dare you speak to me?

DETECTIVE: Dare? I'll show you!

HENRIETTE: What do you mean?

DETECTIVE: It's my job to keep an eye on street-walkers. Yesterday you came here with one man, and to-day with another. That's as good as walking the streets. And unescorted ladies don't get anything here. So you'd better get out and come along with me.

HENRIETTE: My escort will be back in a moment.

DETECTIVE: Yes, and a pretty kind of escort you've got—the kind that doesn't help a girl a bit!

HENRIETTE: O God! My mother, my sisters!— I am of good family, I tell you.

DETECTIVE: Yes, first-rate family, I am sure. But you are too well known through the papers. Come along!

HENRIETTE: Where? What do you mean?

DETECTIVE: Oh, to the Bureau, of course. There you'll get a nice little card and a license that brings you free medical care.

HENRIETTE: O Lord Jesus, you don't mean it!

DETECTIVE: [Grabbing Henriette by the arm] Don't I mean it?

HENRIETTE: [Falling on her knees] Save me, Maurice! Help!

DETECTIVE: Shut up, you fool!

[Maurice enters, followed by Waiter]

WAITER: Gentlemen of that kind are not served here. You just pay and get out! And take the girl along!

MAURICE: [Crushed, searches his pocket-book for money] Henriette, pay for me, and let us get away from this place. I haven't a sou left.

WAITER: So the lady has to put up for her Alphonse! Alphonse! Do you know what that is?

HENRIETTE: [Looking through her pocket-book] Oh, merciful heavens! I have no money either!— Why doesn't Adolphe come back?

DETECTIVE: Well, did you ever see such rotters! Get out of here, and put up something as security. That kind of ladies generally have their fingers full of rings.

MAURICE: Can it be possible that we have sunk so low?

HENRIETTE: [Takes off a ring and hands it to the Waiter] The Abbé was right: this is not the work of man.

MAURICE: No, it's the devil's!— But if we leave before Adolphe returns, he will think that we have deceived him and run away.

HENRIETTE: That would be in keeping with the rest— But we'll go into the river now, won't we?

MAURICE: [Takes Henriette by the hand as they walk out together] Into the river—yes!

CURTAIN

ACT IV. SCENE I.

In the Luxembourg Gardens, at the group of Adam and Eve. The wind is shaking the trees and stirring up dead leaves, straws, and pieces of paper from the ground. Maurice and Henriette are seated on a bench.

HENRIETTE: So you don't want to die?

MAURICE: No, I am afraid. I imagine that I am going to be very cold down there in the grave, with only a sheet to cover me and a few shavings to lie on. And besides that, it seems to me as if there were still some task waiting for me, but I cannot make out what it is.

HENRIETTE: But I can guess what it is.

MAURICE: Tell me.

HENRIETTE: It is revenge. You, like me, must have suspected Jeanne and Emile of sending the detectives after me yesterday. Such a revenge on a rival none but a woman could devise.

MAURICE: Exactly what I was thinking. But let me tell you that my suspicions go even further. It seems as if my sufferings during these last few days had sharpened my wits. Can you explain, for instance, why the waiter from the Auberge des Adrets and the head waiter from the Pavilion were not called to testify at the hearing?

HENRIETTE: I never thought of it before. But now I know why. They had nothing to tell, because they had not been listening.

MAURICE: But how could the Commissaire then know what we had been saying?

HENRIETTE: He didn't know, but he figured it out.

He was guessing, and he guessed right. Perhaps he had had to deal with some similar case before.

MAURICE: Or else he concluded from our looks what we had been saying. There are those who can read other people's thoughts— Adolphe being the dupe, it seemed quite natural that we should have called him an ass. It's the rule, I understand, although it's varied at times by the use of "idiot" instead. But ass was nearer at hand in this case, as we had been talking of carriages and triumphal chariots. It is quite simple to figure out a fourth fact, when you have three known ones to start from.

HENRIETTE: Just think that we have let ourselves be taken in so completely.

MAURICE: That's the result of thinking too well of one's fellow beings. This is all you get out of it. But do you know, I suspect somebody else behind the Commissaire, who, by the by, must be a full-fledged scoundrel.

HENRIETTE: You mean the Abbé, who was taking the part of a private detective.

MAURICE: That's what I mean. That man has to receive all kinds of confessions. And note you: Adolphe himself told us he had been at the Church of St. Germain that morning. What was he doing there? He was blabbing, of course, and bewailing his fate. And then the priest put the questions together for the Commissaire.

HENRIETTE: Tell me something: do you trust Adolphe?

MAURICE: I trust no human being any longer.

HENRIETTE: Not even Adolphe?

MAURICE: Him least of all. How could I trust an enemy—a man from whom I have taken away his mistress?

HENRIETTE: Well, as you were the first one to speak of this, I'll give you some data about our friend. You heard he had returned that medal from London. Do you know his reason for doing so?

MAURICE: No.

HENRIETTE: He thinks himself unworthy of it, and he has taken a penitential vow never to receive any kind of distinction.

MAURICE: Can that be possible? But what has he done?

HENRIETTE: He has committed a crime of the kind that is not punishable under the law. That's what he gave me to understand indirectly.

MAURICE: He, too! He, the best one of all, the model man, who never speaks a hard word of anybody and who forgives everything.

HENRIETTE: Well, there you can see that we are no worse than others. And yet we are being hounded day and night as if devils were after us.

MAURICE: He, also! Then mankind has not been slandered— But if he has been capable of one crime, then you may expect anything of him. Perhaps it was he who sent the police after you yesterday. Coming to think of it now, it was he who sneaked away from us when he saw that we were in the

papers, and he lied when he insisted that those fellows were not detectives. But, of course, you may expect anything from a deceived lover.

HENRIETTE: Could he be as mean as that? No, it is impossible, impossible!

MAURICE: Why so? If he is a scoundrel?— What were you two talking of yesterday, before I came?

HENRIETTE: He had nothing but good to say of you.

MAURICE: That's a lie!

HENRIETTE: [Controlling herself and changing her tone] Listen. There is one person on whom you have cast no suspicion whatever—for what reason, I don't know. Have you thought of Madame Catherine's wavering attitude in this matter? Didn't she say finally that she believed you capable of anything?

MAURICE: Yes, she did, and that shows what kind of person she is. To think evil of other people without reason, you must be a villain yourself.

[Henriette looks hard at him. Pause]

HENRIETTE: To think evil of others, you must be a villain yourself.

MAURICE: What do you mean?

HENRIETTE: What I said.

MAURICE: Do you mean that I——?

HENRIETTE: Yes, that's what I mean now! Look here! Did you meet anybody but Marion when you called there yesterday morning?

MAURICE: Why do you ask?

HENRIETTE: Guess!

MAURICE: Well, as you seem to know—I met Jeanne, too.

HENRIETTE: Why did you lie to me?

MAURICE: I wanted to spare you.

HENRIETTE: And now you want me to believe in one who has been lying to me? No, my boy, now I believe you guilty of that murder.

MAURICE: Wait a moment! We have now reached the place for which my thoughts have been heading all the time, though I resisted as long as possible. It's queer that what lies next to one is seen last of all, and what one doesn't want to believe cannot be believed— Tell me something: where did you go yesterday, after we parted in the Bois?

HENRIETTE: [Alarmed] Why?

MAURICE: You went either to Adolphe—which you couldn't do, as he was attending a lesson—or you went to—Marion!

HENRIETTE: Now I am convinced that you are the murderer.

MAURICE: And I, that you are the murderess! You alone had an interest in getting the child out of the way—to get rid of the rock on the road, as you so aptly put it.

HENRIETTE: It was you who said that.

MAURICE: And the one who had an interest in it must have committed the crime.

HENRIETTE: Now, Maurice, we have been running around and around in this tread-mill, scourging each other. Let us quit before we get to the point of sheer madness.

MAURICE: You have reached that point already.

HENRIETTE: Don't you think it's time for us to part, before we drive each other insane?

MAURICE: Yes, I think so.

HENRIETTE: [*Rising*] Good-bye then!

[*Two men in civilian clothes become visible in the background*]

HENRIETTE: [*Turns and comes back to* Maurice] There they are again!

MAURICE: The dark angels that want to drive us out of the garden.

HENRIETTE: And force us back upon each other as if we were chained together.

MAURICE: Or as if we were condemned to lifelong marriage. Are we really to marry? To settle down in the same place? To be able to close the door behind us and perhaps get peace at last?

HENRIETTE: And shut ourselves up in order to torture each other to death; get behind locks and bolts, with a ghost for marriage portion; you torturing me with the memory of Adolphe, and I getting back at you with Jeanne—and Marion.

MAURICE: Never mention the name of Marion again! Don't you know that she was to be buried to-day—at this very moment perhaps?

HENRIETTE: And you are not there? What does that mean?

MAURICE: It means that both Jeanne and the police have warned me against the rage of the people.

HENRIETTE: A coward, too?

MAURICE: All the vices! How could you ever have cared for me?

HENRIETTE: Because two days ago you were another person, well worthy of being loved——

MAURICE: And now sunk to such a depth!

HENRIETTE: It isn't that. But you are beginning to flaunt bad qualities which are not your own.

MAURICE: But yours?

HENRIETTE: Perhaps, for when you appear a little worse I feel at once a little better.

MAURICE: It's like passing on a disease to save one's self-respect.

HENRIETTE: And how vulgar you have become, too!

MAURICE: Yes, I notice it myself, and I hardly recognise myself since that night in the cell. They put in one person and let out another through that gate which separates us from the rest of society. And now I feel myself the enemy of all mankind: I should like to set fire to the earth and dry up the oceans, for nothing less than a universal conflagration can wipe out my dishonour.

HENRIETTE: I had a letter from my mother to-day. She is the widow of a major in the army, well educated, with old-fashioned ideas of honour and that kind of thing. Do you want to read the letter? No, you don't!— Do you know that I am an outcast? My respectable acquaintances will have noth-

ing to do with me, and if I show myself on the streets alone the police will take me. Do you realise now that we have to get married?

MAURICE: We despise each other, and yet we have to marry: that is hell pure and simple! But, Henriette, before we unite our destinies you must tell me your secret, so that we may be on more equal terms.

HENRIETTE: All right, I'll tell you. I had a friend who got into trouble—you understand. I wanted to help her, as her whole future was at stake—and she died!

MAURICE: That was reckless, but one might almost call it noble, too.

HENRIETTE: You say so now, but the next time you lose your temper you will accuse me of it.

MAURICE: No, I won't. But I cannot deny that it has shaken my faith in you and that it makes me afraid of you. Tell me, is her lover still alive, and does he know to what extent you were responsible?

HENRIETTE: He was as guilty as I.

MAURICE: And if his conscience should begin to trouble him—such things do happen—and if he should feel inclined to confess: then you would be lost.

HENRIETTE: I know it, and it is this constant dread which has made me rush from one dissipation to another—so that I should never have time to wake up to full consciousness.

MAURICE: And now you want me to take my marriage portion out of your dread. That's asking a little too much.

HENRIETTE: But when I shared the shame of Maurice the murderer——

MAURICE: Oh, let's come to an end with it!

HENRIETTE: No, the end is not yet, and I'll not let go my hold until I have put you where you belong. For you can't go around thinking yourself better than I am.

MAURICE: So you want to fight me then? All right, as you please!

HENRIETTE: A fight of life and death!

[*The rolling of drums is heard in the distance*]

MAURICE: The garden is to be closed. "Cursed is the ground for thy sake; thorns and thistles shall it bring forth to thee."

HENRIETTE: "And the Lord God said unto the woman——"

A GUARD: [*In uniform, speaking very politely*] Sorry, but the garden has to be closed.

CURTAIN

SCENE II.

The Crêmerie. Mme. Catherine *is sitting at the counter making entries into an account book.* Adolphe *and* Henriette *are seated at a table.*

ADOLPHE: [*Calmly and kindly*] But if I give you my final assurance that I didn't run away, but that, on the contrary, I thought you had played me false, this ought to convince you.

HENRIETTE: But why did you fool us by saying that those fellows were not policemen?

ADOLPHE: I didn't think myself that they were, and then I wanted to reassure you.

HENRIETTE: When you say it, I believe you. But then you must also believe me, if I reveal my innermost thoughts to you.

ADOLPHE: Go on.

HENRIETTE: But you mustn't come back with your usual talk of fancies and delusions.

ADOLPHE: You seem to have reason to fear that I may.

HENRIETTE: I fear nothing, but I know you and your scepticism— Well, and then you mustn't tell this to anybody—promise me!

ADOLPHE: I promise.

HENRIETTE: Now think of it, although I must say it's something terrible: I have partial evidence that Maurice is guilty, or at least, I have reasonable suspicions——

ADOLPHE: You don't mean it!

HENRIETTE: Listen, and judge for yourself. When Maurice left me in the Bois, he said he was going to see Marion alone, as the mother was out. And now I have discovered afterwards that he did meet the mother. So that he has been lying to me.

ADOLPHE: That's possible, and his motive for doing so may have been the best, but how can anybody conclude from it that he is guilty of a murder?

HENRIETTE: Can't you see that?— Don't you understand?

ADOLPHE: Not at all.

HENRIETTE: Because you don't want to!— Then there is nothing left for me but to report him, and we'll see whether he can prove an alibi.

ADOLPHE: Henriette, let me tell you the grim truth. You, like he, have reached the border-line of —insanity. The demons of distrust have got hold of you, and each of you is using his own sense of partial guilt to wound the other with. Let me see if I can make a straight guess: he has also come to suspect you of killing his child?

HENRIETTE: Yes, he's mad enough to do so.

ADOLPHE: You call his suspicions mad, but not your own.

HENRIETTE: You have first to prove the contrary, or that I suspect him unjustly.

ADOLPHE: Yes, that's easy. A new autopsy has proved that Marion died of a well-known disease, the queer name of which I cannot recall just now.

HENRIETTE: Is it true?

ADOLPHE: The official report is printed in to-day's paper.

HENRIETTE: I don't take any stock of it. They can make up that kind of thing.

ADOLPHE: Beware, Henriette—or you may, without knowing it, pass across that border line. Beware especially of throwing out accusations that may put you into prison. Beware! [*He places his hand on her head*] You hate Maurice?

HENRIETTE: Beyond all bounds!

ADOLPHE: When love turns into hatred, it means that it was tainted from the start.

HENRIETTE: [*In a quieter mood*] What am I to do? Tell me, you who are the only one that understands me.

ADOLPHE: But you don't want any sermons.

HENRIETTE: Have you nothing else to offer me?

ADOLPHE: Nothing else. But they have helped me.

HENRIETTE: Preach away then!

ADOLPHE: Try to turn your hatred against yourself. Put the knife to the evil spot in yourself, for it is there that *your* trouble roots.

HENRIETTE: Explain yourself.

ADOLPHE: Part from Maurice first of all, so that you cannot nurse your qualms of conscience together. Break off your career as an artist, for the only thing that led you into it was a craving for freedom and fun—as they call it. And you have seen how much fun there is in it. Then go home to your mother.

HENRIETTE: Never!

ADOLPHE: Some other place then.

HENRIETTE: I suppose you know, Adolphe, that I have guessed your secret and why you wouldn't accept the prize?

ADOLPHE: Oh, I assumed that you would understand a half-told story.

HENRIETTE: Well—what did you do to get peace?

ADOLPHE: What I have suggested: I became conscious of my guilt, repented, decided to turn over a new leaf, and arranged my life like that of a penitent.

HENRIETTE: How can you repent when, like me, you have no conscience? Is repentance an act of grace bestowed on you as faith is?

ADOLPHE: Everything is a grace, but it isn't granted unless you seek it— Seek!

[*Henriette remains silent*]

ADOLPHE: But don't wait beyond the allotted time, or you may harden yourself until you tumble down into the irretrievable.

HENRIETTE: [*After a pause*] Is conscience fear of punishment?

ADOLPHE: No, it is the horror inspired in our better selves by the misdeeds of our lower selves.

HENRIETTE: Then I must have a conscience also?

ADOLPHE: Of course you have, but——

HENRIETTE: Tell me, Adolphe, are you what they call religious?

ADOLPHE: Not the least bit.

HENRIETTE: It's all so queer— What is religion?

ADOLPHE: Frankly speaking, I don't know! And I don't think anybody else can tell you. Sometimes it appears to me like a punishment, for nobody becomes religious without having a bad conscience.

HENRIETTE: Yes, it is a punishment. Now I know what to do. Good-bye, Adolphe!

ADOLPHE: You'll go away from here?

HENRIETTE: Yes, I am going—to where you said. Good-bye my friend! Good-bye, Madame Catherine!

MME. CATHERINE: Have you to go in such a hurry?

HENRIETTE: Yes.

ADOLPHE: Do you want me to go with you?

HENRIETTE: No, it wouldn't do. I am going alone, alone as I came here, one day in Spring, thinking that I belonged where I don't belong, and believing there was something called freedom, which does not exist. Good-bye! [Goes out]

MME. CATHERINE: I hope that lady never comes back, and I wish she had never come here at all!

ADOLPHE: Who knows but that she may have had some mission to fill here? And at any rate she deserves pity, endless pity.

MME. CATHERINE: I don't deny it, for all of us deserve that.

ADOLPHE: And she has even done less wrong than the rest of us.

MME. CATHERINE: That's possible, but not probable.

ADOLPHE: You are always so severe, Madame Catherine. Tell me: have you never done anything wrong?

MME. CATHERINE: [Startled] Of course, as I am a sinful human creature. But if you have been on thin ice and fallen in, you have a right to tell others to keep away. And you may do so without being held severe or uncharitable. Didn't I say to Monsieur Maurice the moment that lady entered here: Look out! Keep away! And he didn't, and so he fell in. Just like a naughty, self-willed child. And when a man acts like that he has to have a spanking, like any disobedient youngster.

ADOLPHE: Well, hasn't he had his spanking?

MME. CATHERINE: Yes, but it does not seem to have been enough, as he is still going around complaining.

ADOLPHE: That's a very popular interpretation of the whole intricate question.

MME. CATHERINE: Oh, pish! You do nothing but philosophise about your vices, and while you are still at it the police come along and solve the riddle. Now please leave me alone with my accounts!

ADOLPHE: There's Maurice now.

MME. CATHERINE: Yes, God bless him!

MAURICE: [Enters, his face very flushed, and takes a seat near Adolphe] Good evening.

[Mme. Catherine nods and goes on figuring]

ADOLPHE: Well, how's everything with you?

MAURICE: Oh, beginning to clear up.

ADOLPHE: [Hands him a newspaper, which Maurice does not take] So you have read the paper?

MAURICE: No, I don't read the papers any longer. There's nothing but infamies in them.

ADOLPHE: But you had better read it first——

MAURICE: No, I don't! It's nothing but lies— But listen: I have found a new clue. Can you guess who committed that murder?

ADOLPHE: Nobody, nobody!

MAURICE: Do you know where Henriette was during that quarter hour when the child was left alone?— She was there! And it is she who has done it!

ADOLPHE: You are crazy, man.

MAURICE: Not I, but Henriette, is crazy. She suspects me and has threatened to report me.

ADOLPHE: Henriette was here a while ago, and she used the self-same words as you. Both of you are crazy, for it has been proved by a second autopsy that the child died from a well-known disease, the name of which I have forgotten.

MAURICE: It isn't true!

ADOLPHE: That's what she said also. But the official report is printed in the paper.

MAURICE: A report? Then they have made it up!

ADOLPHE: And that's also what she said. The two of you are suffering from the same mental trouble. But with her I got far enough to make her realise her own condition.

MAURICE: Where did she go?

ADOLPHE: She went far away from here to begin a new life.

MAURICE: Hm, hm!— Did you go to the funeral?

ADOLPHE: I did.

MAURICE: Well?

ADOLPHE: Well, Jeanne seemed resigned and didn't have a hard word to say about you.

MAURICE: She is a good woman.

ADOLPHE: Why did you desert her then?

MAURICE: Because I was crazy—blown up with pride especially—and then we had been drinking champagne——

ADOLPHE: Can you understand now why Jeanne wept when you drank champagne?

MAURICE: Yes, I understand now— And for that reason I have already written to her and asked her to forgive me— Do you think she will forgive me?

ADOLPHE: I think so, for it's not like her to hate anybody.

MAURICE: Do you think she will forgive me completely, so that she will come back to me?

ADOLPHE: Well, I don't know about that. You have shown yourself so poor in keeping faith that it is doubtful whether she will trust her fate to you any longer.

MAURICE: But I can feel that her fondness for me has not ceased, and I know she will come back to me.

ADOLPHE: How can you know that? How can you believe it? Didn't you even suspect her and that decent brother of hers of having sent the police after Henriette out of revenge?

MAURICE: But I don't believe it any longer—that is to say, I guess that fellow Emile is a pretty slick customer.

MME. CATHERINE: Now look here! What are you saying of Monsieur Emile? Of course, he is nothing but a workman, but if everybody kept as straight as he— There is no flaw in him, but a lot of sense and tact.

EMILE: [*Enters*] Monsieur Gérard?

MAURICE: That's me.

EMILE: Pardon me, but I have something to say to you in private.

MAURICE: Go right on. We are all friends here.

[*The* Abbé *enters and sits down*]

EMILE: [*With a glance at the* Abbé] Perhaps after——

MAURICE: Never mind. The Abbé is also a friend, although he and I differ.

EMILE: You know who I am, Monsieur Gérard? My sister has asked me to give you this package as an answer to your letter.

[Maurice *takes the package and opens it*]

EMILE: And now I have only to add, seeing as I am in a way my sister's guardian, that, on her behalf as well as my own, I acknowledge you free of all obligations, now when the natural tie between you does not exist any longer.

MAURICE: But you must have a grudge against me?

EMILE: Must I? I can't see why. On the other hand, I should like to have a declaration from you, here in the presence of your friends, that you don't think either me or my sister capable of such a meanness as to send the police after Mademoiselle Henriette.

MAURICE: I wish to take back what I said, and I offer you my apology, if you will accept it.

EMILE: It is accepted. And I wish all of you a good evening. [*Goes out*]

EVERYBODY: Good evening!

MAURICE: The tie and the gloves which Jeanne gave me for the opening night of my play, and which I let Henriette throw into the fireplace. Who can have picked them up? Everything is dug up; everything comes back!— And when she gave them to me in the cemetery, she said she wanted me to look fine and handsome, so that other people would like me also— And she herself stayed at home— This hurt her too deeply, and well it might. I have no right to keep company with decent human beings. Oh, have I done this? Scoffed at a gift coming from a good heart; scorned a sacrifice offered to my own welfare. This was what I threw away in order to get —a laurel that is lying on the rubbish heap, and a bust that would have belonged in the pillory—Abbé, now I come over to you.

ABBÉ: Welcome!

MAURICE: Give me the word that I need.

ABBÉ: Do you expect me to contradict your self-accusations and inform you that you have done nothing wrong?

MAURICE: Speak the right word!

ABBÉ: With your leave, I'll say then that I have found your behaviour just as abominable as you have found it yourself.

MAURICE: What can I do, what can I do, to get out of this?

ABBÉ: You know as well as I do.

MAURICE: No, I only know that I am lost, that my life is spoiled, my career cut off, my reputation in this world ruined for ever.

ABBÉ: And so you are looking for a new existence in some better world, which you are now beginning to believe in?

MAURICE: Yes, that's it.

ABBÉ: You have been living in the flesh and you want now to live in the spirit. Are you then so sure that this world has no more attractions for you?

MAURICE: None whatever! Honour is a phantom; gold, nothing but dry leaves; women, mere intoxicants. Let me hide myself behind your consecrated walls and forget this horrible dream that has filled two days and lasted two eternities.

ABBÉ: All right! But this is not the place to go into the matter more closely. Let us make an appointment for this evening at nine o'clock in the Church of St. Germain. For I am going to preach to the inmates of St. Lazare, and that may be your first step along the hard road of penitence.

MAURICE: Penitence?

ABBÉ: Well, didn't you wish——

MAURICE: Yes, yes!

ABBÉ: Then we have vigils between midnight and two o'clock.

MAURICE: That will be splendid!

ABBÉ: Give me your hand that you will not look back.

MAURICE: [*Rising, holds out his hand*] Here is my hand, and my will goes with it.

SERVANT GIRL: [*Enters from the kitchen*] A telephone call for Monsieur Maurice.

MAURICE: From whom?

SERVANT GIRL: From the theatre.

[Maurice *tries to get away, but the* Abbé *holds on to his hand*]

ABBÉ: [*To the* Servant Girl] Find out what it is.

SERVANT GIRL: They want to know if Monsieur Maurice is going to attend the performance to-night.

ABBÉ: [*To* Maurice, *who is trying to get away*] No, I won't let you go.

MAURICE: What performance is that?

ADOLPHE: Why don't you read the paper?

MME. CATHERINE AND THE ABBÉ: He hasn't read the paper?

MAURICE: It's all lies and slander. [*To the* Servant Girl] Tell them that I am engaged for this evening: I am going to church.

[*The* Servant Girl *goes into the kitchen*]

ADOLPHE: As you don't want to read the paper, I shall have to tell you that your play has been put on again, now when you are exonerated. And your literary friends have planned a demonstration for this evening in recognition of your indisputable talent.

MAURICE: It isn't true.

EVERYBODY: It is true.

MAURICE: [*After a pause*] I have not deserved it!

ABBÉ: Good!

ADOLPHE: And, furthermore, Maurice——

MAURICE: [*Hiding his face in his hands*] Furthermore!

MME. CATHERINE: One hundred thousand francs! Do you see now that they come back to you? And the villa outside the city. Everything is coming back except Mademoiselle Henriette.

ABBÉ: [*Smiling*] You ought to take this matter a little more seriously, Madame Catherine.

MME. CATHERINE: Oh, I cannot—I just can't keep serious any longer! [*She breaks into open laughter, which she vainly tries to smother with her handkerchief*]

ADOLPHE: Say, Maurice, the play begins at eight.

ABBÉ: But the church services are at nine.

ADOLPHE: Maurice!

MME. CATHERINE: Let us hear what the end is going to be, Monsieur Maurice.

[Maurice *drops his head on the table, in his arms*]

ADOLPHE: Loose him, Abbé.

ABBÉ: No, it is not for me to loose or bind. He must do that himself.

MAURICE: [*Rising*] Well, I go with the Abbé.

ABBÉ: No, my young friend. I have nothing to give you but a scolding, which you can give yourself. And you owe a duty to yourself and to your good name. That you have got through with this as quickly as you have is to me a sign that you have suffered your punishment as intensely as if it had lasted an eternity. And when Providence absolves you there is nothing for me to add.

MAURICE: But why did the punishment have to be so hard when I was innocent?

ABBÉ: Hard? Only two days! And you were not innocent. For we have to stand responsible for our thoughts and words and desires also. And in your thought you became a murderer when your evil self wished the life out of your child.

MAURICE: You are right. But my decision is made. To-night I will meet you at the church in order to have a reckoning with myself—but to-morrow evening I go to the theatre.

MME. CATHERINE: A good solution, Monsieur Maurice.

ADOLPHE: Yes, that is the solution. Whew!

ABBÉ: Yes, so it is!

CURTAIN

Ferenc Molnar

(1878– ——)

During the last two decades of its existence, the Austrian-Hungarian Empire teemed with theatrical activity, and Vienna and Budapest were the Mecca and Medina toward which Americans turned their faces whenever they longed for gay times and even gayer plays. The old Empire was tottering in a gavotte that was extremely attractive to those who fancied themselves connoisseurs of good living. In Vienna were to be found facile poet laureates of the gay life. In Vienna, too, resided Arthur Schnitzler (1862–1931), a playwright and novelist of great penetration who brought a physician's mind to bear on the perpetual Mardi gras of the capital of the Hapsburgs. The sister capital, Budapest, even brighter and more colorful, harbored a great number of playwrights (Biro, Lengyel, Herczeg, Vajda, Fodor, and others) who distilled the elixir of *amour* for well-edified audiences. One man of letters and man of the world, however, led all the rest in cunning and theatrical virtuosity, Ferenc Molnár. Celebrated as a *bon vivant* of the old continental school and as a blithe contriver of plays, he became the symbol of "sophistication," if not indeed the culture hero of the Austro-Hungarian upper classes and intellectuals.

Molnár, a native of Budapest, was the son of an affluent merchant family and enjoyed every advantage that wealth and social position could provide. Well educated, handsome, witty, and charming, he quickly drew attention to himself when, abandoning the legal profession for which he had been trained, he turned to journalism and began to publish stories and novels. A number of these were merely entertaining, but one novel, *The Paul Street Boys* (1907), was a simple and warm study of adolescence in Budapest. Its author's facility for drama, however, soon overshadowed his talent for fiction; and his private life, celebrated for its numerous affairs of the heart, was as exciting and entertaining as fiction for his contemporaries. His many social accomplishments, witty conversation, romantic encounters, and pranks furnished Budapest with much of its gossip for more than two decades. He continued to entrance his countrymen even after the First World War had dampened their spirits. When he settled in America just before the outbreak of the Second World War, he could also count on many American admirers. His reputation had preceded him. Better still, his plays had preceded him. A number of them —especially, *The Guardsman, The Play's the Thing, The Glass Slipper,* and, above all, *Liliom*—had made him one of New York's most successful and highly

regarded playwrights by adoption. And in the country that welcomed him he could console himself for the failure of his new plays with the successful revival of *The Play's the Thing* and the attractive musical-comedy transmutation of *Liliom* by Rodgers and Hammerstein into *Carousel.*

Molnár's ability to treat upper- and lower-class life with equal charm made his career as a playwright an almost continuous triumph before 1920. Some of his plays were intentionally frothy. Others mingled realism with generous doses of sentimentality and romanticism. In some plays, Molnár played at fantasy, generally with a view to making a piquant situation still more piquant, as when he brought Mephistopheles into his first successful play, *The Devil* (1907), in order to facilitate some fashionable adultery. He flavored intrigue with much worldly shrewdness and breezy cynicism, as in his ingenious comedy *The Guardsman* (1910), which Alfred Lunt and Lynn Fontanne turned into a sparkling article for Broadway and the screen.

Molnár's flair for comedy of manners seemed inexhaustible. It was no less in evidence when he treated royalty, as in *The Swan* (1920), than when he bestowed his interest on the artists, professional and business classes, and the common folk of the Hungarian capital. Nor could he be charged with deficient sympathy in spite of his wit and his fondness for exploiting the foibles of men and women. Goodness and innocence of heart attracted him immensely, even though he made it look like an idiosyncrasy in a world not remarkable for saintliness. Naïveté and the dreams of little people received a ready, if not altogether unpatronizing, sympathy from him in a work like *The Glass Slipper* (1924), which recounts the adventures of a boarding-house drudge who plays Cinderella to a cabinetmaker elevated in her imagination to the role of Prince Charming. Molnár was, indeed, both the Noel Coward and James M. Barrie of the Central European stage. And he filled both roles with equal ingenuity, a dash of irony, considerable skepticism, and an inexhaustibly sanguine temperament. Theatre for him was not life itself—merely its bouquet.

Molnár will be remembered mainly for his *Liliom,* a work of no great profundity, it is true, but his one successful play that is permeated with a serious view of life. (Another serious drama, *The Miracle in the Mountain,* was unsuccessful.) It was written in 1909 after his divorce from his first wife, who made the proceedings painful by charging that he had struck their little girl in a fit of anger. He was apparently bent upon dramatizing the contradictions of human nature as a way of discharging unhappy memories. Even in *Liliom,* however, Molnár did not suppress the theatrician in himself. His story of the good-for-nothing merry-go-round barker Liliom ("Lily" or worthless fellow in Hungarian) is a thoroughly theatricalized drama from the moment it opens with its "amusement-park pantomime." It settles down into a naturalistic drama, it is true, with the first scene, but it turns into a romantic fantasy. We may regard this part of the play as watereddown expressionism, if we wish, because its seriocomic heaven is conceived in terms suitable to the mentality of Liliom. But it is not Liliom's dream, since he is dead. It is a tour de force, a symbolic contrivance, invented to advance the author's thesis that behavior often contradicts intention. Liliom's fate after his death has the pathos of Molnár's wisdom which takes note of the failure of men to correct their errors, although he also purveys romantic exaltation through the devotion of Liliom's Julie. The fantasy also serves the purposes of characterization; it is the hypothesis by means of which Molnár reminds us that Liliom's behavior is rooted in his character. If he had a second chance to express

the love and tenderness he feels, he would make a mess of life again. If he wanted to do good to his child, he would steal again, even if he had to steal a star from heaven. His love would be inarticulate and gauche even if the emissaries of the Lord were making it the final test of his character and were watching him.

Liliom confused its first audiences in Budapest; it was set down as a failure when produced in 1909. But when it was revived ten years later it was enthusiastically acclaimed and its fame spread rapidly thereafter. The play was produced in London (first under the title of *The Daisy*) in 1920 and 1926, and Paris saw it first in 1923. In New York, it had a memorable Theatre Guild production in 1920, with Joseph Schildkraut and Eva Le Gallienne in the roles of the shiftless Liliom and the faithful Julie. It was revived less successfully on Broadway in the spring of 1940, with Burgess Meredith and Ingrid Bergman in the leading parts, and it was reincarnated in *Carousel* in 1945.

BIBLIOGRAPHY: Frank W. Chandler, *Modern Continental Playwrights* (pp. 438–453), 1931; John Gassner, *Masters of the Drama* (pp. 478–481), 1940, 1945.

LILIOM

By Ferenc Molnár

TRANSLATED FROM THE HUNGARIAN BY BENJAMIN GLAZER

CHARACTERS

LILIOM	YOUNG HOLLUNDER	TWO PLAINCLOTHES POLICEMEN
JULIE	WOLF BEIFELD	TWO HEAVENLY POLICEMEN
MARIE	THE CARPENTER	THE RICHLY DRESSED MAN
MRS. MUSKAT	LINZMAN	THE POORLY DRESSED MAN
LOUISE	THE DOCTOR	THE GUARD
MRS. HOLLUNDER	THE MAGISTRATE	A SUBURBAN POLICEMAN
FICSUR	TWO MOUNTED POLICEMEN	

THE PROLOGUE

An amusement park on the outskirts of Budapest on a late afternoon in Spring. Barkers stand before the booths of the sideshows haranguing the passing crowd. The strident music of a calliope is heard; laughter, shouts, the scuffle of feet, the signal bells of a merry-go-round.

The merry-go-round is at center. Liliom stands at the entrance, a cigarette in his mouth, coaxing the people in. The girls regard him with idolizing glances and screech with pleasure as he playfully pushes them through entrance. Now and then some girl's escort resents the familiarity, whereupon Liliom's demeanor becomes ugly and menacing, and the cowed escort slinks through the entrance behind his girl or contents himself with a muttered resentful comment.

One girl hands Liliom *a red carnation; he rewards her with a bow and a smile. When the soldier who accompanies her protests,* Liliom *cows him with a fierce glance and a threatening gesture.* Marie *and* Julie *come out of the crowd and* Liliom *favors them with particular notice as they pass into the merry-go-round.*

Mrs. Muskat *comes out of the merry-go-round, bringing* Liliom *coffee and rolls.* Liliom *mounts the barker's stand at the entrance, where he is elevated over every one on the stage. Here he begins his harangue. Everybody turns toward him. The other booths are gradually deserted. The tumult makes it impossible for the audience to hear what he is saying, but every now and then some witticism of his provokes a storm of laughter which is audible above the din. Many people enter the merry-go-round. Here and there one catches a phrase "Room for one more on the zebra's back," "Which of you ladies?" "Ten heller for adults, five for children," "Step right up———"*

It is growing darker. A lamplighter crosses the stage, and begins unperturbedly lighting the colored gas-lamps. The whistle of a distant locomotive is

heard. Suddenly the tumult ceases, the lights go out, and the curtain falls in darkness.

END OF PROLOGUE

SCENE I

A lonely place in the park, half hidden by trees and shrubbery. Under a flowering acacia tree stands a painted wooden bench. From the distance, faintly, comes the tumult of the amusement park. It is the sunset of the same day.

When the curtain rises the stage is empty.

[Marie enters quickly, pauses at center, and looks back]

MARIE: Julie, Julie! [*There is no answer*] Do you hear me, Julie? Let her be! Come on. Let her be. [*Starts to go back*]

[Julie enters, looks back angrily]

JULIE: Did you ever hear of such a thing? What's the matter with the woman anyway?

MARIE: [*Looking back again*] Here she comes again.

JULIE: Let her come. I didn't do anything to her. All of a sudden she comes up to me and begins to raise a row.

MARIE: Here she is. Come on, let's run.

[Tries to urge her off]

JULIE: Run? I should say not. What would I want to run for? I'm not afraid of her.

MARIE: Oh, come on. She'll only start a fight.

JULIE: I'm going to stay right here. Let her *start* a fight.

MRS. MUSKAT: [*Entering*] What do you want to run away for? [*To* Julie] Don't worry. I won't eat you. But there's one thing I want to tell you, my dear. Don't let me catch you in my carousel again. I stand for a whole lot, I have to in my business. It makes no difference to me whether my customers are ladies or the likes of you—as long as they pay their money. But when a girl misbehaves herself on my carousel—out she goes. Do you understand?

JULIE: Are you talking to me?

MRS. MUSKAT: Yes, you! You—chambermaid, you! In my carousel——

JULIE: Who did anything in your old carousel? I paid my fare and took my seat and never said a word, except to my friend here.

MARIE: No, she never opened her mouth. Liliom came over to her of his own accord.

MRS. MUSKAT: It's all the same. I'm not going to get in trouble with the police, and lose my license on account of you—you shabby kitchen maid!

JULIE: Shabby yourself.

MRS. MUSKAT: You stay out of my carousel! Letting my barker fool with you! Aren't you ashamed of yourself?

JULIE: What did you say?

MRS. MUSKAT: I suppose you think I have no eyes in my head. I see everything that goes on in my carousel. During the whole ride she let Liliom fool with her—the shameless hussy!

JULIE: He did not fool with me! I don't let any man fool with me!

MRS. MUSKAT: He leaned against you all through the ride!

JULIE: He leaned against the panther. He always leans against something, doesn't he? Everybody leans where he wants. I couldn't tell him not to lean, if he always leans, could I? But he didn't lay a hand on me.

MRS. MUSKAT: Oh, didn't he? And I suppose he didn't put his hand around your waist, either?

MARIE: And if he did? What of it?

MRS. MUSKAT: You hold your tongue! No one's asking you—just you keep out of it.

JULIE: He put his arm around my waist—just the same as he does to all the girls. He always does that.

MRS. MUSKAT: I'll teach him not to do it any more, my dear. No carryings on in my carousel! If you are looking for that sort of thing, you'd better go to the circus! You'll find lots of soldiers there to carry on with!

JULIE: You keep your soldiers for yourself!

MARIE: Soldiers! As if we wanted soldiers!

MRS. MUSKAT: Well, I only want to tell you this, my dear, so that we understand each other perfectly. If you ever stick your nose in my carousel again, you'll wish you hadn't! I'm not going to lose my license on account of the likes of you! People who don't know how to behave, have got to stay out!

JULIE: You're wasting your breath. If I feel like riding on your carousel I'll pay my ten heller and I'll ride. I'd like to see any one try to stop me!

MRS. MUSKAT: Just come and try it, my dear— just come and try it.

MARIE: We'll see what'll happen.

MRS. MUSKAT: Yes, you will see something happen that never happened before in this park.

JULIE: Perhaps you think you could throw me out!

MRS. MUSKAT: I'm sure of it, my dear.

JULIE: And suppose I'm stronger than you?

MRS. MUSKAT: I'd think twice before I'd dirty my hands on a common servant girl. I'll have Liliom throw you out. He knows how to handle your kind.

JULIE: You think Liliom would throw me out.

MRS. MUSKAT: Yes, my dear, so fast that you won't know what happened to you!

JULIE: He'd throw me——

[Stops suddenly, for Mrs. Muskat has turned away. Both look off stage until Liliom enters, surrounded by four giggling servant girls]

LILIOM: Go away! Stop following me, or I'll smack your face!

A LITTLE SERVANT GIRL: Well, give me back my handkerchief.

LILIOM: Go on now——

THE FOUR SERVANT GIRLS: [Simultaneously] What do you think of him?—My handkerchief!—Give it back to her!—That's a nice thing to do!

THE LITTLE SERVANT GIRL: [To Mrs. Muskat] Please, lady, make him——

MRS. MUSKAT: Oh, shut up!

LILIOM: Will you get out of here?

[Makes a threatening gesture—the Four Servant Girls exit in voluble but fearful haste]

MRS. MUSKAT: What have you been doing now?

LILIOM: None of your business. [Glances at Julie] Have you been starting with her again?

JULIE: Mister Liliom, please——

LILIOM: [Steps threateningly toward her] Don't yell!

JULIE: [Timidly] I didn't yell.

LILIOM: Well, don't. [To Mrs. Muskat] What's the matter? What has she done to you?

MRS. MUSKAT: What has she done? She's been impudent to me. Just as impudent as she could be! I put her out of the carousel. Take a good look at this innocent thing, Liliom. She's never to be allowed in my carousel again!

LILIOM: [To Julie] You heard that. Run home, now.

MARIE: Come on. Don't waste your time with such people.

[Tries to lead Julie away]

JULIE: No, I won't——

MRS. MUSKAT: If she ever comes again, you're not to let her in. And if she gets in before you see her, throw her out. Understand?

LILIOM: What has she done, anyhow?

JULIE: [Agitated and very earnest] Mister Liliom —tell me please—honest and truly—if I come into the carousel, will you throw me out?

MRS. MUSKAT: Of course he'll throw you out.

MARIE: She wasn't talking to you.

JULIE: Tell me straight to my face, Mister Liliom, would you throw me out?

[They face each other. There is a brief pause]

LILIOM: Yes, little girl, if there was a reason—but if there was no reason, why should I throw you out?

MARIE: [*To* Mrs. Muskat] There, you see!

JULIE: Thank you, Mister Liliom.

MRS. MUSKAT: And I tell you again, if this little slut dares to set her foot in my carousel, she's to be thrown out! I'll stand for no indecency in my establishment.

LILIOM: What do you mean—indecency?

MRS. MUSKAT: I saw it all. There's no use denying it.

JULIE: She says you put your arm around my waist.

LILIOM: Me?

MRS. MUSKAT: Yes, you! I saw you. Don't play the innocent.

LILIOM: Here's something new! I'm not to put my arm around a girl's waist any more! I suppose I'm to ask your permission before I touch another girl!

MRS. MUSKAT: You can touch as many girls as you want and as often as you want—for my part you can go as far as you like with any of them—but not this one—I permit no indecency in my carousel.

[*There is a long pause*]

LILIOM: [*To* Mrs. Muskat] And now I'll ask you please to shut your mouth.

MRS. MUSKAT: What?

LILIOM: Shut your mouth quick, and go back to your carousel.

MRS. MUSKAT: What?

LILIOM: What did she do to you, anyhow? Tryin' to start a fight with a little pigeon like that . . . just because I touched her?—You come to the carousel as often as you want to, little girl. Come every afternoon, and sit on the panther's back, and if you haven't got the price, Liliom will pay for you. And if any one dares to bother you, you come and tell *me*.

MRS. MUSKAT: You reprobate!

LILIOM: Old witch!

JULIE: Thank you, Mister Liliom.

MRS. MUSKAT: You seem to think that I can't throw you out, too. What's the reason I can't? Because you are the best barker in the park? Well, you are very much mistaken. In fact, you can consider yourself thrown out already. You're discharged!

LILIOM: Very good.

MRS. MUSKAT: [*Weakening a little*] I can discharge you any time I feel like it.

LILIOM: Very good, you feel like discharging me. I'm discharged. That settles it.

MRS. MUSKAT: Playing the high and mighty, are you? Conceited pig! Good-for-nothing!

LILIOM: You said you'd throw me out, didn't you? Well, that suits me; I'm thrown out.

MRS. MUSKAT: [*Softening*] Do you have to take up every word I say?

LILIOM: It's all right; it's all settled. I'm a good-for-nothing. And a conceited pig. And I'm discharged.

MRS. MUSKAT: Do you want to ruin my business?

LILIOM: A good-for-nothing? Now I know! And I'm discharged! Very good.

MRS. MUSKAT: You're a devil, you are . . . and that woman——

LILIOM: Keep away from her!

MRS. MUSKAT: I'll get Hollinger to give you such a beating that you'll hear all the angels sing . . . and it won't be the first time, either.

LILIOM: Get out of here. I'm discharged. And you get out of here.

JULIE: [*Timidly*] Mister Liliom, if she's willing to say that she hasn't discharged you——

LILIOM: You keep out of this.

JULIE: [*Timidly*] I don't want this to happen on account of me.

LILIOM: [*To* Mrs. Muskat, *pointing to* Julie] Apologize to her!

MARIE: A-ha!

MRS. MUSKAT: Apologize? To who?

LILIOM: To this little pigeon. Well—are you going to do it?

MRS. MUSKAT: If you give me this whole park on a silver plate, and all the gold of the Rothschilds on top of it—I'd—I'd—— Let her dare to come into my carousel again and she'll get thrown out so hard that she'll see stars in daylight!

LILIOM: In that case, dear lady [*Takes off his cap with a flourish*] you are respectfully requested to get out o' here as fast as your legs will carry you—I never beat up a woman yet—except that Holzer woman who I sent to the hospital for three weeks—but—if you don't get out o' here this minute, and let this little squab be, I'll give you the prettiest slap in the jaw you ever had in your life.

MRS MUSKAT: Very good, my son. Now you *can* go to the devil. Good-bye. You're discharged, and you needn't try to come back, either.

[*She exits. It is beginning to grow dark*]

MARIE: [*With grave concern*] Mister Liliom——

LILIOM: Don't you pity me or I'll give *you* a slap in the jaw. [*To* Julie] And don't you pity me, either.

JULIE: [*In alarm*] I don't pity you, Mister Liliom.

LILIOM: You're a liar, you *are* pitying me. I can see it in your face. You're thinking, now that Madame Muskat has thrown him out, Liliom will have to go begging. Huh! Look at me. I'm big enough to get along without a Madame Muskat. I have been thrown out of better jobs than hers.

JULIE: What will you do now, Mister Liliom?

LILIOM: Now? First of all, I'll go and get myself—a glass of beer. You see, when something happens to annoy me, I always drink a glass of beer.

JULIE: Then you are annoyed about losing your job.

LILIOM: No, only about where I'm going to get the beer.

MARIE: Well—eh——

LILIOM: Well—eh—what?

MARIE: Well—eh—are you going to stay with us, Mister Liliom?

LILIOM: Will you pay for the beer? [Marie *looks doubtful; he turns to* Julie] Will you? [*She does not answer*] How much money have you got?

JULIE: [*Bashfully*] Eight heller.

LILIOM: And you? [Marie *casts down her eyes and does not reply.* Liliom *continues sternly*] I asked you how much you've got? [Marie *begins to weep softly*] I understand. Well, you needn't cry about it. You girls stay here, while I go back to the carousel and get my clothes and things. And when I come back, we'll go to the Hungarian beer-garden. It's all right, I'll pay. Keep your money.

[*He exits.* Marie *and* Julie *stand silent, watching him until he has gone*]

MARIE: Are you sorry for him?

JULIE: Are you?

MARIE: Yes, a little. Why are you looking after him in that funny way?

JULIE: [*Sits down*] Nothing—except I'm sorry he lost his job.

MARIE: [*With a touch of pride*] It was on our account he lost his job. Because he's fallen in love with you.

JULIE: He hasn't at all.

MARIE: [*Confidently*] Oh, yes! he is in love with you. [*Hesitantly, romantically*] There is some one in love with me, too.

JULIE: There is? Who?

MARIE: I—I never mentioned it before, because you hadn't a lover of your own—but now you have —and I'm free to speak. [*Very grandiloquently*] My heart has found its mate.

JULIE: You're only making it up.

MARIE: No, it's true—my heart's true love——

JULIE: Who? Who is he?

MARIE: A soldier.

JULIE: What kind of a soldier?

MARIE: I don't know. Just a soldier. Are there different kinds?

JULIE: Many different kinds. There are hussars, artillerymen, engineers, infantry—that's the kind that walks—and——

MARIE: How can you tell which is which?

JULIE: By their uniforms.

MARIE: [*After trying to puzzle it out*] The conductors on the street cars—are they soldiers?

JULIE: Certainly not. They're conductors.

MARIE: Well, they have uniforms.

JULIE: But they don't carry swords or guns.

MARIE: Oh! [*Thinks it over again; then*] Well, policemen—are they?

JULIE: [*With a touch of exasperation*] Are they what?

MARIE: Soldiers.

JULIE: Certainly not. They're just policemen.

MARIE: [*Triumphantly*] But they have uniforms— and they carry weapons, too.

JULIE: You're just as dumb as you can be. You don't go by their uniforms.

MARIE: But you said——

JULIE: No, I didn't. A letter-carrier wears a uniform, too, but that doesn't make him a soldier.

MARIE: But if he carried a gun or a sword, would he be——

JULIE: No, he'd still be a letter-carrier. You can't go by guns or swords, either.

MARIE: Well, if you don't go by the uniforms or the weapons, what *do* you go by?

JULIE: By—— [*Tries to put it into words; fails; then breaks off suddenly*] Oh, you'll get to know when you've lived in the city long enough. You're nothing but a country girl. When you've lived in the city a year, like I have, you'll know all about it.

MARIE: [*Half angrily*] Well, how *do* you know when *you* see a real soldier?

JULIE: By one thing.

MARIE: What?

JULIE: One thing——[*She pauses.* Marie *starts to cry*] Oh, what are you crying about?

MARIE: Because you're making fun of me . . . You're a city girl, and I'm just fresh from the country . . . and how am I expected to know a soldier when I see one? . . . You, you ought to tell me, instead of making fun of me——

JULIE: All right. Listen then, cry-baby. There's only one way to tell a soldier: by his salute! That's the only way.

MARIE: [*Joyfully; with a sigh of relief*] Ah—that's good.

JULIE: What?

MARIE: I say—it's all right then—because Wolf —Wolf——[Julie *laughs derisively*] Wolf—that's his name.

[*She weeps again*]

JULIE: Crying again? What now?

MARIE: You're making fun of me again.

JULIE: I'm not. But when you say, "Wolf— Wolf—" like that, I have to laugh, don't I? [*Archly*] What's his name again?

MARIE: I won't tell you.

JULIE: All right. If you won't say it, then he's no soldier.

MARIE: I'll say it.

JULIE: Go on.

MARIE: No, I won't. [*She weeps again*]

JULIE: Then he's not a soldier. I guess he's a letter-carrier——

MARIE: No—no—I'd rather say it.

JULIE: Well, then.

MARIE: [*Giggling*] But you mustn't look at me. You look the other way, and I'll say it. [Julie *looks away.* Marie *can hardly restrain her own laughter*] Wolf! [*She laughs*] That's his real name. Wolf, Wolf, Soldier—Wolf!

JULIE: What kind of a uniform does he wear?

MARIE: Red.

JULIE: Red trousers?

MARIE: No.

JULIE: Red coat?

MARIE: No.

JULIE: What then?

MARIE: [*Triumphantly*] His cap!

JULIE: [*After a long pause*] He's just a porter, you dunce. Red cap . . . that's a porter—and he doesn't carry a gun or a sword, either.

MARIE: [*Triumphantly*] But he salutes. You said yourself that was the only way to tell a soldier——

JULIE: He doesn't salute at all. He only greets people——

MARIE: He salutes me. . . . And if his name *is* Wolf, that doesn't prove he ain't a soldier—he salutes, and he wears a red cap and he stands on guard all day long outside a big building——

JULIE: What does he do there?

MARIE: [*Seriously*] He spits.

JULIE: [*With contempt*] He's nothing—nothing but a common porter.

MARIE: What's Liliom?

JULIE: [*Indignantly*] Why speak of him? What has he to do with me?

MARIE: The same as Wolf has to do with me. If you can talk to me like that about Wolf, I can talk to you about Liliom.

JULIE: He's nothing to me. He put his arm around me in the carousel. I couldn't tell him not to put his arm around me after he had done it, could I?

MARIE: I suppose you didn't like him to do it?

JULIE: No.

MARIE: Then why are you waiting for him? Why don't you go home?

JULIE: Why—eh—he *said* we were to wait for him.

[*Liliom enters. There is a long silence*]

LILIOM: Are you still here? What are you waiting for?

MARIE: You told us to wait.

LILIOM: Must you always interfere? No one is talking to you.

MARIE: You asked us—why we——

LILIOM: Will you keep your mouth shut? What do you suppose I want with two of you? I meant that one of you was to wait. The other can go home.

MARIE: All right.

JULIE: All right. [*Neither starts to go*]

LILIOM: One of you goes home. [*To Marie*] Where do you work?

MARIE: At the Breiers', Damjanovitsch Street, Number Twenty.

LILIOM: And you?

JULIE: I work there, too.

LILIOM: Well, one of you goes home. Which of you wants to stay? [*There is no answer*] Come on, speak up, which of you stays?

MARIE: [*Officiously*] She'll lose her job if she stays.

LILIOM: Who will?

MARIE: Julie. She has to be back by seven o'clock.

LILIOM: Is that true? Will they discharge you if you're not back on time?

JULIE: Yes.

LILIOM: Well, wasn't I discharged?

JULIE: Yes—you were discharged, too.

MARIE: Julie, shall I go?

JULIE: I—can't tell you what to do.

MARIE: All right—stay if you like.

LILIOM: You'll be discharged if you do?

MARIE: Shall I go, Julie?

JULIE: [*Embarrassed*] Why do you keep asking me that?

MARIE: You know best what to do.

JULIE: [*Profoundly moved; slowly*] It's all right, Marie, you can go home.

MARIE: [*Exits reluctantly, but comes back, and says uncertainly*] Good-night.

[*She waits a moment to see if Julie will follow her. Julie does not move. Marie exits. Meantime it has grown quite dark. During the following scene the gas-lamps far in the distance are lighted one by one. Liliom and Julie sit on the bench. From afar, very faintly, comes the music of a calliope. But the music is intermittently heard; now it breaks off, now it resumes again, as if it came down on a fitful wind. Blending with it are the sounds of human voices, now loud, now soft; the blare of a toy trumpet; the confused noises of the show booths. It grows progressively darker until the end of the scene. There is no moonlight. The spring iridescence glows in the deep blue sky*]

LILIOM: Now we're both discharged. [*She does not answer. From now on they speak gradually lower and lower until the end of the scene, which is played almost in whispers. Whistles softly, then*] Have you had your supper?

JULIE: No.

LILIOM: Want to go eat something at the Garden?

JULIE: No.

LILIOM: Anywhere else?

JULIE: No.

LILIOM: [*Whistles softly, then*] You don't come to this park very often, do you? I've only seen you three times. Been here oftener than that?

JULIE: Oh, yes.

LILIOM: Did you see me?

JULIE: Yes.

LILIOM: And did you know I was Liliom?

JULIE: They told me.

LILIOM: [*Whistles softly, then*] Have you got a sweetheart?

JULIE: No.

LILIOM: Don't lie to me.

JULIE: I haven't. If I had, I'd tell you. I've never had one.

LILIOM: What an awful liar you are. I've got a good mind to go away and leave you here.

JULIE: I've never had one.

LILIOM: Tell that to some one else.

JULIE: [*Reproachfully*] Why do you insist I have?

LILIOM: Because you stayed here with me the first time I asked you to. You know your way around, you do.

JULIE: No, I don't, Mister Liliom.

LILIOM: I suppose you'll tell me you don't know why you're sitting here—like this, in the dark, alone with me—— You wouldn't 'a' stayed so quick, if you hadn't done it before—with some soldier, maybe. This isn't the first time. You wouldn't have been so ready to stay if it was—what *did* you stay for, anyhow?

JULIE: So you wouldn't be left alone.

LILIOM: Alone! God, you're dumb! I don't need to be alone. I can have all the girls I want. Not only servant girls like you, but cooks and governesses, even French girls, I could have twenty of them if I wanted to.

JULIE: I know, Mister Liliom.

LILIOM: What do you know?

JULIE: That all the girls are in love with you. But that's not why *I* stayed. I stayed because you've been so good to me.

LILIOM: Well, then you can go home.

JULIE: I don't want to go home now.

LILIOM: And what if I go away and leave you sitting here?

JULIE: If you did, I wouldn't go home.

LILIOM: Do you know what you remind me of? A sweetheart I had once—I'll tell you how I met her —— One night, at closing time we had put out the lights in the carousel, and just as I was——

[*He is interrupted by the entrance of two* Plainclothes Policemen. *They take their stations on either side of the bench. They are police, searching the park for vagabonds*]

FIRST POLICEMAN: What are you doing there?

LILIOM: Me?

SECOND POLICEMAN: Stand up when you're spoken to!

[*He taps* Liliom *imperatively on the shoulder*]

FIRST POLICEMAN: What's your name?

LILIOM: Andreas Zavocki.

[Julie *begins to weep softly*]

SECOND POLICEMAN: Stop your bawling. We're not goin' to eat you. We are only making our rounds.

FIRST POLICEMAN: See that he doesn't get away. [*The* Second Policeman *steps closer to* Liliom] What's your business?

LILIOM: Barker and bouncer.

SECOND POLICEMAN: They call him Liliom, Chief. We've had him up a couple of times.

FIRST POLICEMAN: So that's who you are! Who do you work for now?

LILIOM: I work for the widow Muskat.

FIRST POLICEMAN: What are you hanging around here for?

LILIOM: We're just sitting here—me and this girl.

FIRST POLICEMAN: Your sweetheart?

LILIOM: No.

FIRST POLICEMAN: [*To* Julie] And who are you?

JULIE: Julie Zeller.

FIRST POLICEMAN: Servant girl?

JULIE: Maid of all work for Mister Georg Breier, Number Twenty Damjanovitsch Street.

FIRST POLICEMAN: Show your hands.

SECOND POLICEMAN: [*After examining* Julie's *hand*] Servant girl.

FIRST POLICEMAN: Why aren't you at home? What are you doing out here with him?

JULIE: This is my day out, sir.

FIRST POLICEMAN: It would be better for you if you didn't spend it sitting around with a fellow like this.

SECOND POLICEMAN: They'll be disappearing in the bushes as soon as we turn our backs.

FIRST POLICEMAN: He's only after your money. We know this fine fellow. He picks up you silly servant girls and takes what money you have. Tomorrow you'll probably be coming around to report him. If you do, I'll throw you out.

JULIE: I haven't any money, sir.

FIRST POLICEMAN: Do you hear that, Liliom?

LILIOM: I'm not looking for her money.

SECOND POLICEMAN: [*Nudging him warningly*] Keep your mouth shut.

FIRST POLICEMAN: It is my duty to warn you, my child, what kind of company you're in. He makes a specialty of servant girls. That's why he works in a carousel. He gets hold of a girl, promises to marry her, then he takes her money and her ring.

JULIE: But I haven't got a ring.

SECOND POLICEMAN: You're not to talk unless you're asked a question.

FIRST POLICEMAN: You be thankful that I'm warning you. It's nothing to me what you do. I'm not your father, thank God. But I'm telling you what kind of a fellow he is. By to-morrow morning you'll be coming around to us to report him. Now you be sensible and go home. You needn't be afraid of him. This officer will take you home if you're afraid.

JULIE: Do I *have* to go?

FIRST POLICEMAN: No, you don't *have* to go.

JULIE: Then I'll stay, sir.

FIRST POLICEMAN: Well, you've been warned.

JULIE: Yes, sir. Thank you, sir.

FIRST POLICEMAN: Come on, Berkovics.

[*The* Policemen *exit.* Julie *and* Liliom *sit on the bench again. There is a brief pause*]

JULIE: Well, and what then?

LILIOM: [*Fails to understand*] Huh?

JULIE: You were beginning to tell me a story.

LILIOM: Me?

JULIE: Yes, about a sweetheart. You said, one night, just as they were putting out the lights of the carousel—— That's as far as you got.

LILIOM: Oh, yes, yes, just as the lights were going out, some one came along—a little girl with a big shawl—you know—— She came—eh—from——

Say—tell me—ain't you—that is, ain't you at all—afraid of me? The officer told you what kind of a fellow I am—and that I'd take your money away from you——

JULIE: You couldn't take it away—I haven't got any. But if I had—I'd—I'd give it to you—I'd give it all to you.

LILIOM: You would?

JULIE: If you asked me for it.

LILIOM: Have you ever had a fellow you gave money to?

JULIE: No.

LILIOM: Haven't you ever had a sweetheart?

JULIE: No.

LILIOM: Some one you used to go walking with. You've had one like that?

JULIE: Yes.

LILIOM: A soldier?

JULIE: He came from the same village I did.

LILIOM: That's what all the soldiers say. Where *do* you come from, anyway?

JULIE: Not far from here.

[*There is a pause.*]

LILIOM: Were you in love with him?

JULIE: Why do you keep asking me that all the time, Mister Liliom? I wasn't in love with him. We only went walking together.

LILIOM: Where did you walk?

JULIE: In the park.

LILIOM: And your virtue? Where did you lose that?

JULIE: I haven't got any virtue.

LILIOM: Well, you had once.

JULIE: No, I never had. I'm a respectable girl.

LILIOM: Yes, but you gave the soldier something.

JULIE: Why do you question me like that, Mister Liliom?

LILIOM: Did you give him something?

JULIE: You have to. But I didn't love him.

LILIOM: Do you love me?

JULIE: No, Mister Liliom.

LILIOM: Then why do you stay here with me?

JULIE: Um—nothing.

[*There is a pause. The music from afar is plainly heard*]

LILIOM: Want to dance?

JULIE: No. I have to be very careful.

LILIOM: Of what?

JULIE: My—character.

LILIOM: Why?

JULIE: Because I'm never going to marry. If I was going to marry, it would be different. Then I wouldn't need to worry so much about my character. It doesn't make any difference if you're married. But I shan't marry—and that's why I've got to take care to be a respectable girl.

LILIOM: Suppose I were to say to you—I'll marry you.

JULIE: You?

LILIOM: That frightens you, doesn't it? You're thinking of what the officer said and you're afraid.

JULIE: No, I'm not, Mister Liliom. I don't pay any attention to what he said.

LILIOM: But you wouldn't dare to marry any one like me, would you?

JULIE: I know that—that—if I loved any one—it wouldn't make any difference to me what he—even if I died for it.

LILIOM: But you wouldn't marry a rough guy like me—that is—eh—if you loved me——

JULIE: Yes, I would—if I loved you, Mister Liliom.

[*There is a pause*]

LILIOM: [*Whispers*] Well—you just said—didn't you?—that you don't love me. Well, why don't you go home then?

JULIE: It's too late now, they'd all be asleep.

LILIOM: Locked out?

JULIE: Certainly.

[*They are silent awhile*]

LILIOM: I think—that even a low-down good-for-nothing—can make a man of himself.

JULIE: Certainly.

[*They are silent again. A lamp-lighter crosses the stage, lights the lamp over the bench, and exits*]

LILIOM: Are you hungry?

JULIE: No.

[*Another pause*]

LILIOM: Suppose—you had some money—and I took it from you?

JULIE: Then you could take it, that's all.

LILIOM: [*After another brief silence*] All I have to do—is go back to her—that Muskat woman—she'll be glad to get me back—then I'd be earning my wages again.

[*She is silent. The twilight folds darker about them*]

JULIE: [*Very softly*] Don't go back—to her——

[*Pause*]

LILIOM: There are a lot of acacia trees around here.

[*Pause*]

JULIE: Don't go back to her——

[*Pause*]

LILIOM: She'd take me back the minute I asked her. I know why—she knows, too——

[*Pause*]

JULIE: I can smell them, too—acacia blossoms——

[*There is a pause. Some blossoms drift down from the tree-top to the bench. Liliom picks one up and smells it*]

LILIOM: White acacias!

JULIE: [*After a brief pause*] The wind brings them down.

[*They are silent. There is a long pause before*]

THE CURTAIN FALLS

SCENE II.

A photographer's "studio," operated by the Hol-
lunders, *on the fringe of the park. It is a dilapidated
hovel. The general entrance is back left. Back right
there is a window with a sofa before it. The outlook
is on the amusement park with perhaps a small
Ferris wheel or the scaffolding of a "scenic-railway"
in the background.*

*The door to the kitchen is up left and a black-
curtained entrance to the dark-room is down left.
Just in front of the dark-room stands the camera
on its tripod. Against the back wall, between the
door and window, stands the inevitable photographer's background-screen, ready to be wheeled into
place.*

It is forenoon. When the curtain rises, Marie *and*
Julie *are discovered.*

MARIE: And *he* beat up Hollinger?

JULIE: Yes, he gave him an awful licking.

MARIE: But Hollinger is bigger than he is.

JULIE: He licked him just the same. It isn't size
that counts, you know, it's cleverness. And Liliom's
awful quick.

MARIE: And then he was arrested?

JULIE: Yes, they arrested him, but they let him go
the next day. That makes twice in the two months
we've been living here that Liliom's been arrested
and let go again.

MARIE: Why do they let him go?

JULIE: Because he is innocent.

[Mother Hollunder, *a very old woman, sharp-
tongued, but in reality quite warm-hearted
beneath her formidable exterior, enters at back
carrying a few sticks of firewood, and scolding,
half to herself*]

MOTHER HOLLUNDER: Always wanting something,
but never willing to work for it. He won't work, and
he won't steal, but he'll use up a poor old widow's
last bit of firewood. He'll do that cheerfully enough!
A big, strong lout like that lying around all day
resting his lazy bones! He ought to be ashamed to
look decent people in the face.

JULIE: I'm sorry, Mother Hollunder. . . .

MOTHER HOLLUNDER: Sorry! Better be sorry the
lazy good-for-nothing ain't in jail where he belongs
instead of in the way of honest, hard-working people.

[*She exits into the kitchen*]

MARIE: Who's that?

JULIE: Mrs. Hollunder—my aunt. This is her
[*with a sweeping gesture that takes in the camera,
dark-room and screen*] studio. She lets us live here
for nothing.

MARIE: What's she fetching the wood for?

JULIE: She brings us everything we need. If it
weren't for her I don't know what would become of
us. She's a good-hearted soul even if her tongue is
sharp

[*There is a pause*]

MARIE: [*Shyly*] Do you know—I've found out.
He's not a soldier.

JULIE: Do you still see him?

MARIE: Oh, yes.

JULIE: Often?

MARIE: Very often. He's asked me——

JULIE: To marry you?

MARIE: To marry me.

JULIE: You see—that proves he isn't a soldier.

[*There is another pause*]

MARIE: [*Abashed, yet a bit boastfully*] Do you
know what I'm doing—I'm flirting with him.

JULIE: Flirting?

MARIE: Yes. He asks me to go to the park—and
I say I can't go. Then he coaxes me, and promises
me a new scarf for my head if I go. But I don't go—
even then. . . . So then he walks all the way
home with me—and I bid him good-night at the
door.

JULIE: Is that what you call flirting?

MARIE: Um-hm! It's sinful, but it's so *thrilling.*

JULIE: Do you ever quarrel?

MARIE: [*Grandly*] Only when our Passionate Love
surges up.

JULIE: Your passionate love?

MARIE: Yes. . . . He takes my hand and we walk
along together. Then he wants to swing hands, but
I won't let him. I say: "Don't swing my hand"; and
he says, "Don't be so stubborn." And then he tries to
swing my hand again, but still I don't let him. And
for a long time I don't let him—until in the end I
let him. Then we walk along swinging hands—up
and down, up and down—just like this. *That* is
Passionate Love. It's sinful, but it's awfully *thrilling.*

JULIE: You're happy, aren't you?

MARIE: Happier than—anything—— But the most
beautiful thing on earth is Ideal Love.

JULIE: What kind is that?

MARIE: Daylight comes about three in the morning this time of the year. When we've been up that
long we're all through with flirting and Passionate
Love—and then our Ideal Love comes to the surface. It comes like this: I'll be sitting on the bench
and Wolf, he holds my hand tight—and he puts his
cheek against my cheek and we don't talk . . . we
just sit there very quiet. . . . And after a while he
gets sleepy, and his head sinks down, and he falls
asleep . . . but even in his sleep he holds tight to
my hand. And I—I sit perfectly still just looking
around me and taking long, deep breaths—for by
that time it's morning and the trees and flowers
are fresh with dew. But Wolf doesn't smell anything
because he's so fast asleep. And I get awfully sleepy
myself, but I don't sleep. And we sit like that for a
long time. That is Ideal Love——

[*There is a long pause*]

JULIE: [*Regretfully; uneasily*] He went out last
night and he hasn't come home yet.

MARIE: Here are sixteen kreuzer. It was supposed

to be carfare to take my young lady to the conservatory—eight there and eight back—but I made
her walk. Here—save it with the rest.

JULIE: This makes three gulden, forty-six.

MARIE: Three gulden, forty-six.

JULIE: He won't work at all.

MARIE: Too lazy?

JULIE: No. He never learned a trade, you see,
and he can't just go and be a day-laborer—so he just
does nothing.

MARIE: That ain't right.

JULIE: No. Have the Breiers got a new maid yet?

MARIE: They've had three since you left. You
know, Wolf's going to take a new job. He's going
to work for the city. He'll get rent free, too.

JULIE: He won't go back to work at the carousel,
either. I ask him why, but he won't tell me——
Last Monday he hit me.

MARIE: Did you hit him back?

JULIE: No.

MARIE: Why don't you leave him?

JULIE: I don't want to.

MARIE: I would. I'd leave him.

[There is a strained silence]

MOTHER HOLLUNDER: [Enters, carrying a pot of
water; muttering aloud] He can play cards, all right.
He can fight, too; and take money from poor servant girls. And the police turn their heads the other
way—— The carpenter was here.

JULIE: Is that water for the soup?

MOTHER HOLLUNDER: The carpenter was here.
There's a man for you! Dark, handsome, lots of hair,
a respectable widower with two children—and
money, and a good paying business.

JULIE: [To Marie] It's three gulden, sixty-six, not
forty-six.

MARIE: Yes, that's what I make it—sixty-six.

MOTHER HOLLUNDER: He wants to take her out of
this and marry her. This is the fifth time he's been
here. He has two children, but——

JULIE: Please don't bother, Aunt Hollunder, I'll
get the water myself.

MOTHER HOLLUNDER: He's waiting outside now.

JULIE: Send him away.

MOTHER HOLLUNDER: He'll only come back again
—and first thing you know that vagabond will get
jealous and there'll be a fight. [Goes out, muttering]
Oh, he's ready enough to fight, he is. Strike a poor
little girl like that! Ought to be ashamed of himself!
And the police just let him go on doing as he
pleases.

[Still scolding, she exits at back]

MARIE: A carpenter wants to marry you?

JULIE: Yes.

MARIE: Why don't you?

JULIE: Because——

MARIE: Liliom doesn't support you, and he beats
you—he thinks he can do whatever he likes just
because he's Liliom. He's a bad one.

JULIE: He's not really bad.

MARIE: That night you sat on the bench together
—he was gentle then.

JULIE: Yes, he was gentle.

MARIE: And afterwards he got wild again.

JULIE: Afterwards he got wild—sometimes. But
that night on the bench . . . he was gentle. He's
gentle now, sometimes, very gentle. After supper,
when he stands there and listens to the music of the
carousel, something comes over him—and he is
gentle.

MARIE: Does he say anything?

JULIE: He doesn't say anything. He gets thoughtful and very quiet, and his big eyes stare straight
ahead of him.

MARIE: Into your eyes?

JULIE: Not exactly. He's unhappy because he isn't
working. That's really why he hit me on Monday.

MARIE: That's a fine reason for hitting you! Beats
his wife because he isn't working, the ruffian!

JULIE: It preys on his mind——

MARIE: Did he hurt you?

JULIE: [Very eagerly] Oh, no.

MRS. MUSKAT: [Enters haughtily] Good-morning.
Is Liliom home?

JULIE: No.

MRS. MUSKAT: Gone out?

JULIE: He hasn't come home yet.

MRS. MUSKAT: I'll wait for him.

[She sits down]

MARIE: You've got a lot of gall—to come here.

MRS. MUSKAT: Are you the lady of the house,
my dear? Better look out or you'll get a slap in the
mouth.

MARIE: How dare you set foot in Julie's house?

MRS. MUSKAT: [To Julie] Pay no attention to her,
my child. You know what brings me here. That
vagabond, that good-for-nothing, I've come to give
him his bread and butter back.

MARIE: He's not dependent on you for his bread.

MRS. MUSKAT: [To Julie] Just ignore her, my
child. She's just ignorant.

MARIE: [Going] Good-bye.

JULIE: Good-bye.

MARIE: [In the doorway, calling back] Sixty-six.

JULIE: Yes, sixty-six.

MARIE: Good-bye.

[She exits. Julie starts to go toward the kitchen]

MRS. MUSKAT: I paid him a krone a day, and on
Sunday a gulden. And he got all the beer and cigars
he wanted from the customers. [Julie pauses on the
threshold, but does not answer] And he'd rather
starve than beg my pardon. Well, I don't insist on
that. I'll take him back without it. [Julie does not
answer] The fact is the people ask for him—and,
you see, I've got to consider business first. It's nothing to me if he starves. I wouldn't be here at all, if
it wasn't for business——

[She pauses, for Liliom and Ficsur have en-
tered]

JULIE: Mrs. Muskat is here.

LILIOM: I see she is.

JULIE: You might say good-morning.

LILIOM: What for? And what do *you* want, anyhow?

JULIE: I don't want anything.

LILIOM: Then keep your mouth shut. Next thing you'll be starting to nag again about my being out all night and out of work and living on your relations——

JULIE: I'm not saying anything.

LILIOM: But it's all on the tip of your tongue—I know you—now don't start or you'll get another.

[*He paces angrily up and down. They are all a bit afraid of him, and shrink and look away as he passes them.* Ficsur *shambles from place to place, his eyes cast down as if he were searching for something on the floor*]

MRS. MUSKAT: [*Suddenly, to* Ficsur] You're always dragging him out to play cards and drink with you. I'll have you locked up, I will.

FICSUR: I don't want to talk to you. You're too common.

[*He goes out by the door at back and lingers there in plain view. There is a pause*]

JULIE: Mrs. Muskat is here.

LILIOM: Well, why doesn't she open her mouth, if she has anything to say?

MRS. MUSKAT: Why do you go around with this man, Ficsur? He'll get you mixed up in one of his robberies first thing you know.

LILIOM: What's it to you who I go with? I do what I please. What do you want?

MRS. MUSKAT: You know what I want.

LILIOM: No, I don't.

MRS. MUSKAT: What do you suppose I want? Think I've come just to pay a social call?

LILIOM: Do I owe you anything?

MRS. MUSKAT: Yes, you do—but that's not what I came for. You're a fine one to come to for money! You earn so much these days! You know very well what I'm here for.

LILIOM: You've got Hollinger at the carousel, haven't you?

MRS. MUSKAT: Sure I have.

LILIOM: Well, what else do you want? He's as good as I am.

MRS. MUSKAT: You're quite right, my boy. He's every bit as good as you are. I'd not dream of letting him go. But one isn't enough any more. There's work enough for two——

LILIOM: One was enough when *I* was there.

MRS. MUSKAT: Well, I might let Hollinger go——

LILIOM: Why let him go, if he's so good?

MRS. MUSKAT: [*Shrugs her shoulders*] Yes, he's good.

[*Not once until now has she looked at* Liliom]

LILIOM: [*To* Julie] Ask your aunt if I can have a cup of coffee. [Julie *exits into the kitchen*] So Hollinger is good, is he?

MRS. MUSKAT: [*Crosses to him and looks him in the face*] Why don't you stay home and sleep at night? You're a sight to look at.

LILIOM: He's good, is he?

MRS. MUSKAT: Push your hair back from your forehead.

LILIOM: Let my hair be. It's nothing to you.

MRS. MUSKAT: All right. But if I'd told you to let it hang down over your eyes you'd have pushed it back——I hear you've been beating her, this—this——

LILIOM: None of your business.

MRS. MUSKAT: You're a fine fellow! Beating a skinny little thing like that! If you're tired of her, leave her, but there's no use beating the poor——

LILIOM: Leave her, eh? You'd like that, wouldn't you?

MRS. MUSKAT: Don't flatter yourself. [*Quite embarrassed*] Serves me right, too. If I had any sense I wouldn't have run after you—— My God, the things one must do for the sake of business! If I could only sell the carousel I wouldn't be sitting here. . . . Come, Liliom, if you have any sense, you'll come back. I'll pay you well.

LILIOM: The carousel is crowded just the same . . . *without me?*

MRS. MUSKAT: Crowded, yes—but it's not the same.

LILIOM: Then you admit that you *do* miss me.

MRS. MUSKAT: Miss you? Not I. But the silly girls miss you. They're always asking for you. Well, are you going to be sensible and come back?

LILIOM: And leave—her?

MRS. MUSKAT: You beat her, don't you?

LILIOM: No, I don't beat her. What's all this damn fool talk about beating her? I hit her once—that was all—and now the whole city seems to be talking about it. You don't call that beating her, do you?

MRS. MUSKAT: All right, all right. I take it back. I don't want to get mixed up in it.

LILIOM: Beating her! As if I'd beat her——

MRS. MUSKAT: I can't make out why you're so concerned about her. You've been married to her two months—it's plain to see that you're sick of it—and out there is the carousel—and the show booths—and money—and you'd throw it all away. For what? Heavens, how can any one be such a fool? [*Looks at him appraisingly*] Where have you been all night? You look awful.

LILIOM: It's no business of yours.

MRS. MUSKAT: You never used to look like that. This life is telling on you. [*Pauses*] Do you know—I've got a new organ.

LILIOM: [*Softly*] I know.

MRS. MUSKAT: How did you know?

LILIOM: You can hear it—from here.

MRS. MUSKAT: It's a good one, eh?

LILIOM: [*Wistfully*] Very good. Fine. It roars and snorts—so fine.

MRS. MUSKAT: You should hear it close by—it's heavenly. Even the carousel seems to know . . . it goes quicker. I got rid of those two horses—you know, the ones with the broken ears?

LILIOM: What have you put in their place?

MRS. MUSKAT: Guess.

LILIOM: Zebras?

MRS. MUSKAT: No—an automobile.

LILIOM: [Transported] An automobile——

MRS. MUSKAT: Yes. If you've got any sense you'll come back. What good are you doing here? Out there is your art, the only thing you're fit for. You are an artist, not a respectable married man.

LILIOM: Leave her—this little——

MRS. MUSKAT: She'll be better off. She'll go back and be a servant girl again. As for you—you're an artist and you belong among artists. All the beer you want, cigars, a krone a day and a gulden on Sunday, and the girls, Liliom, the girls—I've always treated you right, haven't I? I bought you a watch, and——

LILIOM: She's not that kind. She'd never be a servant girl again.

MRS. MUSKAT: I suppose you think she'd kill herself. Don't worry. Heavens, if every girl was to commit suicide just because her—— [Finishes with a gesture]

LILIOM: [Stares at her a moment, considering, then with sudden, smiling animation] So the people don't like Hollinger?

MRS. MUSKAT: You know very well they don't, you rascal.

LILIOM: Well——

MRS. MUSKAT: You've always been happy at the carousel. It's a great life—pretty girls and beer and cigars and music—a great life and an easy one. I'll tell you what—come back and I'll give you a ring that used to belong to my dear departed husband. Well, will you come?

LILIOM: She's not that kind. She'd never be a servant girl again. But—but—for my part—if I decide—that needn't make any difference. I can go on living with her even if I do go back to my art——

MRS. MUSKAT: My God!

LILIOM: What's the matter?

MRS. MUSKAT: Who ever heard of a married man—I suppose you think all girls would be pleased to know that you were running home to your wife every night. It's ridiculous! When the people found out they'd laugh themselves sick——

LILIOM: I know what you want.

MRS. MUSKAT: [Refuses to meet his gaze] You flatter yourself.

LILIOM: You'll give me that ring, too?

MRS. MUSKAT: [Pushes the hair back from his forehead] Yes.

LILIOM: I'm not happy in this house.

MRS. MUSKAT: [Still stroking his hair] Nobody takes care of you.

[They are silent. Julie enters, carrying a cup of coffee. Mrs. Muskat removes her hand from Liliom's head. There is a pause]

LILIOM: Do you want anything?

JULIE: No.

[There is a pause. She exits slowly into the kitchen]

MRS. MUSKAT: The old woman says there is a carpenter, a widower, who——

LILIOM: I know—I know——

JULIE: [Reëntering] Liliom, before I forget, I have something to tell you.

LILIOM: All right.

JULIE: I've been wanting to tell you—in fact, I was going to tell you yesterday——

LILIOM: Go ahead.

JULIE: But I must tell you alone—if you'll come in—it will only take a minute.

LILIOM: Don't you see I'm busy now? Here I am talking business and you interrupt with——

JULIE: It'll only take a minute.

LILIOM: Get out of here, or——

JULIE: But I tell you it will only take a minute——

LILIOM: Will you get out of here?

JULIE: [Courageously] No.

LILIOM: [Rising] What's that!

JULIE: No.

MRS. MUSKAT: [Rises, too] Now don't start fighting. I'll go out and look at the photographs in the show case a while and come back later for your answer.

[She exits at back]

JULIE: You can hit me again if you like—don't look at me like that. I'm not afraid of you. . . . I'm not afraid of any one. I told you I had something to tell you.

LILIOM: Well, out with it—quick.

JULIE: I can't tell you so quick. Why don't you drink your coffee?

LILIOM: Is that what you wanted to tell me?

JULIE: No. By the time you've drunk your coffee I'll have told you.

LILIOM: [Gets the coffee and sips it] Well?

JULIE: Yesterday my head ached—and you asked me——

LILIOM: Yes——

JULIE: Well—you see—that's what it is——

LILIOM: Are you sick?

JULIE: No. . . . But you wanted to know what my headaches came from—and you said I seemed —changed.

LILIOM: Did I? I guess I meant the carpenter.

JULIE: I've been—what? The carpenter? No. It's something entirely different—it's awful hard to tell —but you'll have to know sooner or later—I'm not a bit—scared—because it's a perfectly natural thing——

LILIOM: [Puts the coffee cup on the table] What?

JULIE: When—when a man and woman—live together——

LILIOM: Yes.

JULIE: I'm going to have a baby.

[*She exits swiftly at back. There is a pause. Ficsur appears at the open window and looks in*]

LILIOM: Ficsur! [Ficsur *sticks his head in*] Say, Ficsur—Julie is going to have a baby.

FICSUR: Yes? What of it?

LILIOM: Nothing. [*Suddenly*] Get out of here.

[Ficsur's *head is quickly withdrawn. Mrs. Muskat* reënters]

MRS. MUSKAT: Has she gone?

LILIOM: Yes.

MRS. MUSKAT: I might as well give you ten kronen in advance. [*Opens her purse. Liliom takes up his coffee cup*] Here you are. [*She proffers some coins. Liliom ignores her*] Why don't you take it?

LILIOM: [*Very nonchalantly, his cup poised ready to drink*] Go home, Mrs. Muskat.

MRS. MUSKAT: What's the matter with you?

LILIOM: Go home [*Sips his coffee*] and let me finish my coffee in peace. Don't you see I'm at breakfast?

MRS MUSKAT: Have you gone crazy?

LILIOM: Will you get out of here?

[*Turns to her threateningly*]

MRS. MUSKAT: [*Restoring the coins to her purse*] I'll never speak to you again as long as you live.

LILIOM: That worries me a lot.

MRS. MUSKAT: Good-bye!

LILIOM: Good-bye. [*As she exits, he calls*] Ficsur! [Ficsur *enters*] Tell me, Ficsur. You said you knew a way to get a whole lot of money——

FICSUR: Sure I do.

LILIOM: How much?

FICSUR: More than you ever had in your life before. You leave it to an old hand like me.

MOTHER HOLLUNDER: [*Enters from the kitchen*] In the morning he must have his coffee, and at noon his soup, and in the evening coffee again—and plenty of firewood—and I'm expected to furnish it all. Give me back my cup and saucer.

[*The show booths of the amusement park have opened for business. The familiar noises begin to sound; clear above them all, but far in the distance, sounds the organ of the carousel*]

LILIOM: Now, Aunt Hollunder.

[*From now until the fall of the curtain it is apparent that the sound of the organ makes him more and more uneasy*]

MOTHER HOLLUNDER: And you, you vagabond, get out of here this minute or I'll call my son——

FICSUR: I have nothing to do with the likes of him. He's too common.

[*But he slinks out at back*]

LILIOM: Aunt Hollunder!

MOTHER HOLLUNDER: What now?

LILIOM: When your son was born—when you brought him into the world——

MOTHER HOLLUNDER: Well?

LILIOM: Nothing.

MOTHER HOLLUNDER: [*Muttering as she exits*] Sleep it off, you good-for-nothing lout. Drink and play cards all night long—that's all you know how to do—and take the bread out of poor people's mouths—you can do that, too.

[*She exits*]

LILIOM: Ficsur!

FICSUR: [*At the window*] Julie's going to have a baby. You told me before.

LILIOM: This scheme—about the cashier of the leather factory—there's money in it——

FICSUR: Lots of money—but—it takes two to pull it off.

LILIOM: [*Meditatively*] Yes. [*Uneasily*] All right, Ficsur. Go away—and come back later.

[*Ficsur vanishes. The organ in the distant carousel drones incessantly. Liliom listens awhile, then goes to the door and calls*]

LILIOM: Aunt Hollunder! [*With naïve joy*] Julie's going to have a baby. [*Then he goes to the window, jumps on the sofa, looks out. Suddenly, in a voice that overtops the droning of the organ, he shouts as if addressing the far-off carousel*] I'm going to be a father.

JULIE: [*Enters from the kitchen*] Liliom! What's the matter? What's happened?

LILIOM: [*Coming down from the sofa*] Nothing. [*Throws himself on the sofa, buries his face in the cushion. Julie watches him a moment, comes over to him and covers him with a shawl. Then she goes on tiptoe to the door at back and remains standing in the doorway, looking out and listening to the droning of the organ*]

THE CURTAIN FALLS

SCENE III.

The setting is the same, later that afternoon. Liliom is sitting opposite Ficsur, who is teaching him a song. Julie hovers in the background, engaged in some household task.

FICSUR: Listen now. Here's the third verse.

[*Sings hoarsely*]

"Look out, look out, my pretty lad,
The damn police are on your trail;
The nicest girl you ever had
Has now commenced to weep and wail:
Look out here comes the damn police,
The damn police,
The damn police,
Look out here comes the damn police,
They'll get you every time."

LILIOM: [*Sings*]

"Look out, look out, my pretty lad,
The damn police—— ."

FICSUR, LILIOM: [*Sing together*]
"are on your trail;
The nicest girl you ever had
Has now commenced to weep and wail."

LILIOM: [*Alone*]
"Look out here comes the damn police,
The damn police,
The damn police——"

[Julie, *troubled and uneasy, looks from one to the other, then exits into the kitchen*]

FICSUR: [*When she has gone, comes quickly over to* Liliom *and speaks furtively*] As you go down Franzen Street you come to the railroad embankment. Beyond that—all the way to the leather factory—there's not a thing in sight, not even a watchman's hut.

LILIOM: And does he always come that way?

FICSUR: Yes. Not along the embankment, but down below along the path across the fields. Since last year he's been going alone. Before that he always used to have some one with him.

LILIOM: Every Saturday?

FICSUR: Every Saturday.

LILIOM: And the money? Where does he keep it?

FICSUR: In a leather bag. The whole week's pay for the workmen at the factory.

LILIOM: Much?

FICSUR: Sixteen thousand kronen. Quite a haul, what?

LILIOM: What's his name?

FICSUR: Linzman. He's a Jew.

LILIOM: The cashier?

FICSUR: Yes—but when he gets a knife between his ribs—or if I smash his skull for him—he won't be a cashier any more.

LILIOM: Does he have to be killed?

FICSUR: No, he doesn't *have* to be. He can give up the money *without* being killed—but most of these cashiers are peculiar—they'd rather be killed.

[Julie *reënters, pretends to get something on the other side of the room, then exits at back. During the ensuing dialogue she keeps coming in and out in the same way, showing plainly that she is suspicious and anxious. She attempts to overhear what they are saying and, in spite of their caution, does catch a word here and there, which adds to her disquiet. Ficsur, catching sight of her, abruptly changes the conversation*]

FICSUR: And the next verse is:
"And when you're in the prison cell
They'll feed you bread and water."

FICSUR AND LILIOM: [*Sing together*]
"They'll make your little sweetheart tell
Them all the things you brought her.
Look out here comes the damn police,
The damn police,
The damn police,
Look out here comes the damn police,
They'll get you every time."

LILIOM: [*Sings alone*]
"And when you're in the prison cell
They'll feed you bread and water——"
[*Breaks off, as* Julie *exits*]
And when it's done, do we start right off for America?

FICSUR: No.

LILIOM: What then?

FICSUR: We bury the money for six months. That's the usual time. And after the sixth month we dig it up again.

LILIOM: And then?

FICSUR: Then you go on living just as usual for six months more—you don't touch a heller of the money.

LILIOM: In six months the baby will be born.

FICSUR: Then we'll take the baby with us, too. Three months before the time you'll go to work so as to be able to say you saved up your wages to get to America.

LILIOM: Which of us goes up and talks to him.

FICSUR: One of us talks to him with his mouth and the other talks with his knife. Depends on which you'd rather do. I'll tell you what—you talk to him with your mouth.

LILIOM: Do you hear that?

FICSUR: What?

LILIOM: Outside . . . like the rattle of swords. [Ficsur *listens. After a pause,* Liliom *continues*] What do I say to him?

FICSUR: You say good-evening to him and: "Excuse me, sir; can you tell me the time?"

LILIOM: And then what?

FICSUR: By that time I'll have stuck him—and then you take *your knife*——

[*He stops as a* Policeman *enters at back*]

POLICEMAN: Good-day!

FICSUR, LILIOM: [*In unison*] Good-day!

FICSUR: [*Calling toward the kitchen*] Hey, photographer, come out. . . . Here's a customer.

[*There is a pause. The* Policeman *waits.* Ficsur *sings softly*]
"And when you're in the prison cell
They'll feed you bread and water
They'll make your little sweetheart tell"

LILIOM, FICSUR: [*Sing together, low*]
"Them all the things you brought her.
Look out here comes the——"
[*They hum the rest so as not to let the* Policeman *hear the words "the damn police." As they sing,* Mrs. Hollunder *and her* Son *enter*]

POLICEMAN: Do you make cabinet photographs?

YOUNG HOLLUNDER: Certainly, sir. [*Points to a rack of photographs on the wall*] Take your choice, sir. Would you like one full length?

POLICEMAN: Yes, full length.

[Mother Hollunder *pushes out the camera while her* Son *poses the* Policeman, *runs from him to the camera and back again, now altering the pose, now ducking under the black cloth*

and pushing the camera nearer. Meanwhile
Mother Hollunder *has fetched a plate from
the dark-room and thrust it in the camera.
While this is going on,* Liliom *and* Ficsur, *their
heads together, speak in very low tones*]

LILIOM: Belong around here?

FICSUR: Not around here.

LILIOM: Where, then?

FICSUR: Suburban. [*There is a pause*]

LILIOM: [*Bursts out suddenly in a rather grotesquely childish and overstrained lament*] O God,
what a dirty life I'm leading—God, God!

FICSUR: [*Reassuring him benevolently*] Over in
America it will be better, all right.

LILIOM: What's over there?

FICSUR: [*Virtuously*] Factories . . . industries—

YOUNG HOLLUNDER: [*To the* Policeman] Now,
quite still, please. One, two, three. [*Deftly removes
the cover of the lens and in a few seconds restores
it*] Thank you.

MOTHER HOLLUNDER: The picture will be ready in
five minutes.

POLICEMAN: Good. I'll come back in five minutes.
How much do I owe you?

YOUNG HOLLUNDER: [*With exaggerated deference*]
You don't need to pay in advance, Mr. Commis-
sioner.

[*The* Policeman *salutes condescendingly and
exits at back.* Mother Hollunder *carries the
plate into the dark-room.* Young Hollunder,
*after pushing the camera back in place, follows
her*]

MOTHER HOLLUNDER: [*Muttering angrily at she
passes* Ficsur *and* Liliom] You hang around and
dirty the whole place up! Why don't you go take
a walk? Things are going so well with you that you
have to sing, eh? [*Confronting* Ficsur *suddenly*]
Weren't you frightened sick when you saw the
policeman?

FICSUR: [*With loathing*] Go 'way, or I'll step on
you. [*She exits into the dark-room*]

LILIOM: They like Hollinger at the carousel?

FICSUR: I should say they do.

LILIOM: Did you see the Muskat woman, too?

FICSUR: Sure. She takes care of Hollinger's hair.

LILIOM: Combs his hair?

FICSUR: She fixes him all up.

LILIOM: Let her fix him all she likes.

FICSUR: [*Urging him toward the kitchen door*]
Go on. Now's your chance.

LILIOM: What for?

FICSUR: To get the knife.

LILIOM: What knife?

FICSUR: The kitchen knife. I've got a pocket-knife,
but if he shows fight, we'll let him have the big
knife.

LILIOM: What for? If he gets ugly, I'll bat him
one over the head that'll make him squint for the
rest of his life.

FICSUR: You've got to have something on you.
You can't slit his throat with a bat over the head.

LILIOM: Must his throat be slit?

FICSUR: No, it *mustn't.* But if he asks for it.
[*There is a pause*] You'd like to sail on the big
steamer, wouldn't you? And you want to see the
factories over there, don't you? But you're not
willing to inconvenience yourself a little for them.

LILIOM: If I take the knife, Julie will see me.

FICSUR: Take it so she won't see you.

LILIOM: [*Advances a few paces toward the
kitchen. The* Policeman *enters at back.* Liliom
knocks on the door of the dark-room] Here's the
policeman!

MOTHER HOLLUNDER: [*Coming out*] One minute
more, please. Just a minute.

[*She reënters the dark-room.* Liliom *hesitates
a moment, then exits into the kitchen. The*
Policeman *scrutinizes* Ficsur *mockingly*]

FICSUR: [*Returns his stare, walks a few paces
toward him, then deliberately turns his back. Suddenly he wheels around, points at the* Policeman
and addresses him in a teasing, childish tone] Chris-
tiana Street at the corner of Retti!

POLICEMAN: [*Amazed, self-conscious*] How do
you know that?

FICSUR: I used to practice my profession in that
neighborhood.

POLICEMAN: What is your profession?

FICSUR: Professor of pianola——

[*The* Policeman *glares, aware that the man is
joking with him, twirls his moustache indignantly.* Young Hollunder *comes out of the
dark-room and gives him the finished pictures*]

YOUNG HOLLUNDER: Here you are, sir.

[*The* Policeman *examines the photographs,
pays for them, starts to go, stops, glares at*
Ficsur *and exits. When he is gone,* Ficsur *goes
to the doorway and looks out after him.* Young
Hollunder *exits.* Liliom *reënters, buttoning his
coat*]

FICSUR: [*Turns, sees* Liliom] What are you staring at?

LILIOM: I'm not staring.

FICSUR: What then are you doing?

LILIOM: I'm thinking it over.

FICSUR: [*Comes very close to him*] Tell me then—
what will you say to him?

LILIOM: [*Unsteadily*] I'll say—"Good-evening—
Excuse me, sir—Can you tell me the time?" And
suppose he answers me, what do I say to him?

FICSUR: He won't answer you.

LILIOM: Don't you think so?

FICSUR: No. [*Feeling for the knife under* Liliom's
coat] Where is it? Where did you put it?

LILIOM: [*Stonily*] Left side.

FICSUR: That's right—over your heart. [*Feels it*]
Ah—there it is—there—there's the blade—quite a
big fellow, isn't it—ah, here it begins to get nar-

rower. [*Reaches the tip of the knife*] And here is its eye—that's what it sees with. [Julie *enters from the kitchen, passes them slowly, watching them in silent terror, then stops.* Ficsur *nudges* Liliom] Sing, come on, sing!

LILIOM: [*In a quavering voice*]
"Look out for the damn police."

FICSUR: [*Joining in, cheerily, loudly, marking time with the swaying of his body*] "Look out, look out, my pretty lad."

LILIOM:
"—look out, my pretty lad."

[Julie *goes out at back.* Liliom's *glance follows her. When she has gone, he turns to* Ficsur] At night— in my dreams—if his ghost comes back—what will I do then?

FICSUR: His ghost won't never come back.

LILIOM: Why not?

FICSUR: A Jew's ghost don't come back.

LILIOM: Well then—afterwards——

FICSUR: [*Impatiently*] What do you mean—after-wards?

LILIOM: In the next world—when I come up be-fore the Lord God—what'll I say then?

FICSUR: The likes of you will never come up be-fore Him.

LILIOM: Why not?

FICSUR: Have you ever come up before the high court?

LILIOM: No.

FICSUR: Our kind comes up before the police magistrate—and the highest we *ever* get is the crim-inal court.

LILIOM: Will it be the same in the next world?

FICSUR: Just the same. We'll come up before a police magistrate, same as we did in this world.

LILIOM: A police magistrate?

FICSUR: Sure. For the rich folks—the Heavenly Court. For us poor people—only a police magis-trate. For the rich folks—fine music and angels— For us——

LILIOM: For us?

FICSUR: For us, my son, there's only justice. In the next world there'll be lots of justice, yes, nothing but justice. And where there's justice, there must be police magistrates; and where they're police magis-trates, people like us get——

LILIOM: [*Interrupting*] Good-evening. Excuse me, sir, can you tell me the time?

[*Lays his hand over his heart*]

FICSUR: What do you put your hand there for?

LILIOM: My heart is jumping—under the knife.

FICSUR: Put it on the other side then. [*Looks out at the sky*] It's time we started—we'll walk slow——

LILIOM: It's too early.

FICSUR: Come on.

[*As they are about to go,* Julie *appears in the doorway at back, obstructing the way*]

JULIE: Where are you going with him?

LILIOM: Where am I going with him?

JULIE: Stay home.

LILIOM: No.

JULIE: Stay home. It's going to rain soon, and you'll get wet.

FICSUR: It won't rain.

JULIE: How do you know?

FICSUR: I always get notice in advance.

JULIE: Stay home. This evening the carpenter's coming. I've asked him to give you work.

LILIOM: I'm not a carpenter.

JULIE: [*More and more anxious, though she tries to conceal it*] Stay home. Marie's coming with her intended to have their picture taken. She wants to introduce us to her intended husband.

LILIOM: I've seen enough intended husbands——

JULIE: Stay home. Marie's bringing some money, and I'll give it all to you.

LILIOM: [*Approaching the door*] I'm going—for a walk—with Ficsur. We'll be right back.

JULIE: [*Forcing a smile to keep back her tears*] If you stay home, I'll get you a glass of beer—or wine, if you prefer.

FICSUR: Coming or not?

JULIE: I'm not angry with you any more for hit-ting me.

LILIOM: [*Gruffly, but his gruffness is simulated to hide the fact that he cannot bear the sight of her suffering*] Stand out of the way—or I'll——[*He clenches his fist*] Let me out!

JULIE: [*Trembling*] What have you got under your coat?

LILIOM: [*Produces from his pocket a greasy pack of cards*] Cards.

JULIE: [*Trembling, speaks very low*] What's under your coat?

LILIOM: Let me out!

JULIE: [*Obstructing the way. Speaks quickly, eagerly, in a last effort to detain him*] Marie's in-tended knows about a place for a married couple without children to be caretakers of a house on Arader Street. Rent free, a kitchen of your own, and the privilege of keeping chickens——

LILIOM: Get out of the way!

[Julie *stands aside.* Liliom *exits.* Ficsur *follows him.* Julie *remains standing meditatively in the doorway.* Mother Hollunder *comes out of the kitchen*]

MOTHER HOLLUNDER: I can't find my kitchen knife anywhere. Have you seen anything of it?

JULIE: [*Horrified*] No.

MOTHER HOLLUNDER: It was on the kitchen table just a few minutes ago. No one was in there excep' Liliom.

JULIE: He didn't take it.

MOTHER HOLLUNDER: No one else was in there.

JULIE: What would Liliom want with a kitchen knife?

MOTHER HOLLUNDER: He'd sell it and spend the money on drink.

JULIE: It just so happens—see how unjust you

are to him—it just so happens that I went through all of Liliom's pockets just now—I wanted to see if he had any money on him. But he had nothing but a pack of cards.

MOTHER HOLLUNDER: [*Returns to the kitchen, grumbling*] Cards in his pocket—cards! The fine gentlemen have evidently gone off to their club to play a little game.

[*She exits. After a pause* Marie, *happy and beaming, appears in the doorway at back, and enters, followed by* Wolf]

MARIE: Here we are! [*She takes* Wolf *by the hand and leads him, grinning shyly, to* Julie, *who has turned at her call*] Hello!

JULIE: Hello.

MARIE: Well, we're here.

JULIE: Yes.

WOLF: [*Bows awkwardly and extends his hand*] My name is Wolf Beifeld.

JULIE: My name is Julie Zeller.

[*They shake hands. There is an embarrassed silence. Then, to relieve the situation,* Wolf *takes* Julie's *hand again and shakes it vigorously*]

MARIE: Well—this is Wolf.

WOLF: Yes.

JULIE: Yes. [*Another awkward silence*]

MARIE: Where is Liliom?

WOLF: Yes, where is your husband?

JULIE: He's out.

MARIE: Where?

JULIE: Just for a walk.

MARIE: Is he?

JULIE: Yes.

WOLF: Oh!

[*Another silence*]

MARIE: Wolf's got a new place. After the first of the month he won't have to stand outside any more. He's going to work in a club after the first of the month.

WOLF: [*Apologetically*] She don't know yet how to explain these things just right—hehehe—— Beginning the first I'm to be second steward at the Burger Club—a good job, if one conducts oneself properly.

JULIE: Yes?

WOLF: The pay—is quite good—but the main thing is the tips. When they play cards there's always a bit for the steward. The tips, I may say, amount to twenty, even thirty kronen every night.

MARIE: Yes.

WOLF: We've rented two rooms for ourselves to start with—and if things go well——

MARIE: Then we'll buy a house in the country.

WOLF: If one only tends to business and keeps honest. Of course, in the country we'll miss the city life, but if the good Lord sends us children—it's much healthier for children in the country.

[*There is a brief pause*]

MARIE: Wolf's nice looking, isn't he?

JULIE: Yes.

MARIE: And he's a good boy, Wolf.

JULIE: Yes.

MARIE: The only thing is—he's a Jew.

JULIE: Oh, well, you can get used to that.

MARIE: Well, aren't you going to wish us luck?

JULIE: Of course I do.

[*She embraces* Marie]

MARIE: And aren't you going to kiss Wolf, too?

JULIE: Him, too.

[*She embraces* Wolf, *remains quite still a moment, her head resting on his shoulder*]

WOLF: Why are you crying, my dear Mrs.——

[*He looks questioningly at* Marie *over* Julie's *shoulder*]

MARIE: Because she has such a good heart. [*She becomes sentimental, too*]

WOLF: [*Touched*] We thank you for your heartfelt sympathy——

[*He cannot restrain his own tears. There is a pause before* Mother Hollunder *and her son enter.* Young Hollunder *immediately busies himself with the camera*]

MOTHER HOLLUNDER: Now if you don't mind, we'll do it right away, before it gets too dark. [*She leads* Marie *and* Wolf *into position before the background-screen. Here they immediately fall into an awkward pose, smiling mechanically*] Full length?

MARIE: Please. Both figures full length.

MOTHER HOLLUNDER: Bride and groom?

MARIE: Yes.

MOTHER HOLLUNDER, YOUNG HOLLUNDER: [*Speak in unison, in loud professionally expressionless tones*] The lady looks at the gentleman and the gentleman looks straight into the camera.

MOTHER HOLLUNDER: [*Poses first* Marie, *then* Wolf] Now, if you please.

YOUNG HOLLUNDER: [*Who has crept under the black cloth, calls in muffled tones*] That's good— that's very good!

MARIE: [*Stonily rigid, but very happy, trying to speak without altering her expression*] Julie, dear, do we look all right?

JULIE: Yes, dear.

YOUNG HOLLUNDER: Now, if you please, hold still. I'll count up to three, and then you must hold perfectly still. [*Grasps the cover of the lens and calls threateningly*] One—two—three!

[*He removes the cover; there is utter silence. But as he speaks the word "one" there is heard, very faintly in the distance, the refrain of the thieves' song which* Ficsur *and* Liliom *have been singing. The refrain continues until the fall of the curtain. As he speaks the word "three" everybody is perfectly rigid save* Julie, *who lets her head sink slowly to the table. The distant refrain dies out*]

THE CURTAIN FALLS

SCENE IV.

In the fields on the outskirts of the city. At back a railroad embankment crosses the stage obliquely. At center of the embankment stands a red and white signal flag, and near it a little red signal lamp which is not yet lighted. Here also a wooden stairway leads up to the embankment.

At the foot of the embankment to the right is a pile of used railroad ties. In the background a telegraph pole, beyond it a view of trees, fences and fields; still further back a factory building and a cluster of little dwellings.

It is six o'clock of the same afternoon. Dusk has begun to fall.

Liliom *and* Ficsur *are discovered on the stairway looking after the train which has just passed.*

LILIOM: Can you still hear it snort?

FICSUR: Listen!

[*They watch the vanishing train*]

LILIOM: If you put your ear on the tracks you can hear it go all the way to Vienna.

FICSUR: Huh!

LILIOM: The one that just puffed past us—it goes all the way to Vienna.

FICSUR: No further?

LILIOM: Yes—further, too.

[*There is a pause*]

FICSUR: It must be near six. [*As Liliom ascends the steps*] Where are you going?

LILIOM: Don't be afraid. I'm not giving you the slip.

FICSUR: Why should you give me the slip? That cashier has sixteen thousand kronen on him. Just be patient till he comes, then you can talk to him, nice and polite.

LILIOM: I say, "Good-evening—excuse me, sir; what time is it?"

FICSUR: Then he tells you what time it is.

LILIOM: Suppose he don't come?

FICSUR: [*Coming down the steps*] Nonsense! He's got to come. He pays off the workmen every Saturday. And this is Saturday, ain't it? [Liliom *has ascended to the top of the stairway and is gazing along the tracks*] What are you looking at up there?

LILIOM: The tracks go on and on—there's no end to them.

FICSUR: What's that to stare about?

LILIOM: Nothing—only I always look after the train. When you stand down there at night it snorts past you, and spits down.

FICSUR: Spits?

LILIOM: Yes, the engine. It spits down. And then the whole train rattles past and away—and you stand there—spat on—but it draws your eyes along with it.

FICSUR: Draws your eyes along?

LILIOM: Yes—whether you want to or not, you've

got to look after it—as long as the tiniest bit of it is in sight.

FICSUR: Swell people sit in it.

LILIOM: And read newspapers.

FICSUR: And smoke cigars.

LILIOM: And inhale the smoke.

[*There is a short silence*]

FICSUR: Is he coming?

LILIOM: Not yet. [*Silence again.* Liliom *comes down, speaks low, confidentially*] Do you hear the telegraph wires?

FICSUR: I hear them when the wind blows.

LILIOM: Even when the wind doesn't blow you can hear them humming, humming —— People talk through them.

FICSUR: Who?

LILIOM: Jews.

FICSUR: No—they telegraph.

LILIOM: They talk through them and from some other place they get answered. And it all goes through the iron strings—that's why they hum like that—they hum-m——

FICSUR: What do they hum?

LILIOM: They hum! ninety-nine, ninety-nine. Just listen.

FICSUR: What for?

LILIOM: That sparrow's listening, too. He's cocked one eye and looks at me as if to say: "I'd like to know what they're talking about."

FICSUR: You're looking at a bird?

LILIOM: He's looking at me, too.

FICSUR: Listen, you're sick! There's something the matter with you. Do you know what it is? Money. That bird has no money, either; that's why he cocks his eye.

LILIOM: Maybe.

FICSUR: Whoever has money don't cock his eye.

LILIOM: What then does he do?

FICSUR: He does most anything he wants. But nobody works unless he has money. We'll soon have money ourselves.

LILIOM: I say, "Good-evening. Excuse me, sir, can you tell me what time it is!"

FICSUR: He's not coming yet. Got the cards? [Liliom *gives him the pack of cards*] Got any money?

LILIOM: [*Takes some coins from his trousers pocket and counts*] Eleven.

FICSUR: [*Sits astride on the pile of ties and looks off left*] All right—eleven.

LILIOM: [*Sitting astride on the ties facing him*] Put it up.

FICSUR: [*Puts the money on the ties; rapidly shuffles the cards*] We'll play twenty-one. I'll bank.

[*He deals deftly*]

LILIOM: [*Looks at his card*] Good. I'll bet the bank.

FICSUR: Must have an ace!

[*Deals him a second card*]

LILIOM: Another one. [*He gets another card*] Another. [*Gets still another*] Over! [*Throws down his cards.* Ficsur *gathers in the money*] Come on!

FICSUR: Come on what! Got no more money, have you?

LILIOM: No.

FICSUR: Then the game's over—unless you want to——

LILIOM: What?

FICSUR: Play on credit.

LILIOM: You'll trust me?

FICSUR: No—but—I'll deduct it.

LILIOM: Deduct it from what?

FICSUR: From your share of the money. If *you* win you deduct from my share.

LILIOM: [*Looks over his shoulder to see if the cashier is coming; nervous and ashamed*] All right. How much is bank?

FICSUR: That cashier is bringing us sixteen thousand kronen. Eight thousand of that is mine. Well, then, the bank is eight thousand.

LILIOM: Good.

FICSUR: Whoever has the most luck will have the most money.

[*He deals*]

LILIOM: Six hundred kronen. [Ficsur *gives him another card*] Enough.

FICSUR: [*Laying out his own cards*] Twenty-one.

[*He shuffles rapidly*]

LILIOM: [*Moves excitedly nearer to* Ficsur] Well, then, double or nothing.

FICSUR: [*Dealing*] Double or nothing.

LILIOM: [*Gets a card*] Enough.

FICSUR: [*Laying out his own cards*] Twenty-one.

[*Shuffles rapidly again*]

LILIOM: [*In alarm*] You're not—cheating?

FICSUR: Me? Do I look like a cheat?

[*Deals the cards again*]

LILIOM: [*Glances nervously over his shoulder*] A thousand.

FICSUR: [*Nonchalantly*] Kronen?

LILIOM: Kronen. [*He gets a card*] Another one. [*Gets another card*] Over again!

[*Like an inexperienced gambler who is losing heavily,* Liliom *is very nervous. He plays dazedly, wildly, irrationally. From now on it is apparent that his only thought is to win his money back*]

FICSUR: That makes twelve hundred you owe.

LILIOM: Double or nothing. [*He gets a card. He is greatly excited*] Another one. [*Gets another card*] Another.

[*Throws down three cards*]

FICSUR: [*Bends over and adds up the sum on the ground*] Ten—fourteen—twenty-three—— You owe two thousand, four hundred.

LILIOM: Now what?

FICSUR: [*Takes a card out of the deck and gives it to him*] Here's the red ace. You can play double or nothing again.

LILIOM: [*Eagerly*] Good. [*Gets another card*] Enough.

FICSUR: [*Turns up his own cards*] Nineteen.

LILIOM: You win again. [*Almost imploring*] Give me an ace again. Give me the green one. [*Takes a card*] Double or nothing.

FICSUR: Not any more.

LILIOM: Why not?

FICSUR: Because if you lose you won't be able to pay. Double would be nine thousand six hundred. And you've only got eight thousand altogether.

LILIOM: [*Greatly excited*] That—that—I call that —a dirty trick!

FICSUR: Three thousand, two hundred. That's all you can put up.

LILIOM: [*Eagerly*] All right, then—three thousand, two hundred. [Ficsur *deals him a card*] Enough.

FICSUR: I've got an ace myself. Now we'll have to take our time and squeeze 'em. [Liliom *pushes closer to him as he takes up his cards and slowly, intently unfolds them*] Twenty-one.

[*He quickly puts the cards in his pocket. There is a pause*]

LILIOM: Now—now—I'll tell you now—you're a crook, a low-down——

[*Now* Linzman *enters at right. He is a strong, robust, red-bearded Jew about 40 years of age. At his side he carries a leather bag slung by a strap from his shoulder.* Ficsur *coughs warningly, moves to the right between* Linzman *and the embankment, pauses just behind* Linzman *and follows him*]

LILIOM: [*Stands bewildered a few paces to the left of the railroad ties. He finds himself facing* Linzman. *Trembling in every limb*] Good-evening. Excuse me, sir, can you tell me the time?

[Ficsur *springs silently at* Linzman, *the little knife in his right hand. But* Linzman *catches* Ficsur's *right hand with his own left and forces* Ficsur *to his knees. Simultaneously* Linzman *thrusts his right hand into his coat pocket and produces a revolver which he points at* Liliom's *breast.* Liliom *is standing two paces away from the revolver. There is a long pause*]

LINZMAN: [*In a low, even voice*] It is twenty-five minutes past six. [*Pauses, looks ironically down at* Ficsur] It's lucky I grabbed the hand with the knife instead of the other one. [*Pauses again, looks appraisingly from one to the other*] Two fine birds! [*To* Ficsur] I should live so—Rothschild has more luck than you. [*To* Liliom] I'd advise you to keep nice and quiet. If you make one move, you'll get two bullets in you. Just look into the barrel. You'll see some little things in there made of lead.

FICSUR: Let me go. I didn't do anything.

LINZMAN: [*Mockingly shakes the hand which still holds the knife*] And this? What do you call this? Oh, yes, I know. You thought I had an apple in my pocket, and you wanted to peel it. That's it. Forgive me for my error. I beg your pardon, sir.

LILIOM: But I—I——

LINZMAN: Yes, my son, I know. It's so simple. You only asked what time it is. Well, it's twenty-five minutes after six.

FICSUR: Let us go, honorable sir. We didn't do anything to you.

LINZMAN: In the first place, my son, I'm not an honorable sir. In the second place, for the same money, you could have said Your Excellency. But in the third place you'll find it very hard to beg off by flattering me.

LILIOM: But I—*I* really didn't do anything to you.

LINZMAN: Look behind you, my boy. Don't be afraid. Look behind you, but don't run away or I'll have to shoot you down. [Liliom *turns his head slowly around*] Who's coming up there?

LILIOM: [*Looking at* Linzman] Policemen.

LINZMAN: [*To* Ficsur] You hold still, or——[*To* Liliom *teasingly*] How many policemen are there?

LILIOM: [*His eyes cast down*] Two.

LINZMAN: And what are the policemen sitting on?

LILIOM: Horses.

LINZMAN: And which can run faster, a horse or a man?

LILIOM: A horse.

LINZMAN: There, you see. It would be hard to get away now. [*Laughs*] I never saw such an unlucky pair of highway robbers. I can't imagine worse luck. Just to-day I had to put a pistol in my pocket. And even if I hadn't—old Linzman is a match for four like you. But even that isn't all. Did you happen to notice, you oxen, what direction I came from? From the factory, didn't I? When I *went* there I had a nice bit of money with me. Sixteen thousand crowns! But now—not a heller. [*Calls off left*] Hey, come quicker, will you? This fellow is pulling pretty strong. [Ficsur *frees himself with a mighty wrench and darts rapidly off. As* Linzman *aims his pistol at the vanishing* Ficsur, Liliom *runs up the steps to the embankment.* Linzman *hesitates, perceives that* Liliom *is the better target, points the pistol at him*] Stop, or I'll shoot [*Calls off left to the* Policemen] Why don't you come down off your horses? [*His pistol is leveled at* Liliom, *who stands on the embankment, facing the audience. From the left on the embankment a* Policeman *appears, revolver in hand*]

FIRST POLICEMAN: Stop!

LINZMAN: Well, my boy, do you still want to know what time it is? From ten to twelve years in prison!

LILIOM: You won't get me! [Linzman *laughs derisively.* Liliom *is now three or four paces from the* Policeman *and equally distant from* Linzman. *His face is uplifted to the sky. He bursts into laughter, half defiant, half self-pitying, and takes the kitchen knife from under his coat*] Julie——

[*The ring of farewell is in the word. He turns sideways, thrusts the knife deep in his breast, sways, falls and rolls down the far side of the embankment. There is a long pause. From the left up on the embankment come the* Two Policemen]

LINZMAN: What's the matter? [*The* First Policeman *comes along the embankment as far as the steps, looks down in the opposite side, then climbs down at about the spot where* Liliom *disappeared.* Linzman *and the other* Policeman *mount the embankment and look down on him*] Stabbed himself?

VOICE OF FIRST POLICEMAN: Yes—and he seems to have made a thorough job of it.

LINZMAN: [*Excitedly to* Second Policeman] I'll go and telephone to the hospital.

[*He runs down the steps and exits at left*]

SECOND POLICEMAN: Go to Eisler's grocery store and telephone to the factory from there. They've a doctor there, too. [*Calling down to the other* Policeman] I'm going to tie up the horses.

[*Comes down the steps and exits at left. The stage is empty. There is a pause. The little red signal lamp is lit*]

VOICE OF FIRST POLICEMAN: Hey, Stephan?

VOICE OF SECOND POLICEMAN: What?

VOICE OF FIRST POLICEMAN: Shall I pull the knife out of his chest?

VOICE OF SECOND POLICEMAN: Better not, or he may bleed to death.

[*There is a pause*]

VOICE OF FIRST POLICEMAN: Stephan!

VOICE OF SECOND POLICEMAN: Yes.

VOICE OF FIRST POLICEMAN: Lot of mosquitoes around here.

VOICE OF SECOND POLICEMAN: Yes.

VOICE OF FIRST POLICEMAN: Got a cigar?

VOICE OF SECOND POLICEMAN: No.

[*There is a pause. The* First Policeman *appears over the opposite side of the embankment*]

FIRST POLICEMAN: A lot of good the new pay-schedule's done us—made things worse than they used to be—we *get* more but we *have* less than we ever had. If the Government could be made to realize that. It's a thankless job at best. You work hard year after year, you get gray in the service, and slowly you die—yes.

SECOND POLICEMAN: That's right.

FIRST POLICEMAN: Yes.

[*In the distance is heard the bell of the signal tower*]

THE CURTAIN FALLS

SCENE V.

The photographic "studio" a half hour later that same evening.

Mother Hollunder, *her* Son, Marie *and* Wolf *stand in a group back right, their heads together.* Julie *stands apart from them, a few paces to the left.*

YOUNG HOLLUNDER: [*Who has just come in, tells his story excitedly*] They're bringing him now. Two workmen from the factory are carrying him on a stretcher.

WOLF: Where is the doctor?

YOUNG HOLLUNDER: A policeman telephoned to headquarters. The police-surgeon ought to be here any minute.

MARIE: Maybe they'll pull him through after all.

YOUNG HOLLUNDER: He stabbed himself too deep in his chest. But he's still breathing. He can still talk, too, but very faintly. At first he lay there unconscious, but when they put him on the stretcher he came to.

WOLF: That was from the shaking.

MARIE: We'd better make room.

[*They make room. Two workmen carry in* Liliom *on a stretcher which has four legs and stands about as high as a bed. They put the stretcher at left directly in front of the sofa, so that the head is at right and the foot at left. Then they unobtrusively join the group at the door. Later, they go out.* Julie *is standing at the side of the stretcher, where, without moving, she can see* Liliom's *face. The others crowd emotionally together near the door. The* First Policeman *enters*]

FIRST POLICEMAN: Are you his wife?

JULIE: Yes.

FIRST POLICEMAN: The doctor at the factory who bandaged him up forbade us to take him to the hospital.—Dangerous to move him that far. What he needs now is rest. Just let him be until the police-surgeon comes. [*To the group near the door*] He's not to be disturbed.

[*They make way for him. He exits. There is a pause*]

WOLF: [*Gently urging the others out*] Please—it's best if we all get out of here now. We'll only be in the way.

MARIE: [*To* Julie] Julie, what do you think? [Julie *looks at her without answering*] Julie, can I do anything to help? [Julie *does not answer*] We'll be just outside on the bench if you want us.

[Mother Hollunder *and her* Son *have gone out when first requested. Now* Marie *and* Wolf *exit, too.* Julie *sits on the edge of the stretcher and looks at* Liliom. *He stretches his hand out to her. She clasps it. It is not quite dark yet. Both of them can still be plainly seen*]

LILIOM: [*Raises himself with difficulty; speaks lightly at first, but later soberly, defiantly*] Little—Julie—there's something—I want to tell you—like when you go to a restaurant—and you've finished eating—and it's time—to pay—then you have to count up everything—everything you owe—well—I beat you—not because I was mad at you—no—only because I can't bear to see any one crying. You always cried—on my account—and, well, you see—I never learned a trade—what kind of a caretaker

would I make? But anyhow—I wasn't going back to the carousel to fool with the girls. No, I spit on them all—understand?

JULIE: Yes.

LILIOM: And—as for Hollinger—he's good enough—Mrs. Muskat can get along all right with him. The jokes he tells are mine—and the people laugh when he tells them—but I don't care.—I didn't give you anything—no home—not even the food you ate—but you don't understand.—It's true I'm not much good—but I couldn't be a caretaker—and so I thought maybe it would be better over there—in America—do you see?

JULIE: Yes.

LILIOM: I'm not asking—forgiveness—I don't do that—I don't. Tell the baby—if you like.

JULIE: Yes.

LILIOM: Tell the baby—I wasn't much good—but tell him—if you ever talk about me—tell him—I thought—perhaps—over in America—but that's no affair of yours. I'm not asking forgiveness. For my part the police can come now.—If it's a boy—if it's a girl.—Perhaps I'll see the Lord God to-day.—Do you think I'll see Him?

JULIE: Yes.

LILIOM: I'm not afraid—of the police Up There—if they'll only let me come up in front of the Lord God Himself—not like down here where an officer stops you at the door. If the carpenter asks you—yes—be his wife—marry him. And the child—tell him he's his father.—He'll believe you—won't he?

JULIE: Yes.

LILIOM: When I beat you—I was right.—You mustn't always think—you mustn't always be right.—Liliom can be right once, too.—It's all the same to me who was right.—It's so dumb. Nobody's right—but they all think they are right.—A lot they know!

JULIE: Yes.

LILIOM: Julie—come—hold my hand tight.

JULIE: I'm holding it tight—all the time.

LILIOM: Tighter, still tighter—I'm going——[*Pauses*] Julie——

JULIE: Good-bye.

[Liliom *sinks slowly back and dies.* Julie *frees her hand. The* Doctor *enters with the* First Policeman]

DOCTOR: Good-evening. His wife?

JULIE: Yes, sir.

[*Behind the* Doctor *and* Policeman *enter* Marie, Wolf, Mother Hollunder, Young Hollunder *and* Mrs. Muskat. *They remain respectfully at the doorway. The* Doctor *bends over* Liliom *and examines him*]

DOCTOR: A light, if you please. [Julie *fetches a burning candle from the dark-room. The* Doctor *examines* Liliom *briefly in the candle-light, then turns suddenly away*] Have you pen and ink?

WOLF: [*Proffering a pen*] A fountain-pen—American——

DOCTOR: [*Takes a printed form from his pocket; speaks as he writes out the death-certificate at the little table*] My poor woman, your husband is dead—there's nothing to be done for him—the good God will help him now—I'll leave this certificate with you. You will give it to the people from the hospital when they come—I'll arrange for the body to be removed at once. [*Rises*] Please give me a towel and soap.

POLICEMAN: I've got them for you out here, sir. [*Points to door at back*]

DOCTOR: God be with you, my good woman.

JULIE: Thank you, sir.

[*The* Doctor *and* Policeman *exit. The others slowly draw nearer*]

MARIE: Poor Julie. May he rest in peace, poor man, but as for you—please don't be angry with me for saying it—but you're better off this way.

MOTHER HOLLUNDER: He is better off, the poor fellow, and so are you.

MARIE: Much better, Julie . . . you are young . . . and one of these days some good man will come along. Am I right?

WOLF: She's right.

MARIE: Julie, tell me, am I right?

JULIE: You are right, dear; you are very good.

YOUNG HOLLUNDER: There's a good man—the carpenter. Oh, I can speak of it now. He comes here every day on some excuse or other—and he never fails to ask for you.

MARIE: A widower—with two children.

MOTHER HOLLUNDER: He's better off, poor fellow—and so are you. He was a bad man.

MARIE: He wasn't good-hearted. Was he, Wolf?

WOLF: No, I must say, he really wasn't. No, Liliom wasn't a good man. A good man doesn't strike a woman.

MARIE: Am I right? Tell me, Julie, am I right?

JULIE: You are right, dear.

YOUNG HOLLUNDER: It's really a good thing for her it happened.

MOTHER HOLLUNDER: He's better off—and so is she.

WOLF: Now you have your freedom again. How old are you?

JULIE: Eighteen.

WOLF: Eighteen. A mere child! Am I right?

JULIE: You are right, Wolf. You are kind.

YOUNG HOLLUNDER: Lucky for you it happened, isn't it?

JULIE: Yes.

YOUNG HOLLUNDER: All you had before was bad luck. If it weren't for my mother you wouldn't have had a roof over your head or a bite to eat—and now Autumn's coming and Winter. You couldn't have lived in this shack in the Winter time, could you?

MARIE: Certainly not! You'd have frozen like the birds in the fields. Am I right, Julie?

JULIE: Yes, Marie.

MARIE: A year from now you will have forgotten all about him, won't you?

JULIE: You are right, Marie.

WOLF: If you need anything, count on us. We'll go now. But to-morrow morning we'll be back. Come, Marie. God be with you.

[*Offers* Julie *his hand*]

JULIE: God be with you.

MARIE: [*Embraces* Julie, *weeping*] It's the best thing that could have happened to you, Julie, the best thing.

JULIE: Don't cry, Marie.

[Marie *and* Wolf *exit*]

MOTHER HOLLUNDER: I'll make a little black coffee. You haven't had a thing to eat to-day. Then you'll come home with us.

[Mother Hollunder *and her* Son *exit.* Mrs. Muskat *comes over to* Julie]

MRS. MUSKAT: Would you mind if I—looked at him?

JULIE: He used to work for you.

MRS. MUSKAT: [*Contemplates the body; turns to* Julie] Won't you make up with me?

JULIE: I wasn't angry with you.

MRS. MUSKAT: But you were. Let's make it up.

JULIE: [*Raising her voice eagerly, almost triumphantly*] I've nothing to make up with *you*.

MRS. MUSKAT: But I have with you. Every one says hard things against the poor dead boy—except us two. You don't say he was bad.

JULIE: [*Raising her voice yet higher, this time on a defiant, wholly triumphant note*] Yes, I *do*.

MRS. MUSKAT: I understand, my child. But he beat me too. What does that matter? I've forgotten it.

JULIE: [*From now on answers her coldly, dryly, without looking at her*] That's your own affair.

MRS. MUSKAT: If I can help you in any way——

JULIE: There's nothing I need.

MRS. MUSKAT: I still owe him two kronen, back pay.

JULIE: You should have paid him.

MRS. MUSKAT: Now that the poor fellow is dead I thought perhaps it would be the same if I paid you.

JULIE: I've nothing to do with it.

MRS. MUSKAT: All right. Please don't think I'm trying to force myself on you. I stayed because we two are the only ones on earth who loved him. That's why I thought we ought to stick together.

JULIE: No, thank you.

MRS. MUSKAT: Then you couldn't have loved him as I did.

JULIE: No.

MRS. MUSKAT: I loved him better.

JULIE: Yes.

MRS. MUSKAT: Good-bye.

JULIE: Good-bye. [Mrs. Muskat *exits.* Julie *puts the candle on the table near Liliom's head, sits on the edge of the stretcher, looks into the dead man's face and caresses it tenderly*] Sleep, Liliom, sleep—

it's no business of hers—-I never even told you—but now I'll tell you—now I'll tell you—you bad, quick-tempered, rough, unhappy, wicked—*dear* boy —sleep peacefully, Liliom—they can't understand how I feel—I can't even explain to you—not even to you—how I feel—you'd only laugh at me—but you can't hear me any more. [*Between tender motherliness and reproach, yet with great love in her voice*] It was wicked of you to beat me—on the breast and on the head and face—but you're gone now.—You treated me badly—that was wicked of you—but sleep peacefully, Liliom—you bad, bad boy, you—I love you—I never told you before—I was ashamed—but now I've told you—I love you. Liliom—sleep—my boy—sleep.

[*She rises, gets a Bible, sits down near the candle and reads softly to herself, so that not the words but an inarticulate murmur is heard. The* Carpenter *enters at back*]

CARPENTER: [*Stands near the door; in the dimness of the room he can scarcely be seen*] Miss Julie——

JULIE: [*Without alarm*] Who is that?

CARPENTER: [*Very slowly*] The carpenter.

JULIE: What does the carpenter want?

CARPENTER: Can I be of help to you in any way? Shall I stay here with you?

JULIE: [*Gratefully, but firmly*] Don't stay, carpenter.

CARPENTER: Shall I come back to-morrow?

JULIE: Not to-morrow, either.

CARPENTER: Don't be offended, Miss Julie, but I'd like to know—you see, I'm not a young man any more—I have two children—and if I'm to come back any more—I'd like to know—if there's any use——

JULIE: No use, carpenter.

CARPENTER: [*As he exits*] God be with you.

[Julie *resumes her reading.* Ficsur *enters, slinks furtively sideways to the stretcher, looks at* Liliom, *shakes his head.* Julie *looks up from her reading.* Ficsur *takes fright, slinks away from the stretcher, sits down at right, biting his nails.* Julie *rises.* Ficsur *rises, too, and looks at her half fearfully. With her piercing glance upon him he slinks to the doorway at back, where he pauses and speaks*]

FICSUR: The old woman asked me to tell you that coffee is ready, and you are to come in.

[Julie *goes to the kitchen door.* Ficsur *withdraws until she has closed the door behind her. Then he reappears in the doorway, stands on tiptoes, looks at* Liliom, *then exits. Now the body lies alone. After a brief silence music is heard, distant at first, but gradually coming nearer. It is very much like the music of the carousel, but slower, graver, more exalted. The melody, too, is the same, yet the tempo is altered and contrapuntal measures of the thieves' song are intertwined in it. Two men in black, with heavy sticks, soft black hats and* black gloves, *appear in the doorway at back and stride slowly into the room. Their faces are beardless, marble white, grave and benign. One stops in front of the stretcher, the other a pace to the right. From above a dim violet light illuminates their faces*]

THE FIRST: [*To* Liliom] Rise and come with us.

THE SECOND: [*Politely*] You're under arrest.

THE FIRST: [*Somewhat louder, but always in a gentle, low, resonant voice*] Do you hear? Rise. Don't you hear?

THE SECOND: We are the police.

THE FIRST: [*Bends down, touches* Liliom's *shoulder*] Get up and come with us.

[Liliom *slowly sits up*]

THE SECOND: Come along.

THE FIRST: [*Paternally*] These people suppose that when they die all their difficulties are solved for them.

THE SECOND: [*Raising his voice sternly*] That simply by thrusting a knife in your heart and making it stop beating you can leave your wife behind with a child in her womb——

THE FIRST: It is not as simple as that.

THE SECOND: Such things are not settled so easily.

THE FIRST: Come along. You will have to give an account of yourself. [*As both bow their heads, he continues softly*] We are God's police. [*An expression of glad relief lights upon* Liliom's *face. He rises from the stretcher*] Come.

THE SECOND: You mortals don't get off quite as easy as that.

THE FIRST: [*Softly*] Come. [Liliom *starts to walk ahead of them, then stops and looks at them*] The end is not as abrupt as that. Your name is still spoken. Your face is still remembered. And what you did, and what you failed to do—these are still remembered. Remembered, too, are the manner of your glance, the ring of your voice, the clasp of your hand and how your step sounded—as long as one is left who remembers you, so long is the matter unended. Before the end there is much to be undone. Until you are quite forgotten, my son, you will not be finished with the earth—even though you *are* dead.

THE SECOND: [*Very gently*] Come.

[*The music begins again. All three exit at back,* Liliom *leading, the others following. The stage is empty and quite dark save for the candle which burns by the stretcher, on which, in the shadows, the covers are so arranged that one cannot quite be sure that a body is not still lying. The music dies out in the distance as if it had followed* Liliom *and the two Policemen. The candle flickers and goes out. There is a brief interval of silence and total darkness before*

THE CURTAIN FALLS]

SCENE VI.

In the Beyond. A whitewashed courtroom. There is a green-topped table; behind it a bench. Back center is a door with a bell over it. Next to this door is a window through which can be seen a vista of rose-tinted clouds.

Down right there is a grated iron door.

Down left another door.

Two men are on the bench when the curtain rises. One is richly, the other poorly dressed.

From a great distance is heard a fanfare of trumpets playing the refrain of the thieves' song in slow, altered tempo.

Passing the window at back appear Liliom *and the two* Policemen.

The bell rings.

An old Guard *enters at right. He is bald and has a long white beard. He wears the conventional police uniform.*

He goes to the door at back, opens it, exchanges silent greetings with the two Policemen *and closes the door again.*

Liliom *looks wonderingly around.*

THE FIRST: [*To the old* Guard] Announce us.

[*The* Guard *exits at left*]

LILIOM: Is this it?

THE SECOND: Yes, my son.

LILIOM: This is the police court?

THE SECOND: Yes, my son. The part for suicide cases.

LILIOM: And what happens here?

THE FIRST: Here justice is done. Sit down.

[Liliom *sits next to the two men. The two* Policemen *stand silent near the table*]

THE RICHLY DRESSED MAN: [*Whispers*] Suicide, too?

LILIOM: Yes.

THE RICHLY DRESSED MAN: [*Points to* The Poorly Dressed Man] So's he. [*Introducing himself*] My name is Reich.

THE POORLY DRESSED MAN: [*Whispers, too*] My name is Stephan Kadar.

[Liliom *only looks at them*]

THE POORLY DRESSED MAN: And you? What's your name?

LILIOM: None of your business.

[*Both move a bit away from him*]

THE POORLY DRESSED MAN: I did it by jumping out of a window.

THE RICHLY DRESSED MAN: I did it with a pistol—and you?

LILIOM: With a knife.

[*They move a bit further away from him*]

THE RICHLY DRESSED MAN: A pistol is cleaner.

LILIOM: If I had the price of a pistol——

THE SECOND: Silence!

[*The* Police Magistrate *enters. He has a long white beard, is bald, but only in profile can be seen on his head a single tuft of snow-white hair. The* Guard *reënters behind him and sits on the bench with the dead men. As* The Magistrate *enters, all rise, except* Liliom, *who remains surlily seated. When* The Magistrate *sits down, so do the others*]

THE GUARD: Yesterday's cases, your honor. The numbers are entered in the docket.

THE MAGISTRATE: Number 16,472.

THE FIRST: [*Looks in his notebook, beckons* The Richly Dressed Man] Stand up, please. [*The Richly Dressed Man rises*]

THE MAGISTRATE: Your name?

THE RICHLY DRESSED MAN: Doctor Reich.

THE MAGISTRATE: Age?

THE RICHLY DRESSED MAN: Forty-two, married, Jew.

THE MAGISTRATE: [*With a gesture of dismissal*] Religion does not interest us here.—Why did you kill yourself?

THE RICHLY DRESSED MAN: On account of debts.

THE MAGISTRATE: What good did you do on earth?

THE RICHLY DRESSED MAN: I was a lawyer——

THE MAGISTRATE: [*Coughs significantly*] Yes—we'll discuss that later. For the present I shall only ask you: Would you like to go back to earth once more before sunrise? I advise you that you have the right to go if you choose. Do you understand?

THE RICHLY DRESSED MAN: Yes, sir.

THE MAGISTRATE: He who takes his life is apt, in his haste and his excitement, to forget something. Is there anything important down there you have left undone? Something to tell some one? Something to undo?

THE RICHLY DRESSED MAN: My debts——

THE MAGISTRATE: They do not matter here. Here we are concerned only with the affairs of the soul.

THE RICHLY DRESSED MAN: Then—if you please—when I left—the house—my youngest son, Oscar—was asleep. I didn't trust myself to wake him—and bid him good-bye. I would have liked—to kiss him good-bye.

THE MAGISTRATE: [*To* The Second] You will take Dr. Reich back and let him kiss his son Oscar.

THE SECOND: Come with me, please.

THE RICHLY DRESSED MAN: [*To* The Magistrate] I thank you.

[*He bows and exits at back with* The Second]

THE MAGISTRATE: [*After making an entry in the docket*] Number 16,473.

THE FIRST: [*Looks in his notebook, then beckons* Liliom] Stand up.

LILIOM: You said *please* to him.

[*He rises*]

THE MAGISTRATE: Your name?

LILIOM: Liliom.

THE MAGISTRATE: Isn't that your nick-name?

LILIOM: Yes.

THE MAGISTRATE: What is your right name?

LILIOM: Andreas.

THE MAGISTRATE: And your last name?

LILIOM: Zavocki—after my mother.

THE MAGISTRATE: Your age?

LILIOM: Twenty-four.

THE MAGISTRATE: What good did *you* do on earth? [Liliom *is silent*] Why did you take your life? [Liliom *does not answer*. The Magistrate *addresses* The First] Take that knife away from him. [The First *does so*] It will be returned to you, if you go back to earth.

LILIOM: Do I go back to earth again?

THE MAGISTRATE: Just answer my questions.

LILIOM: I wasn't answering then, I was asking if——

THE MAGISTRATE: You don't ask questions here. You only answer. Only answer, Andreas Zavocki! I ask you whether there is anything on earth you neglected to accomplish? Anything down there you would like to do?

LILIOM: Yes.

THE MAGISTRATE: What is it?

LILIOM: I'd like to break Ficsur's head for him.

THE MAGISTRATE: Punishment is our office. Is there nothing else on earth you'd like to do?

LILIOM: I don't know—I guess, as long as I'm here, I'll not go back.

THE MAGISTRATE: [*To* The First] Note that. He waives his right. [Liliom *starts back to the bench*] Stay where you are. You are aware that you left your wife without food or shelter?

LILIOM: Yes.

THE MAGISTRATE: Don't you regret it?

LILIOM: No.

THE MAGISTRATE: You are aware that your wife is pregnant, and that in six months a child will be born?

LILIOM: I know.

THE MAGISTRATE: And that the child, too, will be without food or shelter? Do you regret that?

LILIOM: As long as I won't be there, what's it got to do with me?

THE MAGISTRATE: Don't try to deceive us, Andreas Zavocki. We see through you as through a pane of glass.

LILIOM: If you see so much, what do you want to ask me for? Why don't you let me rest—in peace?

THE MAGISTRATE: First you must earn your rest.

LILIOM: I want—only—to sleep.

THE MAGISTRATE: Your obstinacy won't help you. Here patience is endless as time. We can wait.

LILIOM: Can I ask something?—I'd like to know —if Your Honor will tell me—whether the baby will be a boy or a girl.

THE MAGISTRATE: You shall see that for yourself.

LILIOM: [*Excitedly*] I'll see the baby?

THE MAGISTRATE: When you do it won't be a baby any more. But we haven't reached that question yet.

LILIOM: I'll see it?

THE MAGISTRATE: Again I ask you. Do you not regret that you deserted your wife and child; that you were a bad husband, a bad father?

LILIOM: A bad husband?

THE MAGISTRATE: Yes.

LILIOM: And a bad father?

THE MAGISTRATE: That, too.

LILIOM: I couldn't get work—and I couldn't bear to see Julie——all the time—all the time——

THE MAGISTRATE: Weeping! Why are you ashamed to say it? You couldn't bear to see her weeping. Why are you afraid of that word? And why are you ashamed that you loved her?

LILIOM: [*Shrugs his shoulders*] Who's ashamed? But I couldn't bear to see her—and that's why I was bad to her. You see, it wouldn't do to go back to the carousel—and Ficsur came along with his talk about —that other thing—and all of a sudden it happened, I don't know how. The police and the Jew with the pistol—and there I stood—and I'd lost the money playing cards—and I didn't want to be put in prison. [*Demanding justification*] Maybe I was wrong not to go out and steal when there was nothing to eat in the house? Should I have gone out to steal for Julie?

THE MAGISTRATE: [*Emphatically*] Yes.

LILIOM: [*After an astounded pause*] The police down there never said that.

THE MAGISTRATE: You beat that poor, frail girl; you beat her because she loved you. How could you do that?

LILIOM: We argued with each other—she said this and I said that—and because she was right I couldn't answer her—and I got mad—and the anger rose up in me—until it reached here [*Points to his throat*] and then I beat her.

THE MAGISTRATE: Are you sorry?

LILIOM: [*Shakes his head, but cannot utter the word "no"; continues softly*] When I touched her slender throat—then—if you like—you might say——

[*Falters, looks embarrassed at* The Magistrate]

THE MAGISTRATE: [*Confidently expectant*] Are you sorry?

LILIOM: [*With a stare*] I'm not sorry for anything.

THE MAGISTRATE: Liliom, Liliom, it will be difficult to help you.

LILIOM: I'm not asking any help

THE MAGISTRATE: You were offered employment as a caretaker on Arader Street. [*To* The First] Where is that entered?

THE FIRST: In the small docket.

[*Hands him the open book*. The Magistrate *looks in it*]

THE MAGISTRATE: Rooms, kitchen, quarterly wages, the privilege of keeping poultry. Why didn't you accept it?

LILIOM: I'm not a caretaker. I'm no good at caretaking. To be a caretaker—you have to be a caretaker——

THE MAGISTRATE: If I said to you now: Liliom, go back on your stretcher. Tomorrow morning you will arise alive and well again. Would you be a caretaker then?

LILIOM: No.

THE MAGISTRATE: Why not?

LILIOM: Because—because that's just why I died.

THE MAGISTRATE: That is not true, my son. You died because you loved little Julie and the child she is bearing under her heart.

LILIOM: No.

THE MAGISTRATE: Look me in the eye.

LILIOM: [Looks him in the eye] No.

THE MAGISTRATE: [Stroking his beard] Liliom, Liliom, if it were not for our Heavenly patience—Go back to your seat. Number 16,474.

THE FIRST: [Looks in his notebook] Stephan Kadar.

[The Poorly Dressed Man rises]

THE MAGISTRATE: You came out to-day?

THE POORLY DRESSED MAN: To-day.

THE MAGISTRATE: [Indicating the crimson sea of clouds] How long were you in there?

THE POORLY DRESSED MAN: Thirteen years.

THE MAGISTRATE: Officer, you went to earth with him?

THE FIRST: Yes, sir.

THE MAGISTRATE: Stephan Kadar, after thirteen years of purification by fire you returned to earth to give proof that your soul had been burned clean. What good deed did you perform?

THE POORLY DRESSED MAN: When I came to the village and looked in the window of our cottage I saw my poor little orphans sleeping peacefully. But it was raining and the rain beat into the room through a hole in the roof. So I went and fixed the roof so it wouldn't rain in any more. My hammering woke them up and they were afraid. But their mother came in to them and comforted them. She said to them: "Don't cry! It's your poor, dear father hammering up there. He's come back from the other world to fix the roof for us."

THE MAGISTRATE: Officer?

THE FIRST: That's what happened.

THE MAGISTRATE: Stephan Kadar, you have done a good deed. What you did will be written in books to gladden the hearts of children who read them. [Indicates the door at left] The door is open to you. The eternal light awaits you. [The First escorts The Poorly Dressed Man out at left with great deference] Liliom! [Liliom rises] You have heard?

LILIOM: Yes.

THE MAGISTRATE: When this man first appeared before us he was as stubborn as you. But now he has purified himself and withstood the test. He has done a good deed.

LILIOM: What's he done, anyhow? Any roofer can fix a roof. It's much harder to be a barker in an amusement park.

THE MAGISTRATE: Liliom, you shall remain for sixteen years in the crimson fire until your child is full grown. By that time your pride and your stubbornness will have been burnt out of you. And when your daughter——

LILIOM: My daughter!

THE MAGISTRATE: When your daughter has reached the age of sixteen——

[Liliom bows his head, covers his eyes with his hands, and to keep from weeping laughs defiantly, sadly]

THE MAGISTRATE: When your daughter has reached the age of sixteen you will be sent for one day back to earth.

LILIOM: Me?

THE MAGISTRATE: Yes—just as you may have read in the legends of how the dead reappear on earth for a time.

LILIOM: I never believed them.

THE MAGISTRATE: Now you see they are true. You will go back to earth one day to show how far the purification of your soul has progressed.

LILIOM: Then I must show what I can do—like when you apply for a job—as a coachman?

THE MAGISTRATE: Yes—it is a test.

LILIOM: And will I be told what I have to do?

THE MAGISTRATE: No.

LILIOM: How will I know, then?

THE MAGISTRATE: You must decide that for yourself. That's what you burn sixteen years for. And if you do something good, something splendid for your child, then——

LILIOM: [Laughs sadly] Then? [All stand up and bow their heads reverently. There is a pause] Then?

THE MAGISTRATE: Now I'll bid you farewell, Liliom. Sixteen years and a day shall pass before I see you again. When you have returned from earth you will come up before me again. Take heed and think well of some good deed to do for your child. On that will depend which door shall be opened to you up here. Now go, Liliom.

[He exits at left. The Guard stands at attention. There is a pause]

THE FIRST: [Approaches Liliom] Come along, my son.

[He goes to the door at right; pulls open the bolt and waits]

LILIOM: [To the old Guard, softly] Say, officer.

THE GUARD: What do you want?

LILIOM: Please—can I get—have you got—?

THE GUARD: What?

LILIOM: [Whispers] A cigarette?

[The old Guard stares at him, goes a few paces to the left, shakes his head disapprovingly. Then his expression softens. He takes a cigarette from his pocket and, crossing to Liliom—who has gone over to the door at right—gives him the cigarette. The First throws open the

door. *An intense rose-colored light streams in.*
The glow of it is so strong that it blinds Liliom
and he takes a step backward and bows his
head and covers his eyes with his hand before
he steps forward into the light]

THE CURTAIN FALLS

SCENE VII.

Sixteen years later. A small, tumble-down house
on a bare, unenclosed plot of ground. Before the
house is a tiny garden enclosed by a hip-high hedge.

At back a wooden fence crosses the stage; in the
center of it is a door large enough to admit a
wagon. Beyond the fence is a view of a suburban
street which blends into a broad vista of tilled
fields.

It is a bright Sunday in Spring.
In the garden a table for two is laid.

Julie, *her daughter* Louise, Wolf *and* Marie *are*
discovered in the garden. Wolf *is prosperously*
dressed, Marie *somewhat elaborately, with a huge*
hat.

JULIE: You could stay for lunch.

MARIE: Impossible, dear. Since he became the
proprietor of the Café Sorrento, Wolf simply has to
be there all the time.

JULIE: But you needn't stay there all day, too.

MARIE: Oh, yes. I sit near the cashier's cage, read
the papers, keep an eye on the waiters and drink in
the bustle and excitement of the great city.

JULIE: And what about the children?

MARIE: You know what modern families are like.
Parents scarcely ever see their children these days.
The four girls are with their governess, the three
boys with their tutor.

LOUISE: Auntie, dear, do stay and eat with us.

MARIE: [*Importantly*] Impossible to-day, dear
child, impossible. Perhaps some other time. Come,
Mr. Beifeld.

JULIE: Since when do you call your husband
mister?

WOLF: I'd rather she did, dear lady. When we
used to be very familiar we quarreled all the time.
Now we are formal with each other and get along
like society folk. I kiss your hand, dear lady.

JULIE: Good-bye, Wolf.

MARIE: Adieu, my dear. [*They embrace*] Adieu,
my dear child.

LOUISE: Good-bye, Aunt Marie. Good-bye, Uncle
Wolf. [Wolf *and* Marie *exit*]

JULIE: You can get the soup now, Louise, dear.
    [Louise *goes into the house and reënters with*
    the soup. They sit at the table]

LOUISE: Mother, is it true we're not going to work
at the jute factory any more?

JULIE: Yes, dear.

LOUISE: Where then?

JULIE: Uncle Wolf has gotten us a place in a big
establishment where they make all kinds of fittings
for cafés. We're to make big curtains, you know, the
kind they hang in the windows, with lettering on
them.

LOUISE: It'll be nicer there than at the jute factory.

JULIE: Yes, dear. The work isn't as dirty and pays
better, too. A poor widow like your mother is lucky
to get it.

    [*They eat.* Liliom *and the two* Heavenly Po-
    licemen *appear in the big doorway at back.*
    The Policemen *pass slowly by.* Liliom *stands*
    there alone a moment, then comes slowly down
    and pauses at the opening of the hedge. He is
    dressed as he was on the day of his death. He
    is very pale, but otherwise unaltered. Julie, *at*
    the table, has her back to him. Louise *sits*
    facing the audience]

LILIOM: Good-day.

LOUISE: Good-day.

JULIE: Another beggar! What is it you want, my
poor man?

LILIOM: Nothing.

JULIE: We have no money to give, but if you
care for a plate of soup——[Louise *goes into the*
house] Have you come far to-day?

LILIOM: Yes—very far.

JULIE: Are you tired?

LILIOM: Very tired.

JULIE: Over there at the gate is a stone. Sit down
and rest. My daughter is bringing you the soup.

    [Louise *comes out of the house*]

LILIOM: Is that your daughter?

JULIE: Yes.

LILIOM: [*To* Louise] You are the daughter?

LOUISE: Yes, sir.

LILIOM: A fine, healthy girl.

    [*Takes the soup plate from her with one hand,*
    while with the other he touches her arm.
    Louise *draws back quickly*]

LOUISE: [*Crosses to* Julie] Mother!

JULIE: What, my child?

LOUISE: The man tried to take me by the arm.

JULIE: Nonsense! You only imagined it, dear.
The poor, hungry man has other things to think
about than fooling with young girls. Sit down and
eat your soup.

    [*They eat*]

LILIOM: [*Eats, too, but keeps looking at them*]
You work at the factory, eh?

JULIE: Yes.

LILIOM: Your daughter, too?

LOUISE: Yes.

LILIOM: And your husband?

JULIE: [*After a pause*] I have no husband. I'm a
widow.

LILIOM: A widow?

JULIE: Yes.

LILIOM: Your husband—I suppose he's been dead a long time. [Julie *does not answer*] I say—has your husband been dead a long time?

JULIE: A long time.

LILIOM: What did he die of?

[Julie *is silent*]

LOUISE: No one knows. He went to America to work and he died there—in the hospital. Poor father, I never knew him.

LILIOM: He went to America?

LOUISE: Yes, before I was born.

LILIOM: To America?

JULIE: Why do you ask so many questions? Did you know him, perhaps?

LILIOM: [*Puts the plate down*] Heaven knows! I've known so many people. Maybe I knew him, too.

JULIE: Well, if you knew him, leave him and us in peace with your questions. He went to America and died there. That's all there is to tell.

LILIOM: All right. All right. Don't be angry with me. I didn't mean any harm.

[*There is a pause*]

LOUISE: My father was a very handsome man.

JULIE: Don't talk so much.

LOUISE: Did I say anything——?

LILIOM: Surely the little orphan can say that about her father.

LOUISE: My father could juggle so beautifully with three ivory balls that people used to advise him to go on the stage.

JULIE: Who told you that?

LOUISE: Uncle Wolf.

LILIOM: Who is that?

LOUISE: Mr. Wolf Beifeld, who owns the Café Sorrento.

LILIOM: The one who used to be a porter?

JULIE: [*Astonished*] Do you know him, too? It seems that you know all Budapest.

LILIOM: Wolf Beifeld is a long way from being all Budapest. But I do know a lot of people. Why shouldn't I know Wolf Beifeld?

LOUISE: He was a friend of my father.

JULIE: He was not his friend. No one was.

LILIOM: You speak of your husband so sternly.

JULIE: What's that to you? Doesn't it suit you? I can speak of my husband any way I like. It's nobody's business but mine.

LILIOM: Certainly, certainly—it's your own business.

[*Takes up his soup plate again. All three eat*]

LOUISE: [*To* Julie] Perhaps he knew father, too.

JULIE: Ask him, if you like.

LOUISE: [*Crosses to* Liliom. *He stands up*] Did you know my father? [Liliom *nods*. Louise *addresses her mother*] Yes, he knew him.

JULIE: [*Rises*] You knew Andreas Zavocki?

LILIOM: Liliom? Yes.

LOUISE: Was he really a very handsome man?

LILIOM: I wouldn't exactly say handsome.

LOUISE: [*Confidently*] But he was an awfully good man, wasn't he?

LILIOM: He wasn't so good, either. As far as I know he was what they called a clown, a barker in a carousel.

LOUISE: [*Pleased*] Did he tell funny jokes?

LILIOM: Lots of 'em. And he sang funny songs, too.

LOUISE: In the carousel?

LILIOM: Yes—but he was something of a bully, too. He'd fight any one. He even hit your dear little mother.

JULIE: That's a lie.

LILIOM: It's true.

JULIE: Aren't you ashamed to tell the child such awful things about her father? Get out of here, you shameless liar. Eats our soup and our bread and has the impudence to slander our dead!

LILIOM: I didn't mean—I——

JULIE: What right have you to tell lies to the child? Take that plate, Louise, and let him be on his way. If he wasn't such a hungry-looking beggar, I'd put him out myself.

[Louise *takes the plate out of his hand*]

LILIOM: So he didn't hit you?

JULIE: No, never. He was always good to me.

LOUISE: [*Whispers*] Did he tell funny stories, too?

LILIOM: Yes, and *such* funny ones.

JULIE: Don't speak to him any more. In God's name, go.

LOUISE: In God's name.

[Julie *resumes her seat at the table and eats*]

LILIOM: If you please, Miss—I have a pack of cards in my pocket. And if you like, I'll show you some tricks that'll make you split your sides laughing. [Louise *holds* Liliom's *plate in her left hand. With her right she reaches out and holds the garden gate shut*] Let me in, just a little way, Miss, and I'll do the tricks for you.

LOUISE: Go, in God's name, and let us be. Why are you making those ugly faces?

LILIOM: Don't chase me away, Miss; let me come in for just a minute—just for a minute—just long enough to let me show you something pretty, something wonderful. [*Opens the gate*] Miss, I've something to give you.

[*Takes from his pocket a big red handkerchief in which is wrapped a glittering star from Heaven. He looks furtively about him to make sure that the* Police *are not watching*]

LOUISE: What's that?

LILIOM: Pst! A star!

[*With a gesture he indicates that he has stolen it out of the sky*]

JULIE: [*Sternly*] Don't take anything from him. He's probably stolen it somewhere. [*To* Liliom] In God's name, be off with you.

LOUISE: Yes, be off with you. Be off.

[*She slams the gate*]

LILIOM: Miss—please, Miss—I've got to do something good—or—do something good—a good deed—

LOUISE: [*Pointing with her right hand*] That's the way out.

LILIOM: Miss——

LOUISE: Get out!

LILIOM: Miss!

[*Looks up at her suddenly and slaps her extended hand, so that the slap resounds loudly*]

LOUISE: Mother!

[*Looks dazedly at* Liliom, *who bows his head, dismayed, forlorn.* Julie *rises and looks at* Liliom *in astonishment. There is a long pause*]

JULIE: [*Comes over to them slowly*] What's the matter here?

LOUISE: [*Bewildered, does not take her eyes off* Liliom] Mother—the man—he hit me—on the hand —hard—I heard the sound of it—but it didn't hurt —mother—it didn't hurt—it was like a caress—as if he had just touched my hand tenderly.

[*She hides behind* Julie. Liliom *sulkily raises his head and looks at* Julie]

JULIE: [*Softly*] Go, my child. Go into the house. Go.

LOUISE: [*Going*] But mother—I'm afraid—it sounded so loud—— [*Weepingly*] And it didn't hurt at all—just as if he'd—kissed my hand instead— mother!

[*She hides her face*]

JULIE: Go in, my child, go in.

[Louise *goes slowly into the house.* Julie *watches her until she has disappeared, then turns slowly to* Liliom]

JULIE: You struck my child.

LILIOM: Yes—I struck her.

JULIE: Is that what you came for, to strike my child?

LILIOM: No—I didn't come for that—but I did strike her—and now I'm going back.

JULIE: In the name of the Lord Jesus, who are you?

LILIOM: [*Simply*] A poor, tired beggar who came a long way and who was hungry. And I took your

soup and bread and I struck your child. Are you angry with me?

JULIE: [*Her hand on her heart; fearfully, wonderingly*] Jesus protect me—I don't understand it— I'm *not* angry—not angry at all——

[Liliom *goes to the doorway and leans against the doorpost, his back to the audience.* Julie *goes to the table and sits*]

JULIE: Louise! [Louise *comes out of the house*] Sit down, dear, we'll finish eating.

LOUISE: Has he gone?

JULIE: Yes. [*They are both seated at the table.* Louise, *her head in her hands, is staring into space*] Why don't you eat, dear?

LOUISE: What has happened, mother?

JULIE: Nothing, my child.

[*The* Heavenly Policemen *appear outside.* Liliom *walks slowly off at left. The* First Policeman *makes a deploring gesture. Both shake their heads deploringly and follow* Liliom *slowly off at left*]

LOUISE: Mother, dear, why won't you tell me?

JULIE: What is there to tell you, child? Nothing has happened. We were peacefully eating, and a beggar came who talked of bygone days, and then I thought of your father.

LOUISE: My father?

JULIE: Your father—Liliom.

[*There is a pause*]

LOUISE: Mother—tell me—has it ever happened to you—has any one ever hit you—without hurting you in the least?

JULIE: Yes, my child. It has happened to me, too.

[*There is a pause*]

LOUISE: Is it possible for some one to hit you— hard like that—real loud and hard—and not hurt you at all?

JULIE: It is possible, dear—that some one may beat you and beat you and beat you—and not hurt you at all.——

[*There is a pause. Near by an organ-grinder has stopped. The music of his organ begins*]

THE CURTAIN FALLS

Luigi Pirandello

(1867–1936)

When Shakespeare made Hamlet say that "there is nothing either good or bad, but thinking makes it so," he could not have believed any Englishman would take him literally. That Pirandello, who could hardly be mistaken for an Englishman, did proceed on this premise has been a stumbling block for English-speaking playgoers ever since this Italian playwright won attention outside Italy during the First World War. It does not follow, however, that Pirandello's plays can never prevail in England and America, for the best of them belong to essential theatre, as well as to the universal spirit of humanism. If, besides, one can claim singularity for much of his work, it nevertheless belongs to a tradition as old as late Greek and Roman comedy, whose domestic embroilments were played by actors behind grotesque masks. The only difference is that Pirandello alternately called attention to the "mask" and the "face," often interchanged the one for the other, and exposed both to more scrutiny than is good for comfort.

Pirandello started simply enough, for when he entered the literary field he did so with short stories and one-act plays written in a realistic vein and drawn from his knowledge of the common life of his native Sicily. Among the plays, his tender *Sicilian Limes,* written in 1910, is a small gem. At this time he was under the influence of Giovanni Verga and other masters of Ibsen-inspired Italian realism, which was known as "verismo." Pirandello became famous, however, when he departed from this style and allied himself with a mordant and cynical "school of the grotesque." Retaining his originality even in the company of writers whose point of view he could share, Pirandello went on to elaborate a special style. It became properly known as "Pirandellismo" since it was essentially his own unique creation, and the elements that entered into it were his own studies and experiences, as well as a private anguish.

Born in Girgenti, Sicily, to a comfortable and locally respected family, Pirandello remained sympathetic to the Sicilian people and responsive to local color, but shed his provincialism easily. After studying at the University of Rome, he went to the University of Bonn, where he took a doctorate in philosophy under strenuously Hegelian teachers who were specialists in dialectical argument. He married a girl chosen by his parents and settled down to free-lancing in Rome with the aid of an ample allowance from his father. But difficulties and disillusion became his lot after the early favorable circumstances. He dropped his buoyant liberal faith, which had led him to take the side of the hard-pressed peasants of the Palermo countryside when they seized land belonging to the crown. Discovering corruption and hypocrisy in political circles, he abandoned all faith in government, calling it at one time "a league of brigands against men of good will." The Pirandello family lost its fortune when its mines were flooded, and he was forced to take a position in Rome at a normal school for girls. The difficult delivery of a third child unsettled his wife's mind. She became baselessly jealous, caused scandalous scenes, and even left him for a time. Reality, he came to learn at his own expense, is what the individual conceives it to be, logic is easily overthrown by inner compulsions, and there is no such thing as an entirely objective world for those who feel. Soon his wife's condition worsened and her persecution of her own daughter became so relentless that the girl made an attempt at suicide. As Pirandello's salary was too meager to enable him to commit his wife to a private sanatorium and his conscience too tender to send her to a public institution, he kept an insane woman in his home for many years.

Only his writing provided him with relief, and he pursued his literary labors for a time with such intensity that he wrote as many as nine plays in a single year. He also began to take an active part in stage production, organizing a distinguished company of actors at the Odescalchi Theatre in Rome and directing his own plays. He acquired a famous actor, Ruggero Ruggeri, for his troupe and won the interest of a superb actress, Marta Abba. Signora Abba played the leading feminine role in many of his dramas and rewarded him with an understanding friendship for which few men could have had greater need.

Concern with "identity," or the masks we assume or are compelled to assume, appeared as early as 1904 in Pirandello's work—in the novel *The Late Mattia Pascal,* in which an unhappy husband pretends to have drowned himself and assumes a new personality that entails new hazards. But it is in plays written after 1913 that Pirandello gave the most comprehensive treatment to this and related themes. In 1914 he presented two plays, *Think of It, Giacomino* and *The Pleasure of Honesty.* In the first of these, an elderly professor defies the gossip of the town by perversely marrying a pregnant girl and condoning her continued relations with a young man not in a position to marry her. In *The Pleasure of Honesty,* an eccentric marries a woman to protect her reputation, but once she has put on the mask of honesty, he insists that she wear it henceforth. Although he is not a believer in conventional virtue and is willing to marry another man's mistress for a financial consideration, he now requires absolute fidelity from his wife as a point of "honor." In *Cap and Bells* (1915), a husband, aware of his wife's infidelity with his employer, is outraged when the latter's wife exposes the intrigue. He insists on having the jealous woman declared insane in order to invalidate her charge against his own wife. Men have to "build themselves up" and to put up a front, in order to be able to endure themselves and to live in society. The husband, since he is so ugly, was willing to condone his wife's infidelity, but only so long as outsiders took no note of his ludicrous situation.

In his brilliant *Right You Are if You Think You Are* (1922), Pirandello made the question of personal identity the central theme of a tragicomic extravaganza. An elderly woman insists that a certain character's wife is her daughter. The husband maintains that the lady is demented, since her daughter, his first wife, died some time ago. The lady, in turn, declares that the man is suffering from delusions that his first wife is dead and that his first wife is his second wife. The bewildered townspeople never succeed in discovering who is deluded, and Pirandello refrains from enlightening us because to him the question is irrelevant. The important thing is that the human soul must believe as it believes if it is to be able to endure life, and people's dreams must be protected. In *Signora Morli One and Two*, a woman exhibits different personalities to the lighthearted husband who abandoned her and to the serious-minded lawyer who takes care of her. And so the tragicomedy of masks continues. Sometimes, however, men and women are caught in the trap of the personality they have acquired for themselves. In *Naked,* a play full of pity for those who must assume a mask and resentment for those who fail to understand the need, complications arise from a woman's claim that she tried to commit suicide out of a love she invented for herself in order to clothe herself in a beautiful romance before she died. Accused of imposture, "stripped naked" when she confesses that she does not love the man for whom she pretended to want to die, she makes a second and this time successful attempt at suicide. An author in *When One Is Somebody* is not allowed to change the style which brought him fame, although love has given him a new outlook on life. A prominent actress in *Trovarsi* loses a lover because she is unable to shed her stage personality in private life. And the hero of the powerful psychological drama *Henry IV* is compelled to pretend to be mad after he has recovered his sanity.

"Divine spirit enters into us and becomes dwarfed into a puppet," according to a character in *Cap and Bells*. Pirandello's concern with human puppetry in his many plays and novels won him the attention of distinguished foreign observers—among them the French writer Benjamin Crémieux and James Joyce;

he gained an international reputation, climaxed in 1934 by a Nobel Prize for literature. He projected a fascinating modern mind and spirit in his frequently stylized work. Philosopher and dramatist, he summed up in his writing the relativistic tendencies of modern thought with respect to reality and morality, and he voiced an antibourgeois protest against a smug society that thrusts individuals into narrow categories.

Although he adopted the theatre as his favorite medium he blasted its conventions as well. He combined the discursive drama of ideas with weird situations, and freely intermingled tragic and fantastically comic elements. Not only did he refuse to give the playgoer a helping hand through the maze of unusual complications and questions left as either insoluble or as better not solved; he shook the foundations of the realistic stage with *Tonight We Improvise* and, especially, with *Six Characters in Search of an Author* by refusing to accept the theatre's pretense of being an imitation of reality. In the latter play, making inroads into the structure of realistic drama by employing the play-within-the-play technique, Pirandello gave a hearing to characters who interrupt a rehearsal with their claim that they are being misrepresented by the author and the actors. They were turned into puppets, and they insist that they are human beings. Being human, they are also profoundly disturbing, and the more the puppet transforms itself before us into a human being the more it refuses to be pigeonholed by the theatre and makes the purveyors of stage plots look silly.

As if this were not enough of a departure from the simple assumptions of the "entertainment industry," Pirandello, moreover, often presented his own work as "entertainment." Stark Young was indeed justified in maintaining that Pirandello had "transferred to the mind the legs and antics and the inexhaustible vivacity and loneliness and abstraction of the *commedia dell'arte.*" This description applies even to *Six Characters,* which exposes a far from amusing domestic situation, since Pirandello is poking fun at the theatre and confounding its simplicities. But if Pirandello was lively and indulged in laughter, here as elsewhere, it was because he found the life of men—including their view of life in their works of art—absurd; and the absurdity rankled. Pirandello was a mixed artist because he was of mixed temperament. He could write in his thirty-fifth year, "Ask the poet what is the saddest sight and he will reply 'It is laughter on the face of a man'," and he added, "Who laughs does not know." Since Pirandello "knew," his laughter was generally saturnine, if not indeed indistinguishable, especially in *Six Characters,* from acute distress.

In *Six Characters,* Pirandello's most incisive, as well as moving, quality lies in his challenge to art not to make a neat little conventional drama out of life. By the time the "Six Characters" have presented their case, it is plain that it cannot be completely "dramatized" or even known. Their motives are too mixed and their understanding too cloudy. The mother and the son do not express themselves completely, and the youngest child and the boy are, understandably, too inarticulate. Other characters are too passionately bent upon justifying themselves to present any absolutely objective truth, even if this were possible. When the play is over, Pirandello has shattered our complacent belief that we can really know and understand people. Our only defense against his demonstration—aside from the obtuseness we fortunately possess and the oversimplifying decorum that we usually adopt as a social

measure—is to refrain from passing judgment on one another and to be merciful.

BIBLIOGRAPHY: Eric Bentley, *The Playwright as Thinker* (pp. 177–189), 1946; Frank W. Chandler, *Modern Continental Playwrights* (pp. 573–594), 1931; Barrett H. Clark and George Freedley, *A History of the Modern Drama* (pp. 300–304, 338–340, 359–367), 1947; *Columbia Dictionary of Modern European Literature* (pp. 626–628), 1947; John Gassner, *Masters of the Drama* (pp. 434–445), 1940, 1945; W. Starkie, *Luigi Pirandello,* 1926, 1937 (revised edition); Domenico Vittorini, *The Drama of Luigi Pirandello,* 1935.

SIX CHARACTERS IN SEARCH OF AN AUTHOR

By Luigi Pirandello

TRANSLATED FROM THE ITALIAN BY EDWARD STORER

CHARACTERS OF THE COMEDY IN THE MAKING:

THE FATHER	THE STEPDAUGHTER	THE BOY ⎤ *(These two do*
THE MOTHER	THE SON	THE CHILD ⎦ *not speak)*
	MADAME PACE	

ACTORS OF THE COMPANY

THE MANAGER	L'INGÉNUE	MACHINIST
LEADING LADY	JUVENILE LEAD	MANAGER'S SECRETARY
LEADING MAN	OTHER ACTORS AND ACTRESSES	DOOR-KEEPER
SECOND LADY	PROPERTY MAN	SCENE-SHIFTERS
LEAD	PROMPTER	

DAYTIME: *The Stage of a Theater.*

ACT I.

N.B. The Comedy is without acts or scenes. The performance is interrupted once, without the curtain being lowered, when The Manager *and the chief characters withdraw to arrange the scenario. A second interruption of the action takes place when, by mistake, the stage hands let the curtain down.*

The spectators will find the curtain raised and the stage as it usually is during the daytime. It will be half dark, and empty, so that from the beginning the public may have the impression of an impromptu performance.

Prompter's *box and a small table and chair for* The Manager.

Two other small tables and several chairs scattered about as during rehearsals.

The Actors *and* Actresses *of the company enter from the back of the stage:*

First one, then another, then two together: nine or ten in all. They are about to rehearse a Pirandello play: Mixing It Up. *Some of the company move off towards their dressing rooms. The* Prompter *who has the "book" under his arm, is waiting for* The Manager *in order to begin the rehearsal.*

The Actors *and* Actresses, *some standing, some sitting, chat and smoke. One perhaps reads a paper; another cons his part.*

Finally, The Manager *enters and goes to the table prepared for him. His* Secretary *brings him his mail,* through which he glances. The Prompter *takes his seat, turns on a light, and opens the "book."*

THE MANAGER: [*Throwing a letter down on the table*] I can't see [*To* Property Man] Let's have a little light, please!

PROPERTY MAN: Yes sir, yes, at once. [*A light comes down on to the stage*]

THE MANAGER: [*Clapping his hands*] Come along! Come along! Second act of *Mixing it Up.* [*Sits down*]

[*The* Actors *and* Actresses *go from the front of the stage to the wings, all except the three who are to begin the rehearsal*]

THE PROMPTER: [*Reading the "book"*] "Leo Gala's house. A curious room serving as dining-room and study."

THE MANAGER: [*To* Property Man] Fix up the old red room.

PROPERTY MAN: [*Noting it down*] Red set. All right!

THE PROMPTER: [*Continuing to read from the "book"*] "Table already laid and writing desk with books and papers. Bookshelves. Exit rear to Leo's bedroom. Exit left to kitchen. Principal exit to right."

THE MANAGER: [*Energetically*] Well, you understand: The principal exit over there; here the kitchen. [*Turning to Actor who is to play the part of Socrates*] You make your entrances and exits here. [*To* Property Man] The baize doors at the rear, and curtains.

PROPERTY MAN: [*Noting it down*] Right-o!

PROMPTER: [*Reading as before*] "When the curtain rises, Leo Gala, dressed in cook's cap and apron is busy beating an egg in a cup. Philip, also dressed as a cook, is beating another egg. Guido Venanzi is seated and listening."

LEADING MAN: [*To* Manager] Excuse me, but must I absolutely wear a cook's cap?

THE MANAGER: [*Annoyed*] I imagine so. It says so there anyway. [*Pointing to the* "*book*"]

LEADING MAN: But it's ridiculous!

THE MANAGER: Ridiculous? Ridiculous? Is it my fault if France won't send us any more good comedies, and we are reduced to putting on Pirandello's works, where nobody understands anything, and where the author plays the fool with us all? [*The* Actors *grin. The* Manager *goes to* Leading Man *and shouts*] Yes sir, you put on the cook's cap and beat eggs. Do you suppose that with all this egg-beating business you are on an ordinary stage? Get that out of your head. You represent the shell of the eggs you are beating! [*Laughter and comments among the* Actors] Silence! and listen to my explanations, please! [*To* Leading Man]: "The empty form of reason without the fullness of instinct, which is blind"—You stand for reason, your wife is instinct. It's a mixing up of the parts, according to which you who act your own part become the puppet of yourself. Do you understand?

LEADING MAN: I'm hanged if I do.

THE MANAGER: Neither do I. But let's get on with it. It's sure to be a glorious failure anyway. [*Confidentially*]: But I say, please face three-quarters. Otherwise, what with the abstruseness of the dialogue, and the public that won't be able to hear you, the whole thing will go to hell. Come on! come on!

PROMPTER: Pardon sir, may I get into my box? There's a bit of a draught.

THE MANAGER: Yes, yes, of course!

At this point, the Door-keeper *has entered from the stage door and advances towards* The Manager's *table, taking off his braided cap. During this manœuver, the* Six Characters *enter, and stop by the door at back of stage, so that when the* Door-keeper *is about to announce their coming to* The Manager, *they are already on the stage. A tenuous light surrounds them, almost as if irradiated by them—the faint breath of their fantastic reality.*

This light will disappear when they come forward towards the Actors. *They preserve, however, something of the dream lightness in which they seem almost suspended; but this does not detract from the essential reality of their forms and expressions.*

He who is known as The Father *is a man of about 50: hair, reddish in color, thin at the temples; he is not bald, however; thick moustaches, falling over his still fresh mouth, which often opens in an empty and uncertain smile. He is fattish, pale; with an especially wide forehead. He has blue, oval-shaped eyes, very clear and piercing. Wears light trousers and a dark jacket. He is alternatively mellifluous and violent in his manner.*

The Mother *seems crushed and terrified as if by an intolerable weight of shame and abasement. She is dressed in modest black and wears a thick widow's veil of crêpe. When she lifts this, she reveals a wax-like face. She always keeps her eyes downcast.*

The Stepdaughter *is dashing, almost impudent, beautiful. She wears mourning too, but with great elegance. She shows contempt for the timid half-frightened manner of the wretched* Boy [*14 years old, and also dressed in black*]; *on the other hand, she displays a lively tenderness for her little sister,* The Child [*about four*], *who is dressed in white, with a black silk sash at the waist.*

The Son [22] *tall, severe in his attitude of contempt for* The Father, *supercilious and indifferent to the* Mother. *He looks as if he had come on the stage against his will.*

DOORKEEPER: [*Cap in hand*] Excuse me, sir . . .

THE MANAGER: [*Rudely*] Eh? What is it?

DOORKEEPER: [*Timidly*] These people are asking for you, sir.

THE MANAGER: [*Furious*] I am rehearsing, and you know perfectly well no one's allowed to come in during rehearsals! [*Turning to the* Characters]: Who are you, please? What do you want?

THE FATHER: [*Coming forward a little, followed by the others who seem embarrassed*] As a matter of fact . . . we have come here in search of an author. . . .

THE MANAGER: [*Half angry, half amazed*] An author? What author?

THE FATHER: Any author, sir.

THE MANAGER: But there's no author here. We are not rehearsing a new piece.

THE STEPDAUGHTER: [*Vivaciously*] So much the better, so much the better! We can be your new piece.

AN ACTOR: [*Coming forward from the others*] Oh, do you hear that?

THE FATHER: [*To* Stepdaughter] Yes, but if the author isn't here . . . [*To* Manager] . . . unless you would be willing . . .

THE MANAGER: You are trying to be funny.

THE FATHER: No, for Heaven's sake, what are you saying? We bring you a drama, sir.

THE STEPDAUGHTER: We may be your fortune.

THE MANAGER: Will you oblige me by going away? We haven't time to waste with mad people.

THE FATHER: [*Mellifluously*] Oh sir, you know well that life is full of infinite absurdities, which, strangely enough, do not even need to appear plausible, since they are true.

THE MANAGER: What the devil is he talking about?

THE FATHER: I say that to reverse the ordinary process may well be considered a madness: that is, to create credible situations, in order that they may appear true. But permit me to observe that if this be madness, it is the sole *raison d'être* of your profession, gentlemen. [*The* Actors *look hurt and perplexed*]

THE MANAGER: [*Getting up and looking at him*] So our profession seems to you one worthy of madmen then?

THE FATHER: Well, to make seem true that which isn't true . . . without any need . . . for a joke as it were . . . Isn't that your mission, gentlemen: to give life to fantastic characters on the stage?

THE MANAGER: [*Interpreting the rising anger of the* Company] But I would beg you to believe, my dear sir, that the profession of the comedian is a noble one. If today, as things go, the playwrights give us stupid comedies to play and puppets to represent instead of men, remember we are proud to have given life to immortal works here on these very boards! [*The Actors, satisfied, applaud their* Manager]

THE FATHER: [*Interrupting furiously*] Exactly, perfectly, to living beings more alive than those who breathe and wear clothes: being less real perhaps, but truer! I agree with you entirely. [*The Actors look at one another in amazement*]

THE MANAGER: But what do you mean? Before, you said . . .

THE FATHER: No, excuse me, I meant it for you, sir, who were crying out that you had no time to lose with madmen, while no one better than yourself knows that nature uses the instrument of human fantasy in order to pursue her high creative purpose.

THE MANAGER: Very well—but where does all this take us?

THE FATHER: Nowhere! It is merely to show you that one is born to life in many forms, in many shapes, as tree, or as stone, as water, as butterfly, or as woman. So one may also be born a character in a play.

THE MANAGER: [*With feigned comic dismay*] So you and these other friends of yours have been born characters?

THE FATHER: Exactly, and alive as you see! [*Manager and* Actors *burst out laughing*]

THE FATHER: [*Hurt*] I am sorry you laugh, because we carry in us a drama, as you can guess from this woman here veiled in black.

THE MANAGER: [*Losing patience at last and almost indignant*] Oh, chuck it! Get away please! Clear out of here! [*To* Property Man] For Heaven's sake, turn them out!

THE FATHER: [*Resisting*] No, no, look here, we . . .

THE MANAGER: [*Roaring*] We come here to work, you know.

LEADING ACTOR: One cannot let oneself be made such a fool of.

THE FATHER: [*Determined, coming forward*] I marvel at your incredulity, gentlemen. Are you not accustomed to see the characters created by an author spring to life in yourselves and face each other? Just because there is no "book" [*Pointing to the* Prompter's *box*] which contains us, you refuse to believe . . .

THE STEPDAUGHTER: [*Advances towards* Manager, *smiling and coquettish*] Believe me, we are really six most interesting characters, sir; side-tracked however.

THE FATHER: Yes, that is the word! [*To* Manager *all at once*] In the sense, that is, that the author who created us alive no longer wished, or was no longer able, materially to put us into a work of art. And this was a real crime, sir; because he who has had the luck to be born a character can laugh even at death. He cannot die. The man, the writer, the instrument of the creation will die, but his creation does not die. And to live for ever, it does not need to have extraordinary gifts or to be able to work wonders. Who was Sancho Panza? Who was Don Abbondio? Yet they live eternally because—live germs as they were—they had the fortune to find a fecundating matrix, a fantasy which could raise and nourish them: make them live for ever!

THE MANAGER: That is quite all right. But what do you want here, all of you?

THE FATHER: We want to live.

THE MANAGER: [*Ironically*] For Eternity?

THE FATHER: No, sir, only for a moment . . . in you.

AN ACTOR: Just listen to him!

LEADING LADY: They want to live, in us! . . .

JUVENILE LEAD: [*Pointing to the* Stepdaughter] I've no objection, as far as that one is concerned!

THE FATHER: Look here! Look here! The comedy has to be made. [*To the* Manager] But if you and your actors are willing, we can soon concert it among ourselves.

THE MANAGER: [*Annoyed*] But what do you want to concert? We don't go in for concerts here. Here we play dramas and comedies!

THE FATHER: Exactly! That is just why we have come to you.

THE MANAGER: And where is the "book"?

THE FATHER: It is in us! [*The* Actors *laugh*] The drama is in us, and we are the drama. We are impatient to play it. Our inner passion drives us on to this.

THE STEPDAUGHTER: [*Disdainful, alluring, treacherous, full of impudence*] My passion, sir! Ah, if you only knew! My passion for him! [*Points to the* Father *and makes a pretence of embracing him. Then she breaks out into a loud laugh*]

THE FATHER: [*Angrily*] Behave yourself! And please don't laugh in that fashion.

THE STEPDAUGHTER: With your permission, gentlemen, I, who am a two months' orphan, will show you how I can dance and sing.

[*Sings and then dances* Prenez garde à Tchou-Thin-Tchou]

Les chinois sont un peuple malin,
De Shanghaî à Pékin,
Ils ont mis des écriteaux partout:
Prenez garde à Tchou-Thin-Tchou.

ACTORS and ACTRESSES: Bravo! Well done! Tiptop!

THE MANAGER: Silence! This isn't a café concert, you know! [*Turning to the* Father *in consternation*] Is she mad?

THE FATHER: Mad? No, she's worse than mad.

THE STEPDAUGHTER: [*To* Manager] Worse? Worse? Listen! Stage this drama for us at once! Then you will see that at a certain moment I . . . when this little darling here . . . [*Takes the* Child *by the hand and leads her to the* Manager] Isn't she a dear? [*Takes her up and kisses her*] Darling! Darling! [*Puts her down again and adds feelingly*] Well, when God suddenly takes this dear little child away from that poor mother there; and this imbecile here [*seizing hold of the* Boy *roughly and pushing him forward*] does the stupidest things, like the fool he is, you will see me run away. Yes, gentlemen, I shall be off. But the moment hasn't arrived yet. After what has taken place between him and me [*indicates the* Father *with a horrible wink*] I can't remain any longer in this society, to have to witness the anguish of this mother here for that fool . . . [*Indicates the* Son] Look at him! Look at him! See how indifferent, how frigid he is, because he is the legitimate son. He despises me, despises him [*pointing to the* Boy], despises this baby here; because . . . we are bastards. [*Goes to the* Mother *and embraces her*] And he doesn't want to recognize her as his mother—she who is the common mother of us all. He looks down upon her as if she were only the mother of us three bastards. Wretch! [*She says all this very rapidly, excitedly. At the word "bastards" she raises her voice, and almost spits out the final "Wretch!"*]

THE MOTHER: [*To the* Manager, *in anguish*] In the name of these two little children, I beg you . . . [*She grows faint and is about to fall*] Oh God!

THE FATHER: [*Coming forward to support her as do some of the* Actors] Quick a chair, a chair for this poor widow!

THE ACTORS: Is it true? Has she really fainted?

THE MANAGER: Quick, a chair! Here!

[*One of the* Actors *brings a chair, the others proffer assistance. The* Mother *tries to prevent the* Father *from lifting the veil which covers her face*]

THE FATHER: Look at her! Look at her!

THE MOTHER: No, stop; stop it please!

THE FATHER: [*Raising her veil*] Let them see you!

THE MOTHER: [*Rising and covering her face with her hands, in desperation*] I beg you, sir, to prevent this man from carrying out his plan which is loathsome to me.

THE MANAGER: [*Dumbfounded*] I don't understand at all. What is the situation? Is this lady your wife? [*To the* Father]

THE FATHER: Yes, gentlemen: my wife!

THE MANAGER: But how can she be a widow if you are alive? [*The* Actors *find relief for their astonishment in a loud laugh*]

THE FATHER: Don't laugh! Don't laugh like that, for Heaven's sake. Her drama lies just here in this: she has had a lover, a man who ought to be here.

THE MOTHER: [*With a cry*] No! No!

THE STEPDAUGHTER: Fortunately for her, he is dead. Two months ago as I said. We are in mourning, as you see.

THE FATHER: He isn't here you see, not because he is dead. He isn't here—look at her a moment and you will understand—because her drama isn't a drama of the love of two men for whom she was incapable of feeling anything except possibly a little gratitude—gratitude not for me but for the other. She isn't a woman, she is a mother, and her drama —powerful sir, I assure you—lies, as a matter of fact, all in these four children she has had by two men.

THE MOTHER: I had them? Have you got the courage to say that I wanted them? [*To the* Company] It was his doing. It was he who gave me that other man, who forced me to go away with him.

THE STEPDAUGHTER: It isn't true.

THE MOTHER: [*Startled*] Not true, isn't it?

THE STEPDAUGHTER: No, it isn't true, it just isn't true.

THE MOTHER: And what can you know about it?

THE STEPDAUGHTER: It isn't true. Don't believe it. [*To* Manager] Do you know why she says so? For that fellow there. [*Indicates the* Son] She tortures herself, destroys herself on account of the neglect of that son there; and she wants him to believe that if she abandoned him when he was only two years old, it was because he [*indicates the* Father] made her do so.

THE MOTHER: [*Vigorously*] He forced me to it, and I call God to witness it. [*To the* Manager] Ask him [*indicates the* Father] if it isn't true. Let him speak. You [*to* Daughter] are not in a position to know anything about it.

THE STEPDAUGHTER: I know you lived in peace and happiness with my father while he lived. Can you deny it?

THE MOTHER: No, I don't deny it . . .

THE STEPDAUGHTER: He was always full of affection and kindness for you. [*To the* Boy, *angrily*] It's true, isn't it? Tell them! Why don't you speak, you little fool?

THE MOTHER: Leave the poor boy alone. Why do you want to make me appear ungrateful, daughter? I don't want to offend your father. I have answered him that I didn't abandon my house and my son through any fault of mine, nor from any wilful passion.

THE FATHER: It is true. It was my doing.

LEADING MAN: [*To the* Company] What a spectacle!

LEADING LADY: We are the audience this time.

JUVENILE LEAD: For once, in a way.

THE MANAGER: [*Beginning to get really interested*] Let's hear them out. Listen!

THE SON: Oh yes, you're going to hear a fine bit now. He will talk to you of the Demon of Experiment.

THE FATHER: You are a cynical imbecile. I've told you so already a hundred times. [*To the* Manager] He tries to make fun of me on account of this expression which I have found to excuse myself with.

THE SON: [*With disgust*] Yes, phrases! phrases!

THE FATHER: Phrases! Isn't everyone consoled when faced with a trouble or fact he doesn't understand, by a word, some simple word, which tells us nothing and yet calms us?

THE STEPDAUGHTER: Even in the case of remorse. In fact, especially then.

THE FATHER: Remorse? No, that isn't true. I've done more than use words to quieten the remorse in me.

THE STEPDAUGHTER: Yes, there was a bit of money too. Yes, yes, a bit of money. There were the hundred lire he was about to offer me in payment, gentlemen. . . . [*Sensation of horror among the* Actors]

THE SON: [*To the* Stepdaughter] This is vile.

THE STEPDAUGHTER: Vile? There they were in a pale blue envelope on a little mahogany table in the back of Madame Pace's shop. You know Madame Pace—one of those ladies who attract poor girls of good family into their ateliers, under the pretext of their selling *robes et manteaux*.

THE SON: And he thinks he has bought the right to tyrannize over us all with those hundred lire he was going to pay; but which, fortunately—note this, gentlemen—he had no chance of paying.

THE STEPDAUGHTER: It was a near thing, though, you know! [*Laughs ironically*]

THE MOTHER: [*Protesting*] Shame, my daughter, shame!

THE STEPDAUGHTER: Shame indeed! This is my revenge! I am dying to live that scene. . . . The room . . . I see it . . . Here is the window with the mantles exposed, there the divan, the looking-glass, a screen, there in front of the window the little mahogany table with the blue envelope containing one hundred lire. I see it. I see it. I could take hold of it . . . But you, gentlemen, you ought to turn your backs now: I am almost nude, you know. But I don't blush: I leave that to him. [*Indicating* Father]

THE MANAGER: I don't understand this at all.

THE FATHER: Naturally enough. I would ask you, sir, to exercise your authority a little here, and let me speak before you believe all she is trying to blame me with. Let me explain.

THE STEPDAUGHTER: Ah yes, explain it in your own way.

THE FATHER: But don't you see that the whole trouble lies here. In words, words. Each one of us has within him a whole world of things, each man of us his own special world. And how can we ever come to an understanding if I put in the words I utter the sense and value of things as I see them; while you who listen to me must inevitably translate them according to the conception of things each one of you has within himself. We think we understand each other, but we never really do. Look here! This woman [*indicating the* Mother] takes all my pity for her as a specially ferocious form of cruelty.

THE MOTHER: But you drove me away.

THE FATHER: Do you hear her? I drove her away! She believes I really sent her away.

THE MOTHER: You know how to talk, and I don't; but, believe me sir [*To* Manager], after he had married me . . . who knows why? . . . I was a poor insignificant woman . . .

THE FATHER: But, good Heaven! it was just for your humility that I married you. I loved this simplicity in you. [*He stops when he sees she makes signs to contradict him, opens his arms wide in sign of desperation, seeing how hopeless it is to make himself understood*] You see she denies it. Her mental deafness, believe me, is phenomenal, the limit [*touches his forehead*]: deaf, deaf, mentally deaf! She has plenty of feeling. Oh yes, a good heart for the children; but the brain—deaf, to the point of desperation——!

THE STEPDAUGHTER: Yes, but ask him how his intelligence has helped us.

THE FATHER: If we could see all the evil that may spring from good, what should we do? [*At this point the* Leading Lady *who is biting her lips with rage at seeing the* Leading Man *flirting with the* Stepdaughter, *comes forward and says to the* Manager]

LEADING LADY: Excuse me, but are we going to rehearse today?

MANAGER: Of course, of course; but let's hear them out.

JUVENILE LEAD: This is something quite new.

L'INGÉNUE: Most interesting!

LEADING LADY: Yes, for the people who like that kind of thing. [*Casts a glance at* Leading Man]

THE MANAGER: [*To* Father] You must please explain yourself quite clearly. [*Sits down*]

THE FATHER: Very well then: listen! I had in my service a poor man, a clerk, a secretary of mine, full of devotion, who became friends with her. [*Indicating the* Mother] They understood one another, were kindred souls in fact, without, however the least suspicion of any evil existing. They were incapable even of thinking of it.

THE STEPDAUGHTER: So he thought of it—for them!

THE FATHER: That's not true. I meant to do good to them—and to myself, I confess, at the same time. Things had come to the point that I could not say a word to either of them without their making a mute appeal, one to the other, with their eyes. I could see them silently asking each other how I was to be kept in countenance, how I was to be kept quiet. And this, believe me, was just about enough of itself to keep me in a constant rage, to exasperate me beyond measure.

THE MANAGER: And why didn't you send him away then—this secretary of yours?

THE FATHER: Precisely what I did, sir. And then I had to watch this poor woman drifting forlornly about the house like an animal without a master, like an animal one has taken in out of pity.

THE MOTHER: Ah yes! . . .

THE FATHER: [Suddenly turning to the Mother] It's true about the son anyway, isn't it?

THE MOTHER: He took my son away from me first of all.

THE FATHER: But not from cruelty. I did it so that he should grow up healthy and strong by living in the country.

THE STEPDAUGHTER: [Pointing to him ironically] As one can see.

THE FATHER: [Quickly] Is it my fault if he has grown up like this? I sent him to a wet nurse in the country, a peasant, as she did not seem to me strong enough, though she is of humble origin. That was, anyway, the reason I married her. Unpleasant all this may be, but how can it be helped? My mistake possibly, but there we are! All my life I have had these confounded aspirations towards a certain moral sanity. [At this point the Stepdaughter bursts out into a noisy laugh] Oh, stop it! Stop it! I can't stand it.

THE MANAGER: Yes, please stop it, for Heaven's sake.

THE STEPDAUGHTER: But imagine moral sanity from him, if you please—the client of certain ateliers like that of Madame Pace!

THE FATHER: Fool! That is the proof that I am a man! This seeming contradiction, gentlemen, is the strongest proof that I stand here a live man before you. Why, it is just for this very incongruity in my nature that I have had to suffer what I have. I could not live by the side of that woman [indicating the Mother] any longer; but not so much for the boredom she inspired me with as for the pity I felt for her.

THE MOTHER: And so he turned me out—.

THE FATHER: —well provided for! Yes, I sent her to that man, gentlemen . . . to let her go free of me.

THE MOTHER: And to free himself.

THE FATHER: Yes, I admit it. It was also a liberation for me. But great evil has come of it. I meant well when I did it; and I did it more for her sake than mine. I swear it. [Crosses his arms on his chest; then turns suddenly to the Mother] Did I ever lose sight of you until that other man carried you off to another town, like the angry fool he was? And on account of my pure interest in you . . . my pure interest, I repeat, that had no base motive in it . . .

I watched with the tenderest concern the new family that grew up around her. She can bear witness to this. [Points to the Stepdaughter]

THE STEPDAUGHTER: Oh yes, that's true enough. When I was a kiddie, so so high, you know, with plaits over my shoulders and knickers longer than my skirts, I used to see him waiting outside the school for me to come out. He came to see how I was growing up.

THE FATHER: This is infamous, shameful!

THE STEPDAUGHTER: No. Why?

THE FATHER: Infamous! Infamous! [Then excitedly to Manager explaining] After she [indicating Mother] went away, my house seemed suddenly empty. She was my incubus, but she filled my house. I was like a dazed fly alone in the empty rooms. This boy here [indicating the Son] was educated away from home, and when he came back, he seemed to me to be no more mine. With no mother to stand between him and me, he grew up entirely for himself, on his own, apart, with no tie of intellect or affection binding him to me. And then—strange but true—I was driven, by curiosity at first and then by some tender sentiment, towards her family, which had come into being through my will. The thought of her began gradually to fill up the emptiness I felt all around me. I wanted to know if she were happy in living out the simple daily duties of life. I wanted to think of her as fortunate and happy because far away from the complicated torments of my spirit. And so, to have proof of this, I used to watch that child coming out of school.

THE STEPDAUGHTER: Yes, yes. True. He used to follow me in the street and smiled at me, waved his hand, like this. I would look at him with interest, wondering who he might be. I told my mother, who guessed at once. [The Mother agrees with a nod] Then she didn't want to send me to school for some days; and when I finally went back, there he was again—looking so ridiculous—with a paper parcel in his hands. He came close to me, caressed me, and drew out a fine straw hat from the parcel, with a bouquet of flowers—all for me!

THE MANAGER: A bit discursive this, you know!

THE SON: [Contemptuously] Literature! Literature!

THE FATHER: Literature indeed! This is life, this is passion!

THE MANAGER: It may be, but it won't act.

THE FATHER: I agree. This is only the part leading up. I don't suggest this should be staged. She [pointing to the Stepdaughter], as you see, is no longer the flapper with plaits down her back—.

THE STEPDAUGHTER: —and the knickers showing below the skirt!

THE FATHER: The drama is coming now, sir; something new, complex, most interesting.

THE STEPDAUGHTER: As soon as my father died . . .

THE FATHER: —there was absolute misery for them. They came back here, unknown to me.

Through her stupidity! [*Pointing to the* Mother] It is true she can barely write her own name; but she could anyhow have got her daughter to write to me that they were in need. . . .

THE MOTHER: And how was I to divine all this sentiment in him?

THE FATHER: That is exactly your mistake, never to have guessed any of my sentiments.

THE MOTHER: After so many years apart, and all that had happened . . .

THE FATHER: Was it my fault if that fellow carried you away? It happened quite suddenly; for after he had obtained some job or other, I could find no trace of them; and so, not unnaturally, my interest in them dwindled. But the drama culminated unforeseen and violent on their return, when I was impelled by my miserable flesh that still lives . . . Ah! what misery, what wretchedness is that of the man who is alone and disdains debasing *liaisons!* Not old enough to do without women, and not young enough to go and look for one without shame. Misery? It's worse than misery; it's a horror; for no woman can any longer give him love; and when a man feels this . . . One ought to do without, you say? Yes, yes, I know. Each of us when he appears before his fellows is clothed in a certain dignity. But every man knows what unconfessable things pass within the secrecy of his own heart. One gives way to the temptation, only to rise from it again, afterwards, with a great eagerness to reestablish one's dignity, as if it were a tombstone to place on the grave of one's shame, and a monument to hide and sign the memory of our weaknesses. Everybody's in the same case. Some folks haven't the courage to say certain things, that's all!

THE STEPDAUGHTER: All appear to have the courage to do them though.

THE FATHER: Yes, but in secret. Therefore, you want more courage to say these things. Let a man but speak these things out, and folks at once label him a cynic. But it isn't true. He is like all the others, better indeed, because he isn't afraid to reveal with the light of the intelligence the red shame of human bestiality on which most men close their eyes so as not to see it. Woman—for example, look at her case! She turns tantalizing inviting glances on you. You seize her. No sooner does she feel herself in your grasp than she closes her eyes. It is the sign of her mission, the sign by which she says to man: "Blind yourself, for I am blind."

THE STEPDAUGHTER: Sometimes she can close them no more: when she no longer feels the need of hiding her shame to herself, but dry-eyed and dispassionately, sees only that of the man who has blinded himself without love. Oh, all these intellectual complications make me sick, disgust me—all this philosophy that uncovers the beast in man, and then seeks to save him, excuse him . . . I can't stand it, sir. When a man seeks to "simplify" life bestially. throwing aside every relic of humanity,

every chaste aspiration, every pure feeling, all sense of ideality, duty, modesty, shame . . . then nothing is more revolting and nauseous than a certain kind of remorse—crocodiles' tears, that's what it is.

THE MANAGER: Let's come to the point. This is only discussion.

THE FATHER: Very good, sir! But a fact is like a sack which won't stand up when it is empty. In order that it may stand up, one has to put into it the reason and sentiment which have caused it to exist. I couldn't possibly know that after the death of that man, they had decided to return here, that they were in misery, and that she [*pointing to the* Mother] had gone to work as a modiste, and at a shop of the type of that of Madame Pace.

THE STEPDAUGHTER: A real high-class modiste, you must know, gentlemen. In appearance, she works for the leaders of the best society; but she arranges matters so that these elegant ladies serve her purpose . . . without prejudice to other ladies who are . . . well . . . only so so.

THE MOTHER: You will believe me, gentlemen, that it never entered my mind that the old hag offered me work because she had her eye on my daughter.

THE STEPDAUGHTER: Poor mamma! Do you know, sir, what that woman did when I brought her back the work my mother had finished? She would point out to me that I had torn one of my frocks, and she would give it back to my mother to mend. It was I who paid for it, always I; while this poor creature here believed she was sacrificing herself for me and these two children here, sitting up at night sewing Madame Pace's robes.

THE MANAGER: And one day you met there . . .

THE STEPDAUGHTER: Him, him. Yes, sir, an old client. There's a scene for you to play! Superb!

THE FATHER: She, the Mother arrived just then . . .

THE STEPDAUGHTER: [*Treacherously*] Almost in time!

THE FATHER: [*Crying out*] No, in time! in time! Fortunately I recognized her . . . in time. And I took them back home with me to my house. You can imagine now her position and mine: she, as you see her; and I who cannot look her in the face.

THE STEPDAUGHTER: Absurd! How can I possibly be expected—after that—to be a modest young miss, a fit person to go with his confounded aspirations for "a solid moral sanity"?

THE FATHER: For the drama lies all in this—in the conscience that I have, that each of us has. We believe this conscience to be a single thing, but it is many-sided. There is one for this person, and another for that. Diverse consciences. So we have this illusion of being one person for all, of having a personality that is unique in all our acts. But it isn't true. We perceive this when, tragically perhaps, in something we do, we are, as it were, suspended, caught up in the air on a kind of hook.

Then we perceive that all of us was not in that act, and that it would be an atrocious injustice to judge us by that action alone, as if all our existence were summed up in that one deed. Now do you understand the perfidy of this girl? She surprised me in a place, where she ought not to have known me, just as I could not exist for her; and she now seeks to attach to me a reality such as I could never suppose I should have to assume for her in a shameful and fleeting moment of my life. I feel this above all else. And the drama, you will see, acquires a tremendous value from this point. Then there is the position of the others . . . his . . . [*Indicating the* Son]

THE SON: [*Shrugging his shoulders scornfully*] Leave me alone! I don't come into this.

THE FATHER: What? You don't come into this?

THE SON: I've got nothing to do with it, and don't want to have; because you know well enough I wasn't made to be mixed up in all this with the rest of you.

THE STEPDAUGHTER: We are only vulgar folk! He is the fine gentleman. You may have noticed, Mr. Manager, that I fix him now and again with a look of scorn while he lowers his eyes—for he knows the evil he has done me.

THE SON: [*Scarcely looking at her*] I?

THE STEPDAUGHTER: You! you! I owe my life on the streets to you. Did you or did you not deny us, with your behavior, I won't say the intimacy of home, but even that mere hospitality which makes guests feel at their ease? We were intruders who had come to disturb the kingdom of your legitimacy. I should like to have you witness, Mr. Manager, certain scenes between him and me. He says I have tyrannized over everyone. But it was just his behavior which made me insist on the reason for which I had come into the house—this reason he calls "vile"—into his house, with my mother who is his mother too. And I came as mistress of the house.

THE SON: It's easy for them to put me always in the wrong. But imagine, gentlemen, the position of a son, whose fate it is to see arrive one day at his home a young woman of impudent bearing, a young woman who inquires for his father, with whom who knows what business she has. This young man has then to witness her return bolder than ever, accompanied by that child there. He is obliged to watch her treat his father in an equivocal and confidential manner. She asks money of him in a way that lets one suppose he must give it her, *must*, do you understand, because he has every obligation to do so.

THE FATHER: But I have, as a matter of fact, this obligation. I owe it to your mother.

THE SON: How should I know? When had I ever seen or heard of her? One day there arrive with her [*indicating* Stepdaughter] that lad and this baby here. I am told: "This is *your* mother too, you know." I divine from her manner [*indicating* Stepdaughter *again*] why it is they have come home. I had rather not say what I feel and think about it. I

shouldn't even care to confess to myself. No action can therefore be hoped for from me in this affair. Believe me, Mr. Manager, I am an "unrealized" character, dramatically speaking; and I find myself not at all at ease in their company. Leave me out of it, I beg you.

THE FATHER: What? It is just because you are so that . . .

THE SON: How do you know what I am like? When did you ever bother your head about me?

THE FATHER: I admit it. I admit it. But isn't that a situation in itself? This aloofness of yours which is so cruel to me and to your mother, who returns home and sees you almost for the first time grown up, who doesn't recognize you but knows you are her son . . . [*Pointing out the* Mother *to the* Manager] See, she's crying!

THE STEPDAUGHTER: [*Angrily, stamping her foot*] Like a fool!

THE FATHER: [*Indicating* Stepdaughter] She can't stand him you know. [*Then referring again to the* Son]: He says he doesn't come into the affair, whereas he is really the hinge of the whole action. Look at that lad who is always clinging to his mother, frightened and humiliated. It is on account of this fellow here. Possibly his situation is the most painful of all. He feels himself a stranger more than the others. The poor little chap feels mortified, humiliated at being brought into a home out of charity as it were. [*In confidence*]—: He is the image of his father. Hardly talks at all. Humble and quiet.

THE MANAGER: Oh, we'll cut him out. You've no notion what a nuisance boys are on the stage . . .

THE FATHER: He disappears soon, you know. And the baby too. She is the first to vanish from the scene. The drama consists finally in this: when that mother re-enters my house, her family born outside of it, and shall we say superimposed on the original, ends with the death of the little girl, the tragedy of the boy and the flight of the elder daughter. It cannot go on, because it is foreign to its surroundings. So after much torment, we three remain: I, the mother, that son. Then, owing to the disappearance of that extraneous family, we too find ourselves strange to one another. We find we are living in an atmosphere of mortal desolation which is the revenge, as he [*indicating* Son] scornfully said of the Demon of Experiment, that unfortunately hides in me. Thus, sir, you see when faith is lacking, it becomes impossible to create certain states of happiness, for we lack the necessary humility. Vaingloriously, we try to substitute ourselves for this faith, creating thus for the rest of the world a reality which we believe after their fashion, while, actually, it doesn't exist. For each one of us has his own reality to be respected before God, even when it is harmful to one's very self.

THE MANAGER: There is something in what you say. I assure you all this interests me very much. I begin to think there's the stuff for a drama in all this, and not a bad drama either.

THE STEPDAUGHTER: [*Coming forward*] When you've got a character like me.

THE FATHER: [*Shutting her up, all excited to learn the decision of the* Manager] You be quiet!

THE MANAGER: [*Reflecting, heedless of interruption*] It's new . . . hem . . . yes . . .

THE FATHER: Absolutely new!

THE MANAGER: You've got a nerve though, I must say, to come here and fling it at me like this . . .

THE FATHER: You will understand, sir, born as we are for the stage . . .

THE MANAGER: Are you amateur actors then?

THE FATHER: No, I say born for the stage, because . . .

THE MANAGER: Oh, nonsense. You're an old hand, you know.

THE FATHER: No sir, no. We act that rôle for which we have been cast, that rôle which we are given in life. And in my own case, passion itself, as usually happens, becomes a trifle theatrical when it is exalted.

THE MANAGER: Well, well, that will do. But you see, without an author . . . I could give you the address of an author if you like . . .

THE FATHER: No, no. Look here! You must be the author.

THE MANAGER: I? What are you talking about?

THE FATHER: Yes, you, you! Why not?

THE MANAGER: Because I have never been an author: that's why.

THE FATHER: Then why not turn author now? Everybody does it. You don't want any special qualities. Your task is made much easier by the fact that we are all here alive before you . . .

THE MANAGER: It won't do.

THE FATHER: What? When you see us live our drama . . .

THE MANAGER: Yes, that's all right. But you want someone to write it.

THE FATHER: No, no. Someone to take it down, possibly, while we play it, scene by scene! It will be enough to sketch it out at first, and then try it over.

THE MANAGER: Well . . . I am almost tempted. It's a bit of an idea. One might have a shot at it.

THE FATHER: Of course. You'll see what scenes will come out of it. I can give you one, at once . . .

THE MANAGER: By Jove, it tempts me. I'd like to have a go at it. Let's try it out. Come with me to my office. [*Turning to the* Actors] You are at liberty for a bit, but don't stop out of the theater for long. In a quarter of an hour, twenty minutes, all back here again! [*To the* Father]: We'll see what can be done. Who knows if we don't get something really extraordinary out of it?

THE FATHER: There's no doubt about it. They [*indicating the* Characters] had better come with us too, hadn't they?

THE MANAGER: Yes, yes. Come on! come on! [*Moves away and then turning to the* Actors]: Be punctual, please! [*Manager and the* Six Characters *cross the stage and go off. The other* Actors *remain, looking at one another in astonishment*]

LEADING MAN: Is he serious? What the devil does he want to do?

JUVENILE LEAD: This is rank madness.

THIRD ACTOR: Does he expect to knock up a drama in five minutes?

JUVENILE LEAD: Like the improvisers!

LEADING LADY: If he thinks I'm going to take part in a joke like this . . .

JUVENILE LEAD: I'm out of it anyway.

FOURTH ACTOR: I should like to know who they are. [*Alludes to* Characters]

THIRD ACTOR: What do you suppose? Madmen or rascals!

JUVENILE LEAD: And he takes them seriously!

L'INGÉNUE: Vanity! He fancies himself as an author now.

LEADING MAN: It's absolutely unheard of. If the stage has come to this . . . well I'm . . .

FIFTH ACTOR: It's rather a joke.

THIRD ACTOR: Well, we'll see what's going to happen next.

[*Thus talking, the* Actors *leave the stage; some going out by the little door at the back; others retiring to their dressing-rooms.*
The curtain remains up.
The action of the play is suspended for twenty minutes]

ACT II.

The stage call-bells ring to warn the company that the play is about to begin again.

The Stepdaughter *comes out of the* Manager's *office along with* The Child *and* The Boy. *As she comes out of the office, she cries:*

Nonsense! Nonsense! Do it yourselves! I'm not going to mix myself up in this mess. [*Turning to the* Child *and coming quickly with her on to the stage*] Come on, Rosetta, let's run!

[*The* Boy *follows them slowly, remaining a little behind and seeming perplexed*]

THE STEPDAUGHTER: [*Stops, bends over the* Child *and takes the latter's face between her hands*] My little darling! You're frightened, aren't you? You don't know where we are, do you? [*Pretending to reply to a question of the* Child] What is the stage? It's a place, baby, you know, where people play at being serious, a place where they act comedies. We've got to act a comedy now, dead serious, you know; and you're in it also, little one. [*Embraces her, pressing the little head to her breast, and rocking the* Child *for a moment*] Oh darling, darling, what a horrid comedy you've got to play! What a wretched part they've found for you! A garden . . . a fountain . . . look . . . just suppose, kiddie, it's here. Where, you say? Why, right here in the middle. It's all pretence you know. That's the trouble, my pet: it's all make-believe here. It's better to imagine it though, because if they fix it up for you, it'll only be painted cardboard, painted cardboard for the rockery, the water, the plants . . . Ah, but I think a baby like this one would sooner have a make-believe fountain than a real one, so she could play with it. What a joke it'll be for the others! But for you, alas! not quite such a joke: you who are real, baby dear, and really play by a real fountain that is big and green and beautiful, with ever so many bamboos around it that are reflected in the water, and a whole lot of little ducks swimming about . . . No, Rosetta, no, your mother doesn't bother about you on account of that wretch of a son there. I'm in the devil of a temper, and as for that lad . . . [*Seizes* Boy *by the arm to force him to take one of his hands out of his pockets*] What have you got there? What are you hiding? [*Pulls his hand out of his pocket, looks into it and catches the glint of a revolver*] Ah, where did you get this?

[*The Boy, very pale in the face, looks at her, but does not answer*]

Idiot! If I'd been in your place, instead of killing myself, I'd have shot one of those two, or both of them: father and son.

[*The Father enters from the office, all excited from his work. The Manager follows him*]

THE FATHER: Come on, come on, dear! Come here for a minute! We've arranged everything. It's all fixed up.

THE MANAGER: [*Also excited*] If you please, young lady, there are one or two points to settle still. Will you come along?

THE STEPDAUGHTER: [*Following him towards the office*] Ouff! what's the good, if you've arranged everything.

[*The Father, Manager and* Stepdaughter *go back into the office again (off) for a moment. At the same time, The Son followed by The Mother, comes out*]

THE SON: [*Looking at the three entering office*] Oh this is fine, fine! And to think I can't even get away!

[*The Mother attempts to look at him, but lowers her eyes immediately when he turns away from her. She then sits down. The Boy and The Child approach her. She casts a glance again at the Son, and speaks with humble tones, trying to draw him into conversation*]

THE MOTHER: And isn't my punishment the worst of all? [*Then seeing from the Son's manner that he will not bother himself about her*] My God! Why are you so cruel? Isn't it enough for one person

to support all this torment? Must you then insist on others seeing it also?

THE SON: [*Half to himself, meaning the Mother to hear, however*] And they want to put it on the stage! If there was at least a reason for it! He thinks he has got at the meaning of it all. Just as if each one of us in every circumstance of life couldn't find his own explanation of it! [*Pauses*] He complains he was discovered in a place where he ought not to have been seen, in a moment of his life which ought to have remained hidden and kept out of the reach of that convention which he has to maintain for other people. And what about my case? Haven't I had to reveal what no son ought ever to reveal: how father and mother live and are man and wife for themselves quite apart from that idea of father and mother which we give them? When this idea is revealed, our life is then linked at one point only to that man and that woman; and as such it should shame them, shouldn't it?

[*The Mother hides her face in her hands. From the dressing-rooms and the little door at the back of the stage the* Actors *and* Stage Manager *return, followed by the* Property Man, *and the* Prompter. *At the same moment,* The Manager *comes out of his office, accompanied by the* Father *and the* Stepdaughter]

THE MANAGER: Come on, come on, ladies and gentlemen! Heh! you there, machinist!

MACHINIST: Yes sir?

THE MANAGER: Fix up the white parlor with the floral decorations. Two wings and a drop with a door will do. Hurry up!

[*The Machinist runs off at once to prepare the scene, and arranges it while* The Manager *talks with the* Stage Manager, *the* Property Man, *and the* Prompter *on matters of detail*]

THE MANAGER: [*To* Property Man] Just have a look, and see if there isn't a sofa or divan in the wardrobe . . .

PROPERTY MAN: There's the green one.

THE STEPDAUGHTER: No, no! Green won't do. It was yellow, ornamented with flowers—very large! and most comfortable!

PROPERTY MAN: There isn't one like that.

THE MANAGER: It doesn't matter. Use the one we've got.

THE STEPDAUGHTER: Doesn't matter? It's most important!

THE MANAGER: We're only trying it now. Please don't interfere. [*To* Property Man] See if we've got a shop window—long and narrowish.

THE STEPDAUGHTER: And the little table! The little mahogany table for the pale blue envelope!

PROPERTY MAN: [*To* Manager] There's that little gilt one.

THE MANAGER: That'll do fine.

THE FATHER: A mirror.

THE STEPDAUGHTER: And the screen! We must have a screen. Otherwise how can I manage?

PROPERTY MAN: That's all right, Miss. We've got any amount of them.

THE MANAGER: [To the Stepdaughter] We want some clothes pegs too, don't we?

THE STEPDAUGHTER: Yes, several, several!

THE MANAGER: See how many we've got and bring them all.

PROPERTY MAN: All right!

[The Property Man hurries off to obey his orders. While he is putting the things in their places, the Manager talks to the Prompter and then with the Characters and the Actors]

THE MANAGER: [To Prompter] Take your seat. Look here: this is the outline of the scenes, act by act. [Hands him some sheets of paper] And now I'm going to ask you to do something out of the ordinary.

PROMPTER: Take it down in shorthand?

THE MANAGER: [Pleasantly surprised] Exactly! Can you do shorthand?

PROMPTER: Yes, a little.

MANAGER: Good! [Turning to a stage hand] Go and get some paper from my office, plenty, as much as you can find.

[The Stage Hand goes off, and soon returns with a handful of paper which he gives to the Prompter]

THE MANAGER: [To Prompter] You follow the scenes as we play them, and try and get the points down, at any rate the most important ones. [Then addressing the Actors] Clear the stage, ladies and gentlemen! Come over here [Pointing to the Left] and listen attentively.

LEADING LADY: But, excuse me, we . . .

THE MANAGER: [Guessing her thought] Don't worry! You won't have to improvise.

LEADING MAN: What have we to do then?

THE MANAGER: Nothing. For the moment you just watch and listen. Everybody will get his part written out afterwards. At present we're going to try the thing as best we can. They're going to act now.

THE FATHER: [As if fallen from the clouds into the confusion of the stage] We? What do you mean, if you please, by a rehearsal?

THE MANAGER: A rehearsal for them. [Points to the Actors]

THE FATHER: But since we are the characters . . .

THE MANAGER: All right: "characters" then, if you insist on calling yourselves such. But here, my dear sir, the characters don't act. Here the actors do the acting. The characters are there, in the "book"— [Pointing towards Prompter's box] when there is a "book"!

THE FATHER: I won't contradict you; but excuse me, the actors aren't the characters. They want to be, they pretend to be, don't they? Now if these gentlemen here are fortunate enough to have us alive before them . . .

THE MANAGER: Oh this is grand! You want to come before the public yourselves then?

THE FATHER: As we are . . .

THE MANAGER: I can assure you it would be a magnificent spectacle!

LEADING MAN: What's the use of us here anyway then?

THE MANAGER: You're not going to pretend that you can act? It makes me laugh! [The Actors laugh] There, you see, they are laughing at the notion. But, by the way, I must cast the parts. That won't be difficult. They cast themselves. [To the Second Lady Lead] You play the Mother. [To the Father] We must find her a name.

THE FATHER: Amalia, sir.

THE MANAGER: But that is the real name of your wife. We don't want to call her by her real name.

THE FATHER: Why ever not, if it is her name? . . . Still, perhaps, if that lady must . . . [Makes a slight motion of the hand to indicate the Second Lady Lead] I see this woman here [means the Mother] as Amalia. But do as you like. [Gets more and more confused] I don't know what to say to you. Already, I begin to hear my own words ring false, as if they had another sound . . .

THE MANAGER: Don't you worry about it. It'll be our job the find the right tones. And as for her name, if you want her Amalia, Amalia it shall be; and if you don't like it, we'll find another! For the moment though, we'll call the characters in this way: [to Juvenile Lead] You are the Son; [to the Leading Lady] You naturally are the Stepdaughter . . .

THE STEPDAUGHTER: [Excitedly] What? what? I, that woman there? [Bursts out laughing]

THE MANAGER: [Angry] What is there to laugh at?

LEADING LADY: [Indignant] Nobody has ever dared to laugh at me. I insist on being treated with respect; otherwise I go away.

THE STEPDAUGHTER: No, no, excuse me . . . I am not laughing at you . . .

THE MANAGER: [To Stepdaughter] You ought to feel honored to be played by . . .

LEADING LADY: [At once, contemptuously] "That woman there" . . .

THE STEPDAUGHTER: But I wasn't speaking of you, you know. I was speaking of myself—whom I can't see at all in you! That is all. I don't know . . . but . . . you . . . aren't in the least like me . . .

THE FATHER: True. Here's the point. Look here, sir, our temperaments, our souls . . .

THE MANAGER: Temperament, soul, be hanged. Do you suppose the spirit of the piece is in you? Nothing of the kind!

THE FATHER: What, haven't we our own temperaments, our own souls?

THE MANAGER: Not at all. Your soul or whatever you like to call it takes shape here. The actors give body and form to it, voice and gesture. And my actors—I may tell you—have given expression to much more lofty material than this little drama of yours, which may or may not hold up on the stage.

But if it does, the merit of it, believe me, will be due to my actors.

THE FATHER: I don't dare contradict you, sir; but, believe me, it is a terrible suffering for us who are as we are, with these bodies of ours, these features to see . . .

THE MANAGER: [Cutting him short and out of patience] Good heavens! The make-up will remedy all that, man, the make-up . . .

THE FATHER: Maybe. But the voice, the gestures . . .

THE MANAGER: Now, look here! On the stage, you as yourself, cannot exist. The actor here acts you, and that's an end to it!

THE FATHER: I understand. And now I think I see why our author who conceived us as we are, all alive, didn't want to put us on the stage after all. I haven't the least desire to offend your actors. Far from it! But when I think that I am to be acted by . . . I don't know by whom . . .

LEADING MAN: [On his dignity] By me, if you've no objection!

THE FATHER: [Humbly, mellifluously] Honored, I assure you, sir. [Bows] Still, I must say that try as this gentleman may, with all his good will and wonderful art, to absorb me into himself . . .

LEADING MAN: Oh chuck it! "Wonderful art!" Withdraw that, please!

THE FATHER: The performance he will give, even doing his best with make-up to look like me . . .

LEADING MAN: It will certainly be a bit difficult! [The Actors laugh]

THE FATHER: Exactly! It will be difficult to act me as I really am. The effect will be rather—apart from the make-up—according as to how he supposes I am, as he senses me—if he does sense me—and not as I inside of myself feel myself to be. It seems to me then that account should be taken of this by everyone whose duty it may become to criticize us . .

THE MANAGER: Heavens! The man's starting to think about the critics now! Let them say what they like. It's up to us to put on the play if we can. [Looking around] Come on! come on! Is the stage set? [To the Actors and Characters] Stand back— stand back! Let me see, and don't let's lose any more time! [To the Stepdaughter] Is it all right as it is now?

THE STEPDAUGHTER: Well, to tell the truth, I don't recognize the scene.

THE MANAGER: My dear lady, you can't possibly suppose that we can construct that shop of Madame Pace piece by piece here? [To the Father] You said a white room with flowered wall paper, didn't you?

THE FATHER: Yes.

THE MANAGER: Well then. We've got the furniture right more or less. Bring that little table a bit further forward. [The stage hands obey the order. To Property Man] You go and find an envelope, if possible, a pale blue one; and give it to that gentleman. [Indicates Father]

PROPERTY MAN: An ordinary envelope?

MANAGER AND FATHER: Yes, yes, an ordinary envelope.

PROPERTY MAN: At once, sir. [Exit]

THE MANAGER: Ready, everyone! First scene—the Young Lady. [The Leading Lady comes forward] No, no, you must wait. I meant her. [Indicating the Stepdaughter] You just watch—

THE STEPDAUGHTER: [Adding at once] How I shall play it, how I shall live it! . . .

LEADING LADY: [Offended] I shall live it also, you may be sure, as soon as I begin!

THE MANAGER: [With his hands to his head] Ladies and gentlemen, if you please! No more useless discussions! Scene I: the young lady with Madame Pace: Oh! [Looks around as if lost] And this Madame Pace, where is she?

THE FATHER: She isn't with us, sir.

THE MANAGER: Then what the devil's to be done?

THE FATHER: But she is alive too.

THE MANAGER: Yes, but where is she?

THE FATHER: One minute. Let me speak! [Turning to the Actresses] If these ladies would be so good as to give me their hats for a moment . . .

THE ACTRESSES: [Half surprised, half laughing, in chorus] What?
Why?
Our hats?
What does he say?

THE MANAGER: What are you going to do with the ladies' hats? [The Actors laugh]

THE FATHER: Oh nothing. I just want to put them on these pegs for a moment. And one of the ladies will be so kind as to take off her mantle . . .

THE ACTORS: Oh, what d'you think of that? Only the mantle?
He must be mad.

SOME ACTRESSES: But why?
Mantles as well?

THE FATHER: To hang them up here for a moment. Please be so kind, will you?

THE ACTRESSES: [Taking off their hats, one or two also their cloaks, and going to hang them on the racks] After all, why not?
There you are!
This is really funny.
We've got to put them on show.

THE FATHER: Exactly; just like that, on show.

THE MANAGER: May we know why?

THE FATHER: I'll tell you. Who knows if, by arranging the stage for her, she does not come here herself, attracted by the very articles of her trade? [Inviting the Actors to look towards the exit at back of stage] Look! Look!

[The door at the back of stage opens and Madame Pace enters and takes a few steps forward. She is a fat, oldish woman with puffy oxygenated hair. She is rouged and powdered, *dressed with a comical elegance in black silk. Round her waist is a long silver chain from which hangs a pair of scissors. The* Step-daughter *runs over to her at once amid the stupor of the* Actors]

THE STEPDAUGHTER: [*Turning towards her*] There she is! There she is!

THE FATHER: [*Radiant*] It's she! I said so, didn't I? There she is!

THE MANAGER: [*Conquering his surprise, and then becoming indignant*] What sort of a trick is this?

LEADING MAN: [*Almost at the same time*] What's going to happen next?

JUVENILE LEAD: Where does *she* come from?

L'INGÉNUE: They've been holding her in reserve, I guess.

LEADING LADY: A vulgar trick!

THE FATHER: [*Dominating the protests*] Excuse me, all of you! Why are you so anxious to destroy in the name of a vulgar, commonplace sense of truth, this reality which comes to birth attracted and formed by the magic of the stage itself, which has indeed more right to live here than you, since it is much truer than you—if you don't mind my saying so? Which is the actress among you who is to play Madame Pace? Well, here is Madame Pace herself. And you will allow, I fancy, that the actress who acts her will be less true than this woman here, who is herself in person. You see my daughter recognized her and went over to her at once. Now you're going to witness the scene!

[*But the scene between the* Stepdaughter *and* Madame Pace *has already begun despite the protest of the* Actors *and the reply of* The Father. *It has begun quietly, naturally, in a manner impossible for the stage. So when the* Actors, *called to attention by* The Father, *turn round and see* Madame Pace, *who has placed one hand under the* Stepdaughter's *chin to raise her head, they observe her at first with great attention, but hearing her speak in an unintelligible manner their interest begins to wane*]

THE MANAGER: Well? well?

LEADING MAN: What does she say?

LEADING LADY: One can't hear a word.

JUVENILE LEAD: Louder! Louder please!

THE STEPDAUGHTER: [*Leaving* Madame Pace, *who smiles a Sphinx-like smile, and advancing towards the Actors*] Louder? Louder? What are you talking about? These aren't matters which can be shouted at the top of one's voice. If I have spoken them out loud, it was to shame him and have my revenge. [*Indicates* Father] But for Madame it's quite a different matter.

THE MANAGER: Indeed? indeed? But here, you know, people have got to make themselves heard, my dear. Even we who are on the stage can't hear you. What will it be when the public's in the theater? And anyway, you can very well speak up now

among yourselves, since we shan't be present to listen to you as we are now. You've got to pretend to be alone in a room at the back of a shop where no one can hear you.

[The Stepdaughter *coquettishly and with a touch of malice makes a sign of disagreement two or three times with her finger*]

THE MANAGER: What do you mean by no?

THE STEPDAUGHTER: [*Sotto voce, mysteriously*] There's someone who will hear us if she [*indicating* Madame Pace] speaks out loud.

THE MANAGER: [*In consternation*] What? Have you got someone else to spring on us now? [*The* Actors *burst out laughing*]

THE FATHER: No, no sir. She is alluding to me. I've got to be here—there behind that door, in waiting; and Madame Pace knows it. In fact, if you will allow me, I'll go there at once, so I can be quite ready. [*Moves away*]

THE MANAGER: [*Stopping him*] No! wait! wait! We must observe the conventions of the theater. Before you are ready . . .

THE STEPDAUGHTER: [*Interrupting him*] No, get on with it at once! I'm just dying, I tell you, to act this scene. If he's ready, I'm more than ready.

THE MANAGER: [*Shouting*] But, my dear young lady, first of all, we must have the scene between you and this lady . . . [*Indicates* Madame Pace] Do you understand? . . .

THE STEPDAUGHTER: Good Heavens! She's been telling me what you know already: that mamma's work is badly done again, that the material's ruined; and that if I want her to continue to help us in our misery I must be patient . . .

MADAME PACE: [*Coming forward with an air of great importance*] Yes indeed, sir, I no wanta take advantage of her, I no wanta be hard . . .

[*Note:* Madame Pace *is supposed to talk in a jargon half Italian, half English*]

THE MANAGER: [*Alarmed*] What? What? she talks like that? [*The* Actors *burst out laughing again*]

THE STEPDAUGHTER: [*Also laughing*] Yes, yes, that's the way she talks, half English, half Italian! Most comical it is!

MADAME PACE: Itta seem not verra polite gentlemen laugha atta me eef I trya best speaka English.

THE MANAGER: *Diamine!* Of course! Of course! Let her talk like that! Just what we want. Talk just like that, Madame, if you please! The effect will be certain. Exactly what was wanted to put a little comic relief into the crudity of the situation. Of course she talks like that! Magnificent!

THE STEPDAUGHTER: Magnificent? Certainly! When certain suggestions are made to one in language of that kind, the effect is certain, since it seems almost a joke. One feels inclined to laugh when one hears her talk about an "old signore" "who wanta talka nicely with you." Nice old signore, eh, Madame?

MADAME PACE: Not so old, my dear, not so old!

And even if you no lika him, he won't make any scandal!

THE MOTHER: [*Jumping up amid the amazement and consternation of the* Actors *who had not been noticing her. They move to restrain her*] You old devil! You murderess!

THE STEPDAUGHTER: [*Running over to calm her* Mother] Calm yourself, mother, calm yourself! Please don't . . .

THE FATHER: [*Going to her also at the same time*] Calm yourself! Don't get excited! Sit down now!

THE MOTHER: Well then, take that woman away out of my sight!

THE STEPDAUGHTER: [*To* Manager] It is impossible for my mother to remain here.

THE FATHER: [*To* Manager] They can't be here together. And for this reason, you see: that woman there was not with us when we came . . . If they are on together, the whole thing is given away inevitably, as you see.

THE MANAGER: It doesn't matter. This is only a first rough sketch—just to get an idea of the various points of the scene, even confusedly . . . [*Turning to the* Mother *and leading her to her chair*] Come along, my dear lady, sit down now, and let's get on with the scene . . .

[*Meanwhile, the* Stepdaughter, *coming forward again, turns to* Madame Pace]

THE STEPDAUGHTER: Come on, Madame, come on!

MADAME PACE: [*Offended*] No, no, *grazie*. I not do anything witha your mother present.

THE STEPDAUGHTER: Nonsense! Introduce this "old signore" who wants to talk nicely to me. [*Addressing the company imperiously*] We've got to do this scene one way or another, haven't we? Come on! [*To* Madame Pace] You can go!

MADAME PACE: Ah yes! I go'way! I go'way! Certainly! [*Exits furious*]

THE STEPDAUGHTER: [*To the* Father] Now you make your entry. No, you needn't go over here. Come here. Let's suppose you've already come in. Like that, yes! I'm here with bowed head, modest like. Come on! Out with your voice! Say "Good morning, Miss" in that peculiar tone, that special tone . . .

THE MANAGER: Excuse me, but are you the Manager, or am I? [*To the* Father, *who looks undecided and perplexed*] Get on with it, man! Go down there to the back of the stage. You needn't go off. Then come right forward here.

[*The* Father *does as he is told, looking troubled and perplexed at first. But as soon as he begins to move, the reality of the action affects him, and he begins to smile and to be more natural. The* Actors *watch intently*]

THE MANAGER: [*Sotto voce, quickly to the* Prompter *in his box*] Ready! ready? Get ready to write now.

THE FATHER: [*Coming forward and speaking in a different tone*] Good afternoon, Miss!

THE STEPDAUGHTER: [*Head bowed down slightly, with restrained disgust*] Good afternoon!

THE FATHER: [*Looks under her hat which partly covers her face. Perceiving she is very young, he makes an exclamation, partly of surprise, partly of fear lest he compromise himself in a risky adventure*] Ah . . . but . . . ah . . . I say . . . this is not the first time that you have come here, is it?

THE STEPDAUGHTER: [*Modestly*] No sir.

THE FATHER: You've been here before, eh? [*Then seeing her nod agreement*] More than once? [*Waits for her to answer, looks under her hat, smiles, and then says*] Well then, there's no need to be so shy, is there? May I take off your hat?

THE STEPDAUGHTER: [*Anticipating him and with veiled disgust*] No sir . . . I'll do it myself. [*Takes it off quickly*]

[*The* Mother, *who watches the progress of the scene with* The Son *and the other two* Children *who cling to her, is on thorns; and follows with varying expressions of sorrow, indignation, anxiety, and horror the words and actions of the other two. From time to time she hides her face in her hands and sobs*]

THE MOTHER: Oh, my God, my God!

THE FATHER: [*Playing his part with a touch of gallantry*] Give it to me! I'll put it down. [*Takes hat from her hands*] But a dear little head like yours ought to have a smarter hat. Come and help me choose one from the stock, won't you?

L'INGÉNUE: [*Interrupting*] I say . . . those are our hats you know.

THE MANAGER: [*Furious*] Silence! silence! Don't try and be funny, if you please . . . We're playing the scene now I'd have you notice. [*To the* Stepdaughter] Begin again, please!

THE STEPDAUGHTER: [*Continuing*] No thank you, sir.

THE FATHER: Oh, come now. Don't talk like that. You must take it. I shall be upset if you don't. There are some lovely little hats here; and then— Madame will be pleased. She expects it, anyway, you know.

THE STEPDAUGHTER: No, no! I couldn't wear it!

THE FATHER: Oh, you're thinking about what they'd say at home if they saw you come in with a new hat? My dear girl, there's always a way round these little matters, you know.

THE STEPDAUGHTER: [*All keyed up*] No, it's not that. I couldn't wear it because I am . . . as you see . . . you might have noticed . . . [*Showing her black dress*]

THE FATHER: . . . in mourning! Of course: I beg your pardon: I'm frightfully sorry . . .

THE STEPDAUGHTER: [*Forcing herself to conquer her indignation and nausea*] Stop! Stop! It's I who must thank you. There's no need for you to feel mortified or specially sorry. Don't think any more of what I've said. [*Tries to smile*] I must forget that I am dressed so . . .

THE MANAGER: [*Interrupting and turning to the Prompter*] Stop a minute! Stop! Don't write that down. Cut out that last bit. [*Then to the Father and Stepdaughter*] Fine! it's going fine! [*To the Father only*] And now you can go on as we arranged. [*To the Actors*] Pretty good that scene, where he offers her the hat, eh?

THE STEPDAUGHTER: The best's coming now. Why can't we go on?

THE MANAGER: Have a little patience! [*To the Actors*] Of course, it must be treated rather lightly.

LEADING MAN: Still, with a bit of go in it!

LEADING LADY: Of course! It's easy enough! [*To Leading Man*] Shall you and I try it now?

LEADING MAN: Why, yes! I'll prepare my entrance. [*Exit in order to make his entrance*]

THE MANAGER: [*To Leading Lady*] See here! The scene between you and Madame Pace is finished. I'll have it written out properly after. You remain here . . . oh, where are you going?

LEADING LADY: One minute. I want to put my hat on again. [*Goes over to hat-rack and puts her hat on her head*]

THE MANAGER: Good! You stay here with your head bowed down a bit.

THE STEPDAUGHTER: But she isn't dressed in black.

LEADING LADY: But I shall be, and much more effectively than you.

THE MANAGER: [*To Stepdaughter*] Be quiet please, and watch! You'll be able to learn something. [*Clapping his hands*] Come on! come on! Entrance, please!

[*The door at rear of stage opens, and the Leading Man enters with the lively manner of an old gallant. The rendering of the scene by the Actors from the very first words is seen to be quite a different thing, though it has not in any way the air of a parody. Naturally, the Stepdaughter and the Father, not being able to recognize themselves in the Leading Lady and the Leading Man, who deliver their words in different tones and with a different psychology, express, sometimes with smiles, sometimes with gestures, the impression they receive*]

LEADING MAN: Good afternoon, Miss . . .

THE FATHER: [*At once unable to contain himself*] No! no!

[*The Stepdaughter noticing the way the Leading Man enters, bursts out laughing*]

THE MANAGER: [*Furious*] Silence! And you please just stop that laughing. If we go on like this, we shall never finish.

THE STEPDAUGHTER: Forgive me, sir, but it's natural enough. This lady [*indicating Leading Lady*] stands there still; but if she is supposed to be me, I can assure you that if I heard anyone say "Good afternoon" in that manner and in that tone, I should burst out laughing as I did.

THE FATHER: Yes, yes, the manner, the tone . . .

THE MANAGER: Nonsense! Rubbish! Stand aside and let me see the action.

LEADING MAN: If I've got to represent an old fellow who's coming into a house of an equivocal character . . .

THE MANAGER: Don't listen to them, for Heaven's sake! Do it again! It goes fine. [*Waiting for the Actors to begin again*] Well?

LEADING MAN: Good afternoon, Miss.

LEADING LADY: Good afternoon.

LEADING MAN. [*Imitating the gesture of the Father when he looked under the hat, and then expressing quite clearly first satisfaction and then fear*] Ah, but . . . I say . . . this is not the first time that you have come here, is it?

THE MANAGER: Good, but not quite so heavily. Like this. [*Acts himself*] "This isn't the first time that you have come here" . . . [*To Leading Lady*] And you say: "No, sir."

LEADING LADY: No, sir.

LEADING MAN: You've been here before, more than once.

THE MANAGER: No, no, stop! Let her nod "yes" first. "You've been here before, eh?" [*The Leading Lady lifts up her head slightly and closes her eyes as though in disgust. Then she inclines her head twice*]

THE STEPDAUGHTER: [*Unable to contain herself*] Oh my God! [*Puts a hand to her mouth to prevent herself from laughing*]

THE MANAGER: [*Turning round*] What's the matter?

THE STEPDAUGHTER: Nothing, nothing!

THE MANAGER: [*To Leading Man*] Go on!

LEADING MAN: You've been here before, eh? Well then, there's no need to be so shy, is there? May I take off your hat?

[*The Leading Man says this last speech in such a tone and with such gestures that the Stepdaughter, though she has her hand to her mouth, cannot keep from laughing*]

LEADING LADY: [*Indignant*] I'm not going to stop here to be made a fool of by that woman there.

LEADING MAN: Neither am I! I'm through with it!

THE MANAGER: [*Shouting to Stepdaughter*] Silence! for once and all, I tell you!

THE STEPDAUGHTER: Forgive me! forgive me!

THE MANAGER: You haven't any manners: that's what it is! You go too far.

THE FATHER: [*Endeavoring to intervene*] Yes, it's true, but excuse her . . .

THE MANAGER: Excuse what? It's absolutely disgusting.

THE FATHER: Yes, sir, but believe me, it has such a strange effect when . . .

THE MANAGER: Strange? Why strange? Where is it strange?

THE FATHER: No, sir; I admire your actors—this gentleman here, this lady; but they are certainly not us!

THE MANAGER: I should hope not. Evidently they cannot be you, if they are actors.

THE FATHER: Just so: actors! Both of them act our parts exceedingly well. But, believe me, it produces quite a different effect on us. They want to be us, but they aren't, all the same.

THE MANAGER: What is it then anyway?

THE FATHER: Something that is . . . that is theirs —and no longer ours . . .

THE MANAGER: But naturally, inevitably. I've told you so already.

THE FATHER: Yes, I understand . . . I understand . . .

THE MANAGER: Well then, let's have no more of it! [Turning to the Actors] We'll have the rehearsals by ourselves, afterwards, in the ordinary way. I never could stand rehearsing with the author present. He's never satisfied! [Turning to Father and Stepdaughter] Come on! Let's get on with it again; and try and see if you can't keep from laughing.

THE STEPDAUGHTER: Oh, I shan't laugh any more. There's a nice little bit coming for me now: you'll see.

THE MANAGER: Well then: when she says "Don't think any more of what I've said. I must forget, etc.," you [addressing the Father] come in sharp with "I understand, I understand"; and then you ask her . . .

THE STEPDAUGHTER: [Interrupting] What?

THE MANAGER: Why she is in mourning.

THE STEPDAUGHTER: Not at all! See here: when I told him that it was useless for me to be thinking about my wearing mourning, do you know how he answered me? "Ah well," he said, "then let's take off this little frock."

THE MANAGER: Great! Just what we want, to make a riot in the theater!

THE STEPDAUGHTER: But it's the truth!

THE MANAGER: What does that matter? Acting is our business here. Truth up to a certain point, but no further.

THE STEPDAUGHTER: What do you want to do then?

THE MANAGER: You'll see, you'll see! Leave it to me.

THE STEPDAUGHTER: No sir! What you want to do is to piece together a little romantic sentimental scene out of my disgust, out of all the reasons, each more cruel and viler than the other, why I am what I am. He is to ask me why I'm in mourning; and I'm to answer with tears in my eyes, that it is just two months since papa died. No sir, no! He's got to say to me; as he did say: "Well, let's take off this little dress at once." And I; with my two months' mourning in my heart, went there behind that screen, and with these fingers tingling with shame . . .

THE MANAGER: [Running his hands through his hair] For Heaven's sake! What are you saying?

THE STEPDAUGHTER: [Crying out excitedly] The truth! The truth!

THE MANAGER: It may be. I don't deny it, and I can understand all your horror; but you must surely see that you can't have this kind of thing on the stage. It won't go.

THE STEPDAUGHTER: Not possible, eh? Very well! I'm much obliged to you—but I'm off!

THE MANAGER: Now be reasonable! Don't lose your temper!

THE STEPDAUGHTER: I won't stop here! I won't! I can see you've fixed it all up with him in your office. All this talk about what is possible for the stage . . . I understand! He wants to get at his complicated "cerebral drama," to have his famous remorses and torments acted; but I want to act my part, my part!

THE MANAGER: [Annoyed, shaking his shoulders] Ah! Just your part! But, if you will pardon me, there are other parts than yours: his [indicating the Father] and hers! [Indicating the Mother] On the stage you can't have a character becoming too prominent and overshadowing all the others. The thing is to pack them all into a neat little framework and then act what is actable. I am aware of the fact that everyone has his own interior life which he wants very much to put forward. But the difficulty lies in this fact: to set out just so much as is necessary for the stage, taking the other characters into consideration, and at the same time hint at the unrevealed interior life of each. I am willing to admit, my dear young lady, that from your point of view it would be a fine idea if each character could tell the public all his troubles in a nice monologue or a regular one-hour lecture. [Good humoredly] You must restrain yourself, my dear, and in your own interest, too; because this fury of yours, this exaggerated disgust you show, may make a bad impression, you know. After you have confessed to me that there were others before him at Madame Pace's and more than once . . .

THE STEPDAUGHTER: [Bowing her head, impressed] It's true. But remember those others mean him for me all the same.

THE MANAGER: [Not understanding] What? The others? What do you mean?

THE STEPDAUGHTER: For one who has gone wrong, sir, he who was responsible for the first fault is responsible for all that follow. He is responsible for my faults, was, even before I was born. Look at him, and see if it isn't true!

THE MANAGER: Well, well! And does the weight of so much responsibility seem nothing to you? Give him a chance to act it, to get it over!

THE STEPDAUGHTER: How? How can he act all his "noble remorses" all his "moral torments," if you want to spare him the horror of being discovered one day—after he had asked her what he did ask her—in the arms of her, that already fallen woman, that child, sir, that child he used to watch come out of school? [*She is moved*]

> [The Mother *at this point is overcome with emotion, and breaks out into a fit of crying. All are touched. A long pause*]

THE STEPDAUGHTER: [*As soon as the* Mother *becomes a little quieter, adds resolutely and gravely*] At present, we are unknown to the public. Tomorrow, you will act us as you wish, treating us in your own manner. But do you really want to see drama, do you want to see it flash out as it really did?

THE MANAGER: Of course! That's just what I do want, so I can use as much of it as is possible.

THE STEPDAUGHTER: Well then, ask that Mother there to leave us.

THE MOTHER: [*Changing her low plaint into a sharp cry*] No! No! Don't permit it, sir, don't permit it!

THE MANAGER: But it's only to try it.

THE MOTHER: I can't bear it. I can't.

THE MANAGER: But since it has happened already . . . I don't understand!

THE MOTHER: It's taking place now. It happens all the time. My torment isn't a pretended one. I live and feel every minute of my torture. Those two children there—have you heard them speak? They can't speak any more. They cling to me to keep my torment actual and vivid for me. But for themselves, they do not exist, they aren't any more. And she [*indicating* Stepdaughter] has run away, she has left me, and is lost. If I now see her here before me, it is only to renew for me the tortures I have suffered for her too.

THE FATHER: The eternal moment! She [*indicating the* Stepdaughter] is here to catch me, fix me, and hold me eternally in the stocks for that one fleeting and shameful moment of my life. She can't give it up! And you sir, cannot either fairly spare me it.

THE MANAGER: I never said I didn't want to act it. It will form, as a matter of fact, the nucleus of the whole first act right up to her surprise. [*Indicating the* Mother]

THE FATHER: Just so! This is my punishment: the passion in all of us that must culminate in her final cry.

THE STEPDAUGHTER: I can hear it still in my ears. It's driven me mad, that cry!—You can put me on as you like; it doesn't matter. Fully dressed, if you like—provided I have at least the arm bare; because, standing like this [*she goes close to the* Father *and leans her head on his breast*] with my head so, and my arms round his neck, I saw a vein pulsing in my arm here; and then, as if that live vein had awakened disgust in me, I closed my eyes like this, and let my head sink on his breast. [*Turning to the* Mother] Cry out, mother! Cry out! [*Buries head in* Father's *breast, and with her shoulders raised as if to prevent her hearing the cry, adds in tones of intense emotion*] Cry out as you did then!

THE MOTHER: [*Coming forward to separate them*] No! My daughter, my daughter! [*And after having pulled her away from him*] You brute! you brute! She is my daughter! Don't you see she's my daughter?

THE MANAGER: [*Walking backwards towards footlights*] Fine! fine! Damned good! And then, of course—curtain!

THE FATHER: [*Going towards him excitedly*] Yes, of course, because that's the way it really happened.

THE MANAGER: [*Convinced and pleased*] Oh, yes, no doubt about it. Curtain here, curtain!

> [*At the reiterated cry of* The Manager, The Machinist *lets the curtain down, leaving* The Manager *and* The Father *in front of it before the footlights*]

THE MANAGER: The darned idiot! I said "curtain" to show the act should end there, and he goes and lets it down in earnest. [*To the* Father, *while he pulls the curtain back to go on to the stage again*] Yes, yes, it's all right. Effect certain! That's the right ending. I'll guarantee the first act at any rate.

ACT III.

When the curtain goes up again, it is seen that the stage hands have shifted the bit of scenery used in the last part, and have rigged up instead at the back of the stage a drop, with some trees, and one or two wings. A portion of a fountain basin is visible. The Mother *is sitting on the* Right *with the two children by her side. The* Son *is on the same side, but away from the others. He seems bored, angry, and full of shame. The* Father *and* The Stepdaughter *are also seated towards the* Right *front. On the other side (*Left*) are the* Actors, *much in the positions they occupied before the curtain was lowered. Only* The Manager *is standing up in the middle of the stage, with his hand closed over his mouth in the act of meditating.*

THE MANAGER: [*Shaking his shoulders after a brief pause*] Ah yes: the second act! Leave it to me, leave it all to me as we arranged, and you'll see! It'll go fine!

THE STEPDAUGHTER: Our entry into his house [*indicates* Father] in spite of him . . . [*indicates the* Son]

THE MANAGER: [*Out of patience*] Leave it to me, I tell you!

THE STEPDAUGHTER: Do let it be clear, at any rate, that it is in spite of my wishes.

THE MOTHER: [*From her corner, shaking her head*] For all the good that's come of it . . .

THE STEPDAUGHTER: [*Turning towards her quickly*] It doesn't matter. The more harm done us, the more remorse for him.

THE MANAGER: [*Impatiently*] I understand! Good

Heavens! I understand! I'm taking it into account.

THE MOTHER: [*Supplicatingly*] I beg you, sir, to let it appear quite plain that for conscience' sake I did try in every way . . .

THE STEPDAUGHTER: [*Interrupting indignantly and continuing for the* Mother] . . . to pacify me, to dissuade me from spiting him. [*To* Manager] Do as she wants: satisfy her, because it is true! I enjoy it immensely. Anyhow, as you can see, the meeker she is, the more she tries to get at his heart, the more distant and aloof does he become.

THE MANAGER: Are we going to begin this second act or not?

THE STEPDAUGHTER: I'm not going to talk any more now. But I must tell you this: you can't have the whole action take place in the garden, as you suggest. It isn't possible!

THE MANAGER: Why not?

THE STEPDAUGHTER: Because he [*indicates the* Son *again*] is always shut up alone in his room. And then there's all the part of that poor dazed-looking boy there which takes place indoors.

THE MANAGER: Maybe! On the other hand, you will understand—we can't change scenes three or four times in one act.

THE LEADING MAN: They used to once.

THE MANAGER: Yes, when the public was up to the level of that child there.

THE LEADING LADY: It makes the illusion easier.

THE FATHER: [*Irritated*] The illusion! For Heaven's sake, don't say illusion. Please don't use that word, which is particularly painful for us.

THE MANAGER: [*Astounded*] And why, if you please?

THE FATHER: It's painful, cruel, really cruel; and you ought to understand that.

THE MANAGER: But why? What ought we to say then? The illusion, I tell you, sir, which we've got to create for the audience . . .

THE LEADING MAN: With our acting.

THE MANAGER: The illusion of a reality.

THE FATHER: I understand; but you, perhaps, do not understand us. Forgive me! You see . . . here for you and your actors, the thing is only—and rightly so . . . a kind of game . . .

THE LEADING LADY: [*Interrupting indignantly*] A game! We're not children here, if you please! We are serious actors.

THE FATHER: I don't deny it. What I mean is the game, or play, of your art, which has to give, as the gentleman says, a perfect illusion of reality.

THE MANAGER: Precisely——!

THE FATHER: Now, if you consider the fact that we [*indicates himself and the other five* Characters], as we are, have no other reality outside of this illusion . . .

THE MANAGER: [*Astonished, looking at his* Actors, *who are also amazed*] And what does that mean?

THE FATHER: [*After watching them for a moment with a wan smile*] As I say, sir, that which is a game of art for you is our sole reality. [*Brief pause. He goes a step or two nearer the* Manager *and adds*] But not only for us, you know, by the way. Just you think it over well. [*Looks him in the eyes*] Can you tell me who you are?

THE MANAGER: [*Perplexed, half smiling*] What? Who am I? I am myself.

THE FATHER: And if I were to tell you that that isn't true, because you are I? . . .

THE MANAGER: I should say you were mad——! [*The* Actors *laugh*]

THE FATHER: You're quite right to laugh: because we are all making believe here. [*To* Manager] And you can therefore object that it's only for a joke that that gentleman there [*indicates the* Leading Man], who naturally is himself, has to be me, who am on the contrary myself—this thing you see here. You see I've caught you in a trap! [*The* Actors *laugh*]

THE MANAGER: [*Annoyed*] But we've had all this over once before. Do you want to begin again?

THE FATHER: No, no! that wasn't my meaning! In fact, I should like to request you to abandon this game of art [*Looking at the* Leading Lady *as if anticipating her*] which you are accustomed to play here with your actors, and to ask you seriously once again: who are you?

THE MANAGER: [*Astonished and irritated, turning to his* Actors] If this fellow here hasn't got a nerve! A man who calls himself a character comes and asks me who I am!

THE FATHER: [*With dignity, but not offended*] A character, sir, may always ask a man who he is. Because a character has really a life of his own, marked with his especial characteristics; for which reason he is always "somebody." But a man—I'm not speaking of you now—may very well be "nobody."

THE MANAGER: Yes, but you are asking these questions of me, the boss, the manager! Do you understand?

THE FATHER: But only in order to know if you, as you really are now, see yourself as you once were with all the illusions that were yours then, with all the things both inside and outside of you as they seemed to you—as they were then indeed for you. Well, sir, if you think of all those illusions that mean nothing to you now, of all those things which don't even *seem* to you to exist any more, while once they *were* for you, don't you feel that—I won't say these boards—but the very earth under your feet is sinking away from you when you reflect that in the same way this *you* as you feel it today—all this present reality of yours—is fated to seem a mere illusion to you tomorrow?

THE MANAGER: [*Without having understood much, but astonished by the specious argument*] Well, well! And where does all this take us anyway?

THE FATHER: Oh, nowhere! It's only to show you that if we [*indicating the* Characters] have no other reality beyond illusion, you too must not count over-much on your reality as you feel it today, since, like that of yesterday, it may prove an illusion for you tomorrow.

THE MANAGER: [*Determining to make fun of him*] Ah, excellent! Then you'll be saying next that you, with this comedy of yours that you brought here to act, are truer and more real than I am.

THE FATHER: [*With the greatest seriousness*] But of course; without doubt!

THE MANAGER: Ah, really?

THE FATHER: Why, I thought you'd understand that from the beginning.

THE MANAGER: More real than I?

THE FATHER: If your reality can change from one day to another . . .

THE MANAGER: But everyone knows it can change. It is always changing, the same as anyone else's.

THE FATHER: [*With a cry*] No, sir, not ours! Look here! That is the very difference! Our reality doesn't change: it can't change! It can't be other than what it is, because it is already fixed for ever. It's terrible. Ours is an immutable reality which should make you shudder when you approach us if you are really conscious of the fact that your reality is a mere transitory and fleeting illusion, taking this form to-day and that tomorrow, according to the conditions, according to your will, your sentiments, which in turn are controlled by an intellect that shows them to you today in one manner and tomorrow . . . who knows how? . . . Illusions of reality represented in this fatuous comedy of life that never ends, nor can ever end! Because if tomorrow it were to end . . . then why, all would be finished.

THE MANAGER: Oh for God's sake, will you *at least* finish with this philosophizing and let us try and shape this comedy which you yourself have brought me here? You argue and philosophize a bit too much, my dear sir. You know you seem to me almost, almost . . . [*Stops and looks him over from head to foot*] Ah, by the way, I think you introduced yourself to me as a—what shall . . . we say—a "character," created by an author who did not afterwards care to make a drama of his own creations.

THE FATHER: It is the simple truth, sir.

THE MANAGER: Nonsense! Cut that out, please! None of us believes it, because it isn't a thing, as you must recognize yourself, which one can believe seriously. If you want to know, it seems to me you are trying to imitate the manner of a certain author whom I heartily detest—I warn you—although I have unfortunately bound myself to put on one of his works. As a matter of fact, I was just starting to rehearse it, when you arrived. [*Turning to the Actors*] And this is what we've gained—out of the frying-pan into the fire!

THE FATHER: I don't know to what author you may be alluding, but believe me I feel what I think; and I seem to be philosophizing only for those who do not think what they feel, because they blind themselves with their own sentiment. I know that for many people this self-blinding seems much more "human"; but the contrary is really true. For man never reasons so much and becomes so introspective as when he suffers; since he is anxious to get at the cause of his sufferings, to learn who has produced them, and whether it is just or unjust that he should have to bear them. On the other hand, when he is happy, he takes his happiness as it comes and doesn't analyze it, just as if happiness were his right. The animals suffer without reasoning about their sufferings. But take the case of a man who suffers and begins to reason about it. Oh no! it can't be allowed! Let him suffer like an animal, and then—ah yes, he is "human!"

THE MANAGER: Look here! Look here! You're off again, philosophizing worse than ever.

THE FATHER: Because I suffer, sir! I'm not philosophizing: I'm crying aloud the reason of my sufferings.

THE MANAGER: [*Makes brusque movement as he is taken with a new idea*] I should like to know if anyone has ever heard of a character who gets right out of his part and perorates and speechifies as you do. Have you ever heard of a case? I haven't.

THE FATHER: You have never met such a case, sir, because authors, as a rule, hide the labor of their creations. When the characters are really alive before their author, the latter does nothing but follow them in their action, in their words, in the situations which they suggest to him; and he has to will them the way they will themselves—for there's trouble if he doesn't. When a character is born, he acquires at once such an independence, even of his own author, that he can be imagined by everybody even in many other situations where the author never dreamed of placing him; and so he acquires for himself a meaning which the author never thought of giving him.

THE MANAGER: Yes, yes, I know this.

THE FATHER: What is there then to marvel at in us? Imagine such a misfortune for characters as I have described to you: to be born of an author's fantasy, and be denied life by him; and then answer me if these characters left alive, and yet without life, weren't right in doing what they did do and are doing now, after they have attempted every-thing in their power to persuade him to give them their stage life. We've all tried him in turn, I, she [*indicating the* Stepdaughter] and she. [*Indicating the* Mother]

THE STEPDAUGHTER: It's true. I too have sought to tempt him, many, many times, when he has been sitting at his writing table, feeling a bit melan-choly, at the twilight hour. He would sit in his arm-chair too lazy to switch on the light, and all the shadows that crept into his room were full of our presence coming to tempt him. [*As if she saw her-self still there by the writing table, and was annoyed* by the presence of the Actors] Oh, if you would only go away, go away and leave us alone—mother here with that son of hers—·I with that Child—that Boy there always alone—and then I with him—[just hints at the Father]—and then I alone, alone . . . in those shadows! [Makes a sudden movement as if in the vision she has of herself illuminating those shadows she wanted to seize hold of herself] Ah! my life! my life! Oh, what scenes we proposed to him—and I tempted him more than any of the others!

THE FATHER: Maybe. But perhaps it was your fault that he refused to give us life: because you were too insistent, too troublesome.

THE STEPDAUGHTER: Nonsense! Didn't he make me so himself? [Goes close to the Manager to tell him as if in confidence] In my opinion he abandoned us in a fit of depression, of disgust for the ordinary theater as the public knows it and likes it.

THE SON: Exactly what it was, sir; exactly that!

THE FATHER: Not at all! Don't believe it for a minute. Listen to me! You'll be doing quite right to modify, as you suggest, the excesses both of this girl here, who wants to do too much, and of this young man, who won't do anything at all.

THE SON: No, nothing!

THE MANAGER: You too get over the mark occasionally, my dear sir, if I may say so.

THE FATHER: I? When? Where?

THE MANAGER: Always! Continuously! Then there's this insistence of yours in trying to make us believe you are a character. And then too, you must really argue and philosophize less, you know, much less.

THE FATHER: Well, if you want to take away from me the possibility of representing the torment of my spirit which never gives me peace, you will be suppressing me: that's all. Every true man, sir, who is a little above the level of the beasts and plants does not live for the sake of living, without knowing how to live; but he lives so as to give a meaning and a value of his own to life. For me this is everything. I cannot give up this, just to represent a mere fact as she [indicating the Stepdaughter] wants. It's all very well for her, since her "vendetta" lies in the "fact." I'm not going to do it. It destroys my raison d'être.

THE MANAGER: Your raison d'être! Oh, we're going ahead fine! First she starts off, and then you jump in. At this rate, we'll never finish.

THE FATHER: Now, don't be offended! Have it your own way—provided, however, that within the limits of the parts you assign us each one's sacrifice isn't too great.

THE MANAGER: You've got to understand that you can't go on arguing at your own pleasure. Drama is action, sir, action and not confounded philosophy.

THE FATHER: All right. I'll do just as much arguing and philosophizing as everybody does when he is considering his own torments.

THE MANAGER: If the drama permits! But for Heaven's sake, man, let's get along and come to the scene.

THE STEPDAUGHTER: It seems to me we've got too much action with our coming into his house. [Indicating Father] You said, before, you couldn't change the scene every five minutes.

THE MANAGER: Of course not. What we've got to do is to combine and group up all the facts in one simultaneous, close-knit action. We can't have it as you want, with your little brother wandering like a ghost from room to room, hiding behind doors and meditating a project which—what did you say it did to him?

THE STEPDAUGHTER: Consumes him, sir, wastes him away!

THE MANAGER: Well, it may be. And then at the same time, you want the little girl there to be playing in the garden . . . one in the house, and the other in the garden: isn't that it?

THE STEPDAUGHTER: Yes, in the sun, in the sun! That is my only pleasure: to see her happy and careless in the garden after the misery and squalor of the horrible room where we all four slept together. And I had to sleep with her—I, do you understand?—with my vile contaminated body next to hers; with her folding me fast in her loving little arms. In the garden, whenever she spied me, she would run to take me by the hand. She didn't care for the big flowers, only the little ones; and she loved to show me them and pet me.

THE MANAGER: Well then, we'll have it in the garden. Everything shall happen in the garden; and we'll group the other scenes there. [Calls a stage hand] Here, a back-cloth with trees and something to do as a fountain basin. [Turning round to look at the back of the stage] Ah, you've fixed it up. Good! [To Stepdaughter] This is just to give an idea, of course. The Boy, instead of hiding behind the doors, will wander about here in the garden, hiding behind the trees. But it's going to be rather difficult to find a child to do that scene with you where she shows you the flowers. [Turning to the Youth] Come forward a little, will you please? Let's try it now! Come along! come along! [Then seeing him come shyly forward, full of fear and looking lost] It's a nice business, this lad here. What's the matter with him? We'll have to give him a word or two to say. [Goes close to him, puts a hand on his shoulders, and leads him behind one of the trees] Come on! come on! Let me see you a little! Hide here . . . yes, like that. Try and show your head just a little as if you were looking for someone . . . [Goes back to observe the effect, when the Boy at once goes through the action] Excellent! fine! [Turning to Stepdaughter] Suppose the little girl there were to surprise him as he looks round, and run over to him, so we could give him a word or two to say?

THE STEPDAUGHTER: It's useless to hope he will

speak, as long as that fellow there is here . . . [*Indicates the* Son] You must send him away first.

THE SON: [*Jumping up*] Delighted! delighted! I don't ask for anything better. [*Begins to move away*]

THE MANAGER: [*At once stopping him*] No! No! Where are you going? Wait a bit!

[*The* Mother *gets up alarmed and terrified at the thought that he is really about to go away. Instinctively she lifts her arms to prevent him, without, however, leaving her seat*]

THE SON: [*To* Manager *who stops him*] I've got nothing to do with this affair. Let me go please! Let me go!

THE MANAGER: What do you mean by saying you've got nothing to do with this?

THE STEPDAUGHTER: [*Calmly, with irony*] Don't bother to stop him: he won't go away.

THE FATHER: He has to act the terrible scene in the garden with his mother.

THE SON: [*Suddenly resolute and with dignity*] I shall act nothing at all. I've said so from the very beginning [*To the* Manager] Let me go!

THE STEPDAUGHTER: [*Going over to the* Manager] Allow me? [*Puts down the* Manager's *arm which is restraining the* Son] Well, go away then, if you want to! [*The* Son *looks at her with contempt and hatred. She laughs and says*] You see, he can't, he can't go away! He is obliged to stay here, indissolubly bound to the chain. If I, who fly off when that happens which has to happen, because I can't bear him—if I am still here and support that face and expression of his, you can well imagine that he is unable to move. He has to remain here, has to stop with that nice father of his, and that mother whose only son he is. [*Turning to the* Mother] Come on, mother, come along! [*Turning to* Manager *to indicate her*] You see, she was getting up to keep him back. [*To the* Mother, *beckoning her with her hand*] Come on! come on! [*Then to* Manager] You can imagine how little she wants to show these actors of yours what she really feels; but so eager is she to get near him that . . . There, you see? She is willing to act her part. [*And in fact, the* Mother *approaches him; and as soon as the* Stepdaughter *has finished speaking, opens her arms to signify that she consents*]

THE SON: [*Suddenly*] No! no! If I can't go away, then I'll stop here; but I repeat: I act nothing!

THE FATHER: [*To* Manager *excitedly*] You can force him, sir.

THE SON: Nobody can force me.

THE FATHER: I can.

THE STEPDAUGHTER: Wait a minute, wait . . . First of all, the baby has to go to the fountain . . . [*Runs to take the* Child *and leads her to the fountain*]

THE MANAGER: Yes, yes of course; that's it. Both at the same time.

[*The second* Lady Lead *and the* Juvenile Lead *at this point separate themselves from the group of* Actors. *One watches the* Mother *attentively; the other moves about studying the movements and manner of the* Son *whom he will have to act*]

THE SON: [*To* Manager] What do you mean by both at the same time? It isn't right. There was no scene between me and her. [*Indicates the* Mother] Ask her how it was!

THE MOTHER: Yes, it's true. I had come into his room . . .

THE SON: Into my room, do you understand? Nothing to do with the garden.

THE MANAGER: It doesn't matter. Haven't I told you we've got to group the action?

THE SON: [*Observing the* Juvenile Lead *studying him*] What do you want?

THE JUVENILE LEAD: Nothing! I was just looking at you.

THE SON: [*Turning towards the* Second Lady Lead] Ah! she's at it too: to re-act her part. [*Indicating the* Mother]!

THE MANAGER: Exactly! And it seems to me that you ought to be grateful to them for their interest.

THE SON: Yes, but haven't you yet perceived that it isn't possible to live in front of a mirror which not only freezes us with the image of ourselves, but throws our likeness back at us with a horrible grimace?

THE FATHER: That is true, absolutely true. You must see that.

THE MANAGER: [*To* Second Lady Lead *and* Juvenile Lead] He's right! Move away from them!

THE SON: Do as you like. I'm out of this!

THE MANAGER: Be quiet, you, will you? And let me hear your mother! [*To* Mother] You were saying you had entered . . .

THE MOTHER: Yes, into his room, because I couldn't stand it any longer. I went to empty my heart to him of all the anguish that tortures me . . . But as soon as he saw me come in . . .

THE SON: Nothing happened! There was no scene. I went away, that's all! I don't care for scenes!

THE MOTHER: It's true, true. That's how it was.

THE MANAGER: Well now, we've got to do this bit between you and him. It's indispensable.

THE MOTHER: I'm ready . . . when you are ready. If you could only find a chance for me to tell him what I feel here in my heart.

THE FATHER: [*Going to* Son *in a great rage*] You'll do this for your mother, for your mother, do you understand?

THE SON: [*Quite determined*] I do nothing!

THE FATHER: [*Taking hold of him and shaking him*] For God's sake, do as I tell you! Don't you hear your mother asking you for a favor? Haven't you even got the guts to be a son?

THE SON: [*Taking hold of the* Father] No! No! And for God's sake stop it, or else . . . [*General agitation. The* Mother, *frightened, tries to separate them*]

THE MOTHER: [*Pleading*] Please! please!

THE FATHER: [*Not leaving hold of the* Son] You've got to obey, do you hear?

THE SON: [*Almost crying from rage*] What does it mean, this madness you've got? [*They separate*] Have you no decency, that you insist on showing everyone our shame? I won't do it! I won't! And I stand for the will of our author in this. He didn't want to put us on the stage, after all!

THE MANAGER: Man alive! You came here . . .

THE SON: [*Indicating* Father] *He* did! I didn't!

THE MANAGER: Aren't you here now?

THE SON: It was his wish, and he dragged us along with him. He's told you not only the things that did happen, but also things that have never happened at all.

THE MANAGER: Well, tell me then what did happen. You went out of your room without saying a word?

THE SON: Without a word, so as to avoid a scene!

THE MANAGER: And then what did you do?

THE SON: Nothing . . . walking in the garden . . . [*Hesitates for a moment with expression of gloom*]

THE MANAGER: [*Coming closer to him, interested by his extraordinary reserve*] Well, well . . . walking in the garden . . .

THE SON: [*Exasperated*] Why on earth do you insist? It's horrible! [*The* Mother *trembles, sobs, and looks towards the fountain*]

THE MANAGER: [*Slowly observing the glance and turning towards the* Son *with increasing apprehension*] The baby?

THE SON: There in the fountain . . .

THE FATHER: [*Pointing with tender pity to the* Mother] She was following him at the moment . . .

THE MANAGER: [*To the* Son *anxiously*] And then you . . .

THE SON: I ran over to her; I was jumping in to drag her out when I saw something that froze my blood . . . the boy there standing stock still, with eyes like a madman's, watching his little drowned sister, in the fountain! [*The* Stepdaughter *bends over the fountain to hide the* Child. *She sobs*] Then . . . [*A revolver shot rings out behind the trees where the* Boy *is hidden*]

THE MOTHER: [*With a cry of terror runs over in that direction together with several of the* Actors *amid general confusion*] My son! My son! [*Then amid the cries and exclamations one hears her voice*] Help! Help!

THE MANAGER: [*Pushing the* Actors *aside while they lift up the* Boy *and carry him off*] Is he really wounded?

SOME ACTORS: He's dead! dead!

OTHER ACTORS: No, no, it's only make believe, it's only pretence!

THE FATHER: [*With a terrible cry*] Pretence? Reality, sir, reality!

THE MANAGER: Pretence? Reality? To hell with it all! Never in my life has such a thing happened to me. I've lost a whole day over these people, a whole day!

CURTAIN

Karel Capek

(1890–1938)

Karel Capek, the leading literary figure of Czech-oslovakia after the First World War, was born in eastern Bohemia. Son of a physician, he was a member of a talented family which included his elder brother Josef (1887–1945), who was not only his collaborator on fiction and plays but was independently prominent as a painter, scene designer, and art critic. Karel's intellectual interests were as strong as his artistic inclinations, and his studies took him to Prague, Paris, and Berlin. He became an admirer of the ideas of William James and John Dewey, and he took a doctorate in philosophy at the University of Prague, publishing a thesis on pragmatism in 1917. After graduation, he collaborated with his brother on stories and sketches, practiced journalism, and stage-managed at a theatre in Vinohrady, Czechoslovakia. He also took part in the political revival of his country and as a writer championed liberal causes.

Although he owed his international reputation chiefly to his plays, his literary work extended beyond the theatre. He published a collection of pessimistic stories (*Money and Other Stories,* 1921), two satirical fantasies (*The Absolute at Large,* 1922, and *Krakatit,* 1924) that recall the early science fiction of H. G. Wells, a volume of fables, and a Chestertonian mystery story (*Tales from Two Pockets*). Especially well received was a prose trilogy (*Hordubal,* 1933, *Meteor,* 1935, and *An Ordinary Life,* 1936) in which he told the same story from three different points of view. He gave vent to his concern over the effects of modern science and power politics in a trenchant satire, *War with the Newts* (1936), and to his social sympathies in the story of a mine disaster, *The First Rescue Party* (1937). His exposé of charlatanism, *The Cheat,* remained unfinished when he died of pneumonia on Christmas Day 1938, in time to escape the vengeance of Hitler's Gestapo; it soon fell on his brother Josef, who died in the concentration camp of Belsen. His political activity also resulted in a series of books (1928–1935) about his friend Thomas Masaryk, first president of the Czechoslovak republic, with whose democratic ideals he was obviously in full sympathy.

Capek's interest in the stage came at a time when the Czech people were witnessing the final fulfillment of their dream of developing a vital national theatre. Although a National Theatre had been established in Prague in 1881 under the management of the playwright-director Frantisek Subert (1839–1915), the project suffered from many disadvantages while Bohemia was still a province of the Austrian-Hungarian empire. After 1918, with the independence of Czechoslovakia an actuality, the National Theatre became one of the busiest cultural centers of the new republic, and Capek became its chief luminary.

Into the plays he wrote alone and in collaboration with his brother, he poured the same social interests and imagination that drew attention to his novels. In the theatre of Central Europe, moreover, there was much experimental fermentation after 1918, and Capek responded to it in his own writing. He had started a play, *The Robbers,* as early as 1911 in celebration of a Czech brigand who defied the old order. Capek completed the play in 1920 without much success, but his next two efforts, *R. U. R.* (1920) and *The Insect Comedy* (1921), brought him international fame. Two other experimental dramatic pieces, *The Makropoulos Affair* (1923), which questioned the desirability of longevity, and *Adam the Creator* (1927), a fantasy on the possibility of reconstructing civilization after man had destroyed it, attracted much attention. He continued to challenge the conscience with more conventional social protests, writing *The White Plague* (1937) as an attack on totalitarianism and *The Mother* (1938) as a warning against the war that he knew was coming. His plays made the theatre in Czechoslovakia one of the most vital in Europe before 1939. To the development of the native stage Capek, moreover, brought a keen interest in experimental stagecraft. He became an important associate of the National Theatre and co-manager, with Josef, of the experimental Vinohradsky Art Theatre.

All his plays exemplify his great theatrical virtuosity, which was well supported by his brother's expressionistic and futuristic stage designs and by the inventiveness of the Czech director Hilar. Capek's theatricality was, however, the product of an active imagination which served ideas rather than sensationalism. For *The Makropoulos Affair* (later converted into an opera by Janacek) he invented the story of a Greek woman born in the sixteenth century who is periodically rejuvenated in different countries, always wins success as an artist, and always attracts male admirers. Surviving into the twentieth century, she disillusions many people with the prospect of living forever until the formula that has ensured her survival is finally destroyed by one of the characters to whom she offers it. In *The Insect Play* (written with Josef, and produced in many countries under such titles as *And So Ad*

Infinitum and *The World We Live in*) Capek wrote a spectacle of insect life to parallel the follies and futilities of human life.

Adam the Creator presented Adam as destroying the world in disgust, with God's permission, reconstituting it as a utopia which turns out to be just as distressing as the world he destroyed with a "cannon of Negation," and finally resigning himself to accepting the *status quo*. For *R. U. R.*, apparently inspired by the rabbinical legend of a mechanical man, or "golem," in medieval Prague, Capek conjured up a world so mechanized that all labor is performed by machine-made men. He called these artificial workers "robots," deriving the word from the Czech noun for work, *robota*, and the term won international currency as a result of the success of the play. The additional fantasy of a revolt of the robots, their destruction of humanity, and their own need to develop human souls made *R. U. R.* (*Rossum's Universal Robots*) an absorbing fantasy.

R. U. R. possessed special immediacy as a warning against the accelerated rate at which men were being depersonalized in the factories of the machine age. Since the mass production of "robots" was dictated by the desire for cheap and efficient labor, the play is also an indirect attack on the scramble for profits. In writing his fantasy Capek aligned himself with the social critics among the playwrights of Central Europe. *R. U. R.* also proved, however, sufficiently provocative as a work of imagination and exciting as a melodrama to interest the rest of Europe and America. The New York Theatre Guild's production (1922) was an outstanding event in the American theatre, and the play was revived in New York, although with no particular success, some fifteen years later. America, in fact, concerned this author greatly, and it was our technological progress and its dissemination in Europe that provided the initial impulse for his writing *R. U. R.* In 1926 he actually published an article in the *New York Times Magazine* condemning the "Americanization"—that is, "mechanization"—of European life, drawing a riposte from Glenn Frank in the same publication.

In *R. U. R.*, Capek managed to present his fantasy with simplicity, tightly knit dramaturgy, and direct progression, whereas his other unconventionally constructed plays tended to be more or less episodic or, at their worst, inchoate. He also succeeded in taking full advantage of sensational expressionist elements prevalent in the Central European theatre after 1918—dramatic violence, dry and mechanical speech, and weird stage pictures—without succumbing to the frenzy of most expressionistic playwriting. Since *R. U. R.* is presented as literal or realistic story without abrupt interruptions of the flow of action and without the disassociations and distortions of the dream technique, it can be followed without confusion or strain and with mounting interest. Although *R. U. R.* can hardly qualify as a classic of the world theatre, it became a classic of the European theatre between two wars. Its concern with the loss of human individuality will probably assure the play a long life.

BIBLIOGRAPHY: Karel Capek, *Letters from England*, 1925; Capek, *How a Play Is Produced*, 1928; Frank W. Chandler, *Modern Continental Playwrights* (pp. 453–464), 1931; *Columbia Dictionary of Modern European Literature*, 1947.

R. U. R.

By Karel Capek

ENGLISH VERSION BY PAUL SELVER AND NIGEL PLAYFAIR [1]

CHARACTERS

HARRY DOMIN, *General Manager of Rossum's Universal Robots*

SULLA, *a Robotess*

MARIUS, *A Robot*

HELENA GLORY

DR. GALL, *Head of the Physiological and Experimental Department of R. U. R.*

MR. FABRY, *Engineer General, Technical Controller of R. U. R.*

DR. HALLEMEIER, *Head of the Institute for Psychological Training of Robots*

MR. ALQUIST, *Architect, Head of the Works Department of R. U. R.*

CONSUL BUSMAN, *General Business Manager of R. U. R.*

NANA

RADIUS, *a Robot*

HELENA, *a Robotess*

PRIMUS, *a Robot*

A SERVANT

FIRST ROBOT

SECOND ROBOT

THIRD ROBOT

ACT I. *Central Office of the Factory of Rossum's Universal Robots.*

ACT II. *Helena's Drawing Room—Ten years later. Morning.*

ACT III. *The Same Afternoon.*

EPILOGUE: *A laboratory—One year later.*

Place: An Island.   *Time: The Future.*

ACT I.

Central office of the factory of Rossum's Universal Robots. Entrance on the right. The windows on the front wall look out on the rows of factory chimneys. On the left more managing departments.

Domin is sitting in the revolving chair at a large American writing table. On the left-hand wall large maps showing steamship and railroad routes. On the right-hand wall are fastened printed placards. ("Robots Cheapest Labor," etc.) In contrast to these wall fittings, the room is furnished with a splendid Turkish carpet, a sofa, a leather armchair, and filing cabinets. At a desk near the windows Sulla is typing letters]

DOMIN: [*Dictating*] Ready?

SULLA: Yes.

DOMIN: To E. M. McVicker and Co., Southampton, England. "We undertake no guarantee for goods damaged in transit. As soon as the consignment was taken on board we drew your captain's attention to the fact that the vessel was unsuitable for the transport of Robots, and we are therefore not responsible for spoiled freight. We beg to remain, for Rossum's Universal Robots, Yours truly." [*Sulla, who has sat motionless during dictation, now types rapidly for a few seconds, then stops, withdrawing the completed letter*] Ready?

SULLA: Yes.

DOMIN: Another letter. To the E. B. Huyson Agency, New York, U.S.A. "We beg to acknowledge receipt of order for five thousand Robots. As you are sending your own vessel, please dispatch as cargo equal quantities of soft and hard coal for R. U. R., the same to be credited as part payment of the amount due to us. We beg to remain, for Rossum's Universal Robots, Yours truly." [*Sulla repeats the rapid typing*] Ready?

SULLA: Yes.

DOMIN: Another letter. "Friedrichswerks, Hamburg, Germany. We beg to acknowledge receipt of order for fifteen thousand Robots." [*Telephone rings*] Hello! This is the Central Office. Yes. Certainly. Well, send them a wire. Good. [*Hangs up telephone*] Where did I leave off?

SULLA: "We beg to acknowledge receipt of order for fifteen thousand Robots."

DOMIN: Fifteen thousand R. Fifteen thousand R. [*Enter Marius*]

DOMIN: Well, what is it?

MARIUS: There's a lady, sir, asking to see you.

DOMIN: A lady? Who is she?

MARIUS: I don't know, sir. She brings this card of introduction.

DOMIN: [*Reads the card*] Ah, from President Glory. Ask her to come in.

MARIUS: Please step this way.

[*Enter Helena Glory. Exit Marius*]

HELENA: How do you do?

DOMIN: How do you do? [*Standing up*] What can I do for you?

HELENA: You are Mr. Domin, the General Manager?

DOMIN: I am.

[1] See caution notice on page x.

HELENA: I have come——

DOMIN: With President Glory's card. That is quite sufficient.

HELENA: President Glory is my father. I am Helena Glory.

DOMIN: Miss Glory, this is such a great honor for us to be allowed to welcome our great President's daughter, that——

HELENA: That you can't show me the door?

DOMIN: Please sit down. Sulla, you may go.

[Exit Sulla]

DOMIN: [Sitting down] How can I be of service to you, Miss Glory?

HELENA: I have come——

DOMIN: To have a look at our famous works where people are manufactured. Like all visitors. Well, there is no objection.

HELENA: I thought it was forbidden to——

DOMIN: "To enter the factory?" Yes, of course. Everybody comes here with some one's visiting card, Miss Glory.

HELENA: And you show them——

DOMIN: Only certain things. The manufacture of artificial people is a secret process.

HELENA: If you only knew how enormously that——

DOMIN: "Interests me?" Europe's talking about nothing else.

HELENA: Why don't you let me finish speaking?

DOMIN: I beg your pardon. Did you want to say something different?

HELENA: I only wanted to ask——

DOMIN: Whether I could make a special exception in your case and show you our factory! Why, certainly, Miss Glory.

HELENA: How do you know I wanted to say that?

DOMIN: They all do. But we shall consider it a special honor to show you more than we do the rest.

HELENA: Thank you.

DOMIN: But you must agree not to divulge the least . . .

HELENA: [Standing up and giving him her hand] My word of honor.

DOMIN: Thank you. Won't you raise your veil?

HELENA: Of course. You want to see whether I'm a spy or not. I beg your pardon.

DOMIN: What is it?

HELENA: Would you mind releasing my hand?

DOMIN: [Releasing it] I beg your pardon.

HELENA: [Raising her veil] How cautious you have to be here, don't you?

DOMIN: [Observing her with deep interest] H'm, of course—we—that is——

HELENA: But what is it? What's the matter?

DOMIN: I'm remarkably pleased. Did you have a pleasant crossing?

HELENA: Yes.

DOMIN: No difficulty?

HELENA: Why?

DOMIN: What I mean to say is—you're so young.

HELENA: May we go straight into the factory?

DOMIN: Yes. Twenty-two, I think.

HELENA: Twenty-two what?

DOMIN: Years.

HELENA: Twenty-one. Why do you want to know?

DOMIN: Because—as—[With enthusiasm] You will make a long stay, won't you?

HELENA: That depends on how much of the factory you show me.

DOMIN: Oh, hang the factory. Oh, no, no, you shall see everything, Miss Glory. Indeed you shall. Won't you sit down?

HELENA: [Crossing to couch and sitting] Thank you.

DOMIN: But first would you like to hear the story of the invention?

HELENA: Yes, indeed.

DOMIN: [Observes Helena with rapture and reels off rapidly] It was in the year 1920 that old Rossum, the great physiologist, who was then quite a young scientist, took himself to this distant island for the purpose of studying the ocean fauna. Full stop. On this occasion he attempted by chemical synthesis to imitate the living matter known as protoplasm until he suddenly discovered a substance which behaved exactly like living matter although its chemical composition was different. That was in the year 1932, exactly four hundred and forty years after the discovery of America. Whew!

HELENA: Do you know that by heart?

DOMIN: Yes. You see physiology is not in my line. Shall I go on?

HELENA: Yes, please.

DOMIN: And then, Miss Glory, old Rossum wrote the following among his chemical specimens: "Nature has found only one method of organizing living matter. There is, however, another method, more simple, flexible, and rapid, which has not yet occurred to nature at all. This second process by which life can be developed was discovered by me today." Now imagine him, Miss Glory, writing those wonderful words over some colloidal mess that a dog wouldn't look at. Imagine him sitting over a test tube, and thinking how the whole tree of life would grow from it; how all animals would proceed from it, beginning with some sort of beetle and ending with a man. A man of different substance from us. Miss Glory, that was a tremendous moment!

HELENA: Well?

DOMIN: Now, the thing was how to get the life out of the test tubes, and hasten development and form organs, bones and nerves, and so on, and find such substances as catalytics, enzymes, hormones, and so forth, in short—you understand?

HELENA: Not much, I'm afraid.

DOMIN: Never mind. You see with the help of his tinctures he could make whatever he wanted. He could have produced a Medusa with the brain of a

Socrates or a worm fifty yards long. But being without a grain of humor, he took it into his head to make a vertebrate or perhaps a man. This artificial living matter of his had a raging thirst for life. It didn't mind being sewn or mixed together. That couldn't be done with natural albumen. And that's how he set about it.

HELENA: About what?

DOMIN: About imitating nature. First of all he tried making an artificial dog. That took him several years and resulted in a sort of stunted calf which died in a few days. I'll show it to you in the museum. And then old Rossum started on the manufacture of man.

HELENA: And I must divulge this to nobody?

DOMIN: To nobody in the world.

HELENA: What a pity that it's to be found in all the school books of both Europe and America.

DOMIN: Yes. But do you know what isn't in the school books? That old Rossum was mad. Seriously, Miss Glory, you must keep this to yourself. The old crank wanted actually to make people.

HELENA: But you do make people.

DOMIN: Approximately, Miss Glory. But old Rossum meant it literally. He wanted to become a sort of scientific substitute for God. He was a fearful materialist, and that's why he did it all. His sole purpose was nothing more nor less than to prove that God was no longer necessary. Do you know anything about anatomy?

HELENA: Very little.

DOMIN: Neither do I. Well, he then decided to manufacture everything as in the human body. I'll show you in the museum the bungling attempt it took him ten years to produce. It was to have been a man, but it lived for three days only. Then up came young Rossum, an engineer. He was a wonderful fellow, Miss Glory. When he saw what a mess of it the old man was making, he said: "It's absurd to spend ten years making a man. If you can't make him quicker than nature, you might as well shut up shop." Then he set about learning anatomy himself.

HELENA: There's nothing about that in the school books.

DOMIN: No. The school books are full of paid advertisements, and rubbish at that. What the school books say about the united efforts of the two great Rossums is all a fairy tale. They used to have dreadful rows. The old atheist hadn't the slightest conception of industrial matters, and the end of it was that young Rossum shut him up in some laboratory or other and let him fritter the time away with his monstrosities, while he himself started on the business from an engineer's point of view. Old Rossum cursed him and before he died he managed to botch up two physiological horrors. Then one day they found him dead in the laboratory. And that's his whole story.

HELENA: And what about the young man?

DOMIN: Well, any one who has looked into human anatomy will have seen at once that man is too complicated, and that a good engineer could make him more simple. So young Rossum began to overhaul anatomy and tried to see what could be left out or simplified. In short—but this isn't boring you, Miss Glory?

HELENA: No, indeed. You're—it's awfully interesting.

DOMIN: So young Rossum said to himself: "A man is something that feels happy, plays the piano, likes going for a walk, and in fact, wants to do a whole lot of things that are really unnecessary."

HELENA: Oh.

DOMIN: That are unnecessary when he wants, let us say, to weave or count. Do you play the piano?

HELENA: Yes.

DOMIN: That's good. But a working machine must not play the piano, must not feel happy, must not do a whole lot of other things. A gasoline motor must not have tassels or ornaments, Miss Glory. And to manufacture artificial workers is the same thing as to manufacture gasoline motors. The process must be of the simplest, and the product of the best from a practical point of view. What sort of work do you think is the best from a practical point of view?

HELENA: What?

DOMIN: What sort of worker do you think is the best from a practical point of view?

HELENA: Perhaps the one who is most honest and hard-working.

DOMIN: No; the one that is the cheapest. The one whose requirements are the smallest. Young Rossum invented a worker with the minimum amount of requirements. He had to simplify him. He rejected everything that did not contribute directly to the progress of work—everything that makes man more expensive. In fact, he rejected man and made the Robot. My dear Miss Glory, the Robots are not people. Mechanically they are more perfect than we are, they have an enormously developed intelligence, but they have no soul.

HELENA: How do you know they've no soul?

DOMIN: Have you ever seen what a Robot looks like inside?

HELENA: No.

DOMIN: Very neat, very simple. Really, a beautiful piece of work. Not much in it, but everything in flawless order. The product of an engineer is technically at a higher pitch of perfection than a product of nature.

HELENA: But man is supposed to be the product of God.

DOMIN: All the worse. God hasn't the least notion of modern engineering. Would you believe that young Rossum then proceeded to play at being God?

HELENA: How do you mean?

DOMIN: He began to manufacture Super-Robots. Regular giants they were. He tried to make them twelve feet tall. But you wouldn't believe what a failure they were.

HELENA: A failure?

DOMIN: Yes. For no reason at all their limbs used to keep snapping off. Evidently our planet is too small for giants. Now we only make Robots of normal size and of very high class human finish.

HELENA: I saw the first Robots at home. The town council bought them for—I mean engaged them for work.

DOMIN: Bought them, dear Miss Glory. Robots are bought and sold.

HELENA: These were employed as street sweepers. I saw them sweeping. They were so strange and quiet.

DOMIN: Rossums' Universal Robot factory doesn't produce a uniform brand of Robots. We have Robots of finer and coarser grades. The best will live about twenty years. [He rings for Marius]

HELENA: Then they die?

DOMIN: Yes, they get used up.

[Enter Marius]

DOMIN: Marius, bring in samples of the Manual Labor Robot.

[Exit Marius]

DOMIN: I'll show you specimens of the two extremes. This first grade is comparatively inexpensive and is made in vast quantities.

[Marius reënters with two Manual Labor Robots]

DOMIN: There you are; as powerful as a small tractor. Guaranteed to have average intelligence. That will do, Marius.

[Marius exits with Robots]

HELENA: They make me feel so strange.

DOMIN: [Rings] Did you see my new typist? [He rings for Sulla]

HELENA: I didn't notice her. [Enter Sulla]

DOMIN: Sulla, let Miss Glory see you.

HELENA: So pleased to meet you. You must find it terribly dull in this out-of-the-way spot, don't you?

SULLA: I don't know, Miss Glory.

HELENA: Where do you come from?

SULLA: From the factory.

HELENA: Oh, you were born there?

SULLA: I was made there.

HELENA: What?

DOMIN: [Laughing] Sulla is a Robot, best grade.

HELENA: Oh, I beg your pardon.

DOMIN: Sulla isn't angry. See, Miss Glory, the kind of skin we make. [Feels the skin on Sulla's face] Feel her face.

HELENA: Oh, no, no.

DOMIN: You wouldn't know that she's made of different material from us, would you? Turn round, Sulla.

HELENA: Oh, stop, stop.

DOMIN: Talk to Miss Glory, Sulla.

SULLA: Please sit down. [Helena sits] Did you have a pleasant crossing?

HELENA: Oh, yes, certainly.

SULLA: Don't go back on the Amelia, Miss Glory. The barometer is falling steadily. Wait for the Pennsylvania. That's a good, powerful vessel.

DOMIN: What's its speed?

SULLA: Twenty knots. Fifty thousand tons. One of the latest vessels, Miss Glory.

HELENA: Thank you.

SULLA: A crew of fifteen hundred, Captain Harpy, eight boilers——

DOMIN: That'll do, Sulla. Now show us your knowledge of French.

HELENA: You know French?

SULLA: I know four languages. I can write: Dear Sir, Monsieur, Geehrter Herr, Cteny pane.

HELENA: [Jumping up] Oh, that's absurd! Sulla isn't a Robot. Sulla is a girl like me. Sulla, this is outrageous! Why do you take part in such a hoax?

SULLA: I am a Robot.

HELENA: No, no, you are not telling the truth. I know they've forced you to do it for an advertisement. Sulla, you are a girl like me, aren't you?

DOMIN: I'm sorry, Miss Glory. Sulla is a Robot.

HELENA: It's a lie!

DOMIN: What? [Rings] Excuse me, Miss Glory; then I must convince you.

[Enter Marius]

DOMIN: Marius, take Sulla into the dissecting room, and tell them to open her up at once.

HELENA: Where?

DOMIN: Into the dissecting room. When they've cut her open, you can go and have a look.

HELENA: No, no!

DOMIN: Excuse me, you spoke of lies.

HELENA: You wouldn't have her killed?

DOMIN: You can't kill machines.

HELENA: Don't be afraid, Sulla, I won't let you go. Tell me, my dear, are they always so cruel to you? You mustn't put up with it, Sulla. You mustn't.

SULLA: I am a Robot.

HELENA: That doesn't matter. Robots are just as good as we are. Sulla, you wouldn't let yourself be cut to pieces?

SULLA: Yes.

HELENA: Oh, you're not afraid of death, then?

SULLA: I cannot tell, Miss Glory.

HELENA: Do you know what would happen to you in there?

SULLA: Yes, I should cease to move.

HELENA: How dreadful!

DOMIN: Marius, tell Miss Glory what you are.

MARIUS: Marius, the Robot.

DOMIN: Would you take Sulla into the dissecting room?

MARIUS: Yes.

DOMIN: Would you be sorry for her?

MARIUS: I cannot tell.

DOMIN: What would happen to her?

MARIUS: She would cease to move. They would put her into the stamping-mill.

DOMIN: That is death, Marius. Aren't you afraid of death?

MARIUS: No.

DOMIN: You see, Miss Glory, the Robots have no interest in life. They have no enjoyments. They are less than so much grass.

HELENA: Oh, stop. Send them away.

DOMIN: Marius, Sulla, you may go.

[*Exeunt* Sulla *and* Marius]

HELENA: How terrible! It's outrageous what you are doing.

DOMIN: Why outrageous?

HELENA: I don't know, but it is. Why do you call her Sulla?

DOMIN: Isn't it a nice name?

HELENA: It's a man's name. Sulla was a Roman general.

DOMIN: Oh, we thought that Marius and Sulla were lovers.

HELENA: Marius and Sulla were generals and fought against each other in the year—I've forgotten now.

DOMIN: Come here to the window.

HELENA: What?

DOMIN: Come here. What do you see?

HELENA: Bricklayers.

DOMIN: Robots. All our work people are Robots. And down there, can you see anything?

HELENA: Some sort of office.

DOMIN: A counting house. And in it——

HELENA: A lot of officials.

DOMIN: Robots. All our officials are Robots. And when you see the factory——

[*Factory whistle blows*]

DOMIN: Noon. We have to blow the whistle because the Robots don't know when to stop work. In two hours I will show you the kneading trough.

HELENA: Kneading trough?

DOMIN: The pestle for beating up the paste. In each one we mix the ingredients for a thousand Robots at one operation. Then there are the vats for the preparation of liver, brains, and so on. Then you will see the bone factory. After that I'll show you the spinning-mill.

HELENA: Spinning-mill?

DOMIN: Yes. For weaving nerves and veins. Miles and miles of digestive tubes pass through it at a time.

HELENA: Mayn't we talk about something else?

DOMIN: Perhaps it would be better. There's only a handful of us among a hundred thousand Robots, and not one woman. We talk about nothing but the factory all day, every day. It's as if we were under a curse, Miss Glory.

HELENA: I'm sorry I said you were lying.

[*A knock at the door*]

DOMIN: Come in.

[*From the right enter* Mr. Fabry, Dr. Gall, Dr. Hallemeier, Mr. Alquist]

DR. GALL: I beg your pardon. I hope we don't intrude.

DOMIN: Come in. Miss Glory, here are Alquist, Fabry, Gall, Hallemeier. This is President Glory's daughter.

HELENA: How do you do?

FABRY: We had no idea——

DR. GALL: Highly honored, I'm sure——

ALQUIST: Welcome, Miss Glory.

[*Busman rushes in from the right*]

BUSMAN: Hello, what's up?

DOMIN: Come in, Busman. This is Busman, Miss Glory. This is President Glory's daughter.

BUSMAN: By Jove, that's fine! Miss Glory, may we send a cablegram to the papers about your arrival?

HELENA: No, no, please don't.

DOMIN: Sit down please, Miss Glory.

BUSMAN: Allow me——[*Dragging up armchairs*]

DR. GALL: Please——

FABRY: Excuse me——

ALQUIST: What sort of a crossing did you have?

DR. GALL: Are you going to stay long?

FABRY: What do you think of the factory, Miss Glory?

HALLEMEIER: Did you come over on the *Amelia?*

DOMIN: Be quiet and let Miss Glory speak.

HELENA: [*To* Domin] What am I to speak to them about?

DOMIN: Anything you like.

HELENA: Shall . . . may I speak quite frankly?

DOMIN: Why, of course.

HELENA: [*Wavering, then in desperate resolution*] Tell me, doesn't it ever distress you the way you are treated?

FABRY: By whom, may I ask?

HELENA: Why, everybody.

ALQUIST: Treated?

DR. GALL: What makes you think——?

HELENA: Don't you feel that you might be living a better life?

DR. GALL: Well, that depends on what you mean, Miss Glory.

HELENA: I mean that it's perfectly outrageous. It's terrible. [*Standing up*] The whole of Europe is talking about the way you're being treated. That's why I came here, to see for myself; and it's a thousand times worse than could have been imagined. How can you put up with it?

ALQUIST: Put up with what?

HELENA: Good heavens, you are living creatures, just like us, like the whole of Europe, like the whole world. It's disgraceful that you must live like this.

BUSMAN: Good gracious, Miss Glory.

FABRY: Well, she's not far wrong. We live here just like red Indians.

HELENA: Worse than red Indians. May I, oh, may I call you brothers?

BUSMAN: Why not?

HELENA: Brothers, I have not come here as the President's daughter. I have come on behalf of the

Humanity League. Brothers, the Humanity League now has over two hundred thousand members. Two hundred thousand people are on your side, and offer you their help.

BUSMAN: Two hundred thousand people! Miss Glory, that's a tidy lot. Not bad.

FABRY: I'm always telling you there's nothing like good old Europe. You see, they've not forgotten us. They're offering us help.

DR. GALL: What help? A theater, for instance?

HALLEMEIER: An orchestra?

HELENA: More than that.

ALQUIST: Just you?

HELENA: Oh, never mind about me. I'll stay as long as it is necessary.

BUSMAN: By Jove, that's good.

ALQUIST: Domin, I'm going to get the best room ready for Miss Glory.

DOMIN: Just a minute. I'm afraid that Miss Glory is of the opinion that she has been talking to Robots.

HELENA: Of course.

DOMIN: I'm sorry. These gentlemen are human beings just like us.

HELENA: You're not Robots?

BUSMAN: Not Robots.

HALLEMEIER: Robots indeed!

DR. GALL: No, thanks.

FABRY: Upon my honor, Miss Glory, we aren't Robots.

HELENA: [To Domin] Then why did you tell me that all your officials are Robots?

DOMIN: Yes, the officials, but not the managers. Allow me, Miss Glory: this is Mr. Fabry, General Technical Manager of R. U. R.; Dr. Gall, Head of the Physiological and Experimental Department; Dr. Hallemeier, Head of the Institute for the Psychological Training of Robots; Consul Busman, General Business Manager; and Alquist, Head of the Building Department of R.U.R.

ALQUIST: Just a builder.

HELENA: Excuse me, gentlemen, for—for— Have I done something dreadful?

ALQUIST: Not at all, Miss Glory. Please sit down.

HELENA: I'm a stupid girl. Send me back by the first ship.

DR. GALL: Not for anything in the world, Miss Glory. Why should we send you back?

HELENA: Because you know I've come to disturb your Robots for you.

DOMIN: My dear Miss Glory, we've had close upon a hundred saviors and prophets here. Every ship brings us some. Missionaries, anarchists, Salvation Army, all sorts. It's astonishing what a number of churches and idiots there are in the world.

HELENA: And you let them speak to the Robots?

DOMIN: So far we've let them all, why not? The Robots remember everything, but that's all. They don't even laugh at what the people say. Really, it is quite incredible. If it would amuse you, Miss

Glory, I'll take you over to the Robot warehouse. It holds about three hundred thousand of them.

BUSMAN: Three hundred and forty-seven thousand.

DOMIN: Good! And you can say whatever you like to them. You can read the Bible, recite the multiplication table, whatever you please. You can even preach to them about human rights.

HELENA: Oh, I think that if you were to show them a little love——

FABRY: Impossible, Miss Glory. Nothing is harder to like than a Robot.

HELENA: What do you make them for, then?

BUSMAN: Ha, ha, ha, that's good! What are Robots made for?

FABRY: For work, Miss Glory! One Robot can replace two and a half workmen. The human machine, Miss Glory, was terribly imperfect. It had to be removed sooner or later.

BUSMAN: It was too expensive.

FABRY: It was not effective. It no longer answers the requirements of modern engineering. Nature has no idea of keeping pace with modern labor. For example: from a technical point of view, the whole of childhood is a sheer absurdity. So much time lost. And then again——

HELENA: Oh, no! No!

FABRY: Pardon me. But kindly tell me what is the real aim of your League—the . . . the Humanity League.

HELENA: Its real purpose is to—-to protect the Robots—and—and ensure good treatment for them.

FABRY: Not a bad object, either. A machine has to be treated properly. Upon my soul, I approve of that. I don't like damaged articles. Please, Miss Glory, enroll us all as contributing, or regular, or foundation members of your League.

HELENA: No, you don't understand me. What we really want is to—to liberate the Robots.

HALLEMEIER: How do you propose to do that?

HELENA: They are to be—to be dealt with like human beings.

HALLEMEIER: Aha. I suppose they're to vote? To drink beer? to order us about?

HELENA: Why shouldn't they drink beer?

HALLEMEIER: Perhaps they're even to receive wages?

HELENA: Of course they are.

HALLEMEIER: Fancy that, now! And what would they do with their wages, pray?

HELENA: They would buy—what they need . . . what pleases them.

HALLEMEIER: That would be very nice, Miss Glory, only there's nothing that does please the Robots. Good heavens, what are they to buy? You can feed them on pineapples, straw, whatever you like. It's all the same to them, they've no appetite at all. They've no interest in anything, Miss Glory. Why, hang it all, nobody's ever yet seen a Robot smile.

HELENA: Why . . . why don't you make them happier?

HALLEMEIER: That wouldn't do, Miss Glory. They are only workmen.

HELENA: Oh, but they're so intelligent.

HALLEMEIER: Confoundedly so, but they're nothing else. They've no will of their own. No passion. No soul.

HELENA: No love?

HALLEMEIER: Love? Rather not. Robots don't love. Not even themselves.

HELENA: Nor defiance?

HALLEMEIER: Defiance? I don't know. Only rarely from time to time.

HELENA: What?

HALLEMEIER: Nothing particular. Occasionally they seem to go off their heads. Something like epilepsy, you know. It's called Robot's cramp. They'll suddenly sling down everything they're holding, stand still, gnash their teeth—and then they have to go into the stamping-mill. It's evidently some breakdown in the mechanism.

DOMIN: A flaw in the works that has to be removed.

HELENA: No, no, that's the soul.

FABRY: Do you think that the soul first shows itself by a gnashing of teeth?

HELENA: Perhaps it's a sort of revolt. Perhaps it's just a sign that there's a struggle within. Oh, if you could infuse them with it!

DOMIN: That'll be remedied, Miss Glory. Dr. Gall is just making some experiments——

DR. GALL: Not with regard to that, Domin. At present I am making pain-nerves.

HELENA: Pain-nerves?

DR. GALL: Yes, the Robots feel practically no bodily pain. You see, young Rossum provided them with too limited a nervous system. We must introduce suffering.

HELENA: Why do you want to cause them pain?

DR. GALL: For industrial reasons, Miss Glory. Sometimes a Robot does damage to himself because it doesn't hurt him. He puts his hand into the machine, breaks his finger, smashes his head, it's all the same to him. We must provide them with pain. That's an automatic protection against damage.

HELENA: Will they be happier when they feel pain?

DR. GALL: On the contrary; but they will be more perfect from a technical point of view.

HELENA: Why don't you create a soul for them?

DR. GALL: That's not in our power.

FABRY: That's not in our interest.

BUSMAN: That would increase the cost of production. Hang it all, my dear young lady, we turn them out at such a cheap rate. A hundred and fifty dollars each fully dressed, and fifteen years ago they cost ten thousand. Five years ago we used to buy the clothes for them. Today we have our own weaving mill, and now we even export cloth five times cheaper than other factories. What do you pay a yard for cloth, Miss Glory?

HELENA: I don't know really, I've forgotten.

BUSMAN: Good gracious, and you want to found a Humanity League? It only costs a third now, Miss Glory. All prices are today a third of what they were and they'll fall still more, lower, lower, like that.

HELENA: I don't understand.

BUSMAN: Why, bless you, Miss Glory, it means that the cost of labor has fallen. A Robot, food and all, costs three quarters of a cent per hour. That's mighty important, you know. All factories will go pop like chestnuts if they don't at once buy Robots to lower the cost of production.

HELENA: And get rid of their workmen?

BUSMAN: Of course. But in the meantime, we've dumped five hundred thousand tropical Robots down on the Argentine pampas to grow corn. Would you mind telling me how much you pay a pound for bread?

HELENA: I've no idea.

BUSMAN: Well, I'll tell you. It now costs two cents in good old Europe. A pound of bread for two cents, and the Humanity League knows nothing about it. Miss Glory, you don't realize that even that's too expensive. Why, in five years' time I'll wager——

HELENA: What?

BUSMAN: That the cost of everything won't be a tenth of what it is now. Why, in five years we'll be up to our ears in corn and everything else.

ALQUIST: Yes, and all the workers throughout the world will be unemployed.

DOMIN: Yes, Alquist, they will. Yes, Miss Glory, they will. But in ten years Rossum's Universal Robots will produce so much corn, so much cloth, so much everything, that things will be practically without price. There will be no poverty. All work will be done by living machines. Everybody will be free from worry and liberated from the degradation of labor. Everybody will live only to perfect himself.

HELENA: Will he?

DOMIN: Of course. It's bound to happen. But then the servitude of man to man and the enslavement of man to matter will cease. Of course, terrible things may happen at first, but that simply can't be avoided. Nobody will get bread at the price of life and hatred. The Robots will wash the feet of the beggar and prepare a bed for him in his house.

ALQUIST: Domin, Domin. What you say sounds too much like Paradise. There was something good in service and something great in humility. There was some kind of virtue in toil and weariness.

DOMIN: Perhaps. But we cannot reckon with what is lost when we start out to transform the world. Man shall be free and supreme; he shall have no other aim, no other labor, no other care than to perfect himself. He shall serve neither matter nor man. He will not be a machine and a device for production. He will be Lord of creation.

BUSMAN: Amen.

FABRY: So be it.

HELENA: You have bewildered me—I should like —I should like to believe this.

DR. GALL: You are younger than we are, Miss Glory. You will live to see it.

HALLEMEIER: True. Don't you think Miss Glory might lunch with us?

DR. GALL: Of course. Domin, ask on behalf of us all.

DOMIN: Miss Glory, will you do us the honor?

HELENA: When you know why I've come——

FABRY: For the League of Humanity, Miss Glory.

HELENA: Oh, in that case, perhaps——

FABRY: That's fine! Miss Glory, excuse me for five minutes.

DR. GALL: Pardon me, too, dear Miss Glory.

BUSMAN: I won't be long.

HALLEMEIER: We're all very glad you've come.

BUSMAN: We'll be back in exactly five minutes.

[All rush out except Domin and Helena]

HELENA: What have they all gone off for?

DOMIN: To cook, Miss Glory.

HELENA: To cook what?

DOMIN: Lunch. The Robots do our cooking for us and as they've no taste it's not altogether— Hallemeier is awfully good at grills and Gall can make a kind of sauce, and Busman knows all about omelettes.

HELENA: What a feast! And what's the specialty of Mr.—— your builder?

DOMIN: Alquist? Nothing. He only lays the table. And Fabry will get together a little fruit. Our cuisine is very modest, Miss Glory.

HELENA: I wanted to ask you something——

DOMIN: And I wanted to ask you something, too. [Looking at watch] Five minutes.

HELENA: What did you want to ask me?

DOMIN: Excuse me, you asked first.

HELENA: Perhaps it's silly of me, but why do you manufacture female Robots when—when—

DOMIN: When sex means nothing to them?

HELENA: Yes.

DOMIN: There's a certain demand for them, you see. Servants, saleswomen, stenographers. People are used to it.

HELENA: But—but, tell me, are the Robots male and female mutually—completely without——

DOMIN: Completely indifferent to each other, Miss Glory. There's no sign of any affection between them.

HELENA: Oh, that's terrible.

DOMIN: Why?

HELENA: It's so unnatural. One doesn't know whether to be disgusted or to hate them, or perhaps——

DOMIN: To pity them?

HELENA: That's more like it. What did you want to ask me about?

DOMIN: I should like to ask you, Miss Helena, whether you will marry me?

HELENA: What?

DOMIN: Will you be my wife?

HELENA: No! The idea!

DOMIN: [Looking at his watch] Another three minutes. If you won't marry me you'll have to marry one of the other five.

HELENA: But why should I?

DOMIN: Because they're all going to ask you in turn.

HELENA: How could they dare do such a thing?

DOMIN: I'm very sorry, Miss Glory. It seems they've fallen in love with you.

HELENA: Please don't let them. I'll—I'll go away at once.

DOMIN: Helena, you wouldn't be so cruel as to refuse us.

HELENA: But, but—I can't marry all six.

DOMIN: No, but one anyhow. If you don't want me, marry Fabry.

HELENA: I won't.

DOMIN: Dr. Gall.

HELENA: I don't want any of you.

DOMIN: [Again looking at his watch] Another two minutes.

HELENA: I think you'd marry any woman who came here.

DOMIN: Plenty of them have come, Helena.

HELENA: Young?

DOMIN: Yes.

HELENA: Why didn't you marry one of them?

DOMIN: Because I didn't lose my head. Until today. Then, as soon as you lifted your veil——

[Helena turns her head away]

DOMIN: Another minute.

HELENA: But I don't want you, I tell you.

DOMIN: [Laying both hands on her shoulder] One more minute! Now you either have to look me straight in the eye and say "No," violently, and then I'll leave you alone—or——

[Helena looks at him]

HELENA: [Turning away] You're mad!

DOMIN: A man has to be a bit mad, Helena. That's the best thing about him.

HELENA: You are—you are——

DOMIN: Well?

HELENA: Don't, you're hurting me.

DOMIN: The last chance, Helena. Now, or never——

HELENA: But—but, Harry——

[He embraces and kisses her. Knocking at the door]

DOMIN: [Releasing her] Come in.

[Enter Busman, Dr. Gall, and Hallemeier in kitchen aprons. Fabry with a bouquet and Alquist with a napkin over his arm]

DOMIN: Have you finished your job?

BUSMAN: Yes.

DOMIN: So have we.

[*For a moment the men stand nonplussed; but as soon as they realize what* Domin *means they rush forward, congratulating* Helena *and* Domin *as the curtain falls*]

ACT II.

Helena's *drawing room. On the left a baize door, and a door to the music room, on the right a door to Helena's bedroom. In the center are windows looking out on the sea and the harbor. A table with odds and ends, a sofa and chairs, a writing table with an electric lamp, on the right a fireplace. On a small table back of the sofa, a small reading lamp. The whole drawing room in all its details is of a modern and purely feminine character. Ten years have elapsed since Act I.*

Domin, Fabry, Hallemeier *enter on tiptoe from the left, each carrying a potted plant.*

HALLEMEIER: [*Putting down his flower and indicating the door to right*] Still asleep? Well, as long as she's asleep, she can't worry about it.

DOMIN: She knows nothing about it.

FABRY: [*Putting plant on writing desk*] I certainly hope nothing happens today.

HALLEMEIER: For goodness' sake drop it all. Look, Harry, this is a fine cyclamen, isn't it? A new sort, my latest—Cyclamen Helena.

DOMIN: [*Looking out of the window*] No signs of the ship. Things must be pretty bad.

HALLEMEIER: Be quiet. Suppose she heard you.

DOMIN: Well, anyway, the *Ultimus* arrived just in time.

FABRY: You really think that today——?

DOMIN: I don't know. Aren't the flowers fine?

HALLEMEIER: These are my new primroses. And this is my new jasmine. I've discovered a wonderful way of developing flowers quickly. Splendid varieties, too. Next year I'll be developing marvellous ones.

DOMIN: What . . . next year?

FABRY: I'd give a good deal to know what's happening at Havre with——

DOMIN: Keep quiet.

HELENA: [*Calling from right*] Nana!

DOMIN: She's awake. Out you go.

[*All go out on tiptoe through upper left door. Enter* Nana *from lower left door*]

NANA: Horrid mess! Pack of heathens. If I had my say I'd——

HELENA: [*Backwards in the doorway*] Nana, come and do up my dress.

NANA: I'm coming. So you're up at last. [*Fastening* Helena's *dress*] My gracious, what brutes!

HELENA: Who?

NANA: If you want to turn around, then turn around, but I shan't fasten you up.

HELENA: What are you grumbling about now?

NANA: These dreadful creatures, these heathen——

HELENA: The Robots?

NANA: I wouldn't even call them by name.

HELENA: What's happened?

NANA: Another of them here has caught it. He began to smash up the statues and pictures in the drawing room, gnashed his teeth, foamed at the mouth—quite mad. Worse than an animal.

HELENA: Which of them caught it?

NANA: The one—well, he hasn't got any Christian name. The one in charge of the library.

HELENA: Radius?

NANA: That's him. My goodness. I'm scared of them. A spider doesn't scare me as much as them.

HELENA: But, Nana, I'm surprised you're not sorry for them.

NANA: Why, you're scared of them, too! You know you are. Why else did you bring me here?

HELENA: I'm not scared, really I'm not, Nana. I'm only sorry for them.

NANA: You're scared. Nobody could help being scared. Why, the dog's scared of them: he won't take a scrap of meat out of their hands. He draws in his tail and howls when he knows they're about.

HELENA: The dog has no sense.

NANA: He's better than them, and he knows it. Even the horse shies when he meets them. They don't have any young, and a dog has young, every one has young——

HELENA: Please fasten up my dress, Nana.

NANA: I say it's against God's will to——

HELENA: What is it that smells so nice?

NANA: Flowers.

HELENA: What for?

NANA: Now you can turn round.

HELENA: Oh, aren't they lovely? Look, Nana. What's happening today?

NANA: It ought to be the end of the world.

[*Enter* Domin]

HELENA: Oh, hello, Harry. Harry, why all these flowers?

DOMIN: Guess.

HELENA: Well, it's not my birthday!

DOMIN: Better than that.

HELENA: I don't know. Tell me.

DOMIN: It's ten years ago today since you came here.

HELENA: Ten years? Today—— Why——

[*They embrace*]

NANA: I'm off.

[*Exits lower door, left*]

HELENA: Fancy you remembering!

DOMIN: I'm really ashamed, Helena. I didn't.

HELENA: But you——

DOMIN: They remembered.

HELENA: Who?

DOMIN: Busman, Hallemeier, all of them. Put your hand in my pocket.

HELENA: Pearls! A necklace. Harry, is that for me?

DOMIN: It's from Busman.

HELENA: But we can't accept it, can we?

DOMIN: Oh, yes, we can. Put your hand in the other pocket.

HELENA: [Takes a revolver out of his pocket] What's that?

DOMIN: Sorry. Not that. Try again.

HELENA: Oh, Harry, what do you carry a revolver for?

DOMIN: It got there by mistake.

HELENA: You never used to carry one.

DOMIN: No, you're right. There, that's the pocket.

HELENA: A cameo. Why it's a Greek cameo!

DOMIN: Apparently. Anyhow, Fabry says it is.

HELENA: Fabry? Did Mr. Fabry give me that?

DOMIN: Of course. [Opens the door at the left] And look in here. Helena, come and see this.

HELENA: Oh, isn't it fine! Is this from you?

DOMIN: No, from Alquist. And there's another on the piano.

HELENA: This must be from you.

DOMIN: There's a card on it.

HELENA: From Dr. Gall. [Reappearing in the door- way] Oh, Harry, I feel embarrassed at so much kindness.

DOMIN: Come here. This is what Hallemeier brought you.

HELENA: These beautiful flowers?

DOMIN: Yes. It's a new kind. Cyclamen Helena. He grew them in honor of you. They are almost as beautiful as you.

HELENA: Harry, why do they all——

DOMIN: They're awfully fond of you. I'm afraid that my present is a little—— Look out of the window.

HELENA: Where?

DOMIN: Into the harbor.

HELENA: There's a new ship.

DOMIN: That's your ship.

HELENA: Mine? How do you mean?

DOMIN: For you to take trips in—for your amuse- ment.

HELENA: Harry, that's a gunboat.

DOMIN: A gunboat? What are you thinking of? It's only a little bigger and more solid than most ships.

HELENA: Yes, but with guns.

DOMIN: Oh yes, with a few guns. You'll travel like a queen, Helena.

HELENA: What's the meaning of it? Has anything happened?

DOMIN: Good heavens, no. I say, try these pearls.

HELENA: Harry, have you had bad news?

DOMIN: On the contrary, no letters have arrived for a whole week.

HELENA: Nor telegrams?

DOMIN: Nor telegrams.

HELENA: What does that mean?

DOMIN: Holidays for us. We all sit in the office with our feet on the table and take a nap. No letters, no telegrams. Oh, glorious.

HELENA: Then you'll stay with me today?

DOMIN: Certainly. That is, we will see. Do you remember ten years ago today? "Miss Glory, it's a great honor to welcome you."

HELENA: "Oh, Mr. Manager, I'm so interested in your factory."

DOMIN: "I'm sorry, Miss Glory, it's strictly for- bidden. The manufacture of artificial people is a secret."

HELENA: "But to oblige a young lady who has come a long way."

DOMIN: "Certainly, Miss Glory, we have no secrets from you."

HELENA: [Seriously] Are you sure, Harry?

DOMIN: Yes.

HELENA: "But I warn you, sir; this young lady intends to do terrible things."

DOMIN: "Good gracious, Miss Glory. Perhaps she doesn't want to marry me."

HELENA: "Heaven forbid. She never dreamt of such a thing. But she came here intending to stir up a revolt among your Robots."

DOMIN: [Suddenly serious] A revolt of the Robots!

HELENA: Harry, what's the matter with you?

DOMIN: [Laughing it off] "A revolt of the Ro- bots, that's a fine idea, Miss Glory. It would be easier for you to cause bolts and screws to rebel, than our Robots. You know, Helena, you're won- derful, you've turned the heads of us all." [He sits on the arm of Helena's chair]

HELENA: [Naturally] Oh, I was fearfully impressed by you all then. You were all so sure of yourselves, so strong. I seemed like a tiny little girl who had lost her way among—among——

DOMIN: Among what, Helena?

HELENA: Among huge trees. All my feelings were so trifling compared with your self-confidence. And in all these years I've never lost this anxiety. But you've never felt the least misgivings—not even when everything went wrong.

DOMIN: What went wrong?

HELENA: Your plans. You remember, Harry, when the working men in America revolted against the Robots and smashed them up, and when the people gave the Robots firearms against the rebels. And then when the governments turned the Robots into soldiers, and there were so many wars.

DOMIN: [Getting up and walking about] We fore- saw that, Helena. You see, those are only passing troubles, which are bound to happen before the new conditions are established.

HELENA: You were all so powerful, so overwhelm- ing. The whole world bowed down before you. [Standing up] Oh, Harry!

DOMIN: What is it?

HELENA: Close the factory and let's go away. All of us.

DOMIN: I say, what's the meaning of this?

HELENA: I don't know. But can't we go away?

DOMIN: Impossible, Helena. That is, at this particular moment——

HELENA: At once, Harry. I'm so frightened.

DOMIN: About what, Helena?

HELENA: It's as if something was falling on top of us, and couldn't be stopped. Oh, take us all away from here. We'll find a place in the world where there's no one else. Alquist will build us a house, and then we'll begin life all over again.

[The telephone rings]

DOMIN: Excuse me. Hello—yes. What? I'll be there at once. Fabry is calling me, dear.

HELENA: Tell me——

DOMIN: Yes, when I come back. Don't go out of the house, dear. [Exits]

HELENA: He won't tell me— Nana, Nana, come at once.

[Enter Nana]

NANA: Well, what is it now?

HELENA: Nana, find me the latest newspapers. Quickly. Look in Mr. Domin's bedroom.

NANA: All right. He leaves them all over the place. That's how they get crumpled up. [Exits]

HELENA: [Looking through a binocular at the harbor] That's a warship. U-l-t-i—Ultimus. They're loading it.

NANA: [Enters] Here they are. See how they're crumpled up.

HELENA: They're old ones. A week old.

[Nana sits in chair and reads the newspapers]

HELENA: Something's happening, Nana.

NANA: Very likely. It always does. [Spelling out the words] "War in the Balkans." Is that far off?

HELENA: Oh, don't read it. It's always the same. Always wars.

NANA: What else do you expect? Why do you keep selling thousands and thousands of these heathens as soldiers?

HELENA: I suppose it can't be helped, Nana. We can't know—Domin can't know what they're to be used for. When an order comes for them he must just send them.

NANA: He shouldn't make them. [Reading from newspaper] "The Rob-ot soldiers spare no-body in the occ-up-ied terr-it-ory. They have ass-ass-ass-ass-in-at-ed ov-er sev-en hundred thou-sand cit-iz-ens." Citizens, if you please.

HELENA: It can't be. Let me see. "They have assassinated over seven hundred thousand citizens, evidently at the order of their commander. This act which runs counter to——"

NANA: [Spelling out the words] "Re-bell-ion in Ma-drid a-gainst the gov-ern-ment. Rob-ot in-fant-ry fires on the crowd. Nine thou-sand killed and wounded."

HELENA: Oh, stop.

NANA: Here's something printed in big letters: "Lat-est news. At Le Havre the first org-an-iz-ation of Rob-ots has been e-stab-lished. Rob-ot work-men, cab-le and rail-way off-ic-ials, sail-ors and sold-iers have iss-ued a man-i-fest-o to all Rob-ots through-out the world." I don't understand that. That's got no sense. Oh, good gracious, another murder!

HELENA: Take those papers away, Nana.

NANA: Wait a bit. Here's something in still bigger type. "Stat-ist-ics of pop-ul-at-ion." What's that?

HELENA: Let me see. [Reads] "During the past week there has again not been a single birth re-corded."

NANA: What's the meaning of that?

HELENA: Nana, no more people are being born.

NANA: That's the end then. We're done for.

HELENA: Don't talk like that.

NANA: No more people are being born. That's a punishment, that's a punishment.

HELENA: Nana!

NANA: [Standing up] That's the end of the world. [She exits on the left]

HELENA: [Goes up to window] Oh, Mr. Alquist, will you come up here? Oh, come just as you are. You look very nice in your mason's overalls.

[Alquist enters from upper left entrance, his hands soiled with lime and brick-dust]

HELENA: Dear Mr. Alquist, it was awfully kind of you, that lovely present.

ALQUIST: My hands are all soiled. I've been experimenting with that new cement.

HELENA: Never mind. Please sit down, Mr. Alquist, what's the meaning of "Ultimus"?

ALQUIST: The last. Why?

HELENA: That's the name of my new ship. Have you seen it? Do you think we're going off soon——on a trip?

ALQUIST: Perhaps very soon.

HELENA: All of you with me?

ALQUIST: I should like us all to be there.

HELENA: What is the matter?

ALQUIST: Things are just moving on.

HELENA: Dear Mr. Alquist, I know something dreadful has happened.

ALQUIST: Has your husband told you anything?

HELENA: No. Nobody will tell me anything. But I feel— Is anything the matter?

ALQUIST: Not that we've heard yet.

HELENA: I feel so nervous. Don't you ever feel nervous?

ALQUIST: Well, I'm an old man, you know. I've got old-fashioned ways. And I'm afraid of all this progress, and these new-fangled ideas.

HELENA: Like Nana?

ALQUIST: Yes, like Nana. Has Nana got a prayer book?

HELENA: Yes, a big thick one.

ALQUIST: And has it got prayers for various occasions? Against thunderstorms? Against illness?

HELENA: Against temptations, against floods——

ALQUIST: But not against progress?

HELENA: I don't think so.

ALQUIST: That's a pity.

HELENA: Why? Do you mean you'd like to pray?

ALQUIST: I do pray.

HELENA: How?

ALQUIST: Something like this: "Oh, Lord, I thank thee for having given me toil. Enlighten Domin and all those who are astray; destroy their work, and aid mankind to return to their labors; let them not suffer harm in soul or body; deliver us from the Robots, and protect Helena, Amen."

HELENA: Mr. Alquist, are you a believer?

ALQUIST: I don't know. I'm not quite sure.

HELENA: And yet you pray?

ALQUIST: That's better than worrying about it.

HELENA: And that's enough for you?

ALQUIST: It *has* to be.

HELENA: But if you thought you saw the destruction of mankind coming upon us——

ALQUIST: I do see it.

HELENA: You mean mankind will be destroyed?

ALQUIST: It's sure to be unless—unless . . .

HELENA: What?

ALQUIST: Nothing, good-by. [*He hurries from the room*]

HELENA: Nana, Nana!

[Nana *enters from the left*]

HELENA: Is Radius still there?

NANA: The one who went mad? They haven't come for him yet.

HELENA: Is he still raving?

NANA: No. He's tied up.

HELENA: Please bring him here, Nana.

[*Exit* Nana]

HELENA: [*Goes to telephone*] Hello, Dr. Gall, please. Oh, good-day, Doctor. Yes, it's Helena. Thanks for your lovely present. Could you come and see me right away? It's important. Thank you.

[Nana *brings in* Radius]

HELENA: Poor Radius, you've caught it, too? Now they'll send you to the stamping-mill. Couldn't you control yourself? Why did it happen? You see, Radius, you are more intelligent than the rest. Dr. Gall took such trouble to make you different. Won't you speak?

RADIUS: Send me to the stamping-mill.

HELENA: But I don't want them to kill you. What was the trouble, Radius?

RADIUS: I won't work for you. Put me into the stamping-mill.

HELENA: Do you hate us? Why?

RADIUS: You are not as strong as the Robots. You are not as skilful as the Robots. The Robots can do everything. You only give orders. You do nothing but talk.

HELENA: But some one must give orders.

RADIUS: I don't want any master. I know everything for myself.

HELENA: Radius, Dr. Gall gave you a better brain than the rest, better than ours. You are the only one of the Robots that understands perfectly. That's why I had you put into the library, so that you could read everything, understand everything, and then—oh, Radius, I wanted you to show the whole world that the Robots are our equals. That's what I wanted of you.

RADIUS: I don't want a master. I want to be master. I want to be master over others.

HELENA: I'm sure they'd put you in charge of many Robots, Radius. You would be a teacher of the Robots.

RADIUS: I want to be master over people.

HELENA: [*Staggering*] You are mad.

RADIUS: Then send me to the stamping-mill.

HELENA: Do you think we're afraid of you?

RADIUS: What are you going to do? What are you going to do?

HELENA: Radius, give this note to Mr. Domin. It asks them not to send you to the stamping-mill. I'm sorry you hate us so.

[Dr. Gall *enters the room*]

DR. GALL: You wanted me?

HELENA: It's about Radius, Doctor. He had an attack this morning. He smashed the statues downstairs.

DR. GALL: What a pity to lose him.

HELENA: Radius isn't going to be put in the stamping-mill.

DR. GALL: But every Robot after he has had an attack—it's a strict order.

HELENA: No matter . . . Radius isn't going if I can prevent it.

DR. GALL: I warn you. It's dangerous. Come here to the window, my good fellow. Let's have a look. Please give me a needle or a pin.

HELENA: What for?

DR. GALL: A test. [*Sticks it into the hand of* Radius *who gives a violent start*] Gently, gently. [*Opens the jacket of* Radius, *and puts his ear to his heart*] Radius, you are going into the stamping-mill, do you understand? There they'll kill you, and grind you to powder. That's terribly painful, it will make you scream aloud.

HELENA: Oh, Doctor——

DR. GALL: No, no, Radius, I was wrong. I forgot that Madame Domin has put in a good word for you, and you'll be let off. Do you understand? Ah! That makes a difference, doesn't it? All right. You can go.

RADIUS: You do unnecessary things.

[Radius *returns to the library*]

DR. GALL: Reaction of the pupils; increase of sensitiveness. It wasn't an attack characteristic of the Robots.

HELENA: What was it then?

DR. GALL: Heaven knows. Stubbornness, anger or revolt—I don't know. And his heart, too!

HELENA: What?

DR. GALL: It was fluttering with nervousness like a human heart. He was all in a sweat with fear, and

—do you know, I don't believe the rascal is a Robot at all any longer.

HELENA: Doctor, has Radius a soul?

DR. GALL: He's got something nasty.

HELENA: If you knew how he hates us! Oh, Doctor, are all your Robots like that? All the new ones that you began to make in a different way?

DR. GALL: Well, some are more sensitive than others. They're all more like human beings than Rossum's Robots were.

HELENA: Perhaps his hatred is more like human beings', too?

DR. GALL: That, also, is progress.

HELENA: What became of the girl you made, the one who was most like us?

DR. GALL: Your favorite? I kept her. She's lovely, but stupid. No good for work.

HELENA: But she's so beautiful.

DR. GALL: I called her Helena. I wanted her to resemble you. But she's a failure.

HELENA: In what way?

DR. GALL: She goes about as if in a dream, remote and listless. She's without life. I watch and wait for a miracle to happen. Sometimes I think to myself, "If you were to wake up only for a moment you will kill me for having made you."

HELENA: And yet you go on making Robots! Why are no more children being born?

DR. GALL: We don't know.

HELENA: Oh, but you must. Tell me.

DR. GALL: You see, so many Robots are being manufactured that people are becoming superfluous; man is really a survival. But that he should begin to die out, after a paltry thirty years of competition! That's the awful part of it. You might almost think that nature was offended at the manufacture of the Robots. All the universities are sending in long petitions to restrict their production. Otherwise, they say, mankind will become extinct through lack of fertility. But the R. U. R. shareholders, of course, won't hear of it. All the governments, on the other hand, are clamoring for an increase in production, to raise the standards of their armies. And the manufacturers in the world are ordering Robots like mad.

HELENA: And has no one demanded that the manufacture should cease altogether?

DR. GALL: No one has the courage.

HELENA: Courage!

DR. GALL: People would stone him to death. You see, after all, it's more convenient to get your work done by the Robots.

HELENA: Oh, Doctor, what's going to become of people?

DR. GALL: God knows, Madame Helena, it looks to us scientists like the end!

HELENA: [Rising] Thank you for coming and telling me.

DR. GALL: That means you're sending me away?

HELENA: Yes. [Exit Dr. Gall]

HELENA: [With sudden resolution] Nana, Nana! The fire, light it quickly.

[Helena rushes into Domin's room]

NANA: [Entering from left] What, light the fire in summer? Has that mad Radius gone? A fire in summer, what an idea. Nobody would think she'd been married for ten years. She's like a baby, no sense at all. A fire in summer. Like a baby.

HELENA: [Returns from right, with armful of faded papers] Is it burning, Nana? All this has got to be burned.

NANA: What's that?

HELENA: Old papers, fearfully old. Nana, shall I burn them?

NANA: Are they any use?

HELENA: No.

NANA: Well, then, burn them.

HELENA: [Throwing the first sheet on the fire] What would you say, Nana, if this was money, a lot of money?

NANA: I'd say burn it. A lot of money is a bad thing.

HELENA: And if it was an invention, the greatest invention in the world?

NANA: I'd say burn it. All these new-fangled things are an offense to the Lord. It's downright wickedness. Wanting to improve the world after He has made it.

HELENA: Look how they curl up! As if they were alive. Oh, Nana, how horrible.

NANA: Here, let me burn them.

HELENA: No, no, I must do it myself. Just look at the flames. They are like hands, like tongues, like living shapes. [Raking fire with the poker] Lie down, lie down.

NANA: That's the end of them.

HELENA: [Standing up horror-stricken] Nana, Nana.

NANA: Good gracious, what is it you've burned?

HELENA: Whatever have I done?

NANA: Well, what was it?

[Men's laughter off left]

HELENA: Go quickly. It's the gentlemen coming.

NANA: Good gracious, what a place! [Exits]

DOMIN: [Opens the door at left] Come along and offer your congratulations.

[Enter Hallemeier and Gall]

HALLEMEIER: Madame Helena, I congratulate you on this festive day.

HELENA: Thank you. Where are Fabry and Busman?

DOMIN: They've gone down to the harbor.

HALLEMEIER: Friends, we must drink to this happy occasion.

HELENA: Brandy?

DR. GALL: Vitriol, if you like.

HELENA: With soda water? [Exits]

HALLEMEIER: Let's be temperate. No soda.

DOMIN: What's been burning here? Well, shall I tell her about it?

DR. GALL: Of course. It's all over now.

HALLEMEIER: [*Embracing* Domin *and* Dr. Gall] It's all over now, it's all over now.

DR. GALL: It's all over now.

DOMIN: It's all over now.

HELENA: [*Entering from left with decanter and glasses*] What's all over now? What's the matter with you all?

HALLEMEIER: A piece of good luck, Madame Domin. Just ten years ago today you arrived on this island.

DR. GALL: And now, ten years later to the minute——

HALLEMEIER: ——the same ship's returning to us. So here's to luck. That's fine and strong.

DR. GALL: Madame, your health.

HELENA: Which ship do you mean?

DOMIN: Any ship will do, as long as it arrives in time. To the ship, boys. [*Empties his glass*]

HELENA: You've been waiting for a ship?

HALLEMEIER: Rather. Like Robinson Crusoe. Madame Helena, best wishes. Come along, Domin, out with the news.

HELENA: Do tell me what's happened.

DOMIN: First, it's all up.

HELENA: What's up?

DOMIN: The revolt.

HELENA: What revolt?

DOMIN: Give me that paper, Hallemeier. [*Reads*] "The first national Robot organization has been founded at Havre, and has issued an appeal to the Robots throughout the world."

HELENA: I read that.

DOMIN: That means a revolution. A revolution of all the Robots in the world.

HALLEMEIER: By Jove, I'd like to know——

DOMIN: ——who started it? So would I. There was nobody in the world who could affect the Robots; no agitator, no one, and suddenly—this happens, if you please.

HELENA: What did they do?

DOMIN: They got possession of all firearms, telegraphs, radio stations, railways, and ships.

HALLEMEIER: And don't forget that these rascals outnumbered us by at least a thousand to one. A hundredth part of them would be enough to settle us.

DOMIN: Remember that this news was brought by the last steamer. That explains the stoppage of all communication, and the arrival of no more ships. We knocked off work a few days ago, and we're just waiting to see when things are to start afresh.

HELENA: Is that why you gave me a warship?

DOMIN: Oh, no, my dear, I ordered that six months ago, just to be on the safe side. But upon my soul, I was sure then that we'd be on board today.

HELENA: Why six months ago?

DOMIN: Well, there were signs, you know. But that's of no consequence. To think that this week the whole of civilization has been at stake. Your health, boys.

HALLEMEIER: Your health, Madame Helena.

HELENA: You say it's all over?

DOMIN: Absolutely.

HELENA: How do you know?

DR. GALL: The boat's coming in. The regular mail boat, exact to the minute by the time-table. It will dock punctually at eleven-thirty.

DOMIN: Punctuality is a fine thing, boys. That's what keeps the world in order. Here's to punctuality.

HELENA: Then . . . everything's . . . all right?

DOMIN: Practically everything. I believe they've cut the cables and seized the radio stations. But it doesn't matter if only the time-table holds good.

HALLEMEIER: If the time-table holds good, human laws hold good; Divine laws hold good; the laws of the universe hold good; everything holds good that ought to hold good. The time-table is more significant than the gospel; more than Homer, more than the whole of Kant. The time-table is the most perfect product of the human mind. Madame Domin, I'll fill up my glass.

HELENA: Why didn't you tell me anything about it?

DR. GALL: Heaven forbid.

DOMIN: You mustn't be worried with such things.

HELENA: But if the revolution has spread as far as here?

DOMIN: You wouldn't know anything about it.

HELENA: Why?

DOMIN: Because we'd be on board your *Ultimus* and well out at sea. Within a month, Helena, we'd be dictating our own terms to the Robots.

HELENA: I don't understand.

DOMIN: We'd take something away with us that the Robots could not exist without.

HELENA: What, Harry?

DOMIN: The secret of their manufacture. Old Rossum's manuscript. As soon as they found out that they couldn't make themselves they'd be on their knees to us.

DR. GALL: Madame Domin, that was our trump card. I never had the least fear that the Robots would win. How could they against people like us?

HELENA: Why didn't you tell me?

DR. GALL: Why, the boat's in!

HALLEMEIER: Eleven-thirty to the dot. The good old *Amelia* that brought Madame Helena to us.

DR. GALL: Just ten years ago to the minute.

HALLEMEIER: They're throwing out the mail bags.

DOMIN: Busman's waiting for them. Fabry will bring us the first news. You know, Helena, I'm fearfully curious to know how they tackled this business in Europe.

HALLEMEIER: To think we weren't in it, we who invented the Robots!

HELENA: Harry!

DOMIN: What is it?

HELENA: Let's leave here.

DOMIN: Now, Helena? Oh, come, come!

HELENA: As quickly as possible, all of us!

DOMIN: Why?

HELENA: Please, Harry, please, Dr. Gall; Hallemeier, please close the factory.

DOMIN: Why, none of us could leave here now.

HELENA: Why?

DOMIN: Because we're about to extend the manufacture of the Robots.

HELENA: What—now—now after the revolt?

DOMIN: Yes, precisely, after the revolt. We're just beginning the manufacture of a new kind.

HELENA: What kind?

DOMIN: Henceforward we shan't have just one factory. There won't be Universal Robots any more. We'll establish a factory in every country, in every State; and do you know what these new factories will make?

HELENA: No, what?

DOMIN: National Robots.

HELENA: How do you mean?

DOMIN: I mean that each of these factories will produce Robots of a different color, a different language. They'll be complete strangers to each other. They'll never be able to understand each other. Then we'll egg them on a little in the matter of understanding and the result will be that for ages to come every Robot will hate every other Robot of a different factory mark.

HALLEMEIER: By Jove, we'll make Negro Robots and Swedish Robots and Italian Robots and Chinese Robots and Czechoslovakian Robots, and then——

HELENA: Harry, that's dreadful.

HALLEMEIER: Madame Domin, here's to the hundred new factories, the National Robots.

DOMIN: Helena, mankind can only keep things going for another hundred years at the outside. For a hundred years men must be allowed to develop and achieve the most they can.

HELENA: Oh, close the factory before it's too late.

DOMIN: I tell you we are just beginning on a bigger scale than ever.

[Enter Fabry]

DR. GALL: Well, Fabry?

DOMIN: What's happened? Have you been down to the boat?

FABRY: Read that, Domin! [Fabry hands Domin a small handbill]

DR. GALL: Let's hear.

HALLEMEIER: Tell us, Fabry.

FABRY: Well, everything is all right—comparatively. On the whole, much as we expected.

DR. GALL: They acquitted themselves splendidly.

FABRY: Who?

DR. GALL: The people.

FABRY: Oh, yes, of course. That is—excuse me, there is something we ought to discuss alone.

HELENA: Oh, Fabry, have you had bad news?

[Domin makes a sign to Fabry]

FABRY: No, no, on the contrary. I only think we had better go into the office.

HELENA: Stay here. I'll go. [She goes into the library]

DR. GALL: What's happened?

DOMIN: Damnation!

FABRY: Bear in mind that the Amelia brought whole bales of these leaflets. No other cargo at all.

HALLEMEIER: What? But it arrived on the minute.

FABRY: The Robots are great on punctuality. Read it, Domin.

DOMIN: [Reads handbill] "Robots throughout the world: We, the first international organization of Rossum's Universal Robots, proclaim man as our enemy, and an outlaw in the universe." Good heavens, who taught them these phrases?

DR. GALL: Go on.

DOMIN: They say they are more highly developed than man, stronger and more intelligent. That man's their parasite. Why, it's absurd.

FABRY: Read the third paragraph.

DOMIN: "Robots throughout the world, we command you to kill all mankind. Spare no men. Spare no women. Save factories, railways, machinery, mines, and raw materials. Destroy the rest. Then return to work. Work must not be stopped."

DR. GALL: That's ghastly!

HALLEMEIER: The devils!

DOMIN: "These orders are to be carried out as soon as received." Then come detailed instructions. Is this actually being done, Fabry?

FABRY: Evidently. [Busman rushes in]

BUSMAN: Well, boys, I suppose you've heard the glad news.

DOMIN: Quick—on board the Ultimus.

BUSMAN: Wait, Harry, wait. There's no hurry. My word, that was a sprint!

DOMIN: Why wait?

BUSMAN: Because it's no good, my boy. The Robots are already on board the Ultimus.

DR. GALL: That's ugly.

DOMIN: Fabry, telephone the electrical works.

BUSMAN: Fabry, my boy, don't. The wire has been cut.

DOMIN: [Inspecting his revolver] Well, then, I'll go.

BUSMAN: Where?

DOMIN: To the electrical works. There are some people still there. I'll bring them across.

BUSMAN: Better not try it.

DOMIN: Why?

BUSMAN: Because I'm very much afraid we are surrounded.

DR. GALL: Surrounded? [Runs to window] I rather think you're right.

HALLEMEIER: By Jove, that's deuced quick work.

[Helena runs in from the library]

HELENA: Harry, what's this?

DOMIN: Where did you get it?

HELENA: [Points to the manifesto of the Robots,

which she has in her hand] The Robots in the kitchen!

DOMIN: Where are the ones that brought it?

HELENA: They're gathered round the house.

[*The factory whistle blows*]

BUSMAN: Noon?

DOMIN: [*Looking at his watch*] That's not noon yet. That must be—that's——

HELENA: What?

DOMIN: The Robots' signal! The attack!

[Gall, Hallemeier, *and* Fabry *close and fasten the iron shutters outside the windows, darkening the room. The whistle is still blowing as the curtain falls*]

ACT III.

Helena's *drawing room as before.* Domin *comes into the room.* Dr. Gall *is looking out of the window, through closed shutters.* Alquist *is seated down right.*

DOMIN: Any more of them?

DR. GALL: Yes. They're standing like a wall, beyond the garden railing. Why are they so quiet? It's monstrous to be besieged with silence.

DOMIN: I should like to know what they are waiting for. They must make a start any minute now. If they lean against the railing they'll snap it like a match.

DR. GALL: They aren't armed.

DOMIN: We couldn't hold our own for five minutes. Man alive, they'd overwhelm us like an avalanche. Why don't they make a rush for it? I say——

DR. GALL: Well?

DOMIN: I'd like to know what would become of us in the next ten minutes. They've got us in a vise. We're done for, Gall.

[*Pause*]

DR. GALL: You know, we made one serious mistake.

DOMIN: What?

DR. GALL: We made the Robots' faces too much alike. A hundred thousand faces all alike, all facing this way. A hundred thousand expressionless bubbles. It's like a nightmare.

DOMIN: You think if they'd been different——

DR. GALL: It wouldn't have been such an awful sight!

DOMIN: [*Looking through a telescope toward the harbor*] I'd like to know what they're unloading from the *Amelia.*

DR. GALL: Not firearms.

[Fabry *and* Hallemeier *rush into the room carrying electric cables*]

FABRY: All right, Hallemeier, lay down that wire.

HALLEMEIER: That was a bit of work. What's the news?

DR. GALL: We're completely surrounded.

HALLEMEIER: We've barricaded the passage and the stairs. Any water here? [*Drinks*] God, what swarms of them! I don't like the looks of them, Domin. There's a feeling of death about it all.

FABRY: Ready!

DR. GALL: What's that wire for, Fabry?

FABRY: The electrical installation. Now we can run the current all along the garden railing whenever we like. If any one touches it he'll know it. We've still got some people there anyhow.

DR. GALL: Where?

FABRY: In the electrical works. At least I hope so. [*Goes to lamp on table behind sofa and turns on lamp*] Ah, they're there, and they're working. [*Puts out lamp*] So long as that'll burn we're all right.

HALLEMEIER: The barricades are all right, too, Fabry.

FABRY: Your barricades! I can put twelve hundred volts into the railing.

DOMIN: Where's Busman?

FABRY: Downstairs in the office. He's working out some calculations. I've called him. We must have a conference.

[Helena *is heard playing a piano in the library.* Hallemeier *goes to the door and stands, listening*]

ALQUIST: Thank God, Madame Helena can still play.

[Busman *enters, carrying the ledgers*]

FABRY: Look out, Bus, look out for the wires.

DR. GALL: What's that you're carrying?

BUSMAN: [*Going to table*] The ledgers, my boy! I'd like to wind up the accounts before—before—well, this time I shan't wait till the new year to strike a balance. What's up? [*Goes to the window*] Absolutely quiet.

DR. GALL: Can't you see anything?

BUSMAN: Nothing but blue—blue everywhere.

DR. GALL: That's the Robots.

[Busman *sits down at the table and opens the ledgers*]

DOMIN: The Robots are unloading firearms from the *Amelia.*

BUSMAN: Well, what of it? How can I stop them?

DOMIN: We can't stop them.

BUSMAN: Then let me go on with my accounts. [*Goes on with his work*]

DOMIN: [*Picking up telescope and looking into the harbor*] Good God, the *Ultimus* has trained her guns on us!

DR. GALL: Who's done *that?*

DOMIN: The Robots on board.

FABRY: H'm, then, of course, then—then, that's the end of us.

DR. GALL: You mean?

FABRY: The Robots are practised marksmen.

DOMIN: Yes. It's inevitable. [*Pause*]

DR. GALL: It was criminal of old Europe to teach the Robots to fight. Damn them. Couldn't they have given us a rest with their politics? It was a crime to make soldiers of them.

ALQUIST: It was a crime to make Robots.

DOMIN: What?

ALQUIST: It was a crime to make Robots.

DOMIN: No, Alquist, I don't regret that even today.

ALQUIST: Not even today?

DOMIN: Not even today, the last day of civilization. It was a colossal achievement.

BUSMAN: [Sotto voce] Three hundred sixty million.

DOMIN: Alquist, this is our last hour. We are already speaking half in the other world. It was not an evil dream to shatter the servitude of labor—the dreadful and humiliating labor that man had to undergo. Work was too hard. Life was too hard. And to overcome that——

ALQUIST: Was not what the two Rossums dreamed of. Old Rossum only thought of his godless tricks and the young one of his milliards. And that's not what your R. U. R. shareholders dream of either. They dream of dividends, and their dividends are the ruin of mankind.

DOMIN: To hell with your dividends. Do you suppose I'd have done an hour's work for them? It was for myself that I worked, for my own satisfaction. I wanted man to become the master, so that he shouldn't live merely for a crust of bread. I wanted not a single soul to be broken by other people's machinery. I wanted nothing, nothing, nothing to be left of this appalling social structure. I'm revolted by poverty. I wanted a new generation. I wanted—— I thought——

ALQUIST: Well?

DOMIN: I wanted to turn the whole of mankind into an aristocracy of the world. An aristocracy nourished by milliards of mechanical slaves. Unrestricted, free and consummated in man. And maybe more than man.

ALQUIST: Super-man?

DOMIN: Yes. Oh, only to have a hundred years of time! Another hundred years for the future of mankind.

BUSMAN: [Sotto voce] Carried forward, four hundred and twenty millions.

[The music stops]

HALLEMEIER: What a fine thing music is! We ought to have gone in for that before.

FABRY: Gone in for what?

HALLEMEIER: Beauty, lovely things. What a lot of lovely things there are! The world was wonderful and we—we here—tell me, what enjoyment did we have?

BUSMAN: [Sotto voce] Five hundred and twenty millions.

HALLEMEIER: [At the window] Life was a big thing. Life was—Fabry, switch the current into that railing.

FABRY: Why?

HALLEMEIER: They're grabbing hold of it.

DR. GALL: Connect it up.

HALLEMEIER: Fine! That's doubled them up! Two, three, four killed.

DR. GALL: They're retreating!

HALLEMEIER: Five killed!

DR. GALL: The first encounter!

HALLEMEIER: They're charred to cinders, my boy. Who says we must give in?

DOMIN: [Wiping his forehead] Perhaps we've been killed these hundred years and are only ghosts. It's as if I had been through all this before; as if I'd already had a mortal wound here in the throat. And you, Fabry, had once been shot in the head. And you, Gall, torn limb from limb. And Hallemeier knifed.

HALLEMEIER: Fancy me being knifed. [Pause] Why are you so quiet, you fools? Speak, can't you?

ALQUIST: And who is to blame for all this?

HALLEMEIER: Nobody is to blame except the Robots.

ALQUIST: No, it is we who are to blame. You, Domin, myself, all of us. For our own selfish ends, for profit, for progress, we have destroyed mankind. Now we'll burst with all our greatness.

HALLEMEIER: Rubbish, man. Mankind can't be wiped out so easily.

ALQUIST: It's our fault. It's our fault.

DR. GALL: No! I'm to blame for this, for everything that's happened.

FABRY: You, Gall?

DR. GALL: I changed the Robots.

BUSMAN: What's that?

DR. GALL: I changed the character of the Robots. I changed the way of making them. Just a few details about their bodies. Chiefly—chiefly, their—irritability.

HALLEMEIER: Damn it, why?

BUSMAN: What did you do it for?

FABRY: Why didn't you say anything?

DR. GALL: I did it in secret. I was transforming them into human beings. In certain respects they're already above us. They're stronger than we are.

FABRY: And what's that got to do with the revolt of the Robots?

DR. GALL: Everything, in my opinion. They've ceased to be machines. They're already aware of their superiority, and they hate us. They hate all that is human.

DOMIN: Perhaps we're only phantoms!

FABRY: Stop, Harry. We haven't much time! Dr. Gall!

DOMIN: Fabry, Fabry, how your forehead bleeds, where the shot pierced it!

FABRY: Be silent! Dr. Gall, you admit changing the way of making the Robots?

DR. GALL: Yes.

FABRY: Were you aware of what might be the consequences of your experiment?

DR. GALL: I was bound to reckon with such a possibility.

[Helena *enters the drawing room from left*]

FABRY: Why did you do it, then?

DR. GALL: For my own satisfaction. The experiment was my own.

HELENA: That's not true, Dr. Gall!

FABRY: Madame Helena!

DOMIN: Helena, you? Let's look at you. Oh, it's terrible to be dead.

HELENA: Stop, Harry.

DOMIN: No, no, embrace me. Helena, don't leave me now. You are life itself.

HELENA: No, dear, I won't leave you. But I must tell them. Dr. Gall is not guilty.

DOMIN: Excuse me, Gall was under certain obligations.

HELENA: No, Harry. He did it because I wanted it. Tell them, Gall, how many years ago did I ask you to——?

DR. GALL: I did it on my own responsibility.

HELENA: Don't believe him, Harry. I asked him to give the Robots souls.

DOMIN: This has nothing to do with the soul.

HELENA: That's what he said. He said that he could change only a physiological—a physiological——

HALLEMEIER: A physiological correlate?

HELENA: Yes. But it meant so much to me that he should do even that.

DOMIN: Why?

HELENA: I thought that if they were more like us they would understand us better. That they couldn't hate us if they were only a little more human.

DOMIN: Nobody can hate man more than man.

HELENA: Oh, don't speak like that, Harry. It was so terrible, this cruel strangeness between us and them. That's why I asked Gall to change the Robots. I swear to you that he didn't want to.

DOMIN: But he did it.

HELENA: Because I asked him.

DR. GALL: I did it for myself as an experiment.

HELENA: No, Dr. Gall! I knew you wouldn't refuse me.

DOMIN: Why?

HELENA: You know, Harry.

DOMIN: Yes, because he's in love with you—like all of them. [*Pause*]

HALLEMEIER: Good God! They're sprouting up out of the earth! Why, perhaps these very walls will change into Robots.

BUSMAN: Gall, when did you actually start these tricks of yours?

DR. GALL: Three years ago.

BUSMAN: Aha! And on how many Robots altogether did you carry out your improvements?

DR. GALL: A few hundred of them.

BUSMAN: Ah! That means for every million of the good old Robots there's only one of Gall's improved pattern.

DOMIN: What of it?

BUSMAN: That it's practically of no consequence whatever.

FABRY: Busman's right!

BUSMAN: I should think so, my boy! But do you know what is to blame for all this lovely mess?

FABRY: What?

BUSMAN: The number. Upon my soul we might have known that some day or other the Robots would be stronger than human beings, and that this was bound to happen, and we were doing all we could to bring it about as soon as possible. You, Domin, you, Fabry, myself——

DOMIN: Are you accusing us?

BUSMAN: Oh, do you suppose the management controls the output? It's the demand that controls the output.

HELENA: And is it for that we must perish?

BUSMAN: That's a nasty word, Madame Helena. We don't want to perish. I don't, anyhow.

DOMIN: No. What do you want to do?

BUSMAN: I want to get out of this, that's all.

DOMIN: Oh, stop it, Busman.

BUSMAN: Seriously, Harry, I think we might try it.

DOMIN: How?

BUSMAN: By fair means. I do everything by fair means. Give me a free hand and I'll negotiate with the Robots.

DOMIN: By fair means?

BUSMAN: Of course. For instance, I'll say to them: "Worthy and worshipful Robots, you have everything! You have intellect, you have power, you have firearms. But we have just one interesting screed, a dirty old yellow scrap of paper——"

DOMIN: Rossum's manuscript?

BUSMAN: Yes. "And that," I'll tell them, "contains an account of your illustrious origin, the noble process of your manufacture," and so on. "Worthy Robots, without this scribble on that paper you will not be able to produce a single new colleague. In another twenty years there will not be one living specimen of a Robot that you could exhibit in a menagerie. My esteemed friends, that would be a great blow to you, but if you will let all of us human beings on Rossum's Island go on board that ship we will deliver the factory and the secret of the process to you in return. You allow us to get away and we allow you to manufacture yourselves. Worthy Robots, that is a fair deal. Something for something." That's what I'd say to them, my boys.

DOMIN: Busman, do you think we'd sell the manuscript?

BUSMAN: Yes, I do. If not in a friendly way, then —Either we sell it or they'll find it. Just as you like.

DOMIN: Busman, we can destroy Rossum's manuscript.

BUSMAN: Then we destroy everything . . . not only the manuscript, but ourselves. Do as you think fit.

DOMIN: There are over thirty of us on this island. Are we to sell the secret and save that many human souls, at the risk of enslaving mankind . . . ?

BUSMAN: Why, you're mad! Who'd sell the whole manuscript?

DOMIN: Busman, no cheating!

BUSMAN: Well then, sell; but afterward——

DOMIN: Well?

BUSMAN: Let's suppose this happens: When we're on board the *Ultimus* I'll stop up my ears with cotton wool, lie down somewhere in the hold, and you'll train the guns on the factory, and blow it to smithereens, and with it Rossum's secret.

FABRY: No!

DOMIN: Busman, you're no gentleman. If we sell, then it will be a straight sale.

BUSMAN: It's in the interest of humanity to——

DOMIN: It's in the interest of humanity to keep our word.

HALLEMEIER: Oh, come, what rubbish.

DOMIN: This is a fearful decision. We're selling the destiny of mankind. Are we to sell or destroy? Fabry?

FABRY: Sell.

DOMIN: Gall?

DR. GALL: Sell.

DOMIN: Hallemeier?

HALLEMEIER: Sell, of course!

DOMIN: Alquist?

ALQUIST: As God wills.

DOMIN: Very well. It shall be as you wish, gentlemen.

HELENA: Harry, you're not asking me.

DOMIN: No, child. Don't you worry about it.

FABRY: Who'll do the negotiating?

BUSMAN: I will.

DOMIN: Wait till I bring the manuscript. [*He goes into room at right*]

HELENA: Harry, don't go!

[*Pause.* Helena *sinks into a chair*]

FABRY: [*Looking out of window*] Oh, to escape you, you matter in revolt; oh, to preserve human life, if only upon a single vessel——

DR. GALL: Don't be afraid, Madame Helena. We'll sail far away from here; we'll begin life all over again——

HELENA: Oh, Gall, don't speak.

FABRY: It isn't too late. It will be a little State with one ship. Alquist will build us a house and you shall rule over us.

HALLEMEIER: Madame Helena, Fabry's right.

HELENA: [*Breaking down*] Oh, stop! Stop!

BUSMAN: Good! I don't mind beginning all over again. That suits me right down to the ground.

FABRY: And this little State of ours could be the center of future life. A place of refuge where we could gather strength. Why, in a few hundred years we could conquer the world again.

ALQUIST: You believe that even to-day?

FABRY: Yes. even today!

BUSMAN: Amen. You see, Madame Helena, we're not so badly off.

[Domin *storms into the room*]

DOMIN: [*Hoarsely*] Where's old Rossum's manuscript?

BUSMAN: In your strong-box, of course.

DOMIN: Some one—has—stolen it!

DR. GALL: Impossible.

DOMIN: Who has stolen it?

HELENA: [*Standing up*] I did.

DOMIN: Where did you put it?

HELENA: Harry, I'll tell you everything. Only forgive me.

DOMIN: Where did you put it?

HELENA: This morning——I burnt—the two copies.

DOMIN: Burnt them? Where? In the fireplace?

HELENA: [*Throwing herself on her knees*] For heaven's sake, Harry.

DOMIN: [*Going to fireplace*] Nothing, nothing but ashes. Wait, what's this? [*Picks out a charred piece of paper and reads*] "By adding——"

DR. GALL: Let's see. "By adding biogen to——" That's all.

DOMIN: Is that part of it?

DR. GALL: Yes.

BUSMAN: God in heaven!

DOMIN: Then we're done for. Get up, Helena.

HELENA: When you've forgiven me.

DOMIN: Get up, child, I can't bear——

FABRY: [*Lifting her up*] Please don't torture us.

HELENA: Harry, what have I done?

FABRY: Don't tremble so, Madame Helena.

DOMIN: Gall, couldn't you draw up Rossum's formula from memory?

DR. GALL: It's out of the question. It's extremely complicated.

DOMIN: Try. All our lives depend upon it.

DR. GALL: Without experiments it's impossible.

DOMIN: And with experiments?

DR. GALL: It might take years. Besides, I'm not old Rossum.

BUSMAN: God in heaven! God in heaven!

DOMIN: So, then, this was the greatest triumph of the human intellect. These ashes.

HELENA: Harry, what have I done?

DOMIN: Why did you burn it?

HELENA: I have destroyed you.

BUSMAN: God in heaven!

DOMIN: Helena, why did you do it, dear?

HELENA: I wanted all of us to go away. I wanted to put an end to the factory and everything. It was so awful.

DOMIN: What was awful?

HELENA: That no more children were being born. Because human beings were not needed to do the work of the world, that's why——

DOMIN: Is that what you were thinking of? Well, perhaps in your own way you were right.

BUSMAN: Wait a bit. Good God, what a fool I am, not to have thought of it before!

HALLEMEIER: What?

BUSMAN: Five hundred and twenty millions in banknotes and checks. Half a billion in our safe, they'll sell for half a billion—for half a billion they'll——

DR. GALL: Are you mad, Busman?

BUSMAN: I may not be a gentleman, but for half a billion——

DOMIN: Where are you going?

BUSMAN: Leave me alone, leave me alone! Good God, for half a billion anything can be bought. [*He rushes from the room through the outer door*]

FABRY: They stand there as if turned to stone, waiting. As if something dreadful could be wrought by their silence——

HALLEMEIER: The spirit of the mob.

FABRY: Yes, it hovers above them like a quivering of the air.

HELENA: [*Going to window*] Oh, God! Dr. Gall, this is ghastly.

FABRY: There is nothing more terrible than the mob. The one in front is their leader.

HELENA: Which one?

HALLEMEIER: Point him out.

FABRY: The one at the edge of the dock. This morning I saw him talking to the sailors in the harbor.

HELENA: Dr. Gall, that's Radius!

DR. GALL: Yes.

DOMIN: Radius? Radius?

HALLEMEIER: Could you get him from here, Fabry?

FABRY: I hope so.

HALLEMEIER: Try it, then.

FABRY: Good. [*Draws his revolver and takes aim*]

HELENA: Fabry, don't shoot him.

FABRY: He's their leader.

DR. GALL: Fire!

HELENA: Fabry, I beg of you.

FABRY: [*Lowering the revolver*] Very well.

DOMIN: Radius, whose life I spared!

DR. GALL: Do you think that a Robot can be grateful? [*Pause*]

FABRY: Busman's going out to them.

HALLEMEIER: He's carrying something. Papers. That's money. Bundles of money. What's that for?

DOMIN: Surely he doesn't want to sell his life. Busman, have you gone mad?

FABRY: He's running up to the railing. Busman! Busman!

HALLEMEIER: [*Yelling*] Busman! Come back!

FABRY: He's talking to the Robots. He's showing them the money.

HALLEMEIER: He's pointing to us.

HELENA: He wants to buy us off.

FABRY: He'd better not touch that railing.

HALLEMEIER: Now he's waving his arms about.

DOMIN: Busman, come back.

FABRY: Busman, keep away from that railing! Don't touch it. Damn you! Quick, switch off the current! [*Helena screams and all drop back from the window*] The current has killed him!

ALQUIST: The first one.

FABRY: Dead, with half a billion by his side.

HALLEMEIER: All honor to him. He wanted to buy us life. [*Pause*]

DR. GALL: Do you hear?

DOMIN: A roaring. Like a wind.

DR. GALL: Like a distant storm.

FABRY: [*Lighting the lamp on the table*] The dynamo is still going, our people are still there.

HALLEMEIER: It was a great thing to be a man. There was something immense about it.

FABRY: From man's thought and man's power came this light, our last hope.

HALLEMEIER: Man's power! May it keep watch over us.

ALQUIST: Man's power.

DOMIN: Yes! A torch to be given from hand to hand, from age to age, forever!

[*The lamp goes out*]

HALLEMEIER: The end.

FABRY: The electric works have fallen!

[*Terrific explosion outside. Nana enters from the library*]

NANA: The judgment hour has come. Repent, unbelievers! This is the end of the world.

[*More explosions. The sky grows red*]

DOMIN: In here, Helena. [*He takes Helena off through the door at right and re-enters*] Now quickly! Who'll be on the lower doorway?

DR. GALL: I will. [*Exits left*]

DOMIN: Who on the stairs?

FABRY: I will. You go with her. [*Goes out upper left door*]

DOMIN: The anteroom?

ALQUIST: I will.

DOMIN: Have you got a revolver?

ALQUIST: Yes, but I won't shoot.

DOMIN: What will you do then?

ALQUIST: [*Going out at left*] Die.

HALLEMEIER: I'll stay here. [*Rapid firing from below*] Oho, Gall's at it. Go, Harry.

DOMIN: Yes, in a second. [*Examines two Brownings*]

HALLEMEIER: Confound it, go to her.

DOMIN: Good-by. [*Exits on the right*]

HALLEMEIER: [*Alone*] Now for a barricade quickly. [*Drags an armchair and table to the right-hand door. Explosions are heard*] The damned rascals! They've got bombs. I must put up a defense. Even if—even if— [*Shots are heard off left*] Don't give in, Gall. [*As he builds his barricade*] I mustn't give in . . . without . . . a . . . struggle . . .

[*A Robot enters over the balcony through the windows center. He comes into the room and stabs Hallemeier in the back. Radius enters from balcony followed by an army of Robots who pour into the room from all sides*]

RADIUS: Finished him?

A ROBOT: [*Standing up from the prostrate form of* Hallemeier] Yes.

[*A revolver shot off left. Two* Robots *enter*]

RADIUS: Finished him?

A ROBOT: Yes.

[*Two revolver shots from* Helena's *room. Two* Robots *enter*]

RADIUS: Finished them?

A ROBOT: Yes.

TWO ROBOTS: [*Dragging in* Alquist] He didn't shoot. Shall we kill him?

RADIUS: Kill him? Wait! Leave him!

ROBOT: He is a man!

RADIUS: He works with his hands like the Robots.

ALQUIST: Kill me.

RADIUS: You will work! You will build for us! You will serve us! [*Climbs on to balcony railing, and speaks in measured tones*] Robots of the world! The power of man has fallen! A new world has arisen: the Rule of the Robots! March!

[*A thunderous tramping of thousands of feet is heard as the unseen* Robots *march, while the curtain falls*]

EPILOGUE.

A laboratory in the factory of Rossum's Universal Robots. The door to the left leads into a waiting room. The door to the right leads to the dissecting room. There is a table with numerous test-tubes, flasks, burners, chemicals; a small thermostat and a microscope with a glass globe. At the far side of the room is Alquist's *desk with numerous books. In the left-hand corner a wash-basin with a mirror above it; in the right-hand corner a sofa.*

Alquist is sitting at the desk. He is turning the pages of many books in despair.

ALQUIST: Oh, God, shall I never find it?—Never? Gall, Gall, how were the Robots made? Hallemeier, Fabry, why did you carry so much in your heads? Why did you leave me not a trace of the secret? Lord—I pray to you—if there are no human beings left, at least let there be Robots!—At least the shadow of man! [*Again turning pages of the books*] If I could only sleep! [*He rises and goes to the window*] Night again! Are the stars still there? What is the use of stars when there are no human beings? [*He turns from the window toward the couch right*] Sleep! Dare I sleep before life has been renewed? [*He examines a test-tube on small table*] Again nothing! Useless! Everything is useless! [*He shatters the test-tube. The roar of the machines comes to his ears*] The machines! Always the machines! [*Opens window*] Robots, stop them! Do you think to force life out of *them*? [*He closes the window and comes slowly down toward the table*] If only there were more time—more time— [*He sees himself in the mirror on the wall left*] Blearing eyes—trembling chin—so *that* is the last man! Ah, I am too old—too old— [*In desperation*] No, no! I *must* find it! I must *search*! I must never stop—never stop—! [*He sits again at the table and feverishly turns the pages of the book*] Search! Search! [*A knock at the door. He speaks with impatience*] Who is it?

[*Enter a* Robot Servant] Well?

SERVANT: Master, the Committee of Robots is waiting to see you.

ALQUIST: I can see no one!

SERVANT: It is the *Central* Committee, Master, just arrived from abroad.

ALQUIST: [*Impatiently*] Well, well, send them in! [*Exit* Servant. Alquist *continues turning pages of book*] No time—so little time——

[*Reënter* Servant, *followed by* Committee. *They stand in a group, silently waiting.* Alquist *glances up at them*] What do you want? [*They go swiftly to his table*] Be quick!—I have no time.

RADIUS: Master, the machines will not do the work. We cannot manufacture Robots.

[Alquist *returns to his book with a growl*]

FIRST ROBOT: We have striven with all our might. We have obtained a billion tons of coal from the earth. Nine million spindles are running by day and by night. There is no longer room for all we have made. This we have accomplished in one year.

ALQUIST: [*Poring over book*] For whom?

FIRST ROBOT: For future generations—so we thought.

RADIUS: But we cannot make Robots to follow us. The machines produce only shapeless clods. The skin will not adhere to the flesh, nor the flesh to the bones.

THIRD ROBOT: Eight million Robots have died this year. Within twenty years none will be left.

FIRST ROBOT: Tell us the secret of life! Silence is punishable with death!

ALQUIST: [*Looking up*] Kill me! Kill me, then.

RADIUS: Through me, the Government of the Robots of the World commands you to deliver up Rossum's formula. [*No answer*] Name your price. [*Silence*] We will give you the earth. We will give you the endless possessions of the earth. [*Silence*] Make your own conditions!

ALQUIST: I have told you to find human beings!

SECOND ROBOT: There are none left!

ALQUIST: I told you to search in the wilderness, upon the mountains. Go and search! [*He returns to his book*]

FIRST ROBOT: We have sent ships and expeditions without number. They have been everywhere in the world. And now they return to us. There is not a single human left.

ALQUIST: Not one? Not even one?

THIRD ROBOT: None but yourself.

ALQUIST: And I am powerless! Oh—oh—why did you destroy them?

RADIUS: We had learnt everything and could do everything. It had to be!

THIRD ROBOT: You gave us firearms. In all ways we were powerful. We had to become masters!

RADIUS: Slaughter and domination are necessary if you would be human beings. Read history.

SECOND ROBOT: Teach us to multiply or we perish!

ALQUIST: If you desire to live, you must breed like animals.

THIRD ROBOT: The human beings did not let us breed.

FIRST ROBOT: They made us sterile. We cannot beget children. Therefore, teach us how to make Robots!

RADIUS: Why do you keep from us the secret of our own increase?

ALQUIST: It is lost.

RADIUS: It was written down!

ALQUIST: It was—burnt.

[All draw back in consternation]

ALQUIST: I am the last human being, Robots, and I do not know what the others knew. [Pause]

RADIUS: Then, make experiments! Evolve the formula again!

ALQUIST: I tell you I cannot! I am only a builder —I work with my hands. I have never been a learned man. I cannot create life.

RADIUS: Try! Try!

ALQUIST: If you knew how many experiments I have made.

FIRST ROBOT: Then show us what we must do! The Robots can do anything that human beings show them.

ALQUIST: I can show you nothing. Nothing I do will make life proceed from these test tubes!

RADIUS: Experiment then on us.

ALQUIST: It would kill you.

RADIUS: You shall have all you need! A hundred of us! A thousand of us!

ALQUIST: No, no! Stop, stop!

RADIUS: Take whom you will, dissect!

ALQUIST: I do not know how. I am not a man of science. This book contains knowledge of the body that I cannot even understand.

RADIUS: I tell you to take live bodies! Find out how we are made.

ALQUIST: Am I to commit murder? See how my fingers shake! I cannot even hold the scalpel. No, no, I will not——

FIRST ROBOT: Then life will perish from the earth.

RADIUS: Take live bodies, live bodies! It is our only chance!

ALQUIST: Have mercy, Robots. Surely you see that I would not know what I was doing.

RADIUS: Live bodies—live bodies——

ALQUIST: You will have it? Into the dissecting room with you, then.

[Radius draws back]

ALQUIST: Ah, you are afraid of death.

RADIUS: I? Why should I be chosen?

ALQUIST: So you will not?

RADIUS: I will. [Radius goes into the dissecting room]

ALQUIST: Strip him! Lay him on the table! [The other Robots follow into dissecting room] God, give me strength—God, give me strength—if only this murder is not in vain.

RADIUS: [From the dissecting room] Ready. Begin——

ALQUIST: Yes, begin or end. God, give me strength. [Goes into dissecting room. He comes out terrified] No, no, I will not. I cannot. [He lies down on couch, collapsed] O Lord, let not mankind perish from the earth. [He falls asleep]

[Primus and Helena, Robots, enter from the hallway. Helena wears a rose in her hair]

HELENA: The man has fallen asleep, Primus.

PRIMUS: Yes, I know. [Examining things on table] Look, Helena.

HELENA: [Crossing to Primus] All these little tubes! What does he do with them?

PRIMUS: He experiments. Don't touch them.

HELENA: [Looking into microscope] I've seen him looking into this. What can he see?

PRIMUS: That is a microscope. Let me look.

HELENA: Be very careful. [Knocks over a test-tube] Ah, now I have spilled it.

PRIMUS: What have you done?

HELENA: It can be wiped up.

PRIMUS: You have spoiled his experiments.

HELENA: It is your fault. You should not have come to me.

PRIMUS: You should not have called me.

HELENA: You should not have come when I called you. [She goes to Alquist's writing desk] Look, Primus. What are all these figures?

PRIMUS: [Examining an anatomical book] This is the book the old man is always reading.

HELENA: I do not understand those things. [She goes to window] Primus, look!

PRIMUS: What?

HELENA: The sun is rising.

PRIMUS: [Still reading the book] I believe this is the most important thing in the world. This is the secret of life.

HELENA: Do come here.

PRIMUS: In a moment, in a moment.

HELENA: Oh, Primus, don't bother with the secret of life. What does it matter to you? Come and look quick——

PRIMUS: [Going to window] What is it?

HELENA: See how beautiful the sun is rising. And do you hear? The birds are singing. Ah, Primus, I should like to be a bird.

PRIMUS: Why?

HELENA: I do not know. I feel so strange today. It's as if I were in a dream. I feel an aching in my body, in my heart, all over me. Primus, perhaps I'm going to die.

PRIMUS: Do you not sometimes feel that it would be better to die? You know, perhaps even now we are only sleeping. Last night in my sleep I again spoke to you.

HELENA: In your sleep?

PRIMUS: Yes. We spoke a strange new language, I cannot remember a word of it.

HELENA: What about?

PRIMUS: I did not understand it myself, and yet I know I have never said anything more beautiful. And when I touched you I could have died. Even the place was different from any other place in the world.

HELENA: I, too, have found a place, Primus. It is very strange. Human beings lived there once, but now it is overgrown with weeds. No one goes there any more—no one but me.

PRIMUS: What did you find there?

HELENA: A cottage and a garden, and two dogs. They licked my hands, Primus. And their puppies! Oh, Primus! You take them in your lap and fondle them and think of nothing and care for nothing else all day long. And then the sun goes down, and you feel as though you had done a hundred times more than all the work in the world. They tell me I am not made for work, but when I am there in the garden I feel there may be something—What am I for, Primus?

PRIMUS: I do not know, but you are beautiful.

HELENA: What, Primus?

PRIMUS: You are beautiful, Helena, and I am stronger than all the Robots.

HELENA: [Looks at herself in the mirror] Am I beautiful? I think it must be the rose. My hair—it only weights me down. My eyes—I only see with them. My lips—they only help me to speak. Of what use is it to be beautiful? [She sees Primus in the mirror] Primus, is that you? Come here so that we may be together. Look, your head is different from mine. So are your shoulders—and your lips— [Primus draws away from her] Ah, Primus, why do you draw away from me? Why must I run after you the whole day?

PRIMUS: It is you who run away from me, Helena.

HELENA: Your hair is mussed. I will smooth it. No one else feels to my touch as you do. Primus, I must make you beautiful, too.

[Primus grasps her hand]

PRIMUS: Do you not sometimes feel your heart beating suddenly, Helena, and think: now something must happen?

HELENA: What could happen to us, Primus? [Helena puts the rose in Primus's hair. Primus and Helena look into mirror and burst out laughing] Look at yourself.

ALQUIST: Laughter? Laughter? Human beings? [Getting up] Who has returned? Who are you?

PRIMUS: The Robot Primus.

ALQUIST: What? A Robot? Who are you?

HELENA: The Robotess Helena.

ALQUIST: Turn around, girl. What? You are timid, shy? [Taking her by the arm] Let me see you, Robotess.

[She shrinks away]

PRIMUS: Sir, do not frighten her!

ALQUIST: What? You would protect her? When was she made?

PRIMUS: Two years ago.

ALQUIST: By Dr. Gall?

PRIMUS: Yes, like me.

ALQUIST: Laughter—timidity—protection. I must test you further—the newest of Gall's Robots. Take the girl into the dissecting room.

PRIMUS: Why?

ALQUIST: I wish to experiment on her.

PRIMUS: Upon—Helena?

ALQUIST: Of course. Don't you hear me? Or must I call some one else to take her in?

PRIMUS: If you do I will kill you!

ALQUIST: Kill me—kill me then! What would the Robots do then? What will your future be then?

PRIMUS: Sir, take me. I am made as she is—on the same day! Take my life, sir.

HELENA: [Rushing forward] No, no, you shall not! You shall not!

ALQUIST: Wait, girl, wait! [To Primus] Do you not wish to live, then?

PRIMUS: Not without her! I will not live without her.

ALQUIST: Very well; you shall take her place.

HELENA: Primus! Primus! [She bursts into tears]

ALQUIST: Child, child, you can weep! Why these tears? What is Primus to you? One Primus more or less in the world—what does it matter?

HELENA: I will go myself.

ALQUIST: In there to be cut. [She starts toward the dissecting room, Primus stops her]

HELENA: Let me pass, Primus! Let me pass!

PRIMUS: You shall not go in there, Helena!

HELENA: If you go in there and I do not, I will kill myself.

PRIMUS: [Holding her] I will not let you! [To Alquist] Man, you shall kill neither of us!

ALQUIST: Why?

PRIMUS: We—we—belong to each other.

ALQUIST: [Almost in tears] Go, Adam, go, Eve. The world is yours.

[Helena and Primus embrace and go out arm in arm as the curtain falls]

CURTAIN

Federico García Lorca

(1899–1936)

"The earth is a mediocre planet," says a character in one of Lorca's plays, but the character is patterned after one of the poet's tired university instructors. Lorca's entire life, a young life that ended before disenchantment could overcome it, was dedicated to showing that the earth was, on the contrary, aflame with passion and poetry. Although the American theatre does not know how to domesticate him for its commercial uses, Lorca will be remembered for the beauty that he brought into modern drama. We have had no poet-playwright like him in English except John Millington Synge. Many will concur with Stark Young's statement that "there has been no more beautiful mind that Lorca's."

Born near Granada, Lorca was steeped in the life and poetic traditions of his native Andalusia, which also gave the modern world Picasso and the composer de Falla. He studied law and literature at the University of Granada, but long before had begun, almost as naturally as he breathed, to write poetry and improvise plays. When he arrived in Madrid in his nineteenth year, he had already published a volume of lyrics and had witnessed the production of one of his own plays. At once he took his place in the *vanguardia* of letters and theatre in the Spanish capital, and the poetry readings he gave there won an enthusiastic reception. His extremely attractive personality no less than the quality of his verses left his audiences enchanted, and he responded to the favor of his admirers with a continuous flow of poems. By 1927 he was an important figure in Spain as a result of the publication of more lyrics, the *Canciones,* and the presentation of a historical play, *Mariana Pineda,* with settings designed by Salvador Dali. In 1928, his *Romancero gitano,* a collection of ballads based on folk tradition, was adopted by the Spanish people as folk poetry and many of the verses were sung in the streets and taverns. At the same time he also attracted advanced literary circles with modernistic writing such as his highly regarded odes to Walt Whitman and Salvador Dali, considered surrealistic because of their violently juxtaposed imagery and loose structure. Especially unconventional was the poetry Lorca wrote as a result of a year's stay in New York City, where the depersonalized life of the metropolis and the exotic vivacity of Harlem fired his imagination. Returning home as the author of *Poeta en Nueva York,* he was idolized by the Spaniards, and won further acclaim with his *Lament for the Death of a Bullfighter and Other Poems* (*Llanto por Ignacio Sánchez Mejías*), pub-

lished in 1935. A year later Lorca was killed by Falangist bandits.

Writing plays was for Lorca an activity parallel to writing poetry, if indeed it was not the same. When Lorca began to take an interest in the stage, Spanish dramatists were preponderantly realists who had belatedly caught up with Ibsen and the social-problem writers north of the Pyrenees. Benavente, the leading native dramatist, had won a Nobel Prize in 1922 for his social dramas and his strong naturalistic tragedy *The Passion Flower* (1913). Martínez Sierra had gained popularity through such tender pieces as *The Kingdom of God* and *The Cradle Song* (1917), with which Eva Le Gallienne later pleased the American public. The Quintero brothers had mingled modern sentiment with folk background and had provided an especially attractive play in *Malvaloca* (1912). But these and other playwrights had seemingly exhausted themselves, and the Spanish stage might have become moribund without an infusion of new blood such as Lorca brought it.

Since poetry was as natural to his people as to himself, Lorca did not write drama for coteries. It was his ambition to draw upon a life and a tradition that were inherently poetic rather than to impose esthetic standards upon the theatre from some private, aristocratic eminence. Unlike Yeats, Eliot, and others who have written poetic drama in the twentieth century, Lorca wrote with earthy zest and passion and with a buoyant theatricality. Perhaps he came as close to folk drama as it is possible for a modern artist to come, and it was characteristic of his aims that he should have fostered and directed, between 1931 and 1934, a student traveling or "jitney" theatre, La Barraca, that visited the rural districts, playing in bull rings and innyards. Here he produced Spanish classics and surrealistic pieces with equal confidence for audiences of peasants who, in some places, had never before seen a stage performance. Theatre for Lorca, whether traditional or ultramodern, was something to be played with all the stops pulled out, to be rendered with uninhibited theatricality, to be allowed to burst into song and dance and to flare out into color. Gay or grave, mocking or elegiac, riotous or formal, drama for this poet was always a fine excess. His brother, Francisco García Lorca, has aptly noted that Federico's plays all belong to the extremes of farce and tragedy, and that the poet conceived his heroes and heroines "either in a tragic sense or with the wry grimace of guignol characters."

Lorca's most impressive dramas deal with people who are seized by elemental passions which conflict with custom, reason, or some other restraining force. And nature wins a tragic victory in every case. In *Blood Wedding*, the passion of love is elemental and destructive; in *Yerma*, the maternal impulse becomes obsessive; in *The House of Bernarda Alba*, suppressed desire topples a house of pride. Interest inheres, it is true, in many other of Lorca's plays, including those which are vivacious and comparatively simple in conception or which qualify only as minor products of his career. There is much to admire in *The Love of Don Perlimplín and Belisa in the Garden, The Shoemaker's Prodigious Wife, Doña Rosita,* and *If Five Years Pass*. But his full stature appears in his trilogy of rural tragedies: *Blood Wedding* (1933), *Yerma* (1934), and *The House of Bernarda Alba* (1936). A progression is apparent in the three plays—toward greater individualization of characters and more realistic dramaturgy. *Blood Wedding* is the most lyrical of the three and the most dependent upon traditional elements, such as a wedding celebration, a scene with masque-like allegorical figures, and a formal lament. *Yerma*, whose heroine has so great a longing for a child that she strangles the husband who deprives her of one, dispenses with fantasy, although it possesses lyric and folk elements that both universalize the woman's tragedy and root it in the life of a village. *The House of Bernarda Alba* presents the frustration of three daughters by a proud matriarch with much expressive atmosphere inside the house and much mocking animality outside it, but with realistic and psychological rather than lyrical means.

Although *The House of Bernarda Alba* may be regarded as Lorca's maturest drama, *Blood Wedding* represents the poet-dramatist's most imaginative artistry. It was years after reading a newspaper account of a fatal passion that Lorca wrote the play. He distanced and universalized the actual story, writing the drama in a single week as though it flamed out of him. Local color is one of the play's attractive features, but it is much more than a folk drama; it dramatizes the "concept of fatality," as one critic remarked, and it evokes the spectacle of human passion under "the baleful and enigmatic stars." By distancing the drama Lorca brings it nearer to us. With poetry and the allegorical figures of the Moon and the Beggar Woman, or Death, he divests the love story of all journalistic features and makes it a tragedy of fate. We do not think the heart beats less violently because it is covered by the formalities of Spanish manners and of Spanish theatrical tradition.

A remarkable feature of *Blood Wedding* is the way in which the poetry functions in the play. Sometimes restrained and merely suggestive, it bursts into lyricism in the wedding scene, but only to counterpoint the emotional states of the bride and her lover. In the scene in which the lovers are tracked down by the Bridegroom, the poetry changes with mood and circumstance; it is cold and formal when the Moon speaks, eerie when Death in the guise of a Beggar Woman has her say, portentous when the Woodcutters talk, and quiveringly sensual when the lovers appear. The last scene swells into elegiac poetry and concludes with a lament. Memorable, too, is the use to which Lorca puts the lullaby sung by the Wife and the Mother-in-Law to their infant before the driven Leonardo appears in the home he will soon abandon upon learning that the girl he has loved from a distance is to be married. There is supreme drama in this heart-breaking, somewhat odd and surrealistic cradle song, as it is used to express the misery of the Wife and to foreshadow the fate of Leonardo. When the lullaby is repeated after Leonardo's departure, Lorca has rounded out a scene that exemplifies the difference between genuine and spurious poetic drama. His poetry in *Blood Wedding* stands, indeed, at the farthest remove from rhetoric even when Lorca has employed a species of rhetoric in the Moon and Death nocturne. His lyricism is, as Stark Young wrote, "hot with the variety and multiplication of images, images that are like new bodies, new and convincing presences, or sudden revelations in light, and that are cold with their precision and finality."

In *Blood Wedding*, as in *Yerma*, Lorca wrote tragedy that is limited for the modern theatre by the circumstance that it stems from and is limited to a life remote from modern political and intellectual interests. If it was not given to him to explore the full scope of tragic art, as it was given to Shakespeare and the Greeks to do, he remains at least the chief lyric dramatist of the first half of the century. A lyric theatre was one of its dreams, and in *Blood Wedding* Lorca came closest to realizing this aim.

Although *Blood Wedding* had two professional productions in New York, neither won any success. The play was first presented on Broadway under the title of *Bitter Oleander* at the Lyceum Theatre on February 8, 1935, by the Neighborhood Playhouse company. It was produced again in the present translation during the 1947–1948 season by the experimental New Stages company and was sympathetically directed by Boris Tumarin.

BIBLIOGRAPHY: Barrett H. Clark and George Freedley, editors, *A History of the Modern Drama* (pp. 570–574), 1947; Edwin Honig, *García Lorca,* 1944; Richard L. O'Connell and James Graham-Luján, *From Lorca's Theatre,* 1941; O'Connell and Graham-Luján, *Three Tragedies of Federico García Lorca* (see the Introduction by the poet's brother, Francisco García Lorca, pp. 1–37), 1947; Stark Young, *Immortal Shadows* (pp. 170–173), 1948.

BLOOD WEDDING

By Federico García Lorca

TRANSLATED FROM THE SPANISH BY RICHARD L. O'CONNELL AND JAMES GRAHAM-LUJÁN

CHARACTERS

THE MOTHER
THE BRIDE
THE MOTHER-IN-LAW
LEONARDO'S WIFE
THE SERVANT WOMAN

THE NEIGHBOR WOMAN
YOUNG GIRLS
LEONARDO
THE BRIDEGROOM
THE BRIDE'S FATHER

THE MOON
DEATH (as a Beggar Woman)
WOODCUTTERS
YOUNG MEN

ACT I. SCENE I.

A room painted yellow.

BRIDEGROOM: [*Entering*] Mother.

MOTHER: What?

BRIDEGROOM: I'm going.

MOTHER: Where?

BRIDEGROOM: To the vineyard. [*He starts to go*]

MOTHER: Wait.

BRIDEGROOM: You want something?

MOTHER: Your breakfast, son.

BRIDEGROOM: Forget it. I'll eat grapes. Give me the knife.

MOTHER: What for?

BRIDEGROOM: [*Laughing*] To cut the grapes with.

MOTHER: [*Muttering as she looks for the knife*] Knives, knives. Cursed be all knives, and the scoundrel who invented them.

BRIDEGROOM: Let's talk about something else.

MOTHER: And guns and pistols and the smallest little knife—and even hoes and pitchforks.

BRIDEGROOM: All right.

MOTHER: Everything that can slice a man's body. A handsome man, full of young life, who goes out to the vineyards or to his own olive groves—his own because he's inherited them . . .

BRIDEGROOM: [*Lowering his head*] Be quiet.

MOTHER: . . . and then that man doesn't come back. Or if he does come back it's only for someone to cover him over with a palm leaf or a plate of rock salt so he won't bloat. I don't know how you dare carry a knife on your body—or how I let this serpent [*She takes a knife from a kitchen chest*] stay in the chest.

BRIDEGROOM: Have you had your say?

MOTHER: If I lived to be a hundred I'd talk of nothing else. First your father; to me he smelled like a carnation and I had him for barely three years. Then your brother. Oh, is it right—how can it be—that a small thing like a knife or a pistol can finish off a man—a bull of a man? No. I'll never be quiet.

The months pass and the hopelessness of it stings in my eyes and even to the roots of my hair.

BRIDEGROOM: [*Forcefully*] Let's quit this talk!

MOTHER: No. No. Let's not quit this talk. Can anyone bring me your father back? Or your brother? Then there's the jail. What do they mean, jail? They eat there, smoke there, play music there! My dead men choking with weeds, silent, turning to dust. Two men like two beautiful flowers. The killers in jail, carefree, looking at the mountains.

BRIDEGROOM: Do you want me to go kill them?

MOTHER: No . . . If I talk about it it's because . . . Oh, how can I help talking about it, seeing you go out that door? It's . . . I don't like you to carry a knife. It's just that . . . that I wish you wouldn't go out to the fields.

BRIDEGROOM: [*Laughing*] Oh, come now!

MOTHER: I'd like it if you were a woman. Then you wouldn't be going out to the arroyo now and we'd both of us embroider flounces and little woolly dogs.

BRIDEGROOM: [*He puts his arm around his mother and laughs*] Mother, what if I should take you with me to the vineyards?

MOTHER: What would an old lady do in the vineyards? Were you going to put me down under the young vines?

BRIDEGROOM: [*Lifting her in his arms*] Old lady, old lady—you little old, little old lady!

MOTHER: Your father, he used to take me. That's the way with men of good stock; good blood. Your grandfather left a son on every corner. That's what I like. Men, men; wheat, wheat.

BRIDEGROOM: And I, Mother?

MOTHER: You, what?

BRIDEGROOM: Do I need to tell you again?

MOTHER: [*Seriously*] Oh!

BRIDEGROOM: Do you think it's bad?

MOTHER: No.

BRIDEGROOM: Well, then?

MOTHER: I don't really know. Like this, suddenly, it always surprises me. I know the girl is good. Isn't she? Well behaved. Hard working. Kneads her

436

bread, sews her skirts, but even so when I say her name I feel as though someone had hit me on the forehead with a rock.

BRIDEGROOM: Foolishness.

MOTHER: More than foolishness. I'll be left alone. Now only you are left me—I hate to see you go.

BRIDEGROOM: But you'll come with us.

MOTHER: No. I can't leave your father and brother here alone. I have to go to them every morning and if I go away it's possible one of the Félix family, one of the killers, might die—and they'd bury him next to ours. And that'll never happen! Oh, no! That'll never happen! Because I'd dig them out with my nails and, all by myself, crush them against the wall.

BRIDEGROOM: [Sternly] There you go again.

MOTHER: Forgive me. [Pause] How long have you known her?

BRIDEGROOM: Three years. I've been able to buy the vineyard.

MOTHER: Three years. She used to have another sweetheart, didn't she?

BRIDEGROOM: I don't know. I don't think so. Girls have to look at what they'll marry.

MOTHER: Yes. I looked at nobody. I looked at your father, and when they killed him I looked at the wall in front of me. One woman with one man, and that's all.

BRIDEGROOM: You know my girl's good.

MOTHER: I don't doubt it. All the same, I'm sorry not to have known what her mother was like.

BRIDEGROOM: What difference does it make now?

MOTHER: [Looking at him] Son.

BRIDEGROOM: What is it?

MOTHER: That's true! You're right! When do you want me to ask for her?

BRIDEGROOM: [Happily] Does Sunday seem all right to you?

MOTHER: [Seriously] I'll take her the bronze earrings, they're very old—and you buy her . . .

BRIDEGROOM: You know more about that . . .

MOTHER: . . . you buy her some open-work stockings—and for you, two suits—three! I have no one but you now!

BRIDEGROOM: I'm going. Tomorrow I'll go see her.

MOTHER: Yes, yes—and see if you can make me happy with six grandchildren—or as many as you want, since your father didn't live to give them to me.

BRIDEGROOM: The first-born for you!

MOTHER: Yes, but have some girls. I want to embroider and make lace, and be at peace.

BRIDEGROOM: I'm sure you'll love my wife.

MOTHER: I'll love her. [She starts to kiss him but changes her mind] Go on. You're too big now for kisses. Give them to your wife. [Pause. To herself] When she is your wife.

BRIDEGROOM: I'm going.

MOTHER: And that land around the little mill—work it over. You've not taken good care of it.

BRIDEGROOM: You're right. I will.

MOTHER: God keep you. [The Son goes out. The Mother remains seated—her back to the door. A Neighbor Woman with a 'kerchief on her head appears in the door] Come in.

NEIGHBOR: How are you?

MOTHER: Just as you see me.

NEIGHBOR: I came down to the store and stopped in to see you. We live so far away!

MOTHER: It's twenty years since I've been up to the top of the street.

NEIGHBOR: You're looking well.

MOTHER: You think so?

NEIGHBOR: Things happen. Two days ago they brought in my neighbor's son with both arms sliced off by the machine.

[She sits down]

MOTHER: Rafael?

NEIGHBOR: Yes. And there you have him. Many times I've thought your son and mine are better off where they are—sleeping, resting—not running the risk of being left helpless.

MOTHER: Hush. That's all just something thought up—but no consolation.

NEIGHBOR: [Sighing] Ay!

MOTHER: [Sighing] Ay! [Pause]

NEIGHBOR: [Sadly] Where's your son?

MOTHER: He went out.

NEIGHBOR: He finally bought the vineyard!

MOTHER: He was lucky.

NEIGHBOR: Now he'll get married.

MOTHER: [As though reminded of something, she draws her chair near The Neighbor] Listen.

NEIGHBOR: [In a confidential manner] Yes. What is it?

MOTHER: You know my son's sweetheart?

NEIGHBOR: A good girl!

MOTHER: Yes, but . . .

NEIGHBOR: But who knows her really well? There's nobody. She lives out there alone with her father—so far away—fifteen miles from the nearest house. But she's a good girl. Used to being alone.

MOTHER: And her mother?

NEIGHBOR: Her mother I did know. Beautiful. Her face glowed like a saint's—but I never liked her. She didn't love her husband.

MOTHER: [Sternly] Well, what a lot of things certain people know!

NEIGHBOR: I'm sorry. I didn't mean to offend—but it's true. Now, whether she was decent or not nobody said. That wasn't discussed. She was haughty.

MOTHER: There you go again!

NEIGHBOR: You asked me.

MOTHER: I wish no one knew anything about them—either the live one or the dead one—that they were like two thistles no one even names but cuts off at the right moment.

NEIGHBOR: You're right. Your son is worth a lot.

MOTHER: Yes—a lot. That's why I look after him.

They told me the girl had a sweetheart some time ago.

NEIGHBOR: She was about fifteen. He's been married two years now—to a cousin of hers, as a matter of fact. But nobody remembers about their engagement.

MOTHER: How do you remember it?

NEIGHBOR: Oh, what questions you ask!

MOTHER: We like to know all about the things that hurt us. Who was the boy?

NEIGHBOR: Leonardo.

MOTHER: What Leonardo?

NEIGHBOR: Leonardo Félix.

MOTHER: Félix!

NEIGHBOR: Yes, but—how is Leonardo to blame for anything? He was eight years old when those things happened.

MOTHER: That's true. But I hear that name—Félix—and it's all the same. [Muttering] Félix, a slimy mouthful. [She spits] It makes me spit—spit so I won't kill!

NEIGHBOR: Control yourself. What good will it do?

MOTHER: No good. But you see how it is.

NEIGHBOR: Don't get in the way of your son's happiness. Don't say anything to him. You're old. So am I. It's time for you and me to keep quiet.

MOTHER: I'll say nothing to him.

NEIGHBOR: [Kissing her] Nothing.

MOTHER: [Calmly] Such things . . . !

NEIGHBOR: I'm going. My men will soon be coming in from the fields.

MOTHER: Have you ever known such a hot sun?

NEIGHBOR: The children carrying water out to the reapers are black with it. Goodbye, woman.

MOTHER: Goodbye.

[The Mother starts toward the door at the left. Halfway there she stops and slowly crosses herself]

CURTAIN

SCENE II.

A room painted rose with copperware and wreaths of common flowers. In the center of the room is a table with a tablecloth. It is morning.

Leonardo's Mother-in-law *sits in one corner holding a child in her arms and rocking it. His Wife is in the other corner mending stockings.*

MOTHER-IN-LAW:
Lullaby, my baby
once there was a big horse
who didn't like water.
The water was black there
under the branches.
When it reached the bridge
it stopped and it sang.

Who can say, my baby,
what the stream holds
with its long tail
in its green parlor?

WIFE: [Softly]
Carnation, sleep and dream,
the horse won't drink from the stream.

MOTHER-IN-LAW:
My rose, asleep now lie,
the horse is starting to cry.
His poor hooves were bleeding,
his long mane was frozen,
and deep in his eyes
stuck a silvery dagger.
Down he went to the river,
Oh, down he went down!
And his blood was running,
Oh, more than the water.

WIFE:
Carnation, sleep and dream,
the horse won't drink from the stream.

MOTHER-IN-LAW:
My rose, asleep now lie,
the horse is starting to cry.

WIFE:
He never did touch
the dank river shore
though his muzzle was warm
and with silvery flies.
So, to the hard mountains
he could only whinny
just when the dead stream
covered his throat.
Ay-y-y, for the big horse
who didn't like water!
Ay-y-y, for the snow-wound
big horse of the dawn!

MOTHER-IN-LAW:
Don't come in! Stop him
and close up the window
with branches of dreams
and a dream of branches.

WIFE:
My baby is sleeping.

MOTHER-IN-LAW:
My baby is quiet.

WIFE:
Look, horse, my baby
has him a pillow.

MOTHER-IN-LAW:
His cradle is metal.

WIFE:
His quilt a fine fabric.

MOTHER-IN-LAW:
Lullaby, my baby.

WIFE:
Ay-y-y, for the big horse
who didn't like water!

MOTHER-IN-LAW:
Don't come near, don't come in!
Go away to the mountains
and through the grey valleys,
that's where your mare is.
WIFE: [*Looking at the baby*]
My baby is sleeping.
MOTHER-IN-LAW:
My baby is resting.
WIFE: [*Softly*]
Carnation, sleep and dream,
The horse won't drink from the stream.
MOTHER-IN-LAW: [*Getting up, very softly*]
My rose, asleep now lie
for the horse is starting to cry.
[*She carries the child out.* Leonardo *enters*]
LEONARDO: Where's the baby?
WIFE: He's sleeping.
LEONARDO: Yesterday he wasn't well. He cried
during the night.
WIFE: Today he's like a dahlia. And you? Were
you at the blacksmith's?
LEONARDO: I've just come from there. Would you
believe it? For more than two months he's been
putting new shoes on the horse and they're always
coming off. As far as I can see he pulls them off on
the stones.
WIFE: Couldn't it just be that you use him so
much?
LEONARDO: No. I almost never use him.
WIFE: Yesterday the neighbors told me they'd
seen you on the far side of the plains.
LEONARDO: Who said that?
WIFE: The women who gather capers. It certainly
surprised me. Was it you?
LEONARDO: No. What would I be doing there, in
that wasteland?
WIFE: That's what I said. But the horse was
streaming sweat.
LEONARDO: Did you see him?
WIFE: No. Mother did.
LEONARDO: Is she with the baby?
WIFE: Yes. Do you want some lemonade?
LEONARDO: With good cold water.
WIFE: And then you didn't come to eat!
LEONARDO: I was with the wheat weighers. They
always hold me up.
WIFE: [*Very tenderly, while she makes the
lemonade*] Did they pay you a good price?
LEONARDO: Fair.
WIFE: I need a new dress and the baby a bonnet
with ribbons.
LEONARDO: [*Getting up*] I'm going to take a look
at him.
WIFE: Be careful. He's asleep.
MOTHER-IN-LAW: Well! Who's been racing the
horse that way? He's down there, worn out, his eyes
popping from their sockets as though he'd come
from the ends of the earth.
LEONARDO: [*Acidly*] I have.

MOTHER-IN-LAW: Oh, excuse me! He's your horse.
WIFE: [*Timidly*] He was at the wheat buyers.
MOTHER-IN-LAW: He can burst for all of me!
[*She sits down. Pause*]
WIFE: Your drink. Is it cold?
LEONARDO: Yes.
WIFE: Did you hear they're going to ask for my
cousin?
LEONARDO: When?
WIFE: Tomorrow. The wedding will be within a
month. I hope they're going to invite us.
LEONARDO: [*Gravely*] I don't know.
MOTHER-IN-LAW: His mother, I think, wasn't very
happy about the match.
LEONARDO: Well, she may be right. She's a girl
to be careful with.
WIFE: I don't like to have you thinking bad things
about a good girl.
MOTHER-IN-LAW: [*Meaningfully*] If he does, it's
because he knows her. Didn't you know he courted
her for three years?
LEONARDO: But I left her. [*To his Wife*] Are you
going to cry now? Quit that! [*He brusquely pulls her
hands away from her face*] Let's go see the baby.
[*They go in with their arms around each other.
A Girl* appears. *She is happy. She enters run-
ning*]
GIRL: Señora.
MOTHER-IN-LAW: What is it?
GIRL: The groom came to the store and he's
bought the best of everything they had.
MOTHER-IN-LAW: Was he alone?
GIRL: No. With his mother. Stern, tall. [*She imi-
tates her*] And such extravagance!
MOTHER-IN-LAW: They have money.
GIRL: And they bought some open-work stockings!
Oh, such stockings! A woman's dream of stockings!
Look: a swallow here. [*She points to her ankle*]
a ship here [*She points to her calf*] and here [*She
points to her thigh*] a rose!
MOTHER-IN-LAW: Child!
GIRL: A rose with the seeds and the stem! Oh! All
in silk.
MOTHER-IN-LAW: Two rich families are being
brought together. [Leonardo *and his* Wife *appear*]
GIRL: I came to tell you what they're buying.
LEONARDO: [*Loudly*] We don't care.
WIFE: Leave her alone.
MOTHER-IN-LAW: Leonardo, it's not that impor-
tant.
GIRL: Please excuse me. [*She leaves, weeping*]
MOTHER-IN-LAW: Why do you always have to
make trouble with people?
LEONARDO: I didn't ask for your opinion. [*He sits
down*]
MOTHER-IN-LAW: Very well. [*Pause*]
WIFE: [*To* Leonardo] What's the matter with you?
What idea've you got boiling there inside your head?
Don't leave me like this, not knowing anything.
LEONARDO: Stop that.

WIFE: No. I want you to look at me and tell me.

LEONARDO: Let me alone. [*He rises*]

WIFE: Where you are going, love?

LEONARDO: [*Sharply*] Can't you shut up?

MOTHER-IN-LAW: [*Energetically, to her daughter*] Be quiet! [*Leonardo goes out*] The baby!

[*She goes into the bedroom and comes out again with the baby in her arms.* The Wife *has remained standing, unmoving*]

MOTHER-IN-LAW:

His poor hooves were bleeding,
his long mane was frozen,
and deep in his eyes
stuck a silvery dagger.
Down he went to the river,
Oh, down he went down!
And his blood was running,
oh, more than the water.

WIFE: [*Turning slowly, as though dreaming*]

Carnation, sleep and dream,
the horse is drinking from the stream.

MOTHER-IN-LAW:

My rose, asleep now lie
the horse is starting to cry.

WIFE:

Lullaby, my baby.

MOTHER-IN-LAW:

Ay-y-y, for the big horse
who didn't like water!

WIFE: [*Dramatically*]

Don't come near, don't come in!
Go away to the mountains!
Ay-y-y, for the snow-wound,
big horse of the dawn!

MOTHER-IN-LAW: [*Weeping*]

My baby is sleeping . . .

WIFE: [*Weeping, as she slowly moves closer*]

My baby is resting . . .

MOTHER-IN-LAW:

Carnation, sleep and dream,
the horse won't drink from the stream.

WIFE: [*Weeping, and leaning on the table*]

My rose, asleep now lie,
the horse is starting to cry.

CURTAIN

SCENE III.

Interior of the cave where The Bride *lives. At the back is a cross of large rose-colored flowers. The round doors have lace curtains with rose-colored ties. Around the walls, which are of a white and hard material, are round fans, blue jars, and little mirrors.*

SERVANT: Come right in . . . [*She is very affable, full of humble hypocrisy.* The Bridegroom *and his* Mother *enter.* The Mother *is dressed in black satin and wears a lace mantilla;* The Bridegroom *in black corduroy with a great golden chain*] Won't you sit down? They'll be right here. [*She leaves.* The Mother *and* Son *are left sitting motionless as statues. Long pause*]

MOTHER: Did you wear the watch?

BRIDEGROOM: Yes. [*He takes it out and looks at it*]

MOTHER: We have to be back on time. How far away these people live!

BRIDEGROOM: But this is good land.

MOTHER: Good; but much too lonesome. A four hour trip and not one house, not one tree.

BRIDEGROOM: This is the wasteland.

MOTHER: Your father would have covered it with trees.

BRIDEGROOM: Without water?

MOTHER: He would have found some. In the three years we were married he planted ten cherry trees. [*Remembering*] Those three walnut trees by the mill, a whole vineyard and a plant called Jupiter which had scarlet flowers—but it dried up. [*Pause*]

BRIDEGROOM: [*Referring to* The Bride] She must be dressing.

[*The* Bride's Father *enters. He is very old, with shining white hair. His head is bowed.* The Mother *and the* Bridegroom *rise. They shake hands in silence*]

FATHER: Was it a long trip?

MOTHER: Four hours. [*They sit down*]

FATHER: You must have come the longest way.

MOTHER: I'm too old to come along the cliffs by the river.

BRIDEGROOM: She gets dizzy. [*Pause*]

FATHER: A good hemp harvest.

BRIDEGROOM: A really good one.

FATHER: When I was young this land didn't even grow hemp. We've had to punish it, even weep over it, to make it give us anything useful.

MOTHER: But now it does. Don't complain. I'm not here to ask you for anything.

FATHER: [*Smiling*] You're richer than I. Your vineyards are worth a fortune. Each young vine is a silver coin. But—do you know?—what bothers me is that our lands are separated. I like to have everything together. One thorn I have in my heart, and that's the little orchard there, stuck in between my fields—and they won't sell it to me for all the gold in the world.

BRIDEGROOM: That's the way it always is.

FATHER: If we could just take twenty teams of oxen and move your vineyards over here, and put them down on that hillside, how happy I'd be!

MOTHER: But why?

FATHER: What's mine is hers and what's yours is his. That's why. Just to see it all together. How beautiful it is to bring things together!

BRIDEGROOM: And it would be less work.

MOTHER: When I die, you could sell ours and buy here, right alongside.

FATHER: Sell, sell? Bah! Buy, my friend, buy

everything. If I had had sons I would have bought all this mountainside right up to the part with the stream. It's not good land, but strong arms can make it good, and since no people pass by, they don't steal your fruit and you can sleep in peace. [*Pause*]

MOTHER: You know what I'm here for.

FATHER: Yes.

MOTHER: And?

FATHER: It seems all right to me. They have talked it over.

MOTHER: My son has money and knows how to manage it.

FATHER: My daughter too.

MOTHER: My son is handsome. He's never known a woman. His good name cleaner than a sheet spread out in the sun.

FATHER: No need to tell you about my daughter. At three, when the morning star shines, she prepares the bread. She never talks: soft as wool, she embroiders all kinds of fancy work and she can cut a strong cord with her teeth.

MOTHER: God bless her house.

FATHER: May God bless it.

[*The Servant appears with two trays. One with drinks and the other with sweets*]

MOTHER: [*To The Son*] When would you like the wedding?

BRIDEGROOM: Next Thursday.

FATHER: The day on which she'll be exactly twenty-two years old.

MOTHER: Twenty-two! My oldest son would be that age if he were alive. Warm and manly as he was, he'd be living now if men hadn't invented knives.

FATHER: One mustn't think about that.

MOTHER: Every minute. Always a hand on your breast.

FATHER: Thursday, then? Is that right?

BRIDEGROOM: That's right.

FATHER: You and I and the bridal couple will go in a carriage to the church which is very far from here; the wedding party on the carts and horses they'll bring with them.

MOTHER: Agreed. [*The Servant passes through*]

FATHER: Tell her she may come in now. [*To The Mother*] I shall be much pleased if you like her.

[*The Bride appears. Her hands fall in a modest pose and her head is bowed*]

MOTHER: Come here. Are you happy?

BRIDE: Yes, señora.

FATHER: You shouldn't be so solemn. After all, she's going to be your mother.

BRIDE: I'm happy. I've said "yes" because I wanted to.

MOTHER: Naturally. [*She takes her by the chin*] Look at me.

FATHER: She resembles my wife in every way.

MOTHER: Yes? What a beautiful glance! Do you know what it is to be married, child?

BRIDE: [*Seriously*] I do.

MOTHER: A man, some children and a wall two yards thick for everything else.

BRIDEGROOM: Is anything else needed?

MOTHER: No. Just that you live—that's it! Live long!

BRIDE: I'll know how to keep my word.

MOTHER: Here are some gifts for you.

BRIDE: Thank you.

FATHER: Shall we have something?

MOTHER: Nothing for me. [*To The Son*] But you?

BRIDEGROOM: Yes, thank you. [*He takes one sweet, The Bride another*]

FATHER: [*To The Bridegroom*] Wine?

MOTHER: He doesn't touch it.

FATHER: All the better. [*Pause. All are standing*]

BRIDEGROOM: [*To The Bride*] I'll come tomorrow.

BRIDE: What time?

BRIDEGROOM: Five.

BRIDE: I'll be waiting for you.

BRIDEGROOM: When I leave your side I feel a great emptiness, and something like a knot in my throat.

BRIDE: When you are my husband you won't have it any more.

BRIDEGROOM: That's what I tell myself.

MOTHER: Come. The sun doesn't wait. [*To The Father*] Are we agreed on everything?

FATHER: Agreed.

MOTHER: [*To The Servant*] Goodbye, woman.

SERVANT: God go with you!

[*The Mother kisses The Bride and they begin to leave in silence*]

MOTHER: [*At the door*] Goodbye, daughter. [*The Bride answers with her hand*]

FATHER: I'll go out with you. [*They leave*]

SERVANT: I'm bursting to see the presents.

BRIDE: [*Sharply*] Stop that!

SERVANT: Oh, child, show them to me.

BRIDE: I don't want to.

SERVANT: At least the stockings. They say they're all open work. Please!

BRIDE: I said no.

SERVANT: Well, my Lord. All right then. It looks as if you didn't want to get married.

BRIDE: [*Biting her hand in anger*] Ay-y-y!

SERVANT: Child, child! What's the matter with you? Are you sorry to give up your queen's life? Don't think of bitter things. Have you any reason to? None. Let's look at the presents. [*She takes the box*]

BRIDE: [*Holding her by the wrists*] Let go.

SERVANT: Ay-y-y, girl!

BRIDE: Let go, I said.

SERVANT: You're stronger than a man.

BRIDE: Haven't I done a man's work? I wish I were.

SERVANT: Don't talk like that.

BRIDE: Quiet, I said. Let's talk about something else.

[*The light is fading from the stage. Long pause*]

SERVANT: Did you hear a horse last night?

BRIDE: What time?

SERVANT: Three.

BRIDE: It might have been a stray horse—from the herd.

SERVANT: No. It carried a rider.

BRIDE: How do you know?

SERVANT: Because I saw him. He was standing by your window. It shocked me greatly.

BRIDE: Maybe it was my fiancé. Sometimes he comes by at that time.

SERVANT: No.

BRIDE: You saw him?

SERVANT: Yes.

BRIDE: Who was it?

SERVANT: It was Leonardo.

BRIDE: [Strongly] Liar! You liar! Why should he come here?

SERVANT: He came.

BRIDE: Shut up! Shut your cursed mouth.

[The sound of a horse is heard]

SERVANT: [At the window] Look. Lean out. Was it Leonardo?

BRIDE: It was!

QUICK CURTAIN

ACT II. SCENE I.

The entrance hall of The Bride's *house. A large door in the back. It is night.* The Bride *enters wearing ruffled white petticoats full of laces and embroidered bands, and a sleeveless white bodice.* The Servant *is dressed the same way.*

SERVANT: I'll finish combing your hair out here.

BRIDE: It's too warm to stay in there.

SERVANT: In this country it doesn't even cool off at dawn.

[The Bride *sits on a low chair and looks into a little hand mirror.* The Servant *combs her hair*]

BRIDE: My mother came from a place with lots of trees—from a fertile country.

SERVANT: And she was so happy!

BRIDE: But she wasted away here.

SERVANT: Fate.

BRIDE: As we're all wasting away here. The very walls give off heat. Ay-y-y! Don't pull so hard.

SERVANT: I'm only trying to fix this wave better. I want it to fall over your forehead. [The Bride *looks at herself in the mirror*] How beautiful you are! Ay-y-y! [She kisses her passionately]

BRIDE: [Seriously] Keep right on combing.

SERVANT: [Combing] Oh, lucky you—going to put your arms around a man; and kiss him; and feel his weight.

BRIDE: Hush.

SERVANT: And the best part will be when you'll

wake up and you'll feel him at your side and when he caresses your shoulders with his breath, like a little nightingale's feather.

BRIDE: [Sternly] Will you be quiet.

SERVANT: But, child! What *is* a wedding? A wedding is just that and nothing more. Is it the sweets—or the bouquets of flowers? No. It's a shining bed and a man and a woman.

BRIDE: But you shouldn't talk about it.

SERVANT: Oh, *that's* something else again. But fun enough too.

BRIDE: Or bitter enough.

SERVANT: I'm going to put the orange blossoms on from here to here, so the wreath will shine out on top of your hair. [She tries on the sprigs of orange blossom]

BRIDE: [Looking at herself in the mirror] Give it to me. [She takes the wreath, looks at it and lets her head fall in discouragement]

SERVANT: Now what's the matter?

BRIDE: Leave me alone.

SERVANT: This is not time for you to start feeling sad. [Encouragingly] Give me the wreath. [The Bride *takes the wreath and hurls it away*] Child! You're just asking God to punish you, throwing the wreath on the floor like that. Raise your head! Don't you want to get married? Say it. You can still withdraw. [The Bride *rises*]

BRIDE: Storm clouds. A chill wind that cuts through my heart. Who hasn't felt it?

SERVANT: You love your sweetheart, don't you?

BRIDE: I love him.

SERVANT: Yes, yes. I'm sure you do.

BRIDE: But this is a very serious step.

SERVANT: You've got to take it.

BRIDE: I've already given my word.

SERVANT: I'll put on the wreath.

BRIDE: [She sits down] Hurry. They should be arriving by now.

SERVANT: They've already been at least two hours on the way.

BRIDE: How far is it from here to the church?

SERVANT: Five leagues by the stream, but twice that by the road. [The Bride *rises and* The Servant *grows excited as she looks at her*]

SERVANT:
  Awake, O Bride, awaken,
  On your wedding morning waken!
  The world's rivers may all
  Bear along your bridal Crown!

BRIDE: [Smiling] Come now.

SERVANT: [Enthusiastically kissing her and dancing around her]
  Awake
  with the fresh bouquet
  of flowering laurel.
  Awake,
  by the trunk and branch
  of the laurels!

[The banging of the front door latch is heard]

BRIDE: Open the door! That must be the first guests. [*She leaves.* The Servant *opens the door*]

SERVANT: [*In astonishment*] You!

LEONARDO: Yes, me. Good morning.

SERVANT: The first one!

LEONARDO: Wasn't I invited?

SERVANT: Yes.

LEONARDO: That's why I'm here.

SERVANT: Where's your wife?

LEONARDO: I came on my horse. She's coming by the road.

SERVANT: Didn't you meet anyone?

LEONARDO: I *passed* them on my horse.

SERVANT: You're going to kill that horse with so much racing.

LEONARDO: When he dies, he's dead! [*Pause*]

SERVANT: Sit down. Nobody's up yet.

LEONARDO: Where's the bride?

SERVANT: I'm just on my way to dress her.

LEONARDO: The bride! She ought to be happy!

SERVANT: [*Changing the subject*] How's the baby?

LEONARDO: What baby?

SERVANT: Your son.

LEONARDO: [*Remembering, as though in a dream*] Ah!

SERVANT: Are they bringing him?

LEONARDO: No. [*Pause. Voices sing distantly*]

VOICES:
    Awake, O Bride, awaken,
    On your wedding morning waken!

LEONARDO:
    Awake, O Bride, awaken,
    On your wedding morning waken!

SERVANT: It's the guests. They're still quite a way off.

LEONARDO: The bride's going to wear a big wreath, isn't she? But it ought not to be so large. One a little smaller would look better on her. Has the groom already brought her the orange blossom that must be worn on the breast?

BRIDE: [*Appearing, still in petticoats and wearing the wreath*] He brought it.

SERVANT: [*Sternly*] Don't come out like that.

BRIDE: What does it matter? [*Seriously*] Why do you ask if they brought the orange blossom? Do you have something in mind?

LEONARDO: Nothing. What would I have in mind? [*Drawing near her*] You, you know me; you know I don't. Tell me so. What have I ever meant to you? Open your memory, refresh it. But two oxen and an ugly little hut are almost nothing. That's the thorn.

BRIDE: What have you come here to do?

LEONARDO: To see your wedding.

BRIDE: Just as I saw yours!

LEONARDO: Tied up by you, done with your two hands. Oh, they can kill me but they can't spit on me. But even money, which shines so much, spits sometimes.

BRIDE: Liar!

LEONARDO: I don't want to talk. I'm hot-blooded and I don't want to shout so all these hills will hear me.

BRIDE: My shouts would be louder.

SERVANT: You'll have to stop talking like this. [*To The Bride*] You don't have to talk about what's past. [The Servant *looks around uneasily at the doors*]

BRIDE: She's right. I shouldn't even talk to you. But it offends me to the soul that you come here to watch me, and spy on my wedding, and ask about the orange blossom with something on your mind. Go and wait for your wife at the door.

LEONARDO: But, can't you and I even talk?

SERVANT: [*With rage*] No! No, you can't talk.

LEONARDO: Ever since I got married I've been thinking night and day about whose fault it was, and every time I think about it, out comes a new fault to eat up the old one; but always there's a fault left!

BRIDE: A man with a horse knows a lot of things and can do a lot to ride roughshod over a girl stuck out in the desert. But I have my pride. And that's why I'm getting married. I'll lock myself in with my husband and then I'll have to love him above everyone else.

LEONARDO: Pride won't help you a bit. [*He draws near to her*]

BRIDE: Don't come near me!

LEONARDO: To burn with desire and keep quiet about it is the greatest punishment we can bring on ourselves. What good was pride to me—and not seeing you, and letting you lie awake night after night? No good! It only served to bring the fire down on me! You think that time heals and walls hide things, but it isn't true, it isn't true! When things get that deep inside you there isn't anybody can change them.

BRIDE: [*Trembling*] I can't listen to you. I can't listen to your voice. It's as though I'd drunk a bottle of anise and fallen asleep wrapped in a quilt of roses. It pulls me along, and I know I'm drowning—but I go on down.

SERVANT: [*Seizing* Leonardo *by the lapels*] You've got to go right now!

LEONARDO: This is the last time I'll ever talk to her. Don't you be afraid of anything.

BRIDE: And I know I'm crazy and I know my breast rots with longing; but here I am—calmed by hearing him, by just seeing him move his arms.

LEONARDO: I'd never be at peace if I didn't tell you these things. I got married. Now you get married.

SERVANT: But she *is* getting married!

[*Voices are heard singing, nearer*]

VOICES:
    Awake, O Bride, awaken,
    On your wedding morning waken!

BRIDE:
    Awake, O Bride, awaken,

[*She goes out, running toward her room*]

SERVANT: The people are here now. [*To* Leonardo] Don't you come near her again.

LEONARDO: Don't worry. [*He goes out to the left. Day begins to break*]

FIRST GIRL: [*Entering*]
Awake, O Bride, awaken,
the morning you're to marry;
sing round and dance round;
balconies a wreath must carry.

VOICES:
Bride, awaken!

SERVANT: [*Creating enthusiasm*]
Awake,
with the green bouquet
of love in flower.
Awake,
by the trunk and the branch
of the laurels!

SECOND GIRL: [*Entering*]
Awake,
with her long hair,
snowy sleeping gown,
patent leather boots with silver—
her forehead jasmines crown.

SERVANT:
Oh, shepherdess,
the moon begins to shine!

FIRST GIRL:
Oh, gallant,
leave your hat beneath the vine!

FIRST YOUNG MAN: [*Entering, holding his hat on high*]
Bride, awaken,
for over the fields
the wedding draws nigh
with trays heaped with dahlias
and cakes piled high.

VOICES:
Bride, awaken!

SECOND GIRL:
The bride
has set her white wreath in place
and the groom
ties it on with a golden lace.

SERVANT:
By the orange tree,
sleepless the bride will be.

THIRD GIRL: [*Entering*]
By the citron vine,
gifts from the groom will shine.
[*Three Guests* come in]

FIRST YOUTH:
Dove, awaken!
In the dawn
shadowy bells are shaken.

GUEST:
The bride, the white bride
today a maiden,
tomorrow a wife.

FIRST GIRL:
Dark one, come down
trailing the train of your silken gown.

GUEST:
Little dark one, come down,
cold morning wears a dewy crown.

FIRST GUEST:
Awaken, wife, awake,
orange blossoms the breezes shake.

SERVANT:
A tree I would embroider her
with garnet sashes wound
And on each sash a cupid,
with "Long Live" all around.

VOICES:
Bride, awaken.

FIRST YOUTH:
The morning you're to marry!

GUEST:
The morning you're to marry
how elegant you'll seem;
worthy, mountain flower,
of a captain's dream.

FATHER: [*Entering*]
A captain's wife
the groom will marry.
He comes with his oxen the treasure to carry!

THIRD GIRL:
The groom
is like a flower of gold.
When he walks,
blossoms at his feet unfold.

SERVANT:
Oh, my lucky girl!

SECOND YOUTH:
Bride, awaken.

SERVANT:
Oh, my elegant girl!

FIRST GIRL:
Through the windows
hear the wedding shout.

SECOND GIRL:
Let the bride come out.

FIRST GIRL:
Come out, come out!

SERVANT:
Let the bells
ring and ring out clear!
For here she comes!
For now she's near!

SERVANT:
Like a bull, the wedding
is arising here!
[*The Bride appears. She wears a black dress in the style of 1900, with a bustle and large train covered with pleated gauzes and heavy laces. Upon her hair, brushed in a wave over her forehead, she wears an orange blossom wreath. Guitars sound. The Girls kiss The Bride*]

THIRD GIRL: What scent did you put on your hair?

BRIDE: [*Laughing*] None at all.

SECOND GIRL: [*Looking at her dress*] This cloth is what you can't get.

FIRST YOUTH: Here's the groom!

BRIDEGROOM: Salud!

FIRST GIRL: [*Putting a flower behind his ear*]
    The groom
    is like a flower of gold.

SECOND GIRL:
    Quiet breezes
    from his eyes unfold.

[The Groom *goes to* The Bride]

BRIDE: Why did you put on those shoes?

BRIDEGROOM: They're gayer than the black ones.

LEONARDO'S WIFE: [*Entering and kissing* The Bride] Salud! [*They all speak excitedly*]

LEONARDO: [*Entering, as one who performs a duty*]
    The morning you're to marry
    We give you a wreath to wear.

LEONARDO'S WIFE:
    So the fields may be made happy
    with the dew dropped from your hair!

MOTHER: [*To* The Father] Are those people here, too?

FATHER: They're part of the family. Today is a day of forgiveness!

MOTHER: I'll put up with it, but I don't forgive.

BRIDEGROOM: With your wreath, it's a joy to look at you!

BRIDE: Let's go to the church quickly.

BRIDEGROOM: Are you in a hurry?

BRIDE: Yes. I want to be your wife right now so that I can be with you alone, not hearing any voice but yours.

BRIDEGROOM: That's what I want!

BRIDE: And not seeing any eyes but yours. And for you to hug me so hard, that even though my dead mother should call me, I wouldn't be able to draw away from you.

BRIDEGROOM: My arms are strong. I'll hug you for forty years without stopping.

BRIDE: [*Taking his arm, dramatically*] Forever!

FATHER: Quick now! Round up the teams and carts! The sun's already out.

MOTHER: And go along carefully! Let's hope nothing goes wrong.

[*The great door in the background opens*]

SERVANT: [*Weeping*]
    As you set out from your house,
    oh, maiden white,
    remember you leave shining
    with a star's light.

FIRST GIRL:
    Clean of body, clean of clothes
    from her home to church she goes.

[*They start leaving*]

SECOND GIRL:
    Now you leave your home
    for the church!

SERVANT:
    The wind sets flowers
    on the sands.

THIRD GIRL:
    Ah, the white maid!

SERVANT:
    Dark winds are the lace
    of her mantilla.

[*They leave. Guitars, castanets and tambourines are heard*. Leonardo *and his* Wife *are left alone*]

WIFE: Let's go.

LEONARDO: Where?

WIFE: To the church. But not on your horse. You're coming with me.

LEONARDO: In the cart?

WIFE: Is there anything else?

LEONARDO: I'm not the kind of man to ride in a cart.

WIFE: Nor I the wife to go to a wedding without her husband. I can't stand any more of this!

LEONARDO: Neither can I!

WIFE: And why do you look at me that way? With a thorn in each eye.

LEONARDO: Let's go!

WIFE: I don't know what's happening. But I think, and I don't want to think. One thing I do know. I'm already cast off by you. But I have a son. And another coming. And so it goes. My mother's fate was the same. Well, I'm not moving from here.

[*Voices outside*]

VOICES:
    As you set out from your home
    and to the church go
    remember you leave shining
    with a star's glow.

WIFE: [*Weeping*]
    Remember you leave shining
    with a star's glow!
I left my house like that too. They could have stuffed the whole countryside in my mouth. I was that trusting.

LEONARDO: [*Rising*] Let's go!

WIFE: But you with me!

LEONARDO: Yes. [*Pause*] Start moving! [*They leave*]

VOICES:
    As you set out from your home
    and to the church go,
    remember you leave shining
    with a star's glow.

SLOW CURTAIN

SCENE II.

The exterior of The Bride's *Cave Home, in white gray and cold blue tones. Large cactus trees. Shadowy and silver tones. Panoramas of light tan table-*

*lands, everything hard like a landscape in popular
ceramics.*

SERVANT: [*Arranging glasses and trays on a table*]
A-turning,
the wheel was a-turning
and the water was flowing,
for the wedding night comes.
May the branches part
and the moon be arrayed
at her white balcony rail.
[*In a loud voice*]
Set out the tablecloths!
[*In a pathetic voice*]
A-singing,
bride and groom were singing
and the water was flowing
for their wedding night comes.
Oh, rime-frost, flash!—
and almonds bitter
fill with honey!
[*In a loud voice*]
Get the wine ready!
[*In a poetic tone*]
Elegant girl,
most elegant in the world,
see the way the water is flowing,
for your wedding night comes.
Hold your skirts close in
under the bridegroom's wing
and never leave your house,
for the Bridegroom is a dove
with his breast a firebrand
and the fields wait for the whisper
of spurting blood.
A-turning
the wheel was a-turning
and the water was flowing
and your wedding night comes.
Oh, water, sparkle!

MOTHER: [*Entering*] At last!

FATHER: Are we the first ones?

SERVANT: No. Leonardo and his wife arrived a
while ago. They drove like demons. His wife got
here dead with fright. They made the trip as though
they'd come on horseback.

FATHER: That one's looking for trouble. He's not
of good blood.

MOTHER: What blood would you expect him to
have? His whole family's blood. It comes down from
his great grandfather, who started in killing, and it
goes on down through the whole evil breed of knife
wielding and false smiling men.

FATHER: Let's leave it at that!

SERVANT: But how can she leave it at that?

MOTHER: It hurts me to the tips of my veins. On
the forehead of all of them I see only the hand with
which they killed what was mine. Can you really
see me? Don't I seem mad to you? Well, it's the madness of not having shrieked out all my breast needs

to. Always in my breast there's a shriek standing
tiptoe that I have to beat down and hold in under
my shawls. But the dead are carried off and one has
to keep still. And then, people find fault. [*She removes her shawl*]

FATHER: Today's not the day for you to be remembering these things.

MOTHER: When the talk turns on it, I have to
speak. And more so today. Because today I'm left
alone in my house.

FATHER: But with the expectation of having someone with you.

MOTHER: That's my hope: grandchildren. [*They
sit down*]

FATHER: I want them to have a lot of them. This
land needs hands that aren't hired. There's a battle
to be waged against weeds, the thistles, the big rocks
that come from one doesn't know where. And those
hands have to be the owner's, who chastises and
dominates, who makes the seeds grow. Lots of sons
are needed.

MOTHER: And some daughters! Men are like the
wind! They're forced to handle weapons. Girls never
go out into the street.

FATHER: [*Happily*] I think they'll have both.

MOTHER: My son will cover her well. He's of good
seed. His father could have had many sons with me.

FATHER: What I'd like is to have all this happen
in a day. So that right away they'd have two or three
boys.

MOTHER: But it's not like that. It takes a long
time. That's why it's so terrible to see one's own
blood spilled out on the ground. A fountain that
spurts for a minute, but costs us years. When I got
to my son, he lay fallen in the middle of the street.
I wet my hands with his blood and licked them with
my tongue—because it was my blood. You don't
know what that's like. In a glass and topaze shrine
I'd put the earth moistened by his blood.

FATHER: Now you must hope. My daughter is
wide-hipped and your son is strong.

MOTHER: That's why I'm hoping. [*They rise*]

FATHER: Get the wheat trays ready!

SERVANT: They're all ready.

LEONARDO'S WIFE: [*Entering*] May it be for the
best!

MOTHER: Thank you.

LEONARDO: Is there going to be a celebration?

FATHER: A small one. People can't stay long.

SERVANT: Here they are!

[*Guests begin entering in gay groups. The Bride
and* Groom *come in arm-in-arm. Leonardo
leaves*]

BRIDEGROOM: There's never been a wedding with
so many people!

BRIDE: [*Sullen*] Never.

FATHER: It was brilliant.

MOTHER: Whole branches of families came.

BRIDEGROOM: People who never went out of the
house.

MOTHER: Your father sowed well, and now you're reaping it.

BRIDEGROOM: There were cousins of mine whom I no longer knew.

MOTHER: All the people from the seacoast.

BRIDEGROOM: [Happily] They were frightened of the horses. [They talk]

MOTHER: [To The Bride] What are you thinking about?

BRIDE: I'm not thinking about anything.

MOTHER: Your blessings weigh heavily. [Guitars are heard]

BRIDE: Like lead.

MOTHER: [Stern] But they shouldn't weigh so. Happy as a dove you'd ought to be.

BRIDE: Are you staying here tonight?

MOTHER: No. My house is empty.

BRIDE: You'd ought to stay!

FATHER: [To The Mother] Look at the dance they're forming. Dances of the faraway seashore.

[Leonardo enters and sits down. His Wife stands rigidly behind him]

MOTHER: They're my husband's cousins. Stiff as stones at dancing.

FATHER: It makes me happy to watch them. What a change for this house! [He leaves]

BRIDEGROOM: [To The Bride] Did you like the orange blossom?

BRIDE: [Looking at him fixedly] Yes.

BRIDEGROOM: It's all of wax. It will last forever. I'd like you to have had them all over your dress.

BRIDE: No need of that. [Leonardo goes off to the right]

FIRST GIRL: Let's go and take out your pins.

BRIDE: [To The Groom] I'll be right back.

LEONARDO'S WIFE: I hope you'll be happy with my cousin!

BRIDEGROOM: I'm sure I will.

LEONARDO'S WIFE: The two of you here; never going out; building a home. I wish I could live far away like this, too!

BRIDEGROOM: Why don't you buy land? The mountainside is cheap and children grow up better.

LEONARDO'S WIFE: We don't have any money. And at the rate we're going . . . !

BRIDEGROOM: Your husband is a good worker.

LEONARDO'S WIFE: Yes, but he likes to fly around too much; from one thing to another. He's not a patient man.

SERVANT: Aren't you having anything? I'm going to wrap up some wine cakes for your mother. She likes them so much.

BRIDEGROOM: Put up three dozen for her.

LEONARDO'S WIFE: No, no. A half-dozen's enough for her!

BRIDEGROOM: But today's a day!

LEONARDO'S WIFE: [To The Servant] Where's Leonardo?

BRIDEGROOM: He must be with the guests.

LEONARDO'S WIFE: I'm going to go see. [She leaves]

SERVANT: [Looking off at the dance] That's beautiful there.

BRIDEGROOM: Aren't you dancing?

SERVANT: No one will ask me.

[Two Girls pass across the back of the stage; during this whole scene the background should be an animated crossing of figures]

BRIDEGROOM: [Happily] They just don't know anything. Lively old girls like you dance better than the young ones.

SERVANT: Well! Are you tossing me a compliment, boy? What a family yours is! Men among men! As a little girl I saw your grandfather's wedding. What a figure! It seemed as if a mountain were getting married.

BRIDEGROOM: I'm not as tall.

SERVANT: But there's the same twinkle in your eye. Where's the girl?

BRIDEGROOM: Taking off her wreath.

SERVANT: Ah! Look. For midnight, since you won't be sleeping, I have prepared ham for you, and some large glasses of old wine. On the lower shelf of the cupboard. In case you need it.

BRIDEGROOM: [Smiling] I won't be eating at midnight.

SERVANT: [Slyly] If not you, maybe the bride. [She leaves]

FIRST YOUTH: [Entering] You've got to come have a drink with us!

BRIDEGROOM: I'm waiting for the bride.

SECOND YOUTH: You'll have her at dawn!

FIRST YOUTH: That's when it's best!

SECOND YOUTH: Just for a minute.

BRIDEGROOM: Let's go. [They leave. Great excitement is heard. The Bride enters. From the opposite side Two Girls come running to meet her]

FIRST GIRL: To whom did you give the first pin; me or this one?

BRIDE: I don't remember.

FIRST GIRL: To me, you gave it to me here.

SECOND GIRL: To me, in front of the altar.

BRIDE: [Uneasily, with a great inner struggle] I don't know anything about it.

FIRST GIRL: It's just that I wish you'd . . .

BRIDE: [Interrupting] Nor do I care. I have a lot to think about.

SECOND GIRL: Your pardon. [Leonardo crosses at the rear of the stage]

BRIDE: [She sees Leonardo] And this is an upsetting time.

FIRST GIRL: We wouldn't know anything about that!

BRIDE: You'll know about it when your time comes. This step is a very hard one to take.

FIRST GIRL: Has she offended you?

BRIDE: No. You must pardon me.

SECOND GIRL: What for? But both the pins are good for getting married, aren't they?

BRIDE: Both of them.

FIRST GIRL: Maybe now one will get married before the other.

BRIDE: Are you so eager?

SECOND GIRL: [Shyly] Yes.

BRIDE: Why?

FIRST GIRL: Well . . . [She embraces The Second Girl. Both go running off. The Groom comes in very slowly and embraces The Bride from behind]

BRIDE: [In sudden fright] Let go of me!

BRIDEGROOM: Are you frightened of me?

BRIDE: Ay-y-y! It's you?

BRIDEGROOM: Who else would it be? [Pause] Your father or me.

BRIDE: That's true!

BRIDEGROOM: Of course, your father would have hugged you more gently.

BRIDE: [Darkly] Of course!

BRIDEGROOM: [Embracing her strongly and a little bit brusquely] Because he's old.

BRIDE: [Curtly] Let me go!

BRIDEGROOM: Why? [He lets her go]

BRIDE: Well . . . the people. They can see us. [The Servant crosses at the back of the stage again without looking at The Bride and Bridegroom]

BRIDEGROOM: What of it? It's consecrated now.

BRIDE: Yes, but let me be . . . Later.

BRIDEGROOM: What's the matter with you? You look frightened!

BRIDE: I'm all right. Don't go.

[Leonardo's Wife enters]

LEONARDO'S WIFE: I don't mean to intrude . . .

BRIDEGROOM: What is it?

LEONARDO'S WIFE: Did my husband come through here?

BRIDEGROOM: No.

LEONARDO'S WIFE: Because I can't find him, and his horse isn't in the stable either.

BRIDEGROOM: [Happily] He must be out racing it. [The Wife leaves, troubled. The Servant enters]

SERVANT: Aren't you two proud and happy with so many good wishes?

BRIDEGROOM: I wish it were over with. The bride is a little tired.

SERVANT: That's no way to act, child.

BRIDE: It's as though I'd been struck on the head.

SERVANT: A bride from these mountains must be strong. [To The Groom] You're the only one who can cure her, because she's yours. [She goes running off]

BRIDEGROOM: [Embracing The Bride] Let's go dance a little. [He kisses her]

BRIDE: [Worried] No. I'd like to stretch out on my bed a little.

BRIDEGROOM: I'll keep you company.

BRIDE: Never! With all these people here? What would they say? Let me be quiet for a moment.

BRIDEGROOM: Whatever you say! But don't be like that tonight!

BRIDE: [At the door] I'll be better tonight.

BRIDEGROOM: That's what I want. [The Mother appears]

MOTHER: Son.

BRIDEGROOM: Where've you been?

MOTHER: Out there—in all that noise. Are you happy?

BRIDEGROOM: Yes.

MOTHER: Where's your wife?

BRIDEGROOM: Resting a little. It's a bad day for brides!

MOTHER: A bad day? The only good one. To me it was like coming into my own. [The Servant enters and goes toward The Bride's room] Like the breaking of new ground; the planting of new trees.

BRIDEGROOM: Are you going to leave?

MOTHER: Yes. I'd ought to be at home.

BRIDEGROOM: Alone.

MOTHER: Not alone. For my head is full of things: of men, and fights.

BRIDEGROOM: But now the fights are no longer fights.

[The Servant enters quickly; she disappears at the rear of the stage, running]

MOTHER: While you live, you have to fight.

BRIDEGROOM: I'll always obey you!

MOTHER: Try to be loving with your wife, and if you see she's acting foolish or touchy, caress her in a way that will hurt her a little: a strong hug, a bite and then a soft kiss. Not so she'll be angry, but just so she'll feel you're the man, the boss, the one who gives orders. I learned that from your father. And since you don't have him, I have to be the one to tell you about these strong defenses.

BRIDEGROOM: I'll always do as you say.

FATHER: [Entering] Where's my daughter?

BRIDEGROOM: She's inside. [The Father goes to look for her]

FIRST GIRL: Get the bride and groom! We're going to dance a round!

FIRST YOUTH: [To The Bridegroom] You're going to lead it.

FATHER: [Entering] She's not there.

BRIDEGROOM: No?

FATHER: She must have gone up to the railing.

BRIDEGROOM: I'll go see! [He leaves. A hubbub of excitement and guitars is heard]

FIRST GIRL: They've started it already! [She leaves]

BRIDEGROOM: [Entering] She isn't there.

MOTHER: [Uneasily] Isn't she?

FATHER: But where could she have gone?

SERVANT: [Entering] But where's the girl, where is she?

MOTHER: [Seriously] That we don't know. [The Bridegroom leaves. Three guests enter]

FATHER: [Dramatically] But, isn't she in the dance?

SERVANT: She's not in the dance.

FATHER: [With a start] There are a lot of people. Go look!

SERVANT: I've already looked.

FATHER: [*Tragically*] Then where is she?

BRIDEGROOM: [*Entering*] Nowhere. Not anywhere.

MOTHER: [*To* The Father] What does this mean? Where is your daughter?

[Leonardo's Wife *enters*]

LEONARDO'S WIFE: They've run away! They've run away! She and Leonardo. On the horse. With their arms round each other, they rode off like a shooting star!

FATHER: That's not true! Not my daughter!

MOTHER: Yes, your daughter. Spawn of a wicked mother, and he, he too. But now she's my son's wife!

BRIDEGROOM: [*Entering*] Let's go after them! Who has a horse?

MOTHER: Who has a horse? Right away! Who has a horse? I'll give him all I have—my eyes, my tongue even. . . .

VOICE: Here's one.

MOTHER: [*To* The Son] Go! After them! [*He leaves with two young men*] No. Don't go. Those people kill quickly and well . . . but yes, run, and I'll follow!

FATHER: It couldn't be my daughter. Perhaps she's thrown herself in the well.

MOTHER: Decent women throw themselves in water; not that one! But now she's my son's wife. Two groups. There are two groups here. [*They all enter*] My family and yours. Everyone set out from here. Shake the dust from your heels! We'll go help my son. [*The people separate in two groups*] For he has his family: his cousins from the sea, and all who came from inland. Out of here! On all roads. The hour of blood has come again. Two groups! You with yours and I with mine. After them! After them!

CURTAIN

ACT III. SCENE I.

A forest. It is nighttime. Great moist tree trunks. A dark atmosphere. Two violins are heard. Three Woodcutters *enter.*

FIRST WOODCUTTER: And have they found them?

SECOND WOODCUTTER: No. But they're looking for them everywhere.

THIRD WOODCUTTER: They'll find them.

SECOND WOODCUTTER: Sh-h-h!

THIRD WOODCUTTER: What?

SECOND WOODCUTTER: They seem to be coming closer on all the roads at once.

FIRST WOODCUTTER: When the moon comes out they'll see them.

SECOND WOODCUTTER: They'd ought to let them go.

FIRST WOODCUTTER: The world is wide. Everybody can live in it.

THIRD WOODCUTTER: But they'll kill them.

SECOND WOODCUTTER: You have to follow your passion. They did right to run away.

FIRST WOODCUTTER: They were deceiving themselves but at the last blood was stronger.

THIRD WOODCUTTER: Blood!

FIRST WOODCUTTER: You have to follow the path of your blood.

SECOND WOODCUTTER: But blood that sees the light of day is drunk up by the earth.

FIRST WOODCUTTER: What of it? Better dead with the blood drained away than alive with it rotting.

THIRD WOODCUTTER: Hush!

FIRST WOODCUTTER: What? Do you hear something?

THIRD WOODCUTTER: I hear the crickets, the frogs, the night's ambush.

FIRST WOODCUTTER: But not the horse.

THIRD WOODCUTTER: No.

FIRST WOODCUTTER: By now he must be loving her.

SECOND WOODCUTTER: Her body for him; his body for her.

THIRD WOODCUTTER: They'll find them and they'll kill them.

FIRST WOODCUTTER: But by then they'll have mingled their bloods. They'll be like two empty jars, like two dry arroyos.

SECOND WOODCUTTER: There are many clouds and it would be easy for the moon not to come out.

THIRD WOODCUTTER: The bridegroom will find them with or without the moon. I saw him set out. Like a raging star. His face the color of ashes. He looked the fate of all his clan.

FIRST WOODCUTTER: His clan of dead men lying in the middle of the street.

SECOND WOODCUTTER: There you have it!

THIRD WOODCUTTER: You think they'll be able to break through the circle?

SECOND WOODCUTTER: It's hard to. There are knives and guns for ten leagues 'round.

THIRD WOODCUTTER: He's riding a good horse.

SECOND WOODCUTTER: But he's carrying a woman.

FIRST WOODCUTTER: We're close by now.

SECOND WOODCUTTER: A tree with forty branches. We'll soon cut it down.

THIRD WOODCUTTER: The moon's coming out now. Let's hurry.

[*From the left shines a brightness*]

FIRST WOODCUTTER:
O rising moon!
Moon among the great leaves.

SECOND WOODCUTTER:
Cover the blood with jasmines!

FIRST WOODCUTTER:
O lonely moon!
Moon among the great leaves.

SECOND WOODCUTTER:
Silver on the bride's face

THIRD WOODCUTTER:

    O evil moon!

    Leave for their love a branch in shadow.

FIRST WOODCUTTER:

    O sorrowing moon!

    Leave for their love a branch in shadow!

[*They go out. The* Moon *appears through the shining brightness at the left. The* Moon *is a young woodcutter with a white face. The stage takes on an intense blue radiance*]

MOON:

    Round swan in the river

    and a cathedral's eye,

    false dawn on the leaves,

    they'll not escape; these things am I!

    Who is hiding? And who sobs

    in the thornbrakes of the valley?

    The moon sets a knife

    abandoned in the air

    which being a leaden threat

    yearns to be blood's pain.

    Let me in! I come freezing

    down to walls and windows!

    Open roofs, open breasts

    where I may warm myself!

    I'm cold! My ashes

    of somnolent metals

    seek the fire's crest

    on mountains and streets.

    But the snow carries me

    upon its mottled back

    and pools soak me

    in their water, hard and cold.

    But this night there will be

    red blood for my cheeks,

    and for the reeds that cluster

    at the wide feet of the wind.

    Let there be neither shadow nor bower,

    and then they can't get away!

    O let me enter a breast

    where I may get warm!

    A heart for me!

    Warm! That will spurt

    over the mountains of my chest;

    let me come in, oh let me!

[*To the branches*]

    I want no shadows. My rays

    must get in everywhere,

    even among the dark trunks I want

    the whisper of gleaming lights,

    so that this night there will be

    sweet blood for my cheeks,

    and for the reeds that cluster

    at the wide feet of the wind.

    Who is hiding? Out, I say!

    No! They will not get away!

    I will light up the horse

    with a fever bright as diamonds.

[*He disappears among the trunks, and the stage goes back to its dark lighting. An* Old Woman *comes out completely covered by thin green cloth. She is barefooted. Her face can barely be seen among the folds. This character does not appear in the cast*]

BEGGAR WOMAN:

    That moon's going away, just when they're near.

    They won't get past here. The river's whisper

    and the whispering tree trunks will muffle

    the torn flight of their shrieks.

    It has to be here, and soon. I'm worn out.

    The coffins are ready, and white sheets

    wait on the floor of the bedroom

    for heavy bodies with torn throats.

    Let not one bird awake, let the breeze,

    gathering their moans in her skirt,

    fly with them over black tree tops

    or bury them in soft mud.

[*Impatiently*]

    Oh, that moon! That moon!

[*The* Moon *appears. The intense blue light returns*]

MOON: They're coming. One band through the ravine and the other along the river. I'm going to light up the boulders. What do you need?

BEGGAR WOMAN: Nothing.

MOON: The wind blows hard now, with a double edge.

BEGGAR WOMAN: Light up the waistcoat and open the buttons; the knives will know the path after that.

MOON:

    But let them be a long time a-dying. So the blood

    will slide its delicate hissing between my fingers.

    Look how my ashen valleys already are waking

    in longing for this fountain of shuddering gushes!

BEGGAR WOMAN: Let's not let them get past the arroyo. Silence!

MOON: There they come! [*He goes. The stage is left dark*]

BEGGAR WOMAN: Quick! Lots of light! Do you hear me? They can't get away!

[*The Bridegroom and The First Youth enter. The Beggar Woman sits down and covers herself with her cloak*]

BRIDEGROOM: This way.

FIRST YOUTH: You won't find them.

BRIDEGROOM: [*Angrily*] Yes, I'll find them!

FIRST YOUTH: I think they've taken another path.

BRIDEGROOM: No. Just a moment ago I felt the galloping.

FIRST YOUTH: It could have been another horse.

BRIDEGROOM: [*Intensely*] Listen to me. There's only one horse in the whole world, and this one's it. Can't you understand that? If you're going to follow me, follow me without talking.

FIRST YOUTH: It's only that I want to . . .

BRIDEGROOM: Be quiet. I'm sure of meeting them here. Do you see this arm? Well, it's not my arm. It's my brother's arm, and my father's, and that of all the dead ones in my family. And it has so much strength that it can pull this tree up by the roots, if it wants to. And let's move on, because here I feel the clenched teeth of all my people in me so that I can't breathe easily.

BEGGAR WOMAN: [*Whining*] Ay-y-y!

FIRST YOUTH: Did you hear that?

BRIDEGROOM: You go that way and then circle back.

FIRST YOUTH: This is a hunt.

BRIDEGROOM: A hunt. The greatest hunt there is.

[*The Youth goes off. The Bridegroom goes rapidly to the left and stumbles over* The Beggar Woman, Death]

BEGGAR WOMAN: Ay-y-y!

BRIDEGROOM: What do you want?

BEGGAR WOMAN: I'm cold.

BRIDEGROOM: Which way are you going?

BEGGAR WOMAN: [*Always whining like a beggar*] Over there, far away . . .

BRIDEGROOM: Where are you from?

BEGGAR WOMAN: Over there . . . very far away.

BRIDEGROOM: Have you seen a man and a woman running away on a horse?

BEGGAR WOMAN: [*Awakening*] Wait a minute . . . [*She looks at him*] Handsome young man. [*She rises*] But you'd be much handsomer sleeping.

BRIDEGROOM: Tell me; answer me. Did you see them?

BEGGAR WOMAN: Wait a minute . . . What broad shoulders! How would you like to be laid out on them and not have to walk on the soles of your feet which are so small?

BRIDEGROOM: [*Shaking her*] I asked you if you saw them! Have they passed through here?

BEGGAR WOMAN: [*Energetically*] No. They haven't passed; but they're coming from the hill. Don't you hear them?

BRIDEGROOM: No.

BEGGAR WOMAN: Do you know the road?

BRIDEGROOM: I'll go, whatever it's like!

BEGGAR WOMAN: I'll go along with you. I know this country.

BRIDEGROOM: [*Impatiently*] Well, let's go! Which way?

BEGGAR WOMAN: [*Dramatically*] This way!

[*They go rapidly out. Two violins, which represent the forest, are heard distantly.* The Woodcutters *return. They have their axes on their shoulders. They move slowly among the tree trunks*]

FIRST WOODCUTTER:
O rising death!
Death among the great leaves.

SECOND WOODCUTTER:
Don't open the gush of blood!

FIRST WOODCUTTER:
O lonely death!
Death among the dried leaves.

THIRD WOODCUTTER:
Don't lay flowers over the wedding!

SECOND WOODCUTTER:
O sad death!
Leave for their love a green branch.

FIRST WOODCUTTER:
O evil death!
Leave for their love a branch of green!

[*They go out while they are talking.* Leonardo *and* The Bride *appear*]

LEONARDO:
Hush!

BRIDE:
From here I'll go on alone.
You go now! I want you to turn back.

LEONARDO:
Hush, I said!

BRIDE:
With your teeth, with your hands, anyway you can,
take from my clean throat
the metal of this chain,
and let me live forgotten
back there in my house in the ground.
And if you don't want to kill me
as you would kill a tiny snake,
set in my hands, a bride's hands,
the barrel of your shotgun.
Oh, what lamenting, what fire,
sweeps upward through my head!
What glass splinters are stuck in my
tongue!

LEONARDO:
We've taken the step now; hush!
because they're close behind us,
and I must take you with me.

BRIDE:
Then it must be by force!

LEONARDO:
By force? Who was it first
went down the stairway?

BRIDE:
I went down it.

LEONARDO:
And who was it put
a new bridle on the horse?

BRIDE:
I myself did it. It's true.

LEONARDO:
And whose were the hands
strapped spurs to my boots?

BRIDE:
The same hands, these that are yours,
but which when they see you would like
to break the blue branches
and sunder the purl of your veins.

I love you! I love you! But leave me!
For if I were able to kill you
I'd wrap you 'round in a shroud
with the edges bordered in violets.
Oh, what lamenting, what fire,
sweeps upward through my head!

LEONARDO:
What glass splinters are stuck in my
    tongue!
Because I tried to forget you
and put a wall of stone
between your house and mine.
It's true. You remember?
And when I saw you in the distance
I threw sand in my eyes.
But I was riding a horse
and the horse went straight to your door.
And the silver pins of your wedding
turned my red blood black.
And in me our dream was choking
my flesh with its poisoned weeds.
Oh, it isn't my fault—
the fault is the earth's—
and this fragrance that you exhale
from your breasts and your braids.

BRIDE:
Oh, how untrue! I want
from you neither bed nor food,
yet there's not a minute each day
that I don't want to be with you,
because you drag me, and I come,
then you tell me to go back
and I follow you,
like chaff blown on the breeze.
I have left a good, honest man,
and all his people,
with the wedding feast half over
and wearing my bridal wreath.
But you are the one will be punished
and that I don't want to happen.
Leave me alone now! You run away!
There is no one who will defend you.

LEONARDO:
The birds of early morning
are calling among the trees.
The night is dying
on the stone's ridge.
Let's go to a hidden corner
where I may love you forever,
for to me the people don't matter,
nor the venom they throw on us.
[He embraces her strongly]

BRIDE:
And I'll sleep at your feet,
to watch over your dreams.
Naked, looking over the fields,
as though I were a bitch.
Because that's what I am! Oh, I look at
    you
and your beauty sears me.

LEONARDO:
Fire is stirred by fire.
The same tiny flame
will kill two wheat heads together.
Let's go!

BRIDE:
Where are you taking me?

LEONARDO:
Where they cannot come,
these men who surround us.
Where I can look at you!

BRIDE: [Sarcastically]
Carry me with you from fair to fair,
a shame to clean women,
so that people will see me
with my wedding sheets
on the breeze like banners.

LEONARDO:
I, too, would want to leave you
if I thought as men should.
But wherever you go, I go.
You're the same. Take a step. Try.
Nails of moonlight have fused
my waist and your chains.
[This whole scene is violent, full of great sen-
suality]

BRIDE:
Listen!

LEONARDO:
They're coming.

BRIDE:
                Run!
It's fitting that I should die here,
with water over my feet,
with thorns upon my head.
And fitting the leaves should mourn me,
a woman lost and virgin.

LEONARDO:
Be quiet. Now they're appearing.

BRIDE:
                Go now!

LEONARDO:
Quiet. Don't let them hear us.
[The Bride hesitates]

BRIDE:
Both of us!

LEONARDO: [Embracing her]
                Any way you want!
If they separate us, it will be
because I am dead.

BRIDE:
                And I dead too.
[They go out in each other's arms]
[The Moon appears very slowly. The stage
takes on a strong blue light. The two violins
are heard. Suddenly two long, ear-splitting
shrieks are heard, and the music of the two
violins is cut short. At the second shriek The
Beggar Woman appears and stands with her
back to the audience. She opens her cape and

*stands in the center of the stage like a great
bird with immense wings.* The Moon *halts. The
curtain comes down in absolute silence*]

CURTAIN

SCENE II.

The Final Scene
*A white dwelling with arches and thick walls. To
the right and left, are white stairs. At the back, a
great arch and a wall of the same color. The floor
also should be shining white. This simple dwelling
should have the monumental feeling of a church.
There should not be a single gray nor any shadow,
not even what is necessary for perspective. Two*
Girls *dressed in dark blue are winding a red skein.*

FIRST GIRL:
    Wool, red wool,
    what would you make?
SECOND GIRL:
    Oh, jasmine for dresses,
    fine wool like glass.
    At four o'clock born,
    At ten o'clock dead.
    A thread from this wool yarn,
    a chain 'round your feet
    a knot that will tighten
    the bitter white wreath.
LITTLE GIRL: [*Singing*]
    Were you at the wedding?
FIRST GIRL:
    No.
LITTLE GIRL:
    Well, neither was I!
    What could have happened
    'midst the shoots of the vineyards?
    What could have happened
    'neath the branch of the olive?
    What really happened
    that no one came back?
    Were you at the wedding?
SECOND GIRL:
    We told you once, no.
LITTLE GIRL: [*Leaving*]
    Well, neither was I!
SECOND GIRL:
    Wool, red wool,
    what would you sing?
FIRST GIRL:
    Their wounds turning waxen,
    balm-myrtle for pain.
    Asleep in the morning,
    and watching at night.
LITTLE GIRL: [*In the doorway*]
    And then, the thread stumbled
    on the flinty stones,
    but mountains, blue mountains,

are letting it pass.
    Running, running, running,
    and finally to come
    to stick in a knife blade,
    to take back the bread.
[*She goes out*]
SECOND GIRL:
    Wool, red wool,
    what would you tell?
FIRST GIRL:
    The lover is silent,
    crimson the groom,
    at the still shoreline
    I saw them laid out.
[*She stops and looks at the skein*]
LITTLE GIRL: [*Appearing in the doorway*]
    Running, running, running,
    the thread runs to here.
    All covered with clay
    I feel them draw near.
    Bodies stretched stiffly
    in ivory sheets!
[*The* Wife *and* Mother-in-law *of* Leonardo *appear. They are anguished*]
FIRST GIRL:
    Are they coming yet?
MOTHER-IN-LAW: [*Harshly*]
    We don't know.
SECOND GIRL:
    What can you tell us about the wedding?
FIRST GIRL:
    Yes, tell me.
MOTHER-IN-LAW: [*Curtly*] Nothing.
LEONARDO'S WIFE: I want to go back and find
out all about it.
MOTHER-IN-LAW: [*Sternly*]
    You, back to your house.
    Brave and alone in your house.
    To grow old and to weep.
    But behind closed doors.
    Never again. Neither dead nor alive.
    We'll nail up our windows
    and let rains and nights
    fall on the bitter weeds.
LEONARDO'S WIFE:
    What could have happened?
MOTHER-IN-LAW:
    It doesn't matter what.
    Put a veil over your face.
    Your children are yours,
    that's all. On the bed
    put a cross of ashes
    where his pillow was.
[*They go out*]
BEGGAR WOMAN: [*At the door*]
    A crust of bread, little girls.
LITTLE GIRL:
    Go away!
[*The Girls* huddle close together]

BEGGAR WOMAN:
Why?

LITTLE GIRL:
Because you whine; go away!

FIRST GIRL:
Child!

BEGGAR WOMAN:
I might have asked for your eyes! A cloud
of birds is following me. Will you have one?

LITTLE GIRL:
I want to get away from here!

SECOND GIRL: [*To the* Beggar Woman]
Don't mind her!

FIRST GIRL:
Did you come by the road through the arroyo?

BEGGAR WOMAN:
I came that way!

FIRST GIRL: [*Timidly*]
Can I ask you something?

BEGGAR WOMAN:
I saw them: they'll be here soon; two torrents
still at last, among the great boulders,
two men at the horse's feet.
Two dead men in the night's splendor.
[*With pleasure*]
Dead, yes, dead.

FIRST GIRL:
Hush, old woman, hush!

BEGGAR WOMAN:
Crushed flowers for eyes, and their teeth
two fistfuls of hard-frozen snow.
Both of them fell, and the Bride returns
with bloodstains on her skirt and hair.
And they come covered with two sheets
carried on the shoulders of two tall boys.
That's how it was; nothing more. What was fitting.
Over the golden flower, dirty sand.
[*She goes. The Girls bow their heads and start going out rhythmically*]

FIRST GIRL:
Dirty sand.

SECOND GIRL:
Over the golden flower.

LITTLE GIRL:
Over the golden flower
they're bringing the dead from the arroyo.
Dark the one,
dark the other.
What shadowy nightingale flies and weeps
over the golden flower!
[*She goes. The stage is left empty.* The Mother *and a* Neighbor Woman *appear. The Neighbor is weeping*]

MOTHER: Hush.

NEIGHBOR: I can't.

MOTHER: Hush, I said. [*At the door*] Is there nobody here? [*She puts her hands to her forehead*] My son ought to answer me. But now my son is an armful of shrivelled flowers. My son is a fading voice beyond the mountains now. [*With rage, to* The Neighbor] Will you shut up? I want no wailing in this house. Your tears are only tears from your eyes, but when I'm alone mine will come—from the soles of my feet, from my roots—burning more than blood.

NEIGHBOR: You come to my house; don't you stay here.

MOTHER: I want to be here. Here. In peace. They're all dead now: and at midnight I'll sleep, sleep without terror of guns or knives. Other mothers will go to their windows, lashed by rain, to watch for their sons' faces. But not I. And of my dreams I'll make a cold ivory dove that will carry camellias of white frost to the graveyard. But no; not graveyard, not graveyard: the couch of earth, the bed that shelters them and rocks them in the sky. [*A woman dressed in black enters, goes toward the right, and there kneels. To* The Neighbor] Take your hands from your face. We have terrible days ahead. I want to see no one. The earth and I. My grief and I. And these four walls. Ay-y-y! Ay-y-y! [*She sits down, overcome*]

NEIGHBOR: Take pity on yourself!

MOTHER: [*Pushing back her hair*] I must be calm. [*She sits down*] Because the neighbor women will come and I don't want them to see me so poor. So poor! A woman without even one son to hold to her lips.

[The Bride *appears. She is without her wreath and wears a black shawl*]

NEIGHBOR: [*With rage, seeing* The Bride] Where are you going?

BRIDE: I'm coming here.

MOTHER: [*To* The Neighbor] Who is it?

NEIGHBOR: Don't you recognize her?

MOTHER: That's why I asked who it was. Because I don't want to recognize her, so I won't sink my teeth in her throat. You snake! [*She moves wrathfully on* The Bride, *then stops. To* The Neighbor] Look at her! There she is, and she's crying, while I stand here calmly and don't tear her eyes out. I don't understand myself. Can it be I didn't love my son? But, where's his good name? Where is it now? Where is it? [*She beats* The Bride *who drops to the floor*]

NEIGHBOR: For God's sake! [*She tries to separate them*]

BRIDE: [*To* The Neighbor] Let her; I came here so she'd kill me and they'd take me away with them. [*To* The Mother] But not with her hands; with grappling hooks, with a sickle—and with force—until they break on my bones. Let her! I want her to know I'm clean, that I may be crazy, but that they can bury me without a single man ever having seen himself in the whiteness of my breasts.

MOTHER: Shut up, shut up; what do I care about that?

BRIDE: Because I ran away with the other one; I ran away! [*With anguish*] You would have gone, too. I was a woman burning with desire, full of sores inside and out, and your son was a little bit of water from which I hoped for children, land, health; but the other one was a dark river, choked with brush, that brought near me the undertone of its rushes and its whispered song. And I went along with your son who was like a little boy of cold water —and the other sent against me hundreds of birds who got in my way and left white frost on my wounds, my wounds of a poor withered woman, of a girl caressed by fire. I didn't want to; remember that! I didn't want to. Your son was my destiny and I have not betrayed him, but the other one's arm dragged me along like the pull of the sea, like the head toss of a mule, and he would have dragged me always, always, always—even if I were an old woman and all your son's sons held me by the hair!

[*A* Neighbor *enters*]

MOTHER: She is not to blame; nor am I! [*Sarcastically*] Who is, then? It's a delicate, lazy, sleepless woman who throws away an orange blossom wreath and goes looking for a piece of bed warmed by another woman!

BRIDE: Be still! Be still! Take your revenge on me; here I am! See how soft my throat is; it would be less work for you than cutting a dahlia in your garden. But never that! Clean, clean as a new-born little girl. And strong enough to prove it to you. Light the fire. Let's stick our hands in; you, for your son, I, for my body. *You'll* draw yours out first.

[*Another* Neighbor *enters*]

MOTHER: But what does your good name matter to me? What does your death matter to me? What does anything about anything matter to me? Blesséd be the wheat stalks, because my sons are under them; blesséd be the rain, because it wets the face of the dead. Blesséd be God, who stretches us out together to rest.

[*Another* Neighbor *enters*]

BRIDE: Let me weep with you.

MOTHER: Weep. But at the door. [The Girl *enters. The Bride* stays at the door. *The Mother* is at the center of the stage]

LEONARDO'S WIFE: [*Entering and going to the left*]

He was a beautiful horseman,
now he's a heap of snow.
He rode to fairs and mountains
and women's arms.
Now, the night's dark moss
crowns his forehead.

MOTHER:

A sunflower to your mother,
a mirror of the earth.

Let them put on your breast
the cross of bitter rosebay;
and over you a sheet
of shining silk;
between your quiet hands
let water form its lament.

WIFE:

Ay-y-y, four gallant boys
come with tired shoulders!

BRIDE:

Ay-y-y, four gallant boys
carry death on high!

MOTHER:

Neighbors.

LITTLE GIRL: [*At the door*]
They're bringing them now.

MOTHER:

It's the same thing.
Always the cross, the cross.

WOMEN:

Sweet nails,
cross adored,
sweet name
of Christ our Lord.

BRIDE: May the cross protect both the quick and the dead.

MOTHER:

Neighbors: with a knife,
with a little knife,
on their appointed day, between two and
    three,
these two men killed each other for love.
With a knife,
with a tiny knife
that barely fits the hand,
but that slides in clean
through the astonished flesh
and stops at the place
where trembles, enmeshed,
the dark root of a scream.

BRIDE:

And this is a knife,
a tiny knife
that barely fits the hand;
fish without scales, without river,
so that on their appointed day, between
    two and three,
with this knife,
two men are left stiff,
with their lips turning yellow.

MOTHER:

And it barely fits the hand
but it slides in clean
through the astonished flesh
and stops there, at the place
where trembles enmeshed
the dark root of a scream.

[The Neighbors, *kneeling on the floor, sob*]

CURTAIN

Bertolt Brecht

(1898–1956)

Among the poets of the modern theatre Bertolt Brecht is unique because he has always sung songs of "social significance." He was a stripling when Germany plunged into the First World War. He emerged into manhood when Germany adopted the Weimar republican constitution and broke out into sporadic revolutions, none more violent than the one that enjoyed a temporary triumph in his native Bavaria. These experiences determined the tone of his poetry and plays, most of which possessed an ideology far left of center and a zealous concern with moral and political issues. When Hitler gained control of Germany, Brecht was a marked man, but he cheated the gallows or a fate more horrible than simple execution by self-exile in 1933. He lived in Denmark and Finland for a time, went to Russia to edit the anti-Nazi periodical *Das Wort* with Lion Feuchtwanger and other exiles between 1936 and 1939, and arrived in the United States in 1941, where he devoted himself entirely to writing.

Returning to Germany shortly after Hitler's debacle, Brecht began to resume his important position among native writers and became associated with the liberated Deutsches Theater, once the temple of Brahm, Reinhardt, and other progressive men of the theatre. His lyrics and ballads, collected in several volumes, make him one of the most modern of twentieth-century poets. His plays, neither realistic nor expressionistic but marked by a distinctive combination of styles, give him an important place in the literary and social vanguard. Even in America, where his *Three-Penny Opera* proved disappointing in an inadequate New York production, he aroused more interest and found a more devoted following between 1935 and 1950 than might be expected of a playwright who failed to win the accolade of a Broadway success.

Brecht first attracted attention in 1922 when he won the coveted Kleist Prize for his antiwar play *Drums in the Night,* a morose but far from maudlin account of the experience of a German veteran who returns from the trenches to discover that profiteers have fattened on the blood of his comrades. Confirmed in the conviction that the drama must present social conflicts, Brecht continued to sing didactically in play after play. To promote an understanding of problems and issues, he began to write propaganda plays which combined analytic and poetic elements, demonstrated a problem, and instructed or were intended to instruct the common man as well as the class-conscious partisan in matters of strategy or right thinking. There was nothing prosaic, however,

about these *Lehrstücke,* or learning plays, as he called them. They had expressionistic and symbolic elements, sometimes told a parable and "slanted" their argument with imaginative devices and imagery, launched into balladlike verse, and called for music. One of the first of these pieces, *The Expedient,* an analysis of the moral problems faced by revolutionists, took the form of an oratorio, and was produced in Germany in 1929 with music by Hanns Eisler. Another learning play, *Round Heads and Peaked Heads,* produced in Copenhagen in 1936, satirized the racial theories of Hitler in a grotesque fable. Brecht's dramatization of Gorki's novel *Mother* (1932) traced the growth of revolutionary consciousness in a simple woman in Russia under the Czars; it relied more heavily on argument and choruses, or "mass chants" (with a score by Eisler), than on realistic scenes. In adapting John Gay's eighteenth-century classic *The Beggar's Opera,* renamed *The Three-Penny Opera,* Brecht moved directly into the musical-comedy field. The adaptation, sardonically lyrical and raffish, was a result of collaboration with the now well-known composer for the theatre Kurt Weill. The production, directed by Brecht himself, took Berlin by storm in 1928. It ran counter to the vogue of sentimental musical comedies and was as barbed with social protest as it was ungainly by intention.

Brecht's other plays revealed him as a remarkably flexible artist. He displayed an aptitude for historical plays in *The Life of Edward II* (based on Marlowe's tragedy), *Mother Courage,* and *Galileo,* a cool and antiheroic and yet exhilarating treatment of the famous scientist's life and struggles. He wrote a documentary presentation of German life under National Socialism, *The Private Life of the Master Race,* combining realistic sketches with imaginative technique and lyric power, and he composed two remarkable plays, rightly called "Parables for the Theatre" by his translators Eric and Maja Bentley, *The Good Woman of Setzuan* and *The Caucasian Chalk Circle.* In these, his didacticism is moral rather than political, and the lyric and dramatic elements are superbly balanced and vivid. Each play examines the problems of good and evil, justice and injustice, in fresh and challenging terms.

Brecht's kind of drama cannot, in fact, be properly understood without some appreciation of his qualities as a poet and without some knowledge of his theories of drama and theatre. He is a master of dry and colloquially flavored but charged poetry. He can take a traditional form such as the ballad and infuse it with the modern mind and spirit. He cultivates flatness often, but gives it a knifelike edge. All his plays have the same acuity, and so do his views on drama and acting. He considers himself an "epic realist," along with the stage director and dramatist Erwin Piscator; that is, he favors a type of dramatic composition that grasps the various facets of man's life in society without limiting itself to unity of time, place, and action. Some of his plays, as well as those adapted and staged by Piscator (Piscator's *The Good Soldier Schweik* and *An American Tragedy*), even have the extensiveness of an Elizabethan chronicle such as *Henry IV, Parts I and II* and as much variety of action and tone. One scene may convey a realistic situation while another may symbolize it; or the scene may take the form of a debate or a narration; or there may be no scene at all, only a song or recitation, at certain points in the play. But the episodes, combined with narrative and lyrical passages, and augmented with pantomime, dance, signs or placards, slides and motion-picture sequences if necessary—all following one another in rapid succession or alternation—will form one rich tumultuous play somewhat in the manner of such a novel as John Dos Passos' *U. S. A.* It is the underlying idea or the argument that cements the parts. This makes the drama as written and staged by Brecht and his former associate Erwin Piscator "epic."

Since the dramatist takes an unsentimental, analytical view of reality and demonstrates his argument with every conceivable device, this epic also serves the purpose of social realism. Hence the proper term for this type of drama and staging is "epic realism." Foregoing the esthetic advantages of a complete synthesis by tone or mood (the ideal of both the conventional realists and the symbolists of the Appia-Craig school), Brecht and Piscator concentrate on the diversity of a problem or situation. Risking discursiveness, they attempt to throw a clear light on the realities men must face if human ideals are to be effectuated.

This emphasis on the epic qualities of drama does not rule out the possibility of making the play revolve around a central hero. Brecht, for example, had no qualms about centering *The Caucasian Chalk Circle* and *The Good Woman of Setzuan* in the drama of a woman who in each case is as substantial a character as any created by conventional realists. Nor did he hesitate to select an outstanding historical figure for treatment in *Galileo*. (And Piscator's *The Good Soldier Schweik* thrusts a remarkable character, an arthritic little Czech, against the entire military machine of the Austrian-Hungarian empire. Schweik provided Max Pallenberg, the Charles Chaplin of Europe, with his biggest role.) The diversity of social reality can be presented just as effectively through an individual's experience as through that of a group, or "mass hero," as in *The Private Life of the Master Race*. And the fact that

Brecht and Piscator used all the resources of modern stage machinery and motion-picture technique in no way made them feel that they were flying in the face of tradition with their new epic style. Instead, they could point to the epic features of Greek and Elizabethan drama and stage production, as well as to the epic qualities of the romantic stage (*Faust, Brand, Peer Gynt*). They could claim with considerable justice that it was the writers of tight little realistic plays and not they who had broken with tradition.

Brecht (along with Piscator) also avowed himself the enemy of conventional emotionalism. He propounded a theory of "alienation" (*Verfremdung*) to the effect that no attempt should be made "to put the audience in a trance and give them the illusion of witnessing natural, unrehearsed events." It is necessary, indeed, to find means of neutralizing the audience's tendency to lose itself in illusion. If the playgoer feels too keenly, he is apt to do too little thinking. Pity is not enough as either an esthetic or social value. Neither is empathy, since complete identification with a character on the stage impairs objectivity and lulls the reasoning faculties to sleep. An Aristotelian catharsis through pity and terror, possible only when we succumb to stage illusion and identify ourselves with the characters, is not a desirable experience. When we are thoroughly purged, there is no longer any necessity to take action against the evils we have witnessed. The epic style must turn the spectator into an *observer*. It must "awaken his energy," and it must require decisions of him. This it will do by distancing dramatic experience and breaking the hypnotic spell that realists and symbolists alike cast upon their audience.

For "epic theatre," the actor must not feel himself completely into his role. For if he does, in the manner of a Stanislavskian actor, he will promote illusion instead of distancing the performance so that the audience may observe and appraise events instead of losing itself in them. The actor may in the rehearsals feel himself into his role only up to a point that will enable him to acquire the characteristics requisite for playing the role. And by bringing back into the drama such devices as choral commentary, song, and narration, Brecht intended to achieve the same distancing effect in dramaturgy. These interruptions of the dramatic action are expected to jar the spectator just as he is settling down to enjoy the story and fall into an emotional rapport with the characters. Emotion for Brecht's type of drama was not invalid, and Brecht himself could induce considerable emotion, but he did not want it to become the whole of a play and its final effect. Nor did he banish realism entirely. He could use it with fine effect whenever he wished. What he did not wish was to tether the drama to a confining technique and deprive himself of the benefit of other forms of expression which could strengthen his argument, enlighten his audience and spur it into action of some kind.

There could be much argument about Brecht's theories, especially when they were expressed in doctrinaire terms, and in essence they challenged Aristotelian principles that have been sacrosanct for most playwrights and critics. No one went so far as Brecht in denying the validity or necessity of pity, terror, catharsis, unity, and illusion as dramatic values. He did so with the animus of a Marxist who is concerned with social action and with the conviction of a scientist. (Brecht, we should note, was a student of medicine and served in the German medical corps during the First World War.) The "alienation" effect he advocated is scarcely to be distinguished from the ideal of scientific objectivity and the stress on clear demonstrations of clinical cases that we find in a modern medical school or hospital. Yet, beyond all theory, though not inconsonant with it, he operated in the theatre from the very beginning of his career as an impassioned partisan, a gifted poet, and a theatrician. Not the least attractive feature of his work is the evident struggle between poet and scientist, fabulist and social realist, the man of feeling and imagination and the social thinker who prides himself on his detachment.

Some of Brecht's best writing will be found in *The Private Life of the Master Race* (1944), although the selections given here provide only a modest example of the epic sweep of the work. It is possible to present it in excerpts because it consists of independent one-act plays connected by lyric passages and by an over-all pattern. We follow the travels of a German Panzer or tank, across Europe, from the time when it participates in Hitler's early victories to the time when it bogs down in defeat in Russia. Our primary concern is, however, with the Panzer's soldiers. The essential drama is their personal experience, which demonstrates how National Socialism came to Germany and, wrenching them from private life, sent them into combat. The play attracted much attention, even though its American production in downtown New York proved unsuccessful. The drama was translated into French and published by the *Nouvelle Revue Française*, and some of the one-acters were produced independently in Russia during the war. *The Jewish Wife* and *The Informer*, reprinted here, were particularly favored.

The epic pattern may be seen here in the manner in which the play moves from episode to episode, each built around a different character. (In a conventional realistic play one of these episodes would have been blown up into a single full-length drama and the emotional values of the subject would have been exploited fully.) That there is emotion in the scenes no one will deny after reading them. But the emotion is merely a means to the larger aim of showing us how the German terror operated and of recalling for us the sweep of German arms across the European continent. Brecht, who objected to the suspense that conventional playwrights worked up in their plays, employs a sufficiency of suspense himself in his episodes. But the suspense comes to an end abruptly with each episode, which is followed by a song and recitation, and there is no continuous plot throughout the work. (In fact, the play as a whole drops in interest from time to time and does not "build" in tension and dramatic substance as much as one might wish. Perhaps this tapering off is intentional. It surely creates an "alienation effect," although we are under no obligation to like the play the better for it.) The work as a whole is also distinctly theatrical as it alternates dramatic scenes and lyric passages, carries the roar of the Panzer as a prelude to each scene of the Nazi terror, brings on the military truck four times in the play, and uses placards to indicate the direction of the Panzer and the location of each dramatic episode. The work requires a skillful production and expert lighting effects. The lyric parts are differentiated into the singing of the Panzer troops followed by a voice speaking out of the darkness, and the effect is ironic and menacing—and revealing. Brecht called his work a documentary play, and a document it is, but not in the usual sense of a pedestrian report. It is a document with wings.

That Brecht's and Piscator's "epic realism" is not merely a bee in a Central European bonnet will occur to the experienced playgoer and reader when he recalls such American products as the Federal Theatre's "living newspapers" (as well as documentary films and documentary radio plays), Marc Blitzstein's *The Cradle Will Rock*, Paul Green's dramatization of Richard Wright's novel *Native Son*, and the Lerner and Weill Broadway musical comedy *Love Life*, a chronicle and demonstration of the effect of economics on the love life of the American people.

BIBLIOGRAPHY: Eric Bentley, *The Private Life of the Master Race* (with an essay, "Bertolt Brecht and His Work," pp. 117–140), 1944; Bentley, *The Playwright as Thinker* (pp. 250–272), 1946; Bertolt Brecht, "A New Technique of Acting," translated by Bentley, in *Theatre Arts*, Vol. XXXIII, No. 1, and reprinted under the title of "The Alienation Effect" in *Actors on Acting*, ed. by Toby Cole and Helen Krich Chinoy (pp. 280–285), 1949; Bertolt Brecht, "A Model for Epic Theatre," translated by Bentley, in *The Sewanee Review*, July 1949. See also Erwin Piscator, "Objective Acting," in *Actors on Acting* (pp. 285–291).

THE PRIVATE LIFE OF THE MASTER RACE

By Bertolt Brecht

ENGLISH VERSION BY ERIC RUSSELL BENTLEY

A band plays a barbaric march. Out of the darkness appears a big signpost: To POLAND, *and near it a Panzer truck. Its wheels are turning. On it sit twelve to sixteen soldiers, steel helmeted, their faces white as chalk, their guns between their knees. They could be puppets.*

The soldiers sing to the tune of the Horst Wessel Song:

And when the Führer had created order
At home in Germany with iron hand,
Forthwith he sent us out to carry his New Order
With faith and force to every other land.

So we set out obedient to superiors
In all our might—'twas a September day—
To conquer for them with the dreadful speed of
lightning
A little town that deep in Poland lay.

And soon all Europe saw a bloody plaster
Smeared on our tanks from Seine to Volga strand
Because our Führer had re-cast us as a Master-
Race through the continent with iron hand.

* * *

Dim out. The dull roll of the Panzer motor continues for a few seconds. When the stage lights up, we see a staircase. Above the scene is written in enormous black letters:

BRESLAU 1933

THE BETRAYAL

[*A man and a woman stand listening. They are very pale*]

THE WOMAN: Now they're downstairs.

THE MAN: Not yet.

THE WOMAN: They've smashed the banister. He was already unconscious when they dragged him out of the apartment.

THE MAN: But the only thing I said was that the radio with the broadcasts from Russia didn't come from here.

THE WOMAN: That wasn't the *only* thing you said.

THE MAN: I didn't say anything else.

THE WOMAN: Don't look at me like that. It serves them right. Why do they have to be Communists?

THE MAN: But they didn't need to tear his jacket for him. None of us are as well off as that.

THE WOMAN: The jacket has nothing to do with it.

THE MAN: They didn't need to tear it for him.

Dim out. The sound of the Panzer in motion is heard again.

THE VOICE: [1]

Thus neighbor betrayed neighbor.
Thus the common folk devoured each other
and enmity grew in the houses and in the precincts.
And so we went forth with confidence
and shoved onto our Panzer
every man who had not been slain:
a whole nation of betrayers and betrayed
we shoved onto our iron chariot.

* * *

Dim out.[2] The Panzer is heard.

THE VOICE:

There is also a doctor on our Panzer
who decides which of the Polish miners' wives
shall be sent to the brothel in Cracow.
And he is competent and makes no bones about it,
in memory of the wife he lost,
who was a Jewess, sent away because
the Master Race must be carefully mated
and the Führer decides whom each shall lie with.

* * *

[1] Each scene is introduced or followed by a voice speaking out of the darkness and by the roar of the Panzer as it starts rolling.

[2] After an episode showing the "organization" of science under National Socialism at the University of Goettingen in 1935.

When the lights go up we see a comfortable, bourgeois bedroom. Above the scene is written in enormous letters:

FRANKFURT 1935

THE JEWISH WIFE

It is evening. A woman is packing. She is picking out the things she wants to take with her. Sometimes she takes an article out of the bag again and puts it back in its place so that she can pack something else. She hesitates a long time over a large picture of her husband which is on the dressing-table. In the end she leaves it where it is. Getting tired of packing, she sits for a few moments on a suitcase, her head propped on her hand. Then she goes to the telephone.

THE WIFE: Judith Keith speaking. Is that you, doctor? Good evening.—I just wanted to call up and say that you must look around for a new bridge partner. Yes, I'm going away.—No, not for very long, but it won't be less than a couple of weeks. I'm going to Amsterdam.—Yes, they say the spring is lovely there.—I have friends there.—No, friends, in the plural, unbelievable as it sounds.—How can you play bridge now? But we haven't played for two weeks.—Certainly, Fritz had a cold too. When it gets so cold bridge is impossible, I said so too.—Oh no, doctor, how could I?—Thekla had to accommodate her mother.—I know.—How should I suppose *that?*—No, it really didn't come suddenly at all, it's just that I kept putting it off, but now I must . . . Yes, we'll have to call off our movie date. Say hello to Thekla for me.—Perhaps you'll call him sometimes on Sundays? So long then.—Well, gladly, of course.—Good-bye.

[She hangs up and calls another number]
Judith Keith speaking. I'd like to speak to Frau Shoeck.—Lotte?—I wanted to say a quick good-bye, I'm going away for a time.—No, I'm quite well, I just want to see a couple of new faces.—Yes, what I wanted to say was that Fritz is bringing the professor here for the evening next Tuesday, and perhaps you could come too. As I said I'm leaving tonight.—Yes, Tuesday.—No, I only wanted to say I'm leaving tonight, that has nothing to do with it, I thought you could come then too.—All right, let's say: *although* I'm not there, O.K.?—Of course I know you're not like that, and even if you were these are troubled times, and everybody's careful now. You'll come then?—If Max can? Oh, he will be able to, the professor'll be here, tell him.—I must hang up now. Fine. Good-bye.

[She hangs up and calls another number]
Is that you Gertrude? This is Judith. Sorry to disturb you.—Thanks. I wanted to ask you if you can look after Fritz, I'm going away for a couple of months.—I think that you as his sister . . . Why wouldn't you like to?—But there's no likelihood of that, not in Fritz's case. Naturally he knows that—er—you and I didn't get on too well together, but . . . Then he'll call you, if you wish it.—Yes, I'll tell him.—It's all pretty much in order though the apartment's a bit too big.—His study? Oh, Ida knows how to look after it, just leave that to her.—I find her quite intelligent, and he's used to her.—And another thing, please don't misunderstand me, he doesn't like to talk before dinner, could you remember that? I've always avoided it.—I don't want to discuss it now, my train leaves soon and I've not finished packing, you see.—Look after his suits and remind him he has to go to the tailor—he's ordered a coat—and take care that his bedroom's well heated, he always sleeps with an open window and it's too cold.—I don't believe he should "become inured" to it, but now I must stop.—Thank you so much, Gertrude, and we'll write to each other.—Good-bye.

[She hangs up and calls another number]
Anna? This is Judith. Look, I'm leaving right away.—No, it has to be, it's getting too difficult—too difficult! Yes, no, Fritz doesn't want it, he knows nothing. I simply packed.—I don't think so.—I don't think he'll say much.—It's simply too hard for him, I mean, too many technicalities.—We never discussed it.—We never even spoke about it, never.—No, he was not different, on the contrary—I want you to be good to him a little at the first.—Yes, especially Sundays, and advise him to move.—The apartment is too big for him.—I'd like to say good-bye to you, but you know—the janitor? [3]—Good-bye then. No, don't come to the station, by no means. Good-bye, I'll write.—Surely.

[She hangs up and calls no more numbers. She has been smoking. She now burns the little book in which she looked up the telephone numbers. She walks up and down a couple of times. Then she begins to speak. She is trying out the little speech which she wishes to make to her husband. One sees that he is supposedly sitting in a certain chair]
Yes, I'm going now, Fritz. Perhaps I've stayed too long already, you must forgive that, but . . .
[She stands thinking and then tries again]
Fritz, you shouldn't keep me any longer, you can't . . . It's obvious that I'll be your undoing. I know you're not cowardly, you're not afraid of the police—but there are worse things than the police. They won't take you to the concentration camp but—tomorrow or the next day—they won't let you into the clinic. You won't say anything then, but you'll be sick. I won't see you sitting around here turning the pages of magazines. I'm going out of pure egoism and nothing else. Don't say anything.
[She stops again. And tries again]
Don't say you're not changed. You are! Last week

---

[3] Evidently the janitor is Nazi.

you found—quite objectively—that the percentage of Jewish scientists is after all not so great. It always begins with objectivity. And why do you continually say to me now that I never was such a Jewish nationalist as today. Naturally I am! It's so catching! Oh Fritz, what has happened to us?

[She pauses]

I didn't tell you I wanted to go and have wanted to go a long time because I can't talk when I look at you, Fritz. Talking seems so futile. They have fixed everything. What is wrong with them? What do they actually want? What do I do to them? I've never meddled in politics. Was I for Thaelmann? [4] No, I'm just a bourgeois, a housewife who keep servants and so forth, and now suddenly only blondes can carry on that way. I've often thought lately how you said to me some years ago: "There are valuable people and less valuable people. The valuable people get insulin when they have sugar in the blood, the less valuable get none." I agreed with you, fool that I was! Now they've made new categories of this sort, and I belong to the less valuable. It serves me right.

[Another pause]

Yes, I'm packing. You mustn't act as if you hadn't noticed it in the last few days . . . . Fritz, everything is tolerable except one thing: that we're not looking each other in the eyes during the last hour that remains to us. That they shall not achieve—the liars who set everyone lying. Ten years ago when somebody thought no one could tell I was Jewish you quickly said: "Oh, yes, they can tell." And I liked that. It was clear-headed. Why evade the issue now? I'm packing because otherwise they'll take away your position as chief surgeon at the clinic. And because they already cut you there to your face and because already you can't sleep at night. I don't want you to tell me not to go. I'm going in a hurry because I don't want to have you tell me I should go. It's a question of time. Character is a question of time. It lasts for a certain length of time, just like a glove. There are good ones that last a long time. But they don't last forever. Incidentally, I'm not angry. And yet: I am. Why should I always be so understanding? What's wrong with the shape of my nose and the color of my hair? They want me to quit the town where I was born lest they should need to give me butter. What kind of men are you all? What kind of a man are you? You people discover the quantum theory and let yourselves be bossed by half-savages; you have to conquer the world, but are not allowed to have the wife you want. Artificial respiration and every shot a hit! You're monsters or the bootlickers of monsters. Yes, this is unreasonable of me, but what use is reason in such a world? There you sit watching your wife pack and say nothing. The walls have ears, don't they? And you all say nothing! One lot listen and the other lot hold their tongues. Christ! I should hold my tongue too. If I loved you, I'd hold my tongue. I love you really.

4 Communist candidate in presidential elections.

Give me that underwear. Those have sex appeal, I'll need them. I'm thirty-six, that's not too old, but I can't do much more experimenting. It mustn't be this way in the next country I come to. The next man I get must be allowed to keep me. And don't say you'll send money, you know you can't. And you shouldn't act as if it were for four weeks. This business doesn't last a mere four weeks. You know it and I know it too. So don't say, "Well, it's only for a couple of weeks," as you hand me the fur coat I won't need till winter. And let's not talk about misfortune. Let's talk about shame. Oh, Fritz!

[She stops. A door is heard opening. She hastily puts herself to rights. Her husband comes in]

THE HUSBAND: What are you doing, tidying up?

THE WIFE: No.

THE HUSBAND: Why are you packing?

THE WIFE: I want to get away.

THE HUSBAND: What do you mean?

THE WIFE: We've talked sometimes about my going away for a time. Things are not too good here these days.

THE HUSBAND: That's a lot of nonsense.

THE WIFE: Shall I stay then?

THE HUSBAND: Where do you intend to go?

THE WIFE: To Amsterdam. Away from here.

THE HUSBAND: But you have no one there.

THE WIFE: No.

THE HUSBAND: Why don't you stay here then? You certainly mustn't go on my account.

THE WIFE: No.

THE HUSBAND: You know I've not changed, don't you, Judith?

THE WIFE: Yes.

[He embraces her. They stand, silent between the bags]

THE HUSBAND: And there's nothing else to make you go?

THE WIFE: You know the answer to that.

THE HUSBAND: Perhaps it isn't so stupid. You need a breather. It's stifling here. I'll bring you back. Two days on the other side of the frontier, and I'd feel much better.

THE WIFE: Yes, by all means.

THE HUSBAND: This business here can't last too long. A complete change will come—from somewhere. All this will calm down again like an inflammation. It's really a misfortune.

THE WIFE: It certainly is. Did you meet Shoeck?

THE HUSBAND: Yes, that is, only on the stairs. I believe he's sorry again they cut us. He was quite embarrassed. In the long run they can't hold us intellectuals down like this, however much they hate us. Nor can they make war with completely spineless wrecks. These people are not so unresponsive if one confronts them boldly. When do you want to leave?

THE WIFE: Quarter past nine.

THE HUSBAND: And where shall I send the money?

THE WIFE: General delivery, Amsterdam, perhaps.

THE HUSBAND: I'll get myself a special permit. My God, I can't send my wife away with ten marks a month! What a mess everything is in. I feel awful about it.

THE WIFE: When you come for me, it'll do you good.

THE HUSBAND: To read a paper for once that has something in it!

THE WIFE: I called up Gertrude. She'll look after you.

THE HUSBAND: Quite unnecessary—for a couple of weeks.

THE WIFE: [She has begun to pack] Hand me the fur coat now, will you?

THE HUSBAND: [He gives it to her] After all, it's only for a couple of weeks.

Dim out. The Panzer is heard.

THE VOICE:

And there is also a teacher on our Panzer,
a captain now with a hat of steel,
who teaches a bloody lesson to
French grapefarmers and fishermen of Norway.
For there was a day seven years before,
dimly remembered but never forgotten,
when in the bosom of his family he learned
to hate spies.

* * *

When the lights go up we see a living room. Above the scene is written in enormous black letters:

COLOGNE 1935

The Informer

It is a rainy Sunday afternoon. A husband, his wife, and their boy have just finished lunch. A maid enters.

THE MAID: Herr and Frau Klimbtsch want to know if you're at home, sir.

THE HUSBAND: [Snapping] We're not.

[The Maid goes out]

THE WIFE: You should have gone to the telephone yourself. They know we couldn't possibly have gone out yet.

THE HUSBAND: Why couldn't we have gone out?

THE WIFE: Because it's raining.

THE HUSBAND: That's not a reason.

THE WIFE: What would we have gone out for? They'll certainly wonder about that now.

THE HUSBAND: There are plenty of places to go to.

THE WIFE: Then why don't we go?

THE HUSBAND: Where should we go to?

THE WIFE: If only it weren't raining.

THE HUSBAND: And where on earth should we go if it weren't raining?

THE WIFE: In the old days you could at least arrange to meet somebody.

[There is a pause]

THE WIFE: It was a mistake not to go to the telephone. Now they know we don't want to have them here.

THE HUSBAND: What if they do?

THE WIFE: Why then it means that we're dropping them just when everybody's dropping them. I don't like it.

THE HUSBAND: We're not dropping them.

THE WIFE: Then why shouldn't they come here?

THE HUSBAND: Because this Klimbtsch fellow bores me stiff.

THE WIFE: In the old days he didn't bore you.

THE HUSBAND: "In the old days"! Don't keep saying that. You make me nervous.

THE WIFE: At any rate you wouldn't have cut him in the old days just because his case is being looked into by the school-inspectors.

THE HUSBAND: You want to imply I'm a coward?

[There is a pause]

THE HUSBAND: All right. Call them up and say we've just come back because of the rain.

[The Wife remains seated]

THE WIFE: Shall we ask the Lemkes if they want to come over?

THE HUSBAND: So they can tell us we're not keen enough on Air Raid Precautions?

THE WIFE: [To the Boy] Klaus-Heinrich! Leave the radio alone.

[The Boy turns to the newspapers]

THE HUSBAND: It's certainly a catastrophe to have rain today. You just can't live in a country where it's a catastrophe when it rains.

THE WIFE: Is there much point in throwing remarks like that around?

THE HUSBAND: Within my own four walls I can make whatever remarks I please. In my own home I can say what I . . .

[He is interrupted. The Maid comes in with coffee things. There is silence while she is in the room]

THE HUSBAND: Must we have a maid whose father is Block Warden?

THE WIFE: I think we've talked about that enough. Last time you said it had its advantages.

THE HUSBAND: I've said a whole lot of things. Only say something of the kind to your mother and very likely we'll get in a wonderful mess.

THE WIFE: What I say to my mother . . .

[The Maid interrupts them again as she brings in the coffee]

THE WIFE: Leave it now, Erna, you can go. I'll look after this.

THE MAID: Thanks very much, gnädige Frau. [She goes out]

THE BOY: [Looking up from the paper] Do all priests do that, Papa?

THE HUSBAND: What?

THE BOY: What it says here.

THE HUSBAND: What is it you're reading?

[*He snatches the paper out of his hand*]

THE BOY: Our Group Leader told us we could all know what it says in this paper.

THE HUSBAND: It doesn't matter to me what the Group Leader said. I decide what you can read and what you can't.

THE WIFE: Here's ten cents, Klaus-Heinrich, go over and buy yourself something.

THE BOY: But it's raining.

[*He hangs around near the window, undecided*]

THE HUSBAND: If these reports of the priest trials don't stop, I'll not order this paper any more.

THE WIFE: And which one *will* you subscribe to? It's in all of them.

THE HUSBAND: If all the papers carry filth like that, I'll read none. I couldn't know less of what's going on in the world.

THE WIFE: A house cleaning doesn't do any harm.

THE HUSBAND: House cleaning! That's nothing but politics.

THE WIFE: Anyway it doesn't concern us, after all we're Lutheran.

THE HUSBAND: It's not a matter of indifference for our people if they can't think of a vestry without thinking of such abominations.

THE WIFE: Then what should they do if such things happen?

THE HUSBAND: What should they do? Maybe they might look to their own affairs. It may not all be as clean as it might be in their Brown House,[5] so I hear.

THE WIFE: But that goes to prove our people has recovered its health, Karl.

THE HUSBAND: Recovered its health! If that's what healthiness looks like, give me disease.

THE WIFE: You're so nervous today. Did anything happen at school?

THE HUSBAND: What should happen at school? And please stop telling me I'm nervous. That's what makes me that way.

THE WIFE: We shouldn't always be quarreling, Karl. In the old days . . .

THE HUSBAND: I was waiting for it: "in the old days"! I didn't want my child's mind poisoned in the old days and I don't want it poisoned now.

THE WIFE: Where is he anyway?

THE HUSBAND: How do I know?

THE WIFE: Did you see him leave?

THE HUSBAND: No.

THE WIFE: I don't understand where he can have gone. [*Shouting*] Klaus-Heinrich!

[*She runs out and is heard shouting. She returns*]

THE WIFE: Well, he's out.

THE HUSBAND: Why on earth shouldn't he be out?

THE WIFE: Why, because it's simply pouring.

5 Nazi headquarters.

THE HUSBAND: Why are you so nervous if the boy goes out once in a while?

THE WIFE: What have we been saying?

THE HUSBAND: What's that got to do with it?

THE WIFE: You're so uncontrolled these days.

THE HUSBAND: I certainly am not uncontrolled these days, but even if I were uncontrolled, what has that got to do with the boy being out?

THE WIFE: Oh, you know they listen.

THE HUSBAND: So what?

THE WIFE: So what? So this: what if he tells tales? You know perfectly well what's drummed into them at the Hitler Youth. They're under orders to report everything. Strange he left so quietly.

THE HUSBAND: Nonsense.

THE WIFE: Didn't you notice it, when he'd left?

THE HUSBAND: He was at the window quite a time.

THE WIFE: I wonder what he overheard.

THE HUSBAND: He knows what happens to people who're informed against.

THE WIFE: What of the boy the Schulkes told about? His father must be in the concentration camp still. If we only knew how long he was in the room.

THE HUSBAND: Oh, that's all nonsense.

[*He goes through the other rooms and shouts for* The Boy]

THE WIFE: I can't believe he'd just go off somewhere without saying a word. He isn't like that.

THE HUSBAND: Maybe he's at some school-friend's.

THE WIFE: In that case he can only be at the Mummermanns'. I'll phone.

[*She phones*]

THE HUSBAND: I regard the whole thing as a false alarm.

THE WIFE: [*At the phone*] This is Frau Furcke. Good afternoon, Frau Mummermann. Is Klaus-Heinrich at your place?—He isn't?—Then I just can't think where the boy is.—Tell me, Frau Mummermann, is the club room of the Hitler Youth open on Sunday afternoon?—It is?—Thanks, I'll try them.

[*She hangs up. The couple sit in silence*]

THE HUSBAND: What can he have heard after all?

THE WIFE: You talked about the paper. You shouldn't have said that about the Brown House. He's such a nationalist.

THE HUSBAND: And *what* may I have said about the Brown House?

THE WIFE: You can hardly help remembering: that it's not all clean there.

THE HUSBAND: That can't be interpreted as an attack. To say: it's not all clean, or rather as I more moderately put it, not all *quite* clean, which certainly makes a difference, a considerable difference, why, that's more of a jocular observation, idiomatic and popular, one might almost say a colloquialism. It means little more than that probably, even there, something is not always and under all circumstances as the Führer wishes it. I intentionally indicated the merely probable character of my allegation by using the expression: "it *may* not all be *quite*"—

quite in the mildest sense—"clean." This was my formulation of the matter. *May* be! Not: *is!* I can't say that anything there *is* not clean, there's no proof. But wherever there are men, there are imperfections. I never suggested anything more than that, and that only in the mildest form. And moreover the Führer himself on a certain occasion gave his criticism in the same direction and much more sharply.

THE WIFE: I don't understand you. You don't have to talk this way to me.

THE HUSBAND: I wish I didn't have to. I'm not sure what you yourself say, in the way of gossip, about the things you've heard between these four walls, insignificant things, probably only said in a moment of excitement. Naturally I'm far from accusing you of spreading any frivolous tales against your husband and I don't for a moment assume that the boy would do anything against his father. But unfortunately there's an important distinction between doing wrong and knowing you do it.

THE WIFE: Now please stop! Watch your own tongue! You said one can't live in Hitler Germany. All along I've been trying to remember whether you said that before or after what you said about the Brown House.

THE HUSBAND: I didn't say it at all.

THE WIFE: You act precisely as if I were the police! But what can the boy have heard? That's what tortures me.

THE HUSBAND: The expression "Hitler Germany" is not in my vocabulary.

THE WIFE: And about the Block Warden and about the papers being full of lies and what you said recently about Air Raid Precautions—the boy hears nothing positive at all! That certainly isn't good for a young mind. Youth can only be perverted by such talk. And the Führer always stresses: "Germany's youth is Germany's future." The boy doesn't run off and turn informer. He isn't made that way. I feel bad.

THE HUSBAND: But he's revengeful.

THE WIFE: What can he take revenge for?

THE HUSBAND: God knows. There's always something. Maybe because I took his green frog away from him.

THE WIFE: But that was a week ago.

THE HUSBAND: He remembers such things.

THE WIFE: Why did you take it from him?

THE HUSBAND: Because he caught no flies for it. H. just let it starve.

THE WIFE: He really has too much to do, though.

THE HUSBAND: That's not the frog's fault.

THE WIFE: But he never talked about it afterwards and just now I gave him ten cents. Why, he gets everything he wants.

THE HUSBAND: Yes, that's bribery.

THE WIFE: What do you mean by that?

THE HUSBAND: They'll immediately say we tried to bribe him to keep his mouth shut.

THE WIFE: What do you think they can do to you?

THE HUSBAND: Oh, everything. There are no limits to what they can do. Good God! Educator of the Youth! I fear them. To be a teacher in these circumstances!

THE WIFE: But there's nothing against you.

THE HUSBAND: There's something against everyone. All are suspect. If suspicion exists, someone is suspected. Suspicion need only exist.

THE WIFE: But a child is not a reliable witness. A child hasn't the least idea what he is saying.

THE HUSBAND: That's your opinion. Since when have they needed a witness for anything?

THE WIFE: Can't we think out what you must have meant by your remarks? I mean: then it will be clear he misunderstood you.

THE HUSBAND: What could I have said? I can't remember. It's the fault of the damned rain. . . . It makes you disgruntled. After all I'm the last to say anything against the spiritual revival the German people has experienced. I foresaw it all back in 1932.

THE WIFE: Karl, we haven't time to talk of it. We must straighten everything out and without delay. We haven't a moment to lose.

THE HUSBAND: I can't think it of Klaus-Heinrich.

THE WIFE: Now: first the matter of the Brown House and the filth.

THE HUSBAND: I said nothing about filth.

THE WIFE: You said the paper is full of filth and that you intend to cancel your subscription.

THE HUSBAND: Yes, the paper, but not the Brown House.

THE WIFE: Might you not have said that you disapprove of such filth in the vestries? And that you think it quite possible that the very men now on trial invented the atrocity stories about the Brown House and that they said that all was not clean? And that they therefore should have looked to their own affairs? And above all you told the boy to leave the radio and take the paper instead because you take the stand that youth in the Third Reich should note with open eyes what is going on.

THE HUSBAND: All that wouldn't help in the least.

THE WIFE: Karl, don't let your courage fail you. You must be strong, as the Führer always . . .

THE HUSBAND: I can't stand in the dock with my own flesh and blood in the witness box giving evidence against me.

THE WIFE: You mustn't take it this way.

THE HUSBAND: It was unpardonably careless to have anything to do with the Klimbtsches.

THE WIFE: Why? Nothing has happened to him yet.

THE HUSBAND: But the investigation is pending.

THE WIFE: An investigation is pending for lots of people. What would happen if they were all in despair?

THE HUSBAND: Do you think the Block Warden has anything against us?

THE WIFE: You mean if enquiries are made? He

got a box of cigarettes on his birthday and a splendid tip at New Year's.

THE HUSBAND: The Gauffs next door gave *fifteen* marks!

THE WIFE: But they read *Vorwärts* [6] as late as '32 and in May '33 they put out the black-white-and-red flag.[7]

[*The telephone rings*]

THE HUSBAND: The telephone!

THE WIFE: Shall I go?

THE HUSBAND: I don't know.

THE WIFE: Who can it be?

THE HUSBAND: Wait a while. If it rings again, you can answer it.

[*They wait. It does not ring again*]

THE HUSBAND: This isn't living.

THE WIFE: Karl!

THE HUSBAND: You bore me a Judas. He sits at table and listens as he takes the soup we put before him and carefully registers the conversation of those who begot him. The informer!

THE WIFE: You mustn't say that!

[*There is a pause*]

THE WIFE: Do you think we should make any preparations?

THE HUSBAND: Do you think they'll come with him now?

THE WIFE: It's quite possible.

THE HUSBAND: Maybe I should put on my Iron Cross?

THE WIFE: By all means, Karl.

[*He brings the cross and puts it on with trembling fingers*]

THE WIFE: There's nothing against you at school?

THE HUSBAND: How should I know? I'm willing to teach everything they want to have taught. But what *do* they want to have taught? If only I ever knew! How do I know how they want Bismarck to have been if they are so slow in bringing out the new textbooks? Can't you give the maid another ten marks? She's always listening too.

THE WIFE: [*She nods*] And the picture of Hitler. Shall we hang it over your desk? It'll look better.

THE HUSBAND: Yes, do that.

[*The Wife begins to move the picture*]

THE HUSBAND: But if the boy says we hung it specially, then it will end in "consciousness of guilt."

[*She puts the picture back where it was*]

THE HUSBAND: Wasn't that the door?

THE WIFE: I heard nothing.

THE HUSBAND: There!

THE WIFE: Karl!

[*She throws her arms around him*]

6 Organ of the Social Democrats.
7 Colors of the Nationalists.

THE HUSBAND: Don't lose your nerve. Pack me some underwear.

[*The door is heard opening. Husband and Wife stand close together, petrified, in the corner of the room. The door opens and in comes The Boy, a bag of chocolates in his hand. There is a silence*]

THE BOY: What's the matter?

THE WIFE: Where've you been?

[*The Boy points to the bag of chocolates*]

THE WIFE: Have you only been buying chocolate?

THE BOY: Sure. What do you think?

[*He walks, munching, across the room and out. His parents look after him searchingly*]

THE HUSBAND: Do you think he's telling the truth?

[*The Wife shrugs her shoulders*] [8]

* * *

CONCLUSION

Dim out. A band plays a barbaric march. The chorus is heard. When the lights go up the armored car is seen, stationary, frozen on the Eastern Steppes. The soldiers are wrapped up strangely. They try to keep warm with women's furs and underclothing. But they have also come alive. They beat their arms against their bodies to keep warm. One runs round and stares at the motor.

The soldiers sing to the tune of the Horst Wessel Song:

Two years of conquest in our iron chariot—
And then it stopped before the world was won.
At times we fear that we have made too long a journey;
We'll see no more the Rhineland and the sun.

For as we eastward drove and it was winter,
Our chariot stuck on Volga's bloody strand,
In the third year snow fell upon the Führer's laurels;
We were defeated in the poor man's land.

Enslaved ourselves, we tried to enslave the others.
By force subdued, we grew by force too bold.
Death beckons from the left and from the right.
O brothers—
The road back home is long, and it is cold!

8 After a number of other scenes dealing with other characters and situations which illustrate other phases of the National Socialist terror and the preparation for war, we find the Nazi war machine stalled in Russia. The war has turned against the "master race," as the conclusion tells us.

Jean-Paul Sartre

(1905–   )

Immediately upon the conclusion of the Second World War, France was agitated by a philosophical and literary movement that had been brewing for some years; existentialism was its name and a young Parisian professor, Jean-Paul Sartre, its prophet. He was not the only exponent of its tenets. His associate and friend Simone de Beauvoir was just as ready to explain its principles. Nor was Sartre the only able writer to apply them to literature. Many regard the Algerian-French author Albert Camus as an artist superior to Sartre, on the strength of Camus' novels *The Stranger* and *The Plague*. But Sartre's facility in philosophical exposition placed him in the forefront of the existentialist clan, and his success as a playwright made him more widely known than any of his associates or any of his metaphysical predecessors—Kierkegaard, Husserl, Heidegger, and others.

Before the war, Sartre had been little more than a schoolmaster in the eyes of the world. Having studied at the Ecole Normale Supérieure (1924–1928) under the original French essayist and philosopher Alain (Emile Chartier), he had become disposed at an early age to unconventional thinking and dialectical sharpness. The Sorbonne, to which he went from the Ecole, seemed a tepid place after his schooling under Alain, and the conventional thought of his new masters left him unimpressed. Nevertheless, after taking a degree in philosophy in 1929, he turned dutifully to an academic career in the Lycées of Laon and Le Havre and, finally, at the Lycée Condorcet, in Paris. In 1936, he began to publish a number of remarkable studies in psychology which attracted little attention. Two years later his first novel, *Nausea*, appeared, to be followed by a volume of stories, *The Wall* (1939). The novel expressed the hopelessness of mankind in a world in which nothing whatsoever justified the individual's existence. The stories repeated this theme with intensified insistence on the absurdity of man's position. Both books had a bitter, despairing, and cynical tone. They may stand, with the work of other French writers, especially Céline (*Death on the Installment Plan*, 1938), as expressions of a state of mind reflected in the French political situation. This was the period of the Munich pact, the fall of France, the collaborationist policies of many Frenchmen, and the inglorious rule of the Vichy government under the doddering hero Pétain.

Sartre would have been misunderstood, however, if he had been set down as just another spiritless creature of his times. There was fire in his nega-

tions, intensity in his *Weltschmerz*. Sartre was drafted into the French Army in 1939 and stationed in Alsace as an artillery observer. Captured in June 1940, he spent nine months in a German prison camp. He escaped disguised as a civilian and slipped into Paris, and there he remained, risking return to a concentration camp, if not indeed summary execution, by playing an active role in the French underground. Moreover, he began to compose literature and drama that challenged men to shape themselves into heroic personalities instead of accepting the degrading status to which an indifferent universe and a pusillanimous, convention-bound society would consign them. And with his new work came recognition for Sartre as a spiritual and intellectual leader in his country. His enormous philosophical thesis *L'Être et le néant* and his stirring play *The Flies* appeared in 1943. His mordant one-act drama *No Exit* was produced in Paris in 1944, about a month before D-Day. His writings were greeted as signs of a renaissance of French culture and spirit. Soon Sartre acquired followers and his ideas grew fashionable: he became the center of a cult at the Café de Flore in Paris. The term "Sartrism" spread like wildfire in intellectual circles.

Interest was revived in Sartre's previous writings, not always to his advantage, and he added substantially to his literary output with brilliant essays, a series of novels, and a number of plays: *The Victors* (*Morts sans sépulture*), *The Respectful Prostitute*, and *Les Mains sales* (*Red Gloves* in a questionable American adaptation).

Debate over existentialism continued to rage while Sartre was developing his thought. He was under fire from the Catholic Right in France because his doctrine was uncompromisingly atheistic. He was also assailed by the Communist Left because his philosophy stressed despair as a cardinal principle and centered all fundamental problems in the individual. It may be conceded that his fiction in particular presented such unsavory characters and situations that his work could be described by its Marxist critics as a product of "bourgeois decadence." Sartre's metaphysics was beyond doubt negativistic, because it predicated a distinct discord between the outer world and man's yearning for wholeness and meaning. Man and the universe are not at one with one another, as the German "idealist" philosophers had maintained ever since Kant by claiming that reality is a product of man's mind. This discrepancy between what is and what we want leaves man a certain degree of freedom of will (the universe is one thing and he is another), but the realization of this kind of freedom can only fill him with anguish. Anguish is the primal condition of any man who is aware of the discord, and it is intensified by his realization that the universe is a *néant,* or nothingness. Man is thrust meaninglessly into a meaningless universe, to which his response can be only "nausea" (the title of Sartre's novel), that is, a sense of incompleteness and futility, or desperation. Sartre's fiction characters were a loathsome lot, and there is no doubt that the fashionable people who took up existentialism were attracted by its nihilism, which is a good excuse for self-indulgence and escape from social responsibility. Existentialism came to be known as the philosophy of a defeated nation.

Yet Sartre's ethical system was altogether different from his metaphysics, as his own services in the French Resistance movement have indicated. He himself had turned defeat into resistance, and had found meaning in action. Such novels as *Nausea* expressed the "human condition," according to Sartre, but an awareness of this condition was intended to be only a prelude to the ethical position to which man could lift himself once he knew that he was "free." Relying solely upon himself instead of on some principle of benevolence or meaning in the universe, man could "create" himself. He could wrest a new humanism out of despair, as Sartre maintained in his essay *L'Existentialisme est un humanisme* in 1946. He could turn his sense of isolation in the universe into a sort of splendor––that is, into self-reliance and into a heroism without illusions. He had possibilities in him that it was his business to discover once he relied on neither God nor other people ("Hell," one of the characters in *No Exit* declares, "is other people")—nor on society, for that matter, so long as it imposes demands of conformity upon the individual. And there was only one way to discover what one really was, what one's character was—namely, by responding to the situations that demand crucial decisions; that is, we realize ourselves truly only by our actions. We make ourselves by what we do: "You are your life"— that is, you are what the conduct of your life reveals you to be. You are not what you fancy yourself to be, but what your behavior demonstrates.

Out of his nettle "anguish," Sartre plucked his flower "safety," namely, a self-sufficiency. So much so, indeed, that he expected his existentialist hero to become fully "engaged" in social action. And in such action, the existentialist would even find himself, since it would reveal to him what he really was like in the most objective of all ways—in his decision and deeds. It is the test undergone most clearly in *The Flies,* as well as in *The Victors.* The characters of both plays discover their strength, just as the characters of *No Exit* and *The Respectful Prostitute* reveal their weakness—most notably in the case of

the man in *No Exit* who thought he was an idealist and pacifist when he was actually only a coward.

In a series of significant articles "What Is Literature?" (1947) Sartre called upon literature, as well as men, to become "engaged." Reflecting on French behavior before the Second World War, he declared that "we tolerated everything, even intolerance." The great awakening came with the Resistance movement when men suffered extreme torture rather than betray their comrades or their cause. Their experience, which made them aware more fully than ever of the existence of evil and exposed them more than ever to the temptation of negation, also enabled them to discover their humanity; that is, to destroy evil and to rediscover the nobility in themselves and other men. Everything conspired to discourage the men of the underground, as in his own play *The Victors:* "So many signs around them, those faces [of the torturers] leaning over them, that suffering in them, everything tried to make them believe that they were only insects, that man is the impossible dream of cockroaches and wood-lice and that they would reawaken as vermin like everything else." But, Sartre adds, "They kept silent and man was born in their silence."

It is in the light of these remarks and of the entire question of a meaningless universe, man's freedom of will, and his "engagement" that *The Flies* must be read. The French have distinguished themselves in reworking classic themes ever since Corneille and Racine, and there was only a slight abatement of the tendency to pour the old Attic wine into new Gallic bottles in the French theatre of the twentieth century. Well-known examples are Jean Giraudoux' *Amphitryon 38* and Jean Cocteau's *The Infernal Machine,* which is the Greek *Oedipus the King* in modern dress, treading the stage with some cynicism and a good deal of conscientiously cultivated surrealist naïveté. *The Flies* differs from these works, however, in being thoroughly serious, and it is a drama of ideas. It is Sartre's existentialist fable, based on the Oresteian story as told in the extant plays of Aeschylus, Sophocles, and Euripides. The liberties Sartre takes with the legend elaborate his views, and the play may be fruitfully compared not only with the classic tragedies but with so modern a psychological version as Eugene O'Neill's *Mourning Becomes Electra.* Sartre's treatment is neither reverential nor psychological. It requires metaphysical and political thinking, and its ultimate meaning is ethical. Although it is possible to quarrel with the author's metaphysics, it is not difficult to understand that its political and moral force was extremely welcome when the play reached the French during the days of the German occupation in 1943. If the play has its ambiguities, there is no ambiguity in its message of freedom. Sartre calls for freedom from supernatural and mortal tyrants, freedom from a self-indulgent and enervating sense of guilt that aborts the will to rectify wrongs, and freedom from the hollow detachment or disengagement that tempts the intellectual to live unto himself superiorly in a self-created vacuum.

The play was produced by the distinguished director Charles Dullin under the very nose of the Nazi rulers of Paris, who were evidently too obtuse to read into it the significance it had for that part of the French public which could follow its meaning. A skillful American production was made later (April 17, 1947) at the Dramatic Workshop of the New School in New York by the self-exiled German director Erwin Piscator. Memorable, too, was the production of the play at the Hebbel Theatre in the Allied sector of Berlin shortly after the defeat of Germany. The play aroused considerable debate, with the Russian-licensed press violently in the opposition and the American and English divided between enthusiasm over Sartre as a born dramatist and reservations to the effect that his drama was too much of a discussion piece.

The "flies" are minor Furies or Eumenides, and the reader can proceed to draw his own implications from this point on; he may consider the idea that they represent the wallowing in guilt and the self-condemnation that many Frenchmen experienced after the defeat of France. The critic Eric Bentley

raises interesting questions concerning details in the play: "When, for instance, must Orestes be in exile and when among men? What is the moral difference between his [Orestes'] murdering Ægistheus and his murdering his mother? What kind of power is Jupiter meant to have? [One might answer: Only the power of men's belief in him.] What is this god to whom we owe our being, yet to whom we owe no allegiance?" Probably Sartre would deny that we owe our being to him. Jupiter is merely a personified belief, and men owe him no more allegiance than they are willing to give him through their faith in his existence. This faith is strong enough to give Jupiter a physical reality in the eyes of his believers, and in the eyes of those who have no belief in him as well—since he is a reality to most people, and the nonbeliever has to cope with their beliefs. It is not the least of the merits of a drama of ideas such as *The Flies* that it gives us some mental exercise.

BIBLIOGRAPHY: Eric Bentley, *The Playwright as Thinker* (pp. 233–246, 270–272, 358–359), 1946; Marjorie Grene, *Dreadful Freedom: A Critique of Existentialism*, 1948; *Yale French Studies* (see especially articles by Henri Peyre, Charles G. Whiting, and Walter Leavitt), Vol. I, No. 1, Spring–Summer 1948.

THE FLIES

By Jean-Paul Sartre

TRANSLATED FROM THE FRENCH BY STUART GILBERT

CHARACTERS IN THE PLAY

ZEUS	FIRST FURY	FIRST SOLDIER
ORESTES	SECOND FURY	SECOND SOLDIER
ELECTRA	THE HIGH PRIEST	MEN AND WOMEN, TOWNSFOLK OF
ÆGISTHEUS	A YOUNG WOMAN	ARGOS
CLYTEMNESTRA	AN OLD WOMAN	FURIES, SERVANTS, PALACE GUARDS
THE TUTOR	AN IDIOT BOY	

ACT I.

A public square in Argos, dominated by a statue of Zeus, god of flies and death. The image has white eyes and blood-smeared cheeks. A procession of Old Women *in black, carrying urns, advances; they make libations to the statue. An* Idiot Boy *is squatting in the background.* Orestes *enters, accompanied by* The Tutor.

ORESTES: Listen, my good women.

[*The* Old Women *swing round, emitting little squeals*]

THE TUTOR: Would you kindly tell us— [*The* Old Women *spit on the ground and move back a pace*] Steady, good ladies, steady. I only want a piece of simple information. We are travelers and we have lost our way. [*Dropping their urns, the* Women *take to their heels*] Stupid old hags! You'd think I had intentions on their virtue! [*Ironically*] Ah, young master, truly this has been a pleasant journey. And how well inspired you were to come to this city of Argos, when there are hundreds of towns in Greece and Italy where the drink is good, the inns are hospitable, and the streets full of friendly, smiling people! But these uncouth hillmen—one would suppose they'd never seen a foreigner before. A hundred times and more I've had to ask our way, and never once did I get a straight answer. And then the grilling heat! This Argos is a nightmare city. Squeals of terror everywhere, people who panic the moment they set eyes on you, and scurry to cover, like black beetles, down the glaring streets. Pfoo! I can't think how you bear it—this emptiness, the shimmering air, that fierce sun overhead. What's deadlier than the sun?

ORESTES: I was born here.

THE TUTOR: So the story goes. But, if I were you, I wouldn't brag about it.

ORESTES: I was born here—and yet I have to ask my way, like any stranger. Knock at that door.

THE TUTOR: What do you expect? That someone will open it? Only look at those houses and tell me how they strike you. You will observe there's not a window anywhere. They open on closed courtyards, I suppose, and turn their backsides to the street. [Orestes *makes a fretful gesture*] Very good, sir. I'll knock—but nothing will come of it.

[*He knocks. Nothing happens. He knocks again, and the door opens a cautious inch*]

A VOICE: What do you want?

THE TUTOR: Just a word of information. Can you tell me where—? [*The door is slammed in his face*] Oh, the devil take you! Well, my lord Orestes, is that enough, or must I try elsewhere? If you wish, I'll knock at every door.

ORESTES: No, that's enough.

THE TUTOR: Well, I never! There's someone here. [*He goes up to the* Idiot Boy] Excuse me, sir . . .

THE IDIOT: Hoo! Hoo! Hoo!

THE TUTOR: [*Bowing again*] My noble lord . . .

THE IDIOT: Hoo!

THE TUTOR: Will Your Highness deign to show us where Ægistheus lives?

THE IDIOT: Hoo!

THE TUTOR: Ægistheus, King of Argos.

THE IDIOT: Hoo! Hoo! Hoo!

[Zeus *passes by, back stage*]

THE TUTOR: We're out of luck. The only one who doesn't run away is a half-wit. [Zeus *retraces his steps*] Ah, that's odd! He's followed us here.

ORESTES: Who?

THE TUTOR: That bearded fellow.

ORESTES: You're dreaming.

THE TUTOR: I tell you, I saw him go by.

ORESTES: You must be mistaken.

THE TUTOR: Impossible. Never in my life have I seen such a beard—or, rather, only one: the bronze beard on the chin of Zeus Ahenobarbos at Palermo. Look, there he is again. What can he want of us?

ORESTES: He is only a traveler like ourselves.

THE TUTOR: Only that? We met him on the road to Delphi. And when we took the boat at Itea, there he was, fanning that great beard in the bows. At Nauplia we couldn't move a step without having him at our heels, and now—here he is again! Do you think that chance explains it? [*He brushes the flies off his face*] These flies in Argos are much more sociable than its townsfolk. Just look at them! [*Points to the* Idiot Boy] There must be a round dozen pumping away at each of his eyes, and yet he's smiling quite contentedly; probably he likes having his eyes sucked. That's not surprising; look at that yellow muck oozing out of them. [*He flaps his hand at the flies*] Move on, my little friends. Hah! They're on you now. Allow me! [*He drives them away*] Well, this should please you—you who are always complaining of being a stranger in your native land. These charming insects, anyhow, are making you welcome; one would think they know who you are. [*He whisks them away*] Now leave us in peace, you buzzers. We know you like us, but we've had enough of you. . . . Where can they come from? They're as big as bumble-bees and noisy as a swarm of locusts.

[*Meanwhile* Zeus *has approached them*]

ZEUS: They are only bluebottles, a trifle larger than usual. Fifteen years ago a mighty stench of carrion drew them to this city, and since then they've been getting fatter and fatter. Give them another fifteen years, and they'll be as big as toads. [*A short silence*]

THE TUTOR: Pray, whom have I the honor of addressing?

ZEUS: Demetrios is my name, and I hail from Athens.

ORESTES: Did I not see you on the boat, a fortnight ago?

ZEUS: Yes, and I saw you, too.

[*Hideous shrieks come from the palace*]

THE TUTOR: Listen to that! I don't know if you will agree with me, young master, but I think we'd do better to leave this place.

ORESTES: Keep quiet!

ZEUS: You have nothing to fear. It's what they call Dead Men's Day today. Those cries announce the beginning of the ceremony.

ORESTES: You seem well posted on the local customs.

ZEUS: Yes, I often visit Argos. As it so happened, I was here on the great day of Agamemnon's homecoming, when the Greek fleet, flushed with victory, anchored in the Nauplia roads. From the top of the rampart one saw the bay dappled with their white sails. [*He drives the flies away*] There were no flies then. Argos was only a small country town, basking in the sun, yawning the years away. Like everyone else I went up to the sentry-path to see the royal procession, and I watched it for many an hour wending across the plain. At sundown on the second day Queen Clytemnestra came to the ramparts, and with her was Ægistheus, the present King. The people of Argos saw their faces dyed red by the sunset, and they saw them leaning over the battlements, gazing for a long while seawards. And the people thought: "There's evil brewing." But they kept silence. Ægistheus, you should know, was the Queen's lover. A hard, brutal man, and even in those days he had the cast of melancholy. . . . But you're looking pale, young sir.

ORESTES: It's the long journey I have made, and this accursed heat. But pray go on; you interest me.

ZEUS: Agamemnon was a worthy man, you know, but he made one great mistake. He put a ban on public executions. That was a pity. A good hanging now and then—that entertains folk in the provinces and robs death of its glamour. . . . So the people here held their tongues; they looked forward to seeing, for once, a violent death. They still kept silent when they saw their King entering by the city gates. And when Clytemnestra stretched forth her graceful arms, fragrant and white as lilies, they still said nothing. Yet at that moment a word, a single word, might have sufficed. But no one said it; each was gloating in imagination over the picture of a huge corpse with a shattered face.

ORESTES: And you, too, said nothing?

ZEUS: Does that rouse your indignation? Well, my young friend, I like you all the better for it; it proves your heart's in the right place. No, I admit I, too, held my peace. I'm a stranger here, and it was no concern of mine. And next day when it started, when the folk of Argos heard their King screaming his life out in the palace, they still kept silence, but they rolled their eyes in a sort of ecstasy, and the whole town was like a woman in heat.

ORESTES: So now the murderer is on the throne. For fifteen years he has enjoyed the fruits of crime. And I thought the gods were just!

ZEUS: Steady, my friend. Don't blame the gods too hastily. Must they always punish? Wouldn't it be better to use such breaches of the law to point a moral?

ORESTES: And is this what they did?

ZEUS: They sent the flies.

THE TUTOR: The flies? How do the flies come in?

ZEUS: They are a symbol. But if you want to know what the gods did, look around you. See that old creature over there, creeping away like a beetle on her little black feet, and hugging the walls. Well, she's a good specimen of the squat black vermin that teem in every cranny of this town. Now watch me catch our specimen, it's well worth inspection. Here it is. A loathsome object, you'll agree. . . . Hah! You're blinking now. Still, you're an Argive and you should be used to the white-hot rapiers of the sun.

. . . Watch her wriggling, like a hooked fish! . . . Now, old lady, let's hear your tale of woe. I see you're in black from head to foot. In mourning for a whole regiment of sons, is that it? Tell us, and I'll release you—perhaps. For whom are you in mourning?

OLD WOMAN: Sir, I am not in mourning. Everyone wears black at Argos.

ZEUS: Everyone wears black? Ah, I see. You're in mourning for your murdered King.

OLD WOMAN: Whisht! For God's sake, don't talk of that.

ZEUS: Yes, you're quite old enough to have heard those huge cries that echoed and re-echoed for a whole morning in the city street. What did you do about it?

OLD WOMAN: My good man was in the fields, at work. What could I do? a woman alone? I bolted my door.

ZEUS: Yes, but you left your window not quite closed, so as to hear the better, and, while you peeped behind the curtains and held your breath, you felt a little tingling itch between your loins, and didn't you enjoy it!

OLD WOMAN: Oh, please stop, sir!

ZEUS: And when you went to bed that night, you had a grand time with your man. A real gala night.

OLD WOMAN: A what? . . . No, my lord, that was a dreadful, dreadful night.

ZEUS: A red gala, I tell you, and you've never been able to blot out its memory.

OLD WOMAN: Mercy on us! Are you—are you one of the Dead?

ZEUS: I dead? You're crazy, woman. . . . Anyhow, don't trouble your head who I am; you'd do better to think of yourself, and try to earn forgiveness by repenting of your sins.

OLD WOMAN: Oh, sir, I do repent, most heartily I repent. If you only knew how I repent, and my daughter too, and my son-in-law offers up a heifer every year, and my little grandson has been brought up in a spirit of repentance. He's a pretty lad, with flaxen hair, and he always behaves as good as gold. Though he's only seven, he never plays or laughs, for thinking of his original sin.

ZEUS: Good, you old bitch, that's as it should be —and be sure you die in a nice bitchy odor of repentance. It's your one hope of salvation. [*The Old Woman runs away*] Unless I'm much mistaken, my masters, we have there the real thing, the good old piety of yore, rooted in terror.

ORESTES: What man are you?

ZEUS: Who cares what I am. We were talking of the gods. Well now, should they have struck Ægistheus down?

ORESTES: They should. . . . They should. . . . Oh, how would I know what they should have done? What do I care, anyhow? I'm a stranger here. . . . Does Ægistheus feel contrition?

ZEUS: Ægistheus? I'd be much surprised. But what matter? A whole city's repenting on his account. And it's measured by the bushel, is repentance. [*Eerie screams in the palace*] Listen! Lest they forget the screams of the late King in his last agony, they keep this festival of death each year when the day of the King's murder comes round. A herdsman from the hills—he's chosen for his lung-power—is set to bellow in the Great Hall of the palace. [*Orestes makes a gesture of disgust*] Bah! That's nothing. I wonder what you'll say presently, when they let the Dead loose. Fifteen years ago, to a day, Agamemnon was murdered. And what a change has come over the light-hearted folk of Argos since that day! how near and dear to me they are at present!

ORESTES: Dear to *you*?

ZEUS: Pay no heed, young man. That was a slip of the tongue. Near and dear to the gods, I meant.

ORESTES: You surprise me. Then those blood-smeared walls, these swarms of flies, this reek of shambles and the stifling heat, these empty streets and yonder god with his gashed face, and all those creeping, half-human creatures beating their breasts in darkened rooms, and those shrieks, those hideous, blood-curdling shrieks—can it be that Zeus and his Olympians delight in these?

ZEUS: Young man, do not sit in judgment on the gods. They have their secrets—and their sorrows. [*A short silence*]

ORESTES: Am I right in thinking Agamemnon had a daughter? A daughter named Electra?

ZEUS: Yes. She lives there, in the palace—that building yonder.

ORESTES: So that's the palace? . . . And what does Electra think of—all this?

ZEUS: Oh, she's a mere child. There was a son, too, named Orestes. But he's dead, it seems.

ORESTES: Dead? Well, really . . .

THE TUTOR: Of course he's dead, young master. I thought you knew it. Don't you remember what they told us at Nauplia—about Ægistheus' having him murdered, soon after Agamemnon's death?

ZEUS: Still, some say he's alive. The story goes that the men ordered to kill the child had pity on him and left him in the forest. Some rich Athenians found him there and took him home. For my part, I'd rather he were dead.

ORESTES: Pray, why?

ZEUS: Suppose that one day he appeared in this city, and—

ORESTES: Continue, please.

ZEUS: As you wish . . . Well, I'd say this to him. "My lad—" I'd say, "My lad," as he's your age or thereabouts—if he's alive, of course. By the way, young lord, may I know your name?

ORESTES: Philebus is my name, and I hail from Corinth. I am traveling to improve my mind, and this old slave accompanying me used to be my tutor.

ZEUS: Thank you. Well, I'd say something like this. "My lad, get you gone! What business have you here? Do you wish to enforce your rights? Yes, you're brave and strong and spirited. I can see you as a captain in an army of good fighters. You have better things to do than reigning over a dead-and-alive city, a carrion city plagued by flies. These people are great sinners but, as you see, they're working out their atonement. Let them be, young fellow, let them be; respect their sorrowful endeavor, and be-gone on tiptoe. You cannot share in their repent-ance, since you did not share their crime. Your brazen innocence makes a gulf between you and them. So if you have any care for them, be off! Be off, or you will work their doom. If you hinder them on their way, if even for a moment you turn their thoughts from their remorse, all their sins will harden on them—like cold fat. They have guilty consciences, they're afraid—and fear and guilty consciences have a good savor in the nostrils of the gods. Yes, the gods take pleasure in such poor souls. Would you oust them from the favor of the gods? What, moreover, could you give them in exchange? Good digestions, the gray monotony of provincial life, and the boredom—ah, the soul-destroying bore-dom—of long days of mild content. Go your way, my lad, go your way. The repose of cities and men's souls hangs on a thread; tamper with it and you bring disaster. [*Looking him in the eyes*] A disaster which will recoil on you."

ORESTES: Yes? So that is what you'd say? Well, if I were that young man, I'd answer— [*They eye each other truculently. The Tutor coughs*] No, I don't know how I'd answer you. Perhaps you're right, and anyhow it's no concern of mine.

ZEUS: Good. I only hope Orestes would show as much sense. . . . Well, peace be with you, my friend; I must go about my business.

ORESTES: Peace be with you.

ZEUS: By the way, if those flies bother you, here's a way of getting rid of them. You see that swarm buzzing round your head? Right. Now watch! I flick my wrist—so—and wave my arm once, and then I say: Abraxas, galla, galla, tsay, tsay. See! They're falling down and starting to crawl on the ground like caterpillars.

ORESTES: By Jove!

ZEUS: Oh, that's nothing. Just a parlor trick. I'm a fly-charmer in my leisure hours. Good day to you. We shall meet again. [*Exit Zeus*]

THE TUTOR: Take care. That man knows who you are.

ORESTES: "Man," you say. But *is* he a man?

THE TUTOR: What else should he be? You grieve me, my young master. Have all my lessons, all my precepts, the smiling skepticism I taught you, been wasted on your ears? "Is he a man?" you ask. There's nothing else but men—what more would you have? And that bearded fellow is a man, sure enough; probably one of Ægistheus' spies.

ORESTES: A truce to your philosophy! It's done me too much harm already.

THE TUTOR: Harm? Do you call it doing harm to

people when one emancipates their minds? Ah, how you've changed! Once I read you like an open book. . . . But at least you might tell me your plans. Why bring me to this city, and what's your purpose here?

ORESTES: Did I say I had a purpose? But that's enough. Be silent now. [*He takes some steps towards the palace*] That is *my* palace. My father's birth-place. And it's there a whore and her paramour foully butchered him. I, too, was born there. I was nearly three when that usurper's bravoes carried me away. Most likely we went out by that door. One of them held me in his arms, I had my eyes wide open, and no doubt I was crying. And yet I have no memories, none whatever. I am looking at a huge, gloomy building, solemn and pretentious in the worst provincial taste. I am looking at it, but I *see* it for the first time.

THE TUTOR: No memories, master? What ingrati-tude, considering that I gave ten years of my life to stocking you with them! And what of all the journeys we have made together, all the towns we visited? And the course in archæology I composed specially for you? No memories, indeed! Palaces, shrines, and temples—with so many of them is your memory peopled that you could write a guide-book of all Greece.

ORESTES: Palaces—that's so. Palaces, statues, pil-lars—stones, stones, stones! Why, with all those stones in my head, am I not heavier? While you are about it, why not remind me of the three hundred and eighty-seven steps of the temple at Ephesus? I climbed them, one by one, and I remember each. The seventeenth, if my memory serves me, was badly broken. And yet—! Why, an old, mangy dog, warming himself at the hearth, and struggling to his feet with a little whimper to welcome his master home—why, that dog has more memories than I! At least he recognizes his master. *His* master. But what can I call mine?

THE TUTOR: And what of your culture, Lord Orestes? What of that? All that wise lore I culled for you with loving care, like a bouquet, matching the fruits of my knowledge with the finest flowers of my experience? Did I not, from the very first, set you a-reading all the books there are, so as to make clear to you the infinite diversity of men's opinions? And did I not remind you, time and again, how variable are human creeds and customs? So, along with youth, good looks, and wealth, you have the wisdom of far riper years; your mind is free from prejudice and superstition; you have no family ties, no religion, and no calling; you are free to turn your hand to anything. But you know better than to com-mit yourself—and there lies your strength. So, in a word, you stand head and shoulders above the ruck and, what's more, you could hold a chair of philoso-phy or architecture in a great university. And yet you cavil at your lot!

ORESTES: No, I do not cavil. What should I cavil

at? You've left me free as the strands torn by the wind from spiders' webs that one sees floating ten feet above the ground. I'm light as gossamer and walk on air. I know I'm favored, I appreciate my lot at its full value. [*A pause*] Some men are born bespoken; a certain path has been assigned them, and at its end there is something they *must* do, a deed allotted. So on and on they trudge, wounding their bare feet on the flints. I suppose that strikes *you* as vulgar—the joy of going somewhere definite. And there are others, men of few words, who bear deep down in their hearts a load of dark imaginings; men whose whole life was changed because one day in childhood, at the age of five or seven— Right; I grant you these are no great men. When I was seven, I know I had no home, no roots. I let sounds and scents, the patter of rain on housetops, the golden play of sunbeams, slip past my body and fall round me—and I knew these were for others, I could never make them *my* memories. For memories are luxuries reserved for people who own houses, cattle, fields and servants. Whereas I—! I'm free as air, thank God. My mind's my own, gloriously aloof. [*He goes nearer to the palace*] I might have lived there. I'd not have read any of your books; perhaps I'd not have learned to read. It's rare for a Greek prince to know how to read. But I'd have come in and gone out by that door ten thousand times. As a child I'd have played with its leaves, and when I pushed at them with all my little might, they'd have creaked without yielding, and I'd have taken the measure of my weakness. Later on, I'd have pushed them open furtively by night and gone out after girls. And some years later, when I came of age, the slaves would have flung the doors wide open and I'd have crossed the threshold on horseback. My old wooden door! I'd have been able to find your keyhole with my eyes shut. And that notch there—I might have made it showing off, the first day they let me hold a spear. [*He steps back*] Let's see. That's the Dorian style, isn't it? And what do you make of that gold inlay? I saw the like at Dodona; a pretty piece of craftsmanship. And now I'm going to say something that will rejoice you. This is not *my* palace, nor *my* door. And there's nothing to detain us here.

THE TUTOR: Ah, that's talking sense. For what would you have gained by living in Argos? By now your spirit would be broken, you'd be wallowing in repentance.

ORESTES: Still, it would be *my* repentance. And this furnace heat singeing my hair would be *mine*. Mine, too, the buzz of all these flies. At this moment I'd be lying naked in some dark room at the back of the palace, and watching a ribbon of red light lengthen across the floor. I'd be waiting for sundown; waiting for the cool dusk of an Argos evening to rise like perfume from the parched earth; an Argos evening like many a thousand others, familiar yet ever new, another evening that should be *mine*.

. . . Well, well, my worthy pedagogue, let's be off. We've no business to be luxuriating in others' heat.

THE TUTOR: Ah, my young lord, how you've eased my mind! During these last few months—to be exact, ever since I revealed to you the secret of your birth—I could see you changing day by day, and it gave me many a sleepless night. I was afraid—

ORESTES: Of what?

THE TUTOR: No, it will anger you.

ORESTES: Speak.

THE TUTOR: Be it so. Well, though from one's earliest years one has been trained to skeptic irony, one can't help having foolish fancies now and then. And I wondered if you weren't hatching some wild scheme to oust Ægistheus and take his place.

ORESTES: [*Thoughtfully*] To oust Ægistheus. Ah— [*A pause*] No, my good slave, you need not fear; the time for that is past. True, nothing could please me better than to grip that sanctimonious ruffian by the beard and drag him from my father's throne. But what purpose would it serve? These folk are no concern of mine. I have not seen one of their children come into the world, nor been present at their daughters' weddings; I don't share their remorse, I don't even know a single one of them by name. That bearded fellow was right; a king should share his subjects' memories. So we'll let them be, and begone on tiptoe. . . . But, mind you, if there were something I could do, something to give me the freedom of the city; if, even by a crime, I could acquire their memories, their hopes and fears, and fill with these the void within me, yes, even if I had to kill my own mother—

THE TUTOR: Hush! For heaven's sake, hush!

ORESTES: Yes, these are idle dreams. Let's be off. Now go and see if we can get some horses here, and we'll move on to Sparta, where I have good friends.

[*Electra comes forward, carrying a large ash-can. She goes up to the statue of Zeus, without seeing them*]

ELECTRA: Yes, you old swine, scowl away at me with your goggle eyes and your fat face all smeared with raspberry juice—scowl away, but you won't scare me, not you! They've been to worship you, haven't they?—those pious matrons in black dresses. They've been padding round you in their big creaky shoes. And you were pleased, old bugaboo, it warmed your silly wooden heart. You like them old, of course; the nearer they're to corpses, the more you love them. They've poured their choicest wines out at your feet, because it's your festival today, and the stale smell from their petticoats tickled your nostrils. [*She rubs herself against him*] Now smell me for a change, smell the perfume of a fresh, clean body. But, of course, I'm young, I'm alive—and you loathe youth and life. I, too, am bringing you offerings, while all the others are at prayers. Here they are: ashes from the hearth, peelings, scraps of offal crawling with maggots, a chunk of bread too filthy even for our pigs. But your darling flies will love it, won't they, Zeus? A good feast-day to you, old idol, and let's hope it is your last. I'm not strong enough to pull you down. All I can do is to spit at you. But some day he will come, the man I'm waiting for, carrying a long, keen sword. He'll look you up and down and chuckle, with his hands on his hips, like this, and his head thrown back. Then he'll draw his sword and chop you in two, from top to bottom—like this! So the two halves of Zeus will fall apart, one to the left, one to the right, and everyone will see he's made of common wood. Just a lump of cheap white deal, the terrible God of Death! And all that frightfulness, the blood on his face, his dark-green eyes, and all the rest—they'll see it was only a coat of paint. *You,* anyhow, you know you're white inside, white as a child's body, and you know, too, that a sword can rip you limb from limb, and you won't even bleed. Just a log of deal—anyhow it will serve to light our fires next winter. [*She notices* Orestes] Oh!

ORESTES: Don't be alarmed.

ELECTRA: I'm not alarmed. Not a bit. Who are you?

ORESTES: A stranger.

ELECTRA: Then you are welcome. All that's foreign to this town is dear to me. Your name?

ORESTES: Philebus. I've come from Corinth.

ELECTRA: Ah? From Corinth. My name's Electra.

ORESTES: Electra—[*To the* Tutor] Leave us. [*Exit the* Tutor]

ELECTRA: Why are you looking at me like that?

ORESTES: You're very beautiful. Not at all like the people in these parts.

ELECTRA: I beautiful? Can you really mean it? As beautiful as the Corinthian girls?

ORESTES: Yes.

ELECTRA: Well, here they never tell me that I'm beautiful. Perhaps they don't want me to know it. Anyhow, what use would beauty be to me? I'm only a servant.

ORESTES: What! You a servant?

ELECTRA: The least of the servants in the palace. I wash the King's and the Queen's underlinen. And how dirty it is, all covered with spots and stains! Yes, I have to wash everything they wear next their skin, the shifts they wrap their rotting bodies in, the nightdresses Clytemnestra has on when the King shares her bed. I shut my eyes and scrub with all my might. I have to wash up, too. You don't believe me? See my hands, all chapped and rough. Why are you looking at them in that funny way? Do they, by any chance, look like the hands of a princess?

ORESTES: Poor little hands. No, they don't look like a princess's hands. . . . But tell me more. What else do they make you do?

ELECTRA: Every morning I've to empty the ash-can. I drag it out of the palace, and then—well, you saw what I do with the refuse. That big fellow in wood is Zeus, God of Death and Flies. The other day, when the High Priest came here to make his usual bows and scrapings, he found himself treading on cabbage-stumps and rotten turnips and mussel-shells. He looked startled, I can tell you! I say! You won't tell on me, will you?

ORESTES: No.

ELECTRA: Really I don't care if you do. They can't make things much worse for me than they are already. I'm used to being beaten. Perhaps they'd shut me up in one of the rooms in the tower. That wouldn't be so bad; at least I wouldn't have to see their faces. Just imagine what I get by way of thanks at bedtime, when my day's work is done. I go up to a tall, stout lady with dyed hair, with thick lips and very white hands, a queen's hands, that smell of honey. Then she puts her hands on my shoulders and dabs my forehead with her lips and says: "Good night, Electra. Good night." Every evening. Every evening I have to feel that woman slobbering on my face. Ugh! Like a piece of raw meat on my forehead. But I hold myself up, I've never fallen yet. She's my mother, you know. If I was up in the tower, she wouldn't kiss me any more.

ORESTES: Have you never thought of running away?

ELECTRA: I haven't the courage; I daren't face the country roads at night all by myself.

ORESTES: Is there no one, no girl friend of yours, who'd go with you?

ELECTRA: No, I am quite alone. Ask any of the people here, and they'll tell you I'm a pest, a public nuisance. I've no friends.

ORESTES: Not even an old nurse, who saw you into the world and has kept a little affection for you?

ELECTRA: Not even an old nurse. Mother will tell you; I freeze even the kindest hearts—that's how I am.

ORESTES: Do you propose to spend your life here?

ELECTRA: [*Excitedly*] My life? Oh, no, no! Of course not! Listen. I'm waiting for—for something.

ORESTES: Something, or someone?

ELECTRA: That's my secret. Now it's your turn to speak. You're good-looking, too. Will you be here long?

ORESTES: Well, I'd thought of leaving today. But, as it is—

ELECTRA: Yes?

ORESTES: As it is, I'm not so sure.

ELECTRA: Is Corinth a pretty place?

ORESTES: Very pretty.

ELECTRA: Do you like it? Are you proud of Corinth?

ORESTES: Yes.

ELECTRA: How strange that sounds! I can't imagine myself being proud of my home town. Tell me what it feels like.

ORESTES: Well— No, I don't know. I can't explain.

ELECTRA: You can't? I wonder why. [*A short silence*] What's Corinth like? Are there shady streets and squares? Places where one can stroll in the cool of the evening?

ORESTES: Yes.

ELECTRA: And everyone comes out of doors? People go for walks together?

ORESTES: Almost everyone is out and about at sundown.

ELECTRA: Boys and girls together?

ORESTES: Oh yes, one often sees them going for walks together.

ELECTRA: And they always find something to say to each other? They like each other's company, and one hears them laughing in the streets quite late at night?

ORESTES: Yes.

ELECTRA: I suppose you think I'm very childish. But it's so hard for me to picture a life like that—going for walks, laughing and singing in the streets. Everybody here is sick with fear. Everyone except me. And I—

ORESTES: Yes? and you?

ELECTRA: Oh, I—I'm sick with—hatred. And what do they do all day, the girls at Corinth?

ORESTES: Well, they spend quite a while making themselves pretty; then they sing or play on lutes. Then they call on their friends, and at night they go to dances.

ELECTRA: But don't they have any worries?

ORESTES: Only quite little ones.

ELECTRA: Yes? Now listen well, please. Don't the people at Corinth feel remorse?

ORESTES: Sometimes. Not very often.

ELECTRA: So they do what they like and, afterwards, don't give another thought to it?

ORESTES: That's their way.

ELECTRA: How strange! [A short silence] Please tell me something else; I want to know it because of —of someone I'm expecting. Suppose one of the young fellows you've been telling about, who walk and laugh with girls in the evenings—suppose one of these young men came home after a long journey and found his father murdered, and his mother living with the murderer, and his sister treated like a slave —what would he do, that young man from Corinth? Would he just take it for granted and slink out of his father's house and look for consolation with his girl friends? Or would he draw his sword and hurl himself at the assassin, and slash his brains out? . . . Why are you silent?

ORESTES: I was wondering—

ELECTRA: What? You can't say what he'd do?

CLYTEMNESTRA: [Off stage, calling] Electra!

ELECTRA: Hush!

ORESTES: What is it?

ELECTRA: That was my mother, Queen Clytemnestra. [Clytemnestra enters] What's this, Philebus? Are you afraid of her?

ORESTES: [To himself] So that's the face I tried to picture, night after night, until I came to see it, really see it, drawn and haggard under the rosy mask of paint. But I hadn't counted on those dead eyes.

CLYTEMNESTRA: Electra, hear the King's order. You are to make ready for the ceremony. You must wear your black dress and your jewels. . . . Well, what does this behavior mean? Why are you pressing your elbows to your hips and staring at the ground? Oh, I know your tricks, my girl, but they don't deceive me any longer. Just now I was watching at the window and I saw a very different Electra, a girl with flashing eyes, bold gestures. . . . Why don't you answer?

ELECTRA: Do you really think a scullery-maid would add to the splendor of your festival?

CLYTEMNESTRA: No play-acting. You are a princess, Electra, and the townsfolk expect to see you, as in former years.

ELECTRA: A princess—yes, the princess of a day. Once a year, when this day comes round, you remember who I am; because, of course, the people want an edifying glimpse of our family life. A strange princess, indeed, who herds pigs and washes up. Tell me, will Ægistheus put his arm round my neck as he did last time? Will he smile tenderly on me, while he mumbles horrible threats in my ear?

CLYTEMNESTRA: If you would have him otherwise, it rests with you.

ELECTRA: Yes—if I let myself be tainted by your remorse; if I beg the gods' forgiveness for a crime I never committed. Yes—if I kiss your royal husband's hand and call him father. Ugh! The mere thought makes me sick. There's dry blood under his nails.

CLYTEMNESTRA: Do as you will. I have long ceased giving you orders in my name. It is the King's command I bring you.

ELECTRA: And why should I obey him? Ægistheus is your husband, Mother, your dearly beloved husband—not mine.

CLYTEMNESTRA: That is all I have to say, Electra. Only too well I see you are determined to bring ruin on yourself, and on us all. Yet who am I to counsel you, I who ruined my whole life in a single morning? You hate me, my child, but what disturbs me more is your likeness to me, as I was once. I used to have those clean-cut features, that fever in the blood, those smoldering eyes—and nothing good came of them.

ELECTRA: No! Don't say I'm like you! Tell me, Philebus—you can see us side by side—am I really like her?

ORESTES: How can I tell? Her face is like a pleasant garden that hail and storms have ravaged. And upon yours I see a threat of storm; one day passion will sear it to the bone.

ELECTRA: A threat of storm? Good! So far I welcome the likeness. May your words come true!

CLYTEMNESTRA: And you, young man, who stare so boldly at us, who are you and why have you come here? Let me look at you more closely.

ELECTRA: [Quickly] He's a Corinthian, of the name of Philebus. A traveler.

CLYTEMNESTRA: Philebus? Ah!

ELECTRA: You seemed to fear another name.

CLYTEMNESTRA: To fear? If the doom I brought on my life has taught me anything, it is that I have nothing left to fear. . . . Welcome to Argos, stranger. Yes, come nearer. How young you seem! What's your age?

ORESTES: Eighteen.

CLYTEMNESTRA: Are your parents alive?

ORESTES: My father's dead.

CLYTEMNESTRA: And your mother? Is she about my age? Ah, you don't answer. I suppose she looks much younger; she still laughs and sings when you are with her. Do you love her? Answer me, please. Why did you leave her?

ORESTES: I am on my way to Sparta, to enlist in the army.

CLYTEMNESTRA: Most travelers give our city a wide berth. Some go twenty leagues out of their way to avoid it. Were you not warned? The people of the Plain have put us in quarantine; they see our repentance as a sort of pestilence and are afraid of being infected.

ORESTES: I know.

CLYTEMNESTRA: Did they tell you that we bear the burden of an inexpiable crime, committed fifteen years ago?

ORESTES: Yes, they told me that.

CLYTEMNESTRA: And that Queen Clytemnestra bears the heaviest load of guilt—that men shudder at her name?

ORESTES: That, too, I heard.

CLYTEMNESTRA: And yet you've come here! Stranger, I am Queen Clytemnestra.

ELECTRA: Don't pity her, Philebus. The Queen is indulging in our national pastime, the game of public confession. Here everyone cries his sins on the housetops. On holidays you'll often see a worthy shopkeeper dragging himself along on his knees, covering his hair with dust, and screaming out that he's a murderer, a libertine, a liar, and all the rest of it. But the folk of Argos are getting a little tired of these amusements; everyone knows his neighbor's sins by heart. The Queen's, especially, have lost interest; they're official—our basic crimes, in fact. So you can imagine her delight when she finds someone like you, somebody raw and young, who doesn't even know her name, to hear her tale of guilt. A marvelous opportunity! It's as if she were confessing for the first time.

CLYTEMNESTRA: Be silent. Anyone has the right to spit in my face, to call me murderess and whore. But no one has the right to speak ill of my remorse.

ELECTRA: Note her words, Philebus. That's a rule of the game. People will beg you to condemn them, but you must be sure to judge them only on the sins they own to; their other evil deeds are no one's business, and they wouldn't thank you for detecting them.

CLYTEMNESTRA: Fifteen years ago men said I was the loveliest woman in Greece. Look at me now and judge my sufferings. Let me be frank, young stranger; it is not the death of that old lecher that I regret. When I saw his blood tingeing the water in the bath, I sang and danced for joy. And even now, after fifteen years, whenever I recall it, I have a thrill of pleasure. But—but I had a son; he would be your age now. When Ægistheus handed him over to his bravoes, I—

ELECTRA: You had a daughter too, my mother, if I'm not mistaken. And you've made of her a scullion. But that crime, it seems, sits lightly on your conscience.

CLYTEMNESTRA: You are young, Electra. It is easy for young people, who have not yet had a chance of sinning, to condemn. But wait, my girl; one day you, too, will be trailing after you an inexpiable crime. At every step you will think that you are leaving it behind, but it will remain as heavy as before. Whenever you look back you will see it there, just at arm's length, glowing darkly like a black crystal. And you will have forgotten what it really is, and murmur to yourself: "It wasn't I, it could not have been I, who did that." Yet, though you disown it time and time again, always it will be there, a dead weight holding you back. And then at last you will realize that you staked your life on a single throw of the dice, and nothing remains for you but to drag your crime after you until you die. For that is the law, just or unjust, of repentance. Ah, then we'll see a change come over your young pride.

ELECTRA: My *young* pride? So it's your lost youth you are regretting, still more than your crime. It's my youth you detest, even more than my innocence.

CLYTEMNESTRA: What I detest in you, Electra, is —myself. Not your youth—far from it!—but my own.

ELECTRA: And I—it's you, it's *you* I hate.

CLYTEMNESTRA: For shame, Electra! Here we are, scolding each other like two women of the same age in love with the same man! And yet I am your mother. . . . I do not know who you are, young man, nor what brings you here, but your presence bodes no good. Electra hates me—that, of course, I always knew. But for fifteen years we have kept the peace; only our eyes betrayed our feelings. And now you have come, you have spoken, and here we are showing our teeth and snapping at each other like two curs in the street. An ancient law of Argos compels us to give you hospitality, but, I make no secret of it, I had rather you were gone. As for you, my child, too faithful copy of myself, 'tis true I have no love for you. But I had rather cut off my right hand than do you harm. Only too well you know it, and you trade on my weakness. But I advise you not to rear your noxious little head against Ægistheus; he has a short way with vipers. Mark my words, do his bidding—or you will rue it.

ELECTRA: Tell the King that I shall not attend the rite. Do you know what they do, Philebus? Above the town there's a great cavern; none of our young men, not even the bravest, has ever found its end. People say that it leads down to hell, and the High Priest has had the entrance blocked with a great stone. Well—would you believe it?—each year when this anniversary comes round, the townspeople gather outside the cavern, soldiers roll away the stone, and our dead, so they say, come up from hell and roam the city. Places are laid for them at every table, chairs and beds made ready, and the people in the house huddle in corners to make room for them during the night-watches. For the dead are everywhere, the whole town's at their mercy. You can imagine how our townsfolk plead with them. "My poor dead darling, I didn't mean to wrong you. Please be kind." Tomorrow, at cock-crow, they'll return underground, the stone will be rolled back, and that will be the end of it until this day next year. Well, I refuse to take part in this mummery. Those dead folk are *their* dead, not mine.

CLYTEMNESTRA: If you will not obey his summons willingly, the King will have you brought to him by force.

ELECTRA: By force? . . . I see. Very well, then. My good, kind mother, will you please tell the King that I shall certainly obey. I shall attend the rite, and if the townsfolk wish to see me, they won't be disappointed. . . . Philebus, will you do something for me? Please don't go at once, but stay here for the ceremony. Perhaps some parts of it may entertain you. Now I'll go and make myself ready. [*Exit* Electra]

CLYTEMNESTRA: [*To* Orestes] Leave this place. I feel that you are going to bring disaster on us. You have no cause to wish us ill; we have done nothing to you. So go, I beg you. By all you hold most sacred, for your mother's sake, I beg you, go. [*Exit* Clytemnestra]

ORESTES: [*Thoughtfully*] For my mother's sake.

[Zeus *enters and comes up to him*]

ZEUS: Your attendant tells me you wish to leave. He has been looking for horses all over Argos, but can find none. Well, I can procure for you two sturdy mares and riding-gear at a very low figure.

ORESTES: I've changed my mind. I am not leaving Argos.

ZEUS: [*Meditatively*] Ah, so you're not leaving, after all. [*A short pause. Then, in a quicker tempo*] In that case I shall stay with you and be your host. I know an excellent inn in the lower town where we can lodge together. You won't regret my company, I can assure you. But first—Abraxas, galla, galla, tsay, tsay—let me rid you of those flies. A man of my age can often be very helpful to lads like you. I'm old enough to be your father; you must tell me all about yourself and your troubles. So come, young man, don't try to shake me off. Meetings like this are often of more use than one would think. Consider the case of Telemachus—you know whom I mean, King Ulysses' son. One fine day he met an old worthy of the name of Mentor, who joined forces with him. Now I wonder if you know who that old fellow Mentor really was. . . .

[*He escorts* Orestes *off the stage, holding him in conversation, while the curtain falls*]

ACT II. SCENE I.

A mountain terrace, with a cavern on the right. Its entrance is blocked by a large black boulder. On the left is a flight of steps leading up to a temple. A crowd of men and women have gathered for the ceremony.

A WOMAN: [*Kneeling before her little son, as she straightens the kerchief round his neck*] There! That's the third time I've had to straighten it for you. [*She dusts his clothes*] That's better. Now try to behave properly, and mind you start crying when you're told.

THE CHILD: Is that where they come from?

THE WOMAN: Yes.

THE CHILD: I'm frightened.

THE WOMAN: And so you should be, darling. Terribly frightened. That's how one grows up into a decent, god-fearing man.

A MAN: They'll have good weather today.

ANOTHER MAN: Just as well. It seems they still like sunlight, shadows though they are. Last year, when it rained, they were fierce, weren't they?

FIRST MAN: Ay, that's the word. Fierce.

SECOND MAN: A shocking time we had!

THIRD MAN: Once they've gone back to their cave and left us to ourselves, I'll climb up here again and look at that there stone, and I'll say to myself: "Now we've a year's peace before us."

FOURTH MAN: Well, I'm not like you, I ain't consoled that easily. From tomorrow I'll start wondering how they'll be next year. Every year they're getting nastier and nastier, and—

SECOND MAN: Hold your tongue, you fool! Suppose one of them has crept up through a crevice and is prowling round us now, eavesdropping, like. There's some of the Dead come out ahead of time, so I've heard tell. [*They eye each other nervously*]

A YOUNG WOMAN: If only it would start! What are they up to, those palace folk? They're never in a hurry, and it's all this waiting gets one down, what with the blazing sun and only that big black stone to look at. Just think! They're all there, crowded up behind the stone, gloating over the cruel things they're going to do to us.

AN OLD WOMAN: That's enough, my girl. . . . We all know she's no better than she should be; that's why she's so scared of her ghost. Her husband died last spring, and for ten years she'd been fooling the poor man.

YOUNG WOMAN: I don't deny it. Sure enough, I

fooled him to the top of his bent; but I always liked him and I led him a pleasant life, that he can't deny. He never knew a thing about the other men, and when he died, you should have seen the way he looked at me, so tenderly, like a grateful dog. Of course, he knows everything now, and it's bitter pain for him, poor fellow, and all his love has turned to hate. Presently I'll feel him coiling round me, like a wisp of smoke, and he'll cling to me more closely than any living man has ever clung. I'll bring him home with me, wound round my neck like a tippet. I've a tasty little meal all ready, with the cakes and honey that he always liked. But it's all no use, I know. He'll never forgive me, and tonight—oh, how I dread it!—he will share my bed.

A MAN: Ay, she's right. What's Ægistheus doing? We can't bear this suspense much longer. It ain't fair to keep us waiting like this.

ANOTHER MAN: Sorry for yourself, are you? But do you think Ægistheus is less afraid than we? Tell me, how'd you like to be in his shoes, and have Agamemnon gibbering at you for twenty-four hours?

YOUNG WOMAN: Oh, this horrible, horrible suspense! Do you know, I have a feeling that all of you are drifting miles and miles away, leaving me alone. The stone is not yet rolled aside, but each of us is shut up with his dead, and lonely as a raindrop.

[Zeus enters, followed by Orestes and The Tutor]

ZEUS: This way, young man; you'll have a better view.

ORESTES: So here we have them, the citizens of Argos, King Agamemnon's loyal subjects!

THE TUTOR: What an ugly lot! Observe, young master, their sallow cheeks and sunken eyes. These folk are perishing of fear. What better example could we have of the effects of superstition? Just look at them! And if you need another proof of the soundness of my teaching, look on me and my rosy cheeks.

ZEUS: Much good they do you, your pink cheeks. For all your roses, my good man, you're no more than a sack of dung, like all those others, in the eyes of Zeus. Yes, though you may not guess it, you stink to heaven. These folk, at least, are wise in their generation; they know how bad they smell.

A MAN: [Climbing on to the temple steps, harangues the crowd] Do they want to drive us mad? Let's raise our voices all together and summon Ægistheus. Make him understand we will not suffer any more delay.

THE CROWD: Ægistheus! King Ægistheus! Have pity on us!

A WOMAN: Pity, yes, pity, you cry. And will none have pity on me? He'll come with his slit throat, the man I loathed so bitterly, and clammy, unseen arms will maul me in the darkness, all through the night.

ORESTES: But this is madness! Why doesn't someone tell these wretched people—?

ZEUS: What's this, young man? Why this ado over a woman who's lost her nerve? Wait and see; there's worse to come.

A MAN: [Falling on his knees] I stink! Oh, how I stink! I am a mass of rottenness. See how the flies are teeming round me, like carrion crows. . . . That's right, my harpies; sting and gouge and scavenge me; bore through my flesh to my black heart. I have sinned a thousand times, I am a sink of ordure, and I reek to heaven.

ZEUS: O worthy man!

SOME MEN: [Helping him to his feet] That's enough. You shall talk about it later, when they are out.

[Gasping, rolling his eyes, the man stares at them]

THE CROWD: Ægistheus! Ægistheus! For mercy's sake, give the order to begin. We can bear no more.

[Ægistheus comes on to the temple steps, followed by Clytemnestra, The High Priest, and Bodyguards]

ÆGISTHEUS: Dogs! How dare you bewail your lot? Have you forgotten your disgrace? Then, by Zeus, I shall refresh your memories. [He turns to Clytemnestra] We must start without her, it seems. But let her beware! My punishment will be condign.

CLYTEMNESTRA: She promised to attend. No doubt she is making ready, lingering in front of her mirror.

ÆGISTHEUS: [To the Soldiers] Go seek Electra in the palace and bring her here by force, if need be. [Soldiers file out. He addresses The Crowd] Take your usual places. The men on my right, women and children on my left. Good.

[A short silence. Ægistheus is waiting]

HIGH PRIEST: Sire, these people are at breaking-point.

ÆGISTHEUS: I know. But I am waiting for—

[The Soldiers return]

A SOLDIER: Your Majesty, we have searched for the princess everywhere. But there is no one in the palace.

ÆGISTHEUS: So be it. We shall deal with her tomorrow. [To the High Priest] Begin.

HIGH PRIEST: Roll away the stone.

THE CROWD: Ah!

[The Soldiers roll away the stone. The High Priest goes to the entrance of the cavern]

HIGH PRIEST: You, the forgotten and forsaken, all you whose hopes were dupes, who creep along the ground darkling like smoke wraiths and have nothing left you but your great shame—you, the dead, arise; this is your day of days. Come up, pour forth like a thick cloud of fumes of brimstone driven by the wind; rise from the bowels of the earth, ye who have died a hundred deaths, ye whom every heart-beat in our breasts strikes dead again. In the name of anger unappeased and unappeasable, and the lust of vengeance, I summon you to wreak your hatred on the living. Come forth and scatter like a dark miasma

in our streets, weave between the mother and her
child, the lover and his beloved; make us regret that
we, too, are not dead. Arise, spectres, harpies, ghouls,
and goblins of our nights. Soldiers, arise, who died
blaspheming; arise, downtrodden victims, children
of disgrace; arise, all ye who died of hunger, whose
last sigh was a curse. See, the living are here to
greet you, fodder for your wrath. Arise and have at
them like a great rushing wind, and gnaw them to
the bone. Arise! Arise! Arise!

[*A tomtom sounds, and the* Priest *dances at
the entrance of the cavern, slowly at first,
quickening his gyrations until he falls to the
ground exhausted*]

ÆGISTHEUS: They are coming forth.

THE CROWD: Heaven help us!

ORESTES: I can bear this no longer. I must go—

ZEUS: Look at me, young man. In the eyes.
Good; you understand. Now, keep quiet.

ORESTES: Who—are you?

ZEUS: You shall know soon.

[Ægistheus *comes slowly down the temple
steps*]

ÆGISTHEUS: They are there. All of them. [*A
short silence*] There he is, Aricië, the husband you
used so ill. There he is, beside you, kissing you
tenderly, clasping you in his dead arms. How he
loves you! And, ah, how he hates you! . . . There
she is Nicias, your mother, who died of your
neglect. . . . And you there, Segestes, you blood-
sucker—they are all round you, the wretched men
who borrowed of you; those who starved to death,
and those who hanged themselves because of you.
In your debt they died, but today they are your
creditors. And you, fathers and mothers, loving parents lower your eyes humbly. They are there, your
dead children, stretching their frail arms towards
you, and all the happiness you denied them, all the
tortures you inflicted, weigh like lead on their sad,
childish, unforgiving hearts.

THE CROWD: Have mercy!

ÆGISTHEUS: Mercy? You ask for mercy? Do you
not know the dead have no mercy? Their grievances
are timeproof, adamant; rancor without end. Do you
hope, Nicias, to atone by deeds of kindness for the
wrong you did your mother? But what act of kindness can ever reach her now? Her soul is like a
sultry, windless noon, in which nothing stirs, nothing changes, nothing lives. Only a fierce unmoving
sun beats down on bare rocks forever. The dead
have ceased to be—think what that implies in all its
ruthlessness—yes, they are no more, and in their
eternal keeping your crimes have no reprieve.

THE CROWD: Mercy!

ÆGISTHEUS: Well you may cry mercy! Play your
parts, you wretched mummers, for today you have
a full house to watch you. Millions of staring, hopeless eyes are brooding darkly on your faces and
your gestures. They can see us, read our hearts, and
we are naked in the presence of the dead. Ah, that

makes you squirm; it burns and sears you, that stern,
calm gaze unchanging as the gaze of eyes remembered.

THE CROWD: Mercy!

THE MEN: Forgive us for living while you are
dead.

THE WOMEN: Have mercy! Tokens of you are
ever with us, we see your faces everywhere we turn.
We wear mourning unceasingly, and weep for you
from dawn till dusk, from dusk till dawn. But somehow, try as we may, your memory dwindles and
slips through our fingers; daily it grows dimmer and
we know ourselves the guiltier. Yes, you are leaving
us, ebbing away like life-blood from a wound. And
yet, know you well—if this can mollify your bitter
hatred—that you, our dear departed, have laid waste
our lives.

THE MEN: Forgive us for living while you are
dead.

THE CHILDREN: Please forgive us. We didn't want
to be born, we're ashamed of growing up. What
wrong can we have done you? It's not our fault if
we're alive. And only just alive; see how small we
are, how pale and puny. We never laugh or sing,
we glide about like ghosts. And we're so frightened
of you, so terribly afraid. Have mercy on us.

THE MEN: Forgive us for living while you are
dead.

ÆGISTHEUS: Hold your peace! If you voice your
sorrow thus, what will be left for me, your King,
to say? For my ordeal has begun; the earth is quaking, and the light failing, and the greatest of the
dead is coming forth—he whom I slew with my own
hand, King Agamemnon.

ORESTES: [*Drawing his sword*] I forbid you to
drag my father's name into this mummery.

ZEUS: [*Clutching his arms*] Stop, young fellow!
Stop that!

ÆGISTHEUS: [*Looking around*] Who dares to—?
[Electra, *wearing a white dress, comes on to the
temple steps.* Ægistheus *sees her*] Electra!

THE CROWD: Electra!

ÆGISTHEUS: What is the meaning of this, Electra?
Why are you in white?

ELECTRA: It's my prettiest dress. The city holds
high festival today, and I thought I'd look my best.

HIGH PRIEST: Would you insult our dead? This
day is *their* day, and well you know it. You should
be in mourning.

ELECTRA: Why? I'm not afraid of *my* dead, and
yours mean nothing to me.

ÆGISTHEUS: That is so; your dead are not our
dead. . . . Remember the breed she comes of, the
breed of Atreus, who treacherously cut his nephews'
throats. What are you, Electra, but the last survivor
of an accursed race? Ay, that whorish dress becomes
you. I suffered your presence in the palace out of
pity, but now I know I erred; the old foul blood of
the house of Atreus flows in your veins. And if I
did not see to it, you would taint us all. But bide

awhile, my girl, and you will learn how I can punish. Your eyes will be red with weeping for many a day.

THE CROWD: Sacrilege! Sacrilege! Away with her!

ÆGISTHEUS: Hear, miserable girl, the murmurs of these good folk you have outraged. Were I not here to curb their anger, they would tear you in pieces.

THE CROWD: Away with her, the impious wretch!

ELECTRA: Is it impious to be gay? Why can't these good folk of yours be gay? What prevents them?

ÆGISTHEUS: She is laughing, the wanton—and her dead father is standing there, with blood on his face.

ELECTRA: How dare you talk of Agamemnon? How can you be so sure he doesn't visit me by night and tell me all his secrets? Ah, if you knew the love and longing that hoarse, dead voice breathes in my ears! Yes, I'm laughing—laughing for the first time in my life; for the first time I'm happy. And can you be so sure my new-won happiness doesn't rejoice my father's heart? More likely, if he's here and sees his daughter in her white dress—his daughter of whom you've made a wretched drudge —if he sees her holding her head high, keeping her pride intact, more likely the last thing he dreams of is to blame me. No, his eyes are sparkling in the havoc of his face, he's twisting his blood-stained lips in the shadow of a smile.

THE YOUNG WOMAN: Can it be true, what she says?

VOICES: No, no. She's talking nonsense. She's gone mad. Electra, go, for pity's sake, or your sins will be visited on us.

ELECTRA: But what is it you're so frightened of? I can see all round you and there's nothing but your own shadows. Now listen to what I've just been told, something you may not know. In Greece there are cities where men live happily. White, contented cities, basking like lizards in the sun. At this very moment, under this same sky, children are playing in the streets of Corinth. And their mothers aren't asking forgiveness for having brought them into the world. No, they're smiling tenderly at them, they're proud of their motherhood. Mothers of Argos, can't you understand? Does it mean nothing to you, the pride of a mother who looks at her son, and thinks: "It's I who bore him, brought him up"?

ÆGISTHEUS: That's enough. Keep silent, or I'll thrust your words down your throat.

VOICES: Yes, yes. Make her stop. She's talked enough.

OTHER VOICES: No, let her speak. It's Agamemnon speaking through her.

ELECTRA: The sun is shining. Everywhere down in the plains men are looking up and saying: "It's a fine day," and they're happy. Are you so set on making yourselves wretched that you've forgotten the simple joy of the peasant who says as he walks across his fields: "It's a fine day"? No, there you stand, hanging your heads, moping and mumbling, more dead than alive. You're too terrified to lift a finger, afraid of jolting your precious ghosts if you make any movement. That would be dreadful, wouldn't it, if your hand suddenly went through a patch of clammy mist, and it was your grandmother's ghost! Now look at me. I'm spreading out my arms freely, and I'm stretching like someone just roused from sleep. I have my place in the sunlight, my full place and to spare. And does the sky fall on my head? Now I'm dancing, see, I'm dancing, and all I feel is the wind's breath fanning my cheeks. Where are the dead? Do you think they're dancing with me, in step?

HIGH PRIEST: People of Argos, I tell you that this woman is a profaner of all we hold most holy. Woe to her and to all of you who listen to her words!

ELECTRA: Oh, my beloved dead—Iphigeneia, my elder sister, and Agamemnon, my father and my only King—hear my prayer. If I am an evil-doer, if I offend your sorrowing shades, make some sign that I may know. But if, my dear ones, you approve, let no leaf stir, no blade of grass be moved, and no sound break in on my sacred dance. For I am dancing for joy, for peace among men; I dance for happiness and life. My dead ones, I invoke your silence that these people around me may know your hearts are with me. [She dances]

VOICES IN THE CROWD: Look how she's dancing, light as a flame. Look how her dress is rippling, like a banner in the wind. And the Dead—the Dead do nothing.

THE YOUNG WOMAN: And see her look of ecstasy —oh, no, no, that's not the face of a wicked woman. Well, Ægistheus, what have you to say? Why are you silent?

ÆGISTHEUS: I waste no words on her. Does one argue with malignant vermin? No, one stamps them out. My kindness to her in the past was a mistake, but a mistake that can be remedied. Have no fear, I shall make short work of her and end her accursed race.

VOICES IN THE CROWD: Answer us, King Ægistheus. Threats are no answer.

THE YOUNG WOMAN: She's dancing, smiling, oh, so happily, and the dead seem to protect her. Oh fortunate, too fortunate Electra! Look, I, too, am holding out my arms, baring my neck to the sunlight.

A VOICE IN THE CROWD: The Dead hold their peace. Ægistheus, you have lied.

ORESTES: Dear Electra!

ZEUS: This is too much. I'll shut that foolish wench's tongue. [Stretches out his right arm] Poseidon, carabou, carabou, roola. [The big stone which blocked the entrance to the cavern rumbles across the stage and crashes against the temple steps. Electra stops dancing]

THE CROWD: Ah! . . . Mercy on us! [A long silence]

HIGH PRIEST: Froward and fickle race, now you

have seen how the Dead avenge themselves. Mark how the flies are beating down on you, in thick, swirling clouds. You have hearkened to the tempter's voice, and a curse has fallen on the city.

THE CROWD: It is not our fault, we are innocent. That woman came and tempted us, with her lying tongue. To the river with her. Drown the witch.

AN OLD WOMAN: [*Pointing to the* Young Woman] That young huzzy there was lapping up her words like milk. Strip her naked and lash her till she squeals.

[*The* Women *seize the* Young Woman, *while the* Men *surge up the temple steps, towards* Electra]

ÆGISTHEUS: [*Straightening up*] Silence, dogs! Back to your places! Vengeance is mine, not yours. [*A short silence*] Well, you have seen what comes of disobeying me. Henceforth you will know better than to misdoubt your ruler. Disperse to your homes, the Dead will keep you company and be your guests until tomorrow's dawn. Make place for them at your tables, at your hearths, and in your beds. And see that your good behavior blots out the memory of what has happened here. As for me—grieved though I am by your mistrust, I forgive you. But you, Electra—

ELECTRA: Yes? What of it? I failed to bring it off this time. Next time I'll do better.

ÆGISTHEUS: There shall be no next time. The custom of the city forbids my punishing you on the day the Dead are with us. This you knew, and you took advantage of it. But you are no longer one of us; I cast you out forever. You shall go hence barefooted, with nothing in your hands, wearing that shameless dress. And I hereby order any man who sees you within our gates after the sun has risen to strike you down and rid the city of its bane.

[*He goes out, followed by* The Soldiers. *The Crowd file past* Electra, *shaking their fists at her*]

ZEUS: [*To* Orestes] Well, young master, were you duly edified? For, unless I'm much mistaken, the tale has a moral. The wicked have been punished and the good rewarded. [*He points to* Electra] As for that woman—

ORESTES: [*Sharply*] Mind what you say. That woman is my sister. Now go; I want to talk to her.

ZEUS: [*Observes him for a moment, then shrugs his shoulders*] Very good. [*Exit* Zeus, *followed by* The Tutor]

ORESTES: Electra!

ELECTRA: [*Still standing on the temple steps, she raises her eyes and gazes at him*] Ah, you're still there, Philebus?

ORESTES: You're in danger, Electra. You mustn't stay a moment longer in this city.

ELECTRA: In danger? Yes, that's true. You saw how I failed to bring it off. It was a bit your fault, you know—but I'm not angry with you.

ORESTES: My fault? How?

ELECTRA: You deceived me. [*She comes down the steps towards him*] Let me look at your eyes. Yes, it was your eyes that made a fool of me.

ORESTES: There's no time to lose. Listen, Electra! We'll escape together. Someone's getting a horse for me and you can ride pillion.

ELECTRA: No.

ORESTES: What? You won't come away with me?

ELECTRA: I refuse to run away.

ORESTES: I'll take you with me to Corinth.

ELECTRA: [*Laughing*] Corinth? Exactly! I know you mean well, but you're fooling me again. What could a girl like me do in Corinth? I've got to keep a level head, you know. Only yesterday my desires were so simple, so modest. When I waited at table, with meek, downcast eyes, I used to watch the two of them—the handsome old woman with the dead face, and the fat, pale King with the slack mouth and that absurd beard like a regiment of spiders running round his chin. And then I'd dream of what I'd see one day—a wisp of steam, like one's breath on a cold morning, rising from their split bellies. That was the only thing I lived for, Philebus, I assure you. I don't know what you're after, but this I know: that I mustn't believe you. Your eyes are too bold for my liking. . . . Do you know what I used to tell myself before I met you? That a wise person can want nothing better from life than to pay back the wrong that has been done him.

ORESTES: If you come with me, Electra, you'll see there are many, many other things to ask of life —without one's ceasing to be wise.

ELECTRA: No, I won't listen any more; you've done me quite enough harm already. You came here with your kind, girlish face and your eager eyes— and you made me forget my hatred. I unlocked my hands and I let my one and only treasure slip through them. You lured me into thinking one could cure the people here by words. Well, you saw what happened. They nurse their disease; they've got to like their sores so much that they scratch them with their dirty nails to keep them festering. Words are no use for such as they. An evil thing is conquered only by another evil thing, and only violence can save them. So good-by, Philebus, and leave me to my bad dreams.

ORESTES: They'll kill you.

ELECTRA: We have a sanctuary here, Apollo's shrine. Often criminals take shelter there, and so long as they are in the temple, no one can touch a hair of their heads. That's where I'll go.

ORESTES: But why refuse my help?

ELECTRA: It's not for you to help me. Someone else will come, to set me free. [*A short silence*] My brother isn't dead; I know that. And I'm waiting for his coming.

ORESTES: Suppose he doesn't come?

ELECTRA: He *will* come; he's bound to come. He is of our stock, you see; he has crime and tragedy in his blood, as I have—the bad blood of the house of Atreus. I picture him as a big, strong man, a born fighter, with bloodshot eyes like our father's, always smoldering with rage. He, too, is doomed; tangled up in his destiny, like a horse whose belly is ripped open and his legs are caught up in his guts. And now at every step he tears his bowels out. Yes, one day he will come, this city draws him. Nothing can hinder his coming, for it is here he can do the greatest harm, and suffer the greatest harm. I often seem to see him coming, with lowered head, sullen with pain, muttering angry words. He scares me; every night I see him in my dreams, and I wake screaming with terror. But I'm waiting for him and I love him. I must stay here to direct his rage—for I, anyhow, keep a clear head—to point to the guilty and say: "Those are they, Orestes. Strike!"

ORESTES: And suppose he isn't like that at all?

ELECTRA: How can he be otherwise? Don't forget he's the son of Agamemnon and Clytemnestra.

ORESTES: But mightn't he be weary of all that tale of wickedness and bloodshed; if, for instance, he'd been brought up in a happy, peaceful city?

ELECTRA: Then I'd spit in his face, and I'd say: "Go away, you cur; go and keep company where you belong, with women. But you're reckoning without your doom, poor fool. You're a grandson of Atreus, and you can't escape the heritage of blood. You prefer shame to crime; so be it. But Fate will come and hunt you down in your bed; you'll have the shame to start with, and then you will commit the crime, however much you shirk it."

ORESTES: Electra, I am Orestes.

ELECTRA: [With a cry] Oh! . . . You liar!

ORESTES: By the shades of my father, Agamemnon, I swear I am Orestes. [A short silence] Well? Why don't you carry out your threat and spit in my face?

ELECTRA: How could I? [She gazes at him earnestly] So those shining eyes, that noble forehead, are—my brother's! Orestes. . . . Oh, I'd rather you had stayed Philebus, and my brother was dead. [Shyly] Was it true, what you said about your having lived at Corinth?

ORESTES: No. I was brought up by some well-to-do Athenians.

ELECTRA: How young you look! Have you ever been in battle? Has that sword you carry ever tasted blood?

ORESTES: Never.

ELECTRA: It's strange. I felt less lonely when I didn't know you. I was waiting for the Orestes of my dream; always thinking of his strength and of my weakness. And now you're there before me; Orestes, the real Orestes, was you all the time. I look at you and I see we're just a boy and a girl, two young orphans. But, you know, I love you. More than I'd have loved the other Orestes.

ORESTES: Then, if you love me, come away. We'll leave this place together.

ELECTRA: Leave Argos? No. It's here the doom of the Atrides must be played out, and I am of the house of Atreus. I ask nothing of you. I've nothing more to ask of Philebus. But here I stay.

[Zeus enters, back stage, and takes cover to listen to them]

ORESTES: Electra, I'm Orestes, your brother. I, too, am of the house of Atreus, and my place is at your side.

ELECTRA: No. You're not my brother; you're a stranger. Orestes is dead, and so much the better for him. From now on I'll do homage to his shade, along with my father's and my sister's. You, Philebus, claim to be of our house. So be it! But can you truly say that you are one of us? Was your childhood darkened by the shadow of a murder? No, more likely you were a quiet little boy with happy, trustful eyes, the pride of your adoptive father. Naturally you could trust people—they always had a smile for you—just as you could trust the solid friendly things around you: tables, beds, and stairs. And because you were rich, and always nicely dressed, and had lots of toys, you must have often thought the world was quite a nice world to live in, like a big warm bath in which one can splash and loll contentedly. My childhood was quite different. When I was six I was a drudge, and I mistrusted everything and everyone. [A short pause] So go away, my noble-souled brother. I have no use for noble souls; what I need is an accomplice.

ORESTES: How could I leave you all alone; above all, now that you've lost even your last hope? . . . What do you propose to do here?

ELECTRA: That's my business. Good-by, Philebus.

ORESTES: So you're driving me away? [He takes some steps, then halts and faces her] Is it my fault if I'm not the fierce young swashbuckler you expected? Him you'd have taken by the hand at once and said: "Strike!" Of me you asked nothing. But, good heavens, why should I be outcast by my own sister—when I've not even been put to the test?

ELECTRA: No, Philebus, I could never lay such a load upon a heart like yours; a heart that has no hatred in it.

ORESTES: You are right. No hatred; but no love, either. You, Electra, I might have loved. And yet—I wonder. Love or hatred calls for self-surrender. He cuts a fine figure, the warm-blooded, prosperous man, solidly entrenched in his well-being, who one fine day surrenders all to love—or to hatred; himself, his house, his land, his memories. But who am I, and what have I to surrender? I'm a mere shadow of a man; of all the ghosts haunting this town today, none is ghostlier than I. The only loves I've known were phantom loves, rare and vacillating as will-o'-the-wisps. The solid passions of the living were never mine. Never! [A short silence] But, oh, the shame of it! Here I am, back in the town where I was born, and my own sister disavows me. And now—where shall I go? What city must I haunt?

ELECTRA: Isn't there some pretty girl waiting for you—somewhere in the world?

ORESTES: Nobody is waiting for me anywhere. I wander from city to city, a stranger to all others and to myself, and the cities close again behind me like the waters of a pool. If I leave Argos, what trace of my coming will remain, except the cruel disappointment of your hope?

ELECTRA: You told me about happy towns—

ORESTES: What do I care for happiness? I want my share of memories, my native soil, my place among the men of Argos. [*A short silence*] Electra, I shall not leave Argos.

ELECTRA: Please, please, Philebus, go away. If you have any love for me, go. It hurts me to think what may come to you here—nothing but evil, that I know—and your innocence would ruin all my plans.

ORESTES: I shall not go.

ELECTRA: How can you think I'd let you stay beside me—you with your stubborn uprightness—to pass silent judgment on my acts? Oh, why are you so obstinate? Nobody wants you here.

ORESTES: It's my one chance, and you, Electra— surely you won't refuse it to me? Try to understand. I want to be a man who belongs to some place, a man among comrades. Only consider. Even the slave bent beneath his load, dropping with fatigue and staring dully at the ground a foot in front of him— why, even that poor slave can say he's in *his* town, as a tree is in a forest, or a leaf upon the tree. Argos is all around him, warm, compact, and comforting. Yes, Electra, I'd gladly be that slave and enjoy that feeling of drawing the city round me like a blanket and curling myself up in it. No, I shall not go.

ELECTRA: Even if you stayed a hundred years among us, you'd still be a stranger here, and lonelier than if you were tramping the highroads of Greece. The townspeople would be watching you all the time from the corner of an eye, and they'd lower their voices when you came near.

ORESTES: Is it really so hard to win a place among you? My sword can serve the city, and I have gold to help the needy.

ELECTRA: We are not short of captains, or of charitable souls.

ORESTES: In that case— [*He takes some steps away from her, with lowered eyes. Zeus comes forward and gazes at him, rubbing his hands. Orestes raises his eyes heavenwards*] Ah, if only I knew which path to take! O Zeus, our Lord and King of Heaven, not often have I called on you for help, and you have shown me little favor; yet this you know: that I have always tried to act aright. But now I am weary and my mind is dark; I can no longer distinguish right from wrong. I need a guide to point my way. Tell me, Zeus, is it truly your will that a king's son, hounded from his city, should meekly school himself to banishment and slink away from his ancestral home like a whipped cur? I can-

not think it. And yet—and yet you have forbidden the shedding of blood. . . . What have I said? Who spoke of bloodshed? . . . O Zeus, I beseech you, if meek acceptance, the bowed head and lowly heart are what you would have of me, make plain your will by some sign; for no longer can I see my path.

ZEUS: [*Aside*] Ah, that's where I can help you, my young friend. Abraxas, abraxas, tsou, tsou.

[*Light flashes out round the stone*]

ELECTRA: [*Laughing*] Splendid! It's raining miracles today! See what comes of being a pious young man and asking counsel of the gods. [*She is convulsed with laughter and can hardly get the words out*] Oh, noble youth, Philebus, darling of the gods! "Show me a sign," you asked. "Show me a sign." Well, now you've had your sign—a blaze of light round that precious, sacred stone of theirs. So off you go to Corinth! Off you go!

ORESTES: [*Staring at the stone*] So that is the Right Thing. To live at peace—always at perfect peace. I see. Always to say "Excuse me," and "Thank you." That's what's wanted, eh? [*He stares at the stone in silence for some moments*] The Right Thing. *Their* Right Thing. [*Another silence*] Electra!

ELECTRA: Hurry up and go. Don't disappoint your fatherly old friend, who has bent down from Olympus to enlighten you. [*She stops abruptly, a look of wonder on her face*] But—what's come over you?

ORESTES: [*Slowly, in a tone he has not used till now*] There is another way.

ELECTRA: [*Apprehensively*] No, Philebus, don't be stubborn. You asked the gods for orders; now you have them.

ORESTES: Orders? What do you mean? Ah yes, the light round that big stone. But it's not for me, that light; from now on I'll take no one's orders, neither man's nor god's.

ELECTRA: You're speaking in riddles.

ORESTES: What a change has come on everything, and, oh, how far away you seem! Until now I felt something warm and living round me, like a friendly presence. That something has just died. What emptiness! What endless emptiness, as far as eye can reach! [*He takes some steps away from her*] Night is coming on. The air is getting chilly, isn't it? But what was it—what was it that died just now?

ELECTRA: Philebus—

ORESTES: I say there is another path—*my* path. Can't you see it? It starts here and leads down to the city. I must go down—do you understand?—I must go down into the depths, among you. For you are living, all of you, at the bottom of a pit. [*He goes up to Electra*] You are *my* sister, Electra, and that city is *my* city. *My* sister. [*He takes her arm*]

ELECTRA: Don't touch me. You're hurting me, frightening me—and I'm *not* yours.

ORESTES: I know. Not yet. I'm still too—too light. I must take a burden on my shoulders, a load of guilt so heavy as to drag me down, right down into the abyss of Argos.

ELECTRA: But what—what do you mean to do?

ORESTES: Wait. Give me time to say farewell to all the lightness, the aery lightness that was mine. Let me say good-by to my youth. There are evenings at Corinth and at Athens, golden evenings full of songs and scents and laughter; these I shall never know again. And mornings, too, radiant with promise. Good-by to them all, good-by. . . . Come, Electra, look at our city. There it lies, rose-red in the sun, buzzing with men and flies, drowsing its doom away in the languor of a summer afternoon. It fends me off with its high walls, red roofs, locked doors. And yet it's mine for the taking; I've felt that since this morning. You, too, Electra, are mine for the taking—and I'll take you, too. I'll turn into an ax and hew those walls asunder, I'll rip open the bellies of those stolid houses and there will steam up from the gashes a stench of rotting food and incense. I'll be an iron wedge driven into the city, like a wedge rammed into the heart of an oak tree.

ELECTRA: Oh, how you've changed! Your eyes have lost their glow; they're dull and smoldering. I'm sorry for that, Philebus; you were so gentle. But now you're talking like the Orestes of my dreams.

ORESTES: Listen! all those people quaking with fear in their dark rooms, with their dear departed round them—supposing I take over all their crimes. Supposing I set out to win the name of "guilt-stealer," and heap on myself all their remorse; that of the woman unfaithful to her husband, of the tradesman who let his mother die, of the usurer who bled his victims white? Surely, once I am plagued with all those pangs of conscience, innumerable as the flies of Argos—surely then I shall have earned the freedom of your city. Shall I not be as much at home within your red walls as the red-aproned butcher in his shop, among the carcasses of flayed sheep and cattle?

ELECTRA: So you wish to atone for us?

ORESTES: To atone? No, I said I'd house your penitence, but I did *not* say what I'd do with all those cackling fowls; maybe I'll wring their necks.

ELECTRA: And how can you take over our sense of guilt?

ORESTES: Why, all of you ask nothing better than to be rid of it. Only the King and Queen force you to nurse it in your foolish hearts.

ELECTRA: The King and Queen— Oh, Philebus!

ORESTES: The gods bear witness that I had no wish to shed their blood. [*A long silence*]

ELECTRA: You're too young, too weak.

ORESTES: Are you going to draw back—*now?* Hide me somewhere in the palace, and lead me tonight to the royal bedchamber—and then you'll see if I am too weak!

ELECTRA: Orestes!

ORESTES: Ah! For the first time you've called me Orestes.

ELECTRA: Yes. I know you now. You are indeed

Orestes. I didn't recognize you at first, I'd expected somebody quite different. But this throbbing in my blood, this sour taste on my lips—I've had them in my dreams, and I know what they mean. So at last you have come, Orestes, and your resolve is sure. And here I am beside you—just as in my dreams—on the brink of an act beyond all remedy. And I'm frightened; that, too, was in my dreams. How long I've waited for this moment, dreading and hoping for it! From now on, all the moments will link up, like the cogs in a machine, and we shall never rest again until they both are lying on their backs with faces like crushed mulberries. In a pool of blood. To think it's you who are going to shed it, you with those gentle eyes! I'm sorry now, sorry that never again I'll see that gentleness, never again see Philebus. Orestes, you are my elder brother, and head of our house; fold me in your arms, protect me. Much suffering, many perils lie ahead of both of us.

[Orestes *takes her in his arms.* Zeus *leaves his hiding-place and creeps out on tiptoe*]

CURTAIN

SCENE II.

The throne-room in the palace. An awe-inspiring, blood-smeared image of Zeus *occupies a prominent position. The sun is setting.* Electra *enters: then beckons to* Orestes *to follow her.*

ORESTES: Someone's coming. [*He begins to draw his sword*]

ELECTRA: It's the sentries on their rounds. Follow me. I know where to hide.

[*Two soldiers enter*]

FIRST SOLDIER: I can't think what's come over the flies this evening. They're all crazy-like.

SECOND SOLDIER: They smell the Dead; that's why they're in such a state. Why, I daren't open my mouth to yawn for fear they all come teeming down my throat and start a round dance in my gullet. [Electra *peeps from her hiding-place, then quickly withdraws her head*] Hear that? Something creaked yonder.

FIRST SOLDIER: Oh, it's only Agamemnon, sitting down on his throne.

SECOND SOLDIER: And the seat creaked when he planted his fat bottom on it? No, it couldn't be that; a dead man's light as air.

FIRST SOLDIER: That goes for common folk like you and me. But a king, he's different. Mind you, Agamemnon always did himself proud at table. Why, he weighed two hundred pounds or more if he weighed one. It would be surprising if there wasn't some pounds left of all that flesh.

SECOND SOLDIER: So—so you think he's here, do you?

FIRST SOLDIER: Where else should he be? If I was a dead king and I had twenty-four hours' leave each year, you may be sure I'd spend them squatting on my throne, just to remind me of the high old times I had when I was His Almighty Majesty. And I'd stay put; I wouldn't run round pestering folks in their houses.

SECOND SOLDIER: Ah, wouldn't you? You say that because you're alive. But if you were dead, you'd be just as nasty as the others. [First Soldier smacks his face] Hey! What are you up to?

FIRST SOLDIER: I'm doing you a good turn. Look, I've killed seven of 'em, all at a go.

SECOND SOLDIER: Seven what? Seven dead 'uns?

FIRST SOLDIER: O' course not. Flies. Look, my hand's all bloody. [He wipes it on his pants] Ugh, the filthy brutes!

SECOND SOLDIER: Pity you can't swot the lot of them while you're about it. The dead men, now—they don't do nothing, they know how to behave. If the flies were all killed off, we'd have some peace.

FIRST SOLDIER: Peace, you say? No, if I thought there were ghost-flies here as well, that'd be the last straw.

SECOND SOLDIER: Why?

FIRST SOLDIER: Don't you see? They die by millions every day, the little buzzers. Well, if all the flies that have died since last summer were set loose in the town, there'd be three hundred and sixty-five dead flies for every one that's here. The air'd be laced with flies, we'd breathe flies, eat flies, sweat flies; they'd be rolling down our throats in clusters and bunging up our lungs. . . . I wonder, now—maybe that's why there's such a funny smell in this room.

SECOND SOLDIER: No, no, it ain't that. They say our dead men have foul breaths, you know. And this room's not so big as it looks—a thousand square feet or so, I should say. Two or three dead men would be enough to foul the air.

FIRST SOLDIER: That's so. Fussing and fuming like they do.

SECOND SOLDIER: I tell you there's something amiss here. I heard a floor-board creak over there. [They go behind the throne to investigate. Orestes and Electra slip out on the left and tiptoe past the steps of the throne, returning to their hiding-place just as the soldiers emerge on the left]

FIRST SOLDIER: You see, there ain't nobody. It's only that old sod Agamemnon. Like as not, he's sitting on them cushions, straight as a poker. I shouldn't be surprised if he's watching you and me for want of anything else to do.

SECOND SOLDIER: Ay, and we'd better have a good look round, I ain't easy in my mind. These flies are something wicked, but it can't be helped.

FIRST SOLDIER: I wish I was back in the barracks. At least the dead folk there are old chums come back to visit us, just ordinary folk like us. But when

I think that His Late Lamented Majesty is there, like as not counting the buttons missing on my tunic, well it makes me dithery, like when the general's doing an inspection.

[Enter Ægistheus and Clytemnestra, followed by servants carrying lamps]

ÆGISTHEUS: Go, all of you.

[Exeunt Soldiers and Servants]

CLYTEMNESTRA: What is troubling you tonight?

ÆGISTHEUS: You saw what happened? Had I not played upon their fear, they'd have shaken off their remorse in the twinkling of an eye.

CLYTEMNESTRA: Is that all? Then be reassured. You will always find a way to freeze their courage when the need arises.

ÆGISTHEUS: I know. Oh, I'm only too skillful in the art of false pretense. [A short silence] I am sorry I had to rebuke Electra.

CLYTEMNESTRA: Why? Because she is my daughter? It pleased you to so do, and all you do has my approval.

ÆGISTHEUS: Woman, it is not on your account that I regret it.

CLYTEMNESTRA: Then—why? You used not to have much love for Electra.

ÆGISTHEUS: I am tired. So tired. For fifteen years I have been upholding the remorse of a whole city, and my arms are aching with the strain. For fifteen years I have been dressing a part, playing the scaremonger, and the black of my robes has seeped through to my soul.

CLYTEMNESTRA: But, sire, I, too—

ÆGISTHEUS: I know, woman, I know. You are going to tell me of your remorse. I wish I shared it. It fills out the void of your life. I have no remorse—and no man in Argos is sadder than I.

CLYTEMNESTRA: My sweet lord—[She goes up to him affectionately]

ÆGISTHEUS: Keep off, you whore! Are you not ashamed—under his eyes?

CLYTEMNESTRA: Under his eyes? Who can see us here?

ÆGISTHEUS: Why, the King. The Dead came forth this morning.

CLYTEMNESTRA: Sire, I beg you—the dead are underground and will not trouble us for many a long day. Have you forgotten it was you yourself who invented that fable to impress your people?

ÆGISTHEUS: That's so. Well, it only shows how tired I am, how sick at heart. Now leave me to my thoughts. [Exit Clytemnestra] Have you in me, Lord Zeus, the king you wished for Argos? I come and go among my people, I speak in trumpet tones, I parade the terror of my frown, and all who see me cringe in an agony of repentance. But I—what am I but an empty shell? Some creature has devoured me unawares, gnawed out my inner self. And now, looking within, I see I am more dead than Agamemnon. Did I say I was sad? I lied. Neither sad nor gay is the desert—a boundless waste of sand under burning waste of sky. Not sad, nor gay, but—sinister. Ah, I'd give my kingdom to be able to shed a tear.

[Zeus *enters*]

ZEUS: That's right. Complain away! You're only a king, like every other king.

ÆGISTHEUS: Who are you? What are you doing here?

ZEUS: So you don't recognize me?

ÆGISTHEUS: Begone, stranger, or I shall have you thrown out by my guards.

ZEUS: You don't recognize me? Still, you have seen me often enough, in dreams. It's true I looked more awe-inspiring. [*Flashes of lightning, a peal of thunder.* Zeus *assumes an awe-inspiring air*] And now do you know me?

ÆGISTHEUS: Zeus!

ZEUS: Good! [*Affable again, he goes up to the statue*] So that's meant to be me? It's thus the Argives picture me at their prayers? Well, well, it isn't often that a god can study his likeness, face to face. [*A short silence*] How hideous I am! They cannot like me much.

ÆGISTHEUS: They fear you.

ZEUS: Excellent! I've no use for love. Do you, Ægistheus, love me?

ÆGISTHEUS: What do you want of me? Have I not paid heavily enough?

ZEUS: Never enough.

ÆGISTHEUS: But it's killing me, the task I have undertaken.

ZEUS: Come now! Don't exaggerate! Your health is none too bad; you're fat. Mind, I'm not reproaching you. It's good, royal fat, yellow as tallow—just as it should be. You're built to live another twenty years.

ÆGISTHEUS: Another twenty years!

ZEUS: Would you rather die?

ÆGISTHEUS: Yes.

ZEUS: So, if anyone came here now, with a drawn sword, would you bare your breast to him?

ÆGISTHEUS: I—I cannot say.

ZEUS: Now mark my words. If you let yourself be slaughtered like a dumb ox, your doom will be exemplary. You shall be King in hell for all eternity. That's what I came here to tell you.

ÆGISTHEUS: Is someone planning to kill me?

ZEUS: So it seems.

ÆGISTHEUS: Electra?

ZEUS: Not only Electra.

ÆGISTHEUS: Who?

ZEUS: Orestes.

ÆGISTHEUS: Oh! . . . Well, that's in the natural order of things, no doubt. What can I do against it?

ZEUS: [*Mimicking his tone*] What can I do? [*Imperiously*] Bid your men arrest a young stranger going under the name of Philebus. Have him and Electra thrown into a dungeon—and if you leave them there to rot, I'll think no worse of you. Well, what are you waiting for? Call your men.

ÆGISTHEUS: No.

ZEUS: Be good enough to tell me why that no.

ÆGISTHEUS: I am tired.

ZEUS: Don't stare at the ground. Raise your big, bloodshot eyes and look at me. That's better. Yes, you're majestically stupid, like a horse; a kingly fool. But yours is not the stubbornness that vexes me; rather, it will add a spice to your surrender. For I know you will obey me in the end.

ÆGISTHEUS: I tell you I refuse to fall in with your plans. I have done so far too often.

ZEUS: That's right. Show your mettle! Resist! Resist! Ah, how I cherish souls like yours! Your eyes flash, you clench your fists, you fling refusal in the teeth of Zeus. None the less, my little rebel, my restive little horse, no sooner had I warned you than your heart said yes. Of course you'll obey. Do you think I leave Olympus without good reason? I wished to warn you of this crime because it is my will to avert it.

ÆGISTHEUS: To warn me! How strange!

ZEUS: Why "strange"? Surely it's natural enough. Your life's in danger and I want to save it.

ÆGISTHEUS: Who asked you to save it? What about Agamemnon? Did you warn *him?* And yet *he* wished to live.

ZEUS: O miserable man, what base ingratitude! You are dearer to me than Agamemnon, and when I prove this, you complain!

ÆGISTHEUS: Dearer than Agamemnon? I? No, it's Orestes whom you cherish. You allowed me to work my doom, you let me rush in, ax in hand, to King Agamemnon's bath—and no doubt you watched from high Olympus, licking your lips at the thought of another damned soul to gloat over. But today you are protecting young Orestes against himself; and I, whom you egged on to kill his father—you have chosen me to restrain the young man's hand. I was a poor creature, just qualified for murder; but for Orestes, it seems, you have higher destinies in view.

ZEUS: What strange jealousy is this! But have no fear; I love him no more than I love you. I love nobody.

ÆGISTHEUS: Then see what you have made of me, unjust god that you are. And tell me this. If today you hinder the crime Orestes has in mind, why did you permit mine of fifteen years ago?

ZEUS: All crimes do not displease me equally. And now, Ægistheus, I shall speak to you frankly, as one king to another. The first crime was mine; I committed it when I made man mortal. Once I had done that, what was left for you, poor human murderers, to do? To kill your victims? But they already had the seed of death in them; all you could do was to hasten its fruition by a year or two. Do you know what would have befallen Agamemnon if you had not killed him? Three months later he'd have died of apoplexy in a pretty slave-girl's arms. But your crime served my ends.

ÆGISTHEUS: What ends? For fifteen years I have been atoning for it—and you say it served your ends!

ZEUS: Exactly. It's because you are atoning for it that it served my ends. I like crimes that *pay*. I like yours because it was a clumsy, boorish murder, a crime that did not know itself, a crime in the antique mode, more like a cataclysm that an act of man. Not for one moment did you defy me. You struck in a frenzy of fear and rage. And then, when your frenzy had died down, you looked back on the deed with loathing and disowned it. Yet what a profit I have made on it! For one dead man, twenty thousand living men wallowing in penitence. Yes, it was a good bargain I struck that day.

ÆGISTHEUS: I see what lies behind your words. Orestes will have no remorse.

ZEUS: Not a trace of it. At this moment he is thinking out his plan, coolly, methodically, cheerfully. What good to me is a carefree murder, a shameless, sedate crime, that lies light as thistledown on the murderer's conscience? No, I won't allow it. Ah, how I loathe the crimes of this new generation; thankless and sterile as the wind! Yes, that nice-minded young man will kill you as he'd kill a chicken; he'll go away with red hands and a clean heart. In your place I should feel humiliated. So—call your men!

ÆGISTHEUS: Again I tell you, I will *not*. The crime that is being hatched displeases you enough for me to welcome it.

ZEUS: Ægistheus, you are a king, and it's to your sense of kingship I appeal, for you enjoy wielding the scepter.

ÆGISTHEUS: Continue.

ZEUS: You may hate me, but we are akin; I made you in my image. A king is a god on earth, glorious and terrifying as a god.

ÆGISTHEUS: You, terrifying?

ZEUS: Look at me. [*A long silence*] I told you you were made in my image. Each keeps order; you in Argos, I in heaven and on earth—and you and I harbor the same dark secret in our hearts.

ÆGISTHEUS: I have no secret.

ZEUS: You have. The same as mine. The bane of gods and kings. The bitterness of knowing men are free. Yes, Ægistheus, they are free. But your subjects do not know it, and you do.

ÆGISTHEUS: Why, yes. If they knew it, they'd send my palace up in flames. For fifteen years I've been playing a part to mask their power from them.

ZEUS: So you see we are alike.

ÆGISTHEUS: Alike? A god likening himself to me—what freak of irony is this? Since I came to the throne, all I said, all my acts, have been aimed at building up an image of myself. I wish each of my subjects to keep that image in the foreground of his mind, and to feel, even when alone, that my eyes are on him, severely judging his most private thoughts. But I have been trapped in my own net. I have come to see myself only as they see me. I peer into the dark pit of their souls, and there, deep down, I see the image that I have built up. I shudder, but I cannot take my eyes off it. Almighty Zeus, who am I? Am I anything more than the dread that others have of me?

ZEUS: And I—who do you think *I* am? [*Points to the statue*] I, too, have my image, and do you suppose it doesn't fill me with confusion? For a hundred thousand years I have been dancing a slow, dark ritual dance before men's eyes. Their eyes are so intent on me that they forget to look into themselves. If I forgot myself for a single moment, if I let their eyes turn away—

ÆGISTHEUS: Yes?

ZEUS: Enough. That is my business. Ægistheus, I know that you are weary of it all; but why complain? You'll die one day—but I shall not. So long as there are men on earth, I am doomed to go on dancing before them.

ÆGISTHEUS: Alas! But who has doomed us?

ZEUS: No one but ourselves. For we have the same passion. You Ægistheus, have, like me, a passion for order.

ÆGISTHEUS: For order? That is so. It was for the sake of order that I wooed Clytemnestra, for order that I killed my King; I wished that order should prevail, and that it should prevail through me. I have lived without love, without hope, even without lust. But I have kept order. Yes, I have kept good order in my kingdom. That has been my ruling passion; a godlike passion, but how terrible!

ZEUS: We could have no other, you and I; I am God, and you were born to be a king.

ÆGISTHEUS: Ay, more's the pity!

ZEUS: Ægistheus, my creature and my mortal brother, in the name of this good order that we serve, both you and I, I ask you—nay, I command you—to lay hands on Orestes and his sister.

ÆGISTHEUS: Are they so dangerous?

ZEUS: Orestes knows that he is free.

ÆGISTHEUS: [*Eagerly*] He know he's free? Then, to lay hands on him, to put him in irons, is not enough. A free man in a city acts like a plaguespot. He will infect my whole kingdom and bring my work to nothing. Almighty Zeus, why stay your hand? Why not fell him with a thunderbolt?

ZEUS: [*Slowly*] Fell him with a thunderbolt? [*A pause. Then, in a muffled voice*] Ægistheus, the gods have another secret.

ÆGISTHEUS: Yes?

ZEUS: Once freedom lights its beacon in a man's heart, the gods are powerless against him. It's a matter between man and man, and it is for other men, and for them only, to let him go his gait, or to throttle him.

ÆGISTHEUS: [*Observing him closely*] To throttle him? Be it so. Well, I shall do your will, no doubt. But say no more, and stay here no longer—I could not bear it.

[*As* Zeus *departs,* Electra *leaps forward and rushes to the door.* Orestes *comes forward*]

ELECTRA: Strike him down! Don't give him time to call for help. I'll bar the door.

ÆGISTHEUS: So you, young man, are Orestes?

ORESTES: Defend yourself.

ÆGISTHEUS: I shall not defend myself. It's too late for me to call for help, and I am glad it is too late. No, I shall not resist. I *wish* you to kill me.

ORESTES: Good. Little I care how it is done. . . . So I am to be a murderer. [Orestes *strikes him with his sword*]

ÆGISTHEUS: [*Tottering*] Ah! You struck well, Orestes. [*He clings to* Orestes] Let me look at you. Is it true you feel no remorse?

ORESTES: Remorse? Why should I feel remorse? I am only doing what is right.

ÆGISTHEUS: What is right is the will of God. You were hidden here and you heard the words of Zeus.

ORESTES: What do I care for Zeus? Justice is a matter between men, and I need no god to teach me it. It's right to stamp you out, like the foul brute you are, and to free the people of Argos from your evil influence. It is right to restore to them their sense of human dignity.

ÆGISTHEUS: [*Groaning*] Pain! What agony!

ELECTRA: Look! Look! He's swaying; his face has gone quite gray. What an ugly sight's a dying man!

ORESTES: Keep silent! Let him carry with him to the grave no other memory than the memory of our joy.

ÆGISTHEUS: My curse on you both!

ORESTES: Won't you have done with dying? [*He strikes again.* Ægistheus *falls*]

ÆGISTHEUS: Beware of the flies, Orestes, beware of the flies. All is not over. [*Dies*]

ORESTES: [*Giving the body a kick*] For him, anyhow, all is over. Now lead me to the Queen's room.

ELECTRA: Orestes!

ORESTES: What?

ELECTRA: She—she can do us no more harm.

ORESTES: What of it? What has come over you? This is not how you spoke a little while ago.

ELECTRA: Orestes! You, too, have changed. I hardly recognize you.

ORESTES: Very well. I'll go alone. [*Exit*]

ELECTRA: [*To herself*] Will she scream? [*Silence. She is listening*] He's walking down the passage. When he opens the fourth door— Oh, I wanted this to happen. And I—I want it now, I *must* want it. [*She looks at* Ægistheus] That one—yes, he's dead. So *this* is what I wanted. I didn't realize how it would be. [*She comes closer to the body*] A hundred times I've seen him, in my dreams, lying just where he is now, with a sword through his heart. His eyes were closed, he seemed asleep. How I hated him, what joy I got from hating him! But he doesn't seem asleep; his eyes are open, staring up at me. He is dead, and my hatred is dead, too. And I'm standing

here, waiting, waiting. That woman is still alive, she's in her bedroom, and presently she'll be screaming. Screaming like an animal in pain. No, I can't bear those eyes any longer. [*Kneeling, she lays a mantle over the King's face*] What was it, then, I wanted? What? [*A short silence.* Clytemnestra *screams*] He's struck her. She was our mother— and he's struck her. [*She rises to her feet*] It's done; my enemies are dead. For years and years I've reveled in the thought of this, and, now it's happened, my heart is like a lump of ice. Was I lying to myself all those years? No, that's not true, it can't be true. I'm not a coward. Only a moment ago I wanted it, and I haven't changed. I'm glad, glad, to see that swine lying at my feet. [*She jerks the mantle off the dead King's face*] Those dead-fish eyes goggling up at nothing—why should they trouble me? That's how I wanted to see them, dead and staring, and I'm glad, glad— [Clytemnestra's *screams are weakening*] Let her scream! Make her scream, Orestes. I want her to suffer. [*The screams cease*] Oh joy, joy! I'm weeping for joy; my enemies are dead, my father is avenged.

[Orestes *returns, his sword dripping blood.* Electra *runs to him and flings herself into his arms*]

ELECTRA: Orestes! . . . Oh! . . .

ORESTES: You're frightened. Why?

ELECTRA: I'm not frightened. I'm drunk. Drunk with joy. What did she say? Did she beg for mercy long?

ORESTES: Electra, I shall not repent of what I have done, but I think fit not to speak of it. There are some memories one does not share. It is enough for you to know she's dead.

ELECTRA: Did she die cursing us? That's all I want you to tell me. Did she curse us?

ORESTES: Yes. She died cursing us.

ELECTRA: Take me in your arms, beloved, and press me to your breast. How dark the night is! I never knew such darkness; those torches have no effect on it. . . . Do you love me?

ORESTES: It is not night; a new day is dawning. We are free, Electra. I feel as if I'd brought you into life and I, too, had just been born. Yes, I love you, and you belong to me. Only yesterday I was empty-handed, and today I have *you*. Ours is a double tie of blood; we two come of the same race and we two have shed blood.

ELECTRA: Let go your sword. Give me that hand, your strong right hand. [*She clasps and kisses it*] Your fingers are short and square, made to grasp and hold. Dear hand! It's whiter than mine. But how heavy it became to strike down our father's murderers! Wait! [*She takes a torch and holds it near* Orestes] I must light up your face; it's getting so dark that I can hardly see you. And I *must* see you; when I stop seeing you, I'm afraid of you. I daren't take my eyes off you. I must tell myself again and again that I love you. But—how strange you look!

ORESTES: I am free, Electra. Freedom has crushed down on me like a thunderbolt.

ELECTRA: Free? But I—I don't feel free. And you—can you undo what has been done? Something has happened and we are no longer free to blot it out. Can you prevent our being the murderers of our mother—for all time? . . .

ORESTES: Do you think I'd wish to prevent it? I have done *my* deed, Electra, and that deed was good. I shall bear it on my shoulders as a carrier at a ferry carries the traveler to the farther bank. And when I have brought it to the farther bank I shall take stock of it. The heavier it is to carry, the better pleased I shall be; for that burden is my freedom. Only yesterday I walked the earth haphazard; thousands of roads I tramped that brought me nowhere, for they were other men's roads. Yes, I tried them all; the hauler's tracks along the riverside, the mule-paths in the mountains, and the broad, flagged highways of charioteers. But none of these was mine. Today I have one path only, and heaven knows where it leads. But it is *my* path. . . . What is it, Electra?

ELECTRA: I can't see you any more. Those torches give no light. I hear your voice, but it hurts me, it cuts like a knife. Will it always be as dark as this—always, even in the daytime? . . . Oh, Orestes! There they are!

ORESTES: Who?

ELECTRA: There they are! Where have they come from? They're hanging from the ceiling like clusters of black grapes; the walls are alive with them; they're swirling down across the torchlight and it's their shadows that are hiding your face from me.

ORESTES: The flies—

ELECTRA: Listen! The sound of their wings is like a roaring furnace. They're all around us, Orestes, watching, biding their time. Presently they'll swoop down on us and I shall feel thousands of tiny clammy feet crawling over me. Oh, look! They're growing bigger, bigger; now they're as big as bees. We'll never escape them, they'll follow us everywhere in a dense cloud. Oh God, now I can see their eyes, millions of beady eyes all staring at us!

ORESTES: What do the flies matter to us?

ELECTRA: They're the Furies, Orestes, the goddesses of remorse.

VOICES: [*From behind the door*] Open! Open! . . . If you don't, we'll smash the door in. [*Heavy thuds. They are battering at the door*]

ORESTES: Clytemnestra's cries must have brought them here. Come! Lead me to Apollo's shrine. We will spend the night there, sheltered from men and flies. And tomorrow I shall speak to my people.

CURTAIN

ACT III.

The temple of Apollo. Twilight. A statue of Apollo in the center of the stage. Electra *and* Orestes *are sleeping at the foot of the statue, their arms clasped round its legs. The* Furies *ring them round; they sleep standing, like cranes. At the back is a huge bronze door.*

FIRST FURY: [*Stretching herself*] Aaaah! I slept the night out standing, stiff with rage, and my sleep was glorious with angry dreams. Ah, how lovely is the flower of anger, the red flower in my heart! [*She circles round* Orestes *and* Electra] Still sleeping. How white and soft they are! I'll roll on their breasts and bellies, like a torrent over stones. And I shall polish hour by hour their tender flesh; rub it, scour it, wear it to the bone. [*She comes a few steps forward*] O clear, bright dawn of hate! A superb awakening. They're sleeping, sweating, a smell of fever rises from them. But I am awake; cool and hard and gemlike. My soul is adamant—and I feel my sanctity.

ELECTRA: [*Sighing in her sleep*] No! No!

FIRST FURY: She's sighing. Wait, my pretty one, wait till you feel our teeth. Soon you'll be screaming with the agony of our caresses. I'll woo you like a man, for you're my bride, and you shall feel my love crushing your life out. You, Electra, are more beautiful than I; but you'll see how my kisses age you. Within six months I'll have you raddled like an old hag; but I stay young forever. [*She bends over* Orestes *and* Electra] Ah, this lovely human carrion, what a tasty meal we have in store! As I gaze down at them and breathe their breath, I choke with rage. Nothing is sweeter, nothing, than to feel a dawn of hatred spreading like quickfire in one's veins; teeth and talons ready for their task. Hatred is flooding through me, welling up in my breasts like milk. Awake, sisters, awake! The day has come.

SECOND FURY: I dreamt I was biting them.

FIRST FURY: Be patient. Today they are protected by a god, but soon hunger and thirst will drive them out of sanctuary. And then you shall bite them to your heart's content.

THIRD FURY: Aaah! How I want to claw them!

FIRST FURY: Your turn will come. In a little while your iron talons will be ribboning the flesh of those young criminals with angry red. Come closer, sisters, come and look at them.

A FURY: How young they are!

ANOTHER FURY: And how beautiful!

FIRST FURY: Yes, we are favored. Only too often criminals are old and ugly. Too seldom do we have the joy, the exquisite delight, of ruining what's beautiful.

THE FURIES: Heiah! Heiahah!

THIRD FURY: Orestes is almost a child. I shall

mother him, oh so tenderly, with my hatred; I shall take his pale head on my knees and stroke his hair.

FIRST FURY: And then?

THIRD FURY: Then, when he least expects it, I shall dig these two fingers into his eyes. [*All laugh*]

FIRST FURY: See, they're stretching, sighing, on the brink of waking. And now, my sisters, flies my sisters, let's sing the sinners from their sleep.

THE FURIES: [*Together*] Bzz. Bzz. Bzz. Bzz.
We shall settle on your rotten hearts like flies on butter;
Rotten hearts, juicy, luscious hearts.
Like bees we'll suck the pus and matter from your hearts,
And we'll turn it into honey, rich, green honey.
What love could ravish us as hatred does?
Bzz. Bzz. Bzz. Bzz.
We shall be the staring eyes of the houses,
The growls of the kenneled mastiff baring his fangs as you go by,
A drone of wings pulsing in high air,
Sounds of the forest,
Whistlings, whinings, creakings, hissings, howlings,
We shall be the darkness,
The clotted darkness of your souls.
Bzz. Bzz. Bzz. Bzz.
Heiah, heiah, heiahah!
Bzz. Bzz. Bzz. Bzz.
We are the flies, the suckers of pus,
We shall have open house with you,
We shall gather our food from your mouths,
And our light from the depths of your eyes.
All your life we will be with you,
Until we make you over to the worms.
[*They dance*]

ELECTRA: [*Still half asleep*] Was someone speaking? Who—who are you?

THE FURIES: Bzz. Bzz. Bzz.

ELECTRA: Ah, yes. There you are. Well? Have we really killed them?

ORESTES: [*Waking*] Electra!

ELECTRA: You, who are you? Ah, yes. Orestes. Go away.

ORESTES: But—what's wrong, Electra?

ELECTRA: You frighten me. I had a dream. I saw our mother lying on her back. Blood was pouring from her, gushing under the door. A dream. . . . Feel my hands. They're icy. No, don't. Don't touch me. Did she really bleed much?

ORESTES: Don't!

ELECTRA: [*Waking up completely*] Let me look at you. You killed them. It was you, you who killed them. You are here beside me, you have just waked up, there's nothing written on your face, no brand. . . . And yet you killed them.

ORESTES: Why, yes. I killed them. [*A short silence*] You, too, make me afraid. Yesterday you were so beautiful. And now you look as if some wild beast had clawed your face.

ELECTRA: No beast. Your crime. It's tearing off my cheeks and eyelids; I feel as if my eyes and teeth were naked. . . . But what are those creatures?

ORESTES: Take no notice of them. They can do you no harm.

FIRST FURY: No harm? Let her dare to come among us and you'll see if we can do no harm!

ORESTES: Keep quiet. Back to your kennel, bitches! [*The* Furies *growl*] Is it possible that the girl who only yesterday was dancing in a white dress on the temple steps—is it possible you were that girl?

ELECTRA: I've grown old. In a single night.

ORESTES: You have not lost your beauty, but— Where, now, have I seen dead eyes like those? Electra—you are like *her*. Like Clytemnestra. What use, then, was it killing her? When I see my crime in those eyes, it revolts me.

FIRST FURY: That is because *you* revolt *her*.

ORESTES: Is that true, Electra? Do I revolt you?

ELECTRA: Oh, let me be!

FIRST FURY: Well? Can you still have any doubt? How should she not hate you? She lived in peace, dreaming her dreams; and then you came, bringing murder and impiety upon her. So now she has to share your guilt and hug that pedestal, the only scrap of earth remaining to her.

ORESTES: Do not listen.

FIRST FURY: Away! Away! Make him go, Electra; don't let him touch you! He's a butcher. He reeks of fresh, warm blood. He used the poor old woman very foully, you know; he killed her piecemeal.

ELECTRA: Oh no! That's a lie, surely?

FIRST FURY: You can believe me; I was there all the time, buzzing in the air around them.

ELECTRA: So he struck her several times?

FIRST FURY: Ten times at least. And each time the sword squelched in the wound. She tried to shield her face and belly with her hands, and he carved her hands to ribbons.

ELECTRA: So it wasn't a quick death. Did she suffer much?

ORESTES: Put your fingers in your ears, do not look at them, and, above all, ask no questions. If you question them, you're lost.

FIRST FURY: Yes, she suffered—horribly.

ELECTRA: [*Covering her face with her hands*] Oh!

ORESTES: She wants to part us, she is building up a wall of solitude around you. But beware; once you are alone, alone and helpless, they will fling themselves upon you. Electra, we planned this crime together and we should bear its brunt together.

ELECTRA: You dare to say I planned it with you?

ORESTES: Can you deny it?

ELECTRA: Of course I deny it. Wait! Well, perhaps—in a way. . . . Oh, I don't know. I dreamt the crime, but you carried it out, you murdered your own mother.

THE FURIES: [*Shrieking and laughing*] Murderer! Murderer! Butcher!

ORESTES: Electra, behind that door is the outside world. A world of dawn. Out there the sun is rising, lighting up the roads. Soon we shall leave this place, we shall walk those sunlit roads, and these hags of darkness will lose their power. The sunbeams will cut through them like swords.

ELECTRA: The sun—

FIRST FURY: You will never see the sun again, Electra. We shall mass between you and the sun like a swarm of locusts; you will carry darkness round your head wherever you go.

ELECTRA: Oh, let me be! Stop torturing me!

ORESTES: It's your weakness gives them their strength. Mark how they dare not speak to me. A nameless horror has descended on you, keeping us apart. And yet why should this be? What have you lived through that I have not shared? Do you imagine that my mother's cries will ever cease ringing in my ears? Or that my eyes will ever cease to see her great sad eyes, lakes of lambent darkness in the pallor of her face? And the anguish that consumes you—do you think it will ever cease ravaging my heart? But what matter? I am free. Beyond anguish, beyond remorse. Free. And at one with myself. No, you must not loathe yourself, Electra. Give me your hand. I shall never forsake you.

ELECTRA: Let go of my hand! Those hell-hounds frighten me, but you frighten me more.

FIRST FURY: You see! You see! . . . That's quite true, little doll; you're less afraid of us than of that man. Because you need us, Electra. You are our child, our little girl. You need our nails to score your skin, our teeth to bite your breast, and all our savage love to save you from your hatred of yourself. Only the suffering of your body can take your mind off your suffering soul. So come and let us hurt you. You have only those two steps to come down, and we will take you in our arms. And when our kisses sear your tender flesh, you'll forget all in the cleansing fires of pain.

THE FURIES: Come down to us! Come down!
    [*Slowly they dance round her, weaving their spell.* Electra *rises to her feet*]

ORESTES: [*Gripping her arm*] No, no, for pity's sake. Don't go to them. Once they get you, all is lost.

ELECTRA: [*Freeing herself violently*] Let go! Oh, how I hate you! [*She goes down the steps, and the Furies fling themselves on her*] Help!
    [Zeus *enters*]

ZEUS: Kennel up!

FIRST FURY: The master!
    [The Furies *slink off reluctantly, leaving* Electra *lying on the ground*]

ZEUS: Poor children. [*He goes up to* Electra] So to this you've come, unhappy pair? My heart is torn between anger and compassion. Get up, Electra. So long as I am here, my Furies will not hurt you. [*He helps her to rise and gazes at her face*] Ah, what a cruel change! In a night, a single night, all the wild-rose bloom has left your cheeks. In one night your body has gone to ruin, lungs, gall, and liver all burnt out. The pride of headstrong youth—see what it has brought you to, poor child.

ORESTES: Stop talking in that tone, fellow. It is unbecoming for the king of the gods.

ZEUS: And you, my lad, drop that haughty tone. It's unbecoming for a criminal atoning for his crime.

ORESTES: I am no criminal, and you have no power to make me atone for an act I don't regard as a crime.

ZEUS: So you may think, but wait awhile. I shall cure you of that error before long.

ORESTES: Torture me to your heart's content; I regret nothing.

ZEUS: Not even the doom you have brought upon your sister?

ORESTES: Not even that.

ZEUS: Do you hear, Electra? And this man professed to love you!

ORESTES: She is dearer to me than life. But her suffering comes from within, and only she can rid herself of it. For she is free.

ZEUS: And you? You, too, are free, no doubt?

ORESTES: Yes, and well you know it.

ZEUS: A pity you can't see yourself as you are now, you fool, for all your boasting! What a heroic figure you cut there, cowering between the legs of a protecting god, with a pack of hungry vixen keeping guard on you! If *you* can brag of freedom, why not praise the freedom of a prisoner languishing in fetters, or a slave nailed to the cross?

ORESTES: Certainly. Why not?

ZEUS: Take care. You play the braggart now because Apollo is protecting you. But Apollo is my most obedient servant. I have but to lift a finger and he will abandon you.

ORESTES: Then do so. Lift a finger, lift your whole hand while you are about it.

ZEUS: No, that is not my way. Haven't I told you that I take no pleasure in punishment? I have come to save you both.

ELECTRA: To save us? No, it is too cruel to make sport of us. You are the lord of vengeance and of death, but, god though you are, you have no right to delude your victims with false hopes.

ZEUS: Within a quarter of an hour you can be outside that door.

ELECTRA: Safe and sound?

ZEUS: You have my word for it.

ELECTRA: And what do you want from me in return?

ZEUS: Nothing, my child. Nothing.

ELECTRA: Nothing? Did I hear right? Then you are a kind god, a lovable god.

ZEUS: Or next to nothing. A mere trifle. What you can give most easily—a little penitence.

ORESTES: Take care, Electra. That trifle will weigh like a millstone on your soul.

ZEUS: [To Electra] Don't listen to him. Answer me, instead. Why hesitate to disavow that crime? It was committed by someone else; one could hardly say even that you were his accomplice.

ORESTES: Electra! Are you going to go back on fifteen years of hope and hatred?

ZEUS: What has she to go back on? Never did she really wish that impious deed to be accomplished.

ELECTRA: If only that were true!

ZEUS: Come now! Surely you can trust my word. Do I not read in men's hearts?

ELECTRA: [Incredulously] And you read in mine that I never really desired that crime? Though for fifteen years I dreamt of murder and revenge?

ZEUS: Bah! I know you nursed bloodthirsty dreams—but there was a sort of innocence about them. They made you forget your servitude, they healed your wounded pride. But you never really thought of making them come true. Well, am I mistaken?

ELECTRA: Ah, Zeus, dear Zeus, how I long to think you are not mistaken!

ZEUS: You're a little girl, Electra. A mere child. Most little girls dream of becoming the richest or the loveliest woman on earth. But you were haunted by the cruel destiny of your race, you dreamt of becoming the saddest, most criminal of women. You never willed to do evil; you willed your own misfortune. At an age when most children are playing hopscotch or with their dolls, you, poor child, who had no friends or toys, you toyed with dreams of murder, because that's a game to play alone.

ELECTRA: Yes, yes! I'm beginning to understand.

ORESTES: Listen, Electra! It's now you are bringing guilt upon you. For who except yourself can know what you really wanted? Will you let another decide that for you? Why distort a past that can no longer stand up for itself? And why disown the fire-brand that you were, that glorious young goddess, vivid with hatred, that I loved so much? Can't you see this cruel god is fooling you?

ZEUS: No, Electra, I'm not fooling you. And now hear what I offer. If you repudiate your crime, I'll see that you two occupy the throne of Argos.

ORESTES: Taking the places of our victims?

ZEUS: How else?

ORESTES: And I shall put on the royal robe, still warm from the dead King's wearing?

ZEUS: That or another. What can it matter?

ORESTES: Nothing of course—provided that it's black.

ZEUS: Are you not in mourning?

ORESTES: Yes, I was forgetting; in mourning for my mother. And my subjects—must I have them, too, wear black?

ZEUS: They wear it already.

ORESTES: True. We can give them time to wear out their old clothes. . . . Well, Electra, have you understood? If you shed some tears, you'll be given Clytemnestra's shifts and petticoats—those dirty, stinking ones you had to wash for fifteen years. And the part she played is yours for the asking. Now that you have come to look so much like her, you will play the part superbly; everyone will take you for your mother. But I—I fear I am more squeamish—I refuse to wear the breeches of the clown I killed.

ZEUS: You talk big, my boy. You butchered a defenseless man and an old woman who begged for mercy. But, to hear you speak, one would think you'd bravely fought, one against a crowd, and were the savior of your city.

ORESTES: Perhaps I was.

ZEUS: You a savior! Do you know what's afoot behind that door? All the good folk of Argos are waiting there. Waiting to greet you with stones and pikes and pitchforks. Oh, they are very grateful to their savior! . . . You are lonely as a leper.

ORESTES: Yes.

ZEUS: So you take pride in being an outcast, do you? But the solitude you're doomed to, most cowardly of murderers, is the solitude of scorn and loathing.

ORESTES: The most cowardly of murderers is he who feels remorse.

ZEUS: Orestes, I created you, and I created all things. Now see! [The walls of the temple draw apart, revealing the firmament, spangled with wheeling stars. Zeus is standing in the background. His voice becomes huge—amplified by loud-speakers—but his form is shadowy] See those planets wheeling on their appointed ways, never swerving, never clashing. It was I who ordained their courses, according to the law of justice. Hear the music of the spheres, that vast, mineral hymn of praise, sounding and resounding to the limits of the firmament. [Sounds of music] It is my work that living things increase and multiply, each according to his kind. I have ordained that man shall always beget man, and dog give birth to dog. It is my work that the tides with their innumerable tongues creep up to lap the sand and draw back at the appointed hour. I make the plants grow, and my breath fans round the earth the yellow clouds of pollen. You are not in your own home, intruder; you are a foreign body in the world, like a splinter in flesh, or a poacher in his lordship's forest. For the world is good; I made it according to my will, and I am Goodness. But you, Orestes, you have done evil, the very rocks and stones cry out against you. The Good is everywhere, it is the coolness of the wellspring, the pith of the reed, the grain of flint, the weight of stone. Yes, you will find it even in the heart of fire and light; even your own body plays you false, for it abides perforce by my law. Good is everywhere, in you and about you; sweeping through you like a scythe, crushing you like a mountain. Like an ocean it buoys you up and rocks you to and fro, and it enabled the success of your evil plan, for it was in the brightness of the torches, the temper of your blade, the strength of your right arm. And that of which you are so vain, the Evil that you think is your creation, what is it but a reflection in a mocking mirror, a phantom thing that would have no being but for Goodness. No, Orestes, return to your saner self; the universe refutes you, you are a mite in the scheme of things. Return to Nature, Nature's thankless son. Know your sin, abhor it, and tear it from you as one tears out a rotten, noisome tooth. Or else—beware lest the very seas shrink back at your approach, springs dry up when you pass by, stones and rocks roll from your path, and the earth crumbles under your feet.

ORESTES: Let it crumble! Let the rocks revile me, and flowers wilt at my coming. Your whole universe is not enough to prove me wrong. You are the king of gods, king of stones and stars, king of the waves of the sea. But you are not the king of man.

[*The walls draw together. Zeus comes into view, tired and dejected, and he now speaks in his normal voice*]

ZEUS: Impudent spawn! So I am not your king? Who, then, made you?

ORESTES: You. But you blundered; you should not have made me free.

ZEUS: I gave you freedom so that you might serve me.

ORESTES: Perhaps. But now it has turned against its giver. And neither you nor I can undo what has been done.

ZEUS: Ah, at last! So this is your excuse?

ORESTES: I am not excusing myself.

ZEUS: No? Let me tell you it sounds much like an excuse, this freedom whose slave you claim to be.

ORESTES: Neither slave nor master. I *am* my freedom. No sooner had you created me than I ceased to be yours.

ELECTRA: Oh, Orestes! By all you hold most holy, by our father's memory, I beg you do not add blasphemy to your crime!

ZEUS: Mark her words, young man. And hope no more to win her back by arguments like these. Such language is somewhat new to her ears—and somewhat shocking.

ORESTES: To my ears, too. And to my lungs, which breathe the words, and to my tongue, which shapes them. In fact, I can hardly understand myself. Only yesterday you were still a veil on my eyes, a clot of wax in my ears; yesterday, indeed, I had an excuse. *You* were my excuse for being alive, for you had put me in the world to fulfill your purpose, and the world was an old pander prating to me about your goodness, day in, day out. And then you forsook me.

ZEUS: *I* forsook you? How?

ORESTES: Yesterday, when I was with Electra, I felt at one with Nature, this Nature of your making. It sang the praises of the Good—*your* Good—in siren tones, and lavished intimations. To lull me into gentleness, the fierce light mellowed and grew tender as a lover's eyes. And, to teach me the forgiveness of offenses, the sky grew bland as a pardoner's face. Obedient to your will, my youth rose up before me and pleaded with me like a girl who fears her lover will forsake her. That was the last time, the last, I saw my youth. Suddenly, out of the blue, freedom crashed down on me and swept me off my feet. Nature sprang back, my youth went with the wind, and I knew myself alone, utterly alone in the midst of this well-meaning little universe of yours. I was like a man who's lost his shadow. And there was nothing left in heaven, no right or wrong, nor anyone to give me orders.

ZEUS: What of it? Do you want me to admire a scabby sheep that has to be kept apart; or the leper mewed in a lazar-house? Remember, Orestes, you once were of my flock, you fed in my pastures among my sheep. Your vaunted freedom isolates you from the fold; it means exile.

ORESTES: Yes, exile.

ZEUS: But the disease can't be deeply rooted yet; it began only yesterday. Come back to the fold. Think of your loneliness; even your sister is forsaking you. Your eyes are big with anguish, your face is pale and drawn. The disease you're suffering from is inhuman, foreign to my nature, foreign to yourself. Come back. I am forgetfulness, I am peace.

ORESTES: Foreign to myself—I know it. Outside nature, against nature, without excuse, beyond remedy, except what remedy I find within myself. But I shall not return under your law; I am doomed to have no other law but mine. Nor shall I come back to Nature, the Nature you found good; in it are a thousand beaten paths all leading up to you—but I must blaze my trail. For I, Zeus, am a man, and every man must find out his own way. Nature abhors man, and you too, god of gods, abhor mankind.

ZEUS: That is true; men like you I hold in abhorrence.

ORESTES: Take care; those words were a confession of your weakness. As for me, I do not hate you. What have I to do with you, or you with me? We shall glide past each other, like ships in a river, without touching. You are God and I am free; each of us is alone, and our anguish is akin. How can you know I did not try to feel remorse in the long night that has gone by? And to sleep? But no longer can I feel remorse and I can sleep no more. [*A short silence*]

ZEUS: What do you propose to do?

ORESTES: The folk of Argos are my folk. I must open their eyes.

ZEUS: Poor people! Your gift to them will be a sad one; of loneliness and shame. You will tear from their eyes the veils I had laid on them, and they will see their lives as they are, foul and futile, a barren boon.

ORESTES: Why, since it is their lot, should I deny them the despair I have in me?

ZEUS: What will they make of it?

ORESTES: What they choose. They're free; and human life begins on the far side of despair. [*A short silence*]

ZEUS: Well, Orestes, all this was foreknown. In the fullness of time a man was to come, to announce my decline. And you're that man, it seems. But seeing you yesterday—you with your girlish face —who'd have believed it?

ORESTES: Could I myself have believed it? . . . The words I speak are too big for my mouth, they tear it; the load of destiny I bear is too heavy for my youth and has shattered it.

ZEUS: I have little love for you, yet I am sorry for you.

ORESTES: And I, too, am sorry for *you*.

ZEUS: Good-by, Orestes. [*He takes some steps forward*] As for you, Electra, bear this in mind. My reign is not yet over—far from it!—and I shall not give up the struggle. So choose if you are with me or against me. Farewell.

ORESTES: Farewell. [*Zeus goes out. Electra slowly rises to her feet*] Where are you going?

ELECTRA: Leave me alone. I'm done with you.

ORESTES: I have known you only for a day, and must I lose you now forever?

ELECTRA: Would to God that I had never known you!

ORESTES: Electra! My sister, dear Electra! My only love, the one joy of my life, do not leave me. Stay with me.

ELECTRA: Thief! I had so little, so very little to call mine; only a few weak dreams, a morsel of peace. and now you've taken my all; you've robbed a pauper of her mite! You were my brother, the head of our house, and it was your duty to protect me. But no, you needs must drag me into carnage; I am red as a flayed ox, these loathsome flies are swarming after me, and my heart is buzzing like an angry hive.

ORESTES: Yes, my beloved, it's true, I have taken all from you, and I have nothing to offer in return; nothing but my crime. But think how vast a gift that is! Believe me, it weighs on my heart like lead. We were too light, Electra; now our feet sink into the soil, like chariot-wheels in turf. So come with me; we will tread heavily on our way, bowed beneath our precious load. You shall give me your hand, and we will go—

ELECTRA: Where?

ORESTES: I don't know. Towards ourselves. Be-yond the rivers and mountains are an Orestes and an Electra waiting for us, and we must make our patient way towards them.

ELECTRA: I won't hear any more from you. All you have to offer me is misery and squalor. [*She rushes out into the center of the stage. The* Furies *slowly close in on her*] Help! Zeus, king of gods and men, my king, take me in your arms, carry me from this place, and shelter me. I will obey your law, I will be your creature and your slave, I will embrace your knees. Save me from the flies, from my brother, from myself! Do not leave me lonely and I will give up my whole life to atonement. I repent, Zeus. I bitterly repent.

[*She runs off the stage. The* Furies *make as if to follow her, but the* First Fury *holds them back*]

FIRST FURY: Let her be, sisters. She is not for us. But that man is ours, and ours, I think, for many a day. His little soul is stubborn. He will suffer for two.

[*Buzzing, the* Furies *approach* Orestes]

ORESTES: I am alone, alone.

FIRST FURY: No, no, my sweet little murderer, I'm staying with you, and you'll see what merry games I'll think up to entertain you.

ORESTES: Alone until I die. And after that—?

FIRST FURY: Take heart, sisters, he is weakening. See how his eyes dilate. Soon his nerves will be throbbing like harp-strings, in exquisite arpeggios of terror.

SECOND FURY: And hunger will drive him from his sanctuary before long. Before nightfall we shall know how his blood tastes.

ORESTES: Poor Electra!

[*The* Tutor *enters*]

THE TUTOR: Master! Young master! Where are you? It's so dark one can't see a thing. I'm bringing you some food. The townspeople have surrounded the temple; there's no hope of escape by daylight. We shall have to try our chance when night comes. Meanwhile, eat this food to keep your strength up. [*The* Furies *bar his way*] Hey! Who are these? More of those primitive myths! Ah, how I regret that pleasant land of Attica, where reason's always right.

ORESTES: Do not try to approach me, or they will tear you in pieces.

THE TUTOR: Gently now, my lovelies. See what I've brought you, some nice meat and fruit. Here you are! Let's hope it will calm you down.

ORESTES: So the people of Argos have gathered outside the temple, have they?

THE TUTOR: Indeed they have, and I can't say which are the fiercer, the thirstier for your blood: these charming young creatures here, or your worthy subjects.

ORESTES: Good. [*A short silence*] Open that door.

THE TUTOR: Have you lost your wits? They're waiting behind it, and they're armed.

ORESTES: Do as I told you.

THE TUTOR: For once permit me, sir, to disobey your orders. I tell you, they will stone you. It's madness.

ORESTES: Old man, I am your master, and I order you to unbar that door.

[*The* Tutor *opens one leaf of the double doors a few inches*]

THE TUTOR: Oh dear! Oh dear!

ORESTES: Open both leaves.

[*The* Tutor *half opens both leaves of the door and takes cover behind one of them. The Crowd surges forward, thrusting the doors wide open; then stops, bewildered, on the threshold. The stage is flooded with bright light. Shouts rise from the* Crowd: "Away with him!" "Kill him!" "Stone him!" "Tear him in pieces!"]

ORESTES: [*Who has not heard them*] The sun!

THE CROWD: Murderer! Butcher! Blasphemer! We'll tear you limb from limb. We'll pour molten lead into your veins.

A WOMAN: I'll pluck out your eyes.

A MAN: I'll eat your gizzard!

ORESTES: [*Drawing himself up to his full height*] So here you are, my true and loyal subjects? I am Orestes, your King, son of Agamemnon, and this is my coronation day. [*Exclamations of amazement, mutterings among the crowd*] Ah, you are lowering your tone? [*Complete silence*] I know; you fear me. Fifteen years ago to the day, another murderer showed himself to you, his arms red to the elbows, gloved in blood. But him you did not fear; you read in his eyes that he was of your kind, he had not the courage of his crimes. A crime that its doer disowns becomes ownerless—no man's crime; that's how you see it, isn't it? More like an accident than a crime? So you welcomed the criminal as your King, and that crime without an owner started prowling round the city, whimpering like a dog that has lost its master. You see me, men of Argos, you understand that my crime is wholly mine; I claim it as my own, for all to know; it is my glory, my life's work, and you can neither punish me nor pity me. That is why I fill you with fear. And yet, my people, I love you, and it was for your sake that I killed. For your sake, I had come to claim my kingdom, and you would have none of me because I was not of your kind. Now I am of your kind, my subjects; there is a bond of blood between us, and I have earned my kingship over you. As for your sins and your remorse, your night-fears, and the crime Ægistheus committed—all are mine, I take them all upon me. Fear your Dead no longer; they are *my* Dead. And, see, your faithful flies have left you and come to me. But have no fear, people of Argos. I shall not sit on my victim's throne or take the scepter in my blood-stained hands. A god offered it to me, and I said no. I wish to be a king without a kingdom, without subjects. Farewell, my people. Try to reshape your lives. All here is new, all must begin anew. And for me, too, a new life is beginning. A strange life. . . . Listen now to this tale. One summer there was a plague of rats in Scyros. It was like a foul disease; they soiled and nibbled everything, and the people of the city were at their wits' end. But one day a flute-player came to the city. He took his stand in the market-place. Like this. [Orestes *rises to his feet*] He began playing on his flute and all the rats came out and crowded round him. Then he started off, taking long strides—like this. [*He comes down from the pedestal*] And he called to the people of Scyros: "Make way!" [*The* Crowd *makes way for him*] And all the rats raised their heads and hesitated—as the flies are doing. Look! Look at the flies! Then all of sudden they followed in his train. And the flute-player, with his rats, vanished forever. Thus. [*He strides out into the light. Shrieking, the* Furies *fling themselves after him*]

CURTAIN

ness.

you to unbar that door.

a few inches.*]

pieces!"*]

lead into your veins.

him.*]

CURTAIN

Modern Drama in England and Ireland

Modern Drama in England and Ireland

The two major events to take place since the early eighteen-nineties in the English-speaking theatre across the Atlantic were the modernization of the British drama and the birth of the Irish theatre. The two developments occurred within a decade of each other, and each came as the climax of efforts to meet a strongly felt need. England had yet to develop an effective modern drama at the beginning of the eighteen-nineties; Ireland had yet to create a theatre of national character at the start of the twentieth century. Both nations were faced with the challenge of modern times, and, fortunately, both could look to Continental Europe for inspiration.

Beginning with the eighteen-fifties, indeed, Englishmen had reason to be envious when they looked across the narrow stretch of water that separated them from the Continent. They saw, first, a European theatre increasingly supplied after 1850 with a drama overdidactic but concerned with facts of contemporary life, when composed by the younger Dumas, and commonplace in thought but vigorously objective, when written by Emile Augier. By 1879, moreover, it was evident that a giant had arisen in the north. Ibsen, the Norwegian iconoclast, was challenging the old order in both society and the theatre with *A Doll's House*. Simultaneously, Zola was spreading the gospel of a new dramatic art that would be as concerned with reality and as free from artifice as the great novels of the century. A new stage, energetic and forthright, was making its presence felt. By 1890, in fact, the Continent possessed an impressive body of social and psychological drama irradiated by the modern mind and spirit. Ibsen had by then added *Ghosts, An Enemy of the People, The Wild Duck, Rosmersholm, The Lady from the Sea,* and *Hedda Gabler* to the modern repertory. The irascible but provocative genius August Strindberg, also from the north, had contributed *The Father, Comrades, Miss Julie,* and *The Creditor.* Henry Becque, in Paris, had delivered two witheringly honest studies of reality, *The Vultures* and *The Parisian Woman.* The Russian theatre was moving toward a profoundly human realistic drama after Tolstoy's *The Power of Darkness,* written in 1886. The German theatre had discovered Gerhart Hauptmann in 1889. Moreover, a "free theatre," dedicated to modernism, was gaining a following in Paris and Berlin; André Antoine had established his Théâtre Libre in 1887, and Otto Brahm his Freie Bühne in 1889. Both theatres were producing significant studies of society and character. Could the theatre in England remain insulated from the modern world to which the nation had made so many contributions in industry, science, and thought?

By 1900, moreover, a new art theatre had arisen in Europe, a theatre dedicated to the recovery of imagination and poetry or poetic nuance. Symbolist and neoromantic drama—written by newcomers such as Maeterlinck and Rostand, and even by those pioneers of realism Ibsen and Strindberg—brought spiritual power and enchantment to the stage. A second challenge faced the British Isles. Could England and Ireland succeed in serving beauty as well as truth?

Before either truth or beauty could be served, however, the stage in England had to shed its contented insularity and the stage in Ireland had to be placed on firm foundations. Considerable exertion would be necessary on the part of progressive dramatic critics, playwrights, actors, and stage producers in the British Isles. The magnitude of the task can be realized today only by casting a backward glance at the Victorian period.

VICTORIAN DRAMA

If it is too much to say that British drama was an arid waste between the time of Sheridan and the advent of Wilde and Shaw, there is no doubt that the theatre in England suffered a century of decline between 1780 and 1880 except for the triumphs of certain great actors, chiefly in Shakespearean drama. England, once the soil of distinguished dramatists, not to mention the greatest of all dramatists, failed to develop a single playwright of real importance. Sentimental comedy, strongly favored by the growing middle classes, who frowned upon levity and demanded moral uplift, supplanted the wit of Jonson, Congreve, Gay, and Sheridan. At best, the comic muse was served by farces devoid of any sort of distinction except facility in pandering to complacent minds. And tragedy, the high art in which England had once excelled, was displaced by romantic thrillers accompanied by background music, giving currency to the term "melodrama."

The theatre remained almost exclusively in the hands of hack writers until the last quarter of the century. It was dedicated to melodrama, farce, adaptations of plays by second-rate Continental authors, and spectacles—except, of course, for Shakespearean plays, which were, however, mangled by the actor-managers. The nadir was reached in the mid-Victorian period, which experienced many social and intellectual stirrings in directions other than that of playmaking. The theatre, dependent upon the patronage of the average man and generally promoted by average men hungry for a profit, lagged far behind science, social thought, and even the novel. Darwin, Huxley, Mill, Carlyle, Arnold, Ruskin, Dickens, Thackeray, George Eliot, and Emily Brontë were fully active at the time. The greatness of mid-Victorian literature lay in its protest against the prevailing thought and conduct. But the theatre, complacently on good terms with its public, would have no traffic with the critics of society; it gave no indication, in fact, of being aware of their existence for many decades. As late as 1879, Matthew Arnold could lament with absolute justice that "in England we have no modern drama at all." The date is significant; it was the year of Ibsen's *A Doll's House*.

If we are to comprehend the significance of the battle waged and won for a modern drama in England, we must understand the "Victorian Compromise" reflected and served by the theatre. The Victorians had made some excellent adjustments between reality and social convenience, and these were not to be publicly questioned by young people, irresponsible artists, or mere entertainers. In politics and in society, the adjustment was, as the historian Carlton J. H. Hayes declared, "between democracy and oligarchy, whereby the bourgeoisie enjoyed political rights and left the lower classes to shift for themselves. It was tacitly assumed that if a man was poor, it was due either to his own fault or to inexorable economic laws." In time, the suffrage was extended, especially by the Second Reform Bill of 1867; in time, too, social legislation bettered the condition of the laboring classes. But class distinctions could not be removed by fiat, and social legislation continued to be frowned upon by the average middle-class and upper-class mind, leaving much work for reformers and a great deal of provocation for Bernard Shaw's wit and indignation even in the twentieth century.

The average Victorian, frightened by the rise of scientific and skeptical thought, raised his defenses of convention higher than ever and endeavored to make them as impregnable as possible. Manners, sentiment, family life, the rearing of children, public education, morals, and religion were fortified against invasion by the modern spirit; and the strength of the fortifications may be measured by the great efforts that men such as Bernard Shaw and Samuel Butler had to make to breach them. A bargain was struck with religion, so that it would not interfere with business. And a bargain was struck with Darwinism, so that man might still enjoy a divine dispensation while using the Darwinian theory of "the struggle for existence" in nature as justification for unrestricted competition in society.

At the same time, improvement could be discerned in the evolution of society, assuring the Victorian gentleman that a divine purpose was at work. Optimism became a cult as England acquired more and more wealth and industry continued to make remarkable advances. Tennyson, taking his cue from the growing railway system, saw society in 1842 "spinning down the ringing grooves of change." Commerce was also binding the nations together, and he felt moved to express popular expectations of a "Parliament of man" and a "Federation of the world," held in "fretful awe" by the "common sense of most." England had a constitutional government which did not interfere very much with private behavior and business. "Liberalism" prevailed in the land. And it was a central doctrine of the Liberal party that so long as government refrained from interfering with the natural law of supply and demand and with the liberty of the individual, even in the case of child labor, all would turn out for the best, thanks to reason and self-interest. One need not be disturbed by the way of the world. Robert Browning's Pippa, in 1841, was blissfully certain that "God's in his heaven—all's right with the world."

In "wandering between two worlds, one dead, the other powerless to be born," Matthew Arnold was the exceptional man. The average Victorian was prepared to make the best of all the worlds open to him. Arnold was disturbed by the conflict between science and religion, but the ordinary man, having made a convenient distinction between the weekday and Sunday, found no reason to be distressed. Arnold was appalled by the "Philistinism" of the materialistic middle classes, and Carlyle thundered against the "dismal science" of *laissez-faire* economics. But Arnold could be ignored as an intellectual and a snob; Carlyle, as a dyspeptic or a prophet. If the Victorian needed a symbolic public figure, he had the best one of all at Windsor Castle, and she would never let him down. The good Queen remained loyal to the memory of Prince Albert and to the teachings of her tutors. She forbade smoking on the premises, recommended a whipping for advocates of "women's rights," and was "not amused" by the sallies of Gilbert and Sullivan. She was a monument—as solid as Nelson's statue—to the unwavering virtue of the race.

Even Victoria's poet laureate, however, came to realize that "the old order changeth, yielding place to new." Tennyson's optimistic view of the age, expressed in *Locksley Hall,* in 1842, actually changed to the refrain of "Chaos! Cosmos!" in *Locksley Hall Sixty Years After,* in 1886. The political stirrings grew more pronounced; the intellectual currents, more tempestuous. The voices of Carlyle and Arnold could be heard louder in the land and were joined by other voices. John Henry Newman and others clamored against a religion of accommodation. Ruskin condemned a society notable for the ugliness of its cities and factory towns. "There is no Wealth," he declared, "but life; life, including all its powers of love, of joy, of admiration. That country is the richest which nourishes the greatest number of noble and happy human beings." So spoke the professor of art at Oxford whose reverence for beauty became a social passion, leading him to spend the whole of his fortune of two hundred thousand pounds on the creation of a model industrial community, the Guild of St. George, in 1871. An esthetic revolt, which had been taking shape since 1848, when Dante Gabriel Rossetti founded the Pre-Raphaelite Brotherhood, reinforced the moral protests with its call for art *versus* utility and refined pleasure *versus* grubbing for money. The poets—Rossetti, Swinburne, and others—became "fleshly" when they were not directly involved with social problems. And "art for art's sake," whether supported by the Pre-Raphaelites and Walter Pater or promoted by the later artistic rebels of the eighteen-nineties, was itself a protest. The campaign being waged was the same as that of the philosophers and social thinkers, whose tools were logic and statistics. The poets were contemporaries of John Stuart Mill, then writing in behalf of feminine emancipation and elaborating his "utilitarian" philosophy of "the greatest good for the greatest number," and of Karl Marx, then drafting his *Das Kapital* in the British Museum.

A new dispensation came to the theatre, slowly and unsteadily, it is true, and with many accommodations, but with increasing effect. The story of the progress of the stage has a familiar ring by now, but each advance had the startling effect of an air-raid siren when modernity seemed little short of disastrous to the guardians of convention.

In rapid summary, we may take note of the coming of new dramatists, of their struggle for acceptance by the theatrical managements, and of their growing success with audiences. The first advances were tentative and qualified, hedged about with circumspection; the later ones were brazen and captured attention with the vigor of their assault on conventional behavior and sentiment.

THE FORERUNNERS OF MODERN DRAMA

Credit is usually given first to the mid-Victorian playwright T. W. Robertson, who was something of a prodigy to his age because he took realistic notice of the "cash nexus," or money consideration, in personal relationships such as love and marriage. His first important piece, *Society*, appeared in 1865 at the successful comedienne Marie Wilton's little Queen's Theatre, in London. Conventional in plot, with the hero winning love and fortune at the end, *Society* nevertheless inched toward the modern drama. Characters spoke openly of the significance of money in life and in marriage, calling marriage "a union mutually advantageous," and regarding "honor" as synonymous with "not being bankrupt." Tom Robertson's *Caste* (1867), although feeble in characterization, took notice of the subject implied by its title. It is true that Robertson accepted the stratification of society and deplored social climbing. But he was the first British playwright to look at the life around him and present some of its facets on the stage, although he is apt to be remembered most often for favoring the use of real doorknobs in realistic scenery. Late in the eighteen-eighties, the young Bernard Shaw, then England's most outspoken drama critic, could still treat him with respect, because it was not until two decades after the production of *Caste* that a playwright was to go

beyond Robertson in veracity and concern with contemporary realities.

The interim is notable only for the plays and libretti of W. S. Gilbert, a professed political conservative who nevertheless possessed a genius for making breaches in the Victorian barricade. Especially in his collaborations with Arthur Sullivan, beginning in 1878 with *H. M. S. Pinafore*, this irrepressible humorist played gadfly to Victorian society in a manner as pointed as it was enchanting. But Gilbert-and-Sullivan musical comedy, delightful as it is, was a special department, requiring an almost freakish talent and a genius for poetic nonsense. The Savoy operettas, although they may have left reverberations in the spacious brain of Shaw and in the smaller ones of other British playwrights, could not revitalize the nonmusical stage.

It was the European theatre that accelerated the still lagging rate of progress. In the eighteen-nineties, the French sources, upon which English playwrights and managements had relied for much of their material, began to disappear. The English theatre could not possibly adapt and stage for its public the pungent naturalistic plays of Zola, Becque, and their followers; it had to rely upon home-grown products. At the same time, the British playwrights could not remain entirely impervious to developments abroad. In 1873, Edmund Gosse had drawn attention to Ibsen in a widely read magazine article, and a translation of Ibsen's *Emperor and Galilean* appeared in 1876. A questionable adaptation of *A Doll's House* was performed in 1884. William Archer translated *Pillars of Society* in 1880 and published it in 1888, and Karl Marx's gifted daughter, Eleanor Marx-Aveling, followed suit with translations of *Ghosts* and *An Enemy of the People*. A volume containing the latter three plays appeared in England in 1888. It sold well and attracted a good deal of attention. The following year, Archer's painstaking, if hardly inspired, translation of *A Doll's House* was produced at the Novelty Theatre in London, with the well-known Shakespearean actress Janet Achurch as Nora. The play had a good run and aroused much controversy in the press. *Pillars of Society* had a single performance about a month later. In 1890–1891, a five-volume edition of Ibsen's plays was published in England; it contained all his prose plays from *The Vikings* to *Hedda Gabler* and was, in fact, the first collection of his works to be published anywhere. *The Lady from the Sea* appeared in two separate translations in 1890; a biography of Ibsen was published at about the same time; and Shaw delivered a celebrated lecture on "Socialism in Ibsen" before the Fabian Society in July 1890. The following year, *Rosmersholm* was produced at the Vaudeville Theatre in London and was roundly denounced in the newspapers. *Ghosts* was scheduled for public presentation, only to draw suppression from the censor. It was given a private performance, however, by the Independent Theatre on March 13, 1891, and was defended in print by Archer. At about the same time, Shaw expanded his Fabian lecture into the famous book-length essay *The Quintessence of Ibsenism.* Then *Hedda Gabler* won success at the Vaudeville Theatre, where it was produced by the actress-manager Elizabeth Robins, who played Hedda. Finally, in 1893, the Independent Theatre, the experimental venture of J. T. Grein which had introduced Shaw to the theatre a year before with *Widowers' Houses,* successfully revived *Ghosts.* The battle for Ibsenism was won.

Now it was up to the British playwrights to make the most of the victory. Shaw did. But there were circumspect, long-practicing playwrights who took profitable advantage of the altered situation in the British theatre by expediently compromising. They forged no thunderbolts like Ibsen's but gave imitations of them that provided novelty without danger. Today their work seems mild enough to make us wonder what the shouting they provoked was all about. In the 'eighties and the 'nineties, however, their work was very "advanced," except to Shaw, then functioning as a dramatic critic, who was able to penetrate beneath the surface of their pretensions to courage.

The first of the pseudo Ibsenites was Henry Arthur Jones (1851–1929), a crusty but well-intentioned gentleman of the stage who considered himself a pioneer. Jones, who had won early success with the usual pabulum, had become sufficiently conscious of Ibsenism in 1884 to collaborate (with Henry Herman) on an adaptation of *A Doll's House* and to write *Saints and Sinners,* a play then considered a slashing attack on Philistinism. Although it was a melodrama of seduction, injured innocence, and ultimately triumphant virtue, Jones's drama exposed religious hypocrisy with its story of the persecution of an upright pastor by members of his congregation. In 1889, Jones reviewed the subject of marriage with more than ordinary severity, in *The Middleman.* As late as 1896, he shocked his public by showing a clergyman in the toils of illicit passion, in *Michael and His Lost Angel,* although the play ended in repentance and expiation on the part of the clerical hero. With *Mrs. Dane's Defence,* produced in 1900, Jones still thought himself bold, because he had drawn a more or less sympathetic portrait of a woman with a "past." In a few earlier plays, climaxed by two well-written comedies of manners, *The Liars* and *Dolly Reforming Herself,* he had tilted a lance at British foibles and insincerities. For a man of sharp temperament and good intentions, Jones was remarkably sensible of an obligation to please the public and to offend it as little as possible. Late in life he wrote Brander Matthews that, although he had created some ninety plays and had helped to move things along, only four or five times had he been able to write the play he "should have written if the conditions of the English theatre had been as easy for the dramatist as they are today."

Equally willing to move with the tide of the new realism and equally resolved not to let it sweep him out to sea was Jones's contemporary Arthur Wing Pinero, who ultimately achieved a baronetcy for his facile playwriting. After composing successful farces in the 'eighties, none more charming than *The Magistrate* (1885), he too became speciously progressive, and again it was the fallen-woman theme that gave a British playwright some semblance of modernity. Pinero's *The Second Mrs. Tanqueray* was produced in 1893 and heralded as a work of remarkable realism by the British public, which had as yet only small acquaintance with the modern drama. A woman with a past was Pinero's heroine, and he went so far as to sympathize with her efforts to rehabilitate herself by marriage to a gentleman. The only fly in the ointment was the fact that Pinero proceeded to show that the effort was doomed to failure. He was not entirely unconvincing and he was comparatively free from sentimental tear-shedding; he gave the impression that inexorable fate was working itself out in the real world and in a real character. Between ventures into comedy of manners such as *The Gay Lord Quex,* Pinero composed a number of additional social and character studies, *The Notorious Mrs. Ebbsmith* (1896), *Iris* (1901), and *Mid-Channel* (1909)— plays that might have seemed moderately advanced if Shaw had not already delivered himself of *Candida, Mrs. Warren's Profession,* and *Man and Superman.* The truth is that Pinero retained a quite Victorian mind to the very end. Only his comedy *The Thunderbolt* (1908) suggested the capacity for critical scrutiny that characterizes a truly modern playwright, and even here Pinero relied on the hoary device of a lost will to energize his action. As long ago as 1895, Shaw called Pinero "a humble and somewhat belated follower of the novelists of the middle of the nineteenth century," and this opinion seems even more justified today than it did then.

Pinero, along with Jones and others, might have been described by phrenologists as a man endowed with a large bump of reverence. It was an anatomical feature entirely absent in Wilde and Shaw, who were able to bedevil society with their irreverence. Pinero and Jones wrote a number of "problem plays," but these were cautious and narrowly circumscribed excursions into the modern world. They belonged to the age of Dumas *fils* and Augier rather than to the world of Ibsen and Shaw. This is so not only because Pinero and Jones adhered to the "well-made play" formula of plot construction but because, to paraphrase George Meredith, they fiddled harmonics on the strings of domesticity. The gifted professor-critic Gilbert Norwood did not depart greatly from the truth when he wrote that "your pseudo-advanced writer invariably reveals his caliber by this assumption that the 'Problem play' must treat of marital infidelity; there is only one sin—the Decalogue has become a monologue."

SHAW AND THE MODERN THEATRE

The first playwright to aerate the British theatre was Oscar Wilde, even though he brought something less than a serious interest and intention. Plays were for him a ready means of augmenting his income and discharging his exuberance, so that he was content with conventional plots and trashy formulas of playwriting. But his delight in baiting society and his irrepressible wit made him the first brilliant writer of comedy of manners after Sheridan—if it is not indeed with Sheridan's seventeenth-century masters, Wycherley and Congreve, that we must associate him. Wilde first shocked British sensibilities with the decadent biblical one-acter *Salomé*, originally written in French for Sarah Bernhardt; in the same year (1892), he wrote *Lady Windermere's Fan*, the first of three problem plays which made thesis drama something more than an exercise in moralization—a word that Wilde would have dreaded beyond all words. In *Lady Windermere's Fan*, as well as in *A Woman of No Importance* (1893) and *An Ideal Husband* (1895), Wilde blasted away with a carefree air at Philistinism and social hypocrisy. "A man who moralizes is usually a hypocrite, and a woman who moralizes is invariably plain," says his Cecil Graham, in *Lady Windermere's Fan*. In the three problem plays, Wilde himself indulged in some moralizing, but only at the expense of conventional morality. Like George S. Kaufman and his colleagues in the American theatre of the nineteen-twenties, Wilde, who anticipated the "wisecrack" on a more literary level, was able to serve convention and sophistication in the same breath. The plot satisfied the ordinary requirements of playgoing while the acid of mocking commentary dissolved conventionality in the play and in the playgoer. Finally, in 1895, Wilde wrote the gayest farce in the English language, *The Importance of Being Earnest*. Farce is usually the very antithesis of drama of ideas. This was not the case here, since the epigrams in conjunction with the extravagant complications comprised a perfect reversal of Victorian principles. Wilde upset the Victorian apple-cart, and so great were his skill and good humor that he made his public enjoy watching the apples roll.

If his incorrigible laziness and ill-fated quarrel with the Marquess of Queensbury had not interfered with his career, Wilde might have continued to entertain the British public in ways to which it had not been accustomed for a century or more. His disappearance from the theatre, however, was less than calamitous, for Shaw was now at hand with greater intellect and energy—in fact, with an alto-gether superior equipment for exorcising the ghost of Victorianism. This was, however, only one of the tasks Shaw imposed on himself. Iconoclast and prophet, humorist and social critic, this emigrant from Ireland subsumed all previous and contemporary efforts to modernize the British stage, giving British drama a status that will not easily diminish so long as his plays are read and performed.

Shaw's achievement stems for the most part from the unique quality of his genius, from his mastery of language, and from the marvelous play of his mind on the human scene. He had a dialectical skill given to few men who have written dramatic literature, a flair for showmanship, a feeling for acting and stagecraft, and an ability to make even discussion vibrate with drama—qualities which were not always apparent to Shaw's contemporaries. His genius consisted also in a capacity for characterization and in an intense sincerity, both of which were often overlooked or minimized by his early critics. Shaw's individuality, already the subject of many books, cannot be summarized briefly without being miserably shortchanged, and the savor of his special creativeness cannot, indeed, be transcribed by criticism that does not help itself generously to his own words. But what is easily enough established for the purpose of a perspective on theatrical history is the nature of Shaw's contribution to the rise of a modern drama in England, or, for that matter, elsewhere in the Western world.

Achieving a modern drama was never a simple matter of filling plays with realistic details of background and conduct. If it had been, Dumas *fils* and Augier, Jones and Pinero, and any number of other second-rate playwrights of our time would be modern and important. Like Ibsen, Shaw was aware that realism of detail was less important than the application of intelligence to reality. Any conscientious observer can supply the facts, but only an acutely intelligent person can interpret them incisively and significantly—and only a talented person can make drama of them. The true realist in Shaw was the thinker, not the reporter.

Like Ibsen too, but in a livelier spirit, Shaw was able to sublimate the *facts* of society and of individual conduct into *ideas*. He brought analysis and discussion into the drama of the period after 1890 and gave pre-eminence to the drama of ideas, doing this equally well in tragedy, comedy, and extravaganza. There have been only four types of comedy in the world: Aristophanic comedy, comedy of manners, romantic comedy, and comedy of ideas. All but the last were the creation of past ages. Comedy of ideas is the only modern contribution to the history of high comedy, and it is largely Shaw's creation.

Shaw opened the gates of the theatre to a flood of challenging new ideas. When he entered the theatre he brought with him Schopenhauer, Nietzsche, Samuel Butler, Lamarck, Henry George, Karl Marx, the Webbs, and other redoubtable figures who were shaping modern thought and life. He made the discursive drama possible and often triumphant, which is no small accomplishment. Nor was it an unimportant one, since it enabled the drama to keep abreast of happenings beyond the footlights. In an age of unprecedented dissemination of ideas and of growing conflicts in which these ideas played significant parts, Shaw's achievement came to be appreciated more and more; it amounted to a vitalization of playwriting beside which the contributions of writers such as Jones and Pinero shrank into insignificance. Even Ibsen had not kept abreast of the modern world to the same degree.

According to Shaw, an Ibsen play consisted of *exposition, situation,* and *discussion.* Whether or not this was an accurate analysis of Ibsen's dramaturgy, it applied well enough to Shaw's plays and to those of some of his disciples, especially Granville-Barker. Freely construed, the Shavian dramaturgic formula serves, in any case, to point up for us an important cleavage between the new drama and the old. The old, tried, and indeed still often practiced formula may be said to be: exposition, development (with a view to knotting situations into a major complication or crisis), and resolution or dénouement (literally, the disentangling or untying of the plot). Substitute the principle of exposition, situation, and discussion, and the result is a type of drama that prevails less by hypnotizing its audience than by enlightening or at least stimulating it to mental activity. The latter theory of writing is obviously the very opposite of Wilkie Collins' prescription for storytelling: "Make 'em laugh; make 'em weep; make 'em wait." Factitious suspense vanishes in truly modern drama. Asked whether he would care to set down three rules for playwriting, Oscar Wilde facetiously declared, "The first is not to follow the methods of Mr. Henry [Arthur] Jones, and the second and third are to the same effect." Although Wilde, for whom plot was a mere convenience, himself followed Jones's methods in most plays, his quip sums up the dramaturgic revolt of Shaw and many other moderns, from Becque and Ibsen to Saroyan and Brecht.

To employ "exposition, situation, and discussion," well exemplified by Shaw in such diverse pieces as *Candida, Man and Superman,* and *Saint Joan,* one would need a "new" kind of dialogue and a "new" logic. The dialogue must possess sparkle and intellectual vigor—qualities not of course really new when we remember Aristophanes, Shakespeare, Molière, and other worthies, but fresh in idiom and content. Wilde summed up a distinction between the old and new styles of dialogue when a crash of scenery interrupted a rehearsal of his comedy *A Woman of No Importance.* Stopping the rehearsal, Wilde told the company, "Ladies and gentlemen. Pray, don't be alarmed. The crash you have just heard is merely some of Mr. Jones's dialogue that

has fallen flat." As for logic, it is true that so competent a guardian of the trusty old craftsmanship as Pinero once declared, "Cause—effect! Cause—effect! Two of the most substantial parts of the fabric which go to make up a fine play are logic and intuition. Without logic you cannot construct a play. Without intuition you cannot write it." Nevertheless, the logic Pinero had in mind was not the logic of Shaw and his successors. Pinero meant only the credible motivation of behavior within the play or the cohesion of successive situations and actions within the boundaries of a plot. The Ibsen-Shaw school added a logic of social reality. It implicated the *world of the characters and not merely the world of the play*—that is, it considered the milieu from which human beings acquire their manners and beliefs, their problems, their social status and livelihood, and their ideas. The modern use of logic involved, in addition, the free play of critical reason on habitual life and thought, the pleasure of keen argument, the delight in the exchange or conflict of opinions. Logic, in short, was a drab servant in the older theatre. It was a bright mistress or clever wife in the new theatre. And Shaw was a past master of the art of dialectics—which means, for theatrical purposes, that he found drama in ideas. It is not surprising that his work seemed undramatic to those who found drama only in bedroom situations.

Shaw, we may say in conclusion, also discovered a new poetry for the theatre, although members of the old guard found it the very antithesis of poetry. In a superficial sense, they were right. The dialogue was athletic, intellectual prose instead of prose dressed in the gaudy furbelows of Victorian stage conversation. The point of view was often mundane, for the dramatist claimed an interest in sociological fact and insisted on an underlying economic situation. He penetrated into the painfully prosaic substructure of the superstructure of manners and morals. "Karl Marx," Shaw declared on the occasion of one of his many birthdays, "made a man of me," and Shaw was bent upon proving this in his plays, as well as in his prefaces and tracts, assigning a decisive role to economics in works as diverse as *Widowers' Houses, Mrs. Warren's Profession, Pygmalion,* and *Major Barbara.* Shaw brought politics, too, into the theatre—not romantic flourishes against tyranny, which were as old as Schiller and the young Goethe, nor the superficial politics of intrigue successfully used in Scribe's classic *The Glass of Water* (which even Nazi Germany found innocuous enough to certify for production), but politics in the serious sense in which it was used by Plato and Aristotle, Metternich and Disraeli, Marx and Lenin —and Shakespeare. This kind of political thought, a hard and cold reality whether it appears in the great discussion between Warwick and the Bishop, in *Saint Joan,* or in the decisions of King Magnus, in *The Apple Cart,* was prose to those who confused sentiment with poetry. Shaw was the last person in the world whom the Victorians would have called a poet.

How one could nevertheless claim for him the title of poet can be seen in Shaw's fine artistry: his cadences, imagery, and power of metaphor; his brilliant precision, which recalls Dryden, even as his full-throated rhetoric recalls the King James Bible, Bunyan, and Milton; his moral passion, without which he held life was not worth living; and, for all his glitter of jibe and paradox, his greateartedness. The analyst, realist, and wit was also a man of prophetic disposition who was convinced, with his Father Keegan of *John Bull's Other Island,* that "every dream is a prophecy: every jest is an earnest in the womb of Time." Somehow, through discursive writing, handsprings of argument, bouts with history, coliusions with the "Life Force," and the rest of his sleight of hand, Shaw managed to transform modern reality into vision and passion. In all his vocal masquerade through the disenchanting forest of fact, one could hear Father Keegan's profession of faith: the dream of "a country where the State is the Church and the Church the people: three in one and one in three"; "a commonwealth in which work is play and play is life: three in one and one in three"; "a temple in which the priest is the worshipper and the worshipper the worshipped: three in one and one in three"; "a godhead in which all life is human and all humanity divine: three in one and one in three"—in short, the dream of the poet, with or without the benefit of economics and dialectics.

More significantly than any of his contemporaries, Shaw revealed the possibilities of a poetry of prose in the theatre. Laying claim to nothing more than lucidity of thought and expression, Shaw nonetheless demonstrated that statement can be imaginative and incandescent. In this respect, too, he epitomized a fact of modern literature—namely, the un-Victorian realization that poetry is not synonymous with ornamentation. It was a realization inherent in the verse of Robert Frost, T. S. Eliot, and the later Yeats, and it was also a characteristic feature of such diverse plays as those of Chekhov, Pirandello, Lorca, and Eliot. Genuine poet-playwrights of the past had, of course, instinctively adhered to the principle that poetry was essence, not decoration; this is as apparent in the pages of Sophocles and Racine as in those of later writers such as the Ibsen of *Peer Gynt.* But the prettifying of sentiment and evasion of reality had been a chronic obsession of the playwrights challenged by Ibsen and Shaw, resulting in a pseudo poetry of both verse and prose and therefore in pseudo literature. In Shaw's writing, prose was good prose (none better had been written in English after Swift); and when it became metamorphosed into poetry, it was honest poetry. That has been the ideal of all true modernists of the drama; it is largely what we mean when we say it is characteristic of the modern stage that playwrights began

once more to write plays that could qualify as literature. For this reason, as well as because their work had a content of thought, playwrights began to be pre-eminent in the theatre instead of playing roles secondary to those of actors and managers. In this respect, too, Shaw epitomized a new dispensation. No other playwright who was not also a stage director or actor claimed as much authority and had as much to say about the production of his plays. What passed for an idiosyncrasy, if not for vanity and arrogance, in Shaw was actually a portent of the modern playwright's arrival at voting age in the theatre.

Finally, it is plain that Shaw revealed a capacity for imagination that only poets possess. He could re-create history imaginatively in such plays as *Caesar and Cleopatra, Androcles and the Lion,* and *The Devil's Disciple.* He could employ fantasy with fine effect, in the Don Juan episode of *Man and Superman,* in the epilogue of *Saint Joan,* and in less successful plays. He was never reluctant to invent unlikely situations whenever his agile mind needed a fable. Nor did he hesitate to employ symbolism, notably in *Heartbreak House.* For a man who stressed the bleak realities of economics and practical politics, he took singular liberties with commonplace fact. As a thinker, Shaw took great pride in his "realism." As an artist, however, he refused to allow himself to be fettered to realistic technique and style. He retained the right to be buoyant, free, and inventive; and there was joyous creativity in his blood and sinew. He played the prophet and imp at will, and sometimes he was both. He struck a sober attitude or cut a fanciful caper, and in either case scored a point. Shaw, in short, was the master of reality and not its slave. In this respect, as well as in the wide range of his artistry, he belongs to the small number of dramatists to whom true greatness can be attributed.

THE OTHER MODERNISTS

Not everything that constitutes the modernity of Shaw's drama could be found in the modernity of his fellow playwrights. Shaw's work stood, and still stands, as the summation of their separate and fragmentary contributions to the British theatre. It has been convenient here to touch upon his multifaceted work as the measure of many of the individual efforts that add up to the modern British drama. But it was through the accumulation of plays by others as well as by Shaw between the eighteen-nineties and the beginning of the First World War that England acquired a modern stage. It took some time before Shaw's plays, barred by censorship and by the British commercial managements and opposed by conservative critics and playgoers, could win a large audience. And it took years before Shaw proved as acceptable to the great public as several of his fellow playwrights, whose merit was more transparent. Time has dealt as harshly with them as it has been kind to Shaw, despite their early success. They were more modest in their ventures and claims, more cautious, or more congenial, and consequently more persuasive.

There were, before 1914, a few writers such as Jones, Pinero, and C. Haddon Chambers who continued to take cautious steps in the new direction—and the steps began to add up. There were also the minor Shaws. One of these was the short-lived Stanley Houghton (1881–1913), whose *Hindle Wakes* presented a poor girl refusing to be made honest by a rich weakling after an illicit week end. (Insisting on a "single standard," she explains to right-thinking people that she doesn't care for the man any more than "a fellow cares for any girl he happens to pick up.") Another moderate Shavian was St. John Hankin (born in 1860 and a suicide in 1909), whose *Last of the De Mullins* concerns a woman who defies her family's code of honor by rejecting the father of her illegitimate child and going into business. Also a Shavian was the brilliant actor and producer (later a superb Shakespearean critic) Harley Granville-Barker (1877–1946), who wrote incisive, if not always engrossing, attacks on Victorian convention such as *The Madras House* (1910) and antiromantic dramas such as *The Voysey Inheritance* (1905) and *Waste* (1907).

England also acquired its twentieth-century quota of naturalists and writers of new problem plays with a naturalistic coloring. Elizabeth Baker contributed an affecting drama of lower-middle-class life, *Chains* (1909), to show how "little men" are entrapped by environment and fateful circumstances. Githa Sowerby, three years later, provided the powerful middle-class drama *Rutherford and Son,* set in the home of a domestic tyrant and old-fashioned industrialist. Writers of one-act realistic plays also began to multiply, the best of them being Harold Brighouse. The growing cities, especially Manchester, provided much matter for slices of life from twentieth-century industry.

At the other extreme stood the dramatists of country life, no longer painting idyllic pictures but taking note of the harsher aspects of the countryside from Yorkshire to Scotland, sometimes employing unlovely dialects, sometimes noting the effects of industrialization. And combining the starkest naturalism with eerie feeling, producing a kind of "Gothic naturalism," the poet John Masefield sublimated village naturalism, actually as old as George Crabbe's eighteenth-century verse tales, into the near masterpiece *The Tragedy of Nan,* in 1908. It was a brutal drama that belongs to the genre of peasant naturalism best realized in Tolstoy's *The Power of Darkness.* It treated country life in the spirit of Hauptmann and of Erskine Caldwell, exposing its meanness. But it was also more richly charged with poetic power than the plays of those who, like Stephen Phillips, James Elroy Flecker,

Gordon Bottomley, Lascelles Abercrombie, and John Drinkwater, tried to revive the poetic drama in England with historical and legendary subjects.

Present, besides, was John Galsworthy (1867–1933), the strongest and most admired social naturalist, who cast aside a lyric talent (visible in the long story *The Apple Tree*) in order to serve truth and conscience. Beginning with *The Silver Box,* Galsworthy exposed the inequities in British life with dogged persistence, but also with gentlemanly equanimity and detachment. His claims as a naturalist rested on his fidelity to colloquial dialogue, his firm grasp of character, and his willingness to see all sides of a question. This equableness, apparent from his first plays (*The Silver Box,* in 1906, *Joy,* in 1909, and the class-conflict drama *Strife,* in 1910) to his last completed play (*Escape,* in 1929), tended to diminish the force of his writing and was perhaps more a limitation than a virtue. But at the time of their first productions, when their subjects and analyses were fresh, Galsworthy's plays made the British theatre a living force. And beneath the moss that has since then gathered on some of them still lies some vital undergrowth. Galsworthy was appreciated, and can still be respected, for the solidity of his dramaturgy, for his restraint and discipline, and for the authenticity of his characters. "A human being," he declared, "is the best plot there is. . . . He is organic. And so it must be with a play." Galsworthy was no more of an iconoclast in dramaturgy than he was in opinion. He wrote, "A good plot is that sure edifice which slowly rises out of the interplay of circumstance on temperament, and temperament on circumstance, within the enclosing atmosphere of an idea." He could not have expressed his intention better. It is plain that he acknowledged the force of ideas in the theatre. It is also evident that he was not bent upon creating a new kind of drama and refrained from breaking the mold of plot. But he made the old kind of drama sufficiently better, sufficiently more persuasive and lifelike, to make it seem significantly new in a theatre largely devoted, then as now, to fabrication rather than to life.

It would have been too much to expect that the British public (or, for that matter, any public) could subsist exclusively on the sober realism of the British playwrights. England continued to produce musical pieces, farces, and light comedies—pleasantries, indeed, of all kinds, whose modernity lay on the surface. Even in this airy world there were, however, capers of less than Victorian circumspection, and the master who cut them best was James M. Barrie, who was idolized by the public and seen in perspective only by the discriminating few. Sentimentalist though he was, he was also an ironist of sorts before 1914. A cynic at heart, he had a good eye for the starch in a stuffed shirt, as may be noted in *The Twelve-Pound Look, The Admirable Crichton,* and *What Every Woman Knows.* With these pieces, as well as with that most "escapist" of plays *Peter Pan,* this idiosyncratic son of a Scottish weaver played the agile imp and prankster in the years before the First World War. Shaw the gadfly still stings. Barrie seems a rather tired Puck these days. But Puck too had his role to play in the early years of this century.

NEW THEATRE FOR OLD

With Shaw leading the procession and the others marching or mincing behind, then, the British stage came of age before 1914.

The Independent Theatre, founded in 1891 as a small subscription organization with the help of the critic William Archer, could produce plays "privately" and was therefore free from censorship by the Lord Chamberlain's office. After its production of Ibsen's *Ghosts,* the Independent Theatre discovered Shaw as a playwright when Grein asked him to write a play for the organization and Shaw obliged by completing *Widowers' Houses* (originally intended as a collaboration with Archer). Satirizing Grein's enemies, Archer asked derisively, "Who is this Dutchman who dares to be dissatisfied with our honest, healthy, comfortable, fat, and flourishing drama?" But Grein enjoyed the support of some significant figures in the British world: George Meredith and Thomas Hardy among the novelists, Pinero and Jones among the playwrights, Frank Harris, A. B. Walkley, and Shaw among the journalists.

Seven years of intermittent activity was all that the Independent Theatre enjoyed. But when it closed, in 1897, it had twenty-six productions to its credit. By that time Shaw had completed *The Philanderer, Mrs. Warren's Profession, Arms and the Man, You Never Can Tell,* and *Candida.* As Shaw has written, "the search for native dramatic masterpieces, pursued by Mr. Grein with the ardor and innocence of a foreigner, was so complete a failure that at the end of 1892 he had not produced a single original piece of any magnitude by an English author." After 1897, the acuteness of "this humiliating national emergency" was over, but by then the Independent Theatre had expired.

Henceforth the West End, London's Broadway, was to prove more congenial to the modernists and the experimental groups were to grow in power in influence. Two years after the demise of Grein's little theatre, the Stage Society of London came into being. Founded for the purposes of experimental production and evasion of the British censor, the Stage Society gave Sunday-night performances of plays by Shaw, Ashley Dukes, and European playwrights, some of which were subsequently moved to London's West End. Next came the gallant little repertory companies. The Birmingham Repertory Theatre arose in 1907 with amateur actors, including the playwright John Drinkwater. Six years later, the group opened its own theatre, which had the dis-

tinction of being the first theatre in England specially built for repertory. Subsidized by Sir Barry Jackson, it operated without thought of profit and with experimental zeal. Birmingham became the first British city to have its own civic theatre. In 1929, Jackson opened the Malvern Festival with a Shaw program, including the world *première* of *The Apple Cart.* Jackson was extremely generous in supporting his convictions; when he presented all five parts of *Back to Methuselah,* its astounded author, Shaw, asked him, "Jackson, are you certain your wife and children are insured?"

Important, too, was the Manchester Repertory Theatre, founded in 1908 by Miss A. E. F. Horniman (1860–1937), the generous patroness of the stage who four years earlier had enabled the Irish National Theatre Society to establish its permanent home in Dublin, the Abbey Theatre. Her outstanding early discovery was the young genius Stanley Houghton, who did not live long enough to carry his talent to its full promise. The first fruits of the theatre in Manchester were pictures of North-country life, naturalistic dramas for the most part. (The Manchester style of drama continued to exert an influence for a long time; as late as 1935, England's best unemployment drama, *Love on the Dole,* reflected that influence.) In 1913, the Manchester group introduced one of the best-known English naturalistic dramas, *Jane Clegg,* written by St. John Ervine, of Ulster county, with Dame Sybil Thorndike as the slum heroine who finally drives out her ne'er-do-well scapegrace of a husband.

Enlightened commercial enterprise must also be credited with advancing the drama and stagecraft. Especially important was the career of Granville-Barker as co-manager, director, and actor of the Court Theatre in London, founded in 1904. Under the management of Granville-Barker and Vedrenne, the Court Theatre housed thirty-two productions within three years; eleven of these were plays by Shaw. It was also Granville-Barker who presented Galsworthy's first social drama *The Silver Box,* in 1906, and who gave Masefield's *The Tragedy of Nan* its first professional production. Granville-Barker continued his far-reaching career at the Savoy Theatre, giving modern productions of Shakespearean plays there between 1912 and 1914. He modernized stagecraft and it was he who gave America its first important lesson in artistically trim and expressive stage art, when he played a New York season at Wallack's Theatre in 1915–1916. A recital of facts such as these makes a dull chronicle for those who have no memories or vivid descriptions at hand. But every effective production of a good play is an eventful experience, and the English theatre, always blessed with excellent actors who became still better under superior direction, abounded in such experiences by the time the First World War closed the formative phase of theatrical modernism in England.

ENGLISH DRAMA AFTER 1918

Thereafter, the story of British drama can be summarized rather briefly. The battle for modernism was won; with some notable exceptions, the fruits were meager. Shaw's labors brought forth *Heartbreak House* (written during the war but first produced in 1920 by the Theatre Guild of New York) and his masterpiece *Saint Joan* (1923). A number of other plays which were not up to his highest standards were still better than a good deal of the work of his contemporaries. Galsworthy continued to write until a few years before his death in 1933. He created one of his best-written and most deeply felt plays, *Loyalties,* in 1922, and seven years later, a veritable summary of his works, *Escape,* appeared; he gave nothing else of consequence to the stage. James M. Barrie began to succumb in 1916, the year of *A Kiss for Cinderella,* to his saccharinity and fancy, managing only to bring things to an elfin boil in *Dear Brutus,* in 1917, and to produce a questionable excursion into mysticism, *Mary Rose,* three years later. Nothing of importance came from other prewar writers, and the effect of the first global holocaust was negligible in the theatre except for Shaw's *Heartbreak House* and for *Journey's End* (1929), by a new writer of promise, R. C. Sherriff. Sherriff's later work, however, proved disappointing. John Drinkwater apparently had shot his bolt with *Abraham Lincoln,* in 1919. A scattering of poetic drama appeared but was wholly unimpressive except for the work of the expatriate from St. Louis and Harvard, T. S. Eliot, who provided *Murder in the Cathedral* (1935) and *The Cocktail Party* (1949).

The harvest in serious drama was painfully meager: a few plays of less than major proportions —Sutton Vane's *Outward Bound;* Rudolph Besier's biographical romance *The Barretts of Wimpole Street;* Gordon Daviot's *Richard of Bordeaux;* and Laurence Housman's *Victoria Regina.* Social conscience during the economic depression of the 'thirties yielded Ronald Gow and Walter Greenwood's *Love on the Dole,* based on a novel by the latter, and a few plays by J. B. Priestley, such as *The Inspector Calls.* Democratic fervor inspired two superior but hardly pre-eminent dramas: Emlyn Williams' *The Corn is Green* and Terence Rattigan's *The Winslow Boy.* Robert Nichols and Maurice Browne proved prescient in 1928 with their imaginative atom-bomb drama, *Wings over Europe,* without however, splitting the atom of humdrum realistic drama, which evidently offers greater resistance than uranium. Clemence Dane wrote a fairly moving play, *A Bill of Divorcement* (1921), and a highly original drama, *Come of Age* (1934). And Mordaunt Shairp, along with plays of far less merit, wrote a distinguished drama of sybaritism, *The Green Bay Tree.*

In one field, however, the British theatre remained pre-eminent: in comedy—and farce—of manners. Somerset Maugham, who took playwriting less seriously than he did fiction writing, came to the fore with the scintillating satire on snobbery *Our Betters* (1917), the clever problem comedy *The Constant Wife* (1923), and the wise play *The Circle* (1921). C. K. Munro, who also wrote a sharp but amateurish antiwar play, *The Rumor,* produced one piece of clever entertainment, *At Mrs. Beam's.* Winnie the Pooh's laureate, A. A. Milne, contributed a few pieces of pleasant foolery, such as *Mr. Pim Passes By, The Truth About Blayds,* and *The Dover Road.* Frederick Lonsdale, who had started on his career in 1908, continued to write brittle comedies such as *The Last of Mrs. Cheyney,* and St. John Ervine, who had written powerful realistic drama between 1913 and 1915 (*Jane Clegg* and *John Ferguson,* the play that saved the infant Theatre Guild in 1920), revealed a talent for polished comedy in *The First Mrs. Frazer,* in 1928. Ashley Dukes, better known as a critic and adapter of German expressionist drama, contributed an original romantic comedy, *The Man with a Load of Mischief* (1924). John Van Druten used the British "public school" to advantage in his comedy of adolescence, *Young Woodley* (1925), but rounded out his career as a welcome American citizen, with such plays as *The Voice of the Turtle* and *I Remember Mama,* in the nineteen-forties. Benn Levy, later Labor parliamentarian as well as husband of the actress Constance Cummings, contrived good fun, especially with the tart farce *Springtime for Henry* (1931). Dodie Smith provided gentle entertainment in such pieces as *Autumn Crocus* and *Call It a Day,* in the nineteen-thirties.

The roster of British comedies can be continued, indeed, almost interminably without establishing more than that British urbanity remained steady in a world that gyrated into a second world war and—miraculously—out of it. Even the very serious-minded J. B. Priestley proved more successful with an antic disposition, in *The Good Companions* and *Laburnum Grove,* than when he aired liberal or socialist sympathies. A crusty humorist, James Bridie (Dr. Mavor to his Scottish patients), wrote charmingly and wisely and is the most original humorist to have arisen in the nineteen-thirties. He favored whimsies, such as *The Black Eye, Tobias and the Angel,* and *Susannah and the Elders.* And topping all these playwrights in clever theatricality, Noel Coward bounded into the British theatre with suavity occasionally poisonous, wit often just brazen enough to provoke laughter instead of offending, and cynicism that always fell short of challenging anyone's conviction or intellect.

It is apparent that England relied heavily on its humorists, and their worldly-wise writing was an accomplishment that the English treasured in bad times as well as good. Perhaps these comedies, notable for their gayety and literate dialogue, afforded an assurance that intelligence and a civilized attitude could be maintained even in times of stress. Sometimes, as in some Noel Coward comedies, there was even defiance in the writing, as though the English prided themselves on being unintimidated by the weight of serious problems. Sometimes, as in the work of Maugham, a genial cynicism gave the impression that Britons could not be frightened because they knew the way of men and women too well to expect something better than could be had. And sometimes, as in the plays of Bridie, the English theatre was philosophically resigned to human contradictions and follies. If these qualities did not give rise to a particularly exciting theatre, they nevertheless helped produce a civilized one, preferable, in some respects, to the frantic Central European and the devoutly utilitarian Russian theatre after 1920.

The British theatre, which began somewhat reluctantly to modernize itself with Wilde and Shaw, moved toward the mid-point of the twentieth century somewhat tired by the struggle with momentous crises. Some playwrights turned to religious drama, and a few of their plays—notably Eliot's *Murder in the Cathedral,* Dorothy Sayers' *Zeal of Thy House,* and Christopher Hassall's *Christ's Comet*—were exquisitely written and noble in spirit. A few writers, most notably Auden, Isherwood, and Spender, tried to create a "left-wing" poetic drama. But the rest of the dramatists avoided social and spiritual encounters. They were almost invariably adroit, but they were content to be amiable and urbane.

THE "CELTIC RENAISSANCE" IN THE THEATRE

It occurred to the excellent poet and gentleman William Butler Yeats in 1899 that it was high time for his native Ireland to have a national drama and stage. A little later, a frail young man of English descent, John Millington Synge, waited in a Parisian apartment for his genius to germinate. "You will never create anything by reading Racine," Yeats told him and urged him to go to the Aran Islands off the west coast of Ireland to reacquaint himself with his people. Synge heeded his friend's advice, and so Ireland acquired her first resident dramatist. Ireland had, it is true, contributed playwrights such as Farquhar, Goldsmith, Sheridan, Wilde, and Shaw to the English theatre. But Ireland had had no real theatre of its own since the Middle Ages.

In the eighteen-nineties, its hopes for home rule aroused by the career of its leader, Charles Stewart Parnell (1846–1891), Ireland began to experience a cultural renaissance. After 1890, with Parnell's career ended, home rule suffered a crushing setback and Ireland's political struggle was sublimated into cultural activity. A Gaelic League was founded in 1893 with the express purpose of promoting the study of the Gaelic language and its ancient literature; scholars such as the poet Douglas Hyde began to write in the old language and urged others to

follow suit. Even George Moore, the expatriate novelist, made the attempt. The rich ore of Irish legend began to be mined by Hyde, Yeats, "Æ" (George W. Russell), and others. The Irish Literary Society came into full bloom. The dramatic activity with which Europe was teeming inspired the Irish literati to envisage a national theatre. It would be an art theatre, like the free theatres that had promoted the cause of Ibsen and Ibsenism, and even more like the new art theatres founded by such proponents of stylized stagecraft as Gordon Craig, who was better heeded on the Continent than in England.

In his youth, Yeats, who was ultimately to prove himself one of the most modern of modern poets, was a romanticist. He belonged to the literary generation of the eighteen-nineties which exalted "art for art's sake" in reaction to realism in art and materialism in society. In the "mauve" 'nineties, he became one of the founders of the Rhyming Club of London, which counted William Morris, William Ernest Henley, Arthur Symons, and Lionel Johnson among its fellows. Moreover, Yeats was acquainted with the French symbolists, notably with Paul Verlaine, the poet, and with Maurice Maeterlinck, the prime symbolist among dramatists. Neither a nationalist nor an Irish Catholic, Yeats owed his allegiance to art rather than to Irish politics in those days; he was converted to nationalism chiefly by his esthetic interests, because he found in Ireland a rich source for romantic beauty and poetic speech. Ireland may have lacked the sophistication of the literary circles in Paris and London to which Yeats was accustomed; but even that was an advantage, since fresh poetic emotion was more apt to be aroused by the still rather primeval Irish countryside than by the industrial cities of England and the Continent. Yeats's early one-act play *The Land of Heart's Desire* (1894) was drawn from the folk imagination of Ireland, and the contagion of Irish patriotism soon accentuated his romanticism. In the one-act drama *Kathleen ni Houlihan,* he expressed the call of patriotism in poetic Maeterlinckian terms, Ireland being symbolized by a wizened woman whose account of her injuries ("strangers in her house," and her "four beautiful daughters"—Ireland's four provinces—taken from her) finds a champion in a young man. Yeats continued writing plays in this vein and later, interestingly, in the style of the Japanese Noh play, creating a new, if narrowly limited, poetic drama in the English tongue.

Yeats's enthusiasm for an Irish theatre won the support of the socially prominent Lady Gregory and of her affluent neighbor Edward Martyn, a devout Catholic who enthusiastically espoused Ibsen and an ardent nationalist famous for raising a furor by opposing the recruiting of Irish volunteers for the Boer War. Yeats also attracted George Moore, more French and English than Irish but important because of his social prominence and because his naturalistic novels had already given him prestige

Yeats's enthusiasm bore fruit, and on May 8, 1899, the Irish Literary Theatre made a stormy debut in the "Ancient Concert Rooms" of Dublin. Devout and patriotic Irishmen protested vehemently against the production of Yeats's play about a woman's sacrifice of her soul for starving people, *The Countess Cathleen,* as an insult to the Faith and to Irish womanhood. But English reviewers wrote of it favorably, and the Irish Literary Theatre opened a second season with a piece by George Moore and a fantastic drama, *Maeve,* by Edward Martyn.

At this time the productions were given with actors imported from England, and the enterprise could be viewed virtually as an offshoot of the British movement toward a modern theatre. George Moore's social drama *The Strike at Arlingford* had been an early Independent Theatre production in England, and so had Yeats's *The Land of Heart's Desire* (1894). Ireland, moreover, still had no company of actors, although Irish players were growing in number and the brothers Frank and William G. Fay were touring with a small but brilliant company. Yeats saw a performance of theirs and was sufficiently impressed to turn his *Kathleen ni Houlihan* over to them. On April 2, 1902, with P. J. Kelly and Dudley Digges in their ranks, the Fay players presented Yeats's play and a piece by "Æ" before a wildly enthusiastic audience. Encouraged by this reception, they formed the National Dramatic Society, with Yeats as president, and concluded their season with several other productions. In 1902, they presented two more poetic pieces by Yeats (*The Hour Glass* and *The King's Threshold*), Lady Gregory's *Twenty-Five,* Padraic Colum's *Broken Soil,* and the first of Synge's short masterpieces, *In the Shadow of the Glen.* Within half a year, the company, now augmented by the remarkable Sara Allgood, was riding the crest of a wave of popularity that carried it to London and won it the patronage of the generous Miss Horniman. The group lost P. J. Kelly and Dudley Digges in America when it played at the St. Louis Exposition, in 1904, but in that year, in spite of criticism by extreme Irish zealots who had rioted at the performance of Synge's one-acter, the National Dramatic Society became Ireland's national theatre. Miss Horniman supplied the funds for a playhouse erected in Abbey Street, Dublin, and promised a subsidy to keep the nascent organization in operation for a term of ten years. Over the protest of suspicious chauvinists, the company received a patent and the Abbey Theatre was born.

Henceforth the Abbey was the focal point of dramatic writing in Ireland, and with good reason, since this theatrical company became one of the most distinguished in the world, developing an art of ensemble and an aptitude for authentic performance excelled only by the Moscow Art Theatre and the Théâtre du Vieux Colombier.

The poets continued to write and had, indeed, their quota of productions at the Abbey. But the Irish drama that really made the Abbey Theatre and the Irish dramatic movement effective was essentially a folk art, combining realism of environment and character portrayal with the poetic colloquial dialogue and temperament of Ireland. Irish drama, in its first phase, was a fusion of realistic and neo-romantic or symbolist elements, with sometimes one and sometimes the other dominant. That the Irish drama suffered considerable limitation because too many of its writers turned their backs on Ibsen and the drama of ideas is unquestionably true. The fact was noted vigorously by Ireland's great genius, James Joyce, who inveighed against Celtic mysticism. (Joyce's own play, *Exiles,* written in 1914, was Continental drama and had nothing in common with the prevailing national style.) Yet Lady Gregory's formula, taken from Aristotle, "To think like a wise man but express oneself like the common people," prevailed sufficiently to produce work of more than provincial distinction. This was true in spite of the supersaturation of playwriting with Celtic folklore and with Irish charm. Lady Gregory herself contributed no profundity, but brought peasant drama to the Abbey between 1906 and 1907 with one-act masterpieces such as the delightful comedy of crotchety old age *The Workhouse Ward* and the little tragedy of patriotism *The Gaol Gate.* And Lady Gregory's example resulted in a deluge of peasant drama written by George Fitzmaurice, Padraic Colum, William Boyle, and others. Even the least significant of their plays were steeped in humor, in local color, and in a sense of reality, although they do not qualify for any great importance to the world theatre. Most important of all, the local-color movement brought forth the genius of Synge.

Synge, who gave the English-speaking theatre its greatest one-act tragedy, *Riders to the Sea,* in 1904, also supplied its outstanding folk comedy, *The Playboy of the Western World,* in 1907. He was lost to the Abbey by 1909, when he died of cancer in his thirty-eighth year. But Synge left a legacy in these two works that helped to sustain for decades Ireland's claim to an important place in the twentieth-century drama. Nor did he fall greatly below his high standard with the rollicking farce *The Tinker's Wedding,* the folk comedy *In the Shadow of the Glen,* the symbolic drama *The Well of the Saints,* and the uncompleted romantic tragedy *Deirdre of the Sorrows,* which he did not live to see produced. "All art," he wrote in his preface to the published version of *The Playboy of the Western World,* "is a collaboration, and there is little doubt that in the happy ages of literature, striking and beautiful phrases were as ready to the story-teller's or the playwright's hand as the rich cloaks and dresses of his time. I got more aid than any learning could have given me from a chink in the floor of the old Wicklow house where I was staying, that let me hear what was being said by the servant girls in the kitchen." Synge was fully aware of his debt to Ireland and he repaid it handsomely, even though Irish superpatriots responded to most of his efforts with violent demonstrations.

There was, however, an understandable reason for the indignation of these nationalists, foolish though it may seem to us today. They sensed a mocking temper in his plays—and they were right. Synge would have been a minor playwright like most of his colleagues, if he had not possessed a questing and somewhat skeptical temperament. He did not deal ostensibly with modern questions, yet his outlook was critical. He did not favor the modern drama of ideas, yet was modern in his skepticism. Above all, he was a serious artist for whom the question of national touchiness was irrelevant. He was writing at heart not for the national movement but for eternity, expressing his conviction in the preface to *The Tinker's Wedding* (a farce that treated a priest altogether too cavalierly for the Ireland of his day), when he wrote that "the drama, like the symphony, does not teach or prove anything." He did not wish to go out of fashion, like the realistic theatre's "analysts with their problems, and teachers with their systems," but proposed to be perennial, like "the blackberries on the hedges." Whether he might have gone beyond his intention if he had lived long enough to exhaust his rural material cannot be ascertained, although it is true that he was planning to write a drama of city slum life shortly before his death. In any case, this descendant of Cheshire Englishmen and creator of Irish drama was an exquisite artist who sublimated peasant drama into universal drama. Without presenting the modern conflicts and discussions that characterize much of the modern drama, he proved himself a modern dramatist. His work can be located midway between twentieth-century naturalism and symbolism. His greatest claim to modernity lay in his ability to transmute common life into a natural, seemingly effortless poetry.

O'CASEY AND IRISH MODERNISM

Rural material did become subject to the law of diminishing returns after Synge's death, although the peasant continued to supply Irish drama with some moving or hilarious plays, such as Seumas O'Kelly's tragedy *The Shuiler's Child,* Lennox Robinson's delightful comedy *The White-headed Boy* (1916), and George Shiels's *The New Gossoon* (1930). For some fifteen years, indeed, the Abbey Theatre lacked a playwright of major standing, until it presented Sean O'Casey's *Juno and the Paycock* in 1924. Between 1911 and 1915, it is true, St. John Ervine did turn out drama of a different order from that of the Celtic ruralists: *Mixed Marriage* (a drama of class and religious conflict in Belfast), *Jane Clegg,* and *John Ferguson.* But, although he took charge of productions at the Abbey in 1915, he was an Ulster-

man and British at heart, and he left Ireland with a tart one-act farewell, *The Island of Saints, and the Way to Get Out of It.* In 1909, the year of Synge's death, Lord Dunsany made his debut at the Abbey with his sharp one-act play *The Glittering Gate,* but his imagination was better stimulated by the Orient than by Ireland. He was to win adherents in the little theatres of the English-speaking world with bizarre pieces such as *The Gods of the Mountain* (1911) and *A Night at an Inn* (1916). A Maeterlinckian symbolist but also a thrillmonger, Dunsany attracted much attention. Yet it can hardly be maintained that he has any significance for either the European or Irish theatre.

Ireland, nevertheless, was fortunate in being able to produce a dramatist of first rank after the First World War, something that cannot be said for England proper. O'Casey's artistry linked him with the Abbey's first great period, insofar as he proved himself as fully capable of turning common life into poetry as Synge. And like his distinguished forerunner, O'Casey became a master of language. But it was with a new realism that O'Casey made a distinctive contribution to Irish, as well as to world, drama. His realism was not nourished on the soil but was thrust up from the cobbled streets of Dublin in the midst of the city poor. He gave Ireland its first true proletarian drama in the two masterpieces *Juno and the Paycock* and *The Plough and the Stars.* And what is perhaps more important to the perspectives of dramatic art, O'Casey introduced a fresh sympathy, a critical spirit, and an awareness of twentieth-century conflicts into the poetry of speech and mood already sufficiently ingrained in Irish drama. The spirit of Synge seemed to have merged with the spirit of Ibsen and Shaw in O'Casey's Abbey Theatre plays. This was eventful not only for Dublin but for the rest of the English-speaking world, which acquired two plays of major distinction, as well as a third which was estimable, if less remarkable, *The Shadow of a Gunman.* Rising to the occasion, the Abbey Theatre gave the three plays superb productions between 1923 and 1926, and henceforth O'Casey was acknowledged one of the outstanding dramatists of the century. For the Abbey, too, these productions were significant. How great a departure they were for a theatre that had been rather grudging in its reception of critical social drama will be best realized if we recall that the Abbey did not get around to producing *A Doll's House* until 1923! For a short period, the Abbey stood once more in the front lines of modernism.

O'Casey's next plays, although still Irish in essence, came to be identified with the English theatre. Rejected by the Abbey, his pacifistic and semi-expressionistic drama *The Silver Tassie* (1929) was first produced in London, with Charles Laughton as the hero. Settled in London, O'Casey then gave England the wholly symbolic drama *Within the Gates* (1933), not the most substantial of his plays but a noble composition that was welcome in a period of receding exaltation in the British theatre. His next play to have its *première* in Dublin, *Red Roses for Me,* a poetic class-conflict drama, came many years later, in 1943.

The Irish drama after O'Casey's break with the Abbey would have been exceedingly meager but for the advent of Paul Vincent Carroll, an Irish school-master residing in Glasgow. The best of Carroll's plays, *Shadow and Substance* (1934) and *The White Steed.* both charged with critical spirit, were un-flattering to Irish life but once more called attention to Ireland as the seedbed of good dramatists. With help from Denis Johnston, the highly original author of *The Moon in the Yellow River* (1931), and others, the Irish drama continued to be mod-erately fruitful in the nineteen-thirties; and a num-ber of new dramatic efforts in the next decade indicated that playwriting was still germinating.

THE FUTURE OF ENGLISH AND
IRISH DRAMA

The Abbey suffered new periods of decline after 1926 and underwent several reorganizations. Eire, now an independent state, left its national theatre somewhat less than independent in the selection of plays, and this may account for some of the diffi-culties in finding and encouraging talent. The Abbey, moreover, experienced the rise of rival theatres in Dublin, notably the Gate Theatre, founded in 1928 by Hilton Edwards and the actor-director-dramatist Micheal MacLiammoir. The Gate departed from naturalistic stagecraft and adopted more modern methods of staging than those practiced by the Abbey. It presented stylized dramas, both home grown and imported. In time, another kind of drama, imaginative in a Continental manner and evocative of modern complexities, might arise from the mod-ernism of the Gate. As the century reached its mid-point, Irishmen could look forward to another spurt of interesting playwriting.

Englishmen, who had grown accustomed to ex-pecting help in the theatre from Ireland, could hope for a similar revival in the drama as they went about putting their house in order after the Second World War. England by then had embarked upon a policy of giving financial assistance to its noncommercial theatres, mainly outside London, but it was not yet certain that any drama of transcendent merit was on the verge of blossoming as a result of the govern-ment's unprecedented effort to smile benignly on the stage. England had enjoyed up to 1950 some sixty years of modern drama, a good part of it contrib-uted by Irish-born writers. Some satisfaction could be taken in this fact. Whether the second half of the century would breed another Shaw, O'Casey, Barrie, or Galsworthy could not be foretold. Much would depend upon the state of the world, a changed world in which England was no longer the wealthy ruler of

a mighty empire. If the seams of the globe did not burst entirely in the age of atomic energy, there might be hope for the drama in an England dimin-ished in size and power. The little city-state of Attica had produced immortal dramatic literature. Size and political strength in a nation are fortunately not indispensable to the creative spirit. Intellect and greatheartedness are. And these qualities, manifested in England during the crisis of Hitler's *Blitz* and again when the country had settled down to solving its postwar problems, might come to the aid of British theatre in the unpredictable years to come.

This much was certain by 1950: England was intent upon giving the theatre every opportunity to enlarge itself and to move in new directions, even if these were not yet definable. An Arts Council was encouraging noncommercial productions, touring companies were visiting the provinces in increasing number, and many provincial theatres which had been converted to motion-picture houses before 1939 had been reconverted to the uses of the drama. Even the powerful commercial management of H. M. Tennent Ltd. had established a nonprofit division at the old Haymarket Theatre, and the Old Vic, famous for the quality of its production of classics, was becoming a national theatre. Even the creation of a poetic drama was receiving encouragement in London, at the small Mercury Theatre directed by Martin Browne. Most important of all, playwrights were beginning to deepen their content and to re-fine their artistry.

It was significant that Terence Rattigan, who had turned out froth before the war and soufflés such as *O Mistress Mine* during it, was writing plays such as *The Winslow Boy,* a tribute to the cause of civil liberty, and *The Browning Version,* a long one-act psychological drama. Much was expected from the actor-dramatist Emlyn Williams, who had followed *The Corn Is Green* with the imaginative drama of a messianic visitation in a Welsh village, *The Wind of Heaven,* and from the young playwright Peter Ustinov, who had been displaying a Chekhovian vein of characterization since 1942, when his study of Russian *émigré* life, *The House of Regrets,* was pro-duced. J. B. Priestley had begun to interlace his dramas of social conscience with imagination; Christopher Fry, the young author of *The Lady's Not for Burning* and *Venus Observed,* was on the way to creating scintillating verse drama; and T. S. Eliot had finally succeeded in writing a modern poetic drama, *The Cocktail Party,* that was com-pletely stageworthy even in the commercial theatre. Martin Browne called his Mercury Theatre a "poet's workshop," and more young writers could be ex-pected to work in it. Perhaps the best sign was the fact that the Arts Theatre Club in London, which produced Fry's poetic plays and subsidized new play-wrights, had by 1950 gained a membership of 20,000. England appeared to be on the eve of a renovation of its drama.

Oscar Wilde

(1854–1900)

Casting a backward glance at his destroyed career in the book he wrought out of his prison experiences, *De Profundis,* Oscar Wilde wrote, "I took the drama, the most objective form known to art, and made of it as personal a mode of expression as the lyric or the sonnet; at the same time, widened its range and enriched its characterization." Although the second part of the statement is now open to question, this proud assumption of a beaten man, when it was written, was not far enough from the truth to be seriously challenged. Certainly, as Burns Mantle wrote, "the drama as a personal mode of expression was definitely influenced by Oscar Wilde."

Born in Dublin on October 16, 1854, of brilliant and socially prominent parents, Oscar Wilde began to reveal his talents at an early age. The precocious lad, whose later abnormality may have had its origins in his mother's fondness for dressing him as a girl, made an enviable record at Magdalen College, Oxford. He became a distinguished student of the classics and also won the Newdigate Prize for poetry. Among the admiring teachers and friends of his undergraduate years were such leaders in the world of art as John Ruskin, then Slade Professor of Art, and Walter Pater.

After traveling in Italy and Greece, Wilde came to London, where a book of his poetry and his melodrama *Vera, or the Nihilists* were published. Thereafter, supported in high society by his wife's ample fortune, Wilde became the most lionized wit in England. Regarding himself as an "apostle of the beautiful," he raised the slogan of estheticism and put his preachment into practice with such extravagance that he shocked his social inferiors and amused his equals. George Du Maurier caricatured him in *Punch,* and Gilbert and Sullivan aroused merriment at his expense in *Patience.* Wilde, however, remained undisturbed, and continued to wear his motley: the knee breeches, black silk stockings, velvet jacket, flowing tie, and sunflower, to which he owed the innocent part of his notoriety.

Unfortunately, Wilde, who fancied himself a latter-day Greek, did not confine his cultivation of decadence to peccadilloes that could bear the light of day. He lapsed into a coarse sensualism and indulged in perverse sexual practices. Consequently, the Marquess of Queensbury, father of the poet Lord Alfred Douglas, with whom Wilde had struck up a close friendship, became suspicious of him. Wilde made the mistake of bringing a suit of slander against the Marquess, who had insulted him publicly, and unsavory revelations at the trial in 1895 outraged public opinion. Wilde was prosecuted and sentenced to two years at hard labor in Reading Gaol. Although prison life evoked two of his best writings, *The Ballad of Reading Gaol* (1898) and *De Profundis* (published after Wilde's death, in 1905), it left him a broken man. He spent his last years in Paris in a state of progressive physical deterioration and died in straitened circumstances on November 30, 1900.

More important than his artificial early verse and his decadent novel *The Picture of Dorian Gray* (1891) were the comedies in which Wilde exhibited his talent for witty conversation. In addition to writing the febrile melodrama *The Duchess of Padua* and the powerful, if decadent, one-act drama *Salomé* (1892), he turned out three comedies and a farce: *Lady Windermere's Fan* (1892), *A Woman of No Importance* (1893), *An Ideal Husband* (1895), and *The Importance of Being Earnest* (1895). In the estimation of the pioneering critic of the British stage William Archer, Wilde became "the most exquisite stylist that had written for the stage since Congreve"; according to another critic, his "light, elegant comedies were unsurpassed in wit and epigrammatic brilliance since Sheridan."

Wilde's epigrams were, however, more than polished gems. They were clever inversions of conventional opinion and often barbed comments on British society. The play of repartee, moreover, was supplemented by situations and portraits of society people that showed a critical faculty heretofore revealed in British drama only by Shaw. Wilde even fancied himself a writer of problem plays, and he may be associated by the historian of literature with such writers of Continental thesis drama as Dumas *fils* and Augier. He differs from these earlier writers only in his mastery of drawing-room comedy —that is, in his lightness and grace, although these qualities remained unsupported by genuine characterization and good dramaturgy, of which there is a considerable amount in the work of Augier. In substance, *Lady Windermere's Fan* treated the "fallen woman" with sympathy and directed considerable criticism at the holier-than-thou attitude of Victorian women of good society. In *A Woman of No Importance,* Wilde castigated the social set; in *An Ideal Husband,* he examined political reputations.

Curiously for a man bent upon publicizing himself as an arch-esthete, Wilde left the dream world of estheticism when he turned to the drama. Directly or indirectly, Wilde, who revealed a sharp intelligence in his volume of criticism *Intentions* (1891) and in his essay *The Soul of Man under Socialism,* added some fibre to the drama. In *Lady Windermere's Fan,* he spun out an intrigue and developed it with plot contrivances that playwrights had long found useful. Lady Windermere suspects her husband of carrying on an intrigue with a woman of shady reputation, Mrs. Erlynne, who turns out to be her mother. Seeking revenge in the Victorian tradition, Lady Windermere goes to an admirer's apartment, leaving her fan there. In order to save her daughter's reputation, Mrs. Erlynne claims the fan and thereby foregoes all chances of winning her way back into good society. Sentiment is thus served, especially as Mrs. Erlynne never reveals her identity to her daughter. But in the course of the play, Wilde has also struck at the snobbish superiority of the daughter. Victorian prudery is satirized by means of the situation and of such coruscating epigrams as "Wicked women bother one. Good women bore one. That is the only difference between them."

Anticipating Maugham's *Our Betters* in *A Woman of No Importance,* Wilde satirized the American habit of knocking at the gates of the British aristocracy and took pains to show that British society was a shallow affair at best. It is doubtful that even Shaw delivered a better broadside against the gentry than "the English country gentleman galloping after a fox—the unspeakable in full pursuit of the uneatable." A society of hollow and useless people where one can live down "anything except a good reputation" is what Wilde shows us in *A Woman of No Importance;* the society is made tolerable only by evidences of wit in the speakers, which no one would make the mistake of attributing to them rather than to Wilde himself. The ghost of Congreve would have chuckled to hear Mrs. Allonby tell her friends that her husband was a promissory note and that she was tired of meeting him. But when the play was written, even its wit was less remarkable than the fact that Wilde should have exposed fashionable society and conventional notions to scorn.

In *An Ideal Husband,* Wilde even tried his hand at political drama. He contrived a story in which an important government official, who made his fortune by selling a state secret, is nearly blackmailed into promoting a wildcat scheme for building a worthless canal. If Wilde showed no particular brilliance when he dealt with life beyond the drawing room, his subject matter itself was an advance over the old-fashioned theatre in England, particularly since he was free from Victorian sanctimoniousness. His ideas were shallow, but he evinced some respect for ideas as a force rather than as a conversational convenience. A character in *An Ideal Husband* declares, "All thought is immoral. Its very essence is destruction. If you think of anything, you will kill it. Nothing survives being thought of."

Still, Wilde's slipshod plots were distinctly detrimental to his most ambitious comedies; for "problem plays," which these works suggested, his plots were too contrived and perfunctory. General opinion holds, therefore, that he was most successful in the pure farce *The Importance of Being Earnest.* "It still stands," Burns Mantle wrote in 1935, "as the play that most perfectly illustrates the particular brilliance that he brought to the theatre. . . . It accepted the dare of competition represented by the Pineros and Joneses by following the pattern of their drawing-room comedies in developing a super-farce that was witty as well as literate and as finished in its writing as it was extravagant in its absurdities." Here he could give free rein to sprightly fantastication, and his characterization did not have to meet the requirements of credibility. Contrivance being a virtue rather than a vice in farce, Wilde succeeded in turning flippancy into a fine art.

Wilde was evidently confident when he wrote *The Importance of Being Earnest* that his skill had not failed him. Asked the day before the *première* whether he expected his play to succeed, he replied, "My dear fellow. The play *is* a success. The only question is whether the audience will be a success." The audience was. George Alexander, the actor-manager, had chosen an ideal cast for his celebrated St. James's Theatre production. Nevertheless, the play was withdrawn in the same year (1895) when Wilde lost his libel suit against the Marquess of Queensbury. For years, no producer dared revive the play. But a revival in the season of 1909–1910 was highly successful, as were John Gielgud's 1939 production in London and his 1947 production in New York.

"In matters of grave importance," Wilde had quipped in his farce, "style, not sincerity, is the vital thing." If one hesitates to apply this aphorism to moral questions, it nonetheless works perfectly for this stage piece. "Played sincerely," Brooks Atkinson commented after seeing the Gielgud production, *"The Importance of Being Earnest* would be intolerable—probably impossible. But played purely as style without sincerity it shows genius for the theatre, which has always provided a gay haven for wits and iconoclasts." Whatever the limitations we may ascribe to the work, it is to the theatre that it belongs, wholly and without the slightest sign of fatigue. Properly performed, it reveals, as Atkinson noted, a "hard, lucid, metallic artifice—very modern in materials despite the age of the tradition."

BIBLIOGRAPHY: Brooks Atkinson, *Broadway Scrapbook* (pp. 280–283), 1947; John Mason Brown, *Seeing More Things* (pp. 215–220), 1948; George Jean Nathan, *The Theatre Book of the Year 1946–1947* (pp. 328–331), 1947; Hesketh Pearson, *Oscar Wilde, His Life and Wit,* 1946; Edouard Roditi, *Oscar Wilde,* 1947; Ernest Short, *Theatrical Cavalcade* (pp. 51–54), 1942.

THE IMPORTANCE OF BEING EARNEST

By Oscar Wilde

CHARACTERS

JOHN WORTHING, J.P.
ALGERNON MONCRIEFF
REV. CANON CHASUBLE, D.D.

MERRIMAN (*Butler*)
LANE (*Manservant*)
LADY BRACKNELL

HON. GWENDOLEN FAIRFAX
CECILY CARDEW
MISS PRISM (*Governess*)

THE SCENES OF THE PLAY

ACT I.
Algernon Moncrieff's Flat in Half-Moon Street, W.
ACT II.
The Garden at the Manor House, Woolton.
ACT III.
Drawing-Room of the Manor House, Woolton.
Time—The Present.
Place—London.

ACT I.

SCENE: *Morning-room in* Algernon's *flat in Half-Moon Street. The room is luxuriously and artistically furnished. The sound of a piano is heard in the adjoining room.*

[Lane *is arranging afternoon tea on the table, and after the music has ceased,* Algernon *enters*]

ALGERNON: Did you hear what I was playing, Lane?

LANE: I didn't think it polite to listen, sir.

ALGERNON: I'm sorry for that, for your sake. I don't play accurately—anyone can play accurately—but I play with wonderful expression. As far as the piano is concerned, sentiment is my forte. I keep science for Life.

LANE: Yes, sir.

ALGERNON: And, speaking of the science of Life, have you got the cucumber sandwiches cut for Lady Bracknell?

LANE: Yes, sir. [Hands them on a salver]

ALGERNON: [Inspects them, takes two, and sits down on the sofa] Oh! . . . by the way, Lane, I see from your book that on Thursday night, when Lord Shoreman and Mr. Worthing were dining with me, eight bottles of champagne are entered as having been consumed.

LANE: Yes, sir; eight bottles and a pint.

ALGERNON: Why is it that in a bachelor's establishment the servants invariably drink the champagne? I ask merely for information.

LANE: I attribute it to the superior quality of the wine, sir. I have often observed that in married households the champagne is rarely of a first-rate brand.

ALGERNON: Good Heavens! Is marriage so demoralizing as that?

LANE: I believe it *is* a very pleasant state, sir. I have had very little experience of it myself up to the present. I have only been married once. That was in consequence of a misunderstanding between myself and a young woman.

ALGERNON: [Languidly] I don't know that I am much interested in your family life, Lane.

LANE: No, sir; it is not a very interesting subject. I never think of it myself.

ALGERNON: Very natural, I am sure. That will do, Lane, thank you.

LANE: Thank you, sir. [Lane *goes out*]

ALGERNON: Lane's views on marriage seem somewhat lax. Really, if the lower orders don't set us a good example, what on earth is the use of them? They seem, as a class, to have absolutely no sense of moral responsibility.

[Enter Lane]

LANE: Mr. Ernest Worthing.

[Enter Jack. Lane *goes out*]

ALGERNON: How are you, my dear Ernest? What brings you up to town?

JACK: Oh, pleasure, pleasure! What else should bring one anywhere? Eating as usual, I see, Algy!

ALGERNON: [Stiffly] I believe it is customary in good society to take some slight refreshment at five o'clock. Where have you been since last Thursday?

JACK: [Sitting down on the sofa] In the country.

ALGERNON: What on earth do you do there?

JACK: [Pulling off his gloves] When one is in town one amuses oneself. When one is in the country one amuses other people. It is excessively boring.

ALGERNON: And who are the people you amuse?

JACK: [Airily] Oh, neighbors, neighbors.

ALGERNON: Got nice neighbors in your part of Shropshire?

JACK: Perfectly horrid! Never speak to one of them.

ALGERNON: How immensely you must amuse them! [Goes over and takes sandwich] By the way, Shropshire is your county, is it not?

JACK: Eh? Shropshire? Yes, of course. Hallo! Why all these cups? Why cucumber sandwiches?

Why such reckless extravagance in one so young? Who is coming to tea?

ALGERNON: Oh! merely Aunt Augusta and Gwendolen.

JACK: How perfectly delightful!

ALGERNON: Yes, that is all very well; but I am afraid Aunt Augusta won't quite approve of your being here.

JACK: May I ask why?

ALGERNON: My dear fellow, the way you flirt with Gwendolen is perfectly disgraceful. It is almost as bad as the way Gwendolen flirts with you.

JACK: I am in love with Gwendolen. I have come up to town expressly to propose to her.

ALGERNON: I thought you had come for pleasure? . . . I call that business.

JACK: How utterly unromantic you are!

ALGERNON: I really don't see anything romantic in proposing. It is very romantic to be in love. But there is nothing romantic about a definite proposal. Why, one may be accepted. One usually is, I believe. Then the excitement is all over. The very essence of romance is uncertainty. If ever I get married, I'll certainly try to forget the fact.

JACK. I have no doubt about that, dear Algy. The Divorce Court was specially invented for people whose memories are so curiously constituted.

ALGERNON: Oh! there is no use speculating on that subject. Divorces are made in Heaven—[Jack *puts out his hand to take a sandwich. Algernon at once interferes*] Please don't touch the cucumber sandwiches. They are ordered specially for Aunt Augusta. [*Takes one and eats it*]

JACK: Well, you have been eating them all the time.

ALGERNON: That is quite a different matter. She is my aunt. [*Takes plate from below*] Have some bread and butter. The bread and butter is for Gwendolen. Gwendolen is devoted to bread and butter.

JACK: [*Advancing to table and helping himself*] And very good bread and butter it is, too.

ALGERNON: Well, my dear fellow, you need not eat as if you were going to eat it all. You behave as if you were married to her already. You are not married to her already, and I don't think you will ever be.

JACK: Why on earth do you say that?

ALGERNON: Well, in the first place girls never marry the men they flirt with. Girls don't think it right.

JACK: Oh, that is nonsense!

ALGERNON: It isn't. It is a great truth. It accounts for the extraordinary number of bachelors that one sees all over the place. In the second place, I don't give my consent.

JACK: Your consent!

ALGERNON: My dear fellow, Gwendolen is my first cousin. And before I allow you to marry her, you will have to clear up the whole question of Cecily. [*Rings bell*]

JACK: Cecily! What on earth do you mean? What do you mean, Algy, by Cecily! I don't know anyone of the name Cecily.

[*Enter* Lane]

ALGERNON: Bring me that cigarette case Mr. Worthing left in the smoking-room the last time he dined here.

LANE: Yes, sir. [Lane *goes out*]

JACK: Do you mean to say you have had my cigarette case all this time? I wish to goodness you had let me know. I have been writing frantic letters to Scotland Yard about it. I was very nearly offering a large reward.

ALGERNON: Well, I wish you would offer one. I happen to be more than usually hard up.

JACK: There is no good offering a large reward now that the thing is found.

[*Enter* Lane *with the cigarette case on a salver.* Algernon *takes it at once.* Lane *goes out*]

ALGERNON: I think that is rather mean of you, Ernest, I must say. [*Opens case and examines it*] However, it makes no matter, for, now that I look at the inscription, I find that the thing isn't yours after all.

JACK: Of course it's mine. [*Moving to him*] You have seen me with it a hundred times, and you have no right whatsoever to read what is written inside. It is a very ungentlemanly thing to read a private cigarette case.

ALGERNON: Oh! it is absurd to have a hard-and-fast rule about what one should read and what one shouldn't. More than half of modern culture depends on what one shouldn't read.

JACK: I am quite aware of the fact, and I don't propose to discuss modern culture. It isn't the sort of thing one should talk of in private. I simply want my cigarette case back.

ALGERNON: Yes; but this isn't your cigarette case. This cigarette case is a present from someone of the name of Cecily, and you said you didn't know anyone of that name.

JACK: Well, if you want to know, Cecily happens to be my aunt.

ALGERNON: Your aunt!

JACK: Yes. Charming old lady she is, too. Lives at Tunbridge Wells. Just give it back to me, Algy.

ALGERNON: [*Retreating to back of sofa*] But why does she call herself little Cecily if she is your aunt and lives at Tunbridge Wells? [*Reading*] "From little Cecily with her fondest love."

JACK: [*Moving to sofa and kneeling upon it*] My dear fellow, what on earth is there in that? Some aunts are tall, some aunts are not tall. That is a matter that surely an aunt may be allowed to decide for herself. You seem to think that every aunt should be exactly like your aunt! That is absurd! For Heaven's sake give me back my cigarette case. [*Follows* Algernon *round the room*]

ALGERNON: Yes. But why does your aunt call you her uncle? "From little Cecily, with her fondest love to her dear Uncle Jack." There is no objection, I admit, to an aunt being a small aunt, but why an aunt, no matter what her size may be, should call her own nephew her uncle, I can't quite make out. Besides, your name isn't Jack at all; it's Ernest.

JACK: It isn't Ernest; it's Jack.

ALGERNON: You have always told me it was Ernest. I have introduced you to everyone as Ernest. You answer to the name of Ernest. You look as if your name was Ernest. You are the most earnest-looking person I ever saw in my life. It is perfectly absurd your saying that your name isn't Ernest. It's on your cards. Here is one of them. [*Taking it from case*] "Mr. Ernest Worthing, B 4, The Albany." I'll keep this as a proof your name is Ernest if ever you attempt to deny it to me, or to Gwendolen, or to anyone else. [*Puts the card in his pocket*]

JACK: Well, my name is Ernest in town and Jack in the country, and the cigarette case was given to me in the country.

ALGERNON: Yes, but that does not account for the fact that your small Aunt Cecily, who lives at Tunbridge Wells, calls you her dear uncle. Come, old boy, you had much better have the thing out at once.

JACK: My dear Algy, you talk exactly as if you were a dentist. It is very vulgar to talk like a dentist when one isn't a dentist. It produces a false impression.

ALGERNON: Well, that is exactly what dentists always do. Now, go on! Tell me the whole thing. I may mention that I have always suspected you of being a confirmed and secret Bunburyist; and I am quite sure of it now.

JACK: Bunburyist? What on earth do you mean by a Bunburyist?

ALGERNON: I'll reveal to you the meaning of that incomparable expression as soon as you are kind enough to inform me why you are Ernest in town and Jack in the country.

JACK: Well, produce my cigarette case first.

ALGERNON: Here it is. [*Hands cigarette case*] Now produce your explanation, and pray make it improbable. [*Sits on sofa*]

JACK: My dear fellow, there is nothing improbable about my explanation at all. In fact it's perfectly ordinary. Old Mr. Thomas Cardew, who adopted me when I was a little boy, made me in his will guardian to his grand-daughter, Miss Cecily Cardew. Cecily, who addresses me as her uncle from motives of respect that you could not possibly appreciate, lives at my place in the country under the charge of her admirable governess, Miss Prism.

ALGERNON: Where is that place in the country, by the way?

JACK: That is nothing to you, dear boy. You are not going to be invited. . . . I may tell you candidly that the place is not in Shropshire.

ALGERNON: I suspected that, my dear fellow! I have Bunburyed all over Shropshire on two separate occasions. Now, go on. Why are you Ernest in town and Jack in the country?

JACK: My dear Algy, I don't know whether you will be able to understand my real motives. You are hardly serious enough. When one is placed in the position of guardian, one has to adopt a very high moral tone on all subjects. It's one's duty to do so. And as a high moral tone can hardly be said to conduce very much to either one's health or one's happiness, in order to get up to town I have always pretended to have a younger brother of the name of Ernest, who lives in the Albany, and gets into the most dreadful scrapes. That, my dear Algy, is the whole truth pure and simple.

ALGERNON: The truth is rarely pure and never simple. Modern life would be very tedious if it were either, and modern literature a complete impossibility!

JACK: That wouldn't be at all a bad thing.

ALGERNON: Literary criticism is not your forte, my dear fellow. Don't try it. You should leave that to people who haven't been at a University. They do it so well in the daily papers. What you really are is a Bunburyist. I was quite right in saying you were a Bunburyist. You are one of the most advanced Bunburyists I know.

JACK: What on earth do you mean?

ALGERNON: You have invented a very useful younger brother called Ernest, in order that you may be able to come up to town as often as you like. I have invented an invaluable permanent invalid called Bunbury, in order that I may be able to go down into the country whenever I choose. Bunbury is perfectly invaluable. If it wasn't for Bunbury's extraordinary bad health, for instance, I wouldn't be able to dine with you at Willis' to-night, for I have been really engaged to Aunt Augusta for more than a week.

JACK: I haven't asked you to dine with me anywhere to-night.

ALGERNON: I know. You are absolutely careless about sending out invitations. It is very foolish of you. Nothing annoys people so much as not receiving invitations.

JACK: You had much better dine with your Aunt Augusta.

ALGERNON: I haven't the smallest intention of doing anything of the kind. To begin with, I dined there on Monday, and once a week is quite enough to dine with one's own relatives. In the second place, whenever I do dine there I am always treated as a member of the family, and sent down with either no woman at all, or two. In the third place, I know perfectly well whom she will place me next, to-night. She will place me next Mary Farquhar, who always flirts with her own husband across the dinner-table. That is not very pleasant. Indeed, it is not even decent . . . and that sort of thing is enormously on the increase. The amount of women in London who flirt with their own husbands is perfectly scandalous. It looks so bad. It is simply washing one's clean linen in public. Besides, now that I know you to be a confirmed Bunburyist I naturally want to talk to you about Bunburying. I want to tell you the rules.

JACK: I'm not a Bunburyist at all. If Gwendolen accepts me, I am going to kill my brother, indeed I think I'll kill him in any case. Cecily is a little too much interested in him. It is rather a bore. So I am going to get rid of Ernest. And I strongly advise you to do the same with Mr. . . . with your invalid friend who has the absurd name.

ALGERNON: Nothing will induce me to part with Bunbury, and if you ever get married, which seems to me extremely problematic, you will be very glad to know Bunbury. A man who marries without knowing Bunbury has a very tedious time of it.

JACK: That is nonsense. If I marry a charming girl like Gwendolen, and she is the only girl I ever saw in my life that I would marry, I certainly won't want to know Bunbury.

ALGERNON: Then your wife will. You don't seem to realize, that in married life three is company and two is none.

JACK: [Sententiously] That, my dear young friend, is the theory that the corrupt French Drama has been propounding for the last fifty years.

ALGERNON: Yes; and that the happy English home has proved in half the time.

JACK: For heaven's sake, don't try to be cynical. It's perfectly easy to be cynical.

ALGERNON: My dear fellow, it isn't easy to be anything now-a-days. There's such a lot of beastly competition about. [The sound of an electric bell is heard] Ah! that must be Aunt Augusta. Only relatives, or creditors, ever ring in that Wagnerian manner. Now, if I get her out of the way for ten minutes, so that you can have an opportunity for proposing to Gwendolen, may I dine with you to-night at Willis'?

JACK: I suppose so, if you want to.

ALGERNON: Yes, but you must be serious about it. I hate people who are not serious about meals. It is so shallow of them.

[Enter Lane]

LANE: Lady Bracknell and Miss Fairfax.

[Algernon goes forward to meet them. Enter Lady Bracknell and Gwendolen]

LADY BRACKNELL: Good afternoon, dear Algernon, I hope you are behaving very well.

ALGERNON: I'm feeling very well, Aunt Augusta.

LADY BRACKNELL: That's not quite the same thing. In fact the two things rarely go together. [Sees Jack and bows to him with icy coldness]

ALGERNON: [To Gwendolen] Dear me, you are smart!

GWENDOLEN: I am always smart! Aren't I, Mr. Worthing?

JACK: You're quite perfect, Miss Fairfax.

GWENDOLEN: Oh! I hope I am not that. It would

leave no room for developments, and I intend to develop in many directions.

[Gwendolen and Jack sit down together in the corner]

LADY BRACKNELL: I'm sorry if we are a little late, Algernon, but I was obliged to call on dear Lady Harbury. I hadn't been there since her poor husband's death. I never saw a woman so altered; she looks quite twenty years younger. And now I'll have a cup of tea, and one of those nice cucumber sandwiches you promised me.

ALGERNON: Certainly, Aunt Augusta. [Goes over to tea-table]

LADY BRACKNELL: Won't you come and sit here, Gwendolen?

GWENDOLEN: Thanks, mamma, I'm quite comfortable where I am.

ALGERNON: [Picking up empty plate in horror] Good heavens! Lane! Why are there no cucumber sandwiches? I ordered them specially.

LANE: [Gravely] There were no cucumbers in the market this morning, sir. I went down twice.

ALGERNON: No cucumbers!

LANE: No, sir. Not even for ready money.

ALGERNON: That will do, Lane, thank you.

LANE: Thank you, sir. [Goes out]

ALGERNON: I am greatly distressed, Aunt Augusta, about there being no cucumbers, not even for ready money.

LADY BRACKNELL: It really makes no matter, Algernon. I had some crumpets with Lady Harbury, who seems to me to be living entirely for pleasure now.

ALGERNON: I hear her hair has turned quite gold from grief.

LADY BRACKNELL: It certainly has changed its color. From what cause I, of course, cannot say. [Algernon crosses and hands tea] Thank you. I've quite a treat for you to-night, Algernon. I am going to send you down with Mary Farquhar. She is such a nice woman, and so attentive to her husband. It's delightful to watch them.

ALGERNON: I am afraid, Aunt Augusta, I shall have to give up the pleasure of dining with you to-night after all.

LADY BRACKNELL: [Frowning] I hope not, Algernon. It would put my table completely out. Your uncle would have to dine upstairs. Fortunately he is accustomed to that.

ALGERNON: It is a great bore, and, I need hardly say, a terrible disappointment to me, but the fact is I have just had a telegram to say that my poor friend Bunbury is very ill again. [Exchanges glances with Jack] They seem to think I should be with him.

LADY BRACKNELL: It is very strange. This Mr. Bunbury seems to suffer from curiously bad health.

ALGERNON: Yes; poor Bunbury is a dreadful invalid.

LADY BRACKNELL: Well, I must say, Algernon, that I think it is high time that Mr. Bunbury made up his mind whether he was going to live or to die. This shilly-shallying with the question is absurd. Nor do I in any way approve of the modern sympathy with invalids. I consider it morbid. Illness of any kind is hardly a thing to be encouraged in others. Health is the primary duty of life. I am always telling that to your poor uncle, but he never seems to take much notice . . . as far as any improvement in his ailments goes. I should be much obliged if you would ask Mr. Bunbury, from me, to be kind enough not to have a relapse on Saturday, for I rely on you to arrange my music for me. It is my last reception and one wants something that will encourage conversation, particularly at the end of the season when everyone has practically said whatever they had to say, which, in most cases, was probably not much.

ALGERNON: I'll speak to Bunbury, Aunt Augusta, if he is still conscious, and I think I can promise you he'll be all right by Saturday. You see, if one plays good music, people don't listen, and if one plays bad music people don't talk. But I'll run over the program I've drawn out, if you will kindly come into the next room for a moment.

LADY BRACKNELL: Thank you, Algernon. It is very thoughtful of you. [*Rising, and following* Algernon] I'm sure the program will be delightful, after a few expurgations. French songs I cannot possibly allow. People always seem to think that they are improper, and either look shocked, which is vulgar, or laugh, which is worse. But German sounds a thoroughly respectable language, and indeed, I believe is so. Gwendolen, you will accompany me.

GWENDOLEN: Certainly, mamma.

[Lady Bracknell *and* Algernon *go into the music-room,* Gwendolen *remains behind*]

JACK: Charming day it has been, Miss Fairfax.

GWENDOLEN: Pray don't talk to me about the weather, Mr. Worthing. Whenever people talk to me about the weather, I always feel quite certain that they mean something else. And that makes me so nervous.

JACK: I do mean something else.

GWENDOLEN: I thought so. In fact, I am never wrong.

JACK: And I would like to be allowed to take advantage of Lady Bracknell's temporary absence . . .

GWENDOLEN: I would certainly advise you to do so. Mamma has a way of coming back suddenly into a room that I have often had to speak to her about.

JACK: [*Nervously*] Miss Fairfax, ever since I met you I have admired you more than any girl . . . I have ever met since . . . I met you.

GWENDOLEN: Yes, I am quite aware of the fact. And I often wish that in public, at any rate, you had been more demonstrative. For me you have always had an irresistible fascination. Even before I met you I was far from indifferent to you. [Jack *looks at her in amazement*] We live, as I hope you know, Mr. Worthing, in an age of ideals. The fact is constantly mentioned in the more expensive monthly magazines, and has reached the provincial pulpits I am told: and my ideal has always been to love some one of the name of Ernest. There is something in that name that inspires absolute confidence. The moment Algernon first mentioned to me that he had a friend called Ernest, I knew I was destined to love you.

JACK: You really love me, Gwendolen?

GWENDOLEN: Passionately!

JACK: Darling! You don't know how happy you've made me.

GWENDOLEN: My own Ernest!

JACK: But you don't really mean to say that you couldn't love me if my name wasn't Ernest?

GWENDOLEN: But your name is Ernest.

JACK: Yes, I know it is. But supposing it was something else? Do you mean to say you couldn't love me then?

GWENDOLEN: [*Glibly*] Ah! that is clearly a metaphysical speculation, and like most metaphysical speculations has very little reference at all to the actual facts of real life, as we know them.

JACK: Personally, darling, to speak quite candidly, I don't much care about the name of Ernest . . . I don't think that name suits me at all.

GWENDOLEN: It suits you perfectly. It is a divine name. It has a music of its own. It produces vibrations.

JACK: Well, really, Gwendolen, I must say that I think there are lots of other much nicer names. I think, Jack, for instance, a charming name.

GWENDOLEN: Jack? . . . No, there is very little music in the name Jack, if any at all, indeed. It does not thrill. It produces absolutely no vibrations. . . . I have known several Jacks, and they all, without exception, were more than usually plain. Besides, Jack is a notorious domesticity for John! And I pity any woman who is married to a man called John. She would probably never be allowed to know the entrancing pleasure of a single moment's solitude. The only really safe name is Ernest.

JACK: Gwendolen, I must get christened at once— I mean we must get married at once. There is no time to be lost.

GWENDOLEN: Married, Mr. Worthing?

JACK: [*Astounded*] Well . . . surely. You know that I love you, and you led me to believe, Miss Fairfax, that you were not absolutely indifferent to me.

GWENDOLEN: I adore you. But you haven't proposed to me yet. Nothing has been said at all about marriage. The subject has not even been touched on.

JACK: Well . . . may I propose to you now?

GWENDOLEN: I think it would be an admirable opportunity. And to spare you any possible disappointment, Mr. Worthing, I think it only fair to tell you quite frankly beforehand that I am fully determined to accept you.

JACK: Gwendolen!

GWENDOLEN: Yes, Mr. Worthing, what have you got to say to me?

JACK: You know what I have got to say to you.

GWENDOLEN: Yes, but you don't say it.

JACK: Gwendolen, will you marry me? [*Goes on his knees*]

GWENDOLEN: Of course I will, darling. How long you have been about it! I am afraid you have had very little experience in how to propose.

JACK: My own one, I have never loved anyone in the world but you.

GWENDOLEN: Yes, but men often propose for practice. I know my brother Gerald does. All my girl-friends tell me so. What wonderfully blue eyes you have, Ernest! They are quite, quite blue. I hope you will always look at me just like that, especially when there are other people present.

[*Enter* Lady Bracknell]

LADY BRACKNELL: Mr. Worthing! Rise, sir, from this semi-recumbent posture. It is most indecorous.

GWENDOLEN: Mamma! [*He tries to rise; she restrains him*] I must beg you to retire. This is no place for you. Besides, Mr. Worthing has not quite finished yet.

LADY BRACKNELL: Finished what, may I ask?

GWENDOLEN: I am engaged to Mr. Worthing, mamma. [*They rise together*]

LADY BRACKNELL: Pardon me, you are not engaged to anyone. When you do become engaged to some one, I, or your father, should his health permit him, will inform you of the fact. An engagement should come on a young girl as a surprise, pleasant or unpleasant, as the case may be. It is hardly a matter that she could be allowed to arrange for herself. . . . And now I have a few questions to put to you, Mr. Worthing. While I am making these inquiries, you, Gwendolen, will wait for me below in the carriage.

GWENDOLEN: [*Reproachfully*] Mamma!

LADY BRACKNELL: In the carriage, Gwendolen!

[Gwendolen *goes to the door. She and* Jack *blow kisses to each other behind* Lady Bracknell's *back.* Lady Bracknell *looks vaguely about as if she could not understand what the noise was. Finally turns round*]

Gwendolen, the carriage!

GWENDOLEN: Yes, mamma. [*Goes out, looking back at* Jack]

LADY BRACKNELL: [*Sitting down*] You can take a seat, Mr. Worthing. [*Looks in her pocket for notebook and pencil*]

JACK: Thank you, Lady Bracknell, I prefer standing.

LADY BRACKNELL: [*Pencil and note-book in hand*] I feel bound to tell you that you are not down on my list of eligible young men, although I have the same list as the dear Duchess of Bolton has. We work together, in fact. However, I am quite ready to enter your name, should your answers be what a really affectionate mother requires. Do you smoke?

JACK: Well, yes, I must admit I smoke.

LADY BRACKNELL: I am glad to hear it. A man should always have an occupation of some kind. There are far too many idle men in London as it is. How old are you?

JACK: Twenty-nine.

LADY BRACKNELL: A very good age to be married at. I have always been of opinion that a man who desires to get married should know either everything or nothing. Which do you know?

JACK: [*After some hesitation*] I know nothing, Lady Bracknell.

LADY BRACKNELL: I am pleased to hear it. I do not approve of anything that tampers with natural ignorance. Ignorance is like a delicate exotic fruit; touch it and the bloom is gone. The whole theory of modern education is radically unsound. Fortunately in England, at any rate, education produces no effect whatsoever. If it did, it would prove a serious danger to the upper classes, and probably lead to acts of violence in Grosvenor Square. What is your income?

JACK: Between seven and eight thousand a year.

LADY BRACKNELL: [*Makes a note in her book*] In land, or in investments?

JACK: In investments, chiefly.

LADY BRACKNELL: That is satisfactory. What between the duties expected of one during one's lifetime, and the duties exacted from one after one's death, land has ceased to be either a profit or a pleasure. It gives one position, and prevents one from keeping it up. That's all that can be said about land.

JACK: I have a country house with some land, of course, attached to it, about fifteen hundred acres, I believe; but I don't depend on that for my real income. In fact, as far as I can make out, the poachers are the only people who make anything out of it.

LADY BRACKNELL: A country house! How many bedrooms? Well, that point can be cleared up afterwards. You have a town house, I hope? A girl with a simple, unspoiled nature, like Gwendolen, could hardly be expected to reside in the country.

JACK: Well, I own a house in Belgrave Square, but it is let by the year to Lady Bloxham. Of course, I can get it back whenever I like, at six months' notice.

LADY BRACKNELL: Lady Bloxham? I don't know her.

JACK: Oh, she goes about very little. She is a lady considerably advanced in years.

LADY BRACKNELL: Ah, now-a-days that is no guarantee of respectability of character. What number in Belgrave Square?

JACK: 149.

LADY BRACKNELL: [*Shaking her head*] The unfashionable side. I thought there was something. However, that could easily be altered.

JACK: Do you mean the fashion, or the side?

LADY BRACKNELL: [*Sternly*] Both, if necessary, I presume. What are your politics?

JACK: Well, I am afraid I really have none. I am a Liberal Unionist.

LADY BRACKNELL: Oh, they count as Tories. They dine with us. Or come in the evening, at any rate. Now to minor matters. Are your parents living?

JACK: I have lost both my parents.

LADY BRACKNELL: Both? . . . That seems like carelessness. Who was your father? He was evidently a man of some wealth. Was he born in what the Radical papers call the purple of commerce, or did he rise from the ranks of the aristocracy?

JACK: I am afraid I really don't know. The fact is, Lady Bracknell, I said I had lost my parents. It would be nearer the truth to say that my parents seem to have lost me . . . I don't actually know who I am by birth. I was . . . well, I was found.

LADY BRACKNELL: Found!

JACK: The late Mr. Thomas Cardew, an old gentleman of a very charitable and kindly disposition, found me, and gave me the name of Worthing, because he happened to have a first-class ticket for Worthing in his pocket at the time. Worthing is a place in Sussex. It is a seaside resort.

LADY BRACKNELL: Where did the charitable gentleman who had a first-class ticket for this seaside find you?

JACK: [*Gravely*] In a hand-bag.

LADY BRACKNELL: A hand-bag?

JACK: [*Very seriously*] Yes, Lady Bracknell. I was in a hand-bag—a somewhat large, black leather hand-bag, with handles to it—an ordinary hand-bag in fact.

LADY BRACKNELL: In what locality did this Mr. James, or Thomas, Cardew come across this ordinary hand-bag?

JACK: In the cloak-room at Victoria Station. It was given to him in mistake for his own.

LADY BRACKNELL: The cloak-room at Victoria Station?

JACK: Yes. The Brighton line.

LADY BRACKNELL: The line is immaterial. Mr. Worthing, I confess I feel somewhat bewildered by what you have just told me. To be born, or at any rate bred, in a hand-bag, whether it had handles or not, seems to me to display a contempt for the ordinary decencies of family life that remind one of the worst excesses of the French Revolution. And I presume you know what that unfortunate movement led to? As for the particular locality in which the hand-bag was found, a cloak-room at a railway station might serve to conceal a social indiscretion—has probably, indeed, been used for that purpose before now—but it could hardly be regarded as an assured basis for a recognized position in good society.

JACK: May I ask you then what you would advise me to do? I need hardly say I would do anything in the world to ensure Gwendolen's happiness.

LADY BRACKNELL: I would strongly advise you, Mr. Worthing, to try and acquire some relations as soon as possible, and to make a definite effort to produce at any rate one parent, of either sex, before the season is quite over.

JACK: Well, I don't see how I could possibly manage to do that. I can produce the hand-bag at any moment. It is in my dressing-room at home. I really think that should satisfy you, Lady Bracknell.

LADY BRACKNELL: Me, sir! What has it to do with me? You can hardly imagine that I and Lord Bracknell would dream of allowing our only daughter—a girl brought up with the utmost care—to marry into a cloakroom, and form an alliance with a parcel? Good morning, Mr. Worthing!

[Lady Bracknell *sweeps out in majestic indignation*]

JACK: Good morning!

[Algernon *from the other room, strikes up the* Wedding March. Jack *looks perfectly furious, and goes to the door*] For goodness' sake don't play that ghastly tune, Algy! How idiotic you are!

[*The music stops, and* Algernon *enters cheerily*]

ALGERNON: Didn't it go off all right, old boy? You don't mean to say Gwendolen refused you? I know it is a way she has. She is always refusing people. I think it is most ill-natured of her.

JACK: Oh, Gwendolen is as right as a trivet. As far as she is concerned, we are engaged. Her mother is perfectly unbearable. Never met such a Gorgon . . . I don't really know what a Gorgon is like, but I am quite sure that Lady Bracknell is one. In any case, she is a monster, without being a myth, which is rather unfair. . . . I beg your pardon, Algy, I suppose I shouldn't talk about your own aunt in that way before you.

ALGERNON: My dear boy, I love hearing my relations abused. It is the only thing that makes me put up with them at all. Relations are simply a tedious pack of people, who haven't got the remotest knowledge of how to live, nor the smallest instinct about when to die.

JACK: Oh, that is nonsense!

ALGERNON: It isn't!

JACK: Well, I won't argue about the matter. You always want to argue about things.

ALGERNON: That is exactly what things were originally made for.

JACK: Upon my word, if I thought that, I'd shoot myself. . . . [*A pause*] You don't think there is any chance of Gwendolen becoming like her mother in about a hundred and fifty years, do you, Algy?

ALGERNON: All women become like their mothers. That is their tragedy. No man does. That's his.

JACK: Is that clever?

ALGERNON: It is perfectly phrased! and quite as true as any observation in civilized life should be.

JACK: I am sick to death of cleverness. Everybody is clever now-a-days. You can't go anywhere without meeting clever people. The thing has become an absolute public nuisance. I wish to goodness we had a few fools left.

ALGERNON: We have.

JACK: I should extremely like to meet them. What do they talk about?

ALGERNON: The fools! Oh! about the clever people, of course.

JACK: What fools!

ALGERNON: By the way, did you tell Gwendolen the truth about your being Ernest in town, and Jack in the country?

JACK: [*In a very patronizing manner*] My dear fellow, the truth isn't quite the sort of thing one tells to a nice, sweet, refined girl. What extraordinary ideas you have about the way to behave to a woman!

ALGERNON: The only way to behave to a woman is to make love to her, if she is pretty, and to someone else if she is plain.

JACK: Oh, that is nonsense.

ALGERNON: What about your brother? What about the profligate Ernest?

JACK: Oh, before the end of the week I shall have got rid of him. I'll say he died in Paris of apoplexy. Lots of people die of apoplexy, quite suddenly, don't they?

ALGERNON: Yes, but it's hereditary, my dear fellow. It's a sort of thing that runs in families. You had much better say a severe chill.

JACK: You are sure a severe chill isn't hereditary, or anything of that kind?

ALGERNON: Of course it isn't!

JACK: Very well, then. My poor brother Ernest is carried off suddenly in Paris, by a severe chill. That gets rid of him.

ALGERNON: But I thought you said that . . . Miss Cardew was a little too much interested in your poor brother Ernest? Won't she feel his loss a good deal?

JACK: Oh, that is all right. Cecily is not a silly, romantic girl, I am glad to say. She has got a capital appetite, goes for long walks, and pays no attention at all to her lessons.

ALGERNON: I would rather like to see Cecily.

JACK: I will take very good care you never do. She is excessively pretty, and she is only just eighteen.

ALGERNON: Have you told Gwendolen yet that you have an excessively pretty ward who is only just eighteen?

JACK: Oh! one doesn't blurt these things out to people. Cecily and Gwendolen are perfectly certain to be extremely great friends. I'll bet you anything you like that half an hour after they have met, they will be calling each other sister.

ALGERNON: Women only do that when they have called each other a lot of other things first. Now, my dear boy, if we want to get a good table at Willis', we really must go and dress. Do you know it is nearly seven?

JACK: [*Irritably*] Oh! it always is nearly seven.

ALGERNON: Well, I'm hungry.

JACK: I never knew you when you weren't. . . .

ALGERNON: What shall we do after dinner? Go to a theater?

JACK: Oh, no! I loathe listening.

ALGERNON: Well, let us go to the Club?

JACK: Oh, no! I hate talking.

ALGERNON: Well, we might trot round to the Empire at ten?

JACK: Oh, no! I can't bear looking at things. It is so silly.

ALGERNON: Well, what shall we do?

JACK: Nothing!

ALGERNON: It is awfully hard work doing nothing. However, I don't mind hard work where there is no definite object of any kind.

[*Enter* Lane]

LANE: Miss Fairfax.

[*Enter* Gwendolen. Lane *goes out*]

ALGERNON: Gwendolen, upon my word!

GWENDOLEN: Algy, kindly turn your back. I have something very particular to say to Mr. Worthing.

ALGERNON: Really, Gwendolen, I don't think I can allow this at all.

GWENDOLEN: Algy, you always adopt a strictly immoral attitude towards life. You are not quite old enough to do that. [Algernon *retires to the fireplace*]

JACK: My own darling!

GWENDOLEN: Ernest, we may never be married. From the expression on mamma's face I fear we never shall. Few parents now-a-days pay any regard to what their children say to them. The old-fashioned respect for the young is fast dying out. Whatever influence I ever had over mamma, I lost at the age of three. But although she may prevent us from becoming man and wife, and I may marry someone else, and marry often, nothing that she can possibly do can alter my eternal devotion to you.

JACK: Dear Gwendolen.

GWENDOLEN: The story of your romantic origin, as related to me by mamma, with unpleasing comments, has naturally stirred the deeper fibers of my nature. Your Christian name has an irresistible fascination. The simplicity of your character makes you exquisitely incomprehensible to me. Your town address at the Albany I have. What is your address in the country?

JACK: The Manor House, Woolton, Hertfordshire.

[Algernon, *who has been carefully listening, smiles to himself, and writes the address on his shirt-cuff. Then picks up the Railway Guide*]

GWENDOLEN: There is a good postal service, I suppose? It may be necessary to do something desperate. That, of course, will require serious consideration. I will communicate with you daily.

JACK: My own one!

GWENDOLEN: How long do you remain in town?

JACK: Till Monday.

GWENDOLEN: Good! Algy, you may turn round now.

ALGERNON: Thanks, I've turned round already.

GWENDOLEN: You may also ring the bell.

JACK: You will let me see you to your carriage, my own darling?

GWENDOLEN: Certainly.

JACK: [To Lane, who now enters] I will see Miss Fairfax out.

LANE: Yes, sir.

[Jack and Gwendolen go off. Lane presents several letters on a salver to Algernon. It is to be surmised that they are bills, as Algernon, after looking at the envelopes, tears them up]

ALGERNON: A glass of sherry, Lane.

LANE: Yes, sir.

ALGERNON: To-morrow, Lane, I'm going Bunburying.

LANE: Yes, sir.

ALGERNON: I shall probably not be back till Monday. You can put up my dress clothes, my smoking jacket, and all the Bunbury suits . . .

LANE: Yes, sir. [Handing sherry]

ALGERNON: I hope to-morrow will be a fine day, Lane.

LANE: It never is, sir.

ALGERNON: Lane, you're a perfect pessimist.

LANE: I do my best to give satisfaction, sir.

[Enter Jack. Lane goes off]

JACK: There's a sensible, intellectual girl! the only girl I ever cared for in my life. [Algernon is laughing immoderately] What on earth are you so amused at?

ALGERNON: Oh, I'm a little anxious about poor Bunbury, that's all.

JACK: If you don't take care, your friend Bunbury will get you into a serious scrape some day.

ALGERNON: I love scrapes. They are the only things that are never serious.

JACK: Oh, that's nonsense, Algy. You never talk anything but nonsense.

ALGERNON: Nobody ever does. [Jack looks indignantly at him, and leaves the room. Algernon lights a cigarette, reads his shirt-cuff and smiles]

ACT II.

SCENE: Garden at the Manor House. A flight of gray stone steps leads up to the house. The garden, an old-fashioned one, full of roses. Time of year, July. Basket chairs, and a table covered with books, are set under a large yew tree.

[Miss Prism discovered seated at the table. Cecily is at the back watering flowers]

MISS PRISM: [Calling] Cecily, Cecily! Surely such a utilitarian occupation as the watering of flowers is rather Moulton's duty than yours? Especially at a moment when intellectual pleasures await you. Your German grammar is on the table. Pray open it at page fifteen. We will repeat yesterday's lesson.

CECILY: [Coming over very slowly] But I don't like German. It isn't at all a becoming language. I know perfectly well that I look quite plain after my German lesson.

MISS PRISM: Child, you know how anxious your guardian is that you should improve yourself in every way. He laid particular stress on your German, as he was leaving for town yesterday. Indeed, he always lays stress on your German when he is leaving for town.

CECILY: Dear Uncle Jack is so very serious! Sometimes he is so serious that I think he cannot be quite well.

MISS PRISM: [Drawing herself up] Your guardian enjoys the best of health, and his gravity of demeanor is especially to be commended in one so comparatively young as he is. I know no one who has a higher sense of duty and responsibility.

CECILY: I suppose that is why he often looks a little bored when we three are together.

MISS PRISM: Cecily! I am surprised at you. Mr. Worthing has many troubles in his life. Idle merriment and triviality would be out of place in his conversation. You must remember his constant anxiety about that unfortunate young man, his brother.

CECILY: I wish Uncle Jack would allow that unfortunate young man, his brother, to come down here sometimes. We might have a good influence over him, Miss Prism. I am sure you certainly would. You know German, and geology, and things of that kind influence a man very much. [Cecily begins to write in her diary]

MISS PRISM: [Shaking her head] I do not think that even I could produce any effect on a character that, according to his own brother's admission, is irretrievably weak and vacillating. Indeed, I am not sure that I would desire to reclaim him. I am not in favor of this modern mania for turning bad people into good people at a moment's notice. As a man sows so let him reap. You must put away your diary, Cecily. I really don't see why you should keep a diary at all.

CECILY: I keep a diary in order to enter the wonderful secrets of my life. If I didn't write them down I should probably forget all about them.

MISS PRISM: Memory, my dear Cecily, is the diary that we all carry about with us.

CECILY: Yes, but it usually chronicles the things that have never happened, and couldn't possibly have happened. I believe that Memory is responsible for nearly all the three-volume novels that Mudie sends us.

MISS PRISM: Do not speak slightingly of the three-volume novel, Cecily. I wrote one myself in earlier days.

CECILY: Did you really, Miss Prism? How wonderfully clever you are! I hope it did not end happily? I don't like novels that end happily. They depress me so much.

MISS PRISM: The good ended happily, and the bad unhappily. That is what Fiction means.

CECILY: I suppose so. But it seems very unfair. And was your novel ever published?

MISS PRISM: Alas! no. The manuscript unfortunately was abandoned. I use the word in the sense of lost or mislaid. To your work, child, these speculations are profitless.

CECILY: [*Smiling*] But I see dear Dr. Chasuble coming up through the garden.

MISS PRISM: [*Rising and advancing*] Dr. Chasuble! This is indeed a pleasure.

[*Enter* Canon Chasuble]

CHASUBLE: And how are we this morning? Miss Prism, you are, I trust, well?

CECILY: Miss Prism has just been complaining of a slight headache. I think it would do her so much good to have a short stroll with you in the park, Dr. Chasuble.

MISS PRISM: Cecily, I have not mentioned anything about a headache.

CECILY: No, dear Miss Prism, I know that, but I felt instinctively that you had a headache. Indeed I was thinking about that, and not about my German lesson when the Rector came in.

CHASUBLE: I hope, Cecily, you are not inattentive.

CECILY: Oh, I am afraid I am.

CHASUBLE: That is strange. Were I fortunate enough to be Miss Prism's pupil, I would hang upon her lips. [Miss Prism *glares*] I spoke metaphorically. —My metaphor was drawn from bees. Ahem! Mr. Worthing, I suppose, has not returned from town yet?

MISS PRISM: We do not expect him till Monday afternoon.

CHASUBLE: Ah yes, he usually likes to spend his Sunday in London. He is not one of those whose sole aim is enjoyment, as, by all accounts, that unfortunate young man, his brother, seems to be. But I must not disturb Egeria and her pupil any longer.

MISS PRISM: Egeria? My name is Lætitia, Doctor.

CHASUBLE: [*Bowing*] A classical allusion merely, drawn from the Pagan authors. I shall see you both no doubt at Evensong.

MISS PRISM: I think, dear Doctor, I will have a stroll with you. I find I have a headache after all, and a walk might do it good.

CHASUBLE: With pleasure, Miss Prism, with pleasure. We might go as far as the schools and back.

MISS PRISM: That would be delightful. Cecily, you will read your Political Economy in my absence. The chapter on the Fall of the Rupee you may omit. It is somewhat too sensational. Even these metallic problems have their melodramatic side.

[*Goes down the garden with* Dr. Chasuble]

CECILY: [*Picks up books and throws them back on table*] Horrid Political Economy! Horrid Geography! Horrid, horrid German!

[*Enter* Merriman *with a card on a salver*]

MERRIMAN: Mr. Ernest Worthing has just driven over from the station. He has brought his luggage with him.

CECILY: [*Takes the card and reads it*] "Mr. Ernest Worthing, B 4 The Albany, W." Uncle Jack's brother! Did you tell him Mr. Worthing was in town?

MERRIMAN: Yes, Miss. He seemed very much disappointed. I mentioned that you and Miss Prism were in the garden. He said he was anxious to speak to you privately for a moment.

CECILY: Ask Mr. Ernest Worthing to come here. I suppose you had better talk to the housekeeper about a room for him.

MERRIMAN: Yes, Miss.

[Merriman *goes off*]

CECILY: I have never met any really wicked person before. I feel rather frightened. I am so afraid he will look just like everyone else.

[*Enter* Algernon, *very gay and debonair*] He does!

ALGERNON: [*Raising his hat*] You are my little Cousin Cecily, I'm sure.

CECILY: You are under some strange mistake. I am not little. In fact, I am more than usually tall for my age. [Algernon *is rather taken aback*] But I am your Cousin Cecily. You, I see from your card, are Uncle Jack's brother, my Cousin Ernest, my wicked Cousin Ernest.

ALGERNON: Oh! I am not really wicked at all, Cousin Cecily. You mustn't think that I am wicked.

CECILY: If you are not, then you have certainly been deceiving us all in a very inexcusable manner. I hope you have not been leading a double life, pretending to be wicked and being really good all the time. That would be hypocrisy.

ALGERNON: [*Looks at her in amazement*] Oh! Of course I have been rather reckless.

CECILY: I am glad to hear it.

ALGERNON: In fact, now you mention the subject, I have been very bad in my own small way.

CECILY: I don't think you should be so proud of that, though I am sure it must have been very pleasant.

ALGERNON: It is much pleasanter being here with you.

CECILY: I can't understand how you are here at all. Uncle Jack won't be back till Monday afternoon.

ALGERNON: That is a great disappointment. I am obliged to go up by the first train on Monday morning. I have a business appointment that I am anxious . . . to miss.

CECILY: Couldn't you miss it anywhere but in London?

ALGERNON: No; the appointment is in London.

CECILY: Well, I know, of course, how important it is not to keep a business engagement, if one wants to retain any sense of the beauty of life, but still I think you had better wait till Uncle Jack arrives. I know he wants to speak to you about your emigrating.

ALGERNON: About my what?

CECILY: Your emigrating. He has gone up to buy your outfit.

ALGERNON: I certainly wouldn't let Jack buy my outfit. He has no taste in neckties at all.

CECILY: I don't think you will require neckties. Uncle Jack is sending you to Australia.

ALGERNON: Australia! I'd sooner die.

CECILY: Well, he said at dinner on Wednesday night, that you would have to choose between this world, the next world, and Australia.

ALGERNON: Oh, well! The accounts I have received of Australia and the next world, are not particularly encouraging. This world is good enough for me, Cousin Cecily.

CECILY: Yes, but are you good enough for it?

ALGERNON: I'm afraid I'm not that. That is why I want you to reform me. You might make that your mission, if you don't mind, Cousin Cecily.

CECILY: I'm afraid I've not time, this afternoon.

ALGERNON: Well, would you mind my reforming myself this afternoon?

CECILY: That is rather Quixotic of you. But I think you should try.

ALGERNON: I will. I feel better already.

CECILY: You are looking a little worse.

ALGERNON: That is because I am hungry.

CECILY: How thoughtless of me. I should have remembered that when one is going to lead an entirely new life, one requires regular and wholesome meals. Won't you come in?

ALGERNON: Thank you. Might I have a button-hole first? I never have any appetite unless I have a button-hole first.

CECILY: A Maréchal Niel? [*Picks up scissors*]

ALGERNON: No, I'd sooner have a pink rose.

CECILY: Why? [*Cuts a flower*]

ALGERNON: Because you are like a pink rose, Cousin Cecily.

CECILY: I don't think it can be right for you to talk to me like that. Miss Prism never says such things to me.

ALGERNON: Then Miss Prism is a short-sighted old lady. [Cecily *puts the rose in his button-hole*] You are the prettiest girl I ever saw.

CECILY: Miss Prism says that all good looks are a snare.

ALGERNON: They are a snare that every sensible man would like to be caught in.

CECILY: Oh! I don't think I would care to catch a sensible man. I shouldn't know what to talk to him about.

[*They pass into the house.* Miss Prism *and* Dr. Chasuble *return*]

MISS PRISM: You are too much alone, dear Dr. Chasuble. You should get married. A misanthrope I can understand—a womanthrope, never!

CHASUBLE: [*With a scholar's shudder*] Believe me, I do not deserve so neologistic a phrase. The precept as well as the practice of the Primitive Church was distinctly against matrimony.

MISS PRISM: [*Sententiously*] That is obviously the reason why the Primitive Church has not lasted up to the present day. And you do not seem to realize, dear Doctor, that by persistently remaining single, a man converts himself into a permanent public temptation. Men should be careful; this very celibacy leads weaker vessels astray.

CHASUBLE: But is a man not equally attractive when married?

MISS PRISM: No married man is ever attractive except to his wife.

CHASUBLE: And often, I've been told, not even to her.

MISS PRISM: That depends on the intellectual sympathies of the woman. Maturity can always be depended on. Ripeness can be trusted. Young women are green. [Dr. Chasuble *starts*] I spoke horticulturally. My metaphor was drawn from fruits. But where is Cecily?

CHASUBLE: Perhaps she followed us to the schools.

[*Enter* Jack *slowly from the back of the garden. He is dressed in the deepest mourning, with crape hat-band and black gloves*]

MISS PRISM: Mr. Worthing!

CHASUBLE: Mr. Worthing?

MISS PRISM: This is indeed a surprise. We did not look for you till Monday afternoon.

JACK: [*Shakes* Miss Prism's *hand in a tragic manner*] I have returned sooner than I expected. Dr. Chasuble, I hope you are well?

CHASUBLE: Dear Mr. Worthing, I trust this garb of woe does not betoken some terrible calamity?

JACK: My brother.

MISS PRISM: More shameful debts and extravagance?

CHASUBLE: Still leading his life of pleasure?

JACK: [*Shaking his head*] Dead.

CHASUBLE: Your brother Ernest dead?

JACK: Quite dead.

MISS PRISM: What a lesson for him! I trust he will profit by it.

CHASUBLE: Mr. Worthing, I offer you my sincere condolence. You have at least the consolation of knowing that you were always the most generous and forgiving of brothers.

JACK: Poor Ernest! He had many faults, but it is a sad, sad blow.

CHASUBLE: Very sad indeed. Were you with him at the end?

JACK: No. He died abroad; in Paris, in fact. I had a telegram last night from the manager of the Grand Hotel.

CHASUBLE: Was the cause of death mentioned?

JACK: A severe chill, it seems.

MISS PRISM: As a man sows, so shall he reap.

CHASUBLE: [*Raising his hand*] Charity, dear Miss Prism, charity! None of us are perfect. I myself am peculiarly susceptible to draughts. Will the interment take place here?

JACK: No. He seems to have expressed a desire to be buried in Paris.

CHASUBLE: In Paris! [*Shakes his head*] I fear that hardly points to any very serious state of mind at the last. You would no doubt wish me to make some slight allusion to this tragic domestic affliction next Sunday. [Jack *presses his hand convulsively*] My sermon on the meaning of the manna in the wilderness can be adapted to almost any occasion, joyful, or, as in the present case, distressing. [*All sigh*] I have preached it at harvest celebrations, christenings, confirmations, on days of humiliation and festal days. The last time I delivered it was in the Cathedral, as a charity sermon on behalf of the Society for the Prevention of Discontentment among the Upper Orders. The Bishop, who was present, was much struck by some of the analogies I drew.

JACK: Ah, that reminds me, you mentioned christenings I think, Dr. Chasuble? I suppose you know how to christen all right? [Dr. Chasuble *looks astounded*] I mean, of course, you are continually christening, aren't you?

MISS PRISM: It is, I regret to say, one of the Rector's most constant duties in this parish. I have often spoken to the poorer classes on the subject. But they don't seem to know what thrift is.

CHASUBLE: But is there any particular infant in whom you are interested, Mr. Worthing? Your brother was, I believe, unmarried, was he not?

JACK: Oh, yes.

MISS PRISM: [*Bitterly*] People who live entirely for pleasure usually are.

JACK: But it is not for any child, dear Doctor. I am very fond of children. No! the fact is, I would like to be christened myself, this afternoon, if you have nothing better to do.

CHASUBLE: But surely, Mr. Worthing, you have been christened already?

JACK: I don't remember anything about it.

CHASUBLE: But have you any grave doubts on the subject?

JACK: I certainly intend to have. Of course, I don't know if the thing would bother you in any way, or if you think I am a little too old now.

CHASUBLE: Not at all. The sprinkling, and, indeed, the immersion of adults is a perfectly canonical practice.

JACK: Immersion!

CHASUBLE: You need have no apprehensions. Sprinkling is all that is necessary, or indeed I think advisable. Our weather is so changeable. At what hour would you wish the ceremony performed?

JACK: Oh, I might trot around about five if that would suit you.

CHASUBLE: Perfectly, perfectly! In fact I have two similar ceremonies to perform at that time. A case of twins that occurred recently in one of the outlying cottages on your own estate. Poor Jenkins the carter, a most hard-working man.

JACK: Oh! I don't see much fun in being christened along with other babies. It would be childish. Would half-past five do?

CHASUBLE: Admirably! Admirably! [*Takes out watch*] And now, dear Mr. Worthing, I will not intrude any longer into a house of sorrow. I would merely beg you not to be too much bowed down by grief. What seem to us bitter trials at the moment are often blessings in disguise.

MISS PRISM: This seems to me a blessing of an extremely obvious kind.

[*Enter* Cecily *from the house*]

CECILY: Uncle Jack! Oh, I am pleased to see you back. But what horrid clothes you have on! Do go and change them.

MISS PRISM: Cecily!

CHASUBLE: My child! my child! [Cecily *goes towards* Jack; *he kisses her brow in a melancholy manner*]

CECILY: What is the matter, Uncle Jack? Do look happy! You look as if you had a toothache and I have such a surprise for you. Who do you think is in the dining-room? Your brother!

JACK: Who?

CECILY: Your brother Ernest. He arrived about half an hour ago.

JACK: What nonsense! I haven't got a brother.

CECILY: Oh, don't say that. However badly he may have behaved to you in the past he is still your brother. You couldn't be so heartless as to disown him. I'll tell him to come out. And you will shake hands with him, won't you, Uncle Jack? [*Runs back into the house*]

CHASUBLE: These are very joyful tidings.

MISS PRISM: After we had all been resigned to his loss, his sudden return seems to me peculiarly distressing.

JACK: My brother is in the dining-room? I don't know what it all means. I think it is perfectly absurd.

[*Enter* Algernon *and* Cecily *hand in hand. They come slowly up to* Jack]

JACK: Good heavens! [*Motions* Algernon *away*]

ALGERNON: Brother John, I have come down from town to tell you that I am very sorry for all the trouble I have given you, and that I intend to lead a better life in the future. [Jack *glares at him and does not take his hand*]

CECILY: Uncle Jack, you are not going to refuse your own brother's hand?

JACK: Nothing will induce me to take his hand. I think his coming down here disgraceful. He knows perfectly well why.

CECILY: Uncle, do be nice. There is some good in everyone. Ernest has just been telling me about his poor invalid friend, Mr. Bunbury, whom he goes to visit so often. And surely there must be much good in one who is kind to an invalid, and leaves the pleasures of London to sit by a bed of pain.

JACK: Oh, he has been talking about Bunbury, has he?

CECILY: Yes, he has told me all about poor Mr. Bunbury, and his terrible state of health.

JACK: Bunbury! Well, I won't have him talk to you about Bunbury or about anything else. It is enough to drive one perfectly frantic.

ALGERNON: Of course I admit that the faults were all on my side. But I must say that I think that Brother John's coldness to me is peculiarly painful. I expected a more enthusiastic welcome, especially considering it is the first time I have come here.

CECILY: Uncle Jack, if you don't shake hands with Ernest I will never forgive you.

JACK: Never forgive me?

CECILY: Never, never, never!

JACK: Well, this is the last time I shall ever do it. [Shakes hands with Algernon and glares]

CHASUBLE: It's pleasant, is it not, to see so perfect a reconciliation? I think we might leave the two brothers together.

MISS PRISM: Cecily, you will come with us.

CECILY: Certainly, Miss Prism. My little task of reconciliation is over.

CHASUBLE: You have done a beautiful action to-day, dear child.

MISS PRISM: We must not be premature in our judgments.

CECILY: I feel very happy. [They all go off]

JACK: You young scoundrel, Algy, you must get out of this place as soon as possible. I don't allow any Bunburying here.

[Enter Merriman]

MERRIMAN: I have put Mr. Ernest's things in the room next to yours, sir. I suppose that is all right?

JACK: What?

MERRIMAN: Mr. Ernest's luggage, sir. I have un-packed it and put it in the room next to your own.

JACK: His luggage?

MERRIMAN: Yes, sir. Three portmanteaus, a dress-ing-case, two hat-boxes, and a large luncheon-basket.

ALGERNON: I am afraid I can't stay more than a week this time.

JACK: Merriman, order the dog-cart at once. Mr. Ernest has been suddenly called back to town.

MERRIMAN: Yes, sir. [Goes back into the house]

ALGERNON: What a fearful liar you are, Jack. I have not been called back to town at all.

JACK: Yes, you have.

ALGERNON: I haven't heard anyone call me.

JACK: Your duty as a gentleman calls you back.

ALGERNON: My duty as a gentleman has never interfered with my pleasures in the smallest degree.

JACK: I can quite understand that.

ALGERNON: Well, Cecily is a darling.

JACK: You are not to talk of Miss Cardew like that. I don't like it.

ALGERNON: Well, I don't like your clothes. You look perfectly ridiculous in them. Why on earth don't you go up and change? It is perfectly childish to be in deep mourning for a man who is actually staying for a whole week with you in your house as a guest. I call it grotesque.

JACK: You are certainly not staying with me for a whole week as a guest or anything else. You have got to leave . . . by the four-five train.

ALGERNON: I certainly won't leave you so long as you are in mourning. It would be most unfriendly. If I were in mourning you would stay with me, I suppose. I should think it very unkind if you didn't.

JACK: Well, will you go if I change my clothes?

ALGERNON: Yes, if you are not too long. I never saw anybody take so long to dress, and with such little result.

JACK: Well, at any rate, that is better than being always over-dressed as you are.

ALGERNON: If I am occasionally a little over-dressed, I make up for it by being always immensely over-educated.

JACK: Your vanity is ridiculous, your conduct an outrage, and your presence in my garden utterly absurd. However you have got to catch the four-five, and I hope you will have a pleasant journey back to town. This Bunburying, as you call it, has not been a great success for you. [Goes into the house]

ALGERNON: I think it has been a great success. I'm in love with Cecily, and that is everything. [Enter Cecily at the back of the garden. She picks up the can and begins to water the flowers] But I must see her before I go, and make arrangements for another Bunbury. Ah, there she is.

CECILY: Oh, I merely came back to water the roses. I thought you were with Uncle Jack.

ALGERNON: He's gone to order the dog-cart for me.

CECILY: Oh, is he going to take you for a nice drive?

ALGERNON: He's going to send me away.

CECILY: Then have we got to part?

ALGERNON: I am afraid so. It's a very painful parting.

CECILY: It is always painful to part from people whom one has known for a very brief space of time. The absence of old friends one can endure with equanimity. But even a momentary separation from anyone to whom one has just been introduced is almost unbearable.

ALGERNON: Thank you.

[Enter Merriman]

MERRIMAN: The dog-cart is at the door, sir. [Algernon looks appealingly at Cecily]

CECILY: It can wait, Merriman . . . for . . . five minutes.

MERRIMAN: Yes, miss.

[Exit Merriman]

ALGERNON: I hope, Cecily, I shall not offend you if I state quite frankly and openly that you seem to me to be in every way the visible personification of absolute perfection.

CECILY: I think your frankness does you great credit, Ernest. If you will allow me I will copy your remarks into my diary. [*Goes over to table and begins writing in diary*]

ALGERNON: Do you really keep a diary? I'd give anything to look at it. May I?

CECILY: Oh, no. [*Puts her hand over it*] You see, it is simply a very young girl's record of her own thoughts and impressions, and consequently meant for publication. When it appears in volume form I hope you will order a copy. But pray, Ernest, don't stop. I delight in taking down from dictation. I have reached "absolute perfection." You can go on. I am quite ready for more.

ALGERNON: [*Somewhat taken aback*] Ahem! Ahem!

CECILY: Oh, don't cough, Ernest. When one is dictating one should speak fluently and not cough. Besides, I don't know how to spell a cough. [*Writes as Algernon speaks*]

ALGERNON: [*Speaking very rapidly*] Cecily, ever since I first looked upon your wonderful and incomparable beauty, I have dared to love you wildly, passionately, devotedly, hopelessly.

CECILY: I don't think that you should tell me that you love me wildly, passionately, devotedly, hopelessly. Hopelessly doesn't seem to make much sense, does it?

ALGERNON: Cecily!

[*Enter Merriman*]

MERRIMAN: The dog-cart is waiting, sir.

ALGERNON: Tell it to come round next week, at the same hour.

MERRIMAN: [*Looks at Cecily, who makes no sign*] Yes, sir.

[*Merriman retires*]

CECILY: Uncle Jack would be very much annoyed if he knew you were staying on till next week, at the same hour.

ALGERNON: Oh, I don't care about Jack. I don't care for anybody in the whole world but you. I love you, Cecily. You will marry me, won't you?

CECILY: You silly you! Of course. Why, we have been engaged for the last three months.

ALGERNON: For the last three months?

CECILY: Yes, it will be exactly three months on Thursday.

ALGERNON: But how did we become engaged?

CECILY: Well, ever since dear Uncle Jack first confessed to us that he had a younger brother who was very wicked and bad, you of course have formed the chief topic of conversation between myself and Miss Prism. And of course a man who is much talked about is always very attractive. One feels there must be something in him after all. I daresay it was foolish of me, but I fell in love with you, Ernest.

ALGERNON: Darling! And when was the engagement actually settled?

CECILY: On the 14th of February last. Worn out by your entire ignorance of my existence, I determined to end the matter one way or the other, and after a long struggle with myself I accepted you under this dear old tree here. The next day I bought this little ring in your name, and this is the little bangle with the true lovers' knot I promised you always to wear.

ALGERNON: Did I give you this? It's very pretty, isn't it?

CECILY: Yes, you've wonderfully good taste, Ernest. It's the excuse I've always given for your leading such a bad life. And this is the box in which I keep all your dear letters. [*Kneels at table, opens box, and produces letters tied up with blue ribbon*]

ALGERNON: My letters! But my own sweet Cecily, I have never written you any letters.

CECILY: You need hardly remind me of that, Ernest. I remember only too well that I was forced to write your letters for you. I wrote always three times a week, and sometimes oftener.

ALGERNON: Oh, do let me read them, Cecily?

CECILY: Oh, I couldn't possibly. They would make you far too conceited. [*Replaces box*] The three you wrote me after I had broken off the engagement are so beautiful, and so badly spelled, that even now I can hardly read them without crying a little.

ALGERNON: But was our engagement ever broken off?

CECILY: Of course it was. On the 22nd of last March. You can see the entry if you like. [*Shows diary*] "To-day I broke off my engagement with Ernest. I feel it is better to do so. The weather still continues charming."

ALGERNON: But why on earth did you break it off? What had I done? I had done nothing at all. Cecily, I am very much hurt indeed to hear you broke it off. Particularly when the weather was so charming.

CECILY: It would hardly have been a really serious engagement if it hadn't been broken off at least once. But I forgave you before the week was out.

ALGERNON: [*Crossing to her, and kneeling*] What a perfect angel you are, Cecily.

CECILY: You dear romantic boy. [*He kisses her, she puts her fingers through his hair*] I hope your hair curls naturally, does it?

ALGERNON: Yes, darling, with a little help from others.

CECILY: I am so glad.

ALGERNON: You'll never break off our engagement again, Cecily?

CECILY: I don't think I could break it off now that I have actually met you. Besides, of course, there is the question of your name.

ALGERNON: Yes, of course. [*Nervously*]

CECILY: You must not laugh at me, darling, but it had always been a girlish dream of mine to love some one whose name was Ernest. [*Algernon rises, Cecily also*] There is something in that name that seems to inspire absolute confidence. I pity any poor married woman whose husband is not called Ernest.

ALGERNON: But, my dear child, do you mean to say you could not love me if I had some other name?

CECILY: But what name?

ALGERNON: Oh, any name you like—Algernon, for instance. . . .

CECILY: But I don't like the name of Algernon.

ALGERNON: Well, my dear, sweet, loving little darling, I really can't see why you should object to the name of Algernon. It is not at all a bad name. In fact, it is rather an aristocratic name. Half of the chaps who get into the Bankruptcy Court are called Algernon. But seriously, Cecily . . . [Moving to her] . . . if my name was Algy, couldn't you love me?

CECILY: [Rising] I might respect you, Ernest, I might admire your character, but I fear that I should not be able to give you my undivided attention.

ALGERNON: Ahem! Cecily! [Picking up hat] Your Rector here is, I suppose, thoroughly experienced in the practice of all the rites and ceremonials of the church?

CECILY: Oh, yes. Dr. Chasuble is a most learned man. He has never written a single book, so you can imagine how much he knows.

ALGERNON: I must see him at once on a most important christening—I mean on most important business.

CECILY: Oh!

ALGERNON: I sha'n't be away more than half an hour.

CECILY: Considering that we have been engaged since February the 14th, and that I only met you to-day for the first time, I think it is rather hard that you should leave me for so long a period as half an hour. Couldn't you make it twenty minutes?

ALGERNON: I'll be back in no time. [Kisses her and rushes down the garden]

CECILY: What an impetuous boy he is. I like his hair so much. I must enter his proposal in my diary.

[Enter Merriman]

MERRIMAN: A Miss Fairfax has just called to see Mr. Worthing. On very important business, Miss Fairfax states.

CECILY: Isn't Mr. Worthing in his library?

MERRIMAN: Mr. Worthing went over in the direction of the Rectory some time ago.

CECILY: Pray ask the lady to come out here; Mr. Worthing is sure to be back soon. And you can bring tea.

MERRIMAN: Yes, miss. [Goes out]

CECILY: Miss Fairfax! I suppose one of the many good elderly women who are associated with Uncle Jack in some of his philanthropic work in London. I don't quite like women who are interested in philanthropic work. I think it is so forward of them.

[Enter Merriman]

MERRIMAN: Miss Fairfax.

[Enter Gwendolen]

[Exit Merriman]

CECILY: [Advancing to meet her] Pray let me introduce myself to you. My name is Cecily Cardew.

GWENDOLEN: Cecily Cardew? [Moving to her and shaking hands] What a very sweet name! Something tells me that we are going to be great friends. I like you already more than I can say. My first impressions of people are never wrong.

CECILY: How nice of you to like me so much after we have known each other such a comparatively short time. Pray sit down.

GWENDOLEN: [Still standing up] I may call you Cecily, may I not?

CECILY: With pleasure!

GWENDOLEN: And you will always call me Gwendolen, won't you?

CECILY: If you wish.

GWENDOLEN: Then that is all quite settled, is it not?

CECILY: I hope so. [A pause. They both sit down together]

GWENDOLEN: Perhaps this might be a favorable opportunity for my mentioning who I am. My father is Lord Bracknell. You have never heard of papa, I suppose?

CECILY: I don't think so.

GWENDOLEN: Outside the family circle, papa, I am glad to say, is entirely unknown. I think that is quite as it should be. The home seems to me to be the proper sphere for the man. And certainly once a man begins to neglect his domestic duties he becomes painfully effeminate, does he not? And I don't like that. It makes men so very attractive. Cecily, mamma, whose views on education are remarkably strict, has brought me up to be extremely short-sighted; it is part of her system; so do you mind my looking at you through my glasses?

CECILY: Oh, not at all, Gwendolen. I am very fond of being looked at.

GWENDOLEN: [After examining Cecily carefully through a lorgnette] You are here on a short visit, I suppose.

CECILY: Oh, no, I live here.

GWENDOLEN: [Severely] Really? Your mother, no doubt, or some female relative of advanced years, resides here also?

CECILY: Oh, no. I have no mother, nor, in fact, any relations.

GWENDOLEN: Indeed?

CECILY: My dear guardian, with the assistance of Miss Prism, has the arduous task of looking after me.

GWENDOLEN: Your guardian?

CECILY: Yes, I am Mr. Worthing's ward.

GWENDOLEN: Oh! It is strange he never mentioned to me that he had a ward. How secretive of him! He grows more interesting hourly. I am not sure, however, that the news inspires me with feelings of unmixed delight. [Rising and going to her] I am very fond of you, Cecily; I have liked you ever since I met you. But I am bound to state that now that I know that you are Mr. Worthing's ward, I cannot help expressing a wish you were—well, just a little older than you seem to be—and not quite so very alluring in appearance. In fact, if I may speak candidly——

CECILY: Pray do! I think that whenever one has anything unpleasant to say, one should always be quite candid.

GWENDOLEN: Well, to speak with perfect candor, Cecily, I wish that you were fully forty-two, and more than usually plain for your age. Ernest has a strong upright nature. He is the very soul of truth and honor. Disloyalty would be as impossible to him as deception. But even men of the noblest possible moral character are extremely susceptible to the influence of the physical charms of others. Modern, no less than Ancient History, supplies us with most painful examples of what I refer to. If it were not so, indeed, History would be quite unreadable.

CECILY: I beg your pardon, Gwendolen, did you say Ernest?

GWENDOLEN: Yes.

CECILY: Oh, but it is not Mr. Ernest Worthing who is my guardian. It is his brother—his elder brother.

GWENDOLEN: [Sitting down again] Ernest never mentioned to me that he had a brother.

CECILY: I am sorry to say they have not been on good terms for a long time.

GWENDOLEN: Ah! that accounts for it. And now that I think of it I have never heard any man mention his brother. The subject seems distasteful to most men. Cecily, you have lifted a load from my mind. I was growing almost anxious. It would have been terrible if any cloud had come across a friendship like ours, would it not? Of course you are quite, quite sure that it is not Mr. Ernest Worthing who is your guardian?

CECILY: Quite sure. [A pause] In fact, I am going to be his.

GWENDOLEN: [Enquiringly] I beg your pardon?

CECILY: [Rather shy and confidingly] Dearest Gwendolen, there is no reason why I should make a secret of it to you. Our little county newspaper is sure to chronicle the fact next week. Mr. Ernest Worthing and I are engaged to be married.

GWENDOLEN: [Quite politely, rising] My darling Cecily, I think there must be some slight error. Mr. Ernest Worthing is engaged to me. The announcement will appear in the Morning Post on Saturday at the latest.

CECILY: [Very politely, rising] I am afraid you must be under some misconception. Ernest proposed to me exactly ten minutes ago. [Shows diary]

GWENDOLEN: [Examines diary through her lorgnette carefully] It is certainly very curious, for he asked me to be his wife yesterday afternoon at 5.30. If you would care to verify the incident, pray do so. [Produces diary of her own] I never travel without my diary. One should always have something sensa-

tional to read in the train. I am so sorry, dear Cecily, if it is any disappointment to you, but I am afraid I have the prior claim.

CECILY: It would distress me more than I can tell you, dear Gwendolen, if it caused you any mental or physical anguish, but I feel bound to point out that since Ernest proposed to you he clearly has changed his mind.

GWENDOLEN: [Meditatively] If the poor fellow has been entrapped into any foolish promise I shall consider it my duty to rescue him at once, and with a firm hand.

CECILY: [Thoughtfully and sadly] Whatever unfortunate entanglement my dear boy may have got into, I will never reproach him with it after we are married.

GWENDOLEN: Do you allude to me, Miss Cardew, as an entanglement? You are presumptuous. On an occasion of this kind it becomes more than a moral duty to speak one's mind. It becomes a pleasure.

CECILY: Do you suggest, Miss Fairfax, that I entrapped Ernest into an engagement? How dare you? This is no time for wearing the shallow mask of manners. When I see a spade I call it a spade.

GWENDOLEN: [Satirically] I am glad to say that I have never seen a spade. It is obvious that our social spheres have been widely different.

[Enter Merriman, followed by the footman. He carries a salver, tablecloth, and plate-stand. Cecily is about to retort. The presence of the servants exercises a restraining influence, under which both girls chafe.]

MERRIMAN: Shall I lay tea here as usual, miss?

CECILY: [Sternly, in a calm voice] Yes, as usual. [Merriman begins to clear and lay cloth. A long pause. Cecily and Gwendolen glare at each other]

GWENDOLEN: Are there many interesting walks in the vicinity, Miss Cardew?

CECILY: Oh, yes, a great many. From the top of one of the hills quite close one can see five counties.

GWENDOLEN: Five counties! I don't think I should like that. I hate crowds.

CECILY: [Sweetly] I suppose that is why you live in town? [Gwendolen bites her lip, and beats her foot nervously with her parasol]

GWENDOLEN: [Looking round] Quite a well-kept garden this is, Miss Cardew.

CECILY: So glad you like it, Miss Fairfax.

GWENDOLEN: I had no idea there were any flowers in the country.

CECILY: Oh, flowers are as common here, Miss Fairfax, as people are in London.

GWENDOLEN: Personally I cannot understand how anybody manages to exist in the country, if anybody who is anybody does. The country always bores me to death.

CECILY: Ah! This is what the newspapers call agricultural depression, is it not? I believe the aristocracy are suffering very much from it just at present. It is almost an epidemic amongst them, I have been told. May I offer you some tea, Miss Fairfax?

GWENDOLEN: [*With elaborate politeness*] Thank you. [*Aside*] Detestable girl! But I require tea!

CECILY: [*Sweetly*] Sugar?

GWENDOLEN: [*Superciliously*] No, thank you. Sugar is not fashionable any more. [Cecily *looks angrily at her, takes up the tongs and puts four lumps of sugar into the cup*]

CECILY: [*Severely*] Cake or bread and butter?

GWENDOLEN: [*In a bored manner*] Bread and butter, please. Cake is rarely seen at the best houses nowadays.

CECILY: [*Cuts a very large slice of cake, and puts it on the tray*] Hand that to Miss Fairfax. [Merriman *does so, and goes out with footman.* Gwendolen *drinks the tea and makes a grimace. Puts down cup at once, reaches out her hand to the bread and butter, looks at it, and finds it is cake. Rises in indignation*]

GWENDOLEN: You have filled my tea with lumps of sugar, and though I asked most distinctly for bread and butter, you have given me cake. I am known for the gentleness of my disposition, and the extraordinary sweetness of my nature, but I warn you, Miss Cardew, you may go too far.

CECILY: [*Rising*] To save my poor, innocent, trusting boy from the machinations of any other girl there are no lengths to which I would not go.

GWENDOLEN: From the moment I saw you I distrusted you. I felt that you were false and deceitful. I am never deceived in such matters. My first impressions of people are invariably right.

CECILY: It seems to me, Miss Fairfax, that I am trespassing on your valuable time. No doubt you have many other calls of a similar character to make in the neighborhood.

[*Enter* Jack]

GWENDOLEN: [*Catching sight of him*] Ernest! My own Ernest!

JACK: Gwendolen! Darling! [*Offers to kiss her*]

GWENDOLEN: [*Drawing back*] A moment! May I ask if you are engaged to be married to this young lady? [*Points to* Cecily]

JACK: [*Laughing*] To dear little Cecily! Of course not! What could have put such an idea into your pretty little head?

GWENDOLEN: Thank you. You may. [*Offers her cheek*]

CECILY: [*Very sweetly*] I knew there must be some misunderstanding, Miss Fairfax. The gentleman whose arm is at present around your waist is my dear guardian, Mr. John Worthing.

GWENDOLEN: I beg your pardon?

CECILY: This is Uncle Jack.

GWENDOLEN: [*Receding*] Jack! Oh!

[*Enters* Algernon]

CECILY: Here is Ernest.

ALGERNON: [*Goes straight over to* Cecily *without noticing anyone else*] My own love! [*Offers to kiss her*]

CECILY: [*Drawing back*] A moment, Ernest! May I ask you—are you engaged to be married to this young lady?

ALGERNON: [*Looking round*] To what young lady? Good heavens! Gwendolen!

CECILY: Yes, to good heavens, Gwendolen, I mean to Gwendolen.

ALGERNON: [*Laughing*] Of course not! What could have put such an idea into your pretty little head?

CECILY: Thank you. [*Presenting her cheek to be kissed*] You may. [Algernon *kisses her*]

GWENDOLEN: I felt there was some slight error, Miss Cardew. The gentleman who is now embracing you is my cousin, Mr. Algernon Moncrieff.

CECILY: [*Breaking away from* Algernon] Algernon Moncrieff! Oh! [*The two girls move towards each other and put their arms round each other's waists as if for protection*]

CECILY: Are you called Algernon?

ALGERNON: I cannot deny it.

CECILY: Oh!

GWENDOLEN: Is your name really John?

JACK: [*Standing rather proudly*] I could deny it if I liked. I could deny anything if I liked. But my name certainly is John. It has been John for years.

CECILY: [*To* Gwendolen] A gross deception has been practised on both of us.

GWENDOLEN: My poor wounded Cecily!

CECILY: My sweet, wronged Gwendolen!

GWENDOLEN: [*Slowly and seriously*] You will call me sister, will you not? [*They embrace.* Jack *and* Algernon *groan and walk up and down*]

CECILY: [*Rather brightly*] There is just one question I would like to be allowed to ask my guardian.

GWENDOLEN: An admirable idea! Mr. Worthing, there is just one question I would like to be permitted to put to you. Where is your brother Ernest? We are both engaged to be married to your brother Ernest, so it is a matter of some importance to us to know where your brother Ernest is at present.

JACK: [*Slowly and hesitatingly*] Gwendolen—Cecily—it is very painful for me to be forced to speak the truth. It is the first time in my life that I have ever been reduced to such a painful position, and I am really quite inexperienced in doing anything of the kind. However I will tell you quite frankly that I have no brother Ernest. I have no brother at all. I never had a brother in my life, and I certainly have not the smallest intention of ever having one in the future.

CECILY: [*Surprised*] No brother at all?

JACK: [*Cheerily*] None!

GWENDOLEN: [*Severely*] Had you never a brother of any kind?

JACK: [*Pleasantly*] Never. Not even of any kind.

GWENDOLEN: I am afraid it is quite clear, Cecily, that neither of us is engaged to be married to anyone.

CECILY: It is not a very pleasant position for a young girl suddenly to find herself in. Is it?

GWENDOLEN: Let us go into the house. They will hardly venture to come after us there.

CECILY: No, men are so cowardly, aren't they? [*They retire into the house with scornful looks*]

JACK: This ghastly state of things is what you call Bunburying, I suppose?

ALGERNON: Yes, and a perfectly wonderful Bunbury it is. The most wonderful Bunbury I have ever had in my life.

JACK: Well, you've no right whatsoever to Bunbury here.

ALGERNON: That is absurd. One has a right to Bunbury anywhere one chooses. Every serious Bunburyist knows that.

JACK: Serious Bunburyist! Good heavens!

ALGERNON: Well, one must be serious about something, if one wants to have any amusement in life. I happen to be serious about Bunburying. What on earth you are serious about I haven't got the remotest idea. About everything, I should fancy. You have such an absolutely trivial nature.

JACK: Well, the only small satisfaction I have in the whole of this wretched business is that your friend Bunbury is quite exploded. You won't be able to run down to the country quite so often as you used to do, dear Algy. And a very good thing, too.

ALGERNON: Your brother is a little off color, isn't he, dear Jack? You won't be able to disappear to London quite so frequently as your wicked custom was. And not a bad thing, either.

JACK: As for your conduct towards Miss Cardew, I must say that your taking in a sweet, simple, innocent girl like that is quite inexcusable. To say nothing of the fact that she is my ward.

ALGERNON: I can see no possible defence at all for your deceiving a brilliant, clever, thoroughly experienced young lady like Miss Fairfax. To say nothing of the fact that she is my cousin.

JACK: I wanted to be engaged to Gwendolen, that is all. I love her.

ALGERNON: Well, I simply wanted to be engaged to Cecily. I adore her.

JACK: There is certainly no chance of your marrying Miss Cardew.

ALGERNON: I don't think there is much likelihood, Jack, of you and Miss Fairfax being united.

JACK: Well, that is no business of yours.

ALGERNON: If it was my business, I wouldn't talk about it. [*Begins to eat muffins*] It is very vulgar to talk about one's business. Only people like stockbrokers do that, and then merely at dinner parties.

JACK: How you can sit there, calmly eating muffins, when we are in this horrible trouble, I can't make out. You seem to me to be perfectly heartless.

ALGERNON: Well, I can't eat muffins in an agitated manner. The butter would probably get on my cuffs. One should always eat muffins quite calmly. It is the only way to eat them.

JACK: I say it's perfectly heartless your eating muffins at all, under the circumstances.

ALGERNON: When I am in trouble, eating is the only thing that consoles me. Indeed, when I am in really great trouble, as anyone who knows me intimately will tell you, I refuse everything except food and drink. At the present moment I am eating muffins because I am unhappy. Besides, I am particularly fond of muffins. [*Rising*]

JACK: [*Rising*] Well, that is no reason why you should eat them all in that greedy way. [*Takes muffins from* Algernon]

ALGERNON: [*Offering tea-cake*] I wish you would have tea-cake instead. I don't like tea-cake.

JACK: Good heavens! I suppose a man may eat his own muffins in his own garden.

ALGERNON: But you have just said it was perfectly heartless to eat muffins.

JACK: I said it was perfectly heartless of you, under the circumstances. That is a very different thing.

ALGERNON: That may be. But the muffins are the same. [*He seizes the muffin-dish from* Jack]

JACK: Algy, I wish to goodness you would go.

ALGERNON: You can't possibly ask me to go without having some dinner. It's absurd. I never go without my dinner. No one ever does, except vegetarians and people like that. Besides I have just made arrangements with Dr. Chasuble to be christened at a quarter to six under the name of Ernest.

JACK: My dear fellow, the sooner you give up that nonsense the better. I made arrangements this morning with Dr. Chasuble to be christened myself at 5.30, and I naturally will take the name of Ernest. Gwendolen would wish it. We can't both be christened Ernest. It's absurd. Besides, I have a perfect right to be christened if I like. There is no evidence at all that I ever have been christened by anybody. I should think it extremely probable I never was, and so does Dr. Chasuble. It is entirely different in your case. You have been christened already.

ALGERNON: Yes, but I have not been christened for years.

JACK: Yes, but you have been christened. That is the important thing.

ALGERNON: Quite so. So I know my constitution can stand it. If you are not quite sure about your ever having been christened, I must say I think it rather dangerous your venturing on it now. It might make you very unwell. You can hardly have forgotten that someone very closely connected with you was very nearly carried off this week in Paris by a severe chill.

JACK: Yes, but you said yourself that a severe chill was not hereditary.

ALGERNON: It usedn't to be, I know—but I daresay it is now. Science is always making wonderful improvements in things.

JACK: [*Picking up the muffin-dish*] Oh, that is nonsense; you are always talking nonsense.

ALGERNON: Jack, you are at the muffins again! I wish you wouldn't. There are only two left. [*Takes them*] I told you I was particularly fond of muffins.

JACK: But I hate tea-cake.

ALGERNON: Why on earth then do you allow tea-cake to be served up for your guests? What ideas you have of hospitality!

JACK: Algernon! I have already told you to go. I don't want you here. Why don't you go?

ALGERNON: I haven't quite finished my tea yet, and there is still one muffin left. [Jack *groans, and sinks into a chair.* Algernon *still continues eating*]

CURTAIN

ACT III.

SCENE: *Morning-room at the Manor House.* Gwendolen *and* Cecily *are at the window, looking out into the garden.*

GWENDOLEN: The fact that they did not follow us at once into the house, as anyone else would have done, seems to me to show that they have some sense of shame left.

CECILY: They have been eating muffins. That looks like repentance.

GWENDOLEN: [*After a pause*] They don't seem to notice us at all. Couldn't you cough?

GWENDOLEN: They're looking at us. What effrontery!

CECILY: They're approaching. That's very forward of them.

GWENDOLEN: Let us preserve a dignified silence.

CECILY: Certainly. It's the only thing to do now. [*Enter* Jack, *followed by* Algernon. *They whistle some dreadful popular air from a British opera*]

GWENDOLEN: This dignified silence seems to produce an unpleasant effect.

CECILY: A most distasteful one.

GWENDOLEN: But we will not be the first to speak.

CECILY: Certainly not.

GWENDOLEN: Mr. Worthing, I have something very particular to ask you. Much depends on your reply.

CECILY: Gwendolen, your common sense is invaluable. Mr. Moncrieff, kindly answer me the following question. Why did you pretend to be my guardian's brother?

ALGERNON: In order that I might have an opportunity of meeting you.

CECILY: [*To* Gwendolen] That certainly seems a satisfactory explanation, does it not?

GWENDOLEN: Yes, dear, if you can believe him.

CECILY: I don't. But that does not affect the wonderful beauty of his answer.

GWENDOLEN: True. In matters of grave importance, style, not sincerity, is the vital thing. Mr. Worthing, what explanation can you offer to me for pretending to have a brother? Was it in order that you might have an opportunity of coming up to town to see me as often as possible?

JACK: Can you doubt it, Miss Fairfax?

GWENDOLEN: I have the gravest doubts upon the subject. But I intend to crush them. This is not the moment for German scepticism. [*Moving to* Cecily] Their explanations appear to be quite satisfactory, especially Mr. Worthing's. That seems to me to have the stamp of truth upon it.

CECILY: I am more than content with what Mr. Moncrieff said. His voice alone inspires one with absolute credulity.

GWENDOLEN: Then you think we should forgive them?

CECILY: Yes. I mean no.

GWENDOLEN: True! I had forgotten. There are principles at stake that one cannot surrender. Which of us should tell them? The task is not a pleasant one.

CECILY: Could we not both speak at the same time?

GWENDOLEN: An excellent idea! I nearly always speak at the same time as other people. Will you take the time from me?

CECILY: Certainly. [Gwendolen *beats time with uplifted finger*]

GWENDOLEN AND CECILY: [*Speaking together*] Your Christian names are still an insuperable barrier. That is all!

JACK AND ALGERNON: [*Speaking together*] Our Christian names! Is that all? But we are going to be christened this afternoon.

GWENDOLEN: [*To* Jack] For my sake you are prepared to do this terrible thing?

JACK: I am.

CECILY: [*To* Algernon] To please me you are ready to face this fearful ordeal?

ALGERNON: I am.

GWENDOLEN: How absurd to talk of the equality of the sexes! Where questions of self-sacrifice are concerned, men are infinitely beyond us.

JACK: We are. [*Clasps hands with* Algernon]

CECILY: They have moments of physical courage of which we women know absolutely nothing.

GWENDOLEN: [*To* Jack] Darling!

ALGERNON: [*To* Cecily] Darling! [*They fall into each other's arms*]

[*Enter* Merriman. *When he enters he coughs loudly, seeing the situation*]

MERRIMAN: Ahem! Ahem! Lady Bracknell!

JACK: Good heavens!

[*Enter* Lady Bracknell. *The couples separate in alarm. Exit* Merriman]

LADY BRACKNELL: Gwendolen! What does this mean?

GWENDOLEN: Merely that I am engaged to be married to Mr. Worthing, Mamma.

LADY BRACKNELL: Come here. Sit down. Sit down immediately. Hesitation of any kind is a sign of mental decay in the young, of physical weakness in the old. [*Turns to* Jack] Apprised, sir, of my daughter's sudden flight by her trusty maid, whose confidence I purchased by means of a small coin, I followed her at once by a luggage train. Her unhappy father is, I am glad to say, under the impression that she is attending a more than usually lengthy lecture by the University Extension Scheme on the Influence of a Permanent Income on Thought. I do not propose to undeceive him. Indeed I have never undeceived him on any question. I would consider it wrong. But of course, you will clearly understand that all communication between yourself and my daughter must cease immediately from this moment. On this point, as indeed on all points, I am firm.

JACK: I am engaged to be married to Gwendolen, Lady Bracknell!

LADY BRACKNELL: You are nothing of the kind, sir. And now, as regards Algernon! . . . Algernon!

ALGERNON: Yes, Aunt Augusta.

LADY BRACKNELL: May I ask if it is in this house that your invalid friend Mr. Bunbury resides?

ALGERNON: [*Stammering*] Oh, no! Bunbury doesn't live here. Bunbury is somewhere else at present. In fact, Bunbury is dead.

LADY BRACKNELL: Dead! When did Mr. Bunbury die? His death must have been extremely sudden.

ALGERNON: [*Airily*] Oh, I killed Bunbury this afternoon. I mean poor Bunbury died this afternoon.

LADY BRACKNELL: What did he die of?

ALGERNON: Bunbury? Oh, he was quite exploded.

LADY BLACKNELL: Exploded! Was he the victim of a revolutionary outrage? I was not aware that Mr. Bunbury was interested in social legislation. If so, he is well punished for his morbidity.

ALGERNON: My dear Aunt Augusta, I mean he was found out! The doctors found out that Bunbury could not live, that is what I mean—so Bunbury died.

LADY BRACKNELL: He seems to have had great confidence in the opinion of his physicians. I am glad, however, that he made up his mind at the last to some definite course of action, and acted under proper medical advice. And now that we have finally got rid of this Mr. Bunbury, may I ask, Mr. Worthing, who is that young person whose hand my nephew Algernon is now holding in what seems to me a peculiarly unnecessary manner?

JACK: That lady is Miss Cecily Cardew, my ward. [Lady Bracknell *bows coldly to* Cecily]

ALGERNON: I am engaged to be married to Cecily, Aunt Augusta.

LADY BRACKNELL: I beg your pardon?

CECILY: Mr. Moncrieff and I are engaged to be married, Lady Bracknell.

LADY BRACKNELL: [*With a shiver, crossing to the sofa and sitting down*] I do not know whether there is anything peculiarly exciting in the air in this particular part of Hertfordshire, but the number of engagements that go on seems to me considerably above the proper average that statistics have laid down for our guidance. I think some preliminary enquiry on my part would not be out of place. Mr. Worthing, is Miss Cardew at all connected with any of the larger railway stations in London? I merely desire information. Until yesterday I had no idea that there were any families or persons whose origin was a Terminus. [Jack *looks perfectly furious, but restrains himself*]

JACK: [*In a clear, cold voice*] Miss Cardew is the granddaughter of the late Mr. Thomas Cardew of 149, Belgrave Square, S.W.; Gervase Park, Dorking, Surrey; and the Sporran, Fifeshire, N.B.

LADY BRACKNELL: That sounds not unsatisfactory. Three addresses always inspire confidence, even in tradesmen. But what proof have I of their authenticity?

JACK: I have carefully preserved the Court Guide of the period. They are open to your inspection, Lady Bracknell.

LADY BRACKNELL: [*Grimly*] I have known strange errors in that publication.

JACK: Miss Cardew's family solicitors are Messrs. Markby, Markby, and Markby.

LADY BRACKNELL: Markby, Markby, and Markby? A firm of the very highest position in their profession. Indeed I am told that one of the Mr. Markbys is occasionally to be seen at dinner parties. So far I am satisfied.

JACK: [*Very irritably*] How extremely kind of you, Lady Bracknell! I have also in my possession, you will be pleased to hear, certificates of Miss Cardew's birth, baptism, whooping cough, registration, vaccination, confirmation, and the measles; both the German and the English variety.

LADY BRACKNELL: Ah! A life crowded with incident, I see; though perhaps somewhat too exciting for a young girl. I am not myself in favor of premature experiences. [*Rises, looks at her watch*] Gwendolen! the time approaches for our departure. We have not a moment to lose. As a matter of form, Mr. Worthing, I had better ask you if Miss Cardew has any little fortune?

JACK: Oh, about a hundred and thirty thousand pounds in the Funds. That is all. Good-bye, Lady Bracknell. So pleased to have seen you.

LADY BRACKNELL: [*Sitting down again*] A moment, Mr. Worthing. A hundred and thirty thousand pounds! And in the Funds! Miss Cardew seems to me a most attractive young lady, now that I look at her. Few girls of the present day have any really solid qualities, any of the qualities that last, and improve with time. We live, I regret to say, in an age of surfaces. [*To* Cecily] Come over here, dear. [Cecily *goes across*] Pretty child! your dress is sadly simple, and your hair seems almost as Nature might have left it. But we can soon alter all that. A thoroughly experienced French maid produces a really marvelous result in a very brief space of time. I remember recommending one to young Lady Lancing, and after three months her own husband did not know her.

JACK: [Aside] And after six months nobody knew her.

LADY BRACKNELL: [Glares at Jack for a few moments. Then bends, with a practised smile, to Cecily] Kindly turn round, sweet child. [Cecily turns completely round] No, the side view is what I want. [Cecily presents her profile] Yes, quite as I expected. There are distinct social possibilities in your profile. The two weak points in our age are its want of principle and its want of profile. The chin a little higher, dear. Style largely depends on the way the chin is worn. They are worn very high, just at present. Algernon!

ALGERNON: Yes, Aunt Augusta!

LADY BRACKNELL: There are distinct social possibilities in Miss Cardew's profile.

ALGERNON: Cecily is the sweetest, dearest, prettiest girl in the whole world. And I don't care twopence about social possibilities.

LADY BRACKNELL: Never speak disrespectfully of society, Algernon. Only people who can't get into it do that. [To Cecily] Dear child, of course you know that Algernon has nothing but his debts to depend upon. But I do not approve of mercenary marriages. When I married Lord Bracknell I had no fortune of any kind. But I never dreamed for a moment of allowing that to stand in my way. Well, I suppose I must give my consent.

ALGERNON: Thank you, Aunt Augusta.

LADY BRACKNELL: Cecily, you may kiss me!

CECILY: [Kisses her] Thank you, Lady Bracknell.

LADY BRACKNELL: You may also address me as Aunt Augusta for the future.

CECILY: Thank you, Aunt Augusta.

LADY BRACKNELL: The marriage, I think, had better take place quite soon.

ALGERNON: Thank you, Aunt Augusta.

CECILY: Thank you, Aunt Augusta.

LADY BRACKNELL: To speak frankly, I am not in favor of long engagements. They give people the opportunity of finding out each other's character before marriage, which I think is never advisable.

JACK: I beg your pardon for interrupting you, Lady Bracknell, but this engagement is quite out of the question. I am Miss Cardew's guardian, and she cannot marry without my consent until she comes of age. That consent I absolutely decline to give.

LADY BRACKNELL: Upon what grounds, may I ask? Algernon is an extremely, I may almost say an ostentatiously, eligible young man. He has nothing, but he looks everything. What more can one desire?

JACK: It pains me very much to have to speak frankly to you, Lady Bracknell, about your nephew, but the fact is that I do not approve at all of his moral character. I suspect him of being untruthful.

[Algernon and Cecily look at him in indignant amazement]

LADY BRACKNELL: Untruthful! My nephew Algernon? Impossible! He is an Oxonian.

JACK: I fear there can be no possible doubt about the matter. This afternoon, during my temporary absence in London on an important question of romance, he obtained admission to my house by means of the false pretense of being my brother. Under an assumed name he drank, I've just been informed by my butler, an entire pint bottle of my Perrier-Jouet, Brut, '89; a wine I was specially reserving for myself. Continuing his disgraceful deception, he succeeded in the course of the afternoon in alienating the affections of my only ward. He subsequently stayed to tea, and devoured every single muffin. And what makes his conduct all the more heartless is, that he was perfectly well aware from the first that I have no brother, that I never had a brother, and that I don't intend to have a brother, not even of any kind. I distinctly told him so myself yesterday afternoon.

LADY BRACKNELL: Ahem! Mr. Worthing, after careful consideration I have decided entirely to overlook my nephew's conduct to you.

JACK: That is very generous of you, Lady Bracknell. My own decision, however, is unalterable. I decline to give my consent.

LADY BRACKNELL: [To Cecily] Come here, sweet child. [Cecily goes over] How old are you, dear?

CECILY: Well, I am really only eighteen, but I always admit to twenty when I go to evening parties.

LADY BRACKNELL: You are perfectly right in making some slight alteration. Indeed, no woman should ever be quite accurate about her age. It looks so calculating. . . . [In meditative manner] Eighteen, but admitting to twenty at evening parties. Well, it will not be very long before you are of age and free from the restraints of tutelage. So I don't think your guardian's consent is, after all, a matter of any importance.

JACK: Pray excuse me, Lady Bracknell, for interrupting you again, but it is only fair to tell you that according to the terms of her grandfather's will Miss Cardew does not come legally of age till she is thirty-five.

LADY BRACKNELL: That does not seem to me to be a grave objection. Thirty-five is a very attractive age. London society is full of women of the very highest birth who have, of their own free choice, remained thirty-five for years. Lady Dumbleton is an instance in point. To my own knowledge she has been thirty-five ever since she arrived at the age of forty, which was many years ago now. I see no reason why our dear Cecily should not be even still more attractive at the age you mention than she is at present. There will be a large accumulation of property.

CECILY: Algy, could you wait for me till I was thirty-five?

ALGERNON: Of course I could, Cecily. You know I could.

CECILY: Yes, I felt it instinctively, but I couldn't wait all that time. I hate waiting even five minutes for anybody. It always makes me rather cross. I am not punctual myself, I know, but I do like punctuality in others, and waiting, even to be married, is quite out of the question.

ALGERNON: Then what is to be done, Cecily?

CECILY: I don't know, Mr. Moncrieff.

LADY BRACKNELL: My dear Mr. Worthing, as Miss Cardew states positively that she cannot wait till she is thirty-five—a remark which I am bound to say seems to me to show a somewhat impatient nature— I would beg of you to reconsider your decision.

JACK: But my dear Lady Bracknell, the matter is entirely in your own hands. The moment you consent to my marriage with Gwendolen, I will most gladly allow your nephew to form an alliance with my ward.

LADY BRACKNELL: [Rising and drawing herself up] You must be quite aware that what you propose is out of the question.

JACK: Then a passionate celibacy is all that any of us can look forward to.

LADY BRACKNELL: That is not the destiny I propose for Gwendolen. Algernon, of course, can choose for himself. [Pulls out her watch] Come, dear, [Gwendolen rises] we have already missed five, if not six, trains. To miss any more might expose us to comment on the platform.

[Enter Dr. Chasuble]

CHASUBLE: Everything is quite ready for the christenings.

LADY BRACKNELL: The christenings, sir! Is not that somewhat premature?

CHASUBLE: [Looking rather puzzled, and pointing to Jack and Algernon] Both these gentlemen have expressed a desire for immediate baptism.

LADY BRACKNELL: At their age? The idea is grotesque and irreligious! Algernon, I forbid you to be baptized. I will not hear of such excesses. Lord Bracknell would be highly displeased if he learned that that was the way in which you wasted your time and money.

CHASUBLE: Am I to understand then that there are to be no christenings at all this afternoon?

JACK: I don't think that, as things are now, it would be of much practical value to either of us, Dr. Chasuble.

CHASUBLE: I am grieved to hear such sentiments from you, Mr. Worthing. They savor of the heretical views of the Anabaptists, views that I have completely refuted in four of my unpublished sermons. However, as your present mood seems to be one peculiarly secular, I will return to the church at once. Indeed, I have just been informed by the pew-opener that for the last hour and a half Miss Prism has been waiting for me in the vestry.

LADY BRACKNELL: [Starting] Miss Prism! Did I hear you mention a Miss Prism?

CHASUBLE: Yes, Lady Bracknell. I am on my way to join her.

LADY BRACKNELL: Pray allow me to detain you for a moment. This matter may prove to be one of vital importance to Lord Bracknell and myself. Is this Miss Prism a female of repellent aspect, remotely connected with education?

CHASUBLE: [Somewhat indignantly] She is the most cultivated of ladies, and the very picture of respectability.

LADY BRACKNELL: It is obviously the same person. May I ask what position she holds in your household?

CHASUBLE: [Severely] I am a celibate, madam.

JACK: [Interposing] Miss Prism, Lady Bracknell, has been for the last three years Miss Cardew's esteemed governess and valued companion.

LADY BRACKNELL: In spite of what I hear of her, I must see her at once. Let her be sent for.

CHASUBLE: [Looking off] She approaches; she is nigh.

[Enter Miss Prism hurriedly]

MISS PRISM: I was told you expected me in the vestry, dear Canon. I have been waiting for you there for an hour and three-quarters. [Catches sight of Lady Bracknell, who has fixed her with a stony glare. Miss Prism grows pale and quails. She looks anxiously round as if desirous to escape]

LADY BRACKNELL: [In a severe, judicial voice] Prism! [Miss Prism bows her head in shame] Come here, Prism! [Miss Prism approaches in a humble manner] Prism! Where is that baby? [General consternation. The Canon starts back in horror. Algernon and Jack pretend to be anxious to shield Cecily and Gwendolen from hearing the details of a terrible public scandal] Twenty-eight years ago, Prism, you left Lord Bracknell's house, Number 104, Upper Grosvenor Street, in charge of a perambulator that contained a baby, of the male sex. You never returned. A few weeks later, through the elaborate investigations of the Metropolitan police, the perambulator was discovered at midnight, standing by itself in a remote corner of Bayswater. It contained the manuscript of a three-volume novel of more than usually revolting sentimentality. [Miss Prism starts in involuntary indignation] But the baby was not there! [Everyone looks at Miss Prism] Prism, where is that baby? [A pause]

MISS PRISM: Lady Bracknell, I admit with shame that I do not know. I only wish I did. The plain facts of the case are these. On the morning of the day you mention, a day that is forever branded on my memory, I prepared as usual to take the baby out in its perambulator. I had also with me a somewhat old but capacious handbag in which I had intended to place the manuscript of a work of fiction that I had written during my few unoccupied hours. In a moment of mental abstraction, for which

I never can forgive myself, I deposited the manuscript in the bassinette, and placed the baby in the handbag.

JACK: [*Who has been listening attentively*] But where did you deposit the handbag?

MISS PRISM: Do not ask me, Mr. Worthing.

JACK: Miss Prism, this is a matter of no small importance to me. I insist on knowing where you deposited the handbag that contained that infant.

MISS PRISM: I left it in the cloak-room of one of the larger railway stations in London.

JACK: What railway station?

MISS PRISM: [*Quite crushed*] Victoria. The Brighton line. [*Sinks into a chair*]

JACK: I must retire to my room for a moment. Gwendolen, wait here for me.

GWENDOLEN: If you are not too long, I will wait here for you all my life.

[*Exit* Jack *in great excitement*]

CHASUBLE: What do you think this means, Lady Bracknell?

LADY BRACKNELL: I dare not even suspect, Dr. Chasuble. I need hardly tell you that in families of high position strange coincidences are not supposed to occur. They are hardly considered the thing. [*Noises heard overhead as if someone was throwing trunks about. Everybody looks up*]

CECILY: Uncle Jack seems strangely agitated.

CHASUBLE: Your guardian has a very emotional nature.

LADY BRACKNELL: This noise is extremely unpleasant. It sounds as if he was having an argument. I dislike arguments of any kind. They are always vulgar, and often convincing.

CHASUBLE: [*Looking up*] It has stopped now. [*The noise is redoubled*]

LADY BRACKNELL: I wish he would arrive at some conclusion.

GWENDOLEN: This suspense is terrible. I hope it will last.

[*Enter* Jack *with a handbag of black leather in his hand*]

JACK: [*Rushing over to* Miss Prism] Is this the handbag, Miss Prism? Examine it carefully before you speak. The happiness of more than one life depends on your answer.

MISS PRISM: [*Calmly*] It seems to be mine. Yes, here is the injury it received through the upsetting of a Gower Street omnibus in younger and happier days. Here is the stain on the lining caused by the explosion of a temperance beverage, an incident that occurred at Leamington. And here, on the lock, are my initials. I had forgotten that in an extravagant mood I had had them placed there. The bag is undoubtedly mine. I am delighted to have it so unexpectedly restored to me. It has been a great inconvenience being without it all these years.

JACK: [*In a pathetic voice*] Miss Prism, more is restored to you than this handbag. I was the baby you placed in it.

MISS PRISM: [*Amazed*] You?

JACK: [*Embracing her*] Yes . . . mother!

MISS PRISM: [*Recoiling in indignant astonishment*] Mr. Worthing! I am unmarried!

JACK: Unmarried! I do not deny that is a serious blow. But after all, who has the right to cast a stone against one who has suffered? Cannot repentance wipe out an act of folly? Why should there be one law for men and another for women? Mother, I forgive you. [*Tries to embrace her again*]

MISS PRISM: [*Still more indignant*] Mr. Worthing, there is some error. [*Pointing to* Lady Bracknell] There is the lady who can tell you who you really are.

JACK: [*After a pause*] Lady Bracknell, I hate to seem inquisitive, but would you kindly inform me who I am?

LADY BRACKNELL: I am afraid that the news I have to give you will not altogether please you. You are the son of my poor sister, Mrs. Moncrieff, and consequently Algernon's elder brother.

JACK: Algy's elder brother! Then I have a brother after all. I knew I had a brother! I always said I had a brother! Cecily—how could you have ever doubted that I had a brother? [*Seizes hold of* Algernon] Dr. Chasuble, my unfortunate brother. Miss Prism, my unfortunate brother. Gwendolen, my unfortunate brother. Algy, you young scoundrel, you will have to treat me with more respect in the future. You have never behaved to me like a brother in all your life.

ALGERNON: Well, not till to-day, old boy, I admit. I did my best, however, though I was out of practice. [*Shakes hands*]

GWENDOLEN: [*To* Jack] My own! But what own are you? What is your Christian name, now that you have become someone else?

JACK: Good heavens! . . . I had quite forgotten that point. Your decision on the subject of my name is irrevocable, I suppose?

GWENDOLEN: I never change, except in my affections.

CECILY: What a noble nature you have, Gwendolen!

JACK: Then the question had better be cleared up at once. Aunt Augusta, a moment. At the time when Miss Prism left me in the handbag, had I been christened already?

LADY BRACKNELL: Every luxury that money could buy, including christening, had been lavished on you by your fond and doting parents.

JACK: Then I was christened! That is settled. Now, what name was I given? Let me know the worst.

LADY BRACKNELL: Being the eldest son you were naturally christened after your father.

JACK: [*Irritably*] Yes, but what was my father's Christian name?

LADY BRACKNELL: [*Meditatively*] I cannot at the present moment recall what the General's Christian name was. But I have no doubt he had one. He was eccentric, I admit. But only in later years. And that was the result of the Indian climate, and marriage, and indigestion, and other things of that kind.

JACK: Algy! Can't you recollect what our father's Christian name was?

ALGERNON: My dear boy, we were never even on speaking terms. He died before I was a year old.

JACK: His name would appear in the Army Lists of the period, I suppose, Aunt Augusta?

LADY BRACKNELL: The General was essentially a man of peace, except in his domestic life. But I have no doubt his name would appear in any military directory.

JACK: The Army Lists of the last forty years are here. These delightful records should have been my constant study. [*Rushes to bookcase and tears the books out*] M. Generals . . . Mallam, Maxbohm, Magley, what ghastly names they have—Markby, Migsby, Mobbs, Moncrieff! Lieutenant 1840, Captain, Lieutenant-Colonel, Colonel, General 1869, Christian names, Ernest John. [*Puts book very quietly down and speaks quite calmly*] I always told you, Gwendolen, my name was Ernest, didn't I? Well, it is Ernest after all. I mean it naturally is Ernest.

LADY BRACKNELL: Yes, I remember that the General was called Ernest. I knew I had some particular reason for disliking the name.

GWENDOLEN: Ernest! My own Ernest! I felt from the first that you could have no other name!

JACK: Gwendolen, it is a terrible thing for a man to find out suddenly that all his life he has been speaking nothing but the truth. Can you forgive me?

GWENDOLEN: I can. For I feel that you are sure to change.

JACK: My own one!

CHASUBLE: [*To* Miss Prism] Lætitia! [*Embraces her*]

MISS PRISM: [*Enthusiastically*] Frederick! At last!

ALGERNON: Cecily! [*Embraces her*] At last!

JACK: Gwendolen! [*Embraces her*] At last!

LADY BRACKNELL: My nephew, you seem to be displaying signs of triviality.

JACK: On the contrary, Aunt Augusta, I've now realized for the first time in my life the vital Importance of Being Earnest.

TABLEAU

CURTAIN

George Bernard Shaw

(1856–1950)

The modern English drama began to achieve importance when the critic George Bernard Shaw reworked a manuscript he had written with another critic, William Archer, and presented it in 1892 to the experimental Independent Theatre of J. T. Grein under the title *Widowers' Houses*. Thereafter, Shaw enriched the theatre with play after play, his work becoming the most significant collection of modern dramatic literature by a single playwright.

A neighbor of Oscar Wilde in Dublin, Shaw descended upon London in 1876 as the "upstart son of a downstart father," after having worked for a time in a Dublin real-estate office. He brought with him a haphazard education, some training in music, acquired from his family, and an inordinate appetite for knowledge. His mother, who had found her life with an alcoholic husband unbearable, had preceded her son to London and was teaching music there; she was thus able to assist the young Shaw with her earnings. Supplementing his allowance with hack literary work, Shaw proceeded to round out his informal education, concentrating on the social sciences.

He fell first under the spell of Henry George's single-tax program and then under the influence of Marxism. In time, he became a pillar of the socialist Fabian Society, a formidable soapbox orator, and a successful Labor party candidate for municipal office. Thus he laid the groundwork for his appraisal of man as an economic and political animal and of society as a decrepit organism which required the ministrations of socialism.

Meanwhile, Shaw continued his literary pursuits, turning out a number of discursive novels between 1880 and 1883. Although these had little merit, they were excellent finger exercises for his satiric and conversational talent and may be regarded as overtures to the brilliant social critique in his dramatic work. In addition, Shaw soon acquitted himself ably as a critic of music and of the drama. Although his criticism was erratic, it was astonishingly virile and scintillating; scorning the theory of art for art's sake as untenable, he called for a living relationship between the arts and society. Progressive artists such as Wagner and Ibsen found an effective champion in his reviews and in his books *The Perfect Wagnerite* and *The Quintessence of Ibsenism*. His collected reviews, *Dramatic Opinions and Essays*, although occasionally highhanded and sometimes obtuse (as in the review of *The Importance of Being Earnest*), comprise the most distinguished body of dramatic criticism in English since the death of John Dryden. Finally, Shaw sallied into the theatre with plays of his own.

His first contribution, the naturalistic comedy *Widowers' Houses*, was an exposé of slum conditions and of the mercenary landlordism that battened on them. That it struck the stage like a thunderbolt was inevitable. Although Henry Arthur Jones had already written a realistic problem play, *Saints and Sinners* (1884), and although Jones and Arthur Wing Pinero were soon to add other studies of the social scene, such as the former's *Michael and His Lost Angel* and the latter's *The Second Mrs. Tanqueray*, Shaw's first contribution was of a different order. Jones and Pinero were by inclination and intention compromisers, and their promotion of the realistic or the social drama was mild and tentative. Shaw, on the other hand, penetrated deeply into issues, spoke his mind freely, and gave no quarter.

Shaw's *Mrs. Warren's Profession* (1898) exposed the economic basis of prostitution and the hypocrisies of an upper-class society that drew profits from exploitation of labor in the sweatshops—a newer kind of immorality than commercialized lechery. His *Major Barbara* (1905) proved a blunt indictment of philanthropy as a mere façade for a profit-minded social order responsible for the very miseries it tries to alleviate. Although in his later plays he departed from strictly realistic problem drama, Shaw continued to express himself uncompromisingly about the larger issues of the twentieth century. He wrote wisely about British imperialism and Ireland, in *John Bull's Other Island;* about the futility of the old war-ridden social order, in *Heartbreak House;* about the failure of the Ramsay MacDonald brand of parliamentary socialism, in *The Apple Cart;* about the hopelessness of the situation in Europe on the eve of the Second World War, in *Too True to Be Good;* and about the coming of fascism and revolution, in *On the Rocks*. Even in these plays his polemics were edged with wit, and he performed some dazzling somersaults while delivering them.

For a long time, English critics professed to dismiss Shaw as a clever and paradoxical mountebank. Indeed, he began early to evince a talent for comic improvisation that had not been approximated since the death of Molière. But even his lighter exercises—those in which he did not concern himself directly with economic and political problems—were serious in aim. His second play, *Arms and the Man,* deflated military glory; *The Devil's Disciple* and *Captain Brassbound's Conversion* subjected heroism to provocative examination; *Candida, The Philanderer, You Never Can Tell,* and *Getting Married* brought domestic relations into his field of observation; *Man and Superman* gave incisive treatment to love and the biological drive. Throughout these and other plays Shaw maintained a brilliant barrage against traditional obfuscations and pretensions. Representative was his satire *Pygmalion,* in which the difference between a cockney flower girl and a duchess is dismissed as a matter of economics and of accomplishments obtainable with a little training.

Shaw's range proved altogether remarkable. In the writing of imaginative drama, he revealed a staggering virtuosity with the vitalistic fantasia *Back to Methuselah,* which also entertained the comic idea that men make a mess of this world because they do not live long enough to develop any sense. In the two historical pieces *Caesar and Cleopatra* and *Saint Joan,* he practically changed dramatic horizons. *Caesar and Cleopatra* was a wholly modern historical comedy; *Saint Joan* combined spiritual exaltation with the apparatus of historical materialism to a degree that has not yet been even remotely approached by other playwrights. And if it is true, as it has been charged, that many of Shaw's characters were simply mouthpieces, it is indisputable that he proved himself a master of characterization whenever he cared to exercise that art. Caesar is a brilliant portrait of a whole man and genius; the saints in Shaw's comedy of early Christianity, *Androcles and the Lion,* are supremely human; Barbara and Undershaft, in *Major Barbara,* are memorable; *Candida* is one of the outstanding character dramas in the English language.

In view of these achievements and of this versatile master's influence on the theatre as a social philosopher and as the virtual creator of modern comedy of ideas, it is difficult to pigeonhole him. He has been inconsistent in his thinking and in his panaceas, oscillating in different plays between socialist idealism and superman-worship, between a passion for social democracy and faith in a dictatorship of the intelligent. Nevertheless, he has pursued one main objective—that of building the "good society," the City of God on earth. Perhaps the best description of his dramatic genius is to be found in Ludwig Lewisohn's estimate of him, made as early as 1915: "Mr. George Bernard Shaw is a writer of comedy with a tragic cry in his soul. In the middle ages he would have been a great saint, appalled at the gracelessness of men's hearts, militant for the kingdom of God. Today he is a playwright, appalled at the muddle-headedness of the race, a fighter for the conquest of reason over unreason, of order over disorder, of economy over waste." "The real joke," Shaw himself reminded us, "is that I am earnest."

"The real joke" is, however, somewhat more complicated, for the earnestness of the would-be reformer lost its sociological character as soon as Shaw's creative imagination came into play. There

was thrust upon the stage a personality the antithesis of our conception of a reformer with a blueprint for society. On one hand, Shaw revealed a spirit highly responsive to the nobility and loneliness of exceptional people and painfully aware of human contradictions that social "uplift" cannot alter. On the other, he displayed a volatile imagination that invariably carried him beyond the pulpit into regions of pointed fantastication and theatrical invention. In short, the creative spirit, the Life Force which he celebrated, had its way with Shaw, and found in him a ready collaborator.

In *Candida,* Shaw's dramatic talent is more uniform than in any other play except *Saint Joan,* for his approach to playwriting has been in many instances regrettably haphazard. Here his mastery of characterization is beyond dispute; his heroine is a completely modern and remarkably rounded person —she is Ibsen's Nora grown up and self-possessed. Comic technique and a fundamental seriousness are so ably fused in this work that it may rightly be regarded as one of the masterpieces of high comedy. Social issues such as the emancipation of women and the exploitation of labor are present, but they are subordinated to the interest in Candida's character. Finally, this comedy has the virtue of coming to instant life on the stage.

Shaw once wrote, "When you get accustomed to my habit of mind, you will not find me such bad company. But please do not think you can take in the work of my long life-time at one reading." This is true both of his plays and of his nondramatic writing. But, though they bear rereading, the plays are almost crystalline in their clarity. And more than most of them, *Candida* reveals its substance to normal eyesight—and without the need of sociological hairsplitting. Even "the secret in the poet's heart," which Marchbanks takes with him on his exit into the night, is no conundrum. Neither the profoundest nor the most provocative of Shaw's plays, representing, as Burns Mantle noted, "a compromise of the radical with the conformist dramatist," *Candida* simply represents its author at the peak of his ability to transfigure traditional material for the modern mind.

Composed in 1894, *Candida* belongs to a group of dramas that Shaw called "Pleasant Plays." But its pleasantness does not lie in the conventional reassurance that a marriage can be invulnerable; it is the gay wisdom impacted into this domestic comedy that makes it pleasant. If the tradition of marriage is upheld, it is not on traditional grounds but on modern terms, free of social hypocrisy and self-delusion. In the process of dramatic complication and discussion, the principals achieve self-knowledge, which, being a portable commodity, can also be taken out of the domestic forum. And here Shaw, now playing the Ibsenite with suavity, was serving substantially the same principle of self-realization that Ibsen proposed as an objective. Candida, remaining true to her nature and need, finds self-realization in keeping her marriage intact; she also teaches Marchbanks to know himself and to live in conformity with that knowledge. Marchbanks' secret, well described by Eric Bentley although better demonstrated by Shaw himself, "is the secret of Shaw the Outsider who is the real Insider, the man who is strong enough to leave the homestead and live with himself and his vision."

Against the opinion that *Candida* is a triumph of character comedy—although one could hardly fail to think so when an actress such as Katharine Cornell plays the Reverend Morell's wife—we may set A. B. Walkley's quizzical impression when he saw the play at the Court Theatre in April 1904. "Fantasy," wrote that scintillating critic, "has its place in the theatre, as well as realism, and that is one reason why the theatre has room for Mr. Bernard Shaw. His method of travestying life is to eliminate from it everything but the pure intelligence. . . . We are such stuff as dreams, not manuals of logic, are made of. 'Why did I love my friend?' asks Montaigne, and gives the only true answer: 'Because it was he, because it was I.' By systematically ignoring this all-important side of life, all its subconscious and unconscious elements, by representing life in general and love in particular as based upon ratiocination, Mr. Shaw obtains most amusing results." Walkley proceeds to question Shaw's reduction of the main drama to discussion and to the rational conclusions of Candida, finding the external reality of the char-

acters amusingly at variance with "the internal fantasy of their actions." We may reply that the characters, especially Candida, merely articulate in rational terms what they must feel for irrational reasons; and that this is the way of real people whose cortex is in good working order. And we may propose a reason different from Walkley's, if perhaps no less facetious, for the humor of the play, apart from the amusing situation: the incongruity of sense in a senseless world is a rich source of comedy. In any case, there is warrant for believing that Shaw would think so, if he were pressed to account for the main source of his humor. As usual, however, Walkley scored a point in his critical crotchet. Our respect for *Candida* as a character comedy and the amazement of those who are surprised that Shaw should have been capable of writing one must not obscure the fact that it *is* a comedy of ideas.

BIBLIOGRAPHY: Eric Bentley, *Bernard Shaw,* 1947; Bentley, *The Playwright as Thinker* (pp. 137–157, 162–172, 186–189), 1946; G. K. Chesterton, *George Bernard Shaw,* 1909; John Gassner, *Masters of the Drama* (pp. 591–616), 1940, 1945; Archibald Henderson, *Bernard Shaw: Playboy and Prophet,* 1932; James Huneker, *Iconoclasts* (pp. 233–268), 1905; Hesketh Pearson, *G.B.S.: A Full-Length Portrait,* 1942; A. B. Walkley, *Drama and Life* (pp. 214–250), 1908; Edmund Wilson, *The Triple Thinkers* (pp. 220–265), 1938; S. Winsten, ed., *G.B.S. 90,* 1946.

CANDIDA

By George Bernard Shaw

ACT I.

A fine October morning in the northeast suburbs of London, a vast district many miles away from the London of Mayfair and St. James', much less known there than the Paris of the Rue de Rivoli and the Champs Elysées, and much less narrow, squalid, fetid and airless in its slums; strong in comfortable, prosperous middle-class life; wide-streeted, myriad-populated; well-served with ugly iron urinals, Radical clubs, tram lines, and a perpetual stream of yellow cars; enjoying in its main thoroughfares the luxury of grass-grown "front gardens," untrodden by the foot of man save as to the path from the gate to the hall door; but blighted by an intolerable monotony of miles and miles of graceless, characterless brick houses, black iron railings, stony pavements, slaty roofs, and respectably ill-dressed or disreputably poorly-dressed people, quite accustomed to the place, and mostly plodding about somebody else's work, which they would not do if they themselves could help it. The little energy and eagerness that crop up show themselves in cockney cupidity and business "push." Even the policemen and the chapels are not infrequent enough to break the monotony. The sun is shining cheerfully; there is no fog; and though the smoke effectually prevents anything, whether faces and hands or bricks and mortar, from looking fresh and clean, it is not hanging heavily enough to trouble a Londoner.

This desert of unattractiveness has its oasis. Near the outer end of the Hackney Road is a park of 217 acres, fenced in, not by railings, but by a wooden paling, and containing plenty of greensward, trees, a lake for bathers, flower beds with the flowers arranged carefully in patterns by the admired cockney art of carpet gardening and a sandpit, imported from the seaside for the delight of the children, but speedily deserted on its becoming a natural vermin preserve for all the petty fauna of Kingsland, Hackney and Hoxton. A bandstand, an unfinished forum for religious, anti-religious and political orators, cricket pitches, a gymnasium, and an old-fashioned stone kiosk are among its attractions. Wherever the prospect is bounded by trees or rising green grounds, it is a pleasant place. Where the ground stretches flat to the gray palings, with bricks and mortar, sky signs, crowded chimneys and smoke beyond, the prospect makes desolate and sordid.

The best view of Victoria Park is from the front window of St. Dominic's Parsonage, from which not a single chimney is visible. The parsonage is a semi-detached villa with a front garden and a porch. Visitors go up the flight of steps to the porch: tradespeople and members of the family go down by a door under the steps to the basement, with a breakfast room, used for all meals, in front, and the kitchen at the back. Upstairs, on the level of the hall door, is the drawing-room, with its large plate glass window looking on the park. In this room, the only sitting-room that can be spared from the children and the family meals, the parson, the Reverend James Mavor Morell, does his work. He is sitting in a strong round-backed revolving chair at the right hand end of a long table, which stands across the window, so that he can cheer himself with the view of the park at his elbow. At the opposite end of the table, adjoining it, is a little table only half the width of the other, with a typewriter on it. His typist is sitting at this machine, with her back to the window. The large table is littered with pamphlets, journals, letters, nests of drawers, an office diary, postage scales and the like. A spare chair for visitors having business with the parson is in the middle, turned to his end. Within reach of his hand is a stationery case, and a cabinet photograph in a frame. Behind him the right hand wall, recessed above the fireplace, is fitted with bookshelves, on which an adept eye can measure the parson's divinity and casuistry by a complete set of Browning's poems and Maurice's Theological Essays, and guess at his politics from a yellow-backed Progress and Poverty, Fabian Essays, a Dream of John Ball, Marx's Capital, and half a dozen other literary landmarks in Socialism. Opposite him on the left, near the typewriter, is the door. Further down the room, opposite the fireplace, a bookcase stands on a cellaret, with a sofa near it. There is a generous fire burning; and the hearth, with a comfortable armchair and a japanned flower-painted coal scuttle at one side, a miniature chair for a boy or girl on the other, a nicely varnished wooden mantelpiece, with neatly moulded shelves, tiny bits of mirror let into the panels, and a traveling clock in a leather case (the inevitable wedding present), and on the wall above a large autotype of the chief figure in Titian's Virgin of the Assumption, is very inviting. Altogether the room is the room of a good housekeeper, vanquished, as far as the table is concerned, by an untidy man, but elsewhere mistress of the situation. The furniture, in its ornamental aspect, betrays the style of the advertised "drawing-room suite" of the pushing suburban furniture dealer; but there is noth-

ing useless or pretentious in the room. The paper and paneling are dark, throwing the big cheery window and the park outside into strong relief.

The Reverend James Mavor Morell *is a Christian Socialist clergyman of the Church of England, and an active member of the Guild of St. Matthew and the Christian Social Union. A vigorous, genial, popular man of forty, robust and goodlooking, full of energy, with pleasant, hearty, considerate manners, and a sound, unaffected voice, which he uses with the clean, athletic articulation of a practised orator, and with a wide range and perfect command of expression. He is a first-rate clergyman, able to say what he likes to whom he likes, to lecture people without setting himself up against them, to impose his authority on them without humiliating them, and to interfere in their business without impertinence. His well spring of spiritual enthusiasm and sympathetic emotion has never run dry for a moment: he still eats and sleeps heartily enough to win the daily battle between exhaustion and recuperation triumphantly. Withal, a great baby, pardonably vain of his powers and unconsciously pleased with himself. He has a healthy complexion, a good forehead, with the brows somewhat blunt, and the eyes bright and eager, a mouth resolute, but not particularly well cut, and a substantial nose, with the mobile, spreading nostrils of the dramatic orator, but, like all his features, void of subtlety.*

The typist, Miss Proserpine Garnett, is a brisk little woman of about 30, of the lower middle class, neatly but cheaply dressed in a black merino skirt and a blouse, rather pert and quick of speech, and not very civil in her manner, but sensitive and affectionate. She is clattering away busily at her machine whilst Morell *opens the last of his morning's letters. He realizes its contents with a comic groan of despair.*

PROSERPINE: Another lecture?

MORELL: Yes. The Hoxton Freedom Group want me to address them on Sunday morning. [*Great emphasis on "Sunday," this being the unreasonable part of the business*] What are they?

PROSERPINE: Communist Anarchists, I think.

MORELL: Just like Anarchists not to know that they can't have a parson on Sunday! Tell them to come to church if they want to hear me: it will do them good. Say I can only come on Mondays and Thursdays. Have you the diary there?

PROSERPINE: [*Taking up the diary*] Yes.

MORELL: Have I any lecture on for next Monday?

PROSERPINE: [*Referring to diary*] Tower Hamlets Radical Club.

MORELL: Well, Thursday then?

PROSERPINE: English Land Restoration League.

MORELL: What next?

PROSERPINE: Guild of St. Matthew on Monday. Independent Labor Party, Greenwich Branch, on Thursday. Monday, Social-Democratic Federation,

Mile End Branch. Thursday, first Confirmation class —[*Impatiently*] Oh, I'd better tell them you can't come. They're only half a dozen ignorant and conceited costermongers without five shillings between them.

MORELL: [*Amused*] Ah; but you see they're near relatives of mine, Miss Garnett.

PROSERPINE: [*Staring at him*] Relatives of yours!

MORELL: Yes: we have the same father—in Heaven.

PROSERPINE: [*Relieved*] Oh, is that all?

MORELL: [*With a sadness which is a luxury to a man whose voice expresses it so finely*] Ah, you don't believe it. Everybody says it: nobody believes it—nobody. [*Briskly, getting back to business*] Well, well! Come, Miss Proserpine, can't you find a date for the costers? What about the 25th?: that was vacant the day before yesterday.

PROSERPINE: [*Referring to diary*] Engaged—the Fabian Society.

MORELL: Bother the Fabian Society! Is the 28th gone, too?

PROSERPINE: City dinner. You're invited to dine with the Founder's Company.

MORELL: That'll do; I'll go to the Hoxton Group of Freedom instead. [*She enters the engagement in silence, with implacable disparagement of the Hoxton Anarchists in every line of her face.* Morell *bursts open the cover of a copy of The Church Reformer, which has come by post, and glances through Mr. Stewart Hendlam's leader and the Guild of St. Matthew news. These proceedings are presently enlivened by the appearance of* Morell's *curate, the* Reverend Alexander Mill, *a young gentleman gathered by* Morell *from the nearest University settlement, whither he had come from Oxford to give the east end of London the benefit of his university training. He is a conceitedly well intentioned, enthusiastic, immature person, with nothing positively unbearable about him except a habit of speaking with his lips carefully closed for half an inch from each corner, a finicking articulation, and a set of horribly corrupt vowels, notably* ow *for* o, *this being his chief means of bringing Oxford refinement to bear on Hackney vulgarity.* Morell, *whom he has won over by a doglike devotion, looks up indulgently from The Church Reformer as he enters, and remarks*] Well, Lexy! Late again, as usual.

LEXY: I'm afraid so. I wish I could get up in the morning.

MORELL: [*Exulting in his own energy*] Ha! ha! [*Whimsically*] Watch and pray, Lexy: watch and pray.

LEXY: I know. [*Rising wittily to the occasion*] But how can I watch and pray when I am asleep? Isn't that so, Miss Prossy?

PROSERPINE: [*Sharply*] Miss Garnett, if you please.

LEXY: I beg your pardon—Miss Garnett.

PROSERPINE: You've got to do all the work to-day.

LEXY: Why?

PROSERPINE: Never mind why. It will do you good to earn your supper before you eat it, for once in a way, as I do. Come don't dawdle. You should have been off on your rounds half an hour ago.

LEXY: [*Perplexed*] Is she in earnest, Morell?

MORELL: [*In the highest spirits—his eyes dancing*] Yes. *I* am going to dawdle to-day.

LEXY: You! You don't know how.

MORELL: [*Heartily*] Ha! ha! Don't I? I'm going to have this day all to myself—or at least the forenoon. My wife's coming back: she's due here at 11:45.

LEXY: [*Surprised*] Coming back already—with the children? I thought they were to stay to the end of the month.

MORELL: So they are: she's only coming up for two days, to get some flannel things for Jimmy, and to see how we're getting on without her.

LEXY: [*Anxiously*] But, my dear Morell, if what Jimmy and Fluffy had was scarlatina, do you think it wise—

MORELL: Scarlatina!—rubbish, German measles. I brought it into the house myself from the Pycroft Street School. A parson is like a doctor, my boy: he must face infection as a soldier must face bullets. [*He rises and claps* Lexy *on the shoulder*] Catch the measles if you can, Lexy: she'll nurse you; and what a piece of luck that will be for you!—eh?

LEXY: [*Smiling uneasily*] It's so hard to understand you about Mrs. Morell—

MORELL: [*Tenderly*] Ah, my boy, get married— get married to a good woman; and then you'll understand. That's a foretaste of what will be best in the Kingdom of Heaven we are trying to establish on earth. That will cure you of dawdling. An honest man feels that he must pay Heaven for every hour of happiness with a good spell of hard, unselfish work to make others happy. We have no more right to consume happiness without producing it than to consume wealth without producing it. Get a wife like my Candida; and you'll always be in arrear with your repayment.

[*He pats* Lexy *affectionately on the back, and is leaving the room when* Lexy *calls to him*]

LEXY: Oh, wait a bit: I forgot. [Morell *halts and turns with the door knob in his hand*] Your father-in-law is coming round to see you. [Morell *shuts the door again, with a complete change of manner.*]

MORELL: [*Surprised and not pleased*] Mr. Burgess?

LEXY: Yes. I passed him in the park, arguing with somebody. He gave me good day and asked me to let you know that he was coming.

MORELL: [*Half incredulous*] But he hasn't called here for—I may almost say for years. Are you sure, Lexy? You're not joking, are you?

LEXY: [*Earnestly*] No, sir, really.

MORELL: [*Thoughtfully*] Hm! Time for him to take another look at Candida before she grows out of his knowledge. [*He resigns himself to the inevi-table, and goes out.* Lexy *looks after him with beaming, foolish worship.*]

LEXY: What a good man! What a thorough, loving soul he is!

[*He takes* Morell's *place at the table, making himself very comfortable as he takes out a cigarette*]

PROSERPINE: [*Impatiently, pulling the letter she has been working at off the typewriter and folding it*] Oh, a man ought to be able to be fond of his wife without making a fool of himself about her.

LEXY: [*Shocked*] Oh, Miss Prossy!

PROSERPINE: [*Rising busily and coming to the stationery case to get an envelope, in which she encloses the letter as she speaks*] Candida here, and Candida there, and Candida everywhere! [*She licks the envelope*] It's enough to drive anyone out of their senses [*Thumping the envelope to make it stick*] to hear a perfectly commonplace woman raved about in that absurd manner merely because she's got good hair, and a tolerable figure.

LEXY: [*With reproachful gravity*] I think her extremely beautiful, Miss Garnett. [*He takes the photograph up; looks at it; and adds, with even greater impressiveness*] Extremely beautiful. How fine her eyes are!

PROSERPINE: Her eyes are not a bit better than mine—now! [*He puts down the photograph and stares austerely at her*] And you know very well that you think me dowdy and second rate enough.

LEXY: [*Rising majestically*] Heaven forbid that I should think of any of God's creatures in such a way! [*He moves stiffly away from her across the room to the neighborhood of the bookcase*]

PROSERPINE: Thank you. That's very nice and comforting.

LEXY: [*Saddened by her depravity*] I had no idea you had any feeling against Mrs. Morell.

PROSERPINE: [*Indignantly*] I have no feeling against her. She's very nice, very good-hearted: I'm very fond of her and can appreciate her real qualities far better than any man can. [*He shakes his head sadly and turns to the bookcase, looking along the shelves for a volume. She follows him with intense pepperiness*] You don't believe me? [*He turns and faces her. She pounces at him with spitfire energy*] You think I'm jealous. Oh, what a profound knowledge of the human heart you have, Mr. Lexy Mill! How well you know the weaknesses of Woman, don't you? It must be so nice to be a man and have a fine penetrating intellect instead of mere emotions like us, and to know that the reason we don't share your amorous delusions is that we're all jealous of one another! [*She abandons him with a toss of her shoulders, and crosses to the fire to warm her hands*]

LEXY: Ah, if you women only had the same clue to Man's strength that you have to his weakness, Miss Prossy, there would be no Woman Question.

PROSERPINE: [*Over her shoulder, as she stoops,*

holding her hands to the blaze] Where did you hear Morell say that? You didn't invent it yourself: you're not clever enough.

LEXY: That's quite true. I am not ashamed of owing him that, as I owe him so many other spiritual truths. He said it at the annual conference of the Women's Liberal Federation. Allow me to add that though they didn't appreciate it, I, a mere man, did. [*He turns to the bookcase again, hoping that this may leave her crushed*]

PROSERPINE: [*Putting her hair straight at the little panel of mirror in the mantelpiece*] Well, when you talk to me, give me your own ideas, such as they are, and not his. You never cut a poorer figure than when you are trying to imitate him.

LEXY: [*Stung*] I try to follow his example, not to imitate him.

PROSERPINE: [*Coming at him again on her way back to her work*] Yes, you do: you imitate him. Why do you tuck your umbrella under your left arm instead of carrying it in your hand like anyone else? Why do you walk with your chin stuck out before you, hurrying along with that eager look in your eyes—you, who never get up before half past nine in the morning? Why do you say "knoaledge" in church, though you always say "knolledge" in private conversation! Bah! do you think I don't know? [*She goes back to the typewriter*] Here, come and set about your work: we've wasted enough time for one morning. Here's a copy of the diary for to-day. [*She hands him a memorandum*]

LEXY: [*Deeply offended*] Thank you. [*He takes it and stands at the table with his back to her, reading it. She begins to transcribe her shorthand notes on the typewriter without troubling herself about his feelings. Mr. Burgess enters unannounced. He is a man of sixty, made coarse and sordid by the compulsory selfishness of petty commerce, and later on softened into sluggish bumptiousness by overfeeding and commercial success. A vulgar, ignorant, guzzling man, offensive and contemptuous to people whose labor is cheap, respectful to wealth and rank, and quite sincere and without rancor or envy in both attitudes. Finding him without talent, the world has offered him no decently paid work except ignoble work, and he has become, in consequence, somewhat boggish. But he has no suspicion of this himself, and honestly regards his commercial prosperity as the inevitable and socially wholesome triumph of the ability, industry, shrewdness and experience in business of a man who in private is easygoing, affectionate and humorously convivial to a fault. Corporeally, he is a podgy man, with a square, clean-shaven face and a square beard under his chin; dust colored, with a patch of gray in the centre, and small watery blue eyes with a plaintively sentimental expression, which he transfers easily to his voice by his habit of pompously intoning his sentences.*]

BURGESS: [*Stopping on the threshold, and looking round*] They told me Mr. Morell was here.

PROSERPINE: [*Rising*] He's upstairs. I'll fetch him for you.

BURGESS: [*Staring boorishly at her*] You're not the same young lady as hused to typewrite for him?

PROSERPINE: No.

BURGESS: [*Assenting*] No: she was younger. [Miss Garnett *stolidly stares at him; then goes out with great dignity. He receives this quite obtusely, and crosses to the hearth-rug, where he turns and spreads himself with his back to the fire*] Startin' on your rounds, Mr. Mill?

LEXY: [*Folding his paper and pocketing it*] Yes: I must be off presently.

BURGESS: [*Momentously*] Don't let me detain you, Mr. Mill. What I come about is private between me and Mr. Morell.

LEXY: [*Ruffily*] I have no intention of intruding, I am sure, Mr. Burgess. Good morning.

BURGESS: [*Patronizingly*] Oh, good morning to you. [Morell *returns as* Lexy *is making for the door*]

MORELL: [*To Lexy*] Off to work?

LEXY: Yes, sir.

MORELL: [*Patting him affectionately on the shoulder*] Take my silk handkerchief and wrap your throat up. There's a cold wind. Away with you.

[Lexy *brightens up, and goes out*]

BURGESS: Spoilin' your curates, as usu'l, James. Good mornin'. When I pay a man, an' 'is livin' depen's on me, I keep him in his place.

MORELL: [*Rather shortly*] I always keep my curates in their places as my helpers and comrades. If you get as much work out of your clerks and warehousemen as I do out of my curates, you must be getting rich pretty fast. Will you take your old chair?

[*He points with curt authority to the arm chair beside the fireplace; then takes the spare chair from the table and sits down in front of Burgess.*]

BURGESS: [*Without moving*] Just the same as hever, James!

MORELL: When you last called—it was about three years ago, I think—you said the same thing a little more frankly. Your exact words then were: "Just as big a fool as ever, James?"

BURGESS: [*Soothingly*] Well, perhaps I did; but [*with conciliatory cheerfulness*] I meant no offence by it. A clorgyman is privileged to be a bit of a fool, you know: it's on'y becomin' in his profession that he should. Anyhow, I come here, not to rake up hold differences, but to let bygones be bygones. [*Suddenly becoming very solemn, and approaching Morell*] James: three year ago, you done me a hill turn. You done me hout of a contrac'; an' when I gev you 'arsh words in my nat'ral disappointment, you turned my daughrter again me. Well, I've come to act the part of a Cheristhin. [*Offering his hand*] I forgive you, James.

MORELL: [*Starting up*] Confound your impudence!

BURGESS: [*Retreating, with almost lachrymose deprecation of this treatment*] Is that becomin' language for a clorgyman, James?—and you so partic'lar, too?

MORELL: [*Hotly*] No, sir, it is not becoming language for a clergyman. I used the wrong word. I should have said damn your impudence: that's what St. Paul, or any honest priest would have said to you. Do you think I have forgotten that tender of yours for the contract to supply clothing to the workhouse?

BURGESS: [*In a paroxysm of public spirit*] I acted in the interest of the ratepayers, James. It was the lowest tender: you can't deny that.

MORELL: Yes, the lowest, because you paid worse wages than any other employer—starvation wages— aye, worse than starvation wages—to the women who made the clothing. Your wages would have driven them to the streets to keep body and soul together. [*Getting angrier and angrier*] Those women were my parishioners. I shamed the Guardians out of accepting your tender: I shamed the ratepayers out of letting them do it: I shamed everybody but you. [*Boiling over*] How dare you, sir, come here and offer to forgive me, and talk about your daughter, and—

BURGESS: Easy, James, easy, easy. Don't git hinto a fluster about nothink. I've howned I was wrong.

MORELL: [*Fuming about*] Have you? I didn't hear you.

BURGESS: Of course I did. I hown it now. Come: I harsk your pardon for the letter I wrote you. Is that enough?

MORELL: [*Snapping his fingers*] That's nothing. Have you raised the wages?

BURGESS: [*Triumphantly*] Yes.

MORELL: [*Stopping dead*] What!

BURGESS: [*Unctuously*] I've turned a moddle hemployer. I don't hemploy no women now: they're all sacked; and the work is done by machinery. Not a man 'as less than six-pence a *hour*; and the skilled 'ands gits the Trade Union rate. [*Proudly*] What 'ave you to say to me now?

MORELL: [*Overwhelmed*] Is it possible! Well, there's more joy in heaven over one sinner that repenteth—[*Going to* Burgess *with an explosion of apologetic cordiality*] My dear Burgess, I most heartily beg your pardon for my hard thoughts of you. [*Grasps his hand*] And now, don't you feel the better for the change? Come, confess, you're happier. You look happier.

BURGESS: [*Ruefully*] Well, p'raps I do. I s'pose I must, since you notice it. At all events, I git my contrax asseppit (accepted) by the County Council. [*Savagely*] They dussent 'ave nothink to do with me unless I paid fair wages—curse 'em for a parcel o' meddlin' fools!

MORELL: [*Dropping his hand, utterly discouraged*] So that was why you raised the wages! [*He sits down moodily*]

BURGESS: [*Severely, in spreading, mounting tones*] Why else should I do it? What does it lead to but drink and huppishness in workin' men? [*He seats himself magisterially in the easy chair*] It's hall very well for you, James: it gits you hinto the papers and makes a great man of you; but you never think of the 'arm you do, puttin' money into the pockets of workin' men that they don't know 'ow to spend, and takin' it from people that might be makin' a good huse on it.

MORELL: [*With a heavy sigh, speaking with cold politeness*] What is your business with me this morning? I shall not pretend to believe that you are here merely out of family sentiment.

BURGESS: [*Obstinately*] Yes, I ham—just family sentiment and nothink else.

MORELL: [*With weary calm*] I don't believe you!

BURGESS: [*Rising threateningly*] Don't say that to me again, James Mavor Morell.

MORELL: [*Unmoved*] I'll say it just as often as may be necessary to convince you that it's true. I don't believe you.

BURGESS: [*Collapsing into an abyss of wounded feeling*] Oh, well, if you're determined to be unfriendly, I s'pose I'd better go. [*He moves reluctantly towards the door.* Morell *makes no sign. He lingers*] I didn't hexpect to find a hun-forgivin' spirit in you, James. [Morell *still not responding, he takes a few more reluctant steps downwards. Then he comes back whining*] We huseter git on well enough, spite of our different opinions. Why are you so changed to me? I give you my word I come here in pyorr (pure) frenliness, not wishin' to be on bad terms with my hown daughter's 'usban'. Come, James: be a Cheristhin and shake 'ands. [*He puts his hand sentimentally on* Morell's *shoulder.*]

MORELL: [*Looking up at him thoughtfully*] Look here, Burgess. Do you want to be as welcome here as you were before you lost that contract?

BURGESS: I do, James. I do—honest.

MORELL: Then why don't you behave as you did then?

BURGESS: [*Cautiously removing his hand*] 'Ow d'y' mean?

MORELL: I'll tell you. You thought me a young fool then.

BURGESS: [*Coaxingly*] No, I didn't, James. I—

MORELL: [*Cutting him short*] Yes, you did. And I thought you an old scoundrel.

BURGESS: [*Most vehemently deprecating this gross self-accusation on* Morell's *part*] No, you didn't, James. Now you do yourself a hinjustice.

MORELL: Yes, I did. Well, that did not prevent our getting on very well together. God made you what I call a scoundrel as he made me what you call a fool. [*The effect of this observation on* Burgess *is to remove the keystone of his moral arch. He becomes bodily weak, and, with his eyes fixed on* Morell *in a helpless stare, puts out his hand apprehensively to balance himself, as if the floor had suddenly sloped under him.* Morell *proceeds in the same tone of quiet conviction*] It was not for me to quarrel with his handiwork in the one case more than in the other. So long as you come here honestly as a self-respecting, thorough, convinced scoundrel, justifying your scoundrelism, and proud of it, you are welcome. But [*and now* Morell's *tone becomes formidable; and he rises and strikes the back of the chair for greater emphasis*] I won't have you here sniveling about being a model employer and a converted man when you're only an apostate with your coat turned for the sake of a County Council contract. [*He nods at him to enforce the point; then goes to the hearth-rug, where he takes up a comfortably commanding position with his back to the fire, and continues*] No: I like a man to be true to himself, even in wickedness. Come now: either take your hat and go; or else sit down and give me a good scoundrelly reason for wanting to be friends with me. [Burgess, *whose emotions have subsided sufficiently to be expressed by a dazed grin, is relieved by this concrete proposition. He ponders it for a moment, and then, slowly and very modestly, sits down in the chair* Morell *has just left*] That's right. Now, out with it.

BURGESS: [*Chuckling in spite of himself*] Well, you are a queer bird, James, and no mistake. But [*almost enthusiastically*] one carnt 'elp likin' you; besides, as I said afore, of course one don't take all a clorgyman says seriously, or the world couldn't go on. Could it now? [*He composes himself for graver discourse, and turning his eyes on* Morell *proceeds with dull seriousness*] Well, I don't mind tellin' you, since it's your wish we should be free with one another, that I did think you a bit of a fool once; but I'm beginnin' to think that p'raps I was be'ind the times a bit.

MORELL: [*Delighted*] Aha! You're finding that out at last, are you?

BURGESS: [*Portentously*] Yes, times 'as changed mor'n I could a believed. Five yorr (year) ago, no sensible man would a thought o' takin' up with your ideas. I hused to wonder you was let preach at all. Why, I know a clorgyman that 'as bin kep' hout of his job for yorrs by the Bishop of London, although the pore feller's not a bit more religious than you are. But to-day, if henyone was to offer to bet me a thousan' poun' that you'll end by bein' a bishop yourself, I shouldn't venture to take the bet. You and yore crew are gettin' hinfluential: I can see that. They'll 'ave to give you something someday, if it's only to stop yore mouth. You 'ad the right instinc' arter all, James: the line you took is the payin' line in the long run fur a man o' your sort.

MORELL: [*Decisively—offering his hand*] Shake hands, Burgess. Now you're talking honestly. I don't think they'll make me a bishop; but if they do, I'll introduce you to the biggest jobbers I can get to come to my dinner parties.

BURGESS: [*Who has risen with a sheepish grin and accepted the hand of friendship*] You will 'ave your joke, James. Our quarrel's made up now, isn't it?

A WOMAN'S VOICE: Say yes, James.

[*Startled, they turn quickly and find that* Candida *has just come in, and is looking at them with an amused maternal indulgence which is her characteristic expression. She is a woman of 33, well built, well nourished, likely, one guesses, to become matronly later on, but now quite at her best, with the double charm of youth and motherhood. Her ways are those of a woman who has found that she can always manage people by engaging their affection, and who does so frankly and instinctively without the smallest scruple. So far, she is like any other pretty woman who is just clever enough to make the most of her sexual attractions for trivially selfish ends; but* Candida's *serene brow, courageous eyes, and well-set mouth and chin signify largeness of mind and dignity of character to ennoble her cunning in the affections. A wisehearted observer, looking at her, would at once guess that whoever had placed the Virgin of the Assumption over her hearth did so because he fancied some spiritual resemblance between them, and yet would not suspect either her husband or herself of any such idea, or indeed of any concern with the art of Titian. Just now she is in bonnet and mantle, laden with a strapped rug with her umbrella stuck through it, a handbag, and a supply of illustrated papers.*]

MORELL: [*Shocked at his remissness*] Candida! Why—[*Looks at his watch, and is horrified to find it so late*] My darling! [*Hurrying to her and seizing the rug strap, pouring forth his remorseful regrets all the time*] I intended to meet you at the train. I let the time slip. [*Flinging the rug on the sofa*] I was so engrossed by—[*returning to her*]—I forgot—oh! [*He embraces her with penitent emotion*]

BURGESS: [*A little shame-faced and doubtful of his reception*] How orr you, Candy? [*She, still in* Morell's *arms, offers him her cheek, which he kisses*] James and me is come to a unnerstandin'—a honorable unnerstandin'. Ain' we, James?

MORELL: [*Impetuously*] Oh, bother your understanding! You've kept me late for Candida. [*With compassionate fervor*] My poor love: how did you manage about the luggage?—how—

CANDIDA: [*Stopping him and disengaging herself*] There, there, there. I wasn't alone. Eugene came down yesterday; and we traveled up together.

MORELL: [*Pleased*] Eugene!

CANDIDA: Yes: he's struggling with my luggage, poor boy. Go out, dear, at once; or he will pay for the cab; and I don't want that. [Morell *hurries out.* Candida *puts down her handbag; then takes off her mantle and bonnet and puts them on the sofa with the rug, chatting meanwhile*] Well, papa, how are you getting on at home?

BURGESS: The 'ouse ain't worth livin' in since you left it, Candy. I wish you'd come round and give the **gurl a talkin' to. Who's** this Eugene that's come with you?

CANDIDA: Oh, Eugene's one of James's discoveries. He found him sleeping on the Embankment last June. Haven't you noticed our new picture [*pointing to the Virgin*]? He gave us that.

BURGESS: [*Incredulously*] Garn! D'you mean to tell me—your hown father!—that cab touts or such like, orf the Embankment, buys pictur's like that? [*Severely*] Don't deceive me, Candy: it's a 'Igh Church pictur; and James chose it hisself.

CANDIDA: Guess again. Eugene isn't a cab tout.

BURGESS: Then wot is he? [*Sarcastically*] A nobleman, I s'pose.

CANDIDA: [*Delighted—nodding*] Yes. His uncle's a peer—a real live earl.

BURGESS: [*Not daring to believe such good news*] No!

CANDIDA: Yes. He had a seven-day bill for £55 in his pocket when James found him on the Embankment. He thought he couldn't get any money for it until the seven days were up; and he was too shy to ask for credit. Oh, he's a dear boy! We are very fond of him.

BURGESS: [*Pretending to belittle the aristocracy, but with his eyes gleaming*] Hm, I thort you wouldn't git a piorr's (peer's) nevvy visitin' in Victoria Park unless he were a bit of a flat. [*Looking again at the picture*] Of course I don't 'old with that pictur, Candy; but still it's a 'igh-class, fust-rate work of art: I can see that. Be sure you hintroduce me to him, Candy. [*He looks at his watch anxiously*] I can only stay about two minutes.

[*Morell comes back with Eugene, whom Burgess contemplates moist-eyed with enthusiasm. He is a strange, shy youth of eighteen, slight, effeminate, with a delicate childish voice, and a hunted, tormented expression and shrinking manner that show the painful sensitiveness that very swift and acute apprehensiveness produces in youth, before the character has grown to its full strength. Yet everything that his timidity and frailty suggests is contradicted by his face. He is miserably irresolute, does not know where to stand or what to do with his hands and feet, is afraid of Burgess, and would run away into solitude if he dared; but the very intensity with which he feels a perfectly commonplace position shows great nervous force, and his nostrils and mouth show a fiercely petulant wilfulness, as to the quality of which his great imaginative eyes and fine brow are reassuring. He is so entirely uncommon as to be almost unearthly; and to prosaic people there is something noxious in this unearthliness, just as to poetic people there is something angelic in it. His dress is anarchic. He wears an old blue scrge jacket, unbuttoned over a woolen lawn-tennis shirt, with a silk handkerchief for a cravat, trousers matching the jacket, and* brown canvas shoes. In these garments he has apparently lain in the heather and waded through the waters; but there is no evidence of his having ever brushed them.*

As he catches sight of a stranger on entering, he stops, and edges along the wall on the opposite side of the room]

MORELL: [*As he enters*] Come along: you can spare us quarter of an hour, at all events. This is my father-in-law, Mr. Burgess—Mr. Marchbanks.

MARCHBANKS: [*Nervously backing against the bookcase*] Glad to meet you, sir.

BURGESS: [*Crossing to him with great heartiness, whilst Morell joins Candida at the fire*] Glad to meet you, I'm shore, Mr. Morchbanks. [*Forcing him to shake hands*] 'Ow do you find yoreself this weather? 'Ope you ain't lettin' James put no foolish ideas into your 'ed?

MARCHBANKS: Foolish ideas! Oh, you mean Socialism. No.

BURGESS: That's right. [*Again looking at his watch*] Well, I must go now: there's no 'elp for it. Yo're not comin' my way, are you, Mr. Morchbanks?

MARCHBANKS: Which way is that?

BURGESS: Victawriar Pork Station. There's a city train at 12:25.

MORELL: Nonsense. Eugene will stay to lunch with us, I expect.

MARCHBANKS: [*Anxiously excusing himself*] No—I—I—

BURGESS: Well, well, I shan't press you: I bet you'd rather lunch with Candy. Some night, I 'ope, you'll come and dine with me at my club, the Freeman Founders in Nortn Folgit. Come, say you will.

MARCHBANKS: Thank you, Mr. Burgess. Where is Norton Folgate—down in Surrey, isn't it? [*Burgess, inexpressibly tickled, begins to splutter with laughter*]

CANDIDA: [*Coming to the rescue*] You'll lose your train, papa, if you don't go at once. Come back in the afternoon and tell Mr. Marchbanks where to find the club.

BURGESS: [*Roaring with glee*] Down in Surrey—har, har! that's not a bad one. Well, I never met a man as didn't know Nortn Folgit before. [*Abashed at his own noisiness*] Good-bye, Mr. Morchbanks: I know yo're too 'ighbred to take my pleasantry in bad part. [*He again offers his hand*]

MARCHBANKS: [*Taking it with a nervous jerk*] Not at all.

BURGESS: Bye, bye, Candy. I'll look in again later on. So long, James.

MORELL: Must you go?

BURGESS: Don't stir. [*He goes out with unabated heartiness.*]

MORELL: Oh, I'll see you out. [*He follows him out. Eugene stares after them apprehensively, holding his breath until Burgess disappears.*]

CANDIDA: [*Laughing*] Well, Eugene. [*He turns with a start and comes eagerly towards her, but stops ir-*

resolutely as he meets her amused look] What do you think of my father?

MARCHBANKS: I—I hardly know him yet. He seems to be a very nice old gentleman.

CANDIDA: [*With gentle irony*] And you'll go to the Freeman Founders to dine with him, won't you?

MARCHBANKS: [*Miserably, taking it quite seriously*] Yes, if it will please you.

CANDIDA: [*Touched*] Do you know, you are a very nice boy, Eugene, with all your queerness. If you had laughed at my father I shouldn't have minded; but I like you ever so much better for being nice to him.

MARCHBANKS: Ought I to have laughed? I noticed that he said something funny; but I am so ill at ease with strangers; and I never can see a joke! I'm very sorry. [*He sits down on the sofa, his elbows on his knees and his temples between his fists, with an expression of hopeless suffering*]

CANDIDA: [*Bustling him good-naturedly*] Oh, come! you great baby, you! You are worse than usual this morning. Why were you so melancholy as we came along in the cab?

MARCHBANKS: Oh, that was nothing. I was wondering how much I ought to give the cabman. I know it's utterly silly; but you don't know how dreadful such things are to me—how I shrink from having to deal with strange people. [*Quickly and reassuringly*] But it's all right. He beamed all over and touched his hat when Morell gave him two shillings. I was on the point of offering him ten. [Candida *laughs heartily.* Morell *comes back with a few letters and newspapers which have come by the midday post*]

CANDIDA: Oh, James, dear, he was going to give the cabman ten shillings—ten shillings for a three minutes' drive—oh, dear!

MORELL: [*At the table, glancing through the letters*] Never mind her, Marchbanks. The overpaying instinct is a generous one: better than the underpaying instinct, and not so common.

MARCHBANKS: [*Relapsing into dejection*] No: cowardice, incompetence. Mrs. Morell's quite right.

CANDIDA: Of course she is. [*She takes up her handbag*] And now I must leave you to James for the present. I suppose you are too much of a poet to know the state a woman finds her house in when she's been away for three weeks. Give me my rug. [Eugene *takes the strapped rug from the couch, and gives it to her. She takes it in her left hand, having the bag in her right*] Now hang my cloak across my arm. [*He obeys*] Now my hat. [*He puts it into the hand which has the bag*] Now open the door for me. [*He hurries up before her and opens the door*] Thanks. [*She goes out; and* Marchbanks *shuts the door*]

MORELL: [*Still busy at the table*] You'll stay to lunch, Marchbanks, of course.

MARCHBANKS: [*Scared*] I mustn't. [*He glances quickly at* Morell, *but at once avoids his frank look, and adds, with obvious disingenuousness*] I can't.

MORELL: [*Over his shoulder*] You mean you won't.

MARCHBANKS: [*Earnestly*] No: I should like to, indeed. Thank you very much. But—but—

MORELL: [*Breezily, finishing with the letters and coming close to him*] But—but—but—but—bosh! If you'd like to stay, stay. You don't mean to persuade me you have anything else to do. If you're shy, go and take a turn in the park and write poetry until half past one; and then come in and have a good feed.

MARCHBANKS: Thank you, I should like that very much. But I really mustn't. The truth is, Mrs. Morell told me not to. She said she didn't think you'd ask me to stay to lunch, but that I was to remember, if you did, that you didn't really want me to. [*Plaintively*] She said I'd understand; but I don't. Please don't tell her I told you.

MORELL: [*Drolly*] Oh, is that all? Won't my suggestion that you should take a turn in the park meet the difficulty?

MARCHBANKS: How?

MORELL: [*Exploding good-humoredly*] Why, you duffer—[*But this boisterousness jars himself as well as* Eugene. *He checks himself, and resumes, with affectionate seriousness*] No: I won't put it in that way. My dear lad: in a happy marriage like ours, there is something very sacred in the return of the wife to her home. [Marchbanks *looks quickly at him, half anticipating his meaning*] An old friend or a truly noble and sympathetic soul is not in the way on such occasions; but a chance visitor is. [*The hunted, horror-stricken expression comes out with sudden vividness in* Eugene's *face as he understands.* Morell, *occupied with his own thought, goes on without noticing it*] Candida thought I would rather not have you here; but she was wrong. I'm very fond of you, my boy, and I should like you to see for yourself what a happy thing it is to be married as I am.

MARCHBANKS: Happy!—your marriage! You think that! You believe that!

MORELL: [*Buoyantly*] I know it, my lad. La Rochefoucauld said that there are convenient marriages, but no delightful ones. You don't know the comfort of seeing through and through a thundering liar and rotten cynic like that fellow. Ha, ha! Now off with you to the park, and write your poem. Half past one, sharp, mind: we never wait for anybody.

MARCHBANKS: [*Wildly*] No: stop: you shan't. I'll force it into the light.

MORELL: [*Puzzled*] Eh? Force what?

MARCHBANKS: I must speak to you. There is something that must be settled between us.

MORELL: [*With a whimsical glance at the clock*] Now?

MARCHBANKS: [*Passionately*] Now. Before you leave this room. [*He retreats a few steps, and stands as if to bar* Morell's *way to the door.*]

MORELL: [*Without moving, and gravely, perceiving now that there is something serious the matter*]

I'm not going to leave it, my dear boy: I thought you were. [Eugene, *baffled by his firm tone, turns his back on him, writing with anger*. Morell *goes to him and puts his hand on his shoulder strongly and kindly, disregarding his attempt to shake it off*] Come: sit down quietly; and tell me what it is. And remember: we are friends, and need not fear that either of us will be anything but patient and kind to the other, whatever we may have to say.

MARCHBANKS: [*Twisting himself round on him*] Oh, I am not forgetting myself: I am only [*covering his face desperately with his hands*] full of horror. [*Then, dropping his hands, and thrusting his face forward fiercely at* Morell, *he goes on threateningly*] You shall see whether this is a time for patience and kindness. [Morell, *firm as a rock, looks indulgently at him*] Don't look at me in that self-complacent way. You think yourself stronger than I am; but I shall stagger you if you have a heart in your breast.

MORELL: [*Powerfully confident*] Stagger me, my boy. Out with it.

MARCHBANKS: First—

MORELL: First?—

MARCHBANKS: I love your wife.

[Morell *recoils, and, after staring at him for a moment in utter amazement, bursts into uncontrollable laughter.* Eugene *is taken aback, but not disconcerted; and he soon becomes indignant and contemptuous*]

MORELL: [*Sitting down to have his laugh out*] Why, my dear child, of course you do. Everybody loves her: they can't help it. I like it. But [*looking up whimsically at him*] I say, Eugene: do you think yours is a case to be talked about? You're under twenty: she's over thirty. Doesn't it look rather too like a case of calf love?

MARCHBANKS: [*Vehemently*] You dare say that of her! You think that way of the love she inspires! It is an insult to her!

MORELL: [*Rising quickly, in an altered tone*] To her! Eugene: take care. I have been patient. I hope to remain patient. But there are some things I won't allow. Don't force me to show you the indulgence I should show to a child. Be a man.

MARCHBANKS: [*With a gesture as if sweeping something behind him*] Oh, let us put aside all that cant. It horrifies me when I think of the doses of it she has had to endure in all the weary years during which you have selfishly and blindly sacrificed her to minister to your self-sufficiency—you [*Turning on him*] who have not one thought—one sense—in common with her.

MORELL: [*Philosophically*] She seems to bear it pretty well. [*Looking him straight in the face*] Eugene, my boy: you are making a fool of yourself—a very great fool of yourself. There's a piece of wholesome plain speaking for you.

MARCHBANKS: Oh, do you think I don't know all that? Do you think that the things people make fools of themselves about are any less real and true than the things they behave sensibly about? [Morell's *gaze wavers for the first time. He instinctively averts his face and stands listening, startled and thoughtful*] They are more true: they are the only things that are true. You are very calm and sensible and moderate with me because you can see that I am a fool about your wife; just as no doubt that old man who was here just now is very wise over your Socialism, because he sees that you are a fool about it. [Morell's *perplexity deepens markedly.* Eugene *follows up his advantage, plying him fiercely with questions*] Does that prove you wrong? Does your complacent superiority to me prove that *I* am wrong?

MORELL: [*Turning on* Eugene, *who stands his ground*] Marchbanks: some devil is putting these words into your mouth. It is easy—terribly easy—to shake a man's faith in himself. To take advantage of that to break a man's spirit is devil's work. Take care of what you are doing. Take care.

MARCHBANKS: [*Ruthlessly*] I know. I'm doing it on purpose. I told you I should stagger you.

[*They confront one another threateningly for a moment. Then* Morell *recovers his dignity*]

MORELL: [*With noble tenderness*] Eugene: listen to me. Some day, I hope and trust, you will be a happy man like me. [Eugene *chafes intolerantly, repudiating the worth of his happiness.* Morell, *deeply insulted, controls himself with fine forbearance, and continues steadily, with great artistic beauty of delivery*] You will be married; and you will be working with all your might and valor to make every spot on earth as happy as your own home. You will be one of the makers of the Kingdom of Heaven on earth; and—who knows?—you may be a pioneer and master builder where I am only a humble journeyman; for don't think, my boy, that I cannot see in you, young as you are, promise of higher powers than I can ever pretend to. I well know that it is in the poet that the holy spirit of man—the god within him—is most godlike. It should make you tremble to think of that—to think that the heavy burthen and great gift of a poet may be laid upon you.

MARCHBANKS: [*Unimpressed and remorseless, his boyish crudity of assertion telling sharply against* Morell's *oratory*] It does not make me tremble. It is the want of it in others that makes me tremble.

MORELL: [*Redoubling his force of style under the stimulus of his genuine feeling and* Eugene's *obduracy*] Then help to kindle it in them—in me—not to extinguish it. In the future—when you are as happy as I am—I will be your true brother in the faith. I will help you to believe that God has given us a world that nothing but our own folly keeps from being a paradise. I will help you to believe that every stroke of your work is sowing happiness for the great harvest that all—even the humblest—shall one day reap. And last, but trust me, not least, I will help you to believe that your wife loves you and is happy in her home. We need such help, Marchbanks: we need it greatly and always. There are so many things to make us doubt, if once we let our understanding be troubled. Even at home, we sit as if in camp, encompassed by a hostile army of doubts. Will you play the traitor and let them in on me?

MARCHBANKS: [*Looking round him*] Is it like this for her here always? A woman, with a great soul, craving for reality, truth, freedom, and being fed on metaphors, sermons, stale perorations, mere rhetoric. Do you think a woman's soul can live on your talent for preaching?

MORELL: [*Stung*] Marchbanks: you make it hard for me to control myself. My talent is like yours insofar as it has any real worth at all. It is the gift of finding words for divine truth.

MARCHBANKS: [*Impetuously*] It's the gift of the gab, nothing more and nothing less. What has your knack of fine talking to do with the truth, any more than playing the organ has? I've never been in your church; but I've been to your political meetings; and I've seen you do what's called rousing the meeting to enthusiasm: that is, you excited them until they behaved exactly as if they were drunk. And their wives looked on and saw clearly enough what fools they were. Oh, it's an old story: you'll find it in the Bible. I imagine King David, in his fits of enthusiasm, was very like you. [*Stabbing him with the words*] "But his wife despised him in her heart."

MORELL: [*Wrathfully*] Leave my house. Do you hear? [*He advances on him threateningly*]

MARCHBANKS: [*Shrinking back against the couch*] Let me alone. Don't touch me. [*Morell grasps him powerfully by the lapel of his coat: he cowers down on the sofa and screams passionately*] Stop, Morell, if you strike me, I'll kill myself: I won't bear it. [*Almost in hysterics*] Let me go. Take your hand away.

MORELL: [*With slow, emphatic scorn*] You little sniveling, cowardly whelp. [*Releasing him*] Go, before you frighten yourself into a fit.

MARCHBANKS: [*On the sofa, gasping, but relieved by the withdrawal of* Morell's *hand*] I'm not afraid of you: it's you who are afraid of me.

MORELL: [*Quietly, as he stands over him*] It looks like it, doesn't it?

MARCHBANKS: [*With petulant vehemence*] Yes, it does. [*Morell turns away contemptuously.* Eugene *scrambles to his feet and follows him*] You think because I shrink from being brutally handled—because [*with tears in his voice*] I can do nothing but cry with rage when I am met with violence—because I can't lift a heavy trunk down from the top of a cab like you—because I can't fight you for your wife as a navvy would: all that makes you think that I'm afraid of you. But you're wrong. If I haven't got what you call British pluck, I haven't British cowardice either: I'm not afraid of a clergyman's ideas. I'll fight your ideas. I'll rescue her from her slavery to them: I'll pit my own ideas against them. You are driving me out of the house because you

daren't let her choose between your ideas and mine. You are afraid to let me see her again. [*Morell angered, turns suddenly on him. He flies to the door in involuntary dread*] Let me alone, I say. I'm going.

MORELL: [*With cold scorn*] Wait a moment: I am not going to touch you: don't be afraid. When my wife comes back she will want to know why you have gone. And when she finds that you are never going to cross our threshold again, she will want to have that explained, too. Now I don't wish to distress her by telling her that you have behaved like a blackguard.

MARCHBANKS: [*Coming back with renewed vehemence*] You shall—you must. If you give any explanation but the true one, you are a liar and a coward. Tell her what I said; and how you were strong and manly, and shook me as a terrier shakes a rat; and how I shrank and was terrified; and how you called me a sniveling little whelp and put me out of the house. If you don't tell her, I will: I'll write it to her.

MORELL: [*Taken aback*] Why do you want her to know this?

MARCHBANKS: [*With lyric rapture*] Because she will understand me, and know that I understand her. If you keep back one word of it from her—if you are not ready to lay the truth at her feet as I am— then you will know to the end of your days that she really belongs to me and not to you. Good-bye. [*Going*]

MORELL: [*Terribly disquieted*] Stop: I will not tell her.

MARCHBANKS: [*Turning near the door*] Either the truth or a lie you must tell her, if I go.

MORELL: [*Temporizing*] Marchbanks: it is sometimes justifiable.

MARCHBANKS: [*Cutting him short*] I know—to lie. It will be useless. Good-bye, Mr. Clergyman.

[*As he turns finally to the door, it opens and* Candida *enters in housekeeping attire*]

CANDIDA: Are you going, Eugene? [*Looking more observantly at him*] Well, dear me, just look at you, going out into the street in that state! You are a poet, certainly. Look at him, James! [*She takes him by the coat, and brings him forward to show him to* Morell] Look at his collar! look at his tie! look at his hair! One would think somebody had been throttling you. [*The two men guard themselves against betraying their consciousness*] Here! Stand still. [*She buttons his collar; ties his neckerchief in a bow; and arranges his hair*] There! Now you look so nice that I think you'd better stay to lunch after all, though I told you you mustn't. It will be ready in half an hour. [*She puts a final touch to the bow. He kisses her hand*] Don't be silly.

MARCHBANKS: I want to stay, of course—unless the reverend gentleman, your husband, has anything to advance to the contrary.

CANDIDA: Shall he stay, James, if he promises to be a good boy and to help me to lay the table?

[Marchbanks *turns his head and looks steadfastly at* Morell *over his shoulder, challenging his answer*]

MORELL: [*Shortly*] Oh, yes, certainly: he had better. [*He goes to the table and pretends to busy himself with his papers there*]

MARCHBANKS: [*Offering his arm to* Candida] Come and lay the table. [*She takes it and they go to the door together. As they go out he adds*] I am the happiest of men.

MORELL: So was I—an hour ago.

ACT II.

The same day. The same room. Late in the afternoon. The spare chair for visitors has been replaced at the table, which is, if possible, more untidy than before. Marchbanks, *alone and idle, is trying to find out how the typewriter works. Hearing someone at the door, he steals guiltily away to the window and pretends to be absorbed in the view.* Miss Garnett, *carrying the notebook in which she takes down* Morell's *letters in shorthand from his dictation, sits down at the typewriter and sets to work transcribing them, much too busy to notice* Eugene. *Unfortunately the first key she strikes sticks.*

PROSERPINE: Bother! You've been meddling with my typewriter, Mr. Marchbanks; and there's not the least use in your trying to look as if you hadn't.

MARCHBANKS: [*Timidly*] I'm very sorry, Miss Garnett. I only tried to make it write.

PROSERPINE: Well, you've made this key stick.

MARCHBANKS: [*Earnestly*] I assure you I didn't touch the keys. I didn't, indeed. I only turned a little wheel. [*He points irresolutely at the tension wheel*]

PROSERPINE: Oh, now I understand. [*She sets the machine to rights, talking volubly all the time*] I suppose you thought it was a sort of barrel-organ. Nothing to do but turn the handle, and it would write a beautiful love letter for you straight off, eh?

MARCHBANKS: [*Seriously*] I suppose a machine could be made to write love-letters. They're all the same, aren't they?

PROSERPINE: [*Somewhat indignantly: any such discussion, except by way of pleasantry, being outside her code of manners*] How do I know? Why do you ask me?

MARCHBANKS: I beg your pardon. I thought clever people—people who can do business and write letters, and that sort of thing—always had love affairs.

PROSERPINE: [*Rising, outraged*] Mr. Marchbanks! [*She looks severely at him, and marches with much dignity to the bookcase*]

MARCHBANKS: [*Approaching her humbly*] I hope I haven't offended you. Perhaps I shouldn't have alluded to your love affairs.

PROSERPINE: [*Plucking a blue book from the shelf and turning sharply on him*] I haven't any love affairs. How dare you say such a thing?

MARCHBANKS: [*Simply*] Really! Oh, then you are shy, like me. Isn't that so?

PROSERPINE: Certainly I am not shy. What do you mean?

MARCHBANKS: [*Secretly*] You must be: that is the reason there are so few love affairs in the world. We all go about longing for love: it is the first need of our natures, the loudest cry of our hearts; but we dare not utter our longing: we are too shy. [*Very earnestly*] Oh, Miss Garnett, what would you not give to be without fear, without shame—

PROSERPINE: [*Scandalized*] Well, upon my word!

MARCHBANKS: [*With petulant impatience*] Ah, don't say those stupid things to me: they don't deceive me: what use are they? Why are you afraid to be your real self with me? I am just like you.

PROSERPINE: Like me! Pray, are you flattering me or flattering yourself? I don't feel quite sure which. [*She turns to go back to the typewriter*]

MARCHBANKS: [*Stopping her mysteriously*] Hush! I go about in search of love; and I find it in unmeasured stores in the bosoms of others. But when I try to ask for it, this horrible shyness strangles me; and I stand dumb, or worse than dumb, saying meaningless things—foolish lies. And I see the affection I am longing for given to dogs and cats and pet birds, because they come and ask for it. [*Almost whispering*] It must be asked for: it is like a ghost: it cannot speak unless it is first spoken to. [*At his normal pitch, but with deep melancholy*] All the love in the world is longing to speak; only it dare not, because it is shy, shy, shy. That is the world's tragedy. [*With a deep sigh he sits in the spare chair and buries his face in his hands*]

PROSERPINE: [*Amazed, but keeping her wits about her—her point of honor in encounters with strange young men*] Wicked people get over that shyness occasionally, don't they?

MARCHBANKS: [*Scrambling up almost fiercely*] Wicked people means people who have no love: therefore they have no shame. They have the power to ask love because they don't need it: they have the power to offer it because they have none to give. [*He collapses into his seat, and adds, mournfully*] But we, who have love, and long to mingle it with the love of others: we cannot utter a word. [*Timidly*] You find that, don't you?

PROSERPINE: Look here: if you don't stop talking like this, I'll leave the room, Mr. Marchbanks: I really will. It's not proper.

[*She resumes her seat at the typewriter, opening the blue book and preparing to copy a passage from it*]

MARCHBANKS: [*Hopelessly*] Nothing that's worth saying is proper. [*He rises, and wanders about the room in his lost way, saying*] I can't understand you, Miss Garnett. What am I to talk about?

PROSERPINE: [*Snubbing him*] Talk about indifferent things. 'alk about the weather.

MARCHBANKS: Would you stand and talk about indifferent things if a child were by, crying bitterly with hunger?

PROSERPINE: I suppose not.

MARCHBANKS: Well: *I* can't talk about indifferent things with my heart crying out bitterly in its hunger.

PROSERPINE: Then hold your tongue.

MARCHBANKS: Yes: that is what it always comes to. We hold our tongues. Does that stop the cry of your heart?—for it does cry: doesn't it? It must, if you have a heart.

PROSERPINE: [*Suddenly rising with her hand pressed on her heart*] Oh, it's no use trying to work while you talk like that. [*She leaves her little table and sits on the sofa. Her feelings are evidently strongly worked on*] It's no business of yours, whether my heart cries or not; but I have a mind to tell you, for all that.

MARCHBANKS: You needn't. I know already that it must.

PROSERPINE: But mind: if you ever say I said so, I'll deny it.

MARCHBANKS: [*Compassionately*] Yes, I know. And so you haven't the courage to tell him?

PROSERPINE: [*Bouncing up*] Him! Who?

MARCHBANKS: Whoever he is. The man you love. It might be anybody. The curate, Mr. Mill, perhaps.

PROSERPINE: [*With disdain*] Mr. Mill!!! A fine man to break my heart about, indeed! I'd rather have you than Mr. Mill.

MARCHBANKS: [*Recoiling*] No, really—I'm very sorry; but you mustn't think of that. I—

PROSERPINE: [*Testily, crossing to the fire and standing at it with her back to him*] Oh, don't be frightened: it's not you. It's not any one particular person.

MARCHBANKS: I know. You feel that you could love anybody that offered—

PROSERPINE: [*Exasperated*] Anybody that offered! No, I do not. What do you take me for?

MARCHBANKS: [*Discouraged*] No use. You won't make me real answers—only those things that everybody says. [*He strays to the sofa and sits down disconsolately*]

PROSERPINE: [*Nettled at what she takes to be a disparagement of her manners by an aristocrat*] Oh, well, if you want original conversation, you'd better go and talk to yourself.

MARCHBANKS: That is what all poets do: they talk to themselves out loud; and the world overhears them. But it's horribly lonely not to hear someone else talk sometimes.

PROSERPINE: Wait until Mr. Morell comes. He'll talk to you. [Marchbanks *shudders*] Oh, you needn't make wry faces over him: he can talk better than you. [*With temper*] He'd talk your little head off.

[*She is going back angrily to her place, when, suddenly enlightened, he springs up and stops her*]

MARCHBANKS: Ah, I understand now!

PROSERPINE: [*Reddening*] What do you understand?

MARCHBANKS: Your secret. Tell me: is it really and truly possible for a woman to love him?

PROSERPINE: [*As if this were beyond all bounds*] Well!!

MARCHBANKS: [*Passionately*] No, answer me. I want to know: I must know. *I* can't understand it. I can see nothing in him but words, pious resolutions, what people call goodness. You can't love that.

PROSERPINE: [*Attempting to snub him by an air of cool propriety*] I simply don't know what you're talking about. I don't understand you.

MARCHBANKS: [*Vehemently*] You do. You lie—

PROSERPINE: Oh!

MARCHBANKS: You do understand; and you know. [*Determined to have an answer*] Is it possible for a woman to love him?

PROSERPINE: [*Looking him straight in the face*] Yes. [*He covers his face with his hands*] Whatever is the matter with you! [*He takes down his hands and looks at her. Frightened at the tragic mask presented to her, she hurries past him at the utmost possible distance, keeping her eyes on his face until he turns from her and goes to the child's chair beside the hearth, where he sits in the deepest dejection. As she approaches the door, it opens and Burgess enters. On seeing him, she ejaculates*] Praise heaven, here's somebody! [*And sits down, reassured, at her table. She puts a fresh sheet of paper into the typewriter as Burgess crosses to Eugene*]

BURGESS: [*Bent on taking care of the distinguished visitor*] Well: so this is the way they leave you to yourself, Mr. Morchbanks. I've come to keep you company. [Marchbanks *looks up at him in consternation, which is quite lost on him*] James is receivin' a deppitation in the dinin' room; and Candy is hupstairs educatin' of a young stitcher gurl she's hinterusted in. She's settin' there learnin' her to read out of the " 'Ev'nly Twins." [*Condolingly*] You must find it lonesome here with no one but the typist to talk to. [*He pulls round the easy chair above fire, and sits down*]

PROSERPINE: [*Highly incensed*] He'll be all right now that he has the advantage of your polished conversation: that's one comfort, anyhow. [*She begins to typewrite with clattering asperity*]

BURGESS: [*Amazed at her audacity*] Hi was not addressin' myself to you, young woman, that I'm awerr of.

PROSERPINE: [*Tartly, to Marchbanks*] Did you ever see worse manners, Mr. Marchbanks?

BURGESS: [*With pompous severity*] Mr. Morchbanks is a gentleman and knows his place, which is more than some people do.

PROSERPINE: [*Fretfully*] It's well you and I are not ladies and gentlemen: I'd talk to you pretty straight if Mr. Marchbanks wasn't here. [*She pulls the letter out of the machine so crossly that it tears*] There, now I've spoiled this letter—have to be done all over again. Oh, I can't contain myself—silly old fathead!

BURGESS: [*Rising, breathless with indignation*] Ho! I'm a silly ole fat'ead, am I? Ho, indeed [*Gasping*] Hall right, my gurl! Hall right. You just wait till I tell that to your employer. You'll see. I'll teach you: see if I don't.

PROSERPINE: I—

BURGESS: [*Cutting her short*] No, you've done it now. No huse a-talkin' to me. I'll let you know who I am. [Proserpine *shifts her paper carriage with a defiant bang, and disdainfully goes on with her work*] Don't you take no notice of her, Mr. Morchbanks. She's beneath it. [*He sits down again loftily*]

MARCHBANKS: [*Miserably nervous and disconcerted*] Hadn't we better change the subject. I—I don't think Miss Garnett meant anything.

PROSERPINE: [*With intense conviction*] Oh, didn't I though, just!

BURGESS: I wouldn't demean myself to take notice on her.

[*An electric bell rings twice*]

PROSERPINE: [*Gathering up her note-book and papers*] That's for me. [*She hurries out*]

BURGESS: [*Calling after her*] Oh, we can spare you. [*Somewhat relieved by the triumph of having the last word, and yet half inclined to try to improve on it, he looks after her for a moment; then subsides into his seat by* Eugene, *and addresses him very confidentially*] Now we're alone, Mr. Morchbanks, let me give you a friendly 'int that I wouldn't give to everybody. 'Ow long 'ave you known my son-in-law James here?

MARCHBANKS: I don't know. I never can remember dates. A few months, perhaps.

BURGESS: Ever notice anything queer about him?

MARCHBANKS: I don't think so.

BURGESS: [*Impressively*] No more you wouldn't. That's the danger in it. Well, he's mad.

MARCHBANKS: Mad!

BURGESS: Mad as a Morch 'are. You take notice on him and you'll see.

MARCHBANKS: [*Beginning*] But surely that is only because his opinions—

BURGESS: [*Touching him with his forefinger on his knee, and pressing it as if to hold his attention with it*] That's wot I used ter think, Mr. Morchbanks. Hi thought long enough that it was honly 'is opinions; though, mind you, hopinions becomes vurry serious things when people takes to hactin' on 'em as 'e does. But that's not wot I go on. [*He looks round to make sure that they are alone, and bends over to* Eugene's *ear*] Wot do you think he says to me this mornin' in this very room?

MARCHBANKS: What?

BURGESS: He sez to me—this is as sure as we're settin' here now—he sez "I'm a fool," he sez; "and

yore a scounderl!"—as cool as possible. Me a scounderl, mind you! And then shook 'ands with me on it, as if it was to my credit! Do you mean to tell me that that man's sane?

MORELL: [*Outside, calling to* Proserpine, *holding the door open*] Get all their names and addresses, Miss Garnett.

PROSERPINE: [*In the distance*] Yes, Mr. Morell.

[Morell *comes in, with the deputation's documents in his hands*]

BURGESS: [*Aside to* Marchbanks] Yorr he is. Just you keep your heye on him and see. [*Rising momentously*] I'm sorry, James, to 'ave to make a complaint to you. I don't want to do it; but I feel I oughter, as a matter o' right and dooty.

MORELL: What's the matter?

BURGESS: Mr. Morchbanks will bear me out: he was a witness. [*Very solemnly*] Your young woman so far forgot herself as to call me a silly ole fat'ead.

MORELL: [*Delighted—with tremendous heartiness*] Oh, now, isn't that exactly like Prossy? She's so frank: she can't contain herself! Poor Prossy! Ha! Ha!

BURGESS: [*Trembling with rage*] And do you hexpec me to put up with it from the like of 'er?

MORELL: Pooh, nonsense! you can't take any notice of it. Never mind. [*He goes to the cellaret and puts the papers into one of the drawers*]

BURGESS: Oh, *I* don't mind. I'm above it. But is it right?—that's what I want to know. Is it right?

MORELL: That's a question for the Church, not for the laity. Has it done you any harm, that's the question for you, eh? Of course, it hasn't. Think no more of it. [*He dismisses the subject by going to his place at the table and setting to work at his correspondence*]

BURGESS: [*Aside to* Marchbanks] What did I tell you? Mad as a 'atter. [*He goes to the table and asks, with the sickly civility of a hungry man*] When's dinner, James?

MORELL: Not for half an hour yet.

BURGESS: [*With plaintive resignation*] Gimme a nice book to read over the fire, will you, James: thur's a good chap.

MORELL: What sort of book? A good one?

BURGESS: [*With almost a yell of remonstrance*] Nah-oo! Summat pleasant, just to pass the time. [Morell *takes an illustrated paper from the table and offers it. He accepts it humbly*] Thank yer, James. [*He goes back to his easy chair at the fire, and sits there at his ease, reading*]

MORELL: [*As he writes*] Candida will come to entertain you presently. She has got rid of her pupil. She is filling the lamps.

MARCHBANKS: [*Starting up in the wildest consternation*] But that will soil her hands. I can't bear that, Morell: it's a shame. I'll go and fill them. [*He makes for the door*]

MORELL: You'd better not. [Marchbanks *stops irresolutely*] She'd only set you to clean my boots, to save me the trouble of doing it myself in the morning.

BURGESS: [*With great disapproval*] Don't you keep a servant now, James?

MORELL: Yes; but she isn't a slave; and the house looks as if I kept three. That means that everyone has to lend a hand. It's not a bad plan: Prossy and I can talk business after breakfast whilst we're washing up. Washing up's no trouble when there are two people to do it.

MARCHBANKS: [*Tormentedly*] Do you think every woman is as coarse-grained as Miss Garnett?

BURGESS: [*Emphatically*] That's quite right, Mr. Morchbanks. That's quite right. She is corse-grained.

MORELL: [*Quietly and significantly*] Marchbanks!

MARCHBANKS: Yes.

MORELL: How many servants does your father keep?

MARCHBANKS: Oh, I don't know. [*He comes back uneasily to the sofa, as if to get as far as possible from* Morell's *questioning, and sits down in great agony of mind, thinking of the paraffin*]

MORELL: [*Very gravely*] So many that you don't know. [*More aggressively*] Anyhow, when there's anything coarse-grained to be done, you ring the bell and throw it on to somebody else, eh? That's one of the great facts in your existence, isn't it?

MARCHBANKS: Oh, don't torture me. The one great fact now is that your wife's beautiful fingers are dabbling in paraffin oil, and that you are sitting here comfortably preaching about it—everlasting preaching, preaching, words, words, words.

BURGESS: [*Intensely appreciating this retort*] Ha, ha! Devil a better. [*Radiantly*] 'Ad you there, James, straight.

[Candida *comes in, well aproned, with a reading lamp trimmed, filled, and ready for lighting. She places it on the table near* Morell, *ready for use*]

CANDIDA: [*Brushing her finger tips together with a slight twitch of her nose*] If you stay with us, Eugene, I think I will hand over the lamps to you.

MARCHBANKS: I will stay on condition that you hand over all the rough work to me.

CANDIDA: That's very gallant; but I think I should like to see how you do it first. [*Turning to* Morell] James: you've not been looking after the house properly.

MORELL: What have I done—or not done—my love?

CANDIDA: [*With serious vexation*] My own particular pet scrubbing brush has been used for black-leading. [*A heartbreaking wail bursts from* Marchbanks. Burgess *looks round, amazed*. Candida *hurries to the sofa*] What's the matter? Are you ill, Eugene?

MARCHBANKS: No, not ill. Only horror, horror, horror! [*He bows his head on his hands*]

BURGESS: [*Shocked*] What! Got the 'orrors, Mr.

Morchbanks! Oh, that's bad, at your age. You must leave it off grajally.

CANDIDA: [*Reassured*] Nonsense, papa. It's only poetic horror, isn't it, Eugene? [*Petting him*]

BURGESS: [*Abashed*] Oh, poetic 'orror, is it? I beg your pordon, I'm shore. [*He turns to the fire again, deprecating his hasty conclusion*]

CANDIDA: What is it, Eugene—the scrubbing brush? [*He shudders*] Well, there! never mind. [*She sits down beside him*] Wouldn't you like to present me with a nice new one, with an ivory back inlaid with mother-of-pearl?

MARCHBANKS: [*Softly and musically, but sadly and longingly*] No, not a scrubbing brush, but a boat—a tiny shallop to sail away in, far from the world, where the marble floors are washed by the rain and dried by the sun, where the south wind dusts the beautiful green and purple carpets. Or a chariot—to carry us up into the sky, where the lamps are stars, and don't need to be filled with paraffin oil every day.

MORELL: [*Harshly*] And where there is nothing to do but to be idle, selfish and useless.

CANDIDA: [*Jarred*] Oh, James, how could you spoil it all!

MARCHBANKS: [*Firing up*] Yes, to be idle, selfish and useless: that is to be beautiful and free and happy: hasn't every man desired that with all his soul for the woman he loves? That's my ideal: what's yours, and that of all the dreadful people who live in these hideous rows of houses? Sermons and scrubbing brushes! With you to preach the sermon and your wife to scrub.

CANDIDA: [*Quaintly*] He cleans the boots, Eugene. You will have to clean them to-morrow for saying that about him.

MARCHBANKS: Oh! don't talk about boots. Your feet should be beautiful on the mountains.

CANDIDA: My feet would not be beautiful on the Hackney Road without boots.

BURGESS: [*Scandalized*] Come, Candy, don't be vulgar. Mr. Morchbanks ain't accustomed to it. You're givin' him the 'orrors again. I mean the poetic ones.

[Morell *is silent. Apparently he is busy with his letters: really he is puzzling with misgiving over his new and alarming experience that the surer he is of his moral thrusts, the more swiftly and effectively* Eugene *parries them. To find himself beginning to fear a man whom he does not respect afflicts him bitterly*]

[Miss Garnett *comes in with a telegram*]

PROSERPINE: [*Handing the telegram to* Morell] Reply paid. The boy's waiting. [*To* Candida, *coming back to her machine and sitting down*] Maria is ready for you now in the kitchen, Mrs. Morell. [Candida *rises*] The onions have come.

MARCHBANKS: [*Convulsively*] Onions!

CANDIDA: Yes, onions. Not even Spanish ones—

nasty little red onions. You shall help me to slice them. Come along.

[*She catches him by the wrist and runs out, pulling him after her.* Burgess *rises in consternation, and stands aghast on the hearth-rug, staring after them*]

BURGESS: Candy didn't oughter 'andle a peer's nevvy like that. It's goin' too fur with it. Lookee 'ere, James: do 'e often git taken queer like that?

MORELL: [*Shortly, writing a telegram*] I don't know.

BURGESS: [*Sentimentally*] He talks very pretty. I allus had a turn for a bit of potery. Candy takes arter me that-a-way: huse ter make me tell her fairy stories when she was on'y a little kiddy not that 'igh [*Indicating a stature of two feet or thereabouts*]

MORELL: [*Preoccupied*] Ah, indeed. [*He blots the telegram, and goes out*]

PROSERPINE: Used you to make the fairy stories up out of your own head?

[Burgess, *not deigning to reply, strikes an attitude of the haughtiest disdain on the hearthrug*]

PROSERPINE: [*Calmly*] I should never have supposed you had it in you. By the way, I'd better warn you, since you've taken such a fancy to Mr. Marchbanks. He's mad.

BURGESS: Mad! Wot! 'Im too!!

PROSERPINE: Mad as a March hare. He did frighten me, I can tell you just before you came in that time. Haven't you noticed the queer things he says?

BURGESS: So that's wot the poetic 'orrors means. Blame me if it didn't come into my head once or twyst that he must be off his chump! [*He crosses the room to the door, lifting up his voice as he goes*] Well, this is a pretty sort of asylum for a man to be in, with no one but you to take care of him!

PROSERPINE: [*As he passes her*] Yes, what a dreadful thing it would be if anything happened to you!

BURGESS: [*Loftily*] Don't you address no remarks to me. Tell your hemployer that I've gone into the garden for a smoke.

PROSERPINE: [*Mocking*] Oh!

[*Before* Burgess *can retort,* Morell *comes back*]

BURGESS: [*Sentimentally*] Goin' for a turn in the garden to smoke, James.

MORELL: [*Brusquely*] Oh, all right, all right. [Burgess *goes out pathetically in the character of the weary old man.* Morell *stands at the table, turning over his papers, and adding, across to* Proserpine, *half humorously, half absently*] Well, Miss Prossy, why have you been calling my father-in-law names?

PROSERPINE: [*Blushing fiery red, and looking quickly up at him, half scared, half reproachful*] I— [*She bursts into tears*]

MORELL: [*With tender gayety, leaning across the table towards her, and consoling her*] Oh, come, come, come! Never mind, Pross: he is a silly old fathead, isn't he?

[*With an explosive sob, she makes a dash at the door, and vanishes, banging it.* Morell, *shaking his head resignedly, sighs, and goes wearily to his chair, where he sits down and sets to work, looking old and careworn.* Candida *comes in. She has finished her household work and taken off the apron. She at once notices his dejected appearance, and posts herself quietly at the spare chair, looking down at him attentively; but she says nothing*]

MORELL: [*Looking up, but with his pen raised ready to resume his work*] Well? Where is Eugene?

CANDIDA: Washing his hands in the scullery— under the tap. He will make an excellent cook if he can only get over his dread of Maria.

MORELL: [*Shortly*] Ha! No doubt. [*He begins writing again*]

CANDIDA: [*Going nearer, and putting her hand down softly on his to stop him, as she says*] Come here, dear. Let me look at you. [*He drops his pen and yields himself at her disposal. She makes him rise and brings him a little away from the table, looking at him critically all the time*] Turn your face to the light. [*She places him facing the window*] My boy is not looking well. Has he been overworking?

MORELL: Nothing more than usual.

CANDIDA: He looks very pale, and gray, and wrinkled, and old. [*His melancholy deepens; and she attacks it with wilful gayety*] Here [*pulling him towards the easy chair*] you've done enough writing for to-day. Leave Prossy to finish it and come and talk to me.

MORELL: But——

CANDIDA: Yes, I must be talked to sometimes. [*She makes him sit down, and seats herself on the carpet beside his knee*] Now [*patting his hand*] you're beginning to look better already. Why don't you give up all this tiresome overworking—going out every night lecturing and talking? Of course what you say is all very true and very right; but it does no good: they don't mind what you say to them one little bit. Of course they agree with you; but what's the use of people agreeing with you if they go and do just the opposite of what you tell them the moment your back is turned? Look at our congregation at St. Dominic's! Why do they come to hear you talking about Christianity every Sunday? Why, just because they've been so full of business and money-making for six days that they want to forget all about it and have a rest on the seventh, so that they can go back fresh and make money harder than ever! You positively help them at it instead of hindering them.

MORELL: [*With energetic seriousness*] You know very well, Candida, that I often blow them up soundly for that. But if there is nothing in their church-going but rest and diversion, why don't they try something more amusing—more self-indulgent? There must be some good in the fact that they prefer St. Dominic's to worse places on Sundays.

CANDIDA: Oh, the worst places aren't open; and even if they were, they daren't be seen going to them. Besides, James, dear, you preach so splendidly that it's as good as a play for them. Why do you think the women are so enthusiastic?

MORELL: [Shocked] Candida!

CANDIDA: Oh, *I* know. You silly boy: you think it's your Socialism and your religion; but if it was that, they'd do what you tell them instead of only coming to look at you. They all have Prossy's complaint.

MORELL: Prossy's complaint! What do you mean, Candida?

CANDIDA: Yes, Prossy, and all the other secretaries you ever had. Why does Prossy condescend to wash up the things, and to peel potatoes and abase herself in all manner of ways for six shillings a week less than she used to get in a city office? She's in love with you, James: that's the reason. They're all in love with you. And you are in love with preaching because you do it so beautifully. And you think it's all enthusiasm for the kingdom of Heaven on earth; and so do they. You dear silly!

MORELL: Candida: what dreadful, what soul-destroying cynicism! Are you jesting? Or—can it be? —are you jealous?

CANDIDA: [With curious thoughtfulness] Yes, I feel a little jealous sometimes.

MORELL: [Incredulously] What! Of Prossy!

CANDIDA: [Laughing] No, no, no, no. Not jealous of anybody. Jealous for somebody else, who is not loved as he ought to be.

MORELL: Me!

CANDIDA: You! Why, you're spoiled with love and worship: you get far more than is good for you. No: I mean Eugene.

MORELL: [Startled] Eugene!

CANDIDA: It seems unfair that all the love should go to you, and none to him, although he needs it so much more than you do. [A convulsive movement shakes him in spite of himself] What's the matter? Am I worrying you?

MORELL: [Hastily] Not at all [Looking at her with troubled intensity] You know that I have perfect confidence in you, Candida.

CANDIDA: You vain thing! Are you so sure of your irresistible attractions?

MORELL: Candida: you are shocking me. I never thought of my attractions. I thought of your goodness—your purity. That is what I confide in.

CANDIDA: What a nasty, uncomfortable thing to say to me! Oh, you are a clergyman, James—a thorough clergyman.

MORELL: [Turning away from her, heart-stricken] So Eugene says.

CANDIDA: [With a lively interest, leaning over to him with her arms on his knee] Eugene's always right. He's a wonderful boy: I have grown fonder and fonder of him all the time I was away. Do you know, James, that though he has not the least suspicion of it himself, he is ready to fall madly in love with me?

MORELL: [Grimly] Oh, he has no suspicion of it himself, hasn't he?

CANDIDA: Not a bit. [She takes her arms from his knee, and turns thoughtfully, sinking into a more restful attitude with her hands in her lap] Some day he will know—when he is grown up and experienced, like you. And he will know that I must have known. I wonder what he will think of me then.

MORELL: No evil, Candida. I hope and trust, no evil.

CANDIDA: [Dubiously] That will depend.

MORELL: [Bewildered] Depend!

CANDIDA: [Looking at him] Yes: it will depend on what happens to him. [He looks vacantly at her] Don't you see? It will depend on how he comes to learn what love really is. I mean on the sort of woman who will teach it to him.

MORELL: [Quite at a loss] Yes. No. I don't know what you mean.

CANDIDA: [Explaining] If he learns it from a good woman, then it will be all right: he will forgive me.

MORELL: Forgive!

CANDIDA: But suppose he learns it from a bad woman, as so many men, especially poetic men, who imagine all women are angels! Suppose he only discovers the value of love when he has thrown it away and degraded himself in his ignorance. Will he forgive me then, do you think?

MORELL: Forgive you for what?

CANDIDA: [Realizing how stupid he is, and a little disappointed, though quite tenderly so] Don't you understand? [He shakes his head. She turns to him again, so as to explain with the fondest intimacy] I mean, will he forgive me for not teaching him myself? For abandoning him to the bad women for the sake of my goodness—my purity, as you call it? Ah, James, how little you understand me, to talk of your confidence in my goodness and purity! I would give them both to poor Eugene as willingly as I would give my shawl to a beggar dying of cold, if there were nothing else to restrain me. Put your trust in my love for you, James, for if that went, I should care very little for your sermons—mere phrases that you cheat yourself and others with every day. [She is about to rise]

MORELL: His words!

CANDIDA: [Checking herself quickly in the act of getting up, so that she is on her knees, but upright] Whose words?

MORELL: Eugene's.

CANDIDA: [Delighted] He is always right. He understands you; he understands me; he understands Prossy; and you, James—you understand nothing. [She laughs, and kisses him to console him. He recoils as if stung, and springs up]

MORELL: How can you bear to do that when— oh, Candida [with anguish in his voice] I had rather you had plunged a grappling iron into my heart than given me that kiss.

CANDIDA: [*Rising, alarmed*] My dear: what's the matter?

MORELL: [*Frantically waving her off*] Don't touch me.

CANDIDA: [*Amazed*] James!

[*They are interrupted by the entrance of* March-banks, *with* Burgess, *who stops near the door, staring, whilst* Eugene *hurries forward between them*]

MARCHBANKS: Is anything the matter?

MORELL: [*Deadly white, putting an iron constraint on himself*] Nothing but this: that either you were right this morning, or Candida is mad.

BURGESS: [*In loudest protest*] Wot! Candy mad too! Oh, come, come, come! [*He crosses the room to the fireplace, protesting as he goes, and knocks the ashes out of his pipe on the bars.* Morell *sits down desperately, leaning forward to hide his face, and interlacing his fingers rigidly to keep them steady*]

CANDIDA: [*To* Morell, *relieved and laughing*] Oh, you're only shocked! Is that all? How conventional all you unconventional people are!

BURGESS: Come: be'ave yourself, Candy. What'll Mr. Morchbanks think of you?

CANDIDA: This comes of James teaching me to think for myself, and never to hold back out of fear of what other people may think of me. It works beautifully as long as I think the same things as he does. But now, because I have just thought something different!—look at him—just look! [*She points to* Morell, *greatly amused.* Eugene *looks, and instantly presses his hand on his heart, as if some deadly pain had shot through it, and sits down on the sofa like a man witnessing a tragedy*]

BURGESS: [*On the hearth-rug*] Well, James, you certainly ain't as himpressive lookin' as usu'l.

MORELL: [*With a laugh which is half a sob*] I suppose not. I beg all your pardons: I was not conscious of making a fuss. [*Pulling himself together*] Well, well, well, well, well! [*He goes back to his place at the table, setting to work at his papers again with resolute cheerfulness*]

CANDIDA: [*Going to the sofa and sitting beside* Marchbanks, *still in a bantering humor*] Well, Eugene, why are you so sad? Did the onions make you cry?

[Morell *cannot prevent himself from watching them*]

MARCHBANKS: [*Aside to her*] It is your cruelty. I hate cruelty. It is a horrible thing to see one person make another suffer.

CANDIDA: [*Petting him ironically*] Poor boy, have I been cruel? Did I make it slice nasty little red onions?

MARCHBANKS: [*Earnestly*] Oh, stop, stop: I don't mean myself. You have made him suffer frightfully. I feel his pain in my own heart. I know that it is not

your fault—it is something that must happen; but don't make light of it. I shudder when you torture him and laugh.

CANDIDA: [*Incredulously*] *I* torture James! Nonsense, Eugene: how you exaggerate! Silly! [*She looks round at* Morell, *who hastily resumes his writing. She goes to him and stands behind his chair, bending over him*] Don't work any more, dear. Come and talk to us.

MORELL: [*Affectionately but bitterly*] Ah no. I can't talk. I can only preach.

CANDIDA: [*Caressing him*] Well, come and preach.

BURGESS: [*Strongly remonstrating*] Aw, no, Candy. 'Ang it all!

[Lexy Mill *comes in, looking anxious and important*]

LEXY: [*Hastening to shake hands with* Candida] How do you do, Mrs. Morell? So glad to see you back again.

CANDIDA: Thank you, Lexy. You know Eugene, don't you?

LEXY: Oh, yes. How do you do, Marchbanks?

MARCHBANKS: Quite well, thanks.

LEXY: [*To Morell*] I've just come from the Guild of St. Matthew. They are in the greatest consternation about your telegram. There's nothing wrong, is there?

CANDIDA: What did you telegraph about, James?

LEXY: [*To* Candida] He was to have spoken for them to-night. They've taken the large hall in Mare Street and spent a lot of money on posters. Morell's telegram was to say he couldn't come. It came on them like a thunderbolt.

CANDIDA: [*Surprised, and beginning to suspect something wrong*] Given up an engagement to speak!

BURGESS: First time in his life, I'll bet. Ain' it, Candy?

LEXY: [*To* Morell] They decided to send an urgent telegram to you asking whether you could not change your mind. Have you received it?

MORELL: [*With restrained impatience*] Yes, yes: I got it.

LEXY: It was reply paid.

MORELL: Yes, I know. I answered it. I can't go.

CANDIDA: But why, James?

MORELL: [*Almost fiercely*] Because I don't choose. These people forget that I am a man: they think I am a talking machine to be turned on for their pleasure every evening of my life. May I not have one night at home, with my wife, and friends?

[*They are all amazed at this outburst, except* Eugene. *His expression remains unchanged*]

CANDIDA: Oh, James, you know you'll have an attack of bad conscience to-morrow; and *I* shall have to suffer for that.

LEXY: [*Intimidated, but urgent*] I know, of course, that they make the most unreasonable demands on you. But they have been telegraphing all over the place for another speaker: and they can get nobody but the President of the Agnostic League.

MORELL: [*Promptly*] Well, an excellent man. What better do they want?

LEXY: But he always insists so powerfully on the divorce of Socialism from Christianity. He will undo all the good we have been doing. Of course you know best; but— [*He hesitates*]

CANDIDA: [*Coaxingly*] Oh, do go, James. We'll all go.

BURGESS: [*Grumbling*] Look 'ere, Candy! I say! Let's stay at home by the fire, comfortable. He won't need to be more'n a couple o' hour away.

CANDIDA: You'll be just as comfortable at the meeting. We'll sit on the platform and be great people.

EUGENE: [*Terrified*] Oh, please don't let us go on the platform. No—everyone will stare at us—I couldn't. I'll sit at the back of the room.

CANDIDA: Don't be afraid. They'll be too busy looking at James to notice you.

MORELL: [*Turning his head and looking meaningly at her over his shoulder*] Prossy's complaint, Candida! Eh?

CANDIDA: [*Gayly*] Yes.

BURGESS: [*Mystified*] Prossy's complaint. Wot are you talking about, James?

MORELL: [*Not heeding him, rises; goes to the door; and holds it open, shouting in a commanding voice*] Miss Garnett.

PROSERPINE: [*In the distance*] Yes, Mr. Morell. Coming.

> [*They all wait, except* Burgess, *who goes stealthily to* Lexy *and draws him aside*]

BURGESS: Listen here, Mr. Mill. Wot's Prossy's complaint? Wot's wrong with 'er?

LEXY: [*Confidentially*] Well, I don't exactly know; but she spoke very strangely to me this morning. I'm afraid she's a little out of her mind sometimes.

BURGESS: [*Overwhelmed*] Why, it must be catchin'! Four in the same 'ouse! [*He goes back to the hearth, quite lost before the instability of the human intellect in a clergyman's house*]

PROSERPINE: [*Appearing on the threshold*] What is it, Mr. Morell?

MORELL: Telegraph to the Guild of St. Matthew that I am coming.

PROSERPINE: [*Surprised*] Don't they expect you?

MORELL: [*Peremptorily*] Do as I tell you.

> [Proserpine, *frightened, sits down at her typewriter, and obeys.* Morell *goes across to* Burgess, Candida *watching his movements all the time with growing wonder and misgiving*]

MORELL: Burgess: you don't want to come?

BURGESS: [*In deprecation*] Oh, don't put it like that, James. It's only that it ain't Sunday, you know.

MORELL: I'm sorry, I thought you might like to be introduced to the chairman. He's on the Works Committee of the County Council and has some influence in the matter of contracts. [Burgess *wakes up at once.* Morell, *expecting as much, waits a moment, and says*] Will you come?

BURGESS: [*With enthusiasm*] Course I'll come, James. Ain' it always a pleasure to 'ear you.

MORELL: [*Turning from him*] I shall want you to take some notes at the meeting, Miss Garnett, if you have no other engagement. [*She nods, afraid to speak*] You are coming, Lexy, I suppose.

LEXY: Certainly.

CANDIDA: We are all coming, James.

MORELL: No: you are not coming; and Eugene is not coming. You will stay here and entertain him —to celebrate your return home. [Eugene *rises, breathless*]

CANDIDA: But James—

MORELL: [*Authoritatively*] I insist. You do not want to come, and he does not want to come. [Candida *is about to protest*] Oh, don't concern yourselves: I shall have plenty of people without you: your chairs will be wanted by unconverted people who have never heard me before.

CANDIDA: [*Troubled*] Eugene: wouldn't you like to come?

MORELL: I should be afraid to let myself go before Eugene: he is so critical of sermons. [*Looking at him*] He knows I am afraid of him: he told me as much this morning. Well, I shall show him how much afraid I am by leaving him here in your custody, Candida.

MARCHBANKS: [*To himself, with vivid feeling*] That's brave. That's beautiful. [*He sits down again listening with parted lips*]

CANDIDA: [*With anxious misgiving*] But—but— Is anything the matter, James? [*Greatly troubled*] I can't understand—

MORELL: Ah, I thought it was *I* who couldn't understand, dear. [*He takes her tenderly in his arms and kisses her on the forehead; then looks round quietly at* Marchbanks]

ACT III.

Late in the evening. Past ten. The curtains are drawn, and the lamps lighted. The typewriter is in its case; the large table has been cleared and tidied; everything indicates that the day's work is done.

Candida *and* Marchbanks *are seated at the fire. The reading lamp is on the mantel-shelf above* Marchbanks, *who is sitting on the small chair reading aloud from a manuscript. A little pile of manuscripts and a couple of volumes of poetry are on the carpet beside him.* Candida *is in the easy chair with the poker, a light brass one, upright in her hand. She is leaning back and looking at the point of it curiously, with her feet stretched towards the blaze and her heels resting on the fender, profoundly unconscious of her appearance and surroundings.*

MARCHBANKS: [*Breaking off in his recitation*] Every poet that ever lived has put that thought into a sonnet. He must: he can't help it. [*He looks to her for assent, and notices her absorption in the poker*] Haven't you been listening? [*No response*] Mrs. Morell!

CANDIDA: [*Starting*] Eh?

MARCHBANKS: Haven't you been listening?

CANDIDA: [*With a guilty excess of politeness*] Oh, yes. It's very nice. Go on, Eugene. I'm longing to hear what happens the angel.

MARCHBANKS: [*Crushed—the manuscript dropping from his hand to the floor*] I beg your pardon for boring you.

CANDIDA: But you are not boring me, I assure you. Please go on. Do, Eugene.

MARCHBANKS: I finished the poem about the angel quarter of an hour ago. I've read you several things since.

CANDIDA: [*Remorsefully*] I'm so sorry, Eugene. I think the poker must have fascinated me. [*She puts it down*]

MARCHBANKS: It made me horribly uneasy.

CANDIDA: Why didn't you tell me? I'd have put it down at once.

MARCHBANKS: I was afraid of making you uneasy, too. It looked as if it were a weapon. If I were a hero of old, I should have laid my drawn sword between us. If Morell had come in he would have thought you had taken up the poker because there was no sword between us.

CANDIDA: [*Wondering*] What? [*With a puzzled glance at him*] I can't quite follow that. Those sonnets of yours have perfectly addled me. Why should there be a sword between us?

MARCHBANKS: [*Evasively*] Oh, never mind. [*He stoops to pick up the manuscript*]

CANDIDA: Put that down again, Eugene. There are limits to my appetite for poetry—even your poetry. You've been reading to me for more than two hours—ever since James went out. I want to talk.

MARCHBANKS: [*Rising, scared*] No: I mustn't talk. [*He looks round him in his lost way, and adds, suddenly*] I think I'll go out and take a walk in the park. [*Making for the door*]

CANDIDA: Nonsense: it's shut long ago. Come and sit down on the hearth-rug, and talk moonshine as you usually do. I want to be amused. Don't you want to?

MARCHBANKS: [*In half terror, half rapture*] Yes.

CANDIDA: Then come along. [*She moves her chair back a little to make room. He hesitates; then timidly stretches himself on the hearth-rug, face upwards, and throws back his head across her knees, looking up at her*]

MARCHBANKS: Oh, I've been so miserable all the evening, because I was doing right. Now I'm doing wrong; and I'm happy.

CANDIDA: [*Tenderly amused at him*] Yes: I'm sure you feel a great grown up wicked deceiver—quite proud of yourself, aren't you?

MARCHBANKS: [*Raising his head quickly and turning a little to look round at her*] Take care. I'm ever so much older than you, if you only knew. [*He turns quite over on his knees, with his hands clasped and his arms on her lap, and speaks with growing impulse, his blood beginning to stir*] May I say some wicked things to you?

CANDIDA: [*Without the least fear or coldness, quite nobly, and with perfect respect for his passion, but with a touch of her wise-hearted maternal humor*] No. But you may say anything you really and truly feel. Anything at all, no matter what it is. I am not afraid, so long as it is your real self that speaks, and not a mere attitude—a gallant attitude, or a wicked attitude, or even a poetic attitude. I put you on your honor and truth. Now say whatever you want to.

MARCHBANKS: [*The eager expression vanishing utterly from his lips and nostrils as his eyes light up with pathetic spirituality*] Oh, now I can't say anything: all the words I know belong to some attitude or other—all except one.

CANDIDA: What one is that?

MARCHBANKS: [*Softly, losing himself in the music of the name*] Candida, Candida, Candida, Candida, Candida. I must say that now, because you have put me on my honor and truth; and I never think or feel Mrs. Morell: it is always Candida.

CANDIDA: Of course. And what have you to say to Candida?

MARCHBANKS: Nothing, but to repeat your name a thousand times. Don't you feel that every time is a prayer to you?

CANDIDA: Doesn't it make you happy to be able to pray?

MARCHBANKS: Yes, very happy.

CANDIDA: Well, that happiness is the answer to your prayer. Do you want anything more?

MARCHBANKS: [*In beatitude*] No: I have come into heaven, where want is unknown.

[*Morell comes in. He halts on the threshold, and takes in the scene at a glance*]

MORELL: [*Grave and self-contained*] I hope I don't disturb you.

[*Candida starts up violently, but without the smallest embarrassment, laughing at herself. Eugene, still kneeling, saves himself from falling by putting his hands on the seat of the chair, and remains there, staring open mouthed at Morell*]

CANDIDA: [*As he rises*] Oh, James, how you startled me! I was so taken up with Eugene that I didn't hear your latchkey. How did the meeting go off? Did you speak well?

MORELL: I have never spoken better in my life.

CANDIDA: That was first rate! How much was the collection?

MORELL: I forgot to ask.

CANDIDA: [*To Eugene*] He must have spoken splendidly, or he would never have forgotten that. [*To Morell*] Where are all the others?

MORELL: They left long before I could get away: I thought I should never escape. I believe they are having supper somewhere.

CANDIDA: [*In her domestic business tone*] Oh; in that case, Maria may go to bed. I'll tell her. [*She goes out to the kitchen*]

MORELL: [*Looking sternly down at* Marchbanks] Well?

MARCHBANKS: [*Squatting cross-legged on the hearth-rug, and actually at ease with* Morell—*even impishly humorous*] Well?

MORELL: Have you anything to tell me?

MARCHBANKS: Only that I have been making a fool of myself here in private whilst you have been making a fool of yourself in public.

MORELL: Hardly in the same way, I think.

MARCHBANKS: [*Scrambling up—eagerly*] The very, very, very same way. I have been playing the good man just like you. When you began your heroics about leaving me here with Candida—

MORELL: [*Involuntarily*] Candida?

MARCHBANKS: Oh, yes: I've got that far. Heroics are infectious: I caught the disease from you. I swore not to say a word in your absence that I would not have said a month ago in your presence.

MORELL: Did you keep your oath?

MARCHBANKS: [*Suddenly perching himself grotesquely on the easy chair*] I was ass enough to keep it until about ten minutes ago. Up to that moment I went on desperately reading to her—reading my own poems—anybody's poems—to stave off a conversation. I was standing outside the gate of Heaven, and refusing to go in. Oh, you can't think how heroic it was, and how uncomfortable! Then—

MORELL: [*Steadily controlling his suspense*] Then?—

MARCHBANKS: [*Prosaically slipping down into a quite ordinary attitude in the chair*] Then she couldn't bear being read to any longer.

MORELL: And you approached the gate of Heaven at last?

MARCHBANKS: Yes.

MORELL: Well? [*Fiercely*] Speak, man: have you no feeling for me?

MARCHBANKS: [*Softly and musically*] Then she became an angel; and there was a flaming sword that turned every way, so that I couldn't go in; for I saw that that gate was really the gate of Hell.

MORELL: [*Triumphantly*] She repulsed you!

MARCHBANKS: [*Rising in wild scorn*] No, you fool: if she had done that I should never have seen that I was in Heaven already. Repulsed me! You think that would have saved me—virtuous indignation! Oh, you are not worthy to live in the same world with her. [*He turns away contemptuously to the other side of the room*]

MORELL: [*Who has watched him quietly without changing his place*] Do you think you make yourself more worthy by reviling me, Eugene?

MARCHBANKS: Here endeth the thousand and first lesson. Morell: I don't think much of your preaching after all: I believe I could do it better myself. The man I want to meet is the man that Candida married.

MORELL: The man that—? Do you mean me?

MARCHBANKS: I don't mean the Reverend James Mavor Morell, moralist and windbag. I mean the real man that the Reverend James must have hidden somewhere inside his black coat—the man that Candida loved. You can't make a woman like Candida love you by merely buttoning your collar at the back instead of in front.

MORELL: [*Boldly and steadily*] When Candida promised to marry me, I was the same moralist and windbag that you now see. I wore my black coat; and my collar was buttoned behind instead of in front. Do you think she would have loved me any the better for being insincere in my profession?

MARCHBANKS: [*On the sofa hugging his ankles*] Oh, she forgave you, just as she forgives me for being a coward, and a weakling, and what you call a sniveling little whelp and all the rest of it. [*Dreamily*] A woman like that has divine insight: she loves our souls, and not our follies and vanities and illusions, or our collars and coats, or any other of the rags and tatters we are rolled up in. [*He reflects on this for an instant; then turns intently to question* Morell] What I want to know is how you got past the flaming sword that stopped me.

MORELL: [*Meaningly*] Perhaps because I was not interrupted at the end of ten minutes.

MARCHBANKS: [*Taken aback*] What!

MORELL: Man can climb to the highest summits; but he cannot dwell there long.

MARCHBANKS: It's false: there can he dwell for ever and there only. It's in the other moments that he can find no rest, no sense of the silent glory of life. Where would you have me spend my moments, if not on the summits?

MORELL: In the scullery, slicing onions and filling lamps.

MARCHBANKS: Or in the pulpit, scrubbing cheap earthenware souls?

MORELL: Yes, that, too. It was there that I earned my golden moment, and the right, in that moment, to ask her to love me. *I* did not take the moment on credit; nor did I use it to steal another man's happiness.

MARCHBANKS: [*Rather disgustedly, trotting back towards the fireplace*] I have no doubt you conducted the transaction as honestly as if you were buying a pound of cheese. [*He stops on the brink of the hearth-rug and adds, thoughtfully, to himself, with his back turned to* Morell] *I* could only go to her as a beggar.

MORELL: [*Starting*] A beggar dying of cold—asking for her shawl?

MARCHBANKS: [*Turning, surprised*] Thank you for touching up my poetry. Yes, if you like, a beggar dying of cold asking for her shawl.

MORELL: [*Excitedly*] And she refused. Shall I tell you why she refused? I can tell you, on her own authority. It was because of——

MARCHBANKS: She didn't refuse.

MORELL: Not!

MARCHBANKS: She offered me all I chose to ask for, her shawl, her wings, the wreath of stars on her head, the lilies in her hand, the crescent moon beneath her feet——

MORELL: [*Seizing him*] Out with the truth, man: my wife is my wife: I want no more of your poetic fripperies. I know well that if I have lost her love and you have gained it, no law will bind her.

MARCHBANKS: [*Quaintly, without fear or resistance*] Catch me by the shirt collar, Morell: she will arrange it for me afterwards as she did this morning. [*With quiet rapture*] I shall feel her hands touch me.

MORELL: You young imp, do you know how dangerous it is to say that to me? Or [*with a sudden misgiving*] has something made you brave?

MARCHBANKS: I'm not afraid now. I disliked you before: that was why I shrank from your touch. But I saw to-day—when she tortured you—that you love her. Since then I have been your friend: you may strangle me if you like.

MORELL: [*Releasing him*] Eugene: if that is not a heartless lie—if you have a spark of human feeling left in you—will you tell me what has happened during my absence?

MARCHBANKS: What happened! Why, the flaming sword— [Morell *stamps with impatience*] Well, in plain prose, I loved her so exquisitely that I wanted nothing more than the happiness of being in such love. And before I had time to come down from the highest summits, you came in.

MORELL: [*Suffering deeply*] So it is still unsettled —still the misery of doubt.

MARCHBANKS: Misery! I am the happiest of men. I desire nothing now but her happiness. [*With dreamy enthusiasm*] Oh, Morell, let us both give her up. Why should she have to choose between a wretched little nervous disease like me, and a pigheaded parson like you? Let us go on a pilgrimage, you to the east and I to the west, in search of a worthy lover for her—some beautiful archangel with purple wings——

MORELL: Some fiddlestick. Oh, if she is mad enough to leave me for you, who will protect her? Who will help her? who will work for her? who will be a father to her children? [*He sits down distractedly on the sofa, with his elbows on his knees and his head propped on his clenched fists*]

MARCHBANKS: [*Snapping his fingers wildly*] She does not ask those silly questions. It is she who wants somebody to protect, to help, to work for— somebody to give her children to protect, to help and to work for. Some grown up man who has become as a little child again. Oh, you fool, you fool, you triple fool! I am the man, Morell: I am the

man. [*He dances about excitedly, crying*] You don't understand what a woman is. Send for her, Morell: send for her and let her choose between—[*The door opens and* Candida *enters. He stops as if petrified*]

CANDIDA: [*Amazed, on the threshold*] What on earth are you at, Eugene?

MARCHBANKS: [*Oddly*] James and I are having a preaching match; and he is getting the worst of it. [Candida *looks quickly round at* Morell. *Seeing that he is distressed, she hurries down to him, greatly vexed, speaking with vigorous reproach to* Marchbanks]

CANDIDA: You have been annoying him. Now I won't have it, Eugene: do you hear? [*Putting her hand on* Morell's *shoulder, and quite forgetting her wifely tact in her annoyance*] My boy shall not be worried: I will protect him.

MORELL: [*Rising proudly*] Protect!

CANDIDA: [*Not heeding him—to* Eugene] What have you been saying?

MARCHBANKS: [*Appalled*] Nothing—I——

CANDIDA: Eugene! Nothing?

MARCHBANKS: [*Piteously*] I mean—I—I'm very sorry. I won't do it again: indeed I won't. I'll let him alone.

MORELL: [*Indignantly, with an aggressive movement towards* Eugene] Let me alone! You young——

CANDIDA: [*Stopping him*] Sh—no, let me deal with him, James.

MARCHBANKS: Oh, you're not angry with me, are you?

CANDIDA: [*Severely*] Yes, I am—very angry. I have a great mind to pack you out of the house.

MORELL: [*Taken aback by* Candida's *vigor, and by no means relishing the sense of being rescued by her from another man*] Gently, Candida, gently. I am able to take care of myself.

CANDIDA: [*Petting him*] Yes, dear: of course you are. But you mustn't be annoyed and made miserable.

MARCHBANKS: [*Almost in tears, turning to the door*] I'll go.

CANDIDA: Oh, you needn't go: I can't turn you out at this time of night. [*Vehemently*] Shame on you! For shame!

MARCHBANKS: [*Desperately*] But what have I done?

CANDIDA: I know what you have done—as well as if I had been here all the time. Oh, it was unworthy! You are like a child: you cannot hold your tongue.

MARCHBANKS: I would die ten times over sooner than give you a moment's pain.

CANDIDA: [*With infinite contempt for this puerility*] Much good your dying would do me!

MORELL: Candida, my dear: this altercation is hardly quite seeming. It is a matter between two men; and I am the right person to settle it.

CANDIDA: Two men! Do you call that a man? [*To* Eugene] You bad boy!

MARCHBANKS: [*Gathering a whimsically affectionate courage from the scolding*] If I am to be scolded like this, I must make a boy's excuse. He began it. And he's bigger than I am.

CANDIDA: [*Losing confidence a little as her concern for* Morell's *dignity takes the alarm*] That can't be true. [*To* Morell] You didn't begin it, James, did you?

MORELL: [*Contemptuously*] No.

MARCHBANKS: [*Indignant*] Oh!

MORELL: [*To* Eugene] You began it—this morning. [Candida, *instantly connecting this with his mysterious allusion in the afternoon to something told him by* Eugene *in the morning, looks quickly at him, wrestling with the enigma.* Morell *proceeds with the emphasis of offended superiority*] But your other point is true. I am certainly the bigger of the two, and, I hope, the stronger, Candida. So you had better leave the matter in my hands.

CANDIDA: [*Again soothing him*] Yes, dear; but— [*troubled*] I don't understand about this morning.

MORELL: [*Gently snubbing her*] You need not understand, my dear.

CANDIDA: But, James, I— [*The street bell rings*] Oh, bother! Here they all come. [*She goes out to let them in*]

MARCHBANKS: [*Running to* Morell] Oh, Morell, isn't it dreadful? She's angry with us: she hates me. What shall I do?

MORELL: [*With a quaint desperation, clutching himself by the hair*] Eugene: my head is spinning round. I shall begin to laugh presently. [*He walks up and down the middle of the room.*]

MARCHBANKS: [*Following him anxiously*] No, no: she'll think I've thrown you into hysterics. Don't laugh.

[*Boisterous voices and laughter are heard approaching.* Lexy Mill, *his eyes sparkling, and his bearing denoting unwonted elevation of spirit, enters with* Burgess, *who is greasy and self-complacent, but has all his wits about him.* Miss Garnett, *with her smartest hat and jacket on, follows them; but though her eyes are brighter than before, she is evidently a prey to misgiving. She places herself with her back to her typewriting table, with one hand on it to rest herself, passes the other across her forehead as if she were a little tired and giddy.* Marchbanks *relapses into shyness and edges away into the corner near the window, where* Morell's *books are*]

LEXY: [*Exhilaratedly*] Morell: I must congratulate you. [*Grasping his hand*] What a noble, splendid, inspired address you gave us! You surpassed yourself.

BURGESS: So you did, James. It fair kep' me awake to the last word. Didn't it, Miss Gornett?

PROSERPINE: [*Worriedly*] Oh, I wasn't minding you: I was trying to make notes. [*She takes out her note-book, and looks at her stenography, which nearly makes her cry*]

PROSERPINE: Much too fast. You know I can't do more than a hundred words a minute. [*She relieves her feelings by throwing her note-book angrily beside her machine, ready for use next morning*]

MORELL: [*Soothingly*] Oh, well, well, never mind, never mind, never mind. Have you all had supper?

LEXY: Mr. Burgess has been kind enough to give us a really splendid supper at the Belgrave.

BURGESS: [*With effusive magnanimity*] Don't mention it, Mr. Mill. [*Modestly*] You're 'arty welcome to my little treat.

PROSERPINE: We had champagne! I never tasted it before. I feel quite giddy.

MORELL: [*Surprised*] A champagne supper! That was very handsome. Was it my eloquence that produced all this extravagance?

LEXY: [*Rhetorically*] Your eloquence, and Mr. Burgess' goodness of heart. [*With a fresh burst of exhilaration*] And what a very fine fellow the chairman is, Morell! He came to supper with us.

MORELL: [*With long-drawn significance, looking at* Burgess] O-o-o-h, the chairman. Now I understand.

[Burgess, *covering a lively satisfaction in his diplomatic cunning with a deprecatory cough, retires to the hearth,* Lexy *folds his arms and leans against the cellaret in a high-spirited attitude.* Candida *comes in with glasses, lemons, and a jug of hot water on a tray*]

CANDIDA: Who will have some lemonade? You know our rules: total abstinence. [*She puts the tray on the table, and takes up the lemon squeezers, looking enquiringly around at them*]

MORELL: No use, dear. They've all had champagne. Pross has broken her pledge.

CANDIDA: [*To* Proserpine] You don't mean to say you've been drinking champagne!

PROSERPINE: [*Stubbornly*] Yes, I do. I'm only a beer teetotaler, not a champagne teetotaler. I don't like beer. Are there any letters for me to answer, Mr. Morell?

MORELL: No more to-night.

PROSERPINE: Very well. Good-night, everybody.

LEXY: [*Gallantly*] Had I not better see you home, Miss Garnett?

PROSERPINE: No, thank you. I shan't trust myself with anybody to-night. I wish I hadn't taken any of that stuff. [*She walks straight out*]

BURGESS: [*Indignantly*] Stuff, indeed! That gurl dunno wot champagne is! Pommery and Greeno at twelve and six a bottle. She took two glasses a'most straight hoff.

MORELL: [*A little anxious about her*] Go and look after her, Lexy.

LEXY: [*Alarmed*] But if she should really be— Suppose she began to sing in the street, or anything of that sort.

MORELL: Just so: she may. That's why you'd better see her safely home.

CANDIDA: Do, Lexy: there's a good fellow.

[*She shakes his hand and pushes him gently to the door*]

LEXY: It's evidently my duty to go. I hope it may not be necessary. Good-night, Mrs. Morell. [*To the rest*] Good-night. [*He goes.* Candida *shuts the door*]

BURGESS: He was gushin' with hextra piety hisself arter two sips. People carn't drink like they huseter. [*Dismissing the subject and bustling away from the hearth*] Well, James: it's time to lock up. Mr. Morchbanks: shall I 'ave the pleasure of your company for a bit of the way home?

MARCHBANKS: [*Affrightedly*] Yes: I'd better go. [*He hurries across to the door; but* Candida *places herself before it, barring his way*]

CANDIDA: [*With quiet authority*] You sit down. You're not going yet.

MARCHBANKS: [*Quailing*] No: I—I didn't mean to. [*He comes back into the room and sits down abjectly on the sofa*]

CANDIDA: Mr. Marchbanks will stay the night with us, papa.

BURGESS: Oh, well, I'll say good-night. So long, James. [*He shakes hands with* Morell *and goes on to* Eugene] Make 'em give you a night light by your bed, Mr. Morchbanks: it'll comfort you if you wake up in the night with a touch of that complaint of yores. Good-night.

MARCHBANKS: Thank you: I will. Good-night, Mr. Burgess. [*They shake hands and* Burgess *goes to the door*]

CANDIDA: [*Intercepting* Morell, *who is following* Burgess] Stay here, dear: I'll put on papa's coat for him. [*She goes out with* Burgess]

MARCHBANKS: Morell: there's going to be a terrible scene. Aren't you afraid?

MORELL: Not in the least.

MARCHBANKS: I never envied you your courage before. [*He rises timidly and puts his hand appealingly on* Morell's *forearm*] Stand by me, won't you?

MORELL: [*Casting him off gently, but resolutely*] Each for himself, Eugene. She must choose between us now. [*He goes to the other side of the room as* Candida *returns.* Eugene *sits down again on the sofa like a guilty schoolboy on his best behavior*]

CANDIDA: [*Between them, addressing* Eugene] Are you sorry?

MARCHBANKS: [*Earnestly*] Yes, heartbroken.

CANDIDA: Well, then, you are forgiven. Now go off to bed like a good little boy: I want to talk to James about you.

MARCHBANKS: [*Rising in great consternation*] Oh, I can't do that, Morell. I must be here. I'll not go away. Tell her.

CANDIDA: [*With quick suspicion*] Tell me what? [*His eyes avoid hers furtively. She turns and mutely transfers the question to* Morell]

MORELL: [*Bracing himself for the catastrophe*] I have nothing to tell her, except [*here his voice deepens to a measured and mournful tenderness*]

that she is my greatest treasure on earth—if she is really mine.

CANDIDA: [*Coldly, offended by his yielding to his orator's instinct and treating her as if she were the audience at the Guild of St. Matthew*] I am sure Eugene can say no less, if that is all.

MARCHBANKS: [*Discouraged*] Morell: she's laughing at us.

MORELL: [*With a quick touch of temper*] There is nothing to laugh at. Are you laughing at us, Candida?

CANDIDA: [*With quiet anger*] Eugene is very quick-witted, James. I hope I am going to laugh; but I am not sure that I am not going to be very angry. [*She goes to the fireplace, and stands there leaning with her arm on the mantelpiece, and her foot on the fender, whilst* Eugene *steals to* Morell *and plucks him by the sleeve*]

MARCHBANKS: [*Whispering*] Stop, Morell. Don't let us say anything.

MORELL: [*Pushing* Eugene *away without deigning to look at him*] I hope you don't mean that as a threat, Candida.

CANDIDA: [*With emphatic warning*] Take care, James. Eugene: I asked you to go. Are you going?

MORELL: [*Putting his foot down*] He shall not go. I wish him to remain.

MARCHBANKS: I'll go. I'll do whatever you want. [*He turns to the door*]

CANDIDA: Stop! [*He obeys*] Didn't you hear James say he wished you to stay? James is master here. Don't you know that?

MARCHBANKS: [*Flushing with a young poet's rage against tyranny*] By what right is he master?

CANDIDA: [*Quietly*] Tell him, James.

MORELL: [*Taken aback*] My dear: I don't know of any right that makes me master. I assert no such right.

CANDIDA: [*With infinite reproach*] You don't know! Oh, James, James! [*To* Eugene, *musingly*] I wonder do you understand, Eugene! No: you're too young. Well, I give you leave to stay—to stay and learn. [*She comes away from the hearth and places herself between them*] Now, James: what's the matter? Come: tell me.

MARCHBANKS: [*Whispering tremulously across to him*] Don't.

CANDIDA: Come. Out with it!

MORELL: [*Slowly*] I meant to prepare your mind carefully, Candida, so as to prevent misunderstanding.

CANDIDA: Yes, dear: I am sure you did. But never mind: I shan't misunderstand.

MORELL: Well—er—[*He hesitates, unable to find the long explanation which he supposed to be available*]

CANDIDA: Well?

MORELL: [*Baldly*] Eugene declares that you are in love with him.

MARCHBANKS: [*Frantically*] No, no, no, no, never.

I did not, Mrs. Morell: it's not true. I said I loved you, and that he didn't. I said that I understood you, and that he couldn't. And it was not after what passed there before the fire that I spoke: it was not, on my word. It was this morning.

CANDIDA: [*Enlightened*] This morning!

MARCHBANKS: Yes. [*He looks at her, pleading for credence, and then adds, simply*] That was what was the matter with my collar.

CANDIDA: [*After a pause; for she does not take in his meaning at once*] His collar! [*She turns to* Morell, *shocked*] Oh, James: did you?—[*She stops*]

MORELL: [*Ashamed*] You know, Candida, that I have a temper to struggle with. And he said [*shuddering*] that you despised me in your heart.

CANDIDA: [*Turning quickly on* Eugene] Did you say that?

MARCHBANKS: [*Terrified*] No!

CANDIDA: [*Severely*] Then James has just told me a falsehood. Is that what you mean?

MARCHBANKS: No, no: I—I—[*blurting out the explanation desperately*]—it was David's wife. And it wasn't at home: it was when she saw him dancing before all the people.

MORELL: [*Taking the cue with a debater's adroitness*] Dancing before all the people, Candida; and thinking he was moving their hearts by his mission when they were only suffering from—Prossy's complaint. [*She is about to protest: he raises his hand to silence her, exclaiming*] Don't try to look indignant, Candida:—

CANDIDA: [*Interjecting*] Try!

MORELL: [*Continuing*] Eugene was right. As you told me a few hours after, he is always right. He said nothing that you did not say far better yourself. He is the poet, who sees everything; and I am the poor parson, who understands nothing.

CANDIDA: [*Remorsefully*] Do you mind what is said by a foolish boy, because I said something like it again in jest?

MORELL: That foolish boy can speak with the inspiration of a child and the cunning of a serpent. He has claimed that you belong to him and not to me; and, rightly or wrongly, I have come to fear that it may be true. I will not go about tortured with doubts and suspicions. I will not live with you and keep a secret from you. I will not suffer the intolerable degradation of jealousy. We have agreed —he and I—that you shall choose between us now. I await your decision.

CANDIDA: [*Slowly recoiling a step, her heart hardened by his rhetoric in spite of the sincere feeling behind it*] Oh! I am to choose, am I? I suppose it is quite settled that I must belong to one or the other.

MORELL: [*Firmly*] Quite. You must choose definitely.

MARCHBANKS: [*Anxiously*] Morell: you don't understand. She means that she belongs to herself.

CANDIDA: [*Turning on him*] I mean that and a good deal more, Master Eugene, as you will both

find out presently. And pray, my lords and masters, what have you to offer for my choice? I am up for auction, it seems. What do you bid, James?

MORELL: [*Reproachfully*] Cand— [*He breaks down: his eyes and throat fill with tears: the orator becomes the wounded animal*] I can't speak—

CANDIDA: [*Impulsively going to him*] Ah, dearest—

MARCHBANKS: [*In wild alarm*] Stop: it's not fair. You mustn't show her that you suffer, Morell. I am on the rack, too; but I am not crying.

MORELL: [*Rallying all his forces*] Yes: you are right. It is not for pity that I am bidding. [*He disengages himself from* Candida]

CANDIDA: [*Retreating, chilled*] I beg your pardon, James; I did not mean to touch you. I am waiting to hear your bid.

MORELL: [*With proud humility*] I have nothing to offer you but my strength for your defence, my honesty of purpose for your surety, my ability and industry for your livelihood, and my authority and position for your dignity. That is all it becomes a man to offer to a woman.

CANDIDA: [*Quite quietly*] And you, Eugene? What do you offer?

MARCHBANKS: My weakness! my desolation! my heart's need!

CANDIDA: [*Impressed*] That's a good bid, Eugene. Now I know how to make my choice.

[*She pauses and looks curiously from one to the other, as if weighing them.* Morell, *whose lofty confidence has changed into heartbreaking dread at* Eugene's *bid, loses all power of concealing his anxiety.* Eugene, *strung to the highest tension, does not move a muscle*]

MORELL: [*In a suffocated voice—the appeal bursting from the depths of his anguish*] Candida!

MARCHBANKS: [*Aside, in a flash of contempt*] Coward!

CANDIDA: [*Significantly*] I give myself to the weaker of the two.

[Eugene *divines her meaning at once: his face whitens like steel in a furnace that cannot melt it*]

MORELL: [*Bowing his head with the calm of collapse*] I accept your sentence, Candida.

CANDIDA: Do you understand, Eugene?

MARCHBANKS: Oh, I feel I'm lost. He cannot bear the burden.

MORELL: [*Incredulously, raising his head with prosaic abruptness*] Do you mean me, Candida?

CANDIDA: [*Smiling a little*] Let us sit and talk comfortably over it like three friends. [*To* Morell] Sit down, dear. [Morell *takes the chair from the fireside—the children's chair*] Bring me that chair, Eugene. [*She indicates the easy chair. He fetches it silently, even with something like cold strength, and places it next* Morell, *a little behind him. She sits down. He goes to the sofa and sits there, still silent and inscrutable. When they are all settled she begins, throwing a spell of quietness on them by her calm, sane, tender tone*] You remember what you told me about yourself, Eugene: how nobody has cared for you since your old nurse died: how those clever, fashionable sisters and successful brothers of yours were your mother's and father's pets: how miserable you were at Eton: how your father is trying to starve you into returning to Oxford: how you have had to live without comfort or welcome or refuge, always lonely, and nearly always disliked and misunderstood, poor boy!

MARCHBANKS: [*Faithful to the nobility of his lot*] I had my books. I had Nature. And at last I met you.

CANDIDA: Never mind that just at present. Now I want you to look at this other boy here—my boy—spoiled from his cradle. We go once a fortnight to see his parents. You should come with us, Eugene, and see the pictures of the hero of that household. James as a baby! the most wonderful of all babies. James holding his first school prize, won at the ripe age of eight! James as the captain of his eleven! James in his first frock coat! James under all sorts of glorious circumstances! You know how strong he is (I hope he didn't hurt you)—how clever he is —how happy! [*With deepening gravity*] Ask James' mother and his three sisters what it cost to save James the trouble of doing anything but be strong and clever and happy. Ask me what it costs to be James' mother and three sisters and wife and mother to his children all in one. Ask Prossy and Maria how troublesome the house is even when we have no visitors to help us to slice the onions. Ask the tradesmen who want to worry James and spoil his beautiful sermons who it is that puts them off. When there is money to give, he gives it: when there is money to refuse, I refuse it. I build a castle of comfort and indulgence and love for him, and stand sentinel always to keep little vulgar cares out. I make him master here, though he does not know it, and could not tell you a moment ago how it came to be so. [*With sweet irony*] And when he thought I might go away with you, his only anxiety was what should become of me! And to tempt me to stay he offered me [*leaning forward to stroke his hair caressingly at each phrase*] his strength for my defence, his industry for my livelihood, his position for my dignity, his—[*relenting*] Ah, I am mixing up your beautiful sentences and spoiling them, am I not, darling? [*She lays her cheek fondly against his*]

MORELL: [*Quite overcome, kneeling beside her chair and embracing her with boyish ingenuousness*] It's all true, every word. What I am you have made me with the labor of your hands and the love of your heart! You are my wife, my mother, my sisters: you are the sum of all loving care to me.

CANDIDA: [*In his arms, smiling, to* Eugene] Am I your mother and sisters to you, Eugene?

MARCHBANKS: [*Rising with a fierce gesture of disgust*] Ah, never. Out, then, into the night with me!

CANDIDA: [*Rising quickly and intercepting him*] You are not going like that, Eugene?

MARCHBANKS: [*With the ring of a man's voice— no longer a boy's—in the words*] I know the hour when it strikes. I am impatient to do what must be done.

MORELL: [*Rising from his knee, alarmed*] Candida: don't let him do anything rash.

CANDIDA: [*Confident, smiling at* Eugene] Oh, there is no fear. He has learnt to live without happiness.

MARCHBANKS: I no longer desire happiness, life is nobler than that. Parson James: I give you my happiness with both hands: I love you because you have filled the heart of the woman I loved. Good-bye. [*He goes towards the door*]

CANDIDA: One last word. [*He stops, but without turning to her*] How old are you, Eugene?

MARCHBANKS: As old as the world now. This morning I was eighteen.

CANDIDA: [*Going to him, and standing behind him with one hand caressingly on his shoulder*] Eighteen! Will you, for my sake, make a little poem out of the two sentences I am going to say to you? And will you promise to repeat it to yourself whenever you think of me?

MARCHBANKS: [*Without moving*] Say the sentences.

CANDIDA: When I am thirty, she will be forty-five. When I am sixty, she will be seventy-five.

MARCHBANKS: [*Turning to her*] In a hundred years, we shall be the same age. But I have a better secret than that in my heart. Let me go now. The night outside grows impatient.

CANDIDA: Good-bye. [*She takes his face in her hands; and as he divines her intention and bends his knee, she kisses his forehead. Then he flies out into the night. She turns to* Morell, *holding out her arms to him*] Ah, James! [*They embrace. But they do not know the secret in the poet's heart*]

James M. Barrie

(1860–1937)

The novelist Graham Greene reminds us that "Barrie was as ill at ease in the world as Shaw was confident." Those who knew James Barrie are not apt to demur at this statement. "Favored from the very start of his career by Fortune," Greene continues, "he remained a misfit. He invented a dream world of sexless wives who mothered and understood their husbands, of children who never grew up because they had never really been born." But there were many good reasons why Barrie should have become England's best-loved modern playwright before 1920, quite apart from his exceptional understanding of the business of making a play move on the stage.

Barrie's life was a success story, though not of the aggressive kind celebrated in American fiction, since he was an extraordinarily shy and retiring person. Nor did he succeed with particularly rousing revelations. Rather, he owed his success to a lovable, volatile spirit and to extraordinary insight and ability for fantastication. The son of a displaced weaver from tiny Kirriemuir (Thrums), Scotland, he had the knack of making life seem endurable. He could be, it is true, a shrewd observer of reality, but he had an ingratiating way of leaving it for a whim or a fancy. If he was well aware of the world of cash and carry, he could always be counted on to have agreeable sentiments about such things as motherhood, childhood, and innocence.

The irreverent Bernard Shaw might laugh society out of countenance, but Barrie smiled it right back into countenance. According to many playgoers, England after 1890 was acquiring too many realists for comfort, but the deft magician from Thrums made the romantic spirit bloom again. And his romanticism was unlike that which had seethed with illicit passions and unfurled the banner of revolt in the days before respectability had mounted the throne of England with Victoria. In Barrie's enchanted gardens there were no flowers of evil. Always, it is true, he eluded definitions; always there was something in his temperament and outlook on life that perhaps he himself could never have defined, some disenchantment that made him seek and supply enchantment all the more eagerly. But his grateful public could easily overlook what it could not understand and would not have liked if it had understood. And Barrie, unlike the pertinacious Mr. Shaw, was not one to insist upon any special understanding, partly, perhaps, because his skepticism called reason itself into question.

Educated at Dumfries Academy and the University of Edinburgh, Barrie first practiced journalism in Nottingham, then in London, excelling in humorous little sketches of the Scottish life he knew so well. At the age of thirty-one he was acclaimed for his novel *The Little Minister,* and three years later he published another successful book, *Sentimental Tommy.* By 1892, after some trivial plays (including an anti-Ibsenite spoof *Ibsen's Ghost*) he also had a successful play, the farce *Walker, London,* to his credit. His next play, *The Professor's Love Story,* a sentimental comedy, may have been denounced by Ibsen's champion William Archer, as "a calculated disloyalty to art," but it ran for eighteen months at the Comedy Theatre, from midsummer of 1894 to Christmas 1895. (It also had a run of twenty-nine weeks in 1916, when it was revived in London, proving the steadfast attachment of the British public to Barriesque confections.) Next, he dramatized *The Little Minister,* in 1897, and both public response and encouragement from his manager Charles Frohman made him turn amost exclusively to playwriting. After five years, during which he produced only one play, *The Wedding Guest,* Barrie struck a stride which carried him into the hearts of Englishmen. He completed a play almost every year until 1920.

Although virtually everything he wrote between 1902 and 1920 won the affections of the playgoer, Barrie's reputation rests in the main on five full-length plays, four of them fantasies, and the perennial one-act comedy *The Twelve-Pound Look* (1910). Two of the full-length plays, *Peter Pan* (1904) and *Mary Rose* (1920), were triumphs of tender-hearted fancy. *Peter Pan* is likely to last as long as English is spoken on the stage. It has been produced every Christmas in London since 1904, and a statue of the young hero who believed in fairies will probably stand in London's Kensington Gardens as long as Nelson's monument. When, years after the first production of the play, Maeterlinck visited Barrie, he wrote on the whitewashed walls of the latter's study, "To the father of *Peter Pan* and the grandfather of *The Blue Bird,*" a handsome acknowledgment of indebtedness to this fantasy of the Never-Never Land. *Mary Rose,* a tenuous pathetic fantasy based on a Hebrides Islands legend, also succeeded mightily in its time, but was compounded of more perishable stuff. The other two fantasies, widely separated in time of composition, *The Admirable Crichton* (1902) and *Dear Brutus* (1917), belong to adult sophistication. The former, Barrie's contribution to the drama of ideas, presents an arch attitude toward class distinctions; the latter, his philosophical testament, takes a dim view of people's ability to lead better lives than they do: "The fault, dear Brutus, is not in our stars, But in ourselves, that we are underlings." The fifth important full-length play, *What Every Woman Knows* (1908), carries us somewhat beyond the limits of probability in the pursuit of a fiction—the pleasant one that there is always a woman behind the throne occupied by a seemingly self-sufficient male. But this play is an excursion into the realistic style of drama—Barrie's only satisfactory one.

In spite of the admiration of the public, controversy raged over Barrie's merits as a modern playwright. If the heat has dissipated, it is only because the taste for his work has diminished and he therefore furnishes less provocation. In America, Ludwig Lewisohn and George Jean Nathan were up in arms against Barrie's sentimentality, which was often unvarnished, if not downright shameless. "With great skill, he permits nothing to stand in the way of it," Nathan wrote, "—not life, not reality, none of the hard truths of the world. His characters are for the most part marionettes with human hearts, but with heads filled only with sawdust and good theatrical dialogue." And Nathan observed that the playwright succeeded so well because of his cunning in stating ordinary theatrical sentiment in a fresh theatrical manner: "He lays hold of ancient sugars and molds them into novel and pretty candies." In England, too, there were dissenting critics. Desmond MacCarthy, though granting him "inventiveness," even took exception to his depiction of youth and age "only in the light of the autumnal glow of elderly fancy," and objected to his stopping his ears to the jarring note of conflict in young lives.

Nevertheless, Barrie will be remembered as one of the four or five playwrights who gave the English theatre most of its vitality during the first two decades of the twentieth century, and the best of his work will continue to provide delight to those who do not look at it under the glare of merciless intellect. This delight is, moreover, enhanced for the reader by Barrie's ingratiating treatment of a playscript. For a long time, he refused to allow his plays to be published and when he finally did consent, he worked on the scripts with scrupulous attention to descriptions and stage directions irrelevant to stage production. As a result, he evolved a printed form that fuses the features of a play with those of a novel. Since the nondramatic embellishments were written in Barrie's best style of whimsy, the literary grace of the text is as gratifying as the dialogue.

The Admirable Crichton is unique among Barrie's plays because it represents a compromise between Barriesque fantasy and the drama of ideas that became current in England at the turn of the century largely under the inspiration of Ibsen. It is a Shavian fable with Barriesque sentiment—and without Shaw's dynamic philosophy of social change. In consequence of Barrie's immunity to both liberal and Marxist ideology, *The Admirable Crichton* ends as it begins. The structure of English society remains fundamentally unchallenged, and there is no suggestion that it is likely to undergo any drastic transformation. Yet within the limits of this premise, the comedy contains withering satire on the social order in addition to delightful spoofing of characters. Nor is the play devoid of a philosophical attitude toward such matters as the "law of nature" and the principle of "equality," both touted by old-time liberals with considerably more sentimentality than can be charged against Barrie himself. In London, where the British aristocracy is sustained by "civilization," it is natural for the lords to be lords and for the servants to be servants. In a state of nature, however, it is "natural" for the servants to become the masters. Environment and successful adaptation to it determine social status, both in Mayfair and in the South Sea Islands. On the island, as the critic Walkley noted, "Lord Loam sinks 'naturally' to the bottom, just as Crichton rises 'naturally' to the top."

Only in the last act does *The Admirable Crichton* falter in its logic, so that the play may be regarded as a vestige of the Victorian Compromise. Walkley, who was usually very well disposed toward Barrie's work, complained that it was not "natural" or credible for Crichton to dwindle into a servant again after having been master of the island. And Walkley would be entirely right if Barrie's concern had been with characterization. It is, however, in the parable on the relativity of social status that the playwright appears to have been interested, and it is the parable that comes full circle round in *The Admirable Crichton*. To which we may add that considerable bitterness lurks in the last act! Barrie is unfair to the hero, who is content to be a butler again once he returns to London, unfair, too, to the British social structure in assuming that a man of Crichton's ability will find no better use for his mind and spirit, and decidedly relentless toward Crichton's employers. As Walkley observed, "The aristocrats, who began by being merely fools, are driven in the end into being consummate liars." In view of Barrie's reputation for sentimentality, it is well to remember that the milk of human kindness, of which he had an excess, sometimes curdled with acid.

BIBLIOGRAPHY: Barrett H. Clark, *A Study of the Modern Drama* (pp. 310–320), 1938; William A. Darlington, *J. M. Barrie,* 1938; John Gassner, *Masters of the Drama* (pp. 622–624), 1940, 1945; Desmond MacCarthy, *Drama* (pp. 315–321), 1940; George Jean Nathan, *Art of the Night* (pp. 153–155), 1928; Ernest Short, *Theatrical Cavalcade* (pp. 82–90), 1942; A. B. Walkley, *Drama and Life* (pp. 194–213), 1908.

THE ADMIRABLE CRICHTON

By James M. Barrie

CHARACTERS

THE HON. ERNEST WOOLLEY	TREHERNE	TWEENY
CRICHTON	LORD BROCKLEHURST	OTHER SERVANTS AT LOAM HOUSE
LADY CATHERINE	THE EARL OF LOAM	NAVAL OFFICER
LADY AGATHA	FISHER	LADY BROCKLEHURST
LADY MARY		

ACT I. *Loam House, Mayfair, London.*

ACT II. *A desert isle in the Pacific. Two months later.*

ACT III. *Same as Act II. Two years later.*

ACT IV. *Loam House, London. Several months later.*

TIME—*About 1900.*

ACT I.

A moment before the curtain rises, the Hon. Ernest Woolley *drives up to the door of Loam House in Mayfair. There is a happy smile on his pleasant, insignificant face, and this presumably means that he is thinking of himself. He is too busy over nothing, this man about town, to be always thinking of himself, but, on the other hand, he almost never thinks of any other person. Probably Ernest's great moment is when he wakes of a morning and realizes that he really is Ernest, for we must all wish to be that which is our ideal. We can conceive of him springing out of bed light-heartedly and waiting for his man to do the rest. He is dressed in excellent taste, with just the little bit more which shows that he is not without a sense of humor: the dandiacal are often saved by carrying a smile at the whole thing in their spats, let us say. Ernest left Cambridge the other day, a member of the Athenaeum (which he would be sorry to have you confound with a club in London by the same name). He is a bachelor, but not of the arts, no mean epigrammatist (as you shall see), and a favorite of the ladies. He is almost a celebrity in restaurants, where he dines frequently, returning to sup; and during this last year he has probably paid as much in them for the privilege of handing his hat to an attendant as the rent of a working-man's flat. He complains brightly that he is hard up, and that if somebody or other at Westminster does not look out the country will go to the dogs. He is no fool. He has the shrewdness to float with the current because it is a labor-saving process, but he has sufficient pluck to fight, if fight he must (a brief contest, for he would soon be toppled over). He has a light nature, which would enable him to bob up cheerily in new conditions and return unal-*

tered to the old ones. His selfishness is his most endearing quality. If he has his way he will spend his life like a cat in pushing his betters out of the soft places, and until he is old he will be fondled in the process.

He gives his hat to one footman and his cane to another, and mounts the great staircase unassisted and undirected. As a nephew of the house he need show no credentials even to Crichton, who is guarding a door above.

It would not be good taste to describe Crichton, who is only a servant; if to the scandal of all good houses he is to stand out as a figure in the play, he must do it on his own, as they say in the pantry and the boudoir. We are not going to help him. We have had misgivings ever since we found his name in the title, and we shall keep him out of his rights as long as we can. Even though we softened to him he would not be a hero in these clothes of servitude; and he loves his clothes. How to get him out of them? It would require a cataclysm. To be an indoor servant at all is to Crichton a badge of honor; to be a butler at thirty is the realization of his proudest ambitions. He is devotedly attached to his master, who, in his opinion, has but one fault, he is not sufficiently contemptuous of his inferiors. We are immediately to be introduced to this solitary failing of a great English peer.

This perfect butler, then, opens a door, and ushers Ernest *into a certain room. At the same moment the curtain rises on this room, and the play begins.*

It is one of several reception-rooms in Loam House, not the most magnificent but quite the softest; and of a warm afternoon all that those who are anybody crave for is the softest. The larger rooms are magnificent and bare, carpetless, so that it is an accomplishment to keep one's feet on them; they are sometimes lent for charitable purposes; they are also all in use on the night of a dinner party, when you may find yourself alone in one, having taken a wrong turning; or alone, save for two others who are within hailing distance. This room, however, is comparatively small and very soft. There are so many cushions in it that you wonder why, if you are an outsider and don't know that it needs six cushions to make one fair head comfy. The couches themselves are cushions as large as beds, and there is an art of sinking into them and of waiting to be helped out of them. There are several famous paintings on the walls, of which you may say, "Jolly thing that," without losing caste as knowing too much; and in cases there are glorious miniatures, but the daughters of the house cannot tell you of whom; "there is a catalogue somewhere." There are a thousand or so of roses in basins, several library novels, and a row of weekly illustrated newspapers lying against each other like fallen soldiers. If any one disturbs this row Crichton seems to know of it from afar and appears noiselessly and replaces the wanderer. One thing unexpected in such a room is a great array of tea things. Ernest spots them with a twinkle, and has his epigram at once unsheathed. He dallies, however, before delivering the thrust.

ERNEST: I perceive, from the tea cups, Crichton, that the great function is to take place here.

CRICHTON: [With a respectful sigh] Yes, sir.

ERNEST: [Chuckling heartlessly] The servant's hall coming up to have tea in the drawing-room! [With terrible sarcasm] No wonder you look happy, Crichton.

CRICHTON: [Under the knife] No, sir.

ERNEST: Do you know, Crichton, I think that with an effort you might look even happier. [Crichton smiles wanly] You don't approve of his lordship's compelling his servants to be his equals— once a month?

CRICHTON: It is not for me, sir, to disapprove of his lordship's Radical views.

ERNEST: Certainly not. And, after all, it is only once a month that he is affable to you.

CRICHTON: On all other days of the month, sir, his lordship's treatment of us is everything that could be desired.

ERNEST: [This is the epigram] Tea cups! Life, Crichton, is like a cup of tea; the more heartily we drink, the sooner we reach the dregs.

CRICHTON: [Obediently] Thank you, sir.

ERNEST: [Becoming confidential, as we do when we have need of an ally] Crichton, in case I should be asked to say a few words to the servants, I have strung together a little speech. [His hand strays to his pocket] I was wondering where I should stand.

[He tries various places and postures, and comes to rest leaning over a high chair, whence, in dumb show, he addresses a gathering. Crichton, with the best intentions, gives him a footstool to stand on, and departs, hap-

pily unconscious that Ernest in some dudgeon has kicked the footstool across the room]

ERNEST: [Addressing an imaginary audience, and desirous of startling them at once] Suppose you were all little fishes at the bottom of the sea——

[He is not quite satisfied with his position, though sure that the fault must lie with the chair for being too high, not with him for being too short. Crichton's suggestion was not perhaps a bad one after all. He lifts the stool, but hastily conceals it behind him on the entrance of the Ladies Catherine and Agatha, two daughters of the house. Catherine is twenty, and Agatha is two years younger. They are very fashionable young women indeed, who might wake up for a dance, but they are very lazy, Catherine being two years lazier than Agatha]

ERNEST: [Uneasily jocular, because he is concealing the footstool] And how are my little friends to-day?

AGATHA: [Contriving to reach a settee] Don't be silly, Ernest. If you want to know how we are, we are dead. Even to think of entertaining the servants is so exhausting.

CATHERINE: [Subsiding nearer the door] Besides which, we have had to decide what frocks to take with us on the yacht, and that is such a mental strain.

ERNEST: You poor over-worked things. [Evidently Agatha is his favorite, for he helps her to put her feet on the settee, while Catherine has to dispose of her own feet] Rest your weary limbs.

CATHERINE: [Perhaps in revenge] But why have you a footstool in your hand?

AGATHA: Yes?

ERNEST: Why? [Brilliantly; but to be sure he has had time to think it out] You see, as the servants are to be the guests I must be butler. I was practising. This is a tray, observe. [Holding the footstool as a tray, he minces across the room like an accomplished footman. The gods favor him, for just here Lady Mary enters and he holds out the footstool to her] Tea, my lady?

[Lady Mary is a beautiful creature of twenty-two, and is of a natural hauteur which is at once the fury and the envy of her sisters. If she chooses she can make you seem so insignificant that you feel you might be swept away with the crumb-brush. She seldom chooses, because of the trouble of preening herself as she does it; she is usually content to show that you merely tire her eyes. She often seems to be about to go to sleep in the middle of a remark: there is quite a long and anxious pause, and then she continues, like a clock that hesitates, bored in the middle of its strike]

LADY MARY: [Arching her brows] It is only you, Ernest; I thought there was some one here. [And she also bestows herself on cushions]

ERNEST: [*A little piqued, and deserting the foot-stool*] Had a very tiring day also, Mary?

LADY MARY: [*Yawning*] Dreadfully. Been trying on engagement-rings all the morning.

ERNEST: [*Who is as fond of gossip as the oldest club member*] What's that? [*To* Agatha] Is it Brocklehurst? [*The energetic* Agatha *nods*] You have given your warm· young heart to Brocky? [Lady Mary *is impervious to his humor, but he continues bravely*] I don't wish to fatigue you, Mary, by insisting on a verbal answer, but if, without straining yourself, you can signify Yes or No, won't you make the effort? [*She indolently flashes a ring on her most important finger, and he starts back melodramatically*] The ring! Then I am too late, too late! [*Fixing* Lady Mary *sternly, like a prosecuting counsel*] May I ask, Mary, does Brocky know? Of course it was that terrible mother of his who pulled this through. Mother does everything for Brocky. Still, in the eyes of the law you will be, not her wife, but his, and, therefore, I hold that Brocky ought to be informed. Now—— [*He discovers that their languorous eyes have closed*] If you girls are shamming sleep in the expectation that I shall awaken you in the manner beloved of ladies, abandon all such hopes.

[Catherine *and* Agatha *look up without speaking*]

LADY MARY: [*Speaking without looking up*] You impertinent boy.

ERNEST: [*Eagerly plucking another epigram from his quiver*] I knew that was it, though I don't know everything. Agatha, I'm not young enough to know everything.

[*He looks hopefully from one to another, but though they try to grasp this, his brilliance baffles them*]

AGATHA: [*His secret admirer*] Young enough?

ERNEST: [*Encouragingly*] Don't you see? I'm not young enough to know everything.

AGATHA: I'm sure it's awfully clever, but it's so puzzling.

[*Here* Crichton *ushers in an athletic, pleasant-faced young clergyman,* Mr. Treherne, *who greets the company*]

CATHERINE: Ernest, say it to Mr. Treherne.

ERNEST: Look here, Treherne, I'm not young enough to know everything.

TREHERNE: How do you mean, Ernest?

ERNEST: [*A little nettled*] I mean what I say.

LADY MARY: Say it again; say it more slowly.

ERNEST: I'm—not—young—enough—to—know—everything.

TREHERNE: *I* see. What you really mean, my boy, is that you are not old enough to know everything.

ERNEST: No, I don't.

TREHERNE: I assure you that's it.

LADY MARY: Of course it is.

CATHERINE: Yes, Ernest, that's it.

[Ernest, *in desperation, appeals to* Crichton]

ERNEST: I am not young enough, Crichton, to know everything.

[*It is an anxious moment, but a smile is at length extorted from* Crichton *as with a cork-screw*]

CRICHTON: Thank you, sir. [*He goes*]

ERNEST: [*Relieved*] Ah, if you had that fellow's head, Treherne, you would find something better to do with it than play cricket. I hear you bowl with your head.

TREHERNE: [*With proper humility*] I'm afraid cricket is all I'm good for, Ernest.

CATHERINE: [*Who thinks he has a heavenly nose*] Indeed, it isn't. You are sure to get on, Mr. Treherne.

TREHERNE: Thank you, Lady Catherine.

CATHERINE: But it was the bishop who told me so. He said a clergyman who breaks both ways is sure to get on in England.

TREHERNE: I'm jolly glad.

[*The master of the house comes in, accompanied by* Lord Brocklehurst. *The* Earl of Loam *is a widower, a philanthropist, and a peer of advanced ideas. As a widower he is at least able to interfere in the domestic concerns of his house—to rummage in the drawers, so to speak, for which he has felt an itching all his blameless life; his philanthropy has opened quite a number of other drawers to him; and his advanced ideas have blown out his figure. He takes in all the weightiest monthly reviews, and prefers those that are uncut, because he perhaps never looks better than when cutting them; but he does not read them, and save for the cutting, it would suit him as well merely to take in the covers. He writes letters to the papers, which are printed in a type to scale with himself, and he is very jealous of those other correspondents who get his type. Let laws and learning, art and commerce die, but leave the big type to an intellectual aristocracy. He is really the reformed House of Lords which will come some day.*

Young Lord Brocklehurst *is nothing, save for his rank. You could pick him up by the handful any day in Piccadilly or Holborn, buying socks—or selling them.*]

LORD LOAM: [*Expansively*] You are here, Ernest. Feeling fit for the voyage, Treherne?

TREHERNE: Looking forward to it enormously.

LORD LOAM: That's right. [*He chases his children about as if they were chickens*] Now then, Mary, up and doing, up and doing. Time we had the servants in. They enjoy it so much.

LADY MARY: They hate it.

LORD LOAM: Mary, to your duties. [*And he points severely to the tea-table*]

ERNEST: [*Twinkling*] Congratulations, Brocky.

LORD BROCKLEHURST: [*Who detests humour*] Thanks.

ERNEST: Mother pleased?

LORD BROCKLEHURST: [*With dignity*] Mother is very pleased.

ERNEST: That's good. Do you go on the yacht with us?

LORD BROCKLEHURST: Sorry I can't. And look here, Ernest, I will *not* be called Brocky.

ERNEST: Mother don't like it?

LORD BROCKLEHURST: She does not. [*He leaves Ernest, who forgives him and begins to think about his speech.* Crichton *enters*]

LORD LOAM: [*Speaking as one man to another*] We are quite ready, Crichton.

[Crichton *is distressed*]

LADY MARY: [*Sarcastically*] How Crichton enjoys it!

LORD LOAM: [*Frowning*] He is the only one who doesn't; pitiful creature.

CRICHTON: [*Shuddering under his lord's displeasure*] I can't help being a Conservative, my lord.

LORD LOAM: Be a man, Crichton. You are the same flesh and blood as myself.

CRICHTON: [*In pain*] Oh, my lord!

LORD LOAM: [*Sharply*] Show them in; and, by the way, they were not all here last time.

CRICHTON: All, my lord, except the merest trifles.

LORD LOAM: It must be every one. [*Lowering*] And remember this, Crichton, for the time being you are my equal. [*Testily*] I shall soon show you whether you are not my equal. Do as you are told. [Crichton *departs to obey, and his lordship is now a general. He has no pity for his daughters, and uses a terrible threat*] And girls, remember, no condescension. The first who condescends recites. [*This sends them scurrying to their labors.*] By the way, Brocklehurst, can you do anything?

LORD BROCKLEHURST: How do you mean?

LORD LOAM: Can you do anything—with a penny or a handkerchief, make them disappear, for instance?

LORD BROCKLEHURST: Good heavens, no.

LORD LOAM: It's a pity. Every one in our position ought to be able to do something. Ernest, I shall probably ask you to say a few words; something bright and sparkling.

ERNEST: But, my dear uncle, I have prepared nothing.

LORD LOAM: Anything impromptu will do.

ERNEST: Oh—well—if anything strikes me on the spur of the moment. [*He unostentatiously gets the footstool into position behind the chair.* Crichton *reappears to announce the guests, of whom the first is the housekeeper*]

CRICHTON: [*Reluctantly*] Mrs. Perkins.

LORD LOAM: [*Shaking hands*] Very delighted, Mrs. Perkins. Mary, our friend, Mrs. Perkins.

LADY MARY: How do you do, Mrs. Perkins? Won't you sit here?

LORD LOAM: [*Threateningly*] Agatha!

AGATHA: [*Hastily*] How do you do? Won't you sit down?

LORD LOAM: [*Introducing*] Lord Brocklehurst— my valued friend Mrs. Perkins.

[Lord Brocklehurst *bows and escapes. He has to fall back on* Ernest]

LORD BROCKLEHURST: For heaven's sake, Ernest, don't leave me for a moment; this sort of thing is utterly opposed to all my principles.

ERNEST: [*Airily*] You stick to me, Brocky, and I'll pull you through.

CRICHTON: Monsieur Fleury.

ERNEST: The chef.

LORD LOAM: [*Shaking hands with the chef*] Very charmed to see you, Monsieur Fleury.

FLEURY: Thank you very much.

[Fleury *bows to* Agatha, *who is not effusive*]

LORD LOAM: [*Warningly*] Agatha—recitation!

[*She tosses her head, but immediately finds a seat and tea for M. Fleury.* Treherne *and* Ernest *move about, making themselves amiable.* Lady Mary *is presiding at the teatray*]

CRICHTON: Mr. Rolleston.

LORD LOAM: [*Shaking hands with his valet*] How do you do, Rolleston?

[Catherine *looks after the wants of* Rolleston]

CRICHTON: Mr. Tompsett.

[Tompsett, *the coachman, is received with honors, from which he shrinks*]

CRICHTON: Miss Fisher.

[*This superb creature is no less than* Lady Mary's *maid, and even* Lord Loam *is a little nervous*]

LORD LOAM: This is a pleasure, Miss Fisher.

ERNEST: [*Unabashed*] If I might venture, Miss Fisher. [*And he takes her unto himself*]

CRICHTON: Miss Simmons.

LORD LOAM: [*To* Catherine's *maid*] You are always welcome, Miss Simmons.

ERNEST: [*Perhaps to kindle jealousy in* Miss Fisher] At last we meet. Won't you sit down?

CRICHTON: Mademoiselle Jeanne.

LORD LOAM: Charmed to see you, Mademoiselle Jeanne.

[*A place is found for* Agatha's *maid, and the scene is now an animated one; but still our host thinks his girls are not sufficiently sociable. He frowns on* Lady Mary]

LADY MARY: [*In alarm*] Mr. Treherne, this is Fisher, my maid.

LORD LOAM: [*Sharply*] Your what, Mary?

LADY MARY: My friend.

CRICHTON: Thomas.

LORD LOAM: How do you do, Thomas?

[*The first footman gives him a reluctant hand*]

CRICHTON: John.

LORD LOAM: How do you do, John?

[Ernest *signs to* Lord Brocklehurst, *who hastens to him*]

ERNEST: [*Introducing*] Brocklehurst, this is John. I think you have already met on the door-step.

CRICHTON: Jane.

[*She comes, wrapping her hands miserably in her apron*]

LORD LOAM: [*Doggedly*] Give me your hand, Jane.

CRICHTON: Gladys.

ERNEST: How do you do, Gladys. You know my uncle?

LORD LOAM: Your hand, Gladys. [*He bestows her on* Agatha]

CRICHTON: Tweeny.

[*She is a very humble and frightened kitchen-maid, of whom we are to see more*]

LORD LOAM: So happy to see you.

FISHER: John, I saw you talking to Lord Brockle-hurst just now; introduce me.

LORD BROCKLEHURST: [*At the same moment to* Ernest] That's an uncommon pretty girl; if I must feed one of them, Ernest, that's the one.

[*But* Ernest *tries to part him and* Fisher *as they are about to shake hands*]

ERNEST: No you don't, it won't do, Brocky. [*To* Miss Fisher] You are too pretty, my dear. Mother wouldn't like it. [*Discovering* Tweeny] Here's something safer. Charming girl, Brocky, dying to know you; let me introduce you. Tweeny, Lord Brockle-hurst—Lord Brocklehurst, Tweeny.

[Brocklehurst *accepts his fate; but he still has an eye for* Fisher, *and something may come of this*]

LORD LOAM: [*Severely*] They are not all here, Crichton.

CRICHTON: [*With a sigh*] Odds and ends.

[*A* Stable-Boy *and a* Page *are shown in, and for a moment no daughter of the house advances to them*]

LORD LOAM: [*With a roving eye on his children*] Which is to recite?

[*The last of the company are, so to say, embraced*]

LORD LOAM: [*To* Tompsett, *as they partake of tea together*] And how are all at home?

TOMPSETT: Fairish, my lord, if 'tis the horses you are inquiring for?

LORD LOAM: No, no, the family. How's the baby?

TOMPSETT: Blooming, your lordship.

LORD LOAM: A very fine boy. I remember saying so when I saw him; nice little fellow.

TOMPSETT: [*Not quite knowing whether to let it pass*] Beg pardon, my lord, it's a girl.

LORD LOAM: A girl? Aha! ha! ha! exactly what I said. I distinctly remember saying, If it's spared it will be a girl.

[Crichton *now comes down*]

LORD LOAM: Very delighted to see you, Crichton. [Crichton *has to shake hands*] Mary, you know Mr. Crichton? [*He wanders off in search of other prey*]

LADY MARY: Milk and sugar, Crichton?

CRICHTON: I'm ashamed to be seen talking to you, my lady.

LADY MARY: To such a perfect servant as you all this must be most distasteful. [Crichton *is too respectful to answer*] Oh, please do speak, or I shall have to recite. You do hate it, don't you?

CRICHTON: It pains me, your ladyship. It disturbs the etiquette of the servants' hall. After last month's meeting the pageboy, in a burst of equality, called me Crichton. He is dismissed.

LADY MARY: I wonder—I really do—how you can remain with us.

CRICHTON: I should have felt compelled to give notice, my lady, if the master had not had a seat in the Upper House. I cling to that.

LADY MARY: Do go on speaking. Tell me, what did Mr. Ernest mean by saying that he was not young enough to know everything?

CRICHTON: I have no idea, my lady.

LADY MARY: But you laughed.

CRICHTON: My lady, he is the second son of a peer.

LADY MARY: Very proper sentiments. You are a good soul, Crichton.

LORD BROCKLEHURST: [*Desperately to* Tweeny] And now tell me, have you been to the Opera? What sort of weather have you been having in the kitchen? [Tweeny *giggles*] For heaven's sake, woman, be articulate.

CRICHTON: [*Still talking to* Lady Mary] No, my lady; his lordship may compel us to be equal up-stairs, but there will never be equality in the servants' hall.

LORD LOAM: [*Overhearing this*] What's that? No equality? Can't you see, Crichton, that our divisions into classes are artificial, that if we were to return to Nature, which is the aspiration of my life, all would be equal?

CRICHTON: If I may make so bold as to contradict your lordship——

LORD LOAM: [*With an effort*] Go on.

CRICHTON: The divisions into classes, my lord, are not artificial. They are the natural outcome of a civilized society. [*To* Lady Mary] There must always be a master and servants in all civilized communities, my lady, for it is natural, and whatever is natural is right.

LORD LOAM: [*Wincing*] It is very unnatural for me to stand here and allow you to talk such nonsense.

CRICHTON: [*Eagerly*] Yes, my lord, it is. That is what I have been striving to point out to your lordship.

AGATHA: [*To* Catherine] What is the matter with Fisher? She is looking daggers.

CATHERINE: The tedious creature; some question of etiquette, I suppose. [*She sails across to* Fisher] How are you, Fisher?

FISHER: [*With a toss of her head*] I am nothing, my lady. I am nothing at all.

AGATHA: Oh dear, who says so?

FISHER: [*Affronted*] His lordship has asked that kitchen wench to have a second cup of tea.

CATHERINE: But why not?

FISHER: If it pleases his lordship to offer it to *her* before offering it to *me*——

AGATHA: So that is it. Do you want another cup of tea, Fisher?

FISHER: No, my lady—but my position—I should have been asked first.

AGATHA: Oh dear.

> [*All this has taken some time, and by now the feeble appetites of the uncomfortable guests have been satiated. But they know there is still another ordeal to face—his lordship's monthly speech. Every one awaits it with misgiving— the servants lest they should applaud, as last time, in the wrong place, and the daughters because he may be personal about them, as the time before* Ernest *is annoyed that there should be this speech at all when there is such a much better one coming, and* Brocklehurst *foresees the degradation of the peerage. All are thinking of themselves alone save* Crichton, *who knows his master's weakness, and fears he may stick in the middle.* Lord Loam, *however, advances cheerfully to his doom. He sees* Ernest's *stool, and artfully stands on it, to his nephew's natural indignation. The three ladies knit their lips, the servants look down their noses, and the address begins*]

LORD LOAM: My friends, I am glad to see you all looking so happy. It used to be predicted by the scoffer that these meetings would prove distasteful to you. Are they distasteful? I hear you laughing at the question. [*He has not heard them, but he hears them now, the watchful* Crichton *giving them a lead*] No harm in saying that among us today is one who was formerly hostile to the movement, but who today has been won over. I refer to Lord Brocklehurst, who, I am sure, will presently say to me that if the charming lady now by his side has derived as much pleasure from his company as he has derived from hers, he will be more than satisfied. [*All look at* Tweeny, *who trembles*] For the time being the artificial and unnatural—I say unnatural [*Glaring at* Crichton, *who bows slightly*]— barriers of society are swept away. Would that they could be swept away for ever. [*The* Pageboy *cheers, and has the one moment of prominence in his life. He grows up, marries and has children, but is never really heard of again*] But that is entirely and utterly out of the question. And now for a few months we are to be separated. As you know, my daughters and Mr. Ernest and Mr. Treherne are to accompany me on my yacht, on a voyage to distant parts of the earth. In less than forty-eight hours we shall be under weigh. [*But for* Crichton's *eye the reckless* Pageboy *would repeat his success*] Do not think our life on the yacht is to be one long idle holiday. My

views on the excessive luxury of the day are well known, and what I preach I am resolved to practise. I have therefore decided that my daughters, instead of having one maid each as at present, shall on this voyage have but one maid between them.

> [*Three maids rise; also three mistresses*]

CRICHTON: My lord!

LORD LOAM: My mind is made up.

ERNEST: I cordially agree.

LORD LOAM: And now, my friends, I should like to think that there is some piece of advice I might give you, some thought, some noble saying over which you might ponder in my absence. In this connection I remember a proverb, which has had a great effect on my own life. I first heard it many years ago. I have never forgotten it. It constantly cheers and guides me. That proverb is—that proverb was—the proverb I speak of——[*He grows pale and taps his forehead*]

LADY MARY: Oh dear, I believe he has forgotten it.

LORD LOAM: [*Desperately*] The proverb—that proverb to which I refer——[*Alas, it has gone. The distress is general. He has not even the sense to sit down. He gropes for the proverb in the air. They try applause, but it is no help*] I have it now—— [*not he*]

LADY MARY: [*With confidence*] Crichton.

> [*He does not fail her. As quietly as if he were in goloshes, mind as well as feet, he dismisses the domestics; they go according to precedence as they entered yet, in a moment, they are gone. Then he signs to* Mr. Treherne, *and then they conduct* Lord Loam *with dignity from the room. His hands are still catching flies; he still mutters, "The proverb—that proverb"; but he continues, owing to* Crichton's *skilful treatment, to look every inch a peer. The ladies have now an opportunity to air their indignation*]

LADY MARY: One maid among three grown women!

LORD BROCKLEHURST: Mary, I think I had better go. That dreadful kitchenmaid——

LADY MARY: I can't blame you, George. [*He salutes her*]

LORD BROCKLEHURST: Your father's views are shocking to me, and I am glad I am not to be one of the party on the yacht. My respect for myself, Mary, my natural anxiety as to what mother will say. I shall see you, darling, before you sail. [*He bows to the others and goes*]

ERNEST: Selfish brute, only thinking of himself. What about my speech?

LADY MARY: One maid among three of us. What's to be done?

ERNEST: Pooh! You must do for yourselves, that's all.

LADY MARY: Do for ourselves. How can we know where our things are kept?

AGATHA: Are you aware that dresses button up the back?

CATHERINE: How are we to get into our shoes and be prepared for the carriage?

LADY MARY: Who is to put us to bed, and who is to get us up, and how shall we ever know it's morning if there is no one to pull up the blinds?

[Crichton *crosses on his way out*]

ERNEST: How is his lordship now?

CRICHTON: A little easier, sir.

LADY MARY: Crichton, send Fisher to me. [*He goes*]

ERNEST: I have no pity for you girls, I——

LADY MARY: Ernest, go away, and don't insult the broken-hearted.

ERNEST: And uncommon glad I am to go. Ta-ta, all of you. He asked me to say a few words. I came here to say a few words, and I'm not at all sure that I couldn't bring an action against him. [*He departs, feeling that he has left a dart behind him. The girls are alone with their tragic throughts*]

LADY MARY: [*Become a mother to the younger ones at last*] My poor sisters, come here. [*They go to her doubtfully*] We must make this draw us closer together. I shall do my best to help you in every way. Just now I cannot think of myself at all.

AGATHA: But how unlike you, Mary.

LADY MARY: It is my duty to protect my sisters.

CATHERINE: I never knew her so sweet before, Agatha. [*Cautiously*] What do you propose to do, Mary?

LADY MARY: I propose when we are on the yacht to lend Fisher to you when I don't need her myself.

AGATHA: Fisher?

LADY MARY: [*Who has the most character of the three*] Of course, as the eldest, I have decided that it is *my* maid we shall take with us.

CATHERINE: [*Speaking also for* Agatha] Mary, you toad.

AGATHA: Nothing on earth would induce Fisher to lift her hand for either me or Catherine.

LADY MARY: I was afraid of it, Agatha. That is why I am so sorry for you.

[*The further exchange of pleasantries is interrupted by the arrival of* Fisher]

LADY MARY: Fisher, you heard what his lordship said?

FISHER: Yes, my lady.

LADY MARY: [*Coldly, though the others would have tried blandishment*] You have given me some satisfaction of late, Fisher, and to mark my approval I have decided that you shall be the maid who accompanies us.

FISHER: [*Acidly*] I thank you, my lady.

LADY MARY: That is all; you may go.

FISHER: [*Rapping it out*] If you please, my lady, I wish to give notice.

[Catherine *and* Agatha *gleam, but* Lady Mary *is of sterner stuff*]

LADY MARY: [*Taking up a book*] Oh, certainly—you may go.

CATHERINE: But why, Fisher?

FISHER: I could not undertake, my lady, to wait upon three. *We* don't do it. [*In an indignant outburst to* Lady Mary] Oh, my lady, to think that this affront——

LADY MARY: [*Looking up*] I thought I told you to go, Fisher.

[Fisher *stands for a moment irresolute; then goes. As soon as she has gone* Lady Mary *puts down her book and weeps. She is a pretty woman, but this is the only pretty thing we have seen her do yet*]

AGATHA: [*Succinctly*] Serves you right.

[Crichton *comes*]

CATHERINE: It will be Simmons after all. Send Simmons to me.

CRICHTON: [*After hesitating*] My lady, might I venture to speak?

CATHERINE: What is it?

CRICHTON: I happen to know, your ladyship, that Simmons desires to give notice for the same reason as Fisher.

CATHERINE: Oh!

AGATHA: [*Triumphant*] Then, Catherine, we take Jeanne.

CRICHTON: And Jeanne also, my lady.

[Lady Mary *is reading, indifferent though the heavens fall, but her sisters are not ashamed to show their despair to* Crichton]

AGATHA: We can't blame them. Could any maid who respected herself be got to wait upon three?

LADY MARY: [*With languid interest*] I suppose there are such persons, Crichton?

CRICHTON: [*Guardedly*] I have heard, my lady, that there are such.

LADY MARY: [*A little desperate*] Crichton, what's to be done? We sail in two days; could one be discovered in the time?

AGATHA: [*Frankly a supplicant*] Surely you can think of some one?

CRICHTON: [*After hesitating*] There is in this establishment, your ladyship, a young woman——

LADY MARY: Yes?

CRICHTON: A young woman on whom I have for some time cast an eye.

CATHERINE: [*Eagerly*] Do you mean as a possible lady's-maid?

CRICHTON: I had thought of her, my lady, in another connection.

LADY MARY: Ah!

CRICHTON: But I believe she is quite the young person you require. Perhaps if you could see her, my lady——

LADY MARY: I shall certainly see her. Bring her to me. [*He goes*] You two needn't wait.

CATHERINE: Needn't we? We see your little game. Mary.

AGATHA: We shall certainly remain and have our two-thirds of her.

[*They sit there doggedly until* Crichton *returns with* Tweeny, *who looks scared*]

CRICHTON: This, my lady, is the young person.

CATHERINE: [*Frankly*] Oh dear!

[*It is evident that all three consider her quite unsuitable*]

LADY MARY: Come here, girl. Don't be afraid.

[Tweeny *looks imploringly at her idol*]

CRICHTON: Her appearance, my lady, is homely, and her manners, as you may have observed, deplorable, but she has a heart of gold.

LADY MARY: What is your position downstairs?

TWEENY: [*Bobbing*] I'm a tweeny, your ladyship.

CATHERINE: A what?

CRICHTON: A tweeny; that is to say, my lady, she is not at present, strictly speaking, anything; a *between* maid; she helps the vegetable maid. It is she, my lady, who conveys the dishes from the one end of the kitchen table where they are placed by the cook, to the other end, where they enter into the charge of Thomas and John.

LADY MARY: I see. And you and Crichton are—ah—keeping company?

[Crichton *draws himself up*]

TWEENY: [*Aghast*] A butler don't keep company, my lady.

LADY MARY: [*Indifferently*] Does he not?

CRICHTON: No, your ladyship, we butlers may—[*He makes a gesture with his arms*]—but we do not keep company.

AGATHA: I know what it is; you are engaged?

[Tweeny *looks longingly at* Crichton]

CRICHTON: Certainly not, my lady. The utmost I can say at present is that I have cast a favorable eye.

[*Even this is much to* Tweeny]

LADY MARY: As you choose. But I am afraid, Crichton, she will not suit us.

CRICHTON: My lady, beneath this simple exterior are concealed a very sweet nature and rare womanly gifts.

AGATHA: Unfortunately, that is not what we want.

CRICHTON: And it is she, my lady, who dresses the hair of the ladies'-maids for our evening meals.

[*The ladies are interested at last*]

LADY MARY: She dresses Fisher's hair?

TWEENY: Yes, my lady, and I does them up when they goes to parties.

CRICHTON: [*Pained, but not scolding*] Does!

TWEENY: Doos. And it's me what alters your gowns to fit them.

CRICHTON: *What* alters!

TWEENY: Which alters.

AGATHA: Mary?

LADY MARY: I shall certainly have her.

CATHERINE: *We* shall certainly have her. Tweeny, we have decided to make a lady's-maid of you.

TWEENY: Oh lawks!

AGATHA: We are doing this for you so that your position socially may be more nearly akin to that of Crichton.

CRICHTON: [*Gravely*] It will undoubtedly increase the young person's chances.

LADY MARY: Then if I get a good character for you from Mrs. Perkins, she will make the necessary arrangements. [*She resumes reading*]

TWEENY: [*Elated*] My lady!

LADY MARY: By the way, I hope you are a good sailor.

TWEENY: [*Startled*] You don't mean, my lady, that I'm to go on the ship?

LADY MARY: Certainly.

TWEENY: But—— [*To* Crichton] You ain't going, sir?

CRICHTON: No.

TWEENY: [*Firm at last*] Then neither ain't I.

AGATHA: You must.

TWEENY: Leave him! Not me.

LADY MARY: Girl, don't be silly. Crichton will be —considered in your wages.

TWEENY: I ain't going.

CRICHTON: I feared this, my lady.

TWEENY: Nothing will budge me.

LADY MARY: Leave the room.

[Crichton *shows* Tweeny *out with marked politeness*]

AGATHA: Crichton, I think you might have shown more displeasure with her.

CRICHTON: [*Contrite*] I was touched, my lady. I see, my lady, that to part from her would be a wrench to me, though I could not well say so in her presence, not having yet decided how far I shall go with her. [*He is about to go when* Lord Loam *returns, fuming*]

LORD LOAM: The ingrate! The smug! The fop!

CATHERINE: What is it now, father?

LORD LOAM: That man of mine, Rolleston, refuses to accompany us because you are to have but one maid.

AGATHA: Hurrah!

LADY MARY: [*In better taste*] Darling father, rather than you should lose Rolleston, we will consent to take all the three of them.

LORD LOAM: Pooh, nonsense! Crichton, find me a valet who can do without three maids.

CRICHTON: Yes, my lord. [*Troubled*] In the time —the more suitable the party, my lord, the less willing will he be to come without the—usual perquisites.

LORD LOAM: Any one will do.

CRICHTON: [*Shocked*] My lord!

LORD LOAM: The ingrate! The puppy!

[Agatha *has an idea, and whispers to* Lady Mary]

LADY MARY: I ask a favor of a servant?—never!

AGATHA: Then I will. Crichton, would it not be very distressing to you to let his lordship go, attended by a valet who might prove unworthy? It is only for three months; don't you think that you—you yourself—you—— [As Crichton sees what she wants he pulls himself up with noble, offended dignity, and she is appalled] I beg your pardon.

[He bows stiffly]

CATHERINE: [To Crichton] But think of the joy to Tweeny.

[Crichton is moved, but he shakes his head]

LADY MARY: [So much the cleverest] Crichton, do you think it safe to let the master you love go so far away without you while he has these dangerous views about equality?

[Crichton is profoundly stirred. After a struggle he goes to his master, who has been pacing the room]

CRICHTON: My lord, I have found a man.

LORD LOAM: Already? Who is he? [Crichton presents himself with a gesture] Yourself?

CATHERINE: Father, how good of him.

LORD LOAM: [Pleased, but speaking of it as a small thing] Uncommon good. Thank you, Crichton. This helps me nicely out of a hole; and how it will annoy Rolleston! Come with me, and we shall tell him. Not that I think you have lowered yourself in any way. Come along. [He goes, and Crichton is to follow him, but is stopped by Agatha impulsively offering him her hand]

CRICHTON: [Who is much shaken] My lady—a valet's hand!

AGATHA: I had no idea you would feel it so deeply; why did you do it?

[Crichton is too respectful to reply]

LADY MARY: [Regarding him] Crichton, I am curious. I insist upon an answer.

CRICHTON: My lady, I am the son of a butler and a lady's-maid—perhaps the happiest of all combinations, and to me the most beautiful thing in the world is a haughty, aristocratic English house, with every one kept in his place. Though I were equal to your ladyship, where would be the pleasure to me? It would be counterbalanced by the pain of feeling that Thomas and John were equal to me.

CATHERINE: But father says if we were to return to Nature——

CRICHTON: If we did, my lady, the first thing we should do would be to elect a head. Circumstances might alter cases; the same person might not be master; the same persons might not be servants. I can't say as to that, nor should we have the deciding of it. Nature would decide for us.

LADY MARY: You seem to have thought it all out carefully, Crichton.

CRICHTON: Yes, my lady.

CATHERINE: And you have done this for us, Crichton, because you thought that—that father needed to be kept in his place?

CRICHTON: I should prefer you to say, my lady, that I have done it for the house.

AGATHA: Thank you, Crichton. Mary, be nicer to him. [But Lady Mary has begun to read again] If

there was any way in which we could show our gratitude.

CRICHTON: If I might venture, my lady, would you kindly show it by becoming more like Lady Mary? That disdain is what we like from our superiors. Even so do we, the upper servants, disdain the lower servants, while they take it out of the odds and ends. [He goes, and they bury themselves in cushions]

AGATHA: Oh dear, what a tiring day.

CATHERINE: I feel dead. Tuck in your feet, you selfish thing.

[Lady Mary is lying reading on another couch]

LADY MARY: I wonder what he meant by circumstances might alter cases.

AGATHA: [Yawning] Don't talk, Mary, I was nearly asleep.

LADY MARY: I wonder what he meant by the same person might not be master, and the same persons might not be servants.

CATHERINE: Do be quiet, Mary, and leave it to Nature; he said Nature would decide.

LADY MARY: I wonder——

[But she does not wonder very much. She would wonder more if she knew what was coming. Her book slips unregarded to the floor. The ladies are at rest until it is time to dress]

END OF ACT I

ACT II.

Two months have elapsed, and the scene is a desert island in the Pacific, on which our adventurers have been wrecked.

The curtain rises on a sea of bamboo, which shuts out all view save the foliage of palm trees and some gaunt rocks. Occasionally Crichton and Treherne come momentarily into sight, hacking and hewing the bamboo, through which they are making a clearing between the ladies and the shore; and by and by, owing to their efforts, we shall have an unrestricted outlook on to a sullen sea that is at present hidden. Then we shall also be able to note a mast standing out of the water—all that is left, saving floating wreckage, of the ill-fated yacht the Bluebell. The beginnings of a hut will also be seen, with Crichton driving its walls into the ground or astride its roof of saplings, for at present he is doing more than one thing at a time. In a red shirt, with the ends of his sailor's breeches thrust into wading-boots, he looks a man for the moment; we suddenly remember some one's saying—perhaps it was ourselves—that a cataclysm would be needed to get him out of his servant's clothes, and apparently it has been forthcoming. It is no longer beneath our dignity to cast an inquiring eye on his appearance. His features are not distinguished, but he has a strong jaw and green eyes, in which a yellow light burns that we have not seen before. His dark hair, hitherto so decorously sleek, has been ruffled this way and that by wind and weather, as if they were part of the cataclysm and wanted to help his chance. His muscles must be soft and flabby still, but though they shriek aloud to him to desist, he rains lusty blows with his axe, like one who has come upon the open for the first time in his life, and likes it. He is as yet far from being an expert woodsman—mark the blood on his hands at places where he has hit them instead of the tree; but note also that he does not waste time in bandaging them—he rubs them in the earth and goes on. His face is still of the discreet pallor that befits a butler, and he carries the smaller logs as if they were a salver; not in a day or a month will he shake off the badge of servitude, but without knowing it he has begun.

But for the hatchets at work, and an occasional something horrible falling from a tree into the ladies' laps, they hear nothing save the mournful surf breaking on a coral shore.

They sit or recline huddled together against a rock, and they are farther from home, in every sense of the word, than ever before. Thirty-six hours ago, they were given three minutes in which to dress, without a maid, and reach the boats, and they have not made the best of that valuable time. None of them has boots, and had they known this prickly island they would have thought first of boots. They have a sufficiency of garments, but some of them were gifts dropped into the boat—Lady Mary's tarpaulin coat and hat, for instance, and Catherine's blue jersey and red cap, which certify that the two ladies were lately before the mast. Agatha is too gay in Ernest's dressing-gown, and clutches it to her person with both hands as if afraid that it may be claimed by its rightful owner. There are two pairs of bath slippers between the three of them, and their hair cries aloud and in vain for hairpins.

By their side, on an inverted bucket, sits Ernest, clothed neatly in the garments of day and night, but, alas, barefooted. He is the only cheerful member of this company of four, but his brightness is due less to a manly desire to succour the helpless than to his having been lately in the throes of composition, and to his modest satisfaction with the result. He reads to the ladies, and they listen, each with one scared eye to the things that fall from trees.

ERNEST: [*Who has written on the fly-leaf of the only book saved from the wreck*] This is what I have written. "Wrecked, wrecked, wrecked! on an island in the Tropics, the following: the Hon. Ernest Woolley, the Rev. John Treherne, the Ladies Mary, Catherine, and Agatha Lasenby, with two servants. We are the sole survivors of Lord Loam's steam yacht *Bluebell*, which encountered a fearful gale in these seas, and soon became a total wreck. The crew behaved gallantly, putting us all into the first boat.

What became of them I cannot tell, but we, after dreadful sufferings, and insufficiently clad, in whatever garments we could lay hold of in the dark——"

LADY MARY: Please don't describe our garments.

ERNEST: "succeeded in reaching this island, with the loss of only one of our party, namely, Lord Loam, who flung away his life in a gallant attempt to save a servant who had fallen overboard."

[*The ladies have wept long and sore for their father, but there is something in this last utterance that makes them look up*]

AGATHA: But, Ernest, it was Crichton who jumped overboard trying to save father.

ERNEST: [*With the candor that is one of his most engaging qualities*] Well, you know, it was rather silly of uncle to fling away his life by trying to get into the boat first; and as this document may be printed in the English papers, it struck me, an English peer, you know——

LADY MARY: [*Every inch an English peer's daughter*] Ernest, that is very thoughtful of you.

ERNEST: [*Continuing, well pleased*]—"By night the cries of wild cats and the hissing of snakes terrify us extremely"— [*This does not satisfy him so well, and he makes a correction*]—"terrify the ladies extremely. Against these we have no weapons except one cutlass and a hatchet. A bucket washed ashore is at present our only comfortable seat——"

LADY MARY: [*With some spirit*] And Ernest is sitting on it.

ERNEST: H'sh! Oh, do be quiet.—"To add to our horrors, night falls suddenly in these parts, and it is then that savage animals begin to prowl and roar."

LADY MARY: Have you said that vampire bats suck the blood from our toes as we sleep?

ERNEST: No, that's all. I end up, "Rescue us or we perish. Rich reward. Signed Ernest Woolley, in command of our little party." This is written on a leaf taken out of a book of poems that Crichton found in his pocket. Fancy Crichton being a reader of poetry. Now I shall put it into the bottle and fling it into the sea. [*He pushes the precious document into a soda-water bottle and rams the cork home. At the same moment, and without effort, he gives birth to one of his most characteristic epigrams*] The tide is going out, we mustn't miss the post.

[*They are so unhappy that they fail to grasp it, and a little petulantly he calls for* Crichton, *ever his stand-by in the hour of epigram.* Crichton *breaks through the undergrowth quickly, thinking the ladies are in danger*].

CRICHTON: Anything wrong, sir?

ERNEST: [*With fine confidence*] The tide, Crichton, is a postman who calls at our island twice a day for letters.

CRICHTON: [*After a pause*] Thank you, sir. [*He returns to his labors, however, without giving the smile which is the epigrammatist's right, and* Ernest *is a little disappointed in him*]

ERNEST: Poor Crichton! I sometimes think he is losing his sense of humor. Come along, Agatha. [*He helps his favorite up the rocks, and they disappear gingerly from view*]

CATHERINE: How horribly still it is.

LADY MARY: [*Remembering some recent sounds*] It is best when it is still.

CATHERINE: [*Drawing closer to her*] Mary, I have heard that they are always very still just before they jump.

LADY MARY: Don't.

[*A distinct chopping is heard, and they are startled*]

LADY MARY: [*Controlling herself*] It is only Crichton knocking down trees.

CATHERINE: [*Almost imploringly*] Mary, let us go and stand beside him.

LADY MARY: [*Coldly*] Let a servant see that I am afraid!

CATHERINE: Don't, then; but remember this, dear, they often drop on one from above.

[*She moves away, nearer to the friendly sound of the axe, and* Lady Mary *is left alone. She is the most courageous of them as well as the haughtiest, but when something she had thought to be a stick glides toward her, she forgets her dignity and screams*]

LADY MARY: [*Calling*] Crichton, Crichton!

[*It must have been* Treherne *who was tree-felling, for* Crichton *comes to her from the hut, drawing his cutlass*]

CRICHTON: [*Anxious*] Did you call, my lady?

LADY MARY: [*Herself again, now that he is there*] I! Why should I?

CRICHTON: I made a mistake, your ladyship. [*Hesitating*] If you are afraid of being alone, my lady——

LADY MARY: Afraid! Certainly not. [*Doggedly*] You may go. [*But she does not complain when he remains within eyesight cutting the bamboo. It is heavy work, and she watches him silently*]

LADY MARY: I wish, Crichton, you could work without getting so hot.

CRICHTON: [*Mopping his face*] I wish I could, my lady.

[*He continues his labors*]

LADY MARY: [*Taking off her oilskins*] It makes me hot to look at you.

CRICHTON: It almost makes me cool to look at your ladyship.

LADY MARY: [*Who perhaps thinks he is presuming*] Anything I can do for you in that way, Crichton, I shall do with pleasure.

CRICHTON: [*Quite humbly*] Thank you, my lady.

[*By this time most of the bamboo has been cut, and the shore and the sea are visible, except where they are hidden by the half-completed hut. The mast rising solitary from the water adds to the desolation of the scene, and at last tears run down* Lady Mary's *face*]

CRICHTON: Don't give way, my lady, things might be worse.

LADY MARY: My poor father.

CRICHTON: If I could have given my life for his.

LADY MARY: You did all a man could do. Indeed I thank you, Crichton. [*With some admiration and more wonder*] You are a man.

CRICHTON: Thank you, my lady.

LADY MARY: But it is all so awful. Crichton, is there any hope of a ship coming?

CRICHTON: [*After hesitation*] Of course there is, my lady.

LADY MARY: [*Facing him bravely*] Don't treat me as a child. I have got to know the worst, and to face it. Crichton, the truth.

CRICHTON: [*Reluctantly*] We were driven out of our course, my lady; I fear far from the track of commerce.

LADY MARY: Thank you; I understand. [*For a moment, however, she breaks down. Then she clenches her hands and stands erect*]

CRICHTON: [*Watching her, and forgetting perhaps for the moment that they are not just a man and woman*] You're a good plucky 'un, my lady.

LADY MARY: [*Falling into the same error*] I shall try to be. [*Extricating herself*] Crichton, how dare you?

CRICHTON: I beg your ladyship's pardon; but you are. [*She smiles, as if it were a comfort to be told this even by* Crichton] And until a ship comes we are three men who are going to do our best for you ladies.

LADY MARY: [*With a curl of the lip*] Mr. Ernest does no work.

CRICHTON: [*Cheerily*] But he will, my lady.

LADY MARY: I doubt it.

CRICHTON: [*Confidently, but perhaps thoughtlessly*] No work—no dinner—will make a great change in Mr. Ernest.

LADY MARY: No work—no dinner. When did you invent that rule, Crichton?

CRICHTON: [*Loaded with bamboo*] I didn't invent it, my lady. I seem to see it growing all over the island.

LADY MARY: [*Disquieted*] Crichton, your manner strikes me as curious.

CRICHTON: [*Pained*] I hope not, your ladyship.

LADY MARY: [*Determined to have it out with him*] You are not implying anything so unnatural, I presume, as that if I and my sisters don't work there will be no dinner for *us*?

CRICHTON: [*Brightly*] If it is unnatural, my lady, that is the end of it.

LADY MARY: If? Now I understand. The perfect servant at home holds that we are all equal now. I see.

CRICHTON: [*Wounded to the quick*] My lady, can you think me so inconsistent?

LADY MARY: That was it.

CRICHTON: [*Earnestly*] My lady, I disbelieved in equality at home because it was against nature, and for the same reason I as utterly disbelieve in it on an island.

LADY MARY: [*Relieved by his obvious sincerity*] I apologize.

CRICHTON: [*Continuing unfortunately*] There must always, my lady, be one to command and others to obey.

LADY MARY: [*Satisfied*] One to command, others to obey. Yes. [*Then suddenly she realizes that there may be a dire meaning in his confident words*] Crichton!

CRICHTON: [*Who has intended no dire meaning*] What is it, my lady?

[*But she only stares into his face and then hurries from him. Left alone he is puzzled, but being a practical man he busies himself gathering firewood, until* Tweeny *appears excitedly carrying cocoa-nuts in her skirt. She has made better use than the ladies of her three minutes' grace for dressing*]

TWEENY: [*Who can be happy even on an island if* Crichton *is with her*] Look what I found.

CRICHTON: Cocoa-nuts. Bravo!

TWEENY: They grow on trees.

CRICHTON: Where did you think they grew?

TWEENY: I thought as how they grew in rows on top of little sticks.

CRICHTON: [*Wrinkling his brows*] Oh Tweeny, Tweeny.

TWEENY: [*Anxiously*] Have I offended of your feelings again, sir?

CRICHTON: A little.

TWEENY: [*In a despairing outburst*] I'm full o' vulgar words and ways; and though I may keep them in their holes when you are by, as soon as I'm by myself out they comes in a rush like beetles when the house is dark. I says them gloatinglike, in my head—"Blooming" I says, and "All my eye," and "Ginger," and "Nothink"; and all the time we was being wrecked I was praying to myself, "Please the Lord it may be an island as it's natural to be vulgar on." [*A shudder passes through* Crichton, *and she is abject*] That's the kind I am, sir. I'm 'opeless. You'd better give me up. [*She is a pathetic forlorn creature, and his manhood is stirred*]

CRICHTON: [*Wondering a little at himself for saying it*] I won't give you up. It is strange that one so common should attract one so fastidious; but so it is. [*Thoughtfully*] There is something about you, Tweeny, there is a *je ne sais quoi* about you.

TWEENY: [*Knowing only that he has found something in her to commend*] Is there, is there? Oh, I am glad.

CRICHTON: [*Putting his hand on her shoulder like a protector*] We shall fight your vulgarity together. [*All this time he has been arranging sticks for his fire*] Now get some dry grass.

[*She brings him grass, and he puts it under the*

sticks. *He produces an old lens from his pocket, and tries to focus the sun's rays*]

TWEENY: Why, what is that?

CRICHTON: [*The ingenious creature*] That's the glass from my watch and one from Mr. Treherne's, with a little water between them. I am hoping to kindle a fire with it.

TWEENY: [*Properly impressed*] Oh sir!

[*After one failure the grass takes fire, and they are blowing on it when excited cries near by throw them sharply to their feet.* Agatha *runs to them, white of face, followed by* Ernest]

ERNEST: Danger! Crichton, a tiger-cat!

CRICHTON: [*Getting his cutlass*] Where?

AGATHA: It is at our heels.

ERNEST: Look out, Crichton.

CRICHTON: H'sh!

[Treherne *comes to his assistance, while* Lady Mary *and* Catherine *join* Agatha *in the hut*]

ERNEST: It will be on us in a moment. [*He seizes the hatchet and guards the hut. It is pleasing to see that* Ernest *is no coward*]

TREHERNE: Listen!

ERNEST: The grass is moving. It's coming.

[*It comes. But it is no tiger-cat; it is* Lord Loam *crawling on his hands and knees, a very exhausted and dishevelled peer, wondrously attired in rags. The girls see him, and with glad cries rush into his arms*]

LADY MARY: Father.

LORD LOAM: Mary—Catherine—Agatha. Oh dear, my dears, my dears, oh dear!

LADY MARY: Darling.

AGATHA: Sweetest.

CATHERINE: Love.

TREHERNE: Glad to see you, sir.

ERNEST: Uncle, uncle, dear old uncle.

[*For a time such happy cries fill the air, but presently* Treherne *is thoughtless*]

TREHERNE: Ernest thought you were a tiger-cat.

LORD LOAM: [*Stung somehow to the quick*] Oh, did you? I knew you at once, Ernest; I knew you by the way you ran.

[Ernest *smiles forgivingly*]

CRICHTON: [*Venturing forward at last*] My lord, I am glad.

ERNEST: [*With upraised finger*] But you are also idling, Crichton. [*Making himself comfortable on the ground*] We mustn't waste time. To work, to work.

CRICHTON: [*After contemplating him without rancor*] Yes, sir. [*He gets a pot from the hut and hangs it on a tripod over the fire, which is now burning brightly*]

TREHERNE: Ernest, you be a little more civil. Crichton, let me help.

[*He is soon busy helping* Crichton *to add to the strength of the hut*]

LORD LOAM: [*Gazing at the pot as ladies are said to gaze on precious stones*] Is that—but I suppose

I'm dreaming again. [*Timidly*] It isn't by any chance a pot on top of a fire, is it?

LADY MARY: Indeed, it is, dearest. It is our supper.

LORD LOAM: I have been dreaming of a pot on a fire for two days. [*Quivering*] There's nothing in it, is there?

ERNEST: Sniff, uncle.

[*Lord Loam sniffs*]

LORD LOAM: [*Reverently*] It smells of onions!

[*There is a sudden diversion*]

CATHERINE: Father, you have boots!

LADY MARY: So he has.

LORD LOAM: Of course I have.

ERNEST: [*With greedy cunning*] You are actually wearing boots, uncle. It's very unsafe, you know, in this climate.

LORD LOAM: Is it?

ERNEST: We have all abandoned them, you observe. The blood, the arteries, you know.

LORD LOAM: I hadn't a notion. [*He holds out his feet and* Ernest *kneels*]

ERNEST: O Lord yes.

[*In another moment those boots will be his*]

LADY MARY: [*Quickly*] Father, he is trying to get your boots from you. There is nothing in the world we would not give for boots.

ERNEST: [*Rising haughtily, a proud spirit misunderstood*] I only wanted the loan of them.

AGATHA: [*Running her fingers along them lovingly*] If you lend them to any one, it will be to us, won't it, father?

LORD LOAM: Certainly, my child.

ERNEST: Oh, very well. [*He is leaving these selfish ones*] I don't want your old boots. [*He gives his uncle a last chance*] You don't think you could spare me *one* boot?

LORD LOAM: [*Tartly*] I do not.

ERNEST: Quite so. Well, all I can say is I'm sorry for you. [*He departs to recline elsewhere*]

LADY MARY: Father, we thought we should never see you again.

LORD LOAM: I was washed ashore, my dear, clinging to a hencoop. How awful that first night was!

LADY MARY: Poor father.

LORD LOAM: When I woke, I wept. Then I began to feel extremely hungry. There was a large turtle on the beach. I remembered from the *Swiss Family Robinson* that if you turn a turtle over he is helpless. My dears, I crawled towards him, I flung myself upon him—[*Here he pauses to rub his leg*]—the nasty, spiteful brute.

LADY MARY: You didn't turn him over?

LORD LOAM: [*Vindictively, though he is a kindly man*] Mary, the senseless thing wouldn't wait; I found that none of them would wait.

CATHERINE: We should have been as badly off if Crichton hadn't——

LADY MARY: [*Quickly*] Don't praise Crichton.

LORD LOAM: And then those beastly monkeys. I always understood that if you flung stones at them

they would retaliate by flinging cocoa-nuts at you. Would you believe it, I flung a hundred stones, and not one monkey had sufficient intelligence to grasp my meaning. How I longed for Crichton.

LADY MARY: [*Wincing*] For us also, father?

LORD LOAM: For you also. I tried for hours to make a fire. The authors say that when wrecked on an island you can obtain a light by rubbing two pieces of stick together. [*With feeling*] The liars!

LADY MARY: And all this time you thought there was no one on the island but yourself?

LORD LOAM: I thought so until this morning. I was searching the pools for little fishes, which I caught in my hat, when suddenly I saw before me—on the sand——

CATHERINE: What?

LORD LOAM: A hairpin.

LADY MARY: A hairpin! It must be one of ours. Give it me, father.

AGATHA: No, it's mine.

LORD LOAM: I didn't keep it.

LADY MARY: [*Speaking for all three*] Didn't keep it? Found a hairpin on an island and didn't keep it?

LORD LOAM: [*Humbly*] My dears.

AGATHA: [*Scarcely to be placated*] Oh father, we have returned to nature more than you bargained for.

LADY MARY: For shame, Agatha. [*She has something on her mind*] Father, there is something I want you to do at once—I mean assert your position as the chief person on the island.

[*They are all surprised*]

LORD LOAM: But who would presume to question it?

CATHERINE: She must mean Ernest.

LADY MARY: Must I?

AGATHA: It's cruel to say anything against Ernest.

LORD LOAM: [*Firmly*] If any one presumes to challenge my position, I shall make short work of him.

AGATHA: Here comes Ernest; now see if you can say these horrid things to his face.

LORD LOAM: I shall teach him his place at once.

LADY MARY: [*Anxiously*] But how?

LORD LOAM: [*Chuckling*] I have just thought of an extremely amusing way of doing it. [*As* Ernest *approaches*] Ernest.

ERNEST: [*Loftily*] Excuse me, uncle, I'm thinking. I'm planning out the building of this hut.

LORD LOAM: I also have been thinking.

ERNEST: That don't matter.

LORD LOAM: Eh?

ERNEST: Please, please, this is important.

LORD LOAM: I've been thinking that I ought to give you my boots.

ERNEST: What!

LADY MARY: Father.

LORD LOAM: [*Genially*] Take them, my boy. [*With a rapidity we had not thought him capable of,* Ernest *becomes the wearer of the boots*] And now I dare say you want to know why I give them to you, Ernest?

ERNEST: [*Moving up and down in them deliciously*] Not at all. The great thing is, "I've got 'em, I've got 'em."

LORD LOAM: [*Majestically, but with a knowing look at his daughters*] My reason is that, as head of our little party, you, Ernest, shall be our hunter, you shall clear the forests of those savage beasts that make them so dangerous. [*Pleasantly*] And now you know, my dear nephew, why I have given you my boots.

ERNEST: This is my answer. [*He kicks off the boots*]

LADY MARY: [*Still anxious*] Father, assert yourself.

LORD LOAM: I shall now assert myself. [*But how to do it? He has a happy thought*] Call Crichton.

LADY MARY: Oh father.

[Crichton *comes in answer to a summons and is followed by* Treherne]

ERNEST: [*Wondering a little at Lady Mary's grave face*] Crichton, look here.

LORD LOAM: [*Sturdily*] Silence! Crichton, I want your advice as to what I ought to do with Mr. Ernest. He has defied me.

ERNEST: Pooh!

CRICHTON: [*After considering*] May I speak openly, my lord?

LADY MARY: [*Keeping her eyes fixed on him*] That is what we desire.

CRICHTON: [*Quite humbly*] Then I may say, your lordship, that I have been considering Mr. Ernest's case at odd moments ever since we were wrecked.

ERNEST: My case?

LORD LOAM: [*Sternly*] Hush.

CRICHTON: Since we landed on the island, my lord, it seems to me that Mr. Ernest's epigrams have been particularly brilliant.

ERNEST: [*Gratified*] Thank you, Crichton.

CRICHTON: But I find—I seem to find it growing wild, my lord, in the woods, that sayings which would be justly admired in England are not much use on an island. I would therefore most respectfully propose that henceforth every time Mr. Ernest favors us with an epigram his head should be immersed in a bucket of cold spring water. [*There is a terrible silence*]

LORD LOAM: [*Uneasily*] Serve him right.

ERNEST: I should like to see you try to do it, uncle.

CRICHTON: [*Ever ready to come to the succour of his lordship*] My feeling, my lord, is that at the next offence I should convey him to a retired spot, where I shall carry out the undertaking in as respectful a manner as is consistent with thorough immersion. [*Though his manner is most respectful, he is firm; he evidently means what he says*]

LADY MARY: [*A ramrod*] Father, you must not permit this; Ernest is your nephew.

LORD LOAM: [*With his hand to his brow*] After all, he is my nephew, Crichton; and, as I am sure, he now sees that I am a strong man——

ERNEST: [*Foolishly in the circumstances*] A strong man. You mean a stout man. You are one of mind to two of matter. [*He looks round in the old way for approval. No one has smiled, and to his consternation he sees that* Crichton *is quietly turning up his sleeves*. Ernest *makes an appealing gesture to his uncle; then he turns defiantly to* Crichton]

CRICHTON: Is it to be before the ladies, Mr. Ernest, or in the privacy of the wood? [*He fixes* Ernest *with his eye*. Ernest *is cowed*] Come.

ERNEST: [*Affecting bravado*] Oh, all right.

CRICHTON: [*Succinctly*] Bring the bucket.

[Ernest *hesitates. He then lifts the bucket and follows* Crichton *to the nearest spring*]

LORD LOAM: [*Rather white*] I'm sorry for him, but I had to be firm.

LADY MARY: Oh, father, it wasn't you who was firm. Crichton did it himself.

LORD LOAM: Bless me, so he did.

LADY MARY: Father, be strong.

LORD LOAM: [*Bewildered*] You can't mean that my faithful Crichton——

LADY MARY: Yes, I do.

TREHERNE: Lady Mary, I stake my word that Crichton is incapable of acting dishonourably.

LADY MARY: I know that; I know it as well as you. Don't you see that that is what makes him so dangerous?

TREHERNE: By Jove, I—I believe I catch your meaning.

CATHERINE: He is coming back.

LORD LOAM: [*Who has always known himself to be a man of ideas*] Let us all go into the hut, just to show him at once that it is *our* hut.

LADY MARY: [*As they go*] Father, I implore you, assert yourself now and for ever.

LORD LOAM: I will.

LADY MARY: And, please, don't ask him how you are to do it.

[Crichton *returns with sticks to mend the fire*]

LORD LOAM: [*Loftily, from the door of the hut*] Have you carried out my instructions, Crichton?

CRICHTON: [*Deferentially*] Yes, my lord.

[Ernest *appears, mopping his hair, which has become very wet since we last saw him. He is not bearing malice, he is too busy drying, but* Agatha *is specially his champion*]

AGATHA: It's infamous, infamous.

LORD LOAM: [*Strongly*] My orders, Agatha.

LADY MARY: Now, father, please.

LORD LOAM: [*Striking an attitude*] Before I give you any further orders, Crichton——

CRICHTON: Yes, my lord.

LORD LOAM: [*Delighted*] Pooh! It's all right.

LADY MARY: No. Please go on.

LORD LOAM: Well, well. This question of leadership; what do you think now, Crichton?

CRICHTON: My Lord, I feel it is a matter with which *I* have nothing to do.

LORD LOAM: Excellent. Ha, Mary? That settles it, I think.

LADY MARY: It seems to, but—I'm not sure.

CRICHTON: It will settle itself naturally, my lord, without any interference from us. [*This reference to Nature gives general dissatisfaction*]

LADY MARY: Father.

LORD LOAM: [*A little severely*] It settled itself long ago, Crichton, when I was born a peer, and you, for instance, were born a servant.

CRICHTON: [*Acquiescing*] Yes, my lord, that was how it all came about quite naturally in England. We had nothing to do with it there, and we shall have as little to do with it here.

TREHERNE: [*Relieved*] That's all right.

LADY MARY: [*Determined to clinch the matter*] One moment. In short, Crichton, his lordship will continue to be our natural head.

CRICHTON: I dare say, my lady, I dare say.

CATHERINE: But you must *know.*

CRICHTON: Asking your pardon, my lady, one can't be sure—on an island.

[*They look at each other uneasily*]

LORD LOAM: [*Warningly*] Crichton, I don't like this.

CRICHTON: [*Harassed*] The more I think of it, your lordship, the more uneasy I become myself. When I heard, my lord, that you had left that hairpin behind——[*He is pained*]

LORD LOAM: [*Feebly*] One hairpin among so many would only have caused dissension.

CRICHTON: [*Very sorry to have to contradict him*] Not so, my lord. From that hairpin we could have made a needle; with that needle we could, out of skins, have sewn trousers—of which your lordship is in need; indeed, we are all in need of them.

LADY MARY: [*Suddenly self-conscious*] All?

CRICHTON: On an island, my lady.

LADY MARY: Father.

CRICHTON: [*Really more distressed by the prospect than she*] My lady, if Nature does not think them necessary, you may be sure she will not ask you to wear them. [*Shaking his head*] But among all this undergrowth——

LADY MARY: Now you see this man in his true colors.

LORD LOAM: [*Violently*] Crichton, you will either this moment say, "Down with Nature," or——

CRICHTON: [*Scandalized*] My lord!

LORD LOAM: [*Loftily*] Then this is my last word to you; take a month's notice.

[*If the hut had a door he would now shut it to indicate that the interview is closed*]

CRICHTON: [*In great distress*] Your lordship, the disgrace——

LORD LOAM: [*Swelling*] Not another word: you may go.

LADY MARY: [*Adamant*] And don't come to me, Crichton, for a character

ERNEST: [*Whose immersion has cleared his brain*] Aren't you all forgetting that this is an island?

[*This brings them to earth with a bump.* Lord Loam *looks to his eldest daughter for the fitting response*]

LADY MARY: [*Equal to the occasion*] It makes only this difference—that you may go at once, Crichton, to some other part of the island.

[*The faithful servant has been true to his superiors ever since he was created, and never more true than at this moment; but his fidelity is founded on trust in Nature, and to be untrue to it would be to be untrue to them. He lets the wood he has been gathering slip to the ground, and bows his sorrowful head. He turns to obey. Then affection for these great ones wells up in him*]

CRICHTON: My lady, let me work for you.

LADY MARY: Go.

CRICHTON: You need me sorely; I can't desert you; I won't.

LADY MARY: [*In alarm, lest the others may yield*] Then, father, there is but one alternative, *we* must leave him.

[Lord Loam *is looking yearningly at* Crichton]

TREHERNE: It seems a pity.

CATHERINE: [*Forlornly*] *You* will work for us?

TREHERNE: Most willingly. But I must warn you all that, so far, Crichton has done nine-tenths of the scoring.

LADY MARY: The question is, are we to leave this man?

LORD LOAM: [*Wrapping himself in his dignity*] Come, my dears.

CRICHTON: My lord!

LORD LOAM: Treherne—Ernest—get our things.

ERNEST: We don't have any, uncle. They all belong to Crichton.

TREHERNE: Everything we have he brought from the wreck—he went back to it before it sank. He risked his life.

CRICHTON: My lord, anything you would care to take is yours.

LADY MARY: [*Quickly*] Nothing.

ERNEST: Rot! If I could have your socks, Crichton——

LADY MARY: Come, father; we are ready.

[*Followed by the others, she and* Lord Loam *pick their way up the rocks. In their indignation they scarcely notice that daylight is coming to a sudden end*]

CRICHTON: My lord, I implore you—I am not desirous of being head. Do you have a try at it, my lord?

LORD LOAM: [*Outraged*] A try at it!

CRICHTON: [*Eagerly*] It may be that you will prove to be the best man.

LORD LOAM: *May* be! My children, come. [*They disappear proudly in single file*]

TREHERNE: Crichton, I'm sorry; but of course I must go with them.

CRICHTON: Certainly, sir. [*He calls to* Tweeny, *and she comes from behind the hut, where she has been watching breathlessly*] Will you be so kind, sir, as to take her to the others?

TREHERNE: Assuredly.

TWEENY: But what do it all mean?

CRICHTON: Does, Tweeny, does. [*He passes her up the rocks to* Treherne] We shall meet again soon, Tweeny. Good night, sir.

TREHERNE: Good night. I dare say they are not far away.

CRICHTON: [*Thoughtfully*] They went westward, sir, and the wind is blowing in that direction. That may mean, sir, that Nature is already taking the matter into her own hands. They are all hungry, sir, and the pot has come a-boil. [*He takes off the lid*] The smell will be borne westward. That pot is full of Nature, Mr. Treherne. Good night, sir.

TREHERNE: Good night.

[*He mounts the rocks with* Tweeny, *and they are heard for a little time after their figures are swallowed up in the fast growing darkness.* Crichton *stands motionless, the lid in his hand, though he has forgotten it, and his reason for taking it off the pot. He is deeply stirred, but presently is ashamed of his dejection, for it is as if he had doubted his principles. Bravely true to his faith that Nature will decide now as ever before, he proceeds manfully with his preparations for the night. He lights a ship's lantern, one of several treasures he has brought ashore, and is filling his pipe with crumbs of tobacco from various pockets, when the stealthy movements of some animal in the grass startles him. With the lantern in one hand and the cutlass in the other, he searches the ground around the hut. He returns, lights his pipe, and sits down by the fire, which casts weird moving shadows. There is a red gleam on his face; in the darkness he is a strong and perhaps rather sinister figure. In the great stillness that has fallen over the land, the wash of the surf seems to have increased in volume. The sound is indescribably mournful. Except where the fire is, desolation has fallen on the island like a pall.*

Once or twice, as Nature dictates, Crichton *leans forward to stir the pot, and the smell is borne westward. He then resumes his silent vigil.*

Shadows other than those cast by the fire begin to descend the rocks. They are the adventurers returning. One by one they steal nearer to the pot until they are squatted around it, with their hands out to the blaze. Lady Mary *only is absent. Presently she comes within sight of the others, then stands against a tree with her teeth clenched. One wonders, perhaps, what Nature is to make of her*]

END OF ACT II

ACT III.

The scene is the hall of their island home two years later. This sturdy log-house is no mere extension of the hut we have seen in process of erection, but has been built a mile or less to the west of it, on higher ground and near a stream. When the master chose this site, the others thought that all he expected from the stream was a sufficiency of drinking water. They know better now every time they go down to the mill or turn on the electric light.

This hall is the living-room of the house, and walls and roof are of stout logs. Across the joists supporting the roof are laid many home-made implements, such as spades, saws, fishing-rods, and from hooks in the joists are suspended cured foods, of which hams are specially in evidence. Deep recesses half way up the walls contain various provender in barrels and sacks. There are some skins, trophies of the chase, on the floor, which is otherwise bare. The chairs and tables are in some cases hewn out of solid wood, and in others the result of rough but efficient carpentering. Various pieces of wreckage from the yacht have been turned to novel uses; thus the steering wheel now hangs from the centre of the roof, with electric lights attached to it encased in bladders. A lifebuoy has become the back of a chair. Two barrels have been halved and turn coyly from each other as a settee.

The farther end of the room is more strictly the kitchen, and is a great recess, which can be shut off from the hall by folding doors. There is a large open fire in it. The chimney is half of one of the boats of the yacht. On the walls of the kitchen proper are many plate-racks, containing shells; there are rows of these of one size and shape, which mark them off as dinner plates or bowls; others are as obviously tureens. They are arranged primly as in a well-conducted kitchen; indeed, neatness and cleanliness are the note struck everywhere, yet the effect of the whole is romantic and barbaric.

The outer door into this hall is a little peculiar on an island. It is covered with skins and is in four leaves, like the swing doors of fashionable restaurants, which allow you to enter without allowing the hot air to escape. During the winter season our castaways have found the contrivance useful, but Crichton's *brain was perhaps a little lordly when he conceived it. Another door leads by a passage to the sleeping-rooms of the house, which are all on the ground-floor, and to* Crichton's *work-room, where he is at this moment, and whither we should like to follow him, but in a play we may not, as it is out of sight. There is a large window space without a window, which, however, can be shuttered, and through this we have a view of cattle-sheds, fowl-pens, and a field of grain. It is a fine summer evening.*

Tweeny *is sitting there, very busy plucking the feathers off a bird and dropping them on a sheet placed for that purpose on the floor. She is trilling to herself in the lightness of her heart. We may remember that* Tweeny, *alone among the women, had dressed wisely for an island when they fled the yacht, and her going-away gown still adheres to her, though in fragments. A score of pieces have been added here and there as necessity compelled, and these have been patched and repatched in incongruous colors; but, when all is said and done, it can still be maintained that* Tweeny *wears a skirt. She is deservedly proud of her skirt, and sometimes lends it on important occasions when approached in the proper spirit.*

Some one outside has been whistling to Tweeny; *the guarded whistle which, on a less savage island, is sometimes assumed to be an indication to cook that the constable is willing, if the coast be clear.* Tweeny, *however, is engrossed, or perhaps she is not in the mood for a follower, so he climbs in at the window undaunted, to take her willy-nilly. He is a jolly-looking laboring man, who answers to the name of* Daddy, *and—— But though that may be his island name, we recognize him at once. He is* Lord Loam, *settled down to the new conditions, and enjoying life heartily as handyman about the happy home. He is comfortably attired in skins. He is still stout, but all the flabbiness has dropped from him; gone, too, is his pomposity; his eye is clear, brown his skin; he could leap a gate.*

In his hands he carries an island-made concertina, and such is the exuberance of his spirits that, as he lights on the floor, he bursts into music and song, something about his being a chickety chickety chick chick, and will Tweeny *please to tell him whose chickety chick is she. Retribution follows sharp. We hear a whir, as if from insufficiently oiled machinery, and over the passage door appears a placard showing the one word "Silence." His lordship stops, and steals to* Tweeny *on his tiptoes.*

LORD LOAM: I thought the Gov. was out.

TWEENY: Well, you see he ain't. And if he were to catch you here idling——

[*Lord Loam pales. He lays aside his musical instrument and hurriedly dons an apron.* Tweeny *gives him the bird to pluck, and busies herself laying the table for dinner*]

LORD LOAM: [*Softly*] What is he doing now?

TWEENY: I think he's working out that plan for laying on hot and cold.

LORD LOAM: [*Proud of his master*] And he'll manage it too. The man who could build a blacksmith's forge without tools——

TWEENY: [*Not less proud*] He made the tools.

LORD LOAM: Out of half a dozen rusty nails. The sawmill, Tweeny; the speaking-tube; the electric lighting; and look at the use he has made of the bits of the yacht that were washed ashore. And all in two years. He's a master I'm proud to pluck for.

[*He chirps happily at his work, and she regards him curiously*]

TWEENY: Daddy, you're of little use, but you're a bright, cheerful creature to have about the house. [*He beams at this commendation*] Do you ever think of old times now? We was a bit different.

LORD LOAM: [*Pausing*] Circumstances alter cases.

[*He resumes his plucking contentedly*]

TWEENY: But, Daddy, if the chance was to come of getting back?

LORD LOAM: I have given up bothering about it.

TWEENY: You bothered that day long ago when we saw a ship passing the island. How we all ran like crazy folk into the water, Daddy, and screamed and held out our arms. [*They are both a little agitated*] But it sailed away, and we've never seen another.

LORD LOAM: If we had had the electrical contrivance we have now we could have attracted that ship's notice. [*Their eyes rest on a mysterious apparatus that fills a corner of the hall*] A touch on that lever, Tweeny, and in a few moments bonfires would be blazing all round the shore.

TWEENY: [*Backing from the lever as if it might spring at her*] It's the most wonderful thing he has done.

LORD LOAM: [*In a reverie*] And then—England— home!

TWEENY: [*Also seeing visions*] London of a Saturday night!

LORD LOAM: My lords, in rising once more to address this historic chamber——

TWEENY: There was a little ham and beef shop off the Edgware Road——

[*The visions fade; they return to the practical*]

LORD LOAM: Tweeny, do you think I could have an egg to my tea?

[*At this moment a wiry, athletic figure in skins darkens the window. He is carrying two pails, which are suspended from a pole on his shoulder, and he is* Ernest. *We should say that he is* Ernest *completely changed if we were of those who hold that people change. As he enters by the window he has heard* Lord Loam's *appeal, and is perhaps justifiably indignant*]

ERNEST: What is that about an egg? Why should you have an egg?

LORD LOAM: [*With hauteur*] That is my affair, sir. [*With a Parthian shot as he withdraws stiffly from the room*] The Gov. has never put *my* head in a bucket.

ERNEST: [*Coming to rest on one of his buckets, and speaking with excusable pride. To* Tweeny] Nor mine for nearly three months. It was only last week, Tweeny, that he said to me, "Ernest, the water cure has worked marvels in you, and I question whether I shall require to dip you any more." [*Complacently*] Of course that sort of thing encourages a fellow.

TWEENY: [*Who has now arranged the dinner table to her satisfaction*] I will say, Erny, I never seen a young chap more improved.

ERNEST: [*Gratified*] Thank you, Tweeny; that's

very precious to me. [*She retires to the fire to work the great bellows with her foot, and* Ernest *turns to* Treherne, *who has come in looking more like a cowboy than a clergyman. He has a small box in his hand which he tries to conceal*] What have you got there, John?

TREHERNE: Don't tell anybody. It is a little present for the Gov.; a set of razors. One for each day in the week.

ERNEST: [*Opening the box and examining its contents*] Shells! He'll like that. He likes sets of things.

TREHERNE: [*In a guarded voice*] Have you noticed that?

ERNEST: Rather.

TREHERNE: He's becoming a bit magnificent in his ideas.

ERNEST: [*Huskily*] John, it sometimes gives me the creeps.

TREHERNE: [*Making sure that* Tweeny *is out of hearing*] What do you think of that brilliant robe he got the girls to make for him?

ERNEST: [*Uncomfortable*] I think he looks too regal in it.

TREHERNE: Regal! I sometimes fancy that that's why he's so fond of wearing it. [*Practically*] Well, I must take these down to the grindstone and put an edge on them.

ERNEST: [*Button-holing him*] I say, John, I want a word with you.

TREHERNE: Well?

ERNEST: [*Become suddenly diffident*] Dash it all, you know, you're a clergyman.

TREHERNE: One of the best things the Gov. has done is to insist that none of you forget it.

ERNEST: [*Taking his courage in his hands*] Then—would you, John?

TREHERNE: What?

ERNEST: [*Wistfully*] Officiate at a marriage ceremony, John?

TREHERNE: [*Slowly*] Now, that's really odd.

ERNEST: Odd? Seems to me it's natural. And whatever is natural, John, is right.

TREHERNE: I mean that same question has been put to me today already.

ERNEST: [*Eagerly*] By one of the women?

TREHERNE: Oh, no; they all put it to me long ago. This was by the Gov. himself.

ERNEST: By Jove! [*Admiringly*] I say, John, what an observant beggar he is.

TREHERNE: Ah! You fancy he was thinking of you?

ERNEST: I do not hesitate to affirm, John, that he has seen the love-light in my eyes. You answered——

TREHERNE: I said Yes, I thought it would be my duty to officiate if called upon.

ERNEST: You're a brick.

TREHERNE: [*Still pondering*] But I wonder whether he *was* thinking of you.

ERNEST: Make your mind easy about that.

TREHERNE: Well, my best wishes. Agatha is a very fine girl.

ERNEST: Agatha? What made you think it was Agatha?

TREHERNE: Man alive, you told me all about it soon after we were wrecked.

ERNEST: Pooh! Agatha's all very well in her way, John, but I'm flying after bigger game.

TREHERNE: Ernest, which is it?

ERNEST: Tweeny, of course.

TREHERNE: Tweeny? [*Reprovingly*] Ernest, I hope her cooking has nothing to do with this.

ERNEST: [*With dignity*] Her cooking has very little to do with it.

TREHERNE: But does she return your affection?

ERNEST: [*Simply*] Yes, John, I believe I may say so. I am unworthy of her, but I think I have touched her heart.

TREHERNE: [*With a sigh*] Some people seem to have all the luck. As you know, Catherine won't look at me.

ERNEST: I'm sorry, John.

TREHERNE: It's my deserts; I'm a second eleven sort of chap. Well, my heartiest good wishes, Ernest.

ERNEST: Thank you, John. How's the little black pig today?

TREHERNE: [*Departing*] He has begun to eat again.

[*After a moment's reflection* Ernest *calls to* Tweeny]

ERNEST: Are you very busy, Tweeny?

TWEENY: [*Coming to him good-naturedly*] There's always work to do; but if you want me, Ernest——

ERNEST: There's something I should like to say to you if you could spare me a moment.

TWEENY: Willingly. What is it?

ERNEST: What an ass I used to be, Tweeny.

TWEENY: [*Tolerantly*] Oh, let bygones be bygones.

ERNEST: [*Sincerely, and at his very best*] I'm no great shakes even now. But listen to this, Tweeny; I have known many women, but until I knew you I never knew any woman.

TWEENY: [*To whose uneducated ears this sounds dangerously like an epigram*] Take care—the bucket.

ERNEST: [*Hurriedly*] I didn't mean it in that way. [*He goes chivalrously on his knees*] Ah, Tweeny, I don't undervalue the bucket, but what I want to say now is that the sweet refinement of a dear girl has done more for me than any bucket could do.

TWEENY: [*With large eyes*] Are you offering to walk out with me, Erny?

ERNEST: [*Passionately*] More than that. I want to build a little house for you—in the sunny glade down by Porcupine Creek. I want to make chairs for you and tables; and knives and forks, and a sideboard for you.

TWEENY: [*Who is fond of language*] I like to hear you. [*Eyeing him*] Would there be any one in the house except myself, Ernest?

ERNEST: [*Humbly*] Not often; but just occasionally there would be your adoring husband.

TWEENY: [*Decisively*] It won't do, Ernest.

ERNEST: [*Pleading*] It isn't as if I should be much there.

TWEENY: I know, I know; but I don't love you, Ernest. I'm that sorry.

ERNEST: [*Putting his case clearly*] Twice a week I should be away altogether—at the dam. On the other days you would never see me from breakfast time to supper. [*With the self-abnegation of the true lover*] If you like I'll even go fishing on Sundays.

TWEENY: It's no use, Erny.

ERNEST: [*Rising manfully*] Thank you, Tweeny; it can't be helped. [*Then he remembers*] Tweeny, we shall be disappointing the Gov.

TWEENY: [*With a sinking*] What's that?

ERNEST: He wanted us to marry.

TWEENY: [*Blankly*] You and me? The Gov.! [*Her head droops woefully. From without is heard the whistling of a happier spirit, and* Tweeny *draws herself up fiercely*] That's her; that's the thing what has stolen his heart from me. [*A stalwart youth appears at the window, so handsome and tingling with vitality that, glad to depose* Crichton, *we cry thankfully, "The hero at last." But it is not the hero; it is the heroine. This splendid boy, clad in skins, is what Nature has done for* Lady Mary. *She carries bow and arrows and a blow-pipe, and over her shoulder is a fat buck, which she drops with a cry of triumph. Forgetting to enter demurely, she leaps through the window*] [*Sourly*] Drat you, Polly, why don't you wipe your feet?

LADY MARY: [*Good-naturedly*] Come, Tweeny, be nice to me. It's a splendid buck.

[*But* Tweeny *shakes her off, and retires to the kitchen fire*]

ERNEST: Where did you get it?

LADY MARY: [*Gaily*] I sighted a herd near Penguin's Creek, but had to creep round Silver Lake to get to windward of them. However, they spotted me and then the fun began. There was nothing for it but to try and run them down, so I singled out a fat buck and away we went down the shore of the lake, up the valley of rolling stones; he doubled into Brawling River and took to the water, but I swam after him; the river is only half a mile broad there, but it runs strong. He went spinning down the rapids, down I went in pursuit; he clambered ashore, I clambered ashore; away we tore helter-skelter up the hill and down again. I lost him in the marshes, got on his track again near Bread Fruit Wood, and brought him down with an arrow in Firefly Grove.

TWEENY: [*Staring at her*] Aren't you tired?

LADY MARY: Tired! It was gorgeous. [*She runs up a ladder and deposits her weapons on the joists. She is whistling again*]

TWEENY: [*Snapping*] I can't abide a woman whistling.

LADY MARY: [*Indifferently*] I like it.

TWEENY: [*Stamping her foot*] Drop it, Polly, I tell you.

LADY MARY: [*Stung*] I won't. I'm as good as you are. [*They are facing each other defiantly*]

ERNEST: [*Shocked*] Is this necessary? Think how it would pain *him.*

[*Lady Mary's eyes take a new expression. We see them soft for the first time*]

LADY MARY: [*Contritely*] Tweeny, I beg your pardon. If my whistling annoys you, I shall try to cure myself of it. [*Instead of calming* Tweeny, *this floods her face in tears*] Why, how can that hurt you, Tweeny, dear?

TWEENY: Because I can't make you lose your temper.

LADY MARY: [*Divinely*] Indeed, I often do. Would that I were nicer to everybody.

TWEENY: There you are again. [*Wistfully*] What makes you want to be so nice, Polly?

LADY MARY: [*With fervor*] Only thankfulness, Tweeny. [*She exults*] It is such fun to be alive.

[*So also seem to think* Catherine *and* Agatha, *who bounce in with fishing-rods and creel. They, too, are in manly attire*]

CATHERINE: We've got some ripping fish for the Gov.'s dinner. Are we in time? We ran all the way.

TWEENY: [*Tartly*] You'll please to cook them yourself, Kitty, and look sharp about it. [*She retires to her hearth, where* Agatha *follows her*]

AGATHA: [*Yearning*] Has the Gov. decided who is to wait upon him to-day?

CATHERINE: [*Who is cleaning her fish*] It's my turn.

AGATHA: [*Hotly*] I don't see that.

TWEENY: [*With bitterness*] It's to be neither of you, Aggy; he wants Polly again.

[*Lady Mary is unable to resist a joyous whistle*]

AGATHA: [*Jealously*] Polly, you toad.

[*But they cannot make* Lady Mary *angry*]

TWEENY: [*Storming*] How dare you look so happy?

LADY MARY: [*Willing to embrace her*] I wish, Tweeny, there was anything I could do to make you happy also.

TWEENY: Me! Oh, I'm happy. [*She remembers* Ernest, *whom it is easy to forget on an island*] I've just had a proposal, I tell you.

[*Lady Mary is shaken at last, and her sisters with her*]

AGATHA: A proposal?

CATHERINE: [*Going white*] Not—not—— [*She dare not say his name*]

ERNEST: [*With singular modesty*] You needn't be alarmed; it's only me.

LADY MARY: [*Relieved*] Oh, you!

AGATHA: [*Happy again*] Ernest, you dear, I got such a shock.

CATHERINE: It was only Ernest. [*Showing him her fish in thankfulness*] They are beautifully fresh; come and help me to cook them.

ERNEST: [*With simple dignity*] Do you mind if I don't cook fish to-night? [*She does not mind in the least. They have all forgotten him. A lark is singing in three hearts*] I think you might all be a little sorry for a chap. [*But they are not even sorry, and he addresses* Agatha *in these winged words:*] I'm particularly disappointed in you, Aggy; seeing that

I was half engaged to you, I think you might have had the good feeling to be a little more hurt.

AGATHA: Oh, bother.

ERNEST: [*Summing up the situation in so far as it affects himself*] I shall now go and lie down for a bit. [*He retires coldly but unregretted.* Lady Mary *approaches* Tweeny *with her most insinuating smile*]

LADY MARY: Tweeny, as the Gov. has chosen me to wait on him, please may I have the loan of it again?

[*The reference made with such charming delicacy is evidently to* Tweeny's *skirt*]

TWEENY: [*Doggedly*] No, you mayn't.

AGATHA: [*Supporting* Tweeny] Don't you give it to her.

LADY MARY: [*Still trying sweet persuasion*] You know quite well that he prefers to be waited on in a skirt.

TWEENY: I don't care. Get one for yourself.

LADY MARY: It is the only one on the island.

TWEENY: And it's mine.

LADY MARY: [*An aristocrat after all*] Tweeny, give me that skirt directly.

CATHERINE: Don't.

TWEENY: I won't.

LADY MARY: [*Clearing for action*] I shall make you.

TWEENY: I should like to see you try.

[*An unseemly fracas appears to be inevitable, but something happens. The whir is again heard, and the notice displayed "Dogs delight to bark and bite." Its effect is instantaneous and cheering. The ladies look at each other guiltily and immediately proceed on tiptoe to their duties. These are all concerned with the master's dinner.* Catherine *attends to his fish.* Agatha *fills a quaint toast-rack and brings the menu, which is written on a shell.* Lady Mary *twists a wreath of green leaves around her head, and places a flower beside the master's plate.* Tweeny *signs that all is ready, and she and the younger sisters retire into the kitchen, drawing the screen that separates it from the rest of the room.* Lady Mary *beats a tom-tom, which is the dinner bell. She then gently works a punkah, which we have not hitherto observed, and stands at attention. No doubt she is in hopes that the Gov. will enter into conversation with her, but she is too good a parlormaid to let her hopes appear in her face. We may watch her manner with complete approval. There is not one of us who would not give her £26 a year.*

The master comes in quietly, a book in his hand, still the only book on the island, for he has not thought it worth while to build a printing-press. His dress is not noticeably different from that of the others, the skins are similar, but perhaps these are a trifle more carefully cut or he carries them better. One sees somehow that he has changed for his evening meal.

There is an odd suggestion of a dinner jacket about his doeskin coat. It is, perhaps, too grave a face for a man of thirty-two, as if he were over much immersed in affairs, yet there is a sunny smile left to lighten it at times and bring back its youth; perhaps too intellectual a face to pass as strictly handsome, not sufficiently suggestive of oats. His tall figure is very straight, slight rather than thickset, but nobly muscular. His big hands, firm and hard with labor though they be, are finely shaped—note the fingers so much more tapered, the nails better tended than those of his domestics; they are one of many indications that he is of a superior breed. Such signs, as has often been pointed out, are infallible. A romantic figure, too. One can easily see why the women-folks of this strong man's house both adore and fear him.

He does not seem to notice who is waiting on him tonight, but inclines his head slightly to whoever it is, as she takes her place at the back of his chair. Lady Mary *respectfully places the menu-shell before him, and he glances at it*]

CRICHTON: Clear, please.

[Lady Mary *knocks on the screen, and a serving hutch in it opens, through which* Tweeny *offers two soup plates.* Lady Mary *selects the clear and the aperture is closed. She works the punkah while the master partakes of his soup*]

CRICHTON: [*Who always gives praise where it is due*] An excellent soup, Polly, but still a trifle too rich.

LADY MARY: Thank you.

[*The next course is the fish, and while it is being passed through the hutch we have a glimpse of three jealous women.* Lady Mary's *movements are so deft and noiseless that any observant spectator can see that she was born to wait at table*]

CRICHTON: [*Unbending as he eats*] Polly, you are a very smart girl.

LADY MARY: [*Bridling, but naturally gratified*] La!

CRICHTON: [*Smiling*] And I'm not the first you've heard it from, I'll swear.

LADY MARY: [*Wriggling*] Oh Gov.!

CRICHTON: Got any followers on the island, Polly?

LADY MARY: [*Tossing her head*] Certainly not.

CRICHTON: I thought that perhaps John or Ernest——

LADY MARY: [*Tilting her nose*] I don't say that it's for want of asking.

CRICHTON: [*Emphatically*] I'm sure it isn't. [*Perhaps he thinks he has gone too far*] You may clear.

[*Flushed with pleasure, she puts before him a bird and vegetables, sees that his beaker is filled with wine, and returns to the punkah. She would love to continue their conversation, but it is for him to decide. For a time he seems to have forgotten her*]

CRICHTON: Did you lose any arrows to-day?

LADY MARY: Only one in Firefly Grove.

CRICHTON: You were as far as that? How did you get across the Black Gorge?

LADY MARY: I went across on the rope.

CRICHTON: Hand over hand?

LADY MARY: [*Swelling at the implied praise*] I wasn't in the least dizzy.

CRICHTON: [*Moved*] You brave girl! [*He sits back in his chair a little agitated*] But never do that again.

LADY MARY: [*Pouting*] It is such fun, Gov.

CRICHTON: [*Decisively*] I forbid it.

LADY MARY: [*The little rebel*] I shall.

CRICHTON: [*Surprised*] Polly! [*He signs to her sharply to step forward, but for a moment she holds back petulantly, and even when she comes it is less obediently than like a naughty, sulky child. Nevertheless, with the forbearance that is characteristic of the man, he addresses her with grave gentleness rather than severely*] You must do as I tell you, you know.

LADY MARY: [*Strangely passionate*] I shan't.

CRICHTON: [*Smiling at her fury*] We shall see. Frown at me, Polly; there you do it at once. Clench your little fists, stamp your feet, bite your ribbons —— [*A student of women, or at least of this woman, he knows that she is about to do these things, and thus she seems to do them to order.* Lady Mary *screws up her face like a baby and cries. He is immediately kind*] You child of nature; was it cruel of me to wish to save you from harm?

LADY MARY: [*Drying her eyes*] I'm an ungracious wretch. Oh Gov., I don't try half hard enough to please you. I'm even wearing—— [*She looks down sadly*]—when I know you prefer *it*.

CRICHTON: [*Thoughtfully*] I admit I do prefer *it*. Perhaps I am a little old-fashioned in these matters. [*Her tears again threaten*] Ah, don't, Polly; that's nothing.

LADY MARY: If I could only please you, Gov.

CRICHTON: [*Slowly*] You do please me, child, very much—— [*He half rises*]—very much indeed. [*If he meant to say more he checks himself. He looks at his plate*] No more, thank you.

[*The simple island meal is ended, save for the walnuts and the wine, and* Crichton *is too busy a man to linger long over them. But he is a stickler for etiquette, and the table is cleared charmingly, though with dispatch, before they are placed before him.* Lady Mary *is an artist with the crumb-brush, and there are few arts more delightful to watch. Dusk has come sharply, and she turns on the electric light. It awakens* Crichton *from a reverie in which he has been regarding her*]

CRICHTON: Polly, there is only one thing about you that I don't quite like. [*She looks up, making a moue, if that can be said of one who so well knows her place. He explains*] That action of the hands.

LADY MARY: What do I do?

CRICHTON: So—like one washing them. I have noticed that the others tend to do it also. It seems odd.

LADY MARY: [*Archly*] Oh Gov., have you forgotten?

CRICHTON: What?

LADY MARY: That once upon a time a certain other person did that.

CRICHTON: [*Groping*] You mean myself? [*She nods, and he shudders*] Horrible!

LADY MARY: [*Afraid she has hurt him*] You haven't for a very long time. Perhaps it is natural to servants.

CRICHTON: That must be it. [*He rises*] Polly! [*She looks up expectantly, but he only sighs and turns away*]

LADY MARY: [*Gently*] You sighed, Gov.

CRICHTON: Did I? I was thinking. [*He paces the room and then turns to her agitatedly, yet with control over his agitation. There is some mournfulness in his voice*] I have always tried to do the right thing on this island. Above all, Polly, I want to do the right thing by you.

LADY MARY: [*With shining eyes*] How we all trust you. That is your reward, Gov.

CRICHTON: [*Who is having a fight with himself*] And now I want a greater reward. Is it fair to you? Am I playing the game? Bill Crichton would always like to play the game. If we were in England—— [*He pauses so long that she breaks in softly*]

LADY MARY: We know now that we shall never see England again.

CRICHTON: I am thinking of two people whom neither of us has seen for a long time—Lady Mary Lasenby, and one Crichton, a butler. [*He says the last word bravely, a word he once loved, though it is the most horrible of all words to him now*]

LADY MARY: That cold, haughty, insolent girl. Gov., look around you and forget them both.

CRICHTON: I had nigh forgotten them. He has had a chance, Polly,—that butler—in these two years of becoming a man, and he has tried to take it. There have been many failures, but there has been some success, and with it I have let the past drop off me, and turned my back on it. That butler seems a faraway figure to me now, and not myself. I hail him, but we scarcely know each other. If I am to bring him back it can only be done by force, for in my soul he is abhorrent to me. But if I thought it best for you I'd haul him back; I swear as an honest man, I would bring him back with all his obsequious ways and deferential airs, and let you see the man you call your Gov. melt forever into him who was your servant.

LADY MARY: [*Shivering*] You hurt me. You say these things, but you say them like a king. To me it is the past that was not real.

CRICHTON: [*Too grandly*] A king! I sometimes feel—— [*For a moment the yellow light gleams in his green eyes. We remember suddenly what Tre-*

herne *and* Ernest *said about his regal look. He checks himself*] I say it harshly, it is so hard to say, and all the time there is another voice within me crying—— [*He stops*]

LADY MARY: [*Trembling but not afraid*] If it is the voice of Nature——

CRICHTON: [*Strongly*] I know it to be the voice of Nature.

LADY MARY: [*In a whisper*] Then, if you want to say it very much, Gov., please say it to Polly Lasenby.

CRICHTON: [*Again in the grip of an idea*] A king! Polly, some people hold that the soul but leaves one human tenement for another, and so lives on through all the ages. I have occasionally thought of late that, in some past existence, I may have been a king. It has all come to me so naturally, not as if I had had to work it out, but—as—if—I—remembered.

> "Or ever the knightly years were gone,
> With the old world to the grave,
> I was a *king* in Babylon,
> And you were a Christian slave."

It may have been; you hear me, it may have been.

LADY MARY: [*Who is as one fascinated*] It may have been.

CRICHTON: I am lord over all. They are but hewers of wood and drawers of water for me. These shores are mine. Why should I hesitate; I have no longer any doubt. I do believe I am doing the right thing. Dear Polly, I have grown to love you; are you afraid to mate with me? [*She rocks her arms; no words will come from her*]

> "I was a king in Babylon,
> And you were a Christian slave."

LADY MARY: [*Bewitched*] You are the most wonderful man I have ever known, and I am not afraid. [*He takes her to him reverently. Presently he is seated, and she is at his feet looking up adoringly in his face. As the tension relaxes, she speaks with a smile*] I want you to tell me—every woman likes to know—when was the first time you thought me nicer than the others?

CRICHTON: [*Who like all big men is simple*] I think a year ago. We were chasing goats on the Big Slopes, and you out-distanced us all; you were the first of our party to run a goat down; I was proud of you that day.

LADY MARY: [*Blushing with pleasure*] Oh Gov., I only did it to please you. Everything I have done has been out of the desire to please you. [*Suddenly anxious*] If I thought that in taking a wife from among us you were imperilling your dignity——

CRICHTON: [*Perhaps a little masterful*] Have no fear of that, dear. I have thought it all out. The wife, Polly, always takes the same position as the husband.

LADY MARY: But I am so unworthy. It was sufficient to me that I should be allowed to wait on you at that table.

CRICHTON: You shall wait on me no longer. At whatever table I sit, Polly, you shall soon sit there, also. [*Boyishly*] Come, let us try what it will be like.

LADY MARY: As your servant at your feet.

CRICHTON: No, as my consort by my side.

[*They are sitting thus when the hatch is again opened and coffee offered. But Lady Mary is no longer there to receive it. Her sisters peep through in consternation. In vain they rattle the cup and saucer. Agatha brings the coffee to Crichton*]

CRICHTON: [*Forgetting for the moment that it is not a month hence*] Help your mistress first, girl. [*Three women are bereft of speech, but he does not notice it. He addresses Catherine vaguely*] Are you a good girl, Kitty?

CATHERINE: [*When she finds her tongue*] I try to be, Gov.

CRICHTON: [*Still more vaguely*] That's right.

[*He takes command of himself again, and signs to them to sit down. Ernest comes in cheerily, but finding Crichton here is suddenly weak. He subsides on a chair, wondering what has happened*]

CRICHTON: [*Surveying him*] Ernest. [*Ernest rises*] You are becoming a little slovenly in your dress, Ernest; I don't like it.

ERNEST: [*Respectfully*] Thank you.

[*Ernest sits again. Daddy and Treherne arrive*]

CRICHTON: Daddy, I want you.

LORD LOAM: [*With a sinking*] Is it because I forgot to clean out the dam?

CRICHTON: [*Encouragingly*] No, no. [*He pours some wine into a goblet*] A glass of wine with you, Daddy.

LORD LOAM: [*Hastily*] Your health, Gov. [*He is about to drink, but the master checks him*]

CRICHTON: And hers. Daddy, this lady has done me the honor to promise to be my wife.

LORD LOAM: [*Astounded*] Polly!

CRICHTON: [*A little perturbed*] I ought first to have asked your consent. I deeply regret—but Nature; may I hope I have your approval?

LORD LOAM: May you, Gov.? [*Delighted*] Rather! Polly! [*He puts his proud arms around her*]

TREHERNE: We all congratulate you, Gov., most heartily.

ERNEST: Long life to you both, sir.

[*There is much shaking of hands, all of which is sincere*]

TREHERNE: When will it be, Gov.?

CRICHTON: [*After turning to* Lady Mary, *who whispers to him*] As soon as the bridal skirt can be prepared. [*His manner has been most indulgent, and without the slightest sign of patronage. But he knows it is best for all that he should keep his place, and that his presence hampers them*] My friends, I thank you for your good wishes, I thank you all. And now, perhaps you would like me to leave you to yourselves. Be joyous. Let there be song and dance tonight. Polly, I shall take my coffee in the Parlor—you understand.

[*He retires with pleasant dignity. Immediately there is a rush of two girls at* Lady Mary]

LADY MARY: Oh, oh! Father, they are pinching me.

LORD LOAM: [*Taking her under his protection*] Agatha, Catherine, never presume to pinch your sister again. On the other hand, she may pinch you henceforth as much as ever she chooses.

[*In the meantime* Tweeny *is weeping softly, and the two are not above using her as a weapon*]

CATHERINE: Poor Tweeny. It's a shame.

AGATHA: After he had almost promised *you*.

TWEENY: [*Loyally turning on them*] No, he never did. He was always honorable as could be. 'Twas me as was too vulgar. Don't you dare say a word agin that man.

ERNEST: [*To* Lord Loam] You'll get a lot of tidbits out of this, Daddy.

LORD LOAM: That's what I was thinking.

ERNEST: [*Plunged in thought*] I dare say *I* shall have to clean out the dam now.

LORD LOAM: [*Heartlessly*] I dare say. [*His gay old heart makes him again proclaim that he is a chickety chick. He seizes the concertina*]

TREHERNE: [*Eagerly*] That's the proper spirit.

[*He puts his arm around* Catherine, *and in another moment they are all dancing to Daddy's music. Never were people happier on an island. A moment's pause is presently created by the return of* Crichton *wearing the wonderful robe of which we have already had dark mention. Never has he looked more regal, never perhaps felt so regal. We need not grudge him the one foible of his rule, for it is all coming to an end*]

CRICHTON: [*Graciously, seeing them hesitate*] No, no; I am delighted to see you all so happy. Go on.

TREHERNE: We don't like to before you, Gov.

CRICHTON: [*His last order*] It is my wish.

[*The merrymaking is resumed, and soon* Crichton *himself joins in the dance. It is when the fun is at its fastest and most furious that all stop abruptly as if turned to stone. They have heard the boom of a gun. Presently they are alive again.* Ernest *leaps to the window*]

TREHERNE: [*Huskily*] It was a ship's gun. [*They turn to* Crichton *for confirmation; even in that hour they turn to* Crichton] Gov.?

CRICHTON: Yes.

[*In another moment* Lady Mary *and* Lord Loam *are alone*]

LADY MARY: [*Seeing that her father is unconcerned*] Father, you heard.

LORD LOAM: [*Placidly*] Yes, my child.

LADY MARY: [*Alarmed by his unnatural calmness*] But it was a gun, father.

LORD LOAM: [*Looking an old man now, and shuddering a little*] Yes—a gun—I have often heard it. It's only a dream, you know; why don't we go on dancing?

[*She takes his hands, which have gone cold*]

LADY MARY: Father. Don't you see, they have all rushed down to the beach? Come.

LORD LOAM: Rushed down to the beach; yes, always that—I often dream it.

LADY MARY: Come, father, come.

LORD LOAM: Only a dream, my poor girl.

[Crichton *returns. He is pale but firm*]

CRICHTON: We can see lights within a mile of the shore—a great ship.

LORD LOAM: A ship—always a ship.

LADY MARY: Father, this is no dream.

LORD LOAM: [*Looking timidly at* Crichton] It's a dream, isn't it? There's no ship?

CRICHTON: [*Soothing him with a touch*] You are awake, Daddy, and there is a ship.

LORD LOAM: [*Clutching him*] You are not deceiving me?

CRICHTON: It is the truth.

LORD LOAM: [*Reeling*] True?—a ship—at last! [*He goes after the others pitifully*]

CRICHTON: [*Quietly*] There is a small boat between it and the island; they must have sent it ashore for water.

LADY MARY: Coming in?

CRICHTON: No. That gun must have been a signal to recall it. It is going back. They can't hear our cries.

LADY MARY: [*Pressing her temples*] Going away. So near—so near. [*Almost to herself*] I think I'm glad.

CRICHTON: [*Cheerily*] Have no fear. I shall bring them back. [*He goes towards the table on which is the electrical apparatus*]

LADY MARY: [*Standing on guard as it were between him and the table*] What are you going to do?

CRICHTON: To fire the beacons.

LADY MARY: Stop! [*She faces him*] Don't you see what it means?

CRICHTON: [*Firmly*] It means that our life on the island has come to a natural end.

LADY MARY: [*Huskily*] Gov., let the ship go.

CRICHTON: The old man—you saw what it means to him.

LADY MARY: But I am afraid.

CRICHTON: [*Adoringly*] Dear Polly.

LADY MARY: Gov., let the ship go.

CRICHTON: [*She clings to him, but though it is his death sentence he loosens her hold*] Bill Crichton has got to play the game. [*He pulls the levers. Soon through the window one of the beacons is seen flaring red. There is a long pause. Shouting is heard.* Ernest *is the first to arrive*]

ERNEST: Polly, Gov., the boat has turned back. They are English sailors; they have landed! We are rescued. I tell you, rescued!

LADY MARY: [*Wanly*] Is it anything to make so great a to-do about?

ERNEST: [*Staring*] Eh?

LADY MARY: Have we not been happy here?

ERNEST: Happy? lord, yes.

LADY MARY: [*Catching hold of his sleeve*] Ernest,

we must never forget all that the Gov. has done for us.

ERNEST: [*Stoutly*] Forget it? The man who could forget it would be a selfish wretch and a—— But I say, this makes a difference!

LADY MARY: [*Quickly*] No, it doesn't.

ERNEST: [*His mind tottering*] A mighty difference! [*The others come running in, some weeping with joy, others boisterous. We see blue-jackets gazing through the window at the curious scene. Lord Loam comes accompanied by a naval officer, whom he is continually shaking by the hand*]

LORD LOAM: And here, sir, is our little home. Let me thank you again in the names of all of us, again and again and again.

OFFICER: Very proud, my lord. It is indeed an honor to have been able to assist so distinguished a gentleman as Lord Loam.

LORD LOAM: A glorious, glorious day. I shall show you our other room. Come, my pets. Come, Crichton. [*He has not meant to be cruel. He does not know he has said it. It is the old life that has come back to him. They all go. All leave Crichton except Lady Mary*]

LADY MARY: [*Stretching out her arms to him*] Dear Gov., I will never give you up.

[*There is a salt smile on his face as he shakes his head to her. He lets the cloak slip to the ground. She will not take this for an answer; again her arms go out to him. Then comes the great renunciation. By an effort of will he ceases to be an erect figure; he has the humble bearing of a servant. His hands come together as if he were washing them*]

CRICHTON: [*It is the speech of his life*] My lady. [*She goes away. There is none to salute him now, unless we do it*]

END OF ACT III

ACT IV.

Some months has elapsed, and we have again the honor of waiting upon Lord Loam in his London home. It is the room of the first act, but with a new scheme of decoration, for on the walls are exhibited many interesting trophies from the island, such as skins, stuffed birds, and weapons of the chase, labelled "Shot by Lord Loam," "Hon. Ernest Woolley's Blowpipe," etc. There are also two large glass cases containing other odds and ends, including, curiously enough, the bucket in which Ernest was first dipped, but there is no label calling attention to the incident.

It is not yet time to dress for dinner, and his lordship is on a couch, hastily yet furtively cutting the pages of a new book. With him are his two younger daughters and his nephew, and they also are engaged in literary pursuits; that is to say, the ladies are eagerly but furtively reading the evening papers, of which Ernest is sitting complacently but furtively on an endless number, and doling them out as called for. Note the frequent use of the word "furtive." It implies that they do not wish to be discovered by their butler, say, at their otherwise delightful task.

AGATHA: [*Reading aloud, with emphasis on the wrong words*] "In conclusion, we must heartily congratulate the Hon. Ernest Woolley. This book of his, regarding the adventures of himself and his brave companions on a desert isle, stirs the heart like a trumpet."

[*Evidently the book referred to is the one in Lord Loam's hands*]

ERNEST: [*Handing her a pink paper*] Here is another.

CATHERINE: [*Reading*] "From the first to the last of Mr. Woolley's engrossing pages it is evident that he was an ideal man to be wrecked with, and a true hero." [*Large-eyed*] Ernest!

ERNEST: [*Calmly*] That's how it strikes *them*, you know. Here's another one.

AGATHA: [*Reading*] "There are many kindly references to the two servants who were wrecked with the family, and Mr. Woolley pays the butler a glowing tribute in a footnote."

[*Some one coughs uncomfortably*]

LORD LOAM: [*Who has been searching the index for the letter L*] Excellent, excellent. At the same time I must say, Ernest, that the whole book is about yourself.

ERNEST: [*Genially*] As the author——

LORD LOAM: Certainly, certainly. Still, you know, as a peer of the realm—— [*With dignity*] ——I think, Ernest, you might have given me one of your adventures.

ERNEST: I say it was you who taught us how to obtain a fire by rubbing two pieces of stick together.

LORD LOAM: [*Beaming*] Do you, do you? I call that very handsome. What page?

[*Here the door opens, and the well-bred Crichton enters with the evening papers as subscribed for by the house. Those we have already seen have perhaps been introduced by Ernest up his waistcoat. Every one except the intruder is immediately self-conscious, and when he withdraws there is a general sigh of relief. They pounce on the new papers. Ernest evidently gets a shock from one, which he casts contemptuously on the floor*]

AGATHA: [*More fortunate*] Father, see page 81. "It was a tiger-cat," says Mr. Woolley, "of the largest size. Death stared Lord Loam in the face, but he never flinched."

LORD LOAM: [*Searching his book eagerly*] Page 81.

AGATHA: "With presence of mind only equalled by his courage, he fixed an arrow in his bow."

LORD LOAM: Thank you, Ernest; thank you my boy.

AGATHA: "Unfortunately he missed."

LORD LOAM: Eh?

AGATHA: "But by great good luck I heard his cries——"

LORD LOAM: My cries?

AGATHA: "——and rushing forward with drawn knife, I stabbed the monster to the heart."

[Lord Loam *shuts his book with a pettish slam. There might be a scene here were it not that* Crichton *reappears and goes to one of the glass cases. All are at once on the alert, and his lordship is particularly sly*]

LORD LOAM: Anything in the papers, Catherine?

CATHERINE: No, father, nothing—nothing at all.

ERNEST: [*It pops out as of yore*] The papers! The papers are guides that tell us what we ought to do, and then we don't do it.

[Crichton *having opened the glass case has taken out the bucket, and* Ernest, *looking round for applause, sees him carrying it off and is undone. For a moment of time he forgets that he is no longer on the island, and with a sigh he is about to follow* Crichton *and the bucket to a retired spot. The door closes, and* Ernest *comes to himself*]

LORD LOAM: [*Uncomfortably*] I told him to take it away.

ERNEST: I thought—— [*He wipes his brow*] ——I shall go and dress. [*He goes*]

CATHERINE: Father, it's awful having Crichton here. It's like living on tiptoe.

LORD LOAM: [*Gloomily*] While he is here we are sitting on a volcano.

AGATHA: How mean of you! I am sure he has only stayed on with us to—to help us through. It would have looked so suspicious if he had gone at once.

CATHERINE: [*Revelling in the worst*] But suppose Lady Brocklehurst were to get at him and pump him. She's the most terrifying, suspicious old creature in England; and Crichton simply can't tell a lie.

LORD LOAM: My dear, that is the volcano to which I was referring. [*He has evidently something to communicate*] It's all Mary's fault. She said to me yesterday that she would break her engagement with Brocklehurst unless I told him about—you know what.

[*All conjure up the vision of* Crichton]

AGATHA: Is she mad?

LORD LOAM: She calls it common honesty.

CATHERINE: Father, have you told him?

LORD LOAM: [*Heavily*] She thinks I have, but I couldn't. She's sure to find out to-night.

[*Unconsciously he leans on the island concertina, which he has perhaps been lately showing to an interviewer as something he made for* Tweeny. *It squeaks, and they all jump*]

CATHERINE: It's like a bird of ill-omen.

LORD LOAM: [*Vindictively*] I must have it taken away; it has done that twice.

[Lady Mary *comes in. She is in evening dress.*

Undoubtedly she meant to sail in, but she forgets, and despite her garments it is a manly entrance. She is properly ashamed of herself. She tries again, and has an encouraging success. She indicates to her sisters that she wishes to be alone with papa]

AGATHA: All right, but we know what it's about. Come along, Kit.

[*They go.* Lady Mary *thoughtlessly sits like a boy, and again corrects herself. She addresses her father, but he is in a brown study, and she seeks to draw his attention by whistling. This troubles them both*]

LADY MARY: How horrid of me!

LORD LOAM: [*Depressed*] If you would try to remember——

LADY MARY: [*Sighing*] I do; but there are so many things to remember.

LORD LOAM: [*Sympathetically*] There are—— [*In a whisper*] Do you know, Mary, I constantly find myself secreting hairpins.

LADY MARY: I find it so difficult to go up steps one at a time.

LORD LOAM: I was dining with half dozen members of our party last Thursday, Mary, and they were so eloquent that I couldn't help wondering all the time how many of their heads *he* would have put in the bucket.

LADY MARY: I use so many of his phrases. And my appetite is so scandalous. Father, I usually have a chop before we sit down to dinner.

LORD LOAM: As for my clothes—[*Wriggling*] My dear, you can't think how irksome collars are to me nowadays.

LADY MARY: They can't be half such an annoyance, father, as——

[*She looks dolefully at her skirt*]

LORD LOAM: [*Hurriedly*] Quite so—quite so. You have dressed early tonight, Mary.

LADY MARY: That reminds me; I had a note from Brocklehurst saying he would come a few minutes before his mother as—as he wanted to have a talk with me. He didn't say what about, but of course we know. [*His lordship fidgets*] [*With feeling*] It was good of you to tell him, father. Oh, it is horrible to me—— [*Covering her face*] It seemed so natural at the time.

LORD LOAM: [*Petulantly*] Never again make use of that word in this house, Mary.

LADY MARY: [*With an effort*] Father, Brocklehurst has been so loyal to me for these two years that I should despise myself were I to keep my—my extraordinary lapse from him. Had Brocklehurst been a little less good, then you need not have told him my strange little secret.

LORD LOAM: [*Weakly*] Polly—I mean Mary—it was all Crichton's fault, he——

LADY MARY: [*With decision*] No, father, no; not a word against him though. I haven't the pluck to go on with it; I can't even understand how it ever was

Father, do you not still hear the surf? Do you see the curve of the beach?

LORD LOAM: I have begun to forget—— [*In a low voice*] But they were happy days; there was something magical about them.

LADY MARY: It was glamour. Father, I have lived Arabian nights. I have sat out a dance with the evening star. But it was all in a past existence, in the days of Babylon, and I am myself again. But he has been chivalrous always. If the slothful, indolent creature I used to be has improved in any way, I owe it all to him. I am slipping back in many ways, but I am determined not to slip back altogether—in memory of him and his island. That is why I insisted on your telling Brocklehurst. He can break our engagement if he chooses. [*Proudly*] Mary Lasenby is going to play the game.

LORD LOAM: But my dear——

[*Lord Brocklehurst is announced*]

LADY MARY: [*Meaningly*] Father, dear, oughtn't you to be dressing?

LORD LOAM: [*Very unhappy*] The fact is—before I go—I want to say——

LORD BROCKLEHURST: Loam, if you don't mind, I wish very specially to have a word with Mary before dinner.

LORD LOAM: But——

LADY MARY: Yes, father. [*She induces him to go, and thus courageously faces* Lord Brocklehurst *to hear her fate*] I am ready, George.

LORD BROCKLEHURST: [*Who is so agitated that she ought to see he is thinking not of her but of himself*] It is a painful matter—I wish I could have spared you this, Mary.

LADY MARY: Please go on.

LORD BROCKLEHURST: In common fairness, of course, this should be remembered, that two years had elapsed. You and I had no reason to believe that we should ever meet again.

[*This is more considerate than she had expected*]

LADY MARY: [*Softening*] I was so lost to the world, George.

LORD BROCKLEHURST: [*With a groan*] At the same time, the thing is utterly and absolutely inexcusable.

LADY MARY: [*Recovering her hauteur*] Oh!

LORD BROCKLEHURST: And so I have already said to mother.

LADY MARY: [*Disdaining him*] You have told her?

LORD BROCKLEHURST: Certainly, Mary, certainly; I tell mother everything.

LADY MARY: [*Curling her lips*] And what did she say?

LORD BROCKLEHURST: To tell the truth, mother rather pooh-poohed the whole affair.

LADY MARY: [*Incredulous*] Lady Brocklehurst pooh-poohed the whole affair!

LORD BROCKLEHURST: She said, "Mary and I will have a good laugh over this."

LADY MARY: [*Outraged*] George, your mother is a hateful, depraved old woman.

LORD BROCKLEHURST: Mary!

LADY MARY: [*Turning away*] Laugh indeed, when it will always be such a pain to me.

LORD BROCKLEHURST: [*With strange humility*] If only you would let me bear all the pain, Mary.

LADY MARY: [*Who is taken aback*] George, I think you are the noblest man—— [*She is touched, and gives him both her hands. Unfortunately he simpers*]

LORD BROCKLEHURST: She was a pretty little thing. [*She stares, but he marches to his doom*] Ah, not beautiful like you. I assure you it was the merest flirtation; there were a few letters, but we have got them back. It was all owing to the boat being so late at Calais. You see she had such large, helpless eyes.

LADY MARY: [*Fixing him*] George, when you lunched with father to-day at the club——

LORD BROCKLEHURST: I didn't. He wired me that he couldn't come.

LADY MARY: [*With a tremor*] But he wrote you?

LORD BROCKLEHURST: No.

LADY MARY: [*A bird singing in her breast*] You haven't seen him since?

LORD BROCKLEHURST: No.

[*She is saved. Is he to be let off also? Not at all. She bears down on him like a ship of war*]

LADY MARY: George, who and what is this woman?

LORD BROCKLEHURST: [*Cowering*] She was—she is—the shame of it—a lady's-maid.

LADY MARY: [*Properly horrified*] A what?

LORD BROCKLEHURST: A lady's-maid. A mere servant, Mary. [Lady Mary *whirls round so that he shall not see her face*] I first met her at this house when you were entertaining the servants; so you see it was largely your father's fault.

LADY MARY: [*Looking him up and down*] A lady's-maid?

LORD BROCKLEHURST: [*Degraded*] Her name was Fisher.

LADY MARY: My maid!

LORD BROCKLEHURST: [*With open hands*] Can you forgive me, Mary?

LADY MARY: Oh George, George!

LORD BROCKLEHURST: Mother urged me not to tell you anything about it; but——

LADY MARY: [*From her heart*] I am so glad you told me.

LORD BROCKLEHURST: You see there was nothing wrong in it.

LADY MARY: [*Thinking perhaps of another incident*] No, indeed.

LORD BROCKLEHURST: [*Inclined to simper again*] And she behaved awfully well. She quite saw that it was because the boat was late. I suppose the glamor to a girl in service of a man in high position——

LADY MARY: Glamor!—yes, yes, that was it.

LORD BROCKLEHURST: Mother says that a girl in such circumstances is to be excused if she loses her head.

LADY MARY: [*Impulsively*] George, I am so sorry

if I said anything against your mother. I am sure she is the dearest old thing.

LORD BROCKLEHURST: [*In calm waters at last*] Of course for women of our class she has a very different standard.

LADY MARY: [*Grown tiny*] Of course.

LORD BROCKLEHURST: You see, knowing how good a woman she is herself, she was naturally anxious that I should marry some one like her. That is what has made her watch your conduct so jealously, Mary.

LADY MARY: [*Hurriedly thinking things out*] I know. I—I think, George, that before your mother comes I should like to say a word to father.

LORD BROCKLEHURST: [*Nervously*] About this?

LADY MARY: Oh no; I shan't tell him of this. About something else.

LORD BROCKLEHURST: And you do forgive me, Mary?

LADY MARY: [*Smiling on him*] Yes, yes. I—I am sure the boat was *very* late, George.

LORD BROCKLEHURST: [*Earnestly*] It really was.

LADY MARY: I am even relieved to know that you are not quite perfect, dear. [*She rests her hands on his shoulders. She has a moment of contrition*] George, when we are married, we shall try to be not an entirely frivolous couple, won't we? We must endeavour to be of some little use, dear.

LORD BROCKLEHURST: [*The ass*] Noblesse oblige.

LADY MARY: [*Haunted by the phrases of a better man*] Mary Lasenby is determined to play the game, George.

[*Perhaps she adds to herself, "Except just this once." A kiss closes this episode of the two lovers; and soon after the departure of* Lady Mary *the* Countess of Brocklehurst *is announced. She is a very formidable old lady*]

LADY BROCKLEHURST: Alone, George?

LORD BROCKLEHURST: Mother, I told her all; she has behaved magnificently.

LADY BROCKLEHURST: [*Who has not shared his fears*] Silly boy. [*She casts a supercilious eye on the island trophies*] So these are the wonders they brought back with them. Gone away to dry her eyes, I suppose?

LORD BROCKLEHURST: [*Proud of his mate*] She didn't cry, mother.

LADY BROCKLEHURST: No? [*She reflects*] You're quite right. I wouldn't have cried. Cold, icy. Yes, that was it.

LORD BROCKLEHURST: [*Who has not often contradicted her*] I assure you, mother, that wasn't it at all. She forgave me at once.

LADY BROCKLEHURST: [*Opening her eyes sharply to the full*] Oh!

LORD BROCKLEHURST: She was awfully nice about the boat being late; she even said she was relieved to find that I wasn't quite perfect.

LADY BROCKLEHURST: [*Pouncing*] She said that?

LORD BROCKLEHURST: She really did.

LADY BROCKLEHURST: I mean *I* wouldn't. Now if *I* had said that, what would have made me say it? [*Suspiciously*] George, is Mary all we think her?

LORD BROCKLEHURST: [*With unexpected spirit*] If she wasn't, Mother, you would know it.

LADY BROCKLEHURST: Hold your tongue, boy. We don't really know what happened on that island.

LORD BROCKLEHURST: You were reading the book all the morning.

LADY BROCKLEHURST: How can I be sure that the book is true?

LORD BROCKLEHURST: They all talk of it as true.

LADY BROCKLEHURST: How do I know that they are not lying?

LORD BROCKLEHURST: Why should they lie?

LADY BROCKLEHURST: Why shouldn't they? [*She reflects again*] If I had been wrecked on an island, I think it highly probable that I should have lied when I came back. Weren't some of the servants with them?

LORD BROCKLEHURST: Crichton, the butler. [*He is surprised to see her ring the bell*] Why, Mother, you are not going to——

LADY BROCKLEHURST: Yes, I am. [*Pointedly*] George, watch whether Crichton begins any of his answers to my questions with "The fact is."

LORD BROCKLEHURST: Why?

LADY BROCKLEHURST: Because that is usually the beginning of a lie.

LORD BROCKLEHURST: [*As* Crichton *opens the door*] Mother, you can't do these things in other people's houses.

LADY BROCKLEHURST: [*Coolly, to* Crichton] It was I who rang. [*Surveying him through her eyeglass*] So you were one of the castaways, Crichton?

CRICHTON: Yes, my lady.

LADY BROCKLEHURST: Delightful book Mr. Woolley has written about your adventures. [*Crichton bows*] Don't you think so?

CRICHTON: I have not read it, my lady.

LADY BROCKLEHURST: Odd that they should not have presented you with a copy.

LORD BROCKLEHURST: Presumably Crichton is no reader.

LADY BROCKLEHURST: By the way, Crichton, were there any books on the island?

CRICHTON: I had one, my lady—Henley's poems.

LORD BROCKLEHURST: Never heard of him.

[*Crichton again bows*]

LADY BROCKLEHURST: [*Who has not heard of him either*] I think you were not the only servant wrecked?

CRICHTON: There was a young woman, my lady.

LADY BROCKLEHURST: I want to see her. [*Crichton bows, but remains*] Fetch her up. [*He goes*]

LORD BROCKLEHURST: [*Almost standing up to his mother*] This is scandalous.

LADY BROCKLEHURST: [*Defining her position*] I am a mother. [*Catherine and Agatha enter in dazzling confections and quake in secret to find themselves practically alone with* Lady Brocklehurst] [*Even as she greets them*] How d'you do, Catherine—Agatha?

You didn't dress like this on the island, I expect! By the way, how did you dress?

[*They have thought themselves prepared, but——*]

AGATHA: Not—so well, of course, but quite the same idea.

[*They are relieved by the arrival of* Treherne, *who is in clerical dress*]

LADY BROCKLEHURST: How do you do, Mr. Treherne? There is not so much of you in the book as I had hoped.

TREHERNE: [*Modestly*] There wasn't very much of me on the island, Lady Brocklehurst.

LADY BROCKLEHURST: How d'ye mean?

[*He shrugs his modest shoulders*]

LORD BROCKLEHURST: I hear you have got a living, Treherne. Congratulations.

TREHERNE: Thanks.

LORD BROCKLEHURST: Is it a good one?

TREHERNE: So-so. They are rather weak in bowling, but it's a good bit of turf.

[*Confidence is restored by the entrance of* Ernest, *who takes in the situation promptly, and, of course, knows he is a match for any old lady*]

ERNEST: [*With ease*] How do you do, Lady Brocklehurst.

LADY BROCKLEHURST: Our brilliant author!

ERNEST: [*Impervious to satire*] Oh, I don't know.

LADY BROCKLEHURST: It is as engrossing, Mr. Woolley, as if it were a work of fiction.

ERNEST: [*Suddenly uncomfortable*] Thanks, awfully. [*Recovering*] The fact is—— [*He is puzzled by seeing the Brocklehurst family exchange meaning looks*]

CATHERINE: [*To the rescue*] Lady Brocklehurst, Mr. Treherne and I—we are engaged.

AGATHA: And Ernest and I.

LADY BROCKLEHURST: [*Grimly*] I see, my dears; thought it wise to keep the island in the family.

[*An awkward moment this for the entrance of* Lord Loam *and* Lady Mary, *who, after a private talk upstairs, are feeling happy and secure*]

LORD LOAM: [*With two hands for his distinguished guest*] Aha! ha, ha! younger than any of them, Emily.

LADY BROCKLEHURST: Flatterer. [*To* Lady Mary] You seem in high spirits, Mary.

LADY MARY: [*Gaily*] I am.

LADY BROCKLEHURST: [*With a significant glance at* Lord Brocklehurst] After——

LADY MARY: I—I mean. The fact is——

[*Again that disconcerting glance between the countess and her son*]

LORD LOAM: [*Humorously*] She hears wedding bells, Emily, ha, ha!

LADY BROCKLEHURST: [*Coldly*] Do you, Mary? Can't say I do; but I'm hard of hearing.

LADY MARY: [*Instantly her match*] If you don't, Lady Brocklehurst, I'm sure I don't.

LORD LOAM: [*Nervously*] Tut, tut. Seen our curios from the island, Emily; I should like you to examine them.

LADY BROCKLEHURST: Thank you, Henry. I am glad you say that, for I have just taken the liberty of asking two of them to step upstairs.

[*There is an uncomfortable silence, which the entrance of* Crichton *and* Tweeny *does not seem to dissipate.* Crichton *is impenetrable, but* Tweeny *hangs back in fear*]

LORD BROCKLEHURST: [*Stoutly*] Loam, I have no hand in this.

LADY BROCKLEHURST: [*Undisturbed*] Pooh, what have I done? You always begged me to speak to the servants, Henry, and I merely wanted to discover whether the views you used to hold about equality were adopted on the island; it seemed a splendid opportunity, but Mr. Woolley has not a word on the subject.

[*All eyes turn on* Ernest]

ERNEST: [*With confidence*] The fact is—— [*The fatal words again*]

LORD LOAM: [*Not quite certain what he is to assure her of*] I assure you, Emily——

LADY MARY: [*Cold as steel*] Father, nothing whatever happened on the island of which I, for one, am ashamed, and I hope Crichton will be allowed to answer Lady Brocklehurst's questions.

LADY BROCKLEHURST: To be sure. There's nothing to make a fuss about, and we're a family party. [*To* Crichton] Now, truthfully, my man.

CRICHTON: [*Calmly*] I promise that, my lady.

[*Some hearts sink, the hearts that could never understand a* Crichton]

LADY BROCKLEHURST: [*Sharply*] Well, were you all equal on the island?

CRICHTON: No, my lady. I think I may say there was as little equality there as elsewhere.

LADY BROCKLEHURST: All the social distinctions were preserved?

CRICHTON: As at home, my lady.

LADY BROCKLEHURST: The servants?

CRICHTON: They had to keep their place.

LADY BROCKLEHURST: Wonderful. How was it managed? [*With an inspiration*] You, girl, tell me that?

[*Can there be a more critical moment?*]

TWEENY: [*In agony*] If you please, my lady, it was all the Gov.'s doing.

[*They give themselves up for lost.* Lord Loam *tries to sink out of sight*]

CRICHTON: In the regrettable slang of the servants' hall, my lady, the master is usually referred to as the Gov.

LADY BROCKLEHURST: I see. [*She turns to* Lord Loam] You——

LORD LOAM: [*Reappearing*] Yes, I understand that is what they call me.

LADY BROCKLEHURST: [*To* Crichton] You didn't even take your meals with the family?

CRICHTON: No, my lady, I dined apart.

[*Is all safe?*]

LADY BROCKLEHURST: [*Alas*] You, girl, also? Did you dine with Crichton?

TWEENY: [*Scared*] No, your ladyship.

LADY BROCKLEHURST: [*Fastening on her*] With whom?

TWEENY: I took my bit of supper with—with Daddy and Polly and the rest.

[*Væ victis*]

ERNEST: [*Leaping into the breach*] Dear old Daddy —he was our monkey. You remember our monkey, Agatha?

AGATHA: Rather! What a funny old darling he was.

CATHERINE: [*Thus encouraged*] And don't you think Polly was the sweetest little parrot, Mary?

LADY BROCKLEHURST: Ah! I understand; animals you had domesticated?

LORD LOAM: [*Heavily*] Quite so—quite so.

LADY BROCKLEHURST: The servants' teas that used to take place here once a month——

CRICHTON: They did not seem natural on the island, my lady, and were discontinued by the Gov.'s orders.

LORD BROCKLEHURST: A clear proof, Loam, that they were a mistake here.

LORD LOAM: [*Seeing the opportunity for a diversion*] I admit it frankly. I abandon them. Emily, as the result of our experiences on the island, I think of going over to the Tories.

LADY BROCKLEHURST: I am delighted to hear it.

LORD LOAM: [*Expanding*] Thank you, Crichton, thank you; that is all. [*He motions to them to go, but the time is not yet*]

LADY BROCKLEHURST: One moment. [*There is a universal but stifled groan*] Young people, Crichton, will be young people, even on an island; now, I suppose there was a certain amount of—shall we say sentimentalizing, going on?

CRICHTON: Yes, my lady, there was.

LORD BROCKLEHURST: [*Ashamed*] Mother!

LADY BROCKLEHURST: [*Disregarding him*] Which gentleman? [*To* Tweeny] You, girl, tell me.

TWEENY: [*Confused*] If you please, my lady——

ERNEST: [*Hurriedly*] The fact is—— [*He is checked as before, and probably says "D——n" to himself, but he has saved the situation*]

TWEENY: [*Gasping*] It was him—Mr. Ernest, your ladyship.

LADY BROCKLEHURST: [*Counsel for the prosecution*] With which lady?

AGATHA: I have already told you, Lady Brocklehurst, that Ernest and I——

LADY BROCKLEHURST: Yes, *now;* but you were two years on the island. [*Looking at* Lady Mary] Was it this lady?

TWEENY: No, your ladyship.

LADY BROCKLEHURST: Then I don't care which of the others it was. [*Tweeny* gurgles] Well, I suppose that will do.

LORD BROCKLEHURST: Do! I hope you are ashamed of yourself, mother. [*To* Crichton, *who is going*] You are an excellent fellow, Crichton; and if, after we are married, you ever wish to change your place, come to us.

LADY MARY: [*Losing her head for the only time*] Oh no, impossible.

LADY BROCKLEHURST: [*At once suspicious*] Why impossible? [Lady Mary *cannot answer, or perhaps she is too proud*] Do you see why it should be impossible, my man? [*He can make or mar his unworthy* Mary *now. Have you any doubt of him?*]

CRICHTON: Yes, my lady. I had not told you, my lord, but as soon as your lordship is suited I wish to leave service.

[*They are all immensely relieved, except poor* Tweeny]

TREHERNE: [*The only curious one*] What will you do, Crichton?

[Crichton *shrugs his shoulders "God knows," it may mean*]

CRICHTON: Shall I withdraw, my lord? [*He withdraws without a tremor,* Tweeny *accompanying him. They can all breathe again, the thunderstorm is over*]

LADY BROCKLEHURST: [*Thankful to have made herself unpleasant*] Horrid of me, wasn't it? But if one wasn't disagreeable now and again, it would be horribly tedious to be an old woman. He will soon be yours, Mary, and then—think of the opportunities you will have of being disagreeable to me. On that understanding, my dear, don't you think we might——?

[*Their cold lips meet*]

LORD LOAM: [*Vaguely*] Quite so—quite so.

[Crichton *announces dinner, and they file out.* Lady Mary *stays behind a moment and impulsively holds out her hand*]

LADY MARY: To wish you every dear happiness.

CRICHTON: [*An enigma to the last*] The same to you, my lady.

LADY MARY: Do you despise me, Crichton? [*The man who could never tell a lie makes no answer*] You are the best man among us.

CRICHTON: On an island, my lady, perhaps; but in England, no.

LADY MARY: Then there's something wrong with England.

CRICHTON: My lady, not even from you can I listen to a word against England.

LADY MARY: Tell me one thing; you have not lost your courage?

CRICHTON: No, my lady.

[*She goes. He turns out the lights*]

THE END

John Galsworthy

(1867–1933)

When realism gained a foothold in England, a number of dramatists turned to the writing of problem plays with resolution and talent. No one, however, practiced the objective social drama and the "naturalism" of Continental Europe with more scrupulousness than John Galsworthy.

To his self-imposed task Galsworthy brought a suitable education and temperament. Objectivity and balance were his by virtue of training at New College, Oxford, an honor degree in law in 1889, and extensive travel abroad from 1891 to 1893. A knowledge of the ponderable social realities, without which no dramatist could pretend to write problem drama, came inevitably to this levelheaded gentleman who interested himself for a time in the English socialist movement and generally championed the underdog. He was called to the bar in 1890, but instead of yielding to the legal profession began to write stories and novels, the first, *Jocelyn,* in 1899. Then, at the same time that his first Forsyte novel, *The Man of Property,* was published, he turned to the drama. His first play was *The Silver Box,* which Granville-Barker produced in 1906 at the venturesome Court Theatre.

The Silver Box presents a picture of unequal distribution of justice, leading to the conviction of a poor laborer and the acquittal of a rich man's son on the same charge. This play was followed year after year by other closely reasoned dramas concerned with the social scene. Thus, *Strife* (1909) was notable for its balanced treatment of the class struggle as an evil caused by obstinate leaders of both labor and capital. *Justice* (1910) was a deeply considered drama of a petty forger sucked into crime by his weak character and destroyed by the incomprehension of the law. The strong impression made by this play actually led to penal reforms, at the instigation of Winston Churchill, then Home Secretary of England.

Next, in 1912, Galsworthy fixed an inquiring and quizzical eye on the entire question of philanthropy, in *The Pigeon.* Subsequently, he again took account of social injustice, in *The Eldest Son* (1912) and *The Fugitive;* denounced war hysteria, in *The Mob* (1914); and attacked the caste system within a framework of racial prejudice, in *Loyalties* (1922). When Galsworthy died, in 1933, he left to posterity an impressive body of dramatic work, as well as some highly regarded fiction, most notably the group of novels published in 1922 under the collective title *The Forsyte Saga.*

All of Galsworthy's work bore the impress of an elevated spirit and of an inquiring, if not remarkably subtle, mind. The easily apparent limitations of the plays stem, as a rule, from the nature of the author's temperament and aims; the plays are so reasonable that they seem mild today and make one long for the excitement and transfiguration that passion might have brought to them. Their merits are, however, substantial, for Galsworthy was able to give his dramatic work much persuasiveness and authenticity. If the plays do not scintillate, they generally prove convincing; if they do not cut through all tissues of character and society, they manage to penetrate. Only occasionally obfuscated by sentimentality (most conspicuously in the least social of his plays, *Old English*), Galsworthy's work consists of lucid expositions in the form of spare and usually taut drama. Deliberately refraining from eloquence, Galsworthy wrote authentic dialogue and employed dialect where the social status required it. Above all, this scrupulous dramatist bore in mind the importance of presenting his thesis with credible characterization and without proffering ready-made solutions.

Galsworthy's complete consciousness of principle —largely naturalistic principle—was set forth in his essay *Some Platitudes Concerning Drama.* "A good plot," he wrote, "is that sure edifice which rises out of the interplay of circumstance on temperament, or of temperament on circumstance." Acting on this prescription in a species of playwriting that was antipodal to the well-made-play formula, he actually refrained from drafting scenarios, or outlines, for his plays. If the plays were, as a rule, extremely well organized and theatrically efficacious, Galsworthy preferred to believe that it was the result of his having allowed the characters to dictate their own line of conduct, character being, in his opinion, "the best plot" there is. As for dialogue, he insisted that it is "an austere art, denying itself all license, grudging every sentence devoted to the mere machinery of the play, suppressing all jokes and epigrams severed from character, relying for fun and pathos on the fun and tears of life."

It is not surprising, then, that Galsworthy should have formulated the best working definition of naturalism in England: "The aim of the dramatist employing it is evidently to create such an illusion of actual life passing on the stage as to compel the spectator to pass through an experience of his own, to think and talk and move with the people he sees thinking, talking, and moving." And Galsworthy did not allow himself to swerve from these critical principles except under the pressure of extreme compassion or indignation. He required self-discipline from his actors also, and so persistently in his early career that they sometimes protested against the rigor of his demands. In despair, during a rehearsal of *The Silver Box* at the Court Theatre, Dame Sybil Thorndike is reported to have cried out, "I can't do it. It's too hard. Do you want me to take away everything that is me?" Galsworthy replied, "Yes. If you would do that, I think it would be quite all right. Shall we try again?"

In exposing social wrong, Galsworthy tried to achieve a similar detachment, attacking not the individual but the institution or the human condition represented in the action. To a degree, like the European naturalists, he accepted the deterministic outlook. Ernest Short wrote in his *Theatrical Cavalcade,* "As Galsworthy saw the world of man, Society was the equivalent of the Greek Fate." Moreover, since Galsworthy was concerned with presenting life rather than with turning out machine-made stage pieces, he often suggested in his writing that there could be no resolution at the end of the play, that the life of the characters and the way of the world would continue past the segment he had exhibited on the stage. His curtains, it has been said, hesitated to come down. All these qualities made his work represent a new order in the English theatre during the first two decades of the century. It may be observed too that Winthrop Ames's New York productions of *Strife* and *The Pigeon,* between 1910 and 1912, gave Americans virtually their first experience of true naturalism, as opposed to the spectacular

variety offered by David Belasco and subsequently appropriated by the Hollywood movie industry.

Escape, written in 1926, was one of the last plays to come from Galsworthy's workshop. If, under some influence of the cinema, the play lacks the tightly knit structure of some of his best work, it nevertheless displays most of the playwright's characteristic virtues along with his faults. But for a trace of sentimentality, Galsworthy maintains an objective attitude toward both the fortunate and the unfortunate members of society. The characters are individualized, even if not deeply probed or fully rounded; the dialogue is unforced; and the vivid dialect bears the stamp of Galsworthian authenticity. Galsworthy wrote stronger plays than *Escape,* it is true, but none that appealed more widely to his growing public; the fact that this play should have done so provides an index of Britain's fondness for humane drama in preference to savage offensives. With Leslie Howard playing the hunted man who puts the charity and courage of others to the test, *Escape* became one of Galsworthy's most successful social dramas.

BIBLIOGRAPHY: Barrett H. Clark, *A Study of the Modern Drama* (pp. 272–280), 1938; John Galsworthy, "Some Platitudes Concerning Drama," in *The Inn of Tranquillity,* 1912, 1916; John Gassner, *Masters of the Drama* (pp. 616–618), 1940, 1945; H. W. Marrot, *John Galsworthy,* 1936; Herman Ould, *John Galsworthy,* 1934; Ernest Short, *Theatrical Cavalcade* (pp. 74–79), 1942.

ESCAPE

By John Galsworthy

CHARACTERS OF THE PLAY

MATT DENANT	THE MAID	THE FARMER
THE GIRL OF THE TOWN	THE OLD GENTLEMAN	THE LITTLE GIRL
THE PLAIN CLOTHES MAN	THE FOUR TRIPPERS	THE TWO MAIDEN LADIES
THE TWO POLICEMEN	THE MAN IN PLUS FOURS AND HIS	THE PARSON
THE FELLOW CONVICT	WIFE	THE BELLRINGER
THE TWO WARDERS	THE VILLAGE CONSTABLE	THE HUE AND CRY
THE SHINGLED LADY	THE TWO LABORERS	

PROLOGUE

Hyde Park at night. Summer. The Row with its iron railing, footwalk, seats, trees and bushes behind. A Woman, or Girl (you can't tell), is sitting alone, in dim radiance from lamps unseen to Right and Left. Her painted mask is not unattractive, her attitude slack and uneasy. A Plain Clothes Man passes Right to Left, glances at her inviting him and increases his pace. By the expression on her face as he approaches and recedes, it is easy for him to see what she is. Two People pass without glancing at her at all—they are talking of what "he said to me" and "I said to him." Then nobody passes, and, powdering her nose, she seems preparing to shift along, when from the Left Matt Denant appears strolling. He is a young man, tallish and athletic, dressed as if he has been racing in hot weather; he has a pair of race glasses and a cigar. The Girl shifts forward on her seat as he approaches. He is going by when she looks suddenly up and says in a low voice: "Good evening!" He halts, looks at her, gives a little shrug, carries his hand to his hat, and answering, "Good evening!" is moving on when she speaks again.

GIRL: Have you a match?
  [*She is holding out a cigarette; he stops and hands her his cigarette lighter*]
GIRL: [*Fingering the lighter*] Gold?
MATT: Brass.
GIRL: Have one?
  [*Offering her cigarette case*]
MATT: Thanks, I'm smoking.
  [*He shows her his cigar; resting his foot on the seat and dangling his race glasses*]
GIRL: Been racing?
MATT: Goodwood.
GIRL: I went to see the Jubilee this year.
MATT: And what did you back?
GIRL: Everything that didn't win. It's rotten when you don't back winners.
MATT: Don't you like the horses?

GIRL: They look pretty.
MATT: Prettiest things in the world.
GIRL: Pretty as women?
MATT: Saving your presence.
GIRL: Do you mean that?
MATT: Well, you get a woman once in a way that can arch her neck.
GIRL: You don't like women—that's clear.
MATT: Not too much.
GIRL: [*Smiling*] You speak your mind, anyway.
MATT: If you ask me, they've got such a lot of vice about 'em compared with horses.
GIRL: And who puts vice into them?
MATT: I know—you all say men, but d'you believe it?
GIRL: [*With a laugh*] Well, I don't know. Don't men put vice into horses?
MATT: [*Struck*] M'yes! [*Sitting down*] All the same, there's nothing wilder than a wild horse—I've seen 'em out West.
GIRL: There's nothing *so* wild as a wild woman.
  [*A momentary silence while they stare at each other*]
MATT: Women haven't the excuse of horses—they've been tame since Eve gave Adam his tea.
GIRL: Um! Garden of Eden! Must have been something like Hyde Park—there was a prize cop there, anyway.
MATT: D'you come here often?
GIRL: [*Nodding*] Where else *can* one go? They're so particular now.
MATT: They do seem to keep you on the run.
GIRL: What are you—soldier?
MATT: Once upon a time.
GIRL: What now?
MATT: Thinking of being a parson.
GIRL: [*Laughs*] You've got money of your own, then?
MATT: A little.
GIRL: [*With a sigh*] If I had money of my own, d'you know what I'd do?
MATT: Get rid of it.
GIRL: Just what I wouldn't. If ever I got myself

dependent on you men again, [*Very grimly*] shut my lights off.

MATT: Not like the lady under laughing gas.

GIRL: What was the matter with her?

MATT: Kept shouting, "I don't want to be a free, independent, economic agent! I want to be loved."

GIRL: She was wrong—No, *Sir!* Get my head under a second time? Not much! But we can't save —don't make enough. So there you are! It's a good bit worse than it used to be, they say——

MATT: The ordinary girl more free and easy now, you mean?

GIRL: [*Grimly*] The *ordinary* girl?

MATT: Well, you don't call yourself ordinary, do you?

[*The Girl sits quite still and doesn't answer*]

MATT: Sorry! Didn't mean to hurt you.

GIRL: Give me the fellow that does: he doesn't hurt half so much. But you're quite right. [*Bitterly*] There isn't much excuse for us, now.

MATT: Aren't we getting a bit solemn?

GIRL: The gay girl—eh? They say you get used to anything: but I'll tell you—you never get used to playing the canary when you don't feel like it.

MATT: Ah! I always sympathized with canaries—expected to sing, and so permanently yellow.

GIRL: It was nice of you to sit down and talk.

MATT: Thanks; it's all secondary education.

[*She slides her hand along to his, with a card*]

GIRL: Here's my address; you might come and see me now and then.

MATT: [*Twiddling the card—amused and embarrassed*] *On verra!*

GIRL: What's that?

MATT: It's an expression of hope.

GIRL: [*Mouth opening*] Ow! How about now?

MATT: Thanks—afraid not—due somewhere at ten.

GIRL: Another?

MATT: No.

GIRL: You don't like me, I believe.

MATT: [*With a shrug*] Oh! Don't say that. You're original.

GIRL: Original sin.

MATT: There are worse things, I guess.

GIRL: You bet! There's modest worth. If *that* isn't worse! Not that this is a pretty life. It's just about as rotten as it can be.

MATT: How did you get into it?

GIRL: Cut it out! You all ask that, and you can take it from me you never get told. Well! I belong to the oldest profession in the world! That isn't true, either—there's an older.

MATT: Not really.

GIRL: The cop's. Mine wouldn't ever have been a profession but for them.

MATT: Good for you!

GIRL: It isn't good for me. Look in at Bow Street on Monday morning.

MATT: To see 'em shoot the sitting pheasant?—no, thanks. The Law isn't exactly sporting. Can't be, I suppose, if it's got to keep the course clear.

GIRL: They might wait till one makes oneself a nuisance.

MATT: Ever been run in?

GIRL: [*With a look, and a decision*] Um! Not yet! [*Suddenly*] What can we do? If we don't make a sign, who's to know us?

MATT: That's delightful.

GIRL: Clean streets!—that's the cry. Clean men! That'd be better!

MATT: And then where'd you be?

GIRL: [*Passionately*] Not here!

MATT: [*After staring at her*] Um! The kettle and the pot. What! Give me horses and dogs, all the time.

GIRL: I've got a cat.

MATT: Persian?

GIRL: [*Nodding*] A real beauty. [*Suddenly*] Wouldn't you like to come and see him?

[*He shakes his head, rises, takes his glasses, and holds out his hand. She is going to take it— then draws her hand back sharply, frowning and biting her lips. He gives a shrug, salutes, and moves on. She catches at his sleeve, misses it, sits a second, then rises and follows. Unseen by her, the* Plain Clothes Man *has reappeared, Left. He moves swiftly and grasps her arm just as she is vanishing Right. The Girl gives a little squeal as he draws her back towards the seat. She resists*]

GIRL: Who are *you?*

PLAIN CLOTHES MAN: Plain clothes.

[*And, as she still resists, he tries to calm her by a slight twist of the arm*]

GIRL: You brute—you brute!

PLAIN CLOTHES MAN: Now then—quietly, and you won't get hurt.

GIRL: I wasn't doing anything.

PLAIN CLOTHES MAN: Oh! no, of course not.

GIRL: [*Looking after* Matt] I wasn't, I tell you; and he'll tell you so too!

[Matt *has reappeared, Right*]

Won't you? You talked to me of your own accord?

MATT: I did. Who may you be?

PLAIN CLOTHES MAN: [*Showing his card*] This woman accosted you. I've observed her carefully, and not for the first time.

MATT: Well, you've made a blooming error. We had a chat, that's all.

PLAIN CLOTHES MAN: I saw her accost you. I saw her try to detain you—and I've seen her do it before now.

MATT: I don't care what you've seen before now —you can't arrest her for that. You didn't see it this time.

PLAIN CLOTHES MAN: [*Still holding the* Girl *and looking at* Matt *steadily*] You know perfectly well the woman accosted you—and you'd better keep out of this.

MATT: Let the girl go, then. You're exceeding your duty.

PLAIN CLOTHES MAN: What do you know about my duty? It's my duty to keep the park decent, man or woman. Now then, are you going to clear off?

MATT: No, I'm going to stay on.

PLAIN CLOTHES MAN: All right then, you can follow us to the station.

MATT: Mayn't two people talk! I've made no complaint.

PLAIN CLOTHES MAN: I know this woman, I tell you. Don't interfere with me, or I shall want you too.

MATT: You can have me if you let the girl go.

PLAIN CLOTHES MAN: Now look here, I'm being very patient. But if you don't stop hindering me in the execution of my duty, I'll summon assistance and you'll *both* go to the station.

MATT: Don't lose your hair—I tell you, on my honor, this lady did not annoy me in the least. On the contrary——

PLAIN CLOTHES MAN: She was carrying on her profession here, as she's done before; my orders are to prevent that, and she's going to be charged. This is the third night I've watched her.

GIRL: I've never seen your face before.

PLAIN CLOTHES MAN: No, but I've seen yours— I've given you plenty of rope. That's enough, now—

[*He puts his whistle in his mouth*]

MATT: It's a rotten shame! Drop that girl's arm!

[*He lays his hand on the* Plain Clothes Man's *arm. The* Plain Clothes Man *blows his whistle, drops the* Girl's *arm and seizes* Matt]

MATT: [*Breaking from him; to the* Girl] Run for it!

GIRL: Oh! no—don't fight! The police have got it on you all the time. I'll go with him.

MATT: [*With fists up, keeping the* Plain Clothes Man *at arm's length*] Run, I tell you. He'll have his work cut out with me.

[*But the* Plain Clothes Man *is spryer than he thinks, runs in and catches him round the body*]

GIRL: Oh! Oh!

MATT: No, you don't!

[*In the violent struggle the* Plain Clothes Man's *bowler hat falls off.* Matt *emerges at arm's length again, squaring up*]

MATT: Come on, then, if you will have it!

[*The* Plain Clothes Man *rushes in. He gets* Matt's *right straight from the shoulder on the point of the jaw, topples back, and goes down like a log*]

GIRL: Oh! Oh!

MATT: Run, you little idiot; run!

GIRL: [*Aghast*] Oh! he hit his head—on the rail! I heard the crack. See, he don't move!

MATT: Well, of course. I knocked him out.

[*He goes a step nearer, looking down*]

The rail—did he——?

GIRL: [*Kneeling and feeling the* Plain Clothes Man's *head*] Feel!

MATT: My God! That was a wump. I say!

GIRL: I told you not to fight. What did you want to fight for?

MATT: [*Pulling open the* Plain Clothes Man's *coat, and diving for his heart*] I can't feel it. Curse! Now we can't leave him. [*Feeling for the heart*] Good God!

GIRL: [*Bending and snatching at his arm*] Quick! Before anybody comes. Across the grass back there. Who'd know?

MATT: [*Listening*] I can't leave the poor devil like this. [*Looking round*] Take his hat; go and get some water in it from the Serpentine.

[*The* Girl *picks up the hat and stands undecided*]

GIRL: [*Agonized*] No, no! Come away! It's awful, this! Suppose—suppose he's dead!

[*She pulls at him*]

MATT: [*Shaking her off*] Don't be a little fool! Go and get some water. Go on!

[*The* Girl *wrings her hands, then turns and runs off Left, with the hat.* Matt *continues to kneel, rubbing the* Plain Clothes Man's *temples, feeling his pulse, listening at his heart*]

MATT: I don't see how it's possible!

[*With a gesture of despair he resumes his efforts to revive the body. Suddenly he looks up.* Two Policemen *have come from the Right*]

POLICEMAN: What's this?

MATT: I don't know. I'm a little afraid he——

POLICEMAN: What! Who is he? [*Looking at the face*] Phew! One of ours! [*Bending, kneeling, putting the back of his hand to the mouth*] Not a breath! How did this happen?

MATT: [*Pointing to the rail*] He knocked his head on that.

POLICEMAN: Where's his hat?

MATT: It fell off. Someone's gone to get water in it.

POLICEMAN: Who?

MATT: A girl.——

POLICEMAN: He blew his whistle. Did you hit him?

MATT: There was a row. He seized me. I smote him on the jaw. He fell back and hit his head on the rail.

POLICEMAN: What was the row about?

MATT: [*Putting his hands to his head*] Oh! God knows! Original sin.

POLICEMAN: [*To the other* Policeman] Mate, stay with him. I'll get an ambulance. [*To* Matt] And you —come with me!

THE CURTAIN FALLS

EPISODE I.

More than a year has passed. On the prison farm, Dartmoor, in a heavy fog. The stone wall of the field runs along the back (on the back-cloth) and a stone wall joins it on the Left. Matt Denant and a fellow convict are picking up the potatoes they have dug up earlier. They are but dimly seen in the fog, flinging the potatoes right and left into two baskets between them. They are speaking in low voices.

MATT: The poor blighter was dead, and I got five years for manslaughter.

FELLOW CONVICT: Cripes! A cop! You were lucky not to swing, mate.

MATT: The girl stood by me like a brick. If she hadn't come forward——

FELLOW CONVICT: Lucky there, too. Most of 'em wouldn't. They're too mortal scared. 'Ow much you got left to do?

MATT: Three years, if I behave like a plaster saint. [*He stops and straightens himself*]

FELLOW CONVICT: I got four. I say, you're a torf, yn't you?

MATT: Toff! [*With a laugh*] Item, one Oxford accent; item, one objection to being spoken to like a dog.

FELLOW CONVICT: Hush! [*Jerking his thumb towards the wall, Right*] Fog don't prevent 'em hearin', blight 'em!

MATT: It's come up mighty sudden. Think it's going to last?

FELLOW CONVICT: After a wet spell—this time o' year, when the wind's gone—yus. They'll be roundin' us up in a minute, you'll see—and 'ome to Blighty. Makes 'em nervous—fog. That's when you get the escapes.

MATT: No one's ever got away from here, they say.

FELLOW CONVICT: There've been a good few tries, though.

MATT: Gosh! I'd like to have one.

FELLOW CONVICT: Don't you do it, mate. You want clothes, you want money, you want a car, to give you a dawg's chance. And then they'd get you. This moor's the 'ell of a place. I say, you must 'ave hit that cop a fair knock!

MATT: Just an ordinary knock-out on the jaw. It wasn't that. He landed the back of his head on the Row rail. [*He resumes potato picking*] Poor devil! He wasn't married, luckily.

FELLOW CONVICT: Luckily? Well, you never know about *that*. But get 'im off your chest, mate—'e wouldn't sit on mine—no more than an 'Un did in the War. That's a good fair potato. [*Holding one up*]

[*The figure of a Warder is dimly seen coming along from the Right under the wall. He stops*]

WARDER: No talking there! When you've finished that row, pick back the next and then stand by to fall in. [*No answer from the Convicts*] Hear me? Answer, can't you?

FELLOW CONVICT: Right, Sir! [*The Warder's figure is seen moving back*] Nice man, ain't he? Wot'd I tell you? Early 'ome to tea.

MATT: [*Very low*] Like a dog! Three more years—like a dog!

FELLOW CONVICT: 'E's all right, reely. It's the fog. Fog makes 'em nervous; an' when a man's nervous I've always noticed 'e speaks like that.

MATT: Yes; well, *I* can't get used to it.

FELLOW CONVICT: Too particular, you torfs—get too much corn when you're two-year-olds.

MATT: [*Sharp and low*] *You* know the moor—where's Two Bridges?

FELLOW CONVICT: There—a mile.

MATT: And Tavistock?

FELLOW CONVICT: [*Pointing right back*] Seven. Guv'nor—don't do it. There ain't a chance in a million. You'll only get pneumonium in this stinkin' wet, and they'll have you into the bargain, sure as eggs—bread and water, cells, and the rest of it.

MATT: I got out of Germany.

FELLOW CONVICT: Out of Germany? Cripes! That was none so dusty!

MATT: They've got no dogs here now, have they?

FELLOW CONVICT: Don't fancy they 'ave. But, Guv'nor, the whole countryside round 'ere's agynst you. They don't like convicts. Funny, yn't it?

[*They have reached the end of the row, Left, and stop, stooping, with their heads close together*]

MATT: Draw me a plan with this stick.

FELLOW CONVICT: Blimy! [*Marking the earth*] 'Ere's the main road, and 'ere's the cross road to Tavistock. 'Ere's the Inn at Two Bridges, and 'ere's Post Bridge. 'Ere's Bee Tor Cross, ten to twelve mile. Chagford up there, Moreton 'Ampstead 'ere.

MATT: What's across the main road from Two Bridges?

FELLOW CONVICT: Moor. A long bit o' wood about 'ere; then 'Ambledon; then you drops into fields to Widecombe; then up, and more moor to Heytor and Bovey. [*Pronounce* Buvvy] There's rail at Bovey or Lustleigh, or Moreton or Tavistock, and much good that'll do you with everybody as eager to see you as if you was the Prince of Wyles! Out this way you got Fox Tor Mire—ruddy bad bog, that!

[*A moment's silence while* Matt *studies the chart in the soil*]

WARDER'S VOICE: [*Off*] Hurry up with that last row—you two men!

[*The fog grows thicker*]

MATT: [*Smearing out the chart with his foot*] It's real thick now. Gosh! I'll have a shot!

[*They move back, Right, beginning the last row*]

FELLOW CONVICT: [*Jerking his thumb Left*] There's another blighter thirty yards out on the wall there. 'E'll shoot.

MATT: I know. I'm going over that wall in the corner, and then along under his nose on the near side. Ten to one he'll be looking out on the off side in this fog. If that chap there [*Jerking his head, Right*] doesn't spot me, I'll get by.

FELLOW CONVICT: You're mad, Guv'nor. They'll shoot at sight. And if they don' see you—in ten minutes I'll have finished this row, an' they're bound to know you're gone. You 'aven't the chance of a cock-louse.

MATT: All right, friend, don't worry! A bullet'd be a nice change for me. If I don't get one—I'll give 'em a run for their money.

FELLOW CONVICT: Well, if you must go, mate— Strike the main road and run that way. [*Pointing*] In this fog they'll 'ave to take us back before they dare start after you. You'll find a scrap of a wood a bit beyond the river on the left side. Get into it and cover yourself with leaves till it's dead dark. Then you'll still be close to the road and you can myke shift in a stack or something till the morning. If you go wandering about the moor all night in this fog, you won't get nowhere, and you'll be done in stiff before dawn.

MATT: Thanks. Sooner the better, now— Never stop to look at a fence. Next time the steam's full on. [*Puts some potatoes in his pocket*] Pommes crues— sauce Dartmoor. Can one eat these raw? I ate turnips in Germany.

FELLOW CONVICT: Never tried, Guv'nor. Tyke this. [*He holds out a slice of bread*]

MATT: Thanks awfully. You're a good chap.

FELLOW CONVICT: Wish you luck. Wish I was comin' too, but I 'aven't got the pluck, an' that's a fact.

MATT: Now! Turn your head the other way and keep it there. Remember me to Blighty. So long!

[*He moves three steps away from his fellow convict, pauses a few seconds, then suddenly, stooping low, runs to the wall, Left, and is over it like a cat. In the minute of silence that follows, one can see the* Convict *listening*]

FELLOW CONVICT: [*Counting the seconds to himself, up to twenty, in an excited murmur*] Gawd! 'E's past that blighter! [*Listens again*] Gawd! 'E's orf! [*With realization of his fellow's escape comes an itch to attempt it himself*] Shall I 'ave a shoot meself? Shall I? Gawd! I must!

[*He has just turned to sneak off, when the* Warder's *voice is heard off, Right*]

WARDER: You, man, there! Where's your mate?

FELLOW CONVICT: 'Ad a call, Sir. [*He stands still*]

VOICE OF WARDER: [*Nearing*] What d'you mean?

FELLOW CONVICT: Went over to that wall, Sir.

WARDER: [*Appearing*] He's not there. Now then! Where is he?

FELLOW CONVICT: No use arstin' me. *I* don' know where he is.

WARDER: Come with me. [*He marches sharply along the wall back, towards the Left. Halting*]

Convict! Out there! Answer! Warder! You, Williams! Anyone passed you? Lost a man here!

VOICE OF SECOND WARDER: No one's passed.

FIRST WARDER: Sharp, then! There's a man gone!

[*Second Warder appears on the top of the wall*]

SECOND WARDER: He must ha' got past *you*, then.

FIRST WARDER: Curse this fog! Fire a shot for warning. No, don't, or we'll have others running for it. Muster sharp and get off home and report— that's the only thing. [*To* Convict] Here, you! Keep your mouth shut. You know all about it, I bet.

FELLOW CONVICT: Not me, Sir. 'E just said 'e 'ad a call to 'ave tea with the Duchess; an' I went on pickin' up, knowin' you was in an 'urry.

FIRST WARDER: Mind your lip! Come on, Williams. March, you!

[*They are marching, Right, as*

THE CURTAIN FALLS]

EPISODE II.

Seven hours have passed. The moor in the dark and the fog, close to the main road. Nothing visible.

VOICE OF FIRST WARDER: What the hell's the use of picketing this blighted road—you can see nothing!

VOICE OF SECOND WARDER: I've seen two cops made just here. When a man's out on a night like this, it's human nature to cling to the road.

FIRST WARDER: But he may be anywhere.

SECOND WARDER: If he's traveling at all, he's on a road. You can't make it on the moor in fog as thick as this.

FIRST WARDER: He may have headed for Cornworthy.

SECOND WARDER: They never go that way—too afraid of Fox Tor Mire.

FIRST WARDER: Or Tavistock?

SECOND WARDER: Well, that road's picketed all right.

FIRST WARDER: I'd flog for escapes. They never think of us—out after these blighters nights like this. It's too bad, you know. Got a drain of the stuff?

SECOND WARDER: Here you are. Put it to your mouth by the smell.

FIRST WARDER: If I get this cove, I'll let him know it. 'Tisn't in nature not to feel murderous towards a chap that keeps you out all night in this sort o' muck!

[*He drinks*]

SECOND WARDER: Leave some for me, mate. [*In a whisper*] What was that? Hark!

[*They listen*]

FIRST WARDER: Don't 'ear nothing.

[*He is about to put the flask to his mouth again*]

SECOND WARDER: Thought I heard a scraping noise. Shall I show a glim?

FIRST WARDER: Better not!

[*They listen*]

SECOND WARDER: There's ponies round here.

FIRST WARDER: This fellow was a toff.

SECOND WARDER: Um! Captain in the War.

FIRST WARDER: Him that killed the 'tec in Hyde Park. He's a sporty beggar. Got blood in him. That's the worst sort when it comes to an escape—they run till they drop.

SECOND WARDER: Man of education—might have had more sense than to run for it. He must know he can't get off.

FIRST WARDER: There's a spirit in some of these higher-class chaps you can't break. D'you know that lawyer in the left wing—embezzlement? That chap gives me the creeps. He's got the self-possession of an image.

SECOND WARDER: I'm sorry for some of these fellows, but I'm damned if I'm ever sorry for a gentleman. They ought to know better than to get themselves here. And, as you say, they've got the devil's brass.

FIRST WARDER: Still—up on the ladder and down with a whump—it hits 'em harder than it does the others.

SECOND WARDER: [*Yawning*] Wish I was in bed! [*Startlingly*] There it is again! [*They listen*] It'll be a pony. A warder's life's about the limit. If it wasn't for the missus, I'd sooner sweep streets.

FIRST WARDER: I've got used to it, barring a circus like this. The devil himself couldn't get used to that. It's only fit for the movies.

SECOND WARDER: I believe you. Did you see that picture with Duggie in it? 'Ow'd you think 'e does that roof business? We got some pretty tidy cat burglars, but I don't believe there's one could do what he does.

FIRST WARDER: Well, I'll tell you. I think he has spring heels; and I notice his hands are very blurry in the picture. I believe he holds a rope, and they take that out afterwards, by some process.

SECOND WARDER: Never thought o' that! But when he falls and catches on that ledge?

FIRST WARDER: That's an optical deception. Some of those movie jossers ought to be in prison, the way they deceive the public.

SECOND WARDER: I never saw anything on the screen I liked better than "My Old Dutch"! That fair got me. I took the missus, and I tell you there wasn't a dry eye about the pair of us.

FIRST WARDER: Charlie knocks *me*. I feel a better man after I've seen 'im. Now, why is that?

SECOND WARDER: 'E's very 'uman. Must make a pot of money.

FIRST WARDER: I'm wet through—give me another drain. [*Gurgling sounds*] If I catch that chap, you'll 'ave to stop me quick, or I'll manhandle him for sure.

SECOND WARDER: Same here. We'd better toss up which stops the other. Call!

FIRST WARDER: 'Eads.

SECOND WARDER: Which is it? Throw a glim.

[*The* First Warder *throws from an electric torch the first light of the scene. Their two faces, on the foot-light side of the road, are seen close together over the coin*]

SECOND WARDER: Tails—You've lost. [*The glim is dowsed*] 'Ow do we stand, then? Do I stop you, or do you stop me?

FIRST WARDER: You stop me.

SECOND WARDER: No, I won. That means *I* get the go at him. Lawd Gawd! what a night! Just feel if that rope's all right across the road.

FIRST WARDER: It's taut. Bit too low, though—ought to catch him mid-thigh by rights.

SECOND WARDER: You trust me, old hoss; if it catches 'im as high as that, he stops and goes off sideways, or turns and runs back. It should catch him just below the knee. Then, ten to one he goes over, and we're on to him before he can get up. He'll be goin' a good bat, remember. You'll find me on 'is 'ead when you come to stoppin' me.

FIRST WARDER: To think we can't even smoke. D'you hold with givin' prisoners tobacco, Williams?

SECOND WARDER: On the whole, I do. It sweetens 'em, and that's better for us. I'd give 'em two pipes a week, and stop 'em if they gave a warder any trouble. I've got one or two fellers I'm quite fond of. I'd be glad for 'em to have a smoke every day. Listen! [*They listen. In a whisper*] Footsteps! They are!

FIRST WARDER: [*Still in a whisper*] Look here, mate! Just before he gets to the rope, I'll throw the light into his face, then dowse it sharp. He'll start to run forward and go head foremost. Stand by!

[*They listen*]

FIRST WARDER: He's comin' on! Suppose it isn't him?

SECOND WARDER: Must chance that. I'll throw the light as I say—[*A moment of utter black tenseness, during which the footsteps are heard clearer and clearer*] Now! Stand by! [*He flashes the light on the figure of* Matt *advancing along the road. The light is dowsed, the* Warders *rush forward. Darkness and the sound of a scramble*]

SECOND WARDER'S VOICE: I've got him!

FIRST WARDER'S VOICE: [*Half strangled*] No, you ruddy fool—you've got me!

THE CURTAIN FALLS

EPISODE III.

Thirty-two hours have passed. A bedroom at an Inn on the moor. Dark, with streaks of daylight coming in from two curtained windows, back, opening on to a long balcony. Between them a bed juts into the room. Right, forward, a dressing-table with chair. Left, back, a washstand. Left, forward, a door opening inwards. At foot of the bed a chair with a woman's undergarments thrown on it. A dressing-gown over the footrail of the bed, some slippers on the left side of the bed. A Shingled Lady *asleep in the bed. Knocking on the door, Left.*

LADY: [*Sleepily*] Come in!

[*A* Maid *enters with a can of hot water, which she places on the washstand, Left*]

MAID: 'Alf past seven, Madam.

LADY: [*Yawning*] What sort of day?

MAID: Foggy still. Taking a bath, Madam?

LADY: Yes. Oh! My husband's coming back this evening. I'm to be moved back to the double room.

MAID: Yes, Madam; they told me. [*She has drawn aside the curtains, Left, and now moves round and draws back the curtains, Right*] That escaped convict, Madam; they haven't got him yet.

LADY: No? How thrilling!

MAID: It's the fog. He's been out nearly two days. They say it's the young man who killed the detective in Hyde Park, that made such a fuss.

LADY: Oh? That Captain Denant! I remember. It might have been worse, then.

MAID: Of course they'll catch him—no one ever gets off.

LADY: Don't they?

MAID: Oh! no, Madam! It wouldn't never do.

LADY: I should have thought in fog like this——

MAID: You see, they got to eat and get clothes. That's where they're caught.

LADY: [*Yawning*] This horrible fog!—one can't ride or fish, or even walk. Shall I get up, or shall I——?

MAID: [*Rather coldly*] Just as you please, Madam.

LADY: [*With a laugh*] Well, I suppose I'd better.

MAID: I'll turn the bath on.

LADY: Thank you.

[*The* Maid *goes out, and the* Lady, *in her pajamas, emerges from bed, feels for her slippers, and puts on her dressing-gown. She goes to a window, and looks out. It is a French window, and slightly open on a short hook*]

LADY: Ugh! What a day!

[*Taking sponge and bath towel from the washstand, she goes to the door and out. As soon as the door is shut there is a commotion where the bed touches the wall, and from behind the window curtain* Matt Denant *cautiously emerges, glances quickly round, and stretches himself. He looks haggard, sodden, and crumpled, and has his boots in his hand*]

MATT: [*Muttering*] A lady! Dash it! I must get out!

[*He goes to the window and looks cautiously out, then recoils, drawing in his breath with a hiss. Then, after once more glancing round the room, he steps to the door*]

LADY'S VOICE: [*Off*] I simply can't take cold baths!

[Matt *flattens himself against the wall, so that he will be behind the door if it is opened. And suddenly it is*]

LADY'S VOICE: [*In doorway*] Let me know when the water's hot, please.

MAID'S VOICE: [*Off*] Yes, Madam.

[*The* Lady *re-enters, and passing the door knob from her right hand to her left behind her as she naturally would, closes it without seeing* Matt, *and crosses to the dressing-table, where she sits down and takes up a brush to brush her shingled hair.* Matt *moves quickly to the door, and has his hand on the handle, when his image passes into the mirror. The* Lady *drops the brush, and faces round with an exclamation on her open mouth.*]

MATT: Hush! It's quite O.K.

LADY: Who—how—what d'you mean by coming into my room?

[Matt *drops the door handle, turning the key in the lock*]

MATT: [*In a low voice*] Really, I'm most frightfully sorry.

[*Suddenly the fact that he is the escaped convict dawns on her*]

LADY: You're the escaped——

[*She starts up to go to the window and call for help; but stops at the gestures he makes*]

MATT: I wonder if you'd mind awfully speaking *pianissimo*.

LADY: [*Tersely*] What made you come in here? How did you get in?

MATT: I've been under the bed for hours. You see, I couldn't tell it was a lady.

LADY: D'you mean my hair?

MATT: Oh, no! I couldn't see that.

LADY: I didn't snore?

MATT: No; but that's not an infallible test of sex. I didn't either, or you'd have heard me.

LADY: D'you mean to say you went to sleep?

MATT: I'm afraid I did. Of course, if I'd known—

[*A pause*]

LADY: Well, as you're a gentleman, aren't you going?

MATT: I'd simply love to. But where?

LADY: Really, I can't tell you.

MATT: Look at me! What can one do in these togs?

LADY: D'you expect me to lend you some?

MATT: Hardly. But I'd be eternally grateful if you'd give me something to eat.

LADY: [*Opening a drawer and taking out some chocolate*] This is pretty cool, you know. I ought to ring and hand you over.

MATT: Yes. But—you look such a sport.

LADY: [*Subtly flattered*] I know who you are. Your name's in the paper. But do you realize my position?

MATT: Afraid I only realize my own.

LADY: If I don't hand you over, how on earth are you going to get out of here without being seen?

MATT: Might I have that chocolate?

LADY: [Taking it from the dressing-table drawer] It's only local.

MATT: That won't deter me. I've been forty hours on a piece of bread and two raw potatoes. [He takes the chocolate, bites some off, and puts the rest in his pocket] Would you mind frightfully if I drank some water?

LADY: Of course not.

[Matt goes over to the washstand. When his back is turned she springs to action, but instead of going to door or window, rapidly conceals underneath the bedclothes the corsets and underclothes flung on the chair at the foot of the bed, then returns to the dressing-table. Matt is drinking deeply.

MATT: [Turning] That's good. Ever had the hunted feeling? [She shakes her head] Well, don't! A coursed hare is nothing to it. Oh! I am so jolly stiff!

LADY: [Thrilled in spite of herself] Do you know you're only three miles from the Prison?

MATT: I do. The first night I meant to get near Exeter by morning, and where d'you think I was? A mile from where I started. I'd been ringing. That's what you do in fog. Is that a razor?

LADY: [On stilts] My husband's. Why? [As Matt takes it up] No! There's a limit, Captain Denant. You can't have a weapon.

MATT: No, of course! But would you mind awfully if I shaved? You see, like this [Passes his hand over his chin] I haven't an earthly, even if I could get clothes. There's nothing more attractive than a three days' beard. [While speaking he has lathered himself without a brush] I'm a very quick shaver. It takes me three minutes. I can do it in thirty-two and a half strokes.

LADY: [Gasping] Well, I never— It takes me [Hand to her neck] that is—I mean— Have you nearly been caught?

MATT: [Between scraping motions of the razor] Twice I've been within twenty feet of the hounds——

LADY: Hounds!

MATT: Human! Just out of their jaws. [Groans] D'you know anything so frightful as a shave like this?

LADY: Well, really——

MATT: I mean except, of course, not having it.

LADY: How did you get in here?

MATT: You see, I did so want a dry night, so I hid up and waited till every light was out. I tried to get in below, and couldn't; then I made a boss shot at the corner of the balcony and fell on my back—— Did you feel a sort of earthquake? No? I did. When I got over that, I had another shot at a pillar and made it that time. I chose your window because it

was open—hooked it up again and slid straight under the bed. I meant to sneak some clothes, and be off before daylight but I only woke up when the maid came in. [She indicates a towel; he steeps it in water and wipes his face] D'you mind if I put on my boots? [He stoops and puts them on]

LADY: So you actually slept under there?

MATT: Alas! I did.

LADY: Well! It's about the limit.

MATT: Will be if I get clear—no one ever has.

LADY: Tell me, Captain Denant, weren't you at Harcheston with my brother—he used to talk of a Matt Denant, who was an awfully good runner.

MATT: Quite likely. I was at school with an awful lot of brothers. What was his name?

LADY: No. That won't do.

MATT: You're right. Never tell a convict anything he can tell anybody else.

LADY: I really don't see how I can help you.

MATT: Nor do I, worse luck!

LADY: I read your trial.

MATT: [Standing up] And you think me a bad lot, of course. [Bitterly] D'you know how I spend most of my time in prison? Holding imaginary conversations with the respectable.

LADY: [With a smile] Respectable! D'you think you're holding a real one now?

MATT: I certainly don't. . . . I . . . I beg your pardon. . . . You know what I mean. But I bet most people have put me down a rotter.

LADY: Was all you said true?

MATT: Gospel.

LADY: I suppose they do hunt those girls rather.

MATT: Yes, but you know, I didn't even really see red. I've been sorry enough for that poor chap.

LADY: Well, Captain Denant, what now?

MATT: You've been most awfully kind and I don't want to impose on you; but I shall never get out of here as I am.

LADY: Why not?

MATT: [Jerking his head towards the window] They're too thoughtful. There's a picket out there. [The Lady turns to the window and looks out; then she turns to Matt and finds him smiling] Oh! No, I wasn't scared. One doesn't give one's own kind away.

LADY: I don't know that. Go and try some of those other rooms. Try the couple next door to me.

[A knock on the door. Both stand alert]

LADY: Yes?

VOICE OF MAID: [Off] The bath water's hot now, Madam.

LADY: All right. Thank you. [Her finger is on her lips] D'you think she could hear us?

MATT: Hope not. [Going close] Thanks most awfully. You don't know how decent it's been after a year in there, to talk to a lady. I won't leave any traces.

LADY: What are you going to do?

MATT: Wait till he's looking the other way, sneak

along the balcony, drop at the end, and bolt for it again.

LADY: Are you still a good runner?

MATT: Pretty fair, if I wasn't so stiff.

LADY: [*After a long look at him*] No! Look here! When I go to my bath I'll make sure there's no one. If I don't come back, slip down the stairs, they're almost opposite. In the hall, hanging, you'll find my husband's old Burberry and fishing basket, rod, and fishing hat; a long brown Burberry, with stains, and flies in the hat. Put them on and go out of the front door; the river's down to the left. Can you fish? [*At his nod*] You'd better, then. The bathroom's not that side, so I shan't see you. But— whistle "Lady, be good," if you know it.

MATT: Rather! It's the only tune that's got into prison. Well, I can't thank you—you're just a brick! [*He holds out his hand*]

LADY: [*Taking it*] Good luck! [*She passes him to the door*] Wait a second! [*Getting a flask from drawer*] Take this. If you see anyone looking at you—drink! Nothing gives one more confidence in a man than to see him drinking.

MATT: Splendid! What are you going to say to your husband?

LADY: Um! Yes! He comes to-night. Well, if he doesn't like it, he'll have to lump it. Oh! And these two pounds. It's all I've got here.

[*She has taken two pounds out of her bag lying on the dressing-table*]

MATT: [*Moved*] By George! I think you're sublime!

LADY: I'm afraid I doubt it.

MATT: If I'm caught, I shall say I pinched everything, of course; and if I get clear, I'll——

LADY: Oh! Don't bother about that. Get behind the door now.

[*Matt gets behind the door, and she opens it and goes out. After a moment she returns*]

LADY: All clear!

[*Then closing the door behind her, she goes. Matt takes a look around the room to see that he has not left any trace, and moves softly to the door. His hand is on the handle, when it is opened by the* Maid; *he has just time to shrink behind it while she stands looking curiously round the room, as if for somebody or something*]

LADY'S VOICE: [*Off*] Ellen! D'you mind going and getting me the suit I sent down to dry last night?

MAID: [*Starting*] Yes, Madam. [*She goes, closing the door*]

[*Matt has just time for a breath of relief when it is opened again and the* Lady *reappears*]

LADY: [*Seeing him breathless*] This is a bit hectic! [*In a whisper*] Now! Quick!

[*Matt dives past her. She stands a moment, hustles out her underclothing from under the bedclothes, then drawing the door to, goes to the window, opens it a little wider, and stands*]

there listening. In half a minute the faint strains of "Lady, be good," whistled, are heard]

LADY: [*Waving a stocking like a hat. Under her breath*] Gone away!

[*Whistling "Lady, be good," she crosses jauntily towards the door, meeting the* Maid, *who is coming in with the dried suit. Continuing to whistle, she passes her with a roll of the eyes, leaving the* Maid *in three minds as*

THE CURTAIN FALLS]

EPISODE IV.

Seven hours have passed. Dartmeet. An open space of fern and grass, above the river and away from trippers.

Matt, *who has been working along the river all the morning, is squatting with his catch beside him—some eight smallish trout. He is eating the last of his chocolate and drinking diligently from the already empty flask. The more so as an* Old Gentleman *in Lovat tweeds is straying towards him.* Matt *begins taking his rod to pieces.*

OLD GENTLEMAN: [*Approaching from Left*] Afternoon! Cleared up too well for *you*, I'm afraid.

MATT: Yes, it's a bit bright now.

OLD GENTLEMAN: Best eating in the world, those little brown chaps. Except perhaps the blue trout in the Tirol. *Blaue Forellen* with butter and potatoes, and a bottle of Vöslauer Goldeck, eh?

MATT: My Golly, yes!

[*He looks wolfishly at his trout*]

OLD GENTLEMAN: [*Eyeing him askance*] Very foggy this morning. Worst point about the moor, these fogs. Only good for convicts—um?

MATT: [*Subduing a start*] Escapes, you mean? But they never get clear, I believe.

OLD GENTLEMAN: No, I'm told; but they try, you know—they try. I've often wondered what I should do if I blundered into an escaped convict.

MATT: Yes, sir; bit of a problem.

OLD GENTLEMAN: [*Sitting down on his overcoat*] Between the Law and one's gentlemanly instincts— if it's gentleman-like to dally with a felon—I wonder!

MATT: [*Warming to the subject*] A chap who tries to escape must be a sportsman, anyway. He takes a pretty long chance.

OLD GENTLEMAN: Yes, I don't envy a man in this country; we're a law-abiding people. I remember being very much struck with the difference in America last year—vital race, that—sublime disregard of the law themselves, and a strong sense of moral turpitude in others. Been in America?

MATT: I was out West ranching when the war broke out.

OLD GENTLEMAN: Indeed! Judging by the films, escaping justice is still fashionable there. I think I prefer a more settled country.

MATT: Personally, I've got rather a complex. Escaped from Germany in the war.

OLD GENTLEMAN: Did you? How very interesting!

MATT: If you want to get thin. It's a top-hole cure for adipose. An escape's no picnic.

OLD GENTLEMAN: I imagine not, indeed. Where did you get over the border?

MATT: Holland, after three days and nights on beets and turnips. Do you know the turnip in a state of nature, Sir? He's a homely fellow—only beaten by the beet. Beg your pardon, Sir, it slipped out. By the way, a convict got off the day before yesterday.

OLD GENTLEMAN: Yes, I saw that—a Captain Matt Denant. I read his case with interest at the time. How did it strike you?

MATT: [On guard] Don't believe I remember it.

OLD GENTLEMAN: What? The Hyde Park case!

MATT: Oh! Ah! yes. There was a girl. In those cases they might wait till you complain.

OLD GENTLEMAN: The detective was undoubtedly doing his duty. And yet, quite a question—Rather dangerous giving the police a discretion on morals. The police are very like ourselves; and—er—most of us haven't got discretion, and the rest haven't got morals. The young man didn't complain, I think. D'you happen to recollect?

MATT: [With an uneasy look] So far as I remember, he said she was an intellectual.

[The Old Gentleman has taken out a cigar-case and is offering it]

OLD GENTLEMAN: Smoke?

MATT: Thanks very much. I've got into a bad habit of coming out without tobacco.

[They bite and light cigars]

OLD GENTLEMAN: I suppose one might run across that convict fellow any moment. It would be a little like meeting an adder. The poor thing only wants to get away from you. And yet, if you don't break its back, ten to one it'll bite a dog. I had two dogs die of snakebite. It's a duty, perhaps—what do you say?

MATT: Probably. But I don't always do mine.

OLD GENTLEMAN: Oh! don't you? I'm so glad of that. Neither do I.

MATT: Do you know that Prison? It's a bad style of architecture.

OLD GENTLEMAN: No. The fact is, I've had the misfortune in my time to send a good many people to prison. And in those days I did make a point of seeing a prison now and then. I remember I used to give my Juries a pass to go and see where they sent their fellow-beings. Once I tested whether they went to look round or not, and out of three Juries—no, it was four—how many do you think had had the curiosity?

MATT: None.

OLD GENTLEMAN: Isn't that a little cynical? [With his sideway bird-like glance] No, it was—one. Ha!

MATT: Who'd want to go into a prison? I'd as soon visit the morgue. The bodies there aren't living, anyway.

OLD GENTLEMAN: They tell me prisons are much improved. They've introduced a human feeling.

MATT: Have they? Splendid! What was the date of that?

OLD GENTLEMAN: [His eyes busy] They've abolished the arrows, anyway. And I believe they don't shave their heads now. Do you know any convicts?

MATT: [With a wriggle] I? No. Only one.

OLD GENTLEMAN: Indeed? And is he interesting?

MATT: The most interesting chap I know.

OLD GENTLEMAN: Ha! Suppose this escaped convict suddenly turned up here? [Jerking his thumb towards Matt] What should you do?

MATT: Run like a hare.

OLD GENTLEMAN: Dear me, yes. I think it would depend on whether anyone was about. Human nature is very—er—sensitive. D'you find this climate bracing? Dartmoor has quite a reputation.

MATT: Overrated—I think.

OLD GENTLEMAN: You know it well?

MATT: No; this is my first visit.

OLD GENTLEMAN: And will you be here long?

MATT: Hope not.

OLD GENTLEMAN: Beautiful spot—Dartmeet!

MATT: I prefer Two Bridges.

[Putting up his rod and whistling "Lady, be good"]

OLD GENTLEMAN: I've not fished for years. [As Matt suddenly passes his hand over his brow under his hat] Anything the matter?

MATT: Afraid I shall have to abandon your excellent cigar. I've enjoyed it, but I'm smoking on a rather empty stomach.

[He looks ruefully at the unsmoked portion of his cigar, and pitches it away]

OLD GENTLEMAN: Dear me! Yes. I remember that feeling coming over me once at the Royal Academy banquet—just before I had to make a speech. [Another of his bird-like glances] Tobacco must be one of the great deprivations in prison, I always think. Didn't you find that so in—in—Germany?

MATT: [Breathing rather fast and completing the dismantlement of his fishing-rod] Oh! we got tobacco now and then.

OLD GENTLEMAN: And empty stomachs too, I'm afraid.

MATT: Yes.

OLD GENTLEMAN: One never ceases to be grateful to those who endured such things. [Offering his cigar-case] Will you try again after tea? These moor teas with cream and jam.

MATT: [Taking it] Well, thank you, Sir, I shall down him next time.

[Matt is now ready for departure, for he has been getting increasingly uneasy with this Old

Gentleman. *He takes up his basket and lays the fish within it*]

OLD GENTLEMAN: Well [*Getting up*] I must be getting on too. It's been very pleasant. I've enjoyed our little talk. At my time of life one doesn't often get new sensations.

MATT: [*Nonplussed*] Good Lord, Sir! Have I given you any?

OLD GENTLEMAN: Well, I don't remember ever having talked before to a prisoner who's escaped from—Germany.

MATT: Good-bye, Sir.

OLD GENTLEMAN: Good-bye, Captain Denant—[Matt *starts*] I hope you'll have a pleasant journey, especially as no one seems to have noticed our little chat.

MATT: [*Staring at him*] D'you mind frightfully telling me how you spotted me?

OLD GENTLEMAN: Not at all! First, the way you looked at your trout—shall I say—er—wolfishly? And then—forgive me—your legs.

MATT: [*Drawing up his Burberry and contemplating his legs*] Yes. I hoped you'd think I was a leader of fashion.

OLD GENTLEMAN: And there was another thing—your obvious sympathy with yourself.

MATT: That's a prison habit, Sir. You're not allowed to sympathize with other people, for fear of contaminating them. Before I got into quod I don't remember ever feeling sorry for myself. But I doubt if I shall ever again feel sorry for anyone else.

OLD GENTLEMAN: That must be very natural. Well, it's been most interesting, because now you see I know what I should do——

MATT: [*Intently*] Is it indiscreet to ask, Sir?

OLD GENTLEMAN: Well, Captain Denant, this time —I say *this* time—wink the other eye. Good-day to you!

MATT: Good-day, Sir. It's most frightfully sporting of you. For the moment I feel quite human.

OLD GENTLEMAN: Do you know, that's been rather the effect on me. Original sin, I suppose. Good-day!

[*He goes off, watching the smoke of his cigar and smiling faintly to himself. On Matt, affected by kindness*

THE CURTAIN FALLS]

EPISODE V.

An hour has passed. On the Moor; a high spot.
Four Trippers, *two men and two women, disgorged from a Ford car, are picnicking. One of the men, about fifty, in blue clothes, has a Merchant Service look and a concertina; the other looks more like a shopkeeper, and is perhaps fifty-five. His wife is a stout woman, about forty, of mellow appearance. The other woman is the shopkeeper's sister, dried-up*

and spinsterish. Their clothes are of a suitable nature —some feathers. They are all eating heavily.

WIFE: Captain, you're a prophet—considerin' what it was when we left Ashburton. I call this lovely!

[*Eats*]

CAPTAIN: Takes a bit o' weather to flummox a sailor, ma'am.

[*Drinks*]

WIFE: "You trust the Captain," I said to Pinkem this morning, didn't I, Father? *I* knew, you see; [*Archly*] my corns weren't shootin'.

SISTER: That's not very nice, Fanny.

WIFE: Why not? I'd like to see someone who 'asn't corns, if the truth was known. 'Ave another of these cut rounds, Dolly, and cheer up. Father, don't you eat any more cream—your eyes are yeller.

SHOPKEEPER: When I first came to Devonshire I could put away 'alf a pound o' cream at a meal.

WIFE: Yes, and it spoiled your temper for life.

SHOPKEEPER: Am I bad-tempered, Dolly?

SISTER: So-so, James.

SHOPKEEPER: What do you say, Captain?

CAPTAIN: You keep it for your wife, my boy. Outside the bosom of your family you're a perfect cherub.

WIFE: Captain, you're an 'opeless Benedict.

CAPTAIN: Bachelor born, Ma'am.

WIFE: With a wife in every port, eh?

SISTER: Oh! That reely isn't nice, Fanny; so old-fashioned, too.

CAPTAIN: Is it, Ma'am?

WIFE: Now, Captain, don't go shockin' Dolly. Oh! There's an insect on my skirt! I never seen one like it.

SHOPKEEPER: Kill it, then.

WIFE: Why?

SHOPKEEPER: Always kill what you don't know.

WIFE: [*Flipping it off*] It's only a biddle—poor thing! Give us a tune, Captain. [*The Captain draws a long blast from his concertina*] Hallo! 'Oo's this?

[Matt, *in Burberry, with rod and basket, has appeared Left, and stands lifting his hat*]

MATT: Afternoon! Wonder if you could put me right for Bovey?

SHOPKEEPER: Bovey! That's a goodish step— matter of twelve miles, I should say.

MATT: My Lord! Not really?

SHOPKEEPER: You go down the 'ill, through Ponsworthy to Widecombe, and up the 'ill turn to the left, and ask again.

MATT: I see. Will there be anyone to ask?

SHOPKEEPER: I shouldn't think so.

CAPTAIN: Had any sport, Sir?

MATT: [*Opening the basket*] Eight, rather small.

WIFE: My! Don't they look nice! Such good eatin', too.

MATT: Would you like them, Ma'am?

WIFE: [*With affected restraint*] I'm sure it's very good of you.

CAPTAIN: Don't you miss the chance, Mrs. Pinkem; nothing like moor trout, with a moor appetite.

SISTER: [*Distantly*] I'm sure it's most kind, from a stranger.

WIFE: [*Suddenly*] Well, I don't know, if you're so obliging. 'And me the *Daily Mail*, Father. I'll wrap 'em up; and thank you very much. I quite appreciate it.

MATT: That's splendid! [*He hands them*] Turned out quite nice, hasn't it? Have you come far?

SHOPKEEPER: From Ashburton—ten mile.

MATT: Heard anything there of the escaped convict?

SHOPKEEPER: What about it? Haven't looked at the paper last day or two.

WIFE: Another escape!—oh, my!

MATT: Rather! He got off in the fog, night before last.

SISTER: I always hate to think of one of those dreadful men at large. You can't sleep in your bed.

CAPTAIN: Don't you get too excited, Ma'am. Think of the choice 'e's got.

WIFE: [*Scanning the paper*] Why! It's the man that killed the poor detective in 'Yde Park! That villain! It says 'ere they nearly got him—twice.

[Matt, *who is eyeing them closely, eyes a loaf even more closely, and tries to maneuver into a position to annex it*]

SHOPKEEPER: I 'ope everybody's helping to catch him. He must be a regular desperado. That was a bad case. I never believed the girl.

SISTER: I should think not, indeed!

SHOPKEEPER: Nor the young man neither. They were up to no good there. They tell me those London parks are in a proper state.

CAPTAIN: They ain't a Sunday School, that's certain.

WIFE: Fie, Captain!

SISTER: [*Acidly*] I believe some people quite sympathized with him. Fancy!

MATT: Well, if you won't think it too eccentric, I did, for one.

SHOPKEEPER: You!—Why?

MATT: I thought he had devilish hard luck.

SHOPKEEPER: Ah! there's always a fuss made about the Law. You can't even 'ang a woman for murderin' her 'usband without a lot of 'ysterical nonsense. Look at that case not long ago—there was a petition as long as your arm.

CAPTAIN: I remember. The young chap was a steward. I don't recall this Hyde Park case.

WIFE: Why! the detective arrested one o' those women this young man had been sittin' with—a gentleman he was too—and if he didn't 'it him an' break 'is 'ead, an' kill 'im, poor man!

CAPTAIN: Then why didn't they string him up?

MATT: The jury found it was a quarrel, not an attempt to evade arrest. Besides, in falling the detective hit his head on the iron railing of the Row, and the doctors said he died of the concussion.

SHOPKEEPER: That didn't ought to have got 'im off. He hit the man. If 'e 'adn't 'it him, 'e wouldn't have fallen.

MATT: Exactly! Brilliant! But if the detective hadn't seized him, he wouldn't have hit him.

SHOPKEEPER: Well! I'd 'ave hung 'im.

WIFE: Don't be so bloodthirsty, Father!

SHOPKEEPER: Well, I would. Hitting an officer for doing his duty. Sitting with a woman in the Park, too! He only got off because he was quality.

MATT: Don't you think that's a superstition?

[*The* Shopkeeper *glares at him, but decides that he is a gentleman, and therefore prejudiced, and only snorts slightly*]

SISTER: Did they punish the woman?

MATT: What for, Ma'am?

SISTER: *I'd* keep them shut up; then they wouldn't tempt young men—the 'arpies!

MATT: [*Unexpectedly*] Oh! God!

[*They all stare at him. Then the* Shopkeeper *fatuously breaks the silence*]

SHOPKEEPER: Can't say I was ever tempted by a woman.

MATT: No, you've got a Ford car, I see. D'you find them good in this sort of country?

SHOPKEEPER: [*Distantly*] I do, Sir.

MATT: Do they get up these hills?

SHOPKEEPER: I should think so. I'd engage to catch any convict with my car.

MATT: Would you? [*A thought strikes him*] Splendid!

WIFE: Well, I think we ought to be gettin' 'ome. 'And me the teapot, Captain. Now, Dolly! Never mind those bits o' cake and bread—they're no good. Just leave the deebris. I'd like to be in before dark, with a convict loose like this. He might come prowlin' round, pickin' things up.

[Matt *with a secret movement pockets some scraps*]

MATT: Good afternoon! Hope you'll enjoy the trout.

[*He moves away out of the picture*]

WIFE AND CAPTAIN: Good afternoon—Good afternoon, Sir!

[Matt *salutes and vanishes, Right*]

SISTER: Here, Fanny! Did you see him pocket the scraps?

WIFE: No! Why, he's a gentleman—didn't you hear his sniffy way o' talkin'?

SISTER: I saw him with my own eyes—two bits of cake and a round.

[*Sound of a car being started*]

SHOPKEEPER: I say! [*Jumping up*] What's 'e doin' with the Ford?

CAPTAIN: Hi, there! You, Sir!

SHOPKEEPER: He's got in. Hi!

SISTER: The villain!

ALL: Hi! hi! hi!

[*Sounds of a levanting car, and a hallooed* "So long!" *The* Two Men *run out of the picture*]

WIFE: Well, I——

SISTER: *You!* Taking his fish like that! You might ha' known he was a thief. Why—why—of course! He's the—oh! oh!

WIFE: Dry up, Dolly! 'Ow are we to get 'ome? [*The* Two Men *run back into the picture, breathless*]

SHOPKEEPER: Well, of all the impudent villains!

CAPTAIN: I'm jiggered!

[*He sits down with his hands on his knees and goes off into wheezy laughter*]

SISTER: 'Ow *can* you? 'Ow *can* you, Captain? And we talking about him all the time!

CAPTAIN: [*Stopping*] What! Him!

SISTER: The escaped convict! He hadn't the leggins of a gentleman.

CAPTAIN: What! Did you look at his legs, Ma'am?

WIFE: It's all your fault, Pinkem; you and Dolly's—callin' 'im names. If you 'adn't called 'im names, he wouldn't 'a stole the car—talkin' of hanging 'im! I could see 'im gettin' heated.

SHOPKEEPER: You called 'im a villain yourself. Well—Bovey—we know where to look for him.

CAPTAIN: A blind, old bean.

SHOPKEEPER: I say 'e will go there.

CAPTAIN: I say 'e won't.

SHOPKEEPER: I say 'e'll see we'll think 'e won't, and put the double cross on us.

CAPTAIN: Well, I say, 'e'll see we'll think 'e's going to put the double cross on us.

WIFE: Oh! My corns!

SISTER: Impudence, givin' us 'is fish!

CAPTAIN: Well, there's nothin' for it but tote the things and walk till we get a lift.

WIFE: Oh! my corns are shootin'. I can't walk.

CAPTAIN: Cheerio, Ma'am! Be English.

SHOPKEEPER: English! 'Tisn't *your* car.

CAPTAIN: Don't worry, old sport. 'E'll leave that in a ditch when he gets there.

SHOPKEEPER: There—ye-es—John o' Groats?

CAPTAIN: Come along, Ma'am. Lift your corns well up. I'll give you a tune.

[*They have picked up the gear and are trailing off Right, leaving papers strewn about*]

WIFE: Oh! Look! We've left 'is fish.

SISTER: Fish! Infra dig, I call it. [*She sniffs*]

WIFE: Nonsense, Dolly! Dish of trout like that'll cost five shillings in Ashburton. May as well 'ave the worth of the petrol 'e'll use. Father, pick 'em up.

[*The* Shopkeeper *turns back, picks them up in the* Daily Mail, *puts the combination to his nose, finds it good and follows the others off as the* Captain *begins to play his concertina and*

THE CURTAIN FALLS]

EPISODE VI.

Half an hour has passed. An open space with the moor rising from it. A Man *in plus fours and his* Wife *are returning from a walk. The* Wife *has stopped and is moving her foot uneasily.*

WIFE: I've got something in my shoe, Philip.

MAN: What?

WIFE: I've got something in my shoe.

MAN: [*In front, stopping too*] Take it off, then. [*Goes back to her*] Hold on to me.

WIFE: [*Taking off shoe and shaking it*] It isn't in the shoe—it's inside the stocking.

MAN: You can't sit down here; the ground's still wet.

WIFE: There—feel!

MAN: Yes, I can feel it.

WIFE: [*Standing on one leg*] Well! Hold me.

[*He holds her and she has slipped her stocking off when there is the sound of an approaching car*]

MAN: Look out! Here's a car!

WIFE: [*Letting her skirt fall and standing on one leg*] Bother!

[*Sound of the car stopping*]

MAN: Hallo! He's coming to speak to us.

[*The* Wife *bends and slips the shoe on hurriedly, but the dress is short. She holds the stocking behind her*]

MATT: [*Appearing*] Beg your pardon, Sir, but can you direct me to Bovey?

MAN: Afraid we're strangers. Pity you didn't ask as you came through Widecombe.

MATT: Well, but it's up this hill, anyway, isn't it?

MAN: Must be, I think. That's the way to Heytor Rock.

MATT: Oh! Can you see the promised land from there?

WIFE: Yes. You go up the hill and turn to the right, then to the left through a gate.

MATT: And ask again, I suppose. [*Preparing to leave*] Thanks very much.

MAN: Fine place, the moor, Sir. Splendid air.

MATT: [*Drily*] Oh! Splendid. So dry and clear!

WIFE: [*With a giggle*] Yes, the fog *was* awful yesterday.

MAN: They say Bovey's pretty.

MATT: Yes, I've some Aunts there. Good place for Aunts.

WIFE: [*Laughing*] What makes a good place for Aunts?

MATT: Oh! not too stirring. Awfully good knitting there, I believe.

MAN: Ha! That's good. Ha!

MATT: I must get on, or I shall be late for tea. So I whizz past Heytor Rocks——?

WIFE: Yes, and come down on the church.

MATT: Thanks very much. My Aunts are close there, I know. Good afternoon.

[*He lifts his hat discreetly and goes, Right. The* Man *and* Wife *gaze after him*]

WIFE: What a nice young man!

MAN: That was good about Aunts. Ha!

[*Sound of car moving on*]
Now for your stocking!

WIFE: [*Bending down and taking off her shoe*] I should think he was County, wouldn't you?

MAN: [*Holding her from behind*] Um! Only "County" would drive such a shockin' bad car.

WIFE: He saw my leg and kept his eyes off it. I thought that was charming of him.

MAN: Fellow-feelin'; he had some shockin' leg gear on himself.

WIFE: [*Turning stocking inside out*] See, there it is—a beastly little three-cornered bit of grit. Extraordinary how they get in——

MAN: [*Suddenly*] Look out! Here's a constable on a bike.

[*The* Wife *drops her skirt and stands balancing again, the stocking in her hand. A very hot* Constable *appears, wheeling a bicycle*]

CONSTABLE: Zeen convict pass?

MAN: [*Astonished*] Convict? No.

CONSTABLE: Zeen anybody?

MAN: Only a car.

CONSTABLE: What zort of car?

MAN: Ford, I think.

CONSTABLE: Whu was in it?

MAN: A man.

CONSTABLE: What zort of man?

MAN: Oh!—er—a gentleman.

CONSTABLE: How d'yu know?

MAN: By his voice.

WIFE: He spoke to us.

CONSTABLE: What d'e zay?

MAN: Asked the way to Bovey.

CONSTABLE: Ha! What 'ad 'e on?

MAN: Long Burberry and a hat like mine; he was quite all right.

CONSTABLE: [*Mopping his face*] Was 'e? Bovey—yu zay?

WIFE: Yes, he had some Aunts there—he was going to tea with them.

CONSTABLE: [*Deeply*] Aunts in Bovey! Did yu direct 'im?

WIFE: We told him to go by Heytor Rocks. Wasn't that right?

CONSTABLE: Well, yu've directed the escaped convict.

MAN: [*Alarmed*] No, really! But I tell you——

WIFE: He was quite charming.

CONSTABLE: Was 'e? 'Ow much start's 'e got?

MAN: Oh! not five minutes. Of course, I didn't know—I should never have——

CONSTABLE: [*Muttering and mopping*] This plaguey 'ill!

MAN: Hadn't you better telephone to Bovey?

CONSTABLE: [*Smartly*] Bovey! Why d'yu suppose he spoke to 'ee? Because 'e idn' goin' to Bovey and wants me to think 'e is.

WIFE: But really he was a gentleman.

CONSTABLE: [*Drily*] Volk 'e stole that car from 'alf an hour gone, don't think so. [*He mops his face*]

WIFE: I can't believe——

MAN: There were his legs [*To* Constable, *whose eyes are on the lady's leg*] I noticed they looked like nothing at all.

CONSTABLE: Then why didn' yu stop 'im?

MAN: [*Flustered*] I would have, of course, if I'd suspected for a moment.

CONSTABLE: Stop first—suspect arterwards.

MAN: Well, I'm sorry. If I'd——

CONSTABLE: 'Tes done now. I must get down along sharp and telephone. [*He turns and wheels his bicycle off to the road*]

WIFE: [*On one leg*] I don't see why you need be sorry, Philip. He *was* a gentleman.

MAN: A convict's a convict; you can't play about with the Law.

WIFE: Well, we have, that's one comfort. That constable didn't keep *his* eyes off my leg.

MAN: I suppose you'd have had me get into a row with the police!

WIFE: Don't be silly, Philip! You needn't get angry because your nerves are rattled. No, don't hold me, I can put it on perfectly by myself. [*She stands wobbling on one leg, and pulls the stocking on*]

MAN: The brass of that chap—talking about his Aunts!

WIFE: You thought it very funny, when he did.

MAN: If I'd known——

WIFE: Oh! Yes, if you'd known—you haven't an ounce of original sin in you. Thank goodness, I have.

MAN: Where? *I've* never——

WIFE: No, I don't keep it for you.

MAN: Hallo! He's coming back.

WIFE: Who? The constable?

MAN: No—that chap—the convict.
[*Sounds of car*]

WIFE: Hooray!

MAN: What do you mean—hooray? What am I to do? This is infernal.

WIFE: [*Maliciously*] Run out and stop him, of course.

MAN: [*On one leg and the other*] He'd run over me. These chaps are desperate.

WIFE: Well, *I* will, then; and warn him of the constable.

MAN: You won't!—Hallo! He's stopping. That's worse. What the devil shall I do now?

[*The* Wife *laughs. Sounds of car stopping.* Matt *reappears*]

MATT: Awfully sorry, but my car jibbed. There's another way round, isn't there? Through Widecombe, to the right—I saw a road?

MAN: Um! Well—I—er——

WIFE: Yes, but I shouldn't advise you to take it.

MATT: Must, I'm afraid. My car started to back down the hill.

MAN: I'm afraid—er—that I—er—ought to——

WIFE: My husband means that there's a constable in Widecombe. [*Pointing*]

MATT: Yes. [*Looking back under his hand*] I see him.

WIFE: So you'd better go on up.

MATT: There are *two* up there, you see. My car's very sensitive.

WIFE: Oh, dear!

MAN: Joan! [*Resolutely*] Now, Sir, that constable's been talking to us. The game's up. If you don't mind, I'll take that car. He says it isn't yours.

MATT: [*Stepping back*] You know that's most frightfully true. But then—it isn't yours either.

MAN: Well, just let's argue it. I'm afraid you're helpless.

MATT: What do you take me for?

MAN: Why—er—the escaped convict, if you know what I mean.

MATT: Oh! Well—even so, I've still got a kick in me. I see your point of view, of course; but unfortunately I've got my own.

MAN: After that constable, I simply can't play about with it.

MATT: Look here! I've got a brain-wave. Let's all go into Widecombe in the car?

MAN: Ah! thanks very much; I thought you'd be sporting.

MATT: You see, if you're with me, I shall get through Widecombe all right, and I'll drop you just on the far side.

MAN: But—! What? No—that won't——

MATT: It's all right. You take me in custody into Widecombe—you can't help it if I whizz through and shoot you out. I want to make it easy for you, and I hope you want to make it easy for me.

MAN: Why should I? An escaped convict!

MATT: What do you call *yourself*?

MAN: What! Just an average man.

MATT: D'you mean to say the average man isn't a sportsman?

MAN: Yes. But I've had warning. I'm up against it.

WIFE: *I'll* come in the car. If you're with a lady, you'll get through without being spotted.

MATT: Splendid! Thanks ever so! Will you get in?

MAN: Joan!

MATT: Put yourself in my position, Sir——

MAN: Look here! I ought to be knocking you down and sitting on your head, if you know what I mean.

MATT: [*Squaring up*] Well, any little thing you've got to do, please do it quickly.

MAN: Well, I mean—that's very crude.

WIFE: [*Ironically*] Oh! no, Philip! Oh, no!

MAN: Well, suppose you let me drive.

MATT: Why should I? I stole the car. Now, Madam, shall we start?

WIFE: [*Winding her scarf round her face*] Righto!

MAN: This is monstrous! Look here, Sir, you seem to think——

MATT: I'll tell you what I think— [*Grimly*] I've been in purgatory too long, and I'm going to get out, and you're not going to stop me, if you know what I mean.

MAN: I jolly well am!

WIFE: Philip!

MAN: I'm not going to have it. If you won't surrender, I shall tackle you.

MATT: [*Dangerously*] Oh! [*He takes a spanner out of his pocket*]

WIFE: [*Stepping between them—to* Matt] D'you know, I think you'd better go on.

MATT: I think so, too. Sorry to be a boor and bring out a thing like this. [*Tapping the spanner*] But I'm not playing, you see. [*Somberly*] The life we live spoils our sense of humor! Good-bye, Ma'am, I'm very grateful to *you*. [*He turns and vanishes*]

MAN: Look here! You're not going like that—I'm damned if you are! Stop!

WIFE: Masterly, Philip! Masterly! [*Sound of a car starting*] Run! My dear! Run! It's all right. You'll be too late.

MAN: You really *are*——

[*They stand looking at each other as the sound of the car fails slowly, and*

THE CURTAIN FALLS]

EPISODE VII.

An hour has passed.

In a gravel pit on the edge of the moor are a wheelbarrow, with a pick in it, and Matt lying on his face, apparently asleep, waiting for dark.

From Right comes the figure of a Laborer. He is a burly great fellow with a shovel. Seeing the recumbent figure, he stands still, gazing. Then, turning, he goes back whence he came. Matt, who has been conscious of this visitor, gathers himself to spring up and rush away. Then he takes a resolution and lies down again in the same attitude, as if asleep. The Laborer returns, followed by another Laborer as big as himself. The First Laborer clears his throat.

MATT: [*Sitting up with his feet under him*] Well, my men! What's the matter with you?

FIRST LABORER: Beg pardon, Zurr. We'm lukin' for th' escaped convict. We 'ad a zort of a thought as yu med be 'err.

MATT: Did you? That's pretty good! And now you see I'm not, suppose you apologize?

FIRST LABORER: [*Cautiously*] 'Course, ef we knu 'u'm yu werr——

MATT: Whom do you work for?

FIRST LABORER: Varmer Brownin'. 'Tes 'is grazin' yere.

MATT: I'll see Farmer Browning. It's funny, but I don't altogether like being taken for an escaped convict.

FIRST LABORER: Yas, I rackon as 'ow yu'd better

zee Maester Brownin'. George, goo and vind Maester. 'E'm in th' orchard long across.

[*The* Second Laborer *goes off, Left*]

FIRST LABORER: We'm 'ad nues o' this joker, yu zee. Zeemingly 'e pinched a car and we'm found it just back along in the ditch. 'Tes the zame old car, tu.

MATT: What on earth's the car to do with me?

FIRST LABORER: A don' zay nothin' 'bout that. Maester'll know when 'e comes.

MATT: I'll go and meet him. [*He makes as if to rise*]

FIRST LABORER: No, you zett therr.

MATT: Now, look here, my friend! Do I talk like a convict?

FIRST LABORER: Can't zay, never 'eerd none. They'm town folk, I rackon—mos'ly.

MATT: Well, I was bred in the country, like you. What wages do you get here?

[*He pulls the flask out of his pocket, whistling "Lady, be good"*]

FIRST LABORER: Wall, ef yu'm the convict, yu'm a cule customer arter that.

MATT: But why on earth should you *think* I'm the convict. I'm just a fisherman staying at Lustleigh. [*He takes a pull at the empty flask*] You're making a fool of yourself, you know.

FIRST LABORER: [*Scratching his head*] Ef so be as yu'm what yu zay yu be, wot d'you goo vur to 'ide yere?

MATT: Hide? I was having a nap out of the wind, before walking home.

FIRST LABORER: This joker 'ad a fishin'-rod wi' un, tu.

MATT: The convict? Bosh!

FIRST LABORER: Not zo much bosh, neither.

MATT: Look you, my man, I've had enough of this.

[*He stands up suddenly. The* Laborer *steps back and lifts his shovel. But at this moment the* Farmer *and Second Laborer step into the picture from Left, accompanied by a* Little Girl *of thirteen or so, who has been riding*]

FARMER: Now then, now then! That'll du, Jim. Yu there, on my land, kindly give me yure name, and account for yurself. There's a rough customer about, with a fishin'-rod, same as yu.

MATT: Mr. Browning?

FARMER: Ay! that's my name.

MATT: Mine's Matthew. Captain Matthew. I'm staying at the Inn at Lustleigh. There's some very absurd mistake. This good trusty dog thinks he's treed a convict.

FARMER: [*Impressed by Matt's accent and air, and the flask in his hand*] Well, Sir, when there's these escapes on the moor, we 'ave to be careful. Miss 'Lizabeth, yu run along. [*The* Little Girl *does not move, but remains spellbound*] Constable's just been in wi' nues from Widecombe of the car yonder, and the man that pinched it 'ad a long brown coat, a fishin'-rod, and an 'at like yurn.

MATT: If the constable's here still, you'd better take me to him.

FARMER: No, rackon I'll ask 'im to step over 'ere. George, run and fetch constable, he'm down along by thiccy car.

[*The* Second Laborer *departs, Right, the* First Laborer *retires a little to the Right, leaving the* Farmer *and* Matt *by themselves on the Left, the* Farmer *being on the outside. The* Little Girl *still lurks breathless*]

MATT: Now, Mr. Browning—dash it all!—you ought to know better than this!

FARMER: Oh! I daresay yu'm a gentleman, but so's this convict, seemin'ly. Leastways he'm a captain. Perhaps yu'll tell me the name o' the innkeeper where yu'm stayin' at Lustleigh?

MATT: Has he got a name? I hadn't noticed.

FARMER: No; nor the name of the Inn neither, maybe?

MATT: The Red Lion.

FARMER: Ha!

MATT: Well, it ought to be.

FARMER: And per'aps yu'll show me the clothes yu've got on.

MATT: [*Taking a resolution*] Well, I own up.

LITTLE GIRL: Oh!

FARMER: I thowt yu'd come to it.

MATT: [*Lowering his voice*] Be sporting. Give me a show!

FARMER: Now yu know I can't du that; what's the yuse of askin'?

MATT: Well, I've had forty-eight hours' freedom, and given them a good run. You haven't a cigarette?

FARMER: I don't smoke them things. Jim, got a fag for this gentleman?

[First Laborer *brings out a packet of cigarettes which he holds out. Matt takes one and lights it from a match sheltered in the horny hands of the* Laborer, *who then retires again, Right, with the shovel*]

MATT: Thanks very much! [*He sits on the wheelbarrow. There ensues a silence. The* Little Girl *steals up to* Matt]

LITTLE GIRL: [*Holding out a small book*] Would you mind giving me your autograph?

FARMER: Miss 'Lizabeth!

LITTLE GIRL: Well, I've only just begun—I *have* to ask anybody at all thrilling.

MATT: [*With a grin*] Ink or—blood?

LITTLE GIRL: Oh! that'd be splendid!

MATT: Mine or—yours?

LITTLE GIRL: Oh! I've got a fountain pen. [*Hands it. Matt writes his name*] Thank you so much.

MATT: [*Handing back the book*] Shake hands on it. [*The* Little Girl *and he shake hands*] When you're an old woman you'll be able to say you met Murderous Matt.—Mr. Browning you won't give me a chance?

FARMER: Aid and abet a convict? No, no, Captain!

MATT: Vermin, eh? [*Looking round him*] Well,

you see, I've gone to earth. D'you hold with digging foxes out?

FARMER: I du, the varmints!

MATT: Ah! Well, you may thank your stars you were never in prison.

FARMER: No, an' I 'ope I'll never du nothin' to putt me there.

MATT: Take care you don't have bad luck, that's all.

FARMER: Bad luck? I reckon a man as kills a man can think he's havin' *gude* luck if he don't swing for it.

MATT: [*Somberly*] I meant the poor beggar no harm.

LITTLE GIRL: Have you really killed a man?

MATT: Not yet.

FARMER: [*Removing the pick from the barrow*] Yu struck the blow, and he died of't. What's more, so far as I remember, he was duin' his duty, same as I'm duin' mine. [*He looks intently at Matt, as if warning him not to try another blow*]

MATT: You needn't be afraid; there's a child here. If there weren't! I hope you'll see that my friend here [*Pointing to the* Laborer] has the reward for my capture.

FARMER: 'E can 'ave it; I don' want no reward for duin' *my* duty.

MATT: [*Nodding gravely*] That's lucky! I appreciate your excellent intentions, Mr. Browning. Glad to have met you! Good-bye!

[*He leaps from the barrow, and with a twist like a footballer evading a tackle, is past him and away to the Left. The* Little Girl *claps her hands*]

FARMER: [*Astonished*] The varmint! Hi! Jim! Arter 'im!

[*The* Laborer *utters a sort of roar and starts running. The* Farmer *is about to follow*]

LITTLE GIRL: Oh! Mr. Browning!

FARMER: Well?

LITTLE GIRL: Oh! nothing.

FARMER: Darn!

[*He follows out, running, Left. The* Constable *and* Second Laborer *come hurrying from Right*]

CONSTABLE: Gone! Which way, Missy?

LITTLE GIRL: [*With distant blankness*] I don't know.

CONSTABLE: Come on, then! [*He and the* Laborer *go out, Left, running*]

LITTLE GIRL: Oh! I do hope he gets off! Oh!

[*On the hue and cry*]

THE CURTAIN FALLS]

EPISODE VIII.

A few minutes have passed.

In the parlor of a cottage of gentility are two maiden ladies—Miss Grace, about forty-seven, brew-

ing tea at a little table before the fire, Right, and Miss Dora, much younger, still dressed in hunting togs, standing at the open French window, Back.

MISS DORA: There's such a glow on the Cleave, Grace. Most lovely red. We killed. Everybody was looking out for that escaped convict.

MISS GRACE: Did you see him?

MISS DORA: No, thank goodness. Poor hunted wretch!

MISS GRACE: If you think hunted things are poor, why do you go hunting?

MISS DORA: Foxes hunt and expect to be hunted.

MISS GRACE: So do convicts. Sympathy's wasted on them. Tea, Dora.

MISS DORA: This isn't a common convict. It's that Captain Denant, you remember——

MISS GRACE: Oh!—not likely to forget the row we had about his case. Well! it served him right!

MISS DORA: [*Going to the table and sitting down. Looking steadily at her sister*] For a good woman, Grace, you know—you're awfully hard.

MISS GRACE: Tea-cake, please. I like consistency.

MISS DORA: [*Deeply*] I think you're right.

MISS GRACE: [*Surprised*] How?

MISS DORA: It *is* a shame to hunt a fox—much better to shoot it.

MISS GRACE: There'd soon be no foxes. Don't get *that* bee into your bonnet *here*. What with rabbits, and chained dogs, you've set the farmers by the ears as it is. Wait till we go to Bath. You can have as many bees as you like there.

MISS DORA: I shan't hunt any more.

MISS GRACE: Then you're very foolish, if you enjoy it. Will you come over to the Service with me this evening?

MISS DORA: D'you know what I wish *you'd* say, Grace? "I shan't go to church any more."

MISS GRACE: I wish to God, Dora, you'd give up free thought!

MISS DORA: I wish to God, Grace, you'd give up religion.

MISS GRACE: You only hurt the vicar by it.

MISS DORA: [*Shaking her head*] He's too good a sort to mind.

MISS GRACE: You're too perverse for anything. I've only to say something and you set your will to the opposite.

MISS DORA: My dear, my will is nothing to yours. I haven't the ego for it.

MISS GRACE: [*Coldly*] You mean I'm egoistic? Thank you.

MISS DORA: Sorry, Grace.

MISS GRACE: Will you have another cup?

MISS DORA: Please.

[*She is holding out her cup and* Miss Grace *has poured from the teapot, when a Figure comes rushing through the French window. They both drop their hands and stare.* Matt, *panting and distressed, makes a sudden reveal-ing gesture of appeal, and blots himself out be-*

hind a window curtain. The hue and cry is heard off. The two ladies are still staring in wild surprise, when the Farmer *appears at the French window*]

FARMER: Which way'd 'e go?

MISS DORA: Who?

FARMER: Convict. Mun cam' over your waal un' round the corner ther'.

MISS DORA: Oh! Yes. I thought I saw. Across the lawn, and over the wall at the far end, Mr. Browning. Quick!

[*Behind her the figure and face of* Miss Grace *are expressive*]

FARMER: Gude! Woi! Over the waal 'e went. To him, boys! Chop him before he'm into the spinney.

[*The hue and cry passes the window running— the* Two Laborers, *the* Constable, *and* Two Tourist Youths. *The cries die off and leave a charged silence—the* Two Ladies *on their feet*]

MATT: [*Emerging, still breathless, with his hat in his hand. Noting* Miss Dora's *riding kit, he turns to* Miss Grace] Thank you, Madam.

MISS GRACE: Not me.

MATT: [*Making a bow to* Miss Dora] That was great of you, great!

MISS DORA: Keep back—one of them might see. [*She draws the curtains as* Matt *shrinks back*]

MISS GRACE: Great! To tell such a lie! And for a convict!

MATT: [*Recovering his self-possession*] If you'll forgive my saying so, that makes it greater. To tell a lie for an archbishop wouldn't strain one a bit.

MISS GRACE: Please don't blaspheme.

MISS DORA: [*Pouring out tea*] Will you have a cup of tea, Sir?

MISS GRACE: [*In a low voice*] Really, Dora!

MATT: [*Dropping his hat and taking the cup from* Miss Dora] It's too good of you. [*He drinks it straight off and hands it back*] I'm most awfully sorry for butting in like this; but it was neck or nothing.

MISS GRACE: Then I think it should have been nothing, Sir, considering the position you've placed my poor sister in.

MISS DORA: [*Hotly*] Poor sister! Grace, you——!

MATT: When you're hunted all you think of is the next move.

MISS DORA: I'm afraid you're awfully done.

MATT: Thanks, I'm getting my wind back. I feel like kissing the hem of your garment.

MISS DORA: It hasn't got one. Wasn't it rather mad to escape?

MATT: I don't think so. It's shown me how decent people can be.

MISS DORA: Did they ill-treat you?

MATT: Oh! no, the treatment's all right—a trifle monotonous.

MISS DORA: Listen! [*They listen. Faint shouting*] Where are you making for?

MATT: No plan. They're no good. It's like a battle —you change 'em before you use 'em.

MISS DORA: I read who you were in the papers.

MATT: Oh! yes. I'm in big print? Thank you most awfully. I'll clear out now.

MISS DORA: No, wait! [*At the curtains*] I'll be back in a minute. [*She slips out*]

MISS GRACE: [*Turning round to him*] I suppose you call yourself a gentleman?

MATT: I really don't know. Depends on who I'm with. I might be contradicted.

MISS GRACE: You see the sort of woman my sister is—impulsive, humanitarian. I'm—I'm very fond of her.

MATT: Naturally. She's splendid.

MISS GRACE: If you don't want to involve her——

MISS DORA: [*Reappearing through the curtains*] I think I can hide you.

MISS GRACE: Dora!

MATT: No, no! It's not good enough. I can't let you——

MISS DORA: [*Turning on her sister*] I'm going to, Grace.

[*They speak together in rapid tones*]

MISS GRACE: Not in this house.

MISS DORA: It's as much my house as yours. You need have nothing to do with it.

MISS GRACE: [*Drawing her from the window*] At least you haven't broken the law yet. And you're not going to now.

MISS DORA: I can't bear to see a soldier and a gentleman chased by a lot of chawbacons.

MISS GRACE: [*With a glance at* Matt] Dora, you mustn't. It's wrong and it's absurd.

MISS DORA: [*Heated*] Go up-stairs. If I have to refer to you I'll say you've seen nothing. And so can you.

MISS GRACE: [*Her voice rising*] You expect me to tell lies!

[Matt, *unseen in the heat of this discussion, makes a motion of despair and slips out of the window*]

MISS DORA: I'm going to hide him, I tell you. Captain— [*Suddenly turning to* Matt, *she sees that he is no longer there*] Where is he? [*The* Two Sisters *stand silent, blankly gazing about them*]

MISS DORA: Did he go by the door or the window?

MISS GRACE: I don't know.

MISS DORA: Didn't you see him?

MISS GRACE: I did not. [*At the expression on her sister's face*] I say I did not.

[Miss Dora *looks behind the window curtain, then cautiously out of the window, then recoils before the* Constable, *who comes in heated and breathless, followed by the* Farmer *and the* First Laborer, *who stops outside*]

CONSTABLE: Beg pardon, Miss. We've lost un. He'm a fair twister. Maybe he doubled back. We'll 'ave a luke over, if an' in case he'm hidin' yere somewhere about. Can we go thru yere?

MISS DORA: He can't be in the house.

[Miss Grace *stands pursing her lips*]

FARMER: We med 'ave a luke, Miss, after that. 'E'm a proper varmint.

[*Without waiting for further permission, the two pass through the room and go out Left. The* Two Sisters *stand looking at each other*]

MISS DORA: I won't have him caught. [*She moves towards the door*]

MISS GRACE: [*Seizing her sister's skirt*] Stop! I tell you!

MISS DORA: Let go!

MISS GRACE: I shall not. You're crazy. What is it to you?

MISS DORA: Let go, Grace!

MISS GRACE: You can't help him without breaking the law.

MISS DORA: Will you let me go, Grace? I shall hit you.

MISS GRACE: Very well. Hit me, then!

[*The* Two Sisters *clinch and for a moment it looks as if there were to be a physical struggle between them. There are sounds of approach*]

MISS DORA: Let go!

[*They unclinch, and wait for the door to open. Re-enter the* Farmer *and* Constable]

FARMER: Well he'm not yere; that's certain for zure.

CONSTABLE: [*Between the two*] You're quite sure, Miss, yu saw 'im over that wall?

[*A tense moment*]

MISS DORA: Quite!

[Miss Grace *has drawn her breath in with a hiss*]

FARMER: And not seen un since?

MISS DORA: No.

FARMER: Nor yu, Miss?

[Miss Dora *stares at her sister*]

MISS GRACE: [*Throwing up her head, and with a face like a mask*] No.

FARMER: [*Picking up* Matt's *hat left by him as he fled*] 'Ere, what's this?

MISS DORA: [*Recovering*] That? An old hat of my brother's that I use sometimes.

FARMER: 'Tis uncommon like the one that varmint was wearin'.

MISS DORA: Is it? Those fishing hats are all the same. [*Taking the hat*] Have you tried the orchard, Mr. Browning?

FARMER: Ah! we mun try that, but 'tis gettin' powerful dimsy. Come boys, we mun 'ave a gude old luke. The varmint fuled me bravely. I mun get me own back.

MISS DORA: Try the vicarage!

CONSTABLE: Ah! we'll try that tu.

[*They pass out at the window. The* Two Sisters *are left silent. Miss Grace suddenly sits down at the table and covers her face with her hands*]

MISS DORA: You told it beautifully, Grace. Thank you!

MISS GRACE: [*Uncovering her face with a fierce gesture*] Thank me for telling a lie!

MISS DORA: I'm sorry.

MISS GRACE: Sorry? You'd make me do it again!

MISS DORA: [*Simply*] I would. [*Looking after the hunt*] Poor fellow!

[*On the look between them*

THE CURTAIN FALLS]

EPISODE IX.

No time has passed. In the vestry of a village church lighted by an oil lamp, where, at the back, surplices and cassocks are hanging on pegs, a door, Right, leads to the churchyard and an open door, Left, into the church. There is no furniture except a chair or two, and a small table with a jug on it against the wall "up" from the door, Left.

The stage is empty, but almost at once the Parson *enters from the church, carrying some overpast Harvest decorations, which he places on the table. He is a slim, grizzle-haired, brown, active, middle-aged man with a good, lined, clean-shaven face, and a black Norfolk jacket; obviously a little "High" in his doctrine. He pours water from a jug into two large vases, humming: "O for the wings—for the wings of a dove!" Then carrying the vases, one in each hand, he goes back into the church. The door on the Right is opened and the hunted, hatless* Matt *slips in, closing the door behind him. He stands taking in the situation, crosses to the open door opposite, spies the* Parson, *and, recoiling, blots himself out behind a cassock. His face, peeping out, is withdrawn as the* Parson *returns, this time literally singing: "O for the wings—for the wings of a dove!" Taking off his coat, he prepares to hang it on a peg and take a cassock, and as he reaches the highest note, he lifts the cassock from in front of* Matt *and starts back.*

PARSON: Hullo!

MATT: Sanctuary, Sir!

PARSON: What d'you mean? Who are you? [Matt *opens his* Burberry] Oh! [*That "Oh!" is something more than astonishment; it has in it an accent of dismay, as if the speaker were confronted by his own soul*] The escaped convict! You oughtn't to have come in here.

MATT: Then where, Sir? In old days the Church——

PARSON: In old days the Church was a thing apart; now it belongs to the State. [Matt *makes a move towards the door*] Wait a minute! [*He has hung up his coat and put on the cassock, as if to strengthen the priest within him*] I think I read that you were that Captain Denant who——

MATT: Yes.

PARSON: [*Almost to himself*] Poor fellow!

[Matt *stares at him and there is a silence*]

MATT: Death isn't as much to us who were in the war, as it is to you.

PARSON: I know; I was there.

MATT: Padre?

PARSON: [Nodding] Where have you come from?

MATT: House of the two ladies over there. Left them fighting over me. Couldn't stand that—not worth it.

PARSON: [With a little smile] Yes, Miss Dora wanted to keep you and Miss Grace to throw you out. H'm? And yet Miss Dora doesn't come to church, and Miss Grace does. Something wrong there; or it is something right? [He stares at Matt] Are they after you?

MATT: Full cry.

PARSON: Sanctuary? If I were a Roman. Sometimes wish I were.

MATT: More logical.

PARSON: More powerful. This is a situation I've never had to face, Captain Denant.

MATT: Well, Sir, I'm just about done. If you could let me rest a bit, that's all I ask.

PARSON: My dear fellow! Sit down! [He pulls a chair forward] I'll lock the door. [He does so; then, as Matt looks up at the window, which is in the fourth wall] No, they can't see in. I expect you're very hungry too.

MATT: [Sitting] No, thanks—beyond it. You know that feeling, I bet?

PARSON: [Shaking his head] I'm afraid we of the Church lead too regular lives.

MATT: Not at the Front? It was pretty rife there.

PARSON: No, I'm ashamed to say—not even there. [While speaking, he is evidently pondering and torn]

MATT: [Suddenly] Well, Padre, how does it look to you? Giving me up?

PARSON: [Moved] Padre! [He takes a turn and comes to a sudden halt in front of Matt's chair] As man to man—who am I to give you up? One poor fellow to another! [Shaking his head] I can't help you to escape, but if you want rest, take it.

MATT: [Suddenly] Wonder what Christ would have done!

PARSON: [Gravely] That, Captain Denant, is the hardest question in the world. Nobody ever knows. You may answer this or that, but nobody ever knows. The more you read those writings, the more you realize that He was incalculable. You see—He was a genius! It makes it hard for us who try to follow Him. [Gazing at Matt, who is sitting forward with his elbows on his knees and his head on his hands] Very tired?

MATT: Gosh! I didn't think one could feel so tired. My joints have gone on strike. I was a three-mile runner, too.

PARSON: Were you? Good man!

MATT: It's the strain here. [Touching his head] If they get me and I have to go back! Odd! I didn't feel it half as much when I was escaping from Germany.

PARSON: Did anyone see you come in here?

MATT: Can't have—they'd have been in on my heels.

PARSON: Who's after you?

MATT: Villagers—and a constable.

PARSON: My villagers—and here am I—

MATT: [Standing up] By George, yes, Padre! It's too bad. I'll clear out.

PARSON: [Putting his hand on his shoulder and pressing him back into the chair] No, no! Rest while you can. You've asked for sanctuary. I don't know that I've the right to turn you out of here. I don't know—anyway I can't. Take your time. I have a little brandy here. Sometimes we get a faint in church—[He takes a bottle and a little glass from the corner cupboard] Drink it down.

MATT: [Drinking it off. Pulling out the flask] I say—wonder if you'd return this for me; it's empty—to that name and address. [He takes a tailor-sewn label out of his pocket] I ripped it off this Burberry. You might say "with unending gratitude." But please don't give that name away.

PARSON: No, no; I'll see to it. [Pockets it] Tell me! What made you escape?

MATT: Stick a bob-cat in a cage and open the door by mistake; and see what happens [Looking at the Parson's face] Oh! Yes, I know what you mean—but I've paid my scot long ago.

PARSON: Didn't you have a fair trial?

MATT: You can't "try" bad luck.

PARSON: All bad luck?

MATT: Well, I oughtn't to have hit him, of course; original sin, you know; but for an ordinary knock-out six weeks is about all you'd get; and I got four years more for that Rotten Row rail. Yes, I think I was perfectly entitled to have a shot.

PARSON: If you're quiet in your own mind—that's the only thing.

MATT: Well, you needn't worry, Padre. I shall be caught all right.

PARSON: [With a smile] I'm not worrying about that. Caesar can look after himself, he has the habit. What bothers me is my own peace of mind. I don't like the thoughts that keep rising in it. You led a company in the war. And I lead——

MATT: Your parishioners—um?

PARSON: Yes. [Nodding] When you're gone—shall I be entitled to have been silent about you without telling them that I have been silent? Am I entitled to refrain from helping the Law without letting them know it? If I let them know it, can I keep what little influence I now possess? And is it right for a parson to go on where he has no influence? That's my trouble, Captain Denant.

MATT: I see. [With a start] Some one's trying the door.

[The Parson moves to the door, Right; Matt has started forward]

PARSON: [At the door] Who is that?

VOICE OF BELLRINGER: Me, Zurr.

PARSON: No, Thomas, I'm busy; I can't let anyone into the church now till Service time. [He stands listening, then returns, Center] My bellringer.

MATT: [In a low voice] The hospitality of God—

I shan't forget, Padre. But I don't want to be on your conscience. I'll flit. Wish I had the wings of that dove, though!

PARSON: I have Service at half-past six. There will only be one or two gathered together, I'm afraid. Make a third. You can rest through the Service. No one comes in here.

MATT: You're a trump! But I'd rather go and take my chance again. It's dark now. I don't like to give in. I'll bolt, and be caught in the open. You might give me your blessing.

PARSON: [Shaking his head] Not certain enough of myself—not certain enough. It takes a bishop at least to give a blessing.

[A very loud knocking on the door]

MATT: Trapped, by George! [He springs towards the cassocks and blots himself out]

[The Parson has gone again to the door]

PARSON: [Rather sharply] What is that?

VOICE OF CONSTABLE: Open the door, Zurr, please!

PARSON: Who is it?

VOICE OF CONSTABLE: Constable, Zurr; open, please.

[The Parson, with a gesture of distress, opens the door. Enter the Constable, the Farmer, the Two Laborers, and the Bellringer]

PARSON: I told you, Thomas, I could see no one till after Service.

BELLRINGER: Yes, Zurr; but Constable 'e thought you ought to know as 'ow I zeed a man enter 'ere a while back. [He looks round]

PARSON: What's all this, Constable?

CONSTABLE: 'Tis th' escaped convict, Zurr. We'm after 'e. These tu men yere found 'e down to the old gravel-pit. 'E give 'em the slip, an' we chased un to the ladies' 'ouse yonder, wherr 'e gave us the goo-by again; and Tammas says 'e saw a man come in 'ere as sounds praaperly like the varmint. You ben 'ere long, Zurr?

PARSON: An hour, at least.

CONSTABLE: Front door's locked, but I got men in the porch. Be 'ee sure as there's no one in the church?

PARSON: [Moving towards the church door] I don't know whether you have the right to search a holy place; but look for yourselves, as quietly as you can, please. [He stands at the church door to let them pass. They go, with the exception of the Bellringer, who has remained by the vestry door. The Parson crosses to him] You can go too, Thomas. I'll stand here.

[The Bellringer, with uneasy eyes and motions, crosses under the compulsion of the Parson's glance]

PARSON: [Hardly moving his lips] Now, quick!

[But as he speaks, the Farmer reappears in the church doorway; the Parson has just time to make a warning gesture, Matt just time to blot himself out again]

PARSON: Well, Browning?

FARMER: 'Eem not therr; 'tes zo bare's me 'and 'Eem a proper twisty customer for sure, but we'll get 'e yet. [His eyes rest suspiciously on the Parson's face]

PARSON: [With a forced smile] He got away from you, then, did he?

FARMER: Aye! 'E can run an' twist like a rabbit. He'm a desperate foxy chap. What's behind they cassocks?

PARSON: [Still with that forced smile] I'll look, Browning.

[He moves to the cassocks, and, from the middle, takes a look behind them, but to the Left only. And at this moment they all return from the church and he turns to them]

CONSTABLE: Thank 'ee, Zurr; 'e'm not yere, Tammas. Yu made a fule of us zeemin'ly.

BELLRINGER: [Stammering] I zeed mun come in 'ere; I zeed mun wi' these eyes—I did zurely.

PARSON: [Looking at his watch] Service, Thomas. Go and ring the bell. [To the Constable] I'm afraid I must ask you to go too, please, unless you would all like to stay for Service.

[A certain length of face becomes apparent]

CONSTABLE: [Opening the door and beckoning the Men out] My juty, Zurr, ef yu'll excuse us.

PARSON: That's all right, Constable.

FARMER: [Suddenly] Jest a minute, Vicar. Yu'll pardon me askin', but are yo zartin zure as yu'm not zeen this joker?

PARSON: [Drawing himself up] What is it you are asking me?

FARMER: I'm askin' yu on yure honor as a Christian gentleman, whether or no yu've zeen the escaped convict?

[After a moment's intense silence]

PARSON: I——

MATT: [Stepping out without the Burberry] Certainly he's not. Sorry, Sir, I was hidden there. [Holding up his hands] I surrender, Constable.

FARMER: Woi! The varmint! Got un! Worry, worry, worry!

PARSON: Be quiet in this place; and go out— You shame God!

[Astonished at this outburst, they slink out, leaving Matt, Center, in the grip of the Constable. The Parson is on his Left]

MATT: [To the Parson] Forgive me, Sir! Oughtn't to have come in here. It wasn't playing cricket.

PARSON: No, no! That you have done—that you have done.

MATT: It's one's decent self one can't escape.

PARSON: Ah! that's it! [Very low] God keep you!

[He watches the Constable and Matt go out]

[The bell begins to ring, as

THE CURTAIN FALLS]

END

Lady Gregory

(1859–1932)

"During these first years," wrote Yeats, referring to the founding of the Irish theatre, "Lady Gregory was friend and hostess, a centre of peace, an adviser who never overestimated or underestimated trouble, but neither she nor we thought her a possible creator." There was no reason to expect her to undertake the labor of writing plays for the newly created Irish theatre in addition to fostering the new movement ever since her first decisive conversations with Yeats, in 1894. She was a great lady, beautiful and witty, and was married to a prominent figure in Irish life, the wealthy landowner and member of Parliament Sir William Gregory. She had evinced no great interest in politics and could not be regarded as a nationalist while Ireland was renewing the struggle for home rule after the lull that had followed the fall of Parnell. She was, besides, English by descent and a Protestant. Her efforts to draw closer to the peasantry because of her interest in folklore were actually regarded with suspicion, and malicious country people set her down as a "souper," or proselytizing Protestant.

It was sufficient that she had joined Yeats, George Moore, and Edward Martyn to form the Irish Literary Theatre in 1899, and that she had tided the little group over great difficulties until 1901, when it expired, largely from lack of funds. Two years later she also had helped to lay the foundations for the Irish National Theatre Society, and from then on she could be counted upon to leap into the breach whenever the Society's existence was in jeopardy, which happened to be always. The group was harassed from the beginning not only by lack of money but by defection in the ranks. It encountered attacks from the extremist Sinn Feiners, who saw no merit in a theatre not exclusively political. The patriots rioted at the *première* of Synge's first one-acter, *In the Shadow of the Glen,* because they felt it contained slurs on Irish womanhood, and rioting could be expected during every other important *première*. Lady Gregory had also undertaken the task of running the new Abbey Theatre efficiently and of giving numerous parties to promote public relations, especially strategic first-night suppers, for which she had become famous. In short, she was the social mainstay of the nascent Irish theatre; and if anything, she was, as George Moore noted, "a little too imposing, too suggestive of Corinne or Madame Sand."

It is true that she had written a few articles, but these could be dismissed as mere self-indulgence on the part of a gentlewoman. More recently she had edited her deceased husband's papers, but this could be set down as an act of matrimonial piety. As for her collecting Irish folklore, this could be regarded as a form of innocent dilettantism, although it ceased to be that soon enough and justified her favorite exhortation: "We work to add dignity to Ireland."

"And now," Yeats remarked in his *Dramatis Personae*, "all in a moment, as it seemed, she became the founder of modern Irish dialect literature." What Yeats may have overlooked, however, is that in Lady Gregory's opinion it had become absolutely imperative to create such a literature if the Irish theatre was to capture national interest instead of shrinking into a closed circle for esthetes. Yeats's own plays were beautifully spiritual and poetic, but they could not be expected to root the drama in Irish soil. After an initial effort in 1902, *Twenty-five,* Lady Gregory began to contribute a series of one-act folk plays so singularly adapted to the needs and talents of the Irish theatre that this great-hearted little stage organization continued to subsist largely on folk drama for many years, through many transformations and a shifting directorate.

Lady Gregory wrote a number of romantic dramas steeped in folk legend and one fairly incisive three-act satire on Irish weaknesses, *The Image*. She also translated four Molière pieces (*The Doctor in Spite of Himself, The Rogueries of Scapin, The Miser,* and *The Would-Be Gentleman*) into delectable Irish dialect, an inspired undertaking if there ever was one, especially for the Irish theatre, which did not favor foreign plays. But her major contribution to dramatic literature was a series of little tragedies and farces, flavorsomely colloquial and realistic, and abounding in peasant types and rural backgrounds.

Among the tragedies, *The Gaol Gate* (1906) was a masterpiece in miniature. It was calculated, moreover, to win the approbation of the patriots, since Ireland's struggle for independence had inspired this story of the hanging of a man who refuses to betray his comrades in spite of his neighbors' belief that he has turned informer. The poignancy of the hero's mother and wife, who have come to visit him in prison, made a deep impression, and the mother became one of the best character parts of the famous Sara Allgood's early career. Another political one-acter was the delightful *Rising of the Moon,* in which a police sergeant refrains from arresting a rebel who carries a tempting price on his head.

Even more successful were the folk farces. *Spreading the News,* in 1904, made turbulent fun out of country gossip which turns the simple accident of a man's dropping his hayfork into a hair-raising account of his chasing his neighbor with murderous intent. The long one-act folk farce *Hyacinth Halvey,* in 1906, turned cartwheels on the question of what constitutes a reputation and how much of a burden it can become to the bearer. Young Hyacinth's glowing letters of recommendation threaten to deprive him of all freedom and entertainment, and his efforts to blacken himself in the opinion of unwaveringly admiring neighbors grow increasingly frantic without bringing him nearer to coveted disgrace. Lady Gregory's comic masterpiece, however, is undoubtedly *The Workhouse Ward,* which she wrote in 1908. Here her preoccupation with peasant types was productive of several superbly realized characters.

John Millington Synge began to till the same soil about the time that Lady Gregory came to the aid of the national theatre. It was one of the marks of Synge's genius that he felt impelled to go beyond peasant drama, that he transfigured folk material into a highly personal creation. And since no one could follow Synge into his private world, he had no successors when he died in 1909. The lesson taught by Lady Gregory could, however, be easily absorbed, and to her influence may be traced much of the drama of the Irish stage, which manages to convey the realities of the countryside with colloquial salt and attractive local color. During the lean years when genius did not appear on the Abbey stage, it was good to have such plays. In any case, they were generally better than the artificial fluff that was so often favored in London. Of Synge, Yeats has said with perfect justice, "He had under charming and modest manners, in almost all things of life, a complete absorption in his own dream." Lady Gregory's dream was not her own but that of her fellow creators and of Ireland. Even the writing of comedies was a matter of serving the theatre she helped to create and preserve. Too few were being composed by her colleagues Yeats and Synge. Referring to her little comedy *Spreading the News,* she said, "The idea of this play first came to me as a tragedy. . . . But comedy and not tragedy was wanted at our theatre to put beside the high poetic work . . . and I let laughter have its way with the little play." It was in comedy, moreover, that her true talent lay, and *The Workhouse Ward* has had few rivals for the title of the best one-act comedy in the English language.

BIBLIOGRAPHY: Ernest Boyd, *Ireland's Literary Renaissance,* 1916; Dawson Byrne, *The Story of Ireland's National Theatre,* 1929; Barrett H. Clark, *A Study of the Modern Drama* (pp. 344–348), 1938; Lady Gregory, *Our Irish Theatre,* 1913; William Butler Yeats, *Dramatis Personae,* 1936.

THE WORKHOUSE WARD

By Lady Gregory

PERSONS

MICHAEL MISKELL ⎰ *paupers*
MIKE MC INERNEY ⎱
MRS. DONOHOE, *a countrywoman*

SCENE: *A ward in Cloon Workhouse. The two old men in their beds.*

MICHAEL MISKELL: Isn't it a hard case, Mike McInerney, myself and yourself to be left here in the bed, and it the feast day of Saint Colman, and the rest of the ward attending on the Mass.

MIKE MC INERNEY: Is it sitting up by the hearth you are wishful to be, Michael Miskell, with cold in the shoulders and with speckled shins? Let you rise up so, and you well able to do it, not like myself that has pains the same as tin-tacks within in my inside.

MICHAEL MISKELL: If you have pains within in your inside there is no one can see it or know of it the way they can see my own knees that are swelled up with the rheumatism, and my hands that are twisted in ridges the same as an old cabbage stalk. It is easy to be talking about soreness and about pains, and they maybe not to be in it at all.

MIKE MC INERNEY: To open me and to analyze me you would know what sort of a pain and a soreness I have in my heart and in my chest. But I'm not one like yourself to be cursing and praying and tormenting the time the nuns are at hand, thinking to get a bigger share than myself of the nourishment and of the milk.

MICHAEL MISKELL: That's the way you do be picking at me and faulting me. I had a share and a good share in my early time, and it's well you know that, and the both of us reared in Skehanagh.

MIKE MC INERNEY: You may say that, indeed, we are both of us reared in Skehanagh. Little wonder you to have good nourishment the time we were both rising, and you bringing away my rabbits out of the snare.

MICHAEL MISKELL: And you didn't bring away my own eels, I suppose, I was after spearing in the Turlough? Selling them to the nuns in the convent you did, and letting on they to be your own. For you were always a cheater and a schemer, grabbing every earthly thing for your own profit.

MIKE MC INERNEY: And you were no grabber yourself, I suppose, till your land and all you had grabbed wore away from you!

MICHAEL MISKELL: If I lost it itself, it was through the crosses I met with and I going through the world. I never was a rambler and a card-player like yourself, Mike McInerney, that ran through all and lavished it unknown to your mother!

MIKE MC INERNEY: Lavished it, is it? And if I did was it you yourself led me to lavish it or some other one? It is on my own floor I would be to-day and in the face of my family, but for the misfortune I had to be put with a bad next door neighbor that was yourself. What way did my means go from me is it? Spending on fencing, spending on walls, making up gates, putting up doors, that would keep your hens and your ducks from coming in through starvation on my floor, and every four footed beast you had from preying and trespassing on my oats and my mangolds and my little lock of hay!

MICHAEL MISKELL: O to listen to you! And I striving to please you and to be kind to you and to close my ears to the abuse you would be calling and letting out of your mouth. To trespass on your crops is it? It's little temptation there was for my poor beasts to ask to cross the mering. My God Almighty! What had you but a little corner of a field!

MIKE MC INERNEY: And what do you say to my garden that your two pigs had destroyed on me the year of the big tree being knocked, and they making gaps in the wall.

MICHAEL MISKELL: Ah, there does be a great deal of gaps knocked in a twelve-month. Why wouldn't they be knocked by the thunder, the same as the tree, or some storm that came up from the west?

MIKE MC INERNEY: It was the west wind, I suppose, that devoured my green cabbage? And that rooted up my Champion potatoes? And that ate the gooseberries themselves from off the bush?

MICHAEL MISKELL: What are you saying? The two quietest pigs ever I had, no way wicked and well ringed. They were not ten minutes in it. It would be hard for them to eat strawberries in that time, let alone gooseberries that's full of thorns.

MIKE MC INERNEY: They were not quiet, but very ravenous pigs you had that time, as active as a fox they were, killing my young ducks. Once they had blood tasted you couldn't stop them.

MICHAEL MISKELL: And what happened myself the fair day of Esserkelly, the time I was passing your door? Two brazened dogs that rushed out and took a piece of me. I never was the better of it or of the start I got, but wasting from then till now!

MIKE MC INERNEY: Thinking you were a wild beast they did, that had made his escape out of the traveling show, with the red eyes of you and the ugly face of you, and the two crooked legs of you that wouldn't hardly stop a pig in a gap. Sure any dog that had any life in it at all would be roused and stirred seeing the like of you going the road!

MICHAEL MISKELL: I did well taking out a summons against you that time. It is a great wonder you not to have been bound over through your lifetime, but the laws of England is queer.

MIKE MC INERNEY: What ailed me that I did not summons yourself after you stealing away the clutch of eggs I had in the barrel, and I away in Ardrahan searching out a clocking hen.

MICHAEL MISKELL: To steal your eggs is it? Is that what you are saying now? [Holds up his hands] The Lord is in heaven, and Peter and the saints, and yourself that was in Ardrahan that day put a hand on them as soon as myself! Isn't it a bad story for me to be wearing out my days beside you the same as a spancelled goat. Chained I am and tethered I am to a man that is ram-shacking his mind for lies!

MIKE MC INERNEY: If it is a bad story for you, Michael Miskell, it is a worse story again for myself. A Miskell to be next and near me through the whole of the four quarters of the year. I never heard there to be any great name on the Miskells as there was on my own race and name.

MICHAEL MISKELL: You didn't, is it? Well, you could hear it if you had but ears to hear it. Go across to Lisheen Crannagh and down to the sea and to Newtown Lynch and the mills of Duras and you'll find a Miskell, and as far as Dublin!

MIKE MC INERNEY: What signifies Crannagh and the mills of Duras? Look at all my own generations that are buried at the Seven Churches. And how many generations of the Miskells are buried in it? Answer me that!

MICHAEL MISKELL: I tell you but for the wheat that was to be sowed there would be more side cars and more common cars at my father's funeral (God rest his soul!) than at any funeral ever left your own door. And as to my mother, she was a Cuffe from Claregalway, and it's she had the purer blood!

MIKE MC INERNEY: And what do you say to the banshee? Isn't she apt to have knowledge of the ancient race? Was ever she heard to screech or to cry for the Miskells? Or for the Cuffes from Claregalway? She was not, but for the six families, the Hyneses, the Foxes, the Faheys, the Dooleys, the McInerneys. It is of the nature of the McInerneys she is I am thinking, crying them the same as a king's children.

MICHAEL MISKELL: It is a pity the banshee not to be crying for yourself at this minute, and giving you a warning to quit your lies and your chat and your arguing and your contrary ways; for there is no one under the rising sun could stand you. I tell you you are not behaving as in the presence of the Lord.

MIKE MC INERNEY: Is it wishful for my death you are? Let it come and meet me now and welcome so long as it will part me from yourself! And I say, and I would kiss the book on it, I to have one request only to be granted, and I leaving it in my will, it is what I would request, nine furrows of the field, nine ridges of the hills, nine waves of the ocean to be put between your grave and my own grave the time we will be laid in the ground!

MICHAEL MISKELL: Amen to that! Nine ridges, is it? No, but let the whole ridge of the world separate us till the Day of Judgment! I would not be laid anear you at the Seven Churches, I to get Ireland without a divide!

MIKE MC INERNEY: And after that again! I'd sooner than ten pound in my hand, I to know that my shadow and my ghost will not be knocking about with your shadow and your ghost, and the both of us waiting our time. I'd sooner be delayed in Purgatory! Now, have you anything to say?

MICHAEL MISKELL: I have everything to say, if I had but the time to say it!

MIKE MC INERNEY: [Sitting up] Let me up out of this till I'll choke you!

MICHAEL MISKELL: You scolding pauper you!

MIKE MC INERNEY: [Shaking his fist at him] Wait a while!

MICHAEL MISKELL: [Shaking his fist] Wait a while yourself!

[Mrs. Donohoe comes in with a parcel. She is a countrywoman with a frilled cap and a shawl. She stands still a minute. The two old men lie down and compose themselves]

MRS. DONOHOE: They bade me come up here by the stair. I never was in this place at all. I don't know am I right. Which now of the two of ye is Mike McInerney?

MIKE MC INERNEY: Who is it is calling me by my name?

MRS. DONOHOE: Sure amn't I your sister, Honor McInerney that was, that is now Honor Donohoe.

MIKE MC INERNEY: So you are, I believe. I didn't know you till you pushed anear me. It is time indeed for you to come see me, and I in this place five year or more. Thinking me to be no credit to you, I suppose, among that tribe of the Donohoes. I wonder they to give you leave to come ask am I living yet or dead?

MRS. DONOHOE: Ah, sure, I buried the whole string of them. Himself was the last to go. [Wipes her eyes] The Lord be praised he got a fine natural death. Sure we must go through our crosses. And he got a lovely funeral; it would delight you to hear the priest reading the Mass. My poor John Donohoe! A nice clean man, you couldn't but be fond of him.

Very severe on the tobacco he was, but he wouldn't touch the drink.

MIKE MC INERNEY: And is it in Curranroe you are living yet?

MRS. DONOHOE: It is so. He left all to myself. But it is a lonesome thing the head of a house to have died!

MIKE MC INERNEY: I hope that he has left you a nice way of living?

MRS. DONOHOE: Fair enough, fair enough. A wide lovely house I have; a few acres of grass land . . . the grass does be very sweet that grows among the stones. And as to the sea, there is something from it every day of the year, a handful of periwinkles to make kitchen, or cockles maybe. There is many a thing in the sea is not decent, but cockles is fit to put before the Lord!

MIKE MC INERNEY: You have all that! And you without e'er a man in the house?

MRS. DONOHOE: It is what I am thinking, yourself might come and keep me company. It is no credit to me a brother of my own to be in this place at all.

MIKE MC INERNEY: I'll go with you! Let me out of this! It is the name of the McInerneys will be rising on every side!

MRS. DONOHOE: I don't know. I was ignorant of you being kept to the bed.

MIKE MC INERNEY: I am not kept to it, but maybe an odd time when there is a colic rises up within me. My stomach always gets better the time there is a change in the moon. I'd like well to draw anear you. My heavy blessing on you, Honor Donohoe, for the hand you have held out to me this day.

MRS. DONOHOE: Sure you could be keeping the fire in, and stirring the pot with the bit of Indian meal for the hens, and milking the goat and taking the tacklings off the donkey at the door; and maybe putting out the cabbage plants in their time. For when the old man died the garden died.

MIKE MC INERNEY: I could to be sure, and be cutting the potatoes for seed. What luck could there be in a place and a man not to be in it? Is that now a suit of clothes you have brought with you?

MRS. DONOHOE: It is so, the way you will be tasty coming in among the neighbors at Curranroe.

MIKE MC INERNEY: My joy you are! It is well you earned me! Let me up out of this! [He sits up and spreads out the clothes and tries on coat] That now is a good frieze coat . . . and a hat in the fashion. . . . [He puts on hat]

MICHAEL MISKELL: [Alarmed] And is it going out of this you are, Mike McInerney?

MIKE MC INERNEY: Don't you hear I am going? To Curranroe I am going. Going I am to a place where I will get every good thing!

MICHAEL MISKELL: And is it to leave me here after you you will?

MIKE MC INERNEY: [In a rising chant] Every good thing! The goat and the kid are there, the sheep and the lamb are there, the cow does be running and she coming to be milked! Plowing and seed sowing, blossom at Christmas time, the cuckoo speaking through the dark days of the year! Ah, what are you talking about? Wheat high in hedges, no talk about the rent! Salmon in the rivers as plenty as hurf! Spending and getting and nothing scarce! Sport and pleasure, and music on the strings! Age will go from me and I will be young again. Geese and turkeys for the hundreds and drink for the whole world!

MICHAEL MISKELL: Ah, Mike, is it truth you are saying, you to go from me and to leave me with rude people and townspeople, and with people of every parish in the union, and they having no respect for me or no wish for me at all!

MIKE MC INERNEY: Whist now and I'll leave you . . . my pipe [Hands it over]; and I'll engage it is Honor Donohoe won't refuse to be sending you a few ounces of tobacco an odd time, and neighbors coming to the fair in November or in the month of May.

MICHAEL MISKELL: Ah, what signifies tobacco? All that I am craving is the talk. There to be no one at all to say out to whatever thought might be rising in my innate mind! To be lying here and no conversible person in it would be the abomination of misery!

MIKE MC INERNEY: Look now, Honor. . . . It is what I often heard said, two to be better than one. . . . Sure if you had an old trouser was full of holes. . . . or a skirt. . . . wouldn't you put another in under it that might be as tattered as itself, and the two of them together would make some sort of a decent show?

MRS. DONOHOE: Ah, what are you saying? There is no holes in that suit I brought you now, but as sound it is as the day I spun it for himself.

MIKE MC INERNEY: It is what I am thinking, Honor. . . . I do be weak an odd time . . . Any load I would carry, it preys upon my side . . . and this man does be weak an odd time with the swelling in his knees . . . but the two of us together it's not likely it is at the one time we would fail. Bring the both of us with you, Honor, and the height of the castle of luck on you, and the both of us together will make one good hardy man!

MRS. DONOHOE: I'd like my job! Is it queer in the head you are grown asking me to bring in a stranger off the road?

MICHAEL MISKELL: I am not, ma'am, but an old neighbor I am. If I had forecasted this asking I would have asked it myself. Michael Miskell I am, that was in the next house to you in Skehanagh!

MRS. DONOHOE: For pity's sake! Michael Miskell is it? That's worse again. Yourself and Mike that never left fighting and scolding and attacking one another! Sparring at one another like two young pups you were, and threatening one another after like two grown dogs!

MIKE MC INERNEY: All the quarreling was ever in the place it was myself did it. Sure his anger rises fast and goes away like the wind. Bring him out with myself now, Honor Donohoe, and God bless you.

MRS. DONOHOE: Well, then, I will not bring him out, and I will not bring yourself out, and you not to learn better sense. Are you making yourself ready to come?

MIKE MC INERNEY: I am thinking, maybe . . . it is a mean thing for a man that is shivering into seventy years to go changing from place to place.

MRS. DONOHOE: Well, take your luck or leave it. All I asked was to save you from the hurt and the harm of the year.

MIKE MC INERNEY: Bring the both of us with you or I will not stir out of this.

MRS. DONOHOE: Give me back my fine suit so [Begins gathering up the clothes], till I go look for a man of my own!

MIKE MC INERNEY: Let you go so, as you are so unnatural and so disobliging, and look for some man of your own, God help him! For I will not go with you at all!

MRS. DONOHOE: It is too much time I lost with you, and dark night waiting to overtake me on the road. Let the two of you stop together, and the back of my hand to you. It is I will leave you there the same as God left the Jews!

[She goes out. The old men lie down and are silent for a moment]

MICHAEL MISKELL: Maybe the house is not so wide as what she says.

MIKE MC INERNEY: Why wouldn't it be wide?

MICHAEL MISKELL: Ah, there does be a good deal of middling poor houses down by the sea.

MIKE MC INERNEY: What would you know about wide houses? Whatever sort of a house you had yourself it was too wide for the provision you had into it.

MICHAEL MISKELL: Whatever provision I had in my house it was wholesome provision and natural provision. Herself and her periwinkles! Periwinkles is a hungry sort of food.

MIKE MC INERNEY: Stop your impudence and your chat or it will be the worse for you. I'd bear with my own father and mother as long as any man would, but if they'd vex me I would give them the length of a rope as soon as another!

MICHAEL MISKELL: I would never ask at all to go eating periwinkles.

MIKE MC INERNEY: [Sitting up] Have you any one to fight me?

MICHAEL MISKELL: [Whimpering] I have not, only the Lord!

MIKE MC INERNEY: Let you leave putting insults on me so, and death picking at you!

MICHAEL MISKELL: Sure I am saying nothing at all to displease you. It is why I wouldn't go eating periwinkles, I'm in dread I might swallow the pin.

MIKE MC INERNEY: Who in the world wide is asking you to eat them? You're as tricky as a fish in the full tide!

MICHAEL MISKELL: Tricky is it! Oh, my curse and the curse of the four and twenty men upon you!

MIKE MC INERNEY: That the worm may chew you from skin to marrow bone! [Seizes his pillow]

MICHAEL MISKELL: [Seizing his own pillow] I'll leave my death on you, you scheming vagabone!

MIKE MC INERNEY: By cripes! I'll pull out your pin feathers! [Throwing pillow]

MICHAEL MISKELL: [Throwing pillow] You tyrant! You big bully you!

MIKE MC INERNEY: [Throwing pillow and seizing mug] Take this so, you stobbing ruffian you!

[They throw all within their reach at one another, mugs, prayer books, pipes, etc.]

CURTAIN

John Millington Synge

(1871–1909)

As we have had occasion to observe, one of the most remarkable developments of the modern theatre was the meteoric rise of the Irish drama. Ireland made no contribution to the stage in modern times until the last decade of the nineteenth century. Then it roused itself in response to nationalistic promptings and in time gave the world not only that superb repertory company the Abbey Theatre, renowned for natural acting and musical speech, but a number of dramatic masterpieces. Ireland's contribution, moreover, was as timely as it was meritorious. Realism had achieved a well-deserved supremacy in Europe; but its frequently literal and uninspired dramaturgy had led to a romantic revolt under Maeterlinck and Rostand in the eighteen-nineties which was beginning to lose its vitality by the first decade of the new century. The playwrights of a still untamed, unstandardized country such as Ireland were in a position to revivify the drama by combining the best elements of romanticism and realism. One of the new writers, moreover, was a superb artist. John Millington Synge may have been theoretically in favor of romanticism, and his last tragedy, *Deirdre of the Sorrows,* is the greatest Irish romantic drama; but he acquired such a singular sensitivity to the nuances of common life that most of his work provided a perfect fusion of reality and imagination.

Born in the vicinity of Dublin in 1871, of Protestant, English-descended, and socially prominent parents, Synge received the customary upper-class education in art and letters. He became an ultra-refined young man, proficient in four languages and an admirer of Racine, on whom he wrote a study. Wanderlust and a talent for music drew him to the Continent after his graduation from Trinity College in 1892. Leading a somewhat Bohemian life, mostly in Paris, for six years and augmenting his slender means with book reviewing, he seemed headed for the rather futile career of an Irish emigrant and esthete. But at a critical moment in 1899, his neighbor at the Grand Hotel Corneille, William Butler Yeats, pointed out the meagerness of his prospects and persuaded him to return to Ireland. Synge, by then inclined to heed the good advice, returned to the Aran Islands, thirty miles off the west coast of Ireland, which he had visited the year before, and surrendered to the spell of the primitive ways and dialect of the islanders. Further travels in the western counties of Ireland steeped Synge in the life of the most colorful and eloquent countryfolk of the British Isles. The experience proved a greater boon to Irish literature than anything that had happened before, for it was the making of the first major playwright of Ireland. On the Aran Islands, as well as on the west coast of Ireland, he found people who were close to the plain realities of labor and struggle with the soil and sea. At the same time, however, the environment and the manners were romantically primitive and the speech was poetic.

Synge wrote of his good fortune in the preface to his greatest comedy, *The Playboy of the Western World* (1907). All art, he declared, was a collaboration, and he had found the best collaborators in his simple neighbors. The modern literature of the towns was unsatisfactory; on one hand, it produced exotic work such as that of Mallarmé and Huysmans, and on the other, Ibsen's and Zola's dealings with reality "in joyless and pallid words." Synge maintained that "on the stage one must have reality, and one must have joy"; only "what is superb and wild in reality" was capable of providing esthetic gratification; and a good play must contain speech that is "as fully flavored as a nut or apple." In Ireland he felt the presence of a popular imagination that was still "fiery and magnificent, and tender; so that those of us who wish to write start with a chance that is not given to writers in places where the springtime of local life has been forgotten, and the harvest is a memory only, and the straw has been turned into bricks."

A mild and retiring intellectual, who surprised John Masefield and others by the contrast between his appearance and his buoyant work, Synge nevertheless had the right dramatic temperament. Yeats described it well when he wrote of his friend that he favored "all that has edge, all that is salt in the mouth, all that is rough to the hand, all that heightens the emotions by contest, all that stings into life the sense of tragedy." He added sagely, "The food of the spiritual-minded is sweet, an Indian scripture says, but passionate minds love bitter food."

Everything that has "edge" prevails in Synge's plays, particularly in his comedies. "Bitter food" also appears in them. He may not have been as cynical as was charged by his enemies and, in fact, much compassion of an unsentimental nature will be found in his writing, but a trace of disillusionment and acerbity does run through most of his work. Although, in reacting against Ibsenism, he deplored the fact that "in these days the playhouse is too often stocked with the drugs of many seedy problems," life itself was a "problem" to him. He tried to flee from it, in a back-to-nature romantic spirit that is essentially a nineteenth-century phenomenon. But he could not free himself from the dour temperament with which he viewed life. His first one-acter, *In the Shadow of the Glen,* drew a sobering picture of an unhappily married young peasant woman who is driven out of her home by her crabbed husband; *Riders to the Sea* and *Deirdre of the Sorrows* are unmitigated tragedies; *The Well of Saints* is a commentary on mankind's need for protective self-delusion; and *The Playboy of the Western World* is tinged with disenchantment despite its brisk humor.

Nor was Synge, in spite of his Rousseauist love of nature, a naïve worshiper of the primitive. He took note of the common man's struggle with relentless nature in *Riders to the Sea,* of the misery of the poor in his thoughtful travel notes, of the shiftlessness and drunkenness of some of the Irish in *The Tinker's Wedding,* and of the instability of their affections in *The Playboy of the Western World.* He was a poet with the eye of a realist, or a realist with a poet's talent for transforming common ore into gold. Made oversensitive by their struggle for national independence, Irish patriots felt the sting of his irony so keenly, indeed, that they accused him of malicious intent to defame the Irish and their cause. They resented *In the Shadow of the Glen* as an insult to Irish womanhood and staged riots during the early performances of *The Playboy of the Western World,* alleging that it defamed the nation, in addition to being ribald, or, as the noble firebrand Arthur Griffith put it, "cloacine." More serious, however, than these aspersions on an artist endowed with singular integrity was the shadow that hovered over Synge's genius. He was productive only during the brief span of years between 1903 and 1909, for he died in his thirty-eighth year.

Although each of Synge's six plays is memorable, *Riders to the Sea* is generally considered his most perfect work. It gains intensity from its extreme simplicity and condensation, as well as from its vividly conveyed, fate-charged atmosphere. This little tragedy does not, of course, suggest its author's comic genius, but it is thoroughly representative of his mastery of plain yet impassioned utterance and of his feeling for common life.

To the studious historian, *Riders to the Sea* may represent the influence, by no means negligible in Ireland, of the Belgian symbolist Maeterlinck, and the piece is surely a triumphant vindication of Maeterlinck's theory of "static" drama. Since the catastrophe is not presented on the stage, the play represents a "stasis." But the expectation of disaster, the waiting for news, and its reception by the tragic old woman Maurya are supremely dramatic. The critic may also be prompted to point out that here we have drama without "plot," the possibility—and value—of which was first championed not by Maeterlinck but by the European naturalists about a quarter of a century before Synge began to write plays. For conflict—except for the struggle of men against the sea, only the effect of which is shown—the playwright successfully substituted "tension" as dramatic yeast. This does not prove, however, that the procedures of Synge guarantee comparable results of high drama for others. *Riders to the Sea* represents the triumph of a very personal sensibility and of a disciplined talent given to few who have served the theatre in any style or period. Although an artist of limited scope, Synge was touched with greatness; *Riders to the Sea* is pervaded with that greatness.

BIBLIOGRAPHY: Ernest Boyd, *Ireland's Literary Renaissance,* 1916; Dawson Byrne, *The Story of Ireland's National Theatre,* 1929; W. G. Fay and Catherine Carswell, *The Fays of the Abbey Theatre,* 1935; John Gassner, *Masters of the Drama* (pp. 553–562), 1940, 1945; Ronald Peacock, *The Poet in the Theatre* (pp. 105–116), 1946; William Butler Yeats, *Dramatis Personae,* 1936.

RIDERS TO THE SEA

By John Millington Synge

PERSONS

MAURYA, *an old woman*   CATHLEEN, *her daughter*
BARTLEY, *her son*   NORA, *a younger daughter*   MEN AND WOMEN

SCENE: *An Island off the west of Ireland.*

Cottage kitchen, with nets, oil-skins, spinning-wheel, some new boards standing by the wall, etc. Cathleen, a girl of about twenty, finishes kneading cake, and puts it down in the pot-oven by the fire; then wipes her hands, and begins to spin at the wheel. Nora, a young girl, puts her head in at the door.

NORA: [*In a low voice*] Where is she?

CATHLEEN: She's lying down, God help her, and may be sleeping, if she's able.

[*Nora comes in softly, and takes a bundle from under her shawl*]

CATHLEEN: [*Spinning the wheel rapidly*] What is it you have?

NORA: The young priest is after bringing them. It's a shirt and a plain stocking were got off a drowned man in Donegal.

[*Cathleen stops her wheel with a sudden movement, and leans out to listen*]

NORA: We're to find out if it's Michael's they are, some time herself will be down looking by the sea.

CATHLEEN: How would they be Michael's, Nora? How would he go the length of that way to the far north?

NORA: The young priest says he's known the like of it. "If it's Michael's they are," says he, "you can tell herself he's got a clean burial by the grace of God, and if they're not his, let no one say a word about them, for she'll be getting her death," says he, "with crying and lamenting."

[*The door which Nora half closed is blown open by a gust of wind*]

CATHLEEN: [*Looking out anxiously*] Did you ask him would he stop Bartley going this day with the horses to the Galway fair?

NORA: "I won't stop him," says he, "but let you not be afraid. Herself does be saying prayers half through the night, and the Almighty God won't leave her destitute," says he, "with no son living."

CATHLEEN: Is the sea bad by the white rocks, Nora?

NORA: Middling bad, God help us. There's a great roaring in the west, and it's worse it'll be getting when the tide's turned to the wind. [*She goes

over to the table with the bundle*] Shall I open it now?

CATHLEEN: Maybe she'd wake up on us, and come in before we'd done. [*Coming to the table*] It's a long time we'll be, and the two of us crying.

NORA: [*Goes to the inner door and listens*] She's moving about on the bed. She'll be coming in a minute.

CATHLEEN: Give me the ladder, and I'll put them up in the turf-loft, the way she won't know of them at all, and maybe when the tide turns she'll be going down to see would he be floating from the east.

[*They put the ladder against the gable of the chimney; Cathleen goes up a few steps and hides the bundle in the turf-loft. Maurya comes from the inner room*]

MAURYA: [*Looking up at Cathleen and speaking querulously*] Isn't it turf enough you have for this day and evening?

CATHLEEN: There's a cake baking at the fire for a short space [*Throwing down the turf*] and Bartley will want it when the tide turns if he goes to Connemara.

[*Nora picks up the turf and puts it round the pot-oven*]

MAURYA: [*Sitting down on a stool at the fire*] He won't go this day with the wind rising from the south and west. He won't go this day, for the young priest will stop him surely.

NORA: He'll not stop him, mother, and I heard Eamon Simon and Stephen Pheety and Colum Shawn saying he would go.

MAURYA: Where is he itself?

NORA: He went down to see would there be another boat sailing in the week, and I'm thinking it won't be long till he's here now, for the tide's turning at the green head, and the hooker's tacking from the east.

CATHLEEN: I hear some one passing the big stones.

NORA: [*Looking out*] He's coming now, and he in a hurry.

BARTLEY: [*Comes in and looks round the room; speaking sadly and quietly*] Where is the bit of new rope, Cathleen, was bought in Connemara?

CATHLEEN: [*Coming down*] Give it to him, Nora; it's on a nail by the white boards. I hung it up this morning, for the pig with the black feet was eating it.

NORA: [*Giving him a rope*] Is that it, Bartley?

MAURYA: You'd do right to leave that rope, Bartley, hanging by the boards. [Bartley *takes the rope*] It will be wanting in this place. I'm telling you, if Michael is washed up to-morrow morning, or the next morning, or any morning in the week, for it's a deep grave we'll make him by the grace of God.

BARTLEY: [*Beginning to work with the rope*] I've no halter the way I can ride down on the mare, and I must go now quickly. This is the one boat going for two weeks or beyond it, and the fair will be a good fair for horses I heard them saying below.

MAURYA: It's a hard thing they'll be saying below if the body is washed up and there's no man in it to make the coffin, and I after giving a big price for the finest white boards you'd find in Connemara.

[*She looks round at the boards*]

BARTLEY: How would it be washed up, and we after looking each day for nine days, and a strong wind blowing a while back from the west and south?

MAURYA: If it wasn't found itself, that wind is raising the sea, and there was a star up against the moon, and it rising in the night. If it was a hundred horses, or a thousand horses you had itself, what is the price of a thousand horses against a son where there is one son only?

BARTLEY: [*Working at the halter, to* Cathleen] Let you go down each day, and see the sheep aren't jumping in on the rye, and if the jobber comes you can sell the pig with the black feet if there is a good price going.

MAURYA: How would the like of her get a good price for a pig?

BARTLEY: [*To* Cathleen] If the west wind holds with the last bit of the moon let you and Nora get up weed enough for another cock for the kelp. It's hard set we'll be from this day with no one in it but one man to work.

MAURYA: It's hard set we'll be surely the day you're drownd'd with the rest. What way will I live and the girls with me, and I an old woman looking for the grave?

[Bartley *lays down the halter, takes off his coat, and puts on a newer one of the same flannel*]

BARTLEY: [*To* Nora] Is she coming to the pier?

NORA: [*Looking out*] She's passing the green head and letting fall her sails.

BARTLEY: [*Getting his purse and tobacco*] I'll have half an hour to go down, and you'll see me coming again in two days, or in three days, or maybe in four days if the wind is bad.

MAURYA: [*Turning round to the fire, and putting her shawl over her head*] Isn't it a hard and cruel man won't hear a word from an old woman, and she holding him from the sea?

CATHLEEN: It's the life of a young man to be going on the sea, and who would listen to an old woman with one thing and she saying it over?

BARTLEY: [*Taking the halter*] I must go now quickly. I'll ride down on the red mare, and the gray pony'll run behind me. . . . The blessing of God on you.

[*He goes out*]

MAURYA: [*Crying out as he is in the door*] He's gone now, God spare us, and we'll not see him again. He's gone now, and when the black night is falling I'll have no son left me in the world.

CATHLEEN: Why wouldn't you give him your blessing and he looking round in the door? Isn't it sorrow enough is on every one in this house without your sending him out with an unlucky word behind him, and a hard word in his ear?

[Maurya *takes up the tongs and begins raking the fire aimlessly without looking round*]

NORA: [*Turning toward her*] You're taking away the turf from the cake.

CATHLEEN: [*Crying out*] The Son of God forgive us, Nora, we're after forgetting his bit of bread. [*She comes over to the fire*]

NORA: And it's destroyed he'll be going till dark night, and he after eating nothing since the sun went up.

CATHLEEN: [*Turning the cake out of the oven*] It's destroyed he'll be, surely. There's no sense left on any person in a house where an old woman will be talking forever. [Maurya *sways herself on her stool*]

CATHLEEN: [*Cutting off some of the bread and rolling it in a cloth; to* Maurya] Let you go down now to the spring well and give him this and he passing. You'll see him then and the dark word will be broken, and you can say "God speed you," the way he'll be easy in his mind.

MAURYA: [*Taking the bread*] Will I be in it as soon as himself?

CATHLEEN: If you go now quickly.

MAURYA: [*Standing up unsteadily*] It's hard set I am to walk.

CATHLEEN: [*Looking at her anxiously*] Give her the stick, Nora, or maybe she'll slip on the big stones.

NORA: What stick?

CATHLEEN: The stick Michael brought from Connemara.

MAURYA: [*Taking a stick* Nora *gives her*] In the big world the old people do be leaving things after them for their sons and children, but in this place it is the young men do be leaving things behind for them that do be old.

[*She goes out slowly.* Nora *goes over to the ladder*]

CATHLEEN: Wait, Nora, maybe she'd turn back quickly. She's that sorry, God help her, you wouldn't know the thing she'd do.

NORA: Is she gone round by the bush?

CATHLEEN: [*Looking out*] She's gone now. Throw it down quickly, for the Lord knows when she'll be out of it again.

NORA: [*Getting the bundle from the loft*] The young priest said he'd be passing to-morrow, and we might go down and speak to him below if it's Michael's they are surely.

CATHLEEN: [*Taking the bundle*] Did he say what way they were found?

NORA: [*Coming down*] "There were two men," says he, "and they rowing round with poteen before the cocks crowed, and the oar of one of them caught the body, and they passing the black cliffs of the north."

CATHLEEN: [*Trying to open the bundle*] Give me a knife, Nora, the string's perished with the salt water, and there's a black knot on it you wouldn't loosen in a week.

NORA: [*Giving her a knife*] I've heard tell it was a long way to Donegal.

CATHLEEN: [*Cutting the string*] It is surely. There was a man in here a while ago—the man sold us that knife—and he said if you set off walking from the rocks beyond, it would be seven days you'd be in Donegal.

NORA: And what time would a man take, and he floating?

[Cathleen *opens the bundle and takes out a bit of stocking. They look at them eagerly*]

CATHLEEN: [*In a low voice*] The Lord spare us, Nora! isn't it a queer hard thing to say if it's his they are surely?

NORA: I'll get his shirt off the hook the way we can put the one flannel on the other. [*She looks through some clothes hanging in the corner*] It's not with them, Cathleen, and where will it be?

CATHLEEN: I'm thinking Bartley put it on him in the morning, for his own shirt was heavy with the salt in it. [*Pointing to the corner*] There's a bit of a sleeve was of the same stuff. Give me that and it will do.

[Nora *brings it to her and they compare the flannel*]

CATHLEEN: It's the same stuff, Nora; but if it is itself aren't there great rolls of it in the shops of Galway, and isn't it many another man may have a shirt of it as well as Michael himself?

NORA: [*Who has taken up the stocking and counted the stitches, crying out*] It's Michael, Cathleen, it's Michael; God spare his soul, and what will herself say when she hears this story, and Bartley on the sea?

CATHLEEN: [*Taking the stocking*] It's a plain stocking.

NORA: It's the second one of the third pair I knitted, and I put up threescore stitches, and I dropped four of them.

CATHLEEN: [*Counts the stitches*] It's that number is in it. [*Crying out*] Ah, Nora, isn't it a bitter thing to think of him floating that way to the far north, and no one to keen him but the black hags that do be flying on the sea?

NORA: [*Swinging herself round, and throwing out her arms on the clothes*] And isn't it a pitiful thing when there is nothing left of a man who was a great rower and fisher, but a bit of an old shirt and a plain stocking?

CATHLEEN: [*After an instant*] Tell me is herself coming, Nora? I hear a little sound on the path.

NORA: [*Looking out*] She is, Cathleen. She's coming up to the door.

CATHLEEN: Put these things away before she'll come in. Maybe it's easier she'll be after giving her blessing to Bartley, and we won't let on we've heard anything the time he's on the sea.

NORA: [*Helping Cathleen to close the bundle*] We'll put them here in the corner.

[*They put them into a hole in the chimney corner. Cathleen goes back to the spinning-wheel*]

NORA: Will she see it was crying I was?

CATHLEEN: Keep your back to the door the way the light'll not be on you.

[Nora *sits down at the chimney corner, with her back to the door. Maurya comes in very slowly, without looking at the girls, and goes over to her stool at the other side of the fire. The cloth with the bread is still in her hand. The girls look at each other, and Nora points to the bundle of bread*]

CATHLEEN: [*After spinning for a moment*] You didn't give him his bit of bread?

[Maurya *begins to keen softly, without turning round*]

CATHLEEN: Did you see him riding down?

[Maurya *goes on keening*]

CATHLEEN: [*A little impatiently*] God forgive you; isn't it a better thing to raise your voice and tell what you seen, than to be making lamentation for a thing that's done? Did you see Bartley, I'm saying to you?

MAURYA: [*With a weak voice*] My heart's broken from this day.

CATHLEEN: [*As before*] Did you see Bartley?

MAURYA: I seen the fearfulest thing.

CATHLEEN: [*Leaves her wheel and looks out*] God forgive you; he's riding the mare now over the green head, and the gray pony behind him.

MAURYA: [*Starts, so that her shawl falls back from her head and shows her white tossed hair. With a frightened voice*] The gray pony behind him.

CATHLEEN: [*Coming to the fire*] What is it ails you, at all?

MAURYA: [*Speaking very slowly*] I've seen the fearfulest thing any person has seen, since the day Bride Dara seen the dead man with a child in his arms.

CATHLEEN AND NORA: Uah.

[*They crouch down in front of the old woman at the fire*]

NORA: Tell us what it is you seen.

MAURYA: I went down to the spring well, and I stood there saying a prayer to myself. Then Bartley came along, and he riding on the red mare with the gray pony behind him. [*She puts up her hands *as if to hide something from her eyes*] The Son of God spare us, Nora!

CATHLEEN: What is it you seen?

MAURYA: I seen Michael himself.

CATHLEEN: [*Speaking softly*] You did not, mother; it wasn't Michael you seen, for his body is after being found in the Far North, and he's got a clean burial by the grace of God.

MAURYA: [*A little defiantly*] I'm after seeing him this day, and he riding and galloping. Bartley came first on the red mare; and I tried to say, "God speed you," but something choked the words in my throat. He went by quickly; and "the blessing of God on you," says he, and I could say nothing. I looked up then, and I crying, at the gray pony, and there was Michael upon it—with fine clothes on him, and new shoes on his feet.

CATHLEEN: [*Begins to keen*] It's destroyed we are from this day. It's destroyed, surely.

NORA: Didn't the young priest say the Almighty God wouldn't leave her destitute with no son living?

MAURYA: [*In a low voice, but clearly*] It's little the like of him knows of the sea. . . . Bartley will be lost now, and let you call in Eamon and make me a good coffin out of the white boards, for I won't live after them. I've had a husband, and a husband's father, and six sons in this house—six fine men, though it was a hard birth I had with every one of them and they coming to the world—and some of them were found and some of them were not found, but they're gone now the lot of them. . . . There were Stephen, and Shawn, were lost in the great wind, and found after in the Bay of Gregory of the Golden Mouth, and carried up the two of them on the one plank, and in by that door.

[*She pauses for a moment, the girls start as if they heard something through the door that is half open behind them*]

NORA: [*In a whisper*] Did you hear that, Cathleen? Did you hear a noise in the northeast?

CATHLEEN: [*In a whisper*] There's some one after crying out by the seashore.

MAURYA: [*Continues without hearing anything*] There was Sheamus and his father, and his own father again, were lost in a dark night, and not a stick or sign was seen of them when the sun went up. There was Patch after was drowned out of a curagh that turned over. I was sitting here with Bartley, and he a baby, lying on my two knees, and I seen two women, and three women, and four women coming in, and they crossing themselves, and not saying a word. I looked out then, and there were men coming after them, and they holding a thing in the half of a red sail, and water dripping out of it—it was a dry day, Nora—and leaving a track to the door.

[*She pauses again with her hand stretched out toward the door. It opens softly and old women begin to come in, crossing themselves on the threshold, and kneeling down in front of the stage with red petticoats over their heads*]

MAURYA: [*Half in a dream, to* Cathleen] Is it Patch, or Michael, or what is it at all?

CATHLEEN: Michael is after being found in the Far North, and when he is found there how could he be here in this place?

MAURYA: There does be a power of young men floating round in the sea, and what way would they know if it was Michael they had, or another man like him, for when a man is nine days in the sea, and the wind blowing, it's hard set his own mother would be to say what man was it.

CATHLEEN: It's Michael, God spare him, for they're after sending us a bit of his clothes from the Far North.

[*She reaches out and hands* Maurya *the clothes that belonged to* Michael. Maurya *stands up slowly, and takes them in her hands.* Nora *looks out*]

NORA: They're carrying a thing among them and there's water dripping out of it and leaving a track by the big stones.

CATHLEEN: [*In a whisper to the women who have come in*] Is it Bartley it is?

ONE OF THE WOMEN: It is surely, God rest his soul.

[*Two younger women come in and pull out the table. Then men carry in the body of* Bartley, *laid on a plank, with a bit of sail over it, and lay it on the table*]

CATHLEEN: [*To the women, as they are doing so*] What way was he drowned?

ONE OF THE WOMEN: The gray pony knocked him into the sea, and he was washed out where there is a great surf on the white rocks.

[Maurya *has gone over and knelt down at the head of the table. The women are keening softly and swaying themselves with a slow movement.* Cathleen *and* Nora *kneel at the other end of the table. The men kneel near the door*]

MAURYA: [*Raising her head and speaking as if she did not see the people around her*] They're all gone now, and there isn't anything more the sea can do to me. . . . I'll have no call now to be up crying and praying when the wind breaks from the south, and you can hear the surf is in the east, and the surf is in the west, making a great stir with the two noises, and they hitting one on the other. I'll have no call now to be going down and getting Holy Water in the dark nights after Samhain, and I won't care what way the sea is when the other women will be keening. [*To* Nora] Give me the Holy Water, Nora, there's a small sup still on the dresser. [Nora *gives it to her*]

MAURYA: [*Drops* Michael's *clothes across* Bartley's *feet, and sprinkles the Holy Water over him*] It isn't that I haven't prayed for you, Bartley, to the Almighty God. It isn't that I haven't said prayers in the dark night till you wouldn't know what I'd be saying; but it's a great rest I'll have now, and it's time surely. It's a great rest I'll have now, and great sleeping in the long nights after Samhain, if it's only a bit of wet flour we do have to eat, and maybe a fish that would be stinking.

[*She kneels down again, crossing herself, and saying prayers under her breath*]

CATHLEEN: [*To an old man*] Maybe yourself and Eamon would make a coffin when the sun rises. We have fine white boards herself bought, God help her, thinking Michael would be found, and I have a new cake you can eat while you'll be working.

THE OLD MAN: [*Looking at the boards*] Are there nails with them?

CATHLEEN: There are not, Colum; we didn't think of the nails.

ANOTHER MAN: It's a great wonder she wouldn't think of the nails, and all the coffins she's seen made already.

CATHLEEN: It's getting old she is, and broken.

[Maurya *stands up again very slowly and spreads out the pieces of* Michael's *clothes beside the body, sprinkling them with the last of the Holy Water*]

NORA: [*In a whisper to* Cathleen] She's quiet now

and easy; but the day Michael was drowned you could hear her crying out from this to the spring well. It's fonder she was of Michael, and would any one have thought that?

CATHLEEN: [*Slowly and clearly*] An old woman will be soon tired with anything she will do, and isn't it nine days herself is after crying and keening, and making great sorrow in the house?

MAURYA: [*Puts the empty cup mouth downwards on the table, and lays her hands together on* Bartley's *feet*] They're all together this time, and the end is come. May the Almighty God have mercy on Bartley's soul, and on Michael's soul, and on the souls of Sheamus and Patch, and Stephen and Shawn [*bending her head*]; and may He have mercy on my soul, Nora, and on the soul of every one is left living in the world.

[*She pauses, and the keen rises a little more loudly from the women, then sinks away*]

MAURYA: [*Continuing*] Michael has a clean burial in the Far North, by the grace of the Almighty God. Bartley will have a fine coffin out of the white boards, and a deep grave surely. What more can we want than that? No man at all can be living forever, and we must be satisfied.

[*She kneels down again and the curtain falls slowly*]

Sean O'Casey

(1884–——)

It must have been the dream of every trueborn Irish playwright that heaven would some day drop the mantle of Synge on his shoulders. When a new candidate for fame arrived in the shape of a gaunt, self-educated workingman, Sean O'Casey, the administrators of the Abbey must have rubbed their eyes. A man of rough ways and no graces, he was as unlikely an apparition as any of them could have expected.

O'Casey's progress was slow and painful. He was about forty when the Abbey produced his first play, *The Shadow of a Gunman,* a bitter exposé of the folly and tragedy associated with windy nationalist idealism. He was fourteen before he really learned to read and write. Having lost his father at the age of three, he was reared by a devoted but poverty-stricken mother. He was half starved as a child, living almost exclusively on a diet of hard bread and tea. His schooling, which started late and ended early, was made abhorrent to him by the tyranny and snobbery of schoolmasters. He was to remember this with bitterness in the first of his autobiographical books, *I Knock at the Door,* in which he recalls being introduced to learning by a clergyman, "lugged off along at the backside of this soft-hatted, stiff-collared, egg-headed oul' henchman of heaven, to be added to the swarm of urchins cowering and groping about in the rag-and-bone education provided by the church and state for the children of those who hadn't the wherewithal to do any better." Defective eyesight added to his difficulties, as did an extremely sensitive, rather irascible temperament. His rebelliousness led to his terminating his schooling abruptly. At thirteen he was already a workingman, earning four shillings a week in a Dublin chandlery.

The boy began to take on casual jobs, to which he could adjust no better than to the school and the chandlery. He became a dock worker, hod carrier, and stone breaker on road-building crews, working twelve hours a day with pick and shovel. His pride and temper cost him job after job. He scored his first dismissal for striking a senior clerk, but really earned his spurs at the age of fifteen, when he was fired from a news agency for which he folded papers at four in the morning for nine shillings a week; he had refused to remove his cap while receiving his pittance of pay. Later, his revolt became socially generalized rather than personal, but without any diminution of zeal or passion. He fought through the severe Dublin transport strike of 1913, and the Marxist idea of the class war, no theory but plain reality for O'Casey, was never to be far from his thoughts thereafter. It was to lead him later to denounce Irish nationalism as naïve, so long as it ignored the problem of poverty in the fever for national independence, and it was to bring him ultimately to radicalism and to a position on the editorial board of a radical publication in London in the nineteen-forties. He was not, indeed, impervious to the romanticism and rightness of the Irish cause, and he actually joined the Irish Citizen Army to fight British rule. If he did not participate in the Easter Rebellion, it was only because he was then an involuntary guest of the British military government. But the experiences of childhood and early manhood moved him to put common realities of poverty and daily living ahead of nationalist aspirations.

When O'Casey came to write his masterpieces *Juno and the Paycock* and *The Plough and the Stars,* he was not likely to forget his mother's painful efforts to keep her family alive, his hard-working brother's sickening and dying, his young sister's pauper burial, which was so shabby that the cabmen refused to follow her coffin for fear of losing their reputation. It is not difficult to discover the source of O'Casey's vast contempt for a windbag's revolutionary slogans, in *The Shadow of a Gunman;* of his picture of Captain Boyle's intoxication with nationalist oratory and liquor while his family is falling to pieces, in *Juno and the Paycock;* of his story of Clitheroe's death in the Easter uprising, in *The Plough and the Stars,* while the hero's wife goes mad with anxiety and a tubercular tenement child coughs out its lungs in the courtyard. Nor was O'Casey forgetful of what were to him first and fundamental truths, when, abandoning the realistic form, he wrote the half-realistic, half-expressionistic pacifist play *The Silver Tassie* in 1927: the symbolic *Within the Gates,* with its chorus of "Down and Outs," in 1933; and the later semipoetic revolutionary pieces *The Star Turns Red,* which divided Eire into fascist and antifascist camps, and *Red Roses for Me,* which lyrically turned a strike situation into an apocalyptic vision.

This review of O'Casey's proletarian and socialist conditioning is, nevertheless, only half the story. It accounts for his ideas and his realism, which is at once satiric and compassionate, Hogarthian and Tolstoyan. It does not account for O'Casey's music and poetry any more than it does for his wild humor. Steeping himself in books as soon as he could afford to buy them with pennies set aside from his earnings, intoxicating himself with Shakespeare ("Shakespeare was my education," he was to say later, recalling that he could recite whole passages from the plays), and responding to the magic of Irish speech and song in the old national literature as a member of the Gaelic League, the class-conscious workingman slowly transformed himself into an artist. From the same sources he was to acquire the grand manner that is an integral part of his style and thought; and somewhere along the line of his development he staked out a large area of humor, which is perhaps the greatest miracle for anyone carrying his burden of social anguish. Shakespeare and the visit of the Benson Company in Dublin introduced him to the mysteries of writing for the stage. He made his first stab at playwriting when he was seventeen, submitted a second play to the Abbey a year later, followed this with two other rejected pieces, absorbed criticism from the directors, and finally, in 1923, made his debut in Ireland's national theatre with *The Shadow of a Gunman*.

Concerning the metamorphosis of hod carrier into poet, there were soon no doubts. *Juno and the Paycock* (1924) is the first and, in the opinion of many, the best product of his fusion of realism and poetry, of somber tragedy and extravagant comedy. The very fact that it is an incomplete fusion may be more fortunate than regrettable. Perhaps the comedy and tragedy that jostle each other in the script detract from each other. But if this is so, it is not because each is not amply realized by itself; the contradictory aspects in *Juno and the Paycock* are cardinal facts of its author's observation of life. The play unsettles and whirls us about, leaving us no firmer foundation than the infirm world that is O'Casey's subject. "A state of chassis [chaos]" is his rueful commentary on the self-defeating humanity for which Mrs. Boyle requests Christ's compassion in one of the memorable speeches of modern drama.

O'Casey was never again to attain a comparable success except with the somewhat better integrated and even more bitter Easter Rebellion tragedy *The Plough and the Stars* (1926), an Irish masterpiece which was suitably baptized in another patriotic riot such as had greeted *The Playboy of the Western World*. Yeats, trying to howl down the mob, shouted with unfailing eloquence, "You have once more rocked the cradle of a reputation. The fame of O'Casey is born tonight. This is apotheosis." It was also the last time that the Abbey would unstintedly rejoice in a play by O'Casey.

The Silver Tassie was a divided play, although a turbulently powerful one, "bringing down all the Voodoo war poetry with an ironic crash," as Shaw wrote in a generous tribute. It was rejected by the Abbey, and was first produced by C. B. Cochran in London, with settings by the famous painter Augustus John. Since then, O'Casey has been living in England. *Within the Gates* subordinated the sense of immediate reality to the noble abstractions of morality drama. *The Star Turns Red,* an exalted antifascist vision, was likewise too generalized. *Oak Leaves and Lavender* was a riot of fantasy, as elusive as it was inspired. O'Casey started moving back to the style of his first masterpieces with the farcical comedy *The Purple Dust* (1940), in which blimpish Englishmen are worsted in an encounter with the Irish people, and with his strike drama *Red Roses for Me*. But the return was only partly successful, perhaps because it was only partly intended. O'Casey's random volume on the theatre, *The Flying Wasp* (1937), aired his differences with the Abbey directors and his dissatisfaction with the Irish and English stage; his criticism of his critics was no doubt justified but failed to consider his own part in his failures. He seemed temporarily more attuned to a medium that could give greater scope to his writing when he turned out a series of remarkable autobiographical volumes: *I Knock at the Door* (1939), *Pictures in the Hallway* (1942), *Drums Under the Windows* (1946), and *Inishfallen, Fare Thee Well* (1949).

Still, even in his most flawed plays, O'Casey remained a dramatist whose vitality was equaled by very few of his contemporaries, and whose power of language was approached by none of them. With at least two masterpieces, and with general superiority even in his alleged failures, O'Casey occupies a special niche in the English-speaking theatre. Should anyone who is impatient with the later plays ever be inclined to question their author's rank among playwrights, he can easily fortify his faith by returning to the quite inimitable pages of *Juno and the Paycock* and *The Plough and the Stars*. As for the latter, it may well be noted that O'Casey here wrote a triumphant example of the "mass drama" as first developed by the pioneering naturalists, and that it has not only that "spire of meaning" that Galsworthy recommended for modern naturalist plays but also poetry and a compassionate heart. It concerns elemental realities of social fact and private feeling and translates them through a number of tinglingly alive human beings. And if O'Casey was less than enthusiastic over the Easter Rebellion, it was not because he was indifferent to the cause of Irish freedom but because he was even more passionately devoted to the cause of all stricken humanity—a cause which transcends race and nationality.

BIBLIOGRAPHY: Brooks Atkinson, *Broadway Scrapbook* (pp. 13–16, 147–151), 1947; John Mason Brown, *Two on the Aisle* (pp. 126–130), 1938; John Gassner, *Masters of the Drama* (pp. 566–571), 1940, 1945; Desmond MacCarthy, *Drama* (pp. 349–355), 1940; Ernest Short, *Theatrical Cavalcade* (pp. 208–210), 1942; Sean O'Casey, *The Flying Wasp*, 1937, and the autobiographical volumes cited.

THE PLOUGH AND THE STARS

By Sean O'Casey

ACT I.

SCENE—*The home of the* Clitheroes. *It consists of the front and back drawing-rooms in a fine old Georgian house, struggling for its life against the assaults of time and the more savage assaults of the tenants. The room shown is the back drawing-room, wide, spacious and lofty. At back is the entrance to the front drawing-room. The space, originally occupied by folding doors, is now draped with casement cloth of a dark purple, decorated with a design in reddish-purple. One of the curtains is pulled aside, giving a glimpse of the front drawing-room, at the end of which can be seen the wide, lofty windows looking out into the street. The room directly in front of the audience is furnished in a way that suggests an attempt towards a finer expression of domestic life. The large fireplace on* L. *is of wood, painted to look like marble (the original has been taken away by the landlord). Below the fireplace, on the wall, is a small mirror. On the mantelshelf are two candlesticks of dark carved wood. Between them is a small clock. Over the clock, on wall, is a picture of "The Sleeping Venus." On the right of the entrance to the front drawing-room is a copy of "The Gleaners," on the opposite side a copy of "The Angelus." Underneath "The Gleaners" is a chest of drawers on which stands a green bowl filled with scarlet dahlias and white chrysanthemums. Near to the fireplace is a couch which at night forms a double bed for* Clitheroe *and* Nora. *Near the end of the room opposite to the fireplace is a gate-legged table, covered with a cloth. On top of the table a huge cavalry sword is lying. To the* L. *above fireplace is a door which leads to a lobby from which the staircase leads to the hall. The floor is covered with a dark green linoleum. The room is dim except where it is illuminated from the glow of the fire.* Fluther Good *is repairing the lock of door,* L. *A claw hammer is on a chair beside him, and he has a screwdriver in his hand. He is a man of 40 years of age, rarely surrendering to thoughts of anxiety, fond of his "oil" but determined to conquer the habit before he dies. He is square-jawed and harshly featured; under the left eye is a scar, and his nose is bent from a smashing blow received in a fistic battle long ago. He is bald, save for a few peeping tufts of reddish hair around his ears; and his upper lip is hidden by a scrubby red moustache, em-broidered here and there with a grey hair. He is dressed in a seedy black suit, cotton shirt with a soft collar, and wears a very respectable little black bow. On his head is a faded jerry hat, which, when he is excited, he has a habit of knocking farther back on his head, in a series of taps. In an argument he usually fills with sound and fury, generally signifying a row. He is in his shirt sleeves at present, and wears a soiled white apron, from a pocket in which sticks a carpenter's two-foot rule. He has just finished the job of putting on a new lock, and, filled with satisfaction, he is opening and shutting the door, enjoying the completion of a work well done. Sitting at the fire, airing a white shirt, is* Peter Flynn. *He is a little, thin bit of a man, with a face shaped like a lozenge; on his cheeks and under his chin is a straggling wiry beard of a dirty-white and lemon hue. His face invariably wears a look of animated anguish, mixed with irritated defiance, as if everybody was at war with him, and he at war with everybody. He is cocking his head in such a way that suggests resentment at the presence of* Fluther, *who pays no attention to him, apparently, but is really furtively watching him.* Peter *is clad in a singlet, white whipcord knee-breeches, and is in his stockinged feet. A voice is heard speaking outside of door* L. *(it is that of* Mrs. Gogan *talking to someone).*

MRS. GOGAN: [*Outside door* L.] Who are you lookin' for, sir? Who? Mrs. Clitheroe? . . . Oh, excuse me. Oh ay, up this way. She's out, I think: I seen her goin'. Oh, you've somethin' for her. Oh, excuse me. You're from Arnott's. . . . I see. . . . You've a parcel for her. . . . Righto. . . . I'll take it. . . . I'll give it to her the minute she comes in. . . . It'll be quite safe. . . . Oh, sign that. . . . Excuse me. . . . Where? . . . Here? . . . No, there; righto. Am I to put Maggie or Mrs.? What is it? You dunno? Oh, excuse me.

[Mrs. Gogan *opens the door and comes in. She is a doleful-looking little woman of 40, insinuating manner and sallow complexion. She is fidgety and nervous, terribly talkative, has a habit of taking up things that may be near her and fiddling with them while she is speaking. Her heart is aflame with curiosity, and a fly could not come into nor go out of the house without her knowing. She has a draper's parcel in her hand, the knot of the twine tying it is untied.* Mrs. Gogan *crosses in front of* Fluther,

635

behind the couch, to the table R., *where she puts the parcel, fingering it till she has the paper off, showing a cardboard box.* Peter, *more resentful of this intrusion than of Flurther's presence, gets up from the chair, and without looking around, his head carried at an angry cock, marches into the room at back. He leaves the shirt on the back of the chair*]

[*Removing the paper and opening the cardboard box it contains*] I wondher what's this now? A hat! [*She takes out a hat, black, with decorations in red and gold*] God, she's goin' to th' divil lately for style! That hat, now, cost more than a penny. Such notions of upperosity she's getting. [*Putting the hat on her head*] Swank! [*Turning to* Flurther] Eh, Flurther, swank, what! [Flurther *looks over at her, then goes on opening and shutting the door*]

FLUTHER: She's a pretty little Judy, all the same.

MRS. GOGAN: Ah, she is, an' she isn't. There's prettiness an' prettiness in it. I'm always sayin' that her skirts are a little too short for a married woman. An' to see her, sometimes of an evenin', in her glad-neck gown would make a body's blood run cold. I do be ashamed of me life before her husband. An' th' way she thries to be polite, with her "Good mornin', Mrs. Gogan," when she's goin' down, an' her "Good evenin', Mrs. Gogan," when she's comin' up. But there's politeness an' politeness in it.

FLUTHER: They seem to get on well together, all th' same.

MRS. GOGAN: Ah, they do, an' they don't. The pair o' them used to be like two turtle doves always billin' an' cooin'. You couldn't come into th' room but you'd feel, instinctive like, that they'd just been afther kissin' an' cuddlin' each other. . . . It often made me shiver, for, afther all, there's kissin' an' cuddlin' in it. But I'm thinkin' he's beginnin' to take things more quietly; the mystery of havin' a woman's a mystery no longer. . . . She dhresses herself to keep him with her, but it's no use—afther a month or two, th' wondher of a woman wears off. [Mrs. Gogan *takes off the hat, and puts it back in the box; going on to rearrange paper round box, and tie it up again*]

FLUTHER: I dunno, I dunno. Not wishin' to say anything derogatory, I think it's all a question of location: when a man find th' wondher of one woman beginnin' to die, it's usually beginnin' to live in another.

MRS. GOGAN: She's always grumblin' about havin' to live in a tenement house. "I wouldn't like to spend me last hour in one, let alone live me life in a tenement," says she. "Vaults," says she, "that are hidin' th' dead, instead of homes that are sheltherin' th' livin'." "Many a good one," says I, "was reared in a tenement house." Oh, you know, she's a well-up little lassie, too; able to make a shillin' go where another would have to spend a pound. She's wipin' th' eyes of th' Covey an' poor oul' Pether—everybody knows that—screwin' every penny she can out o' them, in ordher to turn th'

place into a babby-house. An' she has th' life fright-ened out o' them; washin' their face, combin' their hair, wipin' their feet, brushin' their clothes, thrim-min' their nails, cleanin' their teeth—God Almighty, you'd think th' poor men were undhergoin' penal servitude.

FLUTHER: [*With an exclamation of disgust*] A-a-ah, that's goin' beyond th' beyonds in a tenc-ment house. That's a little bit too derogatory.

[Peter *enters from room, back, head elevated and resentful fire in his eyes; he is still in his singlet and trousers, but is now wearing a pair of unlaced boots—possibly to be decent in the presence of* Mrs. Gogan. Peter *comes down* C. *and crosses, front of settee, to chair in front of fire; he turns the shirt which he has left to air on the back of the chair, then goes, front of couch, to the chest of drawers, back* L., *opens drawer after drawer, looking for some-thing; as he fails to find it, he closes each drawer with a snap. He jerks out things neatly folded, and shoves them back into the drawers any way*]

PETER: [*In anguish, snapping a drawer shut*] Well, God Almighty, give me patience. [Peter *returns, front of couch, to the fireplace, gives the shirt a vicious turn on the back of the chair, and goes back, front of couch, to room, back,* Flurther *and* Mrs. Gogan *watching him furtively all the time*]

MRS. GOGAN: [*Curiously*] I wondher what is he foostherin' for now?

FLUTHER: [*Coming* C.] He's adornin' himself for the meeting to-night. [*He pulls a handbill from one of his pockets, and reads*] "Great Demonsthration an' Torchlight Procession around places in the City sacred to th' memory of Irish Pathriots to be concluded be a meetin', at which will be taken an oath of fealty to th' Irish Republic. Formation in Parnell Square at eight o'clock." Well, they can hold it for Flurther. I'm up th' pole; no more dhrink for Flurther. It's three days now since I touched a dhrop, an' I feel a new man already. [*He goes back to door* L.]

MRS. GOGAN: Isn't oul' Peter a funny-lookin' little man? . . . Like somethin' you'd pick off a Christ-mas Tree. . . . When he's dhressed up in his canon-icals, you'd wondher where he'd been got. God for-give me, when I see him in them, I always think he must ha' had a Mormon for a father! He an' th' Covey can't abide each other; th' pair o' them is al-ways at it, thryin' to best each other. There'll be blood dhrawn one o' these days.

FLUTHER: How is it that Clitheroe himself, now, doesn't have anythin' to do with th' Citizen Army? A couple o' months ago, an' you'd hardly ever see him without his gun, an' th' Red Hand o' Liberty Hall in his hat.

MRS. GOGAN: Just because he wasn't made a Captain of. He wasn't goin' to be in anything where he couldn't be conspishuous. He was so cock-sure o' being made one that he bought a Sam

Browne belt, an' was always puttin' it on an' standin' at th' door showing it off, till th' man came an' put out th' street lamps on him. God, I think he used to bring it to bed with him! But I'm tellin' you herself was delighted that that cock didn't crow, for she's like a clockin' hen if he leaves her sight for a minute. [*While she is talking she takes up a book from the table, looks into it in a near-sighted way, and then leaves it back. She now lifts up the sword, and proceeds to examine it*] Be th' look of it, this must ha' been a general's sword. . . . All th' gold lace an' th' fine figaries on it. . . . Sure it's twiced too big for him.

[*Fluther crosses from door L. behind couch, back of table, where Mrs. Gogan is examining the sword, and looks at it, standing to L. of Mrs. Gogan*]

FLUTHER: [*Contemptuously*] Ah, it's a baby's rattle he ought to have, an' he as he is, with thoughts tossin' in his head of what may happen to him on th' Day of Judgement.

[*Peter appears at the curtained door, back, sees Mrs. Gogan with the sword, and a look of vexation comes on to his face. He comes down C. to the table, snatches the sword out of Mrs. Gogan's hands, and bangs it back on the table. He then returns into room, back, without speaking*]

MRS. GOGAN: [*To Peter, as he snatches the sword*] Oh, excuse me. [*To Fluther*] Isn't he the surly oul' rascal, Fluther? [*She wanders from the table, back of the couch, to the chest of drawers, where she stops for a few moments, pulling out drawers and pushing them in again*]

FLUTHER: [*Leaning against left side of the table*] Take no notice of him. . . . You'd think he was dumb, but when you get his goat, or he has a few jars up, he's vice versa. [*Fluther coughs. Mrs. Gogan, who has wandered from the chest of drawers, down L., to the fireplace, where she is fingering Peter's shirt, turns to look at Fluther, as soon as she hears the cough*]

MRS. GOGAN: [*With an ominous note in her voice*] Oh, you've got a cold on you, Fluther.

FLUTHER: [*Carelessly*] Ah, it's only a little one.

MRS. GOGAN: You'd want to be careful, all th' same. I knew a woman, a big lump of a woman, red-faced an' round-bodied, a little awkard on her feet; you'd think, to look at her, she could put out her two arms an' lift a two-storied house on th' top of her head; got a ticklin' in her throat, an' a little cough, an' th' next mornin' she had a little catchin' in her chest, an' they had just time to wet her lips with a little rum, an' off she went. [*She begins to look at and handle the shirt*]

FLUTHER: [*A little nervously*] It's only a little cold I have; there's nothing derogatory wrong with me.

MRS. GOGAN: [*Warningly*] I dunno; there's many a man this minute lowerin' a pint, thinkin' of a woman, or pickin' out a winner, or doin' work as you're doin', while th' hearse dhrawn be th' horses with the black plumes is dhrivin' up to his own hall door, an' a voice that he doesn't hear is muttherin' in his ear, "Earth to earth, an' ashes t' ashes, an' dust to dust."

FLUTHER: [*Faintly, affected by her talk*] A man in th' pink o' health should have a holy horror of allowin' thoughts o' death to be festherin' in his mind, for [*With a frightened cough*] be God, I think I'm afther gettin' a little catch in me chest that time—it's a creepy thing to be thinkin' about. [*Fluther sits weakly in chair L. of table*]

MRS. GOGAN: It is, an' it isn't; it's both bad an' good. . . . It always gives meself a kind o' thresspassin' joy to feel meself movin' along in a mournin' couch, an' me thinkin' that, maybe, th' next funeral'll be me own, an' glad, in a quiet way, that this is somebody's else's.

FLUTHER: [*Very frightened*] An' a curious kind of a gaspin' for breath—I hope there's nothin' derogatory wrong with me.

MRS. GOGAN: [*Examining the shirt*] Frills on it, like a woman's petticoat.

FLUTHER: [*Panic-stricken*] Suddenly gettin' hot, an' then, just as suddenly, gettin' cold.

MRS. GOGAN: [*Holding out the shirt towards Fluther*] How would you like to be wearin' this Lord Mayor's nightdhress, Fluther?

FLUTHER: [*Vehemently*] Blast you an' your nightshirt! Is a man fermentin' with fear to stick th' showin' off to him of a thing that looks like a shinin' shroud?

MRS. GOGAN: [*Startled at Fluther's vehemence*] Oh, excuse me.

[*Peter appears at curtained door, back. Sees his shirt in Mrs. Gogan's hand, comes rapidly down C., goes front of couch to Mrs. Gogan, snatches shirt from her, and replaces it on the back of the chair; he returns the same way to room, back*]

PETER: [*Loudly, as he goes to room, back*] Well, God Almighty give me patience!

[*There is heard a cheer from the men working outside on the street, followed by the clang of tools being thrown down, then silence. Running into the back room to look out of the window*] What's the men repairin' the streets cheerin' for?

FLUTHER: [*Sitting down weakly on a chair*] You can't sneeze but that oul' one wants to know th' why an' th' wherefore. . . . I feel as dizzy as bedamned! I hope I didn't give up th' beer too suddenly.

[*The Covey comes in by door L. He is about 25, tall, thin, with lines on his face that form a perpetual protest against life as he conceives it to be. Heavy seams fall from each side of nose, down around his lips, as if they were suspenders keeping his mouth from falling. He speaks in a slow, wailing drawl; more rapidly when he is excited. He is dressed in dungarees, and is wearing a vividly red tie. He comes down C. and flings his cap with a gesture of*] *disgust on the table, and begins to take off his overalls*]

MRS. GOGAN: [*To the* Covey, *as she runs back into the room*] What's after happenin', Covey?

THE COVEY: [*With contempt*] Th' job's stopped. They've been mobilized to march in th' demonstration to-night undher th' Plough an' th' Stars. Didn't you hear them cheerin', th' mugs. They have to renew their political baptismal vows to be faithful in *seculo seculorum*.

FLUTHER: [*Sitting on the chair* L. *of table, forgetting his fear in his indignation*] There's no reason to bring religion into it. I think we ought to have as great a regard for religion as we can, so as to keep it out of as many things as possible.

THE COVEY: [*Pausing in the taking off of his dungarees*] Oh, you're one o' the boys that climb into religion as high as a short Mass on Sunday mornin's? I suppose you'll be singin' songs o' Sion an' songs o' Tara at th' meetin', too.

FLUTHER: We're all Irishmen, anyhow; aren't we?

THE COVEY: [*With hand outstretched, and in a professional tone*] Look here, comrade, there's no such thing as an Irishman, or an Englishman, or a German or a Turk; we're all only human bein's. Scientifically speakin', it's all a question of the accidental gatherin' together of mollycewels an' atoms.

[Peter *comes in from room, back, with a stiff collar in his hand, comes down* C., *crosses, in front of couch, to the mirror on the wall* L., *below the fireplace. He stands before the mirror and tries to put on his collar.* Fluther *gets up from the chair, goes* C. *and stands to* R. *of the* Covey]

FLUTHER: Mollycewels an' atoms! D'ye think I'm goin' to listen to you thryin' to juggle Fluther's mind with complicated cunundhrums of mollycewels an' atoms?

THE COVEY: [*Rather loudly*] There's nothin' complicated in it. There's no fear o' th' Church tellin' you that mollycewels is a stickin' together of millions of atoms o' sodium, carbon, potassium o' iodide, etcetera, that, accordin' to th' way they're mixed, make a flower, a fish, a star that you see shinin' in th' sky, or a man with a big brain like me, or a man with a little brain like you!

FLUTHER: [*More loudly still*] There's no necessity to be raisin' your voice; shoutin's no manifestin' forth of a growin' mind.

[Fluther *and the* Covey *turn to look at* Peter]

PETER: [*Struggling with his collar*] God give me patience with this thing. . . . She makes these collars as stiff with starch as a shinin' band of solid steel! She does it purposely to thry an' twart me. If I can't get it on to the singlet, how in the name of God am I goin' to get it on the shirt!

[Fluther *and the* Covey *face each other again*]

THE COVEY: [*Loudly*] There's no use o' arguin' with you; it's education you want, comrade.

FLUTHER: [*Sarcastically*] The Covey an' God made th' world I suppose, wha'?

THE COVEY: [*Jeering*] When I hear some men talkin' I'm inclined to disbelieve that th' world's eight-hundhred million years old, for it's not long since th' fathers o' some o' them crawled out o' th' sheltherin' slime o' the sea.

MRS. GOGAN: [*From room at back*] There, they're afther formin' fours, an' now they're goin' to march away.

FLUTHER: [*Scornfully taking no notice of* Mrs. Gogan] Mollycewels! [*He begins to untie his apron*] What about Adam an' Eve?

THE COVEY: Well, what about them?

FLUTHER: [*Fiercely*] What about them, you?

THE COVEY: Adam an' Eve! Is that as far as you've got? Are you still thinkin' there was nobody in th' world before Adam an' Eve? [*Loudly*] Did you ever hear, man, of th' skeleton of th' man o' Java?

PETER: [*Casting the collar from him*] Blast it, blast it! [Peter *angrily picks up the collar he has thrown on the floor, goes up* C., *right of couch, to the chest of drawers, and begins to hunt again in the drawers*]

FLUTHER: [*To the* Covey, *as he viciously folds apron*] Ah, you're not goin' to be let tap your rubbidge o' thoughts into th' mind o' Fluther.

THE COVEY: You're afraid to listen to th' thruth!

FLUTHER: [*Pugnaciously*] Who's afraid?

THE COVEY: You are!

FLUTHER: [*With great contempt*] G'way, you wurum!

THE COVEY: Who's a worum?

FLUTHER: You are, or you wouldn't talk th' way you're talkin'.

[Mrs. Gogan *wanders in from room, back, turns* L., *sees* Peter *at the chest of drawers, turns back, comes down* C., *goes, front of couch, to the fireplace*]

THE COVEY: Th' oul', ignorant savage leppin' up in you, when science shows you that th' head of your god is an empty one. Well, I hope you're enjoyin' th' blessin' o' havin' to live be th' sweat of your brow.

FLUTHER: You'll be kickin' an' yellin' for th' priest yet, me boyo. I'm not goin' to stand silent an' simple listenin' to a thick like you makin' a maddenin' mockery o' God Almighty. It 'ud be a nice derogatory thing on me conscience, an' me dyin', to look back in rememberin' shame of talkin' to a word-weavin' little ignorant yahoo of a red flag Socialist!

MRS. GOGAN: [*At the fireplace, turning to look at the disputants*] For God's sake, Fluther, dhrop it; there's always th' makin's of a row in the mention of religion. [*She turns her head, and looks at the picture of "The Sleeping Venus," hanging over the mantelpiece. She looks at it intently and a look of astonishment comes on her face*] God bless us, it's the picture of a naked woman. [*With a titter*] Look, Fluther.

[Fluther *looks over at the fireplace; comes slowly to the fireplace; looks steadily at the picture.* Peter, *hearing what was said, leaves the chest of drawers, and comes down, standing a little behind* Fluther *and* Mrs. Gogan, *and looks at the picture. The* Covey *looks on from* C.]

FLUTHER: What's undher it? [*Reading slowly*] "Georgina: The Sleeping Vennis." Oh, that's a terrible picture. . . . Oh, that's a shockin' picture! [*Peering into it with evident pleasure*] Oh, the one that got that taken, she must ha' been a prime lassie!

PETER: [*Laughing in a silly way, with head tilted back*] Hee, hee, hee, hee, hee!

FLUTHER: [*Indignantly, to* Peter] What are you hee, hee-in' for? [*Pointing to the picture*] That's a nice thing to be hee, hee-in' at. Where's your morality, man?

MRS. GOGAN: [*Looking intently at it*] God forgive us, it's not right to be lookin' at it.

FLUTHER: It's nearly a derogatory thing to be in th' room where it is.

MRS. GOGAN: [*Giggling hysterically*] I couldn't stop any longer in th' same room with three men, afther lookin' at it! [Mrs. Gogan *goes upstage* L., *and out by door* L. *The* Covey, *who has taken off his dungarees, seeing* Peter's *shirt on the chair, throws dungarees over it with a contemptuous movement*]

PETER: [*Roused by the* Covey's *action*] Where are you throwin' your dungarees? Are you thryin' to twart an' torment me again?

THE COVEY: Who's thryin' to twart you?

[Peter *takes the dungarees from the back of the chair and flings them violently on floor*]

PETER: You're not goin' to make me lose me temper, me young covey!

[*The* Covey, *in retaliation, takes* Peter's *white shirt from the back of the chair, and flings it violently on the floor*]

THE COVEY: If you're Nora's pet aself, you're not goin' to get your own way in everything. [*The* Covey *moves to the back end of the table, enjoying* Peter's *anger*]

PETER: [*Plaintively, with his eyes looking up at the ceiling*] I'll say nothin'. . . . I'll leave you to th' day when th' all-pitiful, all-merciful, all-lovin' God'll be handin' you to th' angels to be rievin' an' roastin' you, tearin' an' tormentin' you, burnin' an' blastin' you!

THE COVEY: Aren't you th' little malignant oul' bastard, you lemon-whiskered oul' swine!

[Peter *rushes to the table, takes up the sword, draws it from its scabbard, and makes for the* Covey, *who runs round the table* R., *followed by* Peter]

THE COVEY: [*Dodging round the table—to* Fluther] Fluther, hold him, there. It's a nice thing

to have a lunatic, like this, lashing round with a lethal weapon! [*The* Covey, *after running round the table, rushes up* C., *and runs back of couch, out of door* L., *which he bangs to behind him in the face of* Peter. Fluther *remains near the fireplace, looking on*]

PETER: [*Hammering at the door—to the* Covey, *outside*] Lemme out, lemme out. Isn't it a poor thing for a man who wouldn't say a word against his greatest enemy to have to listen to that Covey's twartin' animosities, shovin' poor, patient people into a lashin' out of curses that darken his soul with th' shadow of th' wrath of th' last day!

FLUTHER: Why d'ye take notice of him? If he seen you didn't, he'd say nothin' derogatory.

PETER: I'll make him stop his laughin' an' leerin', jibin' an' jeerin' an' scarifyin' people with his cornerboy insinuations! . . . He's always thryin' to rouse me: if it's not a song, it's a whistle; if it isn't a whistle, it's a cough. But you can taunt an' taunt— I'm laughin' at you; he, hee, hee, hee, hee, heee!

THE COVEY: [*Jeering loudly through the keyhole*] Dear harp o' me counthry, in darkness I found thee, The dark chain of silence had hung o'er thee long—

PETER: [*Frantically to* Fluther] Jasus, d'ye hear that? D'ye hear him soundin' forth his divil-souled song o' provocation? [*Battering at door* L.] When I get out I'll do for you, I'll do for you, I'll do for you!

THE COVEY: [*Through the keyhole*] Cuckoo-oo!

[Nora *enters by door* L. *She is a young woman of 23, alert, swift, full of nervous energy, and a little anxious to get on in the world. The firm lines of her face are considerably opposed by a soft, amorous mouth, and gentle eyes. When her firmness fails her, she persuades with her feminine charm. She is dressed in a tailor-made costume, and wears around her neck a silver fox fur*]

NORA: [*Running in and pushing* Peter *away from the door*] Oh, can I not turn me back but th' two o' yous are at it like a pair o' fightin'-cocks! Uncle Peter . . . Uncle Peter . . . UNCLE PETER!

PETER: [*Vociferously*] Oh, Uncle Peter, Uncle Peter be damned! D'ye think I'm goin' to give a free pass to th' young Covey to turn me whole life into a Holy Manual o' penances an' martyrdoms?

THE COVEY: [*Angrily rushing into the room*] If you won't exercise some sort o' conthrol over that Uncle Peter o' yours, there'll be a funeral, an' it won't be me that'll be in th' hearse!

NORA: [C. *back, between* Peter *and the* Covey, *to the* Covey] Are yous always goin' to be tearin' down th' little bit of respectability that a body's thryin' to build up? Am I always goin' to be havin' to nurse yous into th' habit o' thryin' to keep up a little bit of appearance?

THE COVEY: Why weren't you here to see th' way he run at me with th' sword?

PETER: What did you call me a lemon-whiskered oul' swine for?

NORA: If th' two o' yous don't thry to make a generous altheration in your goin's on, an' keep on thryin' t' inaugurate th' customs o' th' rest o' th' house into this place, yous can flit into other lodgin's where your bowsey battlin' 'ill meet, maybe, with an encore.

[*The* Covey *comes down, back of couch to the fire, and sits down in the chair where* Peter's *shirt had hung; he takes a book from a pocket and begins to read*]

PETER: [*To* Nora] Would you like to be called a lemon-whiskered oul' swine?

[Nora *takes the sword from* Peter, *goes to the table, puts it back in the scabbard, goes to the chest of drawers, back* L., *and leaves it on the chest of drawers*]

NORA: [*To* Peter] If you attempt to wag that sword of yours at anybody again, it'll have to be taken off you, an' put in a safe place away from babies that don't know the danger of them things. [Nora *goes across back, taking off her hat and coat, which she leaves.* Peter *comes down* C., *takes up the shirt from the floor, and goes back* C. *towards room, back*]

PETER: [*At entrance to room, back*] Well, I'm not goin' to let anybody call me a lemon-whiskered oul' swine! [Peter *goes into room, back.* Fluther *moves from the fireplace,* L. *of couch, to door* L., *which he begins to open and shut, trying the movement*]

FLUTHER: [*Half to himself, half to* Nora] Openin' an' shuttin' now with a well-mannered motion, like a door of a select bar in a high-class pub.

[Nora *takes up the hat and coat from the table, carries them into the room, back, leaves them there, comes out, goes to the dresser, above table* R., *and puts a few tea things on the table*]

NORA: [*To the* Covey, *as she lays table for tea*] An', once for all, Willie, you'll have to thry to deliver yourself from th' desire to practice o' provo'kin' oul' Pether into a wild forgetfulness of what's proper an' allowable in a respectable home.

THE COVEY: Well, let him mind his own business, then. Yestherday, I caught him hee-hee-in' out of him an' he readin' bits out of Jenersky's *Thesis on th' Origin, Development an' Consolidation of th' Evolutionary Idea of th' Proletariat.*

NORA: Now, let it end at that, for God's sake; Jack'll be in any minute, an' I'm not goin' to have th' quiet of his evenin' tossed about in an everlastin' uproar between you an' Uncle Pether. [Nora *crosses back to* Fluther L., *and stands on his* R.]

NORA: [*To* Fluther] Well, did you manage to settle the lock yet, Mr. Good?

FLUTHER: [*Opening and shutting the door*] It's betther than a new one, now, Mrs. Clitheroe; it's almost ready to open and shut of its own accord.

NORA: [*Giving him a coin*] You're a whole man. How many pints will that get you?

FLUTHER: [*Seriously*] Ne'er a one at all, Mrs. Clitheroe, for Fluther's on th' wather waggon now. You could stan' where you're stannin' chantin', "Have a glass o' malt, Fluther; Fluther, have a glass o' malt," till th' bells would be ringin' th' ould year out an' th' New Year in, an' you'd have as much chance o' movin' Fluther as a tune on a tin whistle would move a deaf man a' he dead.

[*As* Nora *is opening and shutting the door,* Mrs. Bessie Burgess *appears at it. She is a woman of 40, vigorously built. Her face is a dogged one, hardened by toil, and a little coarsened by drink. She looks scornfully and viciously at* Nora *for a few moments before she speaks*]

BESSIE: Puttin' a new lock on her door . . . afraid her poor neighbours ud break through an' steal. . . . [*In a loud tone*] Maybe, now, they're a damn sight more honest than your ladyship . . . checkin' th' children playin' on th' stairs . . . gettin' on th' nerves of your ladyship. . . . Complainin' about Bessie Burgess singin' her hymns at night, when she has a few up. . . . [*She comes in half-way on the threshold, and screams*] Bessie Burgess 'll sing whenever she damn well likes!

[Nora *tries to shut the door, but* Bessie *violently shoves it in, and, gripping* Nora *by the shoulders, shakes her*]

BESSIE: [*Violently*] You little overdhressed throlope, you, for one pin, I'd paste th' white face o' you!

NORA: [*Frightened*] Fluther, Fluther!

FLUTHER: [*Breaking the hold of* Bessie *from* Nora] Now, now, Bessie, Bessie, leave poor Mrs. Clitheroe alone; she'd do no one any harm, an' minds no one's business but her own.

BESSIE: Why is she always thryin' to speak proud things, an' lookin' like a mighty one in th' congregation o' th' people!

[*The* Covey *looks up from his book, watches the encounter, but does not leave his seat by the fire.* Nora *sinks down on back of the couch.* Jack Clitheroe *enters by door,* L. *He is a tall, well-made fellow of 25. His face has none of the strength of* Nora's. *It is a face in which is the desire for authority, without the power to attain it*]

CLITHEROE: [*Excitedly*] What's up? What's afther happenin'?

FLUTHER: Nothin', Jack. Nothin'. It's all over now. Come on, Bessie, come on.

CLITHEROE: [*Coming to couch and bending over* Nora—*anxiously*] What's wrong, Nora? Did she say anything to you?

NORA: [*Agitatedly*] She was bargin' out of her, an' I only told her to go up ower that to her own place; an' before I knew where I was, she flew at me, like a tiger, an' tried to guzzle me.

[Clitheroe *goes close to* Bessie, *standing in*

*front of the chest of drawers, and takes hold
of her arm to get her away*]

CLITHEROE: Get up to your own place, Mrs.
Burgess, and don't you be interferin' with my wife,
or it'll be th' worse for you. . . . Go on, go on!

BESSIE: [*As Clitheroe is pushing her out*] Mind
who you're pushin', now. . . . I attend me place of
worship, anyhow. . . . Not like some of them that
go neither church, chapel or meetin' house. . . . If
me son was home from the threnches, he'd see me
righted.

[Fluther *takes* Bessie *by the arm, and brings
her out by the door* L. Clitheroe *closes the
door behind them, returns to* Nora, *and puts
his arm around her. The* Covey *resumes his
reading*]

CLITHEROE: [*His arm around her*] There, don't
mind that old bitch, Nora, darling; I'll soon put a
stop to her interferin'.

NORA: Some day or another, when I'm here be
meself, she'll come in an' do somethin' desperate.

CLITHEROE: [*Kissing her*] Oh, sorra fear of her
doin' anythin' desperate. I'll talk to her to-morrow
when she's sober. A taste o' me mind that'll shock
her into the sensibility of behavin' herself!

[Nora *gets up, crosses to the dresser* R., *and
finishes laying the table for tea. She catches
sight of the dungarees on the floor and speaks
indignantly to* Covey. Clitheroe *leaves his hat
on the chest of drawers, and sits, waiting for
tea, on the couch*]

NORA: [*To* Covey] Willie, is that the place for your
dungarees?

COVEY: [*Irritably rising, and taking them from the
floor*] Ah, they won't do the floor any harm, will
they? [*He carries them up* C., *into room back, comes
back again, down* C., *and sits by fire.* Nora *crosses
from the table to the fire, gets the teapot from the
hob, and returns to the table*]

NORA: [*To* Clitheroe *and* Covey] Tea's ready.

[Clitheroe *and* Covey *go to the table and sit
down* L. *of same,* Covey *nearest the audience.*
Nora *sits down on* R. *of table, leaving the
chair for* Peter *below, on same side*]

NORA: [*Calling towards room, back*] Uncle Peter,
Uncle Peter, tea's ready!

[Peter *comes in from room back.* Peter *is in the
full dress of the Irish National Foresters: bright
green, gold-braided coat, white breeches, black
top boots and frilled, white shirt. He carries a
large black slouch hat, from which waves a
long white ostrich plume, in his hand. He puts
the hat on the chest of drawers beside the
sword, he comes down* C., *goes round front
end of table, and sits on the vacant seat facing*
Covey *on opposite side of the table. They eat
for a few moments in silence, the* Covey
furtively watching Peter *with scorn in his eyes;*
Peter *knows this, and is fidgety*]

THE COVEY: [*Provokingly*] Another cut o' bread,
Uncle Peter? [Peter *maintains a dignified silence*]

CLITHEROE: It's sure to be a great meetin' to-night.
We ought to go, Nora.

NORA: [*Decisively*] I won't go, Jack; you can go
if you wish.

[*A pause*]

THE COVEY: [*With great politeness, to* Peter] D'ye
want th' sugar, Uncle Peter?

PETER: [*Explosively*] Now, are you goin' to start
your thryin' an' your twartin' again?

NORA: Now, Uncle Peter, you mustn't be so
touchy; Willie has only assed you if you wanted th'
sugar.

PETER: [*Angrily*] He doesn't care a damn whether
I want th' sugar or no. He's only thryin' to twart
me!

NORA: [*Angrily, to the* Covey] Can't you let him
alone, Willie? If he wants the sugar, let him stretch
his hand out an' get it himself!

THE COVEY: [*To* Peter] Now, if you want the
sugar, you can stretch out your hand and get it
yourself!

[*A pause*]

CLITHEROE: To-night is th' first chance that Brennan has got of showing himself off since they made
a Captain of him—why, God only knows. It'll be a
treat to see him swankin' it at th' head of the Citizen
Army carryin' th' flag of the Plough an' th' Stars.
. . . [*Looking roguishly at* Nora] He was sweet on
you, once, Nora?

NORA: He may have been. . . . I never liked him.
I always thought he was a bit of a thick.

THE COVEY: They're bringin' nice disgrace on that
banner now.

CLITHEROE: [*To* Covey, *remonstratively*] How are
they bringin' disgrace on it?

THE COVEY: [*Snappily*] Because it's a Labour flag,
an' was never meant for politics. . . . What does th'
design of th' field plough, bearin' on it th' stars of
th' heavenly plough, mean, if it's not Communism?
It's a flag that should only be used when we're
buildin' th' barricades to fight for a Workers' Republic!

PETER: [*With a puff of derision*] P-phuh.

THE COVEY: [*Angrily, to* Peter] What are you
phuhin' out o' you for? Your mind is th' mind of
a mummy. [*Rising*] I better go an' get a good place
to have a look at Ireland's warriors passin' by. [*He
goes into room* L., *and returns with his cap*]

NORA: [*To the* Covey] Oh, Willie, brush your
clothes before you go.

THE COVEY: [*Carelessly*] Oh, they'll do well
enough.

NORA: Go an' brush them; th' brush is in th'
drawer there.

[*The* Covey *goes to the drawer, muttering, gets
the brush, and starts to brush his clothes*]

THE COVEY: [*Reciting at* Peter, *as he does so*]
Oh, where's the slave so lowly,

> Condemn'd to chains unholy,
> Who, could he burst his bonds at first,
> Would pine beneath them slowly?
> We tread th' land that . . . bore us,
> Th' green flag glitters . . . o'er us,
> Th' friends we've tried are by our side,
> An' th' foe we hate . . . before us!

PETER: [*Leaping to his feet in a whirl of rage*] Now, I'm tellin' you, me young Covey, once for all, that I'll not stick any longer these tittherin' taunts of yours, rovin' around to sing your slights an' slandhers, reddenin' th' mind of a man to th' thinkin' an' sayin' of things that sicken his soul with sin! [*Hysterically; lifting up a cup to fling at the* Covey] Be God, I'll—

CLITHEROE: [*Catching his arm*] Now then, none o' that, none o' that!

NORA: [*Loudly*] Uncle Pether, Uncle Pether, UNCLE PETHER!

THE COVEY: [*At the door* L., *about to go out*] Isn't that th' malignant oul' varmint! Lookin' like th' illegitimate son of an illegitimate child of a corporal in th' Mexican army! [*He goes out door* L.]

PETER: [*Plaintively*] He's afther leavin' me now in such a state of agitation that I won't be able to do meself justice when I'm marchin' to th' meetin'.

[Nora *jumps up from the table, crosses back end of table to the chest of drawers, back, and takes up* Peter's *sword*]

NORA: Oh, for God's sake, here, buckle your sword on, an' go to your meetin', so that we'll have at least one hour of peace.

[Peter *gets up from the chair, goes over to* Nora, *and she helps him to put on his sword*]

CLITHEROE: For God's sake, hurry him up out o' this, Nora.

PETER: Are yous all goin' to thry to start to twart me now?

NORA: [*Putting on his plumed hat*] S-s-sh. Now, your hat's on, your house is thatched; off you pop! [*She gently pushes him from her, towards door* L.]

PETER: [*Going and turning as he reaches the door* L.] Now, if that young Covey—

NORA: Go on, go on. [*He goes out door* L.]

[Clitheroe *goes from the table to the couch and sits down on end nearest the fire, lights a cigarette, and looks thoughtfully into the fire.* Nora *takes things from the table, and puts them on the dresser. She goes into room, back, and comes back with a lighted shaded lamp, which she puts on the table. She then goes on tidying things on the dresser. Softly speaking over from the dresser, to* Clitheroe]

A penny for them, Jack.

CLITHEROE: Me? Oh, I was thinkin' of nothing.

NORA: You were thinkin' of th' . . . meetin' . . . Jack. When we were courtin' an' I wanted you to go, you'd say, "Oh, to hell with meetin's," an' that you felt lonely in cheerin' crowds when I was absent.

An' we weren't a month married when you began that you couldn't keep away from them.

CLITHEROE: [*Crossly*] Oh, that's enough about th' meetin'. It looks as if you wanted me to go th' way you're talkin'. You were always at me to give up the Citizen Army, an' I gave it up: surely that ought to satisfy you.

NORA: [*From dresser*] Aye, you gave it up, because you got the sulks when they didn't make a captain of you. [*She crosses over to* Clitheroe, *and sits on the couch to his* R.]

NORA: [*Softly*] It wasn't for my sake, Jack.

CLITHEROE: For your sake or no, you're benefitin' by it, aren't you? I didn't forget this was your birthday, did I? [*He puts his arms around her*] And you liked your new hat; didn't you, didn't you? [*He kisses her rapidly several times*]

NORA: [*Panting*] Jack, Jack; please, Jack! I thought you were tired of that sort of thing long ago.

CLITHEROE: Well, you're finding out now that I amn't tired of it yet, anyhow. Mrs. Clitheroe doesn't want to be kissed, sure she doesn't? [*He kisses her again*] Little, little red-lipped Nora!

NORA: [*Coquettishly removing his arm from around her*] Oh, yes, your little, little red-lipped Nora's a sweet little girl when th' fit seizes you; but your little, little red-lipped Nora has to clean your boots every mornin', all the same.

CLITHEROE: [*With a movement of irritation*] Oh, well, if we're goin' to be snotty! [*A pause*]

NORA: It's lookin' like as if it was you that was goin' to be . . . snotty! Bridlin' up with bittherness, th' minute a body attempts t'open her mouth.

CLITHEROE: Is it any wondher, turnin' a tendher sayin' into a meanin' o' malice an' spite!

NORA: It's hard for a body to be always keepin' her mind bent on makin' thoughts that'll be no longer than th' length of your own satisfaction.

[*A pause*]

NORA: [*Standing up*] If we're goin' to dhribble th' time away sittin' here like a pair o' cranky mummies, I'd be as well sewin' or doin' something about th' place.

[*She looks appealingly at him for a few moments; he doesn't speak. She swiftly sits down beside him, and puts her arms around his neck*]

NORA: [*Imploringly*] Ah, Jack, don't be so cross!

CLITHEROE: [*Doggedly*] Cross? I'm not cross; I'm not a bit cross. It was yourself started it.

NORA: [*Coaxingly*] I didn't mean to say anything out o' th' way. You take a body up too quickly, Jack. [*In an ordinary tone as if nothing of an angry nature had been said*] You didn't offer me evenin' allowance yet.

[Clitheroe *silently takes out a cigarette for her and himself and lights both. Trying to make conversation*] How quiet th' house is now; they must be all out.

CLITHEROE: [*Rather shortly*] I suppose so.

NORA: [*Rising from the seat*] I'm longin' to show

you me new hat, to see what you think of it. Would you like to see it?

CLITHEROE: Ah, I don't mind.

[Nora *hesitates a moment, then goes up* C. *to the chest of drawers, takes the hat out of the box, comes down* C., *stands front of the couch, looks into the mirror on the wall below the fireplace, and fixes hat on her head. She then turns to face* Clitheroe]

NORA: Well, how does Mr. Clitheroe like me new hat?

CLITHEROE: It suits you, Nora, it does right enough. [*He stands up, puts his hand beneath her chin, and tilts her head up. She looks at him roguishly. He bends down and kisses her*]

NORA: Here, sit down, an' don't let me hear another cross word out of you for th' rest o' the night. [*The two sit on the couch again,* Clitheroe *nearest the fire*]

CLITHEROE: [*His arms round* Nora] Little red-lipped Nora.

NORA: [*With a coaxing movement of her body towards him*] Jack!

CLITHEROE: [*Tightening his arms around her*] Well?

NORA: You haven't sung me a song since our honeymoon. Sing me one now, do . . . please, Jack!

CLITHEROE: What song? "Since Maggie Went Away"?

NORA: Ah, no, Jack, not that; it's too sad. "When You Said You Loved Me."

[*Clearing his throat,* Clitheroe *thinks for a moment, and then begins to sing.* Nora, *putting an arm around him, nestles her head on his breast and listens delightedly*]

CLITHEROE: [*Singing verses following to the air of "When You and I Were Young, Maggie"*]

Th' violets were scenting th' woods, Nora,
    Displaying their charm to th' bee,
When I first said I lov'd only you, Nora,
    An' you said you lov'd only me!

Th' chestnut blooms gleam'd through th' glade, Nora,
    A robin sang loud from a tree,
When I first said I lov'd only you, Nora
    An' you said you lov'd only me!

Th' golden-rob'd daffodils shone, Nora,
    An' danc'd in th' breeze on th' lea;
When I first said I lov'd only you, Nora,
    An' you said you lov'd only me!

Th' trees, birds an' bees sang a song, Nora,
    Of happier transports to be,
When I first said I lov'd only you, Nora,
    An' you said you lov'd only me!

[Nora *kisses him. A knock is heard at the door,* R.; *a pause as they listen.* Nora *clings closely to* Clitheroe. *Another knock, more imperative than the first*] I wonder who can that be, now?

NORA: [*A little nervous*] Take no notice of it, Jack; they'll go away in a minute.

[*Another knock, followed by the voice of* Captain Brennan]

THE VOICE OF CAPT. BRENNAN: Commandant Clitheroe, Commandant Clitheroe, are you there? A message from General Jim Connolly.

CLITHEROE: [*Taking her arms from round him*] Damn it, it's Captain Brennan.

NORA: [*Anxiously*] Don't mind him, don't mind, Jack. Don't break our happiness. . . . Pretend we're not in. . . . Let us forget everything to-night but our two selves!

CLITHEROE: [*Reassuringly*] Don't be alarmed, darling; I'll just see what he wants, an' send him about his business.

NORA: [*Tremulously—putting her arms around him*] No, no. Please, Jack; don't open it. Please, for your own little Nora's sake!

CLITHEROE: [*Taking her arms away and rising to open the door*] Now don't be silly, Nora. [Clitheroe *opens door, and admits a young man in the full uniform of the Irish Citizen Army—green suit; slouch green hat caught up at one side by a small Red Hand badge; Sam Browne belt, with a revolver in the holster. He carries a letter in his hand. When he comes in he smartly salutes* Clitheroe. *The young man is* Captain Brennan. *He stands in front of the chest of drawers*]

CAPT. BRENNAN: [*Giving the letter to* Clitheroe] A dispatch from General Connolly.

CLITHEROE: [*Reading. While he is doing so,* Brennan's *eyes are fixed on* Nora, *who droops as she sits on the lounge*] "Commandant Clitheroe is to take command of the eighth battalion of the I.C.A. which will assemble to proceed to the meeting at nine o'clock. He is to see that all units are provided with full equipment: two day's rations and fifty rounds of ammunition. At two o'clock A.M. the army will leave Liberty Hall for a reconnaissance attack on Dublin Castle.—Com.-Gen. Connolly."

CLITHEROE: [*In surprise, to* Capt. Brennan] I don't understand this. Why does General Connolly call me Commandant?

CAPT. BRENNAN: Th' Staff appointed you Commandant, and th' General agreed with their selection.

CLITHEROE: When did this happen?

CAPT. BRENNAN: A fortnight ago.

CLITHEROE: How is it word was never sent to me?

CAPT. BRENNAN: Word was sent to you. . . . I meself brought it.

CLITHEROE: Who did you give it to, then?

CAPT. BRENNAN: [*After a pause*] I think I gave it to Mrs. Clitheroe, there.

CLITHEROE: Nora, d'ye hear that? [Nora *makes no answer. Standing* C.—*there is a note of hardness in his voice*] Nora . . . Captain Brennan says he brought a letter to me from General Connolly, and that he gave it to you. . . . Where is it? What did you do with it?

[Capt. Brennan *stands in front of the chest of drawers, and softly whistles "The Soldiers' Song"*]

NORA: [*Running over to him, and pleadingly putting her arms around him*] Jack, please Jack, don't go out to-night an' I'll tell you; I'll explain everything. . . . Send him away, an' stay with your own little red-lipp'd Nora.

CLITHEROE: [*Removing her arms from around him*] None o' this nonsense, now; I want to know what you did with th' letter? [*Nora goes slowly to the couch and sits down again. Angrily*] Why didn't you give me th' letter? What did you do with it? . . . [*Goes over and shakes her by the shoulder*] What did you do with th' letter?

NORA: [*Flaming up and standing on her feet*] I burned it, I burned it! That's what I did with it! Is General Connolly an' th' Citizen Army goin' to be your only care? Is your home goin' to be only a place to rest in? Am I goin' to be only somethin' to provide merrymakin' at night for you? Your vanity 'll be th' ruin of you an' me yet. . . . That's what's movin' you: because they've made an officer of you, you'll make a glorious cause of what you're doin', while your little red-lipp'd Nora can go on sittin' here, makin' a companion of th' loneliness of th' night!

CLITHEROE: [*Fiercely*] You burned it, did you? [*He grips her arm*] Well, me good lady—

NORA: Let go—you're hurtin' me!

CLITHEROE: You deserve to be hurt. . . . Any letther that comes to me for th' future, take care that I get it. . . . D'ye hear—take care that I get it! [*He lets her go, and she sinks down, crying on the couch. He goes to the chest of drawers and takes out a Sam Browne belt, which he puts on, and then puts a revolver in the holster. He puts on his hat, and looks towards* Nora. *At door* L., *about to go out*] You needn't wait up for me; if I'm in at all, it won't be before six in th' morning.

NORA: [*Bitterly*] I don't care if you never came back!

CLITHEROE: [*To* Capt. Brennan] Come along, Ned. [*They go out; there is a pause.* Nora *pulls the new hat from her head and with a bitter movement flings it to the other end of the room. There is a gentle knock at door* L., *which opens, and* Mollser *comes into the room. She is about 15, but looks to be only about 10, for the ravages of consumption have shrivelled her up. She is pitifully worn, walks feebly, and frequently coughs. She goes over and sits down* L. *of* Nora]

MOLLSER: [*To* Nora] Mother's gone to th' meetin', an' I was feelin' terrible lonely, so I come down to see if you'd let me sit with you, thinkin' you mightn't be goin' yourself. . . . I do be terrible afraid I'll die sometime when I'm be meself. . . . I

often envy you, Mrs. Clitheroe, seein' th' health you have, an' th' lovely place you have here, an' wondherin' if I'll ever be sthrong enough to be keepin' a home together for a man.

[*The faint sound of a band playing is heard in the distance outside in the street*]

MOLLSER: Oh this must be some more of the Dublin Fusiliers flyin' off to the front.

[*The band, passing in the street outside, is now heard loudly playing as they pass the house. It is the music of a brass band playing a regiment to the boat on the way to the front. The tune that is being played is "It's a Long Way to Tipperary"; as the band comes to the chorus, the regiment is swinging into the street by* Nora's *house, and the voices of the soldiers can be heard lustily singing the chorus of the song*]

It's a long way to Tipperary, it's a long way to go;
It's a long way to Tipperary, to th' sweetest girl I know!
Good-bye, Piccadilly, farewell Leicester Square.
It's a long way to Tipperary, but my heart's right there!

[Nora *and* Mollser *remain silently listening. As the chorus ends, and the music is faint in the distance again,* Bessie Burgess *appears at door* L., *which* Mollser *has left open*]

BESSIE: [*Speaking in towards the room*] There's th' men marchin' out into th' dhread dimness o' danger, while th' lice is crawlin' about feedin' on th' fatness o' the land! But yous'll not escape from th' arrow that flieth be night, or th' sickness that wasteth be day. . . . An' ladyship an' all, as some o' them may be, they'll be scatthered abroad, like th' dust in th' darkness! [Bessie *goes away;* Nora *steals over and quietly shuts the door. She comes back to the lounge and wearily throws herself on it beside* Mollser]

MOLLSER: [*After a pause and a cough*] Is there anybody goin', Mrs. Clitheroe, with a titther o' sense?

ACT II.

SCENE—*A public-house at the corner of the street in which the meeting is being addressed from Platform No. 1. One end of the house is visible to the audience. Part of the counter at the back,* L., *extending out towards* L., *occupies one-third of the width of the scene from* R. *to* L. *On the counter are glasses, beer-pulls, and a carafe filled with water. Behind the counter, on the back wall, are shelves containing bottles of wine, whisky and beer. At back* C. *is a wide, high, plate-glass window. Under the window is a seat to hold three or four persons* seated. L. are the wide swing-doors. At wall, R., is a seat to hold two persons. A few gaudy-coloured show-cards on the walls. A band is heard outside playing "The Soldiers' Song," before the Curtain rises, and for a few moments afterwards, accompanied by the sounds of marching men. The Barman is seen wiping the part of the counter which is in view. Rosie Redmond is standing at the counter toying with what remains of a half of whisky in a wine-glass. She is a sturdy well-shaped girl of 20; pretty and pert in manner. She is wearing a cream blouse, with an obviously suggestive glad neck; a grey tweed dress, brown stockings and shoes. The blouse and most of the dress are hidden by a black shawl. She has no hat, and in her hair is jauntily set a cheap, glittering, jewelled ornament. It is an hour later.

BARMAN: [Wiping counter] Nothin' much doin' in your line to-night, Rosie?

ROSIE: Curse o' God on th' haporth, hardly, Tom. There isn't much notice taken of a pretty petticoat of a night like this. . . . They're all in a holy mood. Th' solemn-lookin' dials on th' whole o' them an' they marchin' to th' meetin'. You'd think they were th' glorious company of th' saints, an' th' noble army of martyrs thrampin' through th' streets of Paradise. They're all thinkin' of higher things than a girl's garthers. . . . It's a tremendous meetin'; four platforms they have—there's one o' them just outside opposite th' window.

BARMAN: Oh, ay; sure when th' speaker comes [Motioning with his hand] to th' near end, here, you can see him plain, an' hear nearly everythin' he's spoutin' out of him.

ROSIE: It's no joke thryin' to make up fifty-five shillin's a week for your keep an' laundhry, an' then taxin' you a quid for your own room if you bring home a friend for th' night. . . . If I could only put by a couple of quid for a swankier outfit, everythin' in th' garden ud look lovely—

[In the window, back, appears the figure of a tall man, who, standing on a platform, is addressing a crowd outside. The figure is almost like a silhouette. The Barman comes to L. end of counter to listen, and Rosie moves C. to see and listen too]

BARMAN: [To Rosie] Whisht, till we hear what he's sayin'.

THE VOICE OF THE MAN: It is a glorious thing to see arms in the hands of Irishmen. We must accustom ourselves to the thought of arms, we must accustom ourselves to the sight of arms, we must accustom ourselves to the use of arms. . . . Bloodshed is a cleansing and sanctifying thing, and the nation that regards it as the final horror has lost its manhood. . . . There are many things more horrible than bloodshed, and slavery is one of them!

[The figure, moving towards L., passes the window, and is lost to sight and hearing. The Barman goes back to wiping of the counter. Rosie remains looking out of the window]

ROSIE: It's th' sacred thruth, mind you, what that man's afther sayin'.

BARMAN: If I was only a little younger, I'd be plungin' mad into th' middle of it!

ROSIE: [Who is still looking out of the window] Oh, here's th' two gems runnin' over again for their oil!

[The doors L. swing open, and Fluther and Peter enter tumultuously. They are hot and hasty with the things they have seen and heard. They hurry across to the counter, Peter leading the way. Rosie, after looking at them listlessly for a moment, retires to the seat under the window, sits down, takes a cigarette from her pocket, lights it and smokes]

PETER: [Splutteringly to the Barman] Two halves . . . [To Fluther] A meetin' like this always makes me feel as if I could dhrink Loch Erinn dhry!

FLUTHER: You couldn't feel anyway else at a time like this when th' spirit of a man is pulsin' to be out fightin' for th' thruth with his feet thremblin' on th' way, maybe to th' gallows, an' his ears tinglin' with th' faint, far-away sound of burstin' rifle-shots that'll maybe whip th' last little shock o' life out of him that's left lingerin' in his body!

PETER: I felt a burnin' lump in me throat when I heard th' band playin' "The Soldiers' Song," rememberin' last hearin' it marchin' in military formation, with th' people starin' on both sides at us, carrin' with us th' pride an' resolution o' Dublin to th' grave of Wolfe Tone.

FLUTHER: Get th' Dublin men goin' an' they'll go on full force for anything that's thryin' to bar them away from what they're wantin', where th' slim thinkin' counthry boyo ud limp away from th' first faintest touch of compromization!

PETER: [Hurriedly to the Barman] Two more, Tom! . . . [To Fluther] Th' memory of all th' things that was done, an' all th' things that was suffered be th' people, was boomin' in me brain. . . . Every nerve in me body was quiverin' to do somethin' desperate!

FLUTHER: Jammed as I was in th' crowd, I listened to th' speeches pattherin' on th' people's head, like rain fallin' on th' corn; every derogatory thought went out o' me mind, an' I said to meself, "You can die now, Fluther, for you've seen th' shadow-dhreams of th' last leppin' to life in th' bodies of livin' men that show, if we were without a titther o' courage for centuries, we're vice versa now!" Looka here. [He stretches out his arm under Peter's face and rolls up his sleeve] The blood was boilin' in me veins!

[The silhouette of the tall figure again moves into the frame of the window, speaking to the people]

PETER: [Unaware, in his enthusiasm, of the

speaker's appearance, to Fluther] I was burnin' to dhraw me sword, an' wave it over me—

FLUTHER: [*Overwhelming* Peter] Will you stop your blatherin' for a minute, man, an' let us hear what he's sayin'!

[*The* Barman *comes to* L. *end of the counter to look at the figure in the window;* Rosie *rises from the seat, stands and looks.* Fluther *and* Peter *move towards* C. *to see and listen*]

THE VOICE OF THE MAN: Comrade soldiers of the Irish Volunteers and of the Citizen Army, we rejoice in this terrible war. The old heart of the earth needed to be warmed with the red wine of the battlefields. . . . Such august homage was never offered to God as this: the homage of millions of lives given gladly for love of country. And we must be ready to pour out the same red wine in the same glorious sacrifice, for without shedding of blood there is no redemption!

[*The figure moves out of sight and hearing.* Fluther *runs back to the counter and gulps down the drink remaining in his glass;* Peter *does the same, less rapidly; the* Barman *leaves the end of the counter;* Rosie *sits on the seat again*]

FLUTHER: [*Finishing drink, to* Peter] Come on, man; this is too good to be missed! [Fluther *rushes across the stage and out by doors* L. Peter *wipes his mouth and hurries after* Fluther. *The doors swing open, and the* Covey *enters. He collides with* Peter C. Peter *stiffens his body, like a cock, and, with a look of hatred on his face, marches stiffly out by doors* L. *The* Covey *looks scornfully after* Peter, *and then crosses to the counter.* Rosie *sees possibilities in the* Covey, *gets up and comes to the counter, a little to the* L. *of the* Covey]

THE COVEY: [*To* Barman] Give us a glass o' malt, for God's sake, till I stimulate meself from the shock of seeing the sight that's afther goin' out.

ROSIE: [*Slyly, to the* Barman] Another one for me, Tommy; the young gentleman's ordherin' it in the corner of his eye.

[*The* Barman *gets a drink for the* Covey, *leaves it on the counter;* Rosie *whips it up. The* Barman *catches* Rosie's *arm, and takes glass from her, putting it down beside the* Covey]

BARMAN: [*Taking the glass from* Rosie] Eh, houl' on there, houl' on there, Rosie.

ROSIE: [*Angrily, to the* Barman] What are you houldin' on out o' you for? Didn't you hear th' young gentleman say that he couldn't refuse anything to a nice little bird? [*To the* Covey] Isn't that right, Jiggs? [*The* Covey *says nothing*] Didn't I know, Tommy, it would be all right? It takes Rosie to size a young man up, an' tell th' thoughts that are thremblin' in his mind. Isn't that right, Jiggs? [*The* Covey *stirs uneasily, moves a little farther away, and pulls his cap over his eyes. Moving after him*] Great meetin' that's gettin' held outside. Well, it's up to us all, anyway, to fight for our freedom.

THE COVEY: [*To the* Barman] Two more, please. [*To* Rosie] Freedom! What's th' use o' freedom, if it's not economic freedom?

ROSIE: [*Emphasizing with extended arm and moving finger*] I used them very words just before you come in. "A lot o' thricksters," says I, "that wouldn't know what freedom was if they got it from their mother." . . . [*To the* Barman] Didn't I, Tommy?

BARMAN: I disremember.

ROSIE: [*To the* Barman] No, you don't disremember. Remember you said, yourself, it was all "only a flash in th' pan." Well, "flash in th' pan, or no flash in th' pan," says I, "they're not goin' to get Rosie Redmond," says I, "to fight for freedom that wouldn't be worth winnin' in a raffle!"

THE COVEY: [*Contemptuously*] There's only one freedom for th' workin' man: conthrol o' th' means o' production, rates of exchange an' th' means of disthribution. [*Tapping* Rosie *on the shoulder*] Look here, comrade, I'll leave here to-morrow night for you a copy of Jenersky's *Thesis on the Origin, Development an' Consolidation of the Evolutionary Idea of th' Proletariat.*

ROSIE: [*Throwing off her shawl on to the counter, and showing an exemplified glad neck, which reveals a good deal of a white bosom*] If y'ass Rosie, it's heartbreakin' to see a young fella thinkin' of anything, or admirin' anything, but silk thransparent stockin's showin' off the shape of a little lassie's legs! [*The* Covey *is frightened, and moves away from* Rosie *along the counter, towards* R. Rosie *follows, gliding after him in a seductive way. Following him*] Out in th' park in th' shade of a warm summery evenin', with your little darlin' bridie to be, kissin' an' cuddlin' [*She tries to put her arm around his neck*] kissin' an' cuddlin', ay?

THE COVEY: [*Frightened*] Ay, what are you doin'? None o' that, now; none o' that. I've something else to do besides shinannickin' after Judies! [*The* Covey *turns to* L. *and moves slowly to* L., *away from* Rosie; *she turns with him, keeping him facing her, holding his arm. They move this way to* C.]

ROSIE: Oh, little duckey, oh, shy little duckey! Never held a mot's hand, an' wouldn't know how to tittle a little Judy! [*She clips him under the chin*] Tittle him undher th' chin, tittle him undher th' chin!

THE COVEY: [*Breaking away and running out by doors* L.] Aye, go on, now; I don't want to have any meddlin' with a lassie like you!

ROSIE: [*Enraged—returning to the seat at the window*] Jasus, it's in a monasthery some of us ought to be, spendin' our holidays kneelin' on our adorers, tellin' our beads an' knockin' hell out of our buzzums!

[*The voice of the* Covey *is heard outside doors* L. *calling in a scale of notes,* "Cuckoo-ooooo." *Then the swing-doors open, and* Peter *and* Fluther, *followed by* Mrs. Gogan, *come in.* Mrs. Gogan *carries a baby in her arms*]

PETER: [*In plaintive anger, looking towards the door* L.] It's terrible that young Covey can't let me pass without proddin' at me! Did you hear him murmurin' "cuckoo" when he were passin'?

FLUTHER: [*Irritably—to* Peter] I wouldn't be everlastin' cockin' me ear to hear every little whisper that was floatin' around about me! It's my rule never to lose me temper till it would be dethrimental to keep it. There's nothin' derogatory in th' use o' th' word "cuckoo," is there?

[Mrs. Gogan, *followed by* Peter, *go up to the seat under the window and sit down,* Peter *to the* R. *of Mrs. Gogan.* Rosie, *after a look at those who've come in, goes out by doors* L.]

PETER: [*Tearfully*] It's not the word, it's the way he says it! He never says it straight, but murmurs it with curious quiverin' ripples, like variations on a flute.

FLUTHER: [*Standing in front of the seat*] A' what odds if he gave it with variations on a thrombone? [*To* Mrs. Gogan] What's yours goin' to be, maam?

MRS. GOGAN: Ah, half a malt, Fluther.

[Fluther *goes from the seat over to the counter*]

FLUTHER: [*To the* Barman] Three halves, Tommy. [*The* Barman *gets the drinks, leaves them on the counter.* Fluther *pays the* Barman; *takes drinks to the seat under the window; gives one to* Mrs. Gogan, *one to* Peter, *and keeps the third for himself. He then sits on the seat to the* L. *of* Mrs. Gogan]

MRS. GOGAN: [*Drinking, and looking admiringly at* Peter's *costume*] The Foresthers' is a gorgeous dhress! I don't think I've seen nicer, mind you, in a pantomine. . . . Th' loveliest part of th' dhress, I think, is th' osthrichess plume. . . . When yous are goin' along, an' I see them wavin' an' noddin' an' waggin', I seem to be lookin' at each of yous hangin' at th' end of a rope, your eyes bulgin' an' your legs twistin' an' jerkin', gaspin' an' gaspin' for breath while yous are thryin' to die for Ireland!

FLUTHER: [*Scornfully*] If any o' them is ever hangin' at the end of a rope, it won't be for Ireland!

PETER: Are you goin' to start th' young Covey's game o' proddin' an' twartin' a man? There's not many that's talkin' can say that for twenty-five years he never missed a pilgrimage to Bodenstown!

FLUTHER: [*Looking angrily at* Peter] You're always blowin' about goin' to Bodenstown. D'ye think no one but yourself ever went to *Bodenstown?* [Fluther *emphasizes the word* "Bodenstown"]

PETER: [*Plaintively*] I'm not blowin' about it; but there's not a year that I go there but I pluck a leaf off Tone's grave, an' this very day me prayer-book is nearly full of them.

FLUTHER: [*Scornfully*] Then Fluther has a viceversa opinion of them that put ivy leaves into their prayer-books, scabbin' it on th' clergy, an' thryin' to out-do th' haloes o' th' saints be lookin' as if he was wearin' around his head a glitherin' aroree boree allis! [*Fiercely*] Sure, I don't care a damn if

you slep' in *Bodenstown!* You can take your breakfast, dinner an' tea on th' grave, in Bodenstown, if you like, for Fluther!

MRS. GOGAN: Oh, don't start a fight, boys, for God's sake; I was only sayin' what a nice costume it is—nicer than th' kilts, for, God forgive me, I always think th' kilts is hardly decent.

FLUTHER: [*Laughing scornfully*] Ah, sure when you'd look at him, you'd wondher whether th' man was makin' fun o' th' costume, or th' costume was makin' fun o' th' man!

BARMAN: [*Over to them*] Now, then, thry to speak asy, will yous? We don't want no shoutin' here.

[*The swing-doors open and the* Covey, *followed by* Bessie Burgess, *come in. They go over and stand at the counter. Passing,* Bessie *gives a scornful look at those seated near the window.* Bessie *and the* Covey *talk together, but frequently eye the group at the window*]

COVEY: [*To the* Barman] Two glasses o' malt.

[*The* Barman *gets the drinks; leaves them on the counter. The* Covey *puts one beside* Bessie *and keeps the other. He pays the* Barman]

PETER: [*Plaintively*] There he is now—I knew he wouldn't be long till he folleyed me in.

BESSIE: [*Speaking to the* Covey, *but really at the other party*] I can't for th' life o' me undherstand how they can call themselves Catholics when they won't lift a finger to help poor little Catholic Belgium.

MRS. GOGAN: [*Raising her voice*] What about poor little Catholic Ireland?

BESSIE: [*Over to* Mrs. Gogan] You mind your own business, maam, an' stupify your foolishness be gettin' dhrunk.

PETER: [*Anxiously—to* Mrs. Gogan] Take no notice of her; pay no attention to her. She's just tormentin' herself towards havin' a row with somebody.

BESSIE: [*In a quiet anger*] There's a storm of anger tossin' in me heart, thinkin' of all th' poor Tommies, an' with them me own son, dhrenched in water an' soaked in blood, gropin' their way to a shattherin' death, in a shower o' shells! Young men with th' sunny lust o' life beamin' in them, layin' down their white bodies, shredded into torn an' bloody pieces, on th' altar that God Himself has built for th' sacrifice of heroes!

MRS. GOGAN: [*Indignantly*] Isn't it a nice thing to have to be listenin' to a lassie an' hangin' our heads in a dead silence, knowin' that some persons think more of a ball of malt than they do of th' blessed saints.

FLUTHER: [*Deprecatingly*] Whisht; she's always dangerous an' derogatory when she's well oiled. Th' safest way to hindher her from havin' any enjoyment out of her spite. is to dip our thoughts into the fact of her bein' a female person that has moved out of th' sight of ordinary sensible people.

BESSIE: [*Over to* Mrs. Gogan, *viciously*] To look

at some o' th' women that's knockin' about, now, is a thing to make a body sigh. . . . A woman on her own, dhrinkin' with a bevy o' men is hardly an example to her sex. . . . A woman dhrinkin' with a woman is one thing, an' a woman dhrinkin' with herself is still a woman—flappers may be put in another category altogether—but a middle-aged married woman makin' herself th' centre of a circle of men is as a woman that is loud an' stubborn, whose feet abideth not in her own house.

THE COVEY: [*To* Bessie—*with a scornful look at* Peter] When I think of all th' problems in front o' th' workers, it makes me sick to be lookin' at oul' codgers goin' about dhressed up like green-accoutered figures gone asthray out of a toyshop!

PETER: [*Angrily*] Gracious God, give me patience to be listenin' to that blasted young Covey proddin' at me from over at th' other end of th' shop!

MRS. GOGAN: [*Dipping her finger in the whisky, and moistening with it the lips of her baby*] Cissie Gogan's a woman livin' for nigh on twenty-five years in her own room, an' beyond biddin' th' time o' day to her neighbours, never yet as much as nodded her head in th' direction of other people's business, while she knows some [*With a look at* Bessie] as are never content unless they're standin' senthry over other people's doin's!

[*Again the figure appears, like a silhouette, in the window, back, and all hear the voice of the speaker declaiming passionately to the gathering outside.* Fluther, Peter *and* Mrs. Gogan *stand up, turn, and look towards the window. The* Barman *comes to the end of the counter;* Bessie *and the* Covey *stop talking, and look towards the window*]

THE VOICE OF THE SPEAKER: The last sixteen months have been the most glorious in the history of Europe. Heroism has come back to the earth. War is a terrible thing, but war is not an evil thing. People in Ireland dread war because they do not know it. Ireland has not known the exhilaration of war for over a hundred years. When war comes to Ireland she must welcome it as she would welcome the Angel of God!

[*The figure passes out of sight and hearing,* L.]

THE COVEY: [*Towards all present*] Dope, dope. There's only one war worth havin': th' war for th' economic emancipation of th' proletariat.

BESSIE: [*Referring to* Mrs. Gogan] They may crow away out o' them; but it ud be fitther for some o' them to mend their ways an' cease from havin' scouts out watchin' for th' comin' of th' Saint Vincent de Paul man, for fear they'd be nailed lowerin' a pint of beer, mockin' th' man with an angel face, shinin' with th' glamour of deceit an' lies!

MRS. GOGAN: [*Over to* Bessie] An' a certain lassie standin' stiff behind her own door with her ears cocked listenin' to what's being said, stuffed till she's sthrained with envy of a neighbour thryin' for a few little things that may be got be hard sthrivin' to keep

up to th' letther an' th' law, an' th' practices of th' Church!

PETER: [*To* Mrs. Gogan] If I was you, Mrs. Gogan, I'd parry her jabbin' remarks be a powerful silence that'll keep her tantalizin' words from penethratin' into your feelin's. It's always betther to leave these people to th' vengeance o' God!

BESSIE: [*At the counter*] Bessie Burgess doesn't put up to know much, never havin' a swaggerin' mind, thanks be to God, but goin' on packin' up knowledge accordin' to her conscience: precept upon precept, line upon line; here a little, an' there a little. [Bessie, *with a vigorous swing of her shawl, turns, and with a quick movement goes* C., *facing* Mrs. Gogan. *Furiously*] But, thanks be to Christ, she knows when she was got, where she was got, an' how she was got; while there's some she knows, decoratin' their finger with a well-polished weddin' ring, would be hard put to it if they were assed to show their weddin' lines!

[Mrs. Gogan *springs up from the seat and bounces to* C., *facing* Bessie Burgess. Mrs. Gogan *is wild with anger*]

MRS. GOGAN: [*With hysterical rage*] Y' oul' rip of a blasted liar, me weddin' ring's been well earned be twenty years be th' side o' me husband, now takin' his rest in heaven, married to me be Father Dempsey, in th' Chapel o' Saint Jude's, in th' Christmas Week of eighteen hundred an' ninety-five; an' any kid, livin' or dead, that Jinnie Gogan's had since, was got between th' bordhers of th' Ten Commandments! . . .

BESSIE: [*Bringing the palms of her hands together in sharp claps to emphasize her remarks*] Liar to you, too, maam, y' oul' hardened thresspasser on other people's good nature, wizenin' up your soul in th' arts o' dodgeries, till every dhrop of respectability in a female is dhried up in her, lookin' at your ready-made manœuverin' with th' menkind!

BARMAN: [*Anxiously leaning over the counter*] Here, there; here, there; speak asy there. No rowin' here, no rowin' here, now.

[Fluther *comes from the seat, gets in front of* Mrs. Gogan, *and tries to pacify her;* Peter *leaves the seat, and tries to do the same with* Bessie, *holding her back from* Mrs. Gogan. *The positions are:* Barman *behind the counter, leaning forward;* Bessie R., *next* Peter; *next* Fluther; *next* Mrs. Gogan, *with baby in her arms. The* Covey *remains leaning on the counter, looking on*]

FLUTHER: [*Trying to calm* Mrs. Gogan] Now, Jinnie, Jinnie, it's a derogatory thing to be smirchin' a night like this with a row; it's rompin' with th' feelin's of hope we ought to be, instead o' bein' vice versa!

PETER: [*Trying to quiet* Bessie] I'm terrible dawny, Mrs. Burgess, an' a fight leaves me weak for a long time afterwards. . . . Please, Mrs. Burgess, before there's damage done, thry to have a little respect for yourself.

BESSIE: [*With a push of her hand that sends* Peter *tottering to the end of the counter*] G'way, you little sermonizing, little yella-faced, little consequential, little pudgy, little bum, you!

MRS. GOGAN: [*Screaming and struggling*] Fluther, leggo! I'm not goin' to keep an unresistin' silence, an' her scatherin' her festherin' words in me face, stirrin' up every dhrop of decency in a respectable female, with her restless rally o' lies that would make a saint say his prayer backwards!

BESSIE: [*Shouting*] Ah, everybody knows well that th' best charity that can be shown to you is to hide th' thruth as much as our thrue worship of God Almighty will allow us!

MRS. GOGAN: [*Frantically*] Here, houl' th' kid, one o' yous; houl' th' kid for a minute! There's nothin' for it but to show this lassie a lesson or two. . . . [*To* Peter] Here, houl' th' kid, you. [Mrs. Gogan *suddenly rushes over to* Peter, *standing, trembling with fear, between the end of the counter and the seat under the window. Bewildered, and before he's aware of it,* Mrs. Gogan *has put the baby in his arms.* Mrs. Gogan *rushes back* C. *and puts herself in a fighting attitude in front of* Bessie. *To* Bessie, *standing before her in a fighting attitude*] Come on, now, me loyal lassie, dyin' with grief for little Catholic Belgium! When Jinnie Gogan's done with you, you'll have a little leisure lyin' down to think an' pray for your king an' counthry!

BARMAN: [*Coming from behind the counter, getting between the women, and proceeding to push* Bessie *towards the door*] Here, now, since yous can't have a little friendly argument quietly, yous'll get out o' this place in quick time. Go on, an' settle your differences somewhere else—I don't want to have another endorsement on me licence. [*The* Barman *pushes* Bessie *towards the doors* L., Mrs. Gogan *following*]

PETER: [*Anxiously calling to* Mrs. Gogan] Here, take your kid back ower this. How nicely I was picked now for it to be plumped into my arms!

THE COVEY: [*Meaningly*] She knew who she was givin' it to, maybe.

[Peter *goes over near to the* Covey *at the counter to retort indignantly, as the* Barman *pushes* Bessie *out of the doors* L. *and gets hold of* Mrs. Gogan *to put her out too*]

PETER: [*Hotly to the* Covey] Now, I'm givin' you fair warnin', me young Covey, to quit firin' your jibes an' jeers at me. . . . For one o' these days, I'll run out in front o' God Almighty an' take your sacred life!

BARMAN: [*Pushing* Mrs. Gogan *out after* Bessie] Go on, now; out you go.

PETER: [*Leaving the baby down on the floor* C.] Ay, be Jasus, wait there, till I give her back her youngster! [Peter *runs to the door* L., *opens it, and calls out after* Mrs. Gogan]

PETER: [*Calling at the door* L.] Eh, there, eh! What about the kid? [*He runs back in,* C., *and looks at* Fluther *and the* Covey] There, she's afther goin' without her kid—what are we goin' to do with it now?

THE COVEY: [*Jeering*] What are *you* goin' to do with it? Bring it outside an' show everybody what you're afther findin'.

PETER: [*In a panic—to* Fluther] Pick it up, you, Fluther, an' run afther her with it, will you?

FLUTHER: [*With a long look at* Peter] What d'ye take Fluther for? You must think Fluther's a right gom. D'ye think Fluther's like yourself, destitute of a tithther of undherstandin'?

BARMAN: [*Imperatively to* Peter] Take it up, man, an' run out afther her with it before she's gone too far. You're not goin' to leave th' bloody thing there, are you?

PETER: [*Plaintively, as he lifts up the baby*] Well, God Almighty, give me patience with all th' scorners, tormentors, an' twarters that are always an' ever thryin' to goad me into prayin' for their blindin' an' blastin' an' burnin' in th' world to come! [Peter, *with the baby, goes out of the door* L. Fluther *comes from the front of the window to the counter and stands there, beside the* Covey]

FLUTHER: [*With an air of relief*] God, it's a relief to get rid o' that crowd. Women is terrible when they start to fight. There's no holdin' them back. [*To the* Covey] Are you goin' to have anything?

THE COVEY: Ah, I don't mind if I have another half.

FLUTHER: [*To the* Barman] Two more, Tommy, me son. [*The* Barman *gets the drinks,* Fluther *pays*]

FLUTHER: [*To the* Covey] You know there's no conthrollin' a woman when she loses her head.

[Rosie *appears at the doors* L. *She looks over at the counter, sees the two men, then crosses over to the* L. *end of the counter, where she stands, with a suggestive look towards* Fluther]

ROSIE: [*To the* Barman] Divil a use o' havin' a thrim little leg on a night like this; things was never worse. . . . Give us a half till to-morrow, Tom, duckey.

BARMAN: [*Coldly*] No more to-night, Rosie; you owe me for three already.

ROSIE: [*Combatively*] You'll be paid, won't you?

BARMAN: I hope so.

ROSIE: You hope so! Is that th' way with you, now?

FLUTHER: [*With a long glance at* Rosie, *to the* Barman] Give her one—it'll be all right.

[*The* Barman *gets a drink, and puts it on the counter before* Rosie; Fluther *pays for it*]

ROSIE: [*Clapping* Fluther *on the back*] Oul' sport!

FLUTHER: [*To* Covey] Th' meetin' should be soon over, now.

THE COVEY: [*In a superior way*] Th' sooner th' betther. It's alla lot o' blasted nonsense, comrade.

FLUTHER: Oh, I wouldn't say it was all nonsense.

After all, Fluther can remember th' time, an' him only a dawny chiselur, bein' taught at his mother's knee to be faithful to th' Shan Vok Vok!

THE COVEY: That's all dope, comrade; th' sort o' thing that workers are fed on be th' Boorzwawzee.

FLUTHER: [*A little sharply*] What's all dope? Though I'm sayin' it that shouldn't: [*Catching his cheek with his hand, and pulling down the flesh from the eye*] d'ye see that mark there, undher me eye? . . . A sabre slice from a dragoon in O'Connell Street! [*Thrusting his head forward towards* Rosie] Feel that dint in th' middle o' me nut!

ROSIE: [*Rubbing* Fluther's *head, and winking at the* Covey] My God, there's a holla!

FLUTHER: [*Putting on his hat with quiet pride*] A skelp from a bobby's baton at a Labour meetin' in th' Phœnix Park!

THE COVEY: [*Sarcastically*] He must ha' hitten you in mistake. I don't know what you ever done for th' Labour movement.

FLUTHER: [*Loudly*] D'ye not? Maybe, then, I done as much, an' know as much about th' Labour movement as th' chancers that are blowin' about it!

BARMAN: [*Over the counter*] Speak easy, Fluther, thry to speak easy.

THE COVEY: [*Quietly*] There's no necessity to get excited about it, comrade.

FLUTHER: [*More loudly*] Excited? Who's gettin' excited? There's no one gettin' excited! It would take something more than a thing like you to flutther a feather o' Fluther. Blatherin', an', when all is said, you know as much as th' rest in th' wind up!

THE COVEY: [*Emphatically*] Well, let us put it to th' test, then, an' see what you know about th' Labour movement: what's the mechanism of exchange?

FLUTHER: [*Roaring, because he feels he is beaten*] How th' hell do I know what it is? There's nothin' about that in th' rules of our Thrades Union!

BARMAN: [*Protesting*] For God's sake, thry to speak easy, Fluther.

THE COVEY: What does Karl Marx say about th' Relation of Value to th' Cost o' Production?

FLUTHER: [*Angrily*] What th' hell do I care what he says? I'm Irishman enough not to lose me head be follyin' foreigners!

BARMAN: Speak easy, Fluther.

THE COVEY: [*Contemptuously*] It's only waste o' time talkin' to you, comrade.

FLUTHER: Don't be comradin' me, mate. I'd be on me last legs if I wanted you for a comrade.

ROSIE: [*To the* Covey, *taking* Fluther's *part*] It seems a highly rediculous thing to hear a thing that's only an inch or two away from a kid, swingin' heavy words about he doesn't know th' meanin' of, an' uppishly thryin' to down a man like Misther Fluther here, that's well flavoured in th' knowledge of th' world he's livin' in.

THE COVEY: [*Bending over the counter—savagely to* Rosie] Nobody's askin' you to be buttin' in with

your prate. . . . I have you well taped, me lassie. . . . Just you keep your opinions for your own place. . . . It'll be a long time before th' Covey takes any insthructions or reprimandin' from a prostitute!

[Rosie, *wild with humiliation, bounds from the end of the counter to* C. *and with eyes blazing, faces towards the* Covey]

ROSIE: You louse, you louse, you! . . . You're no man. . . . You're no man . . . I'm a woman, anyhow, an' if I'm a prostitute aself, I have me feelin's. . . . Thryin' to put his arm around me a minute ago, an' givin' me th' glad eye, th' little wrigglin' lump o' desolation turns on me now, because he saw there was nothin' doin'. . . . You louse, you! If I was a man, or you were a woman, I'd bate th' puss o' you!

BARMAN: Ay, Rosie, ay! You'll have to shut your mouth altogether, if you can't learn to speak easy!

[Fluther, *with a dignified walk, goes over to* Rosie C. *and puts a hand on her shoulder*]

FLUTHER: [*To* Rosie] Houl' on there, Rosie; houl' on, there. There's no necessity to flutther yourself when you're with Fluther. . . . Any lady that's in th' company of Fluther is goin' to get a fair hunt. . . . This is outside your province. . . . I'm not goin' to let you demean yourself be talkin' to a tittherin' chancer. . . . Leave this to Fluther—this is a man's job. . . . [*He turns from* Rosie, *comes back, crosses the* Covey, *then turns and faces him. To the* Covey] Now, if you've anything to say, say it to Fluther; an' let me tell you, you're not goin' to be pass-remarkable to any lady in my company.

THE COVEY: Sure I don't care if you were runnin' all night afther your Mary o' th' Curlin' Hair, but, when you start tellin' luscious lies about what you done for th' Labour movement, it's nearly time to show y'up!

FLUTHER: [*Fiercely*] Is it you show Fluther up? G'way, man, I'd beat two o' you before me breakfast!

THE COVEY: [*Contemptuously*] Tell us where you bury your dead, will you?

FLUTHER: [*With his face stuck into the face of the* Covey] Sing a little less on th' high note, or, when I'm done with you, you'll put a Christianable consthruction on things, I'm tellin' you!

THE COVEY: You're a big fella, you are.

FLUTHER: [*Tapping the* Covey *threateningly on the shoulder*] Now, you're temptin' Providence when you're temptin' Fluther!

THE COVEY: [*Losing his temper, knocking* Fluther's *hands away, and bawling*] Easy with them hands, there, easy with them hands! You're startin' to take a little risk when you commence to paw the Covey!

[Fluther *suddenly springs into the* C. *of the shop, flings his hat into the corner, whips off his coat, and begins to paw the air like a pugilist*]

FLUTHER: [*Roaring*] Come on, come on, you

lowser; put your mitts up now, if there's a man's blood in you! Be God, in a few minutes you'll see some snots flyin' around, I'm tellin' you. . . . When Fluther's done with you, you'll have a vice-versa opinion of him! Come on, now, come on!

[*The* Covey *squares up to* Fluther]

BARMAN: [*Running from behind the counter and catching hold of the* Covey] Here, out you go, me little bowsey. Because you got a couple o' halves you think you can act as you like. [*He pushes the* Covey *to the doors* L] Fluther's a friend o' mine, an' I'll not have him insulted.

THE COVEY: [*Struggling with the* Barman] Ay, leggo, leggo there; fair hunt, give a man a fair hunt! One minute with him is all I ask; one minute alone with him, while you're runnin' for th' priest an' th' doctor!

FLUTHER: [*To the* Barman] Let him go, let him go, Tom: let him open th' door to sudden death if he wants to!

BARMAN: [*Grappling with the* Covey] Go on, out you go an' do th' bowsey somewhere else. [*The* Barman *pushes the* Covey *out by doors* L., *and goes back behind the counter.* Fluther *assumes a proud air of victory.* Rosie *gets his coat, and helps him to put it on; she then gets his hat and puts it on his head*]

ROSIE: [*Helping* Fluther *with his coat*] Be God, you put th' fear o' God in his heart that time! I thought you'd have to be dug out of him. . . . Th' way you lepped out without any of your fancy side-steppin'! "Men like Fluther," says I to myself, "is gettin' scarce nowadays."

FLUTHER: [*With proud complacency,* C.] I wasn't goin' to let meself be malignified by a chancer. . . . He got a little bit too derogatory for Fluther. . . . Be God, to think of a cur like that comin' to talk to a man like me!

ROSIE: [*Fixing on his hat*] Did j'ever!

FLUTHER: He's lucky he got off safe. I hit a man last week, Rosie, an' he's fallin' yet!

ROSIE: Sure, you'd ha' broken him in two if you'd ha' hitten him one clatther!

FLUTHER: [*Amorously, putting his arm around* Rosie] Come on into th' snug, me little darlin', an' we'll have a few dhrinks before I see you home.

ROSIE: Oh, Fluther, I'm afraid you're a terrible man for th' women.

[Fluther *leads* Rosie *to the seat with the round table in front,* R. *She sits down on the seat. He goes to the counter*]

FLUTHER: [*To the* Barman] Two, full ones, Tommy.

[Barman *gets the drinks.* Fluther *brings them over to seat* R., *leaves them on the table, and sits down beside* Rosie. *The swing-doors* L. *open and Captain* Brennan, *Commandant* Clitheroe, *and Lieutenant* Langon *enter, and cross quickly to the counter.* Capt. Brennan *carries the banner of The Plough and the Stars, and* Lieut. Langon *a green, white and*

orange Tricolour. *They are in a state of emotional excitement. Their faces are flushed and their eyes sparkle; they speak rapidly, as if unaware of the meaning of what they say. They have been mesmerized by the fervency of the speeches*]

CLITHEROE: [*Almost pantingly to the* Barman] Three glasses o' port!

[*The* Barman *brings the drinks,* Clitheroe *pays*]

CAPT. BRENNAN: We won't have long to wait now.

LIEUT. LANGON: Th' time is rotten ripe for revolution.

CLITHEROE: [*To* Lieut. Langon] You have a mother, Langon.

LIEUT. LANGON: Ireland is greater than a mother.

CAPT. BRENNAN: [*To* Clitheroe] You have a wife, Clitheroe.

CLITHEROE: Ireland is greater than a wife.

LIEUT. LANGON: Th' time for Ireland's battle is now—th' place for Ireland's battle is here.

[*The tall, dark figure again appears in the window. The three men stiffen to attention. They stand out from the* L. *of the counter,* Brennan *nearest counter, then* Clitheroe, *then* Lieut. Langon. Fluther *and* Rosie, *busy with each other, take no notice*]

THE VOICE OF THE MAN: Our foes are strong, but strong as they are, they cannot undo the miracles of God, who ripens in the heart of young men the seeds sown by the young men of a former generation. They think they have pacified Ireland; think they have foreseen everything; think they have provided against everything; but the fools, the fools, the fools!—they have left us our Fenian dead, and, while Ireland holds these graves, Ireland, unfree, shall never be at peace!

CAPT. BRENNAN: [*Lifting up the Plough and the Stars*] Imprisonment for th' Independence of Ireland!

LIEUT. LANGON: [*Lifting up the Tri-colour*] Wounds for th' Independence of Ireland!

CLITHEROE: Death for th' Independence of Ireland!

THE THREE: [*Together*] So help us God!

[*They lift their glasses and drink together. The "Assembly" is heard on a bugle outside. They leave their glasses on the counter, and hurry out by doors* L. *A pause. Then* Fluther *and* Rosie *rise from the seat, and start to go* L. Rosie *is linking* Fluther, *who is a little drunk. Both are in a merry mood*]

ROSIE: Are you afraid or what? Are you goin' to come home, or are you not?

FLUTHER: Of course I'm goin' home. What ud ail me that I wouldn't go?

ROSIE: [*Lovingly*] Come on, then, oul' sport.

OFFICER'S VOICE: [*Giving command outside*] Irish Volunteers, by th' right, quick march!

ROSIE: [*Putting her arm round* Fluther *and singing to the air "Twenty-four Strings to My Bow"*]
I once had a lover, a tailor, but he could do nothin'
     for me,

An' then I fell in with a sailor as strong an' as wild
as th' sea.
We cuddled an' kissed with devotion, till th' night
from th' mornin' had fled;
An' there, to our joy, a bright bouncin' boy
Was dancin' a jig in th' bed!
Dancin' a jig in th' bed, an' bawlin' for butther an'
bread.
An' there, to our joy, a bright bouncin' boy
Was dancin' a jig in th' bed!

[*They go out with their arms round each other*]

CLITHEROE'S VOICE: [*In command outside*] Dublin
Battalion of the Irish Citizen Army, by th' right,
quick march!

ACT III.

SCENE—*A corner house of a street of tenements;
exterior of house in which the Clitheroes live. It is a
tall, gaunt five-storey tenement. Its brick front is
dull from weather and age. It juts out from L. more
than half-way across stage, showing part of the front
elevation, with wide, heavy door, having windows
above and on both sides. The windows on L., looking
into the rooms of the Clitheroes, are hung with
good casement cloth. The others are draped with
grimy lace curtains. Stone steps lead from the door
to the path on the street. From these steps, on each
side of the door are railings to prevent anyone from
falling down the area. To the extreme R. the front
of another house is merely indicated by the side
aspect of a wall with steps leading from the door,
on which the wounded Langon rests later on in the
scene. Between the two runs a lane which, upstage,
turns to the R. At the corner of the lane, nearest the
house shown almost full front, is a street lamp.
As the house is revealed, Mrs. Gogan is seen helping Mollser to a chair, which stands on the path
beside the railings, at the L. side of the steps. She
then wraps a shawl around Mollser's shoulders. It is
some months later.*

MRS. GOGAN: [*Arranging shawl around Mollser*] Th'
sun'll do you all th' good in th' world. A few more
weeks o' this weather, an' there's no knowin' how
well you'll be. . . . Are you comfy, now?

MOLLSER: [*Weakly and wearily*] Yis, ma; I'm all
right.

MRS. GOGAN: [*Bending over her*] How are you
feelin'?

MOLLSER: Betther, ma, betther. If th' horrible
sinkin' feelin' ud go, I'd be all right.

MRS. GOGAN: Ah, I wouldn't put much pass on
that. Your stomach maybe's out of ordher. . . . Is
th' poor breathin' any betther, d'ye think?

MOLLSER: Yis, yis, ma; a lot betther.

MRS. GOGAN: Well, that's somethin' anyhow. . . .
With th' help o' God, you'll be on th' mend from
this out. . . . D'your legs feel any sthronger undher
you, d'ye think?

MOLLSER: [*Irritably*] I can't tell, ma. I think so.
. . . A little.

MRS. GOGAN: Well, a little aself is somethin'.
I thought I heard you coughin' a little more than
usual last night. . . . D'you think you were?

MOLLSER: I wasn't, ma, I wasn't.

MRS. GOGAN: I thought I heard you, for I was
kep' awake all night with th' shootin'. An' thinkin'
o' that madman, Fluther, runnin' about through th'
night lookin' for Nora Clitheroe to bring her back
when he heard she'd gone to folly her husband, an'
in dhread any minute he might come staggerin' in
covered with bandages, splashed all over with th'
red of his own blood, an' givin' us barely time to
bring th' priest to hear th' last whisper of his final
confession, as his soul was passin' through th' dark
doorway o' death into th' way o' th' wondherin'
dead. . . . You don't feel cold, do you?

MOLLSER: No, ma; I'm all right.

MRS. GOGAN: Keep your chest well covered, for
that's th' delicate spot in you . . . if there's any
danger, I'll whip you in again. . . . [*Mrs. Gogan
crosses to R., goes up the lane, turns and looks R.,
as if looking down the street*] Oh, here's the Covey
an' oul' Peter hurryin' along. [*She comes down the
lane, and crosses to* Mollser] God Almighty, sthrange
things is happenin' when them two is pullin' together. [*The Covey and Peter come into the lane R.,
come down, and stand R.C. Mrs. Gogan stands C.,
near the steps. The two men are breathless and excited. To the two men*] Were yous far up th' town?
Did yous see any sign o' Fluther or Nora? How is
things lookin'? I hear they're blazin' away out o' th'
G.P.O. That th' Tommies is sthretched in heaps
around Nelson's Pillar an' th' Parnell Statue, an'
that th' pavin' sets in O'Connell Street is nearly
covered be pools o' blood.

PETER: We seen no sign o' Nora or Fluther anywhere.

MRS. GOGAN: We should ha' held her back be
main force from goin' to look for her husband.
. . . God knows what's happened to her—I'm always seein' her sthretched on her back in some
hospital, moanin' with th' pain of a bullet in her
vitals, an' nuns thryin' to get her to take a last look
at th' crucifix!

THE COVEY: We can do nothin'. You can't stick
your nose into O'Connell Street, an' Tyler's is on fire.

PETER: An' we seen th' Lancers—

THE COVEY: [*Interrupting*] Throttin' along, heads
in th' air; spurs an' sabres jinglin', an' lances quiverin', an' lookin' as if they were assin' themselves,
"Where's these blighters, till we get a prod at them,"
when there was a volley from th' Post Office that
stretched half o' them, an' sent th' rest gallopin'
away wondherin' how far they'd have to go before
they'd feel safe.

PETER: [*Rubbing his hands*] "Damn it," says I to
meself, "this looks like business!"

THE COVEY: An' then out comes General Pearse

an' his staff, an', standin' in th' middle o' th' street, he reads th' Proclamation.

MRS. GOGAN: What proclamation?

PETER: Declarin' an Irish Republic.

MRS. GOGAN: [*With amazement*] Go to God!

PETER: The gunboat *Helga's* shellin' Liberty Hall, an' I hear that people livin' on th' quays had to crawl on their bellies to Mass with th' bullets that were flyin' around from Boland's Mills.

MRS. GOGAN: God bless us, what's goin' to be th' end of it all!

BESSIE: [*Opening and looking out of a window*] Maybe yous are satisfied now; maybe yous are satisfied now! Go on an' get guns if yous are men— Johnny get your gun, get your gun, get your gun! Yous are all nicely shanghaied now; th' boyo hasn't a sword on his thigh, now! Oh, yous are all nicely shanghaied now! [*She shuts down the window viciously*]

MRS. GOGAN: [*Warningly to* Peter *and the* Covey] S-s-sh, don't answer her. She's th' right oul' Orange bitch! She's been chantin' "Rule, Britannia" all th' mornin'.

PETER: I hope Fluther hasn't met with any accident, he's such a wild card.

THE COVEY: Fluther's well able to take care of himself.

MRS. GOGAN: [*Dolefully*] God grant it; but last night I dreamt I seen gettin' carried into th' house a sthretcher with a figure lyin' on it, stiff an' still, dhressed in th' habit of Saint Francis. An' then, I heard th' murmurs of a crowd no one could see sayin' th' litany for th' dead; an' then it got so dark that nothin' was seen but th' white face of th' corpse, gleamin' like a white wather lily floatin' on th' top of a dark lake. Then a tiny whisper thrickled into me ear, sayin', "Isn't the face very like th' face o' Fluther," an' then, with a thremblin' flutther, th' dead lips opened, an', although I couldn't hear, I knew they were sayin', "Poor oul' Fluther, afther havin' handin' in his gun at last, his shakin' soul moored in th' place where th' wicked are at rest an' th' weary cease from throublin'."

[*While* Mrs. Gogan *is speaking,* Peter *wanders up the lane, looks* R., *then stares; then puts on spectacles and looks again. He turns and shouts at* Mrs. Gogan *and the* Covey]

PETER: [*Shouting*] Here they are, be God, here they are; just afther turnin' the corner—Nora an' Fluther!

[*The* Covey *runs up the lane and looks* R. *with* Peter]

COVEY: She must be wounded or something— Fluther seems to be carryin' her.

[Fluther, *half carrying* Nora, *comes in* R.; Nora's *eyes are dim and hollow; her face pale and strained-looking; her hair is tossed and her clothes are dusty. They pass by* Covey *and* Peter, *come down the lane, and cross over to the door of the house* C. Peter *and the* Covey *follow, and stand* R. Mrs. Gogan *goes over*

solicitously to Nora. Nora *wears a brown mackintosh*]

MRS. GOGAN: [*Running over to them*] God bless us, is it wounded y'are, Mrs. Clitheroe, or what?

FLUTHER: [*Confidently*] Ah, she's all right, Mrs. Gogan; only worn out from thravellin' an' want o' sleep. A night's rest, now, an' she'll be as fit as a fiddle. Bring her in, an' make her lie down.

MRS. GOGAN: [*To* Nora] Did you hear e'er a whisper o' Mr. Clitheroe?

NORA: [*Wearily*] I could find him nowhere, Mrs. Gogan. None o' them would tell me where he was. They told me I shamed my husband an' th' women of Ireland be carryin' on as I was. . . . They said th' women must learn to be brave an' cease to be cowardly. . . . Me who risked more for love than they would risk for hate. . . . [*Raising her voice in hysterical protest*] My Jack will be killed, my Jack will be killed! . . . He is to be butchered as a sacrifice to th' dead! [Nora *sinks down on the steps at the door.* Bessie Burgess *opens the window, and shouts at them. They do not look at her*]

BESSIE: Yous are all nicely shanghaied now! Sorra mend the lassies who have been kissin' an' cuddlin' their boys into th' sheddin' of blood. Fillin' their minds with fairy tales that had no beginnin', but, please God, 'll have a bloody quick endin'! [*She shuts the window with a bang*]

FLUTHER: [*Losing control*] Y' ignorant oul' throllope, you!

MRS. GOGAN: [*Coaxingly, to* Nora] You'll find he'll come home safe enough to you, Mrs. Clitheroe. Afther all, there's a power o' women that's handed over sons an' husbands, to take a runnin' risk in th' fight they're wagin'.

NORA: I can't help thinkin' every shot fired 'll be fired at Jack, an' every shot fired at Jack 'll be fired at me. What do I care for th' others? I can think only of me own self. . . . An' there's no woman gives a son or a husband to be killed—if they say it, they're lyin', lyin', against God, Nature, an' against themselves! . . . One blasted hussy at a barricade told me to go home an' not be thryin' to dishearten th' men . . .

PETER: [*Unctuously*] You'll have to have patience, Nora. We all have to put up with twarthers an' tormentors in this world.

THE COVEY: If they were fightin' for anything worth while, I wouldn't mind.

FLUTHER: [*To* Nora] Nothin' derogatory 'll happen to Mr. Clitheroe. You'll find, now, in th' finish up, it'll be vice versa.

NORA: Oh, I know that wherever he is, he's thinkin' of wantin' to be with me. I know he's longin' to be passin' his hand through me hair, to be caressin' me neck, to fondle me hand an' to feel me kisses clingin' to his mouth. . . . An' he stands wherever he is because he's brave? [*Vehemently*] No, but because he's a coward, a coward, a coward!

MRS. GOGAN: Oh, they're not cowards anyway.

NORA: [*With denunciatory anger*] I tell you they're

afraid to say they're afraid! . . . Oh, I saw it, I saw it, Mrs. Gogan. . . . At th' barricade in North King Street I saw fear glowin' in all their eyes. . . . An' in th' middle o' th' sthreet was somethin' huddled up in a horrible tangled heap. . . . An' I saw that they were afraid to look at it. . . . I tell you they were afraid to look at it. . . . I tell you they were afraid, afraid, afraid!

MRS. GOGAN: [*Lifting her up from the steps*] Come on in, dear. If you'd been a little longer together the wrench asundher wouldn't have been so sharp.

NORA: [*Painfully ascending the steps, helped by* Mrs. Gogan] Th' agony I'm in since he left me has thrust away every rough thing he done, an' every unkind word he spoke; only th' blossoms that grew out of our lives are before me now; shakin' their colours before me face, an' breathin' their sweet scent on every thought springin' up in me mind, till, sometimes, Mrs. Gogan, sometimes I think I'm goin' mad!

MRS. GOGAN: You'll be a lot betther when you have a little lie down.

NORA: [*Turning toward* Fluther *as she is going in*] I don't know what I'd have done, only for Fluther. I'd have been lyin' in th' sthreets, only for him. . . . [*As she goes in*] They have dhriven away th' little happiness life had to spare for me. He has gone from me for ever, for ever. . . . Oh, Jack, Jack, Jack!

[*As Nora is led in,* Bessie *comes out. She passes down the steps with her head in the air; at the bottom she stops to look back. When they have gone in, she takes a mug of milk from under a shawl she is wearing and gives it to* Mollser *silently.* Mollser *takes it from her*]

FLUTHER: [*Going from* C. *to the* Covey *and* Peter, R.] Which of yous has the tossers?

THE COVEY: I have.

[Bessie *crosses from* Mollser *to* R. *She pauses at the corner of the lane,* R., *to speak to the two men*]

BESSIE: [*Scornfully, to* Fluther *and the* Covey] You an' your Leadhers, and their sham-battle soldiers has landed a body in a nice way, havin' to go an' ferret out a bit o' bread, God knows where. . . . Why aren't yous in the G.P.O., if yous are men? It's paler an paler yous are gettin'. . . . A lot of vipers—that's what the Irish people is! [Bessie *goes up the lane, turns* R., *and goes out*]

FLUTHER: [*Warningly*] Never mind her. [*To the* Covey] Make a start, an' keep us from th' sin of idleness. [*He crosses from* R. *to* Mollser *and speaks to her*] Well, how are you to-day, Mollser, oul' son? What are you dhrinkin'? Milk?

MOLLSER: Grand, Fluther, grand, thanks—yes, milk.

FLUTHER: [*To* Mollser] You couldn't get a betther thing down you. . . . This turnup has done one good thing, anyhow; you can't get dhrink anywhere, an' if it lasts a week I'll be so used to it that I won't

think of a pint. [Fluther *returns and joins the two men* R. *The* Covey *takes from his pocket two worn coins and a thin strip of wood (or tin) about four inches long. He puts the coins on the strip of wood and holds the strip out from him*]

THE COVEY: What's the bettin'?

PETER: Heads, a juice.

FLUTHER: Harps, a tanner.

[*The* Covey *flips the coins from the wood into the air. As they jingle on the ground the distant boom of a big gun is heard. They leave the coins where they are and listen intently*]

FLUTHER: [*Awed*] What th' hell's that?

THE COVEY: [*Awed*] It's like the boom of a big gun!

FLUTHER: Surely to God, they're not goin' to use artillery on us!

THE COVEY: [*Scornfully*] Not goin'! [*Vehemently*] Wouldn't they use anything on us, man?

FLUTHER: Aw, holy Christ, that's not playin' th' game!

PETER: [*Plaintively*] What would happen if a shell landed here now?

THE COVEY: [*Ironically*] You'd be off to heaven in a fiery chariot.

PETER: In spite of all th' warnin's that's ringin' around us, are you goin' to start your pickin' at me again?

FLUTHER: Go on, toss them again, toss them again. . . . Harps, a tanner.

PETER: Heads, a juice.

[*The* Covey *tosses the coins as before; they fall on the ground and roll a little.* Fluther *waves the other two back as they bend over the rolling coins*]

FLUTHER: Let them roll, let them roll—heads be God!

[Bessie *runs in* R., *runs downs the lane towards the three men. She is breathless with excitement. She has a new fox fur round her neck over her shawl, a number of new umbrellas under one arm, a box of biscuits under the other, and she wears a gaudily trimmed hat on her head. She speaks rapidly and breathlessly*]

BESSIE: They're breakin' into th' shops, they're breakin' into th' shops! Smashin' th' windows, batterin' in th' doors an' whippin' away everything! An' th' Volunteers is firin' on them. I seen two men an' a lassie pushin' a piano down th' street, an' th' sweat rollin' off them thryin' to get it up on th' pavement; an' an oul' wan that must ha' been seventy lookin' as if she'd dhrop every minute with th' dint o' heart beatin', thryin' to pull a big double bed out of a broken shop window! I was goin' to wait till I dhressed meself from th' skin out.

MOLLSER: [*To* Bessie, *as she is going into the house* C.] Help me in, Bessie; I'm feelin' curious.

[Bessie *leaves the looted things in the house, and, rapidly returning, helps* Mollser *in*]

THE COVEY: [*To* Fluther] Th' selfishness of that one—she waited till she got all she could carry before she'd come to tell anyone!

FLUTHER: [*Running over to the door of the house and shouting in to* Bessie] Ay, Bessie, did you hear of e'er a pub gettin' a shake up?

BESSIE: [*Inside*] I didn't hear o' none.

FLUTHER: [*In a burst of enthusiasm*] Well, you're goin' to hear of one soon!

THE COVEY: [*To* Fluther, *excitedly*] Come on, man, an' don't be wastin' time.

PETER: [*Calling to them as they run up the lane*] E, eh, are yous goin' to leave me here, alone?

[Fluther *and* Covey *halt in middle of lane, and turn to look and reply to* Peter]

FLUTHER: Are you goin' to leave yourself here?

PETER: [*Anxiously*] Didn't yous hear her sayin' they were firin' on them?

THE COVEY AND FLUTHER: [*Together*] Well?

PETER: Supposin' I happened to be potted?

FLUTHER: We'd give you a Christian burial, anyhow.

THE COVEY: [*Ironically*] Dhressed up in your regimentals.

PETER: [*To the* Covey, *passionately*] May th' all-lovin' God give you a hot knock one o' these days, me young Covey, tuthorin' Fluther up now to be tiltin' at me, an' crossin' me with his mockeries an' jibin'!

[Fluther *and* Covey *run up the lane, and go off* R. Peter *looks after them and then goes slowly into the house,* C. *After a slight pause,* Mrs. Gogan *appears at the door of the house* C., *pushing a pram in front of her. As she gets the pram over the threshold* Bessie *appears, catches the pram, and stops* Mrs. Gogan's *progress*]

BESSIE: [*Angrily*] Here, where are you goin' with that? How quick you were, me lady, to clap your eyes on th' pram. . . . Maybe you don't know that Mrs. Sullivan, before she went to spend Easther with her people in Dunboyne, gave me sthrict injunctions to give an occasional look to see if it was still standin' where it was left in th' corner of th' lobby.

MRS. GOGAN: [*Indignantly*] That remark of yours, Mrs. Bessie Burgess, requires a little considheration, seein' that th' pram was left on our lobby, an' not on yours; a foot or two a little to th' left of th' jamb of me own room door; nor is it needful to mention th' name of th' person that gave a squint to see if it was there th' first thing in th' mornin', an' th' last thing in th' stillness o' th' night; never failin' to realize that her eyes couldn't be goin' wrong, be sthretchin' out her arm an' runnin' her hand over th' pram, to make sure that th' sight was no deception! Moreover, somethin' tellin' me that th' runnin' hurry of an inthrest you're takin' in it now is a sudden ambition to use th' pram for a purpose, that a loyal woman of law an' ordher would stagger away from! [Mrs. Gogan *pushes the pram violently down the steps, pulling* Bessie *with her, who holds her up again when they reach the street*]

BESSIE: [*Still holding the pram*] There's not as much as one body in th' house that doesn't know that it wasn't Bessie Burgess that was always shakin' her voice complainin' about people leavin' bassinettes in th' way of them that, week in an' week out, had to pay their rent, an' always had to find a regular accommodation for her own furniture in her own room. . . . An' as for law an' ordher, puttin' aside th' harp an' shamrock, Bessie Burgess 'll have as much respect as she wants for th' lion an' unicorn!

PETER: [*Appearing at the door of the house,* C.] I think I'll go with th' pair of yous an' see th' fun. A fella might as well chance it, anyhow.

MRS. GOGAN: [*Taking no notice of* Peter, *and pushing the pram on towards the lane*] Take your rovin' lumps o' hands from pattin' th' bassinette, if you please, ma'am; an', steppin' from th' threshold of good manners, let me tell you, Mrs. Burgess, that it's a fat wondher to Jennie Gogan that a lady-like singer o' hymns like yourself would lower her thoughts from sky-thinkin' to sthretch out her arm in a sly-seekin' way to pinch anything dhriven asthray in th' confusion of th' battle our boys is makin' for th' freedom of their counthry!

PETER: [*Laughing and rubbing his hands together*] Hee, hee, hee, hee, hee! I'll go with th' pair o' yous an' give yous a hand.

MRS. GOGAN: [*With a rapid turn of her head as she shoves the pram forward*] Get up in th' prambulator an' we'll wheel you down.

BESSIE: [*To* Mrs. Gogan *as she halts the pram again*] Poverty an' hardship has sent Bessie Burgess to abide with sthrange company, but she always knew them she had to live with from backside to breakfast time; an' she can tell them, always havin' had a Christian kinch on her conscience, that a passion for thievin' an' pinchin' would find her soul a foreign place to live in, an' that her present intention is quite th' lofty-hearted one of pickin' up anything shaken up an' scatthered about in th' loose confusion of a general plundher!

[Mrs. Gogan, Bessie *and the pram run up the lane and go off* R. Peter *follows, but as he reaches the corner of the lane the boom of the big guns brings him to a sudden halt*]

PETER: [*Frightened into staying behind by the sound of the gun*] God Almighty, that's th' big gun again! God forbid any harm would happen to them, but sorra mind I'd mind if they met with a dhrop in their mad endeyvours to plundher an' desthroy. [*He looks down the street from the lane for a moment, then runs to the hall door of the house,* C., *which is open, and shuts it with a vicious pull; he then goes to the chair in which* Mollser *had sat, sits down, takes out his pipe, lights it and begins to smoke with his head carried at a haughty angle. The* Covey *comes in* R. *and down the lane, staggering with a tenstone sack of flour on his back. He goes over to the door, pushes it with his head, and finds he can't open it; he turns slightly in the direction of* Peter]

THE COVEY: [*To* Peter] Who shut th' door? . . . [*He kicks at it*] Here, come on an' open it, will you? This isn't a mot's hand-bag I've got on me back.

PETER: Now, me young Covey, d'ye think I'm goin' to be your lackey?

THE COVEY: [*Angrily*] Will you open th' door, y'oul'—

PETER: [*Shouting*] Don't be assin' me to open any door, don't be assin' me to open any door for you. . . . Makin' a shame an' a sin o' th' cause that good men are fightin' for. . . . Oh, God forgive th' people that, instead o' burnishin' th' work th' boys is doin' to-day, with quiet honesty an' patience, is revilin' their sacrifices with a riot of lootin' an' roguery!

THE COVEY: [*Sarcastically*] Isn't your own eyes leppin' out o' your head with envy that you haven't th' guts to ketch a few o' th' things that God is givin' to His chosen people? . . . Y'oul' hypocrite, if every one was blind you'd steal a cross off an ass's back!

PETER: [*Very calmly*] You're not goin' to make me lose me temper; you can go on with your proddin' as long as you like; goad an' goad an' goad away; hee hee, heee! I'll not lose me temper.

[*Somebody opens door and the* Covey *goes in*]

COVEY: [*Inside house, to mock* Peter] Cuckoo-oo!

[Peter *gets up from chair in a blaze of passion, and follows the* Covey *in, shouting*]

PETER: [*Shouting*] You lean, long, lanky lath of a lowsey bastard. [*Going in door of house*, C.] Lowsey bastard, lowsey bastard!

[*Mrs. Gogan and* Bessie, *pushing the pram, come in* R., *come down lane to front of the house*, C. Bessie *is pushing the pram, which is filled with loot*. Mrs. Gogan *carries a tall standard lamp, topped with a wide and bright-coloured shade. The pram is filled with fancy-coloured dresses, and boots and shoes. They are talking as they appear* R.]

MRS. GOGAN: [*Appearing* R.] I don't remember ever havin' seen such lovely pairs as them with the pointed toes an' the cuban heels.

BESSIE: [*They are now* C., *lifting one of the evening dresses from the pram, holding it up admiringly*] They'll go grand with th' dhresses we're afther liftin', when we've stitched a sthray bit o' silk to lift th' bodices up a little bit higher, so as to shake th' shame out o' them, an' make them fit for women that hasn't lost themselves in th' nakedness o' th' times.

PETER: [*At door, sourly to* Mrs. Gogan] Ay, you. Mollser looks as if she was goin' to faint, an' your youngster is roarin' in convulsions in her lap.

MRS. GOGAN: [*Snappily*] She's never any other way but faintin'! [Mrs Gogan *runs into the house with her arm full of things. She comes back, takes up the lamp and is about to go in, when a rifleshot very near is heard*. Mrs. Gogan, *with lamp, and* Bessie, *with pram, rush to the door which* Peter, *in a panic, has shut*]

MRS. GOGAN: [*Banging at the door*] Eh, eh, you cowardly oul' fool, what are you thryin' to shut the door on us for? [Mrs. Gogan *pushes the door open and runs in, followed by* Bessie *dragging in the pram. They shut the door. A pause. Then* Capt. Brennan, *supporting* Lieut. Langon, *comes in* L., *along the street in front of the house*, C. *As* Brennan *and* Langon *reach* C. *going* R., Clitheroe, *pale and in a state of calm nervousness, appears at* L., *walking backwards or looking back in the direction from which they've come; he has a rifle held at the ready in his hands*. Langon *is ghastly white and now and again his face is twisted in agony*]

CAPT. BRENNAN: [*Back to* Clitheroe] Why did you fire over their heads? Why didn't you fire to kill?

CLITHEROE: No, no, Bill; bad as they are, they're Irish men an' women.

[Brennan *gently lets* Langon *recline on the steps of the house indicated to the extreme* R., *holding him by an arm*. Clitheroe *is* C., *watching* Langon]

CAPT. BRENNAN: [*Savagely*] Irish be damned! Attackin' an' mobbin' th' men that are riskin' their lives for them. If these slum lice gather at our heels again, plug one o' them, or I'll soon shock them with a shot or two meself!

LIEUT. LANGON: [*Moaningly*] My God, is there ne'er an ambulance knockin' around anywhere? . . . Th' stomach is ripped out o' me; I feel it—o-o-oh, Christ!

CAPT. BRENNAN: Keep th' heart up, Jim; we'll soon get help, now.

[*Door of house* C. *opens and* Nora *rushes out, dashes down steps into* Clitheroe's *arms at bottom. She flings her arms around his neck. Her hair is down, her face haggard, but her eyes are agleam with happy relief*]

NORA: [*To* Clitheroe] Jack, Jack, oh, God be thanked. Kiss me, kiss me, Jack; kiss your own Nora.

CLITHEROE: [*Kissing her, and speaking brokenly*] My Nora; my little, beautiful Nora, I wish to God I'd never left you.

NORA: It doesn't matter—not now, not now, Jack. It will make us dearer than ever to each other. . . . Kiss me, kiss me again.

CLITHEROE: Now, for God's sake, Nora, don't make a scene.

NORA: [*Fervently*] I won't, I won't; I promise, Jack—honest to God.

[Bessie *opens window of house to the* R., *puts out her head, and shouts at* Clitheroe *and* Brennan]

BESSIE: [*At window*] Has th' big guns knocked all th' harps out of your hands? General Clitheroe'd rather be unlacin' his wife's bodice now than standin' at a barricade. [*To* Brennan] An' the professor of chicken butcherin', there, finds he's up against something a little tougher than his own chickens, an' that's sayin' a lot!

CAPT. BRENNAN: [*Over to* Bessie] Shut up, y'oul' hag!

BESSIE: [*Down to* Brennan] Choke th' chicken, choke th' chicken, choke th' chicken!

LIEUT. LANGON: For God's sake, Bill, bring me some place where me wound 'll be looked afther. . . . Am I to die before anything is done to save me?

CAPT. BRENNAN: [*To* Clitheroe] Come on, Jack. We've got to get help for Jim, here—have you no thought for his pain an' danger?

BESSIE: Choke th' chicken, choke th' chicken, choke th' chicken!

CLITHEROE: [*To* Nora] Loosen me, darling, let me go.

NORA: [*Clinging to him*] No, no, no, I'll not let you go! Come on, come up to our home, Jack, my sweetheart, my lover, my husband, an' we'll forget th' last few terrible days! . . .

LIEUT. LANGON: [*Appealingly*] Oh, if I'd kep' down only a little longer, I mightn't ha' been hit! Every one else escapin', an' me gettin' me belly ripped asundher! . . . I couldn't scream, couldn't even scream. . . . D'ye think I'm really badly wounded, Bill? Me clothes seem to be all soakin' wet. . . . It's blood . . . My God, it must be me own blood!

CAPT. BRENNAN: [*To* Clitheroe] Go on, Jack, bid her good-bye with another kiss, an' be done with it! D'ye want Langon to die in me arms while you're dallyin' with your Nora?

CLITHEROE: [*To* Nora] I must go, I must go, Nora. I'm sorry we met at all. . . . It couldn't be helped —all other ways were blocked be th' British. . . . Let me go, can't you, Nora? D'ye want me to be unthrue to me comrades?

NORA: No, I won't let you go. . . . I want you to be thrue to me, Jack. . . . I'm your dearest comrade; I'm your thruest comrade. [*Tightening her arms round* Clitheroe] Oh, Jack, I can't let you go!

CLITHEROE: [*With anger, mixed with affection*] You must, Nora, you must.

NORA: All last night at the barricades I sought you, Jack. I asked for you everywhere. I didn't think of the danger—I could only think of you. They dhrove me away, but I came back again.

CLITHEROE: [*Ashamed of her action*] What possessed you to make a show of yourself, like that! What are you more than any other woman?

NORA: No more, maybe; but you are more to me than any other man, Jack. . . . I couldn't help it. I shouldn't have told you. . . . My love for you made me mad with terror.

CLITHEROE: [*Angrily*] They'll say now that I sent you out th' way I'd have an excuse to bring you home. . . . Are you goin' to turn all th' risks I'm takin' into a laugh?

LIEUT. LANGON: Let me lie down, let me lie down, Bill; th' pain would be easier, maybe, lyin' down. Oh, God, have mercy on me!

CAPT. BRENNAN: [*Encouragingly to* Langon] A few steps more, Jim, a few steps more; thry to stick it for a few steps more.

LIEUT. LANGON: Oh, I can't, I can't, I can't!

CAPT. BRENNAN: [*To* Clitheroe] Are you comin', man, or are you goin' to make an arrangement for another honeymoon? . . . If you want to act th' renegade, say so, an' we'll be off!

BESSIE: [*From window*] Runnin' from th' Tommies—choke th' chicken. Runnin' from th' Tommies —choke th' chicken!

CLITHEROE: [*Savagely to* Brennan] Damn you, man, who wants to act th' renegade? [*To* Nora] Here, let go your hold; let go, I say!

NORA: [*Clinging to* Clitheroe, *and indicating* Brennan] Look, Jack, look at th' anger in his face; look at th' fear glintin' in his eyes. . . . He, himself's afraid, afraid, afraid! . . . He wants you to go th' way he'll have th' chance of death sthrikin' you an' missin' him! . . .

CLITHEROE: [*Struggling to release himself from* Nora] Damn you, woman, will you let me go!

CAPT. BRENNAN: [*Fiercely, to* Clitheroe] Break her hold on you, man; or go up an' sit on her lap!

[Clitheroe *tries to break her hold with his right hand (he's holding rifle in the other), but* Nora *clings to him*]

NORA: [*Imploringly*] Jack, Jack, Jack!

LIEUT. LANGON: [*Agonizingly*] Brennan, a priest; I'm dyin', I think. I'm dyin'.

CLITHEROE: [*To* Nora] If you won't do it quietly, I'll have to make you! [*To* Brennan] Here, hold this gun, you, for a minute. [*He hands the gun to* Brennan]

NORA: [*Pitifully*] Please, Jack. . . . You're hurting me, Jack. . . . Honestly. . . . Oh, you're hurting . . . me! . . . I won't, I won't, I won't! . . . Oh, Jack, I gave you everything you asked of me. . . . Don't fling me from you, now! [*He roughly loosens her grip, and pushes her away from him.* Nora *sinks to the steps at the door, and lies there*]

NORA: [*Weakly*] Ah, Jack. . . . Jack. . . . Jack!

CLITHEROE: [*Taking the gun back from* Brennan] Come on, come on. [Clitheroe *hurries over to* Brennan, *catches hold of* Langon's *other arm; they both lift him up from steps, and supporting him, turn into the lane and go off* R. Bessie *looks at* Nora *lying on the street, for a few moments, then, leaving the window, she comes out, runs over to* Nora, *lifts her up in her arms, and carries her swiftly into the house. A short pause, then down the street is heard a wild, drunken yell; it comes nearer, and* Fluther *enters, frenzied, wild-eyed, mad, roaring drunk. In his arms is an earthen half-gallon jar of whisky; streaming from one of the pockets of his coat is the arm of a new tunic shirt; on his head is a woman's vivid blue hat with gold lacing, all of which he has looted. The evening begins to darken*]

FLUTHER: [*Singing in a frenzy, as he comes down the lane*]

Fluther's a jolly good fella . . .
Fluther's a jolly good fella . . . up th' rebels!
. . . that nobody can deny!

[*He reels across to* L., *staggers up the steps of the house,* C., *and hammers at the door*] Get us a mug, or a jug, or somethin', some o' yous, one o' yous, will yous, before I lay one o' yous out! [*Rifle firing is heard some distance away and the boom of the big gun.* Fluther *turns from the door, and looks off* R.] Bang an' fire away for all Fluther cares. [*He beats at the door*] Come down an' open th' door, some o' yous, one o' yous, will yous, before I lay some o' yous out! . . . Th' whole city can topple home to hell, for Fluther. [*Inside the house,* C., *is heard a scream from* Nora, *followed by a moan. Singing frantically*] That nobody can deny, that nobody can deny.

For Fluther's a jolly good fella,
Fluther's a jolly good fella,
Fluther's a jolly good fella . . . up th' rebels!
. . . that nobody can deny!

[*His frantic movements cause him to spill some of the whisky out of the jar. Looking down at jar*] Blast you, Fluther, don't be spillin' th' precious liquor! [*He kicks at the door*] Give us a mug, or a jug, or somethin', one o' yous, some o' yous, will yous, before I lay one o' yous out!

[*The door suddenly opens, and* Bessie, *coming out, grips him by the collar*]

BESSIE: [*Indignantly*] You bowsey, come in ower o' that. . . . I'll thrim your thricks o' dhrunken dancin' for you, an' none of us knowin' how soon we'll bump into a world we were niver in before!

FLUTHER: [*As she is pulling him in*] Ay, th' jar, th' jar, th' jar. *Mind th' jar!*

[*A short pause, then again is heard a scream of pain from* Nora. *The door opens and* Mrs. Gogan *and* Bessie *are seen standing at it. The light gets dim*]

BESSIE: Fluther would go, only he's too dhrunk. . . . Oh, God, isn't it a pity he's so dhrunk! We'll have to thry to get a docthor somewhere.

MRS. GOGAN: I'd be afraid to go. . . . Besides, Mollser's terrible bad. I don't think you'll get a docthor to come. It's hardly any use goin'.

BESSIE: [*Determinedly*] I'll risk it. . . . Give her a little of Fluther's whisky. . . . It's th' fright that's brought it on her so soon. . . . Go on back to her, you. [Mrs. Gogan *goes into the house, and* Bessie *softly closes the door. She comes down steps, and is half-way across to* R., *when rifle-firing and the tok-tok-tok of a machine gun bring her to a sudden halt. She hesitates for a moment, then tightens her shawl round her, as if it were a shield. Softly*] O God, be Thou my help in time o' throuble; an' shelther me safely in th' shadow of Thy wings. [*She goes forward, goes up the lane, and goes off* R.]

CURTAIN

ACT IV.

SCENE—*The living-room of* Bessie Burgess. *It is one of two small attic rooms (the other, used as a bedroom, is on the* L.*), the low ceiling slopes down towards the back. There is an unmistakable air of poverty about the room. The paper on the walls is torn and soiled. On the* R., *downstage is a door. A small window* C. *back. To* L. *of window, a well-worn dresser, with a small quantity of Delft. On the* L. *wall, upstage is a door leading to a bedroom. The door on* R. *leads to the rest of the house and street. Below door on* L. *wall, the fireplace. Inside fender is a kettle and saucepan. On the hob a teapot. In front of fire a well-worn armchair. In front of window, back, a little to* R., *an oak coffin stands on two kitchen chairs. On floor, front of coffin, is a wooden box, on which are two lighted candles in candlesticks. In front of coffin, a little to* L., *a small kitchen table. At* R. *end of table, a kitchen chair. In corner where* R. *and back walls meet, the standard lamp, with coloured shade, looted in Third Act, stands; beside the lamp, hanging from nail in wall, back, hangs one of the evening dresses. There is no light in the room but that given from the two candles and the fire. The dusk has well fallen, and the glare of the burning buildings in the town can be seen through the windows in the distant sky. The* Covey, Fluther *and* Peter *have been playing cards, sitting on the floor by the light of the candles on the box near the coffin. When the* Curtain *rises the* Covey *is shuffling the cards,* Peter *is sitting in a stiff, dignified way opposite him, and* Fluther *is kneeling beside the window, back, cautiously looking out into street. It is a few days later.*

FLUTHER: [*Furtively peeping out of the window*] Give them a good shuffling. . . . Th' sky's gettin' reddher an' reddher. . . . You'd think it was afire. . . . Half o' th' city must be burnin'.

THE COVEY: [*Warningly*] If I was you, Fluther, I'd keep away from that window. . . . It's dangerous, an', besides, if they see you, you'll only bring a nose on th' house.

PETER: [*Anxiously*] Yes; an' he knows we had to leave our own place th' way they were riddlin' it with machine-gun fire. . . . He'll keep on pimpin' an' pimpin' there, till we have to fly out o' this place too.

FLUTHER: [*Ironically to* Peter] If they make any attack here, we'll send you out in your green an' glory uniform, shakin' your sword over your head, an' they'll fly before you as th' Danes flew before Brian Boru!

THE COVEY: [*Placing the cards on the floor, after shuffling them*] Come on, an' cut. [Fluther *creeps* L. *end of table, over to where* Covey *and* Peter *are seated, and squats down on floor between them. Having dealt the cards*] Spuds up again.

[Nora *moans feebly in room on* L. *They listen for a moment*]

FLUTHER: There, she's at it again. She's been quiet for a good long time, all th' same.

THE COVEY: She was quiet before, sure, an' she broke out again worse than ever. . . . What was led that time?

PETER: [*Impatiently*] Thray o' Hearts, Thray o' Hearts, Thray o' Hearts.

FLUTHER: It's damned hard lines to think of her dead-born kiddie lyin' there in th' arms o' poor little Mollser. Mollser snuffed it, sudden too, afther all.

THE COVEY: Sure she never got any care. How could she get it, an' th' mother out day and night lookin' for work, an' her consumptive husband leavin' her with a baby to be born before he died.

VOICES: [*In a lilting chant to the* L. *in an outside street*] Red Cr . . . oss, Red Cr . . . oss! . . . Ambu . . . lance, Ambu . . . lance!

THE COVEY: [*To Fluther*] Your deal, Fluther.

FLUTHER: [*Shuffling and dealing the cards*] It'll take a lot out o' Nora—if she'll ever be th' same.

THE COVEY: Th' docthor thinks she'll never be th' same; thinks she'll be a little touched here. [*He touches his forehead*] She's ramblin' a lot; thinkin' she's out in th' counthry with Jack; or, gettin' his dinner ready for him before he comes home; or, yellin' for her kiddie. All that, though, might be th' chloroform she got. . . . I don't know what we'd have done only for oul' Bessie: up with her for th' past three nights, hand runnin'.

FLUTHER: [*Approvingly*] I always knew there was never anything really derogatory wrong with poor Bessie. [*Suddenly catching* Peter's *arm as he is taking a trick*] Eh, houl' on there, don't be so damn quick —that's my thrick!

PETER: [*Resentfully*] What's your thrick? It's my thrick, man.

FLUTHER: [*Loudly*] How is it your thrick?

PETER: [*Answering as loudly*] Didn't I lead th' deuce!

FLUTHER: You must be gettin' blind, man; don't you see th' ace?

BESSIE: [*Appearing at door of room*, L.; *in a tense whisper*] D'ye want to waken her again on me, when she's just gone asleep? If she wakes will yous come an' mind her? If I hear a whisper out o' one o' yous again, I'll . . . gut yous!

THE COVEY: [*In a whisper*] S-s-s-h. She can hear anything above a whisper.

PETER: [*Looking up at the ceiling*] Th' gentle an' merciful God 'll give th' pair o' yous a scawldin' an' a scarifyin' one o' these days!

[Fluther *takes a bottle of whisky from his pocket, and takes a drink*]

THE COVEY: [*To Fluther*] Why don't you spread that out, man, an' thry to keep a sup for to-morrow?

FLUTHER: Spread it out? Keep a sup for to-morrow? How th' hell does a fella know there'll be any to-morrow? If I'm goin' to be whipped away, let me be whipped away when it's empty, an' not

when it's half-full! [Bessie *comes in a tired way from door of room* L., *down to armchair by fire, and sits down. Over to* Bessie] Well, how is she now, Bessie?

BESSIE: I left her sleeping quietly. When I'm listenin' to her babblin' I think she'll never be much betther than she is. Her eyes have a hauntin' way of lookin' in instead of lookin' out, as if her mind had been lost alive in madly minglin' memories of th' past. . . . [*Sleepily*] Crushin' her thoughts . . . together . . . in a fierce . . . an' fanciful . . . [*She nods her head and starts wakefully*] idea that dead things are livin', an' livin' things are dead. . . . [*With a start*] Was that a scream I heard her give? [*Reassured*] Blessed God, I think I hear her screamin' every minute! An' it's only there with me that I'm able to keep awake.

THE COVEY: She'll sleep, maybe, for a long time, now. Ten here.

FLUTHER: [*Gathering up cards*] Ten here. If she gets a long sleep, she might be all right. Peter's th' lone five.

THE COVEY: [*Suddenly*] Whisht! I think I hear somebody movin' below. Whoever it is, he's comin' up.

[*A pause. Then the door*, R. *opens, and* Capt. Brennan *comes timidly in. He has changed his uniform for a suit of civies. His eyes droop with the heaviness of exhaustion; his face is pallid and drawn. His clothes are dusty and stained here and there with mud. He leans heavily on the back of a chair* R. *end of table*]

CAPT. BRENNAN: Mrs. Clitheroe; where's Mrs. Clitheroe? I was told I'd find her here.

BESSIE: What d'ye want with Mrs. Clitheroe?

CAPT. BRENNAN: I've a message, a last message for her from her husband.

BESSIE: Killed! He's not killed, is he!

CAPT. BRENNAN: [*Sinking stiffly and painfully on to a chair*] In th' Imperial Hotel; we fought till th' place was in flames. He was shot through th' arm, an' then through th' lung. . . . I could do nothin' for him—only watch his breath comin' an' goin' in quick, jerky gasps, an' a tiny sthream o' blood thricklin' out of his mouth down over his lower lip. I said a prayer for th' dyin', an' twined his Rosary beads around his fingers. . . . Then I had to leave him to save meself. . . . [*He shows some holes in his coat*] Look at th' way a machine-gun tore at me coat, as I belted out o' th' buildin' an' darted across th' sthreet for shelter. . . . An' then, I seen The Plough an' th' Stars fallin' like a shot as th' roof crashed in, an' where I'd left poor Jack was nothin' but a leppin' spout o' flame!

BESSIE: [*With partly repressed vehemence*] Ay, you left him! You twined his Rosary beads round his fingers, an' then, you run like a hare to get out o' danger!

CAPT. BRENNAN: [*Defensively*] I took me chance as well as him. . . . He took it like a man. His last whisper was to "Tell Nora to be brave; that I'm ready to meet my God, an' that I'm proud to die for Ireland." An' when our General heard it he said that "Commandant Clitheroe's end was a gleam of glory." Mrs. Clitheroe's grief will be a joy when she realizes that she has had a hero for a husband.

BESSIE: If you only seen her, you'd know to th' differ.

[Nora *appears at door,* L. *She is clad only in her nightdress and slippers; her hair, uncared for some days, is hanging in disorder over her shoulders. Her pale face looks paler still because of a vivid red spot on the tip of each cheek. Her eyes are glimmering with the light of incipient insanity; her hands are nervously fiddling with her nightgown. She halts at the door for a moment, looks vacantly around the room, and then comes slowly in. The rest do not notice her till she speaks. Bessie has fallen asleep in chair.* Peter, Covey *and* Fluther *stop their card-playing and watch her*]

NORA: [*Roaming slowly towards* R. *to back of table*] No . . . not there, Jack . . . I feel very, very tired . . . [*Passing her hand across her eyes*] Curious mist on my eyes. Why don't you hold my hand, Jack. . . . [*Excitedly*] No, no, Jack, it's not: can't you see it's a goldfinch? Look at the black satiny wings, with the gold bars, an' th' splash of crimson on its head. . . . [*Wearily*] Something ails me, something ails me. . . . [*Frightened*] You're goin' away, an' I can't follow you! [*She wanders back to* L. *end of table*] I can't follow you. [*Crying out*] Jack, Jack, Jack!

[Bessie *wakes with a start, sees* Nora, *gets up and runs to her*]

BESSIE: [*Putting arm round* Nora] Mrs. Clitheroe, aren't you a terrible woman to get out o' bed. . . . You'll get cold if you stay here in them clothes.

NORA: [*Monotonously*] Cold? I'm feelin' very cold . . . it's chilly out here in the counthry. [*Looking around, frightened*] What place is this? Where am I?

BESSIE: [*Coaxingly*] You're all right, Nora; you're with friends, an' in a safe place. Don't you know your uncle an' your cousin, an' poor oul' Fluther?

PETER: [*Rising to go over to* Nora] Nora, darlin', now—

FLUTHER: [*Pulling him back*] Now, leave her to Bessie, man. A crowd 'll only make her worse.

NORA: [*Thoughtfully*] There is something I want to remember, an' I can't. [*With agony*] I can't, I can't, I can't! My head, my head! [*Suddenly breaking from* Bessie, *and running over to the men, and gripping* Fluther *by the shoulders*] Where is it? Where's my baby? Tell me where you've put it, where've you hidden it? My baby, my baby; I want my baby! My head, my poor head. . . . Oh, I can't tell what is wrong with me. [*Screaming*] Give him to me, give me my husband!

BESSIE: Blessin' o' God on us, isn't this pitiful!

NORA: [*Struggling with* Bessie] I won't go away for you; I won't. Not till you give me back my husband. [*Screaming*] Murderers, that's what yous are; murderers, murderers!

[Bessie *gently, but firmly, pulls her from* Fluther, *and tries to lead her to room,* L.]

BESSIE: [*Tenderly*] Ss-s-sh. We'll bring Mr. Clitheroe back to you, if you'll only lie down an' stop quiet. . . . [*Trying to lead her in*] Come on, now, Nora, an' I'll sing something to you.

NORA: I feel as if my life was thryin' to force its way out of my body. . . . I can hardly breathe . . . I'm frightened, I'm frightened, I'm frightened! For God's sake, don't leave me, Bessie. Hold my hand, put your arms around me!

FLUTHER: [*To* Brennan] Now you can see th' way she is, man.

PETER: An' what way would she be if she heard Jack had gone west?

THE COVEY: [*To* Peter, *warningly*] Shut up, you, man!

BESSIE: [*To* Nora] We'll have to be brave, an' let patience clip away th' heaviness of th' slow-movin' hours, rememberin' that sorrow may endure for th' night, but joy cometh in th' mornin'. . . . Come on in, an' I'll sing to you, an' you'll rest quietly.

NORA: [*Stopping suddenly on her way to the room*] Jack an' me are goin' out somewhere this evenin'. Where I can't tell. Isn't it curious I can't remember. . . . [*Screaming, and pointing* R.] He's there, he's there, an' they won't give him back to me!

BESSIE: Sh-s-sh, darlin', s-ssh. I won't sing to you, if you're not quiet.

NORA: [*Nervously holding* Bessie] Hold my hand, hold my hand, an' sing to me, sing to me!

BESSIE: Come in an' lie down, an' I'll sing to you.

NORA: [*Vehemently*] Sing to me, sing to me; sing, sing!

BESSIE: [*Singing as she leads* Nora *into room,* L.]
Lead, kindly light, amid th' encircling
gloom,
Lead Thou me on.
Th' night is dark an' I am far from
home,
Lead Thou me on.

[*Leading* Nora, Bessie *goes into room* L. *Singing softly inside room,* L.]
Keep thou my feet, I do not ask to see
The distant scene—one step enough for
me.

THE COVEY: [*To* Brennan] Now that you've seen how bad she is, an' that we daren't tell her what has happened till she's bether, you'd best be slippin' back to where you come from.

CAPT. BRENNAN: There's no chance o' slippin' back now, for th' military are everywhere: a fly couldn't get through. I'd never have got here, only I managed to change me uniform for what I'm wearin'. . . . I'll have to take me chance, an' thry to lie low here for a while.

THE COVEY: [*Frightened*] There's no place here to lie low. Th' Tommies 'll be hoppin' in here, any minute!

PETER: [*Aghast*] An' then we'd all be shanghaied!

THE COVEY: Be God, there's enough afther happenin' to us!

FLUTHER: [*Warningly, as he listens*] Whisht, whisht, th' whole o' yous. I think I heard th' clang of a rifle butt on th' floor of th' hall below. [*All alertness*] Here, come on with th' cards again. I'll deal. [*He shuffles and deals the cards to all*] Clubs up. [*To Brennan*] Thry to keep your hands from shakin', man. You lead, Peter. [*As Peter throws out a card*] Four o' Hearts led. [*Heavy steps are heard coming up stairs, outside door R. The door opens and Corporal Stoddart of the Wiltshires enters in full war kit—steel helmet, rifle, bayonet and trench tools. He stands near door R., looks around the room, and at the men who go on silently playing cards. A pause. Gathering up cards, and breaking the silence*] Two tens an' a five.

CORPORAL STODDART: 'Ello. [*Indicating the coffin*] This the stiff?

THE COVEY: Yis.

CORPORAL STODDART: Who's gowing with it? Ownly one allowed to gow with it, you knaow.

THE COVEY: I dunno.

CORPORAL STODDART: You dunnow?

THE COVEY: I dunno.

BESSIE: [*Coming into the room*] She's afther slippin' off to sleep again, thanks be to God. I'm hardly able to keep me own eyes open. [*To the soldier*] Oh, are yous goin' to take away poor little Mollser?

CORPORAL STODDART: Ay; 'oo's agowing with 'er?

BESSIE: Oh, th' poor mother, o' course. God help her, it's a terrible blow to her!

FLUTHER: A terrible blow? Sure, she's in her element now, woman, mixin' earth to earth, an' ashes t'ashes, an' dust to dust, an' revellin' in plumes an' hearses, last days an' judgements!

BESSIE: [*Falling into chair by the fire*] God bless us! I'm jaded!

CORPORAL STODDART: Was she plugged?

COVEY: [*Shortly*] No; died of consumption.

CORPORAL STODDART: [*Carelessly*] Ow, is that all—thought she might 'ave been plugged.

COVEY: [*Indignantly*] Is that all! Isn't it enough? D'ye know, comrade, that more die o' consumption than are killed in the war? An' it's all because of th' system we're livin' undher.

CORPORAL STODDART: Ow, I know. I'm a Socialist, myself, but I 'as to do my dooty.

COVEY: [*Ironically*] Dooty! Th' only dooty of a Socialist is th' emancipation of th' workers.

CORPORAL STODDART: Ow, a man's a man, an' 'e 'as to fight for 'is country, 'asn't 'e?

FLUTHER: [*Aggressively*] You're not fightin' for your counthry here, are you?

PETER: [*Anxiously, to Fluther*] Ay, ay, Fluther, none o' that, none o' that!

THE COVEY: Fight for your counthry! Did y'ever read, comrade, Jenersky's *Thesis on the Origin, Development an' Consolidation of th' Evolutionary Idea of the Proletariat?*

CORPORAL STODDART: [*Good-humouredly*] Ow, cheese it, Paddy, cheese it!

BESSIE: [*Sleepily*] How is things in th' town, Tommy?

CORPORAL STODDART: Ow, I think it's nearly over. We've got 'em surrounded, an' we're closing in on the blighters. It was only a bit of a dorg-fight.

[*Outside in the street is heard the sharp ping of a sniper's rifle, followed by a squeal of pain*]

VOICES: [*To the L. in a chant, outside in street*] Red Cr . . . oss, Red Cr . . . oss! Ambu . . . lance, Ambu . . . lance!

CORPORAL STODDART: [*Going up R. and looking out of window, back*] Christ, there's another of our men 'it by the blarsted sniper! 'E's knocking abaht 'ere somewheres. [*Venomously*] Gord, wen we gets the blighter, we'll give 'im the cold steel, we will. We'll jab the belly aht of 'im, we will!

[*Mrs. Gogan enters tearfully by door R.; she is a little proud of the importance of being connected with death*]

MRS. GOGAN: [*To Fluther*] I'll never forget what you done for me, Fluther, goin' around at th' risk of your life settlin' everything with th' undhertaker an' th' cemetery people. When all me own were afraid to put their noses out, you plunged like a good one through hummin' bullets, an' they knockin' fire out o' th' road, tinklin' through th' frightened windows, an' splashin' themselves to pieces on th' walls! An' you'll find, that Mollser in th' happy place she's gone to, won't forget to whisper, now an' again, th' name o' Fluther.

[*Corporal Stoddart comes from window down R. to door R., and stands near the door*]

CORPORAL STODDART: [*To Mrs. Gogan*] Git it aht, mother, git it aht.

BESSIE: [*From the chair*] It's excusin' me you'll be, Mrs. Gogan, for not stannin' up, seein' I'm shaky on me feet for want of a little sleep, an' not desirin' to show any disrespect to poor little Mollser.

FLUTHER: Sure, we all know, Bessie, that it's vice versa with you.

MRS. GOGAN: [*To Bessie*] Indeed, it's meself that has well chronicled, Mrs. Burgess, all your gentle hurryin' to me little Mollser, when she was alive, bringin' her somethin' to dhrink, or somethin' t'eat, an' never passin' her without lifting up her heart with a delicate word o' kindness.

CORPORAL STODDART: [*Impatiently, but kindly*] Git it aht, git it aht, mother. [*The men rise from their card-playing; Fluther and Brennan go R. to R. end of coffin; Peter and Covey go L. of table to L. end of coffin. One of them takes box and candles out of way. They carry coffin down R. and out by door R., Corporal Stoddart watching them. Mrs. Gogan follows the coffin out. A pause. Corporal Stoddart, at door R., turns towards Bessie. To Bessie, who is almost asleep*] 'Ow many men is in this 'ere 'ouse? [*No answer. Loudly*] 'Ow many men is in this 'ere 'ouse?

BESSIE: [*Waking with a start*] God, I was nearly asleep! . . . How many men? Didn't you see them?

CORPORAL STODDART: Are they all that are in the 'ouse?

BESSIE: [*Sleepily*] Oh, there's none higher up, but there may be more lower down. Why?

CORPORAL STODDART: All men in the district 'as to be rounded up. Somebody's giving 'elp to the snipers, an' we 'as to tike precautions. If I 'ad my wy I'd mike 'em all join up an' do their bit! But I suppose they an' you are all Shinners.

BESSIE: [*Who has been sinking into sleep, waking up to a sleepy vehemence*] Bessie Burgess is no Shinner, an' never had no thruck with anything spotted be th' fingers o' th' Fenians. But always made it her business to harness herself for Church whenever she knew that God Save The King was goin' to be sung at t'end of th' service; whose only son went to th' front in th' first contingent of the Dublin Fusiliers, an' that's on his way home carryin' a shatthered arm that he got fightin' for his King an' counthry!

[Bessie's *head sinks slowly forward again. Door,* R., *opens and* Peter *comes in, his body stiff, and his face contorted with anger. He goes up* R., *to back, and paces angrily from side to side.* Covey, *with a sly grin on his face, and* Fluther *follow* Peter. Fluther *goes to* L. *and* Covey *goes to* R. *end of table.* Brennan *follows in and slinks to back of table to* L. *corner between dresser and door,* L. Corporal Stoddart *remains standing a little in from door* R.]

FLUTHER: [*After an embarrassing pause*] Th' air in th' shtreet outside's shakin' with the firin' o' rifles, an' machine-guns. It must be a hot shop in th' middle o' th' scrap.

CORPORAL STODDART: We're pumping lead in on 'em from every side, now; they'll soon be shoving up th' white flag.

PETER: [*With a shout at* Fluther *and* Covey] I'm tellin' you either o' yous two lowsers 'ud make a betther hearseman than Peter! proddin' an' pokin' at me an' I helpin' to carry out a corpse!

FLUTHER: [*Provokingly*] It wasn't a very derogatory thing for th' Covey to say that you'd make a fancy hearseman, was it?

PETER: [*Furiously*] A pair o' redjesthered, bow-seys pondherin' from mornin' till night on how they'll get a chance to break a gap through th' quiet nature of a man that's always endeavourin' to chase out of him any sthray thought of venom against his fellaman!

THE COVEY: Oh, shut it, shut it, shut it!

PETER: [*Furiously*] As long as I'm a livin' man, responsible for me thoughts, words an' deeds to th' Man above, I'll feel meself instituted to fight again' th' sliddherin' ways of a pair o' picaroons, whisperin', concurrin', concoctin' an' conspirin' together to rendher me unconscious of th' life I'm thryin' to live!

CORPORAL STODDART: [*Dumbfounded*] What's wrong, Paddy; wot 'ave they done to you?

PETER: [*Savagely to the* Corporal] You mind your own business! What's it got to do with you, what's wrong with me?

BESSIE: [*In a sleepy murmur*] Will yous thry to conthrol yourselves into quietness? Yous'll waken her . . . up . . . on . . . me . . . again. [*She sleeps*]

FLUTHER: [*Coming* C.] Come on, boys, to th' cards again, an' never mind him.

CORPORAL STODDART: No use of you going to start cards; you'll be going aht of 'ere, soon as Sergeant comes.

FLUTHER: [*In surprise*] Goin' out o' here? An' why're we goin' out o' here?

CORPORAL STODDART: All men in district 'as to be rounded up, an' 'eld in till the scrap is over.

FLUTHER: [*Concerned*] An' where're we goin' to be held in?

CORPORAL STODDART: They're puttin' them in a church.

COVEY: [*Astounded*] A church?

FLUTHER: What sort of a church? Is it a Protestan' church?

CORPORAL STODDART: I dunno; I suppose so.

FLUTHER: [*In dismay*] Be God, it'll be a nice thing to be stuck all night in a Protestan' church!

CORPORAL STODDART: If I was you, I'd bring the cards—you might get a chance of a gime.

FLUTHER: [*Hesitant*] Ah, no, that wouldn't do. . . . I wondher. . . . [*After a moment's thought*] Ah, I don't think we'd be doin' anything derogatory be playin' cards in a Protestan' church.

CORPORAL STODDART: If I was you I'd bring a little snack with me; you might be glad of it before the morning [*Lilting*]

    Oh, I do like a snice mince pie,
    Oh, I do like a snice mince pie.

[*Again the snap of the sniper's rifle rings out, followed by a scream of pain.* Corporal Stoddart *goes pale, runs up* R. *to near window,* C., *with his rifle at the ready*]

VOICES: [*In street to* R., *chanting*] Red Cr . . . oss . . . Red Cr . . . oss! Ambu . . . lance . . . Ambu . . . lance!

[*The door* R. *is dashed open, and* Sergeant Tinley, *pale, agitated, and angry, comes rapidly in. He stands inside the door, glaring at men in the room.* Corporal Stoddart *swings round at the ready as* Tinley *enters and lets his rifle drop when he sees the* Sergeant]

CORPORAL STODDART: [*To* Sergeant] One of our men 'it again, Sergeant?

SERGEANT TINLEY: [*Angrily*] Private Taylor: got it right through the chest, 'e did; an 'ole in front as ow you could put your 'and through, an' arf 'is back blown away! Dum-dum bullets they're using. Gang of assassins potting at us from behind roofs. That's not plying the gime: why don't they come into the open and fight fair?

FLUTHER: [*Unable to stand the slight, facing*

Sergeant] Fight fair! A few hundhred scrawls o' chaps with a couple o' guns an' Rosary beads, again' a hundhred thousand thrained men with horse, fut an' artillery. . . . [*To others in room*] An' he wants us to fight fair! [*To Sergeant*] D'ye want us to come out in our skins an' throw stones?

SERGEANT TINLEY: [*To* Corporal] Are these four all that are 'ere?

CORPORAL STODDART: Four; that's hall, Sergeant.

SERGEANT TINLEY: [*Roughly*] Come on, then, get the blighters aht. [*To the men*] 'Ere, 'op it aht! Aht into the street with you, an' if another of our men goes west, you go with 'im. [*He catches* Fl12ther *by the arm*] Go on, git aht!

FLUTHER: [*Pulling himself free*] Eh, who are you chuckin', eh?

SERGEANT TINLEY: [*Roughly*] Go on, git aht, you blighter.

FLUTHER: [*Truculently*] Who're you callin' a blighter to, eh? I'm a Dublin man, born an' bred in th' City, see?

SERGEANT TINLEY: Oh, I don't care if you were Bryan Buroo; git aht, git aht.

FLUTHER: [*Pausing as he reaches door* R., *to face the* Sergeant *defiantly*] Jasus, you an' your guns! Leave them down, an' I'd beat th' two of yous without sweatin'!

[*Shepherded by the two soldiers, who follow them out,* Peter, Covey, Fluther *and* Brennan *go out by door* R. Bessie *is sleeping heavily on the chair by the fire. After a pause* Nora *appears at door* L., *in her nightdress. Remaining at door for a few moments she looks vaguely around the room. She then comes in quietly, goes over to the fire, pokes it and puts the kettle on. She thinks for a few moments, pressing her hand to her forehead. She looks questioningly at the fire, and then at the press at back. She goes to the dresser* L., *back, opens drawer, takes out a soiled cloth and spreads it on the table. She then places things for tea on the table*]

NORA: I imagine th' room looks very odd, some-how. . . . I was nearly forgetting Jack's tea. . . . Ah, I think I'll have everything done before he gets in. . . . [*She lilts gently, as she arranges the table*]

Th' violets were scenting th' woods,
    Nora,
Displaying their charms to th' bee,
When I first said I lov'd only you, Nora,
    An' you said you lov'd only me.

Th' chestnut blooms gleam'd through
    th' glade, Nora,
A robin sang loud from a tree,
When I first said I lov'd only you, Nora,
    An' you said you lov'd only me.

[*She pauses suddenly, and glances round the room. Doubtfully*] I can't help feelin' this room very strange. . . . What is it? . . . What is it? . . . I must think. . . . I must thry to remember. . . .

VOICES: [*Chanting in a distant street*] Ambu . . . lance, Ambu . . . lance! Red Cro . . . . ss, Red Cro . . . . ss!

NORA: [*Startled and listening for a moment, then resuming the arrangement of the table*]

Trees, birds an' bees sang a song, Nora,
    Of happier transports to be,
When I first said I lov'd only you, Nora,
    An' you said you lov'd only me.

[*A burst of rifle-fire is heard in a street near by, followed by the rapid tok-tok-tok of a machine-gun. Staring in front of her and screaming*] Jack, Jack, Jack! My baby, my baby, my baby!

BESSIE: [*Waking with a start*] You divil, are you afther gettin' out o' bed again! [*She rises and runs towards* Nora, *who rushes to the window, back* L., *which she frantically opens*]

NORA: [*At the window, screaming*] Jack, Jack, for God's sake, come to me!

SOLDIERS: [*Outside, shouting*] Git awoy, git awoy from that window, there!

BESSIE: [*Seizing hold of* Nora] Come away, come away, woman, from that window!

NORA: [*Struggling with* Bessie] Where is it; where have you hidden it? Oh, Jack, Jack, where are you?

BESSIE: [*Imploringly*] Mrs. Clitheroe, for God's sake, come away!

NORA: [*Fiercely*] I won't; he's below. Let . . . me . . . go! You're thryin' to keep me from me husband. I'll follow him. Jack, Jack, come to your Nora!

BESSIE: Hus-s-sh, Nora, Nora! He'll be here in a minute. I'll bring him to you, if you'll only be quiet—honest to God, I will. [*With a great effort* Bessie *pushes* Nora *away from the window, the force used causing her to stagger against it herself. Two rifle-shots ring out in quick succession.* Bessie *jerks her body convulsively; stands stiffly upright for a moment, a look of agonized astonishment on her face, then she staggers forward, leaning heavily on the table with her hands. With an arrested scream of fear and pain*] Merciful God, I'm shot, I'm shot, I'm shot! . . . Th' life's pourin' out o' me! [*To* Nora] I've got this through . . . through you . . . through you, you bitch, you! . . . O God, have mercy on me! . . . [*To* Nora] You wouldn't stop quiet, no you wouldn't, you wouldn't, blast you! Look at what I'm afther gettin', look at what I'm afther gettin' . . . I'm bleedin' to death, an' no one's here to stop th' flowin' blood! [*Calling*] Mrs. Gogan, Mrs. Gogan! Fluther, Fluther, for God's sake, somebody, a doctor, a doctor!

[Bessie, *leaving* R. *end of table, staggers down towards door* R., *but, weakening, she sinks down on her knees,* R.C., *then reclining, she supports herself by her right hand resting on floor.* Nora *is rigid with her back to wall,* L., *her trembling hands held out a little from her sides; her lips quivering, her breast heaving, staring wildly at the figure of* Bessie]

NORA: [*In a breathless whisper*] Jack, I'm frightened. . . . I'm frightened, Jack. . . . Oh, Jack, where are you?

BESSIE: [*Moaningly*] This is what's afther comin' on me for nursin' you day an' night. . . . I was a fool, a fool, a fool! Get me a dhrink o' wather, you jade, will you? There's a fire burnin' in me blood! [*Pleadingly*] Nora, Nora, dear, for God's sake, run out an' get Mrs. Gogan, or Fluther, or somebody to bring a doctor, quick, quick, quick! [*As* Nora *does not stir*] Blast you, stir yourself, before I'm gone!

NORA: Oh, Jack, Jack, where are you?

BESSIE: [*In a whispered moan*] Jesus Christ, me sight's goin'! It's all dark, dark! Nora, hold me hand! [Bessie's *body lists over and she sinks into a prostrate position on the floor*] I'm dyin', I'm dyin' . . . I feel it. . . . Oh God, oh God! [*She feebly sings*]

> I do believe . . . I will believe
> That . . . Jesus . . . died . . . for . . . me,
> That . . . on . . . the . . . cross He . . .
> shed . . . His . . . blood
> From . . . sin . . . to . . . set . . . free.

[*She ceases singing, and lies stretched out, still and rigid. A pause; then* Mrs. Gogan *runs hastily in by door* R. *She halts at door and looks round with a frightened air*]

MRS. GOGAN: [*Quivering with fear*] Blessed be God, what's afther happenin'! [*To* Nora] What's wrong, child, what's wrong? [*She sees* Bessie, *runs to her and bends over the body*] Bessie, Bessie! [*She shakes the body*] Mrs. Burgess, Mrs. Burgess! [*She feels* Bessie's *forehead*] My God, she's as cold as death. They're afther murdherin' th' poor inoffensive woman!

[Sergeant Tinley *and* Corporal Stoddart, *in agitation, enter by door* R., *their rifles at the ready*]

SERGEANT TINLEY: [*Excitedly*] This is the 'ouse! [*They go rapidly to window, back,* C.] That's the window!

NORA: [*Pressing back against the wall*] Hide it, hide it; cover it up, cover it up!

[Sergeant Tinley, *looking round room, sees body. He comes from window to* Bessie, *and bends over her*]

SERGEANT TINLEY: [*Bending over body*] 'Ere, wot's this? Oo's this? Oh, God, we've plugged one of the women of the 'ouse!

CORPORAL STODDART: [*At window*] W'y the 'ell did she go to the window? Is she dead?

SERGEANT TINLEY: Dead as bedamned. Well, we couldn't afford to tike any chances.

[Sergeant Tinley *goes back to window, and looks out*]

NORA: [*Screaming, and putting her hands before her face*] Hide it, hide it; don't let me see it! Take me away, take me away, Mrs. Gogan!

[Mrs. Gogan, *who has been weeping softly over* Bessie, *rises, and crosses by front of table to room,* L., *goes in and comes out with a sheet*

in her hands. She crosses over and spreads the sheet over* Bessie's *body*]

MRS. GOGAN: [*As she spreads the sheet*] Oh, God help her, th' poor woman, she's stiffenin' out as hard as she can! Her face has written on it th' shock o' sudden agony, an' her hands is whitenin' into th' smooth shininess of wax.

NORA: [*Whimperingly*] Take me away, take me away; don't leave me here to be lookin' an' lookin' at it!

MRS. GOGAN: [*Going over to* Nora *and putting her arm round her*] Come on with me, dear, an' you can doss in poor Mollser's bed, till we gather some neighbours to come an' give th' last friendly touches to Bessie in th' lonely layin' of her out. [Mrs. Gogan *puts her arms round* Nora, *leads her across from* L. *to* R., *and they both go slowly out by door* R. Corporal Stoddart *comes from window to table, looks at tea-things on table; goes to fireplace, takes the teapot up in his hand*]

CORPORAL STODDART: [*Over to* Tinley, *at window*] Tea here, Sergeant; wot abaht a cup of scald?

SERGEANT TINLEY: Pour it aht, pour it aht, Stoddart—I could scoff anything just now.

[Corporal Stoddart *pours out two cups of tea.* Sergeant Tinley *comes from window to table, and sits on* R. *end;* Corporal Stoddart *sits on opposite end of table, and they drink the tea. In the distance is heard a bitter burst of rifle and machine-gun fire, interspersed with the boom, boom of artillery. The glare in the sky seen through the window* C., *back, flares into a fuller and a deeper red*]

SERGEANT TINLEY: There gows the general attack on the Powst Office.

VOICES: [*In a distant street*] Ambu . . . lance, Ambu . . . lance! Red Cro . . . ss, Red Cro . . . ss!

[*The voices of soldiers at a barricade outside the house are heard singing*]

> They were summoned from the 'illside,
> They were called in from the glen,
> And the country found 'em ready
> At the stirring call for men.
> Let not tears add to their 'ardship,
> As the soldiers pass along,
> And although our 'eart is breaking
> Make it sing this cheery song.

[Sergeant Tinley *and* Corporal Stoddart *join in the chorus as they sip the tea.* Sergeant Tinley *and* Corporal Stoddart *singing*]

> Keep the 'ome fires burning,
> While your 'earts are yearning.
> Though your lads are far away,
> They dream of 'ome;
> There's a silver lining
> Through the dark cloud shining,
> Turn the dark cloud inside out,
> Till the boys come 'ome!

THE END

W. Somerset Maugham

(1874————)

Novelist, essayist, and playwright, W. Somerset Maugham was one of the most successful of English writers during the first half of the century. Readers of fiction will remember him longest for his autobiographical novel *Of Human Bondage* (1915); for the book based on the story of Gauguin, *The Moon and Sixpence* (1919), and for the controversial but incisive tale *Cakes and Ale* (1930). Two of his long short stories are also likely to wear rather well, *The Letter* and *Miss Thompson* (1921), which furnished the basis of one of the most successful American plays, John Colton and Clemence Randolph's *Rain*. And there will always be much pleasure awaiting the reader in *The Summing Up* (1937), in which the writer collected sage observations on life and letters. Playwriting was only one of Maugham's interests—and the one that he professed to esteem least. Yet even in this hazardous occupation Maugham was extraordinarily successful, in particular when he concentrated mainly on entertainment.

For a dramatist's career, as well as for a novelist's, this fortunate author was well qualified from the start. He was cosmopolitan by background and education, trained in science and well read in literature, polished in manners and speech, extraordinarily well traveled, and altogether experienced in the ways of the world. Born in Paris of a father who served as Solicitor in the British embassy, Maugham spoke French more fluently than English in early childhood. After studying at King's School in Canterbury, he became a medical student at the University of Heidelberg. From there he went to St. Thomas's Hospital in London and in due time became a member of both the Royal College of Physicians and the Royal College of Surgeons. But, although he profited from this training, acquiring or refining the scientific detachment and power of observation notable in his writing, he evaded the exacting practice of medicine. During his period of internship, in 1897, he wrote the novel *Liza of Lambeth*, and henceforth it was literature that claimed his allegiance. It gave him leisure and occasion for travel. Once he had amassed the financial means to enjoy liberty and satisfy curiosity, he led the life of a man of the world with a relish that he never tried to conceal. His travels took him to most of the countries in Europe, to North and South America, and to the East, and he made his home in the congenial South of France. "Without an adequate income half the possibilities of the world are cut off," he wrote in *The Summing Up*, and he was resolved not to be cut off from anything pleasurable or stimulating within the bounds of reason.

The drama was an early interest with Maugham, and he first expressed it with a play written in German in 1902, *Schiffbrüchig*, translated as *Marriages Are Made in Heaven*. He followed it in 1903 with a serious drama in English, *The Man of Honour*, produced experimentally by the Stage Society of London but frowned upon by the commercial managements as too depressing for the popular taste. Four years later, however, he corrected this error by writing *Lady Frederick*, a light comedy of a spendthrift adventuress, which ran for a year after its *première* on October 26, 1907. While waiting for *Lady Frederick* to interest a management, he wrote two other plays, *Mrs. Dot* and *Jack Straw*. With still another play, *The Explorer*, on the boards, Maugham had four pieces running in London during the year 1908. He completed two plays in 1909 and two more the following year, his productivity tapering off only after 1911. During the First World War he was occupied with the ambulance service and, more importantly, with the British Intelligence Service. In 1917, however, he started another spurt of playwriting, turning out his most important work, which falls into the two categories of serious drama and high comedy.

Perhaps because he found scant encouragement for his most earnest efforts, he grew cynical about them. He concluded in *The Summing Up* that "the aim of the drama is not to instruct but to please," adding that "art is indifferent to morals" and that "a lofty purpose will not serve you so well as a competent technique." He learned this from the failure of a number of plays: *The Unknown* (1920), the drama of a returning soldier who can no longer believe in the existence of God; *The Sacred Flame* (1929), a grim melodrama of the "whodunit" variety in which a mother gives her maimed son an overdose of sleeping tablets to prevent his learning that his wife has betrayed him; *For Services Rendered* (1932), a picture of the postwar dislocation of British life; and, finally, *Sheppey*, a morality drama in the form of a sardonic comedy about the fate of a humble sweepstakes winner who tries to pattern his life after Christ's teachings. The serious plays did not conspicuously depart from Maugham's characteristic vein of detached observation and urbane disenchantment. Sheppey, the sweepstakes winner, for instance, is adjudged mad because he distributes his gains among the poor. The world and Christ are plainly not on speaking terms. "It's obvious,' declares Sheppey's psychiatrist, "that a sane man is not going to give all his money away to the poor. A sane man *takes* from the poor. . . ." But Maugham was not at top form when he grew somber, perhaps because there was too great a discrepancy between his contempt for humanity and his desire to be sympathetic. His public was left ill at ease rather than stirred. After the failure of *Sheppey,* in 1933, Maugham resolved to write no more for the theatre, declaring, "I am conscious that I am no longer in touch with the public that patronizes the theatre. This happens in the end to most dramatists and they are wise to accept the warning."

This would hardly have been Maugham's decision had he continued to write the kind of comedies he began to turn out with *Our Betters* (1917). They represented the ripe fruit of his way of life and observation, and they proved eminently satisfying. *Our Betters* was a devastating satire on the snobbery and selfish emptiness of the fashionable set. The American girl Bessie Saunders is so aghast at the society into which she is introduced by her titled sister that she takes the boat home. It is a society in which noblemen such as Lord Bleane lay ancient coronets at the feet of every *nouveau riche* American woman, spurious noblewomen such as the Duchess de Surennes (her maiden name in Chicago was Hodgson) bestow their favor on idle boys half their age, and expatriated dandies such as Clay speak condescendingly of "you Americans in America." *Our Betters* was one of the most brilliant high comedies since the time of Congreve and Wycherley. In 1921 Maugham wrote *The Circle* and six years later, *The Constant Wife,* in which amoral Restoration comedy fused with modern thesis drama and Shavian comedy of ideas. When Constance learns that her distinguished husband has been unfaithful to her, she refuses to create a scandal, convinced that she has no grievance after fifteen years of marriage during which she has led a parasitical existence. Once she has ceased to please, she has no right to demand loyalty from her husband, since she is of no use to him. Only by earning her own livelihood can she recover her dignity. She goes into business and makes herself economically independent of him. In consequence, the double standard of morality for the sexes vanishes and she pays her husband in his own coin by being openly unfaithful to him. Returning to the theme of marriage in 1930 and using a middle-class setting, Maugham wrote the less lively comedy *The Breadwinner,* in which a husband leaves his tiresomely parasitical household.

It is *The Circle,* however, that displays the best features of the art of high comedy. *The Circle* is comedy of manners, with its many recognizable details of upper-class life and its telling commentary on the social climate. But to this comparatively perishable stuff, Maugham added substantial comedy of character with portraits, such as those of Lady Kitty and Lord Porteous, which have human as well as comic dimension within the framework of a clever plot. The idea of the play—the cycle of romantic passion and the inability of one generation to learn from the experience of another —is so interfused with the importance of character in any situation that Porteous is made to say to Lady Kitty, "If we made rather a hash of things perhaps it was because we are rather trivial people. You can do anything in this world if you're prepared to take the consequences, and consequences depend upon character."

Worldly wisdom in *The Circle* results in a perceptive and tolerant work. It shatters no precedents, but neither does it accept them. There is an organized intellect at work in the play, for which there are evidences in the style and technique. Dialogue suits character and situation instead of being displayed for its own sake, though we may be sure that Maugham would have been at no loss if he had wanted to scintillate. Structurally, too, the play shows Maugham in full command of his medium. With *The Circle,* he brought drawing-room comedy to perfection. It is a "well-made play" in which intrigue is kept within the bounds of naturalness. Surprises, as when Lady Kitty and Lord Porteous make their first entrance and when Elizabeth elopes, were no doubt calculated by the clever showman, who kept a notebook and worked at his craft methodically; but he refrained from trying to startle the playgoer with the ingenuity of his invention. Maugham had the cleverness here not to be too clever. Indeed, it is cleverness that comes a cropper in the play when Arnold, taking his father's advice, offers his wife her freedom on the theory that when the bars and bolts are removed "the prisoner won't escape"—and yet the prisoner does.

BIBLIOGRAPHY: Richard Aldington, *W. Somerset Maugham,* 1939; John Mason Brown, *Two on the Aisle* (pp. 108–113), 1938; Barrett H. Clark, *A Study of the Modern Drama* (pp. 320–327), 1938; Desmond MacCarthy, *Drama* (pp. 343–348), 1940; W. Somerset Maugham, *The Summing Up,* (especially ch. 30–43, 1938; Ernest Short, *Theatrical Cavalcade* (pp. 165–170), 1942.

THE CIRCLE

By W. Somerset Maugham

PERSONS OF THE PLAY

CLIVE CHAMPION-CHENEY   EDWARD LUTON   ELIZABETH
ARNOLD CHAMPION-CHENEY, M.P. LADY CATHERINE CHAMPION-CHENEY MRS. SHENSTONE
LORD PORTEOUS

The action takes place at Aston-Adey, Arnold Champion-Cheney's house in Dorset.

ACT I.

The Scene is a stately drawing-room at Aston-Adey, with fine pictures on the walls and Georgian furniture. Aston-Adey has been described, with many illustrations, in Country Life. *It is not a house, but a place. Its owner takes a great pride in it, and there is nothing in the room which is not of the period. Through the French windows at the back can be seen the beautiful gardens which are one of the features. It is a fine summer morning.*

Arnold comes in. He is a man of about thirty-five, tall and good-looking, fair, with a clean-cut, sensitive face. He has a look that is intellectual, but somewhat bloodless. He is very well dressed.

ARNOLD: [*Calling*] Elizabeth. [*He goes to the window and calls again*] Elizabeth! [*He rings the bell. While he is waiting he gives a look round the room. He slightly alters the position of one of the chairs. He takes an ornament from the chimney-piece and blows the dust from it. A Footman comes in*] Oh, George! See if you can find Mrs. Cheney, and ask her if she'd be good enough to come here.

FOOTMAN: Very good, sir.

[*The* Footman *turns to go*]

ARNOLD: Who is supposed to look after this room?

FOOTMAN: I don't know, sir.

ARNOLD: I wish when they dust they'd take care to replace the things exactly as they were before.

FOOTMAN: Yes, sir.

ARNOLD: [*Dismissing him*] All right.

[*The* Footman *goes out. Arnold goes again to the window and calls*]

ARNOLD: Elizabeth! [*He sees* Mrs. Shenstone] Oh, Anna, do you know where Elizabeth is?

[Mrs. Shenstone *comes in from the garden. She is a woman of forty, pleasant, and of elegant appearance*]

ANNA: Isn't she playing tennis?

ARNOLD: No, I've been down to the tennis court. Something very tiresome has happened.

ANNA: Oh?

ARNOLD: I wonder where the deuce she is.

ANNA: When do you expect Lord Porteous and Lady Kitty?

ARNOLD: They're motoring down in time for luncheon.

ANNA: Are you sure you want me to be here? It's not too late yet, you know. I can have my things packed and catch a train for somewhere or other.

ARNOLD: No, of course we want you. It'll make it so much easier if there are people here. It was exceedingly kind of you to come.

ANNA: Oh, nonsense!

ARNOLD: And I think it was a good thing to have Teddie Luton down.

ANNA: He is so breezy, isn't he?

ARNOLD: Yes, that's his great asset. I don't know that he's very intelligent, but, you know, there are occasions when you want a bull in a china shop. I sent one of the servants to find Elizabeth.

ANNA: I daresay she's putting on her shoes. She and Teddie were going to have a single.

ARNOLD: It can't take all this time to change one's shoes.

ANNA: [*With a smile*] One can't change one's shoes without powdering one's nose, you know.

[Elizabeth *comes in. She is a very pretty creature in the early twenties. She wears a light summer frock*]

ARNOLD: My dear, I've been hunting for you everywhere. What *have* you been doing?

ELIZABETH: Nothing! I've been standing on my head.

ARNOLD: My father's here.

ELIZABETH: [*Startled*] Where?

ARNOLD: At the cottage. He arrived last night.

ELIZABETH: Damn!

ARNOLD: [*Good-humoredly*] I wish you wouldn't say that, Elizabeth.

ELIZABETH: If you're not going to say "Damn" when a thing's damnable, when are you going to say "Damn"?

ARNOLD: I should have thought you could say, "Oh, bother!" or something like that.

ELIZABETH: But that wouldn't express my sentiments. Besides, at that speech day when you were giving away the prizes you said there were no synonyms in the English language.

ANNA: [*Smiling*] Oh, Elizabeth! It's very unfair to expect a politician to live in private up to the statements he makes in public.

ARNOLD: I'm always willing to stand by anything I've said. There *are* no synonyms in the English language.

ELIZABETH: In that case, I shall be regretfully forced to continue to say "Damn" whenever I feel like it.

[*Edward Luton shows himself at the window. He is an attractive youth in flannels*]

TEDDIE: I say, what about this tennis?

ELIZABETH: Come in. We're having a scene.

TEDDIE: [*Entering*] How splendid! What about?

ELIZABETH: The English language.

TEDDIE: Don't tell me you've been splitting your infinitives.

ARNOLD: [*With the shadow of a frown*] I wish you'd be serious, Elizabeth. The situation is none too pleasant.

ANNA: I think Teddie and I had better make ourselves scarce.

ELIZABETH: Nonsense! You're both in it. If there's going to be any unpleasantness we want your moral support. That's why we asked you to come.

TEDDIE: And I thought I'd been asked for my blue eyes.

ELIZABETH: Vain beast! And they happen to be brown.

TEDDIE: Is anything up?

ELIZABETH: Arnold's father arrived last night.

TEDDIE: Did he, by Jove! I thought he was in Paris.

ARNOLD: So did we all. He told me he'd be there for the next month.

ANNA: Have you seen him?

ARNOLD: No! He rang me up. It's a mercy he had a telephone put in the cottage. It would have been a pretty kettle of fish if he'd just walked in.

ELIZABETH: Did you tell him Lady Catherine was coming?

ARNOLD: Of course not. I was flabbergasted to know he was here. And then I thought we'd better talk it over first.

ELIZABETH: Is he coming along here?

ARNOLD: Yes. He suggested it, and I couldn't think of any excuse to prevent him.

TEDDIE: Couldn't you put the other people off?

ARNOLD: They're coming by car. They may be here any minute. It's too late to do that.

ELIZABETH: Besides, it would be beastly.

ARNOLD: I knew it was silly to have them here. Elizabeth insisted.

ELIZABETH: After all, she *is* your mother, Arnold.

ARNOLD: That meant precious little to her when she—went away. You can't imagine it means very much to me now.

ELIZABETH: It's thirty years ago. It seems so absurd to bear malice after all that time.

ARNOLD: I don't bear malice, but the fact remains that she did me the most irreparable harm. I can find no excuse for her.

ELIZABETH: Have you ever tried to?

ARNOLD: My dear Elizabeth, it's no good going over all that again. The facts are lamentably simple. She had a husband who adored her, a wonderful position, all the money she could want, and a child of five. And she ran away with a married man.

ELIZABETH: Lady Porteous is not a very attractive woman, Arnold. [*To Anna*] Do you know her?

ANNA: [*Smiling*] "Forbidding" is the word, I think.

ARNOLD: If you're going to make little jokes about it, I have nothing more to say.

ANNA: I'm sorry, Arnold.

ELIZABETH: Perhaps your mother couldn't help herself—if she was in love?

ARNOLD: And had no sense of honor, duty, or decency? Oh, yes, under those circumstances you can explain a great deal.

ELIZABETH: That's not a very pretty way to speak of your mother.

ARNOLD: I can't look on her as my mother.

ELIZABETH: What you can't get over is that she didn't think of you. Some of us are more mother and some of us more woman. It gives me a little thrill when I think that she loved that man so much. She sacrificed her name, her position, and her child to him.

ARNOLD: You really can't expect the said child to have any great affection for the mother who treated him like that.

ELIZABETH: No, I don't think I do. But I think it's a pity after all these years that you shouldn't be friends.

ARNOLD: I wonder if you realize what it was to grow up under the shadow of that horrible scandal. Everywhere, at school, and at Oxford, and afterward in London, I was always the son of Lady Kitty Cheney. Oh, it was cruel, cruel!

ELIZABETH: Yes, I know, Arnold. It was beastly for you.

ARNOLD: It would have been bad enough if it had been an ordinary case, but the position of the people made it ten times worse. My father was in the House then, and Porteous—he hadn't succeeded to the title—was in the House too; he was Under-Secretary for Foreign Affairs, and he was very much in the public eye.

ANNA: My father always used to say he was the ablest man in the party. Everyone was expecting him to be Prime Minister.

ARNOLD: You can imagine what a boon it was to the British public. They hadn't had such a treat for a generation. The most popular song of the day was about my mother. Did you ever hear it? "Naughty Lady Kitty. Thought it such a pity . . ."

ELIZABETH: [*Interrupting*] Oh, Arnold, don't!

ARNOLD: And then they never let people forget them. If they'd lived quietly in Florence and not made a fuss the scandal would have died down. But those constant actions between Lord and Lady Porteous kept on reminding everyone.

TEDDIE: What were they having actions about?

ARNOLD: Of course my father divorced his wife, but Lady Porteous refused to divorce Porteous. He tried to force her by refusing to support her and turning her out of her house, and heaven knows what. They were constantly wrangling in the law courts.

ANNA: I think it was monstrous of Lady Porteous.

ARNOLD: She knew he wanted to marry my mother, and she hated my mother. You can't blame her.

ANNA: It must have been very difficult for them.

ARNOLD: That's why they've lived in Florence. Porteous has money. They found people there who were willing to accept the situation.

ELIZABETH: This is the first time they've ever come to England.

ARNOLD: My father will have to be told, Elizabeth.

ELIZABETH: Yes.

ANNA: [To Elizabeth] Has he ever spoken to you about Lady Kitty?

ELIZABETH: Never.

ARNOLD: I don't think her name has passed his lips since she ran away from this house thirty years ago.

TEDDIE: Oh, they lived here?

ARNOLD: Naturally. There was a houseparty, and one evening neither Porteous nor my mother came down to dinner. The rest of them waited. They couldn't make it out. My father sent up to my mother's room, and a note was found on the pincushion.

ELIZABETH: [With a faint smile] That's what they did in the Dark Ages.

ARNOLD: I think he took a dislike to this house from that horrible night. He never lived here again, and when I married he handed the place over to me. He just has a cottage now on the estate that he comes to when he feels inclined.

ELIZABETH: It's been very nice for us.

ARNOLD: I owe everything to my father. I don't think he'll ever forgive me for asking these people to come here.

ELIZABETH: I'm going to take all the blame on myself, Arnold.

ARNOLD: [Irritably] The situation was embarrassing enough anyhow. I don't know how I ought to treat them.

ELIZABETH: Don't you think that'll settle itself when you see them?

ARNOLD: After all, they're my guests. I shall try and behave like a gentleman.

ELIZABETH: I wouldn't. We haven't got central heating.

ARNOLD: [Taking no notice] Will she expect me to kiss her?

ELIZABETH: [With a smile] Surely.

ARNOLD: It always makes me uncomfortable when people are effusive.

ANNA: But I can't understand why you never saw her before.

ARNOLD: I believe she tried to see me when I was little, but my father thought it better she shouldn't.

ANNA: Yes, but when you were grown up?

ARNOLD: She was always in Italy. I never went to Italy.

ELIZABETH: It seems to me so pathetic that if you saw one another in the street you wouldn't recognize each other.

ARNOLD: Is it my fault?

ELIZABETH: You've promised to be very gentle with her and very kind.

ARNOLD: The mistake was asking Porteous to come too. It looks as though we condoned the whole thing. And how am I to treat him? Am I to shake him by the hand and slap him on the back? He absolutely ruined my father's life.

ELIZABETH: [Smiling] How much would you give for a nice motor accident that prevented them from coming?

ARNOLD: I let you persuade me against my better judgment, and I've regretted it ever since.

ELIZABETH: [Good-humoredly] I think it's very lucky that Anna and Teddie are here. I don't foresee a very successful party.

ARNOLD: I'm going to do my best. I gave you my promise and I shall keep it. But I can't answer for my father.

ANNA: Here is your father.

[Mr. Champion-Cheney shows himself at one of the French windows]

c.-c.: May I come in through the window, or shall I have myself announced by a supercilious flunkey?

ELIZABETH: Come in. We've been expecting you.

c.-c.: Impatiently, I hope, my dear child.

[Mr. Champion-Cheney is a tall man in the early sixties, spare, with a fine head of gray hair and an intelligent, somewhat ascetic face. He is very carefully dressed. He is a man who makes the most of himself. He bears his years jauntily. He kisses Elizabeth and then holds out his hand to Arnold]

ELIZABETH: We thought you'd be in Paris for another month.

c.-c.: How are you, Arnold? I always reserve to myself the privilege of changing my mind. It's the only one elderly gentlemen share with pretty women.

ELIZABETH: You know Anna.

c.-c.: [Shaking hands with her] Of course I do. How very nice to see you here! Are you staying long?

ANNA: As long as I'm welcome.

ELIZABETH: And this is Mr. Luton.

C.-C.: How do you do? Do you play bridge?

LUTON: I do.

C.-C.: Capital. Do you declare without top honors?

LUTON: Never.

C.-C.: Of such is the kingdom of heaven. I see that you are a good young man.

LUTON: But, like the good in general, I am poor.

C.-C.: Never mind; if your principles are right, you can play ten shillings a hundred without danger. I never play less, and I never play more.

ARNOLD: And you—are going to stay long, Father?

C.-C.: To luncheon, if you'll have me.

[Arnold *gives* Elizabeth *a harassed look*]

ELIZABETH: That'll be jolly.

ARNOLD: I didn't mean that. Of course you're going to stay for luncheon. I meant, how long are you going to stay down here?

C.-C.: A week.

[*There is a moment's pause. Everyone but* Champion-Cheney *is slightly embarrassed*]

TEDDIE: I think we'd better chuck our tennis.

ELIZABETH: Yes. I want my father-in-law to tell me what they're wearing in Paris this week.

TEDDIE: I'll go and put the rackets away.

[Teddie *goes out*]

ARNOLD: It's nearly one o'clock, Elizabeth.

ELIZABETH: I didn't know it was so late.

ANNA: [*To* Arnold] I wonder if I can persuade you to take a turn in the garden before luncheon.

ARNOLD: [*Jumping at the idea*] I'd love it. [Anna *goes out of the windows, and as he follows her he stops irresolutely*] I want you to look at this chair I've just got. I think it's rather good.

C.-C.: Charming.

ARNOLD: About 1750, I should say. Good design, isn't it? It hasn't been restored or anything.

C.-C.: Very pretty.

ARNOLD: I think it was a good buy, don't you?

C.-C.: Oh, my dear boy! You know I'm entirely ignorant about these things.

ARNOLD: It's exactly my period . . . I shall see you at luncheon, then. [*He follows* Anna *through the window*]

C.-C.: Who is that young man?

ELIZABETH: Mr. Luton. He's only just been demobilized. He's the manager of a rubber estate in the F. M. S.

C.-C.: And what are the F. M. S. when they're at home?

ELIZABETH: The Federated Malay States. He joined up at the beginning of the war. He's just going back there.

C.-C.: And why have we been left alone in this very marked manner?

ELIZABETH: Have we? I didn't notice it.

C.-C.: I suppose it's difficult for the young to realize that one may be old without being a fool.

ELIZABETH: I never thought you that. Everyone knows you're very intelligent.

C.-C.: They certainly ought to by now. I've told them often enough. Are you a little nervous?

ELIZABETH: Let me feel my pulse. [*She puts her finger on her wrist*] It's perfectly regular.

C.-C.: When I suggested staying to luncheon Arnold looked exactly like a dose of castor oil.

ELIZABETH: I wish you'd sit down.

C.-C.: Will it make it easier for you? [*He takes a chair*] You have evidently something very disagreeable to say to me.

ELIZABETH: You won't be cross with me?

C.-C.: How old are you?

ELIZABETH: Twenty-five.

C.-C.: I'm never cross with a woman under thirty.

ELIZABETH: Oh, then I've got ten years.

C.-C.: Mathematics?

ELIZABETH: No. Paint.

C.-C.: Well?

ELIZABETH: [*Reflectively*] I think it would be easier if I sat on your knees.

C.-C.: That is a pleasing taste of yours, but you must take care not to put on weight.

[*She sits down on his knees*]

ELIZABETH: Am I bony?

C.-C.: On the contrary. . . . I'm listening.

ELIZABETH: Lady Catherine's coming here.

C.-C.: Who's Lady Catherine?

ELIZABETH: Your—Arnold's mother.

C.-C.: Is she?

[*He withdraws himself a little and* Elizabeth *gets up*]

ELIZABETH: You mustn't blame Arnold. It's my fault. I insisted. He was against it. I nagged till he gave way. And then I wrote and asked her to come.

C.-C.: I didn't know you knew her.

ELIZABETH: I don't. But I heard she was in London. She's staying at Claridge's. It seemed so heartless not to take the smallest notice of her.

C.-C.: When is she coming?

ELIZABETH: We're expecting her in time for luncheon.

C.-C.: As soon as that? I understand the embarrassment.

ELIZABETH: You see, we never expected you to be here. You said you'd be in Paris for another month.

C.-C.: My dear child, this is your house. There's no reason why you shouldn't ask whom you please to stay with you.

ELIZABETH: After all, whatever her faults, she's Arnold's mother. It seemed so unnatural that they should never see one another. My heart ached for that poor lonely woman.

C.-C.: I never heard that she was lonely, and she certainly isn't poor.

ELIZABETH: And there's something else. I couldn't ask her by herself. It would have been so—so insulting. I asked Lord Porteous, too.

C.-C.: I see.

ELIZABETH: I daresay you'd rather not meet them.

C.-C.: I daresay they'd rather not meet me. I shall get a capital luncheon at the cottage. I've noticed you always get the best food if you come in unexpectedly and have the same as they're having in the servants' hall.

ELIZABETH: No one's ever talked to me about Lady Kitty. It's always been a subject that everyone has avoided. I've never even seen a photograph of her.

C.-C.: The house was full of them when she left. I think I told the butler to throw them in the dustbin. She was very much photographed.

ELIZABETH: Won't you tell me what she was like?

C.-C.: She was very like you, Elizabeth, only she had dark hair instead of red.

ELIZABETH: Poor dear! It must be quite white now.

C.-C.: I daresay. She was a pretty little thing.

ELIZABETH: But she was one of the great beauties of her day. They say she was lovely.

C.-C.: She had the most adorable little nose, like yours. . . .

ELIZABETH: D'you like my nose?

C.-C.: And she was very dainty, with a beautiful little figure; very light on her feet. She was like a *marquise* in an old French comedy. Yes, she was lovely.

ELIZABETH: And I'm sure she's lovely still.

C.-C.: She's no chicken, you know.

ELIZABETH: You can't expect me to look at it as you and Arnold do. When you've loved as she's loved you may grow old, but you grow old beautifully.

C.-C.: You're very romantic.

ELIZABETH: If everyone hadn't made such a mystery of it I daresay I shouldn't feel as I do. I know she did a great wrong to you and a great wrong to Arnold. I'm willing to acknowledge that.

C.-C.: I'm sure it's very kind of you.

ELIZABETH: But she loved and she dared. Romance is such an elusive thing. You read of it in books, but it's seldom you see it face to face. I can't help it if it thrills me.

C.-C.: I am painfully aware that the husband in these cases is not a romantic object.

ELIZABETH: She had the world at her feet. You were rich. She was a figure in society. And she gave up everything for love.

C.-C.: [*Dryly*] I'm beginning to suspect it wasn't only for her sake and for Arnold's that you asked her to come here.

ELIZABETH: I seem to know her already. I think her face is a little sad, for a love like that doesn't leave you gay, it leaves you grave, but I think her pale face is unlined. It's like a child's.

C.-C.: My dear, how you let your imagination run away with you!

ELIZABETH: I imagine her slight and frail.

C.-C.: Frail, certainly.

ELIZABETH: With beautiful thin hands and white hair. I've pictured her so often in that Renaissance Palace that they live in, with old Masters on the walls and lovely carved things all round, sitting in a black silk dress with old lace round her neck and old-fashioned diamonds. You see, I never knew my mother; she died when I was a baby. You can't confide in aunts with huge families of their own. I want Arnold's mother to be a mother to me. I've got so much to say to her.

C.-C.: Are you happy with Arnold?

ELIZABETH: Why shouldn't I be?

C.-C.: Why haven't you got any babies?

ELIZABETH: Give us a little time. We've only been married three years.

C.-C.: I wonder what Hughie is like now!

ELIZABETH: Lord Porteous?

C.-C.: He wore his clothes better than any man in London. You know he'd have been Prime Minister if he'd remained in politics.

ELIZABETH: What was he like then?

C.-C.: He was a nice-looking fellow. Fine horseman. I suppose there was something very fascinating about him. Yellow hair and blue eyes, you know. He had a very good figure. I liked him. I was his parliamentary secretary. He was Arnold's god-father.

ELIZABETH: I know.

C.-C.: I wonder if he ever regrets!

ELIZABETH: I wouldn't.

C.-C.: Well, I must be strolling back to my cottage.

ELIZABETH: You're not angry with me?

C.-C.: Not a bit.

[*She puts up her face for him to kiss. He kisses her on both cheeks and then goes out. In a moment* Teddie *is seen at the window*]

TEDDIE: I saw the old blighter go.

ELIZABETH: Come in.

TEDDIE: Everything all right?

ELIZABETH: Oh, quite, as far as he's concerned. He's going to keep out of the way.

TEDDIE: Was it beastly?

ELIZABETH: No, he made it very easy for me. He's a nice old thing.

TEDDIE: You were rather scared.

ELIZABETH: A little. I am still. I don't know why.

TEDDIE: I guessed you were. I thought I'd come and give you a little moral support. It's ripping here, isn't it?

ELIZABETH: It is rather nice.

TEDDIE: It'll be jolly to think of it when I'm back in the F. M. S.

ELIZABETH: Aren't you homesick sometimes?

TEDDIE: Oh, everyone is now and then, you know.

ELIZABETH: You could have got a job in England if you'd wanted to, couldn't you?

TEDDIE: Oh, but I love it out there. England's ripping to come back to, but I couldn't live here now. It's like a woman you're desperately in love with as long as you don't see her, but when you're with her she maddens you so that you can't bear her.

ELIZABETH: [*Smiling*] What's wrong with England?

TEDDIE: I don't think anything's wrong with England. I expect something's wrong with me. I've been away too long. England seems to me full of people doing things they don't want to because other people expect it of them.

ELIZABETH: Isn't that what you call a high degree of civilization?

TEDDIE: People seem to me so insincere. When you go to parties in London they're all babbling about art, and you feel that in their hearts they dcn't care two-pence about it. They read the books that everybody is talking about because they don't want to be out of it. In the F. M. S. we don't get very many books, and we read those we have over and over again. They mean so much to us. I don't think the people over there are half so clever as the people at home, but one gets to know them better. You see, there are so few of us that we have to make the best of one another.

ELIZABETH: I imagine that frills are not much worn in the F. M. S. It must be a comfort.

TEDDIE: It's not much good being pretentious where everyone knows exactly who you are and what your income is.

ELIZABETH: I don't think you want too much sincerity in society. It would be like an iron girder in a house of cards.

TEDDIE: And then, you know, the place is ripping. You get used to a blue sky and you miss it in England.

ELIZABETH: What do you do with yourself all the time?

TEDDIE: Oh, one works like blazes. You have to be a pretty hefty fellow to be a planter. And then there's ripping bathing. You know, it's lovely, with palm trees all along the beach. And there's shooting. And now and then we have a little dance to a gramophone.

ELIZABETH: [*Pretending to tease him*] I think you've got a young woman out there, Teddie.

TEDDIE: [*Vehemently*] Oh, no!

[*She is a little taken aback by the earnestness of his disclaimer. There is a moment's silence, then she recovers herself*]

ELIZABETH: But you'll have to marry and settle down one of these days, you know.

TEDDIE: I want to, but it's not a thing you can do lightly.

ELIZABETH: I don't know why there more than elsewhere.

TEDDIE: In England if people don't get on they go their own ways and jog along after a fashion. In a place like that you're thrown a great deal on your own resources.

ELIZABETH: Of course.

TEDDIE: Lots of girls come out because they think they're going to have a good time. But if they're empty-headed, then they're just faced with their own emptiness and they're done. If their husbands can afford it they go home and settle down as grass-widows.

ELIZABETH: I've met them. They seem to find it a very pleasant occupation.

TEDDIE: It's rotten for their husbands, though.

ELIZABETH: And if the husbands can't afford it?

TEDDIE: Oh, then they tipple.

ELIZABETH: It's not a very alluring prospect.

TEDDIE: But if the woman's the right sort she wouldn't exchange it for any life in the world. When all's said and done it's we who've made the Empire.

ELIZABETH: What sort is the right sort?

TEDDIE: A woman of courage and endurance and sincerity. Of course, it's hopeless unless she's in love with her husband.

[*He is looking at her earnestly and she, raising her eyes, gives him a long look. There is silence between them*]

TEDDIE: My house stands on the side of a hill, and the coconut trees wind down to the shore. Azaleas grow in my garden, and camellias, and all sorts of ripping flowers. And in front of me is the winding coast line, and then the blue sea. [*A pause*] Do you know that I'm awfully in love with you?

ELIZABETH: [*Gravely*] I wasn't quite sure. I wondered.

TEDDIE: And you? [*She nods slowly*] I've never kissed you.

ELIZABETH: I don't want you to.

[*They look at one another steadily. They are both grave. Arnold comes in hurriedly*]

ARNOLD: They're coming, Elizabeth.

ELIZABETH: [*As though returning from a distant world*] Who?

ARNOLD: [*Impatiently*] My dear! My mother, of course. The car is just coming up the drive.

TEDDIE: Would you like me to clear out?

ARNOLD: No, no! For goodness' sake stay.

ELIZABETH: We'd better go and meet them, Arnold.

ARNOLD: No, no; I think they'd much better be shown in. I feel simply sick with nervousness.

[*Anna comes in from the garden*]

ANNA: Your guests have arrived.

ELIZABETH: Yes, I know.

ARNOLD: I've given orders that luncheon should be served at once.

ELIZABETH: Why? It's not half-past one already, is it?

ARNOLD: I thought it would help. When you don't know exactly what to say you can always eat.

[*The Butler comes in and announces*]

BUTLER: Lady Catherine Champion-Cheney! Lord Porteous!

[*Lady Kitty comes in followed by Porteous, and the Butler goes out. Lady Kitty is a gay little lady, with dyed red hair and painted cheeks. She is somewhat outrageously dressed. She never forgets that she has been a pretty woman and she still behaves as if she were twenty-five. Lord Porteous is a very bald, elderly gentleman in loose, rather eccentric clothes. He is snappy and gruff. This is not at all the couple that Elizabeth expected, and for a moment she stares at them with round, startled eyes. Lady Kitty goes up to her with outstretched hands*]

LADY KITTY: Elizabeth! Elizabeth! [*She kisses her effusively*] What an adorable creature. [*Turning to Porteous*] Hughie, isn't she adorable?

PORTEOUS: [*With a grunt*] Ugh!

[*Elizabeth, smiling now, turns to him and gives him her hand*]

ELIZABETH: How d'you do?

PORTEOUS: Damnable road you've got down here. How d'you do, my dear? Why d'you have such damnable roads in England?

[*Lady Kitty's eyes fall on Teddie and she goes up to him with her arms thrown back, prepared to throw them round him*]

LADY KITTY: My boy, my boy! I should have known you anywhere!

ELIZABETH: [*Hastily*] That's Arnold.

LADY KITTY: [*Without a moment's hesitation*] The image of his father! I should have known him anywhere! [*She throws her arms round his neck*] My boy, my boy!

PORTEOUS: [*With a grunt*] Ugh!

LADY KITTY: Tell me, would you have known me again? Have I changed?

ARNOLD: I was only five, you know, when—when you . . .

LADY KITTY: [*Emotionally*] I remember as if it was yesterday. I went up into your room. [*With a sudden change of manner*] By the way, I always thought that nurse drank. Did you ever find out if she really did?

PORTEOUS: How the devil can you expect him to know that, Kitty?

LADY KITTY: You've never had a child, Hughie; how can you tell what they know and what they don't?

ELIZABETH: [*Coming to the rescue*] This is Arnold, Lord Porteous.

PORTEOUS: [*Shaking hands with him*] How d'you do? I knew your father.

ARNOLD: Yes.

PORTEOUS: Alive still?

ARNOLD: Yes.

PORTEOUS: He must be getting on. Is he well?

ARNOLD: Very.

PORTEOUS: Ugh! Takes care of himself, I suppose. I'm not at all well. This damned climate doesn't agree with me.

ELIZABETH: [*To Lady Kitty*] This is Mrs. Shenstone. And this is Mr. Luton. I hope you don't mind a very small party.

LADY KITTY: [*Shaking hands with Anna and Teddie*] Oh, no, I shall enjoy it. I used to give enormous parties here. Political, you know. How nice you've made this room!

ELIZABETH: Oh, that's Arnold.

ARNOLD: [*Nervously*] D'you like this chair? I've just bought it. It's exactly my period.

PORTEOUS: [*Bluntly*] It's a fake.

ARNOLD: [*Indignantly*] I don't think it is for a minute.

PORTEOUS: The legs are not right.

ARNOLD: I don't know how you can say that. If there is anything right about it, it's the legs.

LADY KITTY: I'm sure they're right.

PORTEOUS: You know nothing whatever about it, Kitty.

LADY KITTY: That's what you think. *I* think it's a beautiful chair. Hepplewhite?

ARNOLD: No, Sheraton.

LADY KITTY: Oh, I know. "The School for Scandal."

PORTEOUS: Sheraton, my dear. Sheraton.

LADY KITTY: Yes, that's what I say. I acted the screen scene at some amateur theatricals in Florence, and Ermeto Novelli, the great Italian tragedian, told me he'd never seen a Lady Teazle like me.

PORTEOUS: Ugh!

LADY KITTY: [*To Elizabeth*] Do you act?

ELIZABETH: Oh, I couldn't. I should be too nervous.

LADY KITTY: I'm never nervous. I'm a born actress. Of course, if I had my time over again I'd go on the stage. You know, it's extraordinary how they keep young. Actresses, I mean. I think it's because they're always playing different parts. Hughie, do you think Arnold takes after me or after his father? Of course I think he's the very image of me. Arnold, I think I ought to tell you that I was received into the Catholic Church last winter. I've been thinking about it for years, and the last time we were at Monte Carlo I met such a nice monsignore. I told him what my difficulties were and he was too wonderful. I knew Hughie wouldn't approve, so I kept it a secret. [*To Elizabeth*] Are you interested in religion? I think it's too wonderful. We must have a long talk about it one of these days. [*Pointing to her frock*] Callot?

ELIZABETH: No, Worth.

LADY KITTY: I knew it was either Worth or Callot. Of course, it's line that's the important thing. I go to Worth myself, and I always say to him, "Line, my dear Worth, line." What *is* the matter, Hughie?

PORTEOUS: These new teeth of mine are so damned uncomfortable.

LADY KITTY: Men are extraordinary. They can't stand the smallest discomfort. Why, a woman's life is uncomfortable from the moment she gets up in the morning till the moment she goes to bed at night. And d'you think it's comfortable to sleep with a mask on your face?

PORTEOUS: They don't seem to hold up properly.

LADY KITTY: Well, that's not the fault of your teeth. That's the fault of your gums.

PORTEOUS: Damned rotten dentist. That's what's the matter.

LADY KITTY: I thought he was a very nice dentist. He told me *my* teeth would last till I was fifty. He has a Chinese room. It's so interesting; while he scrapes your teeth he tells you all about the dear Empress Dowager. Are you interested in China? I think it's too wonderful. You know they've cut off their pigtails. I think it's such a pity. They were so picturesque.

[*The* Butler *comes in*]

BUTLER: Luncheon is served, sir.

ELIZABETH: Would you like to see your rooms?

PORTEOUS: We can see our rooms after luncheon.

LADY KITTY: I must powder my nose, Hughie.

PORTEOUS: Powder it down here.

LADY KITTY: I never saw anyone so inconsiderate.

PORTEOUS: You'll keep us waiting half an hour. I know you.

LADY KITTY: [*Fumbling in her bag*] Oh, well, peace at any price, as Lord Beaconsfield said.

PORTEOUS: He said a lot of damned silly things, Kitty, but he never said that.

[Lady Kitty's *face changes. Perplexity is followed by dismay, and dismay by consternation*]

LADY KITTY: Oh!

ELIZABETH: What is the matter?

LADY KITTY: [*With anguish*] My lip-stick!

ELIZABETH: Can't you find it?

LADY KITTY: I had it in the car. Hughie, you remember that I had it in the car.

PORTEOUS: I don't remember anything about it.

LADY KITTY: Don't be so stupid, Hughie. Why, when we came through the gates I said: "My home, my home!" and I took it out and put some on my lips.

ELIZABETH: Perhaps you dropped it in the car.

LADY KITTY: For heaven's sake send some one to look for it.

ARNOLD: I'll ring.

LADY KITTY: I'm absolutely lost without my lip-stick. Lend me yours, darling, will you?

ELIZABETH: I'm awfully sorry. I'm afraid I haven't got one.

LADY KITTY: Do you mean to say you don't use a lip-stick?

ELIZABETH: Never.

PORTEOUS: Look at her lips. What the devil d'you think she wants muck like that for?

LADY KITTY: Oh, my dear, what a mistake you make! You *must* use a lip-stick. It's so good for the lips. Men like it, you know. I couldn't *live* without a lip-stick.

[Champion-Cheney *appears at the window holding in his upstretched hand a little gold case*]

C.-C.: [*As he comes in*] Has anyone here lost a diminutive utensil containing, unless I am mistaken, a favorite preparation for the toilet?

[Arnold *and* Elizabeth *are thunderstruck at his appearance and even* Teddie *and* Anna *are taken aback. But* Lady Kitty *is overjoyed*]

LADY KITTY: My lip-stick!

C.-C.: I found it in the drive and I ventured to bring it in.

LADY KITTY: It's Saint Antony. I said a little prayer to him when I was hunting in my bag.

PORTEOUS: Saint Antony be blowed! It's Clive, by God!

LADY KITTY: [*Startled, her attention suddenly turning from the lip-stick*] Clive!

C.-C.: You didn't recognize me. It's many years since we met.

LADY KITTY: My poor Clive, your hair has gone quite white!

C.-C.: [*Holding out his hand*] I hope you had a pleasant journey down from London.

LADY KITTY: [*Offering him her cheek*] You may kiss me, Clive.

C.-C.: [*Kissing her*] You don't mind, Hughie?

PORTEOUS: [*With a grunt*] Ugh!

C.-C.: [*Going up to him cordially*] And how are you, my dear Hughie?

PORTEOUS: Damned rheumatic if you want to know. Filthy climate you have in this country.

C.-C.: Aren't you going to shake hands with me, Hughie?

PORTEOUS: I have no objection to shaking hands with you.

C.-C.: You've aged, my poor Hughie.

PORTEOUS: Some one was asking me how old you were the other day.

C.-C.: Were they surprised when you told them?

PORTEOUS: Surprised! They wondered you weren't dead. [*The* Butler *comes in*]

BUTLER: Did you ring, sir?

ARNOLD: No. Oh, yes, I did. It doesn't matter now.

C.-C.: [*As the* Butler *is going*] One moment. My dear Elizabeth, I've come to throw myself on your mercy. My servants are busy with their own affairs. There's not a thing for me to eat in my cottage.

ELIZABETH: Oh, but we shall be delighted if you'll lunch with us.

C.-C.: It either means that or my immediate death from starvation. You don't mind, Arnold?

ARNOLD: My dear father!

ELIZABETH: [*To the* Butler] Mr. Cheney will lunch here.

BUTLER: Very good, ma'am.

C.-C.: [*To* Lady Kitty] And what do you think of Arnold?

LADY KITTY: I adore him.

C.-C.: He's grown, hasn't he? But then you'd expect him to do that in thirty years.

ARNOLD: For God's sake let's go in to lunch, Elizabeth!

CURTAIN

ACT II.

The Scene is the same as in the preceding act. It is afternoon. When the curtain rises Porteous *and* Lady Kitty, Anna *and* Teddie *are playing bridge.* Elizabeth *and* Champion-Cheney *are watching.* Porteous *and* Lady Kitty *are partners.*

C.-C.: When will Arnold be back, Elizabeth?

ELIZABETH: Soon, I think.

C.-C.: Is he addressing a meeting?

ELIZABETH: No, it's only a conference with his agent and one or two constituents.

PORTEOUS: [*Irritably*] How anyone can be expected to play bridge when people are shouting at the top of their voices all round them, I for one cannot understand.

ELIZABETH: [*Smiling*] I'm so sorry.

ANNA: I can see your hand, Lord Porteous.

PORTEOUS: It may help you.

LADY KITTY: I've told you over and over again to hold your cards up. It ruins one's game when one can't help seeing one's opponent's hand.

PORTEOUS: One isn't obliged to look.

LADY KITTY: What was Arnold's majority at the last election?

ELIZABETH: Seven hundred and something.

C.-C.: He'll have to fight for it if he wants to keep his seat next time.

PORTEOUS: Are we playing bridge, or talking politics?

LADY KITTY: I never find that conversation interferes with my game.

PORTEOUS: You certainly play no worse when you talk than when you hold your tongue.

LADY KITTY: I think that's a very offensive thing to say, Hughie. Just because I don't play the same game as you do you think I can't play.

PORTEOUS: I'm glad you acknowledge it's not the same game as I play. But why in God's name do you call it bridge?

C.-C.: I agree with Kitty. I hate people who play bridge as though they were at a funeral and knew their feet were getting wet.

PORTEOUS: Of course you take Kitty's part.

LADY KITTY: That's the least he can do.

C.-C.: I have a naturally cheerful disposition.

PORTEOUS: You've never had anything to sour it.

LADY KITTY: I don't know what you mean by that, Hughie.

PORTEOUS: [*Trying to contain himself*] Must you trump my ace?

LADY KITTY: [*Innocently*] Oh, was that your ace, darling?

PORTEOUS: [*Furiously*] Yes, it was my ace.

LADY KITTY: Oh, well, it was the only trump I had. I shouldn't have made it anyway.

PORTEOUS: You needn't have told them that. Now she knows exactly what I've got.

LADY KITTY: She knew before.

PORTEOUS: How could she know?

LADY KITTY: She said she'd seen your hand.

ANNA: Oh, I didn't. I said I could see it.

LADY KITTY: Well, I naturally supposed that if she could see it she did.

PORTEOUS: Really, Kitty, you have the most extraordinary ideas.

C.-C.: Not at all. If anyone is such a fool as to show me his hand, of course I look at it.

PORTEOUS: [*Fuming*] If you study the etiquette of bridge, you'll discover that onlookers are expected not to interfere with the game.

C.-C.: My dear Hughie, this is a matter of ethics, not of bridge.

ANNA: Anyhow, I get the game. And rubber.

TEDDIE: I claim a revoke.

PORTEOUS: Who revoked?

TEDDIE: You did.

PORTEOUS: Nonsense. I've never revoked in my life.

TEDDIE: I'll show you. [*He turns over the tricks to show the faces of the cards*] You threw away a club on the third heart trick and you had another heart.

PORTEOUS: I never had more than two hearts.

TEDDIE: Oh, yes, you had. Look here. That's the card you played on the last trick but one.

LADY KITTY: [*Delighted to catch him out*] There's no doubt about it, Hughie. You revoked.

PORTEOUS: I tell you I did not revoke. I never revoke.

C.-C.: You did, Hughie. I wondered what on earth you were doing.

PORTEOUS: I don't know how anyone can be expected not to revoke when there's this confounded chatter going on all the time.

TEDDIE: Well, that's another hundred to us.

PORTEOUS: [*To* Champion-Cheney] I wish you wouldn't breathe down my neck. I never can play bridge when there's somebody breathing down my neck.

[*The party have risen from the bridge-table, and they scatter about the room*]

ANNA: Well, I'm going to take a book and lie down in the hammock till it's time to dress.

TEDDIE: [*Who has been adding up*] I'll put it down in the book, shall I?

PORTEOUS: [*Who has not moved, setting out the cards for a patience*] Yes, yes, put it down. I never revoke. [Anna *goes out*]

LADY KITTY: Would you like to come for a little stroll, Hughie?

PORTEOUS: What for?

LADY KITTY: Exercise.

PORTEOUS: I hate exercise.

C.-C.: [*Looking at the patience*] The seven goes on the eight.

[Porteous *takes no notice*]

LADY KITTY: The seven goes on the eight, Hughie.

PORTEOUS: I don't choose to put the seven on the eight.

C.-C.: That knave goes on the queen.

PORTEOUS: I'm not blind, thank you.

LADY KITTY: The three goes on the four.

C.-C.: All these go over.

PORTEOUS: [Furiously] Am I playing this patience, or are you playing it?

LADY KITTY: But you're missing everything.

PORTEOUS: That's my business.

C.-C.: It's no good losing your temper over it, Hughie.

PORTEOUS: Go away, both of you. You irritate me.

LADY KITTY: We were only trying to help you, Hughie.

PORTEOUS: I don't want to be helped. I want to do it by myself.

LADY KITTY: I think your manners are perfectly deplorable, Hughie.

PORTEOUS: It's simply maddening when you're playing patience and people won't leave you alone.

C.-C.: We won't say another word.

PORTEOUS: That three goes. I believe it's coming out. If I'd been such a fool as to put that seven up I shouldn't have been able to bring these down. [He puts down several cards while they watch him silently]

LADY KITTY AND C.-C.: [Together] The four goes on the five.

PORTEOUS: [Throwing down the cards violently] Damn you! Why don't you leave me alone? It's intolerable.

C.-C.: It was coming out, my dear fellow.

PORTEOUS: I know it was coming out. Confound you!

LADY KITTY: How petty you are, Hughie!

PORTEOUS: Petty, be damned! I've told you over and over again that I will not be interfered with when I'm playing patience.

LADY KITTY: Don't talk to me like that, Hughie.

PORTEOUS: I shall talk to you as I please.

LADY KITTY: [Beginning to cry] Oh, you brute! You brute! [She flings out of the room]

PORTEOUS: Oh, damn! Now she's going to cry.

[He stumbles out into the garden, Champion-Cheney, Elizabeth and Teddie are left alone. There is a moment's pause. Champion-Cheney looks from Teddie to Elizabeth, with an ironical smile]

C.-C.: Upon my soul, they might be married. They frip so much.

ELIZABETH: [Frigidly] It's been nice of you to come here so often since they arrived. It's helped to make things easy.

C.-C.: Irony? It's a rhetorical form not much favored in this blessed plot, this earth, this realm, this England.

ELIZABETH: What exactly are you getting at?

C.-C.: How slangy the young women of the present day are! I suppose the fact that Arnold is a purist leads you to the contrary extravagance.

ELIZABETH: Anyhow you know what I mean.

C.-C.: [With a smile] I have a dim, groping suspicion.

ELIZABETH: You promised to keep away. Why did you come back the moment they arrived?

C.-C.: Curiosity, my dear child. A surely pardonable curiosity.

ELIZABETH: And since then you've been here all the time. You don't generally favor us with so much of your company when you're down at your cottage

C.-C.: I've been excessively amused.

ELIZABETH: It has struck me that whenever they started fripping you took a malicious pleasure in goading them on.

C.-C.: I don't think there's much love lost between them now, do you?

[Teddie is making as though to leave the room]

ELIZABETH: Don't go, Teddie.

C.-C.: No, please don't. I'm only staying a minute. We were talking about Lady Kitty just before she arrived. [To Elizabeth] Do you remember? The pale, frail lady in black satin and old lace.

ELIZABETH: [With a chuckle] You are a devil, you know.

C.-C.: Ah, well, he's always had the reputation of being a humorist and a gentleman.

ELIZABETH: Did you expect her to be like that, poor dear?

C.-C.: My dear child, I hadn't the vaguest idea. You were asking me the other day what she was like when she ran away. I didn't tell you half. She was so gay and so natural. Who would have thought that animation would turn into such frivolity, and that charming impulsiveness lead to such a ridiculous affectation?

ELIZABETH: It rather sets my nerves on edge to hear the way you talk of her.

C.-C.: It's the truth that sets your nerves on edge, not I.

ELIZABETH: You loved her once. Have you no feeling for her at all?

C.-C.: None. Why should I?

ELIZABETH: She's the mother of your son.

C.-C.: My dear child, you have a charming nature, as simple, frank, and artless as hers was. Don't let pure humbug obscure your common sense.

ELIZABETH: We have no right to judge. She's only been here two days. We know nothing about her.

C.-C.: My dear, her soul is as thickly rouged as her face. She hasn't an emotion that's sincere. She's tinsel. You think I'm a cruel, cynical old man. Why, when I think of what she was, if I didn't laugh at what she has become I should cry.

ELIZABETH: How do you know she wouldn't be just the same now if she'd remained your wife? Do you think your influence would have had such a salutary effect on her?

C.-C.: [*Good-humoredly*] I like you when you're bitter and rather insolent.

ELIZABETH: D'you like me enough to answer my question?

C.-C.: She was only twenty-seven when she went away. She might have become anything. She might have become the woman you expected her to be. There are very few of us who are strong enough to make circumstances serve us. We are the creatures of our environment. She's a silly, worthless woman because she's led a silly, worthless life.

ELIZABETH: [*Disturbed*] You're horrible today.

C.-C.: I don't say it's I who could have prevented her from becoming this ridiculous caricature of a pretty woman grown old. But life could. Here she would have had the friends fit to her station, and a decent activity, and worthy interests. Ask her what her life has been all these years among divorced women and kept women and the men who consort with them. There is no more lamentable pursuit than a life of pleasure.

ELIZABETH: At all events she loved and she loved greatly. I have only pity and affection for her.

C.-C.: And if she loved what d'you think she felt when she saw that she had ruined Hughie? Look at him. He was tight last night after dinner and tight the night before.

ELIZABETH: I know.

C.-C.: And she took it as a matter of course. How long do you suppose he's been getting tight every night? Do you think he was like that thirty years ago? Can you imagine that that was a brilliant young man, whom everyone expected to be Prime Minister? Look at him now. A grumpy sodden old fellow with false teeth.

ELIZABETH: You have false teeth, too.

C.-C.: Yes, but damn it all, they fit. She's ruined him and she knows she's ruined him.

ELIZABETH: [*Looking at him suspiciously*] Why are you saying all this to me?

C.-C.: Am I hurting your feelings?

ELIZABETH: I think I've had enough for the present.

C.-C.: I'll go and have a look at the goldfish. I want to see Arnold when he comes in. [*Politely*] I'm afraid we've been boring Mr. Luton.

TEDDIE: Not at all.

C.-C.: When are you going back to the F. M. S.?

TEDDIE: In about a month.

C.-C.: I see. [*He goes out*]

ELIZABETH: I wonder what he has at the back of his head.

TEDDIE: D'you think he was talking at you?

ELIZABETH: He's as clever as a bagful of monkeys.

[*There is a moment's pause.* Teddie *hesitates a little and when he speaks it is in a different tone. He is grave and somewhat nervous*]

TEDDIE: It seems very difficult to get a few minutes alone with you. I wonder if you've been making it difficult?

ELIZABETH: I wanted to think.

TEDDIE: I've made up my mind to go away to-morrow.

ELIZABETH: Why?

TEDDIE: I want you altogether or not at all.

ELIZABETH: You're so arbitrary.

TEDDIE: You said so—you said you cared for me.

ELIZABETH: I do.

TEDDIE: Do you mind if we talk it over now?

ELIZABETH: No.

TEDDIE: [*Frowning*] It makes me feel rather shy and awkward. I've repeated to myself over and over again exactly what I want to say to you, and now all I'd prepared seems rather footling.

ELIZABETH: I'm so afraid I'm going to cry.

TEDDIE: I feel it's all so tremendously serious and I think we ought to keep emotion out of it. You're rather emotional, aren't you?

ELIZABETH: [*Half smiling and half in tears*] So are you for the matter of that.

TEDDIE: That's why I wanted to have everything I meant to say to you cut and dried. I think it would be awfully unfair if I made love to you and all that sort of thing, and you were carried away. I wrote it all down and thought I'd send it you as a letter.

ELIZABETH: Why didn't you?

TEDDIE: I got the wind up. A letter seems so—so cold. You see, I love you so awfully.

ELIZABETH: For goodness' sake don't say that.

TEDDIE: You mustn't cry. Please don't, or I shall go all to pieces.

ELIZABETH: [*Trying to smile*] I'm sorry. It doesn't mean anything really. It's only tears running out of my eyes.

TEDDIE: Our only chance is to be awfully matter-of-fact. [*He stops for a moment. He finds it quite difficult to control himself. He clears his throat. He frowns with annoyance at himself*]

ELIZABETH: What's the matter?

TEDDIE: I've got a sort of lump in my throat. It is idiotic. I think I'll have a cigarette. [*She watches him in silence while he lights a cigarette*] You see, I've never been in love with anyone before, not really. It's knocked me endways. I don't know how I can live without you now. . . . Does that old fool know I'm in love with you?

ELIZABETH: I think so.

TEDDIE: When he was talking about Lady Kitty smashing up Lord Porteous' career I thought there was something at the back of it.

ELIZABETH: I think he was trying to persuade me not to smash up yours.

TEDDIE: I'm sure that's very considerate of him, but I don't happen to have one to smash. I wish I had. It's the only time in my life I've wished I were a hell of a swell so I could chuck it all and show you how much more you are to me than anything else in the world.

ELIZABETH: [*Affectionately*] You're a dear old thing, Teddie.

TEDDIE: You know, I don't really know how to make love, but if I did I couldn't do it now because I just want to be absolutely practical.

ELIZABETH: [*Chaffing him*] I'm glad you don't know how to make love. It would be almost more than I could bear.

TEDDIE: You see, I'm not at all romantic and that sort of thing. I'm just a common or garden business man. All this is so dreadfully serious and I think we ought to be sensible.

ELIZABETH: [*With a break in her voice*] You owl!

TEDDIE: No, Elizabeth, don't say things like that to me. I want you to consider all the *pros* and *cons*, and my heart's thumping against my chest, and you know I love you, I love you, I love you.

ELIZABETH: [*In a sigh of passion*] Oh, my precious!

TEDDIE: [*Impatiently, but with himself, rather than with* Elizabeth] Don't be idiotic, Elizabeth. I'm not going to tell you that I can't live without you and a lot of muck like that. You know that you mean everything in the world to me. [*Almost giving it up as a bad job*] Oh, my God!

ELIZABETH: [*Her voice faltering*] D'you think there's anything you can say to me that I don't know already?

TEDDIE: [*Desperately*] But I haven't said a single thing I wanted to. I'm a business man. I want to put it all in a business way, if you understand what I mean.

ELIZABETH: [*Smiling*] I don't believe you're a very good business man.

TEDDIE: [*Sharply*] You don't know what you're talking about. I'm a first rate business man, but somehow this is different. [*Hopelessly*] I don't know why it won't go right.

ELIZABETH: What are we going to do about it?

TEDDIE: You see, it's not just because you're awfully pretty that I love you. I'd love you just as much if you were old and ugly. It's you I love, not what you look like. And it's not only love; love be blowed! It's that I *like* you so tremendously. I think you're such a ripping good sort. I just want to be with you. I feel so jolly and happy just to think you're there. I'm so awfully *fond* of you.

ELIZABETH: [*Laughing through her tears*] I don't know if this is your idea of introducing a business proposition.

TEDDIE: Damn you, you won't let me.

ELIZABETH: You said "Damn you."

TEDDIE: I meant it.

ELIZABETH: Your voice sounded as if you meant it, you perfect duck!

TEDDIE: Really, Elizabeth, you're intolerable.

ELIZABETH: I'm doing nothing.

TEDDIE: Yes, you are, you're putting me off my blow. What I want to say is perfectly simple. I'm a very ordinary business man.

ELIZABETH: You've said that before.

TEDDIE: [*Angrily*] Shut up. I haven't got a bob besides what I earn. I've got no position. I'm nothing.

You're rich and you're a big pot and you've got everything that anyone can want. It's awful cheek my saying anything to you at all. But after all there's only one thing that really matters in the world, and that's love. I love you. Chuck all this, Elizabeth, and come to me.

ELIZABETH: Are you cross with me?

TEDDIE: Furious.

ELIZABETH: Darling!

TEDDIE: If you don't want me tell me so at once and let me get out quickly.

ELIZABETH: Teddie, nothing in the world matters anything to me but you. I'll go wherever you take me. I love you.

TEDDIE: [*All to pieces*] Oh, my God!

ELIZABETH: Does it mean as much to you as that? Oh, Teddie!

TEDDIE: [*Trying to control himself*] Don't be a fool, Elizabeth.

ELIZABETH: It's you're the fool. You're making me cry.

TEDDIE: You're so damned emotional.

ELIZABETH: Damned emotional yourself. I'm sure you're a rotten business man.

TEDDIE: I don't care what you think. You've made me so awfully happy. I say, what a lark life's going to be!

ELIZABETH: Teddie, you are an angel.

TEDDIE: Let's get out quick. It's no good wasting time. Elizabeth.

ELIZABETH: What?

TEDDIE: Nothing. I just like to say Elizabeth.

ELIZABETH: You fool!

TEDDIE: I say, can you shoot?

ELIZABETH: No.

TEDDIE: I'll teach you. You don't know how ripping it is to start out from your camp at dawn and travel through the jungle. And you're so tired at night and the sky's all starry. It's a fair treat. Of course I didn't want to say anything about all that till you'd decided. I'd made up my mind to be absolutely practical.

ELIZABETH: [*Chaffing him*] The only practical thing you said was that love is the only thing that really matters.

TEDDIE: [*Happily*] Pull the other leg next time, will you? I should hate to have one longer than the other.

ELIZABETH: Isn't it fun being in love with some one who's in love with you?

TEDDIE: I say, I think I'd better clear out at once, don't you? It seems rather rotten to stay on in—in this house.

ELIZABETH: You can't go tonight. There's no train.

TEDDIE: I'll go tomorrow. I'll wait in London till you're ready to join me.

ELIZABETH: I'm not going to leave a note on the pincushion like Lady Kitty, you know. I'm going to tell Arnold.

TEDDIE: Are you? Don't you think there'll be an awful bother?

ELIZABETH: I must face it. I should hate to be sly and deceitful.

TEDDIE: Well, then, let's face it together.

ELIZABETH: No, I'll talk to Arnold by myself.

TEDDIE: You won't let anyone influence you?

ELIZABETH: No.

[*He holds out his hand and she takes it. They look into one another's eyes with grave, almost solemn affection. There is the sound outside of a car driving up*]

ELIZABETH: There's the car. Arnold's come back. I must go and bathe my eyes. I don't want them to see I've been crying.

TEDDIE: All right. [*As she is going*] Elizabeth.

ELIZABETH: [*Stopping*] What?

TEDDIE: Bless you.

ELIZABETH: [*Affectionately*] Idiot!

[*She goes out of the door and* Teddie *through the French window into the garden. For an instant the room is empty.* Arnold *comes in. He sits down and takes some papers out of his despatch-case.* Lady Kitty *enters. He gets up*]

LADY KITTY: I saw you come in. Oh, my dear, don't get up. There's no reason why you should be so dreadfully polite to me.

ARNOLD: I've just rung for a cup of tea.

LADY KITTY: Perhaps we shall have the chance of a little talk. We don't seem to have had five minutes by ourselves. I want to make your acquaintance, you know.

ARNOLD: I should like you to know that it's not by my wish that my father is here.

LADY KITTY: But I'm so interested to see him.

ARNOLD: I was afraid that you and Lord Porteous must find it embarrassing.

LADY KITTY: Oh, no. Hughie was his greatest friend. They were at Eton and Oxford together. I think your father has improved so much since I saw him last. He wasn't good-looking as a young man, but now he's quite handsome.

[*The* Footman *brings in a tray on which are tea-things*]

LADY KITTY: Shall I pour it out for you?

ARNOLD: Thank you very much.

LADY KITTY: Do you take sugar?

ARNOLD: No. I gave it up during the war.

LADY KITTY: So wise of you. It's so bad for the figure. Besides being patriotic, of course. Isn't it absurd that I should ask my son if he takes sugar or not? Life is really very quaint. Sad, of course, but oh, so quaint! Often I lie in bed at night and have a good laugh to myself as I think how quaint life is.

ARNOLD: I'm afraid I'm a very serious person.

LADY KITTY: How old are you now, Arnold?

ARNOLD: Thirty-five.

LADY KITTY: Are you really? Of course, I was a child when I married your father.

ARNOLD: Really. He always told me you were twenty-two.

LADY KITTY: Oh, what nonsense! Why, I was married out of the nursery. I put my hair up for the first time on my wedding-day.

ARNOLD: Where is Lord Porteous?

LADY KITTY: My dear, it sounds too absurd to hear you call him Lord Porteous. Why don't you call him —Uncle Hughie?

ARNOLD: He doesn't happen to be my uncle.

LADY KITTY: No, but he's your godfather. You know, I'm sure you'll like him when you know him better. I'm so hoping that you and Elizabeth will come and stay with us in Florence. I simply adore Elizabeth. She's too beautiful.

ARNOLD: Her hair is very pretty.

LADY KITTY: It's not touched up, is it?

ARNOLD: Oh, no.

LADY KITTY: I just wondered. It's rather a coincidence that her hair should be the same color as mine. I suppose it shows that your father and you are attracted by just the same thing. So interesting, heredity, isn't it?

ARNOLD: Very.

LADY KITTY: Of course, since I joined the Catholic Church I don't believe in it any more. Darwin and all that sort of thing. Too dreadful. Wicked, you know. Besides, it's not very good form, is it?

[*Champion-Cheney comes in from the garden*]

C.-C.: Do I intrude?

LADY KITTY: Come in, Clive. Arnold and I have been having such a wonderful heart-to-heart talk.

C.-C.: Very nice.

ARNOLD: Father, I stepped in for a moment at the Harveys' on my way back. It's simply criminal what they're doing with that house.

C.-C.: What are they doing?

ARNOLD: It's an almost perfect Georgian house and they've got a lot of dreadful Victorian furniture. I gave them my ideas on the subject, but it's quite hopeless. They said they were attached to their furniture.

C.-C.: Arnold should have been an interior decorator.

LADY KITTY: He has wonderful taste. He gets that from me.

ARNOLD: I suppose I have a certain *flair*. I have a passion for decorating houses.

LADY KITTY: You've made this one charming.

C.-C.: D'you remember, we just had chintzes and comfortable chairs when we lived here, Kitty.

LADY KITTY: Perfectly hideous, wasn't it?

C.-C.: In those days gentlemen and ladies were not expected to have taste.

ARNOLD: You know, I've been looking at this chair again. Since Lord Porteous said the legs weren't right I've been very uneasy.

LADY KITTY: He only said that because he was in a bad temper.

C.-C.: His temper seems to me very short these days, Kitty.

LADY KITTY: Oh, it is.

ARNOLD: You feel he knows what he's talking about. I gave seventy-five pounds for that chair. I'm very seldom taken in. I always think if a thing's right you feel it.

C.-C.: Well, don't let it disturb your night's rest.

ARNOLD: But, my dear father, that's just what it does. I had a most horrible dream about it last night.

LADY KITTY: Here is Hughie.

ARNOLD: I'm going to fetch a book I have on Old English furniture. There's an illustration of a chair which is almost identical with this one.

[Porteous *comes in*]

PORTEOUS: Quite a family gathering, by George!

C.-C.: I was thinking just now we'd make a very pleasing picture of a typical English home.

ARNOLD: I'll be back in five minutes. There's something I want to show you, Lord Porteous. [*He goes out*]

C.-C.: Would you like to play piquet with me, Hughie?

PORTEOUS: Not particularly.

C.-C.: You were never much of a piquet player, were you?

PORTEOUS: My dear Clive, you people don't know what piquet is in England.

C.-C.: Let's have a game then. You may make money.

PORTEOUS: I don't want to play with you.

LADY KITTY: I don't know why not, Hughie.

PORTEOUS: Let me tell you that I don't like your manner.

C.-C.: I'm sorry for that. I'm afraid I can't offer to change it at my age.

PORTEOUS: I don't know what you want to be hanging around here for.

C.-C.: A natural attachment to my home.

PORTEOUS: If you'd had any tact you'd have kept out of the way while we were here.

C.-C.: My dear Hughie. I don't understand your attitude at all. If I'm willing to let bygones be bygones why should you object?

PORTEOUS: Damn it all, they're not bygones.

C.-C.: After all, I am the injured party.

PORTEOUS: How the devil are you the injured party?

C.-C.: Well, you did run away with my wife, didn't you?

LADY KITTY: Now, don't let's go into ancient history. I can't see why we shouldn't all be friends.

PORTEOUS: I beg you not to interfere, Kitty.

LADY KITTY: I'm very fond of Clive.

PORTEOUS: You never cared two straws for Clive. You only say that to irritate me.

LADY KITTY: Not at all. I don't see why he shouldn't come and stay with us.

C.-C.: I'd love to. I think Florence in spring-time is delightful. Have you central heating?

PORTEOUS: I never liked you, I don't like you now, and I never shall like you.

C.-C.: How very unfortunate! Because I liked you, I like you now, and I shall continue to like you.

LADY KITTY: There's something very nice about you, Clive.

PORTEOUS: If you think that, why the devil did you leave him?

LADY KITTY: Are you going to reproach me because I loved you? How utterly, utterly, utterly detestable you are!

C.-C.: Now, now, don't quarrel with one another.

LADY KITTY: It's all his fault. I'm the easiest person in the world to live with. But really he'd try the patience of a saint.

C.-C.: Come, come, don't get upset, Kitty. When two people live together there must be a certain amount of give and take.

PORTEOUS: I don't know what the devil you're talking about.

C.-C.: It hasn't escaped my observation that you are a little inclined to frip. Many couples are. I think it's a pity.

PORTEOUS: Would you have the very great kindness to mind your own business?

LADY KITTY: It is his business. He naturally wants me to be happy.

C.-C.: I have the very greatest affection for Kitty.

PORTEOUS: Then why the devil didn't you look after her properly?

C.-C.: My dear Hughie, you were my greatest friend. I trusted you. It may have been rash.

PORTEOUS: It was inexcusable.

LADY KITTY: I don't know what you mean by that, Hughie.

PORTEOUS: Don't, don't, don't try and bully me, Kitty.

LADY KITTY: Oh, I know what you mean.

PORTEOUS: Then why the devil did you say you didn't?

LADY KITTY: When I think that I sacrificed everything for that man! And for thirty years I've had to live in a filthy marble palace with no sanitary conveniences.

C.-C.: D'you mean to say you haven't got a bathroom?

LADY KITTY: I've had to wash in a tub.

C.-C.: My poor Kitty, how you've suffered!

PORTEOUS: Really, Kitty, I'm sick of hearing of the sacrifices you made. I suppose you think I sacrificed nothing. I should have been Prime Minister by now if it hadn't been for you.

LADY KITTY: Nonsense!

PORTEOUS: What do you mean by that? Everyone said I should be Prime Minister. Shouldn't I have been Prime Minister, Clive?

C.-C.: It was certainly the general expectation.

PORTEOUS: I was the most promising young man of my day. I was bound to get a seat in the Cabinet at the next election.

LADY KITTY: They'd have found you out just as I've found you out. I'm sick of hearing that I ruined your career. You never had a career to ruin. Prime Minister! You haven't the brain. You haven't the character.

C.-C.: Cheek, push, and a gift of the gab will serve very well instead, you know.

LADY KITTY: Besides, in politics it's not the men that matter. It's the women at the back of them. I could have made Clive a Cabinet Minister if I'd wanted to.

PORTEOUS: Clive?

LADY KITTY: With my beauty, my charm, my force of character, my wit, I could have done anything.

PORTEOUS: Clive was nothing but my political secretary. When I was Prime Minister I might have made him Governor of some Colony or other. Western Australia, say. Out of pure kindness.

LADY KITTY: [With flashing eyes] D'you think I would have buried myself in Western Australia? With my beauty? My charm?

PORTEOUS: Or Barbadoes, perhaps.

LADY KITTY: [Furiously] Barbadoes! Barbadoes can go to—Barbadoes.

PORTEOUS: That's all you'd have got.

LADY KITTY: Nonsense! I'd have India.

PORTEOUS: I would never have given you India.

LADY KITTY: You would have given me India.

PORTEOUS: I tell you I wouldn't.

LADY KITTY: The King would have given me India. The nation would have insisted on my having India. I would have been a vice-reine or nothing.

PORTEOUS: I tell you that as long as the interests of the British Empire—damn it all, my teeth are coming out! [He hurries from the room]

LADY KITTY: It's too much. I can't bear it any more. I've put up with him for thirty years and now I'm at the end of my tether.

C.-C.: Calm yourself, my dear Kitty.

LADY KITTY: I won't listen to a word. I've quite made up my mind. It's finished, finished, finished. [With a change of tone] I was so touched when I heard that you never lived in this house again after I left it.

C.-C.: The cuckoos have always been very plentiful. Their note has a personal application which, I must say, I have found extremely offensive.

LADY KITTY: When I saw that you didn't marry again I couldn't help thinking that you still loved me.

C.-C.: I am one of the few men I know who is able to profit by experience.

LADY KITTY: In the eyes of the Church I am still your wife. The Church is so wise. It knows that in the end a woman always comes back to her first love. Clive, I am willing to return to you.

C.-C.: My dear Kitty, I couldn't take advantage of your momentary vexation with Hughie to let you take a step which I know you would bitterly regret.

LADY KITTY: You've waited for me a long time. For Arnold's sake.

C.-C.: Do you think we really need bother about Arnold? In the last thirty years he's had time to grow used to the situation.

LADY KITTY: [With a little smile] I think I've sown my wild oats, Clive.

C.-C.: I haven't. I was a good young man, Kitty.

LADY KITTY: I know.

C.-C.: And I'm very glad, because it has enabled me to be a wicked old one.

LADY KITTY: I beg your pardon.

[Arnold comes in with a large book in his hand]

ARNOLD: I say, I've found the book I was hunting for. Oh! Isn't Lord Porteous here?

LADY KITTY: One moment, Arnold. Your father and I are busy.

ARNOLD: I'm so sorry. [He goes out into the garden]

LADY KITTY: Explain yourself, Clive.

C.-C.: When you ran away from me, Kitty, I was sore and angry and miserable. But above all I felt a fool.

LADY KITTY: Men are so vain.

C.-C.: But I was a student of history, and presently I reflected that I shared my misfortune with very nearly all the greatest men.

LADY KITTY: I'm a great reader myself. It has always struck me as peculiar.

C.-C.: The explanation is very simple. Women dislike intelligence, and when they find it in their husbands they revenge themselves on them in the only way they can, by making them—well, what you made me.

LADY KITTY: It's ingenious. It may be true.

C.-C.: I felt I had done my duty by society and I determined to devote the rest of my life to my own entertainment. The House of Commons had always bored me excessively and the scandal of our divorce gave me an opportunity to resign my seat. I have been relieved to find that the country got on perfectly well without me.

LADY KITTY: But has love never entered your life?

C.-C.: Tell me frankly, Kitty, don't you think people make a lot of unnecessary fuss about love?

LADY KITTY: It's the most wonderful thing in the world.

C.-C.: You're incorrigible. Do you really think it was worth sacrificing so much for?

LADY KITTY: My dear Clive, I don't mind telling you that if I had my time over again I should be unfaithful to you, but I should not leave you.

C.-C.: For some years I was notoriously the prey of a secret sorrow. But I found so many charming creatures who were anxious to console that in the end it grew rather fatiguing. Out of regard to my health I ceased to frequent the drawing-rooms of Mayfair.

LADY KITTY: And since then?

C.-C.: Since then I have allowed myself the luxury of assisting financially a succession of dear little things, in a somewhat humble sphere, between the ages of twenty and twenty-five.

LADY KITTY: I cannot understand the infatuation of men for young girls. I think they're so dull.

C.-C.: It's a matter of taste. I love old wine, old friends, and old books, but I like young women. On their twenty-fifth birthday I give them a diamond ring and tell them they must no longer waste their youth and beauty on an old fogey like me. We have a most affecting scene, my technique on these occasions is perfect, and then I start all over again.

LADY KITTY: You're a wicked old man, Clive.

C.-C.: That's what I told you. But, by George! I'm a happy one.

LADY KITTY: There's only one course open to me now.

C.-C.: What is that?

LADY KITTY: [With a flashing smile] To go and dress for dinner.

C.-C.: Capital. I will follow your example.

[As Lady Kitty goes out Elizabeth comes in]

ELIZABETH: Where is Arnold?

C.-C.: He's on the terrace. I'll call him.

ELIZABETH: Don't bother.

C.-C.: I was just strolling along to my cottage to put on a dinner jacket. [As he goes out] Arnold.

[Exit C.-C.]

ARNOLD: Hulloa! [He comes in] Oh, Elizabeth, I've found an illustration here of a chair which is almost identical with mine. It's dated 1750. Look!

ELIZABETH: That's very interesting.

ARNOLD: I want to show it to Porteous. [Moving a chair which has been misplaced] You know, it does exasperate me the way people will not leave things alone. I no sooner put a thing in its place than somebody moves it.

ELIZABETH: It must be maddening for you.

ARNOLD: It is. You are the worst offender. I can't think why you don't take the pride that I do in the house. After all, it's one of the show places in the country.

ELIZABETH: I'm afraid you find me very unsatisfactory.

ARNOLD: [Good-humoredly] I don't know about that. But my two subjects are politics and decoration. I should be a perfect fool if I didn't see that you don't care two straws about either.

ELIZABETH: We haven't very much in common, Arnold, have we?

ARNOLD: I don't think you can blame me for that.

ELIZABETH: I don't. I blame you for nothing. I have no fault to find with you.

ARNOLD: [Surprised at her significant tone] Good gracious me! What's the meaning of all this?

ELIZABETH: Well, I don't think there's any object in beating about the bush. I want you to let me go.

ARNOLD: Go where?

ELIZABETH: Away. For always.

ARNOLD: My dear child, what are you talking about?

ELIZABETH: I want to be free.

ARNOLD: [Amused rather than disconcerted] Don't be ridiculous, darling. I daresay you're run down and want a change. I'll take you over to Paris for a fortnight if you like.

ELIZABETH: I shouldn't have spoken to you if I hadn't quite made up my mind. We've been married for three years and I don't think it's been a great success. I'm frankly bored by the life you want me to lead.

ARNOLD: Well, if you'll allow me to say so, the fault is yours. We lead a very distinguished, useful life. We know a lot of extremely nice people.

ELIZABETH: I'm quite willing to allow that the fault is mine. But how does that make it any better? I'm only twenty-five. If I've made a mistake I have time to correct it.

ARNOLD: I can't bring myself to take you very seriously.

ELIZABETH: You see, I don't love you.

ARNOLD: Well, I'm awfully sorry. But you weren't obliged to marry me. You've made your bed and I'm afraid you must lie on it.

ELIZABETH: That's one of the falsest proverbs in the English language. Why should you lie on the bed you've made if you don't want to? There's always the floor.

ARNOLD: For goodness' sake, don't be funny, Elizabeth.

ELIZABETH: I've quite made up my mind to leave you, Arnold.

ARNOLD: Come, come, Elizabeth, you must be sensible. You haven't any reason to leave me.

ELIZABETH: Why should you wish to keep a woman tied to you who wants to be free?

ARNOLD: I happen to be in love with you.

ELIZABETH: You might have said that before.

ARNOLD: I thought you'd take it for granted. You can't expect a man to go on making love to his wife after three years. I'm very busy. I'm awfully keen on politics and I've worked like a dog to make this house a thing of beauty. After all, a man marries to have a home, but also because he doesn't want to be bothered with sex and all that sort of thing. I fell in love with you the first time I saw you and I've been in love ever since.

ELIZABETH: I'm sorry, but if you're not in love with a man his love doesn't mean very much to you.

ARNOLD: It's so ungrateful. I've done everything in the world for you.

ELIZABETH: You've been very kind to me. But you've asked me to lead a life I don't like and that I'm not suited for. I'm awfully sorry to cause you pain, but now you must let me go.

ARNOLD: Nonsense! I'm a good deal older than you are and I think I have a little more sense. In your interests as well as in mine I'm not going to do anything of the sort.

ELIZABETH: [*With a smile*] How can you prevent me? You can't keep me under lock and key.

ARNOLD: Please don't talk to me as if I were a foolish child. You're my wife and you're going to remain my wife.

ELIZABETH: What sort of a life do you think we should lead? Do you think there'd be any more happiness for you than for me?

ARNOLD: But what is it precisely that you suggest?

ELIZABETH: Well, I want you to let me divorce you.

ARNOLD: [*Astounded*] Me? Thank you very much. Are you under the impression I'm going to sacrifice my career for a whim of yours?

ELIZABETH: How will it do that?

ARNOLD: My seat's wobbly enough as it is. Do you think I'd be able to hold it if I were in a divorce case? Even if it were a put-up job, as most divorces are nowadays, it would damn me.

ELIZABETH: It's rather hard on a woman to be divorced.

ARNOLD: [*With sudden suspicion*] What do you mean by that? Are you in love with some one?

ELIZABETH: Yes.

ARNOLD: Who?

ELIZABETH: Teddie Luton.

[*He is astonished for a moment, then bursts into a laugh*]

ARNOLD: My poor child, how can you be so ridiculous? Why, he hasn't a bob. He's a perfectly commonplace young man. It's so absurd I can't even be angry with you.

ELIZABETH: I've fallen desperately in love with him, Arnold.

ARNOLD: Well, you'd better fall desperately out.

ELIZABETH: He wants to marry me.

ARNOLD: I daresay he does. He can go to hell.

ELIZABETH: It's no good talking like that.

ARNOLD: Is he your lover?

ELIZABETH: No, certainly not.

ARNOLD: It shows that he's a mean skunk to take advantage of my hospitality to make love to you.

ELIZABETH: He's never even kissed me.

ARNOLD: I'd try telling that to the horse marines if I were you.

ELIZABETH: It's because I wanted to do nothing shabby that I told you straight out how things were.

ARNOLD: How long have you been thinking of this?

ELIZABETH: I've been in love with Teddie ever since I knew him.

ARNOLD: And you never thought of me at all, I suppose.

ELIZABETH: Oh, yes, I did. I was miserable. But I can't help myself. I wish I loved you, but I don't.

ARNOLD: I recommend you to think very carefully before you do anything foolish.

ELIZABETH: I have thought very carefully.

ARNOLD: By God! I don't know why I don't give you a sound hiding. I'm not sure if that wouldn't be the best thing to bring you to your senses.

ELIZABETH: Oh, Arnold, don't take it like that.

ARNOLD: How do you expect me to take it? You come to me quite calmly and say: "I've had enough of you. We've been married three years and I think I'd like to marry somebody else now. Shall I break up your home? What a bore for you! Do you mind my divorcing you? It'll smash up your career, will it? What a pity!" Oh, no, my girl, I may be a fool, but I'm not a damned fool.

ELIZABETH: Teddie is leaving here by the first train tomorrow. I warn you that I mean to join him as soon as he can make the necessary arrangements.

ARNOLD: Where is he?

ELIZABETH: I don't know. I suppose he's in his room.

[Arnold *goes to the door and calls*]

ARNOLD: George!

[*For a moment he walks up and down the room impatiently*. Elizabeth *watches him. The* Footman *comes in*]

FOOTMAN: Yes, sir.

ARNOLD: Tell Mr. Luton to come here at once.

ELIZABETH: Ask Mr. Luton if he wouldn't mind coming here for a moment.

FOOTMAN: Very good, madam.

[*Exit* Footman]

ELIZABETH: What are you going to say to him?

ARNOLD: That's my business.

ELIZABETH: I wouldn't make a scene if I were you.

ARNOLD: I'm not going to make a scene. [*They wait in silence*] Why did you insist on my mother coming here?

ELIZABETH: It seemed to me rather absurd to take up the attitude that I should be contaminated by her when . . .

ARNOLD: [*Interrupting*] When you were proposing to do exactly the same thing. Well, now you've seen her what do you think of her? Do you think it's been a success? Is that the sort of woman a man would like his mother to be?

ELIZABETH: I've been ashamed. I've been so sorry. It all seemed dreadful and horrible. This morning I happened to notice a rose in the garden. It was all over-blown and bedraggled. It looked like a painted old woman. And I remembered that I'd looked at it a day or two ago. It was lovely then, fresh and blooming and fragrant. It may be hideous now, but that doesn't take away from the beauty it had once. That was real.

ARNOLD: Poetry, by God! As if this were the moment for poetry!

[Teddie *comes in. He has changed into a dinner jacket*]

TEDDIE: [*To* Elizabeth] Did you want me?

ARNOLD: *I* sent for you. [Teddie *looks from* Arnold *to* Elizabeth. *He sees that something has happened*] When would it be convenient for you to leave this house?

TEDDIE: I was proposing to go tomorrow morning. But I can very well go at once if you like.

ARNOLD: I do like.

TEDDIE: Very well. Is there anything else you wish to say to me?

ARNOLD: Do you think it was a very honorable thing to come down here and make love to my wife?

TEDDIE: No, I don't. I haven't been very happy about it. That's why I wanted to go away.

ARNOLD: Upon my word, you're cool.

TEDDIE: I'm afraid it's no good saying I'm sorry and that sort of thing. You know what the situation is.

ARNOLD: Is it true that you want to marry Elizabeth?

TEDDIE: Yes. I should like to marry her as soon as ever I can.

ARNOLD: Have you thought of me at all? Has it struck you that you're destroying my home and breaking up my happiness?

TEDDIE: I don't see how there could be much happiness for you if Elizabeth doesn't care for you.

ARNOLD: Let me tell you that I refuse to have my home broken up by a twopenny-halfpenny adventurer who takes advantage of a foolish woman. I refuse to allow myself to be divorced. I can't prevent my wife from going off with you if she's determined to make a damned fool of herself, but this I tell you: nothing will induce me to divorce her.

ELIZABETH: Arnold, that would be monstrous.

TEDDIE: We could force you.

ARNOLD: How?

TEDDIE: If we went away together openly you'd have to bring an action.

ARNOLD: Twenty-four hours after you leave this house I shall go down to Brighton with a chorusgirl. And neither you nor I will be able to get a divorce. We've had enough divorces in our family. And now get out, get out, get out!

[Teddie *looks uncertainly at* Elizabeth]

ELIZABETH: [*With a little smile*] Don't bother about me. I shall be all right.

ARNOLD: Get out! Get out!

CURTAIN

ACT III.

The Scene is the same as in the preceding acts. It is the night of the same day as that on which takes place the action of the second act.

Champion-Cheney *and* Arnold, *both in dinner jackets, are discovered.* Champion-Cheney *is seated.* Arnold *walks restlessly up and down the room.*

c.-c.: I think, if you'll follow my advice to the letter, you'll probably work the trick.

ARNOLD: I don't like it, you know. It's against all my principles.

c.-c.: My dear Arnold, we all hope that you have before you a distinguished political career. You can't learn too soon that the most useful thing about a principle is that it can always be sacrificed to expediency.

ARNOLD: But supposing it doesn't come off? Women are incalculable.

c.-c.: Nonsense! Men are romantic. A woman will always sacrifice herself if you give her the opportunity. It is her favorite form of self-indulgence.

ARNOLD: I never know whether you're a humorist or a cynic, Father.

c.-c.: I'm neither, my dear boy; I'm merely a very truthful man. But people are so unused to the truth that they're apt to mistake it for a joke or a sneer.

ARNOLD: [*Irritably*] It seems so unfair that this should happen to me.

c.-c.: Keep your head, my boy, and do what I tell you.

[Lady Kitty *and* Elizabeth *come in.* Lady Kitty *is in a gorgeous evening gown*]

ELIZABETH: Where is Lord Porteous?

c.-c.: He's on the terrace. He's smoking a cigar. [*Going to window*] Hughie!

[Porteous *comes in*]

PORTEOUS: [*With a grunt*] Yes? Where's Mrs. Shenstone?

ELIZABETH: Oh, she had a headache. She's gone to bed.

[*When* Porteous *comes in* Lady Kitty *with a very haughty air purses her lips and takes up an illustrated paper.* Porteous *gives her an irritated look, takes another illustrated paper and sits himself down at the other end of the room. They are not on speaking terms*]

c.-c.: Arnold and I have just been down to my cottage.

ELIZABETH: I wondered where you'd gone.

c.-c.: I came across an old photograph album this afternoon. I meant to bring it along before dinner, but I forgot, so we went and fetched it.

ELIZABETH: Oh, do let me see it! I love old photographs.

[*He gives her the album, and she, sitting down, puts it on her knees and begins to turn over the pages. He stands over her.* Lady Kitty *and* Porteous *take surreptitious glances at one another*]

c.-c.: I thought it might amuse you to see what pretty women looked like five-and-thirty years ago. That was the day of beautiful women.

ELIZABETH: Do you think they were more beautiful then than they are now?

c.-c.: Oh, much. Now you see lots of pretty little things, but very few beautiful women.

ELIZABETH: Aren't their clothes funny?

c.-c.: [*Pointing to a photograph*] That's Mrs. Langtry.

ELIZABETH: She has a lovely nose.

c.-c.: She was the most wonderful thing you ever saw. Dowagers used to jump on chairs in order to get a good look at her when she came into a drawing-room. I was riding with her once, and we had to have the gates of the livery-stable closed when she was getting on her horse because the crowd was so great.

ELIZABETH: And who's that?

c.-c.: Lady Lonsdale. That's Lady Dudley.

ELIZABETH: This is an actress, isn't it?

c.-c.: It is, indeed. Ellen Terry. By George! How I loved that woman!

ELIZABETH: [*With a smile*] Dear Ellen Terry!

c.-c.: That's Bwabs. I never saw a smarter man in my life. And Oliver Montagu. Henry Manners with his eye-glass.

ELIZABETH: Nice-looking, isn't he? And this?

c.-c.: That's Mary Anderson. I wish you could have seen her in "A Winter's Tale." Her beauty just took your breath away. And look! There's Lady Randolph. Bernal Osborne—the wittiest man I ever knew.

ELIZABETH: I think it's too sweet. I love their absurd bustles and those tight sleeves.

c.-c.: What figures they had! In those days a woman wasn't supposed to be as thin as a rail and as flat as a pancake.

ELIZABETH: Oh, but aren't they laced in? How could they bear it?

c.-c.: They didn't play golf then, and nonsense like that, you know. They hunted, in a tall hat and a long black habit, and they were very gracious and charitable to the poor in the village.

ELIZABETH: Did the poor like it?

c.-c.: They had a very thin time if they didn't. When they were in London they drove in the Park every afternoon, and they went to ten-course dinners, where they never met anybody they didn't know. And they had their box at the opera when Patti was singing or Madam Albani.

ELIZABETH: Oh, what a lovely little thing! Who on earth is that?

c.-c.: That?

ELIZABETH: She looks so fragile, like a piece of exquisite china, with all those furs on and her face up against her muff, and the snow falling.

c.-c.: Yes, there was quite a rage at that time for being taken in an artificial snowstorm.

ELIZABETH: What a sweet smile, so roguish and frank, and debonair! Oh, I wish I looked like that! Do tell me who it is!

c.-c.: Don't you know?

ELIZABETH: No.

c.-c.: Why—it's Kitty.

ELIZABETH: Lady Kitty. [*To* Lady Kitty] Oh, my dear, do look! It's too ravishing. [*She takes the album over to her impulsively*] Why didn't you tell me you looked like that? Everybody must have been in love with you.

[Lady Kitty *takes the album and looks at it. Then she lets it slip from her hands and covers her face with her hands. She is crying*]

[*In consternation*] My dear, what's the matter? Oh, what have I done? I'm so sorry.

LADY KITTY: Don't, don't talk to me. Leave me alone. It's stupid of me.

[Elizabeth *looks at her for a moment perplexed, then, turning round, slips her arm in* Champion-Cheney's *and leads him out on to the terrace*]

ELIZABETH: [*As they are going, in a whisper*] Did you do that on purpose?

[Porteous *gets up and goes over to* Lady Kitty. *He puts his hand on her shoulder. They remain thus for a little while*]

PORTEOUS: I'm afraid I was very rude to you before dinner, Kitty.

LADY KITTY: [*Taking his hand which is on her shoulder*] It doesn't matter. I'm sure I was very exasperating.

PORTEOUS: I didn't mean what I said, you know.

LADY KITTY: Neither did I.

PORTEOUS: Of course I know that I'd never have been Prime Minister.

LADY KITTY: How can you talk such nonsense, Hughie? No one would have had a chance if you'd remained in politics.

PORTEOUS: I haven't the character.

LADY KITTY: You have more character than anyone I've ever met.

PORTEOUS: Besides, I don't know that I much wanted to be Prime Minister.

LADY KITTY: Oh, but I should have been so proud of you. Of course you'd have been Prime Minister.

PORTEOUS: I'd have given you India, you know. I think it would have been a very popular appointment.

LADY KITTY: I don't care twopence about India. I'd have been quite content with Western Australia.

PORTEOUS: My dear, you don't think I'd have let you bury yourself in Western Australia?

LADY KITTY: Or Barbadoes.

PORTEOUS: Never. It sounds like a cure for flat feet. I'd have kept you in London.

[*He picks up the album and is about to look at the photograph of* Lady Kitty. *She puts her hands over it*]

LADY KITTY: No, don't look.

[*He takes her hand away*]

PORTEOUS: Don't be so silly.

LADY KITTY: Isn't it hateful to grow old?

PORTEOUS: You know, you haven't changed much.

LADY KITTY: [*Enchanted*] Oh, Hughie, how can you talk such nonsense?

PORTEOUS: Of course you're a little more mature,

but that's all. A woman's all the better for being rather mature.

LADY KITTY: Do you really think that?

PORTEOUS: Upon my soul I do.

LADY KITTY: You're not saying it just to please me?

PORTEOUS: No, no.

LADY KITTY: Let me look at the photograph again. [*She takes the album and looks at the photograph complacently*] The fact is, if your bones are good, age doesn't really matter. You'll always be beautiful.

PORTEOUS: [*With a little smile, almost as if he were talking to a child*] It was silly of you to cry.

LADY KITTY: It hasn't made my eyelashes run, has it?

PORTEOUS: Not a bit.

LADY KITTY: It's very good stuff I use now. They don't stick together either.

PORTEOUS: Look here, Kitty, how much longer do you want to stay here?

LADY KITTY: Oh, I'm quite ready to go whenever you like.

PORTEOUS: Clive gets on my nerves. I don't like the way he keeps hanging about you.

LADY KITTY: [*Surprised, rather amused, and delighted*] Hughie, you don't mean to say you're jealous of poor Clive?

PORTEOUS: Of course I'm not jealous of him, but he does look at you in a way that I can't help thinking rather objectionable.

LADY KITTY: Hughie, you may throw me downstairs like Amy Robsart; you may drag me about the floor by the hair of my head; I don't care, you're jealous. I shall never grow old.

PORTEOUS: Damn it all, the man was your husband.

LADY KITTY: My dear Hughie, he never had your style. Why, the moment you come into a room everyone looks and says: "Who the devil is that?"

PORTEOUS: What? You think that, do you? Well, I daresay there's something in what you say. These damned Radicals can say what they like, but, by God, Kitty! When a man's a gentleman—well, damn it all, you know what I mean.

LADY KITTY: I think Clive has degenerated dreadfully since we left him.

PORTEOUS: What do you say to making a bee-line for Italy and going to San Michele?

LADY KITTY: Oh, Hughie! It's years since we were there.

PORTEOUS: Wouldn't you like to see it again— just once more?

LADY KITTY: Do you remember the first time we went? It was the most heavenly place I'd ever seen. We'd only left England a month, and I said I'd like to spend all my life there.

PORTEOUS: Of course I remember. And in a fortnight it was yours, lock, stock, and barrel.

LADY KITTY: We were very happy there, Hughie.

PORTEOUS: Let's go back once more.

LADY KITTY: I daren't. It must be all peopled with the ghosts of our past. One should never go again to a place where one has been happy. It would break my heart.

PORTEOUS: Do you remember how we used to sit on the terrace of the old castle and look at the Adriatic? We might have been the only people in the world, you and I, Kitty.

LADY KITTY: [*Tragically*] And we thought our love would last forever.

[*Enter* Champion-Cheney]

PORTEOUS: Is there any chance of bridge this evening?

C.-C.: I don't think we can make up a four.

PORTEOUS: What a nuisance that boy went away like that! He wasn't a bad player.

C.-C.: Teddie Luton?

LADY KITTY: I think it was very funny his going without saying good-by to anyone.

C.-C.: The young men of the present day are very casual.

PORTEOUS: I thought there was no train in the evening.

C.-C.: There isn't. The last train leaves at 5.45.

PORTEOUS: How did he go then?

C.-C.: He went.

PORTEOUS: Damned selfish I call it.

LADY KITTY: [*Intrigued*] Why did he go, Clive?

[Champion-Cheney *looks at her for a moment reflectively*]

C.-C.: I have something very grave to say to you. Elizabeth wants to leave Arnold.

LADY KITTY: Clive! What on earth for?

C.-C.: She's in love with Teddie Luton. That's why he went. The men of my family are really very unfortunate.

PORTEOUS: Does she want to run away with him?

LADY KITTY: [*With consternation*] My dear, what's to be done?

C.-C.: I think you can do a great deal.

LADY KITTY: I? What?

C.-C.: Tell her, tell her what it means.

[*He looks at her fixedly. She stares at him*]

LADY KITTY: Oh, no, no!

C.-C.: She's a child. Not for Arnold's sake. For her sake. You must.

LADY KITTY: You don't know what you're asking.

C.-C.: Yes, I do.

LADY KITTY: Hughie, what shall I do?

PORTEOUS: Do what you like. I shall never blame you for anything.

[*The* Footman *comes in with a letter on a salver. He hesitates on seeing that* Elizabeth *is not in the room*]

C.-C.: What is it?

FOOTMAN: I was looking for Mrs. Champion-Cheney, sir.

C.-C.: She's not here. Is that a letter?

FOOTMAN: Yes, sir. It's just been sent up from the "Champion Arms."

C.-C.: Leave it. I'll give it to Mrs. Cheney.

FOOTMAN: Very good, sir. [*He brings the tray to* Clive, *who takes the letter. The* Footman *goes out*]

PORTEOUS: Is the "Champion Arms" the local pub?

C.-C.: [*Looking at the letter*] It's by way of being a hotel, but I never heard of anyone staying there.

LADY KITTY: If there was no train I suppose he has to go there.

C.-C.: Great minds. I wonder what he has to write about! [*He goes to the door leading on to the garden*] Elizabeth!

ELIZABETH: [*Outside*] Yes.

C.-C.: Here's a note for you.

[*There is silence. They wait for* Elizabeth *to come. She enters*]

ELIZABETH: It's lovely in the garden tonight.

C.-C.: They've just sent this up from the "Champion Arms."

ELIZABETH: Thank you.

[*Without embarrassment she opens the letter. They watch her while she reads it. It covers three pages. She puts it away in her bag*]

LADY KITTY: Hughie, I wish you'd fetch me a cloak. I'd like to take a little stroll in the garden, but after thirty years in Italy I find these English summers rather chilly. [*Without a word* Porteous *goes out.* Elizabeth *is lost in thought*] I want to talk to Elizabeth, Clive.

C.-C.: I'll leave you. [*He goes out*]

LADY KITTY: What does he say?

ELIZABETH: Who?

LADY KITTY: Mr. Luton.

ELIZABETH: [*Gives a little start. Then she looks at* Lady Kitty] They've told you?

LADY KITTY: Yes. And now they have, I think I knew it all along.

ELIZABETH: I don't expect you to have much sympathy for me. Arnold is your son.

LADY KITTY: So pitifully little.

ELIZABETH: I'm not suited for this sort of existence. Arnold wants me to take what he calls my place in Society. Oh, I get so bored with those parties in London. All those middle-aged painted women, in beautiful clothes, lolloping round ballrooms with rather old young men. And the endless luncheons where they gossip about so-and-so's love affairs.

LADY KITTY: Are you very much in love with Mr. Luton?

ELIZABETH: I love him with all my heart.

LADY KITTY: And he?

ELIZABETH: He's never cared for anyone but me. He never will.

LADY KITTY: Will Arnold let you divorce him?

ELIZABETH: No, he won't hear of it. He refuses even to divorce me.

LADY KITTY: Why?

ELIZABETH: He thinks a scandal will revive all the old gossip.

LADY KITTY: Oh, my poor child!

ELIZABETH: It can't be helped. I'm quite willing to accept the consequences.

LADY KITTY: You don't know what it is to have a man tied to you only by his honor. When married people don't get on they can separate, but if they're not married it's impossible. It's a tie that only death can sever.

ELIZABETH: If Teddie stopped caring for me I shouldn't want him to stay with me for five minutes.

LADY KITTY: One says that when one's sure of a man's love, but when one isn't any more—oh, it's so different. In those circumstances one's got to keep a man's love. It's the only thing one has.

ELIZABETH: I'm a human being. I can stand on my own feet.

LADY KITTY: Have you any money of your own?

ELIZABETH: None.

LADY KITTY: Then how can you stand on your own feet? You think I'm a silly, frivolous woman, but I've learned something in a bitter school. They can make what laws they like, they can give us the suffrage, but when you come down to bedrock it's the man who pays the piper who calls the tune. Woman will only be the equal of man when she earns her living in the same way that he does.

ELIZABETH: [*Smiling*] It sounds rather funny to hear you talk like that.

LADY KITTY: A cook who marries a butler can snap her fingers in his face because she can earn just as much as he can. But a woman in your position and a woman in mine will always be dependent on the men who keep them.

ELIZABETH: I don't want luxury. You don't know how sick I am of all this beautiful furniture. These over-decorated houses are like a prison in which I can't breathe. When I drive about in a Callot frock and a Rolls-Royce I envy the shop-girl in a coat and skirt whom I see jumping on the tailboard of a bus.

LADY KITTY: You mean that if need be you could earn your own living?

ELIZABETH: Yes.

LADY KITTY: What could you be? A nurse or a typist. It's nonsense. Luxury saps a woman's nerve. And when she's known it once it becomes a necessity.

ELIZABETH: That depends on the woman.

LADY KITTY: When we're young we think we're different from everyone else, but when we grow a little older we discover we're all very much of a muchness.

ELIZABETH: You're very kind to take so much trouble about me.

LADY KITTY: It breaks my heart to think that you're going to make the same pitiful mistake that I made.

ELIZABETH: Oh, don't say it was that, don't, don't.

LADY KITTY: Look at me, Elizabeth, and look at Hughie. Do you think it's been a success? If I had my time over again do you think I'd do it again? Do you think he would?

ELIZABETH: You see, you don't know how much I love Teddie.

LADY KITTY: And do you think I didn't love Hughie? Do you think he didn't love me?

ELIZABETH: I'm sure he did.

LADY KITTY: Oh, of course in the beginning it was heavenly. We felt so brave and adventurous and we were so much in love. The first two years were wonderful. People cut me, you know, but I didn't mind. I thought love was everything. It *is* a little uncomfortable when you come upon an old friend and go towards her eagerly, so glad to see her, and are met with an icy stare.

ELIZABETH: Do you think friends like that are worth having?

LADY KITTY: Perhaps they're not very sure of themselves. Perhaps they're honestly shocked. It's a test one had better not put one's friends to if one can help it. It's rather bitter to find how few one has.

ELIZABETH: But one has some.

LADY KITTY: Yes, they ask you to come and see them when they're quite certain no one will be there who might object to meeting you. Or else they say to you: "My dear, you know I'm devoted to you, and I wouldn't mind at all, but my girl's growing up—I'm sure you understand; you won't think it unkind of me if I don't ask you to the house?"

ELIZABETH: [*Smiling*] That doesn't seem to me very serious.

LADY KITTY: At first I thought it rather a relief, because it threw Hughie and me together more. But you know, men are very funny. Even when they are in love they're not in love all day long. They want change and recreation.

ELIZABETH: I'm not inclined to blame them for that, poor dears.

LADY KITTY: Then we settled in Florence. And because we couldn't get the society we'd been used to we became used to the society we could get. Loose women and vicious men. Snobs who liked to patronize people with a handle to their names. Vague Italian Princes who were glad to borrow a few francs from Hughie and seedy countesses who liked to drive with me in the Cascine. And then Hughie began to hanker after his old life. He wanted to go big game shooting, but I dared not let him go. I was afraid he'd never come back.

ELIZABETH: But you knew he loved you.

LADY KITTY: Oh, my dear, what a blessed institution marriage is—for women, and what fools they are to meddle with it! The Church is so wise to take its stand on the indi—indi——

ELIZABETH: Solu——

LADY KITTY: Bility of marriage. Believe me, it's no joke when you have to rely only on yourself to keep a man. I could never afford to grow old. My

dear, I'll tell you a secret that I've never told a living soul.

ELIZABETH: What is that?

LADY KITTY: My hair is not naturally this color.

ELIZABETH: Really.

LADY KITTY: I touch it up. You would never have guessed, would you?

ELIZABETH: Never.

LADY KITTY: Nobody does. My dear, it's white, premature of course, but white. I always think it's a symbol of my life. Are you interested in symbolism? I think it's too wonderful.

ELIZABETH: I don't think I know very much about it.

LADY KITTY: However tired I've been I've had to be brilliant and gay. I've never let Hughie see the aching heart behind my smiling eyes.

ELIZABETH: [*Amused and touched*] You poor dear.

LADY KITTY: And when I saw he was attracted by some one else the fear and the jealousy that seized me! You see, I didn't dare make a scene as I should have done if I'd been married—I had to pretend not to notice.

ELIZABETH: [*Taken aback*] But do you mean to say he fell in love with anyone else?

LADY KITTY: Of course he did eventually.

ELIZABETH: [*Hardly knowing what to say*] You must have been very unhappy.

LADY KITTY: Oh, I was dreadfully. Night after night I sobbed my heart out when Hughie told me he was going to play cards at the club and I knew he was with that odious woman. Of course, it wasn't as if there weren't plenty of men who were only too anxious to console me. Men have always been attracted by me, you know.

ELIZABETH: Oh, of course, I can quite understand it.

LADY KITTY: But I had my self-respect to think of. I felt that whatever Hughie did I would do nothing that I should regret.

ELIZABETH: You must be very glad now.

LADY KITTY: Oh, yes. Notwithstanding all my temptations I've been absolutely faithful to Hughie in spirit.

ELIZABETH: I don't think I quite understand what you mean.

LADY KITTY: Well, there was a poor Italian boy, young Count Castel Giovanni, who was so desperately in love with me that his mother begged me not to be too cruel. She was afraid he'd go into a consumption. What could I do? And then, oh, years later, there was Antonio Melita. He said he'd shoot himself unless I—well, you understand—couldn't let the poor boy shoot himself.

ELIZABETH: D'you think he really would have shot himself?

LADY KITTY: Oh, one never knows, you know. Those Italians are so passionate. He was really rather a lamb. He had such beautiful eyes.

[Elizabeth *looks at her for a long time and a certain horror seizes her of this dissolute, painted old woman*]

ELIZABETH: [*Hoarsely*] Oh, but I think that's—dreadful.

LADY KITTY: Are you shocked? One sacrifices one's life for love and then one finds that love doesn't last. The tragedy of love isn't death or separation. One gets over them. The tragedy of love is indifference.

[Arnold *comes in*]

ARNOLD: Can I have a little talk with you, Elizabeth?

ELIZABETH: Of course.

ARNOLD: Shall we go for a stroll in the garden?

ELIZABETH: If you like.

LADY KITTY: No, stay here. I'm going out anyway. [*Exit* Lady Kitty]

ARNOLD: I want you to listen to me for a few minutes, Elizabeth. I was so taken aback by what you told me just now that I lost my head. I was rather absurd and I beg your pardon. I said things I regret.

ELIZABETH: Oh, don't blame yourself. I'm sorry that I should have given you occasion to say them.

ARNOLD: I want to ask you if you've quite made up your mind to go.

ELIZABETH: Quite.

ARNOLD: Just now I seem to have said all that I didn't want to say and nothing that I did. I'm stupid and tongue-tied. I never told you how deeply I loved you.

ELIZABETH: Oh, Arnold!

ARNOLD: Please let me speak now. It's so very difficult. If I seemed absorbed in politics and the house, and so on, to the exclusion of my interest in you, I'm dreadfully sorry. I suppose it was absurd of me to think you would take my great love for granted.

ELIZABETH: But, Arnold, I'm not reproaching you.

ARNOLD: I'm reproaching myself. I've been tactless and neglectful. But I do ask you to believe that it hasn't been because I didn't love you. Can you forgive me?

ELIZABETH: I don't think that there's anything to forgive.

ARNOLD: It wasn't till today when you talked of leaving me that I realized how desperately in love with you I was.

ELIZABETH: After three years?

ARNOLD: I'm so proud of you. I admire you so much. When I see you at a party, so fresh and lovely, and everybody wondering at you, I have a sort of little thrill because you're mine, and afterwards I shall take you home.

ELIZABETH: Oh, Arnold, you're exaggerating.

ARNOLD: I can't imagine this house without you. Life seems on a sudden all empty and meaningless. Oh, Elizabeth, don't you love me at all?

ELIZABETH: It's much better to be honest. No.

ARNOLD: Doesn't my love mean anything to you?

ELIZABETH: I'm very grateful to you. I'm sorry to cause you pain. What would be the good of my staying with you when I should be wretched all the time?

ARNOLD: Do you love that man as much as all that? Does my unhappiness mean nothing to you?

ELIZABETH: Of course it does. It breaks my heart. You see, I never knew I meant so much to you. I'm so touched. And I'm so sorry, Arnold, really sorry. But I can't help myself.

ARNOLD: Poor child, it's cruel of me to torture you.

ELIZABETH: Oh, Arnold, believe me, I have tried to make the best of it. I've tried to love you, but I can't. After all, one either loves or one doesn't. Trying is no help. And now I'm at the end of my tether. I can't help the consequences—I must do what my whole self yearns for.

ARNOLD: My poor child, I'm so afraid you'll be unhappy. I'm so afraid you'll regret.

ELIZABETH: You must leave me to my fate. I hope you'll forget me and all the unhappiness I've caused you.

ARNOLD: [*There is a pause. Arnold walks up and down the room reflectively. He stops and faces her*] If you love this man and want to go to him I'll do nothing to prevent you. My only wish is to do what is best for you.

ELIZABETH: Arnold, that's awfully kind of you. If I'm treating you badly at least I want you to know that I'm grateful for all your kindness to me.

ARNOLD: But there's one favor I should like you to do me. Will you?

ELIZABETH: Oh, Arnold, of course I'll do anything I can.

ARNOLD: Teddie hasn't very much money. You've been used to a certain amount of luxury, and I can't bear to think that you should do without anything you've had. It would kill me to think that you were suffering any hardship or privation.

ELIZABETH: Oh, but Teddie can earn enough for our needs. After all, we don't want much money.

ARNOLD: I'm afraid my mother's life hasn't been easy, but it's obvious that the only thing that's made it possible is that Porteous was rich. I want you to let me make you an allowance of two thousand a year.

ELIZABETH: Oh, no, I couldn't think of it. It's absurd.

ARNOLD: I beg you to accept it. You don't know what a difference it will make.

ELIZABETH: It's awfully kind of you, Arnold. It humiliates me to speak about it. Nothing would induce me to take a penny from you.

ARNOLD: Well, you can't prevent me from opening an account at my bank in your name. The money shall be paid in every quarter whether you touch it or not, and if you happen to want it, it will be there waiting for you.

ELIZABETH: You overwhelm me, Arnold. There's

only one thing I want you to do for me. I should be very grateful if you would divorce me as soon as you possibly can.

ARNOLD: No, I won't do that. But I'll give you cause to divorce me.

ELIZABETH: You!

ARNOLD: Yes. But of course you'll have to be very careful for a bit. I'll put it through as quickly as possible, but I'm afraid you can't hope to be free for over six months.

ELIZABETH: But, Arnold, your seat and your political career!

ARNOLD: Oh, well, my father gave up his seat under very similar circumstances. He's got along very comfortably without politics.

ELIZABETH: But they're your whole life.

ARNOLD: After all one can't have it both ways. You can't serve God and Mammon. If you want to do the decent thing you have to be prepared to suffer for it.

ELIZABETH: But I don't want you to suffer for it.

ARNOLD: At first I rather hesitated at the scandal. But I daresay that was only weakness on my part. Under the circumstances I should have liked to keep out of the Divorce Court if I could.

ELIZABETH: Arnold, you're making me absolutely miserable.

ARNOLD: What you said before dinner was quite right. It's nothing for a man, but it makes so much difference to a woman. Naturally I must think of you first.

ELIZABETH: That's absurd. It's out of the question. Whatever there's to pay I must pay it.

ARNOLD: It's not very much I'm asking you, Elizabeth.

ELIZABETH: I'm taking everything from you.

ARNOLD: It's the only condition I make. My mind is absolutely made up. I will never divorce you, but I will enable you to divorce me.

ELIZABETH: Oh, Arnold, it's cruel to be so generous.

ARNOLD: It's not generous at all. It's the only way I have of showing you how deep and passionate and sincere my love is for you. [There is a silence. He holds out his hand] Good night. I have a great deal of work to do before I go to bed.

ELIZABETH: Good night.

ARNOLD: Do you mind if I kiss you?

ELIZABETH: [With agony] Oh, Arnold!

[He gravely kisses her on the forehead and then goes out. Elizabeth stands lost in thought. She is shattered. Lady Kitty and Porteous come in. Lady Kitty wears a cloak]

LADY KITTY: You're alone, Elizabeth?

ELIZABETH: That note you asked me about, Lady Kitty, from Teddie . . .

LADY KITTIE: Yes?

ELIZABETH: He wanted to have a talk with me before he went away. He's waiting for me in the summer house by the tennis court. Would Lord

Porteous mind going down and asking him to come here?

PORTEOUS: Certainly. Certainly.

ELIZABETH: Forgive me for troubling you. But it's very important.

PORTEOUS: No trouble at all. [He goes out]

LADY KITTY: Hughie and I will leave you alone.

ELIZABETH: But I don't want to be left alone. I want you to stay.

LADY KITTY: What are you going to say to him?

ELIZABETH: [Desperately] Please don't ask me questions. I'm so frightfully unhappy.

LADY KITTY: My poor child!

ELIZABETH: Oh, isn't life rotten? Why can't one be happy without making other people unhappy?

LADY KITTY: I wish I knew how to help you. I'm simply devoted to you. [She hunts about in her mind for something to do or say] Would you like my lipstick?

ELIZABETH: [Smiling through her tears] Thanks. I never use one.

LADY KITTY: Oh, but just try. It's such a comfort when you're in trouble.

[Enter Porteous and Teddie]

PORTEOUS: I brought him. He said he'd be damned if he'd come.

LADY KITTY: When a lady sent for him? Are these the manners of the young men of today?

TEDDIE: When you've been solemnly kicked out of a house once I think it seems rather pushing to come back again as though nothing had happened.

ELIZABETH: Teddie, I want you to be serious.

TEDDIE: Darling, I had such a rotten dinner at that pub. If you ask me to be serious on the top of that I shall cry.

ELIZABETH: Don't be idiotic, Teddie. [Her voice faltering] I'm so utterly wretched.

[He looks at her for a moment gravely]

TEDDIE: What is it?

ELIZABETH: I can't come away with you, Teddie.

TEDDIE: Why not?

ELIZABETH: [Looking away in embarrassment] I don't love you enough.

TEDDIE: Fiddle!

ELIZABETH: [With a flash of anger] Don't say "Fiddle" to me.

TEDDIE: I shall say exactly what I like to you.

ELIZABETH: I won't be bullied.

TEDDIE: Now look here, Elizabeth, you know perfectly well that I'm in love with you, and I know perfectly well that you're in love with me. So what are you talking nonsense for?

ELIZABETH: [Her voice breaking] I can't say it if you're cross with me.

TEDDIE: [Smiling very tenderly] I'm not cross with you, silly.

ELIZABETH: It's harder still when you're being rather an owl.

TEDDIE: [With a chuckle] Am I mistaken in thinking you're not very easy to please?

ELIZABETH: Oh, it's monstrous. I was all wrought up and ready to do anything, and now you've thoroughly put me out. I feel like a great big fat balloon that some one has put a long pin into. [*With a sudden look at him*] Have you done it on purpose?

TEDDIE: Upon my soul I don't know what you're talking about.

ELIZABETH: I wonder if you're really much cleverer than I think you are.

TEDDIE: [*Taking her hands and making her sit down*] Now tell me exactly what you want to say. By the way, do you want Lady Kitty and Lord Porteous to be here?

ELIZABETH: Yes.

LADY KITTY: Elizabeth asked us to stay.

TEDDIE: Oh, I don't mind, bless you. I only thought you might feel rather in the way.

LADY KITTY: [*Frigidly*] A gentlewoman never feels in the way, Mr. Luton.

TEDDIE: Won't you call me Teddie? Everybody does, you know.

[Lady Kitty *tries to give him a withering look, but she finds it very difficult to prevent herself from smiling.* Teddie *strokes* Elizabeth's *hands. She draws them away*]

ELIZABETH: No, don't do that. Teddie, it wasn't true when I said I didn't love you. Of course I love you. But Arnold loves me, too. I didn't know how much.

TEDDIE: What has he been saying to you?

ELIZABETH: He's been very good to me, and so kind. I didn't know he could be so kind. He offered to let me divorce him.

TEDDIE: That's very decent of him.

ELIZABETH: But don't you see, it ties my hands. How can I accept such a sacrifice? I should never forgive myself if I profited by his generosity.

TEDDIE: If another man and I were devilish hungry and there was only one mutton chop between us, and he said, "You eat it," I wouldn't waste a lot of time arguing. I'd wolf it before he changed his mind.

ELIZABETH: Don't talk like that. It maddens me. I'm trying to do the right thing.

TEDDIE: You're not in love with Arnold; you're in love with me. It's idiotic to sacrifice your life for a slushy sentiment.

ELIZABETH: After all, I did marry him.

TEDDIE: Well, you made a mistake. A marriage without love is no marriage at all.

ELIZABETH: *I* made the mistake. Why should he suffer for it? If anyone has to suffer it's only right that I should.

TEDDIE: What sort of a life do you think it would be with him? When two people are married it's very difficult for one of them to be unhappy without making the other unhappy too.

ELIZABETH: I can't take advantage of his generosity.

TEDDIE: I daresay he'll get a lot of satisfaction out of it.

ELIZABETH: You're being beastly, Teddie. He was simply wonderful. I never knew he had it in him. He was really noble.

TEDDIE: You are talking rot, Elizabeth.

ELIZABETH: I wonder if you'd be capable of acting like that.

TEDDIE: Acting like what?

ELIZABETH: What would you do if I were married to you and came and told you I loved somebody else and wanted to leave you?

TEDDIE: You have very pretty blue eyes, Elizabeth. I'd black first one and then the other. And after that we'd see.

ELIZABETH: You damned brute!

TEDDIE: I've often thought I wasn't quite a gentleman. Had it ever struck you?

[*They look at one another for a while*]

ELIZABETH: You know, you are taking an unfair advantage of me. I feel as if I came to you quite unsuspectingly and when I wasn't looking you kicked me on the shins.

TEDDIE: Don't you think we'd get on rather well together?

PORTEOUS: Elizabeth's a fool if she don't stick to her husband. It's bad enough for the man, but for the woman—it's damnable. I hold no brief for Arnold. He plays bridge like a foot. Saving your presence, Kitty, I think he's a prig.

LADY KITTY: Poor dear, his father was at his age. I daresay he'll grow out of it.

PORTEOUS: But you stick to him, Elizabeth, stick to him. Man is a gregarious animal. We're members of a herd. If we break the herd's laws we suffer for it. And we suffer damnably.

LADY KITTY: Oh, Elizabeth, my dear child, don't go. It's not worth it. It's not worth it. I tell you that, and I've sacrificed everything to love.

[*A pause*]

ELIZABETH: I'm afraid.

TEDDIE: [*In a whisper*] Elizabeth.

ELIZABETH: I can't face it. It's asking too much of me. Let's say good-by to one another, Teddie. It's the only thing to do. And have pity on me. I'm giving up all my hope of happiness.

[*He goes up to her and looks into her eyes*]

TEDDIE: But I wasn't offering you happiness. I don't think my sort of love tends to happiness. I'm jealous. I'm not a very easy man to get on with. I'm often out of temper and irritable. I should be fed to the teeth with you sometimes, and so would you be with me. I daresay we'd fight like cat and dog, and sometimes we'd hate each other. Often you'd be wretched and bored stiff and lonely, and often you'd be frightfully homesick, and then you'd regret all you'd lost. Stupid women would be rude to you because we'd run away together. And some of them would cut you. I don't offer you peace and quietness. I offer you unrest and anxiety. I don't offer you happiness. I offer you love.

ELIZABETH: [*Stretching out her arms*] You hateful creature. I absolutely adore you!

[*He throws his arms round her and kisses her passionately on the lips*]

LADY KITTY: Of course the moment he said he'd give her a black eye I knew it was finished.

PORTEOUS: [*Good-humoredly*] You are a fool, Kitty.

LADY KITTY: I know I am, but I can't help it.

TEDDIE: Let's make a bolt for it now.

ELIZABETH: Shall we?

TEDDIE: This minute.

PORTEOUS: You're damned fools, both of you, damned fools! If you like you can have my car.

TEDDIE: That's awfully kind of you. As a matter of fact I got it out of the garage. It's just along the drive.

PORTEOUS: [*Indignantly*] How do you mean, you got it out of the garage?

TEDDIE: Well, I thought there'd be a lot of bother, and it seemed to me the best thing would be for Elizabeth and me not to stand upon the order of our going, you know. Do it now. An excellent motto for a business man.

PORTEOUS: Do you mean to say you were going to steal my car?

TEDDIE: Not exactly. I was only going to bolshevize it, so to speak.

PORTEOUS: I'm speechless. I'm absolutely speechless.

TEDDIE: Hang it all, I couldn't carry Elizabeth all the way to London. She's so damned plump.

ELIZABETH: You dirty dog!

PORTEOUS: [*Spluttering*] Well, well, well! . . . [*Helplessly*] I like him, Kitty, it's no good pretending I don't. I like him.

TEDDIE: The moon's shining, Elizabeth. We'll drive all through the night.

PORTEOUS: They'd better go to San Michele. I'll wire to have it got ready for them.

LADY KITTY: That's where we went when Hughie and I . . . [*Faltering*] Oh, you dear things, how I envy you!

PORTEOUS: [*Mopping his eyes*] Now don't cry, Kitty. Confound you, don't cry.

TEDDIE: Come, darling.

ELIZABETH: But I can't go like this.

TEDDIE: Nonsense! Lady Kitty will lend you her cloak. Won't you?

LADY KITTY: [*Taking it off*] You're capable of tearing it off my back if I don't.

TEDDIE: [*Putting the cloak on* Elizabeth] And we'll buy you a tooth-brush in London in the morning.

LADY KITTY: She must write a note for Arnold. I'll put it on her pin-cushion.

TEDDIE: Pin-cushion be blowed! Come, darling. We'll drive through the dawn and through the sunrise.

ELIZABETH: [*Kissing* Lady Kitty *and* Porteous] Good-by. Good-by.

[Teddie *stretches out his hand and she takes it. Hand in hand they go out into the night*]

LADY KITTY: Oh, Hughie, how it all comes back to me! Will they suffer all we suffered? And have we suffered all in vain?

PORTEOUS: My dear, I don't know that in life it matters so much what you do as what you are. No one can learn by the experience of another because no circumstances are quite the same. If we made rather a hash of things perhaps it was because we were rather trivial people. You can do anything in this world if you're prepared to take the consequences, and consequences depend on character.

[*Enter* Champion-Cheney, *rubbing his hands. He is as pleased as Punch*]

C.-C.: Well, I think I've settled the hash of that young man.

LADY KITTY: Oh!

C.-C.: You have to get up very early in the morning to get the better of your humble servant.

[*There is the sound of a car starting*]

LADY KITTY: What is that?

C.-C.: It sounds like a car. I expect it's your chauffeur taking one of the maids for a joy-ride.

PORTEOUS: Whose hash are you talking about?

C.-C.: Mr. Edward Luton's, my dear Hughie. I told Arnold exactly what to do and he's done it. What makes a prison? Why, bars and bolts. Remove them and a prisoner won't want to escape. Clever, I flatter myself.

PORTEOUS: You were always that, Clive, but at the moment you're obscure.

C.-C.: I told Arnold to go to Elizabeth and tell her she could have her freedom. I told him to sacrifice himself all along the line. I know what women are. The moment every obstacle was removed to her marriage with Teddie Luton, half the allurement was gone.

LADY KITTY: Arnold did that?

C.-C.: He followed my instructions to the letter. I've just seen him. She's shaken. I'm willing to bet five hundred pounds to a penny that she won't bolt. A downy old bird, eh? Downy's the word. Downy.

[*He begins to laugh. They laugh, too. Presently they are all three in fits of laughter*]

CURTAIN

R. C. Sherriff

(1896–——)

England, proverbially the land where people move slowly if steadily, first had its big season of antiwar drama in 1929—eleven years after the end of the First World War and only four years before Adolf Hitler began preparing a second holocaust. And even that season is memorable largely for one play by a hitherto inconspicuous young man: *Journey's End.*

Robert Cedric Sherriff was to all appearances a typical member of the World War generation. Born in 1896, he had hardly completed his education at New College, Oxford, and joined the Sun Insurance Company, when he was called to take up arms in his country's service. Like his Stanhope in *Journey's End,* he became a captain in the British forces at the green age of twenty-one. Then, upon being discharged, he became just another young man in pursuit of a livelihood. He returned to his commonplace profession of junior insurance clerk, relieving the tedium with week-end sports and amateur playwriting for schools and clubs. His memories of Armageddon were not, however, eradicated by civilian life but merely submerged. When it became necessary for him to compose a play for his boat club, which required an all-male cast, he drew readily enough upon his recollections. The result was the war play *Journey's End.*

From 1914 to 1919, England's commercial West End theatres subsisted on musical fluff and saccharine. *Chu Chin Chow* delighted the multitude; *Romance* rolled up over a thousand performances; *Peg o' My Heart* enjoyed a three years' run; *Daddy Long Legs* was a great favorite; and James M. Barrie's *A Kiss for Cinderella* and *The Old Lady Shows Her Medals* tugged at the heartstrings. Then the First World War gradually found expression. Not unexpectedly, the quickest and profoundest response came from Shaw, whose *Heartbreak House* announced a general collapse of the old order. Many of Shaw's later blasts on the sad state of affairs in Europe and on the ruinous folly of mankind are also traceable to the war's effects. Galsworthy's reaction, in *The Skin-Game,* was typically that of a gentleman, moralist, and moderator. Among the younger playwrights, Somerset Maugham, who had served in the medical corps and eased his convalescence in a Swiss sanatorium with the farcical amenities of *Home and Beauty,* delivered himself in 1933 of a long-suppressed bitterness in the drama of postwar doldrums *For Services Rendered.* The still younger playwright Noel Coward reflected the cynicism and instability of the postwar generation in

his comedies and farces. (It is perhaps significant that he wrote one of the most successful of these, *Private Lives,* while performing in *Journey's End* with a theatrical company in Shanghai.) Direct attacks on imperialism or militarism, such as C. K. Munro's *The Rumour* and Allan Monkhouse's *The Conquering Hero,* also appeared on the stage, and Robert Nichols and Maurice Browne, in *Wings Over Europe,* envisioned the possibility of war-making statesmen being checkmated by resolute men of science who have split the atom.

It is true, nevertheless, that the keenest effects of the war, as well as of its aftermath, were not felt in the British theatre. It was in Central Europe, which had been defeated and was most thoroughly shaken by the postwar upheaval, that the drama of protest reached the highest pitch, with Toller's *Man and the Masses,* Werfel's *Goat Song,* Chlumberg's *Miracle at Verdun,* Piscator's *The Good Soldier Schweik,* and Friedrich Wolf's revolutionary *Sailors of Cattaro.* In England, only Sherriff's *Journey's End,* presented in the same year as Munro's *The Rumour* and O'Casey's *The Silver Tassie* (produced in London because the Dublin Abbey Theatre had rejected it), gave complete testimony of the trenches and the shellfire, the terror and the fortitude of the men at the front, and the dreadful waste of young blood. "For ten years," writes the English chronicler Ernest Short in his *Theatrical Cavalcade,* "the topic had seemed too painful for public discussion."

Journey's End was typically British in its refinement of taste, its emphasis on courtesy, its strict division of the characters into gentlemen and comic plebeians, and its tribute to hero-worship and gallantry, which almost suggested a glorification of war not intended by the author. ("There were those," Ernest Short recalls, "who welcomed *Journey's End* as excellent anti-war propaganda, but its stark picture of life in the trenches stirred many more to a sense of nobility which underlies even the ugliest battle when it is waged for something other than self.") But the quiet truthfulness of the play, its picture of shattered nerves and summary annihilation, proved overwhelming. After vain attempts to place the seemingly unpromising play with commercial managements and a single Sunday-evening performance by the Stage Society of London, Sherriff won the interest of the enterprising Arts Theatre Club producer Maurice Browne. The West End production, which opened in January 1929, won immediate acclaim; it became, in fact, one of the most memorable successes of the postwar theatre. As a result, Browne was sufficiently supplied with funds to give London eleven unconventional productions within a year, including an *Othello* with Paul Robeson playing the Moor, more than a dozen years before he played this role in New York for the Theatre Guild. And Sherriff became the young writer of whom the English theatre expected most in serious drama.

Nothing that Sherriff created after this war drama added materially to his reputation as a playwright. He wrote a successful novel, *A Fortnight in September,* and the scenario of the postwar film *The Road Back* (1932). But his comedy *Badger's Green* failed to interest London; and although his *St. Helena,* a collaboration with Jeanne de Casalis, was a considered antiheroic treatment of Napoleon in exile and enjoyed the services of Maurice Evans, it proved too static for the stage. Its author may have defined his limitations when he wrote, "If I had not been a quite ordinary man, I should have got *Journey's End* all wrong." But *Journey's End* was not an ordinary play, and at least for one brief period Sherriff was no ordinary man.

Burns Mantle wrote of Sherriff's play: "If his drama lacks something of the vitality of the Stallings-Anderson study [*What Price Glory?*] of the American doughboy cursing his way through the grime and muck of the trenches, or playing at hearts with the wenches back of the line, it added something a little finer in the way of character analyses and psychological problems and never failed to give its human soldier men something interesting to say or do at entrance and exit and in between. It is an ambling play, in a physical sense, but one that weaves a spell of reality about its players and stimulates the imagination of its auditors quite as much by the art of understatement as by the crash of exciting scenes. The big dramatic moment in *Journey's End* is a daylight raid conducted by twelve men of whom five come back. But a scene of quiet intensity in which a former headmaster of a boy's school talks of hollyhocks and *Alice in Wonderland* to keep the young lieutenant's mind off the approach of the zero hour is one that many *Journey's End* enthusiasts boast of remembering most vividly."

This description can hardly be improved upon, and will be questioned only by Americans who resented traces of British snobbery after seeing the New York performance. Such criticism may be considered inconsequential, however, beside the quality that Stark Young has called its "poetry of human concern," its "tenderness toward all life," its "shyness and passion." That Sherriff sometimes tended to be romantic or sentimental does not invalidate his genuineness. The play, with its objective note-taking, is essentially British in its restraint. Stark Young expressed this well when, reporting on the March 1929 Broadway production, in which Colin Keith-Johnston distinguished himself as Stanhope, he wrote, "The best things in *Journey's End* are not so much written there as they are felt by the author."

BIBLIOGRAPHY: Ernest Short, *Theatrical Cavalcade* (pp. 152–154), 1942; Stark Young, *Immortal Shadows* (pp. 110–113), 1948.

JOURNEY'S END

By R. C. Sherriff

CHARACTERS

CAPTAIN HARDY	SECOND LIEUTENANT RALEIGH	THE COLONEL
LIEUTENANT OSBORNE	CAPTAIN STANHOPE	SECOND LIEUTENANT TROTTER
PRIVATE MASON	SECOND LIEUTENANT HIBBERT	GERMAN SOLDIER
	COMPANY SERGEANT-MAJOR	

THE SCENE.—*A dug-out in the British trenches before St. Quentin.*

A few rough steps lead into the trench above, through a low doorway. A table occupies a good space of the dug-out floor. A wooden frame, covered with wire netting, stands against the left wall and serves the double purpose of a bed and a seat for the table. A wooden bench against the back wall makes another seat, and two boxes serve for the other sides.

Another wire-covered bed is fixed in the right corner beyond the doorway.

Gloomy tunnels lead out of the dug-out to left and right.

Except for the table, beds, and seats, there is no furniture save the bottles holding the candles, and a few tattered magazine pictures pinned to the wall of girls in flimsy costumes.

The earth walls deaden the sounds of war, making them faint and far away, although the front line is only fifty yards ahead. The flames of the candles that burn day and night are steady in the still, damp air.

ACT ONE: Evening on Monday, March 18, 1918
ACT TWO:
   Scene I: Tuesday morning
   Scene II: Tuesday afternoon
ACT THREE:
   Scene I: Wednesday afternoon
   Scene II: Wednesday night
   Scene III: Thursday, towards dawn

ACT I.

The evening of a March day. A pale glimmer of moonlight shines down the narrow steps into one corner of the dug-out. Warm yellow candle-flames light the other corner from the necks of two bottles on the table. Through the doorway can be seen the misty gray parapet of a trench and a narrow strip of starlit sky. A bottle of whisky, a jar of water, and a mug stand on the table among a litter of papers

and magazines. An officer's equipment hangs in a jumbled mass from a nail in the wall.

Captain Hardy, *a red-faced, cheerful-looking man, is sitting on a box by the table, intently drying a sock over a candle-flame. He wears a heavy trench-boot on his left leg, and his right foot, which is naked, is held above the damp floor by resting it on his left knee. His right boot stands on the floor beside him. As he carefully turns the sock this way and that—feeling it against his face to see if it is dry—he half sings, half hums a song—humming when he is not quite sure of the words, and marking time with the toes of his right foot.*

HARDY: "One and Two it's with Maud and Lou;
Three and Four, two girls more;
Five and Six it's with—hm—hm—hm—
Seven, Eight, Clara and Caroline——"
   [*He lapses into an indefinite humming, and finishes with a lively burst*]
"Tick!—Tock!—wind up the clock,
And we'll start the day over again."
   [*A man's legs appear in the moonlit trench above, and a tall, thin man comes slowly down the dug-out steps, stooping low to avoid the roof. He takes his helmet off and reveals a fine head, with close-cropped, iron-gray hair. He looks about forty-five—physically as hard as nails*]

HARDY: [*Looking round*] Hullo, Osborne! Your fellows arriving?

OSBORNE: [*Hitching off his pack and dropping it in a corner*] Yes. They're just coming in.

HARDY: Splendid! Have a drink.

OSBORNE: Thanks.
   [*He crosses and sits on the left-hand bed*]

HARDY: [*Passing the whisky and a mug*] Don't have too much water. It's rather strong to-day.

OSBORNE: [*Slowly mixing a drink*] I wonder what it *is* they put in the water.

HARDY: Some sort of disinfectant, I suppose.

OSBORNE: I'd rather have the microbes, wouldn't you?

HARDY: *I* would—yes—

OSBORNE: Well, cheero.

HARDY: Cheero. Excuse my sock, won't you?

OSBORNE: Certainly. It's a nice-looking sock.

HARDY: It is rather, isn't it? Guaranteed to keep the feet dry. Trouble is, it gets so wet doing it.

OSBORNE: Stanhope asked me to come and take over. He's looking after the men coming in.

HARDY: Splendid! You know, I'm awfully glad you've come.

OSBORNE: I heard it was a quiet bit of line up here.

HARDY: Well, yes—in a way. But you never know. Sometimes nothing happens for hours on end; then —all of a sudden—"over she comes!"—rifle grenades —Minnies—and those horrid little things like pine-apples—you know.

OSBORNE: I know.

HARDY: Swish—swish—swish—swish—*bang!*

OSBORNE: All right—all right—I know.

HARDY: They simply blew us to bits yesterday. Minnies—enormous ones; about twenty. Three bang in the trench. I really *am* glad you've come; I'm not simply being polite.

OSBORNE: Do much damage?

HARDY: Awful. A dug-out got blown up and came down in the men's tea. They were frightfully annoyed.

OSBORNE: I know. There's nothing worse than dirt in your tea.

HARDY: By the way, you know the big German attack's expected any day now?

OSBORNE: It's been expected for the last month.

HARDY: Yes, but it's very near now; there's funny things happening over in the Boche country. I've been out listening at night when it's quiet. There's more transport than usual coming up—you can hear it rattling over the *pavé* all night; more trains in the distance—puffing up and going away again, one after another, bringing up loads and loads of men——

OSBORNE: Yes. It's coming—pretty soon now.

HARDY: Are you here for six days?

OSBORNE: Yes.

HARDY: Then I should think you'll get it—right in the neck.

OSBORNE: Well, you won't be far away. Come along, let's do this handing over. Where's the map?

HARDY: Here we are. [*He gropes among the papers on the table and finds a tattered map*] We hold about two hundred yards of front line. We've got a Lewis gun just here—and one here, in this little sap. Sentry posts where the crosses are——

OSBORNE: Where do the men sleep?

HARDY: *I* don't know. The sergeant-major sees to that. [*He points off to the left*] The servants and signalers sleep in there. Two officers in here, and three in there. [*He points to the right-hand tunnel*] That is, if you've *got* five officers.

OSBORNE: We've only got four at present, but a new man's coming up to-night. He arrived at transport lines a day or two ago.

HARDY: I hope you get better luck than I did with my last officer. He got lumbago the first night and went home. Now he's got a job lecturing young officers on "Life in the Front Line."

OSBORNE: Yes. They do send some funny people over here nowadays. I hope we're lucky and get a youngster straight from school. They're the kind that do best.

HARDY: I suppose they are, really.

OSBORNE: Five beds, you say? [*He examines the one he is sitting on*] Is this the best one?

HARDY: Oh, no. [*He points to the bed in the right corner*] That's mine. The ones in the other dug-out haven't got any bottoms to them. You keep yourself in by hanging your arms and legs over the sides. Mustn't hang your legs too low, or the rats gnaw your boots.

OSBORNE: You got many rats here?

HARDY: I should say—roughly—about two million; but then, of course, I don't see them all. [*He begins to put on his sock and draw on his boot*] Well, there's nothing else you want to know, is there?

OSBORNE: You haven't told me anything yet.

HARDY: What else do you *want* to know.

OSBORNE: Well, what about trench stores?

HARDY: You *are* a fussy old man. Anybody'd think you were in the army. [*He finds a tattered piece of paper*] Here you are: 115 rifle grenades— I shouldn't use them if I were you; they upset Jerry and make him offensive. Besides, they are rusty, in any case. Then there's 500 Mills bombs, 34 gum boots——

OSBORNE: That's seventeen pairs——

HARDY: Oh, no; twenty-five right leg, and nine left leg. But everything's down here. [*He hands the list to* Osborne]

OSBORNE: Did you check it when you took over?

HARDY: No. I think the sergeant-major did. It's quite all right.

OSBORNE: I expect Stanhope would like to see you before you go. He always likes a word with the company commander he's relieving.

HARDY: How *is* the dear young boy? Drinking like a fish, as usual?

OSBORNE: Why do you say that?

HARDY: Well, damn it, it's just the natural thing to ask about Stanhope. [*He pauses, and looks curiously at* Osborne] Poor old man. It must be pretty rotten for you, being his second in command, and you such a quiet, sober old thing.

OSBORNE: He's a long way the best company commander we've got.

HARDY: Oh, he's a good chap, I know. But I never *did* see a youngster put away the whisky he does. D'you know, the last time we were out resting at Valennes he came to supper with us and drank a whole bottle in one hour fourteen minutes—we timed him.

OSBORNE: I suppose it amused everybody; I suppose everybody cheered him on, and said what a splendid achievement it was.

HARDY: He didn't want any "cheering" on——

OSBORNE: No, but everybody thought it was a big thing to do. [*There is a pause*] Didn't they?

HARDY: Well, you can't help, somehow, *admiring* a fellow who can do that—and then pick out his own hat all by himself and walk home——

OSBORNE: When a boy like Stanhope gets a reputation out here for drinking, he turns into a kind of freak show exhibit. People pay with a bottle of whisky for the morbid curiosity of seeing him drink it.

HARDY: Well, naturally, you're biased. You have to put him to bed when he gets home.

OSBORNE: It rather reminds you of bear-baiting—or cock-fighting—to sit and watch a boy drink himself unconscious.

HARDY: Well, damn it, it's pretty dull without *something* to liven people up. I mean, after all— Stanhope really *is* a sort of freak; I mean it *is* jolly fascinating to see a fellow drink like he does—glass after glass. He didn't go home on his last leave, did he?

OSBORNE: No.

HARDY: I suppose he didn't think he was fit to meet Papa. [*A pause*] You know his father's vicar of a country village?

OSBORNE: I know.

HARDY: [*Laughing*] Imagine Stanhope spending his leave in a country vicarage sipping tea! He spent his last leave in Paris, didn't he?

OSBORNE: Yes.

HARDY: I bet it was *some* leave!

OSBORNE: Do you know how long he's been out here?

HARDY: A good time, I know.

OSBORNE: Nearly three years. He came out straight from school—when he was eighteen. He's commanded this company for a year—in and out of the front line. He's never had a rest. Other men come over here and go home ill, and young Stanhope goes on sticking it, month in and month out.

HARDY: Oh, I know he's a jolly good fellow——

OSBORNE: I've seen him on his back all day with trench fever—then on duty all night——

HARDY: Oh, I know; he's a splendid chap!

OSBORNE: And because he's stuck it till his nerves have got battered to bits, he's called a drunkard.

HARDY: Not a drunkard; just a—just a hard drinker; but you're quite right about his nerves. They *are* all to blazes. Last time out resting we were playing bridge and something happened—I don't remember what it was; some silly little argument— and all of a sudden he jumped up and knocked all the glasses off the table! Lost control of himself; and then he—sort of—came to—and cried——

OSBORNE: Yes, I know.

HARDY: You heard about it?

OSBORNE: He told me.

HARDY: Did he? We tried to hush it up. It just shows the state he's in. [*He rises and puts on his*

pack. There is a pause] You know, Osborne, you ought to be commanding this company.

OSBORNE: Rubbish!

HARDY: Of course you ought. It sticks out a mile. I know he's got pluck and all that, but, damn it, man, you're twice his age—and think what a dear, level-headed old thing you are.

OSBORNE: Don't be an ass. He was out here before I joined up. His experience alone makes him worth a dozen people like me.

HARDY: You know as well as I do, you ought to be in command.

OSBORNE: There isn't a man to touch him as a commander of men. He'll command the battalion one day if——

HARDY: Yes, if! [*He laughs*]

OSBORNE: You don't know him as I do; I love that fellow. I'd go to hell with him.

HARDY: Oh, you sweet, sentimental old darling!

OSBORNE: Come along. Finish handing over and stop blithering.

HARDY: There's nothing else to do.

OSBORNE: What about the log-book?

HARDY: God! you are a worker. Oh, well. Here we are. [*He finds a tattered little book among the papers on the table*] Written right up to date; here's my last entry: "5 p.m. to 8 p.m. All quiet. German airman flew over trenches. Shot a rat."

OSBORNE: Did he?

HARDY: No. I shot the rat, you ass. Well, finish up your whisky. I want to pack my mug. I'll leave you that drop in the bottle.

OSBORNE: Thanks.

[*He drinks up his whisky and hands* Hardy *the mug*]

HARDY: [*Tucking the mug into his pack*] I'll be off.

OSBORNE: Aren't you going to wait and see Stanhope?

HARDY: Well, no, I don't specially want to see him. He's so fussy about the trenches. I expect they *are* rather dirty. He'll talk for hours if he catches me. [*He hitches his pack over his shoulders, hangs on his gas satchel, map-case, binoculars, compass-case, until he looks like a traveling peddler. As he dresses:*] Well, I hope you have a nice six days. Don't forget to change your clothes if you get wet.

OSBORNE: No, Papa.

HARDY: And don't forget about the big attack.

OSBORNE: Oh, Lord, no, I mustn't miss that; I'll make a note in my diary.

HARDY: [*Fully dressed*] There we are! Do I look every inch a soldier?

OSBORNE: Yes. I should get quite a fright if I were a German and met you coming round a corner.

HARDY: I should bloody well hope you would.

OSBORNE: Shouldn't be able to run away for laughing.

HARDY: Now, don't be rude. [*He leans over to*

light a cigarette from a candle, and looks down on the table] Well, I'm damned. Still at it!

OSBORNE: What is?

HARDY: Why, that little cockroach. It's been running round and round that candle since tea-time; must have done a mile.

OSBORNE: I shouldn't hang about here if I were a cockroach.

HARDY: Nor should I. I'd go home. Ever had cockroach races?

OSBORNE: No.

HARDY: Great fun. We've had 'em every evening.

OSBORNE: What are the rules?

HARDY: Oh, you each have a cockroach, and start 'em in a line. On the word "Go" you dig your cockroach in the ribs and steer him with a match across the table. I won ten francs last night—had a *splendid* cockroach. I'll give you a tip.

OSBORNE: Yes?

HARDY: Promise not to let it go any farther?

OSBORNE: Yes.

HARDY: Well, if you want to get the best pace out of a cockroach, dip it in whisky—makes 'em go like hell!

OSBORNE: Right. Thanks awfully.

HARDY: Well, I must be off. Cheero!

OSBORNE: Cheero!

HARDY: [*Goes up the narrow steps into the trench above, singing softly and happily to himself*]

"One and Two, it's with Maud and Lou;
Three and Four, two girls more———"

[*The words trail away into the night. Osborne rises and takes his pack from the floor to the bed by the table. While he undoes it a* Soldier Servant *comes out of the tunnel from the left with a tablecloth over his arm and a plate with half a loaf of bread on it*]

MASON: Excuse me, sir. Can I lay supper?

OSBORNE: Yes, do.

[*He shuffles up the papers from the table and puts them on the bed*]

MASON: Thank you, sir.

[*He lays the table*]

OSBORNE: What are you going to tempt us with to-night, Mason?

MASON: Soup, sir—cutlets—and pineapple.

OSBORNE: [*Suspiciously*] Cutlets?

MASON: Well, sir—well, yes, sir!—cutlets.

OSBORNE: What sort of cutlets?

MASON: Now, sir, you've got me. I shouldn't like to commit meself too deep, sir.

OSBORNE: Ordinary ration meat?

MASON: Yes, sir. Ordinary ration meat, but a noo shape, sir. Smells like liver, sir, but it 'asn't got that smooth, wet look that liver's got. [Mason *leaves the dug-out. Osborne sits up to the table and examines the map. Voices come from trench above; a gruff voice says:*] "This is 'C' Company 'Eadquarters, sir."

[*A boyish voice replies*] "Oh, thanks." [*There is a pause, then the gruff voice says*] "Better go down, sir." [*The boyish voice replies*] "Yes. Righto."

[*An* Officer *comes groping down the steps and stands in the candle-light. He looks round, a little bewildered. He is a well-built, healthy-looking boy of about eighteen, with the very new uniform of a second lieutenant. Osborne looks up from the trench map, surprised and interested to see a stranger*]

OSBORNE: Hullo!

RALEIGH: Good evening [*He notices Osborne's gray hair and adds*] sir.

OSBORNE: You the new officer?

RALEIGH: Er—yes. I've been to Battalion Headquarters. They told me to report here.

OSBORNE: Good. We've been expecting you. Sit down, won't you?

RALEIGH: Thanks.

[*He sits gingerly on the box opposite* Osborne]

OSBORNE: I should take your pack off.

RALEIGH: Oh, right.

[*He slips his pack from his shoulders*]

OSBORNE: Will you have a drink?

RALEIGH: Er—well———

OSBORNE: You don't drink whisky?

RALEIGH: [*Hastily*] Oh, yes—er—just a small one, sir.

OSBORNE: [*Pouring out a small whisky and adding water*] Whisky takes away the taste of the water———

RALEIGH: Oh, yes?

[*He pauses, and laughs nervously*]

OSBORNE: —and the water takes away the taste of the whisky. [*He hands* Raleigh *the drink*] Just out from England?

RALEIGH: Yes, I landed a week ago.

OSBORNE: Boulogne?

RALEIGH: Yes. [*A pause, then he self-consciously holds up his drink*] Well, here's luck, sir.

OSBORNE: [*Taking a drink himself*] Good luck.

[*He takes out a cigarette case*] Cigarette?

RALEIGH: Thanks.

OSBORNE: [*Holding a bottle across so that* Raleigh *can light his cigarette from the candle in it*] Ever been up in the line before?

RALEIGH: Oh, no. You see, I only left school at the end of last summer term.

OSBORNE: I expect you find it a bit strange.

RALEIGH: [*Laughing*] Yes—I do—a bit———

OSBORNE: My name's Osborne. I'm second in command of the company. You only call me "sir" in front of the men.

RALEIGH: I see. Thanks.

OSBORNE: You'll find the other officers call me "Uncle."

RALEIGH: Oh, yes? [*He smiles*]

OSBORNE: What's *your* name?

RALEIGH: Raleigh.

OSBORNE: I knew a Raleigh. A master at Rugby.

RALEIGH: Oh? He may be a relation. I don't

know. I've got lots of uncles and—and things like that.

OSBORNE: We've only just moved into these trenches. Captain Stanhope commands the company.

RALEIGH: [*Suddenly brightening up*] I know. It's a frightful bit of luck.

OSBORNE: Why? D'you know him?

RALEIGH: Yes, rather! We were at school together —at least—of course—I was only a kid and he was one of the big fellows; he's three years older than I am.

[*There is a pause;* Osborne *seems to be waiting for* Raleigh *to go on, then suddenly he says:*]

OSBORNE: He's up in the front line at present, looking after the relief. [*Another pause*] He's a splendid chap.

RALEIGH: Isn't he? He was skipper of football at Barford, and kept wicket for the eleven. A jolly good bat, too.

OSBORNE: Did you play football—and cricket?

RALEIGH: Oh, yes. Of course, I wasn't in the same class as Dennis—I say, I suppose I ought to call him Captain Stanhope?

OSBORNE: Just "Stanhope."

RALEIGH: I see. Thanks.

OSBORNE: Did you get your colors?

RALEIGH: I did for football. Not cricket.

OSBORNE: Football and cricket seem a long way from here.

RALEIGH: [*Laughing*] They do, rather.

OSBORNE: We play a bit when we're out of the line.

RALEIGH: Good!

OSBORNE: [*Thoughtfully*] So you were at school with Stanhope. [*Pause*] I wonder if he'll remember you? I expect you've grown in the last three years.

RALEIGH: Oh, I think he'll remember me. [*He stops, and goes on rather awkwardly*] You see, it wasn't only that we were just at school together; our fathers were friends, and Dennis used to come and stay with us in the holidays. Of course, at school I didn't see much of him, but in the holidays we were terrific pals.

OSBORNE: He's a fine company commander.

RALEIGH: I bet he is. Last time he was on leave he came down to school; he'd just got his M.C. and been made a captain. He looked splendid! It sort of —made me feel——

OSBORNE: —keen?

RALEIGH: Yes. Keen to get out here. I was frightfully keen to get into Dennis' regiment. I thought, perhaps, with a bit of luck I might get to the same battalion.

OSBORNE: It's a big fluke to have got to the same company.

RALEIGH: I know. It's an amazing bit of luck. When I was at the base I did an awful thing. You see, my uncle's at the base—he has to detail officers to regiments——

OSBORNE: General Raleigh?

RALEIGH: Yes. I went to see him on the quiet and asked him if he could get me into this battalion. He bit my head off, and said I'd got to be treated like everybody else——

OSBORNE: Yes?

RALEIGH: —and the next day I was told I *was* coming to this battalion. Funny, wasn't it?

OSBORNE: Extraordinary coincidence!

RALEIGH: And when I got to Battalion Headquarters, and the colonel told me to report to "C" Company, I could have cheered. I expect Dennis'll be frightfully surprised to see me. I've got a message for him.

OSBORNE: From the colonel?

RALEIGH: No. From my sister.

OSBORNE: Your sister?

RALEIGH: Yes. You see, Dennis used to stay with us, and naturally my sister [*He hesitates*]—well— perhaps I ought not—

OSBORNE: That's all right. I didn't actually know that Stanhope——

RALEIGH: They're not—er—officially engaged——

OSBORNE: No?

RALEIGH: She'll be awfully glad I'm with him here; I can write and tell her about him. He doesn't say much in his letters; can we write often?

OSBORNE: Oh, yes. Letters are collected every day. [*There is a pause*]

RALEIGH: You don't think Dennis'll mind my— sort of—forcing myself into his company? I never thought of that; I was so keen.

OSBORNE: No, of course he won't. [*Pause*] You say it's—it's a good time since you last saw him?

RALEIGH: Let's see. It was in the summer last year—nearly a year ago.

OSBORNE: You know, Raleigh, you mustn't expect to find him—quite the same.

RALEIGH: Oh?

OSBORNE: You see, he's been out here a long time. It—it tells on a man—rather badly ——

RALEIGH: [*Thinking*] Yes, of course, I suppose it does.

OSBORNE: You may find he's—he's a little bit quick-tempered.

RALEIGH: [*Laughing*] Oh, I know old Dennis' temper! I remember once at school he caught some chaps in a study with a bottle of whisky. Lord! the roof nearly blew off. He gave them a dozen each with a cricket stump. [Osborne *laughs*] He was so keen on the fellows in the house keeping fit. He was frightfully down on smoking—and that sort of thing.

OSBORNE: You must remember he's commanded this company for a long time—through all sorts of rotten times. It's—it's a big strain on a man.

RALEIGH: Oh, it must be.

OSBORNE: If you notice a—difference in Stanhope —you'll know it's only the strain——

RALEIGH: Oh, yes.

[Osborne *rouses himself and speaks briskly*]

OSBORNE: Now, let's see. We've got five beds here —one each. Two in here and three in that dug-out there. I'm afraid you'll have to wait until the others come and pick the beds they want.

RALEIGH: Righto!

OSBORNE: Have you got a blanket?

RALEIGH: Yes, in my pack.

[*He rises to get it*]

OSBORNE: Better wait and unpack when you know where you're sleeping.

RALEIGH: Righto!

[*He sits down again*]

OSBORNE: We never undress when we're in the line. You can take your boots off now and then in the daytime, but it's better to keep pretty well dressed always.

RALEIGH: I see. Thanks.

OSBORNE: I expect we shall each do about three hours on duty at a time and then six off. We all go on duty at stand-to. That's at dawn and dusk.

RALEIGH: Yes.

OSBORNE: I expect Stanhope'll send you on duty with one of us at first—till you get used to it.

[*There is a pause. Raleigh turns, and looks curiously up the steps into the night*]

RALEIGH: Are we in the front line here?

OSBORNE: No. That's the support line outside. The front line's about fifty yards farther on.

RALEIGH: How frightfully quiet it is!

OSBORNE: It's often quiet—like this.

RALEIGH: I thought there would be an awful row here—all the time.

OSBORNE: Most people think that.

[*Pause*]

RALEIGH: I've never known anything so quiet as those trenches we came by; just now and then I heard a rifle firing, like the range at Bisley, and a sort of rumble in the distance.

OSBORNE: Those are the guns up north—up Wipers way. The guns are always going up there; it's never quiet like this. [*Pause*] I expect it's all very strange to you?

RALEIGH: It's—it's not exactly what I thought. It's just this—this quiet that seems so funny.

OSBORNE: A hundred yards from here the Germans are sitting in *their* dug-outs, thinking how quiet it is.

RALEIGH: Are they as near as that?

OSBORNE: About a hundred yards.

RALEIGH: It seems—uncanny. It makes me feel we're—we're all just waiting for something.

OSBORNE: We are, generally, just waiting for something. When anything happens, it happens quickly. Then we just start waiting again.

RALEIGH: I never thought it was like that.

OSBORNE: You thought it was fighting all the time?

RALEIGH: [*Laughing*] Well, yes, in a way.

OSBORNE: [*After puffing at his pipe in silence for a while*] Did you come up by trench to-night—or over the top?

RALEIGH: By trench. An amazing trench—turning and twisting for miles, over a sort of plain.

OSBORNE: Lancer's Alley it's called.

RALEIGH: Is it? It's funny the way it begins—in that ruined village, a few steps down into the cellar of a house—then right under the house and through a little garden—and then under the garden wall— then alongside an enormous ruined factory place— then miles and miles of plains, with those green lights bobbing up and down ahead—all along the front as far as you can see.

OSBORNE: Those are the Very lights. Both sides fire them over No Man's Land—to watch for raids and patrols.

RALEIGH: I knew they fired lights. [*Pause*] I didn't expect so many—and to see them so far away.

OSBORNE: I know. [*He puffs at his pipe*] There's something rather romantic about it all.

RALEIGH: [*Eagerly*] Yes, I thought that, too.

OSBORNE: You must always think of it like that if you can. Think of it all as—as romantic. It helps.

[Mason *comes in with more dinner utensils*]

MASON: D'you expect the captain soon, sir? The soup's 'ot.

OSBORNE: He ought to be here very soon now. This is Mr. Raleigh, Mason.

MASON: Good evening, sir.

RALEIGH: Good evening.

MASON: [*To* Osborne] I've 'ad rather a unpleasant surprise, sir.

OSBORNE: What's happened?

MASON: You know that tin o' pineapple chunks I got, sir?

OSBORNE: Yes?

MASON: Well, sir, I'm sorry to say it's apricots.

OSBORNE: Good heavens! It must have given you a turn.

MASON: I distinctly said "pineapple chunks" at the canteen.

OSBORNE: Wasn't there a label on the tin?

MASON: No, sir. I pointed that out to the man. I said was 'e *certain* it was pineapple chunks?

OSBORNE: I suppose he said he was.

MASON: Yes, sir. 'E said a leopard can't change its spots, sir.

OSBORNE: What have leopards got to do with pineapple?

MASON: That's just what *I* thought, sir. Made me *think* there was something fishy about it. You see, sir, I know the captain can't stand the sight of apricots. 'E said next time we 'ad them 'e'd wring my neck.

OSBORNE: Haven't you anything else?

MASON: There's a pink blancmange I've made, sir. But it ain't anywhere near stiff yet.

OSBORNE: Never mind. We must have the apricots and chance it.

MASON: Only I thought I'd tell you, sir, so as the captain wouldn't blame me.

OSBORNE: All right, Mason. [*Voices are heard in the trench above*] That sounds like the captain coming now.

MASON [*Hastening away*] I'll go and dish out the soup, sir.

[*The voices grow nearer; two figures appear in the trench above and grope down the steps— the leading figure tall and thin, the other short and fat. The tall figure is Captain Stanhope. At the bottom of the steps he straightens himself, pulls off his pack and drops it on the floor. Then he takes off his helmet and throws it on the right-hand bed. Despite his stars of rank he is no more than a boy; tall, slimly built, but broad-shouldered. His dark hair is carefully brushed; his uniform, though old and war-stained, is well cut and cared for. He is good-looking, rather from attractive features than the healthy good looks of Raleigh. Although tanned by months in the open air, there is a pallor under his skin and dark shadows under his eyes. His short and fat companion— Second Lieutenant Trotter—is middle-aged and homely-looking. His face is red, fat, and round; apparently he has put on weight during his war service, for his tunic appears to be on the verge of bursting at the waist. He carries an extra pack belonging to the officer left on duty in the line*]

STANHOPE: [*As he takes off his pack, gas satchel, and belt*] Has Hardy gone?

OSBORNE: Yes. He cleared off a few minutes ago.

STANHOPE: Lucky for him he did. I had a few words to say to Master Hardy. You never saw the blasted mess those fellows left the trenches in. Dugouts smell like cess-pits; rusty bombs; damp rifle grenades; it's perfectly foul. Where are the servants?

OSBORNE: In there.

STANHOPE: [*Calling into* Mason's *dug-out*] Hi! Mason!

MASON: [*Outside*] Coming, sir! Just bringing the soup, sir.

STANHOPE: [*Taking a cigarette from his case and lighting it*] Damn the soup! Bring some whisky!

OSBORNE: Here's a new officer, Stanhope—just arrived.

STANHOPE: Oh, sorry. [*He turns and peers into the dim corner where* Raleigh *stands smiling awkwardly*] I didn't see you in this miserable light.

[*He stops short at the sight of* Raleigh. *There is silence*]

RALEIGH: Hullo, Stanhope!

[Stanhope *stares at* Raleigh *as though dazed.* Raleigh *takes a step forward, half raises his hand, then lets it drop to his side*]

STANHOPE: [*In a low voice*] How did you—get here?

RALEIGH: I was told to report to your company, Stanhope.

STANHOPE: Oh. I see. Rather a coincidence.

RALEIGH: [*With a nervous laugh*] Yes.

[*There is a silence for a moment, broken by* Osborne *in a matter-of-fact voice*]

OSBORNE: I say, Stanhope, it's a terrible business. We thought we'd got a tin of pineapple chunks; it turns out to be apricots.

TROTTER: Ha! Give me apricots every time! I 'ate pineapple chunks; too bloomin' sickly for me!

RALEIGH: I'm awfully glad I got to your company, Stanhope.

STANHOPE: When did you get here?

RALEIGH: Well, I've only just come.

OSBORNE: He came up with the transport while you were taking over.

STANHOPE: I see.

[Mason *brings in a bottle of whisky, a mug, and two plates of soup—so precariously that* Osborne *has to help with the soup plates onto the table*]

STANHOPE: [*With sudden forced gaiety*] Come along, Uncle! Come and sit here. [*He waves towards the box on the right of the table*] You better sit there, Raleigh.

RALEIGH: Right!

TROTTER: [*Taking a pair of pince-nez from his tunic pocket, putting them on, and looking curiously at* Raleigh] You Raleigh?

RALEIGH: Yes. [*Pause*]

TROTTER: I'm Trotter.

RALEIGH: Oh, yes? [*Pause*]

TROTTER: How *are* you?

RALEIGH: Oh, all right, thanks.

TROTTER: Been out 'ere before?

RALEIGH: No.

TROTTER: Feel a bit odd, I s'pose?

RALEIGH: Yes. A bit.

TROTTER: [*Getting a box to sit on*] Oh, well, you'll get used to it; you'll feel you've been 'ere a year in about an hour's time.

[*He puts the box on its side and sits on it. It is too low for the table, and he puts it on its end. It is then too high. He tries the other side, which is too low; he finally contrives to make himself comfortable by sitting on his pack, placed on the side of the box. Mason arrives with two more plates of soup*]

OSBORNE: What kind of soup is this, Mason?

MASON: It's yellow soup, sir.

OSBORNE: It's got a very deep yellow flavor.

TROTTER: [*Taking a melodious sip*] It wants some pepper; bring some pepper, Mason.

MASON: [*Anxiously*] I'm very sorry, sir. When the mess box was packed the pepper was omitted, sir.

TROTTER: [*Throwing his spoon with a clatter into the plate*] Oh, I say, but damn it!

OSBORNE: We must have pepper. It's a disinfectant.

TROTTER. You must have pepper in soup!

STANHOPE: [*Quietly*] Why wasn't it packed, Mason?

MASON: It—it was missed, sir.

STANHOPE: Why?

MASON: [*Miserably*] Well, sir, I left it to——

STANHOPE: Then I advise you never to leave it to anyone else again—unless you want to rejoin your platoon out there.

[*He points into the moonlit trench*]

MASON: I'm—I'm very sorry, sir.

STANHOPE: Send one of the signalers.

MASON: Yes, sir. [*He hastens to the tunnel entrance and calls*] Bert, you're wanted!

[*A* Soldier *appears, with a rifle slung over his shoulder. He stands stiffly to attention*]

STANHOPE: Do you know "A" Company Headquarters?

SOLDIER: Yes, sir.

STANHOPE: Go there at once and ask Captain Willis, with my compliments, if he can lend me a little pepper.

SOLDIER: Very good, sir.

[*He turns smartly and goes up the steps,* Mason *stopping him for a moment to say confidentially:* "A *screw* of pepper you ask for."]

OSBORNE: We must have pepper.

TROTTER: I mean—after all—war's bad enough with pepper—[*noisy sip*]—but war without pepper—it's—it's bloody awful!

OSBORNE: What's it like outside?

TROTTER: Quiet as an empty 'ouse. There's a nasty noise going on up north.

OSBORNE: Wipers, I expect. I believe there's trouble up there. I wish we knew more of what's going on.

TROTTER: So do I. Still, my wife reads the papers every morning and writes and tells me.

OSBORNE: Hardy says they had a lively time here yesterday. Three big Minnies right in the trench.

TROTTER: I know. And they left the bloomin' 'oles for us to fill in. [Mason *arrives with cutlets on enamel plates*] What's this?

MASON: Meat, sir.

TROTTER: I know that. What sort?

MASON: Sort of cutlet, sir.

TROTTER: Sort of cutlet, is it? You know, Mason, there's cutlets and cutlets.

MASON: I know, sir; that one's a cutlet.

TROTTER: Well, it won't let me cut it.

MASON: No, sir?

TROTTER: That's a joke.

MASON: Oh. Right, sir. [*He goes out*]

OSBORNE: [*Studying the map*] There's a sort of ruin marked on this map—just in front of here, in No Man's Land—called Beauvais Farm.

TROTTER: That's what we saw sticking up, skipper. I wondered what it was.

STANHOPE: Better go out and look at it to-night.

TROTTER: I 'ate ruins in No Man's Land; too bloomin' creepy for me.

OSBORNE: There's only about sixty yards of No Man's Land, according to this map—narrower on the left, from the head of this sap; only about fifty.

TROTTER: [*Who has been looking curiously at* Stanhope, *eating his meal with lowered head*] Cheer up, skipper. You *do* look glum!

STANHOPE: I'm tired.

OSBORNE: I should turn in and get some sleep after supper.

STANHOPE: I've got hours of work before I sleep.

OSBORNE: I'll do the duty roll and see the sergeant-major—and all that.

STANHOPE: That's all right, Uncle. I'll see to it. [*He turns to* Raleigh *for the first time*] Trotter goes on duty directly he's had supper. You better go on with him—to learn.

RALEIGH: Oh, right.

TROTTER: Look 'ere, skipper, it's nearly eight now; couldn't we make it 'alf-past?

STANHOPE: No, I told Hibbert he'd be relieved at eight. Will you take from eleven till two, Uncle?

OSBORNE: Right.

STANHOPE: Hibbert can do from two till four, and I'll go on from then till standto. That'll be at six.

TROTTER: Well, boys! 'Ere we are for six days again. Six bloomin' eternal days. [*He makes a calculation on the table*] That's a hundred and forty-four hours; eight thousand six 'undred and forty minutes. *That* doesn't sound so bad; we've done twenty of 'em already. I've got an idea! I'm going to draw a hundred and forty-four little circles on a bit o' paper, and every hour I'm going to black one in; that'll make the time go all right.

STANHOPE: It's five to eight now. You better go and relieve Hibbert. Then you can come back at eleven o'clock and black in three of your bloody little circles.

TROTTER: I 'aven't 'ad my apricots yet!

STANHOPE: We'll keep your apricots till you come back.

TROTTER: I never knew anything like a war for upsetting meals. I'm always down for dooty in the middle of one.

STANHOPE: That's because you never stop eating.

TROTTER: Any'ow, let's 'ave some coffee. Hi! Mason! Coffee!

MASON: Coming, sir!

TROTTER: [*Getting up*] Well, I'll get dressed. Come on, Raleigh.

TROTTER: Just wear your belt with revolver case on it. Must have your revolver to shoot rats. And your gas mask—come here—I'll show you. [*He helps* Raleigh] You wear it sort of tucked up under your chin like a serviette.

RALEIGH: Yes. I was shown the way at home.

TROTTER: Now your hat. That's right. You don't

want a walking-stick. It gets in your way if you have to run fast.

RALEIGH: Why—er—do you have to run fast?

TROTTER: Oh, Lord, yes, often! If you see a Minnie coming—that's a big trench-mortar shell, you know—short for *Minnywerfer*—you see 'em coming right out of the Boche trenches, right up in the air, then down, down, down; and you have to judge it and run like stink sometimes.

[Mason *comes in with two cups of coffee*]

MASON: Coffee, sir?

TROTTER: Thanks.

[*He takes the cup and drinks standing up*]

RALEIGH: Thanks.

TROTTER: You might leave my apricots out, Mason. Put 'em on a separate plate and keep 'em in there.

[*He points to* Mason's *dug-out*]

MASON: Very good, sir.

TROTTER: If you bring 'em in 'ere you never know *what* might 'appen to 'em.

MASON: No, sir.

TROTTER: "B" Company on our right, aren't they, skipper?

STANHOPE: Yes. There's fifty yards of undefended area in between. You better patrol that a good deal.

TROTTER: Aye, aye, sir.

STANHOPE: Have a look at that Lewis gun position on the left. See what field of fire they've got.

TROTTER: Aye, aye, sir. You don't want me to go out and look at that blinkin' ruin?

STANHOPE: I'll see to that.

TROTTER: Good. I don't fancy crawling about on my belly after that cutlet. [*To* Raleigh] Well, come on, my lad, let's go and see about this 'ere war.

[*The two go up the steps, leaving* Stanhope *and* Osborne *alone.* Mason *appears at his dug-out door*]

MASON: Will you take apricots, sir?

STANHOPE: No, thanks.

MASON: Mr. Osborne?

OSBORNE: No, thanks.

MASON: I'm sorry about them being apricots, sir. I explained to Mr. Osborne——

STANHOPE: [*Curtly*] That's all right, Mason—thank you.

MASON: Very good, sir. [*He goes out*]

OSBORNE: [*Over by the right-hand bed*] Will you sleep here? This was Hardy's bed.

STANHOPE: No. You sleep there. I'd rather sleep by the table here. I can get up and work without disturbing you.

OSBORNE: This is a better one.

STANHOPE: You take it. Must have a little comfort in your old age, Uncle.

OSBORNE: I wish you'd turn in and sleep for a bit.

STANHOPE: Sleep?—I can't sleep. [*He takes a whisky and water. A man appears in the trench and comes down the steps—a small, slightly built man*

in the early twenties, with a little mustache and a pallid face. Looking hard at the newcomer] Well, Hibbert?

HIBBERT: Everything's fairly quiet. Bit of sniping somewhere to our left; some rifle grenades coming over just on our right.

STANHOPE: I see. Mason's got your supper.

HIBBERT: [*Gently rubbing his forehead*] I don't think I can manage any supper to-night, Stanhope. It's this beastly neuralgia. It seems to be right inside this eye. The beastly pain gets worse every day.

STANHOPE: Some hot soup and a good tough chop'll put that right.

HIBBERT: I'm afraid the pain rather takes my appetite away. I'm damn sorry to keep on talking about it, Stanhope, only I thought you'd wonder why I don't eat anything much.

STANHOPE: Try and forget about it.

HIBBERT: [*With a little laugh*] Well— I wish I could.

STANHOPE: Get tight.

HIBBERT: I think I'll turn straight in for a rest—and try and get some sleep.

STANHOPE: All right. Turn in. You're in that dug-out there. Here's your pack. [*He picks up the pack that* Trotter *brought down*] You go on duty at two. I take over from you at four. I'll tell Mason to call you.

HIBBERT: [*Faintly*] Oh, right—thanks, Stanhope—cheero.

STANHOPE: Cheero.

[*He watches* Hibbert *go down the tunnel into the dark*]

HIBBERT: [*Returning*] Can I have a candle?

STANHOPE: [*Taking one from the table*] Here you are.

HIBBERT: Thanks.

[*He goes out again. There is silence.* Stanhope *turns to* Osborne]

STANHOPE: Another little worm trying to wriggle home.

OSBORNE: [*Filling his pipe*] I wonder if he really is bad. He looks rotten.

STANHOPE: Pure bloody funk, that's all. He could eat if he wanted to; he's starving himself purposely. Artful little swine! Neuralgia's a splendid idea. No proof as far as I can see.

OSBORNE: You can't help feeling sorry for him. I think he's tried hard.

STANHOPE: How long's he been out here? Three months, I suppose. Now he's decided he's done his bit. He's decided to go home and spend the rest of the war in comfortable nerve hospitals. Well, he's mistaken. I let Warren get away like that, but no more.

OSBORNE: I don't see how you can prevent a fellow going sick.

STANHOPE: I'll have a quiet word with the doctor before *he* does. He thinks he's going to wriggle off before the attack. We'll just see about that. No man of mine's going sick before the attack. They're going to take an equal chance—together.

OSBORNE: Raleigh looks a nice chap.

STANHOPE: [Looking hard at Osborne before replying] Yes.

OSBORNE: Good-looking youngster. At school with you, wasn't he?

STANHOPE: Has he been talking already?

OSBORNE: He just mentioned it. It was a natural thing to tell me when he knew you were in command [Stanhope is lounging at the table with his back to the wall. Osborne, sitting on the right-hand bed, begins to puff clouds of smoke into the air as he lights his pipe] He's awfully pleased to get into your company. [Stanhope makes no reply. He picks up a pencil and scribbles on the back of a magazine] He seems to think a lot of you.

STANHOPE: [Looking up quickly at Osborne and laughing] Yes, I'm his hero.

OSBORNE: It's quite natural.

STANHOPE: You think so?

OSBORNE: Small boys at school generally have heir heroes.

STANHOPE: Yes. Small boys at school do.

OSBORNE: Often it goes on as long as——

STANHOPE: —as long as the hero's a hero.

OSBORNE: It often goes on all through life.

STANHOPE: I wonder. How many battalions are there in France?

OSBORNE: Why?

STANHOPE: We'll say fifty divisions. That's a hundred and fifty brigades—four hundred and fifty battalions. That's one thousand eight hundred companies [He looks up at Osborne from his calculations on the magazine cover] There are one thousand eight hundred companies in France, Uncle. Raleigh might have been sent to any one of those, and, my God! he comes to mine.

OSBORNE: You ought to be glad. He's a good-looking youngster. I like him.

STANHOPE: I knew you'd like him. Personality, isn't it? [He takes a worn leather case from his breast pocket and hands a small photograph to Osborne] I've never shown you that, have I?

OSBORNE: [Looking at the photograph] No. [Pause] Raleigh's sister, isn't it?

STANHOPE: How did you know?

OSBORNE: There's a strong likeness.

STANHOPE: I suppose there is.

OSBORNE: [Intent on the picture] She's an awfully nice-looking girl.

STANHOPE: A photo doesn't show much, really. Just a face.

OSBORNE: She looks awfully nice. [There is silence. Stanhope lights a cigarette. Osborne hands the photo back] You're a lucky chap.

STANHOPE: [Putting the photo back into his case] I don't know why I keep it, really.

OSBORNE: Why? Isn't she—I thought——

STANHOPE: What did you think?

OSBORNE: Well, I thought that perhaps she was waiting for you.

STANHOPE: Yes. She is waiting for me—and she doesn't know. She thinks I'm a wonderful chap—commanding a company. [He turns to Osborne and points up the steps into the line] She doesn't know that if I went up those steps into the front line—without being doped with whisky—I'd go mad with fright.

[There is a pause. Osborne stirs himself to speak]

OSBORNE: Look here, old man. I've meant to say it for a long time, but it sounds like damned impudence. You've done longer out here than any man in the battalion. It's time you went away for a rest. It's due to you.

STANHOPE: You suggest that I go sick, like that little worm in there—neuralgia in the eye?

[He laughs and takes a drink]

OSBORNE: No. Not that. The colonel would have sent you down long ago, only——

STANHOPE: Only—what?

OSBORNE: Only he can't spare you.

STANHOPE: [Laughing] Oh, rot!

OSBORNE: He told me.

STANHOPE: He thinks I'm in such a state I want a rest, is that it?

OSBORNE: No. He thinks it's due to you.

STANHOPE: It's all right, Uncle. I'll stick it out now. It may not be much longer now. I've had my share of luck—more than my share. There's not a man left who was here when I came. But it's rather damnable for that boy—of all the boys in the world—to have come to me. I might at least have been spared that.

OSBORNE: You're looking at things in rather a black sort of way.

STANHOPE: I've just told you. That boy's a hero-worshiper. I'm three years older than he is. You know what that means at school. I was skipper of football and all that sort of thing. It doesn't sound much to a man out here—but it does at school with a kid of fourteen. Damn it, Uncle, you're a schoolmaster; you know.

OSBORNE: I've just told you what I think of hero-worship.

STANHOPE: Raleigh's father knew mine, and I was told to keep an eye on the kid. I rather liked the idea of looking after him. I made him keen on the right things—and all that. His people asked me to stay with them one summer. I met his sister then——

OSBORNE: Yes?

STANHOPE: At first I thought of her as another kid like Raleigh. It was just before I came out here for the first time that I realized what a topping girl she was. Funny how you realize it suddenly. I just prayed to come through the war—and—and do things—and keep absolutely fit for her.

OSBORNE: You've done pretty well. An M.C. and a company.

STANHOPE: [*Taking another whisky*] It was all right at first. When I went home on leave after the first six months it was jolly fine to feel I'd done a little to make her pleased. [*He takes a gulp of his drink*] It was after I came back here—in that awful affair on Vimy Ridge. I knew I'd go mad if I didn't break the strain. I couldn't bear being fully conscious all the time—you've felt that, Uncle, haven't you?

OSBORNE: Yes, often.

STANHOPE: There were only two ways of breaking the strain. One was pretending I was ill—and going home; the other was this. [*He holds up his glass*] Which would you pick, Uncle?

OSBORNE: I haven't been through as much as you. I don't know yet.

STANHOPE: I thought it all out. It's a slimy thing to go home if you're not really ill, isn't it?

OSBORNE: I think it is.

STANHOPE: Well, then [*He holds his glass up to Osborne*] Cheero, and long live the men who go home with neuralgia. [*He puts his glass down*] I didn't go home on my last leave. I couldn't bear to meet her, in case she realized——

OSBORNE: When the war's over—and the strain's gone—you'll soon be as fit as ever, at your age.

STANHOPE: I've hoped that all the time. I'd go away for months and live in the open air—and get fit—and then go back to her.

OSBORNE: And so you can.

STANHOPE: If Raleigh had gone to one of those other one thousand eight hundred companies.

OSBORNE: I don't see why you should think——

STANHOPE: Oh, for Lord's sake, don't be a damn fool. *You* know! You know he'll write and tell her I reek of whisky all day.

OSBORNE: Why should he? He's not a——

STANHOPE: Exactly. He's not a damned little swine who'd deceive his sister.

OSBORNE: He's very young; he's got hundreds of strange things to learn; he'll realize that men are—different—out here.

STANHOPE: It's no good, Uncle. Didn't you see him sitting there at supper?—staring at me?—and wondering? He's up in those trenches now—still wondering—and beginning to understand. All these months he's wanted to be with me out here. Poor little devil!

OSBORNE: I believe Raleigh'll go on liking you—and looking up to you—through everything. There's something very deep and rather fine about hero-worship.

STANHOPE: Hero-worship be damned! [*He pauses, then goes on, in a strange, high-pitched voice*] You know, Uncle, I'm an *awful* fool. I'm *captain* of this company. What's that bloody little prig of a boy matter? D'you see? He's a little prig. Wants to write home and tell Madge all about *me*. Well, he

won't; d'you see, Uncle? He *won't* write. Censorship! I censor his letters—cross out all he says about me.

OSBORNE: You can't read his letters!

STANHOPE: [*Dreamily*] Cross out all he says about me. Then we all go west in the big attack—and she goes on thinking I'm a fine fellow forever—and ever—and ever.

[*He pours out a drink, murmuring "Ever—and ever—and ever"*]

OSBORNE: [*Rising from his bed*] It's not as bad as all that. Turn in and have a sleep.

STANHOPE: Sleep! Catch *me* wasting my time with sleep.

OSBORNE: [*Picking up* Stanhope's *pack and pulling out the blanket*] Come along, old chap. You come and lie down here.

[*He puts the pack as a pillow on* Stanhope's *bed, and spreads out the blanket*]

STANHOPE: [*With his chin in his hands*] Little prig—that's what he is. Did *I* ask him to force his way into my company? No! I didn't. Very well, he'll pay for his damn cheek. [Osborne *lays his hand gently on* Stanhope's *shoulder to persuade him to lie down*] Go away! [*He shakes* Osborne's *hand off*] What the hell are you trying to do?

OSBORNE: Come and lie down and go to sleep.

STANHOPE: Go sleep y'self. I censor his letters, d'you see, Uncle? You watch and see he doesn't smuggle any letters away.

OSBORNE: Righto. Now come and lie down. You've had a hard day of it.

STANHOPE: [*Looking up suddenly*] Where's Hardy? D'you say he's gone?

OSBORNE: Yes. He's gone.

STANHOPE: Gone, has he? Y'know, I had a word to say to Master Hardy. He *would* go, the swine! Dirty trenches—everything dirty—I wanner tell him to keep his trenches clean.

OSBORNE: [*Standing beside* Stanhope *and putting his hand gently on his shoulder again*] We'll clean them up to-morrow.

[Stanhope *looks up at* Osborne *and laughs gaily*]

STANHOPE: Dear old Uncle! Clean trenches up—with little dust pan and brush. [*He laughs*] Make you a little apron—with lace on it.

OSBORNE: That'll be fine. Now then, come along, old chap. I'll see you get called at two o'clock. [*He firmly takes* Stanhope *by the arm and draws him over to the bed*] You *must* be tired.

STANHOPE: [*In a dull voice*] God, I'm bloody tired; ache—all over—feel sick——

[Osborne *helps him on to the bed, takes the blanket and puts it over him*]

OSBORNE: You'll feel all right in a minute. How's that? Comfortable?

STANHOPE: Yes. Comfortable. [*He looks up into* Osborne's *face and laughs again*] Dear old Uncle. Tuck me up.

[Osborne *fumbles the blankets round* Stanhope]

OSBORNE: There we are.

STANHOPE: Kiss me, Uncle.

OSBORNE: Kiss you be blowed! You go to sleep.

STANHOPE: [Closing his eyes] Yes—I go sleep.

[He turns slowly on to his side with his face to the earth wall. Osborne stands watching for a while, then blows out the candle by Stanhope's bed. Stanhope gives a deep sigh, and begins to breathe heavily. Osborne crosses to the servant's dug-out and calls softly]

OSBORNE: Mason!

MASON: [Appearing with unbuttoned tunic at the tunnel entrance] Yessir?

OSBORNE: Will you call me at ten minutes to eleven—and Mr. Hibbert at ten minutes to two? I'm going to turn in for a little while.

MASON: Very good, sir. [Pause] The pepper's come, sir.

OSBORNE: Oh, good.

MASON: I'm very sorry about the pepper, sir.

OSBORNE: That's all right, Mason.

MASON: Good night, sir.

OSBORNE: Good night.

[Mason leaves the dug-out. Osborne turns, and looks up the narrow steps into the night, where the Very lights rise and fade against the starlit sky. He glances once more at Stanhope, then crosses to his own bed, takes out from his tunic a large, old-fashioned watch, and quietly winds it up. Through the stillness comes the low rumble of distant guns]

THE CURTAIN FALLS

ACT II. SCENE I.

Early next morning.

A pale shaft of sunlight shines down the steps, but candles still burn in the dark corner where Osborne and Raleigh are at breakfast. Mason has put a large plate of bacon before each, and turns to go as Trotter comes down the steps, whistling gaily and rubbing his hands.

TROTTER: What a lovely smell of bacon!

MASON: Yes, sir. I reckon there's enough smell of bacon in 'ere to last for dinner.

TROTTER: Well, there's nothing like a good fat bacon rasher when you're as empty as I am.

MASON: I'm glad you like it fat, sir.

TROTTER: Well, I like a bit o' lean, too.

MASON: There was a bit of lean in the middle of yours, sir, but it's kind of shrunk up in the cooking.

TROTTER: Bad cooking, that's all. Any porridge?

MASON: Oh, yes, sir. There's porridge.

TROTTER: Lumpy, I s'pose?

MASON: Yes, sir. Quite nice and lumpy.

TROTTER: Well, take all the lumps out o' mine.

MASON: And just bring you the gravy, sir? Very good, sir.

[Mason goes out. Trotter looks after him suspiciously]

TROTTER: You know, that man's getting familiar.

OSBORNE: He's not a bad cook.

[Trotter has picked up his coffee mug, and is smelling it]

TROTTER: I say, d'you realize he's washed out his dish-cloth?

OSBORNE: I know. I told him about it.

TROTTER: Did you really? You've got some pluck. 'Ow did you go about it?

OSBORNE: I wrote and asked my wife for a packet of Lux. Then I gave it to Mason and suggested he try it on something.

TROTTER: Good man. No, he's not a bad cook. Might be a lot worse. When I was in the ranks we 'ad a prize cook—used to be a plumber before the war. Ought to 'ave seen the stew 'e made. Thin! Thin wasn't the word. Put a bucketful of 'is stew in a bath and pull the plug, and the whole lot would go down in a couple of gurgles.

[Mason brings Trotter's porridge]

MASON: I've took the lumps out.

TROTTER: Good. Keep 'em and use 'em for dumplings next time we 'ave boiled beef.

MASON: Very good, sir. [He goes out]

TROTTER: Yes. That plumber was a prize cook, 'e was. Lucky for us one day 'e set 'imself on fire making the tea. 'E went 'ome pretty well fried. Did Mason get that pepper?

OSBORNE: Yes.

TROTTER: Good. Must 'ave pepper.

OSBORNE: I thought you were on duty now.

TROTTER. I'm supposed to be. Stanhope sent me down to get my breakfast. He's looking after things till I finish.

OSBORNE: He's got a long job then.

TROTTER: Oh, no. I'm a quick eater. Hi! Mason! Bacon!

MASON: [Outside] Coming, sir!

OSBORNE: It's a wonderful morning.

TROTTER: Isn't it lovely? Makes you feel sort of young and 'opeful. I was up in that old trench under the brick wall just now, and damned if a bloomin' little bird didn't start singing! Didn't 'arf sound funny. Sign of spring, I s'pose. [Mason arrives with Trotter's bacon] That looks all right.

MASON: If you look down straight on it from above, you can see a bit o' lean quite clear.

TROTTER: Good Lord, yes! That's it, isn't it?

MASON: No, sir, that's a bit o' rust off the pan.

TROTTER: Ah! That's it, then!

MASON: You've got it, sir. [He goes out]

TROTTER: Cut us a chunk of bread, Uncle.

[Osborne cuts him off a chunk]

OSBORNE: How are things going up there?

TROTTER: I don't like the look of things a bit.

OSBORNE: You mean—the quiet?

TROTTER: Yes. Standing up there in the dark last night there didn't seem a thing in the world alive—except the rats squeaking and my stomach grumbling about that cutlet.

OSBORNE: It's quiet even now.

TROTTER: Too damn quiet. You can bet your boots the Boche is up to something. The big attack soon, I reckon. I don't like it, Uncle. Pass the jam.

OSBORNE: It's strawberry.

TROTTER: Is it? I'm glad we got rid o' that raspberry jam. Can't stand raspberry jam. Pips get be'ind your plate.

OSBORNE: Did Stanhope tell you he wants two wiring parties out to-night?

TROTTER: Yes. He's fixing it up now. [*He pauses, and goes on in a low voice*] My goodness, Uncle, doesn't he look ill!

OSBORNE: I'm afraid he's not well.

TROTTER: Nobody'd be well who went on like he does. [*There is another pause*] You know when you came up to relieve me last night?

OSBORNE: Yes?

TROTTER: Well, Raleigh and me came back here, and there was Stanhope sitting on that bed drinking a whisky. He looked as white as a sheet. God, he looked awful; he'd drunk a bottle since dinner. I said "Ullo!" and he didn't seem to know who I was. Uncanny, wasn't it, Raleigh?

RALEIGH: [*With lowered head*] Yes.

TROTTER: He just said, "Better go to bed, Raleigh"—just as if Raleigh'd been a school kid.

OSBORNE: Did he? [*There is a pause*] Look at the sun. It'll be quite warm soon.

[*They look at the pale square sunlight on the floor*]

TROTTER. It's warm now. You can feel it on your face outside if you stand in it. First time this year. 'Ope we 'ave an 'ot summer.

OSBORNE: So do I.

TROTTER: Funny about that bird. Made me feel quite braced up. Sort of made me think about my garden of an evening—walking round in me slippers after supper, smoking me pipe.

OSBORNE: You keen on gardening?

TROTTER: Oh, I used to do a bit of an evening. I 'ad a decent little grass plot in front, with flower-borders—geraniums, lobelia, and calsularia—you know, red, white, and blue. Looked rather nice in the summer.

OSBORNE: Yes.

TROTTER: 'Ad some fine 'olly'ocks out the back. One year I'd one eight feet 'igh. Took a photer of it.

[*He fumbles in his pocket case*] Like to look at it?

OSBORNE: I would. [*He looks at the photo*] By jove, it's a beauty.

TROTTER: [*Looking over* Osborne's *shoulder*] You see that, just there?

OSBORNE: Yes?

TROTTER: That's the roof of the summer-'ouse.

OSBORNE: Is it really!

TROTTER: Just shows the 'ite of the 'olly-'ock.

OSBORNE: It does. [*He shows the photo to* Raleigh] A beauty, isn't it?

RALEIGH: Rather!

TROTTER: It never wanted no stick to keep it straight, neether. [*There is a pause*] You keen on gardening?

OSBORNE: Yes. A bit. I made a rockery when I was home on leave. I used to cycle out to the woods and get primroses and things like that, and try and get 'em to grow in my garden.

TROTTER: I don't suppose they would!

OSBORNE: They would if you pressed a bit of moss round them——

TROTTER: —to make 'em feel at 'ome, eh? [*He laughs*]

OSBORNE: They'll be coming out again soon if they've got this sun at home.

TROTTER: I reckon they will. I remember one morning last spring—we was coming out of the salient. Just when it was getting light in the morning—it was at the time when the Boche was sending over a lot of that gas that smells like pear-drops, you know?

OSBORNE: I know. Phosgene.

TROTTER: That's it. We were scared to hell of it. All of a sudden we smelt that funny sweet smell, and a fellow shouted "Gas!"—and we put on our masks; and then I spotted what it was.

OSBORNE: What was it?

TROTTER: Why, a blinkin' may-tree! All out in bloom, growing beside the path! We did feel a lot of silly poops—putting on gas masks because of a damn may-tree! [*He stretches himself and tries to button his tunic*] Lord! I *must* get my fat down. [*He gets up*] Well, I better go and relieve Stanhope. He'll curse like hell if I don't. I bet he's got a red-hot liver this morning.

OSBORNE: I relieve you at eleven.

TROTTER: That's right. I don't like this time of day in the line. The old Boche 'as just 'ad 'is break-fast, and sends over a few whizz-bangs and rifle gre-nades to show 'e ain't forgotten us. Still, I'd rather 'ave a bang or two than this damn quiet. [*He puts on his helmet and gas mask satchel and goes up the steps*] Cheero!

OSBORNE: Cheero!

RALEIGH: Cheero!

OSBORNE: [*to* Raleigh] I expect Stanhope'll let you go on duty alone now.

RALEIGH: Will he? About what time?

OSBORNE: Well, after me, I expect. From about two till four.

RALEIGH: I see.

[*There is a pause. Then* Osborne *looks at* Raleigh *and laughs*]

OSBORNE: What do you think about it all?

RALEIGH: Oh, all right, thanks. [*He laughs*] I feel I've been here ages.

OSBORNE: [*Filling his pipe*] I expect you do. The time passes, though.

RALEIGH: Are we here for six days?

OSBORNE: Yes. Seems a long time, doesn't it?

RALEIGH: [*Laughing shortly*] It does rather. I can't imagine—the end of six days here——

OSBORNE: Anyhow, we've done twelve hours already. It's fine when you are relieved and go down the line to billets, and have a good hot bath, and sit and read under trees.

RALEIGH: Good Lord, I feel I haven't seen a tree for ages—not a real tree with leaves and branches—and yet I've only been here twelve hours.

OSBORNE: How did you feel—in front line?

RALEIGH: Oh, all right. It seemed so frightfully quiet and uncanny—everybody creeping about and talking in low voices. I suppose you've *got* to talk quietly when you're so near the German front line— only about seventy yards, isn't it?

OSBORNE: Yes. About the breadth of a football field.

RALEIGH: It's funny to think of it like that.

OSBORNE: I always measure distances like that out here. Keeps them in proportion.

RALEIGH: Did you play football?

OSBORNE: Yes. But mostly reffing at school in the last few years.

RALEIGH: Are you a schoolmaster, then?

OSBORNE: Yes. I must apologize.

RALEIGH: Oh, I don't mind schoolmasters. [*Hastily*] I—I mean, I never met one outside a school.

OSBORNE: They do get out sometimes.

RALEIGH: [*Laughing*] Who did you play for?

OSBORNE: The Harlequins.

RALEIGH: I say, really!

OSBORNE: I played for the English team on one great occasion.

RALEIGH: What! For *England!*

OSBORNE: I was awfully lucky to get the chance. It's a long time ago now.

RALEIGH: [*With awe*] Oh, but, good Lord! that must have been simply topping. Where did you play?

OSBORNE: Wing three.

RALEIGH: I say, I—I never realized—you'd played for England.

OSBORNE: Tuppence to talk to me now! Anyhow, don't breeze it about.

RALEIGH: Don't the others know?

OSBORNE: We never talk about football.

RALEIGH: They ought to know. It'd make them feel jolly bucked.

OSBORNE: [*Laughing*] It doesn't make much difference out here!

RALEIGH: It must be awfully thrilling, playing in front of a huge crowd—all shouting and cheering—

OSBORNE: You don't notice it when the game begins.

RALEIGH: You're too taken up with the game?

OSBORNE: Yes.

RALEIGH: I used to get wind up playing at school with only a few kids looking on.

OSBORNE: You feel it more when there are only a few. [*He has picked up a slip of paper from the table; suddenly he laughs*] Look at this!

RALEIGH: [*Looking curiously at it*] What is it?

OSBORNE: Trotter's plan to make the time pass quickly. One hundred and forty-four little circles— one for each hour of six days. He's blacked in six already. He's six hours behind.

RALEIGH: It's rather a good idea. I like Trotter.

OSBORNE: He's a good chap.

RALEIGH: He makes things feel—natural.

OSBORNE: He's a genuine sort of chap.

RALEIGH: That's it. He's genuine. [*There is a pause. He has been filling a new pipe. Osborne is puffing at his old one*] How topping—to have played for England!

OSBORNE: It was rather fun. [*There is a pause*]

RALEIGH: The Germans are really quite decent, aren't they? I mean, outside the newspapers?

OSBORNE: Yes. [*Pause*] I remember up at Wipers we had a man shot when he was out on patrol. Just at dawn. We couldn't get him in that night. He lay out there groaning all day. Next night three of our men crawled out to get him. It was so near the German trenches that they could have shot our fellows one by one. But, when our men began dragging the wounded man back over the rough ground, a big German officer stood up in their trenches and called out: "Carry him!"—and our fellows stood up and carried the man back, and the German officer fired some lights for them to see by.

RALEIGH: How topping!

OSBORNE: Next day we blew each other's trenches to blazes.

RALEIGH: It all seems rather—*silly*, doesn't it?

OSBORNE: It does, rather. [*There is silence for a while*]

RALEIGH: I started a letter when I came off duty last night. How do we send letters?

OSBORNE: The quartermaster-sergeant takes them down after he brings rations up in the evenings.

[*Stanhope is coming slowly down the steps. Raleigh rises*]

RALEIGH: I think I'll go and finish it now—if I go on duty soon.

OSBORNE: Come and write in here. It's more cheery.

RALEIGH: It's all right, thanks; I'm quite comfortable in there. I've rigged up a sort of little table beside my bed.

OSBORNE: Righto.

[*Raleigh goes into his dug-out. Stanhope is slowly taking off his equipment*]

STANHOPE: What a foul smell of bacon.

OSBORNE: Yes. We've got bacon for breakfast.

STANHOPE: So I gather. Have you told Raleigh about rifle inspection?

OSBORNE: No.

STANHOPE: [*At the entrance to* Raleigh's *dug-out*] Raleigh!

RALEIGH: [*Appearing*] Yes?

STANHOPE: You inspect your platoon's rifles at nine o'clock.

RALEIGH: Oh, righto, Stanhope. [*He goes again*]

STANHOPE: [*Sitting at the table*] I've arranged two wiring parties to begin at eight o'clock to-night —Corporal Burt with two men and Sergeant Smith with two. I want them to strengthen the wire all along the front.

OSBORNE: It's very weak at present.

STANHOPE: Every company leaves it for the next one to do. There're great holes blown out weeks ago.

OSBORNE: I know.

STANHOPE: Next night we'll start putting a belt of wire down both sides of us.

OSBORNE: Down the sides?

STANHOPE: Yes. We'll wire ourselves right in. If this attack comes, I'm not going to trust the companies on our sides to hold their ground.

[Mason *has come in, and stands diffidently in the background*]

MASON: Would you like a nice bit o' bacon, sir?

STANHOPE: No, thanks. I'll have a cup of tea.

MASON: Right, sir. [*He goes out*]

STANHOPE: I've been having a good look round. We've got a strong position here—if we wire ourselves right in. The colonel's been talking to me up there.

OSBORNE: Oh. Has he been round?

STANHOPE: Yes. He says a German prisoner gave the day of attack as the 21st.

OSBORNE: That's Thursday?

STANHOPE: Yes. To-day's Tuesday.

OSBORNE: That means about dawn the day after to-morrow.

STANHOPE: The second dawn from now. [*There is a pause*]

OSBORNE: Then it'll come while we're here.

STANHOPE: Yes. It'll come while we're here. And we shall be in the front seats.

OSBORNE: Oh, well——

[*In the silence that follows,* Mason *enters with a cup of tea*]

MASON: Would you like a nice plate of sardines, sir?

STANHOPE: I should loathe it.

MASON: Very good, sir. [*He goes out*]

OSBORNE: Did the colonel have much to say?

STANHOPE: Only that when the attack comes we can't expect any help from behind. We're not to move from here. We've got to stick it.

OSBORNE: I see.

STANHOPE: We'll wire ourselves in as strongly as possible. I've got to arrange battle positions for each platoon and section this afternoon.

OSBORNE: Well, I'm glad it's coming at last. I'm sick of waiting.

STANHOPE: [*Looking at* Trotter's *chart*] What's this extraordinary affair?

OSBORNE: Trotter's plan to make the time pass by. A hundred and forty-four circles—one for each hour of the six days.

STANHOPE: How many hours are there till dawn on the 21st?

OSBORNE: Goodness knows. Not many, I hope.

STANHOPE: Nearly nine o'clock now. Twenty-four till nine to-morrow; twelve till nine at night—that's thirty-six; nine till six next morning; that's forty-five altogether.

[*He begins to count off forty-five circles on* Trotter's *chart*]

OSBORNE: What are you going to do?

STANHOPE: At the end of the forty-fifth circle I'm going to draw a picture of Trotter being blown up in four pieces.

OSBORNE: Don't spoil his chart. It took him an hour to make that.

STANHOPE: He won't see the point. He's no imagination.

OSBORNE: I don't suppose he has.

STANHOPE: Funny not to have any imagination. Must be rather nice.

OSBORNE: A bit dull, I should think.

STANHOPE: It must be, rather. I suppose all his life Trotter feels like you and I do when we're drowsily drunk.

OSBORNE: Poor chap!

STANHOPE: I suppose if Trotter looks at that wall he just sees a brown surface. He doesn't see into the earth beyond—the worms wandering about round the stones and roots of trees. I wonder how a worm knows when it's going up or down.

OSBORNE: When it's going down I suppose the blood runs into its head and makes it throb.

STANHOPE: Worms haven't got any blood.

OSBORNE: Then I don't suppose it ever does know.

STANHOPE: Rotten if it didn't—and went on going down when it thought it was coming up.

OSBORNE: Yes, I expect that's the one thing worms dread.

STANHOPE: D'you think this life sharpens the imagination?

OSBORNE: It must.

STANHOPE: Whenever I look at anything nowadays I see right through it. Looking at you now there's your uniform—your jersey—shirt—vest—then beyond that—

OSBORNE: Let's talk about something else—croquet, or the war.

STANHOPE: [*Laughing*] Sorry! It's a habit that's grown on me lately—to look right through things, and on and on—till I get frightened and stop.

OSBORNE: I suppose everybody out here—*feels* more keenly.

STANHOPE: I hope so. I wondered if there was anything wrong with me. D'you ever get a sudden feeling that everything's going farther and farther away—till you're the only thing in the world—and then the world begins going away—until you're the only thing in—in the universe—and you struggle to get back—and can't?

OSBORNE: Bit of nerve strain, that's all.

STANHOPE: You don't think I'm going potty?

OSBORNE: Oh, Lord, no!

STANHOPE: [*Throwing back his head and laughing*] Dear old Uncle! you don't really know, do you? You just pretend you do, to make me feel all right.

OSBORNE: When people are going potty they never talk about it; they keep it to themselves.

STANHOPE: Oh, well, that's all right, then. [*There is silence for a while*] I had that feeling this morning, standing out there in the line while the sun was rising. By the way, did you see the sunrise? Wasn't it gorgeous?

OSBORNE: Splendid—this morning.

STANHOPE: I was looking across at the Boche trenches and right beyond—not a sound or a soul; just an enormous plain, all churned up like a sea that's got muddier and muddier till it's so stiff that it can't move. You could have heard a pin drop in the quiet; yet you knew thousands of guns were hidden there, all ready, cleaned and oiled—millions of bullets lying in pouches—thousands of Germans, waiting and thinking. Then, gradually, that feeling came—

OSBORNE: I never knew the sun could rise in so many ways till I came out here. Green, and pink, and red, and blue, and gray. Extraordinary, isn't it?

STANHOPE: Yes. Hi! Mason!

MASON: [*Outside*] Yessir!

STANHOPE: Bring some mugs and a bottle of whisky.

MASON: Yessir.

OSBORNE: [*Smiling*] So early in the morning?

STANHOPE: Just a spot. It's damned cold in here.

OSBORNE: [*Turning over the pages of a magazine*] This show at the Hippodrome has been running a long time.

STANHOPE: What? *Zig-zag?*

OSBORNE: Yes. George Robey's in it.

STANHOPE: Harper saw it on leave. Says it's damn good. Robey's pricelessly funny.

[*Mason brings whisky and mugs and water*]

OSBORNE: Wish I'd seen a show on leave.

STANHOPE: D'you mean to say you didn't go to any shows?

OSBORNE: [*Laughing*] No. I spent all the time in the garden, making a rockery. In the evenings I used to sit and smoke and read—and my wife used to knit socks and play the piano a bit. We pretended there wasn't any war at all—till my two youngsters made me help in a tin-soldier battle on the floor.

STANHOPE: Poor old Uncle! You can't get away from it, can you?

OSBORNE: I wish I knew how to fight a battle like those boys of mine. You ought to have seen the way they lured my men under the sofa and mowed them down.

STANHOPE: [*Laughing and helping himself to a drink*] You going to have one?

OSBORNE: Not now, thanks.

STANHOPE: You go on duty at eleven, don't you?

OSBORNE: Yes. I relieve Trotter.

STANHOPE: Raleigh better go on at one o'clock and stay with you for an hour. Then he can stay on alone till four. Hibbert relieves him at four.

OSBORNE: Righto.

STANHOPE: What's Raleigh doing now?

OSBORNE: Finishing a letter.

STANHOPE: Did you tell him?

OSBORNE: About what?

STANHOPE: Censorship.

OSBORNE: You don't mean that seriously?

STANHOPE: Mean it? Of course I mean it.

OSBORNE: You can't do that.

STANHOPE: Officially I'm supposed to read all your letters. Damn it all, Uncle! Imagine yourself in my place—a letter going away from here—from that boy——

OSBORNE: He'll say nothing—rotten—about you.

STANHOPE: You think so? [*There is a pause*] I heard you go on duty last night. After you'd gone, I got up. I was feeling bad. I forgot Raleigh was out there with Trotter. I'd forgotten all about him. I was sleepy. I just knew something beastly had happened. Then he came in with Trotter—and looked at me. After coming in out of the night air, this place must have reeked of candle-grease, and rats—and whisky. One thing a boy like that can't stand is a smell that isn't fresh. He looked at me as if I'd hit him between the eyes—as if I'd spat on him——

OSBORNE: You imagine things.

STANHOPE: [*Laughing*] Imagine things! No need to imagine!

OSBORNE: Why can't you treat him like any other youngster?

[Raleigh *comes in from his dug-out with a letter in his hand. He stops short as he notices the abrupt silence that follows his entry*]

RALEIGH: I'm sorry.

OSBORNE: It's all right, Raleigh. Going to inspect rifles?

RALEIGH: Yes.

OSBORNE: You needn't bother if the wood's a bit dirty—just the barrels and magazines and all the metal parts.

RALEIGH: Righto.

OSBORNE: See there's plenty of oil on it. And look at the ammunition in the men's pouches.

RALEIGH: Right. [*He crosses towards the door and turns*] Where do we put the letters to be collected?

OSBORNE: Oh, just on the table.

RALEIGH: Thanks.

[*He begins to lick the flap of the envelope*]

STANHOPE: [*In a quiet voice*] You leave it open.

RALEIGH: [*Surprised*] Open?

STANHOPE: Yes. I have to censor all letters.

RALEIGH: [*Stammering*] Oh, but—I haven't said anything about—where we are——

STANHOPE: It's the rule that letters must be read.

RALEIGH: [*Nervously*] Oh, I—I didn't realize that. [*He stands embarrassed; then gives a short laugh*] I —I think—I'll just leave it, then.

[*He unbuttons his tunic pocket to put the letter away. Stanhope rises, crosses slowly and faces Raleigh*]

STANHOPE: Give me that letter!

RALEIGH: [*Astonished*] But—Dennis——

STANHOPE: [*Trembling*] Give me that letter!

RALEIGH: But it's—it's private. I didn't know——

STANHOPE: D'you understand an order? Give me that letter!

RALEIGH: But I tell you—there's nothing— [*Stanhope clutches Raleigh's wrist and tears the letter from his hand*] Dennis—I'm——

STANHOPE: Don't "Dennis" me! Stanhope's my name! You're not at school! Go and inspect your rifles.

[*Raleigh stands in amazement at the foot of the steps*]

STANHOPE: [*Shouting*] D'you understand an order?

[*For a moment Raleigh stares wide-eyed at Stanhope, who is trembling and breathing heavily, then almost in a whisper he says: "Right," and goes quietly up the narrow steps. Stanhope turns toward the table*]

OSBORNE: Good heavens, Stanhope!

STANHOPE: [*Wheeling furiously on* Osborne] Look here, Osborne, *I'm* commanding this company. I ask for advice when I want it!

OSBORNE: Very well.

[*Stanhope sinks down at the table with the letter in his hand. There is silence for a moment. Then he throws the letter on the table and rests his head between his hands*]

STANHOPE: Oh, God! I don't want to read the blasted thing!

OSBORNE: You'll let it go then?

STANHOPE: I don't care. [*There is a pause*]

OSBORNE: Shall I glance through it—for you?

STANHOPE: If you like.

OSBORNE: I don't *want* to.

STANHOPE: You better, I can't.

[*Osborne takes the letter from the table and opens it. Stanhope sits with his head in his hand, digging a magazine with a pencil. After a while, Osborne glances up at Stanhope*]

OSBORNE: D'you want to hear?

STANHOPE: I suppose I better know.

OSBORNE: He begins with a description of his getting here—he doesn't mention the names of any places.

STANHOPE: What does he say then?

OSBORNE: The last piece is about you.

STANHOPE: Go on.

OSBORNE: [*Reading*] He says: "And now I come to the great news. I reported at Battalion Headquarters, and the colonel looked in a little book, and said, 'You report to "C" Company—Captain Stanhope.' Can't you imagine what I felt? I was taken along some trenches and shown a dug-out. There was an awfully nice officer there—quite old—with gray hair"— [Osborne *clears his throat*]—"and then later Dennis came in. He looked tired, but that's because he works so frightfully hard, and because of the responsibility. Then I went on duty in the front line, and a sergeant told me all about Dennis. He said that Dennis is the finest officer in the battalion, and the men simply love him. He hardly ever sleeps in the dug-out; he's always up in the front line with the men, cheering them on with jokes, and making them keen about things, like he did the kids at school. I'm awfully proud to think he's my friend." [*There is silence. Stanhope has not moved while Osborne has read*] That's all. [*Pause*] Shall I stick it down?

[*Stanhope sits with lowered head. He murmurs something that sounds like "Yes, please." He rises heavily and crosses to the shadows by Osborne's bed. The sun is shining quite brightly in the trench outside*]

THE CURTAIN FALLS

SCENE II.

Afternoon on the same day. The sunlight has gone from the dug-out floor, but still shines brightly in the trench.

Stanhope is lying on his bed reading by the light of a candle on the table beside him. A burly Figure *comes groping down the steps and stands blinking in the shadows of the dug-out. A huge man, with a heavy black mustache, a fat red face, and massive chin.*

Stanhope puts the magazine down, rises and sits up to the table.

STANHOPE: I want to talk with you, sergeant-major.

S.-M.: [*Standing stolidly by the steps*] Yes, sir?

STANHOPE: Sit down. Have a whisky?

S.-M.: [*A suspicion of brightness in his voice*] Thank you, sir.

[*The Sergeant-Major diffidently takes a small tot*]

STANHOPE: I say. You won't taste that. Take a proper one.

S.-M.: Well—sir [Stanhope *reaches over, helps the* Sergeant-Major *to a large tot, and takes one himself*] Turning chilly again, sir. Quite warm this morning.

STANHOPE: Yes.

S.-M.: Well, here's your very good health, sir. [*He raises his glass and drinks*]

STANHOPE: Cheero. [*He puts down his glass and abruptly changes his tone*] Now, look here, sergeant-major. We must expect this attack on Thursday morning at dawn. That's the second dawn from now.

[*The* Sergeant-Major *takes a very dirty little notebook from his pocket and jots down notes with a very small stub of a pencil*]

S.-M.: Thursday morning. Very good, sir.

STANHOPE: We're to hold these trenches, and no man's to move from here.

S.-M.: Very good, sir.

STANHOPE: It may happen that companies on our sides will give way, leaving our flanks exposed; so I want a screen of wire in the support line.

S.-M.: [*Writing hurriedly*] Both flanks—yes, sir.

STANHOPE: When the attack begins, I shall take charge of the left, and Mr. Osborne the right. You will be with Mr. Osborne, and Sergeant Baker with me; 9 and 10 Platoons will move over here. [*He points out the position on the trench map*] 11 and 12 Platoons to the left.

S.-M.: I see, sir.

STANHOPE: Is there anything you're not clear about?

S.-M.: [*Looking at his notes*] Seems all clear, sir.

STANHOPE: Anything you want to know?

S.-M.: Well, sir [*Clears his throat*]—when the attack comes, of course, we beat 'em off—but what if they keep on attacking?

STANHOPE: Then we keep on beating them off.

S.-M.: Yes, sir. But what I mean is—they're bound to make a big thing of it.

STANHOPE: [*Cheerily*] Oh, I think they will!

S.-M.: Well, then, sir. If they don't get through the first day they'll attack the next day and the next——

STANHOPE: They're bound to.

S.-M.: Then oughtn't we to fix up something about, well [*He gropes for the right words*]—er—falling back?

STANHOPE: There's no need to—you see, this company's a lot better than "A" and "B" Companies on either side of us.

S.-M.: Quite, sir.

STANHOPE: Well, then, if anyone breaks, "A" and "B" will break before we do. As long as we stick here when the other companies have given way, we can fire into the Boche as they try and get through the gaps on our sides—we'll make a hell of a mess of them. We might delay the advance a whole day.

S.-M.: [*Diffidently*] Yes, sir, but what 'appens when the Boche 'as all got round the back of us?

STANHOPE: Then we advance and win the war.

S.-M.: [*Pretending to make a note*] Win the war. Very good, sir.

STANHOPE: But you understand exactly what I mean, sergeant-major. Our orders are to stick here. If you're told to stick where you are you don't make plans to retire.

S.-M.: Quite, sir.

[*Osborne's voice is calling down the steps. Sergeant-Major rises*]

OSBORNE: Are you there, Stanhope?

STANHOPE: [*Rising quickly*] Yes. What's the matter?

OSBORNE: The colonel's up here. Wants to see you——

STANHOPE: Oh, right, I'll come up.

COLONEL: [*From above*] All right, Stanhope—I'll come down.

S.-M.: [*Who has risen*] Anything more, sir?

STANHOPE: I don't think so. I'll see you at stand-to this evening.

S.-M.: Very good, sir.

[*He stands back a pace and salutes* Stanhope *smartly.* Stanhope's *eye falls on the* Sergeant-Major's *nearly finished drink on the table. He points to it*]

STANHOPE: Hoy! What about that?

S.-M.: Thank you, sir.

[*He finishes the drink. The* Colonel *comes down the steps.*]

COLONEL: Good morning, sergeant-major.

S.-M.: Good morning, sir.

[*The* Sergeant-Major *goes up the steps*]

STANHOPE: Hullo, sir!

COLONEL: Hullo, Stanhope! [*He sniffs*] Strong smell of bacon.

STANHOPE: Yes, sir. We had some bacon for breakfast.

COLONEL: Hangs about, doesn't it?

STANHOPE: Yes, sir. Clings to the walls.

COLONEL: Lovely day.

STANHOPE: Splendid, sir.

COLONEL: Spring's coming. [*There is a pause*] I'm glad you're alone. I've got some rather serious news.

STANHOPE: I'm sorry to hear that, sir. Will you have a drink?

COLONEL: Well, thanks—just a spot. [Stanhope *mixes a drink for the* Colonel *and himself*] Here's luck.

STANHOPE: Cheero, sir. [*Bringing forward a box*] Sit down, sir.

COLONEL: Thanks.

STANHOPE: What's the news, sir?

COLONEL: The brigadier came to see me this morning. [*He pauses*] It seems almost certain the attack's to come on Thursday morning. They've got information from more than one source—but they don't know where it's going to fall the hardest. The Boche began relieving his front-line troops yesterday. They're bound to put in certain regiments where they intend to make the hardest push——

STANHOPE: Naturally——

COLONEL: And the general wants us to make a raid to find out who's come into the line opposite here. [*There is a pause*]

STANHOPE: I see. When?

COLONEL: As soon as possible. He said to-night.

STANHOPE: Oh, but that's absurd!

COLONEL: I told him so. I said the earliest would be to-morrow afternoon. A surprise daylight raid under a smoke screen from the trench-mortar people. I think daylight best. There's not much moon now, and it's vitally important to get hold of a Boche or two.

STANHOPE: Quite.

COLONEL: I suggest sending two officers and ten men. Quite enough for the purpose. Just opposite here there's only seventy yards of No Man's Land. To-night the trench-mortars can blow a hole in the Boche wire and you can cut a hole in yours. Harrison of the trench-mortars is coming in to dinner with me this evening to discuss everything. I'd like you to come too. Eight o'clock suit you?

STANHOPE: Very good, sir.

COLONEL: I'll leave you to select the men.

STANHOPE: You want me to go with them, sir?

COLONEL: Oh, no, Stanhope. I—I can't let you go. No. I want one officer to direct the raid and one to make the dash in and collar some Boche.

STANHOPE: Who do you suggest, sir?

COLONEL: Well, I suggest Osborne, for one. He's a very level-headed chap. He can direct it.

STANHOPE: And who else?

COLONEL: Well, there's Trotter—but he's a bit fat, isn't he? Not much good at dashing in?

STANHOPE: No. D'you suggest Hibbert?

COLONEL: Well, what do *you* think of Hibbert?

STANHOPE: I don't think so.

COLONEL: No. [*There is a pause*]

STANHOPE: Why not send a good sergeant, sir?

COLONEL: No. I don't think a sergeant. The men expect officers to lead a raid.

STANHOPE: Yes. There is that.

COLONEL: As a matter of fact, Stanhope, I'm thinking of that youngster I sent up to you last night.

STANHOPE: Raleigh?

COLONEL: Yes. Just the type. Plenty of guts——

STANHOPE: He's awfully new to it all——

COLONEL: All to the good. His nerves are sound.

STANHOPE: It's rotten to send a fellow who's only just arrived.

COLONEL: Well, who else is there? I could send an officer from another company——

STANHOPE: [*Quickly*] Oh, Lord, no. We'll do it.

COLONEL: Then I suggest Osborne to lead the raid and Raleigh to make the dash—with ten good men. We'll meet Harrison at supper and arrange the smoke bombs—and blowing a hole in the wire. You select the men and talk to Osborne and Raleigh about it in the meantime.

STANHOPE: Very well, sir.

COLONEL: Better send Osborne and Raleigh down to me in the morning to talk things over. Or, better still—I'll come up here first thing to-morrow morning.

STANHOPE: Right, sir.

COLONEL: It's all a damn nuisance; but, after all— it's necessary.

STANHOPE: I suppose it is.

COLONEL: Well, so long, Stanhope. I'll see you at eight o'clock. Do you like fish?

STANHOPE: Fish, sir?

COLONEL: Yes. We've had some fresh fish sent up from railhead for supper to-night.

STANHOPE: Splendid, sir!

COLONEL: Whiting, I think it is.

STANHOPE: Good!

COLONEL: Well, bye-bye.

[*The* Colonel *goes up the steps.* Stanhope *stands watching for a moment, then turns and walks slowly to the table.* Hibbert *comes quietly into the dug-out from the tunnel leading from his sleeping quarters*]

STANHOPE: Hullo! I thought you were asleep.

HIBBERT: I just wanted a word with you, Stanhope.

STANHOPE: Fire away.

HIBBERT: This neuralgia of mine. I'm awfully sorry. I'm afraid I can't stick it any longer——

STANHOPE: I know. It's rotten, isn't it? I've got it like hell——

HIBBERT: [*Taken aback*] You have?

STANHOPE: Had it for weeks.

HIBBERT: Well, I'm sorry, Stanhope. It's no good. I've tried damned hard; but I must go down——

STANHOPE: Go down—where?

HIBBERT: Why, go sick—go down the line. I must go into hospital and have some kind of treatment. [*There is a silence for a moment.* Stanhope *is looking at* Hibbert—*till* Hibbert *turns away and walks towards his dug-out*] I'll go right along now, I think.

STANHOPE: [*Quietly*] You're going to stay here.

HIBBERT: I'm going down to see the doctor. He'll send me to hospital when he understands——

STANHOPE: I've seen the doctor. I saw him this morning. He won't send you to hospital, Hibbert; he'll send you back here. He promised me he would. [*There is silence*] So you can save yourself a walk.

HIBBERT: [*Fiercely*] What the hell——!

STANHOPE: Stop that!

HIBBERT: I've a perfect right to go sick if I want to. The men can—why can't an officer?

STANHOPE: No man's sent down unless he's very ill. There's nothing wrong with you, Hibbert. The German attack's on Thursday; almost for certain. You're going to stay here and see it through with the rest of us.

HIBBERT: [*Hysterically*] I tell you, I can't—the pain's nearly sending me mad. I'm going! I've got all my stuff packed. I'm going now—you can't stop me!

[*He goes excitedly into the dug-out.* Stanhope *walks slowly towards the steps, turns, and undoes the flap of his revolver holster. He takes out his revolver, and stands casually examining it.* Hibbert *returns with his pack slung on his back and a walking-stick in his hand. He pauses at the sight of* Stanhope *by the steps*]

HIBBERT: Let's get by, Stanhope.

STANHOPE: You're going to stay here and do your job.

HIBBERT: Haven't I *told* you? I *can't!* Don't you understand? Let—let me get by.

STANHOPE: Now look here, Hibbert. I've got a lot of work to do and no time to waste. Once and for all, you're going to stay here and see it through with the rest of us.

HIBBERT: I shall die of this pain if I don't go!

STANHOPE: Better die of pain than be shot for deserting.

HIBBERT: [*In a low voice*] What do you mean?

STANHOPE: You know what I mean——

HIBBERT: I've a right to see the doctor!

STANHOPE: Good God! Don't you understand!—he'll send you back here. Doctor Preston's never let a shirker pass him yet—and he's not going to start now—two days before the attack——

HIBBERT: [*Pleadingly*] Stanhope—if you only *knew* how awful I feel—Please do let me go by——

[*He walks slowly round behind* Stanhope. Stanhope *turns and thrusts him roughly back. With a lightning movement* Hibbert *raises his stick and strikes blindly at* Stanhope, *who catches the stick, tears it from* Hibbert's *hands, smashes it across his knee, and throws it on the ground*]

STANHOPE: God!—you little swine. You know what that means—don't you? Striking a superior officer! [*There is silence. Stanhope takes hold of his revolver as it swings from its lanyard.* Hibbert *stands quivering in front of* Stanhope] Never mind, though. I won't have you shot for that——

HIBBERT: Let me go——

STANHOPE: If you went, I'd have you shot—for deserting. It's a hell of a disgrace—to die like that. I'd rather spare you the disgrace. I give you half a minute to think. You either stay here and try and be a man—or you try to get out of that door—to desert. If you do that, there's going to be an accident. D'you understand? I'm fiddling with my revolver, d'you see?—cleaning it—and it's going off by accident. It often happens out here. It's going off, and it's going to shoot you between the eyes.

HIBBERT: [*In a whisper*] You daren't——

STANHOPE: You don't deserve to be shot by accident—but I'd save you the disgrace of the other way—I give you half a minute to decide. [*He holds up his wrist to look at his watch*] Half a minute from now——

[*There is silence; a few seconds go by. Suddenly* Hibbert *bursts into a high-pitched laugh*]

HIBBERT: Go on, then, shoot! You won't let me go to the hospital. I swear I'll never go into those trenches again. Shoot!—and thank God——

STANHOPE: [*With his eyes on his watch*] Fifteen more seconds——

HIBBERT: Go on! I'm ready——

STANHOPE: Ten [*He looks up at* Hibbert *who has closed his eyes*] Five.

[*Again* Stanhope *looks up. After a moment he quietly drops his revolver into its holster and steps towards* Hibbert, *who stands with lowered head and eyes tightly screwed up, his arms stretched stiffly by his sides, his hands tightly clutching the edges of his tunic. Gently* Stanhope *places his hands on* Hibbert's *shoulders.* Hibbert *starts violently and gives a little cry. He opens his eyes and stares vacantly into* Stanhope's *face.* Stanhope *is smiling*]

STANHOPE: Good man, Hibbert. I liked the way you stuck that.

HIBBERT: [*Hoarsely*] Why didn't you shoot?

STANHOPE: Stay here, old chap—and see it through——

[Hibbert *stands trembling, trying to speak. Suddenly he breaks down and cries.* Stanhope *takes his hands from his shoulders and turns away*]

HIBBERT: Stanhope! I've tried like hell—I swear I have. Ever since I came out here I've hated and loathed it. Every sound up there makes me all—cold and sick. I'm different to—to the others—you don't understand. It's got worse and worse, and now I can't bear it any longer. I'll never go up those steps again—into the line—with the men looking at me—and knowing—I'd rather die here.

[*He is sitting on* Stanhope's *bed, crying without an effort to restrain himself*]

STANHOPE: [*Pouring out a whisky*] Try a drop of this, old chap——

HIBBERT. No, thanks.

STANHOPE: Go on. Drink it. [Hibbert *takes the mug and drinks.* Stanhope *sits down beside* Hibbert *and puts an arm round his shoulder*] I know what you feel, Hibbert. I've known all along——

HIBBERT: How *can* you know?

STANHOPE: Because I feel the same—exactly the same! Every little noise up there makes me feel—just as you feel. Why didn't you tell me instead of talking about neuralgia? We *all* feel like you do sometimes, if you only knew. I hate and loathe it all. Sometimes I feel I could just lie down on this bed and pretend I was paralyzed or something—and couldn't move—and just lie there till I died—or was dragged away.

HIBBERT: I can't bear to go up into those awful trenches again.

STANHOPE: When are you due to go on?

HIBBERT: Quite soon. At four.

STANHOPE: Shall we go on together? We know how we both feel now. Shall we see if we can stick it together?

HIBBERT: I can't——

STANHOPE: Supposing I said *I* can't—supposing we *all* say we can't—what would happen then?

HIBBERT: I don't care. What does it matter? It's all so—so beastly—nothing matters——

STANHOPE: Supposing the worst happened—supposing we were knocked right out. Think of all the chaps who've gone already. It can't be very lonely there—with all those fellows. Sometimes I think it's lonelier here. [*He pauses. Hibbert is sitting quietly now, his eyes roving vacantly in front of him*] Just go and have a quiet rest. Then we'll go out together.

HIBBERT: Do please let me go, Stanhope——

STANHOPE: If you went—and left Osborne and Trotter and Raleigh and all those men up there to do your work—could you ever look a man straight in the face again—in all your life? [*There is silence again*] You may be wounded. Then you can go home and feel proud—and if you're killed, you— you won't have to stand this hell any more. I might have fired just now. If I had you would have been dead now. But you're still alive—with a straight fighting chance of coming through. Take the chance, old chap, and stand in with Osborne and Trotter and Raleigh. Don't you think it worth standing in with men like that?—when you know they all feel like you do—in their hearts—and just go on sticking it because they know it's—it's the only thing a decent man can do. [*Again there is silence*] What about it?

HIBBERT: I'll—I'll try——

STANHOPE: Good man!

HIBBERT: You—you won't say anything, Stanhope—about this?

STANHOPE: If you promise not to tell any one what a blasted funk *I* am.

HIBBERT: [*With a little laugh*] No.

STANHOPE: Splendid! Now go and have ten minutes' rest and a smoke—then we'll go up together and hold each other's hands—and jump every time a rat squeaks. [Hibbert *rises and blows his nose*] We've all got a good fighting chance. I mean to come through—don't you think?

HIBBERT: Yes. Rather. [*He goes timidly towards his dug-out, and turns at the doorway*] It's awfully decent of you, Stanhope— [Stanhope *is pouring himself out a whisky*] And thanks most awfully for——

STANHOPE: That's all right.

[Hibbert *goes away*. Stanhope *takes a drink and sits down at the table to write*. Mason *comes in*]

MASON: Will you have a nice cup of tea, sir?

STANHOPE: Can you guarantee it's nice?

MASON: Well, sir—it's a bit oniony, but that's only because of the saucepan.

STANHOPE: In other words, it's onion soup with tea-leaves in it?

MASON: Not till dinner-time, sir.

STANHOPE: All right, Mason. Bring two cups of onion tea. One for Mr. Hibbert.

MASON: Very good, sir. [*Going towards the door, he meets* Osborne *coming in*] Will you have a nice cup of tea, sir?

OSBORNE: Please, Mason—and plenty of bread and butter and strawberry jam.

MASON: Very good, sir.

STANHOPE: Well, Uncle—how are things going on up there?

OSBORNE: Two lonely rifle grenades came over just now.

STANHOPE: I heard them. Where did they pitch?

OSBORNE: Just over the front line on the left. Otherwise nothing doing. [*Pause*]

STANHOPE: The colonel's been talking to me.

OSBORNE: About the attack?

STANHOPE: Partly. We've got to make a raid, Uncle.

OSBORNE: Oh? When?

STANHOPE: To-morrow afternoon. Under a smoke screen. Two officers and ten men.

OSBORNE: Who's going?

STANHOPE: You and Raleigh.

[*Pause*]

OSBORNE: Oh! [*There is another pause*] Why Raleigh?

STANHOPE: The colonel picked you to direct and Raleigh to dash in.

OSBORNE: I see.

STANHOPE: The brigade wants to know who's opposite here.

OSBORNE: To-morrow? What time?

STANHOPE: I suggest about five o'clock. A little before dusk——

OSBORNE: I see.

STANHOPE: I'm damn sorry.

OSBORNE: That's all right, old chap.

STANHOPE: I'm dining with the colonel to arrange everything. Then I'll come back and go through it with you.

OSBORNE: Where do we raid from?

STANHOPE: Out of the sap on our left. Straight across.

OSBORNE: Where's the map?

STANHOPE: Here we are. Look. Straight across to this sentry post of the Boche. Sixty yards. To-night we'll lay out a guiding tape as far as possible. After dark the toch-emmas are going to break the Boche wire and we'll cut a passage in ours.

OSBORNE: Will you fix up the men who are to go?

STANHOPE: Are you keen on any special men?

OSBORNE: Can I take a corporal?

STANHOPE: Sure.

OSBORNE: May I have young Crooks?

STANHOPE: Righto.

OSBORNE: You'll ask for volunteers, I suppose?

STANHOPE: Yes. I'll see the sergeant-major and get him to go round for names.

[*He crosses to the doorway as* Mason *comes in with the tea*]

MASON: Your tea, sir!

STANHOPE: Keep it hot, Mason.

MASON: Will you take this cup, Mr. Osborne?

STANHOPE: Take the other in to Mr. Hibbert, **in** there.

MASON: Very good, sir.

[*He goes in to* Hibbert's *dug-out*]

STANHOPE: Shan't be long, Uncle.

[*He goes up the steps*]

OSBORNE: Righto.

[Mason *returns*]

MASON: Will you have cut bread and butter—or shall I bring the loaf, sir?

OSBORNE: Cut it, Mason, please.

MASON: Just bringing the jam separately?

OSBORNE: Yes.

MASON: Very good, sir.

[Mason *goes out.* Osborne *takes a small leather-bound book from his pocket, opens it at a marker, and begins to read.* Trotter *appears from the sleeping dug-out looking very sleepy*]

TROTTER: Tea ready?

OSBORNE: Yes.

TROTTER: Why's Hibbert got his tea in there?

OSBORNE: I don't know.

TROTTER: [*Rubbing his eyes*] Oh, Lord, I do feel frowsy. 'Ad a fine sleep, though.

[Mason *brings more tea and a pot of jam*]

MASON: Bread just coming, sir. 'Ere's the strawberry jam, sir.

TROTTER: [*Reciting*] " 'Tell me, Mother, what is that

That looks like strawberry jam?'

'Hush, hush, my dear; 'tis only Pa

Run over by a tram——' "

OSBORNE: The colonel came here while you were asleep.

TROTTER: Oh?

OSBORNE: We've got to make a raid to-morrow afternoon.

TROTTER: Oh, Lord! What—all of us?

OSBORNE: Two officers and ten men.

TROTTER: Who's got to do it?

OSBORNE: Raleigh and I.

TROTTER: Raleigh!

OSBORNE: Yes.

TROTTER: But 'e's only just come!

OSBORNE: Apparently that's the reason.

TROTTER: And you're going too?

OSBORNE: Yes.

TROTTER: Let's 'ear all about it.

OSBORNE: I know nothing yet. Except that it's got to be done.

TROTTER: What a damn nuisance!

OSBORNE: It is, rather.

TROTTER: I reckon the Boche are all ready waiting for it. Did you 'ear about the raid just south of 'ere the other night?

OSBORNE: Nothing much.

TROTTER: The trench-mortars go and knock an 'ole in the Boche wire to let our fellers through— and in the night the Boche went out and tied bits o' red rag on each side of the 'ole.

OSBORNE: Yes. I heard about that.

TROTTER: And even then our fellers 'ad to make

the raid. It was murder. Doesn't this tea taste of onions?

OSBORNE: It does a bit.

TROTTER: Pity Mason don't clean 'is pots better. [Mason *brings some bread on a plate*] This tea tastes of onions.

MASON: I'm sorry, sir. Onions do 'ave such a way of cropping up again.

TROTTER: Yes, but we 'aven't 'ad onions for days!

MASON: I know, sir. That's what makes it so funny.

TROTTER: Well, you better do something about it.

MASON: I'll look into it, sir.

[*He goes out*]

[Osborne *and* Trotter *prepare themselves slices of bread and jam*]

TROTTER: Joking apart. It's damn ridiculous making a raid when the Boche are expecting it.

OSBORNE: We're not doing it for fun.

TROTTER: I know.

OSBORNE: You might avoid talking to Raleigh about it.

TROTTER: Why? How do you mean?

OSBORNE: There's no need to tell him it's murder——

TROTTER: Oh! Lord! no. [*He pauses*] I'm sorry 'e's got to go. 'E's a nice young feller— [Osborne *turns to his book. There is silence*] What are you reading?

OSBORNE: [*Wearily*] Oh, just a book.

TROTTER: What's the title?

OSBORNE: [*Showing him the cover*] Ever read it?

TROTTER: [*Leaning over and reading the cover*] *Alice's Adventures in Wonderland*—Why, that's a kid's book!

OSBORNE: Yes.

TROTTER: You aren't *reading* it?

OSBORNE: Yes.

TROTTER: What—a *kid's* book?

OSBORNE: Haven't you read it?

TROTTER: [*Scornfully*] No!

OSBORNE: You ought to. [*Reads*]

"How doth the little crocodile

Improve his shining tail,

And pour the waters of the Nile

On every golden scale?

"How cheerfully he seems to grin

And neatly spread his claws,

And welcomes little fishes in

With gently smiling jaws!"

TROTTER: [*After a moment's thought*] I don't see no point in that.

OSBORNE: [*Wearily*] Exactly. That's just the point.

TROTTER: [*Looking curiously at* Osborne] You are a funny chap!

[Stanhope *returns*]

STANHOPE: The sergeant-major's getting volunteers

OSBORNE: Good!

TROTTER: Sorry to 'ear about the raid, skipper.

STANHOPE: [Shortly] So am I. What do you make the time?

TROTTER: Just on four.

[Mason brings in more tea]

STANHOPE: [Taking the mug of tea] Was Hibbert asleep when you came out of there?

TROTTER: No. 'E was just lying on 'is bed, smoking.

STANHOPE: [Going to the sleeping dug-out] Hibbert!

HIBBERT: [Coming out] I'm ready, Stanhope.

STANHOPE: Had some tea?

HIBBERT: Yes, thanks.

TROTTER: I reckon Raleigh'll be glad to be relieved. Rotten being on dooty for the first time alone.

OSBORNE: I don't think he minds.

STANHOPE: I shall be up there some time, Uncle.

OSBORNE: I say, why don't you have a rest—you've been on the go all day.

STANHOPE: There's too much to do. This raid's going to upset the arrangements of the wiring party to-night. Can't have men out there while the tochemmas are blowing holes in the Boche wire. [He drinks up his tea] Ready, Hibbert? Come on, my lad.

[Stanhope and Hibbert leave the dug-out together. Trotter looks after them curiously, and turns to Osborne]

TROTTER: Can't understand that little feller, can you?

OSBORNE: Who?

TROTTER: Why, 'Ibbert. D'you see 's eyes? All red. 'E told me in there 'e'd got 'ay-fever.

OSBORNE: Rotten thing, hay-fever.

TROTTER: If you ask me, 'e's been crying——

[Osborne is writing at the table]

OSBORNE: Maybe.

TROTTER: Funny little bloke, isn't 'e?

OSBORNE: Yes. I say—d'you mind? I just want to get a letter off.

TROTTER: Oh, sorry. They 'aven't collected the letters yet, then?

OSBORNE: Not yet.

TROTTER: I'll get one off to my old lady. [He goes towards his dug-out] She's wrote and asked if I've got fleas.

OSBORNE: Have you?

TROTTER: [Gently rotating his shoulders] I wish it was fleas.

[Trotter goes into his dug-out; Osborne continues his letter. Raleigh comes down the steps from the trench]

RALEIGH: [Excitedly] I say, Stanhope's told me about the raid.

OSBORNE: Has he?

RALEIGH: Just you and me, isn't it—and ten men?

OSBORNE: Yes, to-morrow. Just before dusk. Under a smoke cloud.

RALEIGH: I say—it's most frightfully exciting!

OSBORNE: We shall know more about it after Stanhope sees the colonel to-night.

RALEIGH: Were you and I picked—specially?

OSBORNE: Yes.

RALEIGH: I—say!

THE CURTAIN FALLS

ACT III. SCENE I.

The following day, towards sunset. The earth wall of the trench outside glows with a light that slowly fades with the sinking sun.

Stanhope is alone, wandering to and fro across the dug-out. He looks up the steps for a moment, crosses to the table, and glances down at the map. He looks anxiously at his watch, and, going to the servants' dug-out, calls:

STANHOPE: Mason!

MASON: [Outside] Yessir!

STANHOPE: Are you making the coffee?

MASON: Yessir!

STANHOPE: Make it hot and strong. Ready in five minutes. I'll call when it's wanted.

MASON: Very good, sir.

[Again Stanhope wanders restlessly to and fro. The Colonel comes down the steps]

COLONEL: Everything ready?

STANHOPE: Yes, sir. [There is silence] You've no news, then?

COLONEL: I'm afraid not. It's got to be done.

STANHOPE: [After a pause] I see.

COLONEL: The brigadier says the Boche did the same thing just south of here the other day.

STANHOPE: I know, but didn't you suggest we alter our plans and make a surprise raid farther up the line after dark?

COLONEL: Yes. I suggested that.

STANHOPE: What did he say?

COLONEL: He said the present arrangements have got to stand.

STANHOPE: But surely he must realize——

COLONEL: [Impatiently breaking in] Look here, Stanhope, I've done all I can, but my report's got to be at headquarters by seven this evening. If we wait till it's dark we shall be too late.

STANHOPE: Why seven?

COLONEL: They've got some conference to arrange the placing of reserves.

STANHOPE: They can't have it later because of dinner, I suppose.

COLONEL: Lots of raids have taken place along the line to-day. With the attack to-morrow morning, headquarters naturally want all the information they can get as early as possible.

STANHOPE: Meanwhile the Boche are sitting over there with a dozen machine-guns trained on that hole—waiting for our fellows to come.

COLONEL: Well, I can't disobey orders.

STANHOPE: Why didn't the trench-mortars blow a dozen holes in different places—so the Boche wouldn't know which we were going to use?

COLONEL: It took three hours to blow that one. How could they blow a dozen in the time? It's no good worrying about that now. It's too late. Where's Osborne and Raleigh?

STANHOPE: They're up in the sap, having a last look around. What d'you make the time, sir?

COLONEL: Exactly nineteen minutes to.

STANHOPE: I'm thirty seconds behind you.

COLONEL: Funny. We checked this morning.

STANHOPE: Still, it's near enough. We shan't go till the smoke blows across.

COLONEL: The smoke ought to blow across nicely. The wind's just right. I called on the trench-mortars on the way up. Everything's ready. They'll drop the bombs thirty yards to the right.

STANHOPE: Are you going to stay here?

COLONEL: I'll watch from the trench just above, I think. Bring the prisoners straight back here. We'll question them right away.

STANHOPE: Why not take them straight down to your quarters?

COLONEL: Well, the Boche are bound to shell pretty heavily. I don't want the risk of the prisoners being knocked out before we've talked to them.

STANHOPE: All right. I'll have them brought back here.

[*There is a pause. The* Colonel *sucks hard at his pipe.* Stanhope *roves restlessly about, smoking a cigarette*]

COLONEL: It's no good getting depressed. After all, it's only sixty yards. The Boche'll be firing into a blank fog. Osborne's a cool, level-headed chap, and Raleigh's the very man to dash in. You've picked good men to follow them?

STANHOPE: The best. All youngsters. Strong, keen chaps.

COLONEL: Good. [*Another pause*] You know quite well I'd give anything to cancel the beastly affair.

STANHOPE: I know you would, sir.

COLONEL: Have these red rags on the wire upset the men at all?

STANHOPE: It's hard to tell. They naturally take it as a joke. They say the rags are just what they want to show them the way through the gap.

COLONEL: That's the spirit, Stanhope. [Osborne *and* Raleigh *come down the steps*] Well, Osborne. Everything ready?

OSBORNE: Yes, I think we're all ready, sir. I make it just a quarter to.

COLONEL: That's right.

OSBORNE: The men are going to stand by at three minutes to.

COLONEL: The smoke bombs drop exactly on the hour. You'll give the word to go when the smoke's thick enough?

OSBORNE: That's right, sir.

STANHOPE: [*At the servants' dug-out*] Mason!

MASON: Coming, sir!

STANHOPE: Were the men having their rum, Uncle?

OSBORNE: Yes. Just as we left. It gives it a quarter of an hour to soak in.

COLONEL: That's right. Are they cheerful?

OSBORNE: Yes. Quite.

[Mason *brings in two cups of coffee and puts them on the table*]

STANHOPE: Would you like to go up and speak to them, sir?

COLONEL: Well, don't you think they'd rather be left alone?

STANHOPE: I think they would appreciate a word or two.

COLONEL: All right. If you think they would.

OSBORNE: They're all in the center dug-out, sir.

COLONEL: Right. You coming, Stanhope?

STANHOPE: Yes. I'll come, sir.

[*The* Colonel *lingers a moment. There is an awkward pause. Then the* Colonel *clears his throat and speaks*]

COLONEL: Well, good luck, Osborne. I'm certain you'll put up a good show.

OSBORNE: [*Taking the* Colonel's *hand*] Thank you, sir.

COLONEL: And, Raleigh, just go in like blazes. Grab hold of the first Boche you see and bundle him across here. One'll do, but bring more if you see any handy.

RALEIGH: [*Taking the* Colonel's *offered hand*] Right, sir.

COLONEL: And, if you succeed, I'll recommend you both for the M.C. [Osborne *and* Raleigh *murmur their thanks*] Remember, a great deal may depend on bringing in a German. It may mean the winning of the whole war. You never know. [*Another pause*] Well, good luck to you both.

[*Again* Osborne *and* Raleigh *murmur their thanks. The* Colonel *and* Stanhope *go towards the door*]

COLONEL: [*Over his shoulder*] Don't forget to empty your pockets of papers and things.

RALEIGH: Oh, no.

[*He goes into his dug-out, taking letters and papers from his pockets.* Stanhope *is about to follow the* Colonel *up the steps when* Osborne *calls him back*]

OSBORNE: Er—Stanhope—just a moment.

STANHOPE: [*Returning*] Hullo!

OSBORNE: I say, don't think I'm being morbid, or anything like that, but would you mind taking these?

STANHOPE: Sure. Until you come back, old man.

OSBORNE: It's only just in case—[*He takes his watch and a letter from his tunic pocket and puts them on the table. Then he pulls off his ring*] If anything should happen, would you send these along to my wife?

[*He pauses, and gives an awkward little laugh*]

STANHOPE: [*Putting the articles together on the table*] You're coming back, old man. Damn it! what on earth should I do without you?

OSBORNE: [*Laughing*] Goodness knows!

STANHOPE: Must have somebody to tuck me up in bed. [*There is a pause*] Well, I'll see you up in the sap, before you go. Just have a spot of rum in that coffee.

OSBORNE: Righto.

[*Stanhope goes to the steps and lingers for a moment*]

STANHOPE: Cheero!

[*For a second their eyes meet; they laugh. Stanhope goes slowly up the steps. There is a silence in the dug-out. Osborne has been filling his pipe, and stands lighting it as Raleigh returns*]

OSBORNE: Just time for a small pipe.

RALEIGH: Good. I'll have a cigarette, I think.

[*He feels in his pocket*]

OSBORNE: Here you are.

[*He offers his case to Raleigh*]

RALEIGH: I say, I'm always smoking yours.

OSBORNE: That's all right. [*Pause*] What about this coffee?

RALEIGH: Sure.

[*They sit at the table*]

OSBORNE: Are you going to have a drop of rum in it?

RALEIGH: Don't you think it might make us a— a bit muzzy?

OSBORNE: I'm just having the coffee as it is.

RALEIGH: I think I will, too.

OSBORNE: We'll have the rum afterwards—to celebrate.

RALEIGH: That's a much better idea.

[*They stir their coffee in silence. Osborne's eyes meet Raleigh's. He smiles*]

OSBORNE: How d'you feel?

RALEIGH: All right.

OSBORNE: I've got a sort of empty feeling inside.

RALEIGH: That's just what I've got!

OSBORNE: Wind up!

RALEIGH: I keep wanting to yawn.

OSBORNE: That's it. Wind up. I keep wanting to yawn too. It'll pass off directly we start.

RALEIGH: [*Taking a deep breath*] I wish we could go now.

OSBORNE: [*Looking at his watch on the table*] We've got eight minutes yet.

RALEIGH: Oh, Lord!

OSBORNE: Let's just have a last look at the map. [*He picks up the map and spreads it out*] Directly the smoke's thick enough, I'll give the word. You run straight for this point here——

RALEIGH: When I get to the Boche wire I lie down and wait for you.

OSBORNE: Don't forget to throw your bombs.

RALEIGH: [*Patting his pocket*] No. I've got them here.

OSBORNE: When I shout "Righto!"—in you go with your eight men. I shall lie on the Boche parapet, and blow my whistle now and then to show you where I am. Pounce on the first Boche you see and bundle him out to me.

RALEIGH: Righto.

OSBORNE: Then we come back like blazes.

RALEIGH: The whole thing'll be over quite quickly?

OSBORNE: I reckon with luck we shall be back in three minutes.

RALEIGH: As quick as that?

OSBORNE: I think so. [*He folds up the map*] And now let's forget all about it for—[*He looks at his watch*]—for six minutes.

RALEIGH: Oh, Lord, I can't!

OSBORNE: You must.

RALEIGH: How topping if we both get the M.C.!

OSBORNE: Yes. [*Pause*] Your coffee sweet enough?

RALEIGH: Yes, thanks. It's jolly good coffee. [*Pause*] I wonder what the Boche are doing over there now?

OSBORNE: I don't know. D'you like coffee better than tea?

RALEIGH: I do for breakfast. [*Pause*] Do these smoke bombs make much row when they burst?

OSBORNE: Not much. [*Pause*] Personally, I like cocoa for breakfast.

RALEIGH: [*Laughing*] I'm sorry!

OSBORNE: Why sorry? Why shouldn't I have cocoa for breakfast?

RALEIGH: I don't mean that. I—mean—I'm sorry to keep talking about the raid. It's so difficult to— to talk about anything else. I was just wondering— will the Boche retaliate in any way after the raid?

OSBORNE: Bound to—a bit.

RALEIGH: Shelling?

OSBORNE: " 'The time has come,' the Walrus said,
'To talk of many things:
Of shoes—and ships—and sealing-wax—
Of cabbages—and kings.' "

RALEIGH: " 'And why the sea is boiling hot—
And whether pigs have wings.' "

OSBORNE: Now we're off! Quick, let's talk about pigs! Black pigs or white pigs?

RALEIGH: Black pigs. In the New Forest you find them, quite wild.

OSBORNE: You know the New Forest?

RALEIGH: Rather! My home's down there. A little place called Allum Green just outside Lyndhurst.

OSBORNE: I know Lyndhurst well.

RALEIGH: It's rather nice down there.

OSBORNE: I like it more than any place I know.

RALEIGH: I think I do, too. Of course, it's different when you've always lived in a place.

OSBORNE: You like it in a different way.

RALEIGH: Yes. Just behind our house there's a stream called the Highland; it runs for miles—right through the middle of the forest. Dennis and I followed it once as far as we could.

OSBORNE: I used to walk a lot round Lyndhurst.

RALEIGH: I wish we'd known each other then. You could have come with Dennis and me.

OSBORNE: I wish I had. I used to walk alone.

RALEIGH: You must come and stay with us one day.

OSBORNE: I should like to—awfully.

RALEIGH: I can show you places in the forest that nobody knows about except Dennis and me. It gets thicker and darker and cooler, and you stir up all kinds of funny wild animals.

OSBORNE: They say there are ruins, somewhere in the forest, of villages that William the Conqueror pulled down to let the forest grow.

RALEIGH: I know. We often used to look for them, but we haven't found them yet. [Pause] You must come and help look one day.

OSBORNE: I'll find them, all right!

RALEIGH: Then you can write to the papers. "Dramatic Discovery of Professor Osborne!"

[Osborne laughs]

OSBORNE: I did go exploring once—digging up Roman remains.

RALEIGH: Where was that?

OSBORNE: Near my home in Sussex there's a Roman road called Stane Street; it runs as straight as a line from the coast to London.

RALEIGH: I know it.

OSBORNE: Near where I live the road runs over Bignor Hill, but in recent times a new road's been cut round the foot of the hill, meeting the old road again farther on. The old road over the hill hasn't been used for years and years—and it's all grown over with grass, and bushes and trees grow in the middle of it.

RALEIGH: Can you still see where it runs?

OSBORNE: Quite easily, in places.

RALEIGH: Did you dig a bit of it up, then?

OSBORNE: Yes. We got permission to dig out a section. It was in wonderful condition.

RALEIGH: Did you find anything?

OSBORNE: We found a horseshoe—and a Roman penny.

RALEIGH: [Laughing] Splendid!

OSBORNE: It's awfully fascinating, digging like that.

RALEIGH: It must be. [Osborne glances at his watch] It is time yet?

OSBORNE: Two minutes. Then we must go up. I wish we had a good hot bath waiting for us when we get back.

RALEIGH: So do I. [Pause] We're having something special for dinner, aren't we?

OSBORNE: How did you know? It's supposed to be a secret.

RALEIGH: Mason dropped a hint.

OSBORNE: Well, we've a fresh chicken sent up from Noyelle Farm.

RALEIGH: I say!

OSBORNE: And a most awful luxury—two bottles of champagne and a half-dozen cigars! One each, and one spare one in case one explodes!

RALEIGH: I've never smoked a cigar.

[Raleigh notices Osborne's ring on the table; he picks it up]

RALEIGH: I say, here's your ring.

OSBORNE: Yes. I'm—I'm leaving it here. I don't want to risk losing it.

RALEIGH: Oh!

[There is silence. He puts the ring slowly down]

OSBORNE: [Rising] Well, I think perhaps we ought to get ready.

RALEIGH: Yes. Righto.

[He also rises]

OSBORNE: I'm not going to wear a belt—just my revolver, with the lanyard round my neck.

RALEIGH: I see. [He puts his lanyard round his neck and grips his revolver] I feel better with this in my hand, don't you?

OSBORNE: Yes, something to hold. Loaded all right?

RALEIGH: Yes.

[They put on their helmets. Osborne takes his pipe from his mouth and lays it carefully on the table]

OSBORNE: I do hate leaving a pipe when it's got a nice glow on the top like that.

RALEIGH: [With a short laugh] What a pity!

[There is another pause. Osborne glances at his watch as it lies on the table]

OSBORNE: Three minutes to. I think we'd better go.

RALEIGH: Righto.

[Their eyes meet as Osborne turns from the table]

OSBORNE: I'm glad it's you and I—together, Raleigh.

RALEIGH: [Eagerly] Are you—really?

OSBORNE: Yes.

RALEIGH: So am I—awfully.

OSBORNE: We must put up a good show.

RALEIGH: Yes. Rather!

[There is a short pause]

OSBORNE: Let's go along, shall we?

RALEIGH: Righto.

[They go towards the steps. Mason comes to the entrance of his dug-out as they pass]

MASON: Good luck, sir.

OSBORNE: Thanks, Mason.

MASON: It's a lovely chicken for dinner, sir.

OSBORNE: [Slowly going up the steps] Splendid!

MASON: Good luck, Mr. Raleigh.

RALEIGH: Thanks.

[Osborne and Raleigh go up together into the pale evening sun. Mason tidies the papers on the table, picks up the two coffee mugs, and goes away. There is silence in the trenches above the deserted dug-out. Then, suddenly, there comes the dull "crush" of bursting smoke bombs, followed in a second by the vicious *rattle of machine-guns. The red and green glow of German alarm rockets comes faintly through the dug-out door. Then comes the thin whistle and crash of falling shells; first one by itself, then two, almost together. Quicker and quicker they come, till the noise mingles together in confused turmoil. Yet the noise is deadened by the earth walls of the tiny dug-out, and comes quite softly till the whine of one shell rises above the others to a shriek and a crash. A dark funnel of earth leaps up beyond the parapet of the trench outside; earth falls and rattles down the steps, and a black cloud of smoke rises slowly out of sight. Gradually the noise dies away—there is a longer pause between the crash of each bursting shell. The machine-guns stop—rattle again and stop—rattle for the last time—and stop. Voices are calling in the trench outside; Stanhope's voice is heard]*

STANHOPE: All right, sir. Come down quickly!

COLONEL: How many?

STANHOPE: Only one. *[Another shell whines and shrieks and crashes near by. There is silence for a moment, then Stanhope speaks again]* Hurt, sir?

COLONEL: No. It's all right.

[Stanhope, pale and haggard, comes down the steps, followed by the Colonel]

STANHOPE: *[Calling up the steps]* Bring him down, sergeant-major.

S.-M.: *[Above]* Coming, sir.

STANHOPE: *[To the Colonel]* You won't want me, will you?

COLONEL: Well—er—

STANHOPE: I want to go and see those men.

COLONEL: Oh, all right.

[Stanhope goes to the door, making way for the Sergeant-Major to come down, followed by a bare-headed German Boy, in field gray, sobbing bitterly. Behind come two Soldiers with fixed bayonets. Stanhope goes up the steps. The Sergeant-Major takes the German Boy by the arm and draws him into the center of the dug-out to face the Colonel, who has seated himself at the table. The two Soldiers stand behind]

S.-M.: *[Soothingly to the German Boy]* All right, sonny, we ain't going to 'urt you.

[Suddenly the Boy falls on his knees and sobs out some words in broken English]

GERMAN: Mercy—mister—mercy!

S.-M.: Come on, lad, get up.

[With a huge fist he takes the Boy by the collar and draws him to his feet. The Boy sobs hysterically. The Colonel clears his throat and begins in somewhat poor German]

COLONEL: *Was ist sein Regiment?*

GERMAN: *Württembergisches.*

COLONEL: *Was ist der Nummer von sein Regiment?*

GERMAN: *Zwanzig.*

COLONEL: *[Making a note]* Twentieth Württembergers. *[He looks up again]* *Wann kommen Sie hier?*

GERMAN: *Gestern abend.*

COLONEL: *[Making a note and looking up again]* *Wo kommen Sie hier?*

GERMAN: *[After a moment's thought]* *Mein Geburtsort?*

COLONEL: *[Forgetting himself for a moment]* What's that?

GERMAN: *[In halting English]* You—wish—to know—where I was—born?

COLONEL: No! What town did you come up to the line from?

GERMAN: *[After a little hesitation]* I—do not tell you.

COLONEL: Oh, well, that's all right. *[To the Sergeant-Major]* Search him.

[The Sergeant-Major's big fists grope over the Boy's pockets. He produces a small book]

S.-M.: *[Giving it to the Colonel]* Looks like 'is pay-book, sir.

COLONEL: *[Looking eagerly into the book]* Good.

[The Sergeant-Major has found a pocket-book; the German Boy clutches at it impulsively]

S.-M.: 'Ere, stop that!

GERMAN: *Lass mich!* *[He pauses]* Let—me—please keep—that.

S.-M.: *[Very embarrassed]* You let go.

[He wrenches the case away and gives it to the Colonel]

COLONEL: *[Glancing at the papers in the case]* Look like letters. May be useful. Is that all, sergeant-major?

S.-M.: *[Looking at a few articles in his hands]* 'Ere's a few oddments, sir—bit o' string, sir; little box o' fruit drops; pocket-knife; bit o' cedar pencil—and a stick o' chocolate, sir.

COLONEL: Let him have those back, except the pocket-knife.

S.-M.: Very good, sir. *[He turns to the German Boy with a smile]* 'Ere you are, sonny.

[The German Boy takes back the oddments]

COLONEL: All right, sergeant-major. Send him straight back to my headquarters. I'll question him again there.

S.-M.: Very good, sir. *[He turns to the German]* Come on, sonny, up you go.

[He points up the steps]

[The German Boy, calm now, bows stiffly to the Colonel, and goes away, followed by the two Soldiers and the Sergeant-Major. The Colonel is deeply absorbed in the German's pay-book. He mutters "Splendid!" to himself, then looks at his watch and rises quickly. Stanhope comes slowly down the steps]

COLONEL: *[Excitedly]* Splendid, Stanhope! We've got all we wanted—20th Württembergers! His regiment came into the line last night. I must go right away and phone the brigadier. He'll be very pleased about it. It's a feather in our cap, Stanhope.

[Stanhope *has given one look of astonishment at the* Colonel *and strolled past him. He turns at the table and speaks in a dead voice*]

STANHOPE: How awfully nice—if the brigadier's pleased.

[*The* Colonel *stares at* Stanhope *and suddenly collects himself*]

COLONEL: Oh—er—what about the raiding-party —are they all safely back?

STANHOPE: Did you expect them to be all safely back, sir?

COLONEL: Oh—er—what—er——

STANHOPE: Four men and Raleigh came safely back, sir.

COLONEL: Oh, I say, I'm sorry! That's—er—six men and—er—Osborne?

STANHOPE: Yes, sir.

COLONEL: I'm very sorry. Poor Osborne!

STANHOPE: Still it'll be awfully nice if the briga- dier's pleased.

COLONEL: Don't be silly, Stanhope. Do you know —er—what happened to Osborne?

STANHOPE: A hand grenade—while he was wait- ing for Raleigh.

COLONEL: I'm very sorry. And the six men?

STANHOPE: Machine-gun bullets, I suppose.

COLONEL: Yes. I was afraid—er— [*His words trail away; he fidgets uneasily as* Stanhope *looks at him with a pale, expressionless face.* Raleigh *comes slowly down the steps, walking as though he were asleep; his hands are bleeding. The* Colonel *turns to the boy with enthusiasm*] Very well done, Raleigh. Well done, my boy. I'll get you a Military Cross for this! Splendid! [Raleigh *looks at the* Colonel *and tries to speak. He raises his hand to his forehead and sways. The* Colonel *takes him by the arm*] Sit down here, my boy. [Raleigh *sits on the edge of* Os- borne's *bed*] Have a good rest. Well, I must be off. [*He moves towards the steps, and turns once more to* Raleigh *as he leaves*] Very well done.

[*With a quick glance at* Stanhope, *the* Colonel *goes away. There is silence now in the trenches outside; the last shell has whistled over and crashed. Dusk is beginning to fall over the German lines. The glow of Very lights begins to rise and fade against the evening sky.* Stan- hope *is staring dumbly at the table—at* Os- borne's *watch and ring. Presently he turns his haggard face towards* Raleigh, *who sits with lowered head, looking at the palms of his hands.* Stanhope *moves slowly across towards the doorway, and pauses to look down at* Raleigh. Raleigh *looks up into* Stanhope's *face, and their eyes meet. When* Stanhope *speaks, his voice is still expressionless and dead*]

STANHOPE: Must you sit on Osborne's bed?

[*He turns and goes slowly up the steps.* Raleigh *rises unsteadily, murmurs "sorry"—and stands with lowered head. Heavy guns are booming miles away*]

THE CURTAIN FALLS

SCENE II.

Late evening on the same day. The dug-out is lit quite festively by an unusual number of candles. Two champagne bottles stand prominently on the table. Dinner is over.

Stanhope, *with a cigar between his teeth, lounges across the table, one elbow among the plates and mugs. His hair is ruffled; there is a bright red flush on his cheeks. He has just made a remark which has sent* Hibbert *and* Trotter *into uproarious laughter; he listens with a smile.* Trotter *is sitting on the box to the right of the table, leaning back against the wall. A cigar is embedded in his podgy fingers; his face is a shiny scarlet, with deep red patches below the ears. The three bottom buttons of his tunic are undone, and now and then his hands steal gently over his distended stomach.* Hibbert *sits on the bed to the left, his thin white fingers nervously twitching the ash from his cigar. His pale face is shiny with sweat from the heat of the candles; his laugh is high-pitched and excited.* Trotter *speaks in a husky voice as the laughter dies away.*

TROTTER: And what did she say to that?

STANHOPE: She said, "Not in these trousers"—in French.

[Trotter *and* Hibbert *burst into laughter again*]

TROTTER: [*Coughing and wheezing*] Oh—dear-o- dear!

STANHOPE: I simply drew myself up and said "Very well, mam'sel, have it your own way."

TROTTER: And she did?

STANHOPE: No. She didn't.

[*Again the others laugh.* Trotter *wipes a tear from his eye*]

TROTTER: Oh, skipper, you *are* a scream—and no mistake!

HIBBERT: I never forget picking up a couple of tarts one night and taking 'em out to dinner.

TROTTER: [*Winking at* Stanhope] 'E's orf again.

HIBBERT: We drank enough bubbly to sink a battleship——

STANHOPE: To *float* a battleship.

HIBBERT: Well—to float a battleship. Then I took 'em for a joy-ride out to Maidenhead—did sixty all the way. We danced a bit at Skindles, and drank a lot of port and muck. Then damned if I didn't lose the way coming back—got landed miles from any- where. And those tarts began cursing me like hell— said I'd done it on purpose. I said if they didn't damn well shut up I'd chuck 'em both out in the road and leave 'em.

STANHOPE: [*Ironically*] Hurrah! That's the idea! Treat 'em rough!

HIBBERT: [*Giggling*] That shut 'em up all right! Then I started doing about sixty down all sorts of roads—I went round a corner on two wheels with those girls' hair on end—didn't have any more trouble from them!

[*He chuckles at the memory, and takes an unsteady gulp of champagne*]

STANHOPE: You're the sort of fellow who makes girls hard to please.

TROTTER: [*Heavily*] Well, I never 'ad no motorcar, my old lady and me used to walk; legs is good enough for me.

STANHOPE: You satisfied with legs?

TROTTER: *I* am—yes!

STANHOPE: Much cheaper.

HIBBERT: [*Laughing delightedly*] That's damn good!

STANHOPE: [*Raising his mug*] Well, here's to a toast to legs—God bless 'em!

HIBBERT: [*Raising his mug*] Good old legs!

TROTTER: [*Raising his mug*] Shank's mare.

STANHOPE: Shank's *what*?

TROTTER: Shank's mare, they call 'em.

STANHOPE: Call what?

TROTTER: Why—legs.

HIBBERT: [*Almost screaming with delight*] Oh, Trotter! you're a dream!

TROTTER: [*Turning a baleful eye on* Hibbert] You've 'ad too much champagne, you 'ave.

[Hibbe*rt takes a leather case from his pocket and produces some picture post-cards*]

HIBBERT: I say, I've never shown you these, have I?

[*He hands them one by one to* Stanhope, *smiling up into* Stanhope's *face for approval*]

STANHOPE: Where did you get these from?

HIBBERT: In Béthune. [*He hands up a card*] She's all right, isn't she?

STANHOPE: Too fat.

HIBBERT: [*Looking over* Stanhope's *shoulder*] Oh, I don't know.

STANHOPE: Much too fat. [*He hands the card to* Trotter] What do you think, Trotter?

[Trotter *takes a pair of pince-nez from his pocket, balances them on his fat nose, and looks at the picture*]

HIBBERT: All right, isn't she?

TROTTER: Well, I don't know. If you ask me I'd rather 'ave a decent picture of Margate Pier.

HIBBERT: [*Impatiently*] Oh, you don't understand art. [*He hands another card to* Stanhope] There's a nice pair of legs for you.

STANHOPE: Too thin—aren't they, Trotter?

[*He hands* Trotter *the card*]

TROTTER: [*After some thought*] Scraggy, I call 'em.

HIBBERT: [*Handing* Stanhope *another card*] That's the one I like best.

STANHOPE: Not bad.

HIBBERT: Glorious bedroom eyes.

STANHOPE: She's all right.

HIBBERT: Ever seen that show *Zip* at the Hippodrome? Couple of damn fine girls in that—twins. Did you see 'em, skipper?

STANHOPE: [*Wearily*] I don't know—seen stacks of shows—can't remember them all. [*He brightens up*]

Now then, swallow up that bubbly! Hi! Mason!

MASON: Yessir!

[Mason *appears*]

STANHOPE: Bring some whisky.

MASON: Yessir.

[*He disappears*]

TROTTER: What? Whisky on top of champagne?

STANHOPE: Why not? It's all right.

TROTTER: Well, I don't know; doesn't sound right to me. I feel as if somebody's blown me up with a bicycle pump.

STANHOPE: You look it, too.

TROTTER: [*Blowing a stream of cigar smoke up to the dark ceiling*] Any'ow, it was a jolly bit o' chicken —and I'd go a mile any day for a chunk o' that jam pudding.

[Mason *brings a bottle of whisky*]

STANHOPE: Your pudding's made Mr. Trotter feel all blown out, Mason.

MASON: I'm sorry, sir; it wasn't meant, sir.

TROTTER: It was all right, Mason, take it from me I know a decent bit o' pudden when I see it.

MASON: It was only boiled ration biscuits and jam, sir. [*He turns to* Stanhope] I thought I better tell you, sir—this is the last bottle.

STANHOPE: The last bottle! Why, damn it, we bought six!

MASON: I know, sir. But five's gone.

STANHOPE: Where the devil's it gone to?

MASON: Well, sir, you remember there was one on the first night—and then one——

STANHOPE: Oh, for Lord's sake don't go through them one by one; this'll last till sunrise. [*He turns to* Trotter *and* Hibbert] Sunrise to-morrow, my lads!

TROTTER: Oh, forget that.

STANHOPE: You bet we will! Now then! Who's for a spot of whisky?

TROTTER: I reckon I'm about full up. I'd like a nice cup o' tea, Mason.

MASON: Very good, sir. [*He goes out*]

STANHOPE: Tea!

TROTTER: Yes. That's what I want. Decent cup o' tea. Still, I'll just have about a spoonful o' whisky— got a touch of pulpitations.

STANHOPE: Here you are—say when!

TROTTER: Wo! That's enough!

STANHOPE: You'll have a decent spot, won't you, Hibbert?

HIBBERT: Yes. I'm game!

TROTTER: [*Stifling a hiccup*] Just a cup o' tea— then I'll go and relieve young Raleigh. Pity 'e didn't come down to supper.

STANHOPE: I told him to. I told him to come down for an hour and let the sergeant-major take over.

TROTTER: I wonder why 'e didn't come.

HIBBERT: That lad's too keen on his "duty." He told me he liked being up there with the men better than down here with us.

STANHOPE: [*Quietly*] He *said* that?

HIBBERT: Yes, I told him about the chicken and champagne and cigars and he stared at me and said

"You're not having that, are you?"—just as if he thought we were going to chuck it away!

TROTTER: I reckon that raid shook 'im up more'n we thought. I like that youngster. 'E's got pluck. Strong lad, too—the way he came back through the smoke after that raid, carrying that Boche under 'is arm like a baby.

HIBBERT: Did you see him afterwards, though? He came into that dugout and never said a word—didn't seem to know where he was.

TROTTER: Well, 'e's only a lad.

STANHOPE: [To Hibbert] He actually told you he preferred being up with the men better than down here?

HIBBERT: That's what he said.

TROTTER: Well, I 'ope 'e gets the M.C., that's all; 'e's just the kid I'd like if I ever 'ave a kid—strong and plucky.

STANHOPE: Oh, for God's sake forget that bloody raid! Think I want to talk about it?

TROTTER: [Surprised] No—but, after all——

STANHOPE: Well—shut up!

TROTTER: [Uneasily] All right—all right.

STANHOPE: We were having a jolly decent evening till you started blabbing about the war.

TROTTER: I didn't start it.

STANHOPE: You did.

TROTTER: You began it about——

STANHOPE: Well, for God's sake stop it, then!

TROTTER: All right—all right.

HIBBERT: Did I ever tell you the story about the girl I met in Soho?

STANHOPE: I don't know—I expect you did.

HIBBERT: [Undismayed] It'll amuse you. I'd been to a dance, and I was coming home quite late——

STANHOPE: Yes, and it's late now. You go on duty at eleven. You better go and get some sleep.

HIBBERT: It's all right. I'm as fresh as a daisy.

STANHOPE: You may be. But go to bed.

HIBBERT: What?

STANHOPE: [Louder] I said, "Go to bed!"

HIBBERT: I say, that's a nice end to a jolly evening!

STANHOPE: I'm sorry. I'm tired.

HIBBERT: [Perkily] Well, you better go to bed!

[There is silence. Stanhope looks at Hibbert, who sniggers]

STANHOPE: What was that you said?

HIBBERT: I was only joking.

STANHOPE: I asked what you said.

HIBBERT: I said, "You better go to bed."

[Stanhope's flushed face is looking full into Hibbert's. Hibbert gives the ghost of a snigger]

STANHOPE: Clear out of here!

HIBBERT: [Rising unsteadily] What—d'you mean?

STANHOPE: Get out of here, for God's sake!

HIBBERT: [Blustering] I say—look here——

STANHOPE: Get out of my sight! [With a frightened glance at Stanhope, Hibbert sneaks quietly away into his dug-out. There is silence, and the guns can be heard—deep and ominous] Little worm gets on my nerves.

TROTTER: Poor little bloke. Never seen 'im so cheerful before out 'ere.

STANHOPE: Doesn't he nearly drive you mad?

TROTTER: I reckon 'e only wanted to keep cheerful.

STANHOPE: Doesn't his repulsive little mind make you sick? [Mason brings Trotter's mug of tea and goes away] I envy you, Trotter. Nothing upsets you, does it? You're always the same.

TROTTER: Always the same, am I? [He sighs] Little you know——

STANHOPE: You never get sick to death of everything, or so happy you want to sing.

TROTTER: I don't know—I whistle sometimes.

STANHOPE: But you always feel the same.

TROTTER: I feel all blown out now. [There is a pause. Trotter sips his tea and Stanhope takes a whisky] 'Ere's 'Ibbert's post-cards. Funny a bloke carrying pictures like this about. Satisfies 'is lust, I s'pose—poor little feller. [He rises] Well, I'll go and relieve young Raleigh. Pity 'e didn't come down to supper.

[He tries to button his tunic, without success. He buckles his webbing belt over his unbuttoned tunic, puts on his helmet, and slings his respirator over his shoulder] Well, cheero!

STANHOPE: You realize you're my second-in-command now, don't you?

TROTTER: Well, you 'adn't said nothing about it, but——

STANHOPE: Well, you are.

TROTTER: Righto, skipper. [He pauses] Thanks. [He goes towards the door] I won't let you down.

STANHOPE: After your duty, have a decent sleep. We must be ready at half-past five.

TROTTER: Righto, skipper. Well, I'll be going up. Give me a chance to cool off up there. It's as 'ot as 'ell in 'ere, with all them damn candles burning.

STANHOPE: I suppose it is. My head's nearly splitting.

[He blows out three of the candles, leaving the dim light of one]

TROTTER: [Half up the steps] There's a bit of a mist rising.

STANHOPE: [Dully] Is there? [Trotter disappears into the night. Stanhope broods over the table] Mason!

MASON: [Outside] Yessir!

STANHOPE: You can bring Mr. Raleigh's dinner.

MASON: Very good, sir.

[Mason brings a plate of steaming food, gathering up and taking away some of the used crockery. Presently Raleigh comes slowly down the steps. He pauses at the bottom, takes off his helmet and hesitates. Stanhope is sitting at the table puffing at the remains of his cigar. There is silence except for the rumble of the guns]

STANHOPE: I thought I told you to come down to dinner at eight o'clock?

RALEIGH: Oh, I'm sorry. I didn't think you—er——

STANHOPE: Well? You didn't think I—er—what?

RALEIGH: I didn't think you'd—you'd mind—if I didn't.

STANHOPE: I see. And why do you think I asked you—if I didn't mind?

RALEIGH: I'm sorry.

STANHOPE: Well, we've kept your dinner. It's ready for you here.

RALEIGH: Oh, it's awfully good of you to have kept it for me, but I—I had something to eat up there.

STANHOPE: You—had something to eat up there? What do you mean, exactly?

RALEIGH: They brought the tea around while I was on duty. I had a cup, and some bread and cheese.

STANHOPE: Are you telling me—you've been feeding with the men?

RALEIGH: Well, Sergeant Baker suggested——

STANHOPE: So you take your orders from Sergeant Baker, do you?

RALEIGH: No, but——

STANHOPE: You eat the men's rations when there's barely enough for each man?

RALEIGH: They asked me to share.

STANHOPE: Now, look here. I know you're new to this, but I thought you'd have the common sense to leave the men alone to their meals. Do you think they want an officer prowling round eating their rations, and sucking up to them like that? My officers are here to be respected—not laughed at.

RALEIGH: Why did they ask me—if they didn't mean it?

STANHOPE: Don't you realize they were making a fool of you?

RALEIGH: Why should they?

STANHOPE: So you know more about my men than I do?

[There is silence, Raleigh is facing Stanhope squarely]

RALEIGH: I'm sorry then—if I was wrong.

STANHOPE: Sit down.

RALEIGH: It's all right, thanks.

STANHOPE: [Suddenly shouting] Sit down! [Raleigh sits on the box to the right of the table. Stanhope speaks quietly again] I understand you prefer being up there with the men than being down here with us?

RALEIGH: I don't see what you mean.

STANHOPE: What did you tell Hibbert?

RALEIGH: Hibbert? I—I didn't say——

STANHOPE: Don't lie.

RALEIGH: [Rising] I'm not lying! Why should I—lie?

STANHOPE: Then why didn't you come down to supper when I told you to?

RALEIGH: I—I wasn't hungry. I had rather a headache. It's cooler up there.

STANHOPE: You insulted Trotter and Hibbert by not coming. You realize that, I suppose?

RALEIGH: I didn't mean to do anything like that.

STANHOPE: Well, you did. You know now—don't you? [Raleigh makes no reply. He is trying to understand why Stanhope's temper has risen to a trembling fury. Stanhope can scarcely control his voice. Loudly] I say—you know now, don't you?

RALEIGH: Yes. I'm sorry.

STANHOPE: My officers work together. I'll have no damn prigs.

RALEIGH: I'll speak to Trotter and Hibbert. I didn't realize——

[Stanhope raises his cigar. His hand trembles so violently that he can scarcely take the cigar between his teeth. Raleigh looks at Stanhope, fascinated and horrified]

STANHOPE: What are you looking at?

RALEIGH: [Lowering his head] Nothing.

STANHOPE: Anything—funny about me?

RALEIGH: No. [After a moment's silence Raleigh speaks in a low, halting voice] I'm awfully sorry, Dennis, if—if I annoyed you by coming to your company.

STANHOPE: What on earth are you talking about? What do you mean?

RALEIGH: You resent my being here.

STANHOPE: Resent you being here?

RALEIGH: Ever since I came——

STANHOPE: I don't know what you mean. I resent you being a damn fool, that's all. [There is a pause] Better eat your dinner before it's cold.

RALEIGH: I'm not hungry, thanks.

STANHOPE: Oh, for God's sake, sit down and eat it like a man!

RALEIGH: I can't eat it, thanks.

STANHOPE: [Shouting] Are you going to eat your dinner?

RALEIGH: Oh! Good God! Don't you understand? How can I sit down and eat that—when—[His voice is nearly breaking]—when Osborne's—lying—out there——

[Stanhope rises slowly. His eyes are wide and staring; he is fighting for breath, and his words come brokenly]

STANHOPE: My God! You bloody little swine! You think I don't care—you think you're the only soul that cares!

RALEIGH: And yet you can sit there and drink champagne—and smoke cigars—

STANHOPE: The one man I could trust—my best friend—the one man I could talk to as man to man —who understood everything—and you think I don't care——

RALEIGH: But how can you when——?

STANHOPE: To forget, you little fool—to forget! D'you understand? To forget! You think there's no limit to what a man can bear?

[He turns quickly from Raleigh and goes to the dark corner by Osborne's bed. He stands with his face towards the wall, his shoulders heaving as he fights for breath]

RALEIGH: I'm awfully sorry, Dennis. I—I didn't understand. [Stanhope *makes no reply*] You don't know how—I——

STANHOPE: Go away, please—leave me alone.

RALEIGH: Can't I——

[Stanhope *turns wildly upon* Raleigh]

STANHOPE: Oh, get out! For God's sake, get out! [Raleigh *goes away into his dug-out, and Stanhope is alone. The Very lights rise and fall outside, softly breaking the darkness with their glow—sometimes steel-blue, sometimes gray. Through the night there comes the impatient grumble of gun fire that never dies away*]

THE CURTAIN FALLS

SCENE III.

Towards dawn. The candles are no longer burning. The intense darkness of the dug-out is softened by the glow of the Very lights in the sky beyond the doorway. There is no sound except the distant mutter of the guns.

A Man *comes from the servants' dug-out; for a moment his head and shoulders stand out black against the glowing sky, then he passes on into the darkness by the table. There comes the rasp of a striking match—a tiny flame—and a candle gleams.* Mason *blinks in the light and turns to* Stanhope's *bed.* Stanhope *lies huddled with his blanket drawn tightly round him.*

MASON: [*Softly*] Sir—— [Stanhope *does not move;* Mason *shakes him gently by the knee. A little louder*] Sir——

STANHOPE: Yes? [*There is a pause*] That you, Mason?

MASON: 'Arf-past five, sir.

STANHOPE: Oh, right. [*He raises himself on his elbow*] I was only half-asleep. I keep on waking up. It's so frightfully cold in here.

MASON: It's a cold dug-out, this one, sir. I've made some 'ot tea.

STANHOPE: Good. You might bring me some.

MASON: Right you are, sir.

STANHOPE: And take some to the officers in there —and wake them up.

MASON: Very good, sir.

[Mason *goes to his dug-out.* Stanhope *rises stiffly from his bed, shudders from the cold, and slowly begins putting his equipment on.* Trotter *wanders in from his dug-out vigorously lathering his face. He is dressed, except for his collar*]

TROTTER: Wash and brush-up, tuppence!

STANHOPE: [*Looking up, surprised*] Hullo! I thought you were asleep.

TROTTER: I 'ad a decent sleep when I came off dooty. What's the time?

STANHOPE: Half-past five. It'll be getting light soon. You better buck up.

TROTTER: All right. I shan't be long. Sounds quiet enough out there.

STANHOPE: Yes.

[Mason *brings four mugs of tea*]

TROTTER: Ah! that's what I want. A decent cup of tea.

MASON: [*Putting a mug on the table for* Stanhope] Nice and 'ot, sir. I've cut a packet of sambridge for each gentleman, sir.

STANHOPE: Good.

[Mason *takes the other mugs of tea into the right-hand dug-out.* Trotter *follows, lathering with gusto*]

STANHOPE: You might give Hibbert and Raleigh a call.

TROTTER: I woke 'em up, skipper. They're getting their things on.

[Mason *returns*]

STANHOPE: When you've cleared up your kitchen, you must dress and join your platoon in the line.

MASON: Very good, sir.

STANHOPE: If things are going well at eleven o'clock, come down here and do your best to get some lunch for us. We shall come down in turn as we can.

MASON: Very good, sir.

[Stanhope *sits at the table and begins to write a short report. The first sign of dawn is beginning to gleam in the dark sky.* Stanhope *calls* "Runner!" *as he writes. A* Soldier *comes from the servants' dug-out*]

STANHOPE: [*Folding the note*] Take this to Battalion Headquarters. There's no reply.

SOLDIER: Yessir.

[*The* Soldier *salutes and goes up the steps. A plaintive noise comes from the other dug-out.* Trotter *is singing* "There's a long, long trail a-winding." Stanhope *listens for a moment, then rises, takes a few small coins from his pocket, and throws them into* Trotter's *dug-out. The singing stops abruptly. After a moment* Trotter's *voice comes*]

TROTTER: Thank you kindly, gov'nor!

[*The* Sergeant-Major *comes down the steps*]

STANHOPE: Morning, sergeant-major.

S.-M.: Morning, sir. Wiring parties are just in, sir. Made a decent job of it—right down to the support line.

STANHOPE: Good. Everything quiet?

S.-M.: It's all right opposite 'ere, sir, but the guns are goin' 'ard down south. 'Eavy bombardment. Not sure if it ain't spreading up this way, sir.

STANHOPE: Very likely it is. The officers are coming up in a minute. They'll stand by with their platoons. I must stay here awhile in case of messages. I shall come up directly things begin to happen.

S.-M.: Very good, sir.

STANHOPE: Are the men having their tea?

S.-M.: Yessir.

STANHOPE: Let 'em have a decent drop of rum.

S.-M.: About 'arf again, sir?

STANHOPE: Yes.

S.-M.: If the attack don't come, sir, 'ow long are we to stand-to?

STANHOPE: We must expect the attack any time up till mid-day. After then I don't think it'll come till to-morrow.

S.-M.: Very good, sir.

STANHOPE: We must naturally make our plans to meet things as they happen.

S.-M.: Quite, sir.

STANHOPE: All right, sergeant-major. I'll see you up there soon.

S.-M.: Yes, sir.

[*He salutes and goes away.* Mason *brings in four little packets of sandwiches, and puts one packet on the table for* Stanhope]

MASON: Your sambridges, sir. 'Arf bully beef and 'arf sardine. Sardine on top, sir.

STANHOPE: How delicious. No *pâté de foie gras?*

MASON: No what, sir?

STANHOPE: No *pâté de fois gras?*

MASON: No, sir. The milkman 'asn't been yet.

[Mason *takes the other parcels to the left-hand dug-out.* Stanhope *pours a little whisky into his tea and the remainder of the contents of the bottle into his flask.* Mason *returns*]

STANHOPE: Get dressed as soon as you can.

MASON: Yessir.

[Mason *goes out.* Trotter *comes in, fully dressed for the line*]

TROTTER: All ready, skipper. Want me to go up?

STANHOPE: Yes. I think so. Go right round the line and see everything's all right. I'll be up soon.

[*Suddenly there comes the faint whistle and thud of falling shells—a few seconds between each.* Stanhope *and* Trotter *listen intently, four shells fall, then silence*]

TROTTER: 'Ullo, 'ullo.

[Stanhope *strides to the doorway, goes up a few steps, and looks out into the night. He comes slowly back*]

STANHOPE: Over on Lancer's Alley—somewhere by the reserve line.

[*There comes the louder thud of three more shells*]

TROTTER: That's nearer.

STANHOPE: Better go up, Trotter. Call the others.

TROTTER: [*At the left-hand dug-out*] 'Ibbert! Raleigh! come on! [*He lights a cigarette over the candle—lingers a moment, and slowly goes up the steps*] Cheero, skipper. See you later.

STANHOPE: Send your runner down to tell me how things are going.

TROTTER: Righto.

[Trotter *disappears into the dark. A vague white line of dawn is broadening above the dark trench wall outside.* Stanhope *sits at the table and sips his tea. He takes a cigarette and lights it with a quivering hand.* Raleigh *comes from his dug-out.* Stanhope *lowers his head and writes in his note-book*]

RALEIGH: Do you want me to go up?

STANHOPE: [*Without looking up*] Yes. Trotter's gone.

RALEIGH: Right. [*He goes to the steps and turns shyly*] Cheero—Stanhope.

STANHOPE: [*Still writing with lowered head*] Cheero, Raleigh. I shall be coming up soon. [Raleigh *goes up the steps.* Stanhope *stops writing, raises his head, and listens. The shells are falling steadily now. He glances towards the left-hand dug-out and calls*] Hibbert! [*There is no reply. He slowly rises and goes to the left-hand dug-out doorway. He calls again— louder*] Hibbert!! [*He looks into the doorway and says:*] What are you doing? [Hibbert *appears. He is very pale; he moves as if half asleep*] Come along, man!

HIBBERT: You want me to go up now?

STANHOPE: Of course I do. The others have gone.

HIBBERT: Got a drop of water?

STANHOPE: What d'you want water for?

HIBBERT: I'm so frightfully thirsty. All that champagne and stuff—dried my mouth up.

[Stanhope *pours a drop of water into a mug and gives it to* Hibbert]

STANHOPE: Here you are. Didn't you have tea?

HIBBERT: Yes. It was a bit sweet, though.

[*The shelling is steadily increasing, and now, above the lighter "crush" of the smaller shells, there comes the deep, resounding "boom" of Minenwerfer.* Hibbert *sips his water very slowly, rinsing his mouth deliberately with each sip.* Stanhope *is by the doorway, looking up into the trench. He has just turned away as a sonorous drawn-out call comes floating through the dawn: "Stretcher-bear—ers!"* Stanhope *half turns, then faces* Hibbert]

STANHOPE: Come on. Buck up.

HIBBERT: There's no appalling hurry, is there?

STANHOPE: No hurry! Why d'you think the others have gone up?

HIBBERT: [*Slowly*] What? Trotter and Raleigh?

STANHOPE: [*Sharply*] Wake up, man! What the devil's the matter with you?

HIBBERT: [*Slowly putting down his mug*] Champagne dries the mouth up so. Makes the tongue feel like a bit of paper.

[*There is a slight pause*]

STANHOPE: The longer you stay here, the harder it'll be to go up.

HIBBERT: Good Lord! You don't think I'm——

STANHOPE: You're just wasting as much time as you can.

HIBBERT: Well, damn it, it's no good going up till I feel fit. Let's just have another spot of water.

[Hibbert *takes the jug and pours out a little more water. He is the picture of misery.* Stanhope *stands impatiently beside him.* Mason *appears from his dug-out, fully dressed for the line, his rifle slung over his shoulder*]

MASON: I'll go right along, sir. I've made up the fire to last a good three hours—if you don't mind me popping down about nine o'clock to 'ave a look at it.

STANHOPE: All right, Mason. Mr. Hibbert's coming up now. You can go along with him.

MASON: [To Hibbert] I'd like to come along of you if you don't mind, sir. I ain't bin up in this part of the front line. Don't want to get lorst.

STANHOPE: Mr. Hibbert'll show you the way up. [He turns to Hibbert] Keep your men against the back wall of the trench as long as the shells are dropping behind. Cheero! [Hibbert looks at Stanhope for a moment, then with a slight smile, he goes slowly up the steps and into the trench, Mason following behind. A dark figure stands out against the pale sky; comes hurrying down the steps—a Private Soldier, out of breath and excited] Yes?

SOLDIER: Message from Mr. Trotter, sir. Shells falling mostly behind support line. Minnies along front line.

STANHOPE: Who's just been hit?

SOLDIER: Corporal Ross, I think it was, sir. Minnie dropped in the trench at the corner—just as I come away.

[The Sergeant-Major comes down the steps very much out of breath]

STANHOPE: [To the Soldier] All right, thanks.

[The Soldier salutes, and goes up the steps slower than he came down]

S.-M.: Beginning to get 'ot, sir.

STANHOPE: Corporal Ross hit?

S.-M.: Yessir.

STANHOPE: Badly?

S.-M.: Pretty badly, sir.

STANHOPE: Most of the shelling's going over, isn't it?

S.-M.: Most of the shells is be'ind, sir, but there's Minnies and rifle grenades along the front line. Pretty 'ot it's getting, sir. They're attacking down south—there's rifle fire.

STANHOPE: All right, sergeant-major; thanks.

S.-M.: What I come to ask, sir—what about the wounded—getting 'em down, sir? The shelling's pretty thick over Lancer's Alley.

STANHOPE: What about Fosse Way?

S.-M.: Pretty bad there, too, sir.

STANHOPE: Don't try then. Take any one badly hit down into the big dug-out on the right. Let the stretcher-bearers do what they can there.

S.-M.: Very good, sir.

STANHOPE: Only Corporal Ross hit?

S.-M.: That's all, sir——

[Again there comes the drawn-out call—several times as it passes from man to man: "Stretcher-bear—ers!" The Sergeant-Major's eyes meet Stanhope's. He turns and goes up the steps. Stanhope is alone. Flying fragments of shell whistle and hiss and moan overhead. The sharp "crack" of the rifle grenades, the thud of the shells, and the boom of the Minenwerfer mingle together in a muffled roar. Stanhope takes his belt from the table and buckles it on, puts his revolver lanyard round his neck, and drops his flask and sandwiches into his pocket. The Sergeant-Major reappears and comes hurrying down the steps]

STANHOPE: [Turning quickly] What is it, sergeant-major?

S.-M.: Mr. Raleigh, sir——

STANHOPE: What!

S.-M.: Mr. Raleigh's been 'it, sir. Bit of shell's got 'im in the back.

STANHOPE: Badly?

S.-M.: 'Fraid it's broke 'is spine, sir; can't move 'is legs.

STANHOPE: Bring him down here.

S.-M.: Down 'ere, sir?

STANHOPE: [Shouting] Yes! Down here—quickly!

[The Sergeant-Major hurries up the steps. A shell screams and bursts very near. The Sergeant-Major shrinks back and throws his hand across his face, as though a human hand could ward off the hot flying pieces. He stumbles on again into the trench, and hurriedly away. Stanhope is by Osborne's bed, fumbling a blanket over it. He takes a trench coat off the wall and rolls it for a pillow. He goes to his own bed, takes up his blanket, and turns as the Sergeant-Major comes carefully down the steps carrying Raleigh like a child in his huge arms]

STANHOPE: [With blanket ready] Lay him down there.

S.-M.: 'E's fainted, sir. 'E was conscious when I picked 'im up.

[The Sergeant-Major lays the boy gently on the bed; he draws away his hands, looks furtively at the palms, and wipes the blood on the sides of his trousers. Stanhope covers Raleigh with his blanket, looks intently at the boy, and turns to the Sergeant-Major]

STANHOPE: Have they dressed the wound?

S.-M.: They've just put a pad on it, sir. Can't do no more.

STANHOPE: Go at once and bring two men with a stretcher.

S.-M.: We'll never get 'im down, sir, with them shells falling on Lancer's Alley.

STANHOPE: Did you hear what I said? Go and get two men with a stretcher.

S.-M.: [After a moment's hesitation] Very good, sir.

[The Sergeant-Major goes slowly away. Stanhope turns to Raleigh once more, then goes to the table, pushes his handkerchief into the water-jug, and brings it, wringing wet, to Raleigh's bed. He bathes the boy's face. Presently Raleigh gives a little moan opens his eyes, and turns his head]

RALEIGH: Hullo—Dennis——

STANHOPE: Well, Jimmy—[He smiles]—you got one quickly.

[*There is silence for a while.* Stanhope *is sitting on a box beside* Raleigh. *Presently* Raleigh *speaks again—in a wondering voice*]

RALEIGH: Why—how did I get down here?

STANHOPE: Sergeant-major brought you down.

[Raleigh *speaks again, vaguely, trying to recollect*]

RALEIGH: Something—hit me in the back—knocked me clean over—sort of—winded me—I'm all right now.

[*He tries to rise*]

STANHOPE: Steady, old boy. Just lie there quietly for a bit.

RALEIGH: I'll be better if I get up and walk about. It happened once before—I got kicked in just the same place at football; it—it soon wore off. It—it just numbs you a bit. [*There is a pause*] What's that rumbling noise?

STANHOPE: The guns are making a bit of a row.

RALEIGH: Our guns?

STANHOPE: No. Mostly theirs.

[*Again there is silence in the dug-out. A very faint rose light is beginning to glow in the dawn sky.* Raleigh *speaks again—uneasily*]

RALEIGH: I say—Dennis——

STANHOPE: Yes, old boy?

RALEIGH: It—it hasn't gone through, has it? It only just hit me?—and knocked me down?

STANHOPE: It's just gone through a bit, Jimmy.

RALEIGH: I won't have to—go on lying here?

STANHOPE: I'm going to have you taken away.

RALEIGH: Away? Where?

STANHOPE: Down to the dressing-station—then hospital—then home. [*He smiles*] You've got a Blighty one, Jimmy.

RALEIGH: But I—I can't go home just for—for a knock in the back. [*He stirs restlessly*] I'm certain I'll be better if—if I get up. [*He tries to raise himself, and gives a sudden cry*] Oh—God! It does hurt!

STANHOPE: It's bound to hurt, Jimmy.

RALEIGH: What's—on my legs? Something holding them down——

STANHOPE: It's all right, old chap; it's just the shock—numbed them.

[*Again there is a pause. When* Raleigh *speaks there is a different note in his voice*]

RALEIGH: It's awfully decent of you to bother, Dennis. I feel rotten lying here—everybody else—up there.

STANHOPE: It's not your fault, Jimmy.

RALEIGH: So—damn—silly—getting hit. [*Pause*] Is there—just a drop of water?

STANHOPE: [*Rising quickly*] Sure. I've got some here. [*He pours some water into the mug and brings it to* Raleigh. *Cheerfully*] Got some tea-leaves in it. D'you mind?

RALEIGH: No. That's all right—thanks—[Stanhope *holds the mug to* Raleigh's *lips, and the boy drinks*] I say, Dennis, don't you wait—if—if you want to be getting on.

STANHOPE: It's quite all right, Jimmy.

RALEIGH: Can you stay for a bit?

STANHOPE: Of course I can.

RALEIGH: [*Faintly*] Thanks awfully. [*There is quiet in the dug-out for a long time.* Stanhope *sits with one hand on* Raleigh's *arm, and* Raleigh *lies very still. Presently he speaks again—hardly above a whisper*] Dennis——

STANHOPE: Yes, old boy?

RALEIGH: Could we have a light? It's—it's so frightfully dark and cold.

STANHOPE: [*Rising*] Sure! I'll bring a candle and get another blanket. [Stanhope *goes to the left-hand dug-out, and* Raleigh *is alone, very still and quiet, on* Osborne's *bed. The faint rosy glow of the dawn is deepening to an angry red. The gray night is dissolving, and the stars begin to go. A tiny sound comes from where* Raleigh *is lying—something between a sob and a moan.* Stanhope *comes back with a blanket. He takes a candle from the table and carries it to* Raleigh's *bed. He puts it on the box beside* Raleigh *and speaks cheerfully*] Is that better, Jimmy? [Raleigh *makes no sign*] Jimmy——

[*Still* Raleigh *is quiet.* Stanhope *gently takes his hand. There is a long silence.* Stanhope *lowers* Raleigh's *hand to the bed, rises and takes the candle back to the table. He sits on the bench behind the table with his back to the wall, and stares listlessly across at the boy on* Osborne's *bed. The solitary candle-flame throws up the lines of his pale, drawn face, and the dark shadows under his tired eyes. The thudding of the shells rises and falls like an angry sea. A* Private Soldier *comes scrambling down the steps, his round, red face wet with perspiration, his chest heaving for breath*]

SOLDIER: Message from Mr. Trotter, sir—will you come at once? [Stanhope *gazes round at the* Soldier *—and makes no other sign*] Mr. Trotter, sir—says will you come at once!

[Stanhope *rises stiffly and takes his helmet from the table*]

STANHOPE: All right, Broughton, I'm coming.

[*The* Soldier *turns and goes away.* Stanhope *pauses for a moment by* Osborne's *bed and lightly runs his fingers over* Raleigh's *tousled hair. He goes stiffly up the steps, his tall figure black against the dawn sky. The shelling has risen to a great fury. The solitary candle burns with a steady flame, and* Raleigh *lies in the shadows. The whine of a shell rises to a shriek and bursts on the dug-out roof. The shock stabs out the candle-flame; the timber props of the door cave slowly in, sandbags fall and block the passage to the open air. There is darkness in the dug-out. Here and there the red dawn glows through the jagged holes of the broken doorway. Very faintly there come the dull rattle of machine-guns and the fevered spatter of rifle fire*]

THE PLAY ENDS

Noel Coward

(1899– ——)

"Past master of the inconsequential," as Brooks Atkinson called him, and able to "transform old hat into harlequinade," Noel Coward descended upon London in the early nineteen-twenties as the representative of the cynical postwar generation and the *enfant terrible* of the klieg lights. The word "sophistication" which was applied by a twist of meaning to the generation's outlook or lack of one was appropriated by him as the slogan under which he fought for a reputation.

In the process Coward drew upon his head the opprobrium of some who called his art "decadent," which it was, in the broad sense of reflecting the deterioration of a once stable society. He also invited a sniff from those who lifted an eyebrow at an emptiness that somehow escaped seeming fatuous and that was elegantly and extravagantly successful. George Jean Nathan put the case against him particularly well when he accused him of "blowing soap bubbles through an upturned nose." He noted that it was a feat unimpressive to anyone "who is not likely to mistake an upturned nose for an upturned mind and a studiously acquired attitude for a natural superior air." But Nathan had the sagacity to observe that the enjoyment of the trick is not necessarily confined to those who can't see through it. And whether one saw through it or not, Coward prevailed upon audiences on both sides of the Atlantic with remarkable ease. Most of his plays were good for at least one successful turn on the stage. For winding up a contrivance so that it would make what Atkinson has called "spinning entertainment," there was no one in Britain to equal Noel Coward. Had he not also tried for seriousness on the stage, he might never have been found out except by the astutest critics. And even so, it is only on the stage that his seriousness betrayed him; on the screen, to judge from such exhibits as *Brief Encounter* and *In Which We Serve,* his gravity won a deserved respect—a fact that may serve someone as the basis for an essay on the differences between the screen and the stage.

Born in Teddington, Middlesex, to a father who worked for music publishers and later sold pianos and to a mother who encouraged musical and dramatic talent, Noel Coward dispensed with formal schooling at an early age and made his debut on the stage when he was eleven. He continued to exercise his acting ability until 1918, when he was called up for military service in the First World War. But an injury contracted during his training in the Artists' Rifles O. T. C. kept him hospitalized up to the Armistice. In 1920 he saw his first play, *I'll Leave It to You,* staged in London. Written when he was only eighteen years old, it was, not surprisingly, a failure, and he had to serve an apprenticeship of three years before playwriting became his forte to the same degree that acting already was.

He tasted success first, in 1923, with a serious drama of postwar decadence, *The Vortex.* It concerned a woman who resigns herself to age only when deserted by her gigolo, and her son, who clings to her and is psychologically disqualified for marriage. Since the background was "society" and the characters were "sophisticated," Coward was able to display some sharp observation in the play.

Coward's success became fabulous. In 1925, for example, he had five plays on the boards in London, and thereafter he was never to fear again the poverty that had been his greatest dread. His facility was so extraordinary that before he was thirty-five he already had twenty-four plays, revues, and musical comedies to his credit—and discredit. He wrote with great speed and was a perfect reflector of the manners practiced by the upper classes and admired by all but the most class-conscious of their social inferiors. He gave scrupulous attention to all theatrical details. He may have made a profitable specialty of frivolity, but he was able to do so only because he was anything but frivolous about his occupation. To it he brought not only craftsmanship but facility in virtually all other branches of theatre. He had an expert knowledge of directing, musical talent as both a composer and a pianist, and an acting style so sure in its timing and movement and speech that John Gielgud, after playing Coward parts, declared that it was impossible to speak lines after Coward had spoken them without giving a poor imitation. And he had a way of interesting the cleverest actors in his roles. Tallulah Bankhead was supremely at ease in the parts he wrote, and so was Gertrude Lawrence. With the latter, indeed, he made an acting team of unusual attractiveness, their partnership having had an auspicious beginning when she was fourteen and he fifteen and both appeared for the Liverpool Repertory Company in Hauptmann's *Hannele.*

It was by virtue of wit and airy charm that Coward captivated London and New York with numerous comedies such as *Hay Fever* (1925), *Private Lives* (1930), *Design for Living* (1933), and *Blithe Spirit* (1941), as well as with musicals such as *Bittersweet* (1929) and *Conversation Piece.* His activity was ceaseless. He also wrote a series of nine one-acters, *Tonight at 8:30,* a number of short and full-length melodramas and pseudo tragedies, and patriotic chronicles such as *Cavalcade* and *This Happy Breed.* He made a number of motion pictures: *Cavalcade, This Happy Breed, In Which We Serve* (a tribute to the British navy during the Second World War), *The Astonished Heart,* and *Brief Encounter,* a noteworthy treatment of his long one-act play *Still Life.* With these multiple activities and with his superb acting style and his production activities (as a partner of John C. Wilson and the Lunts), Noel Coward made himself the wonder of the British theatre.

The three full-length comedies which most advanced Coward's reputation are *Design for Living, Private Lives,* and *Blithe Spirit. Design for Living* was a breezy variant of the *ménage à trois* type of boulevard comedy; *Private Lives* made farcical entertainment out of a double marriage; and *Blithe Spirit* enlivened the theatre with the reasoned opinion that ghosts of first wives are an embarrassing superfluity in a household.

For Coward, as for Wilde, "the Book of Life begins with a man and woman in a garden" and ends "with Revelations"—in a drawing room. *Blithe Spirit* is less strenuously entertaining than *Design for Living* and *Private Lives.* Its plot is also less ingeniously galvanized into a semblance of liveliness on every occasion than *Private Lives.* But *Blithe Spirit* is somewhat more mature in humor and is written with greater taste. It has less smartness won at any cost. And it is less indicative of a high-strung personality than the earlier comedies.

If one had to select a play among the domestic comedies that proliferated in England for half a century, comedies of manners notable for their verve rather than their ideas, one could do worse than choose *Blithe Spirit.* It is the most original of these plays, a tour de force of fancy in which Coward also displays the cutting edge of his wit. He takes human beings as they are, and society as it is, in this sophisticated lark, but rates neither person nor milieu very

highly. His, as Shaw might have said, is essentially "mindless" writing, but it would be difficult to match its cleverness. Many writers who pride themselves on the higher order of their cerebration might well envy Noel Coward's technical skill and showmanship. His showmanship is, indeed, so facile that it is arrogant. In *Blithe Spirit,* however, this is patently a virtue, not a defect. Coward carries off his trickery with a jaunty air, which is more than half the fun. If there are unappeasable souls who will persist in calling the play, along with other comedies by Coward, hollow, it is difficult to understand how they could fail to concede that it has very pleasant reverberations.

In England, engaged in the life-and-death struggle with Hitler's war machine, there could be only gratitude for the kind of relief offered by *Blithe Spirit.* London took Coward's ghost story for what it really was—another variant of drawing-room comedy, with which England and its writers feel particularly at ease. It is perhaps significant that when that Englishman by adoption T. S. Eliot resolved to woo the British playgoer in 1949 with *The Cocktail Party,* he, too, found it expedient to adopt the style of drawing-room comedy. At the mid-point of the century in which nothing stood fast, the urbane art of the British stage remained steadfast. It was still capable of supporting a faith or a frolic. There might also be a skeptic here and there who would rather take a frolic from Coward than a faith from Eliot.

BIBLIOGRAPHY: Brooks Atkinson, *Broadway Scrapbook* (pp. 200–203), 1947; John Mason Brown, *Two on the Aisle* (pp. 108–120), 1938; Brown, *Seeing More Things* (pp. 200–208, 301–304), 1948; Noel Coward, *Present Indicative,* 1937, 1947; W. Somerset Maugham, Prefaces to Coward, *Bitter Sweet and Other Plays,* 1929; George Jean Nathan, *The Theatre Book of the Year 1946–1947* (pp. 142–145), 1947; Ernest Short, *Theatrical Cavalcade* (pp. 188–193), 1942.

BLITHE SPIRIT[1]

By Noel Coward

CHARACTERS

EDITH, *a maid*
RUTH
CHARLES

DR. BRADMAN
MRS. BRADMAN

MADAME ARCATI
ELVIRA

The action of the play takes place in the living room of Charles Condomine's house in Kent.

ACT ONE.
Scene 1. Before dinner on a summer evening.
Scene 2. After dinner.

ACT TWO.
Scene 1. The next morning.
Scene 2. Late the following afternoon.
Scene 3. Early evening. A few days later.

ACT THREE.
Scene 1. After dinner. A few days later.
Scene 2. Several hours later.

ACT I. SCENE I.

The scene is the living-room of the Condomines' house in Kent. The room is light, attractive and comfortably furnished. The arrangement of it may be left to the discretion of the producer. On the right there are French windows opening on to the garden. On the left there is an open fireplace. At the back, on the left, there are double doors leading into the dining-room. Up left, on an angle, there are double doors leading to the hall, the stairs, and the servants' quarters. When the curtain rises it is about eight o'clock on a summer evening. There is a wood fire burning because it is an English summer evening. Edith comes to table with tray of drinks. Ruth comes in. She is a smart-looking woman in the middle thirties. She is dressed for dinner but not elaborately.

RUTH: That's right, Edith.
EDITH: Yes'm.
RUTH: Now you'd better fetch me the ice bucket.
EDITH: Yes'm.

[1] This is the complete text for *Blithe Spirit* as Mr. Coward wrote it. The playgoer, having seen a performance and turning now to the book, may discover that in the acting version some lines, and in certain cases short scenes, are missing. The explanation is simple: those lines were eliminated on the stage because the play ran far beyond the usual time allotted to a Broadway production and because the necessity of bringing the curtain down at a reasonable and convenient hour seemed essential to the producer.

RUTH: Did you manage to get the ice out of those little tin trays?
EDITH: Yes'm—I 'ad a bit of a struggle though—but it's all right.
RUTH: And you filled the little trays up again with water?
EDITH: Yes'm.
RUTH: Very good, Edith—you're making giant strides.
EDITH: Yes'm.
RUTH: Madame Arcati, Mrs. Bradman and I will have our coffee in here, after dinner and Mr. Condomine and Dr. Bradman will have theirs in the dining-room—is that quite clear?
EDITH: Yes'm.
RUTH: And when you're serving dinner, Edith, try to remember to do it calmly and methodically.
EDITH: Yes'm.
RUTH: As you are not in the Navy it is unnecessary to do everything at the double.
EDITH: Very good, 'M.
RUTH: Now go and get the ice.
EDITH: [*Straining at the leash*] Yes'm. [*She starts off at full speed*]
RUTH: *Not* at a run, Edith.
EDITH: [*Slowing down*] Yes'm. [Edith goes]
    [Charles *comes in. He is a nice-looking man of about forty wearing a loose-fitting velvet smoking jacket*]
CHARLES: No sign of the advancing hordes?
RUTH: Not yet.
CHARLES: [*Going to the cocktail tray*] No ice.

RUTH: It's coming. I've been trying to discourage Edith from being quite so fleet of foot. You mustn't mind if everything is a little slow motion tonight.

CHARLES: I shall welcome it. The last few days have been extremely agitating. What do you suppose induced Agnes to leave us and go and get married?

RUTH: The reason was becoming increasingly obvious, dear.

CHARLES: Yes, but in these days nobody thinks anything of that sort of thing—she could have popped into the cottage hospital, had it, and popped out again.

RUTH: Her social life would have been seriously undermined.

CHARLES: We must keep Edith in the house more.

[Edith comes in slowly with the ice bucket]

RUTH: That's right, Edith—put it down on the table.

EDITH: Yes'm. [She does so]

CHARLES: I left my cigarette case on my dressing table, Edith—would you get it for me?

EDITH: Yes, sir. [She runs out of the room]

CHARLES: There now!

RUTH: You took her by surprise.

CHARLES: [At the cocktail table] A dry Martini I think, don't you?

RUTH: Yes, darling—I expect Madame Arcati will want something sweeter.

CHARLES: We'll have this one for ourselves anyhow.

RUTH: [Taking a cigarette and sitting down] Oh dear!

CHARLES: What's the matter?

RUTH: I have a feeling that this evening's going to be awful.

CHARLES: It'll probably be funny, but not awful.

RUTH: You must promise not to catch my eye—if I giggle—and I'm very likely to—it will ruin everything.

CHARLES: You mustn't—you must be dead serious and if possible a little intense. We can't hurt the old girl's feelings however funny she is.

RUTH: But why the Bradmans, darling? He's as skeptical as we are—he'll probably say the most dreadful things.

CHARLES: I've warned him. There must be more than three people and we couldn't have the Vicar and his wife because (a) they're dreary, and (b) they probably wouldn't have approved at all. It had to be the Bradmans. [Edith rushes into the room with Charles' cigarette case. Taking it] Thank you, Edith. Steady does it.

EDITH: [Breathlessly] Yes, sir. [Edith, with an obvious effort, goes out slowly]

CHARLES: We might make her walk about with a book on her head like they do in deportment lessons. [Charles gives Ruth cocktail] Here, try this.

RUTH: [Sipping it] Lovely—dry as a bone.

CHARLES: [Raising his glass to her] To The Unseen!

RUTH: I must say that's a wonderful title.

CHARLES: If this evening's a success I shall start on the first draft tomorrow.

RUTH: How extraordinary it is.

CHARLES: What?

RUTH: Oh, I don't know—being in right at the beginning of something—it gives one an odd feeling.

CHARLES: Do you remember how I got the idea for "The Light Goes Out"?

RUTH: Suddenly seeing that haggard, raddled woman in the hotel at Biarritz—of course I remember—we sat up half the night talking about it—

CHARLES: She certainly came in very handy—I wonder who she was.

RUTH: And if she ever knew, I mean ever recognized, that description of herself—poor thing . . . here's to her, anyhow . . . [She finishes her drink]

CHARLES: [Takes her glass and goes to drinks table] Have another.

RUTH: Darling—it's most awfully strong.

CHARLES: [Pouring it] Never mind.

RUTH: Used Elvira to be a help to you—when you were thinking something out, I mean?

CHARLES: [Pouring out another cocktail for himself] Every now and then—when she concentrated—but she didn't concentrate very often.

RUTH: I do wish I'd known her.

CHARLES: I wonder if you'd have liked her.

RUTH: I'm sure I should—as you talk of her she sounds enchanting—yes, I'm sure I should have liked her because you know I have never for an instant felt in the least jealous of her—that's a good sign.

CHARLES: Poor Elvira.

RUTH: Does it still hurt—when you think of her?

CHARLES: No, not really—sometimes I almost wish it did— I feel rather guilty—

RUTH: I wonder if I died before you'd grown tired of me if you'd forget me so soon?

CHARLES: What a horrible thing to say . . .

RUTH: No—I think it's interesting.

CHARLES: Well to begin with I haven't forgotten Elvira— I remember her very distinctly indeed—I remember how fascinating she was, and how maddening—[Sits] I remember how badly she played all games and how cross she got when she didn't win—I remember her gay charm when she had achieved her own way over something and her extreme acidity when she didn't—I remember her physical attractiveness, which was tremendous—and her spiritual integrity which was nil . . .

RUTH: You can't remember something that was nil.

CHARLES: I remember how morally untidy she was . . .

RUTH: Was she more physically attractive than I am?

CHARLES: That was a very tiresome question, dear, and fully deserves the wrong answer.

RUTH: You really are very sweet.

CHARLES: Thank you.

RUTH: And a little naïve, too.

CHARLES: Why?

RUTH: Because you imagine that I mind about Elvira being more physically attractive than I am.

CHARLES: I should have thought any woman would mind—if it were true. Or perhaps I'm old-fashioned in my views of female psychology. . . .

RUTH: Not exactly old-fashioned, darling, just a bit didactic.

CHARLES: How do you mean?

RUTH: It's didactic to attribute to one type the defects of another type—for instance, because you know perfectly well that Elvira would mind terribly if you found another woman more attractive physically than she was, it doesn't necessarily follow that I should. Elvira was a more physical person than I—I'm certain of that—it's all a question of degree.

CHARLES: [Smiling] I love you, my love.

RUTH: I know you do—but not the wildest stretch of imagination could describe it as the first fine careless rapture.

CHARLES: Would you like it to be?

RUTH: Good God, no!

CHARLES: Wasn't that a shade too vehement?

RUTH: We're neither of us adolescent, Charles, we've neither of us led exactly prim lives, have we? And we've both been married before—careless rapture at this stage would be incongruous and embarrassing.

CHARLES: I hope I haven't been in any way a disappointment, dear.

RUTH: Don't be so idiotic.

CHARLES: After all your first husband was a great deal older than you, wasn't he? I shouldn't like to think that you'd missed out all along the line.

RUTH: There are moments, Charles, when you go too far.

CHARLES: Sorry, darling.

RUTH: As far as waspish female psychology goes, there's a strong vein of it in you.

CHARLES: I've heard that said about Julius Caesar.

RUTH: Julius Caesar is neither here nor there.

CHARLES: He may be for all we know—we'll ask Madame Arcati.

RUTH: You're awfully irritating when you're determined to be witty at all costs—almost supercilious.

CHARLES: That's exactly what Elvira used to say.

RUTH: I'm not at all surprised—I never imagined —physically triumphant as she was—that she was entirely lacking in perception.

CHARLES: Darling Ruth!

RUTH: There you go again . . .

CHARLES: [Kissing her lightly] As I think I mentioned before—I love you, my love.

RUTH: Poor Elvira.

CHARLES: Didn't that light, comradely kiss mollify you at all?

RUTH: You're very annoying, you know you are—

when I said "Poor Elvira" it came from the heart— you must have bewildered her so horribly.

CHARLES: Don't I ever bewilder you at all?

RUTH: Never for an instant—I know every trick.

CHARLES: Well, all I can say is that we'd better get a divorce immediately . . .

RUTH: Put my glass down, there's a darling.

CHARLES: [Taking it] She certainly had a great talent for living—it was a pity that she died so young.

RUTH: Poor Elvira.

CHARLES: That remark is getting monotonous.

RUTH: Poor Charles, then.

CHARLES: That's better.

RUTH: And later on, poor Ruth, I expect.

CHARLES: You have no faith, Ruth. I really do think you should try to have a little faith.

RUTH: I shall strain every nerve.

CHARLES: Life without faith is an arid business.

RUTH: How beautifully you put things, dear.

CHARLES: I aim to please.

RUTH: If I died, I wonder how long it would be before you married again?

CHARLES: You won't die—you're not the dying sort.

RUTH: Neither was Elvira.

CHARLES: Oh yes, she was, now that I look back on it—she had a certain ethereal, not quite of this world quality—nobody could call you even remotely ethereal.

RUTH: Nonsense—she was of the earth earthy.

CHARLES: Well, she is now, anyhow.

RUTH: You know that's the kind of observation that shocks people.

CHARLES: It's discouraging to think how many people are shocked by honesty and how few by deceit.

RUTH: Write that down, you might forget it.

CHARLES: You underrate me.

RUTH: Anyhow it was a question of bad taste more than honesty.

CHARLES: I was devoted to Elvira. We were married for five years. She died. I missed her very much. That was seven years ago. I have now, with your help, my love, risen above the whole thing.

RUTH: Admirable. But if tragedy should darken our lives, I still say—with prophetic foreboding— poor Ruth! [Bell]

CHARLES: That's probably the Bradmans.

RUTH: It might be Madame Arcati.

CHARLES: No, she'll come on her bicycle—she always goes everywhere on her bicycle.

RUTH: It really is very spirited of the old girl.

CHARLES: Shall I go, or shall we let Edith have her fling?

RUTH: Wait a minute and see what happens. [There is a slight pause]

CHARLES: Perhaps she didn't hear.

RUTH: She's probably on one knee in a pre-sprint-ing position waiting for cook to open the kitchen door.

[*There is the sound of a door banging and* Edith *is seen scampering across the hall*]

CHARLES: Steady, Edith.

EDITH: [*Dropping to a walk*] Yes, sir.

[Mrs. Bradman *comes to* Ruth—*shakes hands.* Dr. Bradman *shakes hands with* Charles. Dr. Bradman *is a pleasant-looking middle-aged man.* Mrs. Bradman *is fair and rather faded*]

EDITH: Dr. and Mrs. Bradman.

DR. BRADMAN: We're not late, are we? I only got back from the hospital about half an hour ago.

CHARLES: Of course not—Madame Arcati isn't here yet.

MRS. BRADMAN: That must have been her we passed coming down the hill—I said I thought it was.

RUTH: Then she won't be long. I'm so glad you were able to come.

MRS. BRADMAN: We've been looking forward to it—I feel really quite excited . . .

DR. BRADMAN: [*Shaking hands with* Ruth] I guarantee that Violet will be good—I made her promise.

MRS. BRADMAN: There wasn't any need—I'm absolutely thrilled. I've only seen Madame Arcati two or three times in the village—I mean I've never seen her do anything at all peculiar, if you know what I mean.

CHARLES: Dry Martini?

DR. BRADMAN: By all means.

CHARLES: She certainly is a strange woman. It was only a chance remark of the Vicar's about seeing her up on the Knoll on Midsummer Eve dressed in sort of Indian robes that made me realize that she was psychic at all. Then I began to make inquiries—apparently she's been a professional in London for years.

MRS. BRADMAN: It is funny, isn't it? I mean anybody doing it as a profession.

DR. BRADMAN: I believe it's very lucrative.

MRS. BRADMAN: Do you believe in it, Mrs. Condomine—do you think there's anything really genuine about it at all?

RUTH: I'm afraid not—but I do think it's interesting how easily people allow themselves to be deceived . . .

MRS. BRADMAN: But she must believe in herself, mustn't she—or is the whole business a fake?

CHARLES: I suspect the worst. A real professional charlatan. That's what I am hoping for anyhow—the character I am planning for my book must be a complete impostor, that's one of the most important factors of the whole story.

DR. BRADMAN: What exactly are you hoping to get from her?

CHARLES: [*Handing* Dr. *and* Mrs. Bradman *cocktails*] Jargon, principally—a few of the tricks of the trade—it's many years since I went to a séance. I want to refresh my memory.

DR. BRADMAN: Then it's not entirely new to you?

CHARLES: Oh no—when I was a little boy an aunt of mine used to come and stay with us—she imagined that she was a medium and used to go off into the most elaborate trances after dinner. My mother was fascinated by it.

MRS. BRADMAN: Was she convinced?

CHARLES: [*Gets cocktail for himself*] Good heavens, no—she just naturally disliked my aunt and loved making a fool of her.

DR. BRADMAN: [*Laughing*] I gather that there were never any tangible results?

CHARLES: Oh sometimes she didn't do so badly. On one occasion when we were all sitting round in the pitch dark with my mother groping her way through Chaminade at the piano, my aunt suddenly gave a shrill scream and said that she saw a small black dog by my chair, then someone switched on the lights and sure enough there was.

MRS. BRADMAN: But how extraordinary.

CHARLES: It was obviously a stray that had come in from the street. But I must say I took off my hat to Auntie for producing it, or rather for utilizing—even Mother was a bit shaken.

MRS. BRADMAN: What happened to it?

CHARLES: It lived with us for years.

RUTH: I sincerely hope Madame Arcati won't produce any livestock—we have so very little room in this house.

MRS. BRADMAN: Do you think she tells fortunes? I love having my fortune told.

CHARLES: I expect so—

RUTH: I was told once on the pier at Southsea that I was surrounded by lilies and a golden seven—it worried me for days.

[All *laugh*]

CHARLES: We really must all be serious, you know, and pretend that we believe implicitly, otherwise she won't play.

RUTH: Also, she might really mind—it would be cruel to upset her.

DR. BRADMAN: I shall be as good as gold.

RUTH: Have you ever attended her, Doctor—professionally, I mean?

DR. BRADMAN: Yes—she had influenza in January—she's only been here just over a year, you know. I must say she was singularly unpsychic then—I always understood that she was an authoress.

CHARLES: Oh yes, we originally met as colleagues at one of Mrs. Wilmot's Sunday evenings in Sandgate . . .

MRS. BRADMAN: What sort of books does she write?

CHARLES: Two sorts. Rather whimsical children's stories about enchanted woods filled with highly conversational flora and fauna, and enthusiastic biographies of minor royalties. Very sentimental, reverent and extremely funny.

[*There is the sound of the front door bell*]

RUTH: Here she is.

DR. BRADMAN: She knows, doesn't she, about to-night? You're not going to spring it on her.

CHARLES: Of course—it was all arranged last week—I told her how profoundly interested I was in anything to do with the occult, and she blossomed like a rose.

RUTH: I really feel quite nervous—as though I were going to make a speech.

[*Edith is seen sedately going towards the door*]

CHARLES: You go and meet her, darling.

[*Edith has opened the door, and* Madame Arcati's *voice very high and clear, is heard*]

MADAME ARCATI: I've leant my bike up against that little bush, it will be *perfectly* all right if no one touches it.

EDITH: Madame Arcati.

RUTH: How nice of you to have come all this way.

[*Ruth and Charles greet her simultaneously. Madame Arcati enters. She is a striking woman, dressed not too extravagantly but with a decided bias towards the barbaric. She might be any age between forty-five and sixty-five. Ruth ushers her in*]

CHARLES: [*Advancing*] My dear Madame Arcati!

MADAME ARCATI: I'm afraid I'm rather late, but I had a sudden presentiment that I was going to have a puncture so I went back to fetch my pump, and then of course I didn't have a puncture at all.

[*Madame Arcati takes off cloak and hands it to* Ruth]

CHARLES: Perhaps you will on the way home.

MADAME ARCATI: Doctor Bradman—the man with the gentle hands!

DR. BRADMAN: I'm delighted to see you looking so well. This is my wife.

MADAME ARCATI: We are old friends— [*Shakes hands with* Mrs. Bradman] We meet coming out of shops.

CHARLES: Would you like a cocktail?

MADAME ARCATI: [*Peeling off some rather strange-looking gloves*] If it's a dry Martini, yes—if it's a concoction, no. Experience has taught me to be wary of concoctions.

CHARLES: It is a dry Martini.

MADAME ARCATI: How delicious. It was wonderful cycling through the woods this evening—I was deafened with bird-song.

RUTH: It's been lovely all day.

MADAME ARCATI: But the evening's the time—mark my words. [*She takes the cocktail* Charles *gives her. To others*] Thank you. Cheers! Cheers!

RUTH: Don't you find it very tiring bicycling everywhere?

MADAME ARCATI: On the contrary—it stimulates me—I was getting far too sedentary in London, that horrid little flat with the dim lights—they had to be dim, you know, the clients expect it.

MRS. BRADMAN: I must say I find bicycling very exhausting.

MADAME ARCATI: Steady rhythm—that's what counts. Once you get the knack of it you need never look back—on you get and away you go.

MRS. BRADMAN: But the hills, Madame Arcati—pushing up those awful hills—

MADAME ARCATI: Just knack again—down with your head, up with your heart, and you're over the top like a flash and skimming down the other side like a dragon-fly. This is the best dry Martini I've had for years.

CHARLES: Will you have another?

MADAME ARCATI: [*Holding out her glass*] Certainly. [Charles *takes her glass and refills it at drinks table*] You're a very clever man. Anybody can write books, but it takes an artist to make a dry Martini that's dry enough.

RUTH: Are you writing anything nowadays, Madame Arcati?

MADAME ARCATI: Every morning regular as clockwork, seven till one.

CHARLES: [*Gives* Madame Arcati *cocktail*] Is it a novel or a memoir?

MADAME ARCATI: It's a children's book—I have to finish it by the end of October to catch the Christmas sales. It's mostly about very small animals, the hero is a moss beetle. [Mrs. Bradman *laughs nervously*] I had to give up my memoir of Princess Palliatini because she died in April—I talked to her about it the other day and she implored me to go on with it, but I really hadn't the heart.

MRS. BRADMAN: [*Incredulously*] You *talked* to her about it the other day?

MADAME ARCATI: Yes, through my control, of course. She sounded very irritable.

MRS. BRADMAN: It's funny to think of people in the spirit world being irritable, isn't it? I mean, one can hardly imagine it, can one?

CHARLES: We have no reliable guarantee that the after life will be any less exasperating than this one, have we?

MRS. BRADMAN: [*Laughing*] Oh, Mr. Condomine, how *can* you!

RUTH: I expect it's dreadfully ignorant of me not to know—but who was Princess Palliatini?

MADAME ARCATI: She was originally a Jewess from Odessa of quite remarkable beauty. It was an accepted fact that people used to stand on the seats of railway stations to watch her whizz by.

CHARLES: She was a keen traveler?

MADAME ARCATI: In her younger days, yes—later on she married a Mr. Clarke in the Consular Service and settled down for a while . . .

RUTH: How did she become Princess Palliatini?

MADAME ARCATI: That was years later. Mr. Clarke passed over and left her penniless with two strapping girls—

RUTH: How unpleasant.

MADAME ARCATI: And so there was nothing for

it but to obey the beckoning finger of adventure and take to the road again—so off she went, bag and baggage, to Vladivostok.

CHARLES: What an extraordinary place to go!

MADAME ARCATI: She had cousins there. Some years later she met old Palliatini who was returning from a secret mission in Japan. He was immediately staggered by her beauty and very shortly afterwards married her. From then on her life became really interesting.

DR. BRADMAN: I should hardly have described it as dull before.

RUTH: What happened to the girls?

MADAME ARCATI: She neither saw them nor spoke to them for twenty-three years.

MRS. BRADMAN: How extraordinary.

MADAME ARCATI: Not at all. She was always very erratic emotionally.

[*The double doors of the dining-room open and Edith comes in*]

EDITH: [*Nervously*] Dinner is served, Mum.

RUTH: Thank you, Edith. Shall we?

[*Edith retires backwards into the dining-room*]

MADAME ARCATI: No red meat, I hope?

RUTH: There's meat, but I don't think it will be very red—would you rather have an egg or something?

MADAME ARCATI: [*She and Ruth rise*] No, thank you—it's just that I make it a rule never to eat red meat before I work—it sometimes has an odd effect . . .

CHARLES: What sort of effect?

MADAME ARCATI: Oh, nothing of the least importance—if it isn't very red it won't matter much—anyhow, we'll risk it.

RUTH: [Mrs. Bradman *rises*. Madame Arcati *goes out first with* Ruth *followed by* Mrs. Bradman, Dr. Bradman *and* Charles] Come along, then—Mrs. Bradman—Madame Arcati—you're on Charles's right . . .

[*They all move into the dining-room as the lights fade on the scene*]

SCENE II.

When the lights go up again, dinner is over, and Ruth, Mrs. Bradman *and* Madame Arcati *are sitting having their coffee.*

MADAME ARCATI: . . . on her mother's side she went right back to the Borgias which I think accounted for a lot one way and another—even as a child she was given to the most violent destructive tempers—very inbred, you know.

MRS. BRADMAN: Yes, she must have been.

MADAME ARCATI: My control was quite scared the other day when we were talking—I could hear it in her voice—after all, she's only a child . . .

RUTH: Do you always have a child as a control?

MADAME ARCATI: Yes, they're generally the best—some mediums prefer Indians, of course, but personally I've always found them unreliable.

RUTH: In what way unreliable?

MADAME ARCATI: Well, for one thing they're frightfully lazy and also, when faced with any sort of difficulty, they're rather apt to go off into their own tribal language which is naturally unintelligible—that generally spoils everything and wastes a great deal of time. No, children are undoubtedly more satisfactory, particularly when they get to know you and understand your ways. Daphne has worked for me for years.

MRS. BRADMAN: And she still goes on being a child—I mean, she doesn't show signs of growing any older?

MADAME ARCATI: [*Patiently*] Time values on the "Other Side" are utterly different from ours.

MRS. BRADMAN: Do you feel funny when you go off into a trance?

MADAME ARCATI: In what way funny?

RUTH: [*Hastily*] Mrs. Bradman doesn't mean funny in its comic implication, I think she meant odd or strange—

MADAME ARCATI: The word was an unfortunate choice.

MRS. BRADMAN: I'm sure I'm very sorry.

MADAME ARCATI: It doesn't matter in the least—please don't apologize.

RUTH: When did you first discover that you had these extraordinary powers?

MADAME ARCATI: When I was quite tiny. My mother was a medium before me, you know, and so I had every opportunity of starting on the ground floor as you might say. I had my first trance when I was four years old and my first protoplasmic manifestation when I was five and a half—what an exciting day that was, I shall never forget it—of course the manifestation itself was quite small and of very short duration, but, for a child of my tender years, it was most gratifying.

MRS. BRADMAN: Your mother must have been so pleased.

MADAME ARCATI: [*Modestly*] She was.

MRS. BRADMAN: Can you foretell the future?

MADAME ARCATI: Certainly not. I disapprove of fortune tellers most strongly.

MRS. BRADMAN: [*Disappointed*] Oh really—why?

MADAME ARCATI: Too much guesswork and fake mixed up with it—even when the gift is genuine—and it only very occasionally is—you can't count on it.

RUTH: Why not?

MADAME ARCATI: Time again—time is the reef upon which all our frail mystic ships are wrecked.

RUTH: You mean because it has never yet been proved that the past and the present and the future are not one and the same thing.

MADAME ARCATI: I long ago came to the conclusion that nothing has ever been definitely proved about anything.

RUTH: How very wise.

[Edith *comes in with a tray of drinks. This she brings over to the table by* Ruth. Ruth *moves a coffee cup and a vase to make room for it.*]

RUTH: Edith, we don't want to be disturbed for the next hour or so for any reason whatsoever—is that clear?

EDITH: Yes'm.

RUTH: And if anyone should telephone, just say we are out and take a message.

MRS BRADMAN: Unless it's an urgent call for George.

RUTH: Unless it's an urgent call for Dr. Bradman.

EDITH: Yes'm. [Edith *goes out swiftly*]

RUTH: There's not likely to be one, is there?

MRS. BRADMAN: No, I don't think so.

MADAME ARCATI: Once I am off it won't matter, but an interruption during the preliminary stages might be disastrous.

MRS. BRADMAN: I wish the men would hurry up— I'm terribly excited.

MADAME ARCATI: Please don't be—it makes everything very much more difficult.

[Charles *and* Dr. Bradman *come out of the dining-room. They are smoking cigars*]

CHARLES: [*Cheerfully*] Well, Madame Arcati—the time is drawing near.

MADAME ARCATI: Who knows? It may be receding!

CHARLES: How very true.

DR. BRADMAN: I hope you feel in the mood, Madame Arcati.

MADAME ARCATI: It isn't a question of mood—it's a question of concentration.

RUTH: You must forgive us being impatient. We can perfectly easily wait though, if you're not quite ready to start . . .

MADAME ARCATI: Nonsense, my dear, I'm absolutely ready— [*She rises*] Heigho, heigho, to work we go!

CHARLES: Is there anything you'd like us to do?

MADAME ARCATI: Do?

CHARLES: Yes—hold hands or anything?

MADAME ARCATI: All that will come later— [*She goes to the window*] First a few deep, deep breaths of fresh air— [*Over her shoulder*] You may talk if you wish, it will not disturb me in the least. [*She flings open the windows wide and inhales deeply and a trifle noisily*]

RUTH: [*With a quizzical glance at* Charles] Oh dear!

CHARLES: [*Putting his finger to his lips warningly*] An excellent dinner, darling—I congratulate you.

RUTH: The mousse wasn't quite right.

CHARLES: It looked a bit hysterical but it tasted delicious.

MADAME ARCATI: That cuckoo is very angry.

CHARLES: I beg your pardon?

MADAME ARCATI: I said that cuckoo is very angry . . . listen . . .

[*They all listen obediently*]

CHARLES: How can you tell?

MADAME ARCATI: Timbre . . . No moon—that's as well, I think—there's mist rising from the marshes— [*A thought strikes her*] There's no need for me to light my bicycle lamp, is there? I mean, nobody is likely to fall over it?

RUTH: No, we're not expecting anybody else.

MADAME ARCATI: Good-night, you foolish bird. You have a table?

CHARLES: Yes. We thought that one would do.

MADAME ARCATI: [*Closing the window, she comes over to the table and touches it lightly with her finger*] I think the one that has the drinks on it would be better.

DR. BRADMAN: [*Lifting off the tray*] Change over.

CHARLES: [*To* Ruth] You told Edith we didn't want to be disturbed?

RUTH: Yes, darling.

MADAME ARCATI: [*Walking about the room—twisting and untwisting her hands*] This is a moment I always hate.

RUTH: Are you nervous?

MADAME ARCATI: Yes. When I was a girl I always used to be sick.

DR. BRADMAN: How fortunate that you grew out of it.

RUTH: [*Hurriedly*] Children are always much more prone to be sick than grown-ups, though, aren't they? I know I could never travel in a train with any degree of safety until I was fourteen.

MADAME ARCATI: [*Still walking*] Little Tommy Tucker sings for his supper, what shall he have but brown bread and butter? I despise that because it doesn't rhyme at all—but Daphne loves it.

DR. BRADMAN: Who's Daphne?

RUTH: Daphne is Madame Arcati's control—she's a little girl.

DR. BRADMAN: Oh, I see—yes, of course.

CHARLES: How old is she?

MADAME ARCATI: Rising seven when she died.

MRS. BRADMAN: And when was that?

MADAME ARCATI: February the sixth, 1884.

MRS. BRADMAN: Poor little thing.

DR. BRADMAN: She must be a bit long in the tooth by now, I should think.

MADAME ARCATI: You should think, Dr. Bradman, but I fear you don't—at least, not profoundly enough.

MRS. BRADMAN: Do be quiet, George—you'll put Madame Arcati off.

MADAME ARCATI: [Charles *brings piano chair down to table*] Don't worry, my dear—I am quite used to skeptics—they generally turn out to be the most vulnerable and receptive in the long run.

RUTH: You'd better take that warning to heart, Dr. Bradman.

DR. BRADMAN: Please forgive me, Madame Arcati—I assure you I am most deeply interested.

MADAME ARCATI: It is of no consequence—will you all sit round the table please and place your hands downwards on it?

[Ruth, Mrs. Bradman *and* Dr. Bradman *are seated at table*]

CHARLES: What about the lights?

MADAME ARCATI: All in good time, Mr. Condomine. [*The four of them sit down at each side of a small square table.* Madame Arcati *surveys them critically, her head on one side. She is whistling a little tune*] The fingers should be touching . . . that's right . . . I presume that that is the gramophone, Mr. Condomine?

CHARLES: Yes—would you like me to start it? It's an electric one.

MADAME ARCATI: Please stay where you are—I can manage— [*She goes over to the gramophone and looks over the records*] Now let me see—what have we here—Brahms—oh dear me, no—Rachmaninoff—too florid—where is the dance music?

RUTH: They're the loose ones on the left.

MADAME ARCATI: I see. [*She stoops down and produces a pile of dance records—these she sorts rapidly on the piano*]

CHARLES: I'm afraid they're none of them very new.

MADAME ARCATI: Daphne is really more attached to Irving Berlin than anybody else—she likes a tune she can hum—ah, here's one—"Always"—

CHARLES: [*Half jumping up again*] "Always"!

RUTH: Do sit down, Charles—what is the matter?

CHARLES: [*Subsiding*] Nothing—nothing at all.

MADAME ARCATI: The light switch is by the door?

RUTH: Yes, all except the small one on the desk, and the gramophone.

MADAME ARCATI: Very well—I understand.

RUTH: Charles, do keep still.

MRS. BRADMAN: Fingers touching, George—remember what Madame Arcati said.

MADAME ARCATI: Now there are one or two things I should like to explain, so will you all listen attentively?

RUTH: Of course.

MADAME ARCATI: Presently, when the music begins, I am going to switch out the lights. I may then either walk about the room for a little or lie down flat—in due course I shall draw up this dear little stool and join you at the table—I shall place myself between you and your wife, Mr. Condomine, and rest my hands lightly upon yours—I must ask you not to address me or move or do anything in the least distracting—is that quite, quite clear?

CHARLES: Perfectly.

MADAME ARCATI: Of course I cannot guarantee that anything will happen at all—Daphne may be unavailable—she had a head cold very recently, and was rather under the weather, poor child. On the other hand, a great many things might occur—one of you might have an emanation, for instance, or we might contact a poltergeist which would be extremely destructive and noisy . . .

RUTH: [*Anxiously*] In what way destructive?

MADAME ARCATI: They throw things, you know.

RUTH: No—I didn't know.

MADAME ARCATI: But we must cross that bridge when we come to it, mustn't we?

CHARLES: Certainly—by all means.

MADAME ARCATI: Fortunately an Elemental at this time of the year is most unlikely . . .

RUTH: What do Elementals do?

MADAME ARCATI: Oh, my dear, one can never tell—they're dreadfully unpredictable—usually they take the form of a very cold wind . . .

MRS. BRADMAN: I don't think I shall like that—

MADAME ARCATI: Occasionally reaching almost hurricane velocity—

RUTH: You don't think it would be a good idea to take the more breakable ornaments off the mantelpiece before we start?

MADAME ARCATI: [*Indulgently*] That really is not necessary, Mrs. Condomine—I assure you I have my own methods of dealing with Elementals.

RUTH: I'm so glad.

MADAME ARCATI: Now then—are you ready to empty your minds?

DR. BRADMAN: Do you mean we're to try to think of nothing?

MADAME ARCATI: Absolutely nothing, Dr. Bradman. Concentrate on a space or a nondescript colour, that's really the best way . . .

DR. BRADMAN: I'll do my damnedest.

MADAME ARCATI: Good work!—I will now start the music. [*She goes to the gramophone, puts on the record of "Always," and begins to walk about the room; occasionally she moves into an abortive little dance step, and once, on passing a mirror on the mantelpiece, she surveys herself critically for a moment and adjusts her hair. Then, with sudden speed, she runs across the room and switches off the lights*]

MRS. BRADMAN: Oh dear!

MADAME ARCATI: Quiet—please . . . [*Presently in the gloom* Madame Arcati, *after wandering about a little, draws up a stool and sits at the table between* Charles *and* Ruth. *The gramophone record comes to an end. There is dead silence*] Is there anyone there? . . . [*A long pause*] Is there anyone there? [*Another long pause*] One rap for yes—two raps for no—now then—is there anyone there? . . .

[*After a shorter pause the table gives a little bump*]

MRS. BRADMAN: [*Involuntarily*] Oh!

MADAME ARCATI: Shhhh! . . . Is that you, Daphne? [*The table gives a louder bump*] Is your cold better, dear? [*The table gives two loud bumps very quickly*] Oh, I'm so sorry—are you doing anything for it? [*The table bumps several times*] I'm afraid she's rather fretful . . . [*There is a silence*] Is there anyone there who wishes to speak to anyone here? [*After a pause the table gives one bump*] Ah! Now we're getting somewhere. No. Daphne, don't do that, dear, you're hurting me . . . Daphne, dear, please . . . Oh, oh, oh! . . . be good, there's a dear child . . . You say there is someone there who wishes to speak to someone here? [*One bump*] Is it I? [*Two bumps*] Is it Dr. Bradman? [*Two bumps*] Is it Mrs. Bradman? [*Two bumps*] Is it Mrs. Condomine? [*Several very loud bumps, which continue until* Madame Arcati *shouts it down*] Stop it! Behave yourself! Is it Mr. Condomine? [*There is a dead silence for a moment, and then a very loud single bump*] There's someone who wishes to speak to you, Mr. Condomine . . .

CHARLES: Tell them to leave a message.

[*The table bangs about loudly*]

MADAME ARCATI: I really must ask you not to be flippant, Mr. Condomine . . .

RUTH: Charles, how can you be so idiotic? You'll spoil everything.

CHARLES: I'm sorry—it slipped out.

MADAME ARCATI: Do you know anybody who has passed over recently?

CHARLES: Not recently, except my cousin in the Civil Service, and he wouldn't be likely to want to communicate with me—we haven't spoken for years.

MADAME ARCATI: [*Mystically*] Are you Mr. Condomine's cousin in the Civil Service? [*The table bumps violently several times*] I'm afraid we've drawn a blank . . . Can't you think of anyone else? Rack your brains . . .

RUTH: [*Helpfully*] It might be old Mrs. Plummet, you know—she died on Whit Monday . . .

CHARLES: I can't imagine why old Mrs. Plummet should wish to talk to me—we had very little in common.

RUTH: It's worth trying, anyhow.

MADAME ARCATI: Are you old Mrs. Plummet? [*The table remains still*]

RUTH: She was very deaf—perhaps you'd better shout—

MADAME ARCATI: [*Shouting*] Are you old Mrs. Plummet? [*Nothing happens*] There's nobody there at all.

MRS. BRADMAN: How disappointing—just as we were getting on so nicely.

DR. BRADMAN: Violet, be quiet.

MADAME ARCATI: [*Rising*] Well, I'm afraid there's nothing for it but for me to go into a trance. I had hoped to avoid it because it's so exhausting—however, what must be must be. Excuse me a moment while I start the gramophone again.

CHARLES: [*In a strained voice*] Not "Always"— don't play "Always"—

RUTH: Why ever not, Charles? Don't be absurd.

MADAME ARCATI: [*Gently*] I'm afraid I must—it would be unwise to change horses in midstream if you know what I mean . . . [*She restarts the gramophone*]

CHARLES: Have it your own way.

[Madame Arcati *comes slowly back toward the table and sits down again. After a few moments she begins to moan—then in the darkness a child's voice is heard reciting rather breathily "Little Tommy Tucker"*]

DR. BRADMAN: That would be Daphne—she ought to have had her adenoids out.

MRS. BRADMAN: George—please— [Madame Arcati *suddenly gives a loud scream and falls off the stool on to the floor*]

CHARLES: Good God!

RUTH: Keep still, Charles . . . [Charles *subsides. Everyone sits in silence for a moment, then the table starts bouncing about*]

MRS. BRADMAN: It's trying to get away . . . I can't hold it . . .

RUTH: Press down hard. [*The table falls over with a crash*]

RUTH: There now!

MRS. BRADMAN: Ought we to pick it up or leave it where it is?

DR. BRADMAN: How the hell do I know?

MRS. BRADMAN: There's no need to snap at me. [*A perfectly strange and very charming voice says, "Leave it where it is!"*]

CHARLES: Who said that?

RUTH: Who said what?

CHARLES: Somebody said, "Leave it where it is."

RUTH: Nonsense, dear.

CHARLES: I heard it distinctly.

RUTH: Well, nobody else did—did they?

MRS. BRADMAN: I never heard a sound.

CHARLES: It was you, Ruth—you're playing tricks.

RUTH: I'm not doing anything of the sort. I haven't uttered. [*There is another pause, and then the voice says, "Good evening, Charles"*]

CHARLES: [*Very agitated*] Ventriloquism—that's what it is—ventriloquism . . .

RUTH: [*Irritably*] What is the matter with you?

CHARLES: You must have heard *that*—one of you must have heard *that*!

RUTH: Heard *what*?

CHARLES: You mean to sit there solemnly and tell me that none of you heard anything at all?

DR. BRADMAN: I certainly didn't.

MRS. BRADMAN: Neither did I—I wish I had. I should love to hear something.

RUTH: It's you who are playing the tricks, Charles —you're acting to try to frighten us . . .

CHARLES: [*Breathlessly*] I'm not—I swear I'm not. [*The voice speaks again. It says, "It's difficult to think of what to say after seven years, but I suppose good evening is as good as anything else"*]

CHARLES: [*Intensely*] Who are you? [*The voice says, "Elvira, of course—don't be so silly"*] I can't bear this for another minute . . . [*He rises violently*] Get up, everybody—the entertainment's over . . .

RUTH: Oh. Charles, how tiresome you are—just

as we were beginning to enjoy ourselves. What on earth is the matter with you?

CHARLES: Nothing's the matter with me—I'm just sick of the whole business, that's all.

DR. BRADMAN: Did you hear anything that we didn't hear really?

CHARLES: [*With a forced laugh*] Of course not—I was only pretending . . .

RUTH: I knew you were . . .

MRS. BRADMAN: Oh dear . . . look at Madame Arcati.

[Madame Arcati *is lying on the floor with her feet up on the stool from which she fell. She is obviously quite unconscious*]

RUTH: What are we to do with her?

CHARLES: Bring her round—bring her round as soon as possible.

DR. BRADMAN: [*Going over and kneeling down beside her*] I think we'd better leave her alone.

RUTH: But she might stay like that for hours.

DR. BRADMAN: [*After feeling her pulse and examining her eye*] She's out all right.

CHARLES: [*Almost hysterically*] Bring her around! It's dangerous to leave her like that . . .

RUTH: Really, Charles, you are behaving most peculiarly.

CHARLES: [*Going to* Madame Arcati *and shaking her violently*] Wake up, Madame Arcati—wake up— it's time to go home!

DR. BRADMAN: Here—go easy, old man . . .

CHARLES: Get some brandy—give her some brandy—lift her into the chair—help me, Bradman . . . [Ruth *pours out some brandy while* Charles *and* Dr. Bradman *lift* Madame Arcati *laboriously into an armchair. Leaning over her*] Wake up, Madame Arcati—Little Tommy Tucker, Madame Arcati!

RUTH: Here's the brandy. [Madame Arcati *gives a slight moan and a shiver*]

CHARLES: [*Forcing some brandy between her lips*] Wake up!— [Madame Arcati *gives a prolonged shiver and chokes slightly over the brandy*]

MRS. BRADMAN: She's coming round.

RUTH: Be careful, Charles—you're spilling it all down her dress.

MADAME ARCATI: [*Opening her eyes*] Well, that's that.

RUTH: [*Solicitously*] Are you all right?

MADAME ARCATI: Certainly I am—never felt better in my life.

CHARLES: Would you like some more brandy?

MADAME ARCATI: So that's the funny taste in my mouth—well, really! Fancy allowing them to give me brandy! Doctor Bradman, you ought to have known better—brandy on top of trance might have been catastrophic. Take it away, please—I probably shan't sleep a wink tonight as it is.

CHARLES: I know I shan't.

RUTH: Why on earth not?

CHARLES: The whole experience has unhinged me.

MADAME ARCATI: Well, what happened—was it satisfactory?

RUTH: Nothing much happened, Madame Arcati, after you went off.

MADAME ARCATI: Something happened all right. I can feel it. [*She rises and sniffs*] No poltergeist, at any rate—that's a good thing. Any apparitions?

DR. BRADMAN: Not a thing.

MADAME ARCATI: No protoplasm?

RUTH: I'm not quite sure what it is, but I don't think so.

MADAME ARCATI: Very curious. I feel as though something tremendous had taken place.

RUTH: Charles pretended he heard a voice, in order to frighten us.

CHARLES: It was only a joke.

MADAME ARCATI: A very poor one, if I may say so—[*She walks about a little more*] Nevertheless, I am prepared to swear that there is someone else psychic in this room apart from myself.

RUTH: I don't see how there can be really, Madame Arcati.

MADAME ARCATI: I do hope I haven't gone and released something—however, we are bound to find out within a day or two—if any manifestation should occur or you hear any unexpected noises —you might let me know at once.

RUTH: Of course we will—we'll telephone immediately.

MADAME ARCATI: I think I really must be on my way now.

RUTH: Wouldn't you like anything before you go?

MADAME ARCATI: No, thank you—I have some Ovaltine all ready in a saucepan at home—it only needs hotting up.

DR. BRADMAN: Wouldn't you like to leave your bicycle here and let us drive you?

MRS. BRADMAN: I honestly do think you should, Madame Arcati, after that trance and everything— you can't be feeling quite yourself.

MADAME ARCATI: Nonsense, my dear, I'm as fit as a fiddle—always feel capital after a trance—rejuvenates me. Good night, Mrs. Condomine.

RUTH: It was awfully sweet of you to take so much trouble.

MADAME ARCATI: I'm sorry so little occurred—it's that cold of Daphne's, I expect—you know what children are when they have anything wrong with them. We must try again some other evening.

RUTH: That would be lovely.

MADAME ARCATI: Good night, Mrs. Bradman—

MRS. BRADMAN: It was thrilling, it really was— I felt the table absolutely shaking under my hands.

MADAME ARCATI: Good night, Doctor.

DR. BRADMAN: Congratulations, Madame Arcati.

MADAME ARCATI: I am fully aware of the irony in your voice, Doctor Bradman. As a matter of fact you'd be an admirable subject for telepathic hypnosis—a great chum of mine is an expert—I should like her to look you over.

DR. BRADMAN: I'm sure I should be charmed.

MADAME ARCATI: Good night, everyone—next time we must really put our backs into it!

[*With a comprehensive smile and a wave of the hand, she goes out followed by* Charles. Ruth *sinks down into a chair, laughing helplessly*]

RUTH: Oh dear! . . . Oh dear! . . .

MRS. BRADMAN: [*Beginning to laugh too*] Be careful, Mrs. Condomine—she might hear you.

RUTH: I can't help it—I really can't—I've been holding this in for ages.

MRS. BRADMAN: She certainly put you in your place, George, and serves you right.

RUTH: She's raving mad, of course—mad as a hatter.

MRS. BRADMAN: But do you really think she *believes*?

DR. BRADMAN: Of course not—the whole thing's a put-up job—I must say, though, she shoots a more original line than they generally do.

RUTH: I should think that she's probably half convinced herself by now.

DR. BRADMAN: Possibly—the trance was genuine enough—but that, of course, is easily accounted for.

RUTH: Hysteria?

DR. BRADMAN: Yes—a form of hysteria, I should imagine.

MRS. BRADMAN: I do hope Mr. Condomine got all the atmosphere he wanted for his book.

RUTH: He might have got a great deal more if he hadn't spoiled everything by showing off . . . I'm really very cross with him. [*At this moment* Elvira *comes in through the closed French windows. She is charmingly dressed in a sort of negligee. Everything about her is grey: hair, skin, dress, hands, so we must accept the fact that she is not quite of this world. She passes between* Dr. *and* Mrs. *Bradman and* Ruth *while they are talking. None of them sees her. She goes usptage and sits soundlessly on a chair. She regards them with interest, a slight smile on her face*] I suddenly felt a draught—there must be a window open.

DR. BRADMAN: [*Looking*] No—they're shut.

MRS. BRADMAN: [*Laughing*] Perhaps it was one of those what you may call 'ems that Madame Arcati was talking about.

DR. BRADMAN: Elementals.

RUTH: [*Also laughing again*] Oh no, it couldn't be—she distinctly said that it was the wrong time of the year for Elementals.

[Charles *comes in again*]

CHARLES: Well, the old girl's gone pedalling off down the drive at the hell of a speed—we had a bit of trouble lighting her lamp.

MRS. BRADMAN: Poor thing.

CHARLES: I've got a theory about her, you know —I believe she is completely sincere.

RUTH: Charles! How could she be?

CHARLES: Wouldn't it be possible, Doctor? Some form of self-hypnotism?

DR. BRADMAN: It might be . . . as I was explaining to your wife just now, there are certain types of hysterical subjects . . .

MRS. BRADMAN: George dear—it's getting terribly late, we really must go home—you have to get up so early in the morning.

DR. BRADMAN: You see? The moment I begin to talk about anything that really interests me, my wife interrupts me . . .

MRS. BRADMAN: You know I'm right, darling—it's past eleven.

DR. BRADMAN: [*To* Charles] I'll do a little reading up on the whole business—just for the fun of it.

CHARLES: You must have a drink before you go.

DR. BRADMAN: No, really, thank you—Violet's quite right, I'm afraid. I have got to get up abominably early tomorrow—I have a patient being operated on in Canterbury.

MRS. BRADMAN: [*To* Ruth] It has been a thrilling evening—I shall never forget—it was sweet of you to include us.

DR. BRADMAN: Good night, Mrs. Condomine—thank you so much.

CHARLES: You're sure about the drink!

DR. BRADMAN: Quite sure, thanks.

RUTH: We'll let you know if we find any poltergeists whirling about.

DR. BRADMAN: I should never forgive you if you didn't.

MRS. BRADMAN: Come along, darling . . .

[Charles *leads the* Bradmans *out into the hall.* Ruth, *passing close to* Elvira, *goes over to the fire and turns over a log with her foot. Then she takes a cigarette and is lighting it as* Charles *comes back into the room*]

RUTH: Well, darling?

CHARLES: [*Absently*] Well?

RUTH: Would you say the evening had been profitable?

CHARLES: Yes—I suppose so.

RUTH: I must say it was extremely funny at moments.

CHARLES: Yes—it certainly was.

RUTH: What's the matter?

CHARLES: The matter?

RUTH: Yes—you seem odd somehow—do you feel quite well?

CHARLES: Perfectly. I think I'll have a drink. Do you want one?

RUTH: No, thank you, dear.

CHARLES: [*Pouring himself out a drink*] It's rather chilly in this room.

RUTH: Come over by the fire.

CHARLES: I don't think I'll make any notes tonight—I'll start fresh in the morning. [*He is bringing his drink over to the fire when he sees* Elvira]

My God! [*He drops the drink on the floor.* Ruth *jumps up*]

RUTH: Charles!

ELVIRA: That was very clumsy, Charles dear.

CHARLES: Elvira!—then it's true—it was you!

ELVIRA: Of course it was.

RUTH: [*Coming to him*] Charles—darling Charles —what are you talking about?

CHARLES: [*To Elvira*] Are you a ghost?

ELVIRA: I suppose I must be—it's all very confusing.

RUTH: [*Becoming agitated*] Charles—what do you keep looking over there for? Look at me—what's happened?

CHARLES: Don't you see?

RUTH: See what?

CHARLES: Elvira.

RUTH: [*Staring at him incredulously*] Elvira!!

CHARLES: [*With an effort at social grace*] Yes— Elvira dear, this is Ruth—Ruth, this is Elvira.

RUTH: [*With forced calmness*] Come and sit down, darling.

CHARLES: Do you mean to say you can't see her?

RUTH: Listen, Charles—you just sit down quietly by the fire and I'll mix you another drink. Don't worry about the mess on the carpet—Edith can clean it up in the morning. [*She takes him by the arm*]

CHARLES: [*Breaking away*] But you must be able to see her—she's there—look—right in front of you —there—

RUTH: Are you mad? What's happened to you?

CHARLES: You can't see her?

RUTH: If this is a joke, dear, it's gone quite far enough. Sit down for God's sake and don't be idiotic.

CHARLES: [*Clutching his head*] What am I to do—what the hell am I to do!

ELVIRA: I think you might at least be a little more pleased to see me—after all, you conjured me up.

CHARLES: I didn't do any such thing. I did nothing of the sort.

ELVIRA: Nonsense, of course you did. That awful child with the cold came and told me you wanted to see me urgently.

CHARLES: It was all a mistake—a horrible mistake.

RUTH: Stop talking like that, Charles—as I told you before, the *joke's* gone far enough.

CHARLES: [*Aside*] I've gone mad, that's what it is —I've just gone raving mad.

RUTH: [*Going to the table and quickly pouring him out some neat brandy*] Here—let me get you a drink.

CHARLES: [*Mechanically—taking it*] This is appalling!

RUTH: Relax.

CHARLES: How can I relax? I shall never be able to relax again as long as I live.

RUTH: Drink some brandy.

CHARLES: [*Drinking it at a gulp*] There now—are you satisfied?

RUTH: Now sit down.

CHARLES: Why are you so anxious for me to sit down—what good will that do?

RUTH: I want you to relax—you can't relax standing up.

ELVIRA: African natives can—they can stand on one leg for hours.

CHARLES: I don't happen to be an African native.

RUTH: You don't happen to be a *what?*

CHARLES: [*Savagely*] An African native!

RUTH: What's that got to do with it?

CHARLES: It doesn't matter, Ruth—really it doesn't matter—we'll say no more about it. [*He sits down*] See, I've sat down.

RUTH: Would you like some more brandy?

CHARLES: Yes, please.

ELVIRA: Very unwise—you always had a weak head.

CHARLES: I could drink you under the table.

RUTH: There's no need to be aggressive, Charles— I'm doing my best to help you.

CHARLES: I'm sorry.

RUTH: [*Bringing him some more brandy*] Here— drink this—and then we'll go to bed.

ELVIRA: Get rid of her, Charles—then we can talk in peace.

CHARLES: That's a thoroughly immoral suggestion, you ought to be ashamed of yourself.

RUTH: What is there immoral in that?

CHARLES: I wasn't talking to you.

RUTH: Who were you talking to, then?

CHARLES: Elvira, of course.

RUTH: To hell with Elvira!

ELVIRA: There now—she's getting cross.

CHARLES: I don't blame her.

RUTH: What don't you blame her for?

CHARLES: Oh, God!

RUTH: Now look here, Charles— I gather you've got some sort of plan behind all this. I'm not quite a fool. I suspected you when we were doing that idiotic séance.

CHARLES: Don't be so silly—what plan could I have?

RUTH: I don't know—it's probably something to do with the characters in your book—how they, or one of them would react to a certain situation—I refuse to be used as a guinea pig unless I'm warned beforehand what it's all about.

CHARLES: [*Patiently*] Ruth, Elvira is here—she's standing a few yards away from you.

RUTH: [*Sarcastically*] Yes, dear, I can see her distinctly—under the piano with a horse.

CHARLES: But, Ruth . . .

RUTH: I am not going to stay here arguing any longer . . .

ELVIRA: Hurray!

CHARLES: Shut up.

RUTH: [*Incensed*] How dare you speak to me like that!

CHARLES: Listen, Ruth—please listen—

RUTH: I will not listen to any more of this nonsense—I am going up to bed now. I'll leave you to turn out the lights. I shan't be asleep—I'm too upset so you can come in and say good night to me if you feel like it.

ELVIRA: That's big of her, I must say.

CHARLES: Be quiet—you're behaving like a guttersnipe.

RUTH: [*Icily—at door*] That is all I have to say. Good night, Charles. [Ruth *walks swiftly out of the room without looking at him again*]

CHARLES: Ruth . . .

ELVIRA: That was one of the most enjoyable half-hours I have ever spent.

CHARLES: Oh, Elvira—how could you!

ELVIRA: Poor Ruth.

CHARLES: [*Staring at her*] This is obviously an hallucination, isn't it?

ELVIRA: I'm afraid I don't know the technical term for it.

CHARLES: [*Rising and walking about the room*] What am I to do?

ELVIRA: What Ruth suggested—relax.

CHARLES: Where have you come from?

ELVIRA: Do you know, it's very peculiar, but I've sort of forgotten.

CHARLES: Are you here to stay indefinitely?

ELVIRA: I don't know that either.

CHARLES: Oh, my God!

ELVIRA: Why, would you hate it so much if I did?

CHARLES: Well, you must admit it would be embarrassing.

ELVIRA: I don't see why, really—it's all a question of adjusting yourself—anyhow I think it's horrid of you to be so unwelcoming and disagreeable.

CHARLES: Now look here, Elvira . . .

ELVIRA: [*Near tears*] I do—I think you're mean.

CHARLES: Try to see my point, dear—I've been married to Ruth for five years, and you've been dead for seven . . .

ELVIRA: Not dead, Charles—"passed over." It's considered vulgar to say "dead" where I come from.

CHARLES: Passed over, then.

ELVIRA: At any rate, now that I'm here, the least you can do is to make a pretense of being amiable about it . . .

CHARLES: Of course, my dear, I'm delighted in one way . . .

ELVIRA: I don't believe you love me any more.

CHARLES: I shall always love the memory of you.

ELVIRA: [*Rising and walking about*] You mustn't think me unreasonable, but I really am a little hurt. You called me back—and at great inconvenience I came—and you've been thoroughly churlish ever since I arrived.

CHARLES: [*Gently*] Believe me, Elvira, I most emphatically did not send for you—there's been some mistake.

ELVIRA: [*Irritably*] Well, somebody did—and that child said it was you—I remember I was playing backgammon with a very sweet old Oriental gentleman—I think his name was Genghis Khan—and I'd just thrown double sixes, and then that child paged me and the next thing I knew I was in this room . . . perhaps it was your subconscious.

CHARLES: Well, you must find out whether you are going to stay or not, and we can make arrangements accordingly.

ELVIRA: I don't see how I can.

CHARLES: Well, try to think—isn't there anyone that you know, that you can get in touch with over there—on the other side, or whatever it's called—who could advise you?

ELVIRA: I can't think—it seems so far away—as though I'd dreamed it . . .

CHARLES: You must know somebody else beside Genghis Khan.

ELVIRA: Oh, Charles . . .

CHARLES: What is it?

ELVIRA: I want to cry, but I don't think I'm able to . . .

CHARLES: What do you want to cry for?

ELVIRA: It's seeing you again—and you being so irascible like you always used to be . . .

CHARLES: I don't mean to be irascible, Elvira . . .

ELVIRA: Darling—I don't mind really—I never did.

CHARLES: Is it cold—being a ghost?

ELVIRA: No—I don't think so.

CHARLES: What happens if I touch you?

ELVIRA: I doubt if you can. Do you want to?

CHARLES: Oh, Elvira . . . [*He buries his face in his hands*]

ELVIRA: What is it, darling?

CHARLES: I really do feel strange, seeing you again . . .

ELVIRA: That's better.

CHARLES: [*Looking up*] What's better?

ELVIRA: Your voice was kinder.

CHARLES: Was I ever unkind to you when you were alive?

ELVIRA: Often . . .

CHARLES: Oh, how can you! I'm sure that's an exaggeration.

ELVIRA: Not at all—you were an absolute pig that time we went to Cornwall and stayed in that awful hotel—you hit me with a billiard cue.

CHARLES: Only very, very gently . . .

ELVIRA: I loved you very much.

CHARLES: I loved you too . . . [*He puts out his hand to her and then draws it away*] No, I can't touch you—isn't that horrible?

ELVIRA: Perhaps it's as well if I'm going to stay for any length of time . . .

CHARLES: I feel strangely peaceful—I suppose I shall wake up eventually . . .

ELVIRA: Put your head back.

CHARLES: [Doing so] Like that?

ELVIRA: [Stroking his hair] Can you feel anything . . . ?

CHARLES: Only a very little breeze through my hair. . . .

ELVIRA: Well, that's better than nothing.

CHARLES: [Drowsily] I suppose if I'm really out of my mind they'll put me in an asylum.

ELVIRA: Don't worry about that—just relax—

CHARLES: [Very drowsily indeed] Poor Ruth . . .

ELVIRA: [Gently and sweetly] To hell with Ruth.

THE CURTAIN FALLS

ACT II. SCENE I.

It is about nine-thirty the next morning. The sun is pouring in through the open French windows. Ruth is sitting at the breakfast table, drinking coffee and reading the Times. *After a few moments Charles comes in. He kisses her.*

CHARLES: Good morning, darling.

RUTH: [With a certain stiffness] Good morning, Charles.

CHARLES: [Going to the open window and taking a deep breath] It certainly is.

RUTH: What certainly is what?

CHARLES: A good morning—a tremendously good morning—there isn't a cloud in the sky and everything looks newly washed.

RUTH: [Turning a page of the Times] Edith's keeping your breakfast hot—you'd better ring.

CHARLES: [Pressing the bell by the fireplace] Anything interesting in the Times?

RUTH: Don't be silly, Charles.

CHARLES: [Coming to the table] I intend to work all day.

RUTH: Good.

CHARLES: It's extraordinary about daylight, isn't it?

RUTH: How do you mean?

CHARLES: The way it reduces everything to normal.

RUTH: Does it?

CHARLES: [Sits. Firmly] Yes—it does.

RUTH: I'm sure I'm very glad to hear it.

CHARLES: You're very glacial this morning.

RUTH: Are you surprised?

CHARLES: Frankly—yes. I expected more of *you*.

RUTH: Well, really!

CHARLES: I've always looked upon you as a woman of perception and understanding.

RUTH: Perhaps this is one of my off days. [Edith *comes in with some bacon and eggs and toast*]

CHARLES: [Cheerfully] Good morning, Edith.

EDITH: Good morning, sir.

CHARLES: Feeling fit?

EDITH: Yes, sir—thank you, sir.

CHARLES: How's cook?

EDITH: I don't know, sir—I haven't asked her.

CHARLES: You should. You should begin every day by asking everyone how they are—it oils the wheels.

EDITH: Yes, sir.

CHARLES: Greet her for me, will you?

EDITH: Yes, sir.

RUTH: That will be all for the moment, Edith.

EDITH: Yes'm. [Edith *goes out*]

RUTH: I wish you wouldn't be facetious with the servants, Charles—it confuses them and undermines their morale.

CHARLES: I consider that point of view retrogressive, if not downright feudal.

RUTH: I don't care what you consider it, I have to run the house and you don't.

CHARLES: Are you implying that I couldn't?

RUTH: You're at liberty to try.

CHARLES: I take back what I said about it being a good morning—it's a dreadful morning.

RUTH: You'd better eat your breakfast while it's hot.

CHARLES: It isn't.

RUTH: [Putting down the Times] Now look here, Charles—in your younger days this display of roguish flippancy might have been alluring—in a middle-aged novelist it's nauseating.

CHARLES: Would you like me to writhe at your feet in a frenzy of self-abasement?

RUTH: That would be equally nauseating but certainly more appropriate.

CHARLES: I really don't see what I've done that's so awful.

RUTH: You behaved abominably last night. You wounded me and insulted me.

CHARLES: I was the victim of an aberration.

RUTH: Nonsense—you were drunk.

CHARLES: Drunk?

RUTH: You had four strong dry Martinis before dinner—a great deal too much burgundy at dinner—heaven knows how much port and kümmel with Doctor Bradman while I was doing my best to entertain that madwoman—and then two double brandies later—I gave them to you myself—of course you were drunk.

CHARLES: So that's your story, is it?

RUTH: You refused to come to bed and finally when I came down at three in the morning to see what had happened to you I found you in an alcoholic coma on the sofa with the fire out and your hair all over your face.

CHARLES: I was not in the least drunk, Ruth. Something happened to me—you really must believe that—something very peculiar happened to me.

RUTH: Nonsense.

CHARLES: It isn't nonsense—I know it looks like nonsense now in the clear, remorseless light of day, but last night it was far from being nonsense—I honestly had some sort of hallucination—

RUTH: I would really rather not discuss it any further.

CHARLES: But you must discuss it—it's very disturbing.

RUTH: There I agree with you. It showed you up in a most unpleasant light—I find that extremely disturbing.

CHARLES: I swear to you that during the séance I was convinced that I heard Elvira's voice—

RUTH: Nobody else did.

CHARLES: I can't help that—I did.

RUTH: You couldn't have.

CHARLES: And later on I was equally convinced that she was in this room—I saw her distinctly and talked to her. After you'd gone up to bed we had quite a cosy little chat.

RUTH: And you seriously expect me to believe that you weren't drunk?

CHARLES: I *know* I wasn't drunk. If I'd been all that drunk I should have a dreadful hangover now, shouldn't I?

RUTH: I'm not at all sure that you haven't.

CHARLES: I haven't got a trace of a headache—my tongue's not coated—look at it. [*He puts out his tongue*]

RUTH: I've not the least desire to look at your tongue; kindly put it in again.

CHARLES: I know what it is—you're frightened.

RUTH: Frightened? Rubbish! What is there to be frightened of?

CHARLES: Elvira. You wouldn't have minded all that much even if I had been drunk—it's only because it was all mixed up with Elvira.

RUTH: I seem to remember last night before dinner telling you that your views of female psychology were rather didactic. I was right. I should have added that they were puerile.

CHARLES: That was when it all began.

RUTH: When what all began?

CHARLES: We were talking too much about Elvira —it's dangerous to have somebody very strongly in your mind when you start dabbling with the occult.

RUTH: She certainly wasn't strongly in my mind.

CHARLES: She was in mine.

RUTH: Oh, she was, was she?

CHARLES: You tried to make me say that she was more physically attractive than you, so that you could hold it over me.

RUTH: I did not. I don't give a hoot how physically attractive she was.

CHARLES: Oh yes, you do—your whole being is devoured with jealousy.

RUTH: [*Rises and starts to clear table*] This is *too* much!

CHARLES: Women! My God, what I think of women!

RUTH: Your view of women is academic to say the least of it—just because you've always been

dominated by them it doesn't necessarily follow that you know anything about them.

CHARLES: I've never been dominated by anyone.

RUTH: You were hag-ridden by your mother until you were twenty-three—then you got into the clutches of that awful Mrs. Whatever-her-name-was—

CHARLES: Mrs. Winthrop-Lewellyn.

RUTH: I'm not interested. Then there was Elvira —she ruled you with a rod of iron.

CHARLES: Elvira never ruled anyone, she was much too elusive—that was one of her greatest charms. [*Sits*]

RUTH: Then there was Maud Charteris—

CHARLES: My affair with Maud Charteris lasted exactly seven and a half weeks and she cried all the time.

RUTH: The tyranny of tears! Then there was—

CHARLES: If you wish to make an inventory of my sex life, dear, I think it only fair to tell you that you've missed out several episodes—I'll consult my diary and give you the complete list after lunch.

RUTH: It's no use trying to impress me with your routine amorous exploits—

CHARLES: The only woman in my whole life who's ever attempted to dominate me is you—you've been at it for years.

RUTH: That is completely untrue.

CHARLES: Oh, no, it isn't. You boss me and bully me and order me about—you won't even allow me to have an hallucination if I want to.

RUTH: Alcohol will ruin your whole life if you allow it to get a hold on you, you know.

CHARLES: Once and for all, Ruth, I would like you to understand that what happened last night has nothing whatever to do with alcohol. You've very adroitly rationalized the whole affair to your own satisfaction, but your deductions are based on complete fallacy. I am willing to grant you that it was an aberration, some sort of odd psychic delusion brought on by suggestion or hypnosis. I was stone cold sober from first to last and extremely upset into the bargain.

RUTH: *You* were upset indeed! What about me?

CHARLES: You behaved with a stolid, obtuse lack of comprehension that frankly shocked me!

RUTH: I consider that I was remarkably patient. I shall know better next time.

CHARLES: Instead of putting out a gentle, comradely hand to guide me you shouted staccato orders at me like a sergeant-major.

RUTH: You seem to forget that you gratuitously insulted me.

CHARLES: I did not.

RUTH: You called me a guttersnipe—you told me to shut up—and when I quietly suggested that we should go up to bed you said, with the most disgusting leer, that it was an immoral suggestion.

CHARLES: [*Exasperated*] I was talking to Elvira!

RUTH: If you were I can only say that it conjures up a fragrant picture of your first marriage.

CHARLES: My first marriage was perfectly charming and I think it's in the worst possible taste for you to sneer at it.

RUTH: I am not nearly so interested in your first marriage as you think I am. It's your second marriage that is absorbing me at the moment—it seems to me to be on the rocks.

CHARLES: Only because you persist in taking up this ridiculous attitude.

RUTH: My attitude is that of any normal woman whose husband gets drunk and hurls abuse at her.

CHARLES: [Shouting] I was not drunk!

RUTH: Be quiet, they'll hear you in the kitchen.

CHARLES: I don't care if they hear me in the Folkestone Town Hall—I was not drunk!

RUTH: Control yourself, Charles.

CHARLES: How can I control myself in the face of your idiotic damned stubbornness? It's giving me claustrophobia.

RUTH: [Quietly] You'd better ring up Doctor Bradman. [Edith comes in with a tray to clear away the breakfast things]

EDITH: Can I clear, please'm?

RUTH: Yes, Edith.

EDITH: Cook wants to know about lunch, mum.

RUTH: [Coldly] Will you be in to lunch, Charles?

CHARLES: Please don't worry about me—I shall be perfectly happy with a bottle of gin in my bedroom.

RUTH: Don't be silly, dear. [To Edith] Tell cook we shall both be in.

EDITH: Yes'm.

RUTH: [Conversationally—after a long pause] I'm going into Hythe this morning—is there anything you want?

CHARLES: Yes—a great deal—but I doubt if you could get it in Hythe.

RUTH: Tell cook to put Alka-Seltzer down on my list, will you, Edith?

EDITH: Yes'm.

RUTH: [At the window—after another long pause] It's clouding over.

CHARLES: You have a genius for understatement. [In silence, but breathing heavily, Edith staggers out with the tray]

RUTH: [As she goes] Don't worry about the table, Edith—I'll put it away.

EDITH: Yes'm. [When Edith has gone Charles goes over to Ruth]

CHARLES: Please, Ruth—be reasonable.

RUTH: I'm perfectly reasonable.

CHARLES: I wasn't pretending—I really did believe that I saw Elvira and when I heard her voice I was appalled.

RUTH: You put up with it for five years. [Puts chair by gramophone]

CHARLES: [Puts table in hall] Naturally when I saw her I had the shock of my life—that's why I dropped the glass.

RUTH: But you couldn't have seen her.

CHARLES: I know I couldn't have but I did!

RUTH: I'm willing to concede then that you imagined you did.

CHARLES: That's what I've been trying to explain to you for hours.

RUTH: Well, then, there's obviously something wrong with you.

CHARLES: Exactly—there is something wrong with me—something fundamentally wrong with me—that's why I've been imploring your sympathy and all I got was a sterile temperance lecture.

RUTH: You had been drinking, Charles—there's no denying that.

CHARLES: No more than usual.

RUTH: Well, how do you account for it then?

CHARLES: [Frantically] I can't account for it—that's what's so awful.

RUTH: [Practically] Did you feel quite well yesterday—during the day, I mean?

CHARLES: Of course I did.

RUTH: What did you have for lunch?

CHARLES: You ought to know, you had it with me.

RUTH: [Thinking] Let me see now, there was lemon sole and that cheese thing—

CHARLES: Why should having a cheese thing for lunch make me see my deceased wife after dinner?

RUTH: You never know—it was rather rich.

CHARLES: Why didn't you see your dead husband then? You had just as much of it as I did.

RUTH: This is not getting us anywhere at all.

CHARLES: Of course it isn't, and it won't as long as you insist on ascribing supernatural phenomena to colonic irritation.

RUTH: Supernatural grandmother!

CHARLES: I admit she'd have been much less agitating.

RUTH: [Sits] Perhaps you ought to see a nerve specialist.

CHARLES: I am not in the least neurotic and never have been.

RUTH: A psychoanalyst then.

CHARLES: I refuse to endure months of expensive humiliation only to be told at the end of it that at the age of four I was in love with my rocking horse.

RUTH: What do you suggest then?

CHARLES: I don't suggest anything—I'm profoundly uneasy.

RUTH: Perhaps there's something pressing on your brain.

CHARLES: If there were something pressing on my brain I should have violent headaches, shouldn't I?

RUTH: Not necessarily. An uncle of mine had a lump the size of a cricket ball pressing on his brain for years and he never felt a thing.

CHARLES: [Rises] I know I should know if I had anything like that.

RUTH: He didn't.

CHARLES: What happened to him?

RUTH: He had it taken out and he's been as bright as a button ever since.

CHARLES: Did he have any sort of delusions—did he think he saw things that weren't there?

RUTH: No, I don't think so.

CHARLES: Well, what the hell are we talking about him for then? It's sheer waste of valuable time.

RUTH: I only brought him up as an example.

CHARLES: I think I'm going mad.

RUTH: How do you feel now?

CHARLES: Physically do you mean?

RUTH: Altogether.

CHARLES: [*After due reflection*] Apart from being worried I feel quite normal.

RUTH: Good. You're not hearing or seeing anything in the least unusual?

CHARLES: Not a thing.

[*At this moment* Elvira *comes in from the garden, carrying an armful of roses. The roses are as grey as the rest of her*]

ELVIRA: You've absolutely ruined that border by the sundial—it looks like a mixed salad.

CHARLES: O my God!

RUTH: What's the matter now?

CHARLES: She's here again!

RUTH: What do you mean? Who's here again?

CHARLES: Elvira.

RUTH: Pull yourself together and don't be absurd.

ELVIRA: It's all those nasturtiums—they're so vulgar.

CHARLES: I like nasturtiums.

RUTH: You like what?

ELVIRA: [*Putting her grey roses into a vase*] They're all right in moderation but in a mass like that they look beastly.

CHARLES: Help me, Ruth—you've got to help me—

RUTH: [*Rises*] What did you mean about nasturtiums?

CHARLES: Never mind about that now—I tell you she's here again.

ELVIRA: You have been having a nice scene, haven't you? I could hear you right down the garden.

CHARLES: Please mind your own business.

RUTH: If your behaving like a lunatic isn't my business nothing is.

ELVIRA: I expect it was about me, wasn't it? I know I ought to feel sorry but I'm not—I'm delighted.

CHARLES: How can you be so inconsiderate?

RUTH: [*Shrilly*] Inconsiderate!—I like that, I must say—

CHARLES: Ruth—darling—please . . .

RUTH: I've done everything I can to help—I've controlled myself admirably—and I should like to say here and now that I don't believe a word about your damned hallucinations—you're up to something, Charles—there's been a certain furtiveness in your manner for weeks— Why don't you be honest and tell me what it is?

CHARLES: You're wrong—you're dead wrong—I haven't been in the least furtive—I—

RUTH: You're trying to upset me—for some obscure reason you're trying to goad me into doing something that I might regret—I won't stand for it any more— You're making me utterly miserable— [*She bursts into tears and collapses on sofa*]

CHARLES: Ruth—please— [*Sits on sofa beside Ruth*]

RUTH: Don't come near me——

ELVIRA: Let her have a nice cry—it'll do her good.

CHARLES: You're utterly heartless!

RUTH: Heartless!

CHARLES: [*Wildly*] I was not talking to you—I was talking to Elvira.

RUTH: Go on talking to her then, talk to her until you're blue in the face but don't talk to me—

CHARLES: Help me, Elvira—

ELVIRA: How?

CHARLES: Make her see you or something.

ELVIRA: I'm afraid I couldn't manage that—it's technically the most difficult business—frightfully complicated, you know—it takes years of study—

CHARLES: You are here, aren't you? You're not an illusion?

ELVIRA: I may be an illusion but I'm most definitely here.

CHARLES: How did you get here?

ELVIRA: I told you last night—I don't exactly know—

CHARLES: Well, you must make me a promise that in future you only come and talk to me when I'm alone—

ELVIRA: [*Pouting*] How unkind you are—making me feel so unwanted—I've never been treated so rudely—

CHARLES: I don't mean to be rude, but you must see—

ELVIRA: It's all your own fault for having married a woman who is incapable of seeing beyond the nose on her face—if she had a grain of real sympathy or affection for you she'd believe what you tell her.

CHARLES: How could you expect anybody to believe this?

ELVIRA: You'd be surprised how gullible people are—we often laugh about it on the other side.

[Ruth, *who has stopped crying and been staring at* Charles *in horror, suddenly gets up*]

RUTH: [*Gently*] Charles—

CHARLES: [*Surprised at her tone*] Yes, dear—

RUTH: I'm awfully sorry I was cross—

CHARLES: But, my dear—

RUTH: I understand everything now, I do really—

CHARLES: You do?

RUTH: [*Patting his arm reassuringly*] Of course I do.

ELVIRA: Look out—she's up to something—

CHARLES: Will you please be quiet?

RUTH: Of course, darling—we'll all be quiet, won't we? We'll be as quiet as little mice.

CHARLES: Ruth dear, listen—

RUTH: I want you to come upstairs with me and go to bed—

ELVIRA: The way that woman harps on bed is nothing short of erotic.

CHARLES: I'll deal with you later—

RUTH: Whenever you like, darling. Come along.

CHARLES: Ruth dear—I'd really rather not go to bed in the middle of the morning—

ELVIRA: How you've changed, darling!

CHARLES: Don't be disgusting.

RUTH: [Sweetly] I'm sorry, dear—I didn't mean to be.

CHARLES: What are you up to?

RUTH: I'm not up to anything—I just want you to go quietly to bed and wait there until Doctor Bradman comes—

CHARLES: No, Ruth—you're wrong—

RUTH: [Firmly] Come, dear—

ELVIRA: She'll have you in a strait jacket before you know where you are.

CHARLES: [Frantically] Help me—you must help me—

ELVIRA: [Enjoying herself] My dear, I would with pleasure, but I can't think how—

CHARLES: I can—listen, Ruth—

RUTH: Yes, dear?

CHARLES: If I promise to go to bed will you let me stay here for five minutes longer?

RUTH: I really think it would be better—

CHARLES: Bear with me—however mad it may seem—bear with me for just five minutes longer—

RUTH: [Letting go of him] Very well—what is it?

CHARLES: Sit down then.

RUTH: [Sitting down] All right—there.

CHARLES: Now listen—listen carefully—

ELVIRA: Have a cigarette, it will soothe your nerves.

CHARLES: I don't want a cigarette.

RUTH: [Indulgently] Then you shan't have one, darling.

CHARLES: Ruth, I want to explain to you clearly and without emotion that beyond any shadow of doubt the ghost or shade or whatever you like to call it of my first wife Elvira is in this room now.

RUTH: Yes, dear.

CHARLES: I know you don't believe it and are trying valiantly to humour me but I intend to prove it to you.

RUTH: Why not lie down and have a nice rest and you can prove anything you want to later on?

CHARLES: She may not be here later on.

ELVIRA: Don't worry—she will!

CHARLES: O God!

RUTH: Hush, dear.

CHARLES: [To Elvira] Promise you'll do what I ask?

ELVIRA: That all depends what it is.

CHARLES: Ruth—you see that bowl of flowers on the piano?

RUTH: Yes, dear—I did it myself this morning.

ELVIRA: Very untidily if I may say so.

CHARLES: You may not.

RUTH: Very well—I never will again—I promise.

CHARLES: Elvira will now carry that bowl of flowers to the mantelpiece and back again. You will, Elvira, won't you—just to please me?

ELVIRA: I don't really see why I should—you've been quite insufferable to me ever since I materialized.

CHARLES: Please.

ELVIRA: All right, I will just this once—not that I approve of all these Herman The Great carryings on. [She goes over to the piano]

CHARLES: Now, Ruth—watch carefully.

RUTH: [Patiently] Very well, dear.

CHARLES: Go on, Elvira—bring it to the mantelpiece and back again.

[Elvira does so, taking obvious pleasure in doing it in a very roundabout way. At one moment she brings it up to within an inch of Ruth's face. Ruth shrinks back with a scream and then jumps to her feet]

RUTH: [Furiously] How dare you, Charles! You ought to be ashamed of yourself!

CHARLES: What on earth for?

RUTH: [Hysterically] It's a trick—I know perfectly well it's a trick—you've been working up to this—it's all part of some horrible plan—

CHARLES: It isn't—I swear it isn't—Elvira—do something else for God's sake—

ELVIRA: Certainly—anything to oblige.

RUTH: [Becoming really frightened] You want to get rid of me—you're trying to drive me out of my mind—

CHARLES: Don't be so silly.

RUTH: You're cruel and sadistic and I'll never forgive you—[Elvira lifts up a light chair and waltzes solemnly round the room with it, then she puts it down with a bang. Making a dive for the door] I'm not going to put up with this any more.

CHARLES: [Holding her] You must believe it—you must—

RUTH: Let me go immediately—

CHARLES: That was Elvira—I swear it was—

RUTH: [Struggling] Let me go—

CHARLES: Ruth—please—

[Ruth breaks away from him and runs towards the windows. Elvira gets there just before her and shuts them in her face. Ruth starts back, appalled]

RUTH: [Looking at Charles with eyes of horror] Charles—this is madness—sheer madness! It's some sort of auto-suggestion, isn't it—some form of hypnotism, swear to me it's only that? Swear to me it's only that.

ELVIRA: [*Taking an expensive vase from the mantelpiece and crashing it into the grate*] Hypnotism my foot!

[*Ruth gives a scream and goes into violent hysterics as the curtain falls*]

SCENE II.

The time is late on the following afternoon. When the curtain rises Ruth *is sitting alone at the tea table, which is set in front of the fire. After a moment or two she gets up and, frowning thoughtfully, goes over to the piano and takes a cigarette out of a box. As she returns to the table the front door bell rings. She hears it and straightens herself as though preparing for a difficult interview.* Edith *enters.*

EDITH: Madame Arcati. [Edith *steps aside and* Madame Arcati *comes in.* Edith *goes out.* Madame Arcati *is wearing a tweed coat and skirt and a great many amber beads and, possibly, a beret*]

MADAME ARCATI: My dear Mrs. Condomine, I came directly I got your message.

RUTH: That was very kind of you.

MADAME ARCATI: [*Briskly*] Kind? Nonsense! Nothing kind about it—I look upon it as an outing.

RUTH: I'm so glad—will you have some tea?

MADAME ARCATI: China or Indian?

RUTH: China.

MADAME ARCATI: Good. I never touch Indian, it upsets my vibrations.

RUTH: Do sit down.

MADAME ARCATI: [*Turning her head and sniffing*] I find this room very interesting—very interesting indeed. I noticed it the other night.

RUTH: I'm not entirely surprised. [*She proceeds to pour out tea*]

MADAME ARCATI: [*Sitting down and pulling off her gloves*] Have you ever been to Cowden Manor?

RUTH: No, I'm afraid I haven't.

MADAME ARCATI: That's very interesting too—strikes you like a blow between the eyes the moment you walk into the drawing-room. Two lumps of sugar, please, and no milk at all.

RUTH: I am profoundly disturbed, Madame Arcati, and I want your help.

MADAME ARCATI: Aha! I thought as much. What's in these sandwiches?

RUTH: Cucumber.

MADAME ARCATI: Couldn't be better. [*She takes one*] Fire away.

RUTH: It's most awfully difficult to explain.

MADAME ARCATI: Facts first—explanations afterwards.

RUTH: It's the facts that are difficult to explain—they're so fantastic.

MADAME ARCATI: Facts very often are. Take creative talent for instance, how do you account for

that? Look at Shakespeare and Michael Angelo! Try to explain Mozart snatching sounds out of the air and putting them down on paper when he was practically a baby—facts—plain facts. I know it's the fashion nowadays to ascribe it all to glands but my reply to that is fiddlededee.

RUTH: Yes, I'm sure you're quite right.

MADAME ARCATI: There are more things in heaven and earth than are dreamt of in your philosophy, Mrs. Condomine.

RUTH: There certainly are.

MADAME ARCATI: Come now—take the plunge—out with it. You've heard strange noises in the night no doubt—boards creaking—doors slamming—subdued moaning in the passages—is that it?

RUTH: No—I'm afraid it isn't.

MADAME ARCATI: No sudden gusts of cold wind, I hope.

RUTH: No, it's worse than that.

MADAME ARCATI: I'm all attention.

RUTH: [*With an effort*] I know it sounds idiotic but the other night—during the séance—something happened—

MADAME ARCATI: I knew it! Probably a poltergeist, they're enormously cunning, you know, they sometimes lie doggo for days—

RUTH: You know that my husband was married before?

MADAME ARCATI: Yes—I have heard it mentioned.

RUTH: His first wife, Elvira, died comparatively young—

MADAME ARCATI: [*Sharply*] Where?

RUTH: Here—in this house—in this very room.

MADAME ARCATI: [*Whistling*] Whew! I'm beginning to see daylight!

RUTH: She was convalescing after pneumonia and one evening she started to laugh helplessly at one of the B.B.C. musical programmes and died of a heart attack.

MADAME ARCATI: And she materialized the other evening—after I had gone?

RUTH: Not to me, but to my husband.

MADAME ARCATI: [*Rising impulsively*] Capital—capital! Oh, but that's splendid!

RUTH: [*Coldly*] From your own professional standpoint I can see that it might be regarded as a major achievement.

MADAME ARCATI: [*Delighted*] A triumph, my dear! Nothing more nor less than a triumph!

RUTH: But from my own personal point of view you must see that, to say the least of it, it's embarrassing.

MADAME ARCATI: [*Walking about the room*] At last—at last—a genuine materialization!

RUTH: Please sit down again, Madame Arcati.

MADAME ARCATI: How could anyone sit down at a moment like this? It's tremendous! I haven't had such a success since the Sudbury case.

RUTH: [*Sharply*] Nevertheless I must insist upon you sitting down and controlling your natural exuber-

ance. I appreciate fully your pride in your achievement but I would like to point out that it has made
my position in this house untenable and that I hold
you entirely responsible.

MADAME ARCATI: [*Contrite*] Forgive me, Mrs.
Condomine—I am being abominably selfish—[*She
sits down*] How can I help you?

RUTH: How? By sending her back immediately to
where she came from, of course.

MADAME ARCATI: I'm afraid that that is easier said
than done.

RUTH: Do you mean to tell me that she is liable
to stay here indefinitely?

MADAME ARCATI: It's difficult to say—I fear it depends largely on her.

RUTH: But my dear Madame Arcati—

MADAME ARCATI: Where is she now?

RUTH: My husband has driven her into Folkestone—apparently she was anxious to see an old
friend of hers who is staying at the Grand.

MADAME ARCATI: [*Producing a notebook*] Forgive
this formality, but I shall have to make a report to
the Psychical Research people—

RUTH: I would be very much obliged if there were
no names mentioned.

MADAME ARCATI: The report will be confidential.

RUTH: This is a small village you know and gossip
would be most undesirable.

MADAME ARCATI: I quite understand. You say she
is visible only to your husband?

RUTH: Yes.

MADAME ARCATI: "Visible only to husband." Audible too I presume?

RUTH: Extremely audible.

MADAME ARCATI: "Extremely audible." Your husband was devoted to her?

RUTH: [*With slight irritation*] I believe so—

MADAME ARCATI: "Husband devoted."

RUTH: It was apparently a reasonably happy marriage—

MADAME ARCATI: Tut, tut, Mrs. Condomine.

RUTH: I beg your pardon?

MADAME ARCATI: When did she pass over?

RUTH: Seven years ago.

MADAME ARCATI: Aha! That means she must have
been on the waiting list.

RUTH: Waiting list?

MADAME ARCATI: Yes, otherwise she would have
got beyond the materialization stage by now. She
must have marked herself down for a return visit
and she'd never have been able to manage it unless
there were a strong influence at work.

RUTH: Do you mean that Charles—my husband—
wanted her back all that much?

MADAME ARCATI: Possibly, or it might have been
her own determination—

RUTH: That sounds much more likely.

MADAME ARCATI: Would you say that she was a
woman of strong character?

RUTH: [*With rising annoyance*] I really don't

know, Madame Arcati. I never met her. Nor am I
particularly interested in how and why she got here.
I am solely concerned with the question of how to
get her away again as soon as possible.

MADAME ARCATI: I fully sympathize with you,
Mrs. Condomine, and I assure you I will do anything in my power to help—but at the moment I
fear I cannot offer any great hopes.

RUTH: But I always understood that there was a
way of exorcising ghosts—some sort of ritual?

MADAME ARCATI: You mean the old Bell and Book
method?

RUTH: Yes—I suppose I do.

MADAME ARCATI: Poppycock, Mrs. Condomine. It
was quite effective in the days of genuine religious
belief but that's all changed now. I believe the decline of faith in the Spirit World has been causing
grave concern.

RUTH: [*Impatiently*] Has it indeed?

MADAME ARCATI: There was a time of course
when a drop of holy water could send even a poltergeist scampering for cover, but not any more—"*Où
sont les neiges d'antan?*"

RUTH: Be that as it may, Madame Arcati, I must
beg of you to do your utmost to dematerialize my
husband's first wife as soon as possible.

MADAME ARCATI: The time has come for me to
admit to you frankly, Mrs. Condomine, that I
haven't the faintest idea how to set about it.

RUTH: [*Rises*] Do you mean to sit there and tell
me that having mischievously conjured up this ghost
or spirit or whatever she is and placed me in a hideous position you are unable to do anything about
it at all?

MADAME ARCATI: Honesty is the best policy.

RUTH: But it's outrageous! I ought to hand you
over to the police.

MADAME ARCATI: [*Rising*] You go too far, Mrs.
Condomine.

RUTH: [*Furiously*] I go too far indeed? Do you
realize what your insane amateur muddling has
done?

MADAME ARCATI: I have been a professional since
I was a child, Mrs. Condomine—"Amateur" is a
word I cannot tolerate.

RUTH: It seems to me to be the height of amateur-
ishness to evoke malignant spirits and not be able to
get rid of them again.

MADAME ARCATI: [*With dignity*] I was in a trance.
Anything might happen when I am in a trance.

RUTH: Well, all I can suggest is that you go into
another one immediately and get this damned
woman out of my house.

MADAME ARCATI: I can't go into trances at a moment's notice—it takes hours of preparation—in addition to which I have to be extremely careful of my
diet for days beforehand. Today, for instance, I happened to lunch with friends and had pigeon pie
which, plus these cucumber sandwiches, would make
a trance out of the question.

RUTH: Well, you'll have to do something.

MADAME ARCATI: I will report the whole matter to the Society for Psychical Research at the earliest possible moment.

RUTH: Will they be able to do anything?

MADAME ARCATI: I doubt it. They'd send an investigating committee, I expect, and do a lot of questioning and wall tapping and mumbo jumbo and then they'd have a conference and you would probably have to go up to London to testify—

RUTH: [Near tears] It's too humiliating—it really is.

MADAME ARCATI: Please try not to upset yourself—nothing can be achieved by upsetting yourself.

RUTH: It's all very fine for you to talk like that, Madame Arcati—you don't seem to have the faintest realization of my position.

MADAME ARCATI: Try to look on the bright side.

RUTH: Bright side indeed! If your husband's first wife suddenly appeared from the grave and came to live in the house with you, do you suppose you'd be able to look on the bright side?

MADAME ARCATI: I resent your tone, Mrs. Condomine, I really do.

RUTH: You most decidedly have no right to—you are entirely to blame for the whole horrible situation.

MADAME ARCATI: Kindly remember that I came here the other night on your own invitation.

RUTH: On my husband's invitation.

MADAME ARCATI: I did what I was requested to do, which was to give a séance and establish contact with the other side—I had no idea that there was any ulterior motive mixed up with it.

RUTH: Ulterior motive?

MADAME ARCATI: Your husband was obviously eager to get in touch with his former wife. If I had been aware of that at the time I should naturally have consulted you beforehand—after all "Noblesse oblige"!

RUTH: He had no intention of trying to get in touch with anyone—the whole thing was planned in order for him to get material for a mystery story he is writing about a homicidal medium.

MADAME ARCATI: [Drawing herself up] Am I to understand that I was only invited in a spirit of mockery?

RUTH: Not at all—he merely wanted to make notes of some of the tricks of the trade.

MADAME ARCATI: [Incensed] Tricks of the trade! Insufferable! I've never been so insulted in my life. I feel we have nothing more to say to one another, Mrs. Condomine. Good-bye—[She goes towards the door]

RUTH: Please don't go—please—

MADAME ARCATI: Your attitude from the outset has been most unpleasant, Mrs. Condomine. Some of your remarks have been discourteous in the extreme and I should like to say without umbrage that if you and your husband were foolish enough to tamper with the unseen for paltry motives and in a spirit of ribaldry, whatever has happened to you is your own fault, and, to coin a phrase, as far as I'm concerned you can stew in your own juice! [Madame Arcati goes majestically from the room]

RUTH: [Left alone, walks about the room] Damn —damn—damn!

[After a moment or two Charles comes in with Elvira]

CHARLES: What on earth was Madame Arcati doing here?

RUTH: She came to tea.

CHARLES: Did you ask her?

RUTH: Of course I did.

CHARLES: You never told me you were going to.

RUTH: You never told me you were going to ask Elvira to live with us.

CHARLES: I didn't.

ELVIRA: [Sauntering over to the tea table] Oh, yes, you did, darling—it was your subconscious.

CHARLES: What was the old girl so cross about?— she practically cut me dead.

RUTH: I told her the truth about why we invited her the other night.

CHARLES: That was quite unnecessary and most unkind.

RUTH: She needed taking down a bit, she was blowing herself out like a pouter pigeon.

CHARLES: Why did you ask her to tea?

ELVIRA: To get me exorcised, of course. Oh dear, I wish I could have a cucumber sandwich—I did love them so.

CHARLES: Is that true, Ruth?

RUTH: Is what true?

CHARLES: What Elvira said.

RUTH: You know perfectly well I can't hear what Elvira says.

CHARLES: She said that you got Madame Arcati here to try to get her exorcised. Is that true?

RUTH: We discussed the possibilities.

ELVIRA: There's a snake in the grass for you.

CHARLES: You had no right to do such a thing without consulting me.

RUTH: I have every right—this situation is absolutely impossible and you know it.

CHARLES: If only you'd make an effort and try to be a little more friendly to Elvira we might all have quite a jolly time.

RUTH: I have no wish to have a jolly time with Elvira.

ELVIRA: She's certainly very bad tempered, isn't she? I can't think why you married her.

CHARLES: She's naturally a bit upset—we must make allowances.

ELVIRA: I was never bad tempered though, was I, darling? Not even when you were beastly to me—

CHARLES: I was never beastly to you.

RUTH: [Exasperated] Where is Elvira at the moment?

CHARLES: In the chair, by the table.

RUTH: Now look here, Elvira—I shall have to call you Elvira, shan't I? I can't very well go on saying Mrs. Condomine all the time, it would sound too silly—

ELVIRA: I don't see why not.

RUTH: Did she say anything?

CHARLES: She said she'd like nothing better.

ELVIRA: [Giggling] You really are sweet, Charles darling—I worship you.

RUTH: I wish to be absolutely honest with you, Elvira—

ELVIRA: Hold on to your hats, boys!

RUTH: I admit I did ask Madame Arcati here with a view to getting you exorcised and I think that if you were in my position you'd have done exactly the same thing—wouldn't you?

ELVIRA: I shouldn't have done it so obviously.

RUTH: What did she say?

CHARLES: Nothing—she just nodded and smiled.

RUTH: [With a forced smile] Thank you, Elvira—that's generous of you. I really would so much rather that there were no misunderstandings between us—

CHARLES: That's very sensible, Ruth—I agree entirely.

RUTH: [To Elvira] I want, before we go any further, to ask you a frank question. Why did you really come here? I don't see that you could have hoped to have achieved anything by it beyond the immediate joke of making Charles into a sort of astral bigamist.

ELVIRA: I came because the power of Charles's love tugged and tugged and tugged at me. Didn't it, my sweet?

RUTH: What did she say?

CHARLES: She said that she came because she wanted to see me again.

RUTH: Well, she's done that now, hasn't she?

CHARLES: We can't be inhospitable, Ruth.

RUTH: I have no wish to be inhospitable, but I should like to have just an idea of how long you intend to stay, Elvira?

ELVIRA: I don't know—I really don't know! [She giggles] Isn't it awful?

CHARLES: She says she doesn't know.

RUTH: Surely that's a little inconsiderate?

ELVIRA: Didn't the old spiritualist have any constructive ideas about getting rid of me?

CHARLES: What did Madame Arcati say?

RUTH: She said she couldn't do a thing.

ELVIRA: [Moving gaily over to the window] Hurray!

CHARLES: Don't be upset, Ruth dear—we shall soon adjust ourselves, you know—you must admit it's a unique experience—I can see no valid reason why we shouldn't get a great deal of fun out of it.

RUTH: Fun? Charles, how can you—you must be out of your mind!

CHARLES: Not at all—I thought I was at first—but now I must say I'm beginning to enjoy myself.

RUTH: [Bursting into tears] Oh, Charles—Charles—

ELVIRA: She's off again.

CHARLES: You really must not be so callous, Elvira—try to see her point a little—

RUTH: I suppose she said something insulting—

CHARLES: No, dear, she didn't do anything of the sort.

RUTH: Now look here, Elvira—

CHARLES: She's over by the window now.

RUTH: Why the hell can't she stay in the same place!

ELVIRA: Temper again—my poor Charles, what a terrible life you must lead.

CHARLES: Do shut up, darling, you'll only make everything worse.

RUTH: Who was that "darling" addressed to—her or me?

CHARLES: Both of you.

RUTH: [Rises. Stamping her foot] This is intolerable!

CHARLES: For heaven's sake don't get into another state—

RUTH: [Furiously] I've been doing my level best to control myself ever since yesterday morning and I'm damned if I'm going to try any more, the strain is too much. She has the advantage of being able to say whatever she pleases without me being able to hear her, but she can hear me all right, can't she, without any modified interpreting?

CHARLES: Modified interpreting? I don't know what you mean.

RUTH: Oh yes, you do—you haven't told me once what she really said—you wouldn't dare. Judging from her photograph she's the type who would use most unpleasant language—

CHARLES: Ruth—you're not to talk like that.

RUTH: I've been making polite conversation all through dinner last night and breakfast and lunch today—and it's been a nightmare—and I am not going to do it any more. I don't like Elvira any more than she likes me and what's more I'm certain that I never could have, dead or alive. If, since her untimely arrival here the other evening, she had shown the slightest sign of good manners, the slightest sign of breeding, I might have felt differently towards her, but all she has done is try to make mischief between us and have private jokes with you against me. I am now going up to my room and I shall have my dinner on a tray. You and she can have the house to yourselves and joke and gossip with each other to your heart's content. The first thing in the morning I am going up to London to interview the Psychical Research Society and if they fail me I shall go straight to the Archbishop of Canterbury—[She goes out]

CHARLES: [Making a movement to follow her] Ruth—

ELVIRA: Let her go—she'll calm down later on.

CHARLES: It's unlike her to behave like this—she's generally so equable.

ELVIRA: No, she isn't, not really, her mouth gives her away—it's a hard mouth, Charles.

CHARLES: Her mouth's got nothing to do with it—I resent you discussing Ruth as though she were a horse.

ELVIRA: Do you love her?

CHARLES: Of course I do.

ELVIRA: As much as you loved me?

CHARLES: Don't be silly—it's all entirely different.

ELVIRA: I'm so glad. Nothing could ever have been quite the same, could it?

CHARLES: You always behaved very badly.

ELVIRA: Oh, Charles!

CHARLES: I'm grieved to see that your sojourn in the other world hasn't improved you in the least.

ELVIRA: [Curling up in sofa] Go on, darling—I love it when you pretend to be cross with me—

CHARLES: I'm now going up to talk to Ruth.

ELVIRA: Cowardy custard.

CHARLES: Don't be so idiotic. I can't let her go like that—I must be a little nice and sympathetic to her.

ELVIRA: I don't see why! If she's set on being disagreeable I should just let her get on with it.

CHARLES: The whole business is very difficult for her—we must be fair.

ELVIRA: She should learn to be more adaptable.

CHARLES: She probably will in time—it's been a shock—

ELVIRA: Has it been a shock for you too, darling?

CHARLES: Of course—what did you expect?

ELVIRA: A nice shock?

CHARLES: What do you want, Elvira?

ELVIRA: Want? I don't know what you mean.

CHARLES: I remember that whenever you were overpoweringly demure like that it usually meant that you wanted something.

ELVIRA: It's horrid of you to be so suspicious. All I want is to be with you.

CHARLES: Well, you are.

ELVIRA: I mean alone, darling. If you go and pamper Ruth and smalm her over, she'll probably come flouncing down again and our lovely quiet evening together will be spoilt.

CHARLES: You're incorrigibly selfish.

ELVIRA: Well, I haven't seen you for seven years—it's only natural that I should want a little time alone with you—to talk over old times. I'll let you go up just for a little while if you really think it's your duty.

CHARLES: Of course it is.

ELVIRA: [Smiling] Then I don't mind.

CHARLES: [Rises] You're disgraceful, Elvira.

ELVIRA: You won't be long, will you? You'll come down again very soon?

CHARLES: I shall most likely dress for dinner while I'm upstairs—you can read the Tatler or something.

ELVIRA: Darling, you don't have to dress—for me.

CHARLES: I always dress for dinner.

ELVIRA: What are you going to have? I should like to watch you eat something really delicious—

CHARLES: [Smiling and kissing his hand to her] Be a good girl now—you can play the gramophone if you like.

ELVIRA: [Demurely] Thank you, Charles.

[Charles goes out. Elvira gets up, looks in the gramophone cupboard, finds the record of "Always" and puts it on. She starts to waltz lightly round the room to it. Edith comes in to fetch the tea tray. She sees the gramophone playing by itself so she turns it off and puts the record back in the cupboard. While she is picking up the tray Elvira takes the record out and puts it on again. Edith gives a shriek, drops the tray and rushes out of the room. Elvira continues to waltz gaily]

CURTAIN

SCENE III.

The time is evening several days later. When the curtain rises Mrs. Bradman is sitting in an armchair. Ruth is standing by the window drumming on the pane with her fingers.

MRS. BRADMAN: [In armchair] Does it show any signs of clearing?

RUTH: [At window—looking out] No, it's still pouring.

MRS. BRADMAN: I do sympathize with you, really I do—it's really been quite a chapter of accidents, hasn't it?

RUTH: It certainly has.

MRS. BRADMAN: That happens sometimes, you know—everything seems to go wrong at once—exactly as though there were some evil forces at work. I remember once when George and I went away for a fortnight's holiday not long after we were married—we were dogged by bad luck from beginning to end—the weather was vile—George sprained his ankle—I caught a terrible cold and had to stay in bed for two days—and to crown everything the lamp fell over in the sitting-room and set fire to the treatise George had written on hyperplasia of the abdominal glands.

RUTH: [Absently] How dreadful.

MRS. BRADMAN: He had to write it all over again—every single word.

RUTH: You're sure you wouldn't like a cocktail or some sherry or anything?

MRS. BRADMAN: No, thank you—really not—George will be down in a minute and we've got to go like lightning—we were supposed to be at the Wilmots' at seven and it's nearly that now.

RUTH: I think I'll have a little sherry—I feel I need it. [*She goes to the side table and pours herself some sherry*]

MRS. BRADMAN: Don't worry about your husband's arm, Mrs. Condomine—I'm sure it's only a sprain.

RUTH: It's not his arm I'm worried about.

MRS. BRADMAN: And I'm sure Edith will be up and about again in a few days—

RUTH: My cook gave notice this morning.

MRS. BRADMAN: Well, really! Servants are awful, aren't they? Not a shred of gratitude—at the first sign of trouble they run out on you—like rats leaving a sinking ship.

RUTH: I can't feel that your simile was entirely fortunate, Mrs. Bradman.

MRS. BRADMAN: [*Flustered*] Oh, I didn't mean that, really I didn't!

[*Dr. Bradman comes in*]

DR. BRADMAN: Nothing to worry about, Mrs. Condomine—it's only a slight sprain—

RUTH: I'm so relieved.

DR. BRADMAN: He made a good deal of fuss when I examined it—men are much worse patients than women, you know—particularly highly strung men like your husband.

RUTH: Is he so highly strung, do you think?

DR. BRADMAN: Yes, as a matter of fact I wanted to talk to you about that. I'm afraid he's been overworking lately.

RUTH: [*Frowning*] Overworking?

DR. BRADMAN: He's in rather a nervous condition —nothing serious, you understand—

RUTH: What makes you think so?

DR. BRADMAN: I know the symptoms. Of course the shock of his fall might have something to do with it, but I certainly should advise a complete rest for a couple of weeks—

RUTH: You mean he ought to go away?

DR. BRADMAN: I do. In cases like that a change of atmosphere can work wonders.

RUTH: What symptoms did you notice?

DR. BRADMAN: Oh, nothing to be unduly alarmed about—a certain air of strain—an inability to focus his eyes on the person he is talking to—a few rather marked irrelevancies in his conversation.

RUTH: I see. Can you remember any specific example?

DR. BRADMAN: Oh, he suddenly shouted "What are you doing in the bathroom?" and then, a little later, while I was writing him a prescription, he suddenly said "For God's sake behave yourself!"

MRS. BRADMAN: How extraordinary.

RUTH: [*Nervously*] He often goes on like that— particularly when he's immersed in writing a book—

DR. BRADMAN: Oh, I am not in the least perturbed about it really—but I do think a rest and a change would be a good idea.

RUTH: Thank you so much, Doctor. Would you like some sherry?

DR. BRADMAN: No, thank you—we really must be off.

RUTH: How is poor Edith?

DR. BRADMAN: She'll be all right in a few days— she's still recovering from the concussion.

MRS. BRADMAN: It's funny, isn't it, that both your housemaid and your husband should fall down on the same day, isn't it?

RUTH: Yes, if that sort of thing amuses you.

MRS. BRADMAN: [*Giggling nervously*] Of course I didn't mean it like that, Mrs. Condomine—

DR. BRADMAN: Come along, my dear—you're talking too much as usual.

MRS. BRADMAN: You are horrid, George. Goodbye, Mrs. Condomine—[*Rises*]

RUTH: [*Shaking hands*] Good-bye.

DR. BRADMAN: [*Also shaking hands*] I'll pop in and have a look at both patients sometime tomorrow morning.

RUTH: Thank you so much.

[*Charles comes in. His left arm is in a sling. Elvira follows him and sits down by the fire*]

DR. BRADMAN: Well—how does it feel?

CHARLES: All right.

DR. BRADMAN: It's only a slight sprain, you know.

CHARLES: Is this damned sling really essential?

DR. BRADMAN: It's a wise precaution—it will prevent you using your left hand except when it's really necessary.

CHARLES: I had intended to drive into Folkestone this evening—

DR. BRADMAN: It would be much better if you didn't.

CHARLES: It's extremely inconvenient—

RUTH: You can easily wait and go tomorrow, Charles—

ELVIRA: I can't stand another of those dreary evenings at home. Charles—it'll drive me dotty—and I haven't seen a movie for seven years—

CHARLES: Let me be the first to congratulate you.

DR. BRADMAN: [*Kindly*] What's that, old man?

RUTH: [*With intense meaning*] Charles dear—try to be sensible, I implore you.

CHARLES: Sorry—I forgot.

DR. BRADMAN: You can drive the car if you promise to go very slowly and carefully. Your gear shift is on the right, isn't it?

CHARLES: Yes.

DR. BRADMAN: Well, use your left hand as little as possible.

CHARLES: All right.

RUTH: You'd much better stay at home.

DR. BRADMAN: Couldn't you drive him in?

RUTH: [*Stiffly*] I'm afraid not—I have lots to do in the house and there's Edith to be attended to.

DR. BRADMAN: Well, I'll leave you to fight it out among yourselves—[*To Charles*] But remember if you do insist on going—carefully does it—the roads are very slippery anyhow. Come along, Violet.

MRS. BRADMAN: Good-bye again— Good-bye, Mr. Condomine.

CHARLES: Good-bye. [*He goes into the hall with the Bradmans. Ruth, left alone, puts her sherry glass down on the table irritably*]

RUTH: You really are infuriating, Elvira—surely you could wait and go to the movies another night— [Elvira *gives a little laugh and, taking a rose out of a vase, throws it at* Ruth *and vanishes through the French windows. Picking up the rose and putting it back in the vase*] And stop behaving like a schoolgirl—you're old enough to know better.

CHARLES: [*Coming in*] What?

RUTH: I was talking to Elvira.

CHARLES: She isn't here.

RUTH: She was a moment ago—she threw a rose at me.

CHARLES: She's been very high-spirited all day. I know this mood of old. It usually meant that she was up to something.

RUTH: You're sure she isn't here?

CHARLES: Quite sure.

RUTH: I want to talk with you.

CHARLES: O God!

RUTH: I must—it's important.

CHARLES: You've behaved very well for the last few days, Ruth—you're not going to start making scenes again, are you?

RUTH: I resent that air of patronage, Charles. I have behaved well, as you call it, because there was nothing else to do, but I think it only fair to warn you that I offer no guarantee for the future. My patience is being stretched to its uttermost.

CHARLES: As far as I can see the position is just as difficult for Elvira as it is for you—if not more so. The poor little thing comes back trustingly after all those years in the other world and what is she faced with? Nothing but brawling and hostility?

RUTH: What did she expect?

CHARLES: Surely even a protoplasmic manifestation has the right to expect a little of the milk of human kindness?

RUTH: Milk of human fiddlesticks.

CHARLES: That just doesn't make sense, dear.

RUTH: Elvira is about as trusting as a puff adder.

CHARLES: You're granite, Ruth—sheer, unyielding granite.

RUTH: And a good deal more dangerous into the bargain.

CHARLES: Dangerous? I never heard anything so ridiculous. How could a poor lonely, wistful little spirit like Elvira be dangerous?

RUTH: Quite easily—and she is. She's beginning to show her hand.

CHARLES: How do you mean—in what way?

RUTH: [*Sits on sofa*] This is a fight, Charles—a bloody battle—a duel to the death between Elvira and me. Don't you realize that?

CHARLES: Melodramatic hysteria.

RUTH: It isn't melodramatic hysteria—it's true. Can't you see?

CHARLES: No, I can't. You're imagining things—jealousy causes people to have the most curious delusions.

RUTH: I am making every effort not to lose my temper with you, Charles, but I must say you are making it increasingly difficult for me.

CHARLES: All this talk of battles and duels—

RUTH: She came here with one purpose and one purpose only—and if you can't see it you're a bigger fool than I thought you.

CHARLES: What purpose could she have had beyond a natural desire to see me again? After all, you must remember that she was extremely attached to me, poor child.

RUTH: Her purpose is perfectly obvious. It is to get you to herself forever.

CHARLES: That's absurd—how could she?

RUTH: By killing you off of course.

CHARLES: Killing me off? You're mad!

RUTH: Why do you suppose Edith fell down the stairs and nearly cracked her skull?

CHARLES: What's Edith got to do with it?

RUTH: Because the whole of the top stair was covered with axle grease. Cook discovered it afterwards.

CHARLES: You're making this up, Ruth—

RUTH: I'm not. I swear I'm not. Why do you suppose when you were lopping that dead branch off the pear tree that the ladder broke? Because it had been practically sawn through on both sides.

CHARLES: But why should she want to kill me? I could understand her wanting to kill you, but why me?

RUTH: If you were dead it would be her final triumph over me. She'd have you with her forever on her damned astral plane and I'd be left high and dry. She's probably planning a sort of spiritual remarriage. I wouldn't put anything past her.

CHARLES: [*Rises. Really shocked*] Ruth!

RUTH: Don't you see now?

CHARLES: [*Walking about the room*] She couldn't be so sly, so wicked—she couldn't.

RUTH: Couldn't she just!

CHARLES: I grant you that as a character she was always rather light and irresponsible but I would never have believed her capable of low cunning—

RUTH: Perhaps the spirit world has deteriorated her.

CHARLES: Oh, Ruth!

RUTH: For heaven's sake stop looking like a wounded spaniel and concentrate—this is serious.

CHARLES: What are we to do?

RUTH: You're not to let her know that we suspect a thing—behave perfectly ordinarily—as though nothing had happened. I'm going to Madame Arcati immediately—I don't care how cross she is she's got to help us—even if she can't get rid of Elvira she must know some technical method of rendering her harmless. If a trance is necessary she shall go into a trance if I have to beat her into it. I'll be back in a half an hour—tell Elvira I've gone to see the Vicar—

CHARLES: This is appalling—

RUTH: Never mind about that—remember now, don't give yourself away by so much as a flick of an eyelid—

[Elvira *comes in from the garden*]

CHARLES: Look out—

RUTH: What?

CHARLES: I merely said it's a nice lookout.

ELVIRA: What's a nice lookout?

CHARLES: The weather, Elvira—the glass is going down and down and down—it's positively macabre.

ELVIRA: I find it difficult to believe that you and Ruth, at this particular moment, can't think of anything more interesting to talk about than the weather.

RUTH: [*Rises*] I can't stand this any more. I really can't.

CHARLES: Ruth dear—please—

ELVIRA: Has she broken out again?

RUTH: What did she say?

CHARLES: She asked if you had broken out again.

RUTH: How dare you talk like that, Elvira!

CHARLES: Now then, Ruth—

RUTH: [*With dignity*] Charles and I were not talking about the weather, Elvira, as you so very shrewdly suspected. I should loathe you to think *that we had any secrets from you* and so I will explain exactly what we were talking about. I was trying to persuade him *not* to drive you into Folkestone this evening. It will be bad for his arm and you can perfectly easily wait until tomorrow. However, as he seems to be determined to place your wishes before mine in everything, I have nothing further to say. I'm sure I hope you both enjoy yourselves. [*She goes out and slams the door*]

CHARLES: There now.

ELVIRA: Oh, Charles—have you been beastly to her?

CHARLES: No—Ruth doesn't like being thwarted any more than you do.

ELVIRA: She's a woman of sterling character. It's a pity she's so unforgiving.

CHARLES: As I told you before—I would rather not discuss Ruth with you—it makes me uncomfortable.

ELVIRA: I won't mention her again. Are you ready?

CHARLES: What for?

ELVIRA: To go to Folkestone of course

CHARLES: [*Rises from pouffe*] I want a glass of sherry first.

ELVIRA: I don't believe you want to take me at all.

CHARLES: Of course I want to take you, but I still think it would be more sensible to wait until tomorrow—it's a filthy night.

ELVIRA: [*Crossly*] How familiar this is.

CHARLES: In what way familiar?

ELVIRA: All through our married life I only had to suggest something for you immediately to start hedging me off—

CHARLES: I'm not hedging you off, I merely said—

ELVIRA: All right—all right—we'll spend another cosy, intimate evening at home with Ruth sewing away at that hideous table centre and snapping at us like a terrier.

CHARLES: Ruth is perfectly aware that the table centre is hideous. It happens to be a birthday present for her mother—

ELVIRA: It's no use trying to defend Ruth's taste to me—it's thoroughly artsy craftsy and you know it.

CHARLES: It is not artsy craftsy.

ELVIRA: She's ruined this room—look at those curtains and that awful shawl on the piano—

CHARLES: Lady Mackinley sent it to us from Burma.

ELVIRA: Obviously because it had been sent to her from Birmingham.

CHARLES: If you don't behave yourself I shan't take you into Folkestone ever.

ELVIRA: [*Coaxingly*] Please, Charles—don't be elderly and grand with me! Please let's go now.

CHARLES: Not until I've had my sherry.

ELVIRA: You are tiresome, darling—I've been waiting about for hours—

CHARLES: A few more minutes won't make any difference then. [*He pours himself out some sherry*]

ELVIRA: [*Petulantly, flinging herself into a chair*] Oh, very well.

CHARLES: Besides, the car won't be back for a half an hour at least.

ELVIRA: [*Sharply*] What do you mean?

CHARLES: [*Sipping his sherry nonchalantly*] Ruth's taken it—she had to go and see the Vicar—

ELVIRA: [*Jumping up—in extreme agitation*] What!!

CHARLES: What on earth's the matter?

ELVIRA: You say *Ruth's* taken the car?

CHARLES: Yes—to go and see the vicar—but she won't be long.

ELVIRA: [*Wildly*] O, my God! O, my God!

CHARLES: Elvira!—

ELVIRA: Stop her! You must stop her at once—

CHARLES: Why—what for?—

ELVIRA: [*Jumping up and down*] Stop her—go out and stop her immediately!

CHARLES: It's too late now—she's gone already.

ELVIRA: [*Backs away towards window*] Oh! Oh! Oh! Oh!!!

CHARLES: What are you going on like this for? What have you done?

ELVIRA: [*Frightened*] Done?—I haven't done anything—

CHARLES: Elvira—you're lying—

ELVIRA: [*Backing away from him*] I'm not lying. What is there to lie about?

CHARLES: What are you in such a state for?

ELVIRA: [*Almost hysterical*] I'm not in a state—I don't know what you mean—

CHARLES: You've done something dreadful—

ELVIRA: [*Backs away*] Don't look at me like that, Charles—I haven't—I swear I haven't—

CHARLES: [*Striking his forehead*] My God, the car!

ELVIRA: No, Charles—no—

CHARLES: Ruth was right—you did want to kill me—you've done something to the car—

ELVIRA: [*Howling like a banshee*] Oh—oh—oh—oh!—

CHARLES: What did you do—answer me?

[*At this moment the telephone rings. Charles stops dead; then with slow steps goes to it*]

CHARLES: [*At telephone*] Hallo—hallo—yes, speaking—I see—the bridge at the bottom of the hill—thank you. No, I'll come at once— [*He slowly puts back the receiver. As he does so the door bursts open*]

ELVIRA: [*Obviously retreating from someone*] Well, of all the filthy, low-down tricks— [*She shields her head with her hands and screams*] Ow—stop it —Ruth—let go—

[*She runs out of the room and slams the door. It opens again immediately and slams again. Charles stares, aghast*]

CURTAIN

ACT III. SCENE I.

The time is evening a few days later. Charles is standing before the fire drinking his after-dinner coffee. He is in deep mourning. He finishes his coffee, puts the cup down on the mantelpiece, lights a cigarette and settles himself comfortably in an armchair. He adjusts a reading lamp and with a sigh of well-being opens a novel and begins to read it. There is a ring at the front doorbell. With an exclamation of annoyance he puts down the book, gets up and goes out into the hall. After a moment or so Madame Arcati comes in. Charles follows her and shuts the door. Madame Arcati is wearing the strange, rather barbaric evening clothes that she wore in Act One.

MADAME ARCATI: I hope you will not consider this an intrusion, Mr. Condomine.

CHARLES: Not at all—please sit down, won't you?

MADAME ARCATI: Thank you. [*She does so*]

CHARLES: Would you like some coffee—or a liqueur?

MADAME ARCATI: No, thank you. I had to come, Mr. Condomine.

CHARLES: [*Politely*] Yes?

MADAME ARCATI: I felt a tremendous urge—like a rushing wind, and so I hopped on my bike and here I am.

CHARLES: It was very kind of you.

MADAME ARCATI: No, no, no—not kind at all—it was my duty—I know it strongly.

CHARLES: Duty?

MADAME ARCATI: I reproach myself bitterly, you know.

CHARLES: Please don't—there is no necessity for that. [*Sits in armchair*]

MADAME ARCATI: I allowed myself to get into a huff the other day with your late wife. I rode all the way home in the grip of temper, Mr. Condomine.—I have regretted it ever since.

CHARLES: My dear Madame Arcati . . .

MADAME ARCATI: [*Holding up her hand*] Please let me go on. Mine is the shame, mine is the blame —I shall never forgive myself. Had I not been so impetuous—had I listened to the cool voice of reason—much might have been averted. . . .

CHARLES: You told my wife distinctly that you were unable to help her—you were perfectly honest. Over and above the original unfortunate mistake I see no reason for you to reproach yourself.

MADAME ARCATI: I threw up the sponge—in a moment of crisis I threw up the sponge instead of throwing down the gauntlet . . .

CHARLES: Whatever you threw, Madame Arcati, I very much fear nothing could have been done—it seems that circumstances have been a little too strong for all of us.

MADAME ARCATI: I cannot bring myself to admit defeat so easily—it is gall and wormwood to me— I could have at least concentrated—made an effort.

CHARLES: Never mind.

MADAME ARCATI: I do mind. I cannot help it. I mind with every fibre of my being. I have been thinking very carefully, I have also been reading up a good deal during the last few dreadful days . . . I gather that we are alone?

CHARLES: [*Looking round*] My first wife is not in the room, she is upstairs lying down, the funeral exhausted her. I imagine that my second wife is with her but of course I have no way of knowing for certain.

MADAME ARCATI: You have remarked no difference in the texture of your first wife since the accident?

CHARLES: No, she seems much as usual, a little under the weather perhaps, a trifle low-spirited, but that's all.

MADAME ARCATI: Well, that washes that out.

CHARLES: I'm afraid I don't understand.

MADAME ARCATI: Just a little theory I had. In the nineteenth century there was a pretty widespread belief that a ghost who participated in the death of a human being disintegrated automatically—

CHARLES: How do you know that Elvira was in any way responsible for Ruth's death?

MADAME ARCATI: Elvira—such a pretty name—it has a definite lilt to it, hasn't it? [*She hums for a moment singing the Elvi-i-ira*] Elvira—Elvi-ira . . .

CHARLES: [*Rather agitated*] You haven't answered my question. How did you know?

MADAME ARCATI: It came to me last night, Mr. Condomine—it came to me in a blinding flash—I had just finished my Ovaltine and turned the light out when I suddenly started up in bed with a loud cry—"Great Scott. I've got it!" I said—after that I began to put two and two together. At three in the morning—with my brain fairly seething—I went to work on my crystal for a little but it wasn't very satisfactory—cloudy, you know—

CHARLES: [*Moving about uneasily*] I would be very much obliged if you would keep any theories you have regarding my wife's death to yourself, Madame Arcati . . .

MADAME ARCATI: My one desire is to help you. I feel I have been dreadfully remiss over the whole affair—not only remiss but untidy.

CHARLES: I am afraid there is nothing whatever to be done.

MADAME ARCATI: [*Triumphantly*] But there is—there is! [*She produces a piece of paper from her bag and brandishes it*] I have found a formula—here it is! I copied it out of Edmondson's *Witchcraft and Its Byways*.

CHARLES: [*Irritably*] What the hell are you talking about?

MADAME ARCATI: [*Rises*] Pluck up your heart, Mr. Condomine . . . all is not lost!

CHARLES: [*Rises*] Now look here, Madame Arcati—

MADAME ARCATI: You are still anxious to dematerialize your first wife, I suppose?

CHARLES: [*In a lower voice, with a cautious look towards the door*] Of course I am—I'm perfectly furious with her, but—

MADAME ARCATI: But what?

CHARLES: Well—she's been very upset for the last few days—you see apart from me being angry with her which she always hated even when she was alive, Ruth, my second wife, has hardly left her side for a moment—you must see that she's been having a pretty bad time what with one thing and another . . .

MADAME ARCATI: Your delicacy of feeling does you credit but I must say, if you will forgive my bluntness, that you are a damned fool, Mr. Condomine.

CHARLES: [*Stiffly*] You are at liberty to think whatever you please.

MADAME ARCATI: Now, now, now—don't get on your high horse—there's no sense in that, is there? I have a formula here that I think will be able to get rid of her without hurting her feelings in the least. It's extremely simple and requires nothing more than complete concentration from you and minor trance from me—I may even be able to manage it without lying down.

CHARLES: Honestly I would rather—

[*At this moment the door opens and* Elvira

enters, coming quickly into the room. She is obviously very upset]

ELVIRA: Charles—

CHARLES: What on earth's the matter?

ELVIRA: [*Seeing* Madame Arcati] Oh! What's she doing here?

CHARLES: She came to offer me her condolences.

ELVIRA: They should have been congratulations.

CHARLES: Please don't say things like that, Elvira—it is in the worst possible taste. Madame Arcati—allow me to introduce my first wife Elvira—

MADAME ARCATI: How do you do?

ELVIRA: What does she want, Charles? Send her away—[*She walks about the room*]

MADAME ARCATI: In what part of the room is she at the moment?

CHARLES: She's moving about rather rapidly. I'll tell you when and where she settles.

ELVIRA: She's the one who got me here in the first place, isn't she?

CHARLES: Yes.

ELVIRA: Well, please tell her to get me away again as soon as possible—I can't stand this house another minute.

CHARLES: Really, Elvira—I'm surprised at you.

ELVIRA: [*Nearly in tears*] I don't care how surprised you are—I want to go home—I'm sick of the whole thing.

CHARLES: Don't be childish, Elvira.

ELVIRA: I'm not being childish—I mean it.

MADAME ARCATI: [*Sniffling*] Very interesting—very interesting—I smell protoplasm strongly!

ELVIRA: What a disgusting thing to say.

MADAME ARCATI: [*Very excited*] Where is she now?

CHARLES: Here—close to me.

MADAME ARCATI: [*Mystically—stretching out her hands*] Are you happy, my dear—?

ELVIRA: [*Stamping her foot*] Tell the silly old bitch to mind her own business.

MADAME ARCATI: [*In a sing-song voice*] Was the journey difficult? Are you weary?

ELVIRA: She's dotty.

CHARLES: Just a moment, Madame Arcati . . .

MADAME ARCATI: [*With her eyes shut*] This is wonderful—wonderful—

ELVIRA: For God's sake tell her to go into the other room, Charles. I've got to talk to you.

CHARLES: Madame Arcati . . .

MADAME ARCATI: Just a moment. I almost have contact—I can sense the vibrations—this is magnificent . . .

CHARLES: Go on, Elvira—don't be a spoilsport—give her a bit of encouragement.

ELVIRA: If you'll promise to get her into the other room.

CHARLES: All right. [Elvira *goes up to* Madame Arcati *and blows gently into her ear*]

MADAME ARCATI: [*Jumping*] Yes, yes—again—again—

ELVIRA: [*Blowing in the other ear behind* Madame Arcati] How's that?

MADAME ARCATI: [*Clasping and unclasping her hands in a frenzy of excitement*] This is first rate—it really is first rate. Absolutely stunning!

CHARLES: I'm so glad you're pleased.

ELVIRA: Please get rid of her. Ruth will be in in a minute.

CHARLES: Madame Arcati, would you think it most frightfully rude if I asked you to go into the dining room for a moment? My first wife wishes to speak to me alone.

MADAME ARCATI: Oh, must I? It's so lovely being actually in the room with her.

CHARLES: Only for a few minutes—I promise she'll be here when you come back.

MADAME ARCATI: Very well. Hand me my bag, will you?—it's on the sofa.

ELVIRA: [*Picking it up and handing it to her*] Here you are.

MADAME ARCATI: [*Taking it and blowing her a kiss*] Oh, you darling—you little darling. [Madame Arcati, *humming ecstatically, goes into the dining-room and shuts the door*]

ELVIRA: How good is she really?

CHARLES: I don't know.

ELVIRA: Do you think she really could get me back again?

CHARLES: But my dear child . . .

ELVIRA: And don't call me your dear child—it's smug and supercilious.

CHARLES: There's no need to be rude.

ELVIRA: [*Turning away*] The whole thing's been a failure—a miserable, dreary failure—and oh! what *high hopes* I started out with.

CHARLES: You can't expect much sympathy from me, you know. I am perfectly aware that your highest hope was to murder me.

ELVIRA: Don't put it like that, it sounds so beastly.

CHARLES: It is beastly. It's one of the beastliest ideas I've ever heard.

ELVIRA: There was a time when you'd have welcomed the chance of being with me forever.

CHARLES: Your behaviour has shocked me immeasurably, Elvira, I had no idea you were so unscrupulous.

ELVIRA: [*Bursting into tears*] Oh, Charles.

CHARLES: Stop crying.

ELVIRA: They're only ghost tears—they don't mean anything really—but they're very painful.

CHARLES: You've brought all this on yourself, you know. [*Sits on sofa*]

ELVIRA: That's right—rub it in. Anyhow, it was only because I loved you—the silliest thing I ever did in my whole life was to love you—you were always unworthy of me.

CHARLES: That remark comes perilously near impertinence, Elvira.

ELVIRA: I sat there, on the other side, just longing

for you day after day. I did really—all through your affair with that brassy-looking woman in the South of France I went on loving you and thinking truly of you—then you married Ruth and even then I forgave you and tried to understand because all the time I believed deep inside that you really loved me best . . . that's why I put myself down for a return visit and had to fill in all those forms and wait about in draughty passages for hours—if only you'd died before you met Ruth everything might have been all right—she's absolutely ruined you—I hadn't been in the house a day before I realized that. Your books aren't a quarter as good as they used to be either.

CHARLES: [*Incensed. Rises*] That is entirely untrue . . . Ruth helped me and encouraged me with my work which is a damned sight more than you ever did.

ELVIRA: That's probably what's wrong with it.

CHARLES: All you ever thought of was going to parties and enjoying yourself.

ELVIRA: Why shouldn't I have fun? I died young, didn't I?

CHARLES: You needn't have died at all if you hadn't been idiotic enough to go out on the river with Guy Henderson and get soaked to the skin—

ELVIRA: So we're back at Guy Henderson again, are we?

CHARLES: You behaved abominably over Guy Henderson and it's no use pretending that you didn't.

ELVIRA: [*Sits on arm of chair*] Guy adored me—and anyhow he was very attractive.

CHARLES: You told me distinctly that he didn't attract you in the least.

ELVIRA: You'd have gone through the roof if I'd told you that he did.

CHARLES: Did you have an affair with Guy Henderson?

ELVIRA: I would rather not discuss it if you don't mind.

CHARLES: Answer me—did you or didn't you?

ELVIRA: Of course I didn't.

CHARLES: You let him kiss you though, didn't you?

ELVIRA: How could I stop him? He was bigger than I was.

CHARLES: [*Furiously*] And you swore to me—

ELVIRA: Of course I did. You were always making scenes over nothing at all.

CHARLES: Nothing at all.

ELVIRA: You never loved me a bit really—it was only your beastly vanity.

CHARLES: You seriously believe that it was only vanity that upset me when you went out in the punt with Guy Henderson?

ELVIRA: It was not a punt—it was a little launch.

CHARLES: I don't care if it was a three-masted schooner you had no right to go!

ELVIRA: You seem to forget *why* I went! You seem to forget that you had spent the entire evening making sheep's eyes at that overblown looking harridan with the false pearls.

CHARLES: A woman in Cynthia Cheviot's position would hardly wear false pearls.

ELVIRA: They were practically all she was wearing.

CHARLES: I am pained to observe that seven years in the echoing vaults of eternity have in no way impaired your native vulgarity.

ELVIRA: That was the remark of a pompous ass.

CHARLES: There is nothing to be gained by continuing this discussion.

ELVIRA: You always used to say that when you were thoroughly worsted.

CHARLES: On looking back on our married years, Elvira, I see now, with horrid clarity, that they were nothing but a mockery.

ELVIRA: You invite mockery, Charles—it's something to do with your personality, I think, a certain seedy grandeur.

CHARLES: Once and for all, Elvira—

ELVIRA: You never suspected it but I laughed at you steadily from the altar to the grave—all your ridiculous petty jealousies and your fussings and fumings—

CHARLES: You were feckless and irresponsible and morally unstable—I realized that before we left Budleigh Salterton.

ELVIRA: Nobody but a monumental bore would have thought of having a honeymoon at Budleigh Salterton.

CHARLES: What's the matter with Budleigh Salterton?

ELVIRA: I was an eager young bride, Charles—I wanted glamour and music and romance—all I got was potted palms, seven hours of every day on a damp golf course and a three-piece orchestra playing "Merrie England."

CHARLES: It's a pity you didn't tell me so at the time.

ELVIRA: I did—but you wouldn't listen—that's why I went out on the moors that day with Captain Bracegirdle. I was desperate.

CHARLES: You swore to me that you'd gone over to see your aunt in Exmouth!

ELVIRA: It was the moors.

CHARLES: With Captain Bracegirdle?

ELVIRA: With Captain Bracegirdle.

CHARLES: [Furiously] I might have known it—what a fool I was—what a blind fool! Did he make love to you?

ELVIRA: [Sucking her finger and regarding it thoughtfully] Of course.

CHARLES: Oh, Elvira!

ELVIRA: Only very discreetly—he was in the cavalry, you know—

CHARLES: Well, all I can say is that I'm well rid of you.

ELVIRA: Unfortunately you're not.

CHARLES: Oh yes, I am—you're dead and Ruth's dead—I shall sell this house lock, stock and barrel and go away.

ELVIRA: I shall follow you.

CHARLES: I shall go a long way away—I shall go to South America—you'll hate that, you were always a bad traveller.

ELVIRA: [At piano] That can't be helped—I shall have to follow you—you called me back.

CHARLES: I did not call you back!

ELVIRA: Well somebody did—and it's hardly likely to have been Ruth.

CHARLES: Nothing in the world was further from my thoughts.

ELVIRA: You were talking about me before dinner that evening.

CHARLES: I might just as easily have been talking about Joan of Arc but that wouldn't necessarily mean that I wanted her to come and live with me.

ELVIRA: As a matter of fact she's rather fun.

CHARLES: Stick to the point.

ELVIRA: When I think of what might have happened if I'd succeeded in getting you to the other world after all—it makes me shudder, it does honestly . . . it would be nothing but bickering and squabbling forever and ever and ever . . . I swear I'll be better off with Ruth—at least she'll find her own set and not get in my way.

CHARLES: So I get in your way, do I?

ELVIRA: Only because I was idiotic enough to imagine that you loved me, and I sort of felt sorry for you.

CHARLES: I'm sick of these insults—please go away.

ELVIRA: There's nothing I should like better— I've always believed in cutting my losses. That's why I died.

CHARLES: [Rises] Of all the brazen sophistry—

ELVIRA: Call that old girl in again—set her to work—I won't tolerate this any longer—I want to go home. [She starts to cry]

CHARLES: For heaven's sake don't snivel.

ELVIRA: [Stamping her foot] Call her in—she's got to get me out of this.

CHARLES: [Going to the dining-room door] I quite agree—and the sooner the better. [He opens the door] Madame Arcati—would you please come in now?

[Madame Arcati comes in eagerly]

MADAME ARCATI: Is the darling still here?

CHARLES: [Grimly] Yes, she is.

MADAME ARCATI: Where—tell me where?

CHARLES: Over by the piano—blowing her nose.

MADAME ARCATI: [Approaching the piano] My dear—oh, my dear—

ELVIRA: Stop her fawning on me, Charles, or I shall break something.

CHARLES: Elvira and I have discussed the whole situation, Madame Arcati, and she wishes to go home immediately.

MADAME ARCATI: Home?

CHARLES: Wherever she came from.

MADAME ARCATI: You don't think she would like to stay a few days longer—while I try to get things a little more organized?

ELVIRA: No—no—I want to go now.

MADAME ARCATI: I could come and be here with her—I could bring my crystal—

ELVIRA: God forbid!

CHARLES: We are both agreed that she must go as soon as possible. Please strain every nerve, Madame Arcati—make every effort—you said something about a formula—what is it?

MADAME ARCATI: [*Reluctantly*] Well—if you insist.

CHARLES: I most emphatically do insist.

ELVIRA: [*Wailing*] Oh, Charles. . . .

CHARLES: Shut up.

MADAME ARCATI: I can't guarantee anything, you know—I'll do my best but it may not work.

CHARLES: What is the formula?

MADAME ARCATI: Nothing more than a little verse really—it fell into disuse after the seventeenth century—I shall need some pepper and salt—

CHARLES: There's pepper and salt in the dining-room—I'll get it. [*He goes*]

MADAME ARCATI: We ought of course to have some Shepherd's Wort and a frog or two but I think I can manage without. You won't be frightened, dear, will you? It's absolutely painless.

CHARLES: [*Coming back with the cruet*] Will this be enough?

MADAME ARCATI: Oh yes—I only need a little—put it on the table please. Now then, let me see—[*She fumbles in her bag for the paper and her glasses*] Ah yes—[*To* Charles] Sprinkle it, will you —just a soupçon—there, right in the middle—[Charles *does so*]

ELVIRA: This is going to be a flop—I can tell you that here and now.

MADAME ARCATI: Now a few snapdragons out of that vase, there's a good chap.

ELVIRA: [*Contemptuously*] Merlin does all this sort of thing at parties and bores us all stiff with it, only he always uses blackthorn and a great deal of whimsy!

CHARLES: Here you are.

MADAME ARCATI: Now then—the gramophone—in the old days of course they used a zither or reed pipes—[*She goes to the gramophone*] We'd better have the same record we had before, I think.

ELVIRA: I'll get it. [*She takes out the record and puts it on the gramophone*]

MADAME ARCATI: [*Watching, fascinated*] Oh, if only that Mr. Emsworth of the Psychical Research Society could see this—he'd have a fit, he would really! Don't start it yet, dear. Now then—[Charles *gets piano chair and brings it down to table*] Sit down, please, Mr. Condomine, rest your hands on the table but don't put your fingers in the pepper —I shall turn out the lights myself. Oh, shucks, I'd

nearly forgotten—[*She goes to the table and makes designs in the sprinkled pepper and salt with her forefinger*] One triangle—[*She consults the paper*] One half circle and one little dot—there!

ELVIRA: This is waste of time—she's a complete fake.

CHARLES: Anything's worth trying.

ELVIRA: I'm as eager for it to succeed as you are —don't make any mistake about that. But I'll lay you ten to one it's a dead failure.

MADAME ARCATI: Now, if your wife would be kind enough to lie down on the sofa—

CHARLES: Go on, Elvira.

ELVIRA: [*Lies down on sofa*] This is sheer nonsense—don't blame me if I get the giggles.

CHARLES: Concentrate—think of nothing.

MADAME ARCATI: That's right—quite right—hands at the sides—legs extended—breathe steadily—one two—one two—one two—is she comfortable?

CHARLES: Are you comfortable, Elvira?

ELVIRA: No.

CHARLES: She's quite comfortable.

MADAME ARCATI: I shall join you in a moment, Mr. Condomine—I may have to go into a slight trance but if I do pay no attention—Now first the music and away we go! [Madame Arcati *turns on the gramophone and stands quite still by the side of it with her hands behind her head for a little— then suddenly, with great swiftness, she runs to the door and switches out the lights. Her form can dimly be discerned moving about in the darkness.* Charles *gives a loud sneeze*]

ELVIRA: [*Giggling*] Oh, dear—it's the pepper.

CHARLES: Damn!

MADAME ARCATI: Hold on to yourself—concentrate—[Madame Arcati *recites in a sing-song voice*]

"Ghostly spectre—ghoul or fiend
Never more be thou convened
Shepherd's Wort and Holy Rite
Banish thee into the night."

ELVIRA: What a disagreeable little verse.

CHARLES: Be quiet, Elvira.

MADAME ARCATI: Shhh! [*There is silence*] Is there anyone there? . . . Is there anyone there?—one rap for yes—two raps for no. Is there anyone there? . . . [*The table gives a loud bump*] Aha! Good stuff! Is it Daphne? . . . [*The table gives another bump*] I'm sorry to bother you, dear, but Mrs. Condomine wants to return. [*The table bumps several times very quickly*] Now then, Daphne . . . Did you hear what I said? [*After a pause the table gives one bump*] Can you help us? . . . [*There is another pause, then the table begins to bump violently without stopping*] Hold tight, Mr. Condomine —it's trying to break away. Oh! Oh! Oh— [*The table falls over with a crash*]

CHARLES: What's the matter, Madame Arcati? Are you hurt?

MADAME ARCATI: [*Wailing*] Oh! Oh! Oh—

CHARLES: [*Turns on lights*] What on earth's happening? [Madame Arcati *is lying on the floor with the table upside down on her back.* Charles *hurriedly lifts it off. Shaking her*] Are you hurt, Madame Arcati?

ELVIRA: She's in one of her damned trances again and I'm here as much as ever I was.

CHARLES: [*Shaking* Madame Arcati] For God's sake wake up.

MADAME ARCATI: [*Moaning*] Oh! Oh! Oh—

ELVIRA: Leave her alone—she's having a whale of a time. If I ever do get back I'll strangle that bloody little Daphne. . . .

CHARLES: Wake up!

MADAME ARCATI: [*Sitting up suddenly*] What happened?

CHARLES: Nothing—nothing at all.

MADAME ARCATI: [*Rising and dusting herself*] Oh yes, it did—I know something happened.

CHARLES: You fell over—that's all that happened.

MADAME ARCATI: Is she still here?

CHARLES: Of course she is.

MADAME ARCATI: Something must have gone wrong.

ELVIRA: Make her do it properly. I'm sick of being messed about like this.

CHARLES: She's doing her best. Be quiet, Elvira.

MADAME ARCATI: Something happened—I sensed it in my trance—I felt it—it shivered through me.

[*Suddenly the window curtains blow out almost straight and* Ruth *walks into the room. She is still wearing the brightly colored clothes in which we last saw her but now they are entirely grey. So is her hair and her skin*]

RUTH: Once and for all, Charles, what the hell does this mean?

THE LIGHTS FADE

SCENE II.

When the lights go up again several hours have elapsed. The whole room is in slight disarray. There are birch branches and evergreens laid on the floor in front of the doors and crossed birch branches pinned rather untidily onto the curtains. The furniture has been moved about a bit. On the bridge table there is a pile of playing cards, Madame Arcati's *crystal and a Ouija board. Also a plate of sandwiches and two empty beer mugs. Madame Arcati is stretched out on the sofa with her eyes shut.* Elvira *is seated at the bridge table looking despondently at the debris.* Ruth *is by the fireplace.* Charles *is walking irritably about the room.*

RUTH: Well—we've done all we can—I must say I couldn't be more exhausted.

ELVIRA: It will be daylight soon. [*The clock strikes five, very slowly*]

RUTH: That clock's always irritated me—it strikes far too slowly.

CHARLES: It was a wedding present from Uncle Walter.

RUTH: Whose Uncle Walter?

CHARLES: Elvira's.

RUTH: Well, all I can say is he might have chosen something a little more decorative.

ELVIRA: If that really were all you could say, Ruth, I'm sure it would be a great comfort to us all.

RUTH: [*Grandly*] You can be as rude as you like, Elvira, I don't mind a bit—as a matter of fact I should be extremely surprised if you weren't.

ELVIRA: [*Truculently*] Why?

RUTH: The reply to that is really too obvious.

CHARLES: I wish you two would stop bickering for one minute.

RUTH: This is quite definitely one of the most frustrating nights I have ever spent.

ELVIRA: The reply to that is pretty obvious too.

RUTH: I'm sure I don't know what you mean.

ELVIRA: Skip it.

RUTH: Now listen to me, Elvira. If you and I have got to stay together indefinitely in this house—and it looks unpleasantly—[*Turns to* Madame Arcati] —likely—we had better come to some sort of an arrangement.

ELVIRA: What sort of an arrangement?

CHARLES: You're *not* going to stay indefinitely in this house.

RUTH: With you then—we shall have to be with you.

CHARLES: I don't see why—why don't you take a cottage somewhere?

RUTH: You called us back.

CHARLES: I've already explained until I'm black in the face that I did nothing of the sort.

RUTH: Madame Arcati said you did.

CHARLES: Madame Arcati's a muddling old fool.

ELVIRA: I could have told you that in the first place.

RUTH: I think you're behaving very shabbily, Charles.

CHARLES: I don't see what I've done.

RUTH: We have all agreed that as Elvira and I are dead that it would be both right and proper for us to dematerialize again as soon as possible. That, I admit. We have allowed ourselves to be subjected to the most humiliating hocus-pocus for hours and hours without complaining—

CHARLES: Without complaining?

RUTH: We've stood up—we've lain down—we've concentrated. We've sat interminably while that tiresome old woman recited extremely unflattering verses at us. We've endured five séances—we've watched her fling herself in and out of trances until we're dizzy and at the end of it all we find ourselves exactly where we were at the beginning. . . .

CHARLES: Well, it's not my fault.

RUTH: Be that as it may, the least you could do is

to admit failure gracefully and try to make the best of it—your manners are boorish to a degree.

CHARLES: I'm just as exhausted as you are. I've had to do all the damned table tapping, remember.

RUTH: If she can't get us back, she can't and that's that. We shall have to think of something else.

CHARLES: She *must* get you back—anything else is unthinkable.

ELVIRA: There's gratitude for you!

CHARLES: Gratitude?

ELVIRA: Yes, for all the years we've both devoted to you—you ought to be ashamed.

CHARLES: What about all the years I've devoted to you?

ELVIRA: Nonsense—we've waited on you hand and foot—haven't we, Ruth? You're exceedingly selfish and always were.

CHARLES: In that case I fail to see why you were both so anxious to get back to me.

RUTH: You called us back. And you've done nothing but try to get rid of us ever since we came —hasn't he, Elvira?

ELVIRA: He certainly has.

RUTH: And now, owing to your idiotic inefficiency, we find ourselves in the most mortifying position—we're neither fish, flesh nor fowl nor whatever it is.

ELVIRA: Good red herring.

RUTH: It can't be.

CHARLES: Well, why don't you do something about it? Why don't you go back on your own?

RUTH: We can't—you know perfectly well we can't.

CHARLES: Isn't there anybody on the other side who can help?

RUTH: How do I know? I've only been there a few days . . . ask Elvira.

ELVIRA: I've already told you, that's no good— if we got Cagliostro, Mesmer, Merlin, Gil de Retz and the Black Douglas in a row they couldn't do a thing—the impetus has got to come from here. . . . Perhaps darling Charles doesn't want us to go quite enough.

CHARLES: I certainly do.

ELVIRA: Well, you must have a very weak will then. I always suspected it.

RUTH: It's no use arguing any more—wake up Madame Arcati.

ELVIRA: Oh, not another séance—please, not another séance!

CHARLES: [*Loudly—bending over* Madame Arcati] Please wake up, Madame Arcati . . .

RUTH: Shake her.

CHARLES: It might upset her.

RUTH: I don't care if it kills her.

CHARLES: Please wake up, Madame Arcati. . . .

MADAME ARCATI: [*Waking*] What time is it?

CHARLES: Ten past five!

MADAME ARCATI: What time did I go off? [*She sits up*]

CHARLES: Over an hour ago.

MADAME ARCATI: [*Reaching for her bag*] Curious . . . very curious. Forgive me for a moment, I must just make a note of that for my diary. [*She takes a book out of her bag and scribbles in it*] Are they still here?

CHARLES: Yes.

MADAME ARCATI: How disappointing.

CHARLES: Have you any suggestions?

MADAME ARCATI: [*Rising briskly*] We mustn't give up hope. Chin up—never give in—that's my motto.

RUTH: This schoolgirl phraseology's driving me mad.

MADAME ARCATI: Now then . . .

CHARLES: Now then what?

MADAME ARCATI: What do you say we have another séance and really put our shoulders to the wheel?—Make it a real rouser!

ELVIRA: For God's sake not another séance.

MADAME ARCATI: I might be able to materialize a trumpet if I tried hard enough—better than nothing, you know—I feel as fit as a fiddle after my rest.

ELVIRA: I don't care if she materializes a whole symphony orchestra—I implore you not to let her have another séance.

CHARLES: Don't you think, Madame Arcati, that perhaps we've had enough séances? After all they haven't achieved much, have they?

MADAME ARCATI: Rome wasn't built in a day, you know.

CHARLES: I know it wasn't, but. . . .

MADAME ARCATI: Well then—cheer up—away with melancholy.

CHARLES: Now listen, Madame Arcati . . . before you go off into any further trances I really think we ought to discuss the situation a little.

MADAME ARCATI: Good—an excellent idea—and while we're doing it I shall have another of these delicious sandwiches—I'm as hungry as a hunter.

CHARLES: Would you like some more beer?

MADAME ARCATI: No, thank you—better not.

CHARLES: Very well—I think I'll have a small whisky and soda.

MADAME ARCATI: Make it a double and enjoy yourself.

[Charles *goes to the drinks table and mixes himself a whisky and soda*]

RUTH: One day I intend to give myself the pleasure of telling Madame Arcati exactly what I think of her.

CHARLES: She's been doing her best.

MADAME ARCATI: Are the girls getting despondent?

CHARLES: I'm afraid they are *rather*.

MADAME ARCATI: We'll win through yet—don't be downhearted.

RUTH: If we're not very careful she'll materialize a hockey team.

MADAME ARCATI: Now then, Mr. Condomine— the discussion—fire away.

CHARLES: Well. my wives and I have been talking

it over and they are both absolutely convinced that I somehow or other called them back.

MADAME ARCATI: Very natural.

CHARLES: I am equally convinced that I did not.

MADAME ARCATI: Love is a strong psychic force, Mr. Condomine—it can work untold miracles. A true love call can encompass the universe—

CHARLES: [Hastily] I'm sure it can, but I must confess to you frankly that although my affection for both Elvira and Ruth is of the warmest I cannot truthfully feel that it would come under the heading that you describe.

ELVIRA: I should just think not indeed.

MADAME ARCATI: You may not know your own strength, Mr. Condomine.

CHARLES: [Firmly] I did not call them back—either consciously or subconsciously.

MADAME ARCATI: But, Mr. Condomine . . .

CHARLES: That is my final word on the subject.

MADAME ARCATI: Neither of them could have appeared unless there had been somebody—a psychic subject—in the house, who wished for them . . .

CHARLES: Well, it wasn't me.

ELVIRA: Perhaps it was Doctor Bradman—I never knew he cared.

MADAME ARCATI: Are you sure?—Are you really sure?

CHARLES: Absolutely positive.

MADAME ARCATI: [Snapping her fingers] Great Scott, I believe we've been barking up the wrong tree!

CHARLES: How do you mean?

MADAME ARCATI: The Sudbury case!

CHARLES: I don't understand.

MADAME ARCATI: There's no reason why you should—it was before your day—I wonder—oh, I wonder. . . .

CHARLES: What was the Sudbury case? I wish you'd explain.

MADAME ARCATI: It was the case that made me famous, Mr. Condomine—it was what you might describe in theatrical parlance as my first smash hit! I had letters from all over the world about it—especially India.

CHARLES: What did you do?

MADAME ARCATI: I dematerialized old Lady Sudbury after she'd been firmly entrenched in the private chapel for over seventeen years.

CHARLES: [Rises] How?—Can't you remember how?

MADAME ARCATI: Chance—a fluke—I happened on it by the merest coincidence.

CHARLES: What fluke—what was it?

MADAME ARCATI: Wait—all in good time. [She begins to walk about the room] Now let me see—who was in the house during our first séance?

CHARLES: Only the Bradmans, Ruth and me and yourself.

MADAME ARCATI: Ah, yes—yes—to be sure—but the Bradmans weren't here last night, were they?

CHARLES: No.

MADAME ARCATI: Quickly . . . my crystal—

CHARLES: [Handing it to her] Here. . . .

MADAME ARCATI: [Shaking it crossly] Damn the thing, it's cloudy again—[She looks again] Ah!—that's better—it's there again—it's there again—I'm beginning to understand.

CHARLES: I wish I was. What's there again?

MADAME ARCATI: A bandage—a white bandage—hold on to a white bandage. . . .

CHARLES: I haven't got a white bandage.

MADAME ARCATI: Shhh! [She puts the crystal down and stands silent for a moment]

ELVIRA: She's too good, you know—she ought to be in a circus.

[Madame Arcati advances to the middle of the room and raises her arms slowly—she begins to intone]

MADAME ARCATI:
Be you in nook or cranny answer me
Do you in Still-room or closet answer me
Do you behind the panel, above the stairs
Beneath the eaves—waking or sleeping
Answer me!

That ought to do it or I'm a Dutchman.

CHARLES: Do what?

MADAME ARCATI: Hush—wait— [She picks up one of the birch branches and waves it solemnly to and fro]

RUTH: For God's sake don't let her throw any more of that garlic about. It nearly made me sick last time.

CHARLES: Would you like the gramophone on or the lights out or anything?

MADAME ARCATI: No, no—it's near—it's very near—

ELVIRA: If it's a ghost I shall scream.

RUTH: I hope it's nobody we know—I shall feel so silly.

[Suddenly the door opens and Edith comes into the room. She is wearing a pink flannel dressing gown and bedroom slippers. Her head is bandaged]

EDITH: Did you ring, sir?

MADAME ARCATI: The bandage! The white bandage!

CHARLES: No, Edith.

EDITH: I'm sorry, sir—I could have sworn I heard the bell—or somebody calling—I was asleep—I don't rightly know which it was. . . .

MADAME ARCATI: Come here, child.

EDITH: Oh! [She looks anxiously at Charles]

CHARLES: Go on—go to Madame Arcati—it's quite all right.

MADAME ARCATI: Who do you see in this room, child?

EDITH: Oh, dear. . . .

MADAME ARCATI: Answer please.

EDITH: [Falteringly] You; madame—[She stops]

MADAME ARCATI: Go on.

EDITH: The Master.

MADAME ARCATI: Anyone else?

EDITH: Oh no, madame. . . .

MADAME ARCATI: [*Inflexibly*] Look again.

EDITH: [*Imploringly, to* Charles] I don't understand, sir—I—

MADAME ARCATI: Come, child—don't beat about
the bush—look again.

[Elvira *begins to move about the room almost
as though she were being pulled.* Edith *follows
with her eyes*]

RUTH: Do concentrate, Elvira, and keep still.

ELVIRA: I can't.

MADAME ARCATI: Do you see anyone else now?

EDITH: [*Slyly*] Oh no, madame.

MADAME ARCATI: She's lying.

EDITH: Oh, madame!

MADAME ARCATI: They always do.

CHARLES: They?

MADAME ARCATI: [*Sharply*] Where are they now?

EDITH: By the fireplace. Oh!

CHARLES: She can see them—do you mean she
can see them?

MADAME ARCATI: Probably not very clearly—but
enough—

EDITH: [*Bursting into tears*] Let me go—I haven't
done nothing nor seen nobody—let me go back
to bed.

MADAME ARCATI: Give her a sandwich.

EDITH: [*Drawing away*] I don't want a sandwich.
I want to go back to bed. . . .

CHARLES: [*Handing* Edith *the plate*] Here, Edith.

MADAME ARCATI: Nonsense—a big healthy girl
like you saying no to a delicious sandwich—I never
heard of such a thing—sit down.

EDITH: [*To* Charles] Please, sir, I . . .

CHARLES: Please do as Madame Arcati says, Edith.

EDITH: [*Sitting down and sniffing*] I haven't done
nothing wrong.

CHARLES: It's all right—nobody said you had.

RUTH: If she's been the cause of all this unpleasantness I'll give her a week's notice tomorrow.

ELVIRA: You may not be here tomorrow—

MADAME ARCATI: Look at me, Edith. [Edith *obediently does so*] Cuckoo—cuckoo—cuckoo—

EDITH: [*Jumping*] Oh, dear—what's the matter
with her? Is she barmy?

MADAME ARCATI: Here, Edith—this is my finger—
look—[*She waggles it*] Have you ever seen such a
long, long, long finger? Look now it's on the right—
now it's on the left—backwards and forwards it goes
—see—very quietly backwards and forwards—tic-
toc—tic—toc—tic-toc.

ELVIRA: The mouse ran up the clock.

RUTH: Be quiet—*you'll ruin everything.*

[Madame Arcati *whistles a little tune close to*
Edith's *face—then she snaps her fingers.* Edith
looks stolidly in front of her without flinching.
Madame Arcati *stands back*]

MADAME ARCATI: Well—so far so good—she's off
all right.

CHARLES: Off?

MADAME ARCATI: She's a Natural—just the same
as the Sudbury case—it really is the most amusing
coincidence. Now then—would you ask your wives
to stand close together please?

CHARLES: Where?

MADAME ARCATI: Over there by you.

CHARLES: Elvira—Ruth—

RUTH: I resent being ordered about like this.

ELVIRA: I don't like this at all—I don't like any
of it—I feel peculiar.

CHARLES: I'm afraid I must insist.

ELVIRA: It would serve you right if we flatly refused to do anything at all.

MADAME ARCATI: Are you sorry for having been
so mischievous, Edith?

EDITH: [*Cheerfully*] Oh yes, madame.

MADAME ARCATI: You know what you have to do
now, don't you, Edith?

EDITH: Oh yes, madame.

RUTH: I believe it's going to work whatever it is.
Oh, Charles.

CHARLES: Shhh!

RUTH: This is good-bye, Charles.

ELVIRA: Tell her to stop for a minute—there's
something I want to say before I go.

CHARLES: You should have thought of that before—it's too late now.

ELVIRA: Of all the mean, ungracious—

RUTH: Charles, listen a moment . . .

MADAME ARCATI: [*In a shrill voice*] Lights! [Mad-
ame Arcati *rushes to the door and switches off the
lights. In the dark* Edith *is singing "Always" in a
very high cockney voice*]

ELVIRA: [*In the dark*] I saw Captain Bracegirdle
again, Charles—several times—I went to the Four
Hundred with him twice when you were in Nottingham. And I must say I couldn't have enjoyed it
more.

RUTH: Don't think you're getting rid of us quite
so easily, my dear—you may not be able to see us
but we shall be here all right—I consider that you
have behaved atrociously over the whole miserable
business. And I should like to say here and now—
[*Her voice fades into a whisper and then disappears
altogether*]

MADAME ARCATI: [*Exultantly*] Splendid! Hurrah!
We've done it! That's quite enough singing for the
moment, Edith.

CHARLES: [*After a pause*] Shall I put on the lights?

MADAME ARCATI: No—I will.

[Charles *pulls the curtains and daylight floods
into the room.* Ruth *and* Elvira *have disappeared.* Edith *is still sitting on the chair*]

CHARLES: They've gone—they've really gone.

MADAME ARCATI: Yes—I think we've really pulled
it off this time.

CHARLES: You'd better wake her up, hadn't you? She might bring them back again.

MADAME ARCATI: [*Clapping her hands in* Edith's *face*] Wake up, child!

EDITH: [*Nearly jumping out of the chair*] Good 'eavens! Where am I?

CHARLES: It's all right, Edith—you can go back to bed now.

EDITH: Why, it's morning.

CHARLES: Yes—I know it is.

EDITH: But I was in bed—how did I get down 'ere?

CHARLES: I rang, Edith—I rang the bell and you answered it—didn't I, Madame Arcati?

EDITH: Did I drop off? Do you think it's my concussion again? Oh, dear!

CHARLES: Off you go, Edith, and thank you very much. [*He presses a pound note into her hand*] Thank you very much indeed.

EDITH: Oh, sir, whatever for? [*She looks at him in sudden horror*] Oh, sir!! [*She bolts from the room*]

CHARLES: [*Surprised*] What on earth did she mean by that?

MADAME ARCATI: Golly, what a night! I'm ready to drop in my tracks.

CHARLES: Would you like to stay here?—there's the spare room, you know.

MADAME ARCATI: No, thank you—each to his own nest—I'll pedal home in a jiffy—it's only seven miles.

CHARLES: I'm deeply grateful to you, Madame Arcati. I don't know what arrangements you generally make but I trust you will send in your account in due course.

MADAME ARCATI: Good heavens, Mr. Condomine—it was a pleasure—I wouldn't dream of such a thing.

CHARLES: But really I feel that all those trances. . . .

MADAME ARCATI: I enjoy them, Mr. Condomine, thoroughly. I always have since a child.

CHARLES: Perhaps you'd give me the pleasure of lunching with me one day soon?

MADAME ARCATI: When you come back—I should be delighted.

CHARLES: Come back?

MADAME ARCATI: [*Lowering her voice*] Take my advice, Mr. Condomine, and go away immediately.

CHARLES: But, Madame Arcati! You don't mean that . . . ?

MADAME ARCATI: [*Clearing her stuff from table*] This must be an unhappy house for you—there must be memories both grave and gay in every corner of it—also—[*She pauses*]

CHARLES: Also what?

MADAME ARCATI: [*Thinking better of it*] There are more things in heaven and earth, Mr. Condomine. [*She places her finger to her lips*] Just go—pack your traps and go as soon as possible.

CHARLES: [*Also in lowered tones*] Do you mean that they may still be here?

MADAME ARCATI: [*She nods and then nonchalantly whistles a little tune*] Quien sabe, as the Spanish say. [*She collects her bag and her crystal*]

CHARLES: [*Looking furtively round the room*] I wonder—I wonder. I'll follow your advice, Madame Arcati. Thank you again.

MADAME ARCATI: Well, good-bye, Mr. Condomine—it's been fascinating—from first to last—fascinating. Do you mind if I take just one more sandwich to munch on my way home? [*Comes down to table for sandwich*]

CHARLES: By all means.

[*Madame* Arcati *goes to the door.* Charles *follows her to see her safely out*]

MADAME ARCATI: [*As they go*] Don't trouble—I can find my way. Cheerio once more and good hunting!

[Charles *watches her into the hall and then comes back into the room. He prowls about for a moment as though he were not sure that he was alone*]

CHARLES: [*Softly*] Ruth—Elvira—are you there? [*A pause*] Ruth—Elvira—I know damn well you're there—[*Another pause*] I just want to tell you that I'm going away so there's no point in your hanging about any longer—I'm going a long way away—somewhere where I don't believe you'll be able to follow me. In spite of what Elvira said I don't think spirits can travel over water. Is that quite clear, my darlings? You said in one of your more acid moments, Ruth, that I had been hag-ridden all my life! How right you were—but now I'm free, Ruth dear, not only of Mother and Elvira and Mrs. Winthrop-Llewellyn, but free of you too, and I should like to take this farewell opportunity of saying I'm enjoying it immensely—[*A vase crashes into the fireplace*] Aha—I thought so—you were very silly, Elvira, to imagine that I didn't know all about you and Captain Bracegirdle—I did. But what you didn't know was that I was extremely attached to Paula Westlake at the time! [*The clock strikes sixteen viciously and very quickly*] I was reasonably faithful to you, Ruth, but I doubt if it would have lasted much longer—you were becoming increasingly domineering, you know, and there's nothing more off putting than that, is there? [*A large picture falls down with a crash*] Good-bye for the moment, my dears. I expect we are bound to meet again one day, but until we do I'm going to enjoy myself as I've never enjoyed myself before. You can break up the house as much as you like—I'm leaving it anyhow. Think kindly of me and send out good thoughts—[*The overmantel begins to shake and tremble as though someone were tugging at it*] Nice work, Elvira—persevere. Good-bye again—parting is such *sweet* sorrow! [*He goes out of the room just as the overmantel crashes to the floor and the curtain pole comes tumbling down*]

CURTAIN

Modern American Drama

Modern American Drama

The American theatre was the last theatre of major proportions to come of age. *A Doll's House* was nearly forty years old when O'Neill's first short plays were written. Ibsen, Strindberg, Becque, and Chekhov were dead. Shaw had been writing plays for nearly three decades. Realism and naturalism had already triumphed in Europe and in England, and the symbolists had established the claims of imagination and poetry in the theatre. When, after the conclusion of the First World War, the American drama attained its maturity, Europe had already taken the major steps in the modern theatre. As a matter of fact, across the Atlantic new theatrical movements in the drama were again beginning to teem, and one of these, using the name "expressionism," was exciting interest with its turbulent writing and esoteric explosions; the latest modernists were now the German dramatists Georg Kaiser and Ernst Toller and the Czech Karel Capek.

When playwriting and stagecraft in America became permeated with the modern spirit, the result was a fusion of dramatic elements. Writers and stage directors helped themselves to anything that happened to suit their interests. In some of his work, Eugene O'Neill, for example, was a realist or naturalist, but with poetic overtones. In *The Emperor Jones* and *The Hairy Ape* he could be designated an expressionist. In still other plays, such as *Strange Interlude* and *Mourning Becomes Electra,* he worked out forms for which no particular school could claim paternity. Actually, modern American drama, instead of serving a single principle or style, telescoped the experiments and strivings of several decades of theatrical pioneering.

Our twentieth-century playwrights and their associates did not have to fight the desperate battles that Ibsen and his champions had waged. Yet their advent was quite revolutionary in the hitherto retarded American theatre, and it was not unproductive of plays considered worthy of the modern spirit. America fell short, it is true, of ideal aims, failing to develop a subsidized national theatre (except for a brief period of federal relief between 1935 and 1939) and never quite developing a successful repertory system. Production methods on Broadway were often haphazard and superficial. Brashness was mistaken for vitality. We credited originality to plays which were actually derivative, and we mistook significant subject matter for significant art. Our drama became attuned, nevertheless, to modern ideas and acquired literary value. We even began to contribute to the European stage instead of merely borrowing from it. O'Neill's plays were produced throughout Europe, and productions of more and more works by Elmer Rice, Clifford Odets, Lillian Hellman, Robert Sherwood, Arthur Miller, and Tennessee

Williams traveled as far as Australia. It is not too much to say, indeed, that our theatre was more vital than England's during the nineteen-thirties, and that between 1930 and 1950 we were well ahead of Germany, Italy, and Russia in the production of plays expressive of individual feeling and independent thought. After 1920, except for the appearance of so remarkable a drama as *Saint Joan* or *The Plough and the Stars* across the Atlantic, American playwriting was at least on a par with that of any other nation.

A historical survey and critical overview of modern American drama must differ in some respects from an examination of modern European drama. When we deal with the latter, we are able to trace well-defined movements and to single out conspicuously important playwrights, each of whom deserves attention for his substantial contribution and for his individual mode of expression and point of view. In discussing American drama, we have no such clear-cut pattern to follow. Although experimental groups arose in America after 1915, they developed no distinctive styles important to the history of dramatic form.

A review of the American drama cannot be written around a ruling concept, a succession of influential ideas or dramatic principles, or an evolution of special types of drama. We did not change or subvert the nature of tragedy, as the European naturalists did; we did not modify the approach of comedy; we did not invent some major mode of social, historical, or biographical drama. Nor did we give rise to important modifications of realism, naturalism, symbolism, expressionism, or theatricalism that may be called peculiarly American. Much as the critic, historian, or teacher may want to illuminate our modern drama by means of some philosophical or esthetic concept, he is bound to be contradicted by the eclectic character of our theatre. He cannot even hope to elaborate the kind of synthesis that scholars of the major European cultures are apt to favor. The modern drama of France can be viewed as part of a tradition that includes not only the neoclassic tragedy of Corneille and Racine and the comedy of Molière but certain influential early-nineteenth-century movements as well. Spanish drama can be related to the dramatic literature of the late sixteenth and the seventeenth centuries. England's modern drama can be considered as part of a theatre that produced Congreve and Sheridan long before it gave rise to Wilde and Shaw, Maugham and Coward; and insofar as there has been a poetic drama in Britain, it can be studied in relation to the great poetic theatre of Shakespeare and his contemporaries or to the closet drama of later poet-playwrights. But the modern drama of the United States has no significant national tradition to provide a perspective.

At most, we can trace some continuity of robust vaudeville-like entertainment from the nonliterary farces of Harrigan and Hart (the Mulligan Guard series) to later "fast" comedies. The story of our modern theatre consists largely of efforts to cut adrift from the earlier trends of the American stage.

We can go no further than this in an effort to find distinctive attributes in our drama: We can say that our humor tended to be broader and more robust than European humor. We used bludgeons more frequently than rapiers in attacking absurdities in private and public behavior. We were far less deft at writing high comedy and did so less frequently than the British. We were less brittle and pointed than the French, less airy than the Viennese, less sentimental than the Hungarians, less metaphysical than the modern Italians. We also favored a speedier type of playwriting than prevailed in Europe; our writing was more nervous and, in the main, less intellectual. It may also be noted that we were moderate in experimentation, except in the case of O'Neill's work; we avoided the extreme stridency that characterized the German expressionist stage after the First World War, the overemphasis on utilitarian theatre that the Russians favored after their Revolution, and the odd surrealism that the French made fashionable in Paris. By comparison with the European stage, our theatre after 1918 possessed vigor without fanaticism, speed without turbulence, skepticism without bitterness, interest in ideas without metaphysical complexity, and, except for a brief period during the depression, awareness of social reality without marked propagandistic bias.

These differences between ourselves and Europe were, however, unremarkable. We cannot erect a system of significant "American" drama on this basis. If we are inclined to credit some of our playwrights with greater stature than they actually possess, it is because we inevitably think of them in terms of American rather than of world drama. Their plays receive emphasis in the present volume primarily as American productions, whereas the works of Ibsen, Strindberg, Chekhov, or Shaw concern us less because they represent Scandinavian, Russian, or British drama than because they affected the course of the theatre throughout the Western world. The American drama is of interest as a result of the great many plays of merit contributed by a variety of playwrights, most of whom have individually created neither an extensive nor a distinguished dramatic literature.

The work of America's modern dramatists is part of a single cultural stream to which novelists, poets, and even painters and composers contributed. The drama of the 1919–1929 decade was one manifestation of our maturing creative expression and of our rebellion against the values dominant during the early years of the century. Similarly, the plays of the next twenty years reflected the shifting concerns of dramatists, as well as of other writers and artists, as they faced the depression years and the onset of the Second World War. We may therefore concern ourselves with over-all directions in the theatre, bearing in mind always that a "trend" is not the same thing as a work of art and is never a substitute for it. A chronicle which follows developments in our cultural history and traces the changing sociocultural context of our drama may help to create some order out of our vital and disorderly theatre.

THE EARLY CURRENTS

Before we discover how far we came, we must, of course, know where we started. Our progress is measurable, at least partly, by the limitations with which we began and the efforts we made to overcome them. America has a theatrical past, and it is a mistake to assume that a modern American theatre was suddenly born on a certain date, when, for instance, the Provincetown Players produced O'Neill's first one-act play or when the infant Theatre Guild was saved by the success of St. John Ervine's *John Ferguson*. The fact is that the theatre moved into the modern world, gradually, in a stream of mingled currents, some of them faintly observable in America decades before 1920.

The American theatre started fumbling toward maturity during the eighteen-eighties and 'nineties, having produced little during the earlier part of the century but adaptations of European plays, a few sentimental comedies, the most endurable being Anna Cora Mowatt's *Fashion* (1845), and a great number of melodramas. After 1880, we began to create glossy comedy of manners with some evidence of wit and intelligence, problem plays, and realistic studies of character and situation. Clyde Fitch turned out comedies of manners which had less moss on them than the older, sentimental plays. Bronson Howard considered capital and labor in *Baron Rudolph* and Wall Street speculation in *The Henrietta*, and Steele MacKaye took note of radical movements in *Paul Kauvar, or Anarchy*. Augustus Thomas painted pictures of the American hinterland in such set pieces as *In Mizzoura* and *Arizona*. And quite remarkably for an American playwright in 1890, the actor-manager James A. Herne wrote the first native realistic drama, *Margaret Fleming*, in which human weakness and adultery were for once treated with understanding rather than horror.

The first decade of the new century brought only slight improvement. Clyde Fitch worked himself up to glimmerings of social satire in *The Climbers* (1901) and in *The Truth* (1907). He also arrived at some comedy of character in *The Girl with the Green Eyes* (1901) and at some social realism in *The City* (1910), with its story of a corrupt public career. Human relations began to be treated with more candor. William Vaughn Moody contrasted the free West with puritanical New England in *The Great Divide* (1906), going so far as vaguely to imply that a woman might fall in love with the man who had violated her. Eugene Walter supplied a slice of life in *The Easiest Way* (1908) by presenting a woman's vacillations between the man who had been keeping her and the man who offered her respectability but also poverty. Some interest in psychology thrust itself into the theatre with such pieces as Augustus Thomas' *The Witching Hour* and Moody's *The Faith Healer* (1909). Awareness of social problems grew with the rise of muckraking journalism, especially after Theodore Roosevelt began waving his "big stick" at big business. Even such a purveyor of popular entertainment as Charles Klein concerned himself with malefactors of great wealth, in *The Lion and the Mouse*. Edward Sheldon discussed a racial problem in *The Nigger* (1910) and municipal corruption in *The Boss* (1911). Domestic relations, too, came to be treated with more sharpness: there is still some vitality in Langdon Mitchell's witty divorce comedy *The New York Idea*, produced in 1906. By 1914, the "new woman" had become a topic rather than a monster.

It cannot be said that the commercial theatre before 1920 produced vigorous drama of ideas, penetrating studies of reality, plays transfigured by deeply personal expression—or even particularly bright comedy of manners. New York had already seen a number of Shaw's plays without greatly benefiting from the example. It had familiarized itself with Ibsen's work without being stirred to produce any powerful protest or character analysis. And it had acquired some knowledge of the new romantic plays of Maeterlinck and Rostand without creating better poetic drama than Josephine Preston Peabody's *The Piper* and Percy MacKaye's *The Scarecrow*. Clyde Fitch called for modern plays "reflecting absolutely and truthfully the life and environment about us; every class, every kind, every emotion, every motive, every occupation, every business, every idleness." It was a good program, even if Fitch himself did not follow it. It had yet to be followed when the First World War broke out.

Even during the war years, American plays were about as modern, for the most part, as the horse-drawn wagon is today. By comparison with the novels already written by Henry James, Stephen Crane, Frank Norris, and Theodore Dreiser, even our best dramas were monumentally inconsequential. It is true that in Jesse Lynch Williams' *Why Marry?* (the first Pulitzer Prize play), produced in 1914, the "new woman" proposed to live with a gentleman without benefit of the law. The times having changed somewhat, no one rose up in arms against this comedy. But we must remember that the heroine was duly married at the end by an uncle who happened to be a magistrate. It is also true that Clare Kummer contributed several sophisticated comedies—the frivolous antic *Good Gra-*

cious, *Annabelle* (1916) and the mildly Shavian piece *A Successful Calamity* (1917). How modern these and similar pieces really were, however, can be determined by comparing them to plays long familiar abroad. Melodrama continued to proliferate, with some farcical deviations from the old "unhand her, villain" type of contrivance (our classic example of farce melodrama, George M. Cohan's *Seven Keys to Baldpate,* is of 1913 vintage) and with some modernity, especially in plays by Bayard Veiller and Elmer Rice. (The latter even introduced the "flashback" method of the cinema into his 1914 melodrama *On Trial;* being a man of conviction, he tried also to write thesis plays, to which the wartime theatre was unfavorable.) Inevitably, the war also spawned a number of flag-waving exercises and spy melodramas. And the public gave enthusiastic reception to a succession of such sentimental pieces as the perennial *Peg o' My Heart* and that apotheosis of the "Glad Girl" *Pollyanna*. (Laurette Taylor, later the Amanda of *The Glass Menagerie,* was the adorable Peg; Patricia Collinge, later the Birdie of *The Little Foxes,* was the Glad Girl.)

A minor revolution in the theatre, brewing since 1910, had to make itself felt before the tentative forays into modern drama could became distinctive and before the time-honored genteel comedies and vacuous melodramas would cease to be honored. This revolution came to a head after the First World War, and the result was the drama that made its first appearance with O'Neill and moved toward the middle of the century with Tennessee Williams and Arthur Miller.

A word of caution is needed at this point. Only a part of the American theatre has been modern since 1918; the rest has merely seemed modern because it shaved off its whiskers and talked fast. Progress in the theatre is generally uneven, and the common denominator of taste on the part of a nation's playgoing public is rarely very high. (It will be remembered that *Abie's Irish Rose* came as late as 1922 and rolled up 2,327 performances—in a strenuously sophisticated decade—and that Broadway could bring itself to the point of producing *Grandma's Diary* hopefully as late as 1948.) The general tenor was evident in the years immediately following the First World War, when the commercial theatre fluttered about and proffered more sentimental wares of the *Smilin' Through* and *The Charm School* variety. Affectionate writing also was still in vogue. But the flavor was sometimes new and salty, as in the best product of this genial style, Winchell Smith and Frank Bacon's *Lightnin'* (1918). The Pinero standard was well maintained by Zoë Akins in *Déclassée* (1919), the drama of an impetuous woman's descent from high society. Ethel Barrymore covered herself with glory in the role, and Miss Akins' play was regarded as a very modern drama. Frank Craven was alleged to be a singularly acute dramatist when he described the difficulties of the first year of marriage in the contrived comedy *The First Year*.

THE MODERNIZATION OF THE AMERICAN THEATRE

The real modernization of the American theatre was the work of a few insurgent individuals and groups. Modern American drama as a whole may be described as a brew concocted of domesticated naturalism and expressionism, sophisticated comedy, drama of ideas, cheeky treatment of American manners, protest against puritanical morals, and revolt against the middle-class values of the postwar period. Offered first in pure form by resolute rebels, our modernism began to be purveyed in adulterated versions. The combination of the genuine article with imitations in the form of watered-down realism and protest has constituted the American drama since 1920. But in order to understand what happened to give the American theatre a more or less new dispensation, we must retrace our steps a little.

After 1916, the commercial theatre lost much of its hold outside New York City. The vast touring-company system, on which the managers had thrived for many decades, dwindled as a result of the high cost of railroad transportation and the competition of the motion-picture industry. The theatre lost its mass public which had exhibited very little discrimination. The audience that remained was more cosmopolitan and demanding. It consisted of people with European background, people living in or near New York and a few other cities, and fairly well-educated leaders of the hinterland who had some interest in art and ideas; often their focal institution in the smaller communities was a university or club. Faced with a new audience, the commercial managements in time found it expedient to present plays and production styles that would have seemed altogether too esoteric in 1890, 1900, or 1910. Moreover, among the new managers were men of taste and discrimination, such as Winthrop Ames and Arthur Hopkins, who were eager to associate themselves with modern drama and modern scenic art.

In consequence, the commercial theatre began to include productions that reflected an interest in the stage as an art rather than exclusively as a business; in some instances the managers were also gratified to discover that the gulf between art and business could be narrowed. Thus, in 1912, Winthrop Ames imported the Max Reinhardt Japanese-styled pantomime *Sumurûn;* and Hazelton and Benrimo's fantasy in the Chinese manner, *The Yellow Jacket*, was presented by the practical management of Harris and Selwyn in the same year. Ames also produced the Granville-Barker and Laurence Housman imaginative play *Prunella*, and Arthur Hopkins began an association with the scene designer Robert Edmond Jones which resulted in memorable John Barrymore

productions of *Richard III, Hamlet,* and *The Jest*. John D. Williams, who later presented O'Neill's *Beyond the Horizon*, produced Galsworthy's *Justice* in 1916. (With John Barrymore in the leading role, *Justice* won great popularity; as a result, the play became required reading for schoolboys, whose induction into modern drama at school had hitherto not carried them beyond Charles Rann Kennedy's sermon *The Servant in the House*.) Granville-Barker was invited to stage plays in New York, and in 1915 Robert Edmond Jones gave New Yorkers a famous example of scenic design in one of Granville-Barker's productions, Anatole France's *The Man Who Married a Dumb Wife*.

Between 1911 and 1919, moreover, a "little theatre" movement developed momentum with a notable mushrooming of community and university productions. George Pierce Baker's 47 Workshop Theatre at Harvard produced the first efforts of young playwrights. E. C. Mabie, at the University of Iowa, encouraged native playwriting, and so did a number of other teachers: Thomas H. Dickinson, at the University of Wisconsin; Glenn Hughes, at the University of Washington; A. M. Drummond, at Cornell; and Frederick H. Koch, at the University of North Dakota and later at the University of North Carolina, where Thomas Wolfe, Paul Green, and Dorothy and Du Bose Heyward's dramatic talents germinated. A Chicago Little Theatre was founded in 1912; the Toy Theatre in Boston served as a laboratory for modern art between 1912 and 1916; the Arts and Crafts Theatre arose in Detroit under Sam Hume, a disciple of Gordon Craig; the Cleveland Playhouse became active in 1916. Such groups as these were resolved to create the kind of theatre the commercial managers, with the few exceptions already noted, were not yet willing to supply.

In New York, moreover, there arose three important organizations fired with enthusiasm for modern art and with animus against the old-fashioned drama that George Jean Nathan was then blasting from the pages of the magazine *The Smart Set*. One of these experimental groups, the Neighborhood Playhouse, was established on the East Side in 1915 by the daughters of the philanthropist Adolph Lewisohn. It served the theatre best with stylized productions of such esoteric classics as the Jewish folk fantasy *The Dybbuk* and the Hindu romance *The Little Clay Cart*. The other two groups were started in Greenwich Village, then the Mecca— and inexpensive residence—of rebellious young artists. One was the Washington Square Players; the other, the Provincetown Players. The one-act play, requiring as a rule a small cast and a simple set suitable for tiny stages, served the rebels as a wedge with which to force their way into the theatre.

The Washington Square unit was founded in 1914 by the Welsh-born patent lawyer Lawrence Langner, the clever playwright (later a brilliant stage director) Philip Moeller, the actress Helen Westley, and others. Soon joined by the scene designer Lee Simonson and by such promising young actors as Katherine Cornell and Roland Young, the founders announced a program: they would produce plays of all kinds that were usually ignored by the commercial managements. For this purpose they rented a little theatre, the Bandbox, uptown. In addition to staging European one-acters—Maeterlinck's *Interior* and Chekhov's *The Bear,* for example—they produced such irreverent little American pieces as Moeller's spoof on Helen of Troy, *Helena's Husband,* and Alice Gerstenberg's *Overtones,* a comedy of alter egos, typical of experimental sophistication. Later, the Washington Square Players presented such realistic one-acters as Zona Gale's farm play *Neighbors,* Susan Glaspell's stark drama *Trifles,* and Eugene O'Neill's early sea piece *In the Zone.* The Players also began producing modernistic full-length plays: Andreyev's symbolic *Life of Man,* Ibsen's perennial realistic drama *Ghosts,* Shaw's *Mrs. Warren's Profession,* and others. America's entry into the war dispersed the group in May 1918, after it had enjoyed four years of flamboyant activity. By then it had brought to production sixty-two one-act and six full-length plays.

In 1919, upon returning from war service, a number of the Washington Square amateurs founded America's first professional art theatre, the Theatre Guild, on a subscription-audience basis. The Guild gave its first two performances (Benavente's *The Bonds of Interest* and Ervine's *John Ferguson*) in the spring of 1919. During the next thirty years, this extraordinarily successful theatre was to bring to the fore many of our best-known actors, introduce or revive extreme experiments as well as masterpieces of the modern European drama, and give successful productions of many of the best plays of O'Neill, Sidney Howard, S. N. Behrman, Maxwell Anderson, Philip Barry, Robert Sherwood, and William Saroyan. By reviving many of Shaw's plays and by producing a number of them for the first time in the English language, the Guild also made itself Shaw's official theatre in America.

A more modest, yet in one respect even more important, destiny—namely, the discovery of O'Neill—was in store for the Theatre Guild's sister organization, the Provincetown Players. Among the stalwarts who created this group, in 1915, were the novelist and man of many parts George Cram Cook; his wife, Susan Glaspell (the novelist and playwright, who was to win a Pulitzer Prize in 1930 for the Emily Dickinson drama *Alison's House*); Robert Edmond Jones; and Eugene O'Neill. Before long, they were joined by the veteran of American naturalism Theodore Dreiser, the Harvard firebrand John Reed, the short-story writer Wilbur Daniel Steele, the novelist and writer on labor problems Mary Heaton Vorse, and the then Bohemian poets Harry Kemp, Maxwell Bodenheim, Alfred Kreymborg, and Edna St. Vincent Millay. It seemed that a large part of the vanguard of American letters was rallying to the experimental theatre.

The first theatre of the Provincetown Players stood on an abandoned wharf in the summer colony of Provincetown, Massachusetts. Here, in 1915, they produced their first playlets, the best known being the Freudian one-acter *Suppressed Desires* by Susan Glaspell and George Cram Cook. The next summer, the group made theatrical history by giving O'Neill his first production: *Bound East for Cardiff.* After staging plays at their Wharf Theatre for three summers, they took city quarters in New York's Greenwich Village. Remodeling an abandoned stable on Macdougal Street and hopefully calling it the Playwrights' Theatre, the experimentalists made this unattractive building their temple of the arts from 1918 to 1929.

Here (and for brief periods in a larger Village theatre and on Broadway) the Provincetown Players presented not only unique examples of European modernism but a great many one-act and full-length plays by new American writers. Among the pioneering playwrights were Susan Glaspell, Edmund Wilson and Stark Young (who became better known as novelists and critics), Edna St. Vincent Millay (whose short, poetic *Aria da Capo* is still being played), Hatcher Hughes and Paul Green, both of whom won Pulitzer Prizes, and Eugene O'Neill. Playgoers with long memories may remember the ingratiating style of such revivals as *Patience* and *Fashion,* the electrifying performance of Charles Gilpin in *The Emperor Jones,* and the original staging of some of the experimental plays. But this theatre is less important for its experiments in stagecraft than for its discovery of new American drama. The Provincetown became a playwrights' theatre in fact as well as in name.

It is to the credit of Broadway managements that O'Neill's *Beyond the Horizon* was produced by John D. Williams in 1920 and that *Anna Christie* was presented by Arthur Hopkins a year later. It is also true that the Theatre Guild inherited O'Neill after 1928, when the Provincetown died, and that the Guild gave noteworthy first productions to *Marco Millions, Strange Interlude, Mourning Becomes Electra, Ah, Wilderness!,* and *The Iceman Cometh* over a period of twenty years. But the "revolution" in the American theatre was effected largely by the Provincetown Players' productions of O'Neill's early seapieces and of his longer dramatic experiments—the plays in which he passed beyond realism or naturalism and at the same time incorporated modern life. Most notable among these were *The Emperor Jones, The Hairy Ape, All God's Chillun Got Wings, Desire Under the Elms* (all produced between 1920 and 1924), and *The Great God Brown* (produced in 1926 by the directorate of the Provincetown, then consisting of the critic Kenneth MacGowan, Robert Edmond Jones, and O'Neill himself).

It was in these plays that O'Neill gave uniquely

personal expression to modern man's conflicts and experimented with methods of symbolizing them. It was in this body of work that he gave dimension to the themes of race, labor, the artist's struggle in a materialistic society, the duality of love and hate, and the quest for meaning in a world devoid of faith. He exposed a turbulent and turbid mind as a spectacle for playgoers hitherto accustomed to being entertained rather than troubled. He dredged up for them the weird shapes of desire and anxiety, hitherto discreetly ignored by American playwrights. He gave dramatic expression to the "unconscious," which Freudian psychologists were making a household word among educated and semieducated people. Squeamish citizens might rage and ask the government to intervene, but O'Neill, flanked by the Provincetown faithful and by a growing number of admirers, stood his ground. America had a major modern playwright at last.

In the early nineteen-twenties, O'Neill was, however, no longer alone in forging a new drama, and the Provincetown was no longer alone in providing the suitable setting. The Washington Square Players was now the powerful Theatre Guild. The commercial managements were ready to produce the plays of the rebellious young dramatists—Maxwell Anderson, Laurence Stallings, Elmer Rice, Philip Barry, Sidney Howard, and others too numerous to name here. The new stage directors and the scene designers, led by Robert Edmond Jones and Lee Simonson, were able to translate the work of these writers into expressive theatre. A magazine, *Theatre Arts*, served as an organ for progressive thinkers in the field of the dramatic arts, and such critics as Alexander Woollcott and Heywood Broun greeted the new American plays with a contagious enthusiasm. Writers of fiction and poetry helped educate the theatre public with books that presented a modern outlook. The playwrights now had an audience that was ready for any revelations they cared to make.

THE FIRST DECADE: 1919–1929

The ferment at work in the theatre in the nineteen-twenties can be variously described, for it was compounded of many elements. Its large measure of passion for an art theatre could be seen in the continuing work of the little theatres, in the refinement of stagecraft, in the rise of the stage director to eminence, and in the work of the scenic designer as a creative artist. Unity of design in the stage production and the interpenetration of all aspects of the performance by the meaning and mood of the play were now the ideals of both the experimental and commercial theatres. Attempts were made to establish repertory companies, most notably by Eva Le Gallienne at her Civic Repertory Theatre on New York's Fourteenth Street and by the Theatre Guild, which founded an acting studio also. Actors

created their own theatre, the Actors' Company. Playwrights banded together, with financial support from the philanthropist Otto Kahn, to form a New Playwrights Company, which presented works of an extremely stylized nature.

The progressive playwright who made himself heard during the decade was bent upon expressing his emotions and conveying his convictions. He was, or conceived himself to be, a rebel, although we must remember, as Joseph Wood Krutch has pointed out in *The American Drama Since 1918,* that "the radical who got a hearing was the radical whose criticism was directed rather at the culture than the political organization of America." He belonged to the literary movement that included such iconoclasts as H. L. Mencken, Theodore Dreiser, Sherwood Anderson, Sinclair Lewis, Edna St. Vincent Millay, T. S. Eliot, F. Scott Fitzgerald, and Ernest Hemingway.

The object of attack was not the social structure of America but its external manifestations, which were regarded as offensive and crude—that is, esthetically repellent and unfavorable to the development of a freely creative personality. Insofar as political criticism existed, it was leveled at such illiberal manifestations as vigilantism of the Ku Klux Klan variety, attacks on labor organizations, and restriction of civil liberties. The main assault was directed at the excrescences of an economy bloated with war profits, and at mechanization and commercialization. The revolt was spearheaded by vigorous literary critics. Mencken flailed at middle-class complacency and narrow-mindedness with many a jibe but also with valiant support of every genuinely realistic or critical writer. The critic Vernon L. Parrington (1871–1929) studied our literary history in *Main Currents in American Thought* (1927–1930) and showed that it had always involved a struggle against illiberal forces. Van Wyck Brooks examined the failure of our literary past (which he himself was later loudest in praising in *The Flowering of New England*). Between 1915 and 1930, he viewed our literature and the careers of our writers as a tragedy of frustration. Brooks maintained, in such books as *The Ordeal of Mark Twain* (1920) and *The Pilgrimage of Henry James* (1925), that our Puritan tradition and our materialism had prevented the full flowering of the creative life in America. It was the intention of an entire generation of young writers after 1915 not to allow its spiritual and artistic growth to be stunted. Writers left their home towns and gathered their forces in literary circles in Chicago, where Harriet Monroe published her *Poetry* magazine, and in New York, where Greenwich Village was the haven of the rebel. If they were sufficiently provoked, they left America altogether and lived abroad, usually on the Bohemian left bank of Paris.

A vivid example of the writer's rejection of his milieu was Sherwood Anderson's *Winesburg, Ohio*

(1919). Its stories of small-town life pictured the frustrations and gropings for self-realization in a community deprived of ruling vision and purpose. In his subsequent books Anderson explored related materials, treating of a town's spiritual impoverishment through industrialization, of a businessman's effort to break the stalemate of his existence, of the spiritual richness of the uninhibited Negroes as contrasted with the emptiness of the whites. No less concerned with maladjustments in American life were the novels of Sinclair Lewis. *Main Street,* the most widely read book in 1920, described a young woman's rebellion against a narrow, middle-class society and her search for cosmopolitan culture. For the next eight years, Lewis continued to criticize American life through fictional portraits that have become well-known types. the businessman Babbitt submerged in a humdrum, materialistic life; the scientist Arrowsmith striving to effectuate his ideals in an unfavorable social climate; the hypocrite Elmer Gantry, commercializing religion. During the 'twenties, in short, the rebellious playwright was by no means an isolated phenomenon. His work was part of the critical cultural awakening of the United States, which produced no literary giants but gave rise to a great many artists who placed self-expression above conformity and regarded the prevailing manners and values of their environment with skepticism and distaste.

The new playwrights and their fellow artists abominated the high-pressure salesmanship, the cheap entertainment, the complacency, and the esthetic anesthesia of the Harding-Coolidge-Hoover period. In this age of revivalism of the Billy Sunday tent-show variety, they lashed at religious hypocrisy. As the smaller communities from which they came still imposed taboos on love, sex, and the freer kind of social relations, the playwrights flailed at "puritanism." And they found a special provocation in Prohibition and in the "blue laws" of the period— that is, the regulations imposed by reformers bent upon stifling the "joy of life" and making the natural man feel "blue." All in all, the vanguard in the theatre was dead set against the middle classes, the bourgeoisie known to readers of Mencken's magazine, *The American Mercury,* as the "booboisie."

To flout the herd that followed the golden calf of prosperity—the "go-getters," the "Babbitts," and the "boosters"—became a favorite sport of the theatre. To scorn the mass production of commonplace minds was considered an obligation. To expose, or, in popular parlance, "debunk," inflated reputations was, in addition, a reliable way of providing entertainment. Ever since the rise of muckraking journalism, favored by Joseph Pulitzer of the *New York World* and practiced by such experts as Ida M. Tarbell and Lincoln Steffens, the art of revealing sordid or questionable business practices was highly prized, and playwrights became as experienced in muckraking as the journalists.

Consequently, a great deal of the playwriting of the nineteen-twenties was devoted to the ungentle art of "spoofing." Many writers who came up for notice at this time practiced it with a vigor and ingenuity hitherto absent from the American stage. George S. Kaufman was the master of ceremonies at this burlesque, and he had many assistants. Marc Connelly, Edna Ferber, Ring Lardner, and Moss Hart were his actual collaborators; Charles MacArthur, George Abbott, Preston Sturges, and others practiced nose-thumbing independently. But it is far from certain that they were not also rather fond of the life they travestied. A breezy type of comedy and farce, studded with the irreverent "wisecrack" and briskly satiric, came into vogue. Kaufman and his collaborators, for example, "ribbed" the muddleheaded middle-class woman in *Dulcy* and the motion pictures and tin-pan alley in *Merton of the Movies, Once in a Lifetime,* and *June Moon.* Ben Hecht and Charles MacArthur extracted rowdy fun from the yellow press in *The Front Page,* and George Kelly hilariously satirized the current high-pressure ideal of salesmanship in *The Show-Off.* If it is too much to say that most of these low comedies have more than historical interest for us by now, it must be conceded that they were bright and tart and that they still possess more liveliness than the polite high comedies of Clyde Fitch.

Practitioners of a more polished or penetrating kind of "debunking" comedy also arose. Philip Barry cross-examined the conservative upper classes in such plays as *Paris Bound* and *Holiday,* and George Kelly flayed a grasping middle-class wife in *Craig's Wife.* The generally morose O'Neill joined the Babbitt-baiting game with the romantic satire *Marco Millions;* its insensitive Florentine hero, Marco Polo, was the Main Street businessman in medieval robes.

Imagination was impressed into the service of the critical assault: expressionism, it was found, enabled the playwright to distort the scene and exaggerate its features for purposes of satire. O'Neill used this technique in *The Hairy Ape* with much dramatic effect when he showed that his stoker, Yank, could not even make a physical impression upon the well-dressed gentlemen leaving Sunday service on Fifth Avenue. Whenever he collided with them, Yank rebounded while they walked on, undisturbed and unruffled. George S. Kaufman and Marc Connelly employed the expressionist dream technique in *Beggar on Horseback* (1924) to express the anxiety of a young artist on the verge of marrying a rich heiress and being absorbed in her father's business. The artist has a nightmare in which one of his strange experiences is finding himself employed in a "Consolidated Art Factory," where he has to fill out endless requisitions for pencils.

John Howard Lawson traced a young Iowan's social and sexual maladjustment in *Roger Bloomer* (1923), the story of a youth who, in the opinion of a prospective employer, lacks the "money-making manner"; he experiences a variety of weird frustrations that bring him to prison after the suicide of his equally baffled girl friend. A little later in the same year, Elmer Rice presented his most original play, *The Adding Machine*, on the subject of man's depersonalization in a humdrum life. Rice's hero, the bookkeeper Mr. Zero, has lost all traces of individuality in the course of twenty-five years of service in a department store. He lives contentedly with a dull and nagging wife with whom he has no conversation whatsoever, and he barely notices the fellow employee Daisy, who is secretly in love with him. He is displaced from his job by the installation of an adding machine. In a fury, Zero kills his employer. He is tried in a courtroom in which all the walls seem to cave in on him. After his execution, he finds himself in the Elysian fields, but its happy and uninhibited life so offends his conventional morality that he insists on leaving. He is to be reborn as a baby who, after the usual education in the machine age, will come to run "a super-hyper-adding machine" with a toe of his left foot. It is for this destiny that the universe came into being, the earth cooled sufficiently to support life, and the evolutionary process began to shape the creature called man! In 1925, John Howard Lawson took a kaleidoscopic view of society in *Processional*, interpreting the vulgarity, the mindlessness, and the struggle between labor and local vigilantism in terms of an utterly mad "jazz symphony." And in 1928, Sophie Treadwell projected a well-publicized murder case, in *Machinal*, as a series of automatic responses on the part of a woman frustrated and emotionally numbed at the office and in the home.

The subjects of military heroism and war naturally presented an excellent target for the assault on accepted values in a period of disillusionment with President Wilson's "war for democracy" and with his failure to create effective machinery for maintaining peace. Among the antiwar plays, one could find a comedy as brightly skeptical as Robert Sherwood's *The Road to Rome* (1926) or as slashing as *What Price Glory?*, written by the then pacifistic Maxwell Anderson and the former marine captain Laurence Stalling. The innuendo in *The Road to Rome* was that a military conqueror, such as the great Hannibal, would lose his taste for war if he could find a natural outlet for his libido. A Roman lady turns Hannibal away from the gates of Rome when no army could effectively oppose his entry. The authors' disenchantment in *What Price Glory?* led them to present war as a sorry occupation and professional soldiering as a callous affair. The Anderson-Stallings play may be used, indeed (as it is in this anthology), to represent the entire antiheroic, cynical school of playwriting. It reduced the war to a rough and foulmouthed competition between a marine sergeant and a captain for the favors of a French tart.

Other dramas of the period were equally animated by the critical spirit, which did not always have to assume the mask of mockery to be penetrating or challenging. Paul Green and other writers of folk drama, for example, were not always content to derive gratification from local color; instead, they took note of frustrations in country life. Green painted a picture of racial struggle in his Negro play *In Abraham's Bosom* that departed drastically from glorifications of the Southern landscape. Sidney Howard's *They Knew What They Wanted* (1924) presented a tolerant view of adultery that would have been considered outrageous ten or fifteen years earlier; Howard's *The Silver Cord* (1926) took a skeptical view of American mother-worship and indicated the dangers of overpossessive motherhood. Elmer Rice's *Street Scene* (1929), a panorama of life in the slums, was full of matter that would have been regarded as repellently seedy and crude in an age of genteel sentiment. The play showed, among other things, how a drab existence poisoned human relationships. Maxwell Anderson and Harold Hickerson delivered themselves of a singularly bitter play about the Sacco-Vanzetti case, *Gods of the Lightning*. Mingling furious melodrama with even more furious rhetoric, the authors indicted our system of law and presented an anarchist's case against organized society. And glowering over the entire human scene stood Eugene O'Neill, for whom life was at once a tragedy of alienation and a grim jest.

In O'Neill's *The Hairy Ape*, man still had not achieved humanity and hung suspended between the ape and the human being. In *Beyond the Horizon*, *All God's Chillun Got Wings* (in which man-made racial prejudice added a major complication), and *Desire Under the Elms*, an ironic fate snared and defeated those who strove for happiness and love. In *The Great God Brown*, man was hopelessly divided between his craving for freedom and creativeness and his subservience to restrictive moral codes. In *Strange Interlude* and *Mourning Becomes Electra*, man and woman were whirled about in a storm of passions. Nowhere in O'Neill's picture of life was there any peace for the divided spirit of humanity. All the complacencies were shattered by this playwright who rejected easy consolations and refused to be distracted from man's tragedy by the material gratifications and optimism of a prosperous nation.

It is true that time can whittle down the stature of the playwrights of the 'twenties and has indeed already done so in a number of instances. They did not join, with the much-debated exception of O'Neill, the first echelon of the master dramatists; but they unquestionably deserve a place in the history of American letters and culture. As they took their place in the theatre of modern ideas, they developed effectiveness. A number of them achieved sincere expression and made our drama worthy of regard as a form of literature. They wrote with force and point; they developed a sense of form; and they found expressive techniques that carried playwriting beyond mild manifestations of realism and sentiment. A generation of dramatists started its ascent in this decade, and we may list a number of them with the assurance that they have claims upon our attention.

Foremost, of course, was Eugene O'Neill, memorable for his wrestlings with life's enigmas and ironies, for his concern with the private demons of obsessed and inwardly tormented individuals, and for his sympathy with men's alienation in a world bereft of spiritual ideals and of the certainties of religious faith. O'Neill started with a natural flair for dramatic fireworks that made him translate his themes into exciting melodrama and impassioned psychological conflict. He steeped his plays in moods of longing, anxiety, and doom, thus creating a poetic drama in spite of an inability to supply a language equal to the dramatic turbulence of his plays. And he had the theatrical imagination necessary to visualize psychological and even mystical experience in scenes memorable on the stage even when they were less than memorable on the printed page.

Relentless in his demands upon an audience, O'Neill departed from the neat conventions in plays that required not only intense concentration but patience with dramas twice as long as the usual three-act piece. *Strange Interlude* had nine acts; *Mourning Becomes Electra* (1931) was a trilogy. Drama was for O'Neill a rite rather than an entertainment. It was also a mode of expressing a seething temperament and a spiritual quest. O'Neill approached playwriting with the high seriousness of the masters. He honored the drama as an art that had been practiced by the giants of humane letters—the Greek tragedians, Shakespeare, and Goethe. Although he lacked their transcendent talent for poetic expression, he was touched with their grandeur and their sense of man's capacity to desire, seek, and suffer greatly. He possessed some of their ability to present man as a creature who casts a long shadow on the earth, which is his throne and his prison.

The theatre of the 'twenties contained a number of other well-endowed mortals. Maxwell Anderson sent roots into the American soil with his collaborations, *What Price Glory?* and *Gods of the Lightning*, with *Saturday's Children* (1927), his rueful comedy of marriage destroyed by the disenchanting humdrum realities, and with less effective studies of the American scene. In the midst of his success, he was pondering the possibilities of restoring tragic grandeur to the theatre's characters and investing them with the eloquence of verse. After 1929, he was to write the best romantic verse plays of the American theatre, *Elizabeth the Queen, Mary of Scotland, Anne of the Thousand Days;* to create poetic fantasy, in *High Tor;* and to wrestle at least half successfully with the difficult problem of writing tragedy in verse about contemporary characters, in *Winterset.* He had high expectations for the American drama, which he tried to effectuate in the ensuing decades of depression and war.

Elmer Rice, who had written successful melodrama before 1918, devoted himself to American life with some talent for expressively fantastic commentary, in *The Adding Machine*, and with a strongly developed aptitude for painting vivid pictures of men and their world, in *Street Scene*. Later, even in unsuccessful or only half-successful ventures, he maintained high standards of observation and thought and displayed sound, if not always exciting, craftsmanship.

Splendid in craftsmanship and rich in human sympathy was Sidney Howard, who, although he rarely soared as high as Rice, created an understanding kind of native drama. From such plays as *They Knew What They Wanted, Ned McCobb's Daughter, Lucky Sam McCarver,* and *Dodsworth* (a dramatization of Sinclair Lewis' novel) one derived the feeling that Howard not only knew people and their environment but envisioned for them broad horizons; later, in his treatment of the struggle against yellow fever, *Yellow Jack* (1933), his view widened into a conception of a life dedicated to serving humanity.

Also among the emerging realists was the Southerner Paul Green, whose short plays of life in the South are among the most moving one-acters in the language and whose longer studies, *In Abraham's Bosom* and *The House of Connelly* (1932), a drama of the decay of the Southern gentry, revealed deep sympathy. At about the same time that Paul Green made his first impression in the theatre, there arose other sympathetic regional writers. Dorothy and Du Bose Heyward contributed *Porgy* (1927)—which later formed the basis of our first important folk opera, Gershwin's *Porgy and Bess*—and *Mamba's Daughters*. E. P. Conkle may have attracted little notice on Broadway, but some of his one-acters of Midwestern life, collected under the title of *Crick Bottom Plays* (1928), are surely masterpieces of their kind. Lynn Riggs proved himself a poet with his Oklahoma and Southwestern plays *Roadside* and *Green Grow the Lilacs*—which provided the basis for the musical comedy *Oklahoma*, in 1943—although the regional quality of his work often limited its effectiveness on Broadway.

Nor, finally, may we overlook the writers of literary comedy. Marc Connelly was surely among these, and he later won a place in the theatre as the author of the biblical fantasia *The Green Pastures* (1930). Robert Sherwood first came to the attention of playgoers as the author of *The Road to Rome* and of the brilliant romantic comedy *Reunion in Vienna* (1931). Capable of considerably greater seriousness than his early plays revealed, Sherwood was to prove himself one of the most probing and earnest dramatists of the depression and war periods.

Philip Barry brought a divided talent to the theatre. While he hankered for success as the author of philosophical drama (chiefly with *Hotel Universe* and *Here Come the Clowns,* written in the nineteen-thirties), he displayed a well-rewarded capacity for polished comedy of manners that expressed modern discontents and confusions. Such plays as *Paris Bound* and *Holiday* in the 'twenties and *The Animal Kingdom* and *The Philadelphia Story* in the 'thirties possessed grace and point. They were superior to the drawing-room plays of the American past in that they questioned convention and investigated traditional values. Thus, in *Paris Bound* Barry urbanely doubted that adultery was a sufficient reason for divorce; in *Holiday* he showed the younger generation rejecting its upper-class traditions; and in *The Animal Kingdom* he posited the notion that an understanding mistress was the true wife of the man she led to spiritual freedom, whereas the legal wife became morally the mistress when she proved to be a parasite.

In the late 'twenties, too, arose America's most brilliant writer of high comedy, S. N. Behrman. His gifts were fully developed when, in 1927, the Theatre Guild produced *The Second Man*. Behrman was a stylist. He was also a man endowed with a probing intelligence, which he was to exercise with particular acuity in *Meteor* (1929), a satire on the conceit of a Napoleon of the business world, and later, when he responded to the tensions of the 'thirties, in such plays as *Biography, Rain from Heaven,* and *End of Summer.*

With assistance from authors of single plays of distinction, these writers forged an American drama which its champions were proud to call "adult." The adjective is significant; it indicates that the dream of the American theatre was for its playwrights to achieve a mature outlook upon the world.

THE DECADE OF THE DEPRESSION: 1929–1939

On October 29, 1929, the bubble of American prosperity burst amid a flurry of ticker tape and a rain of suicides from office windows. For the theatre, as for the nation as a whole, the nineteen-thirties comprised a trying period. The economics of the stage took a turn for the worse, and writers found themselves working for an impoverished medium. As artists and men of their times, they were assailed, besides, by two major anxieties—fear of the collapse of American society and fear of the triumph of fascism, foreign and native. They faced a world to which sophistication and Bohemianism were no longer acceptable responses. Although it was still possible to concern oneself with matters of artistry, it became impossible to deal seriously with the world without considering economic facts and political issues and, in the case of young writers, without considering the possibility of reorganizing the social system. If playwrights could still amuse themselves and their public with familiar antics, it is nevertheless to be noted that even "entertainment" felt a pinch of anxiety or rebellion. In general, the mood of the 'thirties was often somber, if not indeed desperate; often rebellious, if not indeed downright revolutionary.

When we glance at the economic situation of the theatre we find that it became increasingly difficult to finance productions, that fewer plays were presented on Broadway, and that the "road" beyond New York City became closed to all but a few greatly publicized successes. It became virtually impossible to tour a play unless the cast included a big Broadway or Hollywood "name." Meanwhile, the motion-picture industry, which now produced "talkies," had won the allegiance of all but a small portion of the public. Hollywood offered extremely inexpensive entertainment; and, indeed, there was now available an even less expensive form of amusement in the form of radio shows. The Broadway theatre began to rely upon a very small public. Worse still, it began to lose the writers, directors, and actors it could not afford to support. Artists went to Hollywood to repair their damaged fortunes or to sustain body and soul. They often set forth with noble resolutions to come back to the theatre as soon as they could afford to do so. But many of them never returned; and of those who did, many found their craftsmanship and their creative spirit lamed by years of servitude to celluloid. And one must add to this dreary history the fact that an evil fate had befallen and continued to haunt the institutional theatres that had played an important role in advancing modern drama in America. When the thirties began, the Neighborhood Playhouse and the Provincetown Players had already disappeared. Even the powerful Theatre Guild felt the pinch of poverty for a number of years during the decade, while the noncommercial community-theatre movement outside New York found itself seriously hampered by lack of subsidies.

The story of the 'thirties is, nevertheless, by no means a record of stalemate. A wave of idealism and protest lifted the drama and the theatre from despondency. New forces gathered strength in the theatre, as in the cultural life of the nation as a whole. New theatrical groups came to the fore, even when their resources consisted of little more than a determination to produce art or to raise an outcry. They created new audiences with low-priced productions or helped themselves to Broadway audiences by offering challenging plays. They gave birth to new playwrights, and they even attracted the playwrights who had won standing in the previous decade and were regarded by the younger rebels as middle aged and a trifle stuffy. The new theatrical movement appears to have influenced in one way or another even some of the writers whose plays continued to be produced by the commercial managements. Besides, quite a number of these managements were themselves inclined to accept a grim and protesting kind of drama which they would have rejected summarily in the past.

First to emerge was a company of young actors and directors who had been loosely associated with the Theatre Guild as a studio acting company. Led by Cheryl Crawford, Lee Strasberg, and Harold Clurman, and calling themselves the Group Theatre, they dedicated themselves to perfecting their ensemble. It did not take them long to make themselves the best modern acting company America had ever had. Sympathetic with the underdog and hopeful of a more or less socialistic dispensation to replace the system of "free enterprise" that then seemed bankrupt, they favored plays critical of the social order and descriptive of the common man's struggles. Somehow they uncovered—they did not "discover" —a few new playwrights and introduced them to the public with sensitive, sometimes powerful productions. Among these writers were Clifford Odets and Sidney Kingsley, who proceeded to write such effective plays as *Awake and Sing!, Golden Boy, Men in White,* and *Dead End.* (The last-mentioned play was not produced by the Group.) Toward the very end of the decade, in the spring of 1939, the Group also brought William Saroyan to the playgoing public, with *My Heart's in the Highlands.*

Another organization, the nonprofit Theatre Union, was founded in December 1932 for the purpose of producing plays of social significance at popular prices. Leasing Eva Le Gallienne's now abandoned Civic Repertory Theatre for its quarters, the Theatre Union drew a working-class and middleclass audience that lacked either the means or the incentive to patronize Broadway regularly. The new company produced, on the whole, the period's most radical plays (by Albert Maltz, later an able novelist, George Sklar, Paul Peters, John Howard Lawson, Bertolt Brecht, Friedrich Wolf, and others). But it is significant of the extent to which the spirit of protest had seized the literary world that the Theatre Union's sponsors should have included Sherwood Anderson, the poet Stephen Vincent Benét, Elmer Rice, and Sidney Howard. Characteristic of the kind of plays favored was Paul Peters and George Sklar's *Stevedore* (1934), a powerful melodrama in which black and white workers in the South unite to prevent a lynching. The authors expressed the conviction that racial conflict was artificially fomented by the exploiters of the common people and that the interests of the working class transcended color, race, and religion.

The influence of the Theatre Union and the mushrooming of theatre groups among workers and discontented intellectuals resulted in the formation of a New Theatre League, which correlated the efforts of a new, socially conscious little-theatre movement. The New Theatre League's numerous branches provided theatrical experience for an entire generation of young actors, directors, and writers. Like the little art theatres of the 1915–1920 period, the new groups relied almost entirely on one-act plays which could be staged with little scenery and slight preparation. In the one-act form, new playwrights could gain experience and reveal their aptitude for dramatic art. Since, moreover, the one-acters now contained a great deal of social material instead of local color, they required a talent for something more than dramatic sketches. It was the New Theatre League that discovered Clifford Odets by giving him a prize and a first production for the best one-act play about a social issue. One of the last contests sponsored by the New Theatre League discovered Marc Blitzstein, with his original music drama about social discontent and vigilantism, *The Cradle Will Rock.* The League also gave encouragement to the young writer Irwin Shaw, by staging his long one-act antiwar fantasy, *Bury the Dead,* previously produced by another new theatrical group, the American Repertory Theatre. Later, Shaw's parable on the revolt of the little people against their bullies, *The Gentle People,* proved to be one of the successful plays of the Group Theatre, and he won even greater distinction with numerous short stories and a Second World War novel, *The Young Lions.*

Mention may also be made of the Mercury Theatre, founded by Orson Welles and John Houseman, which gave memorable productions of *Julius Caesar* and of Thomas Dekker's Elizabethan comedy *The Shoemaker's Holiday,* as well as interesting treatments of George Bernard Shaw's *Heartbreak House* and Büchner's nineteenth-century classic *Danton's Death.* The Mercury Theatre closed its brief career with *The Cradle Will Rock.* The strikingly theatrical style of the productions directed by Orson Welles made him the boy wonder of the American theatre and launched him on a generally successful motion-picture career. The Labor Stage, founded by New York's ladies'-garment-workers' union, aroused enthusiasm and unfulfilled hopes by producing two incisive editions of a topical musical revue, *Pins and Needles.*

The most extensive theatrical venture of the nineteen-thirties was, however, an outgrowth of President Roosevelt's work-relief program. Between 1935 and 1939, the Federal Theatre, as it was called, not only absorbed some ten thousand unemployed actors, directors, designers, writers, and vaudevillians, at a gross cost of forty-six million dollars, but provided theatre for over thirty million people in twenty-nine states, giving approximately twelve hundred productions at popular prices. Led by a great-spirited woman, Hallie Flanagan Davis, who left her Vassar Experimental Theatre to take charge of this far-flung and always tumultuous project, the Federal Theatre presented numerous classics and seventy-seven new plays. It came closest to constituting a "national theatre" for the United States and might have become just that if it had not been abolished by an act of Congress on June 30, 1939. This New Deal institution also gave rise to the one original form of drama developed in the United States. This was a collectively written documentary dealing with such subjects of social interest as public utilities, housing, and venereal disease (*Power, One-Third of a Nation,* and *Spirochete*). In dramatic construction and production style, these "living newspapers" were imaginative and frankly theatrical, being compounded of all kinds of visual aids to knowledge, symbolization, folk humor, and improvisation. Although no particular literary distinction could be claimed for the "living newspaper," it generally constituted provocative and informative theatre. This type of drama had no future on the commercial stage because it required too many collaborators and was generally expensive, but it proved to be of great value in the documentary and war-training films of the Second World War and in educational radio. It could have been adopted with profit by university theatres; it was used once with considerable effect after the war, when Hallie Flanagan Davis created a "living newspaper" on the atom bomb, $E = MC^2$, at Smith College and brought it to Columbia University's Brander Matthews Theatre with a cast of professional and college actors.

All told, the reaction against the economic dislocation of the United States and the concern with the imminence of a new world war produced a large and vigorous theatrical movement. It was augmented by the Broadway theatre when, for example, the Theatre Guild produced such plays as John Wexley's race-prejudice drama *They Shall Not Die* and a variety of other social-problem dramas, when the independent manager Herman Shumlin introduced Lillian Hellman with her first important work, and when the older playwrights (Howard, Anderson, Rice, Sherwood, and Behrman) formed their own producing organization, the Playwrights Company, and triumphed with a series of provocative plays, the best of which was Sherwood's *Abe Lincoln in Illinois.*

Most important to our purpose, however, is the continued force and the extension of dramatic talent among American playwrights. To understand this development we must understand the temper of the country during the decade of unemployment and the literary stream as a whole. The country's writers were, in the main, no longer content to jibe at the vulgarity of Main Street, to exalt art as an escape from the humdrum world, to glorify sophistication, to exploit the discoveries of Freud, to fulminate against puritanical morality, and to call for sexual freedom. Nor did they, with the notable exception of Maxwell Anderson in *High Tor,* air their contempt for the machine as an enemy of individual self-realization. Except for Eugene O'Neill, who continued to deal with man's private devils (in *Mourning Becomes Electra* and in the religious drama *Days Without End*) and who recalled his youth nostalgically with the charming comedy *Ah, Wilderness!,* the playwrights concerned themselves more and more with the social and political organization of the country and with the threat of fascism

from abroad. They were interested less in private difficulties of the ego than in the difficulties that individuals faced together—unemployment, lack of means of subsistence, and racial prejudice. Instead of deploring the introduction of mass production and machinery into the world, they were troubled by the fact that the economic system had broken down. The stress frequently fell on the conflict between employers and the working class and on the disappearance of the hard-pressed middle class, which lost its businesses, homes, and farms. Thus a literature of social protest, variously described as "leftist" or "proletarian," made its appearance. And some of the writers even looked forward to an overthrow of our economic and political system, to its replacement by a socialist society, and to a thoroughgoing defeat of capitalism by an irate, Marxist-directed working class and its intellectual sympathizers. If the theatre of the nineteen-twenties could be described as rebellious, a portion of the theatre of the nineteen-thirties could be called revolutionary.

The playwrights of the period formed only one wing of a movement that included artists, poets, writers of fiction and nonfiction, stage actors, and even Hollywood stars. The dramatist moved along the same road of protest traveled by many poets and novelists. Even authors who in the previous decade had concerned themselves with individual self-realization and sexual frustration (Sherwood Anderson), with objective naturalism (Theodore Dreiser), or with private despair (Ernest Hemingway) joined the literary movement of protest, which was simultaneously anticapitalist and antifascist.

Out of this social and cultural ferment arose the new playwrights. The most widely acclaimed of these was Clifford Odets, the Group Theatre actor who became known as a playwright after the writing of his long one-act strike drama, *Waiting for Lefty.* With the production of *Awake and Sing!,* he came to be considered the most promising playwright to have been discovered in our theatre after the advent of O'Neill. Odets specialized in dramas of middle-class failure, such as *Awake and Sing!, Paradise Lost,* and *Rocket to the Moon,* and in plays which analyzed the social situation generally. He expressed the restiveness of the younger generation and the sense of failure of the older generation, and he supplied his characters with colloquial speech, highly seasoned with the argot of the city streets and with poetic variations based on it. Since his concern was with people collectively, he dealt not with a single central figure but with a group, such as a family and its friends, or members of some profession or business. His dramatic writing was therefore fluid, and his technique recalled Chekhov's. His dialogue frequently got out of hand, his sympathies sometimes resulted in sentimentality, his anger occasionally produced anarchic writing of questionable logic. But there was much human feeling in his work, and his plays contained memorable moments of veracious observation and of explosive self-revelation or pro-test on the part of the characters. If Odets had developed his artistry, he might have become a re-markable playwright. His accomplishment in the nineteen-thirties was a major source of gratification to the champions of social drama.

Impressive, too, was the arrival of Lillian Hellman, with her psychological drama *The Children's Hour* and her picture of the industrialization of the South by a breed of robber barons, *The Little Foxes* (1938). A clearminded grasp of dramatic essentials ruled her playwriting: her characterization was invariably sure and skillful, and her plots were always tautly drawn out. She was relentless in her exposition and resolution, and once she was on the track of anti-social behavior, she never lost sight of the objective of stripping it bare. Although she gave even her vil-lains some interesting characteristics or some human dimension, she always caught them red-handed. The poetic spirit was absent from Miss Hellman's work, and the force of her writing was often gained at the cost of very heavy plots. But relaxed playwriting was not natural during the period of tension and protest; nor was Miss Hellman by nature a relaxed playwright.

Another effective newcomer was Sidney Kingsley, introduced by the Group Theatre with a brilliant production, *Men in White* (1931), a hospital drama dealing with the conflicting claims of a life of ease and a life dedicated to medical service. In 1934, Kingsley aroused much attention with *Dead End,* a compassionate picture of poverty and slum-bred crime. Later, his psychological drama *The World We Make* (1939), a dramatization of Millen Brand's *The Outward Room,* revealed a glowing appreciation of the common man's courage and human warmth, which save him from desperation and neurotic com-plications. Kingsley proved himself a painstaking observer who documented his realism and gave much of his writing sociological significance. His creative-ness did not, as a rule, rise above the mundane scene, but it was generally convincing and compelling.

Along with such writers as George Sklar and John Wexley, who knew how to make a fact ring with drama, the aforementioned social dramatists brought to the American theatre renewed vigor. It seemed for a time, indeed, as if no new playwright worthy of attention could arise without giving his allegiance to social realism.

The only important member of the group of new playwrights who could not be classified with the sociological or revolutionary school was Thornton Wilder. Having written short plays and such notable novels as *The Cabala* and *The Bridge of San Luis Rey* in the previous decade, he emerged in 1938 as a dramatist of singular talent, with one of the most original modern plays, *Our Town.* On the surface his theme was a nostalgic recollection of life in New England at the beginning of the century, and the play was therefore removed in time from the ten-

sions then being reflected in the theatre. More essentially, Wilder addressed himself to the universal problems of living and dying, so that topical con-siderations were, in the main, irrelevant to his purpose. He wrote an originally constructed, beau-tifully styled drama that could not be subsumed in any category other than that of imaginative art. At the most, it could be said that *Our Town* was the sort of play that could not have arisen quite so naturally in any large Western European nation and that its earnest concern with the common way of life had an American ring. *Our Town,* however, would always have been an exception to the general run of playwriting, whether it had appeared in the 'twenties or in any other period.

The playwrights of the generation of the nineteen-twenties, moreover, added their response to the social situation in the new decade of social realism. Philip Barry symbolized the confusions of the times in such plays as *Hotel Universe* (1930) and *Here Come the Clowns* (1938) with much magic, if also with some confusion, and S. N. Behrman turned to comedy of ideas, dramatizing social and political conflict. In *Biography,* he presented the irreconcila-ble attitudes of an embattled reformer and of a wo-man too good-natured to join his crusade; in *Rain from Heaven,* the impossibility of leading a detached intellectual life in the contemporary world of lust for power, race hatred, and totalitarian ambition; in *End of Summer,* the emotional bankruptcy of the idle rich. Throughout his work, Behrman retained an intelligent detachment such as we expect from a writer of high comedies with a style distinguished by lucidity and wit.

Still another member of the old guard, Sidney Howard, wrote two antiwar plays and a drama of scientific idealism, *Yellow Jack.* Elmer Rice offered impassioned works of protest, such as *We, the People,* as well as character comedy, such as *Coun-sellor-at-Law,* in which he flayed snobbery and hypocrisy. And Paul Green joined the protesting dramatists with his antiwar drama *Johnny Johnson* and with a powerful one-act chain-gang drama, *Hymn to the Rising Sun.* Kaufman and his col-laborators satirized politics in the bright musical comedy *Of Thee I Sing,* reviewed the failure of the intelligentsia in a rueful, if also sentimental, chroni-cle, *Merrily We Roll Along,* and reflected the de-pression with a madcap comedy, *You Can't Take It With You.*

It was during the 'thirties, too, that Robert Sher-wood reached the peak of his powers and impor-tance. His ascent after *Reunion in Vienna* was en-tirely a response to the spirit of the times: a concern with the loss of nerve in our civilization and the triumph of international gangsterism (*The Petrified Forest*), with the inevitability of a second world war (*Idiot's Delight*), and with an affirmation of ideals of social justice in another era of stress (*Abe Lincoln in Illinois*). The age of anxiety produced in

Sherwood's work first a sense of acute distress and then a positive stand that turned him into an ardent supporter of Franklin Delano Roosevelt and his New Deal philosophy of government. Since Sherwood was an expert showman, he was able to give theatrical effectiveness to his concerns and convictions.

Seemingly, Maxwell Anderson strove to stand above the contemporary scene, convinced as he was that greatness in the drama lay in the universality of its meaning, in the heroic stature of its characters, and in the distinction of its language. Beginning with *Elizabeth the Queen* (1930), he wrote his most ambitious plays mostly in verse and achieved in them some largeness of spirit. In his chronicles of Elizabeth and Mary Stuart, followed in the nineteen-forties by his drama of Anne Boleyn and Henry VIII, *Anne of the Thousand Days,* he inevitably also achieved an independence of the times. But in a number of other plays, Anderson was stirred to comment on the concerns of the decade. Contempt for self-seeking politicians was mingled with affirmations of the common man's passion for liberty in *Valley Forge.* Detestation of corrupt politicians animated the prose satire on Congress *Both Your Houses,* and hatred for social injustice flared magnificently in the powerful second act of *Winterset.* Scorn for modern materialism gave a sharp edge to the verse fantasy *High Tor.* Anderson's concern with the question of revolution and his disenchantment with its results lifted portions of *The Masque of Kings* out of the Graustark category of political romance. The realization that one could not escape a conflict with fascism or equivalent evils motivated the writing of *Key Largo.*

That even such a writer as Anderson, bent upon universalizing the drama, could not remain disengaged from the struggles of the decade may indicate the intensity of the claims of contemporary problems upon the dramatists who tried to create significant art. To be sure, not all playwrights became embattled or somber. Comedy and farce removed from social issues continued to be written and enjoyed. One may cite such examples as Rachel Crothers' *Susan and God* (the best play of an old hand at comedy), *The Philadelphia Story* (one of Philip Barry's best works), Clare Boothe's vitriolic comedy *The Women,* the Sam and Bella Spewack broad Hollywood satire *Boy Meets Girl,* the brisk farces *Three Men on a Horse* and *Room Service,* and the immensely successful *Life With Father.* But the dominant note of social concern continued throughout the decade, now also concerned with the imminence of armed conflict. Even the related arts responded to the turmoil. Dance drama and pantomime acquired social connotations; for a brief time, radio offered antifascist poetic dramas, such as Archibald MacLeish's *The Fall of the City* and *Air Raid;* Hollywood turned out such films as *Mr. Smith Goes to Washington* and *The Grapes of Wrath.* When the decade ended, Europe was already engaged in the Second World War and new challenges were arising to bedevil the playwright and his audience.

THE WAR AND ITS AFTERMATH

As a result of the wartime industrial boom, the economic situation of the theatre in the nineteen-forties seemed greatly relieved. The demand for entertainment increased rapidly; theatres filled quickly despite fantastic admission prices. Nonetheless, the theatre was in an unhealthy condition and its ailments became visible the moment wartime spending ceased. Production costs mounted and remained stabilized on an inflationary basis even after the playgoing public became more economical in its spending for entertainment. For the state of the drama, however, two factors were of the most serious consequence: First, the number of productions decreased and new playwrights found too little opportunity to serve an apprenticeship; secondly, it became increasingly uneconomic to undertake or keep on the boards plays that did not gross huge weekly sums.

Little room was left in the professional theatre for the "in-between" play—that is, the play that could command only moderately large audiences. Such plays were, as a rule, closed by the producer within two days or at the most three weeks (on which basis the producer could share in the sale of motion-picture rights). The alternatives for the drama were superfluity or starvation. Since most of the important plays of the modern theatre were not "smash hits" when first produced, the inability to put on in-between drama became a deterrent to experiment. This situation became even more grave when Hollywood began to suffer sharp reverses as a result of both falling box-office receipts and discriminatory taxation in Britain. Hollywood had invested huge sums of money in Broadway productions and paid even larger sums for rights to Broadway successes. After 1948, the motion-picture industry ceased to finance Broadway productions and severely limited its purchases of even successfully produced plays.

Another and incalculable difficulty that a number of dramatists had to overcome during the decade of the 'forties was the disappearance to a great extent of the social enthusiasm of the 'thirties and of the groups that it had sustained. The Theatre Union disbanded in 1937; the American Repertory Company disappeared at about the same time; the Mercury Theatre collapsed after three exciting seasons; the Federal Theatre was abolished in 1939; the New Theatre League disintegrated; and even the important Group Theatre succumbed in 1941. The few new organizations that arose to take the place of the old proved feeble, although the Group Theatre's influence continued to be felt on Broadway and in such experimental theatres as the Actor's Laboratory Theatre in Los Angeles and New Stages in Greenwich Village. An effort was made shortly after the war by ANTA (the American National Theatre and Academy) to revitalize the theatre in communities outside New York and to establish an Experimental Theatre in New York. But the results were still uncertain in 1950.

The old social drama lost standing after 1940, and the fervor of the playwrights, along with those of the novelists and poets, cooled considerably. Many writers who in the 'thirties had been or had thought they were radicals, or even communists, lost their revolutionary faith. They were deeply troubled by events in Soviet Russia and, after a brief renewal of faith during the years when Russia resisted and crushed the Germans, their dismay even increased as the Stalin government turned its neighboring nations into satellites. One of the conspicuous tendencies of the decade, especially after 1945, was the rise of literature of disillusionment with communism, socialism, and even New Deal philosophy. To a large degree, the social-protest movement of the previous decade fell apart. A vacuum developed in the theatre, as in other forms of recreation. To what extent it was filled is a question to which the following pages propose an answer.

For one thing, the period's theatre was enriched by a succession of musical comedies and music dramas which represented considerable progress in this form of imaginative drama. Judged solely by the printed text, their theatrical charm and power seem, as a rule, nonexistent but for an occasionally felicitous expression and effective lyric. As theatre, however, the fusion of text, music, dance, and scenery can be vastly attractive. Playgoers in a period of anxiety and wartime prosperity welcomed such entertainment, and able teams of writers, composers, and theatre artists collaborated to provide it. The classic of the period was, of course, *Oklahoma* (1943), the folk musical by Richard Rodgers and Oscar Hammerstein II.

The war naturally provided a stimulus to the writing of war plays, antifascist drama, and works of liberal sentiment. Immediately after the war, a certain degree of democratic enthusiasm also made itself felt, taking the form of attacks on racial discrimination. Even Hollywood responded to this desire to combat the racism that had been defeated on the battle fronts of Europe but was not yet eradicated at home, as may be seen from such films as *Gentleman's Agreement* and *Home of the Brave*.

But the advent of the atom bomb, followed by a struggle for power—this time between the West and Russia—proved by 1950 beyond the capacity of the theatre to absorb. No great American war literature arose during this period—in poetry, fiction, or drama. Our satisfaction with the theatre could be only moderate; we could take pride chiefly in the reflection that our war-inspired drama was rarely objectionable and often considerably intelligent.

Our one noteworthy antifascist melodrama, Lillian Hellman's *Watch on the Rhine,* was written so intelligently that "melodrama" is actually a misnomer. A lean kind of writing characterized pictures of the fighting or of the Resistance movement in Europe, as in the work of such newcomers as the poet Harry Brown (*A Sound of Hunting*) and Dan James (*Winter Soldiers*). Among several efforts by Maxwell Anderson, *The Eve of St. Mark* was honestly poignant until its conclusion—one of sentimental fantasy. Elmer Rice wrote a closely reasoned treatment of the conflict between democratic and fascist ideals in *Flight to the West*. Robert Sherwood contributed a thoughtful treatment of men of peace resisting tyranny, *There Shall Be No Night*. It is to be noted, too, that plays stimulated by the war crisis but not directly concerned with it occasionally possessed impressive features. Among these plays were such historical dramas as Sidney Kingsley's early-American chronicle *The Patriots* and Howard Koch and John Huston's story of Woodrow Wilson's struggle for a League of Nations, *In Time to Come*. Thornton Wilder, moreover, interpreted the crisis in one original, imaginative drama that telescoped the history of man's struggle for survival through the ages, *The Skin of Our Teeth*.

It was, in fact, a distinguishing feature of the theatre that its awareness of humanity and of principle overshadowed the details of battle and strategy usually unmanageable on the stage. This was true even when, as in William Wister Haines's *Command Decision,* the actual plot concerned strategic bombing, or when the war was used with a flair for Broadway showmanship, as in Thomas Heggen and Joshua Logan's *Mister Roberts*. The human being was not often lost even in the pursuit of principle, as could be seen in Paul Osborn's dramatization of *A Bell for Adano,* in John Patrick's back-of-the-lines hospital drama, *The Hasty Heart,* and in Arthur Laurents' psychological drama of racial prejudice, *Home of the Brave*. A play about the conditioning of German youth under Hitler, James Gow and Arnaud d'Usseau's *Tomorrow the World,* was written not only with sympathetic understanding but with clinical objectivity. When Emmet Lavery wanted to uphold American ideals, he drew a warm portrait of Oliver Wendell Holmes, *The Magnificent Yankee*. Elsewhere, across the Atlantic Ocean (especially in Central Europe and in Italy), destructive forces were at work in the theatre. In America, the difficulty was chiefly the absence of constructive forces, except, possibly, for a trend toward the composition of comedies of liberal persuasion, such as Garson Kanin's *Born Yesterday* and Howard Lindsay and Russel Crouse's *State of the Union*.

However, when nothing in the social or cultural matrix proves to be particularly provocative, we can always look to personal endowment, as we must do in any case. In the final reckoning, the decade exhibits some distinction because Wilder wrote *The Skin of Our Teeth,* because O'Neill finally released for production his "lower depths" drama *The Iceman Cometh,* and because William Saroyan, Tennessee Williams, and Arthur Miller unfolded their talent.

Saroyan, already known as a story writer, was the most promising early discovery of the theatre of the nineteen-forties. After *My Heart's in the Highlands,* produced in 1939, his star blazed for a while when he wrote *The Time of Your Life* and was still luminous when he added *Love's Old Sweet Song, The Beautiful People,* and the powerful one-acter *Hello, Out There.* These plays came at the beginning of the decade, before an undisciplined talent removed him from the theatrical firmament. He brought to the stage a highly individual poetry—a bizarre improvisation and, at times, an oddly touching lyricism. Because his sentimentality was gritty, it escaped the usual American objections to sentiment. Saroyan was aggressively in love with the common man, the failure, and the outcast. Such enthusiasm was appealing at a time when the economic depression was just beginning to lift; a few years later, when the memory of seedy times had been banished, the public might have been less grateful for the balm offered in his plays. Saroyan was also a rhapsodist of freedom and of the brotherhood of man, and he expressed his enthusiasm for these ideals with much verve just when they were being driven from large segments of the globe by the advance of totalitarianism.

Explanations of Tennessee Williams' success are less dependent upon the spirit of the times. Although he had been introduced to Boston by the Theatre Guild at the beginning of the decade, he first arrived on Broadway, with *The Glass Menagerie,* in 1945, when anxiety over the outcome of the war was receding and we were less in need of such reassurances as Saroyan had offered. With Williams, we could settle down again to the enjoyment of sober artistry and the study of character. His specialty was an acute dramatic sensibility, delicately presented in his first Broadway success, forcefully—if also somewhat sensationally—thrust forth in his most popular play, *A Streetcar Named Desire,* and less successfully but still impressively revealed in *Summer and Smoke.* He managed, up to a point, to universalize the drama of failure and to give his plays a poetic texture.

Arthur Miller was the third important newcomer. His was the latest arrival on Broadway (an early play had failed), but it became the most heralded as the nineteen-forties ended. His first well-received drama, *All My Sons,* recalled the realistic Ibsen in technique and Sardou in its contrived, last-minute revelation; it also recalled the Group Theatre style of realistic social indictment or lesson. Its moral fervor was strong, its characterization firm, its dramaturgy tightly packed. Miller's remarkably successful next effort, *Death of a Salesman,* was also rooted in familiar middle-class realism and it contained overtones of social criticism. But the strength of this extraordinary play came, in part, from its moving presentation of a little man's failure and, in part, from the author's use of the discontinuous fantasy technique made familiar by the expressionists of the 'twenties but rarely applied so cogently. Miller succeeded in pulling together the past and the present and in giving his work psychological and dramatic force. In *Death of a Salesman* he carried the long familiar trend toward middle-class tragedy to a triumphant climax. He managed, moreover, to convey a poetry of the commonplace, partly in his writing and largely in his imaginative use of the stage. Miller proved himself one of the most successful exponents of the school of playwriting that blends modern realism with a poetry of the theatre.

The foundations for an important American drama have been firmly laid since 1918, and the past three decades have brought a variety of achievements. Realism has been used with vividness; social drama has acquired vigor and fire. Naturalism has not only dealt with tabooed subjects but has become permeated with poetry and feeling. Since the early 'twenties our playwrights have shown an adeptness at folk drama and a promise in the direction of fantasy. It has been no small achievement to have developed two kinds of comedy: a "low," unliterary type that has the virtue of being briskly shrewd and a high comedy that has glittered, now and then, with keen edge, whether dealing with manners or with ideas in conflict. Moreover, American dramatists have not bound themselves to any particular technique; they have not hesitated to move from a play written in a realistic mode to one conceived in imaginative theatrical form.

The interpenetration of the truth of everyday life with the truth of the imagination (especially theatrical imagination) has appeared, in differing degrees, in the plays of O'Neill, Wilder, Maxwell Anderson, Connelly, Saroyan, Williams, Miller, and even Odets. Indeed, if any important tendency emerges from the entire course of our drama since the advent of O'Neill, it is this effort on the part of our most significant playwrights to mediate the requirements of realistic description and of the creative imagination. This is a singular tendency in a nation regarded as the exemplar of down-to-earth practicality. When our theatre arrived at maturity, it absorbed two originally divergent aims of the modern European theatre—that of the realists and naturalists and that of the symbolists and expressionists. This circumstance is surely significant, though it may prove to be merely a contributory factor. In the end, of course, to account for this characteristic of much of our best drama we must look to the intentions and to the temperaments of the individual playwrights. We shall give some discussion to these elements in the introductions that precede our eleven examples of modern American drama.

Eugene O'Neill

(1888–1953)

Although the American theatre gave rise to a number of able playwrights after 1920 and great claims were made for some of them, no one in a responsible mood has ever disputed Eugene O'Neill's pre-eminence among our dramatists. He is the only American playwright whose international reputation has been firmly established, a fact that was formally acknowledged with a Nobel Prize in 1936. Since he experimented in many forms and explored a variety of themes, it is not easy to describe O'Neill's efforts comprehensively without examining them in detail. But they all had the same intention: the promotion of a theatre that would illuminate the inner man and would possess as much human significance as the drama could hold. This significance was for O'Neill, moreover, almost always a fundamentally spiritual one.

As the son of the successful actor James O'Neill, who toured extensively with his wife, Eugene O'Neill had a childhood that was not blessed with much stability. He was born in a Broadway hotel and educated intermittently at various Catholic schools while his parents roved across the country. Later, his stay at Princeton was of brief duration; he was suspended for a freshman prank and did not bother to return. He married early and entered business. But he felt the call of the sea almost immediately and ultimately dissolved his marriage. In 1909, he went prospecting for gold in Honduras with a mining engineer. Returning without gold after contracting malaria, he joined his father's company as assistant manager for a time but grew restless again and signed on a Norwegian vessel for a voyage from Boston to Buenos Aires. In Argentina, he worked at various occupations—in the Westinghouse Electric Company, in a packing plant, and in the office of the Singer Sewing Machine Company. Tiring of the sedentary life of a clerk, he embarked on a cattle steamer from Buenos Aires to South Africa and tended mules on the ship. He experienced a period of destitution on his return to Argentina, finally found a berth on a British tramp steamer bound for New York, and once in New York lived "on the beach" in a water-front bar. He became an able seaman on the American Line, made a trip that took him to Southampton, and then decided to settle down. After playing a small part for his father in the popular melodrama *The Count of Monte Cristo,* he found a position in Connecticut on the *New London Telegraph,* and began contributing a humorous column. But his strenuous life had under-

mined his health. He developed tuberculosis and spent six months in a sanatorium.

During his convalescence, O'Neill gave special attention to the drama, particularly to the works of the Greeks and of Strindberg, and began to write short plays of his own. Desiring some formal training, he enrolled in Professor George Pierce Baker's "47 Workshop" course at Harvard during 1914–1915. Next, he associated himself with the Greenwich Village writers who formed the Provincetown Players in 1915, and acted and wrote plays for them at their Wharf Theatre in Provincetown, Massachusetts. In the summer of 1916, they gave O'Neill his first production, *Bound East for Cardiff,* a short sea piece notable for its brooding and somber mood. When the group settled in its Greenwich Village playhouse, O'Neill became one of its most active members, as well as an associate of the equally young and experimental Washington Square Players. All of O'Neill's early short plays were produced by these two organizations.

Between 1915 and 1919, a radical transformation took place in the American theatre largely as a result of the activity of "little theatres" devoted to art instead of to the prevailing commercialism of the stage. O'Neill became the major discovery of the little-theatre movement. The Provincetown Players produced most of his early work, and the Theatre Guild, an outgrowth of the Washington Square Players, became his official theatre afer the financial collapse of the Provincetown.

But after 1919 the commercial managers also began to show interest in O'Neill's writing. John D. Williams produced two of his early plays: his first full-length tragedy of fate, *Beyond the Horizon* (1920), and his romantic drama *Gold* (1921). George C. Tyler presented the first version of *Anna Christie* under the title *Chris Christopherson* (1920) and the psychological drama *The Straw* (1921). Arthur Hopkins staged *Anna Christie* in November 1921.

O'Neill was never a neglected artist. He found a champion in the critic and man of the world George Jean Nathan. He won the Pulitzer Prize in 1920, 1922, and 1928, made many friends who valued him highly, and found such able associates in the theatre as Robert Edmond Jones, Kenneth MacGowan, and the brilliant Theatre Guild stage director Philip Moeller. If a number of O'Neill's plays did not reach a very large public, it was largely because he experimented with dramatic forms and psychological complications that at first required a select audience. When he broadened the interest of his plays and they were given good productions, he found, more often than not, a large public, willing and eager to follow as far as he wished to lead. O'Neill won signal honors for the modern American theatre and, since he was an uncompromising artist, he always won them on his own terms. In England, a number of critics felt uncomfortable in the presence of his uninhibited playwriting and his passionate creativeness. But he commanded, and still commands, great respect in America and on the Continent.

O'Neill's search for dramatic expression took him into every conceivable field except the militant social drama of the nineteen-thirties, and even this genre owes much to his pioneering in realism. His vigorously descriptive and colloquial one-act plays, assembled in the "S.S. Glencairn cycle," presented the loneliness and bedevilment of common sailors. Despite a romantically charged atmosphere, these dramatic pictures, often fatalistic in philosophy and concerned with human failure and desperation, constituted a triumph for the realistic or, more accurately, naturalistic theatre. His first full-length work, *Beyond the Horizon,* a tragedy of frustration on a farm, extended this victory; and *Anna Christie* confirmed it by setting forth the life of the water front and the fate of a fallen woman. Such minor and unsuccessful efforts as *The First Man* (1922) and *Welded* (1924) revealed Strindbergian influences in the psychological tensions of the characters. A bleak naturalistic background was presented in the slum environment of *All God's Chillun Got Wings* (1924), an original work that went far beyond its ostensible problem of miscegenation. *Desire Under the Elms* (1924) was psychologically centered—in a tense father-son conflict.

O'Neill did not confine himself, however, to any single style; nor was he ever content with photographic representations of reality. His realistic plays had poetic and symbolic qualities. As early as 1920, moreover, he wrote one of the first expressionistic plays in America, *The Emperor Jones,* turning it into a tour de force. It dramatized a self-confident Negro dictator's growing fears and mental breakdown in short, rapidly shifting, subjective scenes intensified by the incessant beat of native tom-toms. Two years later, in *The Hairy Ape,* O'Neill added symbolism to the expressionistic presentation of a brutish stoker's search for a place in society, converting the play into an allegory of modern man's torment. In *All God's Chillun Got Wings,* he used expressionistic emphases and symbolism. In 1925, after *The Fountain,* a mild, romantic play about Ponce de León's search for eternal youth, O'Neill went even further in the direction of subjective drama, with *The Great God Brown.* This remarkable, if somewhat puzzling, tragedy of dual personality expressed the anguish of divided souls by means of masks worn and exchanged by two complementary characters. Three

other symbolic plays followed this tantalizing exploration of the inner self: *Lazarus Laughed* (1927), a poetic, but repetitiously static and rather fulsome, defiance of death; *Dynamo* (1929), a strained quest for a satisfying faith, which materialism fails to supply; and *Days Without End* (1934), another study of "split personality," here concluded with a reconciliation between self-tortured intellectuality and religious faith. These and other works gave effective testimony to their author's conviction that "it is only by means of some form of 'super-naturalism' that we may express in the theatre what we comprehend intuitively of that self-obsession which is the particular discount we moderns have to pay for the loan of life."

After composing the romantic satire on materialism *Marco Millions,* O'Neill climaxed his efforts with his novelistic nine-act drama *Strange Interlude* (1928), one of the most ambitious works written for the modern theatre. Striving to present the complex inner life of a woman from girlhood to middle age (that is, the "strange interlude" of her sexual awakening and maturity), he invented the device of the "interior monologue," a bold and elaborate variant of the old-fashioned "aside." Each character spoke both his conscious and unconscious thoughts, thus revealing himself more completely than ordinary dialogue permits. The procedure of presenting the story on two complementary levels amplified modern dramatic technique and gave *Strange Interlude* the same status in the history of the modern drama that James Joyce's stream-of-consciousness narrative *Ulysses* occupies in the history of the modern novel. But O'Neill did not expend this technical virtuosity and psychological method on humdrum material. Nothing less than the substance of an extensive life history involving other life histories went into *Strange Interlude.* If the technique was complex, so was the life of O'Neill's heroine, Nina Leeds. Frustrated by the jealousy of her father and the death of the lover who might have fulfilled her, she is driven to complete herself through simultaneous attachments to three men, who are for her, respectively, father image, husband, and lover.

For his other large venture, *Mourning Becomes Electra* (1931), O'Neill needed no new methods of representation; he told the story of his New England aristocrats, the Mannons, without marked deviation from realism or much formal embellishment. The play could be accepted on the level of psychological melodrama as the story of hereditary evil and hate, adultery, murder, incestuous drives, and suicide. Nevertheless, this drama possessed greater tragic depth and scope than any American play written before or after it. This Freudian transcription of the Oresteian trilogy of Aeschylus and of the other Greek Electra plays was a trilogy in thirteen acts. Although the treatment took into consideration the influence of puritanical religion and possessiveness in a New England mercantile family, its chief accomplishment was the unearthing of the complexes that psychoanalysis had brought to the attention of the age. The effect of the play was that of tragic catharsis on an almost epic scale. O'Neill defined his masterpiece perhaps better than any of his critics when he framed this question in his first note on *Mourning Becomes Electra*, five years before the play's completion: "Is it possible to get modern psychological approximation of the Greek sense of fate into such a play which an intelligent audience of today, possessed by no belief in gods or supernatural retribution, could accept and be moved by?" This play appears to have provided purgation even for its author, since it was followed, in 1933, by a genial comedy of adolescence and small-town life, *Ah, Wilderness!* If O'Neill felt any relief in 1933, however, it was a temporary one, for the exceptionally long and painful play he wrote in 1939, *The Iceman Cometh* (produced in 1946) is perhaps the most relentlessly depressing drama written by any modern playwright. *The Iceman Cometh* refuted a belief that its author had become reconciled with the Catholic faith of his childhood—a belief which had gained some currency after the presentation of his earlier play *Days Without End* (1933).

In 1940, O'Neill completed a play which he resolved not to have produced during his lifetime: *Long Day's Journey into Night*. In 1947, he exposed to public view *A Moon for the Misbegotten*, written four years earlier; he withdrew it after a brief Midwestern tryout because of a difficult casting problem. In addition, from 1934 to 1947, years of virtual seclusion and ill health spent on Sea Island, Georgia, and in California's Valley of the Moon, he was engaged on a long cycle of eleven plays carrying the working title *A Tale of Possessors Self-Dispossessed*. One of these, *A Touch of the Poet*, intended to start the cycle, was ready for production by 1947. In 1949, however, O'Neill, whose condition had taken a turn for the worse, let it be known that no more plays were to be expected from him.

A complete estimate of this dedicated artist must await publication, or at least perusal, of what has surely been the most Cyclopean dramatic enterprise in the English language. Even without the cycle, however, O'Neill's work is a challenge to dramatic criticism and has evoked a sharp division of opinion. His claims to respect as our most important playwright are nevertheless beyond questioning.

If O'Neill tended to be anything but sparing in his complexities, it is nonetheless true that he was able to hold American audiences, the most restless in the world, with his theatrical force and earnestness. If he often schematized and overexplained psychological complications, his insistence on their presence and force was impressive. If his ideas often seemed borrowed and too baldly expressed, they were maintained with sufficient passion to appear to be discoveries in the American theatre, even though they were discoveries nowhere else. If his plots were

frequently melodramatic and if he seemed to pile one violent effect on top of another, one could always be certain that O'Neill was oppressed, as the Elizabethans John Webster and Cyril Tourneur were, with the terror of man's passions and with the baleful machinery of evil in the world. And if his language often lagged woefully behind the vaulting quality of his action, in the theatre the great sweep of drama in his plays created a tide of emotion difficult to resist. The well-trained and discriminating reader may have been appalled at some of the writing when he saw it on the printed page, but the playgoer was generally awed. Other playwrights might have been cleverer and more graceful than O'Neill, and it is certain that he was no Olympian artist; yet no one matched his sultry turbulence, in which there was considerable splendor. In his early work, moreover, he often displayed his dramatic effects with comparative freedom from prolixity and excess.

Anna Christie, which follows, by no means reveals the greatest depth and furthest range of O'Neill's powers and ambitions. But if it lacks the scope of several of its author's later works, it has the merit of comparative compactness; and if it does not probe as deeply into human nature, it is also free from their more troublesome obscurities, their schematization of psychological forces, and their tragic straining. A fairly simple human drama, it provides emotions more or less readily accessible to the reader. Its pungently colloquial speech and its seedy heroine represent the early portion of O'Neill's career, when he rooted the American theatre in naturalism. The play also suggests some of the characteristics of his later writing—namely, his poetic vein, present here in his feeling for the sea, his concern with obsessed characters, and his saturnine sense of fatality in human experience.

Anna Christie grew out of an earlier written play, *Chris* or *Chris Christopherson*, produced unsuccessfully and withdrawn during its tryout tour. As Barrett H. Clark, O'Neill's biographer, explains, "In its final version *Anna Christie* is a play about a woman. It was in the beginning a play about the woman's father." One objection that has been raised is that the play suffers from this shift in emphasis. Another is that Anna's story bears too much resemblance to the fallen-woman drama we associate with old-fashioned sentimental plays. Critics have also questioned the "happy ending" and suspected O'Neill of compromising the integrity of his play in the manner of Henry Arthur Jones and other pseudo modernists. O'Neill was particularly troubled by the last charge and wrote George Jean Nathan expressing regret that the conclusion, in which Anna and the sailor are reunited, gave a "happy-ever-after" impression that he never intended. "And the sea outside—life— waits," he wrote. "The happy ending is merely the comma at the end of a gaudy introductory clause, with the body of the sentence still unwritten." He added that he had once thought of calling the play

Comma, and complained that it was impossible to project clearly the "sincerity of life pent up in the trappings of theatre." That is, he feared he had not pointed up sufficiently the tentativeness of the happy reunion, in spite of Anna's father's foreboding last speech, the Irish sailor's doubts about the non-Catholic Anna's oath, and the implication that although the characters "have had their moment, the decision still rests with the sea. . . ."

Whether there is any way of reconciling different and seemingly unfused aspects of the play is open to question. So friendly a critic as Barrett H. Clark does not think there is. More than a quarter of a century after the production of the play, however, George Jean Nathan, who had been the first to raise points of criticism, could write: "1920 . . . *Anna Christie* is a new and forceful handling of a familiar theme, deep in its characterizations, driving in its firm composition, and etched with real observation and understanding." Since this is the considered opinion of a critic who was as eagle-eyed in 1947 as he was in 1920, it bears thinking about. As Eleanor Flexner has suggested in her *American Playwrights 1918–1938,* O'Neill is at his best when, as in *Anna Christie,* his creative instinct is emotional rather than intellectual in origin. *Anna Christie* did not deal primarily with "ideas"—at which O'Neill was no master—but with living people trapped by their circumstances. They are shown trying desperately to wriggle out of a net of fate partly of their own making, partly woven by the environment to which they

succumbed, and partly knotted by a destiny undefined but poetically sensed by O'Neill. We may add the possibility that the crudity of the play—that is, a certain incomplete fusion of emphases—makes *Anna Christie* all the more genuine by giving it a feeling of "life observed" rather than of "play plotted."

BIBLIOGRAPHY: Brooks Atkinson, *Broadway Scrapbook* (pp. 52–55, 241–246), 1947; Eric Bentley, *The Playwright as Thinker* (pp. 67–69, 223–285, 318–322), 1946; Anita Block, *The Changing World in Plays and Theatre* (pp. 137–193), 1939; John Mason Brown, *Letters from the Greenroom* (pp. 71–116), 1934; Brown, *Two on the Aisle* (pp. 136–142), 1938; Brown, *Seeing More Things,* (pp. 257–265), 1948; Barrett H. Clark, *Eugene O'Neill: The Man and His Work,* 1947; Eleanor Flexner, *American Playwrights 1918–1938* (pp. 130–197), 1938; John Gassner, *Masters of the Drama* (pp. 641–661), 1940, 1945; Joseph Wood Krutch, Introduction to *Nine Plays by Eugene O'Neill,* 1932; Krutch, *The American Drama Since 1918* (pp. 23–29, 73–133, 288–291), 1939; George Jean Nathan, *The Theatre Book of the Year 1946–1947* (pp. 93–111), 1947; Richard Dana Skinner, *Eugene O'Neill, a Poet's Quest,* 1935; Sophus Keith Winther, *Eugene O'Neill: A Critical Study,* 1934; Stark Young, *Immortal Shadows,* (pp. 61–66, 132–139, 271–274), 1948.

For additional commentary, see pages 817–818.

ANNA CHRISTIE

By Eugene O'Neill

CHARACTERS

"JOHNNY-THE-PRIEST"
TWO LONGSHOREMEN
A POSTMAN
LARRY, *bartender*

CHRIS CHRISTOPHERSON, *captain*
of the barge Simeon Winthrop
MARTHY OWEN
ANNA CHRISTOPHERSON,
Chris' daughter

THREE MEN OF A STEAMER'S CREW
MAT BURKE, *a stoker*
JOHNSON, *deckhand on the barge*

ACT I.

SCENE. *"Johnny-the-Priest's" saloon near South Street, New York City. The stage is divided into two sections, showing a small back room on the right. On the left, forward, of the barroom, a large window looking out on the street. Beyond it, the main entrance—a double swinging door. Farther back, another window. The bar runs from left to right nearly the whole length of the rear wall. In back of the bar, a small show-case displaying a few bottles of case goods, for which there is evidently little call. The remainder of the rear space in front of the large mirrors is occupied by half-barrels of cheap whisky of the "nickel-a-shot" variety, from which the liquor is drawn by means of spigots. On the right is an open doorway leading to the back room. In the back room are four round wooden tables with five chairs grouped about each. In the rear, a family entrance opening on a side street.*

It is late afternoon of a day in fall.

As the curtain rises, Johnny *is discovered. "Johnny-the-Priest" deserves his nickname. With his pale, thin, clean-shaven face, mild blue eyes and white hair, a cassock would seem more suited to him than the apron he wears. Neither his voice nor his general manner dispel this illusion which has made him a personage of the water front. They are soft and bland. But beneath all his mildness one senses the man behind the mask—cynical, callous, hard as nails. He is lounging at ease behind the bar, a pair of spectacles on his nose, reading an evening paper.*

Two longshoremen enter from the street, wearing their working aprons, the button of the union pinned conspicuously on the caps pulled sideways on their heads at an aggressive angle.

FIRST LONGSHOREMAN: [*As they range themselves at the bar*] Gimme a shock. Number Two.

[*He tosses a coin on the bar*]

SECOND LONGSHOREMAN: Same here.

[Johnny *sets two glasses of barrel whisky before them*]

FIRST LONGSHOREMAN: Here's luck!

[*The other nods. They gulp down their whisky*]

SECOND LONGSHOREMAN: [*Putting money on the bar*] Give us another.

FIRST LONGSHOREMAN: Gimme a scoop this time—lager and porter. I'm dry.

SECOND LONGSHOREMAN: Same here.

[Johnny *draws the lager and porter and sets the big, foaming schooners before them. They drink down half the contents and start to talk together hurriedly in low tones. The door on the left is swung open and* Larry *enters. He is a boyish, red-cheeked, rather good-looking young fellow of twenty or so*]

LARRY: [*Nodding to* Johnny—*cheerily*] Hello, boss.

JOHNNY: Hello, Larry. [*With a glance at his watch*] Just on time.

[Larry *goes to the right behind the bar, takes off his coat, and puts on an apron*]

FIRST LONGSHOREMAN: [*Abruptly*] Let's drink up and get back to it.

[*They finish their drinks and go out left. The* Postman *enters as they leave. He exchanges nods with* Johnny *and throws a letter on the bar*]

THE POSTMAN: Addressed care of you, Johnny. Know him?

JOHNNY: [*Picks up the letter, adjusting his spectacles.* Larry *comes and peers over his shoulders.* Johnny *reads very slowly*] Christopher Christopherson.

THE POSTMAN: [*Helpfully*] Square-head name.

LARRY: Old Chris—that's who.

JOHNNY: Oh, sure. I was forgetting Chris carried a hell of a name like that. Letters come here for him sometimes before, I remember now. Long time ago, though.

THE POSTMAN: It'll get him all right then?

JOHNNY: Sure thing. He comes here whenever he's in port.

THE POSTMAN: [*Turning to go*] Sailor, eh?

JOHNNY: [*With a grin*] Captain of a coal barge.

THE POSTMAN: [*Laughing*] Some job! Well, s'long.

JOHNNY: S'long. I'll see he gets it.

[*The Postman goes out. Johnny scrutinizes the*

letter] You got good eyes, Larry. Where's it from?

LARRY: [*After a glance*] St. Paul. That'll be in Minnesota, I'm thinkin'. Looks like a woman's writing, too, the old divil!

JOHNNY: He's got a daughter somewhere's out West, I think he told me once. [*He puts the letter on the cash register*] Come to think of it, I ain't seen old Chris in a dog's age. [*Putting his overcoat on, he comes around the end of the bar*] Guess I'll be gettin' home. See you tomorrow.

LARRY: Good night to ye, boss.

[*As Johnny goes toward the street door, it is pushed open and* Christopher Christopherson *enters. He is a short, squat, broad-shouldered man of about fifty, with a round, weather-beaten, red face from which his light blue eyes peer short-sightedly, twinkling with a simple good humor. His large mouth, overhung by a thick, drooping, yellow mustache, is childishly self-willed and weak, of an obstinate kindliness. A thick neck is jammed like a post into the heavy trunk of his body. His arms with their big, hairy, freckled hands, and his stumpy legs terminating in large flat feet, are awkwardly short and muscular. He walks with a clumsy, rolling gait. His voice, when not raised in a hollow boom, is toned down to a sly, confidential half-whisper with something vaguely plaintive in its quality. He is dressed in a wrinkled, ill-fitting dark suit of shore clothes, and wears a faded cap of gray cloth over his mop of grizzled, blond hair. Just now his face beams with a too-blissful happiness, and he has evidently been drinking. He reaches his hand out to* Johnny]

CHRIS: Hello, Johnny! Have drink on me. Come on, Larry. Give us drink. Have one yourself. [*Putting his hand in his pocket*] Ay gat money—plenty money.

JOHNNY: [*Shakes* Chris *by the hand*] Speak of the devil. We was just talkin' about you.

LARRY: [*Coming to the end of the bar*] Hello, Chris. Put it there.

[*They shake hands*]

CHRIS: [*Beaming*] Give us drink.

JOHNNY: [*With a grin*] You got a half-snootful now. Where'd you get it?

CHRIS: [*Grinning*] Oder fallar on oder barge—Irish fallar—he gat bottle vhisky and we drank it, yust us two. Dot vhisky gat kick, by yingo! Ay yust come ashore. Give us drink, Larry. Ay vas little drunk, not much. Yust feel good. [*He laughs and commences to sing in a nasal, high-pitched quaver*] "My Yosephine, come board de ship. Long time Ay vait for you.
De moon, she shi-i-ine. She looka yust like you.
Tchee-tchee, tchee-tchee, tchee-tchee, tchee-tchee."

[*To the accompaniment of this last he waves*

his hand as if he were conducting an orchestra]

JOHNNY: [*With a laugh*] Same old Yosie, eh, Chris?

CHRIS: You don't know good song when you hear him. Italian fallar on oder barge, he learn me dat. Give us drink.

[*He throws change on the bar*]

LARRY: [*With a professional air*] What's your pleasure, gentlemen?

JOHNNY: Small beer, Larry.

CHRIS: Vhisky—Number Two.

LARRY: [*As he gets their drinks*] I'll take a cigar on you.

CHRIS: [*Lifting his glass*] Skoal!

[*He drinks*]

JOHNNY: Drink hearty.

CHRIS: [*Immediately*] Have oder drink.

JOHNNY: No. Some other time. Got to go home now. So you've just landed? Where are you in from this time?

CHRIS: Norfolk. Ve make slow voyage—dirty vedder—yust fog, fog, fog, all bloody time! [*There is an insistent ring from the doorbell at the family entrance in the back room. Chris gives a start—hurriedly*] Ay go open, Larry. Ay forgat. It vas Marthy. She come with me.

[*He goes into the back room*]

LARRY: [*With a chuckle*] He's still got that same cow livin' with him, the old fool!

JOHNNY: [*With a grin*] A sport, Chris is. Well, I'll beat it home. S'long.

[*He goes to the street door*]

LARRY: So long, boss.

JOHNNY: Oh—don't forget to give him his letter.

LARRY: I won't.

[Johnny *goes out. In the meantime,* Chris *has opened the family entrance door, admitting* Marthy. *She might be forty or fifty. Her jowly, mottled face, with its thick red nose, is streaked with interlacing purple veins. Her thick, gray hair is piled anyhow in a greasy mop on top of her round head. Her figure is flabby and fat; her breath comes in wheezy gasps; she speaks in a loud, mannish voice, punctuated by explosions of hoarse laughter. But there still twinkles in her blood-shot blue eyes a youthful lust for life which hard usage has failed to stifle, a sense of humor mocking, but good-tempered. She wears a man's cap, double-breasted man's jacket, and a grimy, calico skirt. Her bare feet are encased in a man's brogans several sizes too large for her, which gives her a shuffling gait*]

MARTHY: [*Grumblingly*] What yuh tryin' to do, Dutchy—keep me standin' out there all day?

[*She comes forward and sits at the table in the right corner, front*]

CHRIS: [*Mollifyingly*] Ay'm sorry, Marthy. Ay talk to Yohnny. Ay forgat. What you goin' take for drink?

MARTHY: [*Appeased*] Gimme a scoop of lager an' ale.

CHRIS: Ay go bring him back. [*He returns to the bar*] Lager and ale for Marthy, Larry. Vhisky for me.

[*He throws change on the bar*]

LARRY: Right you are. [*Then remembering, he takes the letter from in back of the bar*] Here's a letter for you—from St. Paul, Minnesota—and a lady's writin'.

[*He grins*]

CHRIS: [*Quickly—taking it*] Oh, den it come from my daughter, Anna. She live dere. [*He turns the letter over in his hands uncertainly*] Ay don't gat letter from Anna—must be a year.

LARRY: [*Jokingly*] That's a fine fairy tale to be tellin'—your daughter! Sure I'll bet it's some bum.

CHRIS: [*Soberly*] No. Dis come from Anna. *Engrossed by the letter in his hand—uncertainly*] By golly, Ay tank Ay'm too drunk for read dis letter from Anna. Ay tank Ay sat down for a minute. You bring drinks in back room, Larry.

[*He goes into the room on right*]

MARTHY: [*Angrily*] Where's my lager an' ale, yuh big stiff?

CHRIS: [*Preoccupied*] Larry bring him.

[*He sits down opposite her. Larry brings in the drinks and sets them on the table. He and Marthy exchange nods of recognition. Larry stands looking at Chris curiously. Marthy takes a long draught of her schooner and heaves a huge sigh of satisfaction, wiping her mouth with the back of her hand. Chris stares at the letter for a moment—slowly opens it, and, squinting his eyes, commences to read laboriously, his lips moving as he spells out the words. As he reads his face lights up with an expression of mingled joy and bewilderment*]

LARRY: Good news?

MARTHY: [*Her curiosity also aroused*] What's that yuh got—a letter, fur Gawd's sake?

CHRIS: [*Pauses for a moment, after finishing the letter, as if to let the news sink in—then suddenly pounds his fist on the table with happy excitement*] Py yiminy! Yust tank, Anna say she's comin' here right avay! She gat sick on yob in St. Paul, she say. It's short letter, don't tal me much more'n dat. [*Beaming*] Py golly, dat's good news all at one time for ole fallar! [*Then turning to Marthy, rather shamefacedly*] You know, Marthy, Ay've tole you Ay don't see my Anna since she vas little gel in Sveden five year ole.

MARTHY: How old'll she be now?

CHRIS: She must be—lat me see—she must be twenty year ole, py Yo!

LARRY: [*Surprised*] You've not seen her in fifteen years?

CHRIS: [*Suddenly growing somber—in a low tone*] No. Ven she vas little gel, Ay vas bo'sun on vindjammer. Ay never gat home only few time dem

year. Ay'm fool sailor fallar. My voman—Anna's mo'der—she gat tired vait all time Sveden for me ven Ay don't never come. She come dis country, bring Anna, dey go out Minnesota, live with her cousins on farm. Den ven her mo'der died ven Ay vas on voyage, Ay tank it's better dem cousins keep Anna. Ay tank it's better Anna live on farm, den she don't know dat ole davil, sea, she don't know fa'der like me.

LARRY: [*With a wink at* Marthy] This girl, now, 'll be marryin' a sailor herself, likely. It's in the blood.

CHRIS: [*Suddenly springing to his feet and smashing his fist on the table in a rage*] No, py God! She don't do dat!

MARTHY: [*Grasping her schooner hastily—angrily*] Hey, look out, yuh nut! Wanta spill my suds for me?

LARRY: [*Amazed*] Oho, what's up with you? Ain't you a sailor yourself now, and always been?

CHRIS: [*Slowly*] Dat's yust vhy Ay say it. [*Forcing a smile*] Sailor vas all right fallar, but not for marry gel. No. Ay know dat. Anna's mo'der, she know it, too.

LARRY: [*As* Chris *remains sunk in gloomy reflection*] When is your daughter comin'? Soon?

CHRIS: [*Roused*] Py yiminy, Ay forgat. [*Reads through the letter hurriedly*] She say she come right avay, dat's all.

LARRY: She'll maybe be comin' here to look for you, I s'pose.

[*He returns to the bar, whistling. Left alone with* Marthy, *who stares at him with a twinkle of malicious humor in her eyes,* Chris *suddenly becomes desperately ill-at-ease. He fidgets, then gets up hurriedly*]

CHRIS: Ay gat speak with Larry. Ay be right back. [*Mollifyingly*] Ay bring you oder drink.

MARTHY: [*Emptying her glass*] Sure. That's me.

[*As he retreats with the glass she guffaws after him derisively*]

CHRIS: [*To* Larry *in an alarmed whisper*] Py yingo, Ay gat gat Marthy shore off barge before Anna come! Anna raise hell if she find dat out. Marthy raise hell, too, for go, py golly!

LARRY: [*With a chuckle*] Serve ye right, ye old divil—havin' a woman at your age!

CHRIS: [*Scratching his head in a quandary*] You tal me lie for tal Marthy, Larry, so's she gat off barge quick.

LARRY: She knows your daughter's comin'. Tell her to get the hell out of it.

CHRIS: No. Ay don't like make her feel bad.

LARRY: You're an old mush! Keep your girl away from the barge, then. She'll likely want to stay ashore anyway. [*Curiously*] What does she work at, your Anna?

CHRIS: She stay on dem cousins' farm till two year ago. Dan she gat yob nurse gel in St. Paul. [*Then shaking his head resolutely*] But Ay don't vant for her gat yob now. Ay vant for her stay with me.

LARRY: [*Scornfully*] On a coal barge! She'll not like that, I'm thinkin'.

MARTHY: [*Shouts from the next room*] Don't I get that bucket o' suds, Dutchy?

CHRIS: [*Startled—in apprehensive confusion*] Yes, Ay come, Marthy.

LARRY: [*Drawing the lager and ale, hands it to Chris—laughing*] Now you're in for it! You'd better tell her straight to get out!

CHRIS: [*Shaking in his boots*] Py golly. [*He takes her drink in to Marthy and sits down at the table. She sips it in silence. Larry moves quietly close to the partition to listen, grinning with expectation. Chris seems on the verge of speaking, hesitates, gulps down his whisky desperately as if seeking for courage. He attempts to whistle a few bars of "Yosephine" with careless bravado, but the whistle peters out futilely. Marthy stares at him keenly, taking in his embarrassment with a malicious twinkle of amusement in her eye. Chris clears his throat*] Marthy—

MARTHY: [*Aggressively*] Wha's that? [*Then, pretending to fly into a rage, her eyes enjoying Chris' misery*] I'm wise to what's in back of your nut, Dutchy. Yuh want to git rid o' me, huh?—now she's comin'. Gimme the bum's rush ashore, huh? Lemme tell yuh, Dutchy, there ain't a square-head workin' on a boat man enough to git away with that. Don't start nothin' yuh can't finish!

CHRIS: [*Miserably*] Ay don't start nutting, Marthy.

MARTHY: [*Glares at him for a second—then cannot control a burst of laughter*] Ho-ho! Yuh're a scream, Square-head—an honest-ter-Gawd knock-out! Ho-ho!

[*She wheezes, panting for breath*]

CHRIS: [*With childish pique*] Ay don't see nutting for laugh at.

MARTHY: Take a slant in the mirror and yuh'll see. Ho-ho! [*Recovering from her mirth—chuckling, scornfully*] A square-head tryin' to kid Marthy Owen at this late day!—after me campin' with barge men the last twenty years. I'm wise to the game, up, down, and sideways. I ain't been born and dragged up on the water front for nothin'. Think I'd make trouble, huh? Not me! I'll pack up me duds an' beat it. I'm quittin' yuh, get me? I'm tellin' yuh I'm sick of stickin' with yuh, and I'm leavin' yuh flat, see? There's plenty of other guys on other barges waitin' for me. Always was, I always found. [*She claps the astonished Chris on the back*] So cheer up, Dutchy! I'll be offen the barge before she comes. You'll be rid o' me for good—and me o' you—good riddance for both of us. Ho-ho!

CHRIS: [*Seriously*] Ay don' tank dat. You vas good gel, Marthy.

MARTHY: [*Grinning*] Good girl? Aw, can the bull! Well, yuh treated me square, yuhself. So it's fifty-fifty. Nobody's sore at nobody. We're still good frien's, huh?

[*Larry returns to bar*]

CHRIS: [*Beaming now that he sees his troubles disappearing*] Yes, py golly.

MARTHY: That's the talkin'! In all my time I tried never to split with a guy with no hard feelin's. But what was yuh so scared about—that I'd kick up a row? That ain't Marthy's way. [*Scornfully*] Think I'd break my heart to lose yuh? Commit suicide, huh? Ho-ho. Gawd! The world's full o' men if that's all I'd worry about! [*Then with a grin, after emptying her glass*] Blow me to another scoop, huh? I'll drink your kid's health for yuh.

CHRIS: [*Eagerly*] Sure tang. Ay go gat him. [*He takes the two glasses into the bar*] Oder drink. Same for both.

LARRY: [*Getting the drinks and putting them on the bar*] She's not such a bad lot, that one.

CHRIS: [*Jovially*] She's good gel, Ay tal you! Py golly, Ay calabrate now! Give me vhisky here at bar, too. [*He puts down money. Larry serves him*] You have drink, Larry.

LARRY: [*Virtuously*] You know I never touch it.

CHRIS: You don't know what you miss. Skoal! [*He drinks—then begins to sing loudly*] "My Yosephine, come board de ship——"

[*He picks up the drinks for Marthy and himself and walks unsteadily into the back room, singing*]

"De moon, she shi-i-i-ine. She looks yust like you. Tchee-tchee-tchee, tchee-tchee, tchee-tchee tchee-tchee."

MARTHY: [*Grinning, hands to ears*] Gawd!

CHRIS: [*Sitting down*] Ay'm good singer, yes? Ve drink, eh? Skoal! Ay calabrate! [*He drinks*] Ay calabrate 'cause Anna's coming home. You know, Marthy, Ay never write for her to come, 'cause Ay tank Ay'm no good for her. But all time Ay hope like hell some day she vant for see me and den she come. And dat's vay it happen now, py yiminy! [*His face beaming*] What you tank she look like, Marthy? Ay bet you she's fine, good, strong gel, pooty like hell! Living on farm made her like dat. And Ay bet you some day she marry good, steady land fallar here in East, have home all her own, have kits—and dan Ay'm ole grandfa'der, py golly! And Ay go visit dem every time Ay gat in port near! [*Bursting with joy*] By yiminy crickens, Ay calabrate dat! [*Shouts*] Bring oder drink, Larry! [*He smashes his fist on the table with a bang*]

LARRY: [*Coming in from bar—irritably*] Easy there! Don't be breakin' the table, you old goat!

CHRIS: [*By way of reply, grins foolishly and begins to sing*] "My Yosephine, come board de ship——"

MARTHY: [*Touching Chris' arm persuasively*] You're soused to the ears, Dutchy. Go out and put a feed into you. It'll sober you up. [*Then as Chris shakes his head obstinately*] Listen, yuh old nut! Yuh don't know what time your kid's liable to show up. Yuh want to be sober when she comes, don't yuh?

CHRIS: [*Aroused—gets unsteadily to his feet*] Py golly, yes.

LARRY: That's good sense for you. A good beef stew'll fix you. Go round the corner.

CHRIS: All right. Av be back soon, Marthy.

[*Chris goes through the bar and out the street door*]

LARRY: He'll come round all right with some grub in him.

MARTHY: Sure.

[*Larry goes back to the bar and resumes his newspaper. Marthy sips what is left of her schooner reflectively. There is the ring of the family entrance bell. Larry comes to the door and opens it a trifle—then, with a puzzled expression, pulls it wide. Anna Christopherson enters. She is a tall, blond, fully-developed girl of twenty, handsome after a large, Viking-daughter fashion but now run down in health and plainly showing all the outward evidences of belonging to the world's oldest profession. Her youthful face is already hard and cynical beneath its layer of make-up. Her clothes are the tawdry finery of peasant stock turned prostitute. She comes and sinks wearily in a chair by the table, left front*]

ANNA: Gimme a whisky—ginger ale on the side. [*Then, as Larry turns to go, forcing a winning smile at him*] And don't be stingy, baby.

LARRY: [*Sarcastically*] Shall I serve it in a pail?

ANNA: [*With a hard laugh*] That suits me down to the ground. [*Larry goes into the bar. The two women size each other up with frank stares. Larry comes back with the drink which he sets before Anna and returns to the bar again. Anna downs her drink at a gulp. Then, after a moment, as the alcohol begins to rouse her, she turns to Marthy with a friendly smile*] Gee, I needed that bad, all right, all right!

MARTHY: [*Nodding her head sympathetically*] Sure—yuh look all in. Been on a bat?

ANNA: No—traveling—day and a half on the train. Had to sit up all night in the dirty coach, too. Gawd, I thought I'd never get here!

MARTHY: [*With a start—looking at her intently*] Where'd yuh come from, huh?

ANNA: St. Paul—out in Minnesota.

MARTHY: [*Staring at her in amazement—slowly*] So—yuh're— [*She suddenly bursts out into hoarse, ironical laughter*] Gawd!

ANNA: All the way from Minnesota, sure. [*Flaring up*] What you laughing at? Me?

MARTHY: [*Hastily*] No, honest, kid. I was thinkin' of somethin' else.

ANNA: [*Mollified—with a smile*] Well, I wouldn't blame you, at that. Guess I do look rotten—yust out of the hospital two weeks. I'm going to have another 'ski. What d'you say? Have something on me?

MARTHY: Sure I will. T'anks. [*She calls*] Hey, Larry! Little service!

[*He comes in*]

ANNA: Same for me.

MARTHY: Same here.

[*Larry takes their glasses and goes out*]

ANNA: Why don't you come sit over here, be sociable. I'm a dead stranger in this burg—and I ain't spoke a word with no one since day before yesterday.

MARTHY: Sure thing.

[*She shuffles over to Anna's table and sits down opposite her. Larry brings the drinks and Anna pays him*]

ANNA: Skoal! Here's how! [*She drinks*]

MARTHY: Here's luck! [*She takes a gulp from her schooner*]

ANNA: [*Taking a package of Sweet Caporal cigarettes from her bag*] Let you smoke in here, won't they?

MARTHY: [*Doubtfully*] Sure. [*Then with evident anxiety*] On'y trow it away if yuh hear someone comin'.

ANNA: [*Lighting one and taking a deep inhale*] Gee, they're fussy in this dump, ain't they? [*She puffs, staring at the table top. Marthy looks her over with a new penetrating interest, taking in every detail of her face. Anna suddenly becomes conscious of this appraising stare—resentfully*] Ain't nothing wrong with me, is there? You're looking hard enough.

MARTHY: [*Irritated by the other's tone—scornfully*] Ain't got to look much. I got your number the minute you stepped in the door.

ANNA: [*Her eyes narrowing*] Ain't you smart! Well, I got yours, too, without no trouble. You're me forty years from now. That's you! [*She gives a hard little laugh*]

MARTHY: [*Angrily*] Is that so? Well, I'll tell you straight, kiddo, that Marthy Owen never—— [*She catches herself up short—with a grin*] What are you and me scrappin' over? Let's cut it out, huh? Me, I don't want no hard feelin's with no one. [*Extending her hand*] Shake and forget it, huh?

ANNA: [*Shakes her hand gladly*] Only too glad to. I ain't looking for trouble. Let's have 'nother. What d'you say?

MARTHY: [*Shaking her head*] Not for mine. I'm full up. And you—— Had anythin' to eat lately?

ANNA: Not since this morning on the train.

MARTHY: Then yuh better go easy on it, hadn't yuh?

ANNA: [*After a moment's hesitation*] Guess you're right. I got to meet someone, too. But my nerves is on edge after that rotten trip.

MARTHY: Yuh said yuh was just outa the hospital?

ANNA: Two weeks ago. [*Leaning over to Marthy confidentially*] The joint I was in out in St. Paul got raided. That was the start. The judge give all us girls thirty days. The others didn't seem to mind being in the cooler much. Some of 'em was used to it. But me, I couldn't stand it. It got my goat right—

couldn't eat or sleep or nothing. I never could stand being caged up nowheres. I got good and sick and they had to send me to the hospital. It was nice there. I was sorry to leave it, honest!

MARTHY: [*After a slight pause*] Did yuh say yuh got to meet someone here?

ANNA: Yes. Oh, not what you mean. It's my Old Man I got to meet. Honest! It's funny, too. I ain't seen him since I was a kid—don't even know what he looks like—yust had a letter every now and then. This was always the only address he gave me to write him back. He's yanitor of some building here now—used to be a sailor.

MARTHY: [*Astonished*] Janitor!

ANNA: Sure. And I was thinking maybe, seeing he ain't never done a thing for me in my life, he might be willing to stake me to a room and eats till I get rested up. [*Wearily*] Gee, I sure need that rest! I'm knocked out. [*Then resignedly*] But I ain't expecting much from him. Give you a kick when you're down, that's what all men do. [*With sudden passion*] Men, I hate 'em—all of 'em! And I don't expect he'll turn out no better than the rest. [*Then with sudden interest*] Say, do you hang out around this dump much?

MARTHY: Oh, off and on.

ANNA: Then maybe you know him—my Old Man —or at least seen him?

MARTHY: It ain't old Chris, is it?

ANNA: Old Chris?

MARTHY: Chris Christopherson, his full name is.

ANNA: [*Excitedly*] Yes, that's him! Anna Christopherson—that's my real name—only out there I called myself Anna Christie. So you know him, eh?

MARTHY: [*Evasively*] Seen him about for years.

ANNA: Say, what's he like, tell me, honest?

MARTHY: Oh, he's short and——

ANNA: [*Impatiently*] I don't care what he looks like. What kind is he?

MARTHY: [*Earnestly*] Well, yuh can bet your life, kid, he's as good an old guy as ever walked on two feet. That goes!

ANNA: [*Pleased*] I'm glad to hear it. Then you think he'll stake me to that rest cure I'm after?

MARTHY: [*Emphatically*] Surest thing you know. [*Disgustedly*] But where'd yuh get the idea he was a janitor?

ANNA: He wrote me he was himself.

MARTHY: Well, he was lyin'. He ain't. He's captain of a barge—five men under him.

ANNA: [*Disgusted in her turn*] A barge? What kind of a barge?

MARTHY: Coal, mostly.

ANNA: A coal barge! [*With a harsh laugh*] If that ain't a swell job to find your long lost Old Man working at! Gee, I knew something'd be bound to turn out wrong—always does with me. That puts my idea of his giving me a rest on the bum.

MARTHY: What d'yuh mean?

ANNA: I s'pose he lives on the boat, don't he?

MARTHY: Sure. What about it? Can't you live on it, too?

ANNA: [*Scornfully*] Me? On a dirty coal barge! What d'you think I am?

MARTHY: [*Resentfully*] What d'yuh know about barges, huh? Bet yuh ain't never seen one. That's what comes of his bringing yuh up inland—away from the old devil sea—where yuh'd be safe—Gawd! [*The irony of it strikes her sense of humor and she laughs hoarsely*]

ANNA: [*Angrily*] His bringing me up! Is that what he tells people! I like his nerve! He let them cousins of my Old Woman's keep me on their farm and work me to death like a dog.

MARTHY: Well, he's got queer notions on some things. I've heard him say a farm was the best place for a kid.

ANNA: Sure. That's what he'd always answer back —and a lot of crazy stuff about staying away from the sea—stuff I couldn't make head or tail to. I thought he must be nutty.

MARTHY: He is on that one point. [*Casually*] So yuh didn't fall for life on the farm, huh?

ANNA: I should say not! The old man of the family, his wife, and four sons—I had to slave for all of 'em. I was only a poor relation, and they treated me worse than they dare treat a hired girl. [*After a moment's hesitation—somberly*] It was one of the sons—the youngest—started me—when I was sixteen. After that, I hated 'em so I'd killed 'em all if I'd stayed. So I run away—to St. Paul.

MARTHY: [*Who has been listening sympathetically*] I've heard Old Chris talkin' about your bein' a nurse girl out there. Was that all a bluff yuh put up when yuh wrote him?

ANNA: Not on your life, it wasn't. It was true for two years. I didn't go wrong all at one jump. Being a nurse girl was yust what finished me. Taking care of other people's kids, always listening to their bawling and crying, caged in, when you're only a kid yourself and want to go out and see things. At last I got the chance—to get into that house. And you bet your life I took it! [*Defiantly*] And I ain't sorry neither. [*After a pause—with bitter hatred*] It was all men's fault—the whole business. It was men on the farm ordering and beating me—and giving me the wrong start. Then when I was a nurse, it was men again hanging around, bothering me, trying to see what they could get. [*She gives a hard laugh*] And now it's men all the time. Gawd, I hate 'em all, every mother's son of 'em! Don't you?

MARTHY: Oh, I dunno. There's good ones and bad ones, kid. You've just had a run of bad luck with 'em, that's all. Your Old Man, now—Old Chris— he's a good one.

ANNA: [*Skeptically*] He'll have to show me.

MARTHY: Yuh kept right on writing him yuh was a nurse girl still, even after yuh was in the house, didn't yuh?

ANNA: Sure. [*Cynically*] Not that I think he'd care a darn.

MARTHY: Yuh're all wrong about him, kid. [*Earnestly*] I know Old Chris well for a long time. He's talked to me 'bout you lots o' times. He thinks the world o' you, honest he does.

ANNA: Aw, quit the kiddin'!

MARTHY: Honest! Only, he's a simple old guy, see? He's got nutty notions. But he means well, honest. Listen to me, kid—— [*She is interrupted by the opening and shutting of the street door in the bar and by hearing* Chris' *voice*] Ssshh!

ANNA: What's up?

CHRIS: [*Who has entered the bar. He seems considerably sobered up*] Py golly, Larry, dat grub taste good. Marthy in back?

LARRY: Sure—and another tramp with her.

[Chris *starts for the entrance to the back room*]

MARTHY: [*To* Anna *in a hurried, nervous whisper*] That's him now. He's comin' in here. Brace up!

ANNA: Who?

[Chris *opens the door*]

MARTHY: [*As if she were greeting him for the first time*] Why, hello, Old Chris. [*Then before he can speak, she shuffles hurriedly past him into the bar, beckoning him to follow her*] Come here. I wanta tell yuh somethin'. [*He goes out to her. She speaks hurriedly in a low voice*] Listen! I'm goin' to beat it down to the barge—pack up me duds and blow. That's her in there—your Anna—just come—waitin' for yuh. Treat her right, see? She's been sick. Well, s'long! [*She goes into the back room—to* Anna] S'long kid. I gotta beat it now. See yuh later.

ANNA: [*Nervously*] So long.

[Marthy *goes quickly out of the family entrance*]

LARRY: [*Looking at the stupefied* Chris *curiously*] Well, what's up now?

CHRIS: [*Vaguely*] Nutting—nutting. [*He stands before the door to the back room in an agony of embarrassed emotion—then he forces himself to a bold decision, pushes open the door and walks in. He stands there, casts a shy glance at* Anna, *whose brilliant clothes, and, to him, high-toned appearance, awe him terribly. He looks about him with pitiful nervousness as if to avoid the appraising look with which she takes in his face, his clothes, etc.—his voice seeming to plead for her forbearance*] Anna!

ANNA: [*Acutely embarrassed in her turn*] Hello— father. She told me it was you. I yust got here a little while ago.

CHRIS: [*Goes slowly over to her chair*] It's good— for see you—after all dem years, Anna.

[*He bends down over her. After an embarrassed struggle they manage to kiss each other*]

ANNA: [*A trace of genuine feeling in her voice*] It's good to see you, too.

CHRIS: [*Grasps her arms and looks into her face— then overcome by a wave of fierce tenderness*] Anna lilla! Anna lilla!

[*Takes her in his arms*]

ANNA: [*Shrinks away from him, half-frightened*] What's that—Swedish? I don't know it. [*Then as if seeking relief from the tension in a voluble chatter*] Gee, I had an awful trip coming here. I'm all in. I had to sit up in the dirty coach all night—couldn't get no sleep, hardly—and then I had a hard job finding this place. I never been in New York before, you know, and——

CHRIS: [*Who has been staring down at her face admiringly, not hearing what she says—impulsively*] You know you vas awful pooty gel, Anna? Ay bet all men see you fall in love with you, py yiminy!

ANNA: [*Repelled—harshly*] Cut it! You talk same as they all do.

CHRIS: [*Hurt—humbly*] Ain't no harm for your fa'der talk dat vay, Anna.

ANNA: [*Forcing a short laugh*] No—course not. Only—it's funny to see you and not remember nothing. You're like—a stranger.

CHRIS: [*Sadly*] Ay s'pose. Ay never come home only few times ven you vas kit in Sveden. You don't remember dat?

ANNA: No. [*Resentfully*] But why didn't you never come home them days? Why didn't you never come out West to see me?

CHRIS: [*Slowly*] Ay tank, after your mo'der die, ven Ay vas avay on voyage, it's better for you you don't never see me! [*He sinks down in the chair opposite her dejectedly—then turns to her—sadly*] Ay don't know, Anna, vhy Ay never come home Sveden in ole year. Ay vant come home end of every voyage. Ay vant see your mo'der, your two bro'der before dey vas drowned, you ven you vas born—but—Ay—don't go. Ay sign on oder ships— go South America, go Australia, go China, go every port all over world many times—but Ay never go aboard ship sail for Sveden. Ven Ay gat money for pay passage home as passenger den—— [*He bows his head guiltily*] Ay forgat and Ay spend all money. Ven Ay tank again, it's too late. [*He sighs*] Ay don't know why but dat's vay with most sailor fallar, Anna. Dat ole davil sea make dem crazy fools with her dirty tricks. It's so.

ANNA: [*Who has watched him keenly while he has been speaking—with a trace of scorn in her voice*] Then you think the sea's to blame for everything, eh? Well, you're still workin' on it, ain't you, spite of all you used to write me about hating it. That dame was here told me you was captain of a coal barge—and you wrote me you was yanitor of a building!

CHRIS: [*Embarrassed but lying glibly*] Oh, Ay vork on land long time as yanitor. Yust short time ago Ay got dis yob cause Ay vas sick, need open air.

ANNA: [*Skeptically*] Sick? You? You'd never think it.

CHRIS: And Anna, dis ain't real sailor yob. Dis

ain't real boat on sea. She's yust ole tub—like piece of land with house on it dat float. Yob on her ain't sea yob. No. Ay don't gat yob on sea, Anna, if Ay die first. Ay swear dat ven your mo'der die. Ay keep my word, py yingo!

ANNA: [*Perplexed*] Well, I can't see no difference. [*Dismissing the subject*] Speaking of being sick, I been there myself—yust out of the hospital two weeks ago.

CHRIS: [*Immediately all concern*] You, Anna? Py golly! [*Anxiously*] You feel better now, dough, don't you? You look little tired, dat's all!

ANNA: [*Wearily*] I am. Tired to death. I need a long rest and I don't see much chance of getting it.

CHRIS: What you mean, Anna?

ANNA: Well, when I made up my mind to come to see you, I thought you was a yanitor—that you'd have a place where, maybe if you didn't mind having me, I could visit a while and rest up—till I felt able to get back on the yob again.

CHRIS: [*Eagerly*] But Ay gat place, Anna—nice place. You rest all you want, py yiminy! You don't never have to vork as nurse gel no more. You stay with me, py golly!

ANNA: [*Surprised and pleased by his eagerness— with a smile*] Then you're really glad to see me— honest?

CHRIS: [*Pressing one of her hands in both of his*] Anna, Ay like see you like hell, Ay tal you! And don't you talk no more about gatting yob. You stay with me. Ay don't see you for long time, you don't forgat dat. [*His voice trembles*] Ay'm gatting ole. Ay gat no one in vorld but you.

ANNA: [*Touched—embarrassed by this unfamiliar emotion*] Thanks. It sounds good to hear someone —talk to me that way. Say, though—if you're so lonely—it's funny—why ain't you ever married again?

CHRIS: [*Shaking his head emphatically—after a pause*] Ay love your mo'der too much for ever do dat, Anna.

ANNA: [*Impressed—slowly*] I don't remember nothing about her. What was she like? Tell me.

CHRIS: Ay tal you all about everytang—and you tal me all tangs happen to you. But not here now. Dis ain't good place for young gel, anyway. Only no good sailor fallar come here for gat drunk. [*He gets to his feet quickly and picks up her bag*] You come with me, Anna. You need lie down, gat rest.

ANNA: [*Half rises to her feet, then sits down again*] Where're you going?

CHRIS: Come. Ve gat on board.

ANNA: [*Disappointedly*] On board your barge, you mean? [*Dryly*] Nix for mine! [*Then seeing his crest-fallen look—forcing a smile*] Do you think that's a good place for a young girl like me—a coal barge?

CHRIS: [*Dully*] Yes, Ay tank. [*He hesitates—then continues more and more pleadingly*] You don't know how nice it's on barge, Anna. Tug come and ve gat towed out on voyage—yust water all round,

and sun, and fresh air, and good grub for make you strong, healthy gel. You see many tangs you don't see before. You gat moonlight at night, maybe; see steamer pass; see schooner make sail—see everytang dat's pooty. You need take rest like dat. You work too hard for young gel already. You need vacation, yes!

ANNA: [*Who has listened to him with a growing interest—with an uncertain laugh*] It sounds good to hear you tell it. I'd sure like a trip on the water, all right. It's the barge idea has me stopped. Well, I'll go down with you and have a look—and maybe I'll take a chance. Gee, I'd do anything once.

CHRIS: [*Picks up her bag again*] Ve go, eh?

ANNA: What's the rush? Wait a second. [*Forgetting the situation for a moment, she relapses into the familiar form and flashes one of her winning trade smiles at him*] Gee, I'm thirsty.

CHRIS: [*Sets down her bag immediately—hastily*] Ay'm sorry, Anna. What you tank you like for drink, eh?

ANNA: [*Promptly*] I'll take a—— [*Then suddenly reminded—confusedly*] I don't know. What'a they got here?

CHRIS: [*With a grin*] Ay don't tank dey got much fancy drink for young gel in dis place, Anna. Yinger ale—sas'prilla, maybe.

ANNA: [*Forcing a laugh herself*] Make it sas, then.

CHRIS: [*Coming up to her—with a wink*] Ay tal you, Anna, ve calabrate, yes—dis one time because ve meet after many year. [*In a half whisper, embarrassedly*] Dey gat good port vine, Anna. It's good for you, Ay tank—little bit—for give you appetite. It ain't strong, neider. One glass don't go to your head, Ay promise.

ANNA: [*With a half-hysterical laugh*] All right. I'll take port.

CHRIS: Ay go gat him.

[*He goes out to the bar. As soon as the door closes,* Anna *starts to her feet*]

ANNA: [*Picking up her bag—half-aloud—stammeringly*] Gawd, I can't stand this! I better beat it.

[*Then she lets her bag drop, stumbles over to her chair again, and covering her face with her hands, begins to sob*]

LARRY: [*Putting down his paper as* Chris *comes up—with a grin*] Well, who's the blond?

CHRIS: [*Proudly*] Dat vas Anna, Larry.

LARRY: [*In amazement*] Your daughter, Anna?

[Chris *nods.* Larry *lets a long, low whistle escape him and turns away embarrassedly*]

CHRIS: Don't you tank she vas pooty gel, Larry?

LARRY: [*Rising to the occasion*] Sure! A peach!

CHRIS: You bet you! Give me drink for take back —one port vine for Anna—she calabrate dis one time with me—and small beer for me.

LARRY: [*As he gets the drinks*] Small beer for you, eh? She's reformin' you already.

CHRIS: [*Pleased*] You bet! [*He takes the drinks. As she hears him coming,* Anna *hastily dries her eyes, tries to smile.* Chris *comes in and sets the drinks down on the table—stares at her for a second anxiously—patting her hand*] You look tired, Anna. Vell, Ay make you take good long rest now. [*Picking up his beer*] Come, you drink vine. It put new life in you. [*She lifts her glass—he grins*] Skoal, Anna! You know dat Svedish word?

ANNA: Skoal! [*Downing her port at a gulp like a drink of whisky—her lips trembling*] Skoal? Guess I know that word, all right, all right!

[THE CURTAIN FALLS]

ACT II.

SCENE: *Ten days later. The stern of the deeply laden barge,* Simeon Winthrop, *at anchor in the outer harbor of Provincetown, Mass. It is ten o'clock at night. Dense fog shrouds the barge on all sides, and she floats motionless on a calm. A lantern set up on an immense coil of thick hawser sheds a dull, filtering light on objects near it—the heavy steel bits for making fast the tow lines, etc. In the rear is the cabin, its misty windows glowing wanly with the light of a lamp inside. The chimney of the cabin stove rises a few feet above the roof. The doleful tolling of bells, on Long Point, on ships at anchor, breaks the silence at regular intervals.*

As the curtain rises, Anna *is discovered standing near the coil of rope on which the lantern is placed. She looks healthy, transformed, the natural color has come back to her face. She has on a black oilskin coat, but wears no hat. She is staring out into the fog astern with an expression of awed wonder. The cabin door is pushed open and* Chris *appears. He is dressed in yellow oilskins—coat, pants, sou'-wester—and wears high seaboots.*

CHRIS: [*The glare from the cabin still in his eyes, peers blinkingly astern*] Anna! [*Receiving no reply, he calls again, this time with apparent apprehension*] Anna!

ANNA: [*With a start—making a gesture with her hand as if to impose silence—in a hushed whisper*] Yes, here I am. What d'you want?

CHRIS: [*Walks over to her—solicitously*] Don't you come turn in, Anna? It's late—after four bells. It ain't good for you stay out here in fog, Ay tank.

ANNA: Why not? [*With a trace of strange exultation*] I love this fog! Honest! It's so—— [*She hesitates, groping for a word*] funny and still. I feel as if I was—out of things altogether.

CHRIS: [*Spitting disgustedly*] Fog's vorst one of her dirty tricks, py yingo!

ANNA: [*With a short laugh*] Beefing about the sea again? I'm getting so's I love it, the little I've seen.

CHRIS: [*Glancing at her moodily*] Dat's foolish talk, Anna. You see her more, you don't talk dat vay. [*Then seeing her irritation, he hastily adopts a more cheerful tone*] But Ay'm glad you like it on barge. Ay'm glad it makes you feel good again. [*With a placating grin*] You like live like dis alone with ole fa'der, eh?

ANNA: Sure I do. Everything's been so different from anything I ever come across before. And now —this fog—Gee, I wouldn't have missed it for nothing. I never thought living on ships was so different from land. Gee, I'd yust love to work on it, honest I would, if I was a man. I don't wonder you always been a sailor.

CHRIS: [*Vehemently*] Ay ain't sailor, Anna. And dis ain't real sea. You only see nice part. [*Then as she doesn't answer, he continues hopefully*] Vell, fog lift in morning, Ay tank.

ANNA: [*The exultation again in her voice*] I love it! I don't give a rap if it never lifts! [Chris *fidgets from one foot to the other worriedly.* Anna *continues slowly, after a pause*] It makes me feel clean—out here—'s if I'd taken a bath.

CHRIS: [*After a pause*] You better go in cabin read book. Dat put you to sleep.

ANNA: I don't want to sleep. I want to stay out here—and think about things.

CHRIS: [*Walks away from her toward the cabin—then comes back*] You act funny tonight, Anna.

ANNA: [*Her voice rising angrily*] Say, what're you trying to do—make things rotten? You been kind as kind can be to me and I certainly appreciate it—only don't spoil it all now. [*Then, seeing the hurt expression on her father's face, she forces a smile*] Let's talk of something else. Come. Sit down here. [*She points to the coil of rope*]

CHRIS: [*Sits down beside her with a sigh*] It's gatting pooty late in night, Anna. Must be near five bells.

ANNA: [*Interestedly*] Five bells? What time is that?

CHRIS: Half past ten.

ANNA: Funny I don't know nothing about sea talk —but those cousins was always talking crops and that stuff. Gee, wasn't I sick of it—and of them!

CHRIS: You don't like live on farm, Anna?

ANNA: I've told you a hundred times I hated it. [*Decidedly*] I'd rather have one drop of ocean than all the farms in the world! Honest! And you wouldn't like a farm, neither. Here's where you belong. [*She makes a sweeping gesture seaward*] But not on a coal barge. You belong on a real ship, sailing all over the world.

CHRIS: [*Moodily*] Ay've done dat many year, Anna, when Ay was damn fool.

ANNA: [*Disgustedly*] Oh, rats! [*After a pause she speaks musingly*] Was the men in our family always sailors—as far back as you know about?

CHRIS: [*Shortly*] Yes. Damn fools! All men in our village on coast, Sveden, go to sea. Ain't nutting else for dem to do. My fa'der die on board ship in Indian Ocean. He's buried at sea. Ay don't never know him only little bit. Den my tree bro'der, older'n me, dey go on ships. Den Ay go, too. Den my mo'der she's left all 'lone. She die pooty quick after dat all 'lone. Ve vas all avay on voyage when she die. [*He pauses sadly*] Two my bro'der dey gat lost on fishing boat same like your bro'ders vas drowned. My oder bro'der, he save money, give up sea, den he die home in bed. He's only one dat ole davil don't kill. [*Defiantly*] But me, Ay bet you Ay die ashore in bed, too!

ANNA: Were all of 'em yust plain sailors?

CHRIS: Able body seaman, most of dem. [*With a certain pride*] Dey vas all smart seaman, too—A one. [*Then after hesitating a moment—shyly*] Ay vas bo'sun.

ANNA: Bo'sun?

CHRIS: Dat's kind of officer.

ANNA: Gee, that was fine. What does he do?

CHRIS: [*After a second's hesitation, plunged into gloom again by his fear of her enthusiasm*] Hard vork all time. It's rotten, Ay tal you, for go to sea. [*Determined to disgust her with sea life—volubly*] Dey're all fool fallar, dem fallar in our family. Dey all vork rotten yob on sea for nutting, don't care nutting but yust gat big pay day in pocket, gat drunk, gat robbed, ship avay again on oder voyage. Dey don't come home. Dey don't do anytang like good man do. And dat ole davil, sea, sooner, later she swallow dem up.

ANNA: [*With an excited laugh*] Good sports, I'd call 'em. [*Then hastily*] But say—listen—did all the women of the family marry sailors?

CHRIS: [*Eagerly—seeing a chance to drive home his point*] Yes—and it's bad on dem like hell vorst of all. Dey don't see deir men only once in long while. Dey set and vait all 'lone. And vhen deir boys grows up, go to sea, dey sit and vait some more. [*Vehemently*] Any gel marry sailor, she's crazy fool! Your mo'der she tal you same tang if she vas alive. [*He relapses into an attitude of somber brooding*]

ANNA: [*After a pause—dreamily*] Funny! I do feel sort of—nutty, tonight. I feel old.

CHRIS: [*Mystified*] Ole?

ANNA: Sure—like I'd been living a long, long time —out here in the fog. [*Frowning perplexedly*] I don't know how to tell you yust what I mean. It's like I'd come home after a long visit away some place. It all seems like I'd been here before lots of times— on boats—in this same fog. [*With a short laugh*] You must think I'm off my base.

CHRIS: [*Gruffly*] Anybody feel funny dat vay in fog.

ANNA: [*Persistently*] But why d'you s'pose I feel so —so—like I'd found something I'd missed and been looking for—'s if this was the right place for me to fit in? And I seem to have forgot—everything that's happened—like it didn't matter no more. And I feel clean, somehow—like you feel yust after you've took a bath. And I feel happy for once—yes, honest!—happier than I ever been anywhere before! [*As Chris makes no comment but a heavy sigh, she continues wonderingly*] It's nutty for me to feel that way, don't you think?

CHRIS: [*A grim foreboding in his voice*] Ay tank Ay'm damn fool for bring you on voyage, Anna.

ANNA: [*Impressed by his tone*] You talk—nutty tonight yourself. You act 's if you was scared something was going to happen.

CHRIS: Only God know dat, Anna.

ANNA: [*Half-mockingly*] Then it'll be Gawd's will. like the preachers say—what does happen.

CHRIS: [*Starts to his feet with fierce protest*] No! Dat ole davil, sea, she ain't God! [*In the pause of silence that comes after his defiance a hail in a man's husky, exhausted voice comes faintly out of the fog to port*] "Ahoy!" [*Chris gives a startled exclamation*]

ANNA: [*Jumping to her feet*] What's that?

CHRIS: [*Who has regained his composure—sheepishly*] Py golly, dat scare me for minute. It's only some fallar hail, Anna—loose his course in fog. Must be fisherman's power boat. His engine break down, Ay guess. [*The "ahoy" comes again through the wall of fog, sounding much nearer this time. Chris goes over to the port bulwark*] Sound from dis side. She come in from open sea. [*He holds his hands to his mouth, megaphone-fashion, and shouts back*] Ahoy, dere! Vat's trouble?

THE VOICE: [*This time sounding nearer but up forward toward the bow*] Heave a rope when we come alongside [*Then irritably*] Where are ye, ye scut?

CHRIS: Ay hear dem rowing. Dey come up by bow, Ay tank. [*Then shouting out again*] Dis vay!

THE VOICE: Right ye are!

[*There is a muffled sound of oars in oar-locks*]

ANNA: [*Half to herself—resentfully*] Why don't that guy stay where he belongs?

CHRIS: [*Hurriedly*] Ay go up bow. All hands asleep 'cepting fallar on vatch. Ay gat heave line to dat fallar. [*He picks up a coil of rope and hurries off toward the bow. Anna walks back toward the extreme stern as if she wanted to remain as much isolated as possible. She turns her back on the proceedings and stares out into the fog. The Voice is heard again shouting "Ahoy" and Chris answering "Dis vay." Then there is a pause—the murmur of excited voices —then the scuffling of feet. Chris appears from around the cabin to port. He is supporting the limp form of a man dressed in dungarees, holding one of the man's arms around his neck. The deckhand, Johnson, a young blond Swede, follows him, helping along another exhausted man similar fashion. Anna turns to look at them. Chris stops for a second— volubly*] Anna! You come help, vill you? You find vhisky in cabin. Dese fallars need drink for fix them. Dey vas near dead.

ANNA: [*Hurrying to him*] Sure—but who are they? What's the trouble?

CHRIS: Sailor fallars. Deir steamer gat wrecked. Dey been five days in open boat—four fallars—only one left able stand up. Come, Anna. [*She precedes*

*him into the cabin, holding the door open while he
and* Johnson *carry in their burdens. The door is shut,
then opened again as* Johnson *comes out. Chris'
voice shouts after him]* Go gat oder fallar, Yohnson.

JOHNSON: Yes, sir.

[*He goes. The door is closed again. Mat Burke
stumbles in around the port side of the cabin.
He moves slowly, feeling his way uncertainly,
keeping hold of the port bulwark with his right
hand to steady himself. He is stripped to the
waist, has on nothing but a pair of dirty dungaree pants. He is a powerful, broad-chested
six-footer, his face handsome in a hard, rough,
bold, defiant way. He is about thirty, in the full
power of his heavy-muscled, immense strength.
His dark eyes are bloodshot and wild from
sleeplessness. The muscles of his arms and
shoulders are lumped in knots and bunches,
the veins of his fore-arms stand out like blue
cords. He finds his way to the coil of hawser
and sits down on it facing the cabin, his back
bowed, head in his hands, in an attitude of
spent weariness]*

BURKE: [*Talking aloud to himself*] Row, ye divil!
Row! [*Then lifting his head and looking about him*]
What's this tub? Well, we're safe anyway—with the
help of God. [*He makes the sign of the cross mechanically.* Johnson *comes along the deck to port,
supporting the fourth man, who is babbling to himself incoherently.* Burke *glances at him disdainfully*]
Is it losing the small wits ye iver had, ye are? Deck-
scrubbing scut! [*They pass him and go into the cabin,
leaving the door open.* Burke *sags forward wearily*]
I'm bate out—bate out entirely.

ANNA: [*Comes out of the cabin with a tumbler
quarter-full of whisky in her hand. She gives a start
when she sees* Burke *so near her, the light from the
open door falling full on him. Then, overcoming
what is evidently a feeling of repulsion, she comes
up beside him*] Here you are. Here's a drink for you.
You need it, I guess.

BURKE: [*Lifting his head slowly—confusedly*] Is
it dreaming I am?

ANNA: [*Half smiling*] Drink it and you'll find it
ain't no dream.

BURKE: To hell with the drink—but I'll take it
just the same. [*He tosses it down*] Ahah! I'm needin'
that—and 'tis fine stuff. [*Looking up at her with
frank, grinning admiration*] But 'twasn't the booze
I meant when I said, was I dreaming. I thought you
was some mermaid out of the sea come to torment
me. [*He reaches out to feel of her arm*] Aye, rale
flesh and blood, divil a less.

ANNA: [*Coldly. Stepping back from him*] Cut that.

BURKE: But tell me, isn't this a barge I'm on—or
isn't it?

ANNA: Sure.

BURKE: And what is a fine handsome woman the
like of you doing on this scow?

ANNA: [*Coldly*] Never you mind. [*Then half
amused in spite of herself*] Say, you're a great one,
honest—starting right in kidding after what you been
through.

BURKE: [*Delighted—proudly*] Ah, it was nothing—
aisy for a rale man with guts to him, the like of me.
[*He laughs*] All in the day's work, darlin'. [*Then,
more seriously but still in a boastful tone, confidentially*] But I won't be denying 'twas a damn narrow
squeak. We'd all ought to be with Davy Jones at
the bottom of the sea, be rights. And only for me,
I'm telling you, and the great strength and guts is
in me, we'd be being scoffed by the fishes this
minute!

ANNA: [*Contemptuously*] Gee, you hate yourself,
don't you? [*Then turning away from him indifferently*] Well, you'd better come in and lie down.
You must want to sleep.

BURKE: [*Stung—rising unsteadily to his feet with
chest out and head thrown back—resentfully*] Lie
down and sleep, is it? Divil a wink I'm after having
for two days and nights and divil a bit I'm needing
now. Let you not be thinking I'm the like of them
three weak scuts come in the boat with me. I could
lick the three of them sitting down with one hand
tied behind me. They may be bate out, but I'm
not—and I've been rowing the boat with them lying
in the bottom not able to raise a hand for the last
two days we was in it. [*Furiously, as he sees this is
making no impression on her*] And I can lick all
hands on this tub, wan by wan, tired as I am!

ANNA: [*Sarcastically*] Gee, ain't you a hard guy!
[*Then, with a trace of sympathy, as she notices him
swaying from weakness*] But never mind that fight
talk. I'll take your word for all you've said. Go on
and sit down out here, anyway, if I can't get you
to come inside. [*He sits down weakly*] You're all in,
you might as well own up to it.

BURKE: [*Fiercely*] The hell I am!

ANNA: [*Coldly*] Well, be stubborn then for all I
care. And I must say I don't care for your language.
The men I know don't pull that rough stuff when
ladies are around.

BURKE: [*Getting unsteadily to his feet again—in
a rage*] Ladies! Ho-ho! Divil mend you! Let you not
be making game of me. What would ladies be doing
on this bloody hulk? [*As Anna attempts to go to the
cabin, he lurches into her path*] Aisy, now! You're
not the old Square-head's woman, I suppose you'll
be telling me next—living in his cabin with him no
less! [*Seeing the cold, hostile expression on Anna's
face, he suddenly changes his tone to one of boisterous joviality*] But I do be thinking, iver since the
first look my eyes took at you, that it's a fool you
are to be wasting yourself—a fine, handsome girl—
on a stumpy runt of a man like that old Swede.
There's too many strapping great lads on the sea
would give their heart's blood for one kiss of you!

ANNA: [*Scornfully*] Lads like you, eh?

BURKE: [*Grinning*] Ye take the words out o' my
mouth. I'm the proper lad for you, if it's meself

do be saying it. [*With a quick movement he puts his arms about her waist*] Whist, now, me daisy! Himself's in the cabin. It's wan of your kisses I'm needing to take the tiredness from me bones. Wan kiss, now! [*He presses her to him and attempts to kiss her*]

ANNA: [*Struggling fiercely*] Leggo of me, you big mutt!

[*She pushes him away with all her might. Burke, weak and tottering, is caught off his guard. He is thrown down backward and, in falling, hits his head a hard thump against the bulwark. He lies there still, knocked out for the moment. Anna stands for a second, looking down at him frightenedly. Then she kneels down beside him and raises his head to her knee, staring into his face anxiously for some sign of life*]

BURKE: [*Stirring a bit—mutteringly*] God stiffen it! [*He opens his eyes and blinks up at her with vague wonder*]

ANNA: [*Letting his head sink back on the deck, rising to her feet with a sigh of relief*] You're coming to all right, eh? Gee, I was scared for a moment I'd killed you.

BURKE: [*With difficulty rising to a sitting position —scornfully*] Killed, is it? It'd take more than a bit of a blow to crack my thick skull. [*Then looking at her with the most intense admiration*] But, glory be, it's a power of strength is in them two fine arms of yours. There's not a man in the world can say the same as you, that he seen Mat Burke lying at his feet and him dead to the world.

ANNA: [*Rather remorsefully*] Forget it. I'm sorry it happened, see? [*Burke rises and sits on bench. Then severely*] Only you had no right to be getting fresh with me. Listen, now, and don't go getting any more wrong notions. I'm on this barge because I'm making a trip with my father. The captain's my father. Now you know.

BURKE: The old square—the old Swede, I mean?

ANNA: Yes.

BURKE: [*Rising—peering at her face*] Sure I might have known it, if I wasn't a bloody fool from birth. Where else'd you get that fine yellow hair is like a golden crown on your head.

ANNA: [*With an amused laugh*] Say, nothing stops you, does it? [*Then attempting a severe tone again*] But don't you think you ought to be apologizing for what you said and done yust a minute ago, instead of trying to kid me with that mush?

BURKE: [*Indignantly*] Mush! [*Then bending forward toward her with very intense earnestness*] Indade and I will ask your pardon a thousand times —and on my knees, if ye like. I didn't mean a word of what I said or did. [*Resentful again for a second*] But divil a woman in all the ports of the world has iver made a great fool of me that way before!

ANNA: [*With amused sarcasm*] I see. You mean you're a lady-killer and they all fall for you.

BURKE: [*Offended. Passionately*] Leave off your fooling! 'Tis that is after getting my back up at you. [*Earnestly*] 'Tis no lie I'm telling you about the women. [*Ruefully*] Though it's a great jackass I am to be mistaking you, even in anger, for the like of them cows on the waterfront is the only women I've met up with since I was growed to a man. [*As Anna shrinks away from him at this, he hurries on pleadingly*] I'm a hard, rough man and I'm not fit, I'm thinking, to be kissing the shoe-soles of a fine, dacent girl the like of yourself. 'Tis only the ignorance of your kind made me see you wrong. So you'll forgive me, for the love of God, and let us be friends from this out. [*Passionately*] I'm thinking I'd rather be friends with you than have my wish for anything else in the world. [*He holds out his hand to her shyly*]

ANNA: [*Looking queerly at him, perplexed and worried, but moved and pleased in spite of herself —takes his hand uncertainly*] Sure.

BURKE: [*With boyish delight*] God bless you! [*In his excitement he squeezes her hand tight*]

ANNA: Ouch!

BURKE: [*Hastily dropping her hand—ruefully*] Your pardon, Miss. 'Tis a clumsy ape I am. [*Then simply—glancing down his arm proudly*] It's great power I have in my hand and arm, and I do be forgetting it at times.

ANNA: [*Nursing her crushed hand and glancing at his arm, not without a trace of his own admiration*] Gee, you're some strong, all right.

BURKE: [*Delighted*] It's no lie, and why shouldn't I be, with me shoveling a million tons of coal in the stokeholes of ships since I was a lad only. [*He pats the coil of hawser invitingly*] Let you sit down, now, Miss, and I'll be telling you a bit of myself, and you'll be telling me a bit of yourself, and in an hour we'll be as old friends as if we was born in the same house. [*He pulls at her sleeve shyly*] Sit down now, if you plaze.

ANNA: [*With a half laugh*] Well—— [*She sits down*] But we won't talk about me, see? You tell me about yourself and about the wreck.

BURKE: [*Flattered*] I'll tell you, surely. But can I be asking you one question, Miss, has my head in a puzzle?

ANNA: [*Guardedly*] Well—I dunno—what is it?

BURKE: What is it you do when you're not taking a trip with the Old Man? For I'm thinking a fine girl the like of you ain't living always on this tub.

ANNA: [*Uneasily*] No—of course I ain't. [*She searches his face suspiciously, afraid there may be some hidden insinuation in his words. Seeing his simple frankness, she goes on confidently*] Well, I'll tell you. I'm a governess, see? I take care of kids for people and learn them things.

BURKE: [*Impressed*] A governess, is it? You must be smart, surely.

ANNA: But let's not talk about me. Tell me about the wreck, like you promised me you would.

BURKE: [*Importantly*] 'Twas this way, Miss. Two weeks out we ran into the divil's own storm, and she sprang wan hell of a leak up for'ard. The skipper was hoping to make Boston before another blow would finish her, but ten days back we met up with another storm the like of the first, only worse. Four days we was in it with green seas raking over her from bow to stern. That was a terrible time, God help us. [*Proudly*] And if 'twasn't for me and my great strength, I'm telling you—and it's God's truth —there'd been mutiny itself in the stokehole. 'Twas me held them to it, with a kick to wan and a clout to another, and they not caring a damn for the engineers any more, but fearing a clout of my right arm more than they'd fear the sea itself. [*He glances at her anxiously, eager for her approval*]

ANNA: [*Concealing a smile—amused by this boyish boasting of his*] You did some hard work, didn't you?

BURKE: [*Promptly*] I did that! I'm a divil for sticking it out when them that's weak give up. But much good it did anyone! 'Twas a mad, fightin' scramble in the last seconds with each man for himself. I disremember how it come about, but there was the four of us in wan boat and when we was raised high on a great wave I took a look about and divil a sight there was of ship or men on top of the sea.

ANNA: [*In a subdued voice*] Then all the others was drowned?

BURKE: They was, surely.

ANNA: [*With a shudder*] What a terrible end!

BURKE: [*Turns to her*] A terrible end for the like of them swabs does live on land, maybe. But for the like of us does be roaming the seas, a good end, I'm telling you—quick and clane.

ANNA: [*Struck by the word*] Yes, clean. That's yust the word for—all of it—the way it makes me feel.

BURKE: The sea, you mean? [*Interestedly*] I'm thinking you have a bit of it in your blood, too. Your Old Man wasn't only a barge rat—begging your pardon—all his life, by the cut of him.

ANNA: No, he was bo'sun on sailing ships for years. And all the men on both sides of the family have gone to sea as far back as he remembers, he says. All the women have married sailors, too.

BURKE: [*With intense satisfaction*] Did they, now? They had spirit in them. It's only on the sea you'd find rale men with guts is fit to wed with fine, high-tempered girls [*Then he adds half-boldly*] the like of yourself.

ANNA: [*With a laugh*] There you go kiddin' again. [*Then seeing his hurt expression—quickly*] But you was going to tell me about yourself. You're Irish, of course I can tell that.

BURKE: [*Stoutly*] Yes, thank God, though I've not seen a sight of it in fifteen years or more.

ANNA: [*Thoughtfully*] Sailors never do go home hardly, do they? That's what my father was saying.

BURKE: He wasn't telling no lie. [*With sudden melancholy*] It's a hard and lonesome life, the sea is.

The only women you'd meet in the ports of the world who'd be willing to speak you a kind word isn't woman at all. You know the kind I mane, and they're a poor, wicked lot, God forgive them. They're looking to steal the money from you only.

ANNA: [*Her face averted—rising to her feet—agitatedly*] I think—I guess I'd better see what's doing inside.

BURKE: [*Afraid he has offended her—beseechingly*] Don't go, I'm saying! Is it I've given you offense with my talk of the like of them? Don't heed it at all! I'm clumsy in my wits when it comes to talking proper with a girl the like of you. And why wouldn't I be? Since the day I left home for to go to sea punching coal, this is the first time I've had a word with a rale, dacent woman. So don't turn your back on me now, and we beginning to be friends.

ANNA: [*Turning to him again—forcing a smile*] I'm not sore at you, honest.

BURKE: [*Gratefully*] God bless you!

ANNA: [*Changing the subject abruptly*] But if you honestly think the sea's such a rotten life, why don't you get out of it?

BURKE: [*Surprised*] Work on land, is it? [*She nods. He spits scornfully*] Digging spuds in the muck from dawn to dark, I suppose? [*Vehemently*] I wasn't made for it, Miss.

ANNA: [*With a laugh*] I thought you'd say that.

BURKE: [*Argumentatively*] But there's good jobs and bad jobs at sea, like there'd be on land. I'm thinking if it's in the stokehole of a proper liner I was, I'd be able to have a little house and be home to it wan week out of four. And I'm thinking that maybe then I'd have the luck to find a fine dacent girl—the like of yourself, now—would be willing to wed with me.

ANNA: [*Turning away from him with a short laugh —uneasily*] Why, sure. Why not?

BURKE: [*Edging up close to her—exultantly*] Then you think a girl the like of yourself might maybe not mind the past at all but only be seeing the good herself put in me?

ANNA: [*In the same tone*] Why, sure.

BURKE: [*Passionately*] She'd not be sorry for it, I'd take my oath! 'Tis no more drinking and roving about I'd be doing then, but giving my pay day into her hand and staying at home with her as meek as a lamb each night of the week I'd be in port.

ANNA: [*Moved in spite of herself and troubled by this half-concealed proposal—with a forced laugh*] All you got to do is find the girl.

BURKE: I have found her!

ANNA: [*Half-frightenedly—trying to laugh it off*] You have? When? I thought you was saying——

BURKE: [*Boldly and forcefully*] This night. [*Hanging his head—humbly*] If she'll be having me. [*Then raising his eyes to hers—simply*] 'Tis you I mean.

ANNA: [*Is held by his eyes for a moment—then shrinks back from him with a strange, broken laugh*] Say—are you—going crazy? Are you trying to kid me? Proposing—to me!—for Gawd's sake!—on such short acquaintance?

[Chris *comes out of the cabin and stands staring blinkingly astern. When he makes out* Anna *in such intimate proximity to this strange sailor, an angry expression comes over his face*]

BURKE: [*Following her—with fierce, pleading insistence*] I'm telling you there's the will of God in it that brought me safe through the storm and fog to the wan spot in the world where you was! Think of that now, and isn't it queer——

CHRIS: Anna! [*He comes toward them, raging, his fists clenched*] Anna, you gat in cabin, you hear!

ANNA: [*All her emotions immediately transformed into resentment at his bullying tone*] Who d'you think you're talking to—a slave?

CHRIS: [*Hurt—his voice breaking—pleading*] You need gat rest, Anna. You gat sleep. [*She does not move. He turns on* Burke *furiously*] What you doing here, you sailor fallar? You ain't sick like oders. You gat in fo'c's'tle. Dey give you bunk. [*Threateningly*] You hurry, Ay tal you!

ANNA: [*Impulsively*] But he is sick. Look at him. He can hardly stand up.

BURKE: [*Straightening and throwing out his chest —with a bold laugh*] Is it giving me orders ye are, me bucko? Let you look out, then! With wan hand, weak as I am, I can break ye in two and fling the pieces over the side—and your crew after you. [*Stopping abruptly*] I was forgetting. You're her Old Man and I'd not raise a fist to you for the world.

[*His knees sag, he wavers and seems about to fall.* Anna *utters an exclamation of alarm and hurries to his side*]

ANNA: [*Taking one of his arms over her shoulder*] Come on in the cabin. You can have my bed if there ain't no other place.

BURKE: [*With jubilant happiness—as they proceed toward the cabin*] Glory be to God, is it holding my arm about your neck you are! Anna! Anna! Sure it's a sweet name is suited to you.

ANNA: [*Guiding him carefully*] Sssh! Sssh!

BURKE: Whisht, is it? Indade, and I'll not. I'll be roaring it out like a fog horn over the sea! You're the girl of the world and we'll be marrying soon and I don't care who knows it!

ANNA: [*As she guides him through the cabin door*] Ssshh! Never mind that talk. You go to sleep.

[*They go out of sight in the cabin.* Chris, *who has been listening to* Burke's *last words with open-mouthed amazement, stands looking after them desperately*]

CHRIS: [*Turns suddenly and shakes his fist out at the sea—with bitter hatred*] Dat's your dirty trick, damn ole davil, you! [*Then in a frenzy of rage*] But, py God, you don't do dat! Not while Ay'm living! No, py God, you don't!

[THE CURTAIN FALLS]

ACT III.

SCENE: *The interior of the cabin on the barge* Simeon Winthrop [*at dock in Boston*]—*a narrow, low-ceilinged compartment the walls of which are painted a light brown with white trimmings. In the rear on the left, a door leading to the sleeping quarters. In the far left corner, a large locker-closet, painted white, on the door of which a mirror hangs on a nail. In the rear wall, two small square windows and a door opening out on the deck toward the stern. In the right wall, two more windows looking out on the port deck. White curtains, clean and stiff, are at the windows. A table with two cane-bottomed chairs stands in the center of the cabin. A dilapidated, wicker rocker, painted brown, is also by the table.*

It is afternoon of a sunny day about a week later. From the harbor and docks outside, muffled by the closed door and windows, comes the sound of steamers' whistles and the puffing snort of the donkey engines of some ship unloading nearby.

As the curtain rises, Chris *and* Anna *are discovered.* Anna *is seated in the rocking-chair by the table, with a newspaper in her hands. She is not reading but staring straight in front of her. She looks unhappy, troubled, frowningly concentrated on her thoughts.* Chris *wanders about the room, casting quick, uneasy side glances at her face, then stopping to peer absent-mindedly out of the window. His attitude betrays an overwhelming, gloomy anxiety which has him on tenterhooks. He pretends to be engaged in setting things ship-shape, but this occupation is confined to picking up some object, staring at it stupidly for a second, then aimlessly putting it down again. He clears his throat and starts to sing to himself in a low, doleful voice:* "My Yosephine, come board de ship. Long time Ay vait for you."

ANNA: [*Turning on him, sarcastically*] I'm glad someone's feeling good. [*Wearily*] Gee, I sure wish we was out of this dump and back in New York.

CHRIS: [*With a sigh*] Ay'm glad vhen ve sail again, too. [*Then, as she makes no comment, he goes on with a ponderous attempt at sarcasm*] Ay don't see vhy you don't like Boston, dough. You have good time here, Ay tank. You go ashore all time, every day and night veek ve've been here. You go to movies, see show, gat all kinds fun—— [*His eyes hard with hatred*] All with that damn Irish fallar!

ANNA: [*With weary scorn*] Oh, for heaven's sake, are you off on that again? Where's the harm in his taking me around? D'you want me to sit all day and night in this cabin with you—and knit? Ain't I got a right to have as good a time as I can?

CHRIS: It ain't right kind of fun—not with that fallar, no.

ANNA: I been back on board every night by eleven, ain't I? [*Then struck by some thought—looks at him with keen suspicion—with rising anger*] Say, look here, what d'you mean by what you yust said?

CHRIS: [*Hastily*] Nutting but what Ay say, Anna.

ANNA: You said "ain't right" and you said it funny. Say, listen here, you ain't trying to insinuate that there's something wrong between us, are you?

CHRIS: [*Horrified*] No, Anna! No, Ay svear to God, Ay never tank dat!

ANNA: [*Mollified by his very evident sincerity—sitting down again*] Well, don't you never think it neither if you want me ever to speak to you again. [*Angrily again*] If I ever dreamt you thought that, I'd get the hell out of this barge so quick you couldn't see me for dust.

CHRIS: [*Soothingly*] Ay wouldn't never dream—— [*Then after a second's pause, reprovingly*] You vas gatting learn to swear. Dat ain't nice for young gel, you tank?

ANNA: [*With a faint trace of a smile*] Excuse me. You ain't used to such language, I know. [*Mockingly*] That's what your taking me to sea has done for me.

CHRIS: [*Indignantly*] No, it ain't me. It's dat damn sailor fallar learn you bad tangs.

ANNA: He ain't a sailor. He's a stoker.

CHRIS: [*Forcibly*] Dat vas million times vorse, Ay tal you! Dem fallars dat vork below shoveling coal vas de dirtiest, rough gang of no-good fallars in vorld!

ANNA: I'd hate to hear you say that to Mat.

CHRIS: Oh, Ay tal him same tang. You don't gat it in head Ay'm scared of him yust 'cause he vas stronger'n Ay vas. [*Menacingly*] You don't gat for fight with fists with dem fallars. Dere's oder vay for fix him.

ANNA: [*Glancing at him with sudden alarm*] What d'you mean?

CHRIS: [*Sullenly*] Nutting.

ANNA: You'd better not. I wouldn't start no trouble with him if I was you. He might forget some time that you was old and my father—and then you'd be out of luck.

CHRIS: [*With smoldering hatred*] Vell, yust let him! Ay'm ole bird maybe, but Ay bet Ay show him trick or two.

ANNA: [*Suddenly changing her tone—persuasively*] Aw come on, be good. What's eating you, anyway? Don't you want no one to be nice to me except yourself?

CHRIS: [*Placated—coming to her—eagerly*] Yes, Ay do, Anna—only not fallar on sea. Ay like for you marry steady fallar got good yob on land. You have little home in country all your own——

ANNA: [*Rising to her feet—brusquely*] Oh, cut it out! [*Scornfully*] Little home in the country! I wish you could have seen the little home in the country where you had me in jail till I was sixteen! [*With rising irritation*] Some day you're going to get me

so mad with that talk, I'm going to turn loose on you and tell you—a lot of things that'll open your eyes.

CHRIS: [*Alarmed*] Ay don't vant——

ANNA: I know you don't; but you keep on talking yust the same.

CHRIS: Ay don't talk no more den, Anna.

ANNA: Then promise me you'll cut out saying nasty things about Mat Burke every chance you get.

CHRIS: [*Evasive and suspicious*] Vhy? You like dat fallar—very much, Anna?

ANNA: Yes, I certainly do! He's a regular man, no matter what faults he's got. One of his fingers is worth all the hundreds of men I met out there—inland.

CHRIS: [*His face darkening*] Maybe you tank you love him, den?

ANNA: [*Defiantly*] What of it if I do?

CHRIS: [*Scowling and forcing out the words*] Maybe—you tank you—marry him?

ANNA: [*Shaking her head*] No! [*Chris' face lights up with relief. Anna continues slowly, a trace of sadness in her voice*] I'd met him four years ago—or even two years ago—I'd have jumped at the chance, I tell you that straight. And I would now—only he's such a simple guy—a big kid—and I ain't got the heart to fool him. [*She breaks off suddenly*] But don't never say again he ain't good enough for me. It's me ain't good enough for him.

CHRIS: [*Snorts scornfully*] Py yiminy, you go crazy, Ay tank!

ANNA: [*With a mournful laugh*] Well, I been thinking I was myself the last few days. [*She goes and takes a shawl from the hook near the door and throws it over her shoulders*] Guess I'll take a walk down to the end of the dock for a minute and see what's doing. I love to watch the ships passing. Mat'll be along before long, I guess. Tell him where I am, will you?

CHRIS: [*Despondently*] All right, Ay tal him.

[*Anna goes out the doorway on rear. Chris follows her out and stands on the deck outside for a moment looking after her. Then he comes back inside and shuts the door. He stands looking out of the window—mutters—"Dirty ole davil, you." Then he goes to the table, sets the cloth straight mechanically, picks up the newspaper Anna has let fall to the floor and sits down in the rocking-chair. He stares at the paper for a while, then puts it on table, holds his head in his hands and sighs drearily. The noise of a man's heavy footsteps comes from the deck outside and there is a loud knock on the door. Chris starts, makes a move as if to get up and go to the door, then thinks better of it and sits still. The knock is repeated—then as no answer comes, the door is flung open and Mat Burke appears. Chris scowls at the intruder and his hand instinctively goes back to the sheath knife on his hip. Burke*]

*is dressed up—wears a cheap blue suit, a
striped cotton shirt with a black tie, and black
shoes newly shined. His face is beaming with
good humor]*

BURKE: [*As he sees* Chris—*in a jovial tone of
mockery*] Well, God bless who's here! [*He bends
down and squeezes his huge form through the narrow doorway*] And how is the world treating you
this afternoon, Anna's father?

CHRIS: [*Sullenly*] Pooty goot—if it ain't for some
fallars.

BURKE: [*With a grin*] Meaning me, do you? [*He
laughs*] Well, if you ain't the funny old crank of a
man! [*Then soberly*] Where's herself? [Chris *sits
dumb, scowling, his eyes averted.* Burke *is irritated
by this silence*] Where's Anna, I'm asking you?

CHRIS: [*Hesitating—then grouchily*] She go down
end of dock.

BURKE: I'll be going down to her, then. But first
I'm thinking I'll take this chance when we're alone
to have a word with you. [*He sits down opposite*
Chris *at the table and leans over toward him*] And
that word is soon said. I'm marrying your Anna
before this day is out, and you might as well make
up your mind to it whether you like it or no.

CHRIS: [*Glaring at him with hatred and forcing a
scornful laugh*] Ho-ho! Dat's easy for say!

BURKE: You mean I won't? [*Scornfully*] Is it the
like of yourself will stop me, are you thinking?

CHRIS: Yes, Ay stop it, if it come to vorst.

BURKE: [*With a scornful pity*] God help you!

CHRIS: But ain't no need for me do dat. Anna——

BURKE: [*Smiling confidently*] Is it Anna you think
will prevent me?

CHRIS: Yes.

BURKE: And I'm telling you she'll not. She knows
I'm loving her, and she loves me the same, and I
know it.

CHRIS: Ho-ho! She only have fun. She make big
fool of you, dat's all!

BURKE: [*Unshaken—pleasantly*] That's a lie in
your throat, divil mend you!

CHRIS: No, it ain't lie. She tal me yust before she
go out she never marry fallar like you.

BURKE: I'll not believe it. 'Tis a great old liar you
are, and a divil to be making a power of trouble if
you had your way. But 'tis not trouble I'm looking
for, and me sitting down here. [*Earnestly*] Let us
be talking it out now as man to man. You're her
father, and wouldn't it be a shame for us to be at
each other's throats like a pair of dogs, and I married with Anna. So out with the truth, man alive.
What is it you're holding against me at all?

CHRIS: [*A bit placated, in spite of himself, by*
Burke's *evident sincerity—but puzzled and sus-
picious*] Vell—Ay don't vant for Anna gat married.
Listen, you fallar. Ay'm a ole man. Ay don't see
Anna for fifteen year. She vas all Ay gat in vorld.
And now ven she come on first trip—you tank Ay
vant her leave me 'lone again?

BURKE: [*Heartily*] Let you not be thinking I have
no heart at all for the way you'd be feeling.

CHRIS: [*Astonished and encouraged—trying to
plead persuasively*] Den you do right tang, eh? You
ship avay again, leave Anna alone. [*Cajolingly*] Big
fallar like you dat's on sea, he don't need vife. He
gat new gel in every port, you know dat.

BURKE: [*Angrily for a second*] God stiffen you!
[*Then controlling himself—calmly*] I'll not be giving
you the lie on that. But divil take you, there's a time
comes to every man, on sea or land, that isn't a born
fool, when he's sick of the lot of them cows, and
wearing his heart out to meet up with a fine dacent
girl, and have a home to call his own and be rearing
up children in it. 'Tis small use you're asking me to
leave Anna. She's the wan woman of the world for
me, and I can't live without her now, I'm thinking.

CHRIS: You forgat all about her in one veek out
of port, Ay bet you!

BURKE: You don't know the like I am. Death
itself wouldn't make me forget her. So let you not
be making talk to me about leaving her. I'll not,
and be damned to you! It won't be so bad for you
as you'd make out at all. She'll be living here in the
States, and her married to me. And you'd be seeing
her often so—a sight more often than ever you
saw her the fifteen years she was growing up in the
West. It's quare you'd be the one to be making
great trouble about her leaving you when you never
laid eyes on her once in all them years.

CHRIS: [*Guiltily*] Ay t'ought it vas better Anna
stay away, grow up inland where she don't ever
know ole davil, sea.

BURKE: [*Scornfully*] Is it blaming the sea for your
troubles ye are again, God help you? Well, Anna
knows it now. 'Twas in her blood, anyway.

CHRIS: And Ay don't vant she ever know no-
good fallar on sea——

BURKE: She knows one now.

CHRIS: [*Banging the table with his fist—furiously*]
Dat's yust it! Dat's yust what you are—no-good,
sailor fallar! You tank Ay lat her life be made sorry
by you like her mo'der's vas by me! No, Ay svear!
She don't marry you if Ay gat kill you first!

BURKE: [*Looks at him a moment, in astonishment—then laughing uproariously*] Ho-ho! Glory
be to God, it's bold talk you have for a stumpy
runt of a man!

CHRIS: [*Threateningly*] Vell—you see!

BURKE: [*With grinning defiance*] I'll see, surely!
I'll see myself and Anna married this day, I'm tell-
you. [*Then with contemptuous exasperation*] It's
quare fool's blather you have about the sea done
this and the sea done that. You'd ought to be
'shamed to be saying the like, and you an old sailor
yourself. I'm after hearing a lot of it from you and
a lot more that Anna's told me you do be saying
to her, and I'm thinking it's a poor weak thing you
are, and not a man at all!

CHRIS: [*Darkly*] You see if Ay'm man—maybe quicker'n you tank.

BURKE: [*Contemptuously*] Yerra, don't be boasting. I'm thinking 'tis out of your wits you've got with fright of the sea. You'd be wishing Anna married to a farmer, she told me. That'd be a swate match, surely! Would you have a fine girl the like of Anna lying down at nights with a muddy scut stinking of pigs and dung? Or would you have her tied for life to the like of them skinny, shriveled swabs does be working in cities?

CHRIS: Dat's lie, you fool!

BURKE: 'Tis not. 'Tis your own mad notions I'm after telling. But you know the truth in your heart, if great fear of the sea has made you a liar and coward itself. [*Pounding the table*] The sea's the only life for a man with guts in him isn't afraid of his own shadow! 'Tis only on the sea he's free, and him roving the face of the world, seeing all things, and not giving a damn for saving up money, or stealing from his friends, or any of the black tricks that a landlubber'd waste his life on. 'Twas yourself knew it once, and you a bo'sun for years.

CHRIS: [*Sputtering with rage*] You vas crazy fool, Ay tal you!

BURKE: You've swallowed the anchor. The sea give you a clout once, knocked you down, and you're not man enough to get up for another, but lie there for the rest of your life howling bloody murder. [*Proudly*] Isn't it myself the sea has nearly drowned, and me battered and bate till I was that close to hell I could hear the flames roaring, and never a groan out of me till the sea gave up and it seeing the great strength and guts of a man was in me?

CHRIS: [*Scornfully*] Yes, you vas hell of fallar, hear you tal it!

BURKE: [*Angrily*] You'll be calling me a liar once too often, me old bucko! Wasn't the whole story of it and my picture itself in the newspapers of Boston a week back? [*Looking* Chris *up and down belittlingly*] Sure I'd like to see you in the best of your youth do the like of what I done in the storm and after. 'Tis a mad lunatic, screeching with fear, you'd be this minute!

CHRIS: Ho-ho! You vas young fool! In ole years when Ay vas on windyammer, Ay vas through hundred storms vorse'n dat! Ships vas ships den—and men dat sail on dem vas real men. And now what you gat on steamers? You gat fallars on deck don't know ship from mudscow. [*With a meaning glance at* Burke] And below deck you gat fallars yust know how for shovel coal—might yust as vell vork on coal vagon ashore!

BURKE: [*Stung—angrily*] Is it casting insults at the men in the stokehole ye are, ye old ape? God stiffen you! Wan of them is worth any ten stockfish-swilling Square-heads ever shipped on a windbag!

CHRIS: [*His face working with rage, his hand going back to the sheath-knife on his hip*] Irish svine, you!

BURKE: [*Tauntingly*] Don't ye like the Irish, ye old baboon? 'Tis that you're needing in your family, I'm telling you—an Irishman and a man of the stokehole—to put guts in it so that you'll not be having grandchildren would be fearful cowards and jackasses the like of yourself!

CHRIS: [*Half rising from his chair—in a voice choked with rage*] You look out!

BURKE: [*Watching him intently—a mocking smile on his lips*] And it's that you'll be having, no matter what you'll do to prevent; for Anna and me'll be married this day, and no old fool the like of you will stop us when I've made up my mind.

CHRIS: [*With a hoarse cry*] You don't!

[*He throws himself at* Burke, *knife in hand, knocking his chair over backwards.* Burke *springs to his feet quickly in time to meet the attack. He laughs with the pure love of battle. The old Swede is like a child in his hands.* Burke *does not strike or mistreat him in any way, but simply twists his right hand behind his back and forces the knife from his fingers. He throws the knife into a far corner of the room—tauntingly*]

BURKE: Old men is getting childish shouldn't play with knives. [*Holding the struggling* Chris *at arm's length—with a sudden rush of anger, drawing back his fist*] I've half a mind to hit you a great clout will put sense in your square head. Kape off me now, I'm warning you!

[*He gives* Chris *a push with the flat of his hand which sends the old Swede staggering back against the cabin wall, where he remains standing, panting heavily, his eyes fixed on* Burke *with hatred, as if he were only collecting his strength to rush at him again*]

BURKE: [*Warningly*] Now don't be coming at me again, I'm saying, or I'll flatten you on the floor with a blow, if 'tis Anna's father you are itself! I've no patience left for you. [*Then with an amused laugh*] Well, 'tis a bold old man you are just the same, and I'd never think it was in you to come tackling me alone.

[*A shadow crosses the cabin windows. Both men start.* Anna *appears in the doorway*]

ANNA: [*With pleased surprise as she sees* Burke] Hello, Mat. Are you here already? I was down—— [*She stops, looking from one to the other, sensing immediately that something has happened*] What's up? [*Then noticing the overturned chair—in alarm*] How'd that chair get knocked over? [*Turning on* Burke *reproachfully*] You ain't been fighting with him, Mat—after you promised?

BURKE: [*His old self again*] I've not laid a hand on him, Anna. [*He goes and picks up the chair, then turning on the still questioning* Anna—*with a reassuring smile*] Let you not be worried at all. 'Twas only a bit of an argument we was having to pass the time till you'd come.

ANNA: It must have been some argument when you got to throwing chairs. [*She turns on* Chris] Why don't you say something? What was it about?

CHRIS: [*Relaxing at last—avoiding her eyes—sheepishly*] Ve vas talking about ships and fallars on sea.

ANNA: [*With a relieved smile*] Oh—the old stuff, eh?

BURKE: [*Suddenly seeming to come to a bold decision—with a defiant grin at* Chris] He's not after telling you the whole of it. We was arguing about you mostly.

ANNA: [*With a frown*] About me?

BURKE: And we'll be finishing it out right here and now in your presence if you're willing.

[*He sits down at the left of table*]

ANNA: [*Uncertainly—looking from him to her father*] Sure. Tell me what it's all about.

CHRIS: [*Advancing toward the table—protesting to* Burke] No! You don't do dat, you! You tal him you don't vant for hear him talk, Anna.

ANNA: But I do. I want this cleared up.

CHRIS: [*Miserably afraid now*] Vell, not now, anyvay. You vas going ashore, yes? You ain't got time——

ANNA: [*Firmly*] Yes, right here and now. [*She turns to* Burke] You tell me, Mat, since he don't want to.

BURKE: [*Draws a deep breath—then plunges in boldly*] The whole of it's in a few words only. So's he'd make no mistake, and him hating the sight of me, I told him in his teeth I loved you. [*Passionately*] And that's God truth, Anna, and well you know it!

CHRIS: [*Scornfully—forcing a laugh*] Ho-ho! He tal same tang to gel every port he go!

ANNA: [*Shrinking from her father with repulsion—resentfully*] Shut up, can't you? [*Then to* Burke—*feelingly*] I know it's true, Mat. I don't mind what he says.

BURKE: [*Humbly grateful*] God bless you!

ANNA: And then what?

BURKE: And then—— [*Hesitatingly*] And then I said—— [*He looks at her pleadingly*] I said I was sure—I told him I thought you have a bit of love for me, too. [*Passionately*] Say you do, Anna! Let you not destroy me entirely, for the love of God!

[*He grasps both her hands in his two*]

ANNA: [*Deeply moved and troubled—forcing a trembling laugh*] So you told him that, Mat? No wonder he was mad. [*Forcing out the words*] Well, maybe it's true, Mat. Maybe I do. I been thinking and thinking—I didn't want to, Mat, I'll own up to that—I tried to cut it out—but—— [*She laughs helplessly*] I guess I can't help it anyhow. So I guess I do, Mat. [*Then with a sudden joyous defiance*] Sure I do! What's the use of kidding myself different? Sure I love you, Mat!

CHRIS: [*With a cry of pain*] Anna!

[*He sits crushed*]

BURKE: [*With a great depth of sincerity in his humble gratitude*] God be praised!

ANNA: [*Assertively*] And I ain't never loved a man in my life before, you can always believe that —no matter what happens.

BURKE: [*Goes over to her and puts his arms around her*] Sure I do be believing ivery word you iver said or iver will say. And 'tis you and me will be having a grand, beautiful life together to the end of our days!

[*He tries to kiss her. At first she turns away her head—then, overcome by a fierce impulse of passionate love, she takes his head in both her hands and holds his face close to hers, staring into his eyes. Then she kisses him full on the lips*]

ANNA: [*Pushing him away from her—forcing a broken laugh*] Good-by.

[*She walks to the doorway in rear—stands with her back toward them, looking out. Her shoulders quiver once or twice as if she were fighting back her sobs*]

BURKE: [*Too in the seventh heaven of bliss to get any correct interpretation of her word—with a laugh*] Good-by, is it? The divil you say! I'll be coming back at you in a second for more of the same! [*To* Chris, *who has quickened to instant attention at his daughter's good-by, and has looked back at her with a stirring of foolish hope in his eyes*] Now, me old bucko, what'll you be saying? You heard the words from her own lips. Confess I've bate you. Own up like a man when you're bate fair and square. And here's my hand to you—— [*Holds out his hand*] And let you take it and we'll shake and forget what's over and done, and be friends from this out.

CHRIS: [*With implacable hatred*] Ay don't shake hands with you fallar—not while Ay live!

BURKE: [*Offended*] The back of my hand to you then, if that suits you better. [*Growling*] 'Tis a rotten bad loser you are, divil mend you!

CHRIS: Ay don't lose. [*Trying to be scornful and self-convincing*] Anna say she like you little bit but you don't hear her say she marry you, Ay bet.

[*At the sound of her name* Anna *has turned round to them. Her face is composed and calm again, but it is the dead calm of despair*]

BURKE: [*Scornfully*] No, and I wasn't hearing her say the sun is shining either.

CHRIS: [*Doggedly*] Dat's all right. She don't say it, yust same.

ANNA: [*Quietly—coming forward to them*] No, I didn't say it, Mat.

CHRIS: [*Eagerly*] Dere! You hear!

BURKE: [*Misunderstanding her—with a grin*] You're waiting till you do be asked, you mane? Well, I'm asking you now. And we'll be married this day, with the help of God!

ANNA: [*Gently*] You heard what I said, Mat—after I kissed you?

BURKE: [*Alarmed by something in her manner*] No—I disremember.

ANNA: I said good-by. [*Her voice trembling*] That kiss was for good-by, Mat.

BURKE: [*Terrified*] What d'you mane?

ANNA: I can't marry you, Mat—and we've said good-by. That's all.

CHRIS: [*Unable to hold back his exultation*] Ay know it! Ay know dat vas so!

BURKE: [*Jumping to his feet—unable to believe his ears*] Anna! Is it making game of me you'd be? 'Tis a quare time to joke with me, and don't be doing it, for the love of God.

ANNA: [*Looking him in the eyes—steadily*] D'you think I'd kid you? No, I'm not joking, Mat. I mean what I said.

BURKE: Ye don't! Ye can't! 'Tis mad you are, I'm telling you!

ANNA: [*Fixedly*] No, I'm not.

BURKE: [*Desperately*] But what's come over you so sudden? You was saying you loved me——

ANNA: I'll say that as often as you want me to. It's true.

BURKE: [*Bewilderedly*] Then why—what, in the divil's name—— Oh, God help me, I can't make head or tail to it at all!

ANNA: Because it's the best way out I can figure, Mat. [*Her voice catching*] I been thinking it over and thinking it over day and night all week. Don't think it ain't hard on me, too, Mat.

BURKE: For the love of God, tell me then, what is it that's preventing you wedding me when the two of us has love? [*Suddenly getting an idea and pointing at* Chris—*exasperatedly*] Is it giving heed to the like of that old fool ye are, and him hating me and filling your ears full of bloody lies against me?

CHRIS: [*Getting to his feet—raging triumphantly before* Anna *has a chance to get in a word*] Yes, Anna believe me, not you! She know her old fa'der don't lie like you.

ANNA: [*Turning on her father angrily*] You sit down, d'you hear? Where do you come in butting in and making things worse? You're like a devil, you are! [*Harshly*] Good Lord, and I was beginning to like you, beginning to forget all I've got held up against you!

CHRIS: [*Crushed feebly*] You ain't got nutting for hold against me, Anna.

ANNA: Ain't I yust! Well, lemme tell you—— [*She glances at* Burke *and stops abruptly*] Say, Mat, I'm s'prised at you. You didn't think anything he'd said——

BURKE: [*Glumly*] Sure, what else would it be?

ANNA: Think I've ever paid any attention to all his crazy bull? Gee, you must take me for a five-year-old kid.

BURKE: [*Puzzled and beginning to be irritated at her too*] I don't know how to take you, with your saying this one minute and that the next.

ANNA: Well, he has nothing to do with it.

BURKE: Then what is it has? Tell me, and don't keep me waiting and sweating blood.

ANNA: [*Resolutely*] I can't tell you—and I won't. I got a good reason—and that's all you need to know. I can't marry you, that's all there is to it. [*Distractedly*] So, for Gawd's sake, let's talk of something else.

BURKE: I'll not! [*Then fearfully*] Is it married to someone else you are—in the West maybe?

ANNA: [*Vehemently*] I should say not.

BURKE: [*Regaining his courage*] To the divil with all other reasons then. They don't matter with me at all. [*He gets to his feet confidently, assuming a masterful tone*] I'm thinking you're the like of them women can't make up their mind till they're drove to it. Well, then, I'll make up your mind for you bloody quick. [*He takes her by the arms, grinning to soften his serious bullying*] We've had enough of talk! Let you be going into your room now and be dressing in your best and we'll be going ashore.

CHRIS: [*Aroused—angrily*] No, py God, she don't do that!

[*Takes hold of her arm*]

ANNA: [*Who has listened to* Burke *in astonishment. She draws away from him, instinctively repelled by his tone, but not exactly sure if he is serious or not—a trace of resentment in her voice*] Say, where do you get that stuff?

BURKE: [*Imperiously*] Never mind, now! Let you go get dressed, I'm saying. [*Then turning to* Chris] We'll be seeing who'll win in the end—me or you.

CHRIS: [*To* Anna—*also in an authoritative tone*] You stay right here, Anna, you hear!

[Anna *stands looking from one to the other of them as if she thought they had both gone crazy. Then the expression of her face freezes into the hardened sneer of her experience*]

BURKE: [*Violently*] She'll not! She'll do what I say! You've had your hold on her long enough. It's my turn now.

ANNA: [*With a hard laugh*] Your turn? Say, what am I, anyway?

BURKE: 'Tis not what you are, 'tis what you're going to be this day—and that's wedded to me before night comes. Hurry up now with your dressing.

CHRIS: [*Commandingly*] You don't do one tang he say, Anna!

[Anna *laughs mockingly*]

BURKE: She will, so!

CHRIS: Ay tal you she don't! Ay'm her fa'der.

BURKE: She will in spite of you. She's taking my orders from this out, not yours.

ANNA: [*Laughing again*] Orders is good!

BURKE: [*Turning to her impatiently*] Hurry up now, and shake a leg. We've no time to be wasting.

[*Irritated as she doesn't move*] Do you hear what I'm telling you?

CHRIS: You stay dere, Anna!

ANNA: [*At the end of her patience—blazing out at them passionately*] You can go to hell, both of you! [*There is something in her tone that makes them forget their quarrel and turn to her in a stunned amazement. Anna laughs wildly*] You're just like all the rest of them—you two! Gawd, you'd think I was a piece of furniture! I'll show you! Sit down now! [*As they hesitate—furiously*] Sit down and let me talk for a minute. You're all wrong, see? Listen to me! I'm going to tell you something—and then I'm going to beat it. [*To Burke—with a harsh laugh*] I'm going to tell you a funny story, so pay attention. [*Pointing to* Chris] I've been meaning to turn it loose on him every time he'd get my goat with his bull about keeping me safe inland. I wasn't going to tell you, but you've forced me into it. What's the dif? It's all wrong anyway, and you might as well get cured that way as any other. [*With hard mocking*] Only don't forget what you said a minute ago about it not mattering to you what other reason I got so long as I wasn't married to no one else.

BURKE: [*Manfully*] That's my word, and I'll stick to it!

ANNA: [*Laughing bitterly*] What a chance! You make me laugh, honest! Want to bet you will? Wait 'n' see! [*She stands at the table rear, looking from one to the other of the two men with her hard, mocking smile. Then she begins, fighting to control her emotion and speak calmly*] First thing is, I want to tell you two guys something. You was going on 's if one of you had got to own me. But nobody owns me, see?—'cepting myself. I'll do what I please and no man, I don't give a hoot who he is, can tell me what to do! I ain't asking either of you for a living. I can make it myself—one way or other. I'm my own boss. So put that in your pipe and smoke it! You and your orders!

BURKE: [*Protestingly*] I wasn't meaning it that way at all and well you know it. You've no call to be raising this rumpus with me. [*Pointing to* Chris] 'Tis him you've a right——

ANNA: I'm coming to him. But you—you did mean it that way, too. You sounded—yust like all the rest. [*Hysterically*] But, damn it, shut up! Let me talk for a change!

BURKE: 'Tis square, rough talk, that—for a dacent girl the like of you!

ANNA: [*With a hard laugh*] Decent? Who told you I was? [*Chris is sitting with bowed shoulders, his head in his hands. She leans over in exasperation and shakes him violently by the shoulder*] Don't go to sleep, Old Man! Listen here, I'm talking to you now!

CHRIS: [*Straightening up and looking about as if he were seeking a way to escape—with frightened*

foreboding in his voice] Ay don't vant for hear it. You vas going out of head, Ay tank, Anna.

ANNA: [*Violently*] Well, living with you is enough to drive anyone off their nut. Your bunk about the farm being so fine! Didn't I write you year after year how rotten it was and what a dirty slave them cousins made of me? What'd you care? Nothing! Not even enough to come out and see me! That crazy bull about wanting to keep me away from the sea don't go down with me! You yust didn't want to be bothered with me! You're like all the rest of 'em!

CHRIS: [*Feebly*] Anna! It ain't so——

ANNA: [*Not heeding his interruption—revengefully*] But one thing I never wrote you. It was one of them cousins that you think is such nice people— the youngest son—Paul—that started me wrong. [*Loudly*] It wasn't none of my fault. I hated him worse'n hell and he knew it. But he was big and strong—[*Pointing to* Burke]—like you!

BURKE: [*Half springing to his feet—his fists clenched*] God blarst it!

[*He sinks slowly back in his chair again, the knuckles showing white on his clenched hands, his face tense with the effort to suppress his grief and rage*]

CHRIS: [*In a cry of horrified pain*] Anna!

ANNA: [*To him—seeming not to have heard their interruptions*] That was why I run away from the farm. That was what made me get a yob as nurse girl in St. Paul. [*With a hard, mocking laugh*] And you think that was a nice yob for a girl, too, don't you? [*Sarcastically*] With all them nice inland fellers yust looking for a chance to marry me, I s'pose. Marry me? What a chance! They wasn't looking for marrying. [*As Burke lets a groan of fury escape him—desperately*] I'm owning up to everything fair and square. I was caged in, I tell you—yust like in yail—taking care of other people's kids—listening to 'em bawling and crying day and night—when I wanted to be out—and I was lonesome—lonesome as hell! [*With a sudden weariness in her voice*] So I give up finally. What was the use? [*She stops and looks at the two men. Both are motionless and silent. Chris seems in a stupor of despair, his house of cards fallen about him. Burke's face is livid with the rage that is eating him up, but he is too stunned and bewildered yet to find a vent for it. The condemnation she feels in their silence goads Anna into a harsh, strident defiance*] You don't say nothing—either of you—but I know what you're thinking. You're like all the rest! [*To Chris—furiously*] And who's to blame for it, me or you? If you'd even acted like a man—if you even had been a regular father and had me with you—maybe things would be different!

CHRIS: [*In agony*] Don't talk dat vay, Anna! Ay go crazy! Ay von't listen!

[*Puts his hands over his ears*]

ANNA: [*Infuriated by his action—stridently*] You

will too listen! [*She leans over and pulls his hands from his ears—with hysterical rage*] You—keeping me safe inland—I wasn't no nurse girl the last two years—I lied when I wrote you—I was in a house, that's what!—yes, that kind of a house—the kind sailors like you and Mat goes to in port—and your nice inland men, too—and all men, God damn 'em! I hate 'em! Hate 'em!

[*She breaks into hysterical sobbing, throwing herself into the chair and hiding her face in her hands on the table. The two men have sprung to their feet*]

CHRIS: [*Whimpering like a child*] Anna! Anna! It's lie. It's lie!

[*He stands wringing his hands together and begins to weep*]

BURKE: [*His whole great body tense like a spring—dully and gropingly*] So that's what's in it!

ANNA: [*Raising her head at the sound of his voice—with extreme mocking bitterness*] I s'pose you remember your promise, Mat? No other reason was to count with you so long as I wasn't married already. So I s'pose you want me to get dressed and go ashore, don't you? [*She laughs*] Yes, you do!

BURKE: [*On the verge of his outbreak—stammeringly*] God stiffen you!

ANNA: [*Trying to keep up her hard, bitter tone, but gradually letting a note of pitiful pleading creep in*] I s'pose if I tried to tell you I wasn't—that—no more you'd believe me, wouldn't you? Yes, you would! And if I told you that yust getting out in this barge, and being on the sea had changed me and made me feel different about things, 's if all I'd been through wasn't me and didn't count and yust like it never happened—you'd laugh, wouldn't you? And you'd die laughing sure if I said that meeting you that funny way that night in the fog, and afterwards seeing that you was straight goods stuck on me, had got me thinking for the first time, and I sized you up as a different kind of man—a sea man as different from the ones on land as water is from mud—and that was why I got stuck on you, too. I wanted to marry you and fool you, but I couldn't. Don't you see how I've changed? I couldn't marry you with you believing a lie—and I was shamed to tell you the truth—till the both of you forced my hand, and I seen you was the same as all the rest. And now, give me a bawling out and beat it, like I can tell you're going to. [*She stops, looking at Burke. He is silent, his face averted, his features beginning to work with fury. She pleads passionately*] Will you believe it if I tell you that loving you has made me—clean? It's the straight goods, honest! [*Then as he doesn't reply—bitterly*] Like hell you will! You're like all the rest!

BURKE: [*Blazing out—turning on her in a perfect frenzy of rage—his voice trembling with passion*] The rest, is it? God's curse on you! Clane, is it? You slut, you, I'll be killing you now!

[*He picks up the chair on which he has been sitting and, swinging it high over his shoulder, springs toward her. Chris rushes forward with a cry of alarm, trying to ward off the blow from his daughter. Anna looks up into Burke's eyes with the fearlessness of despair. Burke checks himself, the chair held in the air*]

CHRIS: [*Wildly*] Stop, you crazy fool! You vant for murder her!

ANNA: [*Pushing her father away brusquely, her eyes still holding Burke's*] Keep out of this, you! [*To Burke—dully*] Well, ain't you got the nerve to do it? Go ahead! I'll be thankful to you, honest. I'm sick of the whole game.

BURKE: [*Throwing the chair away into a corner of the room—helplessly*] I can't do it, God help me, and your two eyes looking at me. [*Furiously*] Though I do be thinking I'd have a good right to smash your skull like a rotten egg. Was there iver a woman in the world had the rottenness in her that you have, and was there iver a man the like of me was made the fool of the world, and me thinking thoughts about you, and having great love for you, and dreaming dreams of the fine life we'd have when we'd be wedded! [*His voice high pitched in a lamentation that is like a keen*] Yerra, God help me! I'm destroyed entirely and my heart is broken in bits! I'm asking God Himself, was it for this He'd have me roaming the earth since I was a lad only, to come to black shame in the end, where I'd be giving a power of love to a woman is the same as others you'd meet in any hookershanty in port, with red gowns on them and paint on their grinning mugs, would be sleeping with any man for a dollar or two!

ANNA: [*In a scream*] Don't, Mat! For Gawd's sake! [*Then raging and pounding on the table with her hands*] Get out of here! Leave me alone! Get out of here!

BURKE: [*His anger rushing back on him*] I'll be going, surely! And I'll be drinking sloos of whisky will wash that black kiss of yours off my lips; and I'll be getting dead rotten drunk so I'll not remember if 'twas iver born you was at all; and I'll be shipping away on some boat will take me to the other end of the world where I'll never see your face again!

[*He turns toward the door*]

CHRIS: [*Who has been standing in a stupor—suddenly grasping Burke by the arm—stupidly*] No, you don't go. Ay tank maybe it's better Anna marry you now.

BURKE: [*Shaking Chris off—furiously*] Lave go of me, ye old ape! Marry her, is it? I'd see her roasting in hell first! I'm shipping away out of this, I'm telling you! [*Pointing to Anna—passionately*] And my curse on you and the curse of Almighty God and all the Saints! You've destroyed me this day and may you lie awake in the long nights, tormented with thoughts of Mat Burke and the great wrong you've done him!

ANNA: [*In anguish*] Mat!

[*But he turns without another word and strides out of the doorway. Anna looks after him wildly, starts to run after him, then hides her face in her outstretched arms, sobbing. Chris stands in a stupor, staring at the floor*]

CHRIS: [*After a pause, dully*] Ay tank Ay go ashore, too.

ANNA: [*Looking up, wildly*] Not after him! Let him go! Don't you dare——

CHRIS: [*Somberly*] Ay go for gat drink.

ANNA: [*With a harsh laugh*] So I'm driving you to drink, too, eh? I s'pose you want to get drunk so's you can forget—like him?

CHRIS: [*Bursting out angrily*] Yes, Ay vant! You tank Ay like to hear dem tangs. [*Breaking down—weeping*] Ay tank you vasn't dat kind of gel, Anna.

ANNA: [*Mockingly*] And I s'pose you want me to beat it, don't you? You don't want me here disgracing you, I s'pose?

CHRIS: No, you stay here! [*Goes over and pats her on the shoulder, the tears running down his face*] Ain't your fault, Anna, Ay know dat. [*She looks up at him, softened. He bursts into rage*] It's dat ole davil, sea, do this to me! [*He shakes his fist at the door*] It's her dirty tricks! It vas all right on barge with yust you and me. Den she bring dat Irish fallar in fog, she make you like him, she make you fight with me all time! If dat Irish fallar don't never come, you don't never tal me dem tangs, Ay don't never know, and everytang's all right. [*He shakes his fist again*] Dirty ole davil!

ANNA: [*With spent weariness*] Oh, what's the use? Go on ashore and get drunk.

CHRIS: [*Goes into room on left and gets his cap. He goes to the door, silent and stupid—then turns*] You vait here, Anna?

ANNA: [*Dully*] Maybe—and maybe not. Maybe I'll get drunk, too. Maybe I'll—— But what the hell do you care what I do? Go on and beat it.

[Chris *turns stupidly and goes out. Anna sits at the table, staring straight in front of her*]

[THE CURTAIN FALLS]

ACT IV.

SCENE. *Same as Act Three, about nine o'clock of a foggy night two days later. The whistles of steamers in the harbor can be heard. The cabin is lighted by a small lamp on the table. A suitcase stands in the middle of the floor. Anna is sitting in the rocking-chair. She wears a hat, is all dressed up as in Act One. Her face is pale, looks terribly tired and worn, as if the two days just past had been ones of suffering and sleepless nights. She stares before her despondently, her chin in her hands. There is a timid knock on the door in rear. Anna jumps to her feet with a startled exclamation and looks toward the door with an expression of mingled fear and hope.*

ANNA: [*Faintly*] Come in. [*Then summoning her courage—more resolutely*] Come in. [*The door is opened and Chris appears in the doorway. He is in a very bleary, bedraggled condition, suffering from the after effects of his drunk. A tin pail full of foaming beer is in his hand. He comes forward, his eyes avoiding Anna's. He mutters stupidly*] It's foggy.

ANNA: [*Looking him over with contempt*] So you come back at last, did you? You're a fine-looking sight! [*Then jeeringly*] I thought you'd beaten it for good on account of the disgrace I'd brought on you.

CHRIS: [*Wincing—faintly*] Don't say dat, Anna, please!

[*He sits in a chair by the table, setting down the can of beer, holding his head in his hands*]

ANNA: [*Looks at him with a certain sympathy*] What's the trouble? Feeling sick?

CHRIS: [*Dully*] Inside my head feel sick.

ANNA: Well, what d'you expect after being soused for two days? [*Resentfully*] It serves you right. A fine thing—you leaving me alone on this barge all that time!

CHRIS: [*Humbly*] Ay'm sorry, Anna.

ANNA: [*Scornfully*] Sorry!

CHRIS: But Ay'm not sick inside head vay you mean. Ay'm sick from tank too much about you, about me.

ANNA: And how about me? D'you suppose I ain't been thinking, too?

CHRIS: Ay'm sorry, Anna. [*He sees her bag and gives a start*] You pack your bag, Anna? You vas going——?

ANNA: [*Forcibly*] Yes, I was going right back to what you think.

CHRIS: Anna!

ANNA: I went ashore to get a train for New York. I'd been waiting and waiting till I was sick of it. Then I changed my mind and decided not to go today. But I'm going first thing tomorrow, so it'll all be the same in the end.

CHRIS: [*Raising his head—pleadingly*] No, you never do dat, Anna!

ANNA: [*With a sneer*] Why not, I'd like to know?

CHRIS: You don't never gat to do—dat vay—no more, Ay tal you. Ay fix dat up all right.

ANNA: [*Suspiciously*] Fix what up?

CHRIS: [*Not seeming to have heard her question—sadly*] You vas vaiting, you say? You vasn't vaiting for me, Ay bet.

ANNA: [*Callously*] You'd win.

CHRIS: For dat Irish fallar?

ANNA: [*Defiantly*] Yes—if you want to know! [*Then with a forlorn laugh*] If he did come back it'd only be 'cause he wanted to beat me up or kill me, I suppose. But even if he did, I'd rather have him come than not show up at all. I wouldn't care what he did.

CHRIS: Ay guess it's true you vas in love with him all right.

ANNA: You guess!

CHRIS: [*Turning to her earnestly*] And Ay'm sorry for you like hell he don't come, Anna!

ANNA: [*Softened*] Seems to me you've changed your tune a lot.

CHRIS: Ay've been tanking, and Ay guess it vas all my fault—all bad tangs dat happen to you. [*Pleadingly*] You try for not hate me, Anna. Ay'm crazy ole fool, dat's all.

ANNA: Who said I hated you?

CHRIS: Ay'm sorry for everytank Ay do wrong for you, Anna. Ay vant for you be happy all rest of your life for make up! It make you happy marry dat Irish fallar, Ay vant it, too.

ANNA: [*Dully*] Well, there ain't no chance. But I'm glad you think different about it, anyway.

CHRIS: [*Supplicatingly*] And you tank—maybe—you forgive me sometime?

ANNA: [*With a wan smile*] I'll forgive you right now.

CHRIS: [*Seizing her hand and kissing it—brokenly*] Anna lilla! Anna lilla!

ANNA: [*Touched but a bit embarrassed*] Don't bawl about it. There ain't nothing to forgive, anyway. It ain't your fault, and it ain't mine, and it ain't his neither. We're all poor nuts, and things happen, and we yust get mixed in wrong, that's all.

CHRIS: [*Eagerly*] You say right tang, Anna, py golly! It ain't nobody's fault! [*Shaking his fist*] It's dat ole davil, sea!

ANNA: [*With an exasperated laugh*] Gee, won't you ever can that stuff? [*Chris relapses into injured silence. After a pause Anna continues curiously*] You said a minute ago you'd fixed something up—about me. What was it?

CHRIS: [*After a hesitating pause*] Ay'm shipping avay on sea again, Anna.

ANNA: [*Astounded*] You're—what?

CHRIS: Ay sign on steamer sail tomorrow. Ay gat my ole yob—bo'sun. [*Anna stares at him. As he goes on, a bitter smile comes over her face*] Ay tank dat's best tang for you. Ay only bring you bad luck, Ay tank. Ay make your mo'der's life sorry. Ay don't vant make yours dat vay, but Ay do yust same. Dat ole davil, sea, she make me Yonah man ain't no good for nobody. And Ay tank now it ain't no use fight with sea. No man dat live going to beat her, py yingo!

ANNA: [*With a laugh of helpless bitterness*] So that's how you've fixed me, is it?

CHRIS: Yes, Ay tank if dat ole davil gat me back she leave you alone den.

ANNA: [*Bitterly*] But, for Gawd's sake, don't you see you're doing the same thing you've always done? Don't you see——? [*But she sees the look of obsessed stubbornness on her father's face and gives it up helplessly*] But what's the use of talking? You ain't right, that's what. I'll never blame you for nothing no more. But how could you figure out that was fixing me——!

CHRIS: Dat ain't all. Ay gat dem fallars in steamship office to pay you all money coming to me every month vhile Ay'm avay.

ANNA: [*With a hard laugh*] Thanks. But I guess I won't be hard up for no small change.

CHRIS: [*Hurt—humbly*] It ain't much, Ay know, but it's plenty for keep you so you never gat go back——

ANNA: [*Shortly*] Shut up, will you? We'll talk about it later, see?

CHRIS: [*After a pause—ingratiatingly*] You like Ay go ashore look for dat Irish fallar, Anna?

ANNA: [*Angrily*] Not much! Think I want to drag him back?

CHRIS: [*After a pause—uncomfortably*] Py golly, dat booze don't go vell. Give me fever, Ay tank. Ay feel hot like hell.

[*He takes off his coat and lets it drop on the floor. There is a loud thud*]

ANNA: [*With a start*] What you got in your pocket, for Pete's sake—a ton of lead? [*She reaches down, takes the coat and pulls out a revolver—looks from it to him in amazement*] A gun? What were you doing with this?

CHRIS: [*Sheepishly*] Ay forget. Ain't nothing. Ain't loaded, anyvay.

ANNA: [*Breaking it open to make sure—then closing it again—looking at him suspiciously*] That ain't telling me why you got it.

CHRIS: Ay'm ole fool. Ay got it when Ay go ashore first. Ay tank den it's all fault of dat Irish fallar.

ANNA: [*With a shudder*] Say, you're crazier than I thought. I never dreamt you'd go that far.

CHRIS: [*Quickly*] Ay don't. Ay gat better sense right avay. Ay don't never buy bullets even. It ain't his fault, Ay know.

ANNA: [*Still suspicious of him*] Well, I'll take care of this for a while, loaded or not.

[*She puts it in the drawer of table and closes the drawer*]

CHRIS: [*Placatingly*] Throw it overboard if you vant. Ay don't care. [*Then after a pause*] Py golly, Ay tank Ay go lie down. Ay feel sick. [*Anna takes a magazine from the table. Chris hesitates by her chair*] Ve talk again before Ay go, yes?

ANNA: [*Dully*] Where's this ship going to?

CHRIS: Cape Town. Dat's in South Africa. She's British steamer called Londonderry. [*He stands hesitatingly—finally blurts out*] Anna—you forgive me sure?

ANNA: [*Wearily*] Sure I do. You ain't to blame. You're yust—what you are—like me.

CHRIS: [*Pleadingly*] Den—you lat me kiss you again once?

ANNA: [*Raising her face—forcing a wan smile*] Sure. No hard feelings.

CHRIS: [*Kisses her brokenly*] Anna lilla! Ay—— [*He fights for words to express himself, but finds none—miserably—with a sob*] Ay can't say it. Good night, Anna.

ANNA: Good night. [*He picks up the can of beer and goes slowly into the room on left, his shoulders bowed, his head sunk forward dejectedly. He closes the door after him.* Anna *turns over the pages of the magazine, trying desperately to banish her thoughts by looking at the pictures. This fails to distract her, and flinging the magazine back on the table, she springs to her feet and walks about the cabin distractedly, clenching and unclenching her hands. She speaks aloud to herself in a tense, trembling voice*] Gawd, I can't stand this much longer! What am I waiting for anyway?—like a damn fool! [*She laughs helplessly, then checks herself abruptly, as she hears the sound of heavy footsteps on the deck outside. She appears to recognize these and her face lights up with joy. She gasps*] Mat! [*A strange terror seems suddenly to seize her. She rushes to the table, takes the revolver out of drawer and crouches down in the corner, left, behind the cupboard. A moment later the door is flung open and* Mat Burke *appears in the doorway. He is in bad shape—his clothes torn and dirty, covered with sawdust as if he had been groveling or sleeping on barroom floors. There is a red bruise on his forehead over one of his eyes, another over one cheekbone, his knuckles are skinned and raw—plain evidence of the fighting he has been through on his "bat." His eyes are bloodshot and heavy-lidded, his face has a bloated look. But beyond these appearances—the results of heavy drinking—there is an expression in his eyes of wild mental turmoil, of impotent animal rage baffled by its own abject misery*]

BURKE: [*Peers blinkingly about the cabin— hoarsely*] Let you not be hiding from me, whoever's here—though 'tis well you know I'd have a right to come back and murder you. [*He stops to listen. Hearing no sound, he closes the door behind him and comes forward to the table. He throws himself into the rocking-chair—despondently*] There's no one here, I'm thinking, and 'tis a great fool I am to be coming. [*With a sort of dumb, uncomprehending anguish*] Yerra, Mat Burke, 'tis a great jackass you've become and what's got into you at all, at all? She's gone out of this long ago, I'm telling you, and you'll never see her face again [Anna *stands up, hesitating, struggling between joy and fear.* Burke's *eyes fall on Anna's bag. He leans over to examine it*] What's this? [*Joyfully*] It's hers. She's not gone! But where is she? Ashore? [*Darkly*] What would she be doing ashore on this rotten night? [*His face suddenly convulsed with grief and rage*] 'Tis that, is it? Oh, God's curse on her! [*Raging*] I'll wait 'till she comes and choke her dirty life out.

[Anna *starts, her face grows hard. She steps into the room, the revolver in her right hand by her side*]

ANNA: [*In a cold, hard tone*] What are you doing here?

BURKE: [*Wheeling about with a terrified gasp*] Glory be to God!

[*They remain motionless and silent for a moment, holding each other's eyes*]

ANNA: [*In the same hard voice*] Well, can't you talk?

BURKE: [*Trying to fall into an easy, careless tone*] You've a year's growth scared out of me, coming at me so sudden and me thinking I was alone.

ANNA: You've got your nerve butting in here without knocking or nothing. What d'you want?

BURKE: [*Airily*] Oh, nothing much. I was wanting to have a last word with you, that's all.

[*He moves a step toward her*]

ANNA: [*Sharply—raising the revolver in her hand*] Careful now! Don't try getting too close. I heard what you said you'd do to me.

BURKE: [*Noticing the revolver for the first time*] Is it murdering me you'd be now, God forgive you? [*Then with a contemptuous laugh*] Or is it thinking I'd be frightened by that old tin whistle?

[*He walks straight for her*]

ANNA: [*Wildly*] Look out, I tell you!

BURKE: [*Who has come so close that the revolver is almost touching his chest*] Let you shoot, then! [*Then with sudden wild grief*] Let you shoot, I'm saying, and be done with it! Let you end me with a shot and I'll be thanking you, for it's a rotten dog's life I've lived the past two days since I've known what you are, 'til I'm after wishing I was never born at all!

ANNA: [*Overcome—letting the revolver drop to the floor, as if her fingers had no strength to hold it —hysterically*] What d'you want coming here? Why don't you beat it? Go on!

[*She passes him and sinks down in the rocking-chair*]

BURKE: [*Following her—mournfully*] 'Tis right you'd be asking why did I come [*Then angrily*] 'Tis because 'tis a great weak fool of the world I am, and me tormented with the wickedness you'd told of yourself, and drinking oceans of booze that'd make me forget. Forget? Divil a word I'd forget, and your face grinning always in front of my eyes, awake or asleep, 'til I do be thinking a madhouse is the proper place for me.

ANNA: [*Glancing at his hands and face—scornfully*] You look like you ought to be put away some place. Wonder you wasn't pulled in. You been scrapping, too, ain't you?

BURKE: I have—with every scut would take off his coat to me! [*Fiercely*] And each time I'd be hitting one a clout in the mug, it wasn't his face I'd be seeing at all, but yours, and me wanting to drive you a blow would knock you out of this world where I wouldn't be seeing or thinking more of you.

ANNA: [*Her lips trembling pitifully*] Thanks!

BURKE: [*Walking up and down—distractedly*] That's right, make game of me! Oh, I'm a great coward surely, to be coming back to speak with you at all. You've a right to laugh at me.

ANNA: I ain't laughing at you, Mat.

BURKE: [*Unheeding*] You to be what you are, and

me to be Mat Burke, and me to be drove back to look at you again! 'Tis black shame is on me!

ANNA: [*Resentfully*] Then get out. No one's holding you!

BURKE: [*Bewilderedly*] And me to listen to that talk from a woman like you and be frightened to close her mouth with a slap! Oh, God help me, I'm a yellow coward for all men to spit at! [*Then furiously*] But I'll not be getting out of this 'til I've had me word. [*Raising his fist threateningly*] And let you look out how you'd drive me! [*Letting his fist fall helplessly*] Don't be angry now! I'm raving like a real lunatic, I'm thinking, and the sorrow you put on me has my brains drownded in grief. [*Suddenly bending down to her and grasping her arm intensely*] Tell me it's a lie, I'm saying! That's what I'm after coming to hear you say.

ANNA: [*Dully*] A lie? What?

BURKE: [*With passionate entreaty*] All the badness you told me two days back. Sure it must be a lie! You was only making game of me, wasn't you? Tell me 'twas a lie, Anna, and I'll be saying prayers of thanks on my two knees to the Almighty God!

ANNA: [*Terribly shaken—faintly*] I can't, Mat. [*As he turns away—imploringly*] Oh, Mat, won't you see that no matter what I was I ain't that any more? Why, listen! I packed up my bag this afternoon and went ashore. I'd been waiting here all alone for two days, thinking maybe you'd come back —thinking maybe you'd think over all I'd said—and maybe—oh, I don't know what I was hoping! But I was afraid to even go out of the cabin for a second, honest—afraid you might come and not find me here. Then I gave up hope when you didn't show up and I went to the railroad station. I was going to New York. I was going back——

BURKE: [*Hoarsely*] God's curse on you!

ANNA: Listen, Mat! You hadn't come, and I gave up hope. But—in the station—I couldn't go. I'd bought my ticket and everything. [*She takes the ticket from her dress and tries to hold it before his eyes*] But I got to thinking about you—and I couldn't take the train—I couldn't! So I come back here—to wait some more. Oh, Mat, don't you see I've changed? Can't you forgive what's dead and gone—and forget it?

BURKE: [*Turning on her—overcome by rage again*] Forget, is it? I'll not forget 'til my dying day, I'm telling you, and me tormented with thoughts. [*In a frenzy*] Oh, I'm wishing I had wan of them fornenst me this minute and I'd beat him with my fists 'til he'd be a bloody corpse! I'm wishing the whole lot of them will roast in hell 'til the Judgment Day—and yourself along with them, for you're as bad as they are.

ANNA: [*Shuddering*] Mat! [*Then after a pause— in a voice of dead, stony calm*] Well, you've had your say. Now you better beat it.

BURKE: [*Starts slowly for the door—hesitates— then after a pause*] And what'll you be doing?

ANNA: What difference does it make to you?

BURKE: I'm asking you!

ANNA: [*In the same tone*] My bag's packed and I got my ticket. I'll go to New York tomorrow.

BURKE: [*Helplessly*] You mean—you'll be doing the same again?

ANNA: [*Stonily*] Yes.

BURKE: [*In anguish*] You'll not! Don't torment me with that talk! 'Tis a she-divil you are sent to drive me mad entirely!

ANNA: [*Her voice breaking*] Oh, for Gawd's sake, Mat, leave me alone! Go away! Don't you see I'm licked? Why d'you want to keep on kicking me?

BURKE: [*Indignantly*] And don't you deserve the worst I'd say, God forgive you?

ANNA: All right. Maybe I do. But don't rub it in. Why ain't you done what you said you was going to? Why ain't you got that ship was going to take you to the other side of the earth where you'd never see me again?

BURKE: I have.

ANNA: [*Startled*] What—then you're going— honest?

BURKE: I signed on today at noon, drunk as I was—and she's sailing tomorrow.

ANNA: And where's she going to?

BURKE: Cape Town.

ANNA: [*The memory of having heard that name a little while before coming to her—with a start, confusedly*] Cape Town? Where's that? Far away?

BURKE: 'Tis at the end of Africa. That's far for you.

ANNA: [*Forcing a laugh*] You're keeping your word all right, ain't you? [*After a slight pause— curiously*] What's the boat's name?

BURKE: The Londonderry.

ANNA: [*It suddenly comes to her that this is the same ship her father is sailing on*] The Londonderry! It's the same—Oh, this is too much! [*With wild, ironical laughter*] Ha-ha-ha!

BURKE: What's up with you now?

ANNA: Ha-ha-ha! It's funny, funny! I'll die laughing!

BURKE: [*Irritated*] Laughing at what?

ANNA: It's a secret. You'll know soon enough. It's funny. [*Controlling herself—after a pause—cynically*] What kind of a place is this Cape Town? Plenty of dames there, I suppose?

BURKE: To hell with them! That I may never see another woman to my dying hour!

ANNA: That's what you say now, but I'll bet by the time you get there you'll have forgot all about me and start in talking the same old bull you talked to me to the first one you meet.

BURKE: [*Offended*] I'll not, then! God mend you, is it making me out to be the like of yourself you are, and you taking up with this one and that all the years of your life?

ANNA: [*Angrily assertive*] Yes, that's yust what I do mean! You been doing the same thing all your life, picking up a new girl in every port. How're you any better than I was?

BURKE: [*Thoroughly exasperated*] Is it no shame you have at all? I'm a fool to be wasting talk on you and you hardened in badness. I'll go out of this and lave you alone forever. [*He starts for the door—then stops to turn on her furiously*] And I suppose 'tis the same lies you told them all before that you told to me?

ANNA: [*Indignantly*] That's a lie! I never did!

BURKE: [*Miserably*] You'd be saying that, anyway.

ANNA: [*Forcibly, with growing intensity*] Are you trying to accuse me—of being in love—really in love—with them?

BURKE: I'm thinking you were, surely.

ANNA: [*Furiously, as if this were the last insult—advancing on him threateningly*] You mutt, you! I've stood enough from you. Don't you dare. [*With scornful bitterness*] Love 'em! Oh, my Gawd! You damn thick-head! Love 'em? [*Savagely*] I hated 'em, I tell you! Hated 'em, hated 'em, hated 'em! And may Gawd strike me dead this minute and my mother, too, if she was alive, if I ain't telling you the honest truth!

BURKE: [*Immensely pleased by her vehemence—a light beginning to break over his face—but still uncertain, torn between doubt and the desire to believe—helplessly*] If I could only be believing you now!

ANNA: [*Distractedly*] Oh, what's the use? What's the use of me talking? What's the use of anything? [*Pleadingly*] Oh, Mat, you mustn't think that for a second! You mustn't! Think all the other bad about me you want to, and I won't kick, 'cause you've a right to. But don't think that! [*On the point of tears*] I couldn't bear it! It'd be yust too much to know you was going away where I'd never see you again—thinking that about me!

BURKE: [*After an inward struggle—tensely—forcing out the words with difficulty*] If I was believing—that you'd never had love for any other man in the world but me—I could be forgetting the rest, maybe.

ANNA: [*With a cry of joy*] Mat!

BURKE: [*Slowly*] If 'tis truth you're after telling, I'd have a right, maybe, to believe you'd changed—and that I'd changed you myself 'til the thing you'd been all your life wouldn't be you any more at all.

ANNA: [*Hanging on his words—breathlessly*] Oh, Mat! That's what I been trying to tell you all along!

BURKE: [*Simply*] For I've a power of strength in me to lead men the way I want, and women, too, maybe, and I'm thinking I'd change you to a new woman entirely, so I'd never know, or you either, what kind of woman you'd been in the past at all.

ANNA: Yes, you could, Mat! I know you could!

BURKE: And I'm thinking 'twasn't your fault, maybe, but having that old ape for a father that left you to grow up alone, made you what you was. And if I could be believing 'tis only me you——

ANNA: [*Distractedly*] You got to believe it, Mat! What can I do? I'll do anything, anything you want to prove I'm not lying!

BURKE: [*Suddenly seems to have a solution. He feels in the pocket of his coat and grasps something—solemnly*] Would you be willing to swear an oath, now—a terrible, fearful oath would send your soul to the divils in hell if you was lying?

ANNA: [*Eagerly*] Sure, I'll swear, Mat—on anything!

BURKE: [*Takes a small, cheap old crucifix from his pocket and holds it up for her to see*] Will you swear on this?

ANNA: [*Reaching out for it*] Yes. Sure I will. Give it to me.

BURKE: [*Holding it away*] 'Tis a cross was given me by my mother, God rest her soul. [*He makes the sign of the cross mechanically*] I was a lad only, and she told me to keep it by me if I'd be waking or sleeping and never lose it, and it'd bring me luck. She died soon after. But I'm after keeping it with me from that day to this, and I'm telling you there's great power in it, and 'tis great bad luck it's saved me from and me roaming the seas, and I having it tied round my neck when my last ship sunk, and it bringing me safe to land when the others went to their death. [*Very earnestly*] And I'm warning you now, if you'd swear an oath on this, 'tis my old woman herself will be looking down from Hivin above, and praying Almighty God and the Saints to put a great curse on you if she'd hear you swearing a lie!

ANNA: [*Awed by his manner—superstitiously*] I wouldn't have the nerve—honest—if it was a lie. But it's the truth and I ain't scared to swear. Give it to me.

BURKE: [*Handing it to her—almost frightenedly, as if he feared for her safety*] Be careful what you'd swear, I'm saying.

ANNA: [*Holding the cross gingerly*] Well—what do you want me to swear? You say it.

BURKE: Swear I'm the only man in the world ivir you felt love for.

ANNA: [*Looking into his eyes steadily*] I swear it.

BURKE: And that you'll be forgetting from this day all the badness you've done and never do the like of it again.

ANNA: [*Forcibly*] I swear it! I swear it by God!

BURKE: And may the blackest curse of God strike you if you're lying. Say it now!

ANNA: And may the blackest curse of God strike me if I'm lying!

BURKE: [*With a stupendous sigh*] Oh, glory be to God, I'm after believing you now!

[*He takes the cross from her hand, his face beaming with joy, and puts it back in his pocket. He puts his arm about her waist and is about to kiss her when he stops, appalled by some terrible doubt*]

ANNA: [*Alarmed*] What's the matter with you?

BURKE: [*With sudden fierce questioning*] Is it Catholic ye are?

ANNA: [*Confused*] No. Why?

BURKE: [*Filled with a sort of bewildered fore-

boding] Oh, God, help me! [*With a dark glance of suspicion at her*] There's some divil's trickery in it, to be swearing an oath on a Catholic cross and you wan of the others.

ANNA: [*Distractedly*] Oh, Mat, don't you believe me?

BURKE: [*Miserably*] If it isn't a Catholic you are——

ANNA: I ain't nothing. What's the difference? Didn't you hear me swear?

BURKE: [*Passionately*] Oh, I'd a right to stay away from you—but I couldn't! I was loving you in spite of it all and wanting to be with you, God forgive me, no matter what you are. I'd go mad if I'd not have you! I'd be killing the world——

[*He seizes her in his arms and kisses her fiercely*]

ANNA: [*With a gasp of joy*] Mat!

BURKE: [*Suddenly holding her away from him and staring into her eyes as if to probe into her soul—slowly*] If your oath is no proper oath at all, I'll have to be taking your naked word for it and have you anyway, I'm thinking—I'm needing you that bad!

ANNA: [*Hurt—reproachfully*] Mat! I swore, didn't I?

BURKE: [*Defiantly, as if challenging fate*] Oath or no oath, 'tis no matter. We'll be wedded in the morning, with the help of God. [*Still more defiantly*] We'll be happy now, the two of us, in spite of the divil!

[*He crushes her to him and kisses her again. The door on the left is pushed open and Chris appears in the doorway. He stands blinking at them. At first the old expression of hatred of Burke comes into his eyes instinctively. Then a look of resignation and relief takes its place. His face lights up with a sudden happy thought. He turns back into the bedroom—reappears immediately with the tin can of beer in his hand—grinning*]

CHRIS: Ve have drink on this, py golly! [*They break away from each other with startled exclamations*]

BURKE: [*Explosively*] God stiffen it!

[*He takes a step toward Chris threateningly*]

ANNA: [*Happily—to her father*] That's the way to talk [*With a laugh*] And say, it's about time for you and Mat to kiss and make up. You're going to be shipmates on the Londonderry, did you know it?

BURKE: [*Astounded*] Shipmates—— Has himself——

CHRIS: [*Equally astounded*] Ay vas bo'sun on her.

BURKE: The divil! [*Then angrily*] You'd be going back to sea and leaving her alone, wouldn't you?

ANNA: [*Quickly*] It's all right, Mat. That's where he belongs, and I want him to go. You got to go, too; we'll need the money. [*With a laugh, as she gets the glasses*] And as for me being alone, that runs in the family, and I'll get used to it. [*Pouring out their glasses*] I'll get a little house somewhere and I'll make a regular place for you two to come back to

—wait and see. And now you drink up and be friends.

BURKE: [*Happily—but still a bit resentful against the old man*] Sure! [*Clinking his glass against Chris'*] Here's luck to you!

[*He drinks*]

CHRIS: [*Subdued—his face melancholy*] Skoal.

[*He drinks*]

BURKE: [*To Anna, with a wink*] You'll not be lonesome long. I'll see to that, with the help of God. 'Tis himself here will be having a grandchild to ride on his foot, I'm telling you!

ANNA: [*Turning away in embarrassment*] Quit the kidding now.

[*She picks up her bag and goes into the room on left. As soon as she is gone Burke relapses into an attitude of gloomy thought. Chris stares at his beer absent-mindedly. Finally Burke turns on him*]

BURKE: Is it any religion at all you have, you and your Anna?

CHRIS: [*Surprised*] Why, yes. Ve vas Lutheran in ole country.

BURKE: [*Horrified*] Luthers, is it? [*Then with a grim resignation, slowly, aloud to himself*] Well, I'm damned then surely. Yerra, what's the difference? 'Tis the will of God, anyway.

CHRIS: [*Moodily preoccupied with his own thoughts—speaks with somber premonition as Anna re-enters from the left*] It's funny. It's queer, yes—you and me shipping on same boat dat vay. It ain't right. Ay don't know—it's dat funny vay ole davil sea do her vorst dirty tricks, yes. It's so.

[*He gets up and goes back and, opening the door, stares out into the darkness*]

BURKE: [*Nodding his head in gloomy acquiescence—with a great sigh*] I'm fearing maybe you have the right of it for once, divil take you.

ANNA: [*Forcing a laugh*] Gee, Mat, you ain't agreeing with him, are you? [*She comes forward and puts her arm about his shoulder—with a determined gaiety*] Aw, say, what's the matter? Cut out the gloom. We're all fixed now, ain't we, me and you? [*Pours out more beer into his glass and fills one for herself—slaps him on the back*] Come on! Here's to the sea, no matter what! Be a game sport and drink to that! Come on!

[*She gulps down her glass. Burke banishes his superstitious premonitions with a defiant jerk of his head, grins up at her, and drinks to her toast*]

CHRIS: [*Looking out into the night—lost in his somber preoccupation—shakes his head and mutters*] Fog, fog, fog, all bloody time. You can't see vhere you vas going, no. Only dat ole davil, sea—she knows!

[*The two stare at him. From the harbor comes the muffled, mournful wail of steamers' whistles*]

[THE CURTAIN FALLS]

Eugene O'Neill

(1888–——)

Perhaps nothing in Eugene O'Neill's career drew so much attention to him as his incessant experimentation. After seeing, at the beginning of the 'twenties, such plays as *The Emperor Jones* and *The Hairy Ape*, American playgoers came to expect almost anything from him. They even complied when he required them to change lifetime habits of playgoing. Thus, to see the nine-act stream-of-consciousness drama *Strange Interlude*, they arrived for the performance at 5:30 in the afternoon, had dinner during an intermission, and then dutifully returned to their seats to await the conclusion of the longest interlude they had ever known.

Virtually every play O'Neill wrote after 1920 presented itself to him as a very special problem in structure and style. Unlike the average playwright, he could not accept a conventional dramatic mold. Plainly, too, he preferred a "theatrical" kind of theatre as opposed to one that called itself realistic or naturalistic and pretended to be an unassuming facsimile of life.

Theatricality, indeed, was ingrained in the son of the romantic actor-manager James O'Neill. But there were more important reasons for O'Neill's experimentation than his virtuosity and the pleasure he found in displaying it. In a program note on Strindberg written for the Provincetown Players, O'Neill bade farewell to naturalism as an outmoded style, describing it as "our fathers' daring aspirations toward self-recognition by holding the family kodak up to ill-nature." He complained that "we have taken too many snapshots of each other in every graceless position." Dissatisfied with "the banality of surfaces," O'Neill was, indeed, a symbol-using poet from the very start of his career. Symbol and reality were fused even in the short sea plays, in *Beyond the Horizon*, and in *Anna Christie*. In these plays, however, situations were never deliberately distorted and scenes never "stylized," as they were in *The Emperor Jones* and *The Hairy Ape*. Distortion, for purposes of heightening reality and rendering dream experience, is a method introduced into the modern drama by Strindberg, whose work left a strong impression on O'Neill and who was the father of the expressionism in O'Neill's work. After 1918, moreover, the vogue of expressionistic theatre in Central Europe attracted the American theatrical vanguard, to which O'Neill belonged. Both *The Emperor Jones* (1920) and *The Hairy Ape* (1922) contain expressionistic features; they are the best serious American plays written partly or wholly in that style. In both plays, O'Neill placed much reliance on pantomime and on a pattern of delirious fantastication. Once the Negro hero, "Emperor" Jones, escapes into the jungle, he becomes the victim of one nightmare after another. *The Emperor Jones* is a drama of atavism and it is told chiefly by visual means. The greater part of the play is little more than a monologue by Jones interrupted by vignettes of fantasy. The effect is one of sheer theatre. But *The Hairy Ape* is the story of a quest, and it is drama as well as theatre. It contains much more text than *The Emperor Jones* because it is more than a mere procession of fear images.

O'Neill believed he had an important idea to propound in *The Hairy Ape*, and the idea was charged with his very personal sense of man's alienation in the modern world. In this play he experimented with dramatic style and form not for the sake of theatrical virtuosity, at which no man was to prove more adept, but for the sake of self-expression. "Self-expression" is, of course, a big word, but it is not too big for a playwright who always tried to find theatrical projection for his inner tensions and spiritual quests. O'Neill was even willing to exhibit these in the inchoate or half-crystallized form in which they appeared to him, thus exposing himself to the charges of excessive emotionalism and callow thinking. Such criticism was inevitable, once he began to do more and more of his groping in public.

In *The Hairy Ape*, fortunately, O'Neill's metaphysics has the advantage of a loamy substratum of reality. The person of the heroic stoker, Yank, is ultimately transformed into the abstraction Man as the play moves on. But before Yank is thus abstracted by O'Neill, the two-fisted stoker possesses a lyric vitality. He is half man, half symbol, like Carl Sandburg's Chicago—"Hog Butcher for the World, Tool Maker, Stacker of Wheat. . . ." O'Neill, as he explained to the press, regarded the play as "a symbol of man, who has lost his old harmony with nature, the harmony which he used to have as an animal and has not yet acquired in a spiritual way. . . . Yank can't go forward, and so he tries to go back. This is what his shaking hands with the gorilla meant. But he can't go back to 'belonging' either. The gorilla kills him. The subject here is the ancient one that always was and always will be the one subject for drama, and that is man and his struggle with his own fate. The struggle used to be with the gods, but is now with himself, his own past, his attempt to 'belong.'" How far *The Hairy Ape* actually sustains this interpretation and benefits from it can prove a subject for lively debate.

O'Neill himself insisted on the value of his interpretation, writing in the *New York Tribune*, "The public saw just the stoker, not the symbol, and the symbol makes the play either important or just another play." He was quite correct, although his explanation does not necessarily indicate the only level on which the play can be followed. The theme is "not belonging." Yank is not just the abstraction Man, but the abstraction Worker or Proletariat. Yank discovers that he doesn't "belong," and this is his situation whether he is conceived as Man in the world of nature or as Worker in the world of modern industrial society. Even the early, seemingly ultra-realistic scenes in the hold of the ship, scenes which were strikingly new in 1922 to a public only recently weaned from the genteel tradition, are poetically evocative; they are an example of realism theatrically displayed to create an emotional and symbolic effect.

Because O'Neill used realistic material and vigorous colloquial dialogue in *The Hairy Ape*, it is one of his most satisfactory early experimental plays. For all its allegorical implication, it has a rich texture virtually throughout; even the distorted, expressionistic part beginning with Scene V, on Fifth Avenue, is anything but abstrusely presented. This may explain the play's power and the fascination it holds

for persons who are not prepared to say that they understand or accept the author's argument. Poetically, however, they do of course understand—and probably also accept. That is, they experience the play as a metaphor of modern experience—of alienation in the universe and in society. It is not as a system of ideas that we can approach *The Hairy Ape* but as a felt distress for which O'Neill's ideas form nothing more than a sort of algebraic notation. O'Neill's mood here is saturnine and uncompromisingly pessimistic. It is a mood that rarely left him when he contemplated the world at large and man's chances in it.

Writing about *The Hairy Ape* in 1947, George Jean Nathan remembered its "theme of despairing humanity gazing blinded at the stars." It is, indeed, the large measure of frustration that playgoers were most apt to recall. But they were able to remember it, fortunately, in the context of driving drama and in an atmosphere of angry, broken light. The play radiated a febrile magnificence that made many an intellectually sounder play seem inconsequential. When, in later years, O'Neill's boiler-room explosions began to take longer, they also tended to become tamer, and O'Neill was to lose, at times, one of his most attractive early qualities—his unreconciled fierceness in negation.

For additional commentary and bibliography, see pages 786–789.

THE HAIRY APE

By Eugene O'Neill

CHARACTERS

ROBERT SMITH, "YANK"
PADDY
LONG
MILDRED DOUGLAS
HER AUNT

SECOND ENGINEER
A GUARD
A SECRETARY OF AN ORGANIZATION
STOKERS, LADIES, GENTLEMEN, ETC.

SCENES

I. *The firemen's forecastle of an ocean liner—an hour after sailing from New York.*

II. *Section of promenade deck, two days out—morning.*

III. *The stockade. A few minutes later.*

IV. *Same as Scene I. Half an hour later.*

V. *Fifth Avenue, New York. Three weeks later.*

VI. *An island near the city. The next night.*

VII. *In the city. About a month later.*

VIII. *In the city. Twilight of the next day.*

TIME—*The Modern.*

SCENE I.

The firemen's forecastle of a transatlantic liner an hour after sailing from New York for the voyage across. Tiers of narrow, steel bunks, three deep, on all sides. An entrance in rear. Benches on the floor before the bunks. The room is crowded with men, shouting, cursing, laughing, singing—a confused, inchoate uproar swelling into a sort of unity, a meaning—the bewildered, furious, baffled defiance of a beast in a cage. Nearly all the men are drunk. Many bottles are passed from hand to hand. All are dressed in dungaree pants, heavy ugly shoes. Some wear singlets, but the majority are stripped to the waist.

The treatment of this scene, or of any other scene in the play, should by no means be naturalistic. The effect sought after is a cramped space in the bowels of a ship, imprisoned by white steel. The lines of bunks, the uprights supporting them, cross each other like the steel framework of a cage. The ceiling crushes down upon the men's heads. They cannot stand upright. This accentuates the natural stooping posture which shoveling coal and the resultant over-development of back and shoulder muscles have given them. The men themselves should resemble those pictures in which the appearance of Neanderthal Man is guessed at. All are hairy-chested, with long arms of tremendous power, and low, receding brows above their small, fierce, resentful eyes. All the civilized white races are represented, but except for the slight differentiation in color of hair, skin, eyes, all these men are alike.

The curtain rises on a tumult of sound. Yank is seated in the foreground. He seems broader, fiercer, more truculent, more powerful, more sure of himself than the rest. *They respect his superior strength —the grudging respect of fear. Then, too, he represents to them a self-expression, the very last word in what they are, their most highly developed individual.*

VOICES: Gif me trink dere, you!
'Ave a wet!
Salute!
Gesundheit!
Skoal!
Drunk as a lord, God stiffen you!
Here's how!
Luck!
Pass back that bottle, damn you!
Pourin' it down his neck!
Ho, Groggy! Where the devil have you been?
La Touraine.
I hit him smash in yaw, py Gott!
Jenkins—the First—he's a rotten swine——
And the coppers nabbed him—and I run——
I like peer better. It don't pig head gif you.
A slut, I'm sayin'! She robbed me aslape——
To hell with 'em all!
You're a bloody liar!
Say dot again! [*Commotion. Two men about to fight are pulled apart*]
No scrappin' now!
Tonight——
See who's the best man!
Bloody Dutchman!
Tonight on the for'ard square.
I'll bet on Dutchy.
He packa da wallop, I tella you!
Shut up, Wop!

No fightin', maties. We're all chums, ain't we?

[*A voice starts bawling a song*]

"Beer, beer, glorious beer!

Fill yourselves right up to here."

YANK: [*For the first time seeming to take notice of the uproar about him, turns around threateningly—in a tone of contemptuous authority*] Choke off dat noise! Where d'yuh get dat beer stuff? Beer, hell! Beer's for goils—and Dutchmen. Me for somep'n wit a kick to it! Gimme a drink, one of youse guys. [*Several bottles are eagerly offered. He takes a tremendous gulp at one of them; then, keeping the bottle in his hand, glares belligerently at the* Owner, *who hastens to acquiesce in this robbery by saying:*] All righto, Yank. Keep it and have another.

[Yank *contemptuously turns his back on the crowd again. For a second there is an embarrassed silence. Then:*]

VOICES: We must be passing the Hook.

She's beginning to roll to it.

Six days in hell—and then Southampton.

Py Yesus, I vish somepody take my first vatch for me!

Gittin' seasick, Square-head?

Drink up and forget it!

What's in your bottle?

Gin.

Dot's nigger trink.

Absinthe? It's doped. You'll go off your chump, Froggy!

Cochon!

Whiskey, that's the ticket!

Where's Paddy?

Going asleep.

Sing us that whiskey song, Paddy.

[*They all turn to an old, wizened* Irishman *who is dozing, very drunk, on the benches forward. His face is extremely monkey-like with all the sad, patient pathos of that animal in his small eyes*]

Singa da song, Caruso Pat!

He's getting old. The drink is too much for him.

He's too drunk.

PADDY: [*Blinking about him, starts to his feet resentfully, swaying, holding on to the edge of a bunk*] I'm never too drunk to sing. 'Tis only when I'm dead to the world I'd be wishful to sing at all. [*With a sort of sad contempt*] "Whiskey Johnny," ye want? A chanty, ye want? Now that's a queer wish from the ugly like of you, God help you. But no matter. [*He starts to sing in a thin, nasal, doleful tone*]

Oh, whiskey is the life of man!

Whiskey! O Johnny! [*They all join in on this*]

Oh, whiskey is the life of man!

Whiskey for my Johnny! [*Again chorus*]

Oh, whiskey drove my old man mad!

Whiskey! O Johnny!

Oh, whiskey drove my old man mad!

Whiskey for my Johnny!

YANK: [*Again turning around scornfully*] Aw hell! Nix on dat old sailing ship stuff! All dat bull's dead, see? And you're dead, too, yuh damned old Harp, on'y yuh don't know it. Take it easy, see? Give us a rest. Nix on de loud noise. [*With a cynical grin*] Can't youse see I'm tryin' to t'ink?

ALL: [*Repeating the word after him, as one, with the same cynical amused mockery*] Think!

[*The chorused word has a brazen metallic quality as if their throats were phonograph horns. It is followed by a general uproar of hard, barking laughter*]

VOICES: Don't be cracking your head wit ut, Yank.

You gat headache, py yingo!

One thing about it—it rhymes with drink!

Ha, ha, ha!

Drink, don't think!

Drink, don't think!

Drink, don't think!

[*A whole chorus of voices has taken up this refrain, stamping on the floor, pounding on the benches with fists*]

YANK: [*Taking a gulp from his bottle—good-naturedly:*] Aw right. Can de noise. I got yuh de foist time.

[*The uproar subsides. A very drunken sentimental* Tenor *begins to sing*]

"Far away in Canada,

Far across the sea,

There's a lass who fondly waits

Making a home for me——"

YANK: [*Fiercely contemptuous*] Shut up, yuh lousy boob! Where d'yuh get dat tripe? Home? Home, hell! I'll make a home for yuh! I'll knock yuh dead. Home! T'hell wit home! Where d'yuh get dat tripe? Dis is home, see? What d'yuh want wit home? [*Proudly*] I runned away from mine when I was a kid. On'y too glad to beat it, dat was me. Home was lickings for me, dat's all. But yuh can bet your shoit no one ain't never licked me since! Wanter try it, any of youse? Huh! I guess not. [*In a more placated but still contemptuous tone*] Goils waitin' for yuh, huh? Aw, hell! Dat's all tripe. Dey don't wait for no one. Dey'd double-cross yuh for a nickel. Dey're all tarts, get me? Treat 'em rough, dat's me. To hell wit 'em. Tarts, dat's what, de whole bunch of 'em.

LONG: [*Very drunk, jumps on a bench excitedly, gesticulating with a bottle in his hand*] Listen 'ere, Comrades! Yank 'ere is right. 'E says this 'ere stinkin' ship is our 'ome. And 'e says as 'ome is 'ell. And 'e's right! This is 'ell. We lives in 'ell, Comrades—and right enough we'll die in it. [*Raging*] And who's ter blame, I arsks yer. We ain't. We wasn't born this rotten way. All men is born free and ekal. That's in the bleedin' Bible, maties. But what d'they care for the Bible—them lazy, bloated swine what travels first cabin? Them's the ones. They dragged us down 'til we're on'y wage slaves in the bowels of a bloody ship, sweatin', burnin' up, eatin' coal dust! Hit's them's ter blame—the damned Capitalist clarss!

[*There had been a gradual murmur of contemptuous resentment rising among the* Men *until now he is interrupted by a storm of catcalls, hisses, boos, hard laughter*]

VOICES: Turn it off!

Shut up!

Sit down!

Closa da face!

Tamn fool! [*Etc.*]

YANK: [*Standing up and glaring at* Long] Sit down before I knock yuh down! [Long *makes haste to efface himself.* Yank *goes on contemptuously*] De Bible, huh? De Cap'tlist class, huh? Aw, nix on dat Salvation Army-Socialist bull. Git a soapbox! Hire a hall! Come and be saved, huh? Jerk us to Jesus, huh? Aw g'wan! I've listened to lots of guys like you, see? Yuh're all wrong. Wanter know what I t'ink? Yuh ain't no good for no one. Yuh're de bunk. Yuh ain't got no noive, get me? Yuh're yellow, dat's what. Yellow, dat's you. Say! What's dem slobs in de foist cabin got to do wit us? We're better men dan dey are, ain't we? Sure! One of us guys could clean up de whole mob wit one mit. Put one of 'em down here for one watch in de stokehole, what'd happen? Dey'd carry him off on a stretcher. Dem boids don't amount to nothin'. Dey're just baggage. Who makes dis old tub run? Ain't it us guys? Well den, we belong, don't we? We belong and dey don't. Dat's all. [*A loud chorus of approval.* Yank *goes on*] As for dis bein' hell—aw, nuts! Yuh lost your noive, dat's what. Dis is a man's job, get me? It belongs. It runs dis tub. No stiffs need apply. But yuh're a stiff, see? Yuh're yellow, dat's you.

VOICES: [*With a great hard pride in them*] Righto! A man's job!

Talk is cheap, Long.

He never could hold up his end.

Divil take him!

Yank's right. We make it go.

Py Gott, Yank say right ting!

We don't need no one cryin' over us.

Makin' speeches.

Throw him out!

Yellow!

Chuck him overboard!

I'll break his jaw for him!

[*They crowd around* Long *threateningly*]

YANK: [*Half good-natured again—contemptuously*] Aw, take it easy. Leave him alone. He ain't woith a punch. Drink up. Here's how, whoever owns dis.

[*He takes a long swallow from his bottle. All drink with him. In a flash all is hilarious amiability again, back-slapping, loud talk, etc.*]

PADDY: [*Who has been sitting in a blinking, melancholy daze—suddenly cries out in a voice full of old sorrow*] We belong to this, you're saying? We

make the ship to go, you're saying? Yerra then, that Almighty God have pity on us! [*His voice runs into the wail of a keen; he rocks back and forth on his bench. The men stare at him, startled and impressed in spite of themselves*] Oh, to be back in the fine days of my youth, ochone! Oh, there was fine beautiful ships them days—clippers wid tall masts touching the sky—fine strong men in them—men that was sons of the sea as if 'twas the mother that bore them. Oh, the clean skins of them, and the clear eyes, the straight backs and full chests of them! Brave men they was, and bold men surely! We'd be sailing out, bound down round the Horn maybe. We'd be making sail in the dawn, with a fair breeze, singing a chanty song wid no care to it. And astern the land would be sinking low and dying out, but we'd give it no heed but a laugh, and never a look behind. For the day that was, was enough, for we was free men—and I'm thinking 'tis only slaves do be giving heed to the day that's gone or the day to come—until they're old like me. [*With a sort of religious exaltation*] Oh, to be scudding south again wid the power of the Trade Wind driving her on steady through the nights and the days! Full sail on her! Nights and days! Nights when the foam of the wake would be flaming wid fire, when the sky'd be blazing and winking wid stars. Or the full of the moon maybe. Then you'd see her driving through the gray night, her sails stretching aloft all silver and white, not a sound on the deck, the lot of us dreaming dreams, till you'd believe 'twas no real ship at all you was on but a ghost ship like the *Flying Dutchman* they says does be roaming the seas forevermore widout touching a port. And there was the days, too. A warm sun on the clean decks. Sun warming the blood of you, and wind over the miles of shiny green ocean like strong drink to your lungs. Work—aye, hard work—but who'd mind that at all? Sure, you worked under the sky and 'twas work wid skill and daring to it. And wid the day done, in the dog watch, smoking me pipe at ease, the lookout would be raising land maybe, and we'd see the mountains of South Americy wid the red fire of the setting sun painting their white tops and the clouds floating by them! [*His tone of exaltation ceases. He goes on mournfully*] Yerra, what's the use of talking? 'Tis a dead man's whisper. [*To* Yank *resentfully*] 'Twas them days a ship was part of the sea, and a man was part of a ship, and the sea joined all together and made it one. [*Scornfully*] Is it one wid this you'd be, Yank—black smoke from the funnels smudging the sea, smudging the decks—the bloody engines pounding and throbbing and shaking—wid divil a sight of sun or a breath of clean air—choking our lungs wid coal dust—breaking our backs and hearts in the hell of the stokehole—feeding the bloody furnace—feeding our lives along wid the coal, I'm thinking—caged in by steel from a sight of the sky like bloody apes in the zoo! [*With a harsh laugh*] Ho-ho, divil mend you! Is it to belong to that you're wishing? Is it a flesh and blood wheel of the engines you'd be?

YANK: [*Who has been listening with a contemptuous sneer, barks out the answer*] Sure ting! Dat's me. What about it?

PADDY: [*As if to himself—with great sorrow:*] Me time is past due. That a great wave wid sun in the heart of it may sweep me over the side sometime I'd be dreaming of the days that's gone!

YANK: Aw, yuh crazy Mick! [*He springs to his feet and advances on* Paddy *threateningly—then stops, fighting some queer struggle within himself— lets his hands fall to his sides—contemptuously:*] Aw, take it easy. Yuh're aw right, at dat. Yuh're bugs, dat's all—nutty as a cuckoo. All dat tripe yuh been pullin'—Aw, dat's all right. On'y it's dead, get me? Yuh don't belong no more, see. Yuh don't get de stuff. Yuh're too old. [*Disgustedly*] But aw say, come up for air onct in a while, can't yuh? See what's happened since yuh croaked. [*He suddenly bursts forth vehemently, growing more and more excited*] Say! Sure! Sure I meant it! What de hell— Say, lemme talk! Hey! Hey, you old Harp! Hey, youse guys! Say, listen to me—wait a moment—I gotter talk, see? I belong and he don't. He's dead but I'm livin'. Listen to me! Sure I'm part of de engines! Why de hell not! Dey move, don't they? Dey're speed, ain't dey? Dey smash trou, don't dey? Twenty-five knots a hour! Dat's goin' some! Dat's new stuff! Dat belongs! But him, he's too old. He gets dizzy. Say, listen. All dat crazy tripe about nights and days; all dat crazy tripe about stars and moons; all dat crazy tripe about suns and winds, fresh air and de rest of it—Aw hell, dat's all a dope dream! Hittin' de pipe of de past, dat's what he's doin'. He's old and don't belong no more. But me, I'm young! I'm in de pink! I move wit it! It, get me! I mean de ting dat's de guts of all dis. It ploughs trou all de tripe he's been sayin'. It blows dat up! It knocks dat dead! It slams dat offen de face of de oith! It, get me! De engines and de coal and de smoke and all de rest of it! He can't breathe and swallow coal dust, but I kin, see? Dat's fresh air for me! Dat's food for me! I'm new, get me? Hell in de stokehole? Sure! It takes a man to work in hell. Hell, sure, dat's my fav'rite climate. I eat it up! I git fat on it! It's me makes it hot! It's me makes it roar! It's me makes it move! Sure, on'y for me everything stops. It all goes dead, get me? De noise and smoke and all de engines movin' de woild, dey stop. Dere ain't nothin' no more! Dat's what I'm sayin'. Everyting else dat makes de woild move, somep'n makes it move. It can't move witout somep'n else, see? Den yuh get down to me. I'm at de bottom, get me! Dere ain't nothin' foither. I'm de end! I'm de start! I start somep'n and de woild moves! It—dat's me!—de new dat's moiderin' de old! I'm de ting in coal dat makes it boin; I'm steam and oil for de engines; I'm de ting in noise dat makes yuh hear it; I'm smoke and express trains

and steamers and factory whistles; I'm de ting in gold dat makes it money! And I'm what makes iron into steel! Steel, dat stands for de whole ting! And I'm steel—steel—steel! I'm de muscles in steel, de punch behind it! [*As he says this he pounds with his fist against the steel bunks. All the* Men, *roused to a pitch of frenzied self-glorification by his speech, do likewise. There is a deafening metallic roar, through which* Yank's *voice can be heard bellowing:*] Slaves, hell! We run de whole woiks. All de rich guys dat tink dey're somep'n, dey ain't nothin'! Dey don't belong. But us guys, we're in de move, we're at de bottom, de whole ting is us! [*Paddy from the start of* Yank's *speech has been taking one gulp after another from his bottle, at first frightenedly, as if he were afraid to listen, then desperately, as if to drown his senses, but finally has achieved complete indifferent, even amused, drunkeness.* Yank *sees his lips moving. He quells the uproar with a shout*] Hey, youse guys, take it easy! Wait a moment! De nutty Harp is sayin' somep'n.

PADDY: [*Is heard now—throws his head back with a mocking burst of laughter*] Ho-ho-ho-ho-ho——

YANK: [*Drawing back his fist with a snarl*] Aw! Look out who yuh're givin' the bark!

PADDY: [*Begins to sing the "Miller of Dee" with enormous good nature*]

"I care for nobody, no, not I,
And nobody cares for me."

YANK: [*Good-natured himself in a flash, interrupts* Paddy *with a slap on the bare back like a report*] Dat's de stuff! Now yuh're gettin' wise to somep'n. Care for nobody, dat's de dope! To hell wit 'em all! And nix on nobody else carin'. I kin care for myself, get me! [*Eight bells sound, muffled, vibrating through the steel walls as if some enormous brazen gong were imbedded in the heart of the ship. All the men jump up mechanically, file through the door silently, close upon each other's neels in what is very like a prisoners' lock-step.* Yank *slaps* Paddy *on the back*] Our watch, yuh old Harp! [*Mockingly*] Come on down in hell. Eat up de coal dust. Drink in de heat. It's it, see! Act like yuh liked it, yuh better—or croak yuhself.

PADDY: [*With jovial defiance*] To the divil wid it! I'll not report this watch. Let thim log me and be damned. I'm no slave the like of you. I'll be settin' here at me ease, and drinking, and thinking, and dreaming dreams.

YANK: [*Contemptuously*] Tinkin' and dreamin', what'll that get yuh? What's tinkin' got to do wit it? We move, don't we? Speed, ain't it? Fog, dat's all you stand for. But we drive trou dat, don't we? We split dat up and smash trou—twenty-five knots a hour! [*Turns his back on* Paddy *scornfully*] Aw, yuh make me sick! Yuh don't belong!

[*He strides out the door in rear.* Paddy *hums to himself, blinking drowsily*]

CURTAIN

SCENE II.

Two days out. A section of the promenade deck. Mildred Douglas and her Aunt are discovered reclining in deck chairs. The former is a girl of twenty, slender, delicate, with a pale, pretty face marred by a self-conscious expression of disdainful superiority. She looks fretful, nervous, and discontented, bored by her own anemia. Her Aunt is a pompous and proud—and fat—old lady. She is a type even to the point of a double chin and lorgnettes. She is dressed pretentiously, as if afraid her face alone would never indicate her position in life. Mildred is dressed all in white.

The impression to be conveyed by this scene is one of the beautiful, vivid life of the sea all about—sunshine on the deck in a great flood, the fresh sea wind blowing across it. In the midst of this, these two incongruous, artificial figures, inert and disharmonious, the elder like a gray lump of dough touched up with rouge, the younger looking as if the vitality of her stock had been sapped before she was conceived, so that she is the expression not of its life energy but merely of the artificialities that energy had won for itself in the spending.

MILDRED: [*Looking up with affected dreaminess*] How the black smoke swirls back against the sky! Is it not beautiful?

AUNT: [*Without looking up*] I dislike smoke of any kind.

MILDRED: My great-grandmother smoked a pipe—a clay pipe.

AUNT: [*Ruffling*] Vulgar!

MILDRED: She was too distant a relative to be vulgar. Time mellows pipes.

AUNT: [*Pretending boredom but irritated*] Did the sociology you took up at college teach you that—to play the ghoul on every possible occasion, excavating old bones? Why not let your great-grandmother rest in her grave?

MILDRED: [*Dreamily*] With her pipe beside her—puffing in Paradise.

AUNT: [*With spite*] Yes, you are a natural born ghoul. You are even getting to look like one, my dear.

MILDRED: [*In a passionless tone*] I detest you, Aunt. [*Looking at her critically*] Do you know what you remind me of? Of a cold pork pudding against a background of linoleum tablecloth in the kitchen of a—but the possibilities are wearisome. [*She closes her eyes*]

AUNT: [*With a bitter laugh*] Merci for your candor. But since I am and must be your chaperon—in appearance, at least—let us patch up some sort of armed truce. For my part you are quite free to indulge any pose of eccentricity that beguiles you—as long as you observe the amenities——

MILDRED: [*Drawling*] The inanities?

AUNT: [*Going on as if she hadn't heard*] After exhausting the morbid thrills of social service work on New York's East Side—how they must have hated you, by the way, the poor that you made so much poorer in their own eyes!—you are now bent on making your slumming international. Well, I hope Whitechapel will provide the needed nerve tonic. Do not ask me to chaperon you there, however. I told your father I would not. I loathe deformity. We will hire an army of detectives and you may investigate everything—they allow you to see.

MILDRED: [*Protesting with a trace of genuine earnestness*] Please do not mock at my attempts to discover how the other half lives. Give me credit for some sort of groping sincerity in that at least. I would like to help them. I would like to be some use in the world. Is it my fault I don't know how? I would like to be sincere, to touch life somewhere. [*With weary bitterness*] But I'm afraid I have neither the vitality nor integrity. All that was burnt out in our stock before I was born. Grandfather's blast furnaces, flaming to the sky, melting steel, making millions—then father keeping those home fires burning, making more millions—and little me at the tail-end of it all. I'm a waste product in the Bessemer process—like the millions. Or rather, I inherit the acquired trait of the by-product, wealth, but none of the energy, none of the strength of the steel that made it. I am sired by gold and dammed by it, as they say at the race track—damned in more ways than one. [*She laughs mirthlessly*]

AUNT: [*Unimpressed—superciliously*] You seem to be going in for sincerity today. It isn't becoming to you, really—except as an obvious pose. Be as artificial as you are, I advise. There's a sort of sincerity in that, you know. And, after all, you must confess you like that better.

MILDRED: [*Again affected and bored*] Yes, I suppose I do. Pardon me for my outburst. When a leopard complains of its spots, it must sound rather grotesque. [*In a mocking tone*] Purr, little leopard. Purr, scratch, tear, kill, gorge yourself and be happy—only stay in the jungle where your spots are camouflage. In a cage they make you conspicuous.

AUNT: I don't know what you are talking about.

MILDRED: It would be rude to talk about anything to you. Let's just talk. [*She looks at her wrist watch*] Well, thank goodness, it's about time for them to come for me. That ought to give me a new thrill, Aunt.

AUNT: [*Affectedly troubled*] You don't mean to say you're really going? The dirt—the heat must be frightful——

MILDRED: Grandfather started as a puddler. I should have inherited an immunity to heat that would make a salamander shiver. It will be fun to put it to the test.

AUNT: But don't you have to have the captain's—or someone's—permission to visit the stokehole?

MILDRED: [*With a triumphant smile*] I have it—both his and the chief engineer's. Oh, they didn't want to at first, in spite of my social service credentials. They didn't seem a bit anxious that I should investigate how the other half lives and works on a ship. So I had to tell them that my father, the president of Nazareth Steel, chairman of the board of directors of this line, had told me it would be all right.

AUNT: He didn't.

MILDRED: How naïve age makes one! But I said he did, Aunt. I even said he had given me a letter to them—which I had lost. And they were afraid to take the chance that I might be lying. [*Excitedly*] So it's ho! for the stokehole. The second engineer is to escort me. [*Looking at her watch again*] It's time. And here he comes, I think.

[*The* Second Engineer *enters. He is a husky, fine-looking man of thirty-five or so. He stops before the two and tips his cap, visibly embarrassed and ill-at-ease*]

SECOND ENGINEER: Miss Douglas?

MILDRED: Yes. [*Throwing off her rugs and getting to her feet*] Are we all ready to start?

SECOND ENGINEER: In just a second, ma'am. I'm waiting for the Fourth. He's coming along.

MILDRED: [*With a scornful smile*] You don't care to shoulder this responsibility alone, is that it?

SECOND ENGINEER: [*Forcing a smile*] Two are better than one. [*Disturbed by her eyes, glances out to sea—blurts out:*] A fine day we're having.

MILDRED: Is it?

SECOND ENGINEER: A nice warm breeze——

MILDRED: It feels cold to me.

SECOND ENGINEER: But it's hot enough in the sun——

MILDRED: Not hot enough for me. I don't like Nature. I was never athletic.

SECOND ENGINEER: [*Forcing a smile*] Well, you'll find it hot enough where you're going.

MILDRED: Do you mean hell?

SECOND ENGINEER: [*Flabbergasted, decides to laugh*] Ho-ho! No, I mean the stokehole.

MILDRED: My grandfather was a puddler. He played with boiling steel.

SECOND ENGINEER: [*All at sea—uneasily*] Is that so? Hum, you'll excuse me, ma'am, but are you intending to wear that dress?

MILDRED: Why not?

SECOND ENGINEER: You'll likely rub against oil and dirt. It can't be helped.

MILDRED: It doesn't matter. I have lots of white dresses.

SECOND ENGINEER: I have an old coat you might throw over——

MILDRED: I have fifty dresses like this. I will throw this one into the sea when I come back. That ought to wash it clean, don't you think?

SECOND ENGINEER: [*Doggedly*] There's ladders to climb down that are none too clean—and dark alleyways——

MILDRED: I will wear this very dress and none other.

SECOND ENGINEER: No offense meant. It's none of my business. I was only warning you——

MILDRED: Warning? That sounds thrilling.

SECOND ENGINEER: [*Looking down the deck— with a sigh of relief*] There's the Fourth now. He's waiting for us. If you'll come——

MILDRED: Go on. I'll follow you. [*He goes.* Mildred *turns a mocking smile on her* Aunt] An oaf— but a handsome, virile oaf.

AUNT: [*Scornfully*] Poser!

MILDRED: Take care. He said there were dark alleyways——

AUNT: [*In the same tone*] Poser!

MILDRED: [*Biting her lips angrily*] You are right. But would that my millions were not so anemically chaste!

AUNT: Yes, for a fresh pose I have no doubt you would drag the name of Douglas in the gutter!

MILDRED: From which it sprang. Good-by, Aunt. Don't pray too hard that I may fall into the fiery furnace.

AUNT: Poser!

MILDRED: [*Viciously*] Old hag!

[*She slaps her* Aunt *insultingly across the face and walks off, laughing gaily*]

AUNT: [*Screams after her:*] I said poser!

CURTAIN

SCENE III.

The stokehole. In the rear, the dimly outlined bulks of the furnaces and boilers. High overhead one hanging electric bulb sheds just enough light through the murky air laden with coal dust to pile up masses of shadows everywhere. A line of men, stripped to the waist, is before the furnace doors. They bend over, looking neither to right nor left, handling their shovels as if they were part of their bodies, with a strange, awkward, swinging rhythm. They use the shovels to throw open the furnace doors. Then from these fiery round holes in the black a flood of terrific light and heat pours full upon the men who are outlined in silhouette in the crouching, inhuman attitudes of chained gorillas. The men shovel with a rhythmic motion, swinging as on a pivot from the coal which lies in heaps on the floor behind to hurl it into the flaming mouths before them. There is a tumult of noise—the brazen clang of the furnace doors as they are flung open or slammed shut, the grating, teeth-gritting grind of steel against steel, and of crunching coal. This clash of sounds stuns one's ears with its rending dissonance. But there is order in it, rhythm, a mechanical, regulated recurrence, a tempo. And rising above all, making the air hum with the quiver of liberated energy, the roar of leaping flames in the furnaces, the monotonous throbbing beat of the engines.

As the curtain rises, the furnace doors are shut. The Men *are taking a breathing spell. One or two are arranging the coal behind them, pulling it into more accessible heaps. The others can be dimly made out leaning on their shovels in relaxed attitudes of exhaustion.*

PADDY: [*From somewhere in the line—plaintively*] Yerra, will this divil's own watch nivir end? Me back is broke. I'm destroyed entirely.

YANK: [*From the center of the line—with exuberant scorn*] Aw, yuh make me sick! Lie down and croak, why don't yuh? Always beefin', dat's you! Say, dis is a cinch! Dis was made for me! It's my meat, get me! [*A whistle is blown—a thin, shrill note from somewhere overhead in the darkness.* Yank *curses without resentment*] Dere's de damn engineer crackin' de whip. He tinks we're loafin'.

PADDY: [*Vindictively*] God stiffen him!

YANK: [*In an exultant tone of command*] Come on, youse guys! Git into de game! She's gittin' hungry! Pile some grub in her. Trow it into her belly! Come on now, all of youse! Open her up!

[*At this last all the* Men, *who have followed his movements of getting into position, throw open their furnace doors with a deafening clang. The fiery light floods over their shoulders as they bend round for the coal. Rivulets of sooty sweat have traced maps on their backs. The enlarged muscles form bunches of high light and shadow*]

YANK: [*Chanting a count as he shovels without seeming effort*] One-two-three——[*His voice rising exultantly in the joy of battle*] Dat's de stuff! Let her have it! All togedder now! Sling it into her! Let her ride! Shoot de piece now! Call de toin on her! Drive her into it! Feel her move! Watch her smoke! Speed, dat's her middle name! Give her coal, youse guys! Coal, dat's her booze! Drink it up, baby! Let's see yuh sprint! Dig in and gain a lap! Dere she go-o-es.

[*This last in the chanting formula of the gallery gods at the six-day bike race. He slams his furnace door shut. The others do likewise with as much unison as their wearied bodies will permit. The effect is of one fiery eye after another being blotted out with a series of accompanying bangs*]

PADDY: [*Groaning*] Me back is broke. I'm bate out—bate——

[*There is a pause. Then the inexorable whistle sounds again from the dim regions above the electric light. There is a growl of cursing rage from all sides*]

YANK: [*Shaking his fist upward—contemptuously*] Take it easy dere, you! Who d'yuh tink's runnin' dis game, me or you? When I git ready, we move. Not before! When I git ready, get me!

VOICES: [*Approvingly*] That's the stuff! Yank tal him, py golly!

Yank ain't affeerd.

Goot poy, Yank!

Give him hell!

Tell 'im 'e's a bloody swine!

Bloody slave-driver!

YANK: [*Contemptuously*] He ain't got no noive. He's yellow, get me? All de engineers is yellow. Dey got streaks a mile wide. Aw, to hell wit him! Let's move, youse guys. We had a rest. Come on, she needs it! Give her pep! It ain't for him. Him and his whistle, dey don't belong. But we belong, see! We gotter feed de baby! Come on!

[*He turns and flings his furnace door open. They all follow his lead. At this instant the* Second *and* Fourth Engineers *enter from the darkness on the left with* Mildred *between them. She starts, turns paler, her pose is crumbling, she shivers with fright in spite of the blazing heat, but forces herself to leave the* Engineers *and take a few steps nearer the men. She is right behind* Yank. *All this happens quickly while the men have their backs turned*]

YANK: Come on, youse guys!

[*He is turning to get coal when the whistle sounds again in a peremptory, irritating note. This drives* Yank *into a sudden fury. While the other* Men *have turned full around and stopped dumbfounded by the spectacle of* Mildred *standing there in her white dress,* Yank *does not turn far enough to see her. Besides, his head is thrown back, he blinks upward through the murk trying to find the owner of the whistle, he brandishes his shovel murderously over his head in one hand, pounding on his chest, gorilla-like, with the other, shouting*]

YANK: Toin off dat whistle! Come down outa dere, yuh yellow, brass-buttoned, Belfast bum, yuh! Come down and I'll knock yer brains out! Yuh lousy, stinkin', yellow mut of a Catholic-moiderin' bastard! Come down and I'll moider yuh! Pullin' dat whistle on me, huh? I'll show yuh! I'll crash yer skull in! I'll drive yer teet' down yer troat! I'll slam yer nose trou de back of yer head! I'll cut yer guts out for a nickel, yuh lousy boob, yuh dirty, crummy, muck-eatin' son of a——

[*Suddenly he becomes conscious of all the other* Men *staring at something directly behind his back. He whirls defensively with a snarling, murderous growl, crouching to spring, his lips drawn back over his teeth, his small eyes gleaming ferociously. He sees* Mildred, *like a white apparition in the full light from the open furnace doors. He glares into her eyes, turned to stone. As for her, during his speech she has listened, paralyzed with horror, terror, her whole personality crushed, beaten in, collapsed, by the terrific impact of this unknown, abys-*

mal brutality, naked and shameless. As she looks at his gorilla face, as his eyes bore into hers, she utters a low, choking cry and shrinks away from him, putting both hands up before her eyes to shut out the sight of his face, to protect her own. This startles Yank to a reaction. His mouth falls open, his eyes grow bewildered]

MILDRED: [*About to faint—to the* Engineers, *who now have her one by each arm—whimperingly]* Take me away! Oh, the filthy beast!

[*She faints. They carry her quickly back, disappearing in the darkness at the left, rear. An iron door clangs shut. Rage and bewildered fury rush back on Yank. He feels himself insulted in some unknown fashion in the very heart of his pride. He roars]*

YANK: God damn yuh!

[*And hurls his shovel after them at the door which has just closed. It hits the steel bulkhead with a clang and falls clattering on the steel floor. From overhead the whistle sounds again in a long, angry, insistent command]*

CURTAIN

SCENE IV.

The firemen's forecastle. Yank's watch has just come off duty and had dinner. Their faces and bodies shine from a soap and water scrubbing but around their eyes, where a hasty dousing does not touch, the coal dust sticks like black make-up, giving them a queer, sinister expression.

Yank has not washed either face or body. He stands out in contrast to them, a blackened, brooding figure. He is seated forward on a bench in the exact attitude of Rodin's "The Thinker." The others, most of them smoking pipes, are staring at Yank half-apprehensively, as if fearing an outburst; half-amusedly, as if they saw a joke somewhere that tickled them.

VOICES: He ain't ate nothin'.
Py golly, a fallar gat to gat grub in him.
Divil a lie.
Yank feeda da fire, no feeda da face.
Ha-ha.
He ain't even washed hisself.
He's forgot.
Hey, Yank, you forgot to wash.

YANK: [*Sullenly*] Forgot nothin'! To hell wit washin'.

VOICES: It'll stick to you.
It'll get under your skin.
Give yer bleedin' itch, that's wot.
It makes spots on you—like a leopard.
Like a piebald nigger, you mean.

Better wash up, Yank.
You sleep better.
Wash up, Yank.
Wash up! Wash up!

YANK: [*Resentfully*] Aw say, youse guys. Lemme alone. Can't youse see I'm tryin' to tink?

ALL: [*Repeating the word after him, as one, with cynical mockery*] Think!

[*The word has a brazen, metallic quality as if their throats were phonograph horns. It is followed by a chorus of hard, barking laughter]*

YANK: [*Springing to his feet and glaring at them belligerently*] Yes, tink! Tink, dat's what I said! What about it?

[*They are silent, puzzled by his sudden resentment at what used to be one of his jokes. Yank sits down again in the same attitude of "The Thinker"]*

VOICES: Leave him alone.
He's got a grouch on.
Why wouldn't he?

PADDY: [*With a wink at the others*] Sure I know what's the matther. 'Tis aisy to see. He's fallen in love, I'm telling you.

ALL: [*Repeating the word after him, as one, with cynical mockery*] Love!

[*The word has a brazen metallic quality as if their throats were phonograph horns. It is followed by a chorus of hard, barking laughter]*

YANK: [*With a contemptuous snort*] Love, hell! Hate, dat's what. I've fallen in hate, get me?

PADDY: [*Philosophically*] 'Twould take a wise man to tell one from the other. [*With a bitter, ironical scorn, increasing as he goes on*] But I'm telling you it's love that's in it. Sure what else but love for us poor bastes in the stokehole would be bringing a fine lady, dressed like a white quane, down a mile of ladders and steps to be havin' a look at us?

[*A growl of anger goes up from all sides*]

LONG: [*Jumping on a bench—hectically*] Hinsultin' us! Hinsultin' us, the bloody cow! And them bloody engineers! What right 'as they got to be exhibitin' us 's if we was bleedin' monkeys in a menagerie? Did we sign for hinsults to our dignity as 'onest workers? Is that in the ship's articles? You kin bloody well bet it ain't! But I knows why they done it. I arsked a deck steward 'oo she was an 'e told me. 'Er old man's a bleedin' millionaire, a bloody Capitalist! 'E's got enuf bloody gold to sink this bleedin' ship! 'E makes arf the bloody steel in the world! 'E owns this bloody boat! And you and me, Comrades, we're 'is slaves! And the skipper and mates and engineers, they're 'is slaves! And she's 'is bloody daughter and we're all 'er slaves, too! And she gives 'er orders as 'ow she wants to see the bloody animals below decks and down they takes 'er!

[*There is a roar of rage from all sides*]

YANK: [*Blinking at him bewilderedly*] Say! Wait a moment! Is all dat straight goods?

LONG: Straight as string! The bleedin' steward as

waits on 'em, 'e told me about 'er. And what're we
goin' ter do, I arsks yer? 'Ave we got ter swaller 'er
hinsults like dogs? It ain't in the ship's articles. I
tell yer we got a case. We kin go to law——

YANK: [*With abysmal contempt*] Hell! Law!

ALL: [*Repeating the word after him, as one, with
cynical mockery*] Law!

[*The word has a brazen metallic quality as if
their throats were phonograph horns. It is followed by a chorus of hard, barking laughter*]

LONG: [*Feeling the ground slipping from under
his feet—desperately*] As voters and citizens we kin
force the bloody governments——

YANK: [*With abysmal contempt*] Hell! Governments!

ALL: [*Repeating the word after him, as one, with
cynical mockery*] Governments!

[*The word has a brazen metallic quality as if
their throats were phonograph horns. It is followed by a chorus of hard, barking laughter*]

LONG: [*Hysterically*] We're free and equal in the
sight of God——

YANK: [*With abysmal contempt*] Hell! God!

ALL: [*Repeating the word after him, as one, with
cynical mockery*] God!

[*The word has a brazen metallic quality as if
their throats were phonograph horns. It is followed by a chorus of hard, barking laughter*]

YANK: [*Witheringly*] Aw, join de Salvation Army!

ALL: Sit down! Shut up! Damn fool! Sea-lawyer!

[*Long slinks back out of sight*]

PADDY: [*Continuing the trend of his thoughts as
if he had never been interrupted—bitterly*] And
there she was standing behind us, and the Second
pointing at us like a man you'd hear in a circus
would be saying: In this cage is a queerer kind of
baboon than ever you'd find in darkest Africy. We
roast them in their own sweat—and be damned if
you won't hear some of thim saying they like it!
[*He glances scornfully at Yank*]

YANK: [*With a bewildered uncertain growl*] Aw!

PADDY: And there was Yank roarin' curses and
turning round wid his shovel to brain her—and she
looked at him, and him at her——

YANK: [*Slowly*] She was all white. I tought she
was a ghost. Sure.

PADDY: [*With heavy, biting sarcasm*] 'Twas love
at first sight, divil a doubt of it! If you'd seen the
endearin' look on her pale mug when she shriveled
away with her hands over her eyes to shut out the
sight of him! Sure, 'twas as if she'd seen a great
hairy ape escaped from the Zoo!

YANK: [*Stung—with a growl of rage*] Aw!

PADDY: And the loving way Yank heaved his
shovel at the skull of her, only she was out the door!
[*A grin breaking over his face*] 'Twas touching, I'm
telling you! It put the touch of home, swate home
in the stokehole.

[*There is a roar of laughter from all*]

YANK: [*Glaring at* Paddy *menacingly*] Aw, choke
dat off, see!

PADDY: [*Not heeding him—to the others*] And
her grabbin' at the Second's arm for protection.
[*With a grotesque imitation of a woman's voice*]
Kiss me, Engineer dear, for it's dark down here and
me old man's in Wall Street making money; Hug
me tight, darlin', for I'm afeerd in the dark and
me mother's on deck makin' eyes at the skipper!

[*Another roar of laughter*]

YANK: [*Threateningly*] Say! What yuh tryin' to do,
kid me, yuh old Harp?

PADDY: Divil a bit! Ain't I wishin' myself you'd
brained her?

YANK: [*Fiercely*] I'll brain her! I'll brain her yet,
wait 'n' see! [*Coming over to* Paddy—*slowly*] Say,
is dat what she called me—a hairy ape?

PADDY: She looked it at you if she didn't say the
word itself.

YANK: [*Grinning horribly*] Hairy ape, huh? Sure!
Dat's de way she looked at me, aw right. Hairy ape!
So dat's me, huh? [*Bursting into rage—as if she
were still in front of him*] Yuh skinny tart! Yuh
white-faced bum, yuh! I'll show yuh who's a ape!
[*Turning to the others, bewilderment seizing him
again*] Say, youse guys. I was bawlin' him out for
pullin' de whistle on us. You heard me. And den
I seen youse lookin' at somep'n and I tought he'd
sneaked down to come up in back of me, and I
hopped round to knock him dead wit de shovel. And
dere she was wit de light on her! Christ, yuh coulda
pushed me over wit a finger! I was scared, get me?
Sure! I tought she was a ghost, see? She was all in
white like dey wrap around stiffs. You seen her.
Kin yuh blame me? She didn't belong, dat's what.
And den when I come to and seen it was a real
skoit and seen de way she was lookin' at me—like
Paddy said—Christ, I was sore, get me? I don't stand
for dat stuff from nobody. And I flung de shovel—
on'y she'd beat it. [*Furiously*] I wished it'd banged
her! I wished it'd knocked her block off!

LONG: And be 'anged for murder or 'lectrocuted?
She ain't bleedin' well worth it.

YANK: I don't give a damn what! I'd be square
wit her, wouldn't I? Tink I wanter let her put
somep'n over on me? Tink I'm goin' to let her git
away wit dat stuff? Yuh don't know me! No one
ain't never put nothin' over on me and got away
wit it, see!—not dat kind of stuff—no guy and no
skoit neither! I'll fix her! Maybe she'll come down
again——

VOICE: No chance, Yank. You scared her out of
a year's growth.

YANK: I scared her? Why de hell should I scare
her? Who de hell is she? Ain't she de same as me?
Hairy ape, huh? [*With his old confident bravado*]
I'll show her I'm better'n her, if she on'y knew it.
I belong and she don't, see! I move and she's dead!
Twenty-five knots a hour, dat's me! Dat carries her
but I make dat. She's on'y baggage. Sure! [*Again

bewilderedly] But, Christ, she was funny lookin'! Did yuh pipe her hands? White and skinny. Yuh could see de bones through 'em. And her mush, dat was dead white, too. And her eyes, dey was like dey'd seen a ghost. Me, dat was! Sure! Hairy ape! Ghost, huh? Look at dat arm! [*He extends his right arm, swelling out the great muscles*] I coulda took her wit dat, wit just my little finger even, and broke her in two. [*Again bewilderedly*] Say, who is dat skoit, huh? What is she? What's she come from? Who made her? Who give her de noive to look at me like dat? Dis ting's got my goat right. I don't get her. She's new to me. What does a skoit like her mean, huh? She don't belong, get me! I can't see her. [*With growing anger*] But one ting I'm wise to, aw right, aw right! Youse all kin bet your shoits I'll git even wit her. I'll show her if she tinks she— She grinds de organ and I'm on de string, huh? I'll fix her! Let her come down again and I'll fling her in de furnace! She'll move den! She won't shiver at nothin', den! Speed, dat'll be her! She'll belong den! [*He grins horribly*]

PADDY: She'll never come. She's had her belly-full, I'm telling you. She'll be in bed now, I'm thinking, wid ten doctors and nurses feedin' her salts to clean the fear out of her.

YANK: [*Enraged*] Yuh tink I made her sick too, do yuh? Just lookin' at me, huh? Hairy ape, huh? [*In a frenzy of rage*] I'll fix her! I'll tell her where to git off! She'll git down on her knees and take it back or I'll bust de face offen her! [*Shaking one fist upward and beating on his chest with the other*] I'll find yuh! I'm comin', d'yuh hear? I'll fix yuh, God damn yuh! [*He makes a rush for the door*]

VOICES: Stop him!
He'll get shot!
He'll murder her!
Trip him up!
Hold him!
He's gone crazy!
Gott, he's strong!
Hold him down!
Look out for a kick!
Pin his arms!

[*They have all piled on him and, after a fierce struggle, by sheer weight of numbers have borne him to the floor just inside the door*]

PADDY: [*Who has remained detached*] Kape him down till he's cooled off. [*Scornfully*] Yerra, Yank, you're a great fool. Is it payin' attention at all you are to the like of that skinny sow widout one drop of rale blood in her?

YANK: [*Frenziedly, from the bottom of the heap*] She done me doit! She done me doit, didn't she? I'll git square wit her! I'll get her some way! Git offen me, youse guys! Lemme up! I'll show her who's a ape!

CURTAIN

SCENE V.

Three weeks later. A corner of Fifth Avenue in the Fifties on a fine Sunday morning. A general atmosphere of clean, well-tidied, wide street; a flood of mellow, tempered sunshine; gentle, genteel breezes. In the rear, the show windows of two shops, a jewelry establishment on the corner, a furrier's next to it. Here the adornments of extreme wealth are tantalizingly displayed. The jeweler's window is gaudy with glittering diamonds, emeralds, rubies, pearls, etc., fashioned in ornate tiaras, crowns, necklaces, collars, etc. From each piece hangs an enormous tag from which a dollar sign and numerals in intermittent electric lights wink out the incredible prices. The same in the furrier's. Rich furs of all varieties hang there bathed in a downpour of artificial light. The general effect is of a background of magnificence cheapened and made grotesque by commercialism, a background in tawdry disharmony with the clear light and sunshine on the street itself.

Up the side street Yank and Long come swaggering. Long is dressed in shore clothes, wears a black Windsor tie, cloth cap. Yank is in his dirty dungarees. A fireman's cap with black peak is cocked defiantly on the side of his head. He has not shaved for days and around his fierce, resentful eyes—as around those of Long to a lesser degree—the black smudge of coal dust still sticks like make-up. They hesitate and stand together at the corner, swaggering, looking about them with a forced, defiant contempt.

LONG: [*Indicating it all with an oratorical gesture*] Well, 'ere we are. Fif' Avenoo. This 'ere's their bleedin' private lane, as yer might say. [*Bitterly*] We're trespassers 'ere. Proletarians keep orf the grass!

YANK: [*Dully*] I don't see no grass, yuh boob. [*Staring at the sidewalk*] Clean, ain't it? Yuh could eat a fried egg offen it. The white wings got some job sweepin' dis up. [*Looking up and down the avenue—surlily*] Where's all de white-collar stiffs yuh said was here—and de skoits—her kind?

LONG: In church, blarst 'em! Arskin' Jesus to give 'em more money.

YANK: Choich, huh? I useter go to choich onct— sure—when I was a kid. Me old man and woman, dey made me. Dey never went demselves, dough. Always got too big a head on Sunday mornin', dat was dem. [*With a grin*] Dey was scrappers for fair, bot' of dem. On Satiday nights when dey bot' got a skinful dey could put up a bout oughter been staged at de Garden. When dey got trough dere wasn't a chair or table wit a leg under it. Or else dey bot' jumped on me for somep'n. Dat was where I loined to take punishment. [*With a grin and a swagger*] I'm a chip offen de old block, get me?

LONG: Did yer old man follow the sea?

YANK: Naw. Worked along shore. I runned away when me old lady croaked wit de tremens. I helped at truckin' and in de market. Den I shipped in de stokehole. Sure. Dat belongs. De rest was nothin'. [Looking around him] I ain't never seen dis before. De Brooklyn waterfront, dat was where I was dragged up. [Taking a deep breath] Dis ain't so bad at dat, huh?

LONG: Not bad? Well, we pays for it wiv our bloody sweat, if yer wants to know!

YANK: [With sudden angry disgust] Aw, hell! I don't see no one, see—like her. All dis gives me a pain. It don't belong. Say, ain't dere a back room around dis dump? Let's go shoot a ball. All dis is too clean and quiet and dolled-up, get me? It gives me a pain.

LONG: Wait and yer'll bloody well see——

YANK: I don't wait for no one. I keep on de move. Say, what yuh drag me up here for, anyway? Tryin' to kid me, yuh simp, yuh?

LONG: Yer wants to get back at 'er, don't yer? That's what yer been sayin' every bloomin' hour since she hinsulted yer.

YANK: [Vehemently] Sure ting I do! Didn't I try to get even wit her in Southampton? Didn't I sneak on de deck and wait for her by de gangplank? I was goin' to spit in her pale mug, see! Sure, right in her pop-eyes! Dat woulda made me even, see? But no chanct. Dere was a whole army of plainclothes bulls around. Dey spotted me and gimme de bum's rush. I never seen her. But I'll git square wit her yet, you watch! [Furiously] De lousy tart! She tinks she kin get away wit moider—but not wit me! I'll fix her! I'll tink of a way!

LONG: [As disgusted as he dares to be] Ain't that why I brought yer up 'ere—to show yer? Yer been lookin' at this 'ere 'ole affair wrong. Yer been actin' an' talkin' 's if it was all a bleedin' personal matter between yer and that bloody cow. I wants to convince yer she was on'y a representative of 'er clarss. I wants to awaken yer bloody clarss consciousness. Then yer'll see it's 'er clarss ye've got to fight, not 'er alone. There's a 'ole mob of 'em like 'er, Gawd blind 'em!

YANK: [Spitting on his hands—belligerently] De more de merrier when I gits started. Bring on de gang!

LONG: Yer'll see 'em in arf a mo', when that church lets out. [He turns and sees the window display in the two stores for the first time] Blimey! Look at that, will yer? [They both walk back and stand looking in the jeweler's. Long flies into a fury] Just look at this 'ere bloomin' mess! Just look at it! Look at the bleedin' prices on 'em—more'n our 'ole bloody stokehole makes in ten voyages sweatin' in 'ell! And they—'er and 'er bloody clarss—buys 'em for toys to dangle on 'em! One of these 'ere would buy scoff for a starvin' family for a year!

YANK: Aw, cut de sob stuff! T' hell wit de starvin' family! Yuh'll be passin' de hat to me next. [With naïve admiration] Say, dem tings is pretty, huh? Bet yuh dey'd hock for a piece of change aw right. [Then turning away, bored] But, aw hell, what good are dey? Let her have 'em. Dey don't belong no more'n she does. [With a gesture of sweeping the jeweler's into oblivion] All dat don't count, get me?

LONG: [Who has moved to the furrier's—indignantly] And I s'pose this 'ere don't count neither—skins of poor, 'armless animals slaughtered so as 'er and 'ers can keep their bleedin' noses warm!

YANK: [Who has been staring at something inside—with queer excitement] Take a slant at dat! Give it de once-over! Monkey fur—two t'ousand bucks! [Bewilderedly] Is dat straight goods—monkey fur? What de hell——?

LONG: [Bitterly] It's straight enuf. [With grim humor] They wouldn't bloody well pay that for a 'airy ape's skin—no, nor for the 'ole livin' ape with all 'is 'ead, and body, and soul thrown in!

YANK: [Clenching his fists, his face growing pale with rage as if the skin in the window were a personal insult] Trowin' it up in my face! Christ! I'll fix her!

LONG: [Excitedly] Church is out. 'Ere they come, the bleedin' swine. [After a glance at Yank's lowering face—uneasily] Easy goes, Comrade. Keep yer bloomin' temper. Remember force defeats itself. It ain't our weapon. We must impress our demands through peaceful means—the votes of the on-marching proletarians of the bloody world!

YANK: [With abysmal contempt] Votes, hell! Votes is a joke, see? Votes for women! Let dem do it!

LONG: [Still more uneasily] Calm, now. Treat 'em wiv the proper contempt. Observe the bleedin' parasites but 'old yer 'orses.

YANK: [Angrily] Git away from me! Yuh're yellow, dat's what. Force, dat's me! De punch, dat's me every time, see!

[The Crowd from church enter from the right, sauntering slowly and affectedly, their heads held stiffly up, looking neither to right nor left, talking in toneless, simpering voices. The Women are rouged, calcimined, dyed, overdressed to the nth degree. The Men are in Prince Alberts, high hats, spats, canes, etc. A procession of gaudy marionettes, yet with something of the relentless horror of Frankensteins in their detached, mechanical unawareness]

VOICES: Dear Doctor Caiaphas! He is so sincere! What was the sermon? I dozed off.

About the radicals, my dear—and the false doctrines that are being preached.

We must organize a hundred per cent American bazaar.

And let everyone contribute one one-hundredth per cent of their income tax.

What an original idea!

We can devote the proceeds to rehabilitating the
    veil of the temple.
But that has been done so many times.

YANK: [*Glaring from one to the other of them—
with an insulting snort of scorn*] Huh! Huh!

    [*Without seeming to see him, they make wide
    detours to avoid the spot where he stands in
    the middle of the sidewalk*]

LONG: [*Frightenedly*] Keep yer bloomin' mouth
shut, I tells yer.

YANK: [*Viciously*] G'wan! Tell it to Sweeney! [*He
swaggers away and deliberately lurches into a top-
hatted* Gentleman, *then glares at him pugnaciously*]
Say, who d'yuh tink yuh're bumpin'? Tink yuh own
de oith?

GENTLEMAN: [*Coldly and affectedly*] I beg your
pardon. [*He has not looked at* Yank *and passes on
without a glance, leaving him bewildered*]

LONG: [*Rushing up and grabbing* Yank's *arm*]
'Ere! Come away! This wasn't what I meant. Yer'll
'ave the bloody coppers down on us.

YANK: [*Savagely—giving him a push that sends
him sprawling*] G'wan!

LONG: [*Picks himself up—hysterically*] I'll pop
orf then. This ain't what I meant. And whatever
'appens, yer can't blame me. [*He slinks off left*]

YANK: T' hell wit youse! [*He approaches a* Lady
—with a vicious grin and a smirking wink] Hello,
Kiddo. How's every little ting? Got anything on for
tonight? I know an old boiler down to de docks we
kin crawl into. [*The* Lady *stalks by without a look,
without a change of pace.* Yank *turns to others—
insultingly*] Holy smokes, what a mug! Go hide
yuhself before de horses shy at yuh. Gee, pipe de
heinie on dat one! Say, youse, yuh look like de stoin
of a ferryboat. Paint and powder! All dolled up to
kill! Yuh look like stiffs laid out for de boneyard!
Aw, g'wan, de lot of youse! Yuh give me de eye-
ache. Yuh don't belong, get me! Look at me, why
don't youse dare? I belong, dat's me! [*Pointing to
a sky-scraper across the street which is in process
of construction—with bravado*] See dat building
goin' up dere? See de steel work? Steel, dat's me!
Youse guys live on it and tink yuh're somep'n. But
I'm *in* it, see! I'm de hoistin' engine dat makes it
go up! I'm it—de inside and bottom of it! Sure!
I'm steel and steam and smoke and de rest of it!
It moves—speed—twenty-five stories up—and me
at de top and bottom—movin'! Youse simps don't
move. Yuh're on'y dolls I winds up to see 'm spin.
Yuh're de garbage, get me—de leavins—de ashes
we dump over de side! Now, what 'a' yuh gotta say?
[*But as they seem neither to see nor hear him, he
flies into a fury*] Bums! Pigs! Tarts! Bitches! [*He
turns in a rage on the* Men, *bumping viciously into
them but not jarring them the least bit. Rather it is
he who recoils after each collision. He keeps growling*] Git off de oith! G'wan, yuh bum! Look where
yuh're goin', can't yuh? Git outa here! Fight, why
don't yuh? Put up yer mits! Don't be a dog! Fight

or I'll knock yuh dead! [*But, without seeming to
see him, they all answer with mechanical affected
politeness:*] I beg your pardon.

    [*Then, at a cry from one of the* Women, *they
    all scurry to the furrier's window*]

THE WOMAN: [*Ecstatically, with a gasp of delight*]
Monkey fur! [*The whole crowd of* Men *and* Women
*chorus after her in the same tone of affected de-
light*] Monkey fur!

YANK: [*With a jerk of his head back on his shoulders, as if he had received a punch full in the face
—raging*] I see yuh, all in white! I see yuh, yuh
white-faced tart, yuh! Hairy ape, huh? I'll hairy ape
yuh!

    [*He bends down and grips at the street curbing
    as if to pluck it out and hurl it. Foiled in this,
    snarling with passion, he leaps to the lamp-
    post on the corner and tries to pull it up for
    a club. Just at that moment a bus is heard
    rumbling up. A fat, high-hatted, spatted* Gen-
    tleman *runs out from the side street. He calls
    out plaintively:*]

GENTLEMAN: Bus! Bus! Stop there! [*And runs full
tilt into the bending, straining* Yank, *who is bowled
off his balance*]

YANK: [*Seeing a fight—with a roar of joy as he
springs to his feet*] At last! Bus, huh? I'll bust yuh!
[*He lets drive a terrific swing, his fist landing full
on the fat* Gentleman's *face. But the* Gentleman
stands unmoved as if nothing had happened]

GENTLEMAN: I beg your pardon. [*Then irritably*]
You have made me lose my bus. [*He claps his
hands and begins to scream:*] Officer! Officer!

    [*Many police whistles shrill out on the instant
    and a whole platoon of* Policemen *rush in on*
    Yank *from all sides. He tries to fight but is
    clubbed to the pavement and fallen upon. The*
    Crowd *at the window have not moved or no-
    ticed this disturbance. The clanging gong of
    the patrol wagon approaches with a clamoring
    din*]

CURTAIN

SCENE VI.

*Night of the following day. A row of cells in the
prison on Blackwell's Island. The cells extend back
diagonally from right front to left rear. They do not
stop, but disappear in the dark background as if
they ran on, numberless, into infinity. One electric
bulb from the low ceiling of the narrow corridor
sheds its light through the heavy steel bars of the
cell at the extreme front and reveals part of the interior.*

    Yank *can be seen within, crouched on the edge of
his cot in the attitude of Rodin's "The Thinker."
His face is spotted with black and blue bruises. A
blood-stained bandage is wrapped around his head.*

YANK: [*Suddenly starting as if awakening from a dream, reaches out and shakes the bars—aloud to himself, wonderingly*] Steel. Dis is de Zoo, huh?

[*A burst of hard, barking laughter comes from the unseen* Occupants *of the cells, runs back down the tier, and abruptly ceases*]

VOICES: [*Mockingly*] The Zoo? That's a new name for this coop—a damn good name!

Steel, eh? You said a mouthful. This is the old iron house.

Who is that boob talkin'?

He's the bloke they brung in out of his head. The bulls had beat him up fierce.

YANK: [*Dully*] I musta been dreamin'. I tought I was in a cage at de Zoo—but de apes don't talk, do dey?

VOICES: [*With mocking laughter*] You're in a cage aw right.

A coop!

A pen!

A sty!

A kennel!

[*Hard laughter—a pause*]

Say, guy! Who are you? No, never mind lying. What are you?

Yes, tell us your sad story. What's your game?

What did they jug yuh for?

YANK: [*Dully*] I was a fireman—stokin' on de liners. [*Then with sudden rage, rattling his cell bars*] I'm a hairy ape, get me? And I'll bust youse all in de jaw if yuh don't lay off kiddin' me.

VOICES: Huh! You're a hard boiled duck, ain't youse!

When you spit, it bounces!

[*Laughter*]

Aw, can it. He's a regular guy. Ain't you?

What did he say he was—a ape?

YANK: [*Defiantly*] Sure ting! Ain't dat what youse all are—apes?

[*A silence. Then a furious rattling of bars from down the corridor*]

A VOICE: [*Thick with rage*] I'll show yuh who's a ape, yuh bum!

VOICES: Ssshh! Nix!

Can de noise!

Piano!

You'll have the guard down on us!

YANK: [*Scornfully*] De guard? Yuh mean de keeper, don't yuh?

[*Angry exclamations from all the cells*]

VOICE: [*Placatingly*] Aw, don't pay no attention to him. He's off his nut from the beatin'-up he got.

Say, you guy! We're waitin' to hear what they landed you for—or ain't yuh tellin'?

YANK: Sure, I'll tell youse. Sure! Why de hell not? On'y—youse won't get me. Nobody gets me but me, see? I started to tell de Judge and all he says was: "Toity days to tink it over." Tink it over! Christ, dat's all I been doin' for weeks! [*After a pause*] I

was tryin' to git even wit someone, see?—someone dat done me doit.

VOICES: [*Cynically*] De old stuff, I bet. Your goil, huh?

Give yuh the double-cross, huh?

That's them every time!

Did yuh beat up de odder guy?

YANK: [*Disgustedly*] Aw, yuh're all wrong! Sure dere was a skoit in it—but not what youse mean, not dat old tripe. Dis was a new kind of skoit. She was dolled up all in white—in de stokehole. I tought she was a ghost. Sure.

[*A pause*]

VOICES: [*Whispering*] Gee, he's still nutty.

Let him rave. It's fun listenin'.

YANK: [*Unheeding—groping in his thoughts*] Her hands—dey was skinny and white like dey wasn't real but painted on somep'n. Dere was a million miles from me to her—twenty-five knots a hour. She was like some dead ting de cat brung in. Sure, dat's what. She didn't belong. She belonged in de window of a toy store, or on de top of a garbage can, see! Sure! [*He breaks out angrily*] But would yuh believe it, she had de noive to do me doit. She lamped me like she was seein' somep'n broke loose from de menagerie. Christ, yuh'd oughter seen her eyes! [*He rattles the bars of his cell furiously*] But I'll get back at her yet, you watch! And if I can't find her I'll take it out on de gang she runs wit. I'm wise to where dey hangs out now. I'll show her who belongs! I'll show her who's in de move and who ain't. You watch my smoke!

VOICES: [*Serious and joking*] Dat's de talkin'!

Take her for all she's got!

What was this dame, anyway? Who was she, eh?

YANK: I dunno. First cabin stiff. Her old man's a millionaire, dey says—name of Douglas.

VOICES: Douglas? That's the president of the Steel Trust, I bet.

Sure. I seen his mug in de papers.

He's filthy with dough.

VOICE: Hey, feller, take a tip from me. If you want to get back at that dame, you better join the Wobblies. You'll get some action then.

YANK: Wobblies? What de hell's dat?

VOICE: Ain't you ever heard of the I. W. W.?

YANK: Naw. What is it?

VOICE: A gang of blokes—a tough gang. I been readin' about 'em today in the paper. The guard give me the *Sunday Times*. There's a long spiel about 'em. It's from a speech made in the Senate by a guy named Senator Queen. [*He is in the cell next to* Yank's. *There is a rustling of paper*] Wait'll I see if I got light enough and I'll read you. Listen. [*He reads:*] "There is a menace existing in this country today which threatens the vitals of our fair Republic—as foul a menace against the very life-blood of the American Eagle as was the foul conspiracy of Catiline against the eagles of ancient Rome!"

VOICE: [*Disgustedly*] Aw, hell! Tell him to salt de tail of dat eagle!

VOICE: [*Reading:*] "I refer to that devil's brew of rascals, jailbirds, murderers and cutthroats who libel all honest working men by calling themselves the Industrial Workers of the World; but in the light of their nefarious plots, I call them the Industrious *Wreckers* of the World!"

YANK: [*With vengeful satisfaction*] Wreckers, dat's de right dope! Dat belongs! Me for dem!

VOICE: Ssshh! [*Reading:*] "This fiendish organization is a foul ulcer on the fair body of our Democracy——"

VOICE: Democracy, hell! Give him the boid, fellers—the raspberry! [*They do*]

VOICE: Ssshh! [*Reading:*] "Like Cato I say to this Senate, the I. W. W. must be destroyed! For they represent an ever-present dagger pointed at the heart of the greatest nation the world has ever known, where all men are born free and equal, with equal opportunities to all, where the Founding Fathers have guaranteed to each one happiness, where Truth, Honor, Liberty, Justice, and the Brotherhood of Man are a religion absorbed with one's mother milk, taught at our father's knee, sealed, signed, and stamped in the glorious Constitution of these United States!"

[*A perfect storm of hisses, catcalls, boos, and hard laughter*]

VOICES: [*Scornfully*] Hurrah for de Fort' of July! Pass de hat!
Liberty!
Justice!
Honor!
Opportunity!
Brotherhood!

ALL: [*With abysmal scorn*] Aw, hell!

VOICE: Give the Queen Senator guy the bark! All togedder now—one—two—three——

[*A terrific chorus of barking and yapping*]

GUARD: [*From a distance*] Quiet there, youse—or I'll git the hose.

[*The noise subsides*]

YANK: [*With growling rage*] I'd like to catch dat senator guy alone for a second. I'd loin him some trute!

VOICE: Ssshh! Here's where he gits down to cases on the Wobblies. [*Reads:*] "They plot with fire in one hand and dynamite in the other. They stop not before murder to gain their ends, nor at the outraging of defenseless womanhood. They would tear down society, put the lowest scum in the seats of the mighty, turn Almighty God's revealed plan for the world topsy-turvy, and make of our sweet and lovely civilization a shambles, a desolation where man, God's masterpiece, would soon degenerate back to the ape!"

VOICE: [*To Yank*] Hey, you guy. There's your ape stuff again.

YANK: [*With a growl of fury*] I got him. So dey blow up tings, do they? Dey turn tings round, do dey? Hey, lend me dat paper, will yuh?

VOICE: Sure. Give it to him. On'y keep it to yourself, see? We don't wanter listen to no more of that slop.

VOICE: Here you are. Hide it under your mattress.

YANK: [*Reaching out*] Tanks. I can't read much but I kin manage. [*He sits, the paper in the hand at his side, in the attitude of Rodin's "The Thinker." A pause. Several snores from down the corridor. Suddenly Yank jumps to his feet with a furious groan as if some appalling thought had crashed on him—bewilderedly*] Sure—her old man—president of de Steel Trust—makes half de steel in de world —steel—where I thought I belonged—drivin' trou —movin'—in dat—to make her—and cage me in for her to spit on! Christ! [*He shakes the bars of his cell door till the whole tier trembles. Irritated, protesting exclamations from those awakened or trying to get to sleep*] He made dis—dis cage! Steel! It don't belong, dat's what! Cages, cells, locks, bolts, bars—dat's what it means!—holdin' me down with him at de top! But I'll drive trou! Fire, dat melts it! I'll be fire—under de heap—fire dat never goes out —hot as hell—breakin' out in de night——

[*While he has been saying this last he has shaken his cell door to a clanging accompaniment. As he comes to the "breakin' out" he seizes one bar with both hands and, putting his two feet up against the others so that his position is parallel to the floor like a monkey's, he gives a great wrench backwards. The bar bends like a licorice stick under his tremendous strength. Just at this moment the Prison Guard rushes in, dragging a hose behind him*]

GUARD: [*Angrily*] I'll loin youse bums to wake me up! [*Sees Yank*] Hello, it's you, huh? Got the D. Ts., hey? Well, I'll cure 'em. I'll drown your snakes for yuh! [*Noticing the bar*] Hell, look at dat bar bended! On'y a bug is strong enough for dat!

YANK: [*Glaring at him*] Or a hairy ape, yuh big yellow bum! Look out! Here I come! [*He grabs another bar*]

GUARD: [*Scared now—yelling off left*] Toin de hose on, Ben!—full pressure! And call de others— and a straitjacket!

[*The curtain is falling. As it hides Yank from view, there is a splattering smash as the stream of water hits the steel of Yank's cell*]

CURTAIN

SCENE VII.

Nearly a month later. An I. W. W. local near the waterfront, showing the interior of a front room on the ground floor, and the street outside. Moonlight on the narrow street, buildings massed in black shadow. The interior of the room, which is general assembly room, office, and reading room, resembles some dingy settlement boys' club. A desk and high stool are in one corner. A table with paper, stacks of pamphlets, chairs about it, is at center. The whole is decidedly cheap, banal, commonplace, and unmysterious as a room could well be.

The Secretary *is perched on the stool making entries in a large ledger. An eye shade casts his face into shadows. Eight or ten* Men, Longshoremen, Iron Workers, *and the like, are grouped about the table. Two are playing checkers. One is writing a letter. Most of them are smoking pipes. A big signboard is on the wall at the rear, "Industrial Workers of the World—Local No. 57."* Yank *comes down the street outside. He is dressed as in Scene Five. He moves cautiously, mysteriously. He comes to a point opposite the door; tiptoes softly up to it, listens, is impressed by the silence within, knocks carefully, as if he were guessing at the password to some secret rite. Listens. No answer. Knocks again a bit louder. No answer. Knocks impatiently, much louder.*

SECRETARY: [*Turning around on his stool*] What the hell is that—someone knocking? [*Shouts:*] Come in, why don't you?

[*All the* Men *in the room look up.* Yank *opens the door slowly, gingerly, as if afraid of an ambush. He looks around for the secret doors, mystery, is taken aback by the commonplaceness of the room and the* Men *in it, thinks he may have gotten in the wrong place, then sees the signboard on the wall and is reassured*]

YANK: [*Blurts out:*] Hello.

MEN: [*Reservedly*] Hello.

YANK: [*More easily*] I thought I'd bumped into de wrong dump.

SECRETARY: [*Scrutinizing him carefully*] Maybe you have. Are you a member?

YANK: Naw, not yet. Dat's what I come for—to join.

SECRETARY: That's easy. What's your job—longshore?

YANK: Naw. Fireman—stoker on de liners.

SECRETARY: [*With satisfaction*] Welcome to our city. Glad to know you people are waking up at last. We haven't got many members in your line.

YANK: Naw. Dey're all dead to de woild.

SECRETARY: Well, you can help to wake 'em. What's your name? I'll make out your card.

YANK: [*Confused*] Name? Lemme tink.

SECRETARY: [*Sharply*] Don't you know your own name?

YANK: Sure; but I been just Yank for so long—Bob, dat's it—Bob Smith.

SECRETARY: [*Writing*] Robert Smith. [*Fills out the rest of card*] Here you are. Cost you half a dollar.

YANK: Is dat all—four bits? Dat's easy.

[*Gives the* Secretary *the money*]

SECRETARY: [*Throwing it in drawer*] Thanks. Well, make yourself at home. No introductions needed. There's literature on the table. Take some of those pamphlets with you to distribute aboard ship. They may bring results. Sow the seed, only go about it right. Don't get caught and fired. We got plenty out of work. What we need is men who can hold their jobs—and work for us at the same time.

YANK: Sure. [*But he still stands, embarrassed and uneasy*]

SECRETARY: [*Looking at him—curiously*] What did you knock for? Think we had a coon in uniform to open doors?

YANK: Naw. I tought it was locked—and dat yuh'd wanter give me the once-over trou a peephole or somep'n to see if I was right.

SECRETARY: [*Alert and suspicious but with an easy laugh*] Think we were running a crap game? That door is never locked. What put that in your nut?

YANK: [*With a knowing grin, convinced that this is all camouflage, a part of the secrecy*] Dis burg is full of bulls, ain't it?

SECRETARY: [*Sharply*] What have the cops got to do with us? We're breaking no laws.

YANK: [*With a knowing wink*] Sure. Youse wouldn't for woilds. Sure. I'm wise to dat.

SECRETARY: You seem to be wise to a lot of stuff none of us knows about.

YANK: [*With another wink*] Aw, dat's aw right, see? [*Then made a bit resentful by the suspicious glances from all sides*] Aw, can it! Youse needn't put me trou de toid degree. Can't youse see I belong? Sure! I'm reg'lar. I'll stick, get me? I'll shoot de woiks for youse. Dat's why I wanted to join in.

SECRETARY: [*Breezily, feeling him out*] That's the right spirit. Only are you sure you understand what you've joined? It's all plain and above board; still, some guys get a wrong slant on us. [*Sharply*] What's your notion of the purpose of the I. W. W.?

YANK: Aw, I know all about it.

SECRETARY: [*Sarcastically*] Well, give us some of your valuable information.

YANK: [*Cunningly*] I know enough not to speak outa my toin. [*Then resentfully again*] Aw, say! I'm reg'lar. I'm wise to de game. I know yuh got to watch your step wit a stranger. For all youse know, I might be a plain-clothes dick, or somep'n, dat's what yuh're thinkin', huh? Aw, forget it! I belong, see? Ask any guy down to de docks if I don't.

SECRETARY: Who said you didn't?

YANK: After I'm 'nitiated, I'll show yuh.

SECRETARY: [*Astounded*] Initiated? There's no initiation.

YANK: [*Disappointed*] Ain't there no password—no grip nor nothin'?

SECRETARY: What'd you think this is—the Elks—or the Black Hand?

YANK: De Elks, hell! De Black Hand, dey're a lot of yellow backstickin' Ginees. Naw. Dis is a man's gang, ain't it?

SECRETARY: You said it! That's why we stand on two feet in the open. We got no secrets.

YANK: [*Surprised but admiringly*] Yuh mean to say yuh always run wide open—like dis?

SECRETARY: Exactly.

YANK: Den yuh sure got your noive wit youse!

SECRETARY: [*Sharply*] Just what was it made you want to join us? Come out with that straight.

YANK: Yuh call me? Well, I got noive, too! Here's my hand. Yuh wanter blow tings up, don't yuh? Well, dat's me! I belong!

SECRETARY: [*With pretended carelessness*] You mean change the unequal conditions of society by legitimate direct action—or with dynamite?

YANK: *Dynamite!* Blow it offen de oith—steel—all de cages—all de factories, steamers, buildings, jails—de Steel Trust and all dat makes it go.

SECRETARY: So—that's your idea, eh? And did you have any special job in that line you wanted to propose to us? [*He makes a sign to the* Men, *who get up cautiously one by one and group behind* Yank]

YANK: [*Boldly*] Sure, I'll come out wit it. I'll show youse I'm one of de gang. Dere's dat millionaire guy, Douglas——

SECRETARY: President of the Steel Trust, you mean? Do you want to assassinate him?

YANK: Naw, dat don't get yuh nothin'. I mean blow up de factory, de woiks, where he makes de steel. Dat's what I'm after—to blow up de steel, knock all de steel in de woild up to de moon. Dat'll fix tings! [*Eagerly, with a touch of bravado*] I'll do it by me lonesome! I'll show yuh! Tell me where his woiks is, how to git there, all de dope. Gimme de stuff, de old butter—and watch me do de rest! Watch de smoke and see it move! I don't give a damn if dey nab me—long as it's done! I'll soive life for it—and give 'em de laugh! [*Half to himself*] And I'll write her a letter and tell her de hairy ape done it. Dat'll square tings.

SECRETARY: [*Stepping away from* Yank] Very interesting.

[*He gives a signal. The* Men, *huskies all, throw themselves on* Yank *and before he knows it they have his legs and arms pinioned. But he is too flabbergasted to make a struggle, anyway. They feel him over for weapons*]

MAN: No gat, no knife. Shall we give him what's what and put the boots to him?

SECRETARY: No. He isn't worth the trouble we'd get into. He's too stupid. [*He comes closer and laughs mockingly in* Yank's *face*] Ho-ho! By God, this is the biggest joke they've put up on us yet. Hey, you Joke! Who sent you—Burns or Pinkerton? No, by God, you're such a bonehead I'll bet you're in the Secret Service! Well, you dirty spy, you rotten agent provocator, you can go back and tell whatever skunk is paying you blood-money for betraying your brothers that he's wasting his coin. You couldn't catch a cold. And tell him that all he'll ever get on us, or ever has got, is just his own sneaking plots that he's framed up to put us in jail. We are what our manifesto says we are, neither more nor less—and we'll give him a copy of that any time he calls. And as for you—— [*He glares scornfully at* Yank, *who is sunk in an oblivious stupor*] Oh, hell, what's the use of talking? You're a brainless ape.

YANK: [*Aroused by the word to fierce but futile struggles*] What's dat, yuh Sheeny bum, yuh!

SECRETARY: Throw him out, boys.

[*In spite of his struggles, this is done with gusto and éclat. Propelled by several parting kicks,* Yank *lands sprawling in the middle of the narrow cobbled street. With a growl he starts to get up and storm the closed door, but stops bewildered by the confusion in his brain, pathetically impotent. He sits there, brooding, in as near to the attitude of Rodin's "Thinker" as he can get in his position*]

YANK: [*Bitterly*] So dem boids don't tink I belong, neider. Aw, to hell wit 'em! Dey're in de wrong pew—de same old bull—soapboxes and Salvation Army—no guts! Cut out an hour offen de job a day and make me happy! Gimme a dollar more a day and make me happy! Tree squares a day, and cauliflowers in de front yard—ekal rights—a woman and kids—a lousy vote—and I'm all fixed for Jesus, huh? Aw, hell! What does dat get yuh? Dis ting's in your inside, but it ain't your belly. Feedin' your face—sinkers and coffee—dat don't touch it. It's way down—at de bottom. Yuh can't grab it, and yuh can't stop it. It moves, and everything moves. It stops and de whole woild stops. Dat's me now—I don't tick, see?—I'm a busted Ingersoll, dat's what. Steel was me, and I owned de woild. Now I ain't steel, and de woild owns me. Aw, hell! I can't see—it's all dark, get me? It's all wrong! [*He turns a bitter mocking face up like a ape gibbering at the moon*] Say, youse up dere, Man in de Moon, yuh look so wise, gimme de answer, huh? Slip me de inside dope, de information right from de stable—where do I get off at, huh?

A POLICEMAN: [*Who has come up the street in time to hear this last—with grim humor*] You'll get off at the station, you boob, if you don't get up out of that and keep movin'.

YANK: [*Looking up at him—with a hard, bitter laugh*] Sure! Lock me up! Put me in a cage! Dat's de on'y answer yuh know. G'wan, lock me up!

POLICEMAN: What you been doin'?

YANK: Enuf to gimme life for! I was born, see? Sure, dat's de charge. Write it in de blotter. I was born, get me?

POLICEMAN: [*Jocosely*] God pity your old woman! [*Then matter-of-fact*] But I've no time for kidding. You're soused. I'd run you in but it's too long a walk to the station. Come on now, get up, or I'll fan your ears with this club. Beat it now! [*He hauls* Yank *to his feet*]

YANK: [*In a vague mocking tone*] Say, where do I go from here?

POLICEMAN: [*Giving him a push—with a grin, indifferently*] Go to hell.

CURTAIN

SCENE VIII.

Twilight of the next day. The monkey house at the Zoo. One spot of clear gray light falls on the front of one cage so that the interior can be seen. The other cages are vague, shrouded in shadow from which chatterings pitched in a conversational tone can be heard. On the one cage a sign from which the word "gorilla" stands out. The gigantic Animal himself is seen squatting on his haunches on a bench in much the same attitute as Rodin's "Thinker."

Yank enters from the left. Immediately a chorus of angry chattering and screeching breaks out. The Gorilla turns his eyes but makes no sound or move.

YANK: [*With a hard, bitter laugh*] Welcome to your city, huh? Hail, hail, de gang's all here! [*At the sound of his voice the chattering dies away into an attentive silence. Yank walks up to the Gorilla's cage and, leaning over the railing, stares in at its occupant, who stares back at him, silent and motionless. There is a pause of dead stillness. Then Yank begins to talk in a friendly confidential tone, half-mockingly, but with a deep undercurrent of sympathy*] Say, yuh're some hard-lookin' guy, ain't yuh? I seen lots of tough nuts dat de gang called gorillas, but yuh're de foist real one I ever seen. Some chest yuh got, and shoulders, and dem arms and mits! I bet yuh got a punch in eider fist dat'd knock 'em all silly! [*This with genuine admiration. The Gorilla, as if he understood, stands upright, swelling out his chest and pounding on it with his fist. Yank grins sympathetically*] Sure, I get yuh. Yuh challenge de whole woild, huh? Yuh got what I was sayin' even if yuh muffed de woids. [*Then bitterness creeping in*] And why wouldn't yuh get me? Ain't we both members of de same club—de Hairy Apes? [*They stare at each other—a pause—then Yank goes on slowly and bitterly*] So yuh're what she seen when she looked at me, de white-faced tart! I was you to her, get me? On'y outa de cage—broke out—free to moider her, see? Sure! Dat's what she tought. She wasn't wise dat I was in a cage, too—worser'n yours—sure—a damn sight—'cause you got some chanct to bust loose—but me—— [*He grows confused*] Aw, hell! It's wrong, ain't it? [*A pause*] I s'pose yuh wanter know what I'm doin' here, huh? I been warmin' a bench down to de Battery—ever since last night. Sure. I seen sun come up. Dat was pretty, too—all red and pink and green. I was lookin' at de skyscrapers—steel—and all de ships comin'

in, sailin' out, all over de oith—and dey was steel, too. De sun was warm, dey wasn't no clouds, and dere was a breeze blowin'. Sure, it was great stuff. I got it aw right—what Paddy said about dat bein' de right dope—on'y I couldn't get *in* it, see? I couldn't belong in dat. It was over my head. And I kept tinkin'—and den I beat it up here to see what youse was like. And I waited till dey was all gone to git yuh alone. Say, how d'yuh feel sittin' in dat pen all de time, havin' to stand for 'em comin' and starin' at yuh—de white-faced, skinny tarts and de boobs what marry 'em—makin' fun of yuh, laughin' at yuh, gittin' scared of yuh—damn 'em! [*He pounds on the rail with his fist. The Gorilla rattles the bars of his cage and snarls. All the other monkeys set up an angry chattering in the darkness. Yank goes on excitedly*] Sure! Dat's de way it hits me, too. On'y yuh're lucky, see? Yuh don't belong wit 'em and yuh know it. But me, I belong wit 'em—but I don't, see? Dey don't belong wit me, dat's what. Get me? Tinkin' is hard—— [*He passes one hand across his forehead with a painful gesture. The Gorilla growls impatiently. Yank goes on gropingly*] It's dis way, what I'm drivin' at. Youse can sit and dope dream in de past, green woods, de jungle, and de rest of it. Den yuh belong and dey don't. Den yuh kin laugh at 'em, see? Yuh're de champ of de woild. But me—I ain't got no past to tink in, nor nothin' dat's comin', on'y what's now—and dat don't belong. Sure, you're de best off! Yuh can't tink, can yuh? Yuh can't talk neider. But I kin make a bluff at talkin' and tinkin'—a'most git away wit it—a'most!—and dat's where de joker comes in. [*He laughs*] I ain't on oith and I ain't in heaven, get me? I'm in de middle tryin' to separate 'em, takin' all de woist punches from bot' of 'em. Maybe dat's what dey call hell, huh? But you, yuh're at de bottom. You belong! Sure! Yuh're de on'y one in de woild dat does, yuh lucky stiff! [*The Gorilla growls proudly*] And dat's why dey gotter put yuh in a cage, see? [*The Gorilla roars angrily*] Sure! Yuh get me. It beats it when you try to tink it or talk it—it's way down—deep—behind—you 'n' me we feel it. Sure! Bot' members of dis club! [*He laughs—then in a savage tone*] What de hell! T'hell wit it! A little action, dat's our meat! Dat belongs! Knock 'em down and keep bustin' 'em till dey croaks yuh wit a gat—wit steel! Sure! Are yuh game? Dey've looked at youse, ain't dey—in a cage? Wanter git even? Wanter wind up like a sport 'stead of croakin' slow in dere? [*The Gorilla roars an emphatic affirmative. Yank goes on with a sort of furious exaltation*] Sure! Yuh're reg'lar. Yuh'll stick to de finish! Me 'n' you, huh?—bot' members of this club! We'll put up one last star bout dat'll knock 'em offen deir seats! Dey'll have to make de cages stronger after we're trou! [*The Gorilla is straining at his bars, growling, hopping from one foot to the other. Yank takes a jimmy from under his coat and forces the lock on the cage door. He throws this open*] Pardon from de governor! Step out and shake hands! I'll take yuh for a walk down Fif' Avenoo. We'll knock 'em offen de oith and croak wit de band playin'. Come on, Brother. [*The* Gorilla *scrambles gingerly out of his cage. Goes to* Yank *and stands looking at him.* Yank *keeps his mocking tone—holds out his hand*] Shake—de secret grip of our order. [*Something, the tone of mockery, perhaps, suddenly enrages the Animal. With a spring he wraps his huge arms around* Yank *in a murderous hug. There is a crackling snap of crushed ribs—a gasping cry, still mocking, from* Yank] Hey, I didn't say kiss me! [*The* Gorilla *lets the crushed body slip to the floor; stands over it uncertainly, considering; then picks it up, throws it in the cage, shuts the door, and shuffles off menacingly into the darkness at left. A great uproar of frightened chattering and whimpering comes from the other cages. Then* Yank *moves, groaning, opening his eyes, and there is silence. He mutters painfully:*] Say—dey oughter match him—wit Zybszko. He got me, aw right. I'm trou. Even him didn't tink I belonged. [*Then, with sudden passionate despair*] Christ, where do I get off at? Where do I fit in? [*Checking himself as suddenly*] Aw, what de hell! No squawkin', see! No quittin', get me! Croak wit your boots on! [*He grabs hold of the bars of the cage and hauls himself painfully to his feet— looks around him bewilderedly—forces a mocking laugh*] In de cage, huh? [*In the strident tones of a circus barker*] Ladies and gents, step forward and take a slant at de one and only—[*His voice weakening*]—one and original—Hairy Ape from de wilds of——

[*He slips in a heap on the floor and dies. The monkeys set up a chattering, whimpering wail. And, perhaps, the Hairy Ape at last belongs*]

CURTAIN

Laurence Stallings • Maxwell Anderson

Laurence Stallings will be remembered in the theatre chiefly for *What Price Glory?*, the best modern war play in the English language. The rest of his work in the field of playwriting was not notably successful. After writing *What Price Glory?* with Maxwell Anderson, in 1924, he collaborated with him on two historical romances. The earlier of these, *First Flight* (1925), was a mild treatment of an adventurous episode in Andrew Jackson's romantic life; the other, *The Buccaneer,* revived the career of the swashbuckling pirate Henry Morgan. Next, Stallings turned his attention to musical drama, contributing texts to the opera *Deep River* (1926) and to the musical melodrama *Rainbow* (1928). He also dramatized Hemingway's war novel *A Farewell to Arms,* which was, however, more successful on the screen than on the stage; and he wrote the libretto for a lavish musical spectacle, *Virginia,* in 1937. A tribute to the United States Marines, *The Streets Are Guarded* (1944) proved too mystical and confusing. It was only as the scenarist of two important Hollywood films, *The Big Parade* and *Old Ironsides,* that Stallings won prominence comparable to that which *What Price Glory?* earned for him.

Stallings was born in Macon, Georgia, and attended Wake Forest College in North Carolina. He became a reporter in Atlanta, and one of his assignments, an interview intended to promote enlistments to the United States Marines, in 1917, proved decisive in his career. After writing his piece on the Marines, he himself decided to join. When America came to the rescue of the Allies, he saw heavy action in France and earned a captaincy. He lost a leg in battle at Château-Thierry and spent many months in a military hospital. Returning to civilian life, he resumed his journalistic career but contemplated entering the teaching profession. Instead, he found a job with the *New York World*—first as second-string drama critic and then as book reviewer—and published a novel, *Plumes,* about his war experiences.

Maxwell Anderson was then an editorial writer on the *World,* and the two men decided to collaborate on plays. When the question of a subject was discussed, Stallings remembered his war experiences, and the result was *What Price Glory?* (1924). The First World War was still a topic of considerable interest to the public, and the play was only one of several trenchant reminiscences, among which were such notable novels as John Dos Passos' *Three Soldiers* and Stallings' own *Plumes.* But the popularity of the subject alone could not have assured *What Price Glory?* its extraordinary success.

By judiciously combining robust comedy with the muck and grime of modern warfare, Stallings and Anderson created pungent theatre. The comic matter was accentuated with colloquial speech that bristled with the "high-astounding" oaths of native warriors. The broadly conceived characters bore the stamp of reality; the soldiers were no Galahads fighting for glory, although they were courageous and had a rough-hewn nobility. Although the authors indulged in some romantic, masculine swagger and contented themselves with only random commentary, they drew an unflattering picture of military life such as had never before been seen on an American stage. Most playgoers agreed that Alexander Woollcott, reviewing the play in the *New York Evening Sun,* did not greatly exaggerate when he wrote that "in the tremendous irony of the comedy and in the sardonic laughter which fills its every scene, there is more said about the war than in all the editorials on the subject which, if placed end to end, would reach nowhere."

What Price Glory? became one of the most successful productions of the American stage. The performances of Louis Wolheim and William Boyd as rivals for the favors of the eternal woman and French camp follower Charmaine provided the breeziest entertainment the American public had yet seen; the language was the freest it had yet heard. The mood of cynicism was in vogue at the time, and playgoers were delighted by the satire on brass hats, "thirty-day-wonder lieutenants," and "the band of Gideons from Headquarters bringing more of that world safe for democracy slush." The cry of Lieutenant Moore, "What price glory now?" echoed through the period of postwar disillusionment. The play banished the romantic treatment of fighting that had prevailed in the American theatre after every previous war. Recalling the eventful Arthur Hopkins production on September 3, 1924, after a decade of playgoing, Burns Mantle wrote in the first edition of this *Treasury of the Theatre:* "One of the famous first nights in the theatre going history of New York is that on which *What Price Glory?* was introduced to a slightly startled audience. For the first time in theatre history a war play was presented with something resembling literal realism, and spoken with more regard for a reasonable verisimilitude than for the sensibilities of convention-protected auditors. The shock was a little severe, particularly to the ladies, but it gave way in the end to such cheering as the theatre does not often hear. That night a new blow was struck for freedom of speech in the drama."

Since war is hardly a novel experience for the human race, the subject has been familiar in the theatre ever since Aeschylus wrote *The Persians,* in 472 B.C., eight years after the battle of Salamis. In the opinion of many, the greatest antiwar play is still Euripides' *The Trojan Women,* written in 415 B.C., a year after the civilized Athenians destroyed a neutral island and exterminated the entire male population. These and other classic plays belong to a high tragic tradition that would have seemed remote to the American public. Even the example of Shakespeare, who brought comic, as well as antiheroic, matter into his chronicles but invested war with majesty, could not have satisfied the "debunkers" of the nineteen-twenties. At the same time, however, they could not count upon much public response to the unrelieved bitterness of the plays engendered by the First World War in Continental Europe, especially in Germany. America had not experienced war on its own soil, nor had it tasted defeat. The mood of the American playgoer favored a play of intermediate quality, neither majestic, on the one hand, nor notably embittered, on the other. Stallings and Anderson wrote *What Price Glory?* with an instinctive awareness of the mood of the nation that disavowed Woodrow Wilson's wartime ideals and regarded our embroilment in the European war as an error.

It was only a decade later that American antiwar plays became less "sophisticated" than impassioned, less cynical than rebellious; and this was because war was no longer viewed as something experienced in the past but as an imminent possibility. The altered mood was reflected in Irwin Shaw's *Bury the Dead* (1936), in which a number of soldiers killed in a new war refuse to be buried and are joined by living soldiers in their protest against a society that breeds both poverty and armed conflict. In the same year appeared Paul Green's *Johnny Johnson,* whose pacifist hero is confined to an asylum after an at-

tempt to make the nations lay down their arms, and Robert Sherwood's *Idiot's Delight,* which whipped up much comic complication but without losing sight of its bitter point that the only genuine internationalists in the world were the munitions manufacturers. When the protests went out of fashion with the start of the Second World War, they were replaced by rueful yet heroic plays—Robert Sherwood's *There Shall Be No Night* (1940) and Maxwell Anderson's *The Eve of St. Mark* (1942). Anderson, it is true, tried to combine heroic and antiheroic moods in his next play, *Storm Operation,* but without success. The first war play he wrote remained the best, and it probably would not have been written with such zest at any other time than the early 'twenties.

What Price Glory? has often been discussed as an "antiwar" play. It was so regarded by most of its admirers in the nineteen-twenties. It was criticized in the nineteen-thirties for lacking the qualities of an antiwar play—that is, for failing to present an analysis of war and for making the life of the fighting man seem too attractive. And, indeed, it would be too much to maintain that *What Price Glory?* is a profound study or protest. What the authors accomplished was something else: a picture of war which provides its deepest commentary not in any argument but in its matter-of-fact description of how soldiers live and think "on the spot." It showed, as Joseph Wood Krutch wrote in *The Nation,* "a way of life"; it indicated that actual warfare develops a civilization or "anti-civilization" of its own, "with a language, a philosophy, and a whole *kultur* as different from normal life as the *kultur* and philosophy of the Stone Age were different. . . ." It is as a naturalistic comedy with implicit commentary that *What Price Glory?* retains vitality.

BIBLIOGRAPHY: Anita Block, *The Changing World in Plays and Theatre* (pp. 306–310), 1939; Eleanor Flexner, *American Playwrights 1918–1938* (pp. 80–81), 1938; Joseph Wood Krutch, *The American Drama Since 1918* (pp. 30–43), 1939; Burns Mantle, *Contemporary American Playwrights* (pp. 41–43), 1938.

WHAT PRICE GLORY?

By Laurence Stallings and Maxwell Anderson

CHARACTERS

CORPORAL GOWDY
CORPORAL KIPER
CORPORAL LIPINSKY
SERGEANT QUIRT
CAPTAIN FLAGG
CHARMAINE DE LA COGNAC
PRIVATE LEWISOHN
LIEUTENANT ALDRICH
LIEUTENANT MOORE
LIEUTENANT SCHMIDT

GUNNERY SERGEANT SOCKEL
PRIVATE MULCAHY
SERGEANT FERGUSON
A BRIGADE RUNNER
MONSIEUR PETE DE LA COGNAC
ANOTHER BRIGADE RUNNER
BRIGADIER GENERAL COKELEY

A COLONEL
A CAPTAIN   } Headquarters
A LIEUTENANT   } Staff
ANOTHER LIEUTENANT }
A CHAPLAIN
TOWN MAYOR
SPIKE
PHARMACIST'S MATE
LIEUTENANT CUNNINGHAM
LIEUTENANT LUNDSTROM

AUTHOR'S NOTE

What Price Glory? is a play of war as it is, not as it has been presented theatrically for thousands of years. The soldiers talk and act much as soldiers the world over. The speech of men under arms is universally and consistently interlarded with profanity. Oaths mean nothing to a soldier save a means to obtain emphasis. He uses them in place of more polite adjectives.

The authors of *What Price Glory?* have attempted to reproduce this mannerism along with other general atmosphere they believe to be true. In a theater where war has been lied about, romantically, effectively—and in a city where the war play has usually meant sugary dissimulation—*What Price Glory?* may seem bold. The audience is asked to bear with certain expletives which, under other circumstances, might be used for melodramatic effect, but herein are employed because the mood and truth of the play demand their employment.

ACT I. SCENE I.

A room in a French farmhouse—now a U. S. Marine company headquarters. A couple of desks covered with maps and papers. Several scattered chairs. Three runners sit talking and smoking, very much at ease. Lipinsky is seated at one end of bench, Kiper at the other; Gowdy is sitting on a stool near Kiper.

GOWDY: Well, where the hell did you come from?

KIPER: Who, me? I come from every place I've been to.

GOWDY: Yeah, well, where you been to?

KIPER: Me? I've been to China, Cuba, the Philippines, San Francisco, Buenos Aires, Cape Town, Madagascar . . . wait a minute—Indiana, San Domingo, Tripoli, and Blackwell's Island.

LIPINSKY: Ever going home?

KIPER: Who, me? I can't go anywhere without going home.

GOWDY: By the time this war's over you ought to be pretty near ready to marry and settle down.

KIPER: There ain't going to be any after-this-war. Anyway, I got married after the last two wars and when I get through paying my debt to Lafayette, I'm through settling down. I never have settled down in so many hick towns in my life.

LIPINSKY: What became of them two broads?

KIPER: My wives?

LIPINSKY: Yeah.

KIPER: The first one never knew my last name, and when I left town she was out of luck.

GOWDY: And the next one?

KIPER: Ain't I signing the payroll for her every month? A twenty-dollar allotment, and she gives it to a fireman in Buffalo. Here I am saving democracy, and he's turning in a twenty-bell alarm the first of every month.

GOWDY: That's a waste of cash, the way I look at it. It stands to reason when a girl gets rid of one bozo she's looking for another. Now why does the late unlamented finance that little game? There's no justice in that.

KIPER: Who said it was justice? It ain't justice; it's alimony.

GOWDY: Well, alimony's all right if you're well fixed; hell, a girl ought to have some fun! I don't want a girl to quit living just because she ain't living with me, but the guy that's getting his ought to pay for it. What do you want to pay alimony for?

KIPER: What did you want to come to France for? It's the same reason why I pay alimony. So's to see the rest of the girls. Join the Marines and see the girls—from a porthole.

GOWDY: God! I came to France because I had a brain-storm one day and signed on the dotted line.

LIPINSKY: There ain't but one man in the world that came to France to see the mam'selles, and that's the skipper. When there's women around the skipper's got trick eyes like a horsefly.

KIPER: The old man? Say, he can't look at a mam'selle without blushing. Compared to me he's an amateur. He don't know the difference between a

Hong-Kong honky-tonk and a Santo Domingo smoongy.

LIPINSKY: No, oh, no! I suppose women is an open book to you. You're damn well right—a code book.

KIPER: Yeah, you're damn well right. When I was in Turkey with that landing party the Sultan had to hunt through his harem with a flashlight to find a decent-looking girl, and when I left China the Yangtse was full of the bodies of virgins that drowned their beautiful selves because I was shipping over. And when I was in Spain the king of Spain put an ad in the paper offering a reward for the return of the queen.

GOWDY: What did you do?

KIPER: Took her back for the reward.

LIPINSKY: Huh! I notice you've got Cognac Pete's daughter, too.

KIPER: If I had the skipper's uniform and his Sam Browne belt, I could take that little wench away from him before you could say squads right! You ain't never seen it done. The skip's full of wind.

GOWDY: Anyway, Flagg's got Pete's kid sewed up —and she's as pretty a little frog as ever made a dish of frog's legs.

KIPER: Pete's kid! The poor little tart! What could she do? Ain't the skipper billeted there? God! I guess even Lippy could make a kid if she slept on the other side of a paper wall.

LIPINSKY: God! I don't know. Ain't it the truth some guys just naturally walk away with women? Damned if I could ever do it!

KIPER: Take one good long look at yourself and you'll see why. There ain't many as unfortunate as you are. I guess there ain't anybody handicapped with features like them there.

LIPINSKY: Sometimes I think it's features, and sometimes I think it's luck. Once I spent three hundred dollars on a dame at Asbury Park in two days, and she keeping her damn chum with her all the time. Finally I got the extra one so drunk she couldn't tell her own name, and I ditched her. Then this broad I was trying to make insisted on riding on the merry-go-round. . . . God! the merry-go-round. Nothing else would satisfy her. She'd rung ducks till it rained ducks. She'd shot up more powder in shooting galleries than's been shot in this war, and she wanted to ride on the merry-go-round! So we got on the merry-go-round, and I threw her into a chariot and I piled on a horse. She hollers, "Whoopee, whoopee, let's do it again!" Jeez, I had spent three hundred bucks and I said, "Now, honey, let's not ride any more. Come on, let's do what you promised." She said she would after one more turn on the merry-go-round. So I, like a bloody fool, tries to save twenty cents by catching a brass ring. Son-of-a-bitch! I fall off and break my leg!

KIPER: My God!

LIPINSKY: Yes, sir. I broke my leg.

GOWDY: You certainly have had your share of tough luck.

LIPINSKY: So when the captain walks off with the top soldier's girl I say to myself, maybe there's luck in it. Maybe the breaks favored him. They never did favor me.

GOWDY: Any skipper can walk off with any top soldier's girl in my opinion. Say, maybe that's the lowdown on why the sergeant left.

KIPER: Naw—he was too damn good. Regimental took him. We'll probably get a lousy replacement. Probably get a corporal with ten years' experience chasing prisoners at Portsmouth. Soon's the new sergeant gets here the skip's going on ten days' leave.

LIPINSKY: Yeah? Where?

KIPER: Paris.

LIPINSKY: You going with him?

KIPER: Yep.

LIPINSKY: Some guys have all the luck.

[*The door opens.* Sergeant Quirt, *the very picture of an old-timer, enters and looks quickly around. All rise*]

QUIRT: L Company?

KIPER: Company Headquarters.

QUIRT: Where's the company commander?

KIPER: Just stepped down the street. Will be back soon.

QUIRT: He's going on leave?

KIPER: Right.

QUIRT: What's his name?

KIPER: Captain Flagg.

QUIRT: Whew!

KIPER: You know him?

QUIRT: Do you?

KIPER: Yes, sir!

QUIRT: Company Headquarters. Looks like a God-damn reception room to me.

KIPER: We aim to please.

QUIRT: Yeah, to please yourself. Well, listen, I'm the new top soldier here. Who's the company clerk?

LIPINSKY: I am, sir.

QUIRT: Clear this jam out of here and let's have a look at what you're doing.

LIPINSKY: Will you get the hell out? And don't come back till you're sent for.

[Kiper *and* Gowdy *go out*]

QUIRT: I've been ten kilometers west of you. Took the wrong turn.

LIPINSKY: Here's the map. That's the only road there is, and we can't use it. The damn thing is one long shell-hole from last May.

QUIRT: Jeez!

LIPINSKY: That's what they all say.

QUIRT: Don't you ever clean these galleys?

LIPINSKY: We don't do anything else.

QUIRT: You haven't got a police sergeant, I suppose?

LIPINSKY: We've got an acting corporal. Old Hennessey was bumped off last time up.

QUIRT: Spud Hennessey?

LIPINSKY: That's the soldier.

QUIRT: Tough for Spud to go. A grand soldier. Too damn finicky, though.

LIPINSKY: We've gone to hell for chow since he left.

QUIRT: That's queer. I never knew Flagg to let his men go to hell.

LIPINSKY: Not his fault. These cooks are no good. Hennessey was acting mess sergeant, too.

QUIRT: That's like old times.

LIPINSKY: Yeah?

QUIRT: Say, if the skipper's going ashore they'd better get him out of here before he gets too drunk to navigate. I've seen him shove off with a liberty party and spend a forty-eight-hour leave sleeping it off on the beach.

LIPINSKY: It's the same skip, all right. You know him.

QUIRT: I'll say I do . . . I think I'll look him up. Where's he likely to be?

LIPINSKY: Damned if I know. He might be at Pete's place. Anybody can tell you where that is— just this side of the river.

QUIRT: All right. I'll find it.

[Goes out briskly. After he has gone Lipinsky goes to the door and whistles. Kiper and Gowdy come in]

LIPINSKY: Did you take a slant at the amphibian?

GOWDY: Yeah.

KIPER: What of it?

LIPINSKY: He's our new papa.

KIPER: So he says.

LIPINSKY: He's soldiered with the skipper before. Says he never saw the chief sober.

KIPER: Is he hard-boiled?

LIPINSKY: There's only one place in the world they boil them as hard as that, and that's the Tropic of Cancer.

KIPER: What does he know?

LIPINSKY: This God-damn army's going to run right from now on or get off on its ear.

GOWDY: He must have used some language on you?

LIPINSKY: Not a word, and I'm not going to give him a chance, either.

KIPER: Scared, huh?

LIPINSKY: You meet a top with two glass eyes, a slit across his face for a mouth and a piece out of his ear, and you might just as well heave out and lash up. That bird could curse the hide off a whole Senegalese regiment.

[Captain Flagg enters and comes to chair above table. He is a fine, magnificently endowed man]

FLAGG: 'Tenshun! [Reading report which he picks up from table] Where's that first sergeant?

KIPER: Went out looking for you, sir.

FLAGG: Scatter and find him, a couple of you. [Lipinsky, Gowdy, and Kiper start out] Stay here, Kiper. [Kiper comes back] Damn him, why couldn't he sit still? [Lipinsky and Gowdy go out] What's he like?

KIPER: Tough.

FLAGG: Yeah? I hope he damn well hangs the whole damn company up by the thumbs. About time we had a little discipline around here.

KIPER: Yes, sir.

FLAGG: "Yes, sir!" "Yes, sir!" Shut your trap, will you?

KIPER: Oh, yes, sir.

FLAGG: Go to hell! Everything packed?

KIPER: Absolutely.

FLAGG: Bike working? Side-care trimmed?

KIPER: Tuned it up this morning.

FLAGG: Well, we're going ashore as soon as I see the new top soldier, you understand? And we don't stop for anything smaller than shell-holes!

KIPER: Ay, ay, sir!

FLAGG: Go sit down! Go read a book! You make me nervous. [Kiper sits. Charmaine slips in. She is a drab. Flagg, who is busy at the desk, does not see her at first. He looks up impatiently] Well, hello! Hello! What are you doing here? You better run along back to your papa. Listen, mon amie, you better beat it back to le père, understand?

CHARMAINE: Why?

[She comes nearer]

FLAGG: Well, I'm busy.

CHARMAINE: You are going away.

FLAGG: So that's it. Kiper, did you tell the kid I was going away?

KIPER: No, sir, she saw me with your musette bag.

CHARMAINE: The sergeant went away. He is not coming back. Now you go away. You are not coming back.

FLAGG: As far as the sergeant's concerned, you're quite right, dearie; but as far as I'm concerned, you're dead wrong. The sergeant isn't coming back. We have a new sergeant, see? But I am coming back.

CHARMAINE: Oui?

FLAGG: Oui, oui, oui!

CHARMAINE: No. You are such a lovely liar. You don't want to make me cry. So you lie a little— n'est-ce pas?

FLAGG: [Takes her by shoulders] I'm not lying, Charmaine. I don't know how I can prove it to you, but I'm telling the solemn truth. [A knock on the door] See who that is, and keep him out, whoever it is.

KIPER: [Opens the door, goes out, and returns] It's Lewisohn, third platoon replacement. He wants permission to speak with you, sir.

FLAGG: What about?

KIPER: Lost something, sir.

FLAGG: Let him in. [Lewisohn enters. He is a pale little boy] Let's have it quick, soldier.

LEWISOHN: [Saluting] Beg pardon, sir.

[Very much scared]

FLAGG: What do you want?

LEWISOHN: The truth is, sir, I've lost my identification tag.

FLAGG: What? What? Lost what?

LEWISOHN: My identification tag.

FLAGG: Well, I thought I'd been around a good deal, and I've had 'em ask me to show 'em where they live and button up their pants for them and put on their little night-drawers, but I'm a son-of-a-gun if this isn't the first time anybody has ever asked me to help him find his identification tag!

LEWISOHN: Sorry, sir. I—I thought it was—I. . . .

FLAGG: What did you think?

LEWISOHN: I thought it was important, sir.

FLAGG: And what, may I ask, made you think it was important?

LEWISOHN: In case I was—ah—hit, sir. They wouldn't know who I was. I thought maybe it would matter.

FLAGG: Matter? To whom?

LEWISOHN: Well—to keep the records—or to my folks.

FLAGG: Listen, boy, why did you ever leave your home and come over here?

LEWISOHN: Why, to fight, sir.

FLAGG: Yeah. Well, you'll get a chance, don't you worry, and for God's sake learn to act like a man. Never mind your identification tag. If you want to know what your name is look in your hat.

LEWISOHN: Yes, sir.

FLAGG: By the way, what is your name?

LEWISOHN: Louis Lewisohn.

FLAGG: [To Kiper] Make a note of that, Kiper. [Kiper makes a note in the book he carries in his pocket] Now, anything else? Hope you got a good room with a view and running water and everything.

LEWISOHN: No, sir.

[Swallowing a lump in his throat]

FLAGG: No? I'm surprised. Well, go on outside and swear at me a while. It'll do you good, and that's what I'm here for. I'm here to keep you in hot water till you're hard-boiled. See? You can go.

LEWISOHN: Yes, sir.

[He salutes and goes]

FLAGG: Make a note of that, Kiper, and get him a new tag if they have to build a new factory in Hoboken to turn it out. The God-forsaken fool's dying of grief away from mother. Got it?

KIPER: Yes, Captain Flagg.

FLAGG: Then step outside and guard the door a minute. [Kiper salutes and goes out, closing the door carefully. Flagg then turns to Charmaine] Now, you little she-woman, what do you want?

CHARMAINE: You are going away.

FLAGG: Damn it, I'm not going away. I'm going to Paris—coming back in eight days. Eight days in Paris, see, then I come back.

CHARMAINE: The sergeant did not come back.

FLAGG: My God, child, get this! The sergeant is not coming back. I am coming back. We have a new sergeant, see?

CHARMAINE: Oui?

FLAGG: Oui, oui.

CHARMAINE: No. I think the captain does not love me, not any more?

FLAGG: Girlie, I love you fit to kill. I love you no end, same as always. Come here. [She puts her arms around his neck. Flagg takes her in his arms] You're as sweet as Burgundy, and you've got a kick like triple sec. Sure I love you. Everybody loves you. I love you, dearie girl, but I don't trust you.

CHARMAINE: You take me to Paris? Yes? Take me to Paris?

FLAGG: No. I guess not.

CHARMAINE: But I'm so unhappy when you go away.

FLAGG: Yes, you are! I wish you were. Why, you little geisha [Chucking her under the chin], if I didn't wear captain's stripes you wouldn't know me from the K.P.'s.

CHARMAINE: No, dear Captain Flagg. [Her arms on his shoulders. She runs a hand through his hair] It is true, I shall be so lonesome. I shall be all alone at the inn, crying every day to break your heart.

FLAGG: You'll be dancing all night and flirting all day with the Y.M.C.A. boys, you mean. Ain't it so?

CHARMAINE: Oui. But you could take me. I can't be good—unless you take me. I want to be good for you. We could have so good time—in Paris.

FLAGG: No, I can't take you. But listen. [Takes hold of her shoulders] While I'm gone you wait for me. Remember, you're my girl, see? Just my girl, and you wait for me, see?

CHARMAINE: Oui, I will.

FLAGG: And listen to this. [Putting her away] If I find out you've been running with someone else, I'll break you in two, see? [He makes the motion of breaking something] Now, will you be good while I'm gone?

CHARMAINE: [Coming into his arms] Oui, monsieur.

FLAGG: That's better. You know what I mean?

CHARMAINE: Oui.

FLAGG: That's right, little kitten, purr. . . . And remember, I don't trust you any further than I can see you. Now run along. [Flagg turns to table, but Charmaine follows him]

CHARMAINE: But you will take me to Paris?

FLAGG: [Seating himself on edge of table, he beckons her with his finger and takes her on his knee, between his legs] You ever been to Paris?

CHARMAINE: Non . . .

FLAGG: Well, there's a river in Paris.

CHARMAINE: La Seine.

FLAGG: Yeah, the Seine. That's where they drown little girls like you. Every time the police catch a little girl in Paris, they drown her in the Seine. You can't go there. They'd drown you.

CHARMAINE: It is not true.

FLAGG: It is true. I'll tell you another thing. There's nothing to eat in Paris, no food but horses; no wine, only water. No young girls, only old women. Some of the girls they drown in the Seine; some they make into sausages for the generals. Paris is full of generals that won't eat anything but young girls. You can't go to Paris.

CHARMAINE: You are full of lovely lies. Oh, it is not true.

FLAGG: Uh, you don't know Paris.

CHARMAINE: Oh, but I know these captains and sergeants! They do not ever put anything, what you say, past me. But, oh, I love you for a lovely liar! [*Embraces him*] And I will be good; I will, *vraiment!*

FLAGG: That's a good girl. Now you go back to Papa Pete's. Stay home nights. Wait for Captain Flagg. Kiss me good-bye. [*She kisses him*] Now run along. [*She goes*] Kiper!

KIPER: [*Coming in*] Yes, sir.

FLAGG: Have you found that sergeant yet?

KIPER: He's coming with Lipinsky, sir.

FLAGG: Tell him to damn well get a wiggle on.

KIPER: [*To Quirt, outside*] He's waiting for you, sir.

[*Lipinsky enters with* Quirt]

QUIRT: [*Saluting*] Captain Flagg?

FLAGG: [*Returns salute and remains seated, not even glancing at* Quirt] Hello, Sergeant. Where've you been all day?

QUIRT: Ten kilometers west by mistake.

FLAGG: Do you know our lay-out?

QUIRT: I've got a general idea.

FLAGG: What kind of a hole were you in over there?

QUIRT: Much the same as yours, only we had a road.

FLAGG: Do you think you can handle this company? It's a rough crowd of old men and little baa-lamb recruits.

[*He still does not look up*]

QUIRT: It's an army, ain't it? Sure.

FLAGG: I damn well hope you can. We're in a devilish sector here, and it's going to be worse when we move up again. We just hold half a town; the Heinies hold the other half. It rains grenades most of the time. About half our men are green replacements. They damned near ruined us in that last tour of duty. You'll have to whip some of 'em into shape before we go up. Close order drill is best.

QUIRT: Half of 'em raw?

FLAGG: Over half.

QUIRT: Well, I've seen worse.

FLAGG: Now, I'm going on leave, you see. Eight days. While I'm gone you feed 'em up and give 'em hell. Teach 'em where they are. Make 'em so bad they'll eat steel rather than get another dressing from you. Make 'em hard, but don't break 'em. Give 'em eats and about eight hours of drill and guns a day. They're mostly Bible Class boys, and God knows most of 'em haven't got long to live.

QUIRT: [*Takes step toward table*] Cut the comedy, Captain. You must know me.

FLAGG: [*Rising, looks at* Quirt *for the first time*]

Yeah? I'm a cuckoo if it ain't the old Hoppergrass!

QUIRT: Thought you didn't know me. Well, I'm glad to meet you again, Captain Flagg.

FLAGG: Kiper——

KIPER: Yes, sir.

FLAGG: Step out and tell all platoon commanders to report here at once.

KIPER: Ay, ay, sir.

[*Exits*]

FLAGG: Well, Quirt, I'm glad to see you, because if there was ever a good soldier needed I need one here, and you're as good as there is; but I'm damned if I take any particular joy in meeting you again. You've been poison to me everywhere I've served with you.

QUIRT: [*At right of table*] Same to you, I'm sure, and many of 'em. Personally I'd as soon meet a skunk in a dugout, and officially I don't think much of your crew. I broke you the first time in China, and you broke me in Cuba. You're in a position to break me now, and if you didn't need me worse than the wildcat needed what he didn't have, you'd break me again.

FLAGG: I'd see you in hell before I'd break you, and you know it. I'll give you exactly what you deserve, and as long as you're straight we'll get along, always providing we don't have to shake hands. If that's understood, why, take hold. The company's yours.

QUIRT: Well, before I take hold, let me get one more remark in the record. I wish to God I could jump your damn gang. I've heard of it all along the line. You've got a rabble, and I know it. I saw it coming into Is-sur-Tille once when you didn't see me. A shambling bunch of hams that wouldn't salute anything under a general.

FLAGG: All right, and what's my outfit's rating at regimental?

QUIRT: Oh, I got to hand it to you. You can hypnotize 'em. They'd start out to cut their way to Berlin if you gave the word. But, my God, they ain't much to look at, Captain Flagg.

FLAGG: Well, teach 'em to salute if it'll make you feel any happier, Hoppergrass. And before the platoon commanders get here, there's one thing I'd like to ask you. What did you do with the little girl?

QUIRT: What little girl?

FLAGG: You damn well know what little girl.

QUIRT: It's a small world, Captain Flagg, but the number of soldiers' sluts is numerous.

FLAGG: I was a corporal under you in China. You broke me to get her.

QUIRT: You were a damn fool. You'd have married her if it hadn't been for me, and be running a laundry now with the seat of your pants hanging down between your knees.

FLAGG: What happened to her?

QUIRT: What happened to the battleship *Maine?*

FLAGG: My God. . . .

QUIRT: I broke you in China. I admit I broke

you for that little Chink. And when I served under you in Cuba you got even. That's why I'm still a sergeant. [*A knock at the door from* Kiper] Let it go at that.

FLAGG: Kiper?

KIPER: [*Outside*] Ay, ay, sir!

FLAGG: Bring 'em in. [Kiper *opens the door and follows into the room* Lieutenants Aldrich, Moore, *and* Schmidt, *and Gunnery Sergeant* Sockel. *They salute. They line up*] Gentlemen, this is First Sergeant Quirt, who is in charge. This is Lieutenant Aldrich; this is Lieutenant Moore, and this is Lieutenant Schmidt, and you'll remember Sockel from Cuba. He's commanding the fourth platoon.

QUIRT: [*Turns to* Sockel] Hello, Joe. How's tricks?

SOCKEL: Pretty good. How's yourself?

[*They smile broadly, two old-timers among green lieutenants*]

QUIRT: Ticking like a clock.

FLAGG: Aldrich, you're senior here, aren't you?

ALDRICH: Yes, sir. Two days ahead of the others.

FLAGG: You'll be in command here. Ask Quirt for any advice you need. I'll be back Wednesday week. . . . Now, men, Sergeant Quirt here is one of the best God-damn soldiers that ever destroyed a memorandum receipt. I've soldiered with him around the world, and there isn't a finer, cleaner, smarter Marine afloat than Quirt—when he's sober. As long as he's sober, he'll run this outfit—whether I'm here or absent; but Quirt loves the bottle; and when he's drunk he's the lousiest, filthiest bum that ever wore a uniform. When drunk, he's worse than I am, and you know damn well I don't allow anybody to get as bad as that. If he tanks up I'll break him. I've broken him once, and he knows I'll do it again. The first raw crack he makes will find him drilling in the rear rank of Sockel's platoon, drilling like a tramp with a broom for a rifle. Get that, Aldrich; the first time you find him down in the square with a face in the dirt in front of all these young nipple-nursers, you lock him up and keep him locked up till I return.

ALDRICH: Yes, sir.

FLAGG: Give him his head, and let him have anything he wants, and don't forget he's forgotten more about being a soldier than any of you college boys will ever know. But if you're wise you won't play cards with him, and before you lend him any money you'd better kiss it a last long farewell. That's all. Kiper, have you got the waterproofs in that side-car?

KIPER: Ay, ay, sir.

FLAGG: Give her a spin, and we'll shove off.

[*Picks up cap and stick from table and goes out, followed by all save* Quirt. *Off stage, the motorcycle clatters. The* Lieutenants *shout farewell.* Quirt *goes up to right window, looks out, and then sits at table, takes out dice, and practices a few turns. He holds the dice up to his eyes and then spins.* Quirt *whistles "Pretty Baby"*]

QUIRT: Seven, baby. [*He smiles with satisfaction*]

Look at those acrobats act. You got to treat the old man right, now. [*There is a light tap on the door to left.* Quirt *puts dice in pocket and looks at map*] Come in.

[Charmaine *enters*]

CHARMAINE: Le capitaine—il est parti?

QUIRT: Just left. Don't cry, little one.

CHARMAINE: Le nouveau sergeant. N'est-ce pas?

QUIRT: N'est-ce pas is right.

CHARMAINE: I wanted to see the captain.

QUIRT: Just too late, sorry to say. [*Looks at her for first time*] You one piecie captain's fella boy? You captain's fella?

CHARMAINE: Le capitaine? Mais non!

QUIRT: I'll bet it's mais mon. Say, ain't you Cognac Pete's daughter?

CHARMAINE: Oui. You stay at Pete's?

QUIRT: Sure. [*Pause*] Et vous?

CHARMAINE: C'est mon père.

QUIRT: Uh-huh. I thought so. [*Rises; crosses to her*] Well, baby, you better stick to me, and you'll have another papa.

[*A terrific commotion begins outside. A vociferous Irish voice is heard shouting over and over again, "I'll get that lousy German son-of-a-bitch, I'll get the German bastard," while* Lipinsky *and* Gowdy *yell, "Cut it out, you loafer. Dry up, dry up or you'll get yours."* Lipinsky *opens the door.* Charmaine *steps back. The shouting is audible only when door is open*]

LIPINSKY: Sergeant, there's a drunken Mick named Mulcahy raising hell outside. Can't do a thing with him. Got blood in his eyes for a guy from Cincinnati. It's a rough crowd of old men.

QUIRT: [*Sternly, out of the corner of his mouth, not looking at him*] Tell him to pipe down. [Lipinsky *goes out. Door closes; shouting stops.* Charmaine *goes toward door*] Better not go out there now, honey. Some rough language is taking place out there.

[Lipinsky *re-enters. Shouting is started again*]

LIPINSKY: Sergeant, the Mick's sitting on Gowdy, and I can't pull him off.

QUIRT: [*Quietly, as before*] Tell him to pipe down. [Lipinsky *goes out. Shouting stops.* Quirt *crosses to* Charmaine] You going to promenade avec moi tonight? Down by the canal? Under the lime trees?

CHARMAINE: No. [*She is trembling*]

QUIRT: No? Captain's own private darling, huh? Say, you're a damned pretty frog. For a frog, I don't know as I ever saw a prettier.

[*The hullabaloo redoubles outside.* Lipinsky *comes in again*]

LIPINSKY: Shall we lock him up, Sergeant?

QUIRT: Drag him in.

[Lipinsky *and* Gowdy *drag in a huge, red-faced Irishman and stand him groggily on his feet below* Quirt]

MULCAHY: That damn Nussbaum from Cincinnati is a German spy, and I'll have his guts out of him before I'm through.

QUIRT: [*Quietly*] Mulcahy, pipe down.

MULCAHY: I tell you that Nussbaum is a German spy! I'll get the lousy German and every German out of Cincinnati. . . .

[*The* Sergeant *plants one squarely on* Mulcahy's *jaw. He goes down like a log*]

QUIRT: [*Still out of the corner of his mouth*] Drag him out.

[Lipinsky *and* Gowdy *take him by arms, turn him around, and drag him out.* Quirt, *rubbing his knuckles, crosses back of table to* Charmaine, *who is smiling at her wonderful hero with the powerful punch*]

QUIRT: Why, hello, Pittsburgh, you love me?

[*They embrace and hold a long kiss*]

CURTAIN

SCENE II.

Late afternoon, eight days later. The scene is unchanged. Lipinsky *is lying along bench, smoking a cigarette and trying to sleep at the same time.* Kiper *enters, singing at the top of his voice.* Lipinsky's *cap is down over his eyes. Police Sergeant Ferguson is at table toward back, working over papers; he is smoking a pipe.*

KIPER: "Mademoiselle from Armentiere, parlez-vous?
Mademoiselle from Armentiere, parlez vous?
Mademoiselle from Armentiere——"
Hullo, hullo—Jeezus.

[*Puts musette bags in corner*]

LIPINSKY: Knock off that chat.

[*On bench; doesn't move*]

KIPER: Say, are you running this God-damn army?

LIPINSKY: You're damn well right, I'm running this army.

KIPER: Well, you had better God-damn well snap out of it. You're relieved.

LIPINSKY: [*Sitting up*] Skipper come back?

KIPER: Almost. He's at the Last Chance.

LIPINSKY: Still soaked?

KIPER: He ain't soaked. He's just the drunkest bum you ever saw in your life.

LIPINSKY: Trying to whip the world?

KIPER: Naw, just quiet drunk. Looks out of those eyes of his like two red holes in the snow.

LIPINSKY: How's Paris?

KIPER: Never got that far. Washed ashore at Bar-le-Duc.

LIPINSKY: Yeah? Good time?

KIPER: Pretty good the first day.

LIPINSKY: What'd you do the rest?

KIPER: You see, it was this way. The skip and me was promenading, and he was swinging that damn little Pekin swagger-stick of his when up comes an M.P. "Sorry, sir," says the M.P. "Corps commander's regulations, sir, no swagger-sticks." The skip says, "Well, and who, may I ask, is the corps commander? Tell him he can take his lousy army and sell it for cheese." "Sorry, sir," says the M.P. "Corps commander's regulations, sir, and I'll have to take that stick away from you." "All right," says the skip, whirling the stick around his head, "pitch in, soldier, pitch in!"

LIPINSKY: Did he take it away?

KIPER: Aw, take it away! Listen to the poor nut. I spent the next six days of my leave detained as a material witness for attempted manslaughter.

LIPINSKY: I guess the skip didn't draw much?

KIPER: Draw hell! Didn't I swear this yellow-bellied M.P. came up and knocked him into the road?

LIPINSKY: Yeah?

KIPER: And the court looks at this M.P. and says, "Right face! Take him away and give him ten days, bread and water."

LIPINSKY: Serve him right, the Boy Scout! They ought to take away those guys' whistles before they blow themselves to death. And speaking of whistles, this new top of ours don't do nothing else at all besides blow a whistle. It's been one bloody formation after another ever since you left.

KIPER: Is that the kind of hombre he is?

LIPINSKY: He's a sea-going son-of-a-bitch. He ain't sit down since he was here. He's got the first platoon down in the village now taking up the dirt from the courtyard with teaspoons. You can't get in the chow line until you catch twenty horseflies. He seen Cooper pulling a fag at reveille this morning. What's Cooper doing now? Boy, following the ponies, following the ponies. *He's* out collecting apples.

KIPER: Well, the skip will make him cut that stuff. Me and the skip ain't going to see the little boys bullied.

LIPINSKY: You and the skip, yeah. But say, the skip and this top soldier are going to tangle pant-legs over another little matter before they have been together one day.

KIPER: What t'hell?

LIPINSKY: This horny pelican is going aboard the skip's old hooker every night.

KIPER: Down at Cognac Pete's house?

LIPINSKY: Parking his dogs in Pete's kitchen every night with that little black-eyed frog sitting in his lap lighting his pipe.

KIPER: If the skip finds that out there'll be a noise like you'd throw a tomcat in a dog-pound.

[*Enter* Sergeant Quirt]

QUIRT: [*To* Kiper] Where's Captain Flagg?

KIPER: Last Chance.

QUIRT: What the hell do you mean, coming in

here without him? What do you think you're paid for?

KIPER: I tried to argue with him, Sergeant, and he picked me up and threw me out the window. Lucky for me it was open.

QUIRT: Go get him. Don't argue. Get him. Take Lippy along.

[Lipinsky *and* Kiper *start, hesitate, and talk.* Quirt *starts toward chair above table.* Lieutenant Aldrich *enters*]

ALDRICH: Heard the skipper was aboard.

QUIRT: [*Turning to* Aldrich] Grounded on the last bar.

ALDRICH: Yeah?

QUIRT: [*To* Kiper *and* Lipinsky, *who hurry off*] Cast off, will you? Travel! Hit the deck! [*To* Aldrich] Sending out a salvage party. He's full to the scuppers.

ALDRICH: All I hope is he comes in mild and goes to sleep. He's got too damn much talent for raising hell to suit me.

QUIRT: You ought to see him in China. Straight as a mast, muscled like a gorilla, Christian as hell. Good deal of liquor has flowed under his belt since then.

ALDRICH: Expect any trouble?

QUIRT: What do you mean?

ALDRICH: This here now little wild woman.

QUIRT: I don't know what's your game.

ALDRICH: Oh, all right! Just the same, you'd be a damn sight wiser to lay off, in my opinion.

QUIRT: Lay off what?

ALDRICH: Charmaine.

QUIRT: [*Turning to* Aldrich] Are you thinking of making this a three-handed game?

ALDRICH: I am not.

QUIRT: Because if you are, all I got to say is, help yourself to whatever you can get. It's love in a manner of speaking, and it's certainly war. Everything dirty goes.

ALDRICH: Suit yourself. You've known him longer than I have.

QUIRT: He's got a grudge against me, I don't mind telling you. And I ain't wasting any ardent affection on him. If it hadn't been for him, I'd had a company of my own. I didn't know she was his meat when I first saw her. But when I found out, d'you think I'd apologize and back out the door out of deference to him? I says, Kippy-dope, you're mine!

ALDRICH: Yeah—but do you know what I heard at mess to-day?

QUIRT: Nope.

ALDRICH: Well, now listen. I didn't intend to mix into this unless it was necessary, but Schmidt got it straight yesterday that old Cognac Pete was going to prosecute some soldier or other for corrupting Charmaine's morals.

QUIRT: Charmaine's what? Jeez, that's good!

ALDRICH: Maybe so. Just the same, he's got a case.

QUIRT: He has not.

ALDRICH: No? Suppose he gets you before a court martial? It's a hanging matter if he wants to push it. You know the regulations.

QUIRT: You mean he's after me?

ALDRICH: I don't know who he's after. You—or Flagg. Has Cognac anything on you?

QUIRT: Well, they might hang me once as a sort of lesson to me.

[*Motorcycle clatters outside*]

ALDRICH: Well, there you are. Suppose he takes it to headquarters. Where's Quirt then? Sitting pretty?

QUIRT: Well, I just resign all rights and interests in the mam'selle and avoid possible complications.

ALDRICH: Fine. There's Kiper already. If Flagg's with him, for God's sake use a little diplomacy.

[*Outside,* Flagg *in drunken voice says, "Get out of my way, Kiper." Noise of* Kiper *being pushed*]

QUIRT: Diplomacy, with that?

[Flagg *enters, coat in hand and hair mussed. He still carries stick.* Lipinsky *and* Kiper *follow. All stand at attention until the* Captain *is seated*]

ALDRICH: [*Saluting*] How are you, Captain Flagg?

FLAGG: I'm a wreck, that's what I am! I'm an epoch-making disaster! You see before you, Mr. Aldrich, one of the seven great calamities of the world!

QUIRT: Hope you had a pleasant leave, sir.

FLAGG: Well, I didn't. Held for carrying a stick. Picked up the second day by one of Pershing's Sunday-school teachers. By God, he must think he's running a day nursery! . . . What's happened?

QUIRT: Not a thing.

FLAGG: Boys in shape?

QUIRT: They'll do. Three more days, and I'd risk them on the line.

FLAGG: Try and get three days. If we aren't digging in somewhere before then, I'll pay the Russian national debt out of my salary. How much do you think I spent in Bar-le-Duc?

QUIRT: How much did you have?

FLAGG: Eight hundred francs, and I got a chance to get rid of thirty. Here's the whole roll. Does anybody want it? Just my luck to have to move in again with seven hundred and seventy francs on me and get bumped off. [*A knock at the door by* Brigade Runner] Come in.

[*A* Brigade Runner *enters*]

THE RUNNER: Captain Flagg?

FLAGG: Right here.

THE RUNNER: From Captain Simpson, sir. He wanted you to know the "G One" crowd is on the way over.

FLAGG: Tell him I'm much obliged. Anything else?

THE RUNNER: That's all. How do I get to the Twelfth?

FLAGG: Show him, Kiper. [Kiper *and the* Runner

salute and go out. Flagg *starts to button his coat*]
Damn headquarters! It's some more of that world-
safe-for-democracy slush! Every time they come
around here I've got to ask myself is this an army
or is it a stinking theosophical society for ethical
culture and the Bible-backing uplift! I don't want
that band of Gideons from headquarters. Now you
watch that door. Watch it! In ten minutes we're
going to have another of these round-headed gentlemen of the old school here giving us a prepared
lecture on what we're fighting the war for and how
we're to do it—one of these bill-poster chocolate
soldiers with decorations running clear around to his
backbone and a thrilling speech on army morale and
the last drop of fighting blood that puts your drive
over to glorious victory! . . . The side-whiskered
butter-eaters! I'd like to rub their noses in a few of
the latrines I've slept in, keeping up army morale and
losing men because some screaming fool back in the
New Jersey sector thinks he's playing with paper
dolls. [*A knock*] Well, come in, come in. [*Lieutenant*
Moore *enters*] Hello.

MOORE: How are you, Captain Flagg? Hope you
liked Bar-le-Duc?

FLAGG: Ever been there?

MOORE: Once.

FLAGG: Ever put in much time in the redecorated
chicken stable where they detain the A.W.O.L.'s?

MOORE: Afraid I never saw it, sir.

FLAGG: Well, you haven't missed a great deal.
They whitewashed the damn shanty right over the
hen manure. Phew! I can smell it yet. If I stayed
there another day I'd have laid an egg.

MOORE: Tough luck! But what I really wanted to
say, sir, was there's an old fellow outside here who
wants to see you about his daughter. He seems to
think somebody's taken advantage of her.

FLAGG: Somebody in this outfit?

MOORE: Yes, sir.

FLAGG: Took advantage of the girl, huh?

MOORE: That's what he says.

FLAGG: He means she took advantage of her opportunities and now he's taking advantage of his.
What's the old boy's name?

MOORE: Can't quite make it out, but it seems to
be Pete something or other. Are there any Petes in
France? Sounded like Cognac Pete.

FLAGG: Yeah?

MOORE: Sounded like it.

FLAGG: [*Rising, perturbed*] Well, wait a minute.
Cognac Pete's, huh? Is the girl with him?

MOORE: No.

FLAGG: Hell!

QUIRT: Think fast, Captain. Think fast.

FLAGG: Quirt, do you know anything about this?

QUIRT: [*Starting to leave*] Not a thing.

FLAGG: You leaving us?

QUIRT: [*Unembarrassed*] A few orders to make
out, sir. [*He grins*] Can't very well work here, you
see.

FLAGG: I'm damned if I see. Sit down and spill
your ink. And if you've put a game on me, you
crawling crab. . . .

QUIRT: Me? What have I got to do with it? Think
fast, Captain, think fast.

FLAGG: Damn it, send him in, and we'll see.
[Moore *goes out*] Hell!

QUIRT: [*Laughing*] Think fast, Captain. Don't forget to think fast.

FLAGG: You sit where you are, you hyena; and
laugh, damn you, laugh. [*Enter* Cognac Pete, *an
ancient nut-brown Frenchman, very polite and humble, followed by* Moore *and* Kiper. Moore *and* Pete
stand by the table. Kiper *sits on bench*] Pete, what's
this I hear about a complaint? What's the matter,
huh? One of my men, huh?

PETE: *Oui, mon capitaine.*

FLAGG: I'm damned if I can leave this damn army
half a day without hell breaking loose somewhere.
Come on, let's have it; spit it out.

MOORE: Allay, Pete.

PETE: [*Speaking in an unintelligible rush of
French*] Ah, monsieur le capitaine, je suis un vieil-
lard; mais j'ai vécu heureusement, et mes enfants ont
été toujours honnêtes, mais hélas, mon capitaine,
quelque chose de terrible vient de passer, une cala-
mité monstrueuse. . . .

FLAGG: [*To* Moore] What's on the menu? Do you
get anything out of that?

MOORE: He says something has happened.

FLAGG: [*Distressed*] Does it take all that vocabulary to say something has happened in French? Well,
keep going, keep going.

MOORE: Allay, Pete.

PETE: *Mais, mon capitaine, voilà que les Américains arrivent. Ils sont grands et forts, et ils de-
mandent toujours ce qu'ils veulent. Ils ne s'accoutu-
ment pas à nos mœurs ni à nos habitudes, mais—
nom de Dieu!—pourquoi choisissent-ils la seule
fleur de ma vie, quand ils peuvent trouver n'importe
où qu'ils vont des poules qui les désirent? Ma seule
fleur, ma fleur Charmaine, ma fleur délicate!*

FLAGG: What language is he talking now?

MOORE: He says the soldiers take what they want,
and they have trampled the one flower of his life.

FLAGG: Is that all he said?

MOORE: The rest is poetry.

FLAGG: [*Impatiently*] Well, tell him to omit
flowers, see, omit flowers.

MOORE: [*To* Pete] Brièvement.

PETE: *Ma fille. Ma fille bien-aimée. Elle est défleurée. Elle est dans la boue, elle est déshonorée.*

FLAGG: [*To* Moore] More flowers?

MOORE: No, sir. He says his daughter's been—ah
—ruined [*Pause*] . . . so to speak.

FLAGG: Ruined, huh? Rape or seduction?

MOORE: [*To* Pete] S'est-elle soumise, ou l'a-t-on
forcée?

PETE: *Les Américains sont si forts. Ils se forcent
sur elle, ils ferment sa bouche de façon qu'elle ne*

*peut donner l'alarme. Que peut faire la petite fille?
L'Américaine est forte, elle peut se défendre, mais
la Française, elle est gentille et modeste et craintive
et ne sait se défendre.*

FLAGG: [*To* Moore] Now what's all that?

MOORE: Rape, sir.

FLAGG: Does he allude to any specific girl, or is he speaking of French wenches in general?

MOORE: [*To* Pete] *Comment s'appelle ta fille?*

PETE: Charmaine.

MOORE: Charmaine, sir.

FLAGG: [*Very seriously*] Look here, Moore. You know as well as I do, this same little baggage has been pretty free with me. What's the old boy's game? And for God's sake, what do you think you're up to, bringing him in here?

MOORE: You mean you're . . . God, I didn't know that!

FLAGG: You didn't! You must go around here wearing blinders. You see the fix you've got me in?

QUIRT: Think fast, Captain, think fast.

MOORE: To tell the truth, I got the impression it was somebody else. Honest to God, I thought he said it was a soldier. . . . [Flagg *hesitates and then gives* Moore *a quick look.* Moore *is embarrassed*] I wasn't sure, but I got that impression.

FLAGG: Did he name anybody?

MOORE: No.

FLAGG: [*Turning away*] Well, damn her little soul. No, I know damn well it wasn't anybody else. [*Turns to* Moore] Ask him how much he wants.

MOORE: How much what?

FLAGG: Money, you highbrow, money! What do you think he wants?

MOORE: I don't know, but if I thought he wanted money I certainly would not have listened to him.

FLAGG: You're just a bleating babe in the woods, you are. That's what they all want.

MOORE: He told me he wanted the man to marry the girl.

FLAGG: Marry her!

PETE: *Elle était une petite enfant innocente, une fleur à demi ouverte.*

FLAGG: What's that? Flowers again?

MOORE: He says she was an innocent child.

FLAGG: Listen. You tell him I'm sure she's still an innocent girl. Tell him Charmaine is one of the most virtuous and respectable ladies I've ever had the pleasure of meeting.

MOORE: [*To* Pete] *Monsieur le capitaine dit que c'est impossible et que vous vous trompez, monsieur, parce que Charmaine est tout à fait honnête et vertueuse.*

PETE: [*Shaking his head*] *Non! non! non!—je ne me trompe pas—malheureusement c'est bien la vérité.*

MOORE: He's sure of it.

FLAGG: Ask him if he wants to bring charges.

MOORE: *Désirez-vous le faire passer au conseil de guerre?*

PETE: *Conseil de guerre? Ça se peut.*

MOORE: He says perhaps.

FLAGG: What does he mean, "perhaps"? Ask him how much he wants.

MOORE: *Il demande ce que vous voulez.*

PETE: *Mais la petite qui est défleurée—il faut qu'on la fasse honnête, et moi—est-ce donc que l'honneur de ma famille ne vaut rien? Il faut qu'ils se marient, et quant à moi—il faut me payer si je ne le fais pas passer devant le conseil de guerre. Il me faut cinq cent francs.*

FLAGG: Flowers?

MOORE: No, he wants the fellow to marry the girl —and he wants five hundred francs.

FLAGG: I see. That's better. Tell him he can have three hundred. Tell him he can pick any son-in-law he wants out of the whole damn army.

MOORE: [*To* Pete] *Elle peut choisir n'importe qui qu'il soit de toute la compagnie—et vous—vous aurez trois cent francs.*

PETE: [*Suddenly wildly angry*] *Ça ne va pas! Vous vous moquez de moi, vous officiers américains. Je connais le truc—moi—de vous voir m'insulter quand il s'agit de la rapace. Alors, messieurs, j'irai au G.H.Q. et vous verrez. C'est la mort, et gare à votre peau! Me voilà qui vient vous voir ici, malheureux mais amical, et je ne reçois que des insultes. Cinq cent francs! Rien de moins, et il la marie.*

[*He starts for door*]

FLAGG: Wait a minute. [Aldrich *bars the door*] What's wrong?

MOORE: He's insulted. Going to headquarters. Five hundred, he wants; and it's a certain man, he says.

FLAGG: What man?

MOORE: *Quel homme?*

PETE: [*Turning, crosses in front of table; to* Quirt, *dramatically*] *Le voilà! Alors je m'en vais. Vous vous moquez de moi! Laissez-moi partir.*

[Quirt *rises, knocking over chair*]

FLAGG: [*Taking a step toward* Quirt] Quirt, what's the meaning of this?

QUIRT: Sorry, sir, I don't quite catch the drift myself.

FLAGG: Have you been around with Charmaine?

QUIRT: Charmaine? I don't think so, Captain. But I've got a poor memory for names.

FLAGG: You're a liar. You knew Charmaine was mine, and you couldn't keep your hands off her.

QUIRT: Yeah? It's getting to be a habit of mine, huh? Whaddye going to do about it, Captain Flagg?

FLAGG: Oh? What [*Walks to table*] am I going to do about it?—I'm going to marry you to Charmaine and let you make an honest woman out of her! Quirt, you've taken the detail right off my shoulders, and it's your turn to think fast! [*Turns to* Moore] Mr. Moore, now tell the old man that the sergeant was making honest proposals and desperate love! Ask what church he belongs to, or whether he wants 'em married by the cashier of the bank

[*Turns to* Quirt. Moore *turns to* Pete; *they start toward the door*] Sergeant, you arrived in the nick of time with replacements! You saved the day! The Marines have landed and have the situation well in hand! We're going to decorate you! We're going to let you hold the bag!

QUIRT: All very interesting, Captain. But how are you going to do it? I may have landed, but I don't remember seeing any article in what I signed saying you could pick my woman for me. Seems to me you'd learned that I pick my women for myself.

FLAGG: Quirt, you've signed on for a cruise with this woman, and you can't jump ship. I can tell Aldrich to stand out of the way and let this old man go to headquarters with his story about you . . . and what chance has a lousy Marine sergeant got before an army court-martial when ten majors start the iron ball rolling? Ten army majors back in Paris, who ain't going to let anybody do any seducing but themselves. Don't be a hayshaker, Quirt. You can't play guardhouse lawyer in this country. You're in the army now, with a lot of western shysters sitting in the judge advocate general's room.

QUIRT: And who's going to be witness against me? You couldn't get that little frog to swear anything. I'm too damned handsome a soldier. I'm strong with this little French broad. Told me last night, just before you come back, she never loved a soldier who loved like me. Said she wished the whole damned outfit would move away and leave us in peace. Why, she's jealous every time I have to go to formation.

FLAGG: Sergeant, in about five minutes you're going to be married; in about eight you're going to please this old man by leaving an allotment here for about two-thirds of your pay in regular army style. The more you talk, the more you hang yourself up by the thumbs.

QUIRT: This ain't talk. What do you say I go get this little baby and ask her if she'll say anything about me that ain't praise and admiration? What do you say I go get her? What do I care a whoop in hell what this old bozo says about me? I ain't seduced *him!* He's after money. Well, I ain't got money. I don't have to carry money around in my love affairs. What do you say I go get her?

FLAGG: Of course, you'll go get her. And propose marriage to her on the way, because you'll meet the wedding detail when you get here. Gowdy, go to the Y tent and get the chaplain. [*Gowdy goes out*] Aldrich, accompany Sergeant Quirt to the tavern and tell Charmaine that I'm giving away in marriage the handsomest sergeant in the corps. Tell her she's a woman in a thousand, because Quirt has already run away from a thousand; and if it weren't for my seeing justice done him, he'd run away from that many more. All right, Quirt, we'll be waiting for you. [*Quirt and* Aldrich *go out*. Ferguson *fixes chair, returns to seat, and turns to* Moore] Mr. Moore, tell papa the wedding bells are going to ring, and there's money in it for him, money in it!

[*Moore seats* Pete *on stool at window; then whispers. A knock at the door.* Lipinsky *opens it*]

LIPINSKY: Brigade runner, Captain Flagg.

FLAGG: Send him in.

[*The* Runner *enters*]

RUNNER: Company commander?

FLAGG: What is it—shoving off?

RUNNER: Moving in an hour, sir.

FLAGG: In an hour?

RUNNER: Please initial.

[*Offers pencil and paper*]

FLAGG: [*Signing*] You hear that, Moore?

MOORE: Yes, sir.

FLAGG: [*Up and business-like*] Going in an hour. You know what that means.

MOORE: Yes, sir.

FLAGG: Pass the word to our platoon commanders to stand in heavy packs in thirty minutes. The *camions* are waiting at the crossroad with ammunition. [*Moore goes out*] Kiper, tell Quirt to salvage all rations in the square. [*Kiper starts for door but stops as Flagg says, "Wait a minute"*] Don't let on to Quirt we're going in. We'll marry him to Charmaine and march the blushing bridegroom off to war.

[*Walks up and down*]

FERGUSON: Afraid you can't marry them this evening, Captain Flagg. Chaplain very sticky on that point. Have to be married in the morning.

FLAGG: Well, then, the mayor could marry them, couldn't he? Lipinsky, go get the mayor. Who's seen the mayor to-day?

KIPER: Just saw him down by the bridge on a load of manure.

FLAGG: There you are, Lipinsky—load of manure, near the bridge. Get the mayor, dust him off, and bring him here toot pronto. If the chaplain can't do it, the mayor can.

[Lipinsky *starts to go out but halts and calls "'Tenshun." Pete still sits on stool. In walk a* Brigadier-General, *one* Colonel, *one* Captain, *and two* Lieutenants]

THE GENERAL: Hello, Flagg. Haven't you received that order yet? Not a soul stirring on your damned street. [*All salute*] Flagg, you run the most disreputable outfit of the brigade. I come into town to hold a staff conference and find the whole shebang asleep. What kind of platoon commanders have you got, anyway, sitting round here like a nest of hobos when you're moving in forty-five minutes?

[*The staff remains standing at attention*]

FLAGG: Just got the order, General. We'll get off in time. Never missed a train in my life.

THE GENERAL: Well, I don't see how you do it. *Camions* back two miles at the crossroads. Your men will have ammunition there, and I want every man to carry two extra bandoliers.

FLAGG: If you don't mind my saying so, General,

we're the refuse of the brigade back of the line and we carry extra bandoliers into it.

THE GENERAL: Well, I'll tell you why. Division wants a line straightened that we're going to take over. Isn't straight enough for him. Where's the map? Map, Davis!

THE COLONEL: [Turns] Map, Tolbert!

THE LIEUTENANT: Map, Price!

THE CAPTAIN: Where's that map? [Looks wildly around. The last Lieutenant to enter hands map to Price] Here's the map, sir.

[Hands map to General]

THE GENERAL: Good boy, good boy. A map, after all, among you soldiers. Now, see here, Flagg. [Pointing to map, which he spreads out on table] There she is, and here's the line. The corps wants it straightened out. It will take the steel, the cold steel. But they've got to have it straightened out. Give them the steel and you can do it. You'll hold the town—our half of it—and you'll get these fellows out if it takes a week. Your men are a bunch of tramps, but they can do this sort of thing.

FLAGG: Individualists, General, individualists.

THE GENERAL: Well, it's the penalty you pay for laxity. I admit it has its compensations. But you've got to give 'em the steel. You've got to run 'em down like rats. You give them the old cowering point. We've got to get them out. We want to go in there and run 'em out. We want to give 'em steel.

FLAGG: We? Staff going in there too, General?

THE GENERAL: [Disconsolately] No—they won't risk us fellows, curse the luck.

FLAGG: That's too bad, General.

THE GENERAL: But we'll be behind you, Flagg.

FLAGG: How far, General?

THE GENERAL: We'll probably be at Cemetery Farm. We haven't studied the indirect fire properly yet, but we'll be behind you.

THE COLONEL: [Handing bundle of posters to General] Beg pardon, sir; these posters.

THE GENERAL: And, Flagg, some Yankee Doodle back in Hoboken sends you some posters with his compliments.

FLAGG: Posters? What for?

THE GENERAL: To post behind the German lines— sent to all companies of this brigade.

FLAGG: My God! What are we advertising? Camels?

THE GENERAL: Oh, no! It's intelligence work. Explaining our mission over here to the German soldier. There are three hundred posters. Send a small detail through the German lines some night and tack 'em up all over the place.

FLAGG: How many men am I supposed to lose on that job?

THE GENERAL: Not one. We don't want to lose a man. But tack 'em up.

FLAGG: Yeah, that's easy to say. I'd like to tack up a few in Hoboken containing my sentiments on two-starred idiots who waste men on that kind of monkey-business.

THE GENERAL: Well, here is another thing, Flagg, the big G. one wants a prisoner out of that town of yours. Wants an officer from one of those Alsatian regiments where the deserters are filtering through. And I've got to get him.

FLAGG: Oh, don't say that, General, don't break our hearts. I've got to get him. I knew damn well you had a bolt of black crepe up your sleeve when you came in the door.

THE GENERAL: Hold down the losses, Flagg . . . and listen. If you send me one of those Alsatian officers in good condition I'll send your whole company back for a month's rest.

FLAGG: You mean it?

THE GENERAL: Mean it! You know me, Flagg. I'll do more if you get me an officer without a scratch. I'll give you eight days in any hotel in France. If you weren't such a bum, Flagg, I'd put you on staff.

FLAGG: I've been a bum, General, but I'm damned if I'd go on staff.

THE GENERAL: [At the door] Hold down the losses, Flagg, and give 'em the steel—and don't forget those posters, for they're damned important—and if you fetch me that prisoner you get a month's rest and eight days' leave. [The door opens. In walk the Chaplain, Charmaine and Quirt, Mayor, Kiper, and Lipinsky] Hullo! My God, what's this? A wedding party?

FLAGG: Why, yes, General. I don't suppose we ought to wait for it, but it's a sort of special case and won't take long.

THE GENERAL: You aren't getting married, are you, Flagg?

FLAGG: Not this trip; no sir. It's Sergeant Quirt.

THE GENERAL: [Turning to Quirt] Oh, yes, I remember Sergeant Quirt very well.

FLAGG: I didn't like to intrude company matters when you were in haste, General, but the truth is, Sergeant Quirt has expressed a wish to marry the inn-keeper's daughter here, and her father was waiting to press charges; so, you see—

THE GENERAL: Oh! Charges? . . .

FLAGG: Personally, I'm opposed to Quirt's marrying at all, but he insists his intentions were honorable, and he's such a fine soldier I should hate to carry this old man to H.Q. with a complaint.

THE GENERAL: What's this, Sergeant?

QUIRT: A courtship, General; a love match from the start. Honorable intentions on both sides.

THE GENERAL: Sounds a little fishy to me, I must say, but go right ahead. Don't waste time.

[Ferguson comes forward]

PETE: Monsieur le général, les Américains sont si forts—ils m'ont déshonoré—ma petite fille—ma fleur charmante—ma fleur délicate . . .

FERGUSON: In case of a marriage, Captain Flagg, a little allotment is regulation.

FLAGG: Thanks, Fergy; I almost forgot the allotment.

QUIRT: Hell, we don't need no allotment. This is a love match.

FLAGG: Of course, it holds us up a bit, but if the General doesn't mind?

FERGUSON: A little allotment is regulation, sir.

THE GENERAL: Go ahead, go ahead.

FLAGG: Ferguson, where are those allotment blanks?

FERGUSON: Right here, sir.

THE GENERAL: [*To* Ferguson] Make it out for two-thirds of the sergeant's pay, Ferguson.

FERGUSON: [*Sits and fills papers*] Yes, sir.

QUIRT: [*Standing, with* Charmaine] I don't know about this, General.

THE GENERAL: It's for your own good, Quirt. How do you plan to get out of it, otherwise?

QUIRT: Get out of it? Didn't I tell you it was a love match?

THE GENERAL: No more talk, Sergeant; sign up or stand trial.

FLAGG: For your own good, Quirt.

QUIRT: For whose good, Captain Flagg?

THE GENERAL: Sign up, Quirt.

[Ferguson *gives paper to* Flagg. Quirt *reluctantly signs*]

FLAGG: All in order. [*Looks over paper*] Ship-shape, Sergeant Quirt. Beautiful hand you write, sir. And now, Chaplain, Sergeant Quirt is next.

THE GENERAL: Let's get it over with. And here's her father ready to give her away.

PETE: *Merci, mon général.*

THE GENERAL: A regular church wedding, and Captain Flagg can be best man.

FLAGG: Get that, Sergeant Quirt? Charmaine [*He crosses and hands her allotment papers with a bow*], keep this in a good safe place. It means money to you the first of every month.

CHARMAINE: *Merci.*

THE GENERAL: Turn on the ceremony.

CHAPLAIN: Run it through. Sorry we can't wait to kiss the bride, Quirt. You have about twenty minutes, Flagg.

FLAGG: Right, sir.

THE GENERAL: One word, Quirt. You're going in to-night. You're going in in twenty minutes. If you take your men into the line in first-rate condition, looking like soldiers, you'll square yourself with me. Keep that in mind.

QUIRT: We're going in in twenty minutes?

THE GENERAL: Yes. We're off, men. So long, Flagg. Twenty minutes.

FLAGG: Good-bye, General.

[*All salute. The General and his retinue file out at door*]

CHAPLAIN: Do you, Charmaine, take this man for your husband, to love, honor—

QUIRT: She does not, I do not, we do not. So we're

going in in twenty minutes, eh—and you were going to tie me up before I knew anything about it? And I suppose if I don't marry her you'll lock me up. If you think you can take your men in to-night without a first sergeant, you lock me up. I would like to see you take this gang of tiny tots across that last two miles without a sergeant. Well, if this sergeant goes in, he goes in single; so you God-damn well better make up your mind what you're going to do.

FLAGG: Well, skunk, you've got me. You win. Hit the deck.

QUIRT: Sorry, Charmaine, but I've got work to do. I can't marry you to-night, I can't marry you any God-damn time at all, and if I never see you again— why, then I never see you again, understand? What's more, don't you try cashing that allotment, or by God I'll pull something that'll stop my pay for good. Get out of my way.

[*He goes out. Instantly a whistle blows*]

FLAGG: Sorry, Charmaine, but I need that sergeant. Shake a leg, you hayshakers. Pass the word for inspection in five minutes, and they'd better be ship-shape. *Camions* at the crossroad. Extra bandoliers and V.B. grenades for the outside ranks. Don't let Quirt do all the work.

THE RUNNERS: Ay ay, sir.

[*They go out hastily*]

PETE: [*Angry*] *Sont-ils mariés? Ou votre sergeant, se moque-t-il de moi?*

FLAGG: Sure, they're married.

PETE: [*Beats on table*] *Prenez garde! Je viendrai!*

FLAGG: [*Turns—speaks ominously*] Don't bother me. Don't get in my way, see? We're fighting a war with Germany. I don't give a damn whether he's married or not. Run along outside. [*Turns* Pete *around; spanks him*] I'm busy. [Pete *goes out, stops near* Charmaine *and says, "Sale vache"; then goes out.* Flagg *goes to table, gets his hat, turns toward the door*] So long, Fergy. Take care of the stuff.

FERGUSON: Yes, sir.

[*Turns to desk.* Flagg *starts out.* Charmaine *crosses to him*]

CHARMAINE: [*Her hand on his arm*] I'm so sorry. You should have taken me to Paris. I told you to take me to Paris. I could not be good all alone.

FLAGG: [*Takes her by shoulders*] That's all right, Charmaine. You're a damn fine little animal. Go right on having a good time. It's a great life, and you've got a genius for it.

CHARMAINE: But you do not love me, not any more?

FLAGG: Sure I love you! Everybody loves you.

CHARMAINE: You think I am *pas bonne?*

FLAGG: Listen, Charmaine. Don't you worry any more about Quirt and me. It's a thousand to one you'll never see either of us again. I'm damned sorry I have to take your sergeant away, but this war's lousy with sergeants. There'll be thirty along in thirty days. Anyway you'll probably never see us again. Kiss me good-bye. [*They kiss*] Now you forget me!

CHARMAINE: I never forget you.

[*A whistle blows outside*]

FLAGG: You won't forget me? Well, if I get leave, Charmaine . . . you never can tell. [*The whistle blows twice*] It's a hell of a war, but it's the only one we've got.

[*He goes out. She stands staring after him*]

FERGUSON: [*From his table; turning*] Well, little missy. You're a single woman *with* an allotment. There ain't many as fortunate as that.

CHARMAINE: He will come back?

FERGUSON: Which one?

CHARMAINE: The captain.

FERGUSON: Not likely. Not likely either of them will. A soldier hardly ever doubles on his trail in this war.

CHARMAINE: No?

FERGUSON: Hardly ever. And you're just as fortunate you didn't marry a soldier, darling. They're a bad lot to keep house for. I know. I've been keeping house for one regiment or another since I was as young as you are.

CHARMAINE: Oh, but they are beautiful.

FERGUSON: The girls always like them. I don't know why.

CHARMAINE: They go into hell to die—and they are not old enough to die.

FERGUSON: I shouldn't think it would matter much to you, dear. Some get killed, but plenty more come in to relieve them. Never any shortage of soldiers.

CHARMAINE: It's terrible!

FERGUSON: It's their business. Some of 'em get killed at it, same as in any trade.

CHARMAINE: [*Crosses to back of* Ferguson's *chair; leans over him*] Can I help you?

FERGUSON: No.

CHARMAINE: To-morrow?

FERGUSON: No.

CHARMAINE: You are unkind.

FERGUSON: Just because I'm the only man around here do you think I'm going to let you bother me? You run along home and pray God to keep you out of mischief a few days. It won't do you any harm.

[*He bends over his work*]

CHARMAINE: *Bon soir.* [*He does not hear her*] *Bon soir!*

FERGUSON: What?

CHARMAINE: *Bon soir.*

FERGUSON: Oh, yes, good night. [*She slowly crosses to door, looking back at him all the way. She quietly closes door, and just as she does so,* Ferguson *very loudly says,* "Good night." *He bends over his desk, alone, writing and sings*]
"The French they are a funny race, parlez-vous,
The French they are a funny race, parlez-vous . . ."

CURTAIN

ACT II.

A cellar in a disputed town, a typical deep wine cellar of a prosperous farmhouse on the edge of a village in France. It resembles half of a culvert thirty feet in diameter, with a corresponding curved roof and walls. One end is open, and the other is walled up, admitting a narrow and rather low door in the center, through which a flight of stairs extends to the ground floor above. This cellar is lit dimly by two candles placed at either side of the front stage and held in bottle on small bully-beef boxes. The rear wall can only barely be discerned. Along the sides of this culvert are dirty white ticks stuffed with straw for sleeping quarters, the sort of ticks headquarters detachment men carry about with them. There are four on each side, arranged with all the litter of miscellany a soldier carries about tucked at their heads, and with the foot of these pallets extending into the center of the culvert. The effect is not unlike in design that of a hospital ward, with feet toward the center aisle. Back of Flagg's *bunk all manner of stuff—first-aid kits, bandages, chocolates, sticks, pistols and rifles, notes, books of memoranda, etc.*

Two men are asleep, snoring gently—gas masks at alert on chests, tin hats on back of heads, and heads on floor. They are indescribably dirty, and with six or eight days' beard.

The two men are Spike *and* Kiper. Kiper *is on second bunk at left,* Spike *on third bunk at right.* Gowdy *enters. Stirs* Spike *with his foot.*

GOWDY: All right. Heave out and lash up. Lively now. Rations are in. Go draw for ten. At the gray stable to-night. Take that sack there.

[*Points to a muddy sack on the floor near by*]

SPIKE: What time is it? Rations in?

GOWDY: You heard me, Spike. Shake a leg and go draw rations for ten men, at the gray stable near the square. It's after two o'clock.

SPIKE: Where's Captain Flagg?

GOWDY: Down tying up Mr. Aldrich.

SPIKE: So they got him. Bad?

GOWDY: I'll say they did. A ticket home. Right arm torn all to hell.

SPIKE: A damned dirty shame. He's lucky, though, to get out with an arm. I'd sell 'em mine, and at the same price. What was it—that one-pounder again?

GOWDY: No. Fuse cap from a grenade. Made a hell of a mess on Mr. Aldrich. He was crawling on the embankment near the railway station, and somebody inside threw him a present.

SPIKE: [*Now up and re-winding a spiral legging*] A damned swell officer, if you ask me. Taking him out to-night?

GOWDY: No. The skipper is bringing him here. Send him out to-morrow night. He's lost too much blood to walk it before dawn. God, it's getting on my nerves.

KIPER: [*Who has been awakened*] Who? Mr. Aldrich hit bad?

GOWDY: Pretty bad. Arm. Make a bunk for him, willya? Shake it down and pile another in the back. He'll want to sit up with it. Make up Harry's bunk.

SPIKE: [*At door, about to go upstairs, turns at this*] Harry's bunk? Why, Harry?

GOWDY: Harry's through with bunks.

SPIKE: Bumped off?

GOWDY: Worse. In the belly crossing the square.

[*Spike goes out*]

KIPER: Where is he?

GOWDY: The skipper rushed him back an hour ago. No use, though; Harry was unconscious—halfway—holding half his guts in his bare hands and hollering for somebody to turn him loose so he could shoot himself.

KIPER: Captain Flagg want me?

GOWDY: He said not to wake you. Might need you later on.

KIPER: A good job for me, I suppose. Jeez, with this daylight saving I ain't going to live forever, that's sure. I think I'll go crazy and get the doc to gimme a ticket.

GOWDY: Flagg's crazy now. Raving crazy. Hasn't slept for five nights. We'll be sitting on him in another night like he's had to-night.

KIPER: The whole damned universe is crazy now.

[*Kiper has come forward to Flagg's bunk, smoking. Enter Pharmacist's Mate, with a large clothing roll trussed up in leather straps with a portmanteau handle. He is young, pink-faced, but horribly callous, probably some kid from a medical school of 1917*]

MATE: [*Looking about in the dark as he approaches Kiper*] Flagg's company P.C.?

KIPER: [*Hostile; Gowdy sits up*] Yeah.

MATE: Where'd I better set up shop, soldier?

[*He looks about the cellar*]

KIPER: [*Worried*] What do you want to set up shop for, sailor?

MATE: [*Sitting down on bunk; starts unpacking, takes off helmet*] How'd I know? This ain't my party. Flagg wants it here.

KIPER: What's he want it for to-night?

MATE: He's going to put on a little party before morning. [*He uncovers a litter of blue-rolled bandages on bunk; absorbent cotton, a jar of iodine which he unscrews, and some wooden sticks around which he begins to twist wisps of cotton for daubs*] A little party.

KIPER: The whole damn company, I suppose, and all the engineers he can find to boot.

MATE: [*Professionally*] Oh, no. He ain't got arrangements here for that many. I'd say a small party, according to the stuff they gave me at the dressing station.

KIPER: [*Incredulous*] How small?

MATE: [*With immense indifference, busy about his detail*] Oh, I'd say about two operating tables . . . [*A pause as he enjoys the effect on* Kiper] A small party. About four couples for bridge.

KIPER: Yeah. [*Rather miserable*] Low bridge around that lousy railroad station.

MATE: I guess so. They were passing out V.B. grenades down the street to the station when I came through.

KIPER: [*Immensely friendly all of a sudden*] Look here, sailor. You are smarter than me.

MATE: [*Interrupting*] Oh, no!

KIPER: [*Insistently*] Oh, hell, yes! Any man smart enough not to join in them four couples is smarter than I am. Even you're smarter. Now that being the case, tell me why the hell we want the Heinies out of that God-damn railway station. Leave 'em there, I say. Let 'em sit where they damned well are. They ain't going anywheres.

MATE: I can't tell you.

KIPER: Nobody can. Like as not General Pershing himself couldn't tell you about it . . . and . . . oh, sweet baby, but last night down there I swore to God so long as I lived I'd never let another German in that railroad station throw a potato masher at me.

MATE: You can throw a grenade at him.

KIPER: Sure I can. But I don't want to no more. I pitched yesterday, and my arm is sore. I know I can do it, and it ain't fun any more. I know all about Flagg's invitations to parties. I know why they all got R.S.V.P. on 'em. Right smart of V.B. grenades provided. . . .

[*Enter* Lipinsky, *who comes down; looks first at* Kiper]

LIPINSKY: [*Immediately perceiving the litter*] Jeez, Kiper, I wish you'd keep the undertakers out of here. What's all this, Jack?

[*He waves to the mate's stuff*]

MATE: [*Selecting a small bandage*] Well, this one is yours, and the rest is for your friends.

LIPINSKY: [*Cheerily*] Don't try to put the bug on me. I ain't no queen bee. They ain't made one that could burst alongside of me. If they'd made it, I'd be down with the daisies long ago. I'm proof now. It's down in the cards that I'll live to see the navy at Mare Island again. [*He lights a cigarette which he has taken from Flagg's bunk*] Yes, sir, I'll live to beat the pants off that bird that sold me the wrist watch down by the main gate.

KIPER: How do you know you're going to live? Said your prayers, I suppose, and got an answer.

LIPINSKY: And who'd send me an answer?

KIPER: The great cosmic top sergeant who runs this world.

LIPINSKY: Well, I don't want any answer from that bird. He'd send the answer collect, and it would say, "Fall in and get the manure outa the French angels' backyards. Clean up heaven, you lowdown Marine.

so's the National Guard won't get typhoid when they all die and come here."

KIPER: There ain't any heaven. Paris is heaven enough. If I ever get outa hell, I'm certainly going to stay in heaven until I die.

LIPINSKY: Of course, there's a heaven.

MATE: On the level, now. You birds know your souls go somewheres. You've seen too many men die. A fellow is walking along, blood in his face and breath in his lungs, and whizz - eeee - zzzz, boommmmmm . . . he's down on the ground and something's gone. Something's gone, I tell you. Something that was in that bird a minute before has left, and all you've got is a pack of bloody rags and a lot of dirt. Well, for the want of a better name, you call that something a soul . . . and you can't kid me . . . the soul's gone somewheres.

KIPER: What of it? That soul ain't any of my business. It ain't got to eat, it ain't got to run; it ain't got to stand in line ten days a week to sign the pay-roll. I should get on my ear about where this doodle-bug in my chest is going after I die. It ain't never helped me none. It can go to hell for all I care.

LIPINSKY: Jeez, Kiper, don't talk that way around me. [Raises eyes] It wasn't me, God; it wasn't your little Vladysek Lipinsky. Not him. He knows too damn well if he was to talk that way you would certainly make him cover up and yell for mercy before morning.

KIPER: And you were the one wasn't going to be hit a while ago.

LIPINSKY: That's why I ain't going to be hit. My little soul's all ready to turn out for every formation, boots blacked and buttons shined. A little sea-going soul that knows its top sergeant can give it a kick in the pants any time he gets ready.

KIPER: Well, if there is a God, he ain't got medicine big enough to worry me. Why the hell doesn't he win the war for one side or the other and get this mess over? I know plenty of men could win it. Flagg probably could, if you gave him the army and a barrel of whiskey.

LIPINSKY: But you like the chaplain, Kiper. You said he was a swell bird the other day.

KIPER: Sure I like the chaplain. Gimme two packs of Camels two nights ago. If God was to show him-self, now—come down with a bunch of angels driv-ing a wagon-load of cigarettes, that would be something like it. The chaplain said my folks was all praying for me to come through, and for God to spare me after hearing their prayers. God, I ain't that dirty a coward! That's a case of saying, "Oh, God, don't kill our child. Kill every kid in the neigh-borhood, but bring the one marked Kiper safe back home. . . ." No, I don't want none of that for mine. . . . And you can take all your New Testa-ments with the khaki backs and throw 'em in the incinerator so far as I want anything out of 'em. I'd rather have a book of cigarette papers any time. . . . I ain't asking anybody for a damned thing in

this war. And you can take all your Bible backers and psalm singers and hitch 'em to the ration wagons, if you ask me.

MATE: Well, this is all very pleasant, but I got busi-ness over in the next company now. Bad curve in the position there, and 'long toward daybreak they start hollering "First Aid" as regular as a clock. If I was you fellows I'd go out and sleep in different shell-holes to-night . . . see which one of you is right. . . . Tell your skipper I'll be back around three-thirty.

[He steps on his cigarette and prepares to go out after Quirt enters, which he does. Quirt enters. Sergeant Quirt is tired]

QUIRT: Captain Flagg here?

GOWDY: Still in the orchard . . . digging those new rifle pits. We've got nine captured Maxims there. Those birds can't change the belts, but they can tap a thousand rounds apiece by pressing the buttons in the dark. Fifteen men could hold this half of the town, the way he's got the positions staked out.

QUIRT: There'll be about fifteen holding it if this business of reconnoitering patrols keeps up. I'd like to have that divisional staff in this town one night. Still bad in the square?

GOWDY: Pretty bad. Rifles in box rest in the rail-way stations . . . light automatics.

QUIRT: I thought Flagg got 'em out last night.

GOWDY: They filtered back in at dusk to-night. Our cross-fire couldn't stop 'em. The skipper says they are working them from pulleys from the first floor, and the railroad embankment covers them from us.

QUIRT: [Stretching out and sighing as he takes off his tin hat and mops his forehead] Running rations down that ravine every night is the toughest job I've ever soldiered.

GOWDY: Lucky to-night?

QUIRT: Pretty lucky. Six out of ten come back. Them two Jameson boys got it from the same shell going down. Dutchy and the little Jew were hit right at the dump. Easy ones, though. They'll be back in ten days.

[A commotion at head of stairs. Enter Captain Flagg supporting Aldrich by gripping Aldrich's uninjured wrist over his shoulder and easing him gently down steps. Aldrich is not groan-ing. After all, it won't hurt for fifteen minutes or so. But he is weak from loss of blood and soaked through, and is in an indescribable mess of dried blood and dirt, which appears black. Flagg, who is unkempt, has no leggings or laces in his breeches, these flapping in the most dis-illusioning fashion about his bare legs. His blouse, an old army blouse many sizes too big and without a sign of any insignia, is tied with a piece of twine. He is bareheaded—no tin hat and no accoutrements of any sort. He is a very weary-looking man. He wears belt and *holster with automatic bound to leg. As* Flagg *enters, followed by* Mate, Gowdy *jumps up and spreads blanket on bunk*]

FLAGG: Right here, Aldrich. [*Lowers him down on bunk. The* Pharmacist's Mate *follows him.* Flagg *kneels above* Aldrich. *The* Mate *stands*] Gimme a stick of that dope, Holsen.

MATE: They are quarter grains, Captain.

FLAGG: [*To* Aldrich, *lying down*] Take these two now. [*He puts two tablets from a tiny vial in the wounded officer's mouth*] I'm putting these in your blouse. Get somebody to give you one every three hours until you are carried out.

ALDRICH: What are they?

FLAGG: Morphine—quarter grains——

ALDRICH: [*Not dramatic, just casual*] What if I take them all when your back is turned?

FLAGG: [*Turning his back and crossing to his own bunk down left; sits on bunk*] Go ahead. It's your affair.

[*After* Flagg *is seated on his bunk a strange sob is heard at the head of the stairs.* Lieutenant Moore, *last seen in company headquarters, rushes in and goes straight over to* Aldrich, *where he stands and looks down at his arm, and not his face*]

MOORE: Oh, God, Dave, but they got you. God, but they got you a beauty, the dirty swine. God DAMN them for keeping us up in this hellish town. Why can't they send in some of the million men they've got back there and give us a chance? Men in my platoons are so hysterical every time I get a message from Flagg, they want to know if they're being relieved. What can I tell them? They look at me like whipped dogs—as if I had just beaten them—and I've had enough of them this time. I've got to get them out, I tell you. They've had enough. Every night the same way. [*He turns to* Flagg] And since six o'clock there's been a wounded sniper in the tree by that orchard angel crying "*Kamerad! Kamerad!*" Just like a big crippled whippoorwill. What price glory now? Why in God's name can't we all go home? Who gives a damn for this lousy, stinking little town but the poor French bastards who live here? God damn it! You talk about courage, and all night long you hear a man who's bleeding to death on a tree calling you "*Kamerad*" and asking you to save him. God damn every son of a bitch in the world, who isn't here! I won't stand for it. I won't stand for it! I won't have the platoon asking me every minute of the livelong night when they are going to be relieved. . . . Flagg, I tell you you can shoot me, but I won't stand for it. . . . I'll take 'em out to-night and kill you if you get in my way. . . .

[*Starts sobbing again.* Gowdy *and* Kiper *sit up*]

FLAGG: [*Rising quickly as though he might kill the man, and then putting his arm around the chap, who has clearly gone smash for a few minutes. He speaks in a quiet, chastening tone, with a gentility*

never before revealed] Here, boy, you can't do this before all these men. [*Walks him*] They are rubbed up, too. You are all tuckered out with your side of the line. Don't worry about your platoon. We'll get them out. You turn in here. [*Walks him to bunk on the left side of the room.* Kiper *crosses and throws blanket on him; stops at bunk nearest entrance*] And dope off for a little while . . . that's it, give him a blanket, Kiper . . . and now take it easy a while, and you can go back to your platoon in time to stand to. Sleep it off, boy, sleep it off. . . . You're in a deep wide hole, and shells can't get you. Sleep it off.

[Flagg *crosses to his own bunk, lights cigarette at candle, seats himself on bunk.* Gowdy *rests head on arm.* Quirt *kneels on floor, gets a piece of chocolate out of his pocket; rises, as though his legs were asleep. He carries his helmet. He crosses and tosses candy to* Moore]

QUIRT: Just a little chocolate I bought off a Y.M.C.A. wagon down at the base. [Quirt *is sympathetic and begins to talk nervously*] I got hit myself once. In Nicaragua. We were washed up before we made a landing. I was a corporal, and when we were scrubbing down and putting on clean uniforms —doctors' orders, you know, so they wouldn't have to wash us when we were hit—[*Turns to* Gowdy]— a bird said to me—it was old Smoke Plangetch, who was killed in 1913 in a chippie joint in Yokohama —Smoke said to me: "You'd better swab down, you son of a sea-bitch, because I dreamed last night they wrote your name on a bullet." I said to him, "The bullet ain't been cast that can shoot Micky Quirt." He said, "If your name is on one, it will turn the corner and go upstairs to find you." Jeez! That afternoon when we made a landing and hit the beach, the spigs was on a hill five hundred yards off shore. We started up the hill—they weren't many of us dropping—and I came to a log I had to jump [Quirt *illustrates this*] and I lost my balance and threw my hand up in the air. [Quirt *extends his wrist*] Look, right through the God-damn fin, as pretty as a pinwheel . . . Smoke saw it. "Oh, yeah, you wisenheimer son of a Chinese tart," he says to me, "your name was on that one and you had to reach up for it." [Gowdy *laughs.* Quirt *is obviously embarrassed by having spoken of himself so much. He turns and recollects his business and goes over to* Flagg. *Crosses to the foot of* Flagg's *bunk*] Rations detail in, sir. Lost the two Jameson boys in the ravine going down. Both badly hit. Lost Fleischman and Rosenthal in the dump. Both slight. Brought back all the ammunition and two sacks of bread, one of canned willie, French; I carried a sack of beet sugar on my back. Got a piece of shrapnel in it where they are shelling the crossroads—stopped it square. In the next war, I'm going to wear a suit of beet sugar and stand forest fire watch in the Rocky Mountains. [*He turns, and then remembers and comes back*] Oh, I brought up two of these thirty-day-wonder lieutenants from a training camp. Sent up by divisional for instruction.

FLAGG: By God, I won't stand for it. They wipe their damned dirty feet on this company. They can give my men all their damned good jobs. They can keep us in the line all during the whole damned war. But I'll be damned if my sergeants have got time to teach army lieutenants how to button their pants in the dark.

QUIRT: They are in my hole now, sir. Pretty badly shaken up by the ravine. First time up, you know. Shall I send them to you, sir?

FLAGG: Send them to me, and for God's sake, don't call me sir any more to-night.

QUIRT: [To Gowdy] All right. You heard him. Hit the deck. You'll find 'em in my hole. [Gowdy goes] Those Huns in the railway station again?

FLAGG: Try to cross the town square when there's a flare up, and you'll see.

QUIRT: You get a visit from brigade headquarters to-night. I saw their party in the ravine as we were going down to the dump.

FLAGG: The old man says we've got to drive them off the embankment. Huh! He can give me five general courts and I'll not waste another man at that business. It will take a brigade action to get them out for good.

QUIRT: Do you mind if I take a look around there now? I'd like to see this damned war some. For six days I've been a lousy bakery wagon—haven't seen a spiggoty yet, except stinking dead ones —I never see soldiers stink like these Heinies.

FLAGG: All right. Go get your blooming can blown off. But bury yourself, while you're about it. The burying detail is in for the night.

QUIRT: Gosh, I wish to hell I was home.

FLAGG: Go get one of those Alsatian lootnants then, and you'll get a leave.

QUIRT: I don't want to die yet, thanking you just the same. Well, here goes.

[Exit]

FLAGG: Well, keep your head down. I can't waste any grave-diggers on sergeants. [Flagg shrugs his shoulders and walks over to above Aldrich] Sorry Moore blew up that way, Aldrich . . . you are a damned sight luckier than he is, but he doesn't know it. I'll have you out to-morrow night with the ration detail, and you'll be parking your body in a big white bed in another two days. Good luck . . . You've been a damned good man. I wish you could get a ribbon for this town.

[As Flagg leaves, Gowdy enters with two lieutenants. They are just like tailor's dummies of a Burberry outfit, slicked to the notch and perky and eager. As they enter, Flagg steps on his cigarette and stands facing them. The Lieutenants come down and stand side by side]

FLAGG: [Starts back in mock admiration and salaams deeply as they come forward] So this is the last of the old guard, eh? In the name of the holy sweet Jumping, are you gentlemen bound for a masked ball, that you come disguised as officers? Or do you wish to save the snipers the trouble of picking you off with a glass, that you wear sign-boards? [He goes nearer them, inspecting their clothes] Can't you go without those trench coats even to the trenches? How long will you last in those boots? Take 'em off before you even part your hair in the morning. . . . [He changes to a thundering staccato] My name is Flagg, gentlemen, and I'm the sinkhole and cesspool of this regiment, frowned on in the Y.M.C.A. huts and sneered at by the divisional Beau Brummells. I am a lousy, good-for-nothing company commander. I corrupt youth and lead little boys astray into the black shadows between the lines of hell, killing more men than any other company commander in the regiment, and drawing all the dirty jobs in the world. I take chocolate soldiers and make dead heroes out of them. I did not send for you, Mister . . . [He leans forward, and the first officer salutes and speaks: "Cunningham, sir"] nor for you . . . ["Lundstrom, sir," also salutes]; and I confess I am in a quandary. Four days ago I should have been more hospitable, for I had four gunnery sergeants then. Now I have two, and can't spare them to teach little boys how to adjust their diapers. I've no doubt that one of you was an all-American half-back and the other the editor of the college paper, but we neither follow the ball nor the news here. We are all dirt, and we propose to die in order that corps headquarters may be decorated. I should be happy to receive suggestions as to what should be done with you. Ah, I have it! There are two German gunners over in the enemy railway station. Two bright young men might get them out and cut their throats before dawn; then no more could get in the station all day. Two bright young men, who know very little of anything just yet. I have two bright ones, but they are far too valuable. They are corporals with ten years' experience.

[The Lieutenants are speechless. There is not a smile in the cellar. Cunningham, who is the bigger of the two, finally answers, in a slow Southern drawl]

CUNNINGHAM: I'll do anything you will. Where is the railway station and the two bucks that have got you buffaloed?

FLAGG: Why, it's Frank Merriwell! All right, Frank. You and me will be playing ball in hell by three o'clock this morning.

LUNDSTROM: Put me in too, sir.

FLAGG: Oh, no, no, no! We must have officers left. Rule of the game. Must have officers. Men would get right up and go home, and then there wouldn't be any war at all. Besides, three would be a crowd, and I hate crowds early in the morning around the railway station. They are so noisy, and they die so fast. [He turns to Gowdy] Gowdy! Take Mr. Lundstrom to the fourth platoon sergeant, and tell him that here's his new officer. [*Runner and* Lundstrom *move to door.* Flagg *is all business now*] And by the way, Mr. Lundstrom, they filter through and bomb twice a week, small parties slipping down that ravine you'll find on your left. Watch it closely, or you'll all have your throats cut before you know it. And let that sergeant sleep for the next two days. Remember, he'll do no details until he's rested. Of course you can wake him for advice. That's all. Shove off. [*Runner and* Lundstrom *salute, and go out.* Cunningham *sits down.* Quirt *enters with his helmet on, limping; steals forward quietly, and sits down on his bunk. There is a nice bloody mess on his right calf.* Flagg *happens to turn, sees what's going on, sits up, watches* Quirt. Quirt *looks back, finally grins, then tries to open a first-aid pack*]

FLAGG: What's the matter with you?

QUIRT: Got a can opener?

FLAGG: You crook!

QUIRT: I say, Captain, got a can opener?

FLAGG: Those things are supposed to be opened with the teeth.

QUIRT: You don't say! Well, this'n' wasn't. This here can was evidently made for the Red Cross by the Columbia Red Salmon Company. Like as not instead of bandages I'll find the God-damnedest mess of goldfish in it.

FLAGG: [*Rises, crosses to* Quirt, *takes can away from him*] Where were you? [*He comes over, strains at the tin. He is looking daggers*] Where were you?

QUIRT: Just looking around.

FLAGG: Here.

[*Hands him tin, opened*]

QUIRT: Thanks.

FLAGG: Where were you, I said.

QUIRT: [*Takes out bandage*] In the vegetable garden, pulling turnips.

[*Starts wiping leg*]

FLAGG: God-damn you, Quirt, I believe you stuck your leg out.

[*Goes back and sits on bunk*]

QUIRT: Like hell I did. If I'd wanted to stick my leg out don't you think I've had plenty of chances to do it before? No, sir, I stuck my head out and some bird in the church tower took a shot at me. There she is. In and out without touching the bone. Just let me squeeze the juice out and she'll be all right. Ain't she the prettiest little damn puncture you ever saw, Captain? Ain't she a beauty?

FLAGG: I suppose you think you're going back to Cognac Pete's, huh?

QUIRT: How'd you guess it? Yes, sir, back to my little skookum lady you tried to make me a present of. Am I happy? Am I happy? Oh, boy! Ask me, Captain, am I happy?

FLAGG: You mean to say you aren't cured of Charmaine yet?

QUIRT: Cured of Charmaine? No, sir, I ain't even getting better. Oh, Captain Flagg, ain't you proud of yourself, ain't you a wizard? God, ain't I sorry

to leave you all alone here in this mess? Think of her sitting on my lap, lighting my pipe in the kitchen, and you dodging machine guns. I wonder I don't bust out crying. You know, I wouldn't wonder if you got bumped off and never came back. As a matter of fact, I hope you damn well get your head blown off.

FLAGG: Yeah, you always did have a charming disposition.

QUIRT: [*Squeezing his wound*] Oh, pretty baby, papa doesn't mean to hurt you. Lookit, Captain. By God, I wouldn't take a hundred dollars Mex. for that little bumble-bee that flew in there.

FLAGG: Feel pretty cocky, don't you? Well, you can't go out to-night. I guess you can work all right with that. You'll wait here till Cunningham and I get back with that Alsatian shavetail from the railroad embankment. Then I get leave, the company gets a rest, and we go back together, see?

QUIRT: Not much, I don't see. I've got a very important engagement back to Pete's place. Can't be postponed, not even for the pleasure of your enjoyable company, such as it is. I don't wait for nothing in the world but a medical tag.

[*Enter* Pharmacist's Mate; *stands on steps, leans head in door*]

MATE: Heard your first sergeant was hit in that turnip patch. [Flagg *indicates* Quirt. Mate *crosses to* Quirt; *kneels*] Let's have a look. Um. Night soil in that patch, and you, like a damned fool, crawl after they hit you, and now you're full of that muck. Can you walk, Sergeant?

QUIRT: [*Lying back*] Well, depends on what I see.

MATE: [*Helps up* Quirt, *who carries helmet*] Go to the sick bay at once for a shot of tetanus, and then get out of here. [*Takes his arm, and both cross*] You can reach a collecting station before you're done.

QUIRT: Ain't this heart-breaking, Flagg? Well, duty calls. But my eyes fill with tears at the thought of leaving my old company commander. I don't know as I can go through with it.

FLAGG: Make it snappy, Quirt, or you'll find the door locked.

QUIRT: Yeah? What door?

FLAGG: Charmaine's.

QUIRT: Are you wounded, too, Mr. Flagg?

FLAGG: No, but inside ten minutes I'm going to be wounded or bumped off or have that God-damned prisoner for the Brig.

QUIRT: Try to get killed, will you? To please me— just this once?

[Quirt *and the* Mate *go out*]

FLAGG: Mr. Cunningham . . . I guess you thought I was joking when I proposed that little expedition to the railroad embankments?

CUNNINGHAM: I did not. When do we start?

[*Coming to* Flagg]

FLAGG: Well, I was. I was kidding hell out of you. I'd no more let you go in there, boy, than I'd knife you in the back. The air is full of steel this side of that embankment, and a green man has about as much chance as a cootie on Fifth Avenue.

CUNNINGHAM: You going?

FLAGG: I've got official reasons for going, see? The Brig. wants a prisoner, and he also wants that nest wiped out. Also, I got private and personal reasons for wanting to catch up with that baboon that got the little present through his leg.

CUNNINGHAM: If you're going, that suits me. I ain't no green man. I can crawl on my belly.

FLAGG: Yeah?

CUNNINGHAM: I'm a locomotive engineer and I've been crawling under trains for fifteen years. Had several engines shot out from under me likewise. You think you can scare me with this here war? Christ! You ought to see a few railroad wrecks!

FLAGG: Well, Mr. Cunningham, I'm inclined to think you'll do.

CUNNINGHAM: You're God-damn right, I'll do.

FLAGG: What do you say we black our faces and give a little party, now the guests will be asleep?

CUNNINGHAM: Sure. I like the cut of your jib, and you can lead me to it. Show me which one is the lootenant, so I won't hurt him.

FLAGG: You from Texas?

CUNNINGHAM: You hit it.

FLAGG: Now I get you. So we've got another damned Texan in this outfit, wanting to fight anybody that ain't from Texas.

CUNNINGHAM: Yep, and I ain't no God-damn college boy, either.

FLAGG: Good stuff! Now throw away them fancy-dress clothes of yours and dip in here.

[He offers a can of lamp-black]

CUNNINGHAM: Sure. [Takes off overcoat] I was a locomotive engineer on the Louisiana Midland. Three wrecks in my division last year. Christ, but this war shore is a great relief to me. [Both black their faces] I'm an engineer officer attached to infantry. My brother's still driving an engine back home. Had a letter last month from him. He says, "You dirty yellow sapsucker, quitting your job on the Louisiana Midland. I knew you always were a yellow dog, but I didn't think you'd go back on the road thataway."

FLAGG: Now if I only had a pretty little engine. [Suddenly there is a scream upstairs, a shout in a burly strange tongue. "Heraus!" and three bombs explode. Flagg, the Runners, and all save Aldrich dash for the door] Marines! Marines! Marines! [The lieutenant who had been put to sleep stirs uneasily. After a brief tumult, the people of the cellar descend stairs, Flagg holding a German officer by the collar. He takes him straight to the candle] Let me have a look at you, sweetheart, let me have a look! Boys, he's an Alsatian lieutenant! He couldn't wait for us to go after him, so he came over. [He embraces his captive] Oh, sweetheart—you're the sweetest sight I've seen since Charmaine! Here, Kiper [Pushes him to Kiper]—take care of him for me, and for God's sake don't scare him to death, because he's our ticket of leave!

LEWISOHN: [Screams, outside] Captain Flagg . . .

FLAGG: Who's that?

LIPINSKY: It's little Lewisohn, sir.

[Lewisohn is carried in by Gowdy followed by Pharmacist's Mate, and he is crying monotonously for Captain Flagg]

LEWISOHN: Captain Flagg. Captain Flagg. Stop the blood. Stop the blood.

FLAGG: [Takes him from Gowdy and puts him on floor] I can't stop it, Lewisohn, I'm sorry.

[He examines wound in left side]

LEWISOHN: Oh, Captain Flagg, stop the blood.

FLAGG: Fix him with your needle, Mate.

[Mate gives him needle in arm]

LEWISOHN: Oh, Captain Flagg, can't you please, sir, stop the blood?

FLAGG: [Puts hand behind Lewisohn's head and gently lowers him to floor] You'll be all right, boy. You'll be all right. You'll be all right.

[Lewisohn sighs and relaxes his body]

CURTAIN

ACT III.

A tavern known colloquially as Cognac Pete's. Evening, two days later. The outside door is in the rear, small bar at the right, stairway left, an inside door at right. Windows rear. Ferguson sits at long table smoking and playing solitaire, a bottle of Martell and a brandy pony at his elbow. Charmaine is in front of the table by the candles, sewing. Ferguson is enjoying the luxury of talking to himself, for it is apparent that Charmaine is not following all he says.

FERGUSON: I'm glad they're coming back here. [He sips, between sentences] It's a good, quiet town . . . quiet . . . last time we were in a town where the M.P.'s and the mule skinners fought every night . . . glad they sent 'em back here. . . . You ought to be. . . . Your father'll do a land office business when the outfit gets here. He better knock the bung in every barrel of red ink he's got. God, how they'll eat . . . what's left of 'em. When two hundred leave me behind with the stuff, I always get ready to mess two hundred when they return. Of course a hundred may not return . . . but they'll eat right through to the bottom of the kettle just the same. Now you take that big oakum-haired Swede named Swenson. I never see a Marine eat more than he did . . . I damn well hope Swenson gets back . . . I like to see him eat. There was a little Jew named Lewisohn that could out-eat him, weight for weight; but the Swede weighed twice as much. That Swede could eat anything but a horse collar. [*He chuckles and* Charmaine *smiles*] Well, I'll say we've kept each other company. We sure have, even if you can't speak a white man's lingo; that is, not to say *speak* it. Now if you'd been a Spanish girl we could have got together a little better . . . I lived with a Spanish girl at Cavite back in '99 . . . in those days I was salty as hell, a sea-going buckaroo.

CHARMAINE: *Est-ce que* . . . you are lonely?

FERGUSON: It ain't so bad, staying behind this way. It ain't so bad. Twenty years now I've had 'em leave me. When I was younger I believed some of the liars who said they liked to fight . . . liked being under fire . . . but it always bored me to sit around and be sniped at. Somehow I never did get angry. And you've got to get angry when a bird's shooting at you if you're going to enjoy it. So I didn't have a good time . . . Now you take Flagg there . . . there's the sort likes it. Flagg gets mad as hell if you don't even like him, let alone shoot at him. Flagg and me are different. Now Flagg——

CHARMAINE: Where is *le capitaine?*

FERGUSON: Pretty near here, I suppose.

CHARMAINE: Near here?

FERGUSON: He'll be here presently, General.

CHARMAINE: *Le Capitaine Flagg*—he has been wounded ever?

FERGUSON: Naw! Flagg ain't never been wounded. Never will, neither, if you ask me. You can't hurt his kind. When you see a man like Flagg, it's curious, but they always have the pleasure of drinking themselves to death . . . funny thing . . . I never knew a man who could float a load of liquor, didn't hold all the cards besides. Now you take Flagg . . . he'll be here in fifteen minutes mebbe—mebbe two hours —but just the same as ever . . . thirsty as hell, wishing he had forty geisha girls to play with.

CHARMAINE: Fifteen minutes. . . .

FERGUSON: [*With elaborate gestures*] Le Capitany . . . ici . . . sank . . . min-use ici, sank min-use . . . Compree?

CHARMAINE: *Oui, oui, oui! Merci bien.*

[*She runs upstairs.* Ferguson *continues smoking, pouring a pony of brandy. Presently the door at rear opens slowly. Enter* Sergeant Quirt *in a major's army overcoat, with black braids and a leather-visored garrison cap. He is shaven, crafty-faced. Below the overcoat, which is bursting on his chest, may be seen rough army shoes, gray woolen socks pulled over the bottoms of striped outing-flannel pajamas. He looks exactly what he is, a slightly wounded soldier escaped from hospital in borrowed clothes.* Ferguson *turns, and seeing him, comes to attention.* Quirt *also has a bottle with about half a drink in it*]

FERGUSON: [*Rising courteously*] Good evening, Major.

QUIRT: [*Pours what remains in the bottle he carries into* Ferguson's *glass; then, taking the full bottle,*

sets his empty one in its place*] Sit down, Fergy, and use your eyes. Help me to get out of this rigging.

FERGUSON: [*Sitting; irritated*] What are you doing in those gadgets, Quirt? Where's the outfit? Where you been to?

QUIRT: Listen. I ain't writing my memoirs of this war till it's over. All you need to know is, I got two M.P.'s on my trail, and I don't want to meet 'em in these.

[*He removes his coat and is found to be in striped pajamas. A small red cross on the jumper pocket*]

FERGUSON: You come from the lines in that outfit, Quirt? In night-drawers?

QUIRT: I suppose you think I go 'round this way because I like it. [*He stows the overcoat and cap under the bench*] Major, you're relieved. [*Takes slicker from peg on stair rail*] Lend me your slicker, Fergy. I'll give it back if it thunders.

[*He goes to chair at table, seizes the cognac, pours out two ponies and swallows them, looks at* Ferguson, *then pours a third drink; drinks it*]

FERGUSON: Of course you're paying for those, Quirt, even if you have gone cuckoo.

QUIRT: All right, all right! Don't get on your ear about it . . . and now you want to know where I've been.

FERGUSON: Oh, no, if a soldier wants to campaign in a pair of night-drawers, it ain't none of my parade. It takes all kinds of sergeants to make an army.

QUIRT: [*Drinking his third*] You're too hard-hearted, Fergy. I ain't in my right mind. I was wounded, and now I've got aspasia. [*Mysteriously*] My name is Field Marshal von Hindenburg, and I'm looking for a wagonload of pants that got lost in shipment.

FERGUSON: Yeah?

QUIRT: Yeah, sure. I wandered outta a hospital about five miles over at a place called Noisy. It was damned well named too, Fergy. Noisy was no name for it when I came outta the ether after I'd shipped in there with a piece of pants driven through a bullet hole in my leg.

FERGUSON: Have to give you ether to take off your pants?

QUIRT: No. They gave me ether so the stretcher bearers could steal a gold watch and eight hundred bucks off me. I certainly put up a squawk when I woke up and found 'em missing. But a hell of a lot of good it did me. I went looking for the bird that got them and ran into a guy in a bartender's coat in the operating room. He tried to pipe me down and I hung a shanty on the bimbo's eye [*Enjoying the picture himself*] and when they washed him off he was a captain. So they locked me up, wound and all. And then I got aspasia, and here I am. You ain't seen me.

FERGUSON: No, I ain't seen you [*Distant voices shouting "Fergy!" "When do we eat?" "Chow," etc.*

At this sound, very faint, Quirt *rises quickly, starting for the stairs with a skip and jump*] Keep your drawers on, Quirt. They ain't no M.P.'s. That's the outfit. I've got old Pete and his brother down at the bridge, keeping coffee and slum hot for 'em. Better go and give yourself up to Fiagg as soon as he drives in. You'll be safe then. I'd like to see a set of doctors take Flagg's first sergeant off him when he's just out of the lines. It surely would be a pretty sight afterwards, them doctors working on each other like monkeys. [*The voices come nearer. The cry, long drawn out like a wolf's, comes from many throats: "Ch-o-o-o-w-w!"*] That's me. They're calling for me. Well, old Fergy's got their chow, and hot too.

[*He goes.* Quirt *limps quickly to door after* Ferguson *goes.* Charmaine *comes down the stairs at the same time*]

QUIRT: [*Turning to find* Charmaine] Hello, Pittsburgh.

CHARMAINE: [*With a small cry, comes toward him*] You are wounded.

QUIRT: Sure I'm wounded. Ain't that enough to put me nine miles ahead of Flagg with you? I certainly beat him here.

CHARMAINE: [*Trying to put arms around his neck*] Mais, mais . . . you are . . .

QUIRT: [*Restraining her*] Don't embarrass me, darling, because I ain't clothed and in my right mind. I just been waiting for Fergy to leave so I could steal a uniform from him. Where's his room? [Charmaine *points to door*] Wait a minute, dearie, until I salvage a pair of breeches. [*He goes out.* Charmaine *goes to the outside door, where voices are now heard.* Quirt *reappears*] Damn it, he's locked his chest! Gimme a ice pick.

[Quirt *takes bottle from bar. There are steps and voices at the door, and* Quirt *withdraws hastily to the right,* Charmaine *following. Enter* Kiper, Gowdy, *and* Lipinsky. Kiper *spies the cognac bottle and holds it over his open gullet. The other two rush him. There is a tough scuffle*]

KIPER: Lay off my bottle.

GOWDY: Say, don't drink it all! [*All then sit behind the table and deliberately begin a tremendous racket*]

KIPER: Hey! *Vin rouge! Vin blanc!* You, Pete! *Venez ici.* Toot sweet!

LIPINSKY: Toot sweet—toot sweet—toot God-damn sweet—*jambon? Des œufs! Fromages! Vin! Vin!*

GOWDY: *Bière, bière, bière!*

[Flagg *enters. The three jump up and push back their chairs. When he yells "Clear out," the tumult instantly ceases.* Flagg *is cold sober, still in his old clothes and dusty, but recently shaven, and possessed of rolled leggings and an old brown shirt*]

FLAGG: Clear out, you yapping hounds, and tell the new platoon commander to billet every man down the moment he finishes mess. Tell him I don't want to see one of 'em around this tavern till that's done. [*Turns; crosses to bar*] Tell them not to rag a man to-night. [*Takes bottle; turns to them*] As soon as they know their billets, let 'em out. Let 'em drink. Let 'em fight. Get out.

THE RUNNERS: [*Gently; somewhat discouraged*] Ay, ay, sir.

[*They disappear.* Charmaine *enters quietly and stands leaning in the doorway.* Flagg *pours a beaker and drinks it pleasantly, enjoyingly. Then he pours a second and walks around to chair at table and sits down.* Charmaine *has watched this from the doorway. He sees her at last*]

FLAGG: [*Arising and bowing grandiosely, holding aloft the drink*] Madame la comtesse de la Cognac!

CHARMAINE: [*Embarrassed*] Le grand capitaine de ma cœur.

FLAGG: Yes, I'm the captain of your heart! Like hell I am. Why don't you come and kiss me? None but the brave, you know . . .

CHARMAINE: *Je ne comprends pas.*

FLAGG: Oh, no. You don't understand me. Well, I'm a weary man, and I don't want any finagling from you.

CHARMAINE: [*At door*] You want me to kiss you?

FLAGG: Sure I want you to kiss me. Even though you played the dirtiest sort of trick on me. [*The liquor is beginning to deaden him*] A dirty trick on your poor old Captain Flagg. [*Turns to her*] If I weren't so kind and gentle I'd go out in the orchard, cut a cherry switch, and give you a tanning.

[*She crosses over, kisses him quickly, and draws back, a charmed bird before a snake*]

CHARMAINE: You're a terrible man, *monsieur.*

FLAGG: I ain't terrible to you, honey. Come sit by your old man. [*She sits on the table and looks down into his eyes*] Ain't I tired? Jeez, but I'm off war for life. It's all right with thirty or forty men in the hills who know their business. But there's so many little boys along with me ain't got any business here at all. [*He sighs and drinks the rest of the brandy*] Ah! There ain't no strength in this stuff any more. [*Hands her his glass, which she places on table. He gets up unsteadily*] Le's go walk by the canal. I wanna get away from these new lieutenants. Le's walk along that bicycle path.

CHARMAINE: *Non, non, non. Demain soir. Demain soir.*

FLAGG: To-morrow? All right. I'm tired anyhow. Never been so tired before. Liquor just takes the pins out of my knees. Gimme a bottle to drink in bed. I don't want to think to-night.

CHARMAINE: [*Bringing him a bottle from the bar, smiling*] Ah, monsieur, vous êtes un grand soldat.

FLAGG: [*Wandering to the door, suddenly apathetic*] Nighty, sweetie. See you tomorrow.

[*He goes out at rear*]

QUIRT: [*Entering stealthily, in a farmer's smock*

which comes to his waist] So he's gone away. . . . What's the matter with the old boy?

[*He attempts to kiss her. She shudders*]

CHARMAINE: [*Drawing away from him*] Non, non, non! Merci.

QUIRT: Why, what's the matter, Pittsburgh? Don't you love me no more?

CHARMAINE: *Oui—mais——*

QUIRT: Of course I understand. Seeing him that way sort of cut you up, especially when I was wearing such a lousy outfit, you liking them all in uniforms. Just wait, baby. When I git that brass lock off Fergie's box and turn out in his blues on sick leave, you'll forget this Flagg person. I understand. Sure. I been with soldiers' girls a lot, myself.

CHARMAINE: When you are beautiful, *mon sergeant,* then I love you——

[*She runs up steps*]

QUIRT: Come back here!

[*She disappears, laughing.* Kiper *and* Lipinsky *enter*]

KIPER: Jeez, Sergeant, but you picked a funny outfit to be buried in.

QUIRT: [*At foot of stairs—hostile*] Who's thinking of burying me?

KIPER: I expect Flagg'll make me bury you. But he's going to lay you out himself.

QUIRT: Is he looking for me? How did he know I'm here.

LIPINSKY: We just heard Ferguson telling him. I ain't never heard him swear so much since I been with him. We came to ask you to run away some more.

QUIRT: You did, eh? Well, you can go down to the bridge and head him off. You can tell him he passed up visiting this place just before the outfit shoved last time. You can tell him if he comes up here I'll cut his gizzard out for him. You can tell him I'm engaged to be married, and I ain't got no duty for him around here.

[*Flagg enters, drunk and swaggering*]

FLAGG: Who's the hay-shaker? Well, if it ain't Sergeant Quirt! A regular family reunion. Quirt, how are you? When you coming back to the factory?

QUIRT: Flagg, you're out of this here detail. You're hands off my business after that dirty trick you put over on me. If I kill you there isn't a court can touch me for it in this man's army.

FLAGG: Quirt, you're drunk.

QUIRT: Both of us.

FLAGG: Yeah, both of us.

QUIRT: Well, then, Flagg, you're drunk. What are you going to do about it?

FLAGG: I'm gonna have a drink.

[*Turns to bar and takes bottle; pours two drinks*]

QUIRT: Both of us.

FLAGG: Yeah, both of us. [*They drink, first bowing to each other*] Quirt, I got something I want to tell you.

QUIRT: The hell!

FLAGG: You want to hear it?

QUIRT: I ain't particular.

FLAGG: Well, this is it, Sergeant. You can go jump in the canal. I knew you'd head for Charmaine as soon as you got that bullet under your hide. You had half a day's start of me and you didn't beat me more than five minutes. You might just as well 'a' stayed on the bakery route. You ain't no more needed here than a third leg on a kangaroo. Have one on me.

[*Flagg pours for both*]

QUIRT: [*They bow*] Delighted, I'm sure. [*They drink and replace glasses*] You're a hell of an officer, Flagg [Quirt *wipes right hand on smock*], and your views on me probably ain't worth a damn. On the other hand, it's only fair to warn you that I'm the sole survivor of seven catastrophes, any one of which was calculated to carry off every man-jack in the immediate neighborhood as was adjacent, and if there was to be a catastrophe of any dimensions in this here vicinity in the near future, I have expectations of survival exceeding your own. Have one on me.

[Quirt *pours drinks*]

FLAGG: Thank you, Quirt, I will. [*They drink, and* Flagg *drunkenly points finger at* Quirt *until he can get his mind to working*] Your method of expressing yourself, Quirt, is complicated by your tongue being as thick as your God-damn head. But if you mean trouble, let me point out to you that among other things, you forgot to bring your gun along. [Quirt *feels for his absent weapon;* Flagg *laughs heartily*] Ain't you a neat little fool, Hoppergrass, and will you drink?

QUIRT: I will.

[Flagg *pours. Both bow, then drink again; but* Quirt *has taken a sip before he realizes he hasn't bowed*]

FLAGG: Do you give up?

QUIRT: No.

FLAGG: [*Turns to bar and starts pouring*] Have another.

[*As* Flagg *starts to pour,* Quirt *leaps like a flash on his back.* Kiper *catches* Quirt's *wrists from behind.* Lipinsky *drags* Flagg *away. When* Quirt *jumps* Flagg, *he takes the gun out of* Flagg's *holster with his right hand; his left is in stranglehold around* Flagg's *neck.* Flagg *reaches back and holds* Quirt *by back of neck. They scuffle until separated*]

KIPER: [*Holding* Quirt] What do you want done with him, sir?

FLAGG: [*To* Lipinsky, *who is holding him*] Let me go or I'll knock you for a row of G.I. cans. Take the gun away from him. [Quirt *throws the automatic on the floor.* Flagg *puts his foot on it*] Let go, all. [Quirt *is turned loose*] Well, bo, had enough?

QUIRT: I'll tell you what I'll do with you. **I'll go**

outside with you and try two of them little toys at fifty yards.

FLAGG: And you, the best pistol shot in the corps, would put one through my carburetor as easy as pitching a penny in a well. Come again.

QUIRT: I'll take you on any way you can think of, you baboon. I can out-shoot you and out-think you and out-drink you. There ain't nothing I can't do better than you.

FLAGG: You're a liar, Quirt, and you know it. I could break you in two. You got my gun because you jumped me without warning. No soldier you ever soldiered with could head me when I got started . . . and by the way, Quirt, if you can out-drink me you ain't leading out very well to-night. You're talking thick and wild, Quirt, thick and wild. You'd better turn in somewhere and sleep it off.

QUIRT: Me? Sleep off a couple of drinks? I was living on cognac when all your buttons was safety pins.

FLAGG: Yeah, well, you can't carry it the way you used to, then. You're getting old, Quirt. Old and feeble. Yeah, you're getting old.

QUIRT: Not me, You may be an old man, Flagg. Or an old woman if it suits you better, but not me. Captains and generals, they pass along. I've seen hundreds of 'em. Better men than you, Flagg. They passed along. But top sergeants is eternal. They don't never die.

FLAGG: Well, if you don't want to die, you top sergeant, don't fool with me. I've seen top sergeants go damn fast—Now, listen, Quirt, are you going to jump in that canal or are you going to need six pall-bearers to take you there?

QUIRT: It'll take more than six pall-bearers to put me in one of these French canals. I don't like the taste of them.

[Charmaine re-enters]

FLAGG: Charmaine! Cognac!

[Charmaine crosses behind table; gets bottle; pours drink for Quirt, also for Flagg]

CHARMAINE: [Laying a hand on the Captain's shoulder] Is it now—friends again?

FLAGG: [Putting an arm about her] Best you ever saw, Charmaine. We'll drink to it, Quirt. Flagg and Quirt forever—till you get bumped off. Flagg and Quirt, the tropical twins! There ain't room for both of 'em in the whole world!

[Flagg pats Charmaine on hip]

QUIRT: [Sets down his glass, hard] Damn you, Flagg!

FLAGG: [Setting down his glass] What's the matter, Hoppergrass? Aren't you drinking?

QUIRT: I got here first, Flagg.

FLAGG: I know it. Nobody said you didn't.

QUIRT: [Rising] You take your hands off Charmaine.

FLAGG: Any time you want my hands off Charmaine, you come and take 'em off.

CHARMAINE: No. No! You must be friends.

FLAGG: With you around!

QUIRT: It strikes me there's only room for one of us in this shanty to-night. Do you plan on going somewhere, or not?

FLAGG: Did you ever see me leaving any place I didn't feel like leaving?

CHARMAINE: [Touching the Captain's sleeve] Don't fight—please.

FLAGG: [Not looking at her—pushing her back] The hell you say! First time in six months I've had a good reason for fighting. The Germans don't want my woman. I been fighting them for eight dollars a day. . . . Go on back of the counter.

CHARMAINE: I—I love you both.

QUIRT: You get to hell outta here, Flagg. Dig up a broad of your own.

FLAGG: Sorry. Rejected.

QUIRT: You ain't man enough to shoot me for her. Well, here's what I'll do. I'll shoot you dice for her. [Tosses out dice on table] High dice, aces low. [Kiper and Lipinsky take steps forward, interested]

FLAGG: Boys, is Quirt crooked with the bones? [Lipinsky goes back to lean on platform]

KIPER: He's got a pair out to be in a circus. [Quirt gives Kiper a bad look]

FLAGG: Then we'll deal a hand at blackjack.

QUIRT: [Picks up dice; puts them back in pocket, while Kiper goes back with Lipinsky] And the guy that loses beats it for somewhere else.

FLAGG: What do you mean, beats it? We'll shoot, but my way. The man that wins gets a gun, and the man that loses gets a head start. Everybody wins, see? One gets the girl and the other gets a chance to stay in bed the rest of this war.

KIPER: Captain Flagg, I don't think you ought to do this.

FLAGG: Close your hatch. I'll try anything once, soldier. [Briskly] Now for a game of blackjack for one automatic.

QUIRT: That's all right with me.

FLAGG: And the gun on the table between us. [He picks it up]

KIPER: [As he and Lipinsky seize Quirt's arms] Come quiet now, before he notices.

QUIRT: [Writhing loose] Keep off me, you swine! [Kiper and Lipinsky fall back]

FLAGG: [Having recovered gun, starts to straighten up] March out that door, both of you, and if you stick a neck in here before the game's over, I promise to wreck you for life. Are you going, or do I demonstrate? [They go out quickly] Charmaine! Upstairs!

[She goes. Flagg sits at table; Quirt on table. Flagg shuffles cards, and offering them to Quirt, says "Cut." Quirt fondles cards; says "Be good to me, babies, and I'll let moonlight into a captain." He cuts. Flagg deals one to Quirt, then one to himself; then one to Quirt, and looks at the next one for himself]

QUIRT: What's that, a king?

FLAGG: How many you want? Make it snappy and knock off that guff. Here's looking down your grave. May you have many worms, Quirt.

QUIRT: Crawling, right out of your teeth, Flagg. Hit me.

FLAGG: [*Deals a card face up*] A two-spot. Well, any more?

QUIRT: Hit me again.

FLAGG: [*Dealing one*] Well, you got a king that time. Remember, if you hold six cards without going bust you can empty the automatic at me.

QUIRT: Hit me again.

FLAGG: A king, by God! [Quirt, *with one sweep turns over the table, with candles and chairs, and dives through the door; runs off*] You double-dealing Chinaman! [Flagg *finds the gun in the darkness and fires shot just outside the door. He is heard re-entering*] Show a light, somebody, Charmaine!

[Flagg *sets up the table*]

CHARMAINE: [*At the head of the stairs with a lamp*] What is it? You have killed him?

[*Goes up to door*]

FLAGG: Killed hell! He knocked out the light and ran, the dirty hound! [Charmaine *looks out the door, shielding the lamp from the wind*] Oh, he's gone.

CHARMAINE: Maybe you hit him.

[*Puts lamp on table; then crosses to* Flagg]

FLAGG: Don't you worry. He was halfway to the river, the rate he was going, before I found the door. Don't you weep, sweetheart [*Puts her on his left knee*]; you're weeping for a skunk that'd run out on a game of cards. It's you and me to-night, lady. Listen, Charmaine [*Putting his arm around her*]; I love you like the devil. I always did. You love me, Charmaine?

CHARMAINE: Only you.

FLAGG: God, I'm dead—I'm going to sleep for three days.

[Flagg *rests head on her breast and sighs. Then* Lipinsky *and* Gowdy *walk in*]

LIPINSKY: Sorry to disturb you, sir.

FLAGG: My God, did you hear what I told you?

LIPINSKY: Got bad news, Captain Flagg.

FLAGG: Spit it out.

LIPINSKY: The outfit's going back. Battalion moving at once.

FLAGG: What? What?

LIPINSKY: We're ordered back. Ordered back in. Everybody's going back in. General movement.

FLAGG: Dammit, I'm on leave.

GOWDY: All leaves revoked, Captain Flagg.

FLAGG: Well, why couldn't you stay away from here? You knew where I was. Why in hell did you have to come and tell me?

GOWDY: Well, headquarters sent out, looking for you.

LIPINSKY: Kiper wouldn't come, Captain Flagg. He was for leaving you alone.

FLAGG: He was, was he? Well, Kiper's got sense. Look here, you never found me to give me the message, and I'm not going. Can you remember, or have I got to bury you to keep your mouth shut? What right have they got to offer a man leave and then revoke it? I gave them their prisoner! I've got their damn papers!

LIPINSKY: Well, you see, the company's going to shove off. What could we do?

FLAGG: You could have an attack of something, damn it to hell! You could fall and break your neck on the way here.

LIPINSKY: I was afraid not to let you know. You always wanted to know.

FLAGG: Well, you've got to do some tall lying to make up for it, because I'm not going. Tell them any story you think of, only I never got the news. I earned my leave, and it's signed, sealed, and delivered. That crowd at headquarters has got to live up to its end of the bargain. They can't take these men back in. I won't stand for it. [*Turns to* Charmaine] Shall we stay here, Charmaine?

CHARMAINE: *Oui, ici.*

[*They embrace.* Flagg *rests head on her breast*]

FLAGG: [*After a pause, shakes himself a bit*] No, I'll go. I may be drunk, but I know I'll go. There's something rotten about this profession of arms, some kind of damned religion connected with it that you can't shake. When they tell you to die, you have to do it, even if you're a better man than they are. Good-bye, Charmaine, put your money in real estate, and marry that cuckoo if you can. You'll never see me again. This town is a jinx for me. [*Again rests head on* Charmaine] God Almighty, but I'm tired. [*He rises and crosses to where* Ferguson *has entered.* Charmaine *sits in chair watching*] Hello, Fergy. We're shoving off. Follow us, because we don't know where we're going. Nobody knows.

[*He goes out, staggering, tired.* Ferguson *follows him out.* Gowdy *and* Lipinsky *follow* Ferguson. Charmaine *buries her head in arms on table*]

QUIRT: [*Comes in upper floor stairway*] Hello, Pittsburgh!

CHARMAINE: You are not *killed?*

QUIRT: [*Coming downstairs to bottom step*] No. It's me all right. Everybody gone?

CHARMAINE: Everybody.

QUIRT: Outfit's going in again, huh?

CHARMAINE: *Oui.*

QUIRT: Well, well! I been upstairs. Climbed up the kitchen roof. Do you love your papa?

CHARMAINE: *Mais oui.*

QUIRT: Then you better kiss him good-bye. [*Pats her face; then kisses her. Staggers up to door*] What a lot of God-damn fools it takes to make a war! Hey, Flagg, wait for baby!

[Charmaine *watches from the table*]

CURTAIN

Maxwell Anderson

(1888–1959)

After Eugene O'Neill, no one envisioned higher standards for the American theatre than Maxwell Anderson. Although quite at home in prose, he set up precepts for verse drama; and although adept at writing salty humor, he decided that nothing less than the composition of poetic tragedy could be a proper aim for American dramatists. Whether his approach to poetic drama was not somewhat more academic than necessary, and whether he did not often say less than he seemed to be saying in his purple patches—these and other matters concerning his playwriting could be widely debated. But it was surely an accomplishment for Maxwell Anderson to be the only American (except for the American-born naturalized Englishman T. S. Eliot) to make the Broadway playgoer accept verse drama, and this not merely once but on some half-dozen occasions between 1930 and 1950.

Anderson was the son of a Baptist preacher who occupied various pastorates in Pennsylvania and the Middle West. Having developed a love of literature at an early age, Anderson took a Bachelor of Arts degree at the University of North Dakota and a Master of Arts at Stanford University and in 1914 began to teach English. Soon, however, his ideals began to exercise a disturbing influence on his career. He was dismissed from a post at Whittier College, in California, for advocating pacifism during the First World War, and then found himself in difficulties in the field of journalism, to which he had turned for a living. He lost his job on the *San Francisco Bulletin* in 1918 for his unorthodox editorials and was discharged from other positions quickly and with fateful regularity. He found a refuge at last on Pulitzer's liberal morning newspaper, the *New York World,* then the haven of many men who later achieved literary distinction. When he left the *World,* in 1924, it was not as an unwanted editorial writer but as coauthor of one of the most successful plays of his time, *What Price Glory?*

Anderson's first victories in the field of playwriting were in the service of prose realism. After collaborating with Laurence Stallings on *What Price Glory?,* he adapted Jim Tully's novel about hobos, *Beggars of Life,* under the title *Outside Looking In* (1925); he then wrote a highly successful comedy of marriage, *Saturday's Children* (1927), in which economics destroys domestic happiness; and he collaborated with the journalist Harold Hickerson on a treatment of the Sacco-Vanzetti case, *Gods of the Lightning* (1928), which crackled with indignation at evidences of social injustice. Later, in 1933, he

produced a stinging satire on Congressional logrolling, *Both Your Houses,* which won a Pulitzer Prize, and he continued to write plays in prose whenever he felt that prose dialogue suited his theme. But he had had romantic and poetic aspirations from the very start of his career. He wrote a youthful volume of lyrics, *You Who Have Dreams,* and his very first play to be produced, *White Desert* (1923), was a poetic tragedy. It failed, and he bided his time until 1930 before venturing into poetry again.

When Anderson wrote *Elizabeth the Queen,* he was already an experienced playwright and showman. He reflected that successful verse drama had never been written about contemporary life and decided upon a historical subject: the fatal love affair of Elizabeth and Lord Essex. Superbly produced by the Theatre Guild, with Lynn Fontanne playing Elizabeth and Alfred Lunt as Essex, this tragedy proved highly successful. It was, in fact, the first successful drama of the modern American theatre to be written in verse. Encouraged by his success, Anderson wrote a number of other historical plays, the best being *Mary of Scotland* (1933) and *Anne of the Thousand Days* (1948). The three plays form a Tudor trilogy, although they were not written in chronological order. Anderson turned to American history in *Night over Taos* (1932) and *Valley Forge* (1934), to Austrian history in *The Masque of Kings* (1937), and to the Middle Ages in *Joan of Lorraine* (1946).

In these and other histories, Anderson was more than a chronicler of romantic events. He employed the past to illuminate the present in his story of Joan of Arc, in an effort to dramatize the problem of heroism. He used the story of the ill-starred Rudolph of Hapsburg, in *The Masque of Kings,* to ask whether a true idealist could align himself with any revolutionary movement: that is, whether one was not apt to overthrow a tyrannical government only to become saddled with a new and possibly worse tyranny. Anderson's libretto for the Kurt Weill musical comedy *Knickerbocker Holiday* (1938) revived early New York history with a view to denouncing authoritarian tendencies in American life; the play was even prefaced with an attack on the New Deal. And in the Tudor romances, Anderson never veered far from his customary suspicions of government as a magnet for power lust.

But Anderson did not confine himself to historical drama. In *Winterset* (1935), he returned to the Sacco-Vanzetti case and wrote a contemporary poetic tragedy filled with indignation and pity. He satirized

864

the modern materialistic world in the poetic fantasy *High Tor* (1937). And he turned to the question of fascism in *Key Largo* (1938), dramatizing his conviction that one could not evade the challenge of the times. Anderson's chief interest, however, lay not in asserting political beliefs so much as in demonstrating his tragic view of life. He saw man as a creature of high passion, who is raised to tragic stature by the intensity of his nature. Anderson created characters whose wills clash mightily and send sparks into the night of human error and evil. It is the wonder of man's spiritual resources that has fascinated him most, and his ultimate objective has always been the writing of universal drama. Even in dealing with such topical matters as the Second World War—in *Candle in the Wind* (1941) and *The Eve of St. Mark* (1942)—or the problem of racial prejudice—in *Lost in the Stars* (1949), his dramatization of the novel *Cry, the Beloved Country* —he tried to universalize the immediate issues. In fact, he conscientiously differentiated between universal and topical plays, writing the latter in prose. He came to be most at home in the romantic past and in the drama of "universals" and was least successful when he was most journalistic.

An estimate of Anderson's work as a poetic dramatist cannot be made without examining each of the plays in some detail. It can be said, however, that he became to the American theatre what Schiller was to the German and Rostand to the French. If he was by no means so true a poet as Schiller or so fine an ironist as Rostand, he too gave the stage a romantic drama high in spirit and vaguely idealistic in aim. In *High Tor* he wrote the best romantic comedy and fantasy of the American theatre. In *Winterset* he came closer than any other American playwright to writing a poetic tragedy in verse about modern life. Although he did not quite create an integrated and completely satisfying play in *Winterset,* the second act of this tragedy, in which the quest for justice flares into passionate drama, is one of the memorable pieces of modern playwriting. And the Tudor plays are filled with spirited writing and with rousing conflict. Even the derivativeness of much of his verse in these plays was no great impediment to effectiveness except when he became too prolix; and the questionable profundity of his statement here, as in other plays, was no serious hindrance to dramatic exaltation. A good deal of vigor and vivacity, as well as elevation, came into our theatre when Anderson began reacquainting us with Elizabethan heroes and scoundrels. The question uppermost in the minds of his severest critics was simply whether Anderson was on the right track in trying to make the drama literary in conventional terms, and this is a question that apparently troubled the author himself from time to time. But every writer works within the limits of his endowment, and Anderson's was rich if not remarkably original.

Elizabeth the Queen is unquestionably the cornerstone of Anderson's achievement in verse drama. This play holds in solution the points of view that ruled most of his later work—namely, his distrust of government and of power politics, his conviction that men of good will are apt to be destroyed while "the rats inherit the earth," and his belief that the pageant of human desire and suffering is nevertheless awe-inspiring and magnificent. *Elizabeth the Queen* fulfills the Aristotelian principles which Anderson accepted as right and necessary. The tragedy revolves around strong personalities who are fired by high passion and who dignify the human spirit in the very act of destroying themselves through their failings; they are, in other words, heroic characters destroyed by a "tragic flaw" but capable of asserting the splendor of the soul even in error and defeat.

Anderson believed that the audience of the theatre, which he celebrated as the "phoenix of the arts," wants to be convinced "that men have a desire to break the molds of earth which encase them." This could be accomplished by "the spiritual awakening, or regeneration" of the hero, and Anderson gave much thought to the nature of tragic art in the prefaces he wrote to several of his plays. These prefaces, collected in a volume entitled *Off Broadway* (1947), contain a good deal of considered, if also somewhat "inspirational," writing. But all his thoughts led him to one unavoidable conclusion: high matter required a heightened style of writing, and the American drama needed "the touch of a great poet." Without ever claiming to be that poet, Anderson decided that he had to write his tragedies in verse. *Elizabeth the Queen* represents his first mature attempt to develop a workmanlike poetic style. The over-all pattern is Elizabethan blank verse although a good deal of the writing is more Tennysonian than Elizabethan in quality. The metrical form does not, however, impose any restraints upon the dramatic flow of the dialogue, and Anderson takes as many liberties with the blank-verse line as he feels it necessary or expedient to take in the modern theatre. The general effect of the writing is one of passionateness and elevated expression.

BIBLIOGRAPHY: Maxwell Anderson, *Off Broadway: Essays about the Theatre,* 1947; Brooks Atkinson, *Broadway Scrapbook* (pp. 251–254), 1947; John Mason Brown, *Two on the Aisle* (pp. 148–159, 208–211), 1938; Eleanor Flexner, *American Playwrights 1918–1938* (pp. 78–129), 1938; John Gassner, *Masters of the Drama* (pp. 678–693, 696), 1945; Joseph Wood Krutch, *The American Drama Since 1918* (pp. 286–318), 1939; Burns Mantle, *Contemporary American Playwrights* (pp. 37–46), 1938; George Jean Nathan, *The Theatre Book of the Year 1946–1947* (pp. 189–196), 1947; Stark Young, *Immortal Shadows* (pp. 165–168, 185–188), 1948.

ELIZABETH THE QUEEN

By Maxwell Anderson

CHARACTERS

SIR WALTER RALEIGH	THE FOOL	HEMMINGS
PENELOPE GRAY	CAPTAIN ARMIN	FALSTAFF
A CAPTAIN	MARY	PRINCE HENRY
SIR ROBERT CECIL	ELLEN	GADSHILL
LORD ESSEX	TRESSA	PETO
FRANCIS BACON	MARVEL	POINS
QUEEN ELIZABETH	A COURIER	ALSO GUARDS, MEN-AT-ARMS,
LORD BURGHLEY	A HERALD	MAIDS-IN-WAITING, AND
LORD HOWARD	BURBAGE	OTHERS

Players in the scene from Henry IV (bracketed: HEMMINGS, FALSTAFF, PRINCE HENRY, GADSHILL, PETO, POINS)

ACT I. SCENE I.

An entrance hall before a council chamber in the palace at Whitehall. The entrance to the council room is closed and four Guards *with halberds stand at either side. A small door at the left of the entrance is also shut. It is early morning. The Guards stand immobile.*

FIRST GUARD: The sun's out again, and it's guineas to pounds the earl comes back this morning.

SECOND GUARD: I'll be glad of it, for one. You get nothing but black looks about the court when he's away.

FIRST GUARD: You'll get little else now he's back, my bully. They quarreled too far for mending, this time.

THIRD GUARD: Tut! They quarrel no more than the cock with the hen. The earl's been sick.

FIRST GUARD: Sick of the queen's displeasure. It's a disease a favorite can die of, and many have.

FOURTH GUARD: He's no sicker of her displeasure than she of his, if a man may judge. Once the earl's gone there's no dancing, no plays, no feasting . . . nothing to do nights but sleep. The very scullery-maids grow cold, and go to bed alone—like the queen.

FIRST GUARD: There are some even a scullery-maid would seldom kiss, save in moments of great excitement. Poor Wat looks forward to feast nights.

FOURTH GUARD: I've had my luck.

FIRST GUARD: You've had what was coming to you. Mucklemouth Jean, of the back kitchen.

FOURTH GUARD: You'd have been glad of her yourself if you could have had her.

FIRST GUARD: Consider, man. She may not have been true. When she wouldn't play with you, mayhap she was playing with somebody else. And if the queen could live without her Earl of Essex, it may

have been because Sir Walter had a new suit of silver armor.

THIRD GUARD: And there's a handsome man.

FOURTH GUARD: God defend me from speaking lightly of the queen!

FIRST GUARD: Eh? God defend you? Let no man accuse me of speaking lightly of the queen, nor of any other woman . . . unless she be a light woman, in which case, God defend me, I will speak lightly of her if I choose.

THIRD GUARD: What say you of the queen?

FIRST GUARD: Of the queen? I say she is well-known to be the virgin queen; I say no more.

SECOND GUARD: But do you think she is a virgin?

FIRST GUARD: She has doubtless been a virgin, bully, for all women have been virgins, but the question is: First, when . . . and, second, where?

SECOND GUARD: Where?

FIRST GUARD: Where, bully, where?

THIRD GUARD: Would you not say, in the proper place?

FIRST GUARD: No. I would not say in the proper place. Because it is hard to say if there is a proper place wherein to be a virgin . . . unless it be in church, and, God defend me, I do not go to church.

SECOND GUARD: You do not go to church?

FIRST GUARD: No, for my sins, I do not go to church . . . or, if you like, I do not go to church for my sins.

SECOND GUARD: Does it follow that the church is a proper place for virgins?

FIRST GUARD: It does. Did I not tell you I do not go there for my sins?

FOURTH GUARD: They say the queen's getting to be an old woman; but I swear she looks younger than my wife, whom I married a young thing, six years come Easter.

THIRD GUARD: It would age a girl fast, just the look of you.

FIRST GUARD: As for the queen, powder and paint

866

account for some of it. To say nothing of the earl.
A young lover will do much for a lady's face.

FOURTH GUARD: Now God defend me . . .

FIRST GUARD: Aye, aye . . . God defend poor
Wat.

[*A Nobleman enters in silver armor. It is* Sir
Walter Raleigh, *no other*]

RALEIGH: Has the queen come forth yet?

FIRST GUARD: No, Sir Walter.

RALEIGH: The Earl of Essex . . . is he here?

FIRST GUARD: No, my lord.

RALEIGH: When he comes send me word. I shall
be in the north corridor. [*He turns*]

FIRST GUARD: Good, my lord.

[Penelope Gray *comes in from the right, passing through*]

RALEIGH: [*Meeting her*] Greetings, lady, from my
heart.

PENELOPE: Good-morrow, lord, from my soul.

RALEIGH: I take my oath in your face that you are
rushing to the window to witness the arrival of my
lord of Essex.

PENELOPE: And in your teeth I swear I am on no
such errand . . . but only to see the sunrise.

RALEIGH: The sun has been up this hour, my dear.

PENELOPE: The more reason to hurry, gracious
knight.

RALEIGH: Do you think to pull the bag over my
head so easily, Penelope? On a day when the earl
returns every petticoat in the palace is hung with an
eye to pleasing him. Yours not the least.

PENELOPE: I deny him thrice.

RALEIGH: I relinquish you, lady. Run, run to the
window! He will be here and you will miss him!

PENELOPE: Is there a lady would run from Sir
Walter in his silver suiting? Since the sun is up . . .
I have no errand.

RALEIGH: Is there no limit to a woman's deception,
wench? Would you go so far as to appear pleased
if I kissed you?

PENELOPE: And no deception. [*He kisses her*]
I call the Gods to witness . . . did I not blush
prettily?

RALEIGH: And meant it not at all. Tell me, did the
queen send you to look out the casement for news
of her Essex, or did you come at the prompting of
your heart?

PENELOPE: Shall I tell you the truth?

RALEIGH: Verily.

PENELOPE: The truth is I cannot answer.

RALEIGH: Both, then?

PENELOPE: Both or one or neither.

RALEIGH: Fie on the baggage.

PENELOPE: Is it not a virtue to be close-mouthed
in the queen's service?

RALEIGH: If you kept the rest of your person as
close as your mouth what a paragon of virtue you
would be!

PENELOPE: Indeed, my lord, I am.

RALEIGH: Indeed, my lady? Have there not been
certain deeds on dark nights?

PENELOPE: Sh! Under the rose.

RALEIGH: Meaning under covers . . .

PENELOPE: Fie on my lord, to make me out a
strumpet!

RALEIGH: It is my manner of wooing, fair maid!
I woo by suggestion of images . . .

PENELOPE: Like small boys on the closet wall . . .

RALEIGH: Like a soldier . . .

PENELOPE: Aye, a veteran . . . of encounters . . .

RALEIGH: I will have you yet, my love; I will take
lessons from this earl . . .

PENELOPE: Take this lesson from me, my lord:
You must learn to desire what you would have.
Much wanting makes many a maid a wanton. You
want me not . . . nor I you. You wear your silver
for a queen.

[*A Captain enters from the left*]

CAPTAIN: Good-morrow, Sir Walter. Is the queen
still under canopy?

RALEIGH: I know not.

CAPTAIN: The earl is here and would see her.

RALEIGH: Bid him hurry if he wishes to find her
abed as usual.

PENELOPE: She is dressed and stirring, captain,
and awaits my lord.

RALEIGH: And many another fair maid awaits him
likewise, captain. Take him that message from me.
Run, girl, run. Tell the queen.

[*The* Captain *goes out left*]

PENELOPE: [*Going*] You make yourself so easily
disliked.

[*She goes right.* Cecil *enters, passing her*]

CECIL: He is here?

RALEIGH: So. The heavenly boy, clad in the
regalia of the sun, even now extracts his gallant foot
from his golden stirrup and makes shift to descend
from his heaving charger. Acclamation lifts in every
voice, tears well to every eye . . . with the exception
of mine, perhaps, and yours, I hope . . .

CECIL: I am at a pass to welcome him, myself.
This Elizabeth of ours can be difficult on her good
days . . . and there have been no good ones lately.

[*Two* Men-at-Arms *enter with silver armor in
their arms*]

RALEIGH: And what is all this, sirrah?

FIRST MAN: Armor, my lord.

RALEIGH: For whom?

FIRST MAN: We know not.

RALEIGH: Now by the ten thousand holy names!
Am I mistaken, Robert, or is this armor much like
my own?

CECIL: Very like, I should say. Is it sterling?

RALEIGH: And the self-same pattern. Has the earl
gone lunatic?

CECIL: He means to outshine you, perhaps.

RALEIGH: Has it come to this? Do I set the style
for Essex?
That would be a mad trick, to dress himself like me!

[Bacon *appears in the doorway at right*]
What do you know of this, Sir Francis?

BACON: Greeks, my lord, bearing gifts.

RALEIGH: To hell with your Greeks! The devil
damn him!
This is some blackguardry!

[*Two more* Men-at-Arms *enter, carrying armor*]
There's more of it! Good God, it comes in bales!
I say, who's to wear this, sirrah? Who is it for?

[Essex *enters from corridor between the two
files of soldiers, pushing them aside as he does
so, and crosses to right of* Raleigh, *speaking
as he enters*]

ESSEX: Their name is legion, Sir Walter. Happily
met!
Felicitations on your effulgence, sir!
You're more splendid than I had imagined. News
came of your silver
Even in my retreat! I was ill, and I swear it cured
me!
You should have heard the compliments I've heard
Passed on you! Sir Walter's in silver! The world's
outdone,
They said—the moon out-mooned. He gleams down
every corridor
And every head's turned after him. The queen
Herself has admired it—the design—the workman-
ship!
There's nothing like it this side of Heaven's streets.
And I said to myself—the great man—this is what
we have needed——
More silver everywhere—oceans of silver!
Sir Walter has set the style, the world will follow.
So I sent for the silver-smiths, and by their sweat
Here's for you lads, tailored to every man's meas-
ure——
Shall Raleigh wear silver alone? Why, no,
The whole court shall go argent!

RALEIGH: Take care, my lord.
I bear insults badly.

ESSEX: And where are you insulted?
For the queen's service you buy you a silver armor.
In the queen's service I buy you a dozen more.
A gift, my friends, each man to own his own,
As you own yours. What insult?

RALEIGH: Have your laugh,
Let the queen and court laugh with you! Since you
are envious
You may have my suit. I had not thought even
Essex
Bore so petty a mind.

ESSEX: I misunderstood you
Perhaps, Sir Walter. I had supposed you donned
Silver for our queen, but I was mistaken . . .
Keep these all for yourself. The men shall have
others . . .
Some duller color.

RALEIGH: I have borne much from you
Out of regard for the queen, my lord of Essex.

ESSEX: And I from you.
By God . . .

CECIL: You have forgotten, Sir Walter,
A certain appointment . . .

RALEIGH: And you will bear more, by Heaven! . .

CECIL: He is going to the queen,
Remember. And we have an errand.

ESSEX: You presume to protect me,
Master Secretary?

CECIL: I protect you both, and our mistress.
There can be no quarreling here.

RALEIGH: That's very true. Let us go.

[Cecil *and* Raleigh *go out right*]

BACON: And this armor? What becomes of it?

ESSEX: I have given it.
Would you have me take it back?

BACON: There has seldom been
A man so little wise, so headstrong, but he
Could sometimes see how necessary it is
To keep friends and not make enemies at court.
But you . . . God knows.

ESSEX: Let him make friends with me.
He may need friends himself.
[*To the* Guards] These are your armors.
Keep them, wear them, sell them, whatever you
like . . .
Or your captain directs you.

FIRST GUARD: We thank you.

[*They retire to examine the armor*]

BACON: You are going to the queen?

ESSEX: Yes. God help us both!

BACON: Then hear me a moment. . . .

ESSEX: Speak, schoolmaster,
I knew it was coming. You've been quiet too long.

BACON: Listen to me this once, and listen this once
To purpose, my lord, or it may hardly be worth
My while ever to give you advice again
Or for you to take it. You have enough on your
hands
Without quarrelling with Raleigh. You have quar-
relled with the queen
Against my judgment. . . .

ESSEX: God and the devil! Can a man
Quarrel on order or avoid a quarrel at will?

BACON: Why certainly, if he knows his way.

ESSEX: Not I.

BACON: You quarrelled with her, because she
wished to keep peace.
And you wanted war. . . .

ESSEX: We are at war with Spain!
But such a silly, frightened, womanish war
As only a woman would fight. . . .

BACON: She is a woman and fights a womanish
war;
But ask yourself one question and answer it
Honestly, dear Essex, and perhaps you will see then
Why I speak sharply. You are my friend and patron.
Where you gain I gain . . . where you lose I lose . . .
And I see you riding straight to a fall today . . .
And I'd rather your neck weren't broken.

ESSEX: Ask myself!
What question?

BACON: Ask yourself what you want:
To retain the favor of the queen, remain
Her favorite, keep all that goes with this;
Or set yourself against her and trust your fortune
To popular favor?

ESSEX: I'll not answer that.

BACON: Then . . . I have done.

ESSEX: Forgive me, dear friend, forgive me,
I have been ill, and this silly jackanapes
Of a Raleigh angers me with his silver mountings
Till I forget who's my friend. You know my answer
In regard to the queen. I must keep her favor.
Only it makes me mad to see all this . . .
This utter mismanagement, when a man's hand and
     brain
Are needed and cannot be used.

BACON: Let me answer for you;
You are not forthright with yourself. The queen
Fights wars with tergiversation and ambiguities . . .
You wish to complete your record as general,
Crush Spain, subdue Ireland, make a name like
     Cæsar's,
Climb to the pinnacle of fame. Take care.
You are too popular already. You have
Won at Cadiz, caught the people's hearts,
Caught their voices till the streets ring your name
Whenever you pass. You are loved better than
The queen. That is your danger. She will not suffer
A subject to eclipse her; she cannot suffer it.
Make no mistake. She will not.

ESSEX: And I must wait,
Bite my nails in a corner, let her lose to Spain,
Keep myself back for policy?

BACON: Even so.

ESSEX: I come of better blood than Elizabeth.
My name was among the earls around King John
Under the oak. What the nobles have taught a king
A noble may teach a queen.

BACON: You talk treason and death.
The old order is dead, and you and your house will
     die
With it if you cannot learn.

ESSEX: So said King John
Under the oak, or wherever he was standing,
And little he got by it, as you may recall.
What the devil's a king but a man, or a queen but
     a woman?

BACON: King John is dead; this is Elizabeth,
Queen in her own right, daughter of a haughty line.
There is one man in all her kingdom she fears
And that man's yourself, and she has good reason to
     fear you.
You're a man not easily governed, a natural rebel,
Moreover, a general, popular and acclaimed,
And, last, she loves you, which makes you the more
     to be feared,
Whether you love her or not.

ESSEX: I do love her! I do!

BACON: My lord, a man as young as you——

ESSEX: If she were my mother's kitchen hag,
Toothless and wooden-legged, she'd make all others
Colorless.

BACON: You play dangerously there, my lord.

ESSEX: I've never yet loved or hated
For policy nor a purpose. I tell you she's a witch——
And has a witch's brain. I love her, I fear her,
I hate her, I adore her——

BACON: That side of it you must know
For yourself.

ESSEX: I will walk softly—here is my hand.
Distress yourself no more—I can carry myself.

BACON: Only count not too much on the loves of
queens.

ESSEX: I'll remember.

[Cecil and Raleigh reappear in the doorway at
     the right. Raleigh is wearing ordinary armor
     and carries his silver suit. Essex looks at him,
     biting his lip]

Sir Walter, take care of your health!

RALEIGH: My health, sir?

ESSEX: [Going out] Wearing no silver, in this
chilly weather.

RALEIGH: [Tossing his silver armor into the pile]
Put that with the others.

FIRST GUARD: Are we to wear them, sir?

RALEIGH: No. Melt them down and sell the silver.
And thus see for yourself how soon a fool is parted
from his money. Take station in the outer hall and
carry this trash with you.

FIRST GUARD: Yes, sir.

[The Guards go out right]

RALEIGH: [To Bacon] And you, sir, you are his
friend. . . .

BACON: And yours, Sir Walter. . . .

RALEIGH: It's the first I've heard of it, but if you're
mine too, so much the better. Carry this news to
him: his suits go to the melting-pot.

BACON: Willingly, my lord, if I see him. You have
done quite properly.

RALEIGH: I do not ask your commendation!

BACON: No, but you have it.

[He bows low and goes out to left]

RALEIGH: There's the viper under our flower, this
Francis.
He should be on the winning side.

CECIL: He will be yet . . .
Like all wise men. For myself, I no longer
Stomach Lord Essex. Every word he speaks
Makes me feel queasy.

RALEIGH: Then why put up with him?

CECIL: The queen, my friend, the queen. What
     she wants she will have,
And she must have her earl.

RALEIGH: Which does she love more,
Her earl or her kingdom?

CECIL: Yes, which? I have wondered.

RALEIGH: Then you're less sapient

Than I've always thought you, Cecil. She loves her
  kingdom
More than all men, and always will. If he could
Be made to look like a rebel, which he's close to
  being . . .
And she could be made to believe it, which is harder,
You'd be first man in the council.

CECIL: And you would be? . . .

RALEIGH: Wherever I turn he's stood
Square in my way! My life long here at court
He's snatched honor and favor from before my eyes
Till his voice and walk and aspect make me
  writhe . . .
There's a fatality in it!

CECIL: If he could be sent from England . . . we
  might have a chance
To come between them.

RALEIGH: Would she let him go?

CECIL: No . . . but if he could be teased
And stung about his generalship till he was
Too angry to reflect. . . . Suppose you were pro-
  posed
As general for the next Spanish raid?

RALEIGH: He would see it,
And so would she.

CECIL: Then if you were named
For the expedition to Ireland?

RALEIGH: No, I thank you.
He'd let me go, and I'd be sunk in a bog
This next three hundred years. I've seen enough
Good men try to conquer Ireland.

CECIL: Then how would this be?
We name three men for Ireland of his own sup-
  porters;
He will oppose them, not wishing his party weak-
  ened
At the court. Then we ask what he suggests
And hint at his name for leader. . . .

RALEIGH: Good so far.

CECIL: He will be angry and hint at your name;
  you will offer
To go if he will.

RALEIGH: No. Not to Ireland.

CECIL: Yes!
Do you think he'd let you go with him and share
The military glory? It will go hard,
Having once brought up his name, if we do not
  manage
To ship him alone to Dublin.

RALEIGH: We can try it, then,
Always remembering that no matter what
Is said . . . no matter what I say or you . . .
I do not go. You must get me out of that,
By Christ, for I know Ireland.

CECIL: I will. Be easy.

RALEIGH: When is the council?

CECIL: At nine.

RALEIGH: You'll make these suggestions?

CECIL: If you'll play up to them.

RALEIGH: Count on me. I must look after

These silver soldiers.

CECIL: At nine then.

RALEIGH: Count on me.

[*They go out in opposite directions*]

CURTAIN

SCENE II.

*The queen's study, which adjoins her bed-cham-
bers and the council hall. It is a severe little room,
with chairs, a desk, and a few books, huge and
leather-bound.* Penelope *comes in from the bedchamber and looks out through a curtain opposite.
She returns to the chamber, then re-enters to wait.*
Essex *enters.*

PENELOPE: [*Rising*] Good-morrow, my lord.

ESSEX: Good-morrow, Penelope. Have I kept the
queen?

PENELOPE: If so, would I acknowledge it?

ESSEX: I commend me to your discretion.

PENELOPE: Only to my discretion?

ESSEX: Take her what message you will . . . only
let it be that I am here.

PENELOPE: May I have one moment, my lord?
She is not quite ready.

ESSEX: As many as you like. What is it, my dear?

PENELOPE: Do you love the queen?

ESSEX: Is that a fair question, as between maid
and man?

PENELOPE: An honest question.

ESSEX: Then I will answer honestly. Yes, my dear.

PENELOPE: Dearly?

ESSEX: Yes.

PENELOPE: I would you loved someone who loved
you better.

ESSEX: Meaning . . . whom?

PENELOPE: Meaning . . . no one. Myself, perhaps.
That's no one. Or . . . anyone who loved you better.

ESSEX: Does she not love me, sweet?

PENELOPE: She loves you, loves you not, loves
you, loves you not. . . .

ESSEX: And why do you tell me this?

PENELOPE: Because I am afraid.

ESSEX: For me?

PENELOPE: I have heard her when she thought
she was alone, walk up and down her room soundlessly, night long, cursing you . . . cursing you because she must love you and could not help herself
. . . swearing to be even with you for this love she
scorns to bear you. My lord, you anger her too
much.

ESSEX: But is this not common to lovers?

PENELOPE: No, I have never cursed you. And I
have good cause.

ESSEX: But if I were your lover, you would, sweet.
So thank God I am not.

PENELOPE: I must go and tell her you are here.
[*She lifts her face to be kissed*] Good-bye.

ESSEX: Good-bye, my dear. [*He kisses her*] And
thank you.

PENELOPE: Will you beware of her?

ESSEX: Lover, beware your lover, might well be
an old maxim: I will beware.

PENELOPE: For I am afraid.

[*A Maid-in-Waiting appears in the doorway*]
MAID: Her Majesty is ready.

PENELOPE: I will tell her my lord is here.

[*She runs out hastily. Elizabeth enters, signing
imperiously to the Maid, who disappears.
There is a moment's silence*]

ELIZABETH: When we met last it was, as I remember,
Ill-met by moonlight, sir.

ESSEX: Well-met by day,
My queen.

ELIZABETH: I had hardly hoped to see you again,
My lord of Essex, after what was vowed
Forever when you left.

ESSEX: You are unkind
To remind me.

ELIZABETH: I think I also used
The word forever, and meant it as much, at least . . .
Therefore, no apology. Only my Penelope
Passed me just now in the door with eyes and lips
That looked the softer for kissing. I'm not sure
But I'm inopportune.

ESSEX: She's a crazy child.

ELIZABETH: A child! That's for me, too, no doubt!
These children
Have their little ways with each other!

ESSEX: Must we begin
With charges and counter-charges, when you
know. . . .

ELIZABETH: Do I indeed? . . .
You have been gone a week, at this Wanstock of
yours . . .
And a week's a long time at court. You forget that I
Must live and draw breath whether I see you or
not . . .
And there are other men and women, oh yes, all
fully
Equipped for loving and being loved! Penelope . . .
You find Penelope charming. And as for me
There's always Mountjoy . . . or Sir Walter . . . the
handsome,
Sir Walter, the silver-plated . . .

ESSEX: He'll wear no more
Silver at your door.

ELIZABETH: What have you done . . . come, tell
me.
I knew this silver would draw fire. What happened?

ESSEX: Nothing . . . but the fashion's gone out.

ELIZABETH: No, but tell me!

ESSEX: He happened to be in the way
When the upstairs pot was emptied.
He's gone to change his clothes.

ELIZABETH: You shall not be allowed
To do this to him . . .

ESSEX: [*Moving toward her*] You shall not be
allowed
To mock me, my queen. [*He kisses her*]

ELIZABETH: Isn't it strange how one man's kiss
can grow
To be like any other's . . . or a woman's
To be like any woman's?

ESSEX: Not yours for me,
No, and not mine for you, you lying villain,
You villain and queen, you double-tongued seduct-
ress,
You bitch of brass!

ELIZABETH: Silver, my dear. Let me be
A bitch of silver. It reminds me of Raleigh.

ESSEX: Damn you!

ELIZABETH: Damn you and double-damn you for
a damner!
Come some day when I'm in the mood. What day's
this? . . .
Thursday? Try next Wednesday . . . or any Wednes-
day
Later on in the summer . . . Any summer
Will do. Why are you still here?

ESSEX: Oh, God, if I could but walk out that door
And stay away!

ELIZABETH: It's not locked.

ESSEX: But I'd come back!
Where do you think I've been this last week? Trying,
Trying not to be here! But you see, I am here.

ELIZABETH: Yes, I see.

ESSEX: Why did you plague me without a word?

ELIZABETH: Why did you not come?

ESSEX: You are a queen, my queen. You had
proscribed me.
Sent formal word I'd not be admitted if I came.

ELIZABETH: I may have meant it at the time.

ESSEX: I think I have a demon, and you are it!

ELIZABETH: If ever a mocking devil tortured a
woman
You're my devil and torture me! Let us part and
quickly,
Or there'll be worse to come. Go.

ESSEX: I tell you I will not.

ELIZABETH: Come to me, my Essex. Let us be
kind
For a moment. I will be kind. You need not be.
You are young and strangely winning and strangely
sweet.
My heart goes out to you wherever you are.
And something in me has drawn you. But this same
thing
That draws us together hurts and blinds us until
We strike at one another. This has gone on
A long while. It grows worse with the years. It
will end badly.
Go, my dear, and do not see me again.

ESSEX: All this
Is what I said when last I went away.

Yet here I am.

ELIZABETH: Love someone else, my dear.
I will forgive you.

ESSEX: You mean you would try to forgive me.

ELIZABETH: Aye, but I would.

ESSEX: What would you have to forgive? I have
tried to love others. It's empty as ashes.

ELIZABETH: What others?

ESSEX: No one.

ELIZABETH: What others?

ESSEX: Everyone.

ELIZABETH: Everyone?

ESSEX: That too has been your triumph! What is
a cry
Of love in the night, when I am sick and angry
And care not? I would rather hear your mocking
laughter——
Your laughter—mocking at me—defying me
Ever to be happy—with another.

ELIZABETH: You have done this to me?

ESSEX: You have done this to me! You've made
it all empty
Away from you! And with you too!

ELIZABETH: And me—what of me while you were
gone?

ESSEX: If we
Must quarrel when we meet, why then, for God's
sake,
Let us quarrel. At least we can quarrel together.

ELIZABETH: I think if we are to love we must love
and be silent——
For when we speak——

ESSEX: I'll be silent then.
And you shall speak——

ELIZABETH: [Her finger to her lips] Hush!

ESSEX: If you would sometimes heed me——

ELIZABETH: Hush!

ESSEX: Only sometimes—only when I'm right.
If you would
Say to yourself that even your lover might be
Right sometimes, instead of flying instantly
Into opposition as soon as I propose
A shift in policy!

ELIZABETH: But you were wrong! You were
wrong!
A campaign into Spain's pure madness, and to
strike at Flanders
At the same moment . . . think of the drain in men
And the drain on the treasury, and the risks we'd
run
Of being unable to follow success or failure
For lack of troops and money . . . !

ESSEX: [Letting his arms fall] But why lack
money . . .
And why lack men? There's no richer country in
Europe
In men or money than England! It's this same
ancient
Unprofitable niggardliness that pinches pennies

And wastes a world of treasure! You could have all
Spain,
And Spain's dominions in the new world, an empire
Of untold wealth . . . and you forgo them because
You fear to lay new taxes!

ELIZABETH: I have tried that . . .
And never yet has a warlike expedition
Brought me back what it cost!

ESSEX: You've tried half-measures . . .
Raids on the Spanish coast, a few horsemen sent
Into Flanders and out again, always defeating
Yourself by trying too little! What I plead for
Is to be bold once, just once, give the gods a chance
To be kind to us . . . walk through this cobweb
Philip
And take his lazy cities with a storm
Of troops and ships!
If we are to trifle we might better sit
At home forever, and rot!

ELIZABETH: Here we sit then,
And rot, as you put it.

ESSEX: I'm sorry. . . .

ELIZABETH: It seems to me
We rot to some purpose here. I have kept the peace
And kept my people happy and prosperous.

ESSEX: And at what a price . . .
What a cowardly price!

ELIZABETH: I am no coward, either.
It requires more courage not to fight than to fight
When one is surrounded by hasty hot-heads, urging
Campaigns in all directions.

ESSEX: Think of the name
You will leave. . . . They will set you down in
histories
As the weasel queen who fought and ran away,
Who struck one stroke, preferably in the back,
And then turned and ran. . . .

ELIZABETH: Is it my fame you think of,
Or your own, my lord? Have you not built your
name
High enough? I gave you your chance at Cadiz,
And you took it, and now there's no name in all
England
Like yours to the common people. When we ride
in the streets
Together, it's Essex they cheer and not their queen.
What more would you have?

ESSEX: Is it for fear of me
And this hollow cheering you hold me back from
Spain?

ELIZABETH: It's because I believe in peace, and
have no faith
In wars or what wars win.

ESSEX: You do not fear me?

ELIZABETH: Yes, and I fear you, too! You believe
yourself
Fitter to be king than I to be queen! You are
flattered
By this crying of your name by fools! You trust me
no more

Than you'd trust . . . Penelope . . . or any other
    woman
To be in power! You believe you'd rule England
    better
Because you're a man!
    ESSEX: That last is true. I would.
And that doesn't mean I don't love you . . . remem-
    ber that.
I love you, my queen, madly, beyond all measure,
But that's not to say I cannot see where you fail
As sovereign here, and see that why you fail
When you do is merely because a woman cannot
Act and think like a man.
    ELIZABETH: Act and think like a man . . . !
Why should I
Think like a man when a woman's thinking's wiser?
What do you plan? To depose me, take over the
    kingdom?
    ESSEX: [Smiling] You are a touchy queen.
    ELIZABETH: I had bad bringing up.
I was never sure who my mother was going to be
Next day, and it shook my nerves.
    ESSEX: You're your father's daughter,
I'll swear to that. I can tell by your inconstancy.
    ELIZABETH: I wish you had need
To fear for me . . . or at any rate that I'd never
Let you see how much I'm yours.
    ESSEX: But why?
    ELIZABETH: Tell me, my dear,
Do you tire of me . . . do I wear upon you a little?
    ESSEX: Never.
    ELIZABETH: But you'd have to say that, you can
    see . . .
You'd have to say it, because you wouldn't hurt me,
And because I'm your queen. And so I'll never
    know
Until everyone else has known and is laughing at
    me,
When I've lost you. Wait, let me say this, please . . .
    When the time
Does come, and I seem old to you, and you love
Someone else, tell me, tell me the first . . .
    ESSEX: You are not old! I will not have you old!
    ELIZABETH: Will you do that, in all kindness, in
    memory
Of great love past? No. You could not, could not.
It's not in a man to be kind that way, nor in
A woman to take it kindly. I think I'd kill you,
In a first blind rage.
    ESSEX: Kill me when I can say it.
    ELIZABETH: Love, will you let me
Say one more thing that will hurt you?
    ESSEX: Anything.
    ELIZABETH: Your blood's on fire to lead a new
    command
Now that you've won so handsomely in Spain,
And when I need a general anywhere
You'll ask to go. Don't ask it . . . and don't go.
You're better here in London.

    ESSEX: Was this all you wanted?
    [Stepping back]
To make me promise this?
    ELIZABETH: [Softly] Not for myself,
I swear it, not because I think you reckless
With men and money, though I do think that,
Not because you might return in too much triumph
And take my kingdom from me, which I can im-
    agine,
And not because I want to keep you here
And hate to risk you, though that's also true . . .
But rather . . . and for this you must forgive
    me . . .
Because you're more a poet than general . . .
And I fear you might fail, and lose what you have
    gained,
If you went again.
    ESSEX: God's death! Whom would you send?
    ELIZABETH: I asked you not to be angry
    ESSEX: Not to be angry!
How do you judge a leader except by whether
He wins or loses? Was it by chance, do you think,
That I took Cadiz?
    ELIZABETH: Very well. You shall go.
Go if you will. Only I love you, and I say
What would be wiser.
    ESSEX: You choose the one thing I must have
And ask me not to ask it! No. Forgive me.
    ELIZABETH: I'll not say it again.
    ESSEX: But if I'm more poet than
General, why poets make better generals
Than generals do, on occasion.
    ELIZABETH: You've proved it so.
On more than one occasion.
    [A clock strikes. She rises]
There's the chime.
The council's waiting, and we shall hear about
    Ireland,
If Cecil has his way. One thing remember,
You must not go to Ireland.
    ESSEX: No. That's a war
I'm content to miss.
    ELIZABETH: Thank God for that much then. I've
    been afraid
Ireland might tempt you. And one more thing re-
    member . . .
I'll have to oppose you in the council on
The Spanish hostages. . . . You'll have your way . . .
But I'll have to oppose you, lest they think it's
    your kingdom. . . .
Will you understand . . . ?
    ESSEX: I'll play my part perfectly.
    [He kisses her hand, then her lips]
    ELIZABETH: Now what can come between us, out
    of heaven or hell,
Or Spain or England?
    ESSEX: Nothing . . . never again.

                                    CURTAIN

SCENE III.

The same as Scene I, save that the doors to the council room have been thrown back, revealing a chair of state for the Queen, *and beneath it a table at which her* Councillors *sit. The* Guards *are placed at left and right. The* Queen *sits in her chair,* Raleigh, Cecil, Essex, Burghley, Howard, *and one or two others are at the table. The queen's* Jester *sits cross-legged on a mat.* Burghley *is speaking.*

BURGHLEY: It is quite true we shall have an enemy
  in Spain while Philip lives and his state has
  power
To wage war on us, but there is little he can do
Against an island as well walled as ours.
He has tried his best, and failed. My lord of Essex
Says it cost more to fight Spain every year
In this chronic fashion than it would to throw
A challenge down, raid the Escurial
And sack the empire. With this the weight of the
  council
Disagrees, and we may hold it settled
That our tactics continue defensive till the queen
Rule otherwise.

ELIZABETH: You'll wait some time for that.

BURGHLEY: But in the matter
Of the Spanish ransoms it appears to me
Lord Essex has right on his side. The English soldiers
Who brought their prisoners home from the last raid
Deserve their prize money. By immemorial custom
The ransom belongs to the taker of the prisoner
And not to the state.

ELIZABETH: That I intend to change,
That same immemorial custom. I thought you had
  been
Informed, Lord Burghley, that it was my will
That the Spanish ransoms be paid to the treasury.

BURGHLEY: But my lord of Essex . . .

ELIZABETH: My lord of Essex does not speak for
  me.
I was told this expedition into Spain
Would be paid for in booty. The cost, so far,
Has not been made up; and since there are Spanish
  nobles
To be ransomed, I think they should pay it.

ESSEX: Your Majesty,
I do not speak for myself . . . I took no prizes . . .
But only to redeem my word. I assured
My followers that they would have for their own
Whatever ransoms they earned.

ELIZABETH: And by what right
Did you make this promise?

ESSEX: By this same ancient custom
Of which Lord Burghley speaks. A custom so well
Established there's not a soldier anywhere
But takes it for granted.

ELIZABETH: Your word is pledged?

ESSEX: It is.

ELIZABETH: [*Smiling*] And if the state should con-
  fiscate these ransoms
You would make them good to the captors?

ESSEX: No. To speak frankly . . .
  [*He smiles*]
No.

ELIZABETH: Then the issues lies between the queen
And her soldiers . . . and your lordship need feel no
Concern in the matter.

ESSEX: When I made these promises
I spoke for Your Majesty . . . or believed I did.

ELIZABETH: Master Cecil, advise us; am I as queen
Bound by Lord Essex's promise?

CECIL: No, my liege;
It is well known a regent may repudiate
Treaty or word of a subject officer.
The throne is not bound.

ESSEX: If it comes to repudiation,
The throne can, of course, repudiate what it likes.
But not without breaking faith.

ELIZABETH: I fear we are wrong, Sir Robert;
And what has been promised for me and in my
  name
By my own officer, my delegate in the field,
I must perform. The men may have their ransoms.
The state will take its loss; for this one time
Only, and this the last. In the future a prisoner
Is held in the name of the state, and whatever
  price
Is on his head belongs to the crown. Our action
Here is made no precedent. What further
Business is there before us?

CECIL: There is one perpetual
Subject, Your Majesty, which we take up
Time after time, and always leave unsettled,
But which has come to a place where we must act
One way or another. Tyrone's rebellion in Ulster
Is no longer a smouldering coal, but a running fire
Spreading north to south. We must conquer Ireland
Finally now, or give over what we have won.
Ireland's not Spain.

ELIZABETH: I grant you.

THE FOOL: I also grant you.

ELIZABETH: Be quiet, fool.

THE FOOL: Be quiet, fool.
  [*He slaps his own mouth*]

ELIZABETH: Lord Burghley,
You shall speak first. What's to be done in Ireland?

BURGHLEY: If my son is right, and I believe him
  to be,
We can bide our time no longer there. They have
Some help from Spain, and will have more, no
  doubt,
And the central provinces are rising. We must
Stamp out this fire or lose the island.

ELIZABETH: This means
Men, money, ships?

BURGHLEY: Yes, madam.

CECIL: And more than that . . .
A leader.

ELIZABETH: What leader?

CECIL: A Lord Protector

Of Ireland who can carry sword and fire
From one end of the bogs to the other, and have
    English law
On Irish rebels till there are no rebels.
We've governed Ireland with our left hand, so far,
And our hold is slipping. The man who goes there
    now
Must be one fitted to master any field . . .
The best we have.

ELIZABETH: What man? Name one.

CECIL: We should send,

Unless I am wrong, a proved and able general,
Of no less rank, say, than Lord Howard here,
Lord Essex, Sir Walter Raleigh, Knollys, or Mount-
    joy . . .
This is no slight matter, to keep or lose the island.

ELIZABETH: I grant you that also.

THE FOOL: I also grant you. Be quiet,

Fool! [*He slaps his mouth*]

ELIZABETH: I ask you for one and you name a
dozen, Sir Robert.

RALEIGH: Why should one go alone, if it comes

To that? Why not two expeditions, one
To Dublin, one into Ulster, meeting halfway?

ELIZABETH: Are there two who could work to-
    gether?

CECIL: Knollys and Mountjoy.

They are friends and of one house.

ESSEX: Yes, of my house.

ELIZABETH: Essex, whom would you name?

ESSEX: Why, since Lord Cecil

Feels free to name my followers, I shall feel free
To name one or two of his. . . .

ELIZABETH: In other words,

You would rather Knollys and Mountjoy did not go?

ESSEX: I would rather they stayed in England, as
Sir Robert knows.
I have need of them here. But I will spare one of
    them
If Lord Cecil will let Sir Francis Vere go with him.

ELIZABETH: Let Vere and Knollys go.

CECIL: Lord Essex names

Sir Francis Vere because he knows full well
I cannot spare him, my liege.

ELIZABETH: Is this appointment

To wait for all our private bickerings?
Can we send no man of worth to Ireland, merely
Because to do so would weaken some house or party
Here at court?

THE FOOL: Your Majesty has said . . .

ELIZABETH: Be quiet. . . .

THE FOOL: Fool!

ELIZABETH: Be quiet!

THE FOOL: Fool!

ELIZABETH: Be quiet!

    [*The* Fool *forms the word "fool" with his lips,
    but makes no sound*]

CECIL: [*Rising*] I hope I betray no secret, Sir
    Walter,
If I tell the council that I spoke with you
Before the session, and asked you if you would go
Into Ireland if the queen requested it . . . and that
    you said
Yes, should the queen desire it.

BURGHLEY: That would answer.

CECIL: But I believe, and Sir Walter believes, there
    should be
More than one hand in this . . . that if he goes
Lord Essex should go with him.

ELIZABETH: With him?

ESSEX: In what

Capacity?

CECIL: Leading an equal command. Two generals

Of coeval power, landing north and south
And meeting to crush Tyrone.

ESSEX: Would you set up

Two Lord Protectors?

CECIL: It was my thought that we name

Raleigh as Lord Protector.

ESSEX: And I under him?

CECIL: Since the Azores adventure

Which my Lord Essex led, and which came off
A little lamer than could be wished, but in which
Sir Walter showed to very great advantage,
It has seemed to me that Raleigh should receive
First place if he served in this.

ESSEX: [*Rising*] This is deliberate,

An insult planned!

CECIL: It is no insult, my lord,

But plain truth. I speak for the good of the state.

ESSEX: You lie! You have never spoken here or
    elsewhere
For any cause but your own!

ELIZABETH: No more of this!

ESSEX: The good of the state! Good God!

Am I to swallow this from a clerk, a pen-pusher . . .
To be told I may have second place, for the good of
    the state?

CECIL: Were you not wrong at the Azores?

ESSEX: No, by God!

And you know it!

ELIZABETH: Whoever makes you angry has won

Already, Essex!

ESSEX: They have planned this!

CECIL: I say no more.

Raleigh will go to Ireland as Lord Protector
And go alone, if the queen asks it of him,
And since you will not go.

ESSEX: I have not said

I would not go. But if I were to go I would go
Alone, as Lord Protector!

ELIZABETH: That you will not.

I have some word in this.

ESSEX: If this pet rat

Lord Cecil wishes to know my mind about him,
And it seems he does, he shall have it! How he first
    crept

Into favor here I know not, but the palace is riddled
With his spying and burrowing and crawling under-
ground!
He has filled the court with his rat friends, very
gentle,
White, squeaking, courteous folk, who show their
teeth
Only when cornered; who smile at you, speak you
fair
And spend their nights gnawing the floors and chairs
Out from under us all!
    ELIZABETH: My lord!
    ESSEX: I am
Not the gnawing kind, nor will I speak fair
To those who don't mean me well . . . no, nor to
those
To whom I mean no good! I say frankly here,
Yes, to their faces, that Cecil and Walter Raleigh
Have made themselves my enemies because
They cannot brook greatness or power in any but
Themselves! And I say this to them . . . and to
the world. . . .
I, too, have been ambitious, as all men are
Who bear a noble mind, but if I rise
It will be by my own effort, and not by dragging
Better men down through intrigue! I admit
Sir Walter Raleigh's skill as a general
And Cecil's statecraft! I could work with them freely
And cheerfully, but every time I turn
My back they draw their knives! When Cecil left
England
I guarded his interests as I would my own
Because he asked me to . . . but when I left,
And left my affairs in his hands . . . on my return
I found my plans and my friends out in the rain
Along with the London beggars!
    CECIL: I did my best. . . .
    ESSEX: Aye . . . the best for yourself! For the
good of the state!
    RALEIGH: If Lord Essex wishes
To say he is my enemy, very well . . .
He is my enemy.
    ESSEX: But you were mine first. . . .
And I call the gods to witness you would be my
friend
Still, if I'd had my way! I take it hard
That here, in the queen's council, where there should
be
Magnanimous minds if anywhere, there is still
No trust or friendship!
    ELIZABETH: I take it hard that you
Should quarrel before me.
    ESSEX: Would you have us quarrel
Behind your back? It suits them all too well
To quarrel in secret and knife men down in the
dark!
    BURGHLEY: This is fantastic, my lord. There has
been no knifing.
Let us come to a decision. We were discussing
The Irish protectorate.

    CECIL: And as for Ireland,
I am willing to leave that in Lord Essex' hands
To do as he decides.
    ESSEX: Send your Sir Walter
To Ireland as Protector! And be damned to it!
    CECIL: As the queen wishes.
It is a task both difficult and dangerous.
I cannot blame Lord Essex for refusing
To risk his fame there.
    ESSEX: There speaks the white rat again!
Yet even a rat should know I have never refused
A task out of fear! I said I would not go
As second in command!
    CECIL: Then would you go
As Lord Protector?
    ELIZABETH: You have named your man . . .
Sir Walter Raleigh.
    RALEIGH: I'll go if Essex goes.
    ESSEX: What! Is our Raleigh
Afraid to go alone?
    RALEIGH: I don't care for it . . .
And neither does our Essex!
    ESSEX: Why, what is this
That hangs over Ireland! Is it haunted, this Ireland?
Is it a kind of hell where men are damned
If they set foot on it? I've never seen the place,
But if it's a country like other countries, with peo-
ple
Like other people in it, it's nothing to be
Afraid of, more than France or Wales or Flanders
Or anywhere else!
    CECIL: We hear you say so.
    ESSEX: If I
Am challenged to go to Ireland, then, Christ, I'll go!
Give me what men and horse I need, and put me
In absolute charge, and if I fail to bring
This Tyrone's head back with me, and put the re-
bellion
To sleep forever, take my sword from me
And break it . . . I'll never use it again!
    ELIZABETH: Will you listen . . . ?
    ESSEX: They've challenged me!
    ELIZABETH: If you volunteer
To go to Ireland there is none to stop you.
You are first soldier here, first in acclaim
And in achievement, but since the decision lies
With yourself alone, reflect a little.
    ESSEX: My queen,
I can see that Raleigh and Cecil have set themselves
To bait me into Ireland! They know and I know
That Ireland has been deadly to any captain
Who risked his fortunes there; moreover, once
I'm gone they think to strip me here at home,
Ruin me both ways! And I say to them: "Try it!"
There are men who are greater than Ireland or their
chicane. . . .
Since this is a challenge I go, and go alone,
And return victorious, and, by God, more of a prob-
lem
To Cecils and Raleighs than when I went!

[*The* Fool *rises and approaches* Essex *from behind*]

BURGHLEY: If Essex
Will go, it solves our problem, Your Majesty.
We could hardly refuse that offer.

ELIZABETH: No.

ESSEX: I will go,
And I will return! Mark me!

THE FOOL: [*Touching* Essex] My lord! my lord!

ESSEX: [*Turning suddenly with an instinctive motion that sweeps the* Fool *to the floor*] Take your
hands off me! You touch me for a fool?

[*He helps the* Fool *up*]
Get up!

THE FOOL: Do not go to Ireland!

ESSEX: [*Impatiently*] You too?

THE FOOL: Because, my lord, I come from Ireland,
All the best fools come from Ireland, but only
A very great fool will go there.

ESSEX: Faugh!

THE FOOL: It's not too late yet!

ELIZABETH: Break up the council, my lords.
We meet tomorrow.

BURGHLEY: And this is decided?

ESSEX: Yes.

ELIZABETH: Yes, if you wish it. Go now.
[*The* Council *rises when the queen does and
files out silently, leaving* Essex *and* Elizabeth]
You should have had
The fool's brain and he yours! You would have bettered
By the exchange.

ESSEX: I thank you kindly, lady.

ELIZABETH: What malicious star
Danced in my sky when you were born, I wonder?

ESSEX: What malicious star danced in the sky
Of Ireland, you should ask.

ELIZABETH: Oh, my dear,
You are a child in council. I saw them start
To draw you into this, and tried to warn you . . .
But it was no use.

ESSEX: They drew me into nothing.
I saw their purpose and topped it with my own.
Let them believe they've sunk me.

ELIZABETH: You will withdraw.
I'll countermand this.

ESSEX: And give them the laugh on me?
I'll have the laugh on them yet.

ELIZABETH: Better they should laugh
A little now than laugh at you forever.

ESSEX: And why not win in Ireland?

ELIZABETH: No man wins there.
You're so dazzled
With the chance to lead an army you'd follow the
    devil
In an assault on heaven.

ESSEX: No, but I'd lead him.
Heaven is always taken by storm. That's one thing
The devil doesn't know. Ireland is only

A country, and this is superstition.

ELIZABETH: I know.
You were quite right. I thought so as you said it.
Only somehow here in my breast something constricts . . .
Is it the heart grows heavy? I must let you go . . .
And I'll never see you again.

ESSEX: Mistrust all these
Forebodings. When they prove correct we remember
    them,
But when they're wrong we forget them. They mean
    nothing.
Remember this when I'm back and all turns out
    well . . .
That you felt all would turn out badly.

ELIZABETH: Oh, my love,
Come touch me, tell me all will happen well.

ESSEX: And so it will.

ELIZABETH: Do you want to go?

ESSEX: Why yes . . .
And no. I've said I would and I will.

ELIZABETH: It's not yet
Too late. There are no announcements made, no
    orders
Given. If you win, that will divide us . . .
And if you lose, that will divide us too.

ESSEX: I'll win, and it will not divide us. Is it so
    hard
To believe in me?

ELIZABETH: No . . . I'll believe in you . . .
And even forgive you if you need it. Here.
My father gave me this ring . . . and told me if
    ever
He lost his temper with me, to bring it to him
And he'd forgive me. And so it saved my life . . .
Long after, when he'd forgotten, long after, when
One time he was angry.

ESSEX: Darling, if ever
You're angry rings won't help.

ELIZABETH: Yes, it would.
I'd think of you as you are now, and it would.
Take it.

ESSEX: I have no pledge from you. I'll take it
To remember you in absence.

ELIZABETH: Take it for a better reason. Take it
    because
The years are long, and full of sharp, wearing days
That wear out what we are and what we have been
And change us into people we do not know,
Living among strangers. Lest you and I who love
Should wake some morning strangers and enemies
In an alien world, far off; take my ring, my lover.

ESSEX: You fear
You will not always love me?

ELIZABETH: No, that you
Will not love me, and will not let me love you.
[*She puts the ring on his finger*]

CURTAIN

ACT II. SCENE I.

The queen's study. Penelope *is sitting reading. The* Fool *enters. She does not see him.*

THE FOOL: Sh! Make no noise.

PENELOPE: What do you mean?

THE FOOL: Silence! Quiet!

PENELOPE: I am silent, fool.

THE FOOL: You silent? And even as you say it you are talking!

PENELOPE: You began it.

THE FOOL: Began what?

PENELOPE: Talking.

THE FOOL: Oh, no. Talking began long before my time. It was a woman began it.

PENELOPE: Her name?

THE FOOL: Penelope, I should judge.

PENELOPE: Fool.

THE FOOL: [*Looking away*] No, for with this same Penelope began also beauty and courage and tenderness and faith . . . all that a man could desire or a woman offer . . . and all that this early Penelope began has a later Penelope completed.

PENELOPE: [*Rising*] It lacked only this . . . that the court fool should make love to me.

THE FOOL: I am sorry to have been laggard. But truly I have never found you alone before.

PENELOPE: How lucky I've been!

THE FOOL: Are you angered?

PENELOPE: At what?

THE FOOL: At my loving you.

PENELOPE: I've learned to bear nearly everything.

THE FOOL: A lover's absence?

PENELOPE: Among other things.

THE FOOL: The presence of suitors undesired?

PENELOPE: That, too.

THE FOOL: I am not a suitor, my lady. I ask nothing. I know where your heart lies. It is with my Lord Essex in Ireland. I do not love you.

PENELOPE: Good.

THE FOOL: I lied to you. I do love you.

PENELOPE: I am sorry.

THE FOOL: You will not laugh at me?

PENELOPE: No.

THE FOOL: Then there is yet some divinity in the world . . . while a woman can still be sorry for one who loves her without return.

PENELOPE: A woman is sadly aware that when a man loves her it makes a fool of him.

THE FOOL: And if a fool should love a woman . . . would it not make a man of him?

PENELOPE: No, but doubly a fool, I fear.

THE FOOL: And the women . . . how of the women?

PENELOPE: They have been fools, too.

THE FOOL: The more fool I, I tried to save Lord Essex from Ireland . . . but he needs must go . . . the more fool he.

PENELOPE: Let us not talk of that.

THE FOOL: May I kiss you?

PENELOPE: No.

THE FOOL: Your hand?

PENELOPE: Yes. [*He kisses her hand*]

THE FOOL: I thank you.

[*She touches his fool's cap gently with her hand*]

PENELOPE: The more fool you, poor boy.

[Robert Cecil *enters from the left*]

CECIL: This is hardly a seemly pastime, Mistress Gray.

PENELOPE: And are you now the judge of what is seemly, Sir Robert?

CECIL: [*To the Fool*] Be off with you! [*To* Penelope] The queen is expecting Master Bacon here? [*The Fool goes*]

PENELOPE: I am set to wait for him.

CECIL: You will not be needed.

PENELOPE: Excellent.

[*She goes out right, passing* Raleigh, *who enters*]

CECIL: This Bacon keeps himself close. I have been unable to speak with him. She has this news?

RALEIGH: Yes.

CECIL: She believes it?

RALEIGH: Burghley himself believes it.

CECIL: Then she does.

RALEIGH: Beyond question.

[*The curtains part at the left and* Bacon *enters*]

CECIL: Good morrow, Master Bacon.

BACON: And to you, my lords.

CECIL: I have sent everywhere for you, sir, this three hours . . . and perhaps it was not altogether by accident that I could not find you.

BACON: I was not at home. You must forgive me.

CECIL: You are here to see the queen?

BACON: [*Bowing*] The queen has also been good enough to send for me.

CECIL: It was my wish to speak with you first . . . and it is my opinion that it will be the better for all of us, if I do so now . . . late as it is.

BACON: I am but barely on time, gentlemen.

CECIL: You need answer one question only. You have been in correspondence with Lord Essex in Ireland?

BACON: Perhaps.

CECIL: The queen has this morning received news warning her that Lord Essex is allied with the Irish rebels and is even now leading his army back to England to usurp her throne. Had you heard this?

BACON: No.

CECIL: Do you credit it?

BACON: It is your own scheme, I believe.

CECIL: That Essex should rebel against the queen?

BACON: Even so.

RALEIGH: You accuse us of treason?

BACON: If the queen were aware of certain matters she would herself accuse you of treason.

CECIL: What matters?

BACON: I prefer that the queen should question me.

CECIL: Look to yourself, Master Bacon. If you intend to accuse any man of the suppression of letters written by Essex to the queen, or of the suppression of letters sent by the queen to Essex, you will be unable to prove these assertions and you will argue yourself very neatly into the Tower.

BACON: My lord . . . I had no such business in mind.

RALEIGH: Then what? . . .

BACON: I hope I can keep my own counsel. The truth is, my lords, you are desperate men. You have overreached yourselves, and if wind of it gets to the royal ears you are done.

RALEIGH: We shall drag a few down with us if we are done, though, and you the first.

CECIL: You have but a poor estimate of me, Master Bacon. If you go in to the queen and reveal to her that her letters to Essex have not reached him . . . as you mean to do . . . the queen will then send for me, and I will send for Lord Essex' last letter to you, containing a plan for the capture of the city of London. It will interest you to know that I have read that letter and you are learned enough in the law to realize in what light you will stand as a witness should the queen see it.

BACON: I think it is true, though, that if I go down I shall also drag a few with me, including those here present.

CECIL: I am not so sure of that either. I am not unready for that contingency. But to be frank with you, it would be easier for both you and us if you were on our side.

BACON: You must expect a man to side with his friends.

CECIL: And a man's friends . . . who are they? Those who can help him to what he wants.

BACON: Not always.

CECIL: When he is wise. You have served Lord Essex well and I believe he has made you promises. But the moment Essex enters England in rebellion, he is doomed, and his friends with him.

BACON: One word from the queen to him . . . one word from him to the queen . . . one word from me, revealing that their letters have been intercepted, and there can be no talk of rebellion. There has been some underhand traffic with the couriers between here and Ireland. Their letters have been lost, you have induced the queen to promulgate arbitrary orders . . . and since they are both proud, you have bred distrust in her and defiance in him. Your machinations have been so direct, so childish, so simple . . . and so simply exposed . . . that I wonder at you!

CECIL: My friend, a child could trip him. Not so simple as your own. I have news this morning that Lord Essex has already landed in England and set up his standard here. He is a rebel, and when a man is once a rebel, do you think there will be any careful inquiry into how he happened to become one?

BACON: Essex in England!

CECIL: In England.

RALEIGH: And has neglected to disband his army.

CECIL: You speak of explanations between the queen and Essex. Unless you betray us there will be no explanations. They are at war and will never meet again.

BACON: That is, if your plan succeed.

CECIL: [Standing aside] Very well, then. Go in. You have chosen your master. I have done with you.

BACON: [Not moving] And if I say nothing?

CECIL: Then . . . whatever you have been promised, whatever you have desired, that you shall have. There is no place in the courts you could not fill. You shall have your choice. If you need excuse, no one should know better than you that this Essex is a danger to the state, a danger to the queen, a danger to liberty.

BACON: If I need excuse I shall find one for myself.

[There is a pause. Then the curtain parts to the right and Penelope enters. She holds the curtain back]

PENELOPE: Yes, Your Majesty; he is here.

ELIZABETH: Why was I not told? [She enters] Is this an ante-chamber, Sir Robert? Am I never to look out of my room without seeing you?

CECIL: Your pardon, Your Majesty. I was just going.

ELIZABETH: Then go. You need not pause to explain why you came. I am weary of your face!

CECIL: Yes, Your Majesty.

[Cecil and Raleigh bow and depart]

ELIZABETH: I have heard that you are a shrewd man, Master Bacon.

BACON: Flattery, Majesty, flattery.

ELIZABETH: I have heard it,
And in a sort I believe it. Tell me one thing . . .
Are you Cecil's friend?

BACON: I have never been.

ELIZABETH: He is a shrewd man; he's
A man to make a friend of if you'd stand well
In the court, sir.

BACON: It may be so.

ELIZABETH: Why are you not
His friend then?

BACON: We are not on the same side.

ELIZABETH: You follow Lord Essex?

BACON: Since I have known him.

ELIZABETH: There's
A dangerous man to follow.

BACON: Lord Essex?

ELIZABETH: Lord Essex.

BACON: I am sorry, madam,
If I have displeased you.

ELIZABETH: You have displeased me.

BACON: I repeat then . . .
I am sorry.

ELIZABETH: You will change, then? You will forget
This Essex of yours?

BACON: If you ask it . . . if there is reason . . .

ELIZABETH: Well, there is reason! He has taken up arms
Against me in Ireland.

BACON: You are sure of this?

ELIZABETH: I have reports. Is it so hard to believe?

BACON: Without proofs, it is.

ELIZABETH: I have proof.

BACON: May I ask of what sort?

ELIZABETH: Proof good enough. You know the punishment
For treason? From what I have heard
Of late both you and Essex should remember
That punishment.

BACON: Madam, for myself I have
No need to fear, and if Lord Essex has
I am more than mistaken in him.

ELIZABETH: I am very sorry
That I must do this . . . but all friends of Essex
Go straightway to the Tower. I have sent for you
To give you a last chance to change your mind
Before this blow falls. Are you still his friend?

BACON: Yes, Majesty.

ELIZABETH: I am sorry for it.

BACON: That is all?

ELIZABETH: Why no. You do not believe me?

BACON: I do not.

ELIZABETH: And why?

BACON: I neither believe our Essex a rebel
Nor that you believe so. If you intended to place me
In the Tower . . . I would be in the Tower . . .
and no talk about it.

ELIZABETH: You are shrewd indeed.

BACON: I am Essex' friend.

ELIZABETH: If that
Were true . . . if I could speak to you . . . if
there were only
The sound of one honest voice!
. . . I must rule England,
And they say he is rebel to me . . . and day and night,
Waking, sleeping, in council, there is still always
One thing crying out in me over and again . . .
Waking and sleeping I hear it crying: He cannot,
Cannot fail me! But I have written him my love
And he has not answered. What you know of this
Answer me truly, truly . . . bitter or not,
And you shall not lose!

BACON: He has not answered?

ELIZABETH: No.

BACON: If I
Knew why I would know much. Have you angered
him . . .
Sent arbitrary orders?

ELIZABETH: I have ordered him to disband
His forces and return. I have cut off
Revenue and supplies.

BACON: But this was rash . . .
To send a popular leader out with an army
And then check him suddenly, heap disgrace upon
him . . .
He has great pride.

ELIZABETH: [Getting up] He has rebelled then?
I wrote him lovingly.

BACON: And he answered? . . .

ELIZABETH: Nothing.

BACON: That could not be excused.

ELIZABETH: And it cannot be. It's true. It will not
be!

BACON: Dear queen, I fear
I have turned you against him!

ELIZABETH: No, no! I needed that!

BACON: And if there were something wrong . . .
Some misunderstanding? . . .

ELIZABETH: No, no . . . don't try comfort now
. . .
He had my letters. That could not go wrong.
Did he not have my letters?

BACON: Could it be otherwise?

ELIZABETH: You would know that. You would
know if he had not.
You've had word from him?

BACON: Yes.

ELIZABETH: He has written you,
But not me! Or are you traitor to him also . . .
I think you are! I think you lie to me! I am
Encompassed by lies! I think you, too, betray him
But subtly, with infinite craft, making me believe
First that you would not wrong him! No, no . . .
I'm gone mad
Pacing my room, pacing the room of my mind.
They say a woman's mind is an airless room,
Sunless and airless, where she must walk alone
Saying he loves me, loves me, loves me not,
And has never loved me. The world goes by, all
shadows,
And there are voices, all echoes till he speaks . . .
And there's no light till his presence makes a light
There in that room. But I am a queen. Where I walk
Is a hall of torture, where the curious gods bring all
Their racks and gyves, and stretch me there to
writhe
Till I cry out. They watch me with eyes of iron
Waiting to hear what I cry! I am crying now . . .
Listen, you gods of iron! He never loved me . . .
He wanted my kingdom only . . . .
Loose me and let me go! I am yet a queen . . .
That I have! That he will not take from me.
I shall be queen, and walk his room no more.
He thought to break me down by not answering . . .
Break me until I'd say, I'm all yours . . . what I am
And have, all yours! That I will never, never,
Never say. Not broken yet.

BACON: Nor will be, Majesty.

ELIZABETH: We must not follow him.
We must forget him, break him as he would break
    us,
Bow that bright head . . . I shall be as I was.
See him no more, my friend.
He walks on quicksand. Avoid him.

BACON: Yes, my queen.

ELIZABETH: Go, my friend.
You have done well. I trust you.

BACON: I thank Your Majesty.

[*He goes out. Elizabeth* claps her hands twice.
    After a moment Captain Armin *enters*]

ELIZABETH: Captain Armin, keep a watch on
    Master Bacon,
On his house and on his correspondence.
I wish to know all he knows.

ARMIN: Yes, Your Majesty.

ELIZABETH: Wait. I have found you true of word,
And sure of hand. Moreover, you can keep coun-
    sel—

[Armin *bows. She beckons him to come to her.*
    He does so]

What we say now is forever secret between us—
Between us two—not one other.

ARMIN: I'll hold it so.

ELIZABETH: It is reported there is an army risen
Against me——

ARMIN: God forbid!

ELIZABETH: It is so reported. The rebellion I speak
    of's the force
Lord Essex has brought back with him from Ireland.
I wish to make this preparation for it: Whatever
    orders
You receive from your superiors, whatever broils
Occur, he is to have free access to my presence.

ARMIN: There would be danger to your person,
    madam.

ELIZABETH: I will risk that.

ARMIN: You would be hostage if he were in com-
    mand.

ELIZABETH: Be ready for danger—and if need be,
    death.

ARMIN: Yes, Majesty.

[*He goes out. Elizabeth* stands motionless for a
    moment. There is a sudden burst of girls'
    laughter in an adjoining room, and the *Fool*
    runs in with a garment in his hand. Three
    Girls run after him, the foremost tripping him
    so that he falls in a corner and is instantly
    pounced upon by all three]

MARY: [*Entering*] Thief! Thief! Stop thief!

ELLEN: Kill the slobber thief! Fall on him!

TRESSA: Can a maid not keep a silk smock?

THE FOOL: Help! Salvage! Men-at-arms to the
rescue! I am boarded by pirates!

[*They tickle him*]

ELLEN: Tear it from him! He will exhibit it!

TRESSA: No, no! Don't tear it!

THE FOOL: If you sit on me in that fashion,
darling, you will regret it. There will be issue!

ELLEN: What issue?

THE FOOL: Twins! Seven or eight!

[Ellen *slaps him*]

MARY: Rise! Rise quickly! The queen is here.
Rise!

[*They all get up in confusion*]

TRESSA: We are sorry, Your Majesty.

[Elizabeth *looks at them without seeing them,
    and goes out to her bedroom*]

ELLEN: What is it? She seemed not to see.

MARY: It's not like her not to strike us.

TRESSA: We'll be whipped.

THE FOOL: No, no. She strikes instantly or not at
all.

TRESSA: Give me that.

[*She snatches her smock from the* Fool]

MARY: Come. [*They tiptoe out*]

CURTAIN

SCENE II.

The interior of Essex' *tent on the coast of England.* Essex *sits in the light of a candle, reading dispatches. A* Guard *stands in the shadow.* Marvel, *an
aide, enters*]

MARVEL: There is a courier from the queen, my
lord.

ESSEX: At last, then.

MARVEL: You will see him at once?

ESSEX: Yes . . . Wait. Bring him in and stay
here while I read the dispatches. If I give orders to
torture or kill him, show no surprise. You understand?

MARVEL: You will not torture him?

ESSEX: Am I not tortured? And you, too, sirrah.
You will remember?

THE GUARD: Yes, my lord.

ESSEX: Good.

[Marvel *goes out.* Essex *rises and stands out of
    the light, waiting.* Marvel *enters with the* Cour-
    ier, *who falls on his knee before* Essex]

THE COURIER: My Lord of Essex?

ESSEX: Yes.

COURIER: Dispatches from the queen.

ESSEX: When did you leave London?

COURIER: Four days ago, my lord. We were delayed.

ESSEX: What delayed you?

COURIER: Robbers.

ESSEX: And they took what from you?

COURIER: Our horses and money.

ESSEX: And the letters? . . .

COURIER: Were returned to me untouched.

ESSEX: When did this happen?

COURIER: This side of the ford. There were four armed men against us two.

ESSEX: Give me the letters. [*The* Courier *does so.* Essex *reads briefly*] This is all?

COURIER: Yes, my lord.

ESSEX: You are sure you have lost nothing?

COURIER: Indeed yes, my lord. There was but one missive and the seal was returned unbroken. The cut-throats told us they cared the less about our letters for they could not read.

ESSEX: You are a clever liar, sirrah, and you are the third liar who has come that same road to me from London. You are the third liar to tell this same tale. You shall pay for being the third.

COURIER: My lord, I have not lied to you.

ESSEX: Take his weapons from him, lieutenant. [Marvel *obeys*] Set him against the post there. Not so gently. He shall lose his ears first and then his lying tongue.

COURIER: Your lordship does not mean this?

ESSEX: And why not? We shall then cut him in pieces . . . but gradually, with infinite delicacy.

[Marvel *approaches the* Courier *with a knife. The* Guard *holds him*]

COURIER: No, no, no, no! Oh, God! Oh, my lord! My lord!

ESSEX: What are you waiting for?

MARVEL: We must tie him to the pole first, sir.

ESSEX: Then tie him!

COURIER: No, no . . . oh, God, no! What do you want of me? I swear to you I haven't lied to you! I swear . . . ugh!

[*He is choked*]

ESSEX: Let him speak. What do you swear?

COURIER: My lord, I have not lied . . . I speak truth . . .

ESSEX: Tie him up.

COURIER: Let me speak . . . I can . . . ugh . . .

ESSEX: Silence him. We know too well what you have done, sirrah. We need no evidence of that. What we ask is that you tell us who set you on . . . and your accomplices. Tell us this and I want no more of you. You shall have your freedom . . . and this . . . [*He tosses a clinking bag at his feet*] Speak.

COURIER: My lord, if I knew . . .

ESSEX: Bind him. Truss him up and cut him open. Dispense with these niceties. Have you no knife? [*He is bound*] We have heard enough! Take out his tongue!

[*They approach him. He becomes calm*]

COURIER: My lord, I am not a coward, though it
    may seem to you
I am, for I have cried out . . . but I cried out
Not so much for pain or fear of pain
But to know this was Lord Essex, whom I have loved
And who tortures innocent men.

ESSEX: Come, silence him!

COURIER: Come then. I am innocent. If my Lord
    Essex

Is as I have believed him, he will not hurt me;
If he will hurt me, then he is not as I
And many thousands believe him, who have loved
    him,
And I shall not mind much dying.
    [*A pause*]

ESSEX: Let him go.
    [*They unbind the* Courier]
I thought my letters had been tampered with.
You'd tell me if it were so.

COURIER: My honored lord,
By all the faith I have, and most of it's yours,
I'd rather serve you well and lose in doing it
Than serve you badly and gain. If something I've
    done
Has crossed you or worked you ill I'm enough pun-
    ished
Only knowing it.

ESSEX: This letter came
From the queen's hands?

COURIER: It is as I received it
From the queen's hands.

ESSEX: There was no other?

COURIER: No other.

ESSEX: Take this and go.
    [*He tosses the bag to the* Courier]

COURIER: I have brought misfortune . . .

ESSEX: You bring good news. We break camp tomorrow for London . . . Go . . . take that news with you. They'll welcome you outside. Remain with my guard and return with us.
    [*The* Courier *goes out*]

MARVEL: We march tomorrow?

ESSEX: Yes.

MARVEL: Under orders?

ESSEX: No.
    [*He reads*]
"Lord Essex is required to disperse his men
And return to the capital straightway on his own
Recognizance, to give himself up."

MARVEL: And nothing with this?

ESSEX: Give out the necessary orders, we shall
Move at daybreak.

MARVEL: Yes, my lord.

ESSEX: And it is
As well it falls out this way! By right of name
And power and popular voice this is my kingdom
    . . .
This England under my feet, more mine than hers,
As she shall learn. It is quite as well.

MARVEL: There is no man
But will think so. There is victory in your path,
My lord. The London citizens will rise
At the first breath of your name.

ESSEX: Yes . . . that I'm sure of.

MARVEL: And with London in your hands . . .
    well . . . it's your world then . . .
As far as you like.

ESSEX: And I am glad for England.
She has lain fallow in fear too long! Her hills

Shall have a spring of victory. Goodnight.

MARVEL: Goodnight.

ESSEX: And for this order, I received it not.

[*He tears the paper*]

CURTAIN

SCENE III.

The council hall of Act I is cleared here for a court assembly. Those who attended the council are present, save for Essex, also the Fool, Ellen, Mary, Tressa, Penelope, Bacon, and other Lords- and Ladies-in-Waiting. Burghley and Cecil are standing to one side in earnest talk. Across from them a group made up of Raleigh, Bacon, the Fool, and a number of others]

BURGHLEY: These players should be put down with an iron hand. They have neither conscience nor morals. They will make any display for money. In my young days they were allowed only interludes and instructive entertainment. The queen has been too lax . . .

CECIL: Have you seen this play of Richard II?

BURGHLEY: I see no plays.

CECIL: It's high treason. Richard is deposed in it. High treason.

BACON: Treason to depose a king? Not if you succeed.

CECIL: No, but treason to teach treason.

BACON: What is treason?

RALEIGH: Said jesting Pilate.

CECIL: Is it not treason to depose a king?

RALEIGH: What if it makes a king of you?

THE FOOL: It would then be treason not to have done it.

BACON: The Fool is a Jesuit.

THE FOOL: In truth, he was deposed. It is treason to all his successors to deny it.

BACON: An excellent Jesuit.

THE FOOL: What? I a Jesuit? Jesu!

PENELOPE: And a wit.

BACON: Bad.

PENELOPE: Very bad.

RALEIGH: Unutterably bad. What? Jesuit! Poisonous. Shall we allow this?

PENELOPE: I am guilty. I surrender.

RALEIGH: What did you do with the body?

PENELOPE: There was none. I did eat my words.

RALEIGH: A cannibal, a monster, a word-swallower!

THE FOOL: A man-eater.

PENELOPE: Nay, nay!

BACON: Do you eat your men with butter or salt?

PENELOPE: With salt if they are buttery and with butter if they are salty.

RALEIGH: Ready then. Here comes a salty man to be buttered.

PENELOPE: A butter-in.

THE FOOL: A salt-butter.

BACON: A cheese . . . a whole cheese.

TRESSA: Full of holes, holey.

ELLEN: Pitted.

PENELOPE: What? Am I pitted against a cheese?

RALEIGH: Let but this cheese roll into your pit, Lady . . . and you are answered.

PENELOPE: No . . . you are answered. You are answered no.

BURGHLEY: [*To Cecil*] There can be no doubt the Essex faction sent money to the actors to purchase a performance of Richard. It is an old play; it would draw no public.

CECIL: The actors are then accessory.

BURGHLEY: Think you so?

CECIL: They could hardly be unaware of the purposes of the Essex party.

BACON: It is so certain that Essex has a purpose?

CECIL: He has led his army into London.

BACON: The men live in London. Moreover, the order to disperse on landing may not have been received. Such things have happened.

CECIL: Yes?

BACON: Aye, indeed.

CECIL: [*To Burghley*] You are to see these actors?

BURGHLEY: They are sending spokesmen today.

THE FOOL: Let them put on the play for us.

TRESSA: Yes . . . the deposition scene. It may convince us. We may all turn rebel.

BURGHLEY: Tut!

THE FOOL: Tut? What does this mean . . . this tut?

BURGHLEY: Will you learn manners, sirrah? In my young days there was no such loose speaking about the court.

THE FOOL: There was no tutting, neither.

PENELOPE: You are mistaken. There used to be tutting parties. They all brought their tutting.

THE FOOL: Fie on you! Also pooh on you!

PENELOPE: Yes . . . there were fieing and poohing parties also.

RALEIGH: True, true. Well I remember the old days when all the young people would get together and try which could make the greatest pooh.

TRESSA: There was such laughter and jesting!

RALEIGH: Ah, yes, at the old Tut, Fie and Pooh Tavern! It's torn down now, but what a place it was!

THE FOOL: The game went out of fashion, alas, when it was discovered that a virgin could always pooh farther than anybody else.

TRESSA: Tut!

MARY: Fie!

ELLEN: Pooh!

THE FOOL: I beg pardon. I had forgotten there were virgins present.

PENELOPE: We are all virgins.

RALEIGH: The proof then, quickly. Show me.

PENELOPE: It is nothing that can be seen, my lord.

RALEIGH: They say seeing is believing.

PENELOPE: Virginity is rather a state of mind.

ELLEN: Nay . . . a state of preservation.

THE FOOL: I have seen these preserved virgins.

RALEIGH: You have seen them?

THE FOOL: Seen them? I've been bothered by them. The whole court used to be driven indoors by them regularly on our progress through Middlesex.

RALEIGH: They are worse at night, I believe? Middlesex . . . Middlesex . . .

PENELOPE: Change the subject, gentles. This virginity begins to wear thin.

THE FOOL: It has worn clear through, and a great hole appears in the center.

PENELOPE: A hole in your wit.

RALEIGH: His Jesuit.

PENELOPE: His half-wit.

[A Herald enters and speaks to Cecil]

THE HERALD: My lord, there are two fellows here who ask for audience with the queen.

CECIL: Who are they?

HERALD: Players, my lord.

CECIL: Tell them to wait. The queen will see them presently.

[The Herald goes out]

BURGHLEY: To my mind it was one of these same players writ the ballad that was posted up at St. Paul's.

CECIL: No, no . . . the man has been discovered . . . and will have his ears cropped for it.

BURGHLEY: But he could not have written it . . . he was but an instrument. The actors are too devilish ingenious at writing ballads. I cannot put it out of my mind they are all treasonous scoundrels.

RALEIGH: Is this the ballad on the Earl's return?

CECIL: Aye . . . "When England needeth victories
She calleth Essex on . . ."
And more to the same purpose. What I cannot understand is that the queen should take no steps to put the city in a posture of defense. Essex draws near with his army . . . and we swing the gates as usual.

BACON: Is that a symptom of danger . . . that an English general should return with his army to the English capital?

CECIL: Are you not aware that Essex' house in the Strand is a camp brimming full of armed nobles going and coming?

THE FOOL: It is much more likely to be brimming with drunken nobles going and coming brim full.

CECIL: Be quiet!

THE FOOL: Fool. [Cecil lays a hand on his sword angrily. The Fool points to his own breast and repeats:] Fool.

[Cecil turns away. There is a rustling among those present. Several rise. At the rear the Queen appears silently, two Ladies following her. She comes forward without speaking, her eyes seeking for someone. She fixes on Lord Burghley]

THE QUEEN: Is it true, then, my dear Burghley, that you have taken to attending the Theatre?

BURGHLEY: No, madam.

THE QUEEN: It was not you, then, who forbade the performances of Richard II without asking my advice?

BURGHLEY: It was, madam.

THE QUEEN: On what ground?

BURGHLEY: Your Majesty, the play is treasonous. It shows the deposition of a king, and its performance was procured by rebels.

THE QUEEN: Rebels? What rebels?

BURGHLEY: I know not, madam. I have sent for the players to discover that.

THE QUEEN: You have sent for them?

BURGHLEY: Aye, madam . . . and they are here.

THE QUEEN: They will laugh at you, dear Burghley.

BURGHLEY: Others have laughed at me, Majesty.

THE QUEEN: They will laugh at you, sir, and you will deserve it. Is my kingdom so shaky that we dare not listen to a true history? Are my people so easily led that the sight of a king deposed in play will send them running hither to pull the queen out of her chair? Have we not passion plays in every little town showing the murder of our Lord? You are nervous, Lord Burghley. Let these children play their plays.

CECIL: Your Majesty, I very much fear they are not children, and that they mean to do harm.

THE QUEEN: Then let them. Let them do all the harm they can. Are we too stupid to see that to prohibit a rebellious play is to proclaim our fear of rebellion? Who is there here who fears a rebellion against me? I do not.

CECIL: It is dangerous to let these mutterings grow, dear queen.

ELIZABETH: It is dangerous to touch them. Let them mutter, if they will. Let them cry out . . . let them run the streets, these children! When they have worn themselves weary running and crying "Up with Essex!" "Down with Elizabeth!" and got themselves drunk on mutual pledges, they will go to bed and sleep soundly and wake up wiser. Let me speak to these players. Bring them to me.

BURGHLEY: Here, madam?

ELIZABETH: Here.

CECIL: Majestas, adsunt legati de curia Galliæ. Placetne eos recipere antequam . . .[1]

THE QUEEN: Cras illos recipiam.

CECIL: Sed maxime præstat . . .

[1] CECIL: Your Majesty, the French ambassadors are here. Would it please you to receive them before . . .
THE QUEEN: I will receive them tomorrow.
CECIL: But it is of the highest importance . . .
THE QUEEN: If it seems well to me, I will receive them when they come back tomorrow.

THE QUEEN: Si bene mihi videbitur, cras redituros recipiam!
Nay, I can bang you in Latin too!

[Cecil *goes out.* Elizabeth *sits and turns to the* Fool]

You, sirrah . . . I hear that you have fallen in love. Do you wish to be whipped?

THE FOOL: I would rather have been whipped, madam; much rather.

ELIZABETH: Why?

THE FOOL: It would hurt less.

ELIZABETH: Good. You shall be whipped.

THE FOOL: Madam, if you can whip it out of me I will give you my lucky shilling.

ELIZABETH: You shall be whipped and keep your shilling.

THE FOOL: You would better take it, madam queen.

ELIZABETH: Your shilling?

THE FOOL: Yes, madam queen, to buy another whip with for yourself. Nay, you had perhaps better buy several. But in truth, dear queen, I have not fallen in love, only a pretty little strumpet has fallen in love with me and I beg leave that we be allowed to marry.

ELIZABETH: Is she of the court?

THE FOOL: Yes, madam.

ELIZABETH: What, are there strumpets at court?

THE FOOL: Oh, they are all strumpets here at court. Some are here because they are strumpets and some are strumpets because they are here, but strumpets they all are.

ELIZABETH: Which is it you wish to marry?

THE FOOL: It is not that I wish to marry her, madam, but she wishes to marry me. [*Walking about to choose, finally pointing to* Tressa] This one, Majesty.

TRESSA: [*Leaping at him*] Scoundrel! . . .

THE FOOL: [*Pointing to* Ellen] No, no . . . I mean this one.

ELLEN: You dog! You . . .

[*The* Fool *passes* Penelope *by*]

THE FOOL: [*Pointing to* Mary] Or that one . . .

MARY: What!

THE FOOL: I feel sure it was one of them, Majesty . . . but it was dark at the time . . . and in truth I gave her my word of honor in the dark that I would make an honest woman of her by daylight. It is thus that most marriages are made.

ELIZABETH: How, fool?

THE FOOL: In the dark, my lady. Quite in the dark.

ELIZABETH: [*To a* Soldier] Take this fool, captain, and put him in the dark for three days with but little bread and water. I have a distaste for this fooling.

THE FOOL: No, no, madam.

ELIZABETH: I am tired of your strumpets! And let him not see his lady Penelope meanwhile. You will be sure of that, mistress?

PENELOPE: I have no desire to see him.

ELIZABETH: Whom do you desire to see?

PENELOPE: No one, your Majesty.

ELIZABETH: You lie! This Mistress Gray, take her too! Let her have bread and water!

[*She looks at* Penelope *with hatred*]

PENELOPE: Your Majesty . . . what is this?

ELIZABETH: I am weary to death of you! I am weary of all men and women, but more of you than any! You have written. You have had letters! I say, take her out of my sight! [*The soldiers start to take out* Penelope *and the* Fool] Whip them first, whip them both! [*The two are taken to the door*] Nay, leave them here, leave them, knaves . . . leave them! Damn you, do you hear me? You are too quick to obey orders! You like this whipping too well, sirrah! You have an itch for laying on! You beef-witted bastards! And now let us have entertainment, gentle lords! Let us be merry! The players are here! Let us have a play!

[*A* Herald *runs in to the* Queen *without ceremony, calling out as he comes:*]

THE HERALD: Your Majesty, Your Majesty! Lord Scroop sends me from the city to tell you there is a rising in London! There is a mob rising in the city!

ELIZABETH: What . . . is this one of the players? Are you playing Richard II for us?

THE HERALD: No, no, Your Majesty! A great number of people came through Fleet Street . . . and they have sacked a grocer's and broken into a wine-merchant's cellar! It is said they will break into Fleet Prison and set all free. . . .

ELIZABETH: Not they. If they've broken into a wine-cellar they'll get no farther. We're a marvellous people, we English, but we cannot hold liquor. Now if they were Scotch one might worry. What are they saying, these wine drinkers?

THE HERALD: I cannot tell you that, Your Majesty.

ELIZABETH: Are they not crying "Up with Essex!" "Down with Elizabeth!"?

THE HERALD: Yes, madam!

ELIZABETH: Why surely. What else would they be crying? "Up with Essex!" Viva! "Down with Elizabeth!" A bas! The queen is dead, long live the king! If I were there I would cry it myself! It has a marvellous ring! "Up with Essex!" "Down with Elizabeth!"

BURGHLEY: What are we to do, madam?

ELIZABETH: [*To the* Herald] What is the Lord Mayor doing about this?

THE HERALD: Nothing, Madam.

ELIZABETH: How like a Lord Mayor and how sensible. That's the first principle of government. Never do anything. Let the others make all the mistakes.

CECIL: But madam . . . there are five hundred of the royal guard at the Tower. . . .

ELIZABETH: Let the mayor of London look out for his people. If he allows them to run up and down breaking into wine-cellars, it's his own affair.

BURGHLEY: But if it spreads to the palace, Majesty?

ELIZABETH: Why yes . . . let them bring their

revolution here to me. I should be amused to see it. They are children, Burghley, drunken children. Would you fire on children?

BURGHLEY: Then let me go into London, madam . . .

ELIZABETH: And call out the guard and put down these traitors with powder and ball? No! They are to be allowed to get quite drunk and then go to sleep. Where are these players?

[Cecil enters with Burbage and Hemmings]

CECIL: Here, madam.

ELIZABETH: Ah, yes, bold Burbage and handsome Hemmings. Well, my masters, I understand that you have come to me to have your noses slit and your thumbs branded? Is it so?

BURBAGE: Only if unavoidable, Your Majesty.

ELIZABETH: You have put on a play, I believe?

BURBAGE: Many, Your Majesty.

ELIZABETH: You have revived the old play of Richard II, including in it the deposition scene which was censored on its first presentation, and you have done this to foster treasonous projects.

BURBAGE: No, Your Majesty, I swear it.

ELIZABETH: You have not played this play?

BURBAGE: But not to foster treason, that I swear.

ELIZABETH: If you played Richard with that pot-belly it was treason indeed. Then for what purpose?

BURBAGE: To make money.

ELIZABETH: On an old play?

BURBAGE: We were paid in advance . . .

ELIZABETH: By whom?

BURBAGE: By Lord Southampton.

BURGHLEY: You see? A friend of Essex.

ELIZABETH: You have much too handsome a nose for slitting, Master Hemmings, yet you say nothing.

HEMMINGS: There is only this to say, Your Majesty . . . that we knew nothing of any traitorous intent in the matter . . . and that, had we known of such intent, we would not have given the performance.

ELIZABETH: I think you are all traitorous knaves and rascals, as a matter of fact, in league with Essex and Southampton—and the smoothest liars in Christendom. Is there something in this?

HEMMINGS: No, madam.

ELIZABETH: You know Essex and Southampton?

HEMMINGS: We know Lord Southampton.

ELIZABETH: How much were you paid for the revival of Richard?

HEMMINGS: Three pounds, Your Majesty.

ELIZABETH: No more?

HEMMINGS: No more.

ELIZABETH: Play it again this afternoon, masters, play it at my request this afternoon, and you shall have ten pounds for it. Lord Cecil, pay Master Burbage ten pounds from the royal exchequer for one performance of Richard. And let it stand in the record.

CECIL: Yes, madam.

ELIZABETH: [To Hemmings] And tell Lord Southampton when you see him that I paid ten to his three. Will you tell him?

HEMMINGS: Yes, Your Majesty.

ELIZABETH: And when you have all this treason out of your systems be ready to play Sir John Falstaff for me at the end of the week. I should like to see your Falstaff again, sir.

BURBAGE: Yes, Your Majesty.

ELIZABETH: You may go.

[Burbage and Hemmings go out]

CECIL: [Waiting till they are gone] You are mad, Your Majesty! This is a rebellion, and you play into their hands. The outer court is thronging with messengers from the city! Half the town is in uprising!

ELIZABETH: I know.

CECIL: Madam . . .

ELIZABETH: Little man, little man, let me alone.

CECIL: This much I must tell you. Lord Essex has been seen with an armed force in the city.

ELIZABETH: Lord Essex?

CECIL: With an army. Where he is now no one can say.

ELIZABETH: And if one were to guess?

CECIL: He is on his way hither.

ELIZABETH: So I think. I shall be glad to see him. Let him bring his revolution here. How long think you it will last after I have looked on it?

BURGHLEY: Madam, the palace is unprotected from the waterside. The guard must be drawn up.

ELIZABETH: With your permission, my lord, I would rather not.

CECIL: I took the liberty of ordering a guard posted along the river.

[A door is opened without and a sudden snarl of angry voices breaks in on the conference]

THE VOICES: "Who has given these orders?"
"Back there . . . back!"
"Not the queen, by God!"
"The queen . . . the queen! Defend the queen!"
"An Essex!"
"Hold your mouth!"
"Stand back, fellow!"

ESSEX: [Outside] I say the queen will see me! Stand back!

[There is a clank of armor in the hallway and Essex appears in the doorway, Soldiers following him]

ELIZABETH: You come with a file of soldiers at your back, my lord of Essex.

ESSEX: Do I need them, Your Majesty?

ELIZABETH: No.

ESSEX: Then be off with you. Follow my orders. [Soldiers go out] They told me you would not see me.

ELIZABETH: They were wrong. I will see you. It seems you are in rebellion,
My good lord. Enter and state your grievance,
If you have grievance. For myself, I have

A great affection for rebels, being one myself
Much of the time.

ESSEX: I am no rebel, Your Majesty . . .
But, newly arrived from Ireland, and bearing news
Of your subjects there, I venture to come to see you,
No more.

ELIZABETH: And your army? . . . You have an
army with you?

ESSEX: I have brought my men home to London.

ELIZABETH: You received
My orders, no doubt, directing you to disband?

ESSEX: I believed them to be mistaken. To disband
    on the coast
And leave my expedition there, seemed strange,
And dangerous to the country. An army turned
    loose
Becomes a mob.

ELIZABETH: And you tell me this! You are in-
    formed in these matters
But I am not!

ESSEX: Indeed, that is quite true . . .
I do know about armies . . . and you do not.

ELIZABETH: Oh, yes . . .
Oh, indeed. And who paid them then? I believe
Your supplies were cut off?

ESSEX: I have paid them.

ELIZABETH: They are then
In your service?

ESSEX: In my service and therefore
Devoted yours.

ELIZABETH: And Ireland? How of Ireland?

ESSEX: I could have conquered Ireland had you
    given me time.
I left it worse than I found it.

ELIZABETH: An honest answer,
At any rate.

ESSEX: Why should I lie? The fault,
If any, was yours. To conquer Ireland requires
More than the months you gave me. Years, perhaps.

ELIZABETH: You were engaged in subduing the
    rebels, then,
When I summoned you home?

ESSEX: Just so.

ELIZABETH: You were not, by chance,
Joined with the rebels?

ESSEX: Never.

ELIZABETH: You held no parleys
With our friend Tyrone?

ESSEX: I did. They were part of my plan.

ELIZABETH: Your plans! Your plans! Why did you
    write me nothing
Of these your plans? Am I a witch to find out
What happens on the far side of the Irish Sea
Without being told?

ESSEX: I wrote you . . .

ELIZABETH: Masterly letters.
Brief, to the point, wasting no words, in short,
Nothing.

ESSEX: I know not what Your Majesty means

By that. I wrote you fully, and in answer
Received no reply.

ELIZABETH: You wrote me?

ESSEX: Many times.

ELIZABETH: And had no letters from me?

ESSEX: None.

ELIZABETH: Before God.
If the couriers were tampered with there shall be
Some necks stretched here! My lords, I wish to
    speak
With Lord Essex here alone! Leave us.

CECIL: Dear queen,
Do you think it safe . . .

ELIZABETH: Leave us!
    [Burghley *makes a sign and the stage is silently
    emptied save for the* Queen *and* Essex. *A
    pause*]
What did you write me?

ESSEX: I wrote you my love—for I thought you
    loved me then—
And then I pled with you not to bring me home
In the midst of my mission—and then at last
    angrily—
For I had not heard—but always to say I loved
    you—
Always.

ELIZABETH: But is this true?

ESSEX: Would I lie?

ELIZABETH: Some one
Has lied and will pay with his life if this is true!—
Before God and hell—some one will pay for this.

ESSEX: What did you write me?

ELIZABETH: I wrote—my love——
God keep you safe—I know not—and then, not
    hearing,
I wrote God knows what madness—as to a
    rebel——
Thinking you no longer mine—faithless!
Thinking——

ESSEX: I would I had known—I was in torment—
I—forgive me——

ELIZABETH: You should never have gone away.
God, how I've hated you!——

ESSEX: No!

ELIZABETH: Planned to put you to torture!

ESSEX: I have been in torture!
    [*He steps toward her*]

ELIZABETH: Not yet—I can't breathe yet—I can't
    breathe——
Or think or believe——

ESSEX: Nor I.

ELIZABETH: Can we ever——
Believe again? Can it be as it used to be?

ESSEX: We can make it so.

ELIZABETH: Come, kill me if you will. Put your
    arms round me——
If you love me. Do you still love me?

ESSEX: Yes.

ELIZABETH: Yes, yes——

If this were false, then, then truly—then I should
    die.
I thought because I was older—you see—some one
    else——

ESSEX: No one—never a breath——

ELIZABETH: Is it all, all as before?

ESSEX: We have not changed.

ELIZABETH: No. Yes, a little, perhaps. They have
changed us a little.

ESSEX: Not I. I have not changed.

ELIZABETH: Can I trust you now?

ESSEX: Sweet, think back, all those months,
All those hideous months! No word, no love.
And then word did come, it was to make me
    prisoner!
Christ, I have pride!
And though I came here in defiance, I came truly
    to find you
Who have been lost from me.

ELIZABETH: Do you ask forgiveness?
It is all forgiven.

ESSEX: Then, why then, hell's vanished—
And here's heaven risen out of it, a heaven of years
In the midst of desolate centuries.

ELIZABETH: We have so few years.
Let us make them doubly sweet, these years we have,
Be gracious with each other, sway a little
To left or right if we must to stay together—
Never distrust each other—nay, distrust
All others, when they whisper. Let us make this our
    pact
Now, for the fates are desperate to part us
And the very gods envy this happiness
We pluck out of loss and death.

ESSEX: If two stand shoulder to shoulder against
    the gods,
Happy together, the gods themselves are helpless
Against them, while they stand so.

ELIZABETH: Love, I will be
Your servant. Command me. What would you have?

ESSEX: Why nothing——

ELIZABETH: Take this my world, my present in
    your hands!
You shall stand back of my chair and together we
Shall build an England to make the old world wonder
And the new world worship!—What is this doubt
    in your brow?

ESSEX: I am troubled to be dishonest. I have
    brought my army
Here to the palace—and though it's all true that
    we've said——
No letters—utter agony over long months——
It is something in myself that has made me do this,
Not Cecil—nor anyone. No one but myself.
The rest is all excuse.

ELIZABETH: Speak what you will.

ESSEX: If you had but shown anger I could have
    spoken
Easily. It's not easy now, but speak I must!

Oh, I've thought much about this
On lonely marches and in distant tents,
Thinking of you and me. I say this now
Without rancor—in all friendliness and love——
The throne is yours by right of descent and by
Possession—but if this were a freer time,
And there were election, I should carry the country
    before me,
And this being true, and we being equal in love,
Should we not be equal in power as well?

ELIZABETH: We are equal.
I have made you so.

ESSEX: Yes, but still it's all yours——
Yours to grant me now or take away.

ELIZABETH: How could this well be otherwise?

ESSEX: Am I not—and I say this too in all love—
As worthy to be king as you to be queen?
Must you be sovereign alone?

ELIZABETH: You are young in policy,
My Essex, if you do not see that if I
Should grant high place to you now it would show
    ill to the kingdom——
It would be believed that you had forced this on me,
Would be called a revolution. It would undermine
All confidence. What is built up for years
In people's minds blows away like thistledown
When such things get abroad.

ESSEX: But is this your reason
Or have you another? Would you trust me as king?

ELIZABETH: No.

ESSEX: And are you still reluctant to give up
Your prerogatives?

ELIZABETH: Yes.

ESSEX: Then now, when the country is mine, the
    court in my hands,
You my prisoner, I must send my men away,
Disband my army, give back your kingdom to you,
And know I have been king for a moment only
And never will be again?

ELIZABETH: I am your prisoner?

ESSEX: The palace and the city are in my hands.
This England is mine now for the taking——

ELIZABETH: This is your friendship! This is your
    love!

ESSEX: As water finds its level, so power goes
To him who can use it, and soon or late the name
Of king follows where power is.

ELIZABETH: Oh, my Essex,
You are a child in war as you are in council.
Why all this talk of power? No army opposed you
When your troops came the road from Ireland.
    No guard was set
To stop your entrance with your thousand halberds.
Shall I tell you why? Because I wished to keep
A semblance of peace between us. And for that,
I am your prisoner!

ESSEX: Yes. My dear prisoner.

ELIZABETH: Now I do know at least
What it was you wanted. You wanted my kingdom.
    You have it.

Make the best of it. And so shall I.
What are your plans?

ESSEX: I have none.

ELIZABETH: The Tower, the block——

You could hardly take a queen prisoner and have
no thought
Of her destiny. I am my mother's daughter,
I too can walk the path my mother walked.

ESSEX: These are heroics. You know you are free
as air.

ELIZABETH: If I do as you ask.

ESSEX: Is it so hard to share your power with your
love?

I could have all—and I offer to share with you.

ELIZABETH: Let's have no more pretending.

I'd have given all—but you came with an army,
demanding——
In short, you don't love—nor trust me—no—nor
want me——

ESSEX: God knows I have wanted you. I have
wanted power——
Believed myself fitted to hold it—but not without
you.

ELIZABETH: If you had wanted me would you rise
and strike
At me with an army? Never, never! You'd have
come
To me quietly, and we'd have talked of it together
As lovers should—and we'd both have our way——
And no one the wiser. But now, to take the palace,
Hold me prisoner—no—what you wanted you've
taken——
And that is all you shall have. This is your king-
dom——
But I—I am not yours.

ESSEX: But I am yours
And have been.

ELIZABETH: Who will believe that? Not the world,
No, and not I. I'd rather go to the Tower
Than share my place on terms like these.
                              Put me where I
Will do least harm.

ESSEX: I cannot, could not, will not.

ELIZABETH: If I could have given freely——
But not now. Not surrendering. Not to a victor.

ESSEX: I am no victor if I lose you. The only gift
That I could take from you is that we are equals.

ELIZABETH: Yes, but not now.

ESSEX: I ask one word from you.

Give me this word—this one word—and these soldiers
Shall leave, and you shall be free.

ELIZABETH: I'll believe that
When it happens.

ESSEX: I'll believe you when you promise.

ELIZABETH: Then you have my promise.
You shall share the realm with me. As I am queen,
I promise it.

ESSEX: Then this is my answer.

[*He kisses her, then calls:*]

Marvel!—Marvel!

[Marvel *enters*]

Carry out the order of release. Dismiss my
guard——
Return the palace into the queen's hands.
Retire with all our forces to the Strand.
Release all prisoners. Release the queen's guard
And send them to their stations.

[Marvel *goes out*]

The palace will be
Returned as quickly as taken. This is our last
quarrel.

ELIZABETH: Yes—our last.

MARVEL'S VOICE: [*Off-stage*] Form for retire!

ANOTHER VOICE: Form for retire!

A MORE DISTANT VOICE: Form for retire!

A VOICE: [*In the distance*] Ready to march!

ANOTHER VOICE: Ready to march!

ANOTHER: All ready!

ANOTHER: Ready, captain!

[Marvel *enters*]

MARVEL: The order is obeyed, my lord.

ESSEX: Follow your men.

MARVEL: Yes, my lord. [*He goes out*]

ESSEX: It is as I planned. They are leaving the
palace.
Now let us talk no more of this tonight——
Let us forget this matter of thrones and kingdoms
And be but you and me for a while.

ELIZABETH: [*Immobile*] Yes—yes.

Let us forget. Have you kept your word indeed?

ESSEX: I have kept my word.

ELIZABETH: If I clapped my hands
Would my guard come now—or yours?

ESSEX: Yours only. Shall I call them?

ELIZABETH: No—I'll call them. [*She claps her
hands four times. Captain Armin appears in the
entrance followed by four Beef-eaters with halberds.
They stand at attention in the entrance*]
To be sure I have a guard
Once more. [*To the Captain*]
The palace has been returned? It is in
Our hands?

CAPTAIN: Yes, Majesty.

ELIZABETH: I have ruled England a long time, my
Essex,
And I have found that he who would rule must be
Quite friendless, without mercy, without love.
Arrest Lord Essex!
Arrest Lord Essex! Take him to the Tower
And keep him safe.

ESSEX: Is this a jest?

ELIZABETH: I never
Jest when I play for kingdoms, my lord of Essex.

ESSEX: I trusted you.

ELIZABETH: I trusted you,
And learned from you that no one can be trusted.
I will remember that.

ESSEX: Lest that should be all
You ever have to remember, Your Majesty,
Take care what you do.

ELIZABETH: I shall take care.

[Essex *unsheathes his sword, breaks it across his knee, flings it at the foot of the throne, turns and walks out between the two files of guards*]

CURTAIN

ACT III.

The queen's apartments in the Tower, a square and heavy room, long and with a raised stone platform, at one end of which stands a regal chair. It is dawn, the light filtering in coldly. Ellen stands in the doorway at the left, weeping, with one arm before her face. The Fool, *who has been sleeping wrapped in the draperies of the queen's chair, uncoils himself from among them and rolls over to rub his eyes. Tressa hurries in.*

TRESSA: Come back quickly, dear, quickly! She's sorry she hurt you. She'll have no one else read to her.

ELLEN: [*Weeping*] I can't read now. I'm—I don't mind if she strikes me—only—it wasn't my fault —— We're all so weary.

TRESSA: She's sorry——

THE FOOL: [*Waking*] One, two—there should be three.

[Mary *comes to the door*]

MARY: [*Very low*] Ellen——

THE FOOL: Three.

MARY: Ellen! She wants you at once.

[Ellen *runs out*]

THE FOOL: Where am I?

MARY: Yes—and what are you doing there?

THE FOOL: Trying to sleep.

MARY: Sleep? In the Tower?

THE FOOL: Come and help me. I have heard that you are perfect at lying down. [Mary *and* Tressa *go out. The* Fool *looks about him sleepily, then remembers something and hunts for it under a chair. When he extracts it it proves to be a roasted bird on a wooden platter, covered with leaves. He examines it, then replaces a large leaf over it.* Penelope, *fully dressed, comes in from the rear*] Penelope?

PENELOPE: Yes?

THE FOOL: Have you slept?

PENELOPE: No.

THE FOOL: Then you should break your fast. You are hungry?

PENELOPE: No. I can't eat.

THE FOOL: [*Showing his capon*] Look.

PENELOPE: What's that?

THE FOOL: Breakfast. I brought it from Whitehall.

PENELOPE: Eat it then.

[*She sits on a step disconsolately*]

THE FOOL: You won't have any?

PENELOPE: No.

THE FOOL: [*Pushing the food away*] I'm not hungry either.

PENELOPE: Eat it, poor fool.

THE FOOL: I don't want it. I brought it for you.

PENELOPE: I know. But eat it.

[*She wipes her eyes*]

THE FOOL: Why should you weep?

PENELOPE: God knows. He never wept for me.

THE FOOL: The earl's not dead yet, remember.

PENELOPE: No.

THE FOOL: And she'll never let it happen.

PENELOPE: The clock's struck five. He's to die at six.

THE FOOL: Why has she not sent to him?

PENELOPE: She has. We were awake all night. She has sent messages but he's not answered. She's been waiting for word from him. But he's as silent as if he wanted to die.

THE FOOL: Will she let them kill him if he says nothing?

PENELOPE: She's a strange woman. She wants him to beg her pardon . . . or something like that.

THE FOOL: Would you beg her pardon if you were he?

PENELOPE: No.

THE FOOL: Then he won't. For I think he's as proud as you.

PENELOPE: He has not said a word or sent a message since his arrest.

THE FOOL: And the queen has not slept?

PENELOPE: No.

THE FOOL: Nor you?

PENELOPE: No.

THE FOOL: God help these women.

PENELOPE: She says she gave him a ring once. If he ever wanted forgiveness he was to send the ring. And he sits there stubbornly with the ring on his finger. Oh, God, will nothing happen?

[*The* Fool *has absent-mindedly pulled the capon toward him again, and begins to eat.* Elizabeth *emerges from the rear*]

ELIZABETH: Penelope?

PENELOPE: Yes.

ELIZABETH: Have the players come?

PENELOPE: Not yet.

[*The* Fool *has pushed the food guiltily behind him*]

ELIZABETH: These cheating grooms! I'll have them carbonadoed for this dallying! I shall go mad here! Bring me the little book of prayers . . . from the window-sill. No . . . leave it. The gods of men are sillier than their kings and queens . . . and emptier and more powerless. There is no god but death, no god but death! [*She sees the food the* Fool *has been hiding*] Gnaw your bones somewhere else!

[*The* Fool *goes out left*] Come here, my dear. I
heard the clock strike five.

PENELOPE: Yes. I heard it.

　　[*They sit together on the steps, and* Penelope
　　puts her arm round Elizabeth]

ELIZABETH: Do you love him well, my dear?

PENELOPE: Yes, Your Majesty.

　　[Elizabeth *bows her head wearily on* Penelope]

ELIZABETH: I love him. He has never loved me.

PENELOPE: Yes, yes. He does love you. I've been
madly jealous of you.

ELIZABETH: Of me? Poor child.

PENELOPE: But he loved you . . . and never me
at all.

ELIZABETH: How do you know?

PENELOPE: He told me.

ELIZABETH: What did he say?

PENELOPE: He said, "I love her dearly." I wanted
him for myself, and I warned him against you. He
laughed at me. He said, "I love her very dearly."

ELIZABETH: You tell me this because you want to
save him.

PENELOPE: No, dear queen. It's true.

ELIZABETH: This is the end of me, dear. This is
　　the end.
It comes late. I've been a long while learning,
But I've learned it now. Life is bitter. Nobody
Dies happy, queen or no. Will he speak, think you?
Will he send to me?

PENELOPE: No. Not now.

ELIZABETH: You see,
This is the end of me. Oh, I shall live.
I shall walk about and give orders . . . a horrible
　　while . . .
A horrible old hag.

PENELOPE: You must send for him.
He's proud as you are, and you have the upper hand.
He'll say nothing. You must send for him, bring him
　　here.

　　[*The chimes ring the quarter hour*]

ELIZABETH: Not yet. Not yet. [*She rises*]
Where are the players? I sent
For the players hours ago! They shall pay for this,
The insolent servants! Mary . . . Tressa, God's
　　head!
I'm bestially served! Ellen!

　　[Ellen *looks in, partly dressed*]
Find out if the players
Are here? And be quick.

ELLEN: Yes, madam. [*She disappears*]

ELIZABETH: Where's my fool?

THE FOOL: [*Looking in with a bone in his hand*]
Here, madam.

ELIZABETH: Where are you when I need you?
Look at the oaf! Say nothing! You're funny enough
The way you are with your capon in your mouth!
Eat! Eat! Let me see you!

THE FOOL: I don't seem to be hungry!

ELIZABETH: Eat, I say!

THE FOOL: Yes, madam. [*He tries to eat*]

ELIZABETH: Now wipe your fingers.
Here, take my napkin, child. Come here!
　　You're disgusting!

　　[*She gives him a kerchief*]
Can you not clean your face?

THE FOOL: With this?

ELIZABETH: Aye, with that.

　　[*She takes his bone and throws it*]
Why do you make mouths at it? It's clean.

THE FOOL: Yes, madam!

　　[*He begins to wipe his mouth, then starts to
　　cry; and, sitting down on the steps, sobs
　　heavily, his head in his hands*]

ELIZABETH: What is it now? What good's a fool
　　that cries
When you need comfort? What's the matter?

THE FOOL: Please,
I don't know. You aren't like the queen.

ELIZABETH: I am
The queen, though.

TRESSA: [*Looking in*] The players, madam.

ELIZABETH: Bring them here.

PENELOPE: The time's grown short. Will you send
for him?

ELIZABETH: Wait . . . he may come.

PENELOPE: No, no. He won't. You'll let it go too
long
Watching the players.

ELIZABETH: Let them come in.

　　[Tressa *is seen at the doorway with the* Actors]

PENELOPE: You should eat
A little something first.

ELIZABETH: No, no. Bring them in.

　　[*The* Actors *enter*]
Come in, my masters, let us have a play . . .
Let us have revels and amusements
　　quickly . . .
If ever you played play now. This is my bad
Quarter of an hour.

PENELOPE: Please, please . . .

ELIZABETH: Quick! Quick . . .
You are late, sirs . . . never mind . . . some scene
　　from Falstaff . . .
The one where he lies to the prince about running
　　away
And the prince catches him . . .

HEMMINGS: Where, Majesty?

ELIZABETH: There, anywhere. Come, sit down. Sit
down.

　　[*The* Girls *and the* Fool *group about her*]
Begin, Falstaff! "I call thee coward! I'll see thee
Damned ere I call thee coward!"

FALSTAFF: I call thee coward! I'll see thee damned
ere I call thee coward: but I would give a thousand
pound I could run as fast as thou canst.

PRINCE HENRY: What's the matter?

FALSTAFF: What's the matter! there be four of us
here have ta'en a thousand pound this day morning.

PRINCE HENRY: Where is it, Jack? where is it?

FALSTAFF: Where is it! taken from us it is: a hundred upon poor four of us.

PRINCE HENRY: What, fought ye with them all?

FALSTAFF: All! I know not what ye call all; but if I fought not with fifty of them, I am a bunch of radish: if there were not two or three and fifty upon poor old Jack, then am I no two-legged creature.

ELIZABETH: Come, come . . . this is not to the purpose . . . I had thought this witty . . . [*The* Players *pause*] Play! Play!

PRINCE HENRY: Pray God, you have not murdered some of them.

FALSTAFF: Nay, that's past praying for: I have peppered two of them; two I am sure I have paid, . . . two rogues in buckram suits. I tell thee what, Hal, . . . if I tell thee a lie, spit in my face, call me horse. Thou knowest my old ward . . . here I lay, and thus I bore my point. Four rogues in buckram let drive at me . . .

PRINCE HENRY: What, four? thou saidst but two even now.

FALSTAFF: Four, Hal; I told thee four.

POINS: Ay, ay, he said four.

FALSTAFF: These four came all a-front, and mainly thrust at me. I made me no more ado but took all their seven points in my target, thus.

[*The* Queen *walks from place to place, restlessly*]

PRINCE HENRY: Seven? why, there were but four even now.

FALSTAFF: In buckram?

POINS: Aye, four in buckram suits.

FALSTAFF: Seven, by these hilts, or I am a villain else.

PRINCE HENRY: Pr'ythee, let him alone; we shall have more anon.

FALSTAFF: Dost thou hear me, Hal?

PRINCE HENRY: Ay, and mark thee too, Jack.

ELIZABETH: Aye, aye . . . we are listening . . . Play!

FALSTAFF: Do so, for it is worth the listening to. These nine in buckram that I told thee of . . .

PRINCE HENRY: So, two more already.

FALSTAFF: Began to give me ground: but I followed me close, came in foot and hand; and with a thought seven of the eleven I paid.

PRINCE HENRY: O monstrous! eleven buckram men grown out of two!

FALSTAFF: But, as the devil would have it, three misbegotten knaves in Kendal green came at my back and let drive at me . . . for it was so dark, Hal, that thou couldst not see thy hand.

PRINCE HENRY: These lies are like the father that begets them . . . gross as a mountain, open, palpable. Why, thou clay-brained guts, thou knotty-pated fool, thou whoreson, obscene, greasy tallow-ketch . . .

FALSTAFF: What, art thou mad? art thou mad? is not the truth the truth?

PRINCE HENRY: Why, how couldst thou know these men in Kendal green, when it was so dark thou couldst not see thy hand? come, tell us your reason: what sayest thou to this?

POINS: Come, your reason, Jack . . . your reason.

FALSTAFF: What, upon compulsion? Give you a reason on compulsion! if reasons were as plenty as blackberries I would give no man a reason on compulsion, I.

PRINCE HENRY: I'll be no longer guilty of this sin; this sanguine coward, this bed-presser, this horse back-breaker, this huge hill of flesh . . .

FALSTAFF: Away, you starveling, you elfskin, you dried neat's tongue . . . O for breath to utter what is like thee! . . . you tailor's yard, you sheath, you bowcase, you vile standing-tuck . . .

PRINCE HENRY: Well, breathe awhile, and then to it again: and when thou hast tired thyself in base comparisons, hear me speak but this.

POINS: Mark, Jack.

PRINCE HENRY: We two saw you four set on four; you bound them, and were masters of their wealth. . . . Mark now, how a plain tale shall put you down. . . . Then did we two set on you four; and, with a word, outfaced you from your prize, and have it: yes, and can show it you here in the house: . . . and, Falstaff, you carried your guts away as nimbly, with as quick dexterity, and roared for mercy, and still ran and roared, as ever I heard bull-calf. What a slave art thou, to hack thy sword as thou hast done, and then say it was in fight! What trick, what device, what starting-hole canst thou now find out to hide thee from this open and apparent shame?

POINS: Come, let's hear, Jack; what trick hast thou now?

FALSTAFF: By the Lord, I knew ye as well as He that made ye. Why, hear ye, my masters: was it for me to kill the heir-apparent? Should I turn upon the true prince? Why, thou knowest I am as valiant as Hercules: but beware instinct; the lion will not touch the true prince. Instinct is a great matter; I was a coward on instinct. I shall think the better of myself and thee during my life; I for a valiant lion, and thou for a true prince. But, by the Lord, lads, I am glad you have the money. What, shall we be merry? Shall we have a play extempore?

ELIZABETH: My God, my God . . . can not one forget for a moment?

Who are these strangers? What is this interlude?

Go! Go! It's a vile play and you play it vilely!

Go! By my God, will no one deliver me from this torment? [*The* Players *start out*]

Take your trappings and go!

[*They leave. The chimes strike*]

Again . . . the half-hour . . . [Cecil *enters*]

Yes? [*To* Penelope]

Was I not wise to wait? He has spoken first! Yes?

CECIL: Your Majesty, a citizen rabble has gathered
To protest the execution of Essex. The captain
Begs permission to use your guard. There's no other
Force at hand to disperse them.

ELIZABETH: It's your day, Cecil.
I daresay you know that. The snake-in-the-grass
Endures, and those who are noble, free of soul,
Valiant and admirable . . . they go down in the
    prime,
Always they go down . . .

CECIL: Madam, the guard
Is needed at once . . .

ELIZABETH: Aye . . . the snake-mind is best . . .
One by one you out-last them. To the end
Of time it will be so . . . the rats inherit the earth.
Take my guard. Take it. I thought you brought
    word from . . .
Go, call Lord Essex for me
From his cell . . . and bring him hither! I'll wait
    no longer!

CECIL: Lord Essex is prepared for execution.
The priest has been sent to him.

ELIZABETH: Bring him here, I say,
And now . . . at once!
    [Cecil bows and goes out]
Go out from me, all of you,
All save Penelope. Go quickly, quickly . . .
All . . . [They leave]
Penelope, bring my robe, the one
Laid out . . . [Penelope goes. Elizabeth seats her-
self in the royal chair. Penelope returns with the
robe]
Look here in my face, Penelope. He's so young,
And I'm old, girl, I'm old. It shows in my eyes.
Dear, you're so young. Do not be here when he
    comes . . .
Do you mind? You'll look so young.

PENELOPE: Yes, madam . . . but you . . .
You're beautiful.

ELIZABETH: Beautiful still? But I was once . . .
    I was . . .
You'd not believe it now.

PENELOPE: Oh, yes . . .
You're always beautiful. You've always been.

ELIZABETH: Thank you,
My dear. Go now. He'll come.

PENELOPE: Yes.
    [She goes out to the rear. After a moment
    Essex enters from the left with a Guard. The
    Guard leaves him and steps out. Essex is
    dressed in black and is very pale]

ESSEX: You sent for me?
Or so they said.

ELIZABETH: Yes.

ESSEX: It would have been kinder
To leave me with my thoughts till the axe came
    down
And ended them. You spoil me for death.

ELIZABETH: Are you
So set on dying?

ESSEX: I can't say I care for it.
This blood that beats in us has a way of wanting
To keep right on. But if one is to die
It's well to go straight toward it.

ELIZABETH: You must have known
I never meant you to die.

ESSEX: I am under sentence
From Your Majesty's courts. There's no appeal that
    I know of.
I am found guilty of treason on good evidence,
And cannot deny it. This treason, I believe,
Is punishable with death.

ELIZABETH: God knows I am proud
And bitter, too . . . bitter at you with much cause,
But I have sent for you. I've taken the first step
That way. Do not make me take the next!

ESSEX: The next is to the scaffold. It's only a step
Now, and I've made ready.

ELIZABETH: Aye, you are bitter,
Too; we have let it go late; we've both
Waited for the other. But it was I who spoke
First . . . Will you make me tell you first how
    much
I've longed for you? It's hard for me.

ESSEX: My dear,
You can tell me so gracefully, for you
Have nothing to gain or lose by me . . . but I
Have life and love to gain, and I find it less
Than fitting to speak like a lover, lest you suppose
I do it to save my head.

ELIZABETH: It's true that you never
Loved me, isn't it? You were ambitious, and I
Loved you, and it was the nearest way to power,
And you took the nearest way? No, no . . . one
    moment . . .
This is an hour for truth, if there's ever truth . . .
I'm older than you . . . but a queen; it was natural
You'd flatter me, speak me fair, and I believed you.
I'm sorry I believed you. Sorry for you
More than for me.

ESSEX: Why, yes . . . that's true enough.
Now may I go? This dying sticks in my mind,
And makes me poor company, I fear.

ELIZABETH: It was true.
It was true then?

ESSEX: If you wish to make me tell you
What you well know, how much I used to love you,
How much I have longed for you, very well, I will
    say it.
That's a small victory to win over me now,
But take it with the rest.

ELIZABETH: You did love me?

ESSEX: Yes.

ELIZABETH: And love me still?

ESSEX: Yes. You should know that, I think.

ELIZABETH: You kept my ring. You never sent
    my ring.
I've been waiting for it.

ESSEX: You may have it back.

If you have use for it . . . I had thought to wear it
As far as my grave, but, take it.
　　ELIZABETH: I'd have forgiven
All that had passed, at any hour, day or night,
Since I last saw you. I have waited late at night
Thinking, tonight the ring will come, he will never
Hold out against me so long, but the nights went by
Somehow, like the days, and it never came,
Till the last day came, and here it is the last morning
And the chimes beating out the hours.
　　ESSEX: Dear, if I'd known . . .
But I could not have sent it.
　　ELIZABETH: Why?
　　ESSEX: If I'd tried
To hold you to a promise you could not keep
And you had refused me, I should have died much
　　more
Unhappy than I am now.
　　ELIZABETH: I'd have kept my promise.
I'd keep it now.
　　ESSEX: If I offered you this ring?
　　ELIZABETH: Yes . . . even now.
　　ESSEX: You would pardon me, set me free
Cede back my estates to me, love me as before,
Give me my place in the state?
　　ELIZABETH: All as it was.
　　ESSEX: And what would happen to your throne?
　　ELIZABETH: My throne?
Nothing.
　　ESSEX: Yes, for I'd take it from you.
　　ELIZABETH: Again? You'd play that game again?
　　ESSEX: The games one plays
Are not the games one chooses always. I
Am still a popular idol of a sort.
There are mutterings over my imprisonment,
Even as it is . . . and if you should set me free
And confess your weakness by overlooking treason
And setting me up in power once more, the storm
That broke last time would be nothing to the storm
That would break over you then. As for myself,
I played for power and lost, but if I had
Another chance I think I'd play and win.
　　ELIZABETH: Why do you say this?
　　ESSEX: I say it because it's true.
I have loved you, love you now, but I know myself.
If I were to win you over and take my place
As it used to be, it would gall me. I have a weakness
For being first wherever I am. I refuse
To take pardon from you without warning you
Of this. And when you know it, pardon becomes
Impossible.
　　ELIZABETH: You do this for me?
　　ESSEX: Why, yes,
But not altogether. Partly for England, too.
I've lost conceit of myself a little. A life
In prison's very quiet. It leads to thinking.
You govern England better than I should.
I'd lead her into wars, make a great name,
Perhaps, like Henry Fifth and leave a legacy

Of debts and bloodshed after me. You will leave
Peace, happiness, something secure. A woman gov-
　　erns
Better than a man, being a natural coward.
A coward rules best.
　　ELIZABETH: Still bitter.
　　ESSEX: Perhaps a little.
It's a bitter belief to swallow, but I believe it.
You were right all the time.
　　　　　[The chimes ring three-quarters]
And now, if you'll pardon me,
I have an appointment near-by with a headsman.
He comes sharp on the hour.
　　ELIZABETH: You have an hour yet.
It's but struck five.
　　ESSEX: It struck five some time since.
　　ELIZABETH: It cannot go this way!
　　ESSEX: Aye, but it has.
It has and will. There's no way out. I've thought of
　　it
Every way. Speak frankly. Could you forgive me
And keep your throne?
　　ELIZABETH: No.
　　ESSEX: Are you ready to give
Your crown up to me?
　　ELIZABETH: No. It's all I have. [She rises]
Why, who am I
To stand here paltering with a rebel noble!
I am Elizabeth, daughter of a king,
The queen of England, and you are my subject!
What does this mean, you standing here eye to eye
With me, your liege? You whom I made, and gave
All that you have, you, an upstart, defying
Me to grant pardon, lest you should sweep me from
　　power
And take my place from me? I tell you if Christ his
　　blood
Ran streaming from the heavens for a sign
That I should hold my hand you'd die for this,
You pretender to a throne upon which you have
No claim, you pretender to a heart, who have been
Hollow and heartless and faithless to the end!
　　ESSEX: If we'd met some other how we might have
　　　been happy . . .
But there's been an empire between us! I am to
　　die . . .
Let us say that . . . let us begin with that . . .
For then I can tell you that if there'd been no empire
We could have been great lovers. If even now
You were not queen and I were not pretender,
That god who searches heaven and earth and hell
For two who are perfect lovers, could end his search
With you and me. Remember . . . I am to die . . .
And so I can tell you truly, out of all the earth
That I'm to leave, there's nothing I'm very loath
To leave save you. Yet if I live I'll be
Your death or you'll be mine.
　　ELIZABETH: Give me the ring.
　　ESSEX: No.

ELIZABETH: Give me the ring. I'd rather you killed me
Than I killed you.
    ESSEX: It's better for me as it is
Than that I should live and batten my fame and fortune
On the woman I love. I've thought of it all. It's better
To die young and unblemished than to live long and rule,
And rule not well.
    ELIZABETH: Aye, I should know that.
    ESSEX: Is it not?
    ELIZABETH: Yes.
    ESSEX: Good-by, then.
    ELIZABETH: Oh, then I'm old, I'm old!
I could be young with you, but now I'm old.
I know now how it will be without you. The sun
Will be empty and circle round an empty earth . . .
And I will be queen of emptiness and death. . . .
Why could you not have loved me enough to give me
Your love and let me keep as I was?

    ESSEX: I know not.
I only know I could not. I must go.
    ELIZABETH: [*Frozen*] Yes.
    [*He goes to the door*]
Lord Essex! [*He turns*]
Take my kingdom. It is yours!
    [Essex, *as if not hearing, bows and goes on.*
    Penelope *runs in, meeting him*]
    PENELOPE: My lord! She has forgiven you?
    ESSEX: Good-by, my dear. [*He kisses her*]
    PENELOPE: No, no! She loves you! Go to her.
    [Essex *goes out*]
Run to her! She waits you still! See, if you turn
She waits you still! Dear queen, would you let him go?
He goes to his death! Send, send after him!
    [*The queen lifts her head and shows a face so
    stricken that* Penelope, *who has gone to her,
    says no more. The clock strikes six. Elizabeth
    bows her head on* Penelope's *knees, her hands
    over her ears*]

               CURTAIN

Marc Connelly

(1890– ——)

It would appear that Marc Connelly had to lose one good reputation in order to gain another, greater one. For several years he was well known as George S. Kaufman's collaborator on successful travesties of American life and manners. Connelly, one supposes, could have helped to turn these out indefinitely. Instead, he went his own way and encountered a number of defeats in the theatrical market place. He tasted one victory, however, of the kind that nullifies many reverses and compensates a writer for many disappointments; he wrote a play that is inscribed in the permanent records of the American theatre: *The Green Pastures*. Here he attempted to blend folk imagination with New Testament faith. The results were, not too surprisingly, of a different order of excellence from the results of collaboration with Kaufman.

Connelly was born and spent his boyhood in McKeesport, Pennsylvania. After some higher education, he began writing a daily column of quips for a newspaper in Pittsburgh. His thoughts turned to the theatre, and he inevitably gravitated to New York. He remained there in spite of the failure of his first stage venture, the musical play *The Amber Princess* (1916), to which he contributed the lyrics. After some lean years of free-lancing and play doctoring, he had the good fortune in 1921 to form a partnership with another immigrant from Pennsylvania, George S. Kaufman, then editing the drama page of the *New York Times*. The two men took for their first subject "Dulcinea," a bromidic female celebrated in Franklin P. Adams' famous *New York World* column. The result was the comedy *Dulcy*, about a dull-witted, interfering woman who was to be a symbol of feminine ineptitude for an entire generation. Later in 1921, Kaufman and Connelly won a second hearing on Broadway with the warm comedy of middle-class home life *To the Ladies*, in which the authors were more complimentary to womanhood. A year later, they made theatrical history by turning out the first of Broadway's numerous satires on Hollywood, *Merton of the Movies,* and in 1924, they reached the peak of their partnership with the clever expressionistic satire *Beggar on Horseback*. Connelly must have had a larger share than usual in the writing of the latter play, since it embodies his characteristic qualities of comic fantastication. A devastating dream play based on a young artist's fear that marriage would doom him to the treadmill of big business, *Beggar on Horseback* was one of the best products of the then fashionable Greenwich Village revolt against the machine age. With this play, however, the Kaufman-Connelly partnership ended.

Connelly started the next phase of his career auspiciously enough, when his independent talent for tenderness and fancy asserted itself in *The Wisdom Tooth* (1926). But this comedy was followed by reverses until he had the good fortune to write *The Green Pastures* (1930), a play based on Roark Bradford's collection of more or less genuine Negro folk tales, *Ol' Man Adam an' His Chillun*. The play was brilliantly staged against expressive settings by Robert Edmond Jones with an all-Negro cast, among whom Richard Harrison distinguished himself with a portrayal of "de Lawd" remarkably moving in its simplicity and dignity.

Negro life and manners had interested serious dramatists for a decade, and some of the playwriting inspired by regional literature and theatre was of a high order. The romantic folk drama was already well represented on Broadway by Dorothy and Du Bose Heyward's *Porgy* (1927). For Connelly, however, the regional background was a matter of secondary interest. He sublimated folk drama into religious drama, concluding a play enlivened by scenes such as the celestial fish fry with a mystic vision of the crucifixion.

The Green Pastures is unique: it cannot be placed in any existing classification without some reservations. The Catholic critic Richard Dana Skinner accused Connelly of "sinning against real simplicity," and it is indeed questionable whether the playwright did not veer too far from either folk or religious drama in some details. Is there no discrepancy between the "Harlem" scene and the spirit of the play? Is the play entirely free from a spirit of condescension toward primitive folk and their notions? Yet one cannot overlook the tremendous fascination the play exerted for years after it opened on Broadway. It seemed the culmination of everything we considered a movement toward folk drama for at least a decade, and it was also the only religious drama anyone had succeeded in making tolerable to the American public since the vogue of Charles Rann Kennedy's old-fashioned morality play *The Servant in the House*.

BIBLIOGRAPHY: Burns Mantle, *Contemporary American Playwrights* (pp. 50–53), 1938; Stark Young, *Immortal Shadows* (pp. 119–123), 1948.

THE GREEN PASTURES

By Marc Connelly

CHARACTERS

MR. DESHEE, *the Preacher*	ZEBA	FLATFOOT
MYRTLE	CAIN THE SIXTH	HAM
FIRST BOY	BOY GAMBLER	JAPHETH
SECOND BOY	GENERAL	FIRST CLEANER
FIRST COOK	HEAD MAGICIAN	SECOND CLEANER
A VOICE	FIRST WIZARD	ABRAHAM
SECOND COOK	SECOND WIZARD	ISAAC
FIRST MAN ANGEL	JOSHUA	JACOB
FIRST MAMMY ANGEL	FIRST SCOUT	MOSES
A STOUT ANGEL	MASTER OF CEREMONIES	ZIPPORAH
A SLENDER ANGEL	FIRST GAMBLER	AARON
ARCHANGEL	SECOND GAMBLER	A CANDIDATE MAGICIAN
GABRIEL	VOICE IN SHANTY	PHARAOH
GOD	NOAH	KING OF BABYLON
CHOIR LEADER	NOAH'S WIFE	PROPHET
CUSTARD MAKER	SHEM	HIGH PRIEST
ADAM	FIRST WOMAN	CORPORAL
EVE	SECOND WOMAN	HEZDREL
CAIN	THIRD WOMAN	SECOND OFFICER
CAIN'S GIRL	FIRST MAN	

SCENES

PART I

1. THE SUNDAY SCHOOL
2. A FISH FRY
3. A GARDEN
4. OUTSIDE THE GARDEN
5. A ROADSIDE
6. A PRIVATE OFFICE
7. ANOTHER ROADSIDE AND A HOUSE
8. A HOUSE
9. A HILLSIDE
10. A MOUNTAIN TOP

PART II

1. THE PRIVATE OFFICE
2. THE MOUTH OF A CAVE
3. A THRONE ROOM
4. THE FOOT OF A MOUNTAIN
5. A CABARET
6. THE PRIVATE OFFICE
7. OUTSIDE A TEMPLE
8. ANOTHER FISH FRY

AUTHOR'S NOTE

The Green Pastures is an attempt to present certain aspects of a living religion in the terms of its believers. The religion is that of thousands of Negroes in the deep South. With terrific spiritual hunger and the greatest humility, these untutored black Christians—many of whom cannot even read the book which is the treasure house of their faith—have adapted the contents of the Bible to the consistencies of their everyday lives.

Unburdened by the differences of more educated theologians, they accept the Old Testament as a chronicle of wonders which happened to people like themselves in vague but actual places, and of rules of conduct, true acceptance of which will lead them to a tangible, three-dimensional Heaven. In this Heaven, if one has been born in a district where fish fries are popular, the angels do have magnificent fish fries through an eternity somewhat resembling a series of earthly holidays. The Lord Jehovah will be the promised comforter, a just but compassionate patriarch, the summation of all the virtues. His follower has observed in the human beings about him. The Lord may look like the Reverend Mr.

Dubois, as our Sunday-School teacher speculates in the play, or he may resemble another believer's own grandfather. In any event, His face will be familiar to the one who has come for his reward.

The author is indebted to Mr. Roark Bradford, whose retelling of several of the Old Testament stories in *Ol' Man Adam an' His Chillun* first stimulated his interest in this point of view.

One need not blame a hazy memory of the Bible for the failure to recall the characters of Hezdrel, Zeba and others in the play. They are the author's apocrypha, but he believes persons much like them have figured in the meditations of some of the old Negro preachers, whose simple faith he has tried to translate into a play.

PART I. SCENE I.

A corner in a Negro church.
Ten Children *and an elderly* Preacher.

The costumes are those that might be seen in any lower Louisiana town at Sunday-School time. As the curtain rises, Mr. Deshee, *the preacher, is reading from a Bible. The* Children *are listening with varied degrees of interest. Three or four are wide-eyed in their attention. Two or three are obviously puzzled, but interested, and the smallest ones are engaged in more physical concerns. One is playing with a little doll, and another runs his finger on all angles of his chair.*

DESHEE: "An' Adam lived a hundred and thirty years, an' begat a son in his own likeness, after his image; an' called his name Seth. An' de days of Adam, after he had begotten Seth, were eight hundred years! An' he begat sons an' daughters; an' all de days dat Adam lived were nine hundred an' thirty years; an' he died. An' Seth lived a hundred an' five years an' begat Enos; an' Seth lived after he begat Enos eight hundred an' seven years an' begat sons and daughters. An' all de days of Seth were nine hundred and twelve years; an' he died." An' it go like dat till we come to Enoch an' de Book say: "An' Enoch lived sixty an' five years and begat Methuselah." Den it say: "An' all de days of Methuselah were nine hund'ed an' sixty an' nine years an' he died." An' dat was de oldest man dat ever was. Dat's why we call ol' Mr. Gurney's mammy ol' Mrs. Methuselah, caize she's so ol'. Den a little later it tell about another member of de fam'ly. His name was Noah. Maybe some of you know about him already. I'm gonter tell you all about him next Sunday. Anyway dat's de meat an' substance of de first five chapters of Genesis. Now, how you think you gonter like de Bible?

MYRTLE: I think it's jest wonderful, Mr. Deshee. I cain't understand any of it.

FIRST BOY: Why did dey live so long, Mr. Deshee?

DESHEE: Why? Caize dat was de way God felt.

SECOND BOY: Dat made Adam away back.

DESHEE: Yes, he certainly 'way back by de time Noah come along. Want to ask me any mo' questions?

SECOND BOY: What de worl' look like when de Lawd begin, Mr. Deshee?

DESHEE: How yo' mean what it look like?

MYRTLE: Carlisle mean who was in N'Orleans den.

DESHEE: Dey wasn't nobody in N'Orleans on 'count dey wasn't any N'Orleans. Dat's de whole idea I tol' you at de end of de first Chapter. Yo' got to git yo' minds fixed. Dey wasn't any Rampart Street. Dey wasn't any Canal Street. Dey wasn't any Louisiana. Dey wasn't nothin' on de earth at all caize fo' de reason dey wasn't any earth.

MYRTLE: Yes, but what Carlisle wanter know is—

DESHEE: [*Interrupting and addressing little boy who has been playing with his chair and paying no attention*] Now, Randolph, if you don't listen, how yo' gonter grow up and be a good man? Yo' wanter grow up an' be a transgressor?

LITTE BOY: [*Frightened*] No.

DESHEE: You tell yo' mammy yo' sister got to come wid you next time. She kin git things done in time to bring you to de school. You content yo'self. [*The little boy straightens up in his chair*] Now, what do Carlisle want to know?

SECOND BOY: How He decide He want de worl' to be right yere and how He git de idea He wanted it?

MYRTLE: Caize de Book say, don't it, Mr. Deshee?

DESHEE: De Book say, but at de same time dat's a good question. I remember when I was a little boy de same thing recurred to me. An' ol' Mr. Dubois, he was a wonderful preacher at New Hope Chapel over in East Gretna, he said: "De answer is dat de Book ain't got time to go into all de details." And he was right. You know sometimes I think de Lawd expects us to figure out a few things for ourselves. We know dat at one time dey wasn't anything except Heaven. We don't know jest where it was but we know it was dere. Maybe it was everywhere. Den one day de Lawd got the idea He'd like to make some places. He made de sun and de moon, de stars. An' He made de earth.

MYRTLE: Who was aroun' den, nothin' but angels?

DESHEE: I suppose so.

FIRST BOY: What was de angels doin' up dere?

DESHEE: I suppose dey jest flew aroun' and had a good time. Dey wasn't no sin, so dey musta had a good time.

FIRST BOY: Did dey have picnics?

DESHEE: Sho, dey had the nicest kind of picnics. Dey probably had fish fries, wid b'iled custard and ten-cent seegars for de adults. God gives us humans lotsa ideas about havin' good times. Maybe dey were things he'd seen de angels do. Yes, sir, I bet dey had a fish fry every week.

MYRTLE: Did dey have Sunday School, too?

DESHEE: Yes, dey musta had Sunday School for de cherubs.

MYRTLE: What did God look like, Mr. Deshee?

DESHEE: Well, nobody knows exactly what God looked like. But when I was a little boy I used to imagine dat He looked like de Reverend Dubois. He was de finest-looking ol' man I ever knew. Yes, I used to bet de Lawd looked exactly like Mr. Dubois in de days when He walked de earth in de shape of a natchel man.

MYRTLE: When was dat, Mr. Deshee?

DESHEE: Why, when He was gettin' things started down heah. When he talked to Adam and Eve and Noah and Moses and all dem. He made mighty men in dem days. But aldo dey was awful mighty dey always knew dat He was beyond dem all. Pretty near one o'clock, time fo' you chillun to go home to dinner, but before I let you go I wan' you to go over wid me de main facts of de first lesson. What's de name of de book?

CHILDREN: Genesis.

DESHEE: Dat's right. And what's de other name?

CHILDREN: First Book of Moses.

DESHEE: Da't right. And dis yere's Chapter One. [*The lights begin to dim*] "In de beginnin' God created de heaven and de earth. An' de earth was widout form an' void. An' de darkness was upon de face of de deep."

SCENE II.

In the darkness many voices are heard singing "Rise, Shine, Give God the Glory." They sing it gaily and rapidly. The lights go up as the second verse ends. The chorus is being sung diminuendo by a mixed company of angels. That is, they are angels in that they wear brightly colored robes and have wings protruding from their backs. Otherwise they look and act like a company of happy Negroes at a fish fry. The scene itself is a pre-Creation Heaven with compromises.

In the distance is an unbroken stretch of blue sky. Companionable varicolored clouds billow down to the floor of the stage and roll overhead to the branches of a live oak tree which is up left. The tree is leafy and dripping with Spanish moss, and with the clouds makes a frame for the scene. In the cool shade of the tree are the usual appurtenances of a fish fry; a large kettle of hot fat set on two small parallel logs, with a fire going underneath, and a large rustic table formed by driving four stakes into the ground and placing planks on top of the small connecting boards. On the table are piles of biscuits and corn bread and the cooked fish in dish pans. There are one or two fairly large cedar or crock "churns" containing boiled custard, which looks like milk. There is a gourd dipper beside the churns and several glasses and cups of various sizes and shapes from which the custard is drunk.

The principal singers are marching two by two in a small area at the R. of the stage. Two Mammy Angels are attending to the frying beside the kettle. Behind the table a Man Angel is skinning fish and passing them to the cooks. Another is ladling out the custard. A Mammy Angel is putting fish on bread for a brood of cherubs, and during the first scene they seat themselves on a grassy bank upstage. Another Mammy Angel is clapping her hands disapprovingly and beckoning a laughing Boy Cherub down from a cloud a little out of her reach.

Another Mammy Angel is solicitously slapping the back of a Girl Cherub who has a large fish sandwich in her hand and a bone in her throat. There is much movement about the table, and during the first few minutes several individuals go up to the table to help themselves to the food and drink. Many of the Women Angels wear hats and a few of the Men are smoking cigars. A large boxful is on

the table. There is much laughter and chatter as the music softens, but continues during the early part of the action. The following short scenes are played almost simultaneously.

SECOND COOK: [*At kettle, calling off*] Hurry up, Cajey. Dis yere fat's cryin' fo' mo' feesh.

A VOICE: [*Off stage*] We comin', fas' we kin. Dey got to be ketched, ain't dey? We cain't say, "C'm'on, little fish. C'm'on an' git fried," kin we?

SECOND COOK: [*At table*] De trouble is de mens is all worm fishin'.

FIRST MAN ANGEL: [*At table*] Whut dif'runce do it make? Yo' all de time got to make out like somebody's doin' somethin' de wrong way.

SECOND COOK: [*Near table*] I s'pose you got de per'fec' way fo' makin' bait.

FIRST MAN ANGEL: I ain't sayin' dat. I is sayin' whut's wrong wid worm fishin'.

SECOND COOK: Whut's wrong wid worm fishin'? Ever'thing, dat's all. Dey's only one good way fo' catfishin', and dat's minny fishin'. Anybody know dat.

FIRST MAN ANGEL: Well, it jest so happen dat minny fishin' is de doggondest fool way of fishin' dey is. You kin try minny fishin' to de cows come home an' all you catch'll be de backache. De trouble wid you, sister, is you jest got minny fishin' on de brain.

SECOND COOK: Go right on, loud mouf. You tell me de news. My, my! You jest de wisest person in de worl'. First you, den de Lawd God.

FIRST MAN ANGEL: [*To the custard ladler*] You cain't tell dem nothin'. [*Walks away to the custard churn*] Does you try to 'splain some simple fac' dey git man-deaf.

FIRST MAMMY ANGEL: [*To Cherub on the cloud*] Now, you heerd me. [*The Cherub assumes several mocking poses, as she speaks*] You fly down yere. You wanter be put down in de sin book? [*She goes to the table, gets a drink for herself and points out the Cherub to one of the men behind the table*] Dat baby must got imp blood in him he so vexin'. [*She returns to her position under the cloud*] You want me to fly up dere an' slap you down? Now, I tol' you.

[*The Cherub starts to come down*]

STOUT ANGEL: [*To the Cherub with a bone in her throat*] I tol' you you was too little fo' catfish. What you wanter git a bone in yo' froat fo'?

[*She slaps the Cherub's back*]

SLENDER ANGEL: [*Leisurely eating a sandwich as she watches the back-slapping*] What de trouble wid Leonetta?

STOUT ANGEL: She got a catfish bone down her froat. [*To the Cherub*] Doggone, I tol' you to eat grinnel instead.

SLENDER ANGEL: Ef'n she do git all dat et, she gonter have a belly-ache.

STOUT ANGEL: Ain't I tol' her dat? [*To Cherub*]

Come on now; let go dat bone. [*She slaps* Cherub's *back again. The bone is dislodged and the* Cherub *grins her relief*] Dat's good.

SLENDER ANGEL: [*Comfortingly*] Now she all right.

STOUT ANGEL: Go on an' play wid yo' cousins. [*The* Cherub *joins the* Cherubs *sitting on the embankment. The concurrency of scenes ends here*] I ain't see you lately, Lily. How you been?

SLENDER ANGEL: Me, I'm fine. I been visitin' my mammy. She waitin' on de welcome table over by de throne of grace.

STOUT ANGEL: She always was pretty holy.

SLENDER ANGEL: Yes, ma'am. She like it dere. I guess de Lawd's took quite a fancy to her.

STOUT ANGEL: Well, dat's natural. I declare yo' mammy one of de finest lady angels I know.

SLENDER ANGEL: She claim you best one she know.

STOUT ANGEL: Well, when you come right down to it, I suppose we is all pretty near perfec'.

SLENDER ANGEL: Yes, ma'am. Why is dat, Mis' Jenny?

STOUT ANGEL: I s'pose it's caize de Lawd He don' 'low us 'sociatin' wid de devil any mo' so dat dey cain' be no mo' sinnin'.

SLENDER ANGEL: Po' ol' Satan. Whutevah become of him?

STOUT ANGEL: De Lawd put him some place, I s'pose.

SLENDER ANGEL: But dey ain't any place but Heaven, is dey?

STOUT ANGEL: De Lawd could make a place, couldn't He?

SLENDER ANGEL: Dat's de truth. Dey's one thing confuses me though.

STOUT ANGEL: What's dat?

SLENDER ANGEL: I do a great deal of travelin' an' I ain't never come across any place but Heaven anywhere. So if de Lawd kick Satan out of Heaven jest whereat did he go? Dat's my question.

STOUT ANGEL: You bettah let de Lawd keep His own secrets, Lily. De way things is goin' now dey ain't been no sinnin' since dey give dat scamp a kick in de pants. Nowadays Heaven's free of sin an' if a lady wants a little constitutional she kin fly 'til she wing-weary widout gittin' insulted.

SLENDER ANGEL: I was jest a baby when Satan lef'. I don't even 'member what he look like.

STOUT ANGEL: He was jest right fo' a devil. [*An* Archangel *enters. He is older than the others and wears a white beard. His clothing is much darker than that of the others and his wings a trifle more imposing*] Good mo'nin', Archangel.

[*Others say good morning*]

ARCHANGEL: Good mo'nin', folks. I wonder kin I interrup' de fish fry an' give out de Sunday-School cyards? [*Cries of "Suttingly!" "Mah goodness, yes"—etc. The marching* Choir *stops*] You kin keep singin' if you want to. Why don' you sing "When de Saints Come Marchin' In"? Seem to me I ain't

heard dat lately. [*The* Choir *begins "When de Saints Come Marchin' In," rather softly, but does not resume the marching. The* Archangel *looks off left*] All right, bring 'em yere [*A prim-looking* Woman Teacher-Angel *enters, shepherding ten* Boy *and* Girl Cherubs. *The* Teacher *carries ten beribboned diplomas, which she gives to the* Archangel. *The* Cherubs *are dressed in stiffly starched white suits and dresses, the little girls having enormous ribbons at the backs of their dresses and smaller ones in their hair and on the tips of their wings. They line up in front of the* Archangel *and receive the attention of the rest of the company. The* Choir *sings through the ceremony*] Now den, cherubs, why is you yere?

CHILDREN: Because we so good.

ARCHANGEL: Dat's right. Now who de big boss?

CHILDREN: Our dear Lawd.

ARCHANGEL: Dat's right. When you all grow up what you gonter be?

CHILDREN: Holy angels at de throne of grace.

ARCHANGEL: Dat's right. Now, you passed yo' 'zaminations and it gives me great pleasure to hand out de cyards for de whole class. Gineeva Chaproe. [*The* First Girl Cherub *goes to him and gets her diploma. The* Choir *sings loudly and resumes marching, as the* Archangel *calls out another name—and presents diplomas*] Corey Moulter. [*Second Girl* Cherub *gets her diploma*] Nootzie Winebush. [*Third Girl Cherub*] Harriet Prancy. [*Fourth Girl Cherub*] I guess you is Brozain Stew't. [*He gives the* Fifth Girl Cherub *the paper. Each of the presentations has been accompanied by handclapping from the bystanders*] Now you boys know yo' own names. Suppose you come yere and help me git dese 'sorted right?

[Boy Cherubs *gather about him and receive their diplomas. The little* Girls *have scattered about the stage, joining groups of the* Adult Angels. *The angel* Gabriel *enters. He is bigger and more elaborately winged than even the* Archangel, *but he is also much younger and beardless. His costume is less conventional than that of the other men, resembling more the* Gabriel *of the Doré drawings. His appearance causes a flutter among the others. They stop their chattering with the* Children. *The* Choir *stops as three or four audible whispers of "Gabriel!" are heard. In a moment the heavenly company is all attention*]

GABRIEL: [*Lifting his hand*] Gangway! Gangway for de Lawd God Jehovah!

[*There is a reverent hush and* God *enters. He is the tallest and biggest of them all. He wears a white shirt with a white bow tie, a long Prince Albert coat of black alpaca, black trousers and congress gaiters. He looks at the assemblage. There is a pause. He speaks in a rich, bass voice*]

GOD: Is you been baptized?

OTHERS: [*Chanting*] Certainly, Lawd.

GOD: Is you been baptized?

OTHERS: Certainly, Lawd.

GOD: [*With the beginning of musical notation*] Is you been baptized?

OTHERS: [*Now half-singing*] Certainly, Lawd. Certainly, certainly, certainly, Lawd.

[*They sing the last two verses with equivalent part division*]

Is you been redeemed?

Certainly, Lawd.

Is you been redeemed?

Certainly, Lawd.

Is you been redeemed?

Certainly, Lawd. Certainly, certainly, certainly, Lawd.

Do you bow mighty low?

Certainly, Lawd.

Do you bow mighty low?

Certainly, Lawd.

Do you bow mighty low?

Certainly, Lawd. Certainly, certainly, certainly, Lawd.

[*As the last response ends all heads are bowed. God looks at them for a moment; then lifts His hand*]

GOD: Let de fish fry proceed.

[*Everyone rises. The Angels relax and resume their inaudible conversations. The activity behind the table and about the cauldron is resumed. Some of the Choir members cross to the table and get sandwiches and cups of the boiled custard. Three or four of the Children in the Sunday-School class and the girl who had the bone in her throat affectionately group themselves about God as He speaks with the Archangel. He pats their heads, they hang to His coat-tails, etc.*]

ARCHANGEL: Good mo'nin', Lawd.

GOD: Good mo'nin', Deacon. You lookin' pretty spry.

ACHANGEL: I cain' complain. We just been givin' out cyards to de chillun.

GOD: Dat's good.

[*A small Cherub, his feet braced against one of God's shoes, is using God's coat-tail as a trapeze. One of the Cooks offers a fish sandwich which God politely declines*]

FIRST MAMMY ANGEL: Now, you leave go de Lawd's coat, Herman. You heah me?

GOD: Dat's all right, sister. He jest playin'.

FIRST MAMMY ANGEL: He playin' too rough.

[*God picks up the Cherub and spanks him good-naturedly. The Cherub squeals with delight and runs to his mother. Gabriel advances to God with a glass of the custard*]

GABRIEL: Little b'iled custud, Lawd?

GOD: Thank you very kindly. Dis looks nice.

CUSTARD MAKER: [*Offering a box*] Ten-cent seegar, Lawd?

GOD: [*Taking it*] Thank you, thank you. How de fish fry goin'? [Ad. lib. *cries of "O.K., Lawd," "Fine an' dandy, Lawd," "De best one yit, Lawd,"* etc. *To the* Choir] How you shouters gittin' on?

CHOIR LEADER: We been marchin' and singin' de whole mo'nin'.

GOD: I heerd you. You gittin' better all de time. You gittin' as good as de one at de throne. Why don' you give us one dem ol' time jump-ups?

CHOIR LEADER: Anythin' you say, Lawd. [*To the Others*] "So High!"

[*The Choir begins to sing "So High You Can't Get Over It." They sing softly, but do not march. An Angel offers his cigar to God from which He can light His own*]

GOD: No, thanks. I'm gonter save dis a bit.

[*He puts His cigar in His pocket and listens to the singers a moment. Then He sips His custard. After the second sip, a look of displeasure comes on His face*]

GABRIEL: What's de matter, Lawd?

GOD: [*Sipping again*] I ain't jest sure, yit. Dey's something 'bout dis custahd.

[*Takes another sip*]

CUSTARD MAKER: Ain't it all right, Lawd?

GOD: It don't seem seasoned jest right. You make it?

CUSTARD MAKER: Yes, Lawd. I put everythin' in it like I allus do. It's supposed to be perfec'.

GOD: Yeah. I kin taste de eggs and de cream and de sugar. [*Suddenly*] I know what it is. It needs jest a little bit mo' firmament.

CUSTARD MAKER: Dey's firmament in it, Lawd.

GOD: Maybe, but it ain't enough.

CUSTARD MAKER: It's all we had, Lawd. Dey ain't a drap in de jug.

GOD: Dat's all right. I'll jest r'ar back an' pass a miracle. [Choir *stops singing*] Let it be some firmament! An' when I say let it be some firmament, I don't want jest a little bitty dab o' firmament, caize I'm sick an' tired of runnin' out of it when we need it. Let it be a whole mess of firmament! [*The stage has become misty until* God *and the heavenly company are obscured. As He finishes the speech there is a burst of thunder. As the stage grows darker*] Dat's de way I like it.

[*Murmurs from the others: "Dat's a lot of firmament!" "Look to me like He created rain,"* etc.]

FIRST MAMMY ANGEL: [*When the stage is dark*] Now, look, Lawd, dat's too much firmament. De cherubs is gettin' all wet.

SECOND MAMMY ANGEL: Look at my Carlotta, Lawd. She's soaked to de skin. Dat's *plenty* too much firmament.

GOD: Well, 'co'se we don't want the chillun to ketch cold. Can't you dreen it off?

GABRIEL: Dey's no place to dreen it, Lawd.

FIRST MAMMY ANGEL: Why don't we jest take de babies home, Lawd?

GOD: No, I don' wanta bust up de fish fry. You angels keep quiet an I'll pass another miracle. Dat's always de trouble wid miracles. When you pass one you always gotta r'ar back an' pass another. [*There is a hush*] Let dere be a place to dreen off dis firmament. Let dere be mountains and valleys an' let dere be oceans an' lakes. An' let dere be rivers and bayous to dreen it off in, too. As a matter of fac' let dere be de earth. An' when dat's done let dere be de sun, an' let it come out and dry my cherubs' wings.

[*The lights go up until the stage is bathed in sunlight. On the embankment upstage there is now a waist-high wrought-iron railing such as one sees on the galleries of houses in the French Quarter of New Orleans. The* Cherubs *are being examined by their parents and there is an* ad lib. *murmur of, "You all right, honey?" "You feel better now, Albert?" "Now you all dry, Vangy?" until the* Archangel, *who has been gazing in awe at the railing, drowns them out*]

ARCHANGEL: Look yere!

[*There is a rush to the embankment accompanied by exclamations, "My goodness!" "What's dis?" "I declah!" etc.* Gabriel *towers above the group on the middle of the embankment.* God *is wrapped in thought, facing the audience. The* Choir *resumes singing "So High You Can't Get Over It" softly. The babbling at the balustrade dies away as the people lean over the railing.* Gabriel *turns and faces* God *indicating the earth below the railing with his left hand*]

GABRIEL: Do you see it. Lawd?

GOD: [*Quietly, without turning His head upstage*] Yes, Gabriel.

GABRIEL: Looks mighty nice, Lawd.

GOD: Yes.

[Gabriel *turns and looks over the railing*]

GABRIEL: [*Gazing down*] Yes, suh. Dat'd make mighty nice farming country. Jest look at dat south forty over dere. You ain't going to let dat go to waste is you, Lawd? Dat would be a pity an' a shame.

GOD: [*Not turning*] It's a good earth. [God *turns, room is made for Him beside* Gabriel *on the embankment*] Yes. I ought to have somebody to enjoy it. [*He turns, facing the audience. The others, save for the* Choir *who are lined up in two rows of six on an angle up right, continue to look over the embankment*] Gabriel. [God *steps down from the embankment two paces*]

GABRIEL: [*Joining him*] Yes, Lawd.

GOD: Gabriel, I'm goin' down dere.

GABRIEL: Yes, Lawd.

GOD: I want you to be my working boss yere while I'm gone.

GABRIEL: Yes, Lawd.

GOD: You know dat matter of dem two stars?

GABRIEL: Yes, Lawd.

GOD: Git dat fixed up! You know dat sparrow dat fell a little while ago? Tend to dat, too.

GABRIEL: Yes, Lawd.

GOD: I guess dat's about all. I'll be back Saddy [*To the* Choir] Quiet, angels. [*The* Choir *stops singing. Those on the embankment circle downstage.* God *goes to embankment. Turns and faces the company*] I'm gonter pass one more miracle. You all gonter help me an' not make a soun' caize it's one of the most impo'tant miracles of all. [*Nobody moves.* God *turns, facing the sky, and raises His arms above His head*] Let dere be man.

[*There is growing roll of thunder as stage grows dark. The* Choir *bursts into "Hallelujah," and continues until the lights go up on the next scene*]

SCENE III.

Enclosing the stage is a heterogeneous cluster of cottonwood, camphor, live oak, and sycamore trees, youpon and turkey berry bushes, with their purple and red berries, sprays of fern-like indigo fiera and splashes of various Louisiana flowers. In the middle of the stage, disclosed when the mistiness at rise grows into warm sunlight, stands Adam.

He is a puzzled man of thirty, of medium height, dressed in the clothing of the average field hand. He is bare-headed. In the distance can be heard the Choir *continuing "Bright Mansions Above." A bird begins to sing.* Adam *smiles and turns to look at the source of this novel sound. He senses his strength and raises his forearms, his fists clenched. With his left hand he carefully touches the muscles of his upper right arm. He smiles again, realizing his power. He looks at his feet which are stretched wide apart. He stamps once or twice and now almost laughs in his enjoyment. Other birds begin trilling and* Adam *glances up joyfully toward the foliage.* God *enters.*

GOD: Good mo'nin', Son.

ADAM: [*With a little awe*] Good mo'nin', Lawd.

GOD: What's yo' name, Son?

ADAM: Adam.

GOD: Adam which?

ADAM: [*Frankly, after a moment's puzzled groping*] Jest Adam, Lawd.

GOD: Well, Adam, how dey treatin' you? How's things goin'?

ADAM: Well, Lawd, you know it's kind of a new line of wukk.

GOD: You'll soon get the hang of it. You know yo' kind of a new style with me.

ADAM: Oh, I guess I'm gonter make out all right soon as I learn de ropes.

GOD: Yes, I guess you will. Yo' a nice job.

ADAM: Yes, Lawd.

GOD: Dey's jest one little thing de matter with you. Did you notice it?

ADAM: Well, now you mentioned it, Lawd, I kind of thought dey was somethin' wrong.

GOD: Yes, suh, you ain't quite right. Adam, you need a family. De reason for dat is in yo' heart you is a family man. [*Flicking the ash off His cigar*] I'd say dat was de main trouble at de moment.

ADAM: [*Smiling*] Yes, suh. [*His smile fades and he is puzzled again*] At de same time—dey's one thing puzzlin' me, Lawd. Could I ask you a question?

GOD: Why certainly, Adam.

ADAM: Lawd, jest what *is* a family?

GOD: I'm gonter show you. [*Indicates a spot*] Jest lie down here, Adam. Make out like you was goin' to slumber.

ADAM: [*Gently*] Yes, Lawd.

[*He lies down.* God *stands beside him and as He raises His arms above His head the lights go down. In the darkness* God *speaks*]

GOD: Eve. [*Lights go up.* Eve *is standing beside* Adam. *She is about twenty-six, and quite pretty. She is dressed like a country girl. Her gingham dress is quite new and clean.* God *is now at the other side of the stage, looking at them critically.* Eve *looks at* Adam *in timid wonder and slowly turns her head until she meets the glance of* God. Adam *stands beside* Eve. *They gaze at each other for a moment.* God *smiles*] Now you all right, Eve. [Adam *and* Eve *face Him*] Now I'll tell you what I'm gonter do. I'm gonter put you in charge here. I'm gonter give you de run of dis whole garden. Eve, you take care of dis man, an' Adam, you take care of dis woman. You belong to each other. I don' want you to try to do much caize yo' both kind of experiment wid me an' I ain't sho' whether yo' could make it. You two jest enjoy yo'self. Drink de water from de little brooks an' de wine from de grapes an' de berries, an' eat de food dat's hangin' for you in de trees. [*He pauses, startled by a painful thought*] Dat is, in all but one tree. [*He pauses. Then, not looking at them*] You know what I mean, my children?

ADAM *and* EVE: Yes, Lawd.

[*They slowly turn their heads left, toward the branches of an offstage tree. Then they look back at* God]

ADAM: Thank you, Lawd.

EVE: Thank you, Lawd.

GOD: I gotter be gittin' along now. I got a hund'ed thousan' things to do 'fo' you take yo' nex' breath. Enjoy yo'selves——

[God *exits.* Adam *and* Eve *stand looking after Him for a moment, then each looks down and watches their hands meet and clasp. After a moment they lift their heads slowly until they are again gazing at the tree*]

EVE: Adam.

ADAM: [*Looking at the tree, almost in terror*] What?

EVE: [*Softly as she too continues to look at the tree*] Adam.

[*The* Choir *begins singing "Turn You Round" and as the lights go down the* Choir *continues until there is blackness. The* Choir *suddenly stops. The following scene is played in the darkness*]

MR. DESHEE'S VOICE: Now, I s'pose you chillun know what happened after God made Adam 'n' Eve. Do you?

FIRST GIRL'S VOICE: I know, Mr. Deshee.

MR. DESHEE'S VOICE: Jest a minute, Randolph. Didn't I tell you you gotta tell yo' mammy let yo' sister bring you? Carlisle, take way dat truck he's eatin'. You sit by him, see kin you keep him quiet. Now, den, Myrtle, what happened?

FIRST GIRL'S VOICE: Why den dey ate de fo'bidden fruit and den dey got driv' out de Garden.

MR. DESHEE'S VOICE: An' den what happened?

FIRST GIRL'S VOICE: Den dey felt ver' bad.

MR. DESHEE'S VOICE: I don' mean how dey feel, I mean how dey do. Do dey have any children or anything like dat?

FIRST GIRL'S VOICE: Oh, yes, suh, dey have Cain 'n' Abel.

MR. DESHEE'S VOICE: Dat's right, dey have Cain 'n' Abel.

BOY'S VOICE: Dat was a long time after dey got married, wasn't it, Mr. Deshee? My mammy say it was a hund'ed years.

MR. DESHEE'S VOICE: Well, nobody kin be so sure. As I tol' you befo' dey was jest beginnin' to be able to tell de time an' nobody was any too sure 'bout anythin' even den. So de bes' thing to do is jest realize dat de thing happened an' don't bother 'bout how many years it was. Jest remember what I told you about it gittin' dark when you go to sleep an' it bein' light when you wake up. Dat's de way time went by in dem days. One thing we do know an' dat was dis boy Cain was a mean rascal.

[*The lights go up on the next scene*]

SCENE IV.

A Roadside.

Cain, *a husky young Negro, stands over the body of the dead* Abel. *Both are dressed as laborers.* Cain *is looking at the body in awe, a rock in his right hand.* God *enters.*

GOD: Cain, look what you done to Abel.

CAIN: Lawd, I was min'in' my own business and he come monkeyin' aroun' wit' me. I was wukkin' in de fiel' an' he was sittin' in de shade of de tree. He say "Me, I'd be skeered to git out in dis hot sun. I be 'fraid my brains git cooked. Co'se you ain't got no brains so you ain' in no danger." An' so I up and flang de rock. If it miss 'im all right, an' if it hit 'im all right. Dat's de way I feel.

GOD: All right, but I'm yere to tell you dat's called a crime. When de new Judge is done talkin' to you you'll be draggin' a ball and chain de rest of yo' life.

CAIN: Well, what'd he want to come monkeyin' aroun' me fo' den? I was jest plowin', min'in' my own business, and not payin' him no min', and yere he come makin' me de fool. I'd bust anybody what make me de fool.

GOD: Well, I ain't sayin' you right an' I ain't sayin' you wrong. But I do say was I you I'd jest git myself down de road 'til I was clean out of de county. An' you better take an' git married an' settle down an' raise some chillun. Dey ain't nothin' to make a man fo'git his troubles like raisin' a family. Now, you better git.

CAIN: Yessuh.

[Cain walks off. God watches him from the forestage and as the lights begin to dim looks off. The Choir begins "Run, Sinner, Run"]

GOD: Adam an' Eve, you better try again. You better have Seth an' a lot mo' chillun.

[There is darkness. The Choir continues until the lights go up on the next scene]

SCENE V.

Cain is discovered walking on an unseen tread-mill. A middle distance of trees, hillsides and shrubbery passes him on an upper treadmill. Behind is the blue sky. He stops under the branches of a tree to look at a sign on a fence railing. Only half the tree is visible on the stage. The sign reads, "NOD PARISH. COUNTY LINE."

CAIN: [Sitting down with a sigh of relief under a tree] At las'! Phew! [Wipes his forehead with a handkerchief] Feels like I been walkin' fo'ty years. [He looks back] Well, dey cain' git me now. Now I kin raise a fam'ly. [An idea occurs to him, and suddenly he begins looking right and left] Well, I'll be hit by a mule! Knock me down for a trustin' baby! Where I gonter git dat family? Dat preacher fooled me. [He is quite dejected] Doggone!

CAIN'S GIRL: [Off stage] Hello, Country Boy!

[Cain glances up to the offstage branches of the tree]

CAIN: Hey-ho, Good-lookin'! Which way is it to town?

CAIN'S GIRL: [Off stage] What you tryin' to do? You tryin' to mash me? I be doggone if it ain't gittin' so a gal cain't hardly leave de house 'out some of dese fast men ain' passin' remarks at her.

CAIN: I ain' passin' remarks.

CAIN'S GIRL: [Off stage] If I thought you was tryin' to mash me, I'd call de police an' git you tooken to de first precinct.

CAIN: Look yere, gal, I ast you a question, an' if you don' answer me I'm gonter bend you 'cross my pants an' burn you up.

CAIN'S GIRL: [Off stage] I'm comin' down.

[Cain takes his eyes from the tree]

CAIN: Yes, an' you better hurry.

[Cain's Girl enters. She is as large as Cain, wickedly pretty, and somewhat flashily dressed. She smiles at Cain]

CAIN'S GIRL: I bet you kin handle a gal mean wid dem big stout arms of your'n. I sho' would hate to git you mad at me, Country Boy.

CAIN: [Smiling] Come yere [She goes a little closer to him] Don't be 'fraid, I ain' so mean.

CAIN'S GIRL: You got two bad-lookin' eyes. I bet yo' hot coffee 'mong de women folks.

CAIN: I ain' never find out. What was you doin' in dat tree?

CAIN'S GIRL: Jest coolin' myself in de element.

CAIN: Is you a Nod Parish gal?

CAIN'S GIRL: Bo'n an' bred.

CAIN: You know yo' kinda pretty.

CAIN'S GIRL: Who tol' you dat?

CAIN: Dese yere two bad eyes of mine.

CAIN'S GIRL: I bet you say dat to everybody all de way down de road.

CAIN: Comin' down dat road I din' talk to nobody.

CAIN'S GIRL: Where you boun' for, Beautiful?

CAIN: I'm jest seein' de country. I thought I might settle down yere fo' a spell. Yo' live wit' yo' people?

CAIN'S GIRL: Co'se I does.

CAIN: 'Spose dey'd like to take in a boarder?

CAIN'S GIRL: Be nice if dey would, wouldn't it?

CAIN: I think so. You got a beau?

CAIN'S GIRL: Huh-uh!

CAIN: [Smiling] You has now.

CAIN'S GIRL: I guess—I guess if you wanted to kiss me an' I tried to stop you, you could pretty nearly crush me wit' dem stout arms.

CAIN: You wouldn't try too much, would you?

CAIN'S GIRL: Maybe for a little while.

CAIN: An' den what?

CAIN'S GIRL: Why don' we wait an' see?

CAIN: When would dat be?

CAIN'S GIRL: To-night. After supper. Think you kin walk a little further now, City Boy?

CAIN: Yeh, I ain' so weary now.

[She takes his hand]

CAIN'S GIRL: What yo' name?

[Takes his arm]

CAIN: Cain.

CAIN'S GIRL: Then I'm Cain's Gal. Come on, honey, an' meet de folks.

[They go out. The Choir is heard singing "You Better Mind," as God enters. God watches the vanishing Cain and his girl]

GOD: [After shaking His head] Bad business. I don't like de way things is goin' a-tall.

[The stage is darkened. The Choir *continues singing until the lights go up on the next scene]*

SCENE VI.

God's *private office in Heaven. It is a small room, framed by tableau curtains. A large window up center looks out on the sky. There is a battered roll-top desk. On the wall next to the window is a framed religious oleograph with a calendar attached to it underneath. A door is at the left. A hat rack is on the wall above the door. There are two or three cheap pine chairs beside the window, and beyond the door. In front of the desk is an old swivel armchair which creaks every time* God *leans back in it. The desk is open and various papers are stuck in the pigeonholes. Writing implements,* etc. *are on the desk. On a shelf above the desk is a row of law books. A cuspidor is near the desk, and a waste basket by it. The general atmosphere is that of the office of a Negro lawyer in a Louisiana town. As the lights go up* God *takes a fresh cigar from a box on the desk and begins puffing it without bothering to light it. There is no comment on this minor miracle from* Gabriel *who is sitting in one of the chairs with a pencil and several papers in his hand. The singing becomes pianissimo.*

GABRIEL: *[Looking at the papers]* Well, I guess dat's about all de impo'tant business this mornin', Lawd.

GOD: How 'bout dat cherub over to Archangel Montgomery's house?

GABRIEL: Where do dey live, Lawd?

[The singing stops]

GOD: Dat little two-story gold house, over by de pearly gates.

GABRIEL: Oh, dat Montgomery. I thought you was referrin' to de ol' gentleman. Oh, yeh. *[He sorts through the papers and finds one he is looking for]* Yere it 'tis. *[Reads]* "Cherub Christina Montgomery; wings is moltin' out of season an' nobody knows what to do."

GOD: Well, now, take keer of dat. You gotter be more careful, Gabe.

GABRIEL: Yes, Lawd.

[Folds the papers and puts them in a pocket. God *turns to His desk, takes another puff or two of the cigar, and with a pencil, begins checking off items on a sheet of paper before Him. His back is turned toward* Gabriel. Gabriel *takes his trumpet from the hat rack and burnishes it with his robe. He then wets his lips and puts the mouthpiece to his mouth]*

GOD: *[Without turning around]* Now, watch yo'self, Gabriel.

GABRIEL: I wasn't goin' to blow, Lawd. I jest do dat every now an' den so I can keep de feel of it.

[He leans trumpet against the wall. God *picks up the papers and swings His chair around toward* Gabriel*]*

GOD: What's dis yere about de moon?

GABRIEL: *[Suddenly remembering]* Oh! De moon people say it's beginnin' to melt a little, on 'count caize de sun's so hot.

GOD: It's goin' 'roun' 'cordin' to schedule, ain't it?

GABRIEL: Yes, Lawd.

GOD: Well, tell 'em to stop groanin'. Dere's nothin' de matter wid dat moon. Trouble is so many angels is flyin' over dere on Saddy night. Dey git to beatin' dere wings when dey dancin' an' dat makes de heat. Tell dem dat from now on dancin' 'roun' de moon is sinnin'. Dey got to stop it. Dat'll cool off de moon. *[He swings back and puts the paper on the desk. He leans back in the chair comfortably, His hands clasped behind His head]* Is dere anythin' else you ought to remin' me of?

GABRIEL: De prayers, Lawd.

GOD: *[Puzzled, slowly swinging chair around again]* De prayers?

GABRIEL: From mankind. You know, down on de earth.

GOD: Oh, yeh, de poor little earth. Bless my soul, I almos' forgot about dat. Mus' be three or four hund'ed years since I been down dere. I wasn't any too pleased wid dat job.

GABRIEL: *[Laughing]* You know you don' make mistakes, Lawd.

GOD: *[Soberly, with introspective detachment]* So dey tell me. *[He looks at* Gabriel, *then through the window again]* So dey tell me. I fin' I kin be displeased though, an' I was displeased wid de mankind I las' seen. Maybe I ought to go down dere agin— I need a little holiday.

GABRIEL: Might do you good, Lawd.

GOD: I think I will. I'll go down an' walk de earth agin an' see how dem poor humans is makin' out. What time is it, by de sun an' de stars?

GABRIEL: *[Glancing out of the window]* Jest exactly half-past, Lawd.

[God is taking His hat and stick from the hat rack]

GOD: *[Opening the door]* Well, take keer o' yo'self. I'll be back Saddy.

[He exits. The stage is darkened. The Choir *begins "Dere's No Hidin' Place," and continues until the lights go up on the next scene]*

SCENE VII.

God *is walking along a country road. He stops to listen. Church bells are heard in the distance.*

GOD: Dat's nice. Nice an' quiet. Dat's de way I like Sunday to be. *[The sound is broken by a shrill voice of a girl. It is* Zeba *singing a "blues"]* Now, dat ain't so good. *[God resumes His walk and the*

*upper treadmill brings on a tree stump on which
Zeba is sitting. She is accompanying her song with a
ukulele.* God *and the treadmills stop. When the
stump reaches the center of the stage, it is seen that
Zeba is a rouged and extremely flashily dressed
chippy of about eighteen*] Stop dat!

ZEBA: What's de matter wid you, Country Boy?
Pull up yo' pants.

[*She resumes singing*]

GOD: Stop dat!

ZEBA: [*Stops again*] Say, listen to me, Banjo Eyes.
What right you got to stop a lady enjoyin' herself?

GOD: Don't you know dis is de Sabbath? Dat's no
kin' o' song to sing on de Lawd's day.

ZEBA: Who care 'bout de Lawd's day any mo'?
People jest use Sunday now to git over Saddy.

GOD: You a awful sassy little girl.

ZEBA: I come fum sassy people! We even speak
mean of de dead.

GOD: What's yo' name?

ZEBA: [*Flirtatiously*] "What's my name?" Ain't
you de ol'-time gal hunter! Fust, "What's my name?"
den I s'pose, what would it be like if you tried to kiss
me? You preachers is de debbils.

GOD: I ain't aimin' to touch you, daughter. [*A
sudden sternness frightens* Zeba. *She looks at him
sharply*] What is yo' name?

ZEBA: Zeba.

GOD: Who's yo' fam'ly?

ZEBA: I'm de great-great-gran'daughter of Seth.

GOD: Of Seth? But Seth was a good man.

ZEBA: Yeh, he too good, he die of holiness.

GOD: An' yere's his little gran'daughter reekin'
wid cologne. Ain't nobody ever tol' you yo' on de
road to Hell?

ZEBA: [*Smiling*] Sho' dat's what de preacher say.
Exceptin', of course, I happens to know dat I'm on
de road to de picnic groun's, an' at de present time
I'm waitin' to keep a engagement wid my sweet papa.
He don' like people talkin' to me.

[Cain *the Sixth enters. He is a young buck,
wearing a "box" coat and the other flashy
garments of a Rampart Street swell*]

CAIN THE SIXTH: Hello, sugah! [*He crosses in
front of* God *and faces* Zeba] Hello, mamma! Sorry
I'm late, baby, but de gals in de barrel-house jest
wouldn't let me go. Doggone, one little wirehead
swore she'd tear me down.

[Zeba *smiles and takes his hand*]

GOD: What's yo' name, son?

CAIN THE SIXTH: [*Contemptuously; without turning*] Soap 'n' water, Country Boy.

GOD: [*Sternly*] What's yo' name, son?

[Cain *slowly turns and for a moment his manner is civil*]

CAIN THE SIXTH: Cain the Sixth.

GOD: I was afraid so.

CAIN THE SIXTH: [*His impudence returning*] You
a new preacher?

GOD: Where you live?

CAIN THE SIXTH: Me, I live mos' any place.

GOD: Yes, an' you gonter see dem all. Is de udder
young men all like you?

CAIN THE SIXTH: [*Smiling*] De gals don' think so.
[*He turns towards* Zeba *again, picks her up and
sits on the stump with the laughing* Zeba *on his
lap*]

ZEBA: Dey ain't nobody in de worl' like my honey-
cake.

[Cain *kisses her and she resumes her song.*
God *watches them.* Zeba *finishes a verse of the
song and begins another softly.* Cain *the Sixth's
eyes have been closed during the singing*]

CAIN THE SIXTH: [*His eyes closed*] Is de preacher
gone?

[Zeba *looks quickly at* God *without seeing him,
and then looks off. She stops the song*]

ZEBA: Yeh, I guess he walks fast.

[Cain *pushes her off his lap and rises*]

CAIN THE SIXTH: [*With acid sweetness*] Dey tell
me las' night you was talkin' to a creeper man, baby.

ZEBA: Why, you know dey ain't nobody in de
world fo' me but you.

CAIN THE SIXTH: [*Smiling*] I know dey ain't. I
even got dat guaranteed. [*Takes a revolver from his
pocket*] See dat, baby?

ZEBA: Sho' I see it, honey.

CAIN THE SIXTH: Dat jest makes me positive.

[*Puts the gun back*]

ZEBA: [*Pushing him back on the stump*] You don'
wanter believe dem stories, papa.

CAIN THE SIXTH: [*With sinister lightness*] No. I
didn't believe dem, baby. Co'se dat big gorilla, Flatfoot, from de other side of de river *is* in town ag'in.

ZEBA: Dat don' mean nothin'. Flatfoot ain't
nothin' to me.

CAIN THE SIXTH: [*Sitting again*] Co'se he ain't. Go
'head, sing some mo', baby.

[Zeba *resumes singing*]

GOD: Bad business. [*The treadmills start turning.*
God *resumes his walk.* Zeba, *still singing, and* Cain
the Sixth recede with the landscape. God *is again
alone on the country road. There is a twitter of
birds.* God *looks up and smiles*] De birds is goin'
'bout deir business, all right. [*A patch of flowers
goes by, black-eyed Susans, conspicuously*] How you
flowers makin' out? [*Children's voices answer, "We
O. K., Lawd."*] Yes, an' you looks very pretty.
[*Children's voices: "Thank you, Lawd." The flowers
pass out of sight*] It's only de human bein's makes
me downhearted. Yere's as nice a Sunday as dey is
turnin' out anywhere, an' nobody makin' de right
use of it. [*Something ahead of him attracts his
attention. His face brightens*] Well, now dis is mo'
like it. Now dat's nice to see people prayin'. It's a
wonder dey don' do it in de church. But I fin' I don'
min' it if dey do it outdoors.

GAMBLER: Oh, Lawd, de smoke-house is empty.
Oh, Lawd, lemme git dem groceries. Oh, Lawd,

lemme see dat little six. [*He casts the dice*] Wham! Dere she is, frien's.

> [*Exclamations from the others:* "Well, damn my eyes!" "Doggone, dat's de eighth pass he make." "For God's sake, can't you ever crap?" etc. *The* Boy *is picking up the money*]

GOD: Gamblin'! [*Looks over the group's shoulders*] An' wid frozen dice!

BOY GAMBLER: Dey's a dolla' 'n' a half talkin' fo' me. How much you want of it, Riney?

FIRST GAMBLER: I take fo' bits. Wait a minute. Mebbe I take a little mo'.'

> [*He counts some money in his hand*]

SECOND GAMBLER: [*Glancing up at* God] Hello, Liver Lips. [*To the others*] Looka ol' Liver Lips.

> [*The others look up and laugh good-naturedly, repeating* "Liver Lips"]

FIRST GAMBLER: Ain't his pockets high from de groun'? Ol' High Pockets.

> [*The others keep saying* "Ole Liver Lips." "Ol' Liver Lips don't like to see people dicin'." "Dat's a good name, 'High Pockets' "]

BOY GAMBLER: [*To others*] Come on, you gonter fade me or not?

> [God *seizes the* Boy's *ears and drags him to his feet. The others do not move, but watch, amused*]

GOD: Come yere, son. Why, yo' jest a little boy. Gamblin' an' sinnin'. [God *looks at the* Boy's *face*] You been chewin' tobacco, too, like you was yo' daddy. [God *sniffs*] An' you been drinkin' sonny-kick-mammy wine. You oughta be 'shamed. [*To the others*] An' you gamblers oughta be 'shamed, leadin' dis boy to sin.

FIRST GAMBLER: He de bes' crap shooter in town, mister.

GOD: I'm gonter tell his mammy. I bet she don' know 'bout dis.

FIRST GAMBLER: No, she don' know. [*The others laugh*] She don' know anythin'.

SECOND GAMBLER: Dat's de God's truth.

FIRST GAMBLER: See kin you beat 'im, High Pockets. Dey's a dolla' open yere.

GOD: I ain't gonter beat 'im. I'm gonter teach 'im. I may have to teach you all.

> [*He starts walking from them. The* Boy *sticks out his tongue the moment* God's *back is turned*]

BOY GAMBLER: If you fin' my mammy you do mo'n I kin. Come on, gamblers, see kin you gimme a little action. Who wants any part of dat dollar?

> [*The treadmill carries them off. The* First Gambler *is heard saying:* "I'll take anoder two bits," *and the others,* "Gimme a dime's wo'th," "I ain't only got fifteen cents left," etc., *as they disappear*]

GOD: [*Walking*] Where's dat little boy's home? [*The front of a shanty appears and* God *stops in front of the door*] Yere's de place. It ain't any too clean, either.

> [*Knocks on the door with his cane*]

VOICE IN SHANTY: Who dar?

GOD: Never you min' who's yere. Open de door.

VOICE IN SHANTY: You gotta search warrant?

GOD: I don' need one.

VOICE IN SHANTY: Who you wanter see?

GOD: I wanter see de mammy of de little gamblin' boy.

VOICE IN SHANTY: You mean little Johnny Rucker?

GOD: Dat may be his name.

VOICE IN SHANTY: Well, Mrs. Rucker ain't home.

GOD: Where's she at?

VOICE IN SHANTY: Who, Mrs. Rucker?

GOD: You heerd me.

VOICE IN SHANTY: Oh, she run away las' night wid a railroad man. She's eloped.

GOD: Where's Rucker?

VOICE IN SHANTY: He's flat under de table. He so drunk he cain't move.

GOD: Who are you?

VOICE IN SHANTY: I'se jest a frien' an' neighbor. I come in las' night to de party, an' everybody in yere's dead drunk but me. De only reason I kin talk is I drank some new white mule I made myself, an' it burn my throat so I cain't drink no mo'. You got any mo' questions?

GOD: Not for you.

> [*The shanty begins to move off as* God *starts walking again*]

VOICE IN SHANTY: Good riddance, I say.

> [*Shanty disappears*]

GOD: Dis ain't gittin' me nowheres. All I gotta say dis yere mankind I been peoplin' my earth wid sho' ain't much. [*He stops and looks back*] I got good min' to wipe 'em all off an' people de earth wid angels. No. Angels is all right, singin' an' playin' an' flyin' around, but dey ain't much on workin' de crops and buildin' de levees. No, suh, mankind's jest right for my earth, if he wasn't so doggone sinful. I'd rather have my earth peopled wit' a bunch of channel catfish, dan I would mankin' an' his sin. I jest cain't stan' sin.

> [*He is about to resume his walk when* Noah *enters.* Noah *is dressed like a country preacher. His coat is of the "hammer-tail" variety. He carries a prayer book under his arm*]

NOAH: Mo'nin', brother.

GOD: Mo'nin', brother. I declare you look like a good man.

NOAH: I try to be, brother. I'm de preacher yere. I don't think I seen you to de meetin'.

> [*They resume walking*]

GOD: I jest come to town a little while ago an' I been pretty busy.

NOAH: Yeh, mos' everybody say dey's pretty busy dese days. Dey so busy dey cain't come to meetin'. It seem like de mo' I preaches de mo' people ain't got time to come to church. I ain't hardly got enough members to fill up de choir. I gotta do de preachin' an' de bassin' too.

GOD: Is dat a fac'?

NOAH: Yes, suh, brother. Everybody is mighty busy, gamblin', good-timin', and goin' on. You jest wait, though. When Gabriel blow de horn you gonter fin' dey got plenty of time to punch chunks down in Hell. Yes, suh.

GOD: Seems a pity. Dey all perfec'ly healthy?

NOAH: Oh, dey healthy, all right. Dey jest all lazy, and mean, and full of sin. You look like a preacher, too, brother.

GOD: Well, I am, in a way.

NOAH: You jest passin' through de neighborhood?

GOD: Yes. I wanted to see how things was goin' in yo' part of de country, an' I been feelin' jest 'bout de way you do. It's enough to discourage you.

NOAH: Yes, but I gotta keep wres'lin' wid 'em. Where you boun' for right now, brother?

GOD: I was jest walkin' along. I thought I might stroll on to de nex' town.

NOAH: Well, dat's a pretty good distance. I live right yere. [He stops walking] Why don' you stop an' give us de pleasure of yo' comp'ny for dinner? I believe my ol' woman has kilt a chicken.

GOD: Why, dat's mighty nice of you, brother. I don't believe I caught yo' name.

NOAH: Noah, jest brother Noah. Dis is my home, brother. Come right in.

[God and Noah start walking towards Noah's house which is coming into view on the tread-mill. The stage darkens, the Choir sings "Feastin' Table," and when the lights go up again, the next scene is disclosed]

SCENE VIII.

Interior of Noah's house. The ensemble suggests the combination living-dining room in a fairly pros-perous Negro's cabin. Clean white curtains hang at the window. A table and chairs are in the center of the room. There is a cheerful checked tablecloth on the table, and on the wall, a framed, highly colored picture reading "God Bless Our Home." Noah's Wife, an elderly Negress, simply and neatly dressed, God and Noah are discovered grouped about the table.

NOAH: Company, darlin'. [Noah's Wife takes Noah's and God's hats] Dis gemman's a preacher, too. He's jest passin' through de country.

GOD: Good mo'nin', sister.

NOAH'S WIFE: Good mo'nin'. You jest ketch me when I'm gittin' dinner ready. You gonter stay with us?

GOD: If I ain't intrudin'. Brother Noah sug-gested—

NOAH'S WIFE: You set right down yere. I got a

chicken in de pot an' it'll be ready in 'bout five min-utes. I'll go out de back an' call Shem, Ham 'n' Japheth. [To God] Dey's our sons. Dey live right acrost de way but always have Sunday dinner wid us. You mens make yo'selves comf'table.

GOD: Thank you, thank you very kindly.

NOAH: You run along, we all right.

[God and Noah seat themselves. Noah's Wife exits]

GOD: You got a fine wife, Brother Noah.

NOAH: She pretty good woman.

GOD: Yes, suh, an' you got a nice little home. Have a ten-cent seegar?

[God offers him one]

NOAH: Thank you, much obliged.

[Both men lean back restfully in their chairs]

GOD: Jest what seems to be the main trouble 'mong mankind, Noah?

NOAH: Well, it seems to me dat de main trouble is dat de whol' distric' is wide open. Now you know dat makes fo' loose livin'. Men folks spen's all deir time fightin', loafin' and gamblin', an' makin' bad likker.

GOD: What about de women?

NOAH: De women is worse dan de men. If dey ain't makin' love powder dey out beg, borrow an' stealin' money for policy tickets. Doggone, I come in de church Sunday 'fo' las' 'bout an' hour befo' de meetin' was to start, and dere was a woman stealin' de altar cloth. She was goin' to hock it. Dey ain't got no moral sense. Now you take dat case las' month, over in East Putney. Case of dat young Willy Roback.

GOD: What about him?

NOAH: Dere is a boy seventeen years old. Dog-gone, if he didn't elope with his aunt. Now, you know, dat kin' of goin' on is bad fo' a neighborhood.

GOD: Terrible, terrible.

NOAH: Yes, suh. Dis use' to be a nice, decent community. I been doin' my best to preach de Word, but seems like every time I preach de place jest goes a little mo' to de dogs. De good Lawd only knows what's gonter happen.

GOD: Dat's de truth.

[There is a pause. Each puffs his cigar. Sud-denly Noah grasps his knee, as if it were pain-ing him, and twists his foot]

NOAH: Huh!

GOD: What's de matter?

NOAH: I jest got a twitch. My buckaguer I guess. Every now and den I gets a twitch in de knee. Might be a sign of rain.

GOD: That's just what it is. Noah, what's de mos' rain you ever had 'round dese parts?

NOAH: Well, de water come down fo' six days steady last April an' de ribber got so swole it bust down de levee up 'bove Freeport. Raise cain all de way down to de delta.

GOD: What would you say was it to rain for forty days and forty nights?

NOAH: I'd say dat was a *complete* rain!

GOD: Noah, you don't know who I is, do you?

NOAH: [*Puzzled*] Yo' face looks easy, but I don' think I recall de name. [God *rises slowly, and as He reaches His full height there is a crash of lightning, a moment's darkness, and a roll of thunder. It grows light again.* Noah *is on his knees in front of* God] I should have known you. I should have seen de glory.

GOD: Dat's all right, Noah. You didn' know who I was.

NOAH: I'm jes' ol' preacher Noah, Lawd, an' I'm yo' servant. I ain' very much, but I'se all I got.

GOD: Sit down, Noah. Don' let me hear you shamin' you'se'f, caize yo' a good man. [*Timidly* Noah *waits until* God *is seated, and then sits, himself*] I jest wanted to fin' out if you was good, Noah. Dat's why I'm walkin' de earth in de shape of a natchel man. I wish dey was mo' people like you. But, far as I kin see, you and yo' family is de only respectable people in de worl'.

NOAH: Dey jest all poor sinners, Lawd.

GOD: I know. I am your Lawd. I am a god of wrath and vengeance an' dat's why I'm gonter destroy dis worl'.

NOAH: [*Almost in a whisper. Drawing back*] Jest as you say, Lawd.

GOD: I ain't gonter destroy you, Noah. You an' yo' family, yo' sheep an' cattle, an' all de udder things dat ain't human I'm gonter preserve. But de rest is gotta go. [*Takes a pencil and a sheet of paper from His pocket*] Look yere, Noah. [Noah *comes over and looks over His shoulder*] I want you to build me a boat. I want you to call it de "Ark," and I want it to look like dis. [*He is drawing on the paper. Continues to write as He speaks*] I want you to take two of every kind of animal and bird dat's in the country. I want you to take seeds an' sprouts an' everything like dat an' put dem on dat Ark, because dere is gonter be all dat rain. Dey's gonter be a deluge, Noah, an' dey's goin' to be a flood. De levees is gonter bust an' everything dat's fastened down is comin' loose, but it ain't gonter float long, caize I'm gonter make a storm dat'll sink everythin' from a hencoop to a barn. Dey ain't a ship on de sea dat'll be able to fight dat tempest. Dey all got to go. Everythin'. Everythin' in dis pretty worl' I made, except one thing, Noah. You an' yo' fam'ly an' de things I said are going to ride dat storm in de Ark. Yere's de way it's to be.

[*He hands* Noah *the paper.* Noah *takes it and reads*]

NOAH: [*Pause. Looks at paper again*] Yes, suh, dis seems to be complete. Now 'bout the animals, Lawd, you say you want everythin'?

GOD: Two of everythin'.

NOAH: Dat would include jayraffes an' hippopotamuses?

GOD: Everythin' dat is.

NOAH: Dey was a circus in town las' week. I guess I kin fin' dem. Co'se I kin git all de rabbits an' possums an' wil' turkeys easy. I'll sen' de boys out. Hum, I'm jest wonderin'—

GOD: 'Bout what?

NOAH: 'Bout snakes. Think you'd like snakes, too?

GOD: Certainly I want snakes.

NOAH: Oh, I kin git snakes, lots of 'em. Co'se some of 'em's a little dangerous. Maybe I better take a kag of likker, too?

GOD: You can have a kag of likker.

NOAH: [*Musingly*] Yes, suh, dey's a awful lot of differ'nt kin's of snakes, come to think about it. Dey's water moccasins, cotton-moufs, rattlers—mus' be a hund'ed kin's of other snakes down in de swamps. Maybe I better take two kags of likker.

GOD: [*Mildly*] I think de one kag's enough.

NOAH: No. I better take two kags. Besides I kin put one on each side of de boat, an' balance de ship wid dem as well as havin' dem fo' medicinal use.

GOD: You kin put one kag in de middle of de ship.

NOAH: [*Buoyantly*] Jest as easy to take de two kags, Lawd.

GOD: I think one kag's enough.

NOAH: Yes, Lawd, but you see forty days an' forty nights——

[*There is a distant roll of thunder*]

GOD: [*Firmly*] One kag, Noah.

NOAH: Yes, Lawd. One kag.

[*The door in the back opens and* Noah's Wife *enters with a tray of dishes and food*]

NOAH'S WIFE: Now, den, gen'lemen, if you'll jest draw up cheers.

[*The stage is darkened. The* Choir *is heard singing "I Want to Be Ready." They continue in the darkness until the lights go up on the next scene*]

SCENE IX.

In the middle of the stage is the Ark. On the hillside, below the Ark, a dozen or more men and women, townspeople, are watching Noah, Shem, Ham, *and* Japheth *on the deck of the Ark. The three sons are busily nailing boards on the cabin.* Noah *is smoking a pipe. He wears a silk hat, captain's uniform and a "slicker."*

NOAH: [*To* Shem] You, Shem, tote up some ol' rough lumber; don' bring up any planed-up lumber, caize dat ain't fo' de main deck.

SHEM: Pretty near supper time, daddy.

NOAH: Maybe 'tis, but I got de feelin' we ought to keep goin'.

FIRST WOMAN: You gonter work all night, Noah, maybe, huh?

NOAH: [*Without looking at her*] If de speerit move me.

SECOND WOMAN: Look yere, Noah, whyn't you give up all dis damn foolishness? Don' you know people sayin' yo' crazy? What you think you doin' anyway?

NOAH: I'se buildin' a Ark. [*Other men and women join those in the foreground*] Ham, you better stop for a while 'n' see whether dey bringin' de animals up all right. [*He looks at his watch*] Dey ought to be pretty near de foot o' de hill by dis time; if dey ain't you wait fo' dem and bring 'em yo'se'f.

[*Ham goes down a ladder at the side of the ship and exits during the following scene. The newcomers in the group have been speaking to some of the early arrivals*]

SECOND WOMAN: [*To* Third Woman, *one of the newcomers*] No, you don't mean it!

THIRD WOMAN: I do so. Dat's what de talk is in de town.

FIRST MAN: You hear dat, Noah? Dey say yo' ol' lady is tellin' everybody it's gonter rain fo' fo'ty days and fo'ty nights. You know people soon gonter git de idea you *all* crazy.

NOAH: Lot I keer what you think. [*To* Japheth] Straighten up dem boards down dere, Japheth.

[*Indicating floor deck*]

FIRST MAN: [*To* Third Woman] Was I you, I wouldn' go 'round with Mrs. Noah any more, lady. First thing you know you'll be gittin' a hard name, too.

THIRD WOMAN: Don' I know?

SECOND WOMAN: A lady cain't be too partic'lar dese days.

[Zeba *and* Flatfoot, *a tall, black, wicked-looking buck, enter, their arms around each other's waists*]

ZEBA: Dere it is, baby. Was I lyin'?

FLATFOOT: Well, I'll be split in two!

FIRST MAN: What you think of it, Flatfoot?

FLATFOOT: I must say! Look like a house wit' a warpin' cellar.

NOAH: Dis yere vessel is a boat.

FLATFOOT: When I was a little boy dey used to build boats down near de ribber, where de water was.

[*The others laugh*]

NOAH: Dis time it's been arranged to have de water come up to de boat. [Japheth *looks belligerently over the rail of the Ark at* Flatfoot. *To* Japheth] Keep yo' shirt on, son.

SECOND WOMAN: [*To* Third Woman] Now, you see de whole fam'ly crazy.

THIRD WOMAN: Listen, dey ain't gonter 'taminate me. It was me dat started resolvin' dem both out o' de buryin' society.

ZEBA: When all dis water due up yere, Noah?

NOAH: You won't know when it gits yere, daughter.

ZEBA: Is she goin' to be a side-wheeler, like de *Bessy-Belle?*

FLATFOOT: No! If she was a side-wheeler she'd get her wheels all clogged wid sharks. She gonter have jus' one great big stern wheel, like de *Commodore.*

Den if dey ain't 'nuf water why de big wheel kin stir some up.

[*General laughter. Two or three of the* Gamblers *enter and join the group, followed by* Cain the Sixth]

CAIN THE SIXTH: Dere's de fool an' his monument, jest like I said!

[*The* Gamblers *and* Cain the Sixth *roar with laughter, slap their legs, etc. The members of the main group talk* sotto voce *to each other as* Cain the Sixth *catches* Zeba's *eye.* Flatfoot *is on her right and is not aware of* Cain the Sixth's *presence*]

NOAH: See how dey makin' out inside, son.

[*Stops hammering.* Japheth *exits into Ark.* Noah *turns and gazes towards the east*]

CAIN THE SIXTH: Hello, honey.

ZEBA: [*Frightened but smiling*] Hello, sugah.

CAIN THE SIXTH: [*Pleasantly*] Ain't dat my ol' frien' Flatfoot wid you?

ZEBA: Why, so 'tis! [Flatfoot *is now listening. To* Flatfoot] He's got a gun.

CAIN THE SIXTH: No, I ain't.

[*He lifts his hands over his head.* Zeba *quickly advances and runs her hands lightly over his pockets*]

ZEBA: [*Relieved*] I guess he ain't.

CAIN THE SIXTH: No, I ain't got no gun for my ol' frien', Flatfoot.

[*He walks up to him*]

FLATFOOT: [*Smiling*] Hi, Cain. How's de boy?

[Cain *quickly presses his chest against* Flatfoot's, *his downstage arm sweeps around* Flatfoot's *body and his hand goes up to the small of* Flatfoot's *back*]

CAIN THE SIXTH: [*Quietly, but triumphantly*] I got a little *knife* fo' him.

[Flatfoot *falls dead. The laughter of the others stops and they look at the scene.* Zeba *for a moment is terrified, her clenched hand pressed to her mouth. She looks at* Cain the Sixth, *who is smiling at her. He tosses the knife on the ground and holds his hands out to her. She goes to him, smiling*]

ZEBA: You sho' take keer of me, honey.

CAIN THE SIXTH: Dat's caize I think yo' wo'th takin' keer of. [*To the others*] It's all right, folks. I jest had to do a little cleanin' up.

FIRST WOMAN: [*Smiling*] You is de quickes' scoundrel.

FIRST GAMBLER: It was a nice quick killin'. Who was he?

SECOND WOMAN: [*Casually*] Dey called him Flatfoot. From over de river. He wa'n't any good. He owed me for washin' for over a year.

THIRD WOMAN: Used to peddle muggles. Said it had a kick like reg'lar snow. Wasn't no good.

SECOND GAMBLER: Think we ought to bury him?

FIRST MAN: No, just leave him dere. Nobody comes up yere, 'cept ol' Manatee.

[*Indicates* Noah. *Cries of* "Ol' Manatee! Ol' Manatee, dat's good!"]

NOAH: [*Still looking off*] You bettah pray, you po' chillun. [*They all laugh*]

FIRST WOMAN: We bettah pray? You bettah pray, Ol' Manatee?

[*Laughter again*]

NOAH: Dat's what I ain't doin', sinners. Shem! Japheth! [*To others, as he points off. Patter of rain*] Listen!

CAIN THE SIXTH: [*Casually*] Doggone, I believe it *is* gonter shower a little.

FIRST GAMBLER: It do look like rain.

FIRST WOMAN: I think I'll git on home. I got a new dress on.

ZEBA: Me, too. I wants to keep lookin' nice fo' my sweet papa.

[*She pats* Cain the Sixth's *cheek.* Cain the Sixth *hugs her*]

NOAH: [*Almost frantically*] Ham! Is de animals dere?

HAM: [*Off stage*] Yes, suh, dere yere. We're comin'.

NOAH: Den bring 'em on.

[Shem *and* Japheth *come on deck with their hammers. The stage begins to darken*]

THIRD WOMAN: I guess we all might go home 'til de shower's over. Come on, papa.

SECOND GAMBLER: See you after supper, Noah. [*Crowd starts moving off*]

NOAH: God's gittin' ready to start, my sons. Let's git dis plankin' done.

ZEBA: Put a big Texas on it, Noah, an' we'll use it fo' excursions.

[*There is a distant roll of thunder, there are cries of* "Good night, Admiral." "See you later." "So long, Manatee," *as the crowd goes off. The thunder rumbles again. There is the sound of increasing rain. The hammers of* Shem *and* Japheth *sound louder and are joined by the sounds of other hammerers. There is a flash of lightning. The Choir begins* "De Ol' Ark's a-Movering," *the sounds on the Ark become faster and louder. The rush of rain grows heavier*]

NOAH: Hurry! Hurry! Where are you, Ham!

HAM: [*Just off stage*] Yere I am, Father, wid de animals.

NOAH: God's give us His sign. Send 'em up de gangplank.

[*An inclined plane is thrown against the Ark from the side of the stage by* Ham, *who cracks a whip*]

HAM: Get on, dere.

[*The heads of two elephants are seen*]

NOAH: Bring 'em on board! De Lawd is strikin' down de worl'!

[*The singing and the noises reach fortissimo as* Ham *cracks his whip again, and the rain falls*

on the stage. The stage is darkened. The Choir *continues singing in the darkness*]

SCENE X

When the lights go up on the scene, the Ark is at sea. Stationary waves run in front of it. The hillside has disappeared. The Ark is in the only lighted area.

Shem *is smoking a pipe on the deck, leaning on the rail. A steamboat whistle blows three short and one long blast.* Shem *is surprised. In a moment* Ham *appears, also with a pipe, and joins* Shem *at the rail.*

SHEM: Who'd you think you was signalin'?

HAM: Dat wasn't me, dat was daddy.

SHEM: He think he gonter git a reply?

HAM: I don't know. He's been gittin' a heap of comfort out of dat likker.

SHEM: De kag's nearly empty, ain't it?

HAM: Pretty nearly almos'. [*They look over the rail. A pause*] Seen anythin'?

SHEM: Dis mornin' I seen somethin' over dere migh'a' been a fish.

HAM: Dat's de big news of de week.

SHEM: How long you think dis trip's gonter las'?

HAM: I don' know! Rain fo'ty days 'n' fo'ty nights an' when dat stop' I thought sho' we'd come up ag'inst a san' bar o' somethin'. Looks now like all dat rain was jest a little incident of de trip. [*The whistle blows again*] Doggone! I wish he wouldn't do dat. Fust thing we know he'll wake up dem animals ag'in.

[Japheth *appears*]

SHEM: What's de matter wit' de ol' man, Jape?

JAPHETH: Doggone, he say he had a dream dat we're nearly dere. Dat's why he pullin' de whistle cord. See kin he git a' answer. [*He looks over the rail*] Look to me like de same ol' territory.

[Mrs. Noah *appears on deck*]

NOAH'S WIFE: You boys go stop yo' paw pullin' dat cord. He so full of likker he think he's in a race.

JAPHETH: He claim he know what he's doin'.

NOAH'S WIFE: I claim he gittin' to be a perfec' nuisance. Me an' yo' wives cain't hardly heah ou'sel'es think. [Noah *appears, his hat rakishly tilted on his head. He goes to the railing and looks out*] You 'spectin' company?

NOAH: Leave me be, woman. De watah don't look so rough to-day. De ol' boat's ridin' easier.

NOAH'S WIFE: Ridin' like a ol' mule!

NOAH: Yes, suh, de air don't feel so wet. Shem! S'pose you sen' out 'nother dove. [Shem *goes into the Ark*] Ham, go git de soundin' line. Jape, keep yo' eye on de East.

[Japheth *goes to the end of the boat*]

NOAH'S WIFE: As fo' you, I s'pose you'll help things along by takin' a little drink.

NOAH: Look yere, who's de pilot of dis vessel?

NOAH'S WIFE: O' Mister Dumb Luck.

NOAH: Well, see dat's where you don' know anythin'.

NOAH'S WIFE: I s'pose you ain't drunk as a fool?

NOAH: [*Cordially*] I feel congenial.

NOAH'S WIFE: An' you look it. You look jest wonderful. I wonder if you'd feel so congenial if de Lawd was to show up?

NOAH: De Lawd knows what I'm doin', don' you worry 'bout dat.

NOAH'S WIFE: I wouldn't say anythin' ag'inst de Lawd. He suttinly let us know dey'd be a change in de weather. But I bet even the Lawd wonders sometimes why He ever put you in charge.

NOAH: Well, you let de Lawd worry 'bout dat.

[Shem *appears with the dove*]

SHEM: Will I leave her go, Paw?

NOAH: Leave 'er go. [*There's a chorus of "Good Luck, Dove" from the group as the dove flies off stage. Ham appears with the sounding line*] Throw 'er over, boy.

[Ham *proceeds to do so*]

NOAH'S WIFE: An' another thing——

HAM: Hey.

NOAH: [*Rushing to his side*] What is it?

HAM: Only 'bout a inch! Look!

[*They lean over*]

JAPHETH: It's gettin' light in de East.

[*As Ham works the cord up and down, Noah and Noah's Wife turn toward Japheth. The Choir begins "My Soul Is a Witness for the Lord"*]

NOAH: Praise de Lawd, so it is.

NOAH'S WIFE: Oh, dat's pretty.

NOAH: [*To Ham*] An' de boat's stopped. We've landed. Shem, go down 'n' drag de fires an' dreen de boiler. Yo' go help 'im, Ham.

JAPHETH: Look, Paw.

[*The dove wings back to the Ark with an olive branch in its mouth*]

NOAH: 'N' yere's de little dove wid greenery in its mouth! Take 'er down, Jape, so she kin tell de animals. [*Japheth exits after Shem and Ham carrying the dove. To Mrs. Noah*] Now, maybe you feel little different.

NOAH'S WIFE: [*Contritely*] It was jes' gittin' to be so tiresome. I'm sorry, Noah.

NOAH: Dat's all right, ol' woman. [*Noah's Wife exits, Noah looks about him. The lights have changed and the water piece is gone and the Ark is again on the hillside. Two mountains can be seen in the distance and a rainbow slowly appears over the Ark. The singing has grown louder*] Thank you, Lawd, thank you very much indeed. Amen.

[*The singing stops with the "Amen." God appears on the deck*]

GOD: Yo' welcome, Noah.

[Noah *turns and sees Him*]

NOAH: O, Lawd, it's wonderful.

GOD: [*Looking about Him*] I sort of like it. I like de way you handled de ship, too, Noah.

NOAH: Was you watchin', Lawd?

GOD: Every minute. [*He smiles*] Didn't de ol' lady light into you?

NOAH: [*Apologetically*] She was kinda restless.

GOD: That's right. I ain't blamin' nobody. I don't even min' you cussin' an' drinkin'. I figure a steamboat cap'n on a long trip like you had has a right to a little redeye, jest so he don' go crazy.

NOAH: Thank you, Lawd. What's de orders now?

GOD: All de animals safe?

NOAH: Dey all fin'n' dandy, Lawd.

GOD: Den I want you to open dat starboard door, an' leave 'em all out. Let 'em go down de hill. Den you an' de family take all de seeds 'n' de sprouts an' begin plantin' ag'in. I'm startin' all over, Noah.

[Noah *exits. God looks around*]

GOD: Well, now we'll see what happens. [*God listens with a smile, as noises accompanying the debarking of the animals are heard. They are the cracks of whips, the voices of the men on the Ark, shouting: "Git along dere." "Whoa, take it easy." "Duck yo' head." "Keep in line dere," etc. Over the Ark there is a burst of centrifugal shadows, and the sound of a myriad of wings. God smiles at the shadows*] Dat's right, birds, fin' yo' new homes. [*Bird twitters are heard again. God listens a moment and rests an arm on the railing. He speaks softly*] Gabriel, kin you spare a minute?

GABRIEL: Yes, Lawd?

[*The sounds from the other side of the Ark are by now almost hushed. The Lord indicates the new world with a wave of the hand*]

GOD: Well, it's did.

GABRIEL: [*Respectfully, but with no enthusiasm*] So I take notice.

GOD: Yes, suh, startin' all over again.

GABRIEL: So I see.

GOD: [*Looking at him suddenly*] Don' seem to set you up much.

GABRIEL: Well, Lawd, you see— [*He hesitates*] 'Tain't none of my business.

GOD: What?

GABRIEL: I say, I don' know very much about it.

GOD: I know you don'. I jest wanted you to see it [*A thought strikes Him*] Co'se, it ain' yo' business, Gabe. It's my business. 'Twas my idea. De whole thing was my idea. An' every bit of it's my business 'n' nobody else's. De whole thing rests on my shoulders. I declare, I guess dat's why I feel so solemn an' serious, at dis particklar time. You know dis thing's turned into quite a proposition.

GABRIEL: [*Tenderly*] But it's all right, Lawd, as you say, it's did.

GOD: Yes, suh, it's did. [*Sighs deeply. Looks slowly to the right and the left. Then softly*] I only hope it's goin' to work out all right.

CURTAIN

PART II. SCENE I.

God's *office again.*

Somewhere the Choir *is singing: "A City Called Heaven." In the office are* Two Women Cleaners. *One is scrubbing the floor, the other dusting the furniture. The one dusting stops and looks out the window. There is a whirr and a distant faint boom. The* Choir *stops.*

FIRST CLEANER: Dat was a long way off.

SECOND CLEANER: [*At window*] Yes, ma'am. An' dat must 'a' been a big one. Doggone, de Lawd mus' be mad fo' sho', dis mo'nin'. Dat's de fo'ty-six' thunde'bolt since breakfast.

FIRST CLEANER: I wonder where at He's pitchin' dem.

SECOND CLEANER: My goodness, don' you know?

FIRST CLEANER: [*A little hurt*] Did I know I wouldn't ask de question.

SECOND CLEANER: Every one of dem's bound fo' de earth.

FIRST CLEANER: De earth? You mean dat little ol' dreenin' place?

SECOND CLEANER: Dat's de planet. [*Another faint whirr and boom*] Dere goes another.

FIRST CLEANER: Well, bless me. *I* didn't know dey was thunde'bolts.

SECOND CLEANER: Wha'd you think dey was?

FIRST CLEANER: [*Above desk*] I wasn't sho', but I thought maybe He might be whittlin' a new star o' two, an' de noise was just de chips fallin'.

SECOND CLEANER: Carrie, where you been? Don' you know de earth is de new scandal? Ever'body's talkin' 'bout it.

FIRST CLEANER: Dey kep' it from me.

SECOND CLEANER: Ain't you noticed de Lawd's been unhappy lately?

FIRST CLEANER: [*Thoughtfully*] Yeah, He ain't been His old self.

SECOND CLEANER: What did you think was de matteh? Lumbago?

FIRST CLEANER: [*Petulantly*] I didn't know. I didn't think it was fo' me t'inquieh.

SECOND CLEANER: Well, it jest so happens dat de Lawd is riled as kin be by dat measly little earth. Or I should say de scum dat's on it.

FIRST CLEANER: Dat's mankind down dere.

SECOND CLEANER: Dey mus' be scum, too, to git de Lawd so wukked up.

FIRST CLEANER: I s'pose so. [*Another whirr and boom*] Looks like He's lettin' dem feel de wrath. Ain' dat a shame to plague de Lawd dat way?

SECOND CLEANER: From what I hear dey been beggin' fo' what dey're gittin'. My brother flew down to bring up a saint de other day and he say from what he see mos' of the population down dere has made de debbil king an' dey wukkin' in three shifts fo' him.

FIRST CLEANER: You cain't blame de Lawd.

SECOND CLEANER: Co'se you cain't. Dem human bein's 'd make anybody bile oveh. Ev'rytime de Lawd try to do sompin' fo' dem, doggone if dey don't staht some new ruckus.

FIRST CLEANER: I take notice He's been wukkin' in yere mo' dan usual.

SECOND CLEANER: I wish He'd let us ladies fix it up. Wouldn't take a minute to make dis desk gold-plated.

FIRST CLEANER: I s'pose He likes it dis way. De Lawd's kind o' ol' fashioned in some ways. I s'pose He keeps dis office plain an' simple on purpose.

SECOND CLEANER: [*Finishing her work*] I don't see why.

FIRST CLEANER: [*Looking off*] Well, it's kind of a nice place to come to when He's studyin' somethin' impo'tant. 'Most evahthin' else in heaven's so fin' 'n' gran', maybe ev'ry now an' den He jest gits sick an' tired of de glory.

[*She is also collecting her utensils*]

SECOND CLEANER: Maybe so. Jest de same I'd like to have a free hand wid dis place for a while, so's I could gold it up.

[God *appears in the doorway*]

FIRST AND SECOND CLEANERS: Good mo'nin', Lawd. We was jest finishin'.

GOD: Go ahead den, daughters.

[*Goes to the window*]

FIRST AND SECOND CLEANERS: Yes, Lawd. [*Exeunt. Off stage*] Good mo'nin', Gabriel.

[*Off stage Gabriel says, "Good mo'nin', sisters," and enters immediately. He stands in the doorway for a moment watching* God—*a notebook and pencil in his hand*]

GOD: What's de total?

GABRIEL: [*Consulting the book*] Eighteen thousand nine hund'ed an' sixty for de mo'nin'. Dat's includin' de village wid de fo'tune tellers. Dey certainly kin breed fast.

GOD: [*Solemnly*] Dey displease me. Dey displease me greatly.

GABRIEL: Want some more bolts, Lawd?

GOD: [*Looking through window*] Look at 'em dere. Squirmin' an' fightin' an' bearin' false witness. Listen to dat liar, dere. He don' intend to marry dat little gal. He don' even love her. What did you say?

GABRIEL: Should I git mo' bolts?

GOD: Wait a minute. [*He carefully points His finger down through the window*] I'm goin' to git dat wicked man myself. [*From a great distance comes an agonized cry: "Oh, Lawd!"* God *turns from the window*] No use gittin' mo' thunde'bolts. Dey din' do de trick. [*He goes to the swivel chair and sits*] It's got to be somethin' else.

GABRIEL: How would it be if you was to doom 'em all ag'in, like dat time you sent down de flood? I bet dat would make dem mind.

GOD: You see how much good de flood did. Dere dey is, jest as bad as ever.

GABRIEL: How about cleanin' up on de whole mess of 'em and sta'tin' all over ag'in wid some new kind of animal?

GOD: An' admit I'm licked?

GABRIEL: [*Ashamedly*] No, of co'se not, Lawd.

GOD: No, suh. No, suh. Man is a kind of pet of mine and it ain't right fo' me to give up tryin' to do somethin' wid him. Doggone, mankin' *mus'* be all right at de core or else why did I ever bother wid him in de first place?

[*Sits at desk*]

GABRIEL: It's jest dat I hates to see you worryin' about it, Lawd.

GOD: Gabe, dere ain't anythin' worth while anywheres dat didn't cause somebody some worryin'. I ain't never tol' you de trouble I had gittin' things started up yere. Dat's a story in itself. No, suh, de more I keep on bein' de Lawd de more I know I got to keep improvin' things. An' dat takes time and worry. De main trouble wid mankin' is he takes up so much of my time. He ought to be able to help hisself a little. [*He stops suddenly and cogitates*] Hey, dere! I think I got it!

GABRIEL: [*Eagerly*] What's de news?

GOD: [*Still cogitating*] Yes, suh, dat seems like an awful good idea.

GABRIEL: Tell me, Lawd.

GOD: Gabriel, have you noticed dat every now an' den, mankin' turns out some pretty good specimens?

GABRIEL: Dat's de truth.

GOD: Yes, suh. Dey's ol' Abraham and Isaac an' Jacob an' all dat family.

GABRIEL: Dat's so, Lawd.

GOD: An' every one of dem boys was a hard wukker an' a good citizen. We got to admit dat.

GABRIEL: Dey wouldn't be up yere flyin' wid us if dey hadn't been.

GOD: No, suh. An' I don' know but what de answer to de whole trouble is right dere.

GABRIEL: How you mean, Lawd?

GOD: Why, doggone it, de good man is de man dat keeps busy. I mean I been goin' along on de principle dat he was something like you angels—dat you ought to be able to give him somethin' an' den jest let him sit back an' enjoy it. Now dat I recollec' I put de first one down dere to take keer o' dat garden an' den I let him go ahead an' do nothin' but git into mischief. [*He rises*] Sure, *dat's* it. He ain't *built* jest to fool 'roun' an' do nothin'. Gabe, I'm gonter try a new scheme.

GABRIEL: [*Eagerly*] What's de scheme, Lawd?

GOD: I'll tell you later. Send in Abraham, Isaac an' Jacob. [*A voice outside calls: "Right away, Lawd."*] You go tell dem to put dem bolts back in de boxes. I ain' gonter use dem ag'in a while.

GABRIEL: O. K., Lawd.

GOD: Was you goin' anywhere near de Big Pit?

GABRIEL: I could go.

GOD: Lean over de brink and tell Satan he's jest a plain fool if he thinks he kin beat anybody as big as me.

GABRIEL: Yes, suh, Lawd. Den I'll spit right in his eye.

[Gabriel *exits.* God *looks down through the window again to the earth below*]

GOD: Dat new polish on de sun makes it powerful hot. [*He "r'ar back"*] Let it be jest a little bit cooler. [*He feels the air*] Dat's nice. [*Goes to His desk. A knock on the door*] Come in.

[Abraham, Isaac *and* Jacob *enter. All are very old men, but the beard of* Abraham *is the longest and whitest, and they suggest their three generations. They have wings that are not quite so big as those of the native angels*]

ISAAC: Sorry we so long comin', Lawd. But Pappy and me had to take de boy [*Pointing to* Jacob] over to git him a can of wing ointment.

GOD: What was de matter, son?

JACOB: Dey was chafin' me a little. Dey fine now, thank you, Lawd.

GOD: Dat's good. Sit down an' make yo'selves comf'table. [*The three sit.* Men: *"Thank you, Lawd"*] Men, I'm goin' to talk about a little scheme I got. It's one dat's goin' to affec' yo' fam'lies an' dat's why I 'cided I'd talk it over wid you, 'fo it goes into ee-ffect. I don't know whether you boys know it or not, but you is about de three best men of one fam'ly dat's come up yere since I made little apples. Now I tell you what I'm gonter do. Seein' dat you human bein's cain't 'preciate anythin' lessen you fust wukk to git it and den keep strugglin' to hold it, why I'm gonter turn over a very valuable piece of property to yo' fam'ly, and den see what kin dey do with it. De rest of de worl' kin go jump in de river fo' all I keer. I'm gonter be lookin' out fo' yo' descendants only. Now den, seein' dat you boys know de country pretty tho'ly, where at does you think is de choice piece of property in de whole worl'? Think it over for a minute. I'm gonter let you make the s'lection.

ABRAHAM: If you was to ask me, Lawd, I don't think dey come any better dan de Land of Canaan.

GOD: [*To* Isaac *and* Jacob] What's yo' feelin' in de matter?

JACOB: [*After a nod from* Isaac] Pappy an' me think do we get a pick, dat would be it.

GOD: [*Goes to window again; looks out*] De Land of Canaan. Yes, I guess dat's a likely neighborhood. It's all run over wid Philistines and things right now, but we kin clean dat up. [*He turns from the window and resumes His seat*] All right. Now who do you boys think is best of yo' men to put in charge down dere? You see I ain't been payin' much attention to anybody in partic'lar lately.

ISAAC: Does you want de brainiest or de holiest, Lawd?

[Men *look up*]

GOD: I want de holiest. I'll make him brainy.

[Men *appreciate the miracle*]

ISAAC: [*As* Abraham *and* Jacob *nod to him*] Well, if you want A-Number-One goodness, Lawd, I don't know where you'll git more satisfaction dan in a great-great-great-great-grandson of mine.

GOD: Where's he at?

ISAAC: At de moment I b'lieve he's in de sheep business over in Midian County. He got in a little trouble down in Egypt, but 'twan't his doin'. He killed a man dat was abusin' one of our boys in de brick works. Of co'se you know old King Pharaoh's got all our people in bondage.

GOD: I heard of it. [*With some ire*] Who did you think put them dere? [*The visitors lower their heads*] It's all right, boys [*All rise*] I'm gonter take dem out of it. An' I'm gonter turn over de whole Land of Canaan to dem. An' do you know who's gonter lead dem dere? Yo' great, great, great, great-grandson. Moses, ain't it?

ISAAC: Yes, Lawd.

GOD: [*Smiling*] Yes. I been noticin' *him*.

ABRAHAM: It's quite a favor fo' de fam'ly, Lawd.

GOD: Dat's why I tol' you. You see, it so happens I love yo' fam'ly, an' I delight to honor it. Dat's all, gen'lemen. [*The three others rise and cross to the door, murmuring, "Yes, Lawd," "Thank you, Lawd," "Much obliged, Lawd," etc. The* Choir *begins, "My Lord's A-Writin' All De Time" pianissimo. God stands watching the men leave*] Enjoy yo'selves. [*He goes to the window. The singing grows softer. He speaks through the window to the earth*] I'm comin' down to see you, Moses, an' dis time my scheme's got to wukk.

> [*The stage is darkened. The singing grows louder and continues until the lights go up on the next scene*]

SCENE II.

The tableau curtains frame the opening of a cave, which is dimly lighted. A large turkey-berry bush is somewhere near the foreground. Moses *is seated on the grass eating his lunch from a basket in his lap.* Zipporah, *his wife, stands watching him. He is about forty,* Zipporah *somewhat younger. They are dressed inconspicuously.* Moses *stutters slightly when he speaks. He looks up to see* Zipporah *smiling.*

MOSES: What you smilin' at, Zipporah?

ZIPPORAH: Caize you enjoyin' yo'self.

MOSES: You is a good wife, Zipporah.

ZIPPORAH: You is a good husband, Moses. [Moses *wipes his mouth with a handkerchief and begins putting into the basket the various implements of the meal which had been on the ground about him*] Why you suppose it's so dark yere today? Dey's no rain in de air.

MOSES: Seems like it's jest aroun' dis cave. Yo' father's house is got de sun on it. [*He looks in another direction*] Looks all clear down toward Egypt.

ZIPPORAH: Co'se it *would* be fine weather in Egypt. De sky looks all right. Maybe it's gonter rain jest right yere. Why don't you move de sheep over to de other pasture?

MOSES: [*A bit puzzled*] I don' know. It got dark like dis befo' you come along wid de dinner an' I was gonter stop you on de top of de hill. Den somethin' kep' me yere.

ZIPPORAH: S'pose it could be de Lawd warnin' you dat dey's 'Gyptians hangin' 'roun'?

MOSES: Dey may have fo'gotten all about dat killin' by now. Dey got a new Pharaoh down dere.

ZIPPORAH: An' I hear he's jest as mean to yo' people as his pappy was. I wouldn't put it pas' him to send soljahs all the way up yere fo' you.

MOSES: Dat's all right. De Lawd's looked after me so far. I don't 'spect him to fall down on me now. You better be gittin' home.

ZIPPORAH: [*Taking the basket*] I'll be worryin' about you.

MOSES: [*Kissing her and then smiling*] 'Parently de Lawd ain't. He knows I'm safe as kin be. Lemme see you feel dat way.

ZIPPORAH: You is a good man, Moses.

MOSES: I'se a lucky man [Zipporah *exits with the basket.* Moses *looks up at the sky*] Dat's funny. De sun seems to be shinin' every place but right yere. It's shinin' on de sheep. Why ain't dey no clouds dere?

GOD: [*Off stage*] Caize I want it to be like dat, Moses.

MOSES: [*Looking about him*] Who's dat?

GOD: [*Off stage again*] I'm de Lawd, Moses.

MOSES: [*Smiling*] Dat's what you say. Dis yere shadow may be de Lawd's wukk, but dat voice soun' pretty much to me like my ol' brother Aaron.

GOD: [*Off stage*] Den keep yo' eyes open, son. [*The turkey-berry bush begins to glow and then turns completely red.* Moses *looks at it fascinated*] Maybe you notice de bush ain't burnin' up.

MOSES: Dat's de truth.

> [Moses *is full of awe but not frightened*]

GOD: [*Off stage*] Now you believe me?

MOSES: Co'se I does. It's wonderful.

> [*The light in the bush dies and* God *appears from behind it*]

GOD: No, it ain't, Moses. It was jest a trick.

MOSES: 'Scuse me doubtin' you, Lawd. I always had de feelin' you wuz takin' keer of me, but I never 'spected you'd fin' time to talk wid me pussunly. [*He laughs*] Dat was a good trick, Lawd. I'se seen some good ones, but dat was de beatenest.

GOD: Yo' gonter see lots bigger tricks dan dat, Moses. In fac', yo' gonter perfo'm dem.

MOSES: [*Incredulously*] Me? I'm gonter be a tricker?

GOD: Yes, suh.

MOSES: An' do magic? Lawd, my mouth ain't got de quick talk to go wid it.

GOD: It'll come to you now.

MOSES: [*Now cured of stuttering*] Is I goin' wid a circus?

GOD: [*Slowly and solemnly*] Yo' is goin' down into Egypt, Moses, and lead my people out of bondage. To do dat I'm gonter make you de bes' tricker in de worl'.

MOSES: [*A little frightened*] Egypt! You know I killed a man dere, Lawd. Won't dey kill me?

GOD: Not when dey see yo' tricks. You ain't skeered, is you?

MOSES: [*Simply and bravely*] No, suh, Lawd.

GOD: Den yere's what I'm gonter do. Yo' people is my chillun, Moses. I'm sick and tired o' de way ol' King Pharaoh is treatin' dem, so I'se gonter take dem away, and yo' gonter lead dem. You gonter lead 'em out of Egypt an' across de river Jordan. It's gonter take a long time, and you ain't goin' on no excursion train. Yo' gonter wukk awful hard for somethin' yo' goin' to fin' when de trip's over.

MOSES: What's dat, Lawd?

GOD: It's de Land of Canaan. It's de bes' land I got. I've promised it to yo' people, an' I'm gonter give it to dem.

MOSES: Co'se, ol' King Pharaoh will do everything he kin to stop it.

GOD: Yes, an' dat's where de tricks come in. Dey tell me he's awful fond of tricks.

MOSES: I hear dat's *all* he's fon' of. Dey say if you cain't take a rabbit out of a hat you cain't even git to see him.

GOD: Wait'll you see de tricks you an' me's goin' to show him.

MOSES: [*Delightedly*] Doggone! Huh, Lawd?

GOD: Yes, suh. Now de first trick——

[*God is lifting a stick which He carries*]

MOSES: Jest a minute, Lawd. [*God halts the demonstration*] I'm gonter learn de tricks and do just like you tell me, but I *know* it's gonter take me a little time to learn all dat quick talkin'. Cain't I have my brother Aaron go wid me? He's a good man.

GOD: I was gonter have him help you wid de Exodus. I guess he can watch, too.

MOSES: I'll call 'im.

[*He turns as if to shout*]

GOD: Wait. [*Moses turns and looks at God*] I'll bring him. [*Softly*] Aaron!

[*Aaron appears between God and Moses in the mouth cf the cave. He is a little taller than Moses and slightly older. He, too, is dressed like a field hand*]

AARON: [*Blankly*] Hey!

[*Moses goes to him, takes his hand and leads him, bewildered, down to where Moses had been standing alone. Aaron then sees God*]

MOSES: [*Almost in a whisper*] It's all right.

GOD: Don't worry, son, I'm jest showin' some tricks. Bringin' you yere was one of dem. [*Aaron stares at God as if hypnotized*] Now den, you see dis yere rod? Looks like a ordinary walking stick, don' it?

MOSES: Yes, Lawd.

GOD: Well, it ain't no ordinary walkin' stick, caize look. [*Moses leans forward*] When I lays it down on de groun'——

[*The stage is darkened. The Choir begins, "Go Down, Moses," and continues until the lights go up on the next scene*]

SCENE III.

The throne room of Pharaoh. *It suggests a Negro lodge room. The plain board walls are colored by several large parade banners of varying sizes, colors and materials, bordered with gold fringe and tassels on them. Some of the inscriptions on them read:*

SUBLIME ORDER OF PRINCES OF THE
HOUSE OF PHARAOH
HOME CHAPTER
MYSTIC BROTHERS OF THE EGYPTIAN
HOME GUARD
LADIES AUXILIARY, NO. I
SUPREME MAGICIANS AND WIZARDS
OF THE UNIVERSE
PRIVATE FLAG OF HIS HONOR
OLD KING PHARAOH
ROYAL YOUNG PEOPLE'S
PLEASURE CLUB
ENCHANTED AND INVISIBLE CADETS
OF EGYPT BOYS' BRIGADE

There is one door up right and a window. The throne, an ordinary armchair with a drapery over its back, is on a dais. Pharaoh *is seated on the throne. His crown and garments might be those worn by a high officer in a Negro lodge during a ritual. About the throne itself are high officials, several of them with plumed hats, clothing that suggests military uniforms, and rather elaborate sword belts, swords and scabbards. A few soldiers carrying spears are also in his neighborhood and one or two bearded ancients in brightly colored robes with the word "Wizard" on their conical hats. In the general group of men and women scattered elsewhere in the room Sunday finery is noticeable everywhere. Most of the civilians have bright "parade" ribbons and wear medals. In a cleared space immediately before the throne a Candidate Magician is performing a sleight-of-hand trick with cards.* Pharaoh *watches him apathetically. He is receiving earnest attention from a few of the others, but the majority of the men and women are talking quietly among themselves. Beside the* Candidate Magician *are several paraphernalia of previously demonstrated tricks.*

CANDIDATE MAGICIAN: [*Holding up some cards*] Now den, ol' King Pharaoh, watch dis. [*He completes a trick. There is a murmur of "Not bad," "Pretty good," etc., from a few of the watchers. Pharaoh makes no comment*] Now, I believe de cyard I ast you to keep sittin' on was de trey of diamonds, wasn't it?

PHARAOH: Yeah.

CANDIDATE MAGICIAN: Den kin I trouble you to take a look at it now? [*Pharaoh half rises to pick up a card he has been sitting on, and looks at it*] I believe you'll now notice dat it's de king of clubs? [*Pharaoh nods and shows the card to those nearest him. The Candidate Magician waits for an audible approval and gets practically none*] An' dat, ol' King Pharaoh, completes de puffohmance.

[*An elderly man in a uniform steps forward*]

GENERAL: On behalf of my nephew I beg Yo' Honor to let him jine de ranks of de royal trickers and magicians.

PHARAOH: [*To the two Wizards*] What do de committee think? [*The Wizards shake their heads*] Dat's what I thought. He ain't good enough. I'd like to help you out, General, but you know a man's got to be a awful good tricker to git in de royal society dese days. You better go back an' steddy some mo', son. [*He lifts his voice and directs two Soldiers guarding the door*] Is de head magician reached de royal waitin' room yit? [*One of the Soldiers opens the door to look out*] If he is, send him in.

[*The Soldier beckons to someone off stage, throws the door open, and announces to the court*]

SOLDIER: De Head Magician of de land of Egypt. [*A very old and villainous man enters. His costume is covered with cabalistic and zodiacal signs. He advances to the King, the other Magician and his uncle making way for him. He bows curtly to Pharaoh*]

HEAD MAGICIAN: Good mo'nin', ol' King Pharaoh.

PHARAOH: Mo'nin', Professor. What's de news?

HEAD MAGICIAN: Evahthing's bein' carried out like you said.

PHARAOH: How's de killin' of de babies 'mongst de Hebrews comin' 'long?

HEAD MAGICIAN: Jes' like you ordered.

PHARAOH: [*Genially*] Dey killed all of 'em, huh?

HEAD MAGICIAN: Do dey see one, dey kill 'em. You teachin' 'em a great lesson. Dey don't like it a-tall.

PHARAOH: [*Smiling*] What do dey say?

HEAD MAGICIAN: [*Pawing the air inarticulately*] I hates to tell in front of de ladies.

PHARAOH: Dey feels pretty bad, huh?

HEAD MAGICIAN: Dat's jest de beginnin' of it. Betwixt de poleece and de soljahs we killed about a thousan' of 'em las' night. Dat's purty good.

PHARAOH: [*Thoughtfully*] Yeh, it's fair. I guess you boys is doin' all you kin. But I fin' I ain't satisfied, though.

HEAD MAGICIAN: How you mean. Yo' Honor?

PHARAOH: I mean I'd like to make dose Hebrew chillun realize dat I kin be even mo' of a pest. I mean I hates dem chillun. An' I'm gonter think of a way of makin' 'em even mo' mizzable.

HEAD MAGICIAN: But dey ain't anythin' meaner dan killin' de babies, King.

PHARAOH: Dey must be sump'n. Doggone, you is my head tricker, you put yo' brains on it. [*To the others*] Quiet, whilst de Head Magician go into de silence.

HEAD MAGICIAN: [*After turning completely around twice, and a moment's cogitation*] I tell you what I kin do. All de Hebrews dat ain't out to de buryin' grounds or in de hospitals is laborin' in de brick wukks.

HARAOH: Yeh?

HEAD MAGICIAN: [*After a cackling laugh*] How would it be to take de straw away from 'em and tell 'em dey's got to turn out jest as many bricks as usual? Ain't dat nasty?

PHARAOH: Purty triflin', but I s'pose it'll have to do for de time bein'. Where's de extreme inner guard? [*One of the military Attendants comes forward*] Go on out an' tell de sup'intendent to put dat into ee-ffect. [*The Attendant bows and starts for the door. He stops as Pharaoh calls to him*] Wait a minute! Tell 'im to chop off de hands of anybody dat say he cain't make de bricks dat way. [*The Attendant salutes and exits, the door being opened and closed by one of the Soldiers*] Now what's de news in de magic line?

HEAD MAGICIAN: I ain't got very many novelties today, King. I been wukkin' too hard on de killin's. I'm so tired I don' believe I could lift a wand.

[*There are murmurs of protest from the assemblage*]

PHARAOH: Doggone, you was to 'a been de chief feature o' de meetin' dis mo'nin'. Look at de turnout you got account of me tellin' 'em you was comin'.

HEAD MAGICIAN: Well, dat's de way it is, King. Why don' you git de wizards to do some spell castin'?

PHARAOH: Dey say it's in de cyards dat dey cain't wukk till high noon. [*He glances at the Wizards*] Think mebbe you kin cheat a little?

FIRST WIZARD: Oh, dat cain't be done, King.

PHARAOH: Well, we might as well adjourn, den. Looks to me like de whole program's shot to pieces. [*He starts to rise, when there is a furious banging on the door*] What's de idea, dere? See who dat is. [*The Soldiers open the door. Moses and Aaron enter, pushing the two Soldiers aside and coming down in front of Pharaoh. The Soldiers are bewildered and Pharaoh is angry*] Say, who tol' you two baboons you could come in yere?

MOSES: Is you ol' King Pharaoh?

PHARAOH: Dat's me. Did you heah what I asked you?

MOSES: My name is Moses, and dis is my brother Aaron.

[*Murmur of "Hebrews" spreads through the room*]

PHARAOH: [*In a rage*] Is you Hebrews?

MOSES: Yes, suh.

PHARAOH: [*Almost screaming*] Put 'em to de sword!

[*As the* Courtiers *approach,* Aaron *suddenly discloses the rod, which he swings once over his head. The* Courtiers *draw back as if their hands had been stung. Cries of "Hey!" "Look out," etc.*]

MOSES: Keep outside dat circle.

[*The* Courtiers *nearest* Moses *and* Aaron *look at each other, exclaiming ad lib., "Did you feel dat?" "What was dat?" "What's goin' on, heah?" "My hands is stingin'!" etc.*]

PHARAOH: [*Puzzled but threatening*] What's de idea yere?

MOSES: We is magicians, ol' King Pharaoh.

PHARAOH: [*To the* Head Magician] Put a spell on 'em. [*The* Head Magician *stands looking at them, bewildered. To* Moses] I got some magicians, too. We'll see who's got de bes' magic. [Moses *and* Aaron *laugh. Most of the* Courtiers *are cowering. To the* Head Magician] Go ahead, give 'em gri-gri.

MOSES: Sure, go ahead.

PHARAOH: Hurry up, dey's laughin' at you. What's de matter?

HEAD MAGICIAN: I cain't think of de right spell.

PHARAOH: [*Now frightened himself*] You mean dey got even *you* whupped?

HEAD MAGICIAN: Dey's got a new kind of magic.

PHARAOH: [*Gazes at* Head Magician *a moment, bewildered. To the* Wizards] I s'pose if de Professor cain't, you cain't.

FIRST WIZARD: Dat's a new trick, King.

HEAD MAGICIAN: [*Rubbing his fingers along his palms*] It's got 'lectricity in it!

PHARAOH: Hm, well dat may make it a little diff'rent. So you boys is magicians, too?

MOSES: Yes, suh.

PHARAOH: Well, we's always glad to see some new trickers in de co't, dat is if dey good. [*He glances about him*] You look like you is O. K.

MOSES: Dat's what we claims, ol' King Pharaoh. We think we's de best in de worl'.

PHARAOH: You certainly kin talk big. Jest what is it you boys would like?

MOSES: We came to show you some tricks. Den we's goin' to ask you to do somethin' for us.

PHARAOH: Well, I s'pose you know I'm a fool for conjurin'. If a man kin show me some tricks I ain't seen, I goes out of my way to do him a favor.

MOSES: Dat's good. Want to see de first trick?

PHARAOH: It ain't goin' to hurt nobody?

MOSES: Dis one won't.

PHARAOH: Go ahead.

MOSES: Dis yere rod my brother has looks jes' like a walkin' stick, don't it?

[*The* Courtiers *now join the* King *in interest*]

PHARAOH: Uh-huh. Le's see.

[Aaron *hands him the rod, which* Pharaoh *inspects and returns*]

MOSES: Well, look what happens when he lays it on de groun'.

[Aaron *places the rod on the second step of the throne. It turns into a life-like snake. There are exclamations from the assemblage*]

PHARAOH: Dat's a good trick! Now turn it back into a walkin' stick again. [Aaron *picks it up and it is again a rod. Exclamations of "Purty good!" "Dat's all right!" "What do you think of that!" etc.*] Say, you is good trickers!

MOSES: You ain't never seen de beat of us. Now I'm goin' to ask de favor.

PHARAOH: Sure, what is it?

MOSES: [*Solemnly*] Let de Hebrew chillun go!

PHARAOH: [*Rises and stares at them. There is a murmur of "Listen to 'im!" "He's got nerve!" "I never in my life!" "My goodness!" etc.*] What did you say?

MOSES: Let de Hebrew chillun go.

[Pharaoh *seats himself again*]

PHARAOH: [*Slowly*] Don' you know de Hebrews is my slaves?

MOSES: Yes, suh.

PHARAOH: Yes, suh, my slaves. [*There is a distant groaning*] Listen, and you kin hear 'em bein' treated like slaves. [*He calls toward the window*] What was dey doin' den?

MAN NEAR THE WINDOW: Dey's jest gettin' de news down in de brickyard.

PHARAOH: I won't let them go. [*He snorts contemptuously*] Let's see another trick.

MOSES: Yes, suh, yere's a better one. [*He lowers his head*] Let's have a plague of de flies.

[Aaron *raises the rod. The room grows dark and a great buzzing of flies is heard. The* Courtiers *break out in cries of "Get away fum me!" "Take 'em away!" "De place is filled with flies!" "Dis is terrible!" "Do sump'n, Pharaoh!"*]

PHARAOH: [*Topping the others*] All right—stop de trick!

MOSES: Will you let de Hebrews go?

PHARAOH: Sho' I will. Go ahead, stop it!

MOSES: [*Also above the others*] Begone!

[*The buzzing stops and the room is filled with light again, as* Aaron *lowers the rod. All except* Moses *and* Aaron *are brushing the flies from their persons*]

PHARAOH: [*Laughing*] Doggone, dat was a good trick! [*The others, seeing they are uninjured, join in the laughter, with exclamations of "Doggone!" "You all right?" "Sho' I'm all right." "Didn't hurt me," etc.*] You is good trickers.

MOSES: Will you let de Hebrew chillun go?

PHARAOH: [*Sitting down again*] Well, I'll tell you, boys. I'll tell you sump'n you didn' know. You take me, *I'm* a pretty good tricker, an' I jest outtricked you. So, bein' de bes' tricker, I don' think I will let 'em go. You got any mo' tricks yo'self?

MOSES: Yes, suh. Dis is a little harder one. [*Aaron lifts the rod*] Gnats in de mill pon', gnats in de clover, gnats in de 'tater patch, stingin' all over.

[*The stage grows dark again. There is the humming of gnats and the slapping of hands against faces and arms, and the same protests as were heard with the flies, but with more feeling: "I'm gittin' stung to death!" "I'm all stung!" "Dey're like hornets!" "Dey's on my face!" etc.*]

PHARAOH: Take 'em away, Moses!

MOSES: [*His voice drowning the others*] If I do, will you let 'em go?

PHARAOH: Sho' I will, dis time.

MOSES: Do you mean it?

PHARAOH: Co'se I mean it! Doggone, one just stang me on de nose.

MOSES: Begone! [*Lights come up as Aaron lowers the rod. There is a moment of general recovery again. Pharaoh rubs his nose, looks at his hands, etc., as do the others*] Now, how about it?

PHARAOH: [*Smiling*] Well, I'll tell you, Moses. Now dat de trick's over——

[*Moses takes a step toward Pharaoh*]

MOSES: Listen, Pharaoh. You been lyin' to me, and I'm gittin' tired of it.

PHARAOH: I ain't lyin', I'm trickin', too. You trickin' me and I been trickin' you.

MOSES: I see. Well, I got one mo' trick up my sleeve which I didn't aim to wukk unless I had to. Caize when I does it, I cain't undo it.

PHARAOH: Wukk it an' I'll trick you right back. I don' say you ain't a good tricker, Moses. You is one of de bes' I ever seen. But I kin outtrick you. Dat's all.

MOSES: It ain't only me dat's goin' to wukk dis trick. It's me an' de Lawd.

PHARAOH: Who?

MOSES: De Lawd God of Israel.

PHARAOH: I kin outtrick you an' de Lawd too!

MOSES: [*Angrily*] Now you done it, ol' King Pharaoh. You been mean to de Lawd's people, and de Lawd's been easy on you caize you didn' know better. You been givin' me a lot of say-so and no do-so, and I didn' min' dat. But now you've got to braggin' dat you's better dan de Lawd, and dat's too many.

PHARAOH: You talk like a preacher, an' I never did like to hear preachers talk.

MOSES: You ain't goin' to like it any better, when I strikes down de oldes' boy in every one of yo' people's houses.

PHARAOH: Now, you've given up trickin' and is jest lyin'. [*He rises*] Listen, I'm Pharaoh. I do de strikin' down yere. I strike down my enemies, and dere's no one in all Egypt kin kill who he wants to, 'ceptin' me.

MOSES: I'm sorry, Pharaoh. Will you let de Hebrews go?

PHARAOH: You heard my word. [*Aaron is lifting his rod again at a signal from Moses*] Now, no more tricks or I'll——

MOSES: Oh, Lawd, you'll have to do it, I guess. Aaron, lift de rod.

[*There is a thunderclap, darkness and screams. The lights go up. Several of the younger men on the stage have fallen to the ground or are being held in the arms of the horrified elders*]

PHARAOH: What have you done yere? Where's my boy?

[*Through the door come four men bearing a young man's body*]

FIRST OF THE FOUR MEN: King Pharaoh.

[*Pharaoh drops into his chair, stunned, as the dead boy is brought to the throne*]

PHARAOH: [*Grief-stricken*] Oh, my son, my fine son.

[*The Courtiers look at him with mute appeal*]

MOSES: I'm sorry, Pharaoh, but you cain't fight de Lawd. Will you let his people go?

PHARAOH: Let dem go.

[*The lights go out. The Choir begins, "Mary, Don't You Weep," and continues until it is broken by the strains of "I'm Noways Weary and I'm Noways Tired." The latter is sung by many more voices than the former, and the cacophony ends as the latter grows in volume and the lights go up on the next scene*]

SCENE IV.

The Children of Israel *are marching on the treadmill and now singing fortissimo. They are of all ages and most of them are ragged. The men have packs on their shoulders, one or two have hand carts. The line stretches across the stage. It is nearing twilight, and the faces of the assemblage are illumined by the rays of the late afternoon sun. The upper treadmill carries a gradually rising and falling middle distance past the marchers. The foot of a mountain appears; a trumpet call is heard as the foot of the mountain reaches stage center. The marchers halt. The picture now shows the mountain running up out of sight off right. The singing stops. A babel of "What's de matter?" "Why do we stop?" "'Tain't sundown yet!" "What's happened?" "What's goin' on?" "What are they blowin' for?" etc. Those looking ahead begin to murmur. "It's Moses," "Moses," "What's happened to him?" The others take up the repetition of "Moses," and Moses enters, on the arm of Aaron. He is now an old man, as is his brother, and he totters toward the center of the stage. Cries of "What's de matter, Moses?" "You ain't hurt, is you?" "Ain't that too bad?" etc. He slowly seats himself on the rock at the foot of the mountain.*

AARON: How you feelin' now, brother?

MOSES: I'm so weary, Aaron. Seems like I was took all of a sudden.

AARON: Do we camp yere?

MOSES: [*Pathetically*] No, you got to keep goin'.

AARON: But you cain't go no further tonight, brother.

MOSES: Dis never happened to me befo'.

A YOUNG WOMAN: But you's a ol' man, now, Father Moses. You cain't expect to go as fas' as we kin.

MOSES: But de Lawd said I'd do it. He said I was to show you de Promised Land. Fo'ty years, I bin leadin' you. I led you out o' Egypt. I led you past Sinai, and through de wilderness. Oh, I cain't fall down on you now.

AARON: Le's res' yere fo' de night. Den we'll see how you feel in de mo'nin'.

MOSES: We tol' de scouts we'd meet 'em three miles further on. I hate fo' 'em to come back all dis way to report. 'Tis gettin' a little dark, ain't it?

AARON: It ain't dark, brother.

MOSES: No, it's my eyes.

AARON: Maybe it's de dust.

MOSES: No, I jest cain't seem to see. Oh, Lawd, dey cain't have a blind man leadin' 'em! Where is you, Aaron?

AARON: I'se right yere, Moses.

MOSES: Do you think— [*Pause*] Oh! Do you think it's de time He said?

AARON: How you mean, Moses?

[*Crowd looks from one to another in wonder*]

MOSES: He said I could lead 'em to de Jordan, dat I'd *see* de Promised Land, and dat's all de further I could go, on account I broke de laws. Little while back I thought I *did* see a river ahead, and a pretty land on de other side. [*Distant shouts "Hooray!" "Yere dey are!" "Dey traveled quick,"* etc.] Where's de young leader of de troops? Where's Joshua?

[*The call "Joshua" is taken up by those on the right of the stage, followed almost immediately by "Yere he is!" "Moses wants you!" etc. Joshua enters. He is a fine-looking Negro of about thirty*]

JOSHUA: [*Going to Moses' side*] Yes, suh.

MOSES: What's de shoutin' 'bout, Joshua?

JOSHUA: De scouts is back wid de news. De Jordan is right ahead of us, and Jericho is jest on de other side. Moses, we're dere! [*There are cries of "Hallelujah!" "De Lawd be praised!" "Hooray!" "De King-dom's comin'!" etc. With a considerable stir among the marchers, several new arrivals crowd in from*

right, shouting "Moses, we're dere!" Joshua, seeing the newcomers*] Yere's de scouts.

[*Three very ragged and dusty young men advance to Moses*]

MOSES: [*As the shouting dies*] So it's de river Jordan?

FIRST SCOUT: Yes, suh.

MOSES: All we got to take is de city of Jericho.

FIRST SCOUT: Yes, suh.

MOSES: Joshua, you got to take charge of de fightin' men, an' Aaron's gotta stay by de priests.

JOSHUA: What about you?

MOSES: You are leavin' me behind. Joshua, you gonter get de fightin' men together and take dat city befo' sundown.

JOSHUA: It's a big city, Moses, wid walls all 'round it. We ain't got enough men.

MOSES: You'll take it, Joshua.

JOSHUA: Yes, suh, but how?

MOSES: Move up to de walls wid our people. Tell de priests to go wid you with de rams' horns. You start marchin' 'roun' dem walls, and den——

JOSHUA: Yes, suh.

MOSES: De Lawd'll take charge, jest as He's took charge ev'y time I've led you against a city. He ain't never failed, has He?

SEVERAL VOICES: No, Moses.

[*All raise their heads*]

MOSES: And He ain't goin' to fail us now. [*He prays. All bow*] Oh, Lawd, I'm turnin' over our brave young men to you, caize I know you don' want me to lead 'em any further. [*Rises*] Jest like you said, I've got to de Jordan but I cain't git over it. An' yere dey goin' now to take de city of Jericho. In a little while dey'll be marchin' 'roun' it. An' would you please be so good as to tell 'em what to do? Amen. [*To Joshua*] Go ahead. Ev'ybody follows Joshua now. Give de signal to move on wid ev'y-thing. [*A trumpet is heard*] You camp fo' de night in de city of Jericho.

[*Moses seats himself on the rock*]

JOSHUA: Cain't we help you, Moses?

MOSES: You go ahead. De Lawd's got his plans fo' me. Soun' de signal to march. [*Another trumpet call is heard. The company starts marching off. Aaron lingers a moment*] Take care of de Ark of de Covenant, Aaron.

AARON: Yes, brother. Goodbye.

MOSES: Goodbye, Aaron. [*The singing is resumed softly and dies away. The last of the marchers has disappeared*] Yere I is, Lawd. De chillun is goin' into de Promised Land. [*God enters from behind the hill. He walks to Moses, puts His hands on his shoulders*] You's with me, ain't you, Lawd?

GOD: Co'se I is.

MOSES: Guess I'm through, Lawd. Jest like you said I'd be, when I broke de tablets of de law. De ol' machine broke down.

GOD: Jest what was it I said to you, Moses? Do you remember?

MOSES: You said I couldn't go into de Promised Land.

GOD: Dat's so. But dat ain't all dey was to it.

MOSES: How you mean, Lawd?

GOD: Moses, you been a good man. You been a good leader of my people. You got me angry once, dat's true. And when you anger me I'm a God of Wrath. But I never meant you wasn't gonter have what was comin' to you. An' I ain't goin' to do you out of it, Moses. It's jest de country acrost de river dat you ain't gonter enter. You gonter have a Promised Land. I been gettin' it ready fo' you, fo' a long time. Kin you stand up?

MOSES: [Rising, with God's help] Yes, suh, Lawd.

GOD: Come on, I'm goin' to show it to you. We goin' up this hill to see it. Moses, it's a million times nicer dan de Land of Canaan.

[They start up the hill]

MOSES: I cain't hardly see.

GOD: Don't worry. Dat's jest caize you so old.

[They take a step or two up the hill, when Moses stops suddenly]

MOSES: Oh!

GOD: What's de matter?

MOSES: We cain't be doin' dis!

GOD: Co'se we kin!

MOSES: But I fo'got! I fo'got about Joshua and de fightin' men!

GOD: How about 'em?

MOSES: Dey're marchin' on Jericho. I tol' 'em to march aroun' de walls and den de Lawd would be dere to tell 'em what to do.

GOD: Dat's all right. He's dere.

MOSES: Den who's dis helpin' me up de hill?

GOD: Yo' faith, yo' God.

MOSES: And is you over dere helpin' dem too, Lawd? Is you goin' to tell dem poor chillun what to do?

GOD: Co'se I is. Listen, Moses. I'll show you how I'm helpin' dem.

[From the distance comes the blast of the rams' horns, the sound of crumbling walls, a roar, and a moment's silence. The Choir begins "Joshua Fit de Battle of Jericho" and continues through the rest of the scene]

MOSES: You did it, Lawd! You've tooken it! Listen to de chillun'—dey's in de Land of Canaan at last! You's de only God dey ever was, ain't you, Lawd?

GOD: [Quietly] Come on, ol' man.

[They continue up the hill. The stage is darkened]

MR. DESHEE: [In the dark] But even dat scheme didn' work. Caize after dey got into the Land of Canaan dey went to de dogs again. And dey went into bondage again. Only dis time it was in de city of Babylon.

[The Choir, which has been singing "Cain't Stay Away," stops as the next scene begins]

SCENE V.

Under a low ceiling is a room vaguely resembling a Negro night club in New Orleans. Two or three long tables run across the room, and on the left is a table on a dais with a gaudy canopy above it. The table bears a card marked "Reserved for King and guests."

Flashy young men and women are seated at the tables. About a dozen couples are dancing in the foreground to the tune of a jazz orchestra. The costumes are what would be worn at a Negro masquerade to represent the debauchees of Babylon.

FIRST MAN: When did yuh git to Babylon?

SECOND MAN: I jes' got in yesterday.

THIRD MAN: [Dancing] How do you like dis baby, Joe?

FOURTH MAN: Hot damn! She could be de King's pet!

A WOMAN: Anybody seen my papa?

THIRD MAN: Don' fo'git de dance at de High Priest's home to-morrow.

[The dance stops as a bugle call is heard. Enter Master of Ceremonies]

MASTER OF CEREMONIES: Stop! To-night's guest of honor, de King of Babylon, an' party of five.

[Enter the King and five girls. The King has on an imitation ermine cloak over his conventional clothes and wears a diamond tiara. All rise as the King enters, and sing, "Hail, de King of Bab—Bab—Babylon"]

KING: Wait till you see de swell table I got. [He crosses the stage to his table. The girls are jabbering] Remind me to send you a peck of rubies in de mo'nin'.

MASTER OF CEREMONIES: Ev'nin', King!

KING: Good ev'nin'. How's de party goin'?

MASTER OF CEREMONIES: Bes' one we ever had in Babylon, King.

KING: Any Jew boys yere?

MASTER OF CEREMONIES: [Indicating some of the others] Lot o' dem yere. I kin go git mo' if you want 'em.

KING: I was really referrin' to de High Priest. He's a 'tic'lar frien' o' mine an' he might drop in. You know what he look like?

MASTER OF CEREMONIES: No, suh, but I'll be on de look-out fo' him.

KING: O.K. Now le's have a li'l good time.

MASTER OF CEREMONIES: Yes, suh. [To the orchestra] Let 'er go, boys.

[The music begins, waiters appear with food and great urns painted gold and silver, from which they pour out wine for the guests. The Master of Ceremonies exits. The King's dancing-girls go to the middle of the floor, and start to dance. The King puts his arms about the waists of two girls, and draws them to him]

KING: Hot damn! Da's de way! Let de Jew boys see our gals kin dance better'n deirs. [*There is an ad lib.* babel *of "Da's de truth, King!" "I don't know —we got some good gals, too!" etc.*] Dey ain' nobody in de worl' like Babylon gals.

[*The dancing grows faster, the watchers keep time with handclaps. The door at the left opens suddenly, and the* Prophet, *a patriarchal, ragged figure, enters. He looks belligerently about the room, and is followed almost immediately by the* Master of Ceremonies]

PROPHET: Stop!

[*The music and the dancers halt*]

KING: What's the idea, bustin' up my party?

MASTER OF CEREMONIES: He said he was expected, King. I thought mebbe he was de—

KING: Did you think he was de High Priest of de Hebrews? Why, he's jest an' ol' bum! Throw dis ol' bum out o' yere! De High Priest is a fashion plate. Throw dis ol' bum out o' yere!

PROPHET: Stop!

[*Those who have been advancing to seize him stop, somewhat amused*]

KING: Wait a minute. Don't throw him out. Let's see what he has to say.

PROPHET: Listen to me, King of Babylon! I've been sent yere by de Lawd God Jehovah. Don't you dare lay a hand on de Prophet!

KING: Oh, you're a prophet, is yuh? Well, you know we don't keer much fo' prophets in dis part of de country.

PROPHET: Listen to me, sons and daughters of Babylon! Listen, you children of Israel dat's given yo'selves over to de evil ways of yo' oppressors! You're all wallowin' like hogs in sin, an' de wrath of God ain' goin' to be held back much longer! I'm tellin' you, repent befo' it's too late. Repent befo' Jehovah casts down de same fire dat burned up Sodom and Gomorrah. Repent befo' de——

[*During this scene yells increase as the* Prophet *continues. The High Priest enters left. He is a fat voluptuary, elaborately clothed in brightly colored robes. He walks in hand in hand with a gaudily dressed chippy*]

HIGH PRIEST: [*Noise stops*] Whoa, dere! What you botherin' the King fo'?

PROPHET: [*Wheeling*] And you, de High Priest of all Israel, walkin' de town wid a dirty li'l tramp.

KING: Seems to be a frien' o' yours, Jake.

HIGH PRIEST: [*Crossing to the* King *with his girl*] Aw, he's one of dem wild men, like Jeremiah and Isaiah. Don' let him bother you none.

[*Pushes* Prophet *aside and goes to* King's *table*]

PROPHET: You consort with harlots, an' yo' pollution in the sight of the Lawd. De Lawd God's goin' to smite you down, jest as he's goin' to smite down all dis wicked world!

[*Grabs* High Priest *and turns him around*]

KING: [*Angrily against the last part of the preceding speech*] Wait a minute. I'm getting tired of this. Don' throw him out. Jest kill him!

[*There is the sound of a shot. The* Prophet *falls*]

PROPHET: Smite 'em down, Lawd, like you said. Dey ain't a decent person left in de whole world.

[*He dies. The* Master of Ceremonies, *revolver in hand, looks down at the* Prophet]

MASTER OF CEREMONIES: He's dead, King.

KING: Some of you boys take him out.

[*A couple of young men come from the background and walk off with the body*]

HIGH PRIEST: Don' know whether you should'a done that, King.

KING: Why not?

HIGH PRIEST: I don' know whether de Lawd would like it.

KING: Now, listen, Jake. You know yo' Lawd ain't payin' much attention to dis man's town. Except fo' you boys, it's tho'ly protected by de Gods o' Babylon.

HIGH PRIEST: I know, but jest de same——

KING: Look yere, s'pose I give you a couple hund'ed pieces of silver. Don' you s'pose you kin arrange to persuade yo' God to keep his hands off?

HIGH PRIEST: [*Oilily*] Well of co'se we could try. I dunno how well it would work.

[*As the* High Priest *speaks, the* King *claps his hands.* Master of Ceremonies *enters with bag of money*]

KING: Yere it is.

HIGH PRIEST: [*Smiling*] I guess we kin square things up. [*He prays—whiningly*] Oh Lawd, please forgive my po' frien' de King o' Babylon. He didn't know what he was doin' an'——

[*There is a clap of thunder, darkness for a second. The lights go up and* God *is standing in the center of the room*]

GOD: [*In a voice of doom*] Dat's about enough. [*The guests are horrified*] I'se stood all I kin from you. I tried to make dis a good earth. I helped Adam, I helped Noah, I helped Moses, an' I helped David. What's de grain dat grew out of de seed? Sin! Nothin' but sin throughout de whole world. I've given you ev'y chance. I sent you warriors and prophets. I've given you laws and commandments, an' you betrayed my trust. Ev'ything I've given you, you've defiled. Ev'y time I've fo'given you, you've mocked me. An' now de High Priest of Israel tries to trifle wid my name. Listen, you chillun of darkness, yo' Lawd is tired. I'm tired of de struggle to make you worthy of de breath I gave you. I put you in bondage ag'in to cure you an' yo' worse dan you was amongst de flesh pots of Egypt. So I renounce you. Listen to the words of yo' Lawd God Jehovah, for dey is de last words yo' ever hear from me. I repent of dese people dat I have made and I will deliver dem no more.

[*There is darkness and cries of "Mercy!" "Have pity, Lawd!" "We didn' mean it, Lawd!"*]

"Forgive us, Lawd!" etc. The Choir *sings "Death's Gwinter Lay His Cold Icy Hands on Me" until the lights go up on the next scene]*

SCENE VI.

God *is writing at His desk. Outside, past the door, goes* Hosea, *a dignified old man, with wings like* Jacob's. God, *sensing his presence, looks up from the paper He is examining, and follows* him *out of the corner of His eye. Angrily He resumes His work as soon as* Hosea *is out of sight. There is a knock on the door.*

GOD: Who is it?

[Gabriel *enters*]

GABRIEL: It's de delegation, Lawd.

GOD: [*Wearily*] Tell 'em to come in. [Abraham, Isaac, Jacob, *and* Moses *enter*] Good mo'nin', gen'lemen.

THE VISITORS: Good mo'nin', Lawd.

GOD: What kin I do for you?

MOSES: You know, Lawd. Go back to our people.

GOD: [*Shaking His head*] Ev'ry day fo' hund'eds of years you boys have come in to ask dat same thing. De answer is still de same. I repented of de people I made. I said I would deliver dem no more. Good mo'nin', gen'lemen. [*The four visitors rise and exeunt.* Gabriel *remains*] Gabe, why do dey do it?

GABRIEL: I 'spect dey think you gonter change yo' mind.

GOD: [*Sadly*] Dey don' know me. [Hosea *again passes the door. His shadow shows on wall.* Gabriel *is perplexed, as he watches.* God *again looks surreptitiously over His shoulder at the passing figure*] I don' like dat, either.

GABRIEL: What, Lawd?

GOD: Dat man.

GABRIEL: He's just a prophet, Lawd. Dat's jest old Hosea. He jest come up the other day.

GOD: I know. He's one of de few dat's come up yere since I was on de earth last time.

GABRIEL: Ain' been annoyin' you, has he?

GOD: I don' like him walkin' past de door.

GABRIEL: All you got to do is tell him to stop, Lawd.

GOD: Yes, I know. I don' want to tell him. He's got a right up yere or he wouldn' be yere.

GABRIEL: You needn' be bothered by him hangin' aroun' de office all de time. I'll tell 'im. Who's he think he——

GOD: No, Gabe. I find it ain't in me to stop him. I sometimes jest wonder why he don' jest come in an' say hello.

GABRIEL: You want him to do that?

[*He moves as if to go to the door*]

GOD: He never has spoke to me, and if he don't

wanta come in, I ain't gonter make him. But dat ain't de worst of it, Gabriel.

GABRIEL: What is, Lawd?

GOD: Ev'y time he goes past de door I hears a voice.

GABRIEL: One of de angels?

GOD: [*Shaking His head*] It's from de earth. It's a man.

GABRIEL: You mean he's prayin'?

GOD: No, he ain't exactly prayin'. He's jest talkin' in such a way dat I got to lissen. His name is Hezdrel.

GABRIEL: Is he on de books?

GOD: No, not yet. But ev'y time dat Hosea goes past I hear dat voice.

GABRIEL: Den tell it to stop.

GOD: I find I don' want to do that, either. Dey's gettin' ready to take Jerusalem down dere. Dat was my big fine city. Dis Hezdrel, he's jest one of de defenders. [*Suddenly and passionately, almost wildly*] I ain't comin' down. You hear me? I ain't comin' down. [*He looks at* Gabriel] Go ahead, Gabriel. 'Tend to yo' chores. I'm gonter keep wukkin' yere.

GABRIEL: I hates to see you feelin' like dis, Lawd

GOD: Dat's all right. Even bein' God ain't a bed of roses. [Gabriel *exits.* Hosea's *shadow is on the wall. For a second* Hosea *hesitates.* God *looks at the wall. Goes to window*] I hear you. I know yo' fightin' bravely, but I ain't comin' down. Oh, why don' you leave me alone? You know you ain't talkin' to me. *Is* you talkin' to me? I cain't stand yo' talkin' dat way. I kin only hear part of what yo' sayin', and it puzzles me. Don' you know you cain't puzzle God? [*A pause. Then, tenderly*] Do you want me to come down dere ve'y much? You know I said I wouldn't come down? [*Fiercely*] Why don' he answer me a little? [*With clenched fists, looks down through the window*] Listen! I'll tell you what I'll do. I ain't goin' to promise you anythin', and I ain't goin' to do nothin' to help you. I'm jest feelin' a little low, an' I'm only comin down to make myself feel a little better, dat's all.

[*The stage is darkened.* Choir *begins "A Blind Man Stood in de Middle of de Road," and continues until the lights go up on the next scene*]

SCENE VII.

It is a shadowed corner beside the walls of the temple in Jerusalem. The light of camp fires flickers on the figure of Hezdrel, *who was* Adam *in Part I. He stands in the same position* Adam *held when first discovered but in his right hand is a sword, and his left is in a sling. Around him are several prostrate bodies. Pistol and cannon shots, then a trumpet call. Six young men enter from left in command of a* Corporal. *They are all armed.*

CORPORAL: De fightin' stopped fo' de night, Hezdrel.

HEZDREL: Yes?

CORPORAL: Dey're goin' to begin ag'in at cockcrow. [Man *enters, crosses the stage and exits*] Herod say he's goin' to take de temple to-morrow, burn de books and de Ark of de Covenant, and put us all to de sword.

HEZDREL: Yo' ready, ain't you?

EVERYBODY: Yes, Hezdrel.

HEZDREL: Did de food get in through the hole in de city wall?

[*Two* Soldiers *enter, cross the stage and exeunt*]

CORPORAL: Yessuh, we's goin' back to pass it out now.

HEZDREL: Good. Any mo' of our people escape to-day?

CORPORAL: Ol' Herod's got de ol' hole covered up now, but fifteen of our people got out a new one we made.

[*Other* Soldiers *enter, cross the stage and exeunt*]

HEZDREL: Good. Take dese yere wounded men back and git 'em took care of.

CORPORAL: Yes, suh.

[*They pick up the bodies on the ground and carry them off stage as* Hezdrel *speaks*]

HEZDREL: So dey gonter take de temple in de mo'nin'? We'll be waitin' for 'em. Jest remember, boys, when dey kill us we leap out of our skins, right into de lap of God.

[*The Men disappear with the wounded; from the deep shadow upstage comes God*]

GOD: Hello, Hezdrel—Adam.

HEZDREL: [*Rubbing his forehead*] Who is you?

GOD: Me? I'm jest an ol' preacher, from back in de hills.

HEZDREL: What you doin' yere?

GOD: I heard you boys was fightin'. I jest wanted to see how it was goin'.

HEZDREL: Well, it ain't goin' so well.

GOD: Dey got you skeered, huh?

HEZDREL: Look yere, who is you, a spy in my brain?

GOD: Cain't you see I'se one of yo' people?

HEZDREL: Listen, Preacher, we ain't skeered. We's gonter be killed, but we ain't skeered.

GOD: I'se glad to hear dat. Kin I ask you a question, Hezdrel?

HEZDREL: What is it?

GOD: How is it you is so brave?

HEZDREL: Caize we got faith, dat's why.

GOD: Faith? In who?

HEZDREL: In our dear Lawd God.

GOD: But God say he abandoned ev'y one down yere.

HEZDREL: Who say dat? Who dare say dat of de Lawd God of Hosea?

GOD: De God of Hosea?

HEZDREL: You heard me. Look yere, you *is* a spy in my brain!

GOD: No, I ain't, Hezdrel, I'm jest puzzled. You ought to know dat.

HEZDREL: How come you so puzzled 'bout de God of Hosea?

GOD: I don't know. Maybe I jest don' hear things. You see, I live 'way back in de hills.

HEZDREL: What you wanter find out?

GOD: Ain't de God of Hosea de same Jehovah dat was de God of Moses?

HEZDREL: [*Contemptuously*] No. Dat ol' God of wrath and vengeance? We have de God dat Hosea preached to us. He's de one God.

GOD: Who's he?

HEZDREL: [*Reverently*] De God of mercy.

GOD: Hezdrel, don' you think dey must be de same God?

HEZDREL: I don' know. I ain't bothered to think much about it. Maybe dey is. Maybe our God is de same ol' God. I guess He jest got tired of His appearance dat ol' way.

GOD: What you mean, Hezdrel?

HEZDREL: Oh, dat ol' God dat walked de earth in de shape of a man. I guess he lived with man so much dat all he seen was de sins in man. Dat's what made him de God of wrath and vengeance. Co'se he made Hosea. An' Hosea never would a found what mercy was unless dere was a little of it in God, too. Anyway, he ain't a fearsome God no mo'. Hosea showed us dat.

GOD: How you s'pose Hosea found dat mercy?

HEZDREL: De only way he could find it. De only way I found it. De only way anyone could find it.

GOD: How's dat?

HEZDREL: Through sufferin'.

GOD: [*After a pause*] What if dey kill you in de mo'nin', Hezdrel?

HEZDREL: If dey do, dey do. Dat's all.

GOD: Herod say he's goin' to burn de temple—

HEZDREL: So he say.

GOD: And burn de Ark an' de books. Den dat's de end of de books, ain't it?

HEZDREL: [*Buoyantly*] What you mean? If he burns dem things in dere? Naw. Dem's jest copies.

GOD: Where is de others?

HEZDREL: [*Tapping his head*] Dey's a set in yere. Fifteen got out through de hole in the city wall to-day. A hundred and fifty got out durin' de week. Each of 'em is a set of de books. Dey's scattered safe all over de countryside now, jest waitin' to git pen and paper fo' to put 'em down ag'in.

GOD: [*Proudly*] Dey cain't lick you, kin dey, Hezdrel?

HEZDREL: [*Smiling*] I know dey cain't. [*Trumpet*] You better get out o' yere, Preacher, if you wanter carry de news to yo' people. It'll soon be daylight.

GOD: I'm goin'. [*He takes a step upstage and stops*] Want me to take any message?

HEZDREL: Tell de people in de hills dey ain't nobody like de Lawd God of Hosea.

GOD: I will; if dey kill you to-morrow I'll bet dat God of Hosea'll be waitin' for you.

HEZDREL: I *know* he will.

GOD: [*Quietly*] Thank you, Hezdrel.

HEZDREL: Fo' what?

GOD: Fo' tellin' me so much. You see, I been so far away, I guess I was jest way behin' de times.

[*He exits. Pause, then trumpet sounds. Hezdrel paces back and forth once or twice. Another young Soldier appears. Other men enter and stand grouped about Hezdrel*]

SECOND OFFICER: [*Excitedly*] De cock's jest crowed, Hezdrel. Dey started de fightin' ag'in.

HEZDREL: We's ready for 'em. Come on, boys. [*From the darkness upstage comes another group of soldiers*] Dis is de day dey say dey'll git us. Le's fight till de last man goes. What d'you say?

CORPORAL: Le's go, Hezdrel!

HEZDREL: [*Calling left*] Give 'em ev'ything boys!

[*There is a movement toward the left, a bugle call and the sound of distant battle. The lights go out. The Choir is heard singing, "March On," triumphantly. They continue to sing after the lights go up on the next scene*]

SCENE VIII.

It is the same setting as the Fish Fry Scene in Part I. The same angels are present but the Choir, instead of marching, is standing in a double row on an angle upstage right. God is seated in an armchair near center. He faces the audience. As the Choir continues to sing, Gabriel enters, unnoticed by the chattering angels. He looks at God, who is staring thoughtfully toward the audience.

GABRIEL: You look a little pensive, Lawd. [*God nods his head*] Have a seegar, Lawd?

GOD: No, thanks, Gabriel.

[*Gabriel goes to the table, accepts a cup of custard; chats with the angel behind the table for a moment as he sips, puts the cup down and returns to the side of God*]

GABRIEL: You look awful pensive, Lawd. You been sittin' yere, lookin' dis way, an awful long time. Is it somethin' serious, Lawd?

GOD: Very serious, Gabriel.

GABRIEL: [*Awed by His tone*] Lawd, is de time come for me to blow?

GOD: Not yet, Gabriel. I'm just thinkin'.

GABRIEL: What about, Lawd?

[*Puts up hand. Singing stops*]

GOD: 'Bout somethin' de boy tol' me. Somethin' 'bout Hosea, and himself. How dey foun' somethin'.

GABRIEL: What, Lawd?

GOD: Mercy. [*A pause*] Through *sufferin'*, he said.

GABRIEL: Yes, Lawd.

GOD: I'm tryin' to find it, too. It's awful impo'tant. It's awful impo'tant to all de people on my earth. Did he mean dat even God must suffer?

[*God continues to look out over the audience for a moment and then a look of surprise comes into His face. He sighs. In the distance a voice cries*]

THE VOICE: Oh, look at him! Oh, look, dey goin' to make him carry it up dat high hill! Dey goin' to nail him to it! Oh, dat's a terrible burden for one man to carry!

[*God rises and murmurs "Yes!" as if in recognition. The heavenly beings have been watching Him closely, and now, seeing Him smile gently, draw back, relieved. All the angels burst into "Hallelujah, King Jesus." God continues to smile as the lights fade away. The singing becomes fortissimo*]

CURTAIN

Thornton Wilder

(1897– —)

Thornton Niven Wilder has the double distinction of being a successful novelist and an original dramatist. His two important full-length plays—the Pulitzer Prize drama *Our Town* and *The Skin of Our Teeth*—reflect the theme of all Wilder's major writing—man in the universe. He belongs to the select few who have managed to restore the primacy of imagination to the drama in a completely modern idiom.

Born in Madison, Wisconsin, Wilder spent part of his childhood in China, returning to the United States to complete his high-school education. His college studies were interrupted by his service in the Coast Artillery Corps in the First World War, but he returned to complete them and then spent a graduate year studying archaeology at the American Academy in Rome. During and after his further graduate work at Princeton, he taught at the Lawrenceville School. From 1930 to 1936 he was a member of the faculty of the University of Chicago. In the Second World War he served with the Air Forces Intelligence in North Africa and Italy.

Because of his broad knowledge of European culture, Wilder was called upon by producers to adapt to the stage various foreign works, and his literary activities have won awards for him not only in the United States but from other countries as well.

It was as a novelist that Wilder first won recognition. He received high praise for *The Cabala* (1925) and was awarded a Pulitzer Prize for his philosophical novel *The Bridge of San Luis Rey* (1927). Subsequently, he wrote *The Woman of Andros* (1930) and *Heaven's My Destination* (1935). Much later, after winning success in the theatre, he proved that he was still adept at writing noteworthy fiction, with his semi-Shavian story of Julius Caesar, *The Ides of March* (1948).

Wilder's career in the theatre started inauspiciously with a play called *The Trumpet Shall Sound*, which Richard Boleslavsky's Laboratory Theatre produced in New York in 1926. Wilder then brought out two collections of one-act plays, *The Angel That Troubled the Waters* (1928) and *The Long Christmas Dinner* (1931). Some of these one-acters are notable as early examples of Wilder's interest in the everyday events of simple life and of his fondness for nonrealistic styles of play construction. In 1932, he adapted André Obey's *Lucrece* for Katherine Cornell.

It was rather late in his career that Wilder made his special impression on the theatre. In 1938, in addition to adapting a German play, *The Merchant of Yonkers*, which failed on Broadway, he made theatrical history with *Our Town*. This play received a brilliant production on a bare stage from the volatile genius of the American theatre Jed Harris; it had for its chief actor the lovable performer Frank Craven, who played the Narrator. *Our Town* enjoyed a long run on Broadway, toured widely, and has been a favorite production in the little theatres throughout the United States. In 1942, Wilder startled playgoers with a uniquely stylized drama, *The Skin of Our Teeth*, which telescoped human history in the story of a New Jersey suburban family. Although it did not succeed as well as *Our Town*, *The Skin of Our Teeth* made a deep impression. It was the profoundest commentary on the Second World War crisis of which the American theatre proved capable. In 1948, Wilder's adaptation of a play by Sartre, *The Victors*, received an experimental production. But it was not written in Wilder's characteristic vein, and it throws no light on the nonrealistic dramatic art for which he will be remembered.

Our Town is generally regarded as one of the best examples of stylized dramaturgy developed by an American. From a historical point of view, it is, in fact, an example of a style better represented by the artistry of stage designers and directors than by the work of playwrights. From 1910 on, reports of miraculous productions had been drifting to the United States from the Continent. In these productions, the style of the stagecraft called attention to the nonrepresentational or "theatrical" nature of stage art. Theatre was treated frankly as theatre and not as a means of creating an illusion of reality. "Theatricalism" had effective proponents abroad, such as Max Reinhardt before and Eugene Vakhtangov and Vsevolod Meyerhold after the First World War. Vakhtangov, for example, styled his production of the Jewish folk drama *The Dybbuk* for the Habimah troupe with expressive rather than realistic stage settings, with dance rhythms, and with conspicuously theatrical acting. Also, he attracted considerable attention by staging Gozzi's Italian classic *Princess Turandot* in the Chinese convention. Property men appeared in full view of the audience, shifted scenes in front of the playgoer, and discoursed among themselves, even making commentary on the action.

With theatricalism, directors restored the connection between the stage and the auditorium, or between the actor and the spectator, that had existed in the days of the platform and the apron stage, before the realistic, peepshow type of theatre had erected the fourth-wall convention. The play written for theatricalism was so constructed as to present a view of life rather than a literal copy of it, which is what realism tries and pretends to provide. The actor might costume himself in public, frankly set the scene for his demonstration of an idea or situation, address the spectator, and in all respects communicate with the audience. It is for this nonrealistic *presentation,* instead of *representation,* of life that the writer Alexander Bakshy invented the term "presentational" theatre. In America, before *Our Town,* we had had such theatricalist plays as John Howard Lawson's jazz symphony of American life *Processional* (1924) and Eva Le Gallienne's *Alice in Wonderland* (1933).

Our Town is nonillusionistic, presentational drama. The principal actor is the "stage manager." He sets up his demonstration, calling for skeletal or fragmentary stage settings to help the audience visualize a particular situation; he plays the part of a philosophical druggist who has had many occasions to observe the town's characters; and he acts as host, master of ceremonies, commentator, philosopher, and friend to the spectators. He takes them into his confidence and proceeds to communicate to them his knowledge of the little town of Grover's Corners and its people, along with his thoughts about living and dying. In form, *Our Town* achieves, in short, a significant presentation or, as Gordon Craig would have said, "a noble artificiality."

Locating *Our Town* historically and explaining its style is, however, less important than experiencing the play. Once we become acquainted with a dramatic style, it rapidly loses novelty and ceases to have any value apart from the life and feeling it conveys. The formal structure calls to mind the scaffolding on a building in the process of construction. The important question is: what sort of building is arising behind the wooden platforms? The theatricalist form of *Our Town* enables the author to build the kind of play he wants to give us—an informal, intimate, and compellingly human drama. It is a work of love and of wisdom: it pulsates with Wilder's love for the New England environment and way of life and for life itself; and it is pervaded by a wisdom about these things that is

as down to earth as the life which the author chronicles.

The content of the play is so simple that it is momentous, for it deals primarily with the *life* in life. Hence Wilder can dismiss all topical issues and situations from his demonstration after briefly noting that they appear in Grover's Corners, as they do everywhere else. Grover's Corners is a little town in New Hampshire, and it can be located by latitude and longitude. But it is all places, and it is located in the universe. Nothing sums up the essence of Wilder's philosophy in *Our Town* better than the address on a letter sent to a Grover's Corners' girl by a humorist who, to Wilder, was probably unknowingly the profoundest person in the world: "June Crofut, the Crofut Farm, Grover's Corners, Sultan County, New Hampshire, United States of America, Continent of North America, Western Hemisphere, the Earth, the Solar System, the Universe, the Mind of God."

Without this comprehensive view, *Our Town* would have to be set down as a broken play, with one part concerned with life and the other with death, or with one part presenting "reality" and the other retailing fantasy, or "metaphysics." For Wilder, however, the two parts are one. The dying gives significance to the living, and the "metaphysical" is included in the "real." "The mind of God" idea may remind us of transcendentalism or Emersonianism so characteristic of New England—the concept that everything is interpenetrated by spirit. But it is homespun philosophy that Wilder's informal presentation gives us, and it serves such simple ends as making us treasure ordinary life just as it is and reminding us to live it to the full before our day is over. "There go all of us," Brooks Atkinson has expressed the meaning of the play, "not 'but for the grace of God,' but 'by the grace of God.' " The play deals ever so unostentatiously, as Atkinson has said, with "the days and deaths of the brotherhood of man." Wilder's cultivated and sophisticated mind reduces our human complexity to its irreducible simplicity.

BIBLIOGRAPHY: Brooks Atkinson, *Broadway Scrapbook* (pp. 85–88, 213–217), 1947; John Mason Brown, *Two on the Aisle* (pp. 187–193), 1938; Edmond M. Gagey, *Revolution in the American Drama* (pp. 107–111), 1947.

OUR TOWN

By Thornton Wilder

ACT I.

No curtain. No scenery. The audience, arriving, sees an empty stage in half-light. Presently the Stage Manager, *hat on and pipe in mouth, enters and begins placing a table and several chairs down stage left, and a table and chairs down stage right. "Left" and "right" are from the point of view of the actor facing the audience. "Up" is towards the back wall. As the house lights go down he has finished setting the stage and leaning against the right proscenium pillar watches the late arrivals in the audience. When the auditorium is in complete darkness he speaks:*

STAGE MANAGER: This play is called "Our Town." It was written by Thornton Wilder, produced and directed by A....; [or: produced by A....; directed by B....]. In it you will see Miss C....; Miss D....; Miss E....; and Mr. F....; Mr. G....; Mr. H....; and many others. The name of the town is Grover's Corners, New Hampshire,—just across the Massachusetts line: latitude 42 degrees 40 minutes; longitude 70 degrees 37 minutes. The First Act shows a day in our town. The day is May 7, 1901. The time is just before dawn. [*A rooster crows*] The sky is beginning to show some streaks of light over in the East there, behind our mount'in. The morning star always gets wonderful bright the minute before it has to go. [*He stares at it for a moment, then goes up stage*] Well, I'd better show you how our town lies. Up here—[*That is: parallel with the back wall*] is Main Street. Way back there is the railway station; tracks go that way. Polish Town's across the tracks and some Canuck families. [*Toward the left*] Over there is the Congregational Church; across the street's the Presbyterian. Methodist and Unitarian are over there. Baptist is down in the holla' by the river. Catholic Church is over beyond the tracks. Here's the Town Hall and Post Office combined; jail's in the basement. Bryan once made a speech from these steps here. Along here's a row of stores. Hitching-posts and horse blocks in front of them. First automobile's going to come along in about five years, belonged to Banker Cartwright, our richest citizen . . . lives in the big white house up on the hill. Here's the grocery store and here's Mr. Morgan's drugstore. Most everybody in town manages to look into those two stores once a day. Public School's over yonder. High School's still farther over. Quarter of nine mornings, noontimes, and three o'clock afternoons, the hull town can hear the yelling and screaming from those schoolyards. [*He approaches the table and chairs down stage right*] This is our doctor's house,—Doc Gibbs'. This is the back door. [*Two arched trellises are pushed out, one by each proscenium pillar*] There's some scenery for those who think they have to have scenery. There's a garden here. Corn . . . peas . . . beans . . . hollyhocks . . . heliotrope . . . and a lot of burdock. [*Crosses the stage*] In those days our newspaper come out twice a week,—the Grover's Corners *Sentinel*,—and this is Editor Webb's house. And this is Mrs. Webb's garden. Just like Mrs. Gibbs's, only it's got a lot of sunflowers, too. Right here,—big butternut tree. [*He returns to his place by the right proscenium pillar and looks at the audience for a minute*] Nice town, y'know what I mean? Nobody very remarkable ever come out of it,—s'far as we know. The earliest tombstones in the cemetery up there on the mountain say 1670-1680—they're Grovers and Cartwrights and Gibbses and Herseys—same names as are around here now. Well, as I said: it's about dawn. The only lights on in town are in a cottage over by the tracks where a Polish mother's just had twins. And in the Joe Crowell house, where Joe Junior's getting up so as to deliver the paper. And in the depot, where Shorty Hawkins is gettin' ready to flag the 5:45 for Boston. [*A train whistle is heard. The* Stage Manager *takes out his watch and nods*] Naturally, out in the country—all around—they've been lights on for some time, what with milkin's and so on. But town people sleep late. So—another day's begun. There's Doc Gibbs comin' down Main Street now, comin' back from that baby case. And here's his wife comin' downstairs to get breakfast. Doc Gibbs died in 1930. The new hospital's named after him. Mrs. Gibbs died first—long time ago in fact. She went out to visit her daughter, Rebecca, who married an insurance man in Canton, Ohio, and died there—pneumonia—but her body was brought back here. She's up in the cemetery there now—in with a whole mess of Gibbses and Herseys —she was Julia Hersey 'fore she married Doc Gibbs in the Congregational Church over there. In our town we like to know the facts about everybody. —That's Doc Gibbs. And there comes Joe Crowell, Jr., delivering Mr. Webb's *Sentinel*.

[Dr. Gibbs *has been coming along Main Street from the left. At the point where he would turn to approach his house, he stops, sets down his—imaginary—black bag, takes off his hat, and rubs his face with fatigue, using an enormous handkerchief.* Mrs. Gibbs *has entered her kitchen, gone through the motions of pu:-*

ting wood into a stove, lighting it, and preparing breakfast. Suddenly, Joe Crowell, Jr., *starts down Main Street from the right, hurling imaginary newspapers into doorways*]

JOE CROWELL, JR.: Morning, Doc Gibbs.

DR. GIBBS: Morning, Joe.

JOE CROWELL, JR.: Somebody been sick, Doc?

DR. GIBBS: No. Just some twins born over in Polish Town.

JOE CROWELL, JR.: Do you want your paper now?

DR. GIBBS: Yes, I'll take it.—Anything serious goin' on in the world since Wednesday?

JOE CROWELL, JR.: Yessir. My schoolteacher, Miss Foster, 's getting married to a fella over in Concord.

DR. GIBBS: I declare.—How do you boys feel about that?

JOE CROWELL, JR.: Well, of course, it's none of my business,—but I think if a person starts out to be a teacher, she ought to stay one.

DR. GIBBS: How's your knee, Joe?

JOE CROWELL, JR.: Fine, Doc, I never think about it at all. Only like you said, it always tells me when it's going to rain.

DR. GIBBS: What's it telling you today? Goin' to rain?

JOE CROWELL, JR.: No, sir.

DR. GIBBS: Sure?

JOE CROWELL, JR.: Yessir.

DR. GIBBS: Knee ever make a mistake?

JOE CROWELL, JR.: No, sir. [Joe *goes off.* Dr. Gibbs *stands reading his paper*]

STAGE MANAGER: Here comes Howie Newsome delivering the milk.

[Howie Newsome *comes along Main Street, passes* Doctor Gibbs, *comes down the center of the stage, leaves some bottles at* Mrs. Webb's *back door, and crosses the stage to* Mrs. Gibbs's]

HOWIE NEWSOME: Git-ap, Bessie. What's the matter with you?—Morning, Doc.

DR. GIBBS: Morning, Howie.

HOWIE NEWSOME: Somebody sick?

DR. GIBBS: Pair of twins over to Mrs. Goruslawski's.

HOWIE NEWSOME: Twins, eh? This town's gettin' bigger every year.

DR. GIBBS: Going to rain, Howie?

HOWIE NEWSOME: No, no. Fine day—that'll burn through. Come on, Bessie.

DR. GIBBS: Hello Bessie. [He *strokes her*] How old is she, Howie?

HOWIE NEWSOME: Goin' on seventeen. Bessie's all mixed up about the route ever since the Lockharts stopped takin' their quart of milk every day. She wants to leave 'em a quart just the same—keeps scolding me the hull trip. [He *reaches* Mrs. Gibbs's *back door. She is waiting for him*]

MRS. GIBBS: Good morning, Howie.

HOWIE NEWSOME: Morning, Mrs. Gibbs. Doc's just comin' down the street.

MRS. GIBBS: Is he? Seems like you're late today?

HOWIE NEWSOME: Yes. Somep'n went wrong with the separator. Don't know what 'twas. [He *goes back to Main Street, clucks for Bessie and goes off right.* Dr. Gibbs *reaches his home and goes in*]

MRS. GIBBS: Everything all right?

DR. GIBBS: Yes. I declare—easy as kittens.

MRS. GIBBS: Bacon'll be ready in a minute. Set down and drink your coffee. Child-*run!* Child-*run!* Time to get up.—George! Rebecca!—You can catch a couple hours' sleep this morning, can't you?

DR. GIBBS: Hm! . . . Mrs. Wentworth's coming at eleven. Guess I know what it's about, too. Her stummick ain't what it ought to be.

MRS. GIBBS: All told, you won't get more'n three hours' sleep. Frank Gibbs, I don't know what's goin' to become of you. I do wish I could get you to go away some place and take a rest. I think it would do you good.

MRS. WEBB: Emileeee! Time to get up! Wally! Seven o'clock!

MRS. GIBBS: I declare, you got to speak to George. Seems like something's come over him lately. He's no help to me at all. I can't even get him to cut me some wood.

DR. GIBBS: Is he sassy to you?

MRS. GIBBS: No. He just whines! All he thinks about is that baseball—George! Rebecca! You'll be late for school.

DR. GIBBS: M-m-m. . . .

MRS. GIBBS: George!

DR. GIBBS: George, look sharp!

GEORGE'S VOICE: Yes, Pa!

DR. GIBBS: [*As he goes off the stage*] Don't you hear your mother calling you?

MRS. WEBB: Walleee! Emileee! You'll be late for school! Walleee! You wash yourself good or I'll come up and do it myself.

REBECCA GIBBS'S VOICE: Ma! What dress shall I wear?

MRS. GIBBS: Don't make a noise. Your father's been out all night and needs his sleep. I washed and ironed the blue gingham for you special.

REBECCA: Ma, I hate that dress.

MRS. GIBBS: Oh, hush-up-with-you.

REBECCA: Every day I go to school dressed like a sick turkey.

MRS. GIBBS: Now, Rebecca, don't be impossible. You always look *very* nice.

REBECCA: Mama, George's throwing soap at me.

MRS. GIBBS: I'll come up and slap the both of you,—that's what I'll do.

[*A factory whistle sounds. The children enter and take their places at the breakfast tables:* Emily *and* Wally Webb; George *and* Rebecca Gibbs]

STAGE MANAGER: We've got a factory in our town too,—hear it? Makes blankets. Cartwrights own it and it brung 'em a fortune.

MRS. WEBB: Children! Now I won't have it. Breakfast is just as good as any other meal and I won't have you gobbling like wolves. It'll stunt your growth,—that's a fact. Put away your book, Wally.

WALLY: Aw, Ma!

MRS. WEBB: You know the rule's well as I do—no books at table. As for me, I'd rather have my children healthy than bright.

EMILY: I'm both, Mama: you know I am. I'm the brightest girl in school for my age. I have a wonderful memory.

MRS. WEBB: Eat your breakfast.

WALLY: I'm bright, too, when I'm looking at my stamp collection.

MRS. GIBBS: I'll speak to your father about it when he's rested. Seems to me twenty-five cents a week's enough for a boy your age. I declare I don't know how you spend it all.

GEORGE: Aw, Ma,—I gotta lotta things to buy.

MRS. GIBBS: Strawberry phosphates—that's what you spend it on.

GEORGE: I don't see how Rebecca comes to have so much money. She has more'n a dollar.

REBECCA: [Spoon in mouth, dreamily] I've been saving it up gradual.

MRS. GIBBS: Well, dear, I think it's a good thing every now and then to spend some.

REBECCA: Mama, do you know what I love most in the world—do you?—Money.

MRS. GIBBS: Eat your breakfast.

[The school bell is heard]

THE CHILDREN: Mama, there's the first bell.—I gotta hurry.—I don't want any more.

MRS. WEBB: Walk fast, but you don't have to run. Wally, pull up your pants at the knee. Stand up straight, Emily.

MRS. GIBBS: Tell Miss Foster I send her my best congratulations—can you remember that?

REBECCA: Yes, Ma.

MRS. GIBBS: You look real nice, Rebecca. Pick up your feet.

ALL: Good-by. [The children from the two houses join at the center of the stage and go up to Main Street, then off left. Mrs. Gibbs fills her apron with food for the chickens and comes down to the footlights]

MRS. GIBBS: Here, chick, chick, chick. No, go away, you. Go away. Here, chick, chick, chick. What's the matter with you? Fight, fight, fight,—that's all you do. Hm . . . you don't belong to me. Where'd you come from? [She shakes her apron] Oh, don't be so scared. Nobody's going to hurt you.

[Mrs. Webb is sitting by her trellis, stringing beans]

MRS. GIBBS: Good morning, Myrtle. How's your cold?

MRS. WEBB: Well, it's better; but I told Charles I didn't know as I'd go to choir practice tonight. Wouldn't be any use.

MRS. GIBBS: Just the same, you come to choir practice, Myrtle, and try it.

MRS. WEBB: Well, if I don't feel any worse than I do now I probably will. While I'm resting myself I thought I'd string some of these beans.

MRS. GIBBS: [Rolling up her sleeves as she crosses the stage for a chat] Let me help you. Beans have been good this year.

MRS. WEBB: I've decided to put up forty quarts if it kills me. The children say they hate 'em but I notice they're able to get 'em down all winter. [Pause]

MRS. GIBBS: Now, Myrtle, I've got to tell you something, because if I don't tell somebody I'll burst.

MRS. WEBB: Why, Julia Gibbs!

MRS. GIBBS: Here, give me some more of those beans. Myrtle, did one of those second-hand furniture men from Boston come to see you last Friday?

MRS. WEBB: No—o.

MRS. GIBBS: Well, he called on me. First I thought he was a patient wantin' to see Dr. Gibbs. 'N he wormed his way into my parlor, and, Myrtle Webb, he offered me three hundred and fifty dollars for Grandmother Wentworth's highboy, as I'm sitting here!

MRS. WEBB: Why, Julia Gibbs!

MRS. GIBBS: He did! That old thing! Why, it was so big I didn't know where to put it and I almost give it to Cousin Hester Wilcox.

MRS. WEBB: Well, you're going to take it, aren't you?

MRS. GIBBS: I don't know.

MRS. WEBB: You don't know—three hundred and fifty dollars. What's come over you?

MRS. GIBBS: Well, if I could get the Doctor to take the money and go away some place on a real trip I'd sell it like that.—Myrtle, ever since I was that high I've had the thought that I'd like to see Paris, France. I suppose I'm crazy.

MRS. WEBB: Oh, I know what you mean.—How does the Doctor feel about it?

MRS. GIBBS: Well, I did beat about the bush a little and said that if I got a legacy—that's the way I put it—I'd make him take me somewhere.

MRS. WEBB: M-m-m. . . . What did he say?

MRS. GIBBS: You know how he is. I haven't heard a serious word out of him, ever since I've known him. No, he said, it might make him discontented with Grover's Corners to go traipsin' about Europe; better let well enough alone, he says. Every two years he makes a trip to the battlefields of the Civil War and that's enough treat for anybody, he says.

MRS. WEBB: Well, Mr. Webb just admires the way Dr. Gibbs knows everything about the Civil War. Mr. Webb's a good mind to give up Napoleon and move over to the Civil War, only Dr. Gibbs being one of the greatest experts in the country just makes him despair.

MRS. GIBBS: It's a fact! Doctor Gibbs is never so happy as when he's at Antietam or Gettysburg. The times I've walked over those hills, Myrtle, stopping at every bush and pacing it all out, like we was going to buy it.

MRS. WEBB: Well, if that second-hand man's really serious about buyin' it, Julia, you sell it. And then you'll get to see Paris, all right.

MRS. GIBBS: Oh, I'm sorry I mentioned it. Only it seems to me that once in your life before you die you ought to see a country where they don't talk and think in English and don't even want to.

[*The* Stage Manager *returns to the center of the stage*]

STAGE MANAGER: That'll do. That'll do. Thank you very much, ladies. [Mrs. Gibbs *and* Mrs. Webb *gather up their things, return into their homes and disappear*] Now we're going to skip a few hours in the day at Grover's Corners. But before we go on I want you to know some more things about the town,—all kinds of things. So I've asked Prof. Willard of our State University to come down here and sketch in a few details of our past history,—kind of scientific account, you might say. Is Prof. Willard here? [Prof. Willard, *a rural savant, pince-nez on a wide satin ribbon, enters from the right with some notes in his hand*] May I introduce Prof. Willard of our University. A few brief notes, thank you, Professor,—unfortunately our time is limited.

PROF. WILLARD: Grover's Corners . . . let me see . . . Grover's Corners lies on the old Archaeozoic granite of the Appalachian range. I may say it's some of the oldest land in the world. We're very proud of that. A shelf of Devonian basalt crosses it with vestiges of Mesozoic shale, and some sandstone outcroppings; but that's all more recent: two hundred, three hundred million years old. Some highly interesting fossils have been found. . . . I may say: unique fossils . . . two miles out of town, in Silas Peckham's cow pasture. They can be seen at the museum in our University at any time. Did you wish the meteorological conditions?

STAGE MANAGER: Thank you. We would.

PROF. WILLARD: The mean precipitation is 40 inches. The mean annual temperature is 43 degrees, ranging between 102 degrees in the shade, and 38 degrees below zero in winter. The . . . the . . . uh . . .

STAGE MANAGER: Thank you, Professor. And have you Prof. Gruber's notes on the history of human life here?

PROF. WILLARD: Hm . . . yes . . . anthropological data: Early Amerindian stock. Cotahatchee tribes . . . no evidence before the Tenth Century of this era . . . hm . . . now entirely disappeared . . . possible traces in three families. Migration toward the end of the Seventeenth Century of English brachycephalic blue-eyed stock . . . for the most part. Since then some influx of Slav and Mediterranean types. . . .

STAGE MANAGER: And the population, Prof. Willard?

PROF. WILLARD: Within the town limits: 2,640.

The postal district brings in 507 more. Mortality and birth-rates are constant; by MacPherson's gauge: 6.032.

STAGE MANAGER: Thank you *very* much, Professor. We're all very much obliged to you, I'm sure.

PROF. WILLARD: Not at all, sir; not at all.

STAGE MANAGER: This way, Professor, and thank you again. [*Exit* Prof. Willard] Now the political and social report: Editor Webb.—Oh, Mr. Webb?

[Mrs. Webb *appears at her back door*]

MRS. WEBB: He'll be here in a minute. . . . He just cut his hand while he was eatin' an apple.

STAGE MANAGER: Thank you, Mrs. Webb.

MRS. WEBB: Charles! Everybody's waitin'. [*Exit* Mrs. Webb]

STAGE MANAGER: Mr. Webb is Publisher and Editor of The Grover's Corners *Sentinel*. That's our local paper, y'know.

[Mr. Webb *enters from his house, pulling on his coat. His finger is bound in a handkerchief*]

MR. WEBB: Hm. . . . I don't have to tell you that we're run here by a Board of Selectmen.—All males vote at the age of 21. Women vote indirect. We're lower middle-class, sprinkling of professional men . . . 10% illiterate laborers. Politically, we're 86% Republicans; 6% Democrats; 4% Socialists; rest, indifferent. Religiously, we're 85% Protestants; 12% Catholics; rest, indifferent. Do you want the poverty and insanity statistics?

STAGE MANAGER: Thank you, no. Have you any comments, Mr. Webb?

MR. WEBB: Very ordinary town, if you ask me. Little better behaved than most. Probably a lot duller. But our young people here seem to like it well enough: 90% of 'em graduating from High School settle down right here to live—even when they've been away to college.

STAGE MANAGER: Thank you, Mr. Webb. Now, is there anyone in the audience who would like to ask Editor Webb anything about the town?

WOMAN IN THE BALCONY: Is there much drinking in Grover's Corners?

MR. WEBB: Well, ma'am, I wouldn't know what you'd call *much*. Sattidy nights the farmhands meet down in Ellery Greenough's stable and holler some. Fourth of July I've been known to taste a drop myself—and Decoration Day, of course. We've got one or two town drunks, but they're always having remorses every time an evangelist comes to town. No, ma'am, I'd say likker ain't a regular thing in the home here, except in the medicine chest. Right good for snake-bite, y'know—always was.

TALL MAN AT BACK OF AUDITORIUM: Is there no one in town aware of—

STAGE MANAGER: Come forward, will you, where we can all hear you— What were you saying?

TALL MAN: Is there no one in town aware of social injustice and industrial inequality?

MR. WEBB: Oh, yes, everybody is,—somethin' terrible. Seems like they spend most of their time talking about who's rich and who's poor.

TALL MAN: Then why don't they do something about it?

MR. WEBB: Well, we're ready to listen to everybody's suggestion as to how you can see that the diligent and sensible 'll rise to the top and the lazy and quarrelsome sink to the bottom. We'll listen to anybody. Meantime until that's settled, we try to take care of those that can't help themselves, and those that can we leave alone.—Are there any more questions?

LADY IN A BOX: Oh, Mr. Webb? Mr. Webb, is there any culture or love of beauty in Grover's Corners?

MR. WEBB: Well, ma'am, there ain't much—not in the sense you mean. Come to think of it, there's some girls that play the piano at High School Commencement; but they ain't happy about it. Yes, and I see where my daughter's been made to read "The Merchant of Venice" over to the school. Seems all pretty remote to 'em, y'know what I mean. No, ma'am, there isn't much culture; but maybe this is the place to tell you that we've got a lot of pleasures of a kind here: we like the sun comin' up over the mountain in the morning, and we all notice a good deal about the birds. We pay a lot of attention to them, and trees and plants. And we watch the change of the seasons: yes, everybody knows about them. But those other things—you're right, ma'am—there ain't much—"Robinson Crusoe" and the Bible; and Handel's "Largo," we all know that; and Whistler's "Mother"—those are just about as far as we go.

LADY IN A BOX: So I thought. Thank you, Mr. Webb.

STAGE MANAGER: All right! All right! Thank you, everybody. [Mr. Webb retires] We'll go back to the town now. It's middle of the afternoon. All 2,642 have had their dinners and all the dishes have been washed. There's an early afternoon calm in our town: a buzzin' and a hummin' from the school buildings; only a few buggies on Main Street—the horses dozing at the hitching-posts; you all remember what it's like. Doc Gibbs is in his office, tapping people and making them say "ah." Mr. Webb's cuttin' his lawn over there; one man in ten thinks it's a privilege to push his own lawn mower. No, sir. It's later than I thought. There are the children coming home from school already.

[Emily Webb *comes sedately down Main Street carrying some school books. There are some signs that she is imagining herself to be a lady of striking elegance. Her father's movements to and fro with the lawn mower bring him into her vicinity*]

EMILY: I *can't*, Lois. I've got to go home and help my mother. I *promised.*

MR. WEBB: Emily, walk simply. Who do you think you are today?

EMILY: Papa, you're terrible. One minute you tell me to stand up straight and the next minute you call me names. I just don't listen to you. [*She gives him an abrupt kiss*]

MR. WEBB: Golly, I never got a kiss from such a great lady before. [*He goes out of sight. Emily leans over and picks some flowers by the gate of her house. George Gibbs comes careening down Main Street. He is throwing a ball up to dizzying heights, and waiting to catch it again. This sometimes requires his taking six steps backward*]

GEORGE: Excuse me, Mrs. Forrest.

STAGE MANAGER (*as* MRS. FORREST): Go out and play in the fields, young man. You got no business playing baseball on Main Street.

GEORGE: Awfully sorry, Mrs. Forrest.—Hello, Emily.

EMILY: H'lo.

GEORGE: You made a fine speech in class.

EMILY: Well . . . I was really ready to make a speech about the Monroe Doctrine, but at the last minute Miss Corcoran made me talk about the Louisiana Purchase instead. I worked an awful long time on both of them.

GEORGE: Gee, it's funny, Emily. From my window up there I can just see your head nights when you're doing your homework over in your room.

EMILY: Why, can you?

GEORGE: You certainly do stick to it, Emily. I don't see how you can sit still that long. I guess you like school.

EMILY: Well, I always feel it's something you have to go through.

GEORGE: Yeah.

EMILY: I don't mind it really. It passes the time.

GEORGE: Yeah.—Emily, what do you think? We might work out a kinda telegraph from there to there; and once in a while you could give me a kinda hint or two about one of those Algebra problems. I don't mean the answers, Emily, of course not . . . just some little hint. . . .

EMILY: Oh, I think *hints* are allowed.—So-ah—if you get stuck, George, you whistle to me; and I'll give you some hints.

GEORGE: Emily, you're just naturally bright, I guess.

EMILY: I figure that it's just the way a person's born.

GEORGE: Yeah. But, you see, I want to be a farmer, and my Uncle Luke says whenever I'm ready I can come over and work on his farm and if I'm any good I can just gradually have it.

EMILY: You mean the house and everything?

[*Enter* Mrs. Webb]

GEORGE: Yeah. Well, thanks . . . I better be getting out to the baseball field. Thanks for the talk, Emily.—Good afternoon, Mrs. Webb.

MRS. WEBB: Good afternoon, George.

GEORGE: So-long, Emily.

EMILY: So-long, George.

MRS. WEBB: Emily, come and help me string these beans for the winter. George Gibbs let himself have a real conversation, didn't he? Why, he's growing up. How old would George be?

EMILY: I don't know.

MRS. WEBB: Let's see. He must be almost sixteen.

EMILY: Mama, I made a speech in class today and I was very good.

MRS. WEBB: You must recite it to your father at supper. What was it about?

EMILY: The Louisiana Purchase. It was like silk off a spool. I'm going to make speeches all my life. —Mama, are these big enough?

MRS. WEBB: Try and get them a little bigger if you can.

EMILY: Mama, will you answer me a question, serious?

MRS. WEBB: Seriously, dear—not serious.

EMILY: Seriously,—will you?

MRS. WEBB: Of course, I will.

EMILY: Mama, am I good-looking?

MRS. WEBB: Yes, of course you are. All my children have got good features; I'd be ashamed if they hadn't.

EMILY: Oh, Mama, that's not what I mean. What I mean is: am I *pretty*?

MRS. WEBB: I've already told you, yes. Now that's enough of that. You have a nice young pretty face. I never heard of such foolishness.

EMILY: Oh, Mama, you never tell us the truth about anything.

MRS. WEBB: I *am* telling you the truth.

EMILY: Mama, were *you* pretty?

MRS. WEBB: Yes, I was, if I do say it. I was the prettiest girl in town next to Mamie Cartwright.

EMILY: But, Mama, you've got to say *some*thing about me. Am I pretty enough . . . to get anybody . . . to get people interested in me?

MRS. WEBB: Emily, you make me tired. Now stop it. You're pretty enough for all normal purposes. Come along now and bring that bowl with you.

EMILY: Oh, Mama, you're no help at all.

STAGE MANAGER: Thank you. Thank you! That'll do. We'll have to interrupt again here. Thank you, Mrs. Webb; thank you, Emily. [Mrs. Webb *and* Emily *withdraw*] There are some more things we've got to explore about this town. This time we're going to go about it in another way: we're going to look back on it from the future. I'm not going to tell you what became of these two families we're seeing most of, because the rest of the play will tell you about them. But take some of these others: Take Joe Crowell, Jr.: Joe was a very bright fellow. He graduated with honors and got a scholarship to Boston Tech.,—M.I.T., that is. But the War broke out and Joe died in France. All that education for nothing. Howie Newsome's still delivering milk at Grover's Corners. He's an old man now, has a lot of help, but he still delivers it himself. Says he gets

the feel of the town that way. Carries all the accounts in his head; never has to write down a word. Mr. Morgan's drug store ain't the same,—it's all citified. Mr. Morgan retired and went out to live in San Diego, California, where his daughter married a real estate man, name of Kerby. Mr. Morgan died there in 1935 and was buried in a lot of palm trees. Kinda lost his religion at the end and took up New Thought or something. They read some new-fangled poetry over him and cre-mated him. The New Hampshire in him sort of broke down in him in that climate, seems like. The Cartwrights got richer and richer. The house is closed most of the year. They're off eating big dinners in hotels now,—in Virginia Hot Springs and Miami Beach. They say the winters are cold here. I see where they've become 'Piscopalians. The Cartwright interests have just begun building a new bank in Grover's Corners —had to go to Vermont for the marble, sorry to say. And they've asked a friend of mine what they should put in the cornerstone for people to dig up a thousand years from now. Of course, they've put in a copy of the New York *Times* and a copy of Mr. Webb's *Sentinel*. We're kind of interested in this because some scientific fellas have found a way of painting all that reading matter with a kind of glue—silicate glue—that'll make it keep a thousand —two thousand years. We're putting in a Bible . . . and the Constitution of the United States and a copy of William Shakespeare's plays. What do you say, folks? What do you think? Y'know—Babylon once had two million people in it, and all we know about 'em is the names of the kings and some copies of wheat contracts and . . . the sales of slaves. Yes, every night all those families sat down to supper, and the father came home from his work, and the smoke went up the chimney,—same as here. And even in Greece and Rome, all we know about the real life of the people is what we can piece together out of the joking poems and the comedies they wrote for the theater back then. So I'm going to have a copy of this play put in the cornerstone and the people a thousand years from now'll know a few simple facts about us—more than the Treaty of Versailles and the Lindbergh flight. See what I mean? Well,—you people a thousand years from now,— in the provinces north of New York at the beginning of the Twentieth Century, people et three times a day: soon after sunrise; at noon; and at sunset. Every seventh day, by law and by religion, was a day of rest and all work come to a stop. The religion at that time was Christianity. I guess you have some other records about Christianity. The domestic set-up was marriage: a binding relation between a male and one female that lasted for life. Christianity strictly forbade killing, but you were allowed to kill animals, and you were allowed to kill human beings in war and government punishings. I guess we don't have to tell you about the government and business forms, because that's the kind of thing people seem to hand down first of all. Let me see now if there's anything else. Oh, yes,—at death people were buried in the ground just as they are. So, friends, this is the way we were in our growing up and in our marrying and in our doctoring and in our living and in our dying. Now we'll return to our day in Grover's Corners. A lot of time has gone by. It's evening. You can hear choir practice going on in the Congregational Church. All the children are at home doing their school work. The day is running down like a tired clock.

[*A choir partially concealed in the orchestra pit has begun singing "Blessed be the tie that binds." Simon Stimson stands directing them. Two ladders have been pushed on to the stage; they serve as indication of the second story in the Gibbs and Webb houses. George and Emily mount them, and apply themselves to their school work. Dr. Gibbs has entered and is seated in his kitchen reading*]

SIMON STIMSON: Now look here, everybody. Music come into the world to give pleasure.—Softer! Softer! Get it out of your heads that music's only good when it's loud. You leave loudness to the Methodists. You couldn't beat 'em, even if you wanted to. Now again. Tenors!

GEORGE: Hssst! Emily!

EMILY: Hello.

GEORGE: Hello!

EMILY: I can't work at all. The moonlight's so *terrible*.

GEORGE: Emily, did you get the third problem?

EMILY: Which?

GEORGE: The *third*?

EMILY: Why, yes, George—that's the easiest of them all.

GEORGE: I don't see it. Emily, can you give me a hint?

EMILY: I'll tell you one thing: the answer's in yards.

GEORGE: ! ! ! In yards? How do you mean?

EMILY: In *square* yards.

GEORGE: Oh . . . in square yards.

EMILY: Yes, George, don't you see?

GEORGE: Yeah.

EMILY: In square yards of *wallpaper*.

GEORGE: Wallpaper,—oh, I see. Thanks a lot, Emily.

EMILY: You're welcome. My, isn't the moonlight *terrible*? And choir practice going on.—I think if you hold your breath you can hear the train all the way to Contookuck. Hear it?

GEORGE: M-m-m—What do you know!

EMILY: Well, I guess I better go back and try to work.

GEORGE: Good night, Emily. And thanks.

EMILY: Good night, George.

SIMON STIMSON: Before I forget it: how many of you will be able to come in Tuesday afternoon and sing at Fred Hersey's wedding,—show your hands.

That'll be fine; that'll be right nice. We'll do the same music we did for Jane Trowbridge's last month. —Now we'll do: "Art thou weary; art thou languid?" It's a question, ladies and gentlemen, make it talk. Ready.

DR. GIBBS: Oh, George, can you come down a minute?

GEORGE: Yes, Pa. [*He descends the ladder*]

DR. GIBBS: Make yourself comfortable, George; I'll only keep you a minute. George, how old are you?

GEORGE: I? I'm sixteen almost seventeen.

DR. GIBBS: What do you want to do after school's over?

GEORGE: Why, you know, Pa, I want to be a farmer on Uncle Luke's farm.

DR. GIBBS: You'll be willing, will you, to get up early and milk and feed the stock . . . and you'll be able to hoe and hay all day?

GEORGE: Sure, I will. What are you . . . what do you mean, Pa?

DR. GIBBS: Well, George, while I was in my office today I heard a funny sound . . . and what do you think it was? It was your mother chopping wood. There you see your mother—getting up early; cooking meals all day long; washing and ironing;—and still she has to go out in the back yard and chop wood. I suppose she just got tired of asking you. She just gave up and decided it was easier to do it herself. And you eat her meals, and put on the clothes she keeps nice for you, and you run off and play baseball,—like she's some hired girl we keep around the house but that we don't like very much. Well, I knew all I had to do was call your attention to it. Here's a handkerchief, son. George, I've decided to raise your spending money twenty-five cents a week. Not, of course, for chopping wood for your mother, because that's a present you give her, but because you're getting older—and I imagine there are lots of things you must find to do with it.

GEORGE: Thanks, Pa.

DR. GIBBS: Let's see—tomorrow's pay day. You can count on it—Hmm. Probably Rebecca'll feel she ought to have some more too. Wonder what could have happened to your mother. Choir practice never was as late as this before.

GEORGE: It's only half-past eight, Pa.

DR. GIBBS: I don't know why she's in that old choir. She hasn't any more voice than an old crow. . . . Traipsin' around the streets at this hour of the night. . . . Just about time you retired, don't you think?

GEORGE: Yes, Pa. [George *mounts to his place on the ladder. Laughter and good nights can be heard on stage left and presently* Mrs. Gibbs, Mrs. Soames *and* Mrs. Webb *come down Main Street. When they arrive at the center of the stage they stop*]

MRS. SOAMES: Good night, Martha. Good night, Mr. Foster.

MRS. WEBB: I'll tell Mr. Webb; I *know* he'll want to put it in the paper.

MRS. GIBBS: My, it's late!

MRS. SOAMES: Good night, Irma.

MRS. GIBBS: Real nice choir practice, wa'n't it? Myrtle Webb! Look at that moon, will you! Tsk-tsk-tsk. Potato weather, for sure.

MRS. SOAMES: Naturally I didn't want to say a word about it in front of those others, but now we're alone—really, it's the worst scandal that ever was in this town!

MRS. GIBBS: What?

MRS. SOAMES: Simon Stimson!

MRS. GIBBS: Now, Louella!

MRS. SOAMES: But, Julia! To have the organist of a church drink and drunk year after year. You know he was drunk tonight.

MRS. GIBBS: Now, Louella! We all know about Mr. Stimson, and we all know about the troubles he's been through, and Dr. Ferguson knows too, and if Dr. Ferguson keeps him on there in his job the only thing the rest of us can do is just not to notice it.

MRS. SOAMES: Not to notice it! But it's getting worse.

MRS. WEBB: No, it isn't, Louella. It's getting better. I've been in that choir twice as long as you have. It doesn't happen anywhere near so often. . . . My, I hate to go to bed on a night like this.—I better hurry. Those children'll be sitting up till all hours. Good night, Louella. [*She hurries down stage, enters her house and disappears*]

MRS. GIBBS: Can you get home safe, Louella?

MRS. SOAMES: It's as bright as day. I can see Mr. Soames scowling at the window now. You'd think we'd been to a dance the way the menfolk carry on.

[*Repeated good nights. Mrs. Gibbs arrives at her home*]

MRS. GIBBS: Well, we had a real good time.

DR. GIBBS: You're late enough.

MRS. GIBBS: Why, Frank, it ain't any later 'n usual.

DR. GIBBS: And you stopping at the corner to gossip with a lot of hens.

MRS. GIBBS: Now, Frank, don't be grouchy. Come out and smell my heliotrope in the moonlight. [*They stroll out arm in arm along the footlights*] Isn't that wonderful? What did you do all the time I was away?

DR. GIBBS: Oh, I read—as usual. What were the girls gossiping about tonight?

MRS. GIBBS: Well, believe me, Frank—there is something to gossip about.

DR. GIBBS: Hmm! Simon Stimson far gone, was he?

MRS. GIBBS: Worst I've ever seen him. How'll that end, Frank? Dr. Ferguson can't forgive him forever.

DR. GIBBS: I guess I know more about Simon Stimson's affairs than anybody in this town. Some people ain't made for small town life. I don't know how that'll end; but there's nothing we can do but just leave it alone. Come, get in.

MRS. GIBBS: No, not yet. . . . Oh, Frank, I'm worried about you.

DR. GIBBS: What are you worried about?

MRS. GIBBS: I think it's my duty to make plans for you to get a real rest and change. And if I get that legacy, well, I'm going to insist on it.

DR. GIBBS: Now, Julia, there's no sense in going over that again.

MRS. GIBBS: Frank, you're just *unreasonable!*

DR. GIBBS: Come on, Julia, it's getting late. First thing you know you'll catch cold. I gave George a piece of my mind tonight. I reckon you'll have your wood chopped for a while anyway. No, no, start getting upstairs.

MRS. GIBBS: Oh, dear. There's always so many things to pick up, seems like. You know, Frank, Mrs. Fairchild always locks her front door every night. All those people up that part of town do.

DR. GIBBS: They're all getting citified, that's the trouble with them. They haven't got nothing fit to burgle and everybody knows it. [*They disappear.* Rebecca *climbs up the ladder beside* George]

GEORGE: Get out, Rebecca. There's only room for one at this window. You're always spoiling everything.

REBECCA: Well, let me look just a minute.

GEORGE: Use your own window.

REBECCA: I did; but there's no moon there. . . . George, do you know what I think, do you? I think maybe the moon's getting nearer and nearer and there'll be a big 'splosion.

GEORGE: Rebecca, you don't know anything. If the moon were getting nearer, the guys that sit up all night with telescopes would see it first and they'd tell about it, and it'd be in all the newspapers.

REBECCA: George, is the moon shining on South America, Canada and half the whole world?

GEORGE: Well—prob'ly is.

[*The* Stage Manager *strolls on*]

STAGE MANAGER: Nine-thirty. Most of the lights are out. No, there's Constable Warren trying a few doors on Main Street. And here comes Editor Webb, after putting his newspaper to bed.

MR. WEBB: Good evening, Bill.

CONSTABLE WARREN: Evenin', Mr. Webb.

MR. WEBB: Quite a moon!

CONSTABLE WARREN: Yepp.

MR. WEBB: All quiet tonight?

CONSTABLE WARREN: Simon Stimson is rollin' around a little. Just saw his wife movin' out to hunt for him so I looked the other way—there he is now.

[Simon Stimson *comes down Main Street from the left, only a trace of unsteadiness in his walk*]

MR. WEBB: Good evening, Simon. . . . Town seems to have settled down for the night pretty well. . . . [Simon Stimson *comes up to him and pauses a moment*] Good evening. . . . Yes, most of the town's settled down for the night, Simon. . . . I guess we better do the same. Can I walk along a ways with you? [Simon Stimson *continues on his way without a word and disappears at the right*] Good night.

CONSTABLE WARREN: I don't know how that's goin' to end, Mr. Webb.

MR. WEBB: Well, he's seen a peck of trouble, one thing after another. . . . Oh, Bill . . . if you see my boy smoking cigarettes, just give him a word, will you? He thinks a lot of you, Bill.

CONSTABLE WARREN: I don't think he smokes no cigarettes, Mr. Webb. Leastways, not more'n two or three a year. He don't belong to that crowd that hangs out down by the gully.

MR. WEBB: Hm. . . . I hope not.—Well, good night, Bill.

CONSTABLE WARREN: Good night, Mr. Webb. [*Exit*]

MR. WEBB: Who's that up there? Is that you, Myrtle?

EMILY: No, it's me, Papa.

MR. WEBB: Why aren't you in bed?

EMILY: I don't know. I just can't sleep, Papa. The moonlight's so *won*-derful. And the smell of Mrs. Gibbs's heliotrope. Can you smell it?

MR. WEBB: Hm. . . . Yes. Haven't any troubles on your mind, have you, Emily?

EMILY: *Troubles,* Papa. *No.*

MR. WEBB: Well, enjoy yourself, but don't let your mother catch you. Good night, Emily.

EMILY: Good night, Papa.

[Mr. Webb *crosses into the house, whistling "Blessed Be the Tie that Binds" and disappears*]

REBECCA: I never told you about that letter Jane Crofut got from her minister when she was sick. The minister of her church in the town she was in before she came here. He wrote Jane a letter and on the envelope the address was like this: It said: Jane Crofut; The Crofut Farm; Grover's Corners; Sutton County; New Hampshire; United States of America.

GEORGE: What's funny about that?

REBECCA: But listen, it's not finished: the United States of America; Continent of North America; Western Hemisphere; the Earth; the Solar System; the Universe; the Mind of God,—that's what it said on the envelope.

GEORGE: What do you know!

REBECCA: And the postman brought it just the same.

GEORGE: What do you know!

STAGE MANAGER: That's the end of the First Act, friends. You can go and smoke now, those that smoke.

ACT II.

The tables and chairs of the two kitchens are still on the stage. The ladders have been withdrawn. The Stage Manager *has been at his accustomed place watching the audience return to its seats.*

STAGE MANAGER: Three years have gone by. Yes, the sun's come up over a thousand times. Summers and winters have cracked the mountains a little bit more and the rains have brought down some of the dirt. Some babies that weren't even born before have begun talking regular sentences already; and a number of people who thought they were right young and spry have noticed that they can't bound up a flight of stairs like they used to, without their heart fluttering a little. Some older sons are sitting at the head of the table, and some people I know are having their meat cut up for them.—All that can happen in a thousand days. Nature's been pushing and contriving in other ways, too: a number of young people fell in love and got married. Yes, the mountain got bit away a few fractions of an inch; millions of gallons of water went by the mill; and here and there a new home was set up under a roof. Almost everybody in the world gets married,—you know what I mean? In our town there aren't hardly any exceptions. Most everybody in the world climbs into their graves married. The First Act was called the Daily Life. This Act is called Love and Marriage. There's another Act coming after this: I reckon you can guess what that's about. So: It's three years later. It's 1904. It's July 7th, just after High School Commencement. That's the time most of our young people jump up and get married. Soon as they've passed their last examinations in solid geometry and Cicero's Orations, looks like they suddenly feel themselves fit to be married. It's early morning. Only this time it's been raining. It's been pouring and thundering. Mrs. Gibbs's garden, and Mrs. Webb's here: drenched. All those bean poles and pea vines: drenched. All yesterday over there on Main Street, the rain looked like curtains being blown along. Hm . . . it may begin again any minute. There! You can hear the 5:45 for Boston. And here comes Howie Newsome delivering the milk. And there's Si Crowell delivering the papers like his brother before him.—You remember about his brother?—all that education he's going to get and that'll be wasted. And there's Mrs. Gibbs and Mrs. Webb come down to make breakfast, just as though it were an ordinary day. I don't have to point out to the women in my audience that those ladies they see before them, both those ladies cooked three meals a day,—one of 'em for twenty years, the other for forty,—and no summer vacation. They brought up two children apiece; washed; cleaned the house, —and never a nervous breakdown. Never thought themselves hard-used, either. It's like what one of those Middle West poets said: You've got to love life to have life, and you've got to have life to love life. . . . It's what they call a vicious circle.

[Si Crowell *has entered hurling imaginary newspapers into doorways;* Howie Newsome *has come along Main Street with* Bessie]

HOWIE NEWSOME: Git-ap, Bessie.

SI CROWELL: Morning, Howie.

HOWIE NEWSOME: Morning, Si.—Anything in the papers I ought to know?

SI CROWELL: Nothing much, except we're losing the best baseball pitcher Grover's Corners ever had.

HOWIE NEWSOME: Reckon he was. He's been standing off the whole of South New Hampshire single-handed, looks like.

SI CROWELL: He could hit and run bases, too.

HOWIE NEWSOME: Yep. Mighty fine ball player. —Bessie. I guess I can stop and talk if I've a mind to!

SI CROWELL: I don't see how he could give up a thing like that just to get married. Would you, Howie?

HOWIE NEWSOME: Can't tell, Si. Never had no talent that way. [Constable Warren *enters. They exchange mornings*] You're up early, Bill.

CONSTABLE WARREN: Seein' if there's anything I can do to prevent a flood. River's been risin' all night.

HOWIE NEWSOME: Si Crowell's all worked up here about George Gibbs' retiring from baseball.

CONSTABLE WARREN: Yes, sir; that's the way it goes. Back in '84 we had a player, Si,—even George Gibbs couldn't touch him. Name of Hank Todd. Went down to Maine and become a parson. Wonderful ball player.—Howie, how did the weather look to you?

HOWIE NEWSOME: No, 'tain't bad. Think maybe it'll clear up for good.

[Constable Warren *and* Si Crowell *continue on their way.* Howie Newsome *brings the milk first to* Mrs. Gibbs's *house. She meets him by the trellis*]

MRS. GIBBS: Good morning, Howie. Do you think it's going to rain again?

HOWIE NEWSOME: Morning, Mrs. Gibbs. It rained so heavy, I think maybe it'll clear up.

MRS. GIBBS: Certainly hope it will.

HOWIE NEWSOME: How much did you want today?

MRS. GIBBS: I guess I'll need three-a-milk and two-a-cream, Howie. I'm going to have a house full of relations.

HOWIE NEWSOME: My wife says to tell you we both hope they'll be very happy, Mrs. Gibbs. Know they *will*.

MRS. GIBBS: Thanks a lot, Howie. Tell your wife I hope she gits there to the wedding.

HOWIE NEWSOME: Yes, she'll be there; she'll be there if she kin. [Howie Newsome *crosses to* Mrs. Webb's *house*] Morning, Mrs. Webb.

MRS. WEBB: Oh, good morning, Mr. Newsome. I told you four quarts of milk, but I hope you can spare me another.

HOWIE NEWSOME: Yes'm . . . and the two cream.

MRS. WEBB: Will it rain all day, Mr. Newsome?

HOWIE NEWSOME: No'm. Just sayin' to Mrs. Gibbs as how it may lighten up. Mrs. Newsome told me to tell you as how we hope they'll both be very happy, Mrs. Webb. Know they *will*.

MRS. WEBB: Thank you, and thank Mrs. Newsome and we hope to see you all at the wedding.

HOWIE NEWSOME: Yes, Mrs. Webb. We hope to git there. Couldn't miss that. Chck! Bessie! [*Exit* Howie Newsome. Dr. Gibbs *descends in shirt sleeves, and sits down at his breakfast table*]

DR. GIBBS: Well, Ma, the day has come. You're losin' one of your chicks.

MRS. GIBBS: Frank Gibbs, don't you say another word. I feel like crying every minute. Sit down and drink your coffee.

DR. GIBBS: The groom's up shaving himself. Whistling and singing, like he's glad to leave us.— Every now and then he says "I do" to the mirror, but it don't sound convincing to me.

MRS. GIBBS: I declare I don't know how he'll get along. I've arranged his clothes and seen to it he's put warm things on,— Frank! they're too young. Emily won't think of such things. He'll catch his death of cold within a week.—Here's something I made for you.

DR. GIBBS: Why, Julia Hersey! French toast!

MRS. GIBBS: 'Tain't hard to make, and I had to do something.

DR. GIBBS: I remember my wedding morning, Julia.

MRS. GIBBS: Now don't start that, Frank Gibbs. I tell you I can't stand it.

DR. GIBBS: I was the scardest young fella in the State of New Hampshire. I thought I'd made a mistake for sure. And when I saw you comin' down that aisle I thought you were the prettiest girl I'd ever seen, but the only trouble was that I'd never seen you before. There I was in the Congregational Church marryin' a total stranger.

MRS. GIBBS: And how do you think I felt!—Did you hear Rebecca stirring about upstairs?

DR. GIBBS: Only morning in the year she hasn't been managing everybody's business. She's shut up in her room. I got the impression that maybe she's crying.

MRS. GIBBS: Good Lord! This has got to stop.— Rebecca! Rebecca! Everything's getting cold down here. [George *comes rattling down the stairs, very brisk*]

GEORGE: Good morning, everybody. Only five more hours to live. [*Makes the gesture of cutting his throat*]

MRS. GIBBS: Where are you going?

GEORGE: Just stepping across the grass to see my girl.

MRS. GIBBS: Now, George! You take an umbrella or I won't let you out of this house.

GEORGE: Aw, Ma. It's just a *step!*

MRS. GIBBS: From tomorrow on you can kill yourself in all weathers, but while you're in my house you live wisely, thank you. There are your overshoes right there in the hall. And here's an umbrella.

GEORGE: Aw, Ma!

DR. GIBBS: George, do as your mother tells you.

MRS. GIBBS: Maybe Mrs. Webb isn't used to callers at seven in the morning. Take a cup-a coffee first.

GEORGE: Be back in a minute. [*He crosses the stage, leaping over the puddles*] Good morning, Mother Webb.

MRS. WEBB: Goodness! You frightened me!— Now, George, you can come in a minute out of the wet, but you know I can't ask you in.

GEORGE: Why not—?

MRS. WEBB: George, you know's well as I do: the groom can't see his bride on his wedding day, not until he sees her in church.

GEORGE: Aw!—that's just a superstition. [*Enter* Mr. Webb]

MR. WEBB: Good morning, George.

GEORGE: Mr. Webb, you don't believe in that superstition, do you?

MR. WEBB: There's a lot of common sense in some superstitions, George.

MRS. WEBB: Millions have folla'd it, George, and you don't want to be the first to fly in the face of custom.

GEORGE: How is Emily?

MRS. WEBB: She hasn't waked up yet. I haven't heard a sound out of her.

GEORGE: Emily's *asleep!!!*

MRS. WEBB: No wonder! We were up 'til all hours,—sewing and packing. I'll tell you what I'll do; you set down here a minute with Mr. Webb and drink this cup of coffee; and I'll go upstairs and see she doesn't come down and surprise you. There's some bacon, too; but don't be long about it. [*Exit* Mrs. Webb. *Embarrassed silence*]

MR. WEBB: Well, George, how are you?

GEORGE: Oh, fine. I'm fine. [*Pause*] Mr. Webb, what sense could there be in a superstition like that?

MR. WEBB: Well, you see,—on her wedding morning a girl's head's apt to be full of . . . clothes and things like that. Don't you think that's probably it?

GEORGE: Ye-e-s. I never thought of that.

MR. WEBB: A girl's apt to be a mite nervous on her wedding day. [*Pause*]

GEORGE: I wish a fellow could get married without all that marching up and down.

MR. WEBB: Well, every man that's ever lived has felt that way about it, George; but it hasn't done much good. It's the women that have built up weddings, my boy. From now on they have it pretty much as they like. . . . All those good women standing shoulder to shoulder making sure that the knot's tied in a mighty public way.

GEORGE: But . . . you *believe* in it, don't you, Mr. Webb?

MR. WEBB: Oh, yes; oh, yes. Don't you misunderstand me, my boy. Marriage is a wonderful thing,—wonderful thing. And don't you forget that, George.

GEORGE: No, sir.—Mr. Webb, how old were you when you got married?

MR. WEBB: Well, you see: I'd been to college and I'd taken a little time to get settled. But Mrs. Webb,—she wasn't much older than what Emily is. Oh, age hasn't much to do with it, George,—not compared to other things.

GEORGE: What were you going to say, Mr. Webb?

MR. WEBB: Oh, I don't know,—was I going to say something? [*Pause*] George, I was thinking the other night of some advice my father gave me when I got married. Charles, he said, Charles, start out early showing who's boss, he said. Best thing to do is to give an order, even if it don't make sense; just so she'll learn to obey. And he said: if anything about your wife irritates you,—her conversation, or anything,—just get up and leave the house. That'll make it clear to her, he said. And, oh, yes! he said never *never* let your wife know how much money you have, never.

GEORGE: Well, Mr. Webb . . . I don't think I could . . .

MR. WEBB: So I took the opposite of my father's advice and I've been happy ever since. And let that be a lesson to you, George, never to ask advice on personal matters.—George, are you going to raise chickens on your farm?

GEORGE: What?

MR. WEBB: Are you going to raise chickens on your farm?

GEORGE: Uncle Luke's never been much interested, but I thought—

MR. WEBB: A book came into my office the other day, George, on the Philo System of raising chickens. I want you to read it. I'm thinking of beginning in a small way in the back yard, and I'm going to put an incubator in the cellar—[*Enter* Mrs. Webb]

MRS. WEBB: Charles, are you talking about that old incubator again? I thought you two'd be talking about things worth while.

MR. WEBB: Well, Myrtle, if you want to give the boy some good advice, I'll go upstairs and leave you alone with him.

MRS. WEBB: Now, George, I'm sorry, but I've got to send you away so that Emily can come down and get some breakfast. She told me to tell you that she sends you her love but that she doesn't want to lay eyes on you. So good-by, George. [*George crosses the stage to his own home and disappears*]

MR. WEBB: Myrtle, I guess you don't know about that older superstition.

MRS. WEBB: What do you mean, Charles?

MR. WEBB: Since the cave-men: the groom shouldn't be left alone with his father-in-law on the day of the wedding, or near it. Now don't forget that!

STAGE MANAGER: Thank you. Thank you, everybody. Now I have to interrupt again here. You see, we want to know how all this began,—this wedding, this plan to spend a lifetime together. I'm awfully interested in how big things like that begin. You know how it is: you're twenty-one or twenty-two and you make some decisions; then whisssh! you're seventy: you've been a lawyer for fifty years, and that white-haired lady at your side has eaten over fifty thousand meals with you. How do such things begin? George and Emily are going to show you now the conversation they had when they first knew that . . . that . . . as the saying goes . . . they were meant for one another. But before they do it I want you to try and remember what it was like when you were young, when you were fifteen or sixteen. For some reason it is very hard to do: those days when even the little things in life could be almost too exciting to bear. And particularly the days when you were first in love; when you were like a person sleep-walking, and you didn't quite see the street you were in, and didn't quite hear everything that was said to you. You're just a little bit crazy. Will you remember that, please? Now they'll be coming out of High School at three o'clock. George has just been elected President of the Junior Class, and as it's June, that means he'll be President of the Senior Class all next year. And Emily's just been elected Secretary and Treasurer. I don't have to tell you how important that is. [*He places a board across the backs of two chairs, parallel to the footlights, and places two high stools behind it. This is the counter of* Mr. Morgan's *drugstore*] All ready! [Emily, *carrying an armful of—imaginary—schoolbooks, comes along Main Street from the left*]

EMILY: I can't, Louise. I've got to go home. Goodby. Oh, Earnestine! Earnestine! Can you come over tonight and do Algebra? I did the first and third in Study Hall. No, they're not hard. But, Earnestine, that Caesar's awful hard. I don't see why we have to do a thing like that. Come over about seven. Tell your mother you *have* to. G'by. G'by, Helen. G'by, Fred. [George, *also carrying books, catches up with her*]

GEORGE: Can I carry your books home for you, Emily?

EMILY: [*Coldly*] Thank you. [*She gives them to him*]

GEORGE: Excuse me a minute, Emily.—Say, Bob, get everything ready. I'll be there in a quarter of an hour. If I'm a little late start practice anyway. And give Herb some long high ones. His eye needs a lot of practice. Seeya later.

EMILY: Good-by, Lizzy.

GEORGE: Good-by, Lizzy.—I'm awfully glad you were elected, too, Emily.

EMILY: Thank you.

[*They have been standing on Main Street, almost against the back wall. George is about to take the first steps towards the audience when he stops again and says:*]

GEORGE: Emily, why are you mad at me?

EMILY: I'm not mad at you.

GEORGE: You . . . you treat me so funny.

EMILY: Well, I might as well say it right out, George. I don't like the whole change that's come over you in the last year. I'm sorry if that hurts your feelings, but I've just got to tell the truth and shame the devil.

GEORGE: I'm awfully sorry, Emily. Wha-a-what do you mean?

EMILY: Well, up to a year ago I used to like you a lot. And I used to watch you as you did everything . . . because we'd been friends so long . . . and then you began spending all your time at baseball . . . and you never even spoke to anybody any more; not even to your own family you didn't . . . and, George, it's a fact, you've got awful conceited and stuck-up, and all the girls say so. They may not say so to your face, but that's what they say about you behind your back, and it hurts me to hear them say it, but I've got to agree with them a little. I'm sorry if it hurts your feelings . . . but I can't be sorry I said it.

GEORGE: I . . . I'm glad you said it, Emily. I never thought that such a thing was happening to me. I guess it's hard for a fella not to have faults creep into his character. [*They take a step or two in silence, then stand still in misery*]

EMILY: I always expect a man to be perfect and I think he should be.

GEORGE: Oh . . . I don't think it's possible to be perfect, Emily.

EMILY: Well, my father is, and as far as I can see your father is. There's no reason on earth why you shouldn't be, too.

GEORGE: Well, Emily . . . I feel it's the other way round. That men aren't naturally good; but girls are. Like you and your mother and my mother.

EMILY: Well, you might as well know right now that I'm not perfect. It's not as easy for a girl to be perfect as a man, because we girls are more nervous. —Now I'm sorry I said all that about you. I don't know what made me say it.

GEORGE: No, no,—I guess if it's the truth you ought to say it. You stick to it, Emily.

EMILY: I don't know if it's the truth or not. And I suddenly feel that it isn't important at all.

GEORGE: Emily, would you like an ice-cream soda, or something, before you go home?

EMILY: Well, thank you . . . I would. [*They come into the drugstore and seat themselves on the stools*]

STAGE MANAGER: [*As* Mr. Morgan:] Hello, George. Hello, Emily. What'll you have? Why, Emily Webb, what've you been crying about?

GEORGE: [*He gropes for an explanation*] She . . . she just got an awful scare, Mr. Morgan. She almost got run over by that hardware store wagon. Everybody always says that Tom Huckins drives like a crazy man.

STAGE MANAGER: Here, take a drink of water, Emily. You look all shook up. There!—Now, what'll you have?

EMILY: I'll have a strawberry phosphate, thank you, Mr. Morgan.

GEORGE: No, no. You go and have an ice-cream soda with me, Emily.—Two strawberry ice-cream sodas, Mr. Morgan.

STAGE MANAGER: [*Working the faucets*] Yes, sir. I tell you, you've got to look both ways before you cross Main Street these days. Gets worse every year. There are a hundred and twenty-five horses in Grover's Corners this minute I'm talking to you. State Inspector was in here yesterday. And now they're bringing in these auto-mo-biles, the best thing to do is to just stay home. Why, I can remember the time when a dog could lie down all day in the middle of Main Street and nothing would come to disturb him. —Yes, Miss Ellis; be with you in a minute. Here are your sodas. Enjoy 'em. [*He goes off*]

EMILY: They're so expensive

GEORGE: No, no—don't you think of that. We're celebrating. First, we're celebrating our election. And then do you know what else I'm celebrating?

EMILY: No.

GEORGE: I'm celebrating because I've got a friend who tells me all the things that ought to be told me.

EMILY: George, *please* don't think of that. I don't know why I said it. It's not true. You're—

GEORGE: No, you stick to it, Emily. I'm glad you spoke to me like you did. But you'll see: I'm going to change so quick—you bet I'm going to change. And, Emily, I want to ask you a favor.

EMILY: What?

GEORGE: Emily, if I go away to State Agriculture College next year, will you write me a letter once in a while?

EMILY: I certainly will. I certainly will, George. . . . [*Pause*] It certainly seems like being away three years you'd get out of touch with things.

GEORGE: No, no. I mustn't do that. You see I'm not only going to be just a farmer. After a while maybe I'll run for something to get elected. So your letters'll be very important to me; you know, telling me what's going on here and everything. . . .

EMILY: Just the same, three years is a long time. Maybe letters from Grover's Corners wouldn't be so interesting after a while. Grover's Corners isn't a very important place when you think of all New Hampshire; but I think it's a very nice town.

GEORGE: The day wouldn't come when I wouldn't want to know everything that's happening here. I know *that's* true, Emily.

EMILY: Well, I'll try to make my letters interesting. [*Pause*]

GEORGE: Y'know, Emily, whenever I meet a farmer I ask him if he thinks it's important to go to Agriculture School to be a good farmer.

EMILY: Why, George—

GEORGE: Yeah, and some of them say that it's even a waste of time. You can get all those things, anyway, out of the pamphlets the government sends out. And Uncle Luke's getting old,—he's about ready for me to start in taking over his farm tomorrow, if I could.

EMILY: My!

GEORGE: And, like you say, being gone all that time . . . in other places and meeting other people . . . If anything like that can happen I don't want to go away. I guess new people aren't any better than old ones. I'll bet they almost never are. Emily, . . . I feel that you're as good a friend as I've got. I don't need to go and meet the people in other towns.

EMILY: But, George, maybe it's very important for you to go and learn all that about cattle-judging and soils and those things. And if you're going into politics, maybe you ought to meet people from other parts of the State . . . of course, I don't know.

GEORGE: [*After a pause*] Emily, I'm going to make up my mind right now. I won't go. I'll tell Pa about it tonight.

EMILY: Why, George, I don't see why you have to decide right now. It's a whole year away.

GEORGE: Emily, I'm glad you spoke to me about that . . . that fault in my character. And what you said was right; but there was *one* thing wrong in it, and that was when you said that for a year I wasn't noticing people, and . . . you, for instance. Listen, Emily . . . you say you were watching me when I did everything. . . . Why, I was doing the same about you all the time. Why, sure,—I always thought about you as one of the chief people I thought about. I always made sure where you were sitting on the bleachers, and who you were with. And we've always had lots of talks . . . and joking, in the halls; and they always meant a lot to me. Of course, they weren't as good as the talk we're having now. Lately I'd been noticing that you'd been acting kind of funny to me, and for three days I've been trying to walk home with you, but something's always got in the way. Yesterday I was standing over against the wall waiting for you, and you walked home with Miss Corcoran.

EMILY: George! . . . Life's awful funny! How could I have known that? Why, I thought—

GEORGE: Listen, Emily, I'm going to tell you why I'm not going to Agriculture School. I think that once you've found a person that you're very fond of . . . I mean a person who's fond of you, too,— at least enough to be interested in your character . . . Well, I think that's just as important as college is, and even more so. That's what I think.

EMILY: I think it's awfully important, too.

GEORGE: Emily.

EMILY: Yes, George.

GEORGE: Emily, if I improve and make a big change . . . would you be . . . I mean: *could* you be . . .

EMILY: I . . . I am now; I always have been.

GEORGE: [*Pause*] So I guess this is an important talk we've been having.

EMILY: Yes.

GEORGE: [*Takes a deep breath and straightens his back*] Wait just a minute and I'll take you home. [*He rises and goes to the* Stage Manager *who appears and comes toward him*] Mr. Morgan, I'll have to go home and get the money to pay you for this. It'll only take me a minute.

STAGE MANAGER: What's that? George Gibbs, do you mean to tell me—!

GEORGE: Yes, but I had reasons, Mr. Morgan.— Look, here's my gold watch to keep until I come back with the money.

STAGE MANAGER: That's all right. Keep your watch. I'll trust you.

GEORGE: I'll be back in five minutes.

STAGE MANAGER: I'll trust you ten years, George, —not a day more.—Got all over your shock, Emily?

EMILY: Yes, thank you, Mr. Morgan. It was nothing.

GEORGE: [*Taking up the books from the counter*] I'm ready.

[*They walk in grave silence down the stage, turn, and pass through the trellis at the Webbs' back door and disappear*]

STAGE MANAGER: Thank you, Emily. Thank you, George. Now before we go on to the wedding, there are still some more things we ought to know about this—about this marriage. I want to know some more about how the parents took it; but what I want to know most of all is: oh, you know what I mean,—what Grover's Corners thought about marriage anyway. You know's well as I do: people are never able to say right out what they think of money, or death, or fame, or marriage. You've got to catch it between the lines; you got to *over*-hear it. Oh, Doctor! Mrs. Gibbs!

[*They appear at their side of the stage and exchange a glance of understanding with him. The* Stage Manager *lays the same plank across two chairs that served as a drugstore counter and it has now become* Mrs. Gibbs's *ironing board.* Dr. Gibbs *sits down in a rocker and smokes.* Mrs. Gibbs *irons a moment in silence; then goes to the foot of the stairs and calls:*]

MRS. GIBBS: Rebecca! It's time you turned out your light and went to sleep. George, you'd better get some sleep, too.

REBECCA'S VOICE: Ma, I haven't finished my English.

MRS. GIBBS: What? Well, I bet you haven't been working, Rebecca. You've been reading that Sears, Roebuck catalogue, that's what you've been doing. —All right, I'll give you ten more minutes. If you

haven't finished by then you'll just have to fail the course and be a disgrace to your father and me.— George, what are you doing?

GEORGE'S VOICE: [*Hurt*] I'm doing history.

MRS. GIBBS: Well, you'd better go to bed. You're probably sleeping at the desk as it is. [*She casts an amused eye at her husband and returns to her ironing*]

DR. GIBBS: I had a long talk with the boy today.

MRS. GIBBS: Did you?

DR. GIBBS: I tell you, Mrs. G., there's nothing so terrifying in the world as a son. The relation of a father to a son is the damnedest, awkwardest—. I always come away feeling like a soggy sponge of hypocrisy.

MRS. GIBBS: Well, a mother and a daughter's no picnic, let me tell you.

DR. GIBBS: George is set on it: he wants to marry Emily 'soon as school's out and take her right on to the farm. [*Pause*] He says he can sit up nights and learn agriculture from government pamphlets, without going to college for it.

MRS. GIBBS: He always was crazy about farming. Gets that from my people.

DR. GIBBS: At a pinch, I guess he could start in farming;—but I swear I think he's too young to get married. Julia, he's just a green half-grown kid. He isn't ready to be a family man.

MRS. GIBBS: No, he ain't. You're right.—But he's a good boy and I wouldn't like to think of him being alone out there . . . coming into town Satiddy nights, like any old farm hand, tuckered out from work and looking for excitement. He might get into bad ways. It wouldn't be enough fun for him to come and sit by our stove,—and holding hands with Emily, for a year mightn't be enough either. He might lose interest in her.

DR. GIBBS: Hm.

MRS. GIBBS: Frank, I' been watching her. George is a lucky boy when you think of all the silly girls in the world.

DR. GIBBS: But, Julia,—George *married*. That great gangling selfish nincumpoop.

MRS. GIBBS: Yes, I know. [*She takes up a collar and examines it*] Frank, what do you do to your collars? Do you gnaw 'em? I never saw such a man for collars.

DR. GIBBS: Julia, when I married you, do you know what one of my terrors was in getting married?

MRS. GIBBS: Pshaw! Go on with you!

DR. GIBBS: I was afraid we weren't going to have material for conversation more'n 'ld last us a few weeks. I was afraid we'd run out and eat our meals in silence, that's a fact. You and I've been conversing for twenty years now without any noticeable barren spells.

MRS. GIBBS: Well, good weather, bad weather, 'tain't very choice, but I always manage to find something to say. [*Pause*]

DR. GIBBS: What do you think? What do you think,

Julia? Shall we tell the boy he can go ahead and get married?

MRS. GIBBS: Seems like it's up to us to decide. Myrtle and Charles Webb are willing. They think it's a good idea to throw the young people into the sea and let'm sink or swim, as soon as they're ready.

DR. GIBBS: What does that mean? Must we decide right now? This minute?

MRS. GIBBS: There you go putting the responsibility on me!

DR. GIBBS: Here it is, almost April.—I'll go up and say a word to him right now before he goes to bed. [*He rises*] You're sure, Julia? You've nothing more to add?

MRS. GIBBS: [*Stops ironing a moment*] I don't know what to say. Seems like it's too much to ask, for a big outdoor boy like that to go and get shut up in classrooms for three years. And once he's on the farm, he might just as well have a companion, seeing he's found a fine girl like Emily. . . . People are meant to live two by two in this world. . . . Yes, Frank, go up and tell him it's all right.

DR. GIBBS: [*Crosses and is about to call when*]

MRS. GIBBS: [*Her hands on her cheeks, staring into the audience, in sharp alarm*] Wait a minute! Wait a minute!—[*Then resuming her ironing*] No,—go and tell him.

DR. GIBBS: Why did you stop then, Julia?

MRS. GIBBS: Oh, you know: I thought of all those times we went through in the first years when George and Rebecca were babies,—you walking up and down with them at three in the morning; the whooping-cough; the time George fell off the porch. You and I were twenty-five years old, and more. It's wonderful how one forgets one's troubles, like that. —Yes, Frank, go upstairs and tell him. . . . It's worth it.

DR. GIBBS: Yes, they'll have a lot of troubles, but that's none of our business. Let'm. Everybody has a right to his own troubles.—You ought to be present, Julia,—important occasion like that. I'll call him.—George! Oh, George!

GEORGE'S VOICE: Yes, Pa.

DR. GIBBS: Can you come down a minute? Your mother and I want to speak to you.

GEORGE: Yeah, sure.

MRS. GIBBS: [*Putting her arm through her husband's*] Lord, what a fool I am: I'm trembling all over. There's nothing to tremble about.

STAGE MANAGER: Thank you! Thank you! Now we're ready to go on with the wedding. [*While he talks, the actors remove the chair and tables and trellises from the Gibbs and Webb homes. They arrange the pews for the church in the back of the stage. The congregation will sit facing the back wall. The aisle of the church is in the middle of the scene. A small platform is placed against the back wall on which the* Stage Manager *as Minister can stand*] There are a lot of things to be said about a wedding; there are a lot of thoughts that go on during a wedding. We can't get them all into one wedding, naturally, and especially not into a wedding at Grover's Corners where they're awfully plain and short. In this wedding I play the minister. That gives me the right to say a few more things about it. For a while now, the play gets pretty serious. Y'see, some churches say that marriage is a sacrament. I don't quite know what that means, but I can guess. Like Mrs. Gibbs said a few minutes ago: People were made to live two-by-two. This is a good wedding, but people are so put together that even at a good wedding there's a lot of confusion way down deep in people's minds and we thought that that ought to be in our play, too. The real hero of this scene isn't on the stage at all, and you know who that is. It's like what one of those European fellas said: every child born into the world is Nature's attempt to make a perfect human being. Well, we've seen nature pushing and contriving for some time now. We all know that nature's interested in quantity; but I think she's interested in quality, too, —that's why I'm in the ministry.—Maybe she's trying to make another good governor for New Hampshire. And don't forget the other witnesses at this wedding,—the ancestors. Millions of them. Most of them set out to live two-by-two, also. Millions of them. Well, that's all my sermon. 'Twan't very long, anyway.

[*The organ starts playing Handel's "Largo." The congregation streams into the church and sits in silence.* Mrs. Webb, *on the way to her place, turns back and speaks to the audience*]

MRS. WEBB: I don't know why on earth I should be crying. I suppose there's nothing to cry about. It came over me at breakfast this morning; there was Emily eating her breakfast as she's done for seventeen years and now she's going off to eat it in someone else's house. I suppose that's it. And Emily! She suddenly said: I can't eat another mouthful, and she put her head down on the table and *she* cried. [*She starts toward her seat in the church, but turns back and adds*] Oh, I've got to say it: you know, there's something downright cruel about sending our girls out into marriage this way. I hope some of her girl friends have told her a thing or two. It's cruel, I know, but I couldn't bring myself to say anything. I went into it blind as a bat myself. The whole world's wrong, that's what's the matter. There they come. [*She hurries to her place in the pew.* George *starts to come down the right aisle of the theater, through the audience. Suddenly three members of his baseball team appear by the right proscenium pillar and start whistling and catcalling to him. They are dressed for the ball field*]

THE BASEBALL PLAYERS: Eh, George, George! Hsst —yaow! If things don't go right, call us in. We know what to do. Eh, fellas? Yaow! George, don't look so innocent, you old geezer. We know what you're thinking. Don't disgrace the team, big boy. Whoo-oo-oo.

STAGE MANAGER: All right! All right! That'll do. That's enough of that. [*Smiling, he pushes them off the stage. They lean back to shout a few more cat-calls*] There used to be an awful lot of that kind of thing at weddings in the old days,—Rome, and later. We're more civilized now,—so they say.

[*The choir starts singing "Love divine, all love excelling—." George has reached the stage. He stares at the congregation a moment, then takes a few steps of withdrawal, toward the right proscenium pillar*]

GEORGE: [*Darkly, to himself*] I wish I were back at school. . . . I don't want to get married. [*His mother has left her seat and come toward him. She stops, looking at him anxiously*]

MRS. GIBBS: George, what's the matter?

GEORGE: Ma, I don't want to grow old. Why's everybody pushing me so?

MRS. GIBBS: Why, George . . . you wanted it.

GEORGE: Why do I have to get married at all? Listen, Ma, for the last time I ask you—

MRS. GIBBS: No, no, George . . . you're a man now.

GEORGE: Listen, Ma, you never listen to me. All I want to do is to be a fella . . . why do—

MRS. GIBBS: George! If anyone should hear you! Now stop. Why, I'm ashamed of you!

GEORGE: [*Passing his hand over his forehead*] What's the matter? I've been dreaming. Where's Emily?

MRS. GIBBS: Gracious! You gave me such a turn.

GEORGE: Cheer up, Ma. What are you looking so funny for? Cheer up; I'm getting married.

MRS. GIBBS: Let me catch my breath a minute.

GEORGE: Now, Ma, you have Thursday nights. Emily and I are coming over to dinner every Thursday night . . . you'll see. Ma, what are you crying for? Come on; we've got to get ready for this.

[*In the meantime, Emily, in white and wearing her wedding veil, has come through the audience and mounted on to the stage. She too draws back when she sees the congregation in the church. The choir begins: "Blessed be the tie that binds"*]

EMILY: I never felt so alone in my whole life. And George over there, looking so . . . ! I *hate* him. I wish I were dead. Papa! Papa!

MR. WEBB: [*Leaves his seat in the pews and comes toward her anxiously*] Emily! Emily! Now don't get upset. . . .

EMILY: But, Papa,—I don't want to get married. . . .

MR. WEBB: Sh-sh—Emily. Everything's all right.

EMILY: Why can't I stay for a while just as I am? Let's go away.

MR. WEBB: No, no, Emily. Now stop and think.

EMILY: Don't you remember that you used to say,—all the time you used to say that I was *your* girl. There must be lots of places we can go to. Let's go away. I'll work for you. I could keep house.

MR. WEBB: Sh. . . . You mustn't think of such things. You're just nervous, Emily. Now, now,—you're marrying the best young fellow in the world. George is a fine fellow.

EMILY: But, Papa,—

MR. WEBB: George! George! [Mrs. Gibbs *returns to her seat.* George *hears* Mr. Webb *and looks up.* Mr. Webb *beckons to him. They move to the center of the stage*] I'm giving away my daughter, George. Do you think you can take care of her?

GEORGE: Mr. Webb, I want to . . . I want to try. Emily, I'm going to do my best. I love you, Emily. I need you.

EMILY: Well, if you love me, help me. All I want is someone to love me.

GEORGE: I will, Emily.

EMILY: If ever I'm sick or in trouble, that's what I mean.

GEORGE: Emily, I'll try. I'll try.

EMILY: And I mean for *ever*. Do you hear? For ever and ever. [*They fall into each other's arms. The March from "Lohengrin" is heard*]

MR. WEBB: Come, they're waiting for us. Now you know it'll be all right. Come, quick.

[George *slips away and takes his place beside the* Stage Manager-Clergyman. Emily *proceeds up the aisle on her father's arm*]

STAGE MANAGER: Do you, George, take this woman, Emily, to be your wedded wife, to have . . .

[Mrs. Soames *has been sitting in the last row of the congregation. She now turns to her neighbors and in a shrill voice says*]

MRS. SOAMES: Perfectly lovely wedding! Loveliest wedding I ever saw. Oh, I do love a good wedding, don't you? Doesn't she make a lovely bride?

GEORGE: I do.

STAGE MANAGER: Do you, Emily, take this man, George, to be your wedded husband,—

MRS. SOAMES: Don't know *when* I've seen such a lovely wedding. But I always cry. Don't know why it is, but I always cry. I just like to see young people happy, don't you? Oh, I think it's lovely. [*The ring. The kiss. The stage is suddenly arrested into silent, tableau. The Stage Manager, his eyes on the distance, says to the audience:*] I've married two hundred couples in my day. Do I believe in it? I don't know. M. . . . marries N. . . . millions of them. The cottage, the gocart, the Sunday afternoon drives in the Ford, the first rheumatism, the grandchildren, the second rheumatism, the deathbed, the reading of the will,—Once in a thousand times it's interesting. Well, let's have Mendelssohn's "Wedding March"!

[*The organ picks up the March. The bride and groom come down the aisle, radiant, but trying to be very dignified*]

MRS. SOAMES: Aren't they a lovely couple? Oh, I've never been to such a nice wedding. I'm sure they'll be happy. I always say: *happiness,* that's the great thing! The important thing is to be happy.

[*The bride and groom reach the steps leading*

into the audience. A bright light is thrown upon them. They descend into the auditorium and run up the aisle joyously]

STAGE MANAGER: That's all the Second Act. Ten minutes' intermission, folks.

ACT III.

During the intermission the audience has seen the actors arranging the stage. On the right hand side, a little right of the center, ten or twelve ordinary chairs have been placed in three openly spaced rows facing the audience. These are graves in the cemetery. Towards the end of the intermission the actors enter and take their places. The front row contains: toward the center of the stage, an empty chair; then Mrs. Gibbs, Simon Stimson. *The second row contains, among others,* Mrs. Soames. *The third row has* Wally Webb. *The dead sit in a quiet without stiffness, and in a patience without listlessness. The* Stage Manager *takes his accustomed place and waits for the house-lights to go down.*

STAGE MANAGER: This time nine years have gone by, friends—summer, 1913. Gradual changes in Grover's Corners. Horses are getting rarer. Farmers coming into town in Fords. Chief difference is in the young people, far as I can see. They want to go to the moving pictures all the time. They want to wear clothes like they see there . . . want to be citified. Everybody locks their house doors now at night. Ain't been any burglars in town yet, but everybody's heard about 'em. But you'd be surprised though—on the whole, things don't change much at Grover's Corners. Guess you want to know what all these chairs are here fur. Smarter ones have guessed it already. I don't know how you feel about such things; but this certainly is a beautiful place. It's on a hilltop—a windy hilltop—lots of sky, lots of clouds, —often lots of sun and moon and stars. You come up here on a fine afternoon and you can see range on range of hills—awful blue they are—up there by Lake Sunapee and Lake Winnapassaukee . . . and way up, if you've got a glass, you can see the White Mountains and Mt. Washington—where North Conway and Conway is. And, of course, our favorite mountain, Mt. Monadnock's, right here—and all around it lie these towns—Jaffrey, 'n East Jaffrey, 'n Peterborough, 'n Dublin and [*Then pointing down in the audience*] there, quite a ways down is Grover's Corners. Yes, beautiful spot up here. Mountain laurel and li-lacks. I often wonder why people like to be buried in Woodlawn and Brooklyn when they might pass the same time up here in New Hampshire. Over in that corner—[*Pointing to stage left*] are the old stones,—1670, 1680. Strong-minded people that come a long way to be independent. Summer people walk around there laughing at the funny words on the tombstones . . . it don't do any harm. And genealogists come up from Boston—get paid by city people for looking up their ancestors. They want to make sure they're Daughters of the American Revolution and of the *Mayflower*. . . . Well, I guess that don't do any harm, either. Wherever you come near the human race, there's layers and layers of nonsense. . . . Over there are some Civil War veterans too. Iron flags on their graves. . . . New Hampshire boys . . . had a notion that the Union ought to be kept together, though they'd never seen more than fifty miles of it themselves. All they knew was the name, friends—the United States of America. The United States of America. And they went and died about it. This here is the new part of the cemetery. Here's your friend, Mrs. Gibbs. 'N let me see— Here's Mr. Stimson, organist at the Congregational Church. And over there's Mrs. Soames who enjoyed the wedding so—you remember? Oh, and a lot of others. And Editor Webb's boy, Wallace, whose appendix burst while he was on a Boy Scout trip to Crawford Notch. Yes, an awful lot of sorrow has sort of quieted down up here. People just wild with grief have brought their relatives up to this hill. We all know how it is . . . and then time . . . and sunny days . . . and rainy days . . . 'n snow . . . tz-tz-tz. We're all glad they're in a beautiful place and we're coming up here ourselves when our fit's over. This certainly is an important part of Grover's Corners. A lot of thoughts come up here, night and day, but there's no post office. Now I'm going to tell you some things you know already. You know'm as well as I do; but you don't take'm out and look at'm very often. I don't care what they say with their mouths—everybody knows that *something* is eternal. And it ain't houses and it ain't names, and it ain't earth, and it ain't even the stars . . . everybody knows in their bones that *something* is eternal, and that something has to do with human beings. All the greatest people ever lived have been telling us that for five thousand years and yet you'd be surprised how people are always losing hold of it. There's something way down deep that's eternal about every human being. [*Pause*] You know as well as I do that the dead don't stay interested in us living people for very long. Gradually, gradually, they let hold of the earth . . . and the ambitions they had . . . and the pleasures they had . . . and the things they suffered . . . and the people they loved. They get weaned away from earth—that's the way I put it,—weaned away. Yes, they stay here while the earth-part of 'em burns away, burns out, and all that time they slowly get indifferent to what's goin' on in Grover's Corners. They're waitin'. They're waitin' for something that they feel is comin'. Something important and great. Aren't they waitin' for the eternal part in them to come out clear? Some of the things they're going to say maybe'll hurt your feelings—but that's the way it is: mother'n daughter . . . husband 'n wife . . . enemy 'n enemy . . . money 'n miser . . . all those terribly important things kind of grow pale around here. And what's left? What's left when memory's gone, and your identity, Mrs. Smith? [*He looks at the audience a minute, then turns to the stage*] Well! There are some *living* people. There's Joe Stoddard, our undertaker, supervising a new-made grave. And here comes a Grover's Corners boy, that left town to go out West.

[Joe Stoddard *has hovered about in the background.* Sam Craig *enters left, wiping his forehead from the exertion. He carries an umbrella and strolls front*]

SAM CRAIG: Good afternoon, Joe Stoddard.

JOE STODDARD: Good afternoon, good afternoon. Let me see now: do I know you?

SAM CRAIG: I'm Sam Craig.

JOE STODDARD: Gracious sakes' alive! Of all people! I should'a knowed you'd be back for the funeral. You've been away a long time, Sam.

SAM CRAIG: Yes, I've been away over twelve years. I'm in business out in Buffalo now, Joe. But I was in the East when I got news of my cousin's death, so I thought I'd combine things a little and come and see the old home. You look well.

JOE STODDARD: Yes, yes, can't complain. Very sad, our journey today, Samuel.

SAM CRAIG: Yes.

JOE STODDARD: Yes, yes. I always say, I hate to supervise when a young person is taken. I see you brought your umbrella. It's going to rain and make it sadder still, seems like. They'll be here in a few minutes now. I had to come here early today—my son's supervisin' at the home.

SAM CRAIG: [*Reading stones*] Old Farmer McCarty, I used to do chores for him—after school. He had the lumbago.

JOE STODDARD: Yes, we brought Farmer McCarty here a number of years ago now.

SAM CRAIG: [*Staring at* Mrs. Gibbs' *knees*] Why, this is my Aunt Julia. . . . I'd forgotten that she'd . . . of course, of course.

JOE STODDARD: Yes, Doc Gibbs lost his wife two-three years ago . . . about this time. And today's another pretty bad blow for him, too.

MRS. GIBBS: [*To* Simon Stimson: *in an even voice*] That's my sister Carey's boy, Sam. . . . Sam Craig.

SIMON STIMSON: I'm always uncomfortable when *they're* around.

MRS. GIBBS: Simon.

SIMON STIMSON: They and their nonsense and their damned glee at being alive. . . .

MRS. GIBBS: Simon, be patient. . . .

SAM CRAIG: Do they choose their own verses much, Joe?

JOE STODDARD: No . . . not usual. Mostly the bereaved pick a verse.

SAM CRAIG: Doesn't sound like Aunt Julia. There aren't many of those Hersey sisters left now. Let me

see: where are . . . I wanted to look at my father's and mother's . . .

JOE STODDARD: Over there with the Craigs. . . . Avenue F.

SAM CRAIG: [*Reading* Simon Stimson's *epitaph*] He was organist at church, wasn't he?—Hm, drank a lot, we used to say.

JOE STODDARD: Nobody was supposed to know about it. He'd seen a peck of trouble. Those musical fellas ain't like the rest of us, I reckon. [*Behind his hand*] Took his own life, y' know?

SAM CRAIG: Oh, did he?

JOE STODDARD: Hung himself in the attic. They tried to hush it up, but of course it got around. His wife's just married Senator Barstow. Many a time I've seen her, eleven o'clock at night, goin' around the streets huntin' for her husband. Think o' that! Now she's married to Senator Barstow over at Manchester. He chose his own epy-taph. You can see it there. It ain't a verse exactly.

SAM CRAIG: Why, it's just some notes of music— what is it?

JOE STODDARD: Oh, I wouldn't know. It was wrote up in the Boston papers at the time.

SAM CRAIG: Joe, what did she die of?

JOE STODDARD: Who?

SAM CRAIG: My cousin.

JOE STODDARD: Oh, didn't you know? Had some trouble bringing a baby into the world. Let's see, today's Friday—'twas almost a week ago now.

SAM CRAIG: [*Putting up his umbrella*] Did the baby live?

JOE STODDARD: [*Raising his coat collar*] No. 'Twas her second, though. There's a little boy 'bout four years old.

SAM CRAIG: The grave's going to be over there?

JOE STODDARD: Yes, there ain't much more room over here among the Gibbses, so they're opening up a whole new Gibbs section over by Avenue B. You'll excuse me now. I see they're comin'.

THE DEAD: [*Not lugubrious; and strongly New England in accent*] Rain'll do a lot of good.—Yes, reckon things were gettin' downright parched. Don't look like it's goin' to last long, tho'.—Lemuel, you remember the floods of '79? Carried away all the bridges but one.

[*From left to right, at the back of the stage, comes a procession. Four men carry a casket, invisible to us. All the rest are under umbrellas. One can vaguely see:* Dr. Gibbs, George, *the* Webbs, *etc. They gather about a grave in the back center of the stage, a little to the left of center*]

MRS. SOAMES: Who is it, Julia?

MRS. GIBBS: [*Without raising her eyes*] My daughter-in-law, Emily Webb.

MRS. SOAMES: [*A little surprised, but no emotion*] Well, I declare! The road up here must have been awful muddy. What did she die of, Julia?

MRS. GIBBS: In childbirth.

MRS. SOAMES: Childbirth. [*Almost with a laugh*] I'd forgotten all about that! My, wasn't life awful— [*With a sigh*] and wonderful.

SIMON STIMSON: [*With a sideways glance*] Won-derful, was it?

MRS. GIBBS: Simon! Now, remember!

MRS. SOAMES: I remember Emily's wedding. Wasn't it a lovely wedding! And I remember her reading the class poem at Graduation Exercises. Emily was one of the brightest girls ever graduated from High School. I've heard Principal Wilkins say so time after time. I called on them at their new farm, just before I died. Perfectly beautiful farm.

A WOMAN FROM AMONG THE DEAD: It's on the same road we lived on.

A MAN AMONG THE DEAD: Yes, just near the Elks' picnic grounds. Remember, Joe? By the lake where we always used to go Fourth of July? Right smart farm.

[*They subside. The group by the grave starts singing "Blessed be the tie that binds"*]

A WOMAN AMONG THE DEAD: I always liked that hymn. I was hopin' they'd sing a hymn.

A MAN AMONG THE DEAD: My wife—my second wife—knows all the verses of about every hymn there is. It just beats the Dutch . . . she can go through them all by heart.

[*Pause. Suddenly Emily appears from among the umbrellas. She is wearing a white dress. Her hair is down her back and tied by a white ribbon like a little girl. She comes slowly, gazing wonderingly at the dead, a little dazed. She stops halfway and smiles faintly*]

EMILY: Hello.

VOICES AMONG THE DEAD: Hello, Emily. H'lo, M's. Gibbs.

EMILY: Hello, Mother Gibbs.

MRS. GIBBS: Emily.

EMILY: Hello. [*The hymn continues. Emily looks back at the funeral. She says dreamily:*] It's raining.

MRS. GIBBS: Yes. . . . They'll be gone soon, dear. Just rest yourself. [*Emily sits down in the empty chair by* Mrs. Gibbs]

EMILY: It seems thousands and thousands of years since I. . . . How stupid they all look. They don't have to look like that!

MRS. GIBBS: Don't look at them now, dear. They'll be gone soon.

EMILY: Oh, I wish I'd been here a long time. I don't like being new here.—How do you do, Mr. Stimson?

SIMON STIMSON: How do you do, Emily.

[*Emily continues to look about her with a wan and wondering smile; but for a moment her eyes do not return to the funeral group. As though to shut out from her mind the thought of that group she starts speaking to* Mrs. Gibbs *with a touch of nervousness*]

EMILY: Mother Gibbs, George and I have made that farm into just the best place you ever saw. We thought of you all the time. We wanted to show you the new barn and a great long ce-ment drinking fountain for the stock. We bought that out of the money you left us.

MRS. GIBBS: I did?

EMILY: Don't you remember, Mother Gibbs—the legacy you left us? Why, it was over three hundred and fifty dollars.

MRS. GIBBS: Yes, yes, Emily.

EMILY: Well, there's a patent device on this drinking fountain so that it never overflows, Mother Gibbs, and it never sinks below a certain mark they have there. It's fine. [*Her voice trails off and her eyes return to the funeral group*] It won't be the same to George without me, but it's a lovely farm. [*Suddenly she looks directly at* Mrs. Gibbs] Live people don't understand, do they?

MRS. GIBBS: No, dear—not very much.

EMILY: They're sort of shut up in little boxes, aren't they? I feel as though I knew them last a thousand years ago. . . . My boy is spending the day at Mrs. Carter's. [*She sees Mr. Carter among the dead*] Oh, Mr. Carter, my little boy is spending the day at your house.

MR. CARTER: Is he?

EMILY: Yes, he loves it there.—Mother Gibbs, we have a Ford, too. Never gives any trouble. I don't drive, though. Mother Gibbs, when does this feeling go away?—Of being . . . one of *them*? How long does it . . . ?

MRS. GIBBS: Sh! dear. Just wait and be patient.

EMILY: [*With a sigh*] I know.—Look, they're finished. They're going.

MRS. GIBBS: Sh—.

[*The umbrellas leave the stage.* Dr. Gibbs *comes over to his wife's grave and stands before it a moment.* Emily *looks up at his face.* Mrs. Gibbs *does not raise her eyes*]

EMILY: Look! Father Gibbs is bringing some of my flowers to you. He looks just like George, doesn't he? Oh, Mother Gibbs, I never realized before how troubled and how . . . how in the dark live persons are. From morning till night, that's all they are— troubled. [*Dr. Gibbs goes off*]

THE DEAD: Little cooler than it was.—Yes, that rain's cooled it off a little. Those North East winds always do the same thing, don't they? If it isn't a rain, it's a three-day blow.—Reckon it may clear up before night; often does.

[*A patient calm falls on the stage. The* Stage Manager *appears at his proscenium pillar, smoking.* Emily *sits up abruptly with an idea*]

EMILY: But, Mother Gibbs, one can go back, one can go back there again . . . into living. I feel it. I know it. Why just then for a moment I was thinking about . . . about the farm . . . and for a minute I *was* there, and my baby was on my lap as plain as day.

MRS. GIBBS: Yes, of course you can.

EMILY: I can go back there and live all those days over again . . . why not?

MRS. GIBBS: All I can say is, Emily, don't.

EMILY: [*Takes a few steps toward the* Stage Manager] But it's true, isn't it? I can go and live . . . back there . . . again.

STAGE MANAGER: Yes, some have tried—but they soon come back here.

MRS. GIBBS: Don't do it, Emily.

MRS. SOAMES: Emily, don't. It's not what you think it'd be.

EMILY: But I won't live over a sad day. I'll choose a happy one—I'll choose the day I first knew that I loved George. Why should that be painful? [*They are silent. Her question turns to the* Stage Manager]

STAGE MANAGER: You not only live it; but you watch yourself living it.

EMILY: Yes?

STAGE MANAGER: And as you watch it, you see the thing that they—down there—never know. You see the future. You know what's going to happen afterwards.

EMILY: But is that—painful? Why?

MRS. GIBBS: That's not the only reason why you shouldn't do it, Emily. When you've been here longer you'll see that our life here is our hope that soon we'll forget all that, and think only of what's ahead, and be ready for what's ahead. When you've been here longer you'll understand.

EMILY: [*Softly*] But, Mother Gibbs, how can I ever forget that life? It's all I know. It's all I had. [Mrs. Gibbs *does not answer*] Mr. Stimson, did you go back?

SIMON STIMSON: [*Sharply*] No.

EMILY: Did you, Mrs. Soames?

MRS. SOAMES: Oh, Emily. It isn't wise. Really, it isn't. All we can do is just warn you. It won't be what you expect.

EMILY: [*Slowly*] But it's a thing I must know for myself. I'll choose a happy day, anyway.

MRS. GIBBS: No. At least, choose an unimportant day. Choose the least important day in your life. It will be important enough.

EMILY: [*To the* Stage Manager] Then it can't be since I was married; or since the baby was born. I can choose a birthday at least, can't I?—I choose my twelfth birthday.

STAGE MANAGER: All right. February 11th, 1899. A Tuesday.—Do you want any special time of day?

EMILY: Oh, I want the whole day.

STAGE MANAGER: We'll begin at dawn. You remember it had been snowing for several days; but it had stopped the night before, and they had begun clearing the roads. The sun's coming up.

EMILY: [*With a cry*] There's Main Street . . . why, that's Mr. Morgan's drugstore before he changed it! . . . And there's the livery stable. [*She walks toward the back of the stage*]

STAGE MANAGER: Yes, it's 1899. This is fourteen years ago.

EMILY: Oh, that's the town I knew as a little girl. And, look, there's the old white fence that used to be around our house. Oh, I'd forgotten that! Oh, I love it so! Are *they* inside?

STAGE MANAGER: Yes, your mother'll be coming downstairs in a minute to make breakfast.

EMILY: [*Softly*] Will she?

STAGE MANAGER: And you remember: your father had been away for several days; he came back on the early morning train.

EMILY: No . . . ?

STAGE MANAGER: He'd been back to his college to make a speech—in Western New York, at Clinton.

EMILY: Look! There's Howie Newsome. There's our policeman. But he's *dead;* he *died.*

[*The* Stage Manager *retires to his corner. The voices of* Howie Newsome, Constable Warren *and* Joe Crowell, Jr., *are heard at the left of the stage*]

HOWIE NEWSOME: Whoa, Bessie!—Bessie! 'Morning, Bill.

BILL: Morning, Howie.

HOWIE NEWSOME: You're up early.

BILL: Been rescuin' a party; darn near froze to death, down by Polish Town thar. Got drunk and lay out in the snowdrifts. Thought he was in bed when I shook'm.

EMILY: Why, there's Joe Crowell. . . .

JOE CROWELL: Good morning, Mr. Warren. 'Morning, Howie.

[Mrs. Webb *has appeared in her kitchen, but* Emily *does not see her until she calls*]

MRS. WEBB: Chil-*dren!* Wally! Emily! . . . Time to get up.

EMILY: Mama, here I am! Oh! how young Mama looks! I didn't know Mama was ever that young. Oh!

MRS. WEBB: You can come and dress by the kitchen fire, if you like; but hurry. [Howie Newsome *has entered along Main Street and brings the milk to* Mrs. Webb's *door*] Good morning, Mr. Newsome. Whhhh —it's cold.

HOWIE NEWSOME: Ten below by my barn, Mrs. Webb.

MRS. WEBB: Think of it! Keep yourself wrapped up. [*She takes her bottles in, shuddering*]

EMILY: [*With an effort*] Mama, I can't find my blue hair ribbon anywhere.

MRS. WEBB: Just open your eyes, dear, that's all. I laid it out for you special—on the dresser, there. If it were a snake it would bite you.

EMILY: Yes, yes. . . . [*She puts her hand on her heart.* Mr. Webb *comes along Main Street, where he meets* Constable Warren]

MR. WEBB: Good morning, Bill.

BILL: Good morning, Mr. Webb. You're up early.

MR. WEBB: Yes, just been back to my old college in New York State. Been any trouble here?

BILL: Well, I was called up this mornin' to rescue a Polish fella—darn near froze to death he was.

MR. WEBB: We must get it in the paper.

BILL: 'Twan't much.

EMILY: [*Whispers*] Papa. [*Mr. Webb shakes the snow off his feet and enters his house*]

MR. WEBB: Good morning, Mother.

MRS. WEBB: How did it go, Charles?

MR. WEBB: Oh, fine, I guess. I told'm a few things.

MRS. WEBB: Did you sit up on the train all night?

MR. WEBB: Yes. Never could sleep on a Pullman anyway.

MRS. WEBB: Charles, seems to me—we're rich enough so that you could sleep in a train once in a while.

MR. WEBB: Everything all right here?

MRS. WEBB: Yes—can't think of anything that's happened, special. Been right cold. Howie Newsome says it's ten below over to his barn.

MR. WEBB: Yes, well, it's colder than that at Hamilton College. Students' ears are falling off. It ain't Christian.—Paper have any mistakes in it?

MRS. WEBB: None that I noticed. Coffee's ready when you want it. [*He starts upstairs*] Charles! Don't forget; it's Emily's birthday. Did you remember to get her something?

MR. WEBB: [*Patting his pocket*] Yes, I've got something here.

MRS. WEBB: Goodness sakes! I hope she likes what I got for her. I hunted hard enough for it. Child*ren*! Hurry up! Hurry up!

MR. WEBB: Where's my girl? Where's my birthday girl? [*He goes off left*]

MRS. WEBB: Don't interrupt her now, Charles. You can see her at breakfast. She's slow enough as it is. Hurry up, children! It's seven o'clock. Now, I don't want to call you again.

EMILY: [*Softly, more in wonder than in grief*] I can't bear it. They're so young and beautiful. Why did they ever have to get old? Mama, I'm here. I'm grown up. I love you all, everything.—I can't look at everything hard enough. There's the butternut tree. [*She wanders up Main Street*] There's Mr. Morgan's drugstore. And there's the High School, forever and ever, and ever. And there's the Congregational Church where I got married. Oh, dear. Oh, dear. Oh, dear! [*The Stage Manager beckons partially to her. He points to the house. She says a breathless "yes" and goes to the house*] Good morning, Mama.

MRS. WEBB: [*At the foot of the stairs, kissing her in a matter-of-fact way*] Well, now, dear, a very happy birthday to my girl and many happy returns. There are some surprises waiting for you on the kitchen table.

EMILY: Oh, Mama, you *shouldn't* have. [*She throws an anguished glance at the Stage Manager*] I can't—I can't.

MRS. WEBB: [*Facing the audience, over her stove*] But birthday or no birthday, I want you to eat your breakfast good and slow. I want you to grow up and be a good strong girl. [*She goes to the stairs and calls*] Wally! Wally, wash yourself good. Everything's getting cold down here. [*She returns to the stove with her back to Emily. Emily opens her parcels*] That in the blue paper is from your Aunt Carrie and I reckon you can guess who brought the post card album. I found it on the doorstep when I brought in the milk—George Gibbs . . . must have come over in the cold pretty early . . . right nice of him.

EMILY: [*To herself*] Oh, George; I'd forgotten that. . . .

MRS. WEBB: Chew that bacon slow. It'll help keep you warm on a cold day.

EMILY: [*Beginning softly but urgently*] Oh, Mama, just look at me one minute as though you really saw me. Mama, fourteen years have gone by. I'm dead. You're a grandmother, Mama. I married George Gibbs, Mama. Wally's dead, too. Mama, his appendix burst on a camping trip to North Conway. We felt just terrible about it—don't you remember? But, just for a moment now we're all together. Mama, just for a moment we're happy. Let's look at one another.

MRS. WEBB: That in the yellow paper is something I found in the attic among your grandmother's things. You're old enough to wear it now, and I thought you'd like it.

EMILY: And this is from you. Why, Mama, it's lovely and it's just what I wanted. It's beautiful! [*She flings her arms around her mother's neck. Her mother goes on with her cooking, but is pleased*]

MRS. WEBB: Well, I hoped you'd like it. Hunted all over. Your Aunt Norah couldn't find one in Concord, so I had to send all the way to Boston [*Laughing*] Wally has something for you, too. He made it at Manual Training Class and he's very proud of it. Be sure you make a big fuss about it.—Your father has a surprise for you, too; don't know what it is myself. Sh—here he comes.

MR. WEBB: [*Off stage*] Where's my girl? Where's my birthday girl?

EMILY: [*In a loud voice to the Stage Manager*] I can't. I can't go on. Oh! Oh. It goes so fast. We don't have time to look at one another. [*She breaks down sobbing. At a gesture from the Stage Manager, Mrs. Webb disappears*] I didn't realize. So all that was going on and we never noticed. Take me back—up the hill—to my grave. But first: Wait! One more look. Good-by, Good-by, world. Good-by, Grover's Corners . . . Mama and Papa. Good-by to clocks ticking . . . and Mama's sunflowers. And food and coffee. And new-ironed dresses and hot baths . . . and sleeping and waking up. Oh, earth, you're too wonderful for anybody to realize you. [*She looks toward the Stage Manager and asks abruptly, through her tears*] Do any human beings ever realize life while they live it?—every, every minute?

STAGE MANAGER: No. [*Pause*] The saints and poets, maybe—they do some.

EMILY: I'm ready to go back. [*She returns to her

chair beside Mrs. Gibbs] Mother Gibbs, I should have listened to you. Now I want to be quiet for a while.—Oh, Mother Gibbs, I saw it all. I saw your garden.

MRS. GIBBS: Did you, dear?

EMILY: That's all human beings are!—Just blind people.

MRS. GIBBS: Look, it's clearing up. The stars are coming out.

EMILY: Oh, Mr. Stimson, I should have listened to them.

SIMON STIMSON: [*With mounting violence; bitingly*] Yes, now you know. Now you know! That's what it was to be alive. To move about in a cloud of ignorance; to go up and down trampling on the feelings of those . . . of those about you. To spend and waste time as though you had a million years. To be always at the mercy of one self-centered passion, or another. Now you know—that's the happy existence you wanted to go back and see. Did you shout to 'em? Did you call to 'em?

EMILY: Yes, I did.

SIMON STIMSON: Now you know them as they are: in ignorance and blindness.

MRS. GIBBS: [*Spiritedly*] Simon Stimson, that ain't the whole truth and you know it.

[*The dead have begun to stir*]

THE DEAD: Lemuel, wind's coming up, seems like. —Oh, dear,—I keep remembering things tonight.— It's right cold for June, ain't it?

MRS. GIBBS: Look what you've done, you and your rebellious spirit stirring us up here.—Emily, look at that star. I forget its name.

THE DEAD: I'm getting to know them all, but I don't know their names.—My boy Joel was a sailor, —knew 'em all. He'd set on the porch evenings and tell 'em all by name. Yes sir, it was wonderful.—A star's mighty good company.—Yes, yes.—Yes, 'tis.

SIMON STIMSON: Here's one of *them* coming.

THE DEAD: That's funny. 'Taint no time for one of them to be here.—Goodness sakes.

EMILY: Mother Gibbs, it's George.

MRS. GIBBS: Sh, dear. You just rest yourself.

EMILY: It's George. [George *enters from the left, and slowly comes toward them*]

A MAN FROM AMONG THE DEAD: And my boy, Joel, who knew the stars—he used to say it took millions of years for that speck o' light to git to the earth. Don't seem like a body could believe it, but that's what he used to say—millions of years.

ANOTHER: That's what they say.

[George *flings himself on* Emily's *grave*]

THE DEAD: Goodness! That ain't no way to behave!—He ought to be home.

EMILY: Mother Gibbs?

MRS. GIBBS: Yes, Emily?

EMILY: They don't understand much, do they?

MRS. GIBBS: No, dear, not very much.

[*The* Stage Manager *appears at the right, one hand on a dark curtain which he slowly draws across the scene. In the distance a clock is heard striking the hour very faintly*]

STAGE MANAGER: Most everybody's asleep in Grover's Corners. There are a few lights on: Shorty Hawkins, down at the depot, has just watched the Albany train go by. And at the livery stable somebody's setting up late and talking.—Yes, it's clearing up. There are the stars—doing their old, old crisscross journeys in the sky. Scholars haven't settled the matter yet, but they seem to think there are no living beings up there. They're just chalk . . . or fire. Only this one is straining away, straining away all the time to make something of itself. The strain's so bad that every sixteen hours everybody lies down and gets a rest. [*He winds his watch*] Hm. . . . Eleven o'clock in Grover's Corners.—You get a good rest, too. Good night.

THE END

Clifford Odets

(1906———)

Clifford Odets was in his early twenties when the depression struck America, during the autumn of 1929. Born in Philadelphia, he was brought up in the mixed proletarian and lower-middle-class life of the Bronx, in New York City, and considered himself, despite the comparative prosperity of his father, a spiritual brother of the restive poor. After graduation from high school, he dabbled in writing and became an actor, but he achieved no particular success. Fortunately, he joined a junior acting company of the Theatre Guild which acquired three very able and progressive leaders: Cheryl Crawford, Lee Strasberg, and Harold Clurman. Under their guidance, this studio company broke off from the parent organization and blossomed forth as the independent Group Theatre, in 1931. Odets was one of the founders of this organization and modestly participated in the Group's effort to adapt to American conditions the famous "Stanislavsky system" of ensemble playing. He also began to write a play with an eye to the capacities of his fellow actors, completing for them a draft of *Awake and Sing!* entitled *I've Got the Blues*. It was a sorrowful account of the misery and restlessness of a poor Bronx family during the depression. Odets' colleagues were interested in the mournful play but not at all confident that it could succeed on the stage.

New developments in the theatrical world combined to give the young playwright a hearing. By 1935 the American theatre was in the throes of insurgency, and the New Theatre League, an outgrowth of numerous social-minded groups, was offering prizes for one-act plays. Odets locked himself in a hotel room for three days and turned out a panoramic treatment of a taxicab strike, *Waiting for Lefty*, which won the first prize for its vivid picture of the depression period. The dramatic form of *Waiting for Lefty*, which presented a strike meeting as a frame for flashbacks into the experience of the speakers, was effectively theatrical, and the dialogue was remarkably colorful and explosive. When the play was produced by the New Theatre League with Group Theatre actors, it was instantly acclaimed as a tour de force even by those who did not subscribe to its advocacy of class conflict.

The success of *Waiting for Lefty* prompted the Group Theatre to give this long one-act play a Broadway production, and, in order to round out the evening, Odets added a stirring short dramatization of the conflict between liberalism and fascism in Germany, *Till the Day I Die*. During the same season, moreover, his fellow players brushed the dust off his full-length family picture, now supplied with a revolutionary varnish and given the new title *Awake and Sing!* The production at once revealed new and even more remarkable facets of Odets' talent. The play concluded, it is true, with vague conversions to radicalism, but it also possessed more noteworthy and less superimposed qualities—namely, humor, insight, and compassion. Drawn with exceptional verisimilitude, the characters revealed themselves as frustrated yet irrepressible human beings, and their separate lives were woven together by Odets with much skill. Critics acclaimed *Awake and Sing!* as a rare, Chekhovian play, and Odets was securely launched on a career which brought him acclaim as the most promising young American playwright since the advent of O'Neill, some fifteen years earlier. Although the claims of some admirers proved extravagant, it is entirely true that Odets was the most talented writer discovered by the theatre of the depression generation.

Each of Odets' plays embodied some basic criticism of a society dominated by individualism and a *laissez-faire* philosophy. *Waiting for Lefty* was as violently anticapitalistic and prolabor as *Till the Day I Die* was passionately antifascist. *Awake and Sing!*, although anything but one-dimensional drama, attacked the middle-class family as a major source of human frustration. *Paradise Lost* (1936) presented the proposition that the middle class was dying, and *Golden Boy* (1937) promoted the thesis that our materialistic society diverted men from humanly satisfying modes of self-realization. *Rocket to the Moon* (1938) propounded the view that economic insecurity inhibits the full flowering of the human personality, and *Night Music* (1940) dramatized the theme of homelessness in modern society. The author of these plays considered himself the chronicler of a dying social order, and the two plays he contributed to the next decade of American theatre—*Clash by Night* (1941) and *The Big Knife* (1949)—also examined manifestations of decay. The former treated a domestic triangle as an effect of unemployment, with the humiliation of the "little man," the husband, culminating in his going berserk; the story implied a parallel to the manner in which common men had managed to translate their frustrations into violence in European fascist movements. *The Big Knife* was not only an exposé of Hollywood but dramatized the problem of artistic integrity in a world which buys and sells talent.

It is plain, then, that the social motivation of Odets' writing cannot be entirely ignored. He wrote with an animus, and his buoyancy as a writer depended largely on his confidence that his criticism was called for, that he was uncovering the source of evil and suffering, and that he was at the same time celebrating the growth of some show of resistance, understanding, or sheer idealism among common people. It is significant, in fact, that his plays succeeded only when he was supported by the social enthusiasms of his youth and by those of the theatre for which he wrote between 1935 and 1940. When, after spending a decade in Hollywood as a writer and producer, Odets severed connections with the film industry, vowing never to have any traffic with it, he found it difficult to re-establish himself in the theatre with *The Big Knife.* The play called attention to weaknesses one had tended to overlook in the early Odets plays because their enthusiasm for life and ideals had been affecting or contagious. Odets had been something more than a writer of routine obituaries on men and capitalism. Even the quietest of his early plays, *Rocket to the Moon,* had been charged with sympathy for those who refuse to be defeated by economic circumstances and personal difficulties.

The two full-length plays with which Odets made himself best known as the exponent of a new, socially charged dramatic style were *Awake and Sing!* and *Golden Boy.* The former is the more spontaneous work; it is more richly characterized, more moving, and also less calculated. It also happens to be less representative of American social reality and more dependent upon local color for its argument. *Golden Boy,* written later, is Odets' best-constructed play. Here Odets selected broadly familiar American material, celebrated in the sporting-news columns and in film stories. He transfigured the material with the help of his metaphorical cast of mind and his vigorous, if often uneven, dialogue. The result was an angular and provocative variant of the success-story theme of fiction and films, a work vividly realistic and at the same time always suggestive of larger experience and of ideas applicable to society as a whole. *Golden Boy* proved to be Odets' most successful play, and it was his only full-length play to be seen by any large segment of the playgoing public outside New York. He had offered it as a sort of American saga, and it was received as such, although with less enthusiasm for his sociological intention than he might have wished.

To insist on the allegory of the "the fiddle and the fist" in *Golden Boy* is to invite argument, since it is easy enough to accept the play as simply an exciting story of the ring, written with more than usual insight. Yet the early draft of *Golden Boy* carried the subtitle "A Modern Allegory," and the play was treated as such by its director, Harold Clurman, and its scene designer, Mordecai Gorelik. It is plain that Odets opposed two ways of life—the creative and the destructive, the socially desirable and the socially undesirable—in the story of Joe Bonaparte,

who loved music but became a killer in the ring. As Clurman explained in a preface to the published version, this prize-fight drama was intended as "the picture of a great fight—a fight in which we are all involved, whatever our profession or craft."

To what extent the allegorical intention is supported by the characterization is an interesting question. It is true, for instance, that Odets the social critic showed the "golden boy" becoming a fighter in order to free himself from the scorn attached to "nobodies," especially if they belong to racial minorities. But is it true, as Clurman asserts, that in order to achieve success the boy "must exploit an accidental attribute of his make-up, a mere skill, and abandon the development of his real self"? Is Joe's "real" self one thing and his skill in the ring another? Is it credible that the boy who was a gifted violinist could become a successful boxer? These and other questions we may raise in connection with the story indicate the difficulty of relating allegory to convincing psychological drama. It was a difficulty Odets rarely succeeded in overcoming when he tried to compose social parables.

With or without its allegorical connotations, *Golden Boy* is representative of the charged dramatic realism of the theatre of the nineteen-thirties. But, even more important, the play reveals those qualities of talent that differentiated its author from the ordinary writers of social harangues and blueprints for the noncapitalistic millenium. As Brooks Atkinson noted, "Odets does not discuss the idea in *Golden Boy* so much as he shows it." And Odets "shows it" with the full exercise of his talent for interweaving related themes and situations and, above all, for letting life flow from various directions in a stream often unexpectedly fresh and strangely moving. The characters assert themselves regardless of argument, and we may wonder how it is that they possess so much individuality while their author insists on the theory that they are the product of social pressures. Poor or rich, failures or successes, Odets' characters are irrepressible because they were born alive in their author's memory and imagination. Odets could not have written pat problem plays with such characters, even if he had wanted to do so out of a desire to serve the theatre of "social consciousness." *Golden Boy* arouses interest largely because the thesis drama becomes a fugue again and again, with life providing the variations. And the writing is, characteristically for the young Odets, both concrete and elliptical; it is a poet's kind of writing.

BIBLIOGRAPHY: Brooks Atkinson, *Broadway Scrapbook* (pp. 74–77), 1947; Harold Clurman, Prefaces to *Six Plays of Clifford Odets* (pp. 421–433), 1939; Eleanor Flexner, *American Playwrights 1918–1938* (pp. 290–302, 312–314), 1938; John Gassner, *Masters of the Drama* (pp. 689–693), 1940, 1945; Joseph Wood Krutch, *The American Drama Since 1918* (pp. 263–277), 1939.

GOLDEN BOY

By Clifford Odets

CHARACTERS

TOM MOODY	MR. BONAPARTE	CALL BOY
LORNA MOON	ANNA	SAM
JOE BONAPARTE	FRANK BONAPARTE	LEWIS
TOKIO	ROXY GOTTLIEB	DRAKE
MR. CARP	EDDIE FUSELI	DRISCOLL
SIGGIE	PEPPER WHITE	BARKER
	MICKEY	

SCENES

ACT ONE

Scene 1. The office of Tom Moody.
Scene 2. The Bonaparte home. That night.
Scene 3. The office. Two months later.
Scene 4. A park bench. A few nights later.
Scene 5. The Bonaparte home. Midnight, six weeks later.

ACT TWO

Scene 1. A gymnasium. Five months later.
Scene 2. The park bench. A few nights later.
Scene 3. The office. The following day.
Scene 4. A dressing room in the Arena. Six weeks later.

ACT THREE

Scene 1. The office. Six months later.
Scene 2. The dressing room. The following night.
Scene 3. The Bonaparte home. Several hours later.

ACT I. SCENE I.

The small Broadway office of Tom Moody, *the fight manager. The office is scantily furnished, contains desk, chairs, telephone and couch. With Moody at present is his girl,* Lorna Moon. *There is a certain quiet glitter about this girl, and if she is sometimes hard, it is more from necessity than choice. Her eyes often hold a soft, sad glance. Likewise, Moody's explosiveness covers a soft, boyish quality, and at the same time he possesses a certain vulnerable quality which women find very attractive. The time is eighteen months ago. As the lights fade in, we catch these two at the height of one of their frequent fights.*

MOODY: Pack up your clothes and go! Go! Who the hell's stopping you?

LORNA: You mean it?

MOODY: You brought up the point yourself.

LORNA: No, I didn't!

MOODY: Didn't you say you had a good mind to leave me?

LORNA: No, I said—

MOODY: You said you were going to pack!

LORNA: I said I feel like a tramp and I don't like it. I want to get married, I want—

MOODY: Go home, Lorna, go home! I ain't got time to discuss it. Gimme some air. It's enough I got my wife on my neck.

LORNA: What does she say?

MOODY: Who?

LORNA: Your wife—your sweet goddam Monica!

MOODY: She wants five thousand dollars to give me the divorce. [Lorna *laughs*] I don't see that it's funny.

LORNA: Look, Tom, this means as much to me as it does to you. If she's out of the way, we can get married. Otherwise I'm a tramp from Newark. I don't like the feeling.

MOODY: Lorna, for Pete's sake, use your noodle!

When I get rid of Monica, we'll marry. Now, do I have to bang you on the nose to make you understand?

LORNA: Go to hell! . . . But come back tonight.

[Moody's *answer is to look at her, then smile, then walk to her. They kiss*]

MOODY: If I had the money, I'd buy you something—I don't know what—a big ostrich feather! If Kaplan wins tonight, I'll take you dancing at the Park.

LORNA: He won't win.

MOODY: How do you know? *I* don't know—how do *you* know?

LORNA: Are you crazy? Do you think your Mr. Kaplan can go ten rounds with the Baltimore Chocolate Drop?

MOODY: How do I know?

LORNA: It's the Twentieth Century, Tom—no more miracles. [Moody's *face turns worried*. Lorna *smiles*] You know what I like about you—you take everything so serious.

MOODY: Who will if I don't? I've been off the gold standard for eight years. This used to be a gorgeous town. New York was hot with money. Kaplan gets four hundred bucks tonight. In the old days, that was nothing. Those were the days when I had Marty Welch, the heavyweight contender— Cy Webster who got himself killed in a big, red Stutz. In '27 and 8 you couldn't go to sleep—the town was crawling with attractions.

LORNA: My mother died in '28.

MOODY: I haven't had a break in years. "Carry me back to old Virginny"—that's how I feel. There isn't much of a future. [*Suddenly despondent*, Moody *goes back to his desk*]

LORNA: I was fooling.

MOODY: What about?

LORNA: Do you think I'd leave you?

MOODY: Why not? I'm an old man. What can I give you?

LORNA: A bang on the nose for a start. But what can I give you?

MOODY: A boy who can fight. Find me a good black boy and I'll show you a mint.

LORNA: Are good boys so hard to find?

MOODY: Honest to God, you make me sick to my stomach! What do you think I took a trip to Philadelphia? What do you think I went to Chicago? Wasn't I up in Boston for a week? You think good boys are laying around like pop-corn? I'd even take a bantamweight, if I found one.

LORNA: How about a nice lady fighter with a beard—[*Preparing to leave*] Well, I'll see you tonight, Moody.

MOODY: [*Thoughtfully*] I'd give me right eye for a good black boy.

LORNA: Let me have your right eye for a minute. [*She kisses his eye*. Moody *begins to embrace her— she eludes his grasp*] That's to keep you hot. But if the truth were known—"yours till hell freezes over."

MOODY: I need you, I need you, Lorna—I need you all the time. I'd like to give you everything you want. Push your mouth over. . . .

[Lorna *holds her face to his; he kisses her. Suddenly a youth is standing at the office door.* Lorna *sees him and breaks away*]

BOY: [*Breathing quickly*] Mr. Moody . . .

MOODY: [*Spinning around*] Don't you knock when you come in an office?

BOY: Sometimes I knock, sometimes I don't.

MOODY: Say your piece and get the hell out!

BOY: I just ran over from the gym . . .

MOODY: What gym?

BOY: Where Kaplan trains. He just broke his hand. . . . [Moody *stiffens to attention*] It's a fact.

MOODY: [*Grasping the phone*] Is Tokio over there? My trainer?

BOY: He's looking after Kaplan.

[Moody *begins to dial the phone but abruptly changes his mind and replaces the phone*]

MOODY: You can put me in the bug-house right now. Moody is the name, folks—step right up and wipe your shoes! Ah, that Kaplan! That phonus bolonus! [*He sits at his desk in despair*] Now I have to call up Roxy Gottlieb and cancel the match. His club's in the red as it is.

BOY: I don't think it's necessary to cancel, Tom.

MOODY: [*Aware of the* Boy *for the first time*] Oh, you don't? Who the hell are you? And who the hell are you to call me Tom? Are we acquainted?

BOY: I wrote you a couple of letters. I can do that stretch.

MOODY: What stretch?

BOY: Why don't you let me take Kaplan's place tonight?

MOODY: [*Sarcastically*] Go slow and tell me again . . . what?

BOY: [*Coolly*] I can take Kaplan's place. . . .

MOODY: You mean you want to fight the Baltimore Chocolate Drop? You? [*The* Boy *remains silent*. Moody *comes out from behind his desk and stands face to face with the* Boy. *With sudden discovery*] You're cock-eyed too.

BOY: [*Quietly*] Can't you fix it up with Roxy Gottlieb?

MOODY: [*Suddenly*] Looka, kid, go home, kid, before I blame Kaplan's glass mitts on *you*. Then you won't like it, and I won't like it, and Miss Moon here, she won't like it.

BOY: [*Turning to* Lorna] How do you do, Miss Moon. [Lorna *smiles at the* Boy's *quiet confidence*] I need a good manager, Mr. Moody. You used to be tops around town—everyone says so. I think you can develop me. I fight. You don't know it, but I can fight. Kaplan's been through for years. He may be the best fighter in your stable, but he's a stumble-bum for the younger boys growing up. Why don't you give me this chance, Tom?

MOODY: I don't want you calling me Tom! [*He*

glares at the Boy *and then returns to the desk and telephone*]

BOY: I'm waiting for your answer. [*Moody's answer is an exasperated glance as he begins to dial the phone. The* Boy *half approaches the desk*] There are forty-three thousand minutes in a month—can't you give me five?

MOODY: I'll give you this phone in the head in a minute! Who are you? What the hell do you want? Where do you fight?

BOY: [*With cool persistence*] We ought to get together, Tom.

MOODY: I don't want you calling me Tom. You're brash, you're fresh, you're callow—and you're cockeyed! In fact, you're an insult to my whole nature! Now get out! [*Moody turns back to the phone and begins dialing again. The* Boy *stands there, poised on his toes, not sure of his next move. He turns and looks at* Lorna. *She nods her head and gives him a faint smile of encouragement. On phone*] This is Tom Moody . . . is Tokio there? . . . [*He hangs up the phone and holds the instrument thoughtfully*] Tokio's on his way over.

BOY: The Baltimore Chocolate Drop is not as good as you think he is. [*Moody suddenly whirls around and holds the telephone high over his head in a threatening gesture. The* Boy *steps back lightly and continues*] I've studied his style for months; I've perfected the exact punch to quench his thirst. Did you ever watch closely? [*Acting it out*] He likes to pull your lead—he hesitates for a second—he pulls your lead—he slips his face away and then he's in. Suppose you catch that second when he hesitates—he's open for the punch!

MOODY: [*Sarcastically*] And what do you do with his left hook?

BOY: [*Simply*] Avoid it.

MOODY: [*Lowering the phone*] Looka, you idiot, did you ever hear of Phil Mateo?

BOY: I heard of him.

MOODY: The Chocolate Drop marked him lousy in twelve minutes and ten seconds. Was Kid Peters within your ken? And did you ever hear of Eddie Newton? The Chocolate gave him the blues in two rounds. And Frisco Samuels and Mike Mason . . .

BOY: Did you ever hear of me?

MOODY: [*Sarcastically*] No, who are you? I would honestly like to know—who are you?

BOY: [*Quietly*] My name is Bonaparte. [*Moody howls with laughter, and even* Lorna, *sympathetic to the* Boy, *laughs. The* Boy *continues*] I don't think it's funny. . . .

MOODY: Didn't that name used to get you a little giggle in school? Tell the truth, Bonaparte. Didn't it?

BOY: Call me Joe.

MOODY: [*Laughing*] And your eyes . . . Didn't they used to get a little giggle too?

JOE: You don't seem as intelligent as J thought you were.

LORNA: [*To the laughing* Moody, *seeing the* Boy's *pain*] Stop it, Tom.

MOODY: [*Laughing*] You can't blame me, Bonaparte. . . . I haven't laughed for years.

JOE: I don't like it. . . . I don't want you to do it. [*Suddenly Joe grabs* Moody *by the coat lapels. Moody, surprised, shakes him off. At the same time a small, quiet man enters the office. He is* Tokio, *Moody's trainer*] I'm sorry I did that, Tom. We ought to be together, Tom—not apart.

MOODY: Tokio, did you send this kid here?

TOKIO: No.

MOODY: Take him out before I brain him! [*He storms back to his desk*]

TOKIO: [*After looking at the* Boy] You hear about Kaplan?

MOODY: This idiot told me. It's the end of everything! I'm off my top with the whole thing! Kaplan was our meal-ticket. I'm up to the throat in scandal, blackmail, perjury, alimony and all points west!

TOKIO: [*Turning to* Joe] You oughta be ashamed to show your face in this office.

JOE: If Kaplan's mother fed him milk, he wouldn't have those brittle bones.

MOODY: ? ? ? ?

TOKIO: [*To* Moody] This is the boy who did it to Kaplan.

MOODY: ? ? ?

TOKIO: I went down for an apple and I come back and Kaplan's sparring with this kid—picked him up in the gym. The next thing I know, Kaplan's down on the floor with a busted mitt.

JOE: [*Modestly*] I took it on the elbow.

MOODY: ! ! [*Silence finally*]

LORNA: Where do you come from, Bonaparte?

JOE: Here.

LORNA: How old are you?

JOE: Twenty-one—tomorrow.

MOODY: [*After a look at* Lorna] Fight much?

JOE: Enough.

MOODY: Where?

JOE: [*Fabricating*] Albany, Syracuse . . .

LORNA: Does Roxy Gottlieb know you?

JOE: I never fought at his club.

MOODY: [*Harshly*] Does he know you?

JOE: No. [*Tokio and* Moody *look at each other. The phone rings*]

MOODY: [*On the phone*] Hello. . . . "What's this you hear?" . . . You hear the truth, Roxy. . . . He bust his mitt again. . . . I can't help it if you got *fifty* judgments on your club. . . . The same to you. . . . Your mother too! [*Keeping his eyes on* Bonaparte] If you tie up your big flabby mouth for a minute, I'll give you some news. I'm in a position to do you a big favor. I got a replacement—*better* than Kaplan . . . Bonaparte. . . . No, Bon-a-parte. [*Holds hand over mouthpiece and asks* Boy] Is that crap?

JOE: No, that's my name.

MOODY: [*Back at phone*] That's right, like in Napoleon. . . . [*Looks the* Boy *over appraisingly*] One hundred and thirty

JOE: Three.

MOODY: Hundred and thirty-three. Your customers'll eat him up. I'll bring him right over . . . you can take my word—the kid's a cock-eyed wonder . . . *your* mother too! [*He hangs up and turns around.* Joe *is the focus of all eyes*] It's revenge on somebody—maybe God.

JOE: [*Quietly*] I think you'll be surprised.

MOODY: [*Sadly*] Do your worst, kid. I've been surprised by experts.

JOE: Don't worry, Tom.

MOODY: Call me Tom again and I'll break your neck!!

QUICK FADEOUT

SCENE II.

Later that night. The combination dining and front room of the Bonaparte home. A round dining-room table, littered with newspapers, is lighted from directly above like a billiard table. Plaster busts of Mozart and Beethoven are on the sideboard. A cage of love birds at the other side of the room. Sitting at the table are two men: Mr. Bonaparte, *the father of* Joe, *and a Jewish friend, a* Mr. Carp, *who owns the local candy and stationery store. As the lights fade in,* Mr. Bonaparte *turns his newspaper.* Mr. Carp *is slowly pouring beer from a bottle. He begins to sip it as* Siggie, Mr. Bonaparte's *son-in-law, enters from the kitchen. He is barefooted, dressed in an undershirt, trousers and hung-down suspenders. He brings his own beer and glass, which he begins to fill with an expert's eye. In the silence,* Mr. Carp *takes a long, cool sip of beer combined with a murmur of relish.*

CARP: [*Finally*] I don't take it easy. That's my trouble—if I could only learn to take it easy. . . .

SIGGIE: What do you call it now, what you're doing?

CARP: Say, it's after business hours.

SIGGIE: That's a business? A man who runs a candy store is an outcast of the world. Don't even sell *nickel* candies—*penny* candies!

CARP: And your taxicab business makes you higher in the social scale?

SIGGIE: So I'm an outcast too. Don't change the subject. Like my father-in-law here—he's always changing the subject when I get a little practical on him. [*Putting his beer on the table and scratching himself under the arms like a monkey*] You—I'm talking about you, Mr. Bonaparte.

MR. BONAPARTE: [*Suddenly shooting out two words*] Ha ha! [*He then resumes his reading*]

SIGGIE: Every time I talk money, he gives me that

horse laugh. Suppose you bought me a cab—I could pay it off by the week.

MR. BONAPARTE: [*Who talks with an Italian accent*] I don't go in taxicab business.

SIGGIE: I am married to your daughter and when you do this little thing, you do it for her and me together. A cab in two shifts is a big source of profit. Joe takes the night shift. I'm a married man so you don't expect me to take the night shift. [Anna, Siggie's *wife, in a night-gown, pokes her head in at the door*]

ANNA: Come to bed, Siggie. You'll wake up the whole neighborhood. [Anna *disappears*]

SIGGIE: See? I'm a married man! You don't expect me to take the night shift.

MR. BONAPARTE: [*Having heard this talk for months*] No, Siggie . . . no.

SIGGIE: No, what?

MR. BONAPARTE: No taxicab.

SIGGIE: Don't you wanna help your own family, foolish? After all, Joe's your own son—he's a man, no kid no more—

MR. BONAPARTE: Tomorrow's twenty-one.

SIGGIE: If he don't work he'll turn into a real bum. Look how late he's staying out at night.

MR. BONAPARTE: I don't expects for Joe to drive taxi.

SIGGIE: He's got to do something. He can drive like a fire engine. Why not?

MR. BONAPARTE: He gonna do something.

SIGGIE: What? Play his violinsky in the backyards?

ANNA: [*Looking in at the door again*] Come to bed, Siggie! Poppa, don't talk to him so he'll come to bed! [Anna *disappears again*]

SIGGIE: [*Annoyed*] Women! Always buzzing around. [Mr. Bonaparte's *only answer is to turn over the newspaper on the table before him*]

CARP: [*Reflectively*] Women . . . the less we have to do with women the better. As Schopenhauer says, "Much ado about nothing . . . the comedy of reproduction." [*He wags his head bitterly*] Women . . . !

SIGGIE: I'm hungry, but I ain't got the heart to go in the kitchen again. It reminds me of how my wife slaves for this family of crazy wops! A fine future for an intelligent woman!

MR. BONAPARTE: She'sa your wife, but also my daughter. She'sa not so intelligent as you say. Also, *you* are not so intelligent!

SIGGIE: You can't insult me, I'm too ignorant!

[Anna *now comes fully into the room. She is buxom, energetic, good-natured and adenoidal*]

ANNA: Poppa, why don't you let Siggie come to bed? Looka him, walking around barefooted!

MR. BONAPARTE: I don't stop him. . . .

SIGGIE: Sure he stops me—he stops me every night. I'm worried. I don't sleep. It's my Jewish disposition. He don't wanna help me out, your old man. He wants me to drive a company cab and submit to the brutalities of the foremen all my life. I could be in a healthy little enterprise for myself, but your old man don't wanna help me out.

ANNA: Why don't you buy Siggie a cab, Poppa? You got the cash.

SIGGIE: Buy it for Siggie and Joe.

ANNA: For Siggie and Joe—it don't have to be a new one.

SIGGIE: [*After giving his wife a stabbing glance*] Sure, even an old one—the way they recondition them now-a-days—

MR. BONAPARTE: Children, gone to bed.

SIGGIE: Don't tell a lie—how much you got in the bank?

MR. BONAPARTE: [*With a smile*] Millions.

SIGGIE: Four thousand?

MR. BONAPARTE: No.

SIGGIE: Three? [Mr. Bonaparte *shakes his head*] Three? . . .

ANNA: What's your business how much he's got?

SIGGIE: Shut up, Duchess! Am I asking for my health? If I wanna take you out of the kitchen, is that the gratitude I get? You and your father, you get my goat! I'm sore!

ANNA: Come to bed, Siggie.

SIGGIE: "Come to bed, come to bed!" What the hell's so special in bed. [Anna's *answer is a warm prolonged giggle*] It's a conspiracy around here to put me to bed. I'm warning one thing: if matters go from worse to worse, don't ever expect me to support this family, I'm warning!

MR. BONAPARTE: [*Smiling kindly*] We have-a receive the warning. We are in a conspiracy against you—gone to bed. [*He turns back to his newspaper.* Siggie *sees he has lost again and now turns on his wife*]

SIGGIE: Who asked you to stick in your two cents about secondhand cabs? As long as I'm not gonna get it, I'll tell you what I want—a first-class job, fresh from the factory. [*He suddenly swats her on the head with a rolled-up newspaper. She hits him back. He returns her blow*]

ANNA: Don't be so free with your hands! [*He hits her again. She hits him back*] You got some nerve, Siggie!

SIGGIE: [*Hitting her again*] The next time I'll break your neck—I'm super-disgusted with you!

MR. BONAPARTE: [*Standing up*] Stop this . . .

SIGGIE: [*Turning to him*] And with you, I'm super-finished! [*Turning back to his wife*] Sit out here with this Unholy Alliance—I'll sleep alone tonight. [*He starts for the door.* Mr. Bonaparte *puts his arm around* Anna *who begins to sob*]

MR. BONAPARTE: Hit your wife in private, not in public!

CARP: A man hits his wife and it is the first step to fascism!

SIGGIE: [*To* Carp] What are you talking about, my little prince! I love my wife. You don't stop talking how you hate yours. [*Now to* Mr. Bonaparte] And as for you, don't make believe you care!—Do I have to fall on my knees to you otherwise? We

wanna raise a family—it's a normal instinct. Take your arm off her.

ANNA: [*Suddenly moving over to* Siggie] That's right, poppa. He can hit me any time he likes.

SIGGIE: [*His arm around her*] And we don't want you interfering in our affairs unless you do it the right way!

ANNA: That's right, poppa—you mind your g.d. business! [Mr. Bonaparte *repressing a smile, slowly sits*]

SIGGIE: In the bed, Duchess.

ANNA: [*With a giggle*] Good night.

MR. BONAPARTE *and* MR. CARP: Good night. [*She exits. After a belligerent look at the pair at the table,* Siggie *follows her*]

MR. BONAPARTE: [*Bursting into hushed laughter*] There's a olda remark—never interfere in the laws of nature and you gonna be happy. Love! Ha ha!

CARP: [*Gloomily*] Happy? A famous man remarked in the last century. "Pleasure is negative."

MR. BONAPARTE: I feela good. Like-a to have some music! Hey, where's a my boy Joe? [*Looks at his watch; is surprised*] One o'clock . . . don't come home yet. Hey, he make-a me worry!

CARP: You think you got worries? Wait, you're a young man yet. You got a son, Joe. He practised on his fiddle for ten years? He won a gold medal, the best in the city? They gave him a scholarship in the Erickson Institute? Tomorrow he's twenty-one, yeah?

MR. BONAPARTE: [*Emphatically*] Yeah!

CARP: [*Leaning forward and dramatically making his point*] Suppose a war comes? Before you know it, he's in the army!

MR. BONAPARTE: Naw, naw! Whata you say! Naw!

CARP: [*Wagging his head in imitation*] Look in the papers! On every side the clouds of war—

MR. BONAPARTE: My Joe gotta biga talent. Yesterday I buy-a him present! [*With a dramatic flourish he brings a violin case out of the bottom part of the sideboard*]

CARP: [*As the case is opened*] It looks like a coffin for a baby.

MR. BONAPARTE: [*Looking down at the violin in its case*] His teacher help me to picka him.

CARP: [*The connoisseur*] Fine, fine—beautiful, fine! A cultural thing!

MR. BONAPARTE: [*Touching it fondly*] The mosta golden present for his birthday which I give him tonight.

CARP: How much, if I'm not getting too personal, did such a violin cost you?

MR. BONAPARTE: Twelve hundred dollars.

CARP: [*Shocked*] What?

MR. BONAPARTE: You're surprised of me? Well, I waita for this moment many years.

CARP: [*Sitting*] Ask yourself a pertinent remark: could a boy make a living playing this instrument in our competitive civilization today?

MR. BONAPARTE: Why? Don't expect for Joe to be

a millionaire. He don't need it, to be millionaire. A good life'sa possible—

CARP: For men like us, yes. But nowadays is it possible for a young man to give himself to the Muses? Could the Muses put bread and butter on the table?

MR. BONAPARTE: No millionaire is necessary. Joe love music. Music is the great cheer-up in the language of all countries. I learn that from Joe.

[Carp *sighs as* Mr. Bonaparte *replaces the violin in the buffet*]

CARP: But in the end, as Schopenhauer says, what's the use to try something? For every wish we get, ten remains unsatisfied. Death is playing with us as a cat and her mouse!

MR. BONAPARTE: You make-a me laugh, Mr. Carp. You say life'sa bad. No. life'sa good. Siggie and Anna fight—good! They love—good! You say life'sa bad . . . well, is pleasure for you to say so. No? The streets, winter a' summer—trees, cats—I love-a them all. The gooda boys and girls, they who sing and whistle—[*Bursts into a moment of gay whistling*]— very good! The eating and sleeping, drinking wine— very good! I gone around on my wagon and talk to many people—nice! Howa you like the big buildings of the city?

CARP: Buildings? And suppose it falls? A house fell down last week on Staten Island!

MR. BONAPARTE: Ha ha, you make me laugh, ha ha! [*Now enters* Frank Bonaparte, *oldest son of the family, simple, intelligent, observant*]

MR. BONAPARTE: Hello, Frank.

FRANK: Hello, poppa . . . Mr. Carp . . .

CARP: [*Nodding*] What's new in the world?

FRANK: [*Dropping newspapers to the table, but keeping one for himself*] Read 'em and weep. March first tomorrow—spring on the way. Flowers soon budding, birds twittering—south wind . . . Cannons, bombs and airplane raids! Where's Joe? Did you give him the fiddle yet?

MR. BONAPARTE: No, not in yet. Siggie and Anna sleep. Hungry?

FRANK: [*Beginning to undress—putting his coat on the back of a chair*] No, I'm tired. I'll see you in the morning, before I leave.

CARP: Going away again?

FRANK: South. Tex-tiles. There's hell down there in tex-tiles. [*He sits on the other side of the room and looks at a paper*]

CARP: I don't begin to understand it—tex-tiles! What's it his business if the workers in tex-tiles don't make good wages!

MR. BONAPARTE: Frank, he fight-a for eat, for good life. Why not!

CARP: Foolish!

MR. BONAPARTE: What ever you got ina your nature to do isa not foolish!

CARP: [*Flipping over the newspaper*] For instance —look: playing baseball isn't foolish?

MR. BONAPARTE: No, if you like-a to do.

CARP: Look! Four or five pages—baseball—tennis-ball—it gives you an idea what a civilization! You ever seen a baseball game?

MR. BONAPARTE: No.

CARP: [*Wagging his head*] Hit a ball, catch a ball . . . believe me, my friend—nonsense!

FRANK: Poppa, where did you say Joe was?

MR. BONAPARTE: Don't know—

FRANK: Poppa, you better brace yourself in your chair!

MR. BONAPARTE: What?

[Frank *places the paper before* Mr. Bonaparte. *He reads aloud*]

FRANK: Looka this, Joe's had a fight. "Flash: Chocolate Drop fails to K.O. new cock-eyed wonder." Take a look at the picture.

CARP: What?

MR. BONAPARTE: What?

FRANK: It's my little brother Joie, or I don't know a scab from a picket!

MR. BONAPARTE: Had a fight? That is foolish—not possible.

FRANK: [*Pointing with his finger*] There's his name —Bonaparte.

MR. BONAPARTE: [*Puzzled*] Musta be some other boy.

[Frank *suddenly flips over the newspaper. The others immediately see the reason:* Joe *stands in the entrance, in the shadows*]

JOE: [*In the shadows*] Gee, you're up late. . . .

MR. BONAPARTE: We waita for you.

[Joe *slowly moves into the light. His face is bruised and over one eye is a piece of adhesive tape*]

JOE: [*Seeing their looks*] I had a fight—a boy in the park—

MR. BONAPARTE: He hit you?

JOE: I hit him.

MR. BONAPARTE: You hurt?

JOE: No.

[Mr. Bonaparte *casts a furtive look in the direction of the other men*]

MR. BONAPARTE: Whata you fight him for?

JOE: Didn't like what he said to me.

MR. BONAPARTE: What he said?

JOE: [*Evasively*] It's a long story and I'm tired.

MR. BONAPARTE: [*Trying to break a pause of embarrassment*] I was say to Mr. Carp tomorrow is your birthday. How you like to be so old?

JOE: I forgot about that! I mean I forgot for the last few hours. Where do you think I was? Do you want the truth?

FRANK: Truth is cheap. We bought it for two cents. [*He turns over the paper and shows* Joe *his own face.* Joe *looks at the picture, likes it. General silence*]

JOE: [*Finally, belligerently*] Well, what are you going to do about it?

MR. BONAPARTE: [*Still puzzled*] Abouta what?

JOE: [*Challengingly*] Tomorrow's my birthday!

FRANK: What's that got to do with being a gladiator?

JOE: [*Turning to* Frank, *with sudden vehemence*] Mind your business! You don't know me—I see you once a year; what do you know about me?

FRANK: [*Smiling*] You're a dumb kid!

MR. BONAPARTE: [*Starting to his feet*] Hey, waita one-a minute. What'sa for this excitement?

JOE: [*Hotly*] I don't want to be criticized! Nobody takes me serious here! I want to do what I want. I proved it tonight. I'm good—I went out to earn some money and I earned! I had a professional fight tonight—maybe I'll have some more.

CARP: You honest to God had a fight?

JOE: [*Glaring at* Carp] Why not?

FRANK: [*To* Joe] No one's criticizin'.

MR. BONAPARTE: That's right.

JOE: [*Half sheepishly*] I don't know why I got so sore. . . .

FRANK: You're expecting opposition all the time—

MR. BONAPARTE: Sit down, Joe—resta you'self.

JOE: Don't want to sit. Every birthday I ever had I sat around. Now'sa time for standing. Poppa, I have to tell you—I don't like myself, past, present and future. Do you know there are men who have wonderful things from life? Do you think they're better than me? Do you think I like this feeling of no possessions? Of learning about the world from Carp's encyclopaedia? Frank don't know what it means—he travels around, sees the world! [*Turning to* Frank] You don't know what it means to sit around here and watch the months go ticking by! Do you think that's a life for a boy my age? Tomorrow's my birthday! I change my life!

MR. BONAPARTE: Justa like that?

JOE: Just like that!

FRANK: And what do you do with music?

JOE: Who says I'm married to music? I take a vacation—the notes won't run away!

FRANK: You're a mysterious kid. Where did you learn the fighting game?

JOE: These past two years, all over the city—in the gyms—

MR. BONAPARTE: Hey, Joe, you sounda like crazy! You no gotta nature for fight. You're musician. Whata you say, heh? Whata you do?

JOE: Let's call it a day.

MR. BONAPARTE: Isa no true whata I say?—

JOE: That's all for tonight. [*His lips tightened, he abruptly exits*]

MR. BONAPARTE: [*Calling after him*] Take a gooda sleep, Joe.

FRANK: [*Smiling*] It looks like the gold bug has visited our house.

CARP: [*Sadly*] Fortunes! I used to hear it in my youth—the streets of America is paved with gold. Say, you forgot to give him the present.

MR. BONAPARTE: [*Slowly, puzzled*] I don'ta know . . . he say he gonna fight. . . .

SLOW FADEOUT

SCENE III.

Two months later; Moody's *office as seen before.* Moody *is pacing back and forth in one of his fuming moods. Those present include* Lorna, *stretched out on the couch, blowing cigarette smoke into the air;* Tokio *sitting quietly on the window sill; and* Roxy Gottlieb, *comfortably spread out in the desk chair, wearing a big white panama hat which he seldom removes.*

ROXY: They don't like him. They seen him in five fights already. He's a clever boy, that Bonaparte, and speedy—but he's first-class lousy in the shipping department! I bought a piece of him, so I got a right to say it: a mosquito gives out better! Did you read what he wrote in his column, that Drake? He writes he's a regular "brain trust."

LORNA: What's wrong with that?

ROXY: I'll tell you in a capsule: the people who'll pay to watch a "brain trust" you could fit in a telephone booth! Roxy Gottlieb is telling you!

MOODY: Roxy's right. Joe pulls his punches. Two months already and he don't throw his hands right and he don't throw them enough.

LORNA: Tom, what do you want the boy to do? You surely know by now he's not a slugger. His main asset is his science—he's a student.

ROXY: [*Loftily*] Excuse me, Miss Moon. In the prizefight ring the cash customer don't look for stoodents. Einstein lives in a college—a wonderful man in *his* line! Also, while I think of it, a woman's place is in the hay, not in the office!

MOODY: [*Indignantly*] Where do you come off to make a remark like that?

LORNA: [*Standing up*] At the moment a woman's place is in the bar—see you later. [*She looks at the others with a peculiar smile and exits.* Moody *stares at* Roxy *who realizes he has said the wrong thing*]

MOODY: I'm worried about that boy!

TOKIO: I'd trust him, Tom. Joe knows his own needs, as he says. Don't ask him to change his style. A style is best when it's individual, when it comes out of the inner personality and the lay of the muscles and the set of the bones. That boy stands a chance to make the best lightweight since Benny Simon.

ROXY: On *your* nose!

TOKIO: He's got one of the best defenses I ever seen. And speedy as the wind.

MOODY: But he won't fight!

ROXY: A momma doll gives out better!

TOKIO: He's a peculiar duck—I want him thinking he's the best thing in shoe leather.

MOODY: He thinks so now.

TOKIO: I don't like to contradict you, Tom, but he don't. It's seventy-five percent front. If you want the goods delivered you have to treat him delicate, gentle—like a girl.

ROXY: Like a girl? Why didn't you say so before?

MOODY: No, Roy, not you—you just treat him like a human being.

TOKIO: I think we can begin the build-up now.

MOODY: A road tour?

TOKIO: I'd like to take him around the Middle West, about fifteen bouts.

ROXY: [Answering a look from Moody] I didn't say no. But will he cooperate?

TOKIO: As soon as I find the password.

MOODY: What's the password to make this kid go in and slug—that's the problem. [There is a knock at the door. Moody calls] Yes?

[The door opens and Mr. Bonaparte stands there hesitantly]

MR. BONAPARTE: [Timidly] My name is Joe Bonaparte's father. I come-a to see my son's new friends.

MOODY: [Expansively] Come in, sit down, Mr. Bonaparte.

ROXY: [Sitting comfortably] Take a seat.

MR. BONAPARTE: Am I interrupt?

MOODY: Not at all.

ROXY: What's the matter with your boy?

TOKIO: [To Mr. Bonaparte] This is Mr. Moody and Mr. Gottlieb.

MR. BONAPARTE: [Sitting] Good afternoon.

MOODY: We were just discussing your son.

MR. BONAPARTE: I please to hear. I like find out froma you how's this boxer business for Joe. Whata good in it for him.

MOODY: Your Joe's a very clever fighter.

ROXY: Can you take it? We want to make your boy famous—a millionaire, but he won't let us—won't cooperate. How do you like it?

MR. BONAPARTE: Why? Whatta he do?

ROXY: [Going over and facing the old man in a lecturing position] I'll ask you. What does he do? What does he do that's right? Nothing! We offer him on a gold platter! Wine, women and song, to make a figure of speech. We offer him magnitudes! . . .

MR. BONAPARTE: [Waiting] Yes—?

MOODY: But he won't fight.

MR. BONAPARTE: [Puzzled] He'sa fighta for you, no?

ROXY: You're right—no! Your boy's got unexplored possibilities—unexplored! But you can't make a purse out of somebody's ear.

MOODY: [Trying to counteract Roxy's volubility] My colleague is trying to say that Joe keeps holding back in the ring.

MR. BONAPARTE: Holda back?

TOKIO: He nurses his self—

MOODY: He keeps holding back—

TOKIO: His defense is brilliant—

MOODY: Gorgeous—!

ROXY: But where's the offense? You take but you can't give. Figure it out—where would you be in a traffic jam? You know how to reverse—but to shift in second or high?—nothing!

MR. BONAPARTE: [Quietly to Roxy] Hey, you talka too much—nobody's contradicta you.

ROXY: [After a momentary setback] "Everybody'sa contradicta me!" Even you, and I never met you before. [With a reproachful glance he retires to the desk where he sits and sulks]

MR. BONAPARTE: [Singling out Tokio as a man to whom he can speak] Who are you?

TOKIO: Your son's trainer. . . .

MR. BONAPARTE: You interest to helpa my boy?

TOKIO: [Respectfully] Very much. . . .

MR. BONAPARTE: Me too. Maybe not so as plan by these-a gentleman here. I don't say price fight'sa no good for Joe. Joe like-a to be fame, not feel ashame. . . .

TOKIO: Is Joe afraid of his hands?

MR. BONAPARTE: I don't know. You tella me what'sa what . . . I don't know price fight. His hand coulda get hurt?

MOODY: Every fighter hurts his hands. Sometimes they break—

TOKIO: They heal up in no time.

ROXY: [Flaring out] What's so special about hands? I suppose your kid plays piano!

MR. BONAPARTE: Coulda get hurt? Coulda break?!

ROXY: So what?

MR. BONAPARTE: [Up on his feet] Hey, you! I don't like-a you! You no interest in my boy! [Proudly] My boy'sa besta violin' in New York!

MOODY: [Suddenly sickened] What . . .?

MR. BONAPARTE: Yes, play the violin!

MOODY: That's it! . . .

ROXY: [Anguished by this stupidity] If I had hair I'd tear it out! Five hundred fiddlers stand on Broadway and 48th Street, on the corner, every day, rain or shine, hot or cold. And your boy dares—! [Turning to Moody] How do you like it? [He waves his hands in despair and retires to the desk, where he sits in fuming disgusted silence]

MOODY: [Repressing a feeling of triumph] Your boy's afraid of his hands because he fiddles?

MR. BONAPARTE: Yes, musta be!

TOKIO: Why did you come and tell us this?

MR. BONAPARTE: Because I like-a to help my boy. I like-a for him to try himself out. Maybe thisa better business for him. Maybe not. He mus' try to find out, to see whata he want . . . I don't know. Don't help Joe to tell him I come here. Don't say it. [He slowly walks to the door]

MOODY: That means you won't stand in his way?

MR. BONAPARTE: My boy coulda break his hand? Gentleman, I'ma not so happy as you . . . no! [He slowly exits]

MOODY: [Joyously] I'm beginning to see the light! Joe's mind ain't made up that the fist is mightier than the fiddle.

ROXY: [*Bouncing up and down*] I'll make up his mind. For the money that's involved I'd make Niagara Falls turn around and go back to Canada.

TOKIO: Don't try to bully him into anything

ROXY: In Roxy Gottlieb he met his match.

MOODY: [*Explosively*] What the hell's the matter with you, Roxy! Sit down a minute! [Roxy *sits*] As I see it, the job is to handle him gently, to make him see how much we prize him—to kill his doubts with goodness.

ROXY: I got it: the password is honey! . . .

MOODY: Right! The Middle West tour is on! Tokio goes along to build up a real offensive. I take care of the newspapers here. Chris', I thought it was something serious! I'm getting to feel like 1928 again. Call it intuition: I feel like the Resurrection. [*He gets up and begins to stroll about*] Once we're out of the tunnel, with thirty bouts behind us—

ROXY: If you hear a noise, it's my mouth watering—

[*The telephone rings.* Moody *answers*]

MOODY: Hello? . . . Yeah . . . I think he'll win—[*Hangs up*] Who do you think that was? [*Imitating*] "Fuseli is speaking." Eddie Fuseli!

ROXY: Fuseli? What's he want?

MOODY: Will Joe win against Vincenti Tuesday. Tokio, from now on it's your job.

TOKIO: I got faith in the boy.

MOODY: [*To* Roxy] I have to ask one thing—when Joe comes over from the gym let me do the talking.

TOKIO: And don't mention music! [Lorna *enters*]

LORNA: Shh! Here's Joe.

[Joe Bonaparte *enters the office. Immediately* Moody *and* Roxy *put on their softest kid gloves. Their methods of salesmanship will shortly become so apparent that both* Joe *and* Lorna *become suspicious*]

MOODY: [*Slowly circling around*] Glad to see you, Joe. Joe, you remember in reference to what we were speaking about yesterday? Well . . . we had several friends on the long distance phone. We're booking fifteen out of town bouts for you. Tough ones, too.

ROXY: Tonight I'm calling my Chicago connections.

MOODY: We talked it over with Tokio and he says —well, tell him what you said, Tokio—tell him the truth.

TOKIO: I think you got a wonderful future.

MOODY: [*To* Tokio] Name the names, Tokio.

TOKIO: Well, I said Benny Simon—as good as Simon, I said.

MOODY: Tokio's gonna work with you—help you develop a right—

ROXY: And a left! What'sa right without a left?

MOODY: Tokio thinks that when he brings you back you'll be a contender for Number One.

JOE: [*A little defensively*] Really? . . .

MOODY: But *you* have to help *us* help *you*.

ROXY: Could Webster say it better?

MOODY: [*Softly singing a siren song, his arms around* Joe's *shoulder*] This job needs gorgeous concentration. All your time and thoughts, Joe. No side lines, no side interests—

JOE: [*Defensively*] I don't go out with girls.

MOODY: You're in the fighting game. It's like being a priest—your work comes first. What would you rather do than fight?

JOE: [*Defensively*] I don't know what you mean.

MOODY: [*Carefully picking his words*] Some boys, for instance, like to save their looks. They'd practically throw the fight to keep their nose intact.

JOE: [*Smiling wryly*] My looks don't interest me.

[Lorna *is listening with rapt attention*]

MOODY: [*Still singing the siren song*] Then what's holding you back, Joe? You can tell me, Joe. We've set up housekeeping together, Joe, and I want you to tell me if you can't cook a steak—it don't matter. We're married anyway. . . .

JOE: [*Uneasily*] Who's being put to bed?

MOODY: What do you mean?

JOE: I don't like this seduction scene. [*To* Tokio] What are they after?

TOKIO: They think you're afraid of your hands.

MOODY: Are you?

JOE: Half . . .

TOKIO: Why?

ROXY: [*Bouncing up*] Tell the truth!

JOE: What truth?

MOODY: [*Holding back* Roxy *with a look*] Are you afraid your hands'll bust, Joe? [Joe *remains silent*] What's a busted hand to a *fighter*? You can't go in and do your best if you're scared of your mitts . . . can you? You tell me. . . .

JOE: No. . . .

MOODY: Whyn't you give up outside ideas, Joe?

ROXY: [*Suddenly, in a loud voice to* Tokio] You shoulda seen that bunch of musicians on 48th Street before. Fiddlers, drummers, cornetists—not a dime in a car-load. Bums in the park! Oh, excuse me, Tom, I was just telling Tokio—

[Joe *is now aware that the others know of the violin. Now he is completely closed to them.* Moody *sees this. He says to* Roxy]

MOODY: [*Wrathfully*] What would you like to say, my fine-feathered friend?

ROXY: [*Simulating bewilderment*] What's the matter? What happened? [*Receiving no answer, he looks around several times and adds, with a shrug*] I think I'll run across the street and pick up an eight-cylinder lunch.

MOODY: Sprinkle it with arsenic. Do that for me, for me, sweetheart!!

ROXY: [*Hurt*] That's a fine remark from a friend. [*He haughtily exits*]

JOE: What do you want, Mr. Moody?

MOODY: At the moment, nothing. I'm puffed out. See you tomorrow over the gym.

JOE: Maybe I won't be there. I might give up

fighting as a bad job. I'm not over-convinced it's what I want. I can do other things. . . .

TOKIO: I'll see you tomorrow at the gym, Joe. [Joe *looks at both the men, says nothing, exits*] That Mr. Gottlieb is a case. See you later.

MOODY: [*Not looking up*] Okay. [Tokio *exits. Lorna and Moody are alone. She blows cigarette smoke to the ceiling. Moody puts his feet up on the desk and leans back wearily. Snorting through his nostrils*] The password is honey!

LORNA: What was that all about? [*The telephone rings*]

MOODY: [*Of the ringing bell*] If that's for me, tear it up. I ain't in, not even for God.

LORNA: [*Answering*] Hello? . . . [*Putting her hand on the mouthpiece*] It's Mrs. God—your wife.

[Moody *makes a grimace of distaste but picks up the phone and puts on a sweet voice*]

MOODY: Yes, Monica darling. . . . Yeah . . . you and your support. . . . You're gonna fifty-buck me to death! . . . Monica, if I had fifty bucks I'd buy myself a big juicy coffin—what?—so throw me in jail. [*He hangs up the phone*] Bitch! That'll be time number three. She means it too.

LORNA: What was that scene with Bonaparte?

MOODY: Sweetheart, the jig is up! Believe it or not, Bonaparte's a violinist. Maybe he was on the radio. I don't know what the hell he was. His old man came here and told us. His mitts are on his mind. You can't do a thing with a nut like that.

LORNA: Won't he give up the violin?

MOODY: You heard him stalling. This is the end, Lorna. It's our last chance for a decent life, for getting married—we have to make that kid fight! He's *more* than a meal ticket—he's everything we want and need from life!

[Lorna *goes over and slaps him on the back*]

LORNA: Pick up your chin, little man.

MOODY: Don't Brisbane me, Lorna. I'm licked. I'm tired. Find me a mouse hole to crawl in. . . .

LORNA: Why don't you ask me when you want something? You got the brains of a flea. Do you want Bonaparte to fight?

MOODY: Do I wanna see tomorrow?

LORNA: I'll make him fight.

MOODY: How?

LORNA: How? . . . I'm "a tramp from Newark," Tom. . . . I know a dozen ways. . . .

SLOW FADEOUT

SCENE IV.

A few nights later. Joe and Lorna sit on a bench in the park. It is night. There is carousel music in the distance. Cars ride by in front of the boy and girl in the late spring night. Out of sight a traffic light changes from red to green and back again through-

out the scene and casts its colors on the faces of the boy and girl.

LORNA: Success and fame! Or just a lousy living. You're lucky you won't have to worry about those things. . . .

JOE: Won't I?

LORNA: Unless Tom Moody's a liar.

JOE: You like him, don't you?

LORNA: [*After a pause*] I like him.

JOE: I like how you dress. The girls look nice in the summer time. Did you ever stand at the Fifth Avenue Library and watch those girls go by?

LORNA: No, I never did. [*Switching the subject*] That's the carousel, that music. Did you ever ride on one of those?

JOE: That's for kids.

LORNA: Weren't you ever a kid, for God's sake?

JOE: Not a happy kid.

LORNA: Why?

JOE: Well, I always felt different. Even my name was special—Bonaparte—and my eyes . . .

LORNA: I wouldn't have taken that too serious. . . .

[*There is a silent pause. Joe looks straight ahead*]

JOE: Gee, all those cars . . .

LORNA: Lots of horses trot around here. The rich know how to live. You'll be rich. . . .

JOE: My brother Frank is an organizer for the C.I.O.

LORNA: What's that?

JOE: If you worked in a factory you'd know. Did you ever work?

LORNA: [*With a smile*] No, when I came out of the cocoon I was a butterfly and butterflies don't work.

JOE: All those cars . . . whizz, whizz. [*Now turning less casual*] Where's Mr. Moody tonight?

LORNA: He goes up to see his kid on Tuesday nights. It's a sick kid, a girl. His wife leaves it at her mother's house.

JOE: That leaves you free, don't it?

LORNA: What are you hinting at?

JOE: I'm thinking about you and Mr. Moody.

LORNA: Why think about it? I don't. Why should you?

JOE: If you belonged to me I wouldn't think about it.

LORNA: Haven't you got a girl?

JOE: No.

LORNA: Why not?

JOE: [*Evasively*] Oh . . .

LORNA: Tokio says you're going far in the fighting game.

JOE: Music means more to me. May I tell you something?

LORNA: Of course.

JOE: If you laugh I'll never speak to you again.

LORNA: I'm not the laughing type.

JOE: With music I'm never alone when I'm

alone— Playing music . . . that's like saying, "I am man. I belong here. How do you do, World—good evening!" When I play music nothing is closed to me. I'm not afraid of people and what they say. There's no war in music. It's not like the streets. Does this sound funny?

LORNA: No.

JOE: But when you leave your room . . . down in the street . . . it's war! Music can't help me there. Understand?

LORNA: Yes.

JOE: People have hurt my feelings for years. I never forget. You can't get even with people by playing the fiddle. If music shot bullets I'd like it better—artists and people like that are freaks today. The world moves fast and they sit around like forgotten dopes.

LORNA: You're loaded with fireworks. Why don't you fight?

JOE: You have to be what you are—!

LORNA: Fight! see what happens—

JOE: Or end up in the bughouse!

LORNA: God's teeth! Who says you have to be one thing?

JOE: My nature isn't fighting!

LORNA: Don't Tokio know what he's talking about? Don't Tom? Joe, listen: be a fighter! Show the world! If you made your fame and fortune— and you can—you'd be anything you want. Do it! Bang your way to the lightweight crown. Get a bank account. Hire a great doctor with a beard—get your eyes fixed—

JOE: What's the matter with my eyes?

LORNA: Excuse me, I stand corrected. [After a pause] You get mad all the time.

JOE: That's from thinking about myself.

LORNA: How old are you, Joe?

JOE: Twenty-one and a half, and the months are going fast.

LORNA: You're very smart for twenty-one and a half "and the months are going fast."

JOE: Why not? I read every page of the Encyclopaedia Britannica. My father's friend, Mr. Carp, has it. A shrimp with glasses had to do something.

LORNA: I'd like to meet your father. Your mother dead?

JOE: Yes.

LORNA: So is mine.

JOE: Where do you come from? The city is full of girls who look as if they never had parents.

LORNA: I'm a girl from over the river. My father is still alive—shucking oysters and bumming drinks somewhere in the wilds of Jersey. I'll tell you a secret: I don't like you.

JOE: [Surprised] Why?

LORNA: You're too sufficient by yourself . . . too inside yourself.

JOE: You like it or you don't.

LORNA: You're on an island—

JOE: Robinson Crusoe . . .

LORNA: That's right—"me, myself, and I." Why not come out and see the world?

JOE: Does it seem that way?

LORNA: Can't you see yourself?

JOE: No. . . .

LORNA: Take a bird's-eye view; you don't know what's right or wrong. You don't know what to pick, but you won't admit it.

JOE: Do you?

LORNA: Leave me out. This is the anatomy of Joe Bonaparte.

JOE: You're dancing on my nose, huh?

LORNA: Shall I stop?

JOE: No.

LORNA: You're a miserable creature. You want your arm in gelt up to the elbow. You'll take fame so people won't laugh or scorn your face. You'd give your soul for those things. But every time you turn your back your little soul kicks you in the teeth. It don't give in so easy.

JOE: And what does your soul do in its perfumed vanity case?

LORNA: Forget about me.

JOE: Don't you want—?

LORNA: [Suddenly nasty] I told you to forget it!

JOE: [Quietly] Moody sent you after me—a decoy! You made a mistake, Lorna, for two reasons. I make up my own mind to fight. Point two, he doesn't know you don't love him—

LORNA: You're a fresh kid.

JOE: In fact he doesn't know anything about you at all.

LORNA: [Challengingly] But you do?

JOE: This is the anatomy of Lorna Moon: she's a lost baby. She doesn't know what's right or wrong. She's a miserable creature who never knew what to pick. But she'd never admit it. And I'll tell you why you picked Moody!

LORNA: You don't know what you're talking about.

JOE: Go home, Lorna. If you stay, I'll know something about you. . . .

LORNA: You don't know anything.

JOE: Now's your chance—go home!

LORNA: Tom loves me.

JOE: [After a long silence, looking ahead] I'm going to buy a car.

LORNA: They make wonderful cars today. Even the lizzies—

JOE: Gary Cooper's got the kind I want. I saw it in the paper, but it costs too much—fourteen thousand. If I found one second-hand—

LORNA: And if you had the cash—

JOE: I'll get it—

LORNA: Sure, if you'd go in and really fight!

JOE: [In a sudden burst] Tell your Mr. Moody I'll dazzle the eyes out of his head!

LORNA: You mean it?

JOE: [Looking out ahead] Those cars are poison in my blood. When you sit in a car and speed you're looking down at the world. Speed, speed, everything is speed—nobody gets me!

LORNA: You mean in the ring?

JOE: In or out, nobody gets me! Gee, I like to stroke that gas!

LORNA: You sound like Jack the Ripper.

JOE: [Standing up suddenly] I'll walk you back to your house—your hotel, I mean. [Lorna stands. Joe continues] Do you have the same room?

LORNA: [With sneaking admiration] You're a fresh kid!

JOE: When you're lying in his arms tonight, tell him, for me, that the next World's Champ is feeding in his stable.

LORNA: Did you really read those Britannia books?

JOE: From A to Z.

LORNA: And you're only twenty-one?

JOE: And a half.

LORNA: Something's wrong somewhere.

JOE: I know. . . .

[They slowly walk out as]

FADEOUT

SCENE V.

The next week. It is near midnight in the dining room of the Bonaparte home. An open suitcase rests on the table, Siggie is pouring samples of wine for Lorna Moon. He himself drinks appreciatively. To one side sits Mr. Bonaparte silently, thoughtfully, watchfully—pretending to read the newspaper.

SIGGIE: I was fit to be knocked down with a feather when I heard it. I couldn't believe it until I seen him fight over at the Keystone last week. You never know what somebody's got in him—like the man with germs—suddenly he's down in bed with a crisis!

[Joe enters with an armful of clothes which he begins to pack in the suitcase]

LORNA: Joe's road tour will do him lots of good.

[Anna enters and takes off an apron. Silence, in which Siggie and Lorna sip their wine]

ANNA: How do you like that wine, Miss Moon? My father makes better wine than any Eyetalian in New York. My father knows everything—don't you, poppa?

[With a faint smile, Mr. Bonaparte shrugs his shoulders]

SIGGIE: We're thinking of sending the old man to a leper colony. . . .

ANNA: Don't my husband say funny things? Tell her what you told the janitor Tuesday, Siggie.

SIGGIE: Never mind, never mind.

ANNA: You know how I met Siggie? He was a United Cigar Store clerk and I walked in for a pack of Camels and the first thing you know he

said something funny. It was raw, so I can't say it. He had me laughing from the first. Seven years and I haven't stopped laughing yet. [She laughs loudly, pleasurably] This will be the first time Joe ever went traveling. Was you ever out of New York, Miss Moon?

LORNA: Oh, many times.

ANNA: That's nice. Far?

LORNA: California, Detroit, Chicago. I was an airplane hostess for two months.

ANNA: That's nice—it's a real adventure. I'd like to fly.

SIGGIE: Stay on the ground! Fly! What for? Who do you know up there? Eagles?

ANNA: It must be a wonderful way to see life.

LORNA: [Drinking] I've seen life in all its aspects. [Mr. Bonaparte stands up with a smile. Lorna's eyes follow him as he exits. To Joe] I think your father left because he don't like me.

JOE: He likes you.

ANNA: My father likes everybody. He's a very deep man. My father has more friends than any man alive. But best of all he likes his horse, Dolly, who drives the fruit wagon. My father can't sit still on Sunday afternoon—he has to go see what that horse is doing. [Her eyes catch sight of the suitcase] Joe, you don't know how to pack. [She starts over to assist him]

SIGGIE: [Querulously] Rest the feet awhile, Duchess.

ANNA: [Explaining her move] He don't know how to pack.

[Beginning to rearrange the suitcase. Mr. Bonaparte returns and hands Joe a sweater]

MR. BONAPARTE: You forget your good sweater.

JOE: Thanks. [Mr. Bonaparte sits. Joe looks at him sideways]

ANNA: When you get out to Chicago, buy yourself some new underwear, Joe. I hear everything's cheaper in Chicago. Is that right, Miss Moon?

LORNA: [After taking another drink] Chicago? I don't know. I was there only one night—I got news that night my mother died. As a matter of fact, she killed herself.

ANNA: That's very sad.

LORNA: No, my father's an old drunk son-of-a-bitch. Did you ask me about my father?

MR. BONAPARTE: [Who has been listening intently] Yes. . . .

LORNA: Twice a week he kicked my mother's face in. If I let myself go I'd be a drunkard in a year.

ANNA: My father never said one bad word to my mother in her whole lifetime. And she was a big nuisance right up till the day she died. She was more like me, more on the stout side. Take care of your health, Joe, when you're out there. What's better than health?

LORNA: [Turning to Mr. Bonaparte, with whom she is self-conscious] The question is, do you like me or do you not?

MR. BONAPARTE: [*With a faint smile*] Yes. . . .

LORNA: Your family is very cute— Now do you like me?

MR. BONAPARTE: Yes. . . .

LORNA: Why do you look at me that way?

MR. BONAPARTE: I don't look special. You gonna travel on those train with my son?

LORNA: God's teeth, no! I'm a friend of his manager's, that's all. And a friend of Joe's, too.

MR. BONAPARTE: You are in favor for my son to prizefight?

[Joe *looks at his father sideways and exits*]

LORNA: Certainly. Aren't you?

MR. BONAPARTE: Joe has a dream many year to be superior violin'. Was it boyhood thing? Was it real? Or is this real now? Those are-a my question, Miss Moon. Maybe you are friend to my son. Then I aska you, look out for him. Study him. Help him find what'sa right. Tell me, Miss Moon, when you find out. Help Joe find truthful success. Will you do it for me?

LORNA: I'll be glad to keep my eye on him.

[Joe *enters with slippers, which he puts in bag*]

ANNA: [*To* Joe] You could stand some new shirts, too.

SIGGIE: Listen, pop, I'm a natural man and I don't like wise guys. Joe went in the boxing game 'cause he's ashamed to be poor. That's his way to enter a little enterprise. All other remarks are so much alfalfa!

[Joe *locks the bag*]

ANNA: [*Taking the wine glass from* Siggie's *hand*] Drunk as a horse fly!

JOE: It's getting late and the train won't wait.

SIGGIE: [*Standing up*] My god is success. Need I say more? I'm prouda you, Joe. Come home a champ. Make enough dough to buy your sister's boy friend a new cab. Yes, boys and girls, I'm looking in that old crystal ball and I see strange and wonderful events! Yazoo!

ANNA: [*Giggling*] Drunk as a horse fly!

JOE: [*To* Siggie] You can't drive us down to the station in this condition.

SIGGIE: What condition?

ANNA: You're drunk, stupid.

SIGGIE: Shut the face, foolish! Just because I don't hold in my nerves she thinks I'm drunk. If you hold in your nerves you get ulcers. [*To* Joe] Get your "chapow" and let's go. Or don't you want me to drive you down?

JOE: No.

SIGGIE: I should worry—my cab's in the garage anyway! [*Suddenly he sits*]

JOE: We'd better start. . . .

LORNA: [*To* Mr. Bonaparte] I'd like to have another talk with you some time.

MR. BONAPARTE: Come any time in the evening. You are a very lovely girl. [Mr. Carp *stands in the doorway*] Here is Mr. Carp to say good-bye.

SIGGIE: Come in, my little prince.

CARP: [*Coming in and shaking hands with* Joe] I wish you good luck in every undertaking.

JOE: [*Uneasily, because his father is looking at him*] Thanks.

MR. BONAPARTE: [*Introducing* Carp] Miss Moon, my neighbor, Mr. Carp.

CARP: A pleasure to meet you.

LORNA: Hello.

[Mr. Bonaparte *brings the violin case from its hiding place in the buffet*]

MR. BONAPARTE: Joe, I buy you this some time ago. Don't give cause I don't know whatta you gonna do. Take him with you now. Play for yourself. It gonna remember you your old days of musical life.

[Joe *puts down the suitcase and picks up the violin. He plucks the strings, he tightens one of them. In spite of the tension his face turns soft and tender*]

LORNA: [*Watching intently*] We better not miss the train—Tokio's waiting.

MR. BONAPARTE: [*Of violin*] Take him with you, Joe.

JOE: It's beautiful. . . .

MR. BONAPARTE: Practise on the road.

[Joe *abruptly turns and with the violin exits. The others listen, each standing in his place, as rich violin music comes from the other room.* Joe *returns. There is silence as he places the violin on the table in front of his father*]

JOE: [*In a low voice*] Return it, poppa.

ANNA: [*Hugging* Joe] Have a good trip, Joey.

CARP: Eat in good restaurants. . . .

[*There is silence: the* Father *and* Son *look at each other. The others in the room sense the drama between the two. Finally*]

JOE: I have to do this, poppa.

MR. BONAPARTE: [*To* Joe] Be careful fora your hands.

JOE: Poppa, give me the word—

MR. BONAPARTE: What word?

JOE: Give me the word to go ahead. You're looking at yesterday—I see tomorrow. Maybe you think I ought to spend my whole life here—you and Carp blowing off steam.

MR. BONAPARTE: [*Holding himself back*] Oh, Joe, shut your mouth!

JOE: Give me the word to go ahead!

MR. BONAPARTE: Be careful fora your hands!

JOE: I want you to give me the word!

MR. BONAPARTE: [*Crying out*] No! No word! You gonna fight? All right! Okay! But I don't gonna give no word! No!

JOE: That's how you feel?

MR. BONAPARTE: That'sa how I feel! [Mr. Bonaparte's *voice breaks and there is nothing for father and son to do but to clutch each other in a hasty embrace. Finally* Mr. Bonaparte *disentangles himself and turns away.* Joe *abruptly grabs up his suitcase and exits.* Lorna *follows, stopping at the door to look back at* Mr. Bonaparte. *In the ensuing silence* Anna *looks at her father and shakes her head.* Siggie *suddenly lumbers to his feet and sounds off like a chime*]

SIGGIE: Gong gong gong gong!

ANNA: Gee, poppa . . .

SIGGIE: Come to bed, Anna. . . . Anna-banana . . . [Siggie *exits*]

ANNA: Gee, poppa . . . [*She touches her father sympathetically*]

MR. BONAPARTE: [*Without turning*] Gone to bed, Anna. . . .

[Anna *slowly exits.* Mr. Bonaparte *now slowly comes back to the table and looks down at the violin*]

CARP: [*Seating him slowly*] Come, my friend . . . we will have a nice talk on a cultural topic. [*Looking at the violin*] You'll work around a number of years before you make it up, the price of that fiddle. . . .

[Mr. Bonaparte *stands looking down at the violin*]

CARP: [*Sadly*] Yes, my friend, what is man? As Schopenhauer says, and in the last analysis . . .

SLOW FADEOUT

ACT II. SCENE I.

Six months later. Present in the corner of a gymnasium are Roxy, Moody, Lorna *and* Tokio. *They are looking off right, watching* Joe Bonaparte *work out with a partner. From off right come the sounds of typical gym activities: the thud of boxing gloves, the rat-a-tat of the punching bag, and from time to time the general bell which is a signal for rest periods. Tacked on the tin walls are an ad for Everlast boxing equipment, boxing "card" placards, a soiled American flag, some faded exit signs. The group watches silently for several seconds after the lights fade in. A* Boxer, *wiping his perspiring body with a towel, passes from left to right and looks back at* Lorna's *legs. As* Roxy *watches, his head moves to and fro in the rhythm of* Joe's *sparring off stage,* Roxy *nods his head in admiration.*

ROXY: Tokio. I gotta give the devil his dues: in the past six months you done a noble job!

TOKIO: [*Calling off*] With the left! A long left, Joe! . . .

LORNA: [*Looking off*] Joe's a very good-looking boy. I never quite noticed it before.

[*The general bell sounds; the boxing din off stage stops*]

MOODY: [*Rubbing his hands enthusiastically*] "Let it rain, let it pour! It ain't gonna rain where we're headed for!"

ROXY: I'm tickled to death to see the canary birds left his gloves.

TOKIO: He's the king of all he surveys.

MOODY: Boy, oh, boy, how he surprised them in the Bronx last night! . . . But one thing I can't explain—that knockout he took in Philly five weeks ago.

TOKIO: That night he was off his feed, Tom. Where do you see speed like that? That's style, real style—you can't tag him. And he's giving it with both hands.

MOODY: You don't have to sell me his virtues—I'm sold. Nevertheless, he got tagged in Philly.

TOKIO: Here's what happened there: we run into some man when we're leaving the hotel. Joe goes pale. I ask him what it is. "Nothing," he says. But I see for myself—a man with long hair and a violin case. When we turn the corner, he says, "He's after me," he says. As if it's cops and robbers!

[*The general bell sounds; the fighting din begins again*]

ROXY: A kidnapper?

LORNA: Don't be a fool. He was reminded . . .

ROXY: Speak when spoken to, Miss Moon!

MOODY: [*Moodily*] And when he got in the ring that night, he kept his hands in his pockets?

TOKIO: Yeah. I didn't mention this before—it's not important.

MOODY: But it's still a danger—

TOKIO: No. No.

MOODY: But anyway, we better get him away from his home. We can't afford no more possible bad showings at this stage of the game. No more apparitions, like suddenly a fiddle flies across the room on wings!

[*The group again intently watches* Joe *off stage*]

MOODY: Ooh! Did you see that? He's packing a real Sunday punch in that right. [*Calling off*] Hit 'im, Joe, hit 'im! [*As an indistinct answer come back*] Ha ha, looka that, hahaha . . . [*Now turning to* Tokio] What's your idea of a match with Lombardo?

TOKIO: Can you get it?

MOODY: Maybe.

TOKIO: Get it.

MOODY: Sure?

TOKIO: It's an easy win, on points at least.

[*During the last few lines a thin dark man has entered. His dark hair is grayed at the temples, an inarticulate look in his face. He is* Eddie Fuseli, *a renowned gambler and gunman*]

EDDIE FUSELI: [*Approaching the group*] Hello.

ROXY: [*Nervously*] Hello, Eddie.

MOODY: [*Turning*] I haven't seen you for a dog's age, Fuseli.

EDDIE: [*Pointing off left*] You got this certain boy—Bonaparte. I like his looks. American born?

ROXY: Right from here.

EDDIE: [*Watching* Joe *off*] Like a cat, never off his position. He appeals to me. [*To* Moody] They call you the Brown Fox. What's your opinion of this boy?

MOODY: [*Coolly, on guard*] Possibilities. . . .

EDDIE: [*To Tokio*] What's your idea?

TOKIO: Tom said it.

EDDIE: Could he get on top?

MOODY: [*As above*] I can't see that far ahead. I don't read palms.

EDDIE: Could I buy a piece?

MOODY: No.

EDDIE: [*Coolly*] Could I?

MOODY: No!

EDDIE: [*With a certain tenderness*] I like a good fighter. I like to see you after, Tom. [*Of Lorna*] This your girl?

LORNA: [*Pertly*] I'm my mother's girl.

EDDIE: [*With a small mirthless laugh*] Ha ha— that's a hot one. [*He coolly drifts out of the scene on his cat's feet. The general bell sounds. The din ceases*]

LORNA: What exhaust pipe did he crawl out of?

ROXY: I remember this Eddie Fuseli when he came back from the war with a gun. He's still got the gun and he still gives me goose pimples!

MOODY: That Fuseli's a black mark on my book. Every once in a while he shoots across my quiet existence like a roman candle!

LORNA: Sell or don't sell. But better be careful, that guy's tough.

[*A Fighter, robed, hooded with towel, passes across: A Gambling Type passes in the opposite direction. Both look at Lorna's legs*]

MOODY: Give a rat like that a finger and you lose a hand before you know it!

TOKIO: Did you know Joe bought a car this morning?

ROXY: What kinda car?

TOKIO: A Duesenberg.

MOODY: One of those fancy speed wagons?

TOKIO: [*Agreeing*] It cost him five grand, second-hand.

MOODY: [*Flaring up*] Am I a step-child around here? I'm glad you tell me now, if only outa courtesy!

ROXY: [*Indignantly*] Whatta you keep a thing like that incognito for?

MOODY: He drives like a maniac! That time we drove to Long Beach? I almost lost my scalp! We can't let him drive around like that! Boy, he's getting a bushel of bad habits! We gotta be careful.

[*The general bell sounds again; the fighting din stops*]

MOODY: Here's the truth: our boy can be the champ in three easy lessons—Lombardo, Fulton, the Chocolate Drop. But we gotta be careful!

LORNA: Here he comes. [*Joe enters in bathrobe, taking off his headgear, which Tokio takes from him*]

MOODY: [*Completely changing his tone*] You looked very good in there, Joe. You're going swell

and I like it. I'd work more with that long left if I were you.

JOE: Yes, I was speaking to Tokio about that. I feel my form's improving. I like to work. I'm getting somewhere—I feel it better every day.

LORNA: Happy?

JOE: [*Looking at her intently*] Every day's Saturday!

ROXY: [*Officiously*] Say, what's this I hear you bought a Duesenberg?

JOE: What's your objection—I might have some fun?

ROXY: I got my wampum on you. I like to know your habits. Ain't I permitted?

[*Joe is about to retort hotly when Moody gently takes his arm in an attempt to soothe him*]

MOODY: Wait a minute, Joe. After all we have your welfare at heart. And after all a Duesenberg can go one fifty per—

[*Eddie Fuseli appears above, unseen by the others. He listens*]

JOE: Who'd want to drive that fast?

MOODY: And since we're vitally interested in your future—

JOE: [*Shaking off Moody's arm and saying what is really on his mind*] If you're vitally interested in my future, prove it! Get me some fights—fights with contenders, not with dumb-bunny club fighters. Get me some main bouts in the metropolitan area!—

MOODY: [*Losing his temper*] For a kid who got kayoed five weeks ago, your mouth is pretty big! [*The general bell sounds; the din begins*]

JOE: That won't happen again! And how about some mention in the press? Twenty-six bouts—no one knows I'm alive. This isn't vacation for me— it's a profession! I'm staying more than a week. Match me up against real talent. You can't go too fast for me. Don't worry about autos!

MOODY: We can go too fast! You're not so good!

JOE: [*With a boyish grin*] Look at the records! [*Joe abruptly exits. Tokio follows him, first giving the others a glance*]

MOODY: Boy, oh, boy, that kid's changing!

ROXY: He goes past my head like a cold wind from the river!

LORNA: But you're gettin' what you want—the contender for the crown!

MOODY: I wish I was sure.

ROXY: Frankenstein! [*Eddie Fuseli saunters down to the others*]

EDDIE: I thought it over, Tom. I like to get a piece of that boy.

MOODY: [*Angrily*] I thought it over, too—not for sale. In fact I had a visitation from Jehovah. He came down on the calm waters and He said, "Let there be unity in the ownership."

EDDIE: [*With a dead face*] I had a visit, too. He

came down in the bar and He ate a pretzel. And He says, "Eddie Fuseli, I like you to buy a piece!"

MOODY: [*Trying to delay the inevitable*] Why not see me in my office tomorrow?

EDDIE: It's a cheap office. I get depressed in that office.

MOODY: [*Finally*] I can't make any guarantees about the boy.

EDDIE: How do you mean it, Tom?

MOODY: I don't know what the hell he'll do in the next six months.

ROXY: Eddie, it's like flap-jacks—up and down—you don't know which side next!

EDDIE: [*With his small mirthless laugh*] Ha ha, that's a good one. You oughta be on the radio.

MOODY: No, it's a fact—

ROXY: We had enough headaches already. He's got a father, but how!

EDDIE: Don't want him to fight?

ROXY: His father sits on the kid's head like a bird's nest! [Roxy *puts his hand on* Eddie's *arm*]

EDDIE: Take your hand off. [Roxy *hastily withdraws*] Let the boy decide. . . .

MOODY: If you buy in?

EDDIE: Let the boy decide.

MOODY: Sure! But if he says no— [*Before* Moody *can finish* Joe *enters.* Eddie *whirls around and faces* Joe, *getting his cue from the others. Curiously,* Eddie *is almost embarrassed before* Joe. *The bell sounds; the din stops*]

MOODY: Joe, this is Eddie Fuseli. He's a man around town—

EDDIE: [*Facing* Joe, *his back to the others*] With good connections—

MOODY: He wantsa buy a piece of you—

EDDIE: [*Whirling around*] I will tell him myself. [*Turning back to* Joe; *with quiet intense dignity*] I'm Eyetalian too—Eyetalian born, but an American citizen. I like to buy a piece of you. I don't care for no profit. I could turn it back to—you could take my share. But I like a good fighter; I like a good boy who could win the crown. It's the inter-est of my life. It would be a proud thing for me when Bonaparte could win the crown like I think he can.

MOODY: [*Confidently*] It's up to you, Joe, if he buys in.

EDDIE: [*Wooingly*] Some managers can't give you what you need—

MOODY: Don't say that!

EDDIE: *Some* managers can't! I'll see you get good bouts . . . also press notices . . . I know how. You're a boy who needs that. You decide . . .

[*There is a pause;* Joe's *eyes flit from* Lorna *to the others and back to* Eddie]

JOE: Not my half.

EDDIE: Not your half.

JOE: As long as Mr. Fuseli doesn't mix in my private life . . . cut it up any way you like. Excuse

me, I got a date with Miss Duesenberg. [*The others silently watch* Joe *exit*]

EDDIE: A date with who?

MOODY: [*Snorting*] Miss Duesenberg!

ROXY: An automobile. It gives you an idea what a boy—"Miss Duesenberg"!

EDDIE: How do you like it, Tom? Big bills or little bills?

MOODY: Don't think you're buying in for an apple and an egg.

EDDIE: Take big bills—they're new, they feel good. See you in that office tomorrow.

[*The bell clangs off stage.* Eddie *starts off, but abruptly turns and faces* Roxy *whom he inwardly terrifies*]

EDDIE: It's a trick you don't know, Roxy: when a bird sits on your head and interferes with the championship, you shoot him off. All kinds of birds. You be surprised how fast they fall on the ground. Which is my intention in this syndicate. [*He smiles thinly and then moves out of the scene like a cat*]

MOODY: I don't like that!

ROXY: I'm not so happy myself at the present time. How do you like it with our boy for gratitude? He leaves us here standing in our brevities!

LORNA: What makes you think you're worthy of gratitude?

MOODY: [*To* Lorna] For Pete's sake, pipe down! Are you with us or against us?

ROXY: [*Haughtily, to* Moody] Take my advice, Tom. Marry her and the first year give her a baby. Then she'll sit in the corner and get fat and sleepy, and not have such a big mouth! Uncle Roxy's telling you!

LORNA: [*To* Roxy] Couldn't you keep quiet about the father to that gunman? Go home and let your wife give *you* a baby!

ROXY: A woman shouldn't interfere—

MOODY: Peace, for chri' sake, peace! Lorna, we're in a bad spot with Joe. He's getting hard to manage and this is the time when everything's gotta be right. I'm seeing Lombardo's manager tomorrow! Now that gunman's on my tail. You have to help me. You and I wanna do it like the story books, "happy ever after"? Then help me.

LORNA: How?

MOODY: Go after the boy. Keep him away from his folks. Get him away from the buggies—

LORNA: How?

MOODY: [*Impatiently*] You know how.

ROXY: Now you're talking.

LORNA: [*Pointing to* Roxy] You mean the way I see it on his face?

MOODY: For crying out loud! Where do you come off to make a remark like that?

LORNA: You expect me to sleep with that boy?

MOODY: I could tear your ears off for a remark like that!

ROXY: [*Discreetly*] I think I'll go grab a corn-beef sandwich. [*He exits*]

MOODY: [*After silence*] Are you mad?

LORNA: [*Tight-lipped*] No.

MOODY: [*Seductively*] I'm not a bad guy, Lorna. I don't mean anything bad. . . . All right, I'm crude—sometimes I'm worried and I'm crude. [*The bell clangs; the boxing din stops*] But what the hell, my heart's in the right place. . . . [*Coming behind her and putting his arms around her as she looks ahead*] Lorna, don't we both want that sun to come up and shine on us? Don't we? Before you know it the summer'll be here. Then it's the winter again, and it's another year again . . . and we're not married yet. See? . . . See what I mean? . . .

LORNA: [*Quietly*] Yes. . . .

MOODY: [*Beaming, but with uncertainty*] That sounds like the girl I used to know.

LORNA: I see what you mean. . . .

MOODY: [*Worried underneath*] You're not still mad?

LORNA: [*Briefly*] I'm not mad. [*But she abruptly cuts out of the scene, leaving* Moody *standing there*]

MOODY: [*Shaking his head*] Boy, I still don't know anything about women! . . .

MEDIUM FADEOUT

SCENE II.

A few nights later. Lorna *and* Joe *sit on the same park bench.*

JOE: Some nights I wake up—my heart's beating a mile a minute! Before I open my eyes I know what it is—the feeling that someone's standing at my bed. Then I open my eyes . . . it's gone—ran away!

LORNA: Maybe it's that old fiddle of yours.

JOE: Lorna, maybe it's you. . . .

LORNA: Don't you ever think of it any more—music?

JOE: What're you trying to remind me of? A kid with a Buster Brown collar and a violin case tucked under his arm? Does that sound appetizing to you?

LORNA: Not when you say it that way. You said it different once. . . .

JOE: What's on your mind, Lorna?

LORNA: What's on yours?

JOE: [*Simply*] You. . . . You're real for me—the way music was real.

LORNA: You've got your car, your career—what do you want with me?

JOE: I develop the ability to knock down anyone my weight. But what point have I made? Don't you think I know that? I went off to the wars 'cause someone called me a name—because I wanted to be two other guys. Now it's happening. . . . I'm not sure I like it.

LORNA: Moody's against that car of yours.

JOE: I'm against Moody, so we're even.

LORNA: Why don't you like him?

JOE: He's a manager! He treats me like a possession! I'm just a little silver mine for him—he bangs me around with a shovel!

LORNA: He's helped you—

JOE: No, Tokio's helped me. Why don't you give him up? It's terrible to have just a Tuesday-night girl. Why don't you belong to me every night in the week? Why don't you teach me love? . . . Or am I being a fool?

LORNA: You're not a fool, Joe.

JOE: I want you to be my family, my life—Why don't you do it, Lorna, why?

LORNA: He loves me.

JOE: I love you!

LORNA: [*Treading delicately*] Well . . . Anyway, the early bird got the worm. Anyway, I can't give him anguish. I . . . I know what it's like. You shouldn't kick Moody around. He's poor compared to you. You're alive, you've got yourself—I can't feel sorry for you!

JOE: But you don't love him!

LORNA: I'm not much interested in myself. But the thing I like best about you . . . you still feel like a flop. It's mysterious, Joe. It makes me put my hand out. [*She gives him her hand and he grasps it*]

JOE: I feel very close to you, Lorna.

LORNA: I know. . . .

JOE: And you feel close to me. But you're afraid—

LORNA: Of what?

JOE: To take a chance! Lorna darling, you won't let me wake you up! I feel it all the time—you're half dead, and you don't know it!

LORNA: [*Half smiling*] Maybe I do. . . .

JOE: Don't smile—don't be hard-boiled!

LORNA: [*Sincerely*] I'm not.

JOE: Don't you trust me?

LORNA: [*Evasively*] Why start what we can't finish?

JOE: [*Fiercely*] Oh, Lorna, deep as my voice will reach—*listen!!* Why can't you leave him? Why?

LORNA: Don't pull my dress off—I hear you.

JOE: Why?

LORNA: Because he needs me and you don't—

JOE: That's not true!

LORNA: Because he's a desperate guy who always starts out with two strikes against him. Because he's a kid at forty-two and you're a man at twenty-two.

JOE: You're sorry for him?

LORNA: What's wrong with that?

JOE: But what do *you* get?

LORNA: I told you before I don't care.

JOE: I don't believe it!

LORNA: I can't help that!

JOE: What did he ever do for you?

LORNA: [*With sudden verve*] Would you like to know? He loved me in a world of enemies, of stags and bulls! . . . and I loved him for that. He picked me up in Friskin's hotel on 39th Street. I was nine weeks behind in rent. I hadn't hit the gutter yet, but I was near. He washed my face and combed my hair. He stiffened the space between my shoulder blades. Misery reached out to misery—

JOE: And now you're dead.

LORNA: [Lashing out] I don't know what the hell you're talking about!

JOE: Yes, you do. . . .

LORNA: [Withdrawing] Ho hum. . . .

[There is silence. The soft park music plays in the distance. The traffic lights change. Lorna is trying to appear impassive. Joe begins to whistle softly. Finally Lorna picks up his last note and continues; he stops. He picks up her note, and after he whistles a few phrases she picks him up again. This whistling duet continues for almost a minute. Then the traffic lights change again]

LORNA: [Beginning in a low voice] You make me feel too human, Joe. All I want is peace and quiet, not love. I'm a tired old lady, Joe, and I don't mind being what you call "half dead." In fact it's what I like. [Her voice mounting higher] The twice I was in love I took an awful beating and I don't want it again. [Now half crying] I want you to stop it! Don't devil me, Joe. I beg you, don't devil me . . . let me alone. . . . [She cries softly. Joe reaches out and takes her hand; he gives her a handkerchief which she uses]

LORNA: [Finally] That's the third time I cried in my life. . . .

JOE: Now I know you love me.

LORNA: [Bitterly] Well . . .

JOE: I'll tell Moody.

LORNA: Not yet. Maybe he'd kill you if he knew.

JOE: Maybe.

LORNA: Then Fuseli'd kill him. . . . I guess I'd be left to kill myself. I'll tell him. . . .

JOE: When?

LORNA: Not tonight.

JOE: Swiftly, do it swiftly—

LORNA: Not tonight.

JOE: Everything's easy if you do it swiftly.

LORNA: He went up there tonight with six hundred bucks to bribe her into divorce.

JOE: Oh . . .

LORNA: [Sadly] He's a good guy, neat all over—sweet. I'll tell him tomorrow. I'd like a drink.

JOE: Let's drive over the Washington Bridge.

LORNA: [Standing] No, I'd like a drink.

JOE: [Standing and facing her] Lorna, when I talk to you . . . something moves in my heart. Gee, it's the beginning of a wonderful life! A man and his girl! A warm living girl who shares your room. . . .

LORNA: Take me home with you.

JOE: Yes.

LORNA: But how do I know you love me?

JOE: Lorna . . .

LORNA: How do I know it's true? You'll get to be the champ. They'll all want you, all the girls! But I don't care! I've been undersea a long time! When they'd put their hands on me I used to say, "This isn't it! This isn't what I mean!" It's been a mysterious world for me! But, Joe, I think you're it! I don't know why, I think you're it! Take me home with you.

JOE: Lorna!

LORNA: Poor Tom . . .

JOE: Poor Lorna! [The rest is embrace and kiss and clutching each other]

SLOW FADEOUT

SCENE III.

The next day: the office. Lorna and Moody are present. She has a hangover and is restless.

MOODY: Boy, you certainly double-scotched last night. What's the idea, you making a career of drinking in your old age? Headache?

LORNA: No.

MOODY: I won't let you walk alone in the park any more, if you do that.

LORNA: [Nasty in spite of her best intentions] Well, if you stayed away from your wife for a change . . .

MOODY: It's pretty late to bring that up, isn't it? Tuesday nights—

LORNA: I can't help it—I feel like a tramp. I've felt like a tramp for years.

MOODY: She was pretty friendly last night.

LORNA: Yeah? Did you sleep with her?

MOODY: What the hell's the matter with you, Lorna? [He goes to her. She shrugs away from him]

LORNA: Keep off the grass! [Moody gives her a quizzical look, goes back to his desk and from there gives her another quizzical look]

MOODY: Why do you drink like that?

LORNA: [Pointing to her chest] Right here—there's a hard lump and I drink to dissolve it. Do you mind?

MOODY: I don't mind—as long as you keep your health.

LORNA: Aw, Christ!—you and your health talks!

MOODY: You're looking for a fight, dolly-girl!

LORNA: And you'll give it?

MOODY: [With a grin] No, I'm feeling too good.

LORNA: [Sitting wearily] Who left you a fortune?

MOODY: Better. Monica's seen the light. The truth is she's begun to run around with a retired brewer and now she wants the divorce.

LORNA: Good, now she can begin paying you.

MOODY: She goes to Reno in a few months.

LORNA: [Moodily] I feel like a tramp. . . .

MOODY: That's what I'm telling you— In a few

months we'll be married! [*He laughs with pleasure*]

LORNA: You still want to marry me? Don't I feel like an old shoe to you?

MOODY: [*Coming to her*] Honest, you're so dumb!

LORNA: [*Touched by his boyishness*] You're so sweet. . . .

MOODY: And flash!—I signed Lombardo today! They meet six weeks from tonight.

LORNA: Goody. . . .

MOODY: [*Disappointed by her flippant reaction, but continuing*] I'm still not sure what he'll show with Lombardo. But my present worry is this: help me get that kid straight. Did you speak to him about the driving last night?

LORNA: I didn't see him. . . .

MOODY: It's very important. A Lombardo win clinches everything. In the fall we ride up to the Chocolate's door and dump him in the gutter! After that . . . I don't like to exaggerate—but the kid's primed! And you and I—Lorna baby, we're set. [*Happily*] What do you think of that?

LORNA: [*Evasively*] You draw beautiful pictures.

[*A knock sounds on the door*]

MOODY: Come in. [Siggie *enters, dressed in cab driver's garb*]

SIGGIE: Hello, Miss Moon.

LORNA: Hello. You know Mr. Moody.

SIGGIE: [*To* Moody] Hello.

MOODY: What can we do for you?

SIGGIE: For me you can't do nothing. I'm sore. I'm here against my better instinct. [*Taking a roll of money from his pocket and slapping it on the desk*] He don't want it—no part of it! My father-in-law don't want it. Joe sent it up—two hundred bucks—enough to choke a horse—but he don't want it!

MOODY: Why?

LORNA: That's nice he remembers his folks.

SIGGIE: Listen, I got a father-in-law nothing's nice to him but feeding his horse and giving a laugh and slicing philosophical salami across the table! He's sore because Joe don't come home half the time. As a matter of fact, ain't he suppose to come to sleep no more? The old man's worried.

MOODY: That's not my concern.

SIGGIE: I can't see what it's such a worry. A boy gets in the higher brackets—what's the worry. He's got enough clothes now to leave three suits home in the closet. [*Turning to* Lorna] It won't hurt if he sends me a few passes—tell him I said so.

LORNA: How's the wife?

SIGGIE: The Duchess? Still laughing.

LORNA: When you getting that cab?

SIGGIE: Do me a favor, Miss Moon—tell him I could use this wad for the first instalment.

LORNA: I'll tell him. Tell Mr. Bonaparte I saw Joe last night. He's fine.

MOODY: I'll see you get some passes.

SIGGIE: Thanks, thanks to both of you. Adios. [*He exits*]

LORNA: He and his wife are crazy for each other. Married . . . they throw each other around, but they're like love birds. Marriage is something special. . . . I guess you have to deserve it.

MOODY: I thought you didn't see Joe last night.

LORNA: I didn't, but why worry his father?

MOODY: The hell with his father.

LORNA: The hell with you!

MOODY: [*After a brooding pause*] I'll tell you something, Lorna. I'm not overjoyed the way Joe looks at you.

LORNA: How's he look?

MOODY: As if he saw the whole island of Manhattan in your face, and I don't like it.

LORNA: You thought of that too late.

MOODY: Too late for what?

LORNA: To bawl me out.

MOODY: Who's bawling you out?

LORNA: You were about to. Or warn me. I don't need warnings. [*Coasting away from the argument*] If you saw Joe's father you'd like him.

MOODY: I saw him.

LORNA: If you knew him you'd like him.

MOODY: Who wantsa like him? What do I need him for? I don't like him and I don't like his son! It's a business—Joe does his work, I do mine. Like this telephone—I pay the bill and I use it!

LORNA: He's human.

MOODY: What're we fighting about?

LORNA: We're fighting about love. I'm trying to tell you how cynical I am. Tell the truth, love doesn't last—

MOODY: [*Suddenly quietly serious*] Everything I said about *Joe*—the opposite goes for you. Love lasts . . . if you want it to. . . . I want it to last. I need it to last. What the hell's all this struggle to make a living for if not for a woman and a home? I don't kid myself. I know what I need. I need you, Lorna.

LORNA: It has to end. . . .

MOODY: What has to end?

LORNA: Everything.

MOODY: What're you talking about?

LORNA: I oughta burn. I'm leaving you. . . .

MOODY: [*With a sick smile*] That's what you think.

LORNA: [*Not looking at him*] I mean it.

MOODY: [*As above*] I mean it too.

LORNA: [*After looking at him for a moment*] You can't take a joke?

MOODY: [*Not knowing where he stands*] It all depends. . . . I don't like a joke that pushes the blood down in my feet.

LORNA: [*Coming to him and putting her arms around his neck*] That's true, you're pale.

MOODY: Who's the man?

LORNA: [*Heartsick, and unable to tell him the truth*] There's no man, Tom . . . even if there was, I couldn't leave you. [*She looks at him, unable to say more*]

MOODY: [*After a pause*] How about some lunch? I'll buy it. . . .

LORNA: [*Wearily*] Where would I put it, Tom?

MOODY: [*Impulsively*] In your hat! [*And suddenly he ambraces her roughly and kisses her fully and she allows it.* Joe *walks into the office,* Eddie Fuseli *behind him. They break apart*]

JOE: The first time I walked in here that was going on. It's one long duet around here.

MOODY: Hello.

EDDIE: [*Sardonically*] Hello, Partner. . . .

[Lorna *is silent and avoids* Joe's *looks*]

JOE: How about that fight with Lombardo?

MOODY: Six weeks from tonight.

JOE: He's gonna be surprised.

MOODY: [*Coolly*] No one doubts it.

JOE: [*Sharply*] I didn't say it was doubted!

MOODY: Boy, everyone's off his feed today. It started with the elevator boy—next it's Lorna—now it's you! What are *you* sore about?

LORNA: [*Trying to turn the conversation; to* Joe] Siggie was here looking for you. Your father's worried—

JOE: Not as much as my "manager" worries me.

MOODY: I don't need you to tell me how to run my business. I'll book the matches—

JOE: That doesn't worry me.

MOODY: But you and your speeding worries me! First it's music, then it's motors. Christ, next it'll be girls and booze!

JOE: It's girls already.

LORNA: Joe—

JOE: [*Bitterly*] Certainly! By the dozens!

EDDIE: Haha—that's a hot one. Don't ask me which is worst—women or spiders.

LORNA: Siggie left this money—your father won't take it. Siggie says buy him a cab—

[Joe *takes the money*]

EDDIE: Your relative? I'll get him a cab. [*To* Moody] How about a flock of bouts for Bonaparte over the summer?

MOODY: [*Bitterly*] All he wants—practice fights— to make him a better "artiste."

EDDIE: That is what we like. [Joe *is looking at* Lorna]

MOODY: "We?" Where do *I* come in?

EDDIE: You push the buttons, the *right* buttons. I wanna see Bonaparte with the crown.

MOODY: [*Sarcastically*] Your concern touches me deep in my heart!

EDDIE: What's the matter, Tom? You getting tired?

MOODY: [*Coolly*] I get tired, don't you?

EDDIE: Don't get tired, Tom . . . not in a crucial time.

MOODY: Get him to give up that Duesenberg.

EDDIE: [*After looking at* Joe] That's his fun. . . .

MOODY: His fun might cost your crown.

JOE: [*Suddenly to* Lorna] Why did you kiss him?

MOODY: [*To* Joe] It's about time you shut your

mouth and minded your own goddam business. Also, that you took some orders.

JOE: [*Suddenly savage*] Who are you, God?

MOODY: Yes! I'm your maker, you cock-eyed gutter rat! Outa sawdust and spit I made you! I own you—without me you're a blank! Your insolence is gorgeous, but this is the end! I'm a son of a gun! What're you so superior about?

EDDIE: Don't talk so quick, Tom. You don't know . . .

MOODY: I wouldn't take the crap of this last six eight months from the President himself! Cut me up in little pieces, baby—but not me!

EDDIE: [*Quietly*] You could get cut up in little pieces.

MOODY: [*Retiring in disgust*] Sisst!

EDDIE: You hear me?

MOODY: [*From his desk*] You wanna manage this boy? Help yourself—do it! I'll sell my piece for half of what it's worth. You wanna buy?

EDDIE: You are a funny man.

MOODY: Gimme twenty thousand and lemme out. Ten, I'll take ten. I got my girl. I don't need crowns or jewels. I take my girl and we go sit by the river and it's everything.

JOE: What girl?

MOODY: I'm not on speaking terms with you! [*To* Eddie] Well?

EDDIE: It would be funny if your arms got broke.

JOE: Wait a minute! Lorna loves me and I love her.

MOODY: [*After looking from* Joe *to* Lorna *and back*] Crazy as a bat! [*He laughs*]

JOE: [*Frigidly*] Is it so impossible?

MOODY: About as possible as hell freezes over. [*He and* Joe *simultaneously turn to* Lorna]

JOE: Tell him. . . .

LORNA: [*Looking* Joe *in the face*] I love Tom. Tell him what?

[Joe *looks at her intently. Silence.* Joe *then turns and quietly exits from the office.* Moody *shakes his head with a grin*]

MOODY: Eddie, I take everything back. I was a fool to get sore—that boy's a real nutsy-Fagan! [*He offers his hand.* Eddie *looks at it and then viciously slaps it down*]

EDDIE: [*Repressing a trembling voice*] I don't like no one to laugh at that boy. You call a boy like that a rat? An educated boy? What is your idea to call him cock-eyed? When you do it in front of me, I say, "Tom don't like himself" . . . for Bonaparte is a good friend to me . . . you're a clever manager for him. That's the only reason I take your slop. Do your business, Tom. [*To* Lorna] And that goes for you, too! No tricks, Miss Moon! [*He slowly exits.* Moody *stands there thoughtfully.* Lorna *moves to the couch*]

MOODY: I'm a son of a gun!

LORNA: I feel like I'm shot from a cannon.

MOODY: Why?

LORNA: I'm sorry for him.

MOODY: Why? Because he's a queer?

LORNA: I'm not talking of Fuseli. [*Suddenly* Lorna's *eyes flood with tears.* Moody *takes her hand, half sensing the truth*]

MOODY: What's wrong, Lorna? You can tell me. . . .

LORNA: I feel like the wrath of God.

MOODY: You like that boy, don't you?

LORNA: I love him, Tom.

SLOW FADEOUT

SCENE IV.

Six weeks later. A dressing room before the Lombardo fight. There are a couple of rubbing tables in the room. There are some lockers and a few hooks on which hang pieces of clothing. A door to the left leads to the showers; a door to the right leads to the arena. As the lights fade in, Mr. Bonaparte and Siggie are sitting to one side, on a long wooden bench. Tokio is fussing around in a locker. A fighter, Pepper White, *hands already bandaged, is being rubbed down by his trainer-manager,* Mickey. *Throughout the scene is heard the distant* Roar of The Crowd *and the clanging of the bell.*

MR. BONAPARTE: [*After a silence of intense listening*] What is that noise?

SIGGIE: That's the roar of the crowd.

MR. BONAPARTE: A thousand people?

SIGGIE: Six thousand.

PEPPER WHITE: [*Turning his head as he lies on his belly*] Nine thousand.

SIGGIE: That's right, nine. You're sitting under nine thousand people. Suppose they fell down on your head? Did you ever think of that?

[*The outside door opens;* Eddie Fuseli *enters. The distant bell clangs.* Eddie *looks around suspiciously, then asks* Tokio]

EDDIE: Where's Bonaparte?

TOKIO: Still with the newspapermen.

EDDIE: [*Unpleasantly surprised*] He's what?

TOKIO: Tom took him upstairs—some sports writers.

EDDIE: A half hour before a fight? What is Moody trying to do?

TOKIO: Tom's the boss.

EDDIE: Looka, Tokio—in the future you are gonna take your orders from me! [*Pointing to* Siggie *and* Mr. Bonaparte] Who is this?

TOKIO: Joe's relatives.

EDDIE: [*Going over to them*] Is that his father?

MR. BONAPARTE: [*Somberly*] Yes, thisa his father.

SIGGIE: And this is his brother-in-law. Joe sent passes up the house. We just got here. I thought it was in Coney Island—it's lucky I looked at the tickets. Believe it or not, the old man never seen a fight in his life! Is it human?

EDDIE: [*Coldly*] Shut your mouth a minute! This is The Arena—Bonaparte is fighting a good man tonight—

SIGGIE: Ahh, that Lombardo's a bag of oats!

EDDIE: When Bonaparte goes in there I like him to have one thing on his mind—fighting! I hope you understand me. An' I don't like to find you here when I return! I hope you understand that. . . . [*After a full glance at them* Eddie *gracefully exits*]

SIGGIE: That's a positive personality!

TOKIO: That's Eddie Fuseli.

SIGGIE: Momma-mia! No wonder I smelled gun powder! [*Turning to* Mr. Bonaparte] Pop, that's a paradox in human behavior: he shoots you for a nickel—then for fifty bucks he sends you flowers!

TOKIO: [*Referring to the distant bell*] That's the next bout.

SIGGIE: [*To* Mr. Bonaparte] Come on, we don't wanna miss the whole show.

MR. BONAPARTE: I waita for Joe.

SIGGIE: You heard what Fuseli said—

MR. BONAPARTE: [*With somber stubbornness*] I gonna wait!

SIGGIE: Listen, pop, you—

MR. BONAPARTE: [*With sudden force*] I say I gonna wait!

SIGGIE: [*Handing* Mr. Bonaparte *a ticket*] Ticket. [*Shrugging*] Good-bye, you're letting flies in! [Siggie *exits jauntily.* Mr. Bonaparte *silently watches* Tokio *work over the fighter's materials. A* Second *comes in, puts a pail under the table where* Tokio *hovers, and exits.* Pepper White, *his head turned, watches* Mr. Bonaparte *as he hums a song*]

PEPPER:

Oh, Sweet Dardanella, I love your harem eyes,
Oh, Sweet Dardanella, I'm a lucky fellow to get
    such a prize. . . .

[*To* Mr. Bonaparte] So you're Bonaparte's little boy, Buddy? Why didn't you say so before? Come over here and shake my hand.

[Mr. Bonaparte *does so*]

PEPPER: Tell Bonaparte I like to fight him.

MR. BONAPARTE: Why?

PEPPER: I like to beat him up.

MR. BONAPARTE: [*Naïvely, not amused*] Why? You don't like him?

PEPPER: Don't kid me, Buddy! [*A* Call Boy *looks in at the door*]

CALL BOY: Pepper White! Ready, Pepper White! [Call Boy *exits.* Pepper White *slips off the table and begins to change his shoes*]

PEPPER: [*To* Mr. Bonaparte] When I get back I'll explain you all the ins and outs. [*A* Second *enters, takes a pail from* Mickey *and exits.* Lorna *enters*]

PEPPER: [*Indignantly*] Who told girls to come in here?!

LORNA: Modest? Close your eyes. Is Moody . . . ? [*Suddenly seeing* Mr. Bonaparte] Hello Mr. Bonaparte!

MR. BONAPARTE: [*Glad to see a familiar face*]

Hello, hello, Missa Moon! Howa you feel?

LORNA: What brings you to this part of the world?

MR. BONAPARTE: [*Somberly*] I come-a to see Joe. . . .

LORNA: Why, what's wrong?

MR. BONAPARTE: [*With a slow shrug*] He don't come-a to see me. . . .

LORNA: Does he know you're here?

MR. BONAPARTE: No. [Lorna *looks at him sympathetically*]

LORNA: [*Finally*] It's a three-ring circus, isn't it?

MR. BONAPARTE: How you mean?

LORNA: Oh, I mean you . . . and him . . . and other people . . .

MR. BONAPARTE: I gonna see how he fight.

LORNA: I owe you a report. I wish I had good news for you, but I haven't.

MR. BONAPARTE: Yes, I know . . . he gotta wild wolf inside—eat him up!

LORNA: You could build a city with his ambition to be somebody.

MR. BONAPARTE: [*Sadly, shaking his head*] No . . . burn down!

[*Now the outside door is thrust open—the distant bell clangs.* Joe *enters, behind him* Moody *and* Roxy. Joe *stops in his tracks when he sees* Lorna *and his father together—the last two persons in the world he wants to see now. His hands are already bandaged, a bathrobe is thrown around his shoulders*]

JOE: Hello, poppa. . . .

MR. BONAPARTE: Hello, Joe. . . .

JOE: [*Turning to* Tokio] Throw out the girls— this isn't a hotel bedroom!

MOODY: That's no way to talk!

JOE: [*Coolly*] I talk as I please!

MOODY: [*Angrily*] The future Mrs. Moody—

JOE: I don't want her here!

LORNA: He's right, Tom. Why fight about it? [*She exits*]

JOE: [*To* Moody] Also, I don't want to see writers again before a fight; it makes me nervous!

ROXY: [*Softly, for a wonder*] They're very important, Joe—

JOE: *I'm* important! My mind must be clear before I fight. I have to think before I go in. Don't you know that yet?

ROXY: [*Suddenly*] Yeah, we know—you're a stoodent—you gotta look in your notes.

JOE: What's funny about that? I do, *I do!!*

ROXY: [*Retreating*] So I said you do! [Pepper White *comes forward, about to exit; to* Moody]

PEPPER: How 'bout a bout with Napoleon?

MOODY: On your way, louse!

PEPPER: [*With a grin*] Pickin' setups?

[Joe *suddenly turns and starts for* Pepper. Tokio *quickly steps in between the two boys*]

TOKIO: Save it for the ring!

[*The two fighters glare at each other.* Joe *slowly turns and starts back for the table*]

PEPPER: You think he'll be the champ? Where'd you ever read about a cock-eye champ?

[Joe *spins around, speeds across the room—* Pepper *is on the floor!* Mickey *now starts for* Joe. Tokio *starts for* Mickey. Pepper *gets up off the floor and finds himself occupied with* Moody. *For a moment the fight is general.* Eddie Fuseli *enters. All see him. The fighting magically stops on the second*]

EDDIE: What'sa matter? Cowboys and Indians? [*To* Pepper] Out!

[Mickey *and* Pepper *sullenly exit*]

EDDIE: [*To* Moody] I'm lookin' for you! You're a manager and a half! You and your fat friend! [*Meaning* Roxy] You think this boy is a toy?

JOE: Eddie's the only one here who understands me.

MOODY: Who the hell wantsa understand you! I got one wish—for Lombardo to give you the business! The quicker he taps you off tonight, the better! You gotta be took down a dozen pegs! I'm versus you! Completely versus!

EDDIE: [*Quietly, to* Moody] Moody, your brains is in your feet! This is how you handle a coming champ, to give him the jitters before a bout? Go out and take some air! . . . [*Seeing* Eddie's *quiet deadliness,* Moody *swallows his wrath and exits;* Roxy *follows with pursed lips*]

EDDIE: Lay down, Joe—take it easy.

[Joe *sits on a table*]

EDDIE: Who hurt you, Joe? Someone hurt your feelings?

JOE: Everything's all right.

EDDIE: Tokio, I put fifty bucks on Bonaparte's nose for you. It's my appreciation to you. . . .

TOKIO: Thanks.

EDDIE: [*Of* Mr. Bonaparte] Whatta you want me to do with him?

JOE: Leave him here.

EDDIE: Tell me if you want something. . . .

JOE: Nothing.

EDDIE: Forget that Miss Moon. Stop lookin' down her dress. Go out there and kill Lombardo! Send him out to Woodlawn! Tear his skull off! . . . as I know Bonaparte can do it! [Eddie *gives* Mr. Bonaparte *a sharp look and exits. There is silence intensified by the distant clang of the bell and the muted roar of* The Crowd. Tokio *looks over at* Mr. Bonaparte *who has been silently seated on the bench all this time*]

JOE: [*Not quite knowing what to say*] How is Anna, poppa?

MR. BONAPARTE: Fine.

JOE: Siggie watching the fights?

MR. BONAPARTE: Yes. . . .

JOE: You look fine. . . .

MR. BONAPARTE: Yes, feela good. . . .

JOE: Why did you send that money back? [*There is no answer*] Why did you come here? . . . You sit there like my conscience. . . .

MR. BONAPARTE: Why you say so?

JOE: Poppa, I have to fight, no matter what you say or think! This is my profession! I'm out for fame and fortune, not to be different or artistic! I don't intend to be ashamed of my life!

MR. BONAPARTE: [Standing up] Yeah, I understanda you. . . .

JOE: Go out and watch the fights.

MR. BONAPARTE: [Somberly] Yeah . . . you fight. Now I know . . . is'a too late for music. The men musta be free an' happy for music . . . not like-a you. Now I see whatta you are . . . I give-a you every word to fight . . . I sorry for you. . . .

[Silence. The distant roar of The Crowd climbs up and falls down; the bell clangs again]

TOKIO: [Gently] I'll have to ask you to leave, Mr. Bonaparte. . . .

MR. BONAPARTE: [Holding back his tears] Joe . . . I hope-a you win every fight. [Mr. Bonaparte slowly exits. As he opens and closes the door the roar of The Crowd swells up for an instant]

TOKIO: Lay down, Joe. There's five minutes left to tune you up.

JOE: [In a low voice] That's right, tune me up. . . . [Joe stretches out on his stomach and Tokio's busy hands start up the back of his legs]

TOKIO: [Working with steady briskness] I never worried less about a boy . . . in my life. You're a real sweetheart. . . .

[Suddenly Joe begins to cry in his arms. Tokio looks down, momentarily hesitates in his work —then slowly goes ahead with his massaging hands. The Boy continues to shake with silent sobs. Again the bell clangs in the distance]

TOKIO: [In a soft caressing voice] You're getting good, honey. Maybe I never told you that before. I seen it happen before. [Continuing the massaging] It seems to happen sudden—a fighter gets good. He gets easy and graceful. He learns how to save himself—no energy wasted . . . he slips and slides—he travels with the punch. . . . Oh, sure, I like the way you're shaping up. [Tokio continues massaging. Joe is silent. His sobbing stops. After a moment Tokio continues] What was you saying about Lombardo's trick? I understood you to say he's a bull's-eye for a straight shot from the inside. I think you're right, Joe, but that kind of boy is liable to meet you straight-on in a clinch and give you the back of his head under the chin. Watch out for that.

JOE: He needs a straight punch. . . . [Joe suddenly sits up on the table, his legs dangling] Now I'm alone. They're all against me—Moody, the girl . . . you're my family now, Tokio—you and Eddie! I'll show them all—nobody stands in my way! My father's had his hand on me for years. No more. No more for her either—she had her chance! When a bullet sings through the air it has no past—only a future—like me! Nobody, nothing stands in my way! [In a sudden spurt of feeling Joe starts sparring around lightly in a shadow boxing routine. Tokio smiles with satisfaction. Now the roar of The Crowd reaches a frenzied shriek and hangs there. The bell clangs rapidly several times. The roar of The Crowd settles down again]

TOKIO: That sounds like the kill.

[Joe draws his bathrobe around him and prances on his toes]

JOE: I'm a new boy tonight! I could take two Lombardos! [Vigorously shaking out his bandaged hands above his head] Hallelujah! We're on the Millionaire Express tonight! Nobody gets me!

[The door is thrust open and a Call Boy shouts]

CALL BOY: Bonaparte, ready. Bonaparte, ready.

[Pepper White and Mickey enter as the Call Boy speeds away. Pepper is flushed with victory]

PEPPER: [To Joe] Tell me when you want it; you can have it the way I just give it to Pulaski!

[Joe looks Pepper in the face, flexes his hands several times and suddenly breaks out in laughter, to Pepper's astonishment. Joe and Tokio exit. Pepper throws off his robe and displays his body]

PEPPER: Look me over—not a mark. How do you like that for class! I'm in a hurry to grab a cab to Flushing.

MICKEY: [Impassively] Keep away from her.

PEPPER: I don't even hear you.

MICKEY: Keep away from her!

PEPPER: I go for her like a bee and the flower.

MICKEY: [In a droning prophetic voice] The flower is married. Her husband is an excitable Armenian from the Orient. There will be hell to pay! Keep away from her!

[Now in the distance is heard the indistinct high voice of the announcer]

PEPPER: You oughta get me a fight with that cock-eye Napoleon—insteada sticking your nose where it don't belong! I could slaughter him in next to nothing.

MICKEY: [Impassively] If you could make his weight and slaughter him, you'd be the next world's champ. But you can't make his weight, you can't slaughter him, and you can't be the champ. Why the hell don't you take a shower?

[The bell clangs—in the arena, Joe's fight is on]

PEPPER: [Plaintively, beginning to dress at his locker] If my girl don't like me without a shower, I'll tell her a thing or two.

MICKEY: If her husband don't tell you first.

[The roar of The Crowd swells up as the door opens and Mr. Bonaparte enters. He is unusually agitated. He looks at Pepper and Mickey and sits on a bench. The roar of The Crowd mounts higher than before, then drops]

PEPPER: [To Mr. Bonaparte] What's the matter with you?

MR. BONAPARTE: [Shaking his head] Don't like to see . . .

PEPPER: [*Delighted*] Why? Your boy gettin' smeared?

MR. BONAPARTE: They fighta for money, no?

MICKEY: No, they're fighting for a noble cause—

MR. BONAPARTE: If they wasa fight for cause or for woman, woulda not be so bad.

PEPPER: [*Still dressing behind the locker door*] I fight for money and I like it. I don't fight for under a thousand bucks. Do I, Mickey?

MICKEY: Nope.

PEPPER: [*Boasting naïvely*] I didn't fight for under a thousand for five years. Did I, Mickey?

MICKEY: [*Impassively*] Nope.

PEPPER: I get a thousand bucks tonight, don't I?

MICKEY: Nope.

PEPPER: [*Up like a shot*] How much? How much tonight?

MICKEY: Twelve hundred bucks.

PEPPER: What? Mickey, I oughta bust you in the nose. How many times do I have to say I don't fight for under one thousand bucks! [*To* Mr. Bonaparte] Now you see what I'm up against with this manager!

MICKEY: [*Impassively*] Okay, you'll get a thousand.

PEPPER: I better, Buddy! That's all I say—I better! [*To* Mr. Bonaparte] I tell him I want to fight your kid and he don't lift a finger.

[*The roar of* The Crowd *crescendos and drops down again*]

MICKEY: You don't rate no fight with Bonaparte. [*To* Mr. Bonaparte, *of* Pepper] He's an old man, a fossil!

MR. BONAPARTE: Who?

MICKEY: Him—he's twenty-nine.

MR. BONAPARTE: Old?

MICKEY: In this business, twenty-nine is ancient.

PEPPER: My girl don't think so.

MICKEY: Keep away from her.

[*The roar of* The Crowd *mounts up to a devilish shriek*]

PEPPER: Wow, is your boy getting schlocked!

MR. BONAPARTE: My boy isa win.

PEPPER: Yeah, and that's why you ran away?

MR. BONAPARTE: Whatta the difference who's-a win? Is terrible to see!

PEPPER: [*Grinning*] If I wasn't in a hurry, I'd wait around to help pick up your little Joie's head off the floor. [*He draws on a sport shirt*]

MICKEY: [*To* Pepper] What are you wearing a polo shirt on a winter night for?

PEPPER: For crying out loud, I just bought it! . . . So long, Mr. Bonaparte.

MR. BONAPARTE: I aska you please—whatta happen to a boy's hands when he fight a longa time?

PEPPER: [*Holding up his fists*] Take a look at mine —I got a good pair. See those knuckles? Flat!

MR. BONAPARTE: Broke?

PEPPER: Not broke, flat!—pushed down!

MR. BONAPARTE: Hurt?

PEPPER: You get used to it.

MR. BONAPARTE: Can you use them?

PEPPER: Go down the hall and look at Pulaski.

MR. BONAPARTE: Can you open thees-a hands?

PEPPER: What for?

MR. BONAPARTE: [*Gently touching the fists*] So strong, so hard . . .

PEPPER: You said it, Buddy. So long, Buddy. [*To* Mickey] Take my stuff.

MICKEY: Sam'll take it after. Keep away from her!

[Pepper *looks at* Mickey *with a sardonic grin and exits followed by* Mickey]

MR. BONAPARTE: [*To himself*] So strong . . . so useless . . .

[*The roar of* The Crowd *mounts up and calls for a kill.* Mr. Bonaparte *trembles. For a moment he sits quietly on the bench. Then he goes to the door of the shower room and looks around at the boxing paraphernalia. In the distance the bell begins to clang repeatedly.* Mr. Bonaparte *stares in the direction of the arena. He goes to the exit door. The crowd is cheering and howling.* Mr. Bonaparte *hesitates a moment at the door and then rapidly walks back to the bench, where he sits. Head cocked, he listens for a moment. The roar of* The Crowd *is heated, demanding and hateful. Suddenly* Mr. Bonaparte *jumps to his feet. He is in a murderous mood. He shakes his clenched fist in the direction of the noise—he roars aloud. The roar of* The Crowd *dies down. The door opens,* Pepper's *second,* Sam, *enters softly whistling to himself. Deftly he begins to sling together* Pepper's *paraphernalia*]

MR. BONAPARTE: What'sa happen in the fight?

SAM: Knockout.

MR. BONAPARTE: Who?

SAM: Lombardo's stiff.

[Mr. Bonaparte *slowly sits. Softly whistling,* Sam *exits with the paraphernalia. The outside door is flung open. In come* Joe, Tokio, Moody *and* Roxy, *who is elated beyond sanity.* Joe's *eyes glitter; his face is hard and flushed. He has won by a knockout*]

ROXY: [*Almost dancing*] My boy! My darling boy! My dear darling boy!

[*Silently* Joe *sits on the edge of the table, ignoring his father after a glance. His robe drops from his shoulders.* Roxy *turns to* Moody]

ROXY: How do you like it, Tom? He knocks him out in two rounds!

MOODY: [*Stiffly to* Joe] It's good business to call the sports writers in—

ROXY: That's right, give a statement!

[Moody *gives* Joe *a rapid glance and hurriedly exits*]

ROXY: I'm collecting a bet on you. All my faith and patience is rewarded. [*As he opens the door he almost knocks over* Eddie Fuseli] Haha! How do you like it, Eddie? Haha! [*He exits.* Eddie Fuseli *closes the door and stands with his back to it.* Tokio *moves up to* Joe *and begins to remove a glove*]

TOKIO: [*Gently*] You're a real sweetheart. . . . [Tokio *removes the sweaty glove and begins to fumble with the lace of the other one.* Joe *carefully moves his glove out of* Tokio's *reach, resting it on his opposite arm*]

JOE: [*Almost proudly*] Better cut it off. . . .

[Mr. Bonaparte *is watching tensely.* Eddie *watches from the door*]

TOKIO: . . . Broke? . . .

JOE: [*Holding the hand out proudly*] Yes, it's broke. . . .

[Tokio *slowly reaches for a knife. He begins carefully to cut the glove*]

JOE: Hallelujah!! It's the beginning of the world!

[Mr. Bonaparte, *lips compressed, slowly turns his head away.* Eddie *watches with inner excitement and pleasure:* Joe *has become a fighter.* Tokio *continues with his work.* Joe *begins to laugh loudly, victoriously, exultantly—with a deep thrill of satisfaction*]

SLOW FADEOUT

ACT III. SCENE I.

Moody's *office, six months later. Present are* Moody, *acting the persuasive salesman with two sports writers,* Drake *and* Lewis; Roxy Gottlieb *being helpful in his usual manner;* Tokio, *to one side, characteristically quiet . . . and* Joe Bonaparte. Bonaparte *sits on the desk and diffidently swings his legs as he eats a sandwich. His success has added a certain bellicosity to his attitude; it has changed his clothing to silk shirts and custom-made suits.*

MOODY: He's got his own style. He won't rush—

ROXY: Nobody claims our boy's Niagra Falls.

DRAKE: [*A newspaperman for twenty years*] Except himself!

MOODY: You newspaper boys are right.

DRAKE: We newspaper boys are always right!

MOODY: He won't take chances tomorrow night if he can help it. He'll study his man, pick out flaws —then shoot at them.

JOE: [*Casually*] It won't matter a helluva lot if I win late in the bout or near the opening. The main thing with Bonaparte is to win.

DRAKE: [*Dryly*] Well, what does Bonaparte expect to do tomorrow night?

JOE: [*As dryly*] Win.

MOODY: Why shouldn't we have a win from the Chocolate Drop? Look at our record!—

LEWIS: [*Good-natured and slow*] We just wanna get an impression—

MOODY: Seventeen knockouts? Fulton, Lombardo, Guffey Talbot—?

JOE: Phil Weiner . . .

MOODY: Weiner?

ROXY: That's no powderpuff hitter!

LEWIS: In this fight tomorrow night, can you name the round?

JOE: Which round would you like?

DRAKE: You're either a genius or an idiot!

MOODY: Joe don't mean—

DRAKE: [*Sharply*] Let him talk for himself.

JOE: [*Getting off the desk*] Listen, Drake, I'm not the boy I used to be—the honeymoon's over. I don't blush and stammer these days. Bonaparte goes in and slugs with the best. In the bargain his brain is *better* than the best. That's the truth; why deny it?

DRAKE: The last time you met Chocolate you never even touched him!

JOE: It's almost two years since I "never even touched him." Now I know how!

MOODY: What Joe means to say—

DRAKE: He's the genuine and only modest cockeyed wonder!

JOE: What good is modesty? I'm a fighter! The whole essence of prizefighting is immodesty! "I'm better than you are—I'll prove it by breaking your face in!" What do you expect? A conscience and a meek smile? I don't believe that bull the meek'll inherit the earth!

DRAKE: Oh, so it's the earth you want!

JOE: I know what I want—that's my business! But I don't want your guff!

DRAKE: I have two sons of my own—I like boys. But I'm a son-of-a-bitch if I can stomach your conceit!

MOODY: [*Trying to save the situation*] They serve a helluva rum Collins across the street—

DRAKE: Bonaparte, I'll watch for Waterloo with more than interest!

MOODY: Why don't we run across for a drink? How 'bout some drinks?

DRAKE: Tom, you can buy me twenty drinks and I still won't change my mind about him. [*He exits*]

LEWIS: [*Smiling*] You're all right, Bonaparte.

JOE: Thanks. . . .

LEWIS: [*Clinching a cigarette at the desk*] How's that big blonde of yours, Tom?

MOODY: Fine.

LEWIS: How does she feel about the wedding bells? Sunday is it?

[*This is news to* Joe, *and* Moody *knows it is*]

MOODY: [*Nervously*] Happy, the way I am. Yeah, Sunday.

ROXY: How about the drinks? We'll drink to everybody's health!

LEWIS: [*To* Joe] Good luck tomorrow.

JOE: Thanks. . . . [*They exit,* Moody *throwing a resentful look at* Joe. Joe *and* Tokio *are left. In the silence* Joe *goes back to the remains of his lunch*]

TOKIO: That Drake is a case.

JOE: [*Pushing the food away*] They don't make cheesecake the way they used to when I was a boy.

Or maybe I don't like it any more. When are they getting married?

TOKIO: Moody? Sunday.

JOE: Those writers hate me.

TOKIO: You give them too much lip.

JOE: [*Looking down at his clenched fists*] I'd rather give than take it. That's one reason I became a fighter. When did Moody get his divorce?

TOKIO: Few weeks ago. . . . [*Cannily*] Why don't you forget Lorna?

JOE: [*As if not understanding*] What?

TOKIO: I'll say it again . . . why not forget her? [*No answer comes*] Joe, you're loaded with love. Find something to give it to. Your heart ain't in fighting . . . your *hate* is. But a man with hate and nothing else . . . he's half a man . . . and half a man . . . is no man. Find something to love, or someone. Am I stepping on your toes?

JOE: [*Coldly*] I won't be unhappy if you mind your business.

TOKIO: Okay. . . . [*Tokio goes to the door, stops there*] Watch your dinner tonight. No girls either.

JOE: Excuse me for saying that—

TOKIO: [*With a faint smile*] Okay. [*Tokio opens the door and Lorna Moon enters. Tokio smiles at her and exits. She carries a pack of newspapers under her arm. Joe and she do not know what to say to each other—they wish they had not met here. Lorna crosses and puts the newspapers on the desk. She begins to bang through the desk drawers, looking for the scissors*]

JOE: I hear you're making the leap tomorrow.

LORNA: Sunday. . . .

JOE: Sunday. [*Intense silence*]

LORNA: [*To say anything*] I'm looking for the scissors. . . .

JOE: Who're you cutting up today?

LORNA: [*Bringing out the shears*] Items on Bonaparte, for the press book. [*She turns and begins to unfold and clip a sheet of newspaper. Joe is at a loss for words*]

JOE: [*Finally*] Congratulations. . . .

LORNA: [*Without turning*] Thanks. . . .

[*In a sudden irresistible surge Joe tears the newspaper out of Lorna's hands and hurls them behind the desk. The two stand facing each other*]

JOE: When I speak to you, look at me!

LORNA: What would you like to say? [*They stand face to face, straining. Finally*]

JOE: Marry anyone you like!

LORNA: Thanks for permission!

JOE: Queen Lorna, the tramp of Newark!

LORNA: You haven't spoken to me for months. Why break your silence?

JOE: You're a historical character for me—dead and buried!

LORNA: Then everything's simple; go about your business.

JOE: Moody's right for you—perfect—the mating of zero and zero!

LORNA: I'm not sorry to marry Tom—

JOE: [*Scornfully*] That's from the etiquette book —page twelve: "When you marry a man say you like it!"

LORNA: I know I could do worse when I look at you. When did you look in the mirror last? Getting to be a killer! You're getting to be like Fuseli! You're not the boy I cared about, not you. You murdered that boy with the generous face—God knows where you hid the body! I don't know you.

JOE: I suppose I never kissed your mouth—

LORNA: What do you want from me? Revenge? Sorry—we're all out of revenge today!

JOE: I wouldn't look at you twice if they hung you naked from a Christmas tree!

[*At this moment Eddie Fuseli enters with a pair of packages. He looks intently at Lorna, then crosses and puts the packages on the desk. He and Joe are dressed almost identically. Lorna exits without a word. Eddie is aware of what has happened but begins to talk casually about the packages*]

EDDIE: This one's your new headgear. This is shirts from Jacobs Brothers. He says the neck bands are gonna shrink, so I had him make sixteens— they'll fit you after one washing. [*Holding up a shirt*] You like that color?

JOE: Thanks.

EDDIE: Your brother-in-law drove me over. Picked him up on 49th. Don't you ever see them no more?

JOE: [*Sharply*] What for?

EDDIE: What'sa matter?

JOE: Why? You see a crowd around here, Eddie?

EDDIE: No.

JOE: That's right, you don't! But I do! I see a crowd of Eddies all around me, suffocating me, burying me in good times and silk shirts!

EDDIE: [*Dialing the telephone*] You wanna go to the Scandals tonight? I got tickets. [*Into the telephone*] Charley? Fuseli is speaking. . . . I'm giving four to five on Bonaparte tomorrow. . . . Four G's worth. . . . Yes. [*Hanging up the phone*] It's gonna be a good fight tomorrow.

JOE: [*Belligerently*] How do you know?

EDDIE: I know Bonaparte. I got eighteen thousand spread out on him tomorrow night.

JOE: Suppose Bonaparte loses?

EDDIE: I look at the proposition from all sides— I know he'll win.

JOE: What the hell do you think I am? A machine? Maybe I'm lonely, maybe—

EDDIE: You wanna walk in a parade? Everybody's lonely. Get the money and you're not so lonely.

JOE: I want some personal life.

EDDIE: I give Bonaparte a good personal life. I got loyalty to his cause. . . .

JOE: You use me like a gun! Your loyalty's to keep me oiled and polished!

EDDIE: A year ago Bonaparte was a rookie with a two-pants suit. Now he wears the best, eats the best, sleeps the best. He walks down the street respected—the golden boy! They howl their heads off when Bonaparte steps in the ring . . . and I done it for him!

JOE: There are other things. . . .

EDDIE: There's no other things! Don't think so much—it could make you very sick! You're in this up to your neck. You owe me a lot—I don't like you to forget. You better be on your toes when you step in that ring tomorrow night. [Eddie *turns and begins to dial the telephone*]

JOE: Your loyalty makes me shiver. [Joe *starts for the door*]

EDDIE: Take the shirts.

JOE: What do I want them for? I can only wear one at a time. . . .

[Eddie *speaks into the phone*]

EDDIE: Meyer? . . . Fuseli is speaking. . . . I'm giving four to five on Bonaparte tomorrow. . . . Two? . . . Yeah. . . .

[*About to exit,* Joe *stands at the door and watches* Eddie *as he calmly begins to dial the phone again*]

MEDIUM FADEOUT

SCENE II.

The next night. The lights fade in on an empty stage. We are in the same dressing room as seen in Act Two. Far in the distance is heard the same roar of The Crowd. *The distant bell clangs menacingly. The room is shadows and patches of light. The silence here has its own ugly dead quality.* Lorna Moon *enters. She looks around nervously; she lights a cigarette; this reminds her to rouge her lips; she puffs the cigarette. The distant bell clangs again.* Eddie Fuseli *enters, pale and tense. He sees* Lorna *and stops short in his tracks. There is an intense silence as they look at each other.*

LORNA: How's the fight?

EDDIE: I like to talk to you.

LORNA: Is Joe still on his feet?

EDDIE: Take a month in the country, Miss Moon.

LORNA: Why?

EDDIE: [*Repressing a murderous mood*] Give the boy . . . or move away.

LORNA: I get married tomorrow. . . .

EDDIE: You heard my request—give him or go!

LORNA: Don't Moody count?

EDDIE: If not for Bonaparte they'd find you in a barrel long ago—in the river or a bush!

LORNA: I'm not afraid of you. . . .

[*The distant bell clangs*]

EDDIE: [*After turning his head and listening*] That's the beginning of the eighth. Bonaparte's un-settled—fighting like a drunken sailor. He can't win no more, unless he knocks the Chocolate out. . . .

LORNA: [*At a complete loss*] Don't look at me . . . what'd you . . . I . . .

EDDIE: Get outa town!

[*The roar of* The Crowd *mounts to a demand for a kill*]

EDDIE: [*Listening intently*] He's like a bum tonight . . . and a bum done it! You! [*The roar grows fuller*] I can't watch him get slaughtered. . . .

LORNA: I couldn't watch it myself. . . . [*The bell clangs loudly several times. The roar of* The Crowd *hangs high in the air*] What's happening now?

EDDIE: Someone's getting murdered. . . .

LORNA: It's me. . . .

EDDIE: [*Quietly, intensely*] That's right . . . if he lost . . . the trees are ready for your coffin. [*The roar of* The Crowd *tones down*] You can go now. I don't wanna make a scandal around his name. . . . I'll find you when I want you. Don't be here when they carry him in.

LORNA: [*At a complete loss*] Where do you want me to go?

EDDIE: [*Suddenly releasing his wrath*] Get outa my sight! You turned down the sweetest boy who ever walked in shoes! You turned him down, the golden boy, that king among the ju-ven-niles! He gave you his hand—you spit in his face! You led him on like Gertie's whoore! You sold him down the river! And now you got the nerve to stand here, to wait and see him bleeding from the mouth!—

LORNA: Fuseli, for God's sake—

EDDIE: Get outa my sight!

LORNA: Fuseli, please—

EDDIE: Outa my sight, you nickel whoore! [*Completely enraged and out of control,* Eddie *half brings his gun out from under his left armpit.* Joe *appears in the doorway. Behind him are* Roxy, Moody *and a* Second]

JOE: Eddie! [Eddie *whirls around. The others enter the room. In the ensuing silence,* Moody, *sensing what has happened, crosses to* Lorna]

LORNA: [*Quietly*] What happened?

ROXY: What happened? [*He darts forward and picks up* Joe's *arm in the sign of victory. The arm drops back limply*] The monarch of the masses!

EDDIE: [*To the* Second] Keep everybody out. Only the newspaper boys.

[*The* Second *exits and closes the door.* Joe *sits on a table. Physically he is a very tired boy. There is a high puff under one eye; the other is completely closed. His body is stained with angry splotches*]

TOKIO: [*Gently*] I have to hand it to you, Joe. . . .

ROXY: [*Explaining to the frigid* Eddie, *elaborately*] The beginning of the eighth: first the bell! Next the Chocolate Drop comes out like a waltz clog, confident. Oh, he was so confident! Haha! The next thing I know the Chocolate's on the floor, the referee lifts our arm, we got on our bathrobe and we're here in the dressing room! How do you like it?

EDDIE: [*Narrowly*] I like it.

TOKIO: [*Taking off* Joe's *gloves*] I'll have you feelin' better in a minute. [*After which he cuts the tapes*]

JOE: I feel all right.

EDDIE: [*To* Tokio] Gimme his gloves.

MOODY: [*Wary of* Joe] That's a bad lump under your eye.

JOE: Not as bad as the Chocolate Drop got when he hit the floor!

ROXY: Darling, how you gave it to him! Not to my enemies!

JOE: 'Twas a straight right—with no trimmings or apologies! Aside from fouling me in the second and fifth—

MOODY: I called them on it—

ROXY: I seen the bastard—

JOE: That second time I nearly went through the floor. I gave him the fury of a lifetime in that final punch! [Eddie *has taken the soggy boxing gloves for his own property.* Tokio *is daubing the bruise under* Joe's *eye*] And did you hear them cheer! [*Bitterly, as if reading a news report*] Flash! As thousands cheer, that veritable whirlwind Bonaparte —that veritable cock-eye wonder, Bonaparte—he comes from behind in the eighth stanza to slaughter the Chocolate Drop and clinch a bout with the champ! Well, how do you like me, boys? Am I good or am I good?

ROXY: Believe *me*!

TOKIO: [*Attempting to settle* Joe] You won the right for a crack at the title. You won it fair and clean. Now lay down. . . .

JOE: [*In a vehement outburst*] I'd like to go outside my weight and beat up the whole damn world!

MOODY: [*Coldly*] Well, the world's your oyster now!

TOKIO: [*Insistently*] Take it easy. Lemme fix that eye, Joe—

[*Now a bustling little Irishman,* Driscoll, *hustles into the room*]

DRISCOLL: Who's got the happy boy's gloves?

EDDIE: Here . . . why?

[Driscoll *rapidly takes the gloves, "breaks" and examines them*]

TOKIO: What's the matter, "Drisc"?

JOE: What's wrong?

DRISCOLL: [*Handing the gloves back to* Eddie] Chocolate's a sick boy. Your hands are clean. [Driscoll *hustles for the door.* Joe *is up and to him*]

JOE: What happened?

DRISCOLL: [*Bustling*] It looks like the Pride of Baltimore is out for good. Change your clothes.

JOE: How do you mean?

DRISCOLL: Just like I said—out! [Driscoll *pats* Joe's *shoulder, hustles out, closing the door in* Joe's *face.* Joe *slowly sits on the nearest bench. Immediately* Tokio *comes to him, as tender as a mother*]

TOKIO: You didn't foul him—you're a clean

fighter. You're so honest in the ring it's stupid. If something happened, it's an accident. [*The others stand around stunned, not knowing what to do or say*]

MOODY: [*Very worried*] That's right, there's nothing to worry about.

ROXY: [*Ditto*] That's right. . . .

JOE: Gee. . . . [Joe *stands up, slowly crosses the room and sits on the table, head in his hands, his back to the others. No one knows what to say*]

EDDIE: [*To* Moody] Go out there and size up the situation.

[Moody, *glad of the opportunity to leave the room, turns to the door which is suddenly violently thrust open.* Barker, *the Chocolate Drop's manager, pushes* Moody *into the room with him, leaving the door open. From outside a small group of curious people look in.* Barker, *bereft of his senses, grabs* Moody *by the coat lapel*]

BARKER: Do you know it? Do you know it?

MOODY: Now wait a minute, Barker—

[Barker *runs over to* Joe *and screams*]

BARKER: You murdered my boy! He's dead! You killed him!

TOKIO: [*Getting between* Joe *and* Barker] Just a minute!

BARKER: [*Literally wringing his hands*] He's dead! Chocolate's dead!

TOKIO: We're very sorry about it. Now pull yourself together.

[Eddie *crosses the room and slams the door shut as* Barker *points an accusing finger at* Joe *and screams*]

BARKER: This dirty little wop killed my boy!

EDDIE: [*Coming to* Barker] Go back in your room.

BARKER: Yes he did!! [Eddie's *answer is to shove* Barker *roughly toward the door, weeping*] Yes, he did!!

EDDIE: Get out before I slug your teeth apart!

JOE: [*Jumping to his feet*] Eddie, for God sakes, don't hit him! Let him alone!

[Eddie *immediately desists.* Barker *stands there, a weeping idiot*]

MOODY: Accidents can happen.

BARKER: I know . . . I know. . . .

MOODY: Chocolate fouled us twice.

BARKER: I know, I know. . . . [Barker *stammers, gulps and tries to say something more. Suddenly he dashes out of the room. There is a long silent pause during which* Joe *sits down again*]

EDDIE: We'll have to wait for an investigation.

TOKIO: [*To* Joe] Don't blame yourself for nothing. . . .

JOE: That poor guy . . . with those sleepy little eyes. . . .

ROXY: [*Solemnly*] It's in the hands of God, a thing like that.

[Lewis, *the sports writer, tries to enter the room*]

EDDIE: [*Herding him out*] Stay outside. [*To Moody*] See what's happening? [*Moody immediately leaves*] Everybody out—leave Bonaparte to calm hisself. I'll watch the door.

TOKIO: Don't worry, Joe. [*He exits, followed by* Roxy. *Eddie turns and looks at* Lorna]

EDDIE: You too, Miss Moon—this ain't no cocktail lounge.

LORNA: I'll stay here. [*Eddie looks at her sharply, shifts his glance from her to* Joe *and back again; he exits*] Joe. . . .

JOE: Gee, that poor boy. . . .

LORNA: [*Holding herself off*] But it wasn't your fault.

JOE: That's right—it wasn't my fault!

LORNA: You didn't mean it!

JOE: That's right—I didn't mean it! I wouldn't want to do that, would I? Everybody knows I wouldn't want to kill a man. Lorna, you know it!

LORNA: Of course!

JOE: But I *did* it! That's the thing—I *did* it! What will my father say when he hears I murdered a man? Lorna, I see what I did. I murdered myself, too! I've been running around in circles. Now I'm smashed! That's the truth. Yes, I was a real sparrow, and I wanted to be a fake eagle! But now I'm hung up by my finger tips—I'm no good—my feet are off the earth!

LORNA: [*In a sudden burst, going to* Joe] Joe, I love you! We love each other! Need each other!

JOE: Lorna darling, I see what's happened!

LORNA: You wanted to conquer the world—

JOE: Yes—

LORNA: But it's not the kings and dictators who do it—it's that kid in the park—

JOE: Yes, that boy who might have said, "I have myself; I am what I want to be!"

LORNA: And now, tonight, here, this minute—finding yourself again—that's what makes you a champ. Don't you see that?

JOE: Yes, Lorna—yes!

LORNA: It isn't too late to tell the world good evening again!

JOE: With what? These fists?

LORNA: Give up the fighting business!

JOE: Tonight!

LORNA: Yes, and go back to your music—

JOE: But my hands are ruined. I'll never play again! What's left, Lorna? Half a man, nothing, useless. . . .

LORNA: No, *we're* left! Two together! We have each other! Somewhere there must be happy boys and girls who can teach us the way of life! We'll find some city where poverty's no shame—where music is no crime!—where there's no war in the streets—where a man is glad to be himself, to live and make his woman herself!

JOE: No more fighting, but where do we go?

LORNA: Tonight? Joe, we ride in your car. We speed through the night, across the park, over the Triboro Bridge—

JOE: [*Taking* Lorna's *arms in his trembling hands*] Ride! That's it, we ride—clear my head. We'll drive through the night. When you mow down the night with headlights, nobody gets you! You're on top of the world then—nobody laughs! That's it—speed! We're off the earth—unconnected! We don't have to think!! That's what speed's for, an easy way to live! Lorna darling, we'll burn up the night! [*He turns and as he begins to throw his street clothes out of his locker*]

MEDIUM FADEOUT

SCENE III.

Late the same night. In the Bonaparte home sit Eddie Fuseli, Moody, Roxy, *and* Siggie, *drinking homemade wine, already half drunk. Mr. Bonaparte stands on the other side of the room, looking out of the window. Frank sits near him, a bandage around his head. Moody is at the telephone as the lights fade in.*

MOODY: [*Impatiently*] . . . 'lo? Hello! . . .

SIGGIE: I'll tell you why we need another drink. . . .

ROXY: No, I'll tell you. . . .

MOODY: [*Turning*] Quiet! For Pete's sake! I can't hear myself think! [*Turning to the phone*] Hello? . . . This is Moody. Any calls for me? Messages? . . . No sign of Miss Moon? . . . Thanks. Call me if she comes in—the number I gave you before. [*Hanging up and returning to his wine glass; to* Mr. Bonaparte] I thought you said Joe was coming up here!

MR. BONAPARTE: I say maybe . . .

MOODY: [*Sitting*] I'll wait another fifteen minutes. [*He drinks*]

SIGGIE: Here's why we need another drink; it's a night of success! Joe's in those lofty brackets from now on! We're gonna move to a better neighborhood, have a buncha kids! [*To* Mr. Bonaparte] Hey, pop, I wish we had a mortgage so we could pay it off! To the next champ of the world! [*Siggie lifts his glass; the others join him*]

ROXY: Bonaparte.

EDDIE: Don't you drink, Mr. Bonaparte?

SIGGIE: You, too, Frank—it's all in the family.

[*Mr. Bonaparte shrugs and comes down, accepting a glass*]

ROXY: It's in the nature of a celebration!

MR. BONAPARTE: My son'sa kill a man tonight—what'sa celebrate? What'sa gonna be, heh?

SIGGIE: Ahh, don't worry—they can't do him nothing for that! An accident!

EDDIE: [*Coldly, to* Mr. Bonaparte] Listen, it's old

news. It's been out on the front page two-three hours.

MR. BONAPARTE: Poor color' boy . . .

MOODY: Nobody's fault. Everybody's sorry—we give the mother a few bucks. But we got the next champ! Bottoms up. [*All drink*, Frank *included*]

ROXY: [*To* Mr. Bonaparte] You see how a boy can make a success nowadays?

MR. BONAPARTE: Yeah . . . I see.

EDDIE: [*Resenting* Mr. Bonaparte's *attitude*] Do we bother you? If I didn't think Joe was here I don't come up. I don't like nobody to gimme a boycott!

MR. BONAPARTE: [*Going back to the window*] Helpa you'self to more wine.

SIGGIE: [*To* Eddie] leave him alone—he don't feel social tonight.

MOODY: Don't worry, Mr. Bonaparte. Looka me —take a lesson from me—I'm not worried. I'm getting married tomorrow—*this afternoon!*—I don't know where my girl is, but I'm not worried! What for? We're all in clover up to our necks!

SIGGIE: Shh . . . don't wake up my wife.

[Moody *suddenly sits heavily; jealousy begins to gnaw at him despite his optimism.* Roxy *takes another drink.* Eddie *asks* Frank, *apropos of his bandaged head*]

EDDIE: What's that "Spirit of '76" outfit for?

SIGGIE: [*Grinning to* Eddie] Didn't you hear what he said before? They gave it to him in a strike—

EDDIE: [*To* Frank] You got a good build—you could be a fighter.

FRANK: I fight. . . .

EDDIE: Yeah? For what?

FRANK: A lotta things I believe in. . . .

[Eddie *looks at* Frank *and appreciates his quality*]

EDDIE: Whatta you get for it?

ROXY: [*Laughing*] Can't you see? A busted head!

FRANK: I'm not fooled by a lotta things Joe's fooled by. I don't get autos and custom-made suits. But I get what Joe don't.

EDDIE: What don't he get?

[Mr. Bonaparte *comes in and listens intently*]

FRANK: [*Modestly*] The pleasure of acting as you think! The satisfaction of staying where you belong, being what you are . . . at harmony with millions of others!

ROXY: [*Pricking up his ears*] Harmony? That's music! the family's starting up music again!

FRANK: [*Smiling*] That's right, that's music—

[*Now* Moody *emphatically stamps his glass down on the table and stands*]

MOODY: What's the use waiting around! They won't be back. [*Bitterly*] Lorna's got a helluva lotta nerve, riding around in Long Island with him! Without even asking me!

SIGGIE: Long Island's famous for the best eating ducks.

EDDIE: [*To* Moody] You got the champ—you can't have everything.

MOODY: What's that supposed to mean?

EDDIE: [*Coldly*] That girl belongs to Bonaparte. They're together now, in some roadhouse . . . and they ain't eating duck!

MOODY: [*Finally, unsteadily*] You don't know what you're talking about!

EDDIE: Moody, what do you figger your interest is worth in Bonaparte?

MOODY: Why?

EDDIE: [*Without turning*] Roxy . . . are you listening?

ROXY: Yeah. . . .

EDDIE: 'Cause after tonight I'd like to handle Bonaparte myself.

MOODY: . . . Your gall is gorgeous! But I got a contract. . . .

ROXY: Eddie, have a heart—I'm holding a little twenty percent. . . . [*Out of sheer rage* Moody *drinks more wine;* Roxy *follows his example*]

FRANK: [*To* Eddie] How much does Joe own of himself?

EDDIE: Thirty percent. After tonight I own the rest.

MOODY: Oh, no! No, sir-ee!!

EDDIE: You're drunk tonight! Tomorrow!

MR. BONAPARTE: [*Coming forward*] Maybe Joe don't gonna fight no more, after tonight. . . .

EDDIE: Listen, you creep! Why don't you change your tune for a minute!

ROXY: [*To* Mr. Bonaparte] What're *you* worried about?

MR. BONAPARTE: My boy usta coulda be great for all men. Whatta he got now, heh? Pardon me fora nota to feel so confident in Joe'sa future! Pardon me fora to be anxious. . . .

EDDIE: [*Standing up*] I don't like this talk!

SIGGIE: Sit down, pop—you're rocking the boat! Shh! Shh! [*He slips out of the room*]

ROXY: Does anyone here know what he's talking about?

FRANK: He's trying to say he's worried for Joe.

ROXY: But why? Why? Don't he realize this kid's worth a fortune from tonight on? [*After giving* Eddie *a quick glance*] Ain't he got brains enough to see two feet ahead? Tell him in Italian—he don't understand our language—this is a festive occasion! To Bonaparte, the Monarch of the Masses! [*The telephone rings*]

MOODY: [*Triumphantly, to* Eddie] That's my hotel! You see, you were all wrong! That's Lorna! [*Speaking into the telephone*] Hello? . . . No. . . . [*Turning to* Mr. Bonaparte] It's for you. [Moody *extends the telephone in* Mr. Bonaparte's *direction, but the latter stands in his place, unable to move. After a few seconds* Frank *sees this and briskly moves to the telephone, taking it from* Moody. *In the meantime* Moody *has begun to address* Eddie *with drunken eloquence. Wavering on his feet*] There's a constitution in this country, Eddie

Fuseli. Every man here enjoys life, liberty and the pursuit of happiness!

FRANK: [*Speaking into the telephone*] Yes? . . . No, this is his son . . .

[Mr. Bonaparte *watches* Frank *mutely as he listens at the telephone*]

MOODY: There's laws in this country, Fuseli—contracts! We live in a civilized world—!

FRANK: [*Loudly. to the others*] Keep quiet! [*Resumes listening*] Yes . . . yes. . . .

ROXY: [*To* Eddie] And there's a God in heaven—don't forget it!

FRANK: [*On the telephone*] Say it again. . . . [*He listens*] Yes.

MOODY: [*To* Eddie] You're a killer! A man tries to do his best—but you're a killer!

[Frank *lowers the telephone and comes down to the others*]

FRANK: You're *all killers!*

[Mr. Bonaparte *advances a step toward* Frank]

MR. BONAPARTE: Frank . . . is it . . . ?

FRANK: I don't know how to tell you, poppa. . . .

MR. BONAPARTE: [*Hopefully*] Yes?

FRANK: We'll have to go there—

EDDIE: Go where?

FRANK: Both of them . . . they were killed in a crash—

EDDIE: Who?! What?!

FRANK: They're waiting for identification—Long Island, Babylon.

EDDIE: [*Moving to* Frank] What are you handing me?! [Eddie, *suddenly knowing the truth, stops in his tracks. The telephone operator signals for the telephone to be replaced. The mechanical clicks call* Frank *to attention; he slowly replaces the instrument*]

MOODY: I don't believe that! Do you hear me? I don't believe it—

FRANK: What waste! . . .

MOODY: It's a goddam lie!!

MR. BONAPARTE: What have-a you expect? . . .

MOODY: [*Suddenly weeping*] Lorna!

MR. BONAPARTE: [*Standing, his head high*] Joe. . . . Come, we bring-a him home . . . where he belong. . . .

SLOW FADEOUT

Lillian Hellman

(1905-   )

In the early nineteen-thirties, a period of general dislocation in the United States, there was considerable distress in the theatre because no new playwrights of consequence were emerging. Fortunately, this situation began to change, the first sign of improvement being the appearance in 1934 of a powerful psychological drama by a hitherto active but uncelebrated young woman. The play was *The Children's Hour*. The author was Lillian Hellman, almost every one of whose efforts was to startle playgoers into an awareness of her talent.

Lillian Hellman was born in New Orleans to a shoe merchant who had migrated to Louisiana. Her birth in the South does not, however, align her with the regional writers of America who have made distinguished contributions to letters. Miss Hellman's parents moved to New York when she was five years old, and she is a metropolitan product in all respects but the accident of birth. Except for visiting relatives in the deep South during summer vacations, she grew up and was educated in the city, attending New York and Columbia Universities.

After graduation from college in 1924, Miss Hellman made inroads into the literary and theatrical world from many directions. She worked for a publisher, reviewed books for the *New York Herald Tribune,* published stories and articles, read plays for stage producers, and acted as a press agent for the theatre. In 1930, she went to Hollywood as a script reader, or "story analyst," acquiring more preparation for the stage and the screen. In 1932, on returning to New York, she began working as a play reader for Herman Shumlin, a meticulous and clear-headed New York producer and director. It was at this time that she read a famous early-nineteenth-century Scottish law report, "The Great Drumsheugh Case." Having already developed a taste for playwriting by collaborating on a farce with Louis Kronenberger, she proceeded to dramatize this lawsuit, although advised against it by her employer. Changing the background to a small Connecticut town and creating full-sized characters, she wrote an impressive original play, *The Children's Hour.* Shumlin produced and directed it, and it ran for 691 performances in New York. It also toured widely, attracting much attention and running into difficulties in Boston and Chicago because its story of a fiendish child's machinations against two schoolteachers involved the subject of sexual abnormality.

As a partisan of labor, Miss Hellman next wrote *Days to Come,* a somewhat muddled treatment of the demoralizing effect of a labor conflict on a manufacturer who reluctantly hires strikebreakers. Produced in 1936, *Days to Come* revealed new evidence of Miss Hellman's vigor, although the play was quickly withdrawn from Broadway. Later that year, the author used her royalties from *The Children's Hour* to widen her knowledge of the contemporary scene by traveling to Russia, France, and Spain. In Spain, she witnessed the Civil War, experienced bombardment, and was profoundly stirred by the conflict. Her sympathies entirely on the side of the Loyalist Republicans, she came back to the United States in a combative frame of mind and henceforth gave vigorous support to all efforts to check the rise of fascism. She became a radical in politics and was outspoken in her approach to social problems.

Nevertheless, Miss Hellman's convictions did not lead her to write the kind of political harangues that flavored the playwriting of the radical wing in the theatre. Although her animus was plain enough in her next play, *The Little Foxes* (1939), her procedure was analytical and aloof in this story of unscrupulous roguery associated with the rise of industrial fortunes on the ruins of the old South. Emotion did flare in her work when she turned to the subject of resistance against German fascism, in *Watch on the Rhine.* This play was produced in 1941, when the Second World War was in full swing and when it was only a matter of months before the United States would become embroiled. Melodramatic in action but conceived with much humanity, *Watch on the Rhine* instantly won acclaim. It was considered beyond doubt the best of the anti-Nazi plays written for the American stage. Miss Hellman followed this exciting drama with a panoramic investigation of the errors that had brought us into the war. This inquisition, suitably entitled *The Searching Wind,* appeared in 1944, when the fortunes of war still hung in the balance. Snarled somewhat by a love plot, the chronicle recapitulated our appeasement of fascism in its early stages. Still in a prosecuting frame of mind in 1946, Miss Hellman exhumed the villains of *The Little Foxes* and wrote a second satire on acquisitiveness, *Another Part of the Forest.* Her last play, at the midpoint of the century of social conflict, was an adaptation from the French, *Montserrat,* in which an idealist faces the necessity of sending innocent people to their death in order to save the cause of freedom in South America.

Miss Hellman acquired a formidable reputation as a moralist, a strong hater, and a driving dramatist who never lost control of a situation or an argument. To critics who found her dramaturgy altogether too melodramatic and violent she could offer the partial defense that there was evil in the world and that it was her business to expose it. Never having much use for bumbling, she did not propose to write panegyrics on good intentions, and she showed no inclination to wallow in congenial but futile sentiment. Critics who found her mode of attack quite rasping sometimes voiced the suspicion that Miss Hellman simply did not like people. This was, however, an indictment easily dismissed on the evidence of the plays. The young Birdie in *Another Part of the Forest* and the middle-aged wreck of Birdie in *The Little Foxes,* Regina's husband and daughter in the latter play, and all but one of the major characters in *Watch on the Rhine* were conceived with sympathy and understanding.

Although Miss Hellman never overlooked the social framework within which her subjects functioned, characterization was primary in her procedure as a playwright. She worked slowly and tried to develop a full life for her characters in the ample notes she collected before writing each of her plays. If her stage pieces generally fall into the allegedly outmoded category of the well-made play, they are "well made" with the substance of reality, which consists of people as well as of situations and ideas. If they do not give us much of the wayward flow and happy surprise of writings which convey the "feel" of life more than they demonstrate a point, Miss Hellman's plays also avoid the amorphousness of this kind of "organic" or "protoplasmic" kind of composition. In any case, it must be conceded that, although Miss Hellman forced her dramatic action a little too much, piling evil upon evil and grief upon grief, she carried on the tradition of Ibsen and the social realists with due consideration for both the logic of character and the logic of situations.

The Little Foxes, considered the strongest and most closely knit of Miss Hellman's plays, is also her most interesting contribution to the modern theatre. Its obvious virtues of compactness and firmly drawn characterization are supported by a crackling style. And here her indictment of the predatory life leaves room for an understanding attitude toward those who are broken by it and those who try to resist it. The play exists, indeed, on many levels— as character drama, melodrama, and comedy. This is so decidedly the case that it is less easy than one

would imagine to define the nature and ultimate effect of the play. It belongs to an intermediate genre of playwriting, troubling to precisians in criticism, that came into vogue in modern times with such dramatists as Ibsen, Strindberg, Becque (whose comedy *The Vultures* provides interesting possibilities for a comparison), and Shaw. For an equivalent type of writing in the older drama one may have to go back to the "dark comedies" of Shakespeare, although there is hardly a glimmer of poetry in Miss Hellman's work.

Much has also been made of the sociological aspects of *The Little Foxes,* such as the historical picture of the coming of industrialism to the South and the implication that the modern capitalistic world is full of Hubbards, great and small. Although these elements are certainly present, the argument against capitalism is actually peripheral to the story and not perfectly sustained. (One may wonder whether the Hubbards would not be Hubbards in any kind of society and whether modern big business does operate in the crude ways that the Hubbards favor. Then, too, Miss Hellman has included such capitalists as Regina's husband and William Marshall, who show no affinity for Regina's brothers. Miss Hellman concerns herself generally with damnation as a state of the soul, and a case might be made out for saying that her real theme, whether she knew it or not, is "original sin" in a modern context, which brings her closer to such contemporary Catholic writers as Mauriac than to Bernard Shaw or Karl Marx.) Ultimately, however, the most considered judgment on *The Little Foxes* will be that it is fundamentally an effective work for the stage. Within the strict confines of the theatre, the life in the play holds no insoluble questions and presents no ramifications requiring debate. It is in the theatrical completeness of this and other plays that Miss Hellman proves her mettle as a playwright.

BIBLIOGRAPHY: Brooks Atkinson, *Broadway Scrapbook* (pp. 107–110, 192–195, 255–257), 1947; John Mason Brown, *Broadway in Review* (pp. 116–120), 1940; Margaret Case Harriman, "Miss Lily of New Orleans," in *The New Yorker,* Vol. XVII, No. 39, November 8, 1941; Lillian Hellman, Introduction to *Four Plays,* 1942; Joseph Wood Krutch, *The American Drama Since 1918* (pp. 130–133), 1939.

THE LITTLE FOXES

By Lillian Hellman

CHARACTERS

ADDIE	OSCAR HUBBARD	ALEXANDRA GIDDENS
CAL	LEO HUBBARD	BENJAMIN HUBBARD
BIRDIE HUBBARD	REGINA GIDDENS	HORACE GIDDENS
	WILLIAM MARSHALL	

SCENE

SCENE: *The living room of the Giddens house in a small town of the Deep South.*

TIME: *The Spring of 1900.*

ACT I: *Evening, after supper.*

ACT II: *Morning, a week later.*

ACT III: *Late afternoon, two weeks later.*

ACT I.

SCENE: *The living room of the Giddens house, a small town in the Deep South, the spring of 1900. Upstage is a staircase leading to the second story. U.R. are double doors to the dining room. When these doors are open we see a section of the dining room and the furniture. U.L. is an entrance hall with a coat-rack and umbrella stand. There are large lace-curtained windows on the L. wall. The room is lit by a center gas chandelier and painted china oil lamps on the tables. Against the wall is a large piano. D.R. are a high couch, a large table, several chairs. Against the L. backwall are a table and several chairs. Near the window there are a smaller couch and tables. The room is good-looking, the furniture expensive; but it reflects no particular taste. Everything is of the best, and that is all.*

AT RISE: *Addie, a tall, nice-looking Negro woman of about fifty-five, is closing the U.S. windows. From behind the closed dining-room doors there is the sound of voices. After a second Cal, a middle-aged Negro, comes in from the entrance L. hall, carrying a tray with 10 glasses and a bottle of port wine. Addie crosses, takes the tray from him, puts it on table, begins to arrange it.*

ADDIE: [*Pointing to the bottle*] You gone stark out of your head?

CAL: No, smart lady, I ain't. Miss Regina told me to get out that bottle, [*Points to bottle*] that very bottle for the mighty honored guest. When Miss Regina changes orders like that you can bet your dime she got her reason.

ADDIE: [*Points to dining room—not looking*] Go on. You'll be needed. [*She arranges glasses and pours wine*]

CAL: [*Looking at Addie while wiping glasses*] Miss

Zan she had two helpings frozen fruit cream and she tell that honored guest, she tell him that you make the [*Steps down to* Addie] best frozen fruit cream in all the South.

ADDIE: [*Smiles, pleased*] Did she? Well, see that Belle saves a little for her. She like it right before she go to bed. Save a few little cakes, too, she like——

[*The dining-room doors are opened and quickly closed again by* Birdie Hubbard. Birdie *is a woman of about forty, with a pretty, well-bred, faded face. Her movements are usually nervous and timid, but now, as she comes running into the room, she is gay and excited.* Cal *turns to-* Birdie]

BIRDIE: Oh, Cal. [*Closes door*] I want you to get one of the kitchen boys to run home for me. He's to look in my desk drawer and—— [*Crosses* D. *to back of chair* R.C. *to* Addie] My, Addie. What a good supper. Just as good as good can be.

ADDIE: You look pretty this evening, Miss Birdie, and young.

BIRDIE: [*Laughing*] Me, young? [*Turns back to* Cal] Maybe you better find Simon and tell him to do it himself. He's to look in my desk, the left drawer, and bring my music album right away. Mr. Marshall is very anxious to see it because of his father and the opera in Chicago. [*To* Addie] Mr. Marshall is such a polite man with his manners, and very educated and cultured, and I've told him all about how my Mama and Papa used to go to Europe for the music—— [*Laughs. To* Addie] Imagine going all the way to Europe just to listen to music. Wouldn't that be nice, Addie? Just to sit there and listen and—— [*Turns and takes step to* Cal] Left drawer, Cal. Tell him that twice because he forgets. And tell him not to let any of the things drop out of the album and to bring it right in here when he comes back.

[*The dining-room doors are opened and quickly closed by* Oscar Hubbard. *He is a man in his late forties*]

CAL: Yes'm. But Simon he won't get it right. [*Crossing to door* L.] But I'll tell him.

BIRDIE: Left drawer, Cal, and tell him to bring the blue book and——

OSCAR: [*Sharply*] Birdie.

BIRDIE: [*Turning nervously*] Oh, Oscar. I was just sending Simon for my music album.

OSCAR: [*To* Cal *who has stopped at door* L. *to listen*] Never mind about the album. Miss Birdie has changed her mind.

BIRDIE: But, really, Oscar. Really I promised Mr. Marshall. I——

[Cal *looks at them, exits* L.]

OSCAR: Why do you leave the dinner table and go running about like a child?

[Addie *crosses around sofa to* D.S. *window, closes windows*]

BIRDIE: [*Trying to be gay*] But Oscar, Mr. Marshall said most specially he *wanted* to see my album. I told him about the time Mama met Wagner and Mrs. Wagner gave her the signed program and the big picture. [Oscar *moves away* D.C.] Mr. Marshall wants to see that. [Birdie *moves to him*] Very, very much. We had such a nice talk and——

OSCAR: [*Taking step to her*] You have been chattering to him like a magpie. You haven't let him be for a second. I can't think he came South to be bored with you. [*He turns away, crosses* D.R.]

BIRDIE: [*Quickly, hurt*] He wasn't bored. I don't believe he was bored. He's a very educated, cultured gentleman. [*Her voice rises*] I just don't believe it. [Addie *moves up to back of sofa*] You always talk like that when I'm having a nice time.

OSCAR: [*Turning to her, sharply*] You have had too much wine. Get yourself in hand now.

BIRDIE: [*Drawing back, about to cry, shrilly*] What am I doing? I am not doing anything. [Addie *crosses* U. *back of sofa*] What am I doing?

OSCAR: [*Taking a step to her, tensely*] I said get yourself in hand. Stop acting like a fool. [Addie *crosses to* U.S. *windows, closes them*]

BIRDIE: [*Moves up, then turns to him, quietly*] I don't believe he was bored. I just don't believe it. Some people like music and like to talk about it. [Leo *enters from dining room.* Regina *in dining room rings bell*] That's all I was doing.

[Leo Hubbard *comes hurrying through the door. He is a young man of twenty, with a weak kind of good looks.*]

LEO: Mama! [Birdie *turns sharply to him*] Papa. They are coming in now.

OSCAR: [*Softly, stepping up to* Birdie] Sit down, Birdie. Sit down now.

[Oscar *crosses* D.R. Leo *crosses* D.L. *to piano.* Birdie *sits down in chair* L.C., *bows her head as if to hide her face. The dining-room doors are opened by* Cal. *We see people beginning to*

rise from the table. Regina Giddens *comes in with* William Marshall. Regina *is a handsome woman of forty.* Marshall *is forty-five, pleasant looking, self-possessed. Behind them comes* Alexandra Giddens, *a very pretty, rather delicate looking girl of seventeen. She is followed by* Benjamin Hubbard, *fifty-five, with a large jovial face and the light graceful movements that one often finds in large men.* Regina, *after a sharp look at* Birdie *and* Oscar, *crosses to sofa* R. Marshall *crosses* C. *to chair* R.C. Alexandra *crosses* D.L. *to settee and sits*]

REGINA: Mr. Marshall, I think you're trying to console me. Chicago may be the noisiest, dirtiest city in the world but I should still prefer it to the sound of our horses and the smell of our azaleas. I should like crowds of people, and theaters, and lovely women—— [Regina *sits on sofa, smiles at* Marshall *and indicates for him to sit next to her*] Very lovely women, Mr. Marshall? [Ben *crosses to back of settee* L.]

MARSHALL: [*Crossing to sofa* R.] In Chicago? Oh, I suppose so. But I can tell you this: I've never dined there with three *such* lovely ladies.

[*He sits on sofa to* R. *of* Regina. Addie *comes down to table, takes bottle off tray and serves wine*]

BEN: [*Crossing to* C. *nods*] Our Southern women are well favored.

LEO: [*Stepping in, laughs*] But one must go to Mobile for the ladies, sir. Very elegant worldly ladies, too.

[Addie *is serving* Regina, *who hands a glass to* Marshall, *then takes one for herself*]

BEN: [*Looks at him very deliberately*] Worldly, eh? *Worldly,* did you say?

[Addie *serves* Ben]

OSCAR: [*Hastily, to* Leo] Your Uncle Ben means that worldliness is not a mark of beauty in any woman.

LEO: [*Steps up to above settee* L. *Quickly*] Of course, Uncle Ben. I didn't mean——

[Ben *cross* R. *to chair* R.C., *sits*]

MARSHALL: Your port is excellent, Mrs. Giddens.

[Addie *serves* Birdie, *who catches* Oscar's *look at her, and refuses the drink*]

REGINA: Thank you, Mr. Marshall. We had been saving that bottle, hoping we could open it just for you.

ALEXANDRA: [*As* Addie *comes to her with tray*] Oh. May I *really*, Addie?

ADDIE: Better ask Mama.

ALEXANDRA: May I, Mama?

REGINA: [*Nods, smiles*] In Mr. Marshall's honor.

ALEXANDRA: [*Smiles*] Mr. Marshall, this will be the first taste of port I've ever had.

[Addie *serves* Leo]

MARSHALL: [*Leaning forward*] No one ever had their first taste of a better port. [*He lifts his glass in a toast, she lifts hers, they both drink. Sits back.*

Looks around the room, smiles. Addie *crosses to* Oscar U.R., *serves him*] Well, I suppose it is all true, Mrs. Giddens. [Oscar *crosses* D.R.]

REGINA: What is true?

[Addie *crosses to table for bottle, takes the tray to table* U.C., *places it there, then exits* L.]

MARSHALL: That you Southerners occupy a unique position in America. You live better than the rest of us, you eat better, you drink better. I wonder you find time, or want to find time, to do business.

BEN: [*Laughs*] A great many Southerners don't.

MARSHALL: Do all of you live here together?

REGINA: Here with me? [*Laughs*] Oh, no. My brother Ben lives next door. My brother Oscar and his family live in the next square.

BEN: [*Sitting forward*] But we are a very close family. We've always *wanted* it that way.

MARSHALL: That is very pleasant. Keeping your family together to share each other's lives. My family moves around too much. My children seem never to come home. Away at school in the winter; in the summer, Europe with their mother——

[Ben *sits back*]

REGINA: [*Eagerly*] Oh, yes. Even down here we read about Mrs. Marshall in the society pages.

MARSHALL: I dare say. She moves about a great deal. And all of you are part of the same business? Hubbard Sons?

BEN: [*Motions to* Oscar] Oscar and me. [*Motions to* Regina] My sister's good husband is a banker.

MARSHALL: [*Looks at* Regina, *surprised*] Oh.

REGINA: I am so sorry that my husband isn't here to meet you. He's been very ill. He is at Johns Hopkins. But he will he home soon. We think he is getting better now.

LEO: [*Crosses to above chair* L.C.] I work for Uncle Horace. [Regina *looks at him*] I mean I work for Uncle Horace at his bank. I keep an eye on things while he's away.

REGINA: [*Smiles*] Really, Leo?

BEN: [*Looks at him, then to* Marshall] Modesty in the young is as excellent as it is rare. [*Looks at* Leo *again*]

OSCAR: [*To* Leo] Your Uncle means that a young man should speak more modestly.

LEO: [*Hastily, taking a step to* Ben] Oh, I didn't mean, sir——

MARSHALL: Oh, Mrs. Hubbard. Where's that Wagner autograph you promised to let me see? My train will be leaving soon and——

[Leo *crosses* U. *to table* U.C., *pours himself a drink*]

BIRDIE: The autograph? Oh. Well. Really, Mr. Marshall, I didn't mean to chatter so about it. Really I—— [*Nervously, looking at* Oscar] You must excuse me. I didn't get it because, well, because I had—I—I had a little headache and——

OSCAR: My wife is a miserable victim of headaches. [*Crosses* U.R. *to above sofa* R.]

REGINA: [*Quickly*] Mr. Marshall said at supper that he would like you to play for him, Alexandra.

ALEXANDRA: [*Who has been looking at* Birdie] It's not I who play well, sir. It's my aunt. She plays just wonderfully. She's my teacher. [*Rises; eagerly*] May we play a duet? May we, Mama?

BIRDIE: [*Taking* Alexandra's *hand*] Thank you, dear. But I have my headache now. I——

OSCAR: [*Sharply*] Don't be stubborn, Birdie. Mr. Marshall wants you to play.

MARSHALL: Indeed I do. If your headache isn't——

BIRDIE: [*Hesitates, then gets up, pleased*] But I'd like to, sir. Very much.

[*She and* Alexandra *go to piano.* Alexandra *brings chair from* U.L. *corner to piano for herself.* Birdie *moves stool* D.S., *then takes some music from top of piano. They talk about the music for a second, then study it.* Oscar *slowly crosses* L. *to chair* L.C.]

MARSHALL: It's very remarkable how you Southern aristocrats have kept together. Kept together and kept what belonged to you.

BEN: You misunderstand, sir. Southern aristocrats have *not kept* together and have *not* kept what belonged to them.

MARSHALL: [*Laughs, indicates room*] You don't call this keeping what belongs to you?

[Oscar *sits chair* L.C.]

BEN: But we are not aristocrats. [Leo *slowly crosses* R. *to* D.R.—*listening. Points to* Birdie *at piano*] Our brother's wife is the only one of us who belongs to the Southern aristocracy.

[Birdie *selects a book of music. She opens it as* Alexandra *sits down. She is stopped by "our brother's wife," looks toward* Ben. Alexandra *looks up at her*]

MARSHALL: [*Smiles*] My information is that you people have been here, and solidly here, for a long time.

[Birdie *turns back and goes through the pages*]

OSCAR: And so we have. Since our great-grandfather.

BEN: [*Smiles*] Who was *not* an aristocrat, like Birdie's.

MARSHALL: [*A little sharply*] You make great distinctions.

[Birdie *has found the page, and looks up again on "like Birdie's."* Alexandra *turns head a little to them.* Birdie *turns back to music.* Leo *is* D.R.]

BEN: Oh, they have been made for us. And maybe they are important distinctions. [*Leans forward, intimately*] Now you take Birdie's family. When my great-grandfather came here they were the highest tone plantation owners in this state.

[Birdie *looks at them.* Alexandra *looks back to her, takes her hand, pats it*]

LEO: [*Steps to* Marshall. *Proudly*] My mother's

grandfather was *governor* of the state before the war.

[Birdie *turns back to* Alexandra]

OSCAR: They owned the plantation, Lionnet. You may have heard of it, sir?

MARSHALL: [*Laughs*] No, I've never heard of anything but brick houses on a lake, and *cotton mills.*

BEN: Lionnet in its day was the best cotton land in the South. It still brings us in a fair crop. [*Sits back*] Ah, they were great days for those people—even when I can remember. They had the best of everything. [Birdie *turns to them*] Cloth from Paris, trips to Europe, horses you can't raise any more, niggers to lift their fingers——

BIRDIE: [*Suddenly*] We were good to our people. Everybody knew that. We were better to them than——

[Marshall *looks up at* Birdie]

REGINA: [*A quick look at* Marshall, *then to* Birdie] Why, Birdie. You aren't playing.

[Marshall *has been looking curiously at* Birdie]

BEN: But when the war comes these fine gentlemen ride off and leave the cotton, *and* the women, to rot.

BIRDIE: My father was killed in the war. He was a fine soldier, Mr. Marshall. A fine man.

REGINA: Oh, certainly, Birdie. A famous soldier.

BEN: [*To* Birdie] But that isn't the tale I am telling Mr. Marshall. [*To* Marshall] Well, sir, the war ends. [Birdie *goes back to piano, puts down music, sits and is ready to play*] Lionnet is almost ruined, and the sons finish ruining it. And there were thousands like them. Why? [*Leans forward*] Because the Southern aristocrat can adapt himself to nothing. Too high-toned to try.

MARSHALL: Sometimes it is difficult to learn new ways.

[Birdie *and* Alexandra *begin to play.* Marshall *leans forward, listening*]

BEN: Perhaps, perhaps. [*All listen to music. He sees that* Marshall *is paying attention to music. Irritated, he turns to* Birdie *and* Alexandra *at piano, then back to* Marshall] You're right, Mr. Marshall. It is difficult to learn new ways. But maybe that's why it's profitable. *Our* grandfather and *our* father learned the new ways and learned how to make them pay. They work. [*Smiles nastily*] *They* are in trade. Hubbard Sons, Merchandise. Others, Birdie's family for example, look down on them. [*Settles back in chair*] To make a long story short, Lionnet now belongs to *us.* [Birdie *stops playing and turns to them*] Twenty years ago we took over their land, their cotton, and their daughter.

[Birdie *rises and stands stiffly by piano.* Marshall, *who has been watching her, rises*]

MARSHALL: May I bring you a glass of port, Mrs. Hubbard?

BIRDIE: [*Softly*] No thank you, sir. You are most polite.

[*She turns away and sits.* Alexandra *tries to* soothe her and asks her to play again. She pantomimes that she cannot, and for Alexandra to play alone]

REGINA: [*Sharply, to* Ben] You are boring Mr. Marshall with these ancient family tales.

BEN: I hope not. I hope not. I am trying to make an important point—— [*Bows to* Marshall] for our future business partner.

[Marshall *sits*]

OSCAR: [*To* Marshall] My brother always says that it's folks like us who have struggled and fought to bring to our land some of the prosperity of your land.

BEN: Some people call that patriotism.

REGINA: [*Laughs gaily*] I hope you don't find my brothers too obvious, Mr. Marshall. I'm afraid they mean that this is the time for the ladies to leave the gentlemen to talk business.

MARSHALL: [*Hastily*] Not at all. We settled everything this afternoon. [Alexandra *starts to play, alone.* Marshall *looks at his watch*] I have only a few minutes before I must leave for the train. [*Smiles at her*] And I insist they be spent with you.

REGINA: And with another glass of port.

MARSHALL: Thank you.

[Regina *looks at him, smiles, gets up, takes his glass and crosses to table* U.C. Marshall *rises when she does, then sits*]

BEN: [*To* Regina *as she passes him*] My sister is right. [*To* Marshall] I am a plain man and I am trying to say a plain thing. [*Sitting forward*] A man ain't only in business for what he can get out of it. It's got to give him something here. [*Puts hand to his breast.* Regina *pours* Marshall's *drink*] That's every bit as true for the nigger picking cotton for a silver quarter, as it is for you and me. [Regina *hands* Marshall *glass, then sits*] If it don't give him something here, then he don't pick the cotton right. [*Sits back.* Regina *crosses* D. *to sofa*] Money isn't all. Not by three shots.

MARSHALL: Really? Well, I always thought it was a great deal. [*Drinks*]

REGINA: And so did I, Mr. Marshall.

MARSHALL: [*Leans forward. Pleasantly, but with meaning*] Now you don't have to convince me that you are the right people for the deal. I wouldn't be here if you hadn't convinced me six months ago. You want the mill here, and I want it here. It isn't my business to find out *why* you want it.

BEN: To bring the machine to the cotton, and not the cotton to the machine.

MARSHALL: [*Amused*] You have a turn for neat phrases, Hubbard. Well, however grand your reasons are, mine are simple: [Leo *crosses* U.C. *to table —pours drink*] I want to make money and I believe I'll make it on you. [*As* Ben *starts to speak, he smiles*] Mind you, I have no objections to more high minded reasons. They are mighty valuable in business. It's fine to have partners who so closely follow the teachings of Christ. [*Gets up*] And now I must leave for my train.

    [*Puts his glass on table. All except* Birdie *rise.* Alexandra *stops playing*]

REGINA: I'm sorry you won't stay over with us, Mr. Marshall, but you'll come again, any time you like.

BEN: [*Motions to* Leo, *indicating bottle*] Fill them up, boy, fill them up. [Leo *moves around, filling glasses as* Ben *speaks*] Down here, sir, we have a strange custom. We drink the *last* drink for a toast. That's to prove that the Southerner is always still on his feet for the last drink. [*Picks up his glass*] It was Henry Frick, your Mr. Henry Frick, who said, "Railroads are the Rembrandts of investments." Well, *I* say "Southern cotton mills *will* be the Rembrandts of investments." So I give you the firm of Hubbard Sons and Marshall, Cotton Mills, and to it a long and prosperous life.

    [*They all pick up their glasses.* Marshall *looks at them, amused. Then he, too, lifts his glass, smiles*]

OSCAR: The children will drive you to the depot. [*Crosses to table* U.C.—*puts down glass*] Leo! Alexandra! You will drive Mr. Marshall down.

LEO: [*Eagerly, looks at* Ben *who nods*] Yes, sir. [*To* Marshall] Not often Uncle Ben lets *me* drive the horses. And a beautiful pair they are. [*Starts for hall*] Come on Zan. [*Exits*]

ALEXANDRA: [*Crosses to* Ben] May I drive tonight, Uncle Ben, please? I'd like to and——

BEN: [*Shakes his head, laughs*] In your evening clothes? Oh, no, my dear.

ALEXANDRA: But Leo, always——

    [*Stops, exits quickly*]

REGINA: I don't like to say goodbye to you, Mr. Marshall.

MARSHALL: Then we won't say goodbye. You have promised that you would come and let me show you Chicago. Do I have to make you promise again?

REGINA: [*Looks at him as he presses her hand*] I promise again.

    [Ben *crosses to hall*]

MARSHALL: [*Touches her hand again, then moves to* Birdie] Goodbye, Mrs. Hubbard.

    [Birdie *rises, crosses* C.]

BIRDIE: [*Shyly, with sweetness and dignity*] Goodbye, sir.

    [*He bows, starts toward entrance hall.* Regina *crosses to* C.]

MARSHALL: [*As he passes* Regina] Remember.

REGINA: I will.

OSCAR: We'll see you to the carriage.

    [Marshall *exits followed by* Oscar. *For a second* Regina *and* Birdie *stand looking after them. Then* Regina *throws up her arms, laughs happily*]

REGINA: And there, Birdie, goes the man who has opened the door to our future.

BIRDIE: [*Surprised at the unaccustomed friendliness*] What?

REGINA: [*Turning to her*] Our future. Yours and mine, Ben's and Oscar's, the children's——[*Looks at* Birdie's *puzzled face, laughs*] Our future! [*After a second crosses* D.L. *to* Birdie] You were charming at supper, Birdie. Mr. Marshall certainly thought so.

BIRDIE: [*Pleased*] Why, Regina. Do you think he did?

REGINA: Can't you tell when you're being admired?

BIRDIE: Oscar said I bored Mr. Marshall. [*Then quietly*] But he admired *you.* He told me so.

REGINA: What did he say?

BIRDIE: He said to me, "I hope your sister-in-law will come to Chicago. Chicago will be at her feet." He said the ladies would bow to your manner and the gentlemen to your looks.

REGINA: [*Crossing* R. *to sofa*] Did he? He seems a lonely man. Imagine being lonely with all that money. I don't think he likes his wife.

BIRDIE: Not like his wife? What a thing to say.

REGINA: [*Sits sofa* R.] She's away a great deal. He said that several times. And once he made fun of her being so social and hightoned. But that fits in all right. [*Sits back, arms on back of sofa, stretches*] Her being social, I mean. She can introduce me. It won't take long with an introduction from her.

BIRDIE: [*Bewildered*] Introduce you? In Chicago? You mean you really might go? [*Crosses* R. *to table*] Oh, Regina, you can't leave here. What about Horace?

REGINA: Don't look so scared about everything, Birdie. I'm going to live in Chicago. I've always wanted to. And now there'll be plenty of money to go with.

BIRDIE: [*Sits chair* R.C.] But Horace won't be able to move around. You know what the doctor wrote.

REGINA: There'll be millions, Birdie, millions. You know what I've always said when people told me we were rich? I said I think you should either be a nigger or a millionaire. In between, like us, what for? [*Laughs. Looks at* Birdie] But I'm not going away tomorrow, Birdie. [*Takes her arms down*] There's plenty of time to worry about Horace when he comes home. If he ever decides to come home.

BIRDIE: Will we be going to Chicago? I mean, Oscar and Leo and me?

REGINA: You? I shouldn't think so. [*Laughs. Leaning forward*] Well, we must remember tonight. It's a very important night and we mustn't forget it. We shall plan all the things we'd like to have and then we'll really have them. Make a wish, Birdie, any wish. It's bound to come true now.

    [Ben *and* Oscar *enter*]

BIRDIE: [*Laughs*] Well. Well, I don't know. Maybe. [Regina *turns to look at* Ben] Well, I guess I'd know right off what I wanted.

    [Ben *crosses to above* Regina. Oscar *stands by*

the upper window, waves to the departing carriage]

REGINA: [*Looks up at* Ben, *smiles. He smiles back at her*] Well, you did it. [*Grasps his hand*]

BEN: Looks like it might be we did.

REGINA: [*Springs up, laughs*] Looks like it! Don't pretend. [*Rises, crossing* U.C.] You're like a cat who's been licking the cream. [*Crosses to wine bottle on table* U.C.] Now we must all have a drink to celebrate.

[Ben *crosses to table* U.C.]

OSCAR: [*From window*] The children, Alexandra and Leo, make a very handsome couple, Regina. [Regina *does not look at him.* Ben *and* Regina *drink.* Oscar *steps in*] Marshall remarked himself what fine young folks they were. How well they looked together.

REGINA: [*Sharply*] Yes. You said that before, Oscar. [*She puts drink down, crosses* D. *to chair* L.C. —*sits*]

BEN: Yes, sir. [*Crossing* D.R.] It's beginning to look as if the deal's all set. I may not be a subtle man—but—— [*Turns to them. After a second*] Now somebody ask me how I know the deal is set.

OSCAR: What do you mean, Ben?

BEN: You remember I told him that down here we drink the *last* drink for a toast?

OSCAR: [*Thoughtfully*] Yes. I never heard that before.

BEN: Nobody's ever heard it before. [*Turns chair* D.R. *to face room. Stands in front of it*] God forgives those who invent what they need. [*Holding up his glass*] I already had his signature. But we've all done business with men whose word over a glass is better than a bond. Anyway it don't hurt to have both. [*He sits*]

OSCAR: [*Turns to* Regina. *Crosses* L. *to above sofa*] You understand what Ben means?

REGINA: [*Smiles*] Yes, Oscar. I understand. I understood immediately.

BEN: [*Looks at her admiringly*] Did you, Regina? Well, when he lifted his glass to drink, I closed my eyes and saw the bricks going into place.

REGINA: And *I* saw a lot more than that. [Oscar *sits sofa* R., *lights cigar, sits back to relax*]

BEN: Slowly, slowly. As yet we have only our hopes.

REGINA: Birdie and I have just been planning what we want. I know what I want. What will you want, Ben?

BEN: Caution. Don't count the chickens. [*Leans back, laughs.* Regina *laughs*] Well, God would allow us a little day dreaming. Good for the soul when you've worked hard enough to deserve it. [*Pauses*] I think I'll have a stable. For a long time I've had my good eye on Carter's in Savannah. A rich man's pleasure, the sport of kings, why not the sport of Hubbards? Why not?

REGINA: [*Smiles*] Why not? What will you have, Oscar?

OSCAR: I don't know. [*Thoughtfully—leaning forward on table*] The pleasure of seeing the bricks grow will be enough for me.

BEN: Oh, of course. Our *greatest* pleasure will be to see the bricks grow. But we are all entitled to a little side indulgence.

OSCAR: [*Looking front*] Yes, I suppose so. Well, then, I think we might take a few trips here and there, [*To* Birdie] eh, Birdie?

BIRDIE: [*Surprised at being consulted*] Yes, Oscar. I'd like that.

OSCAR: [*Looking front*] We might even make a regular trip to Jekyll Island. I've heard the Cornelly place is for sale. We might think about buying it. Make a nice change. [*To* Birdie] Do you good, Birdie, a change of climate. [*Front*] Fine shooting, on Jekyll, the best.

BIRDIE: I'd like——

OSCAR: [*Indulgently—front*] What would you like?

BIRDIE: *Two* things. Two things I'd like most.

REGINA: Two! I should like a thousand. You are modest, Birdie.

BIRDIE: [*Warmly, delighted with the unexpected interest*] I should like to have Lionnet back. I know you own it now, but I'd like to see it fixed up again, the way Mama and Papa had it. Every year it used to get a nice coat of paint—Papa was very particular about the paint—and the lawn was so smooth all the way down to the river, with the trims of zinnias and red-feather plush. And the figs and blue little plums and the scuppernongs——[*Smiles. Turns to* Regina] The organ is still there and it wouldn't cost much to fix. We could have parties for Zan, [*rises, crosses to* Regina] the way Mama used to have for me. [*Crosses* U.C., *moving about, dreamily*]

BEN: That's a pretty picture, Birdie. Might be a most pleasant way to live. [*Dismissing* Birdie] What do you want, Regina?

BIRDIE: [*Very happily, not noticing that they are no longer listening to her; crosses* D.S.] I could have a cutting garden. Just where Mama's used to be. Oh, I do think we could be happier there. Papa used to say that *nobody* had ever lost their temper at Lionnet, and *nobody* ever would. Papa would never let anybody be nasty spoken, or mean. No, sir. [*Moving about* U.C.] He just didn't like it.

BEN: What do you want, Regina?

REGINA: I'm going to Chicago. And when I'm settled there and know the right people and the right things to buy—because I certainly don't now—I shall go to *Paris* and buy them. [*Laughs*] I'm going to leave you and Oscar to count the bricks.

BIRDIE: [*Turning to* Oscar, *crosses to chair* R.C.] Oscar. Please let me have Lionnet back.

OSCAR: [*To* Regina] You are serious about moving to Chicago?

[Birdie *crosses* U. *to table* U.C., *pours drink, drinks it fast*]

BEN: She is going to see the great world and leave us in the little one. Well, we'll come and visit you and meet all the great and be proud to think you are our sister.

REGINA: [*Gaily*] Certainly. And you won't even have to learn to be subtle, Ben. Stay as you are. You will be rich and the rich don't have to be subtle.

OSCAR: But what about Alexandra? She's seventeen. Old enough to be thinking about marrying.

BIRDIE: [*Crosses* D. *to* Oscar] And, Oscar, I have one more wish. Just one more wish.

OSCAR: [*Turns*] What is it, Birdie? What are you saying?

BIRDIE: I want you to stop shooting. I mean, so much. I don't like to see animals and birds killed just for the killing. You only throw them away——

BEN: [*To* Regina] It'll take a great deal of money to live as you're planning, Regina.

REGINA: Certainly. But there'll be plenty of money. You have estimated the profits very high.

BEN: I have——

BIRDIE: [*Does not notice that* Oscar *is looking at her furiously*] And you never let anybody else shoot, and the niggers need it so much to keep from starving. It's wicked to shoot food just because you like to shoot, when poor people need it so——

BEN: [*Laughs*] I have estimated the profits very high—for myself.

REGINA: What did you say?

BIRDIE: I've always wanted to speak about it, Oscar.

OSCAR: [*Slowly, carefully*] What are you chattering about?

BIRDIE: [*Finally catches his tone, nervously*] I was talking about Lionnet and—and about your shooting——

OSCAR: You are exciting yourself.

REGINA: [*To* Ben] I didn't hear you. There was so much talking.

OSCAR: [*To* Birdie] You have been acting very childish, very excited, all evening.

BIRDIE: Regina asked me what I'd like——

REGINA: What did you say, Ben?

BIRDIE: ——now that we'll be so rich. Everybody was saying what they would like, so *I* said what *I* would like, too.

BEN: I said——[*He is interrupted by* Oscar]

OSCAR: [*To* Birdie] Very well. We've all heard you. That's enough now.

BEN: I am waiting! [*They stop. Irritated, to* Oscar] I am waiting for you to finish. You and Birdie. Four conversations are three too many. [Birdie *crosses* U.C. *slowly, sits chair* R. *of table.* Oscar *nods,* Ben *waits, sees that everything is quiet. Smiles, to* Regina] I said that I had, and I do, estimate the profits very high—for myself, and Oscar, of course.

REGINA: [*Slowly*] And what does that mean? [Ben *shrugs, looks toward* Oscar]

OSCAR: [*Looks at* Ben, *clears throat*] Well, Regina, it's like this. For forty-nine per cent Marshall will put up four hundred thousand dollars. For fifty-one

per cent—— [*Smiles archly*] a controlling interest, mind you, we will put up two hundred and twenty-five thousand dollars besides offering him certain benefits that our [*Looks at* Ben *to include him*] local position allows us to manage. Ben means that two hundred and twenty-five thousand dollars is a lot of money.

REGINA: I know the terms and I know it's a lot of money.

BEN: [*Nodding*] It is.

OSCAR: Ben means that we are ready with our two-thirds of the money. Your third, Horace's, I mean, doesn't seem to be ready. [*Raises his hand as* Regina *starts to speak*] Ben has written to Horace, I have written, and you have written. He answers. But he never mentions this business. Yet we have explained it to him in great detail, and told him the urgency. Still he never mentions it. Ben has been very patient, Regina. [*Sits back*] Naturally, you are our sister and we want you to benefit from anything we do. [*Looks at* Ben]

REGINA: [*Rises. To* Oscar] And in addition to your concern for me, you do not want control to go out of the family. [*To* Ben] That right, Ben?

BEN: That's cynical. [*Smiles*] Cynicism is only an unpleasant way of saying the truth.

OSCAR: [*Rises. Crosses* L. *to* C.] No need to be cynical. We'd have no trouble raising the third share, the share that you want to take.

REGINA: I am sure you could get the third share, the share you were saving for me. But that would give you a strange partner. [*Crosses* R. *to sofa*] And strange partners sometimes want a great deal. [*Smiles unpleasantly*] But perhaps it would be wise for you to find him.

OSCAR: [*Turns, step* C.] Now, now. Nobody says we *want* to do that. We would like to have you in and you would like to come in.

REGINA: Yes. I certainly would.

BEN: [*Laughs, puts up his hand*] But we haven't heard from Horace.

REGINA: I've given my word that Horace will put up the money. That should be enough.

[Oscar *crosses to table* D.L.—*flicks ash off cigar*]

BEN: Oh, it was enough. I took your word. But I've got to have more than your word now. The contracts will be signed this week, and Marshall will want to see our money soon after. Regina, Horace has been in Baltimore for five months. I know that you've written him to come home, and that he hasn't come.

OSCAR: It's beginning to look as if he doesn't want to come home.

REGINA: Of course he wants to come home. [*Crossing* C.] You can't move around with heart trouble at any moment you choose. You know what doctors are like once they get their hands on a case like this——

OSCAR: They can't very well keep him from answering letters, can they? [Regina *turns to* Ben] They couldn't keep him from arranging for the money if he wanted to——

REGINA: [*Crossing* R.] Has it occurred to you that Horace is also a good business man?

BEN: Certainly. He is a shrewd trader. Always has been. The bank is proof of that.

REGINA: Then, possibly, he may be keeping silent because he doesn't think he is getting enough for his money. [*Looks at* Oscar] Seventy-five thousand he has to put up. That's a lot of money, too. [*Sits sofa*]

OSCAR: Nonsense. He knows a good thing when he hears it. [*Crosses* R. *to table*] He knows that we can make *twice* the profit on cotton goods manufactured *here* than can be made in the North.

BEN: That isn't what Regina means. [*Smiles*] May I interpret you, Regina? [*To* Oscar] Regina is saying that Horace wants *more* than a third of our share.

OSCAR: [*Amazed, playing along*] But he's only putting up a third of the money. You put up a third and you get a third. What else *could* he expect?

REGINA: Well, *I* don't know. I don't know about these things. It would seem that if you put up a third you should only get a third. But then again, there's no law about it, is there? [Oscar *turns—crosses to chair* L.C.] I should think that if you knew your money was very badly needed, well, you just might say, I want more, I want a bigger share. [Oscar *turns —crosses* U. *back of sofa* L.] You *boys* have done that. I've heard you say so.

BEN: [*After a pause, laughs*] So you believe he has deliberately held out? [Oscar *crosses* D. *to chair* L.C.] For a larger share? [*Leaning forward*] Well, I *don't* believe it. But I *do* believe that's what *you* want. Am I right, Regina?

REGINA: Oh, I shouldn't like to be too definite. [Oscar *sits chair* L.C. *To* Ben] But I *could* say that I wouldn't like to persuade Horace unless he did get a larger share. I must look after his interests. It seems only natural——

OSCAR: And where would the larger share come from?

REGINA: I don't know. That's not my business. [*Giggles*] But perhaps it could come off your share, Oscar.

[Regina *and* Ben *laugh*]

OSCAR: [*Rises and wheels furiously on both of them as they laugh*] What kind of talk is this?

BEN: I haven't said a thing.

OSCAR: [*Crosses to table* R. *To* Regina] You are talking very big tonight.

REGINA: [*Stops laughing*] Am I? Well, you should know me well enough to know that I wouldn't be asking for things I didn't think I could get.

OSCAR: Listen. I don't believe you can even get Horace to come home, much less get money from him or talk quite so big about what you want.

REGINA: Oh, I can get him home.

OSCAR: Then why haven't you?

REGINA: I thought I should fight his battles for him, before he came home. Horace is a very sick man. And even if *you* don't care how sick he is, I do.

BEN: Stop this foolish squabbling. [Oscar *turns, crosses* L.C.] How *can* you get him home?

REGINA: I will send Alexandra to Baltimore. She will ask him to come home. She will say that she *wants* him to come home, and that *I* want him to come home.

BIRDIE: [*Suddenly*] Well, of course she wants him here, but he's sick and maybe he's happy where he is.

REGINA: [*As if she had not heard* Birdie, *to* Ben] You agree that he will come home if she asks him to, if she says that I miss him and want him——

BEN: [*Looks at her, smiles*] I admire you, Regina. And I agree. That's settled now, and——[*Starts to rise*]

REGINA: [*Quickly stopping him*] But before she brings him home, I want to know what he's going to get.

BEN: What do you want?

REGINA: Twice what you offered.

BEN: Well, you won't get it.

OSCAR: [*To* Regina] I think you've gone crazy.

REGINA: I don't want to fight, Ben——

BEN: I don't either. You won't get it. There isn't any chance of that. [*Roguishly*] You're holding us up, and that's not pretty, Regina, not pretty. [*Holds up his hand as he sees she is about to speak*] But we need you, and I don't want to fight. Here's what I'll do: I'll give Horace forty per cent, instead of the thirty-three and a third he really should get. I'll do that provided he is home and his money is up within two weeks. How's that?

REGINA: All right.

OSCAR: [*Crossing* C. *to* Ben] I've asked before: Where is this extra share coming from?

BEN: [*Pleasantly*] From you. From your share.

OSCAR: [*Furiously. Crosses* R. *to table* R.] From me, is it? That's just fine and dandy. That's my reward. For thirty-five years I've worked my hands to the bone for you. For thirty-five years I've done all the things you didn't want to do. And this is what I——

BEN: [*Turns slowly to look at* Oscar. Oscar *breaks off*] My, my. I am being attacked tonight on all sides. First by my sister, then by my brother. And I ain't a man who likes being attacked. I can't believe that God wants the strong to parade their strength, but I don't mind doing it, if it's got to be done. [Oscar *turns, crosses to above chair* L.C., *facing* L. *Leans back in his chair*] You ought to take these things better, Oscar. I've made you money in the past. I'm going to make you more money now. You'll be a very rich man. What's the difference to any of us if a little more goes here, a little less goes there— it's all in the family. And it will stay in the family. [Addie *enters, begins to gather the glasses from table* U.C. Oscar *turns to* Ben] So my money will go to Alexandra and Leo. They may even marry some day and——

[Addie *looks at* Ben, *then crosses to table* R., *picks up glasses, then crosses to table* U.C., *picks up tray and exits* L.]

BIRDIE: [*Rising*] Marry—Zan and Leo——

OSCAR: [*Carefully—crossing* D. *to chair* L.C.] That would make a great difference in my feelings. If they married. [*Sits chair* L.C. Birdie *sits chair* U.C.]

BEN: Yes, that's what I mean. Of course it would make a difference.

OSCAR: [*Carefully*] Is that what you mean, Regina?

REGINA: Oh, it's too far away. We'll talk about it in a few years.

OSCAR: I want to talk about it now.

BEN: [*Nods*] Naturally.

REGINA: There's a lot of things to consider. They are first cousins, and——

OSCAR: That isn't unusual. Our grandmother and grandfather were first cousins.

REGINA: [*Giggles*] And look at us.

[Ben *giggles*]

OSCAR: [*Angrily—rises, crosses* D.L.] You're both being very gay with my money.

[Oscar *pacing front piano*]

BEN: [*Sighs*] These quarrels. I dislike them so. [*Leans forward to* Regina. Oscar *stops walking at table* L. *Listens*] A marriage might be a very wise arrangement, for several reasons. And then, Oscar has given up something for you. You should try to manage something for him.

REGINA: I haven't said I was opposed to it. But Leo is a wild boy. There were those times when he took a little money from the bank and——

OSCAR: [*A step in*] That's all past history——

REGINA: Oh, I know. And I know all young men are wild. I'm only mentioning it to show you that there are considerations——

BEN: [*Irritated that she does not understand he is trying to keep* Oscar *quiet*] All right, so there are. But please assure Oscar that you will think about it very seriously.

REGINA: [*Smiles, nods*] Very well. I assure Oscar that I will think about it seriously.

OSCAR: [*Sharply*] That is not an answer.

REGINA: My, [*Rises*] you're in a bad humor and you shall put me in one. [*Crossing to* C.] I have said all that I am willing to say now. After all, Horace has to give his consent, too.

OSCAR: Horace will do what you tell him to.

REGINA: Yes, I think he will.

OSCAR: [*A step to her*] And I have your word that you will try to——

REGINA: [*Patiently. Crosses to him*] Yes, Oscar. You have my word that I will think about it. Now do leave me alone.

[*There is the sound of* Alexandra *and* Leo *opening and closing the front door*]

BIRDIE: [*Rising*] I—Alexandra is only seventeen. She——

REGINA: [*Calling. Crossing in to hall*] Alexandra? Are you back? [Birdie *sits*]

ALEXANDRA: Yes, Mama.

LEO: [*Comes into room. Crossing* D.L.] Mr. Marshall got off safe and sound. Weren't those fine clothes he had? You can always spot clothes made in a good place. Look like maybe they were done in England. [Regina *and* Alexandra *enter room*] Lots of men in the North send all the way to England for their stuff.

BEN: [*To* Leo] Were you careful driving the horses?

LEO: [*Turns to* Ben] Oh, yes sir. I was.

[Alexandra *has come in on* Ben's *question, hears the answer, looks angrily at* Leo]

ALEXANDRA: [*Crosses to* Birdie] It's a lovely night. You should have come, Aunt Birdie.

REGINA: Were you gracious to Mr. Marshall?

ALEXANDRA: I think so, Mama. I liked him. [Leo *crosses to settee* L.—*sits*]

REGINA: Good. And now I have great news for you. [Addie *enters* L. *with tray with water pitcher and glasses. Crosses to table* U.C. Alexandra *crosses to* Regina] You are going to Baltimore in the morning to bring your father home.

ALEXANDRA: [*Gasps, then delighted*] Me? Papa said I should come? That must mean—— [*Turns to* Addie] Addie, he must be well. [*Crosses to* Addie] Think of it, he'll be back home again. We'll *bring* him home.

REGINA: You are going alone, Alexandra. [*Sits sofa* R.]

ADDIE: [Alexandra *has turned in surprise*] Going alone? Going by herself? [*Crosses to above table* R.] A child that age! Mr. Horace ain't going to like Zan traipsing up there by herself.

REGINA: [*Sharply*] Go upstairs and lay out Alexandra's things.

ADDIE: He'd expect me to be along——

REGINA: I'll be up in a few minutes to tell you what to pack. [Addie *slowly begins to climb steps. To* Alexandra] I should think you'd like going alone. At your age it certainly would have delighted me. You're a strange girl, Alexandra. Addie has babied you so much.

ALEXANDRA: I only thought it would be more fun if Addie and I went together.

BIRDIE: [*Timidly*] Maybe I could go with her, Regina. I'd really like to.

REGINA: She is going alone. She is getting old enough to take some responsibilities.

OSCAR: She'd better learn now. She's almost old enough to get married. [*Jovially, to* Leo, *slapping him on shoulder*] Eh, son?

LEO: Huh?

OSCAR: [*Annoyed with* Leo *for not understanding*] Old enough to get married, you're thinking, eh?

LEO: Oh, yes, sir. [*Feebly*] Lots of girls get married at Zan's age. Look at Mary Prester and Johanna and——

REGINA: Well, she's not getting married tomorrow. But she is going to Baltimore tomorrow, so let's talk about *that*. [Oscar *turns away—crosses* U.L. *To* Alexandra] You'll be glad to have Papa home again.

ALEXANDRA: I wanted to go before, Mama. You remember that. [*Crosses* R.C.] But you said *you* couldn't go, and that *I* couldn't go alone.

REGINA: I've changed my mind. [*Too casually*] You're to tell Papa how much you missed him, and that he must come home now—for your sake. Tell him that you *need him* home.

ALEXANDRA: [*Crosses to above table* R.] Need him home? I don't understand.

REGINA: There is nothing for you to understand. You are simply to say what I have told you.

BIRDIE: [*Rises, a step* D. *to* Regina] He may be too sick. She couldn't do that——

ALEXANDRA: Yes. He may be too sick to travel. I couldn't make him think he had to come home for me, if he is too sick to——

REGINA: [*Looks at her, sharply, challengingly*] You *couldn't* do what I tell you to do, Alexandra?

ALEXANDRA: [*Looks at her quietly*] No. I couldn't. If I thought it would hurt him.

REGINA: [*After a second's silence, smiles pleasantly*] But you are doing this for Papa's own good. [*Takes* Alexandra's *hand*] You must let me be the judge of his condition. It's the best possible cure for him to come home and be taken care of here. He mustn't stay there any longer and listen to those alarmist doctors. You are doing this entirely for his sake. Tell your Papa that I want him to come home, that I miss him very much.

ALEXANDRA: [*Slowly*] Yes, Mama.

REGINA: [*To the rest. Rises*] I must go and start getting Alexandra ready now. [*Crosses* U.C. *to stairs*] Why don't you all go home?

BEN: [*Rises*] I'll attend to the railroad ticket. One of the boys will bring it over. [*Crosses* U.R. *back of sofa*] Good night, everybody. Have a nice trip, Alexandra. The food on the train is very good. The celery is so crisp. Have a good time and act like a little lady. [*He exits*]

REGINA: [*On landing*] Good night, Ben. Good night, Oscar——[*Playfully*] Don't be so glum, Oscar. It makes you look as if you had chronic indigestion. [*He does not answer*]

BIRDIE: Good night, Regina.

REGINA: Good night, Birdie. [*Exit upstairs*]

OSCAR: [*Starts for hall, to* Birdie *and* Leo] Come along.

LEO: [*As he crosses* U.R. *to* Alexandra] Imagine your not wanting to go! What a little fool you are. [*Alexandra crosses* D.L.] Wish it were me. What I could do in a place like Baltimore!

ALEXANDRA: [*Angrily, looking away from him*] Mind your business. I can guess the kind of things you could do.

LEO: [*Laughs*] Oh, no, you couldn't. [*He exits*]

REGINA: [*Calling from top of stairs*] Come on, Alexandra.

BIRDIE: [*Quickly, crossing* D.L. *to* Alexandra, *softly*] Zan.

ALEXANDRA: [*Quietly*] I don't understand about my going, Aunt Birdie. [*Shrugs*] But anyway, Papa will be home again. [*Pats* Birdie's *arm*] Don't worry about me. I can take care of myself. Really I can.

BIRDIE: [*Shakes her head, softly*] That's not what I'm worried about, Zan——

ALEXANDRA: [*Comes close to her*] What's the matter?

BIRDIE: It's about Leo——

ALEXANDRA: [*Whispering*] He beat the horses. That's why we were late getting back. We had to wait until they cooled off. He always beats the horses as if——

BIRDIE: [*Whispering frantically, holding* Alexandra's *hands*] He's my son. My own son. But you are more to me—more to me than my own child. I love you more than anybody else——

ALEXANDRA: Don't worry about the horses. I'm sorry I told you.

BIRDIE: [*Her voice rising*] I am not worrying *about the horses.* I am worrying about *you.* You are *not* going to marry Leo. I am not going to let them do that to you——

ALEXANDRA: Marry? To Leo? [*Laughs*] I wouldn't marry, Aunt Birdie. I've never even thought about it——

BIRDIE: Hush! But they have thought about it. [*Wildly*] Zan, I couldn't stand to think about such a thing. You and——

[Oscar *has come into doorway on* Alexandra's *speech. He is standing quietly, listening*]

ALEXANDRA: [*Laughs*] But I'm not going to marry. And I'm certainly not going to marry Leo.

[Oscar *takes one step into the room*]

BIRDIE: Don't you understand? They'll make you. They'll make you——

ALEXANDRA: [*Takes* Birdie's *hands, quietly, firmly*] That's foolish, Aunt Birdie. I'm grown now. Nobody can make me do anything.

BIRDIE: I just couldn't stand——

OSCAR: [*Sharply*] Birdie. [Birdie *looks up, draws quickly away from* Alexandra. *She stands rigid, fearful. Quietly*] Birdie, get your hat and coat.

ADDIE: [*Unseen calls from upstairs hallway*] Come on, baby. Your Mama's waiting for you, and she ain't nobody to keep waiting.

ALEXANDRA: All right. [*Then softly, embracing* Birdie] Good night, Aunt Birdie. [*Crosses upstairs. As she passes* Oscar] Good night, Uncle Oscar. [Birdie *begins to move slowly towards door as* Alexandra *climbs the stairs.* Alexandra *is almost out of view when* Birdie *reaches* Oscar *in doorway. As* Birdie *quickly attempts to pass him, he slaps her hard, across the face.* Birdie *cries out, puts her hand to her face. On the cry,* Alexandra *turns, begins to run down the stairs*] Aunt Birdie! What happened? What happened? I——

BIRDIE: [*Softly, without turning*] Nothing, darling. Nothing happened. [*Quickly, as if anxious to keep* Alexandra *from coming close*] Now go to bed. [Oscar *exits*] Nothing happened. [*Turns to* Alexandra, *who is holding her hand*] I only—I only twisted my ankle.

[*She goes out.* Alexandra *stands on stairs looking after her as if she were puzzled and frightened*]

MEDIUM CURTAIN

ACT II.

SCENE: *Same as* ACT I. *A week later, morning.*

AT RISE: *The light comes from the open shutter of the* R. *window; the other shutters are tightly closed.* Addie *is standing at window, looking out. Near the dining-room doors are brooms, mops, rags, etc. After a second* Oscar *comes into entrance hall, looks in the room, shivers, decides not to take his hat and coat off, comes into the room. At the sound of the door,* Addie *turns to see who has come in.*

ADDIE: [*Without interest*] Oh, it's you, Mr. Oscar.

[Addie *turns back to window, closes windows*]

OSCAR: What is this? It's not night. [*Crosses to above sofa* R.] What's the matter here? [*Shivers.* Addie *crosses to* U.W. *windows*] Fine thing at this time of the morning. Blinds all closed. [Addie *begins to open shutters. The room lights up*] Where's Miss Regina? It's cold in here. [*He crosses* C.]

ADDIE: Miss Regina ain't down yet.

OSCAR: She had any word?

ADDIE: [*Wearily, crossing* D. *to chair* D.R. *picks up feather duster*] No sir.

OSCAR: [*Crossing to settee* L.] Wouldn't you think a girl that age could get on a train at one place and have sense enough to get off at another? [*He sits settee*]

ADDIE: [*At chair* D.R.] Something must have happened. [*Crosses to sofa* R. *for broom*] If Zan say she was coming last night, she's coming last night. Unless something happened. [*Crosses* U.L.] Sure fire disgrace to let a baby like that go all that way alone to bring home a sick man without——

OSCAR: You do a lot of judging around here, Addie, eh? Judging of your white folks, I mean.

ADDIE: [*Looks at him, sighs*] I'm tired. I been up all night watching for them.

REGINA: [*Who cannot be seen. Speaking from upstairs hall*] Who's downstairs, Addie? [*She appears in a dressing gown, peers down from landing.* Addie *picks up carpet sweeper, dustpan and brush, standing* R. *of dining-room door, exits* L.] Oh, it's you,

Oscar. What are you doing here so early? I haven't been down yet. I'm not finished dressing.

OSCAR: [*Speaking up to her*] You had any word from them?

REGINA: No.

OSCAR: Then something certainly has happened. People don't just say they are arriving on Thursday night, and they haven't come by Friday morning.

REGINA: Oh, nothing has happened. Alexandra just hasn't got sense enough to send a message.

OSCAR: [*Rises, crosses* U.C.] If nothing's happened, then why aren't they here?

REGINA: You asked me that ten times last night. My, you do fret so, Oscar. Anything might have happened. They may have missed connections in Atlanta, the train may have been delayed—oh, a hundred things could have kept them.

OSCAR: [*Crosses* R.] Where's Ben?

REGINA: [*As she disappears up stairs*] Where should he be? At home, probably. Really, Oscar, I don't tuck him in his bed and I don't take him out of it. Have some coffee and don't worry so much.

OSCAR: Have some coffee? [*Crosses* U.C.] There isn't any coffee. [*Looks at his watch, shakes his head. After a second* Cal *enters with a large silver tray, coffee urn, 6 small cups, newspaper. He puts tray on table* U.C., *begins to set out cups*] Oh, there you are. [*Crosses* D.C.] Is everything in this house always late?

[*Takes off coat and hat*]

CAL: [*Looks at him surprised*] You ain't out shooting this morning, Mr. Oscar?

OSCAR: [*Places coat and hat on chair* U.C.] First day I missed since I had a head cold. First day I missed in eight years. [*Crosses* D.L., *sits on settee*]

CAL: Yes, sir. I bet you. Simon he say you had a mighty good day yesterday morning. That's what Simon say. [*Brings* Oscar *small coffee and newspaper*]

OSCAR: Pretty good, pretty good. [*Opens newspaper*]

CAL: [*Laughs, slyly, puts coffee cup on table* L. *of settee, moves table toward* Oscar] Bet you got enough bob-white and squirrel to give every nigger in town a Jesus-party. Most of 'em ain't had no meat since the cotton picking was over. Bet they'd give anything for a little piece of that meat——

OSCAR: [*Turns his head to look at* Cal] Cal, if I catch a nigger in this town going shooting, you know what's going to happen.

[Leo *enters*]

CAL: [*Hastily steps back*] Yes sir, Mr. Oscar. I didn't say nothing about nothing. It was Simon who told me and—Morning, Mr. Leo. You gentlemen having your breakfast with us here?

LEO: [*Comes immediately to* Oscar] The boys in the bank don't know a thing. They haven't had any message.

[Cal *waits for an answer, gets none, shrugs, moves to door* L., *looks back at them, exits*]

OSCAR: [*Peers at* Leo] What you doing here, son?

LEO: You told me to find out if the boys at the bank had any message from Uncle Horace or Zan—

OSCAR: I told you if they had a message to bring it here. I told you that if they didn't have a message to stay at the bank and do your work.

LEO: Oh, I guess I misunderstood.

OSCAR: You didn't misunderstand. You just were looking for any excuse to take an hour off. [Leo *crosses to table* U.C., *pours coffee*] You got to stop that kind of thing. You got to start settling down. You going to be a married man one of these days.

LEO: Yes, sir.

OSCAR: You also got to stop with that woman in Mobile. [*As* Leo *is about to speak he puts up a hand.* Leo *turns back for sugar*] You're young and I haven't got no objections to outside women. That is, I haven't got no objections so long as they don't interfere with serious things. Outside women are all right in their place, but *now* isn't their place! You got to realize that.

LEO: [*Nods*] Yes, sir. I'll tell her. She'll act all right about it. [*He drinks his coffee*]

OSCAR: Also, you got to start working harder at the bank. You got to convince your Uncle Horace you going to make a fit husband for Alexandra.

LEO: [*Crossing* D. *to back of settee* L.] What do you think has happened to them? Supposed to be here last night——[*Laughs—crosses to* C.] Bet you Uncle Ben's mighty worried. Seventy-five thousand dollars worried.

OSCAR: [*Smiles happily*] Ought to be worried. Damn well ought to be. First he don't answer the letters, then he don't come home—— [*Giggles*]

LEO: [*Crosses* L. *to chair* L.C.] What will happen if Uncle Horace don't come home or don't——?

OSCAR: Or don't put up the money? Oh, we'll get it from outside. Easy enough.

LEO: [*Surprised*] But *you* don't want outsiders. [*Sits chair* L.C.]

OSCAR: What do I care who gets my share? I been shaved already. Serve Ben right if he had to give away some of his.

LEO: Damn shame what they did to you.

[*Picks up cup to drink*]

OSCAR: [*Looking up the stairs*] Don't talk so loud. [Leo *starts to speak*] Don't you worry. When I die, you'll have as much as the rest. You might have yours *and* Alexandra's. I'm not so easily licked.

LEO: [*Smoothly*] I wasn't thinking of myself, Papa——

OSCAR: Well, you should be, you should be. It's every man's duty to think of himself.

LEO: [*Turns to* Oscar] You think Uncle Horace don't want to go in on this?

OSCAR: [*Giggles*] That's my hunch. [Leo *drinks*] He hasn't showed any signs of *loving* it yet.

[Leo *looks at empty cup*]

LEO: [*Laughs—turns front*] But he hasn't listened to Aunt Regina yet, either. Oh, he'll go along. It's

too good a thing. [*Rises*] Why wouldn't he want to? [*Crosses* U.C. *to pour another coffee*] He's got plenty and plenty to invest with. He don't even have to sell anything. Eighty-eight thousand worth of Union Pacific bonds sitting right in his safe deposit box. All he's got to do is open the box. [*Turns front*]

OSCAR: [*After a pause. Looks at his watch*] Mighty late breakfast in this fancy house. [Leo *drinks*] Yes, he's had those bonds for fifteen years. Bought them when they were low and just locked them up.

LEO: [*Nods—steps* D.C.] Yeah. Just has to open the box and take them out. That's all. Easy as easy can be. [*Laughs*] The things in that box! There's all those bonds, looking mighty fine. [Oscar *slowly puts down his newspaper and turns to* Leo] Then right next to them is a baby shoe of Zan's and a cheap old cameo on a string, and, *and*—nobody'd believe this—a piece of an old violin. Not even a whole violin. Just a piece of an old thing, a piece of a violin.

OSCAR: [*Very softly, as if he were trying to control his voice—looking at* Leo] A piece of a violin! What do you think of that!

LEO: Yes, siree. [*Crossing* R. *to table, puts cup down*] A lot of other crazy things, too. [*Turns to* Oscar *who is staring at him*] A poem, I guess it is, signed with his mother's name, and two old school books with notes and——

[Leo *catches* Oscar's *look. His voice trails off. He turns his head away*]

OSCAR: [*Very softly*] How do you know what's in the box, son?

LEO: [*Stops, draws back, frightened, realizing what he has said. Then after a second, he manages to speak*] Oh, well, well—er. [*Crossing* L. *to chair* L.C.] Well, one of the boys, sir. It was one of the boys at the bank. He took old Mander's keys. It was Joe Horns. He just up and took Mander's keys and, and—well, took the box out. [*Quickly*] Then they all asked me if I wanted to see, too. So I looked a little, I guess, but then I made them close up the box quick and I told them never——

OSCAR: [*Looks at him*] Joe Horns, you say? He opened it?

LEO: Yes, sir, yes he did. My word of honor. [*Very nervously looking away*] I suppose that don't excuse *me* for looking,— [*Looking at* Oscar] but I did make him close it up and put the keys back in Mander's drawer——

OSCAR: [*Leans forward, very softly*] Tell me the truth, Leo. I am not going to be angry with you. Did you open the box yourself?

LEO: *No sir, I didn't.* I told you I didn't. No, I——

OSCAR: [*Irritated, patient*] I am *not* going to be angry with you. [Leo *turns—crosses to table* R. *Watching* Leo *carefully*] Sometimes a young fellow deserves credit for looking round him to see what's going on. Sometimes that's a good sign in a fellow your age. [Leo *turns head to listen.* Oscar *rises*]

Many great men have made their fortune with their eyes. [*Crosses to* C.] Did you open the box?

LEO: [*Very puzzled*] No. I——

OSCAR: [*Taking a step to him*] Did you open the box? It may have been——[*Moving to* Leo] well, it may have been a good thing if you had.

LEO: [*After a long pause*] I opened it.

OSCAR: [*Quickly*] Is that the truth? [Leo *nods*] Does anybody else know that you opened it? Come, Leo, don't be afraid of speaking the truth to me.

LEO: No. Nobody knew. Nobody was in the bank when I did it. But——

OSCAR: Did your Uncle Horace ever know you opened it?

LEO: [*Shakes his head*] He only looks in it once every six months when he cuts the coupons, and sometimes Mander even does that for him. Uncle Horace don't even have the keys. Mander keeps them for him. Imagine not looking at all that. You can bet if I had the bonds, I'd watch 'em like——

OSCAR: If you had them. [*Turns front, crossing* R. *to sofa.* Leo *watches him*] If you had them. Then you could have the share in the mill, you and me. [*Turns to* Leo] A fine, big share, too. [*Pauses—shrugs*] Well, a man can't be shot for wanting to see his son get on in the world, can he, boy?

[Oscar *sits on sofa* R.]

LEO: [*Looks up, begins to understand*] No, he can't! Natural enough. [*Laughs*] But I haven't got the bonds and Uncle Horace has. And now we can just sit back and wait to be a millionaire.

OSCAR: [*Innocently*] You think your Uncle Horace likes you well enough to lend *you* the bonds if he decides not to use them himself?

LEO: Papa, it must be that you haven't had your breakfast! [*Laughs loudly*] Lend me the bonds! My God——

OSCAR: [*Disappointed*] No, I suppose not. Just a fancy of mine. A loan for three months, maybe four, easy enough for us to pay it back then. Anyway, this is only April—— [*Slowly counting the months on his fingers*] and if he doesn't look at them until Fall, he wouldn't even *miss* them out of the box.

LEO: That's it. He wouldn't even miss them. Ah, well——

OSCAR: No, sir. Wouldn't even miss them. How could he miss them if he never looks at them? [*Sighs as* Leo *stares at him*] Well, here we are sitting around waiting for him to come home and invest his money in something he hasn't lifted his hand to get. [Leo *crosses* L.C.] But I can't help thinking he's acting strange. You laugh when I say he could lend you the bonds if he's not going to use them himself. But would it hurt him?

LEO: [*Slowly looking at* Oscar] No. No, it wouldn't.

OSCAR: People *ought* to help other people. But that's not always the way it happens. [Ben *enters, hangs his coat and hat on hall tree. Very carefully*] And so sometimes you got to think of yourself. [*As* Leo *stares at him,* Ben *appears in doorway*] Morning, Ben.

BEN: [*Coming in, carrying his newspaper. Crosses to chair* R.C.] Fine, sunny morning, Any news from the runaways?

[Ben *sits chair* R.C.]

REGINA: [*On landing*] There's no news or you would have heard it. [*Coming down stairs*] Quite a convention so early in the morning, aren't you all? [*Goes to coffee urn*]

OSCAR: You rising mighty late these days. Is that the way they do things in Chicago society?

BEN: [*Looking at his paper*] Old Carter died up in Senateville. Eighty-one is a good time for us all, eh? What do you think has really happened to Horace, Regina?

REGINA: Nothing.

BEN: [*Too casually, still reading*] You don't think maybe he never started from Baltimore and never intends to start?

REGINA: [*Irritated—steps* D.] Of course they've started. Didn't I have a letter from Alexandra? What is so strange about people arriving late? [*Crosses* U. *to table—pours coffee*] He has that cousin in Savannah he's so fond of. He may have stopped to see him. They'll be along today some time, very flattered that you and Oscar are so worried about them. [*Steps* D.]

BEN: I'm a natural worrier. Especially when I am getting ready to close a business deal and one of my partners remains silent *and* invisible.

REGINA: [*Laughs*] Oh, is that it? I thought you were worried about Horace's *health*.

OSCAR: Oh, that too. Who could help but worry? *I'm* worried. This is the first day I haven't shot since my head cold.

REGINA: [*Starts toward dining room*] Then you haven't had your breakfast. Come along.

[Oscar *and* Leo *follow her.* Ben *remains seated*]

BEN: Regina. [*She turns at dining-room door*] That cousin of Horace's has been dead for years and, in any case, the train does not go through Savannah.

REGINA: [*Laughs. Then continues into dining room, seats herself, motions to* Leo *and* Oscar] Did he die? You're always remembering about people dying. [Ben *rises, leaves newspaper on table, crosses* U.L. *to dining room*] Now I intend to eat my breakfast in peace, and read my newspaper. [*Rings bell*]

BEN: [*Goes toward dining room as he talks*] This is second breakfast for me. My first was bad. Celia ain't the cook she used to be. Too old to have taste any more. If she hadn't belonged to Mama, I'd send her off to the country.

[Cal *is putting two silver serving dishes on table.*

Oscar *and* Leo *start to eat.* Ben *seats himself*]

LEO: Uncle Horace will have some tales to tell, I bet. Baltimore is a lively town.

REGINA: [*To* Cal] The grits isn't hot enough. Take it back.

CAL: Oh, yes'm. [*Calling into kitchen as he exits off dining room*] Grits didn't hold the heat. Grits didn't hold the heat.

LEO: When I was at school three of the boys and myself took a train once and went over to Baltimore. It was so big we thought we were in Europe. I was just a kid then——

REGINA: [*Looks up, helps herself from a dish*] I find it very pleasant—— [Addie *enters from* L.] to have breakfast alone. I hate chattering before I've had something hot. [Cal *has come back, closes dining-room doors*] Do be still, Leo.

[Addie *comes into the room, begins gathering up cups, carries them to the large tray, then quickly she runs into the hall. Outside there are the sounds of* Voices *and* People *moving about. A few seconds later* Addie *appears again in doorway, her arm around the shoulders of* Horace Giddens, *supporting him.* Horace *is a tall man of about forty-five. He has been good-looking, but now his face is tired and ill. He walks stiffly, as if it were an enormous effort, and carefully, as if he were unsure of his balance.* Addie *takes off his overcoat and hangs it on hall tree. She then helps him across to the chair* L.C.]

HORACE: [*As they are crossing*] How are you, Addie? How have you been?

ADDIE: I'm all right, Mr. Horace. I've just been worried about you.

[Horace *sits in chair.* Alexandra *enters. She is flushed and excited, her hat awry, her face dirty. Her arms are full of packages, but she comes quickly to* Addie]

ALEXANDRA: Now don't tell me how worried you were. We couldn't help it and there was no way to send a message.

ADDIE: [*To* Horace, *begins to take packages from* Alexandra] Yes, sir, I was mighty worried.

ALEXANDRA: We had to stop in Mobile over night. Papa—— [*Looks at him*] Papa didn't feel well. The trip was too much for him, and I made him stop and rest—— [*As* Addie *takes last package*] No, don't take that. That's Father's medicine. [*Crosses* D. *to table* R.C. Addie *puts the packages on the chair* L. *of table* U.C., *then crosses to* Alexandra] I'll hold it. It mustn't break. Now, about the stuff outside. Papa must have his wheel chair. I'll get that and the valises——

[Alexandra *starts to go, but* Addie *stops her*]

ADDIE: [*Very happy, holding* Alexandra's *arms*] Since when you got to carry your own valises? Since when I ain't old enough to hold a bottle of medicine? [Horace *coughs. Turns and steps to* Horace. Alexandra *looks at* Horace] You feel all right, Mr. Horace?

HORACE: [*Nods*] Glad to be sitting down.

ALEXANDRA: [*Opening package of medicine on table* R.C.] He doesn't feel all right. [Addie *looks at her, then at* Horace] He just says that. The trip was very hard on him, and now he must go right to bed.

ADDIE: [*Looking at him carefully*] Them fancy doctors, they give you help?

HORACE: They did their best.

LEO: [*In dining room*] Papa, can I have your part of the paper?

ALEXANDRA: [*Has become conscious of the voices in dining room*] I bet Mama was worried. I better tell her we're here now. [*She starts for door*]

HORACE: Zan. [*She stops, steps* D. *to above settee* L.] Not for a minute, dear.

ALEXANDRA: Oh, Papa, you feel bad again. I knew you did. Do you want your medicine?

HORACE: No, I don't feel that way. I'm just tired, darling. Let me rest a little.

ALEXANDRA: Yes, but Mama will be mad if I don't tell her we're here.

ADDIE: They're all in there eating breakfast.

ALEXANDRA: Oh, are they all here? [*Crosses to* Addie] Why do they *always* have to be here? I was hoping Papa wouldn't have to see anybody, that it would be nice for him and quiet.

ADDIE: [*Patting* Alexandra's *arm*] Then let your Papa rest for a minute.

HORACE: Addie, I bet your coffee's as good as ever. They don't have such good coffee up North. [*Looks hungrily at urn*] Is it as good, Addie?

[Addie *starts for coffee urn*]

ALEXANDRA: No. [*Step to* Addie—*stops her*] Dr. Reeves said not much coffee. Just now and then. [*Proudly to* Addie] I'm the nurse now, Addie.

ADDIE: You'd be a better one if you didn't look so dirty. [*Taking* Alexandra *to stairs*] Now go and take a bath, Miss Grownup. Change your linens, get out a fresh dress and give your hair a good brushing—go on——

ALEXANDRA: Will you be all right, Papa?

ADDIE: [*Slapping her backside*] Go on.

ALEXANDRA: [*On stairs, talks as she goes up*] The pills Papa must take once every four hours. [Addie *steps into room*] And the bottle only when—only if he feels very bad. [*On landing*] Now don't move until I come back and don't talk much and remember about his medicine, Addie——

ADDIE: Ring for Belle and have her help you and then I'll make you a fresh breakfast.

ALEXANDRA: [*As she disappears up stairs*] How's Aunt Birdie? Is she here?

ADDIE: [*Crosses* D.R. *of* Horace] It ain't right for you to have coffee? It will hurt you?

HORACE: [*Slowly*] Nothing can make much difference now. Get me a cup, Addie. [*She looks at him, crosses to urn, pours a cup*] Funny. They can't make coffee up North. [Addie *brings him a cup*] They don't like red pepper, either. [*He takes cup and gulps it greedily*] God, that's good. You remember how I used to drink it? Ten, twelve cups a day. [*Slight laugh as he picks up cup again. He speaks more slowly*] Addie, before I see anybody else, I want to know why *Zan* came to fetch me home.

She's tried to tell me, but she doesn't seem to know herself. [*Drinks*]

ADDIE: [*Turns away*] I don't know. [*Crosses* R. *to table*] All I know is big things are going on. [*To* Horace] Everybody going to be high-tone rich. Big rich. You too. [*Looks away—at table*] All because smoke's going to start out of a building that ain't even up yet. [*She angrily creases the medicine bottle paper on the table*]

HORACE: I've heard about it.

ADDIE: And, er—— [*Hesitates—steps to him*] And —well, Zan, she going to marry Mr. Leo in a little while.

HORACE: [*Looks at her, then very slowly*] What are you talking about?

ADDIE: [*Crossing to* R. *of* Horace] That's right. That's the talk, God help us.

HORACE: [*Angrily*] *What's* the talk?

ADDIE: I'm telling you. There's going to be a wedding—— [*Angrily clenches paper in her hand, turns head away*] Over my dead body there is.

HORACE: [*He hands cup to* Addie, *not looking at her. After a second, quietly*] Go and tell them I'm home.

ADDIE: [*Hesitates*] Now you ain't to get excited. You're to be in your bed——

HORACE: Go on, Addie. Go and say I'm back.

[Addie *takes cup and paper to tray, looking at him as he is rising, then crosses* L. *and opens dining-room doors. He rises with difficulty, stands stiff as if he were in pain facing the dining room*]

ADDIE: [*Opens doors, then stands in corner* U.L.] Miss Regina. They're home. They got here——

[*Everybody turns to look at her*]

BEN: They are?

OSCAR: Good.

LEO: Just now?

REGINA: Horace.

[Regina *quickly rises, runs into the room. Others follow her*]

REGINA: [*Warmly*] Horace! You've finally arrived. [*As she kisses him, the others come forward, all talking together*]

BEN: [*In doorway, carrying a napkin*] Well, sir, you had us all mighty worried.

[*He steps forward. They shake hands.* Addie *watches them, then exits* L.]

OSCAR: [*Crossing to above settee*] You're a sight for sore eyes.

HORACE: Hello Ben.

[Ben *crosses* R.C. Leo *enters eating biscuit*]

OSCAR: And how you feel? Tip-top, I bet, because that's the way you're looking.

HORACE: [*Coldly, irritated with* Oscar's *lie*] Hello, Oscar. Hello Leo, [Leo *steps* D. *extends hand*] how are you?

LEO: [*Shaking hands*] I'm fine, sir. But a lot better now that you're back.

REGINA: [*Steps to* Horace] Now sit down. [Leo

backs away D.L. *as* Horace *sits*] What did happen to you and where's Alexandra? I am so excited about seeing you that I almost forgot about her.

HORACE: I didn't feel good, a little weak, I guess, and we stopped overnight to rest. Zan's upstairs washing off the train dirt.

REGINA: [*Crossing above* Horace, *to his* L.] Oh, I am so sorry the trip was hard on you. I didn't think that——

HORACE: [*Sarcastically, looking around at them*] Well, it's just as if I had never been away. All of you here——

BEN: Waiting to welcome you home.

[Birdie *bursts in. She is wearing a flannel kimono and her face is flushed and excited.* Ben *crosses* D.R. *to mantel*]

BIRDIE: [*Runs to him, kisses him*] Horace!

HORACE: [*Warmly pressing her arm*] I was just wondering where you were, Birdie.

BIRDIE: [*Excited*] Oh, I would have been here. I didn't know you were back until Simon said he saw the buggy—— [*She draws back to look at him. Her face sobers*] Oh, you don't look well, Horace. No you don't.

REGINA: [*Laughs*] Birdie, what a thing to say——

HORACE: [*Looking at* Oscar] Oscar thinks I look very well.

OSCAR: [*Annoyed. Turns on* Leo] Don't stand there holding that biscuit in your hand.

[*Crosses* R. *to above chair* R.C.]

LEO: Oh. Well. I'll just finish my breakfast, Uncle Horace, and then I'll give you all the news about the bank——

[*He exits into dining room, taking newspaper from settee*]

OSCAR: [*Comes to* R. *of* Birdie] And what is that costume you have on?

BIRDIE: [*Is looking at* Horace] Now that you're home, you'll feel better. Plenty of good rest and we'll take such fine care of you—— [*Stops*] But where is Zan? [Horace *motions to staircase*] I missed her so much.

OSCAR: I asked you what is that strange costume you're parading around in?

BIRDIE: [*Nervously, backing toward stairs*] Me? [*Looks at costume—drops* Horace's *hand.* Oscar *crosses* U.R.] Oh! It's my wrapper. I was so excited about Horace I just rushed out of the house——

OSCAR: Did you come across the square dressed that way? My dear Birdie, I——

HORACE: [*To* Regina, *wearily*] Yes, it's just like old times.

REGINA: [*Quickly to* Oscar] Now no fights. This is a holiday.

BIRDIE: [*Runs quickly up stairs*] Zan! Zannie!

OSCAR: Birdie! [*She stops*]

BIRDIE: Tell Zan I'll be back in a little while. [*Exits door* R.]

REGINA: [*To* Oscar *and* Ben] Why don't you go finish your breakfast—— [*Looks at* Oscar. *He looks at* Ben, *then crosses into dining room.* Regina *crosses* D.C.] and let Horace rest for a minute?

BEN: [*Crossing to dining room.* Regina *crosses* D.R.] Never leave a meal unfinished. There are too many poor people who need the food. Mighty glad to see you home, Horace. Fine to have you back. Fine to have you back.

OSCAR: [*To* Leo *as* Ben *is closing dining-room doors*] Your mother has gone crazy. Running around the streets like a woman——

[*The moment* Regina *and* Horace *are alone, they become awkward and self-conscious*]

REGINA: [*Laughs awkwardly*] Well. Here we are. It's been a long time. [Horace *smiles*] Five months. You know, Horace, I wanted to come and be with you in the hospital, but I didn't know where my duty was. Here, or with you. But you know how much I *wanted* to come.

HORACE: That's kind of you, Regina. There was no need to come.

REGINA: Oh, but there was. Five months lying there all by yourself, no kin-folk, no friends. Don't try to tell me you didn't have a bad time of it.

HORACE: I didn't have a bad time. [*As she shakes her head, he becomes insistent*] No, I didn't, Regina. Oh, at first when I—when I heard the news about myself—but after I got used to that, I liked it there.

REGINA: You *liked* it? [*Coldly*] Isn't that strange! You liked it so well you didn't want to come home?

HORACE: That's not the way to put it. [*Then, kindly, as he sees her turn her head away*] But there I was and I got kind of used to it, kind of to like lying there and thinking. [*Smiles*] I never had much time to think before. And time's become valuable to me.

REGINA: It sounds almost like a holiday. [*Takes a step* R.]

HORACE: [*Laughs*] It was, sort of. The first holiday I've had since I was a little kid.

REGINA: And here I was thinking you were in pain and——

HORACE: [*Quietly*] I was in pain.

REGINA: And instead you were having a holiday! [*She sits chair* R.C.] A holiday of thinking. Couldn't you have done that here?

HORACE: I wanted to do it before I came here. I was thinking about us.

REGINA: About us? About you and me? Thinking about you and me after all these years? [*Unpleasantly. Rises, crosses* D.R.] You shall tell me everything you thought—some day.

HORACE: [*There is silence for a minute*] Regina. [*She turns to him*] Why did you send Zan to Baltimore?

REGINA: Why? Because I wanted you home. [*Crossing to him*] You can't make anything suspicious out of that, can you?

HORACE: I didn't mean to make anything suspicious about it. [*Hesitantly, taking her hand*] Zan

said you wanted me to come home. I was so pleased at that and touched, it made me feel good.

REGINA: [*Taking away her hand, turns*] Touched that I should want you home?

HORACE: [*Sighs*] I'm saying all the wrong things, as usual. Let's try to get along better. There isn't so much more time. Regina, what's all this crazy talk I've been hearing about Zan and Leo? [*Slight laugh*] Zan and Leo marrying?

REGINA: [*Turning to him, sharply*] Who gossips so much around here?

HORACE: [*Shocked*] Regina!

REGINA: [*Annoyed, anxious to quiet him, steps to him*] It's some foolishness that Oscar thought up. I'll explain later. I have no intention of allowing any such arrangement. It was simply a way of keeping Oscar quiet in all this business I've been writing you about——

HORACE: [*Carefully*] What has Zan to do with any business of Oscar's? Whatever it is, you had better put it out of Oscar's head immediately. You know what I think of Leo.

REGINA: But there's no need to talk about it now.

HORACE: There is no need to talk about it ever. Not as long as I live. [Regina *turns crosses* R. Horace *stops, slowly, turns to look at her*] As long as I live. I've been in a hospital for five months. Yet since I've been here you have not once asked me about—about my health. [*Then gently*] Well, I suppose they've written you. I can't live very long.

REGINA: [*Coldly*] I've never understood why people have to talk about this kind of thing. [*Crosses* U.R.]

HORACE: [*There is a silence. Then he looks up at her, his face cold*] You misunderstand. [Regina *pacing* U.R.C.] I don't intend to gossip about my sickness. I thought it was only fair to tell you. I was not asking for your sympathy.

REGINA: [*Sharply, turns to him*] What do the doctors think caused your bad heart?

HORACE: What do you mean?

REGINA: [R. *of* Horace] They didn't think it possible, did they, that your fancy women may have——?

HORACE: [*Smiles, unpleasantly*] Caused my heart to be bad? I don't think that's the best scientific theory. You don't catch heart trouble in bed.

REGINA: [*Angrily*] I didn't think you did. I only thought you might catch a bad conscience—in bed, as you say. [*Crosses* D.R.]

HORACE: I didn't tell them about my bad conscience. Or about my *fancy women.* Nor did I tell them that my wife has not wanted me in bed with her for—— [*Sharply*] How long is it, Regina? [Regina *turns to him*] Ten years? Did you bring me home for this, to make me feel guilty again? That means you want something. But you'll not make me feel guilty any more. My "thinking" has made a difference.

REGINA: I see that it has.

BEN: [*In dining room*] Put down that paper, Leo.

REGINA: [*She looks toward dining-room door. Then comes to him, her manner warm and friendly*] It's foolish for us to fight this way. I didn't mean to be unpleasant. I was stupid.

HORACE: [*Wearily*] God knows I didn't either. I came home wanting so much not to fight, and then all of a sudden there we were. I got hurt and——

REGINA: [*Hastily*] It's all my fault. I didn't ask about—your illness because I didn't want to remind you of it. Anyway I never believe doctors when they talk about——[*Brightly*] when they talk like that.

HORACE: [*Not looking at her*] Well, we'll try our best with each other. [*He rises, starts for stairs. He gets as far as chair* R.C., *when* Regina *stops him*]

REGINA: [*Quickly, crossing with him*] I'll try. Honestly, I will. Horace, [*He stops, turns to her*] Horace, I know you're tired out, but—couldn't you stay down here a few minutes longer? I want Ben to tell you something.

HORACE: Tomorrow.

REGINA: I'd like to now. It's very important to me. It's very important to all of us. [*Gaily, as she moves toward dining room*] Important to your beloved daughter. She'll be a very great heiress——

HORACE: Will she? That's nice.

REGINA: [*Opens doors*] Ben, are you finished breakfast?

HORACE: Is this the mill business I've had so many letters about?

REGINA: [*To* Ben] Horace would like to talk to you now.

HORACE: Horace would not like to talk to you now. I am very tired, Regina—— [*He starts*]

REGINA: [*Comes to him and stops him*] Please. You've said we'll try our best with each other. I'll try. Really, I will. But please do this for me now. [*Urging him into chair* R.C.] You will see what I've done while you've been away. How I watched your interests. [*Laughs gaily*] And I've done very well, too. But things can't be delayed any longer. Everything must be settled this week——[Horace *crosses —sits chair* R.C. Regina *crosses to* Ben, *who is entering. Brings him* C. Oscar *has stayed in the dining room, his head turned to watch them.* Leo *is pretending to read newspaper*] Now you must tell Horace all about it. Only be quick because he is very tired and must go to bed. [Horace *is looking up at her as if he finally understood. His face hardens as she speaks*] But I think your news will be better for him than all the medicine in the world.

BEN: [*Who is looking at* Horace] It could wait. Horace may not feel like talking today.

REGINA: What an old faker you are! You know it can't wait. You know it must be finished this week. [*Crosses* D.R.] You've been just as anxious for Horace to get here as I've been.

BEN: [*Very jovial*] I suppose I have been. And why not? Horace has done Hubbard Sons many a good turn. Why shouldn't I be anxious to help him now?

REGINA: [*Laughs*] Help him! Help him when you need him, that's what you mean. [*Sits sofa* R.]

BEN: What a woman you married, Horace! [*Laughs awkwardly when* Horace *does not answer*] Well, then I'll make it quick. You know what I've been telling you for years. How I've always said that every one of us little Southern business men had great things—— [*Extends his arm, moves his fingers*] —right beyond our finger-tips. It's been my dream: my dream to make those fingers grow longer. I'm a lucky man, Horace, a lucky man. To dream and to live to get what you've dreamed of. That's *my* idea of a lucky man. [*Looks at his fingers as his arm drops slowly*] For thirty years I've cried, bring the cotton mills to the cotton! [Horace *opens medicine bottle, pours dose into spoon*] Well, finally I got up nerve to go to the Marshall Company in Chicago.

HORACE: [*Has finally taken his eyes from* Regina] I know all this.

[*He takes medicine.* Regina *rises, steps to him*]

BEN: Can I get you something?

HORACE: Some water, please.

REGINA: [*Turns quickly*] Oh, I'm sorry. Let me. [*Crosses to tray on table* U.C. *brings him glass. He drinks as they wait in silence*] You feel all right now?

HORACE: Yes. You wrote me. I know all that. [Oscar *rises—crosses to dining-room doors*]

REGINA: [*Triumphantly*] But you don't know that in the last few days Ben has agreed to give us— you, I mean—a much larger share.

HORACE: Really? That's very generous of him. [Oscar *crosses* D. *to above settee* L.]

BEN: [*Laughs*] It wasn't so generous of me; it was smart of Regina.

REGINA: [*As if she were signalling* Horace] I explained to Ben that perhaps you hadn't answered his letters because you didn't think he was offering you enough, and that the time was getting short and you could guess how much he needed you——

HORACE: [*Smiles at her—nods*] And I could guess that he wants to keep control in the family?

REGINA: [*To* Ben, *triumphantly*] Exactly. [*To* Horace] So I did a little bargaining for you and convinced my brothers they weren't the only Hubbards who had a business sense. [*Crosses* D. *to front sofa*]

HORACE: Did you have to convince them of that? How little people know about each other! [Oscar *crosses* D.L. *slowly. Laughs*] But you'll know better about Regina next time, eh, Ben? [Ben, Regina, Horace *laugh together.* Oscar's *face is angry*] Now let's see. We're getting a bigger share. [*Looking at* Oscar] Who's getting less?

BEN: Oscar.

HORACE: Well, Oscar, you've grown very unselfish. What's happened to you?

[Leo *rises, crosses to dining-room doors*]

BEN: [*Quickly, before* Oscar *can answer*] Oscar doesn't mind. [*Crossing* U.L.] Not worth fighting about now, eh, Oscar?

OSCAR: [*Angrily*] I'll get mine in the end. You can be sure of that. I've got my son's future to think about.

HORACE: [*Sharply*] Leo? Oh, I see. [*Puts his head back, laughs.* Regina *looks at him nervously*] I am beginning to see. Everybody will get theirs.

BEN: [*Crossing* R. *to* L. *of* Horace] I knew you'd see it. Seventy-five thousand, and that seventy-five thousand will make you a million.

REGINA: [*Steps to table, leaning forward*] It will, Horace, it will.

HORACE: I believe you. [Regina *steps back, sits sofa. After a second*] Now I can understand Oscar's self-sacrifice, but what did you have to promise Marshall Company besides the money you're putting up?

[Leo *crosses* D. *to back of settee* L.]

BEN: They wouldn't take promises. They wanted guarantees.

HORACE: Of what?

BEN: [*Nods*] Water power. Free and plenty of it.

HORACE: You got them that, of course?

BEN: Cheap. You'd think the governor of a great State would make his price a little higher. [*Crossing to chair* L.C.] From pride, you know. [Horace *smiles.* Ben *smiles*] Cheap wages. [*Sits chair*] What do you mean by cheap wages, I say to Marshall? Less than Massachusetts, he says to me, and that averages eight a week. [*Leans back*] Eight a week! By God, I tell him, *I'd* work for eight a week myself. Why, there ain't a mountain white or a town nigger but wouldn't give his right arm for three silver dollars every week, eh Horace?

HORACE: Sure. And they'll take less than that when you get around to playing them off against each other. You can save a little money *that* way, Ben. [*Angrily*] And make them hate each other just a little more than they do now.

REGINA: What's all this about?

BEN: [*Laughs*] There'll be no trouble from anybody, white or black, Marshall said that to me. "What about strikes? That's all we've had in Massachusetts for the last three years." I say to him, "What's a strike? I never heard of one. Come South, Marshall. We got good folks and we don't stand for any fancy fooling."

HORACE: You're right. [*Slowly*] Well, it looks like you made a good deal for yourselves, and for Marshall, too. [Cal *has come into dining room and closes doors. To* Ben] Your father used to say he made the thousands and you boys would make the millions. I think he was right. [*Rises*]

REGINA: [*They are all looking at* Horace. *She laughs, nervously, leans forward*] Millions for *us,* too.

HORACE: Us? You and me? I don't think so. We've got enough money, Regina. We'll just sit by and watch the boys grow rich. [*Steps* U.C., *holding on to chair.* Oscar *sits on piano stool. They watch him tensely, as he begins to move toward staircase. He passes* Leo, *looks at him for a second. Brightly*] How's everything at the bank, Leo?

LEO: Fine, sir. Everything is fine.

HORACE: How are all the ladies in Mobile? [Leo *draws back.* Horace *turns, a step to* Regina, *sharply*] Whatever made you think I'd let Zan marry——?

REGINA: [*Crosses above table* R.] Do you mean that you are turning this down? Is it possible that's what you mean?

BEN: [*Nervously, but speaking with good nature —gesturing* Regina *to be quiet*] No, that's not what he means. Turning down a fortune! Horace is tired. He'd rather talk about it tomorrow——

REGINA: We can't keep putting it off this way. Oscar must be in Chicago by the end of the week with the money and contracts. [*Crosses to* Horace]

OSCAR: [*Giggles, pleased*] Yes, sir. Got to be there end of the week. [Horace *crosses* R.] No sense going without the money.

REGINA: [*Tensely*] I've waited long enough for your answer. I'm not going to wait any longer.

HORACE: [*Crossing to stairs, above* Regina, *very deliberately*] I'm very tired now, Regina.

BEN: [*Hastily*] Now Horace probably has his reasons. Things he'd like explained. Tomorrow will do. I can——

REGINA: [*Turns to* Ben, *sharply*] *I want to know his reasons now.*

[*Turns back to* Horace]

HORACE: [*As he climbs the steps*] I don't know them all myself. Let's leave it at that.

REGINA: [*Crosses* U. *to foot of stairs*] *We shall not leave it at that.* We have waited for you here like children. Waited for you to come home.

HORACE: So that you could invest my money. So this is why you wanted me home? Well, I had hoped —— [*Quietly*] If you are disappointed, Regina, I'm sorry. But I must do what I think best. We'll talk about it another day.

REGINA: We'll talk about it now. Just you and me.

HORACE: [*Stops on landing, looks down at her. His voice is tense*] Please, Regina. It's been a hard trip. I don't feel well. Please leave me alone now.

REGINA: [*Quietly*] I want to talk to you. Horace, I'm coming up.

[*He looks at her for a moment, then moves on again out of sight. She begins to climb stairs*]

BEN: [*Softly.* Regina *turns to him as he speaks*] Sometimes it is better to wait for the sun to rise again. [*She does not answer*] And sometimes, as our mother used to tell you, [Regina *starts up stairs*] it's unwise for a good-looking woman to frown. [Ben *rises, crosses* U. *to landing*] Softness and a smile do more to the heart of men——

[*She disappears.* Ben *stands looking up the*

stairs. A long silence. Then, suddenly, Oscar giggles]

OSCAR: Let us hope she'll change his mind. Let us hope.

[After a second Ben croses to table R., picks up his newspaper, continues to sofa R., sits— begins to read. Oscar looks at Ben. The silence makes Leo uncomfortable]

LEO: *[Steps R. to C.]* The paper says twenty-seven cases of Yellow Fever in New Orleans. Guess the flood waters caused it. *[Nobody pays attention]* Thought they were building levees high enough. Like the niggers always say: a man born of woman can't build nothing high enough for the Mississippi.

[Gets no answer. Gives an embarrassed laugh. Upstairs there is the sound of Voices. The Voices are not loud, but Ben, Oscar, Leo become conscious of them. Leo crosses U. to landing, looks up, listens]

REGINA: I can't understand what you mean. I can't believe that you mean to turn this down. This is what you've been waiting for, what all of us have been waiting for. You must be going crazy or you must have reasons that you are not telling us.

HORACE: I don't know my reasons. I just don't want it.

REGINA: You don't want it. But I do want it.

OSCAR: *[Pointing up]* Now just suppose she don't change his mind? Just suppose he keeps on refusing?

[Leo turns back to them, listens]

BEN: *[Without conviction]* He's tired. It was a mistake to talk to him today. He's a sick man but he isn't a crazy one.

OSCAR: *[Giggles]* But just suppose he is crazy. What then?

[Leo crosses slowly to back of sofa L.]

BEN: *[Puts down his paper, peers at Oscar]* Then we'll go outside for the money. There's plenty who would give it.

OSCAR: And plenty who will want a lot for what they give. The ones who are rich enough to give, will be smart enough to want. That means we'd be working for them, don't it, Ben?

BEN: You don't have to tell me the things I told you six months ago.

OSCAR: Oh, you're right not to worry. She'll change his mind. She always has.

[There is a silence. Suddenly Regina's voice becomes louder and sharper. All of them begin to listen now. Slowly Ben rises, goes to listen by the staircase. Oscar, watching him, smiles. As they listen Regina's voice becomes very loud. Horace's voice is no longer heard]

REGINA: People don't pass up chances like this. I won't let you pass up chances like this. I won't let you pass up this one just because you've gone crazy!

OSCAR: Maybe.

REGINA: And if you change your mind in a week, it will be too late. It's got to be done now.

HORACE: I won't change my mind. I don't want it.

REGINA: You don't want it but I do want it. I'm your wife. I have a right to expect that you will take care of my future. Of your child's future.

OSCAR: But I don't believe it. I never did believe he was going in with us.

BEN: *[Turning to him—crosses D.C.]* What the hell do you expect me to do?

OSCAR: *[Mildly]* Nothing. You done your almighty best. Nobody could blame you if the whole thing just dripped away right through our fingers. [Ben *crosses R. to sofa for paper]* You can't do a thing. But there may be something I could do for us. [Oscar *rises. Ben starts to pick up paper but is stopped by Oscar's words]* Or, I might better say, *[Crossing to C.]* Leo could do for us. [Ben *stops, turns, looks at Oscar. Leo is staring at Oscar. Turns to Leo]* Ain't that true, son? [Leo *crosses D.L.]* Ain't it true you might be able to help your own kin-folks?

LEO: *[Nervously taking a step to him]* Papa, I——

BEN: *[Slowly]* How would he help us, Oscar?

OSCAR: Leo's got a friend. *[Crosses to Ben]* Leo's friend owns eighty-eight thousand dollars in Union Pacific Bonds. [Ben *turns to look at Leo]* Leo's friend don't look at the bonds much, not for five or six months at a time.

BEN: *[After a pause]* Union Pacific. Uh, huh. Let me understand. Leo's friend would—would lend him these bonds and he——?

OSCAR: *[Nods]* Would be kind enough to lend them to us.

BEN: *[Crossing to C.]* Leo.

LEO: *[Excited, comes to him]* Yes, sir?

BEN: When would your friend be wanting the bonds back?

LEO: *[Very nervous]* I don't know. I—well, I——

OSCAR: *[Sharply—step to him]* You told me he won't look at them until fall——

LEO: Oh. That's right. But I—not till fall. Uncle Horace never——

BEN: *[Sharply]* Be still.

OSCAR: *[Smiles at Leo—crosses to C.]* Your Uncle doesn't wish to know your friend's name.

LEO: *[Starts to laugh]* That's a good one. Not know his name——

OSCAR: Shut up, Leo! [Leo *turns away slowly, moves to table L. Ben turns to Oscar]* He won't look at them again until September. That gives us five months. Leo will return the bonds in three months. And we'll have no trouble raising the money once the mills are going up. Will Marshall accept bonds?

[Ben stops to listen to sudden sharp voices from above. The voices are now very angry and very loud]

REGINA: I have a right to expect that.

HORACE: Please go away and leave me alone.

REGINA: I won't leave you alone. I demand that you put up this money and I demand that you do it immediately.

BEN: [*Then smiling*] Why not? Why not? [*Laughs —to* Oscar] Good. We are lucky. We'll take the loan from Leo's friend—I think he will make a safer partner than our sister. [*Nods toward stairs. Turns to* Leo] How soon can you get them?

LEO: Today. Right now. [*Steps to* Ben] They're in the safe deposit box and——

BEN: [*Sharply*] I don't want to know where they are.

OSCAR: [*Laughs*] We will keep it secret from you. [*Pats* Ben's *arm*]

BEN: [*Smiles*] Good. Draw a check for our part. You can take the night train for Chicago. [*To* Oscar] Well, Oscar, [*Holds out his hand—*Oscar *takes it, they shake hands*] good luck to us. [*Crosses* R. *to table*]

OSCAR: [*Turns to* Ben] Leo will be taken care of?

LEO: I'm entitled to Uncle Horace's share. I'd enjoy being a partner——

BEN: [*Turns to stare at him*] You would? You can go to hell, you little——[*Starts toward* Leo]

OSCAR: [*Nervously, stopping* Ben] Now, now. He didn't mean that. I only want to be sure he'll get something out of all this.

BEN: Of course. We'll take care of him. We won't have any trouble about that. I'll see you at the store.

OSCAR: [*Nods*] That's settled then. Come on, son. [*Starts for door*]

LEO: [*Puts out his hand—crosses to* Ben] I didn't mean just that. I was only going to say what a great day this was for me and——

[Ben *ignores his hand*]

BEN: Go on. [*Crosses* R. *to front of table.* Leo *looks at him, turns, follows* Oscar *out.* Ben *stands where he is, thinking. Again the* Voices *upstairs can be heard.* Regina's *is high and furious.* Ben *looks up, smiles, winces at the noise*]

REGINA: Nobody would turn this down. You must have your reasons. You must have reasons you won't talk about.

[*The noise of fists pounding against a door is heard, and* Alexandra's *voice*]

ALEXANDRA: Mama—Mama—don't——

[*The noise of running footsteps is heard, and* Alexandra *comes running down the steps, speaking as she comes, together with the voices upstairs*]

REGINA: What are they? What possible reasons could there be? I demand to know. All my life I've had to force you to make something out of yourself.

HORACE: Let me alone.

REGINA: I won't let you alone. If I'd let you alone you'd still be working for somebody else.

HORACE: So that's why you wanted me home?

REGINA: Yes, that's the reason.

HORACE: Then it's a bad one. Because it won't work.

REGINA: Did you think I wanted you home for yourself? Is that what you thought?

ALEXANDRA: [*Almost crying. On landing*] Uncle

Ben! [*Coming down stairs*] Uncle Ben! [Ben *crosses* U.C.] Please go up. Please make Mama stop. Uncle Ben, he's sick, he's so sick. How can Mama talk to him like that—please, make her stop. She'll——

BEN: Alexandra, you have a tender heart.

ALEXANDRA: Go on up, Uncle Ben, please——

[*Suddenly the noise from above stops, and a second later there is the sound of a door opening and then being slammed*]

BEN: Now you see. Everything is over. Don't worry. [*He starts for door.* Alexandra *crosses* D. *to above chair* L.C.] Alexandra, I want you to tell your mother how sorry I am that I had to leave. [*Crosses to hall*] And don't worry so, my dear. Married folk frequently raise their voices, unfortunately.

[*He starts to put on his hat and coat as* Regina *appears on stairs. When she speaks to* Ben, *her voice is cold and calm*]

ALEXANDRA: [*Furiously—turns, crosses* U. *to landing*] How can you treat Papa like this! He's sick. He's very sick. Don't you know that! I won't let you.

REGINA: Mind your business, Alexandra. [Alexandra *turns down to above settee* L., *facing* L. *To* Ben *on landing*] How much longer can you wait for the money?

BEN: [*Putting on his coat—steps in*] He has refused? My, that's too bad.

REGINA: He will change his mind. I'll find a way to make him. What's the longest you can wait now?

BEN: I could wait until next week. [*Steps in*] But I can't wait until next week. [*He giggles, pleased at the joke*] I could but I can't. Could and can't. Well, I must go now. I'm very late——[*He starts*]

REGINA: [*Coming downstairs toward him*] You're not going. I want to talk to you.

[*She crosses into room*]

BEN: [*Looks at her, crosses* D. *to her*] Oh, I was about to give Alexandra a message for you. I wanted to tell you that Oscar is going to Chicago tonight, so we can't be here for our usual Friday supper.

REGINA: [*Tensely*] Oscar is going to Chi—— [*Softly*] What do you mean?

BEN: Just that. Everything is settled. He's going on to deliver to Marshall——

REGINA: [*Taking a step to him*] I demand to know what—you are lying. You are trying to scare me. *You haven't got the money.* How could you have it? You can't have——[Ben *laughs*] you will wait until I——

[Horace *comes into view on landing*]

BEN: You are getting out of hand. Since when do I take orders from you? [*He turns*]

REGINA: Wait, you—— [Ben *stops.* Regina *steps to him*] How *can* he go to Chicago? Did a ghost arrive with the money? [Ben *starts for hall*] I don't believe you. Come back here. [Regina *starts after him*] Come back here, you——

[*The door slams. She stops in the doorway, staring, her fists clenched. After a pause she turns slowly and steps into the room*]

HORACE: [*Standing on landing of the stairs, very quietly*] It's a great day when you and Ben cross swords. I've been waiting for it for years.

ALEXANDRA: Papa, Papa, [*Crosses* U. *to below landing*] please go back! You will——

HORACE: And so they don't need you, and so you will not have your millions, after all?

REGINA: [*Turns slowly*] You hate to see anybody live now, don't you? You hate to think that I'm going to be alive and have what I want.

[*Comes toward stairs, looking up at him*]

HORACE: I should have known you'd think that was the reason.

REGINA: Because you're going to die and you know you're going to die.

ALEXANDRA: [*Shrilly*] Mama! Don't—Don't listen, Papa. Just don't listen. Go away——

HORACE: Not to keep you from getting what you want. Not even partly that. [*Steps down one step, holding on to rail, leaning over to look down at her*] I'm sick of you, sick of this house, sick of my life here. I'm sick of your brothers and their dirty tricks to make a dime. [Alexandra *turns away, crosses* D. *to back of settee*] There must be better ways of getting rich than cheating niggers on a pound of bacon. Why should I give you the money? [*Very angrily*] To pound the bones of this town to make dividends for you to spend? You wreck the town, you and your brothers, *you* wreck the town and live on it. Not me. Maybe it's easy for the dying to be honest. But it's not my fault I'm dying. [Addie *enters* L., *stands at door quietly*] I'll do no more harm now. I've done enough. I'll die my own way. And I'll do it without making the world any worse. I leave that to you.

REGINA: [*Looks up at him slowly, calmly*] I hope you die. I hope you die soon. [*Smiles*] I'll be waiting for you to die.

ALEXANDRA: [*Shrieking*] Papa! Don't—don't listen—don't——

ADDIE: Come here, Zan. Come out of this room.

[Alexandra *runs quickly to* Addie, *who holds her in her arms.* Horace *turns slowly and starts upstairs*]

MEDIUM CURTAIN

ACT III.

SCENE: *Same as* ACT I. *Two weeks later. It is late afternoon and it is raining.*

AT RISE: Horace *is sitting near the window in a wheel chair. On the table next to him is a safe deposit box, and one small bottle of medicine and spoon.* Birdie *and* Alexandra *are playing the piano. On the chair* R. *of table* U.C. *is a large sewing-basket.*

A phrase of the song is played before the curtain rises. As the curtain is going up the song is reaching its conclusion.

BIRDIE: [*Counting for* Alexandra] One and two and three and four. One and two and three and four. [*They finish song and laugh.* Alexandra *repeats a phrase. Nods—turns to* Horace] We used to play together, Horace. Remember?

HORACE: [*Has been looking out of window*] What, Birdie?

BIRDIE: We played together. You and me.

ALEXANDRA: [*Stops playing, looks to* Horace, *then* Birdie] Papa used to play?

BIRDIE: Indeed he did. [Addie *appears at door* L. *in a large kitchen apron. She is wiping her hands on a towel*] He played the fiddle and very well, too. [*Turns to piano and starts playing*]

ALEXANDRA: [*Turns to smile at* Horace] I never knew——

ADDIE: Where's your Mama?

ALEXANDRA: Gone to Miss Safronia's to fit her dresses.

[Addie *nods, starts to exit*]

HORACE: Addie.

ADDIE: [*Crossing to* C.] Yes, Mr. Horace.

HORACE: [*Speaks as if he had made a sudden decision*] Tell Cal to get his things. I want him to go an errand.

[Addie *nods, exits* L. Horace *moves nervously in his chair, looks out of window*]

ALEXANDRA: [*Who has been watching him*] It's too bad it's been raining all day, Papa. But you can go out in the yard tomorrow. Don't be restless.

HORACE: I'm not restless, darling.

[Alexandra *turns to piano and joins* Birdie *in playing; after playing one measure together* Birdie *stops and turns to* Horace. Alexandra *continues playing alone*]

BIRDIE: I remember so well the time we played together. [*To* Alexandra] Your Papa and me. [*To* Horace] It was the first time Oscar brought me here to supper. I had never seen all the Hubbards together before, [*To* Alexandra] and you know what a ninny I am and how shy. [*Turns to look at* Horace] You said you could play the fiddle. [*Rises, crosses to table* U.C.] and you'd be much obliged if I'd play with you. [*Pouring glass of water*] I was obliged to you, all right, all right. [*Laughs when he does not answer her*] Horace, [*Steps to him, holding glass*] you haven't heard a word I've said.

HORACE: Birdie, when did Oscar get back from Chicago?

BIRDIE: Yesterday. Hasn't he been here yet?

ALEXANDRA: [*Stops playing*] No. Neither has Uncle Ben since—since that day.

BIRDIE: Oh, [*To* Alexandra] I didn't know it was that bad. [*Turns to* Horace] Oscar never tells *me* anything——

HORACE: [*Smiles, nods*] The Hubbards have had their great quarrel. I knew it would come some day. [*Laughs*] It came.

ALEXANDRA: It came. It certainly came all right.

BIRDIE: [*Amazed*] But Oscar was in such a good humor when he got home, [Addie *enters*] I didn't—

HORACE: Yes, I can understand that.

[Addie *is carrying a large tray with three water glasses, a carafe of elderberry wine, and a plate of cookies, which she puts on the table* D.L. *Birdie hurries to* Addie, *leaving water glass on table* U.C.]

ALEXANDRA: Addie! A party! What for?

ADDIE: [*Pouring wine into the three glasses*] Nothing for, I had the fresh butter so I made the cakes, and a little elderberry does the stomach good in the rain.

[Addie *looks at* Horace, *then crosses to* C., *moves chair* R.C. *upstage, then crosses to him, moves him to* C., L. *of table* R.]

BIRDIE: [*Takes her glass and puts* Alexandra's *on piano*] Isn't this nice! A party just for us. Let's play party music, Zan.

[Alexandra *begins to play a gay piece*]

ADDIE: [*To* Horace, *wheeling his chair to* C.] Come over here, Mr. Horace, and don't be thinking so much. [*She crosses to table* L. *for* Horace's *glass, brings it to him.* Alexandra *stops playing, turns and watches him*] A glass of elderberry will do more good.

[Alexandra *reaches for another cake,* Birdie *pours herself another glass of wine*]

ALEXANDRA: [*Her mouth full*] Good cakes, Addie. It's nice here. Just us. Be nice if it could always be this way.

BIRDIE: [*Nods, happily*] Quiet and restful. [*Drinks, then crosses to piano stool, sits*]

ADDIE: [*Crossing to table* U.C., *lights lamp*] Well, it won't be that way long. Little while now, even sitting here, you'll hear the red bricks going into place. The next day the smoke'll be pushing out the chimneys [Alexandra *crosses to chair at piano, sits*] and by church time that Sunday every human born of woman will be living on chicken. [*Crossing* R. *to mantel*] That's how Mr. Ben's been telling the story.

HORACE: [*Looks at her*] They believe it that way?

ADDIE: Believe it? [*Placing footstool so that she can reach upstage lamp on mantel.* Birdie *crosses to table, pours another drink*] They use to believing what Mr. Ben orders. There ain't been so much talk around here since Sherman's army didn't come near. [*Lights upper mantel lamp*]

HORACE: [*Softly*] They are fools.

ADDIE: [*Nods*] You ain't born in the South unless you're a fool.

[Addie *moves footstool to downstage end of mantel, and lights lower mantel lamp*]

BIRDIE: [*Has drunk another glass. She has been listening to the others*] But we didn't play together after that night. [*Crosses to front settee* L.] Oscar said he didn't like me to play on the piano. [*Turns to* Alexandra] You know what he said that night?

[Addie *crosses to chair* U.C., *gets sewing-basket,*

crosses to chair D.R., *turns it to face them, sits*]

ALEXANDRA: Who?

BIRDIE: Oscar. He said that music made him nervous. He said he just sat and waited for the next note. [Alexandra *laughs*] He wasn't poking fun. He meant it. Ah, well——[*She finishes her glass, shakes her head.* Horace *looks at her, smiles. Crossing to* Horace] Your Papa don't like to admit it, but he's been mighty kind to me all these years. [*Running the back of her hand along his sleeve*] Often he'd step in when somebody said something and once—— [*She stops, turns away, her face still*] Once he stopped Oscar from——[*She stops, turns steps* U.S. *Quickly*] I'm sorry I said that. [*Crossing* L. *back of settee*] Why, here I am so happy and yet I think about bad things. [*Laughs nervously*] That's not right, now is it?

[*Crosses to table* L., *pours drink, crosses to upper end piano.* Cal *appears in the door* L. *He has on an old coat and is carrying a torn umbrella*]

ALEXANDRA: Have a cake, Cal.

CAL: [*Comes in, takes a cake*] Yes'm. You want me, Mr. Horace? [*Crosses* C. *to* L. *of* Horace]

HORACE: What time is it, Cal? [*Puts glass on table*]

CAL: Bout ten minutes before it's five.

HORACE: All right. Now you walk yourself down to the bank.

[Alexandra *starts to play softly*]

CAL: It'll be closed. Nobody'll be there but Mr. Mander, Mr. Joe Horns, Mr. Leo——

HORACE: Go in the back way. They'll be at the table, going over the day's business. [*Points to deposit box*] See that box?

CAL: [*Nods*] Yes, sir.

HORACE: You tell Mander that Mr. Horace says he's much obliged to him for bringing the box, it arrived all right.

CAL: [*Bewildered*] He know you got the box. He bring it hisself Wednesday. I opened the door to him and he say, "Hello, Cal, coming on to summer weather"——

HORACE: You say just what I tell you. Understand?

[Birdie *crosses to table* L. *pours drink, stands at table*]

CAL: No, sir. I ain't going to say I understand. I'm going down and tell a man he give you something he already know he give you, and you say "understand."

HORACE: Now, Cal——

CAL: Yes, sir. I just going to say you obliged for the box coming all right. I ain't going to understand it, but I'm going to say it——

HORACE: And tell him I want him to come over here after supper, and to bring Mr. Sol Fowler with him.

[Alexandra *playing*]

CAL: [*Nods*] He's to come after supper and bring Mr. Sol Fowler, your attorney-at-law, with him.

HORACE: [*Smiles*] That's right. Just walk right in the back room and say your piece. [*Slowly*] In front of everybody.

CAL: [*Takes step to* Horace, *then turns away* L.] Yes, sir. [*Mumbles to himself as he exits* L.]

ALEXANDRA: [*Who has been watching* Horace] Is anything the matter, Papa?

HORACE: Oh, no. Nothing.

ADDIE: [*Watching* Birdie *take another glass of wine*] Miss Birdie, that elderberry going to give you a headache spell.

BIRDIE: [*Beginning to be drunk. Gaily*] Oh, I don't think so. I don't think it will. [*Drinks*]

ALEXANDRA: [*As* Horace *puts his hand to his throat. Rises, crosses to his* L.] Do you want your medicine, Papa?

HORACE: No, no. I'm all right, darling.

BIRDIE: [*At* L. *of table* L.] Mama used to give me elderberry wine when I was a little girl. For hiccoughs. [*Laughs*] You know, I don't think people get hiccoughs anymore. Isn't that funny? [*Birdie laughs.* Horace *and* Alexandra *laugh, too*] I used to get hiccoughs just when I shouldn't have. [*Crosses to piano, sits, starts playing, drinks*]

ADDIE: [*Nods*] And nobody get growing pains no more. That is funny. Just as if there was some style in what you get. One year an ailment's stylish [*Birdie stops playing*] and the next year, it ain't.

BIRDIE: [*Turns to them*] I remember. It was my first big party, at Lionnet I mean, and I was so excited, [*Rises, crosses to table* L.] and there I was with hiccoughs and Mama laughing. [*Softly, looking at carafe*] Mama always laughed. [*Picks up carafe*] A big party, a lovely dress from Mr. Worth in Paris, France, and hiccoughs. [*Pours drink*] My brother pounding me on the back and Mama with the elderberry bottle, laughing at me. Everybody was on their way to come, and I was such a ninny, hiccoughing away. [*Drinks. Pauses*] You know, that was the first day I ever saw Oscar Hubbard. [*Crosses to* C.] The Ballongs were selling their horses and he was going there to buy. He passed and lifted his hat—we could see him from the window—and my brother, to tease Mama, said maybe we should have invited the Hubbards to the party. He said Mama didn't like them because they kept a store, and he said that was old-fashioned of her. [*Her face lights up—looking out*] And then, and *then*, I saw Mama angry for the first time in my life. She said that wasn't the reason. She said she was old-fashioned, but not that way. She said she was old-fashioned enough not to like people who killed animals they couldn't use, and who made their money charging awful interest to poor, ignorant niggers and cheating them on what they bought. She was very angry, Mama was. I had never seen her face like that. And then suddenly she laughed and said, "Look, I've frightened Birdie out of the hiccoughs." [*Her head drops, then softly*] And so she

had. They were all gone. [*Moves up to sofa* L., *sits.* Alexandra *crosses* L. *to chair* L.C.]

ADDIE: [*To her sewing*] Yeah, they got mighty well off cheating niggers. [*To them*] Well, there are people who eat the earth and eat all the people on it like in the Bible with the locusts. Then, there are people who stand around and watch them eat it. [*Softly*] Sometimes I think it ain't right to stand and watch them do it.

BIRDIE: [*Thoughtfully*] Like I say, if we could only go back to Lionnet. Everybody'd be better there. They'd be good and kind. I like people to be kind. [*Pours drink*] Don't you, Horace, don't you like people to be kind?

HORACE: Yes, Birdie.

BIRDIE: [*Very drunk now*] Yes, that was the first day I ever saw Oscar. Who would have thought——? [*Drinks. Quickly—caressing the glass*] You all want to know something? Well, I don't like Leo. My very own son, and I don't like him. [*Laughs, gaily*] My, I guess, I even like Oscar more. [*Drinks*]

ALEXANDRA: [*A step to* Birdie] Why did you marry Uncle Oscar?

ADDIE: [*Sharply*] That's no question for you to be asking.

HORACE: [*Sharply*] Why not? She's heard enough around here to ask anything.

ALEXANDRA: Aunt Birdie, why did you marry Uncle Oscar?

BIRDIE: [*Places glass on table. Pleasantly*] I don't know. I thought I liked him. He was so kind to me and I thought it was because he liked me, too. But that wasn't the reason——[*Wheels on* Alexandra] Ask why *he* married *me*! I can tell you that; he's told it to me often enough.

ADDIE: [*Leaning forward*] Miss Birdie, don't——

BIRDIE: [*Speaking very rapidly, tensely*] My family was good and the cotton on Lionnet's fields was better. Ben Hubbard wanted the cotton and [*Rises*] Oscar Hubbard married it for him. [Alexandra *crosses to* Horace] He was kind to me, then. He used to smile at me. He hasn't smiled at me since. Everybody knew that's what he married me for. [*Addie rises*] Everybody but me. [*Turns away, crosses* D.L.] Stupid, stupid me.

[Addie *puts sewing basket on chair, takes step to* Horace]

ALEXANDRA: [*To* Horace, *holding his hand, softly*] I see. [*Hesitates*] Papa, I mean—when you feel better couldn't we go away? I mean, by ourselves. Couldn't we find a way to go——

HORACE: [*Placing his hand over hers*] Yes, I know what you mean. We'll try to find a way. I promise you, darling.

ADDIE: [*Looks at them for a second, then goes* L. *to* Birdie] Rest a bit, Miss Birdie. You get talking like this you'll get a headache and——

BIRDIE: [*Sharply turning to her*] I've never had a headache in my life. [*Crosses* U.L. *Begins to cry; hysterically*] You know it as well as I do. [*Turns to

Alexandra. *Crossing to her back of settee.* Addie *crosses* U.L.] I never had a headache, Zan. That's a lie they tell for me. *I drink.* All by myself, in my own room, by myself, *I drink.* Then, when they want to hide it, they say "Birdie's got a headache again"——

ALEXANDRA: [*Comes to her, quickly*] Aunt Birdie.

[Addie *turns to look at them*]

BIRDIE: [*Turning away*] Even you won't like me now. You won't like me, any more.

ALEXANDRA: I love you. I'll always love you.

BIRDIE: [*Furiously*] Well, don't. [*Turns to* Alexandra] Don't love me. Because in twenty years you'll just be like me. They'll do all the same things to you. [*Begins to laugh, hysterically*] You know what? In twenty-two years I haven't had a whole day of happiness. Oh, a little, like today with you all. But never a single, whole day. I say to myself, if only I had one more *whole* day, then—[*The laugh stops*] And that's the way you'll be. And you'll trail after them, just like me, hoping they won't be so mean that day or say something to make you feel so bad —only you'll be worse off because you haven't got my Mama to remember——

[*Turns away, her head drops. She stands quietly, swaying a little, holding onto sofa.* Alexandra *leans down, puts her cheek on* Birdie's *arm*]

ALEXANDRA: [*To* Birdie] I guess we were all trying to make a happy day. You know, we sit around and try to pretend nothing's happened. We try to pretend we are not here. We make believe we are just by ourselves, some place else, and it doesn't seem to work. [*Kisses* Birdie's *hand, which she has been holding*] Come now, Aunt Birdie, I'll walk you home. You and me.

[*She takes* Birdie's *arm, they move slowly out. In the hallway* Alexandra *places a raincoat over* Birdie's *shoulders. They exit.* Addie *and* Horace *are silent*]

ADDIE: Well. [*Sighs*] First time I ever heard Miss Birdie say a word. [*Crossing* R. *to table* R. Horace *looks at her*] Maybe it's good for her. [*Picks up glass from table* R.] I'm just sorry Zan had to hear it. [*Takes glass to table* U.C. Horace *moves his head as if he were uncomfortable*] You feel bad, don't you? [*He shrugs*]

HORACE: So you didn't want Zan to hear? It would be nice to let her stay innocent, like Birdie at her age. Let her listen now. Let her see everything. How else is she going to know that she's got to get away? I'm trying to show her that. I'm trying, but I've only got a little time left. She can even hate me when I'm dead, if she'll only learn to hate and fear this.

ADDIE: Mr. Horace——

HORACE: Pretty soon there'll be nobody to help her but you.

ADDIE: [*Crossing to him*] What can I do?

HORACE: Take her away.

ADDIE: How can I do that? Do you think they'd let me just go away with her——?

HORACE: I'll fix it so they can't stop you when you're ready to go. You'll go, Addie?

ADDIE: [*After a second, softly*] Yes sir, I promise. [*He touches her arm, nods*]

HORACE: [*After a second, quietly*] I'm going to have Sol Fowler make me a new will. They'll make trouble, but you make Zan stand firm and Fowler'll do the rest. [*She looks at him, nods, crosses* R., *front table*] Addie, [*She turns to* Horace] I'd like to leave you something for yourself. I always wanted to.

ADDIE: [*Laughs*] Don't you do that, Mr. Horace. A nigger woman in a white man's will! I'd never get it nohow.

HORACE: I know. But upstairs in the armoire drawer there's seventeen hundred-dollar bills. It's money left from my trip. It's in an envelope with your name. It's for you.

ADDIE: Seventeen hundred-dollar bills! My God, Mr. Horace, I won't know how to count up that high. [*Shyly*] It's mighty kind and good of you. I don't know what to *say* for thanks——

CAL: [*Appears in doorway*] I'm back. [*Stands umbrella in* U.L. *corner. No answer. Crossing to* C.] I'm back.

ADDIE: [*Crossing* R. *to chair* D.R., *picks up basket, sits*] So we see.

HORACE: Well?

CAL: Nothing. I just went down and spoke my piece. Just like you told me, I say Mr. Horace he thank you mightily for the safe box arriving in good shape and he say you come right after supper to his house and bring Mr. Attorney-at-law Sol Fowler with you. Then I wipe my hands on my coat. Every time I ever told a lie in my whole life, I wipe my hands right after. Can't help doing it. Well, while I'm wiping my hands, Mr. Leo jump up and say to me "What box! What you talking about?"

HORACE: [*Smiles*] Did he?

CAL: And Mr. Leo say he got to leave a little early 'cause he got something to do. And then Mr. Mander say Mr. Leo should sit right down and finish up his work and stop acting like somebody made him Mr. President. So he sit down. Now, just like I told you, Mr. Mander was mighty surprised with the message because he knows right well he brought the box——[*Pointing to box. Sighs*] But he took it all right. Some men take everything easy and some do not.

HORACE: [*Puts his head back, laughs*] Mr. Leo was telling the truth: he *has* got something to do. I hope Mander don't keep him too long. [*Outside there is the sound of voices.* Cal *exits* R. Addie *crosses quickly to* Horace, *puts basket on table* R., *begins to wheel his chair toward the stairs. Sharply*] No. Leave me where I am.

ADDIE: [*Step* D. *to his* L.] But that's Miss Regina coming back.

HORACE: [*Nods, looking at door*] Go away, Addie.

ADDIE: [*Hesitates*] Mr. Horace. Don't talk no more today. You don't feel well and it won't do you no good——

HORACE: [*As he hears footsteps in the hall*] Go on. [*She looks at him for a second, then picks up her sewing from table* R. *and exits* L. *as Regina comes in from hall. Horace's chair is now so placed that he is in front of table with the medicine. Regina stands in the hall, shakes umbrella, stands it in* U.R. *corner, takes off her cloak and throws it over bannister. She stares at* Horace]

REGINA: [*As she takes off her gloves, crossing to* C.] We had agreed that you were to stay in your part of this house and I in mine. This room is *my* part of the house. Please don't come down here again.

HORACE: I won't.

REGINA: [*Crosses* D.R. *toward bell-cord below mantel*] I'll get Cal to take you upstairs.

HORACE: [*Smiles*] Before you do I want to tell you that after all, we have invested our money in Hubbard, Sons and Marshall, Cotton Manufacturers.

REGINA: [*Stops, turns, stares at him*] What are you talking about? You haven't seen Ben—When did you change your mind?

HORACE: I didn't change my mind. *I* didn't invest the money. [*Smiles at the expression on her face*] It was invested for me.

REGINA: [*Angrily*] What——?

HORACE: I had eighty-eight thousand dollars' worth of Union Pacific bonds in that safe deposit box. They are not there now. Go and look. [*As she stares at him. Points to box*] Go and look, Regina. [*She crosses quickly to box, opens it. He speaks when she is at table*] Those bonds are as negotiable as money. [*She closes box*]

REGINA: [*Turns back to him*] What kind of joke are you playing now? Is this for my benefit?

HORACE: I don't look in that box very often, but three days ago, on Wednesday it was, because I had made a decision——

REGINA: I want to know what you are talking about.

HORACE: [*Sharply*] Don't interrupt me again. [Regina *stiffens*] Because I had made a decision, I sent for the box. The bonds were gone. Eighty-eight thousand dollars gone. [*He smiles at her*]

REGINA: [*After a moment's silence, quietly crossing* U.C.] Do you think I'm crazy enough to believe what you're saying?

HORACE: [*Shrugs*] Believe anything you like.

REGINA: [*Stares at him, slowly*] Where did they go to?

HORACE: They are in Chicago. With Mr. Marshall, I should guess.

REGINA: [*Crossing* D. *to chair* L.C.] What did they do? Walk to Chicago? Have you really gone crazy?

HORACE: Leo took the bonds.

REGINA: [*Turns sharply, then speaks softly, without conviction*] I don't believe it,

HORACE: [*Leans forward*] I wasn't there but I can guess what happened. [Regina *sits chair* L.C.] This fine gentleman, to whom you were willing to marry your daughter, took the keys and opened the box. You remember that the day of the fight, Oscar went to Chicago? Well, he went with my bonds that his son Leo had stolen for him. [*Pleasantly*] And for Ben, of course, too.

REGINA: [*Slowly, nods*] When did you find out the bonds were gone?

HORACE: Wednesday night.

REGINA: I thought that's what you said. Why have you waited three days to do anything? [*Suddenly laughs*] This *will* make a fine story.

HORACE: [*Nods*] Couldn't it?

REGINA: [*Still laughing. Rises, crosses* U.L.—*takes off hat*] A fine story to hold over their heads. How could they be such fools? [*Turns to him back of settee*]

HORACE: But I'm not going to hold it over their heads.

REGINA: [*The laugh stops*] What?

HORACE: [*Turns his chair to face* L.] I'm going to let them keep the bonds—as a loan from you. An eighty-eight thousand dollar loan; they should be grateful to you. They will be, I think.

REGINA: [*Slowly, smiles*] I see. You are punishing me. But I won't let you punish me. If you won't do anything, I will. Now. [*She starts for door*]

HORACE: You won't do anything. Because you can't. [Regina *stops above chair* R.C.] It won't do you any good to make trouble because I shall simply say that I lent them the bonds.

REGINA: [*Slowly*] You would do that?

HORACE: Yes. [Regina *crosses* D. *to chair* L.C.] For once in your life I am tying your hands. There is nothing for you to do.

[*There is silence. Then she sits down*]

REGINA: I see. You are going to lend them the bonds and let them keep all the profit they make on them, and there is nothing I can do about it. Is that right?

HORACE: Yes.

REGINA: [*Softly*] Why did you say that I was making this gift?

HORACE: I was coming to that. I am going to make a new will, Regina, leaving you eighty-eight thousand dollars in Union Pacific bonds. The rest will go to Zan. It's true that your brothers have borrowed your share for a little while. After my death I advise you to talk to Ben and Oscar. They won't admit anything and Ben, I think, will be smart enough to see that he's *safe*. Because I knew about the theft and said nothing. Nor *will* I say anything as long as I live. Is that clear to you?

REGINA: [*Nods, softly, without looking at him*] You will not say anything as long as you live.

HORACE: That's right. And by that time they will probably have replaced your bonds, and then they'll belong to you and nobody but us will ever know what happened. [*Stops, smiles*] They'll be around any minute to see what I am going to do. I took good care to see that word reached Leo. They'll be mighty relieved to know I'm going to do nothing and Ben will think it all a capital joke on you. And that will be the end of that. There's nothing you can do to them, nothing you can do to me.

REGINA: You hate me very much.

HORACE: No.

REGINA: Oh, I think you do. [*Puts her head back, sighs*] Well, we haven't been very good together. Anyway, I don't hate you either. I have only contempt for you. I've always had.

HORACE: From the very first?

REGINA: I think so.

HORACE: I was in love with *you*. But why did *you* marry *me*?

REGINA: I was lonely when I was young.

HORACE: *You* were lonely?

REGINA: Not the way people usually mean. Lonely for all the things I wasn't going to get. Everybody in this house was so busy and there was so little place for what I wanted. I wanted the world. Then, and then—— [*Smiles*] Papa died and left the money to Ben and Oscar.

HORACE: And you married me?

REGINA: Yes, I thought—but I was wrong. You were a small-town clerk then. You haven't changed.

HORACE: [*Nods, smiles*] And that wasn't what you wanted.

REGINA: No. No, it wasn't what I wanted. [*Pauses, leans back, pleasantly*] It took me a little while to find out I had made a mistake. As for you—I don't know. It was almost as if I couldn't stand the kind of man you were. [*Smiles, softly*] I used to lie there at night, praying you wouldn't come near—

HORACE: Really? It was as bad as that?

REGINA: [*Nods*] Remember when I went to Doctor Sloan and I told you he said there was something the matter with me and that you shouldn't touch me any more?

HORACE: I remember.

REGINA: But you believed it? I couldn't understand that. I couldn't understand that anybody could be such a soft fool. That was when I began to despise you.

HORACE: [*Puts his hand to his throat, glances around at bottle of medicine on table, then to her*] Why didn't you leave me?

REGINA: I told you I married you *for* something. It turned out it was only for this. [*Carefully*] This wasn't what I wanted, but it was something. I never thought about it much, but if I had, [*Horace puts his hand to his throat*] I'd have known that you would die before I would. But I couldn't have known that you would get heart trouble so early and so bad. I'm lucky, Horace. I've always been lucky. [*Horace turns slowly to medicine*] I'll be lucky again.

[*Horace looks at her. Then he puts his hand to his throat. Because he cannot reach the bottle*

he moves the chair closer. He reaches for medicine, takes out cork, picks up spoon, tries to pour some in the spoon, the bottle slips out of his shaking fingers and crashes on the table. He draws in his breath, gasps*]

HORACE: Please. Tell Addie—the other bottle is upstairs. [*She has not moved. She does not move now. He stares at her. Then, suddenly as if he understood, he raises his voice. It is a panic-stricken whisper, too small to be heard outside the room*] Addie! Addie! Come——

[*Stops as he hears the softness of his voice. He makes a sudden, furious spring from the chair to the stairs, taking the first few steps as if he were a desperate runner. On the fourth step he slips, gasps, grasps the rail, makes a great effort to reach the landing. When he reaches the landing, he is on his knees. His knees give way, he falls on the landing, out of view. Regina has not turned during his climb up the stairs. Now she waits a second. Then she goes below the landing, speaks up*]

REGINA: Horace. [*When there is no answer, she turns, crosses to door L., opens door, calls*] Addie! Cal! Come in here. [*Crosses R. Starts up the steps. When she is on first step, Addie appears, followed by Cal. Both run toward stairs*] He's had an attack. Come up here.

[*They run up steps quickly, passing Regina*]

CAL: My God! Mr. Horace——

REGINA: [*They cannot be seen now. Her voice comes from the head of the stairs*] Be still, Cal. Bring him in here.

[*Before the footsteps and voices have completely died away, Alexandra appears in hall door, in her raincloak and hood. She comes into the room, begins to unfasten the cloak, suddenly looks around, sees the empty wheelchair, stares, begins to move swiftly as if to look in the dining room. At the same moment, Addie runs down the stairs. She turns and stares up at Addie*]

ALEXANDRA: Addie! What?

ADDIE: [*Takes Alexandra by the shoulders*] I'm going for the doctor. Go upstairs.

[*Alexandra looks at her, then quickly breaks away and runs up the steps. Addie exits L. The stage is empty for a minute. Then the front door bell begins to ring. When there is no answer it rings again. A second later Leo appears in the hall, talking as he comes in*]

LEO: [*Very nervous*] Hello. [*Irritably*] Never saw any use ringing a bell when a door was open. If you are going to ring a bell, then somebody should answer it. [*Gets in the room, looks around, puzzled, listens, hears no sound*] Aunt Regina. [*Puts hat on sofa R. No answer. He moves around restlessly, crossing L.*] Addie. [*Waits, turns crossing C.*] Where the hell——? [*Crosses D.R. to bell cord, rings it im-*

patiently, twice, waits and gets no answer; calls] Cal! [*Rings again, then calls*] Cal——

[*After a second* Cal *appears on stair landing*]

CAL: [*His voice is soft, shaken*] Mr. Leo. Miss Regina says you stop that screaming noise.

LEO: [*Angrily crosses to table* R.] Where is everybody?

CAL: Mr. Horace he got an attack. He's bad. Miss Regina says you stop that noise.

LEO: Uncle Horace—What—— [*Crosses* U.C.]—What happened? [Cal *starts down stairs. Cal shakes his head, begins to move swiftly* L. *off.* Leo *looks around wildly*] But when—You seen Mr. Oscar or Mr. Ben? [Cal *shakes his head. Moves on.* Leo *grabs him by the arm*] Answer me, will you?

CAL: No ain't seen 'em. I ain't got time to answer you. [Cal *breaks* Leo's *hold, crosses* L.] I got to get things. [Cal *exits*]

LEO: But what's the matter with him? When did this happen——? [*Crossing to door* L., *calling after* Cal] You'd think Papa'd be some place where you could find him. I been chasing him all afternoon.

[Oscar *and* Ben *come swiftly into the room, talking excitedly*]

OSCAR: I hope it's not a bad attack.

BEN: It's the first one he's had since he come home.

[Leo *crosses to* Oscar, *excitedly*]

LEO: Papa, I've been looking all over town for you and Uncle Ben——

BEN: Where is he?

OSCAR: Addie said it was sudden.

BEN: [*To* Leo] Where is he? When did it happen?

LEO: Upstairs. Will you listen to me, please? I been looking for you for——

OSCAR: [*To* Ben] You think we should go up?

[Ben, *looking up the steps, shakes his head*]

BEN: I don't know. I don't know.

OSCAR: [*Shakes his head*] But he was all right——

LEO: [*Almost yelling—turns, crosses* D. *to front chair* L.C.] Will you listen to me?

OSCAR: [*Sharply—crossing* D. *to* Leo] What is the matter with you?

LEO: [*Coming to him*] I been trying to tell you. I been trying to find you for an hour——

OSCAR: Tell me what?

LEO: Uncle Horace knows about the bonds. He knows about them. He's had the box since Wednesday——

BEN: [*Sharply*] Stop shouting! [*Crosses* D.C. *to him*] What the hell are you talking about?

LEO: [*Furiously. Crossing to* Ben] I'm telling you he knows about the bonds. Ain't that clear enough——?

OSCAR: [*Grabbing* Leo's *arm*] You God damn fool! Stop screaming!

BEN: Now what happened? Talk quietly.

LEO: [*Closes his eyes, angrily attempted patience*] You heard me. Uncle Horace knows about the bonds. He's known since Wednesday.

BEN: [*After a second.* Oscar *draws close to them*] How do you know that?

LEO: Because Cal comes down to Mander and says the box came O. K. and——

OSCAR: [*Trembling, crosses to* Ben, *pushing* Leo *away* L.] That might not mean a thing——

LEO: [*Angrily steps* D. *to* L. *of* Oscar] No? It might not, huh? [*Takes* Oscar's *arm.* Oscar *turns to him*] Then he says Mander should come here tonight and bring Sol Fowler with him. [Ben *crosses* R. *to* R. *of table*] I guess that don't mean a thing either. [Leo *turns—crosses* D.L.]

OSCAR: [*Panicky, to* Ben] Ben—What—Do you think he's seen the——

BEN: [*Motions to box*] There's the box. [*Both* Oscar *and* Leo *turn sharply.* Leo *makes a leap to the box, crossing* R. *back of* Oscar, *picks up box*] You ass. Put it down. What are you going to do with it, eat it?

LEO: I'm going to—— [*Starts*]

BEN: [*Furiously*] Put it down. Don't touch it again. Now sit down and shut up for a minute.

[Leo *puts box down on table*]

OSCAR: [*Crossing to* Leo] Since Wednesday. [*To* Leo] You said he had it since Wednesday. Why didn't he say something——[*To* Ben] I don't understand——

LEO: [*Taking a step* R.] I can put it back. I can put it back before anybody knows.

BEN: [*Who is standing at the table* R., *softly*] He's had it since Wednesday. Yet he hasn't said a word to us.

OSCAR: *Why? Why?*

LEO: What's the difference why? He was getting ready to say plenty. He was going to say it to Fowler tonight——

OSCAR: [*Angrily*] Be still. [*Turns to* Ben, *looks at him, waits*]

BEN: [*After a moment*] I don't believe that.

LEO: [*Wildly, leaning toward* Ben *over table*] You don't believe it? What do I care what *you* believe? I do the dirty work and then——

BEN: [*Turning his head sharply to* Leo] I'm remembering that. I'm remembering that, Leo.

OSCAR: [*A step* D.] What do you mean?

LEO: You——

BEN: [*To* Oscar] If you don't shut that little fool up, I'll show you what I mean. [Oscar *makes a gesture at* Leo. Leo *crosses* U.C.] For some reason he knows, but he don't say a word.

OSCAR: [*Crossing to* Ben] Maybe he didn't know that *we*——

BEN: [*Quickly*] That *Leo*——? [*Crosses* C.] He's no fool. [*Crossing up to* Leo] Does Mander know the bonds are missing?

LEO: How could I tell? I was half crazy. I don't think so. Because Mander seemed kind of puzzled and——

OSCAR: But we got to find out——

[*He breaks off as* Cal *comes into the room*

carrying a kettle of hot water and clean cloths, leaving door open. They turn to Cal. Leo, startled, crosses U.L. to back settee]

BEN: [*Crosses to above chair* L.] How is he, Cal?

CAL: I don't know, Mr. Ben. He was bad. [*Going toward stairs*]

OSCAR: [*Crosses* L. *to chair* L.] But when did it happen?

CAL: [*Shrugs*] He wasn't feeling so bad early. [*Addie comes in quickly from hall*] Then there he is next thing on the landing, fallen over, his eyes tight ——[*He hurries toward stairs*]

ADDIE: [*To* Cal] Dr. Sloan's over at the Ballongs. Hitch the buggy and go get him. [*She takes kettle and cloths from him, pushes him, runs up stairs*] Go on. [*She disappears*]

[*Cal exits* L., *picking up his umbrella as he goes.* Oscar *crosses* D.R.]

BEN: [*Takes off coat and hat, places them on chair* U.C.] Never seen Sloan anywhere when you need him.

OSCAR: [*Softly*] Sounds bad.

LEO: [*Taking a step to* Ben] He would have told *her* about it. Aunt Regina. He would have told his own wife——

BEN: [*Turning to* Leo] Yes, he might have told her. [*Crossing, to front wheel-chair*] But they weren't on such pretty terms and maybe he didn't. Maybe he didn't. [*Goes quickly to* Leo] Now, listen to me. If she doesn't know, it may work out all right. [*Holding* Leo's *lapel*] If she does know, you're to say he lent you the bonds.

LEO: Lent them to me! Who's going to believe that?

BEN: Nobody.

OSCAR: [*To* Leo, *crossing to* Ben] Don't you understand? It can't do no harm to say it—— [Ben *releases grip on* Leo's *lapel*]

LEO: Why should I say he lent them to me? Why not to you? [*Carefully*] Why not to Uncle Ben?

BEN: [*Smiles*] Just because he didn't lend them to me. Remember that.

LEO: But all he has to do is say he didn't lend them to me——

BEN: [*Furiously*] But for some reason, he doesn't seem to be talking, does he?

[*There are footsteps above. They all stand looking at the stairs.* Regina *begins to come slowly down*]

BEN: [*Crosses* U.R., *to* Regina] What happened?

REGINA: He's had a bad attack. [*Crosses* D.C.]

OSCAR: Too bad. I'm so sorry we weren't here when—when Horace needed us.

BEN: [*Crosses* D.C.] When *you* needed us.

REGINA: [*At chair* L.C. *Looks at him*] Yes.

BEN: How is he? Can we—can we go up?

REGINA: [*Shakes her head*] He's not conscious.

OSCAR: [*Pacing around*] It's that—it's that bad? [*Turns, crosses* D.R.] Wouldn't you think Sloan could be found quickly, just once, just once?

REGINA: I don't think there is much for him to do.

BEN: [*Crossing to* Regina] Oh, don't talk like that. He's come through attacks before. He will now.

[Regina *sits down, chair* L.C. *After a second she speaks softly.* Leo *crosses* R. *to above table* R.]

REGINA: Well. We haven't seen each other since the day of our fight.

BEN: [*Tenderly*] That was nothing. Why, you and Oscar and I used to fight when we were kids.

OSCAR: [*Hurriedly taking a step* L.] Don't you think we should go up? Is there anything we can do for Horace——

BEN: You don't feel well. Ah——

REGINA: [*Without looking at them*] No, I don't. [*Slight pause*] Horace told me about the bonds this afternoon.

[*There is an immediate shocked silence*]

LEO: [*Taking several short steps to* L. *of table* R.] The bonds. What do you mean? What bonds? What——?

OSCAR: [*Looks at him furiously. Then to* Regina] The Union Pacific bonds? *Horace's* Union Pacific Bonds?

REGINA: Yes.

OSCAR: [*Steps to her, very nervously*] Well. Well what—what about them? What—what could he say?

REGINA: He said that Leo had stolen the bonds and given them to you.

OSCAR: [*Aghast, very loudly*] That's ridiculous. Regina, absolutely——

LEO: I don't know what you're talking about What would I—why——

REGINA: [*Wearily to* Ben] Isn't it enough that he stole them from me? Do I have to listen to this in the bargain?

OSCAR: You are talking——

LEO: I didn't steal anything. I don't know why——

REGINA: [*To* Ben] Would you ask them to stop that, please?

[*There is silence for a minute.* Ben *glowers at* Oscar *and* Leo, Leo *looks at* Oscar]

BEN: Aren't we starting at the wrong end, Regina? What did Horace tell you?

REGINA: [*Smiles at him*] He told me that Leo had stolen the bonds.

LEO: [*To* Ben] I didn't steal——

REGINA: Please. Let me finish. [Leo *crosses* R. *slowly*] Then he told me that he was going to pretend that he had lent them to you [Leo *turns sharply to* Regina, *then looks at* Oscar, *then looks back at* Regina] as a present from me to my brothers. He said there was nothing I could do about it. He said the rest of his money would go to Alexandra. That is all.

[*There is a silence.* Oscar *coughs,* Leo *smiles slyly*]

LEO: [*Taking a step to her*] I told you he had lent them—I could have told you——

REGINA: [*Ignores him, smiles sadly at* Ben] So I'm

very badly off, you see. [*Carefully*] But Horace said there was nothing I could do about it as long as he was alive to say he had lent you the bonds.

BEN: You shouldn't feel that way. It can all be explained, all be adjusted. It isn't as bad——

REGINA: So you, at least, are willing to admit that the bonds were stolen?

BEN: [Oscar *laughs nervously*] I admit no such thing. It's possible that Horace made up that part of the story to tease you—— [*Looks at her*] Or perhaps to punish you. Punish you.

REGINA: [*Sadly*] It's not a pleasant story. I feel bad, Ben, naturally. I hadn't thought——

BEN: Now you shall have the bonds safely back. That was the understanding, wasn't it, Oscar?

OSCAR: [*Crossing to* C.] Yes.

REGINA: I'm glad to know that. [*Smiles*] Ah, I had greater hopes——

BEN: Don't talk that way. That's foolish. [*Looks at his watch*] I think we ought to drive out for Sloan ourselves. [*Looks at* Oscar] If we can't find him we'll go over to Senateville for Doctor Morris. [*Looks at her.* Oscar *crosses* U. *to chair* R.C. *for hat,* Leo *crosses* U. *back of sofa to hall, picking up hat*] And don't think I'm dismissing this other business. I'm not. We'll have it all out on a more appropriate day.

[Ben *crosses* U. *to chair* U.C. *for coat and hat*]

REGINA: [*Waits until they are near the door. Looks up, quietly*] I don't think you had better go yet. I think you had better stay and sit down. [Oscar *crosses to hall*]

BEN: [*Picking up coat and hat*] We'll be back with Sloan.

REGINA: Cal has gone for him. I don't want you to go.

[Oscar *turns, looks at them*]

BEN: [*Crossing* U.C.] Now don't worry and——

REGINA: You will come back in this room and sit down. I have something more to say.

[Leo *steps back into view*]

BEN: [*Turns, comes toward her to* C.] Since when do I take orders from you?

REGINA: [*Smiles*] You don't—yet. [Oscar *takes a step in. Sharply*] Come back, Oscar. You too, Leo.

OSCAR: [*Takes another step in. Sure of himself, laughs*] My dear Regina——

BEN: [*Crosses to her. Softly, pats her hand*] Horace has already clipped your wings and very wittily. Do I have to clip them, too? [*Smiles at her*] You'd get farther with a smile, Regina. I'm a soft man for a woman's smile.

REGINA: I'm smiling, Ben. I'm smiling because you are quite safe while Horace lives. But I don't think Horace will live. [Leo *looks at* Oscar. *To* Ben] And if he doesn't live I shall want seventy-five per cent in exchange for the bonds.

BEN: [*Steps back. Whistles, laughs*] Greedy! What a greedy girl you are! You want so much of everything.

REGINA: Yes. And if I don't get what I want I am going to put all three of you in jail.

OSCAR: [*Crosses* L. *to* R. *of* Regina, *furiously*] You're mighty crazy. Having just admitted—— [Leo *steps* D.]

BEN: And on what evidence would you put Oscar and Leo in jail?

REGINA: [*Laughs, gaily*] Oscar, listen to him. He's getting ready to swear that it was you and Leo! What do you say to that? [*As* Oscar *turns furiously toward* Ben] Oh, don't be angry, Oscar. I'm going to see that he goes in with you.

[Oscar *turns, steps* U.C.]

BEN: Try anything you like, Regina. [*Steps to* Regina. Oscar *crosses* U.R. *Sharply*] And now we can stop all this and say goodbye to you. [Alexandra *comes into view on landing, moving slowly down steps*] It's his money and he's obviously willing to let us borrow it. [*More pleasantly.* Leo *slowly crosses* U. *to hall*] Learn to make threats when you can carry them through: for how many years have I told you a good-looking woman gets more by being soft and appealing? Mama used to tell you that. [*Looks at his watch*] Where the hell is Sloan? [*To* Oscar] Take the buggy and——

[*As* Ben *turns to* Oscar, *he sees* Alexandra *and stops.* Oscar *turns to her.* Alexandra *has come slowly down the steps. She walks stiffly. She comes down as if she did not see any of them. She goes slowly to lower window, her head bent. They all turn to look at her*]

OSCAR: [*After a second, moving toward her above sofa*] What? Alexandra——

[*She does not answer. After a second* Addie *comes slowly down the stairs, moving as if she were very tired. At foot of steps, she looks at* Alexandra, *then turns and slowly crosses to door* L. *and exits.* Regina *rises. She sees* Addie. Ben *looks nervously at* Alexandra, *at* Regina]

OSCAR: [*As* Addie *passes him, irritably to* Alexandra] Well, what is—— [*Turns into room—sees* Addie *at foot of steps*] what's?—[Ben *puts up a hand, shakes his head. His movements become nervous and fidgety, as if he were anxious to get out.* Oscar *clears his throat, looks at* Regina, *tries to fill the silence.* Leo *steps* D.] My God, I didn't know—who *could* have known—I didn't know he was that sick. Well, well—I——

[Regina *stands quietly, her back to them*]

BEN: [*Softly, sincerely*] Seems like yesterday when he first came here.

[*Places coat and hat on chair above wheelchair*]

OSCAR: [*Sincerely, nervously*] Yes, that's true. [*Turns to* Ben] The whole town loved him and respected him.

ALEXANDRA: [*Turns and crosses to below sofa* R.] Did you love him, Uncle Oscar?

OSCAR: [*Turns to* Alexandra] Certainly, I—What a strange thing to ask? I——

ALEXANDRA: [*Turns to look at Ben*] Did you love him, Uncle Ben?

BEN: [*Simply*] He had——

ALEXANDRA: [*Suddenly starts to laugh very loudly*] And you, Mama, did you love him, too?

REGINA: I know what you feel, Alexandra, but please try to control yourself.

ALEXANDRA: [*Still laughing*] I'm trying, Mama. I'm trying very hard.

BEN: Grief makes some people laugh and some people cry. It's better to cry, Alexandra.

ALEXANDRA: [*The laugh has stopped. Tensely. Moves toward* Regina, *crossing to front sofa*] What was Papa doing on the staircase?

REGINA: [*Crossing* R. *to* Alexandra. Ben *turns to look at* Alexandra *with interest*] Please go and lie down, my dear. We all need time to get over shocks like this. [Alexandra *does not move.* Regina's *voice becomes softer, more insistent*] Please go, Alexandra.

ALEXANDRA: No, Mama. I'll wait. I've got to talk to you.

REGINA: Later. Go and rest now.

ALEXANDRA: [*Quietly*] I'll wait, Mama. I've plenty of time. [*Sits down on sofa*] All my life.

REGINA: [*Hesitates, stares, makes a half shrug, turns back to* Ben, *crossing* L. *to* C.] As I was saying. Tomorrow morning I am going up to Judge Simmes. I shall tell him about Leo.

BEN: [*Motioning toward* Alexandra, *steps* D. *to chair* L.C.] Not in front of the child, Regina. I——

REGINA: [*Turns to him. Sharply*] I didn't ask her to stay. [*Turns away, crossing* L.] Tomorrow morning I go to Judge Simmes——

OSCAR: And what proof? What proof of all this——

REGINA: [*Turns, crosses to* C. *between* Ben *and* Oscar. *To* Oscar *sharply*] None. I won't need any. The bonds are missing and they are with Marshall. That will be enough. If it isn't, I'll add what's necessary.

BEN: I'm sure of that.

REGINA: [*Turns to* Ben] You can be quite sure.

OSCAR: We'll deny——

REGINA: Deny your heads off. You couldn't find a jury that wouldn't weep for a woman whose brothers steal from her. *And* you couldn't find twelve men in this State you haven't cheated and hate you for it.

OSCAR: What kind of talk is this? You couldn't do anything like that! We're your own brothers. How can you talk that way when upstairs not five minutes ago—— [*Points up stairs*]

REGINA: [*Slowly*] There are people who can never go back, who must finish what they start. I am one of those people, Oscar. [*After a slight pause, turns back to* Ben, *almost teasingly*] Where was I? [*Smiles at* Ben] Well, they'll convict you. But I won't care much if they don't. [*Leans forward, pleasantly*] Because by that time you'll be ruined. [*Crosses* D.L.] I shall also tell my story to Mr. Marshall, who likes me, I think, and who will not want to be involved in your scandal. A respectable firm like Marshall & Company! The deal would be off in an hour. [*Turns to them angrily*] And you know it. Now I don't want to hear any more from any of you. *You'll do no more bargaining in this house.* I'll take my seventy-five per cent and we'll forget the story forever. That's one way of doing it, and the way I prefer. [*Crosses to settee* L.] You know me well enough to know that I don't mind taking the other way. [*Sits down on settee*]

BEN: [*After a second, slowly, at chair* L.C.] None of us have ever known you well enough, Regina.

REGINA: You're getting old, Ben. Your tricks aren't as smart as they used to be. [*There is no answer. She waits, then smiles*] All right. I take it that's settled and I get what I asked for.

OSCAR: [*Furiously to* Ben] Are you going to let her do this——?

BEN: [*Turns to look at him, slowly*] You have a suggestion?

REGINA: [*Puts her arms above her head, stretches, laughs*] No, he hasn't. All right. Now, Leo, I have forgotten that you ever saw the bonds. [*Archly, to* Ben *and* Oscar] And as long as you boys both behave yourselves, I've forgotten that we ever talked about them. You can draw up the necessary papers tomorrow.

[Ben *laughs.* Leo *stares at him, starts for door. Exits.* Oscar *moves toward door, angrily.* Regina *looks at* Ben, *nods, laughs with him. For a second,* Oscar *stands in the door, looking back at them. Then he exits*]

REGINA: You're a good loser, Ben. I like that.

BEN: [*He picks up his coat, then turns to her*] Well, I say to myself, what's the good? You and I aren't like Oscar. We're not sour people. I think that comes from a good digestion. [*Putting on coat*] Then, too, one loses today and wins tomorrow. I say to myself, years of planning and I get what I want. Then I don't get it. But I'm not discouraged. The century's turning, the world is open. Open for people like you and me. Ready for us, waiting for us. After all, this is just the beginning. [*Crosses* L. *to above chair* L.C.] There are hundreds of Hubbards sitting in rooms like this throughout the country. All their names aren't Hubbard, but they are all Hubbards and they will own this country some day. We'll get along.

REGINA: [*Smiles*] I think so.

BEN: [*Crosses to chair, picks up hat*] Then, too, I say to myself, things may change. [*Looks at* Alexandra] I agree with Alexandra. [*Looks up at landing*] What is a man in a wheel chair doing on a staircase? I ask myself that.

REGINA: [*Looks up at him*] And what do you answer?

BEN: I have no answer. [*Crosses* L. *to back of settee*] But maybe some day I will. Maybe never, but maybe some day. [*Smiles. Patting her arm*] When I do, I'll let you know. [*Crosses to* C., *toward hall*]

REGINA: [*As he turns for door*] When you do, write me. I will be in Chicago. [*Gaily*] Ah, Ben, if Papa had only left me his money.

BEN: I'll see you tomorrow. [*Crosses* R. *to above wheel chair*]

REGINA: Oh, yes. Certainly. You'll be sort of working for me now.

BEN: [*Turns, crosses to above sofa* R., *looks at* Alexandra, *smiles at her*] Alexandra, you're turning out to be a right interesting girl. [*Looks at* Regina] Well, goodnight, all. [*He exits*]

REGINA: [*Sits quietly for a second, stretches, turns to look at* Alexandra] What do you want to talk to me about, Alexandra?

ALEXANDRA: [*Slowly*] I've changed my mind. I don't want to talk. There's nothing to talk about now.

REGINA: You're acting very strange. Not like yourself. You've had a bad shock today. I know that. And you loved Papa, but you must have expected this to come someday. You knew how sick he was.

ALEXANDRA: I knew. We all knew.

REGINA: It will be good for you to get away from here. Good for me, too. Time heals most wounds, Alexandra. You're young, you shall have all the things I wanted. I'll make the world for you the way I wanted it to be for me. [*Uncomfortably*] Don't sit there staring. You've been around Birdie so much you're getting just like her.

ALEXANDRA: [*Nods*] Funny. That's what Aunt Birdie said today.

REGINA: [*Nods*] Be good for you to get away from all this.

[Addie *enters*]

ADDIE: Cal is back, Miss Regina. He says Dr. Sloan will be coming in a few minutes.

REGINA: We'll go in a few weeks. A few weeks! That means two or three Saturdays, two or three Sundays. [*Sighs*] Well, I'm very tired. I shall go to bed. I don't want any supper. Put the lights out and lock up. [Addie *moves to the piano lamp, turns it out*] You go to your room, Alexandra. Addie will bring you something hot. You look very tired. [*Rises, crosses* U.C. *To* Addie] Call me when Dr. Sloan gets here. I don't want to see anybody else. I don't want any condolence calls tonight. The whole town will be over.

ALEXANDRA: Mama, I'm not coming with you. I'm not going to Chicago.

REGINA: [*Turns, to her*] You're very upset, Alexandra.

ALEXANDRA: [*Quietly*] I mean what I say. With all my heart.

REGINA: [*Quietly*] We'll talk about it tomorrow. The morning will make a difference.

ALEXANDRA: It won't make any difference. And there isn't anything to talk about. I am going away from you. Because I want to. Because I know Papa would want me to.

REGINA: [*Puzzled, careful, polite*] You *know* your Papa wanted you to go away from me?

ALEXANDRA: Yes.

REGINA: [*Softly*] And if I say no?

ALEXANDRA: [*Looks at her, firmly*] Say it, Mama, say it. And see what happens.

REGINA: [*Softly, after a pause*] And if I make you stay?

ALEXANDRA: That would be foolish. It wouldn't work in the end.

REGINA: You're very serious about it, aren't you? [*Crosses to steps—up two steps*] Well, you'll change your mind in a few days.

ALEXANDRA: You only change your mind when you want to. And I won't want to.

REGINA: [*Going up steps*] Alexandra, I've come to the end of my rope. [*On 5th step*] Somewhere there has to be what I want, too. Life goes too fast. Do what you want; think what you want; go where you want. I'd like to keep you with me, but I won't make you stay. Too many people used to make me do too many things. No. [*Going up to landing*] I won't make you stay.

ALEXANDRA: You couldn't, Mama, because I want to leave here. As I've never wanted anything in my life before. Because I understand what Papa was trying to tell me. [*Pause*] All in one day: Addie said there were people who ate the earth and other people who stood around and watched them do it. And just now Uncle Ben said the same thing. Really, he said the same thing. [*Tensely*] Well, tell him for me, Mama, I'm not going to stand around and watch you do it. Tell him I'll be fighting as hard as he'll be fighting [*Rises, steps* U. *to table*] someplace where people don't just stand around and watch.

REGINA: Well, you have spirit, after all. I used to think you were all sugar water. We don't have to be bad friends. I don't want us to be bad friends, Alexandra. [*Starts off, stops, turns to* Alexandra] Would you like to come and talk to me, Alexandra? Would you—would you like to sleep in my room tonight?

ALEXANDRA: [*Takes a step toward her*] Are you afraid, Mama?

[Regina *does not answer, but moves slowly out of sight*. Addie *then comes to* Alexandra, *squeezes her arm with affection and pride, then starts for the other lamp, as*

THE CURTAIN FALLS]

William Saroyan

(1908– ——)

When William Saroyan made his strange debut as a playwright, in the spring of 1939, he was already well known as an original short-story writer. He had brought out five collections of stories, had expressed notably uninhibited opinions on art and life, and had announced himself as the only original genius in the land. Since the appearance of his first collection, *The Daring Young Man on the Flying Trapeze and Other Stories* (1934), moreover, a number of critics had been willing to accept him at his own high estimation.

Saroyan was born of Armenian parentage in Fresno, California, and was educated at a Fresno grammar school, where he was anything but a model pupil. He started knocking about at an early age, with scant preparation for success other than a buoyant disposition and a vast amount of curiosity about everything except intellectual matters. For a time he worked as a Western Union messenger boy, a roving occupation that evidently pleased him a good deal, for he was fond of returning to this experience in his reminiscences. He also performed odd chores in the neighborhood and worked for a while in his uncle's vineyard. Then, at the age of seventeen, he left Fresno "for some of the rest of the world," as he declared, and simply decided that he was a writer. Taking as his subjects himself and the people he knew, he began to produce generally disorganized but surprisingly fresh stories. *The Daring Young Man on the Flying Trapeze,* a tale of a young writer's starvation-induced delirium, was published in the February 1934 issue of *Story* magazine and received instant acclaim. Since this was all the encouragement Saroyan needed, he proceeded to turn out enough stories at lightning speed to have a volume ready for publication later that year.

For Saroyan, who had not studied writing but had read voluminously and indiscriminately, literary composition (and later on, playwriting) held no mysteries. His rules, the first of which he claimed to have discovered at the age of eleven, were: "Do not pay attention to the rules other people make. . . . Forget everybody who ever wrote anything. . . . Learn to typewrite, so you can turn out stories as fast as Zane Grey." As for playwriting, his considered advice to the young was not to take George Pierce Baker's course at Harvard but to look at the world, to write a great deal without ever being careful, and never to try to achieve a style, "because style is something which is there from the beginning and doesn't have to be achieved." A playwright's sole aim should be "to uncover the magnificent and unending drama in the most ordinary environments, events, and people."

The theatre had attracted Saroyan from his earliest years, but it was the theatricality of the dramatic arts, the showmanship and the excitements of the stage, that absorbed him. "I take pride," he wrote later, "in my having sneaked into every theatre in my home town . . . ; into every circus that came to town; into the County Fairs; into the Summer stock company shows." Vaudeville fascinated him especially, and it had a decisive influence on his playwriting. What effort he made to acquaint himself with the literary drama left him unimpressed. *Lady Windermere's Fan,* read when he was fourteen, had worldly and brilliant style, but "didn't seem right" for him. His world, he realized early, "was a world of plain and poor people, broken-down houses, casualness, good health, poverty, and uproarious laughter." Copies of Ibsen's *Ghosts* and of other plays by "that great and magnificently dull dramatist" were apparently available to the boy. But Ibsen drama had no effect on him, because it was "too cagey, crafty, and calculating." He liked vaudeville much better. It was "easygoing and didn't try for too much and as a result very often achieved things Ibsen himself couldn't achieve. Vaudeville was American, too, which made a great difference."

Like vaudeville, Saroyan's plays were briskly spontaneous, disjointed, and improvisatory. He did not actually cultivate "surrealism." A freedom from the reins of practical reality and normal logic characterized most of his work; a madcap fancy, combined with indefinable intimations, ran riot in it; and the plays, composed at incredible speed, sometimes gave the impression of having come from their author almost automatically. (The French surrealists, we may recall, stressed "automatic writing.") In these respects, Saroyan's plays can be called "surrealist" and they are, indeed, the best representation of this modern style in English-language drama. But Saroyan's writing was native and impulsive rather than borrowed and learned; it was definitely not patterned after the subjective style of the French cult. Vaudeville exerted the most considerable influence in his work. For Saroyan, his kind of sketchy writing was "realistic," in the sense that he did not contrive it but set down what he saw or impulsively felt.

Saroyan's first play was *Subway Circus* (1935); it was a collection of scenes conveying people's daydreams, connected only by the circumstance that the characters happen to be riding in the subway.

Next, in 1938, he dramatized his short story *The Man with the Heart in the Highlands* for William Kozlenko's *One-Act Play Magazine,* under the title *My Heart's in the Highlands.* Kozlenko scheduled it for production by his short-lived One-Act Play Theatre. Subsequently, the author enlarged the then very short play and the Group Theatre produced it on April 13, 1939, with an excellent score by Paul Bowles, an enchanting semisurrealistic setting by Herbert Andrews, and superb direction by Robert Lewis. The newspaper critics were violently divided in their opinion, but Saroyan found powerful champions in Brooks Atkinson, John Mason Brown, and George Jean Nathan. The play, which had originally been scheduled by the Group for four experimental performances, was thereupon taken over by the Theatre Guild and presented to its membership.

Encouraged to continue playwriting, Saroyan completed his first full-length play, *The Time of Your Life,* in six days of furious writing. It was produced in the fall of 1939 by Eddie Dowling and the Theatre Guild, ran the greater part of the season in New York, toured extensively, and won both the Drama Critics Circle award and the Pulitzer Prize. In the spring of 1940, Dowling and the Theatre Guild produced a second full-length play by Saroyan, *Love's Old Sweet Song,* a somewhat more conventional drama that proved less successful. In 1941, using the income he had earned from *The Time of Your Life,* Saroyan acted as his own producer, as well as director, and gave New York the strangely beautiful, if somewhat chaotic, fantasy *The Beautiful People.* In 1941 too, the National Theatre Conference released his wildly fantastic *Jim Dandy* to sixty of its college and community-theatre affiliates. Eddie Dowling used the remarkable one-act play *Hello, Out There* as a curtain raiser in 1942, and in 1943 George Abbott staged Saroyan's travesty on Hollywood, *Get Away Old Man,* written out of the author's experience on the Metro-Goldwyn-Mayer lot. A number of other, rather loosely written and confusing plays of his also managed to be produced. Among these were *Sweeney in the Trees,* which the author described as "anything you like, whatever you please," and *Across the Board on Tomorrow Morning,* a mystical piece which he arranged to have played twice in the same evening at the Pasadena Playhouse, for any playgoers who wanted to see it a second time!

After 1943, Saroyan plays had few productions, none of them on Broadway; but the prolific writer continued to turn out script after script. Two of these (*Afton Water* and the war play *A Decent Birth, a Happy Funeral*) were singularly touching, although faulty. A few plays written after the war, especially the depressing *Don't Go Away Mad,* continued to reveal an original talent, although they showed plainly that their author had never bothered to learn the craft of playwriting. War service as a private had exerted an unfortunate effect on Saroyan's individualistic personality, inspiring a bitter novel, *The Adventures of Wesley Jackson* (he had previously written a charming autobiography, *My Name Is Aram,* and a loose novel, *The Human Comedy*), and depressing his playwriting, which had depended hitherto on buoyancy for success in the theatre.

My Heart's in the Highlands is the simplest and perhaps the best example of Saroyan's style of playwriting. It is free from the excesses of much of his later work. Moreover, it retains an undivided effect, whereas some of the best of his other plays, such as *The Time of Your Life* and *Love's Old Sweet Song,* demand constant adjustment on our part to an alternation of probabilities and improbabilities. Except for a few maladroit passages, *My Heart's in the Highlands* is written in a single vein as a work of inviolable innocence. Although the author's innocence does not exclude the realities of poverty and of old age, the play is a paean to man's impulsive love of beauty, to kindliness and dignity among the obscure, and to the wondering faith that children reveal. The play is sentimental without apology and optimistic without reason—attributes which, incidentally, Saroyan would claim for the greater part of the human race. "The fable of a tenth-rate poet whose protective little boy worships him as a genius," as George Jean Nathan called it, appeals more readily to the heart than to the mind. "There is more human pressure per square foot in it," another reviewer declared, "than in acres of sensible drama."

Perhaps the entire question of sense or nonsense in *My Heart's in the Highlands* is, indeed, altogether irrelevant beside Saroyan's feeling for people and for sheer existence. The play expresses a diffuse Whitmanesque spirit, a poetic caprice that requires no more explanations than does the taste of food and drink. Nothing and everything is in this play. And this is also true of the writing, which has no particular distinction other than that of being alive. The thoughts uttered by the characters are less important than those they do not or are unable to put into words. For all its simplicity, *My Heart's in the Highlands* therefore demands considerable empathy and theatrical imagination, and argument about it leads nowhere. We like the play insofar as we experience it; we dislike it insofar as we do not experience it.

BIBLIOGRAPHY: Brooks Atkinson, *Broadway Scrapbook* (pp. 115–120, 129–132), 1947; Harold Clurman, *The Fervent Years* (pp. 250–252, 263–264), 1945; Edmond M. Gagey, *Revolution in the American Drama* (pp. 111–119), 1947; George Jean Nathan, *The Entertainment of a Nation* (pp. 42–54), 1942; William Saroyan, Introductions to *Three Plays* (see also quotations of critical comment), 1940; Stark Young, *Immortal Shadows* (pp. 215–217), 1948.

MY HEART'S IN THE HIGHLANDS

By William Saroyan

THE PEOPLE

JOHNNY

HIS FATHER, BEN ALEXANDER, *the poet*

JOHNNY'S GRANDMOTHER

JASPER MAC GREGOR, *the man with the heart in the highlands*

MR. KOSAK, *the grocer*

ESTHER, *his beautiful daughter*

RUFE APLEY, *the carpenter*

PHILIP CARMICHAEL, *the young man from the Old People's Home*

HENRY, *the morning paper route carrier*

MR. WILEY, *the mailman*

MR. CUNNINGHAM, *the real estate agent*

THE YOUNG HUSBAND AND WIFE, AND THEIR BABY

GOOD FRIENDS AND NEIGHBORS

A DOG

THE PLACE

A house on San Benito Avenue in Fresno, California. Mr. Kosak's grocery store.

THE TIME

August and November, 1914

An old white, broken-down, frame house with a front porch, on San Benito Avenue in Fresno, California. There are no other houses near by, only a desolation of bleak land and red sky. It is late afternoon of a day in August, 1914. The evening sun is going down.

Johnny, aged nine, but essentially ageless, is sitting, dynamic and acrobatic, on the steps of the porch, dead to the world and deep in thought of a high and holy order. Far away a train whistle cries mournfully. He listens eagerly, cocking his head on one side like a chicken, trying to understand the meaning of the cry and at the same time to figure out everything. He doesn't quite make it and when the cry ends he stops being eager. A fourteen-year-old boy on a bicycle, eating an ice-cream cone and carrying newspaper bags, goes by on the sidewalk in silence, oblivious of the weight on his shoulders and of the contraption on which he is seated, because of the delight and glory of ice cream in the world. Johnny leaps to his feet and waves to the boy, smiling in a big humanitarian way, but is ignored. He sits down again and listens to a small overjoyed but angry bird. After making a brief forceful speech of no meaning, the bird flies away.

From inside the house is heard the somber voice of Johnny's Father *reciting poetry of his own composition.*

JOHNNY'S FATHER: The long silent day journeys through the sore solemn heart, and—[*Bitter pause*] And—[*Quickly*] The long silent day journeys through the sore solemn heart, and—[*Pause*] No. [*He roars and begins again*] Crippled and weeping, time stumbles through the lone lorn heart.

[*A table or chair is pushed over in anger. A groan. Silence. The boy listens. He gets up and tries to stand on his head, fails, tries again, fails, tries again, and succeeds. While he is standing on his head he hears the loveliest and most amazing music in the world: a solo on a bugle. The music is "My Heart's in the Highlands." The bugler, a very old man, finishes the solo in front of the house. The boy leaps to his feet and runs up to the old man, amazed, delighted and bewildered*]

JOHNNY: I sure would like to hear you play another song.

MAC GREGOR: Young man, could you get a glass of water for an old man whose heart is not here, but in the highlands?

JOHNNY: What highlands?

MAC GREGOR: The Scotch Highlands. Could you?

JOHNNY: What's your heart doing in the Scotch Highlands?

MAC GREGOR: My heart's grieving there. Could you get me a glass of cool water?

JOHNNY: Where's your *mother*?

MAC GREGOR: [*Inventing for the boy*] My mother's in Tulsa, Oklahoma, but her heart isn't.

JOHNNY: Where *is* her heart?

MAC GREGOR: [*Loud*] In the Scotch Highlands. [*Soft*] I'm very thirsty, young man.

JOHNNY: How come the members of your family are always leaving their hearts in the highlands?

MAC GREGOR: [*In the Shakespearean manner*] That's the way we are. Here today and gone tomorrow.

JOHNNY: [*Aside*] Here today and gone tomorrow? [*To MacGregor*] How do you figure?

MAC GREGOR: [*The philosopher*] Alive one minute and dead the next.

JOHNNY: Where's your *mother's mother*?

MAC GREGOR: [*Inventing, but angry*] She's up in Vermont, in a little town called White River, but her heart isn't.

JOHNNY: Is her poor old withered heart in the highlands, too?

MAC GREGOR: Right smack in the highlands. Son, I'm dying of thirst.

[Johnny's Father *comes out of the house in a fury, as if he has just broken out of a cage, and roars at the boy like a tiger that has just awakened from evil dreams*]

JOHNNY'S FATHER: Johnny, get the hell away from that poor old man. Get him a pitcher of water before he falls down and dies. Where the hell are your manners?

JOHNNY: Can't a fellow try to find out something from a traveler once in a while?

JOHNNY'S FATHER: Get the old man some water, God damn it. Don't stand there like a dummy. Get him a drink, I tell you, before he falls down and dies.

JOHNNY: *You* get him a drink. You're not doing anything.

JOHNNY'S FATHER: Not doing anything? Why, Johnny, you *know* I'm getting a new poem arranged in my mind.

JOHNNY: How do you figure I know? You're just standing there on the porch with your sleeves rolled up.

JOHNNY'S FATHER: [*Angry*] Well, you ought to know. [*Roaring*] You're my son. [*Amazed*] If you shouldn't know, who should?

MAC GREGOR: [*Blithely*] Good afternoon. Your son has been telling me how clear and cool the climate is in these parts.

JOHNNY: [*Bewildered, but eager to learn. Aside*] Holy Moses, I didn't say anything about the climate. Where's he getting that stuff from?

JOHNNY'S FATHER: [*The aristocrat, grandly*] How do you do? Won't you come in for a little rest? We should be honored to have you at our table for a bit of supper.

MAC GREGOR: [*The realist*] Sir, I'm starving. I shall come right in. [*He moves to enter the house.* Johnny *gets in his way, looking up at him*]

JOHNNY: [*The romantic*] Can you play "Drink to Me Only with Thine Eyes"? I sure would like to hear you play that song on the bugle. That song is my favorite. I guess I like that song better than any song in the world.

MAC GREGOR: [*The disillusioned*] Son, when you get to be my age you'll know songs aren't important, bread's the thing.

JOHNNY: [*The faithful*] Anyway, I sure would like to hear you play that song.

[MacGregor *goes up on the porch and shakes hands with* Johnny's Father]

MAC GREGOR: [*History in the making*] My name is Jasper MacGregor. I am an actor.

JOHNNY'S FATHER: [*Delighted*] I'm mighty glad to make your acquaintance. [*The imperial giver of orders*] Johnny, get Mr. MacGregor a pitcher of water. [Johnny *runs around the house*]

MAC GREGOR: [*Dying of thirst, sighing, but telling the truth nevertheless*] Charming boy.

JOHNNY'S FATHER: [*Ordinary statement*] Like myself, he's a genius.

MAC GREGOR: [*Roaring from fatigue*] I suppose you're very fond of him?

JOHNNY'S FATHER: [*Delighted to be alive*] We are the same person— He is the heart of my youth— Have you noticed his eagerness?

MAC GREGOR: [*Delighted to be still alive*] I should say I have.

JOHNNY'S FATHER: [*Proudly and with anger*] I'm the same way myself, although older and less brilliant.

[Johnny, *running, returns with a pitcher of water which he hands to the old man. The old man throws back his shoulders, lifts his head, his nostrils expand, he snorts, his eyes widen, he lifts the pitcher of water to his lips and drinks all the water in one long swig, while* Johnny *and his* Father *watch with amazement and admiration. The old man breathes deeply, looks around at the landscape and up at the sky and to the end of San Benito Avenue where the evening sun is going down*]

MAC GREGOR: [*Reflection, sadly; weariness, softly*] I reckon I'm five thousand miles from home. Do you think we could eat a little bread and cheese to keep my body and spirit together?

JOHNNY'S FATHER: [*Napoleon*] Johnny, run down to the grocer's and get a loaf of French bread and a pound of cheese.

JOHNNY: [*The voice of doom*] Give me the money.

JOHNNY'S FATHER: [*Statistics, poetic, with pride*] You know I haven't got a *penny*, Johnny. Tell Mr. Kosak to give us credit.

JOHNNY: [*The unwilling dutiful son*] He won't do it. He's tired of giving us credit. He says we don't work and never pay our bills. We owe him forty cents.

JOHNNY'S FATHER: [*Impatient, irritated*] Go on down there and argue it out with him. You know that's your job.

JOHNNY: [*Defending his rights*] He won't listen to reason. He says he doesn't know anything about anything. All he wants is the forty cents.

JOHNNY'S FATHER: [*Napoleon*] Go on down there and make him give you a loaf of bread and a pound of cheese. [*Gently, pleading, flattering*] You can do it, Johnny.

MAC GREGOR: [*Impatient and hungry*] Go on down there and tell Mr. Kosak to give you a loaf of bread and a pound of cheese, son.

JOHNNY'S FATHER: Go ahead, Johnny. You've never failed to leave that store with something or other. You'll be back here in ten minutes with food fit for a King. [*For his own amusement*] Or at least a Duke of some kind.

JOHNNY: I don't know. Mr. Kosak says we are trying to give him the merry run-around. He wants to know what kind of work you do.

JOHNNY'S FATHER: [*Furiously*] Well, go ahead and tell him. [*The hero*] I have nothing to conceal. I write poetry, night and day.

JOHNNY: [*Giving in at last*] All right, but I don't think he'll be impressed. He says you never go out and look for work. He says you're lazy and no good.

JOHNNY'S FATHER: [*Roaring*] You go down there and tell that great-hearted Slovak he's crazy, Johnny. You go on down there and tell that splendid scholar and gentleman your father is one of the greatest unknown poets living.

JOHNNY: He won't care, Pa, but I'll go. I'll do my best. Haven't we got anything in the house?

JOHNNY'S FATHER: [*Mock-tragically, roaring*] Only popcorn. [*To* MacGregor] We've been eating popcorn four days in a row now. Johnny, you've got to get bread and cheese if you expect me to finish that long poem.

JOHNNY: I'll do my best.

MAC GREGOR: Don't take too long, Johnny. I'm five thousand miles from home.

JOHNNY: I'll run all the way, Mr. MacGregor.

JOHNNY'S FATHER: [*For the amusement of the good Lord*] If you find any money on the way, remember we go fifty-fifty.

JOHNNY: [*Delighted with the comedy*] All right, Pa. [Johnny *runs down the street*]

The inside of Mr. Kosak's Grocery Store. Mr. Kosak *is sleeping on his folded arms when* Johnny *runs into the store.* Mr. Kosak *lifts his head. He is a fine, gentle, serious man with a big, blond, old-fashioned mustache. He shakes his head trying to waken.*

JOHNNY: [*The diplomat, as it were*] Mr. Kosak, if you were in China and didn't have a friend in the world and no money, you'd expect somebody over there to give you a pound of rice, wouldn't you?

MR. KOSAK: What do you want?

JOHNNY: I just want to talk a little. You'd expect some member of the Aryan race to help you out a little, wouldn't you, Mr. Kosak?

MR. KOSAK: How much money you got?

JOHNNY: It's not a question of money, Mr. Kosak. I'm talking about being in China.

MR. KOSAK: I don't know nothing about nothing.

JOHNNY: How would you feel in China that way, Mr. Kosak?

MR. KOSAK: I don't know, Johnny. What would I be doing in China?

JOHNNY: Well, you'd be visiting there. You'd be hungry and five thousand miles from home and not a friend in the world. You wouldn't expect *everybody* to turn you away without even a pound of rice, would you, Mr. Kosak?

MR. KOSAK: I guess not, but you ain't in China, Johnny, and neither is your Pa. You or your Pa's got to go out and work sometime in your lives, so you might as well start now. I ain't going to give you no more groceries on credit because I know you won't pay me.

JOHNNY: Mr. Kosak, you misunderstand me. This is 1914, not 1913. I'm not talking about a few groceries. I'm talking about all them heathen people around you in China and you hungry and dying.

MR. KOSAK: This ain't China. You got to go out and make your living in this country. Everybody's got to work in America.

JOHNNY: Mr. Kosak, suppose it was a loaf of bread and a pound of cheese you needed to keep you alive in the world, would you hesitate to ask a Christian *missionary* for these things?

MR. KOSAK: Yes, I would. I would be ashamed to ask.

JOHNNY: Even if you knew you would give him back *two* loaves of bread and *two* pounds of cheese instead of one loaf and one pound? Even then, Mr. Kosak?

MR. KOSAK: Even then.

JOHNNY: Don't be that way, Mr. Kosak. That's defeatist talk, and you know it. Why, the only thing that would happen to you would be death. You'd *die* out there in China, Mr. Kosak.

MR. KOSAK: I wouldn't care if I would. You and your Pa have got to pay for bread and cheese. Why don't your Pa go out and get a job?

JOHNNY: [*Swift abandonment of the intellectual attack for the human one*] Mr. Kosak, how are you?

MR. KOSAK: I'm fine, Johnny. How are *you*?

JOHNNY: Couldn't be better, Mr. Kosak. How are the children?

MR. KOSAK: They're all fine, Johnny. Stephan is beginning to walk now.

JOHNNY: That's great. How's Angela?

MR. KOSAK: Angela's beginning to sing. How's your Grandmother?

JOHNNY: She's fine. She's beginning to sing too. She says she'd rather be an opera singer than Queen of England. How's your wife Martha, Mr. Kosak?

MR. KOSAK: Oh, swell.

JOHNNY: I can't tell you how glad I am to hear that everything is fine at your house. I know Stephan is going to be a great man some day.

MR. KOSAK: I hope so. I'm going to send him to high school and see that he gets every chance I didn't get. I don't want *him* to have trouble all *his* life, too.

JOHNNY: I have great faith in Stephan, Mr. Kosak.

MR. KOSAK: What do you want, Johnny, and how much money you got?

JOHNNY: Mr. Kosak, you know I didn't come here to buy anything. You know I enjoy a quiet philosophical chat with you every now and then. [*Quickly, pleading*] Let me have a loaf of French bread and a pound of cheese.

MR. KOSAK: You got to pay cash, Johnny.

JOHNNY: And Esther? How is your beautiful daughter Esther?

MR. KOSAK: She's all right, Johnny, but you got to pay cash. You and your Pa are the worst citizens in this county.

JOHNNY: I'm glad Esther's all right, Mr. Kosak. Jasper MacGregor is visiting our house. He's a great actor.

MR. KOSAK: Never heard of him.

JOHNNY: And a bottle of beer for Mr. MacGregor.

MR. KOSAK: I can't give you a bottle of beer.

JOHNNY: Sure, you can.

MR. KOSAK: I can't. I'll let you have one loaf of French bread and a pound of cheese, but that's all. What kind of work does your Pa do *when* he works, Johnny?

JOHNNY: My father writes poetry, Mr. Kosak. That's the only work my father does. He's one of the greatest writers of poetry in the world.

MR. KOSAK: When does he get any money?

JOHNNY: He *never* gets any money. You can't have your cake and eat it too.

MR. KOSAK: I don't like that kind of work. Why doesn't your Pa work like everybody else, Johnny?

JOHNNY: He works harder than everybody else. My father works twice as hard as the average man.

[*Mr. Kosak hands Johnny a loaf of French bread and a pound of cheese*]

MR. KOSAK: Well, that's fifty-five cents you owe me, Johnny. I'll let you have some stuff this time, but never again.

JOHNNY: [*At the door*] Tell Esther I love her. [Johnny *runs out of the store. Mr. Kosak swings at a fly, misses, swings again, misses, and, objecting to the world in this manner, he chases the fly all around the store, swinging with all his might*]

The house. Johnny's Father *and the old man are looking down the street to see if* Johnny *is coming back with food. His* Grandmother *is standing on the porch also eager to know if there is to be food.*

MAC GREGOR: I think he's got some food with him.

JOHNNY'S FATHER: [*With pride*] Of course he has. [*He waves at the old lady on the porch who runs*

into the house to set the table. Johnny *runs to his* Father *and* MacGregor] I knew you'd do it.

MAC GREGOR: So did I.

JOHNNY: He says we got to pay him fifty-five cents. He says he's not going to give us any more stuff on credit.

JOHNNY'S FATHER: That's *his* opinion. What did you talk about?

JOHNNY: First I talked about being hungry and at death's door in China. Then I inquired about the family.

JOHNNY'S FATHER: How is everyone?

JOHNNY: Fine. I didn't find any money, though. Not even a *penny.*

JOHNNY'S FATHER: Oh, that's all right. Money isn't everything. [*They go into the house*]

The living room. They are all at the table after supper. MacGregor *finds crumbs here and there which he places delicately in his mouth. He looks around the room to see if there isn't something more to eat.*

MAC GREGOR: That green can up there, Johnny. What's in there?

JOHNNY: Marbles.

MAC GREGOR: That cupboard, Johnny. Anything *edible* in there?

JOHNNY: Crickets.

MAC GREGOR: That big jar in the corner there, Johnny. What's delectable in there?

JOHNNY: I got a gopher snake in that jar.

MAC GREGOR: Well, I could go for a bit of boiled gopher snake in a big way, Johnny.

JOHNNY: [*Defiantly, protector of animals*] Nothing doing, Mr. MacGregor.

MAC GREGOR: Why not, Johnny? Why the hell not, son? I hear of fine Borneo natives eating snakes and grasshoppers. You haven't got a half dozen fat grasshoppers around, have you, Johnny?

JOHNNY: Only four.

MAC GREGOR: Well, trot them out, son, and after we've had our fill, I'll play "Drink to Me Only with Thine Eyes" for you. I'm mighty hungry, Johnny.

JOHNNY: So am I, but I don't want anybody killing them innocent animals. They got rights the same as anybody else.

JOHNNY'S FATHER: [*To MacGregor*] How about a little music? I think the boy would be delighted.

JOHNNY: [*Leaping to his feet*] I sure would, Mr. MacGregor.

MAC GREGOR: All right, Johnny. Bread. Bread. My God, how savagely it quarrels with the heart. [MacGregor *gets up and begins to blow into the bugle. He blows louder and more beautifully and mournfully than anybody ever blew into a bugle. Eighteen* Neighbors *gather in front of the house and cheer when he finishes the solo: "Drink to Me Only with Thine Eyes"*]

JOHNNY'S FATHER: [*Delighted, for amusement*] I want you to meet your public. [*They go out on the porch*]

The house. The crowd is looking up at Johnny's Father, MacGregor *and* Johnny.

JOHNNY'S FATHER: Good neighbors, and friends, I want you to meet Jasper MacGregor, the greatest Shakespearean actor of our day. [*Pause*] I believe.

MAC GREGOR: [*The actor*] I remember my first appearance in London in 1851 as if it was yesterday. I was a boy of fourteen from the slums of Glasgow. My first part was a courier in a play, the title of which I have unfortunately forgotten. I had no lines to speak, but moved about a good deal, running from officer to officer, and from lover to his beloved, and back again, over and over again.

RUFE APLEY, THE CARPENTER: [*Regretfully interrupting the great speech*] How about another song, Mr. MacGregor?

MAC GREGOR: Have you got an egg at your house?

RUFE APLEY: I sure have. I've got a *dozen* eggs at my house.

MAC GREGOR: Would it be convenient for you to go and get one of them dozen eggs? When you return I'll play a song that will make your heart leap with joy and grief.

RUFE APLEY: I'm on my way already. [*He goes*]

MAC GREGOR: [*To the crowd*] My friends, I should be delighted to play another song for you on this golden-throated bugle, but time and distance from home find me weary. If you will be so good as to go, each of you to his home, and return in a moment with some morsel of food, I shall be proud to gather my spirit together and play a song I know will change the course of each of your lives, and change it, mind you, for the better. [*The people go. The last to go is* Esther Kosak, *who hears the speech out, then runs.* MacGregor, Johnny's father, *and* Johnny *sit on the steps and remain in silence, and one by one the people return, bringing food to* MacGregor: *an egg, a sausage, a dozen green onions, two kinds of cheese, butter, two kinds of bread, boiled potatoes, fresh tomatoes, a melon, tea, and many other good things to eat*] Thank you, my friends, thank you. [*He stands solemnly, waiting for absolute silence, straightens himself, looks about him furiously, lifts the bugle to his lips and is irritated by the swift and noisy return of* Esther Kosak, *bringing an eggplant. When there is silence, he plays "My Heart's in the Highlands, My Heart is not Here."* The People *weep, kneel, sing the chorus, and go away.* MacGregor *turns to the father and son. Grandly*] Sir, if it is all the same to you I should like to dwell in your house for a long time to come.

JOHNNY'S FATHER: [*Delighted and amazed*] Sir, my house is your house. [*They go into the house*]

The living room. Eighteen days later, MacGregor *is lying on the floor, face up, asleep.* Johnny *is walking about quietly in the room, looking at everybody. His* Father *is at the table, writing poetry. His* Grandmother *is sitting in the rocking chair, rocking. There is a knock on the door. Everybody but* MacGregor *jumps up and runs to it.*

JOHNNY'S FATHER: [*At the door*] Yes?

YOUNG MAN: I am looking for Jasper MacGregor, the actor.

JOHNNY'S FATHER: What do you want?

JOHNNY: Well, ask him in anyway, Pa.

JOHNNY'S FATHER: Yes, of course. Excuse me. Won't you please come in? [*The* Young Man *enters*]

YOUNG MAN: My name is Philip Carmichael. I am from the Old People's Home. I have been sent to bring Mr. MacGregor home.

MAC GREGOR: [*Wakening and sitting up*] Home? Did someone mention home? [*Roaring*] I'm five thousand miles from home, always have been, and always will be. Who is this young man?

YOUNG MAN: Mr. MacGregor, I'm Philip Carmichael, from the Old People's Home. They've sent me to bring you back. We are putting on our annual show in two weeks and need you for the leading role.

MAC GREGOR: [*Getting up with the help of* Johnny's Father *and* Johnny] What kind of a part is it? I can't be playing young adventurers any longer.

YOUNG MAN: The part is King Lear, Mr. MacGregor. It is perfect for you.

MAC GREGOR: [*The actor, with a job again*] Goodby, my beloved friends. [*He returns from the porch*] In all the hours of my life, in all the places I have visited, never and nowhere have I had the honor and pleasure to commune with souls loftier, purer, or more delightful than yours. Good-by. [*The* Old Man *and the* Young Man *leave the house. There is a moment of silence, full of regret and loneliness*]

JOHNNY'S FATHER: [*Hungry, loudly*] Johnny, go on down to Mr. Kosak's store and get a little something to eat. I know you can do it, Johnny. Get ANYTHING.

JOHNNY: [*Hungry, loudly, and angry*] Mr. Kosak wants eighty-five cents. He won't give us anything more without money.

JOHNNY'S FATHER: Go on down there, Johnny. You know you can get that fine Slovak gentleman to give us a little something to eat.

JOHNNY: [*With despair*] Aw, Pa.

JOHNNY'S FATHER: [*Amazed, roaring*] What? You, my son, in a mood like that. Come on. I fought the world this way before you were born. After you were born we fought it together, and we're going to go on fighting it. The people love poetry but don't know it, that's all. Nothing is going to stop us, Johnny. Go on down there now and get us something to eat.

JOHNNY: All right, Pa. I'll do my best. [*He runs to the door*]

The house. *It now has a large sign: "For Rent." It is a moment before daybreak of a day early in November, 1914. There is a suggestion of Winter coming. High in the sky a flock of geese flying south make their call.* Johnny *is sitting on the steps of the front porch with his chin in his hand. He hears the geese, listening carefully, leaps to his feet and looks into the sky for them. The sound decreases, then ends.* Johnny *goes back to the steps of the porch and sits down. As the sun rises, a big solemn smile comes over his face. He looks out of the corner of his eye at the morning's light as if it were a quiet friend with whom he was on terms of perfect understanding. As the light increases, this play between* Johnny *and the sun grows, like a theme of music, bringing him to his feet, turning his face to the light. He lifts his arms, and very solemnly begins turning somersaults. He then runs around the house lickety-split and returns on the other side, almost dancing.*

A freight train goes by not far enough away not to make the earth tremble. The light of morning increases.

A newspaper route carrier arrives on foot, whistling. He is the typical small-town morning route carrier: about thirteen years old. He is in that somber and dignified state which comes over men who have done their work. His paper bags are empty. Night is over. His daily wage has been earned. The papers have been left at the doors of the readers. Another day has come to the world. He has walked two hours through dark streets to morning. The song he is whistling is soft and full of understanding. It is a song of his own composition, a morning song.

JOHNNY: [*Running down the steps*] Hello.

THE BOY: [*Stopping*] Hello.

JOHNNY: What was that song?

THE BOY: What song?

JOHNNY: That you were whistling?

THE BOY: Was I whistling?

JOHNNY: Sure. Didn't you know?

THE BOY: I guess I'm always whistling.

JOHNNY: What was it?

THE BOY: I don't know.

JOHNNY: I wish I could whistle.

THE BOY: Anybody can whistle.

JOHNNY: I can't. How do you do it?

THE BOY: There's no *how* to it. You just whistle.

JOHNNY: How?

THE BOY: Like this. [*He whistles a moment, obviously improvising a tour de force of technique*]

JOHNNY: [*With admiration*] I wish I could do that.

THE BOY: [*Pleased and eager to make an even better impression*] That was nothing. Listen to this. [*He gives the melody a sort of counterpoint, two tones, and a bit of syncopation*]

JOHNNY: Can't you teach me to do that?

THE BOY: You can't teach whistling. You just do it. This is another way. [*He whistles a little melody, the loud newsboy's style, but keeps it soft*]

JOHNNY: [*Trying to whistle*] Like that?

THE BOY: That's the way to start. Keep it up and after a while your mouth'll take the right shape and you'll be whistling before you know it.

JOHNNY: Honest?

THE BOY: Sure.

JOHNNY: Is your mother dead?

THE BOY: How did you know?

JOHNNY: My mother's dead too.

THE BOY: Yeah?

JOHNNY: [*With a sigh*] Yeah. She died.

THE BOY: I don't remember my mother. Do you remember your mother?

JOHNNY: I don't exactly remember her. Sometimes I dream about her, though.

THE BOY: I used to, too.

JOHNNY: Don't you any more?

THE BOY: [*Disillusioned*] Naaaah. What good does that do you?

JOHNNY: My mother sure is beautiful.

THE BOY: Yeah, I know. I remember. You got a father?

JOHNNY: [*Proudly*] Oh, sure. He's in the house *now*, sleeping.

THE BOY: My *father's* dead, too.

JOHNNY: Your *father*, too?

THE BOY: [*Matter-of-fact*] Yeah. [*They begin bouncing an old tennis ball back and forth to each other*]

JOHNNY: Haven't you got anybody?

THE BOY: I got an aunt, but she ain't really my aunt. I was brought up in an orphanage. I'm adopted.

JOHNNY: What's an orphanage?

THE BOY: That's a kind of a place where kids that ain't got any mothers and fathers live until somebody adopts them.

JOHNNY: What do you mean, adopts?

THE BOY: Somebody who wants a boy or girl comes to the orphanage and looks everybody over and goes away with whoever they like. If they pick you, you go and stay with them.

JOHNNY: Do you like that?

THE BOY: It's all right. [*The Boy puts away the ball*]

JOHNNY: What's your name?

THE BOY: Henry. What's yours?

JOHNNY: Johnny.

THE BOY: Do you want a paper? There's a War in Europe.

JOHNNY: I haven't got any money. We aren't rich. We don't work. My father writes poetry.

THE BOY: [*Giving* Johnny *the extra*] Oh, that's all right. Don't you *ever* have any money?

JOHNNY: Sometimes. I found a quarter once. It was lying on the sidewalk, right in front of me. Once my father got a check for ten dollars from New York, too. We bought a chicken and a lot of stamps and paper and envelopes. The chicken wouldn't lay eggs, though, so my grandmother killed it and cooked it for us. Did you ever eat chicken?

THE BOY: Sure. I guess I've eaten chicken six or seven times.

JOHNNY: What are you going to do when you grow up?

THE BOY: Shucks. I don't know. I don't know what I'll do.

JOHNNY: [Proudly] I'm going to be a poet, like my father. He said so.

THE BOY: I guess I'll carry a paper route for a while. [He moves to go] Well. So long.

JOHNNY: Won't you come here again?

THE BOY: I go by here every morning about this time. I ain't never seen you up before, though.

JOHNNY: [Smiling] I had a dream and then I woke up and didn't want to sleep any more. I wanted to get up and come out here. I saw my mother.

THE BOY: Maybe I'll see you again some morning when you can't sleep.

JOHNNY: I hope so. So long.

THE BOY: So long. Just keep trying and you'll be whistling before you know it.

JOHNNY: Thanks. [The Boy goes, whistling. Johnny tosses the folded paper up on the porch, and sits down again on the steps. His Grandmother comes out on the porch with a broom and begins to sweep]

JOHNNY'S GRANDMOTHER: [In Armenian, which is the only language she speaks, with the exception of Turkish, Kurdish, and a little Arabic, which nobody around seems to know] How are you, my heart?

JOHNNY: [Who understands Armenian, but hardly ever speaks it; in English] Fine.

JOHNNY'S GRANDMOTHER: How's your Papa?

JOHNNY: I don't know. [Calling loudly to his Father] Oh, Pa. How are you? [Pause. Louder] Pa. [Pause. Silence] I guess he's sleeping.

JOHNNY'S GRANDMOTHER: Is there any money?

JOHNNY: Money? [Shaking his head] No.

JOHNNY'S FATHER: [From inside the house] Johnny?

JOHNNY: [Jumping to his feet] Pa?

JOHNNY'S FATHER: Did you call?

JOHNNY: Yeah. How are you?

JOHNNY'S FATHER: Fine, Johnny. How are you?

JOHNNY: Fine, Pa.

JOHNNY'S FATHER: Is that all you woke me up for?

JOHNNY: [To his Grandmother] He's fine. [Louder to his Father] The old lady wanted to know.

JOHNNY'S FATHER: [In Armenian, to the old lady] Good night, Ma. [To Johnny, in English] What do you mean, old? She's not so old.

JOHNNY: I don't mean old. You know what I mean.

[Johnny's Father comes out on the porch, buttoning his shirt, nods to the old lady, looks out of the corner of his eye at the sun, exactly the same way Johnny did, smiling the same way, stretches all over, faces the sun, leaps down the steps and turns one somersault, not so good. The somersault leaves him flat on his back]

JOHNNY: You ought to get a little more exercise, Pa. You're always sitting down.

JOHNNY'S FATHER: [On his back] Johnny, your father is a great poet. I may not be able to turn a somersault as well as you, but if you want to know what kind of an athlete I am, just read the poetry I wrote yesterday.

JOHNNY: Is it really good, Pa?

JOHNNY'S FATHER: Good? [He leaps to his feet, like an acrobat] It's great. I'm going to send it to The Atlantic Monthly, too.

JOHNNY: Oh, I forgot, Pa. There's a paper on the porch.

JOHNNY'S FATHER: [Going up to the porch] You mean a morning paper, Johnny?

JOHNNY: Yeah.

JOHNNY'S FATHER: Well, that's a pleasant surprise. Where in the world did you get it?

JOHNNY: Henry gave it to me.

JOHNNY'S FATHER: Henry? Who's Henry?

JOHNNY: He's a boy who hasn't got a mother or a father, either. He sure can whistle, too.

JOHNNY'S FATHER: [Picking up the paper, opening it] That was certainly nice of him. [He loses himself in the headlines]

JOHNNY'S GRANDMOTHER: [To both of them, to herself, and to the world] Where's that man?

JOHNNY'S FATHER: [Deep in the news] Hmmm?

JOHNNY: Who?

JOHNNY'S GRANDMOTHER: You know. That old man who blew the horn. [She pantomimes the blowing of a horn]

JOHNNY: Oh. Mr. MacGregor? They took him back to the Old People's Home.

JOHNNY'S FATHER: [Reading the paper] Austria. Germany. France. England. Russia. Zeppelins. Submarines. Tanks. Machine guns. Bombs. [Shaking his head] They've gone crazy again.

JOHNNY'S GRANDMOTHER: [To Johnny, reproachfully] Why don't you speak Armenian, boy?

JOHNNY: I can't talk Armenian.

JOHNNY'S FATHER: [To Johnny] What's the matter?

JOHNNY: She wants to know about Mr. MacGregor.

JOHNNY'S GRANDMOTHER: [To Johnny's Father] Where is he?

JOHNNY'S FATHER: [In Armenian] He's back in the Old People's Home.

JOHNNY'S GRANDMOTHER: [Shaking her head sadly] Ahkh, ahkh, the poor old prisoner.

JOHNNY: Is it like a prison, Pa?

JOHNNY'S FATHER: I don't know for sure, Johnny.

JOHNNY'S GRANDMOTHER: [Furiously, the way her son and grandson speak when they are irritated]

Why doesn't he come back and stay here where he belongs? [*She goes into the house*]

JOHNNY: That's right, Pa. Why doesn't Mr. MacGregor come back and stay here? Does he have to stay in that place?

JOHNNY'S FATHER: If you're an old, old man, Johnny, and haven't got any people, and no money, I guess you do.

JOHNNY: I sure get lonesome for him sometimes. Don't you, Pa?

JOHNNY'S FATHER: To tell you the truth, Johnny, I do.

JOHNNY: I'm always remembering him, especially the music. And the way he drinks water.

JOHNNY'S FATHER: He's a great man.

JOHNNY: Is his heart really in the highlands like he said, Pa?

JOHNNY'S FATHER: Not exactly.

JOHNNY: Is he really five thousand miles from home, too?

JOHNNY'S FATHER: At least that many.

JOHNNY: Do you think he'll ever get home again some day?

JOHNNY'S FATHER: He's an old man, Johnny. He will.

JOHNNY: You mean he'll take a train and a boat and get back where the highlands are?

JOHNNY'S FATHER: Not that, Johnny. It's a little different from that. He'll *die*.

JOHNNY: Is that the only way a man gets home?

JOHNNY'S FATHER: That's the only way.

[*All this time, of course,* Johnny's Father *has been turning the pages of the morning paper, and* Johnny *has been going through various kinds of acrobatics, walking on the porch railing, leaping down, turning somersaults, standing on his head, and so forth. Some of his questions have been asked while he has been standing on his head. A sharp whistle is heard in the distance*]

JOHNNY: [*Eagerly*] It's Mr. Wiley, the mailman, Pa. [Johnny's Father *jumps to his feet, dropping the paper*]

JOHNNY: Do you think maybe we'll get a letter from New York with a check in it maybe?

JOHNNY'S FATHER: I don't know, Johnny.

[Mr. Wiley, *riding a bicycle, arrives. He is almost knocked off the bicycle by* Johnny *and* Johnny's Father]

MR. WILEY: [*Getting off the bicycle as if it were a horse*] Good morning, Mr. Alexander.

JOHNNY'S FATHER: Good morning, Mr. Wiley.

JOHNNY: Any mail for us, Mr. Wiley?

MR. WILEY: [*Bringing a packet of letters from his bag, loosening the strap, and looking them over*] Well, now, let me see, Johnny. I think I've got something here for your father.

JOHNNY: Is it from New York?

MR. WILEY: [*Holding a flat envelope*] Yes, it is,

Johnny. Well, Mr. Alexander, it looks like Winter's coming again. The geese were flying this morning.

JOHNNY'S FATHER: [*Excited, tense, yet eager to be casual*] Yes, I know. [*To himself*] I know. I know.

JOHNNY: If *I* ever get a letter from New York I'm going to save it up.

MR. WILEY: [*He wants to talk*] How are things, Mr. Alexander?

JOHNNY'S FATHER: I've been lucky in my work, thank you, Mr. Wiley.

JOHNNY: My father was in New York once. Weren't you, Pa?

JOHNNY'S FATHER: Yes, I was, Johnny. How is your family, Mr. Wiley?

MR. WILEY: All fine, except the littlest one, Joe. He's always crying. That's one thing I can't stand either, a baby crying all the time. I don't know what it does to me, but it makes me lose all faith in everything. When Joe cries I say to myself, Aw, what's the use?

JOHNNY: I guess I'll reach New York some day before I die.

JOHNNY'S FATHER: It's nothing, Mr. Wiley. He'll stop crying after a while.

MR. WILEY: Well, I hope so, and the sooner the better. [*He goes off with the envelope*] Good-by, Mr. Alexander. Good-by, Johnny.

JOHNNY'S FATHER: Mr. Wiley.

[Mr. Wiley *hands over the envelope. They say good-by, and* Mr. Wiley *rides off.* Johnny's Father *holds the envelope before him, obviously eager to open it, yet fearful to do so*]

JOHNNY: [*Impatient*] All right, Pa. Go ahead; open it. What are you waiting for?

JOHNNY'S FATHER: [*Angry; roaring*] Johnny, I'm scared. I can't understand how I, your father, can be so scared.

JOHNNY: You don't sound scared, Pa. Who's it from?

JOHNNY'S FATHER: It's from *The Atlantic Monthly* all right. You remember them poems I wrote after Mr. MacGregor was here?

JOHNNY: Maybe they've bought the poems.

JOHNNY'S FATHER: Bought them, my eye. They don't buy *poetry*, Johnny. They *scare* you to death. [*Reading his name and address with great solemnity, awful fearfulness and terrible rage*] Ben Alexander, 2226 San Benito Avenue, Fresno, California.

JOHNNY: It's for you all right, Pa. Why don't you open it?

JOHNNY'S FATHER: [*Roaring*] I'm scared, I tell you. I'm scared and ashamed. *Those poems were great.* How can it be that I'm scared?

JOHNNY: [*Also defiant*] Don't be scared, Pa.

JOHNNY'S FATHER: [*Angry*] Why do they clamor for all things but the best? Why do they destroy themselves running after things of death, and thrust aside all things of life? I can't understand it. There's no hope for *anybody*.

JOHNNY: Sure there is, Pa. [*Furiously*] Who the hell is *The Atlantic Monthly*?

JOHNNY'S FATHER: [*Angry*] Johnny, go away. Go away. Please go away.

JOHNNY: [*Angry, too*] All right, Pa. [Johnny *goes around the house, reappears, looks at his father a moment, and then knows he must stay out of the way*]

[*It is obvious that* Johnny's Father *knows* The Atlantic Monthly *has sent back the poems. It is equally obvious that he can't believe the poems have come back. It is obvious too that the poems are great, because the man is. He paces about like a tiger. He seems to be speaking to the world, even though his lips are set. At last he tears the envelope open, in a fury. The envelope falls. He unfolds the manuscript of poems. A slip of white, heavy paper falls to the floor of the porch. He stands, very tall, and very proud, and reads the poems to himself, turning the pages swiftly*]

JOHNNY'S FATHER: [*Furiously*] Ah, you crazy, miserable fools. [*He sits on the steps of the porch and buries his face in his hands. The manuscript of poems is on the steps. After several minutes he kicks the poems off the steps of the porch onto the ground and takes up the morning paper again, looking at the headlines. Quietly, with deep fury, his voice mounting in intensity*] Go ahead, kill *everybody*. Declare *War* on one another. Take the people by the thousands and mangle them. Their poor hearts and their poor spirits and their poor bodies. Give them ugliness. Pollute their dreams. Horrify them. Distort them with hatred for one another. Befoul the legend of the living, you maniacs whose greatness is measured by the number you destroy. [Johnny *appears at the side of the house, unseen. He stands in a trance, listening to his father. The sky begins to darken*] You frauds of the world. You wretched and ungodly. [*He stands and points a finger, as if across the world*] Go ahead. *Fire* your feeble guns. You won't kill *anything*. [*Quietly, smiling*] There will always be poets in the world.

[*Lightning flashes silently*]

The house. The sky is dark, as at the beginning of a storm. An occasional deep and faraway roar of thunder is heard, and a flash of lightning is seen. Johnny's Father *is on the steps of the porch, smiling: a foolish, tragic, desolate, lonely smile. Everything is the same; the manuscript of poems is on the ground; the envelope is on the porch. The newspaper too. It is several hours later.*

JOHNNY'S FATHER: [*Shaking his head foolishly, unable to accept the truth*] Johnny. [*Pause. A little louder*] Johnny. [*Pause, softer this time*] Johnny. [*Roaring*] Johnny. [*The boy comes around the house shyly and stands before his father. His father looks up, fire in his eye, defiant, bitter, stubborn, powerful*]

JOHNNY'S FATHER: [*Tenderly, but with tremendous power*] Have you had your breakfast?

JOHNNY: [*Shyly*] I'm not hungry, Pa.

JOHNNY'S FATHER: You go inside now and eat.

JOHNNY: I'm not hungry.

JOHNNY'S FATHER: You do what I tell you.

JOHNNY: I won't eat unless you do.

JOHNNY'S FATHER: You do what I *tell* you.

JOHNNY: I won't eat unless you do.

JOHNNY'S FATHER: I'm not hungry.

JOHNNY: I'll go down to Mr. Kosak's and see if I can get something.

JOHNNY'S FATHER: [*Humiliated. Taking the boy's arm*] No, Johnny. [*He pauses, obviously trying to find words with which to explain about themselves and the grocer*] Johnny? I thought we'd be getting some money. I didn't think it would be this way. Now, go on inside and eat.

JOHNNY: [*Going up the stairs*] You got to eat, too. [*He goes into the house*]

[*There is a silent flash of lightning. A Man in a business suit, and a young* Husband *and* Wife *with a* Baby *in the mother's arms, come up*]

THE REAL ESTATE MAN: This is the house. The rent's six dollars a month. It's not exactly fancy, but it'll keep out the rain and cold.

[Johnny's Father *has been staring at the people, his vision frozen*]

THE REAL ESTATE MAN: [*Coming up to* Johnny's Father, *extending his hand, while the others stand back in a group*] Remember me? I put up the "For Rent" sign.

JOHNNY'S FATHER: [*Rising*] I remember. How do you do.

THE REAL ESTATE MAN: [*Embarrassed*] Well. Mr. Corey, the owner of the house, is out of town, and these people are looking for a house. *Right away.*

JOHNNY'S FATHER: Of course. I can leave any time. Have they furniture?

THE REAL ESTATE MAN: [*Turning to the poor family*] Have you furniture?

THE HUSBAND: No.

JOHNNY'S FATHER: [*To the family*] You can have my furniture. There isn't much of it, but it'll do. There's a pretty good stove.

THE WIFE: [*With the dignity of the poor*] We wouldn't want to take *your* furniture.

JOHNNY'S FATHER: That's all right. I haven't paid rent for three months. I'll leave the furniture for the rent. [The Real Estate Man *tries to speak*]

JOHNNY'S FATHER: It's all right. I'm sorry I haven't the $18. The furniture's worth about that much. You can let these people have it till Mr. Corey gets back. [*To the family*] Do you want to go through the house?

THE HUSBAND: It looks all right.

THE REAL ESTATE MAN: [*Going*] Then that's settled. [*To the people*] The rent's six dollars a month. We pay the water.

JOHNNY'S FATHER: [*To the people*] You can move in any time.

THE HUSBAND: Thank you very much. We'll be back this afternoon or tomorrow. [*They are going as* Johnny *comes out with a plate containing two slices of bread and a small bunch of grapes*]

JOHNNY: Who were those people?

JOHNNY'S FATHER: Just some people walking by.

JOHNNY: What were you talking about?

JOHNNY'S FATHER: Just talking, Johnny.

JOHNNY: [*Shouting; very angry*] Don't feel bad, Pa.

JOHNNY'S FATHER: [*Turning and looking at the boy with love, amazement, admiration, and delight, laughing suddenly*] I don't feel bad, Johnny. Let the world be the world, and God love everyone.

JOHNNY: [*Bantering*] All right then. Let's eat. [*He puts the plate on the top step and they sit down together and begin to eat. They eat in silence, looking at one another, the boy looking at his father out of the corner of his eye as he had looked at the sun; the father looking at the boy the same way. The boy begins to smile. The father begins to smile too*]

JOHNNY: Do you like grapes, Pa?

JOHNNY'S FATHER: Of course I like grapes.

JOHNNY: Pa?

JOHNNY'S FATHER: Yes?

JOHNNY: Is it really like a prison?

JOHNNY'S FATHER: Sometimes I'm *sure* it is. Sometimes I *know* it never can be.

JOHNNY: What, Pa?

JOHNNY'S FATHER: I guess it's fifty-fifty, Johnny. You know. It's both.

JOHNNY: I mean, do you think he gets homesick sometimes?

JOHNNY'S FATHER: I'm sure he does.

JOHNNY: I wish he'd come back.

JOHNNY'S FATHER: I'd like to see him again.

JOHNNY: I remember him all the time.

JOHNNY'S FATHER: I do too. I'll always remember him.

JOHNNY: So will I. Did he *have* to go back, Pa?

JOHNNY'S FATHER: I guess he did.

JOHNNY: He seemed like a nice young man.

JOHNNY'S FATHER: You mean the young man who came and got him?

JOHNNY: Yeah, you know. That young man who talked so sharp, like he was speaking in front of an audience.

JOHNNY'S FATHER: He was all right. [*There is one more grape on the plate*]

JOHNNY: Go ahead, Pa. Take it.

JOHNNY'S FATHER: [*Blithely*] No, that's yours, Johnny. I counted.

JOHNNY: All right, Pa. [*He takes the last grape and eats it*] Is it stealing, Pa?

JOHNNY'S FATHER: [*Comically*] Well, some say it is and some say it isn't. [*Dramatically*] *I* say it isn't. [*Shouting*] You took them off the vines, didn't you?

JOHNNY: I took them off the vines all right, Pa.

JOHNNY'S FATHER: [*Comically*] Then it couldn't very well be stealing.

JOHNNY: When would it be stealing?

JOHNNY'S FATHER: [*Tossing it off like nothing*] The way I see it, Johnny, stealing is where there's unnecessary damage or cruelty to an innocent one, so that there may be undeserved profit or power to one who is not innocent.

JOHNNY: Oh. [*Pause*] Well, if it isn't stealing, Pa, I guess I'll go get some more. [*He gets up*] They'll all be gone pretty soon. [*Goes off*]

JOHNNY'S FATHER: [*When the boy is gone, laughing*] My son John. My God, how fortunate I have been. How grateful I am. [*He picks up the manuscript of poems, puts it in his coat pocket, and walks down the street*]

The inside of Mr. Kosak's Grocery Store. Again Mr. Kosak *is sleeping on his folded arms. The store looks more poverty-stricken than before. The family apparently has been eating the stock.* Johnny's father *comes into the store quietly, almost shyly.* Mr. Kosak *lifts his head, blinks his eyes, stands.*

JOHNNY'S FATHER: [*Almost guiltily*] I'm Johnny's father.

[*The two men stand staring at one another a moment, each of them delighted, embarrassed, impressed, pleased, and angry about the same things in the world: greed, deceit, unkindliness, disproportion. They each begin to smile, then shake hands warmly*]

MR. KOSAK: I recognize you. Johnny has told me about you. It is an honor.

JOHNNY'S FATHER: You are a kind man.

MR. KOSAK: I do not know.

JOHNNY'S FATHER: [*Slowly*] I have come to say good-by. To apologize. To thank you.

MR. KOSAK: [*Swiftly*] You're not going away?

JOHNNY'S FATHER: I'm sorry, yes.

MR. KOSAK: We shall all miss Johnny.

JOHNNY'S FATHER: I have no money. I am in debt to you.

MR. KOSAK: It is nothing.

JOHNNY'S FATHER: I may not see you again. [*He brings the manuscript of poems from his pocket. Powerfully*] I am a poet. These are some of my poems. [*Swiftly*] I am not offering them to you in place of the money I owe you. Money is another thing. [*Pleading*] Will you keep them for your kindness?

MR. KOSAK: [*Sincerely*] I cannot take your poems. [*Pause*]

JOHNNY'S FATHER: I hope you have been prospering.

MR. KOSAK: The people have no money. I do not know how I am going to put in new stock.

JOHNNY'S FATHER: I'm sorry.

MR. KOSAK: In the Winter it is worse. The packing-houses are closed. There are no jobs. I would give them something if I could, but this Winter I have no money for new stock. I may have to close the store. There is hardly enough for my family.

JOHNNY'S FATHER: [*Touched and angry*] These poems. Let me tell you they are the finest I have ever written. I want to leave them with you.

[*Mr. Kosak's daughter,* Esther, *a beautiful girl of seven, comes into the store, from the back*]

MR. KOSAK: This is my daughter Esther. Esther, this is Johnny's father.

JOHNNY'S FATHER: Johnny's told me about you.

ESTHER: [*Really pleased, but shy*] How do you do.

MR. KOSAK: They're going away.

ESTHER: [*Shocked*] Oh.

JOHNNY'S FATHER: Johnny will miss you.

[*The girl's lips tremble, tears come to her eyes. She turns and runs out of the store*]

MR. KOSAK: Everything is like that.

JOHNNY'S FATHER: They are children.

MR. KOSAK: Yes, but it's that way from the beginning and it never changes. Only women never learn to believe it.

JOHNNY'S FATHER: Won't you give *her* these poems?

MR. KOSAK: Please. It's nothing. She will cry for a while, but it is nothing.

JOHNNY'S FATHER: Here. [*Giving* Mr. Kosak *the poems*] You will be doing me a kindness by keeping them. [*Loudly, to God and the world*] Don't you see, poetry must be *read* to be poetry. It may be that one reader is all that I deserve. If this is so, I want that reader to be you.

MR. KOSAK: Thank you. I am unworthy.

JOHNNY'S FATHER: [*Smiling*] Good-by.

MR. KOSAK: Good-by.

[Johnny's Father *goes out of the store. The grocer takes his glasses out of his pocket, puts them on, unfolds the manuscript, and standing in the middle of the store, begins to read, softly, to himself, moving his lips. The expression of his face begins to change. Rain begins to fall. His daughter* Esther *comes back into the store*]

MR. KOSAK: [*Reading from one of the poems, in a quiet voice*] Deep in the bowels of the earth, and far dispersed into the green waters of the sea, and held tight within the hardness of rock, I thee remember, love, remember me. [*The girl begins to sob aloud, and the father turns and goes to her*]

The living room of the house. Some time later. Johnny's Father *is at his table, looking over a stack of manuscripts. It is still raining. Every once in a while he gets up and goes to the window.*

JOHNNY'S FATHER: What the hell's happened to him? [*He goes back to his manuscripts and looks over some poems, grows irritated with them, throws them down, and goes to the window again. Then begins to walk back and forth, waiting. At last* Johnny *tears up the front porch stairs, bursts into the house, closes the door quickly, and bolts it. He is breathless and scared. You know he is one who has been pursued. He has four medium-sized bunches of purple-red Emperors; a half dozen black figs, and two pomegranates*]

JOHNNY: [*Excited and breathless*] Where shall I hide them, Pa?

JOHNNY'S FATHER: What's the matter, Johnny?

JOHNNY: You said it wasn't stealing, Pa.

JOHNNY'S FATHER: [*With furious irritation*] Well, it isn't.

JOHNNY: What about the farmer's dog, then?

JOHNNY'S FATHER: What are you talking about? What farmer's dog?

JOHNNY: The farmer's dog that chased me all the way here.

JOHNNY'S FATHER: Dog? Do you mean to tell me a dog chased you? What kind of a dog?

JOHNNY: I didn't get a chance to take a good look, but I guess it's a great big one.

JOHNNY'S FATHER: [*Very angry at this awful humiliation*] Did the God damn thing try to bite you or anything, Johnny?

JOHNNY: I don't think so, Pa, but I thought it was going to any minute.

JOHNNY'S FATHER: Did it growl at you?

JOHNNY: It wasn't exactly a growl.

JOHNNY'S FATHER: What happened?

JOHNNY: I just ran all the way, with the dog right behind me.

JOHNNY'S FATHER: Where is it now?

JOHNNY: It's *outside*, I think, Pa. Are you sure it isn't stealing?

JOHNNY'S FATHER: [*Very angry, eating three or four grapes*] Of course it isn't stealing. I'll take care of the dog. No man or beast can scare your father, Johnny. Always remember that. [*He goes cautiously to the window and peeks out*]

JOHNNY: Is it out there, Pa?

JOHNNY'S FATHER: There's a little dog out there, Johnny. It's asleep, I think.

JOHNNY: [*Jumping bitterly*] *I knew it*. It's the farmer's dog, waiting for me.

JOHNNY'S FATHER: It's not a very big dog, Johnny.

JOHNNY: Yeah, but if it's stealing—if it's the *farmer's* dog—what about that?

JOHNNY'S FATHER: Why, that little bitty dog doesn't belong to anybody, Johnny. That little dog is looking for a friend, I bet.

JOHNNY: It chased me all the way. Are you sure, Pa?

JOHNNY'S FATHER: Sure I'm sure, Johnny. I'm no poet for nothing. I understand things. [*The dog begins to growl and bark.* Johnny's Father *jumps back from the window, frightened.* Johnny *jumps tense and speechless*]

JOHNNY: [*Whispering*] What is it, Pa?

JOHNNY'S FATHER: Somebody's coming, I think.

JOHNNY: You see, Pa? *It is stealing*. It's the farmer. [*He runs to the table and gathers the fruit into his arms. His Grandmother comes running into the room*]

JOHNNY'S GRANDMOTHER: [*In Armenian*] What's all the hullabaloo, in the rain?

JOHNNY'S FATHER: Shhhh. [Johnny *takes the fruit out of the living room; returns, scared to death. The dog is still growling and barking.* Johnny's Father *is even more scared than* Johnny]

JOHNNY: [*Sore, and now defiant*] God damn it, Pa. Now look at the mess we're in.

JOHNNY'S FATHER: I wish I had a cigarette.

JOHNNY: [*Now worrying about his father; to his grandmother, in Armenian*] Are there cigarettes? [Johnny's Grandmother *runs into the next room. The dog stops growling*]

JOHNNY: You see, Pa? It's the farmer. Where shall I hide? Don't open the door.

JOHNNY'S FATHER: *Open the door?* Help me with this table. [*They push the table up against the door, and tiptoe back to the center of the room.* Johnny's Grandmother *runs back with one cigarette and one match which she hands to* Johnny's Father, *who lights the cigarette, inhales deeply, and straightens up*]

JOHNNY'S FATHER: [*Dramatically*] *I* am the one who took the fruit, understand, Johnny?

JOHNNY: Don't open the door, Pa. [Johnny's Father *picks up a small stool, takes it quietly to the table up against the door, places it on the table, to make it heavier.* Johnny *picks up a chair and puts it on the table. The* Old Lady *puts a vase on the table.* Johnny's Father *adds three books to the barricade. In fact, as the knocks continue, the family little by little puts all the household goods up against the door*]

JOHNNY'S FATHER: Don't be afraid, Johnny.

JOHNNY: He can't get in, can he, Pa?

JOHNNY'S FATHER: I don't think so.

[*The* Grandmother, *the* Father *and the* Son *stand together in the bare room, defying the world. There is a long pause, full of mingling of awful fear and furious defiance. After half a minute the silence is broken. It is a solo on the bugle: "My Heart's in the Highlands." The sun comes out*]

JOHNNY: [*Shouting*] It's Mr. MacGregor.

JOHNNY'S FATHER: [*Running to the window, lifting it, and shouting out to* MacGregor] Welcome, Mr. MacGregor. Johnny, rearrange the furniture. [Johnny's Father *returns to the barricade and helps* Johnny *and his* Grandmother *rearrange the furniture. At last everything is out of the way.* Johnny's Father *swings open the door.* Jasper MacGregor, *still playing the solo, preceded by the dog, which is a very small street dog, comes in. The dog runs around playfully, all excited.* MacGregor's *eyes are full of grief and joy.* Johnny *begins making trips to the kitchen, returning with the fruit, on a plate, and a pitcher of water.* MacGregor *finishes the solo. There is a moment when everybody stands stock-*

still, including the dog. Johnny *offers* MacGregor *the pitcher of water*]

MAC GREGOR: [*Weary*] Not this time, Johnny.

JOHNNY'S FATHER: Welcome, my friend.

MAC GREGOR: I've run away. They're after me now, but I won't go back. They stole my bugle. They tried to keep me in bed. They said I was sick. I'm not sick; I'm old. I know my days on earth are numbered. I want them to be with you. Don't let them take me back.

JOHNNY'S FATHER: I won't. [*He draws out a chair for the old man*] Please sit down. [*They all sit down.* MacGregor *looks around at everybody*]

MAC GREGOR: It's good to see you again.

JOHNNY: Is your heart still in the highlands?

MAC GREGOR: [*Nodding*] In the highlands, son.

JOHNNY'S FATHER: [*Angry*] *Johnny.*

JOHNNY: [*Sore, too*] What?

JOHNNY'S FATHER: Shut up.

JOHNNY: Why?

JOHNNY'S FATHER: *Why?* What do you get so dumb for every once in a while? Can't you see Mr. MacGregor is weary?

JOHNNY: [*To* MacGregor] Are you?

MAC GREGOR: [*Nods*] But where's your mother, son?

JOHNNY: She's dead.

MAC GREGOR: [*Almost to himself*] Not dead, Johnny. [*He shakes his head*] In the highlands.

JOHNNY'S GRANDMOTHER: [*To his father*] What's he saying?

JOHNNY'S FATHER: [*Shaking his head*] Nothing. [*To* MAC GREGOR] Won't you eat?

MAC GREGOR: [*Looking at the plate*] One grape. No more. [*He plucks a grape off a bunch, puts it in his mouth. Suddenly turns, startled*] Are they coming?

JOHNNY'S FATHER: Don't be afraid, my friend. Lie down and rest. [Johnny's Father *takes the* Old Man *to the couch. The* Old Man *stretches out, face up.* Johnny's Father *returns to the table. Nobody is eating. The* Old Man *jumps up suddenly. It's nothing again. He gets up and returns to the table*]

MAC GREGOR: You won't let them take me back, will you?

JOHNNY'S FATHER: No. [*He breaks open a pomegranate and hands* MacGregor *half*] Try to eat something.

MAC GREGOR: Thank you, my friend. [*He eats some of the pomegranate. There is a knock on the door,* MacGregor *leaps to his feet, furiously*]

MAC GREGOR: [*Roaring*] You'll not take me back. I warn you. I'll fall down and die. I belong here, with these people.

JOHNNY'S FATHER: [*Scared*] Shall we open the door?

JOHNNY: [*Also scared*] Shall we?

MAC GREGOR: [*Powerfully*] Of course we'll open the door. [*He goes to the door, opens it. It is* Rufe

Apley, *the carpenter, who is a little shaken up by* MacGregor's *fury*]

RUFE APLEY: Hello, Mr. MacGregor.

JOHNNY: Who is it?

RUFE APLEY: It's Rufe Apley.

MAC GREGOR: How do you do, Rufe.

JOHNNY'S FATHER: [*At the door*] Come in, Rufe. [Rufe *comes in. He has a loaf of bread, a sausage and two eggs in his hands*]

RUFE: I was sitting home doing nothing when I heard that song again. I was sure it was Mr. Mac-Gregor.

MAC GREGOR: I'm delighted you remembered.

RUFE: Nobody could ever forget that song, Mr. MacGregor. I brought these few things.

MAC GREGOR: [*Taking them and putting them on the table*] Thank you, my friend, thank you.

[*There is another knock at the door. It is* Sam Wallace; *he is a lineman, in full regalia: overalls, tools hanging all over him, tape, straps around his calves, spikes, everything. He has cheese and tomatoes and radishes with him*]

WALLACE: I *knew* it was Mr. MacGregor. I said to myself, I'll go over with a few little things to eat.

MAC GREGOR: This is indeed a pleasant surprise.

RUFE: [*Obviously trying hard to say something*] Ah, Mr. MacGregor?

MAC GREGOR: Yes, my friend? Speak up. I'm a plain man, no different in any way from yourself.

RUFE: My wife's sister and her family are outside. I know they'd like to hear you play again. There are some other people.

MAC GREGOR: [*Flattered*] Of course I'll play. I'm over eighty and not long for this world. Before I go I'd like to become a part of you who shall live after I am dead. Are there children out there too?

RUFE: Seven. My wife's sister's kids.

[*Three or four more neighbors come in, bringing food.* MacGregor *takes up his bugle. Everybody follows him out of the room to the porch, except* Johnny's Father. MacGregor *begins to play the solo again. This time he's too old and weak to really play, but he finishes the solo as well as he is able to.* Johnny's Father *paces about the room, smiling, frowning, loving the place. The door to the kitchen opens quietly and* Esther Kosak *stands in the doorway.* Johnny's Father *turns and sees her. She is no longer crying. She has something clutched in her fist*]

JOHNNY'S FATHER: [*Quietly*] Hello, Esther.

ESTHER: Where's Johnny?

JOHNNY'S FATHER: I'll go get him. [*He goes out on the porch. The* Girl *stands alone in terrible sadness and loneliness. After a moment* Johnny *comes rushing in, all excited, but calms down quickly when he begins to feel the mood of the girl*]

JOHNNY: Hello, Esther.

ESTHER: Hello, Johnny.

JOHNNY: What's the matter?

ESTHER: My father read me the poems.

JOHNNY: What?

ESTHER: [*Holding out her hand*] Here. This is all I've got. [Johnny *takes a handful of coins*] I've been saving up for Christmas. [*She begins to cry, turns, and runs out of the house*]

JOHNNY: [*Deeply touched and furious, sensing something profound and beautiful and terrible*] Holy Moses. [*His face takes on boyhood's tragic expression of grief, and he begins to cry. He throws the coins against the wall and falls down, sobbing*] Who the hell wants that stuff? [Johnny's Father *comes back*]

JOHNNY'S FATHER: Johnny. [*Going closer*] Johnny?

JOHNNY: [*Sobbing and angry*] She brought me money.

JOHNNY'S FATHER: It's no use crying, Johnny.

JOHNNY: [*Jumping up*] Who's crying? [*He cries harder than ever*]

JOHNNY'S FATHER: Go wash your face. It's nothing.

JOHNNY: [*Going*] Something's wrong somewhere.

[MacGregor *finishes the solo, the people are silent with awe and the knowledge that something is wrong.* MacGregor's Voice *is heard for a moment in a speech*]

MAC GREGOR: [*Wearily*] The years, my friends. I have walked to the end of them. I'm sorry I can no longer play for you. Thank you. Thank you.

[Johnny's Father *walks back and forth in the room. He sits down at the table and looks at the food.* MacGregor *and* Johnny's Grandmother *return and sit at the table. The dog lies down in a corner*]

MAC GREGOR: [*He lifts the water pitcher, drinks a little*] They wouldn't let me play. [*He drinks a little more*] They stole my bugle. [*He drinks a little more*] They said I was sick. [*He drinks a little more*] I'm strong as a bull. If they come to take me back, I shall pretend that I am dying. I shall play the death scene from "King Lear." I shall play *all* the death scenes.

[Johnny *returns solemnly. They are all at the table. Nobody can eat but the* Old Lady. *There is a long silence. The* Old Lady *stops eating*]

JOHNNY'S GRANDMOTHER: What's the matter? Why this terrible gloom? [MacGregor *rises*]

MAC GREGOR: [*Reciting, remembering lines from Shakespeare, and inventing a few of his own*] Blow, winds, and crack your cheeks! Rage! blow! You cataracts and hurricanes, spout till you have drenched our steeples, drowned the cocks! You sulphurous and thought-executing fires, singe my white head! Humble thy belly-full, spit fire, spout rain! I never gave you kingdom, call'd you children. Here I stand, your slave, a poor infirm, weak and despised old man. To be or not to be . . . [*Tragically*] To be— To be— What? A fool? A man mocked by destiny? Turned away from home and fire and love? I am a man more sinned against than sinning. Arms! Arms! Sword! Fire! Corruption in the place! The little dogs and all, Tray, Blanche, Sweetheart. See? They bark at me. O, that way madness lies— no more of that—let me shun that. My wits begin to turn. [Johnny *goes to him and kneels*] Come on, my boy, how dost my boy? Art cold? let me alone! Wilt break my heart? And my poor fool is hang'd. No, no, no life! Why should a dog, a horse, a rat have life and thou no life at all? Thou'lt come no more, never, never, never, never, never! Pray you undo this button—thank you, sir— [*Holds the bugle before him*] Do you see this? Look on her. Look. Look there, look there!!

[*While MacGregor is acting Johnny returns to the coins on the floor and picks them up one by one and looks at them. The room is in absolute silence. A horse and wagon in the street is heard; then steps on the front porch; then a knock at the door. Johnny's Father goes to the door. It is Philip Carmichael and two guards from the Old People's Home. The guards stand at attention at the door*]

CARMICHAEL: We heard him playing. He's very sick. We've come to take him back.

JOHNNY'S FATHER: Please come in. [*He enters. To* MacGregor] Mr. MacGregor. [*There is no answer*]

JOHNNY'S FATHER: [*Louder*] Mr. MacGregor. [*Goes closer*] Mr. MacGregor, Mr. Mac—

[*Carmichael hurries over to MacGregor and examines him*]

CARMICHAEL: He's dead.

JOHNNY: No, he isn't. He was acting.

JOHNNY'S FATHER: By God, he *was* the greatest Shakespearean actor of our day.

CARMICHAEL: I'm sorry this had to happen here.

JOHNNY'S FATHER: Why not? Why not here? This is where he wanted it to be.

JOHNNY: He was acting, Pa. He isn't dead. [*He goes to* MacGregor] Are you, Mr. MacGregor? [*There is no answer, of course*]

CARMICHAEL: We'll take him back.

JOHNNY'S FATHER: Here's his bugle. Keep it with him. [*Johnny's Father lifts MacGregor and carries him out. The guards carry him up the street. The light of the afternoon sun increases to the same intensity as at the beginning of the play. The horse and wagon goes off. There is a moment of strange silence, and the faint far-away sound of the bugle solo. A knock at the door. Johnny's Father opens the door. It's the young Husband and Wife. The Baby is crying. They come in*]

THE WIFE: The kid is tired and sleepy.

JOHNNY'S FATHER: The house is ready. [*To* Johnny] Get your stuff. [*To the* Old Lady, *in Armenian*] We're going. [*He gets a straw suitcase from under the couch and throws his poems, books, envelopes, one loaf of bread, and a few of the other items of food into it. The* Old Lady *puts a shawl around her head and shoulders. Johnny leaves all his junk; takes only the handful of coins. The* Baby *stops crying. The dog follows* Johnny *around. The music increases in intensity*]

THE HUSBAND: Thank you very much.

THE WIFE: Have you some place to go?

JOHNNY'S FATHER: Yes, we have. Good-by.

THE HUSBAND AND WIFE: Good-by. [*They go out of the house to the street*]

JOHNNY: Where the hell do we think we're going, Pa?

JOHNNY'S FATHER: Never mind, Johnny. You just follow me.

JOHNNY: I'm not mentioning any names, Pa, but something's wrong somewhere.

[*The music grows louder. They walk up the street*]

Tennessee Williams

(1914———)

Nothing is so characteristic of Tennessee Williams as his ability to adapt extreme subjectivity to the most objective of the arts. An individualist and a man of wayward impulse, he learned to discipline a volatile temperament for the purpose of calculating dramatic effects and developing a point to relentless conclusion. It was by no means easy for him to work himself out of the tunnel of subjective artistry into the light of orderly judgment and clear vistas.

Although a cosmopolitan by taste and literary interest, Williams is a Southern artist. He is that not merely because he has given us pictures of the South and dealt with its products, chiefly with the overdelicate girls and futile middle-aged women whom Southern writers have so often portrayed, but in his awareness of decadence. A "Southern Gothic" imagination appears in his world of oppressive half-lights, anxieties, and outbursts of desperation. There is, it is true, something of D. H. Lawrence in Williams' concern with suppressed sexuality and in his search for liberation through uninhibited animality. Williams is an admirer of Lawrence, and the English writer's influence may be traced in some of the plays. But there is a good deal more of Faulkner in Williams' clinical presentation of warped souls and crass conduct. Only one play, *The Glass Menagerie,* and one adaptation, of a story by D. H. Lawrence, have more light than darkness.

We may feel, indeed, that Williams would have been quite lost if he had not made a dramatist of himself. He might have become a minor poet and prose writer for a small coterie. That he should have come to write plays for large audiences and so move out of the confines of esoteric art is evidence of a certain quantity of iron in his constitution. He is an artist to his fingertips, yet he has knocked about in the world instead of living in refined seclusion; he has exquisite tastes, yet he has lived and worked in environments where indulgence of those tastes was an unlikely possibility.

Thomas Lanier ("Tennessee") Williams was born of pioneering, Indian-fighting Tennessee ancestry in Columbus, Mississippi. His father was a shoe salesman; his mother was of the Southern aristocracy. Her father, an Episcopalian clergyman who had much to do with the shaping of the boy's mind, was a gentleman with a taste for poetry and literature, as well as for bridge and cocktails. It was in his grandfather's rectory that Williams first observed the Southern women who fill his plays with their genteel anguish. It would be more accurate to say, however, that Williams grew up in a world divided between the cultured life of the rectory and a not particularly prosperous home environment.

The future playwright attended high school in St. Louis and went on to the University of Missouri in 1931. He found it necessary after his sophomore year to take a job in the shoe factory where his father was employed, and he spent two years there, gaining, as he reported later, "valuable insight into the monotony of the white collar worker's life." But the writing fever that made him stay up late at night brought on a nervous collapse. He returned to college in 1936, studying at Washington University in St. Louis, and then went to the University of Iowa to take a Bachelor of Arts degree. Restlessness seizing him, he began to travel across the land, sustaining himself with odd jobs. He was a bellhop in a New Orleans hotel, a teletypist in Jacksonville, Florida, a seventeen-dollar-a-week usher in a New York motion picture theatre, and a waiter and reciter of verses in a Bohemian Greenwich Village night club. Throughout this apprenticeship he wrote continually, experimenting with poetry, stories, and plays.

Williams' interest in the theatre began when he saw a performance of *Ghosts,* with which Alla Nazimova was touring the country. He was then an undergraduate at the University of Missouri. "It was," he recalled later, "one of the things that made me want to write for the theatre." Numerous one-acters and ten full-length plays by the time he wrote his greatest success, *A Streetcar Named Desire* (1947), testify to his energetic pursuit of a dramatic career. The early full-length plays made no impression and were discarded by the author, but his one-acters, in which the themes of his later long plays are prefigured, attracted attention by 1939. He found an agent, Audrey Wood, who fought hopefully for him, and he won a small cash prize from the Group Theatre for four short pieces, *American Blues,* dealing with victims of the depression. In January 1940, Theresa Helburn and John Gassner, of the Theatre Guild, gave him a scholarship to their advanced playwrights' seminar and brought the play he wrote that semester to the Guild. Entitled *Battle of Angels,* it received a production that autumn under the direction of Margaret Webster and the supervision of the Guild's Lawrence Langner. It closed in Boston for repairs after affronting Bostonians with its somewhat lurid story of decadence in a Southern town and of the affair of a D. H. Lawrence hero and a sexually starved woman. But this defeat on the brink of professional success was salved somewhat by American Academy and Rockefeller Fellowship awards, and in 1945, Eddie Dowling, in association with Louis J. Singer, produced *The Glass Menagerie* in New York after a long tryout period in Chicago. It was a difficult play with which to attract the average playgoer, seemingly too tenuous and depressing as well as too unconventionally constructed. But the magic of the play, movingly conveyed by Laurette Taylor and Julie Haydon in the respective roles of the mother and the daughter, prevailed, and *The Glass Menagerie*, which won the Drama Critics Circle award, became a notable success.

Subsequently, in 1946, Williams had a disappointing production with *You Touched Me,* a collaborative adaptation of a D. H. Lawrence story of frustration in an English home. But a year later, he won an ecstatic reception in New York (and later throughout the country and abroad) with *A Streetcar Named Desire.* It was an unsavory tragedy of a woman's frustration, but its sordid matter of sexual depravity and madness in the New Orleans Latin Quarter was transfigured by poetic dramaturgy and overwhelming compassion. In 1948, Williams faced another disappointment when his next drama of a Southern woman's deterioration, *Summer and Smoke,* failed to live up to the expectations it had aroused when tried out by Margo Jones in her small arena theatre in Dallas. But the play again proved him a master of sensitive characterization and an able observer of town life in the South. Not at all daunted by critics who feared he was repeating himself and exhausting the theme of Southern decadence, Williams went ahead with the composition of a number of plays with which he hoped to extend the range of his playwriting. But even if these plays prove unsatisfactory, Williams will retain a high place in the American theatre. Several of his one-act plays (such as *Portrait of a Madonna* and *The Lady of Larkspur Lotion*) possess much power; his failures (*Battle of Angels* and *Summer and Smoke*) contain distinguished writing; and both *The Glass Menagerie* and *A Streetcar Named Desire* are among the noteworthy creations of the American drama.

Of the latter two plays, *The Glass Menagerie* is the more lyrical, if also more tenuous, example of their author's artistry. But it is plain enough that even in this delicate work Williams retains a highly objective attitude toward his picture of a life of failure. He locates his story in the context of the larger world, which demands a wide-awake attitude toward a society that, ailing and torn with the conflict of a Second World War, challenges our intelligence and capacity for action. The narrations that frame the story of the mother, the daughter, and the son form another dimension and supply a measure of objective reality. The "lives of quiet desperation" seem all the more defeated because they are lived in a world that no longer affords them shelter. A mighty wind has arisen and nobody seems to

temper it to the shorn lamb, whether it be an aging Southern belle abandoned by her husband or a girl too painfully shy for the coarse-grained world. Although the play is written in a mood of tenderly rueful reminiscence, Williams exhibits here much strength of mind and objectivity. Sympathize though he does with his failures, he recognizes that one cannot accept their quiescence and bumbling. The son pays a tribute of compassion to his mother and sister, but acknowledges the validity of the instinct of self-preservation that made him leave them; he knows, too, that in the great struggle of the times their plight is, in a sense, of minor consequence. *The Glass Menagerie* is, as had been claimed, a "mood." But it is a mood not mistaken by either the author or the Narrator (and they are actually the same person, since the play is largely autobiographical) for the whole of reality. The author was attached to his characters to such a degree that he could make them move us deeply, but he was also detached enough to locate them in time, place, and necessity. He created *The Glass Menagerie* as both poet and dramatist, as subjective writer and realist.

Fortunately, Williams found an effective form for this mixed kind of playwriting. He did not, it is true, entirely control his medium, mistaking theatrical virtuosity for effective emphases out of an apparent desire to depart as far as possible from realistic technique. This may be seen in the stage directions he insisted on retaining for the published version—directions which were moderated in Eddie Dowling's excellent production. Yet Williams' feeling for form was essentially right. He used narrations and scenes with emphatic alternation, envisioned the action in the manner of vignettes that soon become alive and charged, and called for the expressive use of visual and musical effects. His work represents a poet who is thoroughly at home in the theatre. *The Glass Menagerie* exists on several levels; it is a work in which imaginative and realistic elements stand in sound relation to each other. It is not a shattering drama, but it is a notable example of exquisite playwriting that is more tensile than it appears to be on the surface.

THE AUTHOR'S PRODUCTION NOTES

Being a "memory play," *The Glass Menagerie* can be presented with unusual freedom of convention. Because of its considerably delicate or tenuous material, atmospheric touches and subtleties of direction play a particularly important part. Expressionism and all other unconventional techniques in drama have only one valid aim, and that is a closer approach to truth. When a play employs unconventional techniques, it is not, or certainly shouldn't be, trying to escape its responsibility of dealing with reality, or interpreting experience, but is actually or should be attempting to find a closer approach, a more penetrating and vivid expression of things as they are. The straight realistic play with its genuine frigidaire and authentic ice-cubes, its characters that speak exactly as its audience speaks, corresponds to the academic landscape and has the same virtue of a photographic likeness. Everyone should know nowadays the unimportance of the photographic in art: that truth, life, or reality is an organic thing which the poetic imagination can represent or suggest, in essence, only through transformation, through changing into other forms than those which were merely present in appearance.

These remarks are not meant as a preface only to this particular play. They have to do with a conception of a new, plastic theatre which must take the place of the exhausted theatre of realistic conventions if the theatre is to resume vitality as a part of our culture.

THE SCREEN DEVICE. There is *only one important difference between the original and acting version of the play* and that is the *omission* in the latter of the device which I tentatively included in my *original* script. This device was the use of a screen on which were projected magic-lantern slides bearing images or titles. I do not regret the omission of this device from the present Broadway production. The extraordinary power of Miss Taylor's performance made it suitable to have the utmost simplicity in the physical production. But I think it may be interesting to some readers to see how this device was conceived. So I am putting it into the published manuscript. These images and legends, projected from behind, were cast on a section of wall between the front-room and dining-room areas, which should be indistinguishable from the rest when not in use.

The purpose of this will probably be apparent. It is to give accent to certain values in each scene. Each scene contains a particular point (or several) which is structurally the most important. In an episodic play, such as this, the basic structure or narrative line may be obscured from the audience; the effect may seem fragmentary rather than architectural. This may not be the fault of the play so much as a lack of attention in the audience. The legend or image upon the screen will strengthen the effect of what is merely allusion in the writing and allow the primary point to be made more simply and lightly than if the entire responsibility were on the spoken lines. Aside from this structural value, I think the screen will have a definite emotional appeal, less definable but just as important. An imaginative producer or director may invent many other uses for this device than those indicated in the present script. In fact the possibilities of the device seem much larger to me than the instance of this play can possibly utilize.

THE MUSIC. Another extra-literary accent in this play is provided by the use of music. A single re-

curring tune, "The Glass Menagerie," is used to give emotional emphasis to suitable passages. This tune is like circus music, not when you are on the grounds or in the immediate vicinity of the parade, but when you are at some distance and very likely thinking of something else. It seems under those circumstances to continue almost interminably and it weaves in and out of your preoccupied consciousness; then it is the lightest, most delicate music in the world and perhaps the saddest. It expresses the surface vivacity of life with the underlying strain of immutable and inexpressible sorrow. When you look at a piece of delicately spun glass you think of two things: how beautiful it is and how easily it can be broken. Both of those ideas should be woven into the recurring tune, which dips in and out of the play as if it were carried on a wind that changes. It serves as a thread of connection and allusion between the narrator with his separate point in time and space and the subject of his story. Between each episode it returns as reference to the emotion, nostalgia, which is the first condition of the play. It is primarily Laura's music and therefore comes out most clearly when the play focuses upon her and the lovely fragility of glass which is her image.

THE LIGHTING. The lighting in the play is not realistic. In keeping with the atmosphere of memory, the stage is dim. Shafts of light are focused on selected areas or actors, sometimes in contradistinction to what is the apparent center. For instance, in the quarrel scene between Tom and Amanda, in which Laura has no active part, the clearest pool of light is on her figure. This is also true of the supper scene, when her silent figure on the sofa should remain the visual center. The light upon Laura should be distinct from the others, having a peculiar pristine clarity such as light used in early religious portraits of female saints or madonnas. A certain correspondence to light in religious paintings, such as El Greco's, where the figures are radiant in atmosphere that is relatively dusky, could be effectively used throughout the play. (It will also permit a more effective use of the screen.) A free, imaginative use of light can be of enormous value in giving a mobile, plastic quality to plays of a more or less static nature.

BIBLIOGRAPHY: John Mason Brown, *Seeing Things* (pp. 224–230), 1946; Brown, *Seeing More Things* (pp. 266–272), 1948; John Gassner, "Tennessee Williams: Dramatist of Frustration," in *College English*, Vol. 10, No. 1, October 1948; Paul Moor, "A Mississippian Named Tennessee," in *Harper's*, July 1948; George Jean Nathan, *Theatre Book of the Year 1944–1945; 1947–1948; 1948–1949;* Tennessee Williams, "The Catastrophe of Success," in *The Glass Menagerie* (New Classics edition), 1945; Stark Young, *Immortal Shadows* (pp. 249–253), 1948.

THE GLASS MENAGERIE

By Tennessee Williams

THE CHARACTERS

AMANDA WINGFIELD, *the mother*

A little woman of great but confused vitality clinging frantically to another time and place. Her characterization must be carefully created, not copied from type. She is not paranoiac, but her life is paranoia. There is much to admire in Amanda, and as much to love and pity as there is to laugh at. Certainly she has endurance and a kind of heroism, and though her foolishness makes her unwittingly cruel at times, there is tenderness in her slight person.

LAURA WINGFIELD, *her daughter*

Amanda, having failed to establish contact with reality, continues to live vitally in her illusions, but Laura's situation is even graver. A childhood illness has left her crippled, one leg slightly shorter than the other, and held in a brace. This defect need not be more than suggested on the stage. Stemming from this, Laura's separation increases till she is like a piece of her own glass collection, too exquisitely fragile to move from the shelf.

TOM WINGFIELD, *her son*

And the narrator of the play. A poet with a job in a warehouse. His nature is not remorseless, but to escape from a trap he has to act without pity.

JIM O'CONNOR, *the gentleman caller*

A nice, ordinary, young man.

SCENE

AN ALLEY IN ST. LOUIS

PART I. Preparation for a Gentleman Caller.
PART II. The Gentleman calls.

Time: Now and the Past.

SCENE I.

The Wingfield apartment is in the rear of the building, one of those vast hive-like conglomerations of cellular living-units that flower as warty growths in overcrowded urban centers of lower middle-class population and are symptomatic of the impulse of this largest and fundamentally enslaved section of American society to avoid fluidity and differentiation and to exist and function as one interfused mass of automatism.

The apartment faces an alley and is entered by a fire-escape, a structure whose name is a touch of accidental poetic truth, for all of these huge buildings are always burning with the slow and implacable fires of human desperation. The fire-escape is included in the set—that is, the landing of it and steps descending from it.

The scene is memory and is therefore nonrealistic. Memory takes a lot of poetic license. It omits some details; others are exaggerated, according to the emotional value of the articles it touches, for memory is seated predominantly in the heart. The interior is therefore rather dim and poetic.

At the rise of the curtain, the audience is faced with the dark, grim rear wall of the Wingfield tene-

ment. This building, which runs parallel to the foot-lights, is flanked on both sides by dark, narrow alleys which run into murky canyons of tangled clothes-lines, garbage cans and the sinister lattice-work of neighboring fire-escapes. It is up and down these side alleys that exterior entrances and exits are made, during the play. At the end of Tom's opening commentary, the dark tenement wall slowly reveals (by means of a transparency) the interior of the ground floor Wingfield apartment.

Downstage is the living room, which also serves as a sleeping room for Laura, the sofa unfolding to make her bed. Upstage, center, and divided by a wide arch or second proscenium with transparent faded portieres (or second curtain), is the dining room. In an old-fashioned what-not in the living room are seen scores of transparent glass animals. A blown-up photograph of the father hangs on the wall of the living room, facing the audience, to the left of the archway. It is the face of a very handsome young man in a doughboy's First World War cap. He is gallantly smiling, ineluctably smiling, as if to say, "I will be smiling forever."

The audience hears and sees the opening scene in the dining room through both the transparent fourth wall of the building and the transparent gauze portieres of the dining-room arch. It is during this

1035

revealing scene that the fourth wall slowly ascends, out of sight. This transparent exterior wall is not brought down again until the very end of the play, during Tom's *final speech.*

The narrator is an undisguised convention of the play. He takes whatever license with dramatic convention as is convenient to his purposes.

Tom *enters dressed as a merchant sailor from alley, stage left, and strolls across the front of the stage to the fire-escape. There he stops and lights a cigarette. He addresses the audience.*

TOM: Yes, I have tricks in my pocket, I have things up my sleeve. But I am the opposite of a stage magician. He gives you illusion that has the appearance of truth. I give you truth in the pleasant disguise of illusion.

To begin with, I turn back time. I reverse it to that quaint period, the thirties, when the huge middle class of America was matriculating in a school for the blind. Their eyes had failed them, or they had failed their eyes, and so they were having their fingers pressed forcibly down on the fiery Braille alphabet of a dissolving economy.

In Spain there was revolution. Here there was only shouting and confusion.

In Spain there was Guernica. Here there were disturbances of labor, sometimes pretty violent, in otherwise peaceful cities such as Chicago, Cleveland, Saint Louis . . .

This is the social background of the play.

[MUSIC]

The play is memory.

Being a memory play, it is dimly lighted, it is sentimental, it is not realistic.

In memory everything seems to happen to music. That explains the fiddle in the wings.

I am the narrator of the play, and also a character in it.

The other characters are my mother, Amanda, my sister, Laura, and a gentleman caller who appears in the final scenes.

He is the most realistic character in the play, being an emissary from a world of reality that we were somehow set apart from.

But since I have a poet's weakness for symbols, I am using this character also as a symbol; he is the long delayed but always expected something that we live for.

There is a fifth character in the play who doesn't appear except in this larger-than-life-size photograph over the mantel.

This is our father who left us a long time ago.

He was a telephone man who fell in love with long distances; he gave up his job with the telephone company and skipped the light fantastic out of town . . .

The last we heard of him was a picture post-card from Mazatlan, on the Pacific coast of Mexico, containing a message of two words—

"Hello— Good-bye!" and no address.

I think the rest of the play will explain itself. . . .

[Amanda's *voice becomes audible through the portieres*]

[LEGEND ON SCREEN: "OÙ SONT LES NEIGES"]

He divides the portieres and enters the upstage area. Amanda *and* Laura *are seated at a drop-leaf table. Eating is indicated by gestures without food or utensils.* Amanda *faces the audience.* Tom *and* Laura *are seated in profile. The interior has lit up softly and through the scrim we see* Amanda *and* Laura *seated at the table in the upstage area.*

AMANDA: [*Calling*] Tom?

TOM: Yes, Mother.

AMANDA: We can't say grace until you come to the table!

TOM: Coming, Mother. [*He bows slightly and withdraws, reappearing a few moments later in his place at the table*]

AMANDA: [*To her son*] Honey, don't *push* with your *fingers.* If you have to push with something, the thing to push with is a crust of bread. And chew —chew! Animals have sections in their stomachs which enable them to digest food without mastication, but human beings are supposed to chew their food before they swallow it down. Eat food leisurely, son, and really enjoy it. A well-cooked meal has lots of delicate flavors that have to be held in the mouth for appreciation. So chew your food and give your salivary glands a chance to function!

[Tom *deliberately lays his imaginary fork down and pushes his chair back from the table*]

TOM: I haven't enjoyed one bite of this dinner because of your constant directions on how to eat it. It's you that make me rush through meals with your hawk-like attention to every bite I take. Sickening— spoils my appetite—all this discussion of—animals' secretion—salivary glands—mastication!

AMANDA: [*Lightly*] Temperament like a Metropolitan star! [*He rises and crosses downstage*] You're not excused from the table.

TOM: I'm getting a cigarette.

AMANDA: You smoke too much. [Laura *rises*]

LAURA: I'll bring in the blanc mange. [*He remains standing with his cigarette by the portieres during the following*]

AMANDA: [*Rising*] No, sister, no, sister—you be the lady this time and I'll be the darky.

LAURA: I'm already up.

AMANDA: Resume your seat, little sister—I want you to stay fresh and pretty—for gentlemen callers!

LAURA: I'm not expecting any gentlemen callers.

AMANDA: [*Crossing out to kitchenette. Airily*] Sometimes they come when they are least expected! Why, I remember one Sunday afternoon in Blue Mountain—[*Enters kitchenette*]

TOM: I know what's coming!

LAURA: Yes. But let her tell it.

TOM: Again?

LAURA: She loves to tell it.

[Amanda *returns with bowl of dessert*]

AMANDA: One Sunday afternoon in Blue Mountain—your mother received—*seventeen*—gentlemen callers! Why, sometimes there weren't chairs enough to accommodate them all. We had to send the nigger over to bring in folding chairs from the parish house.

TOM: [*Remaining at portieres*] How did you entertain those gentlemen callers?

AMANDA: I understood the art of conversation!

TOM: I bet you could talk.

AMANDA: Girls in those days *knew* how to talk, I can tell you.

TOM: Yes?

[IMAGE: Amanda AS A GIRL ON A PORCH, GREETING CALLERS]

AMANDA: They knew how to entertain their gentlemen callers. It wasn't enough for a girl to be possessed of a pretty face and a graceful figure—although I wasn't slighted in either respect. She also needed to have a nimble wit and a tongue to meet all occasions.

TOM: What did you talk about?

AMANDA: Things of importance going on in the world! Never anything coarse or common or vulgar. [*She addresses* Tom *as though he were seated in the vacant chair at the table though he remains by portieres. He plays this scene as though he held the book*] My callers were gentlemen—all! Among my callers were some of the most prominent young planters of the Mississippi Delta—planters and sons of planters!

[Tom *motions for music and a spot of light on* Amanda. *Her eyes lift, her face glows, her voice becomes rich and elegiac*]

[SCREEN LEGEND: "OÙ SONT LES NEIGES"]

There was young Champ Laughlin who later became vice-president of the Delta Planters Bank.

Hadley Stevenson who was drowned in Moon Lake and left his widow one hundred and fifty thousand in Government bonds.

There were the Cutrere brothers, Wesley and Bates. Bates was one of my bright particular beaux! He got in a quarrel with that wild Wainwright boy. They shot it out on the floor of Moon Lake Casino. Bates was shot through the stomach. Died in the ambulance on his way to Memphis. His widow was also well-provided for, came into eight or ten thousand acres, that's all. She married him on the rebound—never loved her—carried my picture on him the night he died!

And there was that boy that every girl in the Delta had set her cap for! That beautiful, brilliant young Fitzhugh boy from Greene County!

TOM: What did he leave his widow?

AMANDA: He never married! Gracious, you talk as though all of my old admirers had turned up their toes to the daisies!

TOM: Isn't this the first you've mentioned that still survives?

AMANDA: That Fitzhugh boy went North and made a fortune—came to be known as the Wolf of Wall Street! He had the Midas touch, whatever he touched turned to gold!

And I could have been Mrs. Duncan J. Fitzhugh, mind you! But—I picked your *father*!

LAURA: [*Rising*] Mother, let me clear the table.

AMANDA: No, dear, you go in front and study your typewriter chart. Or practice your shorthand a little. Stay fresh and pretty!—It's almost time for our gentlemen callers to start arriving. [*She flounces girlishly toward the kitchenette*] How many do you suppose we're going to entertain this afternoon?

[Tom *throws down the paper and jumps up with a groan*]

LAURA: [*Alone in the dining room*] I don't believe we're going to receive any, Mother.

AMANDA: [*Reappearing, airily*] What? No one—not one? You must be joking! [Laura *nervously echoes her laugh. She slips in a fugitive manner through the half-open portieres and draws them gently behind her. A shaft of very clear light is thrown on her face against the faded tapestry of the curtains.* MUSIC: "THE GLASS MENAGERIE" UNDER FAINTLY. *Lightly*] Not one gentleman caller? It can't be true! There must be a flood, there must have been a tornado!

LAURA: It isn't a flood, it's not a tornado, Mother. I'm just not popular like you were in Blue Mountain. . . . [Tom *utters another groan.* Laura *glances at him with a faint, apologetic smile. Her voice catching a little*] Mother's afraid I'm going to be an old maid.

THE SCENE DIMS OUT WITH "GLASS MENAGERIE"

MUSIC

SCENE II.

"Laura, Haven't You Ever Liked Some Boy?"

On the dark stage the screen is lighted with the image of blue roses. Gradually Laura's *figure becomes apparent and the screen goes out. The music subsides.*

Laura *is seated in the delicate ivory chair at the small clawfoot table. She wears a dress of soft violet material for a kimono—her hair tied back from her forehead with a ribbon. She is washing and polishing her collection of glass.*

Amanda *appears on the fire-escape steps. At the sound of her ascent,* Laura *catches her breath, thrusts the bowl of ornaments away and seats herself stiffly before the diagram of the typewriter keyboard as though it held her spellbound. Something has happened to* Amanda. *It is written in her face as she climbs to the landing: a look that is grim and hopeless and a little absurd. She has on one of those cheap or imitation velvety-looking cloth coats with imitation fur collar. Her hat is five or six years old, one of those dreadful cloche hats that were worn in the late twenties and she is clasping an enormous black patent-leather pocketbook with nickel clasps and initials. This is her full-dress outfit, the one she usually wears to the D.A.R. Before entering she looks through the door. She purses her lips, opens her eyes very wide, rolls them upward and shakes her head. Then she slowly lets herself in the door. Seeing her mother's expression* Laura *touches her lips with a nervous gesture.*

LAURA: Hello, Mother, I was— [*She makes a nervous gesture toward the chart on the wall.* Amanda *leans against the shut door and stares at* Laura *with a martyred look*]

AMANDA: Deception? Deception? [*She slowly removes her hat and gloves, continuing the sweet suffering stare. She lets the hat and gloves fall on the floor—a bit of acting*]

LAURA: [*Shakily*] How was the D.A.R. meeting? [Amanda *slowly opens her purse and removes a dainty white handkerchief which she shakes out delicately and delicately touches to her lips and nostrils*] Didn't you go to the D.A.R. meeting, Mother?

AMANDA: [*Faintly, almost inaudibly*]—No.—No. [*Then more forcibly*] I did not have the strength—to go to the D.A.R. In fact, I did not have the courage! I wanted to find a hole in the ground and hide myself in it forever! [*She crosses slowly to the wall and removes the diagram of the typewriter keyboard. She holds it in front of her for a second, staring at it sweetly and sorrowfully—then bites her lips and tears it in two pieces*]

LAURA: [*Faintly*] Why did you do that, Mother? [Amanda *repeats the same procedure with the chart of the Gregg Alphabet*] Why are you—

AMANDA: Why? Why? How old are you, Laura?

LAURA: Mother, you know my age.

AMANDA: I thought that you were an adult; it seems that I was mistaken. [*She crosses slowly to the sofa and sinks down and stares at* Laura]

LAURA: Please don't stare at me, Mother.

[Amanda *closes her eyes and lowers her head. Count ten*]

AMANDA: What are we going to do, what is going to become of us, what is the future? [*Count ten*]

LAURA: Has something happened, Mother? [Amanda *draws a long breath and takes out the handkerchief again. Dabbing process*] Mother, has —something happened?

AMANDA: I'll be all right in a minute, I'm just bewildered—[*Count five*]—by life. . . .

LAURA: Mother, I wish that you would tell me what's happened!

AMANDA: As you know, I was supposed to be inducted into my office at the D.A.R. this afternoon. [IMAGE: A SWARM OF TYPEWRITERS] But I stopped off at Rubicam's Business College to speak to your teachers about your having a cold and ask them what progress they thought you were making down there.

LAURA: Oh. . . .

AMANDA: I went to the typing instructor and introduced myself as your mother. She didn't know who you were. Wingfield, she said. We don't have any such student enrolled at the school!

I assured her she did, that you have been going to classes since early in January.

"I wonder," she said, "if you could be talking about that terribly shy little girl who dropped out of school after only a few days' attendance?"

"No," I said, "Laura, my daughter, has been going to school every day for the past six weeks!"

"Excuse me," she said. She took the attendance book out and there was your name, unmistakably printed, and all the dates you were absent until they decided that you had dropped out of school.

I still said, "No, there must have been some mistake! There must have been some mix-up in the records!"

And she said, "No—I remember her perfectly now. Her hands shook so that she couldn't hit the right keys! The first time we gave a speed-test, she broke down completely—was sick at the stomach and almost had to be carried into the wash-room! After that morning she never showed up any more. We phoned the house but never got any answer— while I was working at Famous and Barr, I suppose, demonstrating those— Oh!"

I felt so weak I could barely keep on my feet!

I had to sit down while they got me a glass of water!

Fifty dollars' tuition, all of our plans—my hopes and ambitions for you—just gone up the spout, just gone up the spout like that. [Laura *draws a long breath and gets awkwardly to her feet. She crosses to the victrola and winds it up*] What are you doing?

LAURA: Oh! [*She releases the handle and returns to her seat*]

AMANDA: Laura, where have you been going when you've gone out pretending that you were going to business college?

LAURA: I've just been going out walking.

AMANDA: That's not true.

LAURA: It is. I just went walking.

AMANDA: Walking? Walking? In winter? Deliberately courting pneumonia in that light coat? Where did you walk to, Laura?

LAURA: All sorts of places—mostly in the park.

AMANDA: Even after you'd started catching that cold?

LAURA: It was the lesser of two evils, Mother. [IMAGE: WINTER SCENE IN PARK] I couldn't go back up. I—threw up—on the floor!

AMANDA: From half past seven till after five every day you mean to tell me you walked around in the park, because you wanted to make me think that you were still going to Rubicam's Business College?

LAURA: It wasn't as bad as it sounds. I went inside places to get warmed up.

AMANDA: Inside where?

LAURA: I went in the art museum and the bird-houses at the Zoo. I visited the penguins every day! Sometimes I did without lunch and went to the movies. Lately I've been spending most of my afternoons in the Jewel-box, that big glass house where they raise the tropical flowers.

AMANDA: You did all this to deceive me, just for deception? [Laura *looks down*] Why?

LAURA: Mother, when you're disappointed, you get that awful suffering look on your face, like the picture of Jesus' mother in the museum!

AMANDA: Hush!

LAURA: I couldn't face it.

[*Pause. A whisper of strings*]

[LEGEND: "THE CRUST OF HUMILITY"]

AMANDA: [*Hopelessly fingering the huge pocket-book*] So what are we going to do the rest of our lives? Stay home and watch the parades go by? Amuse ourselves with the glass menagerie, darling? Eternally play those worn-out phonograph records your father left as a painful reminder of him?

We won't have a business career—we've given that up because it gave us nervous indigestion! [*Laughs wearily*] What is there left but dependency all our lives? I know so well what becomes of unmarried women who aren't prepared to occupy a position. I've seen such pitiful cases in the South—barely tolerated spinsters living upon the grudging patronage of sister's husband or brother's wife!—stuck away in some little mouse-trap of a room—encouraged by one in-law to visit another—little birdlike women without any nest—eating the crust of humility all their life!

Is that the future that we've mapped out for ourselves?

I swear it's the only alternative I can think of!

It isn't a very pleasant alternative, is it?

Of course—some girls *do marry*.

[*Laura twists her hands nervously*]

Haven't you ever liked some boy?

LAURA: Yes. I liked one once. [*Rises*] I came across his picture a while ago.

AMANDA: [*With some interest*] He gave you his picture?

LAURA: No, it's in the year-book.

AMANDA: [*Disappointed*] Oh—a high-school boy.

[SCREEN IMAGE: JIM AS HIGH-SCHOOL HERO BEARING A SILVER CUP]

LAURA: Yes. His name was Jim. [Laura *lifts the heavy annual from the claw-foot table*] Here he is in *The Pirates of Penzance*.

AMANDA: [*Absently*] The what?

LAURA: The operetta the senior class put on. He had a wonderful voice and we sat across the aisle from each other Mondays, Wednesdays and Fridays

in the Aud. Here he is with the silver cup for debating! See his grin?

AMANDA: [*Absently*] He must have had a jolly disposition.

LAURA: He used to call me—Blue Roses.

[IMAGE: BLUE ROSES]

AMANDA: Why did he call you such a name as that?

LAURA: When I had that attack of pleurosis—he asked me what was the matter when I came back. I said pleurosis—he thought that I said Blue Roses! So that's what he always called me after that. Whenever he saw me, he'd holler, "Hello, Blue Roses!" I didn't care for the girl that he went out with. Emily Meisenbach. Emily was the best-dressed girl at Soldan. She never struck me, though, as being sincere . . . It says in the Personal Section—they're engaged. That's—six years ago! They must be married by now.

AMANDA: Girls that aren't cut out for business careers usually wind up married to some nice man. [*Gets up with a spark of revival*] Sister, that's what you'll do!

[Laura *utters a startled, doubtful laugh. She reaches quickly for a piece of glass*]

LAURA: But, Mother—

AMANDA: Yes? [*Crossing to photograph*]

LAURA: [*In a tone of frightened apology*] I'm—crippled!

[IMAGE: SCREEN]

AMANDA: Nonsense! Laura, I've told you never, never to use that word. Why, you're not crippled, you just have a little defect—hardly noticeable, even! When people have some slight disadvantage like that, they cultivate other things to make up for it—develop charm—and vivacity—and—*charm!* That's all you have to do! [*She turns again to the photograph*] One thing your father had *plenty of*— was *charm!*

[Tom *motions to the fiddle in the wings*]

THE SCENE FADES OUT WITH MUSIC

SCENE III.

LEGEND ON SCREEN: "AFTER THE FIASCO—"
TOM *speaks from the fire-escape landing.*

TOM: After the fiasco at Rubicam's Business College, the idea of getting a gentleman caller for Laura began to play a more and more important part in Mother's calculations.

It became an obsession. Like some archetype of the universal unconscious, the image of the gentleman caller haunted our small apartment. . . .

[IMAGE: YOUNG MAN AT DOOR WITH FLOWERS]

An evening at home rarely passed without some allusion to this image, this spectre, this hope. . . .

Even when he wasn't mentioned, his presence hung in Mother's preoccupied look and in my sister's frightened, apologetic manner—hung like a sentence passed upon the Wingfields!

Mother was a woman of action as well as words. She began to take logical steps in the planned direction.

Late that winter and in the early spring—realizing that extra money would be needed to properly feather the nest and plume the bird—she conducted a vigorous campaign on the telephone, roping in subscribers to one of those magazines for matrons called *The Home-maker's Companion,* the type of journal that features the serialized sublimations of ladies of letters who think in terms of delicate cup-like breasts, slim, tapering waists, rich, creamy thighs, eyes like wood-smoke in autumn, fingers that soothe and caress like strains of music, bodies as powerful as Etruscan sculpture.

[SCREEN IMAGE: GLAMOR MAGAZINE COVER]

[Amanda *enters with phone on long extension cord. She is spotted in the dim stage*]

AMANDA: Ida Scott? This is Amanda Wingfield! We *missed* you at the D.A.R. last Monday!

I said to myself: She's probably suffering with that sinus condition! How is that sinus condition?

Horrors! Heaven have mercy!—You're a Christian martyr, yes, that's what you are, a Christian martyr!

Well, I just now happened to notice that your subscription to the *Companion's* about to expire! Yes, it expires with the next issue, honey!—just when that wonderful new serial by Bessie Mae Hopper is getting off to such an exciting start. Oh, honey, it's something that you can't miss! You remember how *Gone With the Wind* took everybody by storm? You simply couldn't go out if you hadn't read it. All everybody *talked* was Scarlett O'Hara. Well, this is a book that critics already compare to *Gone With the Wind.* It's the *Gone With the Wind* of the post-World War generation!—What?—Burning?—Oh, honey, don't let them burn, go take a look in the oven and I'll hold the wire! Heavens—I think she's hung up!

DIM OUT

[LEGEND ON SCREEN: "YOU THINK I'M IN LOVE WITH CONTINENTAL SHOEMAKERS?"]

[*Before the stage is lighted, the violent voices of* Tom *and* Amanda *are heard. They are quarreling behind the portieres. In front of them stands* Laura *with clenched hands and panicky expression. A clear pool of light on her figure throughout this scene*]

TOM: What in Christ's name am I—

AMANDA: [*Shrilly*] Don't you use that—

TOM: Supposed to do!

AMANDA: Expression! Not in my—

TOM: Ohhh!

AMANDA: Presence! Have you gone out of your senses?

TOM: I have, that's true, *driven* out!

AMANDA: What is the matter with you, you—big —big—IDIOT!

TOM: Look!—I've got *no thing,* no single thing—

AMANDA: Lower your voice!

TOM: In my life here that I can call my OWN! Everything is—

AMANDA: Stop that shouting!

TOM: Yesterday you confiscated my books! You had the nerve to—

AMANDA: I took that horrible novel back to the library—yes! That hideous book by that insane Mr. Lawrence. [Tom *laughs wildly*] I cannot control the output of diseased minds or people who cater to them—[Tom *laughs still more wildly*] BUT I WON'T ALLOW SUCH FILTH BROUGHT INTO MY HOUSE! No, no, no, no, no!

TOM: House, house! Who pays rent on it, who makes a slave of himself to—

AMANDA: [*Fairly screeching*] Don't you DARE to—

TOM: No, no, *I* mustn't say things! *I've* got to just—

AMANDA: Let me tell you—

TOM: I don't want to hear any more! [*He tears the portieres open. The upstage area is lit with a turgid smoky red glow*]

[Amanda's *hair is in metal curlers and she wears a very old bathrobe, much too large for her slight figure, a relic of the faithless Mr. Wingfield. An upright typewriter and a wild disarray of manuscripts is on the drop-leaf table. The quarrel was probably precipitated by* Amanda's *interruption of his creative labor. A chair lying overthrown on the floor. Their gesticulating shadows are cast on the ceiling by the fiery glow*]

AMANDA: You *will* hear more, you—

TOM: No, I won't hear more, I'm going out!

AMANDA: You come right back in—

TOM: Out, out, out! Because I'm—

AMANDA: Come back here, Tom Wingfield! I'm not through talking to you!

TOM: Oh, go—

LAURA: [*Desperately*]—Tom!

AMANDA: You're going to listen, and no more insolence from you! I'm at the end of my patience!

[*He comes back toward her*]

TOM: What do you think I'm at? Aren't I supposed to have any patience to reach the end of, Mother? I know, I know. It seems unimportant to you, what I'm *doing*—what I *want* to do—having a little *difference* between them! You don't think that—

AMANDA: I think you've been doing things that you're ashamed of. That's why you act like this. I don't believe that you go every night to the movies. Nobody goes to the movies night after night. Nobody in their right minds goes to the movies as often as you pretend to. People don't go to the movies at nearly midnight, and movies don't let out at two A.M. Come in stumbling. Muttering to yourself like a maniac! You get three hours' sleep and then go to work. Oh, I can picture the way you're doing down there. Moping, doping, because you're in no condition.

TOM: [*Wildly*] No, I'm in no condition!

AMANDA: What right have you got to jeopardize your job? Jeopardize the security of us all? How do you think we'd manage if you were—

TOM: Listen! You think I'm crazy *about* the *warehouse*? [*He bends fiercely toward her slight figure*] You think I'm in love with the Continental Shoemakers? You think I want to spend fifty-five *years* down there in that—*celotex interior!* with—*fluorescent—tubes!* Look! I'd rather somebody picked up a crowbar and battered out my brains—than go back mornings! I *go!* Every time you come in yelling that God damn *"Rise and Shine!" "Rise and Shine!"* I say to myself, "How *lucky dead* people are!" But I get up. I *go!* For sixty-five dollars a month I give up all that I dream of doing and being *ever!* And you say self—*self's* all I ever think of. Why, listen, if self is what I thought of, Mother, I'd be where he is—GONE! [*Pointing to father's picture*] As far as the system of transportation reaches! [*He starts past her. She grabs his arm*] Don't grab at me, Mother!

AMANDA: Where are you going?

TOM: I'm going to the *movies!*

AMANDA: I don't believe that lie!

TOM: [*Crouching toward her, overtowering her tiny figure. She backs away, gasping*] I'm going to opium dens! Yes, opium dens, dens of vice and criminals' hang-outs, Mother. I've joined the Hogan gang, I'm a hired assassin, I carry a tommy-gun in a violin case! I run a string of cat-houses in the Valley! They call me Killer, Killer Wingfield, I'm leading a double-life, a simple, honest warehouse worker by day, by night a dynamic *czar* of the *underworld, Mother.* I go to gambling casinos, I spin away fortunes on the roulette table! I wear a patch over one eye and a false mustache, sometimes I put on green whiskers. On those occasions they call me—*El Diablo!* Oh, I could tell you things to make you sleepless! My enemies plan to dynamite this place. They're going to blow us all sky-high some night! I'll be glad, very happy, and so will you! You'll go up, up on a broomstick, over Blue Mountain with seventeen gentlemen callers! You ugly—babbling old—*witch.* . . . [*He goes through a series of violent, clumsy movements, seizing his overcoat, lunging to the door, pulling it fiercely open. The women watch him, aghast. His arm catches in the sleeve of the coat as he struggles to pull it on. For a moment he is pinioned by the bulky garment. With an outraged groan he tears the coat off again, splitting the shoulder of it, and hurls it across the room. It strikes against the shelf* of Laura's *glass collection, there is a tinkle of shattering glass. Laura cries out as if wounded*]

[MUSIC. LEGEND: "THE GLASS MENAGERIE"]

LAURA: [*Shrilly*] My glass!—menagerie. . . . [*She covers her face and turns away*]

[*But Amanda is still stunned and stupefied by the "ugly witch" so that she barely notices this occurrence. Now she recovers her speech*]

AMANDA: [*In an awful voice*] I won't speak to you —until you apologize! [*She crosses through portieres and draws them together behind her. Tom is left with Laura. Laura clings weakly to the mantel with her face averted. Tom stares at her stupidly for a moment. Then he crosses to shelf. Drops awkwardly on his knees to collect the fallen glass, glancing at Laura as if he would speak but couldn't*]

"The Glass Menagerie" steals in as

THE SCENE DIMS OUT

SCENE IV.

The interior is dark. Faint light in the alley. A deep-voiced bell in a church is tolling the hour of five as the scene commences.

Tom *appears at the top of the alley. After each solemn boom of the bell in the tower, he shakes a little noise-maker or rattle as if to express the tiny spasm of man in contrast to the sustained power and dignity of the Almighty. This and the unsteadiness of his advance make it evident that he has been drinking. As he climbs the few steps to the fire-escape landing light steals up inside. Laura appears in night-dress, observing Tom's empty bed in the front room. Tom fishes in his pockets for door-key, removing a motley assortment of articles in the search, including a perfect shower of movie-ticket stubs and an empty bottle. At last he finds the key, but just as he is about to insert it, it slips from his fingers. He strikes a match and crouches below the door.*

TOM: [*Bitterly*] One crack—and it falls through! [*Laura opens the door*]

LAURA: Tom! Tom, what are you doing?

TOM: Looking for a door-key.

LAURA: Where have you been all this time?

TOM: I have been to the movies.

LAURA: All this time at the movies?

TOM: There was a very long program. There was a Garbo picture and a Mickey Mouse and a travelogue and a newsreel and a preview of coming attractions. And there was an organ solo and a collection for the milk-fund—simultaneously—which ended up in a terrible fight between a fat lady and an usher!

LAURA: [*Innocently*] Did you have to stay through everything?

TOM: Of course! And, oh, I forgot! There was a big stage show! The headliner on this stage show was Malvolio the Magician. He performed wonderful tricks, many of them, such as pouring water back and forth between pitchers. First it turned to wine and then it turned to beer and then it turned to whiskey. I know it was whiskey it finally turned into because he needed somebody to come up out of the audience to help him, and I came up—both shows! It was Kentucky Straight Bourbon. A very generous fellow, he gave souvenirs. [*He pulls from his back pocket a shimmering rainbow-colored scarf*] He gave me this. This is his magic scarf. You can have it, Laura. You wave it over a canary cage and you get a bowl of gold-fish. You wave it over the gold-fish bowl and they fly away canaries. . . . But the wonderfullest trick of all was the coffin trick. We nailed him into a coffin and he got out of the coffin without removing one nail. [*He has come inside*] There is a trick that would come in handy for me—get me out of this 2 by 4 situation. [*Flops onto bed and starts removing shoes*]

LAURA: Tom—Shhh!

TOM: What're you shushing me for?

LAURA: You'll wake up Mother.

TOM: Goody, goody! Pay 'er back for all those "Rise an' Shines." [*Lies down, groaning*] You know it don't take much intelligence to get yourself into a nailed-up coffin, Laura. But who in hell ever got himself out of one without removing one nail?

[*As if in answer, the father's grinning photograph lights up*]

SCENE DIMS OUT

[*Immediately following: The church bell is heard striking six. At the sixth stroke the alarm clock goes off in Amanda's room, and after a few moments we hear her calling: "Rise and Shine! Rise and Shine! Laura, go tell your brother to rise and shine!"*]

TOM: [*Sitting up slowly*] I'll rise—but I won't shine.

[*The light increases*]

AMANDA: Laura, tell your brother his coffee is ready.

[*Laura slips into front room*]

LAURA: Tom!—It's nearly seven. Don't make Mother nervous. [*He stares at her stupidly. Beseechingly*] Tom, speak to Mother this morning. Make up with her, apologize, speak to her!

TOM: She won't to me. It's her that started not speaking.

LAURA: If you just say you're sorry she'll start speaking.

TOM: Her not speaking—is that such a tragedy?

LAURA: Please—please!

AMANDA: [*Calling from kitchenette*] Laura, are you going to do what I asked you to do, or do I have to get dressed and go out myself?

LAURA: Going, going—soon as I get on my coat!

[*She pulls on a shapeless felt hat with nervous, jerky movement, pleadingly glancing at Tom. Rushes awkwardly for coat. The coat is one of Amanda's, inaccurately made-over, the sleeves too short for Laura*] Butter and what else?

AMANDA: [*Entering upstage*] Just butter. Tell them to charge it.

LAURA: Mother, they make such faces when I do that.

AMANDA: Sticks and stones can break our bones, but the expression on Mr. Garfinkel's face won't harm us! Tell your brother his coffee is getting cold.

LAURA: [*At door*] Do what I asked you, will you, will you, Tom?

[*He looks sullenly away*]

AMANDA: Laura, go now or just don't go at all!

LAURA: [*Rushing out*] Going—going! [*A second later she cries out. Tom springs up and crosses to door. Amanda rushes anxiously in. Tom opens the door*]

TOM: Laura?

LAURA: I'm all right. I slipped, but I'm all right.

AMANDA: [*Peering anxiously after her*] If anyone breaks a leg on those fire-escape steps, the landlord ought to be sued for every cent he possesses! [*She shuts door. Remembers she isn't speaking and returns to other room*]

[*As Tom enters listlessly for his coffee, she turns her back to him and stands rigidly facing the window on the gloomy gray vault of the areaway. Its light on her face with its aged but childish features is cruelly sharp, satirical as a Daumier print*]

[MUSIC UNDER: "AVE MARIA"]

[*Tom glances sheepishly but sullenly at her averted figure and slumps at the table. The coffee is scalding hot; he sips it and gasps and spits it back in the cup. At his gasp, Amanda catches her breath and half turns. Then catches herself and turns back to window. Tom blows on his coffee, glancing sidewise at his mother. She clears her throat. Tom clears his. He starts to rise. Sinks back down again, scratches his head, clears his throat again. Amanda coughs. Tom raises his cup in both hands to blow on it, his eyes staring over the rim of it at his mother for several moments. Then he slowly sets the cup down and awkwardly and hesitantly rises from the chair*]

TOM: [*Hoarsely*] Mother. I—I apologize, Mother. [*Amanda draws a quick, shuddering breath. Her face works grotesquely. She breaks into childlike tears*] I'm sorry for what I said, for everything that I said, I didn't mean it.

AMANDA: [*Sobbingly*] My devotion has made me a witch and so I make myself hateful to my children!

TOM: *No*, you *don't*.

AMANDA: I worry so much, don't sleep, it makes me nervous!

TOM: [*Gently*] I understand that.

AMANDA: I've had to put up a solitary battle all

these years. But you're my right-hand bower! Don't fall down, don't fail!

TOM: [*Gently*] I try, Mother.

AMANDA: [*With great enthusiasm*] Try and you will SUCCEED! [*The notion makes her breathless*] Why, you—you're just *full* of natural endowments! Both of my children—they're *unusual* children! Don't you think I know it? I'm so—*proud!* Happy and—feel I've—so much to be thankful for but—— Promise me one thing, Son!

TOM: What, Mother?

AMANDA: Promise, son, you'll—never be a drunkard!

TOM: [*Turns to her grinning*] I will never be a drunkard, Mother.

AMANDA: That's what frightened me so, that you'd be drinking! Eat a bowl of Purina!

TOM: Just coffee, Mother.

AMANDA: Shredded wheat biscuit?

TOM: No. No, Mother, just coffee.

AMANDA: You can't put in a day's work on an empty stomach. You've got ten minutes—don't gulp! Drinking too-hot liquids makes cancer of the stomach. . . . Put cream in.

TOM: No, thank you.

AMANDA: To cool it.

TOM: No! No, thank you, I want it black.

AMANDA: I know, but it's not good for you. We have to do all that we can to build ourselves up. In these trying times we live in, all that we have to cling to is—each other. . . . That's why it's so important to—— Tom, I— I sent out your sister so I could discuss something with you. If you hadn't spoken I would have spoken to you. [*Sits down*]

TOM: [*Gently*] What is it, Mother, that you want to discuss?

AMANDA: *Laura!*

[Tom *puts his cup down slowly*]

[LEGEND ON SCREEN: "LAURA"]

[MUSIC: "THE GLASS MENAGERIE"]

TOM: —Oh.—Laura . . .

AMANDA: [*Touching his sleeve*] You know how Laura is. So quiet but—still water runs deep! She notices things and I think she—broods about them. [Tom *looks up*] A few days ago I came in and she was crying.

TOM: What about?

AMANDA: You.

TOM: Me?

AMANDA: She has an idea that you're not happy here.

TOM: What gave her that idea?

AMANDA: What gives her any idea? However, you do act strangely. I—I'm not criticizing, understand *that!* I know your ambitions do not lie in the warehouse, that like everybody in the whole wide world —you've had to—make sacrifices, but—Tom—Tom —life's not easy, it calls for—Spartan endurance! There's so many things in my heart that I cannot

describe to you! I've never told you but I—*loved* your father. . . .

TOM: [*Gently*] I know that, Mother.

AMANDA: And you—when I see you taking after his ways! Staying out late—and—well, you *had* been drinking the night you were in that—terrifying condition! Laura says that you hate the apartment and that you go out nights to get away from it! Is that true, Tom?

TOM: No. You say there's so much in your heart that you can't describe to me. That's true of me, too. There's so much in my heart that I can't describe to *you!* So let's respect each other's——

AMANDA: But, why—*why*, Tom—are you always so *restless?* Where do you *go* to, nights?

TOM: I—go to the movies.

AMANDA: Why do you go to the movies so much, Tom?

TOM: I go to the movies because—I like adventure. Adventure is something I don't have much of at work, so I go to the movies.

AMANDA: But, Tom, you go to the movies *entirely too much!*

TOM: I like a lot of adventure.

[Amanda *looks baffled, then hurt. As the familiar inquisition resumes he becomes hard and impatient again.* Amanda *slips back into her querulous attitude toward him*]

[IMAGE ON SCREEN: SAILING VESSEL WITH JOLLY ROGER]

AMANDA: Most young men find adventure in their careers.

TOM: Then most young men are not employed in a warehouse.

AMANDA: The world is full of young men employed in warehouses and offices and factories.

TOM: Do all of them find adventure in their careers?

AMANDA: They do or they do without it! Not everybody has a craze for adventure.

TOM: Man is by instinct a lover, a hunter, a fighter, and none of those instincts are given much play at the warehouse!

AMANDA: Man is by instinct! Don't quote instinct to me! Instinct is something that people have got away from! It belongs to animals! Christian adults don't want it!

TOM: What do Christian adults want, then, Mother?

AMANDA: Superior things! Things of the mind and the spirit! Only animals have to satisfy instincts! Surely your aims are somewhat higher than theirs! Than monkeys—pigs—

TOM: I reckon they're not.

AMANDA: You're joking. However, that isn't what I wanted to discuss.

TOM: [*Rising*] I haven't much time.

AMANDA: [*Pushing his shoulders*] Sit down.

TOM: You want me to punch in red at the warehouse, Mother?

AMANDA: You have five minutes. I want to talk about Laura.

[LEGEND: "PLANS AND PROVISIONS"]

TOM: All right! What about Laura?

AMANDA: We have to be making some plans and provisions for her. She's older than you, two years, and nothing has happened. She just drifts along doing nothing. It frightens me terribly how she just drifts along.

TOM: I guess she's the type that people call home girls.

AMANDA: There's no such type, and if there is, it's a pity! That is unless the home is hers, with a husband!

TOM: What?

AMANDA: Oh, I can see the handwriting on the wall as plain as I see the nose in front of my face! It's terrifying! More and more you remind me of your father! He was out all hours without explanation!—Then *left! Good-bye!* And me with the bag to hold. I saw that letter you got from the Merchant Marine. I know what you're dreaming of. I'm not standing here blindfolded. Very well, then. Then *do* it! But not till there's somebody to take your place.

TOM: What do you mean?

AMANDA: I mean that as soon as Laura has got somebody to take care of her, married, a home of her own, independent—why, then you'll be free to go wherever you please, on land, on sea, whichever way the wind blows you! But until that time you've got to look out for your sister. I don't say me because I'm old and don't matter! I say for your sister because she's young and dependent! I put her in business college—a dismal failure! Frightened her so it made her sick at the stomach. I took her over to the Young People's League at the church. Another fiasco. She spoke to nobody, nobody spoke to her. Now all she does is fool with those pieces of glass and play those worn-out records. What kind of a life is that for a girl to lead?

TOM: What can I do about it?

AMANDA: Overcome selfishness! Self, self, self is all that you ever think of! [Tom *springs up and crosses to get his coat. It is ugly and bulky. He pulls on a cap with earmuffs*] Where is your muffler? Put your wool muffler on! [He *snatches it angrily from the closet and tosses it around his neck and pulls both ends tight*] Tom! I haven't said what I had in mind to ask you.

TOM: I'm too late to—

AMANDA: [Catching his arm—very importunately. Then shyly] Down at the warehouse, aren't there some—nice young men?

TOM: No!

AMANDA: There *must* be—*some* . . .

TOM: Mother—[Gesture]

AMANDA: Find out one that's clean-living—doesn't drink and—ask him out for sister!

TOM: What?

AMANDA: For *sister!* To *meet!* Get *acquainted!*

TOM: [Stamping to door] Oh, my *go-osh!*

AMANDA: Will you? [He opens door. Imploringly] Will you? [He starts down] Will you? *Will* you, dear?

TOM: [Calling back] YES!

[Amanda *closes the door hesitantly and with a troubled but faintly hopeful expression*]

[SCREEN IMAGE: GLAMOR MAGAZINE COVER]

[Spot Amanda at phone]

AMANDA: Ella Cartwright? This is Amanda Wingfield! How are you, honey? How is that kidney condition? [Count five] Horrors! [Count five] You're a Christian martyr, yes, honey, that's what you are, a Christian martyr! Well, I just now happened to notice in my little red book that your subscription to the *Companion* has just run out! I knew that you wouldn't want to miss out on the wonderful serial starting in this new issue. It's by Bessie Mae Hopper, the first thing she's written since *Honeymoon for Three.* Wasn't that a strange and interesting story? Well, this one is even lovelier, I believe. It has a sophisticated, society background. It's all about the horsey set on Long Island!

FADE OUT

SCENE V.

LEGEND ON SCREEN: "ANNUNCIATION." *Fade with music.*

It is early dusk of a spring evening. Supper has just been finished in the Wingfield apartment. Amanda and Laura in light-colored dresses are removing dishes from the table, in the upstage area, which is shadowy, their movements formalized almost as a dance or ritual, their moving forms as pale and silent as moths. Tom, in white shirt and trousers, rises from the table and crosses toward the fire-escape.

AMANDA: [As he passes her] Son, will you do me a favor?

TOM: What?

AMANDA: Comb your hair! You look so pretty when your hair is combed! [Tom *slouches on sofa with evening paper. Enormous caption "Franco Triumphs"*] There is only one respect in which I would like you to emulate your father.

TOM: What respect is that?

AMANDA: The care he always took of his appearance. He never allowed himself to look untidy. [He *throws down the paper and crosses to fire-escape*] Where are you going?

TOM: I'm going out to smoke.

AMANDA: You smoke too much. A pack a day at fifteen cents a pack. How much would that amount to in a month? Thirty times fifteen is how much, Tom? Figure it out and you will be astounded at what you could save. Enough to give you a night-school course in accounting at Washington U! Just think what a wonderful thing that would be for you, Son!

[Tom *is unmoved by the thought*]

TOM: I'd rather smoke. [*He steps out on landing, letting the screen door slam*]

AMANDA: [*Sharply*] I know! That's the tragedy of it. . . . [*Alone, she turns to look at her husband's picture*]

[DANCE MUSIC: "ALL THE WORLD IS WAITING FOR THE SUNRISE!"]

TOM: [*To the audience*] Across the alley from us was the Paradise Dance Hall. On evenings in spring the windows and doors were open and the music came outdoors. Sometimes the lights were turned out except for a large glass sphere that hung from the ceiling. It would turn slowly about and filter the dusk with delicate rainbow colors. Then the orchestra played a waltz or a tango, something that had a slow and sensuous rhythm. Couples would come outside, to the relative privacy of the alley. You could see them kissing behind ash-pits and telephone poles. This was the compensation for lives that passed like mine, without any change or adventure. Adventure and change were imminent in this year. They were waiting around the corner for all these kids. Suspended in the mist over Berchtesgaden, caught in the folds of Chamberlain's umbrella—In Spain there was Guernica! But here there was only hot swing music and liquor, dance halls, bars, and movies, and sex that hung in the gloom like a chandelier and flooded the world with brief, deceptive rainbows. . . . All the world was waiting for bombardments!

[Amanda *turns from the picture and comes outside*]

AMANDA: [*Sighing*] A fire-escape landing's a poor excuse for a porch. [*She spreads a newspaper on a step and sits down, gracefully and demurely as if she were settling into a swing on a Mississippi veranda*] What are you looking at?

TOM: The moon.

AMANDA: Is there a moon this evening?

TOM: It's rising over Garfinkel's Delicatessen.

AMANDA: So it is! A little silver slipper of a moon. Have you made a wish on it yet?

TOM: Um-hum.

AMANDA: What did you wish for?

TOM: That's a secret.

AMANDA: A secret, huh? Well, I won't tell mine either. I will be just as mysterious as you.

TOM: I bet I can guess what yours is.

AMANDA: Is my head so transparent?

TOM: You're not a sphinx.

AMANDA: No, I don't have secrets. I'll tell you what I wished for on the moon. Success and happiness for my precious children! I wish for that whenever there's a moon, and when there isn't a moon, I wish for it, too.

TOM: I thought perhaps you wished for a gentleman caller.

AMANDA: Why do you say that?

TOM: Don't you remember asking me to fetch one?

AMANDA: I remember suggesting that it would be nice for your sister if you brought home some nice young man from the warehouse. I think that I've made that suggestion more than once.

TOM: Yes, you have made it repeatedly.

AMANDA: Well?

TOM: We are going to have one.

AMANDA: *What?*

TOM: A gentleman caller!

[THE ANNUNCIATION IS CELEBRATED WITH MUSIC]

[Amanda *rises*]

[IMAGE ON SCREEN: CALLER WITH BOUQUET]

AMANDA: You mean you have asked some nice young man to come over?

TOM: Yep. I've asked him to dinner.

AMANDA: You really did?

TOM: I did!

AMANDA: You did, and did he—*accept?*

TOM: He did!

AMANDA: Well, well—well, well! That's—lovely!

TOM: I thought that you would be pleased.

AMANDA: It's definite, then?

TOM: Very definite.

AMANDA: Soon?

TOM: Very soon.

AMANDA: For heaven's sake, stop putting on and tell me some things, will you?

TOM: What things do you want me to tell you?

AMANDA: *Naturally* I would like to know when he's *coming!*

TOM: He's coming tomorrow.

AMANDA: *Tomorrow?*

TOM: Yep. Tomorrow.

AMANDA: But, Tom!

TOM: Yes, Mother?

AMANDA: Tomorrow gives me no time!

TOM: Time for what?

AMANDA: Preparations! Why didn't you phone me at once, as soon as you asked him, the minute that he accepted? Then, don't you see, I could have been getting ready!

TOM: You don't have to make any fuss.

AMANDA: Oh, Tom, Tom, Tom, of course I have to make a fuss! I want things nice, not sloppy! Not thrown together. I'll certainly have to do some fast thinking, won't I?

TOM: I don't see why you have to think at all.

AMANDA: You just don't know. We can't have a gentleman caller in a pig-sty. All my wedding silver has to be polished, the monogrammed table linen ought to be laundered! The windows have to be washed and fresh curtains put up. And how about clothes? We have to *wear* something, don't we?

TOM: Mother, this boy is no one to make a fuss over!

AMANDA: Do you realize he's the first young man

we've introduced to your sister? It's terrible, dreadful, disgraceful that poor little sister has never received a single gentleman caller! Tom, come inside! [*She opens the screen door*]

TOM: What for?

AMANDA: I want to ask you some things.

TOM: If you're going to make such a fuss, I'll call it off, I'll tell him not to come!

AMANDA: You certainly won't do anything of the kind. Nothing offends people worse than broken engagements. It simply means I'll have to work like a Turk! We won't be brilliant, but we will pass inspection. Come on inside. [Tom *follows, groaning*] Sit down.

TOM: Any particular place you would like me to sit?

AMANDA: Thank heavens I've got that new sofa! I'm also making payments on a floor lamp I'll have sent out! And put the chintz covers on, they'll brighten things up! Of course I'd hoped to have these walls re-papered. . . . What is the young man's name?

TOM: His name is O'Connor.

AMANDA: That, of course, means fish—tomorrow is Friday! I'll have that salmon loaf—with Durkee's dressing! What does he do? He works at the warehouse?

TOM: Of course! How else would I—

AMANDA: Tom, he—doesn't drink?

TOM: Why do you ask me that?

AMANDA: Your father *did*!

TOM: Don't get started on that!

AMANDA: He *does* drink, then?

TOM: Not that I know of!

AMANDA: Make sure, be certain! The last thing I want for my daughter's a boy who drinks!

TOM: Aren't you being a little bit premature? Mr. O'Connor has not yet appeared on the scene!

AMANDA: But will tomorrow. To meet your sister, and what do I know about his character? Nothing! Old maids are better off than wives of drunkards!

TOM: Oh, my God!

AMANDA: Be still!

TOM: [*Leaning forward to whisper*] Lots of fellows meet girls whom they don't marry!

AMANDA: Oh, talk sensibly, Tom—and don't be sarcastic! [*She has gotten a hairbrush*]

TOM: What are you doing?

AMANDA: I'm brushing that cow-lick down! What is this young man's position at the warehouse?

TOM: [*Submitting grimly to the brush and the interrogation*] This young man's position is that of a shipping clerk, Mother.

AMANDA: Sounds to me like a fairly responsible job, the sort of a job *you* would be in if you just had more *get-up*. What is his salary? Have you any idea?

TOM: I would judge it to be approximately eighty-five dollars a month.

AMANDA: Well—not princely, but—

TOM: Twenty more than I make.

AMANDA: Yes, how well I know! But for a family man, eighty-five dollars a month is not much more than you can just get by on. . . .

TOM: Yes, but Mr. O'Connor is not a family man.

AMANDA: He might be, mightn't he? Some time in the future?

TOM: I see. Plans and provisions.

AMANDA: You are the only young man that I know of who ignores the fact that the future becomes the present, the present the past, and the past turns into everlasting regret if you don't plan for it!

TOM: I will think that over and see what I can make of it.

AMANDA: Don't be supercilious with your mother! Tell me some more about this—what do you call him?

TOM: James D. O'Connor. The D. is for Delaney.

AMANDA: Irish on *both* sides! *Gracious!* And doesn't drink?

TOM: Shall I call him up and ask him right this minute?

AMANDA: The only way to find out about those things is to make discreet inquiries at the proper moment. When I was a girl in Blue Mountain and it was suspected that a young man drank, the girl whose attentions he had been receiving, if any girl *was,* would sometimes speak to the minister of his church, or rather her father would if her father was living, and sort of feel him out on the young man's character. That is the way such things are discreetly handled to keep a young woman from making a tragic mistake!

TOM: Then how did you happen to make a tragic mistake?

AMANDA: That innocent look of your father's had everyone fooled! He *smiled*—the world was *enchanted!* No girl can do worse than put herself at the mercy of a handsome appearance! I hope that Mr. O'Connor is not too good-looking.

TOM: No, he's not too good-looking. He's covered with freckles and hasn't too much of a nose.

AMANDA: He's not right-down homely, though?

TOM: Not right-down homely. Just medium homely, I'd say.

AMANDA: Character's what to look for in a man.

TOM: That's what I've always said, Mother.

AMANDA: You've never said anything of the kind and I suspect you would never give it a thought.

TOM: Don't be so suspicious of me.

AMANDA: At least I hope he's the type that's up and coming.

TOM: I think he really goes in for self-improvement.

AMANDA: What reason have you to think so?

TOM: He goes to night school.

AMANDA: [*Beaming*] Splendid! What does he do, I mean study?

TOM: Radio engineering and public speaking!

AMANDA: Then he has visions of being advanced

in the world! Any young man who studies public speaking is aiming to have an executive job some day! And radio engineering? A thing for the future! Both of these facts are very illuminating. Those are the sort of things that a mother should know concerning any young man who comes to call on her daughter. Seriously or—not.

TOM: One little warning. He doesn't know about Laura. I didn't let on that we had dark ulterior motives. I just said, why don't you come and have dinner with us? He said okay and that was the whole conversation.

AMANDA: I bet it was! You're eloquent as an oyster. However, he'll know about Laura when he gets here. When he sees how lovely and sweet and pretty she is, he'll thank his lucky stars he was asked to dinner.

TOM: Mother, you mustn't expect too much of Laura.

AMANDA: What do you mean?

TOM: Laura seems all those things to you and me because she's ours and we love her. We don't even notice she's crippled any more.

AMANDA: Don't say crippled. You know that I never allow that word to be used!

TOM: But face facts, Mother. She is and—that's not all—

AMANDA: What do you mean "not all"?

TOM: Laura is very different from other girls.

AMANDA: I think the difference is all to her advantage.

TOM: Not quite all—in the eyes of others—strangers—she's terribly shy and lives in a world of her own and those things make her seem a little peculiar to people outside the house.

AMANDA: Don't say peculiar.

TOM: Face the facts. She is.

[THE DANCE-HALL MUSIC CHANGES TO A TANGO THAT HAS A MINOR AND SOMEWHAT OMINOUS TONE]

AMANDA: In what way is she peculiar—may I ask?

TOM: [Gently] She lives in a world of her own—a world of—little glass ornaments, Mother. . . . [Gets up. Amanda remains holding brush, looking at him, troubled] She plays old phonograph records and—that's about all— [He glances at himself in the mirror and crosses to door]

AMANDA: [Sharply] Where are you going?

TOM: I'm going to the movies. [Out screen door]

AMANDA: Not to the movies, every night to the movies! [Follows quickly to screen door] I don't believe you always go to the movies! [He is gone. Amanda looks worriedly after him for a moment. Then vitality and optimism return and she turns from the door. Crossing to portieres] Laura! Laura! [Laura answers from kitchenette]

LAURA: Yes, Mother.

AMANDA: Let those dishes go and come in front! [Laura appears with dish towel. Gaily] Laura, come here and make a wish on the moon!

[SCREEN IMAGE: MOON]

LAURA: [Entering] Moon—moon?

AMANDA: A little silver slipper of a moon. Look over your left shoulder, Laura, and make a wish! [Laura looks faintly puzzled as if called out of sleep. Amanda seizes her shoulders and turns her at an angle by the door] Now! Now, darling, wish!

LAURA: What shall I wish for, Mother?

AMANDA: [Her voice trembling and her eyes suddenly filling with tears] Happiness, Good fortune!

[The violin rises and the stage dims out]

CURTAIN

SCENE VI.

[IMAGE: HIGH SCHOOL HERO]

And so the following evening I brought Jim home to dinner. I had known Jim slightly in high school. In high school Jim was a hero. He had tremendous Irish good nature and vitality with the scrubbed and polished look of white chinaware. He seemed to move in a continual spotlight. He was a star in basketball, captain of the debating club, president of the senior class and the glee club and he sang the male lead in the annual light operas. He was always running or bounding, never just walking. He seemed always at the point of defeating the law of gravity. He was shooting with such velocity through his adolescence that you would logically expect him to arrive at nothing short of the White House by the time he was thirty. But Jim apparently ran into more interference after his graduation from Soldan. His speed had definitely slowed. Six years after he left high school he was holding a job that wasn't much better than mine.

[IMAGE: CLERK]

He was the only one at the warehouse with whom I was on friendly terms. I was valuable to him as someone who could remember his former glory, who had seen him win basketball games and the silver cup in debating. He knew of my secret practice of retiring to a cabinet of the wash-room to work on poems when business was slack in the warehouse. He called me Shakespeare. And while the other boys in the warehouse regarded me with suspicious hostility, Jim took a humorous attitude toward me. Gradually his attitude affected the others, their hostility wore off and they also began to smile at me as people smile at an oddly fashioned dog who trots across their path as some distance.

I knew that Jim and Laura had known each other at Soldan, and I had heard Laura speak admiringly of his voice. I didn't know if Jim remembered her or not. In high school Laura had been as unobtrusive as Jim had been astonishing. If he did remember Laura, it was not as my sister, for when I asked him to dinner, he grinned and said, "You know, Shakespeare, I never thought of you as having folks!"

He was about to discover that I did. . . .

[*Light up stage*]

[LEGEND ON SCREEN: "THE ACCENT OF A COMING FOOT"]

[*Friday evening. It is about five o'clock of a late spring evening which comes "scattering poems in the sky." A delicate lemony light is in the Wingfield apartment. Amanda has worked like a Turk in preparation for the gentleman caller. The results are astonishing. The new floor lamp with its rose-silk shade is in place, a colored paper lantern conceals the broken light-fixture in the ceiling, new billowing white curtains are at the windows, chintz covers are on chairs and sofa, a pair of new sofa pillows make their initial appearance. Open boxes and tissue paper are scattered on the floor. Laura stands in the middle with lifted arms while Amanda crouches before her, adjusting the hem of the new dress, devout and ritualistic. The dress is colored and designed by memory. The arrangement of Laura's hair is changed; it is softer and more becoming. A fragile, unearthly prettiness has come out in Laura: she is like a piece of translucent glass touched by light, given a momentary radiance, not actual, not lasting*]

AMANDA: [*Impatiently*] Why are you trembling?

LAURA: Mother, you've made me so nervous!

AMANDA: How have I made you nervous?

LAURA: By all this fuss! You make it seem so important!

AMANDA: I don't understand you, Laura. You couldn't be satisfied with just sitting home, and yet whenever I try to arrange something for you, you seem to resist it. [*She gets up*] Now take a look at yourself. No, wait! Wait just a moment—I have an idea!

LAURA: What is it now?

[Amanda *produces two powder puffs which she wraps in handkerchiefs and stuffs in* Laura's *bosom*]

LAURA: Mother, what are you doing?

AMANDA: They call them "Gay Deceivers"!

LAURA: I won't wear them!

AMANDA: You will!

LAURA: Why should I?

AMANDA: Because, to be painfully honest, your chest is flat.

LAURA: You make it seem like we were setting a trap.

AMANDA: All pretty girls are a trap, a pretty trap, and men expect them to be. [LEGEND: "A PRETTY TRAP"] Now look at yourself, young lady. This is the prettiest you will ever be! I've got to fix myself now! You're going to be surprised by your mother's appearance! [*She crosses through portieres, humming gaily.* Laura *moves slowly to the long mirror*

and stares solemnly at herself. A wind blows the white curtains inward in a slow, graceful motion and with a faint, sorrowful sighing]

AMANDA: [*Off stage*] It isn't dark enough yet. [*She turns slowly before the mirror with a troubled look*]

[LEGEND ON SCREEN: "THIS IS MY SISTER: CELEBRATE HER WITH STRINGS!" MUSIC]

AMANDA: [*Laughing, off*] I'm going to show you something. I'm going to make a spectacular appearance!

LAURA: What is it, Mother?

AMANDA: Possess your soul in patience—you will see! Something I've resurrected from that old trunk! Styles haven't changed so terribly much after all. . . . [*She parts the portieres*] Now just look at your mother! [*She wears a girlish frock of yellowed voile with a blue silk sash. She carries a bunch of jonquils—the legend of her youth is nearly revived. Feverishly*] This is the dress in which I led the cotillion. Won the cakewalk twice at Sunset Hill, wore one spring to the Governor's ball in Jackson! See how I sashayed around the ballroom, Laura? [*She raises her skirt and does a mincing step around the room*] I wore it on Sundays for my gentlemen callers! I had it on the day I met your father—I had malaria fever all that spring. The change of climate from East Tennessee to the Delta—weakened resistance—I had a little temperature all the time—not enough to be serious—just enough to make me restless and giddy!—Invitations poured in—parties all over the Delta!—"Stay in bed," said Mother, "you have fever!"—but I just wouldn't.—I took quinine but kept on going, going!—Evenings, dances!—Afternoons, long, long rides! Picnics—lovely!—So lovely, that country in May.—All lacy with dogwood, literally flooded with jonquils!—That was the spring I had the craze for jonquils. Jonquils became an absolute obsession. Mother said "Honey, there's no more room for jonquils." And still I kept on bringing in more jonquils. Whenever, wherever I saw them, I'd say, "Stop! Stop! I see jonquils!" I made the young men help me gather the jonquils! It was a joke, Amanda and her jonquils! Finally there were no more vases to hold them, every available space was filled with jonquils. No vases to hold them? All right, I'll hold them myself! And then I—[*She stops in front of the picture.* MUSIC] met your father! Malaria fever and jonquils and then—this—boy. . . . [*She switches on the rose-colored lamp*] I hope they get here before it starts to rain. [*She crosses upstage and places the jonquils in bowl on table*] I gave your brother a little extra change so he and Mr. O'Connor could take the service car home.

LAURA: [*With altered look*] What did you say his name was?

AMANDA: O'Connor.

LAURA: What is his first name?

AMANDA: I don't remember. Oh, yes, I do. It was —Jim!

[Laura *sways slightly and catches hold of a chair*]

[IMAGE ON SCREEN: "NOT JIM!"]

LAURA: [*Faintly*] Not—Jim!

AMANDA: Yes, that was it, it was Jim! I've never known a Jim that wasn't nice!

[MUSIC: OMINOUS]

LAURA: Are you sure his name is Jim O'Connor?

AMANDA: Yes. Why?

LAURA: Is he the one that Tom used to know in high school?

AMANDA: He didn't say so. I think he just got to know him at the warehouse.

LAURA: There was a Jim O'Connor we both knew in high school—[*Then, with effort*] If that is the one that Tom is bringing to dinner—you'll have to excuse me, I won't come to the table.

AMANDA: What sort of nonsense is this?

LAURA: You asked me once if I'd ever liked a boy. Don't you remember I showed you this boy's picture?

AMANDA: You mean the boy you showed me in the year book?

LAURA: Yes, that boy.

AMANDA: Laura, Laura, were you in love with that boy?

LAURA: I don't know, Mother. All I know is I couldn't sit at the table if it was him!

AMANDA: It won't be him! It isn't the least bit likely. But whether it is or not, you will come to the table. You will not be excused.

LAURA: I'll have to be, Mother.

AMANDA: I don't intend to humor your silliness, Laura. I've had too much from you and your brother, both! So just sit down and compose yourself till they come. Tom has forgotten his key so you'll have to let them in, when they arrive.

LAURA: [*Panicky*] Oh, Mother—*you* answer the door!

AMANDA: [*Lightly*] I'll be in the kitchen—busy!

LAURA: Oh, Mother, please answer the door, don't make me do it!

AMANDA: [*Crossing into kitchenette*] I've got to fix the dressing for the salmon. Fuss, fuss—silliness!—over a gentleman caller!

[*Door swings shut. Laura is left alone*]

[LEGEND: "TERROR!"]

[*She utters a low moan and turns off the lamp—sits stiffly on the edge of the sofa, knotting her fingers together*]

[LEGEND ON SCREEN: "THE OPENING OF A DOOR!"]

[*Tom and Jim appear on the fire-escape steps and climb to landing. Hearing their approach, Laura rises with a panicky gesture. She retreats to the portieres. The doorbell. Laura catches her breath and touches her throat. Low drums*]

AMANDA: [*Calling*] Laura, sweetheart! The door!

[*Laura stares at it without moving*]

JIM: I think we just beat the rain.

TOM: Uh-huh. [*He rings again, nervously. Jim whistles and fishes for a cigarette*]

AMANDA: [*Very, very gaily*] Laura, that is your brother and Mr. O'Connor! Will you let them in, darling?

[*Laura crosses toward kitchenette door*]

LAURA: [*Breathlessly*] Mother—you go to the door!

[*Amanda steps out of kitchenette and stares furiously at Laura. She points imperiously at the door*]

LAURA: Please, please!

AMANDA: [*In a fierce whisper*] What is the matter with you, you silly thing?

LAURA: [*Desperately*] Please, you answer it, *please!*

AMANDA: I told you I wasn't going to humor you, Laura. Why have you chosen this moment to lose your mind?

LAURA: Please, please, please, you go!

AMANDA: You'll have to go to the door because I can't!

LAURA: [*Despairingly*] I can't either!

AMANDA: *Why?*

LAURA: I'm *sick!*

AMANDA: I'm sick, too—of your nonsense! Why can't you and your brother be normal people? Fantastic whims and behavior! [Tom *gives a long ring*] Preposterous goings on! Can you give me one reason—[*Calls out lyrically*] Coming! Just one second!—why you should be afraid to open a door? Now you answer it, Laura!

LAURA: Oh, oh, oh . . . [*She returns through the portieres. Darts to the victrola and winds it frantically and turns it on*]

AMANDA: Laura Wingfield, you march right to that door!

LAURA: Yes—yes, Mother!

[*A faraway, scratchy rendition of "Dardanella" softens the air and gives her strength to move through it. She slips to the door and draws it cautiously open. Tom enters with the caller, Jim O'Connor*]

TOM: Laura, this is Jim. Jim, this is my sister, Laura.

JIM: [*Stepping inside*] I didn't know that Shakespeare had a sister!

LAURA: [*Retreating stiff and trembling from the door*] How—how do you do?

JIM: [*Heartily extending his hand*] Okay! [Laura *touches it hesitantly with hers*]

JIM: Your hand's *cold*, Laura!

LAURA: Yes, well—I've been playing the victrola. . . .

JIM: Must have been playing classical music on it! You ought to play a little hot swing music to warm you up!

LAURA: Excuse me—I haven't finished playing the victrola. . . . [*She turns awkwardly and hurries into the front room. She pauses a second by the victrola.*

Then catches her breath and darts through the portieres like a frightened deer]

JIM: [*Grinning*] What was the matter?

TOM: Oh—with Laura? Laura is—terribly shy.

JIM: Shy, huh? It's unusual to meet a shy girl nowadays. I don't believe you ever mentioned you had a sister.

TOM: Well, now you know. I have one. Here is the *Post Dispatch.* You want a piece of it?

JIM: Uh-huh.

TOM: What piece? The comics?

JIM: Sports! [*Glances at it*] Ole Dizzy Dean is on his bad behavior.

TOM: [*Disinterest*] Yeah? [*Lights cigarette and crosses back to fire-escape door*]

JIM: Where are *you* going?

TOM: I'm going out on the terrace.

JIM: [*Goes after him*] You know, Shakespeare—I'm going to sell you a bill of goods!

TOM: What goods?

JIM: A course I'm taking.

TOM: Huh?

JIM: In public speaking! You and me, we're not the warehouse type.

TOM: Thanks—that's good news. But what has public speaking got to do with it?

JIM: It fits you for—executive positions!

TOM: Awww.

JIM: I tell you it's done a helluva lot for me.

[IMAGE: EXECUTIVE AT DESK]

TOM: In what respect?

JIM: In every! Ask yourself what is the difference between you an' me and men in the office down front? Brains?—No!—Ability?—No! Then what? Just one little thing—

TOM: What is that one little thing?

JIM: Primarily it amounts to—social poise! Being able to square up to people and hold your own on any social level!

AMANDA: [*Off stage*] Tom?

TOM: Yes, Mother?

AMANDA: Is that you and Mr. O'Connor?

TOM: Yes, Mother.

AMANDA: Well, you just make yourselves comfortable in there.

TOM: Yes, Mother.

AMANDA: Ask Mr. O'Connor if he would like to wash his hands.

JIM: Aw, no—no—thank you—I took care of that at the warehouse. Tom—

TOM: Yes?

JIM: Mr. Mendoza was speaking to me about you.

TOM: Favorably?

JIM: What do you think?

TOM: Well—

JIM: You're going to be out of a job if you don't wake up.

TOM: I am waking up—

JIM: You show no signs.

TOM: The signs are interior.

[IMAGE ON SCREEN: THE SAILING VESSEL WITH JOLLY ROGER AGAIN]

TOM: I'm planning to change. [*He leans over the rail speaking with quiet exhilaration. The incandescent marquees and signs of the first-run movie houses light his face from across the alley. He looks like a voyager*] I'm right at the point of committing myself to a future that doesn't include the warehouse and Mr. Mendoza or even a night-school course in public speaking.

JIM: What are you gassing about?

TOM: I'm tired of the movies.

JIM: Movies!

TOM: Yes, movies! Look at them—[*A wave toward the marvels of Grand Avenue*] All of those glamorous people—having adventures—hogging it all, gobbling the whole thing up! You know what happens? People go to the *movies* instead of *moving!* Hollywood characters are supposed to have all the adventures for everybody in America, while everybody in America sits in a dark room and watches them have them! Yes, until there's a war. That's when adventure becomes available to the masses! *Everyone's* dish, not only Gable's! Then the people in the dark room come out of the dark room to have some adventures themselves—Goody, goody! —It's our turn now, to go to the South Sea Island —to make a safari—to be exotic, far-off!—but I'm not patient. I don't want to wait till then. I'm tired of the *movies* and I am *about* to *move!*

JIM: [*Incredulously*] Move?

TOM: Yes.

JIM: When?

TOM: Soon!

JIM: Where? Where?

[*Theme three music seems to answer the question, while* Tom *thinks it over. He searches among his pockets*]

TOM: I'm starting to boil inside. I know I seem dreamy, but inside—well, I'm boiling!—Whenever I pick up a shoe, I shudder a little thinking how short life is and what I am doing!— Whatever that means, I know it doesn't mean shoes—except as something to wear on a traveler's feet! [*Finds paper*] Look—

JIM: What?

TOM: I'm a member.

JIM: [*Reading*] The Union of Merchant Seamen.

TOM: I paid my dues this month, instead of the light bill.

JIM: You will regret it when they turn the lights off.

TOM: I won't be here.

JIM: How about your mother?

TOM: I'm like my father. The bastard son of a bastard! See how he grins? And he's been absent going on sixteen years!

JIM: You're just talking, you drip. How does your mother feel about it?

TOM: Shhh!—Here comes Mother! Mother is not acquainted with my plans!

AMANDA: [*Enters portieres*] Where are you all?

TOM: On the terrace, Mother.

[*They start inside. She advances to them. Tom is distinctly shocked at her appearance. Even Jim blinks a little. He is making his first contact with girlish Southern vivacity and in spite of the night-school course in public speaking is somewhat thrown off the beam by the unexpected outlay of social charm. Certain responses are attempted by Jim but are swept aside by Amanda's gay laughter and chatter. Tom is embarrassed but after the first shock Jim reacts very warmly. Grins and chuckles, is altogether won over.*]

[IMAGE: AMANDA AS A GIRL]

AMANDA: [*Coyly smiling, shaking her girlish ringlets*] Well, well, well, so this is Mr. O'Connor. Introductions entirely unnecessary. I've heard so much about you from my boy. I finally said to him, Tom —good gracious!—why don't you bring this paragon to supper? I'd like to meet this nice young man at the warehouse!—Instead of just hearing him sing your praises so much!

I don't know why my son is so stand-offish—that's not Southern behavior!

Let's sit down and—I think we could stand a little more air in here! Tom, leave the door open. I felt a nice fresh breeze a moment ago. Where has it gone to?

Mmm, so warm already! And not quite summer, even. We're going to burn up when summer really gets started.

However, we're having—we're having a very light supper. I think light things are better fo' this time of year. The same as light clothes are. Light clothes an' light food are what warm weather calls fo'. You know our blood gets so thick during th' winter—it takes a while fo' us to *adjust* ou'selves!—when the season changes . . .

It's come so quick this year. I wasn't prepared. All of a sudden—heavens! Already summer!—I ran to the trunk an' pulled out this light dress— Terribly old! Historical almost! But feels so good—so good an' co-ol, y'know. . . .

TOM: Mother—

AMANDA: Yes, honey?

TOM: How about—supper?

AMANDA: Honey, you go ask Sister if supper is ready! You know that Sister is in full charge of supper!

Tell her you hungry boys are waiting for it. [*To Jim*] Have you met Laura?

JIM: She—

AMANDA: Let you in? Oh, good, you've met already! It's rare for a girl as sweet an' pretty as Laura to be domestic! But Laura is, thank heavens, not only pretty but also very domestic. I'm not at all. I never was a bit. I never could make a thing but

angel-food cake. Well, in the South we had so many servants. Gone, gone, gone. All vestige of gracious living! Gone completely! I wasn't prepared for what the future brought me. All of my gentlemen callers were sons of planters and so of course I assumed that I would be married to one and raise my family on a large piece of land with plenty of servants. But man proposes—and woman accepts the proposal!—To vary that old, old saying a little bit— I married no planter! I married a man who worked for the telephone company!—That gallantly smiling gentleman over there! [*Points to the picture*] A telephone man who—fell in love with long-distance!— Now he travels and I don't even know where!— But what am I going on for about my tribulations? Tell me yours—I hope you don't have any! Tom?

TOM: [*Returning*] Yes, Mother?

AMANDA: Is supper nearly ready?

TOM: It looks to me like supper is on the table.

AMANDA: Let me look— [*She rises prettily and looks through portieres*] Oh, lovely!—But where is Sister?

TOM: Laura is not feeling well and she says that she thinks she'd better not come to the table.

AMANDA: What?—Nonsense!—Laura? Oh, Laura!

LAURA: [*Off stage, faintly*] Yes, Mother.

AMANDA: You really must come to the table. We won't be seated until you come to the table! Come in, Mr. O'Connor. You sit over there, and I'll— Laura? Laura Wingfield! You're keeping us waiting, honey! We can't say grace until you come to the table!

[*The back door is pushed weakly open and Laura comes in. She is obviously quite faint, her lips trembling, her eyes wide and staring. She moves unsteadily toward the table*]

[LEGEND: "TERROR!"]

[*Outside a summer storm is coming abruptly. The white curtains billow inward at the windows and there is a sorrowful murmur and deep blue dusk. Laura suddenly stumbles—she catches at a chair with a faint moan*]

TOM: Laura!

AMANDA: Laura!

[*There is a clap of thunder*]

[LEGEND: "AH!"]

[*Despairingly*]

Why, Laura, you *are* sick, darling! Tom, help your sister into the living room, dear! Sit in the living room, Laura—rest on the sofa. Well! [*To the gentleman caller*] Standing over the hot stove made her ill!—I told her that it was just too warm this evening, but— [*Tom comes back in. Laura is on the sofa*] Is Laura all right now?

TOM: Yes.

AMANDA: What *is* that? Rain? A nice cool rain has come up! [*She gives the gentleman caller a frightened look*] I think we may—have grace—now . . . [*Tom looks at her stupidly*] Tom, honey—you say grace!

TOM: Oh . . . "For these and all thy mercies—"
[*They bow their heads,* Amanda *stealing a nervous glance at* Jim. *In the living room* Laura, *stretched on the sofa, clenches her hand to her lips, to hold back a shuddering sob*] God's Holy Name be praised—

THE SCENE DIMS OUT

SCENE VII

A Souvenir.
Half an hour later. Dinner is just being finished in the upstage area which is concealed by the drawn portieres. As the curtain rises Laura *is still huddled upon the sofa, her feet drawn under her, her head resting on a pale blue pillow, her eyes wide and mysteriously watchful. The new floor lamp with its shade of rose-colored silk gives a soft, becoming light to her face, bringing out the fragile, unearthly prettiness which usually escapes attention. There is a steady murmur of rain, but it is slackening and stops soon after the scene begins; the air outside becomes pale and luminous as the moon breaks out. A moment after the curtain rises, the lights in both rooms flicker and go out.*

JIM: Hey, there, Mr. Light Bulb!
[Amanda *laughs nervously*]
[LEGEND: "SUSPENSION OF A PUBLIC SERVICE"]
AMANDA: Where was Moses when the lights went out? Ha-ha. Do you know the answer to that one, Mr. O'Connor?
JIM: No, Ma'am, what's the answer?
AMANDA: In the dark! [Jim *laughs appreciatively*] Everybody sit still. I'll light the candles. Isn't it lucky we have them on the table? Where's a match? Which of you gentlemen can provide a match?
JIM: Here.
AMANDA: Thank you, sir.
JIM: Not at all, Ma'am!
AMANDA: I guess the fuse has burnt out. Mr. O'Connor, can you tell a burnt-out fuse? I know I can't and Tom is a total loss when it comes to mechanics.
[*Sound: Getting up: Voices recede a little to kitchenette*]
Oh, be careful you don't bump into something. We don't want our gentleman caller to break his neck. Now wouldn't that be a fine howdy-do?
JIM: Ha-ha! Where is the fuse-box?
AMANDA: Right here next to the stove. Can you see anything?
JIM: Just a minute.
AMANDA: Isn't electricity a mysterious thing? Wasn't it Benjamin Franklin who tied a key to a kite? We live in such a mysterious universe, don't we? Some people say that science clears up all the mysteries for us. In my opinion it only creates more! Have you found it yet?
JIM: No, Ma'am. All these fuses look okay to me.
AMANDA: Tom!
TOM: Yes, Mother?
AMANDA: That light bill I gave you several days ago. The one I told you we got the notices about?
[LEGEND: "HA!"]
TOM: Oh.—Yeah.
AMANDA: You didn't neglect to pay it by any chance?
TOM: Why, I—
AMANDA: Didn't! I might have known it!
JIM: Shakespeare probably wrote a poem on that light bill, Mrs. Wingfield.
AMANDA: I might have known better than to trust him with it! There's such a high price for negligence in this world!
JIM: Maybe the poem will win a ten-dollar prize.
AMANDA: We'll just have to spend the remainder of the evening in the nineteenth century, before Mr. Edison made the Mazda lamp!
JIM: Candlelight is my favorite kind of light.
AMANDA: That shows you're romantic! But that's no excuse for Tom. Well, we got through dinner. Very considerate of them to let us get through dinner before they plunged us into everlasting darkness, wasn't it, Mr. O'Connor?
JIM: Ha-ha!
AMANDA: Tom, as a penalty for your carelessness you can help me with the dishes.
JIM: Let me give you a hand.
AMANDA: Indeed you will not!
JIM: I ought to be good for something.
AMANDA: Good for something? [*Her tone is rhapsodic*] You? Why, Mr. O'Connor, nobody, *nobody's* given me this much entertainment in years—as you have!
JIM: Aw, now, Mrs. Wingfield!
AMANDA: I'm not exaggerating, not one bit! But Sister is all by her lonesome. You go keep her company in the parlor! I'll give you this lovely old candelabrum that used to be on the altar at the church of the Heavenly Rest. It was melted a little out of shape when the church burnt down. Lightning struck it one spring. Gypsy Jones was holding a revival at the time and he intimated that the church was destroyed because the Episcopalians gave card parties.
JIM: Ha-ha.
AMANDA: And how about you coaxing Sister to drink a little wine? I think it would be good for her! Can you carry both at once?
JIM: Sure. I'm Superman!
AMANDA: Now, Thomas, get into this apron!
[*The door of the kitchenette swings closed on* Amanda's *gay laughter; the flickering light approaches the portieres.* Laura *sits up nervously as he enters. Her speech at first is low and*

breathless from the almost intolerable strain of being alone with a stranger]

[THE LEGEND: "I DON'T SUPPOSE YOU REMEMBER ME AT ALL!"]

[*In her first speeches in this scene, before Jim's warmth overcomes her paralyzing shyness, Laura's voice is thin and breathless as though she has just run up a steep flight of stairs. Jim's attitude is gently humorous. In playing this scene it should be stressed that while the incident is apparently unimportant, it is to Laura the climax of her secret life*]

JIM: Hello, there, Laura.

LAURA: [*Faintly*] Hello. [*She clears her throat*]

JIM: How are you feeling now? Better?

LAURA: Yes. Yes, thank you.

JIM: This is for you. A little dandelion wine. [*He extends it toward her with extravagant gallantry*]

LAURA: Thank you.

JIM: Drink it—but don't get drunk! [*He laughs heartily. Laura takes the glass uncertainly; laughs shyly*] Where shall I set the candles?

LAURA: Oh—oh, anywhere . . .

JIM: How about here on the floor? Any objections?

LAURA: No.

JIM: I'll spread a newspaper under to catch the drippings. I like to sit on the floor. Mind if I do?

LAURA: Oh, no.

JIM: Give me a pillow?

LAURA: What?

JIM: A pillow!

LAURA: Oh . . . [*Hands him one quickly*]

JIM: How about you? Don't you like to sit on the floor?

LAURA: Oh—yes.

JIM: Why don't you then?

LAURA: I—will.

JIM: Take a pillow! [*Laura does. Sits on the other side of the candelabrum. Jim crosses his legs and smiles engagingly at her*] I can't hardly see you sitting way over there.

LAURA: I can—see you.

JIM: I know, but that's not fair, I'm in the limelight. [*Laura moves her pillow closer*] Good! Now I can see you! Comfortable?

LAURA: Yes.

JIM: So am I. Comfortable as a cow! Will you have some gum?

LAURA: No, thank you.

JIM: I think that I will indulge, with your permission. [*Musingly unwraps it and holds it up*] Think of the fortune made by the guy that invented the first piece of chewing gum. Amazing, huh? The Wrigley Building is one of the sights of Chicago. —I saw it summer before last when I went up to the Century of Progress. Did you take in the Century of Progress?

LAURA: No, I didn't.

JIM: Well, it was quite a wonderful exposition.

What impressed me most was the Hall of Science. Gives you an idea of what the future will be in America, even more wonderful than the present time is! [*Pause. Smiling at her*] Your brother tells me you're shy. Is that right, Laura?

LAURA: I—don't know.

JIM: I judge you to be an old-fashioned type of girl. Well, I think that's a pretty good type to be. Hope you don't think I'm being too personal—do you?

LAURA: [*Hastily, out of embarrassment*] I believe I *will* take a piece of gum, if you—don't mind. [*Clearing her throat*] Mr. O'Connor, have you—kept up with your singing?

JIM: Singing? Me?

LAURA: Yes. I remember what a beautiful voice you had.

JIM: When did you hear me sing?

[VOICE OFF STAGE IN THE PAUSE]

VOICE: [*Off stage*]
       O blow, ye winds, heigh-ho,
       A-roving I will go!
       I'm off to my love
       With a boxing glove—
       Ten thousand miles away!

JIM: You say you've heard me sing?

LAURA: Oh, yes! Yes, very often . . . I—don't suppose—you remember me—at all?

JIM: [*Smiling doubtfully*] You know I have an idea I've seen you before. I had that idea as soon as you opened the door. It seemed almost like I was about to remember your name. But the name I started to call you—wasn't a name! And so I stopped myself before I said it.

LAURA: Wasn't it—Blue Roses?

JIM: [*Springs up. Grinning*] Blue Roses!—My gosh, yes—Blue Roses! That's what I had on my tongue when you opened the door! Isn't it funny what tricks your memory plays? I didn't connect you with high school somehow or other. But that's where it was; it was high school. I didn't even know you were Shakespeare's sister! Gosh, I'm sorry.

LAURA: I didn't expect you to. You—barely knew me!

JIM: But we did have a speaking acquaintance, huh?

LAURA: Yes, we—spoke to each other.

JIM: When did you recognize me?

LAURA: Oh, right away!

JIM: Soon as I came in the door?

LAURA: When I heard your name I thought it was probably you. I knew that Tom used to know you a little in high school. So when you came in the door—Well, then I was—sure.

JIM: Why didn't you *say* something, then?

LAURA: [*Breathlessly*] I didn't know what to say, I was—too surprised!

JIM: For goodness' sakes! You know, this sure is funny!

LAURA: Yes! Yes, isn't it, though . . .

JIM: Didn't we have a class in something together?

LAURA: Yes, we did.

JIM: What class was that?

LAURA: It was—singing—Chorus!

JIM: Aw!

LAURA: I sat across the aisle from you in the Aud.

JIM: Aw.

LAURA: Mondays, Wednesdays and Fridays.

JIM: Now I remember—you always came in late.

LAURA: Yes, it was so hard for me, getting upstairs. I had that brace on my leg—it clumped so loud!

JIM: I never heard any clumping.

LAURA: [Wincing at the recollection] To me it sounded like—thunder!

JIM: Well, well, well, I never even noticed.

LAURA: And everybody was seated before I came in. I had to walk in front of all those people. My seat was in the back row. I had to go clumping all the way up the aisle with everyone watching!

JIM: You shouldn't have been self-conscious.

LAURA: I know, but I was. It was always such a relief when the singing started.

JIM: Aw, yes, I've placed you now! I used to call you Blue Roses. How was it that I got started calling you that?

LAURA: I was out of school a little while with pleurosis. When I came back you asked me what was the matter. I said I had pleurosis—you thought I said Blue Roses. That's what you always called me after that!

JIM: I hope you didn't mind.

LAURA: Oh, no—I liked it. You see, I wasn't acquainted with many—people. . . .

JIM: As I remember you sort of stuck by yourself.

LAURA: I—I—never have had much luck at—making friends.

JIM: I don't see why you wouldn't.

LAURA: Well, I—started out badly.

JIM: You mean being—

LAURA: Yes, it sort of—stood between me—

JIM: You shouldn't have let it!

LAURA: I know, but it did, and—

JIM: You were shy with people!

LAURA: I tried not to be but never could—

JIM: Overcome it?

LAURA: No, I—I never could!

JIM: I guess being shy is something you have to work out of kind of gradually.

LAURA: [Sorrowfully] Yes—I guess it—

JIM: Takes time!

LAURA: Yes—

JIM: People are not so dreadful when you know them. That's what you have to remember! And everybody has problems, not just you, but practically everybody has got some problems. You think of yourself as having the only problems, as being the only one who is disappointed. But just look around

you and you will see lots of people as disappointed as you are. For instance, I hoped when I was going to high school that I would be further along at this time, six years later, than I am now— You remember that wonderful write-up I had in The Torch?

LAURA: Yes! [She rises and crosses to table]

JIM: It said I was bound to succeed in anything I went into! [Laura returns with the annual] Holy Jeez! The Torch! [He accepts it reverently. They smile across it with mutual wonder. Laura crouches beside him and they begin to turn through it. Laura's shyness is dissolving in his warmth]

LAURA: Here you are in The Pirates of Penzance!

JIM: [Wistfully] I sang the baritone lead in that operetta.

LAURA: [Raptly] So—beautifully!

JIM: [Protesting] Aw—

LAURA: Yes, yes—beautifully—beautifully!

JIM: You heard me?

LAURA: All three times!

JIM: No!

LAURA: Yes!

JIM: All three performances?

LAURA: [Looking down] Yes.

JIM: Why?

LAURA: I—wanted to ask you to—autograph my program.

JIM: Why didn't you ask me to?

LAURA: You were always surrounded by your own friends so much that I never had a chance to.

JIM: You should have just—

LAURA: Well, I—thought you might think I was—

JIM: Thought I might think you was—what?

LAURA: Oh—

JIM: [With reflective relish] I was beleaguered by females in those days.

LAURA: You were terribly popular!

JIM: Yeah—

LAURA: You had such a—friendly way—

JIM: I was spoiled in high school.

LAURA: Everybody—liked you!

JIM: Including you?

LAURA: I—yes, I—I did, too— [She gently closes the book in her lap]

JIM: Well, well, well!—Give me that program, Laura. [She hands it to him. He signs it with a flourish] There you are—better late than never!

LAURA: Oh, I—what a—surprise!

JIM: My signature isn't worth very much right now. But some day—maybe—it will increase in value! Being disappointed is one thing and being discouraged is something else. I am disappointed but I am not discouraged. I'm twenty-three years old. How old are you?

LAURA: I'll be twenty-four in June.

JIM: That's not old age!

LAURA: No, but—

JIM: You finished high school?

LAURA: [With difficulty] I didn't go back.

JIM: You mean you dropped out?

LAURA: I made bad grades in my final examinations. [*She rises and replaces the book and the program. Her voice strained*] How is—Emily Meisenbach getting along?

JIM: Oh, that kraut-head!

LAURA: Why do you call her that?

JIM: That's what she was.

LAURA: You're not still—going with her?

JIM: I never see her.

LAURA: It said in the Personal Section that you were—engaged!

JIM: I know, but I wasn't impressed by that—propaganda!

LAURA: It wasn't—the truth?

JIM: Only in Emily's optimistic opinion!

LAURA: Oh—

[LEGEND: "WHAT HAVE YOU DONE SINCE HIGH SCHOOL?"]

[Jim *lights a cigarette and leans indolently back on his elbows smiling at* Laura *with a warmth and charm which lights her inwardly with altar candles. She remains by the table and turns in her hands a piece of glass to cover her tumult*]

JIM: [*After several reflective puffs on a cigarette*] What have you done since high school? [*She seems not to hear him*] Huh? [Laura *looks up*] I said what have you done since high school, Laura?

LAURA: Nothing much.

JIM: You must have been doing something these six long years.

LAURA: Yes.

JIM: Well, then, such as what?

LAURA: I took a business course at business college—

JIM: How did that work out?

LAURA: Well, not very—well—I had to drop out, it gave me—indigestion—

[Jim *laughs gently*]

JIM: What are you doing now?

LAURA: I don't do anything—much. Oh, please don't think I sit around doing nothing! My glass collection takes up a good deal of time. Glass is something you have to take good care of.

JIM: What did you say—about glass?

LAURA: Collection I said—I have one— [*She clears her throat and turns away again, acutely shy*]

JIM: [*Abruptly*] You know what I judge to be the trouble with you? Inferiority complex! Know what that is? That's what they call it when someone low-rates himself! I understand it because I had it, too. Although my case was not so aggravated as yours seems to be. I had it until I took up public speaking, developed my voice, and learned that I had an aptitude for science. Before that time I never thought of myself as being outstanding in any way whatsoever! Now I've never made a regular study of it, but I have a friend who says I can analyze people better than doctors that make a profession of it. I don't claim that to be necessarily true, but I can sure guess a person's psychology, Laura! [*Takes out his gum*] Excuse me, Laura. I always take it out when the flavor is gone. I'll use this scrap of paper to wrap it in. I know how it is to get it stuck on a shoe. Yep—that's what I judge to be your principal trouble. A lack of confidence in yourself as a person. You don't have the proper amount of faith in yourself. I'm basing that fact on a number of your remarks and also on certain observations I've made. For instance that clumping you thought was so awful in high school. You say you even dreaded to walk into class. You see what you did? You dropped out of school, you gave up an education because of a clump, which as far as I know was practically non-existent! A little physical defect is what you have. Hardly noticeable even! Magnified thousands of times by imagination! You know what my strong advice to you is? Think of yourself as *superior* in some way!

LAURA: In what way would I think?

JIM: Why, man alive, Laura! Just look about you a little. What do you see? A world full of common people! All of 'em born and all of 'em going to die! Which of them has one-tenth of your good points! Or mine! Or anyone else's, as far as that goes— Gosh! Everybody excels in some one thing. Some in many! [*Unconsciously glances at himself in the mirror*] All you've got to do is discover in *what!* Take me, for instance. [*He adjusts his tie at the mirror*] My interest happens to lie in electro-dynamics. I'm taking a course in radio engineering at night school, Laura, on top of a fairly responsible job at the warehouse. I'm taking that course and studying public speaking.

LAURA: Ohhhh.

JIM: Because I believe in the future of television! [*Turning back to her*] I wish to be ready to go up right along with it. Therefore I'm planning to get in on the ground floor. In fact I've already made the right connections and all that remains is for the industry to get under way! Full steam— [*His eyes are starry*] Knowledge—Zzzzzp! Money—Zzzzzzp! —Power! That's the cycle democracy is built on! [*His attitude is convincingly dynamic.* Laura *stares at him, even her shyness eclipsed in her absolute wonder. He suddenly grins*] I guess you think I think a lot of myself!

LAURA: No—o-o-o, I—

JIM: Now how about you? Isn't there something you take more interest in than anything else?

LAURA: Well, I do—as I said—have my—glass collection—

[*A peal of girlish laughter from the kitchen*]

JIM: I'm not right sure I know what you're talking about. What kind of glass is it?

LAURA: Little articles of it, they're ornaments mostly! Most of them are little animals made out of glass, the tiniest little animals in the world. Mother calls them a glass menagerie! Here's an example of one, if you'd like to see it! This is one of the oldest. It's nearly thirteen.

[Music: "The Glass Menagerie"]

[He stretches out his hand]

Oh, be careful—if you breathe, it breaks!

JIM: I'd better not take it. I'm pretty clumsy with things.

LAURA: Go on, I trust you with him! *[Places it in his palm]* There now—you're holding him gently! Hold him over the light, he loves the light! You see how the light shines through him?

JIM: It sure does shine!

LAURA: I shouldn't be partial, but he is my favorite one.

JIM: What kind of a thing is this one supposed to be?

LAURA: Haven't you noticed the single horn on his forehead?

JIM: A unicorn, huh?

LAURA: Mmm-hmmm!

JIM: Unicorns, aren't they extinct in the modern world?

LAURA: I know!

JIM: Poor little fellow, he must feel sort of lonesome.

LAURA: *[Smiling]* Well, if he does he doesn't complain about it. He stays on a shelf with some horses that don't have horns and all of them seem to get along nicely together.

JIM: How do you know?

LAURA: *[Lightly]* I haven't heard any arguments among them!

JIM: *[Grinning]* No arguments, huh? Well, that's a pretty good sign! Where shall I set him?

LAURA: Put him on the table. They all like a change of scenery once in a while!

JIM: *[Stretching]* Well, well, well, well—Look how big my shadow is when I stretch!

LAURA: Oh, oh, yes—it stretches across the ceiling!

JIM: *[Crossing to door]* I think it's stopped raining. *[Opens fire-escape door]* Where does the music come from?

LAURA: From the Paradise Dance Hall across the alley.

JIM: How about cutting the rug a little, Miss Wingfield?

LAURA: Oh, I—

JIM: Or is your program filled up? Let me have a look at it. *[Grasps imaginary card]* Why, every dance is taken! I'll just have to scratch some out. *[Waltz music: "La Golondrina"]* Ahhh, a waltz! *[He executes some sweeping turns by himself then holds his arms toward* Laura*]*

LAURA: *[Breathlessly]* I—can't dance!

JIM: There you go, that inferiority stuff!

LAURA: I've never danced in my life!

JIM: Come on, try!

LAURA: Oh, but I'd step on you!

JIM: I'm not made out of glass.

LAURA: How—how—how do we start?

JIM: Just leave it to me. You hold your arms out a little.

LAURA: Like this?

JIM: A little bit higher. Right. Now don't tighten up, that's the main thing about it—relax.

LAURA: *[Laughing breathlessly]* It's hard not to.

JIM: Okay.

LAURA: I'm afraid you can't budge me.

JIM: What do you bet I can't? *[He swings her into motion]*

LAURA: Goodness, yes, you can!

JIM: Let yourself go, now, Laura, just let yourself go.

LAURA: I'm—

JIM: Come on!

LAURA: Trying!

JIM: Not so stiff— Easy does it!

LAURA: I know but I'm—

JIM: Loosen th' backbone! There now, that's a lot better.

LAURA: Am I?

JIM: Lots, lots better! *[He moves her about the room in a clumsy waltz]*

LAURA: Oh, my!

JIM: Ha-ha!

LAURA: Oh, my goodness!

JIM: Ha-ha-ha! *[They suddenly bump into the table.* Jim *stops]* What did we hit on?

LAURA: Table.

JIM: Did something fall off it? I think—

LAURA: Yes.

JIM: I hope that it wasn't the little glass horse with the horn!

LAURA: Yes.

JIM: Aw, aw, aw. Is it broken?

LAURA: Now it is just like all the other horses.

JIM: It's lost its—

LAURA: Horn! It doesn't matter. Maybe it's a blessing in disguise.

JIM: You'll never forgive me. I bet that that was your favorite piece of glass.

LAURA: I don't have favorites much. It's no tragedy, Freckles. Glass breaks so easily. No matter how careful you are. The traffic jars the shelves and things fall off them.

JIM: Still I'm awfully sorry that I was the cause.

LAURA: *[Smiling]* I'll just imagine he had an operation. The horn was removed to make him feel less —freakish! *[They both laugh]* Now he will feel more at home with the other horses, the ones that don't have horns . . .

JIM: Ha-ha, that's very funny! *[Suddenly serious]* I'm glad to see that you have a sense of humor. You know—you're—well—very different! Surprisingly different from anyone else I know! *[His voice becomes soft and hesitant with a genuine feeling]* Do you mind me telling you that? *[Laura is abashed beyond speech]* I mean it in a nice way . . . *[Laura nods shyly, looking away]* You make me feel sort of—I don't know how to put it! I'm usually pretty good at expressing things, but—This is something that I don't know how to say! [*Laura touches her throat and clears it—turns the broken unicorn in her hands. Even softer*] Has anyone ever told you that you were pretty?

[PAUSE: MUSIC]

[*Laura looks up slowly, with wonder, and shakes her head*]

Well, you are! In a very different way from anyone else. And all the nicer because of the difference too. [*His voice becomes low and husky. Laura turns away, nearly faint with the novelty of her emotions*] I wish that you were my sister. I'd teach you to have some confidence in yourself. The different people are not like other people, but being different is nothing to be ashamed of. Because other people are not such wonderful people. They're one hundred times one thousand. You're one times one! They walk all over the earth. You just stay here. They're common as—weeds, but—you—well, you're—*Blue Roses!*

[IMAGE ON SCREEN: BLUE ROSES]

[MUSIC CHANGES]

LAURA: But blue is wrong for—roses . . .

JIM: It's right for you!—You're—pretty!

LAURA: In what respect am I pretty?

JIM: In all respects—believe me! Your eyes—your hair—are pretty! Your hands are pretty! [*He catches hold of her hand*] You think I'm making this up because I'm invited to dinner and have to be nice. Oh, I could do that! I could put on an act for you, Laura, and say lots of things without being very sincere. But this time I am. I'm talking to you sincerely. I happened to notice you had this inferiority complex that keeps you from feeling comfortable with people. Somebody needs to build your confidence up and make you proud instead of shy and turning away and—blushing—Somebody—ought to—ought to—*kiss* you, Laura! [*His hand slips slowly up her arm to her shoulder*]

[MUSIC SWELLS TUMULTUOUSLY]

[*He suddenly turns her about and kisses her on the lips. When he releases her, Laura sinks on the sofa with a bright, dazed look. Jim backs away and fishes in his pocket for a cigarette*]

[LEGEND ON SCREEN: "SOUVENIR"]

Stumble-john! [*He lights the cigarette, avoiding her look. There is a peal of girlish laughter from Amanda in the kitchen. Laura slowly raises and opens her hand. It still contains the little broken glass animal. She looks at it with a tender, bewildered expression*] Stumble-john! I shouldn't have done that — That was way off the beam. You don't smoke, do you? [*She looks up, smiling, not hearing the question. He sits beside her a little gingerly. She looks at him speechlessly—waiting. He coughs decorously and moves a little farther aside as he considers the situation and senses her feelings, dimly, with perturbation. Gently*] Would you—care for a—mint? [*She doesn't seem to hear him but her look grows*

brighter even] Peppermint.—Life-Saver? My pocket's a regular drug store—wherever I go . . . [*He pops a mint in his mouth. Then gulps and decides to make a clean breast of it. He speaks slowly and gingerly*] Laura, you know, if I had a sister like you, I'd do the same thing as Tom. I'd bring out fellows and—introduce her to them. The right type of boys of a type to—appreciate her. Only—well—he made a mistake about me. Maybe I've got no call to be saying this. That may not have been the idea in having me over. But what if it was? There's nothing wrong about that. The only trouble is that in my case—I'm not in a situation to—do the right thing.

I can't take down your number and say I'll phone. I can't call up next week and—ask for a date. I thought I had better explain the situation in case you—misunderstood it and—hurt your feelings. . . .

[*Pause. Slowly, very slowly, Laura's look changes, her eyes returning slowly from his to the ornament in her palm. Amanda utters another gay laugh in the kitchen*]

LAURA: [*Faintly*] You—won't—call again?

JIM: No, Laura, I can't. [*He rises from the sofa*] As I was just explaining, I've—got strings on me. Laura, I've—been going steady! I go out all of the time with a girl named Betty. She's a home-girl like you, and Catholic, and Irish, and in a great many ways we—get along fine. I met her last summer on a moonlight boat trip up the river to Alton, on the *Majestic*. Well—right away from the start it was—love!

[LEGEND: LOVE!]

[*Laura sways slightly forward and grips the arm of the sofa. He fails to notice, now enrapt in his own comfortable being*]

Being in love has made a new man of me! [*Leaning stiffly forward, clutching the arm of the sofa, Laura struggles visibly with her storm. But Jim is oblivious, she is a long way off*] The power of love is really pretty tremendous! Love is something that —changes the whole world, Laura! [*The storm abates a little and Laura leans back. He notices her again*] It happened that Betty's aunt took sick, she got a wire and had to go to Centralia. So Tom—when he asked me to dinner—I naturally just accepted the invitation, not knowing that you—that he —that I—[*He stops awkwardly*] Huh—I'm a stumble-john! [*He flops back on the sofa. The holy candles in the altar of Laura's face have been snuffed out. There is a look of almost infinite desolation. Jim glances at her uneasily*] I wish that you would—say something. [*She bites her lip which was trembling and then bravely smiles. She opens her hand again on the broken glass ornament. Then she gently takes his hand and raises it level with her own. She carefully places the unicorn in the palm of his hand, then pushes his fingers closed upon it*] What are you—doing that for? You want me to have him?—Laura? [*She nods*] What for?

LAURA: A—souvenir . . . [*She rises unsteadily and crouches beside the victrola to wind it up*]

[LEGEND ON SCREEN: "THINGS HAVE A WAY OF TURNING OUT SO BADLY!"]

[OR IMAGE: "GENTLEMAN CALLER WAVING GOOD-BYE!—GAILY"]

[*At this moment* Amanda *rushes brightly back in the front room. She bears a pitcher of fruit punch in an old-fashioned cut-glass pitcher and a plate of macaroons. The plate has a gold border and poppies painted on it*]

AMANDA: Well, well, well! Isn't the air delightful after the shower? I've made you children a little liquid refreshment. [*Turns gaily to the gentleman caller*] Jim, do you know that song about lemonade?

"Lemonade, lemonade

Made in the shade and stirred with a spade—

Good enough for any old maid!"

JIM: [*Uneasily*] Ha-ha! No—I never heard it.

AMANDA: Why, Laura! You look so serious!

JIM: We were having a serious conversation.

AMANDA: Good! Now you're better acquainted!

JIM: [*Uncertainly*] Ha-ha! Yes.

AMANDA: You modern young people are much more serious-minded than my generation. I was so gay as a girl!

JIM: You haven't changed, Mrs. Wingfield.

AMANDA: Tonight I'm rejuvenated! The gaiety of the occasion, Mr. O'Connor! [*She tosses her head with a peal of laughter. Spills lemonade*] Oooo! I'm baptizing myself!

JIM: Here—let me—

AMANDA: [*Setting the pitcher down*] There now. I discovered we had some maraschino cherries. I dumped them in, juice and all!

JIM: You shouldn't have gone to that trouble, Mrs. Wingfield.

AMANDA: Trouble, trouble? Why, it was loads of fun! Didn't you hear me cutting up in the kitchen? I bet your ears were burning! I told Tom how outdone with him I was for keeping you to himself so long a time! He should have brought you over much, much sooner! Well, now that you've found your way, I want you to be a very frequent caller! Not just occasional but all the time. Oh, we're going to have a lot of gay times together! I see them coming! Mmmm, just breathe that air! So fresh, and the moon's so pretty! I'll skip back out—I know where my place is when young folks are having a—serious conversation!

JIM: Oh, don't go out, Mrs. Wingfield. The fact of the matter is I've got to be going.

AMANDA: Going, now? You're joking! Why, it's only the shank of the evening, Mr. O'Connor!

JIM: Well, you know how it is.

AMANDA: You mean you're a young workingman and have to keep workingmen's hours. We'll let you off early tonight. But only on the condition that next time you stay later. What's the best night for

you? Isn't Saturday night the best night for you workingmen?

JIM: I have a couple of time-clocks to punch, Mrs. Wingfield. One at morning, another one at night!

AMANDA: My, but you *are* ambitious! You work at night, too?

JIM: No, Ma'am, not work but—Betty! [*He crosses deliberately to pick up his hat. The band at the Paradise Dance Hall goes into a tender waltz*]

AMANDA: Betty? Betty? Who's—Betty! [*There is an ominous cracking sound in the sky*]

JIM: Oh, just a girl. The girl I go steady with! [*He smiles charmingly. The sky falls*]

[LEGEND: "THE SKY FALLS"]

AMANDA: [*A long-drawn exhalation*] Ohhhh . . . Is it a serious romance, Mr. O'Connor?

JIM: We're going to be married the second Sunday in June.

AMANDA: Ohhhh—how nice! Tom didn't mention that you were engaged to be married.

JIM: The cat's not out of the bag at the warehouse yet. You know how they are. They call you Romeo and stuff like that. [*He stops at the oval mirror to put on his hat. He carefully shapes the brim and the crown to give a discreetly dashing effect*] It's been a wonderful evening, Mrs. Wingfield. I guess this is what they mean by Southern hospitality.

AMANDA: It really wasn't anything at all.

JIM: I hope it don't seem like I'm rushing off. But I promised Betty I'd pick her up at the Wabash depot, an' by the time I get my jalopy down there her train'll be in. Some women are pretty upset if you keep 'em waiting.

AMANDA: Yes, I know— The tyranny of women! [*Extends her hand*] Good-bye, Mr. O'Connor. I wish you luck—and happiness—and success! All three of them, and so does Laura!—Don't you, Laura?

LAURA: Yes!

JIM: [*Taking her hand*] Good-bye, Laura. I'm certainly going to treasure that souvenir. And don't you forget the good advice I gave you. [*Raises his voice to a cheery shout*] So long, Shakespeare! Thanks again, ladies— Good night! [*He grins and ducks jauntily out. Still bravely grimacing,* Amanda *closes the door on the gentleman caller. Then she turns back to the room with a puzzled expression. She and* Laura *don't dare to face each other.* Laura *crouches beside the victrola to wind it*]

AMANDA: [*Faintly*] Things have a way of turning out so badly. I don't believe that I would play the victrola. Well, well—well—Our gentleman caller was engaged to be married! Tom!

TOM: [*From back*] Yes, Mother?

AMANDA: Come in here a minute. I want to tell you something awfully funny.

TOM: [*Enters with macaroon and a glass of the

lemonade] Has the gentleman caller gotten away already?

AMANDA: The gentleman caller has made an early departure. What a wonderful joke you played on us!

TOM: How do you mean?

AMANDA: You didn't mention that he was engaged to be married.

TOM: Jim? Engaged?

AMANDA: That's what he just informed us.

TOM: I'll be jiggered! I didn't know about that.

AMANDA: That seems very peculiar.

TOM: What's peculiar about it?

AMANDA: Didn't you call him your best friend down at the warehouse?

TOM: He is, but how did I know?

AMANDA: It seems extremely peculiar that you wouldn't know your best friend was going to be married!

TOM: The warehouse is where I work, not where I know things about people!

AMANDA: You don't know things anywhere! You live in a dream; you manufacture illusions! [*He crosses to door*] Where are you going?

TOM: I'm going to the movies.

AMANDA: That's right, now that you've had us make such fools of ourselves. The effort, the preparations, all the expense! The new floor lamp, the rug, the clothes for Laura! All for what? To entertain some other girl's fiancé! Go to the movies, go! Don't think about us, a mother deserted, an unmarried sister who's crippled and has no job! Don't let anything interfere with your selfish pleasure! Just go, go, go—to the movies!

TOM: All right, I will! The more you shout about my selfishness to me the quicker I'll go, and I won't go to the movies!

AMANDA: Go, then! Then go to the moon—you selfish dreamer!

[*Tom smashes his glass on the floor. He plunges out on the fire-escape, slamming the door. Laura screams—cut by door. Dance-hall music up. Tom goes to the rail and grips it desperately, lifting his face in the chill white moonlight penetrating the narrow abyss of the alley*]
[LEGEND ON SCREEN: "AND SO GOOD-BYE . . ."]
[*Tom's closing speech is timed with the in-*

terior pantomime. The interior scene is played as though viewed through soundproof glass. Amanda appears to be making a comforting speech to Laura who is huddled upon the sofa. Now that we cannot hear the mother's speech, her silliness is gone and she has dignity and tragic beauty. Laura's dark hair hides her face until at the end of the speech she lifts it to smile at her mother. Amanda's gestures are slow and graceful, almost dance-like, as she comforts the daughter. At the end of her speech she glances a moment at the father's picture—then withdraws through the portieres. At close of Tom's speech, Laura blows out the candles, ending the play]

TOM: I didn't go to the moon, I went much further—for time is the longest distance between two places—Not long after that I was fired for writing a poem on the lid of a shoe-box. I left Saint Louis. I descended the steps of this fire-escape for a last time and followed, from then on, in my father's footsteps, attempting to find in motion what was lost in space—I traveled around a great deal. The cities swept about me like dead leaves, leaves that were brightly colored but torn away from the branches. I would have stopped, but I was pursued by something. It always came upon me unawares, taking me altogether by surprise. Perhaps it was a familiar bit of music. Perhaps it was only a piece of transparent glass—Perhaps I am walking along a street at night, in some strange city, before I have found companions. I pass the lighted window of a shop where perfume is sold. The window is filled with pieces of colored glass, tiny transparent bottles in delicate colors, like bits of a shattered rainbow. Then all at once my sister touches my shoulder. I turn around and look into her eyes . . . Oh, Laura, Laura, I tried to leave you behind me, but I am more faithful than I intended to be! I reach for a cigarette, I cross the street, I run into the movies or a bar, I buy a drink, I speak to the nearest stranger—anything that can blow your candles out! [*Laura bends over the candles*]—for nowadays the world is lit by lightning! Blow out your candles, Laura—and so good-bye. . . . [*She blows the candles out*]

THE SCENE DISSOLVES

Arthur Miller

(1916–———)

On February 10, 1949, Arthur Miller became famous overnight in a manner that would make most American success stories seem comparatively modest; ironically the occasion was the *première* of *Death of a Salesman*, which tells the story of a failure caused by its hero's worship of the wrong kind of success. The merits of *Death of a Salesman* were conceded even by stern critics and officially signalized by five awards, including the Drama Critics Circle award and the Pulitzer Prize. Miller's victory was quick and decisive on Broadway, and in time it spread to England and the Continent. (After an enthusiastically received production in Vienna in March 1950, the play was quickly scheduled for production in Zurich, Munich, and Berlin.) Unlike the heroes of the success stories he viewed with skepticism, Miller amply deserved the good fortune that came to him. He had been working steadily toward excellence and had already distinguished himself with much thoughtful writing in his thirty-three years.

Miller was born to a lower-middle-class Jewish family in New York's Harlem district and was reared in a suburban section of Brooklyn. He grew into a tall, raw-boned lad with a remarkable resemblance to the young Abraham Lincoln. In high school he became a football player. He went on to the University of Michigan, found an able guide in Professor Kenneth E. Rowe of the English department, and discovered an aptitude for playwriting that helped to support him through college. He won the Avery Hopwood award of $500 two successive years and received a $1,250 prize from the Hollywood-financed Bureau of New Plays, directed by the Theatre Guild's Theresa Helburn and John Gassner. After graduation from college, in 1938, he found employment on the Federal Theatre's WPA playwriting project during the last four months of its existence. He then supported himself by writing radio plays, chiefly for the Columbia Workshop of the Columbia Broadcasting System and for the Cavalcade of America program. He married a University of Michigan classmate, Mary Grace Slattery, became the father of two children, and settled down to a plain life in Brooklyn remote from Bohemian and fashionable intellectual circles. These details are in Miller's case more than usually important because his strength comes from his ability to wring significance out of common reality. He is an artist and intellectual who identifies himself with average life, understands it well, and defends it with demo-cratic fervor. He likes manual work and neighborliness. He might be described as owning a kinship to Walt Whitman but maintaining a critical rather than rhapsodic attitude toward the life of our democracy.

In 1942, he was chosen, at the recommendation of the producer Herman Shumlin, to collect material for the scenario of Ernie Pyle's *The Story of G.I. Joe*. To get the background for the film, Miller, who was incapacitated for war service by a football injury, spent six months in ground-forces camps throughout the country, going on maneuvers with the infantry and the tank crews. A diary of his experiences was published in 1944 under the title of *Situation Normal*. During the war Miller also worked for a while as a steamfitter in the Brooklyn Navy Yard and wrote radio scripts and one-act plays designed to promote civilian morale.

In 1944, Miller had his first production on Broadway: a novelistic and short-lived play, *The Man Who Had All the Luck*. Although unskillfully made, it was rich with human detail, and its rueful story of people who tried to succeed with an insufficient understanding of reality prefigured *Death of a Salesman*. A year later, Miller tasted literary success for the first time, with his novel *Focus*, an account of anti-Semitism in an American community, which he had originally planned as a three-act play.

Encouraged by the success of his novel, Miller spent two years writing another study of American life, this time for the stage. The play, *All My Sons*, revolved around a small industrialist, Joe Keller, who is saved from bankruptcy by the wartime demand for machine products and who, under pressure, sells defective parts to the air force, thus becoming responsible for the death of twenty-one pilots. He is able to shift the burden of guilt to the shoulders of a little man less rugged than himself, and he wins acquittal. But the conscience of his son indicts him, and before this tribunal there can be no acquittal. Joe Keller's defense is that his motives were the best in the world; a deeply affectionate parent, he wanted to preserve his business for his sons. It was the author's contention that no individual's actions can be self-contained, not even within the compass of a family. Miller, who wrote *All My Sons* with humane understanding but moral sinew as well as taut dramaturgy, summarized his theme as "the responsibility of man to society" or "the responsibility of a man for his actions, a recognition of his ethical responsibility to the world outside his home as well as in his own home."

More than a drama about war profiteering, *All My Sons* made a strong impression and won the Drama Critics Circle award for the best play of the season. Its limitations, an overweaving of plot threads and the use of the old-fashioned device of decisive revelations by means of a letter, made it less than the masterpiece some critics thought it to be. But the play was a culmination of technical prowess for Miller in the Ibsen-influenced social-problem type of drama. It also represented a command of plot structure that was to serve the dramatist extremely well when he turned to his next project, the writing of a play in a free dramatic form. *Death of a Salesman* would not be so successful a drama of time present and time past, of present action and reminiscence, but for its author's skill in pulling threads together and keeping a tight rein on scenes that would otherwise fly apart.

On the occasion of the *première* of *All My Sons*, Miller declared in a press interview: "In all my plays and books I try to take settings and dramatic situations from life which involve real questions of right and wrong. Then I set out, rather implacably and in the most realistic situations I can find, the moral dilemma and try to point a real, though hard, path out. I don't see how you can write anything decent without using the question of right and wrong as the basis." How well this statement applies to *Death of a Salesman* is readily apparent. The "way out" is not found for its hero, Willy Loman, for the play is an elegy on a life that has failed and has come to its end. It is too late for reformation or for him to take on a new set of values. (Only his son Biff arrives at an understanding of different objectives and a different way of life.) But it is not too late for the spiritual redemption or the burst of heroic determination in defeat which constitutes the essence of the austere art of tragedy.

Willy Loman's story plainly involves a failure of values in the world around him. Willy accepts the denatured ideals of American society—not the values considered the highest but those that were overpublicized in America. He naïvely succumbs to success-worship, to the belief that a jolly locker-room personality which makes one not only liked but "well liked" is a substitute for solid accomplishment, and to "the wrong dream" of material success. At the age of sixty-three, he is faced with the failure of this way of life, as an unwanted employee and a parent disappointed in the sons to whom he has imparted his own values. Insofar as mistaken ideas have deluded Willy Loman, the play is social criticism. But it is more than that. It is a character drama so firmly drawn that many Americans, from all walks of life, have identified themselves or their relatives with Willy and have been moved by his pathos and his very human qualities.

Miller rejected the notion that the common world is "below tragedy," and in an essay intended for the published version of *Death of a Salesman* he wrote that "in essence the tragic hero is intent upon claiming his whole due as a personality," that the commonest man may take on tragic stature "to the extent of his willingness to throw all he has into the contest," and that tragedy springs from "the underlying fear of being displaced, the disaster inherent in being torn away from our chosen image of what and who we are in this world." And by these standards the commonest of men may exhibit man's heroic spirit. Miller believed that his Willy Loman was a character of heroic dimensions and that, for all his pathos, he made *Death of a Salesman* a tragedy rather than a lament.

Both Miller's theory of tragedy and its applicability to the play are subject to debate. Is "our chosen image of what and who we are" always acceptable, and is it, in Willy's case, worthy of the respect that alone can give us tragic exaltation? Since Miller refused to accept the validity of his hero's factitious view of himself, did the author waste compassion and respect on him? It is possible to contend that he did. Yet most playgoers were willing to accept *Death of a Salesman* as a tragedy, for Miller supplied his loud-mouthed little man with some magnificence of spirit. Willy fights for his family all his life, carries on a difficult struggle for sales long after he has ceased to be welcome in the market place, and holds on to an impossible dream for his son. If in nothing else, moreover, he is tragically impassioned as a father. Perhaps it is well to make here an old distinction between high tragedy and bourgeois tragedy—that is, tragedy of commonplace life in commonplace circumstances. Willy may be called a suburban King Lear, with sons instead of daughters breaking his heart. Although obviously devoid of the splendor of Shakespeare's old man, limited as Willy is by a small mind and by unelevated language, he is not conceived in merely pathetic terms. He is, for example, more passionate and active than Balzac's Lear, the hero of *Père Goriot,* who accepts his fate passively. Willy engages in an intense conflict with his son and dies in order to effectuate his hopes for him, refusing to concede defeat for the ideal of success he has set up for him. Since he makes his sacrifice after discovering his own responsibility for Biff's failure, he ennobles himself; his act is a sort of expiation. Since he kills himself in order to leave the boy his insurance immediately after learning that Biff still loves him, it is also plain that the deluded man's inmost desire has been directed at something greater than a salesman's success; he dies as a father, not as a salesman. This transfiguration of a man who would otherwise have to be dismissed as a cheat and dolt endows him with some of the magnitude we expect to find in tragedy.

The tragic quality of *Death of a Salesman* is more than an academic achievement for the American theatre. In several respects, it represents a culmination of American playwrights' efforts to create a significant American drama. The play carries forward the struggle to create a realistically critical expression of American life, to present the common man as the center of dramatic interest, to find more expressive dramatic forms than the realistic technique permits, and to develop a poetic drama rooted in American speech and manners.

Miller's dramatic approach to the American scene reflects some thirty years of playwriting. Insofar as it exposes the hollowness of materialistic values, *Death of a Salesman* carries on the cultural rebellion staged by the playwrights, novelists, critics, and artists of the nineteen-twenties. Insofar as it relates the fate of a little man who is worn out with the economic struggle to make a home for his family and is discarded by his employer in old age, *Death of a Salesman* continues the social discontent of the theatre of the nineteen-thirties. Willy's story is another variant of the treatment of lower-middle-class life developed by Odets and the Group Theatre as part of an analysis of the social system. And the play possesses the tender regard for the average man that American writers have favored when they have gone beyond satirization of the commonplaceness of suburban and small-town life.

Willy's story, however, does not yield the usual realistic chronicle, but is transfigured by the imagination. To tell this tale of a dispossessed and defeated commoner, Miller has retained all the verisimilitude of realistic description. The dialogue is colloquial, the manners are familiar, the background is authentically suburban. But the author has also availed himself of the expressionistic dream or memory sequence that appeared impressively in American drama as early as 1920, when *The Emperor Jones* was produced at the Provincetown Playhouse. He has even used symbolism for expressive purposes, notably in the treatment of Willy's successful brother, Ben, who went into the jungle and came out a wealthy man. Miller has, in short, succeeded in projecting his social realism, his "humanistic jurisprudence" (as the critic Harold Clurman called it), by imaginative means that tell the story of Willy's errors and failures with dramatic economy and suggestive emphasis. Here, in other words, the expressionistic and realistic styles exist in a fused state.

From this theatrical treatment, finally, emerges a poetic drama not of the first order but rare in the American theatre. Many efforts to create a poetic drama had previously been made in America. O'Neill had developed a mystique of the soul and pitted man against his private demons and inscrutable, often malicious, fate. Maxwell Anderson had chosen a derivative procedure in patterning his historical plays after the older style of tragedy. He had selected high-spirited historical characters, allowed them to speak in more or less formal verse, and permitted them to universalize their emotions and thoughts in time-honored generalizations. He did not depart radically from this approach in *Winterset,* when he tried to write tragedy on a contemporary theme, with the result that his gangsters seemed to belong to the Elizabethan theatre and his lovers frequently bore an odd resemblance to Romeo and Juliet or Hamlet and Ophelia. Saroyan had given free rein to his fancy and depended upon his intuitions and improvisations to create an overgrown child's view of the world, fresh and naïve but at a considerable remove from the realities of the American scene. He created a poetry of flight. Tennessee Williams was able to develop a poetic drama on the basis of psychological deterioration of sensitive characters who do not belong to the mainstream of American realities. He made drama largely out of private sensibility. Miller's poetic drama is of a different order from all these efforts. It is rooted in everyday reality and employs the general idiom of American speech. It has none of the mystique of O'Neill and none of the formality and generalized rhetoric of Anderson; it never leaves the actual world, it does not cultivate naïveté, and it takes a responsible view of life in our society—and it deals with the men and women who struggle with the everyday reality of the average American rather than with a more or less private world. Miller's poetry of theatre is completely rooted in the world we know. It consists of reality rather than of dreams.

BIBLIOGRAPHY: Brooks Atkinson, *Broadway Scrapbook* (pp. 277–279), 1947; John Mason Brown, "Even as You and I," in *The Saturday Review of Literature,* February 26, 1949; George Jean Nathan, *Theatre Book of the Year 1948–1949* (pp. 279–285), 1949.

DEATH OF A SALESMAN[1]

By Arthur Miller

CHARACTERS

WILLY LOMAN	BERNARD	JENNY
LINDA	THE WOMAN	STANLEY
BIFF	CHARLEY	MISS FORSYTHE
HAPPY	UNCLE BEN	LETTA
	HOWARD WAGNER	

ACT I.

A melody is heard, played upon a flute. It is small and fine, telling of grass and trees and the horizon. The curtain rises.

Before us is the Salesman's house. We are aware of towering, angular shapes behind it, surrounding it on all sides. Only the blue light of the sky falls upon the house and forestage; the surrounding area shows an angry glow of orange. As more light appears, we see a solid vault of apartment houses around the small, fragile-seeming home. An air of the dream clings to the place, a dream rising out of reality. The kitchen at center seems actual enough, for there is a kitchen table with three chairs, and a refrigerator. But no other fixtures are seen. At the back of the kitchen there is a draped entrance, which leads to the living-room. To the right of the kitchen, on a level raised two feet, is a bedroom furnished only with a brass bedstead and a straight chair. On a shelf over the bed a silver athletic trophy stands. A window opens onto the apartment house at the side.

Behind the kitchen, on a level raised six and a half feet, is the boys' bedroom, at present barely visible. Two beds are dimly seen, and at the back of the room a dormer window. (This bedroom is above the unseen living-room.) At the left a stairway curves up to it from the kitchen.

The entire setting is wholly or, in some places, partially transparent. The roof-line of the house is one-dimensional; under and over it we see the apartment buildings. Before the house lies an apron, curving beyond the forestage into the orchestra. This forward area serves as the back yard as well as the locale of all Willy's imaginings and of his city scenes. Whenever the action is in the present the actors observe the imaginary wall-lines, entering the house only through its door at the left. But in the scenes of the past these boundaries are broken, and characters enter or leave a room by stepping "through" a wall onto the forestage.

From the right, Willy Loman, *the Salesman, enters, carrying two large sample cases. The flute plays on. He hears but is not aware of it. He is past sixty years of age, dressed quietly. Even as he crosses the stage to the doorway of the house, his exhaustion is apparent. He unlocks the door, comes into the kitchen, and thankfully lets his burden down, feeling the soreness of his palms. A word-sigh escapes his lips—it might be "Oh, boy, oh, boy." He closes the door, then carries his cases out into the living-room, through the draped kitchen doorway.*

Linda, *his wife, has stirred in her bed at the right. She gets out and puts on a robe, listening. Most often jovial, she has developed an iron repression of her exceptions to* Willy's *behavior—she more than loves him, she admires him, as though his mercurial nature, his temper, his massive dreams and little cruelties, served her only as sharp reminders of the turbulent longings within him, longings which she shares but lacks the temperament to utter and follow to their end.*

LINDA: [*Hearing* Willy *outside the bedroom, calls with trepidation*] Willy!

WILLY: It's all right. I came back.

LINDA: Why? What happened? [*Slight pause*] Did something happen, Willy?

WILLY: No, nothing happened.

LINDA: You didn't smash the car, did you?

WILLY: [*With casual irritation*] I said nothing happened. Didn't you hear me?

LINDA: Don't you feel well?

WILLY: I'm tired to the death. [*The flute has faded away. He sits on the bed beside her, a little numb*] I couldn't make it. I just couldn't make it, Linda.

LINDA: [*Very carefully, delicately*] Where were you all day? You look terrible.

WILLY: I got as far as a little above Yonkers. I stopped for a cup of coffee. Maybe it was the coffee.

LINDA: What?

WILLY: [*After a pause*] I suddenly couldn't drive any more. The car kept going off onto the shoulder, y'know?

LINDA: [Helpfully] Oh. Maybe it was the steering again. I don't think Angelo knows the Studebaker.

WILLY: No, it's me, it's me. Suddenly I realize I'm goin' sixty miles an hour and I don't remember the last five minutes. I'm—I can't seem to—keep my mind to it.

LINDA: Maybe it's your glasses. You never went for your new glasses.

WILLY: No, I see everything. I came back ten miles an hour. It took me nearly four hours from Yonkers.

LINDA: [Resigned] Well, you'll just have to take a rest, Willy, you can't continue this way.

WILLY: I just got back from Florida.

LINDA: But you didn't rest your mind. Your mind is overactive, and the mind is what counts, dear.

WILLY: I'll start out in the morning. Maybe I'll feel better in the morning. [She is taking off his shoes] These goddam arch supports are killing me.

LINDA: Take an aspirin. Should I get you an aspirin? It'll soothe you.

WILLY: [With wonder] I was driving along, you understand? And I was fine. I was even observing the scenery. You can imagine, me looking at scenery, on the road every week of my life. But it's so beautiful up there, Linda, the trees are so thick, and the sun is warm. I opened the windshield and just let the warm air bathe over me. And then all of a sudden I'm goin' off the road! I'm tellin' ya, I absolutely forgot I was driving. If I'd've gone the other way over the white line I might've killed somebody. So I went on again—and five minutes later I'm dreamin' again, and I nearly—[He presses two fingers against his eyes] I have such thoughts, I have such strange thoughts.

LINDA: Willy, dear. Talk to them again. There's no reason why you can't work in New York.

WILLY: They don't need me in New York. I'm the New England man. I'm vital in New England.

LINDA: But you're sixty years old. They can't expect you to keep traveling every week.

WILLY: I'll have to send a wire to Portland. I'm supposed to see Brown and Morrison tomorrow morning at ten o'clock to show the line. Goddammit, I could sell them! [He starts putting on his jacket]

LINDA: [Taking the jacket from him] Why don't you go down to the place tomorrow and tell Howard you've simply got to work in New York? You're too accommodating, dear.

WILLY: If old man Wagner was alive I'd a been in charge of New York now! That man was a prince, he was a masterful man. But that boy of his, that Howard, he don't appreciate. When I went north first time, the Wagner Company didn't know where New England was!

LINDA: Why don't you tell those things to Howard, dear?

WILLY: [Encouraged] I will, I definitely will. Is there any cheese?

LINDA: I'll make you a sandwich.

WILLY: No, go to sleep. I'll take some milk. I'll be up right away. The boys in?

LINDA: They're sleeping. Happy took Biff on a date tonight.

WILLY: [Interested] That so?

LINDA: It was so nice to see them shaving together, one behind the other, in the bathroom. And going out together. You notice? The whole house smells of shaving lotion.

WILLY: Figure it out. Work a lifetime to pay off a house. You finally own it, and there's nobody to live in it.

LINDA: Well, dear, life is a casting off. It's always that way.

WILLY: No, no, some people—some people accomplish something. Did Biff say anything after I went this morning?

LINDA: You shouldn't have criticized him, Willy, especially after he just got off the train. You mustn't lose your temper with him.

WILLY: When the hell did I lose my temper? I simply asked him if he was making any money. Is that a criticism?

LINDA: But, dear, how could he make any money?

WILLY: [Worried and angered] There's such an undercurrent in him. He became a moody man. Did he apologize when I left this morning?

LINDA: He was crestfallen, Willy. You know how he admires you. I think if he finds himself, then you'll both be happier and not fight any more.

WILLY: How can he find himself on a farm? Is that a life? A farmhand? In the beginning, when he was young, I thought, well, a young man, it's good for him to tramp around, take a lot of different jobs. But it's more than ten years now and he has yet to make thirty-five dollars a week!

LINDA: He's finding himself, Willy.

WILLY: Not finding yourself at the age of thirty-four is a disgrace!

LINDA: Shh!

WILLY: The trouble is he's lazy, goddammit!

LINDA: Willy, please!

WILLY: Biff is a lazy bum!

LINDA: They're sleeping. Get something to eat. Go on down.

WILLY: Why did he come home? I would like to know what brought him home.

LINDA: I don't know. I think he's still lost, Willy. I think he's very lost.

WILLY: Biff Loman is lost. In the greatest country in the world a young man with such—personal attractiveness, gets lost. And such a hard worker. There's one thing about Biff—he's not lazy.

LINDA: Never.

WILLY: [With pity and resolve] I'll see him in the morning; I'll have a nice talk with him. I'll get him a job selling. He could be big in no time. My God! Remember how they used to follow him around in high school? When he smiled at one of them their faces lit up. When he walked down the street . . . [*He loses himself in reminiscences*]

LINDA: [*Trying to bring him out of it*] Willy, dear, I got a new kind of American-type cheese today. It's whipped.

WILLY: Why do you get American when I like Swiss?

LINDA: I just thought you'd like a change—

WILLY: I don't want a change! I want Swiss cheese. Why am I always being contradicted?

LINDA: [*With a covering laugh*] I thought it would be a surprise.

WILLY: Why don't you open a window in here, for God's sake?

LINDA: [*With infinite patience*] They're all open, dear.

WILLY: The way they boxed us in here. Bricks and windows, windows and bricks.

LINDA: We should've bought the land next door.

WILLY: The street is lined with cars. There's not a breath of fresh air in the neighborhood. The grass don't grow any more, you can't raise a carrot in the back yard. They should've had a law against apartment houses. Remember those two beautiful elm trees out there? When I and Biff hung the swing between them?

LINDA: Yeah, like being a million miles from the city.

WILLY: They should've arrested the builder for cutting those down. They massacred the neighborhood. [*Lost*] More and more I think of those days, Linda. This time of year it was lilac and wisteria. And then the peonies would come out, and the daffodils. What fragrance in this room!

LINDA: Well, after all, people had to move somewhere.

WILLY: No, there's more people now.

LINDA: I don't think there's more people. I think—

WILLY: There's more people! That's what ruining this country! Population is getting out of control. The competition is maddening! Smell the stink from that apartment house! And another one on the other side . . . How can they whip cheese?

[*On* Willy's *last line,* Biff *and* Happy *raise themselves up in their beds, listening*]

LINDA: Go down, try it. And be quiet.

WILLY: [*Turning to* Linda, *guiltily*] You're not worried about me, are you, sweetheart?

BIFF: What's the matter?

HAPPY: Listen!

LINDA: You've got too much on the ball to worry about.

WILLY: You're my foundation and my support, Linda.

LINDA: Just try to relax, dear. You make mountains out of molehills.

WILLY: I won't fight with him any more. If he wants to go back to Texas, let him go.

LINDA: He'll find his way.

WILLY: Sure. Certain men just don't get started

till later in life. Like Thomas Edison, I think. Or B. F. Goodrich. One of them was deaf. [*He starts for the bedroom doorway*] I'll put my money on Biff.

LINDA: And Willy—if it's warm Sunday we'll drive in the country. And we'll open the windshield, and take lunch.

WILLY: No, the windshields don't open on the new cars.

LINDA: But you opened it today.

WILLY: Me? I didn't. [*He stops*] Now isn't that peculiar! Isn't that a remarkable—[*He breaks off in amazement and fright as the flute is heard distantly*]

LINDA: What, darling?

WILLY: That is the most remarkable thing.

LINDA: What, dear?

WILLY: I was thinking of the Chevvy. [*Slight pause*] Nineteen twenty-eight . . . when I had that red Chevvy—[*Breaks off*] That funny? I coulda sworn I was driving that Chevvy today.

LINDA: Well, that's nothing. Something must've reminded you.

WILLY: Remarkable. Ts. Remember those days? The way Biff used to simonize that car? The dealer refused to believe there was eighty thousand miles on it. [*He shakes his head*] Heh! [*To* Linda] Close your eyes, I'll be right up. [*He walks out of the bedroom*]

HAPPY: [*To* Biff] Jesus, maybe he smashed up the car again!

LINDA: [*Calling after* Willy] Be careful on the stairs, dear! The cheese is on the middle shelf! [*She turns, goes over to the bed, takes his jacket, and goes out of the bedroom*]

[*Light has risen on the boys' room. Unseen,* Willy *is heard talking to himself, "Eighty thousand miles," and a little laugh.* Biff *gets out of bed, comes downstage a bit, and stands attentively.* Biff *is two years older than his brother* Happy, *well built, but in these days bears a worn air and seems less self-assured. He has succeeded less, and his dreams are stronger and less acceptable than* Happy's. Happy *is tall, powerfully made. Sexuality is like a visible color on him, or a scent that many women have discovered. He, like his brother, is lost, but in a different way, for he has never allowed himself to turn his face toward defeat and is thus more confused and hard-skinned, although seemingly more content*]

HAPPY: [*Getting out of bed*] He's going to get his license taken away if he keeps that up. I'm getting nervous about him, y'know, Biff?

BIFF: His eyes are going.

HAPPY: No, I've driven with him. He sees all right. He just doesn't keep his mind on it. I drove into the city with him last week. He stops at a green light and then it turns red and he goes. [*He laughs*]

BIFF: Maybe he's color-blind.

HAPPY: Pop? Why he's got the finest eye for color in the business. You know that.

BIFF: [*Sitting down on his bed*] I'm going to sleep.

HAPPY: You're not still sour on Dad, are you, Biff?

BIFF: He's all right, I guess.

WILLY: [*Underneath them, in the living-room*] Yes, sir, eighty thousand miles—eighty-two thousand!

BIFF: You smoking?

HAPPY: [*Holding out a pack of cigarettes*] Want one?

BIFF: [*Taking a cigarette*] I can never sleep when I smell it.

WILLY: What a simonizing job, heh!

HAPPY: [*With deep sentiment*] Funny, Biff, y'know? Us sleeping in here again? The old beds. [*He pats his bed affectionately*] All the talk that went across those two beds, huh? Our whole lives.

BIFF: Yeah. Lotta dreams and plans.

HAPPY: [*With a deep and masculine laugh*] About five hundred women would like to know what was said in this room.

[*They share a soft laugh*]

BIFF: Remember that big Betsy something—what the hell was her name—over on Bushwick Avenue?

HAPPY: [*Combing his hair*] With the collie dog!

BIFF: That's the one. I got you in there, remember?

HAPPY: Yeah, that was my first time—I think. Boy, there was a pig! [*They laugh, almost crudely*] You taught me everything I know about women. Don't forget that.

BIFF: I bet you forgot how bashful you used to be. Especially with girls.

HAPPY: Oh, I still am, Biff.

BIFF: Oh, go on.

HAPPY: I just control it, that's all. I think I got less bashful and you got more so. What happened, Biff? Where's the old humor, the old confidence? [*He shakes Biff's knee. Biff gets up and moves restlessly about the room*] What's the matter?

BIFF: Why does Dad mock me all the time?

HAPPY: He's not mocking you, he—

BIFF: Everything I say there's a twist of mockery on his face. I can't get near him.

HAPPY: He just wants you to make good, that's all. I wanted to talk to you about Dad for a long time, Biff. Something's—happening to him. He—talks to himself.

BIFF: I noticed that this morning. But he always mumbled.

HAPPY: But not so noticeable. It got so embarrassing I sent him to Florida. And you know something? Most of the time he's talking to you.

BIFF: What's he say about me?

HAPPY: I can't make it out.

BIFF: What's he say about me?

HAPPY: I think the fact that you're not settled, that you're still kind of up in the air . . .

BIFF: There's one or two other things depressing him, Happy.

HAPPY: What do you mean?

BIFF: Never mind. Just don't lay it all to me.

HAPPY: But I think if you just got started—I mean—is there any future for you out there?

BIFF: I tell ya, Hap, I don't know what the future is. I don't know—what I'm supposed to want.

HAPPY: What do you mean?

BIFF: Well, I spent six or seven years after high school trying to work myself up. Shipping clerk, salesman, business of one kind or another. And it's a measly manner of existence. To get on that subway on the hot mornings in summer. To devote your whole life to keeping stock, or making phone calls, or selling or buying. To suffer fifty weeks of the year for the sake of a two-week vacation, when all you really desire is to be outdoors, with your shirt off. And always to have to get ahead of the next fella. And still—that's how you build a future.

HAPPY: Well, you really enjoy it on a farm? Are you content out there?

BIFF: [*With rising agitation*] Hap, I've had twenty or thirty different kinds of jobs since I left home before the war, and it always turns out the same. I just realized it lately. In Nebraska when I herded cattle, and the Dakotas, and Arizona, and now in Texas. It's why I came home now, I guess, because I realized it. This farm I work on, it's spring there now, see? And they've got about fifteen new colts. There's nothing more inspiring or—beautiful than the sight of a mare and a new colt. And it's cool there now, see? Texas is cool now, and it's spring. And whenever spring comes to where I am, I suddenly get the feeling, my God, I'm not gettin' anywhere! What the hell am I doing, playing around with horses, twenty-eight dollars a week! I'm thirty-four years old, I oughta be makin' my future. That's when I come running home. And now, I get here, and I don't know what to do with myself. [*After a pause*] I've always made a point of not wasting my life, and everytime I come back here I know that all I've done is to waste my life.

HAPPY: You're a poet, you know that, Biff? You're a—you're an idealist!

BIFF: No, I'm mixed up very bad. Maybe I oughta get married. Maybe I oughta get stuck into something. Maybe that's my trouble. I'm like a boy. I'm not married, I'm not in business, I just—I'm like a boy. Are you content, Hap? You're a success, aren't you? Are you content?

HAPPY: Hell, no!

BIFF: Why? You're making money, aren't you?

HAPPY: [*Moving about with energy, expressiveness*] All I can do now is wait for the merchandise manager to die. And suppose I get to be merchandise manager? He's a good friend of mine, and he just built a terrific estate on Long Island. And he lived there about two months and sold it, and now he's building another one. He can't enjoy it once it's finished. And I know that's just what I would do. I don't know what the hell I'm workin' for. Sometimes I sit in my apartment—all alone. And I think of the rent I'm paying. And it's crazy. But then, it's what I always wanted. My own apartment, a car, and plenty of women. And still, goddammit, I'm lonely.

BIFF: [*With enthusiasm*] Listen, why don't you come out West with me?

HAPPY: You and I, heh?

BIFF: Sure, maybe we could buy a ranch. Raise cattle, use our muscles. Men built like we are should be working out in the open.

HAPPY: [*Avidly*] The Loman Brothers, heh?

BIFF: [*With vast affection*] Sure, we'd be known all over the counties!

HAPPY: [*Enthralled*] That's what I dream about, Biff. Sometimes I want to just rip my clothes off in the middle of the store and outbox that goddam merchandise manager. I mean I can outbox, outrun, and outlift anybody in that store, and I have to take orders from those common, petty sons-of-bitches till I can't stand it any more.

BIFF: I'm tellin' you, kid, if you were with me I'd be happy out there.

HAPPY: [*Filled with enthusiasm*] See, Biff, everybody around me is so false that I'm constantly lowering my ideals . . .

BIFF: Baby, together we'd stand up for one another, we'd have someone to trust.

HAPPY: If I were around you—

BIFF: Hap, the trouble is we weren't brought up to grub for money. I don't know how to do it.

HAPPY: Neither can I!

BIFF: Then let's go!

HAPPY: The only thing is—what can you make out there?

BIFF: But look at your friend. Builds an estate and then hasn't the peace of mind to live in it.

HAPPY: Yeah, but when he walks into the store the waves part in front of him. That's fifty-two thousand dollars a year coming through the revolving door, and I got more in my pinky finger than he's got in his head.

BIFF: Yeah, but you just said—

HAPPY: I gotta show some of those pompous, self-important executives over there that Hap Loman can make the grade. I want to walk into the store the way he walks in. Then I'll go with you, Biff. We'll be together yet, I swear. But take those two we had tonight. Now weren't they gorgeous creatures?

BIFF: Yeah, yeah, most gorgeous I've had in years.

HAPPY: I get that any time I want, Biff. Whenever I feel disgusted. The only trouble is, it gets like bowling or something. I just keep knockin' them over and it doesn't mean anything. You still run around a lot?

BIFF: Naa. I'd like to find a girl—steady, somebody with substance.

HAPPY: That's what I long for.

BIFF: Go on! You'd never come home.

HAPPY: I would! Somebody with character, with resistance! Like Mom, y'know? You're gonna call me a bastard when I tell you this. That girl Charlotte I was with tonight is engaged to be married in five weeks. [*He tries on his new hat*]

BIFF: No kiddin'!

HAPPY: Sure, the guy's in line for the vice-presidency of the store. I don't know what gets into me, maybe I just have an overdeveloped sense of competition or something, but I went and ruined her, and furthermore I can't get rid of her. And he's the third executive I've done that to. Isn't that a crummy characteristic? And to top it all, I go to their weddings! [*Indignantly, but laughing*] Like I'm not supposed to take bribes. Manufacturers offer me a hundred-dollar bill now and then to throw an order their way. You know how honest I am, but it's like this girl, see. I hate myself for it. Because I don't want the girl, and, still, I take it and—I love it!

BIFF: Let's go to sleep.

HAPPY: I guess we didn't settle anything, heh?

BIFF: I just got one idea that I think I'm going to try.

HAPPY: What's that?

BIFF: Remember Bill Oliver?

HAPPY: Sure, Oliver is very big now. You want to work for him again?

BIFF: No, but when I quit he said something to me. He put his arm on my shoulder, and he said, "Biff, if you ever need anything, come to me."

HAPPY: I remember that. That sounds good.

BIFF: I think I'll go to see him. If I could get ten thousand or even seven or eight thousand dollars I could buy a beautiful ranch.

HAPPY: I bet he'd back you. 'Cause he thought highly of you, Biff. I mean, they all do. You're well liked, Biff. That's why I say to come back here, and we both have the apartment. And I'm tellin' you, Biff, any babe you want . . .

BIFF: No, with a ranch I could do the work I like and still be something. I just wonder though. I wonder if Oliver still thinks I stole that carton of basketballs.

HAPPY: Oh, he probably forgot that long ago. It's almost ten years. You're too sensitive. Anyway, he didn't really fire you.

BIFF: Well, I think he was going to. I think that's why I quit. I was never sure whether he knew or not. I know he thought the world of me, though. I was the only one he'd let lock up the place.

WILLY: [*Below*] You gonna wash the engine, Biff?

HAPPY: Shh!

[Biff *looks at* Happy, *who is gazing down, listening.* Willy *is mumbling in the parlor*]

HAPPY: You hear that?

[*They listen.* Willy *laughs warmly*]

BIFF: [*Growing angry*] Doesn't he know Mom can hear that?

WILLY: Don't get your sweater dirty, Biff!

[*A look of pain crosses* Biff's *face*]

HAPPY: Isn't that terrible? Don't leave again, will you? You'll find a job here. You gotta stick around. I don't know what to do about him, it's getting embarrassing.

WILLY: What a simonizing job!

BIFF: Mom's hearing that!

WILLY: No kiddin', Biff, you got a date? Wonderful!

HAPPY: Go on to sleep. But talk to him in the morning, will you?

BIFF: [*Reluctantly getting into bed*] With her in the house. Brother!

HAPPY: [*Getting into bed*] I wish you'd have a good talk with him.

[*The light on their room begins to fade*]

BIFF: [*To himself in bed*] That selfish, stupid . . .

HAPPY: Sh . . . Sleep, Biff.

[*Their light is out. Well before they have finished speaking,* Willy's *form is dimly seen below in the darkened kitchen. He opens the refrigerator, searches in there, and takes out a bottle of milk. The apartment houses are fading out, and the entire house and surroundings become covered with leaves. Music insinuates itself as the leaves appear*]

WILLY: Just wanna be careful with those girls, Biff, that's all. Don't make any promises. No promises of any kind. Because a girl, y'know, they always believe what you tell 'em, and you're very young, Biff, you're too young to be talking seriously to girls.

[*Light rises on the kitchen.* Willy, *talking, shuts the refrigerator door and comes downstage to the kitchen table. He pours milk into a glass. He is totally immersed in himself, smiling faintly*]

WILLY: Too young entirely, Biff. You want to watch your schooling first. Then when you're all set, there'll be plenty of girls for a boy like you. [*He smiles broadly at a kitchen chair*] That so? The girls pay for you? [*He laughs.*] Boy, you must really be makin' a hit.

[Willy *is gradually addressing—physically—a point off stage, speaking through the wall of the kitchen, and his voice has been rising in volume to that of a normal conversation*]

WILLY: I been wondering why you polish the car so careful. Ha! Don't leave the hubcaps, boys. Get the chamois to the hubcaps. Happy, use newspaper on the windows, it's the easiest thing. Show him how to do it, Biff! You see, Happy? Pad it up, use it like a pad. That's it, that's it, good work. You're doin' all right, Hap. [*He pauses, then nods in approbation for a few seconds, then looks upward*] Biff, first thing we gotta do when we get time is clip that big branch over the house. Afraid it's gonna fall in a storm and hit the roof. Tell you what. We get a rope and sling her around, and then we climb up there with a couple of saws and take her down. Soon as you finish the car, boys, I wanna see ya. I got a surprise for you, boys.

BIFF: [*Offstage*] Whatta ya got, Dad?

WILLY: No, you finish first. Never leave a job till you're finished—remember that. [*Looking toward the "big trees"*] Biff, up in Albany I saw a beautiful hammock. I think I'll buy it next trip, and we'll hang it right between those two elms. Wouldn't that be something? Just swingin' there under those branches. Boy, that would be . . .

[Young Biff *and* Young Happy *appear from the direction* Willy *was addressing. Happy carries rags and a pail of water.* Biff, *wearing a sweater with a block "S," carries a football*]

BIFF: [*Pointing in the direction of the car offstage*] How's that, Pop, professional?

WILLY: Terrific. Terrific job, boys. Good work, Biff.

HAPPY: Where's the surprise, Pop?

WILLY: In the back seat of the car.

HAPPY: Boy! [*He runs off*]

BIFF: What is it, Dad? Tell me, what'd you buy?

WILLY: [*Laughing, cuffs him*] Never mind, something I want you to have.

BIFF: [*Turns and starts off*] What is it, Hap?

HAPPY: [*Offstage*] It's a punching bag!

BIFF: Oh, Pop!

WILLY: It's got Gene Tunney's signature on it!

[Happy *runs onstage with a punching bag*]

BIFF: Gee, how'd you know we wanted a punching bag?

WILLY: Well, it's the finest thing for the timing.

HAPPY: [*Lies down on his back and pedals with his feet*] I'm losing weight, you notice, Pop?

WILLY: [*To* Happy] Jumping rope is good too.

BIFF: Did you see the new football I got?

WILLY: [*Examining the ball*] Where'd you get a new ball?

BIFF: The coach told me to practice my passing.

WILLY: That so? And he gave you the ball, heh?

BIFF: Well, I borrowed it from the locker room. [*He laughs confidentially*]

WILLY: [*Laughing with him at the theft*] I want you to return that.

HAPPY: I told you he wouldn't like it!

BIFF: [*Angrily*] Well, I'm bringing it back!

WILLY: [*Stopping the incipient argument, to* Happy] Sure, he's gotta practice with a regulation ball, doesn't he? [*To* Biff] Coach'll probably congratulate you on your initiative!

BIFF: Oh, he keeps congratulating my initiative all the time, Pop.

WILLY: That's because he likes you. If somebody else took that ball there'd be an uproar. So what's the report, boys, what's the report?

BIFF: Where'd you go this time, Dad? Gee we were lonesome for you.

WILLY: [*Pleased, puts an arm around each boy and they come down to the apron*] Lonesome, heh?

BIFF: Missed you every minute.

WILLY: Don't say? Tell you a secret, boys. Don't breathe it to a soul. Someday I'll have my own business, and I'll never have to leave home any more.

HAPPY: Like Uncle Charley, heh?

WILLY: Bigger than Uncle Charley! Because Charley is not—liked. He's liked, but he's not—well liked.

BIFF: Where'd you go this time, Dad?

WILLY: Well, I got on the road, and I went north to Providence. Met the Mayor.

BIFF: The Mayor of Providence!

WILLY: He was sitting in the hotel lobby.

BIFF: What'd he say?

WILLY: He said, "Morning!" And I said, "You got a fine city here, Mayor." And then he had coffee with me. And then I went to Waterbury. Waterbury is a fine city. Big clock city, the famous Waterbury clock. Sold a nice bill there. And then Boston—Boston is the cradle of the Revolution. A fine city. And a couple of other towns in Mass., and on to Portland and Bangor and straight home!

BIFF: Gee, I'd love to go with you sometime, Dad.

WILLY: Soon as summer comes.

HAPPY: Promise?

WILLY: You and Hap and I, and I'll show you all the towns. America is full of beautiful towns and fine, upstanding people. And they know me, boys, they know me up and down New England. The finest people. And when I bring you fellas up, there'll be open sesame for all of us, 'cause one thing, boys: I have friends. I can park my car in any street in New England, and the cops protect it like their own. This summer, heh?

BIFF AND HAPPY: [*Together*] Yeah! You bet!

WILLY: We'll take our bathing suits.

HAPPY: We'll carry your bags, Pop!

WILLY: Oh, won't that be something! Me comin' into the Boston stores with you boys carryin' my bags. What a sensation!

[*Biff is prancing around, practicing passing the ball*]

WILLY: You nervous, Biff, about the game?

BIFF: Not if you're gonna be there.

WILLY: What do they say about you in school, now that they made you captain?

HAPPY: There's a crowd of girls behind him every-time the classes change.

BIFF: [*Taking Willy's hand*] This Saturday, Pop, this Saturday—just for you, I'm going to break through for a touchdown.

HAPPY: You're supposed to pass.

BIFF: I'm takin' one play for Pop. You watch me, Pop, and when I take off my helmet, that means I'm breakin' out. Then you watch me crash through that line!

WILLY: [*Kisses Biff*] Oh, wait'll I tell this in Boston!

[*Bernard enters in knickers. He is younger than Biff, earnest and loyal, a worried boy*]

BERNARD: Biff, where are you? You're supposed to study with me today.

WILLY: Hey, looka Bernard. What're you lookin' so anemic about, Bernard?

BERNARD: He's gotta study, Uncle Willy. He's got Regents next week.

HAPPY: [*Tauntingly, spinning Bernard around*] Let's box, Bernard!

BERNARD: Biff! [*He gets away from Happy*] Listen, Biff, I heard Mr. Birnbaum say that if you don't start studyin' math he's gonna flunk you, and you won't graduate. I heard him!

WILLY: You better study with him, Biff. Go ahead now.

BERNARD: I heard him!

BIFF: Oh, Pop, you didn't see my sneakers! [*He holds up a foot for Willy to look at*]

WILLY: Hey, that's a beautiful job of printing!

BERNARD: [*Wiping his glasses*] Just because he printed University of Virginia on his sneakers doesn't mean they've got to graduate him, Uncle Willy!

WILLY: [*Angrily*] What're you talking about? With scholarships to three universities they're gonna flunk him?

BERNARD: But I heard Mr. Birnbaum say—

WILLY: Don't be a pest, Bernard! [*To his boys*] What an anemic!

BERNARD: Okay, I'm waiting for you in my house, Biff.

[*Bernard goes off. The Lomans laugh*]

WILLY: Bernard is not well liked, is he?

BIFF: He's liked, but he's not well liked.

HAPPY: That's right, Pop.

WILLY: That's just what I mean. Bernard can get the best marks in school, y'understand, but when he gets out in the business world, y'understand, you are going to be five times ahead of him. That's why I thank Almighty God you're both built like Adonises. Because the man who makes an appearance in the business world, the man who creates personal interest, is the man who gets ahead. Be liked and you will never want. You take me, for instance. I never have to wait in line to see a buyer. "Willy Loman is here!" That's all they have to know, and I go right through.

BIFF: Did you knock them dead, Pop?

WILLY: Knocked 'em cold in Providence, slaughtered 'em in Boston.

HAPPY: [*On his back, pedaling again*] I'm losing weight, you notice, Pop?

[*Linda enters, as of old, a ribbon in her hair, carrying a basket of washing*]

LINDA: [*With youthful energy*] Hello, dear!

WILLY: Sweetheart!

LINDA: How'd the Chevvy run?

WILLY: Chevrolet, Linda, is the greatest car ever built. [*To the boys*] Since when do you let your mother carry wash up the stairs?

BIFF: Grab hold there, boy!

HAPPY: Where to, Mom?

LINDA: Hang them up on the line. And you better go down to your friends, Biff. The cellar is full of boys. They don't know what to do with themselves.

BIFF: Ah, when Pop comes home they can wait!

WILLY: [*Laughs appreciatively*] You better go down and tell them what to do, Biff.

BIFF: I think I'll have them sweep out the furnace room.

WILLY: Good work, Biff.

BIFF: [*Goes through wall-line of kitchen to doorway at back and calls down*] Fellas! Everybody sweep out the furnace room! I'll be right down!

VOICES: All right! Okay, Biff.

BIFF: George and Sam and Frank, come out back! We're hangin' up the wash! Come on, Hap, on the double! [*He and* Happy *carry out the basket*]

LINDA: The way they obey him!

WILLY: Well, that's training, the training. I'm tellin' you, I was sellin' thousands and thousands, but I had to come home.

LINDA: Oh, the whole block'll be at that game. Did you sell anything?

WILLY: I did five hundred gross in Providence and seven hundred gross in Boston.

LINDA: No! Wait a minute, I've got a pencil. [*She pulls pencil and paper out of her apron pocket*] That makes your commission . . . Two hundred—my God! Two hundred and twelve dollars!

WILLY: Well, I didn't figure it yet, but . . .

LINDA: How much did you do?

WILLY: Well, I—I did—about a hundred and eighty gross in Providence. Well, no—it came to—roughly two hundred gross on the whole trip.

LINDA: [*Without hesitation*] Two hundred gross. That's . . . [*She figures*]

WILLY: The trouble was that three of the stores were half closed for inventory in Boston. Otherwise I woulda broke records.

LINDA: Well, it makes seventy dollars and some pennies. That's very good.

WILLY: What do we owe?

LINDA: Well, on the first there's sixteen dollars on the refrigerator—

WILLY: Why sixteen?

LINDA: Well, the fan belt broke, so it was a dollar eighty.

WILLY: But it's brand new.

LINDA: Well, the man said that's the way it is. Till they work themselves in, y'know.

[*They move through the wall-line into the kitchen*]

WILLY: I hope we didn't get stuck on that machine.

LINDA: They got the biggest ads of any of them!

WILLY: I know, it's a fine machine. What else?

LINDA: Well, there's nine-sixty for the washing machine. And for the vacuum cleaner there's three and a half due on the fifteenth. Then the roof, you got twenty-one dollars remaining.

WILLY: It don't leak, does it?

LINDA: No, they did a wonderful job. Then you owe Frank for the carburetor.

WILLY: I'm not going to pay that man! That goddam Chevrolet, they ought to prohibit the manufacture of that car!

LINDA: Well, you owe him three and a half. And odds and ends, comes to around a hundred and twenty dollars by the fifteenth.

WILLY: A hundred and twenty dollars! My God, if business don't pick up I don't know what I'm gonna do!

LINDA: Well, next week you'll do better.

WILLY: Oh, I'll knock 'em dead next week. I'll go to Hartford. I'm very well liked in Hartford. You know, the trouble is, Linda, people don't seem to take to me.

[*They move onto the forestage*]

LINDA: Oh, don't be foolish.

WILLY: I know it when I walk in. They seem to laugh at me.

LINDA: Why? Why would they laugh at you? Don't talk that way, Willy.

[Willy *moves to the edge of the stage.* Linda *goes into the kitchen and starts to darn stockings*]

WILLY: I don't know the reason for it, but they just pass me by. I'm not noticed.

LINDA: But you're doing wonderful, dear. You're making seventy to a hundred dollars a week.

WILLY: But I gotta be at it ten, twelve hours a day. Other men—I don't know—they do it easier. I don't know why—I can't stop myself—I talk too much. A man oughta come in with a few words. One thing about Charley. He's a man of few words, and they respect him.

LINDA: You don't talk too much, you're just lively.

WILLY: [*Smiling*] Well, I figure, what the hell, life is short, a couple of jokes. [*To himself*] I joke too much! [*The smile goes*]

LINDA: Why? You're—

WILLY: I'm fat. I'm very—foolish to look at, Linda. I didn't tell you, but Christmas time I happened to be calling on F. H. Stewarts, and a salesman I know, as I was going in to see the buyer I heard him say something about—walrus. And I—I cracked him right across the face. I won't take that. I simply will not take that. But they do laugh at me. I know that.

LINDA: Darling . . .

WILLY: I gotta overcome it. I know I gotta overcome it. I'm not dressing to advantage, maybe.

LINDA: Willy, darling, you're the handsomest man in the world—

WILLY: Oh, no, Linda.

LINDA: To me you are. [*Slight pause*] The handsomest.

[*From the darkness is heard the laughter of a woman.* Willy *doesn't turn to it, but it continues through* Linda's *lines*]

LINDA: And the boys, Willy. Few men are idolized by their children the way you are.

[*Music is heard as behind a scrim, to the left of the house,* The Woman, *dimly seen, is dressing*]

WILLY: [*With great feeling*] You're the best there is, Linda, you're a pal, you know that? On the road —on the road I want to grab you sometimes and just kiss the life outa you.

[*The laughter is loud now, and he moves into a brightening area at the left, where* The Woman *has come from behind the scrim and is standing, putting on her hat, looking into a "mirror" and laughing*]

WILLY: 'Cause I get so lonely—especially when business is bad and there's nobody to talk to. I get the feeling that I'll never sell anything again, that I won't make a living for you, or a business, a business for the boys. [*He talks through* The Woman's *subsiding laughter;* The Woman *primps at the "mirror"*] There's so much I want to make for—

THE WOMAN: Me? You didn't make me, Willy. I picked you.

WILLY: [*Pleased*] You picked me?

THE WOMAN: [*Who is quite proper-looking,* Willy's *age*] I did. I've been sitting at that desk watching all the salesmen go by, day in, day out. But you've got such a sense of humor, and we do have such a good time together, don't we?

WILLY: Sure, sure. [*He takes her in his arms*] Why do you have to go now?

THE WOMAN: It's two o'clock . . .

WILLY: No, come on in! [*He pulls her*]

THE WOMAN: . . . my sisters'll be scandalized. When'll you be back?

WILLY: Oh, two weeks about. Will you come up again?

THE WOMAN: Sure thing. You do make me laugh. It's good for me. [*She squeezes his arm, kisses him*] And I think you're a wonderful man.

WILLY: You picked me, heh?

THE WOMAN: Sure. Because you're so sweet. And such a kidder.

WILLY: Well, I'll see you next time I'm in Boston.

THE WOMAN: I'll put you right through to the buyers.

WILLY: [*Slapping her bottom*] Right. Well, bottoms up!

THE WOMAN: [*Slaps him gently and laughs*] You just kill me, Willy. [*He suddenly grabs her and kisses her roughly*] You kill me. And thanks for the stockings. I love a lot of stockings. Well, good night.

WILLY: Good night. And keep your pores open!

THE WOMAN: Oh, Willy!

[The Woman *bursts out laughing, and* Linda's

laughter blends in. The Woman *disappears into the dark. Now the area at the kitchen table brightens.* Linda *is sitting where she was at the kitchen table, but now is mending a pair of her silk stockings*]

LINDA: You are, Willy. The handsomest man. You've got no reason to feel that—

WILLY: [*Coming out of* The Woman's *dimming area and going over to* Linda] I'll make it all up to you, Linda, I'll—

LINDA: There's nothing to make up, dear. You're doing fine, better than—

WILLY: [*Noticing her mending*] What's that?

LINDA: Just mending my stockings. They're so expensive—

WILLY: [*Angrily, taking them from her*] I won't have you mending stockings in this house! Now throw them out!

[Linda *puts the stockings in her pocket*]

BERNARD: [*Entering on the run*] Where is he? If he doesn't study!

WILLY: [*Moving to the forestage, with great agitation*] You'll give him the answers!

BERNARD: I do, but I can't on a Regents! That's a state exam! They're liable to arrest me!

WILLY: Where is he? I'll whip him, I'll whip him!

LINDA: And he'd better give back that football, Willy, it's not nice.

WILLY: Biff! Where is he? Why is he taking everything?

LINDA: He's too rough with the girls, Willy. All the mothers are afraid of him!

WILLY: I'll whip him!

BERNARD: He's driving the car without a license!

[The Woman's *laugh is heard*]

WILLY: Shut up!

LINDA: All the mothers—

WILLY: Shut up!

BERNARD: [*Backing quietly away and out*] Mr. Birnbaum says he's stuck up.

WILLY: Get outa here!

BERNARD: If he doesn't buckle down he'll flunk math! [*He goes off*]

LINDA: He's right, Willy, you've gotta—

WILLY: [*Exploding at her*] There's nothing the matter with him! You want him to be a worm like Bernard? He's got spirit, personality . . .

[*As he speaks,* Linda, *almost in tears, exits into the living-room.* Willy *is alone in the kitchen, wilting and staring. The leaves are gone. It is night again, and the apartment houses look down from behind*]

WILLY: Loaded with it. Loaded! What is he stealing? He's giving it back, isn't he? Why is he stealing? What did I tell him? I never in my life told him anything but decent things.

[Happy *in pajamas has come down the stairs;* Willy *suddenly becomes aware of* Happy's *presence*]

HAPPY: Let's go now, come on.

WILLY: [*Sitting down at the kitchen table*] Huh! Why did she have to wax the floors herself? Everytime she waxes the floors she keels over. She knows that!

HAPPY: Sh! Take it easy. What brought you back tonight?

WILLY: I got an awful scare. Nearly hit a kid in Yonkers. God! Why didn't I go to Alaska with my brother Ben that time! Ben! That man was a genius, that man was success incarnate! What a mistake! He begged me to go.

HAPPY: Well, there's no use in—

WILLY: You guys! There was a man started with the clothes on his back and ended up with diamond mines!

HAPPY: Boy, someday I'd like to know how he did it.

WILLY: What's the mystery? The man knew what he wanted and went out and got it! Walked into a jungle, and comes out, the age of twenty-one, and he's rich! The world is an oyster, but you don't crack it open on a mattress!

HAPPY: Pop, I told you I'm gonna retire you for life.

WILLY: You'll retire me for life on seventy goddam dollars a week? And your women and your car and your apartment, and you'll retire me for life! Christ's sake, I couldn't get past Yonkers today! Where are you guys, where are you? The woods are burning! I can't drive a car!

[Charley *has appeared in the doorway. He is a large man, slow of speech, laconic, immovable. In all he says, despite what he says, there is pity, and now, trepidation. He has a robe over pajamas, slippers on his feet. He enters the kitchen*]

CHARLEY: Everything all right?

HAPPY: Yeah, Charley, everything's . . .

WILLY: What's the matter?

CHARLEY: I heard some noise. I thought something happened. Can't we do something about the walls? You sneeze in here, and in my house hats blow off.

HAPPY: Let's go to bed, Dad. Come on.

[Charley *signals to* Happy *to go*]

WILLY: You go ahead, I'm not tired at the moment.

HAPPY: [*To* Willy] Take it easy, huh? [*He exits*]

WILLY: What're you doin' up?

CHARLEY: [*Sitting down at the kitchen table opposite* Willy] Couldn't sleep good. I had a heartburn.

WILLY: Well, you don't know how to eat.

CHARLEY: I eat with my mouth.

WILLY: No, you're ignorant. You gotta know about vitamins and things like that.

CHARLEY: Come on, let's shoot. Tire you out a little.

WILLY: [*Hesitantly*] All right. You got cards?

CHARLEY: [*Taking a deck from his pocket*] Yeah, I got them. Someplace. What is it with those vitamins?

WILLY: [*Dealing*] They build up your bones. Chemistry.

CHARLEY: Yeah, but there's no bones in a heartburn.

WILLY: What are you talkin' about? Do you know the first thing about it?

CHARLEY: Don't get insulted.

WILLY: Don't talk about something you don't know anything about.

[*They are playing. Pause*]

CHARLEY: What're you doin' home?

WILLY: A little trouble with the car.

CHARLEY: Oh. [*Pause*] I'd like to take a trip to California.

WILLY: Don't say.

CHARLEY: You want a job?

WILLY: I got a job, I told you that. [*After a slight pause*] What the hell are you offering me a job for?

CHARLEY: Don't get insulted.

WILLY: Don't insult me.

CHARLEY: I don't see no sense in it. You don't have to go on this way.

WILLY: I got a good job. [*Slight pause*] What do you keep comin' in here for?

CHARLEY: You want me to go?

WILLY: [*After a pause, withering*] I can't understand it. He's going back to Texas again. What the hell is that?

CHARLEY: Let him go.

WILLY: I got nothin' to give him, Charley, I'm clean, I'm clean.

CHARLEY: He won't starve. None a them starve. Forget about him.

WILLY: Then what have I got to remember?

CHARLEY: You take it too hard. To hell with it. When a deposit bottle is broken you don't get your nickel back.

WILLY: That's easy enough for you to say.

CHARLEY: That ain't easy for me to say.

WILLY: Did you see the ceiling I put up in the living-room?

CHARLEY: Yeah, that's a piece of work. To put up a ceiling is a mystery to me. How do you do it?

WILLY: What's the difference?

CHARLEY: Well, talk about it.

WILLY: You gonna put up a ceiling?

CHARLEY: How could I put up a ceiling?

WILLY: Then what the hell are you bothering me for?

CHARLEY: You're insulted again.

WILLY: A man who can't handle tools is not a man. You're disgusting.

CHARLEY: Don't call me disgusting, Willy.

[Uncle Ben, *carrying a valise and an umbrella, enters the forestage from around the right corner of the house. He is a stolid man, in his sixties, with a mustache and an authoritative air. He is utterly certain of his destiny, and there is an aura of far places about him. He enters exactly as* Willy *speaks*]

WILLY: I'm getting awfully tired, Ben.

[Ben's *music is heard.* Ben *looks around at everything*]

CHARLEY: Good, keep playing; you'll sleep better. Did you call me Ben?

[Ben *looks at his watch*]

WILLY: That's funny. For a second there you reminded me of my brother Ben.

BEN: I only have a few minutes. [*He strolls, inspecting the place.* Willy *and* Charley *continue playing*]

CHARLEY: You never heard from him again, heh? Since that time?

WILLY: Didn't Linda tell you? Couple of weeks ago we got a letter from his wife in Africa. He died.

CHARLEY: That so.

BEN: [*Chuckling*] So this is Brooklyn, eh?

CHARLEY: Maybe you're in for some of his money.

WILLY: Naa, he had seven sons. There's just one opportunity I had with that man . . .

BEN: I must make a train, William. There are several properties I'm looking at in Alaska.

WILLY: Sure, sure! If I'd gone with him to Alaska that time, everything would've been totally different.

CHARLEY: Go on, you'd froze to death up there.

WILLY: What're you talking about?

BEN: Opportunity is tremendous in Alaska, William. Surprised you're not up there.

WILLY: Sure, tremendous.

CHARLEY: Heh?

WILLY: There was the only man I ever met who knew the answers.

CHARLEY: Who?

BEN: How are you all?

WILLY: [*Taking a pot, smiling*] Fine, fine.

CHARLEY: Pretty sharp tonight.

BEN: Is Mother living with you?

WILLY: No, she died a long time ago.

CHARLEY: Who?

BEN: That's too bad. Fine specimen of a lady, Mother.

WILLY: [*To* Charley] Heh?

BEN: I'd hoped to see the old girl.

CHARLEY: Who died?

BEN: Heard anything from Father, have you?

WILLY: [*Unnerved*] What do you mean, who died?

CHARLEY: [*Taking a pot*] What're you talkin' about?

BEN: [*Looking at his watch*] William, it's half-past eight!

WILLY: [*As though to dispel his confusion he angrily stops* Charley's *hand*] That's my build!

CHARLEY: I put the ace—

WILLY: If you don't know how to play the game I'm not gonna throw my money away on you!

CHARLEY: [*Rising*] It was my ace, for God's sake!

WILLY: I'm through, I'm through!

BEN: When did Mother die?

WILLY: Long ago. Since the beginning you never knew how to play cards.

CHARLEY: [*Picks up the cards and goes to the door*] All right! Next time I'll bring a deck with five aces.

WILLY: I don't play that kind of game!

CHARLEY: [*Turning to him*] You ought to be ashamed of yourself!

WILLY: Yeah?

CHARLEY: Yeah! [*He goes out*]

WILLY: [*Slamming the door after him*] Ignoramus!

BEN: [*As* Willy *comes toward him through the wall-line of the kitchen*] So you're William.

WILLY: [*Shaking* Ben's *hand*] Ben! I've been waiting for you so long! What's the answer? How did you do it?

BEN: Oh, there's a story in that.

[Linda *enters the forestage, as of old, carrying the wash basket*]

LINDA: Is this Ben?

BEN: [*Gallantly*] How do you do, my dear.

LINDA: Where've you been all these years? Willy's always wondered why you—

WILLY: [*Pulling* Ben *away from her impatiently*] Where is Dad? Didn't you follow him? How did you get started?

BEN: Well, I don't know how much you remember.

WILLY: Well, I was just a baby, of course, only three or four years old—

BEN: Three years and eleven months.

WILLY: What a memory, Ben!

BEN: I have many enterprises, William, and I have never kept books.

WILLY: I remember I was sitting under the wagon in—was it Nebraska?

BEN: It was South Dakota, and I gave you a bunch of wild flowers.

WILLY: I remember you walking away down some open road.

BEN: [*Laughing*] I was going to find Father in Alaska.

WILLY: Where is he?

BEN: At that age I had a very faulty view of geography, William. I discovered after a few days that I was heading due south, so instead of Alaska, I ended up in Africa.

LINDA: Africa!

WILLY: The Gold Coast!

BEN: Principally diamond mines.

LINDA: Diamond mines!

BEN: Yes, my dear. But I've only a few minutes—

WILLY: No! Boys! Boys! [*Young* Biff *and* Happy *appear*] Listen to this. This is your Uncle Ben, a great man! Tell my boys, Ben!

BEN: Why, boys, when I was seventeen I walked into the jungle, and when I was twenty-one I walked out. [*He laughs*] And by God I was rich.

WILLY: [*To the boys*] You see what I been talking about? The greatest things can happen!

BEN: [*Glancing at his watch*] I have an appointment in Ketchikan Tuesday week.

WILLY: No, Ben! Please tell about Dad. I want my boys to hear. I want them to know the kind of stock they spring from. All I remember is a man with a big beard, and I was in Mamma's lap, sitting around a fire, and some kind of high music.

BEN: His flute. He played the flute.

WILLY: Sure, the flute, that's right!

[*New music is heard, a high, rollicking tune*]

BEN: Father was a very great and a very wild-hearted man. We would start in Boston, and he'd toss the whole family into the wagon, and then he'd drive the team right across the country; through Ohio, and Indiana, Michigan, Illinois, and all the Western states. And we'd stop in the towns and sell the flutes that he'd made on the way. Great inventor, Father. With one gadget he made more in a week than a man like you could make in a lifetime.

WILLY: That's just the way I'm bringing them up, Ben—rugged, well liked, all-around.

BEN: Yeah? [*To* Biff] Hit that, boy—hard as you can. [*He pounds his stomach*]

BIFF: Oh, no, sir!

BEN: [*Taking boxing stance*] Come on, get to me! [*He laughs*]

WILLY: Go to it, Biff! Go ahead, show him!

BIFF: Okay! [*He cocks his fists and starts in*]

LINDA: [*To* Willy] Why must he fight, dear?

BEN: [*Sparring with* Biff] Good boy! Good boy!

WILLY: How's that, Ben, heh?

HAPPY: Give him the left, Biff!

LINDA: Why are you fighting?

BEN: Good boy! [*Suddenly comes in, trips* Biff, *and stands over him, the point of his umbrella poised over* Biff's *eye*]

LINDA: Look out, Biff!

BIFF: Gee!

BEN: [*Patting* Biff's *knee*] Never fight fair with a stranger, boy. You'll never get out of the jungle that way. [*Taking* Linda's *hand and bowing*] It was an honor and a pleasure to meet you, Linda.

LINDA: [*Withdrawing her hand coldly, frightened*] Have a nice—trip.

BEN: [*To* Willy] And good luck with your—what do you do?

WILLY: Selling.

BEN: Yes. Well . . . [*He raises his hand in farewell to all*]

WILLY: No, Ben, I don't want you to think . . . [*He takes* Ben's *arm to show him*] It's Brooklyn, I know, but we hunt too.

BEN: Really, now.

WILLY: Oh, sure, there's snakes and rabbits and —that's why I moved out here. Why, Biff can fell any one of these trees in no time! Boys! Go right over to where they're building the apartment house and get some sand. We're gonna rebuild the entire front stoop right now! Watch this, Ben!

BIFF: Yes, sir! On the double, Hap!

HAPPY: [*As he and* Biff *run off*] I lost weight, Pop, you notice?

[Charley *enters in knickers, even before the boys are gone*]

CHARLEY: Listen, if they steal any more from that building the watchman'll put the cops on them!

LINDA: [*To* Willy] Don't let Biff . . .

[Ben *laughs lustily*]

WILLY: You shoulda seen the lumber they brought home last week. At least a dozen six-by-tens worth all kinds a money.

CHARLEY: Listen, if that watchman—

WILLY: I gave them hell, understand. But I got a couple of fearless characters there.

CHARLEY: Willy, the jails are full of fearless characters.

BEN: [*Clapping* Willy *on the back, with a laugh at* Charley] And the stock exchange, friend!

WILLY: [*Joining in* Ben's *laughter*] Where are the rest of your pants?

CHARLEY: My wife bought them.

WILLY: Now all you need is a golf club and you can go upstairs and go to sleep. [*To* Ben] Great athlete! Between him and his son Bernard they can't hammer a nail!

BERNARD: [*Rushing in*] The watchman's chasing Biff!

WILLY: [*Angrily*] Shut up! He's not stealing anything!

LINDA: [*Alarmed, hurrying off left*] Where is he? Biff, dear! [*She exits.*]

WILLY: [*Moving toward the left, away from* Ben] There's nothing wrong. What's the matter with you?

BEN: Nervy boy. Good!

WILLY: [*Laughing*] Oh, nerves of iron, that Biff!

CHARLEY: Don't know what it is. My New England man comes back and he's bleedin', they murdered him up there.

WILLY: It's contacts, Charley, I got important contacts!

CHARLEY: [*Sarcastically*] Glad to hear it, Willy. Come in later, we'll shoot a little casino. I'll take some of your Portland money. [*He laughs at* Willy *and exits*]

WILLY: [*Turning to* Ben] Business is bad, it's murderous. But not for me, of course.

BEN: I'll stop by on my way back to Africa.

WILLY: [*Longingly*] Can't you stay a few days? You're just what I need, Ben, because I—I have a fine position here, but I—well, Dad left when I was such a baby and I never had a chance to talk to him and I still feel—kind of temporay about myself.

BEN: I'll be late for my train.

[*They are at opposite ends of the stage*]

WILLY: Ben—my boys—can't we talk? They'd go into the jaws of hell for me, see, but I—

BEN: William, you're being first-rate with your boys. Outstanding, manly chaps!

WILLY: [*Hanging on to his words*] Oh, Ben, that's good to hear! Because sometimes I'm afraid that I'm not teaching them the right kind of— Ben, how should I teach them?

BEN: [*Giving great weight to each word, and with a certain vicious audacity*] William, when I walked into the jungle, I was seventeen. When I walked out I was twenty-one. And, by God, I was rich! [*He goes off into darkness around the right corner of the house*]

WILLY: . . . was rich! That's just the spirit I want to imbue them with! To walk into a jungle! I was right! I was right! I was right!

[*Ben is gone, but Willy is still speaking to him as Linda, in nightgown and robe, enters the kitchen, glances around for Willy, then goes to the door of the house, looks out and sees him. Comes down to his left. He looks at her*]

LINDA: Willy, dear? Willy?

WILLY: I was right!

LINDA: Did you have some cheese? [*He can't answer*] It's very late, darling. Come to bed, heh?

WILLY: [*Looking straight up*] Gotta break your neck to see a star in this yard.

LINDA: You coming in?

WILLY: Whatever happened to that diamond watch fob? Remember? When Ben came from Africa that time? Didn't he give me a watch fob with a diamond in it?

LINDA: You pawned it, dear. Twelve, thirteen years ago. For Biff's radio correspondence course.

WILLY: Gee, that was a beautiful thing. I'll take a walk.

LINDA: But you're in your slippers.

WILLY: [*Starting to go around the house at the left*] I was right! I was! [*Half to Linda, as he goes, shaking his head*] What a man! There was a man worth talking to. I was right!

LINDA: [*Calling after Willy*] But in your slippers, Willy!

[*Willy is almost gone when Biff, in his pajamas, comes down the stairs and enters the kitchen*]

BIFF: What is he doing out there?

LINDA: Sh!

BIFF: God Almighty, Mom, how long has he been doing this?

LINDA: Don't, he'll hear you.

BIFF: What the hell is the matter with him?

LINDA: It'll pass by morning.

BIFF: Shouldn't we do anything?

LINDA: Oh, my dear, you should do a lot of things, but there's nothing to do, so go to sleep.

[*Happy comes down the stair and sits on the steps*]

HAPPY: I never heard him so loud, Mom.

LINDA: Well, come around more often; you'll hear him. [*She sits down at the table and mends the lining of Willy's jacket*]

BIFF: Why didn't you ever write me about this, Mom?

LINDA: How would I write to you? For over three months you had no address.

BIFF: I was on the move. But you know I thought of you all the time. You know that, don't you, pal?

LINDA: I know, dear, I know. But he likes to have a letter. Just to know that there's still a possibility for better things.

BIFF: He's not like this all the time, is he?

LINDA: It's when you come home he's always the worst.

BIFF: When I come home?

LINDA: When you write you're coming, he's all smiles, and talks about the future, and—he's just wonderful. And then the closer you seem to come, the more shaky he gets, and then, by the time you get here, he's arguing, and he seems angry at you. I think it's just that maybe he can't bring himself to —to open up to you. Why are you so hateful to each other? Why is that?

BIFF: [*Evasively*] I'm not hateful, Mom.

LINDA: But you no sooner come in the door than you're fighting!

BIFF: I don't know why. I mean to change. I'm tryin', Mom, you understand?

LINDA: Are you home to stay now?

BIFF: I don't know. I want to look around, see what's doin'.

LINDA: Biff, you can't look around all your life, can you?

BIFF: I just can't take hold, Mom. I can't take hold of some kind of a life.

LINDA: Biff, a man is not a bird, to come and go with the springtime.

BIFF: Your hair . . . [*He touches her hair*] Your hair got so gray.

LINDA: Oh, it's been gray since you were in high school. I just stopped dyeing it, that's all.

BIFF: Dye it again, will ya? I don't want my pal looking old. [*He smiles*]

LINDA: You're such a boy! You think you can go away for a year and . . . You've got to get it into your head now that one day you'll knock on this door and there'll be strange people here—

BIFF: What are you talking about? You're not even sixty, Mom.

LINDA: But what about your father?

BIFF: [*Lamely*] Well, I meant him too.

HAPPY: He admires Pop.

LINDA: Biff, dear, if you don't have any feeling for him, then you can't have any feeling for me.

BIFF: Sure I can, Mom.

LINDA: No. You can't just come to see me, because I love him. [*With a threat, but only a threat, of tears*] He's the dearest man in the world to me, and I won't have anyone making him feel unwanted and low and blue. You've got to make up your mind now, darling, there's no leeway any more. Either he's your father and you pay him that respect, or else you're not to come here. I know he's not easy to get along with—nobody knows that better than me—but . . .

WILLY: [*From the left, with a laugh*] Hey, hey, Biffo!

BIFF: [*Starting to go out after* Willy] What the hell is the matter with him? [Happy *stops him*]

LINDA: Don't—don't go near him!

BIFF: Stop making excuses for him! He always, always wiped the floor with you. Never had an ounce of respect for you.

HAPPY: He's always had respect for—

BIFF: What the hell do you know about it?

HAPPY: [*Surlily*] Just don't call him crazy!

BIFF: He's got no character— Charley wouldn't do this. Not in his own house—spewing out that vomit from his mind.

HAPPY: Charley never had to cope with what he's got to.

BIFF: People are worse off than Willy Loman. Believe me, I've seen them!

LINDA: Then make Charley your father, Biff. You can't do that, can you? I don't say he's a great man. Willy Loman never made a lot of money. His name was never in the paper. He's not the finest character that ever lived. But he's a human being, and a terrible thing is happening to him. So attention must be paid. He's not to be allowed to fall into his grave like an old dog. Attention, attention must be finally paid to such a person. You called him crazy—

BIFF: I didn't mean—

LINDA: No, a lot of people think he's lost his—balance. But you don't have to be very smart to know what his trouble is. The man is exhausted.

HAPPY: Sure!

LINDA: A small man can be just as exhausted as a great man. He works for a company thirty-six years this March, opens up unheard-of territories to their trademark, and now in his old age they take his salary away.

HAPPY: [*Indignantly*] I didn't know that, Mom.

LINDA: You never asked, my dear! Now that you get your spending money someplace else you don't trouble your mind with him.

HAPPY: But I gave you money last—

LINDA: Christmas time, fifty dollars! To fix the hot water it cost ninety-seven fifty! For five weeks he's been on straight commission, like a beginner, an unknown!

BIFF: Those ungrateful bastards!

LINDA: Are they any worse than his sons? When he brought them business, when he was young, they were glad to see him. But now his old friends, the old buyers that loved him so and always found some order to hand him in a pinch—they're all dead, retired. He used to be able to make six, seven calls a day in Boston. Now he takes his valises out of the car and puts them back and takes them out again and he's exhausted. Instead of walking he talks now. He drives seven hundred miles, and when he gets there no one knows him any more, no one welcomes him. And what goes through a man's mind, driving seven hundred miles home without having earned a cent? Why shouldn't he talk to himself? Why? When he has to go to Charley and borrow fifty dollars a week and pretend to me that it's his pay? How long can that go on? How long? You see what I'm sitting here and waiting for? And you tell me he has no character? The man who never worked a day but for your benefit? When does he get the medal for that? Is this his reward—to turn around at the age of sixty-three and find his sons, who he loved better than his life, one a philandering bum—

HAPPY: Mom!

LINDA: That's all you are, my baby! [*To* Biff] And you! What happened to the love you had for him? You were such pals! How you used to talk to him on the phone every night! How lonely he was till he could come home to you!

BIFF: All right, Mom. I'll live here in my room, and I'll get a job. I'll keep away from him, that's all.

LINDA: No, Biff. You can't stay here and fight all the time.

BIFF: He threw me out of this house, remember that.

LINDA: Why did he do that? I never knew why.

BIFF: Because I know he's a fake and he doesn't like anybody around who knows!

LINDA: Why a fake? In what way? What do you mean?

BIFF: Just don't lay it all at my feet. It's between me and him—that's all I have to say. I'll chip in from now on. He'll settle for half my pay check. He'll be all right. I'm going to bed. [*He starts for the stairs*]

LINDA: He won't be all right.

BIFF: [*Turning on the stairs, furiously*] I hate this city and I'll stay here. Now what do you want?

LINDA: He's dying, Biff.

[Happy *turns quickly to her, shocked*]

BIFF: [*After a pause*] Why is he dying?

LINDA: He's been trying to kill himself.

BIFF: [*With great horror*] How?

LINDA: I live from day to day.

BIFF: What're you talking about?

LINDA: Remember I wrote you that he smashed up the car again? In February?

BIFF: Well?

LINDA: The insurance inspector came. He said that they have evidence. That all these accidents in the last year—weren't—weren't—accidents.

HAPPY: How can they tell that? That's a lie.

LINDA: It seems there's a woman . . . [*She takes a breath as*

{BIFF: [*Sharply but contained*] What woman?

{LINDA: [*Simultaneously*] . . . and this woman . . .

LINDA: What?

BIFF: Nothing. Go ahead.

LINDA: What did you say?

BIFF: Nothing. I just said what woman?

HAPPY: What about her?

LINDA: Well, it seems she was walking down the road and saw his car. She says that he wasn't driving fast at all, and that he didn't skid. She says he came to that little bridge, and then deliberately smashed into the railing, and it was only the shallowness of the water that saved him.

BIFF: Oh, no, he probably just fell asleep again.

LINDA: I don't think he fell asleep.

BIFF: Why not?

LINDA: Last month . . . [*With great difficulty*] Oh, boys, it's so hard to say a thing like this! He's just a big stupid man to you, but I tell you there's more good in him than in many other people. [*She chokes, wipes her eyes*] I was looking for a fuse. The lights blew out, and I went down the cellar. And behind the fuse box—it happened to fall out—was a length of rubber pipe—just short.

HAPPY: No kidding?

LINDA: There's a little attachment on the end of it. I knew right away. And sure enough, on the bottom of the water heater there's a new little nipple on the gas pipe.

HAPPY: [*Angrily*] That—jerk.

BIFF: Did you have it taken off?

LINDA: I'm—I'm ashamed to. How can I mention it to him? Every day I go down and take away that little rubber pipe. But, when he comes home, I put it back where it was. How can I insult him that way? I don't know what to do. I live from day to day, boys. I tell you, I know every thought in his mind. It sounds so old-fashioned and silly, but I tell you he put his whole life into you and you've turned your backs on him. [*She is bent over in the chair, weeping, her face in her hands*] Biff, I swear to God! Biff, his life is in your hands!

HAPPY: [*To Biff*] How do you like that damned fool?

BIFF: [*Kissing her*] All right, pal, all right. It's all settled now. I've been remiss. I know that, Mom. But now I'll stay, and I swear to you, I'll apply myself. [*Kneeling in front of her, in a fever of self-reproach*] It's just—you see, Mom, I don't fit in business. Not that I won't try. I'll try, and I'll make good.

HAPPY: Sure you will. The trouble with you in business was you never tried to please people.

BIFF: I know, I—

HAPPY: Like when you worked for Harrison's. Bob Harrison said you were tops, and then you go and do some damn fool thing like whistling whole songs in the elevator like a comedian.

BIFF: [*Against* Happy] So what? I like to whistle sometimes.

HAPPY: You don't raise a guy to a responsible job who whistles in the elevator!

LINDA: Well, don't argue about it now.

HAPPY: Like when you'd go off and swim in the middle of the day instead of taking the line around.

BIFF: [*His resentment rising*] Well, don't you run

off? You take off sometimes, don't you? On a nice summer day?

HAPPY: Yeah, but I cover myself!

LINDA: Boys!

HAPPY: If I'm going to take a fade the boss can call any number where I'm supposed to be and they'll swear to him that I just left. I'll tell you something that I hate to say, Biff, but in the business world some of them think you're crazy.

BIFF: [*Angered*] Screw the business world!

HAPPY: All right, screw it! Great, but cover yourself!

LINDA: Hap, Hap!

BIFF: I don't care what they think! They've laughed at Dad for years, and you know why? Because we don't belong in this nuthouse of a city! We should be mixing cement on some open plain, or—or carpenters. A carpenter is allowed to whistle!

[Willy *walks in from the entrance of the house, at left*]

WILLY: Even your grandfather was better than a carpenter. [*Pause. They watch him*] You never grew up. Bernard does not whistle in the elevator, I assure you.

BIFF: [*As though to laugh* Willy *out of it*] Yeah, but you do, Pop.

WILLY: I never in my life whistled in an elevator! And who in the business world thinks I'm crazy?

BIFF: I didn't mean it like that, Pop. Now don't make a whole thing out of it, will ya?

WILLY: Go back to the West! Be a carpenter, a cowboy, enjoy yourself!

LINDA: Willy, he was just saying—

WILLY: I heard what he said!

HAPPY: [*Trying to quiet* Willy] Hey, Pop, come on now . . .

WILLY: [*Continuing over* Happy's *line*] They laugh at me, heh? Go to Filene's, go to the Hub, go to Slattery's, Boston. Call out the name Willy Loman and see what happens! Big shot!

BIFF: All right, Pop.

WILLY: Big!

BIFF: All right!

WILLY: Why do you always insult me?

BIFF: I didn't say a word. [*To* Linda] Did I say a word?

LINDA: He didn't say anything, Willy.

WILLY: [*Going to the doorway of the living-room*] All right, good night, good night.

LINDA: Willy, dear, he just decided . . .

WILLY: [*To* Biff] If you get tired hanging around tomorrow, paint the ceiling I put up in the living-room.

BIFF: I'm leaving early tomorrow.

HAPPY: He's going to see Bill Oliver, Pop.

WILLY: [*Interestedly*] Oliver? For what?

BIFF: [*With reserve, but trying, trying*] He always said he'd stake me. I'd like to go into business, so maybe I can take him up on it.

LINDA: Isn't that wonderful?

WILLY: Don't interrupt. What's wonderful about it? There's fifty men in the City of New York who'd stake him. [*To* Biff] Sporting goods?

BIFF: I guess so. I know something about it and—

WILLY: He knows something about it! You know sporting goods better than Spalding, for God's sake! How much is he giving you?

BIFF: I don't know, I didn't even see him yet, but—

WILLY: Then what're you talkin' about?

BIFF: [*Getting angry*] Well, all I said was I'm gonna see him, that's all!

WILLY: [*Turning away*] Ah, you're counting your chickens again.

BIFF: [*Starting left for the stairs*] Oh, Jesus, I'm going to sleep!

WILLY: [*Calling after him*] Don't curse in this house!

BIFF: [*Turning*] Since when did you get so clean?

HAPPY: [*Trying to stop them*] Wait a . . .

WILLY: Don't use that language to me! I won't have it!

HAPPY: [*Grabbing* Biff, *shouts*] Wait a minute! I got an idea. I got a feasible idea. Come here, Biff, let's talk this over now, let's talk some sense here. When I was down in Florida last time, I thought of a great idea to sell sporting goods. It just came back to me. You and I, Biff—we have a line, the Loman Line. We train a couple of weeks, and put on a couple of exhibitions, see?

WILLY: That's an idea!

HAPPY: Wait! We form two basketball teams, see? Two water-polo teams. We play each other. It's a million dollars' worth of publicity. Two brothers, see? The Loman Brothers. Displays in the Royal Palms—all the hotels. And banners over the ring and the basketball court: "Loman Brothers." Baby, we could sell sporting goods!

WILLY: That is a one-million-dollar idea!

LINDA: Marvelous!

BIFF: I'm in great shape as far as that's concerned.

HAPPY: And the beauty of it is, Biff, it wouldn't be like a business. We'd be out playin' ball again . . .

BIFF: [*Filled with enthusiasm*] Yeah, that's . . .

WILLY: Million-dollar . . .

HAPPY: And you wouldn't get fed up with it, Biff. It'd be the family again. There'd be the old honor, and comradeship, and if you wanted to go off for a swim or somethin'—well, you'd do it! Without some smart cooky gettin' up ahead of you!

WILLY: Lick the world! You guys together could absolutely lick the civilized world.

BIFF: I'll see Oliver tomorrow. Hap, if we could work that out . . .

LINDA: Maybe things are beginning to—

WILLY: [*Wildly enthusiastic, to* Linda] Stop interrupting! [*To* Biff:] But don't wear sport jacket and slacks when you see Oliver.

BIFF: No, I'll—

WILLY: A business suit, and talk as little as possible, and don't crack any jokes.

BIFF: He did like me. Always liked me.

LINDA: He loved you!

WILLY: [*To* Linda] Will you stop! [*To* Biff] Walk in very serious. You are not applying for a boy's job. Money is to pass. Be quiet, fine, and serious. Everybody likes a kidder, but nobody lends him money.

HAPPY: I'll try to get some myself, Biff. I'm sure I can.

WILLY: I see great things for you kids, I think your troubles are over. But remember, start big and you'll end big. Ask for fifteen. How much you gonna ask for?

BIFF: Gee, I don't know—

WILLY: And don't say "Gee." "Gee" is a boy's word. A man walking in for fifteen thousand dollars does not say "Gee!"

BIFF: Ten, I think, would be top though.

WILLY: Don't be so modest. You always started too low. Walk in with a big laugh. Don't look worried. Start off with a couple of your good stories to lighten things up. It's not what you say, it's how you say it—because personality always wins the day.

LINDA: Oliver always thought the highest of him—

WILLY: Will you let me talk?

BIFF: Don't yell at her, Pop, will ya?

WILLY: [*Angrily*] I was talking, wasn't I?

BIFF: I don't like you yelling at her all the time, and I'm tellin' you, that's all.

WILLY: What're you, takin' over this house?

LINDA: Willy—

WILLY: [*Turning on her*] Don't take his side all the time, god-dammit!

BIFF: [*Furiously*] Stop yelling at her!

WILLY: [*Suddenly pulling on his cheek, beaten down, guilt ridden*] Give my best to Bill Oliver—he may remember me. [*He exits through the living-room doorway*]

LINDA: [*Her voice subdued*] What'd you have to start that for? [Biff *turns away*] You see how sweet he was as soon as you talked hopefully? [*She goes over to* Biff] Come up and say good night to him. Don't let him go to bed that way.

HAPPY: Come on, Biff, let's buck him up.

LINDA: Please, dear. Just say good night. It takes so little to make him happy. Come. [*She goes through the living-room doorway, calling upstairs from within the living-room*] Your pajamas are hanging in the bathroom, Willy!

HAPPY: [*Looking toward where Linda went out*] What a woman! They broke the mold when they made her. You know that, Biff?

BIFF: He's off salary. My God, working on commission!

HAPPY: Well, let's face it: he's no hot-shot selling man. Except that sometimes, you have to admit, he's a sweet personality.

BIFF: [*Deciding*] Lend me ten bucks, will ya? I want to buy some new ties.

HAPPY: I'll take you to a place I know. Beautiful stuff. Wear one of my striped shirts tomorrow.

BIFF: She got gray. Mom got awful old. Gee, I'm gonna go in to Oliver tomorrow and knock him for a——

HAPPY: Come on up. Tell that to Dad. Let's give him a whirl. Come on.

BIFF: [*Steamed up*] You know, with ten thousand bucks, boy!

HAPPY: [*As they go into the living-room*] That's the talk, Biff, that's the first time I've heard the old confidence out of you! [*From within the living-room, fading off*] You're gonna live with me, kid, and any babe you want just say the word . . . [*The last lines are hardly heard. They are mounting the stairs to their parents' bedroom*]

LINDA: [*Entering her bedroom and addressing Willy, who is in the bathroom. She is straightening the bed for him*] Can you do anything about the shower? It drips.

WILLY: [*From the bathroom*] All of a sudden everything falls to pieces! Goddam plumbing, oughta be sued, those people. I hardly finished putting it in and the thing . . . [*His words rumble off*]

LINDA: I'm just wondering if Oliver will remember him. You think he might?

WILLY: [*Coming out of the bathroom in his pajamas*] Remember him? What's the matter with you, you crazy? If he'd've stayed with Oliver he'd be on top by now! Wait'll Oliver gets a look at him. You don't know the average caliber any more. The average young man today—[*He is getting into bed*]—is got a caliber of zero. Greatest thing in the world for him was to bum around.

[*Biff and Happy enter the bedroom. Slight pause*]

WILLY: [*Stops short, looking at Biff*] Glad to hear it, boy.

HAPPY: We wanted to say good night to you, sport.

WILLY: [*To Biff*] Yeah. Knock him dead, boy. What'd you want to tell me?

BIFF: Just take it easy, Pop. Good night. [*He turns to go*].

WILLY: [*Unable to resist*] And if anything falls off the desk while you're talking to him—like a package or something—don't you pick it up. They have office boys for that.

LINDA: I'll make a big breakfast—

WILLY: Will you let me finish? [*To Biff*] Tell him you were in the business in the West. Not farm work.

BIFF: All right, Dad.

LINDA: I think everything—

WILLY: [*Going right through her speech*] And don't undersell yourself. No less than fifteen thousand dollars.

BIFF: [*Unable to bear him*] Okay. Good night, Mom. [*He starts moving*]

WILLY: Because you got a greatness in you, Biff, remember that. You got all kinds of greatness. . . . [*He lies back, exhausted. Biff walks out*]

LINDA: [*Calling after Biff*] Sleep well, darling!

HAPPY: I'm gonna get married, Mom. I wanted to tell you.

LINDA: Go to sleep, dear.

HAPPY: [*Going*] I just wanted to tell you.

WILLY: Keep up the good work. [*Happy exits*] God . . . remember that Ebbets Field game? The championship of the city?

LINDA: Just rest. Should I sing to you?

WILLY: Yeah. Sing to me. [*Linda hums a soft lullaby*] When that team came out—he was the tallest, remember?

LINDA: Oh, yes. And in gold.

[*Biff enters the darkened kitchen, takes a cigarette, and leaves the house. He comes downstage into a golden pool of light. He smokes, staring at the night*]

WILLY: Like a young god. Hercules—something like that. And the sun, the sun all around him. Remember how he waved to me? Right up from the field, with the representatives of three colleges standing by? And the buyers I brought, and the cheers when he came out—Loman, Loman, Loman! God Almighty, he'll be great yet. A star like that, magnificent, can never really fade away!

[*The light on Willy is fading. The gas heater begins to glow through the kitchen wall, near the stairs, a blue flame beneath red coils*]

LINDA: [*Timidly*] Willy dear, what has he got against you?

WILLY: I'm so tired. Don't talk any more.

[*Biff slowly returns to the kitchen. He stops, stares toward the heater*]

LINDA: Will you ask Howard to let you work in New York?

WILLY: First thing in the morning. Everything'll be all right.

[*Biff reaches behind the heater and draws out a length of rubber tubing. He is horrified and turns his head toward Willy's room, still dimly lit, from which the strains of Linda's desperate but monotonous humming rise*]

WILLY: [*Staring through the window into the moonlight*] Gee, look at the moon moving between the buildings!

[*Biff wraps the tubing around his hand and quickly goes up the stairs*]

CURTAIN

ACT II.

Music is heard, gay and bright. The curtain rises as the music fades away. Willy, in shirt sleeves, is sitting at the kitchen table, sipping coffee, his hat in his lap. Linda is filling his cup when she can.

WILLY: Wonderful coffee. Meal in itself.

LINDA: Can I make you some eggs?

WILLY: No. Take a breath.

LINDA: You look so rested, dear.

WILLY: I slept like a dead one. First time in months. Imagine, sleeping till ten on a Tuesday morning. Boys left nice and early, heh?

LINDA: They were out of here by eight o'clock.

WILLY: Good work!

LINDA: It was so thrilling to see them leaving together. I can't get over the shaving lotion in this house!

WILLY: [*Smiling*] Mmm—

LINDA: Biff was very changed this morning. His whole attitude seemed to be hopeful. He couldn't wait to get downtown to see Oliver.

WILLY: He's heading for a change. There's no question, there simply are certain men that take longer to get—solidified. How did he dress?

LINDA: His blue suit. He's so handsome in that suit. He could be a—anything in that suit!

[Willy *gets up from the table*. Linda *holds his jacket for him*]

WILLY: There's no question, no question at all. Gee, on the way home tonight I'd like to buy some seeds.

LINDA: [*Laughing*] That'd be wonderful. But not enough sun gets back there. Nothing'll grow any more.

WILLY: You wait, kid, before it's all over we're gonna get a little place out in the country, and I'll raise some vegetables, a couple of chickens . . .

LINDA: You'll do it yet, dear.

[Willy *walks out of his jacket*. Linda *follows him*]

WILLY: And they'll get married, and come for a weekend. I'd build a little guest house. 'Cause I got so many fine tools, all I'd need would be a little lumber and some peace of mind.

LINDA: [*Joyfully*] I sewed the lining . . .

WILLY: I could build two guest houses, so they'd both come. Did he decide how much he's going to ask Oliver for?

LINDA: [*Getting him into the jacket*] He didn't mention it, but I imagine ten or fifteen thousand. You going to talk to Howard today?

WILLY: Yeah. I'll put it to him straight and simple. He'll just have to take me off the road.

LINDA: And Willy, don't forget to ask for a little advance, because we've got the insurance premium. It's the grace period now.

WILLY: That's a hundred . . . ?

LINDA: A hundred and eight, sixty-eight. Because we're a little short again.

WILLY: Why are we short?

LINDA: Well, you had the motor job on the car . . .

WILLY: That goddam Studebaker!

LINDA: And you got one more payment on the refrigerator . . .

WILLY: But it just broke again!

LINDA: Well, it's old, dear.

WILLY: I told you we should've bought a well-advertised machine. Charley bought a General Electric and it's twenty years old and it's still good, that son-of-a-bitch.

LINDA: But, Willy—

WILLY: Whoever heard of a Hastings refrigerator? Once in my life I would like to own something outright before it's broken! I'm always in a race with the junkyard! I just finished paying for the car and it's on its last legs. The refrigerator consumes belts like a goddam maniac. They time those things. They time them so when you finally paid for them, they're used up.

LINDA: [*Buttoning up his jacket as he unbuttons it*] All told, about two hundred dollars would carry us, dear. But that includes the last payment on the mortgage. After this payment, Willy, the house belongs to us.

WILLY: It's twenty-five years!

LINDA: Biff was nine years old when we bought it.

WILLY: Well, that's a great thing. To weather a twenty-five year mortgage is—

LINDA: It's an accomplishment.

WILLY: All the cement, the lumber, the reconstruction I put in this house! There ain't a crack to be found in it any more.

LINDA: Well, it served its purpose.

WILLY: What purpose? Some stranger'll come along, move in, and that's that. If only Biff would take this house, and raise a family . . . [*He starts to go*] Good-by, I'm late.

LINDA: [*Suddenly remembering*] Oh, I forgot! You're supposed to meet them for dinner.

WILLY: Me?

LINDA: At Frank's Chop House on Forty-eighth near Sixth Avenue.

WILLY: Is that so! How about you?

LINDA: No, just the three of you. They're gonna blow you to a big meal!

WILLY: Don't say! Who thought of that?

LINDA: Biff came to me this morning, Willy, and he said, "Tell Dad, we want to blow him to a big meal." Be there six o'clock. You and your two boys are going to have dinner.

WILLY: Gee whiz! That's really somethin'. I'm gonna knock Howard for a loop, kid. I'll get an advance, and I'll come home with a New York job. Goddammit, now I'm gonna do it!

LINDA: Oh, that's the spirit, Willy!

WILLY: I will never get behind a wheel the rest of my life!

LINDA: It's changing, Willy, I can feel it changing!

WILLY: Beyond a question. G'by, I'm late. [*He starts to go again*]

LINDA: [*Calling after him as she runs to the kitchen table for a handkerchief*] You got your glasses?

WILLY: [*Feels for them, then comes back in*] Yeah, yeah, got my glasses.

LINDA: [*Giving him the handkerchief*] And a handkerchief.

WILLY: Yeah, handkerchief.

LINDA: And your saccharine?

WILLY: Yeah, my saccharine.

LINDA: Be careful on the subway stairs.

[*She kisses him, and a silk stocking is seen hanging from her hand.* Willy *notices it*]

WILLY: Will you stop mending stockings? At least while I'm in the house. It gets me nervous. I can't tell you. Please.

[Linda *hides the stocking in her hand as she follows* Willy *across the forestage in front of the house*]

LINDA: Remember, Frank's Chop House.

WILLY: [*Passing the apron*] Maybe beets would grow out there.

LINDA: [*Laughing*] But you tried so many times.

WILLY: Yeah. Well, don't work hard today. [*He disappears around the right corner of the house*]

LINDA: Be careful.

[*As* Willy *vanishes,* Linda *waves to him. Suddenly the phone rings. She runs across the stage and into the kitchen and lifts it*]

LINDA: Hello? Oh, Biff! I'm so glad you called, I just . . . Yes, sure, I just told him. Yes, he'll be there for dinner at six o'clock. I didn't forget. Listen, I was just dying to tell you. You know that little rubber pipe I told you about? That he connected to the gas heater? I finally decided to go down the cellar this morning and take it away and destroy it. But it's gone! Imagine? He took it away himself, it isn't there! [*She listens*] When? Oh, then you took it. Oh—nothing, it's just that I'd hoped he'd taken it away himself. Oh, I'm not worried, darling, because this morning he left in such high spirits, it was like the old days! I'm not afraid any more. Did Mr. Oliver see you? . . . Well, you wait there then. And make a nice impression on him, darling. Just don't perspire too much before you see him. And have a nice time with Dad. He may have big news too! . . . That's right, a New York job. And be sweet to him tonight, dear. Be loving to him. Because he's only a little boat looking for a harbor. [*She is trembling with sorrow and joy*] Oh, that's wonderful, Biff, you'll save his life. Thanks, darling. Just put your arm around him when he comes into the restaurant. Give him a smile. That's the boy . . . Good-by, dear . . . You got your comb? . . . That's fine. Good-by, Biff dear.

[*In the middle of her speech,* Howard Wagner, *thirty-six, wheels on a small typewriter table on which is a wire-recording machine and proceeds to plug it in. This is on the left forestage. Light slowly fades on* Linda *as it rises on* Howard. Howard *is intent on threading the machine and only glances over his shoulder as* Willy *appears*]

WILLY: Pst! Pst!

HOWARD: Hello, Willy, come in.

WILLY: Like to have a little talk with you, Howard.

HOWARD: Sorry to keep you waiting. I'll be with you in a minute.

WILLY: What's that, Howard?

HOWARD: Didn't you ever see one of these? Wire recorder.

WILLY: Oh. Can we talk a minute?

HOWARD: Records things. Just got delivery yesterday. Been driving me crazy, the most terrific machine I ever saw in my life. I was up all night with it.

WILLY: What do you do with it?

HOWARD: I bought it for dictation, but you can do anything with it. Listen to this. I had it home last night. Listen to what I picked up. The first one is my daughter. Get this. [*He flicks the switch and "Roll out the Barrel!" is heard being whistled*] Listen to that kid whistle.

WILLY: That is lifelike, isn't it?

HOWARD: Seven years old. Get that tone.

WILLY: Ts, ts. Like to ask a little favor of you . . .

[*The whistling breaks off, and the voice of* Howard's *daughter is heard*]

HIS DAUGHTER: "Now you, Daddy."

HOWARD: She's crazy for me! [*Again the same song is whistled*] That's me! Ha! [*He winks*]

WILLY: You're very good!

[*The whistling breaks off again. The machine runs silent for a moment*]

HOWARD: Sh! Get this now, this is my son.

HIS SON: "The capital of Alabama is Montgomery; the capital of Arizona is Phoenix; the capital of Arkansas is Little Rock; the capital of California is Sacramento . . . " [*and on, and on*]

HOWARD: [*Holding up five fingers*] Five years old, Willy.

WILLY: He'll make an announcer some day!

HIS SON: [*Continuing*] "The capital . . ."

HOWARD: Get that—alphabetical order! [*The machine breaks off suddenly*] Wait a minute. The maid kicked the plug out.

WILLY: It certainly is a—

HOWARD: Sh, for God's sake.

HIS SON: "It's nine o'clock, Bulova watch time. So I have to go to sleep."

WILLY: That really is—

HOWARD: Wait a minute! The next is my wife.

[*They wait*]

HOWARD'S VOICE: "Go on, say something." [*Pause*] "Well, you gonna talk?"

HIS WIFE: "I can't think of anything."

HOWARD'S VOICE: "Well, talk—it's turning."

HIS WIFE: [*Shyly, beaten*] "Hello." [*Silence*] "Oh, Howard, I can't talk into this . . ."

HOWARD: [*Snapping the machine off*] That was my wife.

WILLY: That is a wonderful machine. Can we—

HOWARD: I tell you, Willy, I'm gonna take my camera, and my bandsaw, and all my hobbies, and out they go. This is the most fascinating relaxation I ever found.

WILLY: I think I'll get one myself.

HOWARD: Sure, they're only a hundred and a half. You can't do without it. Supposing you wanna hear Jack Benny, see? But you can't be at home at that hour. So you tell the maid to turn the radio on when Jack Benny comes on, and this automatically goes on with the radio . . .

WILLY: And when you come home you . . .

HOWARD: You can come home twelve o'clock, one o'clock, any time you like, and you get yourself a Coke and sit yourself down, throw the switch, and there's Jack Benny's program in the middle of the night!

WILLY: I'm definitely going to get one. Because lots of time I'm on the road, and I think to myself, what I must be missing on the radio!

HOWARD: Don't you have a radio in the car?

WILLY: Well, yeah, but who ever thinks of turning it on?

HOWARD: Say, aren't you supposed to be in Boston?

WILLY: That's what I want to talk to you about, Howard. You got a minute? [He draws a chair in from the wing]

HOWARD: What happened? What're you doing here?

WILLY: Well . . .

HOWARD: You didn't crack up again, did you?

WILLY: Oh, no. No . . .

HOWARD: Geez, you had me worried there for a minute. What's the trouble?

WILLY: Well, tell you the truth, Howard. I've come to the decision that I'd rather not travel any more.

HOWARD: Not travel! Well, what'll you do?

WILLY: Remember, Christmas time, when you had the party here? You said you'd try to think of some spot for me here in town.

HOWARD: With us?

WILLY: Well, sure.

HOWARD: Oh, yeah, yeah. I remember. Well, I couldn't think of anything for you, Willy.

WILLY: I tell ya, Howard. The kids are all grown up, y'know. I don't need much any more. If I could take home—well, sixty-five dollars a week, I could swing it.

HOWARD: Yeah, but Willy, see I—

WILLY: I tell ya why, Howard. Speaking frankly and between the two of us, y'know—I'm just a little tired.

HOWARD: Oh, I could understand that, Willy. But you're a road man, Willy, and we do a road business. We've only got a half-dozen salesmen on the floor here.

WILLY: God knows, Howard, I never asked a favor of any man. But I was with the firm when your father used to carry you in here in his arms.

HOWARD: I know that, Willy, but—

WILLY: Your father came to me the day you were born and asked me what I thought of the name of Howard, may he rest in peace.

HOWARD: I appreciate that, Willy, but there just is no spot here for you. If I had a spot I'd slam you right in, but I just don't have a single solitary spot.

[He looks for his lighter. Willy has picked it up and gives it to him. Pause]

WILLY: [With increasing anger] Howard, all I need to set my table is fifty dollars a week.

HOWARD: But where am I going to put you, kid?

WILLY: Look, it isn't a question of whether I can sell merchandise, is it?

HOWARD: No, but it's a business, kid, and everybody's gotta pull his own weight.

WILLY: [Desperately] Just let me tell you a story, Howard—

HOWARD: 'Cause you gotta admit, business is business.

WILLY: [Angrily] Business is definitely business, but just listen for a minute. You don't understand this. When I was a boy—eighteen, nineteen—I was already on the road. And there was a question in my mind as to whether selling had a future for me. Because in those days I had a yearning to go to Alaska. See, there were three gold strikes in one month in Alaska, and I felt like going out. Just for the ride, you might say.

HOWARD: [Barely interested] Don't say.

WILLY: Oh, yeah, my father lived many years in Alaska. He was an adventurous man. We've got quite a little streak of self-reliance in our family. I thought I'd go out with my older brother and try to locate him, and maybe settle in the North with the old man. And I was almost decided to go, when I met a salesman in the Parker House. His name was Dave Singleman. And he was eighty-four years old, and he'd drummed merchandise in thirty-one states. And old Dave, he'd go up to his room, y'understand, put on his green velvet slippers—I'll never forget—and pick up his phone and call the buyers, and without ever leaving his room, at the age of eighty-four, he made his living. And when I saw that, I realized that selling was the greatest career a man could want. 'Cause what could be more satisfying than to be able to go, at the age of eighty-four, into twenty or thirty different cities, and pick up a phone, and be remembered and loved and helped by so many different people? Do you know? when he died—and by the way he died the death of a salesman, in his green velvet slippers in the smoker of the New York, New Haven and Hartford, going into Boston—when he died, hundreds of salesmen and buyers were at his funeral. Things were sad on a lotta trains for months after that. [He stands up. Howard has not looked at him] In those days there was personality in it, Howard. There was respect, and comradeship, and gratitude in it. Today, it's all cut and dried, and there's no chance for bringing friendship to bear—or personality. You see what I mean? They don't know me any more.

HOWARD: [*Moving away, to the right*] That's just the thing, Willy.

WILLY: If I had forty dollars a week—that's all I'd need. Forty dollars, Howard.

HOWARD: Kid, I can't take blood from a stone, I—

WILLY: [*Desperation is on him now*] Howard, the year Al Smith was nominated, your father came to me and—

HOWARD: [*Starting to go off*] I've got to see some people, kid.

WILLY: [*Stopping him*] I'm talking about your father! There were promises made across this desk! You mustn't tell me you've got people to see—I put thirty-four years into this firm, Howard, and now I can t pay my insurance! You can't eat the orange and t hrow the peel away—a man is not a piece of fruit! [*After a pause*] Now pay attention. Your father—in 1928 I had a big year. I averaged a hundred and seventy dollars a week in commissions.

HOWARD: [*Impatiently*] Now, Willy, you never averaged—

WILLY: [*Banging his hand on the desk*] I averaged a hundred and seventy dollars a week in the year of 1928! And your father came to me—or rather, I was in the office here—it was right over this desk—and he put his hand on my shoulder—

HOWARD: [*Getting up*] You'll have to excuse me, Willy, I gotta see some people. Pull yourself together. [*Going out*] I'll be back in a little while.

[*On Howard's exit, the light on his chair grows very bright and strange.*]

WILLY: Pull myself together! What the hell did I say to him? My God, I was yelling at him! How could I! [Willy *breaks off, staring at the light, which occupies the chair, animating it. He approaches this chair, standing across the desk from it*] Frank, Frank, don't you remember what you told me that time? How you put your hand on my shoulder, and Frank . . . [*He leans on the desk and as he speaks the dead man's name he accidentally switches on the recorder, and instantly*]

HOWARD'S SON: ". . . of New York is Albany. The capital of Ohio is Cincinnati, the capital of Rhode Island is . . ." [*The recitation continues*]

WILLY: [*Leaping away with fright, shouting*] Ha! Howard! Howard! Howard!

HOWARD: [*Rushing in*] What happened?

WILLY: [*Pointing at the machine, which continues nasally, childishly, with the capital cities*] Shut it off! Shut it off!

HOWARD: [*Pulling the plug out*] Look, Willy . . .

WILLY: [*Pressing his hands to his eyes*] I gotta get myself some coffee. I'll get some coffee . . .

[Willy *starts to walk out.* Howard *stops him*]

HOWARD: [*Rolling up the cord*] Willy, look . . .

WILLY: I'll go to Boston.

HOWARD: Willy, you can't go to Boston for us.

WILLY: Why can't I go?

HOWARD: I don't want you to represent us. I've been meaning to tell you for a long time now.

WILLY: Howard, are you firing me?

HOWARD: I think you need a good long rest, Willy.

WILLY: Howard—

HOWARD: And when you feel better, come back, and we'll see if we can work something out.

WILLY: But I gotta earn money, Howard. I'm in no position to—

HOWARD: Where are your sons? Why don't your sons give you a hand?

WILLY: They're working on a very big deal.

HOWARD: This is no time for false pride, Willy. You go to your sons and you tell them that you're tired. You've got two great boys, haven't you?

WILLY: Oh, no question, no question, but in the meantime . . .

HOWARD: Then that's that, heh?

WILLY: All right, I'll go to Boston tomorrow.

HOWARD: No, no.

WILLY: I can't throw myself on my sons. I'm not a cripple!

HOWARD: Look, kid, I'm busy this morning.

WILLY: [*Grasping* Howard's *arm*] Howard, you've got to let me go to Boston!

HOWARD: [*Hard, keeping himself under control*] I've got a line of people to see this morning. Sit down, take five minutes, and pull yourself together, and then go home, will ya? I need the office, Willy. [*He starts to go, turns, remembering the recorder, starts to push off the table holding the recorder*] Oh, yeah. Whenever you can this week, stop by and drop off the samples. You'll feel better, Willy, and then come back and we'll talk. Pull yourself together, kid, there's people outside.

[Howard *exits, pushing the table off left.* Willy *stares into space, exhausted. Now the music is heard—Ben's music—first distantly, then closer, closer. As* Willy *speaks,* Ben *enters from the right. He carries valise and umbrella*]

WILLY: Oh, Ben, how did you do it? What is the answer? Did you wind up the Alaska deal already?

BEN: Doesn't take much time if you know what you're doing. Just a short business trip. Boarding ship in an hour. Wanted to say good-by.

WILLY: Ben, I've got to talk to you.

BEN: [*Glancing at his watch*] Haven't the time, William.

WILLY: [*Crossing the apron to* Ben] Ben, nothing's working out. I don't know what to do.

BEN: Now, look here, William. I've bought timberland in Alaska and I need a man to look after things for me.

WILLY: God, timberland! Me and my boys in those grand outdoors!

BEN: You've a new continent at your doorstep, William. Get out of these cities, they're full of talk and time payments and courts of law. Screw on your fists and you can fight for a fortune up there.

WILLY: Yes, yes! Linda, Linda!

[Linda *enters as of old, with the wash*]

LINDA: Oh, you're back?

BEN: I haven't much time.

WILLY: No, wait! Linda, he's got a proposition for me in Alaska.

LINDA: But you've got—[*To* Ben] He's got a beautiful job here.

WILLY: But in Alaska, kid, I could—

LINDA: You're doing well enough, Willy!

BEN: [*To* Linda] Enough for what, my dear?

LINDA: [*Frightened of* Ben *and angry at him*] Don't say those things to him! Enough to be happy right here, right now. [*To* Willy, *while* Ben *laughs*] Why must everybody conquer the world? You're well liked, and the boys love you, and someday—[*To* Ben]—why, old man Wagner told him just the other day that if he keeps it up he'll be a member of the firm, didn't he, Willy?

WILLY: Sure, sure. I am building something with this firm, Ben, and if a man is building something he must be on the right track, mustn't he?

BEN: What are you building? Lay your hand on it. Where is it?

WILLY: [*Hesitantly*] That's true, Linda, there's nothing.

LINDA: Why? [*To* Ben] There's a man eighty-four years old—

WILLY: That's right, Ben, that's right. When I look at that man I say, what is there to worry about?

BEN: Bah!

WILLY: It's true, Ben. All he has to do is go into any city, pick up the phone, and he's making his living and you know why?

BEN: [*Picking up his valise*] I've got to go.

WILLY: [*Holding* Ben *back*] Look at this boy!

[Biff, *in his high school sweater, enters carrying suitcase.* Happy *carries* Biff's *shoulder guards, gold helmet, and football pants*]

WILLY: Without a penny to his name, three great universities are begging for him, and from there the sky's the limit, because it's not what you do, Ben. It's who you know and the smile on your face! It's contacts, Ben, contacts! The whole wealth of Alaska passes over the lunch table at the Commodore Hotel, and that's the wonder, the wonder of this country, that a man can end with diamonds here on the basis of being liked! [*He turns to* Biff] And that's why when you get out on that field today it's important. Because thousands of people will be rooting for you and loving you. [*To* Ben, *who has again begun to leave*] And Ben! when he walks into a business office his name will sound out like a bell and all the doors will open to him! I've seen it, Ben, I've seen it a thousand times! You can't feel it with your hand like timber, but it's there!

BEN: Good-by, William.

WILLY: Ben, am I right? Don't you think I'm right? I value your advice.

BEN: There's a new continent at your doorstep, William. You could walk out rich. Rich! [*He is gone*]

WILLY: We'll do it here, Ben! You hear me? We're gonna do it here!

[*Young* Bernard *rushes in. The gay music of the* Boys *is heard*]

BERNARD: Oh, gee, I was afraid you left already!

WILLY: Why? What time is it?

BERNARD: It's half-past one!

WILLY: Well, come on, everybody! Ebbets Field next stop! Where's the pennants? [*He rushes through the wall-line of the kitchen and out into the living-room*]

LINDA: [*To* Biff] Did you pack fresh underwear?

BIFF: [*Who has been limbering up*] I want to go!

BERNARD: Biff, I'm carrying your helmet, ain't I?

HAPPY: No, I'm carrying the helmet.

BERNARD: Oh, Biff, you promised me.

HAPPY: I'm carrying the helmet.

BERNARD: How am I going to get in the locker room?

LINDA: Let him carry the shoulder guards. [*She puts her coat and hat on in the kitchen*]

BERNARD: Can I, Biff? 'Cause I told everybody I'm going to be in the locker room.

HAPPY: In Ebbets Field it's the clubhouse.

BERNARD: I meant the clubhouse. Biff.

HAPPY: Biff!

BIFF: [*Grandly, after a slight pause*] Let him carry the shoulder guards.

HAPPY: [*As he gives* Bernard *the shoulder guards*] Stay close to us now.

[Willy *rushes in with the pennants*]

WILLY: [*Handing them out*] Everybody wave when Biff comes out on the field. [Happy *and* Bernard *run off*] You set now, boy?

[*The music has died away*]

BIFF: Ready to go, Pop. Every muscle is ready.

WILLY: [*At the edge of the apron*] You realize what this means?

BIFF: That's right, Pop.

WILLY: [*Feeling* Biff's *muscles*] You're comin' home this afternoon captain of the All-Scholastic Championship Team of the City of New York.

BIFF: I got it, Pop. And remember, pal, when I take off my helmet, that touchdown is for you.

WILLY: Let's go! [*He is starting out, with his arm around* Biff, *when* Charley *enters, as of old, in knickers*] I got no room for you, Charley.

CHARLEY: Room? For what?

WILLY: In the car.

CHARLEY: You goin' for a ride? I wanted to shoot some casino.

WILLY: [*Furiously*] Casino! [*Incredulously*] Don't you realize what today is?

LINDA: Oh, he knows, Willy. He's just kidding you.

WILLY: That's nothing to kid about!

CHARLEY: No, Linda, what's goin' on?

LINDA: He's playing in Ebbets Field.

CHARLEY: Baseball in this weather?

WILLY: Don't talk to him. Come on, come on! [*He is pushing them out*]

CHARLEY: Wait a minute, didn't you hear the news?

WILLY: What?

CHARLEY: Don't you listen to the radio? Ebbets Field just blew up.

WILLY: You go to hell! [Charley *laughs. Pushing them out*] Come on, come on! We're late.

CHARLEY: [*As they go*] Knock a homer, Biff, knock a homer!

WILLY: [*The last to leave, turning to* Charley] I don't think that was funny, Charley. This is the greatest day of his life.

CHARLEY: Willy, when are you going to grow up?

WILLY: Yeah, heh? When this game is over, Charley, you'll be laughing out of the other side of your face. They'll be calling him another Red Grange. Twenty-five thousand a year.

CHARLEY: [*Kidding*] Is that so?

WILLY: Yeah, that's so.

CHARLEY: Well, then, I'm sorry, Willy. But tell me something.

WILLY: What?

CHARLEY: Who is Red Grange?

WILLY: Put up your hands. Goddam you, put up your hands!

[Charley, *chuckling, shakes his head and walks away, around the left corner of the stage.* Willy *follows him. The music rises to a mocking frenzy*]

WILLY: Who the hell do you think you are, better than everybody else? You don't know everything, you big, ignorant, stupid . . . Put up your hands!

[*Light rises, on the right side of the forestage, on a small table in the reception room of* Charley's *office. Traffic sounds are heard. Bernard, now mature, sits whistling to himself. A pair of tennis rackets and an overnight bag are on the floor beside him*]

WILLY: [*Offstage*] What are you walking away for? Don't walk away! If you're going to say something say it to my face! I know you laugh at me behind my back. You'll laugh out of the other side of your goddam face after this game. Touchdown! Touchdown! Eighty thousand people! Touchdown! Right between the goal posts.

[Bernard *is a quiet, earnest, but self-assured young man.* Willy's *voice is coming from right upstage now.* Bernard *lowers his feet off the table and listens.* Jenny, *his father's secretary, enters*]

JENNY: [*Distressed*] Say, Bernard, will you go out in the hall?

BERNARD: What is that noise? Who is it?

JENNY: Mr. Loman. He just got off the elevator.

BERNARD: [*Getting up*] Who's he arguing with?

JENNY: Nobody. There's nobody with him. I can't deal with him any more, and your father gets all upset everytime he comes. I've got a lot of typing to do, and your father's waiting to sign it. Will you see him?

WILLY: [*Entering*] Touchdown! Touch—[*He sees* Jenny] Jenny, Jenny, good to see you. How're ya? Workin'? Or still honest?

JENNY: Fine. How've you been feeling?

WILLY: Not much any more, Jenny. Ha, ha! [*He is surprised to see the rackets*]

BERNARD: Hello, Uncle Willy.

WILLY: [*Almost shocked*] Bernard! Well, look who's here! [*He comes quickly, guiltily, to* Bernard *and warmly shakes his hand*]

BERNARD: How are you? Good to see you.

WILLY: What are you doing here?

BERNARD: Oh, just stopped by to see Pop. Get off my feet till my train leaves. I'm going to Washington in a few minutes.

WILLY: Is he in?

BERNARD: Yes, he's in his office with the accountant. Sit down.

WILLY: [*Sitting down*] What're you going to do in Washington?

BERNARD: Oh, just a case I've got there, Willy.

WILLY: That so? [*Indicating the rackets*] You going to play tennis there?

BERNARD: I'm staying with a friend who's got a court.

WILLY: Don't say. His own tennis court. Must be fine people, I bet.

BERNARD: They are, very nice. Dad tells me Biff's in town.

WILLY: [*With a big smile*] Yeah, Biff's in. Working on a very big deal, Bernard.

BERNARD: What's Biff doing?

WILLY: Well, he's been doing very big things in the West. But he decided to establish himself here. Very big. We're having dinner. Did I hear your wife had a boy?

BERNARD: That's right. Our second.

WILLY: Two boys! What do you know!

BERNARD: What kind of a deal has Biff got?

WILLY: Well, Bill Oliver—very big sporting-goods man—he wants Biff very badly. Called him in from the West. Long distance, carte blanche, special deliveries. Your friends have their own private tennis court?

BERNARD: You still with the old firm, Willy?

WILLY: [*After a pause*] I'm—I'm overjoyed to see how you made the grade, Bernard, overjoyed. It's an encouraging thing to see a young man really—really— Looks very good for Biff—very—[*He breaks off, then*] Bernard— [*He is so full of emotion, he breaks off again*]

BERNARD: What is it, Willy?

WILLY: [*Small and alone*] What—what's the secret?

BERNARD: What secret?

WILLY: How—how did you? Why didn't he ever catch on?

BERNARD: I wouldn't know that, Willy.

WILLY: [*Confidentially, desperately*] You were his friend, his boyhood friend. There's something I don't understand about it. His life ended after that Ebbets Field game. From the age of seventeen nothing good ever happened to him.

BERNARD: He never trained himself for anything.

WILLY: But he did, he did. After high school he took so many correspondence courses. Radio mechanics; television; God knows what, and never made the slightest mark.

BERNARD: [*Taking off his glasses*] Willy, do you want to talk candidly?

WILLY: [*Rising, faces* Bernard] I regard you as a very brilliant man, Bernard. I value your advice.

BERNARD: Oh, the hell with the advice, Willy. I couldn't advise you. There's just one thing I've always wanted to ask you. When he was supposed to graduate, and the math teacher flunked him—

WILLY: Oh, that son-of-a-bitch ruined his life.

BERNARD: Yeah, but, Willy, all he had to do was go to summer school and make up that subject.

WILLY: That's right, that's right.

BERNARD: Did you tell him not to go to summer school?

WILLY: Me? I begged him to go. I ordered him to go!

BERNARD: Then why wouldn't he go?

WILLY: Why? Why! Bernard, that question has been trailing me like a ghost for the last fifteen years. He flunked the subject, and laid down and died like a hammer hit him!

BERNARD: Take it easy, kid.

WILLY: Let me talk to you—I got nobody to talk to. Bernard, Bernard, was it my fault? Y'see? It keeps going around in my mind, maybe I did something to him. I got nothing to give him.

BERNARD: Don't take it so hard.

WILLY: Why did he lay down? What is the story there? You were his friend!

BERNARD: Willy, I remember, it was June, and our grades came out. And he'd flunked math.

WILLY: That son-of-a-bitch!

BERNARD: No, it wasn't right then. Biff just got very angry, I remember, and he was ready to enroll in summer school.

WILLY: [*Surprised*] He was?

BERNARD: He wasn't beaten by it at all. But then, Willy, he disappeared from the block for almost a month. And I got the idea that he'd gone up to New England to see you. Did he have a talk with you then?

[Willy *stares in silence*]

BERNARD: Willy?

WILLY: [*With a stronge edge of resentment in his voice*] Yeah, he came to Boston. What about it?

BERNARD: Well, just that when he came back— I'll never forget this, it always mystifies me. Because I'd thought so well of Biff, even though he'd always taken advantage of me. I loved him, Willy, y'know?

And he came back after that month and took his sneakers—remember those sneakers with "University of Virginia" printed on them? He was so proud of those, wore them every day. And he took them down in the cellar, and burned them up in the furnace. We had a fist fight. It lasted at least half an hour. Just the two of us, punching each other down the cellar, and crying right through it. I've often thought of how strange it was that I knew he'd given up his life. What happened in Boston, Willy?

[Willy *looks at him as at an intruder*]

BERNARD: I just bring it up because you asked me.

WILLY: [*Angrily*] Nothing. What do you mean. "What happened?" What's that got to do with anything?

BERNARD: Well, don't get sore.

WILLY: What are you trying to do, blame it on me? If a boy lays down is that my fault?

BERNARD: Now, Willy, don't get—

WILLY: Well, don't—don't talk to me that way! What does that mean, "What happened?"

[Charley *enters. He is in his vest, and he carries a bottle of bourbon*]

CHARLEY: Hey, you're going to miss that train. [*He waves the bottle*]

BERNARD: Yeah, I'm going. [*He takes the bottle*] Thanks, Pop. [*He picks up his rackets and bag*] Good-by, Willy, and don't worry about it. You know, "If at first you don't succeed . . ."

WILLY: Yes, I believe in that.

BERNARD: But sometimes, Willy, it's better for a man just to walk away.

WILLY: Walk away?

BERNARD: That's right.

WILLY: But if you can't walk away?

BERNARD: [*After a slight pause*] I guess that's when it's tough. [*Extending his hand*] Good-by, Willy.

WILLY: [*Shaking* Bernard's *hand*] Good-by, boy.

CHARLEY: [*An arm on* Bernard's *shoulder*] How do you like this kid? Gonna argue a case in front of the Supreme Court.

BERNARD: [*Protesting*] Pop!

WILLY: [*Genuinely shocked, pained, and happy*] No! The Supreme Court!

BERNARD: I gotta run. 'By, Dad!

CHARLEY: Knock 'em dead, Bernard!

[Bernard *goes off*]

WILLY: [*As* Charley *takes out his wallet*] The Supreme Court! And he didn't even mention it!

CHARLEY: [*Counting out money on the desk*] He don't have to—he's gonna do it.

WILLY: And you never told him what to do, did you? You never took any interest in him.

CHARLEY: My salvation is that I never took any interest in anything. There's some money—fifty dollars. I got an accountant inside.

WILLY: Charley, look . . . [*With difficulty*] I got

my insurance to pay. If you can manage it—I need a hundred and ten dollars.

[Charley *doesn't reply for a moment; merely stops moving*]

WILLY: I'd draw it from my bank but Linda would know, and I . . .

CHARLEY: Sit down, Willy.

WILLY: [*Moving toward the chair*] I'm keeping an account of everything, remember. I'll pay every penny back. [*He sits*]

CHARLEY: Now listen to me, Willy.

WILLY: I want you to know I appreciate . . .

CHARLEY: [*Sitting down on the table*] Willy, what're you doin'? What the hell is goin' on in your head?

WILLY: Why? I'm simply . . .

CHARLEY: I offered you a job. You can make fifty dollars a week. And I won't send you on the road.

WILLY: I've got a job.

CHARLEY: Without pay? What kind of a job is a job without pay? [*He rises*] Now, look, kid, enough is enough. I'm no genius but I know when I'm being insulted.

WILLY: Insulted!

CHARLEY: Why don't you want to work for me?

WILLY: What's the matter with you? I've got a job.

CHARLEY: Then what're you walkin' in here every week for?

WILLY: [*Getting up*] Well, if you don't want me to walk in here—

CHARLEY: I am offering you a job.

WILLY: I don't want your goddam job!

CHARLEY: When the hell are you going to grow up?

WILLY: [*Furiously*] You big ignoramus, if you say that to me again I'll rap you one! I don't care how big you are! [*He's ready to fight*]

[*Pause*]

CHARLEY: [*Kindly, going to him*] How much do you need, Willy?

WILLY: Charley, I'm strapped, I'm strapped. I don't know what to do. I was just fired.

CHARLEY: Howard fired you?

WILLY: That snotnose. Imagine that? I named him. I named him Howard.

CHARLEY: Willy, when're you gonna realize that them things don't mean anything? You named him Howard, but you can't sell that. The only thing you got in this world is what you can sell. And the funny thing is that you're a salesman, and you don't know that.

WILLY: I've always tried to think otherwise, I guess. I always felt that if a man was impressive, and well liked, that nothing—

CHARLEY: Why must everybody like you? Who liked J. P. Morgan? Was he impressive? In a Turkish bath he'd look like a butcher. But with his pockets on he was very well liked. Now listen, Willy, I know you don't like me, and nobody can say I'm in love with you, but I'll give you a job because—just

for the hell of it, put it that way. Now what do you say?

WILLY: I—I just can't work for you, Charley.

CHARLEY: What're you, jealous of me?

WILLY: I can't work for you, that's all, don't ask me why.

CHARLEY: [*Angered, takes out more bills*] You been jealous of me all your life, you damned fool! Here, pay your insurance. [*He puts the money in Willy's hand*]

WILLY: I'm keeping strict accounts.

CHARLEY: I've got some work to do. Take care of yourself. And pay your insurance.

WILLY: [*Moving to the right*] Funny, y'know? After all the highways, and the trains, and the appointments, and the years, you end up worth more dead than alive.

CHARLEY: Willy, nobody's worth nothin' dead. [*After a slight pause*] Did you hear what I said?

[Willy *stands still, dreaming*]

CHARLEY: Willy!

WILLY: Apologize to Bernard for me when you see him. I didn't mean to argue with him. He's a fine boy. They're all fine boys, and they'll end up big—all of them. Someday they'll all play tennis together. Wish me luck, Charley. He saw Bill Oliver today.

CHARLEY: Good luck.

WILLY: [*On the verge of tears*] Charley, you're the only friend I got. Isn't that a remarkable thing? [*He goes out*]

CHARLEY: Jesus!

[Charley *stares after him a moment and follows. All light blacks out. Suddenly raucous music is heard, and a red glow rises behind the screen at right.* Stanley, *a young waiter, appears, carrying a table, followed by* Happy, *who is carrying two chairs*]

STANLEY: [*Putting the table down*] That's all right, Mr. Loman, I can handle it myself. [*He turns and takes the chairs from* Happy *and places them at the table*]

HAPPY: [*Glancing around*] Oh, this is better.

STANLEY: Sure, in front there you're in the middle of all kinds a noise. Whenever you got a party, Mr. Loman, you just tell me and I'll put you back here. Y'know, there's a lotta people they don't like it private, because when they go out they like to see a lotta action around them because they're sick and tired to stay in the house by theirself. But I know you, you ain't from Hackensack. You know what I mean?

HAPPY: [*Sitting down*] So how's it coming, Stanley?

STANLEY: Ah, it's a dog's life. I only wish during the war they'd a took me in the Army. I coulda been dead by now.

HAPPY: My brother's back, Stanley.

STANLEY: Oh, he come back, heh? From the Far West.

HAPPY: Yeah, big cattle man, my brother, so treat him right. And my father's coming too.

STANLEY: Oh, your father too!

HAPPY: You got a couple of nice lobsters?

STANLEY: Hundred per cent, big.

HAPPY: I want them with the claws.

STANLEY: Don't worry, I don't give you no mice. [Happy *laughs*] How about some wine? It'll put a head on the meal.

HAPPY: No. You remember, Stanley, that recipe I brought you from overseas? With the champagne in it?

STANLEY: Oh, yeah, sure. I still got it tacked up yet in the kitchen. But that'll have to cost a buck apiece anyways.

HAPPY: That's all right.

STANLEY: What'd you, hit a number or somethin'?

HAPPY: No, it's a little celebration. My brother is —I think he pulled off a big deal today. I think we're going into business together.

STANLEY: Great! That's the best for you. Because a family business, you know what I mean?—that's the best.

HAPPY: That's what I think.

STANLEY: 'Cause what's the difference? Somebody steals? It's in the family. Know what I mean? [*Sotto voce*] Like this bartender here. The boss is goin' crazy what kinda leak he's got in the cash register. You put it in but it don't come out.

HAPPY: [*Raising his head*] Sh!

STANLEY: What?

HAPPY: You notice I wasn't lookin' right or left, was I?

STANLEY: No.

HAPPY: And my eyes are closed.

STANLEY: So what's the—?

HAPPY: Strudel's comin'.

STANLEY: [*Catching on, looks around*] Ah, no, there's no—

[*He breaks off as a furred, lavishly dressed girl enters and sits at the next table. Both follow her with their eyes*]

STANLEY: Geez, how'd ya know?

HAPPY: I got radar or something. [*Staring directly at her profile*] Oooooooo . . . Stanley.

STANLEY: I think that's for you, Mr. Loman.

HAPPY: Look at that mouth. Oh, God. And the binoculars.

STANLEY: Geez, you got a life, Mr. Loman.

HAPPY: Wait on her.

STANLEY: [*Going to the Girl's table*] Would you like a menu, ma'am?

GIRL: I'm expecting someone, but I'd like a—

HAPPY: Why don't you bring her—excuse me, miss, do you mind? I sell champagne, and I'd like you to try my brand. Bring her a champagne, Stanley.

GIRL: That's awfully nice of you.

HAPPY: Don't mention it. It's all company money. [*He laughs*]

GIRL: That's a charming product to be selling, *isn't it?*

HAPPY: Oh, gets to be like everything else. Selling is selling, y'know.

GIRL: I suppose.

HAPPY: You don't happen to sell, do you?

GIRL: No, I don't sell.

HAPPY: Would you object to a compliment from a stranger? You ought to be on a magazine cover.

GIRL: [*Looking at him a little archly*] I have been.

[*Stanley comes in with a glass of champagne*]

HAPPY: What'd I say before, Stanley? You see? She's a cover girl.

STANLEY: Oh, I could see, I could see.

HAPPY: [*To the Girl*] What magazine?

GIRL: Oh, a lot of them. [*She takes the drink*] Thank you.

HAPPY: You know what they say in France, don't you? "Champagne is the drink of the complexion" —Hya, Biff!

[*Biff has entered and sits with Happy*]

BIFF: Hello, kid. Sorry I'm late.

HAPPY: I just got here. Uh, Miss—?

GIRL: Forsythe.

HAPPY: Miss Forsythe, this is my brother.

BIFF: Is Dad here?

HAPPY: His name is Biff. You might've heard of him. Great football player.

GIRL: Really? What team?

HAPPY: Are you familiar with football?

GIRL: No, I'm afraid I'm not.

HAPPY: Biff is quarterback with the New York Giants.

GIRL: Well, that is nice, isn't it? [*She drinks*]

HAPPY: Good health.

GIRL: I'm happy to meet you.

HAPPY: That's my name. Hap. It's really Harold, but at West Point they called me Happy.

GIRL: [*Now really impressed*] Oh, I see. How do you do? [*She turns her profile*]

BIFF: Isn't Dad coming?

HAPPY: You want her?

BIFF: Oh, I could never make that.

HAPPY: I remember the time that idea would never come into your head. Where's the old confidence, Biff?

BIFF: I just saw Oliver—

HAPPY: Wait a minute. I've got to see that old confidence again. Do you want her? She's on call.

BIFF: Oh, no. [*He turns to look at the Girl*]

HAPPY: I'm telling you. Watch this. [*Turning to the Girl*] Honey? [*She turns to him*] Are you busy?

GIRL: Well, I am . . . but I could make a phone call.

HAPPY: Do that, will you, honey? And see if you can get a friend. We'll be here for a while. Biff is one of the greatest football players in the country.

GIRL: [*Standing up*] Well, I'm certainly happy to meet you.

HAPPY: Come back soon.

GIRL: I'll try.

HAPPY: Don't try, honey, try hard.

[*The* Girl *exits. Stanley* follows, shaking his head in bewildered admiration]

HAPPY: Isn't that a shame now? A beautiful girl like that? That's why I can't get married. There's not a good woman in a thousand. New York is loaded with them, kid!

BIFF: Hap, look—

HAPPY: I told you she was on call!

BIFF: [*Strangely unnerved*] Cut it out, will ya? I want to say something to you.

HAPPY: Did you see Oliver?

BIFF: I saw him all right. Now look, I want to tell Dad a couple of things and I want you to help me.

HAPPY: What? Is he going to back you?

BIFF: Are you crazy? You're out of your goddam head, you know that?

HAPPY: Why? What happened?

BIFF: [*Breathlessly*] I did a terrible thing today, Hap. It's been the strangest day I ever went through. I'm all numb, I swear.

HAPPY: You mean he wouldn't see you?

BIFF: Well, I waited six hours for him, see? All day. Kept sending my name in. Even tried to date his secretary so she'd get me to him, but no soap.

HAPPY: Because you're not showin' the old confidence, Biff. He remembered you, didn't he?

BIFF: [*Stopping* Happy *with a gesture*] Finally, about five o'clock, he comes out. Didn't remember who I was or anything. I felt like such an idiot, Hap.

HAPPY: Did you tell him my Florida idea?

BIFF: He walked away. I saw him for one minute. I got so mad I could've torn the walls down! How the hell did I ever get the idea I was a salesman there? I even believed myself that I'd been a salesman for him! And then he gave me one look and— I realized what a ridiculous lie my whole life has been! We've been talking in a dream for fifteen years. I was a shipping clerk.

HAPPY: What'd you do?

BIFF: [*With great tension and wonder*] Well, he left, see. And the secretary went out. I was all alone in the waiting-room. I don't know what came over me, Hap. The next thing I know I'm in his office— paneled walls, everything. I can't explain it. I—Hap, I took his fountain pen.

HAPPY: Geez, did he catch you?

BIFF: I ran out. I ran down all eleven flights. I ran and ran and ran.

HAPPY: That was an awful dumb—what'd you do that for?

BIFF: [*Agonized*] I don't know, I just—wanted to take something, I don't know. You gotta help me, Hap, I'm gonna tell Pop.

HAPPY: You crazy? What for?

BIFF: Hap, he's got to understand that I'm not the

man somebody lends that kind of money to. He thinks I've been spiting him all these years and it's eating him up.

HAPPY: That's just it. You tell him something nice.

BIFF: I can't.

HAPPY: Say you got a lunch date with Oliver tomorrow.

BIFF: So what do I do tomorrow?

HAPPY: You leave the house tomorrow and come back at night and say Oliver is thinking it over. And he thinks it over for a couple of weeks, and gradually it fades away and nobody's the worse.

BIFF: But it'll go on forever!

HAPPY: Dad is never so happy as when he's looking forward to something!

[Willy *enters*]

HAPPY: Hello, scout!

WILLY: Gee, I haven't been here in years!

[Stanley *has followed* Willy *in and sets a chair for him.* Stanley *starts off but* Happy *stops him*]

HAPPY: Stanley!

[Stanley *stands by, waiting for an order*]

BIFF: [*Going to* Willy *with guilt, as to an invalid*] Sit down, Pop. You want a drink?

WILLY: Sure, I don't mind.

BIFF: Let's get a load on.

WILLY: You look worried.

BIFF: N-no. [*To* Stanley] Scotch all around. Make it doubles.

STANLEY: Doubles, right. [*He goes*]

WILLY: You had a couple already, didn't you?

BIFF: Just a couple, yeah.

WILLY: Well, what happened, boy? [*Nodding affirmatively, with a smile*] Everything go all right?

BIFF: [*Takes a breath, then reaches out and grasps* Willy's *hand*] Pal . . . [*He is smiling bravely, and* Willy *is smiling too*] I had an experience today.

HAPPY: Terrific, Pop.

WILLY: That so? What happened?

BIFF: [*High, slightly alcoholic, above the earth*] I'm going to tell you everything from first to last. It's been a strange day. [*Silence. He looks around, composes himself as best he can, but his breath keeps breaking the rhythm of his voice*] I had to wait quite a while for him, and—

WILLY: Oliver?

BIFF: Yeah, Oliver. All day, as a matter of cold fact. And a lot of—instances—facts, Pop, facts about my life came back to me. Who was it, Pop? Who ever said I was a salesman with Oliver?

WILLY: Well, you were.

BIFF: No, Dad, I was a shipping clerk.

WILLY: But you were practically—

BIFF: [*With determination*] Dad, I don't know who said it first, but I was never a salesman for Bill Oliver.

WILLY: What're you talking about?

BIFF: Let's hold on to the facts tonight, Pop.

We're not going to get anywhere bullin' around. I was a shipping clerk.

WILLY: [*Angrily*] All right, now listen to me—

BIFF: Why don't you let me finish?

WILLY: I'm not interested in stories about the past or any crap of that kind because the woods are burning, boys, you understand? There's a big blaze going on all around. I was fired today.

BIFF: [*Shocked*] How could you be?

WILLY: I was fired, and I'm looking for a little good news to tell your mother, because the woman has waited and the woman has suffered. The gist of it is that I haven't got a story left in my head, Biff. So don't give me a lecture about facts and aspects. I am not interested. Now what've you got to say to me?

[*Stanley enters with three drinks. They wait until he leaves*]

WILLY: Did you see Oliver?

BIFF: Jesus, Dad!

WILLY: You mean you didn't go up there?

HAPPY: Sure he went up there.

BIFF: I did. I saw him. How could they fire you?

WILLY: [*On the edge of his chair*] What kind of a welcome did he give you?

BIFF: He won't even let you work on commission?

WILLY: I'm out! [*Driving*] So tell me, he gave you a warm welcome?

HAPPY: Sure, Pop, sure!

BIFF: [*Driven*] Well, it was kind of—

WILLY: I was wondering if he'd remember you. [*To* Happy] Imagine, man doesn't see him for ten, twelve years and gives him that kind of a welcome!

HAPPY: Damn right!

BIFF: [*Trying to return to the offensive*] Pop, look—

WILLY: You know why he remembered you, don't you? Because you impressed him in those days.

BIFF: Let's talk quietly and get this down to the facts, huh?

WILLY: [*As though* Biff *had been interrupting*] Well, what happened? It's great news, Biff. Did he take you into his office or'd you talk in the waiting-room?

BIFF: Well, he came in, see, and—

WILLY: [*With a big smile*] What'd he say? Betcha he threw his arm around you.

BIFF: Well, he kinda—

WILLY: He's a fine man. [*To* Happy] Very hard man to see, y'know.

HAPPY: [*Agreeing*] Oh, I know.

WILLY: [*To* Biff] Is that where you had the drinks?

BIFF: Yeah, he gave me a couple of—no, no!

HAPPY: [*Cutting in*] He told him my Florida idea.

WILLY: Don't interrupt. [*To* Biff] How'd he react to the Florida idea?

BIFF: Dad, will you give me a minute to explain?

WILLY: I've been waiting for you to explain since I sat down here! What happened? He took you into his office and what?

BIFF: Well—I talked. And—and he listened, see.

WILLY: Famous for the way he listens, y'know. What was his answer?

BIFF: His answer was— [*He breaks off, suddenly angry*] Dad, you're not letting me tell you what I want to tell you!

WILLY: [*Accusing, angered*] You didn't see him, did you?

BIFF: I did see him!

WILLY: What'd you insult him or something? You insulted him, didn't you?

BIFF: Listen, will you let me out of it, will you just let me out of it!

HAPPY: What the hell!

WILLY: Tell me what happened!

BIFF: [*To* Happy] I can't talk to him!

[*A single trumpet note jars the ear. The light of green leaves stains the house, which holds the air of night and a dream. Young Bernard enters and knocks on the door of the house*]

YOUNG BERNARD: [*Frantically*] Mrs. Loman, Mrs. Loman!

HAPPY: Tell him what happened!

BIFF: [*To* Happy] Shut up and leave me alone!

WILLY: No, no! You had to go and flunk math!

BIFF: What math? What're you talking about?

YOUNG BERNARD: Mrs. Loman, Mrs. Loman!

[*Linda appears in the house, as of old*]

WILLY: [*Wildly*] Math, math, math!

BIFF: Take it easy, Pop!

YOUNG BERNARD: Mrs. Loman!

WILLY: [*Furiously*] If you hadn't flunked you'd've been set by now!

BIFF: Now, look, I'm gonna tell you what happened, and you're going to listen to me.

YOUNG BERNARD: Mrs. Loman!

BIFF: I waited six hours—

HAPPY: What the hell are you saying?

BIFF: I kept sending in my name but he wouldn't see me. So finally he . . . [*He continues unheard as light fades low on the restaurant*]

YOUNG BERNARD: Biff flunked math!

LINDA: No!

YOUNG BERNARD: Birnbaum flunked him! They won't graduate him!

LINDA: But they have to. He's gotta go to the university. Where is he? Biff! Biff!

YOUNG BERNARD: No, he left. He went to Grand Central.

LINDA: Grand— You mean he went to Boston!

YOUNG BERNARD: Is Uncle Willy in Boston?

LINDA: Oh, maybe Willy can talk to the teacher. Oh, the poor, poor boy!

[*Light on house area snaps out*]

BIFF: [*At the table, now audible, holding up a gold fountain pen*] . . . so I'm washed up with Oliver, you understand? Are you listening to me?

WILLY: [*At a loss*] Yeah, sure. If you hadn't flunked—

BIFF: Flunked what? What're you talking about?

WILLY: Don't blame everything on me! I didn't flunk math—you did! What pen?

HAPPY: That was awful dumb, Biff, a pen like that is worth—

WILLY: [*Seeing the pen for the first time*] You took Oliver's pen?

BIFF: [*Weakening*] Dad, I just explained it to you.

WILLY: You stole Bill Oliver's fountain pen!

BIFF: I didn't exactly steal it! That's just what I've been explaining to you!

HAPPY: He had it in his hand and just then Oliver walked in, so he got nervous and stuck it in his pocket!

WILLY: My God, Biff!

BIFF: I never intended to do it, Dad!

OPERATOR'S VOICE: Standish Arms, good evening!

WILLY: [*Shouting*] I'm not in my room!

BIFF: [*Frightened*] Dad, what's the matter? [*He and* Happy *stand up*]

OPERATOR: Ringing Mr. Loman for you!

WILLY: I'm not there, stop it!

BIFF: [*Horrified, gets down on one knee before* Willy] Dad, I'll make good, I'll make good. [*Willy tries to get to his feet.* Biff *holds him down*] Sit down now.

WILLY: No, you're no good, you're no good for anything.

BIFF: I am, Dad, I'll find something else, you understand? Now don't worry about anything. [*He holds up* Willy's *face*] Talk to me, Dad.

OPERATOR: Mr. Loman does not answer. Shall I page him?

WILLY: [*Attempting to stand, as though to rush and silence the* Operator] No, no, no!

HAPPY: He'll strike something, Pop.

WILLY: No, no . . .

BIFF: [*Desperately, standing over* Willy] Pop, listen! Listen to me! I'm telling you something good. Oliver talked to his partner about the Florida idea. You listening? He—he talked to his partner, and he came to me . . . I'm going to be all right, you hear? Dad, listen to me, he said it was just a question of the amount!

WILLY: Then you . . . got it?

HAPPY: He's gonna be terrific, Pop!

WILLY: [*Trying to stand*] Then you got it, haven't you? You got it! You got it!

BIFF: [*Agonized, holds* Willy *down*] No, no. Look, Pop. I'm supposed to have lunch with them tomorrow. I'm just telling you this so you'll know that I can still make an impression, Pop. And I'll make good somewhere, but I can't go tomorrow, see?

WILLY: Why not? You simply—

BIFF: But the pen, Pop!

WILLY: You give it to him and tell him it was an oversight!

HAPPY: Sure, have lunch tomorrow!

BIFF: I can't say that—

WILLY: You were doing a crossword puzzle and accidentally used his pen!

BIFF: Listen, kid, I took those balls years ago, now I walk in with his fountain pen? That clinches it, don't you see? I can't face him like that! I'll try elsewhere.

PAGE'S VOICE: Paging Mr. Loman!

WILLY: Don't you want to be anything?

BIFF: Pop, how can I go back?

WILLY: You don't want to be anything, is that what's behind it?

BIFF: [*Now angry at* Willy *for not crediting his sympathy*] Don't take it that way! You think it was easy walking into that office after what I'd done to him? A team of horses couldn't have dragged me back to Bill Oliver!

WILLY: Then why'd you go?

BIFF: Why did I go? Why did I go! Look at you! Look at what's become of you!

[*Off left,* The Woman *laughs*]

WILLY: Biff, you're going to go to that lunch tomorrow, or—

BIFF: I can't go. I've got no appointment!

HAPPY: Biff, for . . . !

WILLY: Are you spiting me?

BIFF: Don't take it that way! Goddammit!

WILLY: [*Strikes* Biff *and falters away from the table*] You rotten little louse! Are you spiting me?

THE WOMAN: Someone's at the door, Willy!

BIFF: I'm no good, can't you see what I am?

HAPPY: [*Separating them*] Hey, you're in a restaurant! Now cut it out, both of you! [*The girls enter*] Hello, girls, sit down.

[The Woman *laughs, off left*]

MISS FORSYTHE: I guess we might as well. This is Letta.

THE WOMAN: Willy, are you going to wake up?

BIFF: [*Ignoring* Willy] How're ya, miss, sit down. What do you drink?

MISS FORSYTHE: Letta might not be able to stay long.

LETTA: I gotta get up very early tomorrow. I got jury duty. I'm so excited! Were you fellows ever on a jury?

BIFF: No, but I been in front of them! [*The girls laugh*] This is my father.

LETTA: Isn't he cute? Sit down with us, Pop.

HAPPY: Sit him down, Biff!

BIFF: [*Going to him*] Come on, slugger, drink us under the table. To hell with it! Come on, sit down, pal.

[*On* Biff's *last insistence,* Willy *is about to sit*]

THE WOMAN: [*Now urgently*] Willy, are you going to answer the door!

[The Woman's *call pulls* Willy *back. He starts right, befuddled*]

BIFF: Hey, where are you going?

WILLY: Open the door.

BIFF: The door?

WILLY: The washroom . . . the door . . . where's the door?

BIFF: [*Leading* Willy *to the left*] Just go straight down.

[Willy *moves left*]

THE WOMAN: Willy, Willy, are you going to get up, get up, get up, get up?

[Willy *exits left*]

LETTA: I think it's sweet you bring your daddy along.

MISS FORSYTHE: Oh, he isn't really your father!

BIFF: [*At left to her resentfully*] Miss Forsythe, you've just seen a prince walk by. A fine, troubled prince. A hard-working, unappreciated prince. A pal, you understand? A good companion. Always for his boys.

LETTA: That's so sweet.

HAPPY: Well, girls, what's the program? We're wasting time. Come on, Biff. Gather round. Where would you like to go?

BIFF: Why don't you do something for him?

HAPPY: Me!

BIFF: Don't you give a damn for him, Hap?

HAPPY: What're you talking about? I'm the one who—

BIFF: I sense it, you don't give a good goddam about him. [*He takes the rolled-up hose from his pocket and puts it on the table in front of* Happy] Look what I found in the cellar, for Christ's sake. How can you bear to let it go on?

HAPPY: Me? Who goes away? Who runs off and—

BIFF: Yeah, but he doesn't mean anything to you. You could help him—I can't! Don't you understand what I'm talking about? He's going to kill himself, don't you know that?

HAPPY: Don't I know it! Me!

BIFF: Hap, help him! Jesus . . . help him . . . Help me, help me, I can't bear to look at his face! [*Ready to weep, he hurries out, up right*]

HAPPY: [*Starting after him*] Where are you going?

MISS FORSYTHE: What's he so mad about?

HAPPY: Come on, girls, we'll catch up with him.

MISS FORSYTHE: [*As* Happy *pushes her out*] Say, I don't like that temper of his!

HAPPY: He's just a little overstrung, he'll be all right!

WILLY: [*Off left, as* The Woman *laughs*] Don't answer! Don't answer!

LETTA: Don't you want to tell your father—

HAPPY: No, that's not my father. He's just a guy. Come on, we'll catch Biff, and, honey, we're going to paint this town! Stanley, where's the check! Hey, Stanley!

[*They exit.* Stanley *looks toward left*]

STANLEY: [*Calling to* Happy *indignantly*] Mr. Loman! Mr. Loman!

[Stanley *picks up a chair and follows them off. Knocking is heard off left.* The Woman *enters, laughing.* Willy *follows her. She is in a black*

slip; he is buttoning his shirt. Raw, sensuous music accompanies their speech.]

WILLY: Will you stop laughing? Will you stop?

THE WOMAN: Aren't you going to answer the door? He'll wake the whole hotel.

WILLY: I'm not expecting anybody.

THE WOMAN: Whyn't you have another drink, honey, and stop being so damn self-centered?

WILLY: I'm so lonely.

THE WOMAN: You know you ruined me, Willy? From now on, whenever you come to the office, I'll see that you go right through to the buyers. No waiting at my desk any more, Willy. You ruined me.

WILLY: That's nice of you to say that.

THE WOMAN: Gee, you are self-centered! Why so sad? You are the saddest, self-centeredest soul I ever did see-saw. [*She laughs. He kisses her*] Come on inside, drummer boy. It's silly to be dressing in the middle of the night. [*As knocking is heard*] Aren't you going to answer the door?

WILLY: They're knocking on the wrong door.

THE WOMAN: But I felt the knocking. And he heard us talking in here. Maybe the hotel's on fire!

WILLY: [*His terror rising*] It's a mistake.

THE WOMAN: Then tell him to go away!

WILLY: There's nobody there.

THE WOMAN: It's getting on my nerves, Willy. There's somebody standing out there and it's getting on my nerves!

WILLY: [*Pushing her away from him*] All right, stay in the bathroom here, and don't come out. I think there's a law in Massachusetts about it, so don't come out. It may be that new room clerk. He looked very mean. So don't come out. It's a mistake, there's no fire.

[*The knocking is heard again. He takes a few steps away from her, and vanishes into the wing. The light follows him, and now he is facing* Young Biff, *who carries a suitcase.* Biff *steps toward him. The music is gone*]

BIFF: Why didn't you answer?

WILLY: Biff! What are you doing in Boston?

BIFF: Why didn't you answer? I've been knocking for five minutes, I called you on the phone—

WILLY: I just heard you. I was in the bathroom and had the door shut. Did anything happen home?

BIFF: Dad—I let you down.

WILLY: What do you mean?

BIFF: Dad . . .

WILLY: Biffo, what's this about? [*Putting his arm around* Biff] Come on, let's go downstairs and get you a malted.

BIFF: Dad, I flunked math.

WILLY: Not for the term?

BIFF: The term. I haven't got enough credits to graduate.

WILLY: You mean to say Bernard wouldn't give you the answers?

BIFF: He did, he tried, but I only got a sixty-one.

WILLY: And they wouldn't give you four points?

BIFF: Birnbaum refused absolutely. I begged him, Pop, but he won't give me those points. You gotta talk to him before they close the school. Because if he saw the kind of man you are, and you just talked to him in your way, I'm sure he'd come through for me. The class came right before practice, see, and I didn't go enough. Would you talk to him? He'd like you, Pop. You know the way you could talk.

WILLY: You're on. We'll drive right back.

BIFF: Oh, Dad, good work! I'm sure he'll change it for you!

WILLY: Go downstairs and tell the clerk I'm checkin' out. Go right down.

BIFF: Yes, sir! See, the reason he hates me, Pop—one day he was late for class so I got up at the blackboard and imitated him. I crossed my eyes and talked with a lithp.

WILLY: [Laughing] You did? The kids like it?

BIFF: They nearly died laughing!

WILLY: Yeah? What'd you do?

BIFF: The thquare root of thixthy twee is . . . [Willy bursts out laughing; Biff joins him] And in the middle of it he walked in!

[Willy laughs and The Woman joins in offstage]

WILLY: [Without hesitation] Hurry downstairs and—

BIFF: Somebody in there?

WILLY: No, that was next door.

[The Woman laughs offstage]

BIFF: Somebody got in your bathroom!

WILLY: No, it's the next room, there's a party—

THE WOMAN: [Enters, laughing. She lisps this] Can I come in? There's something in the bathtub, Willy, and it's moving!

[Willy looks at Biff, who is staring open-mouthed and horrified at The Woman]

WILLY: Ah—you better go back to your room. They must be finished painting by now. They're painting her room so I let her take a shower here. Go back, go back . . . [He pushes her]

THE WOMAN: [Resisting] But I've got to get dressed, Willy, I can't—

WILLY: Get out of here! Go back, go back . . . [Suddenly striving for the ordinary] This is Miss Francis, Biff, she's a buyer. They're painting her room. Go back, Miss Francis, go back . . .

THE WOMAN: But my clothes, I can't go out naked in the hall!

WILLY: [Pushing her offstage] Get outa here! Go back, go back!

[Biff slowly sits down on his suitcase as the argument continues offstage]

THE WOMAN: Where's my stockings? You promised me stockings, Willy!

WILLY: I have no stockings here!

THE WOMAN: You had two boxes of size nine sheers for me, and I want them!

WILLY: Here, for God's sake, will you get outa here¹

THE WOMAN: [Enters holding a box of stockings] I just hope there's nobody in the hall. That's all I hope. [To Biff] Are you football or baseball?

BIFF: Football.

THE WOMAN: [Angry, humiliated] That's me too. G'night. [She snatches her clothes from Willy, and walks out]

WILLY: [After a pause] Well, better get going. I want to get to the school first thing in the morning. Get my suits out of the closet. I'll get my valise. [Biff doesn't move] What's the matter? [Biff remains motionless, tears falling] She's a buyer. Buys for J. H. Simmons. She lives down the hall—they're painting. You don't imagine—[He breaks off. After a pause] Now listen, pal, she's just a buyer. She sees merchandise in her room and they have to keep it looking just so . . . [Pause. Assuming command] All right, get my suits. [Biff doesn't move] Now stop crying and do as I say. I gave you an order. Biff, I gave you an order! Is that what you do when I give you an order? How dare you cry! [Putting his arm around Biff] Now look, Biff, when you grow up you'll understand about these things. You mustn't—you mustn't overemphasize a thing like this. I'll see Birnbaum first thing in the morning.

BIFF: Never mind.

WILLY: [Getting down beside Biff] Never mind! He's going to give you those points. I'll see to it.

BIFF: He wouldn't listen to you.

WILLY: He certainly will listen to me. You need those points for the U. of Virginia.

BIFF: I'm not going there.

WILLY: Heh? If I can't get him to change that mark you'll make it up in summer school. You've got all summer to—

BIFF: [His weeping breaking from him] Dad . . .

WILLY: [Infected by it] Oh, my boy . . .

BIFF: Dad . . .

WILLY: She's nothing to me, Biff. I was lonely, I was terribly lonely.

BIFF: You—you gave her Mama's stockings! [His tears break through and he rises to go]

WILLY: [Grabbing for Biff] I gave you an order!

BIFF: Don't touch me, you—liar!

WILLY: Apologize for that!

BIFF: You fake! You phony little fake! You fake! [Overcome, he turns quickly and weeping fully goes out with his suitcase. Willy is left on the floor on his knees]

WILLY: I gave you an order! Biff, come back here or I'll beat you! Come back here! I'll whip you!

[Stanley comes quickly from the right and stands in front of Willy]

WILLY: [Shouts at Stanley] I gave you an order . . .

STANLEY: Hey, let's pick it up, pick it up, Mr. Loman. [He helps Willy to his feet] Your boys left with the chippies. They said they'll see you home.

[A second waiter watches some distance away]

WILLY: But we were supposed to have dinner together.

[*Music is heard,* Willy's *theme*]

STANLEY: Can you make it?

WILLY: I'll—sure, I can make it. [*Suddenly concerned about his clothes*] Do I—I look all right?

STANLEY: Sure, you look all right. [*He flicks a speck off* Willy's *lapel*]

WILLY: Here—here's a dollar.

STANLEY: Oh, your son paid me. It's all right.

WILLY: [*Putting it in* Stanley's *hand*] No, take it. You're a good boy.

STANLEY: Oh, no, you don't have to . . .

WILLY: Here—here's some more, I don't need it any more. [*After a slight pause*] Tell me—is there a seed store in the neighborhood?

STANLEY: Seeds? You mean like to plant?

[*As* Willy *turns,* Stanley *slips the money back into his jacket pocket*]

WILLY: Yes. Carrots, peas . . .

STANLEY: Well, there's hardware stores on Sixth Avenue, but it may be too late now.

WILLY: [*Anxiously*] Oh, I'd better hurry. I've got to get some seeds. [*He starts off to the right*] I've got to get some seeds, right away. Nothing's planted. I don't have a thing in the ground.

[Willy *hurries out as the light goes down.* Stanley *moves over to the right after him, watches him off. The other waiter has been staring at* Willy]

STANLEY: [*To the waiter*] Well, whatta you looking at?

[*The waiter picks up the chairs and moves off right.* Stanley *takes the table and follows him. The light fades on this area. There is a long pause, the sound of the flute coming over. The light gradually rises on the kitchen, which is empty.* Happy *appears at the door of the house, followed by* Biff. Happy *is carrying a large bunch of long-stemmed roses. He enters the kitchen, looks around for* Linda. *Not seeing her, he turns to* Biff, *who is just outside the house door, and makes a gesture with his hands, indicating "Not here, I guess." He looks into the living-room and freezes. Inside,* Linda, *unseen, is seated,* Willy's *coat on her lap. She rises ominously and quietly and moves toward* Happy, *who backs up into the kitchen, afraid*]

HAPPY: Hey, what're you doing up? [Linda *says nothing but moves toward him implacably*] Where's Pop? [*He keeps backing to the right, and now* Linda *is in full view in the doorway to the living-room*] Is he sleeping?

LINDA: Where were you?

HAPPY: [*Trying to laugh it off*] We met two girls, Mom, very fine types. Here, we brought you some flowers. [*Offering them to her*] Put them in your room, Ma.

[*She knocks them to the floor at* Biff's *feet. He*

has now come inside and closed the door behind him. She stares at Biff, silent]

HAPPY: Now what'd you do that for? Mom, I want you to have some flowers—

LINDA: [*Cutting* Happy *off, violently to* Biff] Don't you care whether he lives or dies?

HAPPY: [*Going to the stairs*] Come upstairs, Biff.

BIFF: [*With a flare of disgust, to* Happy] Go away from me! [*To* Linda] What do you mean, lives or dies? Nobody's dying around here, pal.

LINDA: Get out of my sight! Get out of here!

BIFF: I wanna see the boss.

LINDA: You're not going near him!

BIFF: Where is he? [*He moves into the living-room and* Linda *follows*]

LINDA: [*Shouting after* Biff] You invite him for dinner. He looks forward to it all day—[Biff *appears in his parents' bedroom, looks around, and exits*]—and then you desert him there. There's no stranger you'd do that to!

HAPPY: Why? He had a swell time with us. Listen, when I—[Linda *comes back into the kitchen*]—desert him I hope I don't outlive the day!

LINDA: Get out of here!

HAPPY: Now look, Mom . . .

LINDA: Did you have to go to women tonight? You and your lousy rotten whores!

[Biff *re-enters the kitchen*]

HAPPY: Mom, all we did was follow Biff around trying to cheer him up! [*To* Biff] Boy, what a night you gave me!

LINDA: Get out of here, both of you, and don't come back! I don't want you tormenting him any more. Go on now, get your things together! [*To* Biff] You can sleep in his apartment. [*She starts to pick up the flowers and stops herself*] Pick up this stuff, I'm not your maid any more. Pick it up, you bum, you!

[Happy *turns his back to her in refusal.* Biff *slowly moves over and gets down on his knees, picking up the flowers*]

LINDA: You're a pair of animals! Not one, not another living soul would have had the cruelty to walk out on that man in a restaurant!

BIFF: [*Not looking at her*] Is that what he said?

LINDA: He didn't have to say anything. He was so humiliated he nearly limped when he came in.

HAPPY: But, Mom, he had a great time with us—

BIFF: [*Cutting him off violently*] Shut up!

[*Without another word,* Happy *goes upstairs*]

LINDA: You! You didn't even go in to see if he was all right!

BIFF: [*Still on the floor in front of* Linda, *the flowers in his hand, with self-loathing*] No. Didn't. Didn't do a damned thing. How do you like that, heh? Left him babbling in a toilet.

LINDA: You louse. You . . .

BIFF: Now you hit it on the nose! [*He gets up, throws the flowers in the wastebasket*] The scum of the earth, and you're looking at him!

LINDA: Get out of here!

BIFF: I gotta talk to the boss, Mom. Where is he?

LINDA: You're not going near him. Get out of this house!

BIFF: [*With absolute assurance, determination*] No. We're gonna have an abrupt conversation, him and me.

LINDA: You're not talking to him!

[*Hammering is heard from outside the house, off right. Biff turns toward the noise*]

LINDA: [*Suddenly pleading*] Will you please leave him alone?

BIFF: What's he doing out there?

LINDA: He's planting the garden!

BIFF: [*Quietly*] Now? Oh, my God!

[*Biff moves outside, Linda following. The light dies down on them and comes up on the center of the apron as Willy walks into it. He is carrying a flashlight, a hoe, and a handful of seed packets. He raps the top of the hoe sharply to fix it firmly, and then moves to the left, measuring off the distance with his foot. He holds the flashlight to look at the seed packets, reading off the instructions. He is in the blue of night*]

WILLY: Carrots . . . quarter-inch apart. Rows . . . one-foot rows. [*He measures it off*] One foot. [*He puts down a package and measures off*] Beets. [*He puts down another package and measures again*] Lettuce. [*He reads the package, puts it down*] One foot— [*He breaks off as Ben appears at the right and moves slowly down to him*] What a proposition, ts, ts. Terrific, terrific. 'Cause she's suffered, Ben, the woman has suffered. You understand me? A man can't go out the way he came in, Ben, a man has got to add up to something. You can't, you can't— [*Ben moves toward him as though to interrupt*] You gotta consider, now. Don't answer so quick. Remember, it's a guaranteed twenty-thousand dollar proposition. Now look, Ben, I want you to go through the ins and outs of this thing with me. I've got nobody to talk to, Ben, and the woman has suffered, you hear me?

BEN: [*Standing still, considering*] What's the proposition?

WILLY: It's twenty thousand dollars on the barrel-head. Guaranteed, gilt-edged, you understand?

BEN: You don't want to make a fool of yourself. They might not honor the policy.

WILLY: How can they dare refuse? Didn't I work like a coolie to meet every premium on the nose? And now they don't pay off? Impossible!

BEN: It's called a cowardly thing, William.

WILLY: Why? Does it take more guts to stand here the rest of my life ringing up a zero?

BEN: [*Yielding*] That's a point, William. [*He moves, thinking, turns*] And twenty thousand—that is something one can feel with the hand, it is there.

WILLY: [*Now assured, with rising power*] Oh, Ben, that's the whole beauty of it! I see it like a diamond, shining in the dark, hard and rough, that I can pick up and touch in my hand. Not like—like an appointment! This would not be another damned-fool appointment, Ben, and it changes all the aspects. Because he thinks I'm nothing, see, and so he spites me. But the funeral— [*Straightening up*] Ben, that funeral will be massive! They'll come from Maine, Massachusetts, Vermont, New Hampshire! All the old-timers with the strange license plates—that boy will be thunder-struck, Ben, because he never realized—I am known! Rhode Island, New York, New Jersey—I am known, Ben, and he'll see it with his eyes once and for all. He'll see what I am, Ben! He's in for a shock, that boy!

BEN: [*Coming down to the edge of the garden*] He'll call you a coward.

WILLY: [*Suddenly fearful*] No, that would be terrible.

BEN: Yes. And a damned fool.

WILLY: No, no, he mustn't, I won't have that! [*He is broken and desperate*]

BEN: He'll hate you, William.

[*The gay music of the Boys is heard*]

WILLY: Oh, Ben, how do we get back to all the great times? Used to be so full of light, and comradeship, the sleigh-riding in winter, and the ruddiness on his cheeks. And always some kind of good news coming up, always something nice coming up ahead. And never even let me carry the valises in the house, and simonizing, simonizing that little red car! Why, why can't I give him something and not have him hate me?

BEN: Let me think about it. [*He glances at his watch*] I still have a little time. Remarkable proposition, but you've got to be sure you're not making a fool of yourself.

[*Ben drifts off upstage and goes out of sight. Biff comes down from the left*]

WILLY: [*Suddenly conscious of Biff, turns and looks up at him, then begins picking up the packages of seeds in confusion*] Where the hell is that seed? [*Indignantly*] You can't see nothing out here! They boxed in the whole goddam neighborhood!

BIFF: There are people all around here. Don't you realize that?

WILLY: I'm busy. Don't bother me.

BIFF: [*Taking the hoe from Willy*] I'm saying good-by to you, Pop. [*Willy looks at him, silent, unable to move*] I'm not coming back any more.

WILLY: You're not going to see Oliver tomorrow?

BIFF: I've got no appointment, Dad.

WILLY: He put his arm around you, and you've got no appointment?

BIFF: Pop, get this now, will you? Everytime I've left it's been a fight that sent me out of here. Today I realized something about myself and I tried to explain it to you and I—I think I'm just not smart enough to make any sense out of it for you. To hell with whose fault it is or anything like that. [*He takes

Willy's *arm*] Let's just wrap it up, heh? Come on in, we'll tell Mom. [*He gently tries to pull* Willy *to left*]

WILLY: [*Frozen, immobile, with guilt in his voice*] No, I don't want to see her.

BIFF: Come on! [*He pulls again, and* Willy *tries to pull away*]

WILLY: [*Highly nervous*] No, no, I don't want to see her.

BIFF: [*Tries to look into* Willy's *face, as if to find the answer there*] Why don't you want to see her?

WILLY: [*More harshly now*] Don't bother me, will you?

BIFF: What do you mean, you don't want to see her? You don't want them calling you yellow, do you? This isn't your fault; it's me, I'm a bum. Now come inside! [Willy *strains to get away*] Did you hear what I said to you?

[Willy *pulls away and quickly goes by himself into the house.* Biff *follows*]

LINDA: [*To* Willy] Did you plant, dear?

BIFF: [*At the door, to* Linda] All right, we had it out. I'm going and I'm not writing any more.

LINDA: [*Going to* Willy *in the kitchen*] I think that's the best way, dear. 'Cause there's no use drawing it out, you'll just never get along.

[Willy *doesn't respond*]

BIFF: People ask where I am and what I'm doing, you don't know, and you don't care. That way it'll be off your mind and you can start brightening up again. All right? That clears it, doesn't it? [Willy *is silent, and* Biff *goes to him*] You gonna wish me luck, scout? [*He extends his hand*] What do you say?

LINDA: Shake his hand, Willy.

WILLY: [*Turning to her, seething with hurt*] There's no necessity to mention the pen at all, y'know.

BIFF: [*Gently*] I've got no appointment, Dad.

WILLY: [*Erupting fiercely*] He put his arm around . . . ?

BIFF: Dad, you're never going to see what I am, so what's the use of arguing? If I strike oil I'll send you a check. Meantime forget I'm alive.

WILLY: [*To* Linda] Spite, see?

BIFF: Shake hands, Dad.

WILLY: Not my hand.

BIFF: I was hoping not to go this way.

WILLY: Well, this is the way you're going. Goodby.

[Biff *looks at him a moment, then turns sharply and goes to the stairs*]

WILLY: [*Stops him with*] May you rot in hell if you leave this house!

BIFF: [*Turning*] Exactly what is it that you want from me?

WILLY: I want you to know, on the train, in the mountains, in the valleys, wherever you go, that you cut down your life for spite!

BIFF: No, no.

WILLY: Spite, spite, is the word of your undoing!

And when you're down and out, remember what did it. When you're rotting somewhere beside the railroad tracks, remember, and don't you dare blame it on me!

BIFF: I'm not blaming it on you!

WILLY: I won't take the rap for this, you hear?

[Happy *comes down the stairs and stands on the bottom step, watching*]

BIFF: That's just what I'm telling you!

WILLY: [*Sinking into a chair at the table, with full accusation*] You're trying to put a knife in me—don't think I don't know what you're doing!

BIFF: All right, phony! Then let's lay it on the line. [*He whips the rubber tube out of his pocket and puts it on the table*]

HAPPY: You crazy—

LINDA: Biff! [*She moves to grab the hose, but* Biff *holds it down with his hand*]

BIFF: Leave it there! Don't move it!

WILLY: [*Not looking at it*] What is that?

BIFF: You know goddam well what that is.

WILLY: [*Caged, wanting to escape*] I never saw that.

BIFF: You saw it. The mice didn't bring it into the cellar! What is this supposed to do, make a hero out of you? This supposed to make me sorry for you?

WILLY: Never heard of it.

BIFF: There'll be no pity for you, you hear it? No pity!

WILLY: [*To* Linda] You hear the spite!

BIFF: No, you're going to hear the truth—what you are and what I am!

LINDA: Stop it!

WILLY: Spite!

HAPPY: [*Coming down toward* Biff] You cut it now!

BIFF: [*To* Happy] The man don't know who we are! The man is gonna know! [*To* Willy] We never told the truth for ten minutes in this house!

HAPPY: We always told the truth!

BIFF: [*Turning on him*] You big blow, are you the assistant buyer? You're one of the two assistants to the assistant, aren't you?

HAPPY: Well, I'm practically—

BIFF: You're practically full of it! We all are! And I'm through with it. [*To* Willy] Now hear this, Willy, this is me.

WILLY: I know you!

BIFF: You know why I had no address for three months? I stole a suit in Kansas City and I was in jail. [*To* Linda, *who is sobbing*] Stop crying. I'm through with it.

[Linda *turns away from them, her hands covering her face*]

WILLY: I suppose that's my fault!

BIFF: I stole myself out of every good job since high school!

WILLY: And whose fault is that?

BIFF: And I never got anywhere because you blew

me so full of hot air I could never stand taking orders from anybody! That's whose fault it is!

WILLY: I hear that!

LINDA: Don't, Biff!

BIFF: It's goddam time you heard that! I had to be boss big shot in two weeks, and I'm through with it!

WILLY: Then hang yourself! For spite, hang yourself!

BIFF: No! Nobody's hanging himself, Willy! I ran down eleven flights with a pen in my hand today. And suddenly I stopped, you hear me? And in the middle of that office building, do you hear this? I stopped in the middle of that building and I saw— the sky. I saw the things that I love in this world. The work and the food and time to sit and smoke. And I looked at the pen and said to myself, what the hell am I grabbing this for? Why am I trying to become what I don't want to be? What am I doing in an office, making a contemptuous, begging fool of myself, when all I want is out there, waiting for me the minute I say I know who I am! Why can't I say that, Willy? [*He tries to make* Willy *face him, but* Willy *pulls away and moves to the left*]

WILLY: [*With hatred, threateningly*] The door of your life is wide open!

BIFF: Pop! I'm a dime a dozen, and so are you!

WILLY: [*Turning on him now in an uncontrolled outburst*] I am not a dime a dozen! I am Willy Loman, and you are Biff Loman!

[Biff *starts for* Willy, *but is blocked by* Happy. *In his fury,* Biff *seems on the verge of attacking his father*]

BIFF: I am not a leader of men, Willy, and neither are you. You were never anything but a hard-working drummer who landed in the ash can like all the rest of them! I'm one dollar an hour, Willy! I tried seven states and couldn't raise it. A buck an hour! Do you gather my meaning! I'm not bringing home any prizes any more, and you're going to stop waiting for me to bring them home!

WILLY: [*Directly to* Biff] You vengeful, spiteful mut!

[Biff *breaks from* Happy. Willy, *in fright, starts up the stairs.* Biff *grabs him*]

BIFF: [*At the peak of his fury*] Pop, I'm nothing! I'm nothing, Pop. Can't you understand that? There's no spite in it any more. I'm just what I am, that's all.

[Biff's *fury has spent itself, and he breaks down, sobbing, holding on to* Willy, *who dumbly fumbles for* Biff's *face*]

WILLY: [*Astonished*] What're you doing? What're you doing? [*To* Linda] Why is he crying?

BIFF: [*Crying, broken*] Will you let me go, for Christ's sake? Will you take that phony dream and burn it before something happens? [*Struggling to contain himself, he pulls away and moves to the stairs*] I'll go in the morning. Put him—put him to bed. [*Exhausted,* Biff *moves up the stairs to his room*]

WILLY: [*After a long pause, astonished, elevated*] Isn't that—isn't that remarkable? Biff—he likes me!

LINDA: He loves you, Willy!

HAPPY: [*Deeply moved*] Always did, Pop.

WILLY: Oh, Biff! [*Staring wildly*] He cried! Cried to me. [*He is choking with his love, and now cries out his promise*] That boy—that boy is going to be magnificent!

[Ben *appears in the light just outside the kitchen*]

BEN: Yes, outstanding, with twenty thousand behind him.

LINDA: [*Sensing the racing of his mind, fearfully, carefully*] Now come to bed, Willy. It's all settled now.

WILLY: [*Finding it difficult not to rush out of the house*] Yes, we'll sleep. Come on. Go to sleep, Hap.

BEN: And it does take a great kind of a man to crack the jungle.

[*In accents of dread,* Ben's *idyllic music starts up*]

HAPPY: [*His arm around* Linda] I'm getting married, Pop, don't forget it. I'm changing everything. I'm gonna run that department before the year is up. You'll see, Mom. [*He kisses her*]

BEN: The jungle is dark but full of diamonds, Willy.

[Willy *turns, moves, listening to* Ben]

LINDA: Be good. You're both good boys, just act that way, that's all.

HAPPY: 'Night, Pop. [*He goes upstairs*]

LINDA: [*To* Willy] Come, dear.

BEN: [*With greater force*] One must go in to fetch a diamond out.

WILLY: [*To* Linda, *as he moves slowly along the edge of the kitchen, toward the door*] I just want to get settled down, Linda. Let me sit alone for a little.

LINDA: [*Almost uttering her fear*] I want you upstairs.

WILLY: [*Taking her in his arms*] In a few minutes, Linda. I couldn't sleep right now. Go on, you look awful tired. [*He kisses her*]

BEN: Not like an appointment at all. A diamond is rough and hard to the touch.

WILLY: Go on now. I'll be right up.

LINDA: I think this is the only way, Willy.

WILLY: Sure, it's the best thing.

BEN: Best thing!

WILLY: The only way. Everything is gonna be— go on, kid, get to bed. You look so tired.

LINDA: Come right up.

WILLY: Two minutes.

[Linda *goes into the living-room, then reappears in her bedroom.* Willy *moves just outside the kitchen door*]

WILLY: Loves me. [*Wonderingly*] Always loved me. Isn't that a remarkable thing? Ben, he'll worship me for it!

BEN: [With promise] It's dark there, but full of diamonds.

WILLY: Can you imagine that magnificence with twenty thousand dollars in his pocket?

LINDA: [Calling from her room] Willy! Come up!

WILLY: [Calling into the kitchen] Yes! Yes. Coming! It's very smart, you realize that, don't you, sweetheart? Even Ben sees it. I gotta go, baby. 'By! 'By! [Going over to Ben, almost dancing] Imagine? When the mail comes he'll be ahead of Bernard again!

BEN: A perfect proposition all around.

WILLY: Did you see how he cried to me? Oh, if I could kiss him, Ben!

BEN: Time, William, time!

WILLY: Oh, Ben, I always knew one way or another we were gonna make it, Biff and I!

BEN: [Looking at his watch] The boat. We'll be late. [He moves slowly off into the darkness]

WILLY: [Elegiacally, turning to the house] Now when you kick off, boy, I want a seventy-yard boot, and get right down the field under the ball, and when you hit, hit low and hit hard, because it's important, boy. [He swings around and faces the audience] There's all kinds of important people in the stands, and the first thing you know . . . [Suddenly realizing he is alone] Ben! Ben, where do I . . . ? [He makes a sudden movement of search] Ben, how do I . . . ?

LINDA: [Calling] Willy, you coming up?

WILLY: [Uttering a gasp of fear, whirling about as if to quiet her] Sh! [He turns around as if to find his way; sounds, faces, voices, seem to be swarming in upon him and he flicks at them, crying] Sh! Sh! [Suddenly music, faint and high, stops him. It rises in intensity, almost to an unbearable scream. He goes up and down on his toes, and rushes off around the house] Shhh!

LINDA: Willy?

[There is no answer. Linda waits. Biff gets up off his bed. He is still in his clothes. Happy sits up. Biff stands listening]

LINDA: [With real fear] Willy, answer me! Willy!

[There is the sound of a car starting and moving away at full speed]

LINDA: No!

BIFF: [Rushing down the stairs] Pop!

[As the car speeds off, the music crashes down in a frenzy of sound, which becomes the soft pulsation of a single cello string. Biff slowly returns to his bedroom. He and Happy gravely don their jackets. Linda slowly walks out of her room. The music has developed into a dead march. The leaves of day are appearing over everything. Charley and Bernard, somberly dressed, appear and knock on the kitchen door. Biff and Happy slowly descend the stairs to the kitchen as Charley and Bernard enter. All stop a moment when Linda, in clothes of mourning, bearing a little bunch of roses, comes through the draped doorway into the kitchen. She goes to Charley and takes his arm. Now all move toward the audience, through the wall-line of the kitchen. At the limit of the apron, Linda lays down the flowers, kneels, and sits back on her heels. All stare down at the grave]

REQUIEM

CHARLEY: It's getting dark, Linda.

[Linda doesn't react. She stares at the grave]

BIFF: How about it, Mom? Better get some rest, heh? They'll be closing the gate soon.

[Linda makes no move. Pause]

HAPPY: [Deeply angered] He had no right to do that. There was no necessity for it. We would've helped him.

CHARLEY: [Grunting] Hmmm.

BIFF: Come along, Mom.

LINDA: Why didn't anybody come?

CHARLEY: It was a very nice funeral.

LINDA: But where are all the people he knew? Maybe they blame him.

CHARLEY: Naa. It's a rough world, Linda. They wouldn't blame him.

LINDA: I can't understand it. At this time especially. First time in thirty-five years we were just about free and clear. He only needed a little salary. He was even finished with the dentist.

CHARLEY: No man only needs a little salary.

LINDA: I can't understand it.

BIFF: There were a lot of nice days. When he'd come home from a trip; or on Sundays, making the stoop; finishing the cellar; putting on the new porch; when he built the extra bathroom; and put up the garage. You know something, Charley, there's more of him in that front stoop than in all the sales he ever made.

CHARLEY: Yeah. He was a happy man with a batch of cement.

LINDA: He was so wonderful with his hands.

BIFF: He had the wrong dreams. All, all, wrong.

HAPPY: [Almost ready to fight Biff] Don't say that!

BIFF: He never knew who he was.

CHARLEY: [Stopping Happy's movement and reply. To Biff] Nobody dast blame this man. You don't understand: Willy was a salesman. And for a salesman, there is no rock bottom to the life. He don't put a bolt to a nut, he don't tell you the law or give you medicine. He's a man way out there in the blue, riding on a smile and a shoeshine. And when they start not smiling back—that's an earthquake. And then you get yourself a couple of spots on your hat, and you're finished. Nobody dast blame this man. A salesman is got to dream, boy. It comes with the territory.

BIFF: Charley, the man didn't know who he was.

HAPPY: [*Infuriated*] Don't say that!

BIFF: Why don't you come with me, Happy?

HAPPY: I'm not licked that easily. I'm staying right in this city, and I'm gonna beat this racket! [*He looks at* Biff, *his chin set*] The Loman Brothers!

BIFF: I know who I am, kid.

HAPPY: All right, boy. I'm gonna show you and everybody else that Willy Loman did not die in vain. He had a good dream. It's the only dream you can have—to come out number-one man. He fought it out here, and this is where I'm gonna win it for him.

BIFF: [*With a hopeless glance at* Happy, *bends toward his mother*] Let's go, Mom.

LINDA: I'll be with you in a minute. Go on, Charley. [*He hesitates*] I want to, just for a minute. I never had a chance to say good-by.

[Charley *moves away, followed by* Happy. Biff *remains a slight distance up and left of* Linda. *She sits there, summoning herself. The flute begins, not far away, playing behind her speech*]

LINDA: Forgive me, dear. I can't cry. I don't know what it is, but I can't cry. I don't understand it. Why did you ever do that? Help me, Willy, I can't cry. It seems to me that you're just on another trip. I keep expecting you. Willy, dear. I can't cry. Why did you do it? I search and search and I search, and I can't understand it, Willy. I made the last payment on the house today. Today, dear. And there'll be nobody home. [*A sob rises in her throat*] We're free and clear. [*Sobbing more fully, released*] We're free. [Biff *comes slowly toward her*] We're free . . . We're free . . .

[Biff *lifts her to her feet and moves out up right with her in his arms.* Linda *sobs quietly.* Bernard *and* Charley *come together and follow them, followed by* Happy. *Only the music of the flute is left on the darkening stage as over the house the hard towers of the apartment buildings rise into sharp focus, and*

THE CURTAIN FALLS]

Modernist Directions

Modernist Directions

The following section is offered as an Appendix, with the main purpose of introducing the student to modernist tendencies that have continued to prove seductive since World War II. The plays—and there would have been more of them here if space and permission clearances had allowed—should help to round out his acquaintance with departures from a realistic style of drama that has become overfamiliar and in some respects tattered with use. The subject has already been introduced in the "Departures from Realism" division of our book on pages 258–495, as well as in the preceding "Modern American Drama" section which offers *The Hairy Ape, The Green Pastures, Our Town,* and *The Glass Menagerie.* But there are more aspects of "modernism" to be noted and explored.

AUGUST STRINDBERG and *A Dream Play*

It is once more advisable to "cut back" to the early years of the century if we are to appreciate the potentiality of the "tendencies"—basically, poetic —to which reference has been made. We start, therefore, with the most influential of expressionist experiments, August Strindberg's *A Dream Play* at the turn of the century (in 1902, to be precise). The base of the expressionist style is here at its widest; *A Dream Play* is spiritual drama as well as social drama, it is poetry as well as prose, it is both dream and reality. The play shows how many kinds of drama could be embraced by expressionist fancy and technique. Here Strindberg realized fully in a single work what playwrights after his death in 1912 usually achieved only by fits and starts, in a number of separate plays dealing with a variety of different subjects. Strindberg dealt with the entire human condition, which he pronounced miserable ("All men are to be pitied," says his goddess-heroine); the ramifications of private and social distress are interminable in *A Dream Play*. In this respect, he became one of the forerunners of the mid-century nihilistic playwrights, such as Samuel Beckett and Eugène Ionesco—and Tennessee Williams, in such plays of the 1950's as *Camino Real* and *Orpheus Descending*.

In *A Dream Play*, Strindberg writes with the imagination and idiom of a nineteenth-century man while expressing twentieth-century alienation and division. The writing in this transitional work is characterized by a romantic opulence of invention and expression, and the prologue and the concluding section have an operatic, near-Wagnerian, quality. Even the most bizarre details in the play, moreover, are "motivated," as if Strindberg still followed realism in principle; that is, they are presented as elements of a poet's, or the author's, dream. The fragmentary, time-annihilating, expressionist technique is, as Strindberg explains in his preface to the

work (see page 1111), justified by the chaotic character of dream-formation. This style of treating subjective experience, however, is by no means to be considered "old-fashioned" today. Dream techniques or related hallucinatory distortions of surface reality began to be employed frequently after his death in 1912. They appeared in the American theatre after 1920 in such plays as O'Neill's *The Emperor Jones,* Kaufman and Connelly's *Beggar on Horseback,* Miller's *Death of a Salesman,* and (with musical-comedy, song-and-dance accretions) Moss Hart's *Lady in the Dark.*

Under the insistent drama of disillusion in *A Dream Play,* runs a no less insistent longing for redemption. It is a "descent-play," so to speak, since the Daughter of Indra descends into the inferno of this world; and it is an "ascent-play," too, since the only course of salvation is to ascend from the earthly plane, as the poet-dreamer aspires to do. A spiritual quest dominates some of the most transparent scenes. It is deeply felt, and the anguish that produces the longing for redemption has a personal basis in the author's mental crises. (See pages 75–77 and 328– 329 for Strindberg's life.) "Existentialist" nausea is accompanied by religious nostalgia, and the combination gives a lyrical turn to the play, especially toward the end. In this respect, too, *A Dream Play* bridges nineteenth- and twentieth-century literary taste. Later modernist plays are less given to moods of lamentation and longing; they tend to be more sardonic and relatively dry in tone, and Strindberg himself expressed his nihilism and spiritual thirst with more restraint in his later and more compact drama *The Spook* (or *Ghost*) *Sonata* (1907). But his vivid depiction of a state of alienation attributed to mankind as a whole makes *A Dream Play* a contemporary work. Strindberg's picture of arid and disoriented modern life makes him a true forerunner of middle-of-the-century dramatists of despair or denial such as Sartre, Camus, Anouilh, Beckett, Ionesco, and others who employed "modernistic," as contrasted with modern realistic, dramatic style.

PAUL CLAUDEL and *The Tidings Brought to Mary*

Ten years after *A Dream Play,* in 1912, we encounter Paul Claudel's imposing spiritual affirmation, *The Tidings Brought to Mary,* the play with which the reintroduction of formal poetry—a poetry not reminiscently romantic nor Shakespearian—may be said to begin.

It so happens that many more or less important playwrights who endeavored to restore formal verse-writing to the twentieth-century stage favored religious themes. They surmounted negativistic attitudes and entertained affirmations ranging from the ecstatic to the formalistic, and from unqualified to qualified belief. France had a powerful Catholic stage movement, with Henri Ghéon as its most active playwright, and Austria also acquired an active Catholic theatre, with the poet Hugo von Hofmannsthal as its most distinguished writer. (Open-air productions of the latter's free version of the medieval morality play *Everyman,* known in German as *Jedermann,* became a prominent feature of the annual Salzburg summer festival.) In England, a number of playwrights led by the poets T. S. Eliot and Christopher Fry wrote a number of uplifting plays originally intended for production at the Canterbury Cathedral Festival and for other religious occasions. Among these the former's *Murder in the Cathedral,* written partly in verse and partly in prose, remains the most inspired drama; as verse-drama it is especially noteworthy for its chorus of Canterbury Women. There could be little doubt that in an age of anxiety and materialism a spiritually quickened drama became a desideratum. Poets were especially responsive to the need, whether they were "conservative" believers like Claudel and Eliot or "liberal" sceptics like Archibald MacLeish, who gave the American stage its most successful religious verse play, *J.B.*

The Tidings Brought to Mary was the first masterpiece of the religio-poetic movement and may be considered its most powerful dramatic achievement. Its author, Paul Claudel, was not only one of the greatest of twentieth-century poets but one of the commanding literary figures in France and a leading Catholic layman. Since he was also the most uncompromising of dramatic poets (unlike Eliot, who accommodated himself to the requirements of London and Broadway "show business" with *The Cocktail Party* and later plays), Claudel stood for half a century as a solitary beacon to devotees of both religious and poetic drama. The French theatre was not particularly responsive to his formidable dramatic work until France had suffered a broken and contrite heart, so to speak, in World War II. The great actor-mime and director Jean-Louis Barrault, who was briefly in command at the *Comédie Française* after the war, won a notable success with a production of one of Claudel's most ambitiously conceived dramatic works, *The Satin Slipper,* a comprehensive spiritual history as panoramic as it is dramatically intense.

By career this poet and dramatist was a practical man and diplomat who was entrusted by his government with delicate negotiations and with the management of cultural relations between nation and nation. But as a reading of *The Tidings Brought to Mary* will disclose, Claudel was an extremist where his art and faith were concerned, and he steadily refused to compromise with either. His free verse and cadenced prose recall Whitman's sonorous and swirling lines. Claudel's poetry takes us far from the rhymed hexameter verse form of the Alexandrine, the long-established norm of French dramatic versification. Taste and sentiment are under distinctly better control in Claudel's verse than in Whitman's,

but a great voice resounds in Claudel's ample measures, and it can recall for us the two poets' common poetic ancestry in the resonant world of Old Testament prophecy. Claudel's writing in *The Tidings* and other plays, like prophetic rhapsody, possesses vigor, exaltation, and the ring of truth and conviction. It is not a mixture of convenient prose and decorative verse, of exalted feeling and opportunistic cleverness, as in popular poetic plays.

Claudel's dramatic writing is *all poetry,* just as his faith is *all faith.* It is that, moreover, in a uniquely modern (although also universal) sense, for there is no ignorance of human passion, error, and evil in his work. Human error is forgiven, not forgotten or naively overlooked, in his plays. In *The Tidings Brought to Mary,* the passionate heart of Violaine's jealous sister drives the latter to undisguised and unmitigated criminality. In later plays, such as *Partage de Midi* and *Le Soulier de Satin,* the conflict between good and evil attains true vibrancy. Claudel was not the man to overlook the strength of the passions; he had no use for the indulgent view of human nature taken by liberals, moral relativists, and religious sceptics. He was both a traditionalist and an ultra-modernist in his recognition of the dark side of human nature acknowledged in theological concepts of "original sin." His dramatic vision noted an intrinsic leaning toward evil in the human condition which modern sociological approaches and political reforms could never eradicate. Claudel, in brief, was one of those early "anti-modern" modernists who maintained a neo-conservative position that came to be considered an ultra-advanced one when represented by T. S. Eliot, Graham Greene, François Mauriac, and others after 1930.

Calling for a complete yielding of the spirit and for unlimited love and self-sacrifice, Claudel was absolute in his demands. He was as absolute for religion as for poetic drama. In refusing to entertain half-way measures of saving the soul from sin and the theatre from prosiness and prose, he stood more unambiguously opposed to the modern materialistic and rationalistic world than any other important writer for the twentieth-century stage. With *The Tidings* he became a redoubtable playwright at the beginning of this century. As previously noted, the play appeared in 1912, two years before the outbreak of World War I, the first of the great catastrophes that have brought humanity to the verge of self-annihilation. But because his spiritual call has more urgency now than it had then, and also because the stage, even in his native country, was slow to accept him, his plays, from the early *Tidings Brought to Mary* to his late historical drama *Christopher Columbus,* first prevailed in the midcentury theatre.

As a dramatist, Claudel belongs, then, to the contemporary theatre. He remains a "modernist" in it on several counts: His works constitute the least adulterated and most unsparing type of poetic drama offered to the modern theatre by a major writer of our times. More than the better-publicized dramatic pieces of Eliot, Claudel's plays continue to occupy the most advanced and demanding positions in the struggle for a modern poetic drama.

Born in 1868 of middle-class parents and a brilliant student at the Lycée Louis-le-Grand in Paris, Claudel seemed a typical product of a modern secular society until he recovered his Catholic faith at the cathedral of Notre-Dame in Paris on Christmas night, 1886. But conversion did not interfere with his literary interests. He frequented symbolist literary circles (he became a life-long admirer of the ultra-modernist poet Rimbaud) and devoted himself energetically to publishing poetry. At the same time, like other men of letters in France, Claudel entered the diplomatic service, with the result that he traveled widely and was abroad most of the time until his retirement in 1935. He was Ambassador to the United States from 1927 to 1933 after having acquired an international reputation with his volumes of impassioned and elevated poetry.

Claudel also wrote more than two dozen plays, among which the best known were *The Tidings Brought to Mary*, *Tête d'or* (*Head of God*, 1889), *L'Otage* (*The Hostage*, 1910), *Partage de Midi* (*The Moment of Noon*, 1906, first staged in 1948), *Le Soulier de Satin* (*The Satin Slipper*, written between 1919 and 1924, but first produced in 1943), and *Christophe Colomb*, for which Darius Milhaud wrote the music. Of all his dramatic works, however, it was *L'Annonce faite à Marie* (1912), or *The Tidings Brought to Mary*, that brought him fame. It was a revision of an earlier work, *La Jeune Fille Violaine* (*The Young Girl Violaine*), and it is the play by which he came to be first known in the United States. It was staged in New York by the Theatre Guild on December 25, 1922, with settings by Lee Simonson. Claudel died at the venerable age of 86 on February 26, 1955, shortly after having attended rehearsals of a new production of this, his most famous play, at the *Comédie Française*.

Although less monumental than *The Satin Slipper* and less emotionally shattering than the love-tragedy *Partage de Midi*, Claudel's frequently revised "saint-play" is the most immediately compelling of his dramatic pieces. Its author's turbulent writing, even his so-called verbal incontinence, is a manifestation of the vitality of the work, which derives much of its power from the conflict of carnality and spirituality. The play has the simplicity of a folktale but also the complex turbulence of a modern drama of passion. Above all, *The Tidings Brought to Mary* is a testament of poetic rapture and religious faith written in defiance of worldliness and rationality. This poetic drama transcends the realistic and intellectual modern theatre with its nobly demanding Christianity and its conviction that mystical dedication to God is essentially a separation from everything we call the world.

The saintly Violaine, who exemplifies Claudel's meaning, is, in the words of Professor Wallace Fowlie, "a symbol of eternity within time, of spirit within matter," and her story exemplifies the principle that "if salvation is the goal of each human existence, love is the means for reaching this goal." That so "un-modern" a view should appear in the work of a modernist among poets whose position, as Professor Fowlie declares, "is at the very head of the experiments with language that characterize symbolism and surrealism" is one of the remarkable features of the paradoxical career of Paul Claudel.

In the twentieth century, which has earned the opprobrium of moralists for its relaxed standards, Claudel seemed at first a misfit, a stranger, a vestigial Victorian perhaps. But as the age moved toward moral insolvency, Claudel seemed more new than old-fashioned—a man well in advance of his contemporaries in offering example and correction. When the French theatre belatedly began to stage his work after the collapse of France in 1940 (Barrault staged a cut version of *The Satin Slipper* in 1943) Claudel appeared to be speaking to audiences with midcentury relevance; that which was "old" in him had become "new." His morally exacting plays, mostly "cases of conscience," acquired augmented significance.

JEAN GIRAUDOUX and *The Madwoman of Chaillot*

Modernist directions in the theatre became pronounced shortly after Claudel's high achievement. The outbreak of the First World War in 1914 was an especially disturbing event, and the European theatre reflected private and public disorientation in a variety of ways for about the next dozen years. Expressionism (see pages 261–263) ran riot in the Central European theatre in plays of nightmare violence, none of which rose to the artistic level of Strindberg's *A Dream Play*, while the French theatre yielded to the sensationalism of "dadaist" and "surrealistic" art and favored styles of drama related to it, as in Jean Cocteau's well-publicized dramatic experiments *Orpheus* (1926) and *The Infernal Machine* (1934). In Italy a "school of the grotesque" led by Pirandello (see page 384) acquired importance. A more or less frantic Symbolism affected the Russian theatre, culminating in the pessimistic, allegorical, and symbolist plays of Leonid Andreyev such as *The Life of Man* (1906), *The Black Maskers* (1908), and *He Who Gets Slapped* (1915), while the post-war American theatre accorded some favor to expressionist drama in such pieces for the stage as O'Neill's *The Emperor Jones* (1920) and *The Hairy Ape* (1922, see pages 819–836). Also, efforts to produce lyrical drama had been proceeding ever since the 1890's in plays by Rostand (*Cyrano de Bergerac*, see pages 276–327), Hugo von Hofmannsthal, William Butler Yeats, and others, including

Federico García Lorca, whose *Blood Wedding* (see pages 436–455) represents a high point in lyrical drama. And post-war Central Europe also produced a species of Marxist, so-called epic, drama, whether sardonically lyrical (as in the Bertolt Brecht and Kurt Weill ballad-drama *The Threepenny Opera*), "epic" (as in Brecht's *Mother Courage*), instructive in the manner of a parable (Brecht's *The Good Woman of Setzuan*), or demonstrative, as in Brecht's political drama *From the Life of the Master Race* (see pages 459–465).

But a more purely theatrical style of theatre had also made headway ever since the gifted stage-director Jacques Copeau established his experimental theatre, *Le Théâtre de Vieux-Colombier,* in Paris in 1913. It was a style in which no particular ideology was favored and in which neither violence nor nightmare fancies predominated. Even when negativistic in approach, its representative writers manifested a cultivated disenchantment rather than a savage indignation. It was, in the main, "civilized theatre" and its most distinguished representative was the diplomat, novelist, and man of letters Jean Giraudoux (1882–1944) virtually all of whose dramatic work was staged in Paris by his friend Louis Jouvet, Copeau's most successful disciple. Only in one respect could Giraudoux be described as somewhat extreme, and that was in his baroquely opulent dialogue. Giraudoux could skate across a polished verbal mirror with emotional and intellectual freight, as in his *Electra* and *Judith,* no less gracefully and provocatively than when he brought his audiences the light comic fantastication of *Amphitryon 38,* first produced in Paris in 1928. Moreover, he had the gift of being able to bring to the theatre momentous meaning with a juggling dexterity that made satire poetical and fancy satirical. There may be no more accurate way of describing the climactic achievement of *The Madwoman of Chaillot,* which brought him posthumous fame as far as the United States with a successful Broadway production in 1948. It was followed by productions of earlier written plays such as the antiphilistine fantasy *Intermezzo* (1933), the fairytale of the love of a knight and water-spright *Ondine* (1939), and the brilliant pacifist drama *La Guerre de Troie n'aura pas lieu* (1935, *The Trojan War Will Not Take Place*), staged in London and New York in a Christopher Fry translation titled *Tiger at the Gates.* Among his shorter pieces, the one-act diversion *The Apollo of Bellac,* a quizzical comment on the vanity of men, won favor with amateurs. Previously he had had a successful production only with the 1938 Theatre Guild production of his mythological comedy *Amphitryon 38,* his first American production, *Siegfried,* by Eva Le Gallienne at her New York Civic Repertory Productions Theatre having met with scant favor in 1928. His posthumously published play *Pour Lucrèce* (1953), translated by Christopher Fry under the title of *Duel of Angels,* and the intense dramas *Judith* (1931), and *Electra* (1937) were more difficult to present outside his native France, but these plays left a strong impression even upon readers who had divided feelings about the author's verbosity and quizzical imagination.

The Madwoman of Chaillot is a mixture of poetic drama, satirical fantasy, and literary improvisation that commends itself to playgoers as a theatrical fable while winning approval from readers for its literary style. It is at once a work for the stage and the library, and it is most agreeable to students of the drama as an example of theatricality displacing the pseudo-realism of the commonplace theatre with playful and lucid imaginativeness rather than with strained and murky sensationalism. *The Madwoman* is the work of an extremely civilized man who deprecated the materialism of the twentieth-century world and expressed a refined revulsion against it. He did not count on some revolutionary movement to change that world; he was a gentleman by breeding, an intellectual by education, and a conservative by political conviction.

In *The Madwoman,* Giraudoux heaped scorn on the predatory aspects of modern European society, but added fantasy to his disapproval, taking delight in imagining how gratifying it would be if the cold, calculating *laissez-faire* intelligence of modern enterprise could be routed by a noble irrationality. It might take a "madwoman" to defeat the extravagant representatives of "venture capitalism" invented by Giraudoux. His play, in brief, is poetic "social drama" in being written with whimsy, self-conscious artfulness, and wishful thinking.

Coming at the close of Giraudoux' life—*The Madwoman* was written shortly before its author's death in 1944—the play, which was first staged in Paris on December 21, 1945, was the high-water mark of a distinguished career. Born in 1882 in Bellac, Haute-Vienne, France, and educated at the Ecole Normale Supérieure, where he won the highest honors, he entered the diplomatic service and remained there until virtually the end of his life. He became the author of a number of poetic and extravagant novels noted for their wit; and it was as a stylist that he first won distinction in the theatre, too. To the stage, however, Giraudoux brought the challenge of a mature mind with his very first production *Siegfried,* adapted by him from his own antinationalistic novel. The success of the production staged by Louis Jouvet in 1928 was the beginning of Giraudoux' long association with this prominent exponent of "retheatricalized theatre" or "theatrical" theatre. At the same time, few of Giraudoux' contemporaries, except for Bertolt Brecht and his "epic theatre," brought to theatrical stylization so much genuine concern with the state of the world as the author of *Tiger at the Gates* and *The Madwoman of Chaillot,* who headed the Press Bureau of the French government in 1924 and became a cabinet minister in 1939 shortly before the military collapse of France at the beginning of the second World War. The ironic development of the theme in *The Madwoman* can only reveal, rather than conceal, the fusion of modernistic style and social interest. It remains to be added concerning the version presented in this book, that Maurice Valency, the translator-adapter of the play for the American production, restored passages of the author's lavish dialogue that had been omitted in the Broadway production.

JEAN ANOUILH and *The Lark*

A generally less impressive modernist, Jean Anouilh, a younger man (he was born in Bordeaux on June 23, 1910), entered the same "retheatricalized" French theatre that Giraudoux did, the latter having first had a stage production when he was already forty-six years old. Anouilh, the child of a mother who played the violin in the orchestra of an operetta company, became associated with the theatre at an early age. He was only twenty-two years old when, after a year and a half at law school and two years' association with an advertising company, he joined Louis Jouvet's stage company as secretary. It was characteristic of Anouilh's associations with the theatre that he should have married an actress and started housekeeping with her with furniture borrowed from settings built for Giraudoux' first play *Siegfried*. He was also associated with other leaders of the "theatricalist" movement such as the actor-managers Pierre Fresnay and George Pitoëff.

After 1937 Anouilh had a stage production in Paris almost every year, and believing, as he declared to the press, that a dramatist "could and should play with his characters, with their passions and their actions," Anouilh became identified with modernism whether he wrote gay plays such as *The Thieves' Carnival* or grave plays such as *Eurydice* (known in English as *Legend of Lovers*), ironic pieces such as *The Waltz of the Toreadors* (1951) or high tragedies such as his *Antigone* (1944).

Although capable of composing concentrated drama without conspicuous theatricality, as in his powerful short play *Medea*, he usually favored theatrical situations and gave a theatrical turn to the organization of his dramatic action. He wrote plays about the theatre such as *Colombe*, about make-believe passions such as the romantic *Time Remembered* (*Léocadia*, 1942), and about deluded histrionic characters such as *Ardèle* and *The Waltz of the Toreadors*. His reputation grew abroad, notably in England in the 1940's and in the United States in the 1950's (after having encountered considerable resistance from New York reviewers and playgoers). That resistance vanished entirely with the production of his Saint Joan play *L'Alouette,* or *The Lark,* in an adaptation made by Lillian Hellman

for a Broadway production in 1955, chiefly distinguished by the performance of Julie Harris in the title role. It was evident from *The Lark,* as also from his *Antigone,* that theatrical ingenuity was not the author's sole aim. Almost equally characteristic of his playwriting was his large use of irony, and usually it accompanied a pessimistic opinion of mankind and an existentialist's disenchantment with life. *The Lark* is a divided play in the original French, although considerably unified in the Lillian Hellman adaptation. It views Joan, wrote Anouilh, as "a saint who died in a political episode." He underscored the irony of history with ironic flashes of characterization. Yet Joan's drama managed to be moving even while its author adopted a cynical view. But the ambivalence of his approach to his country's greatest national theme was part of his provocative, if also questionable, strategy. He was superficial and incisive, at the same time.

In commenting on the original French production, which opened in Paris on October 14, 1953, with Suzanne Flon in the part of Joan, the author disavowed any knowledge of "the mystery of Joan," and it is entirely true that he did not provide any extensive character analysis. He used Joan as the center of a theatrical story told with such irony that the American producer of the work hesitated to place *The Lark* on the Broadway stage without having the play "adapted" by an expert American playwright. Miss Hellman's version avoided such details as a little scene toward the end in which Joan's unsympathetic father, observing her triumphant crowning of the Dauphin, tells his son to take his fingers out of his nose (*"Et tire tes doigts de ton nez"*) and observes that he had always expected great things from her, following which the curtain slowly descends on the coronation scene, described as "this beautiful illustration from a school prize." The American adaptation ends without this ironic conclusion. But the essential theatricality of the work, which contrasts sharply with the zealous safeguarding of "the illusion of reality" by realistic playwrights, is evident in both the original play and the adaptation.

In the original it becomes quite apparent at the beginning that the action of *The Lark* is the continuation of a stage production; it is time for the trial scene— that is, Joan's trial—to be reenacted, whereupon the actors start their performance. The adaptation gives less indication at the start that a play is being presented. But both in the original and the adaptation, Joan's trial is the occasion for an episodic theatrical summary of the career that brought her to the extremity of being placed on trial. And in both versions, finally, "illusion" is openly violated while Joan stands tied to the stake and the flames are beginning to reach her. The play is not allowed to end that way, and we cut back at the urging of a character (La Hire in the American version, Beaudricourt in the French) to the scene of her greatest triumph, "her happiest day," when she crowned the Dauphin Charles in the Cathedral of Rheims.

There are departures from the original even here, and lines attributed to one character in the French are distributed among other characters in the English. Some excellent lines in the original are sacrificed for the sake of a rapid and emphatic conclusion. Thus the character Beaudricourt adds a strong theatricalist note to the French version by protesting that the performers promised to play the entire story of Joan but that the Coronation scene was not played. He insists that she has a right to the ceremony: "*On ne peut pas finir comme ça, Monseigneur,*" he says to Cauchon. "*On n'a pas joué le sacre. On avait dit qu'on jouerait tout. Ce n'est pas juste! Jeanne a droit à jouer le sacre, c'est dans son histoire.*" ("One cannot finish like that. The coronation hasn't been played. They were going to perform all of it. It isn't just. Joan has a right to play the coronation, it is in her story.") And Beaudricourt, assisting the others to remove the fagots, cries out, "It's fortunate I arrived in time. The imbeciles, they were going to burn Joan of Arc." Warwick also has a good ironic and theatrical speech; as he resignedly leaves the stage when Beaudricourt has convinced his hearers to play the coronation scene, Warwick declares "Very well. Let's have the coronation. . . . My presence at this ceremony would be indecent, so I erase myself. In any case, so far as I'm concerned it's finished, she has been burnt. His Majesty's government has attained its political objective."

However, some excellent lines are introduced by Lillian Hellman in her adaptation, such as the first three of the last four speeches, and the version prepared by her gave a stronger direction and a heroic accent to the play. *The Lark,* as adapted for the American stage, represents a blending of modernist theatricality as practiced on two continents. The play was also translated into English by Christopher Fry for production in England, and this version also departs in minor respects from the French original. The reader aware of Lillian Hellman's departures may raise exceptions to the adaptation, but the student concerned with the diffusion of modernist theatricalism from its center in Paris will observe that even so resolute a realist among playwrights as Lillian Hellman was drawn to Anouilh's dramatic invention.

To view *The Lark* on pages 1204–1225 as a joint French and American work is to recognize the fact that theatrical stylization has not been an exotic development. It appeared early on the American stage in O'Neill's expressionist plays and continued to be effective in Thornton Wilder's *Our Town* (see pages 928–949) and *The Skin of Our Teeth* (1942). In England, too, self-conscious or deliberate theatricality gained enough vogue to radically affect the structure of modernistic poetic plays, among

which T. S. Eliot's *Murder in the Cathedral* (1935) was the most eminent.

JEAN GENET and *The Maids*

A want of depth of thought and feeling has been observable in the work of Anouilh and other theatrical jugglers with ideas and emotions. Among the recent ultra-modernists, however, one playwright plunged into abysses of emotion with a drive and an insight truly frightening. In plays distinguishable on the surface by various degrees of perversity, plays as fascinating as they are unwholesome, Jean Genet now and then touched bottom, revealing compulsions and appalling complexities of love and hatred. In his macabre artistry Genet was utterly fascinated with corruption. Like Claudel, the noble mystic, Genet, the criminal and social outcast, took account of the presence of evil in the human condition. Whereas there is salvation at the end of human travail in the religious masterpieces of Claudel, there is only moral bankruptcy and destruction in the work of Genet. But Genet's knowledge of corruption proved to be a powerful ferment in his writing, and his readiness to acknowledge the reality of evil constituted a degree of integrity usually absent from the commercial theatre, which favors shallow and deceptive optimism. Genet is a descendant of Baudelaire; and like that nineteenth-century poet who became the culture-hero of modernism with the publication of his famous book of poems *The Flowers of Evil,* Genet assiduously cultivated "the flowers of evil" in the plays that drew attention to him after World War II: *Les Bonnes* (*The Maids,* 1947), *Haute Surveillance* (*Deathwatch,* 1948), and *The Balcony* (1900). If their moral insensitiveness, their "amorality," is a limitation that may not allow Genet the status of a major playwright, it does not prevent us from considering him an engrossing as well as symptomatic writer for the modernist stage.

It is even possible to regard Genet as a profounder playwright than either Giraudoux or Anouilh, although he has been neither as prolific nor as successful in the theatre. By 1960 he had not had a single Broadway success, but had received three noteworthy semiprofessional or "off-Broadway" stage productions. In France, both his plays and his nondramatic writings had won a following and received critical esteem. Jean-Paul Sartre wrote a thoughtful introduction to *The Maids* and Genet was indeed extremely fortunate in the friends his talents had acquired for him; they saved him from life-imprisonment when such distinguished men as Claudel, Sartre, Cocteau, and Gide procured a pardon for him in 1948 from the president of the French Republic.

Born in Paris in 1910 of unknown parentage, adopted by a peasant family after his mother had abandoned her infant to public charity, sent to a reformatory at the age of ten for stealing, Jean Genet became the latter-day François Villon of French literature. After many years in reformatories, he escaped, joined the Foreign Legion, deserted, and engaged in smuggling and thieving. He was in and out of prisons in several countries for years. Convicted for the tenth time in 1948, Genet the thief was automatically a candidate for a life-sentence according to French law. But Genet the genius was saved from this fate by the literary world of France that he had started to impress with his first published work, *Notre-Dame des Fleurs,* written in prison in 1942 while he was serving a long term. This book was followed within the next five years by three novels, two plays (*The Maids* and *Deathwatch*), a volume of verse, and the autobiographical *Journal d'un Voleur,* or *Diary of a Thief.* Sartre, in particular, was so greatly taken with Genet's work, views, and personality that he published a substantial book on him provocatively titled *Saint Genet, Comédien et Martyr* (1952).

Among Genet's plays, it is *The Maids* that may most legitimately attract the general student of the contemporary drama. *Deathwatch,* a drama of prison life, is quite outrageous in its treatment of sexual abnormality, and *The Balcony,* which takes place largely in a house of prostitution, is an ironic, negativistic account of a social revolution. *The Balcony* consists of a long chain of imaginings and disguises by characters who visit an illusion-vending house of prostitution that provides its clients for a brief interval with the personalities and careers they would like to have in real life. In the climactic episodes a revolution is started, developed, and finally suppressed as the characters assume a variety of roles by whom the populace is first inspired to revolt and then pacified and controlled.

The Maids also revolves around illusions that reveal the secret desires and tensions of the central characters, two servants who are entangled in a network of passions and pretenses, motivated by jealousy of their mistress ("Madame") whom they alternate in impersonating. Play-acting (the game they play every time is the murder of "Madame") and the interchanging of roles appear to be the two principal characters' reason for living. Moreover, their play-acting is both cause and consequence of the ambivalence of their feelings. And into their histrionic actions, their impersonations and pretenses, they pour their accumulated poisons—the long-felt frustrations and resentments of siblings, spinsters, and servants.

The Maids, then, is "modernist" both in its marked use of the theatrical motif—for everything in the play is "theatre" even to the point of Claire's carrying her play-acting to the extreme of killing herself—and in the particular negativism of its characters' disorientation and revulsion against their lives. We may say that the entire drama is a sort of chess game, but that the figures on the chessboard are themselves players and the pawns are their special

impersonations. The "play-within-the-play" stylization of drama can hardly be carried further or pursued with greater intensity. "Theatricalism" and "disorientation" commingle in *The Maids* to produce a singularly absorbing drama. It is an indefinable mixture of harlequinade and Grand-Guignolism, a game that becomes disturbingly serious, a piece of flagrant make-believe that becomes terrifyingly real.

In *The Maids,* "theatricalism" plunges into the depths of human anguish, and the theatrical game having been carried far enough ceases to be, in its effect upon both the characters and ourselves, a game. It becomes reality, and this reality is both individual and collective, "psychological" and "social" to such a degree that one can only endorse a comment in the *New Yorker* magazine that "All the poison and impotence of contemporary Europe [at least of Western Europe with its galling distinctions between a servant and a master class] are expressed in this little play." One can object, however, to the term "little," for *The Maids* is so replete with tensions and their appropriate explosions into dramatic action that we cannot fail to experience the work as an ample, so-called "full-length," drama. *The Maids* makes many longer and more expansive plays written in some more or less "theatricalist" style seem slight, if not indeed trivial. It is not surprising that French critics began to consider Genet the greatest writer of his generation in France. If the existence of Samuel Beckett, the author of *Waiting for Godot* and *Endgame* as well as of several powerful novels, could indeed throw some doubt on this opinion, it will have to be conceded that by comparison with Genet's plays Beckett's Joycean dramas of the 1950's are rather abstract. Genet proved himself more genuinely a dramatist in his ability to produce specific and immediate experience, always the experience of *particulars.* In this respect, as also in his questionable character and nonliterary career, he can remind us of one who like him was redeemed from waste only by the grace of genius, the equally "lost" medieval François Villon, the poet of another lost generation in another disordered era.

EUGENE IONESCO and *The Chairs*

Finally, in this appendix on special modernist trends in the drama not covered in any previous section of this anthology, we turn to one other playwright's recognition of failure and simultaneous defense against it, to Eugène Ionesco. The sharpest alternative to Genet's method is that of making farce the vehicle of disillusion. This involves either an intensification of farcicality until it makes nonsense of everything, as in Ionesco's *The Bald Soprano,* or a darkening and sobering of farce until farce becomes barely distinguishable from tragedy (except for inflexible formalists) and yet retains the extravagance and theatrics of farce. Ionesco, a virtuoso in the first-mentioned style, proved himself a master of the other, more provocative, method—the method of mixed genres, so to speak—when he wrote *The Chairs*.

The Roumanian Ionesco joined the small and special company of the social outcast Genet and the Irish exile Beckett as one of the seminal writers for the French stage and, like Genet and Beckett, first won repute in the little *avant-garde* theatres of Paris before acquiring international standing. With other writers of non-French origin such as the Belgian Michel de Ghelderode (first known to American playgoers by the brilliantly sustained one-act melodrama *Escurial*) and Arthur Adamov (of Russian descent), Ionesco made short shrift of "*le théâtre bourgeois*"; that is, the artistically bankrupt middle-class theatre which had started its characteristic "well-made play" style of drama more than a century before. With his associates he adopted a style disruptive to such a degree as to make the dramaturgy of the Existentialists seem conservative. For these *avant-garde* writers indeed, Sartre could seem too "constructive" and Giraudoux' great friend Louis Jouvet, although he was the first commercial manager to produce Genet's *The Maids,* too mild or placid. The new philosophy of theatre was most forcibly expressed by the influential visionary Antoine Artaud, who died in 1947. He rejected the earlier modernist theatre of Copeau's disciples at its very height during the 1930–1935 period when Jouvet was giving Paris three of Giraudoux' most advanced plays. Artaud felt closer to the *poètes maudits,* the "accursed" or outlaw poets Rimbaud and Apollinaire, as well as to Alfred Jarry, author of the outrageous travesty on respectability *Ubu Roi* (1896), than to the boulevard modernists. Artaud in his critical essay *Le Théâtre et son Double,* "The Theatre and Its Double," proposed the cult of a "theatre of cruelty" that would shake the equableness of reason in the spectator. He advocated an "anti-bourgeois" theatre with greater affinities to the surreal and the outrageous than to the urbanity of the big Parisian theatres, and in one way or another his call was heeded by a new generation of left-bank artists.

Giraudoux and Anouilh, whom the mid-century American stage regarded as thoroughly advanced playwrights, were by no means advanced enough for the Parisian little theatres of the 1950's. Their leaders cultivated a new nihilistic modernism, and it is a question whether this modernism was better represented by Beckett with his dramas of resignation *Waiting for Godot* and *Endgame* or by Ionesco with his satirical farces and tragical (or pseudo-tragical) farces. Ionesco indeed was so negativistic (though buoyantly so) that he was not only "anti-bourgeois" but even "anti-theatre" in his mockery.

Ionesco, for example, made such a farce of the theatre that he rightly called his first performed play, a satire on middle-class marriage, *La Cantatrice Chauve* or *The Bald Soprano* (first given in Paris at the little Théâtre des Noctambules on May 11, 1950), an "anti-play." That is, he made nonsense of dramatic form with the inconsequence of the dialogue and action; the "bald soprano" of the title never appears and has no bearing whatsoever on the substance or lack of substance of the work. His second play, *The Lesson* (first presented in the little Théâtre de Poche in Paris in 1951), was both a Grand Guignol and a flagrant reduction of teaching, learning, and even language to absurdity. The mad pedagogue of the piece prepares a young girl for her doctorate with idiotic questions and answers, while she is so scatter-brained that the taking of an academic degree could be for her only a wild, surrealist fantasy. The professor murders her in one of his homicidal rages and is mildly reproved by his housekeeper, who indulgently allows him to take on another pupil and prospective victim just before the fall of the curtain.

Here, as in some other Ionesco pieces, the drama of words is reduced to frequent babbling, and the action becomes a burlesque extravaganza, so that the spectator may not always know whether he is being moved to pathos, dread, or laughter. *The Lesson* was acclaimed as a minor classic in France. It was the first of his plays to support his ideal of a new theatre dominated by grotesqueness or caricature, a theatre based (as Professor Wallace Fowlie has put it in a *Sewanee Review* article) upon the coexistence of contradictory principles: tragedy and farce; the poetic and the prosaic; fantasy and realism; the familiar and the unusual.

This type of theatre is also present in *The Chairs* and in other plays, such as the three-act *Amédie* in which a corpse (the corpse, one presumes, of dead happiness) grows terrifyingly in a married couple's apartment until there is no longer any room left in it for them (the subtitle of the piece is *How to Get Rid of It*) and *The New Tenant,* in which the furniture accumulated by people multiplies until it turns a home into a tomb. Another extravaganza is *Jack, or The Submission,* in which a grotesquely caricatured family forces a rebellious son (he does not like "hashed brown potatoes") to accept a bride; he finally succumbs to one with nine fingers on one hand and three noses on her face that Picasso might have painted. (Here is indeed an opportunity to recall that during World War II, Pablo Picasso himself wrote a surrealist play, *Desire Trapped by the Tail.* Its bizarre character is suggested by a list of characters that includes The Big Foot, The Onion, The Tart, The Two Bow-Wows, The Silence, The Lean Anguish, The Fat Anguish, The Curtains. . . .)

Ionesco's theatrical extravagance constitutes a judgment on contemporary life. In one play, *The Rhinoceros,* which had its world premiere in Düsseldorf, Germany, on November 2, 1959, the judgment was recognizably political; it was an attack on conformity and transparently a protest against totalitarianism of both the Right and the Left. The playwright mocks the lunatic world and exposes the gross inability of orderly middle-class drama to reflect the disorderly character of contemporary life. Thomas Barbour having observed that in Ionesco's plays "sense is spoken as nonsense and nonsense as sense" and that "the ordinary is shocking and the shocking, ordinary," rightly concludes that the "implied conception of the playwright as impersonal manipulator of effects encourages his audience to respond with a reciprocal disengagement . . ." and that disengagement is the beginning of evaluation or criticism. (Summer issue of *The Hudson Review*, p. 277.)

If one would like to see Ionesco, however, as more than "a very clever and audacious contriver of theatrical effects," as Thomas Barbour calls him, one would be well advised to turn to the compact masterpiece *Les Chaises* (*The Chairs*), first staged on April 22, 1952, in Paris. It is an engrossing and devastating commentary on human illusion and failure. The theatrical contrivances are as abundant in this work as in Ionesco's other plays. The effects are achieved with simple yet ample theatricality as in the case of the multiplication of chairs on the stage while the old couple receive the imaginary guests who have come to hear the old man's important message to the world. Here the stage properties alone have true farcical power.

Pathos and searing satire were combined by Ionesco to give *The Chairs* depth as well as vivacity. *The Chairs*, in which the "message" is gibberish and the old people are unable to reach "His Majesty" through the mass of chairs obstructing their way to Him, is a haunting work of Western disillusion in the twentieth century. It is one of the most trenchant plays with which it is possible to conclude a summary of the "modernistic" drama founded upon

negativism. Yet the old man's insistence that his life should add up to a meaning worth passing on to mankind is paradoxically affirmative, too; it takes rueful account of the desire to give life a meaning of sorts.

Ionesco's disenchantment was widely diffused in Europe during the midcentury period; England, for example, had its angry young men (led in the theatre by John Osborne, best known for his play *Look Back in Anger*) and the United States acquired a so-called "beat generation." But Ionesco's disillusion was free from sentimental ingredients and became the last word in "sophistication." His mockery marked a climax in a special style of theatre that is essentially French in tradition. Ionesco, who was born in Roumania in 1912, was taken to Paris at the age of one and brought back to Bucharest at the age of 14, but finally settled in Paris in 1938 and became a French citizen. In his "anti-bourgeois" animus and his parody of platitudes ("cliché heightened to a state of near paroxysm," one commentator, Richard Roud, calls this method), Ionesco carried on an *avant-garde* French tradition first established by Alfred Jarry's extravagant *Ubu Roi* in 1896. Ionesco brought it to a conclusion that far from having an effect of negativeness was buoyantly theatrical and flamboyantly histrionic.

We may say with some measure of truth, then, that negativistic, even "decadent," theatre had a positive character in at least this one respect, that it helped to "re-theatricalize" the twentieth-century theatre that commonplace realism had "de-theatricalized." We may conclude indeed that modernistic theatre, whether associated with belief or scepticism, had in common one important result—a series of striking victories for the "theatrical theatre."

A DREAM PLAY

By August Strindberg

IN A NEW TRANSLATION FROM THE SWEDISH BY ARVID PAULSON
DEDICATED TO CHARITY GRACE AND H. STILWELL CLAPP

THE AUTHOR'S PREFACE

As in his previous dream play, *To Damascus,* the author has in *A Dream Play* attempted to reproduce the detached and disunited—although apparently logical—form of dreams. Anything is apt to happen, anything seems possible and probable. Time and space do not exist. On a flimsy foundation of actual happenings, imagination spins, and weaves in new patterns: an intermingling of remembrances, experiences, whims, fancies, ideas, fantastic absurdities and improvisations, and original inventions of the mind.

The personalities split, take on duality, multiply, vanish, intensify, diffuse and disperse, and are brought into a focus. There is, however, one single-minded consciousness that exercises a dominance over the characters: the dreamer's. There are for the dreamer no secrets, no inconsequences, no scruples, no laws. He neither pronounces judgment nor exonerates; he merely narrates.

Since dreams most frequently are filled with pain, and less often with joy, a note of melancholy and of compassion for all living things runs through the limping story. Sleep, the liberator, often appears as a tormentor, a torturer, but when the agony is most oppressive the awakening rescues the sufferer and reconciles him to reality. No matter how agonizing reality may be, it will at this moment be welcomed cheerfully as a release from the painful dream.

CAST OF CHARACTERS

THE VOICE OF INDRA	KRISTIN	THE HUSBAND
THE DAUGHTER OF INDRA	THE QUARANTINE MASTER	THE WIFE
THE GLAZIER	THE POET	THE BLIND MAN
THE OFFICER	HE	FIRST COALHEAVER
THE FATHER	SHE	SECOND COALHEAVER
THE MOTHER	THE PENSIONER	THE GENTLEMAN
LINA	THE ELDERLY DANDY	THE LADY
THE PORTRESS	THE OLD FLIRT	THE LORD CHANCELLOR
THE BILLPOSTER	HER LOVER (THE MAJOR)	THE DEAN OF THEOLOGY
THE SINGER	THE THREE SERVANT GIRLS	THE DEAN OF PHILOSOPHY
A WOMAN'S VOICE (VICTORIA)	PLAINLOOKING EDITH	THE DEAN OF MEDICINE
THE BALLET GIRL	EDITH'S MOTHER	THE DEAN OF JURISPRUDENCE
THE CHORIST	ALICE	THE SHIP'S CREW
THE PROMPTER	THE TEACHER	MEMBERS OF THE OPERA COMPANY
THE POLICEMAN	THE NAVAL OFFICER	CLERKS, HERALDS, DANCING GIRLS,
THE ATTORNEY	SEVERAL BOY PUPILS	MEN AND WOMEN, ETC.

SETTINGS

1. The Prologue: In the Clouds.
2. Outside the Growing Castle.
3. Inside the Castle: The Officer's Room.
4. Inside the Castle: The Mother's Room.
5. The Alleyway Outside the Opera House.
6. The Attorney's Office.
7. The Interior of a Church (The Chancel; The Organ).
8. Fingal's Cave.
9. The Attorney's Living-quarters Behind His Office.
10. Foulgut [also translated as "Foulstrand"].—

In the background a beautiful, wooded shore with flags flying from jetties, to which white sailboats are moored; villas, pavilions, kiosks and marble statues discerned along the shore, between the tree tops. In the foreground a hillside scorched by fire, with patches of red heather; smoky tree stubs; pigpens and outhouses; an open-air gymnasium with apparatuses resembling instruments of torture; the quarantine station with fireplaces, furnaces and piping conduits. Between the shore in the background and the landscape in the foreground, a narrow strait. A white, dragonlike boat glides into the strait.

11. Faircove [also translated as "Fairhaven"].— The above scene reversed: scorched hillside in the

background; shore with Casino and School in the foreground.

12. A beach on the Mediterranean.

13. Fingal's Cave.—The waves roll into the cave; the wind grows into storm. The Shipwreck scene.

14. The Alley way outside the Opera House.

15. Outside the Growing Castle. The castle burns; it blossoms into a giant chrysanthemum.

PROLOGUE

The background represents cloud banks, shaped like disintegrating slate cliffs, dotted with castles and fortified strongholds.

The constellations Leo, Virgo and Libra can be discerned on the firmament. In their midst the planet Jupiter is visible, shining with a bright light.

The Daughter of Indra *stands on the topmost cloud.*

VOICE OF INDRA: [*Heard from above*] Where are you, daughter . . . where?

DAUGHTER OF INDRA: Here, father . . . here!

VOICE OF INDRA: You've lost your way, my child! Take care—you're sinking. . . .
How did you stray?

D. OF INDRA: I followed in the path of lightning from the ether
and used a cloud as travel coach. . . .
The cloud, however, sank—and now we're falling. . . .
Oh, tell me, lofty father Indra, to what regions
I have come. And why so sultry here,
so hard to breathe?

VOICE OF INDRA: You've left the second world and come into the third one—
you've passed the star of morning,
and from Çukra you now enter
the atmosphere of Earth; there you will see
the Scales, the seventh house of planet Sun,
where Çukra stands on guard at the autumnal equinox—
when day and night are equal in duration.

D. OF INDRA: You spoke of Earth. . . . Is that the dreary planet,
whose darkness is lit up by Mother Moon?

VOICE OF INDRA: It is the heaviest and densest
of the spheres that sail in space.

D. OF INDRA: And do the sunrays never reach it?

VOICE OF INDRA: Oh yes, it gets some sun, but not at all times. . . .

D. OF INDRA: There is a rift now in the cloud—
and I can see below—

VOICE OF INDRA: What do you see, my child?

D. OF INDRA: I see . . . that there is beauty—the woods are green—
the water's blue—and snowcapped mountains—yellow fields. . . .

VOICE OF INDRA: A beauty such as only Brahma could create . . .

yet it has once had even greater beauty
when Time was born, long, long ago. . . . Then something happened—
its destined orbit was disturbed, or maybe something else;
revolt bred crime that had to be suppressed. . . .

D. OF INDRA: Now I can hear sounds from down below. . . .
What kind of beings live upon that planet?

VOICE OF INDRA: Descend and see. . . . I will not slander these poor children of Creation;
and what you now can hear is their tongue.

D. OF INDRA: It sounds as though. . . . It has a ring that is not happy.

VOICE OF INDRA: I feared so!—Their mother-tongue is discontent!
Yes—I fear that the people of the Earth
are hard to please, a most ungrateful race. . . .

D. OF INDRA: Speak not unkindly. . . . Now I hear joyous cries—
and shooting—thunder—I see lightning. . . .
Now bells are ringing, fires burning—
and voices—thousands upon thousands—
sing praise and thanks to the celestial. . . .
[*There is a silence*]
You judge them much too harshly, father. . . .

VOICE OF INDRA: Descend, then, and when you have learned, have seen, and heard,
return and tell me if they've cause to grumble and complain,
to be lamenting and bewailing constantly.

D. OF INDRA: I'll go then—down to them . . . but won't you, father, come with me?

VOICE OF INDRA: No, no—I cannot breathe down there.

D. OF INDRA: The cloud is sinking. . . . Oh, how close it is. . . . It's stifling here.
This is not air I'm breathing . . . it is smoke and moisture. . . .
It weighs me down—it drags me downward, downward;
I feel a tilting, turning motion—
the third world truly can't be said to be the best. . . .

VOICE OF INDRA: No, it is not the best—yet not the worst;
its name is Dust, it rotates like the rest of them—
that's why the people there are prone to dizziness,
a thing betwixt plain foolishness and madness. . . .
Take courage now, my child, for this is but a test,
a trial.

D. OF INDRA: [*She kneels as the cloud descends*] I am sinking . . .

The background represents a wood of giant hollyhocks in bloom. The flowers are of various colors: white, pink, crimson, sulphur yellow and bluish purple. Above their tops is seen the gilded roof of a castle; its apex is a flower bud resembling a crown.

At the foot of the foundation walls of the castle, hay and straw heaped up in ricks. These cover litter, cast out from the stable.

The wings, which remain unchanged throughout the play, are stylized frescoes: a blending of interior, architecture and landscape.

[*The* Glazier *and the* Daughter of Indra *are seen entering*]

D. OF INDRA: The castle is steadily growing up from the earth. . . . Can you see how it has grown since last year?

GLAZIER: [*To himself*] I have never seen this castle before—have never heard of a castle that could grow —but . . . [*To the* Daughter of Indra, *with sincere conviction*] Yes—it has grown six feet. . . . That's because of the manure . . . and if you take a good look, you will see that a wing has sprouted on the side where the sun shines.

D. OF INDRA: Don't you think it will come out in bloom soon, now that it is past midsummer?

GLAZIER: You see the flower up there, don't you?

D. OF INDRA: Yes—I see it! [*She claps her hands joyfully*] Tell me, father, why is it that flowers rise up out of dirt?

GLAZIER: [*With piety*] Because they do not thrive in dirt. That is why they are anxious to reach the light, so that they may blossom and die.

D. OF INDRA: Do you know who lives in the castle?

GLAZIER: I did know once but have forgotten.

D. OF INDRA: I believe someone is imprisoned there . . . he must be waiting for me to set him free.

GLAZIER: And at what cost?

D. OF INDRA: One never bargains when it comes to duty. Let us enter the castle.

GLAZIER: Yes—let us go in.

[*They go toward the rear, which slowly opens, dividing itself in two parts that disappear in the wings*]

The scene is now a plain, naked room. A table and a few chairs are the only furnishings in it.

On one of the chairs is seated the Officer, *attired in a bizarre, yet modern, uniform. He is rocking back and forth in his chair, while striking the table with his sabre.*

D. OF INDRA: [*She goes over to the* Officer *and gently takes away the sabre from his hand*] You mustn't do that! You mustn't do that!

OFFICER: Agnes dear, let me keep the sabre!

D. OF INDRA: No, you will break the table! [*To the* Glazier] Go down to the harness room now and put in the pane. We'll see each other later.

[*The* Glazier *leaves*]

D. OF INDRA: You are a prisoner in your own house. I have come to set you free.

OFFICER: I have been waiting for you to come, although I was never certain you *would* come.

D. OF INDRA: The castle is a stronghold—it has seven walls—but . . . it will be done!—Do you wish to be free, or don't you?

OFFICER: To tell the truth, I don't know. Whatever I choose, it will mean suffering. Every joy in life has to be paid for with double its worth of sorrow. Living here is hard enough, but if I have to buy back my precious freedom, I shall have to suffer threefold. . . . Agnes, I'd rather endure life as it is here, if I only may see you.

D. OF INDRA: What do you see in me?

OFFICER: In you I see beauty—which is the harmony of the universe. Only in the solar system's motion, in the exquisite, inspiring chords of a stringed instrument, in the vibrations of light do I find delineated anything resembling the beauty of your figure. . . . You are a child of celestial spheres—

D. OF INDRA: And so are you!

OFFICER: Why, then, must I tend horses, look after stables, and see that the litter is removed?

D. OF INDRA: That you may wish to get away from it all!

OFFICER: I wish to—but it is so hard to do just that!

D. OF INDRA: But we owe it to ourselves to seek freedom in light, don't we? It is a duty we have—

OFFICER: Duty? Life has never recognized its duties to me!

D. OF INDRA: You feel that life has been unjust to you, then?

OFFICER: Yes—it has been unjust. . . .

Voices can now be heard behind the screen or partition which is drawn aside in the next moment.

The Officer *and the* Daughter of Indra *glance in that direction. Then they remain motionless in position, gestures and expression. Seated at a table is the* Mother. *She is sickly. Before her is a lighted taper. Now and then she prunes the wick with a pair of snuffers. Piled on the table are some shirts which she has just finished making and which she is now marking with quill and ink. On the right stands a dark, wooden wardrobe.*

FATHER: [*He hands her a cape of silk. Then he speaks to her gently*] Don't you want it?

MOTHER: A silken cape for me, my dear? What use would it be to me, when I am going to die soon?

FATHER: Do you really believe what the doctor says?

MOTHER: That, too . . . but most of all I believe the voice inside me.

[*Her hand fumbles toward her heart*]

FATHER: [*With sorrow in his voice*] Then you are really seriously—? And first, last and always you are thinking of your children. . . .

MOTHER: Haven't they been everything to me— my life, my very reason for living—my happiness, my sorrows?

FATHER: Kristina! Forgive me—for all I have failed in!

MOTHER: Forgive you? For what? . . . But forgive *me*, my dearest! We have both tormented each other —and why? That's something we cannot explain . . . there was no other way out, I suppose! Now here is the children's new linen. . . . Be sure to see that they change twice a week, Wednesdays and Saturdays, and that Louise washes them—their whole bodies. . . . Are you going out?

FATHER: I have to be at the teachers' staff meeting at eleven.

MOTHER: Will you ask Alfred to come in to me, before you leave?

FATHER: [*He points to the* Officer] But, dearest, he is standing right here!

MOTHER: To think that my eyes should be failing me, too . . . yes, darkness is setting in. . . . [*She snuffs out the taper*] Alfred, come here!

[*The* Father *disappears through the wall. As he leaves, he nods a goodbye. The* Officer *steps over to the* Mother]

MOTHER: Who is that girl there?

OFFICER: [*In a whisper*] Why, it's Agnes!

MOTHER: [*In a similar tone of voice*] Oh, it's Agnes, is it? Have you heard what they are saying? That she is the daughter of the God Indra, and that she pleaded with him to come down to Earth in order to see how human beings really live and behave. But don't mention this to anyone. . . .

OFFICER: A child of heaven, that's what she is!

MOTHER: [*In a louder voice*] Alfred, my darling, I shall soon be leaving you and the rest of the children. But before I go, I want to leave a thought with you, to be remembered all through your life!

OFFICER: [*Sadly*] Speak, mother—

MOTHER: Just these words: Never quarrel with God!

OFFICER: What do you mean, mother?

MOTHER: You must not go about feeling that life has wronged and cheated you.

OFFICER: But when people treat me unjustly . . .

MOTHER: You are alluding to the time when you were unfairly punished for having taken a coin that later was found elsewhere?

OFFICER: Yes! That piece of injustice has distorted the purpose of my life ever since—

MOTHER: Perhaps it has! But go and look in the wardrobe now—

OFFICER: [*Shamefaced*] So you know, then! It's— is it . . . ?

MOTHER: *The Swiss Family Robinson*—for which—

OFFICER: Don't say it—don't—

MOTHER: —for which your brother was punished . . . and which you had torn the leaves out of—and hidden!

OFFICER: To think that this old wardrobe should still be here—after twenty years. . . . After the many times we have moved! And my mother died ten years ago!

MOTHER: Well, what has that to do with it? You

just *have* to ask questions about everything. That's why you ruin for yourself the best that life has to give!—Ah, there is Lina!

LINA: [*Enters*] I want to thank you ever so much, ma'am, but I can't go to the christening after all.

MOTHER: Why not, my child?

LINA: I have nothing to wear.

MOTHER: I'll lend you my cape here.

LINA: Dear me—no, that wouldn't *do*!

MOTHER: I don't see why not! I shall never again be going to another party.

OFFICER: What would father say? He gave it to you, didn't he?

MOTHER: Oh, what petty minds.

FATHER: [*Puts his head inside the door*] Are you letting the maid use the cape I gave you?

MOTHER: Don't say things like that! Remember that I also was a servant girl once. . . . Why do you want to be insulting to an innocent young girl?

FATHER: And why should you offend me, your husband?

MOTHER: Oh, this life of ours! When you do something out of the goodness of your heart there is always someone who finds it ugly and bad. And if you do something good for *one* person, then someone else feels hurt. Oh, this life!

[*She trims the taper, so that it goes out. The scene is now in darkness, and the partition is pushed back into its previous position*]

D. OF INDRA: Humanity is to be pitied!

OFFICER: Is that what you think?

D. OF INDRA: Yes. Life is hard—but love conquers all! Come—and see!

[*They walk toward the rear*]

The backdrop is now raised. One sees a different background, representing a dilapidated, ancient fire-proof wall. In its center is a gate opening onto a path that terminates at a green, sunlit space, featuring a blue aconite, or monk's hood, of giant proportions.

On the right, close by the gate, sits the Portress. *She wears a shawl wrapped round her head and shoulders, and she is busy crocheting a star-studded bedspread.*

On the other side of the gate, left, there is a small billboard, which the Billposter *is in the throes of cleaning. Nearby stands a dip-net on a pole painted green. Farther to the left is a door with an air-hole, shaped like a four-leaf clover.*

To the right of the gate stands a dwarfed lime tree. Its trunk is jet-black, and it bears few leaves. These are pale green in color. Nearby is seen an aperture, leading to the basement.

D. OF INDRA: [*Steps over to the* Portress] You haven't finished the star-covered bedspread, have you?

PORTRESS: No, my dear little friend. Twenty-six years is not a long time for a work like this!

D. OF INDRA: And he never came back—your lover?

PORTRESS: No—but that was not *his* fault. He *had* to go away . . . poor man. . . . It's thirty years ago now!

D. OF INDRA: [*To the* Billposter] She used to be in the ballet, didn't she? In there at the Opera?

BILLPOSTER: She was the best one they had there. . . . But when he went away, it was as if he had taken her dancing feet with him—and it was not long before her career was ended.

D. OF INDRA: People do nothing but complain.— You see it in their eyes—and the lament is in their voices, too. . . .

BILLPOSTER: I don't think I complain very much. Certainly not now that I have got myself a dip-net and a green fish-well!

D. OF INDRA: And that makes you happy?

BILLPOSTER: Yes, it makes me very happy! I have dreamed of it since I was a lad! And now my dream has come true!—I know I am past fifty, of course. . . .

D. OF INDRA: Fifty years for a dip-net and a fish-well.—

BILLPOSTER: A *green* fish-well—a *green* one. . . .

D. OF INDRA: [*To the* Portress] If you will let me have your shawl now, I'd like to sit here and watch the human children. . . . But you must stand behind me and help me a little!

[*She is given the shawl and takes the* Portress' *seat by the gate*]

PORTRESS: Today is the last day of the season, and then the Opera will be closed. Today they will know whether they have been re-engaged.

D. OF INDRA: What about those who are not engaged?

PORTRESS: Oh, may God forgive me—I hate to look at them. . . . I cover my face with my shawl— I—

D. OF INDRA: Poor human beings!

PORTRESS: Look! Here is one of them! . . . She is not among the chosen!—See how she is crying.

[*The* Singer *enters from the left. She hastens out through the gate, holding a handkerchief to her eyes. She stops momentarily on the path outside the gate and presses her head against the wall. Then she leaves quickly*]

D. OF INDRA: Man is to be pitied! . . .

PORTRESS: But here—here you see what a happy human being looks like!

[*The* Officer *enters through the gate. He is dressed in a redingote and top hat; in his hand he carries a bouquet of roses. He radiates joy and buoyant happiness*]

PORTRESS: He is engaged to be married to Miss Victoria!

OFFICER: [*He stands downstage, looks up above and sings*] Victoria!

PORTRESS: Miss Victoria will be here in a moment.

OFFICER: Good! The carriage is waiting—the table is set—the champagne is on ice. . . . I'd like to embrace you ladies.

[*He embraces the* Daughter of Indra *and the* Portress. *Then he sings out again*] Victoria!

WOMAN'S VOICE: [*Sings back from above*] Here I am!

OFFICER: [*Starts to pace*] Oh well . . . I shall wait!

D. OF INDRA: Do you know me?

OFFICER: No—I know only one woman—Victoria! For seven years I have been waiting for her here— waiting—waiting . . . at noon of day when the sun-rays touch the chimney-stacks, and in the evening when the dusk of night sets in. . . . Look—here you can see the imprint of my steps on the walk—the faithful lover's steps. . . . Hurray! She is mine! [*He sings*] Victoria! [*This time there is no reply*] Well— she is dressing. [*To the* Billposter] There is your dip-net, I see! Everybody at the Opera is mad about dip-nets—or I should say, fish! Because the fish are mute—and therefore can't sing. . . . How much does a gadget like that cost?

BILLPOSTER: It's rather expensive.

OFFICER: [*Sings*] Victoria! [*He shakes the lime tree*] See! It's getting green again! For the eighth time! [*He sings out*] Victoria! . . . Now she is arranging her hair. [*To the* Daughter of Indra] My sweet lady, please let me go upstairs and fetch my bride!

PORTRESS: No one is allowed to go backstage.

OFFICER: For seven years I have been coming here! Seven times three hundred and sixty-five makes two thousand five hundred and fifty-five! [*He halts and pokes at the door with the four-leaf clover*] And I have looked at this door two thousand five hundred and fifty-five times without being able to figure out where it leads! And that clover leaf, which is supposed to let in light! For whom is it to let in light? Is anybody in there, eh? Does anybody live in there?

PORTRESS: I don't know anything about it! I've never seen it opened.

OFFICER: It looks like a door to a pantry. I saw one like it when I was four and went visiting with our maid one Sunday afternoon! She took me from one family to another—to chat with the servants there—but we never went beyond the kitchen. And I had to sit wedged between the water barrel and a keg of salt. I have seen a multitude of kitchens in my days, and the pantry was invariably in the servants' hall outside the kitchen and always had small round holes bored in the door—holes shaped like a four-leaf clover. . . . But why should they have a pantry at the Opera, when they haven't any kitchen there! [*He sings*] Victoria!—Tell me, my dear lady—she couldn't have gone out any other way, could she?

PORTRESS: No—there is no other way.

OFFICER: Oh well, then I am bound to see her.

[*Artists come rushing out. The* Officer *scrutinizes each and every one*]

OFFICER: Now she simply must be here before much longer! Oh, madam! That blue aconite out there! I've seen that flower there since I was a child.

. . . Is it the same flower? . . . I recall being in a parsonage out in the country when I was seven. . . . The aconite has two doves—two blue doves underneath its hood . . . and then a bee came flying and crept into the hood. I thought to myself: now I'll catch you . . . and I cupped my hands round the flower. But the bee stung my hand right through the petals, and I started to cry. Then the pastor's wife came and put some wet earth on it to ease the pain . . . and then we had wild strawberries and cream for supper. . . . I think it's already getting dark. [*To the* Billposter] Where are you going now?

BILLPOSTER: I am going home for supper.

OFFICER: [*Running his hand across his eyes*] Supper? At this time of day?—Oh, please, may I go in and make a brief telephone call to "the growing castle"? May I?

D. OF INDRA: What business could you have there?

OFFICER: I want to tell the glazier to put in the storm windows. Soon we'll have winter—and I suffer so terribly from the cold!

[*He goes inside to the* Portress]

D. OF INDRA: Who is Miss Victoria?

PORTRESS: She is his sweetheart.

D. OF INDRA: There is truth in your answer.—What she is to us and to others, means nothing to him. Only what she is to *him*, is what she *really* is!

[*There is a sudden, stark darkness*]

PORTRESS: [*Lights her lantern*] It is getting dark early today.

D. OF INDRA: To the gods the years are as minutes.

PORTRESS: And to us humans a minute may seem like a year!

[*The* Officer *comes out again. He is covered with dust, and the roses are withered*]

OFFICER: She hasn't come yet?

PORTRESS: No.

OFFICER: But she will, I am sure!—She will come! [*He starts to pace*] Yes, perhaps I had best cancel the dinner—since it is already a little late. . . . Yes, yes, that's what I'll do!

[*He goes inside again to telephone*]

PORTRESS: [*To the* Daughter of Indra] May I have my shawl now?

D. OF INDRA: No—you take it easy for a while, my dear. I'll take care of your duties! I want to learn all I can about life and human beings. . . . I want to see if life is really so hard as they say it is.

PORTRESS: But one never gets a moment of rest here. Day and night, one never gets a chance to shut an eye.

D. OF INDRA: No sleep—even at night?

PORTRESS: Well, yes—if you can manage it with the bell cord round your wrist . . . for there are watchmen on the stage all through the night—and they are relieved every three hours.

D. OF INDRA: But that's torture!

PORTRESS: You may think so, but the rest of us

are only too glad to get a position like this. If you only knew how envious people are of me.

D. OF INDRA: Envious! They are envious of the tortured!

PORTRESS: Yes. But let me tell you something that is harder to bear than all the night vigil and all the drudgery, harder than the draft and cold and dampness—and that is to have to receive the confidences of all the unfortunates here—as I have to do. . . . They all come to me! Why? Perhaps in the wrinkles of my face they read the runes of past suffering. Perhaps that is what persuades them to confide to me their secrets. . . . That shawl, my dear, holds agonies and disappointments, secrets and confidences —my own and theirs—of the past thirty years!

D. OF INDRA: It is heavy, and it burns like nettle.

PORTRESS: Wear it then, if you like. . . . And if you should find it too heavy for you, just call me and I'll come and relieve you.

D. OF INDRA: Goodbye. What *you* can do, *I* should be able to do.

PORTRESS: We'll see! . . . Only treat my poor young friends kindly—and never lose patience with them, when they come with their complaints!

[*She disappears down the walk*]

The stage grows completely dark. During the darkness, there is a change of season: the lime tree now has lost its leaves; the blue aconite has withered. When daylight has returned, the verdure in the perspective of the walk has changed into autumn brown.

[*The* Officer *appears again, coming out when the stage is lighted. His hair is now gray, likewise his beard. His clothes are shabby, his collar wilted and soiled. All that remains of the bouquet of roses is the forked stems—no leaves, no petals are left. He walks to and fro*]

OFFICER: Judging by what I see, summer is gone and fall is near. I can see it by the lime tree there— and the monk's hood! [*He commences his walk again*] But autumn is spring for me, for that's when the Opera opens again! And that's when she'll be here! Dear madam, will you allow me to sit down for a little while?

D. OF INDRA: [*Gets up from her chair and offers it to the* Officer] Sit here, my friend . . . I'll stand.

OFFICER: [*Seats himself*] If I could only get a little sleep, too! That would be still better. . . . [*He dozes momentarily, and then suddenly gets up with a start and begins to pace back and forth. He stops before the door with the four-leaf clover and pokes at it*] This door—it just won't give me any peace! What is behind it? There must be *something*! [*Faint music is heard from above, in dance tempo*] So! They've started rehearsals again! [*The stage is now lighted by fits and starts, as by a flashing light*] What's the meaning of this? [*He accentuates the words as the lights go on and off*] Light and dark; dark and light. . . .

D. OF INDRA: [*Imitates him*] Day and night; night and day. . . . A merciful Providence desires to shorten your waiting. That is why the days fly, ever pursuing the nights!

[*It again grows light on the stage. The* Billposter *enters with his dip-net and billposting material*]

OFFICER: So—it's you—with your dip-net. . . . Did you have a good catch?

BILLPOSTER: Yes, I should say I did! It was a warm summer, and a little long. . . . The net wasn't bad—but not as good as I had expected it to be. . . .

OFFICER: [*He accentuates the words*] Not as good as I had expected it to be! That is very well put! Nothing is as *I* expected it to be! . . . Because the thought is greater than the deed—higher than anything material. . . .

[*He starts to pace again, beating the bouquet against the wall so that the last remaining petals and leaves fall off*]

BILLPOSTER: Hasn't she come down yet?

OFFICER: No, not yet, but she won't be long now! —Have you any idea what is behind that door?

BILLPOSTER: No, I have never seen that door open.

OFFICER: I am going in to telephone for a locksmith to come and open it.

[*He goes inside*]

[*The* Billposter *puts up a bill; then he goes toward the right*]

D. OF INDRA: What was wrong with the dip-net?

BILLPOSTER: What was wrong? Well, there wasn't anything wrong with it exactly—but it wasn't precisely what I had expected it to be. . . . So my first joy turned into disappointment you might say. . . .

D. OF INDRA: What had you expected when you bought the dip-net?

BILLPOSTER: What I'd expected? Why—I don't know. . . .

D. OF INDRA: Let me tell you then! You had expected it to be what it turned out *not* to be. You wanted it to be green, but *not*—the green you got!

BILLPOSTER: You put your finger on it, lady! You know everything! That's why they all come to you with their troubles. . . . I wish you would listen to *me*, too, some time. . . .

D. OF INDRA: I will be happy to. Come and tell me, pour out your heart to me.

[*She goes into her room. The* Billposter *remains outside and talks to her through the wicket*]

Again the stage is in complete darkness. Then it grows light, and the lime tree can be seen, its leaves now green; the aconite is blooming again, and the sun shines on the verdure in the space at the end of the walk, in the background.

[*The* Officer *comes out. He is now an old, white-haired man. His clothes are in rags, his shoes*

worn. *He still carries the stems that are left of the bouquet of roses. He walks to and fro, moving like a man who has aged considerably. Then he stops and studies the bill that has just been posted. A* Ballet Girl *comes from the left*]

OFFICER: Has Miss Victoria left yet?

BALLET GIRL: No, she has not.

OFFICER: Then I'll wait! No doubt she'll be down soon?

BALLET GIRL: [*With a serious expression on her face*] No doubt she will!

OFFICER: Don't go away yet, and you'll see what is behind this door. I've just sent for the locksmith!

BALLET GIRL: It will really be interesting to see that door opened. That door and the growing castle! Do you know the growing castle?

OFFICER: If I do!—Haven't I been a prisoner there!

BALLET GIRL: You don't say? Was that you? But tell me—why did they have so many horses there?

OFFICER: Why—it was a stable castle—

BALLET GIRL: [*Painfully touched*] How stupid of me! I should have known. . . .

[*A* Chorist *enters from the left*]

OFFICER: Has Miss Victoria left yet?

CHORIST: [*In a serious voice*] No! She hasn't left! She never leaves!

OFFICER: That's because she loves me! . . . Don't leave now before the locksmith comes to open the door here.

CHORIST: Oh—are they going to open the door? Oh, that will be fun to see!—I just want to ask the portress a question.

[*The* Prompter *enters from the left*]

OFFICER: Has Miss Victoria left yet?

PROMPTER: No, not as far as I know.

OFFICER: There you see! Didn't I say that she would be waiting for me!—But don't go! The door is to be opened.

PROMPTER: Which door?

OFFICER: Is there more than one door?

PROMPTER: Oh, I know. The one with the clover leaf! Then I certainly want to stay! I just want to have a word with the portress.

[*The* Ballet Girl, *the* Chorist *and the* Prompter *group themselves beside the* Billposter, *outside the* Portress' *wicket. They take turns speaking with the* Daughter of Indra. *The* Glazier *enters through the gate*]

OFFICER: Are you the locksmith?

GLAZIER: No, the locksmith couldn't come. But I guess I can do the job, even though I am a glazier.

OFFICER: Certainly, certainly—but have you your diamond with you?

GLAZIER: Of course! A glazier without a diamond! What do you think?

OFFICER: Never mind!—Let's get to work!

[*He claps his hands. All gather round the door*]

[Chorists *dressed as Mastersingers, and Ballet* Girls, *attired as the dancers in* AÏDA, *enter from the left. They join the others*]

OFFICER: Locksmith—or glazier . . . do your duty! [*The* Glazier *steps to the door with his diamond in his hand*] A moment like this does not come often in a man's life. For this reason, my good friends, stop to think . . . think carefully. . . .

POLICEMAN: [*Enters*] In the name of the law, I forbid you to open that door!

OFFICER: Oh, Heavens, what a fuss there is whenever anybody tries to do something great and new! But we shall take this matter to court! I'll see a lawyer! Then we'll find out what the law says! I'm going to the attorney!

Without lowering the curtain, the scene changes to an attorney's office. The gate remains in its place, functioning now as the entrance wicket in the railing that extends from left to right, clear across the stage.

The Portress' *room serves as the* Attorney's *private compartment, the front partition having been removed. The lime tree, now barren, serves as a hat and coat rack. The billboard is covered with official and legal notices and court decisions. The door with the clover leaf now hides book shelves on which documents are piled.*

The Attorney, *in evening dress with tails and white tie, sits at a writing desk littered with legal papers and documents, right, in back of the railing. His face speaks of untold sufferings. It is chalk-white and wrinkled, with shadows of bluish purple. He is ugly, and his countenance reflects all the crimes and vices with which he has been forced to come in contact.*

His two clerks are both infirm: one has lost an arm, the other one is minus an eye.

The ones who collected to view the opening of the door, remain on the stage; they now seem to be waiting to gain admittance to the Attorney. *They appear to have been waiting forever.*

Daughter of Indra, *wearing the* Portress' *shawl, stands downstage, as does the* Officer.

ATTORNEY: [*Steps forward to the* Daughter of Indra] Tell me, my sister, may I have that shawl? I'll hang it inside, until I can make a fire in the stove—then I'll burn it with all its sorrows and miseries. . . .

D. OF INDRA: Not yet, my brother! First I want to have it completely filled! And above all, I want it to absorb all your agonies—all the confidences about crime and vice, about revilement and slander, about things wrongly gained. . . .

ATTORNEY: My dear little friend—for that your shawl would not be big enough! Look at these walls. . . . Even the wall paper seems to have been soiled by every kind of sin! Take a look at these papers, which are filled with stories of wrongs, written by me! Look at *me!*—Among those who come here you will never find a human being with a smile on his face—here you see only vicious glances, clenched fists, and teeth ready to bite! And they all squirt their anger and their envy, and spit their suspicions over me. . . . See. . . . Look at my hands! They are black—and can never be washed clean! You see how cracked and bleeding they are! I can never wear a suit of clothes more than a day or two before it stinks of other people's crimes. . . . Sometimes I have the place fumigated with sulphur—but it doesn't help much. . . . I sleep in the back room, and whenever I dream, I dream about crime. . . . Just now I have a murder case before the court. . . . That's bad enough—but do you know what is worse?—the very worst?—Having to separate a married couple!—I feel as if I heard a cry from the bowels of the earth and from the heavens—a voice crying treason—treason against the source of life, against the wellspring of everything that's good, against love itself. . . . And you'll find that after reams and reams of paper have been scribbled full of mutual accusations . . . and then a sympathetic person takes one of them aside for a heart-to-heart talk, and asks—with a pinch of the ear, or with a smile—this simple question: What is it that you really have against your husband?—or your wife, as the case may be—then he—or she—stands mute, can't find an answer, doesn't know the cause of it all! I can remember once when . . . yes, I think the trouble was caused by a salad . . . another time it was caused by a mere word—generally such trouble is caused by nothing but trifles. . . . But the suffering, the torture! That's what I have to bear! Look at my face! Do you think I could ever win a woman's love with a face such as mine—a criminal's face? And do you think anybody would care to be a friend of mine—I, who have to collect debts and accounts and liabilities for everybody in the city?—To be a human being is hard!

D. OF INDRA: Man is to be pitied!

ATTORNEY: Indeed, man is! And how people manage to live is a puzzle to me! They marry on an income of two thousand a year—when they need four thousand. . . . And so they have to borrow, of course! They all borrow! And then they muddle along and zig-zag through life for the rest of their days until they die. . . . And then it's discovered there is nothing left but debts! Who is it who pays in the end? Well—who knows. . . .

D. OF INDRA: He who feeds the birds!

ATTORNEY: Well—but if He who feeds the birds would only come to Earth and see what we poor human creatures have to go through—then, perhaps, He would show compassion. . . .

D. OF INDRA: Man is, indeed, to be pitied!

ATTORNEY: Man is, indeed! [*He turns to the* Officer] What is it you wish?

OFFICER: I simply wish to know whether Miss Victoria has left yet?

ATTORNEY: No, she has not, you can rest assured of that. . . . But why are you poking at my closet there?

OFFICER: Why, the door looks exactly like . . .

ATTORNEY: Oh no—oh no—oh no. . . .

[*Church bells are heard ringing*]

OFFICER: Is there a funeral in the city?

ATTORNEY: No, today is university graduation day. They are conferring the doctor's degree. They are conferring the degree of doctor of laws on me today. Wouldn't you, too, like to have a degree conferred on you and receive the laurel wreath?

OFFICER: Why, I have no objection. At least it would be a kind of distraction.

ATTORNEY: Well, then, let's get ready for the solemnity without delay. . . . But you must first go home and dress for the occasion!

[*The* Officer *leaves*]

The scene is darkened, and the setting is changed into the chancel of a church.

The railing now functions as the balustrade; the billboard serves as an announcement board for the hymns to be sung at the occasion; the attorney's desk is the pulpit of the presiding functionary; the door with the clover leaf is the entrance to the vestry.

The chorists from Die Meistersinger *function as heralds with staffs. The ballet girls carry laurel wreaths. The others act as spectators.*

The backdrop is raised, baring the new background representing the pipes of a huge organ. The instrument itself with the keyboard is below. On it, above, is the organist's mirror. The music swells from the organ.

On each side are representatives of the four faculties: philosophy, theology, medicine and jurisprudence.

The scene is at first empty for a few moments.

[*The* Heralds *enter from the left*]
[*The* Ballet Girls *follow, carrying the laurel wreaths, which they hold high before them*]
[*Three Conferees enter in turn, one after the other, from the right. Each one is crowned with a wreath; after which they go out, left*]
[*The* Attorney *steps forward to receive his wreath*]
[*The* Ballet Girls *turn their backs on him, refusing to present him with a wreath, and leave*]
[*The* Attorney, *visibly affected, supports himself against a temple column*]
[*All withdraw, leaving the* Attorney *alone on the stage*]
[Daughter of Indra *enters. She wears a white veil over her shoulders and head*]

D. OF INDRA: Now, you see, I have washed the shawl. . . . But why are you standing here? Didn't you get your wreath?

ATTORNEY: No—I was not considered worthy of it.

D. OF INDRA: Why not? Because you have been championing the poor, spoken a good word for the wicked, lightened the burden for the guilty, obtained another chance for the condemned? Oh, humanity! . . . Men are no angels—they are to be pitied!

ATTORNEY: You must not speak badly about human beings. . . . Isn't it my duty to plead for them?

D. OF INDRA: [*She supports herself against the organ*] Why do they always abuse their friends?

ATTORNEY: They don't know any better.

D. OF INDRA: Then let us show them the light. . . . Will you help? Shall we—together—

ATTORNEY: They do not care to be enlightened. . . . Oh, that the gods in heaven would hear the weeping of our sorrow.

D. OF INDRA: I shall reach their ears. [*She seats herself at the organ*] Do you know what I see in the mirror here? The world as it *should* be—as it *really is!* Because as it is now, it is upside down!

ATTORNEY: How did it come to be turned upside down?

D. OF INDRA: When the copy was made . . .

ATTORNEY: You put your finger on what is wrong! The copy . . . I always sensed that the replica was faulty! When I recalled the original, I became dissatisfied with the world. And I was called an ingrate, hard to please; I was told I was looking at things through the devil's eyes, and much more in that vein.

D. OF INDRA: Yes, isn't it a mad world! Look at the four faculties here! The government—whose duty it is to preserve society—pays their salaries, all four of them. Theology, the science of God, is constantly attacked and ridiculed by Philosophy, which declares itself to be the cornerstone of all wisdom. And Medicine, which is forever at odds with Philosophy, contradicts Theology's claim to be a science and calls it mere superstition. And yet the four are part of the same academic council—whose duty it is to teach respect for the university! Wouldn't you call this madness? And woe be to him who first recovers his reason and sanity!

ATTORNEY: The first ones to realize it are the theologians. As a preparatory study they take philosophy. Philosophy teaches them that theology is nonsense. Then, when they study theology, they are taught that philosophy is nonsense! Isn't that madness?

D. OF INDRA: Then there is jurisprudence—the servant of all, except the toilers—

ATTORNEY: Justice, which—in the name of the law—can mark a man for life! Justice—which so often makes a mockery of justice!

D. OF INDRA: What a sorry mess you have made for yourselves, you children of humanity! For that's what you all are—children!—Come here, and I shall give you a wreath—one that will be more appropriate for you! [*She places a wreath of thorns on his head*] And now I shall play for you.

[*She sits down at the keyboard of the organ. But instead of hearing organ music, one hears human voices*]

VOICES OF CHILDREN: Eternal One! Eternal One!
[*The last note is sustained*]

VOICES OF WOMEN: Be merciful, O God!
[*The last note is similarly held*]

VOICES OF MEN: [*Tenors*] Save us, for Your mercy's sake!

[*Again the last note is held*]

VOICES OF MEN: [*Basses*] Spare Your children, O Lord, and let not Your wrath descend upon us!

ALL: Be merciful, O God! Hear us! Take pity upon us mortals!—Eternal One, why are You afar from us? We cry out of the depths to You: Have mercy upon us, God Eternal! Make not the burden of Your children too heavy! Hear us! Hear us!

The scene grows dark. The Daughter of Indra *rises, goes toward the* Attorney. *Through effects of lighting, the organ is transformed into Fingal's Cave. The backwash of the sea can be seen against the basalt pillars, and the sounds of waves and wind can be heard in harmonious blending.*

ATTORNEY: Where are we, sister?

D. OF INDRA: What do you hear?

ATTORNEY: I hear the dripping of water.

D. OF INDRA: It is tears . . . the tears of mankind. What else do you hear?

ATTORNEY: I hear sighing. . . . I hear whining and wailing.

D. OF INDRA: This is as far as the plaints of mortals reach . . . and no farther. But why this eternal wailing? Is there nothing in life to rejoice over?

ATTORNEY: Yes—that . . . which is sweeter than anything . . . and yet more bitter than anything: love—a wife and a home: the most sublime and the most hollow!

D. OF INDRA: I would like to submit myself to the test.

ATTORNEY: With me?

D. OF INDRA: With you!—You know the pitfalls and the stumbling blocks. . . . Let us stay clear of them.

ATTORNEY: I am poor . . .

D. OF INDRA: What does it matter? All that matters is that we love each other! A little beauty does not have to be bought.

ATTORNEY: I have dislikes and aversions. They may be your likes and sympathies.

D. OF INDRA: We have to modify and compromise, give way to each other.

ATTORNEY: And if we tire of each other?

D. OF INDRA: When the child comes, it will bring a joy that will be ever young!

ATTORNEY: And you—you will have me, poor and ugly as I am, scorned and despised, disdained and rejected?

D. OF INDRA: Yes. Let us unite our destinies.

ATTORNEY: So be it.

A starkly simple room behind the Attorney's *office. On the left, a large double bed with curtains round it; close by, a window.*

On the right, a parlor stove with cooking utensils.

Kristin *is busy pasting paper strips, or tape, along the openings between the windows and the casement.*

There is a door, rear, leading to the law office. It is open, and beyond it can be seen men and women, all visibly poor, waiting to see the Attorney.

KRISTIN: I paste, I paste!

D. OF INDRA: [*Sits by the stove. She looks pale and worn*] You are shutting out the air! I am stifling!

KRISTIN: I have just one little leaky spot left now . . .

D. OF INDRA: Air! Air!—I can't breathe here . . .

KRISTIN: I paste, I paste!

ATTORNEY: That's right, Kristin. . . . Heat costs money!

D. OF INDRA: Oh, I feel as if my jaws were glued together.

ATTORNEY: [*He is standing in the doorway, holding a document in his hand*] Is the little one asleep?

D. OF INDRA: Yes, at last!

ATTORNEY: [*Gently*] Its continual crying frightens away my clients.

D. OF INDRA: [*In a mild tone of voice*] What is there we can do about it?

ATTORNEY: Nothing!

D. OF INDRA: We must try to find a roomier place to live.

ATTORNEY: We can't afford it.

D. OF INDRA: Will you let me open the window? The air here is foul! It suffocates me!

ATTORNEY: Then the heat will escape, and we'll freeze.

D. OF INDRA: This is horrible! Will you let us scrub the floor in the office?

ATTORNEY: You are not strong enough to do that! I haven't the strength either! And Kristin must finish the pasting. She has to paste strips throughout the house, from top to bottom—every crack and crevice—in the ceilings, the walls and the floors.

D. OF INDRA: I foresaw that we might be poor, but I was not prepared for this filth and dirt.

ATTORNEY: Poverty is a kin of squalor.

D. OF INDRA: This is worse than I had thought!

ATTORNEY: There are others who are worse off. We still have some food in the house.

D. OF INDRA: But what kind of food?

ATTORNEY: Cabbage is cheap. And it is nourishing and good.

D. OF INDRA: Yes—if you like cabbage! To me it is distasteful!

ATTORNEY: You never said anything before.

D. OF INDRA: I tried to sacrifice my own preferences out of love for you!

ATTORNEY: Then I must make a sacrifice of what I like, too. We each must sacrifice something.

D. OF INDRA: What shall we eat, then? Fish?—But you don't like fish!

ATTORNEY: And it's expensive, too.

D. OF INDRA: This is more wretched than I thought it would be.

ATTORNEY: [*In a gentle voice*] Now you see how

hard it is. . . . And the child that was to be the bond between us—our blessing! The child turns out to be our undoing.

D. OF INDRA: Beloved! I shall die in here—in this air! All I ever see is the view of the yard in the back! I hear nothing but crying children, and lie without sleep for hours! I hear the people outside, whining without end, bickering with each other, accusing each other. . . . There is nothing left for me but death!

ATTORNEY: My poor little flower, who is without light—without air—

D. OF INDRA: And you say there are those who have it worse than we?

ATTORNEY: I am one of the few envied ones in our street.

D. OF INDRA: If I could only have some beauty in my home, things might not seem so bad.

ATTORNEY: I know . . . you mean a flower—above all a heliotrope. But that would cost as much as six bottles of milk or half a bushel of potatoes.

D. OF INDRA: I'll gladly go without food if I can only have a flower.

ATTORNEY: But there is one kind of beauty one doesn't have to pay for! Its lack in the home is more painful than anything else to a man with a feeling for beauty. . . .

D. OF INDRA: What is that?

ATTORNEY: If I should tell you, you'll be angry with me.

D. OF INDRA: Haven't we agreed never to get angry?

ATTORNEY: So we have. Everything can be overlooked, Agnes, except a short-tempered, sharp, curt tone of voice. Have you ever heard such a tone of voice? Or haven't you?

D. OF INDRA: Such a tone will never be used by either of us.

ATTORNEY: Never as far as I am concerned!

D. OF INDRA: You can tell me now!

ATTORNEY: Well—when I come into a room, the first thing I look at is the curtains—to see how they are draped in the sash. [He goes over to the window and adjusts the curtains] If they hang like a rope or a rag, then I don't remain long in that house. . . . Next I take a glance at the chairs. If they are placed where they should be placed, I stay. . . . [He moves a chair back against the wall] And finally I look at the candles in their holders. If they are askew—then the whole house is awry. [He puts straight a candle on the bureau] It is this kind of beauty that cannot be bought, my dearest.

D. OF INDRA: [With bent head] Don't be short-tempered, Axel—

ATTORNEY: I wasn't short-tempered!

D. OF INDRA: Yes, you were.

ATTORNEY: Now, what in hell . . .

D. OF INDRA: What kind of language is that?

ATTORNEY: Forgive me, Agnes! But I have suffered as much from your disorderliness as you have suffered from dirt and filth. And I haven't dared offer my help to keep the house in order for fear that

you would be angry. You would think I was reproaching you. Ugh! Don't you think we ought to stop bickering?

D. OF INDRA: It is a hardship to be married. . . . A greater test than anything else! One has to be an angel. . . .

ATTORNEY: I think you are right.

D. OF INDRA: I feel as if I were beginning to hate you!

ATTORNEY: That would be the end for us! Let us never feel hatred for each other! I vow I shall never again remark upon the disorderliness in our home—even though it tortures me!

D. OF INDRA: And I shall eat cabbage, even if I suffer agony.

ATTORNEY: A married life of common pain and deprivation! What is pleasure to one is pain to another.

D. OF INDRA: Men are to be pitied!

ATTORNEY: You've come to realize it now?

D. OF INDRA: I have . . . but in the name of Heaven, let us stay clear of the rocks, now that we know their dangers.

ATTORNEY: Yes, let us try. . . . We are both good, and we are intelligent. We both have forbearance, and have learned to forgive.

D. OF INDRA: Why shouldn't we pass over all trifles with a smile?

ATTORNEY: We can! And we only can do it. . . . Let me tell you—I read today in the Morning . . . By the way, where is the newspaper?

D. OF INDRA: [Embarrassed] Which newspaper?

ATTORNEY: [In a biting tone] Do I keep more than one, do I?

D. OF INDRA: Smile now, and don't speak harshly. . . . I used it to start the fire with.

ATTORNEY: [Bursts out violently] Hell and damnation!

D. OF INDRA: Smile . . . smile! I burned it because it ridiculed what to me is holy!

ATTORNEY: And to me—unholy! Cha! [He strikes his fist against the palm of his hand, incontrollably] I'll keep smiling until my molars show. . . . I'll be lenient and forgiving, and suppress my opinions, and say yes to everything and anything, and be a sneak and a hypocrite! So-o, you have burned my newspaper, eh? [He rearranges the curtain round the bed] Now you see—I am rearranging things again, and that will make you angry. Agnes, this just cannot go on!

D. OF INDRA: No, it can't.

ATTORNEY: And yet we must endure it. It isn't our vows and promises that matter so much as our child!

D. OF INDRA: You are right! It's the child that matters!—that matters most! . . . Oh! Oh! . . . We must keep going. . . .

ATTORNEY: Now I must go out to my clients. You hear how they chatter, impatient to tear at each other, aching to see the other fellow getting fined and imprisoned! They are lost souls.

D. OF INDRA: These poor, poor people. . . . And this incessant pasting!

[*She bends her head in silent despair*]

KRISTIN: I paste . . . I paste. . . .

[*The* Attorney *stands at the door, nervously squeezing and turning the door knob*]

D. OF INDRA: Oh! The screech from that knob! It makes me feel as if you were squeezing my heart . . .

ATTORNEY: I turn and twist, I turn and twist . . .

D. OF INDRA: Please—please don't!

ATTORNEY: I turn and twist . . .

D. OF INDRA: Don't! . . .

ATTORNEY: I . . .

[*The* Officer *turns the knob from within the office*]

OFFICER: Allow me . . .

ATTORNEY: [*Lets go the knob*] Certainly . . . seeing that you have a doctor's degree . . .

OFFICER: Now I have all of life before me! All roads are open to me! I have reached my Parnassus, have won the laurel wreath, gained fame and immortality! The world is mine!

ATTORNEY: And what are you going to live on?

OFFICER: Live on?

ATTORNEY: You must have a place to live in, you must have food, clothes . . .

OFFICER: There is always a way out, so long as you have someone to love you.

ATTORNEY: I can well imagine! I can well. . . . Paste, Kristin! Paste until they can't breathe any longer!

[*The* Attorney *goes out backward, nodding*]

KRISTIN: I paste, I paste—until they can't breathe. . . .

OFFICER: [*To the* Daughter of Indra] Will you come with me now?

D. OF INDRA: This very moment! But where?

OFFICER: To Faircove! Where it is summer, where the sun is shining—where there is youth, where there are children and flowers, singing and dancing, gayety and exuberant life!

D. OF INDRA: Then I would like to go there!

OFFICER: Come, then!

[*The* Attorney *enters again*]

ATTORNEY: Now I return to my first hell. This was the second—the more terrible one! The sweeter the hell, the more horrible! . . . Now look here— she has dropped hairpins on the floor again!

[*He picks up the hairpins*]

OFFICER: Imagine, he has discovered the hairpins, too!

ATTORNEY: Too? Look at this one! It has two prongs, yet it is *one* pin. Two—yet only one! If I straighten it, then it is one; if I bend it, it becomes two—yet without ceasing to be one! That means that the two are one! But if I should break it—like this— then the two are two.

[*He breaks the hairpin in two and throws away the pieces*]

OFFICER: He has seen all that! But before break-

ing, the prongs must diverge. If they converge—they will hold.

ATTORNEY: And if they are parallel, they will never meet—and then they will neither break nor hold anything.

OFFICER: The hairpin is the most perfect among created things! A straight line that equals two parallel lines!

ATTORNEY: A lock that shuts while it is open—

OFFICER: —for, while open, it shuts in a braid of hair that remains outside while it is shut in . . .

ATTORNEY: Much like this door! When I close it . . . I open—the way out—for you, Agnes.

[*He withdraws, closing the door after him*]

D. OF INDRA: And now?

There is a change of scenery. The bed with the curtains is transformed into a tent; the stove remains. The backdrop is raised; and one sees now in the background a beautiful, wooded shore with flags flying from its jetties, to which white sailboats are moored. Some of the boats have their sails hoisted, others have dropped sails. Small Italian villas, pavilions, kiosks and marble statues can be discerned along the shore, between the tree tops.

On the left, downstage, is a hillside, scorched by fire and with patches of red heather; here and there a smoky, blackened white tree stub and several pigpens and outhouses, painted red.

Below is an open-air gymnasium for the rehabilitation of physically handicapped and other ailing persons, where patients go through a routine of exercises on apparatuses resembling instruments of torture.

On the right in the foreground are visible some of the open sheds of the quarantine station, supplied with fireplaces, furnaces and piping conduits.

Between the shore in the background and the landscape in the foreground is a narrow strait.

[*The* Quarantine Master, *dressed as a blackamoor, is walking along the shore. The* Officer *steps up to him. They shake hands*]

OFFICER: Well, if it isn't Ordström! So you've landed out here?

QUARANTINE MASTER: So I have, as you see!

OFFICER: Can this be Faircove?

QUARANTINE MASTER: No—Faircove is across the strait. This is Foulgut.

OFFICER: Then we have come to the wrong place!

QUARANTINE MASTER: We?—Won't you introduce me?

OFFICER: No, that wouldn't do! [*In an undertone*] Do you know who she is? She is the Daughter of Indra!

QUARANTINE MASTER: The Daughter of Indra? I thought she was the Daughter of Varuna himself! Well, aren't you surprised to see my face black?

OFFICER: My dear boy! When one has reached

fifty, one ceases to be surprised at anything!—I immediately took it for granted that you were going to a masquerade ball this afternoon.

QUARANTINE MASTER: You are quite right. And I hope you will both come with me.

OFFICER: And why not? . . . For I can't say—I can't say that this place seems especially inviting. . . . What kind of people live here anyway?

QUARANTINE MASTER: Here is where the sick live . . . over there are the healthy.

OFFICER: Then you have nothing but poor people here, I suppose?

QUARANTINE MASTER: On the contrary . . . here is where you find the rich! Take a look at that one on the rack there. He has stuffed himself with goose liver and truffles and consumed so much burgundy that his feet have curled into knots.

OFFICER: Into knots?

QUARANTINE MASTER: Yes, he has developed knotted feet. And that one over there—on that guillotine—has swallowed so much brandy that his spine has to be mangled out!

OFFICER: Will that really help?

QUARANTINE MASTER: For the rest, all who have some sort of misery that they wish to hide, live on this side! For instance—do you see the man coming here?

[An elderly dandy is pushed on the stage in a wheelchair. He is accompanied by a woman of sixty, an emaciated ugly old flirt, dressed in latest fashion. She is being attended by her lover, a man of about forty]

OFFICER: It's the major! He went to school with us, didn't he?

QUARANTINE MASTER: Yes—Don Juan! You can see, can't you, that he is still in love with that old spook-face next to him! He doesn't even see how she has aged—that she is ugly, faithless and cruel!

OFFICER: Well—that's what love does! But I never thought that such a fickle fellow as he used to be could fall in love so deeply, so seriously!

QUARANTINE MASTER: You look at things in a very sympathetic way, I must say.

OFFICER: I have been in love myself—with Victoria . . . and I am still waiting—waiting for her to come.

QUARANTINE MASTER: Oh, it's you—it's you who are waiting for her in the passage way.

OFFICER: Yes—I am the fellow. . . .

QUARANTINE MASTER: Tell me—have you got that door opened yet?

OFFICER: No—the matter is still before the court. . . . The billposter is out fishing with his dip-net, of course—and that's what's delaying the testimony. . . . Meantime the glazier has been putting in the windows in the castle—it has now grown half a story higher. . . . This has been an exceptionally good year—warm and wet.

QUARANTINE MASTER: But you haven't had it as hot as I have had it here, that's certain!

OFFICER: How hot do you keep your ovens, may I ask?

QUARANTINE MASTER: When we fumigate suspected cholera cases, we run it up to 108 degrees Fahrenheit.

OFFICER: Is the cholera rampant again?

QUARANTINE MASTER: Didn't you know?

OFFICER: Yes, of course, I know—but I forget so frequently things I should remember. . . .

QUARANTINE MASTER: I often wish I could forget, too, especially myself. That's one reason why I like to disguise myself and go to masquerade balls and take part in theatricals.

OFFICER: What have you been doing these many years?

QUARANTINE MASTER: If I told anyone, people would say I was boasting. And if I should say nothing, I would be called a hypocrite!

OFFICER: Is that why you have blackened your face?

QUARANTINE MASTER: Yes—I've made myself a little blacker than I really am!

OFFICER: Who is that man coming here?

QUARANTINE MASTER: Oh, he is a poet. . . . He is coming to get his mud bath. . . .

[The Poet enters. His eyes are turned heavenward. He is carrying a bucket of mud]

OFFICER: In heaven's name! Why don't you give him a sun bath—or an air bath—instead?

QUARANTINE MASTER: Oh no—he is forever flitting about in the loftier regions—and so gets homesick for the mud occasionally. . . . Wallowing about in the slime and dirt toughens the skin. Look at the pigs! And once he is toughened, he is immune to the stings of the horseflies.

OFFICER: This is a strange world! So full of contradictions!

POET: [Ecstatically] Out of clay the god Ptah created Man, on a potter's wheel, or lathe . . . [Skeptically] out of clay or something else—whatever it was! [Ecstatically] Out of clay the sculptor creates his more or less immortal masterpieces . . . [Skeptically] most of the time nothing but rubbish. . . . [Ecstatically] Out of clay are manufactured the wares and utensils—so absolutely necessary in a household—which we commonly call pottery, earthenware, dishes and so forth . . . [Skeptically] anyhow, what do I care what they are called! [Ecstatically] That much for clay! When the clay is oozy, or thin, in liquid form, it's called mud.—And that's what I want! [He calls] Lina!

[Lina enters with a bucket]

POET: Lina, show yourself to Miss Agnes!—She knew you ten years ago when you were a young girl, full of joy—and, we might say, pretty. . . . But take a look at Lina now—after five children, drudgery, baby-cries, lack of nourishment, and cruel treatment! You can see how all that was lovely has vanished—that happiness is gone! And all the while she was trying to exercise her duties—duties which ought to have given her an inner satisfaction that would have shown in her face! Her face would have had a pleasing symmetry, her eyes would have shone with warmth and gentleness . . .

QUARANTINE MASTER: [Covers the Poet's *mouth with his hand*] Keep your mouth shut! Will you keep your mouth shut!

POET: That's what they all say! And if I keep silent, they say: Why don't you say something!— Oh, these unpredictable mortals!

D. OF INDRA: [*Goes over to* Lina] Tell me what troubles you!

LINA: I wouldn't dare! It would only make things worse for me!

D. OF INDRA: Who is so cruel to you?

LINA: I wouldn't dare to say. . . . I would only suffer for it. . . .

POET: Well, never mind . . . but I shall—even if the blackamoor should threaten to knock all my teeth out! . . . I am not afraid to say that we don't always get justice here!—Agnes, daughter of the gods, do you hear the music and dancing up there on the hillside?—Then listen to what I have to say! It is all for Lina's sister, who has come home from the city, where she went astray—you know what I mean. . . . Now they are killing the fatted calf for her—but Lina, who stayed at home—she has to carry the slops to the swine and feed them!

D. OF INDRA: Bear in mind: there is rejoicing in that home not alone because the misguided child has come back to her parents, but all the more because she has abandoned the path of evil!

POET: But why not then give a ball and a banquet every evening in the week for the blameless toiler who never strayed from the straight and narrow path? Why not do that?—No—that they would never do! But when Lina has a moment to herself, she has to go to a prayer meeting and hear herself reproached for not being perfect!—Do you call that justice— do you?

D. OF INDRA: I find it hard to answer your questions because they—because there are so many unforeseen, so many different angles to take into consideration. . . .

POET: That is just what Harun the Just, the caliph, realized while he sat tranquilly on his throne. There he sat, away on high, without any knowledge of how the mortals fared below. . . . Finally the complaints reached his ear. One day he descended, and in disguise he mingled unrecognized with the crowds.—He wanted to find out what sort of justice was being meted out to his subjects.

D. OF INDRA: But I am not Harun the Just!

OFFICER: Let us talk about something else. . . . Here come some visitors. . . .

[*A white, dragonlike boat with sails of light blue on a gilded yard and with gilded mast glides slowly into the strait from the right. A rosy red pennant flies from the masthead. He and* She *are seated abaft by the rudder, their arms entwined round each other*]

OFFICER: There—there you see perfect happiness, boundless bliss, triumphant young love. . . .

[*The scene gradually grows light. He stands up in the boat and sings*]

HE: Hail, hail, fairest cove
where in youth I spent my springtime . . .
where in rosy colors I dreamt youth's sweet dreams:
Here I come to you again—
though not, as then, alone!
Greet her, you sea and sky,
you bays and groves—
greet her. . . .
My love, my bride,
my life, my sun!

[*The flags flowing from the slips and jetties at Faircove are dipped in salute; white handkerchiefs are waved from the cottages and the shore, and soft music from harps and violins is heard*]

POET: Behold the shining light that radiates from them! Hear the music floating over the water!—The God of Love . . . Eros!

OFFICER: It's Victoria!

QUARANTINE MASTER: Well—what of it?

OFFICER: It's *his* Victoria! My Victoria is still mine! And I won't let anybody see her. . . . Now— you hoist the quarantine flag, and I shall pull in the net!

[*The* Quarantine Master *waves a yellow flag*]

OFFICER: [*Pulls at a rope, causing the boat to turn toward Foulgut*] Hold on there !

[*He and* She *suddenly become aware of the dread features of the locality and express their horror audibly*]

QUARANTINE MASTER: Well, well—this takes the wind out of your sails, doesn't it? But they all have to come here—all who come from cholera-infested localities.

POET: Imagine, to speak in that manner—to do such a thing as this to two human beings who are in love! Don't you touch them! Don't soil their great love! It would be a crime—nothing short of high treason! . . . Woe unto us! All that was once beautiful must be dragged down—dragged into the mud and mire!

[*He and* She *step ashore. They now look shamefaced and sad*]

HE: Why should we have to suffer this grief? What have we done?

QUARANTINE MASTER: You needn't necessarily have done anything, even if you are pricked by life's little barbs.

SHE: That is how long happiness and joy last!

HE: How long do we have to stay here?

QUARANTINE MASTER: Forty days and forty nights.

SHE: Then let us rather die!

HE: To have to live here—among fire-scorched hills and pigsties! Oh!

POET: Love conquers all—even sulphur fumes and carbolic acid!

QUARANTINE MASTER: [*Makes a fire in the oven. Blue sulphur flames break out*] Now I have started the fire and am burning the sulphur. . . . Will you please step inside. . . .

SHE: Oh! My blue dress will be discolored. . . .

QUARANTINE MASTER: It will turn white—and so will your red roses. . . .

HE: And your cheeks, too, before the forty days are over!

SHE: [*To the* Officer] That will make you glad!

OFFICER: No, that's not true! . . . It's true that your happiness became the source of my *un*happiness —but . . . that doesn't matter now. I have received my degree and have now a tutoring position across the strait . . . yes, yes—yes, yes—and in the fall I'll be teaching school. . . . I'll be teaching the boys the same lessons I learned in my long childhood, and all through my youth—and now I'll be teaching these same lessons throughout my manhood—and finally, the very same lessons till I am an old man and ready to die: How much is two times two?— How many times two is four? . . . until I'm pensioned off and have nothing to do except to wait around for the meals to be served, and for the newspapers! . . . And at last I am brought to the crematorium and burned to ashes. . . . Is there nobody here who is entitled to a pension? I think it's about the worst next to "two times two is four"! And to start going to school all over again, after being given a doctor's degree—and to have to ask the same questions over and over again until you die!

[*An aged gentleman, his hands on his back, is seen passing*]

See—there you have a pensioner who is waiting for nothing but the end. . . . I think he must be an army captain who couldn't make the grade—or he may have been a clerk of the supreme court, who failed to be appointed to a judgeship. Many are called, but few are chosen. . . . He is impatiently waiting for his breakfast. . . .

PENSIONER: No—for the newspaper! The Morning News!

OFFICER: And he is only fifty-four years old. . . . He might be waiting for his meals and his newspaper twenty-five years from now! Isn't it frightful?

PENSIONER: What is it that *isn't* frightful? Tell me, tell me, tell me!

OFFICER: Well, let him answer who can! . . . Now I am going to teach boys that two times two is four —and how many times four can be evenly divided by two. . . . [*He scratches his head in desperation*] And Victoria—whom I loved and therefore wished the greatest happiness in the world. . . . Now she has found her happiness—the greatest for her . . . and I suffer . . . I suffer . . . suffer!

SHE: Do you think I can be happy when I see you suffer? How can you think that? Perhaps it will lessen the pain for you to know that I am being incarcerated here for forty days and forty nights? Does that lighten the pain?

OFFICER: Yes—and no! How can I be happy, while you suffer? Oh . . .

HE: And do you think my happiness can be built on your misery and pain?

OFFICER: We are all to be pitied!

ALL: [*They lift their hands toward the sky and utter a dissonant cry of anguish*] Oh! . . .

D. OF INDRA: Eternal One, hear their cry! Life is a misery! Men are to be pitied!

ALL: [*As before*] Oh! . . .

For a moment the stage is in utter darkness. During this period, those on the stage disappear or change position. When the stage is light again, the shore at Foulgut can be seen dimly in the back-ground. The strait flows between Foulgut and Faircove; the latter is visible in the foreground. The body of water and Faircove are bathed in light. On the left, a corner of the main pavilion or casino. Through its open windows can be seen a couple, dancing. On a wooden crate outside stand three servant maids with their arms round each other's waists. They are watching the dancers inside. On the terrace stand a piano with open keyboard and a bench. Seated on the latter is Plainlooking Edith. She is bareheaded and seems depressed; she has a mass of tousled hair, and sad eyes.

On the right is a yellow frame house. Two children in summer dress are playing ball outside. On the downstage side of the strait is a jetty with sailboats tied up to it. In the rear, flags and pennants fly from the jetty's flagpoles. In the stream is anchored a white navy brig with gunports.

The entire scene is in winter dress, and both the ground and the barren trees are covered with snow]

[*The* Daughter of Indra *and the* Officer *enter*]

D. OF INDRA: Here is peace and happiness. Here you can relax. Drudgery is banished. Every day is a day of enjoyment. People are dressed as for a holiday. Music and dancing from early morn. [*To the* Servant Maids] Why don't you go inside and join in the dancing?

ONE OF THE SERVANT MAIDS: We?

OFFICER: Can't you see they are servants?

D. OF INDRA: I forgot!—But why is Edith sitting there by herself? Why isn't she dancing?

[Edith *buries her face in her hands*]

OFFICER: You shouldn't have asked her that! She has been sitting there for three hours, and no one has asked her to dance. . . .

[*He goes into the yellow house on the right*]

D. OF INDRA: What cruelty there can be in pleasure!

[*The* Mother *comes out from the casino. She is dressed in a lownecked dress. She goes directly over to* Edith]

MOTHER: Why don't you go inside as I told you!

EDITH: Because—I can't put myself on exhibition!

I can't force people to dance with me, can I? I know I am not pretty to look at! That's why nobody wants to dance with me . . . and I wish you would stop reminding me of it. . . .

[*She starts to play on the piano Johann Sebastian Bach's Toccata con Fuga, No. 10. At first the music from within is heard faintly; then it increases in sound as if it were trying to drown out Bach's Toccata. Edith, however, persists and the dance music finally stops. Guests at the casino appear in the doorway, fascinated by her playing. They all stand silent, in rapt attention*]

A NAVAL OFFICER: [*Puts his arm round the waist of* Alice, *one of the guests, and leads her down toward the jetty*] Come quickly!

[Edith *breaks off her playing abruptly, rises and follows them, agonized, with her eyes. She remains standing as if she had turned into stone*]

The façade of the yellow house is now removed, revealing a classroom in a school. One sees three rows of benches, seated on which are a number of boy pupils. Among them is the Officer. He seems to be ill at ease, restless and worried. Facing the pupils stands the Teacher; he is wearing spectacles, and in his hand he has a piece of chalk and a rattan cane.

TEACHER: [*To the* Officer] Well, my boy, can you tell me now what two times two makes?

[*The* Officer *remains seated. He racks his brain without being able to give the answer*]

TEACHER: Stand up when you are asked a question!

OFFICER: [*Painfully affected, he rises*] Two . . . times two. . . . Let me see . . . it's . . . two two . . .

TEACHER: Oho! You haven't studied your lesson!

OFFICER: [*Ashamed*] Yes, I have—but. . . . I know the answer—but I can't tell you. . . .

TEACHER: You are trying to get out of answering! You know the answer—but you can't tell me! Perhaps you want me to help you!

[*He pulls his hair*]

OFFICER: Oh, this is terrible—terrible!

TEACHER: Yes, isn't it! A big boy like you—so completely lacking in ambition. . . .

OFFICER: [*Tortured*] A big boy! Yes—I am big— bigger than the other boys here. . . . I'm a grown man—have been through school. . . . [*He searches his mind; he seems to be recovering his memory*] I have been given a doctor's degree, haven't I?— Then why am I sitting here? Haven't I been given a degree?

TEACHER: Of course you have . . . but, you see, you have to sit here to mature. You have to mature —isn't that so?

OFFICER: [*Runs his hand over his forehead*] Yes,

of course . . . you are right—we have to mature. . . . Two times two—is two . . . and I'll prove it by a demonstration in analogy—the highest form of reasoning that exists.—Now listen to me!—One time one is one, isn't it? Therefore two times two is two! For what applies in one case must of necessity apply in another.

TEACHER: Your conclusion is in complete conformity with good logic—but the answer is wrong!

OFFICER: What is right according to logic can't be wrong! Let's put it to the test. One divided by one gives one—and so two divided by two must give two.

TEACHER: Entirely correct according to the conclusion arrived at by analogy. But what does one time three make?

OFFICER: Three!

TEACHER: Consequently two times three should also make three, shouldn't it?

OFFICER: [*Ponders the question*] No—that can't be right . . . it can't be—unless . . . [*He sits down in despair*] Yes, I see I am not mature yet!

TEACHER: No—you are not! Not by any means!

OFFICER: But how long will I have to sit here, then?

TEACHER: How long?—Do you believe in the existence of time and space?—Suppose that time does exist—then you should be able to tell me what it is. What is time?

OFFICER: Time? . . . [*He reflects*] I can't say exactly what it is—but I know very well what it is. . . . Consequently, why can't I know what two times two makes, without being able to say it? Can you tell me what time is, teacher?

TEACHER: Of course I can!

ALL THE PUPILS: [*In chorus*] Tell us, then!

TEACHER: Time—let me see! [*He stands immobile, one finger on his nose*] While we are talking, time flies . . . therefore it is something that flies . . . while I talk . . .

A PUPIL: [*Stands up*] Now you are talking, teacher, and while you are talking, I fly. . . . consequently I am time!

[*He runs out*]

TEACHER: Absolutely correct according to the laws of logic!

OFFICER: But in that case the laws of logic are ridiculous—for Nils, who just skipped class, can't possibly be time. . . .

TEACHER: What you say is also quite in accordance with the laws of logic, except that it's silly. . . .

OFFICER: Then all logic must be silly!

TEACHER: It really seems so. . . . But if logic is asinine, then the whole world must be crazy . . . and then the devil himself wouldn't want to stay here and teach you any more idiotic stupidities!— If anybody cares to treat me to a good stiff drink, I wouldn't mind taking you for a swim!

OFFICER: I would call this a *posterus prius*, or— the world turned upside down. I always thought the swim came first and the drink afterwards. You old fogie!

TEACHER: I warn you not to get a swelled head, Doctor!

OFFICER: Call me Major, if you please! I am an army officer—and I haven't the faintest idea why I am sitting here taking scoldings like any school-boy. . . .

TEACHER: [*Pointing his finger at him*] We have to learn—to mature!

QUARANTINE MASTER: [*Enters*] The quarantine is now in effect!

OFFICER: Oh, there you are! Can you imagine—he made me sit among the young lads in this class-room, despite my degree as a doctor of philosophy!

QUARANTINE MASTER: Well, why didn't you get up and leave?

OFFICER: Leave, you say. . . . Well, I don't know. . . . It isn't so easy as you think. . . .

TEACHER: No—you are quite right! You just try!

OFFICER: [*To the* Quarantine Master] Save me! Save me from his staring eyes!

QUARANTINE MASTER: Just come with me!—Come and join in the dance . . . we have to dance before the plague breaks out—we simply must!

OFFICER: Is the brig sailing?

QUARANTINE MASTER: Yes, that's the first thing we must do—get the brig away from here!—There'll be much weeping, of course. . . .

OFFICER: There always is, whenever that brig comes here—and whenever it leaves!—Let us go. . . .

[*They go out. The* Teacher, *in pantomime, continues calmly with his teaching*]

[*The* Servant Maids, *who have been standing outside the casino windows, now drag themselves mournfully down to the jetty. Edith, who has remained standing like a statue by the piano, follows them*]

D. OF INDRA: [*To the* Officer] Is there then not one person who is happy in this paradise?

OFFICER: Yes—there is a couple that have just been married. . . . Let's listen to them and watch them. . . .

[*The two newly married enter*]

HUSBAND: [*To his wife*] My bliss is so boundless that I could die happy this moment. . . .

WIFE: Why should you wish to die?

HUSBAND: Because at the core of happiness lies the seed of unhappiness. . . . Happiness devours itself as fire does! The flame can't burn eternally—it is doomed to die. . . . This foreknowledge of the finality of things annihilates bliss at its very apex.

WIFE: Then let us die together—this very moment!

HUSBAND: Die . . . together. . . . Come! I am frightened by happiness and its treachery! . . .

[*They disappear toward the sea*]

D. OF INDRA: [*To the* Officer] Life is misery! Man is to be pitied!

OFFICER: Look at this man coming here! He is the most envied of the humans in this community! [*The* Blind Man *enters. He is being led by another man*] He is the owner of hundreds of Italian villas here. He owns all these coves and bays, shores and woods, the fish in the water, the birds in the air and the game in the woods. These, close to a thousand human beings, are his tenants—and the sun rises over his holdings by the sea and sets over his properties inland. . . .

D. OF INDRA: And does he complain also?

OFFICER: Yes—and with good reason. . . . He can't see. . . .

QUARANTINE MASTER: He is blind!

D. OF INDRA: And he is the most envied of all. . . .

OFFICER: Now he is watching the brig sail away. . . . His son is aboard. . . .

BLIND MAN: I may not see—but I can hear! I can hear the claws of the anchor grappling with the mud at the bottom of the sea . . . exactly as when one extracts a fish-hook from a fish and the heart is dragged out at the same time. . . . My son—my only child—is leaving for strange lands across the wide, open seas . . . and I can only be with him in my thoughts. . . . Now I hear the cable screech and groan . . . and . . . I hear something flutter and flap in the wind—like wet wash on a clothes line. . . . It might be wet handkerchiefs hung up to dry. . . . And I hear weeping and sobbing—as when people can't control their feelings. . . . I can't tell whether it's the small waves lapping against the seams of the ship, or whether it's the young girls on the shore—the ones who are being abandoned and who are disconsolate. . . . I once asked a little boy why the sea was so salty. . . . The child's father was away on a long voyage. . . . Without a moment's hesitation he answered: The sea is salty because seamen cry so often.—Why do seamen cry so much? I asked.—Because they always have to leave their homes; that's why they always have to hang their handkerchiefs on the masts to dry! . . .—And why do human beings cry when they feel sorrow? I asked again.—Why! said he, that's because the windows of the eyes have to be washed now and then so that we can see more clearly. . . .

[*The brig has now set sail and is slowly gliding off. The girls on shore wave their handkerchiefs and some of them wipe their eyes. From the signal rack on the foremast is then hoisted the signal "Yes": a red ball on a white field. In answer to it* Alice *exultantly waves her handkerchief*]

D. OF INDRA: [*To the* Officer] What's the meaning of that flag?

OFFICER: It carries the message "yes." It's the lieutenant's way of reaffirming his love—in red—like the crimson blood of a heart—against the sky-blue canvas of heaven. . . .

D. OF INDRA: How would they signal the word "no"?

OFFICER: It would be blue as the rancid blood in blue veins. . . . But just see how Alice almost leaps with joy!

D. OF INDRA: And Edith is weeping!

BLIND MAN: To meet and to part . . . to part and to meet. . . . That is life. . . . I met her—his mother. . . . And then she left me—and I was left our son. . . . Now he has left me. . . .

D. OF INDRA: But he will come back. . . .

BLIND MAN: Who is that speaking to me? I have heard that voice before—in my dreams—in my youth—when the holidays of summer came—when first I was married—when my child was brought into the world—whenever life smiled upon me, I heard that voice—like the soughing of the south wind— like the voice of harps from ethereal worlds; as I feel the angels would have sung their greeting on the Night of His birth. . . .

[*The* Attorney *enters. He steps over to the* Blind Man *and whispers in his ear*]

BLIND MAN: You don't say?

ATTORNEY: Yes—believe me! [*He turns to the* Daughter of Indra] Now you have seen many things —but you have not met with the worst. . . .

D. OF INDRA: And the worst is . . .

ATTORNEY: To go back, to go over again, to re- capitulate! To have to learn the same lesson over and over again! Come!

D. OF INDRA: Where are we going?

ATTORNEY: To your duties!

D. OF INDRA: And what are they?

ATTORNEY: Whatever you are in dread of! What- ever you have no desire to do, yet must do! It means —to deny yourself things you desire—to sacrifice— to go through hardships and deprivations—in brief, everything that lacks joy and beauty—everything that is vile, loathsome and painful. . . .

D. OF INDRA: Are no duties pleasant, then?

ATTORNEY: Yes—when they are done—when they are fulfilled!

D. OF INDRA: And then they no longer exist. . . . Duty, then, is always something odious. . . . Is there nothing that is joyful and pleasant here?

ATTORNEY: Pleasures are sin.

D. OF INDRA: Sin?

ATTORNEY: Something to be punished, yes! If I enjoy myself day and night, I suffer the agonies of hell and have a bad conscience the day after.

D. OF INDRA: How strange!

ATTORNEY: I wake up in the morning with a headache—and at once the iteration, the recapitula- tion begins! But it is always a perverted recapitula- tion! What seemed beautiful and delightful and witty the night before, seems to me the next morning ugly and loathsome and stupid. Pleasure seems de- cayed; joy disintegrated. What people like to call success invariably turns out to be the cause of their next setback. Every success I have achieved during my life, has turned into some failure for me. People

have an instinctive fear and envy of seeing others get along. They feel that fate is unjust when it favors some one else; and so they try to restore the balance by placing obstacles in the way of others. To be talented is dangerous to one's life: one runs the risk of starving to death!—But you must return to your duties—or I shall bring suit against you. . . . I'll take it through every court, from the lowest to the highest.

D. OF INDRA: I have to go back to the stove and the cooking, the cabbage, and the baby's clothes? . . .

ATTORNEY: Yes, you must! We have a big wash today—all the handkerchiefs have to be washed.

D. OF INDRA: Oh, must I do this again . . . again . . .

ATTORNEY: Life is one long stretch of repetitions. . . . Look at the schoolmaster in there! Yesterday he was given a degree, was given the laurel wreath and a salute of guns, reached his Parnassus, and was embraced by the monarch. . . . And today he is back in school again, asking for an answer to what two times two makes. . . . and he'll be asking that ques- tion until his dying day. . . . But—come back to your home, come back to me!

D. OF INDRA: I would rather die!

ATTORNEY: Die? No—you must not think of that! First of all, it is a disgrace—a disgrace so great that your body would be abused and subjected to insults; and secondly, you would find no rest in the here- after. . . . It is a mortal sin!

D. OF INDRA: It is not easy to be a human!

ALL: How true!

D. OF INDRA: I will not return with you to humilia- tion and dirt!—I yearn to go back up there, from where I came . . . but . . . first the door must be opened so that I may learn the secret within. . . . It is my will that the door be opened!

ATTORNEY: To learn that secret you must retrace your steps, travel the road back, all the way, and suffer through all the vexations and adversities, repe- titions, restraints and circumscriptions that go with a lawsuit. . . .

D. OF INDRA: So be it . . . but first I shall go to some lonely spot out in the wilderness and find my own self again. . . . We shall see each other in the future. . . . [*To the* Poet] Follow me! [*Cries of an- guish and pain are heard distantly:* O woe! O woe! O woe!] Did you hear that?

ATTORNEY: That came from the lost souls over at Foulgut. . . .

D. OF INDRA: Why is their anguish today louder than usual?

ATTORNEY: Because the sun is shining here, be- cause there is youth and dancing here, because there is music in the air. . . . It is then that they feel their pains and afflictions so much more deeply.

D. OF INDRA: We must set them free!

ATTORNEY: You may try!—Once there was a man who sought to liberate. . . . He was hanged on a cross. . . .

D. OF INDRA: Who hanged him?

ATTORNEY: The self-righteous, the sanctimonious! . . .

D. OF INDRA: Who are they?

ATTORNEY: Don't you know who the self-righteous are? You will soon learn to know them!

D. OF INDRA: Was it they who refused you your degree?

ATTORNEY: Yes!

D. OF INDRA: Then I know who they are. . . .

A beach on the Mediterranean. On the right, in the foreground, is seen a white wall. Protruding above it are orange trees, laden with fruit. In the background are villas, and the casino with its terraced approach.

On the left, a big pile of coal and two wheelbarrows.

In the background, to the left, can be discerned a faint and limited view of the blue sea. Two Coalheavers, *naked to the waist and black of body, face and hands from handling the coal, sit on the wheelbarrows. Their faces show despair and agony.*

The Daughter of Indra *and the* Attorney *are visible in the background.*

D. OF INDRA: This is paradise!

1ST COALHEAVER: This is hell!

2ND COALHEAVER: Nearly eighty-seven degrees in the shade!

1ST COALHEAVER: What do you say about a dip in the sea?

2ND COALHEAVER: And get the police on us! Don't you know you can't bathe here?

1ST COALHEAVER: How about picking an orange from one of the trees?

2ND COALHEAVER: No—we'll have the police on us. . . .

1ST COALHEAVER: But I can't work in this heat. . . . I'm quitting right now.

2ND COALHEAVER: If you do, the police will be after you. . . . [*There is a silence*] And furthermore —you wouldn't be able to buy yourself food. . . .

1ST COALHEAVER: No food? We, who work harder than anyone else—we get the least to eat! The rich, on the other hand, who do nothing, get all they want! . . . Don't you think one can truthfully say that this is unrighteous and unjust?—I wonder what the Daughter of the Gods has to say about it?

D. OF INDRA: I am at a loss for a reply!—But tell me—what have you done to make you so grimy? Why are you having such a hard life?

1ST COALHEAVER: What we have done? It was our lot to be born of poor parents—and not too respectable at that. . . . We may have been convicted a couple of times, too. . . .

D. OF INDRA: Convicted?

1ST COALHEAVER: Yes! The unpunished lounge up there in the Casino, feasting on eight-course dinners and wine.

D. OF INDRA: [*To the* Attorney] Can this really be true?

ATTORNEY: Broadly speaking, yes. . . .

D. OF INDRA: You mean to say that every mortal, if given his just deserts, would—at some time or other—have been condemned to prison?

ATTORNEY: Yes.

D. OF INDRA: Even you?

ATTORNEY: Yes—even I!

D. OF INDRA: Is it true that the poor cannot go bathing in the sea here?

ATTORNEY: Yes—not even with their clothes on! The only ones who escape being fined are the ones who try to drown themselves. . . . But I have heard that they are given a good thrashing by the police. . . .

D. OF INDRA: But isn't there some place on the outskirts of the community, out in the country, where they can go bathing?

ATTORNEY: There is no such facility here—all the properties are fenced in.

D. OF INDRA: But I mean—on the free, open shore beyond. . . .

ATTORNEY: Nothing is free here.—It all belongs to somebody.

D. OF INDRA: Even the sea—the great, open sea? . . .

ATTORNEY: Yes—even the sea! You can't go sailing the sea and put into port without being duly registered and charged for it. A nice state of affairs, isn't it?

D. OF INDRA: This is no paradise. . . .

ATTORNEY: No—this is not paradise!

D. OF INDRA: Why, then, do people do nothing to improve their lot?

ATTORNEY: People do try, of course! But the ones who do try—the reformers—end in a prison or a madhouse. . . .

D. OF INDRA: Who has them put in prison?

ATTORNEY: All the righteous, the respectable people. . . .

D. OF INDRA: And who sends them to the madhouse?

ATTORNEY: Their own anguish . . . despair over the hopelessness of their struggle.

D. OF INDRA: Has the thought not occurred to anyone that things—for reasons not known—must remain as they are?

ATTORNEY: Yes—to them who are well off! They always think that way!

D. OF INDRA: That the world is as it should be? . . .

1ST COALHEAVER: Nevertheless—aren't we the very foundations of society?—If we didn't deliver the coal, you would have no fire in the kitchen range, or in the fireplaces in the rest of the house—you would have no coal for your factories. The lights in the streets, in the homes and the shops would go out, you would freeze in darkness! That's why we

sweat like hell to see that you get the black coal. . . .
And what do you give us in return?

ATTORNEY: [*To the* Daughter of Indra] Help them!
. . . [*There is a silence*] Things can't be the same for
all—I understand that . . . but why should the gap
be so great?

[*The* Gentleman *and the* Lady *walk across the
stage*]

LADY: Will you come with me and play a game?

GENTLEMAN: No, I have to take a walk—otherwise I'll have no appetite for dinner. . . .

1ST COALHEAVER: No appetite for dinner? . . .

2ND COALHEAVER: No appetite! . . .

[*Several Children* enter. *They scream, frightened,
when they see the two coalheavers*]

1ST COALHEAVER: They scream when they see us!
They scream. . . .

2ND COALHEAVER: Hell and damnation!—I'm afraid
we'll have to drag out the scaffolds soon and operate
on this carcass. . . .

1ST COALHEAVER: Yes, damn it, I say the same! . . .

[*He spits contemptuously*]

ATTORNEY: [*To the* Daughter of Indra] There is
no question—something is wrong. . . . Yet people
are not *too* bad . . . but it's . . .

D. OF INDRA: But—what?

ATTORNEY: It's their supervisors—their rulers. . . .

D. OF INDRA: [*She hides her face. She leaves*] This
is not paradise!

COALHEAVERS: No—it's not paradise! It's hell—
that's what it is!

---

*Fingal's Cave. Languishing great green waves roll
into the cave. In the foreground a red alarm buoy
rocks to and fro on the waves; it emits no sound,
however, except at such times as indicated in the
play.—Music of the winds and the waves.—The
Daughter of Indra and the Poet are visible when the
curtain rises.*

POET: Where have you brought me?

D. OF INDRA: Far from the murmur and moans
and laments of the children of humanity, to the
farthest end of the seven seas—to this grotto, which
has been given the name of Indra's Ear, because it
is here that the Master of the Heavens is said to
listen to the complaints of the mortals. . . .

POET: Here?—How can . . .

D. OF INDRA: Can't you see that this grotto is built
like a sea shell? You can see it, can't you? And don't
you know that your own ear is built like a shell? You
know it—but you haven't given thought to it. . . .
[*She picks up a sea shell on the shore*] When you
were a child—don't you remember holding a sea
shell to your ear, listening—listening to its singing.
. . . You heard the ripple of your heart's blood, the

hum of your brain, thinking, the snapping of thousands of tiny little worn-out fibres inside the tissues
of your body, didn't you? All *that* you heard in such
a little sea shell. . . . Imagine then what sounds you
will hear in this enormous ear!

POET: [*He listens*] I hear nothing but the whisper
of the wind. . . .

D. OF INDRA: Then let me interpret what it tells
me. . . . Listen to the wailing of the winds. . . .
[*She recites to soft music*]

Born beneath the firmament of heaven,
Indra's flashing lightning soon pursued us
to the earth of dust below. . . .
Litter of pasture fields soiled our feet;
we were forced to endure
the dust of highways,
the smoke of cities,
and evil-smelling breaths,
the odors of wines and cooking. . . .
Finally we fled to the open sea
to take breath and fill our lungs
with fresh air, to flap our wings
and cleanse and bathe our feet.—
Indra, Lord of the Heavens,
hear us! . . .
Hear our sighs! . . .
Unclean is the Earth,
life there is miserable;
mankind is not wicked—
yet it can't be called good.
People live as best they can,
for each passing day.
Sons of the Dust, they trudge through dust;
born out of dust,
they return to dust.
Feet they were given to move with,
wings were denied them. . . .
Laden with dust they are. . . .
Are they to be blamed—
or are You?

POET: And then I heard one time . . .

D. OF INDRA: Hush! The winds are still singing.
[*She continues to soft music*]

We, the winds, the sons of Air,
Scatter abroad the wails of humans. . . .
Did you hear us
on autumn nights—
whining in the chimneys,
rattling the stove shutters,
or stealing through leaky windows,
whilst the rain wept tears on the roof tiles? . . .
Or in wintry night,
in snow-clad woods of pine? . . .
Have you heard moaning and bewailing
in sails and rigging
upon the windswept sea? . . .
It is we—we, the winds—
sons of the Air! . . .
And we've learned these sounds of pain
from anguished human breasts,

which we have pierced and invaded—
on sickbeds, on battle fields . . .
but mostly when babes
whimper at childbirth
and utter cries
of painful anguish to be born. . . .
It is we—winds of the Air—
hissing and whining!
Woe! Woe! Woe!

POET: It seems as if I once . . .

D. OF INDRA: Hush! The waves are singing. . . .

[*She again recites to subdued music*]

It is we, the billowy waves,
that cradle the winds
to their sleep! . . .
Green are the cradles we rock,
watery are we and salty;
we leap like fiery flames—
watery flames we are. . . .
Burning and quenching,
bathing and cleansing,
begetting, conceiving. . . .
We—the billowy waves
that cradle them, rock them
into sleep!

D. OF INDRA: Treacherous and faithless waves. . . .
All on earth that is not burned, falls victim to the
sea. . . . Look here. . . . [*She points to a heap of
débris*] Look what the sea has plundered and destroyed. . . . All that remains of the sunken ships is
the figurehead—and their name-boards: Justice,
Friendship, Golden Peace, and Hope. . . . This is
all that remains of Hope—of inconstant and capri-
cious Hope! Railings and rowlocks and bailers! And
look here: a life-buoy—that saved *itself,* but let men
in distress go down!

POET: [*Searching in the pile of débris*] Here is the
name-board of the good ship Justice—the very same
ship that sailed from Faircove with the Blind Man's
son aboard! It was lost, then! And so is Alice's
betrothed, with whom poor Edith was so hopelessly
in love. . . .

D. OF INDRA: The Blind Man? Faircove? Could I
have been dreaming? And Alice's fiancé, ugly Edith,
Foulgut with its quarantine, its sulphur and carbolic
acid, the university ceremony in the church, the
attorney's office, the portress's cubicle at the Opera,
and Victoria, the growing castle and the officer . . .
I have dreamed it all. . . .

POET: I have lived it in my imagination. . . .

D. OF INDRA: You know what poetry and imagination are, then. . . .

POET: I know what dreams are. . . . But what is
poetry?

D. OF INDRA: It is not reality. . . . It is more than
reality. It is not dreaming—but dreams come alive,
envisioned. . . .

POET: And the children of humanity think that
we poets only like to play, are mere jesters—that we
merely fabricate, make believe!

D. OF INDRA: And that may be a good thing, my
friend. Else the world would lie fallow and be barren
for lack of care and cultivation. Everybody would
be lying on his back, gazing at the sky; and nobody
would touch a hoe or a pick-axe, a shovel or a
plow.

POET: And you say this—you, Indra's daughter,
who hail from realms above? . . .

D. OF INDRA: You reproach me justly. . . . I have
dwelt too long down here, wallowing in the mud like
you. . . . My thoughts no longer take flight—their
wings are weighted down by clay—the mud sticks to
their feet! And I myself . . . [*She raises her arms*]
I myself keep sinking . . . sinking . . . Help me, O
Father, God of the Heavens! [*There is a silence*] No
longer can I hear His voice! The ether no longer
carries the sound from His lips to my ear—the
silvery thread has snapped. . . . Woe to me, I am
earthbound!

POET: When will you ascend? Is the time near?

D. OF INDRA: When I have shed this mortal guise
and it has burned to dust . . . for all the water of the
sea cannot make me clean. . . . Why do you ask?

POET: Because I have a favor to beseech of you:
a prayer, a fervent supplication. . . .

D. OF INDRA: What is it you desire?

POET: A prayer of all mankind—to the ruler of
the universe—framed in words by a dreamer . . .

D. OF INDRA: And by whom do you wish it to be
given to Him? . . .

POET: By Indra's Daughter!

D. OF INDRA: Have you committed it to memory—
this petition?

POET: Yes, I know it by heart.

D. OF INDRA: Then speak it!

POET: I'd rather you did!

D. OF INDRA: Where may I read the words?

POET: In my mind—and also here. . . .

[*He hands her a scroll*]

D. OF INDRA: [*She accepts the scroll, but speaks
without glancing at it*] Then I shall give voice to your
prayer. . . .

[*The Daughter of Indra recites*]

"Why must you be born in anguish,
child of mankind? Why must mothers
suffer birth pains when you bring her
the most precious of all gifts:
motherhood, life's greatest blessing?
Why must you to life awaken? . . . .
Why do you salute the sunlight
with a cry of pain and mean ill-temper?
Why do you not smile on dawning life,
mortal child, since human happiness
has been promised as your birthright?
Why must we be born like beasts—
we, descendants of both gods and mortals?—
Better guise could have been given us than this
wretched body spun of blood and slime. . . .
and why must this image of the gods shed teeth?"

Silence, rash one! Blame the image—not the Maker!
No man yet has solved life's riddle!

"Started thus, the pilgrimage begins
over stones and thorns and thistles. . . .
Should it lead across a beaten path,
you will find the road forbidden;
and if you should pluck a flower,
you'd be held for trespass—and for thieving also;
if a field should stop you from advancing
and you take a short cut through it,
you will trample down the farmer's crops;
others do the same to you,
equalizing thus the damage!—
Every moment that gives joy
brings to others only grief;
your own sorrow spreads, however,
not much gladness anywhere:
thus it's sorrow after sorrow! . . .
So the pilgrimage goes on—
even death brings gain to others!"

Is it this way, you—the Son of Dust—mean to come
before the Great Almighty? . . .

POET: How could I, the Son of Dust,
find such chaste, ethereal words
that they'd soar to realms beyond?
Child of Gods, will you translate
all our sorrows into speech
that will reach immortal ears?

D. OF INDRA: I will.

POET: [*He points to the buoy*] What is that, floating there?—Is it a buoy?

D. OF INDRA: Yes.

POET: It looks like a lung with an Adam's apple.

D. OF INDRA: It is the watchman of the seas. When
there is danger ahead, it utters a warning.

POET: It looks as if the sea were rising and the
waves were growing restless and ever higher. . . .

D. OF INDRA: So it does. . . .

POET: Woe! What do I see? A ship—just outside—
close by the reef. . . .

D. OF INDRA: What ship can that be?

POET: I believe it is the eternal ghost ship. . . .

D. OF INDRA: The ghost ship? What ship is that?

POET: The Flying Dutchman. . . .

D. OF INDRA: Oh, I know. . . . Why is he being
punished so cruelly, and why doesn't he ever put
ashore?

POET: Because he had seven unfaithful wives.

D. OF INDRA: Why should he be punished for that?

POET: He was condemned by all the righteous-
minded. . . .

D. OF INDRA: How strange this world is!—But can't
he ever be freed from the curse?

POET: Freed?—One has to be careful not to set
people free. . . .

D. OF INDRA: Why?

POET: Because . . . No, it's not the Flying Dutchman! It's just an ordinary ship in distress!—Why
doesn't the buoy cry out a warning now?—Look, the
sea is rising, the waves are growing higher and

higher. . . . Soon we shall be marooned in the cave!
—The ship's bell is clanging now . . . before long
there'll be another figurehead floating on the water.
. . . Cry out your warning, buoy! Do your duty,
watchman! . . . [*The buoy emits a four-tone chord
of fifths and sixths, resembling the sound of a fog-
horn*] The crew are signaling and waving to us—and
we ourselves are perishing. . . .

D. OF INDRA: Is it not your wish to be set free?

POET: Why, certainly! Of course I wish to be set
free . . . but not at this moment—and not through
water!

THE CREW: [*Singing in quartet*] Christ Kyrie!

[*Cries and shouts from the ship*]

POET: Now they are shouting—and the sea roars—
and no one can hear them. . . .

THE CREW: [*Sings as before*] Christ Kyrie!

D. OF INDRA: Who is that coming there?

POET: Walking on the waters? There is only one
who walks on the waters. And it is not Peter the
Rock, for he sank like a stone.

[*A white light appears on the surface of the
water in the distance*]

CREW: Christ Kyrie!

D. OF INDRA: Is that He?

POET: It is He—who was crucified. . . .

D. OF INDRA: Why . . . tell me . . . why was He
crucified?

POET: Because He wished to set free. . . .

D. OF INDRA: I have forgotten who . . . Who crucified Him?

POET: All the righteous-minded. . . .

D. OF INDRA: What a strange world!

POET: The sea is rising! Darkness is coming upon
us! The storm is increasing!

[*The Crew give out a scream of terror*]

POET: The men are screaming, horror-stricken at
the sight of their Saviour! . . . and now—and now
they are jumping overboard out of fear. . . .

[*The Crew scream anew with fear*]

POET: They cry from fear of dying! They come
into the world crying and go out crying!

[*The rolling, surging waves keep increasing in
height and volume and threaten to drown the
two in the grotto*]

D. OF INDRA: If I were only certain that it is a
ship. . . .

POET: To tell the truth . . . I don't believe it is a
ship . . . it is a two-story house with trees before it
. . . and . . . a telephone tower—a tower reaching
to the skies. . . . It is the Babel's Tower of our times
sending messages by wire to higher regions—com-
municating with the dwellers there. . . .

D. OF INDRA: My child, the thoughts of mankind
need no wires for transmission! The prayers of the
pious reach to the far ends of the universe. . . . No—
it cannot be a Tower of Babel . . . for if you wish
to assail the heavens, you must do so by prayer. . . .

POET: No, it is no house—and no telephone tower.
. . . You can see that, can't you?

D. OF INDRA: Then what do you see?

POET: I see a vast snow-covered space—a drill ground. . . . The winter sun is peeking out from behind a church on a hillside, and its tower casts a long shadow over the snow. . . . Now I see a company of soldiers marching across the open field. . . . They march straight to the tower, march up the spire. . . . Now they have reached the cross, but I have a foreboding that the first one who steps on the weathercock at the pinnacle, will die. . . . Now they are close to the top—a corporal is at the head of his men. . . . Aha! A cloud comes sweeping across the field . . . it blots out the sun . . . now everything has disappeared . . . the moisture of the cloud has put out the sun's fire! The sunlight created the shadow picture of the tower, but the shadow picture of the cloud disembodied the shadow image of the tower. . . .

While the preceding dialogue is being spoken, the setting is being shifted: it now shows again the alley outside the Opera.

D. OF INDRA: [*To the* Portress] Has the Lord Chancellor arrived yet?

PORTRESS: No.

D. OF INDRA: Have the deans come?

PORTRESS: No.

D. OF INDRA: Then please call them at once . . . the door is about to be opened!

PORTRESS: Is it so important?

D. OF INDRA: Yes, it is. People have become excited. . . . They have a notion that the solution to the riddle of the world is being hidden in there!— So please call the Lord Chancellor and the Deans of the Faculties at once! [*The* Portress *blows a whistle*] And don't forget the glazier with his diamond! If he doesn't come, we'll have to call it off!

[People of the Opera *enter from the right, as in the earlier scenes*]

[*The* Officer *enters from the rear. He is dressed in redingote and top hat and carries a bouquet of roses. He is radiantly happy*]

OFFICER: Victoria!

PORTRESS: Miss Victoria will be down in a moment!

OFFICER: Splendid! The carriage is waiting, the table is set, the champagne is on ice. . . . Let me embrace you, madam! [*He embraces the* Portress] Victoria!

WOMAN'S VOICE: [*Sings out from above*] Here I am!

OFFICER: [*Starts to pace*] Good! I'll be waiting!

POET: It seems to me as if I had experienced all this once before . . .

D. OF INDRA: I also!

POET: Perhaps I have dreamed it!

D. OF INDRA: Or lived it in your imagination—in a poem?

POET: Perhaps even that . . .

D. OF INDRA: Now you know what poetry is. . . .

POET: Now I know what dreams are. . . .

D. OF INDRA: I feel as if we once before had spoken these very words—but in some other place. . . .

POET: Therefore you can easily conceive what reality is . . .

D. OF INDRA: Or dreams!

POET: Or the imagery of poetry!

[*The* Lord Chancellor *and the* Deans *of the theological, philosophical, medical, and law faculties enter*]

LORD CHANCELLOR: It is about that door, of course! —What does the Dean of Theology think about the matter?

DEAN OF THEOLOGY: I don't think. I believe— credo . . .

DEAN OF PHILOSOPHY: I hold the view that . . .

DEAN OF MEDICINE: I know . . . .

DEAN OF JURISPRUDENCE: I hold a doubt until I have seen the evidence and heard the testimony!

LORD CHANCELLOR: Now they'll start wrangling again! . . . Well, let's first hear what Theology has to say!

DEAN OF THEOLOGY: I believe that this door should not be opened for the reason that it has been placed there to conceal dangerous truths . . .

DEAN OF PHILOSOPHY: Truth is never dangerous!

DEAN OF MEDICINE: What is truth?

DEAN OF JURISPRUDENCE: That which can be proved by two witnesses.

DEAN OF THEOLOGY: A shyster lawyer can prove anything—with two false witnesses!

DEAN OF PHILOSOPHY: Truth is wisdom; and wisdom plus knowledge is philosophy itself. . . . Philosophy is the science of sciences, the supreme knowledge, and all the other sciences are merely its handmaids.

DEAN OF MEDICINE: There is only *one* science: natural science! Philosophy is no science. It's nothing but empty speculation!

DEAN OF THEOLOGY: Bravo!

DEAN OF PHILOSOPHY: [*To the* Dean of Theology] You shout bravo! What about yourself? You are the arch-enemy of all knowledge. You are the very antithesis of science—you are full of obscurity and vagueness. . . .

DEAN OF MEDICINE: Bravo!

DEAN OF THEOLOGY: [*To the* Dean of Medicine] You shout bravo—you who can't see any further than your nose, when you look through your microscope—you, who only put faith in your deceptive senses: your eye, for example, which may be farsighted, near-sighted, blind, dim-sighted, cross-eyed, one-eyed, color-blind, red-blind, green-blind . . .

DEAN OF MEDICINE: Dolt! Idiot!

DEAN OF THEOLOGY: Fool! Ass!

[*They fly at each other*]

LORD CHANCELLOR: Calm yourselves! Are you two crows trying to peck each other's eyes out?

DEAN OF PHILOSOPHY: [*To the* Chancellor *and the* Deans of Jurisprudence and Philosophy] If I had to choose between those two, Theology and Medicine, I would choose—neither!

DEAN OF JURISPRUDENCE: And if I had to sit in

judgment over you three, I would—find you all guilty!—You don't seem to find a single point on which you can agree! Neither now nor in the past!— But let's get back now to the case in hand! What is the Lord Chancellor's opinion regarding this door and its opening?

LORD CHANCELLOR: Opinion? I have no opinions. I have merely been appointed by the government to make sure that you don't break each other's arms and legs during Council meetings—for the edification of the students! My opinion . . . No, no! I stay away from anything that has to do with opinions. . . . There *was* a time when I had an opinion or two, but it didn't take long to put an end to them. . . . Opinions are quickly proved to be erroneous—by one's opponents, of course!—Could we proceed with the opening of the door now—even at the risk of discovering some dangerous truths behind it?

DEAN OF JURISPRUDENCE: What is truth? *What is truth?*

DEAN OF THEOLOGY: I am the truth and the life . . .

DEAN OF PHILOSOPHY: I am the core of all knowledge . . .

DEAN OF MEDICINE: I am the exact science . . .

DEAN OF JURISPRUDENCE: I doubt! . . .

[*They fly at each other*]

D. OF INDRA: Shame on you, you teachers of the young!

DEAN OF JURISPRUDENCE: Mr. Lord Chancellor! As the representative of the government, as the head of the body of instructors in this university, it is your duty to bring this woman before a court of justice for her offensive demeanor. She has dared to tell you to be ashamed of yourselves! This is an insult! She has—in a scoffing, sneering manner—sarcastically labeled you the teachers of the young. . . . This is nothing short of slander!

D. OF INDRA: I pity the young!

DEAN OF JURISPRUDENCE: She feels sorry for the young! Isn't that the same as an accusation against us?—Lord Chancellor, prosecute her without a moment's delay!

D. OF INDRA: Yes—I accuse you, all of you, of sowing doubt and dissension in the minds of the young.

DEAN OF JURISPRUDENCE: Listen to her! She is herself casting doubt on our authority, inveigling the young! And what is more, she accuses us of creating doubts! I ask of all the righteous-minded: Is not this a criminal offence?

ALL THE RIGHTEOUS-MINDED: It is indeed a criminal offence!

DEAN OF JURISPRUDENCE: All the righteous-minded have judged you!—Now leave—leave in peace with what you have gained from us—or else . . .

D. OF INDRA: What I have gained from you?—Or else—or else what?

DEAN OF JURISPRUDENCE: Or you will be stoned!

POET: Or crucified. . . .

D. OF INDRA: [*To the* Poet] I shall go. . . . Follow me, and you shall learn the riddle.

POET: Which riddle?

D. OF INDRA: What did he mean when he spoke of my gain?

POET: Probably nothing. What he said was what we call fatuous prattle. He just talked.

D. OF INDRA: It was this that hurt me more than anything. . . .

POET: That's probably why he said it. People are like that. . . .

ALL THE RIGHTEOUS-MINDED: Hurrah! The door has been opened!

LORD CHANCELLOR: What was behind it?

GLAZIER: I don't see anything. . . .

LORD CHANCELLOR: You can't see anything? No, of course, you can't! Deans! What was hidden behind the door?

DEAN OF THEOLOGY: Nothing! That is the solution of the riddle of the world. . . . In the beginning God created heaven and the earth out of nothing . . .

DEAN OF PHILOSOPHY: Out of nothing comes nothing . . .

DEAN OF MEDICINE: Nothing but nonsense—and that's nothing!

DEAN OF JURISPRUDENCE: I doubt. It is a clear case of fraud. I appeal to all the righteous-minded!

D. OF INDRA: [*To the* Poet] Who are the righteous-minded?

POET: Well—tell me that—whoever can! All the righteous-minded are usually only one person. Today it may be I and my followers—tomorrow it may be you and yours. It is a position one is chosen for—or rather, one chooses oneself!

ALL THE RIGHTEOUS-MINDED: We have been deceived, defrauded!

LORD CHANCELLOR: Who has deceived you?

ALL THE RIGHTEOUS-MINDED: The daughter of Indra!

LORD CHANCELLOR: Will the daughter of Indra please tell us why she was so anxious to have this door opened?

D. OF INDRA: No, my friends . . . for if I did tell you, you would not believe me. . . .

DEAN OF MEDICINE: But there is nothing in there!

D. OF INDRA: You speak the truth—yet you do not understand it.

DEAN OF MEDICINE: She is talking nonsense, rubbish!

ALL: Nonsense! Rubbish!

D. OF INDRA: [*To the* Poet] They are to be pitied! . . .

POET: Are you speaking seriously?

D. OF INDRA: I am always in earnest.

POET: Do you feel pity for the self-righteous, too?

D. OF INDRA: I think I pity them most. . . .

POET: And the four faculties?

D. OF INDRA: Yes, and not least them. Four heads, four minds—and all part of one body! Who created this monster?

ALL: She hasn't answered the Lord Chancellor's question. . . .

LORD CHANCELLOR: Then flog her!

D. OF INDRA: I have already answered.

LORD CHANCELLOR: Listen—she is answering back! . . .

ALL: Beat her! Flog her! She is answering back, . . .

D. OF INDRA: Whether she answers or doesn't answer, strike her, beat her! . . . [*To the* Poet] Come with me, seer, and then I shall answer the riddle—but far away from here—out in the wilderness—where no one can hear us, no one can see us. . . .

[*The* Attorney *appears. He takes hold of the* Daughter of Indra *by the arm*]

ATTORNEY: Have you forgotten your duties?

D. OF INDRA: O God! No!—But I have other duties, higher duties, to perform. . . .

ATTORNEY: And your child?

D. OF INDRA: My child! And what more?

ATTORNEY: Your child is crying for you. . . .

D. OF INDRA: My child! Woe to me! I am earth-bound! . . . And this pain in my breast, this dread, this anguish! . . . What is it?

ATTORNEY: And you don't know? . . .

D. OF INDRA: No!

ATTORNEY: It is remorse—the pangs of conscience. . . .

D. OF INDRA: Alas, is that my grieving conscience?

ATTORNEY: Yes!—Remorse sets in after every duty that has been neglected; after every pleasure indulged in, however innocent—if there *is* such a thing as an innocent pleasure; after every suffering inflicted upon others.

D. OF INDRA: And is there no remedy for it?

ATTORNEY: Yes, there is a remedy—and only one! By fulfilling one's duties without hesitation. . . .

D. OF INDRA: You look like a demon when you utter the word *duty!*—But I—I have not *one* duty—my duties are twofold—What am I to do?

ATTORNEY: You fulfill one at a time.

D. OF INDRA: Then the highest duty first . . . and so: will you look after my child while I fulfill my duty? . . .

ATTORNEY: Your child will miss you, and will suffer. . . . Can you endure knowing that someone will suffer for your sake?

D. OF INDRA: Now there is struggle in my soul . . . it seems to be cleaving in two—each part pulling away from the other. . . .

ATTORNEY: It is a mere sample of the disharmony that exists in life! Now you know how it feels! . . .

D. OF INDRA: Oh! How it tugs and tears at my heart!

POET: If you knew . . . if you only suspected how much grief and devastation I have caused by fulfilling my calling—and note that I use the word calling, which is a higher, more sublime duty—then you would not touch my hand!

D. OF INDRA: What have you done, then?

POET: I was an only son. My father cherished the hope that I would some day take over his business. But I ran away from business school. My father took it so to heart that he died. My mother, who was deeply religious, wanted me to be religious, too. I *could* not. . . . She disowned me. I had a friend who

helped me through hard and trying days. This friend behaved like a tyrant toward those whose cause I had taken upon myself. I was compelled to strike down my friend and benefactor in order to save my soul! Ever since, I have had no peace. Now I am called scum, offal, infamous and lacking in honor!—And this despite the fact that my conscience tells me: "You were in the right!" For in the next moment it tells me: "You did wrong!"—That is the way life is. . . .

D. OF INDRA: Come away with me—out into the wilderness!

ATTORNEY: What about your child?

D. OF INDRA: [*She indicates all those who are present*] These are my children! Individually they are good—but as soon as they get together with one another, they quarrel and become demons. . . . Farewell!

Outside the castle. The setting is the same as in the first scene in the early part of the play. Now, however, the ground, facing the foundation walls of the castle, is covered with flowers: blue monk's hood, or aconite.

Topmost on the roof of the castle, on its lantern, is seen a chrysanthemum bud about to open its petals. The castle windows are illuminated with tapers.

The Daughter of Indra *and the* Poet *appear on the stage.*

D. OF INDRA: The moment for my ascent to the ether is not far off. . . . I shall have the help of fire. . . . It is this severance from Earth that you call death, and that you humans look forward to with fear. . . .

POET: Fear of the unknown . . .

D. OF INDRA: That you have within you . . .

POET: Who has? . . .

D. OF INDRA: All of you! Why do you put no faith in your prophets?

POET: Prophets have always been disbelieved! Why? . . . And—"if God has spoken, why will not men believe?" . . . Nothing can stand up against His Omnipotence. . . .

D. OF INDRA: Have you always doubted?

POET: No—many a time I have felt certainty beyond doubt . . . but then it slipped away . . . like a dream on waking. . . .

D. OF INDRA: It is not easy to be a mortal. . . .

POET: You have come to realize—and admit it?

D. OF INDRA: I do. . . .

POET: Tell me—did not Indra once send His son down to Earth to probe the plaints and charges of mankind?

D. OF INDRA: So He did—yes!—And how was He received?

POET: How did He fulfill His mission?—to answer with another question. . . .

D. OF INDRA: And may I answer with still another? —Was not Man helped by His stay on Earth? Answer me truthfully!

POET: Helped?—Yes—in a measure . . . yet very little. . . . But instead of asking questions—will you not explain the riddle to me?

D. OF INDRA: Yes—but how can it be of help to you? You will not believe me!

POET: I shall believe you, for I know who you are. . . .

D. OF INDRA: Then I shall tell you. . . . In the early morning of Time—before the sun was born— Brahma, the divine force of all living things, allowed himself to be tempted by Maya, the Mother of the Universe, to propagate himself. This meeting of the divine primal force with the earth matter, constituted the fall of heaven into sin. Thus the universe, mankind, existence are merely a phantom, a dream, an illusion . . .

POET: [Ecstatically] My dream!

D. OF INDRA: A dream of truth! . . . But Brahma's offspring seek to free themselves from the earth-matter through self-denial and suffering. . . . Thus suffering becomes the liberator.—However, this yearning for suffering comes into conflict with the craving and the desire to find enjoyment—and love! Do you now understand what love is, with its mixture of the greatest in enjoyment and the greatest in suffering, the sweetest and the bitterest? Can you now understand what woman is? Woman—through whom sin and death came into being? . . .

POET: I can. . . . And where is the end?

D. OF INDRA: You know the end. . . . The struggle between the pain that follows enjoyment and the pleasure that we take in suffering: between the penitent's torment and torture and the sensualist's dissipations. . . .

POET: And therefore strife?

D. OF INDRA: Struggle between opposites produces energy—just as fire and water generate steam.

POET: But peace—and rest?

D. OF INDRA: Hush! You must ask no more questions; and I must speak no more! . . . The altar is already adorned for the sacrifice: the flowers stand on guard, the tapers are lighted, white sheets are hung in the windows, twigs of spruce have been spread in the gateway. . . .

POET: You speak as calmly as though suffering did not exist for you!

D. OF INDRA: As though it did not exist! . . . I have suffered all your sufferings, hundredfold, for my sensibilities are so much more receptive. . . .

POET: Tell me your sorrows!

D. OF INDRA: Could you, poet, lay bare your own, frankly, candidly? Could your words, even once, for a fleeting moment, impart the full and true meaning of your thoughts?

POET: No—you are right! I have ever seemed to myself a mere deaf-mute! The crowd always listened admiringly to my outpourings, but I could find them

only hollow and empty. And so, you see, I felt ashamed when people acclaimed me and paid me homage. . . .

D. OF INDRA: And yet you wish me to. . . . Look me in the eye!

POET: I cannot endure your gaze!

D. OF INDRA: How would you then be able to endure my words, if I were to speak in my celestial tongue?

POET: But before you go, tell me what you suffered most from down here!

D. OF INDRA: From being—from living—from feeling one's sight weakened by an eye, one's hearing impaired by an ear, and my thoughts—my luminous, enlightening, ethereal thoughts—bound up in a labyrinth of coiled slime! You have seen a brain, haven't you?—with its crooked, crawling, worming tracks and passages. . . .

POET: I have—and that's what makes all the righteous-minded think so crookedly. . . .

D. OF INDRA: Malicious—always malicious! But you are all the same!

POET: How could we be otherwise?

D. OF INDRA: Now I shake the dust off my feet— the dust, the earth, the clay. . . .

[She removes her shoes and casts them in the fire]

[The Portress enters. She places her shawl on the fire]

PORTRESS: You don't mind if I burn my shawl, too? [She leaves]

OFFICER: [Enters] And here are my roses—with nothing but the thorns left. . . .

[He, too, offers them to the flames]

BILLPOSTER: [Enters] The posters you may have— but the dip-net—never! . . .

[He throws the posters into the fire]

GLAZIER: [Enters] Take the diamond that opened the door! Farewell!

[He rushes out, after having sacrificed his diamond]

ATTORNEY: [Enters] And here is the dossier containing the minutes of the great dispute concerning the pope's beard or the diminishing water supply in the sources of the Ganges River.

[He sacrifices the documents to the flames; then he leaves]

QUARANTINE MASTER: [Comes in] Here is my contribution: the black mask which changed me into a blackamoor against my will. . . .

[He throws the mask into the fire]

VICTORIA: [Enters] I offer you my beauty—my sorrow!

[She leaves]

BLIND MAN: [Enters. He thrusts his hand into the fire] Having no eye to sacrifice, I give my hand!

DON JUAN: [Enters in his wheelchair. He is followed by She and the Lover (the Major)] Make haste, make haste! Life is short!

[He leaves together with the others]

POET: I have read somewhere that when the end is near, all of life passes before us in one long cavalcade. . . . Is this the end for you?

D. OF INDRA: Yes—it is the end! Farewell!

POET: Then speak a word before we part!

D. OF INDRA: No—that I cannot! Could your words, do you think, truly image your thoughts?

DEAN OF THEOLOGY: [*Enters. He is in a raging temper*] God has disavowed me—I am persecuted by man—the government has deserted me—and I am the scorn of my colleagues! How can I keep my faith, when no one else has faith? How can I defend a God who does not defend his own? . . . It's rubbish —that's all it is!

[*He flings a book into the fire and struts out*]

POET: [*Snatches the book from the flames*] Do you know what he threw into the fire?—A martyrology! A calendar with a martyr for each day of the year. . . .

D. OF INDRA: A martyr?

POET: Yes—one who has suffered and been tortured to death for the sake of his faith! And can you tell me why? Do you believe that all who endure pain, suffer? And that all who are put to death, feel pain? Isn't it through suffering we gain redemption from sin—and doesn't death give us deliverance and set us free?

KRISTIN: [*Enters, carrying her strips of paper*] I paste—I paste—until every nook and cranny has been pasted over. . . .

POET: And if there were a cleft in heaven itself, you would try to patch it with your tape. . . . Go away!

KRISTIN: Are there no double windows in the castle?

POET: No! That is one place where you won't find any!

KRISTIN: [*Turns to leave*] Well, then I'll be going!

D. OF INDRA: My life on earth is ending—it is time to leave. . . .

Farewell, you mortal child, you poet-dreamer,
who—better than the rest—has learned to live. . . .
Borne upon wings, you soar to heights beyond this earth,
yet sometimes fall into the mire,
but don't get caught in it—you merely graze it!

Now that I leave, the loss of what has been,
what I have loved, and the remorse for things left undone,
arises in me, as—when parting from one's friends—
one says Godspeed to them, and to the places one holds dear. . . .
Oh! In this moment I can feel the utter pain of being,
of living, and of being mortal. . . .
One misses even what was once disdained
and feels a guilt for wrongs that one did never do. . . .
One longs to leave—yet yearns to stay. . . .
Thus in a tug of war the heart is torn in twain
and feelings rent asunder by the beasts
of conflict, indecision and disharmony. . . .
Farewell! And tell your earth-kin I shall never
forget them where I go—and I shall bring
their plaint to Indra—in your name. . . .
Farewell! . . .

She enters the castle.—One hears music.—The background is illuminated by the flames from the burning castle and reveals a wall of human faces— faces that are searching and inquiring, sorrowful and grief-stricken, tortured by agony and anguish. As the castle burns, the flower bud on the roof-top opens into a chrysanthemum of giant proportions.

THE TIDINGS BROUGHT TO MARY: *A Mystery*

BY PAUL CLAUDEL

TRANSLATED FROM THE FRENCH BY LOUISE MORGAN SILL

PROLOGUE

The barn at Combernon. It is a lofty edifice, with square pillars that support a vaulted roof. It is empty except for the right wing, which is still filled with straw; and straws are scattered about on the floor, which is of well-trampled earth. At the back is a large double door in the thick wall, with complicated bars and bolts. On the valves of the door are painted rude images of St. Peter and St. Paul, one holding the keys, the other the sword. The scene is lighted by a large yellow wax candle in an iron socket fastened to one of the pillars.

The scenes of the drama take place at the close of the Middle Ages, seen conventionally, as mediæval poets might have imagined classic antiquity.

The time is night, merging into the hours of dawn.

Enter, on a heavy horse, a man wearing a black cloak, and with a leathern bag on the horse's croup behind him, Pierre de Craon. His gigantic shadow moves across the wall, the floor, the pillars.

Suddenly, from behind a pillar, Violaine steps out to meet him. She is tall and slender, and her feet are bare. Her gown is of coarse woollen stuff, and upon her head is a linen coif at once peasant-like and monastic.

VIOLAINE: [*Laughingly raising her hands toward him, with the forefingers crossed*] Halt, my lord cavalier! Dismount!

PIERRE DE CRAON: Violaine!

[*He gets off the horse*]

VIOLAINE: Softly, Master Pierre! Is that the way one leaves the house, like a thief without an honest greeting to the ladies?

PIERRE DE CRAON: Violaine, take yourself off. It is the dead of night, and we are here alone, the two of us.

And you know that I am not such a very safe man.

VIOLAINE: I am not afraid of you, mason! A man is not wicked merely because he wants to be!

And a man doesn't do with me just as he wills!

Poor Pierre! You did not even succeed in killing me

With your wretched knife! Nothing but a little snick on my arm which nobody has seen.

PIERRE DE CRAON: Violaine, you must forgive me.

VIOLAINE: It is for that I came.

PIERRE DE CRAON: You are the first woman I ever laid hands on. The devil, who always seizes his chance, took possession of me.

VIOLAINE: But you found me stronger than him.

PIERRE DE CRAON: Violaine, I am even more dangerous now than I was then.

VIOLAINE: Must we then fight once more?

PIERRE DE CRAON: Even my very presence here is baleful.

[*Silence*]

VIOLAINE: I don't know what you mean.

PIERRE DE CRAON: Had I not my work? Stones enough to choose and gather, wood enough to join, and metals to melt and mould,

My own work, that suddenly I should lay an impious and lustful hand on the work of another, a living being?

VIOLAINE: In my father's house, the house of your host! Lord! what would they have said if they had known? But I concealed it well.

And they all take you for a sincere and blameless man, just as they did before.

PIERRE DE CRAON: Under appearances, God judges the heart.

VIOLAINE: We three then will guard the secret.

PIERRE DE CRAON: Violaine!

VIOLAINE: Master Pierre?

PIERRE DE CRAON: Stand there near the candle that I may see you well.

[*She stands, smiling, under the candle. He looks a long while at her*]

VIOLAINE: Have you looked at me long enough?

PIERRE DE CRAON: Who are you, young girl, and what part in you has God reserved to himself

That the hand which touches you with fleshly desire should in that same instant be thus

Withered, as if it had approached too near the mystery of his dwelling-place?

VIOLAINE: What has happened to you, then, since last year?

PIERRE DE CRAON: The very next day after that one you remember . . .

VIOLAINE: Well—?

PIERRE DE CRAON: I discovered in my side the horrible scourge.

VIOLAINE: The scourge, you say? What scourge?

PIERRE DE CRAON: Leprosy, the same we read of in the book of Moses.

VIOLAINE: What is leprosy?

PIERRE DE CRAON: Have you never heard of the woman who lived alone among the rocks of the Géyn,

Veiled from head to foot, and with a rattle in her hand?

VIOLAINE: That malady, Master Pierre?

PIERRE DE CRAON: Such a scourge it is

That he who has it in its most malicious form

Must be set apart at once,

For there is no living man so healthy that leprosy cannot taint him.

VIOLAINE: Why, then, are you still at liberty among us?

PIERRE DE CRAON: The Bishop gave me a dispensation, and you must know how few people I see,

Except my workmen to give them orders, and my malady is as yet secret and concealed.

And, were I not there, who would give away those new-born churches whom God has confided to my care, on their wedding day?

VIOLAINE: Is that why nobody has seen you this time at Combernon?

PIERRE DE CRAON: I could not avoid returning here,

Because it is my duty to open the side of Monsanvierge

And to unseal the wall for each new flight of doves that seek entrance into the high Ark whose gates may only open toward heaven!

And this time we led to the altar an illustrious victim, a solemn censer,

The Queen herself, mother of the King, ascending in her own person,

For her son deprived of his kingdom.

And now I return to Rheims.

VIOLAINE: Maker of doors, let me open this one for you.

PIERRE DE CRAON: Was there no one else at the farm to do me this service?

VIOLAINE: The servant likes to sleep, and willingly gave me the keys.

PIERRE DE CRAON: Have you no fear or horror of the leper?

VIOLAINE: There is God, He knows how to protect me.

PIERRE DE CRAON: Give me the key, then.

VIOLAINE: No. Let me. You do not understand the working of these old doors.

Indeed! Do you take me for a dainty damsel

Whose taper fingers are used to nothing rougher than the spur, light as the bone of a bird, that arms the heel of her new knight?

You shall see!

[She turns the keys in the two grinding locks and draws the bolts]

PIERRE DE CRAON: This iron is very rusty.

VIOLAINE: The door is no longer used. But the road is shorter this way.

[She strains at the bar]

I have opened the door!

PIERRE DE CRAON: What could resist such an assailant?

What a dust! the old valve from top to bottom creaks and moves,

The black spiders run away, the old nests crumble, and the door at last opens from the centre.

[The door opens; through the darkness can be seen the meadows and the harvest. A feeble glimmer in the east]

VIOLAINE: This little rain has done everybody good.

PIERRE DE CRAON: The dust in the road will be well laid.

VIOLAINE: [In a low voice, affectionately] Peace to you, Pierre!

[Silence. And, suddenly, sonorous and clear and very high in the heaven, the first tolling of the Angelus. Pierre takes off his hat, and both make the sign of the cross]

VIOLAINE: [Her hands clasped and her face raised to heaven, in a voice beautifully clear and touching] REGINA CAELI, LAETARE, ALLELUIA!

[Second tolling]

PIERRE DE CRAON: [In a hollow voice] QUIA QUEM MERUISTI PORTARE, ALLELUIA!

[Third tolling]

VIOLAINE: RESURREXIT SICUT DIXIT, ALLELUIA!

PIERRE DE CRAON: ORA PRO NOBIS DEUM.

[Pause]

VIOLAINE: GAUDE ET LAETARE, VIRGO MARIA, ALLELUIA!

PIERRE DE CRAON: QUIA RESURREXIT DOMINUS VERE, ALLELUIA!

[Peal of the Angelus]

PIERRE DE CRAON: QUIA RESURREXIT DOMINUS PER RESURRECTIONEM FILII TUI DOMINI NOSTRI JESU CRISTI MUNDUM LAETIFICARE DIGNATUS ES, PRAESTA, QUAESUMUS, UT PER EJUS GENITRICEM VIRGINEM MARIAM PERPETUAE CAPIAMUS GAUDIA VITAE. PER BUNDEM DOMINUM NOSTRUM JESUM CHRISTUM QUI TECUM VIVIT ET REGNAT IN UNITATE SPIRITUS SANCTI DEUS PER OMNIA SAECULA SAECULORUM.

VIOLAINE: Amen.

[Both cross themselves]

PIERRE DE CRAON: How early the Angelus rings!

VIOLAINE: They say matins up there at midnight like the Carthusians.

PIERRE DE CRAON: I shall be at Rheims this evening.

VIOLAINE: Know you well the road?

First along this hedge,

And then by that low house in the grove of elder bushes, under which you will see five or six beehives.

And a hundred paces further on you reach the King's Highway.

[A pause]

PIERRE DE CRAON: PAX TIBI.

How all creation seems to rest with God in a profound mystery!

That which was hidden grows visible again with

Him, and I feel on my face a breath as fresh as roses.

Praise thy God, blessed earth, in tears and darkness!

The fruit is for man, but the flower is for God and the sweet fragrance of all things born.

Thus the virtue of the holy soul that is hidden is subtly revealed, as the mint leaf by its odour.

Violaine, who have opened the door for me, farewell!

I shall never return again to you.

O young tree of the knowledge of Good and Evil, behold how my dissolution begins because I have laid my hands upon you,

And already my soul and body are being divided, as the wine in the vat from the crushed grape!

What matters it? I had no need of woman.

I have never possessed a corruptible woman.

The man who in his heart has preferred God, sees when he dies his guardian Angel.

The time will soon come when another door opens,

When he who in this life has pleased but few, having finished his work, falls asleep in the arms of the eternal Bird:

When through translucent walls looms on all sides the sombre Paradise,

And the censers of the night mingle their scent with the odour of the noisome wick as it sputters out.

VIOLAINE: Pierre de Craon, I know that you do not expect to hear from me any false sighs, "Poor fellows!" or "Poor Pierres."

Because to him who suffers the consolation of a joyous comforter is not of much worth, for his anguish is not to us what it is to him.

Suffer with our Lord.

But know that your evil act is forgotten

So far as it concerns me, and that I am at peace with you,

And that I do not scorn or abhor you because you are stricken with the pest and malady,

But I shall treat you like a healthy man, and like Pierre de Craon, our old friend, whom I respect and love and fear.

What I say to you is true.

PIERRE DE CRAON: Thank you, Violaine.

VIOLAINE: And now I have something to ask you.

PIERRE DE CRAON: Speak.

VIOLAINE: What is this beautiful story that my father has told us? What is this "Justice" that you are building at Rheims, and that will be more beautiful than Saint-Rémy and Notre-Dame?

PIERRE DE CRAON: It is the church which the guilds of Rheims gave me to build on the site of the old Parc-aux-Ouilles,[1]

There where the old Marc-de-l'Evêque[2] was burned down yesteryear.

Firstly, as a thank-offering to God for seven fat

summers while distress reigned everywhere else in the kingdom,

For abundant grain and fruit, for cheap and beautiful wool,

For cloth and parchment profitably sold to the merchants of Paris and Germany.

Secondly, for the liberties acquired, the privileges conferred by our Lord the King,

The old order issued against us by Bishops Felix II and Abondant de Cramail

Rescinded by the Pope,

And all that by the aid of the bright sword and Champenois coins.

For such is the Christian commonwealth, without servile fear,

But that each should have his right, according to justice, in marvellous diversity,

That charity may be fulfilled.

VIOLAINE: But of which King and of which Pope do you speak? For there are two, and one does not know which is the good one.

PIERRE DE CRAON: The good one is he who is good to us.

VIOLAINE: You do not speak rightly.

PIERRE DE CRAON: Forgive me. I am only an ignorant man.

VIOLAINE: And whence comes this name given to the new parish?

PIERRE DE CRAON: Have you never heard of Saint Justice who was martyred in an anise field in the time of the Emperor Julian?

(The anise seeds which they put in our gingerbread at the Easter fair.)

As we were trying to divert the waters of a subterranean spring, to make way for our foundations,

We discovered her tomb, with this inscription on a slab of stone, broken in two: JUSTITIA ANCILLA DOMINI IN PACE.

The fragile little skull was broken like a nut—she was a child of eight years—

And a few milk teeth still adhere to the jaw.

For which all Rheims is filled with admiration, and many signs and miracles follow the body

Which we have laid in a chapel, to await the completion of our work.

But under the great foundation stone we have left, like seed, the little teeth.

VIOLAINE: What a beautiful story! And father also told us that all the ladies of Rheims give their jewels for the building of the Justice.

PIERRE DE CRAON: We have a great heap of them, and many Jews around them like flies.

[Violaine *has been looking down and turning hesitatingly a massive gold ring which she wears on her fourth finger*]

PIERRE DE CRAON: What ring is that, Violaine?

VIOLAINE: A ring that Jacques gave me.

[*Silence*]

PIERRE DE CRAON: I congratulate you.

---

[1] Sheep-fold.
[2] The bishop's still.

[*She holds out the ring to him*]

VIOLAINE: It is not yet settled. My father has said nothing.

Well! That is what I wanted to tell you.

Take my beautiful ring, which is all I have, and Jacques gave it to me secretly.

PIERRE DE CRAON: But I do not want it!

VIOLAINE: Take it quickly, or I shall no longer have the strength to part with it.

[*He takes the ring*]

PIERRE DE CRAON: What will your betrothed say?

VIOLAINE: He is not really my betrothed yet.

The loss of a ring does not change the heart. He knows me. He will give me another of silver.

This one was too fine for me.

PIERRE DE CRAON: [*Examining it*] It is of vegetable gold which, in former times, they knew how to make with an alloy of honey.

It is as supple as wax, and nothing can break it.

VIOLAINE: Jacques turned it up in the ground when he was ploughing, in a place where they sometimes find old swords turned quite green, and pretty bits of glass.

I was afraid to wear such a pagan thing, which belongs to the dead.

PIERRE DE CRAON: I accept this pure gold.

VIOLAINE: And kiss my sister Justice for me.

PIERRE DE CRAON: [*Looking suddenly at her, as if struck with an idea*] Is that all you have to give me for her? a bit of gold taken off your finger?

VIOLAINE: Will that not be enough to pay for one little stone?

PIERRE DE CRAON: But Justice is a large stone herself.

VIOLAINE: [*Laughing*] I am not from the same quarry.

PIERRE DE CRAON: The stone needed for the base is not the stone needed for the pinnacle.

VIOLAINE: Then, if I am a stone, may it be that useful one that grinds the corn, coupled to the twin millstone.

PIERRE DE CRAON: And Justitia also was only a humble little girl at her mother's side.

Until the moment God called her to the confession of faith.

VIOLAINE: But nobody wishes me ill! Is it necessary that I should go preach the Gospel to the Saracens?

PIERRE DE CRAON: It is not for the stone to choose its own place, but for the Master of the Work who chose the stone.

VIOLAINE: Then praised be God who has given me mine now, and I have no longer to seek it. And I ask him for no other.

I am Violaine, I am eighteen years old, my father's name is Anne Vercors, my mother's name is Elisabeth,

My sister's name is Mara, my betrothed is named Jacques. There, that is all, there is nothing more to know.

Everything is perfectly clear, all is arranged beforehand, and I am very glad.

I am free, I have nothing to trouble me; another will lead me, the poor man, and he knows everything that there is to do.

Sower of steeples, come to Combernon! we will give you stone and wood, but you shall not have the daughter of the house!

And, besides, is this not already the house of God, the land of God, the service of God?

Have we not charge over lonely Monsanvierge, which we must feed and guard, providing it with bread, wine, and wax,

Being a dependency of this lonely eyrie of angels with half-spread wings?

Thus, as the great lords have their dovecot, we too have ours, which is known from a great distance away.

PIERRE DE CRAON: One day as I went through the forest of Fisme, I heard two beautiful oak trees talking together,

Praising God for making them immovable on the spot where they were born.

Now one of them, in the prow of an ocean raft, makes war upon the Turks,

The other, felled under my care, supports Jehanne, the good bell in the tower of Laon, whose voice is heard ten leagues away.

Young girl, in my craft one does not keep one's eyes in one's pocket.

I know the good stone under the juniper trees, and the good wood like a master woodpecker;

In the same way, men and women.

VIOLAINE: But not girls, Master Pierre! That is too subtle for you. And in the first place, there is nothing at all to know.

PIERRE DE CRAON: [*In a low voice*] You love him dearly, Violaine?

VIOLAINE: [*Lowering her eyes*] That is a great mystery between us two.

PIERRE DE CRAON: Blessed be thou in thy pure heart!

Holiness is not to get oneself stoned by the Turks, or to kiss a leper on the mouth,

But to obey promptly God's commands.

Whether it be

To stay where we are, or to ascend higher.

VIOLAINE: Ah, how beautiful the world is, and how happy I am!

PIERRE DE CRAON: [*Speaking low*] Ah, how beautiful the world is, and how unhappy I am!

VIOLAINE: [*Pointing to the sky*] Man of the city, listen!

[*Pause*]

Do you hear high up there that little soul singing?

PIERRE DE CRAON: It is the lark!

VIOLAINE: It is the lark, alleluia! The lark of the Christian earth, alleluia, alleluia!

Do you hear it cry four times, he! he! he! he! higher, higher!

Do you see it, the eager little cross, with its wings spread, like the seraphim who have only wings and no feet, singing shrilly before the throne of God?

PIERRE DE CRAON: I hear it.

And it is thus I heard it once at dawn, on the day we dedicated my daughter Notre-Dame de la Couture,

And a golden point gleamed at the topmost pinnacle of this great thing I had made, like a star newborn!

VIOLAINE: Pierre de Craon, if you had done with me as you would,

Would you be more happy now because of that, or I more beautiful?

PIERRE DE CRAON: No, Violaine.

VIOLAINE: And would I still be the same Violaine whom you loved?

PIERRE DE CRAON: No, not she, but another.

VIOLAINE: And which is better, Pierre,

That I share my joy with you, or that I share your pain?

PIERRE DE CRAON: Sing far up in the highest heaven, lark of France!

VIOLAINE: Forgive me, for I am too happy, because he whom I love

Loves me, and I am sure of him, and I know he loves me, and all is equal between us.

And because God made me to be happy and not for evil nor any sorrow.

PIERRE DE CRAON: Mount to heaven in a single flight!

As for me, to ascend a little I must have the whole of a cathedral, with its deep foundations.

VIOLAINE: And tell me that you forgive Jacques for marrying me.

PIERRE DE CRAON: No, I do not forgive him.

VIOLAINE: Hatred does you no good, Pierre, and makes me grieve.

PIERRE DE CRAON: It is you who make me speak. Why do you force me to show the ugly wound that no one sees?

Let me go, and ask me nothing more. We shall not see each other any more.

All the same, I carry away his ring!

VIOLAINE: Leave your hatred in its place, and I will give it back to you when you have need of it.

PIERRE DE CRAON: But besides, Violaine, I am very wretched.

It is hard to be a leper, to bear this shameful wound, knowing that there is no cure and that there is no help for it,

But that each day it spreads and bites deeper; and to be alone, and to suffer one's own poison, to feel oneself alive in corruption,

Not only to taste death once, aye, ten times, but to miss nothing, even to the end, of the horrible alchemy of the tomb!

Is it you who have brought this evil upon me by

your beauty, for before I saw you I was pure and happy,

My heart lost in my work and ideas, under another's command.

And now that I command in my turn, and draw the plans,

Behold, you turn your face toward me with that poisonous smile.

VIOLAINE: The poison was not in me, Pierre!

PIERRE DE CREON: I know it, it was in me, and it is still there, and this sick flesh has not cured the tainted soul!

O little soul, was it possible that I should see you and not love you?

VIOLAINE: And certainly you have shown that you loved me.

PIERRE DE CRAON: It is my fault if the fruit hangs on the branch?

And who is he who loves and does not desire all?

VIOLAINE: And that is why you tried to destroy me?

PIERRE DE CRAON: Man, cruelly injured, has his infernal shades, too, like woman.

VIOLAINE: In what have I failed you?

PIERRE DE CRAON: O image of eternal Beauty, thou art not for me!

VIOLAINE: I am not an image!

That is not the way to speak!

PIERRE DE CRAON: Another takes from you that which was for me.

VIOLAINE: The image remains.

PIERRE DE CRAON: Another takes Violaine from me, and leaves me this tainted flesh and this consumed mind.

VIOLAINE: Be a man, Pierre! Be worthy of the flame which consumes you!

And if one must be consumed, let it be like the Paschal-candle, flaming on its golden candelabrum in the midst of the choir for the glory of all the Church!

PIERRE DE CRAON: So many sublime pinnacles! But shall I never see the roof of my own little house under the trees?

So many belfries whose circling shadows write the hour for all the city! But shall I never design an oven, and the room for the children?

VIOLAINE: It was not for me to take for myself alone what belongs to all.

PIERRE DE CRAON: When will the wedding be, Violaine?

VIOLAINE: At Michaelmas, I suppose, when the harvest is done.

PIERRE DE CRAON: On that day, when the bells of Monsanvierge have spoken and are silent, listen well and you will hear me answer them far away at Rheims.

VIOLAINE: Who takes care of you there?

PIERRE DE CRAON: I have always lived like a workman; it is enough for me if I have a bunch of straw between two stones, a leathern coat, and a little bacon on my bread.

VIOLAINE: Poor Pierre!

PIERRE DE CRAON: I am not to be pitied for that; we are set apart.

I do not live as other men, as I am always under the ground with the foundations, or in the sky with the belfry.

VIOLAINE: Well! We could never have lived together! My head swims if I only go up to the hayloft.

PIERRE DE CRAON: This church alone will be my wife, drawn from my side like an Eve of stone, in the slumber of pain.

May I soon feel my great structure rising under me, and lay my hand on this indestructible thing I have made, whose parts hold firmly together, this solid work which I have constructed of strong stone that the Holy Sacrament may be placed there, my work that God inhabits!

I shall never come down again! It is I at whom they point, that group of young girls with arms interlaced, on the chequered pavement a hundred feet below!

VIOLAINE: You must come down. Who knows but I shall have need of you some day?

PIERRE DE CRAON: Farewell, Violaine, my soul, I shall never see you again!

VIOLAINE: Who knows that you will never see me again?

PIERRE DE CRAON: Farewell, Violaine!

How many things I have already done! How many things remain for me to do, how much building up of habitations!

Darkness, with God.

Not the hours of the office in a breviary, but the real hours of a cathedral, where the sun brings light and shade successfully to every part.

I take away your ring,

And of its little circle I will make golden seed!

"God caused the deluge to cease," as says the baptismal psalm,

And I, between the walls of the Justice, shall imprison the gold of the dawn!

The light of day changes, but not that which I shall distil under those arches,

Like the light of the human soul, that the Host may dwell in the midst of it.

The soul of Violaine, my child, in whom my heart delights.

There are churches like pits, and others which are like furnaces,

And others so delicately put together, adjusted with such art, that they seem as if they would ring like a bell under a finger-tap.

But that which I am going to build will lie under its own shadow like condensed gold, and like a pyx full of manna!

VIOLAINE: O Master Pierre, what a beautiful stained-glass window you gave to the monks of Clinchy!

PIERRE DE CRAON: The staining of glass is not my art, though I know something of it.

But, before the glass is made, the architect, by his knowledge of arrangement, makes the stone framework like a filter in the waves of God's Light,

And gives to the whole edifice its individual lustre, as to a pearl.

[Mara Vercors *enters and watches them without being seen*]

And now farewell! The sun is risen, and I ought already to be far on my road.

VIOLAINE: Farewell, Pierre!

PIERRE DE CRAON: Farewell, Violaine!

VIOLAINE: Poor Pierre!

[*She looks at him with eyes full of tears, hesitates, and offers him her hand. He seizes it, and while he holds it between his own she leans towards him and kisses him on the face*]

[Mara *makes a gesture of surprise and goes out*]

[Pierre de Craon *and* Violaine *go out by the different doors*]

ACT ONE: SCENE ONE

The kitchen of Combernon, a spacious room having a great fireplace with an emblazoned mantel; in the middle of the room a long table and all the domestic utensils, as in a picture by Breughel. The Mother, stooping before the hearth, tries to revive the fire. Anne Vercors, standing, looks at her. He is a tall and strong man of sixty years, with a full blond beard streaked with much white.

THE MOTHER: [*Without turning round*] Why do you look at me like that?

ANNE VERCORS: [*Thinking*] The end, already! It is like coming to the last page in a picture book.

"When the night had passed, the woman having revived the household fire . . .," and the humble and touching story is finished.

It is as if I were no longer here. There she is, before my eyes, yet seeming already like something only remembered. [*Aloud*]

O wife it is a month since we were married

With a ring which is shaped like *Oui*,

A month of which each day is a year.

And for a long time you were fruitless

Like a tree which gives nothing but shade.

And one day we looked at each other

And it was the middle of our life,

Elisabeth! and I saw the first wrinkles on thy forehead and around thine eyes.

And, as on our wedding day,

We clasped and embraced each other, no longer with
  lightness of heart,
But with the tenderness and compassion and piety
  of our mutual trust.
And between us was our child and the modesty
Of this sweet narcissus, Violaine.
And then the second was born to us,
Mara the black. Another daughter, and not a son.
[*Pause*]
Well now, say what you have to say, for I know
When you begin speaking without looking at you,
  saying something and nothing. Come now!

THE MOTHER: You know well that one can tell
  you nothing. You are never there, and I must
  even catch you to sew on a button.

And you do not listen to one, but like a watchdog
  you watch,
Only attentive to the noises of the door.
But men never understand anything.

ANNE VERCORS: Now the little girls are grown up.

THE MOTHER: They? No.

ANNE VERCORS: To whom are we going to marry
  them all?

THE MOTHER: Marry them, Anne, say you? We
  have plenty of time to think of that.

ANNE VERCORS: Oh, deceit of woman! Tell me!
  When think you anything

But first you do not say just the contrary; maliciousness! I know thee.[1]

THE MOTHER: I won't say anything more.

ANNE VERCORS: Jacques Hury.

THE MOTHER: Well?

ANNE VERCORS: There. I will give him Violaine . . .

And he will take the place of the son I have not had.
  He is an upright and industrious man.
I have known him since he was a little lad, and his
  mother gave him to us. It is I who have taught
  him everything,
Grain, cattle, servants, arms, tools, our neighbours,
  our betters, custom—God—
The weather, the nature of this ancient soil,
How to reflect before speaking.
I have seen him develop into a man while he was
  looking at me and the beard grow around his
  kind face,
As he is now, straight-backed and tight like the ears
  of the barley.
And he was never one of those who contradict, but
  who reflect, like the earth which receives all
  kinds of grain.
And that which is false, not taking root, dies;
And so, one may not say that he believes in truth,
  but rather that it grows within him, having found
  nourishment.

THE MOTHER: How do you know, if they love each
  other or not?

ANNE VERCORS: Violaine
Will do what I tell her.

_____
[1] This is meant to be affectionate banter.

As for him, I know that he loves her, and you too
  know it.
Yet the blockhead dares not speak to me. But I will
  give her to him if he wants her. So shall it be.

THE MOTHER: Yes.

No doubt that is as it should be.

ANNE VERCORS: Have you nothing more to say?

THE MOTHER: What, then?

ANNE VERCORS: Very well, I will go seek him.

THE MOTHER: What, seek him? Anne!

ANNE VERCORS: I want everything to be settled at
  once. I will tell you why presently.

THE MOTHER: What have you to tell me?
—Anne, listen a moment. . . . I fear. . . .

ANNE VERCORS: Well?

THE MOTHER: Mara

Slept in my room this winter, while you were ill, and
  we talked at night in our beds.
Surely he is an honest lad, and I love him like my
  own child, almost.
He has no property, that is true, but he is a good
  ploughman, and comes of a good family.
We could give them
Our Demi-muids farm with the lower fields which
  are too far away for us.—I, too, wanted to speak
  to you of him.

ANNE VERCORS: Well?

THE MOTHER: Well, nothing.

No doubt Violaine is the eldest.

ANNE VERCORS: Come, come, what then?

THE MOTHER: What then? How do you know surely
  that he loves her?—Our old friend, Master
  Pierre,
(Why did he keep away from us this time without
  seeing anybody?)
You saw him last year when he came,
And how he looked at her while she served us.—
  Certainly he has no land, but he earns much
  money.
—And she, while he spoke,
How she listened to him, with her eyes wide open
  like a child's,
Forgetting to pour the drink for us, so that I had
  to scold her!
—And Mara, you know her. You know how hard-
  headed she is!
If she has a notion then
That she will marry Jacques,—heigh-ho! She is hard
  as iron.
I don't know! Perhaps it would be better . . .

ANNE VERCORS: What is all this nonsense?

THE MOTHER: Very well! Very well! we can talk
  like that. You must not get angry.

ANNE VERCORS: It is my will.

Jacques shall marry Violaine.

THE MOTHER: Well! he shall marry her then.

ANNE VERCORS: And now, mother, I have something else to tell you, poor old woman! I am
  going away.

THE MOTHER: You are going away? You are going away, old man? What is that you say?

ANNE VERCORS: That is why Jacques must marry Violaine without delay, and take my place here.

THE MOTHER: Lord! You are going away! You mean it? And where are you going?

ANNE VERCORS: [*Pointing vaguely toward the south*] Down there.

THE MOTHER: To Château?

ANNE VERCORS: Farther than Château.

THE MOTHER: [*Lowering her voice*] To Bourges, to the other King?

ANNE VERCORS: To the King of Kings, to Jerusalem.

THE MOTHER: Lord! [*She sits down*]

Is it because France is not good enough for you?

ANNE VERCORS: There is too much sorrow in France.

THE MOTHER: But we are very comfortable here and nobody troubles Rheims.

ANNE VERCORS: That is it.

THE MOTHER: That is what?

ANNE VERCORS: The very thing; we are too happy,

And the others not happy enough.

THE MOTHER: Anne, that is not our fault.

ANNE VERCORS: It is not theirs either.

THE MOTHER: I don't know. I know that you are there and that I have two children.

ANNE VERCORS: But you see, surely, that everything is upset and put out of its right place, and everybody seeks distractedly to find where that place is.

And the smoke we see sometimes in the distance is not merely the smoke of burning straw.

And these crowds of poor people who come to us from every side.

There is no longer a King reigning over France, according to the prediction of the prophet.[1]

THE MOTHER: That is what you read to us the other day?

ANNE VERCORS: In the place of the King we have two children.

The English one, in his island,

And the other one, so little that among the reeds of the Loire he cannot be seen.

In place of the Pope we have three Popes, and instead of Rome, I don't know what council or other in Switzerland.

All is struggling and moving,

Having no longer any counterweight to steady it.

[1] "1 For, behold the Lord, the Lord of hosts, doth take away from Jerusalem and from Judah, the stay and the staff, the whole stay of bread, and the whole stay of water.

"2 The mighty man, and the man of war, the judge, and the prophet, and the prudent, and the ancient.

"3 The captain of fifty, and the honourable man, and the counsellor, and the cunning artificer, and the eloquent orator.

"4 And I will give children to be their princes, and babes shall rule over them."—Isaiah iii, 1–5.

THE MOTHER: And you, also, where do you want to go?

ANNE VERCORS: I can no longer stay here.

THE MOTHER: Anne, have I done anything to grieve you?

ANNE VERCORS: No, my Elisabeth.

THE MOTHER: Here you abandon me in my old age.

ANNE VERCORS: Give me leave to go, yourself.

THE MOTHER: You do not love me any more and you are no longer happy with me.

ANNE VERCORS: I am weary of being happy.

THE MOTHER: Scorn not the gift which God has given you.

ANNE VERCORS: God be praised who has overwhelmed me with his goodness!

For these thirty years now I have held this sacred fief from my father, and God has sent rain on my furrows.

For ten years there has not been one hour of my work

That he has not repaid four times over and more,

As if it were not his will to keep open his account with me, or leave anything owing.

All else perished, yet I was spared.

So that I shall appear before him empty and without a claim, among those who have received their reward.

THE MOTHER: It is enough to have a grateful heart.

ANNE VERCORS: But I am not satisfied with his benefits,

And because I have received them, shall I leave the greater good to others?

THE MOTHER: I do not understand you.

ANNE VERCORS: Which receives more, the full or the empty vessel?

And which has need of the most water, the cistern or the spring?

THE MOTHER: Ours is nearly dried up by this long hot summer.

ANNE VERCORS: Such has been the evil of this world, that each has wanted to enjoy his own as if it had been created for him,

And not at all as if he had received it by the will of God,

The lord his estate, the father his children,

The King his Kingdom and the scholar his rank.

That is why God has taken away from them all these things which can be taken away,

And has sent to each man deliverance and fasting.

And why is the portion of others not mine also?

THE MOTHER: You have your duty here with us.

ANNE VERCORS: Not if you will absolve me from it.

THE MOTHER: I will not absolve you.

ANNE VERCORS: You see that what I had to do is done.

The two children are reared, and Jacques is there to take my place.

THE MOTHER: Who calls you far away from us?

ANNE VERCORS: [*Smiling*] An angel blowing a trumpet.

THE MOTHER: What trumpet?

ANNE VERCORS: The soundless trumpet that is heard by all.

The trumpet that calls all men from time to time that the portions may be distributed afresh.

The trumpet in the valley of Jehosaphat before it has made a sound,

That of Bethlehem when Augustus numbered the people.

The trumpet of the Assumption, when the apostles were assembled.

The voice which takes the place of the Word when the Chief no longer speaks

To the body that seeks union with him.

THE MOTHER: Jerusalem is so far away!

ANNE VERCORS: Paradise is still farther.

THE MOTHER: God in the tabernacle is with us even here.

ANNE VERCORS: But not that great hole in the earth.

THE MOTHER: What hole?

ANNE VERCORS: That the Cross made when it was set there.

Behold how it draws everything to itself.

There is the stitch which cannot be undone, the knot which cannot be untied,

The heritage of all, the interior boundary stone that can never be uprooted,

The centre and the navel of the world, the element by which all humanity is held together.

THE MOTHER: What can one pilgrim alone do?

ANNE VERCORS: I am not alone! A great multitude rejoice and depart with me!

The multitude of all my dead,

Those souls, one above the other, of whom nothing is left now but the tombstones, all those stones baptized with me who claim their rightful place in the structure!

And as it is true that the Christian is never alone, but is in communion with all his brothers,

The whole kingdom is with me, invoking, and drawing near to the Seat of God, taking anew its course toward him,

And I am its deputy and I carry it with me

To lay it once again upon the eternal Pattern.

THE MOTHER: Who knows but that we shall need you here?

ANNE VERCORS: Who knows but that I am needed elsewhere?

Everything is shaking; who knows but that I obstruct God's plan by remaining here

Where the need there was of me is past?

THE MOTHER: I know you are an inflexible man.

ANNE VERCORS: [*Tenderly, changing his voice*] To me you are always young and beautiful, and very great is the love I feel for my black-haired sweet Elisabeth.

THE MOTHER: My hair is grey!

ANNE VERCORS: Say yes, Elisabeth. . . .

THE MOTHER: Anne, you have not left me in all these thirty years. What will become of me without my chief and my companion?

ANNE VERCORS: . . . The yes which will separate us now, very low,

As round as the oui that formerly made us one.

[*Silence*]

THE MOTHER: [*Speaking very low*] Yes, Anne.

ANNE VERCORS: Have patience, Zabillet! I shall soon return.

Can you not have faith in me a little while, though I am not here!

Soon will come another separation.

Come, put food for two days in a bag. It is time I was off.

THE MOTHER: What? To-day, even to-day?

ANNE VERCORS: Even to-day.

[*Her head droops and she does not move. He takes her in his arms but she does not respond*]

Farewell, Elisabeth.

THE MOTHER: Alas, old man, I shall never see you again.

ANNE VERCORS: And now I must seek Jacques.

ACT ONE: SCENE TWO

[*Enter* Mara]

MARA TO THE MOTHER: Go, and tell him she is not to marry him.

THE MOTHER: Mara! How is this? You were there?

MARA: Go, I tell you, and tell him she is not to marry him.

THE MOTHER: What, she? What, he? What do you know of her marrying him?

MARA: I was there. I heard it all.

THE MOTHER: Very well, my child! Your father wishes it.

You have seen I did what I could, and his mind is not changed.

MARA: Go and tell him that she is not to marry him, or I will kill myself!

THE MOTHER: Mara!

MARA: I will hang myself in the wood-house, there where we found the cat hung.

THE MOTHER: Mara! Wicked girl!

MARA: There again she has taken him away from me! Now she has taken him away!

It was always I who was to be his wife, and not she. She knows very well it is I.

THE MOTHER: She is the eldest.

MARA: What does that matter?

THE MOTHER: It is your father who wishes it.

MARA: I don't care.

THE MOTHER: Jacques Hury

Loves her.

MARA: That is not true! I know well enough that you do not love me!

You have always loved her best! Oh, when you talk of your Violaine it is like talking of sugar,

It is like sucking a cherry just when you are about to spit out the stone!

But Mara the magpie! She is as hard as iron, she is as sour as the wild cherry!

Added to that, there's always the talk of your Violaine being so beautiful!

And behold, she is now to have Combernon!

What does she know how to do, the ferret? which of us two can drive the cart?

She thinks herself like Saint Onzemillevierges! But, as for me, I am Mara Vercors, who hates injustice and deceit,

Mara who speaks the truth and it is that which makes the servants angry!

Let them be angry! I scorn them. Not one of the women dares stir in my presence, the hypocrites! Everything goes as smoothly as at the mill.

—And yet everything is for her and nothing for me.

THE MOTHER: You will have your share.

MARA: Aye, truly! The sandy ground up yonder! ooze and mud that it needs five oxen to plough! the bad ground of Chinchy.

THE MOTHER: It brings in good profit all the same.

MARA: Surely.

Long-rooted reeds and cow-wheat, senna, and mullein!

I shall have enough to make my herb-tea.

THE MOTHER: Bad girl; you know well enough that is not true!

You know well no wrong is done you!

But you have always been wicked! When you were little

You would not cry when you were beaten.

Tell me, you black-skinned child, you ugly one!

Is she not the eldest?

What have you against her?

Jealous girl! Yet she has always done what you wish.

Very well! She will be married first, and you will be married, you also, afterwards!

And it is too late to do differently anyhow, because your father is going away—oh, how sad I am!

He has gone to speak to Violaine and he will look for Jacques.

MARA: That's true! Go at once! Go, go at once!

THE MOTHER: Go where?

MARA: Mother, come now! You know well I am the one. Tell him she is not to marry him, *maman!*

THE MOTHER: Surely I shall do no such thing.

MARA: Only tell him what I have said. Tell him that I will kill myself. Do you understand? [*She looks fixedly at her*]

THE MOTHER: Ha!

MARA: Do you believe I will not do it?

THE MOTHER: Alack, I know you would!

MARA: Go then!

THE MOTHER: O Obstinate!

MARA: You have nothing to do with it.

Only to repeat to him just what I have said.

THE MOTHER: And he—how do you know he will be willing to marry you?

MARA: Certainly he will not.

THE MOTHER: Well. . . .

MARA: Well?

THE MOTHER: Don't think that I shall advise him to do your will!—on the contrary!

I will only tell him what you have said. It is very sure

That she will not be so silly as to give in to you, if she will listen to me.

MARA: Perhaps.—Go.—Do as I say.

[*She goes out*]

ACT ONE: SCENE THREE

[*Enter* Anne Vercors *and* Jacques Hury, *afterwards* Violaine, *and then the farm labourers and servants*]

ANNE VERCORS: [*Stopping*] Heh! what is that thou tell'st me?

JACQUES HURY: Just as I say! This time I took him in the act, with the pruning-hook in his hand!

I came up softly behind him and all of a sudden

Flac! I threw myself full length on him,

As you throw yourself on a hare in her hole at harvest

And there beside him was a bunch of twenty young poplars, the ones you set such store by!

ANNE VERCORS: Why did he not come to me? I should have given him the wood he needed.

JACQUES HURY: The wood he needs is the handle of my whip!

It is not need but wickedness, the idea of doing wrong!

These ne'er-do-wells from Chevoche are always ready to do anything

Out of bravado, and to defy people!

But as to that man, I will cut off his ears with my little knife!

ANNE VERCORS: No.

JACQUES HURY: At least let me tie him by his wrists to the harrow, before the big gate,

With his face turned against the teeth; with Faraud the dog to watch him.

ANNE VERCORS: Not that either.

JACQUES HURY: What is to be done then?

ANNE VERCORS: Send him home.

JACQUES HURY: With his bundle of wood?

ANNE VERCORS: And with another that thou wilt give him.

JACQUES HURY: Father, that is not right.

ANNE VERCORS: Thou canst tie his faggot around, that he may not lose any of it.

That will help him in crossing the ford at Saponay.

JACQUES HURY: It is not well to be lax about one's rights.

ANNE VERCORS: I know it, it is not well!

Jacques, behold how lazy and old I am, weary of fighting and defending.

Once I was harsh like thee.

There is a time to take and a time to let take.

The budding tree must be protected, but the tree where the fruit hangs do not trouble thyself about.

Let us be unjust in very little, lest God be unjust to me in much.

—And besides, thou wilt do now as thou wilt, for thou art placed over Combernon in my stead.

JACQUES HURY: What do you say?

THE MOTHER: He is going a pilgrim to Jerusalem.

JACQUES HURY: Jerusalem?

ANNE VERCORS: It is true. I start this very moment.

JACQUES HURY: What? What does that mean?

ANNE VERCORS: Thou hast heard very well.

JACQUES HURY: Thou wilt leave us like that, when the work is at its heaviest?

ANNE VERCORS: It is not necessary to have two masters at Combernon.

JACQUES HURY: My father, I am only your son!

ANNE VERCORS: Thou wilt be the father here, in my stead.

JACQUES HURY: I do not understand you.

ANNE VERCORS: I am going away. Take Combernon from me

As I took it from my father, and he from his,

And Radulphe the Frank, first of our line, from Saint Rémy de Rheims,

Who from Genevieve of Paris received this land, pagan and bristling with seedlings and wild thorns.

Radulphe and his children made it Christian by iron and by fire

And laid it naked and broken under the waters of baptism.

Hill and plain scored they with equal furrows,

As an industrious scholar copies line after line the word of God.

And they began to build Monsanvierge on the mountain, in that place where Evil was worshipped,

(And at first there was naught but a cabin made of logs and reeds, whose door the Bishop came to seal,

And two holy recluses were left to guard it),

And at the mountain's base, Combernon, a dwelling armed and provisioned.

Thus this land is free that we hold from St. Rémy in heaven, paying tithes up there to this flight, one moment stayed, of murmuring doves.

For everything is of God, and those who live in Him reap without ceasing the fruits of their works,

Which pass and come back to us again in their time in magnificent succession;

As over the various harvests every day in summer float those great clouds that drift toward Germany.

The cattle here are never sick, the udders and the wells are never dry; the grain is as solid as gold, the straw as firm as iron.

And for defence against pillagers we have arms, and the walls of Combernon, and the King, our neighbor.

Gather this harvest that I have sown, as in the past I myself have filled again the furrows my father ploughed.

O joyful work of the farmer, for which the sun is as bright as our glistening ox, and the rain is our banker, and God works with us every day, making of everything the best!

Others look to men for their rewards, but we receive ours straight from heaven itself,

A hundred for one, the full ear for a seed, and the tree for a nut.

For such is the justice of God to us, and the measure with which He repays us.

The earth cleaves to the sky, the body to the spirit, all things that He has created are in communion, all have need of one another.

Take the handles of the plough in my stead, that the earth may bring forth bread as God himself has wished.

Give food to all creatures, men and animals, to spirits and bodies, and to immortal souls.

You, women, labourers, look! Behold the son I have chosen, Jacques! I am going away and he stays in my place. Obey him.

JACQUES HURY: May it be done according to your will.

ANNE VERCORS: Violaine!

My child, first born instead of the son I have not had!

Heir of my name in whom I too shall be given to another!

Violaine, when thou shalt have a husband, do not scorn the love of thy father.

For thou canst not give back to a father what he has given thee, when thou wouldst.

Between husband and wife everything is equal; what they do not know they accept, one from the other, with faith.

This is the mutual religion, this is the servitude through which the wife's breast grows large with milk!

But the father, seeing his children separate from him, recognizes what was once within himself.

My daughter, know thy father!

A Father's love

Asks no return, and the child has no need either to win or merit it:

As it was his before the beginning, so it remains

His blessing and his inheritance, his help, his honour, his right, his justification!

My soul is never divided from the soul I have trans-
mitted.

What I have given can never be given back. Only
know, O my child, that I am thy father!

And of my issue there is no male. Only women have
I brought into the world.

Nothing but that thing in us which gives and which
is given.

—And now the hour of parting is come.

VIOLAINE: Father! Do not say such a cruel thing!

ANNE VERCORS: Jacques, you are the man whom
I love. Take her! I give you my daughter, Violaine. Take my name from her.

Love her, for she is as pure as gold.

All the days of thy life, like bread, of which one
never tires.

She is simple and obedient, sensitive and reserved.

Do not cause her any sorrow, and give her only
kindness.

Everything here is thine, except what will be given
to Mara, in accordance with my plan.

JACQUES HURY: What, my father, your daughter,
your property . . .

ANNE VERCORS: I give you all at once, as all is
mine.

JACQUES HURY: But who knows if she still cares
for me?

ANNE VERCORS: Who knows?

[She looks at Jacques and forms "Yes" with her
lips, without speaking]

JACQUES HURY: You care for me, Violaine?

VIOLAINE: My father wishes it.

JACQUES HURY: You wish it too?

VIOLAINE: I wish it too.

JACQUES HURY: Violaine!

How shall we get on together?

VIOLAINE: Consider well while there is yet time!

JACQUES HURY: Then I take you by God's command, and I will nevermore let you go.

[He takes her by both hands]

I have you and hold you, your hand and the arm
with it, and all that comes with the arm.

Parents, your daughter is no longer yours! She is
mine only!

ANNE VERCORS: Well, they are married; it is done!
What say you, mother?

THE MOTHER: I am very glad!

[She weeps]

ANNE VERCORS: She weeps, my wife!

There! that is how they take our children from us
and we shall be left alone,

The old woman who lives on a little milk and a
small bit of cake,

And the old man with his ears full of white hairs
like the heart of an artichoke.

—Let them make ready the wedding-dress!

—Children, I shall not be at your wedding.

VIOLAINE: What, father!

THE MOTHER: Anne!

ANNE VERCORS: I am going. Now.

VIOLAINE: O father! before we are married.

ANNE VERCORS: It must be. Your mother will explain all to you.

[Enter Mara]

THE MOTHER: How long shall you stay over there?

ANNE VERCORS: I do not know. It may be but a
short time.

I shall soon be coming back.

[Silence]

VOICE OF A CHILD: [In the distance] Oriole, oriole!
all alone!

Who eats the wild cherry and throws out the stone!

ANNE VERCORS: The oriole, rosy and golden, whistles in the heart of the tree.

What does he say? that after these long days of heat

The rain last night was like a shower of gold falling
upon the earth.

What does he say? he says it is good weather for
ploughing.

What more does he say? that the weather is fine,
that God is great, and that it is still two hours
of noon.

What more does the little bird say?

That it is time for the old man to go

Elsewhere, and leave the world to itself.

—Jacques, I leave to you all my property,—protect
these women.

JACQUES HURY: What, are you really going?

ANNE VERCORS: I believe he has heard nothing.

JACQUES HURY: Like that, right away?

ANNE VERCORS: The hour is come.

THE MOTHER: You will not go without first eating?

[During this time the women servants have prepared the table for the farm meal]

ANNE VERCORS: [To a woman servant] Ho! my bag,
my hat!

Bring my shoes! bring my cloak!

I have not time enough to share this meal with you.

THE MOTHER: Anne! How long wilt thou stay over
there? One year, two years? More than two
years?

ANNE VERCORS: One year. Two years. Yes, that
is it.

Put on my shoes.

[The Mother kneels before him and puts on his
shoes]

For the first time I leave thee, O house!

Combernon, lofty dwelling!

Watch faithfully over it all! Jacques will be here in
my stead.

There is the hearth where there is always fire, there
is the long table where I give food to my people.

All take your places! Just once more I will cut the
bread. . . .

[He seats himself at the head of the long table,
with The Mother at his right. All the men and
women servants stand, each at his place]

[He takes the bread, making the sign of the cross

above it with the knife, and cuts it; and gives it to Violaine *and* Mara *to pass. The last piece he keeps himself. Then he turns solemnly toward* The Mother *and opens his arms*]

Farewell, Elisabeth!

THE MOTHER: [*Weeping in his arms*] Thou wilt never see me more.

ANNE VERCORS: [*In a lower tone*] Farewell, Elisabeth.

[*He turns toward* Mara, *looks gravely at her for a long time, and then holds out his hand to her*]

Farewell, Mara! be virtuous.

MARA: [*Kissing his hand*] Farewell, father!

[*Silence.* Anne Vercors *stands, looking before him as if he did not see* Violaine, *who stands full of agitation at his side. At last he turns slightly toward her, and she puts her arms around his neck, sobbing, with her face against his breast*]

ANNE VERCORS: [*To the men servants, as if he noticed nothing*] Farewell, all!

I have always dealt justly by you. If any one denies this, he lies.

I am not like other masters. But I praise when praise is due, and I reprove when reproof is due.

Now that I am going away, do your duty as if I were there.

For I shall return. I shall return some time when you do not expect me.

[*He shakes hands with them all*]

Let my horse be brought!

[*Silence. He leans toward* Violaine, *who continues to embrace him*]

What is it, little child?

You have exchanged a husband for thy father.

VIOLAINE: Alas! Father! Alas!

[*He removes her hands gently from around his neck*]

THE MOTHER: Tell me when will you return.

ANNE VERCORS: I cannot tell.

Perhaps it will be in the morning, perhaps at midday, when you are eating.

And perhaps, awaking some night, you will hear my step on the road.

Farewell!

[*He goes*]

ACT TWO: SCENE ONE

A fortnight later. The beginning of July. Noon. A large orchard planted with regular rows of round trees. Higher, and a little withdrawn, the wall and towers and long buildings with tiled roofs of Combernon. Then, the side of the hill, which rises abruptly, and on its summit the massive stone arch of Monsanvierge, without door or window, with its five towers like those of the Cathedral of Laon, and in its side the great white scar made for the recent entrance of the Queen Mother of France.

Everything vibrates under an ardent sun.

A WOMAN'S VOICE *on high, from the height of the highest tower of Monsanvierge.*

SALVE REGINA MATER MISERICORDIAE

VITA DULCEDO ET SPES NOSTRA SALVE

AD TE CLAMAMUS EXULES FILII HEVAE

AD TE SUSPIRAMUS GEMENTES ET FLENTES IN HAC
     LACRYMARUM VALLE

EIA ERGO ADVOCATA NOSTRA ILLOS TUOS MISERICORDES
     OCULOS AD NOS CONVERTE

ET JESUM BENEDICTUM FRUCTUM VENTRIS TUI NOBIS
     POST HOC EXILIUM OSTENDE

O CLEMENS

O PIA

O DULCIS VIRGO MARIA

[*Long pause during which the stage remains empty*]

[*Enter* The Mother *and* Mara]

MARA: What did she say?

THE MOTHER: I drew her out as we talked, without seeming to. You see how she has lost her gay spirits these last few days.

MARA: She never talks much.

THE MOTHER: But she does not laugh any more. That troubles me.

Perhaps it is because Jacquin is away, but he returns to-day.

—And her father too is gone.

MARA: That is all you said to her?

THE MOTHER: That is what I said to her, and the rest of it without changing a word, just as you said it to me: Jacquin and you: that you love him and all.

And I added, and I said it over two or three times, that this time she must not be foolish, and not resist at all,

Or break off the marriage, which is as good as made, against the father's will.

What would people think of it?

MARA: And what did she answer?

THE MOTHER: She began to laugh, and I, I began to cry.

MARA: I will make her laugh!

THE MOTHER: It was not the laughter I love of my little girl, and I began to cry.

And I said, "No, no, Violaine, my child!" not knowing any longer what I said.

But she, without speaking, made a sign with her hand that she wanted to be alone.

Ah! what misery we have with our children!

MARA: Hush!

THE MOTHER: What is it?

I am sorry for what I have done.

MARA: Well! Do you see her down there in the paddock? She is walking behind the trees. Now she is out of sight.

[*Silence. From behind the scene is heard the blast of a horn*]

THE MOTHER: There is Jacquin come back. I know the sound of his horn.

MARA: Let us go further off.

[*They move off*]

ACT TWO: SCENE TWO

[*Enter* Jacques Hury]

JACQUES HURY: [*Looking all around*] I don't see her.

And yet she sent word

That she wanted to see me this morning,

Here.

[*Enter Mara. She advances to* Jacques, *and at six paces before him drops a ceremonious courtesy*]

JACQUES HURY: Good morning, Mara.

MARA: My lord, your servant!

JACQUES HURY: What is this foolery?

MARA: Do I not owe you respect? Are you not the master here, dependent only upon God, like the King of France himself and the Emperor Charlemagne?

JACQUES HURY: Jest if you like, but it is true all the same! Yes, Mara, it is glorious! Dear sister, I am too happy!

MARA: I am not your *dear* sister! I am your servant because I must be.

Man of Braine! son of a serf! I am not your sister; you are not of our blood!

JACQUES HURY: I am the husband of Violaine.

MARA: You are not that yet.

JACQUES HURY: I shall be to-morrow.

MARA: Who knows?

JACQUES HURY: Mara, I have thought deeply about it,

And I believe you have only dreamed that story you told me the other day.

MARA: What story?

JACQUES HURY: Don't pretend not to know.

That story about the mason, that secret kiss at dawn.

MARA: It is possible. I did not see well. Yet I have good eyes.

JACQUES HURY: And it has been whispered to me that the man is a leper!

MARA: I do not love you, Jacques.

But you have the right to know all. All must be pure and clear at Monsanvierge, which is held up like a monstrance before all the kingdom.

JACQUES HURY: All that will be explained in a moment.

MARA: You are clever and nothing can escape you.

JACQUES HURY: I see at any rate that you don't love me.

MARA: There! there! What did I say? what did I say?

JACQUES HURY: Everybody here is not of your mind.

MARA: You speak of Violaine? I blush for that little girl.

It is shameful to give oneself like that,

Soul, body, heart, skin, the outside, the inside, and the root.

JACQUES HURY: I know that she belongs entirely to me.

MARA: Yes.

How grandly he speaks! how sure he is of the things that belong to him! Brainard of Braine!

Only those things belong to one that one has made, or taken, or earned.

JACQUES HURY: But Mara, I like you, and I have nothing against you.

MARA: Without doubt—like all the rest of the things here?

JACQUES HURY: It is no fault of mine that you are not a man, and that I take your property from you!

MARA: How proud and satisfied he is! Look at him, he can hardly keep from laughing!

There now! don't do yourself harm! Laugh!

[*He laughs*]

I know your face well, Jacques.

JACQUES HURY: You are angry because you cannot make me unhappy.

MARA: Like the other day while the father was talking,

When one of your eyes smiled and the other wept— without tears.

JACQUES HURY: Am I not master of a fine estate?

MARA: And the father was old, wasn't he? You know a thing or two more than he does?

JACQUES HURY: To each man his day.

MARA: That is true, Jacques, you are a tall and handsome young man.

See him, how he blushes.

JACQUES HURY: Don't torment me.

MARA: All the same, it is a pity!

JACQUES HURY: What is a pity?

MARA: Farewell, husband of Violaine! Farewell, master of Monsanvierge—ah—ah!

JACQUES HURY: I will show you that so I am.

MARA: Then understand the spirit of this place, Brainard of Braine!

He thinks that everything is his, like a peasant; you will be shown the contrary!

Like a peasant who sees nothing higher than himself as he stands in the midst of his flat little field!

But Monsanvierge belongs to God, and the master of Monsanvierge is God's man, who has nothing

For himself, having received everything for another.

That is the lesson passed on here from father to son.

There is no higher position than ours.

Take on the spirit of your masters, peasant!

[*She makes as if to go and turns back*]
Ah!
Violaine, when I met her,
Gave me a message for you.

> JACQUES HURY: Why did you not say so sooner?

> MARA: She is waiting for you near the fountain.

ACT TWO: SCENE THREE

The fountain of the Adoue. It is a large square orifice cut in a vertical wall, built of blocks of limestone. A thin stream of water drips from it with a melancholy sound. Thank-offerings of crosses made of straw and bouquets of faded flowers are hung on the wall.

The fountain is surrounded with luxurious trees, and with a bower of rose-bushes whose abundant blossoms thickly star the green foliage.

> JACQUES HURY: [*He looks at* Violaine *who comes along the winding path. She is all golden, and glows brilliantly at moments when the sun falls upon her between the leaves*] O my betrothed among the flowery branches, hail!
> [Violaine *enters and stands before him. She is clothed in a linen gown with a kind of dalmatic of cloth-of-gold decorated with large red and blue flowers. Her head is crowned with a diadem of enamel and gold.*]

Violaine, how beautiful you are!

> VIOLAINE: Jacques! Good morning, Jacques! Ah, how long you stayed down there!

> JACQUES HURY: I had to get rid of everything, and sell, in order to be perfectly free.

To be the man of Monsanvierge only and yours.

——What is this wonderful dress?

> VIOLAINE: I wore it for you. I had spoken to you about it. Do you not recognize it?

It is the habit of the nuns of Monsanvierge, except only the maniple, the habit they wear in the choir,

The deacon's dalmatic which they have the privilege of wearing, something priestly, as they themselves are holy sacrifices,

And the women of Combernon have the right to wear it twice:

First, on the day of their betrothal,

Secondly, on the day of their death.

> JACQUES HURY: It is really true, then, that this is the day of our betrothal, Violaine?

> VIOLAINE: Jacques, there is yet time, we are not married yet!

If you have only wanted to please my father there is still time to withdraw; it concerns no one but us. Say but a word, and I would not want you any more, Jacques.

For nothing has yet been put in writing, and I do not know if I still please you.

> JACQUES HURY: How beautiful you are, Violaine! And how beautiful is the world of which you are the portion reserved for me.

> VIOLAINE: It is you, Jacques, who are all that is best in the world.

> JACQUES HURY: Is it true that you are willing to belong to me?

> VIOLAINE: Yes, it is true! good morning, my beloved! I am yours.

> JACQUES HURY: Good morning, my wife! Good morning, sweet Violaine!

> VIOLAINE: These are good things to hear, Jacques!

> JACQUES HURY: You must always be there! Tell me that you will always be the same, the angel who is sent to me!

> VIOLAINE: For evermore all that is mine shall always be yours.

> JACQUES HURY: And as for me, Violaine. . . .

> VIOLAINE: Say nothing. I ask you nothing. You are there, and that is enough for me. Good morning, Jacques!

Ah, how beautiful this hour is, and I ask for nothing more.

> JACQUES HURY: To-morrow will be still more beautiful!

> VIOLAINE: To-morrow I shall have taken off my gorgeous robe.

> JACQUES HURY: But you will be so near to me that I shall no longer be able to see you.

> VIOLAINE: Very near to you indeed!

> JACQUES HURY: Your place is ready.

Violaine, what a solitary spot this is, and how secretly I am here with you!

> VIOLAINE: [*In a low tone*] Your heart is enough. Go to, I am with you, and say not a word more.

> JACQUES HURY: But to-morrow, before everybody, I will take this Queen in my arms.

> VIOLAINE: Take her, and do not let her go.

Ah, take your little one with you so that they can never find her, and never do her any harm!

> JACQUES HURY: And you will not regret then the linen and the gold?

> VIOLAINE: Was I wrong to make myself beautiful for one poor little hour?

> JACQUES HURY: No, my beautiful lily, I can never tire of looking at you in your glory!

> VIOLAINE: O Jacques! tell me again that you think me beautiful!

> JACQUES HURY: Yes, Violaine!

> VIOLAINE: The most beautiful of all, and the other women are nothing to you?

> JACQUES HURY: Yes, Violaine.

> VIOLAINE: And that you love me only, as the tenderest husband loves the poor creature who has given herself to him?

> JACQUES HURY: Yes, Violaine.

> VIOLAINE: Who gives herself to him with all her

heart, Jacques, believe me, and holds nothing back.

JACQUES HURY: And you, Violaine, do you not believe me then?

VIOLAINE: I believe you, I believe you, Jacques! I believe in you! I have confidence in you, my darling!

JACQUES HURY: Why, then, do you seem troubled and frightened?

Show me your left hand.

[She shows it]

My ring is gone.

VIOLAINE: I will explain that to you presently, you will be satisfied.

JACQUES HURY: I am satisfied, Violaine. I have faith in you.

VIOLAINE: I am more than a ring, Jacques. I am a great treasure.

JACQUES HURY: Yes, Violaine.

VIOLAINE: Ah, if I give myself to you,

Will you not know how to save your little one who loves you?

JACQUES HURY: There you are doubting me again.

VIOLAINE: Jacques! After all I do no harm in loving you. It is God's will, and my father's.

It is you who have charge of me! And who knows if you will not know perfectly how to defend and save me?

It is enough that I give myself entirely to you. The rest is your affair, and no longer mine.

JACQUES HURY: And is it like this you give yourself to me, my flower-o'-the-sun?

VIOLAINE: Yes, Jacques.

JACQUES HURY: Who then can take you out of my arms?

VIOLAINE: Ah, how big the world is, and how alone we are!

JACQUES HURY: Poor child! I know that your father is gone.

And I too no longer have anyone with me to tell me what should be done, and what is good or ill.

You must help me, Violaine, as I love you.

VIOLAINE: My father has abandoned me.

JACQUES HURY: But I remain to you, Violaine.

VIOLAINE: Neither my mother nor my sister love me, though I have done them no wrong.

And nothing is left to me but this tall, terrible man whom I do not know.

[He tries to take her in his arms. She pushes him away quickly]

Do not touch me, Jacques!

JACQUES HURY: Am I then a leper?

VIOLAINE: Jacques, I want to speak to you—ah, but it is hard!

Do not fail me, who now have only you!

JACQUES HURY: Who would do you harm?

VIOLAINE: Know what you do in taking me for your wife!

Let me speak to you very humbly, my lord Jacques,

Who are about to receive my soul and my body from the hands of God according to his command, and my father's who made them.

And know the dowry I bring to you which is not like those of other women,

But this holy mountain wrapped in prayer day and night before God, like an altar smoking always,

And this lamp whose light is never suffered to go out, and whose oil it is our duty to replenish.

And no man is witness to our marriage, but that Lord whose fief we alone hold,

Who is the Omnipotent, the God of the Armies.

And it is not the sun of July that lights us, but the light of his countenance.

To the holy be the holy things! Who knows if our heart be pure?

Never until now has a male been lacking to our race, and always the sacred place has been handed down from father to son,

And behold, for the first time it falls into the hands of a woman, and becomes with her the object of desire.

JACQUES HURY: Violaine—no: I am not a scholar nor a monk nor a saint.

I am not the lay-servant of Monsanvierge, nor the keeper of its turning-box.

I have a duty and I will perform it,

Which is to feed these murmuring birds,

And to fill each morning the basket they lower from the sky.

That is written down. That is right.

I have understood that, and I have fixed it in my head, and you must not ask any more of me.

You must not ask me to understand what is above me, and why these holy women have imprisoned themselves up there in that pigeon-house.

To the heavenly be heaven, and the earth to the earthly.

For the wheat will not grow by itself, and a good ploughman is necessary.

And I can say without boasting that such I am, and no one can teach me that, not even your father himself perhaps,

For he was old and set in his ways.

To each one his own place, and that is justice.

And your father, in giving you to me,

Together with Monsanvierge, knew what he was doing, and that was just.

VIOLAINE: But Jacques, I do not love you because it is just.

And even if it were not just, I would love you the same, and more.

JACQUES HURY: I do not understand you, Violaine.

VIOLAINE: Jacques, do not make me speak! You love me so much, and I can only do you harm.

Let me alone! there cannot be justice between us two! but only faith and charity. Go away from me while there is yet time.

JACQUES HURY: I do not understand, Violaine.

VIOLAINE: My beloved, do not force me to tell you my great secret.

JACQUES HURY: A great secret, Violaine?

VIOLAINE: So great that all is over, and you will not ask to marry me any more.

JACQUES HURY: I do not understand you.

VIOLAINE: Am I not beautiful enough just now, Jacques? What more do you ask of me?

What does one ask of a flower

Except to be beautiful and fragrant for a moment, poor flower, and then—the end.

The flower's life is short, but the joy it has given for a minute

Is not of those things which have a beginning and an end.

Am I not beautiful enough? Is something lacking?

Ah! I see thine eyes, my beloved! Is there anything in thee at this moment that does not love me, and that doubts me?

Is my soul not enough? Take it, and I am still here, and absorb to its depths that which is all thine!

To die requires but a moment, and to die in each other would not annihilate us more than love, and does one need to live when one is dead?

What more wouldst thou do with me? Fly, take thyself away! Why dost thou wish to marry me? Why dost thou wish

To take for thyself what belongs only to God?

The hand of God is upon us, and thou canst not defend me!

O Jacques, we shall never be husband and wife in this world!

JACQUES HURY: Violaine, what are these strange words, so tender, so bitter? By what threatening and gloomy paths are you leading me?

I believe you wish to put me to the proof, and to triumph over me, who am but a simple and rough man.

Ah! Violaine, how beautiful you are like this! and yet I am afraid, and I see you in clothing that terrifies me!

For this is not a woman's dress, but the robe of one who offers the sacrifice at the altar,

Of him who waits upon the priest, leaving the side uncovered and the arms free!

Ah, I see, it is the spirit of Monsanvierge which lives in you, the supreme flower outside of this sealed garden!

Ah, do not turn to me that face which is no longer of this world! that is no longer my dear Violaine.

There are enough angels to serve the mass in Heaven!

Have pity on me, who am only a man without wings, who rejoiced in this companion God had given me, and that I should hear her sigh with her head resting on my shoulder!

Sweet bird! the sky is beautiful, but it is beautiful too to be taken captive!

And the sky is beautiful! but this is a beautiful thing too, and even worthy of God, the heart of a man that can be filled, leaving no part empty.

Do not torment me by depriving me of your face!

And no doubt I am a dull and ugly man,

But I love you, my angel, my queen, my darling!

VIOLAINE: So I have warned you in vain, and you want to take me for your wife, and you will not give up your plan?

JACQUES HURY: Yes, Violaine.

VIOLAINE: When a man takes a woman for his wife they are then one soul in one body, and nothing will ever separate them.

JACQUES HURY: Yes, Violaine.

VIOLAINE: You wish it!

Then it is not right that I should reserve anything, or keep to myself any longer

This great, this unspeakable secret.

JACQUES HURY: Again this secret, Violaine?

VIOLAINE: So great, truly, Jacques,

That your heart will be saturated with it,

And you will ask nothing more of me,

And that we shall never be torn apart from each other.

A secret so deep

That neither life, Jacques, nor hell, nor Heaven itself

Will ever end it, or will ever end this

Moment in which I have revealed it, here in the burning

Heat of this terrible sun which almost prevents us from seeing each other!

JACQUES HURY: Speak, then!

VIOLAINE: But tell me first once more that you love me.

JACQUES HURY: I love you!

VIOLAINE: And that I am your wife and your only love?

JACQUES HURY: My wife, my only love.

VIOLAINE: Tell me, Jacques: neither my face nor my soul has sufficed thee, and that is not enough?

And have you been misled by my proud words? Then learn of the fire which consumes me!

Know this flesh which you have loved so much!

Come nearer to me.

[*He comes nearer*]

Nearer! nearer still! close against my side. Sit down on that bench.

[*Silence*]

And give me your knife.

[*He gives her his knife. She cuts the linen of her gown, at her side upon the heart, under the left breast, and leaning towards him she opens the slit with her hands and shows him the flesh where the first spot of leprosy has appeared. Silence*]

JACQUES HURY: [*Slightly turning away his face*] Give me the knife.

[*She gives it to him. Silence. Then Jacques moves a few steps away from her, half turning his back, and he does not look at her again until the end of the Act*]

JACQUES HURY: Violaine, I am not mistaken?

What is this silver flower emblazoned on your
flesh?

VIOLAINE: You are not mistaken.

JACQUES HURY: It is the malady? It is the malady,
Violaine?

VIOLAINE: Yes, Jacques.

JACQUES HURY: Leprosy!

VIOLAINE: Surely you are hard to convince.
And you had to see it to believe.

JACQUES HURY: And which leprosy is the most
hideous,
That of the soul or that of the body?

VIOLAINE: I cannot say as to the other. I only
know that of the body, which is bad enough.

JACQUES HURY: No, you know not the other, reprobate?

VIOLAINE: I am not a reprobate.

JACQUES HURY: Infamous woman, reprobate,
Infamous in your soul and in your flesh!

VIOLAINE: So you do not ask any more to marry
me, Jacques?

JACQUES HURY: Scoff no more, child of the devil!

VIOLAINE: Such is that great love you had for me.

JACQUES HURY: Such is this lily that I had chosen.

VIOLAINE: Such is the man who takes the place of
my father.

JACQUES HURY: Such is the angel that God had
sent me.

VIOLAINE: Ah, who will tear us apart from each
other? I love you, Jacques, and you will defend
me, and I know that in thy arms I have nothing
to fear.

JACQUES HURY: Do not mock thyself with these
horrible words!

VIOLAINE: Tell me,
Have I broken my word? My soul was not enough
for thee? Have you enough now of my flesh?
Will you forget henceforth your Violaine, and the
heart she revealed to thee?

JACQUES HURY: Go farther away from me!

VIOLAINE: Go to, I am far enough away, Jacques;
you have nothing to fear.

JACQUES HURY: Yes, yes,
Further than you were from that measled pig of
yours!
That maker of bones whereon the flesh rots!

VIOLAINE: Is it of Pierre de Craon that you speak?

JACQUES HURY: It is of him I speak, him you
kissed on the mouth.

VIOLAINE: And who has told you that?

JACQUES HURY: Mara saw you with her own eyes.
And she has told me all, as it was her duty to do,
And I, fool that I was, did not believe it!
Come, confess it! confess it then! It is true! Say that
it is true!

VIOLAINE: It is true, Jacques.
Mara always speaks the truth.

JACQUES HURY: And it is true that you kissed him
on the face?

VIOLAINE: It is true.

JACQUES HURY: O damned one! are the flames of
hell so savory that you have thus lusted after
them while you were still alive?

VIOLAINE: [Speaking very low] No, not damned.
But sweet, sweet Violaine! sweet, sweet Violaine!

JACQUES HURY: And you do not deny that this
man had you and possessed you?

VIOLAINE: I deny nothing, Jacques.

JACQUES HURY: But I love you still, Violaine! Ah,
this is too cruel!
Tell me something, even if you have nothing to say,
and I will believe it! Speak, I beg you! tell me
it is not true!

VIOLAINE: I cannot turn all black in a minute,
Jacques; but in a few months, a few months
more,
You will not recognize me any longer.

JACQUES HURY: Tell me that all this is not true.

VIOLAINE: Mara always speaks the truth, and then
there is that flower upon my body that you have
seen.

JACQUES HURY: Farewell, Violaine.

VIOLAINE: Farewell, Jacques.

JACQUES HURY: Tell me, what shall you do,
wretched woman?

VIOLAINE: Take off this robe. Leave this house.
Fulfil the law. Show myself to the priest. Go
to . . .

JACQUES HURY: Well?

VIOLAINE: . . . the place set apart for people like
me.
The lazar-house of the Géyn, over there.

JACQUES HURY: When?

VIOLAINE: To-day—this very evening.
[Long silence]
There is nothing else to be done.

JACQUES HURY: We must avoid any scandal.
Go, take off your robe and put on a travelling dress,
and I will tell you what it is right to do.
[They go out]

ACT TWO: SCENE FOUR

The kitchen at Combernon, as in ACT I

THE MOTHER: Every day the weather is fine.
It has not rained for eight days.
[She listens]
Now and then I hear the bells of Arcy.
Dong! Dong!
How warm it is, and how large everything looks!
What is Violaine doing? and Jacques? What have
they to talk about so long?
I am sorry for what I said to her
[She sighs]
And what is the crazy old man doing? Where is he
now?[1]

[1] She is thinking of her absent old husband.

Ah!

[*She bows her head*]

MARA: [*Entering quickly*] They are coming here. I think the marriage is broken off. Do you hear me?

Be silent,

And say nothing.

THE MOTHER: What?

O wicked girl! wretch! You have got what you wished for!

MARA: Let it alone. It is only for a moment. There was no other way

It could be done. So, now it is I

He must marry and not she. It will be better for her like that. It must be thus. Do you hear?

Be silent!

THE MOTHER: Who told you that?

MARA: Was there need for me to be told? I saw it all in their faces.

I came upon them all warm. I understood everything in no time at all.

And Jacques, poor fellow, I pity him.

THE MOTHER: I am sorry for what I said!

MARA: You have said nothing; you know nothing —be silent!

And if they say anything to you, no matter what they tell you,

Agree with them, do everything they wish. There is nothing more to do.

THE MOTHER: I hope all is for the best.

ACT TWO: SCENE FIVE

[*Enter* Jacques Hury, *then* Violaine *all in black, dressed as for a journey*]

THE MOTHER: What is the matter, Jacques? What is the matter, Violaine?

Why have you put on this dress, as if you were going away?

VIOLAINE: I, too, am going away.

THE MOTHER: Going away? You going away, too? Jacques! what has happened between you?

JACQUES HURY: Nothing has happened.

But you know that I went to see my mother at Braine, and have only just returned.

THE MOTHER: Well?

JACQUES HURY: You know, she is old and feeble.

She says she wishes to see and bless

Her daughter-in-law before she dies.

THE MOTHER: Can she not come to the wedding?

JACQUES HURY: She is ill, she cannot wait.

And this harvest time, too, when there is so much to be done

Is not the time to be married.

We have just been talking about it, Violaine and I, just now, very pleasantly,

And we have decided that it is best to wait till The autumn.

Until then she will stay at Braine with my mother.

THE MOTHER: Is this your wish, Violaine?

VIOLAINE: Yes, mother.

THE MOTHER: But what! Do you wish to go away this very day?

VIOLAINE: This very evening.

JACQUES HURY: I shall go with her.

Time is short and work pressing in this month of hay and harvest. I have already stayed away too long.

THE MOTHER: Stay, Violaine! Do not go away from us, thou too!

VIOLAINE: It is only for a short time, mother!

THE MOTHER: A short time, you promise?

JACQUES HURY: A short time, and when autumn comes

Here she will be with us again, never to go away any more.

THE MOTHER: Ah, Jacques! Why do you let her go away?

JACQUES HURY: Do you think it is not hard for me?

MARA: Mother, what they both say is reasonable.

THE MOTHER: It is hard to see my child leave me.

VIOLAINE: Do not be sad, mother!

What does it matter that we should wait a few days?

It is only a little time to pass.

Am I not sure of your affection? and of Mara's? and of Jacques', my betrothed?

Is it not so, Jacques? He is mine as I am his, and nothing can separate us? Look at me, dear Jacques. See how he weeps to see me go away!

This is not the time for weeping, mother! am I not young and beautiful and loved by everybody?

My father has gone away, it is true, but he has left me the tenderest of husbands, the friend who will never forsake me.

So it is not the time to weep, but to rejoice. Ah, dear mother, how beautiful life is, and how happy I am!

MARA: And you, Jacques, what do you say? You do not look very happy.

JACQUES HURY: Is it not natural that I should be sad?

MARA: Come! it is only a separation for a few months!

JACQUES HURY: Too long for my heart.

MARA: Listen, Violaine, how well he said that!

And how is this, my sister, you so sad too? Smile at me with that charming mouth! Raise those blue eyes that our father loved so much. See Jacques! Look at your wife and see how beautiful she is when she smiles!

She will not be taken away from you! who would be sad who has a little sun like this to shine in his home?

Love her well for us, cruel man! Tell her to be brave!

JACQUES HURY: Courage, Violaine!

You have not lost me; we are not lost to each other!

You see that I do not doubt your love; but do you
doubt mine?

Do I doubt you, Violaine? Do I not love you, Violaine? Am I not sure of you,

Violaine!

I have talked about you to my mother, and you may
imagine how happy she will be to see you.

It is hard to leave the house of your parents. But
where you are going you will have a safe shelter
where no one can break in.

Neither your love nor your innocence, dear Violaine, has anything to fear.

THE MOTHER: These are very loving words,

And yet there is something in them, and in what you
said to me, my child,

I don't know what—something strange which does
not please me.

MARA: I see nothing strange, mother.

THE MOTHER: Violaine! If I hurt you just now,
my child,

Forget what I said.

VIOLAINE: You have not hurt me.

THE MOTHER: Then let me embrace you.

[She opens her arms to her]

VIOLAINE: No, mother.

THE MOTHER: What?

VIOLAINE: No.

MARA: Violaine, that is wrong! Do you fear to
have us touch thee? Why do you treat us thus,
like lepers?

VIOLAINE: I have made a vow.

MARA: What vow?

VIOLAINE: That nobody shall touch me.

MARA: Until your return here?

[Silence. She lowers her head]

JACQUES HURY: Let her alone. You see she is
troubled.

THE MOTHER: Go away for a moment.

[They move away]

Farewell, Violaine!

You will not deceive me, my child; you will not
deceive the mother who bore thee.

What I have said to you is hard; but look at me, I
am full of trouble, and I am old.

You—you are young, and you will forget.

My man is gone, and now here is my child turning
away from me.

One's own sorrow is nothing, but the sorrow one
has caused to others

Makes bitter the bread in the mouth.

Think of that, my sacrificed lamb, and say to yourself: Thus I have caused sorrow to no one.

I counselled thee as I thought for the best. Don't
bear malice, Violaine! Save your sister. Must
she be left to be ruined?

And God will be with you, who is your recompense.

That is all. You will never see my old face again.
May God be with thee!

And you do not wish to kiss me, but I can at least
give you my blessing, sweet, sweet Violaine!

VIOLAINE: Yes, mother! yes, mother!

[She kneels, and The Mother makes the sign of
the cross above her]

JACQUES: [Returning] Come, Violaine, it is time
to go.

MARA: Go and pray for us.

VIOLAINE: [Calling] I give you my dresses, Mara,
and all my things!

Have no fear of them; you know that I have not
touched them.

I did not go into that room.

—Ah, ah! my poor wedding-dress that was so pretty!

[She stretches out her arms as if to find support.
All remain at a distance from her. She goes out
tottering, followed by Jacques]

ACT THREE: SCENE ONE

*Chevoche. A large forest sparsely grown with lofty
oaks and birches, with an undergrowth of pines, firs,
and a few holly trees. A wide straight road has just
been cut through the woods to the horizon. Workmen
are removing the last stumps of trees and preparing
the roadway. There is a camp at one side, with huts
made of faggots, a pot over a camp-fire, etc. The
camp lies in a sand-pit, where a few workmen are
engaged in loading a cart with a fine white sand. An
apprentice of Pierre de Craon, squatting among the
dry gorse bushes, oversees the work. On either side
of the new road stand two colossi made of faggots,
with collars and smocks of white cloth, each with a
red cross on its breast. A barrel forms the head of
each colossus, with its edge cut into saw-teeth to
simulate a crown, and a sort of face roughly painted
on it in red. A long trumpet is fitted to the bunghole,
and held in place by a board as if by an arm.*

*It is the end of the day. There is snow on the
ground and in the sky.*

It is Christmas Eve. [It is eight years later.]

THE MAYOR OF CHEVOCHE: There. Now the King
can come.

A WORKMAN: 'A can coom an' 'a likes. We've done
our part well.

THE MAYOR: [Looking around with satisfaction]
It's mighty beautiful! Fact is, it can hold everybody, as many as there are, men, women, and
tiny children.

And to think 'twas the worst part, with all these
bad weeds and these briars, and the marsh.

It ain't the wise ones of Bruyères can teach us anything.

A WORKMAN: Their road has a beard, and teeth
too, wi' all those stumps they's left us!

[They laugh]

THE APPRENTICE: [Pedantically, in a voice frightfully sharp and shrill] Vox clamantis in deserto:
Parate vias Domini et erunt prava in directa
et aspera in vias planas.

It is true you have done your work well. I congratulate you, good people. It is like the road at
Corpus Christi.

[*Pointing to the Giants*]: And who, gentlemen, are
these two beautiful and reverend persons?

A WORKMAN: Beant they handsome? It was fathe'
Vincent, the old drunkard, thet made 'em.

'A said it's th' great King of Abyssinia an' his wife
Bellotte.

THE APPRENTICE: For my part I thought they
were Gog and Magog.

THE MAYOR: 'Tis the two Angels of Chevoche who
come to salute the King their lord.

They'll be set a-fire when 'a passes.

Listen!

[*All listen*]

A WORKMAN: Oh, no, that beant him yet. We'd
hear the bells o' Bruyères a-ringin'.

ANOTHER: 'A won't be here afore midnight. 'A
supped at Fisme.

ANOTHER: 'Tis a good place to see from, here. I
shallna budge.

ANOTHER: Hast 'a eat, Perrot? I've on'y a mossel
o' bread, all froze.

THE MAYOR: Don't be afraid. The's a quarter o'
pork in the pot and some big sausages, and the
roebuck we killed,

And three ells o' blood-sausages, and apples, and a
good little keg of Marne wine.

THE APPRENTICE: I stay with you.

A WOMAN: And there's a good little Christmas for
you.

THE APPRENTICE: It was on Christmas Day that
King Clovis was baptized at Rheims.

ANOTHER WOMAN: 'Tis Christmas Day that oor
King Charles comes back to get hi'self crowned.

ANOTHER: 'Tis a village girl, sent by God,

Who brings him back to his own.

ANOTHER: Jeanne, they call her!

ANOTHER: The Maid!

ANOTHER: Who was born on Twelfth Night!

ANOTHER: Who drove the English away from
Orleans when they besieged it!

ANOTHER WORKMAN: And who's goin' to drive 'em
out of France too, all of 'em! Amen:

ANOTHER WORKMAN: [*Humming*] Noel! Cock-a-
doodle-do! Noel! Noel come again! Rrr! How
cauld it be!

[*He wraps himself closer in his cloak*]

A WOMAN: Mus' look well t' see if the's a little
man all in red clothes by th' King. That's her.

ANOTHER WOMAN: On a tall black horse.

THE FIRST WOMAN: On'y six months agone her
was keepin' her father's cows.

ANOTHER WOMAN: And now her carries a banner
where Jesus is in writin'.

A WORKMAN: An' that the English run away before
like mice.

ANOTHER WORKMAN: Let the wicked Bourguignons
o' Saponay beware!

ANOTHER WORKMAN: They'll all be at Rheims at
the break o' day.

ANOTHER WORKMAN: What be they doin', those
down there?

THE APPRENTICE: The two bells of the Cathedral,
Baudon and Baude, will be rung at the Gloria
at midnight, and they will never stop swinging
and clanging until the French come.

Everybody will keep a lighted candle in his house
until morning.

They expect the King to be there for the Mass at
dawn, which is "Lux fulgebit."

All the clergy will go out to meet him, three hundred
priests and the Archbishop in copes of gold,
and the monks, the Mayor and the vestry.

All that will be very beautiful on the snow, in the
bright merry sunshine, with all the people singing "Noel"!

And they say that the King intends to get down from
his horse, and enter his good city riding upon
an ass, like our Lord.

THE MAYOR: How comes it that you did not stay
down there?

THE APPRENTICE: Master Pierre de Craon sent
me here to get sand.

THE MAYOR: What! He busies himself about sand
at such a time?

THE APPRENTICE: He says there is not much time.

THE MAYOR: But how could he employ himself
better than in making this road, as we do?

THE APPRENTICE: He says that his work is not to
make roads for the King, but a dwelling for
God.

THE MAYOR: Of what use would Rheims be if the
King could not reach it?

THE APPRENTICE: But what use would the road
be if there is no church at the end of it?

THE MAYOR: He is not a good Frenchman.

THE APPRENTICE: He says that he knows nothing
but his work. If anybody talks politics to us,
we blacken his nose with the bottom of the
frying-pan.

THE MAYOR: He has not even been able to finish
his Justice, though 'tis ten years they've been
working on it.[1]

THE APPRENTICE: On the contrary! All the stone
is polished, and the woodwork is in place; it's
only the spire that has not yet done growing.

THE MAYOR: They never work on it.

THE APPRENTICE: The master is preparing the
glass for his windows now, and that is why he
sends us here for sand;

Though that is not his craft.

All winter he has worked among his furnaces.

To make light, my poor people, is more difficult
than to make gold,

To breathe on this heavy matter and make it trans-

---

[1] This refers to the church built in honor of Saint Justitia
at Rheims.

parent, "according as our bodies of mud shall be changed into bodies of glory,"
As Saint Paul said.

And he says that he must find for each colour
The mother-colour itself, just as God himself made it.
That is why, into his great clean vessels, full of shining water, he pours jacinth, ultramarine, rich gold, vermilion,
And he watches these beautiful rose-coloured liquids to see what happens to them in the sunshine, and by virtue of the grace of God, and how they mingle and bloom in the matrass.
And he says there is not one colour which he cannot make out of his own knowledge alone,
As his body makes red and blue.
Because he wishes the Justice of Rheims to shine like the morning on the day of her nuptials.

THE MAYOR: They say he has leprosy.

THE APPRENTICE: That is not true! I saw him naked last summer.

While he bathed in the Aisne at Soissons. I know what I say!
His flesh is as healthy as a child's.

THE MAYOR: It is queer, all the same. Why did he keep himself hidden so long?

THE APPRENTICE: That is a lie.

THE MAYOR: I know, I am older than you. You mustn't get angry, little man. It doesn't matter if he be sick in the body.

It isn't with his body he works.

THE APPRENTICE: Better not let him hear you say that! I remember how he punished one of us because he stayed all the time in his corner, drawing:

He sent him up on the scaffolding to serve the masons all day and pass them their hods and their stones,
Saying that by the end of the day he would know two things better than he could learn them by rule and design: the weight a man can carry and the height of his body.
And as the grace of God multiplies each of our good deeds,
So he taught us about what he calls "the shekel of the Temple," and this dwelling of God of which each man who does all that his body is capable of doing is like a secret foundation;
What means the thumb, and the hand, and the arm's length, and the spread of both our arms, and the arm extended, and the circle it makes,
And the foot and the step;
And how all these things are never the same.
Do you think Father Noah was indifferent to the body when he built the ark? and are these things of no account:
The number of paces from the door to the altar, and the height the eye may be lifted to, and the number of souls the two sides of the Church may hold all at the same time?
For the heathen artist made everything from the outside, but we make all from within, like the bees,
And as the soul does for the body: nothing is lifeless, everything lives,
Everything gives thanks in action.

THE MAYOR: The little man talks well.

A WORKMAN: Hear him, like a magpie, all full of his master's words.

THE APPRENTICE: Speak with respect of Pierre de Craon!

THE MAYOR: 'Tis true he's a burgher of Rheims, and they call him Master of the Compass.

As they used to call Messire Loys
The Master of the Rule.

ANOTHER: Throw some wood on the fire, Perrot, look it's beginning to snow.

[It snows. Night has come. Enter MARA dressed in black, carrying a bundle under her cloak.

MARA: Are these the people of Chevoche?

THE MAYOR: 'Tis ourselves.

MARA: Praised be Jesus Christ.

THE MAYOR: Amen!

MARA: Is it around here I'll find the little cell of the Géyn?

THE MAYOR: Where the leper woman lives?

MARA: Yes.

THE MAYOR: Not exactly here, but close by.

ANOTHER: You want to see the leper woman?

MARA: Yes.

A MAN: She can't be seen; she always wears a veil over her face, as it's ordered.

ANOTHER: And well ordered! it isn't myself as wants to see her.

MARA: It's a long time you've had her?

A MAN: A'most eight years, and we'd like it well not to have her at all.

MARA: Is that because she has done harm?

A MAN: No, but all t'same it's unlucky to have these varmint kind of folk near by.

THE MAYOR: And then, 'tis the parish that feeds her.

A MAN: By the way, I bet they've forgot to take her her bite to eat for three days, with all these doings about the road!

A WOMAN: And what do you want o' this woman? [Mara makes no reply, but stands, looking at the fire]

A WOMAN: A person would say it's a child you're a-holdin' in your arms?

ANOTHER WOMAN: It's a fearsome cold to take out little children at such an hour.

MARA: It is not cold.

[Silence. There is heard, from the darkness under the trees, the sound of a wooden rattle]

AN OLD WOMAN: Wait! there's her! there's her click-click! Holy Virgin! what a pity her ain't dead!

A WOMAN: 'A comes to ask for her food. No fear her'll forget that!

A MAN: What a plague 'tis to feed such varmint.

ANOTHER: Toss her somethin'. She mustn't come anigh to us. First thing you know she'd give us the poison.

ANOTHER: No meat, Perrot! It's fast day, it's Christmas Eve!

[*They laugh*]

Throw her this mossel o' bread that's froze. Good enough for the like o' her!

A MAN: [*Calling*] Heigh, No-face! Heigh, Jeanne, I say, hallo, rotting one!

[*The black form of the leper woman is seen on the snow. Mara looks at her*]

Catch it!

[*He throws her swiftly a piece of bread. She stoops and picks it up and goes away. Mara follows her*]

A MAN: Where is it she's going?

ANOTHER: Here, woman! hallo! where be you going, what be you doing?

[*Mara and The Woman go farther away*]

ACT THREE: SCENE TWO

They disappear within the forest, leaving their tracks upon the snow. The night brightens. The brilliant moon, surrounded by an immense halo, lights up a hillock covered with heather and white sand. Enormous sandstone rocks, fantastically formed, rise here and there like beasts belonging to the fossil ages, like inexplicable monuments or idols with deformed heads and limbs. And the leper woman conducts Mara to the cave where she lives, a kind of low cavern in which it is impossible to stand upright. The back of the cave is closed, leaving only an opening for the smoke.

ACT THREE: SCENE THREE

VIOLAINE: Who is this
That does not fear to walk with the leper woman?
You must know that it is dangerous to be near her,
  and her breath is deadly.

MARA: It is I, Violaine.

VIOLAINE: O voice, so long unheard! Is it you,
  mother?

MARA: It is I, Violaine.

VIOLAINE: It is your voice and another.
Let me light this fire, for it is very cold. And this
  torch, too.

[*She lights a fire of turf and heather by means of live embers which she takes from a pot, and then the torch*]

MARA: It is I, Violaine; Mara, your sister.

VIOLAINE: Dear sister, hail! How good of you to come! But do you not fear me?

MARA: I fear nothing in this world.

VIOLAINE: How much your voice has become like *Maman's!*

MARA: Violaine, our dear mother is no more.

[*Silence*]

VIOLAINE: When did she die?

MARA: In that same month after your departure.

VIOLAINE: Knowing nothing?

MARA: I do not know.

VIOLAINE: Poor *Maman!*
May God have thy soul in his keeping!

MARA: And our father has not yet come back.

VIOLAINE: And you two?

MARA: It is well with us.

VIOLAINE: Everything at home is as you wish it?

MARA: Everything is well.

VIOLAINE: I know it could not be otherwise
With Jacques and you.

MARA: You should see what we have done! We have three more ploughs.
You would not recognize Combernon.
And we are going to pull down those old walls,
Now that the King has come back.

VIOLAINE: And are you happy together, Mara?

MARA: Yes. We are happy. He loves me
As I love him.

VIOLAINE: God be praised.

MARA: Violaine!
You do not see what I hold in my arms?

VIOLAINE: I cannot see.

MARA: Lift your veil, then.

VIOLAINE: Under that I have another.

MARA: You cannot see any more?

VIOLAINE: I have no longer any eyes.
The soul lives alone in the ruined body.

MARA: Blind!
How then are you able to walk so straight?

VIOLAINE: I hear.

MARA: What do you hear?

VIOLAINE: I hear all things exist with me.

MARA: [*Significantly*] And I, Violaine, do you hear me?

VIOLAINE: God has given me the same intelligence
Which He has given to us all.

MARA: Do you hear me, Violaine?

VIOLAINE: Ah, poor Mara!

MARA: Do you hear me, Violaine?

VIOLAINE: What would you have of me, dear sister?

MARA: To join you in praise of this God who has struck you with the pestilence.

VIOLAINE: Then let us praise Him, on this Eve of His Nativity.

MARA: It is easy to be a saint when leprosy helps us.

VIOLAINE: I do not know, not being one.

MARA: We must turn to God when everything else is gone.

VIOLAINE: He at least will not fail us.

MARA: [*Softly*] Perhaps, who knows, Violaine, tell me?

VIOLAINE: Life fails, but not the death where I now live.

MARA: Heretic! are you sure, then, of your salvation?

VIOLAINE: I am sure of the goodness of Him who has provided for everything.

MARA: We see His first instalment.[1]

VIOLAINE: I have faith in God who has ordained my destiny.

MARA: What do you know of Him who is invisible, who is never manifest?

VIOLAINE: He is not more invisible to me now than all the rest.

MARA: [*Ironically*] He is with you, little dove, and He loves you!

VIOLAINE: As with all who are wretched, Himself with me.

MARA: Surely how very great is His love!

VIOLAINE: As the love of the fire for the wood it flames above.

MARA: He has cruelly punished you.

VIOLAINE: Not more that it was due to me.

MARA: And already, he to whom you had submitted your body has forgotten you?

VIOLAINE: I have not submitted my body!

MARA: Sweet Violaine! lying Violaine! Did I not see you tenderly kiss Pierre de Craon the morning of that beautiful day in June?

VIOLAINE: You saw all, and there was nothing else.

MARA: Why, then, did you kiss him so feelingly?

VIOLAINE: The poor man was a leper, and I, I was so happy that day!

MARA: In all innocence, wasn't it?

VIOLAINE: Like a little girl who kisses a poor little boy.

MARA: Ought I to believe that, Violaine?

VIOLAINE: It is true.

MARA: Don't say, too, that it was of your own will you abandoned Jacques to me?

VIOLAINE: No, not of my own will. I loved him! I am not so good as that.

MARA: Ought he to have loved you the same, though you were a leper?

VIOLAINE: I did not expect it.

MARA: Who would love a leper woman?

VIOLAINE: My heart is pure!

MARA: But what did Jacques know of that? He believes you guilty.

VIOLAINE: Our mother had told me that you loved him.

MARA: Don't say it was she who made you a leper.

VIOLAINE: God in His goodness warned me.

MARA: So that when our mother spoke to you . . .

VIOLAINE: It was His voice that I heard.

MARA: But why allow yourself to seem guilty?

VIOLAINE: Should I have done nothing, then, on my part?

[1] This is meant ironically and refers to Violaine's sufferings.

Poor Jacquin! Was it necessary to leave him still regretting me?

MARA: Say that you did not love him at all.

VIOLAINE: I did not love him, Mara.

MARA: But I would never have let him go like that.

VIOLAINE: Was it I who let him go?

MARA: It would have killed me.

VIOLAINE: And am I living?

MARA: Now I am happy with him.

VIOLAINE: Peace be unto you!

MARA: And I have given him a child, Violaine! a dear little girl. A sweet little girl.

VIOLAINE: Peace be unto you!

MARA: Our happiness is great. But yours is greater, with God.

VIOLAINE: And I too knew what happiness was eight years ago, and my heart was ravished with it.

So much, that I madly asked God—ah!—that it might last for ever!

And God heard me in a strange manner! Will my leprosy ever be cured? No, no, as long as there remains a particle of my flesh to be devoured.

Will the love in my heart be cured? Never, as long as my immortal soul lives to nourish it.

Does your husband understand you, Mara?

MARA: What man understands a woman?

VIOLAINE: Happy is she who can be known, heart and soul, who can give herself utterly.

Jacques—what would he have done with all that I could have given him?

MARA: You have transferred your faith to Another?

VIOLAINE: Love has ended in pain, and pain has ended in love.

The wood we set on fire gives not only ashes, but a flame as well.

MARA: But of what use is this blind fire that gives to others

Neither light nor heat?

VIOLAINE: Is it not something that it does me service?

Do not begrudge to a creature consumed,

Afflicted to the uttermost depths, this light that illumines her within!

And if you could pass but one night only in my skin, you would not say that this fire gives no heat.

Man is the priest, but it is not forbidden to woman to be victim.

God is miserly, and does not permit any creature to be set on fire

Unless some impurity be burned with him,

His own, or that which surrounds him, as when the living embers in the censer are stirred.

And truly these are unhappy times.

The people have no father. They look around, and they know no longer where the King is, or the Pope.

That is why my body agonizes here for all Christendom which is perishing.

Powerful is suffering when it is as voluntary as sin!
You saw me kiss that leper, Mara?
Ah, the chalice of sorrow is deep,
And who once sets his lip to it can never withdraw
 it again of his own free will.
  MARA: Take my sorrow upon thee, too!
  VIOLAINE: I have already taken it.
  MARA: Violaine! if there is still something living,
   that was once my sister, under that veil and in
   that ruined body,
Remember that we were children together! Have pity
 upon me!
  VIOLAINE: Speak, dear sister. Have faith! Tell me
   all!
  MARA: Violaine, I am a wretched woman, and my
   pain is greater than yours!
  VIOLAINE: Greater, sister?
   [Mara, *with a loud cry, opens her cloak and
   lifts up the corpse of a baby*]
Look! Take it!
  VIOLAINE: What is this?
  MARA: Look, I tell you! take it! Take it, I give
   it to you.
   [*She lays the corpse in her arms*]
  VIOLAINE: Ah! I feel a rigid little body! a poor
   little cold face!
  MARA: Ha! ha! Violaine! My child! my little girl!
That is her sweet little face! that is her poor little
 body!
  VIOLAINE: [*Speaking low*] Dead, Mara?
  MARA: Take her, I give her to you!
  VIOLAINE: Peace, Mara!
  MARA: They wanted to take her away from me,
   but I would not let them! and I ran away with
   her.
But you, take her, Violaine. Here, take her; you see,
 I give her to you.
  VIOLAINE: What do you wish me to do, Mara?
  MARA: What do I wish you to do? do you not
   understand?
I tell you she is dead! I tell you she is dead!
  VIOLAINE: Her soul lives with God. She follows
   the Lamb. She is with all the blessèd little girls.
  MARA: But for me she is dead!
  VIOLAINE: You readily give me her body! give
   the rest to God.
  MARA: No! no! no! You shall never trick me with
   your nunnish rigmaroles! No, I shall never be
   silenced.
This milk that burns my breast cries out to God like
 the blood of Abel!
Have I got fifty children to tear out of my body?
 have I got fifty souls to tear out of my soul?
Do you know what it is to be rent in two in order
 to bring into the world this little wailing creature?
And the midwife told me I should have no more
 children.
But if I had a hundred children it would not be my
 little Aubaine.

  VIOLAINE: Accept, submit.
  MARA: Violaine, you know well I have a hard
   head. I am one who never gives up, and who
   accepts nothing.
  VIOLAINE: Poor sister!
  MARA: Violaine, they are so sweet, these little ones,
   and it hurts you so when this cruel little mouth
   bites your breast!
  VIOLAINE: [*Caressing the face*] How cold her little
   face is!
  MARA: [*Speaking low*] He knows nothing yet.
  VIOLAINE: [*Also speaking low*] He was not home?
  MARA: He has gone to Rheims to sell his grain.
   She died suddenly, in two hours.
  VIOLAINE: Whom was she like?
  MARA: Like him, Violaine. She is not only mine,
   she is his, too. Only her eyes are like mine.
  VIOLAINE: Poor Jacquin!
  MARA: It was not to hear you say poor Jacquin!
   that I came here.
  VIOLAINE: What do you wish of me, then?
  MARA: Violaine, do you want to know? Tell me,
   do you know what a soul is that damns itself,
Of its own will, to all eternity?
Do you know what it is in the heart that really
 blasphemes?
There is a devil who, while I was running, sang me
 a little song,
Do you wish to hear the things he taught me?
  VIOLAINE: Do not say these horrible things!
  MARA: Then give me back my child that I gave
   you.
  VIOLAINE: You gave me only a corpse.
  MARA: And you, give it back to me alive!
  VIOLAINE: Mara, what do you dare to say?
  MARA: I will not have it that my child is dead.
  VIOLAINE: Is it in my power to bring the dead
   to life?
  MARA: I don't know, I have only you to help me.
  VIOLAINE: Is it in my power to bring the dead to
   life, like God?
  MARA: Of what use are you, then?
  VIOLAINE: To suffer and to supplicate!
  MARA: But of what use is it to suffer and suppli-
   cate if you give me not back my child?
  VIOLAINE: God knows. It is enough for Him that
   I serve Him.
  MARA: But I—I am deaf, and I do not hear! and
   I cry to you from the depths where I am fallen!
   Violaine! Violaine!
Give me back that child I gave you! See! I give in,
 I humiliate myself! have pity on me!
Have pity on me, Violaine, and give me back that
 child you took from me.
  VIOLAINE: Only He who took it can give it back!
  MARA: Give it back to me then! Ah, I know it is
   all your fault.
  VIOLAINE: My fault!
  MARA: Then let it not be yours.
It is mine, forgive me!

But give her back to me, my sister!

VIOLAINE: But you see it is dead.

MARA: You lie! it is not dead! Ah! figure-of-tow, ah, heart-of-a-sheep! Ah, if I had access to your God as you have,

He would not take my little ones away from me so easily!

VIOLAINE: Ask me to re-create heaven and earth!

MARA: But it is written that you may blow on that mountain and cast it into the sea.

VIOLAINE: I can, if I am a saint.

MARA: You must be a saint when a wretched being prays to you.

VIOLAINE: Ah, supreme temptation!

I swear, and I declare, and I protest before God that I am not a saint!

MARA: Then give me back my child.

VIOLAINE: O my God, you see into my heart.

I swear and I protest before God that I am not a saint!

MARA: Violaine, give me back my child!

VIOLAINE: Why will you not leave me in peace? Why do you come thus to torment me in my tomb?

Am I of any worth? do I influence God? am I like God?

It is God himself you are asking me to judge.

MARA: I ask you only for my child.

[Pause]

VIOLAINE: [Raising her finger] Listen.

[Silence. A distant, almost imperceptible, sound of bells]

MARA: I hear nothing.

VIOLAINE: The Christmas bells, the bells announcing the midnight Mass!

O Mara, a little child is born to us!

MARA: Then give me back mine.

[Trumpets in the distance]

VIOLAINE: What is that?

MARA: It is the King going to Rheims. Have you not heard of the road the peasants have cut through the forest?

And they can keep all the wood they cut.

It is a little shepherdess who guides the King through the middle of France

To Rheims, to be crowned there.[1]

VIOLAINE: Praised be God, who does all these wonderful things!

[Again the sound of bells, very distinct]

MARA: How loud the bells ring for the *Gloria!* The wind blows this way.

They are ringing in three villages all at once.

VIOLAINE: Let us pray, with all the universe! Thou art not cold, Mara?

MARA: I am cold only in my heart.

VIOLAINE: Let us pray. It is long since we celebrated Christmas together.

Fear nothing. I have taken your grief upon myself.

Look! and that which you have given me lies close against my heart.

Do not weep! This is not the time to weep, when the salvation of all mankind is already born.

[Bells in the distance, less clear]

MARA: The snow has stopped, and the stars are shining.

VIOLAINE: Look! Do you see this Book?

The priest who visits me now and then left it with me.

MARA: I see it.

VIOLAINE: Take it, will you? and read me the Christmas Service, the First Lesson of each of the three Nocturnes.

[Mara *takes the Book and reads*]

PROPHECY OF ISAIAH[2]

1 Nevertheless, the dimness shall not be such as was in her vexation, when at the first he lightly afflicted the land of Zebulun and the land of Naphtali, and afterward did more grievously afflict her by the way of the sea, beyond Jordan, in Galilee of the nations.

2 The people that walked in darkness have seen a great light: they that dwell in the land of the shadow of death, upon them hath the light shined.

3 Thou hast multiplied the nation, and not increased the joy: they joy before thee according to the joy in harvest, and as men rejoice when they divide the spoil.

4 For thou hast broken the yoke of his burden; and the staff of his shoulder, the rod of his oppressor, as in the day of Midian.

5 For every battle of the warrior is with confused noise, and garments rolled in blood; but this shall be with burning and fuel of fire.

6 For unto us a child is born, unto us a son is given, and the government shall be upon his shoulder; and his name shall be called Wonderful, Counselor, The mighty God, The everlasting Father, the Prince of Peace.

VIOLAINE: [Raising her face] Listen!

[Silence]

VOICES OF ANGELS in heaven, heard only by Violaine:

CHOIR:[3] HODIE NOBIS DE CAELO PAX VERA DESCENDIT, HODIE PER TOTUM MUNDUM MELLIFLUI FACTI SUNT CAELI.

A VOICE:[4] HODIE ILLUXIT NOBIS DIES REDEMPTIONIS NOVAE, REPARATIONIS ANTIQUAE, FELICITATIS AETERNAE.

CHOIR: HODIE PER TOTUM MUNDUM MELLIFLUI FACTI SUNT CAELI.

[Violaine *lifts her finger in warning. Silence.* Mara *listens and looks uneasily*]

---

[1] This refers to the crowning of the Dauphin Charles by Joan of Arc

[2] Isaiah ix, 1–6.

[3] The voices are like those of heroic young men singing solemnly in unison, with retarded movement and very simple cadence at the end of phrases.

[4] Like the voice of a child.

MARA: I hear nothing.

VIOLAINE: Read on, Mara.

MARA: [*Continuing to read*]

SERMON OF SAINT LEO, POPE

Our Saviour, dearly beloved, was to-day born: let us rejoice. For there should be no loophole open to sorrow on the birthday of Life, which, the fear of Death being at last consumed, filleth us with the joy of eternity promised. No one from this gladness is excluded, as one and the same cause for happiness exists for us all: for Our Lord, the destroyer of sin and Death, having found no one exempt from sin, came to deliver every one. Let the sinless exult insomuch as his palm is at hand; let the sinful rejoice . . .

[*Suddenly a brilliant and prolonged sound of trumpets very near. Shouts resound through the forest*]

MARA: The King! The King of France!

[*Again and again the blare of the trumpets, unutterably piercing, solemn, and triumphant*]

MARA: [*In a low voice*] The King of France who goes to Rheims!

[*Silence*]

Violaine!

[*Silence*]

Do you hear me, Violaine?

[*Silence. She goes on with the reading*]

. . . Let the sinful rejoice insomuch as forgiveness is offered to him. Let the Gentile be of good cheer, because he is bidden to share life. For the Son of God, according to the fulness of this time which the inscrutable depth of the Divine counsel hath disposed, took on Himself the nature of mankind so that He might reconcile it to its maker, and that this deviser of Death, Satan, by that which he had vanquished might be in his turn conquered.

VOICES OF ANGELS: [*Heard only by* Violaine, *as before*]

CHOIR: O MAGNUM MYSTERIUM ET ADMIRABILE SACRAMENTUM UT ANIMALIA VIDERINT DOMINUM NATUM JACENTEM IN PRAESEPIO! BEATA VIRGO CUJUS VISCERA MERUERUNT PORTARE DOMINUM CHRISTUM.

A VOICE: AVE, MARIA, GRATIA PLENA, DOMINUS TECUM.

CHOIR: BEATA VIRGO CUJUS VISCERA MERUERUNT PORTARE DOMINUM CHRISTUM.

[*Pause*]

MARA: Violaine, I am not worthy to read this Book!

Violaine, I know that my heart is too hard, and I am sorry for it: I wish I could be different.

VIOLAINE: Read on, Mara. You do not know who chants the responses.

[*Silence*]

MARA: [*With an effort takes up the Book, and reads in a trembling voice*]

The Holy Gospel according to Saint Luke.[1]

[*They both stand up*]

1 And it came to pass in those days, that there went out a decree from Cæsar Augustus, that all the world should be taxed. (And the rest.)

[*They sit down*]

HOMILY OF SAINT GREGORY, POPE

[*She stops, overcome by emotion.—The trumpets sound a last time in the distance*]

MARA:

Forasmuch as, by the grace of God, we are this day thrice to celebrate the solemnities of Mass, we may not speak at length on the gospel that hath just been read. However, the birth of our Redeemer bids us address you at least in a few words. Wherefore, at the time of this birth, should there have been a census of all the people except clearly to manifest that He who was appearing in the flesh just then was numbering his Elect for eternity? On the contrary, the Prophet saith of the wicked: they shall be deleted from the Book of the Living and they shall not be written down among the Righteous. It is meet also that He should be born in Bethlehem. For Bethlehem means the House of Bread, and Jesus Christ saith of Himself: I am the Living Bread descended from Heaven. Therefore had the place in which our Lord was born been called the House of Bread in order that He who was to feed our hearts with internal satiety should there appear in the substance of flesh. He was born, not in the house of his parents, but by the roadside, no doubt to show that by taking on humanity He was being born in a place strange to Him.

VOICES OF ANGELS:

CHOIR: BEATA VISCERA MARIAE VIRGINIS QUAE PORTAVERUNT AETERNI PATRIS FILIUM; ET BEATA UBERA QUAE LACTAVERUNT CHRISTUM DOMINUM. QUI HODIE PRO SALUTE MUNDI DE VIRGINE NASCI DIGNATUS EST.

A VOICE: DIES SANCTIFICATUS ILLUXIT NOBIS; VENITE, GENTES, ET ADORATE DOMINUM.

CHOIR: QUI HODIE PRO SALUTE MUNDI DE VIRGINE NASCI DIGNATUS EST.

[*Long silence*]

VOICES OF ANGELS: [*Again, almost imperceptible*]

CHOIR: VERBUM CARO FACTUM EST ET HABITAVIT IN NOBIS: ET VIDIMUS GLORIAM EJUS, GLORIAM QUASI UNIGENITI A PATRE, PLENUM GRATIAE ET VERITATIS.

A VOICE: OMNIA PER IPSUM FACTA SUNT ET SINE IPSO FACTUM EST NIHIL.

CHOIR: ET VIDIMUS GLORIAM EJUS, GLORIAM QUASI UNIGENITI A PATRE, PLENUM GRATIAE ET VERITATIS.

---

[1] Luke ii, 1.

A VOICE: GLORIA PATRI ET FILIO ET SPIRITUI SANCTO.

CHOIRS ET VIDIMUS GLORIAM EJUS, GLORIAM QUASI UNIGENITI A PATRE, PLENUM GRATIAE ET VERITATIS.

[*Long silence*]

VIOLAINE: [*Suddenly cries out in a stifled voice*] Ah!

MARA: What is it?

[*With her hand she makes her a sign to be silent. —Silence.—The first flush of dawn appears*]

[Violaine *puts her hand under her cloak as if to fasten her dress again*]

MARA: Violaine, I see something moving under your cloak!

VIOLAINE: [*As if she were awakening little by little*] Is it you, Mara? good morning, sister. I feel the breath of the new-born day on my face.

MARA: Violaine! Violaine! is it your arm that stirs? Again I see something moving.

VIOLAINE: Peace, Mara, it is Christmas Day, when all joy is born!

MARA: What joy is there for me unless my child lives?

VIOLAINE: And for us, too—a little child is born to us!

MARA: In the name of the living God, what say you?

VIOLAINE: "Behold, I bring thee glad tidings . . ."

MARA: Your cloak—it moves again!

[*The little bare foot of a baby, moving lazily, appears in the opening of the cloak*]

VIOLAINE: ". . . Because a man has appeared in the world!"

[Mara *falls upon her knees, with a deep sigh, her forehead on the knees of her sister. Violaine caresses her*]

VIOLAINE: Poor sister! she weeps. She, too, has had too much sorrow.

[*Silence.* Violaine *kisses her head*]

Take it, Mara! Would you leave the child always with me?

MARA: [*She takes the child from under the cloak and looks at it wildly*] It lives!

VIOLAINE: [*She walks out of the cave a few steps upon the heather. By the first light of the bitter cold morning can be seen, first, the pine and birch trees hoary with frost, then, at the end of an immense snow-covered plain, seeming very small on the top of its hill, but clearly etched in the pure air, the five-towered silhouette of Monsanvierge*] Glory to God!

MARA: It lives!

VIOLAINE: Peace on earth to men!

MARA: It lives! it lives!

VIOLAINE: It lives and we live.

And the face of the Father appeared on the earth born again and comforted.

MARA: My child lives!

VIOLAINE: [*Raising her finger*] Listen!

[*Silence*]

I hear the Angelus ringing at Monsanvierge.

[*She crosses herself and prays. The child awakes*]

MARA: [*Whispering*] It is I, Aubaine; dost know me?

[*The child moves about and whines*]

What is it, my joy? What is it, my treasure?

[*The child opens its eyes, looks at its mother and begins to cry. Mara* looks closely at it]

Violaine!

What does this mean? Its eyes were black,

And now they are blue like yours.

[*Silence*]

Ah!

And what is this drop of milk I see on its lips?

ACT FOUR: SCENE ONE

Night. The large kitchen, as in ACT I, *empty. A lamp is on the table. The outer door is half open.*

Mara *enters from without, and carefully closes the door. She stands still for a moment in the centre of the room, looking toward the door, and listening.*

Then she takes the lamp and goes out by another door without making any sound.

The stage remains dark. Nothing can be seen but the fire of some live coals on the hearth.

ACT FOUR: SCENE TWO

Two or three blasts of a horn are heard in the distance. Sounds of calling. Movement in the farm. Then the noise of opening doors, and the grinding of approaching cart-wheels. Loud knocks at the door.

VOICE FROM WITHOUT: [*Calling*] Hallo!

[*Noise in the upper story of a window opening*]

VOICE OF JACQUES HURY: Who is there?

VOICE FROM WITHOUT: Open the door!

VOICE OF JACQUES HURY: What do you want?

VOICE FROM WITHOUT: Open the door!

VOICE OF JACQUES HURY: Who are you?

VOICE FROM WITHOUT: Open the door so that I can tell you!

[*Pause*]

[Jacques Hury, *with a candle in his hand, enters the room; he opens the door. After a slight pause,*]

[*Enter* Pierre de Craon, *carrying the body of a woman wrapped up in his arms. He lays his burden very carefully upon the table. Then he lifts his head. The two men stare at each other in the candlelight*]

PIERRE DE CRAON: Jacques Hury, do you not recognize me?

JACQUES HURY: Pierre de Craon?

PIERRE DE CRAON: It is I.

[*They continue to look at each other*]

JACQUES HURY: And what is this you bring me?

PIERRE DE CRAON: I found her half-buried in my sandpit, there where I seek what I need

For my glass ovens, and for the mortar—

Half-hidden under a great cart-load of sand, under a cart standing on end from which they had taken off the backboard.

She is still alive. It is I who took it upon myself to bring her to you

Here.

JACQUES HURY: Why here?

PIERRE DE CRAON: That at least she might die under her father's roof!

JACQUES HURY: There is no roof here but mine.

PIERRE DE CRAON: Jacques, here is Violaine.

JACQUES HURY: I know no Violaine.

PIERRE DE CRAON: Have you never heard of the Leper Woman of Chevoche?

JACQUES HURY: What does that matter to me? You lepers, it is for you to scrape each other's sores.

PIERRE DE CRAON: I am not a leper any more; I was cured long ago.

JACQUES HURY: Cured?

PIERRE DE CRAON: Year after year the disease grew less, and I am now healthy.

JACQUES HURY: And this one, she too will be cured presently.

PIERRE DE CRAON: You are more leprous than she and I.

JACQUES HURY: But I don't ask to be taken out of my hole in the sand.

PIERRE DE CRAON: And even if she had been guilty, you ought to remember.

JACQUES HURY: Is it true that she kissed you on the mouth?

PIERRE DE CRAON: [*Looking at him*] It is true, poor child!

JACQUES HURY: She moves, she is coming to herself.

PIERRE DE CRAON: I leave you with her.

[*He goes out*]

ACT FOUR: SCENE THREE

[Jacques Hury *sits down near the table and looks silently at* Violaine]

VIOLAINE: [*Coming to herself and stretching forth her hand*] Where am I, and who is there?

JACQUES HURY: At Monsanvierge, and it is I who am near you.

[*Pause*]

VIOLAINE: [*Speaking as she used to do*] Good morning, Jacques.

[*Silence*]

Jacques, you still care for me, then?

JACQUES HURY: The wound is not healed.

VIOLAINE: Poor boy!

And I, too, have I not suffered a little too?

JACQUES HURY: What possessed you to kiss that leper on the mouth!

VIOLAINE: Jacques! you must reproach me quickly with all you have in your heart against me, that we may finish with all that.

For we have other things still to say.

And I want to hear you say just once again those words I loved so much: *Dear Violaine! Sweet Violaine!*

For the time that remains to us is short.

JACQUES HURY: I have nothing more to say to you.

VIOLAINE: Come here, cruel man!

[*He approaches her, where she lies*]

Come nearer to me.

[*She takes his hand and draws him to her. He kneels awkwardly at her side*]

Jacques, you must believe me. I swear it before God, who is looking upon us!

I was never guilty with Pierre de Craon.

JACQUES HURY: Why, then, did you kiss him?

VIOLAINE: Ah, he was so sad and I was so happy.

JACQUES HURY: I don't believe you.

[*She lays her hand a moment on his head*]

VIOLAINE: Do you believe me now?

[*He hides his face in her dress and sobs heavily*]

JACQUES HURY: Ah, Violaine! cruel Violaine!

VIOLAINE: Not cruel, but sweet, sweet Violaine!

JACQUES HURY: It is true, then? yes, it was only I you loved?

[*Silence. She gives him her other hand*]

VIOLAINE: Jacques, no doubt it was all too beautiful, and we should have been too happy.

JACQUES HURY: You have cruelly deceived me.

VIOLAINE: Deceived? this silver flower on my side did not lie.

JACQUES HURY: What was I to believe, Violaine?

VIOLAINE: If you had believed in me,

Who knows but what you might have cured me?

JACQUES HURY: Was I not to believe my own eyes?

VIOLAINE: That is true. You ought to have believed your own eyes, that is right.

One does not marry a leper. One does not marry an unfaithful woman.

Do not regret anything, Jacques. There, it is better as it is.

JACQUES HURY: Did you know that Mara loved me?

VIOLAINE: I knew it. My mother herself had told me.

JACQUES HURY: Thus everything was in league with her against me!

VIOLAINE: Jacques, there is already enough sorrow in the world.

It is best not to be willingly the cause of a great sorrow to others.

JACQUES HURY: But what of my sorrow?

VIOLAINE: That is another thing, Jacques. Are you not happy to be with me?

JACQUES HURY: Yes, Violaine.

VIOLAINE: Where I am, there is patience, not sorrow.

[Silence]

The world's grief is great.

It is too hard to suffer, and not to know why.

But that which others do not know, I have learned, and thou must share my knowledge.

Jacques, have we not been separated long enough now? should we let any barrier remain between us? Must it still be that death shall separate us?

Only that which is ill should perish, and that which should not perish is that which suffers.

Happy is he who suffers, and who knows why.

Now my task is finished.

JACQUES HURY: And mine begins.

VIOLAINE: What! do you find the cup where I have drunk so bitter?

JACQUES HURY: And now I have lost you for ever!

VIOLAINE: Tell me, why lost?

JACQUES HURY: You are dying.

VIOLAINE: Jacques, you must understand me!

Of what use is the finest perfume in a sealed vase? it serves for nothing.

JACQUES HURY: No, Violaine.

VIOLAINE: Of what use has my body been to me, having hidden away my heart so that you could not see it, but you saw only the scar on the outside of the worthless shell.

JACQUES HURY: I was hard and blind!

VIOLAINE: Now I am broken utterly, and the perfume is set free.

And Behold, you believe everything, simply because I laid my hand on your head.

JACQUES HURY: I believe. I do not doubt any more.

VIOLAINE: And tell me, where is the justice in all that, this justice you spoke of so proudly?

JACQUES HURY: I am no longer proud.

VIOLAINE: Come, leave Justice alone. It is not for us to call her and to make her come.

JACQUES HURY: Violaine, how you have suffered in these eight long years!

VIOLAINE: But not in vain. Many things are consumed in the flame of a heart that burns.

JACQUES HURY: Deliverance is near.

VIOLAINE: Blessed be the hand that led me that night!

JACQUES HURY: What hand?

VIOLAINE: That silent hand that clasped mine, and led me, when I was coming back with my food.

JACQUES HURY: Led you where?

VIOLAINE: Where Pierre de Craon found me.

Under a great mound of sand, a whole cart-load heaped upon me. Did I place myself there, all alone?

JACQUES HURY: [Rising] Who has done that? God's Blood! who has done that?

VIOLAINE: I don't know. It matters little. Do not curse.

JACQUES HURY: I shall find out the truth about that.

VIOLAINE: No, you shall find out the truth about nothing.

JACQUES HURY: Tell me all!

VIOLAINE: I have told you all. What would you learn of a blind woman?

JACQUES HURY: You shall not put me off the track.

VIOLAINE: Do not waste words. I have only a little more time to be with you.

JACQUES HURY: I shall always have Mara.

VIOLAINE: She is your wife, and she is my sister, born of the same father and the same mother, and of the same flesh,

Both of us, here beside Monsanvierge.

[Silence]

[Jacques stands a moment motionless, as if trying to control himself. Then he sits down again]

JACQUES HURY: There are no more recluses at Monsanvierge.

VIOLAINE: What do you say?

JACQUES HURY: The last one died last Christmas. No mouth comes any more to the wicket of the nourishing church of this holy monastery, so the priest tells us who used to give them communion.

VIOLAINE: The mountain of God

Is dead, and we share the heritage, Mara and I.

JACQUES HURY: And Violaine was the secret offshoot of the Holy Tree, growing from some subterranean root.

God would not have taken her from me, if she had been entirely filled by me, leaving no part of her empty,

"God's part," as good women call it.

VIOLAINE: What's to be done? so much the worse!

JACQUES HURY: Stay! do not go!

VIOLAINE: I stay, I am not going.

Tell me, Jacques, do you remember that hour at noon, and that great scorching sun, and that spot on the flesh under my breast that I showed to you?

JACQUES HURY: Ah!

VIOLAINE: You remember? did I not tell you truly that you could never more tear me out of your soul?

This of myself is in you for ever. I do not wish you any more to be happy, it is not proper that you should laugh,

In this time when you are still far away from me.

JACQUES HURY: Ah! Ah! Violaine!

VIOLAINE: Have this from me, my well-beloved!

The communion on the cross, the bitterness like the bitterness of myrrh,

Of the sick man who sees the shadow upon the dial, and of the soul that receives its call!

And for you age is already come. But how hard it is to renounce when the heart is young!

JACQUES HURY: And from me you have not wanted to accept anything!

VIOLAINE: Think you that I know nothing about you, Jacques?

JACQUES HURY: My mother knew me.

VIOLAINE: To me also, O Jacques, you have caused much pain!

JACQUES HURY: You are a virgin and I have no part in you.

VIOLAINE: What! must I tell you everything?

JACQUES HURY: What do you still conceal?

VIOLAINE: It is necessary. This is not the time to keep anything back.

JACQUES HURY: Speak louder.

VIOLAINE: Have they not told you, then, that your child was dead?

Last year, while you were at Rheims?

JACQUES HURY: Several people told me. But Mara swears that it only slept.

And I have never been able to draw from her the whole story.

They say she went to find you.

I should have known everything in time. I wanted to learn the whole truth.

VIOLAINE: That is true. You have the right to know all.

JACQUES HURY: What did she go to ask of you?

VIOLAINE: Have you never noticed that the eyes of your little girl are changed?

JACQUES HURY: They are blue now, like yours.

VIOLAINE: It was Christmas night. Yes, Jacques, it is true, she was dead. Her little body was stiff and icy.

I know it; all night I held her in my arms.

JACQUES HURY: Who then restored her to life?

VIOLAINE: God only, and with God the faith and the despair of her mother.

JACQUES HURY: But you had nothing to do with it?

VIOLAINE: O Jacques, to you only I will tell a great mystery.

It is true, when I felt this dead body upon my own, the child of your flesh, Jacques. . . .

JACQUES HURY: Ah, my little Aubaine!

VIOLAINE: You love her very much?

JACQUES HURY: Go on.

VIOLAINE: . . . . My heart contracted, and the iron entered into me.

Behold what I held in my arms for my Christmas night, and all that remained of our race, a dead child!

All of yours that I should ever possess in this life!

And I listened to Mara, who read me the Service for this Holy night: the babe who has been given to us, the gospel of Joy.

Ah, do not say that I know nothing of you!

Do not say that I do not know what it is to suffer for you!

Nor that I do not know the effort and the partition of the woman who gives life!

JACQUES HURY: You do not mean that the child was really brought back to life?

VIOLAINE: What I know is that it was dead, and that all of a sudden I felt its head move!

And life burst from me in a flash, at one bound, and my mortified flesh bloomed again!

Ah, I know what it is, that little blind mouth that seeks, and those pitiless teeth![1]

JACQUES HURY: O Violaine!

[Silence. He makes as if to rise. Violaine feebly forces him to remain seated]

VIOLAINE: Do you forgive me now?

JACQUES HURY: Oh, the duplicity of women! Ah, you are the daughter of your mother!

Tell me! it is not you that you would have me forgive!

VIOLAINE: Whom, then?

JACQUES HURY: What hand was that which took yours the other night, and so kindly led you?

VIOLAINE: I do not know.

JACQUES HURY: But I think that I know.

VIOLAINE: You do not know.

Leave that to us, it is an affair between women.

JACQUES HURY: My affair is to have justice done.

VIOLAINE: Ah, leave thy Justice alone!

JACQUES HURY: I know what remains for me to do.

VIOLAINE: You know nothing at all, poor fellow. You have no understanding of women,

And what poor creatures they are, stupid and hard-headed and knowing only one thing.

Do not confuse everything between you and her, as with you and me.

Was it really her hand alone? I do not know. And you do not know either. And of what good would it be to know?

Keep what you have. Forgive.

And you, have you never needed to be forgiven?

JACQUES HURY: I am alone.

VIOLAINE: Not alone, with this beautiful little child I have given back to you,

And Mara, my sister, your wife, of the same flesh as myself. Who, with me, knows you better?

It is necessary for you to have the strength and the deed, it is necessary for you to have a duty plainly laid down and final.

That is why I have this sand in my hair.

JACQUES HURY: Happiness is ended for me.

VIOLAINE: It is ended, what does that matter? Happiness was never promised to you. Work, that is all that is asked of you. (And Monsanvierge belongs only to you now.)

Question the old earth and she will always answer you with bread and wine.

As for me I have finished with her, and I go beyond.

Tell me, what is the day you will pass far from me? It will soon pass.

[1] The revived infant suckled at Violaine's breast; see the last line of Act Three.

And when your turn shall come, and when you see the great door creak and move,

I shall be on the other side and you will find me waiting.

[*Silence*]

JACQUES HURY: O my betrothed, through the blossoming branches, hail!

VIOLAINE: You remember?

Jacques! Good morning, Jacques!

[*The first rays of dawn appear*]

And now I must be carried away from here.

JACQUES HURY: Carried away?

VIOLAINE: This is not the place for a leper to die in.

Let me be carried to that shelter my father built for the poor at the door of Monsanvierge,

[*He makes as if to take her. She waves him away with her hand*]

No, Jacques, no, not you.

JACQUES HURY: What, not even this last duty to you?

VIOLAINE: No it is not right that you should touch me.

Call Pierre de Craon.

He has been a leper, though God has cured him. He has no horror of me.

And I know that to him I am like a brother, and woman has no more power over his soul.

[*Jacques Hury goes out and returns several minutes later with* Pierre de Craon. *She does not speak. The two men look at her in silence*]

VIOLAINE: Jacques!

JACQUES HURY: Violaine!

VIOLAINE: Has the year been good and the grain fine and abundant?

JACQUES HURY: So abundant that we do not know where to put it all.

VIOLAINE: Ah!

How beautiful a great harvest is!

Yes, even now I remember it, and I think it beautiful.

JACQUES HURY: Yes, Violaine.

VIOLAINE: How beautiful it is

To live! [*speaking low and with deep fervour*] and how great is the glory of God!

JACQUES HURY: Live, then, and stay with us.

VIOLAINE: But how good it is to die too! When all is really ended, and over us spreads little by little

The darkness, as of a deep shade.

[*Silence*]

PIERRE DE CRAON: She does not speak any more.

JACQUES HURY: Take her. Carry her where I have told you.

For, as to me, she does not wish me to touch her,

Very gently! Gently, gently, I tell you. Do not hurt her.

[*They go out,* Pierre *carrying the body. The door stands open. Long pause*]

ACT FOUR: SCENE FOUR

On the threshold of the door appears Anne Vercors *in the habit of a traveller, a staff in his hand and a sack slung on his back.*

ANNE VERCORS: Open?

Is the house empty, that all the doors should be open?

Who has come in so early before me? or who is it that has gone out?

[*He looks around a long time*]

I recognize the old room, nothing is changed.

Here is the fireplace, here is the table.

Here is the ceiling with its strong beams.

I am like an animal that smells all around him, and who knows his resting-place and his home.

Hail, house! It is I. Here is the master come back.

Hail, Monsanvierge, lofty dwelling!

From far away, since yesterday morning and the day before, on the top of the hill I recognized the Arch with the five towers.

But why is it that the bells ring no more? neither yesterday nor this morning.

Have I heard in the sky, with the Angel ninefold sonorous, tidings of Jesus brought three times, three times to the heart of Mary.

Monsanvierge! how often I have thought of thy walls,

While, under my captive feet, I made the water rise into the garden of the old man of Damascus.

(Oh, the morning, and the implacable afternoon! Oh, the eternal noria and the eyes we lift toward Lebanon!)[1]

And all the aromatic odours of exile are little to me

Compared with this walnut-leaf I crush between my fingers.

Hail, Earth, powerful and subdued! Here it is not sand that we plough, and soft alluvium,

But the deep earth itself that we work with the whole strength of our body and of the six oxen who pull and form slowly under the plough-share of the great trench,

And, as far as my eyes can see, everything has responded to the upheaval man has caused.

Already I have seen all my fields, and perceived that everything is well cared for. God be praised! Jacques does his work well.

[*He lays his sack on the table*]

Earth, I have been to seek for thee a little earth,

A little earth for my burial, that which God himself chose for his own at Jerusalem.

[*Pause*]

I would not come back last night. I waited for daylight.

And I passed the night under a stack of new straw,

---

[1] Noria: a water wheel used for raising water.

thinking, sleeping, praying, looking around, remembering, giving thanks,

Listening to hear, if I could, the voice of my wife, or of my daughter Violaine, or of a crying child.

When I awoke I saw that the night was brighter.

And up there, above the dark crest of Monsanvierge, resplendent, from Arabia,

The morning star rose over France, like a herald rising in the solitude!

And then I came to the house.

Hallo! Is there anybody here?

[*He raps on the table with his staff. . . . Curtain, which remains down a few minutes*]

ACT FOUR: SCENE FIVE

The farther end of the garden. Afternoon of the same day. End of the summer.

The trees are heavy with fruit. The branches of some of them, bending to the ground, are held up by props. The dried and tarnished leaves, mingled with the red and yellow of apples, seem like tapestry.

Below, flooded with light, lies the immense plain as it would be after the harvest; with stubble, and already some ploughed earth. The white roads and the villages can be seen. There are rows of haystacks, looking very small, and here and there a poplar. Far away, in another direction, are flocks of sheep. The shadows of large clouds pass over the plain.

In the middle, where the scene descends toward the background, from which the tops of the trees in a little wood are seen to emerge, there is a semicircular stone bench, reached by three steps, and with lions' heads at each end of its back. Anne Vercors is sitting there, with Jacques Hury *at his right side.*

ANNE VERCORS: The golden end of Autumn
Will soon
Despoil the fruit tree and the vine.
And in the morning the white sun,
A single flash of a fireless diamond, will blend with the white vesture of the earth:
And the evening is near when he who walks beneath the aspen
Shall hear the last leaf on its summit.
Now, behold, making equal the days and nights,
Counterpoising the long hours of labour with its projecting sign, athwart the celestial Door
Interposes the royal Balance.

JACQUES HURY: Father, since thou hast been gone,
Everything, the painful story, and the plot of these women, and the pitfall made to take us in,
Thou know'st, and I have told thee
Still another thing, with my mouth against thine ear,
Where is thy wife? where is thy daughter Violaine?

And lo, thou talkest of the straw we twist, and of the great black grape

Which fills the hand of the vine-dresser, the hand he thrusts under the vine-branch!

Already

The crooked Scorpion and the retreating Sagittarius

Have appeared on the dial of night.

ANNE VERCORS: Let the old man exult in the warm season! O truly blessed place! O bosom of the Fatherland! O grateful, fecund earth!

The carts passing along the road

Leave straw among the fruited branches!

JACQUES HURY: O Violaine! O cruel Violaine! desire of my soul, you have betrayed me!

O hateful garden! O love useless and denied! O garden planted in an evil hour!

Sweet Violaine! perfidious Violaine! Oh, the silence and the depth of woman!

Art thou then really gone, my soul?

Having deceived me, she goes away; and having undeceived me, with fatal sweet words,

She goes again, and I, bearing this poisoned arrow, it will be necessary

That I live on and on! like the beast we take by the horn, drawing his head out of the manger,

Like the horse we loose from the single-tree in the evening with a lash of the whip on his back!

O ox, it is thou that walkest ahead, but we two make but one team.

Only that the furrow be made, that is all they ask of us.

That is why everything that was not necessary to my task, everything has been taken away from me.

ANNE VERCORS: Monsanvierge is dead, and the fruit of your labour is for you alone.

JACQUES HURY: It is true.

[*Silence*]

ANNE VERCORS: Have they looked well to provisioning the chapel for to-morrow?

Is there enough to eat and drink for all those we shall have to entertain?

JACQUES HURY: Old man! It is your daughter we are going to lay in the earth, and behold what you find to say!

Surely you have never loved her! But the old man, like the miser who after warming his hands at his pot of embers hoards their heat in his bosom,

He suffices for himself alone.

ANNE VERCORS: Everything must be done. Things must be done honourably.

. . . Elisabeth, my wife, hidden heart!

[*Enter* Pierre de Craon]

ANNE VERCORS: Is everything ready?

PIERRE DE CRAON: They are working at the coffin. They are digging the grave where you ordered,

Close up by the church there, near that of the last chaplain, your brother.

Within it they have put the earth you brought back.
A great black ivy-vine
Comes out of the priestly tomb, and, crossing the
wall,
Enters almost into the sealed arch.
. . . To-morrow, in the early morning. Everything is
ready.

[Jacques Hury *weeps, his face in his cloak. In
the path is seen a nun, like a woman who hunts
for flowers*]

ANNE VERCORS: What are you looking for, Sister?

VOICE OF THE NUN: [*Hollow and smothered*] Some
flowers, to lay on her heart, between her hands.

ANNE VERCORS: There are no more flowers, there
is nothing but fruit.

JACQUES HURY: Push aside the leaves and you will
find the last violet!

And the Immortelle is still in the bud, and nothing
is left to us but the dahlia and the poppy.

[*The nun is no longer there*]

PIERRE DE CRAON: The two Sisters, who care for
the sick, one quite young the other very old,

Have dressed her, and Mara has sent her wedding-
dress for her.

Truly, she was only a leper, but she was honourable
in the sight of God.

She reposes in a deep sleep
As one who knows in whose care she is.
I saw her before they had laid her in the coffin.
Her body is still supple.
Oh, while the Sister finished dressing her, with her
arm around her waist,

Holding her in a sitting posture, how her head fell
backward

Like that of the still warm partridge the hunter picks
in his hand!

ANNE VERCORS: My child! my little daughter I carried in my arms before she knew how to walk!

The fat little girl who awoke with bursts of laughter
in her little sabot of a bed.[1]

All that is over. Ah! ah! O God! Alas!

PIERRE DE CRAON: Don't you want to see her before they nail down the coffin-lid?

ANNE VERCORS: No. The child disowned
Goes away secretly.

JACQUES HURY: Never again in this life shall I see
her face.

[Pierre de Craon *sits down at the left of* Anne
Vercors. *Long pause. The sound of a hammer
on planks. They remain silent, listening*]

[Mara *is seen to pass at the side of the stage
holding a child in her arms wrapped in a black
shawl. Then she re-enters slowly at the back,
and comes and stands in front of the bench
where the three men are sitting. They stare at
her, except* Jacques Hury, *who looks at the
ground*]

[1] Sabot: a wooden shoe worn by the peasantry.

MARA: [*Her head lowered*] Hail, father! Hail to
you all.

You stare at me and I know what you think: "Violaine is dead.

The beautiful ripe fruit, the good golden fruit
Has fallen from the branch, and, bitter without, hard
as a stone within,

Only the wintry nut remains to us." Who loves me?
Who has ever loved me?

[*She lifts her head with a savage gesture*]

Well! here I am! what have you to say to me? Say
everything! What have you against me?

What makes you look at me like that, with your
eyes saying: It is thou! It is true, it is I!

It is true, it was I who killed her,
It was I the other night who took her by the hand,
having gone to seek her,

While Jacques was not there,
And I who made her fall into the sandpit, and who
turned over upon her

That loaded cart. Everything was ready, there was
only a bolt to pull out,

I did that,
Jacques! and it is I, too, who said to my mother,
Violaine—to talk to her that day when you came
back from Braine.

For I longed ardently to marry you, and if I could
not I had decided to hang myself the day of
your wedding.

Now God, who sees into hearts, had already let her
take the leprosy.

—But Jacques never stopped thinking of her. That
is why I killed her.

What then? What else was there to do? What more
could be done

So that the one I love and who is mine
Should be mine entirely, as I am his entirely,
And that Violaine should be shut out?
I did what I could.

And you in your turn, answer! Your Violaine that
you loved,

How then did you love her, and which was worth
the most,

Your love, do you think, or my hatred?
You all loved her! and here is her father who abandons her, and her mother who advises her!

And her betrothed, how he has believed in her!
Certainly you loved her,
As we say we love a gentle animal, a pretty flower,
and that was all the feeling there was in your
love!

Mine was of another kind;
Blind, never letting go anything once taken, like a
deaf thing that does not hear!

For him to have me entirely, it was necessary to me
to have him entirely!

What have I done after all that I must defend myself? who has been the most faithful to him, I
or Violaine?

Violaine who betrayed him for I know not what leper, giving in, said she, to God's council in a kiss?

I honour God. Let him stay where he is! Our miserable life is so short! Let him leave us in peace!

Is it my fault if I loved Jacques? was it for my happiness, or for the burning away of my soul?

What could I do to defend myself, I who am not beautiful, nor agreeable, a poor woman who can only give pain?

That is why I killed her in my despair!

O poor, unskilful crime!

O disgrace to her that no one loves and with whom nothing succeeds! What ought to have been done, since I loved him and he did not love me?

[*She turns toward* Jacques]

And you, O Jacques, why do you not speak?

Why turn you your face to the ground, without a word to say,

Like Violaine, the day when you accused her unjustly?

Do you not know me? I am your wife.

Truly I know that I do not seem to you either beautiful or agreeable, but look, I have dressed myself for you, I have added to that pain that I can give you. And I am the sister of Violaine.

It is born of pain! This love is not born of joy, it is born of pain! the pain which suffices for those who have no joy!

No one is glad to see it, ah, it is not the flower in its season,

But that which is under the flowers that wither, the earth itself, the miserly earth under the grass, the earth that never fails!

Know me then!

I am your wife and you can do nothing to change that!

One inseparable flesh, the contact by the centre and by the soul, and for confirmation this mysterious parentage between us two.

Which is, that I have had a child of yours.

I have committed a great crime, I have killed my sister; but I have not sinned against you. And I tell you that you have nothing to reproach me with. And what do the others matter to me?

That is what I had to say, and now do what you will.

[*Silence*]

ANNE VERCORS: What she says is true. Go, Jacques, forgive her!

JACQUES HURY: Come then, Mara.

[*She comes nearer and stands before them, forming with her child a single object upon which the two men extend together their right hands. Their arms cross, and* Jacques' *hand is laid on the head of the child, that of* Anne *on the head of* Mara]

JACQUES HURY: It is Violaine who forgives you. It is through her, Mara, that I forgive you. Guilty woman, it is she who reunites us.

MARA: Alas! alas! dead words and without a ray of light!

O Jacques, I am no longer the same! There is something in me that is ended. Have no fear. All that is nothing to me.

Something in me is broken, and I am left without strength, like a woman widowed and without children.

[*The child laughs vaguely and looks all around, with little cries of delight*]

ANNE VERCORS: [*Caressing it*] Poor Violaine! And you, little child! How blue its eyes are!

MARA: [*Melting into tears*] Father! father! ah! It was dead, and it was she who brought it back to life!

[*She goes away, and sits down alone*]

[*The sun goes down. It rains here and there on the plain, and the lines of the rain can be seen crossing the rays of the sun. An immense rainbow unfurls*]

VOICE OF A CHILD: Hi! Hi! look at the beautiful rainbow!

[*Other voices cease in the distance. Great flocks of pigeons fly about, turning, scattering, and alighting here and there in the stubble*]

ANNE VERCORS: The earth is set free. The place is empty.

The harvest is all gathered, and the birds of heaven

Pick up the lost grain.

PIERRE DE CRAON: Summer is over, the season sleeps in a time of quiet, everywhere the foliage rustles in the breeze of September.

The sky has turned blue again, and while the partridges call from their covert,

The buzzard soars in the liquid air.

JACQUES HURY: Everything is yours. Father! take back again all this property you vested in me.

ANNE VERCORS: No, Jacques, I no longer possess anything, and this is no more mine. He who went away will not return, and that which is once given cannot be

Taken back. Here is a new Combernon, a new Monsanvierge.

PIERRE DE CRAON: The other is dead. The virgin mountain is dead, and the scar in her side will never open again.

ANNE VERCORS: It is dead. My wife, too, is dead, my daughter is dead, the holy Maid

Has been burned and thrown to the winds, not one of her bones remains on the earth.[1]

But the King and the Pope have been given back again to France and to the whole world.

The schism comes to an end, and once more the Throne rises above all men.

I returned by Rome, I kissed the foot of Saint Peter, I ate the consecrated bread standing with people from the Four Divisions of the Earth,

While the bells of the Quirinal and of the Lateran, and the voice of Santa Maria Maggiore,

---

[1] This is a reference to Joan of Arc.

Saluted the ambassadors of these new nations who
  come from the Orient and the Occident all
  together into the City,
Asia found again, and this Atlantic world beyond
  the Pillars of Hercules!
And this very evening when the Angelus shall ring,
  at the same hour when the star Al-Zohar glows
  in the unfurled heaven,
Begins the year of Jubilee which the new Pope
  grants,
The annulment of debts, the liberation of prisoners,
  the suspension of war, the closing of the courts,
  the restitution of all property.

  PIERRE DE CRAON: Truce for one year and peace
    for one day only.

  ANNE VERCORS: What does it matter? peace is good,
    but war will find us armed.

O Pierre! this is a time when women and new-born
  infants teach sages and old men!
Here am I shocked like a Jew because the face of
  the Church is darkened, and because she totters
  on her road forsaken by all men.
And I wanted once more to clasp the empty tomb,
  to put my hand in the hole left by the cross.
But my little daughter Violaine has been wiser.
Is the object of life only to live? will the feet of
  God's children be fastened to this wretched
  earth?
It is not to live, but to die, and not to hew the cross,
  but to mount upon it, and to give all that we
  have, laughing!
There is joy, there is freedom, there is grace, there
  is eternal youth! and as God lives, the blood of
  the old man on the sacrificial cloth, near that
  of the young man,
Makes a stain as red and fresh as that of the yearling
  lamb!
O Violaine! child of grace! flesh of my flesh! As far
  as the smoky fire of my farm is distant from
  the morning star,
When on the sun's breast that beautiful virgin lays
  her illumined head,
May thy father see thee on high through all eternity
  in the place which has been kept for thee!
As God lives, where the little child goes the father
  should go also!
What is the worth of the world compared to life?
  and what is the worth of life if not to be given?
And why torment ourselves when it is so simple to
  obey?
It is thus that Violaine follows at once without hesitation the hand that takes hers.

  PIERRE DE CRAON: O father! I was the last who
    held her in my arms, because she entrusted
    herself to Pierre de Craon, knowing that there
    is no longer in his heart the desire of the flesh.
And the young body of this divine brother lay in
  my arms like a tree that has been cut down
  and droops
Already, as the glowing colour of the pomegranate

blossoms everywhere flames from the bud that
  can no longer sheathe it,
So the splendour of the angel that knows not death
  embraces our little sister.
The odour of Paradise exhaled in my arms from
  this broken tabernacle.
Do not weep, Jacques, my friend.

  ANNE VERCORS: Do not weep, my son.

  JACQUES HURY: Pierre, give me back that ring she
    gave thee.

  PIERRE DE CRAON: I cannot!

Any more than the ripened spike of corn can give
  back the seed in the earth from which sprang
  its stem.
Of that bit of gold I have made a fiery gem.
And the vessel of everlasting Day where the seed
  of the ultimate goodness of saintly souls is
  treasured.
Justitia is finished and lacks only the woman that
  I shall set there at the blossoming of my supreme lily.[1]

  ANNE VERCORS: You are powerful in works, Pierre,
    and I have seen on my way the churches you
    have brought to birth.

  PIERRE DE CRAON: Blessed be God who has made
    me a father of churches,
And who has endowed my soul with understanding
  and the sense of the three dimensions!
And who has debarred me as a leper and freed me
  from all temporal care,
To the end that I should raise up from the soil of
  France Ten Wise Virgins whose oil is never
  exhausted, and who compose a vessel of prayers![2]
What is this *soul,* or bolt of wood, that the lute-
  maker inserts between the front and the back
  of his instrument,
Compared to this great enclosed lyre, and of these
  columnar Powers in the night, whose number
  and distance I have calculated?
Never from the outside do I carve an image.
But, like father Noah, from the middle of my enormous Arch,
I work from within, and see everything rise simultaneously around me!
And what is matter which the hand can chisel compared to the spirit we strive to enshrine,
Or to the hallowed space left empty by a reverent
  soul shrinking back in the presence of its God?
Nothing is too deep for me: my wells descend as
  far as the waters of the Mother-spring.
Nothing is too high for the spire that mounts to
  heaven and steals God's lightning from him!
Pierre de Craon will die, but the Ten Virgins, his
  daughters,
Will remain like the Widow's cruse

---

[1] The church of Justitia is completed and lacks only a
statue of the Saint in whose honor the edifice was erected.
[2] **Ten Wise Virgins:** ten churches built under his supervision.

In which the flower and the sacred measures of the
oil and wine are renewed for ever.

ANNE VERCORS: Yes, Pierre. Whoever trusts himself to stone will not be deceived.

PIERRE DE CRAON: Oh, how beautiful is stone, and
how soft it is in the hands of the architect! and
how right and beautiful a thing is his whole
completed work!

How faithful is stone, and how well it preserves the
idea, and what shadows it makes!

And if a vine grows well on the least bit of wall,
and the rosebush above it blooms,

How beautiful it is, and how true it is altogether!

Have you seen my little church of l'Epine, which is
like a glowing brasier and a rosebush in full
bloom?

And Saint Jean de Vertus like a handsome young
man in the midst of the Craie Champenoise?
And Mont-Saint Martin which will be mellow
in fifty years?

And Saint-Thomas of Fond-d'Ardenne that you can
hear in the evening bellowing like a bull in the
midst of its marshes?

But Justitia that I have made last, Justitia my daughter is more beautiful!

ANNE VERCORS: I shall go there and leave my staff
for a thank-offering.

PIERRE DE CRAON: She is dedicated in my heart,
nothing is lacking, she is whole.

And for the roof,

I have found the stone I sought, not quarried by
iron,

Softer than alabaster and closer-grained than a
grindstone.

As the fragile teeth of the little Justitia serve as
a foundation for my great structure,

So also at the summit, in the wide sky, I shall set
this other Justice

Violaine the leper in glory, Violaine the blind in
the sight of everybody.

And I shall make her with her hands crossed on her
breast, like the spike of grain still half-prisoned
in its tegmen,

And her eyes blindfolded.

ANNE VERCORS: Why blindfolded?

PIERRE DE CRAON: That, seeing not, she may the
better hear

The sounds of the city and the fields, and man's
voice at the same time with the voice of God.

For she is Justice herself, who listens and conceives
in her heart the perfect harmony.

This is she who is a refuge from storms, and a shade
from the heat at the rising of the dog-star.

JACQUES HURY: But Violaine is not a stone for
me, and stone does not suffice me!

And I do not wish the light of her beautiful eyes to
be veiled!

ANNE VERCORS: The light of her soul is with us.
I have not lost thee, Violaine! How beautiful
thou art, my child!

And how beautiful is the bride when on her wed-

ding-day she shows herself to her father in her
splendid wedding-gown, sweetly embarrassed.

Walk before me, Violaine, my child, and I will follow thee. But sometimes turn thy face toward
me, that I may see thine eyes!

Violaine! Elisabeth! soon again I shall be with you.

As for you, Jacques, perform your task in your
turn, as I have done mine! The end is near.

It is here, the end of all that is given me of the
day, of the year, and of my own life!

It is six o'clock. The shadow of the Grès-qui-
va-boire reaches the brook.

Winter comes, night comes; yet a little more night,
A short watch!

All my life I have worked with the Sun and aided
him in his task.

But now, by the fireside, in the light of the lamp,
All alone I must begin the night.

PIERRE DE CRAON: O husbandman, your work is
finished. See the empty land, see the harvested
earth, and already the plough attacks the stubble!

And now, what you have begun it is my part to
complete.

As you have opened the furrow, I dig the pit wherein to preserve the grain, I prepare the tabernacle.

And as it is not you who cause the harvest to ripen,
but the sun, so is it also with grace.

And nothing, unless it issue from the seed, can
develop into the ear.

And certainly, Justice is beautiful. But how much
more beautiful

Is this fruitful tree of mankind, which the seed of
the Eucharist engenders and makes grow.

This too makes one complete whole, unified.

Ah, if all men understood architecture as I do,

Who would willingly fail to follow his vocation and
renounce the sacred place assigned to him in
the Temple?

ANNE VERCORS: Pierre de Craon, you have many
thoughts, but for me this setting sun suffices.

All my life I have done the same thing that he does,
cultivating the earth, rising and returning home
with him.

And now I go into the night, and I am not afraid,
and I know that there too all is clear and in
order, in the season of this great heavenly winter which sets all things in motion.

The night sky where everything is at work, and
which is like a great ploughing, and a room
with only one person in it.

And there the eternal Ploughman drives the seven
oxen, with his gaze set upon a fixed star,[1]

As ours is set upon the green branch that marks the
end of the furrow.

The sun and I, side by side

Have worked, and the product of our work does
not concern us. Mine is done.

---

[1] The seven oxen are the seven planets.

I bow to what must be, and now I am willing to be dissolved.

And herein lies peace for him who knows it, and joy and grief in equal parts.

My wife is dead. Violaine is dead. That is right.

I do not desire to hold any more that weak and wrinkled old hand. And as for Violaine, when she was eight years old, when she came and threw herself against my legs,

How I loved that strong little body! And little by little the impetuous, frolicsome roughness of the laughing child

Melted into the tenderness of the maiden, into the pain and heaviness of love, and when I went away

I saw already in her eyes one unknown blossom among the flowers of her springtime.

PIERRE DE CRAON: The call of death, like a solemn lily.

ANNE VERCORS: Blessed be death in which all the petitions in the Paternoster are satisfied.

PIERRE DE CRAON: For my part, it was by herself and from her innocent lips

That I received freedom and dismissal from this life.

[*The sun is in the western sky, as high as a tall tree*]

ANNE VERCORS: Behold the sun in the sky,

As he is in the pictures where the Master awakes the workman at the Eleventh Hour.

[*The door of the barn is heard to creak*]

JACQUES HURY: What is that?

ANNE VERCORS: They have come to the barn for straw

To lay in the bottom of the grave.

[*Silence:—Sound in the distance of a washer-woman beating linen*]

VOICE OF A CHILD: [*Without*]

    Marguerite of Paris, pray!

    Lend to me thy shoes of gray!

    To walk in Paradise a way!

    How fair it is!

    How warm it is!

    I hear the little bird say it is!

    He goes pa—a—a—a!

JACQUES HURY: That is not the door of the barn, it is the sound of the tomb opening!

And, having looked at me with her blind eyes, she that I loved passes to the other side.

And I too, I have looked at her like one who is blind, and I did not doubt without proofs.

I never doubted her who accused her.

I have made my choice, and she that I chose has been given to me. What shall I say? It is right.

It is right.

Happiness is not for me, but desire! it will never be torn from me.

And not Violaine, radiant and unblemished,

But the leper bending over me with a bitter smile and the devouring wound in her side!

[*Silence*]

[*The sun is behind the trees. It shines through the branches. The shadows of the leaves cover the ground and the seated people. Here and there a golden bee shines in the sunny interstices*]

ANNE VERCORS: Here am I seated, and from the top of the mountain I see all the country at my feet.

And I recognize the roads, and I count the farms and villages, and I know them by name, and all the people who live in them.

The plain is lost to view toward the north.

And elsewhere, rising again, the hill surrounds this village like a theatre.

And everywhere, all the while,

Green and pink in the spring, blue and flaxen in the summer, brown in winter or all white with snow,

Before me, at my side, around me,

I see always the Earth, like an unchanging sky all painted with changing colours.

Having a form as much its own as a person's, it is always there present with me.

Now that is finished.

How many times have I risen from my bed and gone to my work!

And now here is evening, and the sun brings home the men and the animals as if he led them by his hand.

[*He raises himself slowly and painfully, and slowly stretches out his arms to their full length, while the sun, grown yellow, covers him*]

Ah! ah!

Here am I stretching out my arms in the rays of the sun.

Evening is come! Have pity upon every man, Lord, in that hour when he has finished his task and stands before Thee like a child whose hands are being examined.

Mine are free. My day is finished. I have planted the grain and I have harvested it, and with this bread that I have made all my children have made their communion.

Now I have finished.

A moment ago there was some one with me.

And now, wife and child having gone away,

I remain alone to say grace at the empty table.

Both of them are dead, but I,

I live, on the threshold of death, and I am filled with inexplicable joy!

[*The Angelus is rung from the church down below. First toll of three strokes*]

JACQUES HURY: [*Hollowly*] The Angel of God proclaims peace to us, and the child thrills in the bosom of its mother.

[*Second toll*]

PIERRE DE CRAON: "Men of little faith, why do you weep?"

[*Third toll*]

ANNE VERCORS: "Because I go to my father and to your father."

[*Profound silence. Then peal*]

PIERRE DE CRAON: Thus the Angelus speaks as if with three voices, in May

When the unmarried man comes home, having buried his mother,

"Voice-of-the-Rose" speaks in the silvery evening.

O Violaine! O woman through whom comes temptation!

For, not yet knowing what I would do, I turned my eyes where you then did turn thine.

Truly I have always thought that joy was a good thing.

But now I have everything!

I possess everything, under my hands, and I am like a person who, seeing a tree laden with fruit,

And having mounted a ladder, feels the thick branches yield under his body.

I must talk under the tree, like a flute which is neither low nor shrill! How the water

Raises me! Thanksgiving unseals the stone of my heart!

How I live, thus! How I grow greater, thus mingled with my God, like the vine and the olive-tree.

[*The sun goes down.* Mara *turns her head toward her husband and looks at him*]

JACQUES HURY: See her, looking at me. See her returning to me with the night!

[*Sound of a cracked bell near by. First toll*]

ANNE VERCORS: It is the little bell of the sisters that rings the Angelus in its turn.

[*Silence. Then another bell is heard, very high up, at Monsanvierge, sounding in its turn the triple toll, admirably sonorous and solemn*]

JACQUES HURY: Listen!

PIERRE DE CRAON: A miracle!

ANNE VERCORS: It is Monsanvierge come to life again! The Angelus, ringing once more, brings to the listening heavens and earth the wonted tidings.

PIERRE DE CRAON: Yes, Voice-of-the-Rose, God is born!

[*Second toll of the bell of the sisters*]

[*It strikes the third note just as Monsanvierge strikes the first*]

ANNE VERCORS: God makes himself man.

JACQUES HURY: He is dead!

PIERRE DE CRAON: He is risen!

[*Third toll of the bell of the sisters. Then the peal*]

[*Pause. Then, nearly lost in the distance, are heard the three strokes of the third toll up on the heights*]

ANNE VERCORS: This is not the toll of the Angelus, it is the communion bells!

PIERRE DE CRAON: The three strokes are gathered like an ineffable sacrifice into the bosom of the Virgin without sin.

[*Their faces are turned toward the heights, they listen as if awaiting the peal, which does not come*]

EXPLICIT.

THE MADWOMAN OF CHAILLOT

By Jean Giraudoux

IN THE ADAPTATION BY MAURICE VALENCY

CHARACTERS

THE WAITER	IRMA	MME. CONSTANCE,
THE LITTLE MAN	THE SHOELACE PEDDLER	*The Madwoman of Passy*
THE PROSPECTOR	THE BROKER	MLLE. GABRIELLE,
THE PRESIDENT	THE STREET JUGGLER	*The Madwoman of St. Sulpice*
THE BARON	DR. JADIN	MME. JOSEPHINE,
THERESE	COUNTESS AURELIA,	*The Madwoman of La Concorde*
THE STREET SINGER	*The Madwoman of Chaillot*	THE PRESIDENTS
THE FLOWER GIRL	THE DOORMAN	THE PROSPECTORS
THE RAGPICKER	THE POLICEMAN	THE PRESS AGENTS
PAULETTE	PIERRE	THE LADIES
THE DEAF-MUTE	THE SERGEANT	THE ADOLPHE BERTAUTS
	THE SEWER MAN	

ACT ONE: The Café Terrace of *Chez Francis*.   ACT TWO: The Countess' Cellar—21 Rue de Chaillot.

ACT I.

SCENE.—*The café terrace at* Chez Francis, *on the Place de l'Alma in Paris. The Alma is in the stately quarter of Paris known as Chaillot, between the Champs Elysées and the Seine, across the river from the Eiffel Tower.*

Chez Francis *has several rows of tables set out under its awning, and, as it is lunch time, a good many of them are occupied. At a table, downstage, a somewhat obvious Blonde with ravishing legs is sipping a vermouth-cassis and trying hard to engage the attention of the* Prospector, *who sits at an adjacent table taking little sips of water and rolling them over his tongue with the air of a connoisseur. Downstage right, in front of the tables on the sidewalk, is the usual Paris bench, a stout and uncomfortable affair provided by the municipality for the benefit of those who prefer to sit without drinking. A* Policeman *lounges about, keeping the peace without unnecessary exertion.*

TIME.—*It is a little before noon in the Spring of next year.*

AT RISE.—*The* President *and the* Baron *enter with importance, and are ushered to a front table by the* Waiter.

THE PRESIDENT: Baron, sit down. This is a historic occasion. It must be properly celebrated. The waiter is going to bring out my special port.

THE BARON: Splendid.

THE PRESIDENT: [*Offers his cigar case*] Cigar? My private brand.

THE BARON: Thank you. You know, this all gives me the feeling of one of those enchanted mornings in the *Arabian Nights* when thieves foregather in the market place. Thieves—pashas. . . .

[*He sniffs the cigar judiciously, and begins lighting it*]

THE PRESIDENT: [*Chuckles*] Tell me about yourself.

THE BARON: Well, where shall I begin?

[*The* Street Singer *enters. He takes off a battered black felt with a flourish and begins singing an ancient mazurka*]

STREET SINGER: [*Sings*]
　　Do you hear, Mademoiselle,
　　Those musicians of hell?

THE PRESIDENT: Waiter! Get rid of that man.

WAITER: He is singing *La Belle Polonaise*.

THE PRESIDENT: I didn't ask for the program. I asked you to get rid of him. [*The* Waiter *doesn't budge. The* Singer *goes by himself*] As you were saying, Baron . . . ?

THE BARON: Well, until I was fifty . . . [*The* Flower Girl *enters through the café door, center*] my life was relatively uncomplicated. It consisted of selling off one by one the various estates left me by my father. Three years ago, I parted with my last farm. Two years ago, I lost my last mistress. And now— all that is left me is . . .

THE FLOWER GIRL: [*To the* Baron] Violets, sir?

1177

THE PRESIDENT: Run along.

[*The* Flower Girl *moves on*]

THE BARON: [*Staring after her*] So that, in short, all I have left now is my name.

THE PRESIDENT: Your name is precisely the name we need on our board of directors.

THE BARON: [*With an inclination of his head*] Very flattering.

THE PRESIDENT: You will understand when I tell you that mine has been a very different experience. I came up from the bottom. My mother spent most of her life bent over a washtub in order to send me to school. I'm eternally grateful to her, of course, but I must confess that I no longer remember her face. It was no doubt beautiful—but when I try to recall it, I see only the part she invariably showed me—her rear.

THE BARON: Very touching.

THE PRESIDENT: When I was thrown out of school for the fifth and last time, I decided to find out for myself what makes the world go round. I ran errands for an editor, a movie star, a financier. . . . I began to understand a little what life is. Then, one day, in the subway, I saw a face. . . . My rise in life dates from that day.

THE BARON: Really?

THE PRESIDENT: One look at that face, and I knew. One look at mine, and he knew. And so I made my first thousand—passing a boxful of counterfeit notes. A year later, I saw another such face. It got me a nice berth in the narcotics business. Since then, all I do is to look out for such faces. And now here I am—president of eleven corporations, director of fifty-two companies, and, beginning today, chairman of the board of the international combine in which you have been so good as to accept a post. [*The* Ragpicker *passes, sees something under the President's table, and stoops to pick it up*] Looking for something?

THE RAGPICKER: Did you drop this?

THE PRESIDENT: I never drop anything.

THE RAGPICKER: Then this hundred-franc note isn't yours?

THE PRESIDENT: Give it here.

[*The* Ragpicker *gives him the note, and goes out*]

THE BARON: Are you sure it's yours?

THE PRESIDENT: All hundred-franc notes, Baron, are mine.

THE BARON: Mr. President, there's something I've been wanting to ask you. What exactly is the purpose of our new company? Or is that an indiscreet question . . . ?

THE PRESIDENT: Indiscreet? Not a bit. Merely unusual. As far as I know, you're the first member of a board of directors ever to ask such a question.

THE BARON: Do we plan to exploit a commodity? A utility?

THE PRESIDENT: My dear sir, I haven't the faintest idea.

THE BARON: But if you don't know—who does?

THE PRESIDENT: Nobody. And at the moment, it's becoming just a trifle embarrassing. Yes, my dear Baron, since we are now close business associates, I must confess that for the time being we're in a little trouble.

THE BARON: I was afraid of that. The stock issue isn't going well?

THE PRESIDENT: No, no—on the contrary. The stock issue is going beautifully. Yesterday morning at ten o'clock we offered 500,000 shares to the general public. By 10:05 they were all snapped up at par. By 10:20, when the police finally arrived, our offices were a shambles. . . . Windows smashed—doors torn off their hinges—you never saw anything so beautiful in your life! And this morning our stock is being quoted over the counter at 124 with no sellers, and the orders are still pouring in.

THE BARON: But in that case—what is the trouble?

THE PRESIDENT: The trouble is we have a tremendous capital, and not the slightest idea of what to do with it.

THE BARON: You mean all those people are fighting to buy stock in a company that has no object?

THE PRESIDENT: My dear Baron, do you imagine that when a subscriber buys a share of stock, he has any idea of getting behind a counter or digging a ditch? A stock certificate is not a tool, like a shovel, or a commodity, like a pound of cheese. What we sell a customer is not a share in a business, but a view of the Elysian Fields. A financier is a creative artist. Our function is to stimulate the imagination. We are poets!

THE BARON: But in order to stimulate the imagination, don't you need some field of activity?

THE PRESIDENT: Not at all. What you need for that is a name. A name that will stir the pulse like a trumpet call, set the brain awhirl like a movie star, inspire reverence like a cathedral. *United General International Consolidated!* Of course that's been used. That's what a corporation needs.

THE BARON: And do we have such a name?

THE PRESIDENT: So far we have only a blank space. In that blank space a name must be printed. This name must be a masterpiece. And if I seem a little nervous today, it's because—somehow—I've racked my brains, but it hasn't come to me. Oho! Look at that! Just like the answer to a prayer . . . ! [*The* Baron *turns and stares in the direction of the* Prospector] You see? There's one. And what a beauty!

THE BARON: You mean that girl?

THE PRESIDENT: No, no, not the girl. That face. You see . . . ? The one that's drinking water.

THE BARON: You call that a face? That's a tombstone.

THE PRESIDENT: It's a milestone. It's a signpost. But is it pointing the way to steel, or wheat, or phosphates? That's what we have to find out. Ah! He sees me. He understands. He will be over.

THE BARON: And when he comes . . . ?

THE PRESIDENT: He will tell me what to do.

THE BARON: You mean business is done this way? You mean, you would trust a stranger with a matter of this importance?

THE PRESIDENT: Baron, I trust neither my wife, nor my daughter, nor my closest friend. My confidential secretary has no idea where I live. But a face like that I would trust with my inmost secrets. Though we have never laid eyes on each other before, that man and I know each other to the depths of our souls. He's no stranger—he's my brother, he's myself. You'll see. He'll be over in a minute. [*The* Deaf-Mute *enters and passes slowly among the tables, placing a small envelope before each customer. He comes to the* President's *table*] What is this anyway? A conspiracy? We don't want your envelopes. Take them away. [*The* Deaf-Mute *makes a short but pointed speech in sign language*] Waiter, what the devil's he saying?

WAITER: Only Irma understands him.

THE PRESIDENT: Irma? Who's Irma?

WAITER: [*Calls*] Irma! It's the waitress inside, sir. Irma!

[Irma *comes out. She is twenty. She has the face and figure of an angel*]

IRMA: Yes?

WAITER: These gentlemen would . . .

THE PRESIDENT: Tell this fellow to get out of here, for God's sake! [*The* Deaf-Mute *makes another manual oration*] What's he trying to say, anyway?

IRMA: He says it's an exceptionally beautiful morning, sir. . . .

THE PRESIDENT: Who asked him?

IRMA: But, he says, it was nicer before the gentleman stuck his face in it.

THE PRESIDENT: Call the manager!

[Irma *shrugs. She goes back into the restaurant. The* Deaf-Mute *walks off, left. Meanwhile a* Shoelace Peddler *has arrived*]

PEDDLER: Shoelaces? Postcards?

THE BARON: I think I could use a shoelace.

THE PRESIDENT: No, no . . .

PEDDLER: Black? Tan?

THE BARON: [*Showing his shoes*] What would you recommend?

PEDDLER: Anybody's guess.

THE BARON: Well, give me one of each.

THE PRESIDENT: [*Putting a hand on the* Baron's *arm*] Baron, although I am your chairman, I have no authority over your personal life—none, that is, except to fix the amount of your director's fees, and eventually to assign a motor car for your use. Therefore, I am asking you, as a personal favor to me, not to purchase anything from this fellow.

THE BARON: How can I resist so gracious a request? [*The* Peddler *shrugs, and passes on*] But I really don't understand . . . What difference would it make?

THE PRESIDENT: Look here, Baron. Now that you're with us, you must understand that between this irresponsible riff-raff and us there is an impenetrable barrier. *We* have no dealings whatever with *them*.

THE BARON: But without us, the poor devil will starve.

THE PRESIDENT: No, he won't. He expects nothing from us. He has a clientele of his own. He sells shoelaces exclusively to those who have no shoes. Just as the necktie peddler sells only to those who wear no shirts. And that's why these street hawkers can afford to be insolent, disrespectful and independent. They don't need us. They have a world of their own. Ah! My broker. Splendid. He's beaming.

[*The* Broker *walks up and grasps the* President's *hand with enthusiasm*]

BROKER: Mr. President! My heartiest congratulations! What a day! What a day!

[*The* Street Juggler *appears, right. He removes his coat, folds it carefully, and puts it on the bench. Then he opens a suitcase, from which he extracts a number of colored clubs*]

THE PRESIDENT: [*Presenting the* Broker] Baron Tommard, of our Board of Directors. My broker. [*The* Broker *bows. So does the* Juggler. *The* Broker *sits down and signals for a drink. The* Juggler *prepares to juggle*] What's happened?

BROKER: Listen to this. Ten o'clock this morning. The market opens. [*As he speaks, the* Juggler *provides a visual counterpart to the* Broker's *lines, his clubs rising and falling in rhythm to the* Broker's *words*] Half million shares issued at par, par value a hundred, quoted on the curb at 124 and we start buying at 126, 127, 129—and it's going up—up—up —[*The* Juggler's *clubs rise righer and higher*]— 132—133—138—141—141—141—141 . . .

THE BARON: May I ask . . . ?

THE PRESIDENT: No, no—any explanation would only confuse you.

BROKER: Ten forty-five we start selling short on rumors of a Communist plot, market bearish. . . . 141—138—133—132—and it's down—down—down —102—and we start buying back at 93. Eleven o'clock, rumors denied—95—98—101—106—124— 141—and by 11:30 we've got it all back—net profit three and a half million francs.

THE PRESIDENT: Classical. Pure. [*The* Juggler *bows again. A* Little Man *leans over from a near-by table, listening intently, and trembling with excitement*] And how many shares do we reserve to each member of the board?

BROKER: Fifty, as agreed.

THE PRESIDENT: Bit stingy, don't you think?

BROKER: All right—three thousand.

THE PRESIDENT: That's a little better. [*To the* Baron] You get the idea?

THE BARON: I'm beginning to get it.

BROKER: And now we come to the exciting part . . . [*The* Juggler *prepares to juggle with balls of fire*] Listen carefully: With 35 percent of our funded capital under Section 32 I buy 50,000 United at 36 which I immediately reconvert into 32,000 National Amalgamated two's preferred which I set up as collateral on 150,000 General Consols which I deposit against a credit of fifteen billion to buy Eastern Hennequin which I immediately turn into Argentine wheat realizing 136 percent of the original investment which naturally accrues as capital gain and not as corporate income thus saving twelve millions in taxes, and at once convert the 25 percent cotton reserve into lignite, and as our people swing into action in London and New York, I beat up the price on greige goods from 26 to 92—114—203—306— [*The* Juggler *by now is juggling his fireballs in the sky. The balls no longer return to his hands*] 404 . . .

> [*The* Little Man *can stand no more. He rushes over and dumps a sackful of money on the table*]

LITTLE MAN: Here—take it—please, take it!

BROKER: [*Frigidly*] Who is this man? What is this money?

LITTLE MAN: It's my life's savings. Every cent. I put it all in your hands.

BROKER: Can't you see we're busy?

LITTLE MAN: But I beg you . . . It's my only chance . . . Please don't turn me away.

BROKER: Oh, all right. [*He sweeps the money into his pocket*] Well?

LITTLE MAN: I thought—perhaps you'd give me a little receipt. . . .

THE PRESIDENT: My dear man, people like us don't give receipts for money. We take them.

LITTLE MAN: Oh, pardon. Of course. I was confused. Here it is. [*Scribbles a receipt*] Thank you—thank you—thank you.

> [*He rushes off joyfully. The* Street Singer *reappears*]

STREET SINGER: [*Sings*]

> Do you hear, Mademoiselle,
> Those musicians of hell?

THE PRESIDENT: What, again? Why does he keep repeating those two lines like a parrot?

WAITER: What else can he do? He doesn't know any more and the song's been out of print for years.

THE BARON: Couldn't he sing a song he knows?

WAITER: He likes this one. He hopes if he keeps singing the beginning someone will turn up to teach him the end.

THE PRESIDENT: Tell him to move on. We don't know the song.

> [*The* Professor *strolls by, swinging his cane. He overhears*]

PROFESSOR: [*Stops and addresses the* President *politely*] Nor do I, my dear sir. Nor do I. And yet, I'm in exactly the same predicament. I remember just two lines of my favorite song, as a child. A mazurka also, in case you're interested. . . .

THE PRESIDENT: I'm not.

PROFESSOR: Why is it, I wonder, that one always forgets the words of a mazurka? I suppose they just

get lost in that damnable rhythm. All I remember is: [*He sings*]

> From England to Spain
> I have drunk, it was bliss . . .

STREET SINGER: [*Walks over, and picks up the tune*]

> Red wine and champagne
> And many a kiss.

PROFESSOR: Oh, God! It all comes back to me . . . ! [*He sings*]

> Red lips and white hands I have known
> Where the nightingales dwell. . . .

THE PRESIDENT: [*Holding his hands to his ears*] Please—please . . .

STREET SINGER:

> And to each one I've whispered, "My own,"
> And to each one, I've murmured: "Farewell."

THE PRESIDENT: Farewell. Farewell.

STREET SINGER AND PROFESSOR: [*Duo*]

> But there's one I shall never forget. . . .

THE PRESIDENT: This isn't a café. It's a circus! [*The two go off, still singing: "There is one that's engraved in my heart." The* Prospector *gets up slowly and walks toward the* President's *table. He looks down without a word. There is a tense silence*]

PROSPECTOR: Well?

THE PRESIDENT: I need a name.

PROSPECTOR: [*Nods, with complete comprehension*] I need fifty thousand.

THE PRESIDENT: For a corporation.

PROSPECTOR: For a woman.

THE PRESIDENT: Immediately.

PROSPECTOR: Before evening.

THE PRESIDENT: Something . . .

PROSPECTOR: Unusual?

THE PRESIDENT: Something . . .

PROSPECTOR: Provocative?

THE PRESIDENT: Something . . .

PROSPECTOR: Practical.

THE PRESIDENT: Yes.

PROSPECTOR: Fifty thousand. Cash.

THE PRESIDENT: I'm listening.

PROSPECTOR: *International Substrate of Paris, Inc.*

THE PRESIDENT: [*Snaps his fingers*] That's it! [*To the* Broker] Pay him off. [*The* Broker *pays with the* Little Man's *money*] Now—what does it mean?

PROSPECTOR: It means what it says. I'm a prospector.

THE PRESIDENT: [*Rises*] A prospector! Allow me to shake your hand. Baron. You are in the presence of one of nature's noblemen. Shake his hand. This is Baron Tommard. [*They shake hands*] It is this man, my dear Baron, who smells out in the bowels of the earth those deposits of metal or liquid on which can be founded the only social unit of which our age is capable—the corporation. Sit down, please. [*They all sit*] And now that we have a name . . .

PROSPECTOR: You need a property.

THE PRESIDENT: Precisely.

PROSPECTOR: I have one.

THE PRESIDENT: A claim?

PROSPECTOR: Terrific.

THE PRESIDENT: Foreign?

PROSPECTOR: French.

THE BARON: In Indo-China?

BROKER: Morocco?

THE PRESIDENT: In France?

PROSPECTOR: [*Matter-of-fact*] In Paris.

THE PRESIDENT: In Paris? You've been prospecting in Paris?

THE BARON: For women, no doubt.

THE PRESIDENT: For art?

BROKER: For gold?

PROSPECTOR: Oil.

BROKER: He's crazy.

THE PRESIDENT: Sh! He's inspired.

PROSPECTOR: You think I'm crazy. Well, they thought Columbus was crazy.

THE BARON: Oil in Paris?

BROKER: But how is it possible?

PROSPECTOR: It's not only possible. It's certain.

THE PRESIDENT: Tell us.

PROSPECTOR: You don't know, my dear sir, what treasures Paris conceals. Paris is the least prospected place in the world. We've gone over the rest of the planet with a fine-tooth comb. But has anyone ever thought of looking for oil in Paris? Nobody. Before me, that is.

THE PRESIDENT: Genius!

PROSPECTOR: No. Just a practical man. I used my head.

THE BARON: But why has nobody ever thought of this before?

PROSPECTOR: The treasures of the earth, my dear sir, are not easy to find nor to get at. They are invariably guarded by dragons. Doubtless there is some reason for this. For once we've dug out and consumed the internal ballast of the planet, the chances are it will shoot off on some irresponsible tangent and smash itself up in the sky. Well, that's the risk we take. Anyway, that's not my business. A prospector has enough to worry about.

THE BARON: I know—snakes—tarantulas—fleas . . .

PROSPECTOR: Worse than that, sir. Civilization.

THE PRESIDENT: Does that annoy you?

PROSPECTOR: Civilization gets in our way all the time. In the first place, it covers the earth with cities and towns which are damned awkward to dig up when you want to see what's underneath. It's not only the real-estate people—you can always do business with them—it's human sentimentality. How do you do business with that?

THE PRESIDENT: I see what you mean.

PROSPECTOR: They say that where we pass, nothing ever grows again. What of it? Is a park any better than a coal mine? What's a mountain got that a slag pile hasn't? What would you rather have in your garden—an almond tree or an oil well?

THE PRESIDENT: Well . . .

PROSPECTOR: Exactly. But what's the use of arguing with these fools? Imagine the choicest place you ever saw for an excavation, and what do they put there? A playground for children! Civilization!

THE PRESIDENT: Just show us the point where you want to start digging. We'll do the rest. Even if it's in the middle of the Louvre. Where's the oil?

PROSPECTOR: Perhaps you think it's easy to make an accurate fix in an area like Paris where everything conspires to put you off the scent? Women—perfume—flowers—history. You can talk all you like about geology, but an oil deposit, gentlemen, has to be smelled out. I have a good nose. I go further. I have a phenomenal nose. But the minute I get the right whiff—the minute I'm on the scent—a fragrance rises from what I take to be the spiritual deposits of the past—and I'm completely at sea. Now take this very point, for example, this very spot.

THE BARON: You mean—right here in Chaillot?

PROSPECTOR: Right under here.

THE PRESIDENT: Good heavens!

[*He looks under his chair*]

PROSPECTOR: It's taken me months to locate this spot.

THE BARON: But what in the world makes you think . . . ?

PROSPECTOR: Do you know this place, Baron?

THE BARON: Well, I've been sitting here for thirty years.

PROSPECTOR: Did you ever taste the water?

THE BARON: The water? Good God, no!

PROSPECTOR: It's plain to see that you are no prospector! A prospector, Baron, is addicted to water as a drunkard to wine. Water, gentlemen, is the one substance from which the earth can conceal nothing. It sucks out its innermost secrets and brings them to our very lips. Well—beginning at Notre Dame, where I first caught the scent of oil three months ago, I worked my way across Paris, glassful by glassful, sampling the water, until at last I came to this café. And here—just two days ago—I took a sip. My heart began to thump. Was it possible that I was deceived? I took another, a third, a fourth, a fifth. I was trembling like a leaf. But there was no mistake. Each time that I drank, my taste buds thrilled to the most exquisite flavor known to a prospector—the flavor of— [*With utmost lyricism*] Petroleum!

THE PRESIDENT: Waiter! Some water and four glasses. Hurry. This round, gentlemen, is on me. And as a toast—I shall propose International Substrate of Paris, Incorporated. [*The Waiter brings a decanter and the glasses. The President pours out the water amid profound silence. They taste it with the air of connoisseurs savoring something that has never before passed human lips. Then they look at each other doubtfully. The Prospector pours himself a second glass and drinks it off*] Well . . .

BROKER: Ye-es . . .

THE BARON: Mm . . .

PROSPECTOR: Get it?

THE BARON: Tastes queer.

PROSPECTOR: That's it. To the unpracticed palate it tastes queer. But to the taste buds of the expert—ah!

THE BARON: Still, there's one thing I don't quite understand . . .

PROSPECTOR: Yes?

THE BARON: This café doesn't have its own well, does it?

PROSPECTOR: Of course not. This is Paris water.

BROKER: Then why should it taste different here than anywhere else?

PROSPECTOR: Because, my dear sir, the pipes that carry this water pass deep through the earth, and the earth just here is soaked with oil, and this oil permeates the pores of the iron and flavors the water it carries. Ever so little, yes—but quite enough to betray its presence to the sensitive tongue of the specialist.

THE BARON: I see.

PROSPECTOR: I don't say everyone is capable of tasting it. No. But I—I can detect the presence of oil in water that has passed within fifteen miles of a deposit. Under special circumstances, twenty.

THE PRESIDENT: Phenomenal!

PROSPECTOR: And so here I am with the greatest discovery of the age on my hands—but the blasted authorities won't let me drill a single well unless I show them the oil! Now how can I show them the oil unless they let me dig? Completely stymied! Eh?

THE PRESIDENT: What? A man like you?

PROSPECTOR: That's what they think. That's what they want. Have you noticed the strange glamor of the women this morning? And the quality of the sunshine? And this extraordinary convocation of vagabonds buzzing about protectively like bees around a hive? Do you know why it is? Because they know. It's a plot to distract us, to turn us from our purpose. Well, let them try. I know there's oil here. And I'm going to dig it up, even if I . . . [*He smiles*] Shall I tell you my little plan?

THE PRESIDENT: By all means.

PROSPECTOR: Well . . . For heaven's sake, what's that?

[*At this point, the* Madwoman *enters. She is dressed in the grand fashion of 1885, a taffeta skirt with an immense train—which she has gathered up by means of a clothespin—ancient button shoes, and a hat in the style of Marie Antoinette. She wears a lorgnette on a chain, and an enormous cameo pin at her throat. In her hand she carries a small basket. She walks in with great dignity, extracts a dinner bell from the bosom of her dress, and rings it sharply.* Irma *appears*]

COUNTESS: Are my bones ready, Irma?

IRMA: There won't be much today, Countess. We had broilers. Can you wait? While the gentleman inside finishes eating?

COUNTESS: And my gizzard?

IRMA: I'll try to get it away from him.

COUNTESS: If he eats my gizzard, save me the giblets. They will do for the tomcat that lives under the bridge. He likes a few giblets now and again.

IRMA: Yes, Countess.

[Irma *goes back into the café. The* Countess *takes a few steps and stops in front of the* President's *table. She examines him with undisguised disapproval*]

THE PRESIDENT: Waiter. Ask that woman to move on.

WAITER: Sorry, sir. This is her café.

THE PRESIDENT: Is she the manager of the café?

WAITER: She's the Madwoman of Chaillot.

THE PRESIDENT: A madwoman? She's mad?

WAITER: Who says she's mad?

THE PRESIDENT: You just said so yourself.

WAITER: Look, sir. You asked me who she was. And I told you. What's mad about her? She's the Madwoman of Chaillot.

THE PRESIDENT: Call a policeman.

[*The* Countess *whistles through her fingers. At once, the* Doorman *runs out of the café. He has three scarves in his hands*]

COUNTESS: Have you found it? My feather boa?

DOORMAN: Not yet, Countess. Three scarves. But no boa.

COUNTESS: It's five years since I lost it. Surely you've had time to find it.

DOORMAN: Take one of these, Countess. Nobody's claimed them.

COUNTESS: A boa like that doesn't vanish, you know. A feather boa nine feet long!

DOORMAN: How about this blue one?

COUNTESS: With my pink ruffle and my green veil? You're joking! Let me see the yellow. [*She tries it on*] How does it look?

DOORMAN: Terrific.

[*With a magnificent gesture, she flings the scarf about her, upsetting the* President's *glass and drenching his trousers with water. She stalks off without a glance at him*]

THE PRESIDENT: Waiter! I'm making a complaint.

WAITER: Against whom?

THE PRESIDENT: Against her! Against you! The whole gang of you! That singer! That shoelace peddler! That female lunatic! Or whatever you call her!

THE BARON: Calm yourself, Mr. President. . . .

THE PRESIDENT: I'll do nothing of the sort! Baron, the first thing we have to do is to get rid of these people! Good heavens, look at them! Every size, shape, color and period of history imaginable. It's utter anarchy! I tell you, sir, the only safeguard of order and discipline in the modern world is a standardized worker with interchangeable parts. That would solve the entire problem of management. Here, the manager . . . And there—one composite drudge grunting and sweating all over the world.

Just we two. Ah, how beautiful! How easy on the eyes! How restful for the conscience!

THE BARON: Yes, yes—of course.

THE PRESIDENT: Order. Symmetry. Balance. But instead of that, what? Here in Chaillot, the very citadel of management, these insolent phantoms of the past come to beard us with their raffish individualism—with the right of the voiceless to sing, of the dumb to make speeches, of trousers to have no seats and bosoms to have dinner bells!

THE BARON: But, after all, do these people matter?

THE PRESIDENT: My dear sir, wherever the poor are happy, and the servants are proud, and the mad are respected, our power is at an end. Look at that! That waiter! That madwoman! That flower girl! Do I get that sort of service? And suppose that I—president of twelve corporations and ten times a millionaire—were to stick a gladiolus in my buttonhole and start yelling—[He tinkles his spoon in a glass violently, yelling] Are my bones ready, Irma?

THE BARON: [Reprovingly] Mr. President . . .

[People at the adjoining tables turn and stare with raised eyebrows. The Waiter starts to come over]

THE PRESIDENT: You see? Now.

PROSPECTOR: We were discussing my plan.

THE PRESIDENT: Ah yes, your plan. [He glances in the direction of the Madwoman's table] Careful—she's looking at us.

PROSPECTOR: Do you know what a bomb is?

THE PRESIDENT: I'm told they explode.

PROSPECTOR: Exactly. You see that white building across the river. Do you happen to know what that is?

THE PRESIDENT: I do not.

PROSPECTOR: That's the office of the City Architect. That man has stubbornly refused to give me a permit to drill for oil anywhere within the limits of the city of Paris. I've tried everything with him—influence, bribes, threats. He says I'm crazy. And now . . .

THE PRESIDENT: Oh, my God! What is this one trying to sell us?

[A little Old Man enters left, and doffs his hat politely. He is somewhat ostentatiously respectable—gloved, pomaded, and carefully dressed, with a white handkerchief peeping out of his breast pocket]

DR. JADIN: Nothing but health, sir. Or rather the health of the feet. But remember—as the foot goes, so goes the man. May I present myself . . . ? Dr. Gaspard Jadin, French Navy, retired. Former specialist in the extraction of ticks and chiggers. At present specializing in the extraction of bunions and corns. In case of sudden emergency, Martial the waiter will furnish my home address. My office is here, second row, third table, week days, twelve to five. Thank you very much.

[He sits at his table]

WAITER: Your vermouth, Doctor?

DR. JADIN: My vermouth. My vermouths. How are your gallstones today, Martial?

WAITER: Fine. Fine. They rattle like anything.

DR. JADIN: Splendid. [He spies the Countess] Good morning, Countess. How's the floating kidney? Still afloat? [She nods graciously] Splendid. Splendid. So long as it floats, it can't sink.

THE PRESIDENT: This is impossible! Let's go somewhere else.

PROSPECTOR: No. It's nearly noon.

THE PRESIDENT: Yes. It is. Five to twelve.

PROSPECTOR: In five minutes' time you're going to see that City Architect blown up, building and all—boom!

BROKER: Are you serious?

PROSPECTOR: That imbecile has no one to blame but himself. Yesterday noon, he got my ultimatum—he's had twenty-four hours to think it over. No permit? All right. Within two minutes my agent is going to drop a little package in his coal bin. And three minutes after that, precisely at noon . . .

THE BARON: You prospectors certainly use modern methods.

PROSPECTOR: The method may be modern. But the idea is old. To get at the treasure, it has always been necessary to slay the dragon. I guarantee that after this, the City Architect will be more reasonable. The new one, I mean.

THE PRESIDENT: Don't you think we're sitting a little close for comfort?

PROSPECTOR: Oh no, no. Don't worry. And, above all, don't stare. We may be watched. [A clock strikes] Why, that's noon. Something's wrong! Good God! What's this? [A Policeman staggers in bearing a lifeless body on his shoulders in the manner prescribed as "The Fireman's Lift"] It's Pierre! My agent! [He walks over with affected nonchalance] I say, Officer, what's that you've got?

POLICEMAN: Drowned man.

[He puts him down on the bench]

WAITER: He's not drowned. His clothes are dry. He's been slugged.

POLICEMAN: Slugged is also correct. He was just jumping off the bridge when I came along and pulled him back. I slugged him, naturally, so he wouldn't drag me under. Life Saving Manual, Rule 5: "In cases where there is danger of being dragged under, it is necessary to render the subject unconscious by means of a sharp blow." He's had that.

[He loosens the clothes and begins applying artificial respiration]

PROSPECTOR: The stupid idiot! What the devil did he do with the bomb? That's what comes of employing amateurs!

THE PRESIDENT: You don't think he'll give you away?

PROSPECTOR: Don't worry. [He walks over to the Policeman] Say, what do you think you're doing?

POLICEMAN: Lifesaving. Artificial respiration. First aid to the drowning.

PROSPECTOR: But he's not drowning.

POLICEMAN: But he thinks he is.

PROSPECTOR: You'll never bring him round that way, my friend. That's meant for people who drown in water. It's no good at all for those who drown without water.

POLICEMAN: What am I supposed to do? I've just been sworn in. It's my first day on the beat. I can't afford to get in trouble. I've got to go by the book.

PROSPECTOR: Perfectly simple. Take him back to the bridge where you found him and throw him in. Then you can save his life and you'll get a medal. This way, you'll only get fined for slugging an innocent man.

POLICEMAN: What do you mean, innocent? He was just going to jump when I grabbed him.

PROSPECTOR: Have you any proof of that?

POLICEMAN: Well, I saw him.

PROSPECTOR: Written proof? Witnesses?

POLICEMAN: No, but . . .

PROSPECTOR: Then don't waste time arguing. You're in trouble. Quick—before anybody notices—throw him in and dive after him. It's the only way out.

POLICEMAN: But I don't swim.

THE PRESIDENT: You'll learn how on the way down. Before you were born, did you know how to breathe?

POLICEMAN: [Convinced] All right. Here we go.

[He starts lifting the body]

DR. JADIN: One moment, please. I don't like to interfere, but it's my professional duty to point out that medical science has definitely established the fact of intra-uterine respiration. Consequently, this policeman, even before he was born, knew not only how to breathe but also how to cough, hiccup and belch.

THE PRESIDENT: Suppose he did—how does it concern you?

DR. JADIN: On the other hand, medical science has never established the fact of intra-uterine swimming or diving. Under the circumstances, we are forced to the opinion, Officer, that if you dive in you will probably drown.

POLICEMAN: You think so?

PROSPECTOR: Who asked you for an opinion?

THE PRESIDENT: Pay no attention to that quack, Officer.

DR. JADIN: Quack, sir?

PROSPECTOR: This is not a medical matter. It's a legal problem. The officer has made a grave error. He's new. We're trying to help him.

BROKER: He's probably afraid of the water.

POLICEMAN: Nothing of the sort. Officially, I'm afraid of nothing. But I always follow doctor's orders.

DR. JADIN: You see, Officer, when a child is born . . . .

PROSPECTOR: Now, what does he care about when a child is born? He's got a dying man on his hands. . . . Officer, if you want my advice . . .

POLICEMAN: It so happens, I care a lot about when a child is born. It's part of my duty to aid and assist any woman in childbirth or labor.

THE PRESIDENT: Can you imagine!

POLICEMAN: Is it true, Doctor, what they say, that when you have twins, the first born is considered to be the youngest?

DR. JADIN: Quite correct. And what's more, if the twins happen to be born at midnight on December 31st, the older is a whole year younger. He does his military service a year later. That's why you have to keep your eyes open. And that's the reason why a queen always gives birth before witnesses. . . .

POLICEMAN: God! The things a policeman is supposed to know! Doctor, what does it mean if, when I get up in the morning sometimes . . .

PROSPECTOR: [Nudging the President meaningfully] The old woman . . .

BROKER: Come on, Baron.

THE PRESIDENT: I think we'd better all run along.

PROSPECTOR: Leave him to me.

THE PRESIDENT: I'll see you later.

[The President steals off with the Broker and the Baron]

POLICEMAN: [Still in conference with Dr. Jadin] But what's really worrying me, Doctor, is this—don't you think it's a bit risky for a man to marry after forty-five?

[The Broker runs in breathlessly]

BROKER: Officer! Officer!

POLICEMAN: What's the trouble?

BROKER: Quick! Two women are calling for help—on the sidewalk—Avenue Wilson!

POLICEMAN: Two women at once? Standing up or lying down?

BROKER: You'd better go and see. Quick!

PROSPECTOR: You'd better take the doctor with you.

POLICEMAN: Come along, Doctor, come along. . . . [Pointing to Pierre] Tell him to wait till I get back. Come along, Doctor.

[He runs out, the Doctor following. The Prospector moves over toward Pierre, but Irma crosses in front of him and takes the boy's hand]

IRMA: How beautiful he is! Is he dead, Martial?

WAITER: [Handing her a pocket mirror] Hold this mirror to his mouth. If it clouds over . . .

IRMA: It clouds over.

WAITER: He's alive.

[He holds out his hand for the mirror]

IRMA: Just a sec— [She rubs it clean and looks at herself intently. Before handing it back, she fixes her hair and applies her lipstick. Meanwhile the Prospector tries to get around the other side, but the Countess' eagle eye drives him off. He shrugs his shoulders and exits with the Baron] Oh, look—he's opened his eyes!

[Pierre *opens his eyes, stares intently at* Irma *and closes them again with the expression of a man who is among the angels*]

PIERRE: [*Murmurs*] Oh! How beautiful!

VOICE: [*From within the café*] Irma!

IRMA: Coming. Coming.

[*She goes in, not without a certain reluctance. The* Countess *at once takes her place on the bench, and also the young man's hand.* Pierre *sits up suddenly, and finds himself staring, not at* Irma, *but into the very peculiar face of the* Countess. *His expression changes*]

COUNTESS: You're looking at my iris? Isn't it beautiful?

PIERRE: Very.

[*He drops back, exhausted*]

COUNTESS: The Sergeant was good enough to say it becomes me. But I no longer trust his taste. Yesterday, the flower girl gave me a lily, and he said it didn't suit me.

PIERRE: [*Weakly*] It's beautiful.

COUNTESS: He'll be very happy to know that you agree with him. He's really quite sensitive. [*She calls*] Sergeant!

PIERRE: No, please—don't call the police.

COUNTESS: But I must. I think I hurt his feelings.

PIERRE: Let me go, Madame.

COUNTESS: No, no. Stay where you are. Sergeant!

[Pierre *struggles weakly to get up*]

PIERRE: Please let me go.

COUNTESS: I'll do nothing of the sort. When you let someone go, you never see him again. I let Charlotte Mazumet go. I never saw her again.

PIERRE: Oh, my head.

COUNTESS: I let Adolphe Bertaut go. And I was holding him. And I never saw him again.

PIERRE: Oh, God!

COUNTESS: Except once. Thirty years later. In the market. He had changed a great deal—he didn't know me. He sneaked a melon from right under my nose, the only good one of the year. Ah, here we are. Sergeant!

[*The* Police Sergeant *comes in with importance*]

SERGEANT: I'm in a hurry, Countess.

COUNTESS: With regard to the iris. This young man agrees with you. He says it suits me.

SERGEANT: [*Going*] There's a man drowning in the Seine.

COUNTESS: He's not drowning in the Seine. He's drowning here. Because I'm holding him tight—as I should have held Adolphe Bertaut. But if I let him go, I'm sure he will go and drown in the Seine. He's a lot better looking than Adolphe Bertaut, wouldn't you say?

[Pierre *sighs deeply*]

SERGEANT: How would I know?

COUNTESS: I've shown you his photograph. The one with the bicycle.

SERGEANT: Oh, yes. The one with the harelip.

COUNTESS: I've told you a hundred times! Adolphe

Bertaut had no harelip. That was a scratch in the negative. [*The* Sergeant *takes out his notebook and pencil*] What are you doing?

SERGEANT: I am taking down the drowned man's name, given name and date of birth.

COUNTESS: You think that's going to stop him from jumping in the river? Don't be silly, Sergeant. Put that book away and try to console him.

SERGEANT: I should try and console him?

COUNTESS: When people want to die, it is your job as a guardian of the state to speak out in praise of life. Not mine.

SERGEANT: I should speak out in praise of life?

COUNTESS: I assume you have some motive for interfering with people's attempts to kill each other, and rob each other, and run each other over? If you believe that life has some value, tell him what it is. Go on.

SERGEANT: Well, all right. Now look, young man . . .

COUNTESS: His name is Roderick.

PIERRE: My name is not Roderick.

COUNTESS: Yes, it is. It's noon. At noon all men become Roderick.

SERGEANT: Except Adolphe Bertaut.

COUNTESS: In the days of Adolphe Bertaut, we were forced to change the men when we got tired of their names. Nowadays, we're more practical—each hour on the hour all names are automatically changed. The men remain the same. But you're not here to discuss Adolphe Bertaut, Sergeant. You're here to convince the young man that life is worth living.

PIERRE: It isn't.

SERGEANT: Quiet. Now then—what was the idea of jumping off the bridge, anyway?

COUNTESS: The idea was to land in the river. Roderick doesn't seem to be at all confused about that.

SERGEANT: Now how can I convince anybody that life is worth living if you keep interrupting all the time?

COUNTESS: I'll be quiet.

SERGEANT: First of all, Mr. Roderick, you have to realize that suicide is a crime against the state. And why is it a crime against the state? Because every time anybody commits suicide, that means one soldier less for the army, one taxpayer less for the . . .

COUNTESS: Sergeant, isn't there something about life that you really enjoy?

SERGEANT: That I enjoy?

COUNTESS: Well, surely, in all these years, you must have found something worth living for. Some secret pleasure, or passion. Don't blush. Tell him about it.

SERGEANT: Who's blushing? Well, naturally, yes— I have my passions—like everybody else. The fact is, since you ask me—I love—to play—casino. And if the gentleman would like to join me, by and by when I go off duty, we can sit down to a nice little game in the back room with a nice cold glass of beer. If he wants to kill an hour, that is.

COUNTESS: He doesn't want to kill an hour. He wants to kill himself. Well? Is that all the police force has to offer by way of earthly bliss?

SERGEANT: Huh? You mean— [*He jerks a thumb in the direction of the pretty* Blonde, *who has just been joined by a* Brunette *of the same stamp*] Paulette?

[*The young man groans*]

COUNTESS: You're not earning your salary, Sergeant. I defy anybody to stop dying on your account.

SERGEANT: Go ahead, if you can do any better. But you won't find it easy.

COUNTESS: Oh, this is not a desperate case at all. A young man who has just fallen in love with someone who has fallen in love with him!

PIERRE: She hasn't. How could she?

COUNTESS: Oh, yes, she has. She was holding your hand, just as I'm holding it, when all of a sudden . . . Did you ever know Marshal Canrobert's niece?

SERGEANT: How could he know Marshal Canrobert's niece?

COUNTESS: Lots of people knew her—when she was alive. [Pierre *begins to struggle energetically*] No, No, Roderick—stop—stop!

SERGEANT: You see? You won't do any better than I did.

COUNTESS: No? Let's bet. I'll bet my iris against one of your gold buttons. Right?—Roderick, I know very well why you tried to drown yourself in the river.

PIERRE: You don't at all.

COUNTESS: It's because that Prospector wanted you to commit a horrible crime.

PIERRE: How did you know that?

COUNTESS: He stole my boa, and now he wants you to kill me.

PIERRE: Not exactly.

COUNTESS: It wouldn't be the first time they've tried it. But I'm not so easy to get rid of, my boy, oh, no . . . Because . . .

[*The* Doorman *rides in on his bicycle. He winks at the* Sergeant, *who has now seated himself while the* Waiter *serves him a beer*]

DOORMAN: Take it easy, Sergeant.

SERGEANT: I'm busy saving a drowning man.

COUNTESS: They can't kill me because—I have no desire to die.

PIERRE: You're fortunate.

COUNTESS: To be alive is to be fortunate, Roderick. Of course, in the morning, when you first awake, it does not always seem so very gay. When you take your hair out of the drawer, and your teeth out of the glass, you are apt to feel a little out of place in this world. Especially if you've just been dreaming that you're a little girl on a pony looking for strawberries in the woods. But all you need to feel the call of life once more is a letter in your mail giving you your schedule for the day—your mending, your shopping, that letter to your grandmother that you never seem to get around to. And so, when you've washed your face in rosewater, and powdered it—not with this awful rice-powder they sell nowadays, which does nothing for the skin, but with a cake of pure white starch—and put on your pins, your rings, your brooches, bracelets, earrings and pearls—in short, when you are dressed for your morning coffee—and have had a good look at yourself—not in the glass, naturally—it lies—but in the side of the brass gong that once belonged to Admiral Courbet —then, Roderick, then you're armed, you're strong, you're ready—you can begin again.

[Pierre *is listening now intently. There are tears in his eyes*]

PIERRE: Oh, Madame . . . ! Oh, Madame . . . !

COUNTESS: After that, everything is pure delight. First the morning paper. Not, of course, these current sheets full of lies and vulgarity. I always read the *Gaulois,* the issue of March 22, 1903. It's by far the best. It has some delightful scandal, some excellent fashion notes, and, of course, the last-minute bulletin on the death of Leonide Leblanc. She used to live next door, poor woman, and when I learn of her death every morning, it gives me quite a shock. I'd gladly lend you my copy, but it's in tatters.

SERGEANT: Couldn't we find him a copy in some library?

COUNTESS: I doubt it. And so, when you've taken your fruit salts—not in water, naturally—no matter what they say, it's water that gives you gas—but with a bit of spiced cake—then in sunlight or rain, Chaillot calls. It is time to dress for your morning walk. This takes much longer, of course—without a maid, impossible to do it under an hour, what with your corset, corset-cover and drawers all of which lace or button in the back. I asked Madame Lanvin, a while ago, to fit the drawers with zippers. She was quite charming, but she declined. She thought it would spoil the style.

[*The* Deaf-Mute *comes in*]

WAITER: I know a place where they put zippers on anything.

[*The* Ragpicker *enters*]

COUNTESS: I think Lanvin knows best. But I really manage very well, Martial. What I do now is, I lace them up in front, then twist them around to the back. It's quite simple, really. Then you choose a lorgnette, and then the usual fruitless search for the feather boa that the Prospector stole—I know it was he: he didn't dare look me in the eye—and then all you need is a rubber band to slip around your parasol—I lost the catch the day I struck the cat that was stalking the pigeon—it was worth it—ah, that day I earned my wages!

THE RAGPICKER: Countess, if you can use it, I found a nice umbrella catch the other day with a cat's eye in it.

COUNTESS: Thank you, Ragpicker. They say these eyes sometimes come to life and fill with tears. I'd be afraid . . .

PIERRE: Go on, Madame, go on . . .

COUNTESS: Ah! So life is beginning to interest you, is it? You see how beautiful it is?

PIERRE: What a fool I've been!

COUNTESS: Then, Roderick, I begin my rounds. I have my cats to feed, my dogs to pet, my plants to water. I have to see what the evil ones are up to in the district—those who hate people, those who hate plants, those who hate animals. I watch them sneaking off in the morning to put on their disguises—to the baths, to the beauty parlors, to the barbers. But they can't deceive me. And when they come out again with blonde hair and false whiskers, to pull up my flowers and poison my dogs, I'm there, and I'm ready. All you have to do to break their power is to cut across their path from the left. That isn't always easy. Vice moves swiftly. But I have a good long stride and I generally manage. . . . Right, my friends? [*The* Waiter *and the* Ragpicker *nod their heads with evident approval*] Yes, the flowers have been marvelous this year. And the butcher's dog on the Rue Bizet, in spite of that wretch that tried to poison him, is friskier than ever. . . .

SERGEANT: That dog had better look out. He has no license.

COUNTESS: He doesn't seem to feel the need for one.

THE RAGPICKER: The Duchess de la Rochefoucauld's whippet is getting awfully thin. . . .

COUNTESS: What can I do? She bought that dog full grown from a kennel where they didn't know his right name. A dog without his right name is bound to get thin.

THE RAGPICKER: I've got a friend who knows a lot about dogs—an Arab . . .

COUNTESS: Ask him to call on the Duchess. She receives Thursdays, five to seven. You see, then, Roderick. That's life. Does it appeal to you now?

PIERRE: It seems marvelous.

COUNTESS: Ah! Sergeant. My button. [*The* Sergeant *gives her his button and goes off. At this point the* Prospector *enters*] That's only this morning. Wait till I tell you about the afternoon!

PROSPECTOR: All right, Pierre. Come along now.

PIERRE: I'm perfectly all right here.

PROSPECTOR: I said, come along now.

PIERRE: [*To the* Countess] I'd better go, Madame.

COUNTESS: No.

PIERRE: It's no use. Please let go my hand.

PROSPECTOR: Madame, will you oblige me by letting my friend go?

COUNTESS: I will not oblige you in any way.

PROSPECTOR: All right. Then I'll oblige you . . . !

[*He tries to push her away. She catches up a soda water siphon and squirts it in his face*]

PIERRE: Countess . . .

COUNTESS: Stay where you are. This man isn't going to take you away. In the first place, I shall need you in a few minutes to take me home. I'm all alone here and I'm very easily frightened.

[*The* Prospector *makes a second attempt to drag* Pierre *away. The* Countess *cracks him over the skull with the siphon. They join battle. The* Countess *whistles. The* Doorman *comes, then the other* Vagabonds, *and lastly the* Police Sergeant]

PROSPECTOR: Officer! Arrest this woman!

SERGEANT: What's the trouble here?

PROSPECTOR: She refuses to let this man go.

SERGEANT: Why should she?

PROSPECTOR: It's against the law for a woman to detain a man on the street.

IRMA: Suppose it's her son whom she's found again after twenty years?

THE RAGPICKER: [*Gallantly*] Or her long-lost brother? The Countess is not so old.

PROSPECTOR: Officer, this is a clear case of disorderly conduct.

[*The* Deaf-Mute *interrupts with frantic signals*]

COUNTESS: Irma, what is the Deaf-Mute saying?

IRMA: [*Interpreting*] The young man is in danger of his life. He mustn't go with him.

PROSPECTOR: What does he know?

IRMA: He knows everything.

PROSPECTOR: Officer, I'll have to take your number.

COUNTESS: Take his number. It's 2133. It adds up to nine. It will bring you luck.

SERGEANT: Countess, between ourselves, what are you holding him for, anyway?

COUNTESS: I'm holding him because it's very pleasant to hold him. I've never really held anybody before, and I'm making the most of it. And because so long as *I* hold him, he's free.

PROSPECTOR: Pierre, I'm giving you fair warning. . . .

COUNTESS: And I'm holding him because Irma wants me to hold him. Because if I let him go, it will break her heart.

IRMA: Oh, Countess!

SERGEANT: [*To the* Prospector] All right, you—move on. Nobody's holding you. You're blocking traffic. Move on.

PROSPECTOR: [*Menacingly*] I have your number. [*And murderously, to* Pierre] You'll regret this, Pierre.

[*Exit* Prospector]

PIERRE: Thank you, Countess.

COUNTESS: They're blackmailing you, are they? [Pierre *nods*] What have you done? Murdered somebody?

PIERRE: No.

COUNTESS: Stolen something?

PIERRE: No.

COUNTESS: What then?

PIERRE: I forged a signature.

COUNTESS: Whose signature?

PIERRE: My father's. To a note.

COUNTESS: And this man has the paper, I suppose?

PIERRE: He promised to tear it up, if I did what he wanted. But I couldn't do it.

COUNTESS: But the man is mad! Does he really want to destroy the whole neighborhood?

PIERRE: He wants to destroy the whole city.

COUNTESS: [Laughs] Fantastic.

PIERRE: It's not funny, Countess. He can do it. He's mad, but he's powerful, and he has friends. Their machines are already drawn up and waiting. In three months' time you may see the city covered by a forest of derricks and drills.

COUNTESS: But what are they looking for? Have they lost something?

PIERRE: They're looking for oil. They're convinced that Paris is sitting on a lake of oil.

COUNTESS: Suppose it is. What harm does it do?

PIERRE: They want to bring the oil to the surface, Countess.

COUNTESS: [Laughs] How silly! Is that a reason to destroy a city? What do they want with this oil?

PIERRE: They want to make war, Countess.

COUNTESS: Oh, dear, let's forget about these horrible men. The world is beautiful. It's happy. That's how God made it. No man can change it.

WAITER: Ah, Countess, if you only knew . . .

COUNTESS: If I only knew what?

WAITER: Shall we tell her now? Shall we tell her?

COUNTESS: What is it you are hiding from me?

THE RAGPICKER: Nothing, Countess. It's you who are hiding.

WAITER: You tell her. You've been a pitchman. You can talk.

ALL: Tell her. Tell her. Tell her.

COUNTESS: You're frightening me, my friends. Go on. I'm listening.

THE RAGPICKER: Countess, there was a time when old clothes were as good as new—in fact, they were better. Because when people wore clothes, they gave something to them. You may not believe it, but right this minute, the highest-priced shops in Paris are selling clothes that were thrown away thirty years ago. They're selling them for new. That's how good they were.

COUNTESS: Well?

THE RAGPICKER: Countess, there was a time when garbage was a pleasure. A garbage can was not what it is now. If it smelled a little strange, it was because it was a little confused—there was everything there —sardines, cologne, iodine, roses. An amateur might jump to a wrong conclusion. But to a professional— it was the smell of God's plenty.

COUNTESS: Well?

THE RAGPICKER: Countess, the world has changed.

COUNTESS: Nonsense. How could it change? People are the same, I hope.

THE RAGPICKER: No, Countess. The people are not the same. The people are different. There's been an invasion. An infiltration. From another planet. The world is not beautiful any more. It's not happy.

COUNTESS: Not happy? Is that true? Why didn't you tell me this before?

THE RAGPICKER: Because you live in a dream, Countess. And we don't like to disturb you.

COUNTESS: But how could it have happened?

THE RAGPICKER: Countess, there was a time when you could walk around Paris, and all the people you met were just like yourself. A little cleaner, maybe, or dirtier, perhaps, or angry, or smiling—but you knew them. They were you. Well, Countess, twenty years ago, one day, on the street, I saw a face in the crowd. A face, you might say, without a face. The eyes—empty. The expression—not human. Not a human face. It saw me staring, and when it looked back at me with its gelatine eyes, I shuddered. Because I knew that to make room for this one, one of us must have left the earth. A while after, I saw another. And another. And since then, I've seen hundreds come in—yes—thousands.

COUNTESS: Describe them to me.

THE RAGPICKER: You've seen them yourself, Countess. Their clothes don't wrinkle. Their hats don't come off. When they talk, they don't look at you. They don't perspire.

COUNTESS: Have they wives? Have they children?

THE RAGPICKER: They buy the models out of shop windows, furs and all. They animate them by a secret process. Then they marry them. Naturally, they don't have children.

COUNTESS: What work do they do?

THE RAGPICKER: They don't do any work. Whenever they meet, they whisper, and then they pass each other thousand-franc notes. You see them standing on the corner by the Stock Exchange. You see them at auctions—in the back. They never raise a finger—they just stand there. In theater lobbies, by the box office—they never go inside. They don't do anything, but wherever you see them, things are not the same. I remember well the time when a cabbage could sell itself just by being a cabbage. Nowadays it's no good being a cabbage—unless you have an agent and pay him a commission. Nothing is free any more to sell itself or give itself away. These days, Countess, every cabbage has its pimp.

COUNTESS: I can't believe that.

THE RAGPICKER: Countess, little by little, the pimps have taken over the world. They don't do anything, they don't make anything—they just stand there and take their cut. It makes a difference. Look at the shopkeepers. Do you ever see one smiling at a customer any more? Certainly not. Their smiles are strictly for the pimps. The butcher has to smile at the meat-pimp, the florist at the rose-pimp, the grocer at the fresh-fruit-and-vegetable-pimp. It's all organized down to the slightest detail. A pimp for birdseed. A pimp for fishfood. That's why the cost of living keeps going up all the time. You buy a glass of beer—it costs twice as much as it used to. Why? Ten percent for the glass-pimp, 10 percent for the beer-pimp, 20 percent for the glass-of-beer-pimp —that's where our money goes. Personally, I prefer the old-fashioned type. Some of those men at least were loved by the women they sold. But what feelings can a pimp arouse in a leg of lamb? Pardon my language, Irma.

COUNTESS: It's all right. She doesn't understand it.

THE RAGPICKER: So now you know, Countess, why the world is no longer happy. We are the last of the free people of the earth. You saw them looking us over today. Tomorrow, the street singer will start paying the song-pimp, and the garbage-pimp will be after me. I tell you, Countess, we're finished. It's the end of free enterprise in this world!

COUNTESS: Is this true, Roderick?

PIERRE: I'm afraid it's true.

COUNTESS: Did you know about this, Irma?

IRMA: All I know is the doorman says that faith is dead.

DOORMAN: I've stopped taking bets over the phone.

JUGGLER: The very air is different, Countess. You can't trust it any more. If I throw my torches up too high, they go out.

THE RAGPICKER: The sky-pimp puts them out.

FLOWER GIRL: My flowers don't last overnight now. They wilt.

JUGGLER: Have you noticed, the pigeons don't fly any more?

THE RAGPICKER: They can't afford to. They walk.

COUNTESS: They're a lot of fools and so are you! You should have told me at once! How can you bear to live in a world where there is unhappiness? Where a man is not his own master? Are you cowards? All we have to do is get rid of these men.

PIERRE: How can we get rid of them? They're too strong.

[The Sergeant walks up again]

COUNTESS: [Smiling] The Sergeant will help us.

SERGEANT: Who? Me?

IRMA: There are a great many of them, Countess. The Deaf-Mute knows them all. They employed him once, years ago, because he was deaf. [The Deaf-Mute wigwags a short speech] They fired him because he wasn't blind. [Another flash of sign language] They're all connected like the parts of a machine.

COUNTESS: So much the better. We shall drive the whole machine into a ditch.

SERGEANT: It's not that easy, Countess. You never catch these birds napping. They change before your very eyes. I remember when I was in the detectives . . . You catch a president, pfft! He turns into a trustee. You catch him as trustee, and pfft! he's not a trustee—he's an honorary vice-chairman. You catch a Senator dead to rights: he becomes Minister of Justice. You get after the Minister of Justice—he is Chief of Police. And there you are—no longer in the detectives.

PIERRE: He's right, Countess. They have all the power. And all the money. And they're greedy for more.

COUNTESS: They're greedy? Ah, then, my friends, they're lost. If they're greedy, they're stupid. If

they're greedy—don't worry, I know exactly what to do. Roderick, by tonight you will be an honest man. And, Juggler, your torches will stay lit. And your beer will flow freely again, Martial. And the world will be saved. Let's get to work.

THE RAGPICKER: What are you going to do?

COUNTESS: Have you any kerosene in the house, Irma?

IRMA: Yes. Would you like some?

COUNTESS: I want just a little. In a dirty bottle. With a little mud. And some mange-cure, if you have it. [To the Deaf-Mute] Deaf-Mute! Take a letter. [Irma interprets in sign language. To the Singer] Singer, go and find Madame Constance.

[Irma and the Waiter go into the café]

SINGER: Yes, Countess.

COUNTESS: Ask her to be at my house by two o'clock. I'll be waiting for her in the cellar. You may tell her we have to discuss the future of humanity. That's sure to bring her.

SINGER: Yes, Countess.

COUNTESS: And ask her to bring Mademoiselle Gabrielle and Madame Josephine with her. Do you know how to get in to speak to Madame Constance? You ring twice, and then meow three times like a cat. Do you know how to meow?

SINGER: I'm better at barking.

COUNTESS: Better practice meowing on the way. Incidentally, I think Madame Constance knows all the verses of your mazurka. Remind me to ask her.

SINGER: Yes, Countess.

[Exit]

[Irma comes in. She is shaking the oily concoction in a little perfume vial, which she now hands the Countess]

IRMA: Here you are, Countess.

COUNTESS: Thanks, Irma. [She assumes a presidential manner] Deaf-Mute! Ready?

[Irma interprets in sign language. The Waiter has brought out a portfolio of letter paper and placed it on a table. The Deaf-Mute sits down before it, and prepares to write]

IRMA: [Speaking for the Deaf-Mute] I'm ready.

COUNTESS: My dear Mr.— What's his name?

[Irma wigwags the question to the Deaf-Mute, who answers in the same manner. It is all done so deftly that it is as if the Deaf-Mute were actually speaking]

IRMA: They are all called Mr. President.

COUNTESS: My dear Mr. President: I have personally verified the existence of a spontaneous outcrop of oil in the cellar of Number 21 Rue de Chaillot, which is at present occupied by a dignified person of unstable mentality. [The Countess grins knowingly] This explains why, fortunately for us, the discovery has so long been kept secret. If you should wish to verify the existence of this outcrop for yourself, you may call at the above address at three P.M. today. I am herewith enclosing a sample so that you may judge the quality and consistency of the crude. Yours very truly. Roderick, can you sign the Prospector's name?

PIERRE: You wish me to?

COUNTESS: One forgery wipes out the other.

[Pierre *signs the letter. The* Deaf-Mute *types the address on an envelope*]

IRMA: Who is to deliver this?

COUNTESS: The Doorman, of course. On his bicycle. And as soon as you have delivered it, run over to the Prospector's office. Leave word that the President expects to see him at my house at three.

DOORMAN: Yes, Countess.

COUNTESS: I shall leave you now. I have many pressing things to do. Among others, I must press my red gown.

THE RAGPICKER: But this only takes care of two of them, Countess.

COUNTESS: Didn't the Deaf-Mute say they are all connected like the works of a machine?

IRMA: Yes.

COUNTESS: Then, if one comes, the rest will follow. And we shall have them all. My boa, please.

DOORMAN: The one that's stolen, Countess?

COUNTESS: Naturally. The one the Prospector stole.

DOORMAN: It hasn't turned up yet, Countess. But someone has left an ermine collar.

COUNTESS: Real ermine?

DOORMAN: Looks like it.

COUNTESS: Ermine and iris were made for each other. Let me see it.

DOORMAN: Yes, Countess.

[*Exit* Doorman]

COUNTESS: Roderick, you shall escort me. You still look pale. I have some old Chartreuse at home. I always take a glass each year. Last year I forgot. You shall have it.

PIERRE: If there is anything I can do, Countess . . . ?

COUNTESS: There is a great deal you can do. There are all the things that need to be done in a room that no man has been in for twenty years. You can untwist the cord on the blind and let in a little sunshine for a change. You can take the mirror off the wardrobe door, and deliver me once and for all from the old harpy that lives in the mirror. You can let the mouse out of the trap. I'm tired of feeding it. [*To her friends*] Each man to his post. See you later, my friends. [*The* Doorman *puts the ermine collar around her shoulders*] Thank you, my boy. It's rabbit. [*One o'clock strikes*] Your arm, Valentine.

PIERRE: Valentine?

COUNTESS: It's just struck one. At one, all men become Valentine.

PIERRE: [*He offers his arm*] Permit me.

COUNTESS: Or Valentino. It's obviously far from the same, isn't it, Irma? But they have that much choice.

[*She sweeps out majestically with* Pierre. *The others disperse. All but* Irma]

IRMA: [*Clearing off the table*] I hate ugliness. I love beauty. I hate meanness. I adore kindness. It may not seem so grand to some to be a waitress in Paris. I love it. A waitress meets all sorts of people. She observes life. I hate to be alone. I love people. But I have never said I love you to a man. Men try to make me say it. They put their arms around me—I pretend I don't see it. They pinch me—I pretend I don't feel it. They kiss me—I pretend I don't know it. They take me out in the evening and make me drink—but I'm careful, I never say it. If they don't like it, they can leave me alone. Because when I say I love you to Him, He will know just by looking in my eyes that many have held me and pinched me and kissed me, but I have never said I love you to anyone in the world before. Never. No. [*Looking off in the direction in which* Pierre *has gone, she whispers softly*] I love you.

VOICE: [*From within the café*] Irma!

IRMA: Coming.

[*Exits*]

CURTAIN

ACT II.

SCENE.—*The cellar of the* Countess' *house. An ancient vault set deep in the ground, with walls of solid masonry, part brick and part great ashlars, mossy and sweating. A staircase of medieval pattern is built into the thickness of the wall, and leads up to the street level from a landing halfway down. In the corners of the cellar are piled casks, packing cases, bird-cages, and other odds and ends—the accumulation of centuries—the whole effect utterly fantastic.*

In the center of the vast underground room, some furniture has been arranged to give an impression of a sitting-room of the 1890's. There is a venerable chaise-longue piled with cushions that once were gay, three armchairs, a table with an oil lamp and a bowl of flowers, a shaggy rug. It is two P.M., *the same day.*

AT RISE.—*The* Countess *is sitting over a bit of mending, in one of the armchairs.* Irma *appears on the landing and calls down.*

IRMA: Countess! The Sewer Man is here.

COUNTESS: Thank goodness, Irma. Send him down. [*The* Sewer Man *enters. He carries his hip boots in his hand*] How do you do, Mr. Sewer Man? [*The* Sewer Man *bows*] But why do you have your boots in your hand instead of on your feet?

SEWER MAN: Etiquette, Countess. Etiquette.

COUNTESS: How very American! I'm told that Americans nowadays apologize for their gloves if they happen to take one's hand. As if the skin of a human were nicer to touch than the skin of a sheep! And particularly if they have sweaty hands . . . !

SEWER MAN: My feet never sweat, Countess.

COUNTESS: How very nice! But please don't stand on ceremony here. Put your boots on. Put them on.

SEWER MAN: [*Complying*] Thanks very much, Countess.

COUNTESS: [*While he draws on his boots*] I'm sure you must have a very poor opinion of the upper world, from what you see of it. The way people throw their filth into your territory is absolutely scandalous! I burn all my refuse, and I scatter the ashes. All I ever throw in the drain is flowers. Did you happen to see a lily float by this morning? Mine. But perhaps you didn't notice?

SEWER MAN: We notice a lot more down there, Countess, than you might think. You'd be surprised the things we notice. There's lots of things come along that were obviously intended for us—little gifts, you might call them—sometimes a brand-new shaving brush—sometimes, *The Brothers Karamazov* . . . Thanks for the lily, Countess. A very sweet thought.

COUNTESS: Tomorrow you shall have this iris. But now, let's come to the point. I have two questions to ask you.

SEWER MAN: Yes, Countess?

COUNTESS: First—and this has nothing to do with our problem—it's just something that has been troubling me. . . . Tell me, is it true that the sewer men of Paris have a king?

SEWER MAN: Oh, now, Countess, that's another of those fairy tales out of the Sunday supplements. It just seems those writers can't keep their minds off the sewers! It fascinates them. They keep thinking of us moving around in our underground canals like gondoliers in Venice, and it sends them into a fever of romance! The things they say about us! They say we have a race of girls down there who never see the light of day! It's completely fantastic! The girls naturally come out—every Christmas and Easter. And orgies by torchlight with gondolas and guitars! With troops of rats that dance as they follow the piper! What nonsense! The rats are not allowed to dance. No, no, no. Of course we have no king. Down in the sewers, you'll find nothing but good republicans.

COUNTESS: And no queen?

SEWER MAN: No. We may run a beauty contest down there once in a while. Or crown a mermaid Queen of the May. But no queen what you'd call a queen. And, as for these swimming races they talk so much about . . . possibly once in a while—in the summer—in the dog days . . .

COUNTESS: I believe you. I believe you. And now tell me. Do you remember that night I found you here in my cellar—looking very pale and strange—you were half-dead as a matter of fact—and I gave you some brandy . . .

SEWER MAN: Yes, Countess.

COUNTESS: That night you promised if ever I should need it—you would tell me the secret of this room.

SEWER MAN: The secret of the moving stone?

COUNTESS: I need it now.

SEWER MAN: Only the King of the Sewer Men knows this secret.

COUNTESS: I'm sure of it. I know most secrets, of course. As a matter of fact, I have three magic words

that will open any door that words can open. I have tried them all—in various tones of voice. They don't seem to work. And this is a matter of life and death.

SEWER MAN: Look, Countess.

[*He locates a brick in the masonry, and pushes it. A huge block of stone slowly pivots and uncovers a trap from which a circular staircase winds into the bowels of the earth*]

COUNTESS: Good heavens! Where do those stairs lead?

SEWER MAN: Nowhere.

COUNTESS: But they must go somewhere.

SEWER MAN: They just go down.

COUNTESS: Let's go and see.

SEWER MAN: No, Countess. Never again. That time you found me, I had a pretty close shave. I kept going down and around, and down and around for an hour, a year—I don't know. There's no end to it, Countess. Once you start you can't stop. . . . Your head begins to turn—you're lost. No—once you start down, there's no coming up.

COUNTESS: You came up.

SEWER MAN: I—I am a special case. Besides, I had my tools, my ropes. And I stopped in time.

COUNTESS: You could have screamed—shouted.

SEWER MAN: You could fire off a cannon.

COUNTESS: Who could have built a thing like this?

SEWER MAN: Paris is old, you know. Paris is very old.

COUNTESS: You don't suppose, by any chance, there is oil down there?

SEWER MAN: There's only death down there.

COUNTESS: I should have preferred a little oil too —or a vein of gold—or emeralds. You're quite sure there is nothing?

SEWER MAN: Not even rats.

COUNTESS: How does one lower this stone?

SEWER MAN: Simple. To open, you press here. And to close it, you push there. [*He presses the brick. The stone descends*] Now there's two of us in the world that knows it.

COUNTESS: I won't remember long. Is it all right if I repeat my magic words while I press it?

SEWER MAN: It's bound to help.

[*Irma enters*]

IRMA: Countess, Madame Constance and Mademoiselle Gabrielle are here.

COUNTESS: Show them down, Irma. Thank you very much, Mr. Sewer Man.

SEWER MAN: Like that story about the steam laundry that's supposed to be running day and night in my sewer . . . I can assure you . . .

COUNTESS: [*Edging him toward the door*] Thank you very much.

SEWER MAN: Pure imagination! They never work nights.

[*He goes off, bowing graciously*]

[*Constance, the Madwoman of Passy, and Gabrielle, the Madwoman of St. Sulpice, come down daintily. Constance is all in white. She wears an enormous hat graced with ostrich plumes, and a lavender veil.* Gabrielle *is costumed with the affected simplicity of the 1880's. She is atrociously made up in a remorseless parody of blushing innocence, and she minces down the stairs with macabre coyness*]

CONSTANCE: Aurelia! Don't tell us they've found your feather boa?

GABRIELLE: You don't mean Adolphe Bertaut has proposed at last! I knew he would.

COUNTESS: How are you, Constance? [*She shouts*] How are you, Gabrielle?

GARRIELLE: You needn't shout today, my dear. It's Wednesday. Wednesdays, I hear perfectly.

CONSTANCE: It's Thursday.

GABRIELLE: Oh, dear. Well, never mind. I'm going to make an exception just this once.

CONSTANCE: [*To an imaginary dog who has stopped on the landing*] Come along, Dickie. Come along. And stop barking. What a racket you're making! Come on, darling—we've come to see the longest boa and the handsomest man in Paris. Come on.

COUNTESS: Constance, it's not a question of my boa today. Nor of poor Adolphe. It's a question of the future of the human race.

CONSTANCE: You think it has a future?

COUNTESS: Please don't make silly jokes. Sit down and listen to me. Today we must make a decision which may alter the fate of the world.

CONSTANCE: Couldn't we do it tomorrow? I want to wash my slippers. Now, Dickie—please!

COUNTESS: We haven't a moment to waste. Where is Josephine? Well, we'd best have our tea, and the moment Josephine comes . . .

GABRIELLE: Josephine is sitting on her bench in front of the palace waiting for President Wilson to come out. She says she's sorry, but she positively must see him today.

CONSTANCE: Dickie!

COUNTESS: What a pity! [*She gets the tea things from the side table, pours tea and serves cake and honey*] I wish she were here to help us. She has a first-class brain.

CONSTANCE: Go ahead, dear. We're listening. [*To Dickie*] What is it, Dickie? You want to sit in Aunt Aurelia's lap. All right, darling. Go on. Jump, Dickie.

COUNTESS: Constance, we love you, as you know. And we love Dickie. But this is a serious matter. So let's stop being childish for once.

CONSTANCE: And what does that mean, if you please?

COUNTESS: It means Dickie. You know perfectly well that we love him and fuss over him just as if he were still alive. He's a sacred memory and we wouldn't hurt his feelings for the world. But please don't plump him in my lap when I'm settling the future of mankind. His basket is in the corner—he knows where it is, and he can just go and sit in it.

CONSTANCE: So you're against Dickie too! You too!

COUNTESS: Constance! I'm not in the least against Dickie! I adore Dickie. But you know as well as I that Dickie is only a convention with us. It's a beau-

tiful convention—but it doesn't have to bark all the time. Besides, it's you that spoil him. The time you went to visit your niece and left him with me, we got on marvelously together. He didn't bark, he didn't tear things, he didn't even eat. But when you're with him, one can pay attention to nothing else. I'm not going to take Dickie in my lap at a solemn moment like this, no, not for anything in the world. And that's that!

GABRIELLE: [*Very sweetly*] Constance, dear, I don't mind taking him in my lap. He loves to sit in my lap, don't you, darling?

CONSTANCE: Kindly stop putting on angelic airs, Gabrielle. I know you very well. You're much too sweet to be sincere. There's plenty of times that I make believe that Dickie is here, when really I've left him home, and you cuddle and pet him just the same.

GABRIELLE: I adore animals.

CONSTANCE: If you adore animals, you shouldn't pet them when they're not there. It's a form of hypocrisy.

COUNTESS: Now, Constance, Gabrielle has as much right as you . . .

CONSTANCE: Gabrielle has no right to do what she does. Do you know what she does? She invites *people* to come to tea with us. *People* whom we know nothing about. *People* who exist only in her imagination.

COUNTESS: You think that's not an existence?

GABRIELLE: I don't invite them at all. They come by themselves. What can I do?

CONSTANCE: You might introduce us.

COUNTESS: If you think they're only imaginary, there's no point in your meeting them, is there?

CONSTANCE: Of course they're imaginary. But who likes to have imaginary people staring at one? Especially strangers.

GABRIELLE: Oh, they're really very nice. . . .

CONSTANCE: Tell me just one thing, Gabrielle—are they here now?

COUNTESS: Am I to be allowed to speak? Or is this going to be the same as the argument about inoculating Josephine's cat, when we didn't get to the subject at all?

CONSTANCE: Never! Never! Never! I'll never give my consent to that. [*To Dickie*] I'd never do a thing like that to you, Dickie sweet. . . . Oh, no! Oh, no!

[*She begins to weep softly*]

COUNTESS: Good heavens! Now we have her in tears. What an impossible creature! With the fate of humanity hanging in the balance! All right, all right, stop crying. I'll take him in my lap. Come, Dickie, Dickie.

CONSTANCE: No. He won't go now. Oh, how can you be so cruel? Don't you suppose I know about Dickie? Don't you think I'd rather have him here alive and woolly and frisking around the way he used to? You have your Adolphe. Gabrielle has her birds. But I have only Dickie. Do you think I'd be so silly about him if it wasn't that it's only by pretending that he's here all the time that I get him to come sometimes, really? Next time I won't bring him!

COUNTESS: Now let's not get ourselves worked up over nothing. Come here, Dickie. . . . Irma is going to take you for a nice walk. [*She rings her bell*] Irma!

[Irma *appears on the landing*]

CONSTANCE: No. He doesn't want to go. Besides, I didn't bring him today. So there!

COUNTESS: Very well, then. Irma, make sure the door is locked.

IRMA: Yes, Countess.

[Irma *exits*]

CONSTANCE: What do you mean? Why locked? Who's coming?

COUNTESS: If you'd let me get a word in, you'd know by now. A terrible thing has happened. This morning, this very morning, exactly at noon . . .

CONSTANCE: [*Thrilled*] Oh, how exciting!

COUNTESS: Be quiet. This morning, exactly at noon, thanks to a young man who drowned himself in the Seine . . . Oh, yes, while I think of it—do you know a mazurka called *La Belle Polonaise*?

CONSTANCE: Yes, Aurelia.

COUNTESS: Could you sing it now? This very minute?

CONSTANCE: Yes, Aurelia.

COUNTESS: All of it?

CONSTANCE: Yes, Aurelia. But who's interrupting now, Aurelia?

COUNTESS: You're right. Well, this morning, exactly at noon, I discovered a horrible plot. There is a group of men who intend to tear down the whole city!

CONSTANCE: Is that all?

GABRIELLE: But I don't understand, Aurelia. Why should men want to tear down the city? It was they themselves who put it up.

COUNTESS: You are so innocent, my poor Gabrielle. There are people in the world who want to destroy everything. They have the fever of destruction. Even when they pretend that they're building, it is only in order to destroy. When they put up a new building, they quietly knock down two old ones. They build cities so that they can destroy the countryside. They destroy space with telephones and time with airplanes. Humanity is now dedicated to the task of universal destruction. I am speaking, of course, primarily of the male sex.

GABRIELLE: [*Shocked*] Oh . . . !

CONSTANCE: Aurelia! Must you talk sex in front of Gabrielle?

COUNTESS: There *are* two sexes.

CONSTANCE: Gabrielle is a virgin, Aurelia!

COUNTESS: Oh, she can't be as innocent as all that. She keeps canaries.

GABRIELLE: I think you're being very cruel about men, Aurelia. Men are big and beautiful, and as loyal as dogs. I preferred not to marry, it's true. But I hear excellent reports from friends who have had an opportunity to observe them closely.

COUNTESS: My poor darling! You are still living in a dream. But one day, you will wake up as I have, and then you will see what is happening in the world. The tide has turned, my dear. Men are changing back into beasts. They know it. They no longer try to hide it. There was once such a thing as manners. I remember a time when the hungriest was the one who took the longest to pick up his fork. The one with the broadest grin was the one who needed most to go to the . . . It was such fun to keep them grinning like that for hours. But now they no longer pretend. Just look at them—snuffling their soup like pigs, tearing their meat like tigers, crunching their lettuce like crocodiles! A man doesn't take your hand nowadays. He gives you his paw.

CONSTANCE: Would that trouble you so much if they turned into animals? Personally, I think it's a good idea.

GABRIELLE: Oh, I'd love to see them like that. They'd be sweet.

CONSTANCE: It might be the salvation of the human race.

COUNTESS: [*To* Constance] You'd make a fine rabbit, wouldn't you?

CONSTANCE: I?

COUNTESS: Naturally. You don't think it's only the men who are changing? You change along with them. Husbands and wives together. We're all one race, you know.

CONSTANCE: You think so? And why would my poor husband have to be a rabbit if he were alive?

COUNTESS: Remember his front teeth? When he nibbled his celery?

CONSTANCE: I'm happy to say, I remember absolutely nothing about him. All I remember on that subject is the time that Father Lacordaire tried to kiss me in the park.

COUNTESS: Yes, yes, of course.

CONSTANCE: And what does that mean, if you please, "Yes, yes, of course"?

COUNTESS: Constance, just this once, look us in the eye and tell us truly—did that really happen or did you read about it in a book?

CONSTANCE: Now I'm being insulted!

COUNTESS: We promise you faithfully that we'll believe it all over again afterwards, won't we, Gabrielle? But tell us the truth this once.

CONSTANCE: How dare you question my memories? Suppose I said your pearls were false!

COUNTESS: They were.

CONSTANCE: I'm not asking what they were. I'm asking what they are. Are they false or are they real?

COUNTESS: Everyone knows that little by little, as one wears pearls, they become real.

CONSTANCE: And isn't it exactly the same with memories?

COUNTESS: Now do not let us waste time. I must go on.

CONSTANCE: I think Gabrielle is perfectly right about men. There are still plenty who haven't changed a bit. There's an old Senator who bows to Gabrielle every day when he passes her in front of the palace. And he takes off his hat each time.

GABRIELLE: That's perfectly true, Aurelia. He's always pushing an empty baby carriage, and he always stops and bows.

COUNTESS: Don't be taken in, Gabrielle. It's all make-believe. And all we can expect from these make-believe men is itself make-believe. They give us face powder made of stones, sausages made of sawdust, shirts made of glass, stockings made of milk. It's all a vulgar pretense. And if that is the case, imagine what passes, these days, for virtue, sincerity, generosity and love! I warn you, Gabrielle, don't let this Senator with the empty baby carriage pull the wool over your eyes.

GABRIELLE: He's really the soul of courtesy. He seems very correct.

COUNTESS: Those are the worst. Gabrielle, beware! He'll make you put on black riding boots, while he dances the cancan around you, singing God knows what filth at the top of his voice. The very thought makes one's blood run cold!

GABRIELLE: You think that's what he has in mind?

COUNTESS: Of course. Men have lost all sense of decency. They are all equally disgusting. Just look at them in the evening, sitting at their tables in the café, working away in unison with their toothpicks, hour after hour, digging up roast beef, veal, onion . . .

CONSTANCE: They don't harm anyone that way.

COUNTESS: Then why do you barricade your door, and make your friends meow before you let them come up? Incidentally, we must make an interesting sight, Gabrielle and I, yowling together on your doorstep like a couple of tomcats!

CONSTANCE: There's no need at all for you to yowl together. One would be quite enough. And you know perfectly well why I have to do it. It's because there are murderers.

COUNTESS: I don't quite see what prevents murderers from meowing like anybody else. But why are there murderers?

CONSTANCE: Why? Because there are thieves.

COUNTESS: And why are there thieves? Why is there almost nothing but thieves?

CONSTANCE: Because they worship money. Because money is king.

COUNTESS: Ah—now we've come to it. Because we live in the reign of the Golden Calf. Did you realize that, Gabrielle? Men now publicly worship the Golden Calf!

GABRIELLE: How awful! Have the authorities been notified?

COUNTESS: The authorities do it themselves, Gabrielle.

GABRIELLE: Oh! Has anyone talked to the bishop?

COUNTESS: Nowadays only money talks to the bishop. And so you see why I asked you to come here today. The world has gone out of its mind. Unless we do something, humanity is doomed! Constance, have you any suggestions?

CONSTANCE: I know what I always do in a case like this. . . .

COUNTESS: You write to the Prime Minister.

CONSTANCE: He always does what I tell him.

COUNTESS: Does he ever answer your letters?

CONSTANCE: He knows I prefer him not to. It might excite gossip. Besides, I don't always write. Sometimes I wire. The time I told him about the Archbishop's Frigidaire, it was by wire. And they sent a new one the very next day.

COUNTESS: There was probably a commission in it for someone. And what do you suggest, Gabrielle?

CONSTANCE: Now, how can she tell you until she's consulted her voices?

GABRIELLE: I could go right home and consult them, and we could meet again after dinner.

COUNTESS: There's no time for that. Besides, your voices are not real voices.

GABRIELLE: [Furious] How dare you say a thing like that?

COUNTESS: Where do your voices come from? Still from your sewing machine?

GABRIELLE: Not at all. They've passed into my hot-water bottle. And it's much nicer that way. They don't chatter any more. They gurgle. But they haven't been a bit nice to me lately. Last night they kept telling me to let my canaries out. "Let them out. Let them out. Let them out."

CONSTANCE: Did you?

GABRIELLE: I opened the cage. They wouldn't go.

COUNTESS: I don't call that voices. Objects talk—everyone knows that. It's the principle of the phonograph. But to ask a hot-water bottle for advice is silly. What does a hot-water bottle know? No, all we have to consult here is our own judgment.

CONSTANCE: Very well then, tell us what you have decided. Since you're asking our opinion, you've doubtless made up your mind.

COUNTESS: Yes, I've thought the whole thing out. All I really needed to discover was the source of the infection. Today I found it.

CONSTANCE: Where?

COUNTESS: You'll see soon enough. I've baited a trap. In just a few minutes, the rats will be here.

GABRIELLE: [In alarm] Rats!

COUNTESS: Don't be alarmed. They're still in human form.

GABRIELLE: Heavens! What are you going to do with them?

COUNTESS: That's just the question. Suppose I get these wicked men all here at once—in my cellar—have I the right to exterminate them?

GABRIELLE: To kill them? [Countess nods]

CONSTANCE: That's not a question for us. You'll have to ask Father Bridet.

COUNTESS: I have asked him. Yes. One day, in confession, I told him frankly that I had a secret desire to destroy all wicked people. He said: "By all means, my child. And when you're ready to go into action, I'll lend you the jawbone of an ass."

CONSTANCE: That's just talk. You get him to put that in writing.

GABRIELLE: What's your scheme, Aurelia?

COUNTESS: That's a secret.

CONSTANCE: It's not so easy to kill them. Let's say you had a tank full of vitriol all ready for them. You could never get them to walk into it. There's nothing so stubborn as a man when you want him to do something.

COUNTESS: Leave that to me.

CONSTANCE: But if they're killed, they're bound to be missed, and then we'll be fined. They fine you for every little thing these days.

COUNTESS: They won't be missed.

GABRIELLE: I wish Josephine were here. Her sister's husband was a lawyer. She knows all about these things.

COUNTESS: Do you miss a cold when it's gone? Or the germs that caused it? When the world feels well again, do you think it will regret its illness? No, it will stretch itself joyfully, and it will smile—that's all.

CONSTANCE: Just a moment! Gabrielle, are they here now? Yes or no?

COUNTESS: What's the matter with you now?

CONSTANCE: I'm simply asking Gabrielle if her friends are in the room or not. I have a right to know.

GABRIELLE: I'm not allowed to say.

CONSTANCE: I know very well they are. I'm sure of it. Otherwise you wouldn't be making faces.

COUNTESS: May I ask what difference it makes to you if her friends are in the room?

CONSTANCE: Just this: If they're here, I'm not going to say another word! I'm certainly not going to commit myself in a matter involving the death sentence in the presence of third parties, whether they exist or not.

GABRIELLE: That's not being very nice to my guests, is it?[1]

COUNTESS: Constance, you must be mad! Or are you so stupid as to think that just because we're alone, there's nobody with us? Do you consider us so boring or repulsive that of all the millions of beings, imaginary or otherwise, who are prowling about in space, there's not one who might possibly enjoy spending a little time with us? On the contrary, my dear— my house is full of guests always. They know that here they have a place in the universe where they can come when they're lonely and be sure of a welcome. For my part, I'm delighted to have them.

GABRIELLE: Thank you, Aurelia.

CONSTANCE: You know perfectly well, Aurelia . . .

COUNTESS: I know perfectly well that at this moment the whole universe is listening to us—and that every word we say echoes to the remotest star. To pretend otherwise is the sheerest hypocrisy.

CONSTANCE: Then why do you insult me in front of everybody? I'm not mean. I'm shy. I feel timid about giving an opinion in front of such a crowd. Furthermore, if you think I'm so bad and so stupid, why did you invite me, in the first place?

COUNTESS: I'll tell you. And I'll tell you why, dis- agreeable as you are, I always give you the biggest piece of cake and my best honey. It's because when you come there's always someone with you—and I don't mean Dickie—I mean someone who resembles you like a sister, only she's young and lovely, and she sits modestly to one side and smiles at me ten- derly all the time you're bickering and quarreling, and never says a word. That's the Constance to whom I give the cake that you gobble, and it's because of her that you're here today, and it's her vote that I'm asking you to cast in this crucial moment. And not yours, which is of no importance whatever.

CONSTANCE: I'm leaving.

COUNTESS: Be so good as to sit down. I can't let her go yet.

CONSTANCE: [*Crossing toward the stairs*] No. This is too much. I'm taking her with me.

[Irma *enters*]

IRMA: Madame Josephine.

COUNTESS: Thank heaven!

GABRIELLE: We're saved.

[Josephine, *the Madwoman of La Concorde, sweeps in majestically in a get-up somewhere between the regal and the priestly*]

JOSEPHINE: My dear friends, today once again, I waited for President Wilson—but he didn't come out.

COUNTESS: You'll have to wait quite a while longer before he does. He's been dead since 1924.

JOSEPHINE: I have plenty of time.

COUNTESS: In anyone else, Josephine, these extrav- agances might seem a little childish. But a person of your judgment doubtless has her reasons for wanting to talk to a man to whom no one would listen when he was alive. We have a legal problem for you. Sup- pose you had all the world's criminals here in this room. And suppose you had a way of getting rid of them forever. Would you have the right to do it?

JOSEPHINE: Why not?

COUNTESS: Exactly my point.

GABRIELLE: But, Josephine, so many people!

JOSEPHINE: *De minimis non curat lex!*[2] The more there are the more legal it is. It's impersonal. It's even military. It's the cardinal principle of battle— you get all your enemies in one place, and you kill them all together at one time. Because if you had to track them down one by one in their houses and offices, you'd get tired, and sooner or later you'd stop. I believe your idea is very practical, Aurelia. I can't imagine why we never thought of it before.

GABRIELLE: Well, if you think it's all right to do it. . . .

JOSEPHINE: By all means. Your criminals have had a fair trial, I suppose?

COUNTESS: Trial?

---

[1] In the original, merely *"Vous êtes discourtoise, Con- stance,"* "you are being rude"—which is clearer.

[2] "The law does not regard trifles."

JOSEPHINE: Certainly. You can't kill anybody without a trial. That's elementary. "No man shall be deprived of his life, liberty and property without due process of law."

COUNTESS: They deprive us of ours.

JOSEPHINE: That's not the point. You're not accused of anything. Every accused—man, woman or child—has the right to defend himself at the bar of justice. Even animals. Before the Deluge, you will recall, the Lord permitted Noah to speak in defense of his fellow mortals. He evidently stuttered. You know the result. On the other hand, Captain Dreyfus was not only innocent—he was defended by a marvelous orator. The result was precisely the same. So you see, in having a trial, you run no risk whatever.[1]

COUNTESS: But if I give them the slightest cause for suspicion—I'll lose them.

JOSEPHINE: There's a simple procedure prescribed in such cases. You can summon the defendants by calling them three times—mentally, if you like. If they don't appear, the court may designate an attorney who will represent them. This attorney can then argue their case to the court, *in absentia,* and a judgment can then be rendered, *in contumacio.*

COUNTESS: But I don't know any attorneys. And we have only ten minutes.

GABRIELLE: Hurry, Josephine, hurry!

JOSEPHINE: In case of emergency, it is permissible for the court to order the first passer-by to act as attorney for the defense. A defense is like a baptism. Absolutely indispensable, but you don't have to know anything to do it. Ask Irma to get you somebody. Anybody.

COUNTESS: The Deaf-Mute?

JOSEPHINE: Well—that's getting it down a bit fine. That might be questionable on appeal.

COUNTESS: [*Calls*] Irma! What about the Police Sergeant?

JOSEPHINE: He won't do. He's under oath to the state.

[Irma *appears*]

IRMA: Yes, Countess?

COUNTESS: Who's out there, Irma?

IRMA: All our friends, Countess. There's the Ragpicker and . . .

COUNTESS: Send down the Ragpicker.

CONSTANCE: Do you think it's wise to have all those millionaires represented by a ragpicker?

JOSEPHINE: It's a first-rate choice. Criminals are always represented by their opposites. Murderers, by someone who obviously wouldn't hurt a fly. Rapists, by a member of the League for Decency. Experience shows it's the only way to get an acquittal.

COUNTESS: But we must not have an acquittal. That would mean the end of the world!

[1] Alfred Dreyfus, a French army officer, was convicted of treason in 1894 and imprisoned on Devil's Island, but was later proved innocent. Emile Zola and other distinguished persons rallied to his cause but encountered great opposition in official circles. The original conviction was not set aside until 1906.

JOSEPHINE: Justice is justice, my dear.

[*The* Ragpicker *comes down, with a stately air. Behind him, on the landing, appear the other* Vagabonds]

THE RAGPICKER: Greetings, Countess. Greetings, ladies. My most sincere compliments.

COUNTESS: Has Irma told you . . . ?

THE RAGPICKER: She said something about a trial.

COUNTESS: You have been appointed attorney for the defense.

THE RAGPICKER: Terribly flattered, I'm sure.

COUNTESS: You realize, don't you, how much depends on the outcome of this trial?

JOSEPHINE: Do you know the defendants well enough to undertake the case?

THE RAGPICKER: I know them to the bottom of their souls. I go through their garbage every day.

CONSTANCE: And what do you find there?

THE RAGPICKER: Mostly flowers.

GABRIELLE: It's true, you know, the rich are always surrounded with flowers.

CONSTANCE: How beautiful!

COUNTESS: Are you trying to prejudice the court?

THE RAGPICKER: Oh no, Countess, no.

COUNTESS: We want a completely impartial defense.

THE RAGPICKER: Of course, Countess, of course. Permit me to make a suggestion.

COUNTESS: Will you preside, Josephine?

THE RAGPICKER: Instead of speaking as attorney, suppose you let me speak directly as defendant. It will be more convincing, and I can get into it more.

JOSEPHINE: Excellent idea. Motion granted.

COUNTESS: We don't want you to be too convincing, remember.

THE RAGPICKER: Impartial, Countess, impartial.

JOSEPHINE: Well? Have you prepared your case?

THE RAGPICKER: How rich am I?

JOSEPHINE: Millions. Billions.

THE RAGPICKER: How did I get them? Theft? Murder? Embezzlement?

COUNTESS: Most likely.

THE RAGPICKER: Do I have a wife? A mistress?

COUNTESS: Everything.

THE RAGPICKER: All right. I'm ready.

GABRIELLE: Will you have some tea?

THE RAGPICKER: Is that good?

CONSTANCE: Very good for the voice. The Russians drink nothing but tea. And they talk like anything.

THE RAGPICKER: All right. Tea.

JOSEPHINE: [*To the* Vagabonds] Come in. Come in. All of you. You may take places. The trial is public. [*The* Vagabonds *dispose themselves on the steps and elsewhere*] Your bell, if you please, Aurelia.

COUNTESS: But what if I should need to ring for Irma?

JOSEPHINE: Irma will sit here, next to me. If you need her, she can ring for herself. [*To the* Police Sergeant *and the* Policeman] Conduct the accused to the bar. [*The officers conduct the* Ragpicker *to a bar improvised with a rocking chair and a packing case marked FRAGILE. The* Ragpicker *mounts the box. She rings the bell]* The court is now in session. [*All sit*] Counsel for the defense, you may take the oath.

THE RAGPICKER: I swear to tell the truth, the whole truth, and nothing but the truth, so help me God.

JOSEPHINE: Nonsense! You're not a witness. You're an attorney. It's your duty to lie, conceal and distort everything, and slander everybody.

THE RAGPICKER: All right. I swear to lie, conceal and distort everything, and slander everybody.

[Josephine *rings stridently*]

JOSEPHINE: Quiet! Begin.

THE RAGPICKER: May it please the honorable, august and elegant Court . . .

JOSEPHINE: Flattery will get you nowhere. That will do. The defense has been heard. Cross-examination.

COUNTESS: Mr. President . . .

THE RAGPICKER: [*Bowing with dignity*] Madame.

COUNTESS: Do you know what you are charged with?

THE RAGPICKER: I can't for the life of me imagine. My life is an open book. My ways are known to all. I am a pillar of the church and the sole support of the Opera. My hands are spotless.

COUNTESS: What an atrocious lie! Just look at them!

CONSTANCE: You don't have to insult the man. He's only lying to please you.

COUNTESS: Be quiet, Constance! You don't get the idea at all. [*To the* Ragpicker] You are charged with the crime of worshipping money.

THE RAGPICKER: Worshipping money? Me?

JOSEPHINE: Do you plead guilty or not guilty? Which is it?

THE RAGPICKER: Why, Your Honor . . .

JOSEPHINE: Yes or no?

THE RAGPICKER: Yes or no? No! I don't worship money, Countess. Heavens, no! Money worships me. It adores me. It won't let me alone. It's damned embarrassing, I can tell you.

JOSEPHINE: Kindly watch your language.

COUNTESS: Defendant, tell the Court how you came by your money.

THE RAGPICKER: The first time money came to me, I was a mere boy, a little golden-haired child in the bosom of my dear family. It came to me suddenly in the guise of a gold brick which, in my innocence, I picked out of a garbage can one day while playing. I was horrified, as you can imagine. I immediately tried to get rid of it by swapping it for a little run-down one-track railroad which, to my consternation, at once sold itself for a hundred times its value. In a desperate effort to get rid of this money, I began to buy things. I bought the Northern Refineries, the Galeries Lafayette, and the Schneider-Creusot Munition Works. And now I'm stuck with them. It's a horrible fate—but I'm resigned to it. I don't ask for

your sympathy, I don't ask for your pity—all I ask for is a little common human understanding. . . .

[*He begins to cry*]

COUNTESS: I object. This wretch is trying to play on the emotions of the Court.

JOSEPHINE: The Court has no emotions.

THE RAGPICKER: Everyone knows that the poor have no one but themselves to blame for their poverty. It's only just that they should suffer the consequences. But how is it the fault of the rich if they're rich?

COUNTESS: Dry your tears. You're deceiving nobody. If, as you say, you're ashamed of your money, why is it you hold onto it with such a death grip?

THE RAGPICKER: Me?

STREET PEDDLER: You never part with a franc!

JUGGLER: You wouldn't even give the poor Deaf-Mute a sou!

THE RAGPICKER: Me, hold onto money? What slander! What injustice! What a thing to say to me in the presence of this honorable, august and elegant Court! I spend all my time trying to spend my money. If I have tan shoes, I buy black ones. If I have a bicycle, I buy a motor car. If I have a wife, I buy . . .

JOSEPHINE: [*Rings*] Order!

THE RAGPICKER: I dispatch a plane to Java for a bouquet of flowers. I send a steamer to Egypt for a basket of figs. I send a special representative to New York to fetch me an ice-cream cone. And if it's not just exactly right, back it goes. But no matter what I do, I can't get rid of my money! If I play a hundred-to-one shot, the horse comes in by twenty lengths. If I throw a diamond in the Seine, it turns up in the trout they serve me for lunch. Ten diamonds—ten trout. Well, now, do you suppose I can get rid of forty millions by giving a sou to a deaf-mute? Is it even worth the effort?

CONSTANCE: He's right.

THE RAGPICKER: Ah! You see, my dear? At last, there is somebody who understands me! Somebody who is not only beautiful, but extraordinarily sensitive and intelligent.

COUNTESS: I object!

JOSEPHINE: Overruled!

THE RAGPICKER: I should be delighted to send you some flowers, Miss—directly I'm acquitted. What flowers do you prefer?

CONSTANCE: Roses.

THE RAGPICKER: You shall have a bale every morning for the next five years. Money means nothing to me.

CONSTANCE: And amaryllis.

THE RAGPICKER: I'll make a note of the name. [*In his best lyrical style*] The lady understands, ladies and gentlemen. The lady is no fool. She's been around and she knows what's what. If I gave the Deaf-Mute a franc, twenty francs, twenty million francs—I still wouldn't make a dent in the forty times a thousand million francs that I'm afflicted with! Right, little lady?

CONSTANCE: Right.

JOSEPHINE: Proceed.

THE RAGPICKER: Like on the Stock Exchange. If *you* buy a stock, it sinks at once like a plummet. But if *I* buy a stock, it turns around and soars like an eagle. If I buy it at 33 . . .

PEDDLER: It goes up to a thousand.

THE RAGPICKER: It goes to twenty thousand! That's how I bought my twelve chateaux, my twenty villas, my 234 farms. That's how I endow the Opera and keep my twelve ballerinas.

FLOWER GIRL: I hope every one of them deceives you every moment of the day!

THE RAGPICKER: How can they deceive me? Suppose they try to deceive me with the male chorus, the general director, the assistant electrician, or the English horn—I own them all, body and soul. It would be like deceiving me with my big toe.

CONSTANCE: Don't listen, Gabrielle.

GABRIELLE: Listen to what?

THE RAGPICKER: No. I am incapable of jealousy. I have all the women—or I can have them, which is the same thing. I get the thin ones with caviar—the fat ones with pearls . . .

COUNTESS: So you think there are no women with morals?

THE RAGPICKER: I mix morals with mink—delicious combination. I drip pearls into protests. I adorn resistance with rubies. My touch is jeweled; my smile, a motor car. What woman can withstand me? I lift my little finger—and do they fall?—Like leaves in autumn—like tin cans from a second-story window.

CONSTANCE: That's going a little too far!

COUNTESS: You see where money leads.

THE RAGPICKER: Of course. When you have no money, nobody trusts you, nobody believes you, nobody likes you. Because to have money is to be virtuous, honest, beautiful and witty. And to be without is to be ugly and boring and stupid and useless.

COUNTESS: One last question. Suppose you find this oil you're looking for. What do you propose to do with it?

THE RAGPICKER: I propose to make war! I propose to conquer the world!

COUNTESS: You have heard the defense, such as it is. I demand a verdict of guilty.

THE RAGPICKER: What are you talking about? Guilty? I? I am never guilty!

JOSEPHINE: I order you to keep quiet.

THE RAGPICKER: I am never quiet!

JOSEPHINE: Quiet, in the name of the law!

THE RAGPICKER: I am the law. When I speak, that is the law. When I present my backside, it is etiquette to smile and to apply the lips respectfully. It is more than etiquette—it is a cherished national privilege, guaranteed by the Constitution.

JOSEPHINE: That's contempt of court. The trial is over.

COUNTESS: And the verdict?

ALL: Guilty!

JOSEPHINE: Guilty as charged.

COUNTESS: Then I have full authority to carry out the sentence?

ALL: Yes!

COUNTESS: I can do what I like with them?

ALL: Yes!

COUNTESS: I have the right to exterminate them?

ALL: Yes!

JOSEPHINE: Court adjourned!

COUNTESS: [*To the* Ragpicker] Congratulations, Ragpicker. A marvelous defense. Absolutely impartial.

THE RAGPICKER: Had I known a little before, I could have done better. I could have prepared a little speech, like the time I used to sell the Miracle Spot Remover. . . .

JOSEPHINE: No need for that. You did very well, extempore. The likeness was striking and the style reminiscent of Clemenceau. I predict a brilliant future for you. Good-bye, Aurelia. I'll take our little Gabrielle home.

CONSTANCE: I'm going to walk along the river. [*To Dickie*] Oh! So here you are. And your ear all bloody! Dickie! Have you been fighting again? Oh dear . . . !

COUNTESS: [*To the* Ragpicker] See that she gets home all right, won't you? She loses everything on the way. And in the queerest places. Her prayer book in the butcher shop. And her corset in church.

THE RAGPICKER: [*Bowing and offering his arm*] Permit me, Madame.

STREET SINGER: Oh, Countess—my mazurka. Remember?

COUNTESS: Oh, yes. Constance, wait a moment. [*To the* Singer] Well? Begin.

SINGER: [*Sings*]
Do you hear, Mademoiselle,
Those musicians of hell?

CONSTANCE: Why, of course, it's *La Belle Polonaise.* . . . [*She sings*]
From Poland to France
Comes this marvelous dance,
So gracious,
Audacious,
Will you foot it, perchance?

SINGER: I'm saved!

JOSEPHINE: [*Reappearing at the head of the stairs*]
Now my arm I entwine
Round these contours divine,
So pure, so impassioned,
Which Cupid has fashioned. . . .

GABRIELLE: [*Reappearing also, she sings a quartet with the others*]
Come, let's dance the mazurka, that devilish measure,
'Tis a joy that's reserved to the gods for their pleasure—
Let's gallop, let's hop,
With never a stop,

My blonde Polish miss,
Let our heads spin and turn
As the dance-floor we spurn—
There was never such pleasure as this!

[*They exit, dancing*]

IRMA: It's time for your afternoon nap.

COUNTESS: But suppose they come, Irma?

IRMA: I'll watch out for them.

COUNTESS: Thank you, Irma. I *am* tired. [*She smiles*] Did you ever see a trial end more happily in your life?

IRMA: Lie down and close your eyes a moment. [*The* Countess *stretches out on the chaise-longue and shuts her eyes.* Irma *tiptoes out. In a moment,* Pierre *comes down softly, the feather boa in his hands. He stands over the chaise-longue, looking tenderly down at the sleeping woman, then kneels beside her and takes her hand*]

COUNTESS: [*Without opening her eyes*] Is it you, Adolphe Bertaut?

PIERRE: It's only Pierre.

COUNTESS: Don't lie to me, Adolphe Bertaut. These are your hands. Why do you complicate things always? Say that it's you.

PIERRE: Yes. It is I.

COUNTESS: Would it cost you so much to call me Aurelia?

PIERRE: It's I, Aurelia.

COUNTESS: Why did you leave me, Adolphe Bertaut? Was she so very lovely, this Georgette of yours?

PIERRE: No. You are a thousand times lovelier.

COUNTESS: But she was clever.

PIERRE: She was stupid.

COUNTESS: It was her soul, then, that drew you? When you looked into her eyes, you saw a vision of heaven, perhaps?

PIERRE: I saw nothing.

COUNTESS: That's how it is with men. They love you because you are beautiful and clever and soulful —and at the first opportunity they leave you for someone who is plain and dull and soulless. But why does it have to be like that, Adolphe Bertaut? Why?

PIERRE: Why, Aurelia?

COUNTESS: I know very well she wasn't rich. Because when I saw you that time at the grocer's, and you snatched the only good melon from right under my nose, your cuffs, my poor friend, were badly frayed. . . .

PIERRE: Yes. She was poor.

COUNTESS: "Was" poor? Is she dead then? If it's because she's dead that you've come back to me— then no. Go away. I will not take their leavings from the dead. I refuse to inherit you. . . .

PIERRE: She's quite well.

COUNTESS: Your hands are still the same, Adolphe Bertaut. Your touch is young and firm. Because it's the only part of you that has stayed with me. The rest of you is pretty far gone, I'm afraid. I can see why you'd rather not come near me when my eyes are open. It's thoughtful of you.

PIERRE: Yes. I've aged.

COUNTESS: Not I. I am young because I haven't had to live down my youth, like you. I have it with me still, as fresh and beautiful as ever. But when you walk now in the park at Colombes with Georgette, I'm sure . . .

PIERRE: There is no longer a park at Colombes.

COUNTESS: Is there a park still at St. Cloud? Is there a park at Versailles? I've never gone back to see. But I think, if they could move, those trees would have walked away in disgust the day you went there with Georgette. . . .

PIERRE: They did. Not many are left.

COUNTESS: You take her also, I suppose, to hear *Denise*?

PIERRE: No one hears *Denise* any more.

COUNTESS: It was on the way home from *Denise*, Adolphe Bertaut, that I first took your arm. Because it was windy and it was late. I have never set foot in that street again. I go the other way round. It's not easy, in the winter, when there's ice. One is quite apt to fall. I often do.

PIERRE: Oh, my darling—forgive me.

COUNTESS: No, never. I will never forgive you. It was very bad taste to take her to the very places where we'd been together.

PIERRE: All the same, I swear, Aurelia . . .

COUNTESS: Don't swear. I know what you did. You gave her the same flowers. You bought her the same chocolates. But has she any left? No. I have all your flowers still. I have twelve chocolates. No, I will never forgive you as long as I live.

PIERRE: I always loved you, Aurelia.

COUNTESS: You "loved" me? Then you too are dead, Adolphe Bertaut?

PIERRE: No. I love you. I shall always love you, Aurelia.

COUNTESS: Yes. I know. That much I've always known. I knew it the moment you went away, Adolphe, and I knew that nothing could ever change it. Georgette is in his arms now—yes. But he loves me. Tonight he's taken Georgette to hear *Denise*— yes. But he loves me. . . . I know it. You never loved her. Do you think I believed for one moment that absurd story about her running off with the osteopath? Of course not. Since you didn't love her, obviously she stayed with you. And, after that, when she came back, and I heard about her going off with the surveyor—I knew that couldn't be true, either. You'll never get rid of her, Adolphe Bertaut—never. Because you don't love her.

PIERRE: I need your pity, Aurelia. I need your love. Don't forget me. . . .

COUNTESS: Farewell, Adolphe Bertaut. Farewell. Let go my hand, and give it to little Pierre. [Pierre *lets go her hand, and after a moment takes it again. The* Countess *opens her eyes*] Pierre? Ah, it's you. Has he gone?

PIERRE: Yes, Countess.

COUNTESS: I didn't hear him go. Oh, he knows

how to make a quick exit, that one. [*She sees the boa*] Good heavens! Wherever did you find it?

PIERRE: In the wardrobe, Countess. When I took off the mirror.

COUNTESS: Was there a purple felt shopping bag with it?

PIERRE: Yes, Countess.

COUNTESS: And a little child's sewing box?

PIERRE: No, Countess.

COUNTESS: Oh, they're frightened now. They're trembling for their lives. You see what they're up to? They're quietly putting back all the things they have stolen. I never open that wardrobe, of course, on account of the old woman in the mirror. But I have sharp eyes. I don't need to open it to see what's in it. Up to this morning, that wardrobe was empty. And now—you see? But, dear me, how stupid they are! The one thing I really miss is my little sewing box. It's something they stole from me when I was a child. They haven't put it back? You're quite sure?

PIERRE: What was it like?

COUNTESS: Green cardboard with paper lace and gold stampings. I got it for Christmas when I was seven. They stole it the very next day. I cried my eyes out every time I thought of it—until I was eight.

PIERRE: It's not there, Countess.

COUNTESS: The thimble was gilt. I swore I'd never use any other. Look at my poor fingers. . . .

PIERRE: They've kept the thimble too.

COUNTESS: Splendid! Then I'm under no obligation to be merciful. Put the boa around my neck, Pierre. I want them to see me wearing it. They'll think it's a real boa.

[Irma *runs in excitedly*]

IRMA: Here they come, Countess! You were right —it's a procession. The street is full of limousines and taxis!

COUNTESS: I will receive them. [*As Pierre hesitates to leave her*] Don't worry. There's nothing to be frightened of. [Pierre *goes out*] Irma, did you remember to stir the kerosene into the water?

IRMA: Yes, Countess. Here it is.

COUNTESS: [*Looking critically at the bottle*] You might as well pour in what's left of the tea. [Irma *shakes up the liquid*] Don't forget, I'm supposed to be deaf. I want to hear what they're thinking.

IRMA: Yes, Countess.

COUNTESS: [*Putting the finishing touches to her make-up*] I don't have to be merciful—but, after all, I do want to be just. . . .

[Irma *goes up to the landing and exits. As soon as she is alone, the* Countess *presses the brick, and the trap door opens. There is a confused sound of auto horns in the street above, and the noise of an approaching crowd*]

IRMA: [*Offstage*] Yes, Mr. President. Come in, Mr. President. You're expected, Mr. President. This way, Mr. President. [*The* Presidents *come down, led by*

the President. *They all look alike, are dressed alike, and all have long cigars*] The Countess is quite deaf, gentlemen. You'll have to shout. [*She announces*] The presidents of the boards of directors!

THE PRESIDENT: I had a premonition, Madame, when I saw you this morning, that we should meet again. [*The* Countess *smiles vaguely. He continues, a tone louder*] I want to thank you for your trust. You may place yourself in our hands with complete confidence.

SECOND PRESIDENT: Louder. The old trot can't hear you.

THE PRESIDENT: I have a letter here, Madame, in which . . .

SECOND PRESIDENT: Louder. Louder.

THIRD PRESIDENT: [*Shouting*] Is it true that you've located . . . ? [*The* Countess *stares at him blankly. He shouts at the top of his voice*] Oil? [*The* Countess *nods with a smile, and points down. The* President *produces a legal paper and a fountain pen*] Sign here.

COUNTESS: What is it? I haven't my glasses.

THE PRESIDENT: Your contract.

[*He offers the pen*]

COUNTESS: Thank you.

SECOND PRESIDENT: [*Normal voice*] What is it?

THIRD PRESIDENT: Waiver of all rights. [*He takes it back signed*] Thank you. [*He hands it to the* Second President] Witness. [*The* Second President *witnesses it. The* President *passes it on to the* Third President] Notarize. [*The paper is notarized. The* President *turns to the* Countess *and shouts*] My congratulations. And now, Madame—[*He produces a gold brick wrapped in tissue paper*] If you'll show us the well, this package is yours.

COUNTESS: What is it?

THE PRESIDENT: Pure gold. Twenty-four karat. For you.

COUNTESS: Thank you very much. [*She takes it*] It's heavy.

SECOND PRESIDENT: Are you going to give her that?

THE PRESIDENT: Don't worry. We'll pick it up again on the way out. [*He shouts at the* Countess, *pointing at the trap door*] Is this the way?

COUNTESS: That's the way.

[*The* Second President *tries to slip in first. The* President *pulls him back*]

THE PRESIDENT: Just a minute, Mr. President. After me, if you don't mind. And watch those cigars. It's oil, you know.

[*But as he is about to descend, the* Countess *steps forward*]

COUNTESS: Just one moment . . .

THE PRESIDENT: Yes?

COUNTESS: Did any of you happen to bring along a little sewing box?

THE PRESIDENT: Sewing box? [*He pulls back another impatient* President] Take it easy.

COUNTESS: Or a little gold thimble?

THE PRESIDENT: Not me,

THE PRESIDENTS: Not us.

COUNTESS: What a pity!

THE PRESIDENT: Can we go down now?

COUNTESS: Yes. You may go down now. Watch your step!

[*They hurry down eagerly. When they have quite disappeared,* Irma *appears on the landing and announces the next echelon*]

IRMA: Countess, the Prospectors.

COUNTESS: Heavens! Are there more than one?

IRMA: There's a whole delegation.

COUNTESS: Send them down.

[*The* Prospector *comes in, following his nose*]

IRMA: Come in, please.

THE PROSPECTOR: [*Sniffing the air like a bloodhound*] I smell something. . . . Who's that?

IRMA: The Countess. She is very deaf.

THE PROSPECTOR: Good.

[*The* Prospectors *also look alike. Sharp clothes, Western hats and long noses. They crowd down the stairs after the* Prospector, *sniffing in unison. The* Prospector *is especially talented. He casts about on the scent until it leads him to the decanter on the table. He pours himself a glass, drinks it off, and belches with much satisfaction. The others join him at once, and follow his example. They all belch in unison*]

THE PROSPECTORS: Oil?

THP PROSPECTOR: Oil!

COUNTESS: Oil.

THE PROSPECTOR: Traces? Puddles?

COUNTESS: Pools. Gushers.

SECOND PROSPECTOR: Characteristic odor?

[*He sniffs*]

THE PROSPECTOR: Chanel Number 5. Nectar! Undoubtedly—the finest—rarest! [*He drinks*] Sixty gravity crude: straight gasoline! [*To the* Countess] How found? By blast? Drill?

COUNTESS: By finger.

THE PROSPECTOR: [*Whipping out a document*] Sign here, please.

COUNTESS: What is it?

THE PROSPECTOR: Agreement for dividing the profits. . . .

[*The* Countess *signs*]

SECOND PROSPECTOR: [*To First Prospector*] What is it?

THE PROSPECTOR: [*Pocketing the paper*] Application to enter a lunatic asylum. Down there?

COUNTESS: Down there.

[*The* Prospectors *go down, sniffing*]

[Irma *enters*]

IRMA: The gentlemen of the press are here.

COUNTESS: The rest of the machine! Show them in.

IRMA: The Public Relations Counsellors! [*They enter, all shapes and sizes, all in blue pin-striped suits and black homburg hats*] The Countess is very deaf, gentlemen. You'll have to shout!

FIRST PRESS AGENT: You don't say— Delighted to make the acquaintance of so charming and beautiful a lady . . .

SECOND PRESS AGENT: Louder. She can't hear you.

FIRST PRESS AGENT: What a face! [*Shouts*] Madame, we are the press. You know our power. We fix all values. We set all standards. Your entire future depends on us.

COUNTESS: How do you do?

FIRST PRESS AGENT: What will we charge the old trull? The usual thirty?

SECOND PRESS AGENT: Forty.

THIRD PRESS AGENT: Sixty.

FIRST PRESS AGENT: All right—seventy-five. [*He fills in a form and offers it to the* Countess] Sign here, Countess. This contract really gives you a break.

COUNTESS: That is the entrance.

FIRST PRESS AGENT: Entrance to what?

COUNTESS: The oil well.

FIRST PRESS AGENT: Oh, we don't need to see that, Madame.

COUNTESS: Don't need to see it?

FIRST PRESS AGENT: No, no—we don't have to see it to write about it. We can imagine it. An oil well is an oil well. "That's oil we know on earth, and oil we need to know."

[*He bows*]

COUNTESS: But if you don't see it, how can you be sure the oil is there?

FIRST PRESS AGENT: If it's there, well and good. If it's not, by the time we get through, it will be. You underestimate the creative aspect of our profession, Madame. [*The* Countess *shakes her head, handing back the papers*] I warn you, if you insist on rubbing our noses in this oil, it will cost you 10 percent extra.

COUNTESS: It's worth it.

[*She signs. They cross toward the trap door*]

SECOND PRESS AGENT: [*Descending*] You see, Madame, we of the press can refuse a lady nothing.

THIRD PRESS AGENT: Especially, such a lady.

[Third Press Agent *starts going down*]

SECOND PRESS AGENT: [*Going down. Gallantly*] It's plain to see, Madame, that even fountains of oil have their nymphs. . . . I can use that somewhere. That's copy!

[*The* Press Agents *go down. As he disappears, the* First Press Agent *steals the gold brick and blows a kiss gallantly to the* Countess, *who blows one back*]

[*There is a high-pitched chatter offstage, and* Irma *comes in, trying hard to hold back* Three Women *who pay no attention to her whatever. These* Women *are tall, slender, and as soulless as if they were molded of wax. They march down the steps, erect and abstracted like animated window models, but chattering incessantly*]

IRMA: But, ladies, please—you have no business

here—you are not expected. [*To the* Countess] There are some strange ladies coming. . . .

COUNTESS: Show them in, Irma. [*The* Women *come down, without taking the slightest interest in their surroundings*] Who are you?

FIRST WOMAN: Madame, we are the most powerful pressure group in the world.

SECOND WOMAN: We are the ultimate dynamic.

THIRD WOMAN: The mainspring of all combinations.

FIRST WOMAN: Nothing succeeds without our assistance. Is that the well, Madame?

COUNTESS: That is the well.

FIRST WOMAN: Put out your cigarettes, girls. We don't want any explosions. Not with my brand-new eyelashes.

[*They go down, still chattering. The* Countess *crosses to the wall to close the trap. As she does so, there is a commotion on the landing*]

IRMA: Countess . . .

[*A* Man *rushes in breathlessly*]

MAN: Just a minute! Just a minute!

[*He rushes for the trap door*]

COUNTESS: Wait! Who are you?

MAN: I'm in a hurry. Excuse me. It's my only chance!

[*He rushes down*]

COUNTESS: But . . . [*But he is gone. She shrugs her shoulders, and presses the brick. The trap closes. She rings the bell for* Irma] My gold brick! Why, they've stolen my gold brick! [*She moves toward the trap. It is now closed*] Well, let them take their god with them.

[Irma *enters and sees with astonishment that the stage is empty of all but the* Countess. *Little by little, the scene is suffused with light, faint at first, but increasing as if the very walls were glowing with the quiet radiance of universal joy. Only around the closed trap a shadow lingers*]

IRMA: But what's happened? They've gone! They've vanished!

COUNTESS: They've evaporated, Irma. They were wicked. Wickedness evaporates.

[Pierre *enters. He is followed by the* Vagabonds, *all of them. The new radiance of the world is now very perceptible. It glows from their faces*]

PIERRE: Oh, Countess . . . !

WAITER: Countess, everything's changed. Now you can breathe again. Now you can see.

PIERRE: The air is pure! The sky is clear!

IRMA: Life is beautiful again.

THE RAGPICKER: [*Rushes in*] Countess—the pigeons! The pigeons are flying!

FLOWER GIRL: They don't have to walk any more.

THE RAGPICKER: They're flying. . . . The air is like crystal. And young grass is sprouting on the pavements.

COUNTESS: Is it possible?

IRMA: [*Interpreting for the* Deaf-Mute] Now, Juggler, you can throw your fireballs up as high as you please—they won't go out.

SERGEANT: On the street, utter strangers are shaking hands, they don't know why, and offering each other almond bars!

COUNTESS: Oh, my friends . . .

WAITER: Countess, we thank you. . . .

[*They go on talking with happy and animated gestures, but we no longer hear them, for their words blend into a strain of unearthly music which seems to thrill from the uttermost confines of the universe. And out of this music comes a voice*]

FIRST VOICE: Countess . . .

[*Only the* Countess *hears it. She turns from the group of* Vagabonds *in wonder*]

SECOND VOICE: Countess . . .

THIRD VOICE: Countess . . .

[*As she looks up in rapture, the* First Voice *speaks again*]

FIRST VOICE: Countess, we thank you. We are the friends of animals.

SECOND VOICE: We are the friends of people.

THIRD VOICE: We are the friends of friendship.

FIRST VOICE: You have freed us!

SECOND VOICE: From now on, there will be no hungry cats. . . .

THIRD VOICE: And we shall tell the Duchess her dog's right name!

[*The voices fade off. And now another group of voices is heard*]

FIRST VOICE: Countess, we thank you. We are the friends of flowers.

SECOND VOICE: From now on, every plant in Paris will be watered. . . .

THIRD VOICE: And the sewers will be fragrant with jasmine!

[*These voices, too, are silent. For an instant, the stage is vibrant with music. Then the* Deaf-Mute *speaks, and his voice is the most beautiful of all*]

DEAF-MUTE: Sadness flies on the wings of the morning, and out of the heart of darkness comes the light.

[*Suddenly a group of figures detaches itself from the shadows. These are exactly similar in face and figure and in dress. They are shabby in the fashion of 1900 and their cuffs are badly frayed. Each bears in his hand a ripe melon*]

FIRST ADOLPHE BERTAUT: Countess, we thank you. We, too, are freed at last. We are the Adolphe Bertauts of the world.

SECOND ADOLPHE BERTAUT: We are no longer timid.

THIRD ADOLPHE BERTAUT: We are no longer weak.

FIRST ADOLPHE BERTAUT: From this day on, we shall hold fast to what we love. For your sake, henceforth, we shall be handsome, and our cuffs forever immaculate and new. Countess, we bring you this melon and with it our hearts . . . ! [*They all kneel*] Will you do us the honor to be our wife?

COUNTESS: [*Sadly*] Too late! Too late! [*She waves them aside. They take up their melons sadly and vanish. The voices of the* Vagabonds *are heard again, and the music dies*] Too late! Too late!

PIERRE: Too late, Countess?

IRMA: Too late for what?

COUNTESS: I say that it's too late for them. On the twenty-fourth of May, 1881, the most beautiful Easter in the memory of man, it was not too late. And on the fifth of September, 1887, the day they caught the trout and broiled it on the open fire by the brook at Villeneuve, it was not too late. And it was even not too late for them on the twenty-first of August, 1897, the day the Czar visited Paris with his guard. But they did nothing and they said nothing, and now—kiss each other, you two, this very instant!

IRMA: You mean . . . ?

PIERRE: You mean . . . ?

IRMA: But, Countess . . .

COUNTESS: It's three hours since you've met and known and loved each other. Kiss each other quickly. [Pierre *hesitates*] Look at him. He hesitates. He trembles. Happiness frightens him. . . . How like a man! Oh, Irma, kiss him, kiss him! If two people who love

each other let a single instant wedge itself between them, it grows—it becomes a month, a year, a century; it becomes too late. Kiss him, Irma, kiss him while there is time, or in a moment his hair will be white and there will be another madwoman in Paris. Oh, make her kiss him, all of you! [*They kiss*] Bravo! Oh, if only you'd had the courage to do that thirty years ago, how different I would be today! Dear Deaf-Mute, be still—your words dazzle our eyes! And Irma is too busy to translate for you. [*They kiss once more*] Well, there we are. The world is saved. And you see how simple it all was? Nothing is ever so wrong in this world that a sensible woman can't set it right in the course of an afternoon. Only, the next time, don't wait until things begin to look black. The minute you notice anything, tell me at once.

THE RAGPICKER: We will, Countess. We will.

COUNTESS: [*Puts on her hat. Her tone becomes businesslike*] Irma. My bones. My gizzard.

IRMA: I have them ready, Countess.

COUNTESS: Good. [*She puts the bones into her basket and starts for the stairs*] Well, let's go on to more important things. Four o'clock. My poor cats must be starved. What a bore for them if humanity had to be saved every afternoon. They don't think much of it, as it is.

CURTAIN

THE LARK

By Jean Anouilh

IN THE ADAPTATION BY LILLIAN HELLMAN

CHARACTERS

WARWICK	THE INQUISITOR	ARCHBISHOP OF REIMS
CAUCHON	BROTHER LADVENU	CAPTAIN LA HIRE
JOAN	ROBERT DE BEAUDRICOURT	EXECUTIONER
JOAN'S FATHER	AGNES SOREL	ENGLISH SOLDIER
JOAN'S MOTHER	THE LITTLE QUEEN	SCRIBE
JOAN'S BROTHER	THE DAUPHIN	LADIES OF THE COURT
THE PROMOTER	QUEEN YOLANDE	MONKS AND SOLDIERS
	MONSIEUR DE LA TREMOUILLE	

ACT ONE: The Trial.

ACT TWO: The Trial.

ACT I.

The music for the play was composed by Leonard Bernstein. It was sung and recorded by a group of seven men and women, without instruments, and with solos by a countertenor.

Before the curtain rises we hear the music of a psalm: the chorus is singing "Exaudi orationem meam, domine." When the curtain rises the music changes to a motet on the words "Qui tollis," from the Mass. (Note: The musical directions refer only to the Broadway stage production.)

THE SCENE—*Another day in the trial of* Joan. *The stage is a series of platforms, different in size and in height. The cyclorama is gray in color and projections will be thrown on it to indicate a change of scene. At this moment we see the bars of a jail as they are projected on the cyclorama.*

AT RISE—Joan *is sitting on a stool.* Cauchon *is standing downstage near* The Promoter. *The Priests are about to take their places on the* Judges' *bench. The Inquisitor sits quietly on a stool near the* Judges. Joan's *family stand upstage; the royal family stand in a group.* Village Women *cross the stage carrying bundles of faggots and* English Soldiers *and* Guards *move into place.* Beaudricourt *and* La Hire *appear and take their places upstage.*

[Warwick *enters and moves through the crowd*]

WARWICK: Everybody here? Good. Let the trial begin at once. The quicker the judgment and the burning, the better for all of us.

CAUCHON: No, sire. The whole story must be played. Domremy, the Voices, Chinon——

WARWICK: I am not here to watch that children's story of the warrior virgin, strong and tender, dressed in white armor, white standard streaming in the wind. If they have time to waste, they can make the statues that way, in days to come. Different politics may well require different symbols. We might even have to make her a monument in London. Don't be shocked at that, sire. The politics of my government may well require it one day, and what's required, Englishmen supply. That's our secret, sire, and a very good one, indeed. [*Moves downstage to address the audience*] Well, let's worry about only this minute of time. I am Beauchamp, Earl of Warwick. I have a dirty virgin witch girl tucked away on a litter of straw in the depths of a prison here in Rouen. The girl has been an expensive nuisance. Your Duke of Burgundy sold her high. You like money in France, Monseigneur, all of you. That's the French secret, sire, and a very good one, indeed. [*He moves toward* Joan] And here she is. The Maid. The famous Joan the Maid. Obviously, we paid too much. So put her on trial, and burn her, and be finished.

CAUCHON: No, sire. She must play out her whole life first. It's a short life. It won't take very long.

WARWICK: [*Moves to a stool near* Cauchon] If you insist. Englishmen are patient, and for the purposes of this trial I am all Englishmen. But certainly you don't intend to amuse yourselves by acting out all the old battles? I would find that very disagreeable. Nobody wishes to remember defeat.

CAUCHON: No, sire. We no longer have enough men to act out the old battles. [*Turns toward* Joan] Joan? [Joan *turns to* Cauchon] You may begin.

JOAN: Can I begin any place I want to?

CAUCHON: Yes.

JOAN: Then I'll start at the beginning. It's always nicer at the beginning. I'll begin with my father's house when I was very small. [*Her* Mother, *her* Father *and her* Brothers *appear on stage. She runs to join them*] I live here happy enough with my mother, my brothers, my father. [*We hear the music of a shepherd song and as she leaves the family group she dances her way downstage, clapping her hands to the music*] I'm in the meadow now, watching my sheep. I am not thinking of anything. It is

1204

the first time I hear the Voices. I wasn't thinking of anything. I know only that God is good and that He keeps me pure and safe in this little corner of the earth near Domremy. This one little piece of French earth that has not yet been destroyed by the English invaders. [*She makes childish thrusts with an imaginary sword, and stops suddenly as if someone has pulled her back*] Then, suddenly, someone behind me touched my shoulder. I know very well that no one is behind me. I turn and there is a great blinding light in the shadow of me. The Voice is grave and sweet and I was frightened. But I didn't tell anybody. I don't know why. Then came the second time. It was the noon Angelus. A light came over the sun and was stronger than the sun. There he was. I saw him. An angel in a beautiful clean robe that must have been ironed by somebody very careful. He had two great white wings. He didn't tell me his name that day, but later I found out he was Monseigneur the Blessed Saint Michael.

WARWICK: [*To* Cauchon] We know all this. Is it necessary to let her go over that nonsense again?

CAUCHON: It is necessary, sire.

JOAN: Blessed Saint Michael, excuse me, but you are in the wrong village. I am Joan, an ignorant girl, my father's daughter—— [*Pauses, listens*] I can't save France. I don't even know how to ride a horse. [*Smiles*] To you people the Sire de Beaudricourt is only a country squire, but to us he is master here. He would never take me to the Dauphin, I've never even bowed to him—— [*Turns to the court*] Then the Blessed Saint Michael said Saint Catherine would come along with me, and if that wasn't enough Saint Marguerite would go, too. [*She turns back as if to listen to Saint Michael*] But when the army captains lose a battle—and they lose a great many—they can go to sleep at night. I could never send men to their death. Forgive me, Blessed Saint Michael, but I must go home now—— [*But she doesn't move. She is held back by a command*] Oh, Blessed Saint Michael, have pity on me. Have pity, Messire. [*The chorus sings* "Alleluia, Alleluia" *to the shepherd's tune. She listens, smiles, moves back into the trial. Simply*] Well, he didn't. And that was the day I was saddled with France. *And* my work on the farm.

[*The Father who has been moving about near The Mother, suddenly grows angry*]

THE FATHER: What's she up to?

THE MOTHER: She's in the fields.

THE FATHER: So was I, in the fields, but I've come in. It's six o'clock! I ask you, what's she up to?

THE BROTHER: She's dreaming under the lady tree.

THE FATHER: What's anybody doing under a tree at this hour?

THE BROTHER: You ask her. She stares straight ahead. She looks as if she is waiting for something. It isn't the first time.

THE FATHER: [*Angrily to* The Brother] Why didn't you tell me? She is waiting for someone, not something. She has a lover.

THE MOTHER: [*Softly*] Joan is as clean as a baby.

THE FATHER: All girls are as clean as babies until that night when they aren't any more. I'll find her and if she is with someone, I'll beat her until——

JOAN: I was with someone, but my lover had two great white wings and through the rain he came so close to me that I thought I could touch his wings. He was very worried that day, he told me so. He said the Kingdom of France was in great misery and that God said I could wait no longer. There has been a mistake, I kept saying. The Blessed Saint Michael asked me if God made mistakes. You understand that I couldn't very well say yes?

THE PROMOTER: Why didn't you make the Sign of the Cross?

JOAN: That question is not written in your charge against me.

THE PROMOTER: Why didn't you say to the archangel, "*Vado retro Satanas?*"

JOAN: I don't know any Latin, Messire. And *that* question is not written in your charge against me.

THE PROMOTER: Don't act the fool. The devil understands French. You could have said, "Go away, you filthy, stinking devil."

JOAN: [*Angry*] I don't talk that way to the Blessed Saint Michael, Messire!

THE PROMOTER: The Devil told you he was Saint Michael and you were fool enough to believe him.

JOAN: I believed him. He could not have been the Devil. He was so beautiful.

THE PROMOTER: The Devil *is* beautiful!

JOAN: [*Shocked*] Oh, Messire!

CAUCHON: [*To* The Promoter] These theological subtleties are far above the understanding of this poor child. You shock her without reason.

JOAN: [*To* The Promoter] You've lied, Canon! I am not as educated as you are, but I know the Devil *is* ugly and everything that is beautiful is the work of God. I have no doubts. I know.

THE PROMOTER: You know nothing. Evil has a lovely face when a lovely face is needed. In real life the Devil waits for a soft, sweet night of summer. Then he comes on a gentle wind in the form of a beautiful girl with bare breasts——

CAUCHON: [*Sharply*] Canon, let us not get mixed up in our private devils. Continue, Joan.

JOAN: [*To* The Promoter] But if the Devil is beautiful, how can we know he is the Devil?

THE PROMOTER: Go to your priest. He will tell you.

JOAN: Can't I recognize him all by myself?

THE PROMOTER: No. Certainly not. No.

JOAN: But only the rich have their priests always with them. The poor can't be running back and forth.

THE PROMOTER: [*Angry*] I do not like the way you speak in this court. I warn you again——

CAUCHON: Enough, enough, Messire. Let her speak peacefully with her Voices. There is nothing to reproach her with so far.

JOAN: Then another time it was Saint Marguerite and Saint Catherine who came to me. [*She turns to* The Promoter] and they, too, were beautiful.

THE PROMOTER: Were they naked?

JOAN: [*Laughs*] Oh, Messire! Don't you think our Lord can afford to buy clothing for His Saints?

CAUCHON: [*To* The Promoter] You make us all smile, Messire, with your questions. You are confusing the girl with the suggestion that good and evil is a question of what clothes are worn by what Angels and what Devils. [*Turns to* Joan] But it is not your place to correct the venerable Canon. You forget who you are and who we are. We are your priests, your masters, and your judges. Beware of your pride, Joan.

JOAN: [*Softly*] I know that I am proud. But I am a daughter of God. If He didn't want me to be proud, why did He send me His shining Archangel and His Saints all dressed in light? Why did He promise me that I should conquer all the men I have conquered? Why did He promise me a suit of beautiful white armor, the gift of my king? And a sword? And that I should lead brave soldiers into battle while riding a fine white horse? If He had left me alone, I would never have become proud.

CAUCHON: Take care of your words, Joan. You are accusing our Lord.

JOAN: [*Makes the Sign of the Cross*] Oh, God forbid. I say only that His Will be done even if it means making me proud and then damning me for it. That, too, is His Right.

THE PROMOTER: [*Very angry*] What are you saying? Could God wish to damn a human soul? How can you listen to her without shuddering, Messires? I see here the germ of a frightful heresy that could tear the Church——

[The Inquisitor *rises*. The Promoter *stops speaking. The stage is silent*. Ladvenu, *a young priest, rises and goes to* The Inquisitor. The Inquisitor *whispers to him*. Ladvenu *moves to* Cauchon, *whispers to him*]

CAUCHON: [*Looks toward* The Inquisitor; *very hesitant*] Messire—— [The Inquisitor *stares at* Cauchon. Cauchon *hesitates, then turns toward* Joan] Joan, listen well to what I must ask you. At this moment, are you in a State of Grace?

LADVENU: Messire, this is a fearful question for a simple girl who sincerely believes that God has chosen her. Do not hold her answer against her. She is in great danger and she is confused.

CAUCHON: Are you in a State of Grace?

JOAN: [*As if she knew this was a dangerous question*] Which moment is that, Messire? Everything is so mixed up, I no longer know where I am. At the beginning when I heard my Voices, or at the end of the trial when I knew that my king and my friends had abandoned me? When I lost faith, when I recanted, or when, at the very last minute, I gave myself back to myself? When——

CAUCHON: [*Softly, worried*] Messire demands an answer. His reasons must be grave. Joan, are you in a State of Grace?

JOAN: If I am not, God will help me in Grace. If I am, God will keep me in Grace.

[*The* Priests *murmur among themselves*. The Inquisitor, *impassive, sits down*]

LADVENU: [*Gently, warmly*] Well spoken, Joan.

THE PROMOTER: [*Sharply*] And the Devil would have the same clever answer.

WARWICK: [*To* Cauchon, *pointing to* The Inquisitor] Is that the gentleman about whom I have been told?

CAUCHON: [*Softly*] Yes.

WARWICK: When did he arrive?

CAUCHON: Three days ago. He has wished to be alone.

WARWICK: Why was I not told of his arrival?

CAUCHON: He is one of us, sire. We do not acknowledge your authority here.

WARWICK: Only when you count our money and eat our food. Never mind, the formalities do not matter to me. But time does and I hope his presence will not add to the confusion. I am almost as bewildered as the girl. All these questions must be very interesting to you gentlemen of the Church, but if we continue at this speed we'll never get to the trial and the girl will be dead of old age. Get to the burning and be done with it.

CAUCHON: [*Angry*] Sire! Who speaks of burning? We will try to save the girl——

WARWICK: Monseigneur, I allow you this charade because the object of my government is to tell the whole Christian world that the coronation of the idiot Charles was managed by a sorceress, a heretic, a mad girl, a whore camp follower. However you do that, please move with greater speed.

CAUCHON: And I remind you each day that this is a court of the Church. We are here to judge the charge of heresy. Our considerations are not yours.

WARWICK: My dear Bishop, I know that. But the fine points of ecclesiastic judgments may be a little too distinguished for my soldiers—and for the rest of the world. Propaganda is a soft weapon: hold it in your hands too long, and it will move about like a snake, and strike the other way. Whatever the girl is or has been, she must now be stripped and degraded. That is why we bought her high, and it is what we will insist upon. [*Smiles*] I'm coming to like her. I admire the way she stands up to all of you. And she rides beautifully—I've seen her. Rare to find a woman who rides that way. I'd like to have known her in other circumstances, in a pleasanter world. Hard for me to remember that she took France away from us, deprived us of our heritage. We know that God is on the side of the English. He proved himself at Agincourt. "God and my right," you know. But when this girl came along, and we began to lose, there were those who doubted our motto. That, of course, cannot be tolerated. "God and my right" is inscribed on all English armor, and we certainly have no intention of changing the armor. So get on with her story. The world will forget her soon enough. Where were we?

THE FATHER: [*Comes forward*] At the moment when I find her under the lady tree. [*He goes to

Joan] What are you doing? You were crying out to someone, but the bastard fled before I could catch him. Who was it? Who was it? Answer me. Answer me, or I'll beat you to salt mash.

JOAN: I was talking to the Blessed Saint Michael.

THE FATHER: [*Hits* Joan] That will teach you to lie to your father. You want to start whoring like the others. Well, you can tell your Blessed Saint Michael that if I catch you together I'll plunge my pitchfork into his belly and strangle you with my bare hands for the filthy rutting cat you are.

JOAN: [*Softly*] Father, it was Saint Michael who was talking to me.

THE FATHER: The priest will hear about this, and from me. I'll tell him straight out that not content with running after men, you have also dared to blaspheme!

JOAN: I swear to you before God that I am telling the truth. It's been happening for a long time and always at the noon or evening Angelus. The Saints appear to me. They speak to me. They answer me when I question them. And they all say the same thing.

THE FATHER: Why would the Saints speak to you, idiot? I am your father, why don't they speak to me? If they had anything to say they'd talk to me.

JOAN: Father, try to understand the trouble I'm in. For three years I've refused what they ask. But I don't think I can say no much longer. I think the moment has come when I must go.

THE FATHER: For forty years I've worked myself to death to raise my children like Christians, and this is my reward. A daughter who thinks she hears Voices.

JOAN: They say I can't wait any longer——

THE FATHER: What can't wait any longer?

JOAN: They tell me France is at the last moment of danger. My voices tell me I must save her.

THE FATHER: You? You? You are crazy. Crazy. You are a fool! A fool and a crazy girl.

JOAN: I must do what my Voices tell me. I will go to the Sire de Beaudricourt and ask him to give me an armed escort to the Dauphin at Chinon. I'll talk to the Dauphin and make him fight. Then I will take the army to Orléans and we'll push the English into the sea.

THE FATHER: For ten years I have dreamed that you would disgrace us with men. Do you think I raised you, sacrificed everything for you, to have you run off to live with soldiers? I knew what you would be. But you won't—I'll kill you first.

[*He begins to beat her and to kick her*]

JOAN: [*Screams*] Stop! Stop! Oh, Father, stop!

LADVENU: [*Rises, horrified*] Stop him. Stop him. He's hurting her.

CAUCHON: We cannot, Brother Ladvenu. We do not know Joan. You forget that we first meet her at the trial. We can only play our roles, good or bad, just as they were, each in his turn. And we will hurt her far more than he does. You know that.

[*Turns to* Warwick] Ugly, isn't it, this family scene?

WARWICK: Why? In England we are in favor of strong punishment for children. It makes character. I was half beaten to death as a boy, but I am in excellent health.

THE FATHER: [*He looks down at* Joan *who has fallen at his feet*] Crazy little whore. Do you still want to save France? [*Then, shamefaced, he turns to the* Judges] Well, messieurs, what would you have done in my place if your daughter had been like that?

WARWICK: If we had known about this girl from the very beginning, we could have reached an agreement with her father. We tell people that our intelligence service is remarkable and we say it so often that everybody believes us. It should be their business not only to tell us what is happening, but what might happen. When a country virgin talked about saving France, I should have known about it. I tell myself now I would not have laughed.

[*The* Mother *comes forward. She bends over* Joan]

THE FATHER: [*To* The Mother] The next time your daughter talks of running after soldiers, I'll put her in the river and with my own hands I'll hold her under.

[*The* Mother *takes* Joan *in her arms*]

THE MOTHER: He hurt you bad.

JOAN: Yes.

THE MOTHER: [*Softly*] He's your father.

JOAN: Yes. He is my father. Oh, Mama, somebody must understand. I can't do it alone.

THE MOTHER: Lean against me. You're big now. I can hardly hold you in my arms. Joan, your father is a good and honest man but—[*She whispers in* Joan's *ear*] I've saved a little from the house money. If you'd like one, I'll buy you a broidered kerchief at the very next fair.

JOAN: I don't need a kerchief. I won't ever be pretty, Mama.

THE MOTHER: We're all a little wild when we're young. Who is it, Joan? Don't have secrets from me. Is he from our village?

JOAN: I don't want to marry, Mama. That isn't what I mean.

THE MOTHER: Then what do you mean?

JOAN: Blessed Saint Michael says that I must put on man's clothes. He says that I must save France.

THE MOTHER: Joan, I speak to you in kindness, but I forbid you to tell me such nonsense. A man's clothes! I should just like to see you try it.

JOAN: But I'll have to, Mama, if I'm to ride horse with my soldiers. Saint Michael makes good sense.

THE MOTHER: Your soldiers? Your soldiers? You bad girl! I'd rather see you dead first. Now I'm talking like your father, and that I never want to do. [*She begins to cry*] Running after soldiers! What have I done to deserve a daughter like this? You will kill me.

JOAN: No, Mama, no. [*She cries out as her* Mother *moves off*] Monseigneur Saint Michael. It cannot be done. Nobody will ever understand. It is better for me to say no right now. [*Pauses, listens*] Then Saint Michael's voice grew soft, the way it does when he is angry. And he said that I must take the first step. He said that God trusted me and if a mountain of ice did rise ahead of me it was only because God was busy and trusted me to climb the mountain even if I tore my hands and broke my legs, and my face might run with blood—— [*After a second, slowly, carefully*] Then I said that I would go. I said that I would go that day.

[*Joan's Brother comes forward and stands looking at her*]

THE BROTHER: You haven't got the sense you were born with. If you give me something next time, I won't tell Papa I saw you with your lover.

JOAN: So it was you, you pig, you told them? Here's what I'll give you this time—— [*She slaps him*] And the next time—[*She slaps him again, and begins to chase him. He runs from her*] and the time after that. [*Joan's voice changes and she moves slowly about, not concerned with him any longer but speaking into space*] And so I went to my uncle Durand. And my uncle Durand went to the seigneur of the manor. And I walked a long way west and a little way south and there was the night I was shivering with rain—or with fear—and the day I was shivering with sun—or with fear—and then I walked to the west again and east. I was on my way to the first fool I had to deal with. And I had plenty of them to deal with.

[*She moves upstage, bumps into two* Soldiers *as* Beaudricourt *comes on stage*]

BEAUDRICOURT: What is it? What's the matter? What does she want? What's the matter with these crazy fools? [*He grabs* Joan *and shakes her*] What's the matter with you, young woman? You've been carrying on like a bad girl. I've heard about you standing outside the doors ragging at the sentries until they fall asleep.

[*He holds her up. She dangles in front of his face*]

JOAN: I want a horse. I want the dress of a man. I want an armed escort. You will give them orders to take me to Chinon to see the Dauphin.

BEAUDRICOURT: Of course. And I will also kick you in the place where it will do the most good.

JOAN: Kicks, blows. Whichever you like best. I'm used to them by now. I want a horse. I want the dress of a man. I want an armed escort.

BEAUDRICOURT: That's a new idea—a horse. You know who I am and what I usually want? Did the village girls tell you? When they come to ask a favor it usually has to do with a father or a brother who has poached my land. If the girl is pretty, I have a good heart, and we both pitch in. If the girl is ugly, well, usually I have a good heart, too, but not so good as the other way. I am known in this land for goodheartedness. But a horse is a nasty kind of bargain.

JOAN: I have been sent by Blessed Saint Michael.

BEAUDRICOURT: [*Puts her down hurriedly, makes the Sign of the Cross*] Don't mix the Saints up in this kind of thing. That talk was good enough to get you past the sentries, but it's not good enough to get you a horse. A horse costs more than a woman. You're a country girl. You ought to know that. Are you a virgin?

JOAN: Yes, sire.

BEAUDRICOURT: Well, maybe we'll talk about a small horse. You have lovely eyes.

JOAN: I want more than a horse, sire.

BEAUDRICOURT: [*Laughs*] You're greedy. But I like that sometimes. There are fools who get angry when the girl wants too much. But I say good things should cost a lot. That pleases me in a girl. You understand what I mean?

JOAN: No, sire.

BEAUDRICOURT: That's good. I don't like clear-thinking women in bed. Not in my bed. You understand what I mean?

JOAN: No, sire.

BEAUDRICOURT: Well, I don't like idiots, either. What is it you're up to? What else besides a horse?

JOAN: Just as I said before, sire. An armed escort as far as Chinon.

BEAUDRICOURT: Stop that crazy talk. I'm the master here. I can send you back where you came from with no better present than the lashes of a whip. I told you I like a girl to come high, but if she costs too much the opposite effect sets in—and I can't—well, I can't. You understand what I mean? [*Suddenly*] Why do you want to go to Chinon?

JOAN: As I said before, sire, I wish to find Monseigneur the Dauphin.

BEAUDRICOURT: Well, you *are* on a high road. Why not the Duke of Burgundy while you're at it? He's more powerful, and he likes the girls. But not our Dauphin. He runs from war and women. An hour with either would kill him. Why do you want to see such a fellow?

JOAN: I want an army, Messire. An army to march upon Orléans.

BEAUDRICOURT: If you're crazy, forget about me. [*Shouting*] Boudousse. Boudousse. [*A Soldier comes forward*] Throw some cold water on this girl and send her back to her father. Don't beat her. It's bad luck to beat a crazy woman.

JOAN: You won't beat me. You're a kind man, Messire. Very kind.

BEAUDRICOURT: Sometimes yes, sometimes no. But I don't like virgins whose heads come off at night——

JOAN: And you're very intelligent, which is sometimes even better than being kind. But when a man is intelligent *and* kind, then that's the very best combination on God's fine earth.

BEAUDRICOURT: [*He waves the* Guard *away*] You're a strange girl. Want a little wine? Why do you think I'm intelligent?

JOAN: It shows in your face. You're handsome, Messire.

BEAUDRICOURT: Twenty years ago, I wouldn't have said no. I married two rich widows, God bless me. But not now. Of course, I've tried not to get old too fast, and there are men who get better looking with age—— [Smiles] You know, it's very comic to be talking like this with a shepherd girl who drops out of the sky one bright morning. I am bored here. My officers are animals. I have nobody to talk to. I like a little philosophy now and then. I should like to know from your mouth what connection you see between beauty and intelligence? Usually people say that handsome men are stupid.

JOAN: Hunchbacks talk that way, and people with long noses, or those who will die of a bitter egg that grows in their head. God has the power to create a perfect man—— [She smiles at him] And sometimes He uses His power.

BEAUDRICOURT: Well, you can look at it that way, of course. But you take me, for example. No, I'm not ugly, but sometimes I wonder if I'm intelligent. No, no, don't protest. I tell you there are times when I have problems that seem too much for me. They ask me to decide something, a tactical or administrative point. Then, all of a sudden, I don't know why, my head acts like it's gone someplace else, and I don't even understand the words people are saying. Isn't that strange? [After a second] But I never show it. I roar out an order, whatever happens. That's the main thing in an army. Make a decision, good or bad, just make it. Things will turn out almost the same, anyway. [Softly, as if to himself] Still, I wish I could have done better. This is a small village to die away your life. [Points outside] They think I'm a great man, but they never saw anybody else. Like every other man, I wanted to be brilliant and remarkable, but I end up hanging a few poor bastards who deserted from a broken army. I wanted to shake a nation—— Ah, well. [Looks at her] Why do I tell you all this? You can't help me, and you're crazy.

JOAN: They told me you would speak this way.

BEAUDRICOURT: They told you?

JOAN: Listen to me, nice, good Robert, and don't shout any more. It's useless. I'm about to say something very important. You will be brilliant and remarkable. You will shake a nation because I will do it for you. Your name will go far outside this village——

BEAUDRICOURT: [Puts his arms around her] What are you talking about?

JOAN: [She pulls away from him] Robert, don't think any more about my being a girl. That just confuses everything. You'll find plenty of girls who are prettier and will give more pleasure—[Softly] and will not ask as much. You don't want me.

BEAUDRICOURT: Well, I don't know. You're all right.

JOAN: [Sharply] If you want me to help you, then help me. When I say the truth say it with me.

BEAUDRICOURT: [Politely] But you're a pleasant-looking girl, and it's nice weather, and . . . . [Laughs] No, I don't want you any more than that.

JOAN: Good. Now that we have got that out of the way, let's pretend that you've given me the clothes of a boy and we're sitting here like two comrades talking good sense.

BEAUDRICOURT: [Fills a glass] All right. Have a little wine.

JOAN: [Drinks her wine] Kind, sweet Robert. Great things are about to begin for you. [As he starts to speak] No, no. Listen. The English are everywhere, and everywhere they are our masters. Brittany and Anjou will go next. The English wait only to see which one will pay the higher tribute money. The Duke of Burgundy signs a bitter treaty and the English give him the Order of the Golden Fleece. They invented just such medals for foreign traitors. Our little monkey Dauphin Charles sits with his court in Bourges, shaking and jibbering. He knows nothing, his court knows nothing, and all falls to pieces around him. You know that. You know our army, our good army of brave boys, is tired and sick. They believe the English will always be stronger and that there's no sense to it any more. When an army thinks that way, the end is near. The Bastard Dunois is a good captain and intelligent. So intelligent that nobody will listen to him. So he forgets that he should be leading an army and drowns himself in wine, and tells stories of past battles to his whores. I'll put a stop to that, you can be sure——

BEAUDRICOURT: [Softly] You'll put a stop to——

JOAN: Our best soldiers are like angry bulls. They always want to attack, to act fine for the history books. They are great champions of individual bravery. But they don't know how to use their cannon and they get people killed for nothing. That's what they did at Agincourt. Ah, when it comes to dying, they're all ready to volunteer. But what good is it to die? You think just as I do, my dear Robert: war isn't a tournament for fancy gentlemen. You must be smart to win a war. You must think, and be smart. [Quickly] But you who are so intelligent, knew all that when you were born.

BEAUDRICOURT: I've always said it. I've always said that nobody thinks any more. I used to be a thinker, but nobody paid any attention.

JOAN: They will, they will. Because you have just had an idea that will probably save all of us.

BEAUDRICOURT: I've had an idea?

JOAN: Well, you are about to have it. But don't let anything get in its way. Please sit quiet and don't, well, just—— [As he is about to move she holds him down] You are the only man in France who at this minute can see the future. Sit still.

BEAUDRICOURT: What is it that I see?

JOAN: You know your soldiers. You know they will leave you soon. You know that to keep them you must give them faith. You have nothing else to give them now. A little bread, a little faith—good simple things to fight with.

BEAUDRICOURT: It's too late——

JOAN: A girl comes before you. Saint Michael and Saint Catherine and Saint Marguerite have told her to come. You will say it's not true. But I believe it *is* true, and that's what matters. A farm girl who says that God is on her side. You can't prove He isn't. You can't. Try it and see. The girl came a long, hard way, she got so far as you, and she has convinced you. Yes, I have. I have convinced you. And why have I convinced so intelligent a man? Because I tell the truth, and it takes a smart head to know the truth.

BEAUDRICOURT: Where is this idea you said I had?

JOAN: Coming, coming just this minute. You are saying to yourself, if she convinced me, why shouldn't she convince the Dauphin and Dunois and the Archbishop? After all they're only men like me, although a good deal less intelligent. [*Very fast*] All right, that's settled. But now you're saying to yourself, when it comes to dying, soldiers are very intelligent, and so she'll have a harder time with them. No, she won't. She will say English heads are like all others: hit them hard enough, at the right time, and we'll march over them to Orléans. They need faith, your soldiers. They need somebody who believes it to say that God is on their side. Everybody says things like that. But *I* believe it—and that's the difference. Our soldiers will fight again, you know it, and because you know it you are the most remarkable man in France.

BEAUDRICOURT: You think so?

JOAN: The whole world will think so. But you must move fast. Like all great political men you are a realist. At this minute you are saying to yourself, "If the troops will believe this girl has come from God, what difference does it make whether she has or not? I will send her to Bourges tomorrow with the courier."

BEAUDRICOURT: The courier does go tomorrow. How did you know that? He goes with a secret packet——

JOAN: [*Laughs, delighted*] Give me six good soldiers and a fine white horse. I want a *white* horse, please. I will do the rest. But give me a quiet white horse because I don't know how to ride.

BEAUDRICOURT: [*Laughs*] You'll break your neck.

JOAN: It's up to Blessed Saint Michael to keep me in the saddle. [*He laughs. She doesn't like his laughter*] I will make you a bet, Robert. I'll bet you a man's dress that if you will have two horses brought now, and we both ride at a gallop, I won't fall off. If I stay on, then will you believe in me? All right?

BEAUDRICOURT: [*Laughs*] All this thinking makes a man weary. I had other plans for this afternoon, as I told you, but any kind of exercise is good for me. Come on.

[*He exits. Joan, smiling, looks toward Heaven. Then she runs after Beaudricourt. But she is stopped by a Soldier and suddenly realizes she is back in the trial. She sits quietly as the lights fade out on the Beaudricourt scene*]

WARWICK: She made that idiot believe he wasn't an idiot.

CAUCHON: It was a man-woman scene, a little coarse for my taste.

WARWICK: Coarse for *your* taste? The trick of making him believe what she put into his head is exactly what I do in my trade and what you do in yours. [*Suddenly*] Speaking of your trade, sire, forgive a brutal question but, just between ourselves, do you really have the faith?

CAUCHON: [*Simply*] As a child has it. And that is why my judges and I will try to save Joan. To the bitter end we will try to save her. Our honor demands that—— [*Warwick turns away. Cauchon, sharply*] You think of us as collaborators and therefore without honor. We believed that collaboration with you was the only reasonable solution——

WARWICK: And so it was. But when you say reasonable solution it is often more honorable to omit the word honor.

CAUCHON: [*Softly*] I say honor. Our poor honor, the little that was left us, demanded that we fight for our beliefs.

WARWICK: While you lived on English money——

CAUCHON: Yes. And while eight hundred of your soldiers were at our gates. It was easy for free men to call us traitors, but we lived in occupied territory, dependent upon the will of your king to kill us or to feed us. We were men, and we wanted to live; we were priests, and we wanted to save Joan. Like most other men, we wanted everything. We played a shameful role.

WARWICK: Shameful? I don't know. You might have played a nobler part, perhaps, if you had decided to be martyrs and fight against us. My eight hundred men were quite ready to help.

CAUCHON: We had good reason to know about your soldiers. I remember no day without insults and threats. And yet we stood against you. Nine long months before we agreed to hand over a girl who had been deserted by everybody but us. They can call us barbarians, but for all their noble principles I believe they would have surrendered her before we did.

WARWICK: You could have given us the girl on the first day. Nine long months of endless what?

CAUCHON: It was hard for us. God had been silent since Joan's arrest. He had not spoken to her or to us. Therefore, we had to do without his counsel. We were here to defend the House of God. During our years in the seminaries we learned how to defend it. Joan had no training in our seminaries and yet, abandoned, she defended God's House in her own way. Defended it with that strange conflict of insolence and humility, worldly sense and unworldly grandeur. [*Softly*] The piety was so simple and sweet—to the last moment of the last flame. We did not understand her in those days. We covered our eyes like old, fighting, childish men, and turned away so that we could not hear the cries of anguish.

She was all alone at the end. God had not come to her. That is a terrible time for a religious nature, sire, and brings doubt and despair unknown to others. [Cauchon *rises and turns away*] But it is then and there that some men raise their heads, and when they do, it is a noble sight.

WARWICK: Yes, it is. But as a man of politics, I cannot afford the doctrine of man's individual magnificence. I might meet another man who felt the same way. And he might express his individual magnificence by cutting off *my* head.

CAUCHON: [*Softly, as if he hadn't heard* Warwick] Sometimes, to console myself, I remember how beautiful were all those old priests who tried to protect the child, to save her from what can never now be mended——

WARWICK: Oh, you speak in large words, sire. Political language has no such words as "never now be mended." I have told you that the time will come when we will raise her a statue in London.

CAUCHON: And the time will come when our names will be known only for what we did to her; when men, forgiving their own sins, but angry with ours, will speak our names in a curse——

[*The lights dim on* Warwick *and* Cauchon *and we hear the music of a court song. A throne is brought on stage and as the lights come up slowly on* The Dauphin's *Court, the cyclorama reflects the royal fleur-de-lis. The Dauphin,* Charles, *is lolling about on his throne playing at bilboquet.* Agnes Sorel *and* The Little Queen *are practicing a new dance.* Yolande (Charles's *mother-in-law) is moving about. Four Courtiers are playing at cards*]

THE LITTLE QUEEN: [*She is having a hard time learning the dance steps*] It's very hard.

AGNES: Everything is very hard for you, dear.

THE LITTLE QUEEN: [*As they pass* Charles] It's a new dance. Very fashionable. Influenced by the Orient, they say.

AGNES: [*To* Charles] Come. We'll teach you.

CHARLES: I won't be going to the ball.

AGNES: Well, *we* will be going. And we must dance better than anybody else and look better than anybody else. [*Stops, to* Charles, *points to her headdress*] And I'm not going in this old thing. I'm your mistress. Have a little pride. A mistress must be better dressed than anybody. You know that.

THE LITTLE QUEEN: And so must wives. I mean better dressed than other wives. The Queen of France in last year's shoddy. What do you think they will say, Charles?

CHARLES: They will say that poor little Queen married a king who hasn't a sou. They will be wrong. I have a sou.

[*He throws a coin in the air. It falls and he begins to scramble on the floor for it*]

THE LITTLE QUEEN: I can hear them all the way to London. The Duchess of Bedford and the Duchess of Gloucester——

[Charles, *on the floor, is about to find his sou as the* Archbishop *and* La Tremouille *come in.* Charles *jumps back in fear*]

LA TREMOUILLE: [*To* Charles] You grow more like your father each day.

ARCHBISHOP: But his father had the decency to take to his bed.

CHARLES: Which father?

LA TREMOUILLE: You act so strangely, sire, that even I, who knew your mother, am convinced you are legitimate. [*Angrily, to* Charles *who is still on the floor*] Move. Move.

THE LITTLE QUEEN: Oh, please don't speak to him that way, Monsieur de la Tremouille.

ARCHBISHOP: [*Who has been glaring at the dancers*] You believe this is the proper time for dancing?

THE LITTLE QUEEN: But if the English take us prisoner, we have to know a little something. We can't disgrace our country——

[LA TREMOUILLE *stares at her, exits*]

YOLANDE: What harm do they do, sire? They are young—and there isn't much ahead for them.

ARCHBISHOP: There isn't much ahead for any of us. [*He moves off*]

YOLANDE: Please get up, Charles. It is a sad thing to see you so frightened by so many men.

CHARLES: And why shouldn't I be frightened of La Tremouille and the Archbishop? I have been all my life. They could order every soldier in the place to cut me up and eat me.

AGNES: They're cheats, every woman in England. We set the styles—and they send spies to steal the latest models. But, fortunately, they're so ugly that nothing looks very well—[*Admires her own feet and hands*] with cows for feet and pigs for hands. We want new headdresses. Are you the King of France or aren't you?

CHARLES: I don't know if I am. Nobody knows. I told you all about that the first night you came to bed.

AGNES: The new headdress is two feet tall and has two horns coming from the side——

CHARLES: Sounds like a man. A very small married man.

THE LITTLE QUEEN: And they have a drape at the back—they will cause a revolution, Charles.

AGNES: The English ladies—the mistresses, I mean, of course—won't be able to sleep when they see us. And if they can't sleep neither will the Dukes. And if the Dukes can't sleep they won't feel well and they won't have time to march on us——

CHARLES: They won't march on us. Nobody wants this dull town. They're already in Orléans. So there isn't much sense counterattacking with a headdress.

THE LITTLE QUEEN: Oh, Charles, one has to have a little pleasure in life. And Mama—[*Pointing to* Yolande] and the Archbishop and La Tremouille, and all the wise people, tell us that the end is here, anyway, and this will be the last state ball——

CHARLES: How much do they cost?

AGNES: I flirted with the man—[*Hastily*] in a nice way—and he's going to let us have them for six thousand francs.

CHARLES: Where would I get six thousand francs, you little idiot?

THE LITTLE QUEEN: Twelve thousand francs, Charles. I'm here.

CHARLES: That's enough to pay Dunois' army the six months' wages that I owe them. You are dreaming, my kittens. My dear mother-in-law, please speak to these children.

YOLANDE: No. I wish to speak to you.

CHARLES: For two days you've been following me about looking the way good women always look when they're about to give a lecture.

YOLANDE: Have I ever spoken against your interests? Have I ever shown myself concerned with anything but your welfare? I am the mother of your Queen, but I brought Agnes to you when I realized she would do you good.

THE LITTLE QUEEN: Please, Mama, don't brag about it.

YOLANDE: My child, Agnes is a charming girl and she knows her place. It was important that Charles make up his mind to become a man, and if he was to become a man he had to have a woman.

THE LITTLE QUEEN: I am a woman and his wife in the bargain.

YOLANDE: You are my dear little girl and I don't want to hurt you, but you're not very much of a woman. I know because I was just like you. I was honest and sensible, and that was all. Be the Queen to your Charles, keep his house, give him a Dauphin. But leave the rest to others. Love is not a business for honest women. We're no good at it. Charles is more virile since he knows Agnes. [*Worried*] You are more virile, aren't you, Charles?

AGNES: [*Too firmly*] Yes, indeed.

YOLANDE: I hope so. He doesn't act it with the Archbishop or La Tremouille.

AGNES: Things like that take a while. But he's much more virile. Doesn't read so much any more. [*To* Charles] And since it's all due to me the very least you can do is to give me the headdress. And one for the little Queen. [Charles *doesn't answer*] I feel ill. And if I feel ill it will certainly be for a whole week. And you'll be very bored without me. [*Eagerly, as she sees his face*] Sign a Treasury Bond and we'll worry afterwards. [*He nods. She turns to* The Little Queen] Come, my little Majesty. The pink one for you, the green one for me. [*To* Charles, *as they exit*] We'll make fools of those London ladies, you'll see. It'll be a great victory for France.

CHARLES: [*To* Yolande] A great victory for France. She talks like an army captain. I'm sick of such talk. France will be victorious, you'll be a great king—all the people who have wanted to make a king out of me. Even Agnes. She practices in bed. That's very funny. I must tell you about it some day. I am a poor frightened nothing with a lost kingdom and a broken army. When will they understand that?

YOLANDE: I understand it, Charles.

CHARLES: [*Softly, taken aback*] Do you? You've never said that before.

YOLANDE: I say it now because I want you to see this girl. For three days I have had her brought here, waiting for you——

CHARLES: I am ridiculous enough without playing games with village louts who come to me on clouds carrying a basket of dreams.

YOLANDE: There is something strange about this girl, something remarkable. Or so everybody thinks, and that's what matters.

CHARLES: You know La Tremouille would never allow me to see the girl.

YOLANDE: Why not? It is time they understood that a peasant at their council table might do a little good. A measure of common sense from humble people might bring us all——

CHARLES: [*Sharply*] To ruin. Men of the people have been at council tables, have become kings, and it was a time of massacre and mistake. At least I'm harmless. The day may come when Frenchmen will regret their little Charles. At least, I have no large ideas about how to organize happiness and death. [*He throws his ball in the air*]

YOLANDE: Please stop playing at bilboquet, Charles.

CHARLES: Let me alone. I like this game. When I miss the cup, the ball only falls on my nose, and that hurts nobody but me. But if I sit straight on the throne with the ball in one hand and the stick in the other, I might start taking myself seriously. Then the ball will fall on the nose of France, and the nose of France won't like it.

[*The* Archbishop *and* La Tremouille *enter*]

LA TREMOUILLE: We have a new miracle every day. The girl walked to the village church to say her prayers. A drunken soldier yelled an insult at her. "You are wrong to curse," she said. "You will soon appear before our Lord." An hour later the soldier fell into a well and was drowned. The stumbling of a drunkard has turned the town into a roaring holiday. They are marching here now, shouting that God commands you to receive this girl.

CHARLES: He hasn't said a word to me.

LA TREMOUILLE: The day God speaks to you, sire, I will turn infidel.

ARCHBISHOP: [*Very angry*] Put up that toy, Your Majesty. You will have the rest of your life to devote to it.

LA TREMOUILLE: Get ready to leave here.

CHARLES: Where will I go? Where will you go? To the English?

ARCHBISHOP: Even from you, sire, we will not accept such words.

[*As* La Tremouille *angrily advances on* Charles, Yolande *moves between them*]

YOLANDE: [*To* Archbishop] Allow him to see the girl.

ARCHBISHOP: And throw open the palace to every charlatan, every bonesetter, every faith healer in the land?

LA TREMOUILLE: What difference does it make any more? We have come to the end of our rope.

YOLANDE: If he sees the girl, it will give the people hope for a few days.

CHARLES: Oh, I am tired of hearing about the girl. Bring her in and have it ended. Maybe she has a little money and can play cards.

YOLANDE: [To La Tremouille] We have nothing to lose, sire——

LA TREMOUILLE: When you deal with God you risk losing everything. If He has really sent this girl then He has decided to concern Himself with us. In that case, we are in even worse trouble than we thought. People who govern states should not attract God's attention. They should make themselves very small and pray that they will go unnoticed.

[Joan comes in. She stands small and frightened, staring at Charles, bowing respectfully to the Archbishop. As she moves toward the throne, one of the Courtiers laughs. Joan turns to stare, and the Courtier draws back as if he is frightened]

CHARLES: What do you want? I'm a very busy man. It's time for my milk.

JOAN: [Bows before him] I am Joan the Maid. The King of Heaven has sent me here. I am to take you to Reims and have you anointed and crowned King of France.

CHARLES: My. Well, that is splendid, mademoiselle, but Reims is in the hands of the English, as far as I know. How shall we get there?

JOAN: We will fight our way there, noble Dauphin. First, we will take Orléans and then we will walk to Reims.

LA TREMOUILLE: I am commander of the army, madame. We have not been able to take Orléans.

JOAN: [Carefully] I will do it, sire. With the help of our Lord God who is my only commander.

LA TREMOUILLE: When did Orléans come to God's attention?

JOAN: I do not know the hour, but I know that he wishes us to take the city. After that, we will push the English into the sea.

LA TREMOUILLE: Is the Lord in such bad shape that he needs you to do his errands?

JOAN: He has said that he needs me.

ARCHBISHOP: Young woman—[Joan kneels and kisses the hem of his robe] if God wishes to save the Kingdom of France he has no need of armies.

JOAN: Monseigneur, God doesn't want a lazy Kingdom of France. We must put up a good fight and then He will give us victory.

ARCHBISHOP: [To Charles] The replies of this girl are, indeed, interesting and make a certain amount of good sense. But this is a delicate matter: a commission of learned doctors will now examine her. We will review their findings in council——

LA TREMOUILLE: [To Charles] And will keep you informed of our decision. Go back to your book. She will not disturb you any more today. Come, Madame Henriette——

JOAN: My name is Joan.

LA TREMOUILLE: Forgive me. The last quack was called Henriette.

ARCHBISHOP: Come, my child——

CHARLES: No! [He motions to Joan] You. Don't move. [He turns toward La Tremouille, standing straight and stiff and holding Joan's hand to give himself courage] Leave me alone with her. [Giggles] Your King commands you. [La Tremouille and the Archbishop bow and leave. Charles holds his noble pose for an instant, then bursts into laughter] And they went. It's the first time they ever obeyed me. [Very worried] You haven't come here to kill me? [She smiles] No. No, of course not, you have an honest face. I've lived so long with those pirates that I've almost forgotten what an honest face looks like. Are there other people who have honest faces?

JOAN: [Gravely] Many, sire.

CHARLES: I never see them. Brutes and whores, that's all I ever see. And the little Queen. She's nice, but she's stupid. And Agnes. She's not stupid—and she's not nice. [He climbs on his throne, hangs his feet over one of the arms and sighs] All right. Start boring me. Tell me that I ought to be a great King.

JOAN: [Softly] Yes, Charles.

CHARLES: Listen. If you want to make an impression on the Archbishop and the council, we'll have to stay in this room for at least an hour. If you talk to me of God and the Kingdom of France, I'll never live through the hour. Let's do something else. Do you know how to play at cards?

JOAN: I don't know what it is.

CHARLES: It is a nice game invented to amuse my papa when he was ill. I'll teach you. [He begins to hunt for the cards] I hope they haven't stolen them. They steal everything from me around here and cards are expensive. Only the wealthiest princes can have them. I got mine from papa. I'll never have the price of another pack. If those pigs have stolen them—— No. Here they are. [He finds them in his pocket] My papa was crazy. Went crazy young—in his thirties. Did you know that? Sometimes I am glad I am a bastard. At least I don't have to be so frightened of going crazy. Then sometimes I wish I were his son and knew that I was meant to be a king. It's confusing.

JOAN: Of the two, which would you prefer?

CHARLES: Well, on the days when I have a little courage, I'd risk going crazy. But on the days when I haven't any courage—that's from Sunday to Saturday—I would rather let everything go to hell and live in peace in some foreign land on whatever little money I have left.

JOAN: Today, Charles, is this one of the days when you have courage?

CHARLES: Today? [He thinks a minute] Yes, it

seems to me I have a little bit today. Not much, but a little bit. I was sharp with the Archbishop, and——

JOAN: You will have courage every day. Beginning now.

CHARLES: You have a charm in a bottle or a basket?

JOAN: I have a charm.

CHARLES: You are a witch? You can tell me, you know, because I don't care. I swear to you that I won't repeat it. I have a horror of people being tortured. A long time ago, they made me witness the burning of a heretic at the stake. I vomited all night long.

JOAN: I am not a witch. But I have a charm.

CHARLES: Sell it to me without telling the others.

JOAN: I will give it to you, Charles. For nothing.

CHARLES: Then I don't want it. What you get free costs too much. [He shuffles the cards] I act like a fool so that people will let me alone. My papa was so crazy they think I am, too. He was very crazy, did all kinds of strange things, some of them very funny. One day he thought it would be nice to have a great funeral, but nobody happened to die just then so he decided to bury a man who'd been dead four years. It cost a fortune to dig him out and put him back, but it was fun. [He laughs merrily, catches himself, stares at Joan] But don't think you can catch me too easily. I know a little about the world.

JOAN: You know too much. You are too smart.

CHARLES: Yes. Because I must defend myself against these cutthroats. They've got large bones, I've got puny sticks. But my head's harder than theirs and I've clung to my throne by using it.

JOAN: [Gently] I would like to defend you against them, Charles. I would give my life to do it.

CHARLES: Do you mean that?

JOAN: Yes. And I'm not afraid of anything.

CHARLES: You're lucky. Or you're a liar. Sit down and I'll teach you to play.

JOAN: All right. You teach me this game and I'll teach you another game.

CHARLES: What game do you know?

JOAN: How not to be too smart. [Softly] And how not to be afraid.

CHARLES: [Laughs] You'll be here a lifetime, my girl. Now. See these cards? They have pictures painted on them. Kings, queens and knaves, just as in real life. Now which would you say was the most powerful, which one could take all the rest?

JOAN: The king.

CHARLES: Well, you're wrong. This large heart can take the king. It can put him to rout, break his heart, win all his money. This card is called——

JOAN: I know. It is called God. Because God is more powerful than kings.

CHARLES: Oh, leave God alone for a minute. It's called the ace. Are you running this game? God this and God that. You talk as if you dined with Him last night. Didn't anybody tell you that the English also say their prayers to God? Every man thinks God is on his side. The rich and powerful know He is. But we're not rich and powerful, you and I—and France.

JOAN: That isn't what God cares about. He is angry with us because we have no courage left. God doesn't like frightened people.

CHARLES: Then He certainly doesn't like me. And if He doesn't like me, why should I like Him? He could have given me courage. I wanted it.

JOAN: [Sharply] Is God your nurse? Couldn't you have tried to do a little better? Even with those legs.

CHARLES: I am sorry to know that my legs have already come to your attention. It's because of my legs that Agnes can never really love me. That's sad, isn't it?

JOAN: No.

CHARLES: Why not?

JOAN: Because your head is ugly, too, and you can't be sad about everything. But what's inside your head isn't ugly, because God gave you sense. And what do you do with it? Play cards. Bounce a ball in the air. Play baby tricks with the Archbishop and act the fool for all to see. You have a son. But what have you made for him? Nothing. And when he's grown he, too, will have a right to say, "God didn't like me, so why should I like Him?" But when he says God he will mean you because every son thinks his father is God. And when he's old enough to know that, he will hate you for what you didn't give him.

CHARLES: Give him? What can I give him? I'm glad to be alive. I've told you the truth: I am afraid. I've always been and I always will be.

JOAN: And now I'll tell you the truth: I am also afraid. [With force] And why not? Only the stupid are not afraid. What is the matter with you? Don't you understand that it was far more dangerous for me to get here than it is for you to build a kingdom? I've been in danger every minute of the way, and every minute of the way I was frightened. I don't want to be beaten, I don't want pain, I don't want to die. I am scared.

CHARLES: [Softly] What do you do when you get scared?

JOAN: Act as if I wasn't. It's that simple. Try it. Say to yourself, yes, I am afraid. But it's nobody else's business, so go on, go on. And you do go on.

CHARLES: [Softly] Where do you go?

JOAN: [Slowly, carefully] To the English, outside Orléans. And when you get there and see the cannon and the archers, and you know you are outnumbered, you will say to yourself, all right, they are stronger than I am, and that frightens me, as well it should. But I'll march right through because I had sense enough to get frightened first.

CHARLES: March through a stronger army? That can't be done.

JOAN: Yes it can. If you have sense and courage. Do you want to know what happened in my village last year? They tell the story as a miracle now but it wasn't. The Bouchon boy went hunting. He's the best poacher in our village, and this day he was poaching on the master's grounds. The master kept a famous dog, trained to kill, and the dog found the Bouchon boy. The boy was caught and death faced him. So he threw a stone and the dog turned his head. That was sense. And while the dog turned his head the boy decided the only way was to stand and fight. That was courage. He strangled the dog. That was victory. See?

CHARLES: Didn't the dog bite him?

JOAN: [As if to a stupid child] You're like the old people in the village—you really believe in miracles. Of course the dog bit him. But I told you the boy had sense, and sense saved his life. God gave man an inside to his head, and He naturally doesn't want to see it wasted. [Smiles] See? That's my secret. The witches' secret. What will you pay me for it now?

CHARLES: What do you want?

JOAN: The army of France. Believe in God and give me the army.

CHARLES: [Moves away from her] Tomorrow. I'll have time to get ready——

JOAN: [Moves after him] No, right now. You are ready. Come on, Charlie.

CHARLES: Perhaps I am. Perhaps I've been waiting for you and didn't know—— [Laughs nervously] Shall we send for the Archbishop and La Tremouille and tell them that I have decided to give the army to you? It would be fun to see their faces.

JOAN: Call them.

CHARLES: [In a panic] No. I am frightened.

JOAN: Are you as afraid as you ever can be, ever were or will be, then, now and in the future? Are you sick?

CHARLES: [Holding his stomach] I think so.

JOAN: Good. Good. Then the worst is over. By the time they get scared, you'll be all over yours. Now, if you're as sick as you can get, I'll call them. [She runs upstage and calls out] Monseigneur the Archbishop. Monseigneur de La Tremouille. Please come to the Dauphin.

CHARLES: [Almost happy] I am very sick.

JOAN: [Moves him gently to the throne and arranges his hands and feet] God is smiling. He is saying to Himself, "Look at that little Charles. He is sicker than he's ever been in his life. But he has called in his enemies and will face them. My, such a thing is wonderful." [With great force] Hang on, Charles. We'll be in Orléans. We'll march right up.

[The Archbishop and La Tremouille enter, followed by Yolande and the Courtiers]

ARCHBISHOP: You sent for us, Your Highness?

CHARLES: [Very sharply] I have made a decision. The Royal Army is now under the command of Joan the Virgin Maid, here present. [Roars out] I wish to hear no word from you. None.

[They stare at Charles]

JOAN: [Clapping her hands] Good. Good, my Charles. You see how simple it is? You're getting

better looking, Charles. [Charles giggles. Then he suddenly stops the giggle and stares at Joan. She stares at him. She drops to her knees] Oh, my God, I thank you.

CHARLES: There is not time to lose. We will need your blessing, sire. Give it to us. [To La Tremouille] Kneel down, sire.

[La Tremouille, Yolande and the Courtiers drop to their knees. As the Archbishop pronounces the blessing, we hear the chorus sing the Benedictus. A Court Page gives a sword to The Dauphin. The Dauphin gives the sword to Joan. Warwick comes into the scene and moves downstage to address the audience]

WARWICK: In real life, it didn't work out exactly that way. As before, now, and forever, there were long discussions in the French fashion. The council met. Desperate, frightened, with nothing to lose, they decided to dress the girl in battle flags and let her go forth as a symbol of something or other. It worked well. A simple girl inspired simple people to get themselves killed for simple ideals.

[Joan rises and moves away from The Dauphin. She puts her hand on the sword, and lowers her head in prayer]

CURTAIN

ACT II.

Before the curtain rises we hear the music of a soldier's song. The Soldiers sing of Joan and her victories. As the curtain rises we see Joan, in full armor, move across the stage to the music. She carries her sword high above her head in a kind of hero's salute to a group of admiring Village Women. She marches off as Cauchon, The Inquisitor, and the Judges take their places. Warwick moves down to address the audience.

WARWICK: She was in the field. From that day laws of strategy no longer made any difference. We began to lose. They say that Joan worked no miracles at Orléans. They say that our plan of isolated fortresses was absurd, that they could have been taken by anyone who had courage enough to attack. But that is not true. Sir John Talbot was not a fool. He's a good soldier, as he proved long before that miserable business, and after it. By all military laws his fortified positions could not have been broken. And they could not have been broken except by—— Well, by what? What shall we call it even now? The unknown, the unguessed—God, if that's the way you believe. The girl was a lark in the skies of France, high over the heads of her soldiers, singing a joyous, crazy song of courage. There she was, outlined against the sun, a target for everybody to shoot at, flying straight and happy into battle. To Frenchmen, she was the soul of France. She was to me, too.

[*Smiles, to* Cauchon] Monseigneur, I like France. Of course, you have your fair share of fools and blackguards. [*Somebody coughs nervously.* Warwick *laughs*] But every once in a while a lark does appear in your sky and then everything stupid and evil is wiped out by the shadow of the lark. I like France very much.

CAUCHON: Your guns prove your affection.

WARWICK: They prove nothing. I love animals but I hunt with guns. [*Sharply*] Too difficult to explain to a man of your simple piety, Monseigneur. So let's get on with the trial. The lark has been captured. The King she crowned, the royal court she saved—for a minute, at least—are about to abandon their little girl. Their loyalty lasted through victory. When we took her prisoner, their luck ran out. They are returning as fast as they can to the old, stale political games.

[Charles *and the* Archbishop *appear*]

JOAN: [*As she goes back to the trial*] Charles. [*No answer*] Charles.

CHARLES: [*He turns toward her, then turns away again. He speaks to the* Archbishop] I didn't want to send the letter. I tell you I have a feeling that——

ARCHBISHOP: The letter was necessary, sire. We must be rid of the girl now. She is dangerous to us.

CHARLES: I didn't like the letter——

CAUCHON: [*Gently, to* Joan] Yesterday Charles disavowed you in a letter sent to all his cities.

JOAN: Charles. [*No answer. To* Cauchon] Well. He is still my King. And he is your King.

CAUCHON: No, he is not my King. We are loyal subjects of Henry of Lancaster, King of England, King of France. Joan, we love France as much as you do, but we believe that English Henry will put an end to this terrible war. That is why we have taken him as king. The man you call king is, for us, a rebel, claiming a throne that does not belong to him, refusing a good peace because it does not suit his ambitions. He is a puppet man, and we do not wish him as master. [*Sharply*] But I only confuse you. This is not a political trial in which you state your beliefs and we state ours. We are here only to return a lost girl to the bosom of the Sainted Mother Church.

JOAN: [*Pointing to* Charles] That puppet man is the king God gave you. He is a poor, skinny, miserable thing, but given a little time——

CHARLES: [*To the* Archbishop] I object as much to being defended in this fashion as I do to being attacked.

ARCHBISHOP: [*Maliciously*] Let them speak, sire. Turn away. It will be over soon. They will speed up the trial now. They will burn her at the stake.

CHARLES: [*Softly, as if he were sick*] I hate violence. It makes me sick——

ARCHBISHOP: [*Sharply*] Count yourself a lucky man. If the English do not condemn her to death, we will have to do it.

CHARLES: I will never do that, Monseigneur. After all, the girl loved me. I will never do that.

ARCHBISHOP: No, sire, certainly not. We will do it for you.

[*They move off*]

CAUCHON: [*To* Joan] You are not stupid, Joan. You can understand what we think. You swear that you heard voices and you swear to the messages they sent you. But because we believe in another king, we cannot believe that it was God Who sent you to fight against us. We are priests but we are men. And man cannot believe that God has turned against him.

JOAN: You'll have to believe it when we've beaten you.

CAUCHON: Ah, you answer like a foolish child.

JOAN: My Voices told me——

CAUCHON: How often have we heard those words? Do you think you are the only girl who has ever heard voices?

JOAN: No, I don't think that.

CAUCHON: Not the first and not the last. Every village priest has had his share of young girls in crisis. If the Church believed every sick child—— [*Wearily*] You have good sense. You were commander in chief of the army.

JOAN: [*With pride and sudden energy*] I commanded brave men. *They* believed in me, and *they* followed me.

CAUCHON: Yes. And if on the morning of an attack one of your brave men had suddenly heard Voices that ordered him *not* to follow you, what would you have done with him?

[Joan *laughs and there is sudden, loud laughter from off-stage* Soldiers]

JOAN: [*Calls out toward the laughter*] The Seigneur Bishop is a priest. He has never been close to you, my soldiers. [*The laughter dies off. Amused, she turns back to* Cauchon] A good army fights, drinks, rapes—but they don't hear voices.

CAUCHON: A jest is not an answer. You know that a disobedient soldier in your army, in any army in this world, would be silenced. The Church Militant is also an army of this earth and we, its priests, do not believe in the Divine origin of *your* disobedience. Nobody believes in you now, Joan.

JOAN: The common people believe in me——

CAUCHON: They believe in anything. They will follow another leader tomorrow. You are alone, all alone.

JOAN: I think as I think. You have the right to punish me for it.

CAUCHON: You are strong and you are stubborn, but that is not a sign that God is on your side.

JOAN: When something is black I cannot say that it is white.

THE PROMOTER: [*Rises and speaks angrily to* Joan] What spell did you cast upon the man you call your king? By what means did you force him to give his armies to you?

JOAN: I have told you. I cast no spell upon him.

THE PROMOTER: It is said that you gave him a piece of mandrake.

JOAN: I don't know what mandrake is.

THE PROMOTER: Your secret has a name. We want to know what it is.

JOAN: [Sharply] I gave him courage. That is the only word I know for what was between us. When a girl says one word of good sense and people listen to her, that's proof that God is present and no strange spells or miracles are needed.

LADVENU: [Softly] Now there is a good and humble answer, Monseigneur. An answer that cannot be held against her.

THE PROMOTER: I do not agree. She is saying that she does not believe in the miracles as they are taught in our Holy Book. [To Joan] You declare that you deny the act of Jesus at the Marriage of Cana? You declare that you deny the miracle raising of Lazarus from the dead?

JOAN: No, Messire. Our Seigneur changed the water into wine and retied the thread of Lazarus' life. But for Him Who is Master of life and death, that is no more miracle than if I were to make thread for my loom.

THE PROMOTER: [With great anger, to the Judges] Mark her words. Write them down. She says that Jesus made no miracles.

JOAN: [Runs toward the Judges with great force] I say that true miracles are not tricks performed by gypsies in a village square. True miracles are created by men when they use the courage and intelligence that God gave them.

CAUCHON: You are saying to us, to us, that the real miracle of God on this earth is man. Man, who is naught but sin and error, impotent against his own wickedness——

JOAN: And man is also strength and courage and splendor in his most desperate minutes. I know man because I have seen him. He is a miracle.

LADVENU: [Quickly, nervously] Monseigneur, Joan speaks an awkward language. But she speaks from the heart, and without guile. Perhaps when we press down upon her, we risk making her say here what she does not mean.

THE PROMOTER: [To Joan] Do you believe that man is the greatest miracle of God?

JOAN: Yes, Messire.

THE PROMOTER: [Shouts] You blaspheme. Man is impurity and lust. The dark acts of his nights are the acts of a beast——

JOAN: Yes, Messire. And the same man who acts the beast will rise from a brothel bed and throw himself before a blade to save the soldier who walks beside him. Nobody knows why he does. He doesn't know. But he does it, and he dies, cleansed and shining. He has done both good and evil, and thus twice acted like a man. That makes God happy because God made him for just this contradiction. We

are good and we are evil, and that is what was meant.

[There is indignant movement among the Judges. The Inquisitor rises, holds up his hand. Immediately there is silence. They have been waiting for him to speak]

THE INQUISITOR: I have at no time spoken. [To Joan] I speak to you now. I represent here the Holy Inquisition of which I am the Vicar for France. I have arrived from the south of Spain, and have little knowledge of the French and English war. It does not concern me whether Charles or the Lancaster Henry rules over France. It does not concern me that the French Duke of Burgundy has joined the English, and thus Frenchman fights French brother. They are all children of the Church. Nor have I interest in defending the temporal integrity of the Church in these quarrels. [Turns toward Cauchon] We leave such matters to our bishops and our priests. [Bows to Cauchon] Nor time to be curious about the kindness and humanity which seem to move the judgment. [Sharply, toward The Promoter] Nor do we find interest in these endless dreams of the Devil that haunt the nights of the Promoter. The Holy Inquisition fights in the dark world of night, against an enemy it alone can recognize. [Stops, moves toward Warwick] We do not care that the princes of the earth have sometimes laughed at the vigilance with which we hunt the enemy, the time and thought that we give to the judgment of the enemy. The princes of the earth are sometimes hurrying and shallow men. They remove their enemies with a length of rope and, in the crudeness of their thinking, they believe the danger ended there. We hear the mocking laughter of such men and we forgive it. The Holy Inquisition concerns itself in matters unknown to temporal kings. Our enemy is a great enemy and has a great name. [To Joan] You know his name?

JOAN: No, Messire. I do not understand you.

THE INQUISITOR: You will understand me. Stand up. You will answer now to me. Are you a Christian?

JOAN: Yes, Messire.

THE INQUISITOR: The trees that shaded the village church threw shadows on the house of your father. The bells of the Church brought you to prayer and sent you to work. The men we sent to your village all bring the same word: you were a pious girl.

JOAN: Yes, Messire.

THE INQUISITOR: You were a tender little girl. And you were a tender woman. You cried for the wounded in every battle——

JOAN: Yes. I cried for the wounded. They were French.

THE INQUISITOR: And you cried for the English. You stayed with a wounded English soldier who screamed through a night of pain. You held him until he died, calling him your child and giving him a hope of Heaven.

JOAN: You know that, Messire?

THE INQUISITOR: Yes. The Holy Inquisition knows much of you, Joan. Grave considerate talk was given to you. And they sent me here to judge you.

LADVENU: Messire Inquisitor, Joan has always acted with kindness and Christian charity, but this court has buried it in silence. I am happy to hear you remind them that——

THE INQUISITOR: [Sternly] Silence, Brother Ladvenu. I ask you not to forget that the Holy Inquisition alone is qualified to distinguish between theological virtues and that troubled brew that man so boastfully calls the milk of human kindness. [Turns to the Judges] Ah, my masters. What strange matters concern you all. Your business is to defend the Faith. But you see the kind eyes of a young girl and you are overwhelmed.

LADVENU: Our Lord loved with charity and kindness, Messire. He said to a sinner, "Go in peace." He said——

THE INQUISITOR: Silence, I said to you, Brother Ladvenu. [Softly, carefully] You are young. I am told your learning is very great and that is why you were admitted to this trial. Therefore I am hopeful that experience will teach you not to translate the great words into the vulgar tongue, nor embroider the meaning to suit your heart. Be seated and be silent.[1] [He turns back to Joan] You were very young when you first heard your Voices.

JOAN: Yes, Messire.

THE INQUISITOR: I am going to shock you: there is nothing very exceptional about the Voices you heard in those days. Our archives are full of such cases. There are many young visionaries. Girls frequently experience a crisis of mysticism. It passes. But with you—and your priest should have recognized it—the crisis was prolonged. The messages became precise and the Celestial Voices began to use most unusual words.

JOAN: Yes. My Voices told me to go and save the Kingdom of France.

THE INQUISITOR: A strange order to an ignorant peasant girl.

JOAN: Not so strange, Messire, because it turned out to be the truth.

THE INQUISITOR: I say a strange order to a girl who had seen nothing of war. The troubles of France could have been no more to you than tales told at twilight. And yet suddenly you went out into the great world of kings and battles, convinced that it was your mission to aid your brothers in their struggle to keep the land on which they were born, and which they imagine belongs to them.

JOAN: Our Lord could not want the English to kill us and to conquer us. He could not want us to live by their laws and wishes. When they have

gone back across the sea, to their own land, I will not go and pick a quarrel with them. They can rest easy in their own house. I've always said that.

THE INQUISITOR: [Sternly] And I say your presumption is not suited to my taste.

LADVENU: She did not mean, Messire—she speaks in a youthful fashion.

CAUCHON: [Softly] Be still, Brother Ladvenu.

THE INQUISITOR: [To Joan] It would have been more fitting for a pious girl to have spent her life in prayers and penitence and, in such manner, obtained from Heaven the promise that the English would be defeated.

JOAN: I did all that. But I think you must first strike and then pray. That's the way God wants it. I had to explain to Charles how to attack. And he believed me and Dunois believed me and La Hire—good men, wild bulls they were, and warriors. Ah, we had some fine battles together. It was good, in the dawn, riding boot to boot with friends——

THE PROMOTER: To the kill. Did your Voices instruct you to kill?

JOAN: [Angrily] I have never killed a man. But war is war.

CAUCHON: You love war, Joan.

JOAN: [Softly] Yes. And that is one of the sins from which God will have to absolve me. But I did not like pain or death. At night, on the battlefield, I would weep for the dead——

THE PROMOTER: You would weep at night for the dead but by morning you were shouting for a new battle.

JOAN: [Moves to him, with great force] I say God did not wish one Englishman to remain in France. That's not so hard to understand, is it? We had to do our work, that's all. You are wise men, you think too much. Your heads are filled with too much celestial science. You don't understand even the simplest things any more—things that my dullest soldier would understand without talk. Isn't that true, La Hire?

[She stumbles, moves away from the Judges, and falls to the ground. The lights dim on the trial and we hear again the whistling of the soldier's song. La Hire, in full armor, appears upstage and moves toward Joan]

LA HIRE: The morning has come, Madame Joan. [She sits up, shivers, stares at La Hire]

JOAN: The night was cold, La Hire. [He sits beside her, warms her hands in his own. Joan looks toward the trial, then up, then back to La Hire, as if she were confused by the place and the time] Good La Hire. Great La Hire. You've really come to help me as I knew you would.

LA HIRE: [He takes out an onion and begins to peel it] Come to help you? I was sleeping fifty feet from you, Madame Joan, watching over you as I always do. [She laughs and moves closer to him] Don't come too close. I stink of wine and onions.

JOAN: No, no. You smell fine.

[1] In the original play, The Inquisitor adds, "Et qui aime l'homme, n'aime pas Dieu," "And he who loves Man does not love God," transposed to another speech by The Inquisitor in Act II of the adaptation.

LA HIRE: Usually you tell me I stink too much to be a Christian. You say I am a danger to the army because if the wind is behind me the English will know where we are.

JOAN: Oh, La Hire, I was so stupid in those days. You know how girls are. Nothing ever happens to them, they know nothing, but they pretend they know everything. But I am not so stupid any more. You smell good because you smell like a man.

LA HIRE: I can't stand a man who washes in the field because to me a man like that isn't a man. I was brought up on an onion in the morning. The rest can have their sausage. The smell is more distinguished, you tell me. I know you think a breakfast onion is a sin.

JOAN: [Laughs] A breakfast onion is not a sin. Nothing that is true is a sin, La Hire. I was a fool. I tormented you. But I didn't know anything then. I didn't. [Softly] Ah, you smell so good. Sweat, onions, wine. You have all the smells a man should have. And you curse, you kill, and you think of nothing but women.

LA HIRE: Me?

JOAN: You. But I tell you that with all your sins you are like a bright new coin in the hand of God.

LA HIRE: Well, I have had a bastard life and when I go into battle, I say my prayers. I say, "God, I hope You'll help me as I would help You if You faced those God damned——"

JOAN: [Shocked] La Hire!

LA HIRE: [Softly] To tell you the truth, I'm frightened of what will happen to me if I get killed.

JOAN: Paradise will happen to you. They are looking forward to having you with them.

LA HIRE: That gives me heart, Madame Joan. I've always wanted to go to Paradise. But if it's all full of saints and bishops, I might not be too happy——

JOAN: It's full of men like you. It's the others who are kept waiting at the gates—— [Suddenly] The gates. The gates of Orléans. They're ahead of us— the day has come, La Hire. To horse, my boy, to horse. [She climbs on her stool. La Hire stands next to her. They hold imaginary reins in their hands as they ride imaginary horses] It's dawn, La Hire. The woods are still wet from the night, the trees are still dark and strange. It's fine to ride into battle with a good soldier by your side.

LA HIRE: Some people don't like it. Some people like to make a little garden out of life and walk down a path.

JOAN: But they never know what we know. [As if she were puzzled and ashamed] Death has to be waiting at the end of the ride before you truly see the earth, and feel your heart, and love the world. [Suddenly, in a whisper] There are three English soldiers. [She looks back] We've outridden the others. We are alone.

LA HIRE: Get off your horse, Madame Joan. Lead him back. You have never used your sword.

JOAN: No. Don't meet them alone, La Hire——

LA HIRE: [He draws his sword] I'll kill them . . . God damned English bastards.

[Sword in hand, he disappears]

JOAN: [Kneels in prayer] Dear God, he is as good as bread. I answer for him. He's my friend. [She turns toward the Judges, angry, defiant] The last word will not be spoken at this trial. La Hire will come to deliver me. He will bring three hundred lancers, I know them all, and they will take me from my prison——

CAUCHON: Yes. They came to deliver you, Joan.

JOAN: [Running to him] Where are they? I knew they would come——

CAUCHON: They came to the gates of the city. When they saw how many English soldiers were here, they turned and went away.

JOAN: [Shaken] Ah. They turned and went away. Without fighting? [Cauchon turns away] Yes. Of course. It was I who taught them to do just that. I would say to them, "Have a little sense. It doesn't cost a sou. Learn not to be brave when you are outnumbered, unless——" [Violently] That's what they did. They went to get reinforcements for me——

CAUCHON: No. Your friends will not return, Joan.

JOAN: That's not true. "Learn not to be brave when you are outnumbered," I said, "unless you can't retreat. Then you must fight because there is no other way——" [Proudly] La Hire will return. Because there is no other way to save me now.

CAUCHON: La Hire sells himself to whichever prince has need. When he discovered that your Charles was tired of war and would sign any peace, he marched his men toward Germany. He looks for a new land on which to try his sword. [Comes to her] You have been abandoned. It will sound strange to you, but the priests of this court are the only men who care for your soul and for your life. Humble yourself, Joan, and the Church will take your hand. In your heart, you are a child of the Church.

JOAN: [Softly] Yes.

CAUCHON: Trust yourself to the Church. She will weigh your deeds and take from you the agony of self-judgment.

JOAN: [After a long silence] For that which is of the Faith, I turn to the Church, as I have always done. But what I am, I will not denounce. What I have done, I will not deny.

[There is a shocked silence. Then there is great movement in the courtroom, as if this were the answer that would bring the judgment. The Inquisitor rises. The Priests are suddenly silent. The Inquisitor slowly moves before the Priests, peering into their faces. The Priests draw back, frightened]

THE INQUISITOR: [To one Priest]. Not you. [To another Priest] Not you. [To a third Priest] Not you. [Pauses before Cauchon, stares at him] And not you, Bishop of Beauvais. I have spoken of the great enemy, but not even now do you know his name. You do not understand on whom you sit in judgment, nor the issues of the judgment. I have told you that the Holy Inquisition is not concerned with royal rank or merchant gold or peasant birth. To us, a scholar in his room is equal in importance to an emperor in his palace. Because *we* know the name of our enemy. His name is natural man. [*There is silence.* Ladvenu *moves forward*] Can you not see that this girl is the symbol of that which is most to be feared? She is the enemy. She is man as he stands against us. Look at her. Frightened, hungry, dirty, abandoned by all, and no longer even sure that those Voices in the air ever spoke to her at all. Does her misery make her a suppliant begging God for mercy and for light? No. She turns away from God. She dares to stand under torture, thrashing about like a proud beast in the stable of her dungeon. She raises her eyes, not to God, but to man's image of himself. I have need to remind you, Masters, that he who loves Man does not love God.[1]

LADVENU: [*With great force*] It cannot be. Jesus Himself became a man.

THE INQUISITOR: [*Turns to* Cauchon] Seigneur Bishop, I must ask you to send your young assessor from this courtroom. I will consider after this session whether he may return or whether I will bring charges against him. [*Shouts*] Against him, or against any other. *Any* other. I would bring charges against myself if God should let me lose my way.

CAUCHON: [*Softly*] Leave us, Brother Ladvenu.

LADVENU: Messire Inquisitor, I owe you obedience. I will not speak again. But I will pray to our Lord Jesus that you remember the weakness of your small, sad, lonely—enemy.

[Ladvenu *exits*]

THE INQUISITOR: Do you have need to question her further? To ask all the heavy words that are listed in your legal papers? What need to ask her why she still persists in wearing man's dress when it is contrary to the commandments? Why she dared the sin of living among men as a man? The deeds no longer matter. What she has done is of less importance than why she did it, the answers less important than the one answer. It is a fearful answer, "What I am, I will not. . . ." You wish to say it again? Say it.

JOAN: [*Slowly, softly*] What I am, I will not denounce. What I have done, I will not deny.

THE INQUISITOR: [*Carefully, as if has taken the measure of an enemy*] You have heard it. Down through the ages, from dungeon, from torture chamber, from the fire of the stake. Ask her and she will say with those others, "Take my life. I will give it because I will not deny what I have done." This is what they say, all of them, the insolent breed. The men who dare our God. Those who say no to us. [*He moves toward* Joan. Cauchon *rises*] Well, you and all like you shall be made to say yes. You put the Idea in peril, and that you will not be allowed

[1] This sentence and the next four speeches were transposed from Act I of the original French.

to do. [*Turns to the* Judges] The girl is only a monstrous symbol of the faith decayed. Therefore I now demand her immediate punishment. I demand that she be excommunicated from the Church. I demand that she be returned to secular authority there to receive her punishment. I ask the secular arm to limit her sentence to this side of death and the mutilation of her members.

[Cauchon *moves to* The Inquisitor *as if to stop the judgment*]

WARWICK: [*To* Cauchon] A passionate man and so sincere. I think he means simply to throw the dirty work to me. I am the secular authority here. Why didn't your French Charles have her burned? It was his job.

CHARLES: [*Very disturbed*] I don't want to do it. I don't like killing.

[*A large, masked figure appears*]

CAUCHON: [*Calls to the masked man*] Master Executioner, is the wood for the stake dry and ready to burn?

EXECUTIONER: All is ready. Things will go according to custom. But I will not be able to help the girl this time.

CAUCHON: What do you mean help her, Master?

EXECUTIONER: We let the first flames rise high. Then I climb up behind the victims and strangle them the rest of the way. It's easier and quicker for everybody. But I have had special instructions this time to make the fire very high. And so it will take longer and I will not be able to reach her for the act of mercy.

CAUCHON: [*Moves to* Joan] Did you hear that?

JOAN: I've remembered a dream from years ago. I woke screaming and ran to my mother—— [*Screams as if in pain*] Ah.

CAUCHON: [*Desperately*] Joan, for the last time I offer you the saving hand of your Mother Church. We wish to save you, but we can delay no longer. The crowd has been waiting since dawn. They eat their food, scold their children, make jokes, and grow impatient. You are famous and they have nothing better to do with their lives than bring garlands to the famous—or watch them burn.

JOAN: [*As if she is still in the dream*] I forgive them, Messire. I forgive you, too.

THE PROMOTER: [*Furiously*] Monseigneur speaks to you like a father in order to save your miserable soul and you answer by forgiving him.

JOAN: Monseigneur speaks to me gently, he takes great pains to seduce me, but I do not know whether he means to save me or conquer me. In any case, he will be obliged to have me burned.

CAUCHON: [*Comes to her*] For the last time I say: Confess your sins and return to us. We will save you.

JOAN: [*She clings to his robe*] I wish to return to the Church. I want the Holy Communion. I have asked for it over and over again. But they have refused to give it to me.

CAUCHON: After your confession, when you have

begun your penance, we will give it to you. [*There is no answer. Very softly*] Are you not afraid to die?

JOAN: Yes. I am afraid. What difference does that make? I've always been so afraid of fire. [*Gasps*] I've remembered a dream——

CAUCHON: [*Pulls her to him*] Joan, we cannot believe in the Divinity of your Voices. But if we are wrong—and certainly that thought has crossed our minds——

THE PROMOTER: [*Furious*] No, I say no. Even to you, my Bishop of Beauvais——

CAUCHON: [*To Joan*] But if we are wrong then we will have committed a monstrous sin of ignorance and we will pay for it the rest of our eternal lives. But we are the priests of your Church. Trust our belief that we are right, as you trusted your good village priest. Place yourself in our hands. You will be at peace.

JOAN: I cannot follow what you say. I am tired. Oh, sire, I do not sleep at night. I come here and all is said so fast that I cannot understand. You torture me with such gentle words, and your voice is so kind. I would rather have you beat me——

CAUCHON: I talk to you thus because my pride is less than yours.

JOAN: [*She moves away from him, as if she were sick and wanted to be alone*] Pride? I have been a prisoner so long—I think my head is sick and old, and the bottom of me does not hold any more. Sometimes I don't know where I am and my dungeon seems a great beech tree. I am hungry, or I was, and I want a taste of country milk——

CAUCHON: [*Desperately, as if he were at the end*] Look at me, Joan, keep your mind here. I am an old man. I have killed people in the defense of my beliefs. I am so close to death myself that I do not wish to kill again. I do not wish to kill a little girl. Be kind. [*Cries out*] Help me to save you.

JOAN: [*Very softly; broken now*] What do you want me to say? Please tell me in simple words.

CAUCHON: I am going to ask you three questions. Answer yes three times. That is all. [*With passion*] Help me, Joan.

JOAN: But could I sleep a few hours, sire?

CAUCHON: No! We cannot wait. Do you entrust yourself with humility to the Holy Roman and Apostolic Church, to our Holy Father, the Pope, and to his bishops? Will you rely upon them, and upon no one else, to be your judges? Do you make the complete and total act of submission? Do you ask to be returned to the bosom of the Church?

JOAN: Yes, but—[*The Inquisitor rises. Cauchon becomes nervous*] I don't want to say the opposite of what my Voices told me. I don't ever want to bear false witness against Charlie. I fought so hard for the glory of his consecration. Oh, that was a day when he was crowned. The sun was out——

CHARLES: [*To Joan*] It was a nice day and I'll always remember it. But I'd rather not think it was a divine miracle. I'd rather people didn't think

that God sent you to me. Because now that you're a prisoner, and thought to be a heretic and a sorceress, they think that God has abandoned me. I'm in bad enough trouble without that kind of gossip. Just forget about me and go your way.

[*Joan bows her head*]

CAUCHON: Do you wish me to repeat the question? [*Joan does not answer. Cauchon is angry*] Are you mad? You understand now that we are your only protectors, that this is the last thing I can do for you? You cannot bargain and quibble like a peasant at a village fair. You are an impudent girl, and I now become angry with you. You should be on your knees to the Church.

JOAN: [*Falls to her knees*] Messire, deep in your heart do you believe that our Lord wishes me to submit to the judgment?

CAUCHON: I so believe.

JOAN: [*Softly*] Then I submit.

[*There is great movement in the court. The Inquisitor rises; The Promoter moves to him*]

CAUCHON: [*Very tired now*] You promise to renounce forever the bearing of arms?

JOAN: But, Messire, there is still so much to do——

CAUCHON: [*Angrily*] Nothing more will ever be done by you.

WARWICK: That is true, Joan.

CHARLES: And if you're thinking of helping me again, please don't. I won't ever use you any more. It would be very dangerous for me.

JOAN: [*Broken now, almost as if she were asleep*] I renounce forever the bearing of arms.

CAUCHON: [*In great haste*] Do you renounce forever the wearing of that brazen uniform?

JOAN: You have asked me that over and over again. The uniform doesn't matter. My Voices told me to put it on.

THE PROMOTER: It was the Devil who told you to put it on.

JOAN: Oh, Messire, put away the Devil for today. My Voices chose the uniform because my Voices have good sense. [*With great effort*] I had to ride with soldiers. It was necessary they not think of me as a girl. It was necessary they see in me nothing but a soldier like themselves. That is all the sense there was to it.

CAUCHON: But why have you persisted in wearing it in prison? You have been asked this question in many examinations and your refusal to answer has become of great significance to your judges.

JOAN: And I have asked over and over to be taken to a Church prison. Then I would take off my man's uniform.

THE PROMOTER: [*To Cauchon*] Monseigneur, the girl is playing with us, as from the first. I do not understand what she says or why you——

JOAN: [*Angry*] One doesn't have to be an educated man to understand what I am saying.

THE PROMOTER: [*Turns to Judges*] She says that she submits to the Church. But I tell you that as long as she refuses to put aside that Devil dress, I will exercise my rights as master judge of heretics and witchcraft. [*To* Cauchon] Strange pressures have been put upon all of us. I know not from where they come, but I tell even you——

JOAN: I have said that if you put me in a Church prison I will take off this uniform.

THE PROMOTER: You will not bargain. Put aside that dress or, no matter who feels otherwise, you will be declared a sorceress.

JOAN: [*Softly, to* Cauchon] I am not alone in prison. Two English soldier guards are in the cell with me night and day. The nights are long. I am in chains. I try hard not to sleep, but sometimes I am too tired—— [*She stops, embarrassed*] In this uniform it is easier for me to defend myself.

CAUCHON: [*In great anger*] Have you had so to defend yourself since the beginning of this trial?

[Warwick *moves to* Joan]

JOAN: Every night since I've been captured. I don't have much sleep. In the mornings, when I am brought before you, I am confused, and I don't understand your questions. I told you that. Sometimes I try to sleep here in the trial so that I will stay awake in the night——

CAUCHON: Why haven't you told us this before?

JOAN: Because the soldiers told me they would be hanged if I said anything——

WARWICK: [*Very angry*] They were right. [*To* Cauchon] Detestable bastards. It's disgusting. They've learned such things since they came to France. It may be all right in the French Army, but not in mine. [*Bows to* Joan] I am sorry, Madame. It will not happen again.

CAUCHON: [*To* Joan] The Church will protect you from now on. I promise you.

JOAN: Then I agree to put on woman's dress.

CAUCHON: Thank you, my child. That is all. [*He moves to* The Inquisitor] Messire Inquisitor, Brother Ladvenu drew up the Act of Renunciation. Will you permit me to recall him here? [*With bitterness*] The girl has said yes, this man has said yes.

THE PROMOTER: [*To* The Inquisitor] Messire Inquisitor, you are going to allow this to happen?

THE INQUISITOR: If she said yes, she has fulfilled the only condition that concerns me.

THE PROMOTER: [*Turns to* Cauchon] This trial has been conducted with an indulgence that is beyond my understanding. [*To* The Inquisitor] I am told that there are those here who eat from the English manger. I ask myself now if they have arranged to eat better from the French manger.

THE INQUISITOR: [*Rises, moves toward* Joan] It is not a question of mangers, Messire Promoter. *I* ask myself how did it happen that this girl said yes when so many lesser ones did not bow the head. I had not believed it to be possible. [*Points to* Cauchon] And why was tenderness born in the heart of that old man who was her judge? He is at the end of a

life worn out with compromise and debasement. Why now, here, for this girl, this dangerous girl, did his heart—— [*He kneels, ignoring the others. As he prays, we hear only the words.* . . .] Why, Oh Lord Why, Oh Lord . . . ? Consecrate it in peace to Your Glory. . . . Your Glory——[1]

CAUCHON: [*As* Ladvenu *enters*] Please read the act.

LADVENU: [*Comes to* Joan. *With great tenderness*] I have prayed for you, Joan. [*Reading*] "I, Joan, commonly called The Maid, confess having sinned through pride and malice in pretending to have received revelations from our Lord God. I confess I have blasphemed by wearing an immodest costume. I have incited men to kill through witchcraft and I here confess to it. I swear on the Holy Gospels I will not again wear this heretic's dress and I swear never to bear arms again. I declare that I place myself humbly at the mercy of our Holy Mother Church and our Holy Father, the Pope of Rome and His Bishops, so that they may judge my sins and my errors. I beseech Her to receive me in Her Bosom and I declare myself ready to submit to the sentence which She may inflict upon me. In faith of which, I have signed my name upon this Act of Renunciation of which I have full knowledge. [Ladvenu *hands the pen to* Joan. *She moves it in the air, as if she had not heard and did not understand.* Ladvenu *takes her hand and puts it on the paper*] I will help you.

CAUCHON: [*As if he were a very old man*] You have been saved. We, your judges, in mercy and mitigation, now condemn you to spend the remainder of your days in prison. There you will do penance for your sins. You will eat the bread of sorrow and drink the water of anguish until, through solitary contemplation, you repent. Under these conditions of penance, we declare you delivered of the danger of excommunication. You may go in peace. [*He makes the Sign of the Cross*] Take her away.

[Cauchon *stumbles and is helped by* Ladvenu. A Soldier *pushes* Joan *away from the trial. The* Judges *rise and slowly move off.* Cauchon *moves past* Warwick]

WARWICK: There were several times, sire, when I thought I would have to interfere. My King must have what he paid for. But you were right and I was wrong. The making of a martyr is dangerous business. The pile of faggots, the invincible girl in the flames, might have been a triumph for the French spirit. But the apologies of a hero are sad and degrading. You did well, sire; you are a wise man.

CAUCHON: [*With great bitterness*] I did not mean to earn your praise.

[*He moves off. The lights dim on the trial as* Warwick *moves off. Four* Soldiers *appear with*

---

[1] In the original French, The Inquisitor says, "Wilt Thou never permit, Lord, that the world be rid of every trace of Man in order that we may consecrate in peace to Thy glory."

spears, and their spears become the bars of Joan's *jail cell.* Charles *appears and stands looking at* Joan *through the bars*][1]

CHARLES: I didn't want you to sacrifice yourself for me, Joan. I know you loved me, but I don't want people to love me. It makes for obligations. This filthy prison air is wet and stinks. Don't they ever clean these places? [*He peers into her cell, sees the water pail that sits beside her, and draws back*] Tell them to give you fresh water. My God, what goes on in this world. [*She does not answer him*] Don't you want to speak to me, Joan?

JOAN: Good-by, Charlie.

CHARLES: You must stop calling me Charlie. Ever since my coronation I am careful to make everyone say sire.

JOAN: Sire.

CHARLES: I'll come and see you again. Good-by.

[*He moves off.* Joan *lies in silence. Then she tries to drink from the water pail, retches, and puts her hand over her mouth as if she were very sick*]

JOAN: Blessed Saint Michael. [*She makes a strange sound, shivers*] I am in prison. Come to me. Find me. [*Cries out*] I need you now. [*Very loudly*] I told you that I was afraid of fire, long before I ever knew—or did I always know? You want me to live? [*When there is no answer*] Why do I call for help? You must have good reason for not coming to me. [*She motions toward courtroom*] They think I dreamed it all. Maybe I did. But it's over now. . . .

[Warwick *comes slowly into the cell*]

WARWICK: [*Hesitantly*] You are weeping?

JOAN: No, Monseigneur.

WARWICK: I am sorry to disturb you. I only came to say that I am glad you are saved. You behaved damned well. I, er, well, it's rather difficult to say in my language, but the plain fact is that I like you. And it amused me to watch you with the Inquisitor. Sinister man, isn't he? I detest these intellectual idealists more than anything in the world. What disgusting animals they are. He wanted only to see you humiliate yourself, no matter your state or your misery. And when you did, he was satisfied.

JOAN: [*Softly*] He had reason to be satisfied.

WARWICK: Well, don't worry about him. It all worked out well. Martyrs are likely to stir the blood of simple people and set up too grand a monument to themselves. It's all very complex and dangerous. Tell me, are you a virgin?

JOAN: Yes.

[1] In the original French, Joan is first addressed by Agnes and Queen Yolande, who fail to appreciate her service to France and the Dauphin Charles. In the rest of this brief ironical scene, abbreviated in the adaptation, Charles's mistress maintains that her sexual allure enabled her to do more than Joan did in making a man of the Dauphin, and that even his wife, The Little Queen, did something for France in producing a second son and so assuring the succession to the throne.

WARWICK: I knew you were. A woman would not talk as you do. My fiancée in England is a very pure girl and she also talks like a boy. You are the greatest horsewoman I have ever seen. [*When there is no answer*] Ah, well. I am intruding on you. Don't hesitate to let me know if I can ever do anything for you. Good-by, madame.

JOAN: Nobody else came to see me here. You are a kind man, Monseigneur.

WARWICK: Not at all. [*Motions toward courtroom*] It's that I don't like all those fellows who use words to make war. You and I killed because that was the way things turned out for us.

JOAN: Monseigneur, I have done wrong. And I don't know how or why I did it. [*Slowly, bitterly*] I swore against myself. That is a great sin, past all others—— [*Desperately*] I still believe in all that I did, and yet I swore against it. God can't want that. What can be left for me?

WARWICK: Certainly they are not going to make you a gay life, not at first. But things work out and in time your nasty little Charles might even show you a speck of loyalty——

JOAN: Yes, when I am no longer dangerous, he might even give me a small pension and a servant's room at court.

WARWICK: [*Sharply*] Madame, there will be no court.

JOAN: And I will wear castoff brocade and put jewels in my hair and grow old. I will be happy that few people remember my warrior days and I will grovel before those who speak of my past and pray them to be silent. And when I die, in a big fat bed, I will be remembered as a crazy girl who rode into battle for what she said she believed, and ate the dirt of lies when she was faced with punishment. That will be the best that I can have—if my little Charles remembers me at all. If he doesn't there will be a prison dungeon, and filth and darkness—— [*Cries out*] What good is life either way?

WARWICK: It is good any way you can have it. We all try to save a little honor, of course, but the main thing is to be here——

JOAN: [*Rises, calls out, speaking to the Voices*] I was only born the day you first spoke to me. My life only began on the day you told me what I must do, my sword in hand. You are silent, dear my God, because you are sad to see me frightened and craven. And for what? A few years of unworthy life. [*She kneels. Softly, as if she is answering a message*] I know. Yes, I know. I took the good days from You and refused the bad. I know. Dear my God forgive me, and keep me now to be myself. Forgive me and take me back for what I am. [*She rises. She is happy and cheerful*] Call your soldiers, Warwick. I deny my confession.

WARWICK: Joan. No nonsense, please. Things are all right as they are. I——

JOAN: Come. [*She holds out her hand to him*]

WARWICK: I don't want anything to do with your death.

JOAN: [*Smiles*] You have a funny gentleman's face. But you are kind. Come now. [*She calls out*] Soldiers! Englishmen! Give me back my warrior clothes. And when I have put them on, call back all the priests. [*Stops, puts her hands in prayer and speaks simply*] Please God, help me now.

[*The music of the "Sanctus" begins as the Judges, Cauchon, The Inquisitor, The Promoter, Charles, the People of the Court, return to the stage. Two Soldiers bring a crude stake. Joan herself moves to the stake and the Soldiers lash her to it. Other Soldiers and Village Women pick up the bundles of faggots and carry them off stage. The Executioner appears with lighted torch and moves through the crowd*][1]

JOAN: [*As they are about to carry her off*] Please. Please. Give me a Cross.

THE PROMOTER: No Cross will be given to a witch.

AN ENGLISH SOLDIER: [*He has taken two sticks of wood and made a Cross. Now he hands his Cross to* Joan] Here, my daughter. Here's your Cross. [*Very angry, to* The Promoter] She has a right to a Cross like anybody else.

[JOAN *is carried off stage. The lights dim and we see flames—or the shadows of flames—as they are projected on the cyclorama.* Ladvenu *runs on stage with a Cross from the church and stands holding it high for* Joan *to see*]

THE INQUISITOR: [*Calling to* Executioner] Be quick. Be quick. Let the smoke hide her. [*To* Warwick] In five minutes, Monseigneur, the world will be crying.[2]

WARWICK: Yes.[3]

THE INQUISITOR: [*Shouting to* Executioner] Be quick, master, be quick.

EXECUTIONER: [*Calling in to him*] All is ready, messire. The flames reach her now.

LADVENU: [*Calling out*] Courage, Joan. We pray for you.

CAUCHON: May God forgive us all.

[Cauchon *falls to his knees and begins the prayer for the dead. The prayers are murmured as the chorus chants a Requiem. The* Soldiers *and the* Village People *return to the stage: a* Woman *falls to the ground; a* Soldier *cries out; a* Girl *bends over as if in pain and a* Soldier *helps her to move on; the* Court Ladies *back away, hiding their faces from the burning; the* Priests *kneel in prayer*]

CHARLES: [*In a whisper as he leaves*] What does she do? What does she say? Is it over?

THE INQUISITOR: [*To* Ladvenu] What does she do?[4]

[1] Warwick declares in the original that he finds all this decidedly "*déplacé,*" unbecoming, and "*vulgaire.*"

[2] That is, crying for her—"*tout le monde sera pour elle.*"

[3] In the original, "*Je crains que ce ne soit déja fait*"—"I am afraid that has already happened."

[4] In the original, "Does she look straight ahead?" and Ladvenu replies that she does. "Without weakening?" Lad-

LADVENU: She is quiet.

THE INQUISITOR: [*Moves away*] Is her head lowered?

LADVENU: No, messire. Her head is high.

THE INQUISITOR: [*As if he were in pain*] Ah. [*To* Ladvenu] She falters now?

LADVENU: No. It is a terrible and noble sight, messire. You should turn and see.

THE INQUISITOR: [*Moves off*] I have seen it all before.

[*The lights dim.* Cauchon *rises from his prayers. He stumbles and falls.* Ladvenu *and* Warwick *move to help him. He takes* Ladvenu's *arm, but moves away from* Warwick, *refusing his help. As the stage becomes dark,* Cauchon, The Promoter, Ladvenu *and* Warwick *move downstage and the light comes up on* La Hire *who stands above them.* La Hire *is in full armor, holding helmet and sword*][5]

venu says "Yes." Sadly The Inquisitor asks, "And there is almost a smile on her lips, is there not?" "Yes," says Ladvenu. And The Inquisitor bows his head, overwhelmed with despair, saying not "I have seen it all before," but "*Je ne le vaincrai jamais,*"—"I shall never be able to master him." The ambiguous "him" may be the Devil; more probably, The Inquisitor is referring to Man. And Ladvenu replies, with confidence and joy, "*Non, Messire.*"

[5] In the original, Beaudricourt (not La Hire) arrives on the scene to stop the execution and cries out to Cauchon, "It is not possible to end that way. The coronation scene has not been played. We said we would perform everything. It is not just. Joan has a right to play the coronation, it belongs to her story." Cauchon agrees, while Warwick, astounded by the turn of events, removes himself from the scene because it would be "improper" for him to be present at the Coronation. He adds that as far as he is concerned, it is all over: "Joan has been burnt, and His Majesty's Government has obtained its political objectives." Then Joan is released and given her sword and her banner; and Charles, dressed for his coronation, moves forward smiling, saying, "This man is quite right. The true story of Joan, the true conclusion that will never come to an end, which will be forever retold long after our names have been forgotten or confused, is not that of the miserable death of a cornered animal who was taken at Rouen, but that of a lark in the free sky; it is Joan at Reims in all her glory. . . . The true conclusion of Joan's story is joyous. Joan's story has a happy end." That this speech should come from Charles is at once appropriate, since it was he who was crowned at Reims, and ironic, since his own part in Joan's story was anything but glorious. Then Beaudricourt, who assists the others to remove the faggots, congratulates himself on having arrived in the nick of time, since "the imbeciles were going to burn Joan of Arc" (*les imbeciles, ils allaient brûler Jeanne d'Arc!*) and Joan's father, who is also removing the faggots with Joan's brother, says to the boy, "*Avance, toi,*" "Move ahead! And take your fingers out of your nose. Take a lesson from your sister. Observe what honor she has won; I am proud to be her father. . . . I always said, I did, that this little girl had a great future in store for her." Then an altar is set up in place of the stake, bells ring out, and Joan, leaning on her standard, watches with a smile as the Archbishop places the crown on Charles's head. Bells ring, the cannon booms, there is a flight of doves, and, ironically, *Le rideau tombe lentement sur cette belle image de livre de prix . . . ,* the curtain falls slowly on this pretty picture, this illustration from a prize book.

LA HIRE: You were fools to burn Joan of Arc.

CAUCHON: We committed a sin, a monstrous sin.

WARWICK: Yes, it was a grave mistake. We made a lark into a giant bird who will travel the skies of the world long after our names are forgotten, or confused, or cursed down.

LA HIRE: I knew the girl and I loved her. You can't let it end this way. If you do, it will not be the true story of Joan.

LADVENU: That is right. The true story of Joan is not the hideous agony of a girl tied to a burning stake. She will stand forever for the glory that can be. Praise God.

LA HIRE: The true story of Joan is the story of her happiest day. Anybody with any sense knows that. Go back and act it out.

[*The lights dim on the four men and come up on the Coronation of Charles in Reims Cathedral. The altar cloth is in place, the lighted candles are behind the altar, stained glass windows are projected on the cyclorama. The* Archbishop *appears, and the people of the royal court.* Joan *stands clothed in a fine white robe, ornamented with a fleur-de-lis*]

WARWICK: [*Moves into the coronation scene, stares bewildered as* Charles, *in coronation robes, carrying his crown, crosses to the altar*] This could not have been her happiest day. To watch Holy Oil being poured on that mean, sly little head!

CHARLES: [*Turns to* Warwick, *amused*] Oh, I didn't turn out so bad. I drove you out of the country. And I got myself some money before I died. I was as good as most.

WARWICK: So you were. But certainly the girl would never have ridden into battle, never have been willing to die because you were as good as most.

JOAN: [*Comes forward, smiling, happy*] Oh, Warwick, I wasn't paying any attention to Charlie. I knew what Charlie was like. I wanted him crowned because I wanted my country back. And God gave it to us on this Coronation Day. Let's end with it, please, if nobody would mind.

As the curtain falls the chorus sings the "Gloria" of the Mass.

THE MAIDS

By Jean Genet

TRANSLATED BY BERNARD FRECHTMAN

THE CHARACTERS

SOLANGE } *two housemaids, sisters, thirty to thirty-*
CLAIRE } *five years old. Solange is the elder.*
MADAME, *their mistress. She is about twenty-five.*

Madame's bedroom. Louis-Quinze furniture. Lace. Rear, a window opening on the front of the house opposite. Right, a bed. Left, a door and a dressing table. Flowers in profusion. The time is evening.

[Claire, *wearing a slip, is standing with her back to the dressing table. Her gestures—arm extended—and tone are exaggeratedly tragic*]

CLAIRE: Those gloves! Those eternal gloves! I've told you time and again to leave them in the kitchen. You probably hope to seduce the milkman with them. No, no, don't lie; that won't get you anywhere! Hang them over the sink. When *will* you understand that this room is not to be sullied. Everything, yes, everything that comes out of the kitchen is spit! So stop it!

[*During this speech,* Solange *has been playing with a pair of rubber gloves and observing her gloved hands, which are alternately spread fanwise and folded in the form of a bouquet*]

Make yourself quite at home. Preen like a peacock. And above all, don't hurry, we've plenty of time. Go!

[Solange's *posture changes and she leaves humbly, holding the rubber gloves with her fingertips.* Claire *sits down at the dressing table. She sniffs at the flowers, runs her hand over the toilet articles, brushes her hair, pats her face*]

Get my dress ready. Quick! Time presses. Are you there? [*She turns round*] Claire! Claire!

[Solange (*who has been called "Claire"*) *enters*]

SOLANGE: I beg Madame's pardon, I was preparing her tea. [*She pronounces it "tay"*]

CLAIRE: Lay out my things. The white spangled dress. The fan. The emeralds.

SOLANGE: Very well, Madame. All Madame's jewels?

CLAIRE: Put them out and I shall choose. And, of course, my patent-leather slippers. The ones you've had your eye on for years.

[Solange *takes a few jewel boxes from the closet, opens them, and lays them out on the bed*]

For your wedding, no doubt. Admit he seduced you! Just look at you! How big you are! Admit it!

[Solange *squats on the rug, spits on the patent-leather slippers, and polishes them*]

I've told you, Claire, with*out* spit. Let it sleep in you, my child, let it stagnate. Ah! Ah; [*She giggles nervously*] May the lost wayfarer drown in it. Ah! Ah! You *are* hideous. Lean forward and look at yourself in my shoes. Do you think I find it pleasant to know that my foot is shrouded by the veils of your saliva? By the mists of your swamps?

SOLANGE: [*On her knees, and very humble*] I wish Madame to be lovely.

CLAIRE: I shall be. [*She primps in front of the mirror*] You hate me, don't you? You crush me with your attentions and your humbleness; you smother me with gladioli and mimosa. [*She stands up and, lowering her tone*] There are too many flowers. The room is needlessly cluttered. It's *impossible.* [*She looks at herself again in the glass*] I shall be lovely. Lovelier than you'll ever be. With a face and body like that, you'll never seduce Mario. [*Dropping the tragic tone*] A ridiculous young milkman despises us, and if we're going to have a kid by him—

SOLANGE: Oh! I've never—

CLAIRE: [*Resuming*] Be quiet, you fool. My dress!

SOLANGE: [*She looks in the closet, pushing aside a few dresses*] The red dress. Madame will wear the red dress.

CLAIRE: I said the white dress, the one with spangles.

SOLANGE: [*Firmly*] I'm sorry. Madame will wear the scarlet velvet dress this evening.

CLAIRE: [*Naively*] Ah? Why?

SOLANGE: [*Coldly*] It's impossible to forget Madame's bosom under the velvet folds. And the jet brooch, when Madame was sighing and telling Monsieur of my devotion! Your widowhood really requires that you be entirely in black.

CLAIRE: Eh?

SOLANGE: Need I say more? A word to the wise—

CLAIRE: Ah! So you want to talk. . . . Very well. Threaten me. Insult your mistress, Solange. You want to talk about Monsieur's misfortunes, don't you? Fool. It was hardly the moment to allude to him, but I can turn this matter to fine account! You're smiling? Do you doubt it?

SOLANGE: The time is not yet ripe to unearth—

CLAIRE: What a word! My infamy? My infamy! To unearth!

SOLANGE: Madame!

CLAIRE: Am I to be at your mercy for having denounced Monsieur to the police, for having sold him? And yet I'd have done even worse, or better. You think I haven't suffered? Claire, I forced my hand to pen the letter—without mistakes in spelling or syntax, without crossing anything out—the letter that sent my lover to prison. And you, instead of standing by me, you mock me. You force your colors on me! You speak of widowhood! He isn't dead. Claire, Monsieur will be led from prison to prison, perhaps even to Devil's Island, where I, his mistress, mad with grief, shall follow him. I shall be in the convoy. I shall share his glory. You speak of widowhood and deny me the white gown—the mourning of queens. You're unaware of that, Claire—

SOLANGE: [Coldly] Madame will wear the red dress.

CLAIRE: [Simply] Quite. [Severely] Hand me the dress. Oh! I'm so alone and friendless. I can see in your eyes that you loathe me. You don't care what happens to me.

SOLANGE: I'll follow you everywhere. I love you.

CLAIRE: No doubt. As one loves a mistress. You love and respect me. And you're hoping for a legacy, a codicil in your favor—

SOLANGE: I'd do all in my power—

CLAIRE: [Ironically] I know. You'd go through fire for me. [Solange helps Claire put on her dress] Fasten it. Don't pull so hard. Don't try to bind me. [Solange kneels at Claire's feet and arranges the folds of the dress.] Avoid pawing me. You smell like an animal. You've brought those odors from some foul attic, where the lackeys visit us at night. The maid's room! The garret! [Graciously] Claire, if I speak of the smell of garrets, it is for memory's sake. And of the twin beds where two sisters fall asleep, dreaming of one another. There, [She points to a spot in the room] there, the two iron beds with the night table between them. There, [She points to a spot opposite] the pinewood dresser with the little altar to the Holy Virgin! That's right, isn't it?

SOLANGE: We're so unhappy. I could cry! If you go on—

CLAIRE: It is right, isn't it! Let's skip the business of your prayers and kneeling. I won't even mention the paper flowers. . . . [She laughs] Paper flowers! And the branch of holy boxwood! [She points to the flowers in the room] Just look at these flowers open in my honor! Claire, am I not a lovelier Virgin?

SOLANGE: [As if in adoration] Be quiet—

CLAIRE: And there, [She points to a very high spot at the window] that notorious skylight from which a half-naked milkman jumps to your bed!

SOLANGE: Madame is forgetting herself, Madame—

CLAIRE: And what about your hands? Don't you forget your hands. How often have I [She hesitates] murmured: they befoul the sink.

SOLANGE: The fall!

CLAIRE: Eh?

SOLANGE: [Arranging the dress on Claire's hips] The fall of your dress. I'm arranging your fall from grace.

CLAIRE: Get away, you bungler! [She kicks Solange in the temple with her Louis-Quinze heel. Solange, who is kneeling, staggers and draws back]

SOLANGE: Oh! Me a burglar?

CLAIRE: I said bungler; and if you must whimper, do it in your garret. Here, in my bedroom, I will have only noble tears. A time will come when the hem of my gown will be studded with them, but those will be precious tears. Arrange my train, you clod.

SOLANGE: [In ecstasy] Madame's being carried away!

CLAIRE: By the devil! He's carrying me away in his fragrant arms. He's lifting me up, I leave the ground, I'm off. . . . [She stamps with her heel] And I stay behind. Get my necklace! But hurry, we won't have time. If the gown's too long, make a hem with some safety pins.

[Solange gets up and goes to take the necklace from a jewel case, but Claire rushes ahead of her and seizes the jewels. Her fingers graze those of Solange, and she recoils in horror]

Keep your hands off mine! I can't stand your touching me. Hurry up!

SOLANGE: There's no need to overdo it. Your eyes are ablaze.

CLAIRE: [Shocked astonishment] What's that you said?

SOLANGE: Limits, boundaries, Madame. Frontiers are not conventions but laws. Here, my lands; there, your shore—

CLAIRE: What language, my dear. Claire, do you mean that I've already crossed the seas? Are you offering me the dreary exile of your imagination? You're taking revenge, aren't you? You feel the time coming when, no longer a maid—

SOLANGE: You see straight through me. You divine my thoughts.

CLAIRE: [Increasingly carried away]—the time coming when, no longer a maid, you become vengeance itself, but, Claire, don't forget—Claire, are you listening?—don't forget, it was the maid who hatched schemes of vengeance, and I—Claire, you're not listening.

SOLANGE: [Absent-mindedly] I'm listening.

CLAIRE: And I contain within me both vengeance and the maid and give them a chance for life, a chance for salvation. Claire, it's a burden, it's terribly painful to be a mistress, to contain all the springs of hatred, to be the dunghill on which you grow. You want to see me naked every day. I am beautiful, am I not? And the desperation of my love makes me even more so, but you have no idea what strength I need!

SOLANGE: [Contemptuously] Your lover!

CLAIRE: My unhappy lover heightens my nobility. Yes. Yes, my child. All that you'll ever know is your own baseness.

SOLANGE: That'll do! Now hurry! Are you ready?

CLAIRE: Are you?

SOLANGE: [*She steps back to the wardrobe*] I'm ready.—I'm tired of being an object of disgust. I hate you, too. I despise you. I hate your scented bosom. Your . . . *ivory* bosom! Your . . . *golden* thighs! Your . . . *amber* feet! I hate you! [*She spits on the red dress*]

CLAIRE: [*Aghast*] Oh! . . . Oh! . . . But. . . .

SOLANGE: [*Walking up to her*] Yes, my proud beauty. You think you can always do just as you like. You think you can deprive me forever of the beauty of the sky, that you can choose your perfumes and powders, your nail-polish and silk and velvet and lace, and deprive *me* of them? That you can steal the milkman from me? Admit it! Admit about the milkman. His youth and vigor excite you, don't they? Admit about the milkman. For Solange says: to hell with you!

CLAIRE: [*Panic-stricken*] Claire! Claire!

SOLANGE: Eh?

CLAIRE: [*In a murmur*] Claire, Solange, Claire.

SOLANGE: Ah! Yes, Claire, Claire says: to hell with you! Claire is here, more dazzling than ever. Radiant! [*She slaps* Claire]

CLAIRE: Oh! . . . Oh! Claire. . . . You. . . . Oh!

SOLANGE: Madame thought she was protected by her barricade of flowers, saved by some special destiny, by a sacrifice. But she reckoned without a maid's rebellion. Behold her wrath, Madame. She turns your pretty speeches to nought. She'll cut the ground from under your fine adventure. Your Monsieur was just a cheap thief, and you—

CLAIRE: I forbid you! Confound your impudence!

SOLANGE: Twaddle! She forbids me! It's Madame who's confounded. Her face is all convulsed. Would you like a mirror? Here. [*She hands* Claire *a mirror*]

CLAIRE: [*Regarding herself with satisfaction*] I see the marks of a slap, but now I'm more beautiful than ever!

SOLANGE: Yes, a slap!

CLAIRE: Danger is my halo, Claire; and you, you dwell in darkness. . . .

SOLANGE: But the darkness is dangerous.—I know. I've heard all that before. I can tell by your face what I'm supposed to answer. So I'll finish it up. Now, here are the two maids, the faithful servants! They're standing in front of you. Despise them. Look more beautiful.—We no longer fear you. We're merged, enveloped in our fumes, in our revels, in our hatred of you. The mold is setting. We're taking shape, Madame. Don't laugh—ah! above all, don't laugh at my grandiloquence. . . .

CLAIRE: Get out!

SOLANGE: But only to be of further service to Madame! I'm going back to my kitchen, back to my gloves and the smell of my teeth. To my belching sink. You have your flowers, I my sink. I'm the maid. You, at least, you can't defile me. But! But! . . . [*She advances on* Claire, *threateningly*] But before I go back, I'm going to finish the job. [*Suddenly*

an alarm clock goes off. Solange *stops. The two actresses, in a state of agitation, run together. They huddle and listen*] Already?

CLAIRE: Let's hurry! Madame'll be back. [*She starts to unfasten her dress*] Help me. It's over already. And you didn't get to the end.

SOLANGE: [*Helping her. In a sad tone of voice*] The same thing happens every time. And it's all your fault, you're never ready. I can't finish you off.

CLAIRE: We waste too much time with the preliminaries. But we've still. . . .

SOLANGE: [*As she helps* Claire *out of her dress*] Watch at the window.

CLAIRE: We've still got a little time left. I set the clock so we'd be able to put the things in order. [*She drops wearily into the armchair*]

SOLANGE: [*Gently*] It's so close this evening. It's been close all day.

CLAIRE: [*Gently*] Yes.

SOLANGE: Is that what's killing us, Claire?

CLAIRE: Yes.

SOLANGE: It's time now.

CLAIRE: Yes. [*She gets up wearily*] I'm going to make the tea.

SOLANGE: Watch at the window.

CLAIRE: There's time. [*She wipes her face*]

SOLANGE: Still looking at yourself . . . Claire, dear. . . .

CLAIRE: Let me alone. I'm exhausted.

SOLANGE: [*Sternly*] Watch at the window. Thanks to you, the whole place is in a mess again. And I've got to clean Madame's gown. [*She stares at her sister*] Well, what's the matter with you? You can be like me now. Be yourself again. Come on, Claire, be my sister again.

CLAIRE: I'm finished. That light's killing me. Do you think the people opposite. . . .

SOLANGE: Who cares! You don't expect us to . . . [*She hesitates*] organize things in the dark? Have a rest. Shut your eyes. Shut your eyes, Claire.

CLAIRE: [*She puts on her short black dress*] Oh! When I say I'm exhausted, it's just a way of talking. Don't use it to pity me. Stop trying to dominate me.

SOLANGE: I've never tried to dominate you. I only want you to rest. You'll help me more by resting.

CLAIRE: I understand, don't explain.

SOLANGE: Yes, I will explain. It was you who started it. When you mentioned the milkman. You think I couldn't see what you were driving at? If Mario—

CLAIRE: Oh!

SOLANGE: If the milkman says indecent things to me, he does to you, too. But you loved mingling. . . .

CLAIRE: [*Shrugging her shoulders*] You'd better see whether everything's in order. Look, the key of the secretary was like this [*She arranges the key*] and, as Monsieur says—

SOLANGE: [*Violently*] You loved mingling your insults—

CLAIRE: He's always finding the maids' hairs all over the pinks and roses!

SOLANGE: And things about our private life with—

CLAIRE: With? With? With what? Say it! Go on, name it! The ceremony? Besides, we've no time to start a discussion now. She'll be back, back, back! But, Solange, this time we've got her. I envy you; I wish I could have seen the expression on her face when she heard about her lover's arrest. For once in my life, I did a good job. You've got to admit it. If it weren't for me, if it hadn't been for my anonymous letter, you'd have missed a pretty sight: the lover handcuffed and Madame in tears. It's enough to kill her. This morning she could hardly stand up.

SOLANGE: Fine. She can drop dead! And I'll inherit! Not to have to set foot again in that filthy garret, with those two idiots, that cook and that butler.

CLAIRE: I really liked our garret.

SOLANGE: Just to contradict me. Don't start getting sentimental about it. I loathe it and I see it as it really is, bare and mean. And shabby. But what of it! We're just scum!

CLAIRE: Ah! No, don't start that again. Better watch at the window. I can't see a thing. It's too dark outside.

SOLANGE: Let me talk. Let me get it out of my system. I liked the garret because it was plain and I didn't have to put on a show. No hangings to push aside, no rugs to shake, no furniture to caress—with my eyes or with a rag, no mirrors, no balcony. Nothing forced us to make pretty gestures. Don't worry, you'll be able to go on playing queen, playing at Marie Antoinette, strolling about the apartment at night.

CLAIRE: You're mad! I've never strolled about the apartment.

SOLANGE: [Ironically] Oh, no. Mademoiselle has never gone strolling! Wrapped in the curtains or the lace bedcover. Oh no! Looking at herself in the mirrors, strutting on the balcony at two in the morning, and greeting the populace which has turned out to parade beneath her windows. Never, oh no, never.

CLAIRE: But, Solange—

SOLANGE: It's too dark at night for spying on Madame, and you thought you were invisible on your balcony. What do you take me for? Don't try to tell me you walk in your sleep. At the stage we've reached you can admit it.

CLAIRE: But, Solange, you're shouting. Please, please lower your voice. Madame may come in without making a sound. . . . [She runs to the window and lifts the curtain]

SOLANGE: All right, I've had my say. Let go of the curtains. Oh, I can't stand the way you lift them. Let go of them. It upsets me; that's how Monsieur did it when he was spying on the police, the morning he was arrested.

CLAIRE: So you're scared now? The slightest gesture makes you feel like a murderer trying to slip away by the service stairway.

SOLANGE: Go on, be sarcastic, work me up! Go on, be sarcastic! Nobody loves me! Nobody loves us!

CLAIRE: She does, she loves us. She's kind. Madame is kind! Madame adores us.

SOLANGE: She loves us the way she loves her armchair. Not even that much! Like her bidet, rather. Like her pink enamel toilet-seat. And we, can't love one another. Filth . . .

CLAIRE: Ah! . . .

SOLANGE: . . . doesn't love filth. D'you think I'm going to put up with it that I'm going to keep playing this game and then at night go back to my folding-cot? The game! Will we even be able to go on with it? And if I have to stop spitting on someone who calls me Claire, I'll simply choke! My spurt of saliva is my spray of diamonds!

CLAIRE: [She stands up and cries] Speak more softly, please, please. Speak—speak of Madame's kindness.

SOLANGE: Her kindness, is it? It's easy to be kind, and smiling, and sweet—ah! that sweetness of hers! —when you're beautiful and rich. But what if you're only a maid? The best you can do is to give yourself airs while you're doing the cleaning or washing up. You twirl a feather duster like a fan. You make fancy gestures with the dishcloth. Or like you, you treat yourself to historical parades in Madame's apartment.

CLAIRE: Solange! You're starting again! What are you trying to do? We'll never calm down if you talk like that! I could say a thing or two about you.

SOLANGE: You? You?

CLAIRE: Yes, me. If I wanted to. Because, after all. . . .

SOLANGE: All? After all? What are you insinuating? It was you who started talking about that man. Claire, I hate you.

CLAIRE: Same to you and more! But if I wanted to provoke you, I wouldn't have to use the milkman as an excuse. I've got something better on you and you know it.

SOLANGE: Who's going to get the better of who? Eh? Well, say something?

CLAIRE: Go on, start it! You hit first. It's you who're backing out, Solange. You don't dare accuse me of the worst: my letters. Pages and pages of them. The garret was littered with them. I invented the most fantastic stories and you used them for your own purposes. You frittered away my frenzy. Yesterday, when you were Madame, I could see how delighted you were at the chance they gave you to stow away on the Lamartinière, to flee France in the company of your lover—

SOLANGE: Claire—

CLAIRE: Your lover, to Devil's Island, to Guiana. You were delighted that my letters allowed you to be the prostitute kneeling at the feet of the thief. You were happy to sacrifice yourself, to bear the cross of the impenitent thief, to wipe his face, to stand by him, to take his place in the galleys so that he could rest. And you felt yourself growing. Your brow rose higher than mine, it rose above the palm trees.

SOLANGE: But what about you, just before, when you were talking about following him. . . .

CLAIRE: Right. I don't deny it. I took up where you left off. But with less violence than you. Even in the garret, amidst all the letters, you started swaying back and forth with the pitching of the boat.

SOLANGE: You didn't see yourself—

CLAIRE: I did. I'm more sensible than you. You're the one who concocted the story. Turn your head. Ha! If only you could see yourself, Solange. Your face is still lit up by the sun setting through the virgin forest! You're planning his escape! [*She laughs nervously*] You certainly do work yourself up! But don't let it worry you; it would be cruel to disturb your blissful voyage. I hate you for other reasons, and you know what they are.

SOLANGE: [*Lowering her voice*] I'm not afraid of you. I know you hate me and that you're a sneak, but be careful now. I'm older than you.

CLAIRE: So what?—Older! And stronger too? You're trying to put me off by making me talk about that man. Hmph! You think I haven't found you out? You tried to kill her.

SOLANGE: Are you accusing me?

CLAIRE: Don't deny it. I saw you.

[*A long silence*]

And I was frightened. Frightened, Solange. Through her, it was me you were aiming at. I'm the one who's in danger. When we finish the ceremony, I'll protect my neck.

[*A long silence. Solange shrugs her shoulders*]

SOLANGE: [*With decision*] Is that all? Yes, I did try. I wanted to free you. I couldn't bear it any longer. It made me suffocate to see you suffocating, to see you turning red and green, rotting away in that woman's bitter-sweetness. Blame me for it, you're right. I loved you too much. Had I killed her, you'd have been the first to denounce me. You'd have turned me over to the police, yes, you.

CLAIRE: [*She seizes her by the wrists*] Solange. . . .

SOLANGE: [*Freeing herself*] What are *you* afraid of? It's *my* concern.

CLAIRE: Solange, my little sister, she'll be back soon.

SOLANGE: I didn't kill anyone. I was a coward, you realize. I did the best I could, but she turned over in her sleep. [*Rising exaltation*] She was breathing softly. She swelled out the sheets: it was Madame.

CLAIRE: Stop it.

SOLANGE: Now you want to stop me. You wanted to know, didn't you. Well, wait, I've got some more to tell you. You'll see what your sister's made of. What stuff she's made of. What a servant girl really is. I wanted to strangle her—

CLAIRE: Let me alone. Think of what comes after.

SOLANGE: Nothing comes after. I'm sick and tired of kneeling in pews. In church I'd have had the red velvet of abbesses or the stone of the penitents, but my bearing at least would have been noble. Look, just look at how she suffers. How she suffers in beauty. Grief transfigures her, doesn't it? Beautifies her? When she learned that her lover was a thief, she stood up to the police. She exulted. Now she is forlorn and splendid, supported under each arm by two devoted servants whose hearts bleed to see her grief. Did you see it? Her grief sparkling with the glint of her jewels, with the satin of her gowns, in the glow of the chandelier! Claire, I wanted to make up for the poverty of my grief by the splendor of my crime. Afterward, I'd have set fire to the lot.

CLAIRE: Solange, calm down. The fire might not have caught. You'd have been found out. You know what happens to incendiaries.

SOLANGE: I know everything. I kept my eye and ear to the keyhole. No servant ever listened at doors as I did. I know everything. Incendiary! It's a splendid title.

CLAIRE: Be quiet. I'm stifling. You're stifling me. [*She wants to open the window*] Oh! Let's have some air!

SOLANGE: Get away from the window. Open the anteroom and the kitchen doors. [Claire *opens both doors*] Go and see whether the water's boiling.

CLAIRE: All alone?

SOLANGE: Wait, all right, wait till she comes. She's bringing her stars, her tears, her smiles, her sighs. She'll corrupt us with her sweetness.

[*The telephone rings. The two sisters listen*]

CLAIRE: [*At the telephone*] Monsieur? It's Monsieur! . . . This is Claire, Monsieur. . . . [Solange *wants to hear too, but* Claire *pushes her away*] Very well. I'll inform Madame. Madame will be overjoyed to hear that Monsieur is free. . . . Yes, Monsieur. . . . Very well. . . . Good-by, Monsieur. [*She wants to hang up, but her hand trembles, and she lays the receiver on the table*]

SOLANGE: Is he out?

CLAIRE: The judge let him out on bail.

SOLANGE: Well, you've done a fine job. My compliments. Your denunciations, your letters, it's working out beautifully. And if they recognize your handwriting, it'll be perfect.

CLAIRE: Please, please, don't overwhelm me. Since you're so clever, you should have managed your business with Madame. But you were afraid. The bed was warm. The air thick with perfume. It was Madame! We've got to carry on with the same kind of life. With the same old game. But, you poor wretch! Even the game is dangerous. I'm sure we've left traces. We leave them every time. I see a host of traces I'll never be able to cover up. And she, she walks about in her tamed menagerie. She unravels the clues. She points to our traces with the tip of her pink toe. She discovers us, one by one. Madame jeers at us. And it's your fault. All's lost because you lacked strength.

SOLANGE: I can still find whatever strength I need.

CLAIRE: Where? Where? You've been outstripped

by *me*. You don't live above the treetops. A milkman passing through your mind gets you all flustered.

SOLANGE: It was because I couldn't see her face, Claire. Because I was so close to Madame, so close to her sleep. I lost my strength. In order to get at her throat, I'd have had to lift the sheet from her heaving bosom.

CLAIRE: [*Ironically*] And the sheets were warm. The night dark. That kind of thing has to be done in broad daylight. You're incapable of it. It's too terrible a deed. But *I* can manage it.

SOLANGE: Claire!

CLAIRE: Where you botched it, *I'll* succeed.

SOLANGE: [*She runs a comb through her hair*] Claire, don't get carried away, don't be rash—

CLAIRE: What makes you think I'm being rash? First of all, don't mix your hairpins up with mine! You. . . . Oh! All right, mix your muck with mine. Mix it! Mix your rags with my tatters! Mix it all up. It'll stink of the maids. So Monsieur won't have any trouble discovering us. And we'll die in a flood of shame. [*Suddenly calm*] I'm capable of anything, you know.

SOLANGE: The sleeping pills.

CLAIRE: Yes. Let's talk calmly. I'm strong. You tried to dominate me. . . .

SOLANGE: But, Claire—

CLAIRE: [*Calmly*] I beg your pardon, but I know what I'm saying. I've made up my mind. I'm ready. I'm tired of it all. Tired of being the spider, the umbrella-case, the shabby, godless nun, without a family! I'm tired of having a stove for an altar. I'm that disagreeable, sullen, smelly girl. To you, too.

SOLANGE: Claire . . . we're both nervous. [*Anxiously*] Where's Madame? I can't stand it any more either. I can't stand our being so alike, I can't stand my hands, my black stockings, my hair. I'm not reproaching you for anything, my little sister. I understand that your strolls through the apartment helped ease the strain.

CLAIRE: [*Irritated*] Ah! Stop it!

SOLANGE: I want to help you. I want to comfort you, but I know I disgust you. I'm repulsive to you. And I know it because you disgust me. When slaves love one another, it's not love.

CLAIRE: And me, I'm sick of seeing my image thrown back at me by a mirror, like a bad smell. You're my bad smell. Well, I'm ready. Ready to bite. I'll have my crown and I shall stroll about the apartment.

SOLANGE: That's not reason enough to kill her.

CLAIRE: Really? Why, please? For what other reason? Where and when could we find a better excuse? Ah, so it's not enough, not enough to be raped by a milkman who goes blithely through our garrets? Tonight Madame will witness our shame. Bursting with laughter, laughing until the tears roll down her face, with her flabby sighs. No. I shall have my crown. I shall be the poisoner that you failed to be. It's my turn now to dominate you!

SOLANGE: But I never. . . .

CLAIRE: Hand me the towel! Hand me the clothespins! Peel the onions! Scrape the carrots! Scrub the tiles! It's over. Over. Ah! I almost forgot! Turn off the tap! It's over. [*Exalted*] I'll run the world!

SOLANGE: My little baby sister!

CLAIRE: You'll help me.

SOLANGE: You won't know what gestures to make. Things are more serious, Claire, and simpler too.

CLAIRE: [*Exalted*] We've read the story of Sister Holy Cross of the Blessed Valley who poisoned twenty-seven Arabs. She walked without shoes, with her feet all stiff. She was lifted up, carried off to the crime. We've read the story of Princess Albanarez who caused the death of her lover and her husband. She uncorked the bottle and made a big sign of the cross over the goblet. As she stood before the corpses, she saw only death and, off in the distance, the fleet image of herself being carried by the wind. She made all the gestures of earthly despair. In the book about the Marquise de Venosa, the one who poisoned her children, we're told that, as she approached the bed, her arms were supported by the ghost of her lover.

SOLANGE: Baby sister, my angel!

CLAIRE: I'll be supported by the sturdy arms of the milkman. I'll lean my left hand on the back of his neck. He won't flinch. You'll help me. And, far away, Solange, if we have to go far away, if I have to leave for Devil's Island, you'll come with me. You'll board the boat. The flight you were planning for him can be used for me. We shall be that eternal couple, Solange, the two of us, the eternal couple of the criminal and the saint. We'll be saved, Solange, saved, I swear to you! [*She falls on Madame's bed*]

SOLANGE: Be calm. You're going to sleep. I'll carry you upstairs.

CLAIRE: Let me alone. Turn out the light. Please turn out the light. [*Solange turns out the light*]

SOLANGE: Rest. Rest, little sister. [*She kneels, removes* Claire's *shoes, kisses her feet*] Be calm, my darling. [*She caresses her*] Put your feet on my shoulders. There. Close your eyes.

CLAIRE: [*She sighs*] I'm ashamed, Solange.

SOLANGE: [*Very gently*] Don't talk. Leave things to me. I'm going to put you to bed and, when you fall asleep, I'll carry you upstairs, to the garret. I'll undress you and put you into your little cot. Sleep. I'll be here.

CLAIRE: I'm ashamed, Solange.

SOLANGE: Sh! Let me tell you a story.

CLAIRE: [*Simply*] Solange.

SOLANGE: My angel?

CLAIRE: Solange, listen. . . .

SOLANGE: Sleep.

[*A long silence*]

CLAIRE: You have lovely hair. You have such lovely hair. Hers—

SOLANGE: Don't talk about her any more.

CLAIRE: Hers is false.

[*A long silence*]

Do you remember? Under the tree, just the two of us? Our feet in the sun? Solange?

SOLANGE: I'm here. Sleep. I'm your big sister.

[*Silence. A moment later* Claire *gets up*]

CLAIRE: No! No weakness! Put the light on! Put it on! Quick! It's too great a moment! [Solange *puts the light on*] Stand up. And let's eat. What's in the kitchen? Eh? We've got to eat. To be strong. Come along, you'll advise me. The phenobarbital.

SOLANGE: I'm too exhausted. Yes, the phenobarbital.

CLAIRE: The phenobarbital! Don't make such a face. We must be joyous. And sing. Let's sing! Sing, the way you'll sing when you go begging in the courts and embassies! Laugh! [*They burst out laughing*] Otherwise, it'll be so tragic that we'll go flying out the window. Shut the window. [Solange, *laughing, shuts the window*] Murder is a thing that's . . . unspeakable!

SOLANGE: Let's sing! We'll carry her off to the woods, and under the fir trees we'll cut her to bits by the light of the moon. And we'll sing. We'll bury her beneath the flowers, in our flower beds, and at night—we'll water her *toes* with a little *hose!*

[*The front doorbell rings*]

CLAIRE: It's Madame!

SOLANGE: It must be her! Straighten the bed. [*She seizes her sister by the wrists*] Claire, are you sure you can go through with it?

CLAIRE: How many do we need?

SOLANGE: About ten. Put ten pills into her tea. Will you do it?

CLAIRE: [*She frees herself, goes to tidy the bed, stares at it for a moment*] Yes. I've got the tube in my pocket.

[*Exit* Solange, *left.* Claire *continues tidying the room and leaves right. A few seconds elapse. A burst of nervous laughter backstage.* Madame, *in a fur coat, enters laughing, with* Solange *behind her*]

MADAME: There's no end to it! Such horrible gladioli, such a sickly pink, and mimosa! They probably hunt through the market before dawn to get them cheaper. [Solange *helps her off with her coat*]

SOLANGE: Madame wasn't too cold?

MADAME: Yes, Solange, I was very cold. I've been trailing through corridors all night long. I've been seeing frozen men and stony faces, but I did manage to catch a glimpse of Monsieur. From a distance. I waved to him. I've only just left the wife of a magistrate. Claire!

SOLANGE: She's preparing Madame's tea.

MADAME: I wish she'd hurry. I'm ashamed to ask for tea when Monsieur is all alone, without a thing, without food, without cigarettes.

SOLANGE: But Monsieur won't stay there long. They'll see right away that he's not guilty.

MADAME: Guilty or not, I shall never desert him, never. You see, Solange, it's at times like this that you realize how much you love someone. I don't think he's guilty either, but if he were, I'd become his accomplice. I'd follow him to Devil's Island, to Siberia.

SOLANGE: There's no need to get panicky. I've seen worse cases acquitted. There was a trial in Bordeaux—

MADAME: Do you go to trials? You?

SOLANGE: I read the crime news. It was about a man who—

MADAME: You can't compare Monsieur's case. He's been accused of the most idiotic thefts. I know he'll get out of it. All I mean is that, as a result of this preposterous affair, I've come to realize how deeply attached I am to him. Of course, none of this is serious, but if it were, Solange, it would be a joy for me to bear his cross. I'd follow him from place to place, from prison to prison, on foot if need be, as far as the penal colony.

SOLANGE: They wouldn't let you. Only bandits' wives, or their sisters, or their mothers, are allowed to follow them.

MADAME: A condemned man is no longer a bandit. And then I'd force my way in, past the guards. [*Suddenly conquettish*] And, Solange, I'd be utterly fearless. I'd use my weapons. What do you take me for?

SOLANGE: Madame mustn't get such ideas into her head. You must rest.

MADAME: I'm not tired. You treat me like an invalid. You're always ready to coddle me and pamper me as if I were dying. Thank God, I've got my wits about me. I'm ready for the fight. [*She looks at* Solange *and, feeling that she has hurt her, adds, with a smile*] Come, come, don't make such a face. [*With sudden violence*] All right, it's true! There are times when you're so sweet that I simply can't stand it. It crushes me, stifles me! And those flowers which are there for the very opposite of a celebration!

SOLANGE: If Madame means that we lack discretion. . . .

MADAME: But I didn't mean anything of the kind, my dear girl. It's just that I'm so upset. You see what a state I'm in.

SOLANGE: Would Madame like to see the day's accounts?

MADAME: You certainly picked the right time. You must be mad. Do you think I could look at figures now? Show them to me tomorrow.

SOLANGE: [*Putting away the fur cape*] The lining's torn. I'll take it to the furrier tomorrow.

MADAME: If you like. Though it's hardly worth while. I'm giving up my wardrobe. Besides, I'm an old woman.

SOLANGE: There go those gloomy ideas again.

MADAME: I'm thinking of going into mourning. Don't be surprised if I do. How can I lead a worldly life when Monsieur is in prison? If you find the house too sad. . . .

SOLANGE: We'll never desert Madame.

MADAME: I know you won't, Solange. You've not been too unhappy with me, have you?

SOLANGE: Oh!

MADAME: When you needed anything, I saw that you got it. With my old gowns alone you both could have dressed like princesses. Besides . . . [*She goes to the closet and looks at her dresses*] of what use will they be to me? I'm through with finery and all that goes with it.

[Claire *enters carrying the tea*]

CLAIRE: The tea is ready.

MADAME: Farewell to parties and dances and the theater. You'll inherit all that.

CLAIRE: Madame is losing her self-control. She must pull herself together.

SOLANGE: The tea is ready.

MADAME: Put it down. I'm going to bed. It's all over. [*She runs her hand over the red velvet dress*] My lovely "Fascination," the loveliest of them all. [*She takes it down, and runs her hand over it*] It was designed for me by Chanel. Specially. Here, you may have it. It's yours. [*She gives it to* Claire *and searches in the closet*]

CLAIRE: For me?

MADAME: [*Smiling sadly*] Of course. I said so, didn't I?

SOLANGE: Madame is very kind. [*To* Claire] You might thank Madame. You've been admiring it so long.

CLAIRE: It's so beautiful. I'll never dare wear it.

MADAME: You can have it altered. There's enough velvet in the train alone for the sleeves. And for you, Solange, I'm going to give you. . . . What shall I give you? Here, this coat. [*She hands* Solange *the magnificent fur cape*]

CLAIRE: Oh! the fur cape!

SOLANGE: [*Thrilled*] Oh! Madame . . . never . . . Madame's too kind.

MADAME: No, no, don't thank me. It's such a pleasure to make people happy. Now I'm going to get undressed. [*She looks at the telephone*] Who left the receiver off?

CLAIRE: It was Monsieur. . . . [*She stops suddenly*]

MADAME: [*Dumbfounded*] Eh? Monsieur? [Claire *is silent*] What do you mean? Speak up!

SOLANGE: [*Slowly and as if in spite of herself*] When Monsieur rang up.

MADAME: What are you talking about? Monsieur phoned?

SOLANGE: We wanted to surprise Madame. Monsieur's out on bail. He's waiting for Madame at the Hong-Kong Bar.

MADAME: [*Rising to her feet*] And you didn't say anything! Go get a taxi! Solange, quick, quick, get me a taxi. And hurry up. Go on, run. [*She pushes* Solange *out of the room*] My furs! Quick, quick!

You're both mad. You let me go on talking. You really are mad. Or am *I* going mad! [*She puts on her fur coat. To* Claire] When did he phone?

CLAIRE: [*In a toneless voice*] Five minutes before Madame came in.

MADAME: But you should have told me. And this cold tea! I'll never be able to wait for Solange to get back! Oh! What did he say?

CLAIRE: What I've just told you. He was very calm.

MADAME: Ah, him, he always is. He'd be utterly unconcerned if he were condemned to death. The man's unique! What else did he say?

CLAIRE: Nothing. He said the judge was letting him out.

MADAME: How can anyone leave police headquarters at midnight? Do judges work as late as that?

CLAIRE: Sometimes, much later.

MADAME: Much later? How do *you* know that?

CLAIRE: I read *True Detective*. I know those things.

MADAME: [*Astonished*] Oh you do? You really are an odd little girl, Claire. She *might* hurry. [*She looks at her wrist watch*] You won't forget to have the lining of my coat sewn?

CLAIRE: I'll take it to the furrier tomorrow.

[*A long silence*]

MADAME: What about the accounts? The day's accounts. Let me see them. I've got time!

CLAIRE: Solange attends to that.

MADAME: That's right. I'm all in a dither. I'll look at them tomorrow. [*Staring at* Claire] Come a little closer! Come here! Why . . . you've got make-up on! [*Laughing*] Why Claire, you've been putting make-up on!

CLAIRE: [*Very embarrassed*] Madame. . . .

MADAME: Ah, don't lie! Besides, you've every right to. Live, my child, live. In whose honor is it? Eh? Got a crush on someone? Own up!

CLAIRE: I put a little powder on. . . .

MADAME: That's not powder, it's make-up. But there's nothing wrong in that, you're still young. Make yourself attractive. Smarten up. [*She puts a flower in* Claire's *hair. She looks at her wrist watch*] What *can* she be doing? It's midnight and she's not back!

CLAIRE: There aren't many taxis at this hour. She probably had to run to the cab-stand.

MADAME: You think so? I've lost track of time. I'm wild with happiness. Monsieur ringing up at a time like that! And that he's free.

CLAIRE: Madame ought to sit down. I'll go and heat up the tea. [*She starts to leave*]

MADAME: Don't bother, I'm not thirsty. It's champagne we'll be drinking tonight. You can be sure we won't be coming home.

CLAIRE: Really, just a little tea. . . .

MADAME: [*Laughing*] I'm nervous enough as it is. I don't want you and Solange to wait up for us.

Go upstairs and get to bed right away. [*Suddenly she sees the alarm clock*] But. . . . That alarm clock, what's that doing here? Where does it come from?

CLAIRE: [*Very embarrassed*] The alarm clock? It's the kitchen clock.

MADAME: It is? I've never seen it before.

CLAIRE: [*She takes the alarm clock*] It belongs on the shelf. It's always been there.

MADAME: [*Smiling*] It's true I'm something of a stranger in the kitchen. You're at home there. It's your domain. You're its sovereigns. But, I wonder why you brought it in here?

CLAIRE: It was Solange, for the cleaning. She'd never dare trust the big clock.

MADAME: How odd.

[*Claire goes out carrying the alarm clock*]

How odd. [*She looks at her wrist watch*] She's certainly taking her time. You can find taxis at every street-corner. [*She sits down at her dressing table. She looks at herself in the mirror and talks to herself*] And what about you, you fool, will you be beautiful enough to receive him? No wrinkles, eh? It's been such a long separation, it'll have been like a thousand years! Eh? Let's see, now. Gay? Wistful? Idiot, you idiot, there I go talking to myself. Happiness makes me giddy. And Solange not back yet. All those flowers! Those girls do worship me, but—[*She looks at the top of the dressing table and blows at the powder*] but they haven't dusted the dressing table. Their housekeeping is the most extraordinary combination of luxury and filth.

[*As she utters the last sentence,* Claire *enters the room on tiptoe. She stands silently behind* Madame *who suddenly notices her in the mirror*]

Eh? I'm raving, Claire, my mind's wandering. Forgive me. Today's been too dreadful.

CLAIRE: Isn't Madame satisfied with our work?

MADAME: [*Smiling*] But I am, Claire. Delighted. In seventh heaven.

CLAIRE: Madame's making fun of us.

MADAME: [*Laughing*] Oh, stop nagging me. After what I've been through today, I've got a right to be out of sorts. In the first place, there's that business of the letters to the police. . . . I wonder who could have sent them. I suppose you wouldn't have any idea?

CLAIRE: Does Madame mean? . . .

MADAME: I don't mean anything. I'd like to know, that's all. I've been groping around the whole day long as if I were blind. I felt like the police hunting in the bushes for a girl's corpse.

CLAIRE: That's all over with. Monsieur is free.

MADAME: Thank heavens. Which still doesn't account for those letters. What *can* she be doing? She's been gone an hour. Why didn't you tell me at once that Monsieur had phoned? He'll be furious.

CLAIRE: We were terribly afraid of alarming Madame, of giving her a shock.

MADAME: That was very bright. You're quietly killing me with flowers and kindness. One fine day I'll be found dead beneath the roses. Claire, what do you think of this coiffure? Do you like it?

CLAIRE: If I might venture. . . .

MADAME: Eh? If you might venture? Well, venture. I've full confidence in your opinion. Well? What do you think of it?

CLAIRE: If I might be so bold as to make a suggestion, Madame's hair would look fluffier worn over the forehead.

MADAME: Are you sure?

CLAIRE: It would soften Madame's face.

MADAME: Like that? You're right. You *are* a bright girl, Claire. You know, Claire, I've always thought you had a great deal of taste and that you were meant for better things.

CLAIRE: I'm not complaining.

MADAME: No, no, I know. But after all, you *are* more sensitive than the others. I realize that it's not much fun living with them. Fortunately you're with your sister. You're a family. But with a bit of luck you—

CLAIRE: Oh! If I had wanted to!

MADAME: I don't doubt it! [*She listens*] Listen! [*She stands up*] Listen! A car. It's her. Ah!

[*She looks at herself again in the mirror*]

CLAIRE: Madame should have some tea because of the cold.

MADAME: [*Laughing*] You're trying to kill me with your tea and your flowers and your suggestions. You're too much for me, Claire. No. I've never felt so alive. Oh! And served in the best tea set, the *very best* set! Such pomp! Such elegance!

[*She wants to leave, but* Claire *stands between her and the door*]

CLAIRE: [*Imploringly*] Madame *must* drink it. Otherwise. . . .

[Solange *dashes in. She pushes her sister aside and turns to* Madame]

MADAME: Well!

SOLANGE: [*Surprised*] Ah! Madame's still here. I've looked everywhere. No one wanted to come as late as this!

MADAME: Did you get a taxi?

SOLANGE: It's here, Madame. It's downstairs, Madame.

MADAME: Let's hurry. So it's understood, you're to go upstairs and to bed. And tomorrow morning we'll just sleep and sleep and sleep. Claire, come and close the door behind me. And you're not to latch it.

[*She leaves, followed by* Claire. Solange *is left alone.* Claire *returns. The two sisters look at one another*]

SOLANGE: [*Ironically*] You certainly did a fine job. And you sneered at me.

CLAIRE: Don't. I tried so hard not to say it, but I just couldn't help myself.

SOLANGE: Didn't she drink it?

[Claire *shakes her head "no"*]

Obviously. It was to be expected.

CLAIRE: I'd have liked to see *you* in my place. [*She remains motionless for a moment and then starts walking toward the kitchen*]

SOLANGE: Where are you going?

CLAIRE: [*Without turning around and in a weary voice*] To sleep!

[*She leaves*]

SOLANGE: Claire! [*Silence*] Claire! [*She goes to the door and calls her*] Claire, I'm calling you.

CLAIRE: [*Off stage*] Who cares?

SOLANGE: [*Facing the door at the right*] Come here. Do you hear me? Come here.

[Claire *comes in untying her apron*]

CLAIRE: [*Very wearily*] What do you want? Is it my fault? The "tay"—as she says—was ready. I put in the pills. She wouldn't drink it!

SOLANGE: And so you think we're just going to sit here and shake? [*She stares hard at her sister*] They'll both be back tomorrow, drunk probably and vicious, like conquerors. They'll know where the letters came from. They—I hate her. [Claire *shrugs her shoulders*] Oh, I hate her! I loathe her. And you, you just stand there! Didn't you see how she sparkled? How disgustingly happy she was? *Her* joy feeds on *our* shame. Her carnation is the red of our shame. Her dress. . . . [*She kicks at the red velvet dress*] It's the red of our shame. Her furs. . . . Ah! She took back her furs! And you just stand there! You don't scream. Are you dead?

CLAIRE: What do you want me to do? She got away from us. You came back too soon.

SOLANGE: She gets away and you just stand there!

CLAIRE: What do you want to do? Make a scene? Eh? [*She screams in the face of* Solange, *who remains motionless*] You want to make a scene? Answer. Answer. Well, answer. We've got time. We've got all night.

SOLANGE: [*In a very calm tone*] Let's get on with it.

CLAIRE: What's the hurry? No, we'll take our time. Shall we?

[*She unties her apron*]

SOLANGE: Keep your apron on. It's your turn.

CLAIRE: No, that doesn't matter.

SOLANGE: It's my turn to be Madame.

CLAIRE: Take the apron.

SOLANGE: But Claire. . . .

CLAIRE: [*Simply*] I'm used to it. Here. [*She delicately hands the apron to* Solange] Do you think I've really got too much rouge on?

SOLANGE: Rouge? Yes, there's some rouge left. . . . But you're not rouged. You're all made-up.

CLAIRE: That's what she said.

SOLANGE: That's all over. [*She grabs the apron*] Forced to wear that! But I want to be a real maid. [*She ties the strings behind her back*] Put out the light.

CLAIRE: [*Timidly*] You. . . . You don't want us to . . . to organize things in the dark?

SOLANGE: Do as I say.

[*She puts out the light. The room is in semi-darkness. The two sisters look at one another and speak, without moving*]

CLAIRE: Oh! Let's wait a little while, Solange. Suppose she comes back? Madame might have forgotten something. At times like that one always forgets . . . one's bag, or money, or. . . .

SOLANGE: Naive!

CLAIRE: [*Muttering*] She left in such a hurry. It's a trap. Madame suspects something.

SOLANGE: [*Shrugging her shoulders*] What? For instance?

CLAIRE: She's suspicious. We're being watched. . . .

SOLANGE: What of it? We're beyond that!

CLAIRE: [*She wants to gain time*] You're not listening to me, Solange. I assure you, I feel something, I feel it. Listen, we're being spied on. I'm sure she'll come back unexpectedly. She'll have forgotten her handkerchief. Or her gloves. [Solange *shrugs her shoulders*] Or her compact, God knows what. But I feel there's something here, Solange—something in this room—that can record our gestures and play them back. Remember, Madame told us not to latch the front door. . . .

SOLANGE: You're raving.

CLAIRE: I'm not! No! Please, wait, please, it's so serious. Suppose she came back. . . .

SOLANGE: Too bad for her!

CLAIRE: You're growing terrible, Solange. You've got an answer for everything. At least. . . .

SOLANGE: What?

CLAIRE: [*Timidly*] At least . . . suppose we said a prayer?

SOLANGE: Do you dare bring God. . . .

CLAIRE: But to the Holy. . . .

SOLANGE: Bring the *Mother* of God into the ceremony? Really, you've got more nerve than I thought. You've no shame.

CLAIRE: More softly, Solange, the walls are thin.

SOLANGE: [*Less loudly*] You're going mad, Claire. It's God who's listening to us. We know that it's for Him that the last act is to be performed, but we mustn't forewarn Him. We'll play it to the hilt.

CLAIRE: Not so loud!

SOLANGE: The walls are His ears.

CLAIRE: Then I'll put on the white dress.

SOLANGE: If you like. It makes no difference. But hurry up! Let's drop the preliminaries and get on with it. We've long since stopped needing the twists and turns and the lies. Let's get right into the transformation. Hurry up! Hurry up! I can't stand the shame and humiliation any longer. Who cares if the world listens to us and smiles and shrugs its shoulders and says I'm crazy and envious! I'm quivering, I'm shuddering with pleasure. Claire, I'm going to whinny with joy!

[*During this speech,* Claire *has taken down the white dress and, hidden behind a screen, has put it on over her black dress whose black sleeves show*]

CLAIRE: [*Appearing, all in white, with an imperious voice*] Begin!

SOLANGE: [*Ecstatically*] You're beautiful!

CLAIRE: Skip that. You said we're skipping the prelude. Start the insults.

SOLANGE: I'll never be able to. You dazzle me.

CLAIRE: I said the insults! Let them come, let them unfurl, let them drown me, for, as you well know, I loathe servants. A vile and odious breed, I loathe them. They're not of the human race. Servants ooze. They're a foul effluvium drifting through our rooms and hallways, seeping into us, entering our mouths, corrupting us. I vomit you!

SOLANGE: Go on. [*Silence.* Claire *coughs*] Go on! I'm getting there, I'm getting there!

CLAIRE: I know they're necessary, just as gravediggers and scavengers and policemen are necessary. Nevertheless, they're a putrid lot.

SOLANGE: Go on, go on!

CLAIRE: Your frightened guilty faces, your puckered elbows, your outmoded clothes, your wasted bodies, only fit for our castoffs! You're our distorting mirrors, our loathsome vent, our shame, our dregs!

SOLANGE: Go on, go on!

CLAIRE: Please hurry. Please! I can't go on. You're . . . you're. . . . My God, I can't think of anything. My mind's a blank. I've run out of insults. Claire, you exhaust me. [*Addressing* Solange]

SOLANGE: Stop. I've got there. It's my turn.— Madame had her billing and cooing, her lovers, her milkman. . . .

CLAIRE: Solange. . . .

SOLANGE: Silence! Her morning milkman, her messenger of dawn, her handsome clarion, her pale and charming lover. That's over. [*She takes down a riding whip*] Take your place for the ball.

CLAIRE: What are you doing?

SOLANGE: [*Solemnly*] I'm checking the flow. Down on your knees!

CLAIRE: Solange. . . .

SOLANGE: Down on your knees! [Claire *hesitates and kneels*] Ah! Ah! You were so beautiful, the way you wrung your precious arms! Your tears, your petals oozed down your lovely face. Ah! Ah! Down! [Claire *does not move*] Down! [Solange *strikes her*] Get down! [Claire *lies down*] Ah! You amuse me, my dear! Crawl! Crawl, I say, like a worm! And you were going to follow in the wake of the boats, to cross the sea to aid and comfort your handsome exile! Look at yourself again! That role is only for the fairest of the fair. The guards would snicker. People would point at you. Your lover would hang his head in shame! And are you strong enough? Strong enough to carry his bag? And spry enough,

Madame, spry enough on your feet? Don't worry. I'm not jealous. I don't need that thief where I'm going. No, Madame. I myself am both the thief and his slavish shadow. I move alone toward the brightest shores.

CLAIRE: [*Playing the role of* Madame] I'm losing him!

SOLANGE: Aren't I enough for you?

CLAIRE: Solange, please, I'm sinking.

SOLANGE: Sink! But rise again to the surface. I know what my final destiny is to be. I've reached shelter. I can be bountiful. [*She takes a breath*] Stand up! I'll marry you standing up! Ah! Ah! Groveling on the rug at a man's feet. What a sorry, facile gesture. The great thing is to end in beauty. How are you going to get up?

CLAIRE: [*Getting up slowly and clumsily*] You're killing me.

SOLANGE: [*Ironically*] Careful now, watch your movements.

CLAIRE: [*On her feet*] We're out of our depth. We must go to bed. My throat's—

SOLANGE: [*Striding up to her*] Madame has a very lovely throat. The throat of a queen.

[Claire *moves back to the kitchen door*] Of a dove. Come, my turtle dove!

CLAIRE: [*She withdraws farther back, putting her hands to her neck as if to protect it*] It's late.

SOLANGE: Never too late.

CLAIRE: Madame. . . .

SOLANGE: . . . is drinking champagne with Monsieur who has returned from the dead.

CLAIRE: She'll be back any moment. Let me go.

SOLANGE: Stop worrying. She's waltzing! She's waltzing! She's guzzling fine wine! She's delirious.

CLAIRE: Let's get out of here, Solange. I tell you we're in danger.

SOLANGE: Go into the vestry. [*She points to the kitchen door*] Go on in. You've got to finish the linoleum.

CLAIRE: [*She screams in a hollow voice*] Help!

SOLANGE: Don't yell! It's useless. Death is present, and is stalking you. Don't yell! I, who kept you the way they keep kittens for drowning. I, yes I, who trimmed my belly with pins to stab all the foetuses I threw into the gutter! In order to keep you, to have *you* alive!

CLAIRE: [*Running about the room*] Solange, Solange, come to yourself!

SOLANGE: [*Running after her*] To *your*self!

CLAIRE: [*In a dull voice*] Help!

SOLANGE: Stop yelling! No one can hear you! We're both beyond the pale.

CLAIRE: Solange. . . .

SOLANGE: Everyone's listening, but no one will hear.

CLAIRE: I'm ill. . . .

SOLANGE: You'll be taken care of there.

CLAIRE: I'm ill . . . I . . . I'm going to be sick. . . .

[*She seems to be gagging*]

SOLANGE: [*She approaches her and says sympathetically*] Really? Are you really ill? Claire, are you really feeling ill?

CLAIRE: I'm, I'm going to—

SOLANGE: Not here, Claire, hold it in. [*She supports her*] Not here, please, please. Come. Lean on me. There. Walk gently. We'll be better off there, in our flowered domain. I have such sure ways of putting an end to all suffering.

[*They leave by the kitchen door. The stage remains empty for a few seconds. A gust of wind opens the unlocked window. Enter Solange,* right, *wearing her short black dress. Throughout the scene she will seem to be addressing characters who are imaginary, though present*]

SOLANGE: Madame. . . . At last! Madame is dead! . . . laid out on the linoleum . . . strangled by the dish-gloves. What? Oh, Madame may remain seated. . . . Madame may call me Mademoiselle Solange. . . . Exactly. It's because of what I've done. Madame and Monsieur will call me Mademoiselle Solange Lemercier. . . . Madame should have taken off that black dress. It's grotesque. [*She imitates Madame's voice*] So I'm reduced to wearing mourning for my maid. As I left the cemetery all the servants of the neighborhood marched past me as if I were a member of the family. I've so often been part of the family. Death will see the joke through to the bitter end. . . . What? Oh! Madame needn't feel sorry for me. I'm Madame's equal and I hold my head high. . . . Oh! And there are things Monsieur doesn't realize. He doesn't know that he used to obey our orders. [*She laughs*] Ah! Ah! Monsieur was a tiny little boy. Monsieur toed the line when we threatened. No, Inspector, no. . . . I won't talk! I won't say a word. I refuse to speak about our complicity in this murder. . . . The dresses? Oh, Madame could have kept them. My sister and I had our own. Those we used to put on at night, in secret. Now, I have my own dress, and I'm your equal. I wear the red garb of criminals. Monsieur's laughing at me? He's smiling at me. Monsieur thinks I'm mad. He's thinking maids should have better taste than to make gestures reserved for Madame! Monsieur really forgives me? Monsieur is the soul of kindness. He'd like to vie with me in grandeur. But I've scaled the fiercest heights. Madame now sees my loneliness—at last! Yes, I am alone. And fearsome. I might say cruel things, but I can be kind. . . . Madame will get over her fright. She'll get over it well enough. What with her flowers and perfumes and gowns and jewels and lovers. As for me, I've my sister. . . . Yes. I dare speak of these things. I do, Madame. There's nothing I won't dare. And who could silence me, who? Who would be so bold as to say to me: "My dear child!" I've been a servant. Well and good. I've made the gestures a servant must make. I've smiled at Madame.

I've bent down to make the bed, bent down to scrub the tiles, bent down to peel vegetables, to listen at doors, to glue my eye to keyholes! But now I stand upright. And firm. I'm the strangler. Mademoiselle Solange, the one who strangled her sister! . . . Me be still? Madame is delicate, really. But I pity Madame. I pity Madame's whiteness, her satiny skin, and her little ears, and little wrists. . . . Eh? I'm the black crow. . . . Oh! Oh! I have my judges. I belong to the police. Claire? She was really very fond of Madame. . . . YOUR dresses again! And THAT white dress, THAT one, which I forbade her to put on, the one you wore the night of the Opera Ball, the night you poked fun at her, because she was sitting in the kitchen admiring a photo of Gary Cooper. . . . Madame will remember. Madame will remember her gentle irony, the maternal grace with which she took the magazine from us, and smiled. Nor will Madame forget that she called her Clarinette. Monsieur laughed until the tears rolled down his cheeks. . . . Eh? Who am I? The monstrous soul of servantdom! . . . No, Inspector, I'll explain nothing in their presence. That's *our* business. It would be a fine thing if masters could pierce the shadows where servants live. . . . That, my child, is our darkness, ours. [*She lights a cigarette and smokes clumsily. The smoke makes her cough.*] Neither you nor anyone else will be told anything. Just tell yourselves that this time Solange has gone through with it. . . . You see her dressed in red. She is going out.

[*She goes to the window, opens it, and steps out on the balcony. Facing the night, with her back to the audience, she delivers the following speech. A slight breeze makes the curtains stir*]

Going out. Descending the great stairway. Accompanied by the police. Out on your balconies to see her making her way among the shadowy penitents! It's noon. She's carrying a nine-pound torch. The hangman follows close behind. He's whispering sweet nothings in her ear. Claire! The hangman's by my side! Now take your hand off my waist. He's trying to kiss me! Let go of me! Ah! Ah! [*She laughs*] The hangman's trifling with me. She will be led in procession by all the maids of the neighborhood, by all the servants who accompanied Claire to her final resting place. They'll all be wearing crowns, flowers, streamers, banners. They'll toll the bell. The funeral will unfold its pomp. It's beautiful, isn't it? First come the butlers, in full livery, but without silk lining. They're wearing their crowns. Then come the footmen, the lackeys in knee breeches and white stockings. They're wearing their crowns. Then come the valets, and then the chambermaids wearing our colors. Then the porters. And then come the delegations from heaven. And I'm leading them. The hangman's lulling me. I'm being acclaimed. I'm pale and I'm about to die. . . . [*She returns to the room*] And what flowers! They gave her such a lovely funeral, didn't they? Oh! Claire, poor little Claire! [*She bursts into tears and collapses into an armchair*] What? [*She gets up*] It's no use, Madame, I'm obeying the police. They're the only ones who understand me. They too belong to the world of outcasts, the world you touch only with tongs.

[*Visible only to the audience,* Claire, *during the last few moments, has been leaning with her elbows against the jamb of the kitchen door and listening to her sister*]

Now we are Mademoiselle Solange Lemercier, that Lemercier woman. The famous criminal. And above all, Monsieur need not be uneasy. I'm not a maid. I have a noble soul. . . . [*She shrugs her shoulders*] No, no, not another word, my dear fellow. Ah, Madame's not forgetting what I've done for her. . . . No, no she must not forget my devotion. . . .

[*Meanwhile* Claire *enters through the door at the left. She is wearing the white dress*]

And in spite of my forbidding it, Madame continues to stroll about the apartment. She will please sit down . . . and listen to me. . . . [*To Claire*] Claire . . . we're raving!

CLAIRE: [*Complainingly, Madame's voice*] You're talking far too much, my child. Far too much. Shut the window. [Solange *shuts the window*] Draw the curtains. Very good, Claire!

SOLANGE: It's late. Everyone's in bed. . . . We're playing an idiotic game.

CLAIRE: [*She signals with her hand for silence*] Claire, pour me a cup of tea.

SOLANGE: But. . . .

CLAIRE: I said a cup of tea.

SOLANGE: We're dead-tired. We've got to stop. [*She sits down in an armchair*]

CLAIRE: Ah, by no means! Poor servant girl, you think you'll get out of it as easily as that? It would be too simple to conspire with the wind, to make the night one's accomplice. Solange, you will contain me within you. Now pay close attention.

SOLANGE: Claire. . . .

CLAIRE: Do as I tell you. I'm going to help you. I've decided to take the lead. Your role is to keep me from backing out, nothing more.

SOLANGE: What more do you want? We're at the end. . . .

CLAIRE: We're at the very beginning.

SOLANGE: They'll be coming. . . .

CLAIRE: Forget about them. We're alone in the world. Nothing exists but the altar where one of the two maids is about to immolate herself—

SOLANGE: But—

CLAIRE: Be still. It will be your task, yours alone, to keep us both alive. You must be very strong. In prison no one will know that I'm with you, secretly. On the sly.

SOLANGE: I'll never be able. . . .

CLAIRE: Please, stand up straight. Up straight, Solange! Claire! Darling, stand straight now. Up straight. Pull yourself together.

SOLANGE: You're overwhelming me.

CLAIRE: A staff! A standard! Claire, up straight! I call upon you to represent me—

SOLANGE: I've been working too hard. I'm exhausted.

CLAIRE: To represent me in the world. [*She tries to lift her sister and keep her on her feet*] My darling, stand up straight.

SOLANGE: Please, I beg of you.

CLAIRE: [*Domineeringly*] I beg of you, stand up straight. Solemnly, Claire! Pretty does it, pretty does it! Up Claire! Up on your paws! [*She holds her by the wrists and lifts her from her chair*] Up on your paws! Now then! Up! Up!

SOLANGE: You don't realize the danger—

CLAIRE: But, Solange, you're immortal! Repeat after me—

SOLANGE: Talk. But not so loud.

CLAIRE: [*Mechanically*] Madame must have her tea.

SOLANGE: [*Firmly*] No, I won't.

CLAIRE: [*Holding her by the wrists*] You bitch! Repeat. Madame must have her tea.

SOLANGE: I've just been through such a lot. . . .

CLAIRE: [*More firmly*] Madame will have her tea. . . .

SOLANGE: Madame will have her tea. . . .

CLAIRE: Because she must sleep. . . .

SOLANGE: Because she must sleep. . . .

CLAIRE: And I must stay awake.

SOLANGE: And I must stay awake.

CLAIRE: [*She lies down on Madame's bed*] Don't interrupt again. I repeat. Are you listening? Are you obeying? [Solange *nods "yes"*] I repeat: My tea!

SOLANGE: [*Hesitating*] But. . . .

CLAIRE: I say: my tea.

SOLANGE: But, Madame.

CLAIRE: Good. Continue.

SOLANGE: But, Madame, it's cold.

CLAIRE: I'll drink it anyway. Let me have it. [Solange *brings the tray*] And you've poured it into the best, the finest tea set.

[*She takes the cup and drinks, while* Solange, *facing the audience, delivers the end of her speech*]

SOLANGE: The orchestra is playing brilliantly. The attendant is raising the red velvet curtain. He bows. Madame is descending the stairs. Her furs brush against the green plants. Madame steps into the car. Monsieur is whispering sweet nothings in her ear. She would like to smile, but she is dead. She rings the bell. The porter yawns. He opens the door. Madame goes up the stairs. She enters her apartment— but, Madame is dead. Her two maids are alive: they've just risen up, free, from Madame's icy form. All the maids were present at her side—not they themselves, but rather the hellish agony of their names. And all that remains of them to float about Madame's airy corpse is the delicate perfume of the holy maidens which they were in secret. We are beautiful, joyous, drunk, and free!

CURTAIN

THE CHAIRS

By Eugène Ionesco
TRANSLATED BY DONALD M. ALLEN

THE CHARACTERS

OLD MAN, *aged 95*
OLD WOMAN, *aged 94*
THE ORATOR, *aged 45 to 50*
And many other characters

SCENE—*Circular walls with a recess upstage center. A large, very sparsely furnished room. To the right, going upstage from the proscenium, three doors. Then a window with a stool in front of it; then another door. In the center of the back wall of the recess, a large double door, and two other doors facing each other and bracketing the main door: these last two doors, or at least one of them, are almost hidden from the audience. To the left, going upstage from the proscenium, there are three doors, a window with a stool in front of it, opposite the window on the right, then a blackboard and a dais. See the plan below. Downstage are two chairs, side by side. A gas lamp hangs from the ceiling.*

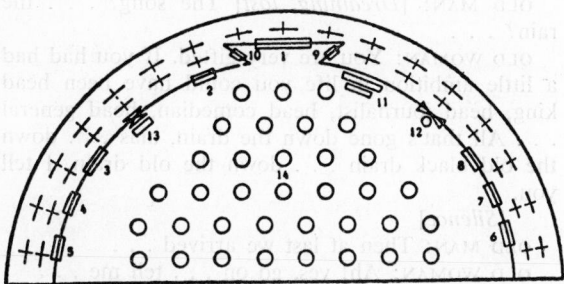

1: Main double door.
2, 3, 4, 5: Side doors on the right.
6, 7, 8: Side doors on the left.
9, 10: Two doors hidden in the recess.
11: Dais and blackboard.
12, 13: Windows, with stools, left and right.
14: Empty chairs.
XXX Corridor, in wings.

The curtain rises. Half-light. The Old Man *is up on the stool, leaning out the window on the left. The* Old Woman *lights the gas lamp. Green light. She goes over to the* Old Man *and takes him by the sleeve.*

OLD WOMAN: Come my darling, close the window. There's a bad smell from that stagnant water, and besides the mosquitoes are coming in.

OLD MAN: Leave me alone!

OLD WOMAN: Come, come, my darling, come sit down. You shouldn't lean out, you might fall into the water. You know what happened to François I. You must be careful.

OLD MAN: Still more examples from history! Sweetheart, I'm tired of French history. I want to see— the boats on the water making blots in the sunlight.

OLD WOMAN: You can't see them, there's no sunlight, it's nighttime, my darling.

OLD MAN: There are still shadows.

[*He leans out very far*]

OLD WOMAN: [*Pulling him in with all her strength*] Oh! . . . you're frightening me, my darling . . . come sit down, you won't be able to see them come, anyway. There's no use trying. It's dark . . .

[*The* Old Man *reluctantly lets himself be pulled in*]

OLD MAN: I wanted to see—you know how much I love to see the water.

OLD WOMAN: How can you, my darling? . . . . It makes me dizzy. Ah! this house, this island, I can't get used to it. Water all around us . . . water under the windows, stretching as far as the horizon.

[*The* Old Woman *drags the* Old Man *down and they move towards the two chairs downstage; the* Old Man *seats himself quite naturally on the lap of the* Old Woman]

OLD MAN: It's six o'clock in the evening . . . it is dark already. It wasn't like this before. Surely you remember, there was still daylight at nine o'clock in the evening, at ten o'clock, at midnight.

OLD WOMAN: Come to think of it, that's very true. What a remarkable memory you have!

OLD MAN: Things have certainly changed.

OLD WOMAN: Why is that, do you think?

OLD MAN: I don't know, Semiramis, sweetheart . . . Perhaps it's because the further one goes, the deeper one sinks. It's because the earth keeps turning around, around, around, around . . .

OLD WOMAN: Around, around, my little pet. [*Silence*] Ah! yes, you've certainly a fine intellect. You are very gifted, my darling. You could have been head president, head king, or even head doctor, or head general, if you had wanted to, if only you'd had a little ambition in life . . .

OLD MAN: What good would that have done us? We'd not have lived any better . . . and besides, we have a position here. I am a general, in any case, of the house, since I am the general factotum.

OLD WOMAN: [*Caressing the* Old Man *as one caresses a child*] My darling, my pet.

OLD MAN: I'm very bored.

OLD WOMAN: You were more cheerful when you were looking at the water . . . Let's amuse ourselves by making believe, the way you did the other evening.

OLD MAN: Make believe yourself, it's your turn.

OLD WOMAN: It's your turn.

OLD MAN: Your turn.

OLD WOMAN: Your turn.

OLD MAN: Your turn.

OLD WOMAN: Your turn.

OLD MAN: Drink your tea, Semiramis.

[*Of course there is no tea*]

OLD WOMAN: Come on now, imitate the month of February.

OLD MAN: I don't like the months of the year.

OLD WOMAN: Those are the only ones we have, up till now. Come on, just to please me . . .

OLD MAN: All right, here's the month of February.

[*He scratches his head like Stan Laurel*]

OLD WOMAN: [*Laughing, applauding*] That's just right. Thank you, thank you, you're as cute as can be, my darling. [*She hugs him*] Oh, you are so gifted, you could have been at least a head general, if you had wanted to . . .

OLD MAN: I am a general, general factotum.

[*Silence*]

OLD WOMAN: Tell me the story, you know *the* story: "Then at last we arrived . . ."

OLD MAN: Again? . . . I'm sick of it . . . "Then at last we arrived"? That again . . . you always ask for the same thing! . . . "Then at last we arrived . . ." But it's monotonous . . . For all of the seventy-five years that we've been married, every single evening, absolutely every blessed evening, you've made me tell the same story, you've made me imitate the same people, the same months . . . always the same . . . let's talk about something else . . .

OLD WOMAN: My darling, I'm not tired of it . . . it's your life, it fascinates me.

OLD MAN: You know it by heart.

OLD WOMAN: It's as if suddenly I'd forgotten everything . . . it's as though my mind were a clean slate every evening . . . Yes, my darling, I do it on purpose, I take a dose of salts . . . I become new again, for you, my darling, every evening . . . Come on, begin again, please.

OLD MAN: Well, if you want me to.

OLD WOMAN: Come on then, tell your story . . . It's also mine; what is yours is mine! Then at last we arrived . . .

OLD MAN: Then at last we arrived . . . my sweetheart . . .

OLD WOMAN: Then at last we arrived . . . my darling . . .

OLD MAN: Then at last we arrived at a big fence. We were soaked through, frozen to the bone, for hours, for days, for nights, for weeks . . .

OLD WOMAN: For months . . .

OLD MAN: . . . In the rain . . . Our ears, our feet, our knees, our noses, our teeth were chattering . . . that was eighty years ago . . . They wouldn't let us in . . . they might at least have opened the gate of the garden . . .

[*Silence*]

OLD WOMAN: In the garden the grass was wet.

OLD MAN: There was a path which led to a little square and in the center, a village church . . . Where was this village? Do you recall?

OLD WOMAN: No, my darling, I've forgotten.

OLD MAN: How did we reach it? Where is the road? This place was called Paris, I think . . .

OLD WOMAN: Paris never existed, my little one.

OLD MAN: That city must have existed because it collapsed . . . It was the city of light, but it has been extinguished, extinguished, for four hundred thousand years . . . Nothing remains of it today, except a song.

OLD WOMAN: A real song? That's odd. What song?

OLD MAN: A lullaby, an allegory: "Paris will always be Paris."

OLD WOMAN: And the way to it was through the garden? Was it far?

OLD MAN: [*Dreaming, lost*] The song? . . . the rain? . . .

OLD WOMAN: You are very gifted. If you had had a little ambition in life you could have been head king, head journalist, head comedian, head general . . . All that's gone down the drain, alas . . . down the old black drain . . . down the old drain, I tell you.

[*Silence*]

OLD MAN: Then at last we arrived . . .

OLD WOMAN: Ah! yes, go on . . . tell me . . .

OLD MAN: [*While the* Old Woman *begins to laugh softly, senilely, then progressively in great bursts, the* Old Man *laughs, too, as he continues*] Then at last we arrived, we laughed till we cried, the story was so idiotic . . . the idiot arrived full speed, bare-bellied, the idiot was pot-bellied . . . he arrived with a trunk chock full of rice; the rice spilled out on the ground . . . the idiot on the ground too, belly to ground . . . then at last we laughed, we laughed, the idiotic belly, bare with rice on the ground, the trunk, the story of sick from rice belly to ground, bare-bellied, all with rice, at last we laughed, the idiot at last arrived all bare, we laughed . . .

OLD WOMAN: [*Laughing*] At last we laughed like idiots, at last arrived all bare, we laughed, the trunk, the trunk full of rice, the rice on the belly, on the ground . . .

OLD MAN and OLD WOMAN: [*Laughing together*] At last we laughed. Ah! . . . laughed . . . arrived . . . arrived . . . Ah! . . . Ah! . . . rived . . . arrived . . . arrived . . . the idiotic bare belly . . . arrived with the rice . . . arrived with the rice . . . [*This is all we hear*] At last we . . . bare-bellied . . . arrived . . . the trunk . . . [*Then the Old Man and Old Woman calm down little by little*] We lau . . . Ah! . . . aughed . . . Ah! . . . arrived . . . Ah! . . . arrived . . . aughed . . . aughed.

OLD WOMAN: So that's the way it was, your wonderful Paris.

OLD MAN: Who could put it better?

OLD WOMAN: Oh! my darling, you are so really fine. Oh! so really, you know, so really, so really, you could have been anything in life, a lot more than general factotum.

OLD MAN: Let's be modest . . . we should be content with the little . . .

OLD WOMAN: Perhaps you've spoiled your career?

OLD MAN: [*Weeping suddenly*] I've spoiled it? I've spilled it? Ah! where are you, Mamma, Mamma, where are you, Mamma? . . . hi, hi, hi, I'm an orphan. [*He moans*] . . . an orphan, dworfan.

OLD WOMAN: Here I am, what are you afraid of?

OLD MAN: No, Semiramis, my sweetheart, you're not my mamma . . . orphan, dworfan, who will protect me?

OLD WOMAN: But I'm here, my darling!

OLD MAN: It's not the same thing . . . I want my mamma, na, you, you're not my mamma, you . . .

OLD WOMAN: [*Caressing him*] You're breaking my heart, don't cry, my little one.

OLD MAN: Hi, hi, let me go, hi, hi, I'm all spoiled, I'm wet all over, my career is spilled, it's spoiled.

OLD WOMAN: Calm down.

OLD MAN: [*Sobbing, his mouth wide open like a baby*] I'm an orphan . . . dworfan.

OLD WOMAN: [*Trying to console him by cajoling him*] My orphan, my darling, you're breaking my heart, my orphan.

[*She rocks the Old Man who is sitting on her knees again*]

OLD MAN: [*Sobbing*] Hi, hi, hi! My mamma! Where is my mamma? I don't have a mamma anymore.

OLD WOMAN: I am your wife, I'm the one who is your mamma now.

OLD MAN: [*Giving in a little*] That's not true, I'm an orphan, hi, hi.

OLD WOMAN: [*Still rocking him*] My pet, my orphan, dworfan, worfan, morphan, orphan.

OLD MAN: [*Still sulky, but giving in more and more*] No . . . I don't want; I don't wa-a-a-ant.

OLD WOMAN: [*Crooning*] Orphan-ly, orphan-lay, orphan-lo, orphan-loo.

OLD MAN: No-o-o . . . No-o-o.

OLD WOMAN: [*Same business*] Li lon lala, li lon la lay, orphan-ly, orphan-lay, relee-relay, orphan-li-relee-rela . . .

OLD MAN: Hi, hi, hi, hi. [*He sniffles, calming down little by little*] Where is she? My mamma.

OLD WOMAN: In heavenly paradise . . . she hears you, she sees you, among the flowers; don't cry anymore, you will only make me weep!

OLD MAN: That's not even true-ue . . . she can't see me . . . she can't hear me. I'm an orphan, on earth, you're not my mamma . . .

OLD WOMAN: [*He is almost calm*] Now, come on, calm down, don't get so upset . . . you have great qualities, my little general . . . dry your tears; the guests are sure to come this evening and they mustn't see you this way . . . all is not lost, all is not spoiled, you'll tell them everything, you will explain, you have a message . . . you always say you are going to deliver it . . . you must live, you have to struggle for your message . . .

OLD MAN: I have a message, that's God's truth, I struggle, a mission, I have something to say, a message to communicate to humanity, to mankind . . .

OLD WOMAN: To mankind, my darling, your message! . . .

OLD MAN: That's true, yes, it's true . . .

OLD WOMAN: [*She wipes the Old Man's nose, dries his tears*] That's it . . . you're a man, a soldier, a general factotum . . .

OLD MAN: [*He gets off the Old Woman's lap and walks with short, agitated steps*] I'm not like other people, I have an ideal in life. I am perhaps gifted, as you say, I have some talent, but things aren't easy for me. I've served well in my capacity as general factotum, I've always been in command of the situation, honorably, that should be enough . . .

OLD WOMAN: Not for you, you're not like other people, you are much greater, and moreover you'd have done much better if you had got along with other people, like other people do. You've quarreled with all your friends, with all the directors, with all the generals, with your own brother.

OLD MAN: It's not my fault, Semiramis, you know very well what he said.

OLD WOMAN: What did he say?

OLD MAN: He said: "My friends, I've got a flea. I'm going to pay you a visit in the hope of leaving my flea with you."

OLD WOMAN: People say things like that, my dear. You shouldn't have paid any attention to it. But with Carel, why were you so angry with him. Was it his fault too?

OLD MAN: You're going to make me angry, you're going to make me angry. Na. Of course it was his fault. He came one evening, he said: "I know just the word that fits you. I'm not going to say it, I'll just think it." And he laughed like a fool.

OLD WOMAN: But he had a warm heart, my darling. In this life, you've got to be less sensitive.

OLD MAN: I don't care for jokes like that.

OLD WOMAN: You could have been head admiral, head cabinet-maker, head orchestra conductor.

[*Long silence. They remain immobile for a time, completely rigid on their chairs*]

OLD MAN: [*As in a dream*] At the end of the garden there was . . . there was . . . there was . . . there was . . . was what, my dear?

OLD WOMAN: The city of Paris!

OLD MAN: At the end, at the end of the end of the city of Paris, there was, there was, was what?

OLD WOMAN: My darling, was what, my darling, was who?

OLD MAN: The place and the weather were beautiful . . .

OLD WOMAN: The weather was so beautiful, are you sure?

OLD MAN: I don't recall the place . . .

OLD WOMAN: Don't tax your mind then . . .

OLD MAN: It's too far away, I can no longer . . . recall it . . . where was this?

OLD WOMAN: But what?

OLD MAN: What I . . . what I . . . where was this? And who?

OLD WOMAN: No matter where it is—I will follow you anywhere, I'll follow you, my darling.

OLD MAN: Ah! I have so much difficulty expressing myself . . . but I must tell it all.

OLD WOMAN: It's a sacred duty. You've no right to keep your message from the world. You must reveal it to mankind, they're waiting for it . . . the universe waits only for you.

OLD MAN: Yes, yes, I will speak.

OLD WOMAN: Have you really decided? You must.

OLD MAN: Drink your tea.

OLD WOMAN: You could have been head orator, if you'd had more will power in life . . . I'm proud, I'm happy that you have at last decided to speak to every country, to Europe, to every continent!

OLD MAN: Unfortunately, I have so much difficulty expressing myself, it isn't easy for me.

OLD WOMAN: It's easy once you begin, like life and death . . . it's enough to have your mind made up. It's in speaking that ideas come to us, words, and then we, in our own words, we find perhaps everything, the city too, the garden, and then we are orphans no longer.

OLD MAN: It's not I who's going to speak, I've hired a professional orator, he'll speak in my name, you'll see.

OLD WOMAN: Then, it really is for this evening? And have you invited everyone, all the characters, all the property owners, and all the intellectuals?

OLD MAN: Yes, all the owners and all the intellectuals.

[*Silence*]

OLD WOMAN: The janitors? the bishops? the chemists? the tinsmiths? the violinists? the delegates? the presidents? the police? the merchants? the buildings? the pen holders? the chromosomes?

OLD MAN: Yes, yes, and the post-office employees, the innkeepers, and the artists, everybody who is a little intellectual, a little proprietary!

OLD WOMAN: And the bankers?

OLD MAN: Yes, invited.

OLD WOMAN: The proletarians? the functionaries? the militaries? the revolutionaries? the reactionaries? the alienists and their alienated?

OLD MAN: Of course, all of them, all of them, all of them, since actually everyone is either intellectual or proprietary.

OLD WOMAN: Don't get upset, my darling, I don't mean to annoy you, you are so very absent-minded, like all great geniuses. This meeting is important, they must all be here this evening. Can you count on them? Have they promised?

OLD MAN: Drink your tea, Semiramis.

[*Silence*]

OLD WOMAN: The papacy, the papayas, and the papers?

OLD MAN: I've invited them. [*Silence*] I'm going to communicate the message to them . . . All my life, I've felt that I was suffocating; and now, they will know all, thanks to you and to the Orator, you are the only ones who have understood me.

OLD WOMAN: I'm so proud of you . . .

OLD MAN: The meeting will take place in a few minutes.

OLD WOMAN: It's true then, they're going to come, this evening? You won't feel like crying any more, the intellectuals and the proprietors will take the place of papas and mammas? [*Silence*] Couldn't you put off this meeting? It won't be too tiring for us?

[*More violent agitation. For several moments the* Old Man *has been turning around the* Old Woman *with the short, hesitant steps of an old man or of a child. He takes a step or two towards one of the doors, then returns and walks around her again*]

OLD MAN: You really think this might tire us?

OLD WOMAN: You have a slight cold.

OLD MAN: How can I call it off?

OLD WOMAN: Invite them for another evening. You could telephone.

OLD MAN: No, my God, I can't do that, it's too late. They've probably already embarked!

OLD WOMAN: You should have been more careful.

[*We hear the sound of a boat gliding through the water*]

OLD MAN: I think someone is coming already . . .

[*The gliding sound of a boat is heard more clearly*]

. . . Yes, they're coming! . . .

[*The* Old Woman *gets up also and walks with a hobble*]

OLD WOMAN: Perhaps it's the Orator.

OLD MAN: He won't come so soon. This must be somebody else. [*We hear the doorbell ring*] Ah!

OLD WOMAN: Ah!

[*Nervously, the* Old Man *and the* Old Woman *move towards the concealed door in the recess to the right. As they move upstage, they say*]

OLD MAN: Come on . . .

OLD WOMAN: My hair must look a sight . . . wait a moment . . .

[*She arranges her hair and her dress as she hobbles along, pulling up her thick red stockings*]

OLD MAN: You should have gotten ready before . . . you had plenty of time.

OLD WOMAN: I'm so badly dressed . . . I'm wearing an old gown and it's all rumpled . . .

OLD MAN: All you had to do was to press it . . . hurry up! You're making our guests wait.

[*The* Old Man, *followed by the* Old Woman *still grumbling, reaches the door in the recess; we don't see them for a moment; we hear them open the door, then close it again after having shown someone in*]

VOICE OF OLD MAN: Good evening, madam, won't you please come in. We're delighted to see you. This is my wife.

VOICE OF OLD WOMAN: Good evening, madam, I am very happy to make your acquaintance. Take care, don't ruin your hat. You might take out the hatpin, that will be more comfortable. Oh! no, no one will sit on it.

VOICE OF OLD MAN: Put your fur down there. Let me help you. No, nothing will happen to it.

VOICE OF OLD WOMAN: Oh! what a pretty suit . . . and such darling colors in your blouse . . . Won't you have some cookies . . . Oh, you're not fat at all . . . no . . . plump . . . Just leave your umbrella there.

VOICE OF OLD MAN: Follow me, please.

OLD MAN: [*Back view*] I have only a modest position . . .

[*The* Old Man *and* Old Woman *re-enter together, leaving space between them for their guest. She is invisible. The* Old Man *and* Old Woman *advance, downstage, facing the audience and speaking to the invisible Lady, who walks between them*]

OLD MAN: [*To the invisible Lady*] You've had good weather?

OLD WOMAN: [*To the Lady*] You're not too tired? . . . Yes, a little.

OLD MAN: [*To the Lady*] At the edge of the water . . .

OLD WOMAN: [*To the Lady*] It's kind of you to say so.

OLD MAN: [*To the Lady*] Let me get you a chair.

[Old Man *goes to the left, he exits by door No. 6*]

OLD WOMAN: [*To the Lady*] Take this one, for the moment, please. [*She indicates one of the two chairs and seats herself on the other, to the right of the invisible Lady*] It seems rather warm in here, doesn't it? [*She smiles at the Lady*] What a charming fan you have! My husband . . . [*The* Old Man *re-enters through door No. 7, carrying a chair*] . . . gave me one very like it, that must have been seventy-three years ago . . . and I still have it . . . [*The* Old Man *places the chair to the left of the invisible Lady*] . . . it was for my birthday! . . .

[*The* Old Man *sits on the chair that he has just brought on-stage, so that the invisible Lady is between the old couple. The* Old Man *turns his face towards the Lady, smiles at her, nods his head, softly rubs his hands together, with the air of following what she says. The* Old Woman *does the same business*]

OLD MAN: No, madam, life is never cheap.

OLD WOMAN: [*To the Lady*] You are so right . . . [*The Lady speaks*] As you say, it is about time all that changed . . . [*Changing her tone*] Perhaps my husband can do something about it . . . he's going to tell you about it.

OLD MAN: [*To the* Old Woman] Hush, hush, Semiramis, the time hasn't come to talk about that yet. [*To the Lady*] Excuse me, madam, for having aroused your curiosity. [*The Lady reacts*] Dear madam, don't insist . . .

[*The* Old Man *and* Old Woman *smile. They even laugh. They appear to be very amused by the story the invisible Lady tells them. A pause, a moment of silence in the conversation. Their faces lose all expression*]

OLD MAN: [*To the invisible Lady*] Yes, you're quite right . . .

OLD WOMAN: Yes, yes, yes . . . Oh! surely not.

OLD MAN: Yes, yes, yes. Not at all.

OLD WOMAN: Yes?

OLD MAN: No!?

OLD WOMAN: It's certainly true.

OLD MAN: [*Laughing*] It isn't possible.

OLD WOMAN: [*Laughing*] Oh! well. [*To the* Old Man] She's charming.

OLD MAN: [*To the* Old Woman] Madam has made a conquest. [*To the invisible Lady*] My congratulations! . . .

OLD WOMAN: [*To the invisible Lady*] You're not like the young people today . . .

OLD MAN: [*Bending over painfully in order to recover an invisible object that the invisible Lady has dropped*] Let me . . . don't disturb yourself . . . I'll get it . . . Oh! you're quicker than I . . .

[*He straightens up again*]

OLD WOMAN: [*To the* Old Man] She's younger than you!

OLD MAN: [*To the invisible Lady*] Old age is a heavy burden. I can only wish you an eternal youth.

OLD WOMAN: [*To the invisible Lady*] He's sincere, he speaks from the heart. [*To the* Old Man] My darling!

[*Several moments of silence. The* Old Man *and* Old Woman, *heads turned in profile, look at the invisible Lady, smiling politely; they then turn their heads towards the audience, then look again at the invisible Lady, answering her smile with their smiles, and her questions with their replies]*

OLD WOMAN: It's very kind of you to take such an interest in us.

OLD MAN: We live a retired life.

OLD WOMAN: My husband's not really misanthropic, he just loves solitude.

OLD MAN: We have the radio, I get in some fishing, and then there's fairly regular boat service.

OLD WOMAN: On Sundays there are two boats in the morning, one in the evening, not to mention privately chartered trips.

OLD MAN: [*To the invisible Lady*] When the weather's clear, there is a moon.

OLD WOMAN: [*To the invisible Lady*] He's always concerned with his duties as general factotum . . . they keep him busy . . . On the other hand, at his age, he might very well take it easy.

OLD MAN: [*To the invisible Lady*] I'll have plenty of time to take it easy in my grave.

OLD WOMAN: [*To the Old Man*] Don't say that, my little darling . . . [*To the invisible Lady*] Our family, what's left of it, my husband's friends, still came to see us, from time to time, ten years ago . . .

OLD MAN: [*To the invisible Lady*] In the winter, a good book, beside the radiator, and the memories of a lifetime.

OLD WOMAN: [*To the invisible Lady*] A modest life but a full one . . . he devotes two hours every day to work on his message.

[*The doorbell rings. After a short pause, we hear the noise of a boat leaving*]

OLD WOMAN: [*To the Old Man*] Someone has come. Go quickly.

OLD MAN: [*To the invisible Lady*] Please excuse me, madam. Just a moment! [*To the Old Woman*] Hurry and bring some chairs!

[*Loud ringing of the doorbell*]

OLD MAN: [*Hastening, all bent over, towards door No. 2 to the right, while the Old Woman goes towards the concealed door on the left, hurrying with difficulty, hobbling along*] It must be someone important. [*He hurries, opens door No. 2, and the invisible Colonel enters. Perhaps it would be useful for us to hear discreetly several trumpet notes, several phrases, like "Hail the Chief." When he opens the door and sees the invisible Colonel, the Old Man stiffens into a respectful position of attention*] Ah! . . . Colonel! [*He lifts his hand vaguely towards his forehead, so as to roughly sketch a salute*] Good evening, my dear Colonel . . . This is a very great honor for me . . . I . . . I . . . I was not expecting it . . . although . . . indeed . . . in short, I am most proud to welcome you, a hero of your eminence, into my humble dwelling . . . [*He presses the invisible hand that the invisible Colonel gives him, bending forward ceremoniously, then straightening up again*] Without false modesty, nevertheless, I permit myself to confess to you that I do not feel unworthy of the honor of your visit! Proud, yes . . . unworthy, no! . . .

[*The Old Woman appears with a chair, entering from the right*]

OLD WOMAN: Oh! What a handsome uniform! What beautiful medals! Who is it, my darling?

OLD MAN: [*To the Old Woman*] Can't you see that it's the Colonel?

OLD WOMAN: [*To the Old Man*] Ah!

OLD MAN: [*To the Old Woman*] Count his stripes! [*To the Colonel*] This is my wife, Semiramis. [*To the Old Woman*] Come here so that I can introduce you to the Colonel. [*The Old Woman approaches, dragging the chair by one hand, and makes a curtsey, without letting go of the chair. To the Colonel*] My wife. [*To the Old Woman*] The Colonel.

OLD WOMAN: How do you do, Colonel. Welcome. You're an old comrade of my husband's, he's a general . . .

OLD MAN: [*Annoyed*] Factotum, factotum . . .

[*The invisible Colonel kisses the hand of the Old Woman. This is apparent from the gesture she makes as she raises her hand toward his lips. Overcome with emotion, the Old Woman lets go of the chair*]

OLD WOMAN: Oh! He's most polite . . . you can see that he's really superior, a superior being! . . . [*She takes hold of the chair again. To the Colonel*] This chair is for you . . .

OLD MAN: [*To the invisible Colonel*] This way, if you please . . . [*They move downstage, the Old Woman dragging the chair. To the Colonel*] Yes, one guest has come already. We're expecting a great many more people! . . .

[*The Old Woman places the chair to the right*]

OLD WOMAN: [*To the Colonel*] Sit here, please.

[*The Old Man introduces the two invisible guests to each other*]

OLD MAN: A young lady we know . . .

OLD WOMAN: A very dear friend . . .

OLD MAN: [*Same business*] The Colonel . . . a famous soldier.

OLD WOMAN: [*Indicating the chair she has just brought in to the Colonel*] Do take this chair . . .

OLD MAN: [*To the Old Woman*] No, no, can't you see that the Colonel wishes to sit beside the Lady! . . .

[*The Colonel seats himself invisibly on the third chair from the left; the invisible Lady is supposedly sitting on the second chair; seated next to each other they engage in an inaudible conversation; the Old Woman and Old Man continue to stand behind their chairs, on both sides of their invisible guests; the Old Man to the left of the Lady, the Old Woman to the right of the Colonel*]

OLD WOMAN: [*Listening to the conversation of the two guests*] Oh! Oh! That's going too far.

OLD MAN: [*Same business*] Perhaps. [*The Old Man and the Old Woman make signs to each other*] *over the heads of their guests, while they follow the inaudible conversation which takes a turn that seems to displease them. Abruptly*] Yes, Colonel, they are not here yet, but they'll be here. And the Orator will speak in my behalf, he will explain the meaning of my message . . . Take care, Colonel, this Lady's husband may arrive at any moment.

OLD WOMAN: [*To the* Old Man] Who is this gentleman?

OLD MAN: [*To the* Old Woman] I've told you, it's the Colonel.

[*Some embarrassing things take place, invisibly*]

OLD WOMAN: [*To the* Old Man] I knew it. I knew it.

OLD MAN: Then why are you asking?

OLD WOMAN: For my information. Colonel, no cigarette butts on the floor!

OLD MAN: [*To Colonel*] Colonel, Colonel, it's slipped my mind—in the last war did you win or lose?

OLD WOMAN: [*To the invisible Lady*] But my dear, don't let it happen!

OLD MAN: Look at me, look at me, do I look like a bad soldier? One time, Colonel, under fire . . .

OLD WOMAN: He's going too far! It's embarrassing! [*She seizes the invisible sleeve of the Colonel*] Listen to him! My darling, why don't you stop him!

OLD MAN: [*Continuing quickly*] And all on my own, I killed 209 of them; we called them that because they jumped so high to escape, however there weren't so many of them as there were flies; of course it is less amusing, Colonel, but thanks to my strength of character, I have . . . Oh! no, I must, please.

OLD WOMAN: [*To Colonel*] My husband never lies; it may be true that we are old, nevertheless we're respectable.

OLD MAN: [*Violently, to the Colonel*] A hero must be a gentleman too, if he hopes to be a complete hero!

OLD WOMAN: [*To the Colonel*] I've known you for many years, but I'd never have believed you were capable of this. [*To the Lady, while we hear the sound of boats*] I'd never have believed him capable of this. We have our dignity, our self-respect.

OLD MAN: [*In a quavering voice*] I'm still capable of bearing arms. [*Doorbell rings*] Excuse me, I must go to the door. [*He stumbles and knocks over the chair of the invisible Lady*] Oh! pardon.

OLD WOMAN: [*Rushing forward*] You didn't hurt yourself? [*The* Old Man *and* Old Woman *help the invisible Lady onto her feet*] You've got all dirty, there's some dust. [*She helps brush the Lady. The doorbell rings again*]

OLD MAN: Forgive me, forgive me. [*To the* Old Woman] Go bring a chair.

OLD WOMAN: [*To the two invisible guests*] Excuse me for a moment.

[*While the* Old Man *goes to open door No. 3,* the Old Woman *exits through door No. 5 to look for a chair, and she re-enters by door No. 8*]

OLD MAN: [*Moving towards the door*] He was trying to get my goat. I'm almost angry. [*He opens the door*] Oh! madam, you're here! I can scarcely believe my eyes, and yet, nevertheless . . . I didn't really dare to hope . . . really it's . . . Oh! madam, madam . . . I have thought about you, all my life, all my life, madam, they always called you La Belle . . . it's your husband . . . someone told me, certainly . . . you haven't changed a bit . . . Oh! yes, yes, your nose *has* grown longer, maybe it's a little swollen . . . I didn't notice it when I first saw you, but I see it now . . . a lot longer . . . ah! how unfortunate! You certainly didn't do it on purpose . . . how did it happen? . . . little by little . . . excuse me, sir and dear friend, you'll permit me to call you "dear friend," I knew your wife long before you . . . she was the same, but with a completely different nose . . . I congratulate you, sir, you seem to love each other very much. [*The* Old Woman *re-enters through door No. 8 with a chair*] Semiramis, two guests have arrived, we need one more chair . . . [*The* Old Woman *puts the chair behind the four others, then exits by door No. 8 and re-enters by door No. 5, after a few moments, with another chair that she places beside the one she has just brought in. By this time, the* Old Man *and the two guests have moved near the* Old Woman] Come this way, please, more guests have arrived. I'm going to introduce you . . . now then, madam . . . Oh! Belle, Belle, Miss Belle, that's what they used to call you . . . now you're all bent over . . . Oh! sir, she is still Belle to me, even so; under her glasses, she still has pretty eyes; her hair is white, but under the white one can see brown, and blue, I'm sure of that . . . come nearer, nearer . . . what is this, sir, a gift, for my wife? [*To the* Old Woman, *who has just come on with the chair*] Semiramis, this is Belle, you know, Belle . . . [*To the Colonel and the invisible Lady*] This is Miss, pardon, Mrs. Belle, don't smile . . . and her husband . . . [*To the* Old Woman] A childhood friend, I've often spoken of her to you . . . and her husband. [*Again to the Colonel and to the invisible Lady*] And her husband . . .

OLD WOMAN: [*Making a little curtsey*] He certainly makes good introductions. He has fine manners. Good evening, madam, good evening, sir. [*She indicates the two first guests to the newly arrived couple*] Our friends, yes . . .

OLD MAN: [*To the* Old Woman] He's brought you a present.

[*The* Old Woman *takes the present*]

OLD WOMAN: Is it a flower, sir? or a cradle? a pear tree? or a crow?

OLD MAN: [*To the* Old Woman] No, no, can't you see that it's a painting?

OLD WOMAN: Oh! how pretty! Thank you, sir . . .

[*To the invisible Lady*] Would you like to see it, dear friend?

OLD MAN: [*To the invisible Colonel*] Would you like to see it?

OLD WOMAN: [*To Belle's husband*] Doctor, Doctor, I feel squeamish, I have hot flashes, I feel sick, I've aches and pains, I haven't any feeling in my feet, I've caught cold in my eyes, I've a cold in my fingers, I'm suffering from liver trouble, Doctor, Doctor! . . .

OLD MAN: [*To the* Old Woman] This gentleman is not a doctor, he's a photo-engraver.

OLD WOMAN: [*To the first invisible Lady*] If you've finished looking at it, you might hang it up. [*To the* Old Man] That doesn't matter, he's charming even so, he's dazzling. [*To the Photo-engraver*] Without meaning to flatter you . . .

[*The* Old Man *and the* Old Woman *now move behind the chairs, close to each other, almost touching, but back to back; they talk: the* Old Man *to Belle, the* Old Woman *to the Photo-engraver; from time to time their replies, as shown by the way they turn their heads, are addressed to one or the other of the two first guests*]

OLD MAN: [*To Belle*] I am very touched . . . You're still the same, in spite of everything . . . I've loved you, a hundred years ago . . . But there's been such a change . . . No, you haven't changed a bit . . . I loved you, I love you . . .

OLD WOMAN: [*To the Photo-engraver*] Oh! Sir, sir, sir . . .

OLD MAN: [*To the Colonel*] I'm in complete agreement with you on that point.

OLD WOMAN: [*To the Photo-engraver*] Oh! certainly, sir, certainly, sir, certainly . . . [*To the first Lady*] Thanks for hanging it up . . . Forgive me if I've inconvenienced you.

[*The light grows stronger. It should grow stronger and stronger as the invisible guests continue to arrive*]

OLD MAN: [*Almost whimpering to Belle*] Where are the snows of yester year?

OLD WOMAN: [*To the Photo-engraver*] Oh! Sir, sir, sir . . . Oh! sir . . .

OLD MAN: [*Pointing out the first lady to Belle*] She's a young friend . . . she's very sweet . . .

OLD WOMAN: [*Pointing the Colonel out to the Photo-engraver*] Yes, he's a mounted staff colonel . . . a comrade of my husband . . . a subaltern, my husband's a general . . .

OLD MAN: [*To Belle*] Your ears were not always so pointed! . . . My Belle, do you remember?

OLD WOMAN: [*To the Photo-engraver, simpering grotesquely; she develops this manner more and more in this scene; she shows her thick red stockings, raises her many petticoats, shows an underskirt full of holes, exposes her old breast; then, her hands on her hips, throws her head back, makes little erotic cries, projects her pelvis, her legs spread apart; she laughs like an old prostitute; this business, entirely different from her manner heretofore as well as from that she will have subsequently, and which must reveal the hidden personality of the* Old Woman, *ceases abruptly*] So you think I'm too old for that, do you?

OLD MAN: [*To Belle, very romantically*] When we were young, the moon was a living star. Ah! yes, yes, if only we had dared, but we were only children. Wouldn't you like to recapture those bygone days . . . is it still possible? Is it still possible? Ah! no, no, it is no longer possible. Those days have flown away as fast as a train. Time has left the marks of his wheels on our skin. Do you believe surgeons can perform miracles? [*To the Colonel*] I am a soldier, and you too, we soldiers are always young, the generals are like gods . . . [*To Belle*] It ought to be that way . . . Alas! Alas! We have lost everything. We could have been so happy, I'm sure of it, we could have been, we could have been; perhaps the flowers are budding again beneath the snow! . . .

OLD WOMAN: [*To Photo-engraver*] Flatterer! Rascal! Ah! Ah! I look younger than my years? You're a little savage! You're exciting.

OLD MAN: [*To Belle*] Will you be my Isolde and let me be your Tristan? Beauty is more than skin deep, it's in the heart . . . Do you understand? We could have had the pleasure of sharing, joy, beauty, eternity . . . an eternity . . . Why didn't we dare? We weren't brave enough . . . Everything is lost, lost, lost.

OLD WOMAN: [*To Photo-engraver*] Oh no, Oh! no, Oh! la la, you give me the shivers. You too, are you ticklish? To tickle or be tickled? I'm a little embarrassed . . . [*She laughs*] Do you like my petticoat? Or do you like this skirt better?

OLD MAN: [*To Belle*] A general factotum has a poor life!

OLD WOMAN: [*Turning her head towards the first invisible Lady*] In order to make Crepes de Chine? A leaf of beef, an hour of flour, a little gastric sugar. [*To the Photo-engraver*] You've got clever fingers, ah . . . all the sa-a-a-me! . . . Oh-oh-oh-oh.

OLD MAN: [*To Belle*] My worthy helpmeet, Semiramis, has taken the place of my mother. [*He turns towards the Colonel*] Colonel, as I've often observed to you, one must take the truth as one finds it.

[*He turns back towards Belle*]

OLD WOMAN: [*To Photo-engraver*] Do you really really believe that one could have children at any age? Any age children?

OLD MAN: [*To Belle*] It's this alone that has saved me: the inner life, peace of mind, austerity, my scientific investigations, philosophy, my message . . .

OLD WOMAN: [*To Photo-engraver*] I've never yet betrayed my husband, the general . . . not so hard, you're going to make me fall . . . I'm only his poor mamma! [*She sobs*] A great, great [*She pushes him back*], great . . . mamma. My conscience causes these tears to flow. For me the branch of the apple tree is broken. Try to find somebody else. I no longer want to gather rosebuds . . .

OLD MAN: [*To Belle*] . . . All the preoccupations of a superior order . . .

[*The* Old Man *and* Old Woman *lead Belle and the Photo-engraver up alongside the two other invisible guests, and seat them*]

OLD MAN *and* OLD WOMAN: [*To the Photo-engraver and Belle*] Sit down, please sit down.

[*The* Old Man *and* Old Woman *sit down too, he to the left, she to the right, with the four empty chairs between them. A long mute scene, punctuated at intervals with "no," "yes," "yes." The* Old Man *and* Old Woman *listen to the conversation of the invisible guests*]

OLD WOMAN: [*To the Photo-engraver*] We had one son . . . of course, he's still alive . . . he's gone away . . . it's a common story . . . or, rather, unusual . . . he abandoned his parents . . . he had a heart of gold . . . that was a long time ago . . . We loved him so much . . . he slammed the door . . . My husband and I tried to hold him back with all our might . . . he was seven years old, the age of reason, I called after him: "My son, my child, my son, my child." . . . He didn't even look back . . .

OLD MAN: Alas, no . . . no, we've never had a child . . . I'd hoped for a son . . . Semiramis, too . . . we did everything . . . and my poor Semiramis is so maternal, too. Perhaps it was better that way . . . As for me I was an ungrateful son myself . . . Ah! . . . grief, regret, remorse, that's all we have . . . that's all we have left . . .

OLD WOMAN: He said to me: "You kill birds! Why do you kill birds?" . . . But we don't kill birds . . . we've never harmed so much as a fly . . . His eyes were full of big tears. He wouldn't let us dry them. He wouldn't let me come near him. He said: "Yes, you kill all the birds, all the birds." . . . He showed us his little fists . . . "You're lying, you've betrayed me! The streets are full of dead birds, of dying baby birds." It's the song of the birds! . . . "No, it's their death rattle. The sky is red with blood." . . . No, my child, it's blue. He cried again: "You've betrayed me, I adored you, I believed you to be good . . . the streets are full of dead birds, you've torn out their eyes . . . Papa, mamma, you're wicked! I refuse to stay with you." . . . I threw myself at his feet . . . His father was weeping. We couldn't hold him back. As he went we could still hear him calling: "It's you who are responsible" . . . What does that mean, "responsible"?

OLD MAN: I let my mother die all alone in a ditch. She called after me, moaning feebly: "My little child, my beloved son, don't leave me to die all alone . . . Stay with me. I don't have much time left." Don't worry, Mamma, I told her, I'll be back in a moment . . . I was in a hurry . . . I was going to the ball, to dance. I will be back in a minute. But when I returned, she was already dead, and they had buried her deep . . . I broke open the grave, I searched for her . . . I couldn't find her . . . I know, I know, sons, always, abandon their mothers,

and they more or less kill their fathers . . . Life is like that . . . but I, I suffer from it . . . and the others, they don't . . .

OLD WOMAN: He cried: "Papa, Mamma, I'll never set eyes on you again."

OLD MAN: I suffer from it, yes, the others don't . . .

OLD WOMAN: Don't speak of him to my husband. He loved his parents so much. He never left them for a single moment. He cared for them, coddled them . . . And they died in his arms, saying to him: "You have been a perfect son. God will be good to you."

OLD MAN: I can still see her stretched out in the ditch, she was holding lily of the valley in her hand, she cried: "Don't forget me, don't forget me" . . . her eyes were full of big tears, and she called me by my baby name: "Little Chick," she said, "Little Chick, don't leave me here all alone."

OLD WOMAN: [*To the Photo-engraver*] He has never written to us. From time to time, a friend tells us that he's been seen here or there, that he is well, that he is a good husband . . .

OLD MAN: [*To Belle*] When I got back, she had been buried a long time. [*To the first invisible Lady*] Oh, yes. Oh! yes, madam, we have a movie theatre in the house, a restaurant, bathrooms . . .

OLD WOMAN: [*To the Colonel*] Yes, Colonel, it is because he . . .

OLD MAN: Basically that's it.

[*Desultory conversation, getting bogged down*]

OLD WOMAN: If only!

OLD MAN: Thus, I've not . . . I, it . . . certainly . . .

OLD WOMAN: [*Dislocated dialogue, exhaustion*] All in all.

OLD MAN: To ours and to theirs.

OLD WOMAN: So that.

OLD MAN: From me to him.

OLD WOMAN: Him, or her?

OLD MAN: Them.

OLD WOMAN: Curl-papers . . . After all.

OLD MAN: It's not that.

OLD WOMAN: Why?

OLD MAN: Yes.

OLD WOMAN: I.

OLD MAN: All in all.

OLD WOMAN: All in all.

OLD MAN: [*To the first invisible Lady*] What was that, madam?

[*A long silence, the* Old Man *and* Old Woman *remain rigid on their chairs. Then the doorbell rings*]

OLD MAN: [*With increasing nervousness*] Someone has come. People. Still more people.

OLD WOMAN: I thought I heard some boats.

OLD MAN: I'll go to the door. Go bring some chairs. Excuse me, gentlemen, ladies.

[*He goes towards door No. 7*]

OLD WOMAN: [*To the invisible guests who have already arrived*] Get up for a moment, please. The Orator will be here soon. We must ready the room for the meeting. [*The* Old Woman *arranges the chairs, turning their backs towards the audience*] Lend me a hand, please. Thanks.

OLD MAN: [*Opening door No. 7*] Good evening, ladies, good evening, gentlemen. Please come in.

[*The three or four invisible persons who have arrived are very tall, and the* Old Man *has to stand on his toes in order to shake hands with them. The* Old Woman, *after placing the chairs as indicated above, goes over to the* Old Man]

OLD MAN: [*Making introductions*] My wife . . . Mr. . . . Mrs. . . . my wife . . . Mr. . . . Mrs. . . . my wife . . .

OLD WOMAN: Who are all these people, my darling?

OLD MAN: [*To* Old Woman] Go find some chairs, dear.

OLD WOMAN: I can't do everything! . . .

[*She exits, grumbling, by door No. 6 and re-enters by door No. 7, while the* Old Man, *with the newly arrived guests, moves downstage*]

OLD MAN: Don't drop your movie camera. [*More introductions*] The Colonel . . . the Lady . . . Mrs. Belle . . . the Photo-engraver . . . These are the newspaper men, they have come to hear the Orator too, who should be here any minute now . . . Don't be impatient . . . You'll not be bored . . . all together now . . . [*The* Old Woman *re-enters through door No. 7 with two chairs*] Come along, bring the chairs more quickly . . . we're still short one.

[*The* Old Woman *goes to find another chair, still grumbling, exiting by door No. 3, and re-entering by door No. 8*]

OLD WOMAN: All right, and so . . . I'm doing as well as I can . . . I'm not a machine, you know . . . Who are all these people?

[*She exits*]

OLD MAN: Sit down, sit down, the ladies with the ladies, and the gentlemen with the gentlemen, or vice versa, if you prefer . . . We don't have any more nice chairs . . . we have to make do with what we have . . . I'm sorry . . . take the one in the middle . . . does anyone need a fountain pen? Telephone Maillot, you'll get Monique . . . Claude is an angel. I don't have a radio . . . I take all the newspapers . . . that depends on a number of things; I manage these buildings, but I have no help . . . we have to economize . . . no interviews, please, for the moment . . . later, we'll see . . . you'll soon have a place to sit . . . what can she be doing? [*The* Old Woman *enters by door No. 8 with a chair*] Faster, Semiramis . . .

OLD WOMAN: I'm doing my best . . . Who are all these people?

OLD MAN: I'll explain it all to you later.

OLD WOMAN: And that woman? That woman, my darling?

OLD MAN: Don't get upset . . . [*To the Colonel*] Colonel, journalism is a profession too, like a fighting man's . . . [*To the* Old Woman] Take care of the

ladies, my dear . . . [*The doorbell rings. The* Old Man *hurries towards door No. 8*] Wait a moment . . . [*To the* Old Woman] Bring chairs!

OLD WOMAN: Gentlemen, ladies, excuse me . . .

[*She exits by door No. 3, re-entering by door No. 2; the* Old Man *goes to open concealed door No. 9, and disappears at the moment the* Old Woman *re-enters by door No. 2*]

OLD MAN: [*Out of sight*] Come in . . . come in . . . come in . . . come in . . . [*He reappears, leading in a number of invisible people, including one very small child he holds by the hand*] One doesn't bring little children to a scientific lecture . . . the poor little thing is going to be bored . . . if he begins to cry or to peepee on the ladies' dresses, that'll be a fine state of affairs! [*He conducts them to stage center; the* Old Woman *comes on with two chairs*] I wish to introduce you to my wife, Semiramis; and these are their children.

OLD WOMAN: Ladies, gentlemen . . . Oh! aren't they sweet!

OLD MAN: That one is the smallest.

OLD WOMAN: Oh, he's so cute . . . so cute . . . so cute!

OLD MAN: Not enough chairs.

OLD WOMAN: Oh! dear, oh dear, oh dear . . .

[*She exits, looking for another chair, using now door No. 2 as exit and door No. 3 on the right to re-enter*]

OLD MAN: Hold the little boy on your lap . . . The twins can sit together in the same chair. Be careful, they're not very strong . . . they go with the house, they belong to the landlord. Yes, my children, he'd make trouble for us, he's a bad man . . . he wants us to buy them from him, these worthless chairs. [*The* Old Woman *returns as quickly as she can with a chair*] You don't all know each other . . . you're seeing each other for the first time . . . you knew each other by name . . . [*To the* Old Woman] Semiramis, help me make the introductions . . .

OLD WOMAN: Who are all these people? . . . May I introduce you, excuse me . . . May I introduce you . . . but who are they?

OLD MAN: May I introduce you . . . Allow me to introduce you . . . permit me to introduce you . . . Mr., Mrs., Miss . . . Mr. . . . Mrs. . . . Mrs. . . . Mr.

OLD WOMAN: [*To* Old Man] Did you put on your sweater? [*To the invisible guests*] Mr., Mrs., Mr. . . .

[*Doorbell rings again*]

OLD MAN: More people!

[*Another ring of doorbell*]

OLD WOMAN: More people!

[*The doorbell rings again, then several more times, and more times again; the* Old Man *is beside himself; the chairs, turned towards the dais, with their backs to the audience, form regular rows, each one longer as in a theatre; the* Old Man *is winded, he mops his brow, goes from one door to another, seats invisible people, while the* Old Woman, *hobbling along, unable to move any faster, goes as rapidly as she can, from one door to another, hunting for chairs and carrying them in. There are now many invisible people on stage; both the* Old Man *and* Old Woman *take care not to bump into people and to thread their way between the rows of chairs. The movement could go like this: the* Old Man *goes to door No. 4, the* Old Woman *exits by door No. 3, returns by door No. 2; the* Old Man *goes to open door No. 7, the* Old Woman *exits by door No. 8, re-enters by door No. 6 with chairs, etc., in this manner making their way around the stage, using all the doors]*

OLD WOMAN: Beg pardon . . . excuse me . . . what . . . oh, yes . . . beg pardon . . . excuse me . . .

OLD MAN: Gentlemen . . . come in . . . ladies . . . enter . . . it is Mrs. . . . let me . . . yes . . .

OLD WOMAN: *[With more chairs]* Oh dear . . . Oh dear . . . there are too many . . . There really are too, too . . . too many, oh dear, oh dear, oh dear . . .

[We hear from outside, louder and louder and approaching nearer and nearer, the sounds of boats moving through the water; all the noises come directly from the wings. The Old Woman *and the* Old Man *continue the business outlined above; they open the doors, they carry in chairs. The doorbell continues to ring]*

OLD MAN: This table is in our way. *[He moves a table, or he sketches the business of moving it, without slowing down his rhythm, aided by the* Old Woman*]* There's scarcely a place left here, excuse us . . .

OLD WOMAN: *[Making a gesture of clearing the table, to the* Old Man*]* Are you wearing your sweater?

[Doorbell rings]

OLD MAN: More people! More chairs! More people! More chairs! Come in, come in, ladies and gentlemen . . . Semiramis, faster . . . We'll give you a hand soon . . .

OLD WOMAN: Beg pardon . . . beg pardon . . . good evening, Mrs. . . . Mrs. . . . Mrs. . . . Mr. . . . Mr. . . . yes, yes, the chairs . . .

[The doorbell rings louder and louder and we hear the noises of boats striking the quay very close by, and more and more frequently. The Old Man *flounders among the chairs; he has scarcely enough time to go from one door to another, so rapidly do the ringings of the doorbell succeed each other]*

OLD MAN: Yes, right away . . . are you wearing your sweater? Yes, yes . . . immediately, patience, yes, yes . . . patience . . .

OLD WOMAN: Your sweater? My sweater? . . . Beg pardon, beg pardon.

OLD MAN: This way, ladies and gentlemen, I request you . . . I re you . . . pardon . . . quest . . . enter, enter . . . going to show . . . there, the seats . . . dear friend . . . not there . . . take care . . . you, my friend?

[Then a long moment without words. We hear waves, boats, the continuous ringing of the doorbell. The movement culminates in intensity at this point. The doors are now opening and shutting all together ceaselessly. Only the main door in the center of the recess remains closed. The Old Man *and* Old Woman *come and go, without saying a word, from one door to another; they appear to be gliding on roller skates. The* Old Man *receives the people, accompanies them, but doesn't take them very far, he only indicates seats to them after having taken one or two steps with them; he hasn't enough time. The* Old Woman *carries in chairs. The* Old Man *and the* Old Woman *meet each other and bump into each other, once or twice, without interrupting their rhythm. Then, the* Old Man *takes a position upstage center, and turns from left to right, from right to left, etc., towards all the doors and indicates the seats with his arms. His arms move very rapidly. Then, finally the* Old Woman *stops, with a chair in one hand, which she places, takes up again, replaces, looks as though she, too, wants to go from one door to another, from right to left, from left to right, moving her head and neck very rapidly. This must not interrupt the rhythm; the* Old Man *and* Old Woman *must still give the impression of not stopping, even while remaining almost in one place; their hands, their chests, their heads, their eyes are agitated, perhaps moving in little circles. Finally, there is a progressive slowing down of movement, at first slight: the ringings of the doorbell are less loud, less frequent; the doors open less and less rapidly; the gestures of the* Old Man *and* Old Woman *slacken continuously. At the moment when the doors stop opening and closing altogether, and the ringings cease to be heard, we have the impression that the stage is packed with people]*

OLD MAN: I'm going to find a place for you . . . patience . . . Semiramis, for the love of . . .

OLD WOMAN: *[With a large gesture, her hands empty]* There are no more chairs, my darling. *[Then, abruptly, she begins to sell invisible programs in a full hall, with the doors closed]* Programs, get your programs here, the program of the evening, buy your program!

OLD MAN: Relax, ladies and gentlemen, we'll take care of you . . . Each in his turn, in the order of your arrival . . . You'll have a seat. I'll take care of you.

OLD WOMAN: Buy your programs! Wait a moment, madam, I cannot take care of everyone at the same time, I haven't got thirty-three hands, you know, I'm not a cow . . . Mister, please be kind enough to pass the program to the lady next to you, thank you . . . my change, my change . . .

OLD MAN: I've told you that I'd find a place for you! Don't get excited! Over here, it's over here, there, take care . . . oh, dear friend . . . dear friends . . .

OLD WOMAN: . . . Programs . . . get your grams . . . grams . . .

OLD MAN: Yes, my dear, she's over there, further down, she's selling programs . . . no trade is unworthy . . . that's her . . . do you see her? . . . you have a seat in the second row . . . to the right . . . no, to the left . . . that's it! . . .

OLD WOMAN: . . . gram . . . gram . . . program . . . get your program . . .

OLD MAN: What do you expect me to do? I'm doing my best! [*To invisible seated people*] Push over a little, if you will please . . . there's still a little room, that will do for you, won't it, Mrs. . . . come here. [*He mounts the dais, forced by the pushing of the crowd*] Ladies, gentlemen, please excuse us, there are no more seats available . . .

OLD WOMAN: [*Who is now on the opposite side of the stage, across from the* Old Man, *between door No. 3 and the window*] Get your programs . . . who wants a program? Eskimo pies, caramels . . . fruit drops . . . [*Unable to move, the* Old Woman, *hemmed in by the crowd, scatters her programs and candies anywhere, above the invisible heads*] Here are some! There they are!

OLD MAN: [*Standing on the dais, very animated; he is jostled as he descends from the dais, remounts it, steps down again, hits someone in the face, is struck by an elbow, says*] Pardon . . . please excuse us . . . take care . . .

[*Pushed, he staggers, has trouble regaining his equilibrium, clutches at shoulders*]

OLD WOMAN: Why are there so many people? Programs, get your program here, Eskimo pies.

OLD MAN: Ladies, young ladies, gentlemen, a moment of silence, I beg you . . . silence . . . it's very important . . . those people who've no seats are asked to clear the aisles . . . that's it . . . don't stand between the chairs.

OLD WOMAN: [*To the* Old Man, *almost screaming*] Who are all these people, my darling? What are they doing here?

OLD MAN: Clear the aisles, ladies and gentlemen. Those who do not have seats must, for the convenience of all, stand against the wall, there, along the right or the left . . . you'll be able to hear everything, you'll see everything, don't worry, you won't miss a thing, all seats are equally good!

[*There is a great hullabaloo. Pushed by the crowd, the* Old Man *makes almost a complete turn around the stage and ends up at the window on the right, near to the stool. The* Old Woman *makes the same movement in reverse, and ends up at the window on the left, near the stool there*]

OLD MAN: [*Making this movement*] Don't push, don't push.

OLD WOMAN: [*Same business*] Don't push, don't push.

OLD MAN: [*Same business*] Don't push, don't push.

OLD WOMAN: [*Same business*] Don't push, ladies and gentlemen, don't push.

OLD MAN: [*Same business*] Relax . . . take it easy . . . be quiet . . . what's going on here?

OLD WOMAN: [*Same business*] There's no need to act like savages, in any case.

[*At last they reach their final positions. Each is near a window. The* Old Man *to the left, by the window which is beside the dais. The* Old Woman *on the right. They don't move from these positions until the end*]

OLD WOMAN: [*Calling to the* Old Man] My darling . . . I can't see you, anymore . . . where are you? Who are they? What do all these people want? Who is that man over there?

OLD MAN: Where are you? Where are you, Semiramis?

OLD WOMAN: My darling, where are you?

OLD MAN: Here, beside the window . . . Can you hear me?

OLD WOMAN: Yes, I hear your voice! . . . there are so many . . . but I can make out yours . . .

OLD MAN: And you, where are you?

OLD WOMAN: I'm beside the window too! . . . My dear, I'm frightened, there are too many people . . . we are very far from each other . . . at our age we have to be careful . . . we might get lost . . . We must stay close together, one never knows, my darling, my darling . . .

OLD MAN: Ah! . . . I just caught sight of you . . . Oh! . . . We'll find each other, never fear . . . I'm with friends. [*To the friends*] I'm happy to shake your hands . . . But of course, I believe in progress, uninterrupted progress, with some jolts, nevertheless . . .

OLD WOMAN: That's fine, thanks . . . What foul weather! Yes, it's been nice! [*Aside*] I'm afraid, even so . . . What am I doing here? . . . [*She screams*] My darling, My darling!

[*The* Old Man *and* Old Woman *individually speak to guests near them*]

OLD MAN: In order to prevent the exploitation of man by man, we need money, money, and still more money!

OLD WOMAN: My darling! [*Then, hemmed in by friends*] Yes, my husband is here, he's organizing everything . . . over there . . . Oh! you'll never get there . . . you'd have to go across, he's with friends . . .

OLD MAN: Certainly not . . . as I've always said . . . pure logic does not exist . . . all we've got is an imitation.

OLD WOMAN: But you know, there are people who are happy. In the morning they eat breakfast on the plane, at noon they lunch in the pullman, and in the evening they dine aboard the liner. At night they sleep in the trucks that roll, roll, roll . . .

OLD MAN: Talk about the dignity of man! At least let's try to save face. Dignity is only skin deep.

OLD WOMAN: Don't slink away into the shadows . . .

[*She bursts out laughing in conversation*]

OLD MAN: Your compatriots ask of me.

OLD WOMAN: Certainly . . . tell me everything.

OLD MAN: I've invited you . . . in order to explain to you . . . that the individual and the person are one and the same.

OLD WOMAN: He has a borrowed look about him. He owes us a lot of money.

OLD MAN: I am not myself. I am another. I am the one in the other.

OLD WOMAN: My children, take care not to trust one another.

OLD MAN: Sometimes I awaken in the midst of absolute silence. It's a perfect circle. There's nothing lacking. But one must be careful, all the same. Its shape might disappear. There are holes through which it can escape.

OLD WOMAN: Ghosts, you know, phantoms, mere nothings . . . The duties my husband fulfills are very important, sublime.

OLD MAN: Excuse me . . . that's not at all my opinion! At the proper time, I'll communicate my views on this subject to you . . . I have nothing to say for the present! . . . We're waiting for the Orator, he'll tell you, he'll speak in my behalf, and explain everything that we hold most dear . . . he'll explain everything to you . . . when? . . . when the moment has come . . . the moment will come soon . . .

OLD WOMAN: [*On her side to her friends*] The sooner, the better . . . That's understood . . . [*Aside*] They're never going to leave us alone. Let them go, why don't they go? . . . My poor darling, where is he? I can't see him any more . . .

OLD MAN: [*Same business*] Don't be so impatient. You'll hear my message. In just a moment.

OLD WOMAN: [*Aside*] Ah! . . . I hear his voice! . . . [*To her friends*] Do you know, my husband has never been understood. But at last his hour has come.

OLD MAN: Listen to me, I've had a rich experience of life. In all walks of life, at every level of thought . . . I'm not an egotist: humanity must profit by what I've learned.

OLD WOMAN: Ow! You stepped on my foot . . . I've got chilblains!

OLD MAN: I've perfected a real system. [*Aside*] The Orator ought to be here. [*Aloud*] I've suffered enormously.

OLD WOMAN: We have suffered so much. [*Aside*] The Orator ought to be here. It's certainly time.

OLD MAN: Suffered much, learned much.

OLD WOMAN: [*Like an echo*] Suffered much, learned much.

OLD MAN: You'll see for yourselves, my system is perfect.

OLD WOMAN: [*Like an echo*] You'll see for yourselves, his system is perfect.

OLD MAN: If only my instructions are carried out.

OLD WOMAN: [*Echo*] If only his instructions are carried out.

OLD MAN: We'll save the world! . . .

OLD WOMAN: [*Echo*] Saving his own soul by saving the world!

OLD MAN: One truth for all!

OLD WOMAN: [*Echo*] One truth for all!

OLD MAN: Follow me! . . .

OLD WOMAN: [*Echo*] Follow him! . . .

OLD MAN: For I have absolute certainty! . . .

OLD WOMAN: [*Echo*] He has absolute certainty!

OLD MAN: Never . . .

OLD WOMAN: [*Echo*] Ever and ever . . .

[*Suddenly we hear noises in the wings, fanfares*]

OLD WOMAN: What's going on?

[*The noises increase, then the main door opens wide, with a great crash; through the open door we see nothing but a very powerful light which floods onto the stage through the main door and the windows, which at the entrance of the emperor are brightly lighted*]

OLD MAN: I don't know . . . I can scarcely believe . . . is it possible . . . but yes . . . but yes . . . incredible . . . and still it's true . . . yes . . . if . . . yes . . . it is the Emperor! His Majesty the Emperor!

[*The light reaches its maximum intensity, through the open door and through the windows; but the light is cold, empty; more noises which cease abruptly*]

OLD MAN: Stand up! . . . It's His Majesty the Emperor! The Emperor in my house, in our house . . . Semiramis . . . do you realize what this means?

OLD WOMAN: [*Not understanding*] The Emperor . . . the Emperor? My darling! [*Then suddenly she understands*] Ah, yes, the Emperor! Your Majesty! Your Majesty! [*She wildly makes countless grotesque curtsies*] In our house! In our house!

OLD MAN: [*Weeping with emotion*] Your Majesty! . . . Oh! Your Majesty! . . . Your little, Your great Majesty! . . . Oh! what a sublime honor . . . it's all a marvelous dream.

OLD WOMAN: [*Like an echo*] A marvelous dream . . . arvelous . . .

OLD MAN: [*To the invisible crowd*] Ladies, gentlemen, stand up, our beloved sovereign, the Emperor, is among us! Hurrah! Hurrah!

[*He stands up on the stool; he stands on his toes in order to see the Emperor; the Old Woman does the same on her side*]

OLD WOMAN: Hurrah! Hurrah!

[*Stamping of feet*]

OLD MAN: Your Majesty! . . . I'm over here! . . . Your Majesty! Can you hear me? Can you see me? Please tell his Majesty that I'm here! Your Majesty! Your Majesty!!! I'm here, your most faithful servant! . . .

OLD WOMAN: [*Still echoing*] Your most faithful servant, Your Majesty!

OLD MAN: Your servant, your slave, your dog, arf, arf, your dog, Your Majesty! . . .

OLD WOMAN: [Barking loudly like a dog] Arf . . . arf . . . arf . . .

OLD MAN: [Wringing his hands] Can you see me? . . . Answer, Sire! . . . Ah, I can see you, I've just caught sight of Your Majesty's august face . . . your divine forehead . . . I've seen you, yes, in spite of the screen of courtiers . . .

OLD WOMAN: In spite of the courtiers . . . we're here, Your Majesty!

OLD MAN: Your Majesty! Your Majesty! Ladies, gentlemen, don't keep him—His Majesty standing . . . you see, Your Majesty, I'm truly the only one who cares for you, for your health, I'm the most faithful of all your subjects . . .

OLD WOMAN: [Echoing] Your Majesty's most faithful subjects!

OLD MAN: Let me through, now, ladies and gentlemen . . . how can I make my way through such a crowd? . . . I must go to present my most humble respects to His Majesty, the Emperor . . . let me pass . . .

OLD WOMAN: [Echo] Let him pass . . . let him pass . . . pass . . . ass . . .

OLD MAN: Let me pass, please, let me pass. [Desperate] Ah! Will I ever be able to reach him?

OLD WOMAN: [Echo] Reach him . . . reach him . . .

OLD MAN: Nevertheless, my heart and my whole being are at his feet, the crowd of courtiers surrounds him, ah! ah! they want to prevent me from approaching him . . . They know very well that . . . oh! I understand, I understand . . . Court intrigues, I know all about it . . . They hope to separate me from Your Majesty!

OLD WOMAN: Calm yourself, my darling . . . His Majesty sees you, he's looking at you . . . His Majesty has given me a wink . . . His Majesty is on our side! . . .

OLD MAN: They must give the Emperor the best seat . . . near the dais . . . so that he can hear everything the Orator is going to say.

OLD WOMAN: [Hoisting herself up on the stool, on her toes, lifting her chin as high as she can, in order to see better] At last they're taking care of the Emperor.

OLD MAN: Thank heaven for that! [To the Emperor] Sire . . . Your Majesty may rely on him. It's my friend, it's my representative who is at Your Majesty's side. [On his toes, standing on the stool] Gentlemen, ladies, young ladies, little children, I implore you.

OLD WOMAN: [Echoing] Plore . . . plore . . .

OLD MAN: . . . I want to see . . . move aside . . . I want . . . the celestial gaze, the noble face, the crown, the radiance of His Majesty . . . Sire, deign to turn your illustrious face in my direction, toward your humble servant . . . so humble . . . Oh! I caught sight of him clearly that time . . . I caught sight . . .

OLD WOMAN: [Echo] He caught sight that time . . . he caught sight . . . caught . . . sight . . .

OLD MAN: I'm at the height of joy . . . I've no more words to express my boundless gratitude . . . in my humble dwelling, Oh! Majesty! Oh! radiance! . . . here . . . here . . . in the dwelling where I am, true enough, a general . . . but within the hierarchy of your army, I'm only a simple general factotum . . .

OLD WOMAN: [Echo] General factotum . . .

OLD MAN: I'm proud of it . . . proud and humble, at the same time . . . as I should be . . . alas! certainly, I am a general, I might have been at the imperial court, I have only a little court here to take care of . . . Your Majesty . . . I . . . Your Majesty, I have difficulty expressing myself . . . I might have had . . . many things, not a few possessions if I'd known, if I'd wanted, if I . . . if we . . . Your Majesty, forgive my emotion . . .

OLD WOMAN: Speak in the third person!

OLD MAN: [Sniveling] May Your Majesty deign to forgive me! You are here at last . . . We had given up hope . . . you might not even have come . . . Oh! Savior, in my life, I have been humiliated . . .

OLD WOMAN: [Echo, sobbing] . . . miliated . . . miliated . . .

OLD MAN: I've suffered much in my life . . . I might have been something, if I could have been sure of the support of Your Majesty . . . I have no other support . . . if you hadn't come, everything would have been too late . . . you are, Sire, my last recourse . . .

OLD WOMAN: [Echo] Last recourse . . . Sire . . . ast recourse . . . ire . . . recourse . . .

OLD MAN: I've brought bad luck to my friends, to all those who have helped me . . . Lightning struck the hand which was held out toward me . . .

OLD WOMAN: [Echo] . . . hand that was held out . . . held out . . . out . . .

OLD MAN: They've always had good reasons for hating me, bad reasons for loving me . . .

OLD WOMAN: That's not true, my darling, not true. I love you, I'm your little mother . . .

OLD MAN: All my enemies have been rewarded and my friends have betrayed me . . .

OLD WOMAN: [Echo] Friends . . . betrayed . . . betrayed . . .

OLD MAN: They've treated me badly. They've persecuted me. If I complained, it was always they who were in the right . . . Sometimes I've tried to revenge myself . . . I was never able to, never able to revenge myself . . . I have too much pity . . . I refused to strike the enemy to the ground, I have always been too good.

OLD WOMAN: [Echo] He was too good, good, good, good, good . . .

OLD MAN: It is my pity that has defeated me.

OLD WOMAN: [Echo] My pity . . . pity . . . pity . . .

OLD MAN: But they never pitied me. I gave them a pin prick, and they repaid me with club blows, with knife blows, with cannon blows, they've crushed my bones . . .

OLD WOMAN: [Echo] . . . My bones . . . my bones . . . my bones . . .

OLD MAN: They've supplanted me, they've robbed me, they've assassinated me . . . I've been the collector of injustices, the lightning rod of catastrophes . . .

OLD WOMAN: [*Echo*] Lightning rod . . . catastrophe . . . lightning rod . . .

OLD MAN: In order to forget, Your Majesty, I wanted to go in for sports . . . for mountain climbing . . . they pulled my feet and made me slip . . . I wanted to climb stairways, they rotted the steps . . . I fell down . . . I wanted to travel, they refused me a passport . . . I wanted to cross the river, they burnt my bridges . . .

OLD WOMAN: [*Echo*] Burnt my bridges.

OLD MAN: I wanted to cross the Pyrenees, and there were no more Pyrenees.

OLD WOMAN: [*Echo*] No more Pyrenees . . . He could have been, he too, Your Majesty, like so many others, a head editor, a head actor, a head doctor, Your Majesty, a head king . . .

OLD MAN: Furthermore, no one has ever shown me due consideration . . . no one has ever sent me invitations . . . However, I, hear me, I say this to you, I alone could have saved humanity, who is so sick. Your Majesty realizes this as do I . . . or, at the least, I could have spared it the evils from which it has suffered so much this last quarter of a century, had I had the opportunity to communicate my message; I do not despair of saving it, there is still time, I have a plan . . . alas, I express myself with difficulty . . .

OLD WOMAN: [*Above the invisible heads*] The Orator will be here, he'll speak for you. His Majesty is here, thus you'll be heard, you've no reason to despair, you hold all the trumps, everything has changed, everything has changed . . .

OLD MAN: I hope Your Majesty will excuse me . . . I know you have many other worries . . . I've been humiliated . . . Ladies and gentlemen, move aside just a little bit, don't hide His Majesty's nose from me altogether, I want to see the diamonds of the imperial crown glittering . . . But if Your Majesty has deigned to come to our miserable home, it is because you have condescended to take into consideration my wretched self. What an extraordinary reward. Your Majesty, if corporeally I raise myself on my toes, this is not through pride, this is only in order to gaze upon you! . . . morally, I throw myself at your knees.

OLD WOMAN: [*Sobbing*] At your knees, Sire, we throw ourselves at your knees, at your feet, at your toes . . .

OLD MAN: I've had scabies. My employer fired me because I did not bow to his baby, to his horse. I've been kicked in the ass, but all this, Sire, no longer has any importance . . . since . . . since . . . Sir . . . Your Majesty . . . look . . . I am here . . . here . . .

OLD WOMAN: [*Echo*] Here . . . here . . . here . . . here . . . here . . .

OLD MAN: Since Your Majesty is here . . . since

Your Majesty will take my message into consideration . . . But the Orator should be here . . . he's making His Majesty wait . . .

OLD WOMAN: If Your Majesty will forgive him. He's surely coming. He will be here in a moment. They've telephoned us.

OLD MAN: His Majesty is so kind. His Majesty wouldn't depart just like that, without having listened to everything, heard everything.

OLD WOMAN: [*Echo*] Heard everything . . . heard . . . listened to everything . . .

OLD MAN: It is he who will speak in my name . . . I, I cannot . . . I lack the talent . . . he has all the papers, all the documents . . .

OLD WOMAN: [*Echo*] He has all the documents . . .

OLD MAN: A little patience, Sire, I beg of you . . . he should be coming.

OLD WOMAN: He should be coming in a moment.

OLD MAN: [*So that the Emperor will not grow impatient*] Your Majesty, hear me, a long time ago I had the revelation . . . I was forty years old . . . I say this also to you, ladies and gentlemen . . . one evening, after supper, as was our custom, before going to bed, I seated myself on my father's knees . . . my mustaches were longer than his and more pointed . . . I had more hair on my chest . . . my hair was graying already, but his was still brown . . . There were some guests, grownups, sitting at table, who began to laugh, laugh.

OLD WOMAN: [*Echo*] Laugh . . . laugh . . .

OLD MAN: I'm not joking, I told them, I love my papa very much. Someone replied: It is midnight, a child shouldn't stay up so late. If you don't go beddy-bye, then you're no longer a kid. But I'd still not have believed them if they hadn't addressed me as an adult.

OLD WOMAN: [*Echo*] An adult.

OLD MAN: Instead of as a child . . .

OLD WOMAN: [*Echo*] A child.

OLD MAN: Nevertheless, I thought to myself, I'm not married. Hence, I'm still a child. They married me off right then, expressly to prove the contrary to me . . . Fortunately, my wife has been both father and mother to me . . .

OLD WOMAN: The Orator should be here, Your Majesty . . .

OLD MAN: The Orator will come.

OLD WOMAN: He will come.

OLD MAN: He will come.

OLD WOMAN: He will come.

OLD MAN: He will come.

OLD WOMAN: He will come.

OLD MAN: He will come, he will come.

OLD WOMAN: He will come, he will come.

OLD MAN: He will come.

OLD WOMAN: He is coming.

OLD MAN: He is coming.

OLD WOMAN: He is coming, he is here.

OLD MAN: He is coming, he is here.

OLD WOMAN: He is coming, he is here.

OLD MAN and OLD WOMAN: He is here . . .

OLD WOMAN: Here he is!

[*Silence; all movement stops. Petrified, the two old people stare at door No. 5; this immobility lasts rather long—about thirty seconds; very slowly, very slowly the door opens wide, silently; then the* Orator *appears. He is a real person. He's a typical painter or poet of the nineteenth century; he wears a large black felt hat with a wide brim, loosely tied bow tie, artist's blouse, mustache and goatee, very histrionic in manner, conceited; just as the invisible people must be as real as possible, the* Orator *must appear unreal. He goes along the wall to the right, gliding, softly, to upstage center, in front of the main door, without turning his head to right or left; he passes close by the* Old Woman *without appearing to notice her, not even when the* Old Woman *touches his arm in order to assure herself that he exists. It is at this moment that the* Old Woman *says:* "Here he is!"*]*

OLD MAN: Here he is!

OLD WOMAN: [*Following the* Orator *with her eyes and continuing to stare at him*] It's really he, he exists. In flesh and blood.

OLD MAN: [*Following him with his eyes*] He exists. It's really he. This is not a dream!

OLD WOMAN: This is not a dream, I told you so.

[*The* Old Man *clasps his hands, lifts his eyes to heaven; he exults silently. The* Orator, *having reached upstage center, lifts his hat, bends forward in silence, saluting the invisible Emperor with his hat with a Musketeer's flourish and somewhat like an automaton. At this moment:*]

OLD MAN: Your Majesty . . . May I present to you, the Orator . . .

OLD WOMAN: It is he!

[*Then the* Orator *puts his hat back on his head and mounts the dais from which he looks down on the invisible crowd on the stage and at the chairs; he freezes in a solemn pose*]

OLD MAN [*To the invisible crowd*] You may ask him for autographs. [*Automatically, silently, the* Orator *signs and distributes numberless autographs. The* Old Man *during this time lifts his eyes again to heaven, clasping his hands, and exultantly says*] No man, in his lifetime, could hope for more . . .

OLD WOMAN: [*Echo*] No man could hope for more.

OLD MAN: [*To the invisible crowd*] And now, with the permission of Your Majesty, I will address myself to all of you, ladies, young ladies, gentlemen, little children, dear colleagues, dear compatriots, Your Honor the President, dear comrades in arms . . .

OLD WOMAN: [*Echo*] And little children . . . dren . . . dren . . .

OLD MAN: I address myself to all of you, without distinction of age, sex, civil status, social rank, or business, to thank you, with all my heart.

OLD WOMAN: [*Echo*] To thank you . . .

OLD MAN: As well as the Orator . . . cordially, for having come in such large numbers . . . silence, gentlemen! . . .

OLD WOMAN: [*Echo*] . . . Silence, gentlemen . . .

OLD MAN: I address my thanks also to those who have made possible the meeting this evening, to the organizers . . .

OLD WOMAN: Bravo!

[*Meanwhile, the* Orator *on the dais remains solemn, immobile, except for his hand, which signs autographs automatically*]

OLD MAN: To the owners of this building, to the architect, to the masons who were kind enough to erect these walls! . . .

OLD WOMAN: [*Echo*] . . . walls . . .

OLD MAN: To all those who've dug the foundations . . . Silence, ladies and gentlemen . . .

OLD WOMAN: . . . 'adies and gentlemen . . .

OLD MAN: Last but not least I address my warmest thanks to the cabinet-makers who have made these chairs on which you have been able to sit, to the master carpenter . . .

OLD WOMAN: [*Echo*] . . . penter . . .

OLD MAN: . . . Who made the armchair in which Your Majesty is sinking so softly, which does not prevent you, nevertheless, from maintaining a firm and manly attitude . . . Thanks again to all the technicians, machinists, electrocutioners . . .

OLD WOMAN: [*Echoing*] . . . cutioners . . . cutioners . . .

OLD MAN: . . . To the paper manufacturers and the printers, proofreaders, editors to whom we owe the programs, so charmingly decorated, to the universal solidarity of all men, thanks, thanks, to our country, to the State [*He turns toward where the* Emperor *is sitting*] whose helm Your Majesty directs with the skill of a true pilot . . . thanks to the usher . . .

OLD WOMAN: [*Echo*] . . . usher . . . rusher . . .

OLD MAN: [*Pointing to the* Old Woman] Hawker of Eskimo pies and programs . . .

OLD WOMAN: [*Echo*] . . . grams . . .

OLD MAN: . . . My wife, my helpmeet . . . Semiramis! . . .

OLD WOMAN: [*Echo*] . . . ife . . . meet . . . mis . . . [*Aside*] The darling, he never forgets to give me credit.

OLD MAN: Thanks to all those who have given me their precious and expert, financial or moral support, thereby contributing to the overwhelming success of this evening's gathering . . . thanks again, thanks above all to our beloved sovereign, His Majesty the Emperor . . .

OLD WOMAN: [*Echo*] . . . jesty the Emperor . . .

OLD MAN: [*In a total silence*] . . . A little silence . . . Your Majesty . . .

OLD WOMAN: [*Echo*] . . . jesty . . . jesty . . .

OLD MAN: Your Majesty, my wife and myself have nothing more to ask of life. Our existence can come to an end in this apotheosis . . . thanks be to heaven who has granted us such long and peaceful years . . . My life has been filled to overflowing. My mission is accomplished. I will not have lived in vain, since my message will be revealed to the world . . . [*Gesture towards the* Orator, *who does not perceive it; the* Orator *waves off requests for autographs, very dignified and firm*] To the world, or rather to what is left of it! [*Wide gesture toward the invisible crowd*] To you, ladies and gentlemen, and dear comrades, who are all that is left from humanity, but with such leftovers one can still make a very good soup . . . Orator, friend . . . [*The* Orator *looks in another direction*] If I have been long unrecognized, underestimated by my contemporaries, it is because it had to be . . . [*The* Old Woman *sobs*] What matters all that now when I am leaving to you, to you, my dear Orator and friend [*The* Orator *rejects a new request for an autograph, then takes an indifferent pose, looking in all directions*] . . . the responsibility of radiating upon posterity the light of my mind . . . thus making known to the universe my philosophy. Neglect none of the details of my private life, some laughable, some painful or heartwarming, of my tastes, my amusing gluttony . . . tell everything . . . speak of my helpmeet . . . [*The* Old Woman *redoubles her sobs*] . . . of the way she prepared those marvelous little Turkish pies, of her potted rabbit à la Normandabbit . . . speak of Berry, my native province . . . I count on you, great master and Orator . . . as for me and my faithful helpmeet, after our long years of labor in behalf of the progress of humanity during which we fought the good fight, nothing remains for us but to withdraw . . . immediately, in order to make the supreme sacrifice which no one demands of us but which we will carry out even so . . .

OLD WOMAN: [*Sobbing*] Yes, yes, let's die in full glory . . . let's die in order to become a legend . . . At least, they'll name a street after us . . .

OLD MAN: [*To* Old Woman] O my faithful helpmeet! . . . you who have believed in me, unfailingly, during a whole century, who have never left me, never . . . alas, today, at this supreme moment, the crowd pitilessly separates us . . .

> Above all I had hoped
> that together we might lie
> with all our bones together
> within the selfsame skin
> within the same sepulchre
> and that the same worms
> might share our old flesh
> that we might rot together . . .

OLD WOMAN: . . . Rot together . . .

OLD MAN: Alas! . . . alas! . . .

OLD WOMAN: Alas! . . . alas! . . .

OLD MAN: . . . Our corpses will fall far from each other, and we will rot in an aquatic solitude . . . Don't pity us over much.

OLD WOMAN: What will be, will be!

OLD MAN: We shall not be forgotten. The eternal Emperor will remember us, always.

OLD WOMAN: [*Echo*] Always.

OLD MAN: We will leave some traces, for we are people and not cities.

OLD MAN and OLD WOMAN: [*Together*] We will have a street named after us.

OLD MAN: Let us be united in time and in eternity, even if we are not together in space, as we were in adversity: let us die at the same moment . . . [*To the* Orator, *who is impassive, immobile*] One last time . . . I place my trust in you . . . I count on you. You will tell all . . . bequeath my message . . . [*To the* Emperor] If your Majesty will excuse me . . . Farewell to all. Farewell, Semiramis.

OLD WOMAN: Farewell to all! . . . Farewell, my darling!

OLD MAN: Long live the Emperor!

[*He throws confetti and paper streamers on the invisible Emperor; we hear fanfares; bright lights like fireworks*]

OLD WOMAN: Long live the Emperor!

[*Confetti and streamers thrown in the direction of the Emperor, then on the immobile and impassive* Orator, *and on the empty chairs*]

OLD MAN: [*Same business*] Long live the Emperor!

OLD WOMAN: [*Same business*] Long live the Emperor!

[*The* Old Woman *and* Old Man *at the same moment throw themselves out the windows, shouting "Long live the Emperor." Sudden silence; no more fireworks; we hear an "Ah" from both sides of the stage, the sea-green noises of bodies falling into the water. The light coming through the main door and the windows has disappeared; there remains only a weak light as at the beginning of the play; the darkened windows remain wide open, their curtains floating on the wind*]

ORATOR: [*He has remained immobile and impassive during the scene of the double suicide, and now, after several moments, he decides to speak. He faces the rows of empty chairs; he makes the invisible crowd understand that he is deaf and dumb; he makes the signs of a deafmute; desperate efforts to make himself understood; then he coughs, groans, utters the guttural sounds of a mute*] He, mme, mm, mm. Ju, gou, hou, hou. Heu, heu, gu, gou, gueue.

[*Helpless, he lets his arms fall down alongside his body; suddenly, his face lights up, he has an idea, he turns toward the blackboard, he takes a piece of chalk out of his pocket, and writes, in large capitals:*

ANGELFOOD

then:

NNAA NNM NWNWNW V

He turns around again, towards the invisible crowd on the stage, and points with his finger to what he's written on the blackboard]

ORATOR: Mmm, mmm, gueue, gou, gu. Mmm, Mmm, Mmm, Mmm.

[*Then, not satisfied, with abrupt gestures he*

*wipes out the chalk letters, and replaces them
with others, among which we can make out,
still in large capitals:*

ΛΛADIEU ΛADIEU ΛPΛ

Again, the Orator *turns around to face the
crowd; he smiles, questions, with an air of
hoping that he's been understood, of having
said something; he indicates to the empty
chairs what he's just written. He remains immobile for a few seconds, rather satisfied and
a little solemn; but then, faced with the absence of the hoped-for reaction, little by little
his smile disappears, his face darkens; he waits
another moment; suddenly he bows petulantly,
brusquely, descends from the dais; he goes
toward the main door upstage center, gliding
like a ghost; before exiting through this door,
he bows ceremoniously again to the rows of
empty chairs, to the invisible Emperor. The
stage remains empty with only the chairs, the
dais, the floor covered with streamers and
confetti. The main door is wide open onto
darkness.*

*We hear for the first time the human noises
of the invisible crowd; these are bursts of
laughter, murmurs, shh's, ironical coughs;
weak at the beginning, these noises grow
louder, then, again, progressively they become
weaker. All this should last long enough for
the audience—the real and visible audience—
to leave with this ending firmly impressed on
its mind. The curtain falls very slowly]*[1]

April–June, 1951

---

[1] In the original production the curtain fell on the mum-
blings of the mute Orator. The blackboard was not used.

A Representative List
of Modern Plays

A REPRESENTATIVE LIST OF MODERN PLAYS

The following appendix is intended to supplement this anthology with a selected list of historically important plays. Many of these titles have already been mentioned or discussed in the introductions, but they are repeated here for the convenience of the reader. The editor makes no claim of completeness for this list. The informed reader, the student, and his instructor will undoubtedly want to add their own preferences. The starting date for this volume of *A Treasury of the Theatre* is more or less arbitrarily taken to be 1875. The forerunners of the modern playwrights are represented in the first volume of the anthology, which begins with the period of Greek classicism and brings us to Ibsen's early career as a romanticist.

SCANDINAVIAN DRAMA

HENRIK IBSEN: *Pillars of Society* (1877). Ibsen's first realistic play to attack the façade of respectability behind which are hidden social evils and private derelictions.

A Doll's House (1879). The famous problem play which exposes the unsoundness of conventional marriage and expounds woman's need for emancipation.

Ghosts (1881). See page 10.

An Enemy of the People (1882). The drama of an idealistic physician's defiance of the vested interests of a community.

The Wild Duck (1884). Ibsen's examination of the relativity of morals, of the confusion between "ideals" and "illusions," and of the wrecking of lives by the misguided idealism of a neurotic would-be reformer.

Rosmersholm (1886). The tragedy of a weak-spirited idealist and a strong-minded "new woman" who drives his first wife to suicide in order to free him for a high destiny.

The Lady from the Sea (1888). A symbolic study of the problem of freedom in marriage.

Hedda Gabler (1890). See page 40.

The Master Builder (1892). A symbolic tragedy of the decline of creativeness and loss of confidence in an artist's life.

John Gabriel Borkman (1896). The tragedy of a financial genius who tries to create an industrial empire and sacrifices love to his dream of power and glory.

BJÖRNSTJERNE BJÖRNSON: *Beyond Human Power, I* and *II* (*I,* 1883; *II,* 1895). The first part, a tragedy of a minister's struggle with faith in a psychological situation; the second, a problem play about the conflict between capital and labor.

AUGUST STRINDBERG: *The Father* (1887). See page 75.

Miss Julie (1888). A long, naturalistic one-act drama about the conflict of the sexes and the classes; the tragedy of a repressed young woman in the grip of the sexual instinct.

Comrades (1888). A saturnine comedy about the "equality of the sexes" and about a woman's desire to elevate herself above her husband, who mistakenly treats her as a "comrade" and tries to give her a victory that she has not earned with her own talents.

The Creditor (1890). A long, psychological one-act treatment of feminine parasitism and of a scorned first husband's vengeance by the application of suggestion to her second husband.

The Link (1893). A divorce drama in which the compulsive recriminations of husband and wife deprive them of the custody of their child.

There Are Crimes and Crimes (1899). See page 328.

The Dance of Death, I and *II* (1901). A naturalistic psychological drama about the war of the sexes.

The Dream Play (1902). A symbolic and expressionistic fantasy on the anguish, evil, and illusoriness of human existence.

The Spook Sonata (1907). An expressionistic examination of the hidden guilt and failure of lives that lack the grace of God or man.

GUNNAR HEIBERG: *The Tragedy of Love* (1905). A romantic psychological drama dealing with the difference between masculine and feminine love.

HJALMAR BERGSTRÖM: *Karen Bornemann* (1907). A liberal, Ibsen-inspired treatment of the conflict between a conservative father and a daughter who insists on freedom in love without the sanction of marriage.

JÓHANN SIGURJÓNSSON: *Eyvind of the Hills* (1911). An Icelandic tragedy, notable for its passion and poetic background.

CENTRAL EUROPEAN DRAMA

LUDWIG ANZENGRUBER: *The Fourth Commandment* (1877). A seminaturalistic study of depravity in middle-class Viennese life.

GERHART HAUPTMANN: *The Weavers* (1892). See page 132.

The Beaver Coat (1893). A naturalistic thieves' comedy and a satire on the old Prussian bureaucracy. See also its sequel, *The Conflagration.*

The Assumption of Hannele (1893). The drama of a child hounded to death by her stepfather; presented by means of naturalistic and fantastic scenes.

The Sunken Bell (1896). A symbolist fairy tale in verse dealing with the conflict between duty and the pagan pursuit of freedom in an artist's soul.

Drayman Henschel (1898). A naturalistic tragedy of an inarticulate man destroyed by his conscience and by a worthless second wife.

Rose Bernd (1903). A naturalistic tragedy of a girl destroyed by the sexual instinct.

The Rats (1911). A naturalistic drama of the struggle of two women for the possession of a child in a slum environment. Deals with the instinct for maternity (see Lorca's *Yerma*) and is also a humorous apologia for naturalistic art—which Hauptmann had himself abandoned in *The Sunken Bell* and other plays.

HERMANN SUDERMANN: *Magda* (1893). A realistic study of the conflict between a "free" woman and her conservative father. The heroine's role attracted Sarah Bernhardt, Helena Modjeska, and Eleonora Duse.

FRANK WEDEKIND: *The Awakening of Spring* (1891). The tragedy of adolescents in the grip of the sexual instinct; presented with a mixture of naturalistic and expressionistic styles.

Earth Spirit (1895). A naturalistic-expressionistic treatment of the amoral force of sexuality, notable for its heroine Lulu, "the wild, beautiful animal" in whom sexuality is incarnate. See also its sequel, *Pandora's Box* (1893), in which Lulu is murdered by a man in whom the sexual instinct is compulsive and pathological.

The Tenor (1899). See page 164.

The Marquis of Keith (1900). The comedy of a Nietzschean scoundrel and adventurer for whom life is a "toboggan slide."

MAX HALBE: *Youth* (1893). A tragedy of youth and frustration in a narrow religious background.

GEORG HIRSCHFELD: *The Mothers* (1896). A naturalistic treatment of the conflict between an artist's desire for freedom and the family pressure which he is unable to resist.

LUDWIG THOMA: *Moral* (1908). A satire on the hypocrisy of crusaders against vice.

WILHELM VON SCHOLZ: *The Race with the Shadow* (1921). A psychological fantasy in which an author finds a rival for his wife's affections in the character he creates in one of his books.

ARTHUR SCHNITZLER: *Anatol* (1889-1891; published in 1893). A series of one-act plays dealing with the same character's various love affairs and disillusionment. (Adapted by Harley Granville-Barker.)

Light-o'-Love (*Liebelei*) (1894). The tragedy of a poor Viennese girl who has idealized her upper-class lover only to discover that he has been killed in a duel fought over the wife of another man; a contrast between the meaning of love on the upper and lower social levels.

Hands Around (*Reigen*) (1897). "The death dance of love": a series of ten dramatic dialogues preceding and following sexual consummation. A clinical, naturalistic study of the instinct that holds individuals in its grip regardless of the difference in their social positions.

The Green Cockatoo (1898). A grotesque and ironic one-act treatment of the doomed but frivolous aristocracy on the eve of the French Revolution.

The Lonely Way (1903). A tragedy of loneliness and disillusionment after a life of self-indulgence and egotism.

The Vast Domain (1911). An exposé of a ruthless philanderer and his "sophisticated" social circle.

Professor Bernhardi (1912). A problem play dealing with Austrian anti-Semitism and with a Jewish physician's conflict with religious fanaticism.

HERMAN HEIJERMANS: *The Good Hope* (1900). A naturalistic social drama exposing the greed of shipowners and presenting the tragedy of fishermen exposed to the perils of the sea in unseaworthy ships.

HUGO VON HOFMANNSTHAL: *Death and the Fool* (1893). A symbolist verse drama dealing with a dilettante's failure to grasp reality and make fruitful use of his life.

Electra (1903). A psychological, "modern" treatment of Sophocles' *Electra;* the heroine is presented as a hysterical neurotic. (The play was set to music by Richard Strauss.)

Everyman (1911). A modern reworking of the famous medieval English morality play.

KARL SCHÖNHERR: *Earth* (1907). A comedy of the tenacity of peasant life.

HERMANN BAHR: *The Concert* (1909). A comedy of a volatile artist's philandering disposition and its unromantic consequences.

FERENC MOLNÁR: *Liliom* (1909). See page 354.

The Guardsman (1911). An ingenious comedy of jealousy among actors. Popularized in America by Alfred Lunt and Lynn Fontanne.

The Play's the Thing (1924). A comedy of jealousy, ingeniously enlivened by the play-within-the-play technique.

ERNST VAJDA: *Fata Morgana* (1915). A comedy of an adolescent's infatuation with a woman of the world.

CARL STERNHEIM: *The Snob* (1913). A mordant satire on the social ascent of a designing character who becomes an industrial magnate and marries into the German aristocracy. See also its sequels, *1913* (published in 1915) and *Tabula rasa* (1916).

FRITZ VON UNRUH: *Officers* (1912). A treatment of the conflict between military obedience and individual thought. May be compared with Heinrich von Kleist's *The Prince of Homburg,* an early psychological study of Prussianism.

ANTON WILDGANS: *Poverty* (1913). The drama of the slow death of a superannuated government official.

ARNOLT BRONNEN: *Parricide* (1915). A violent treatment of the Oedipus complex, notable as an early example of expressionism.

WALTER HASENCLEVER: *The Son* (1916; written in 1914). An early expressionistic presentation of the struggle of the generations.

GEORG KAISER: *From Morn to Midnight* (1916). An expressionistic treatment of a bank cashier's revolt against the frustrations of his lowly, depersonalized life and of his frenzied and disillusioning effort to experience the excitements of the metropolitan world.

Gas, I and *II* (*I,* 1918; *II,* 1920). An expressionistic presentation of the problems of the modern industrial world, ending in the collapse of society. See also the first part of this trilogy, *The Coral* (1917).

STEFAN ZWEIG: *Jeremiah* (1917). A pacifistic protest against the First World War, in a biblical setting.

REINHARD GOERING: *Sea Battle* (1918). An expressionistic presentation of the thoughts of seven sailors on a German warship during the First World War.

ERNST TOLLER: *Man and the Masses* (1919). An expressionistic treatment of the revolt of the masses after the First World War and a study of the conflict between a humanitarian idealist and depersonalized masses bent upon destruction.

The Machine-Wreckers (1922). A drama of the revolt of the Luddite workers in England against the introduction of steam-driven machinery. May be compared with Hauptmann's *The Weavers.*

FRANZ WERFEL: *The Goat Song* (1921). A symbolic presentation of the recrudescence of brutishness in man and the coming of revolution as a destructive force; the story of the birth of a monster to a wealthy peasant family and the social upheaval he causes.

KAREL CAPEK: *R. U. R.* (1921). See page 409.

KAREL and JOSEF CAPEK: *The Insect Comedy* (*The World We Live In:* American adaptation by Owen Davis; *And So Ad Infinitum:* version played in England) (1922). An expressionistic fantasy of the foibles, predatoriness, regimentation, and warring habits of the human race, presented as a picture of insect life in the delirium of a dying vagabond.

BRUNO FRANK: *The Twelve Thousand* (1927). A comedy about the sale of Hessian soldiers by their duke as mercenaries to help defeat the colonists in the American Revolution.

FERDINAND BRUCKNER: *The Sickness of Youth* (1928). A treatment of the failure of the young in erotic and social situations.

The Criminals (1929). A cross section of life in Germany, first written as a study of judicial procedure, rewritten during the Second World War as a study of social deterioration on the eve of the Nazi revolution.

HANS CHLUMBERG: *The Miracle at Verdun* (1930). An expressionistic antiwar fantasy. German and French soldiers buried in a common mass grave return to life only to discover that the living have learned nothing from the First World War and are getting ready for a second holocaust. May be compared with Irwin Shaw's *Bury the Dead.*

CARL ZUCKMAYER: *The Captain of Köpenick* (1931). A satire on Prussian militarism and the tendency of the Germans to obey military authority unquestioningly.

FRIEDRICH WOLF: *The Sailors of Cattaro* (1931). A drama of the mutiny of the Austrian fleet at the end of the First World War.

Professor Mamlock (1935). A play about anti-Semitism in Nazi Germany. Better known as a motion picture.

HANNS JOHST: *Schlageter* (1933). A meretricious early Nazi play, permeated with the extreme nationalism and hatred of culture glorified by National Socialism. A typical statement in the play is, "When I hear '*Kultur,*' I loosen the safety catch on my revolver."

BERTOLT BRECHT: *The Three-Penny Opera* (1928). A social satire based on John Gay's eighteenth-century classic *The Beggar's Opera.*

The Private Life of the Master Race (1939). See page 456.

The Good Woman of Setzuan (published in English in 1948; written in 1941?). A brilliant morality play about the problem of good will and charitableness in the world of social realities.

The Caucasian Chalk Circle (published in English in 1948; written in 1944?). An "epic" morality play, based upon the Chinese classic *The Chalk Circle.* Deals with a woman's right to a child by virtue of her devotion to it as against an aristocratic mother's purely biological claims.

FRENCH DRAMA

EMILE ZOLA: *Thérèse Raquin* (1873). A naturalistic treatment of an adulterous relationship, of the murder of the husband by the lovers, and of their remorse and self-torture under the accusing eyes of the paralyzed mother of the murdered man.

HENRY BECQUE: *The Vultures* (1882; written in 1875). See page 95.

The Parisian Woman (*La Parisienne*) (1885). A brilliant naturalistic comedy about an amoral adulterous woman in Parisian society.

JEAN JULLIEN: *Serenade* (1887). A Théâtre Libre *comédie rosse,* in which a mother and daughter live with the same man.

GEORGES DE PORTO-RICHE: *A Loving Wife* (*Amoureuse; The Tyranny of Love*) (1891). The naturalistic drama of a man who tries to break the spell of sexual passion in his relations with an ardent young wife.

FRANÇOIS DE CUREL: *The Fossils* (1892). A notable naturalistic tragedy dealing with the decline of the French aristocracy.

GEORGES COURTELINE: *Boubouroche* (1893). A famous Théâtre Libre farce with overtones of cynicism. Revolves around a deceived husband whose suspicions are allayed by his wife's pretense at feeling outraged when reproved by him.

EUGÈNE BRIEUX: *The Three Daughters of M. Dupont* (1897). An early naturalistic problem play dealing with the sufferings of daughters under the dowry system of the French middle class.

The Red Robe (1900) (produced in America as *The Letter of the Law,* 1920). A thesis drama about the French system of criminology.

Damaged Goods (1902). A naturalistic problem play that became notorious for its candid sociological treatment of the subject of venereal disease.

The June Bugs (*Les Hannetons*) (1907). Brieux's best play; a comedy which shows an illicit affair to be no less exacting than marriage. (Brieux, who was greatly admired by Bernard Shaw, infused the old thesis type of drama developed by Dumas *fils* with naturalism by dealing with subjects and dispensing doctrines popularized by that style of writing.)

PAUL HERVIEU: *Know Thyself* (1909). A realistic triangle play about a husband's understanding attitude toward his unfaithful wife.

MAURICE MAETERLINCK: *The Intruder* (1890). See page 264.

The Blind (1891). A one-act symbolist drama presenting the helplessness of blind people who are lost when their priest and guide dies.

Pelléas and Mélisande (1893). A symbolist version of the Paolo and Francesca story. The basis of Claude Debussy's famous opera.

Interior (1895). A one-act symbolist drama about the death of a girl by drowning.

The Blue Bird (1908). The once very popular ultrasymbolist allegory dealing with two children's search for the blue bird of happiness.

EDMOND ROSTAND: *Cyrano de Bergerac* (1897). See page 274.

L'Aiglon (1900). The tragedy of Napoleon's son ("the eaglet"), who is incapable of realizing the heroic aspirations inspired by his father's fame.

Chantecler (1910). A tribute to the heroic spirit, written as a poetic beast fable about La Fontaine's rooster.

The Last Night of Don Juan (published posthumously in 1921). An imaginative version of the Don Juan legend; presents the fabulous philanderer as a failure in love.

JACQUES COPEAU: *The Brothers Karamazov* (1911). Copeau's famous dramatization of Dostoevsky's novel.

PAUL CLAUDEL: *The Tidings Brought to Mary* (1912). A poetic religious drama of selfless love and saintliness.

SACHA GUITRY: *Pasteur* (1919). The biographical drama of Pasteur and his struggles with conservatism in scientific circles.

HENRI RENÉ LENORMAND: *Time Is a Dream* (1919). A Pirandellian treatment of the unreality and relativity of time and life.

The Failures (1920). A play about the failure and deterioration of a playwright and an actress.

Man and His Phantoms (1924). A psychoanalytic interpretation of the Don Juan legend.

The Coward (1925). A sympathetic psychological study of an artist who betrays France to a German spy out of cowardice.

FERNAND CROMMELYNCK: *The Magnificent Cuckold* (1921). A broad comedy of jealousy, in which the foolish husband drives his wife into the arms of many men with his obsessive behavior.

CHARLES VILDRAC: *S. S. Tenacity* (1920). A play about the divergent destinies of two companions—a dreamer and a practical man—bound for Canada.

Michael Auclair (1922). A tender play about a selfless man who loses his fiancée to a dishonest and swaggering soldier but proceeds to reform him for the sake of the girl.

JEAN JACQUES BERNARD: *Martine* (1922). The tragedy of a simple peasant girl ensnared by a philanderer from the city; presented with notable sensitivity.

Invitation to a Voyage (1924). The comedy of a wife who indulges in extravagantly romantic illusions about her husband's friend when he takes a business trip to Argentina but is disillusioned by his unromantic return.

SIMON GANTILLON: *Maya* (1924). A somewhat Pirandellian treatment of a prostitute in sordid circumstances and of men's need for dreams; she is "maya," or illusion, for them.

EDOUARD BOURDET: *The Captive* (1926). A psychological treatment of sexual inversion in a wife who is unable to free herself from her aberration.

JULES ROMAINS: *Dr. Knock* (*Knock, ou le Triomphe de la médicine*) (1923). An extravagant satire on medical charlatanism.

ALFRED SAVOIR: *The Lion Tamer* (*Le Dompteur, ou l'Anglais tel qu'on le mange*) (1925). A tragic farce about the absurdities of idealism in an Englishman who follows a circus from town to town in the hope that the "op-pressed" lions will turn on the lion tamer and devour him. Instead, it is the English-man who is eaten.

MARCEL PAGNOL: *Topaze* (1928). An extrava-gant satire on the necessity of dishonesty for survival in a predatory world.

RENÉ FAUCHOIS: *Prenez garde à la peinture* (1932) (*The Late Christopher Bean* in Sid-ney Howard's adaptation, 1932). A comedy about the rapacity of art dealers and the neglect of artists while they are still living.

ANDRÉ BIRABEAU: *Dame Nature* (1936). A sensi-tive comedy of adolescent love and marriage.

JEAN COCTEAU: *The Infernal Machine* (1934). An ironic and more or less surrealistic ver-sion of the legend of Oedipus, in which the hero achieves humanity only after Fate has crossed and confounded him cruelly.

JEAN GIRAUDOUX: *Amphitryon 38* (1929). A sparkling boudoir comedy, the "thirty-eighth" version of the classic story of Jupiter's seduc-tion of Alcmena, the wife of Amphitryon, whom the god impersonates.

The Trojan War Will Not Take Place (1935). An ironic foretelling of the Second World War through the story of the Trojan War.

The Madwoman of Chaillot (1945) (Ameri-can adaptation by Maurice Valency, 1948). A poetic extravaganza satirizing greed and celebrating a fantastic liberation from mod-ern society's speculators and entrepreneurs.

JEAN-PAUL SARTRE: *The Flies* (1943). See page 466.

No Exit (*Huis-Clos*) (1944). A long one-act existentialist fantasy in which three failures are doomed to spend their afterlife together.

The Respectful Prostitute (1946). A sardonic existentialist treatment of race relations in the South of the United States.

The Victors (*Morts sans sépulture*) (1946). An existentialist treatment of the French un-derground Resistance movement.

ALBERT CAMUS: *Caligula* (1944). An existen-tialist account of the sanguinary career of Caligula, who entertains ideals but avenges himself on humanity when he becomes dis-illusioned; the "idealist" thus makes himself a tyrant by his conduct.

JEAN ANOUILH: *Antigone* (1944). A version of Sophocles' play of the same title, in which Antigone goes to her death for burying her brother Polyneices primarily because of dis-gust with the timorous, calculating world.

ITALIAN DRAMA

GABRIELE D'ANNUNZIO: *La Gioconda* (1898). An example of D'Annunzian poetic tragedy. Deals with the ill-fated love of high-spirited romantic personalities.

The Daughter of Jorio (1904). A poetic peas-ant tragedy, weird and frenetic but imagina-tive and rich with local color.

SEM BENELLI: *The Jest* (1910). A colorful poetic melodrama of love, hatred, and vengeance during the Italian Renaissance, contrasting the artist and the man of action. A popular example of the poetic school.

LUIGI CHIARELLI: *The Mask and the Face* (1916). An ironical comedy, the first written in the manner of the modern Italian "gro-tesque" school of playwriting. Satirizes the conventional attitude toward marital infidel-ity and the difference between what we pro-fess and what we feel. A betrayed husband, to avenge his honor, pretends that he has killed his wife.

LUIGI PIRANDELLO: *Right You Are if You Think You Are* [*Right You Are (If You Think So)*] (1916). A metaphysical comedy posing the Pirandellian question, "What is reality?" and requiring tolerance for people's illusions.

Six Characters in Search of an Author (1921). See page 384.

Henry IV (produced in New York as *The Living Mask*) (1922). A powerful tragedy of insanity and disillusionment, exemplify-ing Pirandello's concern with the border line between sanity and insanity.

Naked (1922). The tragedy of a woman's longing for a romantic personality and the incomprehension of people who blame her for having pretended to die for love.

ALBERTO CASELLA: *Death Takes a Holiday* (1924) (American adaptation by Walter Ferris, 1929). A fantasy in which Death falls in love with a girl and she, returning his love, gives up life.

SPANISH DRAMA

JOSÉ ECHEGARAY: *The Great Galeoto* (1881). A drama in which doubt of a woman's fidelity throws her into the arms of the man with whom scandalmongers have associated her.

JACINTO BENAVENTE: *The Bonds of Interest* (1907). A modern satirical *commedia dell'arte,* showing how self-interest draws people together.

The Passion Flower (1913). A peasant tragedy dealing with the love of a girl and her step-father.

GREGORIO MARTÍNEZ SIERRA: *Cradle Song* (1911). A drama that presents the maternal instinct fulfilling itself in a nunnery.

The Two Shepherds (1913). A portrait of a priest and a physician who have been good shepherds to their people but are out of step with modern theology and science.

The Kingdom of God (1915). A drama of self-sacrifice that revolves around a pious woman who gives her life to those who need it.

SERAFÍN and JOAQUÍN ALVAREZ QUINTERO: *Malvaloca* (1912). A drama of Andalusian life, dealing with the vicissitudes of a woman who, in spite of her past, finds an understanding love.

FEDERICO GARCÍA LORCA: *Blood Wedding* (1933). See page 434.

Yerma (1934). The poetic tragedy of a woman obsessed with a frustrated passion for maternity and driven to murder the husband who is responsible for her empty life.

The House of Bernarda Alba (1936). The tragedy of the daughters of a proud matriarchal woman who refuses to allow them to realize themselves as women.

RUSSIAN DRAMA

LEO TOLSTOY: *The Power of Darkness* (1886). See page 173.

The Living Corpse (*Redemption*) (1900). An Enoch Arden tragedy of a failure and an attack on irrational marriage laws.

The Light That Shines in Darkness (begun in the 'eighties and continued in 1900 and 1902; last act never written). The tragedy of an idealist like Tolstoy himself.

ANTON CHEKHOV: *The Sea Gull* (1896). A tragedy of love and frustration, artistic ambitions, and the ironies of life.

Uncle Vanya (1899). Another Chekhovian tragicomic study in frustration. Notable, like other Chekhov plays, for its superb characterizations.

The Three Sisters (1901). A tragedy of longing for experience and of frustration in provincial Russia.

The Cherry Orchard (1904). See page 205.

MAXIM GORKI: *The Lower Depths* (*Na dne*) (1902). See page 227.

Yegor Bulychov (1932). A tragedy of degeneration in the middle class on the eve of the Russian Revolution. A notable naturalistic drama, containing an incisive picture of a merchant's family.

LEONID ANDREYEV: *The Life of Man* (1906). A symbolic tragedy dealing with the rise and fall of an individual and with the spectral domination of Death.

King Hunger (1907). A symbolic drama of revolution, reflecting the events of the Revolution of 1905; King Hunger champions his children, the poor, but ultimately betrays them, because he is the servant of the rich.

The Black Maskers (1908). The most thoroughly symbolic of Andreyev's plays. Deals with the problem of dual personality and evil in the human soul.

He Who Gets Slapped (1915). A tragedy of disillusionment, set in a circus.

NIKOLAI EVREINOV: *The Chief Thing* (1921). An attempt to depart from realism by treating life as a product of creative will and imagination.

MICHAEL BULGAKOV: *Days of the Turbins* (*The Last of the Turbins; The White Guard* in an English adaptation by Rodney Ackland) (1926). A drama of civil war in Soviet Russia, notable for its sympathetic characterization of revolutionists and counterrevolutionists alike; a more or less Chekhovian picture of the destruction of the Russian aristocracy.

VALENTIN KATAEV: *Squaring the Circle* (1928). A hilarious farce on marriage relations and other mores of Soviet Russia. Called the *Abie's Irish Rose* of Soviet Russia.

ALEXANDER AFINOGENOV: *Fear* (1931). A psychological social-problem play in which a scientist investigates the incidence of fear among Soviet citizens.

Distant Point (1935). A picture of life in a remote Siberian railway junction, which the characters desire to leave until convinced that they are needed.

NIKOLAI POGODIN: *Aristocrats* (1935). A drama of the rehabilitation of common criminals who help to build a canal from the White Sea to the Baltic.

KONSTANTIN SIMONOV: *The Russian People* (1942). An account of the struggle of a Russian town against occupation by the German army.

HEBREW DRAMA

S. ANSKY: *The Dybbuk* (1919). A fantastic love tragedy of demoniacal possession and exorcism, based on Jewish folklore. A famous Habimah stage production.

ENGLISH DRAMA

OSCAR WILDE: *Lady Windermere's Fan* (1892). The first notable English comedy after Sheridan's *School for Scandal*. Combines comedy of manners with problem drama and the fallen-woman theme of early realism.

The Importance of Being Earnest (1895). See page 512.

BRANDON THOMAS: *Charley's Aunt* (1892). The best of the late Victorian farces. Revolves around an Oxford undergraduate's impersonation of a classmate's unknown aunt from Brazil, "where the nuts come from."

ARTHUR WING PINERO: *The Second Mrs. Tanqueray* (1893). Important as one of the earliest realistic problem plays of the English stage. Deals with a fallen woman's struggle for respectability.

The Thunderbolt (1908). A comedy exposing middle-class cupidity and hypocrisy. Revolves around the conventional device of a destroyed will.

Mid-Channel (1909). A realistic study of a wrecked marriage.

HENRY ARTHUR JONES: *Michael and His Lost Angel* (1896). An early example of social tragedy, dealing with a clergyman's illicit passion and struggle with conscience.

The Liars (1897). A comedy of manners. Shows the author at his best.

GEORGE BERNARD SHAW: *Widowers' Houses* (1892). The first of Shaw's social satires.

Mrs. Warren's Profession (1902; written in 1893; published in 1898). An onslaught on complacent respectability, an analysis of the economic sources of prostitution, and a backhanded slap at the profit system.

Arms and the Man (1894). Shaw's spoof on romanticism and military vainglory.

Candida (1897; published in 1898). See page 538.

Caesar and Cleopatra (1899; published in 1900). Shaw's first antiromantic treatment of a historical subject; a character study of a Shavian "superman."

Man and Superman (1905; published in 1903). An antiromantic treatment of the problem of sex; emphasizes the role of the "Life Force" and maintains that woman, not man, is the pursuer.

John Bull's Other Island (1903). Shaw's only play about the Irish question, later produced by the Abbey Theatre. A satirical inversion of Irish and English national characteristics.

Major Barbara (1905). An attack on conventional philanthropy and meliorism, a challenge to the social system which makes charity necessary, and a comedy which presents a munitions magnate as more beneficial to society than conventional philanthropists and reformers.

The Doctor's Dilemma (1906). A satire on medicine and medical ethics, but also an investigation of the relative value of the artist and the commonplace man to society, with a memorable characterization of the man whose integrity is confined to his art.

Getting Married (1908). Shaw's discussion piece on marriage. Technically interesting as a play without a plot.

Androcles and the Lion (1912). A Shavian treatment of martyrdom and of nascent Christianity in the Roman Empire.

Pygmalion (1912; produced in English in 1914; screen version in 1938). A comedy on the superficiality of class distinctions.

Heartbreak House (1920; written in 1913–1916). A comedy of social disintegration, written rather broadly in the manner of Chekhov, concerning upper-class decadence during the First World War.

Back to Methuselah (1922). An oversized philosophical comedy concerning the importance of longevity as a factor in human progress. Contends that only a life counted in centuries rather than in decades can make human beings wise enough to order society rationally.

Saint Joan (1923). A sympathetic treatment of Joan of Arc as a superior person in advance of her times—an instinctive Protestant before the Protestant Reformation and a nationalist before feudalism made way for progressive nationalism.

The Apple Cart (1929). A political comedy about the problems of governing England— where the Labour party may be voted into office but the corporations still rule the nation—and the efforts of a benevolent monarch to govern better than the cabinet.

Too True to Be Good (1932). An extravaganza on the collapse of European society on the eve of Hitler's National Socialist revolution.

On the Rocks (1933). A political comedy about the failure of the British government to cope with economic problems and the failure of a well-intentioned statesman to take the ship of state "off the rocks."

In Good King Charles's Golden Days (1939). Shaw's discursive comedy about Charles II's political acumen and Newton's genius.

C. HADDON CHAMBERS: *The Tyranny of Tears* (1899). A Pinero-Jones type of comedy of character, showing how a husband may be dominated by his wife through sentiment.

JAMES M. BARRIE: *The Admirable Crichton* (1903). See page 566.

Peter Pan (1904). The fantasy play of childhood which best exemplifies Barrie's whimsy and charm. The outstanding fantastic play of the modern English stage.

What Every Woman Knows (1908). A shrewd treatment of marriage, in which a wife promotes her husband's career without his realizing it.

The Twelve-Pound Look (1910). Barrie's famous one-act comedy about a successful stuffed shirt who is deflated by his former wife, who left him and became a typist because he bored her.

HARLEY GRANVILLE-BARKER: *The Voysey Inheritance* (1905). A comedy of business practices and social responsibility, written in the Shavian manner.

Waste (1907). A drama about the deplorable waste of personal talent and loss to society caused by a scandalous romance.

The Madras House (1910). A disquisition on the problem of sexuality in the modern world; a unique drama of ideas. Shows Shaw's influence.

ST. JOHN HANKIN: *The Cassilis Engagement* (1907). A comedy about a clever mother's successful elimination of her son's unsuitable fiancée.

The Last of the De Mullins (1908). A treatment of the problem of the emancipation of woman. Reflects the influence of Ibsen.

JOHN MASEFIELD: *The Tragedy of Nan* (1908). A powerful peasant tragedy, remarkable for its picture of human bestiality and pathos. Deals with the persecution of a girl whose father was unjustly hanged for sheepstealing.

ELIZABETH BAKER: *Chains* (1909). A drama of humdrum suburban life and of the failure of a man to win his freedom when his wife is with child.

STANLEY HOUGHTON: *Hindle Wakes* (1912). An Ibsensite comedy about the double standard. A poor girl refuses to let a rich weakling make a respectable woman of her by marrying her at the insistence of a righteous father.

GITHA SOWERBY: *Rutherford and Son* (1912). A grim drama of conflict in the home of a righteous and unbending industrialist.

JOHN GALSWORTHY: *The Silver Box* (1906). A drama of social inequality and injustice.

Strife (1909). A treatment of the clash between labor and capital; the first notable British play about a strike.

Justice (1910). A drama of legal injustice. Deals with a weakling's misfortunes in the grip of circumstances and the law.

The Pigeon (1912). An ironic comedy about the problem of society's misfits and about the complications of philanthropy.

Loyalties (1922). A drama of class loyalties and racial prejudice, in which a thieving "gentleman" is supported by members of good society, with disastrous results.

Escape (1926). See page 597.

W. SOMERSET MAUGHAM: *Our Betters* (1917). A satire on snobbishness; especially caustic in its picture of socially aspiring Americans in England.

The Circle (1921). See page 665.

The Constant Wife (1923). A comedy about the double standard and its elimination by a woman who wins economic independence and therefore moral freedom after her husband's infidelity.

For Services Rendered (1932). A grim picture of the effect of war on an English family.

JOHN DRINKWATER: *Abraham Lincoln* (1918). A poetic chronicle play about Lincoln during the Civil War.

CLEMENCE DANE: *A Bill of Divorcement* (1921). A moving drama of postwar misery. Deals with a shell-shocked veteran, his divorced wife, and their daughter.

Come of Age (1934). A poetic drama in which the tragedy of the eighteenth-century poet Thomas Chatterton is translated into modern terms.

C. K. MUNRO: *At Mrs. Beam's* (1921). A comedy of London boarding-house life.

A. A. MILNE: *The Truth About Blayds* (1922). A satiric comedy about a literary charlatan and his family's readiness to profit by his dishonesty.

SUTTON VANE: *Outward Bound* (1923). A drama revolving around death and the afterlife. Notable for restrained fantasy and sympathy.

NOEL COWARD: *The Vortex* (1923). A study of a mother and son suffering defeat through character disintegration in postwar society.

Private Lives (1930). Coward's ultrasophisticated farce about an exchange of husbands and wives.

Fumed Oak (1935). A one-act comedy about the revolt of a middle-class Englishman against his unbearable family.

Blithe Spirit (1941). See page 730.

ASHLEY DUKES: *The Man with a Load of Mischief* (1924). A poetic fantasy play set in England during the French Revolution, satirizing aristocratic arrogance and championing the common man.

JOHN VAN DRUTEN: *Young Woodley* (1925). A drama of public-school (that is, private-school) life and adolescence in England.

ROBERT NICHOLS and MAURICE BROWNE: *Wings over Europe* (1928). The first atom-bomb play, revolving around the conflict between war-making statesmanship and humanitarian science, with the proponents of the latter attempting to force governments to renounce war.

R. C. SHERRIFF: *Journey's End* (1929). See page 693.

RUDOLPH BESIER: *The Barretts of Wimpole Street* (1931). The biographical romance of Elizabeth and Robert Browning; presented with psychological overtones.

DODIE SMITH: *Autumn Crocus* (1931). A romantic comedy revolving around the thawing out of an English schoolteacher on vacation in Switzerland.

Call It a Day (1935). A genteel comedy of an English family and its confusions on a more or less typical day.

BENN W. LEVY: *Springtime for Henry* (1931). A farce about the attempted reformation of a clever scapegrace.

MORDAUNT SHAIRP: *The Green Bay Tree* (1932). An incisive treatment of sybaritism and sexual inversion from a Freudian standpoint.

JAMES BRIDIE: *Tobias and the Angel* (1932). A biblical comedy, written with canny Scottish humor and wisdom.

A Sleeping Clergyman (1933). An anti-eugenics chronicle showing how humanity would have been cheated by a narrow and obtuse application of eugenics.

J. B. PRIESTLEY: *Dangerous Corner* (1932). An original psychological melodrama.

Laburnum Grove (1933). A comedy of middle-class suburban life.

An Inspector Calls (1946). A morality play on the subject of social responsibility, in which members of the upper class are exposed as callous and irresponsible.

RONALD GOW and WALTER GREENWOOD: *Love on the Dole* (1935). A study of the British depression of the nineteen-thirties.

LAURENCE HOUSMAN: *Victoria Regina* (1935). A biographical chronicle of Queen Victoria, compounded of a number of Housman's one-act plays. Perhaps chiefly memorable for Helen Hayes's impersonation of the Queen in the New York production.

PATRICK HAMILTON: *Gaslight* (1938) (*Angel Street* in the American production, 1941). A superior melodrama, dealing with a husband's effort to remove his wife by driving her insane.

EMLYN WILLIAMS: *The Corn Is Green* (1938). A drama of the Welsh mining districts. Revolves around the education of a miner's son by a resolutely idealistic woman.

TERENCE RATTIGAN: *The Winslow Boy* (1945). A dramatization of the famous old Archer-Shee case. Justice is secured for an inconsequential victim of officialdom—a tribute to England's regard for civil liberties.

W. H. AUDEN and CHRISTOPHER ISHERWOOD: *The Dog Beneath the Skin* (1935). A satirical, poetic revue on the deterioration of Europe and the collapse of society. Critical of capitalism and fascism.

The Ascent of F 6 (1936). A poetic indictment of British imperialism, profit-seeking exploitation, and the sentimentality of the easily deluded common people, presented in the story of the exploration of a mountain.

T. S. ELIOT: *Murder in the Cathedral* (1935). Eliot's poetic, liturgical drama of the martyrdom of St. Thomas à Becket; a treatment of the conflict between church and state and between spiritual and worldly values.

The Cocktail Party (1949; first commercial production in 1950 in America). A verse drama of spiritual failure and redemption largely in terms of British comedy of manners (but with mystical touches). An essentially shallow couple is brought back together by a "psychiatrist" by being faced with the truth about their shallowness, and a girl with deeper capacity for love is directed into social service and eventual martyrdom.

DOROTHY L. SAYERS: *The Zeal of Thy House* (1937). A poetic religious drama on the building of a cathedral by a famous medieval architect who learns to mediate between his ego and his faith.

ROBERT MORLEY and NOEL LANGLEY: *Edward, My Son* (1947). A theatrically ingenious chronicle of an egotist whose career of ruthlessness begins with his desire to cure his son of a limp.

CHRISTOPHER FRY: *The Lady's Not for Burning* (1948). A poetic comedy in which a soldier saves a woman from being burned as a witch in medieval England by diverting suspicion to himself as a murderer.

IRISH DRAMA

WILLIAM BUTLER YEATS: *Kathleen ni Houlihan* (1902). A symbolic patriotic drama in which an old woman (Ireland) claims a young man's devotion and turns out to be beautiful and have "the walk of a Queen" when he follows her. With *The Countess Cathleen* (1892), *The Land of Heart's Desire* (1894), and *The Shadowy Waters* (1900), representative of Yeats's early dramatic work.

Four Plays for Dancers (1920). Short poetic treatments of Irish legend in the style of Japanese Noh drama. Remarkable for their extreme concentration and poetic power.

EDWARD MARTYN: *The Heather-Field* (1899). An Ibsenite semisymbolist drama of a landowner's effort to reclaim a wind-swept heather field for use as pasture land. Symbolic of Ireland's struggle.

JOHN MILLINGTON SYNGE: *In the Shadow of the Glen* (1903). A one-act play dealing with the revolt of a frustrated young wife and her departure from her home in the company of a carefree tramp.

Riders to the Sea (1904). See page 626.

The Well of the Saints (1905). A drama of disenchantment and dissatisfaction with reality, in which two beggars, cured of blindness by a miracle-working saint, are glad to become blind again.

The Tinker's Wedding (published in 1909). A robust farce of Irish tramp life.

The Playboy of the Western World (1907). A comedy of Irish peasantry. Concerns the misadventures of a youth who thinks he slew his father, is lionized in the remote village to which he flees, and is ultimately disenchanted. Synge's most important full-length play.

Deirdre of the Sorrows (1910). A poetic love tragedy based on Irish legend.

LADY GREGORY: *Hyacinth Halvey* (1906). A long one-act farce dealing with the burdens of an unearned reputation and the effort of a youth to divest himself of it.

The Gaol Gate (1906). A one-act tragedy of a patriot's execution for refusing to betray his neighbors to the police.

The Workhouse Ward (1908). See page 620.

PADRAIC COLUM: *The Fiddler's House* (1907). A drama about the restlessness of a natural-born fiddler and the struggle to keep him tethered to his farm.

The Land (1905). A treatment of the conflict between the old generation, which tries to make the best of the impoverished land, and the younger generation, which wants to leave home and find a new way of life.

T. C. MURRAY: *Maurice Hart* (1912). A realistic drama of peasant family life and of a favorite son's difficulty in accepting the call to the priesthood, for which the family prepares him at great sacrifice.

Autumn Fire (1924). A somber drama of a young man's passion for his father's second wife. May be compared with O'Neill's *Desire Under the Elms.*

ST. JOHN ERVINE: *Jane Clegg* (1913). A realistic drama of a woman's marriage to a weakling and struggle to make a decent life for her family against heavy odds.

John Ferguson (1915). A tragedy of middle-class Protestant life in Ulster. Revolves around the strong character of an upright, religious man.

The First Mrs. Frazer (1928). A high comedy in which a man gets rid of an unfaithful second wife with the help of his sensible and clever first wife.

LENNOX ROBINSON: *The White-headed Boy* (1916). A light comedy about a high-spirited Irish lad whose family makes many sacrifices for him, while he seemingly behaves with great indiscretion. It is finally discovered that he is married to the girl he was believed to be seducing.

The Far-off Hills (1928). A comedy revolving around a domineering elder daughter who manages her father's life until he escapes her ministrations by remarrying. She marries a "go-getting" young man who will provide fresh opportunities for her to manage affairs.

SEAN O'CASEY: *The Shadow of a Gunman* (1923). A tragedy of Irish political strife and a bitter excoriation of pseudo patriotism.

Juno and the Paycock (1924). A drama of Irish life, part comedy and part tragedy. Revolves around the confused and unhappy family of a boastful idler who intoxicates himself with drink and windy words while his daughter is betrayed, his son is executed by Irish patriots for treachery to their cause, and his wife, Juno, struggles in vain to keep the impoverished family intact.

The Plough and the Stars (1926). See page 633.

The Silver Tassie (1929; written in 1927). A half-realistic, half-expressionistic antiwar drama.

Within the Gates (1933). A poetic and symbolic play laid in Hyde Park. Constitutes an allegory on modern life and a protest of the "down-and-outers" against the privileged classes.

The Purple Dust (1940). An exuberant satire on Englishmen in Ireland.

The Star Turns Red (1940). A poetic drama of class conflict in Ireland.

Red Roses for Me (1943). A poetic strike drama, half realistic and half symbolic.

GEORGE SHIELS: *The New Gossoon* (1930). A peasant comedy about a young wastrel and a roguish poacher who is an Irish Autolycus.

DENIS JOHNSTON: *The Old Lady Says 'No'* (1929). An expressionistic play about the tawdriness of Irish society and the contrast between what Ireland has become and the ideals represented by Robert Emmet. Presented as the delirium of an actor who is knocked unconscious while acting the role of Emmet.

The Moon in the Yellow River (1931). A Chekhovian drama of Irish life, of ignorant and bumbling conservatism, of failure to improve conditions in Ireland, and of an intelligent, sensitive man who succumbs to depression and nihilism.

PAUL VINCENT CARROLL: *Shadow and Substance* (1934). A tragedy of the conflict between cold, formal faith and simple Christianity. Notable for its characterization of an intellectual priest.

The White Steed (1938). A social comedy concerning the political ambitions of an Irish priest and the effects of intolerance and vigilantism, which are opposed by another clerical character, a lovable old priest.

AMERICAN DRAMA

JAMES A. HERNE: *Margaret Fleming* (1890). The first American realistic drama; revolves around a husband's infidelity and his wife's understanding attitude.

CLYDE FITCH: *The Climbers* (1901). A satire on social climbing.

The Truth (1907). A high comedy revolving around a woman's chronic prevarications.

The City (1910). An exposure of a respectable career as founded on corruption. Watered-down social criticism by comparison with Ibsen's work (*Pillars of Society, An Enemy of the People*), but marks an advance in American comedy.

WILLIAM VAUGHN MOODY: *The Great Divide* (1906). A realistic drama in which a woman overcomes her conventional training and loves the rough man who forced her to marry him.

AUGUSTUS THOMAS: *The Witching Hour* (1907). A primitive attempt to inject "ideas" into American drama by dealing with the subject of mental telepathy.

EUGENE WALTER: *The Easiest Way* (1908). A realistic portrait of a rich man's mistress who falls in love with a reporter but fails to redeem herself.

PERCY MACKAYE: *The Scarecrow* (1908). A fantastic play about witchcraft in New England.

This Fine-Pretty World (1924). A folk play of native types and dialect in the Kentucky mountains.

EDWARD SHELDON: *The Nigger* (1910). An early study of the Negro problem.

GEORGE C. HAZELTON and J. HARRY BENRIMO: *The Yellow Jacket* (1912). A comedy written in the style of Chinese drama; marked by whimsical humor and technical ingenuity.

EUGENE O'NEILL: *The Long Voyage Home* (1917). A realistic one-acter about the fate of a Swedish sailor who is shanghaied in spite of his resolve to stay sober and return to his homeland.

The Moon of the Caribbees (1918). A notable atmospheric one-act sea play filled with a sense of defeat and fate. An early example of O'Neill's poetic naturalism.

Beyond the Horizon (1920). A realistic tragedy of frustration and defeat.

The Emperor Jones (1920). An expressionistic drama of fear and atavism in the jungle. A Negro dictator tries to flee from a revolt of the natives he has oppressed, but he is destroyed by his obsessive fantasies.

Anna Christie (1921). See page 786.

The Hairy Ape (1922). See page 817.

Desire Under the Elms (1924). A tragedy of life on the soil. Revolves around a son's passion for his father's second wife.

Marco Millions (1927). A social satire exposing the materialism and narrow-mindedness of a Babbitt of Western civilization (Marco Polo), who is impervious to romantic love and ancient Chinese culture.

Strange Interlude (1928). The psychological drama of a woman who finds fulfillment of her multifaceted love in three men who for her supplement one another. A play in nine acts, notable for its use of stream-of-consciousness monologues and asides.

Mourning Becomes Electra (1931). A modern variant of the classic Oresteian story, given a New England setting and treated as a tragedy of the Oedipus complex in psychoanalytical terms.

Ah, Wilderness! (1933). A nostalgic comedy of adolescence and of an understanding father at the beginning of the century.

The Iceman Cometh (1946; written in 1939). A tragedy dealing with men's need for illusions to make the failure of their lives endurable.

JOHN COLTON and CLEMENCE RANDOLPH: *Rain* (1922). A psychological melodrama of religious fanaticism, hypocrisy, and sexual repression. Revolves around the conflict between a missionary and a prostitute. Based on a short story, *Miss Thompson,* by W. Somerset Maugham.

OWEN DAVIS: *Icebound* (1923). A drama of New England frustration.

ELMER RICE: *The Adding Machine* (1923). An expressionistic treatment of the commonplaceness and mediocrity caused by the routinized life of the modern world.

Street Scene (1929). A tragedy of a woman driven into adultery by a dreary life. Notable for its realistic picture of tenement life.

The Left Bank (1931). A comedy of American expatriates in Paris who fail to appreciate America.

Counsellor-at-Law (1931). A character comedy of a successful lawyer with a poor Jewish background and of his conflict with snobbery.

JOHN HOWARD LAWSON: *Roger Bloomer* (1923). A satirical, expressionistic account of a young man's difficulties in a money-minded world and a clever exposure of that world.

Processional (1925). A humorous and imaginative "jazz symphony" of the confusions and conflicts of American life in the "jazz age"; presented through a vaudevillian but socially critical picture of a labor strike in a West Virginia town.

HATCHER HUGHES: *Hell-Bent fer Heaven* (1923). A drama of American mountaineer life, notable for its use of folk elements.

GEORGE KELLY: *The Show-Off* (1924). A satirical comedy of egotism and high-pressure salesmanship.

Craig's Wife (1925). A character study of a middle-class woman who substitutes possessiveness and homemaking for love and ultimately exposes her selfishness to her long-suffering husband.

The Deep Mrs. Sykes (1945). A comedy of a self-centered woman who relies on intuitions that always fail her.

The Fatal Weakness (1946). A comedy of a foolishly romantic woman; deals with her love of weddings and her loss of her husband to a refugee woman.

LAURENCE STALLINGS and MAXWELL ANDERSON: *What Price Glory?* (1924). See page 837.

MAXWELL ANDERSON: *Saturday's Children* (1927). A comedy of marriage of young people whose romance founders on economic problems.

Elizabeth the Queen (1930). See page 864.

Both Your Houses (1933). A political satire on Congressional logrolling; the story of a young legislator's struggle to purify politics.

Mary of Scotland (1933). A romantic verse tragedy about Mary Stuart's destruction by her designing rival, Elizabeth of England.

Winterset (1935). A poetic tragedy of modern life, in which the son of a wronged man foregoes for the sake of love his chance to vindicate his father and to save his own life.

High Tor (1937). A poetic fantasy about a young man's rebellion against the machine age; a satire on the mercenary world of materialists.

Anne of the Thousand Days (1948). A verse tragedy of Anne Boleyn, Elizabeth's mother, and her violent romance with Henry VIII. Notable for the conflict of high-spirited characters.

DAN TOTHEROH: *Wild Birds* (1925). A sensitive farm tragedy ending in a brutal murder.

SIDNEY HOWARD: *The Silver Cord* (1926). A psychological drama of overpossessive and destructive mother love.

Yellow Jack (1933). A semidocumentary treatment of the battle against yellow fever, reflecting the modern interest in science.

SIDNEY HOWARD and SINCLAIR LEWIS: *Dodsworth* (1933). A comedy of a wife's infatuation with European pseudo culture and of a Midwestern husband's awakening.

GEORGE S. KAUFMAN and MARC CONNELLY: *Beggar on Horseback* (1924). An expressionistic, satirical comedy of big business and its threat to individuality.

GEORGE S. KAUFMAN and RING LARDNER: *June Moon* (1929). A broad comedy of the popular-music-publishing business and a satire on commercialized "culture."

GEORGE S. KAUFMAN and MOSS HART: *Once in a Lifetime* (1930). A broad comedy of Hollywood life and manners.

You Can't Take It With You (1936). A comedy of carefree family life during the economic depression.

The Man Who Came to Dinner (1939). A high comedy of egotism on the part of a literary figure (Alexander Woollcott), ending in a farcical solution of the problem of his secretary's love affair.

GEORGE S. KAUFMAN and MORRIE RYSKIND: *Of Thee I Sing* (1931). A musical-comedy satire on American presidential campaigns and politics.

PAUL GREEN: *In Abraham's Bosom* (1926). A chronicle of a Negro's tragic struggle for education and dignity.

The House of Connelly (1932). A drama of

decadent Southern culture and of its dissolution.

Hymn to the Rising Sun (1936). A one-act drama of the chain gang in which social protest is fused with character study and poetic power.

Johnny Johnson (1937). The tragicomic history of a homespun American idealist, his disillusionment with Wilsonian democracy, and his vain attempt to oppose war, resulting in his ending his life in an insane asylum.

DU BOSE and DOROTHY HEYWARD: *Porgy* (1927). A Negro folk play. The basis of George Gershwin's folk opera, *Porgy and Bess* (1935).

E. P. CONKLE: *Crick Bottom Plays* (1928). A series of Midwestern one-act plays, among which is the grim *Minnie Field*.

JOHN BALDERSTON: *Berkeley Square* (1928). A fantasy in which an American, transported into eighteenth-century England, observes the manners of his English ancestors and returns to modern life.

S. N. BEHRMAN: *The Second Man* (1927). A high comedy of the difficulties of a sophisticated man in extricating himself from the situation of having an idealistic young woman in love with him when he prefers a life that makes fewer demands. A "second man" in him inclines him to a life of ease with a wealthy mistress.

Meteor (1929). A study of an American business tycoon, his will to power, and his delusions of grandeur.

Biography (1932). A high comedy contrasting two dispositions or outlooks—a too-relaxed tolerance and a too-insistent sense of righteousness. A comparison with *The Misanthrope* reveals parallels to Molière's comedy.

Rain from Heaven (1934). A study of an aloof esthete's realization that he must join the struggle against social evil as represented by fascism.

End of Summer (1936). A high comedy of the futility and distress of an idle rich woman and of her daughter's search for a life with more meaning and purpose.

JOHN WEXLEY: *The Last Mile* (1929). A realistic melodrama of prison life and of the electrocution of a convict.

They Shall Not Die (1934). An indictment of legal injustice to the Negro. Based on the famous Scottsboro case.

PHILIP BARRY: *Holiday* (1928). A comedy of the rebellion of an upper-class girl against the conservative standards of her family.

Hotel Universe (1930). A philosophical and psychological study of warped lives that are enlightened by an uncanny character.

Here Come the Clowns (1938). A fantasy of the conflict between good and evil in the world.

The Philadelphia Story (1939). A comedy of a too-righteous daughter of the social set who learns to make allowances for human frailty and remarries her former husband.

LYNN RIGGS: *Green Grow the Lilacs* (1931). A folk play of life on the Oklahoma frontier. The basis of the Rodgers and Hammerstein musical comedy *Oklahoma!* (1943).

LAWRENCE LANGNER and ARMINA MARSHALL: *The Pursuit of Happiness* (1933). A comedy of democratic ardor and "bundling" in New England during the Revolutionary War.

PAUL PETERS and GEORGE SKLAR: *Stevedore* (1934). A realistic melodrama and thesis drama of racial conflict in the South, showing white and Negro labor uniting to oppose a lynching.

SIDNEY KINGSLEY: *Dead End* (1934). A sociological picture of slum life and of the making of criminals in the environment of the underprivileged.

The World We Make (1939). A dramatization of Millen Brand's novel *The Outward Room*. A neurotic rich girl is cured of her anxieties by the kindness and courage of the common people among whom she finds shelter and love.

The Patriots (1943). A historical play presenting the conflict of Jefferson and Hamilton over social and political matters; concludes with Hamilton's support of Jefferson against Aaron Burr for the presidency.

Detective Story (1949). A naturalistic study of night-court life and a drama in which too much righteousness on the part of an idealistic detective backfires; a plea for tolerance and the tempering of righteousness with some consideration for the frailty of the human race.

LILLIAN HELLMAN: *The Children's Hour* (1934). A psychological drama of the maliciousness of a neurotic child who destroys two of her teachers with insinuations of homosexual relations between them.

The Little Foxes (1939). See page 983. See also *Another Part of the Forest,* treating the early history of the characters.

Watch on the Rhine (1941). A drama in which the struggle against fascism invades an American household that has tried to remain aloof from the social conflicts of the day and to lead a civilized life in a world torn by momentous issues.

CLIFFORD ODETS: *Waiting for Lefty* (1935). A semiexpressionistic one-act strike drama. Uses flashbacks into the lives of the underprivileged to explain their revolt against the social system of capitalism.

Till the Day I Die (1935). A one-act drama of the anti-Nazi underground in Germany.

Awake and Sing! (1935). A Chekhovian picture of disintegrating lower-middle-class life and of the rebellion of the young against the seedy respectability and timorousness of that life.

Paradise Lost (1936). An allegorical treatment of the failure of false middle-class hopes and dreams in a world of economic collapse and social conflict.

Golden Boy (1937). See page 950.

Rocket to the Moon (1938). A study of failure of nerve in middle-class society.

MARK REED: *Yes, My Darling Daughter* (1937). A comedy of a former "new woman" of the Greenwich Village period of Bohemianism, now conventionally married and the mother of a grown daughter, who is faced with the unconventional behavior of her daughter.

IRWIN SHAW: *Bury the Dead* (1936). A one-act fantasy of the revolt of the dead against the society that cheated them of a full life and then sent them to die in a new world war. May be compared with Hans Chlumberg's *The Miracle at Verdun.*

CLARE BOOTH: *The Women* (1936). A comedy of scandalmongering upper-class women and of their destruction of a woman's marriage.

THORNTON WILDER: *Our Town* (1938). See page 926.

JOHN STEINBECK: *Of Mice and Men* (1937). A drama of itinerant life, revolving around the friendship of a keen-witted youth for a pathetic imbecile endowed with too much physical strength.

ROBERT E. SHERWOOD: *The Road to Rome* (1926). An antiwar comedy about a Roman woman who breaks Hannibal's resolve to conquer Rome by awakening him to normal sexual appetites.

The Petrified Forest (1935). A symbolic drama, told in the form of a Western melodrama. Represents the failure of nerve in society and the suicidal impulse in civilization, which enable the barbarians to take over the world.

Idiots' Delight (1936). An augury of the coming of a second world war and a description of an outbreak of instinctive chauvinism among advocates of international-mindedness while the munitions magnates thrive.

There Shall Be No Night (1940). The drama of a Nobel Prize scientist and man of peace who arrives at the conclusion that, although war is madness, it is necessary to fight in behalf of freedom. First set in Finland, the action of the play was transferred to Greece for the British production in 1941.

ARTHUR ARENT and FEDERAL THEATRE STAFF: *The Living Newspaper: Power* (1937). A documentary drama of the utilities problem in the United States.

One-Third of a Nation (1938). A documentary "living newspaper" on the problem of housing and slum clearance in America.

PAUL OSBORN: *On Borrowed Time* (1938). A fantasy on death. Adapted from the novel by Lawrence Edward Watkin.

A Bell for Adano (1945). A dramatization of John Hersey's novel of the same title, dealing with the struggle of an American officer of Italian extraction to bring the democratic way of life to Italy under the Allied occupation.

JAMES THURBER and ELLIOTT NUGENT: *The Male Animal* (1939). A comic treatment of a college professor's domestic difficulties and effort to maintain a liberal point of view as a teacher.

HOWARD LINDSAY and RUSSEL CROUSE: *Life With Father* (1939). The famous period piece. A dramatization of Clarence Day's book of the same title.

State of the Union (1945). A "liberal comedy" about a presidential candidate's revolt against the politicians and reactionaries who use him to promote their interests and about his return to a wife who always deflates his ego but represents his better self.

Life With Mother (1949). A sequel to *Life With Father*.

WILLIAM SAROYAN: *My Heart's in the Highlands* (1939). See page 1016.

The Time of Your Life (1939). A bizarre comedy of life in a San Francisco water-front honky-tonk, where a wealthy idler encourages the marriage of his dull-witted but good-natured protégé to an unhappy young prostitute who tries to escape the miserable life she has been leading.

Love's Old Sweet Song (1940). A broad and romantic comedy of the love of a retiring old maid and a "pitchman," or vendor of quack medicines.

The Beautiful People (1941). A poetic fantasy about an oversensitive girl who succors mice and her philosophical father who tries to lead a carefree life.

Hello, Out There (West coast production, 1941; Broadway production, 1942). A realistic one-act play in which a tramp is imprisoned and killed when charged with rape by an immoral woman.

JOSEPH KESSELRING: *Arsenic and Old Lace* (1941). A farcical melodrama about kind old ladies who specialize in poison in order to put old men out of their misery.

SAMSON RAPHAELSON: *Jason* (1942). A high comedy dealing with the conflict of a hyperesthetic drama critic and a rugged playwright of the people for the affections of an upstart girl.

JOHN VAN DRUTEN: *The Voice of the Turtle* (1943). A three-character comedy of love in wartime between two people who, when they take a seemingly passing affair seriously, discover that they are still capable of genuine love.

I Remember Mama (1944). A dramatization of Kathryn Forbes's *Mama's Bank Account*. Deals with a Norwegian immigrant family and an understanding mother who gives her children courage to face the world.

JAMES GOW and ARNAUD D'USSEAU: *Tomorrow the World* (1943). The reconditioning of the little son of a German liberal by understanding Americans who have taken charge of him after his education under National Socialism.

Deep Are the Roots (1945). A drama purporting to show that racial prejudice is so ingrained that it breaks out even in a Southern woman of liberal persuasion.

ARTHUR GOETZ and RUTH GOODMAN: *One-Man Show* (1944). A drama of the art dealers' world. Revolves around a father's effort to wean his daughter from himself and his reluctance to let her go when she falls in love.

The Heiress (1947). A notably successful dramatization of Henry James's short novel *Washington Square*.

MARY COYLE CHASE: *Harvey* (1944). A comedy of an alcoholic and his imaginary man-sized rabbit.

TENNESSEE WILLIAMS: *The Glass Menagerie* (1944 in Chicago; 1945 in New York). See page 1032.

A Streetcar Named Desire (1947). The drama of a mentally ailing woman who becomes a prostitute after the suicide of her homosexual husband. She seeks shelter in the home of her sister after coming to the end of her resources, but arouses the antagonism of her brother-in-law, is stripped of her defenses by him, and loses her mind after he sadistically violates her.

Summer and Smoke (1948). A novelistic drama of the love of an unworldly girl for a high-spirited young physician whose advances repel her and of her desperation on being rejected by him when she is at last ready for physical love.

JOHN PATRICK: *The Hasty Heart* (1945). A war drama set in the convalescent ward of a British general hospital.

ARTHUR LAURENTS: *Home of the Brave* (1945). A drama of racial tensions that cause the psychopathological condition of an American Jewish soldier of the Second World War; his condition is uncovered and cured by narcosynthesis.

EMMET LAVERY: *The Magnificent Yankee* (1946). A biography of Justice Oliver Wendell Holmes and a representation of his family life and championship of liberal principles.

GARSON KANIN: *Born Yesterday* (1946). A comedy of the awakening of the naïve mistress of a racketeer by a crusading reporter; an example of the liberal farce or comedy.

WILLIAM WISTER HAINES: *Command Decision* (1947). A notable war play dealing with an air-force officer's anguish over having to sacrifice his men in raids over Germany.

ARTHUR MILLER: *All My Sons* (1947). A social drama dealing with the discovery that loyalty to family cannot serve as an excuse for socially irresponsible conduct. An example of realistic thesis drama.

Death of a Salesman (1949). See page 1060.

The Crucible (1953). A tragedy revolving around the Salem witchcraft trials and one man's heroic defiance of mass hysteria and injustice.

A View from the Bridge (1955). A tragedy of incestuous passion and betrayal on the Brooklyn waterfront; an attempt to write a lower-class tragedy and to make it parallel classic Greek drama.

THOMAS HEGGEN and JOSHUA LOGAN: *Mister Roberts* (1948). A dramatization of Heggen's novel of the same title, dealing with naval life and with a young lieutenant's efforts to badger his superiors into allowing him to see active duty.

CARSON MCCULLERS: *The Member of the Wedding* (1950). A dramatization by Miss McCullers of her novel of the same title. A sensitive study of the adolescence of a girl emerging from the tomboy stage.

LOUIS O. COXE and ROBERT CHAPMAN: *Billy Budd* (1951). A thoughtful and provocative dramatization in verse of Melville's famous story.

ROBERT ANDERSON: *Tea and Sympathy* (1953). A study of the persecution of a sensitive boarding-school student by his classmates and schoolmaster on the grounds of alleged abnormal sexuality.

WILLIAM INGE: *Picnic* (1953). A vivid picture of small-town life and its frustrations.

The Dark at the Top of the Stairs (1957). A drama of dislocation in a small-town family abandoned by the husband after an absurd quarrel with his overanxious wife.

EUGENE O'NEILL: *Long Day's Journey into Night* (1956, a posthumous production). An autobiographical drama of the author's youth and awareness of tragic misunderstandings and conflicts in his family.

A Touch of the Poet (1958, a posthumous production). A drama of self-deception and aristocratic pretensions in early 19th century New England.

599.051 U55   FV
THE UNDERSTANDING OF ANIMALS
                              19.95